The
Necessary
Shakespeare

The Necessary Shakespeare

Second Edition

Edited by

David Bevington

The University of Chicago

PEARSON
Longman

New York   San Francisco   Boston
London   Toronto   Sydney   Tokyo   Singapore   Madrid
Mexico City   Munich   Paris   Cape Town   Hong Kong   Montreal

Vice President and Editor-in-Chief: Joseph Terry
Development Manager: Janet Lanphier
Executive Marketing Manager: Ann Stypuloski
Senior Supplements Editor: Donna Campion
Media Supplements Editor: Nancy Garcia
Managing Editor: Valerie Zaborski
Project Coordination and Electronic Page Makeup: Electronic Publishing Services Inc., NYC
Cover Designer/Manager: Wendy Ann Fredericks
Cover Illustration: *The Flower Portrait,* from the RSC Collection with permission of the Governors of the Royal Shakespeare Company.
      (Background photo) Siede Preis/Getty Images.
Part Opening Photos: Universiteitsbibliotheek Utrecht
Photo Researcher: Photosearch, Inc.
Manufacturing Buyer: Lucy Hebard
Printer and Binder: Hamilton Printing
Cover Printer: Lehigh Press, Inc.

Library of Congress Cataloging-in-Publication Data

Shakespeare, William, 1564-1616.
  [Selections. 2005]
  The necessary Shakespeare / edited by David Bevington.— 2nd ed.
    p. cm.
  Includes bibliographical references and index.
  ISBN 0-321-27250-1
  I. Bevington, David M. II. Title.

PR2759.B64 2005
822.3'3—dc22

                                                    2004007876

Please visit our website at http://www.ablongman.com.

ISBN 0-321-27250-1

  3 4 5 6 7 8 9 10—HT—07 06 05

CONTENTS

Preface   vi

Shakespeare's World: A Visual Portfolio   following page lxxx

PREFACE

The Necessary Shakespeare distills the best, the oftenest read, the most often produced of Shakespeare's great plays. By publishing this selection in a compact paperback edition, my hope is to expose a new broader student audience to the work of perhaps the greatest author in the history of the English language.

Of the thirty-eight or so plays and various poems written by or attributed to Shakespeare, this collection offers twenty plays and the sonnets. I have made these selections based on the response of Shakespeare instructors across the country who indicated which works are truly "necessary" in the undergraduate classroom. I have also tried to select plays that are frequently performed or widely available on film or video.

I include seven romantic comedies, four English history plays, seven of the great tragedies, and two romances. Cutting is always a thankless task, and I have omitted some works that some readers will miss: *Troilus and Cressida, The Second Part of King Henry the Fourth, Coriolanus,* and *Cymbeline* might well be on such a list. Even so, I hope that this collection does represent the best and best known of his work. It covers Shakespeare's favorite genres; it shows his development from the early *The Taming of the Shrew* and *Richard the Third* to the late *The Tempest;* it shows him as an amazing poet as well as dramatist. My hope is that such a volume will find a real use in personal libraries and classrooms.

The arrangement of the plays in this volume under the categories of comedies, histories, tragedies, and romances is close to that of the First Folio of 1623, in which Shake-

speare's plays were grouped under three categories of comedies, histories, and tragedies (the romances were included under "comedies"). They were published posthumously by two of his erstwhile colleagues in the acting company known as the King's men. The poems and sonnets were published separately.

My edition of *The Complete Works of Shakespeare* (fifth edition, Longman, 2003) is still available for more complete coverage. Over the course of its publishing history, I have profited greatly from the consultation of various friends and colleagues at colleges and universities all over the world. In each case I showed the consultant all the materials I had prepared—the Shakespeare text, the commentary notes, the textual notes, the introduction—and sought that person's aid in revision. These friends have aided me through progressive reconsiderations of the work. Other colleagues helped me with the plays and poems omitted from this present volume. I want to extend my warmest thanks to all.

In this present edition, I have also selected from the front matter and appendices of the 2003 edition of *The Complete Works of Shakespeare.* The choices here are an attempt to respond to the desires of representative readers and users of the volume. They helped me decide that we should keep the introductory material on life in Shakespeare's England, the drama before Shakespeare, London theatres and dramatic companies, Shakespeare's life and work, Shakespeare's language, and Shakespeare criticism. All of these sections have been brought up to date, especially the materials on Shakespeare criticism. I have added substantially to the bibliography, to make it as up-to-date as possible.

In the appendices, I have kept the material on Canon, Dates, and Early Texts, and on sources. A new essay on "Shakespeare in Performance," by Professor Lois Potter of the University of Delaware, brings performance history up to date with an emphasis on film and television. I have revised the bibliographies to focus on the works contained in this edition. I have recast the index. Readers and teachers seem to appreciate having an index, although many editions do not include one. I have kept this as part of the volume.

KEY FEATURES OF THIS EDITION

- **Thoroughly revised and updated notes and glosses** provide contemporary readers the support they need to understand Elizabethan language and idioms in accessible and clear modern language, line by line.
- **A richly illustrated general introduction** provides readers with the historical and cultural background required to understand Shakespeare's works in context.
- **"Shakespeare's World: A Visual Portfolio"** provides 16 pages of full color illustrations to help readers visualize Renaissance life and culture and to trace the his-

tory of significant performances on stage and screen. Nearly half of these color images are new to this edition, including a selection of stills from recent films of Shakespeare's plays.

- **Significantly revised introductory essays on each of the plays and poems** offer new insight into major themes, cultural issues, and critical conflicts.
- **Updated appendices** include the most recent information on sources, textual choices, performance history, dating of the works, and bibliographic resources.

SUPPLEMENTS

The following supplements are available free when ordered with this text. Please consult your local Longman representative if you would like to set up a value pack.

Evaluating a Performance, **by Mike Greenwald,** informs students about stage and theatrical performance and helps them to become more critical viewers of dramatic productions (ISBN 0-321-09541-3).

Screening Shakespeare: Using Film to Understand the Plays, **by Michael Greer,** is a brief, practical guide to select feature films of the most commonly taught plays (ISBN 0-321-19479-9).

David Bevington
2004

GENERAL INTRODUCTION

LIFE IN SHAKESPEARE'S ENGLAND

England during Shakespeare's lifetime (1564–1616) was a proud nation with a strong sense of national identity, but it was also a small nation by modern standards. Probably not more than five million people lived in the whole of England, considerably fewer than now live in London. England's territories in France were no longer extensive, as they had been during the fourteenth century and earlier; in fact, by the end of Queen Elizabeth's reign (1558–1603), England had virtually retired from the territories she had previously controlled on the Continent, especially in France. Wales was a conquered principality. England's overseas empire in America had scarcely begun, with the Virginia settlement established in the 1580s. Scotland was not yet a part of Great Britain; union with Scotland would not take place until 1707, despite the fact that King James VI of Scotland assumed the English throne in 1603 as James I of England. Ireland, although declared a kingdom under English rule in 1541, was more a source of trouble than of economic strength. The last years of Elizabeth's reign, especially from 1597 to 1601, were plagued by the rebellion of the Irish under Hugh O'Neill, Earl of Tyrone. Thus, England of the sixteenth and early seventeenth centuries was both small and isolated.

THE SOCIAL AND ECONOMIC BACKGROUND

By and large, England was a rural land. Much of the kingdom was still wooded, though timber was being used increasingly in manufacturing and shipbuilding. The area of the Midlands, today heavily industrialized, was at that time still a region of great trees, green fields, and clear streams. England's chief means of livelihood was agriculture. This part of the economy was generally in a bad way, however, and people who lived off the land did not share in the prosperity of many Londoners. A problem throughout the sixteenth century was that of "enclosure": the conversion by rich landowners of croplands into pasturage. Farmers and peasants complained bitterly that they were being dispossessed and starved for the benefit of livestock. Rural uprisings and food riots were common, to the dismay of the authorities. Some Oxfordshire peasants arose in 1596, threatening to massacre the gentry and march on London; other riots had occurred in 1586 and 1591. There were thirteen riots in Kent alone during Elizabeth's reign. Unrest continued into the reign of James I, notably the Midlands' rising of 1607. Although the government did what it could to inhibit enclosure, the economic forces at work were too massive and too inadequately understood to be curbed by governmental fiat. The absence of effective bureaucracies or agencies of coercion compounded the difficulty of governmental control. Pasture used large areas with greater efficiency than crop farming, and required far less labor. The wool produced

This detail from a 1572 map of London shows closely packed buildings intersected with throroughfares, with gardens and open spaces on the outskirts.

"Enclosure" was a problem throughout the sixteenth century in England. Crop lands were converted into pasturage. The livelihood of the plowman was threatened by the pasturing of sheep and the growing production of wool.

by the pasturing of sheep was needed in ever increasing amounts for the manufacture of cloth.

The wool industry also experienced occasional economic difficulties, to be sure; overexpansion in the early years of the sixteenth century created a glutted market that collapsed disastrously in 1551, producing widespread unemployment. Despite such fluctuations and reversals, however, the wool industry at least provided handsome profits for some landowners and middlemen. Mining and manufacture in coal, iron, tin, copper, and lead, although insignificant by modern standards, also were expanding at a significant rate. Trading companies exploited the rich new resources of the Americas, as well as of eastern Europe and the Orient. Queen Elizabeth aided economic development by keeping England out of war with her continental enemies as long as possible,

despite provocations from those powers and despite the eagerness of some of her advisers to retaliate.

Certainly England's economic condition was better than the economic condition of the rest of the Continent; an Italian called England "the land of comforts." Yet although some prosperity did exist, it was not evenly distributed. Especially during Shakespeare's first years in London, in the late 1580s and the 1590s, the gap between rich and poor grew more and more extreme. Elizabeth's efforts at peacemaking were no longer able to prevent years of war with the Catholic powers of the Continent. Taxation grew heavier, and inflation proceeded at an unusually rapid rate during this period. A succession of bad harvests compounded the miseries of those who dwelled on the land. When the hostilities on the Continent ceased for a time in about 1597, a wave of returning veterans added to unemployment and crime. The rising prosperity experienced by Shakespeare and other fortunate Londoners was undeniably real, but it

Sixteenth-century London was a city teeming with activity. Pedestrians were often forced to make way for the livestock being driven through the streets.

London Bridge, lined with shops, houses, and severed heads on poles, provided a colorful route for those traveling between the north and south banks of the Thames. A number of Elizabethan theaters, including the Globe, were located on the south bank.

was not universal. Nowhere was the contrast between rich and poor more visible than in London.

London

Sixteenth-century London was at once more attractive and less attractive than twenty-first-century London. It was full of trees and gardens; meadows and cultivated lands reached in some places to its very walls. Today we can perhaps imagine the way in which it bordered clear streams and green fields when we approach from a distance some noncommercial provincial city such as Lincoln, York, or Hereford. Partly surrounded by its ancient wall, London was by no means a large metropolis. With 190,000 to 200,000 inhabitants in the city proper and its suburbs, it was nonetheless the largest city of Europe, and its dominance among English cities was even more striking; in 1543–1544, London paid thirty times the subsidy of Norwich, then the second-largest city in the kingdom (15,000 inhabitants). Although London's population had expanded into the surrounding area in all directions, the city proper stretched along the north bank of the Thames River from the old Tower of London on the east to St. Paul's Cathedral and the Fleet Ditch on the west—a distance of little more than a mile. Visitors approaching London from the south bank of the Thames (the Bankside) and crossing London Bridge could see virtually all of this exciting city lying before them. London Bridge itself was one of the major attractions of the city, lined with shops and richly decorated on occasion for the triumphal entry of a king or queen.

Yet London had its grim and ugly side as well. On London Bridge could sometimes be seen the heads of exe-

The taverns of Cheapside in London were popular and occasionally rowdy.

cuted traitors. The city's houses were generally small and crowded; its streets were often narrow and filthy. In the absence of sewers, open ditches in the streets served to collect and carry off refuse. Frequent epidemics of the bubonic plague were the inevitable result of unsanitary conditions and medical ignorance. Lighting of the streets at night was generally nonexistent, and the constabulary was notoriously unreliable. Shakespeare gives us unforgettable satires of night watchmen and bumbling police officials in *Much Ado About Nothing* (Dogberry and the night watch) and *Measure for Measure* (Constable Elbow). Prostitution thrived in the suburbs, conveniently located, although beyond the reach of the London authorities. Again, we are indebted to Shakespeare for a memorable portrayal in *Measure for Measure* of just such a demimonde (Mistress Overdone the bawd, Pompey her pimp, and various customers). Houses of prostitution were often found in the vicinity of the public theaters, since the theaters also took advantage of suburban locations to escape the stringent regulations imposed by London's Lord Mayor and Council of Aldermen. The famous Globe Theatre, for example, was on the south bank of the Thames, a short distance west of London Bridge. Anoth-

er theatrical building (called simply "The Theatre"), used earlier by Shakespeare and the Lord Chamberlain's players, was located in Finsbury Fields, a short distance across Moorfields from London's northeast corner. The suburbs also housed various con games and illegal operations, some of them brilliantly illustrated (and no doubt exaggerated) in Ben Jonson's *The Alchemist* (1610).

Roughly half of London's total population, perhaps 100,000 people, lived within its walls, and as many more in the suburbs. The royal palace of Whitehall, Westminster Abbey (then known as the Abbey Church of St. Peter), the Parliament House, and Westminster Hall were well outside London, two miles or so to the west on the Thames River. They remain today in the same location, in Westminster, although the metropolis of London has long since surrounded these official buildings.

Travel

Travel was still extremely painful and slow because of the poor condition of the roads. Highway robbers were a constant threat. (The celebrated highway robbery in Shakespeare's *1 Henry IV* takes place at Gads Hill, on the main road between London and Canterbury.) English inns seem to have been good, however, and certainly much better than the inns of the Continent. Travel on horseback was the most common method of transportation, and probably the most comfortable, since coach building was a new and imperfect art. Coaches of state, some of which we see in prints and pictures of the era, were lumbering affairs, no doubt handsome enough in processions, but springless, unwieldly, and hard to pull. Carts and wagons were used for carrying merchandise, but packsaddles were safer and quicker. Under such difficulties, no metropolitan area such as London could possibly have thrived in the interior. London depended for its commercial greatness upon the Thames River and its access to the North Sea.

Commerce

When Elizabeth came to the English throne in 1558, England's chief foreign trade was with Antwerp, Bruges, and other Belgian cities. Antwerp was an especially important market for England's export of wool cloth. This market was seriously threatened, however, since the Low Countries were under the domination of the Catholic King of Spain, Philip II. When Philip undertook to punish his Protestant subjects in the Low Countries for their religious heresy, many of Elizabeth's counselors and subjects urged her to come to the defense of England's Protestant neighbors and trading allies. Elizabeth held back. Philip's armies attacked Antwerp in 1576 and again in 1585, putting an end to the commercial ascendancy of that great northern European metropolis. Perhaps as many as one-third of Antwerp's merchants and artisans settled in London, bringing with them their

expert knowledge of commerce and manufacture. The influx of so many skilled workers and merchants into London produced problems of unemployment and overcrowding but contributed nevertheless to London's emergence as a leading port of trade.

English ships assumed a dominant position in Mediterranean trade, formerly carried on mainly by the Venetians. In the Baltic Sea, England competed successfully in trade that had previously been controlled by the Hanseatic League. Bristol thrived on commerce with Ireland and subsequently on trade with the Western Hemisphere. Boston and Hull increased their business with Scandinavian ports. The Russia Company was founded in 1555; the Levant Company became the famous East India Company in 1600; and the Virginia Company opened up trade with the New World in the Western Hemisphere. Fisheries were developed in the North Sea, in the waters north of Ireland, and off the banks of Newfoundland. Elizabeth and her ministers encouraged this commercial expansion.

The Poor Laws and Apprenticeship

Despite the new prosperity experienced by many Elizabethans, especially in London, unemployment remained a serious problem. The suppresssion of the monasteries in 1536–1539, as part of Henry VIII's reformation of the Catholic Church, had dispossessed a large class of persons who were not easily reemployed. Other causes of unemployment, such as the periodic collapse of the wool trade, dispossession of farm workers by enclosure of land, the sudden influx of skilled artisans from Antwerp, and the return of army veterans, have already been mentioned. Elizabethan parliaments attempted to cope with the problem of unemployment but did so in ways that seem unduly harsh today. Several laws were passed between 1531, when the distinction between those poor needing charity and those unwilling to work first became law, and 1597–1598. The harshest of the laws was that of 1547, providing that vagabonds be branded and enslaved for two years; escape was punishable by death or life enslavement. This act was repealed in 1549, but subsequent acts of 1572 and 1576 designated ten classes of vagrants and required municipal authorities to provide work for the healthy unemployed of each town or parish. This localization of responsibility laid the basis for what has been known historically as the "poor rate" (a local tax levied for the support of the poor) and for that sinister institution, the workhouse. The provisions of this act remained in force for centuries. The most comprehensive laws were those of the Parliament of 1597–1598, which repeated many provisions of earlier acts and added harsh, punitive penalties intended to send vagabonds back to the parishes in which they had been born or had last worked. After 1597, no begging was permitted; the poor were supposed to be provided for by the "poor rate" already established.

BY PERMISSION OF THE BRITISH LIBRARY

Although some Elizabethans rose to great wealth, poverty and unemployment were widespread.

Regulations for apprentices were no less strict. An act of Parliament of 1563, known as the Statute of Artificers, gave the craft trades of England—still organized as medieval guilds—virtually complete authority over the young persons apprenticed to a trade. The law severely limited access to apprenticeship to sons of families with estates worth at least forty shillings of income. Apprenticeship usually began between the ages of fourteen and seventeen, and lasted for a period of not less than seven years. During this time, the young worker lived with the family of the employer. Without such an extensive apprenticeship, entry into the skilled crafts was virtually impossible. Apprenticeships were not open, however, in all guilds, and the law courts subsequently ruled that apprenticeship rules did not apply to crafts developed after 1563, so that exceptions did exist. All able-bodied workers not bound to crafts were supposed to work in agriculture. Acting companies, such as the company Shakespeare joined, were not technically organized as guilds, though the boys who played women's parts were in some cases at least bound by the terms of apprenticeship; a number of the adult actors belonged to one London guild or another and could use that status to apprentice boys. We do not know whether Shakespeare actually served such an indenture before becoming a full member of his acting company.

Social Change

The opportunities for rapid economic advance in Elizabethan England, though limited almost entirely to those who were already prosperous, did produce social change and a quality of restlessness in English society. "New men" at court were an increasing phenomenon under the Tudor monarchs, especially Henry VII and Henry VIII, who tended to rely on loyal counselors of humble origin rather than on the once-too-powerful nobility. Cardinal Wolsey, for example, rose from obscurity to become the most mighty subject of Henry VIII's realm, with a newly built residence (Hampton Court) rivaling the splendor of the King's own palaces. He was detested as an upstart by old aristocrats, such as the Duke of Norfolk, and his sudden fall was as spectacular as had been his rise to power. The Earl of Leicester, Queen Elizabeth's first favorite, was a descendant of the Edmund Dudley who had risen from unpretentious beginnings to great eminence under Henry VII, Queen Elizabeth's grandfather. Although Queen Elizabeth did not contribute substantially to the new aristocracy—she created only three peers from 1573 onward—new and influential families were numerous throughout the century. Conversely, the ancient families discovered that they were no longer entrusted with positions of highest authority. To be sure, the aristocracy remained at the apex of England's social structure. New aspirants to power emulated the aristocracy by purchasing land and building splendid residences, rather than defining themselves as a rich new "middle class." Bourgeois status was something the new men put behind them as quickly as they could. Moreover, social mobility could work in both directions: upward and downward. Many men were quickly ruined by the costly and competitive business of seeking favor at the Tudor court. The poor, in a vast majority, enjoyed virtually no rights at all. Nonetheless, the Elizabethan era was one of greater opportunity for rapid social and economic advancement among persons of wealth than England had heretofore known.

Increased economic contacts with the outside world inevitably led to the importation of new styles of living. Such new fashions, together with the rapid changes now possible in social position, produced a reaction of dismay from those who feared the destruction of traditional English values. Attitudes toward Italy veered erratically between condemnation and admiration: on the one hand, Italy was the home of the Catholic Church and originator of many supposedly decadent fashions, whereas, on the other hand, Italy was the cradle of humanism and the country famed for Venice's experiment in republican government. To many conservative Englishmen, the word *Italianate* connoted a whole range of villainous practices, including diabolical methods of torture and revenge: poisoned books of devotion that would kill the unsuspecting victims who kissed them, ingeniously contrived chairs that would close upon the person who sat in them, and the like. The revenge plays of Shakespeare's contemporaries, such as *Antonio's Revenge* by John Marston, *The Revenger's Tragedy* probably by Thomas Middleton, and *The White Devil* by John Webster, offer spectacular caricatures of the so-called Italianate style in murder. The name of Italy was also associated with licentiousness, immorality, and outlandish fashions in clothes. France, too, was accused of encouraging such extravagances in dress as ornamented headdresses, stiffly pleated ruffs, padded doublets, puffed or double sleeves, and richly decorated hose. Rapid changes in fashion added to the costliness of being up to date and thereby increased the outcry against vanity in dress. Fencing, dicing, the use of cosmetics, the smoking of tobacco, the drinking of imported wines, and almost every vice known to humanity were attributed by angry moralists to the corrupting influence from abroad.

Not all Englishmen deplored continental fashion, of course. Persons of advanced taste saw the importation of European styles as a culturally liberating process. Fashion thus became a subject of debate between moral traditionalists and those who welcomed the new styles. The controversy was a bitter one, with religious overtones, in which the reformers' angry accusations became increasingly extreme. This attack on changing fashion was, in fact, an integral part of the Puritan movement. It therefore stressed the sinfulness, not only of extravagance in clothing, but also of the costliness in building great

This brothel scene, featuring gambling or dicing, illustrates some of the vices that were attributed to the corrupting influence from abroad.

houses and other such worldly pursuits. Those whose sympathies were Puritan became more and more disaffected with the cultural values represented by the court, and thus English society drifted further and further toward irreconcilable conflict.

Shakespeare's personal views on this controversy are hard to determine and do not bear importantly on his achievement as an artist. Generally, however, we can observe that his many references to changes in fashion cater neither to the avant-garde nor to reactionary traditionalists. Shakespeare's audience was, after all, a broadly national one. It included many well-informed Londoners who viewed "Italianate" fashion neither with enthusiasm nor with alarm, but with satiric laughter. Such spectators would certainly have seen the point, for example, in Mercutio's witty diatribe at the expense of the new French style in fencing. The object of his scorn is Tybalt, who, according to Mercutio, "fights as you sing prick song" and fancies himself to be "the very butcher of a silk button." "Is not this a lamentable thing," asks Mercutio rhetorically, "that we should be thus afflicted with these strange flies, these fashionmongers, these pardon-me's, who stand so much on the new form that they cannot sit at ease on the old bench?" (*Romeo and Juliet*, 2.4.20–35). In a similar vein, Shakespeare's audience would have appreciated the joking in *The Merchant of Venice* about England's servile imitation of continental styles in clothes. "What say you, then, to Falconbridge, the young baron of England?" asks Nerissa of her mistress Portia concerning one of Portia's many suitors. Portia replies, "How oddly he is suited! I think he bought his doublet in Italy, his round hose in France, his bonnet in Germany, and his behavior everywhere" (1.2.64–74). Court butterflies in Shakespeare's plays who bow and scrape and fondle their plumed headgear, like Le Beau in *As You Like It* and Osric in *Hamlet*, are the objects of ridicule. Hotspur in *1 Henry IV*, proud northern aristocrat

that he is, has nothing but contempt for an effeminate courtier, "perfumèd like a milliner," who has come from King Henry to discuss the question of prisoners (1.3.36). Throughout Shakespeare's plays, the use of cosmetics generally has the negative connotation of artificial beauty used to conceal inward corruption, as in Claudius's reference to "the harlot's cheek, beautied with plast'ring art" (*Hamlet*, 3.1.52). Yet Shakespeare's treatment of newness in fashion is never shrill in tone. Nor does he fail in his dramas to give an honorable place to the ceremonial use of wealth and splendid costuming. His plays thus avoid both extremes in the controversy over changing fashions, though they give plentiful evidence as to the liveliness and currency of the topic.

Shakespeare also reflects a contemporary interest in the problem of usury, especially in *The Merchant of Venice*. Although usury was becoming more and more of a necessity, emotional attitudes toward it changed only slowly. The traditional moral view condemned usury as forbidden by Christian teaching; on the other hand, European governments of the sixteenth century found themselves increasingly obliged to borrow large sums of money. The laws against usury were alternatively relaxed and enforced, according to the economic exigencies of the moment. Shakespeare's plays capture the Elizabethan ambivalence of attitude toward this feared but necessary practice (see Introduction to *The Merchant of Venice*). Similarly, most Englishmen had contradictory attitudes toward what we today would call the law of supply and demand in the marketplace. Conservative moralists complained bitterly when merchants exploited the scarcity of some commodity by forcing up prices; the practice was denounced as excessive profit taking and declared to be sinful, like usury. In economic policy, then, as in matters of changing fashion or increased social mobility, many Englishmen were ambivalent about the perennial conflict between the old order and the new.

Tudor mansions were often splendid, with impressive gardens and terraces. Shown here is Little Moreton Hall, in Cheshire, built in 1559.

Elizabethan Houses

Those fortunate Englishmen who grew wealthy in the reign of Elizabeth took special pleasure in building themselves fine new houses with furnishings to match. Chimneys were increasingly common, so that smoke no longer had to escape through a hole in the roof. Pewter, or even silver dishes, took the place of the wooden spoon and trencher. Beds, and even pillows, became common. Carpets were replacing rushes as covering for the floors; wainscoting, tapestries or hangings, and pictures appeared on the walls; and glass began to be used extensively for windows.

Despite the warnings of those moralists who preached against the vanity of worldly acquisition, domestic comfort made considerable progress in Elizabethan England. Many splendid Tudor mansions stand today, testifying to the important social changes that had taken place between the strife-torn fifteenth century and the era of relative peace under Elizabeth. The battlement, the moat, the fortified gate, and the narrow window used for archery or firearms generally disappeared in favor of handsome gardens and terraces. At the lower end of the social scale, the agricultural laborers who constituted the great mass of the English population were generally poor, malnourished, and uneducated, but they seem to have enjoyed greater physical security than did their ancestors in the fifteenth century, and no longer needed to bring their cows, pigs, and poultry into their dwellings at night in order to protect them from thieves. City houses, of which many exist today, were often large and imposing structures, three or four stories in height, and framed usually of strong oak with the walls filled in with brick and plaster. Although the frontage on the streets of London was usually narrow, many houses had trees and handsome gardens at the rear. Of course London also had its plentiful share of tenements for the urban poor.

With the finer houses owned by the fortunate elite came features of privacy that had been virtually unknown to previous generations. Life in the household of a medieval lord had generally focused on the great hall, which could serve variously as the kitchen, dining hall, and sitting room for the entire family and its retainers. The men drank in the hall in the evenings and slept there at night. The new dwellings of prosperous Elizabethans, on the other hand, featured private chambers into which the family and the chief guests could retire.

The Elizabethans built well. Not only do we still admire their houses, but also we can see from their oriel windows and stained glass, their broad staircases, their jewels, and their costumes that they treasured the new beauty of their lives made possible by the culture of the Renaissance. Although the graphic and plastic arts did not thrive in England to the same extent as in Italy, France, and the Low Countries, England made lasting achievements in architecture, as well as in music, drama, and all forms of literature.

THE POLITICAL AND RELIGIOUS BACKGROUND

England under the Tudors suffered from almost unceasing religious conflict. The battle over religion affected every aspect of life and none more so than politics. At the very beginning of the Tudor reign, to be sure, England's problem was not religious but dynastic. Henry VII, the first of the Tudor kings, brought an end to the devastating civil wars of the fifteenth century with his overthrow of Richard III at the battle of Bosworth Field in 1485. The civil wars thus ended were the so-called Wars of the Roses, between the Lancastrian House of Henry VI (symbolized by the red rose) and the Yorkist House of Edward IV (symbolized by the white rose). Shakespeare chose these eventful struggles as the subject for his first series of English history plays, from *Henry VI* in three parts to *Richard III*. The House of Lancaster drew its title from John of Gaunt, Duke of Lancaster, father of Henry IV and great-grandfather of Henry VI; the House of York drew its title from Edmund Langley, Duke of York, great-grandfather of Edward IV and Richard III. Because John of Gaunt and Edmund Langley had been brothers, virtually all the noble contestants in this War of the Roses were cousins of one another, caught in a remorseless dynastic struggle for control of the English crown. Many of them lost their lives in the fighting. By 1485, England was exhausted from civil conflict. Although Henry VII's own

On Sundays crowds gathered to listen to the sermon at St. Paul's Cathedral, the subject of this anonymous painting dated 1616.

dynastic claim to the throne was weak, he managed to suppress factional opposition and to give England the respite from war so desperately needed. His son, Henry VIII, inherited a throne in 1509 that was more secure than it had been in nearly a century.

Henry VIII's notorious marital difficulties, however, soon brought an end to dynastic security and civil accord. Moreover, religious conflict within the Catholic Church was growing to the extent that a break with Rome appeared inevitable. Henry's marriage troubles precipitated that momentous event. Because he divorced his first wife, Katharine of Aragon, in 1530 without the consent of Rome, he was excommunicated by the pope. His response in 1534 was to have himself proclaimed "Protector and only Supreme Head of the Church and Clergy of England." This decisive act signaled the beginning of the Reformation in England, not many years after Martin Luther's momentous break with the papacy in 1517 and the consequent beginning of Lutheran Protestantism on the Continent. In England, Henry's act of defiance split the Church and the nation. Many persons chose Sir Thomas More's path of martyrdom rather than submit to Henry's new title as supreme head of the English church. Henry's later years did witness a period of retrenchment in religion, after the downfall of Thomas Cromwell in 1540, and indeed Henry's break with Rome had had its origin in political and marital strife as well as in matters of dogma and liturgy. Nevertheless, the establishment of an English church was now an accomplished fact. The accession of Henry's ten-year-old son Edward VI in 1547 gave reformers an opportunity to bring about rapid changes in English Protestantism. Archbishop Cranmer's forty-two articles of religion (1551) and his prayer book laid the basis for the Anglican Church of the sixteenth century.

The death of the sickly Edward VI in 1553 brought with it an intense crisis in religious politics and a temporary reversal of England's religious orientation. The Duke of Northumberland, Protector and virtual ruler of England in Edward's last years, attempted to secure a Protestant succession and his own power by marrying his son to Lady Jane Grey, a granddaughter of Henry VII, whom Edward had named heir to the throne, but the proclamation of Lady Jane as Queen ended in failure. She was executed, as were her husband and father-in-law. For five years, England returned to Catholicism under the rule of Edward's elder sister Mary, daughter of the Catholic Queen Katharine of Aragon. The crisis accompanying such changes of government during this midcentury period was greatly exacerbated by the fact that all three of Henry VIII's living children were considered illegitimate by one faction or another of the English people. In Protestant eyes, Mary was the daughter of the divorced Queen Katharine, whose marriage to Henry had never been valid because she had previous-

ly been the spouse of Henry VIII's older brother Arthur. This Arthur had died at a young age, in 1502, shortly after his state marriage to the Spanish princess. If, as the Protestants insisted, Arthur had consummated the marriage, then Katharine's subsequent union with her deceased husband's brother was invalid, and Henry was free, instead, to marry Anne Boleyn—the mother-to-be of Elizabeth. In Catholic eyes, however, both Elizabeth and her brother Edward VI (son of Jane Seymour, Henry VIII's third wife) were the bastard issue of Henry's bigamous marriages; Henry's one and only true marriage in the Catholic faith was that to Katharine of Aragon. Edward and Elizabeth were regarded by many Catholics, at home and abroad, not only as illegitimate children, but also as illegitimate rulers, to be disobeyed and even overthrown by force. Thus, dynastic and marital conflicts became matters of grave political consequence.

Because of these struggles, Elizabeth's accession to the throne in 1558 remained an uncertainty until the last moment. Once she actually became ruler, England returned once more to the Protestant faith. Even then, tact and moderation were required to prevent open religious war. Elizabeth's genius at compromise prompted her to seek a middle position for her church, one that combined an episcopal form of church government (owing no allegiance to the pope) with an essentially traditional form of liturgy and dogma. As much as was practicable, she left matters up to individual conscience; she drew the line, however, where matters of conscience tended to "exceed their bounds and grow to be matter of faction." In practice, this meant that she did not tolerate avowed Catholics on the religious right or Protestant sects who denied the doctrine of the Trinity on the religious left. The foundation for this so-called Elizabethan compromise was the thirty-nine articles, adopted in 1563 and based in many respects upon Cranmer's forty-two articles of 1551. The compromise did not please everyone, of course, but it did achieve a remarkable degree of consensus during Elizabeth's long reign.

Queen Elizabeth and Tudor Absolutism

Elizabeth had to cope with a religiously divided nation and with extremists of both the right and the left who wished her downfall. She was a woman, in an age openly skeptical of women's ability or right to rule. Her success in dealing with such formidable odds was in large measure the result of her personal style as a monarch. Her combination of imperious will and femininity and her brilliant handling of her many contending male admirers have become legendary. She remained unmarried throughout her life, in part, at least, because marriage would have upset the delicate balance she maintained among rival groups, both foreign and domestic. Marriage

The Knights of the Garter belonged to the highest order of knighthood; many were influential courtiers and favorites of Queen Elizabeth. A masterful politician, Elizabeth remained unmarried throughout her life. A marriage would have upset the political balance and would have committed her to one foreign nation or to one constituency at home.

would have committed her irretrievably to either one foreign nation or to one constituency at home. She chose instead to bestow her favor on certain courtiers, notably Robert Dudley (whom she elevated to be the Earl of Leicester) and, after Leicester's death in 1588, Robert Devereux, second Earl of Essex. Her relationship with these men, despite her partiality to them, was marked by her outbursts of tempestuous jealousy. In addition, she relied on the staid counsel of her hard-working ministers: Lord Burghley, Sir Francis Walsingham, Burghley's son Robert Cecil, and a few others.

In her personal style as monarch, Elizabeth availed herself of the theory of absolute supremacy. Under all the Tudors, England was nominally at least an absolute monarchy in an age when many of England's greatest rivals—France, Spain, the Holy Roman Empire—were also under absolutist rule. "Absolutism" meant that the monarch served for life, could not legally be removed from office, and was normally succeeded by his eldest son—all of this bolstered by claims of divine sanction, though the claims were frequently contested. The rise of absolutism throughout Renaissance Europe was the result of an increase of centralized national power and a corresponding decrease in autonomous baronial influence. Henry VII's strong assertion of his royal authority

at the expense of the feudal lords corresponded roughly in time with the ascendancy of Francis I of France (1515) and Charles V of the Holy Roman Empire (1519). Yet England had long enjoyed a tradition of rule by consensus. When Elizabeth came to the throne, England was already in some ways a "limited" monarchy. Parliament, and especially the members of the House of Commons, claimed prerogatives of their own and were steadily gaining in both experience and power. In the mid-1560s, for example, the Commons made repeated attempts to use parliamentary tax-levying authority as a means of obliging Elizabeth to name a Protestant successor to the throne. The attempt, despite its failure to achieve its immediate goal, was significant; the Commons had shown that they were a force to be reckoned with. Even though Elizabeth made skillful rhetorical use of the theory of absolutism, portraying herself as God's appointed deputy on earth, her idea of absolutism should not be confused with despotism. To be sure, Elizabeth learned to avoid parliamentary interference in her affairs whenever possible; there were only thirteen sessions of Parliament in her forty-five years of rule. Still, Parliament claimed the right to establish law and to levy taxes on which the monarchy had to depend. Elizabeth needed all her considerable diplomatic skills in dealing with her parliaments and with the English people, who were self-reliant and proud of their reputation for independence. Elizabeth had more direct authority over her Privy Council, since she could appoint its members herself, yet even here she consulted faithfully with them on virtually everything she did. Nor were her closest advisers reluctant to offer her advice. Many vocal leaders in her government, including Walsingham and Leicester, urged the Queen during the 1570s and 1580s to undertake a more active military role on the Continent against the Catholic powers. So did her later favorite, the Earl of Essex. With remarkable tact, she managed to retain the loyalty of her militant and sometimes exasperated counselors, and yet to keep England out of war with Spain until that country actually launched an invasion attempt in 1588 (the Great Armada).

Catholic Opposition

During her early years, Elizabeth sought through her religious compromise to ease the divisions of her kingdom and attempted to placate her enemies abroad (notably Philip of Spain) rather than involve England in a costly war. For about twelve years, while England's economy gained much-needed strength, this policy of temporizing succeeded. Yet Elizabeth's more extreme Catholic oppo-

nents at home and abroad could never be reconciled to the daughter of that Protestant "whore," Anne Boleyn. England's period of relative accommodation came to an end in 1569 and 1570, with Catholic uprisings in the north and with papal excommunication of the English Queen. As a declared heretic, Elizabeth's very life was in danger; her Catholic subjects were encouraged by Rome to disobey her and to seek means for her violent overthrow.

Conspirators did, in fact, make attempts on the Queen's life, notably in the so-called Babington conspiracy of 1586, named for one of the chief participants. This plot, brought to light by Secretary of State Walsingham, sought to place Mary, Queen of Scots on the English throne in Elizabeth's stead. Mary was Elizabeth's kinswoman; Mary's grandmother, sister to Henry VIII, had been married to James IV of Scotland. So long as Elizabeth remained childless, Mary was a prominent heir to the English throne. Catholics pinned their hopes on her succession, by force if necessary; Protestant leaders urged Elizabeth to marry and give birth to a Protestant heir or at least to name a Protestant successor. Mary had abdicated the Scottish throne in 1567 after the sensational murder of her Catholic counselor David Rizzio, the murder of Mary's husband, the Earl of Darnley (in which Mary was widely suspected to have taken part), and her subsequent

Along with the defeat of the Spanish Armada in 1588, the 1587 beheading of Mary, Queen of Scots, shown holding a crucifix and surrounded by official witnesses in this contemporary illustration, virtually ended any serious Catholic challenge to Elizabeth's throne.

marriage to Darnley's slayer, the Earl of Bothwell. Taking refuge in England, Mary remained a political prisoner and the inevitable focus of Catholic plotting against Elizabeth for approximately two decades. She, in fact, assented in writing to Babington's plot against Elizabeth. All that long while Elizabeth resisted demands from her Protestant advisers that she execute her kinswoman and thereby end a constant threat to the throne; Elizabeth was reluctant to kill a fellow monarch and agreed fully with Mary's son James that "anointing by God cannot be defiled by man." Nonetheless, Mary's clear involvement in the Babington conspiracy led to the so-called Bond of Association, in which thousands of Englishmen pledged to prevent the succession of any person plotting Elizabeth's death, and then at last to Mary's execution in 1587. By that time, Spain was mounting an invasion against England, the Great Armada of 1588, and Elizabeth's temporizing tactics were no longer feasible. The long years of peace had done their work, however, and England was considerably stronger and more resolute than thirty years before. With Elizabeth's tacit approval, Sir Francis Drake and other naval commanders carried the fighting to Spain's very shore and to her American colonies. The war with Spain continued from 1588 until about 1597.

Elizabeth's great compromise dealt not only with the political dangers of opposition but also with the more cen-tral theological issues. England was sorely divided, as was much of Europe, on such matters as whether Christ's body was transubstantially present in the Mass, as Catholic faith maintained; whether good works were efficacious in salvation or whether people could be saved by God's grace alone, as the Reformers insisted; whether a portion of humankind was predeterminately damned, as the Calvinists believed; and the like. During the turbulent years of the Reformation, many people died for their faith. In general, the Elizabethan compromise insisted on allegiance to the English throne, church, and ecclesiastical hierarchy but allowed some latitude in matters of faith. The degree of elaboration in vestments and ritual was also an explosive issue on which the English church attempted to steer a central and pragmatic course, although conflicts inevitably arose within the church itself.

Protestant Opposition

The threat from the Protestant left was no less worrisome than that from the Catholic right. Protestant reformers had experienced their first taste of power at the time of Henry VIII's break with Rome in 1534. Under Thomas Cromwell, Cardinal Wolsey's successor as the King's chief minister, the monasteries were suppressed and William Tyndale's English Bible was authorized. The execution of Cromwell introduced a period of conservative retrenchment, but the accession of Edward VI in 1547 brought reform once more into prominence. Thereafter, Mary's Catholic reign drove most of the reformers into exile on the Continent. When they returned after 1558, many had been made more radical by their continental experience.

To be sure, reform covered a wide spectrum, from moderation to radicalism. Some preferred to work within the existing hierarchical structure of church and state, whereas others were religious separatists. Only the more radical groups, such as the Brownists and Anabaptists, endorsed ideas of equality and communal living. The abusive epithet "Puritan," applied indiscriminately to all reformers, tended to obscure the wide range of difference in the reform movement. The reformers were, to some extent, united by a dislike for formal ritual and ecclesiastical garments, by a preference for a simple and pious manner of living, and by a belief in the literal word of the Bible rather than the traditional teachings of the church fathers. They stressed personal responsibility in religion and were Calvinist in their emphasis on human depravity and the need for grace through election. Yet at first only the more radical were involved in a movement to separate entirely from the established English church.

The radicals on the religious left, even if they represented at first only a minority of the reformers, posed a serious threat to Elizabeth's government. Their program bore an ironic resemblance to that of the Catholic opposition on the religious right. In their theoretical writings, the extreme reformers justified overthrow of what they considered to be tyrannical rule, just as Catholic spokesmen had absolved Elizabeth's subjects of obedience to her on the grounds that she was illegitimate. Both extremes appealed to disobedience in the name of a higher religious law, as enunciated in Romans 13:1–2: "For there is no power but of God." Among the reforming theoreticians was John Ponet, whose *Short Treatise of Politic Power* (1556) argued that a monarch is subject to a social contract and must rule according to laws that are equally subscribed to by Parliament, the clergy, and the people.

The Doctrine of Passive Obedience

Elizabeth's government countered such assaults on its authority, from both the right and the left, with many arguments, of which perhaps the most central was that of passive obedience. This doctrine condemned rebellion under virtually all circumstances. Its basic assumption was that the king or queen is God's appointed deputy on earth. To depose such a monarch must therefore be an act of disobedience against God's will. Since God is all-wise and all-powerful, his placing of an evil ruler in power must proceed from some divine intention, such as the punishment of a wayward people. Rebellion against

God's "scourge" merely displays further disobedience to God's will. A people suffering under a tyrant must wait patiently for God to remove the burden, which he will surely do when the proper time arrives.

This doctrine was included in the official book of homilies of the Church of England and was read from the pulpit at regular intervals. The best-known such homily, entitled *Against Disobedience and Willful Rebellion,* had been preceded by such tracts as William Tyndale's *Obedience of a Christian Man* (1528); a book of homilies, published in 1547, including an "Exhortation Concerning Good Order and Obedience"; Thomas Cranmer's *Notes for a Sermon on the Rebellion of 1549;* and Hugh Latimer's *Sermon on the Lord's Prayer* (1552). Shakespeare heard such homilies often, and he expresses their ideas through several of his characters, such as John of Gaunt and the Bishop of Carlisle in *Richard II* (1.2.37–41, 4.1.115–50). This is not to say that he endorses such ideas, for he sets them in dramatic opposition to other and more heterodox concepts. We can say, nevertheless, that Shakespeare's audience would have recognized in Gaunt's speeches a clear expression of a familiar and officially correct position.

The Political Ideas of Machiavelli

The orthodoxies of the Elizabethan establishment were under attack, not only from the Catholic right and the Protestant left, but also from a new and revolutionary point of view that set aside all criteria of religious morality. Tudor defense of order was based, as we have seen, on the assumption that the monarch rules in accord with a divine plan, a higher Law of Nature to which every just ruler is attuned. Political morality must be at one with religious morality. Catholic and Protestant critiques of the Tudor establishment made similar assumptions, even though they appealed to revolution in the name of that religious morality. To Niccolò Machiavelli, on the other hand, politics was a manipulative science best governed by the dictates of social expediency. His philosophy did not, as many accusingly charged, lead necessarily to the cynical promotion of mere self-interest. Nevertheless, he did argue, in his *Discourses* and *The Prince,* that survival and political stability are the first obligations of any ruler. Machiavelli regarded religion as a tool of the enlightened ruler rather than as a morally absolute guide. He extolled in his ideal leader the quality of *virtù*—a mixture of cunning and forcefulness. He saw history as a subject offering practical lessons in the kind of pragmatic statecraft he proposed.

Machiavelli was a hated name in England, and most of his works were never available in an English printed edition during Shakespeare's lifetime. (The *Florentine History* was translated in 1595; *The Prince* was not translated until 1640.) Nevertheless, his writings were available in Italian, French, and Latin editions, and in manuscript English translations. His ideas certainly had a profound impact on the England of the 1590s. Marlowe caricatures the Italian writer in his *The Jew of Malta,* but he clearly was fascinated by what Machiavelli had to say. Shakespeare, too, reveals a complex awareness. However much he may lampoon the Machiavellian type of conscienceless villain in *Richard III,* he shows us more plausible pragmatists in *Richard II* and *1 Henry IV.* Conservative theories of the divine right of kings are set in debate with the more heterodox ambitions of Henry Bolingbroke (who then adopts the most orthodox of political vocabularies once he is king). Bolingbroke is not a very attractive figure, but he does succeed politically where Richard has failed.

Shakespeare thus reveals himself as less a defender of the established order than as a great dramatist able to give sympathetic expression to the aspirations of all sides in a tense political struggle. His history plays have been variously interpreted either as defenses of monarchy or as subtle pleas for rebellion, but the consensus today is that the plays use political conflict as a way of probing the motivations of social behavior. To be sure, the plays do stress the painful consequences of disorder and present, on the whole, an admiring view of monarchy (especially in *Henry V*), despite the manifest limitations of that institution. Certainly, we can sense that Shakespeare's history plays were written for a generation of Englishmen who had experienced political crisis and who could perceive issues of statecraft in Shakespeare's plays that were relevant to England's struggles in the 1580s and the 1590s. The play of *King John,* for example, deals with a king whose uncertain claim to the throne is challenged by France and the papacy in the name of John's nephew, Arthur; Elizabeth faced a similar situation in her dilemma over her kinswoman, Mary, Queen of Scots. Elizabeth also bitterly acknowledged the cogency of a popular analogy comparing her reign with that of King Richard II, and, when Shakespeare's play about Bolingbroke's overthrow of Richard was apparently revived for political purposes shortly before the Earl of Essex's abortive rebellion against Elizabeth in 1601, Shakespeare's acting company had some explaining to do to the authorities (see Introduction to *Richard II*). Nevertheless, Shakespeare's attitudes toward the issues of his own day are ultimately unknowable and unimportant, since his main concern seems to have been with the dramatization of political conflict rather than with the urging of a polemical position.

Shakespeare on Religion

Our impressions of Shakespeare's personal sympathies in religion are similarly obscured by his refusal to use his art for polemical purposes. To be sure, members of his mother's family in Warwickshire seem to have remained loyal to Catholicism, and his father John Shakespeare may conceivably have undergone financial and other difficulties in Stratford for reasons of faith. (See "Shakespeare's Family" below, in the section on Shakespeare's Life and Work.) Certainly Shakespeare himself displays a familiarity with some Catholic practices and theology, as when the Ghost of Hamlet's father speaks of being "Unhousled, disappointed, unaneled" (i.e., not having received last rites) at the time of his murder (*Hamlet,* 1.5.78). Nonetheless, we see in his plays a spectrum of religious attitudes portrayed with an extraordinary range of insight. In matters of doctrine, his characters are at various times acquainted with Catholic theology or with the controversy concerning salvation by faith or good works (see *Measure for Measure,* 1.2.24–5), and yet a consistent polemical bias is absent. Some Catholic prelates are schemers, like Pandulph in *King John.* Ordinarily, however, Shakespeare's satirical digs at ecclesiastical pomposity and hypocrisy have little to do with the Catholic question. Cardinal Beaufort in *1 Henry VI* is a political maneuverer, but so are many of his secular rivals. Cardinal Wolsey in *Henry VIII* is motivated by personal ambition, rather than by any sinister conspiracy of the international church. Many of Shakespeare's nominally Catholic clerics, such as Friar Laurence in *Romeo and Juliet* or Friar Francis in *Much Ado About Nothing,* are gentle and well-intentioned people, even if occasionally bumbling. We can certainly say that Shakespeare consistently avoids the chauvinistic anti-Catholic baiting so often found in the plays of his contemporaries.

The same avoidance of extremes can be seen in his portrayal of Protestant reformers, though the instances in this case are few. Malvolio in *Twelfth Night* is fleetingly compared with a "puritan" (2.3.139–46), although Shakespeare insists that no extensive analogy can be made. Angelo in *Measure for Measure* is sometimes thought to be a critical portrait of the Puritan temperament. Even if this were so, Shakespeare's satire is extremely indirect compared with the lampoons written by his contemporaries Ben Jonson and Thomas Dekker.

Stuart Absolutism

Queen Elizabeth's successor, James I of the Scottish house of Stuarts, reigned from 1603 to 1625. Even more than Elizabeth, he was a strong believer in the divinely appointed authority of kings; whereas she had insisted on divine sanction, James and his successor Charles called it a divine right. Although James succeeded easily to the throne in 1603, since he was Protestant with a legitimate claim of descent from Henry VIII, the English people did not take to this foreigner from the north. James was eccentric in his personal habits, and the English were always inclined to be suspicious of the Scots in any case. As a result, James was less successful in dealing with the heterogeneous and antagonistic forces that Elizabeth had kept in precarious balance. At the Hampton Court Conference of 1604, relations quickly broke down between James and the Puritan wing of the church, so that even its more moderate adherents joined forces with the separatists. James had similar difficulties with an increasingly radical group in the House of Commons. In the widening rift between the absolutists and those who defended the supremacy of Parliament, James's court moved toward the right. Catholic sympathies at court became common. Civil war was still a long way off and by no means inevitable; the beheading of King Charles I (James's son) would not occur until 1649. Still, throughout James's reign, the estrangement between the right and the left was becoming more and more uncomfortable. The infamous Gunpowder Plot of 1605, in which Guy Fawkes and other Catholic conspirators were accused of having plotted to blow up the houses of Parliament, raised hysteria to a new intensity. Penal laws against papists were harshly enforced. The Parliament of 1614 included in its membership John Pym, Thomas Wentworth, and John Eliot—men who were to become turbulent spokesmen against taxes imposed without parliamentary grant, imprisonment without the stating of specific criminal charges, and other purported abuses of royal power. The polarization of English society naturally affected the London theaters. Popular London audiences (generally sympathetic with religious reform) eventually grew disaffected with the stage, while even the popular acting companies came under the increasing domination of the court. Shakespeare's late plays reflect the increasing influence of a courtly audience.

THE INTELLECTUAL BACKGROUND

Renaissance Cosmology

In learning, as in politics and religion, Shakespeare's England was a time of conflict and excitement. Medieval ideas of a hierarchical and ordered creation were under attack but were still widely prevalent, and were used to justify a hierarchical order in society itself. According to the so-called Ptolemaic system of the universe, formulated by Ptolemy of Alexandria in the second century A.D., the earth stood at the center of creation. Around it moved, in nine concentric spheres, the heavenly bodies of the visible universe, in order as follows (from the earth outward): the moon, Mercury, Venus, the sun, Mars, Jupiter, Saturn, the fixed stars on a single plane, and lastly the *primum mobile,* imparting motion to the whole system. (See the accompanying illustration.) Some commentators proposed alternate arrangements or speculated as to the existence of one or two additional spheres, in particular a "crystalline sphere" between the fixed stars and the *primum mobile.* These additional spheres were needed to cope with matters not adequately explained in Ptolema-

ic astronomy, such as the precession of the equinoxes. More troublesomely, the seemingly erratic retrograde motion of the planets—that is, the refusal of Mars and other planets to move around the earth in steady orbit—called forth increasingly ingenious theories, such as Tycho Brahe's scheme of epicycles. Still, the conservative appeal of the earth-centered cosmos remained very strong. How could one suppose that the earth was not at the center of the universe?

The *primum mobile* was thought to turn the entire universe around the earth once every twenty-four hours. Simultaneously, the individual heavenly bodies moved more slowly around the earth on their individual spheres, constantly changing position with respect to the fixed stars. The moon, being the only heavenly body that seemed subject to change in its monthly waxing and waning, was thought to represent the boundary between the unchanging universe and the incessantly changing world. Beneath the moon, in the "sublunary" sphere, all creation was subject to death as a result of Adam's fall from grace; beyond the moon lay perfection. Hell was imagined to exist deep within the earth, as in Dante's *Inferno,* or else outside the *primum mobile* and far below the created universe in the realm of chaos, as in Milton's *Paradise Lost.*

Heaven or the Empyrean stood, according to most Ptolemaic systems, at the top of the universe. Between heaven and earth dwelled the nine angelic orders, each associated with one of the nine concentric spheres. According to a work attributed to Dionysius the Areopagite, *On the Heavenly Hierarchy* (fifth century A.D.), the nine angelic orders consisted of three hierarchies. Closest to God were the contemplative orders of Seraphim, Cherubim, and Thrones; next, the intermediate orders of Dominions, Powers, and Virtues; and finally the active orders of Principalities, Archangels, and Angels. These last served as God's messengers and intervened from time to time in the affairs of mortals. Ordered life among humans, although manifestly imperfect when compared with the eternal bliss of the angelic orders, still modeled itself on that platonic idea of perfect harmony. Thus the state, the church, and the family all resembled one another because they resembled (however distantly) the kingdom of God. Richard Hooker, in his *Of the Laws of Ecclesiastical Polity* (1594–1597), defends the established Church of England in terms that emanate from a comparable idea of a divine, creative, and ordering law of nature "Whose seat is the bosom of God, whose voice the harmony of the world."

The devils of hell were fallen angels, with Satan as their leader. Such evil spirits might assume any number of shapes, such as demons, goblins, wizards, or witches. Believers in evil spirits generally made no distinction between orthodox Christian explanations of evil and the more primitive folklore of witchcraft. Belief in witchcraft was widespread indeed; King James I took the matter

Ptolemy's earth-centered system of the universe (top) was challenged by the sun-centered system of Copernicus (bottom) with the publishing of De revolutionibus orbium coelestium *in 1543. Shakespeare, like other major poets of the English Renaissance, poetically represents the universe in cosmic terms as described by Ptolemy, but also reflects uncertainties generated by the new cosmology.*

very seriously. So did Reginald Scot's *The Discovery of Witchcraft* (1584), though its author also attempted to confute what he regarded as ignorant superstition and charlatanism. Throughout Shakespeare's lifetime, belief and skepticism about such matters existed side by side.

A similar ambiguity pertained to belief in the Ptolemaic universe itself. All major poets of the Renaissance, including Shakespeare, Spenser, and Milton (who completed *Paradise Lost* after 1660), represented the universe in cosmic terms essentially as described by Ptolemy. Yet Nicolaus Copernicus's revolutionary theory of a sun-centered solar system (*De revolutionibus orbium coelestium,* published on the Continent in 1543) and the discovery of a new star in Cassiopeia in 1572 stimulated much new thought. Galileo Galilei, born in the same year as Shakespeare (1564), published in 1610 the results of his telescopic examinations of the moon, thereby further confirming Copernicus's hypothesis. Although the news of Galileo's astounding discovery came too late to affect any but the latest of Shakespeare's plays, a sense of excitement and dislocation was apparent throughout most of the years of his writing career. Thomas Nashe, in 1595, referred familiarly to Copernicus as the author "who held that the sun remains immobile in the center of the world, and that the earth is moved about the sun" (Nashe, *Works,* ed. R. B. McKerrow, 1904–1910, 3.94). John Donne lamented in 1611–1612 that the "new philosophy" (i.e., the new science) "calls all in doubt." Skeptical uncertainty about the cosmos was on the rise. The poetic affirmations in Renaissance art of traditional ideas of the cosmos can best be understood as a response to uncertainty—a statement of faith in an age of increasing skepticism.

Alchemy and Medicine

In all areas of Renaissance learning, the new and the old science were juxtaposed. Alchemy, for example, made important contributions to learning, despite its superstitious character. Its chief goal was the transformation of base metals into gold, on the assumption that all metals were ranked on a hierarchical scale and could be raised from lower to higher positions on that scale by means of certain alchemical techniques. Other aims of alchemy included the discovery of a universal cure for diseases and of a means for preserving life indefinitely. Such aims encouraged quackery and prompted various exposés, such as Chaucer's "The Canon's Yeoman's Tale" (late fourteenth century) and Jonson's *The Alchemist* (1610). Yet many of the procedures used in alchemy were essentially chemical procedures, and the science of chemistry received a valuable impetus from constant experimentation. Queen Elizabeth was seriously interested in alchemy throughout her life.

In physics, medicine, and psychology, as well, older concepts vied with new. Traditional learning apportioned

Alchemists employed relatively sophisticated equipment in their futile search for the "philosopher's stone," a reputed substance supposed to possess the property of changing other metals into gold and silver.

all physical matter into four elements: earth, air, fire, and water. Each of these was thought to be a different combination of the four "qualities" of the universe: hot, cold, moist, and dry. Earth combined cold and dry; air, hot and moist; fire, hot and dry; and water, cold and moist. Earth and water were the baser or lower elements, confined to the physical world; fire and air were aspiring elements, tending upward. Humans, as a microcosm of the larger universe, contained in themselves the four elements. The individual's temperament, or "humor" or "complexion," depended on which "humor" predominated in that person. The four humors in humans corresponded to the four elements of physical matter. The blood was hot and moist, like air; yellow bile or choler was hot and dry, like fire; phlegm was cold and moist, like water; and black bile was cold and dry, like earth. A predominance of blood in an individual created a sanguine or cheerful temperament (or humor), yellow bile produced a choleric or irascible temperament, phlegm produced a phlegmatic or stolid temperament, and black bile produced a melancholic temperament. Diet could affect the balance among these humors, since an excess of a particular food would stimulate overproduction of one humor. The stomach and the liver, which converted food into humors, were regarded as the seat of human passions. The spleen was thought to be the seat of laughter, sudden impulse, or caprice, and also melancholy. (Hotspur, in *1 Henry IV,* is said to be "governed by a spleen," 5.2.19.) Strong emotional reactions could be explained in terms of the physiology of the humors: in anger, the blood rushed to the head and thereby produced a flush of red color and staring eyes; in fear, the blood migrated to the heart and thus left the face and liver pale, and so on. Sighs supposedly cost the heart a

drop of blood, while wine could refortify it (as Falstaff insists in 2 *Henry IV,* 4.3.90–123). The signs of youth were warmth and moisture, as in Desdemona's "hot and moist" hand (*Othello,* 3.4.39); those of age were "a moist eye, a dry hand, a yellow cheek, a white beard, a decreasing leg, an increasing belly" (*2 Henry IV,* 1.2.179–81). A common remedy for illness was to let blood and thereby purge the body of unwanted humors.

The name traditionally associated with such theories was that of Galen, the most celebrated of ancient writers on medicine (c. 130 A.D.). A more revolutionary name was that of Paracelsus, a famous German physician (c. 1493–1541) who attacked the traditional medical learning of his time and urged a more unfettered pragmatic research into pharmacy and medicine. Such experimentalism bore fruit in the anatomical research of Vesalius (1514–1564) and in William Harvey's investigations of the circulation of the blood (c. 1616). Nevertheless, the practice of medicine in Renaissance times remained under the

The four humors of black bile, blood, yellow bile or choler, and phlegm, as shown in this illustration from an illuminated manuscript, were believed to govern the human personality by producing a disposition toward melancholic, sanguine, choleric, or phlegmatic temperaments.

influence of the "humors" theory until quite late, and its ideas are found throughout Shakespeare's writings.

Learning

In learning generally, and in theories of education, new ideas conflicted with old. The curriculum of schools and colleges in the Renaissance was inherited largely from the Middle Ages and displayed many traditional characteristics. The curriculum consisted of the seven Liberal Arts: a lower division, called the trivium, comprised of grammar, rhetoric, and logic; and an upper division, called the quadrivium, comprised of arithmetic, geometry, astronomy, and music. In addition, there were the philosophical studies associated chiefly with Aristotle: natural philosophy, ethics, and metaphysics.

Aristotle's name had a towering influence in medieval times and remained important to the Renaissance as well. Even among his Renaissance admirers, however, Aristotle proved more compelling in practical matters than in the abstract scholastic reasoning associated with his name in the Middle Ages. The Italian Aristotelians whose work made its way into England were interested primarily in the science of human behavior. Aristotelian ethics was for them a practical subject, telling people how to live usefully and well and how to govern themselves politically. Rhetoric was the science of persuasion, enabling people to use eloquence for socially useful goals. Poetry was a kind of rhetoric, a language of persuasion which dramatists, too, might use for morally pragmatic ends.

At the same time, new thinkers were daring to attack Aristotle by name as a symbol of traditional medieval thought. The attack was not always fair to Aristotle himself, whose work had been bent to the *a priori* purposes of much medieval scholasticism. Nevertheless, his name had assumed such symbolic importance that he had to be confronted directly. The Huguenot logician Petrus Ramus (1515–1572), defiantly proclaiming that "everything that Aristotle taught is false," argued for rules of logic as derived from observation. He urged, for example, that his students learn about rhetoric from observing in detail Cicero's effect on his listeners, rather than by the rote practice of syllogism. Actually, Ramus's thought was less revolutionary in its concepts of logic than in the tremendous ferment of opinion caused by his iconoclastic teaching.

A basic issue at stake in the anti-Aristotelian movement was that of traditional authority versus independent observation. How do people best acquire true knowledge—through the teachings of their predecessors or through their own discovery? The issue had profound implications for religious truth as well: should individuals heed the collective wisdom of the earthly church or read the Bible with their individual perceptions as their guide? Is "reason" an accretive wisdom handed down by authority or a quality of the individual soul? Obviously, a middle ground exists between the two extremes, and no new thinker of the Renaissance professed to abandon entirely the use of ancient authority. For men like Henricus Agrippa (1486–1535) and Sir Francis Bacon (1561–1626), however, scholastic tradition had exerted its oppressive influence far too long. Authority needed to be examined critically and scientifically. Bacon, in his *The Advancement of Learning* (1605), fought against the blind acceptance of ancient wisdom and argued that "knowledge derived from Aristotle, and exempted from liberty of examination, will not rise again higher than the knowledge of Aristotle." Sir Walter Ralegh and others joined in the excited new search for what human "reason" could discover when set free from scholastic restraint. Such belief in the perfectibility of human reason owed some of its inspiration to Italian Neoplatonic humanists like Giovanni Pico della Mirandola (1463–1494), who, in his *Oration on the Dignity of Man*, celebrated a human race "constrained by no limits" in accordance with the potential of its own free will. The new learning did not seem to trouble these men in their religious faith, although a tension between scientific observation and faith in miracles was to become plentifully evident in the seventeenth century.

The Nature of Humankind

Medieval thought generally assigned to humankind a uniquely superior place in the order of creation on earth. That assumption of superiority rested on biblical and patristic teachings about the hierarchy of creation, in which humanity stood at the apex of physical creation nearest God and the angels. Humankind was thus supreme on earth in the so-called chain of being. Human reason, though subject to error because of sinfulness, enabled humans to aspire toward divinity. Humans were, in the view of medieval philosophers, the great amphibians, as well as the microcosm of the universe, part bestial and part immortal, doomed by Adam's fall to misery and death in this life but promised eternal salvation through Christ's atonement. Right reason, properly employed, could lead to the truths of revealed Christianity and thus give humankind a glimpse of the heavenly perfection one day to be ours. Renaissance Neoplatonism, as expounded, for example, in the writings of Marsilio Ficino, Pico della Mirandola, and Baldassare Castiglione (in *The Courtier*, translated by Sir Thomas Hoby in 1561), offered humanity a vision of a platonic ladder, extending from the perception of physical beauty to contemplation of the platonic idea of beauty and finally to the experiencing of God's transcendent love.

Protestant thought of the Renaissance did not wholly disagree with this formulation, but it did place a major new emphasis on human reprobation. The idea was not new, for Saint Augustine (354–430) had insisted on human depravity and our total dependence on God's inscrutable grace, but, in the years of the Reformation, this theology took on a new urgency. Martin Luther (1483–1540), by rejecting veneration of the Virgin Mary and the saints, and by taking away the sacraments of confession and penance, by which individual Christians could seek the institutional comforts of the Catholic Church, exposed the individual sinner to agonies of conscience that could result in a sense of alienation and loss. The rewards were great for those who found new faith in God's infinite goodness, but the hazards of predestinate damnation were fearsome to those who were less sure of their spiritual welfare. Luther's God was inscrutable, majestic, and infallible. Luther's God decreed salvation for the elect and damnation for all others, and His will could not be challenged or questioned. The individual was to blame for sin, even though God hardened the hearts of the reprobate. John Calvin (1509–1564) placed even greater stress on predestinate good and evil and insisted that the grace of salvation was founded on God's freely given mercy that humans could not possibly deserve. Salvation was God's to give or withhold as He

wished; humans might not repine that in His incomprehensible wisdom God has "barred the door of life to those whom He has given over to damnation." Faced with such a view of human spiritual destiny, the individual Christian's lot was one of potential tragedy. The human soul was a battleground of good and evil.

Michel de Montaigne (1533–1592), Shakespeare's great French contemporary, provided a very different and heterodox way of thinking about human imperfection. In his "Apology for Raymond Sebond" and other of his essays, Montaigne questioned the assumption of humanity's superiority to the animal kingdom, and in doing so gave Shakespeare a fundamentally different way to consider the nature of humankind—a way that reflects itself, for example, in Hamlet's observations on humans as "quintessence of dust." Montaigne stressed humans' arrogance, vanity, and frailty. He was unconvinced of humanity's purported moral superiority to the animals and argued that animals are no less endowed with a soul. Montaigne undermined, in other words, the hierarchy in which the human race was the unquestioned master of the physical world, just as Copernican science overturned the earth-centered cosmos

This guide, graphically setting forth the ideals to which every English gentlewoman and gentleman should aspire, illustrates the Renaissance concept that outward deportment and accomplishments should correctly and invariably mirror a person's inner nature.

and Machiavelli's political system dismissed as an improbable fiction the divinely constituted hierarchy of the state. Montaigne's very choice of the essay as his favorite literary form bespeaks his commitment to attempts and explorations, rather than to definite solutions; etymologically, the very word "essay" signifies an exploration or inquiry. Montaigne was not alone in his skepticism about human nature; his ideas had much in common with Bernardino Telesio's *De Rerum Natura* and with the writings of the Italian Giordano Bruno. Montaigne was followed in the seventeenth century by that overpowering iconoclast, Thomas Hobbes, who extended the concept of mechanical laws governing human society and human psychology. Hobbes postdates Shakespeare, to be sure, but one has only to consider Iago's philosophy of the assertive individual will (in *Othello*) or Edmund's contempt for his father Gloucester's astrological pieties (in *King Lear*) to see the enormous impact on Shakespeare of the new heterodoxies of his age. Shakespeare makes us aware that skeptical thought can be used by dangerous men like Iago, Edmund, and Richard III to promote their own villainies in a world no longer held together by the certitudes of traditional faith, but he also shows us the gullibility of some traditionalists and the abuses of power that can be perpetrated in the name of ancient and divine privilege by a king like Richard II. Above all, Shakespeare delights in the play of mind among competing ideas, inviting us to wonder, for example, if Caliban in *The Tempest* is not invested with natural qualities that Prospero, his Christian colonizer, does not sufficiently understand, and whether some of the other supposedly civilized Europeans who come to Caliban's island do not have a great deal to learn from its uncivilized beauty.

THE DRAMA BEFORE SHAKESPEARE

When William Shakespeare made his first acquaintance with the professions of acting and playwriting in the late 1580s, the English theater was already a flourishing institution with a long and complex history. In order to understand what opportunities it offered Shakespeare, we need to look briefly at that history.

The Liturgical Drama

The sixth-century Catholic Church had been largely responsible for closing down the late Roman theater, with its bloody gladiatorial contests and its pervasive moral decadence. Thereafter, for about four centuries the theater officially did not exist in western Europe. Paradoxically, it was the Church in the tenth century that sponsored the beginnings of a new dramatic form within the liturgy (the prescribed form of worship) of the Church itself. This dramatic activity perhaps began as an insertion into the regular service of a "trope" or musical composition designed to be sung antiphonally by members of a monastic community. The earliest of these may have been composed for Easter morning, at the supremely important moment of Christ's Resurrection. The Mass itself had long displayed semidramatic characteristics, and the first Easter expansions must not have seemed particularly revolutionary to anyone involved. The simplest of the early tropes (though perhaps not the first), composed at St. Gall in Switzerland some time early in the tenth century, consists merely of a chanted interrogation, "*Quem quaeritis in sepulchro, Christicolae?*" ("Whom do you seek in the sepulcher, O followers of Christ?"), and a chanted response, "*Jesum Nazarenum crucifixum, o caelicolae*" ("Jesus of Nazareth who was crucified, O heaven-dwellers"), followed by an announcement that Christ is risen as he had predicted. From other early texts of this sort, we can guess that this simple antiphon was accompanied by some stylized semidramatic assignment of roles to members of the religious community as the three Marys visiting Christ's tomb and as the angels guarding the tomb. At any rate, tenth-century tropes of Easter soon included use of simple costumes, physical movement toward the tomb, and appropriate gestures.

Other actions were appropriate to such a dramatic representation of the Resurrection: the visit of the disciples to the sepulchre, the appearance of Christ as a gardener to Mary Magdalene, and his appearance to the disciples on the road to Emmaus. Moreover, other seasons of the year afforded similar opportunities, especially Christmas; the crèche was already a venerable custom, and Christmas tropes may have originated as early as Easter tropes or possibly even earlier.

In any event, Christmas liturgical dramatic activity grew apace, perhaps more rapidly than at Easter because of the sacred inhibitions associated with the Resurrection. By the twelfth century, Christmas liturgical drama had become lengthy and complex, including not only the visit of the shepherds and the Magi but also the slaughter of the innocents and the flight into Egypt. Simultaneously, liturgical plays were developed for other festivals in the liturgical calendar. Some were in the vernacular: by the end of the twelfth century, an Anglo-Norman poet had written a play of Adam featuring the creation of humankind, the expulsion from the garden of Eden, the slaughter of Abel by Cain, and a lengthy procession of prophets announcing the advent of Christ. Such early vernacular plays may well have influenced the development of Latin liturgical drama. The twelfth century also saw a play about Daniel in the lions' den, various Saint Nicholas plays in which that popular saint performed miracles, a play at Tegernsee about the Antichrist, a play about the conversion of Saint Paul, and many others. In other words, by 1200 or thereabouts, the liturgical drama had produced plays of considerable length and complexity for numerous religious festivals throughout the year. Montecassino in Italy had a complex Passion play by this date. The late twelfth or early thirteenth century saw the performance at Benediktbeuren in Germany of the impressive "Carmina Burana" plays for Easter and Christmas.

The Corpus Christi Play

Although one might suppose that these liturgical plays would be gathered together into larger cycles of the divine history of the world, compilations of this sort do not seem generally to have taken place. Liturgical plays continued to be performed individually at appropriate times in the Church calendar. Most religious communities owned and produced one or two such plays year after year, but no communities owned or produced very many such plays. The plays were numerous but scattered throughout western Europe.

What appears to have happened instead of the forming of liturgical plays into a cycle is that the various craft guilds of certain towns, especially in England, banded together with the ecclesiastical authorities to produce a summer festival that would be both civic and religious in nature. One impetus was the institution of the feast of Corpus Christi in the early fourteenth century. The feast was designed to honor the Eucharist (the sacrament of the Lord's Supper) in a joyous mood, uninhibited by the somber reflections on Christ's crucifixion that are appropriate to Passion Week. The date chosen, the Thursday after Trinity Sunday, came during a slack period in the liturgical calendar in very late spring. In May or June the days of the year are longest, and the English weather is generally cooperative. The cycles that thus originated were performed on other festivals of the early summer season besides Corpus Christi day, but that festival has given its name to the genre.

Corpus Christi plays were often performed either in procession on moving pageant wagons or in arena theaters with scaffolds located around the acting area. This illustration shows a procession around a square in Brussels in 1615, using staging methods perhaps not unlike those in use in England during the fifteenth and sixteenth centuries.

The feast of Corpus Christi regularly featured elaborate processions through town, and, indeed, these processions may have preceded the plays themselves. Various guilds were usually assigned events in the divine history of the world for which they undertook to present dramatized renditions. The plays written for such guilds had to be numerous in most towns, since there were many guilds: the York cycle, for example, had forty-eight plays; the so-called Towneley cycle (probably misnamed, perhaps acted at Wakefield), thirty-two; the so-called N-Town or *Ludus Coventriae* cycle (perhaps acted in the vicinity of Lincoln), forty-three. The texts were evidently not translations from the Latin liturgical drama but were English compositions often based on medieval narrative accounts of the divine history of the world. Such versions contained much patristic and legendary material, as well as straightforward biblical narrative; for example, the account of Christ's harrowing of hell, based on the apocryphal Gospel of Saint Thomas rather than on the Bible itself, had become an accepted part of the story. More noncanonical still are accounts of Mary's childhood and of her marriage to Joseph. The cycles varied somewhat as to content, but they tended to choose many of the same traditional stories embodied in Church liturgy. The main figures in these favorite stories—Abel, Noah, Abraham, and Isaac—were often seen as "typological," that is, prefiguring by their piety and suffering the advent of Christ himself.

The common core of most cycles included the following: the creation, the fall of Adam and expulsion from Paradise, Cain's slaying of Abel, Noah's flood, Abraham and Isaac, Moses, the prophets, the Annunciation, the visit of the shepherds and the Magi, the flight into Egypt, the slaughter of the innocents, the baptism, the temptation in the wilderness, the raising of Lazarus, the entry into Jerusalem and the entire Passion sequence, the burial, the harrowing of hell, the Resurrection, Christ's appearances to the disciples, his Ascension, and the day of doom. Other subjects were often added, such as the story of Pentecost, the assumption of the blessed Virgin Mary, and the coming of Antichrist.

Sometimes these medieval "pageants" were acted by individual craft guilds on pageant wagons before a series of audiences gathered at fixed locales throughout the town. Recent investigations have shown, however, the formidable difficulties involved in performing a complete cycle of plays in narrow streets, with each pageant having to wait in line until the preceding pageant had finished. Street processions remained common but may, in some cases, have involved displays in *tableau vivant* rather than a full performance of each play. Certainly, in some towns the plays themselves were acted, not on pageant wagons, but in the round, in arena theaters with several scaffolds on the periphery or even in the center of the acting area. Scaffolds variously represented heaven and hell, Pilate's judgment hall, the house of the Last Supper, and the like.

In the marketplace or in the cathedral close, the pageants may have been ranged in order about the open space so that the spectators themselves could move from scene to scene. Multiple-place staging certainly existed in London and in the south of England, and was the regular form of the mystery-play stage on the Continent. (The Corpus Christi plays are sometimes called "mystery" plays, since they were acted by the "mystery" or trade guilds.)

As many as twenty full-scope plays, mostly of the Corpus Christi type, may have existed at one time in England, though the complete texts of only four have been preserved. The York, Towneley, and N-Town cycles have already been mentioned; a fourth extant cycle was acted at Chester. In addition, two fragments exist of a cycle acted at Coventry, one each from Norwich and Newcastle-on-Tyne, and several other single scenes from places not located. A Cornish cycle, written in Celtic, presents some Old Testament episodes and a Passion sequence more like certain continental religious dramas than the English plays we have been discussing.

Shakespeare probably saw Corpus Christi plays in his youth, before they were suppressed by Protestant authorities, and he appears to recollect them at times in his plays. When Hamlet says disparagingly of bombastic acting that "it out-herods Herod" (*Hamlet*, 3.2.14), he is thinking of the stage bully of the slaughter of the innocents who, in the Coventry version, "ragis in the pagond [pageant] and in the strete also." Herod was indeed legendary for his rant. The Porter in *Macbeth* is surely alluding to Christ's harrowing of hell when he complains, "But this place is too cold for hell. / I'll devil-porter it no further" (2.3.16–17). The medieval heritage adds a remarkable dimension to this scene: Macbeth's castle becomes a kind of hell, as the Porter jokingly observes, and Macduff's arrival takes on an aspect of deliverance through which Macbeth and his "fiend-like Queen" (5.8.70) will be brought to account. Henry V has Herod in mind again in his speech to the beleaguered citizens of Harfleur, when he bids them surrender lest they see their naked infants "spitted upon pikes" and the childrens' mothers howling in grief "as did the wives of Jewry / At Herod's bloody-hunting slaughtermen" (3.3.38–41). More broadly, the cosmic structure of the cycle plays, bound together in their many episodes by an overarching narrative of divine history, offered a model of construction that Shakespeare would apply in modified form to his writing of English history plays.

Saints' Plays and Morality Plays

Saints' plays were also widely current in England, although few examples survive today. These dramas resembled the Corpus Christi cycles in their staging and their panoramic religious spectacle, but they differed from the cycles in that they told about the lives and miracles of individual saints and martyrs rather than, as in the cycles, telling the entire divine history of the human race as incorporated chiefly in the Old and New Testaments. Some particular cases, to be sure, incorporated features of both saints' lives and Corpus Christi drama. The story of Mary Magdalene, for example, was derived in part from the biblical accounts of her meetings with Christ, but the narrative had been enormously expanded to include legendary reports of her travels and miraculous deeds as a saint. St. Paul was another biblical figure whose sudden conversion and subsequent travels gave to his story the characteristics of a typical saint's life. As a group, however, saints' plays offered more emphasis on miraculous conversion from sin to grace and on the wondrous intervention of saints in the lives of ordinary people than did the Corpus Christi cycles.

Shakespeare's debt to saints' plays is indirect and hard to demonstrate. Some of his history plays reveal a pattern of conversion followed by glorious acts, as in the saga of Henry V, but this story was inherent in the myth of Henry V that Shakespeare inherited. Comedies of repentance, such as *Measure for Measure* and *The Winter's Tale,* show us a pattern of redemptive sorrow and renewal in which the protagonist is given an almost miraculous second chance. Shakespeare's late romances are especially illuminated by this tradition of conversion narratives. We cannot be sure, however, that he encountered such stories through saints' plays (which were suppressed by the English Reformation), since nondramatic sources, such as the Legenda Aurea or Golden Legend of the lives of the saints, were more immediately available to him.

Shakespeare's awareness of the morality play is easier to prove. Indeed, this genre had survived well enough into the late sixteenth century to make a significant impact on the plays of Shakespeare, Ben Jonson, and oth-

ers. The morality play chose as its distinctive mode the allegorical rendition of humanity's spiritual journey through life to an eventual preparation for death and judgment before God. Allegory was not unknown in the cycles or in the saints' plays, but it became the staple of the morality play. The earliest texts, from the sixteenth century, include *The Castle of Perseverance, Mankind,* and *Everyman.* Although the last of these focuses atypically on the moment of death, more typical early morality plays tell a story of spiritual struggle and eventual triumph over sin. This simple plot had an advantage over the cycles and saints' plays in that it could be adapted to the religious and social controversies of the era. The Corpus Christi cycles and saints' plays were, after all, tied to biblical or legendary events; when Reformation authorities sought to suppress the "idolatrous" representation of God on stage or banned worship of the Virgin Mary and the saints, the cycles and saints' plays were doomed. Even though they were occasionally staged late enough in the sixteenth century for Shakespeare to have seen performances, they belonged chiefly to an earlier, pre-Reformation era. The morality play, on the other hand, thrived on controversy. Its plot of soul struggle between the forces of good and evil for the allegiance of Mankind or Everyman, and his wavering progress toward eventual salvation, could and did frequently serve as a vehicle for portraying many social phenomena of the sixteenth century.

In John Skelton's political morality play called *Magnificence* (1515–1518), for example, the protagonist is a representative king figure who must choose between evil counselors urging fiscal extravagance on the one hand and wise counselors urging fiscal prudence on the other hand. The plot, telling of the King's temptation and his choosing of the wrong path before he is finally awakened to his folly, is essentially that of nonpolitical morality

Four allegorical characters in the morality play Hickescorner *were Contemplation, Perseverance, Imagination, and Free Will.*

plays, such as *Hickescorner* or *Youth* (c. 1513–1520), in which the human protagonist inevitably succumbs to temptation but is eventually rescued through divine guidance. The issues in Skelton's play have embraced secular as well as spiritual concerns, while the simple story line and the dramatic structure have remained virtually unchanged. The study of a "historical" type, in this case a king, enables such a play to comment on contemporary history and yet appeal simultaneously to a universal moral pattern. Skelton's play may allude indirectly to the fiscal recklessness of Henry VIII under Cardinal Wolsey's persuasive tutelage, but it discusses fiscal responsibility in general terms that also apply to any king—or to any human. Shakespeare's English history plays, especially the early plays about Henry VI and Richard III, owe an important debt to the tradition of the political morality, as exemplified by *Magnificence*.

Shakespeare's history play *King John* studies a king who had actually been the protagonist of the first play to represent an English monarch, *King Johan*, by John Bale (1538, later revised). Although Shakespeare may not have consulted Bale's play directly, Bale still had made an impressive contribution to the English history play by demonstrating how the morality structure could be used in the analysis of political crises. His play is an avowedly Protestant tract in the guise of a morality play, depicting its historical protagonist as a victim of Catholic duplicity and hence an example of what sixteenth-century England had to fear from its Catholic enemies. Later popular plays, combining a morality structure with a passionate interest in history and contemporary political theory, include Thomas Preston's *Cambises* (1560–1561) and John Pickering's *Horestes* (1567).

During the Reformation, the morality play was used polemically by both the Protestants and the Catholics. Dramatists were often commissioned by governmental authorities to write plays for public performance by touring actors as weapons of ideological persuasion. In Protestant plays, such as *Lusty Juventus* (c. 1547–1553) or *New Custom* (c. 1570), the villainous Vices were depicted as Catholic tempters; in Catholic plays, such as *Respublica* (1553, during the reign of Queen Mary), the Vices were Protestant. The protean flexibility of the morality formula enabled it to adapt itself to many different situations in this way. Polemical drama put ideology ahead of artistic concern, to be sure, but constant experimentation with new forms provided the popular drama of midcentury England with much-needed practical experience. One permutation of the Reformation morality play, for example, proved of considerable importance to the development of English tragedy. In some Protestant morality plays that Calvinistically stress humankind's innate depravity, such as William Wager's *Enough Is as Good as a Feast* (c. 1559–1570) and Nathaniel Woodes's *The Conflict of Conscience* (1570–1581), spiritual struggle ends in fail-

ure rather than in triumph for the human protagonist. Among the great English tragedies of the late sixteenth century, Christopher Marlowe's *Doctor Faustus* (c. 1588) is most obviously indebted to such dramatic renditions of spiritual despair, but Shakespeare's *Macbeth* and other plays may also have learned something from a native homiletic tradition in tragedy.

In staging and acting, as well, the morality play served as an important transition from late medieval religious drama to the drama of the late sixteenth century. In its origins, as seen, for example, in *The Castle of Perseverance* (early fifteenth century), the morality play had been staged like many of the cycles or saints' plays, such as *Mary Magdalene,* that is, in the round, with an open acting area surrounded by acting scaffolds on the periphery. The morality play developed great flexibility in its staging, however, just as it had developed flexibility in its approach to contemporary political or social issues. *Mankind* (c. 1471) required only an acting platform, raised probably on trestles to a height of four or five feet, and a curtain backdrop through which the actors could enter and exit. A stage of this simplicity could be carried anywhere in England and set up at a moment's notice—on a village green, in a town hall, or in the banqueting hall of a lord's manor. The troupe acting *Mankind* was vastly more efficient and transportable than the company of twenty-two or more actors required for *The Castle of Perseverance; Mankind* required only six actors.

Troupes of four or five men and one boy apprentice (for women's roles) were quite standard in early Tudor England. Similar or even smaller troupes enacted folk plays and miracle plays, the texts of which are regrettably not as extensively preserved as those of morality plays. Such troupes traveled the length and breadth of the country, and dominated the field of popular entertainment from the late fifteenth century until Shakespeare's day. They were, in fact, the professional ancestors of the Shakespearean acting company. Under the direction of their leading player, who often acted the part of Vice since it was usually the choice role of the morality play, the actors were organized as repertory companies able to perform a number of plays on short notice and to present a remarkably large number of roles by the doubling of parts. They grew slowly in size as they prospered, but they retained their traditional organization. The best of the troupes gravitated to London, where, in 1576, a troupe of perhaps six or eight men and two boys founded England's first permanent theater. Shakespeare's company, the Lord Chamberlain's men (later the King's men), was only slightly larger than this, with perhaps ten actors who were partners or "sharers" in the company, two or more boys, and a few hired hands. Shakespeare's early plays, moreover, were sometimes structured for presentation by just such a company, much as earlier popular plays had been structured, with considerable doubling of

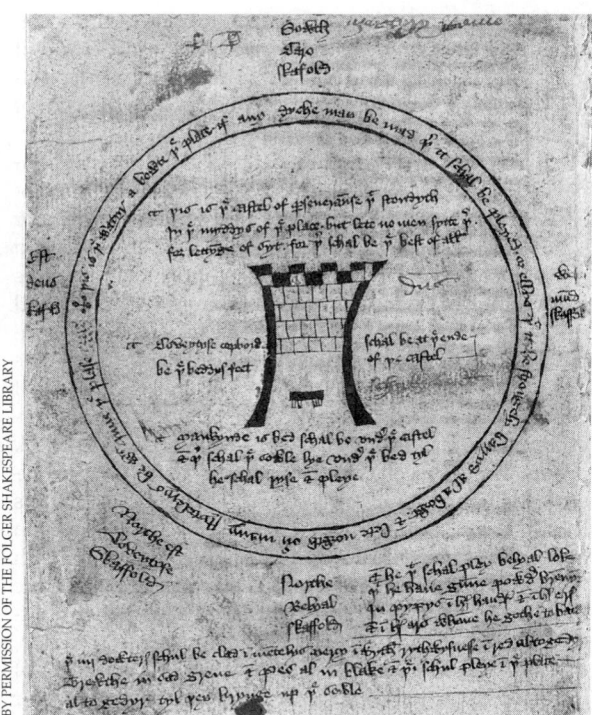

A fifteenth-century diagram for the presentation of The Castle of Perseverance *shows the scaffolds surrounding the open acting area with the castle in the center.*

parts and with a multiplicity of episodes allowing for the sequential presentation of numerous minor roles. The early history plays about Henry VI and Richard III are especially illustrative of this structural tradition.

Shakespeare's references to morality drama suggest a real familiarity. Prince Hal jestingly caricatures Falstaff as "that roasted Manningtree ox with the pudding in his belly, that reverend Vice, that grey iniquity, that father ruffian, that vanity in years . . . that old whitebearded Satan" (*1 Henry IV,* 2.4.447–58). Manningtree in Essex appears to have been renowned for its annual fair at which plays were acted and great-sized oxen were roasted; the Vice, as we have seen, was the chief comic tempter of most morality plays. Falstaff himself refers to the Vice's traditional dagger of lath in his contemptuous remarks about Justice Shallow: "And now is this Vice's dagger become a squire" (*2 Henry IV,* 3.2.317–18). Feste, in *Twelfth Night,* exits at one point with a promise to the audience that he will return soon "Like to the old Vice" with his "dagger of lath" and "his rage and his wrath" (4.2.120–31). Kent, in *King Lear,* speaks of Goneril as having taken "Vanity the puppet's part against the royalty of her father" (2.2.36–7), as though she were a personified representation of Pride in a morality play. The evocation of that

genre strengthens our perception that good and evil are indeed battling over Lear's destiny on a cosmic scale. Richard III explicitly compares himself to "the formal Vice, Iniquity" in his use of sinister double entendres and his boasting to the audience of his cleverness 3.1.82–3).

Shakespeare's specific references to late medieval drama are less important, however, than his larger indebtedness to it. His use of a structural tradition of episodic multiplicity and of alternation between seriousness and comedy is especially evident in the early history plays. Of equal significance is his indebtedness to the Vice, the comic tempter of the morality play whose sinister but fascinating techniques of evil persuasion had become an enduring part of Tudor popular drama. The Vice's boastful and chortling brand of villainy is still clearly recognizable, though transmuted into superb poetry, in the insinuations of Richard III, Aaron the Moor (in *Titus Andronicus*), Iago (in *Othello*), and Edmund (in *King Lear*). As Bernard Spivack has argued, in his *Shakespeare and the Allegory of Evil,* Shakespeare's secular vision of the contest between good and evil for human souls owes much to the morality tradition and to other forms of medieval drama.

Early Tudor Humanist Drama

The development of the morality play and of other medieval drama, briefly sketched in the preceding sections, tells only one part of the story of sixteenth-century drama. The trend we have observed in morality drama, toward the depiction of contemporary English life, manifested itself also in other kinds of plays that were not so plainly derived from the religious drama of the Middle Ages. A relatively new influence was that of classical and neoclassical drama, from the ancient classical world and from Renaissance Europe. Important, too, were the secular kinds of dramatic entertainment that had flourished in the English court even before the advent of neoclassicism. Early Tudor drama for courtly and well-educated audiences was heterogeneous because it reflected so many diverse impulses: the intensified renewal of classical learning that had come about through the activities of the new humanists, the ferment of ideologies introduced by the Reformation, the increase in social mobility in the Tudor court, and the like. In varying proportions, the courtly and intellectual drama of the period borrowed from the English morality play, from courtly pastimes such as the "disguising" (a kind of masque) and the dialogue or *débat,* from secular farce and romance, from classical and neoclassical literature, and even from the Corpus Christi cycles and saints' plays. The mixture, experimental and often uneven, was nonetheless stimulating, because it attempted to fuse English culture with the thought of neoclassical Europe. This drama was usually staged in courtly surroundings, such as the banqueting halls of the aristocracy. (See "The

Tudor Hall" below, in the section on London Theaters and Dramatic Companies.)

Especially important in the development of this early Tudor drama were the humanists who associated themselves with Sir Thomas More and his patron Cardinal Morton. These men were, like their counterparts in Italy and elsewhere on the Continent, intensely devoted to the revival of classical learning in all its aspects—art, architecture, literary texts, historical knowledge, and politics—and thus to the enhancement of the human spirit. Their shared ideals can be seen in the plays that they wrote or sponsored. Henry Medwall, chaplain to Cardinal Morton, wrote a morality play called *Nature* (c. 1490–1501) that reveals an interest in Aristotelian ethics, as well as in traditional Christian ideas of salvation. Medwall also wrote *Fulgens and Lucrece* (c. 1490–1500), the earliest extant play in England to use an ancient Roman setting and a secular romantic love plot. The heroine, Lucrece, chooses the love of a virtuous but untitled "new" man at court in preference to a haughty and degenerate aristocrat. This *débat* was derived from *De Vera Nobilitate* by Buonaccorso of Pistoia, an ardent Italian humanist. Despite its ancient setting and romantic plot, it is also unmistakably relevant to the struggle between "new" men and old aristocrats in the court of Henry VII. Both of Medwall's plays were printed by John Rastell, another humanist in the service of Cardinal Morton. Rastell, who married More's sister, wrote a humanist interlude called *The Nature of the Four Elements* (c. 1517–1518), in which he excitedly discussed the latest scientific theories concerning the roundness of the world and other such new ideas. He is probably the author of *Of Gentleness and Nobility* (c. 1527–1530) as well, a play that iconoclastically asks whether monarchy and the inheritance of property are not social evils that ideally ought to be abolished. The influence of Thomas More's *Utopia* on this play is unmistakable.

John Heywood, son-in-law of John Rastell, was the most important and versatile dramatist of the humanist group. All his plays, except *Witty and Witless*, which has been preserved only in manuscript, were printed by John Rastell or his son, William Rastell. Heywood's plays fall into two groups: the courtly disputations, such as *The Play of Love, The Play of the Weather,* and *Witty and Witless* (c. 1525–1533), and the more popular farces that may have been intended for popular audiences as well, such as *The Pardoner and the Friar, The Four PP,* and *John John the Husband* (c. 1513–1533). In the first group, *Weather* reveals a characteristic attention to humanist and courtly themes. In an obvious analogy to the Tudor concept of an absolutist yet benevolent monarchy, the various petitioners of the play complain to Jupiter about the weather but are finally persuaded to be grateful for the mixed weather that is provided them. Heywood is suggesting, in other words, that the English monarchy must bestow its favors impartially on all classes of persons and that all subjects ought to recognize the essential soundness of the social order as it presently exists. Heywood's second group of plays, on the other hand, eschews such courtly and political themes for a broader slapstick comedy in the vein of Chaucerian fabliau and French farce.

In addition to these humanist plays written by members of the Sir Thomas More circle, the learned drama of early Tudor England included many plays written for schoolboys or for the choristers attached to royal and noble households. The plays written under such auspices tended to reveal a much stronger interest in classical and neoclassical drama than did the plays written for popular audiences. Schoolmasters wrote dramatic texts derived from the classics for educational purposes; at court, sophisticated audiences were interested in the latest dramatic fashions from Italy or France. Ancient Greek drama did not receive nearly so much attention, however, as the Latin drama of Terence (c. 186–159 B.C.), Plautus (c. 254–184 B.C.), and Seneca (c. 4 B.C. –65 A.D.). These Latin authors had long been used as schoolboys' texts, though they were frequently expurgated or allegorized into the terms of Christian morality in order to render them suitable for schoolboys' sensibilities. This academic tradition, on the Continent and in England, produced a number of imitative plays that could be acted by boys as part of their training in classical languages. Some plays, such as John Palsgrave's *Acolastus* (1540), were intended to be read rather than acted. Many others were Latin biblical plays in classical guise, such as Thomas Watson's *Absalom* (c. 1535–1544) and George Buchanan's *Jephthes* (1540–1545).

At court and in noble households, choristers were becoming noted for their acting ability. They performed chiefly during seasons of revels, such as in the Christmas season. They did not appear commercially before public audiences during the early Tudor period, as did the players of moralities and popular interludes. The Children of the Royal Chapel are known to have presented plays as early as 1506. The boys of St. Paul's School acted before King Henry VIII in 1528. Later, in the 1570s and 1580s, these children's groups were organized into professional acting companies. Children's plays were generally written by schoolmasters or choirmasters. The plays were heavily influenced by continental traditions and often depicted themes, such as that of the Prodigal Son, that were congenial to boys of school age. *Nice Wanton* (1547–1553) offers an instance of this sort. Biblical themes were common and were sometimes used to urge a political lesson in the presence of a courtly audience. *Godly Queen Hester* (1525–1529), for example, seems to defend the cause of Katharine of Aragon and to denounce the machinations of Cardinal Wolsey. *Jacob and Esau* (1547–1553) draws an unflattering comparison between the unregenerate Esau and those who refuse to abandon the Catholic faith. Classical subjects were, of course, much in

By permission of the british library

Early Tudor drama employed the talents of boy actors on stage such as this company, the Children of the Royal Chapel.

demand as a way of educating youth, as in *Appius and Virginia* (1559–1567) and in Richard Edwards's *Damon and Pythias* (c. 1565).

Early Comedy

Schoolboys' drama was also vitally important in the development of classical or "regular" comedy on the English stage. Native morality drama was often highly comic, to be sure, especially in its depiction of the resourceful and scheming Vice; but English drama still had much to learn from classical examples about play construction and about the presentation of various types of characters. Perhaps the two best-known early English "regular" comedies were *Ralph Roister Doister* and *Gammer Gurton's Needle*.

Ralph Roister Doister, by Nicholas Udall, at one time headmaster of Eton, was acted probably between 1552 and 1554 by boy actors. Its staging is essentially that of neoclassical comedy, with two houses facing onto a street. The play employs a classical five-act structure and preserves the unities of time and place. (According to classical and neoclassical theory, a play's action should be limited to one location—a city, for example—and to a single day.) Stock comic types include the *miles gloriosus,* or braggart soldier, and the parasite. At the same time, Udall has transformed his heroine, usually a courtesan in Plautus's racy comedies, into a winsomely pious Englishwoman named Christian Custance. Ralph Roister Doister, the braggardly type for whom the play is named, is foiled in his mean-spirited determination to win Christian Custance away from her true love, Gawin Goodluck. Almost all the characters virtuously conspire to expose Ralph for his effrontery and pretended bravery; even Matthew Merrygreek, the fun-loving parasite, proves ultimately to be on the side of decency and fair play. Throughout, Udall has adapted Roman comedy to English customs and mores.

Gammer Gurton's Needle, written by William Stevenson, fellow of Christ's College, Cambridge, at about the same time as *Roister Doister,* is similarly designed for student acting. Stock Roman characters are transformed into hearty English types. Diccon the Bedlam, who engineers the farcical action of the lost needle, resembles not only the Roman parasite but also the English natural fool or zany. To some extent, he also reminds us of the mischievous and inventive Vice of the morality play. Other characters are even less purely Roman in their origin: Hodge, the clownish servant; Dame Chat, the shrewish neighbor; and Dr. Rat, the impoverished and ill-trained clergyman who spends most of his time drinking and complaining about his wretched lot. The play is an educated college man's indulgent laugh at his country neighbors. Yet the play is, like *Ralph Roister Doister,* classically structured into five acts, with a single stage setting that preserves the unities of time and place.

In 1566, the members of Gray's Inn saw a production of George Gascoigne's *Supposes,* translated from the Italian of Ariosto (1509). Because it was a translation and not an English adaptation, this play preserves essentially in their original form the stock character types of neoclassical comedy: the parasite, the pantaloon or miserly aged rival in love, the overly watchful father, the clever servant, the bawdy nurse, and so on. The heroine, though no longer a Roman courtesan, as in the comedies of the much-imitated Latin dramatist Plautus, is nonetheless a self-possessed and sophisticated young woman who conducts a secret affair for some time without being detected by her father. The mores of this continental play must have seemed challengingly cosmopolitan to its fashionable courtly and intellectual audience. Just as importantly, the play offered graceful prose language as its medium, rather than the homely English verse of *Ralph Roister Doister* and *Gammer Gurton's Needle. Supposes* provided a new model for neoclassical comedy and was to become (with some of its continental morality anglicized) a source for Shakespeare's *The Taming of the Shrew.* Indeed, Shakespeare learned much about play construction, dialogue, and characterization from neoclassical comedies of this sort; perhaps his earliest comedy, *The Comedy of Errors,* owes a great deal to Plautus and to neoclassical imitators of that Latin comic writer. Another early Italian comedy in English, *The Bugbears,* was adapted from Grazzini's *La Spiritata* and acted in about 1563–1565 by boy actors.

Early Tragedy

In early English tragedy, as in early comedy, native and neoclassical traditions coalesced and sometimes clashed. Native conceptions of tragedy had partly originated in two great medieval commonplaces: the "wheel of fortune" and the "fall of princes." Both were incorporated in Chaucer's "The Monk's Tale" and its source, Boccaccio's *De Casibus Virorum Illustrium,* which presented moral examples from the lives of famous men. Chaucer had defined "tragedy" as the story of a great person "that stood in greet prosperitee, / And is yfallen out of heigh degree / Into myserie, and endeth wrecchedly." His examples, taken from Boccaccio, included Lucifer, Adam, Samson, Hercules, Julius Caesar, and others. These were men or evil beings who had either fallen through sinful pride or had been brought low through the inevitable turn of fortune's wheel. Both types of tragedy illustrated to the medieval mind the folly of trusting to worldly expectations. The "fall of princes" tradition was extended into Elizabethan times through John Lydgate's Chaucerian imitation, *The Fall of Princes,* and its Tudor sequel, *The Mirror for Magistrates* (1559, with many subsequent revisions and enlargements). The morality play contributed a pattern similar to that of Satan's tragic fall through pride; and, although the mankind figure of early morality plays invariably was recovered to God's grace by the end of the play, some early Elizabethan Calvinistic moralities (such as *Enough Is as Good as a Feast* or *The Longer Thou Livest the More Fool Thou Art*) featured human protagonists who were eternally damned. As we have already seen, Elizabethan moralities of this sort anticipated the tragic pattern of Marlowe's *Doctor Faustus.*

Native traditions of tragedy evolved quite independent of classical tragic drama and were, in some ways, strikingly different from it. Christian morality often served as a major explanation of the cause of tragic fall in medieval tragedy. Moreover, the focus was broad and cosmic, as in *Doctor Faustus.* Scenes of comic depravity often alternated with scenes of tragic seriousness, especially in the morality plays. Classical tragedy, on the other hand, usually focused on a moment of crisis in the protagonist's life and presented this crisis in its full, tragic intensity without the undercutting of comic effect. In classical tragedy generally, narrative interest was subordinated to dramatic or lyrical interest. Unity of action, as understood by Renaissance theorists of drama, necessarily included unity of time and place. Thus, the gap between native and classical tragedy was potentially vast.

Perhaps the earliest tragedy based on classical models in England was Thomas Norton and Thomas Sackville's *Gorboduc,* presented before Queen Elizabeth at Whitehall on January 18, 1562. The play attempted to offer Queen Elizabeth political advice on the need for naming a Protestant successor, by way of a cautionary example in the fratricidal strife between Gorboduc's two sons. Although Sir Philip Sidney later complained about the play's violation of the unities in the fifth act, he praised it otherwise as "an exact model of all tragedies." To be sure, native concepts of tragedy are observable in *Gorboduc,* especially in its use of an ancient British setting and in its moral and Christian explanations of the causes of tragedy. Nevertheless, the classical element predominates.

This classical element is basically Senecan. Ancient Greek tragedy was relatively unknown to Elizabethan England except through Seneca's Roman adaptations. Seneca's ten plays were all translated into English by 1581 and had long been read in the schools as models of rhetoric (just as Terence and Plautus were also read). Seneca's plays were, in fact, closet dramas, intended to be recited rather than acted. Seneca provided *Gorboduc* with a model for its long declamatory speeches, its occasional passages of stichomythia (rapid one-line exchange of dialogue), its five-act structure punctuated by dumb shows, and its supernatural agents prognosticating doom. Moreover, *Gorboduc's* blank verse, created to approximate the Latin meters of Seneca, set a style for blank verse tragedy that dominated the English stage throughout Shakespeare's career. (Blank verse had been used shortly before *Gorboduc* by the Earl of Surrey in his translations from Virgil's *Aeneid,* but never before in drama.) *Gorboduc* also made an important contribution to the English history play by its use of chronicle materials in a tragic setting.

Other Senecan plays followed, written at first for gentlemanly audiences of the universities and the Inns of Court, rather than for the popular stage. One such was George Gascoigne's *Jocasta* (1566). In 1588, eight gentlemen of Gray's Inn, including Thomas Hughes and Francis Bacon, presented before the Queen a drama similar in form to *Gorboduc,* called *The Misfortunes of Arthur.* This tragedy borrows from Seneca not only chorus, messengers, and machinery but also ideas, sentiments, and heightened language. Like *Gorboduc, The Misfortunes of Arthur* is somewhat free with the classical unities. Also, it is based upon the chronicle history of Britain, which was to become one of the chief sources of subject matter for English tragedy.

Another principal source for tragic writers was the Italian short story, which, because it was also impassioned and serious, offered many themes to writers of tragedy. *Gismond of Salerne* dramatizes a well-known Italian tale and, like *Gorboduc* and *The Misfortunes of Arthur,* is Senecan in form and nature. It was acted before the Queen in 1566 or 1568. In the same storehouse of narrative,

Shakespeare was later to find his source for *Othello*, as well as for such comedies as *The Merchant of Venice* and *Measure for Measure*. *Romeo and Juliet* was based on an English poem which in turn drew from an Italian source.

Sir Philip Sidney as Dramatic Critic

The kind of tragedy that Shakespeare and other popular dramatists wrote in the late sixteenth and early seventeenth centuries is not rigorously classical. It preserves many of the elements of English tragedy already enumerated: a broad narrative focus, frequent violations or total ignoring of the classical unities of time and place, the inclusion of comedy, and the like. Tragedy of this sort might never have developed in England to so high a point or might never have been accepted as the prevailing form of tragedy but for two things: in the first place, few Elizabethan dramatists learned their craft by studying the classical rules; in the second place, the Elizabethan audience, with a taste for native English drama, demanded new, varied, and sensational plots, accompanied by vaudeville clownery and songs. Such popular drama was often condemned by those critics who were familiar with classical literature, but to have made English tragedy conform with classical rules would have meant changing its nature. In France, where in Shakespeare's time the drama came under the control of the court and the learned classes, tragedy developed according to classical rules into the drama of Corneille and Racine; in England, on the other hand, Shakespeare and his contemporaries created a kind of tragedy particularly their own.

The most famous neoclassical critic of the age, Sir Philip Sidney, took vigorous exception to the kind of tragedy in vogue during the 1580s. His views are set forth in *The Defence of Poesy*, written in 1581 or slightly later:

Our tragedies and comedies not without cause cried out against, observing rules neither of honest civility nor skillful poetry, excepting *Gorboduc*—again I say of those that I have seen. Which notwithstanding as it is full of stately speeches and well-sounding phrases, climbing to the height of Seneca his style, and as full of notable morality, which it doth most delightfully teach, and so obtain the very end of poesy, yet in truth it is very defective in the circumstances, which grieves me, because it might not remain as an exact model of all tragedies. For it is faulty both in place and time, the two necessary companions of all corporal actions. For where the stage should alway represent but one place, and the uttermost time presupposed in it should be, both by Aristotle's precept and common reason, but one day, there is both many days and many places inartificially imagined.

But if it be so in *Gorboduc*, how much more in all the rest? where you shall have Asia of the one side and Afric of the other, and so many other under-kingdoms, that the player, when he comes in, must ever begin with telling where he is, or else the tale will not be conceived. Now you shall have three ladies walk to gather flowers, and then we must believe the stage to be a garden. By and by we hear news of shipwreck in the same place; then we are to blame if we accept it not for a rock. Upon the back of that comes out a hideous monster with fire and smoke, and then the miserable beholders are bound to take it for a cave. While in the meantime two armies fly in, represented with four swords and bucklers, and then what hard heart will not receive it for a pitched field?

Now of time they are much more liberal. For ordinary it is that two young princes fall in love; after many traverses she is got with child, delivered of a fair boy; he is lost, groweth a man, falleth in love, and is ready to get another child,—and all this in two hours space; which how absurd it is in sense even sense may imagine, and art hath taught, and all ancient examples justified, and at this day the ordinary players in Italy will not err in....

Later he tells us that English plays are "neither right tragedies nor right comedies"; instead, they mingle clowns and kings with "neither decency nor discretion."

To be sure, Sidney's criticism is never narrowly classical; in the essay as a whole, he affirms the power of the artist to range freely in the world of wit and imagination and to create artifacts that are more universally "true" than either philosophy or history. At the same time, his strictures against the contemporary English stage do invoke classical ideals of unity that many dramatists and audiences ignored. Popular audiences of the time seem to have had no more difficulty imagining the lapse of twenty years than the lapse of two hours. Nor were they troubled by scenic shifts from one continent to another, or by shifts in tone from the comic to the pathetic, the grotesque, or the tragic. Because native English drama had never paid much attention to classical precept, it worked out its own sense of cohesion according to different criteria of multiplicity, alternating effects, sudden juxtapositions, typological recurrence, and the like.

John Lyly, George Peele, and Robert Greene

In facing the problem of understanding just what Elizabethan drama was and how it became what it was, we must recognize that the classification of drama into comedy and tragedy by the ancients does not tell the whole story. Even when we add the history or chronicle play to these two divisions of drama, we have, at best, a rough classification that leaves out a great deal and implies that these three forms were sharply discriminated. In fact, Elizabethan drama is, generally speaking, a blend of many elements. Nearly all Elizabethan tragedies have in them comic scenes and by-plots; most comedies have in them serious issues that might conceivably result in disaster; and history plays are often capable of being classified as comedies or as tragedies. To appreciate further this protean quality of genre in early Elizabethan drama, we might consider the varied works of a number of dramatists whose practice was successful on the stage and who influenced Shakespeare and his immediate contemporaries. Of these, John Lyly is one of the most important.

John Lyly (1554?–1606), grandson of the grammarian William Lyly or Lilly, educated at Oxford and Cambridge, first acquired fame not as a dramatist, but as a writer of prose. His *Euphues, The Anatomy of Wit,* published in 1578, and its sequel, *Euphues and His England* (1580), stand as the most sensational and brilliant effort in the struggle of English Renaissance prose to acquire a conscious artistic manner. The style is, to a remarkable extent, composed of rhetorical devices: antithesis, personification, rhetorical question, metaphor, simile, and, above all, balance reinforced by alliteration. Recondite tidbits and fanciful legends about natural history are garnered from Plutarch, Pliny, and many other writers. The overall result is a kind of handbook for the courtier, the lover, the traveler, and the statesman. Lyly's deliberately outrageous style was imitated by dozens of other writers, including Robert Greene and Thomas Lodge, and seems to have set a new fashion of smart speech in the court of Queen Elizabeth. "Euphuism" itself had a vast influence on the style of the drama and other literature, both in poetry and in prose. Shakespeare is one of those who imitated and also ridiculed euphuistic speech. (For amusing examples of Shakespeare's parodying of the euphuistic style, see Falstaff's speech in *1 Henry IV,* 2.4.396 ff., beginning "for though the camomile, the more it is trodden on the faster it grows, yet youth, the more it is wasted the sooner it wears," or Don Armado's love letter in *Love's Labor's Lost,* 4.1.61 ff.: "Shall I command thy love? I may. Shall I enforce thy love? I could. Shall I entreat thy love? I will," and so on.)

Lyly was also the author of at least eight comedies, written to suit the taste of the court and possibly all acted before the Queen by the children of the Chapel Royal or of St. Paul's School. The plays are often courtly debates in the tradition of Medwall's *Fulgens and Lucrece,* with much combat of wits and philosophical argument. These comedies are also sufficiently modeled on Plautus or Terence to indicate that the characteristic features of Latin comedy by this time (1580–1590) had become naturalized on the English stage. *Mother Bombie,* for example, is an adaptation of Latin comedy, containing such stock figures as the pedant, the rascally servant, the duped parent, the parasite, and the aged lover, although, as usual, in Lyly the clownery has an English flavor as well.

Indeed, however much Lyly may recall classical Latin comedy, he is most important as the inventor of a fanciful type of love comedy to which Shakespeare was significantly indebted in several of his plays. Lyly's *Sappho and Phao, Endymion,* and *Midas* have romantic plots derived from Ovidian mythology. *Galatea* uses a pastoral setting for its love story and male disguises for the heroines, as in *As You Like It. Love's Metamorphosis* and *The Woman in the Moon* are also pastoral comedies. *Campaspe,* like *The Merchant of Venice,* portrays conflicts of love and friendship. Lyly's flattery of Queen Elizabeth through topical allegory and his appeal to a courtly clientele are, to be sure, modes that Shakespeare does not generally adopt. On the other hand, Shakespeare learned a good deal from Lyly's sensitive portrayal of the psychology of love. The depiction is often wryly comic: Lyly's men abase themselves before women, vacillate between idealization and misogyny, and not infrequently fail as wooers—much as the young lords do in Shakespeare's most Lylyan play, *Love's Labor's Lost.* Shakespeare's lovers generally work toward a more successful and realistic completion of romantic expectations, but Shakespeare's interest in love comedy began, in part, with what Lyly had achieved.

George Peele (1558?–1597) was also active as a dramatist around the time that Shakespeare first came to London. Peele's *The Arraignment of Paris* (1581) offers a quality of blank verse not previously seen in comedy and shows how classical legend could be adapted to a thoroughly English celebration of the nation and its Queen. *The Old Wives' Tale* (c. 1588–1594) is a seemingly naive but actually skillful medley of folk legends in the spirit of popular romance. *David and Bethsabe* (c. 1581–1594) dramatizes a familar biblical narrative in terms of erotic love and kingly power. Peele also contributed importantly to the new and burgeoning genre of the English history play with his *Edward I* (1590–1593); it is, like other history plays of the Armada era, jingoistically anti-Spanish and features a popular folk-hero king who understands and respects the proud local customs of his people. *The Battle of Alcazar* (1588–1589), another play of the Armada era, revels in the exotic world of Africa and the Middle East, in the vaunting heroic vein of Christopher Marlowe's *Tamburlaine.* Peele also devised two London civic pageants.

Robert Greene (1558–1592), more than any other dramatist, opened up for Shakespeare the world of Greek romance—the kind of fiction ultimately derived from Heliodorus, Achilles Tatius, and other protonovelists of the Mediterranean world in the second through fourth centuries. The Greeks of that era were the merchants, traders, sailors, and schoolmasters of the Roman Empire, and the early form of prose romance they created was a reflection of the adventurous life they lived. This romantic fiction reveled in strange and improbable encounters, piracies, the exposure of infant children to the elements and their eventual restoration as grown-ups to their aging parents, the separation and reunion of indistinguishable twins, and many other plot devices rendered familiar to us in the writings of Renaissance authors for whom this kind of sensationalism was every bit as interesting and worthy of imitation as the classics of Virgil and Ovid. Stories of the Greek kind, translated into various languages and ultimately into English, were to serve as models for a number of Shakespeare's late romances, especially *Pericles, The Winter's Tale,* and *Cymbeline.* Indeed, the plot of *The Winter's Tale* came to Shakespeare by way of Greene's prose romance, *Pandosto*.

From Greek romantic fiction, Greene devised a type of plucky romantic heroine for his plays and novels that Shakespeare was to develop further in his comedies. The society depicted by Greek romance gave women great liberty, and, like them, Greene's heroines are independent, witty, and resourceful, though at the same time feminine. Greene's dramas are almost the first modern productions in which women are in any degree represented as assuming a relatively dignified station in a mutually supportive love relationship with a man.

Greene also borrowed from Greek romantic fiction, and from other sources, especially for pastoral fiction. His plays, particularly *James IV* and *Friar Bacon and Friar Bungay* (c. 1589–1592), give us that blend of the pastoral and the romantic which the world has enjoyed in *As You Like It* and *Love's Labor's Lost*. *Friar Bacon* is particularly noteworthy for its multiple plot, its resourceful heroine, and its embracing of serious issues in a comic world. Greene must be regarded as the first great master of plot in English comedy.

Greene may also have written *George a Greene, the Pinner of Wakefield* (1587–1593), a play that exalts the virtues of England's yeoman class in defiance of the aristocracy and all foreign foes. The hero, George, is a patriot, a scorner of hereditary titles, and a representative of the common people against vested interests. As a new breed of English folk hero, he is so invincible that even Robin Hood must yield to his authority. The appeal of this dream of power to the artisans and yeomen in Greene's popular audiences must have been heady indeed.

Shortly before he fell victim to the notorious debaucheries of his bohemian existence (he was reported to have died from a surfeit of pickled herring and Rhenish wine), Greene wrote many pamphlets, some about London roguery, some about his own hard usage at the hands of the world. In one of the latter, *Greene's Groatsworth of Wit Bought with a Million of Repentance* (1592), he gave us our first personal reference to Shakespeare. (See "The Only Shake-scene in a Country" in the biographical account of Shakespeare's life and work, below.) Shakespeare was, of course, not the only dramatist to be influenced by Greene; Anthony Munday, Thomas Dekker, and most of the popular dramatists of the next decade were similarly indebted to Greene's example.

Thomas Kyd and Christopher Marlowe

While romantic comedy was being shaped and developed in the hands of Lyly, Peele, and Greene, Senecan tragedy was also finding its proponents on the English stage. Lucius Annaeus Seneca (c. 4 B.C.–65 A.D.), a Roman statesman and stoic philosopher during the reign of the emperor Nero, wrote tragedies of a severely formal cast based on the tragedies of Aeschylus, Sophocles, and Euripides. Although never performed in Seneca's lifetime and indeed written as "closet" dramas, they became immensely influential on dramatists of later generations, especially during the Renaissance on the Continent and in England. The greatest genius in adapting Senecan action to the English theater was Thomas Kyd (1558–1594). His influence on his contemporaries and on later dramatists was immense; *The Spanish Tragedy* (c. 1583–1587) was probably acted more times during the sixteenth century than any other English play and became a pattern for subsequent revenge drama. Although Senecan tradition by no means accounts for all of the play's successful qualities, it remains a central part. Kyd catches the unabashed brutality and horror of the Senecan story and reveals it openly. Instead of having the action reported as taking place off the stage, as in Seneca and in most classical tragedy, he presents it directly. For tales of Greek mythology, he substitutes a modern story

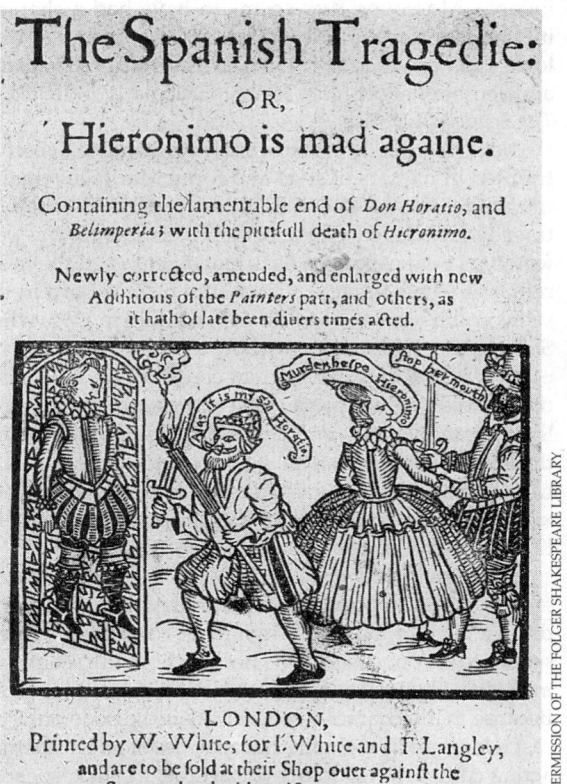

BY PERMISSION OF THE FOLGER SHAKESPEARE LIBRARY

Thomas Kyd's The Spanish Tragedy *was perhaps the most popular play of the sixteenth century; it was performed more than any other English drama of the time.* The Spanish Tragedy *served as a pattern and influenced subsequent revenge drama—including Shakespeare's* Hamlet.

of love, conspiracy, murder, and political intrigue. He retains the Senecan ghost, the revenge motive, the spirit of stoicism, and a modified form of the chorus. The play deals both seriously and sensationally with the conflicting codes of revenge and Christian faith in God's providence. The protagonist Hieronimo, confronted with his son's murder and seemingly unable to obtain justice through the state, finds his pleas to the heavens unanswered and turns instead to a revenge that hardens his spirit and requires his own violent death as payment. The action is presided over by the spirit of Revenge, a choruslike figure whose aims share nothing in common with Christian views of justice and mercy. *The Spanish Tragedy* is also noteworthy for a style that is a tour de force of rhetorical figures, such as anaphora and oxymoron—an achievement both imitated and mocked by later dramatists. Probably Kyd is also the author of the first dramatic version of the story of Hamlet.

Kyd's work gave rise to a series of revenge plays, not only in his own time, but also later, in 1600 and the years following, when the revenge tragedy again became fashionable. Moreover, Kyd seems to have had a shaping influence on Greene and on Marlowe. For example, Marlowe's *The Jew of Malta* (c. 1589), in its verbal extravagance and sensational intrigue, seems particularly indebted to *The Spanish Tragedy*.

Nevertheless, however much Kyd may have contributed in matters of style and form, Marlowe remains the leader in the great English type of Elizabethan tragedy. He shaped the genre that subsequently was perfected by Shakespeare. His achievement is all the more remarkable when we consider that he was born in the same year as Shakespeare (1564) and died in 1593, when Shakespeare had written no more than six or seven of his earliest plays. Marlowe's great contribution to English drama was a type of protagonist expressing something of the aspiration of the very Renaissance itself. Tamburlaine thirsts for world conquest; Dr. Faustus would go to the utmost bounds of knowledge and the power which knowledge gives; and Barabas in *The Jew of Malta* sets no limit to his longing for wealth.

Structurally, *Tamburlaine* (1587–1588) is a good deal closer to the English popular morality play than to classical drama. Each of the play's two parts consists of a linear sequence of conquests by the humbly born but seemingly invincible Tamburlaine, until at last death ends his glory. Because many characters appear in one episode only, the cast is large and yet within the capacities of an Elizabethan acting company. Doubling of parts, as in Shakespeare's early history plays, is both common and necessary. Structural unity is achieved through thematic repetition rather than through a narrowing of the narrative focus. At the same time, the language of *Tamburlaine* is rich and new in its vibrant appeal to limitless human aspiration. The Elizabethan playgoer is invited to forget moral considerations

in evaluating the play's ruthless hero and to revel instead in the intoxicating spectacle of a baseborn shepherd "threat'ning the world with high astounding terms."

A profound ambivalence permeates all of Marlowe's plays and gives them a restless, brilliant energy that is characteristic of the times for which they were written. Tamburlaine is both a remorseless butcher of his enemies and a superhuman quester. He is fierce, mysterious, oriental, exotic, unknowable; as the projection of a universal human dream of aspiration, he is to be both admired and feared. Barabas in *The Jew of Malta* is at once colossally rich and colossally evil. Similarly, the protagonist of *Doctor Faustus* (c. 1588–1589) is both a sinner who falls from grace and a noble but doomed Overreacher (as Harry Levin describes him), daring like Icarus to fly toward the sun. In medieval and Christian orthodox terms, Faustus is guilty of pride, the deadliest of the Deadly Sins; but in Renaissance terms he at least fleetingly resembles Prometheus, challenging the hierarchy of an oppressive and outmoded universe. In its free mixture of comedy and tragedy and its wholesale disregard of the classical unities, *Doctor Faustus* brilliantly demonstrates

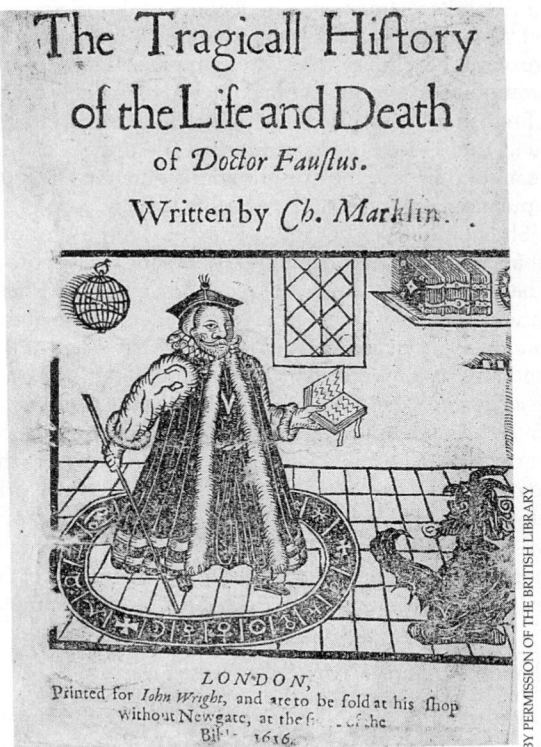

The title page of the 1616 edition of Christopher Marlowe's Doctor Faustus *shows Faustus's conjuration of the devil. The play illustrates native rather than classical traditions of tragedy in its disregard of the unities and its free use of comedy.*

what the native and homiletic tradition of tragedy had to offer Shakespeare.

Edward II, perhaps Marlowe's last play (1591–1593), is ambivalent toward its paired central figures, Edward and Mortimer Junior. At first, the effeminate King seems chiefly in the wrong, while his baronial opponents lament England's decline. Toward the end of the play, however, the King becomes the sympathetic victim of a power-mad and Machiavellian Mortimer. Queen Isabella also changes radically from a long-suffering, neglected wife into a scheming adulteress. This shift in sympathy from the barons to King Edward is structurally much like that of Shakespeare's *Richard II*, and, unquestionably, Marlowe's history play had a profound effect on Shakespeare. Yet Marlowe's tone, as in his other plays, remains one of naturalistic amorality. He wryly regards England's political struggles as one more manifestation of the restlessness and ambition afflicting all mortal endeavors. His world is one of constant turmoil in which persons of insatiable will assert themselves and rise to the top, at whatever cost to themselves and to society. Shakespeare's world is basically different, even though he learned a great deal from Marlowe's tragic vision.

Marlowe first gave to English tragedy its realization of character and, still more, its dignity and seriousness. He endowed English drama with a spirit of aspiration. His enthusiasm for beauty of language, shared by Spenser, Greene, Peele, and others, provided a rich heritage for the young Shakespeare. Not the least among Marlowe's gifts to English drama was a new and more flexible blank-verse style. In the following prologue to *Tamburlaine the Great*, Part I, Marlowe does not treat each blank-verse line as a separate unit but runs the sense on from line to line in order to produce what might be described as a blank-verse paragraph, a thing most necessary to drama if it is to represent widely varying emotions, thoughts, and characters:

> From jigging veins of rhyming mother-wits,
> And such conceits as clownage keeps in pay,
> We'll lead you to the stately tent of war,
> Where you shall hear the Scythian Tamburlaine
> Threat'ning the world with high astounding terms,
> And scourging kingdoms with his conquering sword.
> View but his picture in this tragic glass,
> And then applaud his fortunes as you please.

This is not only a manifesto of tragic seriousness; it is also, in spite of its elevated style, one of the first examples in English tragedy of vigorous, natural, straightforward expression. Tamburlaine in his utterances is a typical Renaissance poet on the themes of both love and war, as can be seen in the following evocation of the aspiring mind:

> If all the pens that ever poets held
> Had fed the feeling of their masters' thoughts,
> And every sweetness that inspired their hearts,
> Their minds, and muses on admirèd themes;
> If all the heavenly quintessence they still
> From their immortal flowers of poesy,
> Wherein, as in a mirror, we perceive
> The highest reaches of a human wit;
> If these had made one poem's period,
> And all combined in beauty's worthiness,
> Yet should there hover in their restless heads
> One thought, one grace, one wonder, at the least,
> Which into words no virtue can digest.

—*Tamburlaine*, Pt. I, 5.1.161–73

Shakespeare's Dramatic Heritage

Shakespearean tragedy began, roughly speaking, with marked indebtedness to the tragic writing of Marlowe and Kyd: poetry, character, and style from Marlowe; motive, plot, and tragic intensity from Kyd. No evidence suggests that Shakespeare was ever particularly aware of, or influenced by, Aristotelian theories of tragedy. His wish was to hold "the mirror up to nature" and show "virtue her feature, scorn her own image, and the very age and body of the time his form and pressure" (*Hamlet*, 3.2.22–4). Sometimes he approximated Aristotelian ideals in his plays (most nearly, perhaps, in *Othello, Macbeth,* and *Coriolanus*), but not by conscious design. Nor was he a slavish borrower from Marlowe and Kyd, even in his early tragedies, such as *Titus Andronicus*. Greene and many others sought to imitate Marlowe in tragedy, with but indifferent success. Shakespeare, Marlowe's only successful imitator, soon outdistanced Marlowe in those very qualities for which he was indebted to him.

Similarly, the elements of Shakespearean comedy are, in part, derived from Lyly, Peele, and Greene. The contributions of Lyly and Peele were those of style, setting, and movement. Greene, primarily a writer of romance, an adapter of Greek romantic fiction, furnished the element of love and adventure that makes so many Elizabethan plays delightful merely as stories. He also put upon the stage the witty, independent-minded woman, often in boy's clothes, who gives point and naturalness to love intrigue whether in serious drama or in comedy. Not only did Shakespeare, who was a far greater genius than any of them, combine the elements of the comedies of these men and better the instruction, but, as his career went on, he realized on a broad scale the possibilities of the comic point of view in the representation of human life and character.

In the English history play, though he may have learned much from Marlowe, Peele, and others, Shakespeare was clearly an innovator as well. His early history plays on the reigns of Henry VI and Richard III were among the earliest such plays seen in London and were (at least some of them) enormous stage successes. Even here, however, we can see how much Shakespeare learned from such earlier plays as *Gorboduc* and *The Troublesome Reign of King John*.

LONDON THEATERS AND DRAMATIC COMPANIES

Throughout Shakespeare's life, the propriety of acting any plays at all was a matter of bitter controversy. Indeed, when one considers the power and earnestness of the opposition, one is surprised that such a wealth of dramatic excellence could come into being and that Shakespeare's plays should reflect so little the anger and hostility generated by this continuing conflict.

Religious and Moral Opposition to the Theater

From the 1570s onward, and even earlier, the city fathers of London revealed an ever-increasing distrust of the public performance of plays. They fretted about the dangers of plague and of riotous assembly. They objected to the fact that apprentices idly wasted their time instead of working in their shops. And always the municipal authorities suspected immorality. Thus, by an order of the Common Council of London, dated December 6, 1574, the players were put under severe restrictions.

The order cites the reasons. The players, it was charged, had been acting in the innyards of the city, which in consequence were haunted by great multitudes of people, especially youths. These gatherings had been the occasions of frays and quarrels, "evil practices of incontinency in great inns"; the players published "uncomely and unshamefast speeches and doings," withdrew the Queen's subjects from divine service on Sundays and holidays, wasted the money of "poor and fond persons," gave opportunity to pick pockets, uttered "busy and seditious matters," and injured and maimed people by the falling of their scaffolds and by weapons and powder used in plays. The order goes on to state the Common Council's fear that if the plays, which had been forbidden on account of the plague, should be resumed, God's wrath would manifest itself by an increase of the infection. Therefore, no innkeeper, tavernkeeper, or other person might cause or suffer to be openly played "any play, interlude, comedy, tragedy, matter, or show" which had not been first licensed by the mayor and the Court of Aldermen.

The mayor and aldermen did not always state their case plainly, because Queen Elizabeth was a patron of the players, and because the players had friends and patrons in the Privy Council and among the nobility; sometimes,

however, they did so quite boldly. One sees the case against plays stated syllogistically in the following words of Thomas White, a preacher at Paul's Cross in 1577:

Look but upon the common plays of London, and see the multitude that flocketh to them and followeth them! Behold the sumptuous theater houses, a continual monument of London prodigality and folly! But I understand they are now forbidden because of the plague. I like the policy well if it hold still, for a disease is but botched and patched up that is not cured in the cause, and the cause of plagues is sin, if you look to it well, and the cause of sin are plays. Therefore the cause of plagues are plays. (From *A Sermon preached at Paul's Cross . . . in the Time of the Plague*, 1578.)

Moved, no doubt, by the prohibition of the Common Council, James Burbage, with a company of actors under the patronage of the Earl of Leicester, leased a site in Shoreditch, a London suburb in Middlesex, beyond the immediate jurisdiction of the official enemies in the Common Council, whose authority extended only to the city limits. By 1576, he had completed the Theatre. Perhaps he called it "the Theatre" because it had no competitor (other than the Red Lion, established in 1567 and used seemingly as a playing place for feasts and festival days in the performance style of Corpus Christi and saints' plays). Burbage erected what may have been England's first permanent commercial theatrical building. In general, the building combined features of the innyard and the animal-baiting house, having a central and probably paved courtyard open to the sky (like an innyard) and surrounding galleries on all sides (like an animal-baiting house). Burbage erected a stage at one side of the circular arena and put dressing rooms behind it to form the "tiring house" or backstage area for the actors; the facade of this "tiring house" served as a visible backdrop to the stage itself. Burbage's Theatre became the model for other public playhouses, such as the Curtain, the Swan, and the Globe, which were constructed later.

By building his playhouse in Shoreditch, Burbage gained immunity from the London authorities. The city fathers could not suppress plays or control them with perfect success if they were performed in Middlesex, or in the "liberty" of Blackfriars and similar districts exempted by charters from London's civic authority (see "London's Private Theaters," below), or (in the case of later playhouses) on the Bankside across the Thames in Surrey. In order to get at them in these suburban regions, the city authorities had to petition the Queen's Privy Council to give orders to the magistrates and officers of the law in these counties. The Queen's Privy Council, although always on the most polite terms with the Lord Mayor and his brethren of the city and always open to the argument that the assemblage of crowds caused the spread of the plague, was to a much less degree in sympathy with the moral scruples of the city. Current arguments for the plays,

The George Inn of Southwark, England, London's only surviving galleried inn, was destroyed by fire in 1676 but rebuilt the following year with two galleries instead of the original three. Despite these changes, the George Inn gives us the best picture we have of the kind of space in which traveling companies could mount their plays on bare platform stages.

derived from the works of scholars, poets, and playwrights, were numerous and often heard: namely, that classical antiquity gave precedent for dramatic spectacles; that by drawing a true picture of both the bad and the good in life, plays enabled people to choose the good; that people should have wholesome amusement; and that plays provided livelihood for loyal subjects of the Queen.

Of these arguments, to be sure, the Privy Council made little use, resting the case for plays instead on what was, no doubt, an unanswerable argument: that since the players were to appear before Her Majesty, especially during the Christmas/Shrovetide period, the players needed practice in order to prepare themselves to please the royal taste. A good deal of politic fencing ensued, and, so far as orders, complaints, and denunciations were concerned, the reforming opposition had much the better of it. The preachers thundered against plays. Pamphleteers denounced all matters pertaining to the stage: Stephen Gosson in *The School of Abuse, Containing a Pleasant Invective Against Poets, Pipers, Players, Jesters and Suchlike Caterpillars of a Commonwealth* (1579) and other works; Philip

Stubbes in *The Anatomy of Abuses* (1583); and finally and most furiously of all, William Prynne in *Histrio-Mastix: The Players' Scourge or Actor's Tragedy* (1633). Gosson spoke of plays as "the inventions of the devil, the offerings of idolatry, the pomp of worldlings, the blossoms of vanity, the root of apostacy, food of iniquity, riot and adultery." "Detest them," he warned. "Players are masters of vice, teachers of wantonness, spurs to impurity, the sons of idleness."

At first, such diatribes represented an extreme reforming opinion obviously not shared by a majority of London viewers. They kept coming to plays, and the flourishing public theaters attracted the talents of the age's leading dramatists. An ominous note of polarization was sounded, however, early in the reign of James I (1603–1625) when the rift between the Puritans and the court broke into open antagonism. After about 1604, when James alienated the Puritans at the Hampton Court Conference, the split between popular audiences and the best drama of the age became increasingly evident. Shakespeare's company, now the King's men, gravitated, whether through choice or necessity, toward the precinct of the court. Although the public theater, with its capacity for large audiences, continued to serve as a lively center of theatrical activity, Puritan opposition to the stage gathered momentum. Many dramatists, in turn, grew more satirical of London customs and more attuned to courtly tastes. Eventually, Puritan hostility to the theater was at least part of the motive behind Parliament's order to close the theaters in 1642.

The Public Theaters

A year or more after Burbage built the Theatre in 1576, the Curtain was put up near it by Philip Henslowe, or possibly by Henry Laneman, or Lanman. About ten years later, Philip Henslowe built the Rose, the first playhouse on the Bankside (the southern bank of the Thames River). In 1599, James Burbage's sons Richard and Cuthbert dismantled the Theatre because of trouble about the lease of the land and rebuilt it as the Globe on the Bankside. This Globe playhouse burned on June 29, 1613, from the discharge of cannon backstage during a performance of *All Is True*, a play thought to be identical with Shakespeare's *Henry VIII*. The Globe was rebuilt, probably in its original polygonal form, that is, essentially round with a large number of sides. In 1600, Henslowe built the Fortune as a theater for the Lord Admiral's men, who were chief rivals to the Lord Chamberlain's men. The companies were differently organized, in that the Lord Chamberlain's men were joint sharers in their own enterprise and owners of their own theatrical building, whereas Henslowe owned the Fortune (and the Rose before it) and served as landlord to the Admiral's men—no doubt profiting handsomely from their activities.

Various records of these theatrical buildings have survived. One such record is the Fortune contract, preserved at Dulwich College among other invaluable papers of Philip Henslowe, theatrical entrepreneur and father-in-law of the famous Edward Alleyn of the Lord Admiral's men. The contract for building the Fortune was let to the same contractor who had built the new Globe, and, since the specifications required that the Fortune should be like the Globe in all its main features, except that it was to be square instead of polygonal, we may gain from these specifications an idea of the Globe. A second documentary record is a drawing of the Swan, a Bankside theater, accompanying a description of the playhouse by Johannes De Witt, who visited London in 1596. The drawing, which was discovered in the University Library at Utrecht, is the work of one Van Buchell and may be based on drawings by De Witt himself. Besides the Fortune contract and the Swan drawing, we have two or three little pictures of the Elizabethan public stage on the title pages of published plays, the most important being that on the title page of William Alabaster's *Roxana* (1632). Just recently, in 1989, the discovery and excavation of the

foundations of the Rose playhouse and partial excavation of the Globe playhouse foundations in Southwark, together with the construction of a modern replica of the Globe playhouse near the site of these two theaters, have added invaluable archeological information about the dimensions of that acting arena.

The London Public Stage

From these documents and pictures and from scattered references to the theaters, as well as from extended studies of stage directions and scenic conditions in plays themselves, we have a fairly clear idea of the public stage in London. Its features are these: a pit about seventy feet in diameter, usually circular and open to the sky; surrounding this, galleries in three tiers, containing the most expensive seats; and a rectangular stage, about forty-three by twenty-seven feet, wider than it was deep, raised about five and one-half feet above the surface of the yard, sometimes built on trestles so that it could be removed if the house was also customarily used for bearbaiting and bullbaiting. The flat, open stage usually contained one trapdoor. Part of the stage was afforded some protection from the weather by a brightly decorated wooden roof supported by posts, constituting the "heavens." Above this roof was a "hut," perhaps containing suspension gear for ascents and descents. (The Rose appears originally to have been generally smaller than what is described here, with a stage that tapered toward the front to a width of only twenty-five feet or so. The building was somewhat expanded in 1592 but was still small compared with other theaters. The original building shows no certain evidence of a roof over the stage supported by pillars, but the later building appears to have had roof pillars at the front of the stage.)

At the back of the stage was a partition wall, the "tiring-house facade," with at least two doors in it connecting the stage with the actors' dressing rooms or "tiring house." In the Rose, the tiring-house facade seems to have curved with the polygonal shape of the theater building, but in the DeWitt drawing the Swan facade looks perfectly straight across. Some theaters appear to have had no more than two doors, left and right, as shown in the Swan drawing; other theaters may have had a third door in the center. The arrangement of the Globe playhouse in this important matter cannot be finally determined, although some particular scenes from Shakespeare's plays seem to demand a third door. In any case, the so-called inner stage, long supposed to have stood at the rear of the Elizabeth stage, almost certainly did not exist. A more modest "discovery space" could be provided at one of the curtained doors when needed, as for example in *The Tempest* when Ferdinand and Miranda are suddenly "discovered" at their game of chess by Prospero. Such scenes never called for extensive action within the

This drawing of an Elizabethan public stage appeared on the title page of the published version of William Alabaster's play Roxana *(1632).*

This diagram of the Swan Theatre (left) by Van Buchell (c. 1596), based on the observations of Johannes De Witt, shows features of the public playhouse shared by James Burbage's Theatre and the Globe. A modern sketch of the Swan Theatre (right) shows the open, encircling roof and a full view of the tiring house. Like the Globe and other open theaters, the design of the Swan seems to resemble the Elizabethan innyard with an added stage.

discovery space, however, and, indeed, the number of such discoveries in Elizabethan plays is very few. Well-to-do spectators who may have been seated in the gallery above the rear of the stage could not see into the discovery space. Accordingly, it was used sparingly and only for brief visual effects. Otherwise, the actors performed virtually all their scenes on the open stage. Sometimes curtains were hung over the tiring-house facade between the doors to facilitate scenes of concealment, as when Polonius and Claudius eavesdrop on Hamlet and Ophelia.

An upper station was sometimes used as an acting space, but not nearly so often as was once supposed. The gallery seats above the stage, sometimes known as the "Lord's room," were normally sold to well-to-do spectators. (We can see such spectators in the Swan drawing and in Alabaster's *Roxana*.) Occasionally, these box seats could be used by the actors, as when Juliet appears at her window (it is never called a balcony). In military sequences, as in the *Henry VI* plays, the tiring-house facade could represent the walls of a besieged city, with the city's defenders appearing "on the walls" (i.e., in the gallery above the stage) in order to parley with the besieging enemy standing below on the main stage. Such scenes were relatively infrequent, however, and usually required only a small number of persons to be aloft. A music room,

when needed, could be located in one of the gallery boxes over the stage, but public theaters did not emulate the private stages with music rooms and music between the acts until some time around 1609.

The use of scenery was almost wholly unknown on the Elizabethan public stage, although we do find occasional hints of the use of labels to designate a certain door or area as a fixed location (as, perhaps, in *The Comedy of Errors*). For the most part, the scene was unlimited and the concept of space was fluid. No proscenium arch or curtain stood between the actors and the audience, and so the action could not be easily interrupted. Only belatedly did the public companies adopt the private-theater practice of entr'acte music, as we have seen. Most popular Elizabethan plays were written to be performed nonstop. Five-act structure had little currency, especially at first, and the occasional act divisions in the published versions of Shakespeare's plays may be nonauthorial. Acting tempo was brisk. The Prologue of *Romeo and Juliet* speaks of "the two hours' traffic of our stage." Plays were performed in the afternoons and had to be completed by dark in order to allow the audience to return safely to London. During the winter season, playing time was severely restricted. Outbreaks of plague often occasioned the closing of the theaters, especially in warm weather.

Elizabethan dancers, shown above, perform on a stage below a gallery of musicians. Imported stage designs from Italy made more use of perspective scenery than did the commercial theaters.

A capacity audience for the popular theaters came to about 2,000 to 3,000 persons. (The recently excavated Rose playhouse foundations suggest an audience there of around 2,000.) For the most part, the audience was affluent, consisting chiefly of the gentry and of London's substantial mercantile citizenry who paid two to three pence or more for gallery seats or the "Lord's room," but the ample pit or yard also provided room for small shopkeepers and artisans who stood for a penny. The spectators were lively, demanding, and intelligent. Although Shakespeare does allow Hamlet to refer disparagingly on one occasion to the "groundlings" who "for the most part are capable of nothing but inexplicable dumbshows and noise" (*Hamlet*, 3.2.11–12), Shakespeare appealed to the keenest understanding of his whole audience, thereby achieving a breadth of vision seldom found in continental courtly drama of the same period. The vitality and financial success of the Elizabethan public theater is without parallel in English history. The city of London itself, in 1600 or so, had only about 100,000 inhabitants, yet throughout Shakespeare's career several companies were competing simultaneously for this audience and constantly producing new plays. Most new plays ran for only a few performances, so that the acting companies were always in rehearsal with new shows. The actors needed phenomenal memories and a gift of improvisation as well. Their acting seems to have been of a high caliber, despite the speed with which they worked. Among other things, many of them were expert fencers and singers.

The London public stage inherited many of its practices from native and medieval traditions. The fluid, open stage, with spectators on four sides, recalled the arena staging of many early Corpus Christi cycles, saints' plays, and morality plays. The adult professional companies were, as we have seen, descended from the itinerant troupes that had acted their plays throughout England in guildhalls, private residences, monastic houses and schools, and perhaps occasionally outdoors on booth stages (though the evidence for this last possible venue is scarce). The Elizabethan tiring-house facade and platform stage may have owed much to the kinds of theatrical space that touring actors had known, and perhaps to the arrangement of a booth stage and a trestle platform set up against one wall of an innyard where the guests of the inn could enjoy a performance, along with standing spectators in the yard. When the itinerant actors had set up their plays in noblemen's banqueting halls or at court, at any rate, they encountered another space that had an important influence on their concept of a theater: the Tudor hall. We must next examine the significance of this indoor theatrical setting.

The Tudor Hall

The Tudor banqueting hall played a major part in the staging of much early Tudor drama. Medwall's *Fulgens and Lucrece,* one of the earliest such plays, was written to be performed during the intervals of a state banquet. The patrician guests were seated at tables, while servingmen bustled to and fro or stood crowded together at the doors in the hall "screen." This screen or partition traversed the lower end of the rectangular hall, providing a passageway to the kitchens and to the outside. Its doors—often two, sometimes three—were normally curtained to prevent drafts. This arrangement of the doors bears an interesting resemblance to that of many playhouses in late Elizabethan England, both public and private. Moreover, hall screens and passageways were normally surmounted by a gallery, where musicians could play—an architectural feature markedly resembling the upper galleries of late Elizabethan theaters. Could the Tudor hall screen provide a natural facade for dramatic action? Perhaps it did, although records from Shakespeare's era only rarely document an actual performance in front of the screen, whereas performances were common at the upper end of the hall in front of the dais or in the midst of the hall, where the persons of highest social rank sitting on the dais would have had the best view. The actors of *Fulgens and Lucrece* clearly made use of the doorways in the hall screen, sometimes joking with the servingmen as the actors pushed their way into the hall, but they probably acted in the center, among the spectators' tables. John Heywood's *Play of the Weather* calls for a similar *mise en scène*. Although this ready-made "stage" sufficed for most Tudor plays, the actors sometimes provided additional stage structures; *Weather,* for example, calls for a throne room into which Jupiter can retire without leaving the hall. Similar structures could represent a shop, an orchard, a mountain, or what have you.

Guild and town halls, where players on tour performed before the mayor and council (and sometimes a wider public), provided a similar physical environment except that we cannot be sure that such spaces had galleries in the sixteenth century. Since the gallery is not necessary for many Tudor plays, the players may well have gained experience in halls of this kind that influenced their techniques of staging once they had gravitated to London.

Although both medieval and continental drama offered traditions of multiple staging, in which a series of simultaneously visible and adjacent structures would represent as fixed locations all the playing areas needed for the performance of a play, Tudor indoor staging seems to have made less use of this method than was once supposed. Nor did the various indoor theaters of Tudor England make extensive use of neoclassical staging from Italy, with its street scene in perspective created by means of lath-and-canvas stage "houses." Italian scenery of this sort came into use sooner in the court masque than in regular drama. Nevertheless, we do find in the Tudor indoor theater a neoclassical tendency toward a fixed locale, in preference to the unlimited open stage. *Gammer Gurton's Needle*, for example, acted probably in a university hall, seems to have used one stage structure, or possibly one door, to represent Gammer's house throughout the action, and another to represent Dame Chat's house. Shakespeare may have been influenced by this kind of fixed-locale staging in *The Comedy of Errors*. (Alan Nelson's *Early Cambridge Theaters*, 1994, is an important resource for school staging.)

The Private Stage

Despite such influences on the public stage, the most significant contribution of the Tudor hall and its hall screen was to the so-called private stage of the late Elizabethan period—"private" in the sense of being intended for a more select and courtly audience than that which frequented the "public" theaters. In the 1570s, choir boys began performing professionally to courtly and intellectual audiences in London. The choir boys had long performed plays for the royal and noble households to which they were attached, but in the 1570s they were, in effect, organized into professional acting companies. Sebastian Westcote and the Children of Paul's may have originated this enterprise. Their theater was apparently

The Tudor banqueting hall provided a place to "stage" much early Tudor drama. The actors performed on the floor among the tables of the guests. The Middle Temple Hall, shown here, later served as the location for a performance of Shakespeare's Twelfth Night *on February 2, 1602. The Middle Temple is one of the Inns of Court, where young men studied law and occasionally relaxed by staging dramatic entertainments.*

some indoor hall in the vicinity of St. Paul's in London, outfitted much like the typical domestic Tudor hall to which the boys had grown accustomed. Comparable indoor "private" theaters soon followed at Blackfriars and Whitefriars.

At some point, a low stage was constructed in front of the hall screen, and seats were provided for all the spectators. Many of these seats were in the "pit," or what we would call the "orchestra," facing toward the stage at one end of the rectangular room. Other seats were in galleries along both sides of the room; these were quite elaborate in the so-called Second Blackfriars of 1596 and provided two or three tiers of seats. Elegant box seats stood at either side of the stage itself. The Second Blackfriars had a permanently built tiring house to the rear of the stage, with probably three doors. Above it was a gallery used variously as a lord's room, a music room, and an upper station for occasional acting.

The private theater flourished during the 1580s and again after 1598–1599, having been closed down during most of the 1590s because of its satirical activities. Although it was a commercial theater, it was "private" in its clientele, because its high price of admission (sixpence) excluded those who could stand in the yards of the "public" theaters for a penny (roughly the equivalent of an hour's wage for a skilled worker). Plays written for the more select audiences of the "private" theaters tended to be more satirical and oriented to courtly values than those written for the "public" theaters, although the distinction is by no means absolute.

A reconstruction of the Second Blackfriars, featuring a rectangular stage, a tiring house with three doors, and a gallery.

COURTESY: C. WALTER HODGES

London Private Theaters

The important private theaters of Shakespeare's London were two in the precinct, or "liberty," of Blackfriars, an early one in Whitefriars about which little is known, a later one there, and a theater at Paul's, the exact location and nature of which is not known. In the thirteenth century, the mother house of the Dominican friars, or Blackfriars, was established on the sloping ground between St. Paul's Cathedral and the river. It was a sizable institution, ultimately covering about five acres of ground. It stood on the very border of the city and, after the custom of the time, was made a liberty; that is to say, it had its own local government and was removed from the immediate jurisdiction of the city of London. After the suppression of the friary and the confiscation of its lands, the jealousy existing between the Privy Council, representing the crown, and the mayor and aldermen, representing the city and probably also the rights of property holders, prevented the district of the Blackfriars from losing its political independence of the municipality. It was still a liberty and therefore attractive to players and other persons wishing to avoid the London authorities. At the same time, aristocrats residing in the area required protection, and the crown had certain rights still in its control.

From 1576 to 1584, the Children of the Queen's Chapel, one of the two most important companies of boy actors, had used a hall in the precinct of Blackfriars in which to act their plays. Here were acted at least some of John Lyly's plays. In 1596, James Burbage purchased property in this precinct and seems to have spent a good deal of money in its adaptation for use as an indoor theater (the so-called Second Blackfriars). He probably appreciated its advantages over Cripplegate or the Bankside of greater proximity to London and of protection against the elements, particularly for use in winter. But the aristocratic residents of the Blackfriars by petition to the Privy Council prevented him from making use of his theater. Plays within the city proper had only recently been finally and successfully prohibited, and the petitioners no doubt objected to their intrusion into Blackfriars on the grounds that the plays and their crowds were a nuisance.

Burbage's new indoor theater may have lain idle from the time of its preparation until 1600; but, in any case, in that year it became the scene of many plays. It was let by lease for the use of the Children of the Chapel, who in 1604 became the Children of the Queen's Revels. Their theater managers brought into their service a number of new dramatists—Ben Jonson, John Marston, George Chapman, and later John Webster. The vogue of the plays acted by the Children of the Chapel was so great as to damage the patronage of the established companies and to compel them to go on the road. Out of this rivalry between the children and the adult actors arose that open competition alluded to in *Hamlet* (2.2.328–362) and sometimes referred to today as the "War of the Theaters." The skirmishes were relatively brief, arising in part from a clash of personalities among Jonson, Marston, and Thomas Dekker, but the debate between public and private acting companies was significant as an indication of whether London drama would continue to play to large popular audiences or would increasingly turn to a more courtly clientele. In 1608, the Burbage interests secured the evacuation of the lease, so that the theater in Blackfriars became the winter playhouse of Shakespeare's company from that time forward.

System of Patronage

In 1572, common players of interludes, along with minstrels, bearwards, and fencers, were included within the hard terms of the act for the punishment of vagabonds, provided that such common players were not enrolled as the servants of a baron of the realm or of some honorable person of greater degree. The result was a system of patronage of theatrical companies in Elizabethan and Jacobean times, according to which players became the "servants" of some nobleman or of some member of the royal family.

By the time Shakespeare came to London in the late 1580s, many of these companies were already in existence, some of which long antedated the passage of the act of 1572. Provincial records of the visits of players, to be sure, sometimes failed to distinguish actors from acrobats or other public performers who were similarly organized. Nonetheless, we have evidence that various companies of players performed in London and elsewhere in the late 1580s under the patronage of the Queen, the Earl of Worcester, the Earl of Leicester, the Earl of Oxford, the Earl of Sussex, the Lord Admiral, and Charles, Lord Howard of Effingham. These companies were eventually much reduced in number; usually only three adult companies acted at any given time in London during Shakespeare's prime. In addition, the children's companies, privately controlled, acted intermittently but at times very successfully. The most important of these were the Children of the Chapel and Queen's Revels and the Children of Paul's, but there were also boy players of Windsor, Eton College, the Merchant Taylors, Westminster, and other schools.

Shakespeare and the London Theatrical Companies

We know that by 1592 Shakespeare had arrived in London and had achieved sufficient notice as a young playwright to arouse the resentment of a rival dramatist, Robert Greene. In that year, shortly before he died, Greene—or possibly his editor after Greene's death—lashed out at an "upstart crow, beautified with our feathers," who had had the audacity to fancy himself "the only Shake-scene in a country" (*Groats-worth of Wit*). This petulant outburst was plainly directed at Shakespeare, since Greene included in his remarks a parody of some lines from *3 Henry VI*. As a university man and an established dramatist, Greene seems to have resented the intrusion into his profession of a mere player who was not university trained. This "upstart crow" was achieving a very real success on the London stage. Shakespeare had probably already written *The Comedy of Errors, Love's Labor's Lost, The Two Gentlemen of Verona*, the *Henry VI* plays, and *Titus Andronicus*, and perhaps also *Richard III* and *The Taming of the Shrew*.

For which acting company or companies had he written these plays, however? By 1594, we know that Shakespeare was an established member of the Lord Chamberlain's company, important enough, in fact, to have been named, along with Will Kempe and Richard Burbage, as payee for court performances on December 26 and 28 of 1594. But when had he joined the Chamberlain's men, and for whom had he written and acted previously? These are the problems of the so-called dark years, during which Shakespeare came to London (perhaps around 1587) and got started on his career.

One prestigious acting company he could have joined was the Earl of Leicester's company, led by James Burbage, father of Shakespeare's later colleague, Richard Burbage. Leicester was a favorite minister of Queen Elizabeth until his death in 1588, and his company of actors received from the Queen in 1574 an extraordinary patent to perform plays anywhere in England, despite all local prohibitions, provided that the plays were approved beforehand by the master of the Queen's Revels. Since an act of 1572 had outlawed all unlicensed troupes, Leicester's men and similar companies attached to important noblemen were given a virtual monopoly over public acting. In 1576, Burbage built the Theatre for his company in the northeast suburbs of London. This group also toured the provinces: Leicester's company visited Stratford-upon-Avon in 1587. Conceivably, Shakespeare served an apprenticeship in this company, though no evidence exists to prove a connection. Leicester's company had lost some of its prominence in 1583, when several of its best men joined the newly formed Queen's men, with Richard Tarlton as its most famous actor. The remaining members of Leicester's company disbanded in 1588 upon the death of the Earl, and many of its principal actors ultimately became part of Lord Strange's company. These probably included George Bryan, Will Kempe, and Thomas Pope, all of whom subsequently went on to become Lord Chamberlain's men.

Lord Strange's (The Earl of Derby's) Men

The Queen's men gained an extraordinary prominence in the 1580s, as Scott McMillin and Sally-Beth MacLean have shown in the *Queen's Men and Their Plays* (1998). This acting group was assembled under royal sponsorship as an instrument of furthering the Protestant Reformation through its performances of plays, and did so with notable success, although it then declined rapidly in the early 1590s chiefly because as a touring company it was unprepared to compete with the new companies that learned how to succeed in the metropolis by staging a wide variety of plays in a fixed London theater. Prominent among the acting companies to which Shakespeare could have belonged when he came to London, probably in the late 1580s, were Lord Strange's men, the Lord Admiral's men, the Earl of Pembroke's men, and the Earl of Sussex's men. Scholars have long speculated that Shakespeare may have joined the company of Ferdinando Stanley, Lord Strange (who in 1593 became the Earl of Derby). The names of George Bryan, Will Kempe, and Thomas Pope appear on a roster of Strange's company in 1593, along with those of John Heminges and Augustine Phillips. All of these men later became part of the Lord Chamberlain's company, most of them when it was first formed in 1594. Shakespeare's name does not appear on the 1593 Lord Strange's list (which was a license for touring in the provinces), but he may possibly have stayed in London to attend to his writing while the company toured. Certainly, an important number of his later associates belonged to this group.

During the years from 1590 to 1594, some of Lord Strange's men appear to have joined forces on occasion with Edward Alleyn and others of the Admiral's men. This impressive combination of talents enjoyed a successful season in 1591–1592, with six performances at court. Alleyn's father-in-law, Philip Henslowe, recorded in his *Diary* the performances of the combined players in early 1592, probably at the Rose Theatre. Their repertory included a *Harey the vj* and a *Titus & Vespacia*. The latter play is, however, no longer thought to have any connection with Shakespeare's *Titus Andronicus;* and the *Harey the vj* may or may not have been Shakespeare's, since *3 Henry VI* was (according to its 1595 title page) acted by Pembroke's men, rather than Lord Strange's men. If Shakespeare was a member of the Strange-Admiral's combination in 1591–1592, we are at a loss to explain why Henslowe's 1592 list records so many performances of plays by Marlowe, Greene, Kyd, and others, but none that are certainly by Shakespeare. On the other hand, the *Harey the vj* may be his, and the title page of the 1594 Quarto of *Titus Andronicus* does list the Earl of Derby's men as performers of the play, in addition to the Earl of Pembroke's and the Earl of Sussex's men. (Lord Strange's men became officially known as the Earl of Derby's men when Lord Strange was made an earl in September 1593.) At any rate, the company disbanded when the Earl died in April 1594, leaving them without a patron. The connection with the Admiral's men was discontinued, with Alleyn returning to the Admiral's men and the rest of the

Clowns were enormously popular on the Elizabethan stage. Of the many Elizabethan clowns whose names are known to us, Richard Tarlton is one of the most famous. (Will Kempe, in Shakespeare's company, the Lord Chamberlain's men, is another; see pp. lxviii–lxix.) Tarlton is shown here inside an elaborate letter T, dancing a jig with his pipe and tabor. Such jigs were often used at the conclusion of a play.

group forming a new company under the patronage of Henry Carey, first Lord Hunsdon, the Lord Chamberlain.

The Earl of Pembroke's Men

The other company to which Shakespeare is most likely to have belonged prior to 1594 is the Earl of Pembroke's company. This group came to grief in 1593–1594, evidently as a result of virulent outbursts of the plague, which had kept the theaters closed during most of 1592 and 1593. Pembroke's men were forced to tour the provinces and then to sell a number of their best plays to the booksellers. Henslowe wrote to Alleyn in September 1593 of the extreme financial plight of Pembroke's company: "As for my lord of Pembroke's [men], which you desire to know where they be, they are all at home and has been this five or six weeks, for they cannot save their charges [expenses] with travel, as I hear, and were fain to pawn their parell [apparel] for their charge." Soon thereafter this company disbanded.

Pembroke's men were associated with a significant number of Shakespeare's early plays. Among the playbooks they evidently sold in 1593–1594 were *The Taming of a Shrew* and *The True Tragedy of Richard Duke of York*. The first of these was published in 1594 with the assertion that it had been "sundry times acted by the Right Honorable the Earle of Pembroke his Servants." Although the text of this quarto is not Shakespeare's play as we know it but, instead, an anonymous version, most scholars now feel certain that it was an imitation of Shakespeare's play and that the work performed by Pembroke's men was, in fact, Shakespeare's. The same conclusion pertains to a performance in 1594 of *"the Tamynge of a Shrowe"* at Newington Butts, a playhouse south of London Bridge. Henslowe's *Diary* informs us that the actors on this occasion were either the Lord Chamberlain's or the Lord Admiral's men. The probability, then, is that Shakespeare's *The Taming of the Shrew* passed from Pembroke's men to the Chamberlain's men when Pembroke's company collapsed in 1593–1594.

The True Tragedy of Richard Duke of York, published in 1595, was a seemingly unauthorized quarto of Shakespeare's *3 Henry VI.* Its title page declared that it had been "sundry times acted by the Right Honorable the Earl of Pembroke his Servants." Probably they acted *2 Henry VI* as well, to which part three was a sequel. In addition, the 1594 Quarto of *Titus Andronicus* mentions on its title page the Earl of Pembroke's servants, although the Earl of Derby's and the Earl of Sussex's men are named there as well. Thus, Pembroke's men performed as many as four of Shakespeare's early plays—more than we can assign to any other known company. Nevertheless, their claim to Shakespeare remains uncertain. We simply do not know who acted several of Shakespeare's earliest plays, such as *The Comedy of Errors, Love's Labor's Lost,* and *The Two Gentlemen of Verona.* Lord Strange's (Derby's) men, as we have seen, did act something called *Harey the vj* and are named on the 1594 title page of *Titus Andronicus.* Sussex's men may conceivably have owned for a time some early Shakespearean plays that later went to the Lord Chamberlain's men, such as *Titus Andronicus.* The Queen's men, although associated with no known Shakespeare play, other than the old *King Lear* (acted jointly with Sussex's men in 1593), were a leading company during the years in question. All we can say for sure is that the difficulties of 1592–1593 with the plague and the death of the Earl of Derby in 1594 led to a major reshuffling of the London acting companies. From this reshuffling emerged in 1594 the Lord Chamberlain's company, with Shakespeare and Richard Burbage (whose earlier history is also difficult to trace) as two of its earliest and most prominent members.

SHAKESPEARE'S LIFE AND WORK

THE EARLY YEARS, 1564–C. 1594

Stratford-upon-Avon

About Shakespeare's place of birth, Stratford-upon-Avon, there is no doubt. He spent his childhood there and returned periodically throughout his life. During most or all of his long professional career in London, his wife and children lived in Stratford. He acquired property and took some interest in local affairs. He retired to Stratford and chose to be buried there. Its Warwickshire surroundings lived in his poetic imagination.

The Stratford of Shakespeare's day was a "handsome small market town" (as described by William Camden) of perhaps 1,500 inhabitants, with fairly broad streets and half-timbered houses roofed with thatch. It could boast of a long history and an attractive setting on the river Avon. A bridge of fourteen arches, built in 1496 by Sir Hugh Clopton, Lord Mayor of London, spanned the river. Beside the Avon stood Trinity Church, built on the site of a Saxon monastery. The chapel of the Guild of the Holy Trinity, dating from the thirteenth century, and an old King Edward VI grammar school were buildings of note. Strat-

The earliest written reference to William Shakespeare is this record of his christening in the register of Holy Trinity Church at Stratford, April 26, 1564. The entry reads, "Gulielmus filius Johannes Shakspere."

REPRODUCED FROM THE 1930 ORDNANCE SURVEY MAP

The town of Stratford-upon-Avon as Shakespeare knew it. The house in which he is considered to have been born is on Henley Street; the larger house he purchased in 1597, New Place, is on Chapel Street.

ford had maintained a grammar school at least since 1424 and probably long before that. It was a town without the domination of clergy, aristocracy, or great wealth. It lay in a rich agricultural region, in the county of Warwickshire. To the north of Stratford lay the Forest of Arden.

Shakespeare's Family

The family that bore the name of Shakespeare was well distributed throughout England, but was especially numerous in Warwickshire. A name "Saquespee," in various spellings, is found in Normandy at an early date. It means, according to J. Q. Adams, "to draw out the sword quickly." That name, in the form "Sakspee," with many variants, is found in England; also the name "Saksper," varying gradually to the form "Shakespeare." It may have been wrought into that form by the obvious military meaning of "one who shakes the spear."

Our first substantial records of the family begin with Richard Shakespeare, who was, in all probability, Shakespeare's grandfather, a farmer living in the village of

Snitterfield four miles from Stratford. He was a tenant on the property of Robert Arden of Wilmcote, a wealthy man with the social status of gentleman. Richard Shakespeare died about 1561, possessed of an estate valued at the very respectable sum of thirty-eight pounds and seventeen shillings.

His son John made a great step forward in the world by his marriage with Mary Arden, daughter of his father's landlord. John Shakespeare had some property of his own and through his wife acquired a good deal more. He moved from Snitterfield to Stratford at some date before 1552. He rose to great local importance in Stratford and bought several houses, among which was the one on Henley Street traditionally identified as Shakespeare's birthplace. William Shakespeare was born in 1564 and was baptized on April 26. The exact date of his birth is not known, but traditionally we celebrate it on April 23, the feast day of St. George, England's patron saint. (The date is at least plausible in view of the practice of baptizing infants shortly after birth.) The house in which Shakespeare was probably born, though almost entirely rebuilt and changed in various and unknown ways during the years that have intervened since Shakespeare's birth, still stands. It is of considerable size, having four rooms on the ground floor, and must, therefore, have been an important business house in the Stratford of those days. John Shakespeare's occupation seems to have been that of a tanner and glover; that is, he cured skins, made gloves and some other leather goods, and sold them in his shop. He was also a dealer in wool, grain, malt, and other farm produce.

The long story, beginning in 1552, of John Shakespeare's success and misfortunes in Stratford is attested to by many borough records. He held various city offices. He was ale taster (inspector of bread and malt), burgess (petty constable), affeeror (assessor of fines), city chamberlain (treasurer), alderman, and high bailiff of the town—the highest municipal office in Stratford. At some time around 1576, he applied to the Herald's office for the right to bear arms and style himself a gentleman. This petition was later to be renewed and successfully carried through to completion by his famous son. In 1577 or 1578, however, when William was as yet only thirteen or fourteen years old, John Shakespeare's fortunes began a sudden and mysterious decline. He absented himself from council meetings. He had to mortgage his wife's property and showed other signs of being in financial difficulty. He became involved in serious litigation and was assessed heavy fines. Although he kept his position on the corporation council until 1586 or 1587, he was finally replaced as alderman because of his failure to attend. Conceivably, John Shakespeare's sudden difficulties were the result of persecution for his Catholic faith, since John's wife's family had remained loyal to Catholicism, and the old faith was being attacked with new vigor in the Warwickshire

This house on Henley Street in Stratford is considered to have been the birthplace of Shakespeare. Its considerable size shows what must have been an important house of business. Shakespeare's father dealt chiefly in leather goods, though he also traded in wool, grain, and other farm produce.

region in 1577 and afterwards. This hypothesis is unsubstantial, however, especially in view of the fact that some Catholics and Puritans seemed to have held posts of trust and to have remained prosperous in Stratford during this period. In the last analysis, we have little evidence as to John Shakespeare's religious faith or as to the reasons for his sudden reversal of fortune.

The family of Shakespeare's mother could trace its ancestry back to the time of William the Conqueror, and Shakespeare's father, in spite of his troubles, was a citizen of importance. John Shakespeare made his mark, instead of writing his name, but so did other men of the time who we know could read and write. His offices, particularly that of chamberlain, and the various public functions he discharged indicate that he must have had some education.

Shakespeare in School

Nicholas Rowe, who published in 1709 the first extensive biographical account of Shakespeare, reports the tradition that Shakespeare studied "for some time at a Free-School." Although the list of students who actually attended the King's New School at Stratford-upon-Avon in the late sixteenth century has not survived, we cannot doubt that Rowe is reporting accurately. Shakespeare's father, as a leading citizen of Stratford, would scarcely have spurned the benefits of one of Stratford's most prized institutions. The town had had a free school since the thirteenth century, at first under the auspices of the Church. During the reign of King Edward VI (1547–1553), the Church lands were expropriated by the crown and the town of Stratford was granted a corporate charter. At this time, the school was reorganized as the King's New School, named in honor of the reigning monarch. It prospered. Its teachers, or "masters," regularly held degrees from Oxford during Shakespeare's childhood and received salaries that were superior to those of most comparable schools.

Much has been learned about the curriculum of such a school. A child would first learn the rudiments of reading and writing English by spending two or three years in a "petty" or elementary school. The child learned to read from a "hornbook," a single sheet of paper mounted on a board and protected by a thin transparent layer of horn, on which was usually printed the alphabet in small and capital letters and the Lord's Prayer. The child would also practice an ABC book with catechism. When the child had demonstrated the ability to read satisfactorily, the child was admitted, at about the age of seven, to the grammar school proper. Here the day was a rigorous one, usually extending from 6 A.M. in the summer or 7 A.M. in the winter until 5 P.M. Intervals for food or brief

The interior of the Stratford grammar school: a late and not very reliable tradition claims that Shakespeare's desk was third from the front on the left-hand side.

recreation came at midmorning, noon, and midafternoon. Holidays occurred at Christmas, Easter, and Whitsuntide (usually late May and June), comprising perhaps forty days in all through the year. Discipline was strict, and physical punishment was common.

Latin formed the basis of the grammar school curriculum. The scholars studied grammar, read ancient writers, recited, and learned to write in Latin. A standard text was the *Grammatica Latina* by William Lilly or Lyly, grandfather of the later Elizabethan dramatist John Lyly. The scholars also became familiar with the *Disticha de Moribus* (moral proverbs) attributed to Cato, *Aesop's Fables,* the *Eclogues* of Baptista Spagnuoli Mantuanus or Mantuan (alluded to in *Love's Labor's Lost*), the *Eclogues* and *Aeneid* of Virgil, the comedies of Plautus or Terence (sometimes performed in Latin by the children), Ovid's *Metamorphoses* and other of his works, and possibly some Horace and Seneca.

Shakespeare plentifully reveals in his dramatic writings an awareness of many of these authors, especially Plautus (in *The Comedy of Errors*), Ovid (in *A Midsummer Night's Dream* and elsewhere), and Seneca (in *Titus Andronicus*). Although he often consulted translations of these authors, he seems to have known the originals as well. He had, in Ben Jonson's learned estimation, "small Latin and less Greek"; the tone is condescending, but the statement does concede that Shakespeare had some of both. He would have acquired some Greek in the last years of his grammar schooling. By twentieth-century standards, Shakespeare had a fairly comprehensive amount of training in the ancient classics, certainly enough to account for the general, if unscholarly, references we find in the plays.

Shakespeare's Marriage

When Shakespeare was eighteen years old, he married Anne Hathaway, a woman eight years his senior. (The inscription on her grave states that she was sixty-seven when she died in August 1623.) The bishop's register of

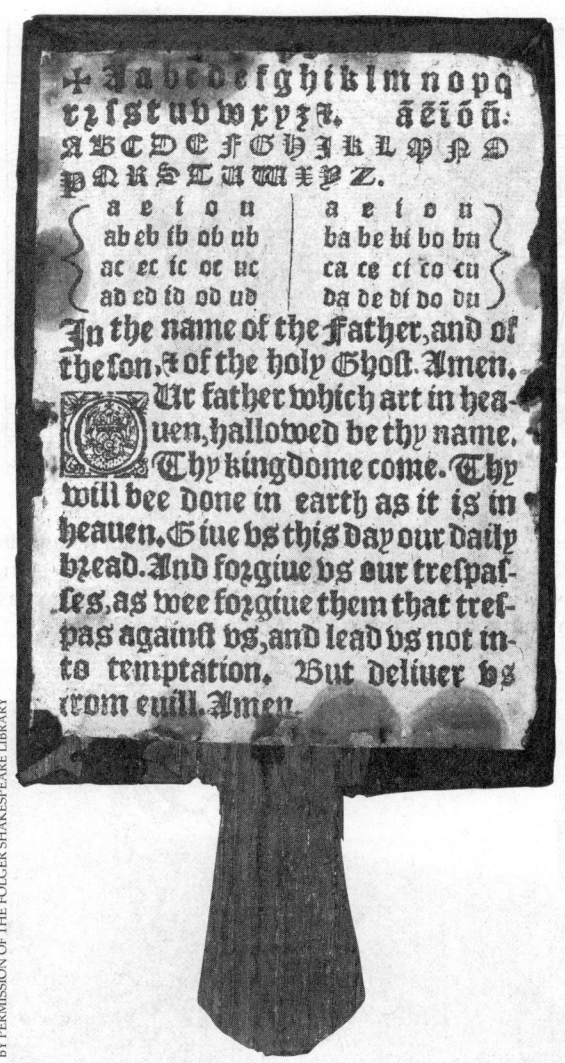

BY PERMISSION OF THE FOLGER SHAKESPEARE LIBRARY

The hornbook pictured here—showing the alphabet and the Lord's Prayer—was part of a child's education in Shakespeare's time.

ing of the banns rather than the usual three. (The reading of the banns, or announcement in church of a forthcoming marriage, usually on three successive Sundays, enabled any party to object to the marriage if he or she knew of any legal impediment.) Since the reading of all banns was suspended for long periods during Advent (before Christmas) and Lent (before Easter), a couple intending to marry shortly before Christmas might have had to wait until April before the banns could be read thrice. Accordingly, the bishop not uncommonly granted a license permitting couples to marry during the winter season with only one reading of the banns. To obtain such a license, two friends of the bride's family had to sign a bond obligating themselves to pay the bishop up to forty pounds, should any impediment to the marriage result in a legal action against the bishop for having issued the license.

The actual record of the marriage in a parish register has not survived, but presumably the couple were married shortly after obtaining the license. They may have been married in Temple Grafton, where Anne had relatives. The couple took up residence in Stratford. Anne was already pregnant at the time of the marriage, for she gave birth to a daughter, Susanna, on May 26, 1583. The birth of a child six months after the wedding may explain the need for haste the previous November. These circumstances, and Anne's considerable seniority in age to William, have given rise to much speculation about matters that can never be satisfactorily resolved. We do know that a formal betrothal in the presence of witnesses could legally validate a binding relationship, enabling a couple to consummate their love without social stigma. We know also that Shakespeare dramatized the issue of premarital contract and pregnancy in *Measure for Measure*. Whether Shakespeare entered into such a formal relationship with Anne is, however, undiscoverable.

On February 2, 1585, Shakespeare's only other children, the twins Hamnet and Judith, were baptized in Stratford Church. The twins seem to have been named after Shakespeare's friends and neighbors, Hamnet Sadler, a baker, and his wife, Judith.

The Seven "Dark" Years

From 1585, the year in which his twins were baptized, until 1592, when he was first referred to as an actor and dramatist of growing importance in London, Shakespeare's activities are wholly unknown. Presumably, at some time during this period he made his way to London and entered its theatrical world, but otherwise we can only record traditions and guesses as to what he did between the ages of 21 and 28.

One of the oldest and most intriguing suggestions comes from John Aubrey, who, in collecting information in the late seventeenth century about actors and drama-

Worcester, the central city of the diocese, shows for November 27, 1582, the issue of a bishop's license for the marriage of William Shakespeare and Anne "Whately"; the bond of sureties issued next day refers to her as "Hathaway." She has been identified with all reasonable probability as Agnes (or Anne) Hathaway, daughter of the then recently deceased Richard Hathaway of the hamlet of Shottery, a short distance from Stratford.

The obtaining of a license was not normally required for a marriage. William Shakespeare and Anne Hathaway seem to have applied for a license on this occasion because they wished to be married after only one read-

A schoolroom in Tudor England.

tists for his "Minutes of Lives," sought the help of one William Beeston. John Dryden believed Beeston to be "the chronicle of the stage," and Aubrey seems also to have had a high opinion of Beeston's theatrical knowledge. In his manuscript, Aubrey made a note to himself: "W. Shakespeare—quaere [i.e., inquire of] Mr. Beeston, who knows most of him." Aubrey then cites Beeston as his authority for this tradition about Shakespeare:

The substantial farmhouse owned by the Hathaways of Shottery, originally known as "Hewland" but now almost universally famous as Anne Hathaway's Cottage.

Though, as Ben Jonson says of him, that he had but little Latin and less Greek, he understood Latin pretty well, for he had been in his younger years a schoolmaster in the country.

Beeston had been a theatrical manager all his life. He was the son of the actor Christopher Beeston, who had been a member of Shakespeare's company, probably from 1596 until 1602, and who therefore had occasion to know Shakespeare well.

Shakespeare's own grammar school education would not have qualified him to be the master of a school, but he could have served as "usher" or assistant to the master. The idea that Shakespeare may have taught in this way is not unattractive. Although, as we have seen, he had some acquaintance with Plautus, Ovid, and other classical writers through his own grammar school reading, a stint as schoolmaster would have made these authors more familiar and readily accessible to him when he began writing his plays and nondramatic poems. His earliest works—*The Comedy of Errors, Love's Labor's Lost, Titus Andronicus, Venus and Adonis, The Rape of Lucrece*—show most steadily and directly the effect of his classical reading. Schoolteaching experience might have encouraged his ambitions to be a writer, like Marlowe or Greene, who went to London not to be actors but to try their hands at poetry and playwriting. All in all, however, it seems more probable that Shakespeare became a young actor rather than a schoolteacher.

Another tradition about the years from 1585 to 1592 asserts that Shakespeare served part of an apprenticeship in Stratford. This suggestion comes to us from one John Dowdall, who, traveling through Warwickshire in 1693, heard the story from an old parish clerk who was showing him around the town of Stratford. According to this parish clerk, Shakespeare had been bound as apprentice to a butcher but ran away from his master to London where he was received into a playhouse as "servitor." John Aubrey records a similar tradition: "When he [Shakespeare] was a boy he exercised his father's trade." Aubrey believed this trade to have been that of a butcher. Moreover, says Aubrey, "When he killed a calf, he would do it in a high style, and make a speech." No other evidence confirms, however, that Shakespeare was a runaway apprentice. The allusion to "killing a calf" may, instead, refer to an ancient rural amusement in which the slaughter of a calf was staged behind a curtain for the entertainment of visitors at county fairs. Conceivably, Shakespeare's participation in such a game during his youth may have given rise to the tradition that he had been a butcher's apprentice.

Another legend, that of Shakespeare's deer stealing, has enjoyed wide currency. We are indebted for this story to the Reverend Richard Davies, who, some time between 1688 and 1709, jotted down some gossipy interpolations in the manuscripts of the Reverend William Fulman. (Fulman himself was an antiquarian who had collected a number of notes about Shakespeare and Stratford.) According to Davies, Shakespeare was "much given to all unluckiness in stealing venison and rabbits, particularly from Sir —— Lucy, who had him oft whipped and sometimes imprisoned and at last made him fly his native country, to his great advancement." This tradition has led to speculation by Nicholas Rowe that Justice Shallow of *2 Henry IV* and *The Merry Wives of Windsor* is a satirical portrait of Sir Thomas Lucy of Charlecote Hall and that Shakespeare even composed an irreverent ballad about Lucy that added to the urgency of Shakespeare's departure for London. In fact, however, there is no compelling reason to believe that Shallow is based on Lucy, on Justice William Gardiner of Surrey (as Leslie Hotson insists), or on any live Elizabethan. We don't know that Shakespeare ever drew contemporary portraits in his plays, as is sometimes alleged; is Polonius in *Hamlet* Lord Burghley, for example, or is he Shakespeare's original portrait of a minister of state who is also a busybody? Nor do we know if the deer-slaying incident took place at all. It makes interesting fiction but unreliable biography.

Shakespeare's Arrival in London

Because of the total absence of reliable information concerning the seven years from 1585 to 1592, we do not know how Shakespeare got his start in the theatrical world. He may have joined one of the touring companies that came to Stratford and then accompanied the players to London. Edmund Malone offered the unsupported statement (in 1780) that Shakespeare's "first office in the theater was that of prompter's attendant." Presumably, a young man from the country would have had to begin at the bottom. Shakespeare's later work certainly reveals an intimate and practical acquaintance with technical matters of stagecraft. In any case, his rise to eminence as an actor and a writer seems to have been rapid. He was fortunate also in having at least one prosperous acquaintance in London, Richard Field, formerly of Stratford and the son of an associate of Shakespeare's father. Field was a printer, and in 1593 and 1594 he published two handsome editions of Shakespeare's first serious poems, *Venus and Adonis* and *The Rape of Lucrece*.

"The Only Shake-scene in a Country"

The first allusion to Shakespeare after his Stratford days is a vitriolic attack on him. It occurs in *Greene's Groatsworth of Wit Bought with a Million of Repentance,* written by Robert Greene during the last months of his wretched existence (he died in poverty in September 1592). A famous passage in this work lashes out at the actors of the public theaters for having deserted Greene and for bestowing their favor instead on a certain upstart dramatist. The passage warns three fellow dramatists and University Wits, Christopher Marlowe, Thomas Nashe, and George Peele, to abandon the writing of plays before they fall prey to a similar ingratitude. The diatribe runs as follows:

> . . . Base minded men all three of you, if by my misery you be not warned. For unto none of you (like me) sought those burs to cleave—those puppets, I mean, that spake from our mouths, those antics garnished in our colors. Is it not strange that I, to whom they all have been beholding, is it not like that you, to whom they all have been beholding, shall (were ye in that case as I am now) be both at once of them forsaken? Yes, trust them not. For there is an upstart crow, beautified with our feathers, that with his "Tiger's heart wrapped in a player's hide" supposes he is as well able to bombast out a blank verse as the best of you, and, being an absolute *Johannes Factotum,* is in his own conceit the only Shake-scene in a country.

The "burs" here referred to are the actors who have forsaken Greene in his poverty for the rival playwright "Shake-scene"—an obvious hit at Shakespeare. The sneer at a *"Johannes Factotum"* suggests another dig at Shakespeare for being a jack-of-all-trades—actor, playwright, poet, and theatrical handyman in the directing and producing of plays. The most unmistakable reference to Shakespeare, however, is to be found in the burlesque line, "Tiger's heart wrapped in a player's hide," modeled after "Oh, tiger's heart wrapped in a woman's hide!" from *3 Henry VI* (1.4.137). Shakespeare's success as a dramatist had led to an envious outburst from an older, disappointed rival. (Did Shakespeare possibly have this attack in mind some years later when he has Polonius object, in *Hamlet,* 2.2.111–12, "'beautified' is a vile phrase"?)

Soon after Greene's death, Henry Chettle, who had seen the manuscript through the press (and who today some believe to have written the attack himself), issued an apology in his *Kind-Heart's Dream* that may refer to Shakespeare. The apology begins with a disclaimer of all personal responsibility for the incident and with Chettle's insistence that he has neither known nor wishes to know Marlowe (whom Greene's pamphlet had accused of atheism). Toward another unidentified playwright, on the other hand, Chettle expresses genuine concern and regret that Chettle had not done more to soften the acerbity of Greene's vitriol:

> The other, whom at that time I did not so much spare as since I wish I had, for that, as I have moderated the heat of living writers and might have used my own discretion (especially in such a case, the author being dead), that I did not I am as sorry as if the original fault had been my fault; because myself have seen his demeanor no less civil than he excellent in the quality he professes. Besides, divers of worship have reported his uprightness of dealing, which argues his honesty and his facetious grace in writing that approves his art.

If the unnamed person here is to be understood as Shakespeare, it represents him in a most attractive light. Chettle freely admits to having been impressed by this person's civility. He praises the dramatist as "excellent in the quality he professes," that is, excellent as an actor. Chettle notes with approval that the man he is describing enjoys the favor of certain persons of importance, some of whom have borne witness to his uprightness in dealing. *Greene's Groatsworth of Wit,* then, with its rancorous attack on Shakespeare, has paradoxically led to the plausible inference (though not certain in its identification) that in 1592 Shakespeare was regarded as a man of pleasant demeanor, honest reputation, and acknowledged skill as an actor and writer.

Dramatic Apprenticeship

By the end of the year 1594, when after the long plague the theatrical companies were again permitted to act before London audiences, we find Shakespeare as a member of the Lord Chamberlain's company. Probably he had already written *The Comedy of Errors, Love's Labor's Lost, The Two Gentlemen of Verona, the Henry VI* plays, and *Titus Andronicus.* (A *Love's Labor's Won,* mentioned by Francis Meres in 1598, is possibly either a lost play or an alternate title for one of the extant comedies.) He may also have completed *The Taming of the Shrew, A Midsummer Night's Dream, Richard III, King John,* and *Romeo and Juliet.* Although some scholars still question his authorship in part or all of *Titus* and the *Henry VI* plays, no one questions that they are from the period around 1590.

Shakespeare's early development is hard to follow because of difficulties in exact dating of the early plays and because some of the texts (such as *Love's Labor's Lost*) may have been later revised. As a learner making rapid progress in the skill of his art, Shakespeare was also subjected to outside influences that can only partly be determined. Among these influences, we may be sure, were the plays of his contemporary dramatists. If we could define these influences and form an idea of the kinds of plays acceptable on the stage during Shakespeare's early period, we could better understand the milieu in which he began his work.

Fortunately, we know a fair amount concerning the dramatic repertory in London during Shakespeare's early years. Henslowe's *Diary,* for example, records the daily performances of plays by the Lord Strange's men, in conjunction with the Admiral's men, from February 19, 1592 to June 22, 1592. Many of their plays unfortunately are lost, but enough of them are preserved to indicate the sorts of drama then in vogue. The Strange-Admiral's repertory included Christopher Marlowe's *The Jew of Malta,* Robert Greene's *Orlando Furioso* and *Friar Bacon and Friar Bungay,* Robert Greene and Thomas Lodge's *A Looking Glass for London and England,* Thomas Kyd's *The*

Spanish Tragedy, the anonymous *A Knack to Know a Knave,* and possibly George Peele's *The Battle of Alcazar,* and Shakespeare's *1 Henry VI.* We find, in other words, a tragedy with a villain as hero, a romantic comedy masquerading as a heroic play, a love comedy featuring a lot of magic, a biblical moral, England's first great revenge tragedy, a popular satiric comedy aimed at dissolute courtiers and usurers, a history play about Portugal's African empire, and an English history play. The titles of other works now lost suggest a similar amalgam of widely differing genres.

Comparatively few plays may have been written during the period when plays were forbidden because of the long plague of 1592–1594. When the Lord Chamberlain's men and the Lord Admiral's men acted under Henslowe's management at the suburban theater of Newington Butts from June 3–13, 1594, their repertories seem to have consisted largely of old plays. In this brief period, they are thought to have acted *Titus Andronicus, Hamlet* (the pre-Shakespearean version), *The Taming of a Shrew* (quite possibly Shakespeare's version), *The Jew of Malta,* a lost play called *Hester and Ahasuerus,* and others.

The Lord Admiral's men probably moved soon afterwards in 1594 to the Rose on the Bankside, across the river Thames from the city of London, where they continued to play under Henslowe's management until 1603. During the years 1594–1597, Henslowe kept in his *Diary* a careful record of their plays and of the sums of money taken in. This circumstance enables us to know a great deal more about the repertory of Shakespeare's rival company than we can ever know about his own. When the Lord Admiral's men began again in 1594, they had five of Marlowe's plays. They seem also to have had Peele's *Edward I,* Kyd's *The Spanish Tragedy,* and a Henry V play. They may also have had plays by both Greene and Peele (Henslowe's chaotic spelling makes it hard to determine), although some of the principal dramas of these two authors had probably ceased to be acted.

We do not know as much about the repertory of the Lord Chamberlain's company as we do about that of the Lord Admiral's men. We know enough, however, to be sure that in 1594 both companies were acting the same sorts of plays that had been on the boards in 1592. We have, therefore, grounds for assuming that, in spite of the loss of many plays (some of which may have been important), the chief contemporary influences upon Shakespeare during his early period were those of Marlowe, Greene, Peele, and Kyd. As an actor possibly in Lord Strange's company or the Earl of Pembroke's company, he would have been familiar with their plays.

Shakespeare learned also from Lyly, though perhaps more from reading Lyly's plays than from actually seeing or performing in them. The boy actors for whom Lyly wrote were forced by the authorities to suspend acting in about 1591 because of their tendency toward controversial satire, and a number of Lyly's plays were printed at that time. As a theatrical figure, therefore, Lyly belonged really to the previous decade.

The Early Plays

Although Shakespeare's genius manifests itself in his early work, his indebtedness to contemporary dramatists and to classical writers is also more plainly evident than in his later writings. His first tragedy, *Titus Andronicus* (c. 1589–1592), is more laden with quotations and classical references than any other tragedy he wrote. Its genre owes much to the revenge play that had been made so popular by Thomas Kyd. Like Kyd, Shakespeare turns to Seneca but also reveals on stage a considerable amount of sensational violence in a manner that is distinctly not classical. For his first villain, Aaron the Moor, Shakespeare borrows some motifs from the morality play and its gleefully sinister tempter, the Vice. Shakespeare may also have had in mind the boastful antics of Marlowe's Vicelike Barabas, in *The Jew of Malta.* Certainly, Shakespeare reveals an extensive debt in his early works to Ovid and to the vogue of Ovidian narrative poetry in the early 1590s, as, for example, in his repeated allusions to the story of Philomela and Tereus (in *Titus Andronicus*) and in his Ovidian poems, *Venus and Adonis* and *The Rape of Lucrece* (1593, 1594).

Shakespeare was still questing for a suitable mode in tragedy and was discovering that the English drama of the 1590s offered no single, clear model. His only other early tragedy, *Romeo and Juliet* (c. 1594–1596), proved to be as different a tragedy from *Titus Andronicus* as could be imagined. Revenge is still prominent in *Romeo and Juliet* but is ultimately far less compelling a theme than the brevity of love and the sacrifice the lovers make of themselves to one another. Shakespeare's source is not the revenge drama of Seneca or Kyd, but a romantic love narrative derived from the fiction of Renaissance Italy. Elements of comedy so predominate in the play's first half that one senses a closer affinity to *A Midsummer Night's Dream* than to *The Spanish Tragedy.*

Shakespeare discovered his true bent more quickly in comedy than in tragedy. Again, however, he experimented with a wide range of models and genres. *The Comedy of Errors* (c. 1589–1594) brings together elements of two plots from the Latin drama of Plautus. The character types and situations are partly derivative, but Shakespeare still reveals an impressive skill in plot construction. *Love's Labor's Lost* (c. 1588–1597) is Shakespeare's most Lylyan early comedy, with its witty debates and its amicable, if brittle, war between the sexes. The play also features an array of humorous characters, including a clownish bumpkin, a country slut, a fantastic courtier, a pedant, a country curate, and the like, whose mannerisms and wordplay add to the rich feast of language in a play that

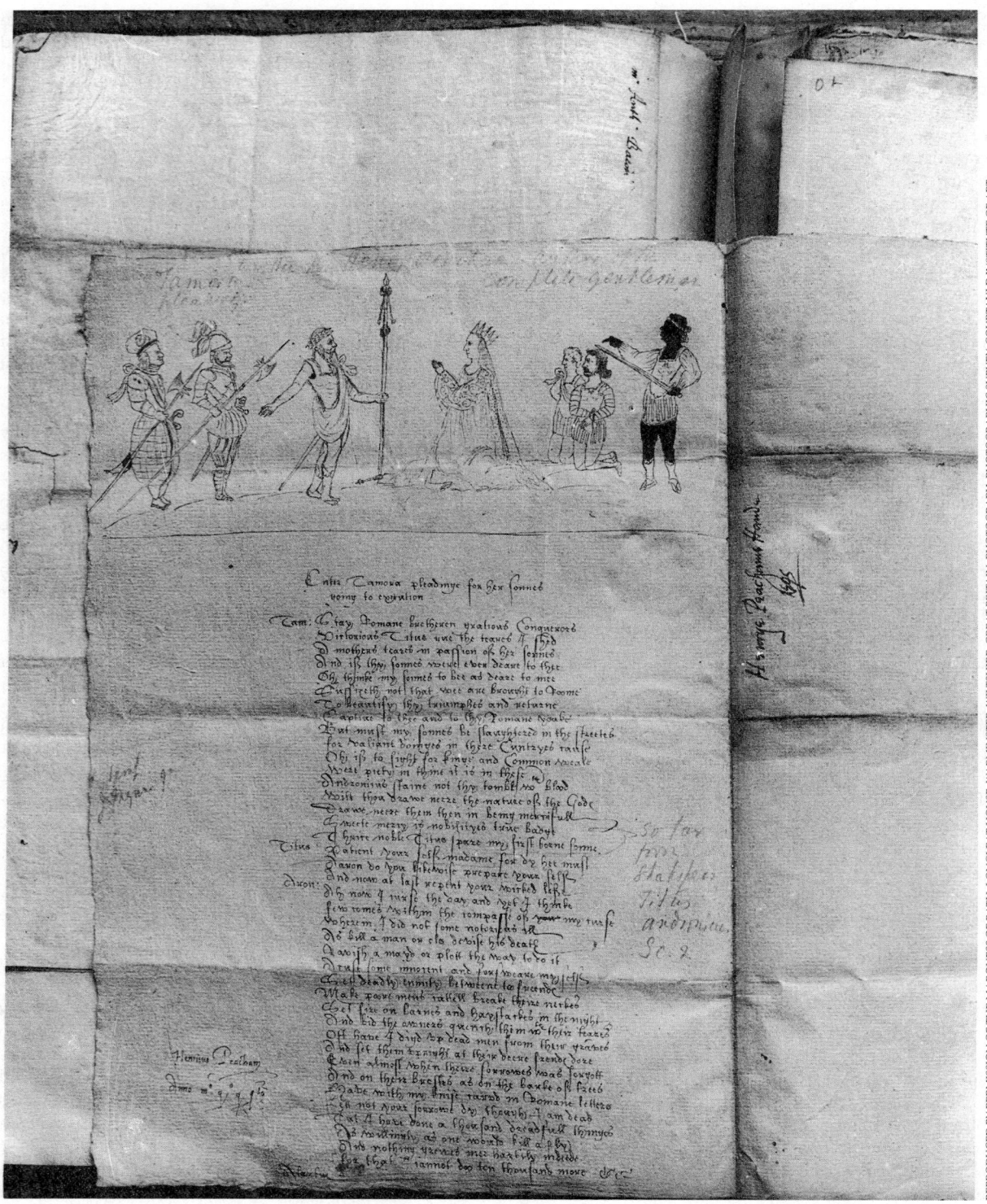

A contemporary illustration of Titus Andronicus, the earliest of Shakespeare's tragedies. Shakespeare's early plays demonstrated that he was more than a slavish imitator of predecessors such as Kyd and Marlowe.

THE GREAT POND AT ELVETHAM
arranged for the Second Day's Entertainment.

A. Her Majestie's presence seate and traine.   B. Nereus and his followers.   C. The pinnace of Neæra and her musicke.   D. The Ship-ile.
E. A boate with musicke, attending on the pinnace of Neæra.   F. The Fort-mount.   G. The Snaile-mount.   H. The Roome of Estate.
I. Her Majestie's Court.   K. Her Majestie's Wardrop.   L. The place whence Silvanus and his companie issued.

An entertainment presented by the Earl of Hertford to Queen Elizabeth during her visit to Elvetham in 1591 is seemingly referred to by Shakespeare in A Midsummer Night's Dream, *2.1.157–64. The scene shows an elaborate water pageant in honor of the Queen, who appears enthroned at the left of the picture.*

centers its attention on proper and improper styles. *The Two Gentlemen of Verona* (c. 1590–1594) and *The Taming of the Shrew* (c. 1590–1593) are derived from Italianate romantic fiction and comedy. In both, Shakespeare skillfully combines simultaneous plots that offer contrasting views on love and friendship. (*The Taming of the Shrew* makes effective use of a "frame" plot involving a group of characters who serve as audience for the rest of the play.) *A Midsummer Night's Dream* (c. 1595), with its four brilliantly interwoven actions involving court figures, lovers, fairies, and Athenian tradesmen, shows us Shakespeare already at the height of his powers in play construction, even though the comic emphasis on love's irrationality in this play is still in keeping with Shakespeare's early style. The early comedies do not ignore conflict and danger, as we see in the threatened execution of Egeon in

The Comedy of Errors and the failure of courtships in *Love's Labor's Lost,* but these plays do not as yet fully explore the social dilemmas of *The Merchant of Venice*, the narrowly averted catastrophe of *Much Ado About Nothing,* or the melancholy vein of *As You Like It* and *Twelfth Night.* On stage, early comedies such as *The Comedy of Errors* and *The Taming of the Shrew* are as hilariously funny as anything Shakespeare ever wrote.

Shakespeare's early history plays show a marked affinity with those of Marlowe, Peele, and Greene. Yet today Shakespeare is given more credit for pioneering in the genre of the English history play than he once was. If all the *Henry VI* plays (c. 1589–1592) are basically his, as scholars now often allow, he had more imitators in this genre than predecessors. He scored a huge early success with the heroic character of Lord Talbot in *1 Henry VI,* and by the time Richard Duke of Gloucester had emerged from the *Henry VI* plays to become King Richard III, Shakespeare's fame as a dramatist was assured. He had, of course, learned much from Marlowe's "mighty line" in *Tamburlaine* (1587–1588) and perhaps from Peele's *The Battle of Alcazar* (1588–1589). The anonymous *Famous Victories of Henry V* (1583–1588) must have preceded and influenced his work. Even so, Shakespeare had done much more than simply "beautify" himself with the "feathers" of earlier dramatists, as Greene (or Chettle) enviously charged. Even in his earliest work, Shakespeare already displayed an extraordinary ability to transcend the models from which he learned.

SHAKESPEARE IN THE THEATER, C. 1594–1601

By the year 1594, Shakespeare had already achieved a considerable reputation as a poet and dramatist. We should not be surprised that many of his contemporaries thought of his nondramatic writing as his most significant literary achievement. Throughout his lifetime, in fact, his contemporary fame rested, to a remarkable degree, on his nondramatic poems, *Venus and Adonis, The Rape of Lucrece,* and the *Sonnets* (which were circulated in manuscript prior to their unauthorized publication in 1609). One of the earliest tributes suggesting the importance of the poems is found in an anonymous commendatory verse prefixed to Henry Willobie's *Willobie His Avisa* (1594). It summarizes the plot and theme of *The Rape of Lucrece*:

> Though *Collatine* have dearly bought,
> To high renown, a lasting life,
> And found—that most in vain have sought—
> To have a fair and constant wife,
>   Yet Tarquin plucked his glittering grape,
>   And Shakespeare paints poor Lucrece' rape.

Richard Barnfield, in his *Poems in Divers Humors* (1598), praised the "honey-flowing vein" of Shakespeare's *Venus and Adonis* and *The Rape of Lucrece.*

Yet Shakespeare's plays were also highly regarded by his contemporaries, even if those plays were accorded a literary status below that given to the narrative and lyrical poems. Francis Meres insisted, in 1598, that Shakespeare deserved to be compared not only with Ovid for his verse but also with Plautus and Seneca for his comedies and tragedies:

As the soul of Euphorbus was thought to live in Pythagoras, so the sweet, witty soul of Ovid lives in mellifluous and honey-tongued Shakespeare: witness his *Venus and Adonis,* his *Lucrece,* his sugared sonnets among his private friends, etc.

As Plautus and Seneca are accounted the best for comedy and tragedy among the Latins, so Shakespeare among the English is the most excellent in both kinds for the stage: for comedy, witness his *Gentlemen of Verona,* his *Errors,* his *Love's*

Labor's Lost, his *Love's Labor's Won,* his *Midsummer Night's Dream,* and his *Merchant of Venice;* for tragedy, his *Richard the II, Richard the III, Henry the IV, King John, Titus Andronicus,* and his *Romeo and Juliet.*

Comedy and tragedy were, after all, literary forms sanctioned by classical precept. By calling some of Shakespeare's English history plays "tragedies," Meres endowed them with the respectability of an ancient literary tradition, recognizing, too, that many of Shakespeare's historical plays culminate in the death of an English king.

John Weever, too, in his epigram *Ad Gulielmum Shakespeare* in *Epigrams in the Oldest Cut and Newest Fashion* (1599), mentioned not only the ever-popular narrative poems but also *Romeo and Juliet* and a history play about one of the Richards:

> Honey-tongued Shakespeare! When I saw thine issue,
> I swore Apollo got them and none other:
> Their rosy-tainted features clothed in tissue,
> Some heaven-born goddess said to be their mother;
> Rose-cheeked Adonis, with his amber tresses,
> Fair fire-hot Venus, charming him to love her;
> Chaste Lucretia virgin-like her dresses,
> Proud lust-stung Tarquin seeking still to prove her;
> *Romeo, Richard*—more whose names I know not.
> Their sugared tongues and power-attractive beauty
> Say they are saints, although that saints they show not,
> For thousands vows to them subjective duty;
> They burn in love thy children. Shakespeare het them.
> Go, woo thy muse more nymphish brood beget them.

Even Gabriel Harvey, an esteemed classical scholar and friend of Edmund Spenser, considered Shakespeare's play *Hamlet* to be worthy of no less praise than the best of the Ovidian poems. Harvey's comments are to be found in a marginal note to a copy of Speght's *Chaucer,* written down some time between 1598 and 1601:

The younger sort takes much delight in Shakespeare's *Venus and Adonis,* but his *Lucrece* and his tragedy of *Hamlet, Prince of Denmark* have it in them to please the wiser sort.

Shakespeare's growing fame was even such that his dramatic characters began to enter into the intellectual life of the time. The name of Falstaff became a byword almost as soon as he made his appearance on the stage. The references were not always friendly. A play written to be performed by the rival Admiral's company in answer to *1 Henry IV,* called *Sir John Oldcastle* (1599), took Falstaff to task for being a "pampered glutton" and an "aged counsellor to youthful sin." Evidently, the authors of this attack were offended by the fact that Falstaff had been named "Oldcastle" in an early version of *1 Henry IV,* thereby dishonoring the name of one whom many Puritans regarded as a martyr to their cause (see the Introduction to *1 Henry IV*). Generally, however, the references

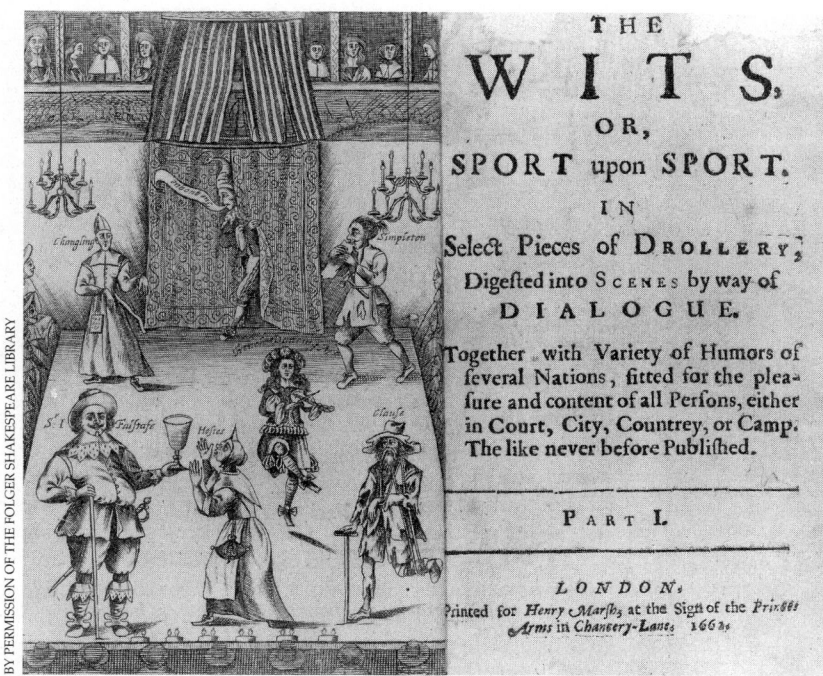

Falstaff and Mistress Quickly are shown here in a composite theatrical illustration of about 1662. The engraving, used as the frontispiece to Francis Kirkman's The Wits, or Sport upon Sport, *also shows other theatrical types. Visible are candelabras and footlights for stage lighting and a curtained area used perhaps for "discoveries." Spectators are visible in the gallery above, as they are also in the De Witt drawing of the Swan Theatre on p. xlvi and in Alabaster's* Roxana *on p. xlv.*

during this period to Falstaff and his cronies were fond. In a letter to a friend in London, for example, Sir Charles Percy fretted jocosely that his prolonged stay in the country among his rustic neighbors might cause him to "be taken for Justice Silence or Justice Shallow" (1600). In another letter, from the Countess of Southampton to her husband (written seemingly in 1599), Falstaff's name had become so familiar that it was used apparently as a privately understood substitute for the name of some real person in an item of court gossip:

All the news I can send you, that I think will make you merry, is that I read in a letter from London that Sir John Falstaff is by his Mistress Dame Pintpot made father of a godly miller's thumb, a boy that's all head and very little body; but this is a secret.

Shakespeare's immense popularity as a dramatist was bound to invite some resentment. One irreverent reaction is found in the so-called *Parnassus* trilogy (1598–1603). The three plays in this series consist of *The Pilgrimage to Parnassus* and *The Return from Parnassus,* in two parts, all of which were acted by the students of St. John's College, Cambridge.

These *Parnassus* plays take a mordantly satirical view of English life around 1600, from the point of view of university graduates attempting to find gainful employment. The graduates discover, to their vocal dismay, that they must seek the patronage of fashion-mongering courtiers, complacent justices of the peace, professional acting com-

panies who offer them pitifully small wages, and the like. One especially foolish patron, to whom the witty Ingenioso applies for a position, is a poetaster named Gullio. This courtly fop aspires to be a fashionable poet himself, and agrees to hire Ingenioso if the latter will help him with his verse writing. In fact, however, as Ingenioso scornfully observes in a series of asides, Gullio's verses are "nothing but pure Shakespeare and shreds of poetry that he hath gathered at the theaters." Most of all, Gullio loves to plagiarize from *Venus and Adonis* and *Romeo and Juliet.* With unparalleled presumption, he actually requests Ingenioso to compose poems "in two or three divers veins, in Chaucer's, Gower's and Spenser's and Mr. Shakespeare's," which Gullio will then pass off as his own inspiration. When Ingenioso does so extempore, producing, among other things, a fine parody of *Venus and Adonis,* Gullio is as delighted as a child. Although he admires Spenser, Chaucer, and Gower, Gullio confesses that Shakespeare is his favorite; he longs to hang Shakespeare's portrait "in my study at the court" and vows he will sleep with *Venus and Adonis* under his pillow (*The Return from Parnassus,* Part I, 1009–1217). Later on (lines 1875–1880), some university graduates trying out as actors in Shakespeare's company are requested to recite a few famous lines from the beginning of *Richard III*—lines that, in the satirical context of this play, sound both stereotyped and bombastic. Shakespeare's fame made him an easy target for university "wits" who regarded the theater of London

Henry Fuseli's nineteenth-century interpretation of Falstaff shows him in the tavern in Eastcheap with Doll Tearsheet on his lap while Prince Hal and Poins, disguised as tapsters, enter from behind. Falstaff is perhaps saying, "Peace, good Doll, do not speak like a death's-head" (2 Henry IV, 2.4.232–3).

as lowbrow. Still, the portrait throughout is more satirical of those who plagiarize and idolize Shakespeare than of the dramatist's own work. In their backhanded tribute, the *Parnassus* authors make plain that Shakespeare was a household name even at the universities.

Shakespeare's Career and Private Life

During the years from 1594 to 1601, Shakespeare seems to have prospered as an actor and writer for the Lord Chamberlain's men. Whether he had previously belonged to Lord Strange's company or to the Earl of Pembroke's company, or possibly to some other group, is uncertain, but we know that he took part in 1594 in the general reorganization of the companies, out of which emerged the Lord Chamberlain's company. In 1595, his name appeared, for the first time, in the accounts of the Treasurer of the Royal Chamber as a member of the Chamberlain's company of players, which had presented two comedies before Queen Elizabeth at Greenwich in the Christmas season of 1594. This company usually performed at the Theatre, northeast of London, from 1594

until 1599, when they moved to the Globe playhouse south of the Thames. They seem to have been the victors in the intense economic rivalry between themselves and the Lord Admiral's company at the Rose playhouse under Philip Henslowe's management. Fortunately for all the adult companies, the boys' private theatrical companies were shut down during most of the 1590s. Shakespeare's company enjoyed a phenomenal success, and in short time it became the most successful theatrical organization in England.

The nucleus of the Chamberlain's company in 1594 was the family of Burbage. James Burbage, the father, was owner of the Theatre, Cuthbert Burbage was a manager, and Richard Burbage became the principal actor of the troupe. Together the Burbages owned five "shares" in the company, entitling them to half the profits. Shakespeare and four other principal actors—John Heminges, Thomas Pope, Augustine Phillips, and Will Kempe—owned one share each. Not only was Shakespeare a full sharing actor, but also he was the principal playwright of the company. He was named as a chief actor in the 1616 edition of Ben Jonson's *Every Man in His Humor,* performed by the Chamberlain's company in 1598. Later tradition reports, with questionable reliability, that Shakespeare specialized in "kingly parts" or in the roles of older men, such as Adam in *As You Like It* and the Ghost in *Hamlet.* Shakespeare was more celebrated as a playwright than as an actor, and his acting responsibilities may well have diminished as his writing reputation grew. The last occasion on which he is known to have acted was in Jonson's *Sejanus* in 1603.

His prosperity appears in the first record of his residence in London. The tax returns, or Subsidy Rolls, of a parliamentary subsidy granted to Queen Elizabeth for the year 1596 show that Shakespeare was a resident in the parish of St. Helen's, Bishopsgate, near the Theatre, and was assessed at the respectable sum of five pounds. By the next year, Shakespeare had evidently moved to Southwark, near the Bear Garden, for the returns from

First among the actors in Shakespeare's company was Richard Burbage (1567–1619). He played Hamlet, Othello, King Lear, and presumably other major roles including Macbeth, Antony, Coriolanus, and Prospero.

Bishopsgate show his taxes delinquent. He was later located and the taxes paid.

In 1596, Shakespeare suffered a serious personal loss: the death of his only son Hamnet, at the age of eleven. Hamnet was buried at Stratford in August.

Shakespeare acquired property in Stratford during these years, as well as in London. In 1597 he purchased New Place, a house of importance and one of the two largest in the town. Shakespeare's family entered the house as residents shortly after the purchase and continued to live there until long after Shakespeare's death. The last of his family, his granddaughter, Lady Bernard, died in 1670, and New Place was sold.

Shakespeare was also interested in the purchase of land at Shottery in 1598. He was listed among the chief holders of corn and malt in Stratford that same year and sold a load of stone to the Stratford corporation in 1599.

No less suggestive of Shakespeare's rapid rise in the world is his acquisition of the right to bear arms, or, in other words, his establishment in the rank and title of gentleman. The Herald's College in London preserves two drafts of a grant of arms to Shakespeare's father, devised by one William Dethick and dated October 20, 1596. Although we may certainly believe that the application was put forward by William Shakespeare, John Shakespeare was still living, and the grant was drawn up in the father's name. The device for Shakespeare's coat of arms makes a somewhat easy use of the meaning of his name:

Gold on a bend sables, a spear of the first steeled argent. And for his crest of cognizance a falcon, his wings displayed argent, standing on a wreath of his colors, supporting a spear, gold

steeled as aforesaid, set upon a helmet with mantles and tassels, as hath been accustomed and doth more plainly appear depicted on this margent.

According to one of the documents in the grant, John Shakespeare, at the height of his prosperity as a Stratford burgher, had applied twenty years before to the Herald's College for authority to bear arms. The family may not have been able to meet the expense of seeing the application through, however, until William Shakespeare had made his fortune. The grant of heraldic honors to John Shakespeare was confirmed in 1599.

A lawsuit during this period gives us a rather baffling glimpse into Shakespeare's life in the theater. From a writ discovered by Leslie Hotson (*Shakespeare Versus Shallow*, 1931) in the records of the Court of the Queen's Bench, Michaelmas term 1596, we learn that a person named William Wayte sought "for fear of death" to have William Shakespeare, Francis Langley, and two unknown women bound over to keep the peace. Earlier in the same term, moreover, Francis Langley had sworn out a similar writ against this same William Wayte and his stepfather William Gardiner, a justice of the peace in Surrey. Langley was owner of the Swan playhouse on the bankside, near the later-built Globe. His quarrel with Gardiner and Wayte appears to have jeopardized all the acting companies that performed plays south of the Thames, for William Gardiner's jurisdiction included the Bankside theater district. Gardiner and Wayte vengefully tried to drive the theaters out of the area. Possibly Shakespeare's company acted occasionally at the Swan in 1596. Hotson speculates that Shakespeare retaliated by immortalizing

This recreation of what New Place purportedly looked like during Shakespeare's ownership suggests that it must have indeed been an imposing structure. It was warmed by ten fireplaces and had surrounding grounds that included two gardens and two barns.

Gardiner and Wayte as Shallow and Slender in *The Merry Wives of Windsor*. The date of 1596 is too early for that play, and we do not know that Shakespeare drew contemporary portraits in his drama, but we can wonder if lawsuits of this sort gave him no very high opinion of the law's delay and the insolence of office.

During this period Shakespeare's plays began to appear occasionally in print. His name was becoming such a drawing card that it appeared on the title pages of the Second and Third Quartos of *Richard II* (1598), the Second Quarto of *Richard III* (1598), *Love's Labor's Lost* (1598), and the Second Quarto of *1 Henry IV* (1599).

In 1599, the printer William Jaggard sought to capitalize unscrupulously on Shakespeare's growing reputation by bringing out a slender volume of twenty or twenty-one poems called *The Passionate Pilgrim*, attributed to Shakespeare. In fact, only five of the poems were assuredly his, and none of them was newly composed for the occasion. Three came from *Love's Labor's Lost* (published in 1598) and two from Shakespeare's as yet unpublished sonnet sequence.

Contemporary Drama

Shakespeare was without doubt the leading dramatist of the period from 1594 to 1601, not only in our view, but also in that of his contemporaries. The earlier group of dramatists from whom he had learned so much—Lyly, Greene, Marlowe, Peele, Kyd, Nashe—were either dead or no longer writing plays. The group of dramatists who were to rival him in the 1600s and eventually surpass him in contemporary popularity had not yet become well known.

Ben Jonson's early career is obscure. He may have written an early version of his *A Tale of a Tub* in 1596 and *The Case Is Altered* in 1597, though both were later revised. Unquestionably, his first major play was *Every Man in His Humor* (1598), in which Shakespeare acted. This comedy did much to establish the new vogue of comedy of humors, a realistic and satirical kind of drama featuring "humors" characters whose personalities are dominated by some exaggerated trait. We are invited to laugh at the country simpleton, the jealous husband, the overly careful father, the cowardly braggart soldier, the poetaster, and the like. Shakespeare responded to the vogue of humors comedy in his *Henry IV* plays and *The Merry Wives*. Jonson followed his great success with *Every Man Out of His Humor* (1599), an even more biting vision of human folly. George Chapman also deserves important credit for the establishment of humors comedy, with his *The Blind Beggar of Alexandria* (1596) and *An Humorous Day's Mirth* (1597).

Despite the emergence of humors comedy, however, with its important anticipations of Jacobean and even Restoration comedy of manners, the prevailing comedy to be seen on the London stage between 1595 and 1601 was romantic comedy. William Haughton wrote *Englishmen for My Money* in 1598. Thomas Dekker's *Old Fortunatus*, the dramatization of a German folktale, appeared in 1599. Dekker's *The Shoemaker's Holiday* (1599), despite its seemingly realistic touches of life among the apprentices of London, is a thoroughly romanticized saga of rags to riches. A young aristocrat disguises himself as a shoemaker to woo a mayor's daughter; love conquers social rank, and the King himself sentimentally blesses the union. Thomas Heywood wrote heroical romances and comedies, perhaps including *Godfrey of Boulogne* (1594), although most of his early works have disappeared. The boys' private theaters were closed during most of the 1590s, until 1598–1599, and thus the child actors could not perform the satirical comedies at which they were so adept.

Patriotic history drama also continued to flourish on the public stage during those years when Shakespeare wrote his best history plays. Heywood wrote the two parts of *Edward IV* between 1592 and 1599. The anonymous *Edward III* appeared in 1595 or earlier, enough in the vein of Shakespeare's histories that it is sometimes attributed (albeit on uncertain and impressionistic grounds) to him. *Sir Thomas More*, by Munday, Dekker, Chettle, and perhaps Heywood, was written sometime in the later 1590s and very probably revised by Shakespeare himself. Chettle and Munday wrote a trilogy of plays about *Robert, Earl of Huntingdon*, or Robin Hood (1598–1599), on themes that remind us of Shakespeare's *As You Like It*. These plays were performed by the Admiral's men, who also produced the two parts of *Sir John Oldcastle* (1599–1600) by Drayton, Hathway, Munday, and others, in rivalry with Shakespeare's *Henry IV* plays.

Shakespeare's Work

Shakespeare thus wrote his greatest history plays for an audience that knew the genre well. The history play had first become popular just at the start of Shakespeare's career, during the patriotic aftermath of the defeat of the Spanish Armada (1588). Shakespeare himself did much to establish the genre. He wrote first his four-play series dealing with the Lancastrian wars of the fifteenth century, and then went backwards in historical time to King John's reign and to the famous reigns of Henry IV and Henry V.

His romantic comedies were also written for audiences that knew what to expect from the genre. From the comedies of Greene, Peele, Munday, and the rest, as well as Shakespeare himself, Elizabethan audiences were thoroughly familiar with such conventions as fairy charms, improbable adventures in forests, heroines disguised as young men, shipwrecks, love overcoming differences in social rank, and the like. Yet the conventions also demanded more than mere horseplay or foolish antics. Plays of this sort customarily affirmed "wholesome" moral values and appealed to generosity and decency. They were written, like the history plays, for a socially diversified, though generally intelligent and well-to-do, audience.

Several critical terms have been used to suggest the special quality of Shakespeare's comedies during this period of the later 1590s. "Romantic comedy" implies first of all a story in which the main action is about love, but it can also imply elements of the improbable and the miraculous. (The difference between the "romantic comedies" of the later 1590s and the "romances" of Shakespeare's last years, 1606–1613, is that, in part at least, romantic comedy seeks to "make wonder familiar," whereas the romances seek to make the familiar wonderful.) "Philosophical comedy" emphasizes the moral and sometimes Christian idealism underlying many of these comedies of the 1590s: the quest for deep and honest understanding between men and women in *Much Ado About Nothing,* the awareness of an eternal and spiritual dimension to love in *The Merchant of Venice,* and the theme of love as a mysterious force able to regenerate a corrupted social world from which it has been banished in *As You Like It.* "Love-game comedy" pays particular attention to the witty battle of the sexes that we find in several of these plays. "Festive comedy" urges the celebratory nature of comedy, especially in *Twelfth Night* and the *Henry IV* plays, in which Saturnalian revelry must contend against grim and disapproving forces of sobriety. "Comedy of forgiveness," although applicable to only a limited number of plays of this period (especially *Much Ado*), stresses the unexpected second chance that the world of comedy extends to even the most undeserving of heroes; Claudio is forgiven his ill treatment of Hero, although the play's villain, Don John, is not.

SHAKESPEARE IN THE THEATER, C.1601–1608

When the Globe, the most famous of the London public playhouses, was built in 1599, one-half interest in the property was assigned to the Burbage family, especially to the brothers Cuthbert and Richard Burbage. The other half was divided among five actor-sharers: Shakespeare, Will Kempe, Thomas Pope, Augustine Phillips, and John Heminges. Kempe left the company, however, in 1599 and subsequently became a member of the Earl of Worcester's men. His place as leading comic actor was taken by Robert Armin, an experienced man of the theater and occasional author, whose comic specialty was the role of the wise fool. We can observe in Shakespeare's plays the effects of Kempe's departure and of Armin's arrival. Kempe had apparently specialized in clownish and rustic parts, such as those of Dogberry in *Much Ado,* Lancelot Gobbo in *The Merchant of Venice,* and Bottom in *A Midsummer Night's Dream.* (We know that he played Dogberry because his name appears in the early Quarto, derived from the play manuscript; similar evidence links his name to the role of Peter in *Romeo and Juliet.*) For Armin, on the other hand, Shakespeare evidently created such roles as Touchstone in *As You Like It,* Feste in *Twelfth Night,* Lavatch in *All's Well That Ends Well,* and the Fool in *King Lear.*

Other shifts in personnel can sometimes be traced in Shakespeare's plays, especially changes in the number and ability of the boy actors (whose voices would suddenly start to crack at puberty). Shakespeare makes an amusing point about the relative size of two boy actors, for example, in *A Midsummer Night's Dream* and in *As You Like It*; this option may have been available to him only at certain times. On the other hand, not all changes in the company roster can be related meaningfully to Shake-

Among the members of Shakespeare's acting company were John Lowin, William Sly, and Nathaniel Field.

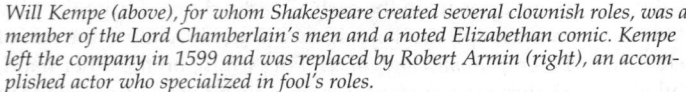

Will Kempe (above), for whom Shakespeare created several clownish roles, was a member of the Lord Chamberlain's men and a noted Elizabethan comic. Kempe left the company in 1599 and was replaced by Robert Armin (right), an accomplished actor who specialized in fool's roles.

speare's dramatic development. Augustine Phillips, who died in 1605, was a full actor-sharer of long standing in the company, but his "type" of role was probably not sharply differentiated from that of several of his associates. Shakespeare's plays, after all, involve many important supporting roles, and versatility in the undertaking of such parts must have been more common than specialization. (Phillips is remembered also for his last will and testament: he left a bequest of "a thirty shillings piece in gold" to "my fellow, William Shakespeare," and similar bequests to other members of the troupe.)

With the reopening of the boys' acting companies in 1598–1599, a serious economic rivalry sprang up between them and the adult companies. The Children of the Chapel Royal occupied the theater in Blackfriars, and the Children of Paul's probably acted in their own singing school in St. Paul's churchyard. Their plays exploited a new vogue for satire. The satiric laughter was often directed at the city of London and its bourgeois inhabitants: socially ambitious tradesmen's wives, Puritan zealots, and the like. Other favorite targets included parvenu knights at court, would-be poets, and hysterical governmental officials. The price of admission at the private theaters was considerably higher than at the Globe or Rose, so the clientele tended to be more fashionable. Sophisticated authors like Ben Jonson, George Chapman, and John Marston tended to find writing for the boy actors more rewarding literarily than writing for the adult players.

One manifestation of the rivalry between public and private theaters was the so-called War of the Theaters, or Poetomachia. In part, this was a personal quarrel between

Jonson on one side and Marston and Thomas Dekker on the other. Underlying this quarrel, however, was a serious hostility between a public theater and one that catered more to the elite. Dekker, with Marston's encouragement, attacked Jonson as a literary dictator and snob—one who subverted public decency. Jonson replied with a fervent defense of the artist's right to criticize everything that the artist sees wrong. The major plays in the exchange (1600–1601) were Jonson's *Cynthia's Revels*, Dekker and Marston's *Satiromastix*, and Jonson's *The Poetaster*.

Shakespeare allows Hamlet to comment on the theatrical rivalry (2.2.330–62), with seeming regret for the fact that the boys have been overly successful and that many adult troupes have been obliged to tour the provinces. Most of all, though, Hamlet's remarks deplore the needless bitterness on both sides. The tone of kindly remonstrance makes it seem unlikely that Shakespeare took an active part in the fracas. To be sure, in the Cambridge play *2 Return from Parnassus* (1601–1603), the character called Will Kempe does assert that his fellow actor, Shakespeare, had put down the famous Ben Jonson:

Why, here's our fellow Shakespeare puts them all down, ay, and Ben Jonson, too. O, that Ben Jonson is a pestilent fellow! And he brought up Horace giving the poets a pill, but our fellow Shakespeare hath given him a purge that made him bewray his credit (lines 1809–1813).

Nevertheless, no play exists in which Shakespeare did put down Jonson, and the reference may be instead to *Satiromastix,* which was performed by Shakespeare's company. Or perhaps "put down" means simply "surpassed." In fact, Shakespeare and Jonson remained on cordial terms, despite their differences in artistic outlook.

Upon the death of Queen Elizabeth in 1603 and the accession to the throne of King James I, Shakespeare's company added an important new success to their already great prosperity. According to a document of instruction from King James to his Keeper of the Privy Seal, dated May 19, 1603, and endorsed as "The Players' Privilege," the acting company that had formerly been the Lord Chamberlain's men now became the King's company. The document names Shakespeare, Richard Burbage, Augustine Phillips, John Heminges, Henry Condell, Will Sly, Robert Armin, Richard Cowley, and Lawrence Fletcher—the last, an actor who had played before the King and the Scottish court in 1599 and 1601. These players are accorded the usual privileges of exercising their art anywhere within the kingdom and are henceforth to be known as the King's company. The principal members of the troupe also were appointed to the honorary rank of Grooms of the Royal Chamber. We therefore find them duly recorded in the Accounts of the Master of the Wardrobe on March 15, 1604, as recipients of the customary grants of red cloth, so that they, dressed in the royal livery, might take part in the approaching coronation procession of King James. The same men are mentioned in these grants as in the Players' Privilege. Shakespeare's name stands second in the former document and first in the latter. In a somewhat similar manner, the King's players, as Grooms of the Royal Chamber, were called in attendance on the Spanish ambassador at Somerset House in August 1604.

The Revels Accounts of performances at court during the winter season of 1604–1605 contain an unusually full entry, listing several of Shakespeare's plays. The list includes *Othello, The Merry Wives of Windsor, Measure for Measure, "The play of Errors," Love's Labor's Lost, Henry V,* and *The Merchant of Venice.* The last play was "again commanded by the King's majesty," and so was performed a second time. This list also sporadically notes the names of "the poets which made the plays," ascribing three of these works to "Shaxberd." (Probably the final *d* is an error for *e*, since the two characters are easily confused in Elizabethan handwriting; the word represents "Shaxbere" or "Shaxpere.") The entire entry was once called into question as a possible forgery but is now generally regarded as authentic.

A number of records during this period show us glimpses of Shakespeare as a man of property. On May 1, 1602, John and William Combe conveyed to Shakespeare one hundred and seven acres of arable land, plus twenty acres of pasture in the parish of Old Stratford, for the sizable payment of three hundred and twenty pounds. The deed was delivered to Shakespeare's brother Gilbert and not to the poet, who was probably at that time occupied in London. On September 28 of the same year, Shake-

speare acquired the title to "one cottage and one garden by estimation a quarter of an acre," located opposite his home (New Place) in Stratford.

Shakespeare made still other real-estate investments in his home town. In 1605 he purchased an interest in the tithes of Stratford and adjacent villages from one Ralph Hubaud for the considerable sum of four hundred and forty pounds. The purchasing of tithes was a common financial transaction in Shakespeare's time, though unknown today. Tithes were originally intended for the support of the Church but had, in many cases, become privately owned and hence negotiable. The owners of tithes paid a fixed rental sum for the right to collect as many of these taxes as they could, up to the total amount due under the law. Shakespeare seems, on this occasion in 1605, to have bought from Ralph Hubaud a one-half interest, or "moiety," in certain tithes of Stratford and vicinity. Later, probably in 1609, Shakespeare was one of those who brought a bill of complaint before the Lord Chancellor, requesting that certain other titheholders be required to come into the High Court of Chancery and make answer to the complaints alleged, namely, that they had not paid their proportional part of an annual rental of twenty-seven pounds, thirteen shillings, and four pence on the whole property in the tithes to one Henry Barker. This Barker had the theoretical right to foreclose on the entire property if any one of the forty-two titheholders failed to contribute his share of the annual fee. The suit was, in effect, a friendly one, designed to ensure that all those who were supposed to contribute did so on an equitable and businesslike basis.

We learn from the Stratford Registers of baptism, marriage, and burial of the changes in Shakespeare's family during this period. His father died in 1601, his brother Edmund in 1607, and his mother in 1608. On June 5, 1607, his daughter Susanna was married to Dr. John Hall in Holy Trinity Church, Stratford. Their first child, and Shakespeare's first grandchild, Elizabeth, was christened in the same church on February 21, 1608.

Shakespeare's Reputation, 1601–1608

Allusions to Shakespeare are frequent during this period of his life. One amusing reference is not literary but professes to tell about Shakespeare's prowess as a lover and rival of his good friend and theatrical colleague, Richard Burbage. Perhaps the joke was just a good bawdy story and should not be taken too seriously, but it is nonetheless one of the few anecdotes that date from Shakespeare's lifetime. Our informant is John Manningham, a young law student, who notes in his commonplace book in 1602 the following:

13 March 1601 [1602] . . . Upon a time, when Burbage played Richard III there was a citizen grew so far in liking with him

that, before she went to the play, she appointed him to come that night unto her by the name of Richard the Third. Shakespeare, overhearing their conclusion, went before, and was entertained and at his game ere Burbage came. Then message being brought that Richard the Third was at the door, Shakespeare caused return to be made that William the Conqueror was before Richard the Third. Shakespeare's name William.

Other allusions of the time are more literary. Shakespeare's greatness is, by this time, taken for granted. Anthony Scoloker, for example, in his epistle prefatory to *Diaphantus, or the Passions of Love* (1604), attempts to describe an excellent literary work in this way:

It should be like the never-too-well read Arcadia . . . or to come home to the vulgar's element, like friendly Shakespeare's tragedies, where the comedian rides, when the tragedian stands on tip-toe. Faith, it should please all, like Prince Hamlet.

The antiquarian William Camden includes Shakespeare's name among his list of England's greatest writers in his *Remains of a Greater Work Concerning Britain* (1605):

These may suffice for some poetical descriptions of our ancient poets. If I would come to our time, what a world could I present to you out of Sir Philip Sidney, Edmund Spenser, Samuel Daniel, Hugh Holland, Ben Jonson, Thomas Campion, Michael Drayton, George Chapman, John Marston, William Shakespeare, and other most pregnant wits of these our times, whom succeeding ages may justly admire.

An attempt to use one of Shakespeare's plays for political purposes had some potentially serious repercussions. Two days before the abortive rebellion of the Earl of Essex on February 7, 1601, Shakespeare's company was commissioned to perform a well-known play in its repertory about King Richard II. This play must almost surely have been Shakespeare's. Evidently, the purpose of this extraordinary performance was to awaken public sympathy for Essex by suggesting that Queen Elizabeth was another Richard II, surrounded by corrupt favorites and deaf to the pleas of her subjects. Essex's avowed intention was to remove from positions of influence those men whom he considered his political enemies. Fortunately, Shakespeare's company was later exonerated of any blame in the affair (see the Introduction to *Richard II*).

Perhaps no other allusion to Shakespeare during this period can suggest so well as the following quotation the extent to which Shakespeare's plays had become familiar to English citizens everywhere. The quotation is taken from the notes of a certain Captain Keeling, commander of the East India Company's ship *Dragon*, off Sierra Leone, in the years 1607 and 1608:

1607, Sept. 5. I sent the interpreter, according to his desire, aboard the *Hector*, where he broke fast, and after came aboard me, where we gave the tragedy of *Hamlet*.

30. Captain Hawkins dined with me, where my companions acted *King Richard the Second*.

[March 31.] I invited Captain Hawkins to a fish dinner and had *Hamlet* acted aboard me, which I permit to keep my people from idleness and unlawful games or sleep.

Other Drama of the Period

Even without Shakespeare, the early Jacobean drama in England would rank as one of the most creative periods in the history of all theater. (The word *Jacobean* is derived from *Jacobus*, the Latin form of the name of King James I.) Shakespeare's earlier contemporaries—Lyly, Greene, Marlowe, Peele, Kyd—were dead or silent, but another generation of playwrights was at hand. George Chapman, John Marston, and Ben Jonson all began writing plays shortly before 1600. So did Thomas Dekker and Thomas Heywood, whose dramatic output, often in collaboration, would prove to be considerable. Francis Beaumont, John Fletcher, Cyril Tourneur, and Thomas Middleton emerged into prominence in about 1606 or 1607. John Webster collaborated with Dekker and others in such plays as *Westward Ho* and *Sir Thomas Wyatt* around 1604, although he did not write his great tragedies until 1609–1614. Lesser talents, such as Henry Chettle, Anthony Munday, Henry Porter, John Day, and William Haughton, continued to pour forth an abundant supply of workmanlike plays. As Shakespeare's career developed, therefore, he enjoyed the fellowship and, no doubt, the rivalry of a remarkably gifted and diverse group of practicing dramatists.

Early Jacobean drama is, on the whole, characteristically different from the late Elizabethan drama that had preceded it. Other dramatists besides Shakespeare mirror his shift of focus from romantic comedies and patriotic histories to "problem" plays and tragedies. The boys' companies, reopening in 1598–1599 after virtually a decade of silence, did much to set the new tone. They avoided almost entirely the English history play, with its muscularly heroic style, so unsuited for the acting capabilities of boys. Besides, sophisticated audiences were sated with jingoistic fare, and even in the public theaters the genre had pretty well run its course. The fashion of the moment turned instead to revenge tragedy and satiric comedy.

The Jacobean revenge play owed much of its original inspiration to Thomas Kyd's *The Spanish Tragedy* (c. 1587), with its influential conventions: the intervention of supernatural forces, the feigned madness of the avenger, his difficulty in ascertaining the true facts of the murder, his morbid awareness of the conflict between human injustice and divine justice, his devising of a play within the play, and his invention of ingenious methods of slaughter in the play's gory ending. Kyd may also have written an early version of *Hamlet* featuring similar motifs. Shakespeare confronted cosmic issues of justice and human depravity in his revenge tragedy, *Hamlet* (c. 1599–1601), as indeed Kyd had done, but most followers of Kyd preferred to revel in the sensationalism of the genre. Some private-theater dramatists, such as Marston, subjected the conventions of the genre to caricature. Marston's revenge plays, written chiefly for Paul's boys and (after 1604) for the Children of the Queen's Revels, include *Antonio's Revenge* (1599–1601) and *The Malcontent* (1600–1604). These dramas are marked by flamboyantly overstated cynicism and are, in many ways, as close to satire as they are to tragedy. Marston had, in fact, made his first reputation as a nondramatic satirist, with *The Metamorphosis of Pygmalion's Image* and *The Scourge of Villainy* in 1598. His plays represent a continuation in dramatic form of the techniques of the Roman satirist. The typical Marstonian avenger, such as Malevole in *The Malcontent,* is an exaggeratedly unattractive authorial spokesman, pouring forth venomous hatred upon the loathsome and degenerate court in which he finds himself.

Similar in their exaggerated pursuit of the grotesque and the morbid are Cyril Tourneur's *The Atheist's Tragedy* (1607–1611) and a play formerly attributed to Tourneur but probably by Thomas Middleton, *The Revenger's Tragedy* (1606–1607). These plays are brilliant in the plotting of impossible situations and in the invention of cunning Italianate forms of torture and murder. Any sympathetic identification with the characters of these plays is sacrificed in the interests of technical virtuosity. As a result, the plays are more ironic than cathartic in their effect; we are overwhelmed by life's dark absurdities rather than ennobled by a vision of humanity's tragic grandeur. *The Tragedy of Hoffman, or A Revenge for a Father* by Henry Chettle (Admiral's men, 1602) is similarly grotesque and lacking in sympathy for its revenger hero. To be sure, George Chapman's *Bussy D'Ambois* (1600–1604) and its sequel, *The Revenge of Bussy D'Ambois* (1607–1612), are thoughtful plays about human aspiration, in the vein of Marlowe's *Tamburlaine,* but even these plays employ a good deal of Senecan bloody melodrama.

The revenge play enjoyed a great popularity on the public stage and (in a caricatured form) on the private stage. The public theater did, however, cater also to its Puritan-leaning audiences with more pious and moral tragedy. *Arden of Feversham* (c. 1591) is a good early example of what has come to be called domestic or homiletic tragedy. In the studiously plain style of a broadside ballad, it sets forth the facts of an actual murder that had occurred in 1551 and had been reported in Holinshed's *Chronicles.* The play interprets those events earnestly and providentially. The most famous play in the genre of domestic tragedy is Thomas Heywood's *A Woman Killed with Kindness* (1603). It tells, not of a murder, but of an adultery, for which the goodhearted but offending wife must be perpetually banished by her grieving husband. The play succeeds in elevating the private sorrows of its ordinary characters to tragic stature. The moral stances appear to be unambiguous: adultery is a heinous offense but can be transcended by Christian forgiveness; dueling is evil. Still, a mix of sympathies is perhaps reflective of shifting public attitudes toward the role of women in marriage. Other plays in the vein of domestic tragedy include *A Yorkshire Tragedy* (1605–1608), *The Miseries of Enforced Marriage* (1605–1606), and *Two Lamentable Tragedies* (c. 1594–1598).

In comedy, the greatest writer of the period besides Shakespeare was Ben Jonson. His predilection was toward the private theater, though he continued to write occasionally for the public stage as well. To an ever-increasing extent, he fixed his satirical gaze on those values and institutions which Thomas Heywood cherished: the city of London, its bourgeois citizens, its traditional approach to morality, and its religious zeal. *Every Man Out of His Humor* (1599), written for the Chamberlain's men, features a foolish uxorious citizen, his socially aspiring wife, and her fashionmongering lover—humors types that were to appear again and again in the genre of satirical comedy known as "city comedy." (See Brian Gibbons, *Jacobean City Comedy,* 1968.) *Volpone* (1605–1606), though technically not a London city comedy, since it purportedly takes place in Venice, castigates greed among lawyers, businessmen, and other professional types. *The Alchemist* (1610) ridicules the affectations of petty shopkeepers, lawyers' clerks, Puritan divines, and others. *Bartholomew Fair* (1614) and *The Alchemist* give us Jonson's most memorable indictment of the Puritans.

Numerous other writers contributed to humors comedy and city comedy. George Chapman probably deserves more credit than he usually receives for having helped determine the shape of humors comedy in his *The Blind Beggar of Alexandria* (1596), *An Humorous Day's Mirth* (1597), *All Fools* (1599–1604), *May-Day* (1601–1609), *The Gentleman Usher* (1602–1604), and others. Francis Beaumont, assisted perhaps by John Fletcher, ridicules London grocers and apprentices for their naive tastes in romantic chivalry in *The Knight of the Burning Pestle* (1607–1610). Some satire in this vein, to be sure, is reasonably good-humored. *Eastward Ho* (1605), by Chapman, Jonson, and Marston, is genially sympathetic toward the lifestyle of the small shopkeeper, even though the play contains a good deal of satire directed at social climbing and sharp business practices. Thomas Dekker's collaboration with Thomas Middleton on *The Honest Whore* (Part I, 1604) gives us an amused and yet warm portrayal of a linen draper who succeeds in business by insisting that the customer is always right. Dekker often shows a wry but generous appreciation of bourgeois ethics, as in *The Shoemaker's Holiday* (1599). Yet even he turns against the Puritans in *If This Be Not a Good Play, the Devil Is in It* (1611–1612).

Marston shows his talent for city comedy in *The Dutch Courtesan* (1603–1605). Perhaps the most ingratiating and truly funny of the writers of city comedy, however, is Middleton. His *A Trick to Catch the Old One* (1604–1607) illustrates the tendency of Jacobean comedy to move away both from Shakespeare's romantic vein and Jonson's morally satirical vein toward a more lighthearted comedy of manners, anticipating the style of Restoration comedy. One of Middleton's most hilarious and philosophically unpretentious plays, though plotted with great ingenuity of situation, is *A Mad World, My Masters* (1604–1607). *Michaelmas Term*, written about the same time, exposes the sharp practices of usurers and lawyers. All these Middleton plays were written for Paul's boys.

Romantic comedy, though overshadowed by humors and city comedy during the 1600s, still held forth at the public theaters. A leading exponent was Thomas Heywood, in such plays as *The Fair Maid of the West*, or *A Girl Worth Gold* (1597–1610). Heywood also wrote English history plays designed to prove the sturdiness and historical importance of the London citizenry he so loved, as in *Edward IV* (1597–1599), *The Four Prentices of London* (c. 1600), and *If You Know Not Me You Know Nobody* (1605). Classical tragedy also continued to be written, despite the vogue of revenge tragedy. Ben Jonson rather dogmatically illustrated his classical theories of tragedy in *Sejanus* (1603) and *Catiline* (1611). Samuel Daniel wrote *Philotas* in 1604 and a revision of his *Cleopatra* in 1607. Heywood's *The Rape of Lucrece* appeared in 1606–1608. These are not, however, the immortal tragedies for which the Jacobean period is remembered.

Shakespeare's Work, 1601–1608

Shakespeare's plays of this period are characteristically Jacobean in their fascination with the dark complexities of sexual jealousy, betrayal, revenge, and social conflict. The comedies are few in number and lack the joyous affirmation we associate with *Twelfth Night* and earlier plays. *Measure for Measure,* for example, is not about young men and women happily in love, but about premarital sex and the insoluble problems that arise when vice-prone men attempt to legislate morality for their fellow mortals. Angelo, self-hating and out of emotional control, is a tragic hero providentially rescued from his own worst self. The Duke and Isabella must use ethically dubious means—the bed trick—to effect their virtuous aims. Comedy in the play deals darkly in terms of prostitution, slander, and police inefficiency.

All's Well That Ends Well, though less grim than *Measure for Measure* in its confrontation of human degeneracy, does apply a similar bed trick as its central plot device. Just as important, the obstacles to love are internal and psychological, rather than external; that is, the happy union of Bertram and Helena is delayed, not by parental objections or by accident (as in *Romeo and Juliet* and *A Midsummer Night's Dream*), but by Bertram's unreadiness for the demands of a mature marital relationship. *Troilus and Cressida* is a play in which love is paralyzed by a combination of external and internal forces. Troilus must hand Cressida over to the Greeks because his code of honor bids him put his country's cause before his own, and yet that code of "honor" is based on Paris's rape of Helen. Cressida simply gives herself up to Diomedes, knowing she is not strong enough to stand alone in a moral wilderness. The combatants in the greatest war in all history turn out to be petty bickerers who play nasty games on one another and sulk when their reputations are impugned. The cause for which both sides fight is squalid and senseless.

Raphael Holinshed's Chronicles of England, Scotland, and Ireland, *which was published (1577, 2nd edition in 1587) before Shakespeare's career began, served as principal historic source for many plays, including* Macbeth, King Lear, *and* Cymbeline, *as well as the history plays. Here, in a woodcut from the* Chronicles, *Macbeth and Banquo are shown encountering the three weird sisters.*

In *Hamlet,* Shakespeare explores similar dilemmas posed by human carnality. Women, in Hamlet's misogynistic angst, are too often frail; men are too often importunate and brutal. How is a thoughtful person to justify his or her own existence? Should one struggle actively against injustice and personal wrong? How can one know what is really true or foresee the complex results of action? How, in *Othello,* can the protagonist resist temptation and inner weakness, prompting him to destroy the very thing on which his happiness depends? Is Macbeth tempted to sin by the weird sisters and his wife, or is the choice to murder Duncan ultimately his? To what extent is humanity responsible for its tragic fate? Most of all, in *King Lear,* are the heavens themselves indifferent to human bestiality? Must Cordelia die? Yet, despite these overwhelmingly pessimistic questions, and the tragic consequences they imply for all human life, Shakespeare's "great" tragedies affirm at least the nobility of humanity's striving to know itself, and the redeeming fact that human goodness does exist (in Desdemona, Duncan, Cordelia), even if those who practice goodness are often slaughtered.

The Roman or classical tragedies are something apart from the "great" tragedies. They are more ironic in tone, more dispiriting, though they, too, affirm an essential nobility in humanity. Brutus misguidedly leads a revolution against Caesar but dies loyal to his great principles. Timon of Athens proves the appalling ingratitude of his fellow creature and resolutely cuts himself off from all human contact. Coriolanus proclaims himself an enemy of the Roman people and seeks to destroy them for their ingratitude, though he is compromised and destroyed at last by his promptings of human feeling. Antony, too, is pulled apart by an irreconcilable conflict. Yet, in this play at least, Shakespeare achieves, partly through the greatness of Cleopatra, a triumph over defeat that seems to offer a new resolution of humanity's tragic dilemma.

THE LATE YEARS: 1608–1616

In the summer of 1608, Shakespeare's acting company signed a twenty-one-year lease for the use of the Blackfriars playhouse, an indoor and rather intimate, artificially lighted theater inside the city of London, close to the site of St. Paul's cathedral. A private theater had existed on this spot since 1576, when the Children of the Chapel and then Paul's boys began acting their courtly plays for paying spectators in a building that had once belonged to the Dominicans, or Black Friars. James Burbage had begun construction in 1596 of the so-called Second Blackfriars theater in the same building. Although James encountered opposition from the residents of the area and died before he could complete the work, James's son Richard did succeed in opening the new theater in 1600. At first, he leased it (for twenty-one

years) to a children's company, but when that company was suppressed in 1608 for offending the French ambassador in a play by George Chapman, Burbage seized the opportunity to take back the unexpired lease and to set up Blackfriars as the winter playhouse for his adult company, the King's men. By this time, the adult troupes could plainly see that they needed to cater more directly to courtly audiences than they once had done. Their popular audiences were becoming increasingly disenchanted with the drama. Puritan fulminations against the stage gained in effect, especially when many playwrights refused to disguise their satirical hostility toward Puritans and the London bourgeoisie.

Several of Shakespeare's late plays may have been acted both at the Globe and at Blackfriars. The plays he wrote after 1608–1609—*Cymbeline, The Winter's Tale,* and *The Tempest*—all show the distinct influence of the dramaturgy of the private theaters. Also, we know that an increasing number of Shakespeare's plays were acted at the court of King James. *Othello, King Lear,* and *The Tempest* are named in court revels accounts, and *Macbeth* dramatizes Scottish history with a seemingly explicit reference to King James as the descendant of Banquo who bears the "twofold balls and treble scepters" (4.1.121); James had received a double coronation as King of England and Scotland, and took seriously his assumed title as King of Great Britain, France, and Ireland. On the other hand, Shakespeare's plays certainly continued to be acted at the Globe to the very end of his career. The 1609 Quarto of *Pericles* advertises that it was acted "by his Majesty's Servants, at the Globe on the Bankside." The 1608 Quarto of *King Lear* mentions a performance at court and assigns the play to "his Majesty's servants playing usually at the Globe on the Bankside." Simon Forman saw *Macbeth, Cymbeline,* and *The Winter's Tale* at the Globe. Finally, a performance of *Henry VIII* on June 29, 1613, resulted in the burning of the Globe to the ground, though afterwards it soon was rebuilt.

Shakespeare's last plays, written with a view to Blackfriars and the court, as well as to the Globe, are now usually called "romances" or "tragicomedies," or sometimes both. Although they were not known by these terms in Shakespeare's day—they were grouped with the comedies in the First Folio of 1623, except for *Cymbeline,* which was placed among the tragedies—the very ambiguity about the genre in this arrangement is suggestive of an uncertainty as to whether they were seen as predominantly comic or tragic. The term "romance" suggests a return to the kind of story Robert Greene had derived from Greek romance: tales of adventure, long separation, and tearful reunion, involving shipwreck, capture by pirates, riddling prophecies, children set adrift in boats or abandoned on foreign shores, the illusion of death and subsequent restoration to life, the revelation of the identity of long-lost children by birthmarks, and the like. The term "tragicomedy" suggests

This section of Wenceslaus Hollar's "Long View" of London dates from 1647, some years after Shakespeare's death, but gives nonetheless a fine view of two theater buildings on the south bank of the Thames River, across from the city. The two labels of "The Globe" and "Beere bayting" should in fact be reversed; the Globe (rebuilt in 1613) appears to the left and below the bearbaiting arena.

a play in which the protagonist commits a seemingly fatal error or crime, or (as in *Pericles*) suffers an extraordinarily adverse fortune to test his patience; in either event, he must experience agonies of contrition and bereavement until he is providentially delivered from his tribulations. The tone is deeply melancholic and resigned, although suffused also with a sense of gratitude for the harmonies that are mysteriously restored.

The appropriateness of such plays to the elegant atmosphere of Blackfriars and the court is subtle but real. Although one might suppose at first that old-fashioned naiveté would seem out of place in a sophisticated milieu, the naiveté is only superficial. Tragicomedy and pastoral romance were, in the period from 1606 to 1610, beginning to enjoy a fashionable courtly revival. The leading practitioners of the new genre were Beaumont and Fletcher, though Shakespeare made a highly significant contribution. Perhaps sophisticated audiences responded to pastoral and romantic drama as the nostalgic evocation of an idealized past, a chivalric "golden world" fleetingly recovered through an artistic journey back to naiveté and innocence. The evocation of such a world demands the kind of studied but informal artifice we find in many tragicomic plays of the period: the elaborate masques and allegorical shows, the descents of enthroned gods from the heavens (as in *Cymbeline*), the use of quaint Chorus figures like Old Gower or Time (in *Pericles* and *The Winter's Tale*), and the quasi-operatic blend of music and spectacle. At their best, such plays powerfully compel belief in the artistic world thus artificially created. The very improbability of the story becomes, paradoxically, part of the means by which an audience must "awake its faith" in a mysterious truth.

Shakespeare did not merely ape the new fashion in tragicomedy and romance. In fact, he may have done much to establish it. His *Pericles*, written seemingly in about 1606–1608 for the public stage before Shakespeare's company acquired Blackfriars, anticipated many important features, not only of Shakespeare's own later romances, but also of Beaumont and Fletcher's *The Maid's Tragedy* and *Philaster* (c. 1608–1611). Still, Shakespeare was on the verge of retirement, and the future belonged to Beaumont and Fletcher. Gradually, Shakespeare disengaged himself, spending more and more time in Stratford. His last-known stint as an actor was in Jonson's *Sejanus* in 1603. Some time in 1611 or 1612, he probably gave up his lodgings in London, though he still may have returned for such occasions as the opening performance of *Henry VIII* in 1613. He continued to be one of the proprietors of the newly rebuilt Globe, but his involvement in its day-to-day operations dwindled.

Shakespeare's Reputation, 1608–1616

Shakespeare's reputation among his contemporaries was undiminished in his late years, even though Beaumont and Fletcher were the new rage at the Globe and Blackfriars. Among those who apostrophized Shakespeare was John Davies of Hereford in *The Scourge of Folly* (entered in the Stationers' Register in 1610):

> To our English Terence, Mr. Will Shakespeare.
>
> Some say, good Will, which I, in sport, do sing:
> Hadst thou not played some kingly parts in sport,
> Thou hadst been a companion for a king,
> And been a king among the meaner sort.
> Some others rail. But, rail as they think fit,
> Thou hast no railing, but a reigning, wit.
> And honesty thou sow'st, which they do reap,
> So to increase their stock which they do keep.

The following sonnet is from *Run and a Great Cast* (1614) by Thomas Freeman:

> To Master W. Shakespeare.
>
> Shakespeare, that nimble Mercury thy brain

Lulls many hundred Argus-eyes asleep,
So fit, for all thou fashionest thy vein,
At th' horse-foot fountain thou hast drunk full deep.
Virtue's or vice's theme to thee all one is.
Who loves chaste life, there's *Lucrece* for a teacher;
Who list read lust, there's *Venus and Adonis*,
True model of a most lascivious lecher.
Besides, in plays thy wit winds like Meander,
Whence needy new composers borrow more
Than Terence doth from Plautus or Menander.
But to praise thee aright, I want thy store.
   Then let thine own works thine own worth upraise,
   And help t' adorn thee with deservèd bays.

Ben Jonson took a more critical view, though he also admired Shakespeare greatly. In the Induction to his *Bartholomew Fair* (1631 edition), Jonson compared the imaginary world he presented in his play with the more improbable fantasies of romantic drama:

If there be never a servant-monster i' the fair, who can help it? He [the author, Jonson] says; nor a nest of antics? He is loath to make Nature afraid in his plays, like those that beget tales, Tempests, and suchlike drolleries to mix his head with other men's heels.

From this, one judges that Jonson had in mind not only *The Tempest* but also Shakespeare's other late romances. He similarly protested in the Prologue to his 1616 edition of *Every Man in His Humor* that his own playwriting was free of the usual romantic claptrap:

Where neither Chrous wafts you o'er the seas,
Nor creaking throne comes down the boys to please,
Nor nimble squib is seen to make afeard
The gentlewomen, nor rolled bullet heard
To say it thunders, nor tempestuous drum
Rumbles to tell you when the storm doth come.

Still, Shakespeare's reputation was assured. John Webster paid due homage, in his note To the Reader accompanying *The White Devil* (1612), to "the right happy and copious industry of M. *Shakespeare*, M. *Dekker*, & M. *Heywood*," along with Chapman, Jonson, Beaumont, and Fletcher.

Records of the Late Years

Shakespeare's last recorded investment in real estate was the purchase of a house in Blackfriars, London, in 1613. There is no indication he lived there, for he had retired to Stratford. He did not pay the full purchase price of one hundred and forty pounds, and the mortgage deed executed for the unpaid balance furnishes one of the six unquestioned examples of his signature.

John Combe, a wealthy bachelor of Stratford and Shakespeare's friend, left him a legacy of five pounds in his will at the time of Combe's death in 1613. At about the same time, John's kinsman William Combe began a controversial attempt to enclose Welcombe Common, that is, to convert narrow strips of arable land to pasture. Presumably, Combe was interested in a more efficient means of using the land. Enclosure was, however, an explosive issue, since many people feared they would lose the right to farm the land and would be evicted to make room for cattle and sheep. Combe attempted to guarantee Shakespeare and other titheholders that they would lose no money. He offered similar assurances to the Stratford Council, but the townspeople were adamantly opposed. Shakespeare was consulted by letter as a leading titheholder. The letter is lost, but, presumably, it set forth the Council's reasons for objecting to enclosure. Shakespeare's views on the controversy remain unknown. Eventually, the case went to the Privy Council, where Combe was ordered to restore the land to its original use.

One of the most interesting documents from these years consists of the records of a lawsuit entered into in 1612 by Stephen Belott against his father-in-law, Christopher Mountjoy, a Huguenot maker of women's ornamental headdresses who resided on Silver Street, St. Olave's parish, London. Belott sought to secure the payment of a dower promised him at the time of his marriage to Mountjoy's daughter. In this suit, Shakespeare was summoned as a witness and made deposition on five interrogatories. From this document we learn that Shakespeare was a lodger in Mountjoy's house at the time of the marriage in 1604 and probably for some time before that, since he states in his testimony that he had known Mountjoy for more than ten years. Shakespeare admitted that, at the solicitation of Mountjoy's wife, he had acted as an intermediary in the arrangement of the marriage between Belott and Mountjoy's daughter. Shakespeare declared himself unable, however, to recall the exact amount of the portion or the date on which it was to have been paid. Shakespeare's signature to his deposition is authentic and one of the best samples of his handwriting that we have.

In January of 1615 or 1616, Shakespeare drew up his last will and testament with the assistance of his lawyer Francis Collins, who had aided him earlier in some of his transactions in real estate. On March 25, 1616, Shakespeare revised his will in order to provide for the marriage of his daughter Judith and Thomas Quiney in that same year. Shakespeare's three quavering signatures, one on each page of this document, suggest that he was in failing health. The cause of his death on April 23 is not known. An intriguing bit of Stratford gossip is reported by John Ward, vicar of Holy Trinity in Stratford from 1662 to 1689, in his diary: "Shakespeare, Drayton, and Ben Jonson had a merry meeting, and it seems drank too hard, for Shakespeare died of a fever there contracted." The report comes fifty years after Shakespeare's death, however, and is hardly an expert medical opinion.

The will disposes of all the property of which Shakespeare is known to have died possessing, the greater share of it going to his daughter Susanna. His recently married daughter Judith received a dowry, a provision for any children that might be born of her marriage, and other gifts. Ten pounds went to the poor of Stratford; Shakespeare's sword went to Mr. Thomas Combe; twenty-six shillings and eight pence apiece went to Shakespeare's fellow actors Heminges, Burbage, and Condell to buy them mourning rings; and other small bequests went to various other friends and relatives.

An interlineation contains the bequest of Shakespeare's "second best bed with the furniture," that is, the hangings, to his wife. Anne's name appears nowhere else in the will. Some scholars, beginning with Edmund Malone, have taken this reference as proof of an unhappy marriage, confirming earlier indications, such as the hasty wedding to a woman who was William's senior by eight years and his prolonged residence in London for twenty years or more seemingly without his family. The evidence is inconclusive, however. Shakespeare certainly supported his family handsomely, acquired much property in Stratford, and retired there when he might have remained still in London. Although he showed no great solicitude for Anne's well-being in the will, her rights were protected by law; a third of her husband's estate went to her without having to be mentioned in the will. New Place was to be the home of Shakespeare's favorite daughter Susanna, wife of the distinguished Dr. John Hall. Anne Shakespeare would make her home with her daughter and, with her dower rights secured by law, would be quite as wealthy as she would need to be.

The date of Shakespeare's death (April 23, 1616) and his age (his fifty-third year) are inscribed on his monument. This elaborate structure, still standing in the chancel of Trinity Church, Stratford, was erected some time before 1623 by the London stonecutting firm of Gheerart Janssen and his sons. Janssen's shop was in Southwark, near the Globe, and may have been familiar to the actors. The bust of Shakespeare is a conventional sort of statuary for its time. Still, it is one of the only two contemporary likenesses we have. The other is the Droeshout engraving of Shakespeare in the Folio of 1623.

The epitaph on the monument reads as follows:

Iudicio Phylium, genio Socratem, arte Maronem;
Terra tegit, populus maeret, Olympus habet.
Stay passenger. Why goest thou by so fast?
Read, if thou canst, whom envious Death hath placed
Within this monument: Shakespeare, with whom
Quick Nature died, whose name doth deck this tomb
Far more than cost, sith all that he hath writ
Leaves living art but page to serve his wit.
                              Obiit anno domini 1616,
                              Aetatis 53, die 23 April.

These lines, of which the beginning Latin couplet compares Shakespeare with Nestor (King of Pylos) for wise judgment, Socrates for genius, and Virgil (Maro) for poetic art, and avers that the earth covers him, people grieve for him, and Mount Olympus (that is, heaven) has him, indicate the high reputation he enjoyed at the time of his death. More widely known, perhaps, are the four lines inscribed over Shakespeare's grave near the north wall of the chancel. A local tradition assigns them to Shakespeare himself and implies that he wrote them "to suit the capacity of clerks and sextons," whom he wished apparently to frighten out of the idea of opening the grave to make room for a new occupant:

Good friend, for Jesus' sake forbear
To dig the dust enclosèd here.
Blest be the man that spares these stones,
And curst be he that moves my bones.

Whether Shakespeare actually wrote these lines cannot, however, be determined.

Other Dramatists

The most significant new development in the drama of the period from about 1608 to 1616, apart from Shakespeare's

THE NATIONAL ARCHIVES, LONDON PROB 1/4 E3

As with so many other things in his life, the curious terms of Shakespeare's will have led to endless and provocative conjecture.

new interest in romance and tragicomedy, was the emergence of the famous literary partners Francis Beaumont and John Fletcher. Beaumont, the son of a distinguished lawyer, studied for a while at Oxford and then at the Inner Temple before drifting into a literary career. In 1613, he married an heiress and retired almost completely from the theater. John Fletcher was the son of Richard Fletcher, Queen Elizabeth's chaplain and later Bishop of London. The young man probably studied at Cambridge. The father died in 1596 heavily in debt, leaving the young Fletcher to support a family of eight children. Fletcher became a professional writer, earning his living as chief dramatist for the King's men. He was Shakespeare's successor. Fletcher's cousins, Giles and Phineas Fletcher, gained some reputation as poets. Beaumont and Fletcher, who were close friends, regarded themselves also as poets and as members of the "tribe of Ben"—the disciples of the great Ben Jonson who often gathered together at the Mermaid Tavern for an evening of witty literary conversation.

> What things have we seen
> Done at the Mermaid! heard words that have been
> So nimble, and so full of subtle flame,
> As if that every one from whence they came
> Had meant to put his whole wit in a jest,
> And had resolved to live a fool the rest
> Of his dull life!

(Master Francis Beaumont's Letter to Ben Jonson)

Beaumont and Fletcher actually collaborated on only about seven plays: *The Woman Hater,* a comedy (1606); *The Maid's Tragedy*, a tragedy (1608–1611); *Philaster,* a tragicomedy (1608–1610); *Cupid's Revenge,* a tragedy (c. 1607–1612); *The Coxcomb,* a comedy (1608–1610); *A King and No King,* a tragicomedy (1611); *The Scornful Lady,* a tragicomedy (1613–1616); and perhaps one or two others. They may have collaborated on *The Knight of the Burning Pestle* (c. 1607–1610), though it was chiefly Beaumont's. Beaumont also wrote *Mask of the Inner Temple and Gray's Inn* (1613). Fletcher unassisted wrote *The Faithful Shepherdess* (1608–1609), *The Night Walker* (c. 1611), *Bonduca* (1611–1614), *Valentinian* (1610–1614), and others. He also collaborated with several other writers, including Massinger, Middleton, Field, and Rowley. Importantly, he seems to have collaborated with Shakespeare on *The Two Noble Kinsmen* (1613–1616) and, probably, on *Henry VIII.* Eventually, most of these various dramatic enterprises were gathered together in 1647 as the works of Beaumont and Fletcher. They have remained known as such ever since, partly because the original collaboration of these two men did so much to set a new style in coterie drama.

The plays they wrote together, such as *The Maid's Tragedy* and *Philaster,* offer an interesting comparison with Shakespeare's contemporary writing in a similar genre.

Beaumont and Fletcher often employ exotic settings, like Rhodes or Sicily. In such an environment, refined aristocratic characters are caught in dynastic struggles or in a rarified conflict between love and honor. They must cope with stereotyped villains, such as tyrants or shamelessly lustful courtiers. The sentiments are lofty, the rhetoric is mannered; elaborately contrived situations are offered with no pretense of verisimilitude. The characters live according to lofty chivalric codes and despise ill breeding above all else. In the plotting of the tragicomic reversal, the audience is sometimes deliberately deceived into believing something that is not true, so that the sudden happy outcome arrives as a theatrically contrived surprise. Disguising and masking are common motifs. The audience is deliberately made aware throughout of the play's theatrical artifice, statuesque scene building, and titillating sensationalism.

Although Shakespeare wrote no tragedies after *Coriolanus,* great tragedy did continue to appear on the Jacobean stage. John Webster wrote his two most splendid plays, *The White Devil* and *The Duchess of Malfi,* between 1609 and 1614. Both contain elements of the still-popular revenge tradition. They also manage to achieve a vision of triumphant human dignity in defeat that merits comparison with Shakespeare's greatest tragic achievement. Still to come were *The Changeling* (1622) by Thomas Middleton and William Rowley, *Women Beware Women* (c. 1620–1627) by Middleton, *'Tis Pity She's a Whore* (1629?–1633) by John Ford, and others. Although these tragedies are more concerned with the grotesque than are Shakespeare's great tragedies, and more obsessed with abnormal human psychology (incest, werewolfism, and the like), they are nonetheless sublime achievements in art. The genius of the age for tragedy did not die with Shakespeare. During Shakespeare's last years, George Chapman was also writing his best tragedies, including *Charles Duke of Byron* in 1608, *The Revenge of Bussy D'Ambois* in about 1610, and *Chabot, Admiral of France* between 1611 and 1622. Ben Jonson's *Catiline His Conspiracy,* a classical tragedy, appeared in 1611; Marston's *The Insatiate Countess,* in about 1610.

The Anti-Stratfordian Movement

What we know of Shakespeare's life is really quite considerable. The information we have is just the kind one would expect. It hangs together and refers to one man and one career. Though lacking in the personal details we should like to have, it is both adequate and plausible. Yet the past hundred years or so have seen the growth of a tendency to doubt Shakespeare's authorship of the plays and poems ascribed to him. The phenomenon is sometimes called the "anti-Stratfordian" movement, since its attack is leveled at the literary credentials of the man who was born in Stratford and later became an actor in London.

Although based on no reliable evidence, the movement has persisted long enough to become a kind of myth. It also has the appeal of a mystery thriller: who really wrote Shakespeare's plays? A brief account must be made here of the origins of the anti-Stratfordian movement.

Beginning in the late eighteenth century, and especially in the mid nineteenth century, a few admirers of Shakespeare began to be troubled by the scantiness of information about England's greatest author. As we have already seen, good reasons exist for the scarcity: the great London fire of 1666 that destroyed many records, the relatively low social esteem accorded to popular dramatists during the Elizabethan period, and the like. Also, we do actually know more about Shakespeare than about most of his contemporaries in the theater, despite the difficulties imposed by the passage of time. Still, some nineteenth-century readers saw only that they knew far less about Shakespeare than about many authors of more recent date.

Moreover, the impressions of the man did not seem to square with his unparalleled literary greatness. William Shakespeare had been brought up in a small country town; were his parents cultured folk or even literate? No record of his schooling has been preserved; was Shakespeare himself able to read and write, much less write immortal plays and poems? The anti-Stratfordians did not deny the existence of a man called Shakespeare from Stratford-upon-Avon, but they found it incredible that such a person should be connected with the works ascribed to him. Mark Twain, himself an anti-Stratfordian, was fond of joking that the plays were not by Shakespeare but by another person of the same name. Beneath the humor in this remark lies a deep-seated mistrust: how could a country boy have written so knowledgeably and eloquently about the lives of kings and queens? Where could such a person have learned so much about the law, about medicine, about the art of war, about heraldry? The puzzle seemed a genuine one, even though no one until the late eighteenth century had thought to question Shakespeare's authorship of the plays—least of all his colleagues and friends, such as Ben Jonson, who admitted that Shakespeare's classical learning was "small" but insisted that Shakespeare was an incomparable genius.

The first candidate put forward in the anti-Stratfordian cause as the "real" author of the plays was Sir Francis Bacon, a reputable Elizabethan writer with connections at court and considerable cultural attainments. Yet the ascription of the plays to Bacon was based on no documentary evidence. It relied, instead, on the essentially snobbish argument that Bacon was better born and purportedly better educated than Shakespeare—an argument that appealed strongly to the nineteenth century in which a university education was becoming more and more a distinctive mark of the cultivated person. The assertion of Bacon's authorship was also based on a conspiratorial theory of history; that is, its believers had to assume the existence of a mammoth conspiracy in Elizabethan times in which Shakespeare would allow his name to be used by Bacon as a *nom de plume* and in which Shakespeare's friends, such as Ben Jonson, would take part. (Jonson knew Shakespeare too well, after all, to have been duped for a period of almost twenty years.) The motive for such an arrangement, presumably, was that Bacon did not deign to lend his dignified name to the writing of popular plays (since they were considered subliterary) and so chose a common actor named Shakespeare to serve as his alter ego. This theory of an elaborate hoax involving England's greatest literary giant has proved powerfully attractive to modern writers like Mark Twain who have sometimes referred to themselves as rebels against the cultural "Establishment" of their own times.

The claim that Bacon wrote Shakespeare's works was soon challenged in the name of other prominent Elizabethans: the Earl of Oxford, the Earl of Southampton, Anthony Bacon, the Earl of Rutland, the Earl of Devonshire, Christopher Marlowe, and others. Since documentary claims as to Bacon's authorship of the Shakespearen canon were nonexistent, other Elizabethans could be proposed to fill his role just as satisfactorily as Bacon himself. The anti-Stratfordian movement gained momentum and came to include several prominent persons, including Delia Bacon and Sigmund Freud, as well as Mark Twain. One of the appeals of the anti-Stratfordian movement in recent years has proved to be a kind of amateur sleuthing or scholarship, carried on by professional lawyers, doctors, and the like, who have explored Shakespeare's interest in law and medicine as a hobby and have convinced themselves that Shakespeare's wisdom in these subjects entitles him to claim a better birth than that of a glover's son from Stratford. Ingenious efforts at "deciphering" hidden meanings in the works have been adduced to prove one authorship claim or another. The academic "Establishments" of modern universities have been accused of perpetuating Shakespeare's name out of mere vested self-interest: Shakespeare scholarship is an industry, and its busy workers need to preserve their source of income.

We must ask in all seriousness, however, whether such assertions are not offering answers to nonexistent questions. Responsible scholarship has admirably dispelled the seeming mystery of Shakespeare's humble beginnings. T. W. Baldwin, for example, in *William Shakespeare's Petty School* (1943) and *William Shakspere's Small Latine and Lesse Greeke* (1944), has shown just what sort of classical training Shakespeare almost surely received in the free grammar school of Stratford. It is precisely the sort of training that would have enabled him to use classical authors as he does, with the familiarity of one who likes to read. His Latin and Greek were passable but not strong; he often consulted modern translations, as well as classical originals. Just as importantly, Shakespeare's social background was, in fact, typical of many of the greatest writers of the English Renaissance. He earned his living by his writing, and thus had one of the strongest of motives for success. So did his contemporaries Marlowe (who came from a shoemaker's family) and Jonson (whose stepfather was a brickmason). Greene, Peele, Nashe, and many others sold plays and other writings for a livelihood. Although a few wellborn persons, such as Bacon and Sir Philip Sidney, also made exceptional contributions to literature, and although a number of courtiers emulated Henry VIII and Elizabeth as gifted amateurs in the arts, the court was not the direct or major source of England's literary greatness. Most courtiers were not, like Shakespeare, professional writers. A man like Bacon lacked Shakespeare's connection with a commercial acting company. Surely the theater was a more relevant "university" for Shakespeare than Oxford or Cambridge, where most of his studies would have been in ancient languages and in divinity.

SHAKESPEARE'S LANGUAGE: HIS DEVELOPMENT AS POET AND DRAMATIST

LANGUAGE AND ARTISTIC DEVELOPMENT

One indication of Shakespeare's greatness is his extraordinary development. As he worked through his writing career of more than twenty years, he constantly explored new themes, perfected genres and moved on to new ones, and saw ever more deeply into the human condition. Many of the works that have made him immortal were not written until he was nearly forty years old or more. The study of his development is, in itself, an interesting and complex subject. It is one that requires an accurate dating of his plays and poems.

The First Folio, published in 1623 as the first "complete edition" of Shakespeare's plays in the large and handsome folio format for which the printed sheet was folded only once, gives no help in determining the order of composition of Shakespeare's plays. They are arranged in three groups—comedies, histories, and tragedies—without regard for dates of composition. The first comedy in the Folio is *The Tempest,* known to be one of Shakespeare's latest plays; the second is *The Two Gentlemen of Verona,* one of the earliest. The histories are arranged in order of the English kings whose reigns they treat, although Shakespeare clearly did not write them in that order. The tragedies show no discernible arrangement by date. Information about dating can partially be recovered from the fact that eighteen of the thirty-six plays in the First Folio had previously been published in single quarto volumes at various times, with dates on their title pages. *Pericles,* which

was not included in the First Folio, appeared in quarto format in 1609. (The quarto format required that the printed sheet be folded twice, resulting in a smaller page than that of a folio volume.) All the quarto editions, except *Romeo and Juliet* and *Love's Labor's Lost,* were entered in the Register of the Stationers' Company of London; two other plays, *As You Like It* (entered in the Stationers' Register in 1600) and *Antony and Cleopatra* (S.R. 1608), although not printed in quarto, were entered in the Stationers' Register possibly in order to forestall publication by printers who had no right to them. The date of entry of a play in the register indicates that, at least by that time, the play was in existence. The quarto editions also have certain information on their title pages regarding date, author, and publisher, and sometimes tell what theatrical company acted the play. Other kinds of external evidence of date include references to Shakespeare's plays in diaries, journals, or accounts of the period, and quotations from his plays in the literary works of Elizabethan and Jacobean writers. Allusions in Shakespeare's plays themselves to contemporary events, although difficult to prove beyond dispute, can sometimes be helpful. See Appendix 1, at the end of this volume, for a detailed discussion on "Canon, Dates, and Early Texts" of each of Shakespeare's plays.

Once Shakespeare's plays have been arranged in approximate chronological order on the basis of the kinds of external evidence already described, we can perceive that his style underwent a continuous development from his earliest work to the end of his career as a dramatist. Matters of style are not easy to talk about precisely, and we can hardly expect to be able to date a particular passage as having been written in 1604, say, as distinguished from 1602. Overall, on the other hand, the early and late Shakespeare are strikingly distinguishable. Take, for example, the following two passages. One is from the Duke of Clarence's description of his dream in *Richard III* (1.4.21–33), written in about 1591–1594, near the start of Shakespeare's career:

> Oh, Lord, methought what pain it was to drown!
> What dreadful noise of waters in my ears!
> What sights of ugly death within my eyes!
> Methoughts I saw a thousand fearful wracks;
> Ten thousand men that fishes gnawed upon;
> Wedges of gold, great anchors, heaps of pearl,
> Inestimable stones, unvalued jewels,
> All scattered in the bottom of the sea.
> Some lay in dead men's skulls, and in the holes
> Where eyes did once inhabit there were crept,
> As 'twere in scorn of eyes, reflecting gems,
> That wooed the slimy bottom of the deep
> And mocked the dead bones that lay scattered by.

The second is Prospero's description of his magic in *The Tempest* (5.1.33–50), from about 1610–1611 when Shakespeare was on the verge of retirement:

Ye elves of hills, brooks, standing lakes, and groves,
And ye that on the sands with printless foot
Do chase the ebbing Neptune, and do fly him
When he comes back; you demi-puppets that
By moonshine do the green sour ringlets make,
Whereof the ewe not bites; and you whose pastime
Is to make midnight mushrooms, that rejoice
To hear the solemn curfew; by whose aid,
Weak masters though ye be, I have bedimmed
The noontide sun, called forth the mutinous winds,
And twixt the green sea and the azured vault
Set roaring war; to the dread rattling thunder
Have I given fire, and rifted Jove's stout oak
With his own bolt; the strong-based promontory
Have I made shake, and by the spurs plucked up
The pine and cedar; graves at my command
Have waked their sleepers, oped, and let 'em forth
By my so potent art.

These two passages have been chosen for comparison, in part because they are both set speeches in blank verse, rich in formal characteristics. Put side by side, they reveal a stylistic shift that we can observe in other less formal poetry and even in prose. The shift is away from rhetorical balance toward a freedom from verse restraint, a deliberate syncopation of blank verse rhythms, and a complication of syntax.

Completely regular blank verse, invariably consisting of ten syllables to each unrhymed line, with an accent falling on every other syllable, soon becomes monotonous. The iambic pattern can, however, be varied by a number of subtle changes. Extra syllables, accented and unaccented, can be added to the line, or a line may occasionally be short by one or more syllables. The regular alternation of accented and unaccented syllables, producing the effect of five iambic "feet" in each line (each foot consisting of an accented and an unaccented syllable), can be interrupted by the occasional inversion of a foot. Pauses, or caesuras, may occur at several points in the line. Most importantly, the line can be "end-stopped"—with a strong pause at the end of the line—or "run on" without interruption into the next line. Variations of this sort can transform blank verse from a formal and rhetorical vehicle into one that is highly conversational and supple.

Shakespeare increasingly abandons formal end-stopped verse for a fluid and more conversational style. In the preceding two passages, the first introduces a grammatical stop at the end of every line, except the ninth, whereas the second passage tends to run on past the end of the line; it does so in all but the fifth and tenth lines. Similarly, the passage from *The Tempest* is more apt to introduce a grammatical pause in the middle of a verse line, whereas the passage from *Richard III* stops between clauses in midline only in line 9. Shakespeare's later style is freer in its use of so-called feminine ends at the ends of

lines, that is, endings with an unstressed syllable added on to the final stress of the iambic pattern; "fly him," "pastime," and "thunder" are good examples of this. A corollary of Shakespeare's increased use of feminine line endings and nonstopped blank verse is that the lines of his later verse are more apt to end in conjunctions, prepositions, auxiliary verbs, possessive pronouns, and other lightly stressed words. The *Richard III* passage generally ends in strong verbs and nouns, such as "drown," "ears," "eyes," and so on, whereas the *Tempest* passage makes use of "that," "up," and "forth."

Stylistic traits such as these can be quantified to demonstrate a fairly steady course of progression from the early to later plays. Early plays have low percentages of run-on lines in relation to the total number of lines: *1 Henry VI* has 10.4 percent, *2 Henry VI* 11.4 percent, *3 Henry VI* 9.5 percent, *The Comedy of Errors* 12.9 percent, and *The Two Gentlement of Verona* 12.4 percent, whereas *Cymbeline* has 46.0 percent, *The Winter's Tale* 37.5 percent, *The Tempest* 41.5 percent, and *Henry VIII* 46.3 percent. Feminine or "double" endings run from a total of 9 in *Love's Labor's Lost* and 29 in *A Midsummer Night's Dream* to 708 in *Coriolanus*, 726 in *Cymbeline,* and 1,195 in *Henry VIII*. The actual number of light or weak endings increases from none in *The Comedy of Errors* and *The Two Gentlemen of Verona* to 104 in *Coriolanus*, 130 in *Cymbeline,* and 100 in *The Tempest*.

Other stylistic characteristics, though not discernible in the two examples from *Richard III* and *The Tempest*, spell out a similar development toward flexibility. For example, Shakespeare increasingly divides a verse line between two or more speakers. *The Comedy of Errors* and *1 Henry VI* do so hardly at all, whereas in *Cymbeline* the figures rise to a remarkable 85 percent of all instances in which one speaker stops speaking and another begins; *The Winter's Tale* does so in 87.6 percent of such instances, and *The Tempest*, in 84.5 percent.

Shakespeare's use of prose in his plays depends, to a significant extent, on genre, especially in his early work. At the start of his career, Shakespeare seldom uses prose, except in the speeches of clowns, servants, and rustics, whereas blank verse is his common vehicle of expression in speeches of heightened oratory or dramatic seriousness. *1 Henry VI* and *3 Henry VI, King John,* and *Richard II* are essentially written throughout in verse—usually blank verse. Prose is more common in the early comedies because of the presence of the Dromios, Christopher Sly, and Bottom the Weaver, but the love scenes are generally in verse. Poetry is important to the lyric plays of the mid-1590s, such as *The Merchant of Venice, A Midsummer Night's Dream,* and *Romeo and Juliet*. Prose assumes a major function, on the other hand, in plays of comic wit in the later 1590s, including *1 Henry IV* (45 percent), *2 Henry IV* (54 percent), *Much Ado About Nothing* (74 percent), and *The Merry Wives of Windsor* (81 percent), and here we see that comedy is used not for wisecracking servants so much as

Shakespeare's World
A Visual Portfolio

GLOBE. SOUTHWARKE.

PLATE 1. The Globe Theater. *This eighteenth-century watercolor is based on Claes Janszoon de Visscher's* View of London *(1616). Built in 1599, the Globe was about 80 feet in diameter and accommodated between two and three thousand spectators. Southwark, on the south bank of the Thames river, was also home to the Rose and Swan theaters.*

PLATE 2. London in Shakespeare's Time. *In this anonymous seventeenth-century painting, the theaters of Southwark are clearly visible in the left foreground, flags flying. London Bridge crosses the River Thames into the city, where St Paul's Cathedral dominates the central skyline. The Tower of London is visible on the right. The many boats on the Thames are evidence of the vital role the river played in the city's emerging importance in national and international trade.*

PLATE 3. The Painting of a Lifetime. *This painting of the life of Sir Henry Unton (1557?–1596), probably commissioned by his widow, shows the important events of his life. In the lower right, we see him at birth, in his mother's arms. Above that, we see him as a student at Oxford. The top center depicts his travels to Europe and his expedition to the Netherlands ("Low Countries") under the command of the Earl of Leicester. Below that, we see various scenes in Wadley House, his residence, including a feast with masquers in festive dress, led in procession by Diana and Mercury. His death and burial are pictured in the lower left corner.*

PLATE 4. Queen Elizabeth I. *Few monarchs have ever influenced an age so pervasively and left their stamp on it so permanently as did Elizabeth I during her reign from 1558-1603. Elizabeth is celebrated in this portrait that commemorates the English defeat of the Spanish Armada in 1588. A mythology developed around the Queen, linked to her virginity and devotion to her people. With her right hand on the globe, she is shown here in all her glory as the empress of the world.*

PLATE 5. King James I. *James I, King of England from 1603–1625, was the first of the Stuart dynasty. His name is linked to one of the most creative periods in the history of the theater: that of the Jacobean drama. "Jacobean" is derived from* Jacobus, *the Latin word for James.*

PLATE 6. Social Class in Shakespeare's Time. *Social classes and fashions in Shakespeare's day were clearly defined. People were required by English law to dress according to their social status. Shown here are a workman (top), carrying his tools; "a presumptuous woman" (center), gaudily attired beyond her appointed station; and a "gentleman" (bottom), privileged to wear his apparel.*

PLATE 7. Ben Jonson. *Chief dramatic rival for public acclaim during Shakespeare's later years was Ben Jonson (1572–1637). Jonson, a poet, playwright, and literary critic, was a noted scholar of classical literature and a good friend of Shakespeare. The First Folio of 1623 contains a poetic eulogy of Shakespeare written by Jonson.*

PLATE 8. Edward Alleyn. *Edward Alleyn (1566–1626) won great acclaim in the roles of Tamburlaine and Doctor Faustus, among many others. As leading player of Lord Strange's men and then the Lord Admiral's men, he became a prominent rival of Richard Burbage of the Lord Chamberlain's men. This was the company in which Shakespeare served as actor-sharer and playwright, starting in 1594. Alleyn was also the founder of Dulwich College.*

PLATE 9. Falstaff and Crew. *William Hogarth's painting, "Falstaff Examining His Recruits from Henry IV," dates from 1730. Sir John Falstaff was one of Shakespeare's most popular characters, appearing in parts 1 and 2 of* Henry IV *as well as* The Merry Wives of Windsor. *Falstaff, in the red jacket and feathered hat, here reviews his ragged recruits in a scene from* 2 Henry IV *(3.2).*

PLATE 10. *A Midsummer Night's Dream. Peter Brook's brilliantly revisionary stage production for the Royal Shakespeare Company in 1970 set* A Midsummer Night's Dream *in a brightly lit white box peopled with jugglers and athletic trapeze artists who tumbled and dashed about after one another with abandon. Here, Titania, under the spell of a love potion, embraces the weaver, Bottom, whom Puck has mischievously given an ass's ears and a clown nose. (The clown nose is Brook's invention; Shakespeare's script calls for an ass's head.)*

PLATE 11. *Coriolanus. Caius Marcius (Ian McKellen), about to be glorified with the surname "Coriolanus" for his triumph over the army of Aufidius at Corioles, is hoisted aloft by his triumphant soldiers in Act 1 of Peter Hall's* Coriolanus *at the National Theatre, London, in 1985.*

PLATE 12. *Much Ado About Nothing. Beatrice (Emma Thompson) and Benedick (Kenneth Branagh) in Branagh's 1993 film of* Much Ado About Nothing. *In this scene, (5.2) Beatrice asks Benedick whether or not he has followed through on his promise to challenge Claudio.*

PLATE 13. *Twelfth Night. The four lovers in their festive wedding clothes at the very end of Trevor Nunn's film of* Twelfth Night *(1996). Olivia (Helena Bonham Carter) is on the left, with Sebastian (Steven Mackintosh), Viola (Imogen Stubbs), and Orsino (Toby Stephens), left to right.*

PLATE 14. *Henry V.* Laurence Olivier as King Henry V, about to sail for France at the end of Act 2, Scene 2. "Cheerly to sea! The signs of war advance! / No king of England, if not king of France!" Note how the colorful, patriotic imagery of Olivier's 1944 film contrasts with the gritty realism of Branagh's 1989 film, in Plate 17.

PLATE 15. *Richard III.* Ian McKellen in director Richard Loncraine's 1995 film. In Act 1, Scene 1, Richard appears to be celebrating the Yorkist victory over the Lancastrians, though we as audience perceive the mockery and malice in his words, "Now is the winter of our discontent / Made glorious summer by this son of York." Set in pre-WWII England, Loncraine's film imagines England to be taken over by fascists with Richard Duke of Gloucester as their evil genius.

PLATE 16. *King Lear.* Laurence Olivier as King Lear in Granada Television's 1983 production. See Act 4, Scene 6: Enter Lear [mad, fantastically dressed with wild flowers]. *This was to be Olivier's last performance; he was terminally ill with cancer when this production was televised.*

PLATE 17. *Henry V.* King Henry V (Kenneth Branagh), exhausted yet triumphant after his victory over the French at the Battle of Agincourt, surveys the carnage of war amid his devoted followers in Act 4. Compare this image, from Branagh's 1989 film, to Olivier's more nationalistic view in Plate 14.

PLATE 18. *Hamlet. Hamlet (Mel Gibson) and Ophelia (Helena Bonham Carter) in Franco Zeffirelli's 1990 film of* Hamlet. *In Zeffirelli's direction, this scene from Act 3 takes place without any words being spoken. While Polonius watches, Hamlet grabs Ophelia, looks into her eyes, sighs, and leaves.*

PLATE 19. *Hamlet. Hamlet (Ethan Hawke) and Ophelia (Julia Stiles) in Michael Almereyda's* Hamlet *(2000). Almereyda's* Hamlet *is set in present-day New York City, and in this scene from Act 3, Ophelia is wearing a surveillance microphone (so that Polonius can eavesdrop electronically). Hamlet reaches to embrace her and discovers the wire.*

PLATE 20. *Romeo and Juliet. Juliet (Olivia Hussey) and Romeo (Leonard Whiting), near the end of Franco Zeffirelli's 1968 film. Juliet is about to stab herself with Romeo's dagger: "This is thy sheath. There rust, and let me die"* (5.3.170).

PLATE 21. *Romeo and Juliet. Claire Danes as Juliet in Baz Luhrmann's 1996 film,* William Shakespeare's Romeo + Juliet. *Juliet prepares to take the sleeping potion the Friar has given her, not sure that it may not be poison. "What if this mixture not work at all? / Shall I be married then tomorrow morning?"* (4.3.21-2).

PLATE 22. *Othello.* *Othello (Laurence Fishburne) and Iago (Kenneth Branagh) in Oliver Parker's 1997 film. Iago's insinuations begin their poisonous work, destroying Othello's peace of mind by urging Othello to suspect his wife Desdemona of infidelity. 3.3.178-80: "Oh, beware, my lord, of jealousy. / It is the green-eyed monster which doth mock / The meat it feeds on."*

PLATE 23. *Shakespeare in Love.* *"Will Shakespeare" (Joseph Fiennes) suffers from writer's block in his frustrating attempt to write a play called "Romeo and Ethel the Pirate's Daughter."*

for Falstaff, Beatrice, and Benedick. Thereafter, prose is essential to Shakespeare's comic world. It also takes on a major function in *Hamlet* (31 percent), as, for instance, when Hamlet converses with his onetime friends Rosencrantz and Guildenstern, when he plagues Polonius with his satirical wit, or when he philosophizes with Horatio, though verse is, of course, appropriate for the soliloquies and the moments of confrontation with Claudius. In the other great tragedies as well, prose has become for Shakespeare an instrument of limitless flexibility. Although the mixture of prose and blank verse is thus hard to quantify in any steady progression of percentages, the pattern of increased versatility is undeniable. Many of the late plays make less use of prose because of their choice of subject, but all excel in prose comic scenes for Autolycus, Caliban, and many others.

In his use of rhyme, as well, Shakespeare's practice changes from the early to late plays. Early plays and those of the lyric period, such as *A Midsummer Night's Dream* and *Romeo and Juliet*, use a great deal of rhyme, whereas late plays, such as *The Tempest*, use practically none. The commonest form of rhyme is the iambic pentameter measure rhymed in couplet, as when Phoebe, quoting Marlowe's *Hero and Leander*, says in *As You Like It* (3.5.81–2):

> Dead shepherd, now I find thy saw of might,
> "Who ever loved that loved not at first sight?"

Shakespeare does not limit his use of rhyme to the couplet, however. *Romeo and Juliet* and *Love's Labor's Lost* each contains a number of complete sonnets, as well as rhymed sequences made up of a quatrain followed by a couplet, and a good deal of alternate rhyme. Doggerel lines of verse appear in some of the early plays.

One quite formal use of the rhymed couplet does not conform to the statistical pattern that we observe generally in the use of rhyme. Because the Elizabethan theater lacked a front curtain to mark a pause between scenes in a play, Elizabethan dramatists often gave emphasis to a scene ending by means of a rhymed couplet. Possibly the device served also as a cue to those actors backstage who were waiting to begin the next scene. At any rate, the use of scene-ending couplets is common in some plays that otherwise make little use of rhyme. For example, Act 1, scene 5 of *Hamlet* virtually ends with the following concluding statement by the protagonist:

> The time is out of joint. O cursèd spite,
> That ever I was born to set it right!

Apart from this convention, however, use of rhyme in Shakespeare is normally indicative of early style. His lovers in the early plays often speak in rhyme; later, they tend to use prose.

Impossible to quantify, but no less significant in any study of the evolution of Shakespeare's art, is his use of imagery. Images are key to his poetic imagination, and, in part, they can be appreciated out of chronological context, because Shakespeare's mind dwells incessantly on certain image clusters: the family as a metaphor for the state, the garden as an image of social order and disorder, images of medicine and healing applied to the ills of the individual and the commonwealth, images of sexual desire and activity, images of hunting and of other sports, biblical images (Eden, Cain and Abel, Christ's ministry, his Passion, the Last Judgment, etc.), mythological allusions (Danae, Actaeon, Phaethon, Noah, Niobe), and many others. Patterns of imagery have been well studied by Caroline Spurgeon in her *Shakespeare's Imagery and What It Tells Us* (1935), Maurice Charney in *The Function of Imagery in the Drama* (1961), and others. In addition, we can see throughout Shakespeare's career the evolution of an imagistic style, as convincingly demonstrated by Wolfgang Clemen in *The Development of Shakespeare's Imagery* (1951). The early Shakespeare uses figures of speech for decoration and amplification, and learns only gradually to integrate these figures into a presentation of theme, subject, and individual character. In Shakespeare's later work, simile is often transformed into metaphor and assumes an organic function in relation to the entire play. By the end of his career, virtually every aspect of his style has been transformed from one of formal and rhetorical regularity to one of vast flexibility and range.

SHAKESPEARE'S ENGLISH

Pronunciation

How would Shakespeare's plays have sounded to our ears? The distance between Shakespearean and modern English is clearly not as great as in the case of Chaucer, and yet significant differences remain. Spoken English, especially in the pronunciation of vowel sounds, has undergone many striking changes since the early seventeenth century. We can assume that however much Shakespeare's own speech may have been colored by his Warwickshire boyhood, his acting company as a whole was most heavily influenced by London dialect. This form of English had become notably more dominant than in Chaucer's day, though it also included an admixture of northern, eastern, and southern forms because of the cosmopolitan character of the city. Shakespeare often pokes fun at regional dialects in his plays, especially at Welsh, Scottish, and Irish, and at the accents of Frenchmen or other foreigners attempting to speak English (see, for example, *Henry V* and *The Merry Wives of Windsor*).

Reconstructing how early modern English would have sounded is, to be sure, not always easy, since dialect did vary substantially from region to region, and since the ascertaining of pronunciations is often based on rhymes when we cannot be sure how either word in a rhyming pair was pronounced and cannot safely assume that rhymes were exact. Nevertheless, here, in summary form, are some approximate suggestions for pronouncing words in Shakespeare that are not similarly pronounced today. These examples can be applied to similar words: for example, *way* and *say* have the same vowel sound as *day; night,* the same vowel sound as *wide.*

> *folk* (sound the *l*)
> *gnaw* (sound the *g*)
> *knife* (sound the *k; i* as in *wide,* below)
> *brush* (rhymes with *push; r* somewhat trilled)
> *dull* (rhymes with *pull*)
> *seam* (pronounced *same,* with open *a*)
> *old* (pronounced *auld*)
> *now* (pronounced *noo*)
> *house* (pronounced *hoos*)
> *soul* (pronounced *saul*)
> *know* (pronounced *knaw,* with sounded *k*)
> *own* (pronounced *awn*)
> *tune* (pronounced *tiwn*)
> *rule* (pronounced *riwl; r* somewhat trilled)
> *day* (pronounced *die*)
> *time* (pronounced *toime*)
> *wide* (pronounced *woide*)
> *join* (rhymes with *line*)
> *creeping* (pronounced *craypin,* with open *a*)
> *dissention* (in four syllables, without *sh* sound)
> *persuasion* (in four syllables, without *zh* sound)

A matter of more practical importance than phonetic changes is that of differences in Shakespeare's English and ours in the accentuation of syllables. Many cases of variable stress can be found in which he seems to have been at liberty to accent the word in two different ways; in other cases, words were customarily accented on a different syllable from that in current speech. For example, the following accentuations are either usual or frequent: *aspect´, charac´ter, com´mendable, com´plete, con´cealed, con´fessor, consort´* (as a noun), *contract´* (noun), *de´testable, dis´tinct, envy´, for´lorn, hu´mane, instinct´, ob´scure, persev´er, pi´oner, ple´beians, portents´, pur´sue, record´* (noun), *reven´ue, se´cure, sinis´ter, welcome´.*

Not only are *-tion* and *-sion* regularly pronounced as two syllables, but the same situation causes other words in which *e* or *i* stand before vowels to be uttered in Shakespeare's language with one more syllable than in ours; for example, *oce-an, courti-er, marri-age.* We may even have *cre-ature, tre-asure,* and *venge-ance.* Nasals and liquids are frequently pronounced as if an extra vowel were introduced between them and a preceding letter. Accordingly, we have *wrest(e)ler, Eng(e)land, assemb(e)ly,* and *ent(e)rance,* as well as *de-ar, you(e)r,* and *mo-re.* Final *-er*

often has a greater syllabic importance than it has in later poetry. Final *-(e)s* in the genitive singular and the plural of nouns not ending in an *-s* sound may constitute a separate syllable; for example, "To show his teeth as white as whale's bone" (*Love's Labor's Lost,* 5.2.333).

The study of metrics is fraught with peril. Knowledge of syllabification can often be circular in that it has to assume a kind of metrical regularity in the line of a verse. Even so, in scanning of Shakespeare's verse it helps to ascertain as accurately as we can how many syllables he intended a given word to have. As compared to modern-day English, a Shakespearean word may have (1) an additional syllable, or (2) one fewer syllables, or (3) two adjoining syllables in adjoining words that coalesce or elide. Spelling may not always indicate these differences to a modern reader.

1. The following lines give us extra-syllable words in *moon's, juggler, entrance,* and *complexion*:

   > I do wander everywhere,
   > Swifter than the moon's sphere.
   > (*A Midsummer Night's Dream,* 2.1.6–7)

   > O me! You juggler! You cankerblossom!
   > (*A Midsummer Night's Dream,* 3.2.282)

   > After the prompter, for our entrance.
   > (*Romeo and Juliet,* 1.4.8)

   > Mislike me not for my complexion.
   > (*The Merchant of Venice,* 2.1.1)

   Similarly, the words *captain, monstrous, esperance, this* (this is), *George* (*Richard III,* 5.5.9), *valiant, villain,* and *jealous* sometimes have extra syllables in pronunciation.

2. In the following line, *marry* is elided into one syllable:

   > Good mother, do not *marry* me to yond fool.
   > (*The Merry Wives of Windsor,* 3.4.83)

   Similarly, the words *lineal, journeying, carrion, celestial, herald, royal, malice, absolute, perjury, madame, needle, taken, heaven, spirit, devil, gentleman, unpeople, forward, gather, innocent, violet, Africa, eagle, listen,* and *venomous* have usually one fewer syllables than in current English.

3. The following examples are of elision between the syllables of adjoining words:

   > Why should I joy in *an abortive* birth?
   > (*Love's Labor's Lost,* 1.1.104)

   > The *lover, all* as frantic,
   > (*A Midsummer Night's Dream,* 5.1.10)

   > Romans, *do me* right.
   > (*Titus Andronicus,* 1.1.204)

Differences in accentuation and lengthening or shortening of words thus have great importance in the reading and scanning of Shakespeare's verse. Shortening of words by elision or by slurring is common in Shakespeare, but at least in this matter modern practice forms a good guide. Syllables ending in vowels are not infrequently elided before words beginning with a vowel, as in "How cáme / we ashóre" (*The Tempest*, 1.2.159) and "too hárd / a knót / for mé / t' un*tie*" (*Twelfth Night*, 2.2.41). Syncopation, or the omission of a syllable, often occurs in words with *r*, as in "I wár-*rant* / it wíll" (*Hamlet*, 1.2.248); and in final *-er, -el,* and *-le,* as in "Trável you / farre ón" (*The Taming of the Shrew*, 4.2.74). The following words and other similar ones may be treated as monosyllabic in Shakespeare's verse: *whether, ever, hither, other, father, evil, having.* Almost any unaccented syllable of a polysyllabic word (especially if it contains an *i*) may be softened and ignored. This syncopation is frequent in polysyllabic words and proper names: "Thoughts spécu / latíve" (*Macbeth*, 5.4.19) and "Did sláy / this Fórtinbras; / who by / a seáled /compáct" (*Hamlet*, 1.1.90). Other occasions for slurring, as listed by Abbott in his *Shakespearian Grammar*, are light vowels preceded by heavy vowels, as in *power, dying,* and so on; plurals and possessives of nouns ending in an *s* sound, as in *empress'* and *Mars';* final *-ed* following *d* or *t,* as in "you háve / exceéde*d* / all prómise" (*As You Like It*, 1.2.234); and the *-est* of superlatives (pronounced *-st*) after dentals and liquids, as "the stérn'st / good-níght" (*Macbeth*, 2.2.4) and "thy éldest / son's són" (*King John*, 2.1.177).

Grammar and Rhetoric

Shakespeare's grammar presents but few differences in forms from the grammar of current modern English. The *-eth* ending in the third person singular of the present tense, indicative mood, was very commonly used, especially in serious prose. Shakespeare frequently uses this older form, especially *hath, doth,* and *saith,* but seems to prefer the form in *-s* or *-es.* In a few cases, he also seems to use the old northern plural in *-s* or *-es* in the third person of the present indicative, as " . . . at those springs, / On chaliced flowers that *lies*" (*Cymbeline*, 2.3.22–3). He does not always agree with modern usage in the forms of the past tenses and the perfect participles of the verbs that he employs. He retains some lost forms of the strong verbs, sometimes ignores distinctions we make between the past tense and the perfect participle, and treats some verbs as weak (or regular) which are now strong (or irregular). For example, he uses *arose* for *arisen, swam* for *swum, foughten* for *fought, gave* for *given, took* for *taken, sprung* for *sprang, writ* for *wrote, blowed* for *blew, weaved* for *wove,* and *shaked* for *shaken.* Forms like *degenerate* for *degenerated* and *exhaust* for *exhausted* are especially common. A few instances are to be found of

the archaic *y-* with the past participle, as in *yclad.* For the possessive case of the neuter personal pronoun *it*, Shakespeare normally uses the regular form at that time, *his*; but he also uses the possessive form *it,* and in his plays first published in the First Folio in 1623 we find several occurrences of the new form *its.* Shakespeare uses the old form *moe,* as well as *more,* and *enow* as the plural of *enough,* though these forms have been modernized in this edition because they are used so inconsistently. He uses *near* and *next* along with *nearer* and *nearest,* as the comparative and superlative of *nigh.* These are the most obvious of the formal differences between Shakespeare's grammar and our own.

The functional differences are more considerable. Elizabethan language exercised an extraordinary freedom, even for English, in the use of one part of speech for another. Shakespeare uses verbs, adjectives, adverbs, and pronouns as nouns. He makes verbs out of nouns and adjectives and, of course, uses nouns as adjectives, for this is a distinguishing characteristic of English speech, but he also uses adverbs, verbs, and prepositional phrases as adjectives, as in "Looks he as freshly as he did . . . ?" (*As You Like It*, 3.2.227). Almost any adjective may be freely used as an adverb, as in "And in my house you shall be friendly lodged" (*The Taming of the Shrew*, 4.2.109). He makes active words—both adjectives and verbs—discharge a passive function, as in "the sightless [invisible] couriers of the air" (*Macbeth*, 1.7.23) and "this aspect of mine / Hath feared the valiant," that is, caused the valiant to be afraid (*The Merchant of Venice*, 2.1.8–9). He makes wider use of the infinitive as a verbal noun or as a gerundive participle than do we: "This to be true / I do engage my life" (*As You Like It*, 5.4.164–5), "My operant powers their functions leave to do" (*Hamlet*, 3.2.172), "Nor do I now make moan to be abridged" (*The Merchant of Venice*, 1.1.126), and "You might have saved me my pains, to have taken [by having taken] it away yourself" (*Twelfth Night*, 2.2.5–7). The functions of prepositions in Elizabethan English were so various that one can only refer the student to the notes to the text or to a dictionary.

In certain other features, however, as, for example, in the use of modal auxiliaries, Shakespeare's language is as restricted and conventional as ours is at formal levels, or even more so. *Shall* is regularly used in Shakespeare to express something inevitable in future time and is, therefore, the usual future tense for all persons. *Will*, which originally expressed intention, determination, or willingness, was, to be sure, beginning to encroach on *shall* for the expression of futurity in the second and third persons, but its use usually still retains in Shakespeare a consciousness of its original meaning. *Should* and *would* had their original senses of obligation and volition, respectively, and had other peculiarities, then as now, of considerable difficulty. The subjunctive mood was vital to

Shakespeare as a means of expressing condition, doubt, concession, command, wish, or desire, and, in dependent clauses, indefinitiveness, purpose, or sometimes simple futurity. Note the following examples:

> But if my father *had* not scanted me . . .
> Yourself, renownèd prince, then *stood* as fair.
> (*The Merchant of Venice*, 2.1.17, 20)

> *Live* a thousand years,
> I *shall* not find myself so apt to die.
> (*Julius Caesar*, 3.1.161–2)

> Lest your retirement do *amaze* your friends.
> (*1 Henry IV*, 5.4.6)

> *'Twere* best he speak no harm of Brutus here.
> (*Julius Caesar*, 3.2.70)

> *Melt* Egypt into Nile, and kindly creatures
> *Turn* all to serpents!
> (*Antony and Cleopatra*, 2.5.79–80)

> Yet were it true
> To say this boy *were* like me.
> (*The Winter's Tale*, 1.2.134–5)

> And may direct his course as *please* himself.
> (*Richard III*, 2.2.129)

Some other features of Shakespeare's grammar are as follows: he often omits the relative pronoun; he often uses the nominative case of the pronoun for the accusative case, and vice versa; he uses *him, her, me,* and *them* as true reflexives to mean *himself, herself, myself,* and *themselves;* he employs double negatives and double comparatives and superlatives; he shows a consciousness in the use of *thee* and *thou* of their application to intimates and inferiors and of their insulting quality when addressed to strangers (e.g., "If thou 'thou'-est him some thrice, it shall not be amiss," *Twelfth Night*, 3.2.43–4); he employs *which* to refer to both persons and things; and he does not discriminate closely between *ye*, nominative, and *you*, objective. He makes frequent use of the dative constructions, that is, the objective forms of the pronouns, *me, thee, you, him, her,* and so on, without prepositions where the meaning is "by me," "for me," "with me," "to me," "of me," and the like. For example:

> I am appointed *him* [by him] to murder you.
> (*The Winter's Tale*, 1.2.411)

> She looks *us* [to us] like
> A thing made more of malice than of duty.
> (*Cymbeline*, 3.5.32–3)

One prominent feature of Shakespeare's grammar is his use of the ethical dative, a construction in which the pronoun is generally used to indicate the person interested in the statement. In *King John* (3.4.146), the phrase "John lays you plots," means something like "John lays plots which you may profit by." In the following, *me* means "to my detriment" or "to my disadvantage":

> See how this river comes *me* cranking in
> And cuts *me* from the best of all my land
> A huge half-moon.
> (*1 Henry IV*, 3.1.95–7)

"Whip *me* such honest knaves" (*Othello*, 1.1.51) means "In my judgment such knaves should be whipped." In Quickly's description of Mistress Page, the dative *you* is equivalent to "mark you," "take notice":

> . . . a civil modest wife, and one, I tell you, that will not
> miss *you* morning nor evening prayer, as any is in Windsor.
> (*The Merry Wives of Windsor*, 2.2.92–4)

At times, however, the ethical dative is idiomatic and virtually without equivalent meaning in modern English; the sense of the passage is best obtained by omitting the pronoun.

Shakespeare, like other Renaissance poets, makes extensive use of the forms and figures of rhetoric. He is fond, for example, of using the abstract for the concrete, as in the words addressed by Surrey to Cardinal Wolsey: "Thou scarlet sin" (*Henry VIII*, 3.2.255). Transpositions are numerous, as are inversions, ellipses, and broken or confused constructions, as in the following examples:

> That thing you speak of,
> I took it for a man. (*Absolute construction.*)
> (*King Lear*, 4.6.77–8)

> Souls and bodies hath he divorced three. (*Transposition of adjective.*)
> (*Twelfth Night*, 3.4.238–9)

> A happy gentleman in blood and lineaments. (*Transposition of adjectival phrase.*)
> (*Richard II*, 3.1.9)

> Your state of fortune and your due of birth. (*Transposition of pronoun.*)
> (*Richard III*, 3.7.120)

> She calls me proud, and [says] that she could not love me. (*Ellipsis.*)
> (*As You Like It*, 4.3.17)

> Returning were as tedious as [to] go o'er. (*Ellipsis.*)
> (*Macbeth*, 3.4.139)

> They call him Doricles, and boasts himself
> To have a worthy feeding. (*Ellipsis of nominative.*)
> (*The Winter's Tale*, 4.4.168–9)

Of all men else I have avoided thee. (*Confusion of two constructions.*)

(*Macbeth,* 5.8.4)

The venom of such looks, we fairly hope,
Have lost their quality. (*Confusion of number arising from proximity.*)

(*Henry V,* 5.2.18–19)

Rather proclaim it, Westmorland, through my host
That he which hath no stomach to this fight,
Let him depart. (*Construction changed by change of thought.*)

(*Henry V,* 4.3.34–6)

For always I am Caesar. (*Inversion of adverb.*)

(*Julius Caesar,* 1.2.212)

Shakespeare often uses rhetorical figures for symmetrical effects, especially in the early, ornamental style of *Richard III* and the nondramatic poems. Following are definitions of some of the most popular figures he uses, with illustrations from *Venus and Adonis:*

1. *Parison.* The symmetrical repetition of words in grammatically parallel phrases: "How love makes young men thrall, and old men dote" (line 837).
2. *Isocolon.* The symmetrical repetition of sounds and words in phrases of equal length, as in the previous example, and in this: "Or as the wolf doth grin before he barketh, / Or as the berry breaks before it staineth" (lines 459–60). Parison and isocolon are frequently combined.
3. *Anaphora.* The symmetrical repetition of a word at the beginning of a sequence of clauses or sentences, often at the beginning of lines. Anaphora is frequently combined with parison and isocolon, as in the second example already given, and in this: " 'Give me my hand,' saith he. 'Why dost thou feel it?' / 'Give me my heart,' saith she, 'and thou shalt have it' " (lines 373–4).
4. *Antimetabole.* The symmetrical repetition of words in inverted order: "She clepes him king of graves and grave for kings" (line 995).
5. *Anadiplosis.* The beginning of a phrase with the final words of the previous phrase: "O, thou didst kill me; kill me once again!" (line 499).
6. *Epanalepsis.* The symmetrical repetition of a word or words at the beginning and ending of a line: "He sees his love, and nothing else he sees" (line 287).
7. *Ploce.* The insistent repetition of a word within the same line or phrase: "Then why not lips on lips, since eyes in eyes?" (line 120).
8. *Epizeuxis.* An intensified form of ploce, repeating the word without another intervening word: " 'Ay me!' she cries, and twenty times, 'Woe, woe!' / And twenty echoes twenty times cry so" (lines 833–4).
9. *Antanaclasis.* The shifting of a repeated word from one meaning to another: "My love to love is love but to disgrace it," or " 'Where did I leave?' 'No matter where,' quoth he, / 'Leave me' " (lines 412, 715–6).

For other figures and illustrations, see Sister Miriam Joseph, *Shakespeare's Use of the Arts of Language* (1947) and Brian Vickers, "Shakespeare's Use of Rhetoric," in *A New Companion to Shakespeare Studies,* edited by Kenneth Muir and S. Schoenbaum (1971).

Vocabulary

Renaissance English was hospitable to foreign importation. Many words taken directly from Latin became a permanent part of the language, serving to enrich its power to express thought and its rhythmical capabilities; others were ultimately discarded. The principal borrowings were in the realm of learning and culture. Such words usually retained a vital sense of their original Latin meaning. Sometimes such words have not replaced native words of the same meaning, so that we have such pairs of synonyms as *acknowledge* and *confess,* just as Shakespeare had *wonder* and *admiration.* Because of this Latin heritage, even a slight knowledge of Latin is a great advantage in the correct understanding of Elizabethan writers, since many Latin borrowings have taken on since the sixteenth century a different shade of meaning from that in which they were borrowed. The Latin sense of *aggravate* ("to add weight to") still struggles for recognition; but *apparent* no longer means primarily "visible to sight," and *intention* does not convey the idea of "intentness." The *Oxford English Dictionary* (*OED*) provides a wealth of information about derivations and changes in meaning.

Latin words were often taken over in their Latin forms, as *objectum* and *subjectum, statua* and *aristocratia,* and later were made to conform to English spelling and stress, though a few, such as *decorum,* still have a Latin form. French continued to be drawn upon and sometimes caused a new Latin borrowing to be adopted in a French form, just as, on the other hand, such words as *adventure* were supplied with a *d* to make them conform to Latin spelling. This principle is illustrated in the pedantry of Holofernes when he objects (*Love's Labor's Lost,* 5.1.20) to "det" as the pronunciation of "debt." Spanish, Italian, and Dutch also supplied many terms. Spanish gave words having to do with commerce, religion, and the New World, such as *mosquito, alligator, ambuscado,* and *grandee.* From Italian came terms of art, learning, and dueling: *bandetto, portico, canto, stoccato.* The Dutch contributed many nautical and oriental words.

These foreign borrowings were a part of what might be called the linguistic ambition of the age, a desire for forcible expression. Language was in a plastic state, so that it had an unparalleled freedom in both vocabulary and form. With this freedom, to be sure, came some confusion, since the Elizabethan era saw few efforts at grammatical precision. Such efforts were later to be made by the age of Dryden and the Royal Society, and by learned men ever since, prompted by an awareness that English was too vague and irregular for use as a means of scientific expression. Still, we readily perceive that English profited from its Renaissance expansion and its subsequent absorption with Shakespeare and the English Bible. It gained, for example, an increased facility in making compounds. Shakespeare, with his *cloud-capped towers* and his *home-keeping wits,* was a genius at this. Also from Shakespeare's time came the English adaptability in the use of prefixes, such as *dis-, re-,* and *en-,* and of suffixes, such as *-ful, -less, -ness,* and *-hood.*

EDITIONS AND EDITORS OF SHAKESPEARE

The earliest complete edition of Shakespeare's plays was the so-called First Folio of 1623, sponsored by Shakespeare's theatrical colleagues, John Heminges and Henry Condell. (A "folio" book was one in which the printing sheets were folded only once, each producing two "leaves," or four rather large printed pages of about 13 ½ × 8 ¼ inches. In a "quarto" book, the sheets were folded twice, producing eight pages on four leaves half the folio size.) The First Folio brought together eighteen plays that had previously been published individually in quarto volumes and eighteen plays that had never before been published. It did not include Shakespeare's nondramatic poetry, of which *Venus and Adonis* and *The Rape of Lucrece* had been published in 1593–1594 and the sonnets in 1609. Nor did it include *Pericles, The Two Noble Kinsmen,* and *Edward III.*

The nature of the early printed texts, and their relationship to what Shakespeare actually wrote, is a complex subject requiring some understanding of the physical process by which Elizabethan plays were written, prepared for staging, licensed, and printed. What sorts of manuscripts lie behind the various printed early editions we have, and how were those manuscripts modified successively by scribes, governmental officials, theatrical producers, actors, editors, compositors, proofreaders, and editors of subsequent editions? The problem is amplified by the fact that none of Shakespeare's manuscripts survives today. Consequently, textual critics can only theorize about the kinds of printer's copy that appear to underlie the printed texts we have. The resulting theories are necessarily conjectural, and they appear increasingly so in an age that general-

ly is wary of attempts to construct an authorial presence in a literary work. What follows here is an attempt to set forth what was once a widely adopted theory of textual origins, as devised by A. W. Pollard, R. B. McKerrow, W. W. Greg, Fredson Bowers, and others. Although, as we shall see, the various hypotheses about manuscript sources and types of quartos do not always account for the evidence, the theory itself still represents a once-prevailing set of assumptions against which the new textual scholarship offers its objections and qualifications, and hence needs to be laid out here. A good place to begin is with the hypothetical reconstruction of manuscripts.

Manuscripts

Most often, it seems, Elizabethan dramatic companies obtained a play by commissioning a known professional dramatist to write a new play, to revise an old one, or to collaborate with another author. Usually, the company paid the dramatist a flat fee. Shakespeare, on the other hand, was a "sharer" in the Chamberlain's (later the King's) company; that is, he was part owner and took a share of the profits. He may then have written plays not for a fee but as his chief contribution to the company's activities. Whatever the financial arrangement between author and company, in any case, the play became the property of the acting company, and the author gave up his individual right to sell it elsewhere. Moreover, he ordinarily wrote the play with a view not to publication, but to performance. Occasionally, a literary-minded author like Ben Jonson would see his plays through the press (and be scoffed at for his pretentiousness). Shakespeare, however, almost certainly did not do this. The quarto texts of his plays that appeared during his lifetime show no trace of having been prepared for the reader. They are playhouse documents.

When Shakespeare had finished writing a play, very likely in consultation with his fellow players, he presumably submitted a readable manuscript to his acting company. A certain amount of deletion, interlineation, inconsistency, and illegibility was inevitable. Authors' manuscripts became the property of the acting company and might be turned over to the printer when the company decided to sell its rights in a play. The company presumably would prefer to hold on to its theatrical copy of the play and to dispose of the authors' manuscript as of little further value if they chose to have a play printed. Such a supposed manuscript naturally would pose some difficulties for the compositor.

Since we lack manuscript copy for any printed play by Shakespeare or indeed generally by other playwrights, the business of determining from the printed plays themselves any clear evidence of their having been printed from mansucript copy is uncertain and provisional. Textual scholars like Greg and Bowers used to be more confident of such deductions than now seems tenable. Nonetheless, some educated guesswork as to whether the play was printed from authors' mansucript, or from a transcript of that mansucript, or from manuscript that had been marked up by the prompter for theatrical use, can be provisionally helpful in thinking about the nature of the printed text and what kinds of printing errors it might be especially prone to. Appendix 1 in this volume records, play by play, a summary of speculation concerning the kinds of manuscript lying behind the printed texts. The characterizations in Appendix 1 should be viewed with skepticism in light of these difficulties.

Among the Shakespearean quarto texts thought by Greg and others to have been based on authorial manuscripts are the first quartos of *Titus Andronicus, Love's Labor's Lost, A Midsummer Night's Dream, Richard II, The Merchant of Venice, Much Ado About Nothing,* and *1* and *2 Henry IV,* and the second quartos of *Romeo and Juliet* and *Hamlet.* Three more first quartos—*Troilus and Cressida, Othello,* and *King Lear*—were also thought to be based on authorial papers, each as an anomolous case. In addition, the First Folio contains several newly printed plays thought to be based on authorial manuscripts or transcripts thereof, including *The Comedy of Errors, The Taming of the Shrew, All's Well That Ends Well, Timon of Athens, Coriolanus,* and *Henry VIII.*

We might expect printed texts based on authorial papers to be close to what Shakespeare wrote but also to contain errors of transcription resulting from difficulties of deletion, illegibility, and the like encountered by the printers as they read their copy. Some printed texts presumably based on authorial manuscripts do indeed seem to preserve Shakespeare's work in an early state of composition: *Timon of Athens,* for example, seems never to have been finished by Shakespeare, since the text we have retains glaring inconsistencies and redundancies that he presumably would have straightened out in a final version. *Love's Labor's Lost* and *Romeo and Juliet* contain uncanceled duplicatory passages. On the other hand, *The Merchant of Venice, Richard II,* and the *Henry IV* plays are very good texts, and *Much Ado* is almost ready for stage production; the names of two actors appear among the speech prefixes, although other irregularities suggest that the manuscript was in the last stages of authorial revision. The hypothesis therefore represents a whole spectrum of states from unrevised manuscript to a text that has been thoroughly worked over.

In addition to the fact that we lack an existing manuscript for any of Shakespeare's plays, we need to recognize that hypothesizing a distinction between texts based on authorial papers and those based on theatrical copy is entirely prone to compromise and unclear distinctions. Authors' papers may well have been used sometimes by the acting company without recopying and without extensive annotation for purposes of production. Authors might well think in terms of production needs and add stage directions intended for the players; Shakespeare was, after all, a member of his acting company. Play texts that scholars have tentatively classified as based on authorial manuscripts not infrequently contain details that sound like something the prompter would want to add, and conversely texts that are presumed to be based on theatrical copy are not infrequently careless of details that one might have supposed a prompter would have wished to remedy or clarify for the acting company.

Given all these formidable difficulties, we must be cautious. In theory, an author's manuscript is thought to be identifiable behind the printed text through some of the following characteristics: vagueness in specifying the number of supernumeraries needed for a scene, lack of precision in the marking of entrances and especially exits, authorial stage directions that tend to describe stage business or the emotional states of the characters, speech prefixes that inconsistently refer to a character both by personal name and generic title, and so on. Thus, in *Love's Labor's Lost,* Navarre, Armado, and Holofernes are at times referred to as King, Braggart, and Pedant; Navarre is also called Ferdinand.

Licensing for Performance

Before one of Shakespeare's plays could go into production, it had to be licensed by the Master of the Revels, an officer of the royal household responsible for supervising court entertainments. Since the beginning of Elizabeth's reign, and even earlier, dramatic performances throughout England had been made subject to governmental control. Elizabeth had authorized municipal and other local governments to scrutinize plays performed within their jurisdictions. In the vicinity of London, however, where municipal hostility toward the theater was particularly strong, she took the unusual step in 1581 of transferring licensing power to her own Master of the Revels. Since many public plays came to court, as we have seen, Elizabeth was inclined to protect the players against the city authorities in this way and to adopt the useful fiction that public performances were rehearsals of plays intended for her ultimate benefit.

The Master of the Revels did occasionally censor Shakespeare's plays. For example, the scene of Richard II's deposition, omitted from the three earliest quarto editions of the play, may have been disallowed for acting during Elizabeth's lifetime. (She was sensitive to a widespread and libelous analogy comparing her with

John Heminges and Henry Condell, Shakespeare's fellow actors, gathered contents for the First Folio, published in 1623. They collected thirty-six plays in the volume, omitting Pericles *and* The Two Noble Kinsmen. Troilus and Cressida *is included in most copies of the First Folio but is not listed here in the contents.*

A CATALOGVE

of the feuerall Comedies, Hiftories, and Tragedies contained in this Volume.

COMEDIES.

The Tempeft.	Folio 1.
The two Gentlemen of Verona.	20
The Merry Wiues of Windfor.	38
Meafure for Meafure.	61
The Comedy of Errours.	85
Much adoo about Nothing.	101
Loues Labour loft.	122
Midfommer Nights Dreame.	145
The Merchant of Venice.	163
As you Like it.	185
The Taming of the Shrew.	208
All is well, that Ends well.	230
Twelfe-Night, or what you will.	255
The Winters Tale.	304

HISTORIES.

The Life and Death of King John.	Fol. 1.
The Life & death of Richard the fecond.	23
The Firft part of King Henry the fourth.	46
The Second part of K. Henry the fourth.	74
The Life of King Henry the Fift.	69
The Firft part of King Henry the Sixt.	96
The Second part of King Hen. the Sixt.	120
The Third part of King Henry the Sixt.	147
The Life & Death of Richard the Third.	173
The Life of King Henry the Eight.	205

TRAGEDIES.

The Tragedy of Coriolanus.	Fol. 1.
Titus Andronicus.	31
Romeo and Juliet.	53
Timon of Athens.	80
The Life and death of Julius Cæfar.	109
The Tragedy of Macbeth.	131
The Tragedy of Hamlet.	152
King Lear.	283
Othello, the Moore of Venice.	310
Anthony and Cleopater.	346
Cymbeline King of Britaine.	369

Richard.) More often, one suspects, the mere threat of censorship was sufficient to keep the London dramatic companies in line. The Tudor establishment had no intention of tolerating openly seditious criticism in the drama. Generally, the Master of the Revels was more concerned with questions of religion and politics than with morals. Edmund Tilney served as Master of the Revels from 1579 to 1610, when he was succeeded by his deputy, Sir George Buc. In 1622, the office passed to Sir Henry Herbert.

The Playbook

The document on which the Master of the Revels affixed his seal of approval was the playbook, often referred to in recent scholarship as the "prompt-book" or "prompt-copy," that is, the version prepared by the acting company for use in actual production. Sometimes this version may have been a fair copy of the manuscript, readied for stage performance, that is, with the odd technical inconsistency weeded out and with briefer but sometimes incomplete stage directions added marginally. One possibility is that the author's last draft might be converted into a playbook. Whatever manuscript was thus used, McKerrow once supposed that the playbook would undertake to normalize any inconsistent speech prefixes (such as those already noted in *Love's Labor's Lost*), in order to avoid confusion for actors and stage managers, but this supposition is not well supported by evidence from extant manuscripts. Perhaps the prompter would add some stage directions, concentrating on such technical matters as entrances and occasional specific effects. In *Julius Caesar*, for example, we find such stage directions as *"Enter Brutus in his orchard," "Thunder and lightning. Enter Julius Caesar in his nightgown,"* and *"Brutus goes into the pulpit."* We cannot be sure, however, that these are not authorial stage directions, and, indeed, recent evidence suggests that the acting company often did rather little to an authorial manuscript to ready it for production. Shakespeare was an acting member of his own company and must have known what his colleagues wanted, so that revision of his final draft need not have been extensive. Examination of existing playbooks by dramatists other than Shakespeare suggests that such playbooks were annotated in a variety of ways: sometimes with actors' names, sometimes with warnings for entrances and props, sometimes with calls for sound effects, and sometimes with stage directions repeated in more visible locations in the margins and highlighted with rules. Seldom does annotation follow a now-recoverable pattern within a manuscript or across various manuscripts. The category of "playbook" is not as certain today as it seemed to Greg and others.

Comparatively few of Shakespeare's printed texts are thought to be derived from playbooks, actually, since the playbook, bearing the official license of the Master of the Revels, was an invaluable document if the play was ever to be revived. Of the nineteen Shakespearean plays published in quarto prior to 1623, not one seems to have been printed from a playbook. Nevertheless, the First Folio does contain a few plays seemingly printed from playbooks or transcripts of playbooks, including *As You Like It, Twelfth Night, Julius Caesar,* and *Macbeth* (in a cut version). Two more plays—*The Two Gentlemen of Verona* and *The Merry Wives of Windsor*—were evidently printed from transcriptions by Ralph Crane of playbooks. Three other plays, *1 Henry VI, Antony and Cleopatra,* and *Cymbeline,* have been thought to contain some annotations by the stage adapter.

Playbooks are presumably not as likely to correspond with the author's intentions as his own papers, and indeed, some playbooks probably reflect changes occurring in the theater over a period of years. A playbook might be altered for the revival of an old favorite or might even represent a cut performance intended to be taken on tour—as perhaps in the case of *Macbeth*. Such a text might incorporate non-Shakespearean material; *Macbeth* contains songs and lines attributed to Thomas Middleton.

Playbooks were presumably also used to copy out individual parts for each actor. Although such actors' "rolls," as they were called, could conceivably have been used to assemble a printed text, no Shakespearean play is known to have been printed in this fashion. A few plays, such as *The Two Gentlemen of Verona* and *The Winter's Tale*, were once thought to have been made up out of actors' rolls, since the texts of these plays generally omit stage directions and group characters' names at the head of each scene; however, these traits are now known to be the identifying characteristics of the professional scrivener named Ralph Crane. Apparently, Crane was employed to prepare copies (also including *The Tempest, The Merry Wives of Windsor*, and *Measure for Measure*) for the printers of the First Folio.

The Question of "Unauthorized" Quartos

An acting company presumably had some concern to get its plays into print, chiefly for the purpose of advertising. The acting company's name almost invariably appears prominently on the title page of a play—which, until the seventeenth century, often provided no playwright's name. At the same time, other copies of plays might well exist besides those owned by acting companies, and copies such as these might conceivably find their way into print. According to Humphrey

Moseley's "The Stationer to the Readers" in the Beaumont and Fletcher Folio (1646), actors sometimes sold patrons transcripts of what was acted. Copies might be obtained by other means. If a bookseller chose to risk the capital to print a play that he had somehow obtained, he might then present his copy of it at Stationers' Hall and enter it in the Stationers' Register, or the official record book of the London Company of Stationers (i.e., booksellers). By paying a fee, usually sixpence, he reserved the right to publish the work he had thus entered. Indeed, even if a book was printed without having been entered in the Stationers' Register, it evidently received the protection of copyright by the very act of printing. Copyright had considerable legal force. Although authors and acting companies could not copyright their plays, the stationers or booksellers enjoyed a tight monopoly. Their London Company of Stationers had a patent from the crown to restrict the number of presses operating in London, the number of books that could be printed, and so on.

A. W. Pollard was followed by many twentieth-century textual critics in imagining that the acting companies were concerned to keep their plays out of print as long as the plays could hold the stage and in further imagining that the stationers were desperate to get plays into print in whatever form, however corrupt, to feed a presumably bottomless market of playreaders. Consequently Pollard and his followers have argued that acting companies protected themselves by entering into agreements with cooperative booksellers. The acting companies, according to this theory, might allow a friendly bookseller or a printer to register a play for later publication. For example, on July 22, 1598, the printer James Roberts entered in the Stationers' Register "a booke of the Marchaunt of Venyce, or otherwise called the Jewe Of Venyce, Prouided, that yt bee not prynted by the said James Robertes or anye other whatsoeuer without lycence first had from the Right honorable the lord Chamberlen." This is what is generally known as a "staying entry," since Roberts agrees to "stay" or withhold publication pending further authorization from the acting company's patron. Similar entries occur in August 1600 for *Much Ado About Nothing, As You Like It*, and *Henry V*, although a Quarto of *Henry V* appeared in August 1600. The argument that such staying entries were designed to forestall the activities of less scrupulous publishers has been exploded, however, by Peter Blayney ("The Publication of Playbooks," in *A New History of Early English Drama*, ed. John D. Cox and David Scott Kastan, 1997), who shows that a large proportion of books in the Stationers' Register was given only conditional entrance. Moreover, Blayney's research, indicating how small was the proportion of plays in the overall publication schedule of London

publishers, calls into question the idea that stationers were so hungry for plays that they would resort to any means to get them. All in all, Pollard's theory that the printers of the so-called bad quartos were somehow unscrupulous has been thoroughly challenged.

How much credence should we give to complaints that corrupt texts of plays were somehow stolen to be put into print? A prefatory letter "To the great Variety of Readers" of the First Folio signed by Heminges and Condell complains that "before" publication of the Folio, readers "were abused with divers stolen and surreptitious copies, maimed and deformed by the frauds and stealths of injurious imposters." Thomas Heywood similarly protests against unauthorized editions of his plays, which "have (unknown to me, and without any of my direction) accidentally come into the printer's hands, and therefore so corrupt and mangled (copied only by the ear) that I have been unable to know them" (Preface to *The Rape of Lucrece*, 1608).

How were such corrupt and mangled texts obtained? Heywood says they were "copied only by the ear." Elsewhere, in *Pleasant Dialogues and Dramas* (1637), he complains about the pirating of one of his plays "by stenography." Yet the stenographic hypothesis may not account for most cases of reported texts. The apparently corrupted texts we have seem to rely instead on the use of memory.

Most such texts, according to W. W. Greg, were put together by "memorial reconstruction." The agents sometimes may have been one or more actors, especially temporary actors hired to perform minor roles, rather than actor-sharers. Possibly, one or more such minor actors got together and slowly recited what they could remember of a play, while a scribe took down what they recited. The reporter or reporters of a pirated text can sometimes tentatively be identified by the relative accuracy of certain roles. For example, the actor who perhaps played the minor part of Marcellus in *Hamlet* may have helped in the memorial reconstruction of some of the first act of the unauthorized quarto of that play.

A quarto put together in some part by memorial reconstruction reveals itself by certain characteristics, although the matter of identification is in some dispute. Such a text tends to give a fairly accurate rendition of the overall plot but garbles some speeches, transfers or misplaces lines of dialogue or even whole scenes, borrows scraps of phrases from other plays in which the actor-reporters may have acted, mislineates blank verse or crudely versifies passages of prose, ad-libs freely in half-remembered parts of the play, and so on. A memorially reported quarto is always shorter than the regular version. Visual impressions are often vivid, since the actor-reporters are remembering things they have seen on stage. The stage directions tend to be more frequent and more detailed than in either an author's manuscript or a playbook.

The theory of memorial reconstruction was once thought to have application to dozens of plays from Shakespeare's time. Now it is thought to explain, although only in part, the origin of the 1602 Quarto of *The Merry Wives of Windsor* (the text for which Greg originally devised the fullest elaboration of the theory), and, in even smaller part, the origin of the 1603 Quarto of *Hamlet*. The theory has also been attached to the Quarto versions of *2 Henry VI* and *3 Henry VI* known as *The First Part of the Contention betwixt the Two Famous Houses of York and Lancaster* and *The True Tragedy of Richard Duke of York* (1594 and 1595), as well as to the 1597 Quarto of *Romeo and Juliet*, the 1600 Quarto of *Henry V* (1600), and the 1609 Quarto of *Pericles* (the only substantive text we have of this play), but the application of the theory to these texts is very hard to maintain. The title page of the Second Quarto of *Romeo and Juliet* in 1599, advertising itself as "New corrected, augmented, and amended," does suggest a desire to correct the earlier Quarto, but need not necessitate a theory of memorial reconstruction for that earlier edition. A similar phrase, "Newly corrected and augmented," appeared on the title page of the 1598 Quarto of *Love's Labor's Lost*, implying an earlier edition in need of improvement, but if such an edition ever existed, it has disappeared.

A few texts seem to have been put together by unusual circumstances that somewhat resemble memorial reconstruction, so that the number of quartos to be characterized as "bad" remains in dispute. *The Taming of the Shrew* was not printed until the Folio of 1623, but a Quarto did appear in 1594 of a very similar play, called *The Taming of a Shrew*. Its place names and characters' names are different from those of the Folio version, and the language differs throughout. Some scholars still regard the play as a source for Shakespeare. Nevertheless, the generally held view today is that *A Shrew* is a special kind of pirated text, one in which a rival dramatist has changed the language and the names of the characters to make the work seem his own. A different sort of anomaly is seen in *Richard III*. The 1597 Quarto may be one in which the acting company had a hand, putting together an acting version for performance on tour when the original text was not available. Whatever the circumstances, we can see that the category of so-called "bad" quartos is problematic as to how many quartos belong in this group and how their various defects may have come about. Nonetheless, A. W. Pollard's distinction between "good" and "bad" continues to be embraced in some form by some textual critics today.

The So-Called "Good" Quartos

The so-called "good" quartos, according to Pollard's theory, were based generally on Shakespeare's own drafts or on transcripts of them. Good first quartos, as thus defined, include *Titus Andronicus* (1594), *Richard II* (1597), *1 Henry IV* (1598), *Love's Labor's Lost* (1598), *Romeo and Juliet* (1599), *2 Henry IV* (1600), *A Midsummer Night's Dream* (1600), *The Merchant of Venice* (1600), *Much Ado About Nothing* (1600), *Hamlet* (1604–1605), *Troilus and Cressida* (1609, printed seemingly without permission of Shakespeare's company), and the late First Quarto of *Othello* (1622). This is a short list and is sporadic in its time schedule; booksellers, it seems, were wary of plays as investments. Once a play had appeared in print, it sometimes sold well and sometimes not. *Richard II* went through five quartos before the Folio of 1623. At the other extreme, we have *2 Henry IV*, issued in only one quarto prior to 1623; possibly the printers ran off a large number of copies in anticipation of heavy sales, or perhaps, as Peter Blayney argues, the book-buying market may have been glutted with plays. Some quarto texts continued to appear after the Folio of 1623.

Licensing for Printing

Before a play could be printed, it had to be licensed. The licensing agency responsible for printed matter was a panel of London clergymen known as the "correctors of the press," operating under the authority of the Privy Council, the Bishop of London, the Archbishop of Canterbury, and the Lord Chamberlain. In 1606, Parliament passed a law forbidding references to the Deity in the performance of plays. This legislation, though not aimed at publication per se, had a visible effect on printed texts. Plays printed before 1606 and then revised for subsequent publication after that date show the effects of this censorship.

The Pavier Collection of 1619

A few years before the Shakespearean First Folio appeared in 1623, a bookseller named Thomas Pavier and a printer named William Jaggard made an apparent attempt to collect Shakespeare's plays. Pavier already owned the publishing rights to *Henry V*, for in August 1600 he had received assignment of rights to the memorially reconstructed Quarto of the play published in that year. He brought out a Second Quarto of *Henry V* in 1602 and a Third (printed by Jaggard) in 1619 as part of his anthologizing project. In 1602, Pavier had also obtained the rights to *The First Part of the Contention* and *The True Tragedy of Richard Duke of York*, now generally regarded as the unauthorized quartos of *2* and *3 Henry VI*. Pavier issued them in 1619 under the combined title *The Whole Contention between the Two Famous Houses, Lancaster and York*, printed by Jaggard. Pavier also included in his collection two pseudo-Shakespearean plays to which he owned the rights, *A Yorkshire Tragedy* and *Sir John Oldcastle*, and five Shakespearean plays to which he may have obtained rights or which he considered to be unowned: *A Midsummer Night's Dream, The Merchant of Venice, The Merry Wives of Windsor, King Lear*, and *Pericles*.

Pavier's evident intention was to publish these ten plays in a single volume, and, indeed, two such copies exist today—one in the Folger Library and one in the Lewis Collection at Texas Christian University. Pavier's scheme was frustrated, however, seemingly by the Lord Chamberlain at the instigation of Shakespeare's company. Pavier chose the expedient of publishing his plays separately, some with fraudulently early dates and names of publishers on their title pages in an apparent attempt to obscure the fact of new publication. Whether Pavier's texts contain any textual authority is a vexing question. They are, for the most part, copied from earlier quartos, and yet at times (in *Henry V, The Contention*, and *The True Tragedy*), they anticipate Folio readings in departing from their printed copy, and in the latter half of *King Lear*, the Pavier Quarto anticipates Folio line divisions. Possibly, this evidence points to an infusion of new manuscript source material into the Pavier quartos, but it may instead reflect a consultation of the Pavier quartos during the printing of the Folio.

Publishing Rights for the 1623 Folio

Pavier's dubious and abortive undertaking may possibly have given impetus to a more legitimate edition of Shakespeare's collected plays, some seven years after the author's death, although Shakespeare's company may already have been contemplating such an honor to its famous playwright. Ben Jonson's folio collection of plays in 1616 had established a major precedent for such a volume, despite the scorn of those who regarded all plays as subliterary. The large and tomelike folio format, normally reserved for edifying religious tracts, the "works" of classical authorities, and the like, might now be used also for a collection of plays.

The first task facing the supervisors of the Folio collection, Heminges and Condell, was the assembling of publishing rights to those eighteen Shakespearean plays that had already appeared in print. The most efficient means of doing so was to form a syndicate of publishers who already owned the rights to a large number of the plays. The colophon at the very end of the First Folio names those who took part: "Printed at the charges of W. Jaggard, Ed. Blount, I. Smithweeke, and W. Aspley, 1623." William Jaggard had succeeded to the printing business of James Roberts in 1608. Despite Jaggard's part in the printing of the Pavier quartos of 1619, he evident-

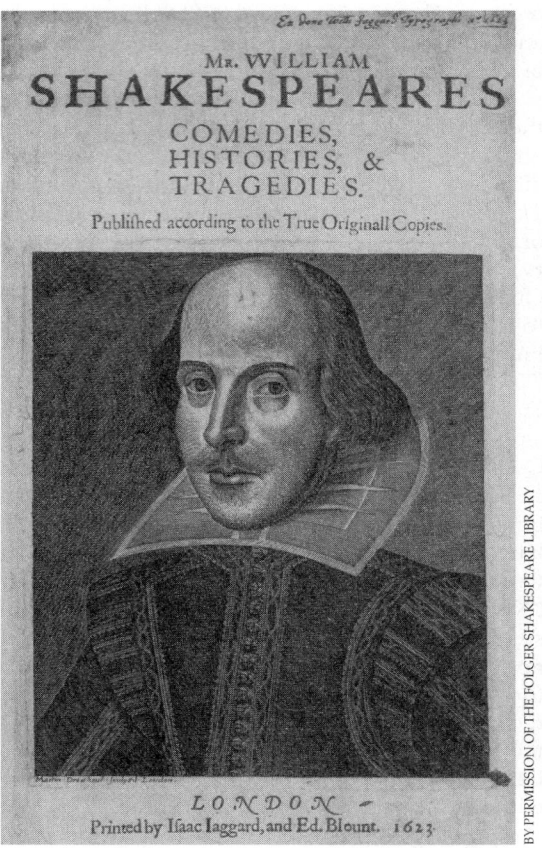

Martin Droeshout's engraving on the title page of the First Folio is one of only two authentic likenesses of Shakespeare in existence.

ly remained on good terms with Shakespeare's company and became (together with his son Isaac) the printer of the 1623 Folio. (William Jaggard died in November 1623, but his son continued to carry on the business as he had during his father's blindness.) Edward Blount had registered *Antony and Cleopatra* and *Pericles* in 1608, though he seems to have overlooked the fact, for *Antony* was reregistered in 1623, and *Pericles* never appeared in the Folio. John Smethwick had received from Nicholas Ling the rights to *Love's Labor's Lost, Romeo and Juliet*, and *Hamlet* in 1607. William Aspley owned the rights to *Much Ado About Nothing* and *2 Henry IV*. One other previously published play, *A Midsummer Night's Dream*, was "derelict" or no longer assigned to a publisher.

Some further negotiations must still have been necessary, with Richard Bonian and Henry Walley for *Troilus and Cressida*, with Nathaniel Butter for *King Lear*, with Thomas Pavier for *2 and 3 Henry VI, Titus Andronicus*, and *Henry V*, perhaps also with Edward White for *Titus Andronicus*, with Matthew Law for *Richard III, Richard II*, and *1 Henry IV*, with Thomas Heyes for *The Merchant of*

Venice, with Arthur Johnson for *The Merry Wives of Windsor,* and with Thomas Walkley for *Othello.* The last-minute inclusion of *Troilus and Cressida* between the histories and the tragedies with incomplete pagination may suggest that Bonian and Walley held out for a long time.

Eighteen plays had never before been printed. To secure rights to these plays, Messrs. Blount and Isaac Jaggard caused the following entry to be made in the Stationers' Register on November 8, 1623:

Mr. Blount, Isaac Jaggard: Entered for their copy under the hands of Mr. Dr. Worrall and Mr. Cole, Warden, Mr. William Shakespeare's Comedies, Histories, and Tragedies, so many of the said copies as are not formerly entered to other men, viz.: Comedies: *The Tempest, The Two Gentlemen of Verona, Measure for Measure, The Comedy of Errors, As You Like It, All's Well That Ends Well, Twelfth Night, The Winter's Tale.* Histories: *The Third Part of Henry the Sixth, Henry the Eighth.* Tragedies: *Coriolanus, Timon of Athens, Julius Caesar, Macbeth, Antony and Cleopatra, Cymbeline.*

The Stationers' Register list includes only sixteen names, since *The Taming of the Shrew* and *King John* were considered to have been published previously: *The Taming of a Shrew* and *The Troublesome Reign of King John,* now generally regarded as an adaptation and a source, respectively, had appeared in print in 1594 and 1591. Two plays on the list had actually been registered previously: *As You Like It* and *Antony and Cleopatra.* "The Third Part of Henry the Sixth" refers to *1 Henry VI,* since the other two *Henry VI* plays had already been published as quartos.

The Texts Used for the 1623 Folio

In addition to securing publishing rights, Heminges and Condell and their associates had the further task of selecting copy from which the printers were to set up their work. In the case of the eighteen as yet unpublished plays, the editors selected various manuscripts: the author's draft, or, just as likely, a transcript of it for *All's Well,* perhaps the playbook for *As You Like It,* a scribal transcript for *Twelfth Night,* and so on. Perhaps the editors planned at first to give the printers clean new transcriptions of such plays, for the first four plays in the Folio—*The Tempest, The Two Gentlemen of Verona, The Merry Wives of Windsor,* and *Measure for Measure*—were all printed from copies made by the professional scribe Ralph Crane. If the editors had planned to continue this practice throughout the volume, however, they abandoned it after the fourth play and turned instead to a variety of sorts of copy. An alternative explanation is that the editors had these four clean copies on hand and chose to begin the volume with them simply because they were available and ready for the printer.

The complicated choices involved plays that had already been published. Printers, then as now, preferred to work from printed copy because of its legibility.

Although one might suppose that Heminges and Condell would have set aside unauthorized quartos entirely, they did not always do so, perhaps because the manuscript alternatives were illegible or defective. In other cases, the editors had to make a more subtle choice between a "good" quarto and a still better manuscript. What the editors sometimes did in such cases was to use the inferior printed text but to annotate it by reference to a superior manuscript. This process of annotation might vary widely in its degree of thoroughness.

The use of inferior quartos as copy was, to be sure, unusual. The Folio text of *Henry V* seems to have been sporadically contaminated by the Third Quarto, which was derived from the Quarto of 1600, but probably the Third Quarto did not, in fact, serve as printer's copy. On the other hand, the Folio text of *2 Henry VI* may actually have been set in part from pages of the Third Quarto, derived from the First Quarto, and some editors argue that the same is basically true of *3 Henry VI.* Even in these questionable cases, an attempt seems to have been made to overcome the limitations of the defective quarto copy.

More often, one of the good quartos was corrected by checking it against a manuscript source. The Folio text of *Titus Andronicus,* for example, was evidently derived from a copy of the Third Quarto, but that copy may have been corrected by reference to some other copy, perhaps the playbook. In any case, a portion of Act 3 that is missing from all the early quartos must have been derived from some manuscript source. In some cases, later quartos supplied material missing from earlier ones. In still other instances, as in *Richard III, Troilus and Cressida, Othello, King Lear, Hamlet,* and *2 Henry IV,* the relationship of Quarto text to the Folio text is extraordinarily complicated. See Appendix 1 for statements on the texts of each play.

The Printing of the 1623 Folio

The printing of the 1623 Folio continued from April 1621 to December 1623 in the printing shop of William and Isaac Jaggard. The compositors who actually set the type were, according to Charlton Hinman (*The Printing and Proof-Reading of the First Folio of Shakespeare,* 2 vols., 1963), five in number. For convenient reference, they are designated as compositors A through E. A and B were the principal workmen. E was evidently an inept apprentice, unfortunately brought into the project just in time to work on several of the tragedies. Still other compositors have been proposed since Hinman's time, namely, F, H, I, and J, at least some of which are problematic—F likely being D, and J almost certainly A. (See Peter W. M. Blayney, *The First Folio of Shakespeare,* Folger Shakespeare Library, Washington, D.C., 1991.)

Compositors had to rely on their ability to memorize large segments of their copy—perhaps whole lines of verse—at a time, since they needed to look at the type they were setting manually. Hence, they were apt to make mistakes based on imperfect remembering. Less skillful compositors not infrequently introduced errors by transposing words in a line, substituting a new word for what was in the copy, or maiming the scansion of a line of verse by adding or subtracting syllables.

Compositors were largely responsible for the "pointing" or punctuation of the text. They also usually imposed their own spelling practices on their copy. No copy editor went over the materials first to normalize spelling, and the compositors were free to normalize as they chose. They occasionally used variant spellings to "justify" prose lines. Elizabethan spelling was, in any case, chaotic by our standards. The modern textual business of identifying compositors relies mainly on discovering the characteristic spelling habits of each.

Rather than setting their pages in numbered sequence right through an entire play, as we would assume, the compositors of the Folio used a system known as "casting off": that is, they estimated the amount of copy needed to fill a page of type and divided the whole text up into portions of the estimated correct length. They could then begin by setting pages six and seven, and would immediately start printing these two pages side by side on the same "forme" or side of a sheet. (When three large sheets are folded once and gathered together, the result is a "quire" of twelve pages, with pages one and twelve printed on the outer side or "forme" of the outermost sheet, pages two and eleven on the inner forme of that same sheet, pages three and ten on the outer forme of the middle sheet, and so on.) Since type was expensive and in limited supply in a printing shop, the type had to be redistributed into the type cases as soon as the requisite number of copies of any forme had been run off. Casting off enabled the printers to print and redistribute the type of pages six and seven without having to wait for all the intervening pages to be set up also. (The reappearance of distributed type is, in fact, one clue by which Hinman was able to discover that the Folio had been set up throughout by casting off rather than by printing in sequence.)

Despite the advantages of flexibility, casting off had its disadvantages. If a compositor discovered he had been given too little copy for a page of text, he had to stretch his material by heavy "leading" or spacing. If, on the other hand, he discovered he had been given too much copy for a page, he had to crowd his lines, print verse as prose, or even eliminate words and lines. Knowledge of this sort of printing information is useful to modern editors, since it enables them to determine when the compositors may have interfered with the text that Shakespeare wrote.

When a compositor had completed one entire forme, consisting of two pages of text to be printed on one side of a large printing sheet, the forme went into the press and the requisite number of copies was run off by hand.

One side of the sheet, either the inner or outer forme, was printed at a time. Proofreading, or "press correction," may have been done in part by checking the "foul proof" before the press run began, but further proofreading took place while the printing continued. At first, a number of sides of the sheet would be printed in their uncorrected state, that is, entirely unproofread. When the press corrector found more errors, the presses would be stopped so that the errors might be corrected, after which printing would continue. Such interruptions might occur several times. Uncorrected or partially corrected sheets were not destroyed, however; paper was too costly for that. Later, when the stacks of sheets printed on one side were printed on the other side, errors would again be corrected as printing continued. Ultimately, when the sheets were gathered by threes into a quire of twelve pages and then sewn into a complete volume, no single copy of the Folio was apt to be exactly like another. In fact, the many copies of the First Folio extant today differ from one another in their press variants. Even though we might regard this as evidence of carelessness, Jaggard's work on the First Folio seems to have been scrupulous when judged by the standards of the day.

At a guess, about 750 copies of the First Folio were printed and sold for as much as twenty shillings, though the price could vary depending on markup; the cost of an unbound copy, retail, may have been around fifteen shillings. Approximately 230 copies survive today, of which seventy-nine bound folios, not all complete copies, plus some fragments, are to be found in the collection of the Folger Library, Washington, D.C.

The Later Folios

When, after nine years, the first edition of the Folio had been sold out, a second edition was printed in 1632 by Thomas Cotes. He had succeeded to the Jaggards' business after the death of Isaac in 1627. The Second Folio merely reprinted the text of the First Folio together with a considerable number of editorial emendations. These have no independent textual authority, although some of the more commonsense suggestions have since been adopted by modern editors. A third edition appeared in 1663, based on the second. A second issue of this same third edition in 1664 included seven new plays: *Pericles, The London Prodigal, Thomas Lord Cromwell, Sir John Oldcastle, The Puritan, A Yorkshire Tragedy*, and *Locrine*. Of these, only *Pericles* has gained general acceptance in the Shakespeare canon (see Appendix 1 and the Introduction to the play). A fourth edition of the Folio in 1685, based on the third, also included the seven new plays. Like the second and third editions, this fourth edition offered many emendations or new errors not based on any textual authority.

Later Editions

The first editor of Shakespeare in the modern sense of the term was Nicholas Rowe. His six-volume edition of 1709 (reedited in eight volumes in 1714) was based on the Fourth Folio, to which the publisher Jacob Tonson had acquired the rights. Rowe began many practices we now regard as standard for a reader's edition. He provided a complete list of *dramatis personae* for each play, whereas the earlier folios had done so only sporadically. Similarly, he extended the practice of announcing the locale at the beginning of a scene. He marked entrances and exits with more care than in the folios and provided more extensive division of the plays into acts and scenes. Although he did not consult Shakespeare's early texts, Rowe did offer a number of textual emendations. He also modernized spelling and punctuation.

Alexander Pope was Shakespeare's next editor. Pope's text, completed in 1725 in six volumes (2nd edition, 1728), was printed from a copy of Rowe's edition with Pope's annotations. Pope excluded *Pericles* and the spurious plays that had been added to the Third Folio, although a companion volume containing these plays appeared with the second edition of 1728, lacking Pope's name and perhaps not authorized by him. He completed Rowe's task of indicating locale for each of the scenes, and also completed the division of the text into acts and scenes. In fact, Pope used the "continental" system of marking a new scene whenever a major character comes on stage, so that his text contained many more scenes than did other editions. Most importantly, Pope regarded Shakespeare's text as something to be "improved," because it had been written in a barbaric age for irresponsible actors all too ready to take liberties with the text, and for ignorant spectators. Although he claimed to have consulted the early quartos, Pope excised parts of Shakespeare's text that he considered vulgar, regularized lines that struck him as defective, eliminated anachronisms he regarded as indecorous, and the like. Pope's edition reflected the "refined" eighteenth-century view of Shakespeare as a very rough diamond in need of polishing. Some of the "improvements" are convincing and have been adopted by more recent editors, but most are sophistications that, for a time, moved Shakespearean editing away from the purpose of recovering what Shakespeare had actually written.

A corrective was in order. Lewis Theobald took up the challenge, though he was to be rewarded for his pains by being crowned the King of Dullness in Pope's *The Dunciad* (1728 version). Theobald's edition appeared in 1733 and was later reissued several times. He was the first editor to consult the folios and quartos. He did not, however, wholly recognize the textual value of those quartos. He also failed to base his text directly on the earliest substantive texts; instead, he annotated a copy of Pope's edition, just as Pope had annotated Rowe and Rowe had annotated

the Fourth Folio. Despite his consultation of the early texts and his occasional brilliance as an emender, therefore, Theobald inevitably perpetuated more errors than he eliminated from the Rowe-Pope tradition.

The convention of relying on one's predecessor's edition continued to afflict eighteenth-century editing of Shakespeare. Sir Thomas Hanmer (1743–1744) and William Warburton (1747) contributed some emendations that are used today but tended to follow their predecessors. (This Warburton is not, however, the John Warburton whose cook is said to have burned a number of now-lost early editions of plays by using them to line pie plates.) Even Dr. Johnson (1765), who set a standard of conservatism in admitting emendations to the Shakespearean text, based his edition almost entirely on Theobald's of 1757, with only occasional use of Warburton's. Johnson's account of the text took an unfriendly view toward the interference of scribes, players, and printers; he shared Pope's dismay at the conditions under which Shakespeare wrote but mistrusted Pope's poetic "improvements" as too subjective.

Only with Edward Capell (1768) did an eighteenth-century editor finally base his text on the original Folio and quartos. Capell amassed an admirable collection of quartos and was the first to recognize that they might sometimes be preferred as copy text to the Folio itself. Unlike his eighteenth-century predecessors, who generally dismissed the quartos as based on playbooks and hence contaminated by theatrical revision, Capell thought that they usually represented Shakespeare's own drafts. At the same time, Capell's principle of selection was too eclectic in that he was ready to choose any early reading, whether from the first printing or a derivative one, so long as it offered what he regarded as an improvement. Capell's work heavily influenced George Steevens's 1773 revision of Dr. Johnson's text.

Edmund Malone, at first a collaborator with Steevens and later his rival, issued a ten-volume edition in 1790. Malone reintroduced *Pericles*, which Pope and subsequent editors had eliminated along with the spurious plays of the Third Folio. Malone brought to his editing an extensive knowledge of Elizabethan documents, such as the Stationers' Register, Henslowe's *Diary*, and the records of the Master of the Revels. His most important contribution to theory of editing was to grant authority only to the earliest printing of any version of a play—a principle that he had trouble applying in some cases, however, because the false-dated Pavier quartos had yet to be sorted out. He left uncompleted a variorum edition recording all textual variants; this edition was finished in 1821 by James Boswell, son of Dr. Johnson's biographer, and became known as the Third Variorum because Isaac Reed's earlier editions (1803, 1813) had called themselves the First and Second Variorums. The so-called New Variorum Shakespeare continued this tradition under Henry Howard Furness, beginning in 1871.

Nineteenth-century editions were numerous. One of the most famous and influential was the "bowdlerized" or expurgated *Family Shakespeare* of the Rev. Thomas Bowdler, done with the assistance of his daughter Henrietta; first appearing in 1807 and then in 1818, it soon extended its influence throughout the English-speaking world. Other editions included those of S. W. Singer (1826, 1855–1856), John Payne Collier (1842–1844, 1858, 1875–1878), Charles Knight (1838–1843, 1842–1844, 1867), Alexander Dyce (1857, 1864–1867, 1875–1876), Howard Staunton (1858–1860), Nikolaus Delius (1854–1861, 1864), H. N. Hudson (1851–1856, 1880–1881), Thomas Keightley (1864), and Charles and Mary Cowden Clarke (1864–1868). Editors from this period were generally absorbed with reading different printed versions as if they represented different authorial versions and with an unresolved debate as to whether the "bad" quarto of *Hamlet*, among others, represented authorial versions or else derivative and corrupt versions of fuller texts.

The outstanding scholarly edition of the nineteenth century was the so-called Cambridge Shakespeare of William George Clark and William Aldis Wright (1863–1866), issued in 1864 in a single volume known as the Globe text. Although its choice of copy texts has been challenged in two or three instances by twentieth-century bibliographical research, the Globe text was soundly edited for its day and soon established itself as definitive. Its act and scene divisions and its line numbering became standards of reference for concordances, works of literary criticism, and the like.

Later nineteenth- and early twentieth-century editions included those of W. J. Rolfe (1871–1896), Appleton Morgan (1888), F. A. Marshall and others (The Henry Irving Shakespeare, 1888–1890), Sir Israel Gollancz (The Temple Shakespeare, 1894–1895), W. J. Craig (1891), C. H. Herford (1899), and Helen Porter and Charlotte Clarke (1903–1914). Influential American editions included those of W. A. Neilson (1906) and George Lyman Kittredge (1936).

The twentieth century has seen an enormous increase in the information available on bibliographical matters: printing-house procedures, the mechanics of book production, watermarks, printer's ornaments, Elizabethan handwriting, spelling, punctuation, and the like. Prominent among bibliographical studies are those that laid the basis for the standard "received" theories of editorial scholarship discussed previously. These include A. W. Pollard's *Shakespeare's Folios and Quartos* (1909) and *Shakespeare's Hand in the Play of Sir Thomas More* (1923); R. B. McKerrow's *An Introduction to Bibliography for Literary Students* (1927) and *Prolegomena for the Oxford Shakespeare* (1939) in which, near the end of his life, McKerrow dissents from much of what became the standard "received" theory of Greg; W. W. Greg's *Principles of Emendation in Shakespeare* (1928) and *The Editorial Problem in Shakespeare* (3rd edition, 1954); and E. K. Chambers's *William Shake-*

speare: A Study of Facts and Problems (1930). No less important are Alice Walker's *Textual Problems of the First Folio* (1953) and Fredson Bowers's *Bibliography and Textual Criticism* (1964). An updated survey of problems and methods is to be found in Philip Gaskell's *A New Introduction to Bibliography* (1972). Significant studies also have appeared on individual plays, such as that of Peter Alexander on the *Henry VI* plays and *Richard III*, Madeleine Doran also on *Henry VI*, J. Dover Wilson on *Hamlet*, George Williams on *Romeo and Juliet*, G. I. Duthie on *King Lear*, and Peter Blayney on *King Lear*.

During the twentieth century, bibliographical theories have, of course, continued to evolve. Sidney Lee, early in the century, still held by and large to Dr. Johnson's view that Heminges and Condell were right to denigrate the quartos because some of them offered such apparently deficient texts (a totalizing view of the quartos based on only a handful of them) and that the Folio was equally suspect because Heminges and Condell, though having denigrated the quartos, persisted in using some of them as printer's copy. Only in the 1930s and afterward did a consensus begin to develop as to how Shakespeare's play texts got transmitted into print. Pollard's distinction between good and bad quartos, although it relied too much on the notion that the printers of the bad quartos were unscrupulous and led to disagreement as to which quartos might, in fact, be categorized as "bad," established the system of classification that continues, albeit with increasing reservations, to be used today.

Two main challenges face bibliographical scholars currently. The first asks whether the categories proposed by Pollard, Greg, and others, for all their being well established, are, in fact, viable. William B. Long and Paul Werstine have shown with disconcerting precision that many supposed "foul paper" characteristics are to be found in supposed playbooks, and the reverse, so that it is often virtually impossible to determine what was the nature of the copy underlying a printed text. (See, for example, William B. Long, "'A bed for woodstock': A Warning for the Unwary," *Medieval and Renaissance Drama in England*, 2, 1985, pp. 91–118, and Paul Werstine, "Plays in Manuscript," *A New History of Early English Drama*, eds. John D. Cox and David Scott Kastan, New York, 1997, pp. 481–97). Empirical research, based in part on surviving manuscripts by dramatists other than Shakespeare, suggests that manuscripts annotated for use in the theater contain little of the normalization and regularization that Greg and McKerrow argued they would. Perhaps most decisively against Greg and McKerrow is the observation that neither the perfectly regularized and completely annotated playbook nor the first-and-final authorial draft called "foul papers" seems to be represented among extant manuscripts of Shakespeare's period. And, although theories of memorial reconstruction appear still to be useful, not even the theory of memorial reconstruction of a "bad" quarto by an actor or actors quite stands up as a complete explanation of the origin of such a quarto, because there are always discrepancies in the fit between the role(s) of the alleged reporter(s) and the quality of the reproduction of the play text. Steven Urkowitz and others challenge the category of "bad" quartos entirely by attempting to show how theatrical the readings in those quartos sometimes can be represented to be. (See, for example, Steven Urkowitz, "Five Women Eleven Ways: Changing Images of Shakespearean Characters in the Earliest Texts," *Images of Shakespeare*, ed. Werner Habicht et al., 1988, pp. 292–304.)

The other challenge is the hypothesis of authorial revision, especially with regard to *King Lear, Hamlet, Troilus and Cressida, 2 Henry IV, The Contention, The True Tragedy, Richard III, Henry V, Othello*, and, to a lesser extent, *1 Henry IV* and *Richard II*. The case for Shakespeare as a conscious reviser is being made more and more strongly than ever before by Gary Taylor, Stanley Wells, Michael Warren, and others, and it is an argument that, of course, affects the issue of what text to edit. Is the Folio *King Lear* an authorial revision? If so, its claim to precedence over the Quarto version is strong. If, on the other hand, it represents theatrical revision, involving the acting company, then Shakespeare's role is less determinable. Does this uncertainty matter, or should we prefer the theatrically revised versions in any case? Were cuts made for reasons of length? Did actors have trouble with certain lines and wish to see them dropped or altered? Did actors' improvisations sometimes make their way into the text? In what ways did censorship contribute to revision? Were there other practical considerations at work, such as provincial touring, to which Shakespeare may have been asked to accede? Do we want a text that comes closest to what Shakespeare may originally have written, or do we want the product as it emerged from the process of rehearsal and revival? The Folio and Quarto versions of *King Lear* are so unlike each other that we must realize we have been given the play in two states, both arguably authoritative. An edition can choose to print both, as in the new Oxford Shakespeare, but perhaps at the cost of making life unreasonably difficult for many readers and certainly at the cost of added paper. How is an editor to address the question of what is most useful for readers and students? The answer must depend in part on what any given edition is for and what audience it is addressing.

Textual controversies such as these have led to new twentieth-century editions of Shakespeare in which the textual method has been measurably advanced. Among the most significant are the New Cambridge Shakespeare of Sir Arthur Quiller-Couch and J. Dover Wilson, and the still-continuing Arden Shakespeare under a succession of general editors, including W. J. Craig, R. H. Case, Una Ellis-Fermor, Harold Jenkins, Harold Brooks, Richard Proudfoot, Ann Thompson, and David Scott Kastan. Peter Alexander's edition of 1951 is often cited as a standard text.

It was soon followed by C. J. Sisson's edition of 1954 and the London Shakespeare of John Munro, 1958. College editions reedited from original texts include the Pelican Shakespeare, under the general editorship of Alfred Harbage (1956–1969, currently appearing in newly edited individual texts by Stephen Orgel, A. R. Braunmuller, Russ McDonald, and others); the revision of Kittredge's edition by Irving Ribner (1971); the Signet Classic Shakespeare, under the general editorship of Sylvan Barnet (1972); the Riverside Shakespeare (1974, 2nd edition 1997), of which G. Blakemore Evans is the textual editor; this present edition; the still-continuing English New Penguin Shakespeare under the general editorship of T. J. B. Spencer and Stanley Wells; the Bantam Shakespeare, edited by David Bevington (1988); and The New Folger Library Shakespeare, edited by Barbara A. Mowat and Paul Werstine, currently appearing in individual paperbacks. Two major editorial undertakings of the 1980s are the controversial and impressive Oxford Shakespeare in several formats (a one-volume modern-spelling edition and a one-volume old-spelling edition, 1986; a *Textual Companion*, 1987; and individual editions of the plays and poems by various editors, still forthcoming, all under the general editorship of Stanley Wells and Gary Taylor), and the New Cambridge Shakespeare (in individual one-volume editions, still forthcoming, under the general editorship of Philip Brockbank, Brian Gibbons, and A. R. Braunmuller).

Norton has also issued its Norton *Facsimile of The First Folio* of Shakespeare, prepared by Charlton Hinman from the Folios of the Folger Library (1968, updated by Peter Blayney, 1991). Older facsimiles of the First Folio are available in libraries, such as that prepared by Sidney Lee (1902) and J. Dover Wilson (in separate plays), but the Norton facsimile unquestionably sets a new standard of excellence. Facsimiles of the quartos are also available, including those prepared for the Oxford University Press by W. W. Greg and Charlton Hinman, those published as Malone Society Reprints, and, most recently, a one-volume set edited by Kenneth Muir and Michael Allen, chiefly from the holdings of the Huntington Library. They are also available from Early English Books Online. Xerox copies of early printed books, such as Shakespearean quartos, are to be found in many libraries through the S.T.C. (Short Title Catalogue) series of University Microfilms. Photographic copies of early texts are also frequently available on microfilm and online.

SHAKESPEARE CRITICISM

In his own time, Shakespeare achieved a reputation for immortal greatness that is astonishing when we consider the low regard in which playwrights were then generally held. Francis Meres compared him to Ovid, Plautus, and Seneca, and proclaimed Shakespeare to be England's most excellent writer in both comedy and tragedy. John Weever spoke of "honey-tongued Shakespeare." The number of such praising allusions is high. Even Ben Jonson, a learned writer strongly influenced by the classical tradition, lauded Shakespeare as "a monument without a tomb," England's best poet, exceeding Chaucer, Spenser, Beaumont, Kyd, and Marlowe. In tragedy, Jonson compared Shakespeare with Aeschylus, Euripides, and Sophocles; in comedy, he insisted Shakespeare had no rival even in "insolent Greece or haughty Rome." This tribute appeared in Jonson's commendatory poem written for the Shakespeare First Folio of 1623.

To be sure, Jonson had more critical things to say about Shakespeare. Even in the Folio commendatory poem, Jonson could not resist a dig at Shakespeare's "small Latin, and less Greek." To William Drummond of Hawthornden, he objected that Shakespeare "wanted art" because in a play (*The Winter's Tale*) he "brought in a number of men saying they had suffered shipwreck in Bohemia, where there is no sea near by some hundred miles." In *Timber*, or *Discoveries*, Jonson chided Shakespeare for his unrestrained facility in writing. "The players have often mentioned it as an honor to Shakespeare, that in his writing, whatsoever he penned he never blotted out [a] line. My answer hath been, would he had blotted a thousand." In a preface to his own play, *Every Man in His Humor* (1616 edition), Jonson satirized English history plays (such as Shakespeare's) that "with three rusty swords, / And help of some few foot-and-half-foot words, / Fight over York and Lancaster's long jars, / And in the tiring-house bring wounds to scars." He also jeered at plays lacking unity of time in which children grow to the age of sixty or older and at nonsensical romantic plays featuring fireworks, thunder, and a chorus that "wafts you o'er the seas."

These criticisms are all of a piece. As a classicist himself, Jonson held in high regard the classical unities. He deplored much English popular drama, including some of Shakespeare's plays, for their undisciplined mixture of comedy and tragedy. Measured against his cherished ideals of classical decorum and refinement of language, Shakespeare's histories and the late romances—*Pericles, Cymbeline, The Winter's Tale,* and *The Tempest*—seemed irritatingly naive and loose-jointed. Yet Jonson knew that Shakespeare had an incomparable genius, superior even to his own. Jonson's affection and respect for Shakespeare seem to have been quite unforced. In the midst of his critical remarks in *Timber*, he freely conceded that "I loved the man, and do honor his memory (on this side idolatry) as much as any. He was indeed honest, and of an open and free nature, had an excellent fantasy, brave notions, and gentle expressions."

The Age of Dryden and Pope

Jonson's attitude toward Shakespeare lived on into the Restoration period of the late seventeenth century. A commonplace of that age held it proper to "admire" Ben Jonson but to "love" Shakespeare. Jonson was the more correct poet, the better model for imitation. Shakespeare often had to be rewritten according to the sophisticated tastes of the Restoration (see Appendix 3 for an account of Restoration stage adaptations of Shakespeare), but he was also regarded as a natural genius. Dryden reflected this view in his *Essay of Dramatic Poesy* (1668) and his *Essay on the Dramatic Poetry of the Last Age* (1672). Dryden condemned *The Winter's Tale, Pericles,* and several other late romances for "the lameness of their plots" and for their "ridiculous incoherent story" which is usually "grounded on impossibilities." Not only Shakespeare, he charged, but several of his contemporaries "neither understood correct plotting nor that which they call *the decorum of the stage*." Had Shakespeare lived in the Restoration, Dryden believed, he would doubtless have written "more correctly" under the influence of a language that had become more "courtly" and a wit that had grown more "refined." Shakespeare, he thought, had limitless "fancy" but sometimes lacked "judgment." Dryden regretted that Shakespeare had been forced to write in "ignorant" times and for audiences who "knew no better." Like Jonson, nevertheless, Dryden had the magnanimity to perceive that Shakespeare transcended his limitations. Shakespeare, said Dryden, was "the man who of all modern and perhaps ancient poets had the largest and most comprehensive soul." From a classical writer, this was high praise indeed.

Alexander Pope's edition of Shakespeare (1725) was based upon a similar estimate of Shakespeare as an untutored genius. Pope freely "improved" Shakespeare's language, rewriting lines and excising those parts he considered vulgar, in order to rescue Shakespeare from the barbaric circumstances of his Elizabethan milieu. Other critics of the Restoration and early eighteenth century who stressed Shakespeare's "natural" genius and imaginative powers were John Dennis, Joseph Addison, and the editors Nicholas Rowe and Lewis Theobald.

The Age of Johnson

Shakespeare was not without his detractors during the late seventeenth and early eighteenth centuries; after all, classical criticism tended to distrust imagination and fancy. Notable among the harsher critics of the Restoration period was Thomas Rymer, whose *Short View of Tragedy* (1692) included a famous attack on *Othello* for making too much out of Desdemona's handkerchief. In the eighteenth century, Voltaire spoke out sharply against Shakespeare's violation of the classical unities, though Voltaire also had some admiring things to say.

The most considered answer to such criticism in the later eighteenth century was that of Dr. Samuel Johnson, in his edition of Shakespeare's plays and its great preface

(1765). Shakespeare, said Johnson, is the poet of nature who "holds up to his readers a faithful mirror of manners and of life. His characters are not modified by the customs of particular places, unpracticed by the rest of the world. . . . In the writings of other poets a character is too often an individual; in those of Shakespeare it is commonly a species." Johnson's attitudes were essentially classical in that he praised Shakespeare for being universal, for having provided a "just representation of general nature," and for having stood the test of time. Yet Johnson also magnanimously praised Shakespeare for having transcended the classical rules. Johnson triumphantly vindicated the mixture of comedy and tragedy in Shakespeare's plays and the supposed indecorum of his characters.

Of course, Johnson did not praise everything he saw. He objected to Shakespeare's loose construction of plot, careless huddling together of the ends of his plays, licentious humor, and, above all, the punning wordplay. He deplored Shakespeare's failure to satisfy the demands of poetic justice, especially in *King Lear,* and he regretted that Shakespeare seemed more anxious to please than to instruct. Still, Johnson did much to free Shakespeare from the constraint of an overly restrictive classical approach to criticism.

The Age of Coleridge

With the beginning of the Romantic period, in England and on the Continent, Shakespeare criticism increasingly turned away from classical precept in favor of a more spontaneous and enthusiastic approach to Shakespeare's creative genius. The new Shakespeare became indeed a rallying cry for those who now deplored such "regular" dramatic poets as Racine and Corneille. Shakespeare became a seer, a bard with mystic powers of insight into the human condition. Goethe, in *Wilhelm Meister* (1796), conceived of Hamlet as the archetypal "Romantic" poet: melancholic, delicate, and unable to act.

Critical trends in England moved toward similar conclusions. Maurice Morgann, in his *Essay on the Dramatic Character of Sir John Falstaff* (1777), glorified Falstaff into a rare individual of courage, dignity, and—yes—honor. To do so, Morgann had to suppress much evidence as to Falstaff's overall function in the *Henry IV* plays. Dramatic structure, in fact, did not interest him; his passion was "character," and his study of Falstaff reflected a new Romantic preoccupation with character analysis. Like other character critics who followed him, Morgann tended to move away from the play itself and into a world where the dramatic personage being considered might lead an independent existence. What would it have been like to know Falstaff as a real person? How would he have behaved on occasions other than those reported by Shakespeare? Such questions fascinated Morgann and others because they led into grand speculations about

human psychology and philosophy. Shakespeare's incomparably penetrating insights into character prompted further investigations of the human psyche.

Other late eighteenth-century works devoted to the study of character included Lord Kames's *Elements of Criticism* (1762), Thomas Whately's *Remarks on Some of the Characters of Shakespeare* (1785), William Richardson's *Philosophical Analysis and Illustration of Some of Shakespeare's Remarkable Characters* (1774), and William Jackson's *Thirty Letters on Various Subjects* (1782). Morgann spoke for this school of critics when he insisted, "It may be fit to consider them [Shakespeare's characters] rather as historic than dramatic beings; and, when occasion requires, to account for their conduct from the whole of character, from general principles, from latent motives, and from policies not avowed."

Samuel Taylor Coleridge, the greatest of the English Romantic critics, was profoundly influenced by character criticism, both English and continental. He himself made important contributions to the study of character. His conception of Hamlet, derived in part from Goethe and Hegel, as one who "vacillates from sensibility, and procrastinates from thought, and loses the power of action in the energy of resolve," was to dominate nineteenth-century interpretations of Hamlet. His insight into Iago's evil nature—"the motive-hunting of a motiveless malignity"— was also influential.

Nevertheless, Coleridge did not succumb to the temptation, as did so many character critics, of ignoring the unity of an entire play. Quite to the contrary, he affirmed in Shakespeare an "organic form" or "innate" sense of shape, developed from within, that gave new meaning to Shakespeare's fusion of comedy and tragedy, his seeming anachronisms, his improbable fictions, and his supposedly rambling plots. Coleridge heaped scorn on the eighteenth-century idea of Shakespeare as a "natural" but untaught genius. He praised Shakespeare not for having mirrored life, as Dr. Johnson had said, but for having created an imaginative world attuned to its own internal harmonies. He saw Shakespeare as an inspired but deliberate artist who fitted together the parts of his imaginative world with consummate skill. "The judgment of Shakespeare is commensurate with his genius."

In all this, Coleridge was remarkably close to his German contemporary and rival, August Wilhelm Schlegel, who insisted that Shakespeare was "a profound artist, and not a blind and wildly luxuriant genius." In Shakespeare's plays, said Schlegel, "The fancy lays claim to be considered as an independent mental power governed according to its own laws." Between them, Coleridge and Schlegel utterly inverted the critical values of the previous age, substituting "sublimity" and "imagination" for universality and trueness to nature.

Other Romantic critics included William Hazlitt (*Characters of Shakespear's Plays,* 1817), Charles Lamb (*On* the *Tragedies of Shakespeare,* 1811), and Thomas De Quincey (*On the Knocking at the Gate in Macbeth,* 1823). Hazlitt reveals a political liberalism characteristic of a number of Romantic writers in his skeptical view of Henry V's absolutism and his imperialist war against the French. John Keats has some penetrating things to say in his letters about Shakespeare's "negative capability," or his ability to see into characters' lives with an extraordinary self-effacing sympathy. As a whole, the Romantics were enthusiasts of Shakespeare, and sometimes even idolaters. Yet they consistently refused to recognize him as a man of the theater. Lamb wrote, "It may seem a paradox, but I cannot help being of opinion that the plays of Shakespeare are less calculated for performance on a stage than those of almost any other dramatist whatever." Hazlitt similarly observed: "We do not like to see our author's plays acted, and least of all, *Hamlet.* There is no play that suffers so much in being transferred to the stage." These hostile attitudes toward the theater reflected, in part, the condition of the stage in nineteenth-century England. In part, however, these attitudes were the inevitable result of character criticism, or what Lamb called the desire "to know the internal workings and movements of a great mind, of an Othello or a Hamlet for instance, the *when* and the *why* and the *how far* they should be moved." This fascination with character swept everything before it during the Romantic period.

A. C. Bradley and the Turn of the Century

The tendency of nineteenth-century criticism, then, was to exalt Shakespeare as a poet and a philosopher rather than as a playwright, and as a creator of immortal characters whose "lives" might be studied as though existing independent of a dramatic text. Not infrequently, this critical approach led to a biographical interpretation of Shakespeare through his plays, on the assumption that what he wrote was his own spiritual autobiography and a key to his own fascinating character. Perhaps the most famous critical study in this line was Edward Dowden's *Shakspere: A Critical Study of His Mind and Art* (1875), in which he traced a progression from Shakespeare's early exuberance and passionate involvement through brooding pessimism to a final philosophical calm.

At the same time, the nineteenth century also saw the rise of a more factual and methodological scholarship, especially in the German universities. Dowden, in fact, reflected this trend as well, for one of the achievements of philological study was to establish with some accuracy the dating of Shakespeare's plays and thus make possible an analysis of his artistic development. Hermann Ulrici's *Über Shakespeares dramatische Kunst* (1839) and Gottfried Gervinus's edition of 1849 were among the earliest studies to interest themselves in Shakespeare's chronological development.

The critic who best summed up the achievement of nineteenth-century Shakespeare criticism was A. C. Bradley, in his *Shakespearean Tragedy* (1904) and other studies. *Shakespearean Tragedy* dealt with the four "great" tragedies: *Hamlet, Othello, King Lear,* and *Macbeth.* Bradley revealed his Romantic tendencies in his focus on psychological analysis of character, but he also brought to his work a scholarly awareness of the text that had been missing in some earlier character critics. His work continues to have considerable influence today, despite modern tendencies to rebel against nineteenth-century idealism. To Bradley, Shakespeare's tragic world was ultimately explicable and profoundly moral. Despite the overwhelming impression of tragic waste in *King Lear,* he argued, we as audience experience a sense of compensation and completion that implies an ultimate pattern in human life. "Good, in the widest sense, seems thus to be the principle of life and health in the world; evil, at least in these worst forms, to be a poison. The world reacts against it violently, and, in the struggle to expel it, is driven to devastate itself." Humanity must suffer because of its fatal tendency to pursue some extreme passion, but humanity learns through suffering about itself and the nature of its world. We as audience are reconciled to our existence through purgative release; we smile through our tears. Cordelia is wantonly destroyed, but the fact of her transcendent goodness is eternal. Although in one sense she fails, said Bradley, she is "in another sense superior to the world in which [she] appears; is, in some way which we do not seek to define, untouched by the doom that overtakes [her]; and is rather set free from life than deprived of it."

Historical Criticism

The first major twentieth-century reaction against character criticism was that of the so-called historical critics. (On the later critical movement known as the New Historicism, see below, following "Jan Kott and the Theater of the Absurd.") These critics insisted on a more hardheaded and skeptical appraisal of Shakespeare through better understanding of his historical milieu: his theater, his audience, and his political and social environment. In good part, this movement was the result of a new professionalism of Shakespearean studies in the twentieth century. Whereas earlier critics—Dryden, Pope, Johnson, and Coleridge—had generally been literary amateurs in the best sense, early twentieth-century criticism became increasingly the province of those who taught in universities. Historical research became a professional activity. Bradley himself was Professor of English Literature at Liverpool and Oxford, and did much to legitimize the incorporation of Shakespeare into the humanities curriculum. German scholarship produced the first regular periodical devoted to Shakespeare studies, *Shakespeare-Jahrbuch,* to be followed in due course in England and

America by *Shakespeare Survey* (beginning in 1948), *Shakespeare Quarterly* (1950), and *Shakespeare Studies* (1965).

From the start, historical criticism took a new look at Shakespeare as a man of the theater. Sir Walter Raleigh (Professor of English Literature at Oxford, not to be confused with his Elizabethan namesake) rejected the Romantic absorption in psychology and turned his attention instead to the artistic methods by which plays affect theater-going spectators. The poet Robert Bridges insisted that Shakespeare had often sacrificed consistency and logic for primitive theatrical effects designed to please his vulgar audience. Bridges's objections were often based on serious lack of information about Shakespeare's stage, but they had a healthy iconoclastic effect nonetheless on the scholarship of his time. In Germany, Levin Schücking pursued a similar line of reasoning in his *Character Problems in Shakespeare's Plays* (1917, translated into English in 1922). Schücking argued that Shakespeare had disregarded coherent structure and had striven instead for vivid dramatic effect ("episodic intensification") in his particular scenes. Schücking's *The Meaning of Hamlet* (1937) explained the strange contradictions of that play as resulting from primitive and brutal Germanic source materials which Shakespeare had not fully assimilated.

A keynote for historical critics of the early twentieth century was the concept of artifice or convention in the construction of a play. Perhaps the leading spokesman for this approach was E. E. Stoll, a student of G. L. Kittredge of Harvard University, himself a leading force in historical scholarship in America. Stoll vigorously insisted, in such works as *Othello: An Historical and Comparative Study* (1915), *Hamlet: An Historical and Comparative Study* (1919), and *Art and Artifice in Shakespeare* (1933), that a critic must never be sidetracked by moral, psychological, or biographical interpretations. A play, he argued, is an artifice arising out of its historical milieu. Its conventions are implicit agreements between playwright and spectator. They alter with time, and a modern reader who is ignorant of Elizabethan conventions is all too apt to be misled by his own post-Romantic preconceptions. For example, a calumniator like Iago in *Othello* is conventionally supposed to be believed by the other characters on stage. We do not need to speculate about the "realities" of Othello's being duped, and, in fact, we are likely to be led astray by such Romantic speculations. Stoll went so far as to affirm, in fact, that Shakespearean drama intentionally distorts reality through its theatrical conventions in order to fulfill its own existence as artifice. *Hamlet* is not a play about delay but a revenge story of a certain length, containing many conventional revenge motifs, such as the ghost and the "mousetrap" scheme used to test the villain, and deriving many of its circumstances from Shakespeare's sources; delay is a conventional device needed to continue the story to its conclusion.

Stoll's zeal led to excessive claims for historical criticism, as one might expect in the early years of a pioneering movement. At its extreme, historical criticism came close to implying that Shakespeare was a mere product of his environment. Indeed, the movement owed many of its evolutionist assumptions to the supposedly scientific "social Darwinism" of Thomas Huxley and other late nineteenth-century social philosophers. In more recent years, however, the crusading spirit has given way to a more moderate historical criticism that continues to be an important part of Shakespearean scholarship.

Alfred Harbage, for example, in *As They Liked It* (1947) and *Shakespeare and the Rival Traditions* (1952), has analyzed the audience for which Shakespeare wrote and the rivalry between popular and elite theaters in the London of his day. Harbage sees Shakespeare as a popular dramatist writing for a highly intelligent, enthusiastic, and socially diversified audience. More recently, in *The Privileged Playgoers of Shakespeare's London, 1576–1642* (1981), Ann Jennalie Cook has qualified Harbage's view, arguing that Shakespeare's audience was, for the most part, affluent and well connected. G. E. Bentley has amassed an invaluable storehouse of information about *The Jacobean and Caroline Stage* (1941–1968), just as E. K. Chambers earlier had collected documents and data on *The Elizabethan Stage* (1923). Other studies by these historical scholars include Chambers's *William Shakespeare: A Study of Facts and Problems* (1930), and Bentley's *Shakespeare and His Theatre* (1964) and *The Profession of Dramatist in Shakespeare's Time* (1971). T. W. Baldwin exemplifies the historical scholar who, like Stoll, claims too much for the method; nevertheless, much information on Shakespeare's schooling, reading, and professional theatrical life is available in such works as *William Shakspere's Small Latine and Lesse Greeke* (1944) and *The Organization and Personnel of the Shakespearean Company* (1927). Hardin Craig uses historical method in *An Interpretation of Shakespeare* (1948).

Historical criticism has contributed greatly to our knowledge of the staging of Shakespeare's plays. George Pierce Baker, in *The Development of Shakespeare as a Dramatist* (1907), continued the line of investigation begun by Walter Raleigh. Harley Granville-Barker brought to his *Prefaces to Shakespeare* (1930, 1946) a wealth of professional theatrical experience of his own. Ever since his time, the new theatrical method of interpreting Shakespeare has been based to an ever increasing extent on a genuine revival of interest in Shakespearean production. John Dover Wilson shows an awareness of the stage in *What Happens in Hamlet* (1935) and *The Fortunes of Falstaff* (1943). At its best, as in John Russell Brown's *Shakespeare's Plays in Performance* (1966), in John Styan's *Shakespeare's Stagecraft* (1967), in Michael Goldman's *Shakespeare and the Energies of Drama* (1972), and in Alan Dessen's *Elizabethan Drama and the Viewer's Eye* (1977) and his *Recovering Shakespeare's Theatrical Vocabulary* (1995), this critical method reveals many insights into the text that are hard to obtain without an awareness of theatrical technique.

Supporting this theatrical criticism, historical research has learned a great deal about the physical nature of Shakespeare's stage. J. C. Adams's well-known model of the Globe Playhouse, as presented in Irwin Smith's *Shakespeare's Globe Playhouse: A Modern Reconstruction* (1956), is now generally discredited in favor of a simpler building, as reconstructed by C. Walter Hodges (*The Globe Restored*, 1953, 2nd edition, 1968), Bernard Beckerman (*Shakespeare at the Globe*, 1962, 2nd edition, 1967), Richard Hosley ("The Playhouses and the Stage" in *A New Companion to Shakespeare Studies*, edited by K. Muir and S. Schoenbaum, 1971, and several other good essays), T. J. King (*Shakespearean Staging*, 1599–1642, 1971), and others. Information on the private theaters, such as the Blackfriars, where Shakespeare's plays were also performed, appears in William Armstrong, *The Elizabethan Private Theatres* (1958); Richard Hosley, "A Reconstruction of the Second Blackfriars" (*The Elizabethan Theatre*, 1969); Glynne Wickham, *Early English Stages* (1959–1972); and others. For further information on innyard theaters and on courtly or private theaters, see the contributions of Herbert Berry, D. F. Rowan, W. Reavley Gair, and others cited in the bibliography at the end of this volume.

A related pursuit of historical criticism has been the better understanding of Shakespeare through his dramatic predecessors and contemporaries. Willard Farnham, in *The Medieval Heritage of Elizabethan Tragedy* (1936), traces the evolution of native English tragedy through the morality plays of the early Tudor period. J. M. R. Margeson's *The Origins of English Tragedy* (1967) broadens the pattern to include still other sources for Elizabethan ideas on dramatic tragedy. Bernard Spivack, in *Shakespeare and the Allegory of Evil* (1958), sees Iago, Edmund, Richard III, and other boasting villains in Shakespeare as descendants of the morality Vice. In *Shakespeare and the Idea of the Play* (1962), Anne Righter (Barton) traces the device of the play-within-the-play and the metaphor of the world as a stage back to medieval and classical ideas of dramatic illusion. Irving Ribner's *The English History Play in the Age of Shakespeare* (1959, revised 1965) examines Shakespeare's plays on English history in the context of the popular Elizabethan genre to which they belonged. Robert Weimann's *Shakespeare and the Popular Tradition in the Theatre* (translated from the German in 1978) is a Marxist study in the social dimension of dramatic form and function. Many other studies of this sort could be cited, including Glynne Wickham's *Shakespeare's Dramatic Heritage* (1969), Oscar J. Campbell's *Shakespeare's Satire* (1943), M. C. Bradbrook's *Themes and Conventions of Elizabethan Tragedy* (1935), and S. L. Bethell's *Shakespeare and the Popular Dramatic Tradition* (1944).

Another important concern of historical criticism has been the relationship between Shakespeare and the ideas of his age—cosmological, philosophical, and political. Among the first scholars to study Elizabethan cosmology were Hardin Craig in *The Enchanted Glass* (1936) and A. O. Lovejoy in *The Great Chain of Being* (1936). As their successor, E. M. W. Tillyard provided in *The Elizabethan World Picture* (1943) a definitive view of the conservative and hierarchical values that Elizabethans were supposed to have espoused. In *Shakespeare's History Plays* (1944), Tillyard extended his essentially conservative view of Shakespeare's philosophical outlook to the histories, arguing that they embody a "Tudor myth" and thereby lend support to the Tudor state. Increasingly, however, critics have disputed the extent to which Shakespeare in fact endorsed the "establishment" values of the Elizabethan world picture. Theodore Spencer, in *Shakespeare and the Nature of Man* (1942), discusses the impact on Shakespeare of radical new thinkers like Machiavelli, Montaigne, and Copernicus. In political matters, Henry A. Kelly's *Divine Providence in the England of Shakespeare's Histories* (1970) has challenged the existence of a single "Tudor myth" and has argued that Shakespeare's history plays reflect contrasting political philosophies set dramatically in conflict with one another. M. M. Reese's *The Cease of Majesty* (1961) also offers a graceful corrective to Tillyard's lucid but occasionally one-sided interpretations. Revisions in this direction continue in the work of the so-called new historicists and cultural materialists, to be discussed below.

Historical criticism has also yielded many profitable specialized studies, in which Shakespeare is illuminated by a better understanding of various sciences of his day. Lily Bess Campbell approaches Shakespearean tragedy through Renaissance psychology in *Shakespeare's Tragic Heroes: Slaves of Passion* (1930). Paul Jorgensen uses Elizabethan documents on the arts of war and generalship in his study *Shakespeare's Military World* (1956). Many similar studies examine Shakespeare in relation to law, medicine, and other professions.

"New" Criticism

As we have seen, historical criticism is still an important part of Shakespeare criticism; for better or worse, it is the stuff of some research-oriented universities and their Ph.D. programs. Since its beginning, however, historical criticism has had to face a critical reaction, generated, in part, by its own utilitarian and fact-gathering tendencies. The suggestions urged by Stoll and others that Shakespeare was the product of his cultural and theatrical environment tended to obscure his achievement as a poet. Amassing of information about Shakespeare's reading or his theatrical company often seemed to inhibit the scholar from responding to the power of words and images.

Such at any rate was the rallying cry of the *Scrutiny* group in England, centered on F. R. Leavis, L. C. Knights, and Derek Traversi, and the "new" critics in America, such as Cleanth Brooks. The new critics demanded close attention to the poetry without the encumbrance of historical research. Especially at first, the new critics were openly hostile to any criticism distracting readers from the text. The satirical force of the movement can perhaps best be savored in L. C. Knights's "How Many Children Had Lady Macbeth?" (1933), prompted by the learned appendices in Bradley's *Shakespearean Tragedy*: "When was the murder of Duncan first plotted? Did Lady Macbeth really faint? Duration of the action in *Macbeth*. Macbeth's age. 'He has no children.'"

In part, the new critical movement was (and still is) a pedagogical movement, a protest against the potential dryness of historical footnoting and an insistence that classroom study of Shakespeare ought to focus on a response to his language. Cleanth Brooks's "The Naked Babe and the Cloak of Manliness" (in *The Well Wrought Urn*, 1947) offers to the teacher a model of close reading that focuses on imagery and yet attempts to see a whole vision of the play through its language. G. Wilson Knight concentrates on imagery and verbal texture, sometimes to the exclusion of the play as a whole, in his *The Wheel of Fire* (1930), *The Imperial Theme* (1931), *The Shakespearian Tempest* (1932), *The Crown of Life* (1947), and others. William Empson is best known for his *Seven Types of Ambiguity* (1930) and *Some Versions of Pastoral* (1935). Derek Traversi's works include *An Approach to Shakespeare* (1938), *Shakespeare: The Last Phase* (1954), *Shakespeare: From Richard II to Henry V* (1957), and *Shakespeare: The Roman Plays* (1963). Perhaps the greatest critic of this school has been L. C. Knights, whose books include *Explorations* (1946), *Some Shakespearean Themes* (1959), *An Approach to Hamlet* (1960), and *Further Explorations* (1965). T. S. Eliot's perceptive and controversial observations have also had an important influence on critics of this school. Other studies making good use of the new critical method include Robert Heilman's *This Great Stage* (1948) and *Magic in the Web* (1956). Many of these critics are concerned not only with language but also with the larger moral and structural implications of Shakespeare's plays as discovered through a sensitive reading of the text.

More specialized studies of Shakespearean imagery and language include Caroline Spurgeon's *Shakespeare's Imagery and What It Tells Us* (1935). Its classifications are now recognized to be overly statistical and restricted in definition, but the work has nonetheless prompted valuable further study. Among later works are Sister Miriam Joseph's *Shakespeare's Use of the Arts of Language* (1947, partly reprinted in *Rhetoric in Shakespeare's Time*, 1962), Wolfgang Clemen's *The Development of Shakespeare's Imagery* (1951), and M. M. Mahood's *Shakespeare's Wordplay* (1957). The study of prose has not received as much attention as that of poetry, although Brian Vickers's *The Artistry of Shakespeare's Prose* (1968) and Milton Crane's *Shakespeare's Prose* (1951) make significant contributions. See also Edward Armstrong's *Shakespeare's Imagination* (1963) and Kirby Farrell's *Shakespeare's Creation: The Language of Magic and Play* (1975).

A more recent development in studies of Shakespeare's imagery has led to the examination of visual images in the theater as part of Shakespeare's art. Reginald Foakes ("Suggestions for a New Approach to Shakespeare's Imagery," *Shakespeare Survey*, 5, 1952, 81–92) and Maurice Charney (*Shakespeare's Roman Plays: The Function of Imagery in the Drama*, 1961) were among the first to notice that Caroline Spurgeon and other "new" critics usually excluded stage picture in their focus on verbal image patterns. Yet Shakespeare's extensive involvement with the practicalities of theatrical production might well lead one to suspect that he arranges his stage with care and that the plays are full of hints as to how he communicates through visual means. Costume, properties, the theater building, the blocking of actors in visual patterns onstage, expression, movement—all of these contribute to the play's artistic whole. Francis Fergusson analyzes the way in which the Elizabethan theatrical building provides *Hamlet* with an eloquently expressive idea of order and hierarchy, against which are ironically juxtaposed Claudius's acts of killing a king and marrying his widow (*The Idea of a Theater*, 1949). Other studies of stage imagery include Ann Pasternak Slater's *Shakespeare the Director* (1982) and David Bevington's *Action Is Eloquence: Shakespeare's Language of Gesture* (1984).

Another call for expansion of the occasionally narrow limits of "new" criticism comes from the so-called Chicago school of criticism, centered on R. S. Crane, Richard McKeon, Elder Olson, Bernard Weinberg, and others, who, in the 1950s and 1960s, espoused a formal or structural approach to criticism, using Aristotle as its point of departure. Crane was reacting to the new critics who, in his view, restricted the kinds of answers they could obtain by limiting themselves to one methodology. Critics hostile to the Chicago school have responded, to be sure, that Crane's own approach tends to produce its own dogmatism. Formalist analyses of Shakespeare plays are to be found, for example, in the work of W. R. Keast, Wayne Booth, and Norman Maclean; see *Critics and Criticism*, edited by R. S. Crane (1952) and the bibliography at the back of this book.

Psychological Criticism

In a sense, Freudian and other psychological criticism continues the "character" criticism of the nineteenth century. Freudian critics sometimes follow a character into a world outside the text, analyzing Hamlet (for instance) as though he were a real person whose childhood traumas can be inferred from the symptoms he displays. The most famous work in this vein is *Hamlet and Oedipus* (1910, revised 1949), by Freud's disciple, Ernest Jones. According to Jones, Hamlet's delay is caused by an oedipal trauma. Hamlet's uncle, Claudius, has done exactly what Hamlet himself incestuously and subconsciously wished to do: kill his father and marry his mother. Because he cannot articulate these forbidden impulses to himself, Hamlet is paralyzed into inactivity. Jones's critical analysis thus assumes, as did such Romantic critics as Coleridge, that the central problem of *Hamlet* is one of character and motivation: why does Hamlet delay? (Many modern critics would deny that this is a problem or would insist, at least, that by setting such a problem, Jones has limited the number of possible answers. Avi Erlich proposes an entirely different psychological reading of the play in *Hamlet's Absent Father*, 1977.) Psychological criticism sometimes also reveals its affinities with nineteenth-century character criticism in its attempt to analyze Shakespeare's personality through his plays, as though the works constituted a spiritual autobiography. The terminology of psychological criticism is suspect to some readers because it is at least superficially anachronistic when dealing with a Renaissance writer. The terminology is also sometimes overburdened with technical jargon.

Nonetheless, psychological criticism has afforded many insights into Shakespeare not readily available through other modes of perception. Jones's book makes clear the intensity of Hamlet's revulsion toward women as a result of his mother's inconstancy. At a mythic level, Hamlet's story certainly resembles that of Oedipus, and Freudian criticism is often at its best when it shows us this universal aspect of the human psyche. Freudian terminology need not be anachronistic when it deals with timeless truths. Psychological criticism can reveal to us Shakespeare's preoccupation with certain types of women in his plays, such as the domineering and threatening masculine type (Joan of Arc, Margaret of Anjou) or, conversely, the long-suffering and patient heroine (Helena in *All's Well*, Hermione in *The Winter's Tale*). Psychological criticism is perhaps most useful in studying family relationships in Shakespeare. It also has much to say about the psychic or sexual connotations of symbols. Influential books include Norman O. Brown's *Life Against Death: The Psychoanalytical Meaning of History* (1959) and Norman Holland's *Psychoanalysis and Shakespeare* (1966) and *The Shakespearean Imagination* (1964).

Richard Wheeler's *Turn and Counter-Turn: Shakespeare's Development and the Problem Comedies* (1981) applies psychoanalytic method to a study of Shakespeare's development, in which, as Wheeler sees it, the sonnets and the problem plays are pivotal as Shakespeare turns from the safely contained worlds of romantic comedy (with non-threatening heroines) and the English history play (in which women are generally denied anything more than a marginal role in state affairs) to the tragedies, in which sexual conflict is shown in all its potentially terrifying destructiveness. Wheeler's completion of C. L. Barber's *The Whole Journey: Shakespeare's Power of Development* (1986) continues the study of Shakespeare's development in the late plays. The dichotomies of gender and genre urged in these studies and continued by Linda Bamber (*Comic Women, Tragic Men: A Study of Gender and Genre in Shakespeare*, 1982), among others, have been challenged by Jonathan Goldberg in his essay, "Shakespearean Inscriptions: The Voicing of Power," in *Shakespeare and the Question of Theory* (edited by Patricia Parker and Geoffrey Hartman, 1985). A collection of essays under the editorship of Murray Schwartz and Coppélia Kahn, *Representing Shakespeare* (1980), affords a sample of work by Janet Adelman, David Willbern, Meredith Skura, David Sundelson, Madelon Gohlke Sprengnether, Joel Fineman, and others.

Much psychoanalytic criticism of the 1980s has sought to displace Freud's emphasis upon the relation of son and father in the oedipal triangle in favor of attention to the mother and child preoedipal relation; a model here is the work of Karen Horney (e.g., *Neurosis and Human Growth: The Struggle Toward Self-Realization*, 1950). Jacques Lacan (*Écrits*, translated by Alan Sheridan, 1977) and Erik Erikson (*Childhood and Selfhood*, 1978) are also prominent theorists in the post-Freudian era. Despite such changes, the psychoanalytic critic still attempts to discover in the language of the play the means by which he or she can reconstruct an early stage in the development of one or more of the dramatic characters.

Mythological Criticism

Related to psychological criticism is the search for archetypal myth in literature, as an expression of the "collective unconscious" of the human race. Behind such an approach lie the anthropological and psychological assumptions of Jung and his followers. One of the earliest studies of this sort was Gilbert Murray's *Hamlet and Orestes* (1914), analyzing the archetype of revenge for a murdered father. Clearly this custom goes far back into tribal prehistory and emerges in varying but interrelated forms in many different societies. This anthropological universality enables us to look at Hamlet as the heightened manifestation of an incredibly basic story. *Hamlet* gives shape to urgings that are a part of our innermost social being. The struggle between the civilized and the primitive goes on in us as in the play *Hamlet*.

The vast interdisciplinary character of mythological criticism leaves it vulnerable to charges of speculativeness and glib theorizing. At its best, however, mythological criticism can illuminate the nature of our responses as audience to a work of art. Northrop Frye argues, in *A Natural Perspective* (1965), that we respond to mythic patterns by imagining ourselves participating in them communally. The Greek drama emerged, after all, from

Dionysiac ritual. All drama celebrates in one form or another the primal myths of vegetation, from the death of the year to the renewal or resurrection of life. In his most influential book, *Anatomy of Criticism* (1957), Frye argues that mythic criticism presents a universal scheme for the investigation of all literature, or all art, since art is itself the ordering of our most primal stirrings. Frye sees in drama (as in other literature) a fourfold correspondence to the cyclical pattern of the year: comedy is associated with spring, romance with summer, tragedy with autumn, and satire with winter. Historically, civilization moves through a recurrent cycle from newness to decadence and decay; this cycle expresses itself culturally in a progression from epic and romance to tragedy, to social realism, and, finally, to irony and satire before the cycle renews itself. Thus, according to Frye, the genres of dramatic literature (and of other literary forms as well) have an absolute and timeless relationship to myth and cultural history. That is why we as audience respond so deeply to form and meaning as contained in genre. C. L. Barber, in *Shakespeare's Festive Comedy* (1959), makes a similar argument: our enjoyment of comedy arises from our intuitive appreciation of such "primitive" social customs as Saturnalian revels, May games, and fertility rites. John Holloway offers an anthropological study of Shakespeare's tragedies in *The Story of the Night* (1961).

Frye's critical system has not been without its detractors. For example, Frederick Crews (*Psychoanalysis and Literary Process,* 1970) argues that Frye's system is too self-contained in its ivory tower and too much an abstract artifact of the critical mind to be "relevant" to the social purposes of art. Nevertheless, Frye continues to be one of the most influential critics of the late twentieth century.

Typological Criticism

Another controversy of the later twentieth century has to do with the Christian interpretation of Shakespeare. Do the images and allusions of Shakespeare's plays show him to be deeply immersed in a Christian culture inherited from the Middle Ages? Does he reveal a typological cast of mind, so common in medieval literature, whereby a story can suggest through analogy a universal religious archetype? For example, does the mysterious Duke in *Measure for Measure* suggest to us a God figure, hovering unseen throughout the play to test human will and then to present humanity with an omniscient but merciful judgment? Is the wanton slaughter of the good Cordelia in *King Lear* reminiscent of the Passion of Christ? Can Portia in *The Merchant of Venice* be seen as an angelic figure descending from Belmont into the fallen human world of Venice? Often the operative question we must ask is: "How far should such analogy be pursued?" Richard II unquestionably likens himself to Christ betrayed by the disciples, and at times the play evokes images of Adam

banished from Paradise, but do these allusions coalesce into a sustained analogy?

Among the most enthusiastic searchers after Christian meaning are J. A. Bryant, in *Hippolyta's View* (1961); Roy Battenhouse, in *Shakespearean Tragedy: Its Art and Christian Premises* (1969); and R. Chris Hassel, in *Renaissance Drama and the English Church* (1979) and *Faith and Folly in Shakespeare: Romantic Comedies* (1980). Their efforts have encountered stern opposition, however. One notable dissenter is Roland M. Frye, whose *Shakespeare and Christian Doctrine* (1963) argues that Shakespeare cannot be shown to have known much Renaissance theology and that, in any case, his plays are concerned with human drama rather than with otherworldly questions of damnation or salvation. Frye's argument stresses the incompatibility of Christianity and tragedy, as do also D. G. James's *The Dream of Learning* (1951) and Clifford Leech's *Shakespeare's Tragedies and Other Studies in Seventeenth-Century Drama* (1950). Virgil Whitaker's *The Mirror Up to Nature* (1965) sees religion as an essential element in Shakespeare's plays but argues that Shakespeare uses the religious knowledge of his audience as a shortcut to characterization and meaning, rather than as an ideological weapon. The controversy will doubtless long continue, even though the typological critics have had to assume a defensive posture.

Jan Kott and the Theater of the Absurd

At an opposite extreme from the Christian idealism of most typological critics is the iconoclasm of those who have been disillusioned by recent events in history. One who brilliantly epitomizes political disillusionment in the aftermath of World War II, especially in Eastern Europe, is Jan Kott. The evocative debunking of romantic idealism set forth in his *Shakespeare Our Contemporary* (1964, translated from the Polish) has enjoyed enormous influence since the 1960s, especially in the theater. Kott sees Shakespeare as a dramatist of the absurd and the grotesque. In this view, Shakespearean plays are often close to "black" comedy or comedy of the absurd, as defined by Antonin Artaud (*The Theatre and Its Double,* 1958) and Jerzy Grotowski (*Towards a Poor Theatre,* 1968). Indeed, Kott has inspired productions that expose traditional values to skepticism and ridicule. Portia and Bassanio in *The Merchant of Venice* become scheming adventurers; Henry V becomes a priggish warmonger. History is for Kott a nightmare associated with his country's experience in World War II, and Shakespeare's modernity can be seen in his sardonic portrayal of political opportunism and violence. Even *A Midsummer Night's Dream* is a play of disturbingly erotic brutality, Kott argues. Here is an interpretation of Shakespeare that was bound to have an enormous appeal in a world confronted by the assassinations of the Kennedys and Martin Luther King, Jr.; by incessant war in the Middle East, Southeast Asia, and much of the third world; by the threat of nuclear annihilation and ecological disaster; and by political leadership generally perceived as interested only in the public-relations techniques of self-preservation. An essentially ironic view of politics and, more broadly, of human nature has informed a good deal of criticism since Kott's day and has led to the dethronement of E. M. W. Tillyard and his essentially positive view of English patriotism and heroism in the history plays.

New Historicism and Cultural Materialism

A more recent way of investigating Shakespeare through the demystifying perspective of modern experience—the so-called new historicism— has focused on the themes of political self-fashioning and role playing in terms of power and subversion. This critical school has paid close attention to historians and cultural anthropologists like Lawrence Stone (*The Crisis of the Aristocracy,* 1558–1641, 1965) and Clifford Geertz (*Negara: The Theatre State in Nineteenth-Century Bali,* 1980), who explore new ways of looking at the relationship between historical change and the myths generated to bring it about or to retain power. Geertz analyzes the way in which the ceremonies and myths of political rule can, in effect, become a self-fulfilling reality; kings and other leaders, acting out their roles in ceremonials designed to encapsulate the myth of their greatness and divine origin, essentially become what they have created in their impersonations of power. Such a view of political authority is an inherently skeptical one, seeing government as a process of manipulating illusions. When Shakespeare's English history plays—or indeed any plays dealing with conflicts of authority—are analyzed in these terms, subversion and containment become important issues. Do the plays of Shakespeare and other Renaissance dramatists celebrate the power of the Tudor monarchs, or do they question and undermine assumptions of hierarchy? Did Elizabethan drama serve to increase skepticism and pressure for change, or was it, conversely, a way of easing that pressure so that the power structure could remain in force?

The "new historicism" is a name applied to a kind of literary criticism practiced in America, prominently by Stephen Greenblatt. Especially influential have been his *Renaissance Self-Fashioning* (1980), *Shakespearean Negotiations* (1988), and his editing of the journal *Representations*. Those who pursue similar concerns, including Louis Montrose, Stephen Orgel, Richard Helgerson, Don E. Wayne, Frank Whigham, Richard Strier, Jonathan Goldberg, David Scott Kastan, and Steven Mullaney, share Greenblatt's goals to a greater or lesser extent and think of themselves only with important reservations as "new historicists"; the term is misleadingly categorical, and Greenblatt, among others, is eager to enlarge the

parameters of the method rather than to allow it to harden into an orthodoxy. (Greenblatt, in fact, prefers the term "poetics of culture" to "new historicism," even though the latter phrase remains better known.) Still, these critics do generally share a number of common concerns. Among the ways in which new historicists seek to separate themselves from earlier historical critics is by denying that the work of art is a unified and self-contained product of an independent creator in masterful control of the meaning of the work. Instead, the new historicists represent the work as shot through with the multiple and contradictory discourses of its time. New historicists also deny the notion that art merely "reflects" its historical milieu; instead, they argue that art is caught up in, and contributes to, the social practices of its time. Although the boundary between new and old historical criticism is often hard to draw, in general the new historicists are apt to be skeptical of the accepted canon of literary texts and are drawn to a markedly politicized reading of Renaissance plays. One finds everywhere in the new historicism a deep ambivalence toward political authority.

Mikhail Bakhtin's provocative ideas on carnival (*L'Oeuvre de François Rabelais et la Culture Populaire du Moyen Age,* 1970) have had an important influence in new historical circles, as reflected, for example, in the work of Michael Bristol (*Carnival and Theatre: Plebeian Culture and the Structure of Authority in Renaissance England,* 1985), Peter Stallybrass, Gail Paster, and others. Like new historicism, this critical approach looks at so-called high cultural entertainment, including Shakespeare, in relation to the practices of popular culture, thereby breaking down the distinction between "high" and "popular." Literary and nonliterary texts are subjected to the same kind of serious scrutiny. Popular origins of the theater receive new attention, as in Robert Weimann's *Shakespeare and the Popular Tradition in the Theater: Studies in the Social Dimension of Dramatic Form and Function* (published in German in 1967 and in English translation in 1978).

Cultural materialism, in Britain, takes an analogous approach to the dethroning of canonical texts and the emphasis on art as deeply implicated in the social practices of its time but differs from American new historicism on the issue of change. New historicism is sometimes criticized for its lack of a model for change and for its reluctant belief, instead (in Greenblatt's formulation especially), that all attempts at subversion through art are destined to be contained by power structures in society; art permits the expression of heterodox points of view, but only as a way of letting off steam, as it were, and thereby easing the pressures for actual radical change. British cultural materialism, in contrast, is more avowedly committed not only to radical political interpretation but also to rapid political change, partly in response to what are perceived to be more deeply rooted class differences than are found in

America. Jonathan Dollimore's *Radical Tragedy* (1984) and *Political Shakespeare* (1985), edited by Dollimore and Alan Sinfield, enlist the dramatist on the side of class struggle. So do *Alternative Shakespeares*, edited by John Drakakis (1985), and Terry Eagleton's *Shakespeare and Society* (1967) and *William Shakespeare* (1986). Raymond Williams, not himself a Shakespearean critic, is an acknowledged godfather of the movement.

Feminist Criticism

Feminist criticism is such an important and diverse field that it has necessarily and productively reached into a number of related disciplines, such as cultural anthropology and its wealth of information about family structures. In his *The Elementary Structures of Kinship* (1949, translated 1969) and other books, Claude Lévi-Strauss analyzes the way in which men, as fathers and as husbands, control the transfer of women from one family to another in an "exogamous" marital system designed to strengthen commercial and other ties among men. Recent feminist criticism has had a lot to say about patriarchal structures in the plays and poems of Shakespeare, some of it building upon Lévi-Strauss's analysis of patriarchy; see, for example, Karen Newman, "Portia's Ring: Unruly Women and Structures of Exchange in *The Merchant of Venice*," *Shakespeare Quarterly*, 38 (1987), 10–33, and Lynda Boose, "The Father and the Bride in Shakespeare," *PMLA*, 97 (1982), 325–47. Coppélia Kahn has examined the ideology of rape in *The Rape of Lucrece*, showing how the raped woman is devalued by the shame that attaches to her husband, even though she is innocent (*Shakespeare Studies*, 9, 1976, 45–72).

Another important source of insight for feminist criticism is the anthropological work on rites of passage by Arnold Van Gennep (*The Rites of Passage*, translated by M. B. Vizedom and G. L. Caffee, 1960) and Victor Turner (*The Ritual Process*, 1969), among others. The focus here is on the dangers of transition at times of birth, puberty, marriage, death, and other turning points of human life. Feminist criticism, in dealing with such crises of transition, concerns itself not only with women's roles but also, more broadly, with gender relations, with family structures, and with the problems that males encounter in their quest for mature sexual identity. Coppélia Kahn's *Man's Estate; Masculine Identity in Shakespeare* (1981) looks particularly at the difficulty of the male in confronting the hazards of maturity. Robert Watson's *Shakespeare and the Hazards of Ambition* (1984) also looks at the male in the political context of career and self-fashioning. Marjorie Garber's *Coming of Age in Shakespeare* (1981) takes a broad look at maturation.

As these titles suggest, the models are often psychological, as well as anthropological. One focus of feminist criticism is the role of women in love and marriage. Feminist critics disagree among themselves as to whether the portrait painted by Shakespeare and other Elizabethan dramatists is a hopeful one, as argued, for example, by Juliet Dusinberre in *Shakespeare and the Nature of Women* (1975, 1996), or repressive, as argued by Lisa Jardine in *Still Harping on Daughters: Women and Drama in the Age of Shakespeare* (1983). Recent historians add an important perspective, especially Lawrence Stone in his *The Family, Sex, and Marriage in England, 1500–1800* (1977). Did the Protestant emphasis on marriage as a morally elevated and reciprocal relationship have the paradoxical effect of arousing in men an increased hostility and wariness toward women and a resulting increase in repression and violence? Or, as David Underdown suggests, should we look to economic explanations of hostility and wariness toward women in the Renaissance? His studies indicate that repression of women is greatest in regions of the country where their place in the economy offers the possibility of their having some control over family finances. (See *Revel, Riot, and Rebellion: Popular Culture in England, 1603–1660*, 1985, pp. 73–105, especially p. 99.)

Certainly, recent criticism has paid a lot of attention to male anxieties about women in Shakespeare's plays, as various male protagonists resolve to teach women a lesson (*The Taming of the Shrew*), succumb to dark fantasies of female unfaithfulness (*Much Ado About Nothing, Othello*), or are overwhelmed by misogynistic revulsion (*Hamlet, King Lear*). It is as though Shakespeare, in his plays and poems, works through the problems that men experience throughout their lives in their relationships with women, from the insecurities of courtship to the desire for possession and control in marriage, and from jealous fears of betrayal to the longing for escape into middle-age sexual adventure (as in *Antony and Cleopatra*). The late plays show us the preoccupation of the aging male with the marriages of his daughters (another form of betrayal) and with the approach of death.

Recently, feminist criticism has begun to increase its historical consciousness. Critics such as Gail Paster, Jean Howard, Phyllis Rackin, Dympna Callaghan, Lorraine Helms, Jyotsna Singh, Alison Findlay, Lisa Jardine, and Karen Newman focus on the construction of gender in early modern England in terms of social and material conditions, abandoning the nonhistorical psychological model of earlier feminist criticism. See the bibliography at the end of this book for feminist studies by these and other feminist critics, including Catherine Belsey, Carol Neely, Peter Erickson, Meredith Skura, Marianne Novy, Margo Hendricks, Kim Hall, Philippa Berry, Frances Dolan, Mary Beth Rose, Valerie Traub, Susan Zimmerman, Lynda Boose, and Ania Loomba. Gender studies concerned with issues of same-sex relationships have made important contributions in recent years, in the work of Bruce Smith,

Laurie Shannon, Jonathan Goldberg, Stephen Orgel, Leonard Barkan, Mario DiGangi, and others.

Poststructuralism and Deconstruction

A major influence today in Shakespeare criticism, as in virtually all literary criticism of recent date, is the school of analysis known as poststructuralism or deconstruction; the terms, though not identical, significantly overlap. This school derives its inspiration originally from the work of certain French philosophers and critics, chief among whom are Ferdinand de Saussure, a specialist in linguistics, Michel Foucault, a historian of systems of discourse, and Jacques Derrida, perhaps the most highly visible exponent and practitioner of deconstruction. The ideas of these men were first introduced into American literary criticism by scholars at Yale such as Geoffrey Hartman, J. Hillis Miller, and Paul de Man. The ideas are controversial and difficult.

Poststructuralism and deconstruction begin with an insistence that language is a system of difference—one in which the signifiers (such as words and gestures) are essentially arbitrary to the extent that "meaning" and "authorial intention" are virtually impossible to fix precisely; that is, language enjoys a potentially infinite subjectivity. To an extent, this approach to the subjectivity of meaning in a work of art resembles "new" criticism in its mistrust of "message" in literature, but the new method goes further. It resists all attempts at paraphrase, for example, insisting that the words of a text cannot be translated into other words without altering something vital; indeed, there is no way of knowing if an author's words will strike any two readers or listeners in the same way. The very concept of an author has been challenged by Michel Foucault ("What Is an Author?" in *Language, Counter-Memory, Practice,* edited by Donald F. Bouchard, 1977). Deconstruction proclaims that there is no single identifiable author in the traditional sense; instead of a single text, we have a potentially infinite number of texts.

Both the theory and practice of deconstruction remain highly controversial. Although poststructuralism and deconstruction owe a debt to the general philosophical theory of signs and symbols known as semiotics, in which the function of linguistic signs is perceived to be artificially constructed, the new method also calls into question the very distinctions on which the discipline of semiotics is based. Derrida builds upon the work of Saussure and yet goes well beyond him in an insistence that words (signifiers) be left in play rather than attached to their alleged meaning (signifieds). Frank Lentricchia (*After the New Criticism,* 1980) takes the Yale school critics to task for interpreting Derrida in too formalist and apolitical a sense. Despite disagreements among theorists, nevertheless, the approach has deeply influenced Shakespeare criticism as a whole by urging critics to consider the suppleness with which signifiers (words) in the Shakespearean text are converted by listeners and readers into some approximation of meaning.

The ramifications of poststructuralism and deconstruction are increasingly felt in other forms of criticism, even those at least nominally at odds with poststructuralist assumptions. Some radical textual critics, for example, are fascinated by the unsettling prospects of the deconstructed text. What does one edit and how does one go about editing when words are to be left in play, to the infinite regress of meaning? The problems are acutely examined in a collection of essays called *The Division of the Kingdom,* edited by Gary Taylor and Michael Warren, on the two early and divergent texts of *King Lear* (1983). The method of linguistic analysis known as "speech-act theory," developed by the philosopher Warren Austin as a way of exploring how we perform certain linguistic acts when we swear oaths or make asseverations and the like, is sharply at variance with deconstruction in its premises about a correlation between speech and intended meaning, and yet it, too, can help us understand the instability of spoken or written language in Shakespeare. Joseph Porter's *The Drama of Speech Acts* (1979), for example, looks at ways in which Shakespeare's characters in the plays about Henry IV and Henry V reveal, through their language of oath making and oath breaking, asseveration, and the like, their linguistic adaptability or lack of adaptability to historical change. Richard II resists historical change in the very way he speaks; Prince Hal embraces it. A third related field of analysis that is interested in the instability of meaning in Shakespeare's texts is metadramatic criticism, where the focus is on ways in which dramatic texts essentially talk about the drama itself, about artistic expression, and about the artist's quest for immortality in art. James Calderwood's *Shakespearean Metadrama* (1971) is an influential example.

At its extreme, then, deconstructive criticism comes close to undermining all kinds of "meaningfulness" in artistic utterance and to being thus at war with other methods of interpretation. Still, deconstruction continues to remain influential, because it also usefully challenges complacent formulations of meaning and because it promotes such a subtle view of linguistic complexity.

At its best, late twentieth-century criticism transcends the splintering effect of a heterogeneous critical tradition to achieve a synthesis that is at once unified and multiform in its vision. The pluralistic approach aims at overall balance and a reinforcement of one critical approach through the methodology of another. Many of the works already cited in this introduction refuse to be constricted by methodological boundaries. The best historical criticism makes use of close explication of the text where appropriate; image patterns can certainly reinforce mythological patterns; typological interpretation, when sensibly applied, serves the cause of image study. Some fine books are so eclectic in their method that one hesitates to apply the label of any one critical school. Among such works are Maynard Mack's *King Lear in Our Time* (1965), David Young's *Something of Great Constancy: The Art of A Midsummer Night's Dream* (1966), R. G. Hunter's *Shakespeare and the Comedy of Forgiveness* (1965), Janet Adelman's *The Common Liar: An Essay on "Antony and Cleopatra"* (1973), Stanley Cavell's "The Avoidance of Love: A Reading of King Lear," in *Must We Mean What We Say?* (1969, reprinted in *Disowning Knowledge in Six Plays of Shakespeare,* 1987), and Paul Jorgensen's *Our Naked Frailties: Sensational Art and Meaning in Macbeth* (1971).

Into the Twenty-First Century

The sense of where we are in the twenty-first century in Shakespeare criticism reflects the uncertainties and guardedly hopeful expectations of the academic profession as a whole. The period of the 1970s and 1980s, described previously, was one of extraordinary ferment, brought on by a host of developments: the Vietnam War and its aftermath, the assassinations of the Kennedys and Martin Luther King, the impact of French linguistic and philosophical thought on American intellectual writing, the frustrations of many academics with Reaganomics and their consequent fascination with British Marxism, emerging demands on behalf of minorities and women, a revolution in social and sexual mores accompanied by a backlash in the name of "family values," conflict over American foreign policy in the Middle East (Israel, Iraq), and much more. The result was what must be regarded as a genuine revolution in methods of critical analysis and reading. The literary text became multivalent, ambiguous, deconstructed, dethroned as a unique artifact, and was seen, instead, as a product of and contributing to its social and intellectual environment. The author became a construction of criticism and of a new kind of literary history.

Shakespeare studies have taken a lead in all of this new exploration. Although one of the postmodern demands has been for a recanonizing of literature in favor of newer literature, works by women and minorities, and works from countries other than Britain and the United States instead of the traditional canon of dead white European males, Shakespeare not only has survived this recanonization but also has become more prominent than ever. Other Renaissance writers such as Ben Jonson, John Webster, Thomas Dekker, Thomas Nashe, John Lyly, Edmund Spenser, and even Christopher Marlowe, John Milton, and John Donne have been the victims of declining enrollments in classes generally, but Shakespeare triumphs. Why?

One compelling answer is that Shakespeare is simply indispensable to postmodern critical inquiry. His texts are so extraordinarily responsive that new questions put to them—about the changing role of women, about cynicism in the political process, about the protean near-indeterminacy of meaning in language—evoke insights that are hard to duplicate in other literary texts. Shakespeare does not seem out of date. The very impulse of so much recent criticism to claim Shakespeare as "our contemporary," attuned to our own skepticisms and disillusionment and even despair (as in the writings of Jan Kott, for example), attests to his unparalleled engagement with the issues about which we care so deeply. Even those who argue that Shakespeare exhibits the male hang-ups of a patriarchal society and that he is a social snob who glorifies aristocracy and warfare do not see Shakespeare as a writer who is out of touch with the values of our contemporary society but, rather, as one who gives eloquent testimonial to structures that were alive in our cultural past and with which we sense a continuum today even if outward circumstances have changed. The best scholarship does not condemn Shakespeare for believing in kingship or for sometimes showing men as victorious in the battle of the sexes; instead, that criticism is interested in the whole process of the literary text's participation in the creation of culture. Even when recent scholarship is concerned with examining class and gender issues to clarify some of the systematic oppressiveness of early modern culture, it does so generally in an attempt to negotiate the relationship of the present to the past, rather than assuming a superiority in our modern world's approaches to issues of class, gender, and ethnicity.

To be sure, a number of Shakespeare's plays are in trouble today because they make us uncomfortable about these issues. *The Merchant of Venice* is, in the eyes of many, almost unproduceable, because the anti-Semitic emotions it explores are so distasteful. It is less often assigned now in classrooms than it once was, even though, when it is taught or produced onstage, it can lead to extraordinarily searching discussions of painful but real issues. The same is true of *The Taming of the Shrew,* which is being taken from the shelves of more than a few libraries because of its apparent flaunting of sexist behavior toward women. *Othello* offends some readers and viewers because of its racist language and, in the view of some, racial stereotypes. Yet, the power of Shakespeare's language continues to exert its spell despite, and in part because of, these troubling conflicts over the role of dramatic art in modern society.

The world of Shakespeare criticism today, after two decades or so of revolution, is seemingly one of consolidation. At a March 1995 meeting of the Shakespeare Association of America in Chicago, many conferees wondered: Where is the profession going? What are the hot new issues? Who are the new critics that no one wants to miss? And, in fact, there seemed to be little dramatic excitement of this sort, little agreement as to any discernible new trend. To some, this is frustrating. Where does one turn for real creativity after a thoroughgoing revolution such as we have experienced?

To others, a time of stocktaking is potentially healthy. There seems to be relatively little interest in turning the clock back; postmodernism and indeterminacy have changed the critical landscape for better and for worse. Now that this new landscape begins to seem familiar, however, new members of the profession seem less anxious to resolve their own identity crises in terms of affiliating with some critical school or other. The critical challenges are there, not so stridently new as they were ten years ago, and adaptable to various uses.

The result is increasing variety in the kinds of critical work being done. Some of it is recognizably traditional, dealing with stage history and conditions of performance during Shakespeare's lifetime, as, for example, in T. J. King, *Casting Shakespeare's Plays: London Actors and Their Roles* (1992); William Ingram, *The Business of Playing: The Beginnings of the Adult Professional Theater in Elizabethan London* (1992); David Bradley, *From Text to Performance in the Elizabethan Theatre: Preparing the Play for the Stage* (1992); David Mann, *The Elizabethan Player: Contemporary Stage Representation* (1991); John H. Astington, ed., *The Development of Shakespeare's Theater* (1992); Andrew Gurr, *Playgoing in Shakespeare's London* (1987, 2nd edition, 1996) and *The Shakespearian Playing Companies* (1996); and Roslyn Lander Knutson, *The Repertory of Shakespeare's Company, 1594–1613* (1991). Background and historical studies of the conditions that helped produce Shakespeare's theater can sometimes be informatively revisionist in the sense of toppling cherished older notions without at the same time being postmodern in approach. Examples here might include Richard Dutton, *Mastering the Revels: The Regulation and Censorship of English Renaissance Drama* (1991); Scott McMillin and Sally-Beth MacLean, *The Queen's Men and Their Plays* (1998); and Leeds Barroll, *Politics, Plague, and Shakespeare's Theater: The Stuart Years* (1991).

Other studies are more openly revisionist in a postmodern vein, sometimes in dealing with hypotheses about bibliography and textual studies, as in Margreta de Grazia, *Shakespeare Verbatim: The Reproduction of Authenticity and the 1790 Apparatus* (1991) and Grace Ioppolo, *Revising Shakespeare* (1991). The New Folger Library Shakespeare, edited by Barbara Mowat and Paul Werstine (1992—), gives a more measured approach. The Arden Shakespeare is currently bringing out new critical editions of all the plays in individual volumes (Arden 3), as are the New Cambridge Shakespeare and the Oxford Shakespeare. Occasionally a conservative counterblast is heard, as in Brian Vickers's entertaining, learned, and feisty polemic, *Appropriating Shakespeare: Contemporary Critical Quarrels* (1993). A forum of essays edited by Ivo Kamps, called *Shakespeare Left and Right,* gives us a chance to weigh arguments from various sides.

What the contemporary critical scene does best is to free critics to be who they are and to write without paying dues to any particular affiliation. The results are refreshingly diverse. Among the books that show this spread of critical approaches are Karen Newman, *Fashioning Femininity and the English Renaissance Drama* (1991); Bruce R. Smith, *Homosexual Desire in Shakespeare's England* (1991); Janet Adelman, *Suffocating Mothers: Fantasies of Maternal Origin in Shakespeare's Plays, "Hamlet" to "The Tempest"* (1992); Alan Sinfield, *Faultlines: Cultural Materialism and the Politics of Dissident Reading* (1992); Valerie Traub, *Desire and Anxiety: Circulations of Sexuality in Shakespearean Drama* (1992); Richard Burt, *Licensed by Authority: Ben Jonson and the Discourses of Censorship* (1993); Linda Charnes, *Notorious Identity: Materializing the Subject in Shakespeare* (1993); Lars Engle, *Shakespearean Pragmatism: Market of His Time* (1993); Gail Kern Paster, *The Body Embarrassed: Drama and the Disciplines of Shame in Early Modern England* (1993); Meredith Anne Skura, *Shakespeare the Actor and the Purposes of Playing* (1993); Frances E. Dolan, *Dangerous Familiars: Representations of Domestic Crime in England, 1550–1700* (1994); Kim F. Hall, *Things of Darkness: Economies of Race and Gender in Early Modern England* (1994); Jean Howard, *The Stage and Social Struggle in Early Modern England* (1994); Robert Watson, *The Rest Is Silence: Death as Annihilation in the English Renaissance* (1994); Katharine Eisaman Maus, *Inwardness and Theatre in the English Renaissance Drama* (1995); Louis Montrose, *The Purpose of Playing: Shakespeare and the Cultural Politics of the Elizabethan Theatre* (1996); Patricia Parker, *Shakespeare from the Margins: Language, Culture, Context* (1996); Jean E. Howard and Phyllis Rackin, *Engendering a Nation: A Feminist Account of Shakespeare's English Histories* (1997); Anthony B. Dawson and Paul Yachnin, *The Culture of Playgoing in Shakespeare's England* (2001); David Scott Kastan, *Shakespeare and the Book* (2001); Mary Beth Rose, *Gender and Heroism in Early Modern English Literature* (2002); and Stephen Orgel, *The Authentic Shakespeare* (2002). For other suggestions, see recent entries in the bibliography at the back of this volume.

The Comedies

The Taming of the Shrew

The Taming of the Shrew (c. 1592–1594) shows Shakespeare's comic genius at its best. At the same time, it shares with his other early plays an anticipation of the directions that his genius is to take in *Much Ado about Nothing* and other comedies of the later 1590s. By skillfully juxtaposing two plots and an induction, or framing plot, it offers contrasting views on the battle of the sexes. This debate on the nature of the love relationship will continue through many later comedies. The play also adroitly manipulates the device of mistaken identity, as in *The Comedy of Errors,* inverting appearance and reality, dreaming and waking, and the master-servant relationship in order to create a transformed Saturnalian world anticipating that of *A Midsummer Night's Dream* and *Twelfth Night.*

The induction sets up the theme of illusion, using an old motif known as "The Sleeper Awakened" (as found, for example, in *The Arabian Nights*). This device frames the main action of the play, giving to it an added perspective. *The Taming of the Shrew* purports, in fact, to be a play within a play, an entertainment devised by a witty nobleman as a practical joke on a drunken tinker, Christopher Sly. The jest is to convince Sly that he is not Sly at all, but an aristocrat suffering delusions. Outlandishly dressed in new finery, Sly is invited to witness a play from the gallery over the stage. In a rendition called *The Taming of a Shrew* (printed in 1594 and now generally thought to be taken from an earlier version of Shakespeare's play, employing a good deal of conscious originality along with some literary borrowing and even plagiarism), the framing plot concludes by actually putting Sly back out on the street in front of the alehouse where he was found. He awakes, recalls the play as a dream, and proposes to put the vision to good use by taming his own wife. Whether this ending reflects an epilogue now lost from the text of Shakespeare's play cannot be said, but it does reinforce the idea of the play as Sly's fantasy. Like Puck at the end of *A Midsummer Night's Dream,* urging us to

dismiss what we have seen as the product of our own slumbering, Sly continually reminds us that the play is only an illusion or shadow.

With repeated daring, Shakespeare calls attention to the contrived nature of his artifact, the play. When, for example, Sly is finally convinced that he is, in fact, a noble lord recovering from madness and lustily proposes to hasten off to bed with his long-neglected wife, we are comically aware that the "wife" is an impostor, a young page in disguise. Yet this counterfeiting of roles is no more unreal than the employment of Elizabethan boy-actors for the parts of Katharina and Bianca in the "real" play. As we watch Sly watching a play, levels of meaning intersect in this evocative fashion. Again, the paintings offered to Sly by his new attendants call attention to art's ability to confound illusion and reality. In one painting, Cytherea is hidden by reeds "Which seem to move and wanton with her breath / Even as the waving sedges play wi'th'wind," and, in another painting, Io appears "As lively painted as the deed was done" (Induction, 2.50–6). Sly's function, then, is that of the naive observer who inverts illusion and reality in his mind, concluding that his whole previous life of tinkers and alehouses and Cicely Hackets has been unreal. As his attendants explain to him, "These fifteen years you have been in a dream, / Or when you waked, so waked as if you slept." We as audience laugh at Sly's naiveté, and yet we, too, are moved and even transformed by an artistic vision that we know to be illusory.

Like Sly, many characters in the main action of the play are persuaded, or contrive, to be what they are not. Lucentio and Tranio exchange roles of master and servant. Bianca's supposed tutors are, in fact, her wooers, using their lessons to disguise messages of love. Katharina is prevailed upon by her husband, Petruchio, to declare that the sun is the moon and that an old gentleman (Vincentio) is a fair young maiden. Vincentio is publicly informed that he is an impostor and that the "real" Vincentio (the Pedant) is at that very moment looking at him out of the window of his son Lucentio's house. This last ruse does not fool the real Vincentio, but it nearly succeeds in fooling everyone else. Baptista Minola is about to commit Vincentio to jail for the infamous slander of asserting that the supposed Lucentio is only a servant in disguise. Vincentio, as the newly arrived stranger, is able to see matters as they really are, but the dwellers of Padua have grown so accustomed to the mad and improbable fictions of their life that they are not easily awakened to reality.

Such illusions have the effect of challenging the norms of social order. If a servant can playact at being the master so successfully that no one can tell the difference, are we to understand that social distinctions are mere arbitrary constructions? If Sly can become a lord by wearing the right clothes and speaking blank verse (as in the Induction, 2.68 and following), might audience members similarly raise their status? The theater promotes such skeptical questions, since it is in the business of dressing actors up as persons of whatever rank the playwright chooses. Surely one of the pleasures of theatrical performance for Elizabethan audiences was that of dreaming of social advancement or social control. At the same time, this theater treats such a liberating experience as holiday or farcical nightmare, and as Saturnalian escape; we realize as audience that we will return to the norms of our daily lives after having visited an imagined space where anything is possible.

Shakespeare multiplies his devices of illusion by combining two entirely distinct plots, each concerned, at least in part, with the comic inversion of appearance and reality: the shrew-taming plot involving Petruchio and Kate, and the more conventional romantic plot involving Lucentio and Bianca. The latter plot is derived from the *Supposes* of George Gascoigne, a play first presented at Gray's Inn (one of the Inns of Court) in 1566, as translated from Ariosto's neoclassical comedy, *I Suppositi,* 1509. (Ariosto's work, in turn, was based upon Terence's *Eunuchus* and Plautus's *Captivi.*) The "Supposes" are mistaken identities or misunderstandings, the kind of hilarious farcical mix-ups with which Shakespeare had already experimented in *The Comedy of Errors.* Shakespeare has, as usual, both romanticized his source and moralized it in a characteristically English way. The heroine, who in the Roman comedy of Plautus and Terence would have been a courtesan, and who in *Supposes* is made pregnant by her clandestine lover, remains thoroughly chaste in Shakespeare's comedy. Consequently, she has no need for a pander, or go-between, such as the bawdy Duenna or Nurse of *Supposes.* The satire directed at the heroine's unwelcome old wooer Gremio is far less savage than in *Supposes,* where the "pantaloon," Dr. Cleander, is a villainously corrupt lawyer epitomizing the depravity of "respectable" society. Despite Shakespeare's modifications, however, the basic plot remains an effort to foil parental authority. The young lovers, choosing

each other for romantic reasons, must fend off the materialistic calculations of their parents.

In a stock situation of this sort, the character types are also conventional. Gremio, the aged wealthy wooer, is actually labeled a "pantaloon" in the text (3.1.36–7) to stress his neoclassical ancestry. (Lean and foolish old wooers of this sort were customarily dressed in pantaloons, slippers, and spectacles on the Italian stage.) Gremio is typically "the graybeard," and Baptista Minola is "the narrow-prying father" (3.2.145–6). Even though Shakespeare renders these characters far less unattractive than in *Supposes,* their worldly behavior still invites reprisal from the young. Since Baptista Minola insists on selling his daughter Bianca to the highest bidder, it is fitting that her wealthiest suitor (the supposed Lucentio) should turn out in the end to be a penniless servant (Tranio) disguised as a man of affluence and position. In his traditional role as the clever servant of neoclassical comedy, Tranio skillfully apes the mannerisms of respectable society. He can deal in the mere surfaces—clothes or reputation—out of which a man's social importance is created, and can even furnish himself with a rich father. Gremio and Baptista deserve to be foiled, because they accept the illusion of respectability as real.

Even the romantic lovers of this borrowed plot are largely conventional. To be sure, Shakespeare emphasizes their virtuous qualities and their sincerity. He adds Hortensio (not in *Supposes*) to provide Lucentio with a genuine, if foolish, rival and Bianca with two wooers closer to her age than old Gremio. Lucentio and Bianca deserve their romantic triumph; they are self-possessed, witty, and steadfast to each other. Yet we know very little about them, nor have they seen deeply into each other. Lucentio's love talk is laden with conventional images in praise of Bianca's dark eyes and scarlet lips. At the play's end, he discovers, to his surprise, that she can be willful, even disobedient. Has her appearance of virtue concealed something from him and from us? Because the relationship between these lovers is superficial, they are appropriately destined to a superficial marriage as well. The passive Bianca becomes the proud and defiant wife.

By contrast, Petruchio and Kate are the more interesting lovers, whose courtship involves mutual self-discovery. Admittedly, we must not overstate the case. Especially at first, these lovers are also stock types: the shrew tamer and his proverbially shrewish wife. (The word *shrew,* originally signifying a wicked or malignant man, often applied to the devil or to a malignant planet, had come to mean a scolding or turbulent wife.) Although Shakespeare seems not to have used any single source for this plot, he was well acquainted with crude, misogynistic stories demonstrating the need for putting women in their place. In a ballad called *A Merry Jest of a Shrewd and Curst Wife, Lapped in Morel's Skin* (printed c. 1550), for example, the husband tames his shrewish wife by flaying her bloody with birch rods and then wrapping her in the freshly salted skin of a plow horse named Morel. (This shrewish wife, like Kate, has an obedient and gentle younger sister who is their father's favorite.) Other features of Shakespeare's plot can be found in similar tales: the tailor scolded for devising a gown of outlandish fashion (Gerard Legh's *Accidence of Armory,* 1562), the wife obliged to agree with her husband's assertion of some patent falsehood (Don Juan Manuel's *El Conde Lucanor,* c. 1335), and the three husbands' wager on their wives' obedience (*The Book of the Knight of La Tour-Landry,* printed 1484). In the raw spirit of this sexist tradition, so unlike the refined Italianate sentiment of his other plot, Shakespeare introduces Petruchio as a man of reckless bravado who is ready to marry the ugliest or sharpest-tongued woman alive so long as she is rich. However much he may be later attracted by Kate's fiery spirit, his first attraction to her is crassly financial. Kate is, moreover, a troublesomely defiant young woman at first, described by the men who know her as "intolerable curst / And shrewd and froward," and aggressive in her bullying of Bianca. She and Petruchio meet as grotesque comic counterparts.

At the play's end, the traditional pattern of male dominance and female acquiescence is still prominent. Kate is allowed food, sleep, and sex only when she yields to a socially ordained patriarchal framework in which a husband is the princely ruler of his wife. Kate is not like the young heroines of many other Shakespearean comedies (Portia in *The Merchant of Venice* and Rosalind in *As You Like It,* for example) who wittily guide their immature and overly romantic young men toward a pragmatic view of love and marriage; in this play, Kate is the one who must be mastered by the self-assured male. Her shrewishness is an open threat to male control in the marital bond, and, accordingly, the play's comic finale celebrates containment of this threat in her, along with a sharp reminder of the resistance to be endured by other husbands who have failed to tame their shrews.

Within this male-oriented frame of reference, however, Petruchio and Kate are surprisingly like Benedick and Beatrice of *Much Ado About Nothing.* Petruchio, for all his rant, is increasingly drawn to Kate by her spirit. As wit-combatants, they are worthy of one another's enmity—or love. No one else in the play is a fit match for either of them. Kate, too, is attracted to Petruchio, despite her war of words. Her anger is part defensive protection, part testing of his sincerity. If she is contemptuous of the wooers she has seen till now, she has good reason to be. We share her condescension toward the aged Gremio or the laughably inept Hortensio. She rightly fears that her father wishes to dispose of her so that he may auction off Bianca to the wealthiest competitor. Kate's jaded view of such marriage brokering is entirely defensible. Not surprisingly, she first views Petruchio, whose professed intentions are far from reassuring, as another mere adventurer in love. She is impressed by his "line" in wooing her but needs to test his constancy and sincerity. Marriage for her

would be a serious step, since social convention allows a dominant role for the husband; can she hope that she and Petruchio will arrive at some sort of understanding in which her role as wife and partner will be an honorable one? She puts down most men with a shrewish manner that challenges their very masculinity; Petruchio is the first man to counter her wit and energy with his own. Can she learn to live with this man?

Kate's rejection of men has not left her very happy, however genuine her disdain is for most of those who have come to woo. Petruchio's "schooling" can be seen as addressing that unhappiness, even if his purpose is unremittingly masculine in its assumption that a rebellious wife has to be "tamed" as one would tame a hawk. Having wooed and partly won her, Petruchio tests her with his late arrival at the marriage, his unconventional dress, and his crossing all her desires. Like the hawk-tamer, Petruchio uses harsh physical means, including deprivation of food and drink. He treats Kate as his chattel, and never wavers in his certainty that he is right to do so. Other males applaud his success and wish only to follow his example. The resolution is in these terms manifestly more sexist than in *Much Ado About Nothing*; it is as though Shakespeare works his way through the problems of sexual conflict from this early, very masculine play to a more complex and mutual accommodation in his later comedies.

At the same time, it is possible to see *The Taming of the Shrew* as a play in which a genuine accommodation is reached, even if it is on the man's terms with the woman being given no choice. The play may encourage the view that Petruchio's treatment of Kate, no matter how temporarily harsh, is ultimately benign in its intent. Petruchio, by his outlandish behavior of overturning tables and scolding servants, shows Kate an ugly picture of what her refractoriness is like. He succeeds by insisting on what, arguably, she may desire too: a well-defined relationship tempered by mutual respect and love. In this interpretation, Kate may gain something by the play's end. Her closing speech, with its fine blend of irony and self-conscious hyperbole, together with its seriousness of concern, can be read as expressing the way in which her independence of spirit and her newfound acceptance of a domestic rule are successfully fused, enabling her to gain widespread applause instead of opprobrium.

This is by no means the only way of reading the final scene, as modern productions often make clear: Kate emerges in various stage productions as more or less contented, or as simply resigned, or as cruelly brainwashed, or as only playing the role of obedient wife to get what she wants. The uncertainty of interpretation is one of the great pleasures and challenges today, in a world for which ideas about marriage have manifestly shifted since Shakespeare wrote. Even so, the play offers common ground in its appreciation for the seriousness of the issue and in its wonderful transparency as a text that offers itself up for rival interpretations.

The Taming of the Shrew

[*Dramatis Personae*

CHRISTOPHER SLY, *a tinker and beggar,*
HOSTESS *of an alehouse,*
A LORD,
A PAGE, SERVANTS, HUNTSMEN,
PLAYERS,

} *Persons in the Induction*

BAPTISTA, *a rich gentleman of Padua*
KATHARINA, *the shrew, also called Katharine and Kate, Baptista's elder daughter*
BIANCA, *Baptista's younger daughter*

PETRUCHIO, *a gentleman of Verona, suitor to Katharina*
GRUMIO, *Petruchio's servant*
CURTIS, NATHANIEL, PHILIP, JOSEPH, NICHOLAS, PETER, *and other servants of Petruchio*

GREMIO, *elderly suitor to Bianca*
HORTENSIO, *suitor to Bianca*
LUCENTIO, *son of Vincentio, in love with Bianca*
TRANIO, *Lucentio's servant*
BIONDELLO, *Lucentio's servant*
VINCENTIO, *a gentleman of Pisa*
A PEDANT *(or Merchant) of Mantua*
A WIDOW, *courted by Hortensio*

A TAILOR
A HABERDASHER
AN OFFICER
Other Servants of Baptista and Lucentio

SCENE: *Padua, and Petruchio's country house in Italy; the Induction is located in the countryside and at a Lord's house in England*]

[Induction.1]

Enter Beggar (Christopher Sly) and Hostess.

SLY I'll feeze you, in faith. 1
HOSTESS A pair of stocks, you rogue! 2
SLY You're a baggage. The Slys are no rogues. Look in 3
the chronicles; we came in with Richard Conqueror. 4
Therefore *paucas pallabris*, let the world slide. Sessa! 5
HOSTESS You will not pay for the glasses you have
burst?
SLY No, not a denier. Go by, Saint Jeronimy, go to thy 8
cold bed and warm thee. 9

HOSTESS I know my remedy; I must go fetch the third- 10
borough.   [*Exit.*] 11
SLY Third, or fourth, or fifth borough, I'll answer him 12
by law. I'll not budge an inch, boy. Let him come, and 13
kindly.   *Falls asleep.* 14

Wind horns [within]. Enter a Lord from hunting, with his train.

LORD

Huntsman, I charge thee, tender well my hounds. 15
Breathe Merriman—the poor cur is embossed— 16
And couple Clowder with the deep-mouthed brach. 17
Saw'st thou not, boy, how Silver made it good 18
At the hedge corner, in the coldest fault? 19

Induction.1. Location: Before an alehouse and, subsequently, before the Lord's house nearby. (See lines 75, 135.)
1 feeze you i.e., fix you, get even with you   **2 A . . . stocks** i.e., I'll have you put in the stocks   **3 baggage** contemptible woman or prostitute   **4 Richard** (Sly's mistake for "William.")   **5 *paucas pallabris*** i.e., *pocas palabras*, "few words." (Spanish.)   **Sessa** (Of doubtful meaning; perhaps "be quiet," "cease," or "let it go.")   **8 denier** French copper coin of little value.   **Go . . . Jeronimy** (Sly's variation of an often quoted line from Kyd's *The Spanish Tragedy*, urging caution.)   **8–9 go . . . thee** (Perhaps a proverb; see *King Lear*, 3.4.46–7.)

10–11 thirdborough constable.   **12 Third** (Sly shows his ignorance; the *third* in "thirdborough" derives from the Old English word *frith*, "peace.")   **13 by law** in the law courts.   **14 kindly** welcome. (Said ironically.)   **14.1 *Wind*** Blow   **14.2 *train*** retinue.   **15 tender** care for   **16 Breathe Merriman** Give the dog Merriman time to recover its breath.   **embossed** foaming at the mouth from exhaustion   **17 couple** leash together.   **deep-mouthed brach** bitch hound with the deep baying voice.   **18 made it good** i.e., picked up the lost scent   **19 in the coldest fault** when the scent was lost by a *fault* or break in the scent.

I would not lose the dog for twenty pound.

FIRST HUNTSMAN
Why, Bellman is as good as he, my lord.
He cried upon it at the merest loss,   22
And twice today picked out the dullest scent.
Trust me, I take him for the better dog.

LORD
Thou art a fool. If Echo were as fleet,
I would esteem him worth a dozen such.
But sup them well and look unto them all.   27
Tomorrow I intend to hunt again.

FIRST HUNTSMAN   I will, my lord.

LORD [seeing Sly]
What's here? One dead, or drunk? See, doth he
    breathe?

SECOND HUNTSMAN [examining Sly]
He breathes, my lord. Were he not warmed with ale,
This were a bed but cold to sleep so soundly.

LORD
Oh, monstrous beast, how like a swine he lies!
Grim death, how foul and loathsome is thine image!   34
Sirs, I will practice on this drunken man.   35
What think you, if he were conveyed to bed,
Wrapped in sweet clothes, rings put upon his fingers,   37
A most delicious banquet by his bed,   38
And brave attendants near him when he wakes,   39
Would not the beggar then forget himself?

FIRST HUNTSMAN
Believe me, lord, I think he cannot choose.   41

SECOND HUNTSMAN
It would seem strange unto him when he waked.

LORD
Even as a flatt'ring dream or worthless fancy.   43
Then take him up, and manage well the jest.
Carry him gently to my fairest chamber,
And hang it round with all my wanton pictures.
Balm his foul head in warm distillèd waters,   47
And burn sweet wood to make the lodging sweet.
Procure me music ready when he wakes,
To make a dulcet and a heavenly sound.   50
And if he chance to speak, be ready straight,   51
And with a low submissive reverence   52
Say, "What is it Your Honor will command?"
Let one attend him with a silver basin
Full of rosewater and bestrewed with flowers;
Another bear the ewer, the third a diaper,   56
And say, "Will 't please Your Lordship cool your
    hands?"
Someone be ready with a costly suit,
And ask him what apparel he will wear;
Another tell him of his hounds and horse,   60
And that his lady mourns at his disease.   61

Persuade him that he hath been lunatic,
And when he says he is, say that he dreams,   63
For he is nothing but a mighty lord.
This do, and do it kindly, gentle sirs.   65
It will be pastime passing excellent,   66
If it be husbanded with modesty.   67

FIRST HUNTSMAN
My lord, I warrant you we will play our part
As he shall think by our true diligence   69
He is no less than what we say he is.

LORD
Take him up gently, and to bed with him,
And each one to his office when he wakes.   72
        [Some bear out Sly.] Sound trumpets [within].
Sirrah, go see what trumpet 'tis that sounds.   73
                              [Exit a Servingman.]
Belike some noble gentleman that means,   74
Traveling some journey, to repose him here.

        Enter [a] Servingman.

How now? Who is it?

SERVINGMAN   An't please Your Honor, players 76
That offer service to Your Lordship.

        Enter Players.

LORD
Bid them come near.—Now, fellows, you are welcome.

PLAYERS   We thank Your Honor.

LORD
Do you intend to stay with me tonight?

FIRST PLAYER
So please Your Lordship to accept our duty.   81

LORD
With all my heart. This fellow I remember
Since once he played a farmer's eldest son.—
'Twas where you wooed the gentlewoman so well.
I have forgot your name, but sure that part
Was aptly fitted and naturally performed.

SECOND PLAYER
I think 'twas Soto that Your Honor means.

LORD
'Tis very true. Thou didst it excellent.
Well, you are come to me in happy time,   89
The rather for I have some sport in hand   90
Wherein your cunning can assist me much.   91
There is a lord will hear you play tonight.
But I am doubtful of your modesties,   93
Lest, overeyeing of his odd behavior—   94
For yet His Honor never heard a play—
You break into some merry passion   96

---

22 cried . . . loss bayed to signal his recovery of the scent after it had been completely lost   **27 sup them well** feed them a good supper
34 image likeness (since sleep was regarded as a likeness of death).
35 practice on play a joke on   **37 sweet** perfumed   **38 banquet** light repast   **39 brave** finely arrayed   **41 cannot choose** is bound to.
43 fancy flight of imagination.   **47 Balm** Bathe, anoint   **50 dulcet** melodious   **51 straight** at once   **52 reverence** bow   **56 ewer** jug, pitcher.
diaper towel   **60 horse** horses   **61 disease** i.e., mental derangement.

63 when . . . is i.e., when he says he must be mad indeed. (The *is* is stressed.)   **65 kindly** naturally (and thus persuasively).   **gentle** kind
66 passing surpassingly   **67 husbanded with modesty** managed with decorum.   **69 As** so that.   **by** as a result of   **72 office** duty
73 Sirrah (Usual form of address to inferiors.)   **74 Belike** Perhaps
76 An't If it   **81 So please** If it please.   **duty** expression of respect and dutiful service.   **89 happy** opportune   **90 The rather for** the more so since   **91 cunning** professional skill   **93 doubtful** apprehensive.   **modesties** discretion, self-control   **94 overeyeing of** witnessing   **96 merry passion** outburst of laughter

And so offend him; for I tell you, sirs,
If you should smile, he grows impatient.

FIRST PLAYER
Fear not, my lord, we can contain ourselves,
Were he the veriest antic in the world.   100

LORD [to a Servingman]
Go, sirrah, take them to the buttery,   101
And give them friendly welcome every one.
Let them want nothing that my house affords.   103

Exit one with the Players.

Sirrah, go you to Barthol'mew my page,
And see him dressed in all suits like a lady.   105
That done, conduct him to the drunkard's chamber,
And call him "madam," do him obeisance.   107
Tell him from me, as he will win my love,   108
He bear himself with honorable action
Such as he hath observed in noble ladies
Unto their lords by them accomplishèd.   111
Such duty to the drunkard let him do
With soft low tongue and lowly courtesy,
And say, "What is't Your Honor will command,
Wherein your lady and your humble wife
May show her duty and make known her love?"
And then with kind embracements, tempting kisses,
And with declining head into his bosom,
Bid him shed tears, as being overjoyed
To see her noble lord restored to health,
Who for this seven years hath esteemèd him   121
No better than a poor and loathsome beggar.
And if the boy have not a woman's gift
To rain a shower of commanded tears,
An onion will do well for such a shift,   125
Which in a napkin being close conveyed   126
Shall in despite enforce a watery eye.   127
See this dispatched with all the haste thou canst.
Anon I'll give thee more instructions.   129

Exit a Servingman.

I know the boy will well usurp the grace,   130
Voice, gait, and action of a gentlewoman.
I long to hear him call the drunkard husband,
And how my men will stay themselves from laughter 133
When they do homage to this simple peasant.
I'll in to counsel them. Haply my presence   135
May well abate the overmerry spleen   136
Which otherwise would grow into extremes.

[*Exeunt.*]

❧

[Induction.2]

*Enter aloft the drunkard [Sly], with attendants;
some with apparel, basin, and ewer and other
appurtenances; and Lord.*

SLY   For God's sake, a pot of small ale.   1

FIRST SERVINGMAN
Will't please Your Lordship drink a cup of sack?   2

SECOND SERVINGMAN
Will't please Your Honor taste of these conserves? 3

THIRD SERVINGMAN
What raiment will Your Honor wear today?

SLY   I am Christophero Sly. Call not me "Honor" nor
"Lordship." I ne'er drank sack in my life; and if you
give me any conserves, give me conserves of beef.   7
Ne'er ask me what raiment I'll wear, for I have no
more doublets than backs, no more stockings than   9
legs, nor no more shoes than feet—nay, sometimes
more feet than shoes, or such shoes as my toes look 11
through the overleather.   12

LORD
Heaven cease this idle humor in Your Honor!   13
Oh, that a mighty man of such descent,
Of such possessions and so high esteem,
Should be infusèd with so foul a spirit!

SLY   What, would you make me mad? Am not I Christopher Sly, old Sly's son of Burton-heath, by birth a 18
peddler, by education a cardmaker, by transmutation 19
a bearherd, and now by present profession a tinker? 20
Ask Marian Hacket, the fat alewife of Wincot, if she 21
know me not. If she say I am not fourteen pence on 22
the score for sheer ale, score me up for the lyingest 23
knave in Christendom. What, I am not bestraught: 24
here's—

THIRD SERVINGMAN
Oh, this it is that makes your lady mourn!

SECOND SERVINGMAN
Oh, this is it that makes your servants droop!

LORD
Hence comes it that your kindred shuns your house,
As beaten hence by your strange lunacy.   29
Oh, noble lord, bethink thee of thy birth.
Call home thy ancient thoughts from banishment,   31
And banish hence these abject lowly dreams.
Look how thy servants do attend on thee,
Each in his office ready at thy beck.   34

Induction.2. Location: A bedchamber in the Lord's house.
0.1 *aloft* i.e., in the gallery over the rear facade of the stage   **1 small**
weak (and therefore cheap)   **2 sack** sweet Spanish wine (suited for a
gentleman to drink).   **3 conserves** candied fruit.   **7 conserves of
beef** preserved (salted) beef.   **9 doublets** men's jackets   **11 as** that
12 overleather upper leather of the shoe.   **13 idle humor** foolish
whim   **18 Burton-heath** (Perhaps Barton on the Heath, about sixteen
miles from Stratford, the home of Shakespeare's aunt.)   **19 cardmaker** maker of cards or combs used to prepare wool for spinning
20 bearherd keeper of a performing bear.   **tinker** pot mender.
21 alewife woman who keeps an alehouse.   **Wincot** small village about
four miles from Stratford. (The parish register shows that there were
Hackets living there in 1591.)   **22–3 on the score** in debt (since such
reckonings were originally notched or scored on a stick)   **23 sheer**
nothing but.   **score me up for** reckon me to be   **24 bestraught** distracted   **29 As** as if   **31 ancient** former   **34 beck** nod.

100 veriest antic oddest buffoon or eccentric   **101 buttery** pantry, or
a room for storing liquor (in butts) and other provisions   **103 want**
lack   **105 in all suits** in every detail. (With a pun on *suits* of clothes.)
107 do him obeisance show him dutiful respect.   **108 him** i.e., the
page Bartholomew.   **as he will** if he wishes to   **111 by them accomplishèd** performed by the ladies.   **121 him** himself   **125 shift** purpose   **126 napkin** handkerchief.   **close** secretly   **127 in despite** i.e.,
notwithstanding a natural inclination to laugh rather than cry
129 Anon Soon   **130 usurp** assume   **133 And how** i.e., and to see
how   **135 I'll in** I'll go in   **136 spleen** mood. (The spleen was the
supposed seat of laughter and anger.)

Wilt thou have music? Hark, Apollo plays,   *Music.* 35
And twenty cagèd nightingales do sing.
Or wilt thou sleep? We'll have thee to a couch,
Softer and sweeter than the lustful bed
On purpose trimmed up for Semiramis.   39
Say thou wilt walk; we will bestrew the ground.   40
Or wilt thou ride? Thy horses shall be trapped,   41
Their harness studded all with gold and pearl.
Dost thou love hawking? Thou hast hawks will soar
Above the morning lark. Or wilt thou hunt?
Thy hounds shall make the welkin answer them   45
And fetch shrill echoes from the hollow earth.

FIRST SERVINGMAN
Say thou wilt course, thy greyhounds are as swift   47
As breathèd stags, ay, fleeter than the roe.   48

SECOND SERVINGMAN
Dost thou love pictures? We will fetch thee straight
Adonis painted by a running brook,   50
And Cytherea all in sedges hid,   51
Which seem to move and wanton with her breath,   52
Even as the waving sedges play wi'th'wind.

LORD
We'll show thee Io as she was a maid,   54
And how she was beguilèd and surprised,
As lively painted as the deed was done.   56

THIRD SERVINGMAN
Or Daphne roaming through a thorny wood,   57
Scratching her legs that one shall swear she bleeds,
And at that sight shall sad Apollo weep,
So workmanly the blood and tears are drawn.   60

LORD
Thou art a lord, and nothing but a lord.
Thou hast a lady far more beautiful
Than any woman in this waning age.   63

FIRST SERVINGMAN
And till the tears that she hath shed for thee
Like envious floods o'errun her lovely face,   65
She was the fairest creature in the world;
And yet she is inferior to none.   67

SLY
Am I a lord? And have I such a lady?
Or do I dream? Or have I dreamed till now?
I do not sleep: I see, I hear, I speak,
I smell sweet savors, and I feel soft things.
Upon my life, I am a lord indeed,
And not a tinker nor Christopher Sly.
Well, bring our lady hither to our sight,

And once again a pot o'th' smallest ale.

SECOND SERVINGMAN
Will 't please Your Mightiness to wash your hands?
Oh, how we joy to see your wit restored!   77
Oh, that once more you knew but what you are!   78
These fifteen years you have been in a dream,
Or when you waked, so waked as if you slept.

SLY
These fifteen years! By my fay, a goodly nap.   81
But did I never speak of all that time?   82

FIRST SERVINGMAN
Oh, yes, my lord, but very idle words;
For though you lay here in this goodly chamber,
Yet would you say ye were beaten out of door,
And rail upon the hostess of the house,   86
And say you would present her at the leet   87
Because she brought stone jugs and no sealed quarts.   88
Sometimes you would call out for Cicely Hacket.

SLY
Ay, the woman's maid of the house.

THIRD SERVINGMAN
Why, sir, you know no house, nor no such maid,
Nor no such men as you have reckoned up,
As Stephen Sly, and old John Naps of Greet,   93
And Peter Turf, and Henry Pimpernel,
And twenty more such names and men as these,
Which never were, nor no man ever saw.

SLY
Now Lord be thankèd for my good amends!   97

ALL
Amen.

Enter [the Page as a] lady, with Attendants.

SLY   I thank thee. Thou shalt not lose by it.   98

PAGE
How fares my noble lord?

SLY   Marry, I fare well, 99
For here is cheer enough. Where is my wife?

PAGE
Here, noble lord. What is thy will with her?

SLY
Are you my wife, and will not call me husband?
My men should call me "lord"; I am your goodman.   103

PAGE
My husband and my lord, my lord and husband;
I am your wife in all obedience.

SLY
I know it well.—What must I call her?

---

35 **Apollo** i.e., as god of music   39 **Semiramis** legendary queen of Assyria, famous for her voluptuousness.   40 **bestrew** i.e., scatter rushes on   41 **trapped** adorned   45 **welkin** sky, heavens   47 **course** hunt the hare   48 **breathèd** in good physical condition, with good wind.   **roe** small, swift deer.   50 **Adonis** a young huntsman with whom Venus is vainly in love. (See Ovid's *Metamorphoses*, Book 10, and Shakespeare's poem, *Venus and Adonis*.)   51 **Cytherea** one of the names for Venus (because of her association with the island of Cythera).   **sedges** grassy marsh plants   52 **wanton** play seductively   54 **Io** a woman who, according to Ovid, was seduced by Jove concealed in a mist and afterwards transformed into a heifer   56 **as** as if   57 **Daphne** a wood nymph beloved by Apollo, changed by Diana into a laurel tree to preserve her from Apollo's assault (*Metamorphoses*, Book 1)   60 **workmanly** skillfully   63 **waning** degenerate   65 **envious** spiteful   67 **yet** even today

77 **wit** mental faculties   78 **knew but** only knew   81 **fay** faith   82 **of** during   86 **house** tavern   87 **present** bring accusation against.   **leet** manorial court   88 **sealed quarts** quart containers officially stamped as a guarantee of that capacity. (The irregular stoneware quarts might be used to cheat customers.)   93 **Stephen . . . Greet** (A Stephen Sly lived in Stratford during Shakespeare's day. *Greet* is a Gloucestershire hamlet not far from Stratford. The Folio reading, "Greece," is an easy misreading if Shakespeare wrote "Greete.")   97 **amends** recovery   98 **Thou . . . it** i.e., I will reward your solicitude toward me.   99 **Marry** (A mild oath, derived from "by Mary.")   **fare well** (1) am fine (2) have plenty of good *cheer* (line 100), refreshment   103 **goodman** (A homely term for "husband.")

LORD   Madam.

SLY   Al'ce madam, or Joan madam?

LORD

Madam, and nothing else. So lords call ladies.

SLY

Madam wife, they say that I have dreamed
And slept above some fifteen year or more.

PAGE

Ay, and the time seems thirty unto me,
Being all this time abandoned from your bed.   112

SLY

'Tis much.—Servants, leave me and her alone.—
Madam, undress you and come now to bed.

PAGE

Thrice-noble lord, let me entreat of you
To pardon me yet for a night or two,
Or, if not so, until the sun be set.
For your physicians have expressly charged,
In peril to incur your former malady,
That I should yet absent me from your bed.
I hope this reason stands for my excuse.

SLY   Ay, it stands so that I may hardly tarry so long. But   122
I would be loath to fall into my dreams again. I will
therefore tarry in despite of the flesh and the blood.

Enter a [Servingman as] messenger.

SERVINGMAN

Your Honor's players, hearing your amendment,
Are come to play a pleasant comedy,
For so your doctors hold it very meet,   127
Seeing too much sadness hath congealed your blood,
And melancholy is the nurse of frenzy.
Therefore they thought it good you hear a play
And frame your mind to mirth and merriment,
Which bars a thousand harms and lengthens life.

SLY   Marry, I will let them play it. Is not a comonty a   133
Christmas gambold or a tumbling-trick?   134

PAGE

No, my good lord, it is more pleasing stuff.

SLY   What, household stuff?   136

PAGE   It is a kind of history.   137

SLY   Well, we'll see 't. Come, madam wife, sit by my side
and let the world slip; we shall ne'er be younger.   139
                    [They sit over the stage.] Flourish.

❧

1.1

Enter Lucentio and his man, Tranio.

LUCENTIO

Tranio, since for the great desire I had
To see fair Padua, nursery of arts,   2
I am arrived fore fruitful Lombardy,   3
The pleasant garden of great Italy,
And by my father's love and leave am armed
With his good will and thy good company,
My trusty servant, well approved in all,   7
Here let us breathe and haply institute   8
A course of learning and ingenious studies.   9
Pisa, renownèd for grave citizens,
Gave me my being, and my father first—   11
A merchant of great traffic through the world,   12
Vincentio, come of the Bentivolii.   13
Vincentio's son, brought up in Florence,   14
It shall become to serve all hopes conceived   15
To deck his fortune with his virtuous deeds.   16
And therefore, Tranio, for the time I study,   17
Virtue and that part of philosophy
Will I apply that treats of happiness   19
By virtue specially to be achieved.
Tell me thy mind, for I have Pisa left
And am to Padua come as he that leaves
A shallow plash to plunge him in the deep,   23
And with satiety seeks to quench his thirst.

TRANIO

Mi perdonate, gentle master mine.   25
I am in all affected as yourself,   26
Glad that you thus continue your resolve
To suck the sweets of sweet philosophy.
Only, good master, while we do admire
This virtue and this moral discipline,
Let's be no stoics nor no stocks, I pray,   31
Or so devote to Aristotle's checks   32
As Ovid be an outcast quite abjured.   33
Balk logic with acquaintance that you have,   34
And practice rhetoric in your common talk.   35
Music and poesy use to quicken you;   36

---

112 **abandoned** banished   122 **stands** (1) is the case (2) punningly, "is giving me an erection." The joke picks up on *stands,* meaning "serves," in line 121.   127 **meet** suitable   133 **Marry . . . play it** (Perhaps the Folio punctuation should be emended to "Marry, I will. Let them play it.")   **comonty** (Sly's approximation of "comedy.")   134 **gambold** (Sly's version of "gambol," frolicsome merrymaking and leaping about.)   136 **household stuff** i.e., domestic doings.   137 **history** story.   139.1 *They sit over the stage* (Possibly the Lord and some servingmen exeunt here or at line 113. At 1.1.249 ff., a servingman, the Page, and Sly speak, while the Lord is no longer heard from.)

1.1 Location: Padua. A street before Baptista's house.
2 Padua . . . arts (Padua's was one of the most renowned of universities during Shakespeare's time.)   **3 am arrived fore** have arrived at, or at the gates of, before. (Padua is not in Lombardy, but imprecise maps may have allowed Shakespeare to think of Lombardy as comprising all of northern Italy.)   **7 approved** tested and proved trustworthy   **8 breathe** pause, settle down.   **haply institute** begin, as circumstances permit   **9 ingenious** i.e., "ingenuous," liberal, befitting a wellborn person   **11 first** i.e., before me   **12 of great traffic** involved in extensive trade   **13 come of** descended from   **14–16 Vincentio's . . . deeds** It will befit Vincentio's son, brought up in Florence, to fulfill all the hopes of his family by adding virtuous deeds to what fortune has bestowed on him.   **17 for . . . study** for my term of study   **19 apply** study.   **treats of** discusses, concerns   **23 plash** pool   **25 Mi perdonate** Pardon me   **26 affected** disposed   **31 stocks** persons devoid of feeling, like wooden posts. (With a play on *stoics.*)   **32 devote** devoted.   **checks** restraints   **33 As** so that.   **Ovid** Latin love poet. (Used here to typify amorous light entertainment, as contrasted with the constraining philosophic study of Aristotle.)   **34 Balk logic** Argue, bandy words.   **acquaintance** acquaintances   **35 common talk** ordinary conversation.   **36 Music . . . you** Use music and poetry to refresh yourself

The mathematics and the metaphysics,
Fall to them as you find your stomach serves you.   38
No profit grows where is no pleasure ta'en.
In brief, sir, study what you most affect.   40
LUCENTIO
Gramercies, Tranio, well dost thou advise.   41
If, Biondello, thou wert come ashore,   42
We could at once put us in readiness
And take a lodging fit to entertain
Such friends as time in Padua shall beget.
But stay awhile, what company is this?
TRANIO
Master, some show to welcome us to town.   47

Enter Baptista with his two daughters, Katha-
rina and Bianca; Gremio, a pantaloon; [and]
Hortensio, suitor to Bianca. Lucentio [and]
Tranio stand by.

BAPTISTA
Gentlemen, importune me no farther,
For how I firmly am resolved you know:
That is, not to bestow my youngest daughter
Before I have a husband for the elder.
If either of you both love Katharina,
Because I know you well and love you well,
Leave shall you have to court her at your pleasure.
GREMIO
To cart her rather. She's too rough for me.   55
There, there, Hortensio, will you any wife?
KATHARINA [*to Baptista*]
I pray you, sir, is it your will
To make a stale of me amongst these mates?   58
HORTENSIO
"Mates," maid? How mean you that? No mates for
    you,
Unless you were of gentler, milder mold.
KATHARINA
I'faith, sir, you shall never need to fear;
Iwis it is not halfway to her heart.   62
But if it were, doubt not her care should be
To comb your noddle with a three-legged stool,   64
And paint your face, and use you like a fool.   65
HORTENSIO
From all such devils, good Lord deliver us!
GREMIO   And me too, good Lord!
TRANIO [*aside to Lucentio*]
Husht, master, here's some good pastime toward.   68

That wench is stark mad or wonderful froward.   69
LUCENTIO [*aside to Tranio*]
But in other's silence do I see
Maid's mild behavior and sobriety.
Peace, Tranio!
TRANIO [*aside to Lucentio*]
Well said, master. Mum, and gaze your fill.
BAPTISTA
Gentlemen, that I may soon make good
What I have said—Bianca, get you in.
And let it not displease thee, good Bianca,
For I will love thee ne'er the less, my girl.
KATHARINA   A pretty peat! It is best   78
Put finger in the eye, an she knew why.   79
BIANCA
Sister, content you in my discontent.—
Sir, to your pleasure humbly I subscribe.   81
My books and instruments shall be my company,
On them to look and practice by myself.
LUCENTIO [*aside to Tranio*]
Hark, Tranio, thou mayst hear Minerva speak.   84
HORTENSIO
Signor Baptista, will you be so strange?   85
Sorry am I that our good will effects   86
Bianca's grief.
GREMIO   Why will you mew her up,   87
Signor Baptista, for this fiend of hell,
And make her bear the penance of her tongue?   89
BAPTISTA
Gentlemen, content ye. I am resolved.
Go in, Bianca.   [*Exit Bianca.*]
And for I know she taketh most delight   92
In music, instruments, and poetry,
Schoolmasters will I keep within my house
Fit to instruct her youth. If you, Hortensio,
Or, Signor Gremio, you know any such,
Prefer them hither; for to cunning men   97
I will be very kind, and liberal
To mine own children in good bringing up.
And so farewell.—Katharina, you may stay,
For I have more to commune with Bianca.   *Exit.* 101
KATHARINA
Why, and I trust I may go too, may I not?
What, shall I be appointed hours,   103
As though, belike, I knew not what to take,   104
And what to leave? Ha!   *Exit.* 105
GREMIO   You may go to the devil's dam. Your gifts are 106
so good, here's none will hold you.—Their love is not 107

---

38 stomach inclination, appetite   **40 affect** find pleasant.   **41 Gra-mercies** Many thanks   **42 Biondello** (Lucentio apostrophizes his absent servant.)   **come ashore** (Padua, though inland, is given a harbor by Shakespeare, unless he is thinking of the canals that crossed northern Italy in the sixteenth century.)   **47.2** *pantaloon* foolish old man, a stock character in Italian comedy   **55 cart** carry in a cart through the streets by way of punishment or public exposure. (With a play on *court*.)   **58 stale** laughingstock. (With a play on the meaning "harlot," since a harlot might well be carted.)   **mates** rude fellows. (But Hortensio takes the word in the sense of "husband.")   **62 Iwis . . . heart** indeed, marriage is not even halfway suited to my inclination. (Katharina speaks of herself in the third person here and in line 63.)   **64 comb your noddle** rake your head   **65 paint** i.e., make red with scratches   **68 toward** in prospect.

69 wonderful froward incredibly perverse.   **78–9 A . . . why** i.e., A fine spoiled darling she is! She does well to put on a show of weeping, knowing what's good for her. (Said sardonically.)   **81 pleasure** will.   **subscribe** submit.   **84 Minerva** goddess of wisdom   **85 strange** distant, unfeeling.   **86 effects** causes   **87 mew** coop (as one would a falcon)   **89 her . . . her** i.e., Bianca . . . Katharina's   **92 for** because   **97 Prefer** recommend.   **cunning** skillful, learned   **101 commune** discuss   **103 appointed hours** given a timetable   **104–5 As . . . leave?** as though, forsooth, I didn't know how to choose for myself?   **106 dam** mother.   **gifts** endowments. (Said ironically.)   **107 hold** detain.   **Their love** i.e., The love of women

so great, Hortensio, but we may blow our nails to-   108
gether and fast it fairly out. Our cake's dough on both   109
sides. Farewell. Yet, for the love I bear my sweet   110
Bianca, if I can by any means light on a fit man to teach
her that wherein she delights, I will wish him to   112
her father.

HORTENSIO   So will I, Signor Gremio. But a word, I pray.
Though the nature of our quarrel yet never brooked   115
parle, know now, upon advice, it toucheth us both,   116
that we may yet again have access to our fair mistress
and be happy rivals in Bianca's love, to labor and effect
one thing specially.

GREMIO   What's that, I pray?

HORTENSIO   Marry, sir, to get a husband for her sister.

GREMIO   A husband? A devil.

HORTENSIO   I say a husband.

GREMIO   I say a devil. Think'st thou, Hortensio, though
her father be very rich, any man is so very a fool to be   125
married to hell?

HORTENSIO   Tush, Gremio, though it pass your patience   127
and mine to endure her loud alarums, why, man, there   128
be good fellows in the world, an a man could light on   129
them, would take her with all faults, and money   130
enough.

GREMIO   I cannot tell. But I had as lief take her dowry   132
with this condition: to be whipped at the high cross   133
every morning.

HORTENSIO   Faith, as you say, there's small choice in
rotten apples. But come, since this bar in law makes us   136
friends, it shall be so far forth friendly maintained till
by helping Baptista's eldest daughter to a husband we
set his youngest free for a husband, and then have to't   139
afresh. Sweet Bianca! Happy man be his dole! He that   140
runs fastest gets the ring. How say you, Signor   141
Gremio?

GREMIO   I am agreed, and would I had given him the
best horse in Padua to begin his wooing that would
thor-oughly woo her, wed her, and bed her and rid the
house of her! Come on.   *Exeunt ambo. Manent*   146
                               Tranio and Lucentio.

TRANIO
I pray, sir, tell me, is it possible
That love should of a sudden take such hold?

LUCENTIO
Oh, Tranio, till I found it to be true,
I never thought it possible or likely.
But see, while idly I stood looking on,

I found the effect of love in idleness,   152
And now in plainness do confess to thee,
That art to me as secret and as dear   154
As Anna to the Queen of Carthage was,   155
Tranio, I burn, I pine, I perish, Tranio,
If I achieve not this young modest girl.
Counsel me, Tranio, for I know thou canst;
Assist me, Tranio, for I know thou wilt.

TRANIO
Master, it is no time to chide you now.
Affection is not rated from the heart.   161
If love have touched you, naught remains but so,
"Redime te captum quam queas minimo."   163

LUCENTIO
Gramercies, lad. Go forward. This contents;   164
The rest will comfort, for thy counsel's sound.   165

TRANIO
Master, you looked so longly on the maid,   166
Perhaps you marked not what's the pith of all.   167

LUCENTIO
Oh, yes, I saw sweet beauty in her face,
Such as the daughter of Agenor had,   169
That made great Jove to humble him to her hand,   170
When with his knees he kissed the Cretan strand.   171

TRANIO
Saw you no more? Marked you not how her sister
Began to scold and raise up such a storm
That mortal ears might hardly endure the din?

LUCENTIO
Tranio, I saw her coral lips to move,
And with her breath she did perfume the air.
Sacred and sweet was all I saw in her.

TRANIO [*aside*]
Nay, then, 'tis time to stir him from his trance.—
I pray, awake, sir. If you love the maid,
Bend thoughts and wits to achieve her. Thus it stands:
Her elder sister is so curst and shrewd   181
That till the father rid his hands of her,
Master, your love must live a maid at home,   183
And therefore has he closely mewed her up,
Because she will not be annoyed with suitors.   185

LUCENTIO
Ah, Tranio, what a cruel father's he!
But art thou not advised he took some care   187
To get her cunning schoolmasters to instruct her?   188

TRANIO
Ay, marry, am I, sir; and now 'tis plotted.

108–9 blow . . . together i.e., twiddle our thumbs, wait patiently
109 fast . . . out abstain as best we can   **109–10 Our cake's . . . sides**
i.e., We're both out of luck, getting nowhere.   **112 wish** commend
115-16 brooked parle tolerated conference   **116 advice** reflection.
toucheth concerns   **125 very a** utterly a   **127 pass** exceed
128 alarums i.e., loud, startling noises. (In military terms, a call to
arms.)   **129 an** if   **130 would** who would   **132 I cannot tell** i.e., I
don't know about that, don't know what to say.   **had as lief** would
as willingly   **133 high cross** cross set on a pedestal in a marketplace
or center of a town   **136 bar in law** legal impediment, i.e., Baptista's
refusal to receive suitors for Bianca   **139 have to't** renew combat
140 Happy . . . dole! i.e., May happiness be the reward of him who
wins! (Proverbial.)   **141 the ring** (An allusion to the sport of riding at
the ring, with quibble on "wedding ring" and also sexual sense, "vul-
var ring.")   **146 s.d. ambo** both.   ***Manent*** They remain onstage

152 love in idleness i.e., (1) desire bred by idleness (2) a popular name
for the pansy, thought to induce love   **154 secret** trusted, intimate
155 Anna confidante of her sister Dido, Queen of Carthage, beloved of
Aeneas   **161 rated** driven away by chiding   **163 *Redime . . . minimo***
Buy yourself out of bondage for as little as you can. (From Terence's
Eunuchus as quoted in William Lilly's *Latin Grammar*.)   **164 Gramercies** Thanks   **165 The rest** The rest of what you have to say   **166 so
longly** (1) for such a long time (2) so longingly   **167 marked** noted.
pith core, essence   **169 daughter of Agenor** Europa, beloved of Jove;
Jove took the form of a bull in order to abduct her   **170 him** himself
171 kissed i.e., knelt on   **181 curst and shrewd** shrewish and ill-
natured   **183 must . . . home** must remain unattached, unmated
185 Because so that   **187 advised** aware (that)   **188 cunning** expert

LUCENTIO
　I have it, Tranio.
TRANIO　　　　　　Master, for my hand,   190
　Both our inventions meet and jump in one.   191
LUCENTIO
　Tell me thine first.
TRANIO　　　　　　You will be schoolmaster
　And undertake the teaching of the maid:
　That's your device.
LUCENTIO　　　　　It is. May it be done?
TRANIO
　Not possible; for who shall bear your part
　And be in Padua here Vincentio's son,
　Keep house and ply his book, welcome his friends,   197
　Visit his countrymen, and banquet them?
LUCENTIO
　Basta, content thee, for I have it full.   199
　We have not yet been seen in any house,
　Nor can we be distinguished by our faces
　For man or master. Then it follows thus:
　Thou shalt be master, Tranio, in my stead,
　Keep house, and port, and servants, as I should.   204
　I will some other be, some Florentine,
　Some Neapolitan, or meaner man of Pisa.   206
　'Tis hatched and shall be so. Tranio, at once
　Uncase thee. Take my colored hat and cloak.   208
　When Biondello comes, he waits on thee,
　But I will charm him first to keep his tongue.   210
TRANIO　　So had you need.
　In brief, sir, sith it your pleasure is,   212
　And I am tied to be obedient—
　For so your father charged me at our parting,
　"Be serviceable to my son," quoth he,
　Although I think 'twas in another sense—
　I am content to be Lucentio,
　Because so well I love Lucentio.
　　　　　　　　　　　　　　　[They exchange clothes.]
LUCENTIO
　Tranio, be so, because Lucentio loves.
　And let me be a slave t'achieve that maid
　Whose sudden sight hath thralled my wounded eye.   221

　　　　　　　Enter Biondello.

　Here comes the rogue.—Sirrah, where have you been?
BIONDELLO
　Where have I been? Nay, how now, where are you?
　Master, has my fellow Tranio stol'n your clothes?
　Or you stol'n his? Or both? Pray, what's the news?
LUCENTIO
　Sirrah, come hither. 'Tis no time to jest,
　And therefore frame your manners to the time.   227
　Your fellow Tranio here, to save my life,
　Puts my apparel and my countenance on,   229

　And I for my escape have put on his;
　For in a quarrel since I came ashore,
　I killed a man, and fear I was descried.   232
　Wait you on him, I charge you, as becomes,   233
　While I make way from hence to save my life.
　You understand me?
BIONDELLO　　　　　　I, sir?—Ne'er a whit.   235
LUCENTIO
　And not a jot of Tranio in your mouth.
　Tranio is changed into Lucentio.
BIONDELLO
　The better for him. Would I were so, too!
TRANIO
　So could I, faith, boy, to have the next wish after,
　That Lucentio indeed had Baptista's youngest
　　daughter.
　But, sirrah, not for my sake, but your master's, I
　　advise
　You use your manners discreetly in all kind of com-
　　panies.
　When I am alone, why, then I am Tranio,
　But in all places else your master Lucentio.
LUCENTIO　　Tranio, let's go.
　One thing more rests, that thyself execute: 246
　To make one among these wooers. If thou ask me
　　why,
　Sufficeth my reasons are both good and weighty.   248
　　　　　　　　　　　　　　　　　　　　　　Exeunt.

　　　　　The presenters above speak.

FIRST SERVINGMAN
　My lord, you nod. You do not mind the play.   249
SLY　　Yes, by Saint Anne, do I. A good matter, surely.
　Comes there any more of it?
PAGE [as lady]　　My lord, 'tis but begun.
SLY　　'Tis a very excellent piece of work, madam lady.
　Would 'twere done!　　　　　　They sit and mark.   254

　　　　　　　　　　　❖

[1.2]

　　　　　Enter Petruchio and his man, Grumio.

PETRUCHIO
　Verona, for a while I take my leave
　To see my friends in Padua, but of all   2
　My best belovèd and approvèd friend,
　Hortensio; and I trow this is his house.   4
　Here, sirrah Grumio, knock, I say.
GRUMIO　　Knock, sir? Whom should I knock? Is there any
　man has rebused Your Worship?   7
PETRUCHIO　　Villain, I say, knock me here soundly.   8

---

190 for my hand (A mild oath.)　191 inventions plans.　jump tally,
agree　197 keep . . . book entertain guests and pursue his studies
199 Basta Enough.　full i.e., fully thought out.　204 port state, style
of living　206 meaner of a lower social class　208 Uncase thee
Remove your outer garments.　210 charm i.e., command, persuade
212 sith since　221 Whose . . . thralled the sudden sight of whom has
captured　227 frame adapt, suit　229 countenance bearing, manner

232 descried observed.　233 as becomes as is suitable　235 I, sir
(Lucentio may hear this as "Ay, sir.")　Ne'er a whit Not in the least.
246 rests remains to be done　248 Sufficeth it suffices that
248.2 presenters characters of the Induction, whose role it is to "present" the play proper　249 mind attend to　254 s.d. mark observe
1.2. Location: Padua. Before Hortensio's house.
2 of all above all　4 trow believe　7 rebused (A blunder for
"abused.")　8 Villain i.e., Wretch. (A term of abuse.)　me i.e., for me.
(But Grumio, perhaps intentionally, misunderstands.)

GRUMIO   Knock you here, sir? Why, sir, what am I, sir, that I should knock you here, sir?

PETRUCHIO
Villain, I say, knock me at this gate,   11
And rap me well, or I'll knock your knave's pate.

GRUMIO
My master is grown quarrelsome. I should knock
   you first,   13
And then I know after who comes by the worst.   14

PETRUCHIO   Will it not be?   15
Faith, sirrah, an you'll not knock, I'll ring it.   16
I'll try how you can *sol fa* and sing it.   17
                                    He wrings him by the ears.

GRUMIO
Help, masters, help! My master is mad.   18

PETRUCHIO
Now knock when I bid you, sirrah villain.

                   Enter Hortensio.

HORTENSIO   How now, what's the matter? My old
friend Grumio and my good friend Petruchio? How
do you all at Verona?

PETRUCHIO
Signor Hortensio, come you to part the fray?
Con tutto il cuore ben trovato, may I say.   24

HORTENSIO
Alla nostra casa ben venuto,   25
Molto onorato signor mio Petruchio.—   26
Rise, Grumio, rise. We will compound this quarrel.   27

GRUMIO   Nay, 'tis no matter, sir, what he 'leges in Latin. 28
If this be not a lawful cause for me to leave his service!
Look you, sir: he bid me knock him and rap him
soundly, sir. Well, was it fit for a servant to use his
master so, being perhaps, for aught I see, two-and- 32
thirty, a pip out?   33
Whom would to God I had well knocked at first!
Then had not Grumio come by the worst.

PETRUCHIO
A senseless villain! Good Hortensio,
I bade the rascal knock upon your gate,
And could not get him for my heart to do it.   38

GRUMIO   Knock at the gate? Oh, heavens! Spake you
not these words plain, "Sirrah, knock me here, rap me
here, knock me well, and knock me soundly"? And
come you now with "knocking at the gate"?   42

PETRUCHIO
Sirrah, begone, or talk not, I advise you.

HORTENSIO
Petruchio, patience. I am Grumio's pledge.   44
Why, this's a heavy chance twixt him and you,   45
Your ancient, trusty, pleasant servant Grumio.   46
And tell me now, sweet friend, what happy gale
Blows you to Padua here from old Verona?

PETRUCHIO
Such wind as scatters young men through the world
To seek their fortunes farther than at home,
Where small experience grows. But in a few,   51
Signor Hortensio, thus it stands with me:
Antonio, my father, is deceased,
And I have thrust myself into this maze,
Happily to wive and thrive as best I may.   55
Crowns in my purse I have, and goods at home,   56
And so am come abroad to see the world.

HORTENSIO
Petruchio, shall I then come roundly to thee   58
And wish thee to a shrewd, ill-favored wife?   59
Thou'dst thank me but a little for my counsel.
And yet I'll promise thee she shall be rich,
And very rich. But thou'rt too much my friend,
And I'll not wish thee to her.

PETRUCHIO
Signor Hortensio, twixt such friends as we
Few words suffice. And therefore, if thou know
One rich enough to be Petruchio's wife—
As wealth is burden of my wooing dance—   67
Be she as foul as was Florentius' love,   68
As old as Sibyl, and as curst and shrewd   69
As Socrates' Xanthippe, or a worse,   70
She moves me not, or not removes, at least,   71
Affection's edge in me, were she as rough   72
As are the swelling Adriatic seas.
I come to wive it wealthily in Padua;
If wealthily, then happily in Padua.

GRUMIO   Nay, look you, sir, he tells you flatly what his
mind is. Why, give him gold enough and marry him
to a puppet or an aglet-baby, or an old trot with ne'er 78
a tooth in her head, though she have as many diseases
as two-and-fifty horses. Why, nothing comes amiss, so   80
money comes withal.   81

---

44 pledge surety.   **45 this's . . . chance** this is a sad occurrence
46 ancient long-standing.   **pleasant** merry   **51 in a few** in short
55 Happily with good luck. (*Happily* and *haply* were not always distinguished.)   **56 Crowns** Gold coins   **58 come roundly** speak
plainly   **59 shrewd** shrewish.   **ill-favored** ill-natured (? Kate is not
"ugly," the usual meaning of this term; see line 85.)   **67 burden**
undersong, i.e., basis   **68 foul** ugly.   **Florentius' love** (An allusion
to John Gower's version in *Confessio Amantis* of the fairy tale of the
knight who promises to marry an ugly old woman if she solves the
riddle he must answer. After the fulfillment of all promises, she
becomes young and beautiful. Another version of this story is
Chaucer's "Tale of the Wife of Bath," from *The Canterbury Tales*.)
69 Sibyl prophetess of Cumae, to whom Apollo gave as many
years of life as she held grains of sand in her hand   **70 Xanthippe**
the philosopher's notoriously shrewish wife   **71 moves** affects,
disturbs. (Setting up wordplay on *removes*.)   **72 Affection's edge**
the keen edge of desire   **78 aglet-baby** small figure carved on the
metal tip of a lace, i.e., a tiny baby.   **trot** hag   **80 so** provided
81 withal with it.

11 gate door   **13–14 I should . . . worst** i.e., You're asking me to hit
you—and I know who then will get the worst of it.   **15 Will it not
be?** i.e., Aren't you going to do what I said?   **16 an** if.   **ring it** sound
loudly, using a circular knocker or a bell. (With a pun on *wring*.)
17 I'll . . . sing it i.e., I'll make you cry out. (To *sol fa* is to sing a scale.)
18 masters i.e., sirs. (Addressed to the audience.)   **24 Con . . . trovato**
With all my heart, well met   **25–6 Alla . . . Petruchio** Welcome to our
house, my much-honored Petruchio. (Italian.)   **27 compound** settle
28 'leges alleges   **32–3 two . . . out** i.e., drunk, or not quite right in
the head. (Derived from the card game called *one-and-thirty*.)
33 a pip a spot on a playing card. (Hence, *a pip out* means "off by
one," or "one in excess of thirty one.")   **38 for my heart** i.e., for my
life   **42 come you now with** do you now change your tune to

HORTENSIO
  Petruchio, since we are stepped thus far in,
  I will continue that I broached in jest.   83
  I can, Petruchio, help thee to a wife
  With wealth enough, and young and beauteous,
  Brought up as best becomes a gentlewoman.
  Her only fault, and that is faults enough,
  Is that she is intolerable curst   88
  And shrewd, and froward, so beyond all measure   89
  That, were my state far worser than it is,   90
  I would not wed her for a mine of gold.
PETRUCHIO
  Hortensio, peace! Thou know'st not gold's effect.
  Tell me her father's name and 'tis enough;
  For I will board her, though she chide as loud   94
  As thunder when the clouds in autumn crack.   95
HORTENSIO
  Her father is Baptista Minola,
  An affable and courteous gentleman.
  Her name is Katharina Minola,
  Renowned in Padua for her scolding tongue.
PETRUCHIO
  I know her father, though I know not her,
  And he knew my deceasèd father well.
  I will not sleep, Hortensio, till I see her;
  And therefore let me be thus bold with you
  To give you over at this first encounter,   104
  Unless you will accompany me thither.
GRUMIO [*to Hortensio*]   I pray you, sir, let him go while
  the humor lasts. O' my word, an she knew him as well 107
  as I do, she would think scolding would do little good
  upon him. She may perhaps call him half a score
  knaves or so. Why, that's nothing; an he begin once,
  he'll rail in his rope tricks. I'll tell you what, sir: an she 111
  stand him but a little, he will throw a figure in her face 112
  and so disfigure her with it that she shall have no more 113
  eyes to see withal than a cat. You know him not, sir. 114
HORTENSIO
  Tarry, Petruchio, I must go with thee,
  For in Baptista's keep my treasure is.   117
  He hath the jewel of my life in hold,   118
  His youngest daughter, beautiful Bianca,
  And her withholds from me and other more,   120
  Suitors to her and rivals in my love,
  Supposing it a thing impossible,
  For those defects I have before rehearsed,   123
  That ever Katharina will be wooed.
  Therefore this order hath Baptista ta'en,   125
  That none shall have access unto Bianca

Till Katharine the curst have got a husband.
GRUMIO   Katharine the curst!
  A title for a maid of all titles the worst.
HORTENSIO
  Now shall my friend Petruchio do me grace,   130
  And offer me disguised in sober robes
  To old Baptista as a schoolmaster
  Well seen in music, to instruct Bianca,   133
  That so I may by this device at least
  Have leave and leisure to make love to her,   135
  And unsuspected court her by herself.

    Enter Gremio [with a paper], and Lucentio dis-
    guised [as a schoolmaster].

GRUMIO   Here's no knavery! See, to beguile the old 137
  folks, how the young folks lay their heads together!
  Master, master, look about you. Who goes there, ha?
HORTENSIO
  Peace, Grumio, it is the rival of my love.
  Petruchio, stand by awhile.   [*They stand aside.*]
GRUMIO [*aside*]
  A proper stripling and an amorous!   142
GREMIO [*to Lucentio*]
  Oh, very well, I have perused the note.   143
  Hark you, sir, I'll have them very fairly bound—
  All books of love, see that at any hand—   145
  And see you read no other lectures to her.   146
  You understand me. Over and beside
  Signor Baptista's liberality,
  I'll mend it with a largess. Take your paper too,   149
    [*giving Lucentio the note*]
  And let me have them very well perfumed,   150
  For she is sweeter than perfume itself
  To whom they go to. What will you read to her?
LUCENTIO
  Whate'er I read to her, I'll plead for you
  As for my patron, stand you so assured,
  As firmly as yourself were still in place—   155
  Yea, and perhaps with more successful words
  Than you, unless you were a scholar, sir.
GREMIO
  Oh, this learning, what a thing it is!
GRUMIO [*aside*]
  Oh, this woodcock, what an ass it is!   159
PETRUCHIO   Peace, sirrah!
HORTENSIO [*coming forward*]
  Grumio, mum!—God save you, Signor Gremio.
GREMIO
  And you are well met, Signor Hortensio.   162
  Trow you whither I am going? To Baptista Minola. 163

---

83 that I broached what I began   **88–9 intolerable . . . froward** intolerably ill-natured and willful   **90 state** estate   **94 board** woo aggressively, accost, have intercourse with, rape   **95 crack** make an explosive noise.   **104 give you over** leave you   **107 humor** whim. **O' my word, an** On my word, if   **111 he'll . . . tricks** i.e., he has tricks up his sleeve to answer her scolding.   **112–14 he will . . . cat** i.e., he will utterly dazzle and disable her with his rhetorical tricks. (A *figure* is a figure of speech.)   **117 keep** (1) place to store treasure (2) keeping **118 in hold** (1) in his custody (2) in his stronghold   **120 And . . . more** and witholds her from me and others besides   **123 rehearsed** related, described   **125 this order** these measures

130 grace a favor   **133 seen** skilled   **135 make love to** woo **137 Here's no knavery!** (Said sarcastically.)   **142 proper stripling** handsome young fellow. (Said ironically, in reference to Gremio.) **143 note** (Evidently, a list of books for Bianca's tutoring.) **145 see** see to.   **at any hand** in any case   **146 read . . . lectures** teach no other lessons   **149 mend** improve, increase.   **largess** gift of money.   **150 them** i.e., the books   **155 as** as if.   **still in place** present all the time   **159 woodcock** (A bird easily caught; proverbially stupid.)   **162 you are well met** i.e., how opportune to meet you just now   **163 Trow** Know

I promised to inquire carefully
About a schoolmaster for the fair Bianca,
And by good fortune I have lighted well   166
On this young man, for learning and behavior
Fit for her turn, well read in poetry   168
And other books—good ones, I warrant ye.

HORTENSIO
'Tis well. And I have met a gentleman
Hath promised me to help me to another,   171
A fine musician to instruct our mistress.
So shall I no whit be behind in duty
To fair Bianca, so beloved of me.

GREMIO
Beloved of me, and that my deeds shall prove.

GRUMIO [*aside*]   And that his bags shall prove.   176

HORTENSIO
Gremio, 'tis now no time to vent our love.   177
Listen to me, and if you speak me fair,   178
I'll tell you news indifferent good for either.   179
Here is a gentleman whom by chance I met,
Upon agreement from us to his liking,   181
Will undertake to woo curst Katharine,
Yea, and to marry her, if her dowry please.

GREMIO   So said, so done, is well.   184
Hortensio, have you told him all her faults?

PETRUCHIO
I know she is an irksome brawling scold.
If that be all, masters, I hear no harm.   187

GREMIO
No? Say'st me so, friend? What countryman?

PETRUCHIO
Born in Verona, old Antonio's son.
My father dead, his fortune lives for me,
And I do hope good days and long to see.   191

GREMIO
Oh, sir, such a life with such a wife were strange.   192
But if you have a stomach, to't, i' God's name.   193
You shall have me assisting you in all.
But will you woo this wildcat?

PETRUCHIO   Will I live?

GRUMIO
Will he woo her? Ay, or I'll hang her.

PETRUCHIO
Why came I hither but to that intent?
Think you a little din can daunt mine ears?
Have I not in my time heard lions roar?
Have I not heard the sea, puffed up with winds,
Rage like an angry boar chafèd with sweat?
Have I not heard great ordnance in the field,   202
And heaven's artillery thunder in the skies?

Have I not in a pitchèd battle heard   204
Loud 'larums, neighing steeds, and trumpets' clang?   205
And do you tell me of a woman's tongue,
That gives not half so great a blow to hear
As will a chestnut in a farmer's fire?   208
Tush, tush! Fear boys with bugs.

GRUMIO   For he fears none.   209

GREMIO   Hortensio, hark.
This gentleman is happily arrived,   211
My mind presumes, for his own good and ours.

HORTENSIO
I promised we would be contributors
And bear his charge of wooing, whatsoe'er.   214

GREMIO
And so we will, provided that he win her.

GRUMIO
I would I were as sure of a good dinner.   216

        *Enter Tranio, brave [as Lucentio], and
        Biondello.*

TRANIO
Gentlemen, God save you. If I may be bold,
Tell me, I beseech you, which is the readiest way
To the house of Signor Baptista Minola?

BIONDELLO   He that has the two fair daughters, is't he
you mean?

TRANIO   Even he, Biondello.   221

GREMIO
Hark you, sir, you mean not her to—

TRANIO
Perhaps him and her, sir. What have you to do?   224

PETRUCHIO
Not her that chides, sir, at any hand, I pray.   225

TRANIO
I love no chiders, sir.—Biondello, let's away.

LUCENTIO [*aside*]
Well begun, Tranio.

HORTENSIO   Sir, a word ere you go.
Are you a suitor to the maid you talk of, yea or no?

TRANIO
An if I be, sir, is it any offense?

GREMIO
No, if without more words you will get you hence.

TRANIO
Why, sir, I pray, are not the streets as free
For me as for you?

GREMIO   But so is not she.

TRANIO
For what reason, I beseech you?

GREMIO   For this reason, if you'll know,
That she's the choice love of Signor Gremio.

---

166 **lighted** alighted   168 **Fit for her turn** suited to her needs. (Something that is true in more ways than Gremio realizes.)   171 **Hath . . . another** who has promised to help me to obtain another   176 **bags** moneybags   177 **vent** express   178 **speak me fair** deal with me courteously   179 **indifferent** equally   181 **Upon . . . liking** who, if we agree to terms satisfactory to him   184 **So . . . is well** i.e., That's all very well, when his deeds match his words (which may not be soon).   187 **masters** good sirs   191 **And . . . see** and I hope to see many happy days.   192 **were** would be   193 **a stomach** an appetite, inclination   202 **ordnance** artillery.   **field** battlefield

204 **a pitchèd battle** a planned battle set in orderly array (unlike a skirmish)   205 **'larums** calls to arms   208 **chestnut** (Chestnuts roasted will pop open or explode with a loud report.)   209 **Fear . . . bugs.** Frighten children with bugbears, bogeymen.   211 **happily** fortunately, just when needed   214 **charge** expense   216.1 *brave* elegantly dressed   221 **Even he** Yes, precisely, he   224 **Perhaps . . . do?** i.e., Perhaps I mean to woo both Baptista Minola and Katharine, sir. What's that to you?   225 **at any hand** on any account

HORTENSIO
　That she's the chosen of Signor Hortensio.
TRANIO
　Softly, my masters! If you be gentlemen,
　Do me this right: hear me with patience.
　Baptista is a noble gentleman,
　To whom my father is not all unknown;　239
　And were his daughter fairer than she is,
　She may more suitors have, and me for one.
　Fair Leda's daughter had a thousand wooers;　242
　Then well one more may fair Bianca have,
　And so she shall. Lucentio shall make one,
　Though Paris came in hope to speed alone.　245
GREMIO
　What, this gentleman will out-talk us all!
LUCENTIO
　Sir, give him head. I know he'll prove a jade.　247
PETRUCHIO
　Hortensio, to what end are all these words?
HORTENSIO [to Tranio]
　Sir, let me be so bold as ask you,　249
　Did you yet ever see Baptista's daughter?
TRANIO
　No, sir, but hear I do that he hath two,
　The one as famous for a scolding tongue
　As is the other for beauteous modesty.
PETRUCHIO
　Sir, sir, the first's for me. Let her go by.　254
GREMIO
　Yea, leave that labor to great Hercules,
　And let it be more than Alcides' twelve.　256
PETRUCHIO
　Sir, understand you this of me, in sooth:　257
　The youngest daughter, whom you hearken for,　258
　Her father keeps from all access of suitors,
　And will not promise her to any man
　Until the elder sister first be wed.
　The younger then is free, and not before.
TRANIO
　If it be so, sir, that you are the man
　Must stead us all, and me amongst the rest;　264
　And if you break the ice and do this feat,
　Achieve the elder, set the younger free
　For our access, whose hap shall be to have her　267
　Will not so graceless be to be ingrate.　268
HORTENSIO
　Sir, you say well, and well you do conceive.　269
　And since you do profess to be a suitor,
　You must, as we do, gratify this gentleman,　271

　To whom we all rest generally beholding.　272
TRANIO
　Sir, I shall not be slack. In sign whereof,
　Please ye we may contrive this afternoon,　274
　And quaff carouses to our mistress' health,　275
　And do as adversaries do in law—　276
　Strive mightily, but eat and drink as friends.
GRUMIO, BIONDELLO
　Oh, excellent motion! Fellows, let's be gone.　278
HORTENSIO
　The motion's good indeed, and be it so.
　Petruchio, I shall be your ben venuto.　Exeunt. 280

❧

[2.1]

　　*Enter Katharina and Bianca [with her hands
　　tied].*

BIANCA
　Good sister, wrong me not, nor wrong yourself,
　To make a bondmaid and a slave of me.
　That I disdain. But for these other goods,　3
　Unbind my hands, I'll pull them off myself,　4
　Yea, all my raiment, to my petticoat,
　Or what you will command me will I do,
　So well I know my duty to my elders.
KATHARINA
　Of all thy suitors here I charge thee tell
　Whom thou lov'st best. See thou dissemble not.
BIANCA
　Believe me, sister, of all the men alive
　I never yet beheld that special face
　Which I could fancy more than any other.
KATHARINA
　Minion, thou liest. Is't not Hortensio?　13
BIANCA
　If you affect him, sister, here I swear　14
　I'll plead for you myself but you shall have him.　15
KATHARINA
　Oh, then belike you fancy riches more.　16
　You will have Gremio to keep you fair.　17
BIANCA
　Is it for him you do envy me so?
　Nay, then, you jest, and now I well perceive
　You have but jested with me all this while.
　I prithee, sister Kate, untie my hands.
KATHARINA (*strikes her*)
　If that be jest, then all the rest was so.

　　Enter Baptista.

239 all entirely　242 Leda's daughter Helen of Troy　245 Though . . .
alone even if Paris (who abducted Helen from her husband,
Menelaus) were to come in hopes of succeeding above all others.
247 Sir . . . jade Sir, give him a loose bridle; i.e., let him talk freely. I
know he'll prove to be a worthless horse, soon tired.　249 as ask as
to ask　254 Let her go by Pass over her.　256 And . . . twelve (Hercules, called *Alcides* because he was the reputed grandson of Alcaeus,
had to perform twelve huge labors.)　257 of me from me.　sooth
truth　258 hearken for seek to win　264 Must stead who must help
267 whose hap he whose good fortune　268 to be ingrate as to be
ungrateful.　269 conceive understand.　271 gratify this gentleman
reward Petruchio

272 beholding beholden, indebted.　274 contrive manage our affairs,
pass the time (?)　275 quaff carouses drink toasts　276 adversaries
opposing lawyers　278 motion suggestion.　280 ben venuto welcome, i.e., host.
2.1. Location: Padua. Baptista's house.
3 for as for.　goods i.e., clothes, jewels, love tokens　4 Unbind if you
will unbind　13 Minion Hussy　14 affect love　15 but . . . him if
necessary for you to win him.　16 belike perhaps　17 fair resplendent with finery.

BAPTISTA

Why, how now, dame, whence grows this
    insolence?—
Bianca, stand aside. Poor girl, she weeps.
Go ply thy needle, meddle not with her.—   25
For shame, thou hilding of a devilish spirit,   26
Why dost thou wrong her that did ne'er wrong thee?
When did she cross thee with a bitter word?   28

KATHARINA

Her silence flouts me, and I'll be revenged.   29
            [*She*] *flies after Bianca.*

BAPTISTA

What, in my sight? Bianca, get thee in.   *Exit* [*Bianca*].

KATHARINA

What, will you not suffer me? Nay, now I see   31
She is your treasure, she must have a husband;
I must dance barefoot on her wedding day,   33
And for your love to her lead apes in hell.   34
Talk not to me. I will go sit and weep
Till I can find occasion of revenge.   [*Exit.*]

BAPTISTA

Was ever gentleman thus grieved as I?
But who comes here?   38

    Enter Gremio, Lucentio [*as a schoolmaster*] *in the
    habit of a mean man, Petruchio, with* [*Hortensio as
    a musician, and*] *Tranio* [*as Lucentio*] *with his boy
    [Biondello] bearing a lute and books.*

GREMIO   Good morrow, neighbor Baptista.

BAPTISTA   Good morrow, neighbor Gremio. God save
you, gentlemen.

PETRUCHIO

And you, good sir. Pray, have you not a daughter
Called Katharina, fair and virtuous?

BAPTISTA

I have a daughter, sir, called Katharina.

GREMIO

You are too blunt. Go to it orderly.   45

PETRUCHIO

You wrong me, Signor Gremio; give me leave.—   46
I am a gentleman of Verona, sir,
That, hearing of her beauty and her wit,
Her affability and bashful modesty,
Her wondrous qualities and mild behavior,
Am bold to show myself a forward guest
Within your house, to make mine eye the witness
Of that report which I so oft have heard.
And, for an entrance to my entertainment,   54
I do present you with a man of mine,
            [*presenting Hortensio*]
Cunning in music and the mathematics,   56

To instruct her fully in those sciences,   57
Whereof I know she is not ignorant.
Accept of him, or else you do me wrong.   59
His name is Litio, born in Mantua.

BAPTISTA

You're welcome, sir, and he, for your good sake.
But for my daughter Katharine, this I know,   62
She is not for your turn, the more my grief.

PETRUCHIO

I see you do not mean to part with her,
Or else you like not of my company.   65

BAPTISTA

Mistake me not, I speak but as I find.
Whence are you, sir? What may I call your name?

PETRUCHIO

Petruchio is my name, Antonio's son,
A man well known throughout all Italy.

BAPTISTA

I know him well. You are welcome for his sake.   70

GREMIO

Saving your tale, Petruchio, I pray,   71
Let us that are poor petitioners speak too.
Bacare! You are marvelous forward.   73

PETRUCHIO

Oh, pardon me, Signor Gremio, I would fain be doing. 74

GREMIO

I doubt it not, sir, but you will curse your wooing.—
Neighbors, this is a gift very grateful, I am sure of   76
it. [*To Baptista*] To express the like kindness, myself, that have been more kindly beholding to you
than any, freely give unto you this young scholar
[*presenting Lucentio*], that hath been long studying at
Rheims, as cunning in Greek, Latin, and other languages, as the other in music and mathematics. His   82
name is Cambio. Pray, accept his service.   83

BAPTISTA   A thousand thanks, Signor Gremio.—Welcome, good Cambio. [*To Tranio*] But, gentle sir,
methinks you walk like a stranger. May I be so bold to
know the cause of your coming?

TRANIO

Pardon me, sir, the boldness is mine own,
That, being a stranger in this city here,
Do make myself a suitor to your daughter,
Unto Bianca, fair and virtuous.
Nor is your firm resolve unknown to me
In the preferment of the eldest sister.   93
This liberty is all that I request,
That, upon knowledge of my parentage,   95
I may have welcome 'mongst the rest that woo,
And free access and favor as the rest.   97

---

25 **meddle not with** have nothing to do with   26 **hilding** vicious
(hence worthless) beast   28 **cross** contradict, thwart   29 **flouts**
mocks, insults   31 **suffer me** let me have my own way.   33, 34 **dance
. . . day, lead . . . hell** (Popularly supposed to be the fate of old maids.)
38.2 *habit* dress.   *mean* of low social station. (Said here of a schoolmaster.)   45 **orderly** in a properly orderly manner   46 **give me leave**
excuse me, let me do this my way.   54 **entrance** entrance fee.
entertainment reception.   56 **Cunning** skillful

57 **sciences** subjects, branches of knowledge   59 **Accept of** Accept
62 **for** as for   65 **like not of** do not like   70 **know** know of. (See also
lines 104–5.)   71 **Saving** With all due respect for   73 *Bacare!* Stand
back!   74 **fain** gladly.   **doing** getting on with the business. (With
sexual suggestion.)   76 **grateful** pleasing   82 **the other** i.e., Hortensio   83 **Cambio** (In Italian, appropriately, the word means "change"
or "exchange.")   93 **In the preferment of** in the precedence you give
to   95 **upon knowledge of** when you know about   97 **favor** leave,
permission

And toward the education of your daughters
I here bestow a simple instrument,
And this small packet of Greek and Latin books.
If you accept them, then their worth is great.
              [*Biondello brings forward the lute and books.*]

BAPTISTA
Lucentio is your name? Of whence, I pray?   102

TRANIO
Of Pisa, sir, son to Vincentio.

BAPTISTA
A mighty man of Pisa. By report
I know him well. You are very welcome, sir.
[*To Hortensio*] Take you the lute, [*to Lucentio*] and
   you the set of books;
You shall go see your pupils presently.—
Holla, within!

           Enter a Servant.

              Sirrah, lead these gentlemen
To my daughters, and tell them both
These are their tutors. Bid them use them well.
         [*Exit Servant, with Lucentio and Hortensio.*]
We will go walk a little in the orchard,
And then to dinner. You are passing welcome,   112
And so I pray you all to think yourselves.

PETRUCHIO
Signor Baptista, my business asketh haste,
And every day I cannot come to woo.
You knew my father well, and in him me,
Left solely heir to all his lands and goods,
Which I have bettered rather than decreased.
Then tell me, if I get your daughter's love,
What dowry shall I have with her to wife?

BAPTISTA
After my death the one half of my lands,
And in possession twenty thousand crowns.   122

PETRUCHIO
And for that dowry I'll assure her of   123
Her widowhood, be it that she survive me,   124
In all my lands and leases whatsoever.
Let specialties be therefore drawn between us,   126
That covenants may be kept on either hand.

BAPTISTA
Ay, when the special thing is well obtained,
That is, her love; for that is all in all.

PETRUCHIO
Why, that is nothing, for I tell you, father,   130
I am as peremptory as she proud-minded;
And where two raging fires meet together,
They do consume the thing that feeds their fury.
Though little fire grows great with little wind,
Yet extreme gusts will blow out fire and all.
So I to her, and so she yields to me,   136

For I am rough and woo not like a babe.

BAPTISTA
Well mayst thou woo, and happy be thy speed!   138
But be thou armed for some unhappy words.

PETRUCHIO
Ay, to the proof, as mountains are for winds,   140
That shakes not, though they blow perpetually.   141

      Enter Hortensio [as Litio], with his head broke.

BAPTISTA
How now, my friend, why dost thou look so pale?

HORTENSIO
For fear, I promise you, if I look pale.   143

BAPTISTA
What, will my daughter prove a good musician?

HORTENSIO
I think she'll sooner prove a soldier.   145
Iron may hold with her, but never lutes.   146

BAPTISTA
Why then, thou canst not break her to the lute?   147

HORTENSIO
Why, no, for she hath broke the lute to me.
I did but tell her she mistook her frets,   149
And bowed her hand to teach her fingering,
When, with a most impatient devilish spirit,
"Frets, call you these?" quoth she, "I'll fume with
   them."
And with that word she struck me on the head,
And through the instrument my pate made way;
And there I stood amazèd for a while,   155
As on a pillory, looking through the lute,   156
While she did call me rascal fiddler
And twangling Jack, with twenty such vile terms,   158
As had she studied to misuse me so.   159

PETRUCHIO
Now, by the world, it is a lusty wench!   160
I love her ten times more than e'er I did.
Oh, how I long to have some chat with her!

BAPTISTA [*to Hortensio*]
Well, go with me, and be not so discomfited.
Proceed in practice with my younger daughter;   164
She's apt to learn and thankful for good turns.—
Signor Petruchio, will you go with us,
Or shall I send my daughter Kate to you?

PETRUCHIO
I pray you, do.   *Exeunt. Manet Petruchio.*
         I'll attend her here,   168
And woo her with some spirit when she comes.

---

102 **Lucentio . . . name?** (Baptista may have learned this information from a note accompanying the books and lute.)   112 **passing** exceedingly   122 **in possession** in immediate possession   123 **for** in exchange for   124 **widowhood** i.e., widow's share of the estate. **be it that she** if she should   126 **specialties** terms of contract   130 **father** father-in-law   136 **So I** i.e., So I behave, like an extreme gust of wind

138 **happy . . . speed!** may fortune give you success!   140 **to the proof** i.e., in armor, proof against her shrewishness   141 **shakes** shake.   141.1 *broke* with a bleeding cut. (Hortensio usually appears on stage with his head emerging through a broken lute.)
143 **promise** assure   145 **I think . . . soldier** i.e., She's better suited for the manly career of soldiering.   146 **hold with** hold out against   147 **break** train. (With pun in the next line.)   149 **frets** ridges or bars on the fingerboard of the lute. (But Kate puns on the sense of "fume," "be indignant.")   155 **amazèd** bewildered   156 **As on a pillory** as if with my head in a wooden collar used as punishment   158 **Jack** knave   159 **As . . . so** as if she had planned how to abuse me so.   160 **lusty** lively   164 **practice** instruction   168 s.d. *Manet* He remains onstage

Say that she rail, why then I'll tell her plain
She sings as sweetly as a nightingale.
Say that she frown, I'll say she looks as clear   172
As morning roses newly washed with dew.
Say she be mute and will not speak a word,
Then I'll commend her volubility
And say she uttereth piercing eloquence.   176
If she do bid me pack, I'll give her thanks,   177
As though she bid me stay by her a week.
If she deny to wed, I'll crave the day   179
When I shall ask the banns and when be married.   180
But here she comes; and now, Petruchio, speak.

Enter Katharina.

Good morrow, Kate, for that's your name, I hear.
KATHARINA
Well have you heard, but something hard of hearing.   183
They call me Katharine that do talk of me.
PETRUCHIO
You lie, in faith, for you are called plain Kate,
And bonny Kate, and sometimes Kate the curst;
But Kate, the prettiest Kate in Christendom,
Kate of Kate Hall, my superdainty Kate,
For dainties are all Kates, and therefore, Kate,   189
Take this of me, Kate of my consolation: 190
Hearing thy mildness praised in every town,
Thy virtues spoke of, and thy beauty sounded,   192
Yet not so deeply as to thee belongs,
Myself am moved to woo thee for my wife.   194
KATHARINA
Moved? In good time! Let him that moved you hither 195
Remove you hence. I knew you at the first
You were a movable.
PETRUCHIO   Why, what's a movable?   197
KATHARINA
A joint stool.
PETRUCHIO   Thou hast hit it. Come, sit on me.   198
KATHARINA
Asses are made to bear, and so are you.   199
PETRUCHIO
Women are made to bear, and so are you.
KATHARINA
No such jade as you, if me you mean.   201
PETRUCHIO
Alas, good Kate, I will not burden thee,   202

For knowing thee to be but young and light.   203
KATHARINA
Too light for such a swain as you to catch,   204
And yet as heavy as my weight should be.
PETRUCHIO
Should be? Should—buzz!
KATHARINA   Well ta'en, and like a buzzard. 206
PETRUCHIO
Oh, slow-winged turtle, shall a buzzard take thee?
KATHARINA
Ay, for a turtle, as he takes a buzzard.
PETRUCHIO
Come, come, you wasp, i'faith you are too angry.   209
KATHARINA
If I be waspish, best beware my sting.
PETRUCHIO
My remedy is then to pluck it out.
KATHARINA
Ay, if the fool could find it where it lies.
PETRUCHIO
Who knows not where a wasp does wear his sting?
In his tail.
KATHARINA   In his tongue.
PETRUCHIO   Whose tongue?
KATHARINA
Yours, if you talk of tales, and so farewell.   217
PETRUCHIO
What, with my tongue in your tail? Nay, come again.
Good Kate, I am a gentleman—
KATHARINA   That I'll try.
                                She strikes him.
PETRUCHIO
I swear I'll cuff you if you strike again.
KATHARINA   So may you lose your arms.
If you strike me, you are no gentleman,
And if no gentleman, why then no arms.   223
PETRUCHIO
A herald, Kate? Oh, put me in thy books!   224
KATHARINA   What is your crest, a coxcomb?   225
PETRUCHIO
A combless cock, so Kate will be my hen.   226
KATHARINA
No cock of mine. You crow too like a craven.   227

---

172 **clear** serene   176 **piercing** moving   177 **pack** begone   179 **deny** refuse.   **crave the day** ask her to name the day   180 **ask the banns** have a reading of the required announcement in church of a forthcoming marriage   183 **heard, hard** (Pronounced nearly alike.)
189 **all Kates** (With a quibble on "cates," confections, delicacies.)
190 **of me** from me.   **consolation** comfort   192 **sounded** proclaimed. (With a quibble on "plumbed," as indicated by *deeply* in the next line.)
194 **moved** impelled. (Followed by wordplay on the more literal meaning of *move* and *remove*.)   195 **In good time!** Forsooth! Indeed!
197 **movable** (1) one easily changed or dissuaded (2) an article of furniture.   198 **A joint stool** a well-fitted stool made by an expert craftsman.   199 **bear** carry. (With puns in the following lines suggesting "bear children" and "support a man during sexual intercourse.")
201 **jade** an ill-conditioned horse   202 **burden** (1) oppress with a heavy load—a term appropriate to *asses* and *bear* in line 199, since asses are beasts of *burden* (2) lie on during sexual intercourse, impregnate. (See notes on lines 199 and 203.)

203 **For knowing** because I know.   **light** (1) of delicate stature (2) lascivious (3) lacking a *burden* (see previous line) in the musical sense of lacking a bass undersong or accompaniment (4) elusive (in the following line).   204 **swain** young rustic in love   206 **Should . . . buzz!** (Petruchio puns on *be* and "bee," and uses *buzz* in perhaps three senses: [1] an interjection of impatience or contempt [2] a bee's sound [3] a rumor being buzzed about, to which, he implies, Kate had better listen.)   **buzzard** (1) figuratively, a fool (2) in the next line, an inferior kind of hawk, fit only to overtake a slow-winged *turtle* or turtledove, as Petruchio might overtake Kate (3) a buzzing insect, caught by a turtledove.   209 **wasp** i.e., waspish, scolding woman. (But suggested by *buzzard*, buzzing insect.)   217 **talk of tales** i.e., idly tell stories. (With pun on "tail.")   223 **no arms** no coat of arms. (With pun on *arms* as limbs of the body.)   224 **books** (1) books of heraldry, heraldic registers (2) grace, favor.   225 **crest** (1) armorial device (2) a rooster's comb, setting up the joke on *coxcomb*, the cap of the court fool
226 **A combless cock** i.e., A gentle rooster. (With suggestion of the male sexual organ.)   **so** provided that   227 **a craven** a cock that is not "game" or willing to fight.

PETRUCHIO
  Nay, come, Kate, come. You must not look so sour.
KATHARINA
  It is my fashion when I see a crab.   229
PETRUCHIO
  Why, here's no crab, and therefore look not sour.
KATHARINA   There is, there is.
PETRUCHIO
  Then show it me.
KATHARINA   Had I a glass, I would.
PETRUCHIO   What, you mean my face?
KATHARINA   Well aimed of such a young one.   234
PETRUCHIO
  Now, by Saint George, I am too young for you.
KATHARINA
  Yet you are withered.
PETRUCHIO   'Tis with cares.
KATHARINA   I care not.
PETRUCHIO
  Nay, hear you, Kate. In sooth, you scape not so.   237
KATHARINA
  I chafe you if I tarry. Let me go.   238
PETRUCHIO
  No, not a whit. I find you passing gentle.   239
  'Twas told me you were rough, and coy, and sullen,   240
  And now I find report a very liar,   241
  For thou art pleasant, gamesome, passing courteous,   242
  But slow in speech, yet sweet as springtime flowers. 243
  Thou canst not frown, thou canst not look askance,   244
  Nor bite the lip, as angry wenches will,
  Nor hast thou pleasure to be cross in talk;   246
  But thou with mildness entertain'st thy wooers,   247
  With gentle conference, soft and affable.   248
  Why does the world report that Kate doth limp?
  Oh, sland'rous world! Kate like the hazel twig
  Is straight and slender, and as brown in hue
  As hazelnuts, and sweeter than the kernels.
  Oh, let me see thee walk. Thou dost not halt.   253
KATHARINA
  Go, fool, and whom thou keep'st command.   254
PETRUCHIO
  Did ever Dian so become a grove   255
  As Kate this chamber with her princely gait?
  Oh, be thou Dian, and let her be Kate,
  And then let Kate be chaste and Dian sportful!   258
KATHARINA
  Where did you study all this goodly speech?   259
PETRUCHIO
  It is extempore, from my mother wit.   260

KATHARINA
  A witty mother! Witless else her son.   261
PETRUCHIO   Am I not wise?   262
KATHARINA   Yes, keep you warm.   263
PETRUCHIO
  Marry, so I mean, sweet Katharine, in thy bed.
  And therefore, setting all this chat aside,
  Thus in plain terms: your father hath consented
  That you shall be my wife; your dowry 'greed on;
  And will you, nill you, I will marry you.   268
  Now, Kate, I am a husband for your turn,   269
  For by this light, whereby I see thy beauty—
  Thy beauty that doth make me like thee well—
  Thou must be married to no man but me.

        Enter Baptista, Gremio, [and] Tranio [as
        Lucentio].

  For I am he am born to tame you, Kate,
  And bring you from a wild Kate to a Kate   274
  Conformable as other household Kates.   275
  Here comes your father. Never make denial;
  I must and will have Katharine to my wife.
BAPTISTA
  Now, Signor Petruchio, how speed you with my
    daughter?   278
PETRUCHIO
  How but well, sir, how but well?
  It were impossible I should speed amiss.
BAPTISTA
  Why, how now, daughter Katharine, in your dumps? 281
KATHARINA
  Call you me daughter? Now, I promise you,   282
  You have showed a tender fatherly regard,
  To wish me wed to one half-lunatic,
  A madcap ruffian and a swearing Jack,   285
  That thinks with oaths to face the matter out.   286
PETRUCHIO
  Father, 'tis thus: yourself and all the world
  That talked of her have talked amiss of her.
  If she be curst, it is for policy,   289
  For she's not froward, but modest as the dove.   290
  She is not hot, but temperate as the morn.
  For patience she will prove a second Grissel,   292
  And Roman Lucrece for her chastity.   293
  And to conclude, we have 'greed so well together
  That upon Sunday is the wedding day.

---

229 **crab** crab apple.   234 **aimed of** guessed for.   **young** i.e., inexperienced. (But Petruchio picks up the word in the sense of "strong," "virile.")   237 **scape** escape   238 **chafe** irritate, arouse   239 **passing** very. (Also in line 242.)   240 **coy** disdainful   241 **a very** an utter   242 **pleasant, gamesome** merry, spirited   243 **But slow** never anything but slow   244 **askance** scornfully   246 **cross in talk** always contradicting   247 **entertain'st** receive   248 **conference** conversation   253 **halt** limp.   254 **whom thou keep'st command** i.e., order about those whom you employ, your servants, not me.   255 **Dian** Diana, goddess of the hunt and of chastity.   **become** adorn   258 **sportful** amorous.   259 **study** memorize   260 **mother wit** native intelligence.

261 **Witless . . . son** i.e., Without the intelligence inherited from her, he would have none at all.   262–3 **wise . . . warm** (An allusion to the proverbial phrase "enough wit to keep oneself warm.")   268 **will you, nill you** whether you're willing or not   269 **for your turn** to suit you   274 **wild Kate** (With a quibble on "wildcat.")   275 **Conformable** compliant   278 **speed** fare, get on   281 **in your dumps** in low spirits.   282 **promise** assure   285 **Jack** ill-mannered fellow   286 **face** brazen   289 **policy** cunning, ulterior motive   290 **froward** willful, perverse   292 **Grissel** patient Griselda, the epitome of wifely patience and devotion (whose story was told by Chaucer in "The Clerk's Tale" of *The Canterbury Tales* and earlier by Boccaccio and Petrarch)   293 **Roman Lucrece** Lucretia, a Roman lady who took her own life after her chastity had been violated by the Tarquin prince, Sextus. (Shakespeare tells the story in *The Rape of Lucrece*.)

KATHARINA
I'll see thee hanged on Sunday first.

GREMIO Hark, Petruchio, she says she'll see thee
hanged first.

TRANIO
Is this your speeding? Nay then, good night our part!   299

PETRUCHIO
Be patient, gentlemen. I choose her for myself.
If she and I be pleased, what's that to you?
'Tis bargained twixt us twain, being alone,
That she shall still be curst in company.
I tell you, 'tis incredible to believe
How much she loves me. Oh, the kindest Kate!
She hung about my neck, and kiss on kiss
She vied so fast, protesting oath on oath,   307
That in a twink she won me to her love.
Oh, you are novices! 'Tis a world to see   309
How tame, when men and women are alone,
A meacock wretch can make the curstest shrew.—   311
Give me thy hand, Kate. I will unto Venice
To buy apparel gainst the wedding day.—   313
Provide the feast, father, and bid the guests.
I will be sure my Katharine shall be fine.   315

BAPTISTA
I know not what to say. But give me your hands.
God send you joy, Petruchio! 'Tis a match.

GREMIO, TRANIO
Amen, say we. We will be witnesses.

PETRUCHIO
Father, and wife, and gentlemen, adieu.
I will to Venice. Sunday comes apace.
We will have rings, and things, and fine array;
And kiss me, Kate. We will be married o'Sunday.   322
Exeunt Petruchio and Katharine [separately].

GREMIO
Was ever match clapped up so suddenly?   323

BAPTISTA
Faith, gentlemen, now I play a merchant's part,   324
And venture madly on a desperate mart.   325

TRANIO
'Twas a commodity lay fretting by you;   326
'Twill bring you gain, or perish on the seas.

BAPTISTA
The gain I seek is quiet in the match.

GREMIO
No doubt but he hath got a quiet catch.   329
But now, Baptista, to your younger daughter.
Now is the day we long have looked for.
I am your neighbor, and was suitor first.

TRANIO
And I am one that love Bianca more
Than words can witness, or your thoughts can guess.

GREMIO
Youngling, thou canst not love so dear as I.

TRANIO
Graybeard, thy love doth freeze.

GREMIO   But thine doth fry.
Skipper, stand back. 'Tis age that nourisheth.   337

TRANIO
But youth in ladies' eyes that flourisheth.

BAPTISTA
Content you, gentlemen, I will compound this strife.   339
'Tis deeds must win the prize, and he of both   340
That can assure my daughter greatest dower   341
Shall have my Bianca's love.
Say, Signor Gremio, what can you assure her?

GREMIO
First, as you know, my house within the city
Is richly furnishèd with plate and gold,   345
Basins and ewers to lave her dainty hands;   346
My hangings all of Tyrian tapestry;   347
In ivory coffers I have stuffed my crowns;   348
In cypress chests my arras counterpoints,   349
Costly apparel, tents, and canopies,   350
Fine linen, Turkey cushions bossed with pearl,   351
Valance of Venice gold in needlework,   352
Pewter and brass, and all things that belongs
To house or housekeeping. Then at my farm
I have a hundred milch kine to the pail,   355
Sixscore fat oxen standing in my stalls,
And all things answerable to this portion.   357
Myself am struck in years, I must confess,   358
And if I die tomorrow, this is hers,
If whilst I live she will be only mine.

TRANIO
That "only" came well in.—Sir, list to me:
I am my father's heir and only son.
If I may have your daughter to my wife,
I'll leave her houses three or four as good,
Within rich Pisa walls, as any one
Old Signor Gremio has in Padua,
Besides two thousand ducats by the year   367
Of fruitful land, all which shall be her jointure.—   368
What, have I pinched you, Signor Gremio?

GREMIO
Two thousand ducats by the year of land!
[Aside] My land amounts not to so much in all.—
That she shall have, besides an argosy   372

---

337 **Skipper** Flighty fellow   339 **compound** settle   340 **deeds**
(1) actions (2) legal deeds.   **he of both** the one of you two   341
dower portion of a husband's estate settled on his wife in his will.
(Also at line 387 and 4.4.45.)   345 **plate** silver utensils   346 **ewers to
lave** pitchers to wash   347 **hangings** draperies hung on beds and
walls.   **Tyrian** dark red or purple   348 **crowns** five-shilling coins
349 **arras counterpoints** counterpanes of tapestry   350 **tents** bed curtains   351 **Turkey** Turkish.   **bossed** embossed   352 **Valance** fringes
of drapery around the canopy or bed frame   355 **milch kine to the
pail** dairy cattle   357 **answerable to** on the same scale as   358 **struck**
advanced   367 **ducats** gold coins   368 **Of** from.   **jointure** marriage
settlement.   372 **argosy** merchant vessel of the largest size

---

299 **speeding** success.   **good night our part** good-bye to what we
hoped to get.   307 **vied** went me one better, kiss for kiss   309 **a
world** worth a whole world   311 **meacock** cowardly   313 **gainst** in
anticipation of   315 **fine** elegantly dressed.   322 **kiss me** (Petruchio
probably kisses her.)   323 **clapped up** settled (by a shaking of hands)
324 **Faith** In faith   325 **desperate mart** risky venture.   326 **lay fretting** i.e., which lay in storage being destroyed by moths, weevils, or
spoilage. (With a pun on "chafing.")   329 **quiet catch** (Said ironically;
Gremio is sure that Kate will be anything but quiet.)

That now is lying in Marseilles road. 373
[*To Tranio*] What, have I choked you with an argosy?

TRANIO
Gremio, 'tis known my father hath no less
Than three great argosies, besides two galliases 376
And twelve tight galleys. These I will assure her, 377
And twice as much, whate'er thou off'rest next.

GREMIO
Nay, I have offered all. I have no more,
And she can have no more than all I have.
[*To Baptista*] If you like me, she shall have me and
mine.

TRANIO
Why then, the maid is mine from all the world,
By your firm promise. Gremio is outvied. 383

BAPTISTA
I must confess your offer is the best;
And, let your father make her the assurance, 385
She is your own; else, you must pardon me.
If you should die before him, where's her dower?

TRANIO
That's but a cavil. He is old, I young. 388

GREMIO
And may not young men die, as well as old?

BAPTISTA
Well, gentlemen, I am thus resolved:
On Sunday next, you know
My daughter Katharine is to be married.
Now, on the Sunday following shall Bianca
Be bride [*to Tranio*] to you, if you make this assurance;
If not, to Signor Gremio.
And so I take my leave, and thank you both. *Exit.*

GREMIO
Adieu, good neighbor.—Now I fear thee not.
Sirrah, young gamester, your father were a fool
To give thee all, and in his waning age
Set foot under thy table. Tut, a toy! 400
An old Italian fox is not so kind, my boy. *Exit.*

TRANIO
A vengeance on your crafty withered hide!
Yet I have faced it with a card of ten. 403
'Tis in my head to do my master good.
I see no reason but supposed Lucentio
Must get a father, called supposed Vincentio—
And that's a wonder. Fathers commonly
Do get their children; but in this case of wooing, 408
A child shall get a sire, if I fail not of my cunning.
Exit.

❧

3.1

Enter Lucentio [as Cambio], Hortensio [as Litio], and Bianca.

LUCENTIO
Fiddler, forbear. You grow too forward, sir.
Have you so soon forgot the entertainment
Her sister Katharine welcomed you withal?

HORTENSIO
But, wrangling pedant, this is 4
The patroness of heavenly harmony.
Then give me leave to have prerogative, 6
And when in music we have spent an hour,
Your lecture shall have leisure for as much. 8

LUCENTIO
Preposterous ass, that never read so far
To know the cause why music was ordained! 10
Was it not to refresh the mind of man
After his studies or his usual pain? 12
Then give me leave to read philosophy, 13
And, while I pause, serve in your harmony. 14

HORTENSIO
Sirrah, I will not bear these braves of thine. 15

BIANCA
Why, gentlemen, you do me double wrong
To strive for that which resteth in my choice.
I am no breeching scholar in the schools; 18
I'll not be tied to hours nor 'pointed times,
But learn my lessons as I please myself.
And, to cut off all strife, here sit we down.
[*To Hortensio*] Take you your instrument, play you the
whiles; 22
His lecture will be done ere you have tuned.

HORTENSIO
You'll leave his lecture when I am in tune?

LUCENTIO
That will be never. Tune your instrument.
[*Hortensio moves aside and tunes.*]

BIANCA   Where left we last?
LUCENTIO   Here, madam. [*He reads.*]
    "Hic ibat Simois; hic est Sigeia tellus; 28
    Hic steterat Priami regia celsa senis." 29
BIANCA   Conster them. 30
LUCENTIO   "Hic ibat," as I told you before, "Simois," I
am Lucentio, "hic est," son unto Vincentio of Pisa, "Sigeia
tellus," disguised thus to get your love; "Hic
steterat," and that Lucentio that comes a-wooing,
"Priami," is my man Tranio, "regia," bearing my port, 35
"celsa senis," that we might beguile the old panta- 36
loon. 37

---

373 **road** roadstead, harbor.   376 **galliases** heavy, low-built vessels
377 **tight** watertight   383 **outvied** outbidden.   385 **let** provided
388 **but a cavil** merely a frivolous objection.   400 **Set . . . toy!** i.e.,
become a dependent in your household. Tut, nonsense!   403 **faced . . .
ten** brazened it out with only a ten-spot of cards.   408 **get** beget.
(With a play on *get*, "obtain," in line 406.)

3.1. Location: The same.
4 this i.e., Bianca   **6 prerogative** precedence   **8 lecture** lesson
10 To know as to know   **12 usual pain** regular labors.   **13 read** teach
14 serve in present, serve up   **15 braves** insults   **18 breeching
scholar** i.e., schoolboy liable to be whipped   **22 the whiles** meantime
28–9 Hic . . . senis Here flowed the river Simois; here is the Sigeian
land; here stood the lofty palace of old Priam. (Ovid, *Heroides*, 1.33–4.)
30 Conster Construe   **35 bearing my port** i.e., pretending to be me
36–7 pantaloon foolish old man, i.e., Gremio

HORTENSIO   Madam, my instrument's in tune.
BIANCA   Let's hear. [*He plays.*] Oh, fie! The treble jars.
LUCENTIO   Spit in the hole, man, and tune again.   40
                                        [*Hortensio moves aside.*]
BIANCA   Now let me see if I can conster it: "*Hic ibat
Simois,*" I know you not, "*hic est Sigeia tellus,*" I trust
you not; "*Hic steterat Priami,*" take heed he hear us not,
"*regia,*" presume not, "*celsa senis,*" despair not.
HORTENSIO
     Madam, 'tis now in tune.   [*He plays again.*]
LUCENTIO   All but the bass.
HORTENSIO
     The bass is right, 'tis the base knave that jars.
     [*Aside*] How fiery and forward our pedant is!
     Now, for my life, the knave doth court my love.
     Pedascule, I'll watch you better yet.   49
BIANCA [*to Lucentio*]
     In time I may believe, yet I mistrust.
LUCENTIO
     Mistrust it not, for, sure, Aeacides   51
     Was Ajax, called so from his grandfather.
BIANCA
     I must believe my master; else, I promise you,
     I should be arguing still upon that doubt.
     But let it rest.—Now, Litio, to you:
     Good master, take it not unkindly, pray,
     That I have been thus pleasant with you both.   57
HORTENSIO [*to Lucentio*]
     You may go walk, and give me leave awhile.
     My lessons make no music in three parts.
LUCENTIO
     Are you so formal, sir? Well, I must wait.   60
     [*Aside*] And watch withal; for, but I be deceived,   61
     Our fine musician groweth amorous.
                                        [*He moves aside.*]
HORTENSIO
     Madam, before you touch the instrument,
     To learn the order of my fingering,   64
     I must begin with rudiments of art,
     To teach you gamut in a briefer sort,   66
     More pleasant, pithy, and effectual
     Than hath been taught by any of my trade.
     And there it is in writing, fairly drawn.   69
                                        [*He gives her a paper.*]
BIANCA
     Why, I am past my gamut long ago.

HORTENSIO
     Yet read the gamut of Hortensio.
BIANCA [*reads*]
     "*Gamut* I am, the ground of all accord,   72
     A re, to plead Hortensio's passion;
     B mi, Bianca, take him for thy lord,   74
     C fa ut, that loves with all affection.   75
     D sol re, one clef, two notes have I;   76
     E la mi, show pity, or I die."   77
     Call you this gamut? Tut, I like it not.
     Old fashions please me best; I am not so nice   79
     To change true rules for odd inventions.

                    Enter a [*Servant as*] *messenger.*

SERVANT
     Mistress, your father prays you leave your books
     And help to dress your sister's chamber up.
     You know tomorrow is the wedding day.
BIANCA
     Farewell, sweet masters both. I must be gone.
LUCENTIO
     Faith, mistress, then I have no cause to stay.
                    [*Exeunt Bianca, Servant, and Lucentio.*]
HORTENSIO
     But I have cause to pry into this pedant.
     Methinks he looks as though he were in love.
     Yet if thy thoughts, Bianca, be so humble
     To cast thy wandering eyes on every stale,   89
     Seize thee that list. If once I find thee ranging,   90
     Hortensio will be quit with thee by changing.   *Exit.*   91

                                ❧

[3.2]

                    Enter Baptista, Gremio, Tranio [*as Lucentio*],
                    Katharine, Bianca, [*Lucentio as Cambio*], *and
                    others, attendants.*

BAPTISTA [*to Tranio*]
     Signor Lucentio, this is the 'pointed day
     That Katharine and Petruchio should be married,
     And yet we hear not of our son-in-law.
     What will be said? What mockery will it be,   4
     To want the bridegroom when the priest attends   5
     To speak the ceremonial rites of marriage?
     What says Lucentio to this shame of ours?

---

40 Spit in the hole i.e., to make the peg stick   **49** *Pedascule* (A word contemptuously coined by Hortensio, presumably the vocative of an invented Latinism, *pedasculus,* "little pedant.")   **51 Mistrust** (Lucentio plays upon Bianca's *mistrust* in line 50, in which she expresses skepticism about his secret wooing; his answer seeks to reassure her, while at the same time in "Litio's" hearing he seems to emphasize the truth of his instruction as he goes on with his lesson from the *Heroides.* Her reply is ambiguous in the same way.)   **Aeacides** descendant of Aeacus, King of Aegina, father of Telamon and grandfather of Ajax   **57 pleasant** merry   **60 formal** precise   **61 but** unless   **64 order** method   **66 gamut** the scale, from the alphabet name (*gamma*) of the first note plus *ut,* its syllable name, now commonly called *do.* (The *gamut* of Hortensio begins on G instead of on C.)   **69 drawn** set out, copied.

72 ground bass note, foundation.   **accord** harmony   **74** *B mi* (With a suggestion of "be my.")   **75** *fa ut* (The note C is the fourth note, or *fa,* of a scale based on G but is the first note, *ut,* or *do,* of the more universal major scale based on C. Similarly, D is the fifth note, or *sol,* in the G scale but is the second, or *re,* in the C scale; similarly, with E as sixth and third.)   **76 two notes** (Hinting at Hortensio's disguise.)   **77** *E la mi* (Suggesting "Ill am I.")   **79 nice** capricious   **89 stale** ridiculous rival   **90 Seize . . . list** let him who wants you have you.   **ranging** inconstant. (The metaphor is that of a straying hawk.)   **91 be quit** get even.   **changing** loving another.
3.2. Location: Padua. Before Baptista's house.
4 What . . . said? What will people say?   **5 want** lack

KATHARINA
No shame but mine. I must, forsooth, be forced
To give my hand opposed against my heart
Unto a mad-brain rudesby full of spleen,   10
Who wooed in haste and means to wed at leisure.
I told you, I, he was a frantic fool,
Hiding his bitter jests in blunt behavior.
And, to be noted for a merry man,   14
He'll woo a thousand, 'point the day of marriage,
Make friends, invite, and proclaim the banns,   16
Yet never means to wed where he hath wooed.
Now must the world point at poor Katharine
And say, "Lo, there is mad Petruchio's wife,
If it would please him come and marry her!"

TRANIO
Patience, good Katharine, and Baptista, too.
Upon my life, Petruchio means but well,
Whatever fortune stays him from his word.   23
Though he be blunt, I know him passing wise;   24
Though he be merry, yet withal he's honest.   25

KATHARINA
Would Katharine had never seen him, though!
                                             Exit weeping.

BAPTISTA
Go, girl, I cannot blame thee now to weep,
For such an injury would vex a very saint,
Much more a shrew of thy impatient humor.

              Enter Biondello.

BIONDELLO   Master, master! News, and such old news   30
as you never heard of!
BAPTISTA   Is it new and old too? How may that be?
BIONDELLO   Why, is it not news to hear of Petruchio's
coming?
BAPTISTA   Is he come?
BIONDELLO   Why, no, sir.
BAPTISTA   What, then?
BIONDELLO   He is coming.
BAPTISTA   When will he be here?
BIONDELLO   When he stands where I am and sees you
there.
TRANIO   But say, what to thine old news?   42
BIONDELLO   Why, Petruchio is coming in a new hat and
an old jerkin; a pair of old breeches thrice turned; a   44
pair of boots that have been candle-cases, one buckled,   45
another laced; an old rusty sword ta'en out of the town
armory, with a broken hilt, and chapeless; with two   47
broken points; his horse hipped, with an old mothy   48

saddle and stirrups of no kindred; besides, possessed   49
with the glanders and like to mose in the chine, trou-   50
bled with the lampass, infected with the fashions, full   51
of windgalls, sped with spavins, rayed with the yel-   52
lows, past cure of the fives, stark spoiled with the stag- 53
gers, begnawn with the bots, swayed in the back and   54
shoulder-shotten; near-legged before, and with a half-   55
cheeked bit and a headstall of sheep's leather which,   56
being restrained to keep him from stumbling, hath   57
been often burst and now repaired with knots; one
girth six times pieced, and a woman's crupper of   59
velour, which hath two letters for her name fairly   60
set down in studs, and here and there pieced
with packthread.   62
BAPTISTA   Who comes with him?
BIONDELLO   Oh, sir, his lackey, for all the world capari- 64
soned like the horse; with a linen stock on one leg and   65
a kersey boot-hose on the other, gartered with a red   66
and blue list; an old hat, and the humor of forty fan-   67
cies pricked in 't for a feather—a monster, a very mon-   68
ster in apparel, and not like a Christian footboy or a
gentleman's lackey.
TRANIO
'Tis some odd humor pricks him to this fashion;   71
Yet oftentimes he goes but mean-appareled.   72
BAPTISTA   I am glad he's come, howsoe'er he comes.
BIONDELLO   Why, sir, he comes not.
BAPTISTA   Didst thou not say he comes?
BIONDELLO   Who? That Petruchio came?
BAPTISTA   Ay, that Petruchio came.
BIONDELLO   No, sir, I say his horse comes, with him on
his back.
BAPTISTA   Why, that's all one.   80
BIONDELLO
Nay, by Saint Jamy,

---

10 rudesby unmannerly fellow.   **spleen** i.e., changeable temper
14 to be noted for in order to get a reputation as   **16 banns** wedding
announcement   **23 Whatever . . . word** whatever accident keeps him
from fulfilling his promise.   **24 passing** exceedingly   **25 merry**
given to joking   **30 old** rare; and referring to Petruchio's old clothes
42 to about   **44 jerkin** man's jacket.   **turned** i.e., with the material
reversed to get more wear   **45 candle-cases** i.e., discarded boots,
used only as a receptacle for candle ends   **47 chapeless** without the
chape, the metal plate or mounting of a scabbard, especially that
which covers the point   **48 points** tagged laces for attaching hose to
doublet.   **hipped** lamed in the hip. (Almost all the diseases here
named are described in Gervase Markham's *How to Choose, Ride,
Train, and Diet both Hunting Horses and Running Horses . . . Also a Discourse of Horsemanship*, probably first published in 1593.)

49 of no kindred that don't match   **50 glanders** contagious disease in
horses causing swelling beneath the jaw and mucous discharge from
the nostrils   **50 mose in the chine** suffer from glanders   **51 lampass** a
thick, spongy flesh growing over a horse's upper teeth and hindering
his eating.   **fashions** i.e., farcins, or farcy, a disease like glanders.
52 windgalls soft tumors or swellings generally found on the fetlock
joint, so called from having been supposed to contain air.   **sped** far
gone.   **spavins** a disease of the hock, marked by a small bony enlargement inside the leg.   **rayed** bespattered, defiled   **52–3 yellows** jaundice   **53 fives** avives, a glandular disease causing swelling behind the
ear   **53–4 stark . . . staggers** completely destroyed by a disease causing
palsylike staggering   **54 bots** parasitic worms   **55 shoulder-shotten**
with sprained or dislocated shoulder.   **near-legged before** with knock-
kneed forelegs   **55–6 half-cheeked bit** one to which the bridle is
attached halfway up the cheek or sidepiece and thus not giving sufficient control over the horse   **56 headstall** part of the bridle over the
head.   **sheep's leather** (i.e., of inferior quality; pigskin was used for
strongest harness)   **57 restrained** drawn back   **59 girth** saddle-strap
passing under the horse's belly.   **pieced** mended.   **crupper** leather
loop passing under the horse's tail and fastened to the saddle
60 velour velvet.   **two . . . name** her initials   **62 packthread** twine for
securing parcels.   **64–5 for . . . caparisoned** in all respects outfitted
65 stock stocking   **66 kersey boot-hose** overstocking of coarse material
for wearing under boots   **67 list** strip of cloth   **67–8 the humor . . .
feather** a trite motto incised in it instead of a feather   **68 pricked**
pinned.   **for** in place of   **71 humor pricks** whim that spurs   **72 mean-
appareled** poorly dressed   **80 all one** the same thing.

I hold you a penny,   82
A horse and a man
Is more than one,
And yet not many.

    Enter Petruchio and Grumio.

PETRUCHIO
  Come, where be these gallants? Who's at home?
BAPTISTA   You are welcome, sir.
PETRUCHIO   And yet I come not well.   88
BAPTISTA   And yet you halt not.   89
TRANIO
  Not so well appareled as I wish you were.
PETRUCHIO
  Were it better, I should rush in thus.   91
  But where is Kate? Where is my lovely bride?
  How does my father? Gentles, methinks you frown.
  And wherefore gaze this goodly company,
  As if they saw some wondrous monument,   95
  Some comet, or unusual prodigy?   96
BAPTISTA
  Why, sir, you know this is your wedding day.
  First were we sad, fearing you would not come,
  Now sadder that you come so unprovided.   99
  Fie, doff this habit, shame to your estate,   100
  An eyesore to our solemn festival!
TRANIO
  And tell us, what occasion of import
  Hath all so long detained you from your wife
  And sent you hither so unlike yourself?
PETRUCHIO
  Tedious it were to tell, and harsh to hear.
  Sufficeth I am come to keep my word,   106
  Though in some part enforcèd to digress,   107
  Which at more leisure I will so excuse
  As you shall well be satisfied withal.
  But where is Kate? I stay too long from her.
  The morning wears; 'tis time we were at church.
TRANIO
  See not your bride in these unreverent robes.
  Go to my chamber. Put on clothes of mine.
PETRUCHIO
  Not I, believe me. Thus I'll visit her.
BAPTISTA
  But thus, I trust, you will not marry her.
PETRUCHIO
  Good sooth, even thus. Therefore ha' done with
    words.   116
  To me she's married, not unto my clothes.
  Could I repair what she will wear in me   118
  As I can change these poor accoutrements,
  'Twere well for Kate and better for myself.

But what a fool am I to chat with you,
When I should bid good morrow to my bride
And seal the title with a lovely kiss!   *Exit.* 123
TRANIO
  He hath some meaning in his mad attire.
  We will persuade him, be it possible,
  To put on better ere he go to church.
BAPTISTA
  I'll after him, and see the event of this.   127
    Exit [with all but Tranio and Lucentio].
TRANIO
  But, sir, to love concerneth us to add   128
  Her father's liking, which to bring to pass,
  As I before imparted to Your Worship,   130
  I am to get a man—whate'er he be
  It skills not much, we'll fit him to our turn—   132
  And he shall be Vincentio of Pisa
  And make assurance here in Padua
  Of greater sums than I have promisèd.
  So shall you quietly enjoy your hope
  And marry sweet Bianca with consent.
LUCENTIO
  Were it not that my fellow schoolmaster
  Doth watch Bianca's steps so narrowly,
  'Twere good, methinks, to steal our marriage,   140
  Which once performed, let all the world say no,
  I'll keep mine own, despite of all the world.
TRANIO
  That by degrees we mean to look into,
  And watch our vantage in this business.   144
  We'll overreach the graybeard, Gremio,
  The narrow-prying father, Minola,   146
  The quaint musician, amorous Litio,   147
  All for my master's sake, Lucentio.

    Enter Gremio.

  Signor Gremio, came you from the church?
GREMIO
  As willingly as e'er I came from school.
TRANIO
  And is the bride and bridegroom coming home?
GREMIO
  A bridegroom, say you? 'Tis a groom indeed,   152
  A grumbling groom, and that the girl shall find.
TRANIO
  Curster than she? Why, 'tis impossible.
GREMIO
  Why, he 's a devil, a devil, a very fiend.
TRANIO
  Why, she's a devil, a devil, the devil's dam.   156

---

82 **hold** wager 88 **I come not well** i.e., I am not made to feel welcome; or, I come admittedly not well appareled. 89 **halt** limp, move slowly 91 **Were it** Even if it (my apparel) were. **rush** come quickly. (Referring to *halt not* in line 89.) 95 **monument** portent 96 **prodigy** omen. 99 **unprovided** ill equipped 100 **habit** outfit. **estate** position, station 106 **Sufficeth** It is enough that 107 **digress** i.e., deviate 116 **Good sooth** i.e., Yes, indeed 118 **Could . . . me** If I could amend in my character what she'll have to put up with

123 **lovely** loving 127 **event** outcome 128 **to love . . . add** besides obtaining the love of the lady, it behooves us to add 130 **to Your Worship** (Tranio privately drops the fiction that he is Lucentio's master.) 132 **skills** matters 140 **steal our marriage** elope 144 **watch our vantage** look out for our best opportunity, advantage 146 **narrow-prying** suspicious, watchful 147 **quaint** skillful 152 **'Tis a groom indeed** A fine bridegroom he is. (Said ironically, with pun on the sense of "servant," "rough fellow.") 156 **dam** mother.

GREMIO

   Tut, she's a lamb, a dove, a fool to him.   157
   I'll tell you, Sir Lucentio. When the priest
   Should ask if Katharine should be his wife,   159
   "Ay, by Gog's wouns," quoth he, and swore so loud   160
   That all amazed the priest let fall the book,
   And as he stooped again to take it up,
   This mad-brained bridegroom took him such a cuff   163
   That down fell priest and book, and book and priest.
   "Now take them up," quoth he, "if any list."   165

TRANIO

   What said the wench when he rose again?

GREMIO

   Trembled and shook, forwhy he stamped and swore   167
   As if the vicar meant to cozen him.   168
   But after many ceremonies done
   He calls for wine. "A health!" quoth he, as if
   He had been aboard, carousing to his mates   171
   After a storm; quaffed off the muscatel
   And threw the sops all in the sexton's face,   173
   Having no other reason
   But that his beard grew thin and hungerly   175
   And seemed to ask him sops as he was drinking.   176
   This done, he took the bride about the neck
   And kissed her lips with such a clamorous smack
   That at the parting all the church did echo.
   And I seeing this came thence for very shame,
   And after me, I know, the rout is coming.   181
   Such a mad marriage never was before. *Music plays.*
   Hark, hark! I hear the minstrels play.

      Enter Petruchio, Kate, Bianca, Hortensio [as Litio],
      Baptista, [with Grumio, and train].

PETRUCHIO

   Gentlemen and friends, I thank you for your pains.
   I know you think to dine with me today,
   And have prepared great store of wedding cheer;
   But so it is my haste doth call me hence,
   And therefore here I mean to take my leave.

BAPTISTA

   Is't possible you will away tonight?

PETRUCHIO

   I must away today, before night come.
   Make it no wonder. If you knew my business,   191
   You would entreat me rather go than stay.
   And, honest company, I thank you all   193
   That have beheld me give away myself
   To this most patient, sweet, and virtuous wife.
   Dine with my father, drink a health to me,
   For I must hence; and farewell to you all.

TRANIO

   Let us entreat you stay till after dinner.

PETRUCHIO

   It may not be.

GREMIO   Let me entreat you.

PETRUCHIO

   It cannot be.

KATHARINA   Let me entreat you.

PETRUCHIO

   I am content.

KATHARINA   Are you content to stay?

PETRUCHIO

   I am content you shall entreat me stay;
   But yet not stay, entreat me how you can.

KATHARINA

   Now, if you love me, stay.

PETRUCHIO   Grumio, my horse.   204

GRUMIO   Ay, sir, they are ready. The oats have eaten the   205
   horses.   206

KATHARINA   Nay, then,
   Do what thou canst, I will not go today,
   No, nor tomorrow—not till I please myself.
   The door is open, sir; there lies your way.
   You may be jogging whiles your boots are green.   211
   For me, I'll not be gone till I please myself.   212
   'Tis like you'll prove a jolly, surly groom,   213
   That take it on you at the first so roundly.   214

PETRUCHIO

   Oh, Kate, content thee. Prithee, be not angry.

KATHARINA

   I will be angry. What hast thou to do?—   216
   Father, be quiet. He shall stay my leisure.   217

GREMIO

   Ay, marry, sir, now it begins to work.   218

KATHARINA

   Gentlemen, forward to the bridal dinner.
   I see a woman may be made a fool
   If she had not a spirit to resist.

PETRUCHIO

   They shall go forward, Kate, at thy command.—
   Obey the bride, you that attend on her.
   Go to the feast, revel and domineer,   224
   Carouse full measure to her maidenhead,   225
   Be mad and merry, or go hang yourselves.
   But for my bonny Kate, she must with me.   227
   Nay, look not big, nor stamp, nor stare, nor fret;   228
   I will be master of what is mine own.
   She is my goods, my chattels; she is my house,
   My household stuff, my field, my barn,
   My horse, my ox, my ass, my anything;   232
   And here she stands, touch her whoever dare.

---

157 **a fool to** i.e., a pitiable weak creature compared with
159 **Should ask** came to the point (in the service) where he is directed
to ask   160 **Gog's wouns** God's (Christ's) wounds   163 **took** gave,
struck   165 **list** choose   167 **forwhy** for   168 **cozen** cheat
171 **aboard** aboard ship   173 **sops** cakes or bread soaked in the wine
175 **hungerly** hungry looking, having a starved or famished look
176 **And . . . drinking** and seemed to invite the throwing in his face of
what Petruchio was drinking.   181 **rout** crowd, wedding party
191 **Make it no wonder** Don't be surprised.   193 **honest** worthy, kind

204 **horse** horses.   205–6 **oats . . . horses** (A comic inversion.)
211 **be . . . green** (Proverbial for "getting an early start," with a sarcastic allusion to his unseemly attire.)   **green** fresh, new.   212 **For** As
for   213 **like** likely.   **jolly** (Said sarcastically.)   214 **take it on you**
i.e., throw your weight around.   **roundly** unceremoniously.
216 **What . . . do?** What business is it of yours?   217 **stay my leisure**
wait until I am ready.   218 **now . . . work** now it starts.   224 **domineer** feast riotously   225 **to her maidenhead** to her loss of virginity
227 **for** as for   228 **big** threatening   232 **ox . . . anything** (This catalogue of a man's possessions is from the Tenth Commandment.)

I'll bring mine action on the proudest he   234
That stops my way in Padua.—Grumio,
Draw forth thy weapon. We are beset with thieves.   236
Rescue thy mistress, if thou be a man.—
Fear not, sweet wench, they shall not touch thee, Kate!
I'll buckler thee against a million.   239

    Exeunt Petruchio, Katharina, [and Grumio].

BAPTISTA
Nay, let them go—a couple of quiet ones!

GREMIO
Went they not quickly, I should die with laughing.

TRANIO
Of all mad matches never was the like.

LUCENTIO
Mistress, what's your opinion of your sister?

BIANCA
That, being mad herself, she's madly mated.

GREMIO
I warrant him, Petruchio is Kated.   245

BAPTISTA
Neighbors and friends, though bride and bridegroom
   wants   246
For to supply the places at the table,   247
You know there wants no junkets at the feast.   248
Lucentio, you shall supply the bridegroom's place,
And let Bianca take her sister's room.

TRANIO
Shall sweet Bianca practice how to bride it?   251

BAPTISTA
She shall, Lucentio.—Come, gentlemen, let's go.

    Exeunt.

    ❖

[4.1]

   Enter Grumio.

GRUMIO   Fie, fie on all tired jades, on all mad masters,   1
and all foul ways! Was ever man so beaten? Was ever   2
man so rayed? Was ever man so weary? I am sent be-   3
fore to make a fire, and they are coming after to warm
them. Now, were not I a little pot and soon hot, my   5
very lips might freeze to my teeth, my tongue to the
roof of my mouth, my heart in my belly, ere I should
come by a fire to thaw me. But I with blowing the fire   8
shall warm myself; for, considering the weather, a
taller man than I will take cold.—Holla, ho! Curtis!   10

   Enter Curtis.

CURTIS   Who is that calls so coldly?

GRUMIO   A piece of ice. If thou doubt it, thou mayst
slide from my shoulder to my heel with no greater a
run but my head and my neck. A fire, good Curtis!   14

CURTIS   Is my master and his wife coming, Grumio?

GRUMIO   Oh, ay, Curtis, ay, and therefore fire, fire! Cast   16
on no water.   17

CURTIS   Is she so hot a shrew as she's reported?

GRUMIO   She was, good Curtis, before this frost. But,
thou know'st, winter tames man, woman, and beast;
for it hath tamed my old master and my new mistress
and myself, fellow Curtis.

CURTIS   Away, you three-inch fool! I am no beast.   23

GRUMIO   Am I but three inches? Why, thy horn is a foot,   24
and so long am I, at the least. But wilt thou make a fire,   25
or shall I complain on thee to our mistress, whose
hand—she being now at hand—thou shalt soon feel,
to thy cold comfort, for being slow in thy hot office?   28

CURTIS   I prithee, good Grumio, tell me, how goes the
world?

GRUMIO   A cold world, Curtis, in every office but thine,
and therefore fire. Do thy duty, and have thy duty, for   32
my master and mistress are almost frozen to death.

CURTIS   There's fire ready, and therefore, good Grumio,
the news.

GRUMIO   Why, "Jack boy, ho, boy!" and as much news   36
as wilt thou.

CURTIS   Come, you are so full of coney-catching.   38

GRUMIO   Why, therefore fire, for I have caught extreme
cold. Where's the cook? Is supper ready, the house
trimmed, rushes strewed, cobwebs swept, the serv-   41
ingmen in their new fustian, the white stockings, and   42
every officer his wedding garment on? Be the Jacks   43
fair within, the Jills fair without, the carpets laid, and   44
everything in order?

CURTIS   All ready; and therefore, I pray thee, news.

GRUMIO   First, know my horse is tired, my master and
mistress fallen out.   48

CURTIS   How?

GRUMIO   Out of their saddles into the dirt—and thereby   50
hangs a tale.   51

---

234 action (1) lawsuit (2) attack   **236 Draw** (Perhaps Petruchio and Grumio actually draw their swords.)   **239 buckler** shield, defend   **245 Kated** (Gremio's invention for "mated and matched with Kate.")   **246–7 wants For to supply** are not present to fill   **248 there wants no junkets** there is no lack of sweetmeats   **251 bride it** play the bride.   **4.1. Location: Petruchio's country house. A table is set out, with seats.**
1 jades ill-conditioned horses   **2 ways** roads.   **3 rayed** bespattered.   **5 a little . . . hot** (Proverbial expression for a person of small stature soon angered.)   **8 come by** find   **10 taller** (With play on the meaning "better," "finer.")

14 run running start   **16–17 Cast . . . water** (Alludes to the round "Scotland's burning," in which the phrase "Fire, fire!" is followed by "Pour on water, pour on water.")   **23 three-inch fool** (Another reference to Grumio's size.)   **I am no beast** (Curtis protests being called *fellow* by Grumio, since Grumio in line 20 has paralleled himself with *beast*.)   **24–5 Why . . . least** (Grumio hints that Curtis is a beast with a prominent *horn*, and hence a cuckold; suggesting too that Grumio's *horn*, i.e., *penis*, is as long as Curtis's or longer.)   **28 hot office** i.e., duty of providing a fire.   **32 have thy duty** have what's coming to you, your due   **36 Jack . . . boy** (The first line of another round or catch.)   **38 coney-catching** cheating, trickery. (With wordplay on *catch*, or round, like "Jack boy, ho, boy" in line 36.)
41 rushes (Used to cover the floor.)   **42 fustian** coarse cloth of cotton and flax   **43 officer** household servant.   **Jacks** (1) servingmen (2) drinking vessels, usually of leather and hence needing to be clean *within*   **44 Jills** (1) maidservants (2) "gills," drinking vessels holding a quarter pint, often of metal and hence in need of polishing *without*. (Grumio may joke that the maidservants cannot be expected to be clean *within*.)   **48 fallen out** quarreling. (But with a pun on the literal sense in line 50.)   **50–1 thereby hangs a tale** there's quite a story to tell about that. (But with a risible suggestion of hanging by one's tail.)

CURTIS   Let's ha 't, good Grumio.   52
GRUMIO   Lend thine ear.
CURTIS   Here.
GRUMIO   There.   [*He cuffs Curtis.*]
CURTIS   This 'tis to feel a tale, not to hear a tale.
GRUMIO   And therefore 'tis called a sensible tale, and   57
this cuff was but to knock at your ear and beseech
listening. Now I begin: Imprimis, we came down a   59
foul hill, my master riding behind my mistress—   60
CURTIS   Both of one horse?   61
GRUMIO   What's that to thee?
CURTIS   Why, a horse.
GRUMIO   Tell thou the tale. But hadst thou not crossed   64
me, thou shouldst have heard how her horse fell and
she under her horse; thou shouldst have heard in how
miry a place, how she was bemoiled, how he left her   67
with the horse upon her, how he beat me because her
horse stumbled, how she waded through the dirt to
pluck him off me, how he swore, how she prayed that
never prayed before, how I cried, how the horses ran
away, how her bridle was burst, how I lost my
crupper, with many things of worthy memory, which   73
now shall die in oblivion and thou return unexperi-
enced to thy grave.
CURTIS   By this reckoning he is more shrew than she.
GRUMIO   Ay, and that thou and the proudest of you all
shall find when he comes home. But what talk I of   78
this? Call forth Nathaniel, Joseph, Nicholas, Philip,
Walter, Sugarsop, and the rest. Let their heads be
sleekly combed, their blue coats brushed, and their   81
garters of an indifferent knit; let them curtsy with their   82
left legs, and not presume to touch a hair of my
master's horsetail till they kiss their hands. Are they
all ready?
CURTIS   They are.
GRUMIO   Call them forth.
CURTIS   [*calling*]   Do you hear, ho? You must meet my
master to countenance my mistress.   89
GRUMIO   Why, she hath a face of her own.
CURTIS   Who knows not that?
GRUMIO   Thou, it seems, that calls for company to
countenance her.
CURTIS   I call them forth to credit her.   94

Enter four or five Servingmen.

GRUMIO   Why, she comes to borrow nothing of them.
NATHANIEL   Welcome home, Grumio!
PHILIP   How now, Grumio?
JOSEPH   What, Grumio!
NICHOLAS   Fellow Grumio!
NATHANIEL   How now, old lad?

GRUMIO   Welcome, you; how now, you; what, you; fellow, you—and thus much for greeting. Now, my
spruce companions, is all ready, and all things neat?   103
NATHANIEL   All things is ready. How near is our
master?
GRUMIO   E'en at hand, alighted by this; and therefore
be not—Cock's passion, silence! I hear my master.   107

Enter Petruchio and Kate.

PETRUCHIO
Where be these knaves? What, no man at door
To hold my stirrup nor to take my horse?   109
Where is Nathaniel, Gregory, Philip?
ALL SERVANTS   Here, here, sir, here, sir.
PETRUCHIO
Here, sir! Here, sir! Here, sir! Here, sir!
You loggerheaded and unpolished grooms!
What, no attendance? No regard? No duty?
Where is the foolish knave I sent before?   115
GRUMIO
Here, sir, as foolish as I was before.
PETRUCHIO
You peasant swain, you whoreson, malt-horse
drudge!   117
Did I not bid thee meet me in the park
And bring along these rascal knaves with thee?
GRUMIO
Nathaniel's coat, sir, was not fully made,
And Gabriel's pumps were all unpinked i'the heel.   121
There was no link to color Peter's hat,   122
And Walter's dagger was not come from sheathing.   123
There were none fine but Adam, Ralph, and Gregory;   124
The rest were ragged, old, and beggarly.
Yet, as they are, here are they come to meet you.
PETRUCHIO
Go, rascals, go and fetch my supper in.
                                    Exeunt Servants.
[*He sings.*] "Where is the life that late I led?   128
Where are those—" Sit down, Kate, and welcome.—   129
                                [*They sit at table.*]
Soud, soud, soud, soud!   130

Enter Servants with supper.

Why, when, I say?—Nay, good sweet Kate, be
merry.—   131
Off with my boots, you rogues! You villains, when?
                    [*A Servant takes off Petruchio's boots.*]
[*He sings.*] "It was the friar of orders gray,   133
As he forth walkèd on his way—"   134

103 spruce lively, trim in appearance   **107 Cock's passion** By God's
(Christ's) suffering   **109 hold my stirrup** i.e., help me dismount
115 before ahead. (With pun in next line on "previously.")
117 swain rustic.   **whoreson . . . drudge** worthless plodding work
animal, such as would be used on a treadmill to grind malt.
121 pumps low cut shoes.   **unpinked** lacking in eyelets or in ornamental tracing in the leather   **122 link** blacking made from burnt
"links" or torches   **123 sheathing** being fitted with a sheath.
124 fine well clothed   **128–9 Where . . . those** (A fragment of a lost
ballad, probably lamenting the man's loss of freedom in marriage.)
130 Soud (A nonsense song, or expression of impatience, or perhaps
"food!")   **131 when** (An exclamation of impatience.)   **133–4 "It . . .
way"** (A fragment of a lost ballad, probably bawdy.)

52 ha 't have it   **57 sensible** (1) capable of being felt (2) showing
good sense   **59 Imprimis** In the first place   **60 foul** muddy   **61 of**
on   **64 crossed** thwarted, interrupted   **67 bemoiled** befouled with
mire   **73 crupper.** (See 3.2.59.)   **of worthy** worthy of   **78 what** why
81 blue coats (Usual dress for servingmen.)   **82 indifferent** well-
matched, identical   **89 countenance** pay respects to. (With a following pun on the meaning "face.")   **94 credit** pay respects to. (With
another pun following, on "extend financial credit.")

Out, you rogue! You pluck my foot awry.   135
                    [*He kicks the Servant.*]
Take that, and mend the plucking of the other.—   136
Be merry, Kate.—Some water, here. What, ho!

        Enter one with water.

Where's my spaniel Troilus? Sirrah, get you hence,
And bid my cousin Ferdinand come hither—
                            [*Exit Servant.*]
One, Kate, that you must kiss and be acquainted with.
Where are my slippers? Shall I have some water?
Come, Kate, and wash, and welcome heartily.
        [*A Servant offers water, but spills some.*]
You whoreson villain, will you let it fall?
                    [*He strikes the Servant.*]

KATHARINA
Patience, I pray you, 'twas a fault unwilling.   144
PETRUCHIO
A whoreson, beetleheaded, flap-eared knave!—   145
Come, Kate, sit down. I know you have a stomach.   146
Will you give thanks, sweet Kate, or else shall I?—   147
What's this? Mutton?
FIRST SERVANT   Ay.
PETRUCHIO   Who brought it?
PETER   I.
PETRUCHIO
'Tis burnt, and so is all the meat.
What dogs are these? Where is the rascal cook?
How durst you, villains, bring it from the dresser   151
And serve it thus to me that love it not?
There, take it to you, trenchers, cups, and all.   153
            [*He throws the meat, etc., at them.*]
You heedless jolt-heads and unmannered slaves!   154
What, do you grumble? I'll be with you straight.   155
                        [*They run out.*]

KATHARINA
I pray you, husband, be not so disquiet.
The meat was well, if you were so contented.   157
PETRUCHIO
I tell thee, Kate, 'twas burnt and dried away,
And I expressly am forbid to touch it;
For it engenders choler, planteth anger,   160
And better 'twere that both of us did fast,
Since, of ourselves, ourselves are choleric,   162
Than feed it with such overroasted flesh.
Be patient. Tomorrow 't shall be mended,
And for this night we'll fast for company.   165
Come, I will bring thee to thy bridal chamber.   166
                                        Exeunt.

        Enter Servants severally.

NATHANIEL   Peter, didst ever see the like?
PETER   He kills her in her own humor.   168

        Enter Curtis.

GRUMIO   Where is he?
CURTIS   In her chamber,
Making a sermon of continency to her,   171
And rails, and swears, and rates, that she, poor soul, 172
Knows not which way to stand, to look, to speak,
And sits as one new risen from a dream.
Away, away! For he is coming hither.   [*Exeunt.*]

        Enter Petruchio.

PETRUCHIO
Thus have I politicly begun my reign,   176
And 'tis my hope to end successfully.
My falcon now is sharp and passing empty,   178
And till she stoop she must not be full-gorged,   179
For then she never looks upon her lure.
Another way I have to man my haggard,   181
To make her come and know her keeper's call:
That is, to watch her, as we watch these kites   183
That bate and beat and will not be obedient.   184
She ate no meat today, nor none shall eat.
Last night she slept not, nor tonight she shall not.
As with the meat, some undeservèd fault
I'll find about the making of the bed,
And here I'll fling the pillow, there the bolster,
This way the coverlet, another way the sheets.
Ay, and amid this hurly I intend   191
That all is done in reverent care of her.
And in conclusion she shall watch all night,   193
And if she chance to nod I'll rail and brawl,
And with the clamor keep her still awake.
This is a way to kill a wife with kindness;
And thus I'll curb her mad and headstrong humor.   197
He that knows better how to tame a shrew,
Now let him speak. 'Tis charity to show.   *Exit.* 199

                    ❧

[4.2]

        *Enter Tranio [as Lucentio] and Hortensio
        [as Litio].*

TRANIO
Is't possible, friend Litio, that Mistress Bianca
Doth fancy any other but Lucentio?
I tell you, sir, she bears me fair in hand.   3

135 **Out** (Exclamation of anger or reproach.) 136 **mend the plucking of** do a better job of pulling off   144 **unwilling** not intentional. 145 **beetleheaded** i.e., blockheaded (since a *beetle* is a pounding tool) 146 **stomach** appetite. (With a suggestion also of "temper.") 147 **give thanks** say grace   151 **dresser** one who "dresses" or prepares the food; or, sideboard   153 **trenchers** wooden dishes or plates 154 **jolt-heads** blockheads   155 **with you straight** after you at once (to get even for this).   157 **if . . . contented** if you had chosen to be pleased with it.   160 **choler** the humor or bodily fluid, hot and dry in character, that supposedly produced ill temper and was thought to be aggravated by the eating of roast meat   162 **of ourselves** by our natures   165 **for company** together.   166.2 *severally* separately

168 **He . . . humor** He subdues her shrewishness with his own greater shrewishness.   171 **sermon of continency** lecture on self-restraint 172 **rates** scolds.   **that** so that   176 **politicly** with skillful calculation 178 **sharp** hungry.   **passing** very   179 **stoop** fly down to the lure 181 **man** tame, assert masculine authority over.   **haggard** wild female hawk; hence, an intractable woman   183 **watch her** keep her watching, i.e., awake.   **kites** a kind of hawk. (With a pun on *Kate*.) 184 **bate and beat** beat the wings impatiently and flutter away from the hand or perch   191 **hurly** commotion.   **intend** pretend 193 **watch** stay awake   197 **humor** disposition.   199 **'Tis charity to show** This is to perform an act of Christian benevolence. (On the rhyme with *shrew*, see also the play's final lines.) 4.2. Location: Padua. Before Baptista's house. 3 **bears . . . hand** gives me encouragement, leads me on.

HORTENSIO
Sir, to satisfy you in what I have said,   4
Stand by and mark the manner of his teaching.
                   [They stand aside.]

Enter Bianca [and Lucentio as Cambio].

LUCENTIO
Now, mistress, profit you in what you read?   6
BIANCA
What, master, read you? First resolve me that.   7
LUCENTIO
I read that I profess, *The Art to Love.*   8
BIANCA
And may you prove, sir, master of your art!
LUCENTIO
While you, sweet dear, prove mistress of my heart!
            [They move aside and court each other.]
HORTENSIO *[to Tranio, coming forward]*
Quick proceeders, marry! Now, tell me, I pray,   11
You that durst swear that your mistress Bianca
Loved none in the world so well as Lucentio.
TRANIO
Oh, despiteful love! Unconstant womankind!   14
I tell thee, Litio, this is wonderful.   15
HORTENSIO
Mistake no more. I am not Litio,
Nor a musician, as I seem to be,
But one that scorn to live in this disguise   18
For such a one as leaves a gentleman   19
And makes a god of such a cullion.   20
Know, sir, that I am called Hortensio.
TRANIO
Signor Hortensio, I have often heard
Of your entire affection to Bianca;   23
And since mine eyes are witness of her lightness,   24
I will with you, if you be so contented,
Forswear Bianca and her love forever.
HORTENSIO
See how they kiss and court! Signor Lucentio,
Here is my hand, and here I firmly vow
                   [giving his hand]
Never to woo her more, but do forswear her,
As one unworthy all the former favors
That I have fondly flattered her withal.   31
TRANIO
And here I take the like unfeignèd oath,
Never to marry with her though she would entreat.
Fie on her, see how beastly she doth court him!
HORTENSIO
Would all the world but he had quite forsworn!   35

For me, that I may surely keep mine oath,   36
I will be married to a wealthy widow,
Ere three days pass, which hath as long loved me
As I have loved this proud disdainful haggard.   39
And so farewell, Signor Lucentio.
Kindness in women, not their beauteous looks,
Shall win my love. And so I take my leave,
In resolution as I swore before.   *[Exit.]*   43
TRANIO *[as Lucentio and Bianca come forward again]*
Mistress Bianca, bless you with such grace
As 'longeth to a lover's blessèd case!   45
Nay, I have ta'en you napping, gentle love,   46
And have forsworn you with Hortensio.
BIANCA
Tranio, you jest. But have you both forsworn me?
TRANIO
Mistress, we have.
LUCENTIO   Then we are rid of Litio.
TRANIO
I' faith, he'll have a lusty widow now,   50
That shall be wooed and wedded in a day.
BIANCA   God give him joy!
TRANIO   Ay, and he'll tame her.
BIANCA   He says so, Tranio?
TRANIO
Faith, he is gone unto the taming-school.
BIANCA
The taming-school! What, is there such a place?
TRANIO
Ay, mistress, and Petruchio is the master,
That teacheth tricks eleven-and-twenty long   58
To tame a shrew and charm her chattering tongue.

Enter Biondello.

BIONDELLO
Oh, master, master, I have watched so long
That I am dog-weary, but at last I spied
An ancient angel coming down the hill   62
Will serve the turn.
TRANIO   What is he, Biondello?   63
BIONDELLO
Master, a marcantant, or a pedant,   64
I know not what, but formal in apparel,
In gait and countenance surely like a father.
LUCENTIO   And what of him, Tranio?
TRANIO
If he be credulous and trust my tale,
I'll make him glad to seem Vincentio,
And give assurance to Baptista Minola

---

4 satisfy convince **6 read** (Evidently, both Bianca and "Cambio" carry books.) **7 resolve** answer **8 I read . . . *Love*** I read what I practice, Ovid's *Ars Amatoria.* **11 proceeders** (1) workers, doers (2) candidates for academic degrees (as suggested by the phrase *master of your art* in line 9) **14 despiteful** cruel **15 wonderful** cause for wonder. **18 scorn** scorns **19 such a one** i.e., Bianca **20 cullion** base fellow. (Referring to "Cambio"; literally, *cullion* means "testicle.") **23 entire** sincere **24 lightness** wantonness **31 fondly** foolishly **35 Would . . . forsworn!** i.e., May everyone in the world forsake her except the penniless "Cambio," and may she thus get what she deserves!

36 For As for **39 haggard** wild hawk. **43 In resolution** determined **45 'longeth** belongs **46 ta'en you napping** taken you by surprise **50 lusty** merry, lively **58 eleven . . . long** i.e., right on the money. (Alluding to the card game called "one-and-thirty" referred to at 1.2.32–3.) **62 ancient angel** i.e., fellow of the good old stamp. (Literally, an "angel" or gold coin bearing the stamp of the archangel Michael and thus distinguishable from more recent debased coinage.) **63 Will . . . turn** who will serve our purposes. **64 marcantant** merchant. **pedant** schoolmaster. (Though at lines 90–1 he speaks more like a merchant.)

As if he were the right Vincentio.
Take in your love, and then let me alone.   72

                    [*Exeunt Lucentio and Bianca.*]

         Enter a Pedant.

PEDANT
    God save you, sir!
TRANIO   And you sir! You are welcome.
    Travel you farre on, or are you at the farthest?   74
PEDANT
    Sir, at the farthest for a week or two,
    But then up farther, and as far as Rome,
    And so to Tripoli, if God lend me life.
TRANIO
    What countryman, I pray?
PEDANT   Of Mantua.
TRANIO
    Of Mantua, sir? Marry, God forbid!
    And come to Padua, careless of your life?
PEDANT
    My life, sir? How, I pray? For that goes hard.   81
TRANIO
    'Tis death for anyone in Mantua
    To come to Padua. Know you not the cause?
    Your ships are stayed at Venice, and the Duke,   84
    For private quarrel twixt your Duke and him,
    Hath published and proclaimed it openly.
    'Tis marvel, but that you are but newly come,
    You might have heard it else proclaimed about.
PEDANT
    Alas, sir, it is worse for me than so,   89
    For I have bills for money by exchange   90
    From Florence, and must here deliver them.
TRANIO
    Well, sir, to do you courtesy,
    This will I do, and this I will advise you—
    First, tell me, have you ever been at Pisa?
PEDANT
    Ay, sir, in Pisa have I often been,
    Pisa renownèd for grave citizens.
TRANIO
    Among them know you one Vincentio?
PEDANT
    I know him not, but I have heard of him;
    A merchant of incomparable wealth.
TRANIO
    He is my father, sir, and, sooth to say,
    In count'nance somewhat doth resemble you.
BIONDELLO [*aside*]   As much as an apple doth an oy-
    ster, and all one.   103
TRANIO
    To save your life in this extremity,
    This favor will I do you for his sake;
    And think it not the worst of all your fortunes
    That you are like to Sir Vincentio.

His name and credit shall you undertake,   108
And in my house you shall be friendly lodged.
Look that you take upon you as you should.   110
You understand me, sir. So shall you stay
Till you have done your business in the city.
If this be courtesy, sir, accept of it.
PEDANT
    Oh, sir, I do, and will repute you ever   114
    The patron of my life and liberty.
TRANIO
    Then go with me to make the matter good.   116
    This, by the way, I let you understand:
    My father is here looked for every day
    To pass assurance of a dower in marriage   119
    Twixt me and one Baptista's daughter here.
    In all these circumstances I'll instruct you.
    Go with me to clothe you as becomes you.

                                        Exeunt.

                    ❧

4.[3]

         Enter Katharina and Grumio.

GRUMIO
    No, no, forsooth, I dare not for my life.
KATHARINA
    The more my wrong, the more his spite appears.   2
    What, did he marry me to famish me?
    Beggars that come unto my father's door
    Upon entreaty have a present alms;   5
    If not, elsewhere they meet with charity.
    But I, who never knew how to entreat,
    Nor never needed that I should entreat,
    Am starved for meat, giddy for lack of sleep,
    With oaths kept waking, and with brawling fed.
    And that which spites me more than all these wants,
    He does it under name of perfect love,
    As who should say, if I should sleep or eat   13
    'Twere deadly sickness or else present death.
    I prithee, go and get me some repast,
    I care not what, so it be wholesome food.   16
GRUMIO   What say you to a neat's foot?   17
KATHARINA
    'Tis passing good. I prithee, let me have it.   18
GRUMIO
    I fear it is too choleric a meat.
    How say you to a fat tripe finely broiled?
KATHARINA
    I like it well. Good Grumio, fetch it me.
GRUMIO
    I cannot tell. I fear 'tis choleric.   22
    What say you to a piece of beef and mustard?

72 **let me alone** leave things to me.   74 **farre** farther   81 **goes hard** is serious indeed.   84 **stayed** detained   89 **than so** than that 90 **bills . . . exchange** promissory notes   103 **all one** no matter.

108 **credit** reputation   110 **take upon you** play your part   114 **repute you** regard you as   116 **make . . . good** carry out the plan.   119 **pass assurance** convey a legal guarantee
4.3. Location: Petruchio's house. A table is set out, with seats.
2 **my wrong** the wrong done to me   5 **present** immediate. (As in line 14.)   13 **As who** as if one   16 **so** so long as   17 **neat's** ox's   18 **passing** extremely   22 **I cannot tell** I don't know what to say.

KATHARINA
A dish that I do love to feed upon.

GRUMIO
Ay, but the mustard is too hot a little.

KATHARINA
Why then, the beef, and let the mustard rest.   26

GRUMIO
Nay then, I will not. You shall have the mustard,
Or else you get no beef of Grumio.

KATHARINA
Then both, or one, or anything thou wilt.

GRUMIO
Why then, the mustard without the beef.

KATHARINA
Go, get thee gone, thou false, deluding slave,
                                        [She] beats him.
That feed'st me with the very name of meat!   32
Sorrow on thee and all the pack of you,
That triumph thus upon my misery!
Go, get thee gone, I say.

        Enter Petruchio and Hortensio with meat.

PETRUCHIO
How fares my Kate? What, sweeting, all amort?   36

HORTENSIO
Mistress, what cheer?

KATHARINA   Faith, as cold as can be.

PETRUCHIO
Pluck up thy spirits; look cheerfully upon me.
Here, love, thou see'st how diligent I am
To dress thy meat myself and bring it thee.   40
I am sure, sweet Kate, this kindness merits thanks.
What, not a word? Nay, then thou lov'st it not,
And all my pains is sorted to no proof.—   43
Here, take away this dish.

KATHARINA   I pray you, let it stand.

PETRUCHIO
The poorest service is repaid with thanks,
And so shall mine before you touch the meat.

KATHARINA   I thank you, sir.

HORTENSIO
Signor Petruchio, fie, you are to blame.
Come, Mistress Kate, I'll bear you company.

PETRUCHIO [aside to Hortensio]
Eat it up all, Hortensio, if thou lovest me.—
Much good do it unto thy gentle heart!
Kate, eat apace. And now, my honey love,
Will we return unto thy father's house
And revel it as bravely as the best,   54
With silken coats and caps and golden rings,
With ruffs, and cuffs, and farthingales, and things,   56
With scarves, and fans, and double change of brav'ry,   57
With amber bracelets, beads, and all this knav'ry.

What, hast thou dined? The tailor stays thy leisure,   59
To deck thy body with his ruffling treasure.   60

        Enter Tailor [with a gown].

Come, tailor, let us see these ornaments.
Lay forth the gown.

        Enter Haberdasher [with a cap].

                        What news with you, sir?

HABERDASHER
Here is the cap Your Worship did bespeak.   63

PETRUCHIO
Why, this was molded on a porringer—   64
A velvet dish. Fie, fie, 'tis lewd and filthy.   65
Why, 'tis a cockle or a walnut shell,   66
A knack, a toy, a trick, a baby's cap.   67
Away with it! Come, let me have a bigger.

KATHARINA
I'll have no bigger. This doth fit the time,   69
And gentlewomen wear such caps as these.

PETRUCHIO
When you are gentle, you shall have one too,   71
And not till then.

HORTENSIO [aside]   That will not be in haste.

KATHARINA
Why, sir, I trust I may have leave to speak,
And speak I will. I am no child, no babe.
Your betters have endured me say my mind,   75
And if you cannot, best you stop your ears.
My tongue will tell the anger of my heart,
Or else my heart, concealing it, will break.
And rather than it shall, I will be free
Even to the uttermost, as I please, in words.

PETRUCHIO
Why, thou say'st true. It is a paltry cap,
A custard-coffin, a bauble, a silken pie.   82
I love thee well in that thou lik'st it not.

KATHARINA
Love me or love me not, I like the cap,
And it I will have, or I will have none.

                            [Exit Haberdasher.]

PETRUCHIO
Thy gown? Why, ay. Come, tailor, let us see't.
Oh, mercy, God, what masquing stuff is here?   87
What's this, a sleeve? 'Tis like a demicannon.   88
What, up and down carved like an apple tart?   89
Here's snip, and nip, and cut, and slish and slash,
Like to a censer in a barber's shop.   91
Why, what i' devil's name, tailor, call'st thou this?

---

26 let . . . rest i.e., forget about the mustard.   32 very mere   36 all
amort dejected, dispirited.   40 dress prepare   43 is . . . proof have
proved to be to no purpose.   54 bravely splendidly   56 farthingales
hooped petticoats   57 bravery finery

59 stays awaits   60 ruffling treasure finery trimmed with ruffles.
63 bespeak order.   64 porringer porridge bowl   65 lewd vile
66 cockle cockleshell   67 trick trifle   69 fit the time suit the current
fashion   71 gentle mild. (Petruchio plays on Kate's gentlewomen,
line 70, i.e., women of high social station.)   75 endured me say
suffered me to say   82 custard-coffin pastry crust for a custard
87 masquing i.e., suited only for a masque   88 demicannon large
cannon.   89 What . . . tart? What, carved from one end to the other
with slits like those in the crust of an apple tart? (Such slits in gowns
were designed to reveal the fabric underneath.)   91 censer perfum-
ing pan having an ornamental lid

HORTENSIO [*aside*]

     I see she's like to have neither cap nor gown.   93

TAILOR

     You bid me make it orderly and well,

     According to the fashion and the time.

PETRUCHIO

     Marry, and did. But if you be remembered,   96

     I did not bid you mar it to the time.

     Go hop me over every kennel home,   98

     For you shall hop without my custom, sir.

     I'll none of it. Hence, make your best of it.

KATHARINA

     I never saw a better fashioned gown,

     More quaint, more pleasing, nor more

       commendable.   102

     Belike you mean to make a puppet of me.   103

PETRUCHIO

     Why, true, he means to make a puppet of thee.

TAILOR

     She says Your Worship means to make a puppet of her.

PETRUCHIO

     Oh, monstrous arrogance! Thou liest, thou thread,

       thou thimble,   106

     Thou yard, three-quarters, half-yard, quarter, nail!   107

     Thou flea, thou nit, thou winter cricket, thou!   108

     Braved in mine own house with a skein of thread?   109

     Away, thou rag, thou quantity, thou remnant,   110

     Or I shall so be-mete thee with thy yard   111

     As thou shalt think on prating whilst thou liv'st!   112

     I tell thee, I, that thou hast marred her gown.

TAILOR

     Your Worship is deceived. The gown is made

     Just as my master had direction.

     Grumio gave order how it should be done.

GRUMIO   I gave him no order. I gave him the stuff.   117

TAILOR

     But how did you desire it should be made?

GRUMIO   Marry, sir, with needle and thread.

TAILOR

     But did you not request to have it cut?

GRUMIO   Thou hast faced many things.   121

TAILOR   I have.

GRUMIO   Face not me. Thou hast braved many men;   123

     brave not me. I will neither be faced nor braved. I say   124

     unto thee, I bid thy master cut out the gown, but I did

     not bid him cut it to pieces. Ergo, thou liest.   126

TAILOR   Why, here is the note of the fashion to testify.

                         [*He displays his bill.*]

PETRUCHIO   Read it.

GRUMIO   The note lies in 's throat if he say I said so.   129

TAILOR [*reads*]   "Imprimis, a loose-bodied gown—"   130

GRUMIO   Master, if ever I said loose-bodied gown,   131

     sew me in the skirts of it and beat me to death with a

     bottom of brown thread. I said a gown.   133

PETRUCHIO   Proceed.

TAILOR [*reads*]   "With a small compassed cape—"   135

GRUMIO   I confess the cape.

TAILOR [*reads*]   "With a trunk sleeve—"   137

GRUMIO   I confess two sleeves.

TAILOR [*reads*]   "The sleeves curiously cut."   139

PETRUCHIO   Ay, there's the villainy.

GRUMIO   Error i'the bill, sir, error i'the bill. I commanded

     the sleeves should be cut out and sewed up again, and

     that I'll prove upon thee, though thy little finger be   143

     armed in a thimble.

TAILOR   This is true that I say. An I had thee in place   145

     where, thou shouldst know it.   146

GRUMIO   I am for thee straight. Take thou the bill, give   147

     me thy mete-yard, and spare not me.   148

HORTENSIO   God-a-mercy, Grumio, then he shall have   149

     no odds.   150

PETRUCHIO   Well, sir, in brief, the gown is not for me.

GRUMIO   You are i'the right, sir, 'tis for my mistress.

PETRUCHIO   Go, take it up unto thy master's use.   153

GRUMIO [*to the Tailor*]   Villain, not for thy life! Take up

     my mistress' gown for thy master's use!

PETRUCHIO   Why sir, what's your conceit in that?   156

GRUMIO

     Oh, sir, the conceit is deeper than you think for: 157

     Take up my mistress' gown to his master's use!

     Oh, fie, fie, fie!

PETRUCHIO [*aside to Hortensio*]

     Hortensio, say thou wilt see the tailor paid.

     [*To Tailor*] Go, take it hence. Begone, and say no more.

HORTENSIO [*aside to the Tailor*]

     Tailor, I'll pay thee for thy gown tomorrow.

     Take no unkindness of his hasty words.

     Away, I say. Commend me to thy master.

                           Exit Tailor.

PETRUCHIO

     Well, come, my Kate. We will unto your father's

     Even in these honest, mean habiliments.   166

     Our purses shall be proud, our garments poor,

     For 'tis the mind that makes the body rich;

     And as the sun breaks through the darkest clouds,

---

93 like likely   **96 Marry . . . remembered** I did indeed. But if you recollect   **98 hop . . . home** hop on home over every street gutter   **102 quaint** elegant   **103 Belike** Perhaps   **106–10 thou thread . . . remnant** Petruchio attacks the tailor's proverbial thinness and effeminacy using metaphors from tailoring.   **107 nail** a measure of length for cloth: 2 ¼ inches.   **108 nit** louse egg   **109 Braved** Defied. **with** by   **110 quantity** fragment   **111 be-mete** measure, i.e., thrash. **yard** yardstick   **112 think on prating** i.e., remember this thrashing and think twice before talking so again   **117 stuff** material.   **121 faced** trimmed, decked   **123 Face** Bully. **braved** dressed finely   **124 brave** defy   **126 Ergo** Therefore

129 lies in 's throat i.e., lies utterly   **130 Imprimis** First   **131 loose-bodied gown** (Grumio plays on *loose*, "wanton"; a gown fit for a prostitute.)   **133 bottom** i.e., ball or skein. (A weaver's term for the bobbin.)   **135 compassed** flared, cut on the bias so as to fall in a circle   **137 trunk** full, wide   **139 curiously** elaborately   **143 prove upon thee** prove by fighting you   **145–6 in place where** in a suitable place   **147 bill** (1) the note ordering the gown (2) a weapon, a halberd   **148 mete-yard** measuring stick   **149 God-a-mercy** Thanks   **150 no odds** no advantage. (The contest between Grumio and the Tailor will be evenly matched.)   **153 take it up** take it away. **use** i.e., whatever use he can make of it. (But Grumio deliberately misinterprets both expressions in a bawdy sense.)   **156 conceit** idea   **157 deeper** more serious. (But continuing the sexual idea of lifting up the dress and entering for sexual "use," as in lines 155 and 158.)   **166 honest, mean habiliments** respectable, plain clothes.

So honor peereth in the meanest habit.   170
What, is the jay more precious than the lark
Because his feathers are more beautiful?
Or is the adder better than the eel
Because his painted skin contents the eye?   174
Oh, no, good Kate; neither art thou the worse
For this poor furniture and mean array.   176
If thou account'st it shame, lay it on me.
And therefore frolic; we will hence forthwith,
To feast and sport us at thy father's house.
[_To Grumio_] Go call my men, and let us straight
   to him;
And bring our horses unto Long Lane end.
There will we mount, and thither walk on foot.
Let's see, I think 'tis now some seven o'clock,
And well we may come there by dinnertime.   184

KATHARINA
I dare assure you, sir, 'tis almost two,
And 'twill be suppertime ere you come there.

PETRUCHIO
It shall be seven ere I go to horse.
Look what I speak, or do, or think to do,   188
You are still crossing it.—Sirs, let 't alone.   189
I will not go today, and ere I do,
It shall be what o'clock I say it is.

HORTENSIO [_aside_]
Why, so this gallant will command the sun.   192
                                      [_Exeunt._]

                    ❧

[4.4]

_Enter Tranio [as Lucentio], and the Pedant
dressed like Vincentio [booted]._

TRANIO
Sir, this is the house. Please it you that I call?

PEDANT
Ay, what else? And but I be deceived,   2
Signor Baptista may remember me,   3
Near twenty years ago, in Genoa—   4

TRANIO
Where we were lodgers at the Pegasus.—   5
'Tis well; and hold your own in any case   6
With such austerity as 'longeth to a father.

             Enter Biondello.

PEDANT
I warrant you. But, sir, here comes your boy.
'Twere good he were schooled.   9

TRANIO
Fear you not him.—Sirrah Biondello,
Now do your duty throughly, I advise you.   11
Imagine 'twere the right Vincentio.   12

BIONDELLO   Tut, fear not me.   13

TRANIO
But hast thou done thy errand to Baptista?

BIONDELLO
I told him that your father was at Venice
And that you looked for him this day in Padua.

TRANIO [_giving money_]
Thou'rt a tall fellow. Hold thee that to drink.   17
Here comes Baptista. Set your countenance, sir.   18

    _Enter Baptista, and Lucentio [as Cambio].
    [The] Pedant [stands] bareheaded._

Signor Baptista, you are happily met.   19
[_To the Pedant_] Sir, this is the gentleman I told you of.
I pray you, stand good father to me now;
Give me Bianca for my patrimony.

PEDANT   Soft, son!—   23
Sir, by your leave, having come to Padua
To gather in some debts, my son Lucentio
Made me acquainted with a weighty cause
Of love between your daughter and himself;
And, for the good report I hear of you   28
And for the love he beareth to your daughter
And she to him, to stay him not too long,   30
I am content, in a good father's care,
To have him matched. And if you please to like   32
No worse than I, upon some agreement
Me shall you find ready and willing
With one consent to have her so bestowed;   35
For curious I cannot be with you,   36
Signor Baptista, of whom I hear so well.

BAPTISTA
Sir, pardon me in what I have to say.
Your plainness and your shortness please me well.
Right true it is your son Lucentio here
Doth love my daughter, and she loveth him,
Or both dissemble deeply their affections.
And therefore, if you say no more than this,
That like a father you will deal with him
And pass my daughter a sufficient dower,   45
The match is made, and all is done.
Your son shall have my daughter with consent.

TRANIO
I thank you, sir. Where then do you know best   48
We be affied and such assurance ta'en   49
As shall with either part's agreement stand?   50

170 **peereth . . . habit** peeps through the humblest attire.
174 **painted** colorfully patterned   176 **furniture** furnishings of attire
184 **dinnertime** i.e., about noon.   188 **Look what** Whatever
189 **still crossing** always contradicting or defying   192 **so** at this rate
4.4. Location: Padua. Before Baptista's house.
0.2 **booted** (signifying travel)   2 **but** unless   3–4 **Signor . . . Genoa**
(The Pedant rehearses what he is to say.)   5 **Where . . . Pegasus**
(Tranio is coaching the Pedant in further details of his story.)   **the
Pegasus** i.e., an inn, so named after the famous winged horse of classical myth.   6 **hold your own** play your part   9 **schooled** i.e.,
rehearsed in his part.

11 **throughly** thoroughly   12 **right** real   13 **fear not me** don't worry
about my doing my part   17 **tall** fine.   **Hold . . . drink** Take that and
buy a drink.   18 **Set your countenance** i.e., Put on the expression of
an austere father (line 7).   19 **happily** fortunately   23 **Soft** i.e.,
Steady, take it easy   28 **for** because of   30 **to stay him not** not to
keep him waiting   32 **like** i.e., approve of the match   35 **one** i.e.,
firm   36 **curious** overly particular   45 **pass** settle on, give
48–50 **Where . . . stand?** Where in your view is the best place for
us to be betrothed and for legal assurances to be made that will
confirm an agreement satisfactory to both parties?

BAPTISTA
Not in my house, Lucentio, for you know
Pitchers have ears, and I have many servants.
Besides, old Gremio is heark'ning still,   53
And happily we might be interrupted.   54

TRANIO
Then at my lodging, an it like you.   55
There doth my father lie, and there this night   56
We'll pass the business privately and well.   57
Send for your daughter by your servant here.
                    [*He indicates Lucentio, and winks at him.*]
My boy shall fetch the scrivener presently.   59
The worst is this, that at so slender warning
You are like to have a thin and slender pittance.   61

BAPTISTA
It likes me well. Cambio, hie you home,
And bid Bianca make her ready straight.
And if you will, tell what hath happened:
Lucentio's father is arrived in Padua,
And how she's like to be Lucentio's wife.
                    [*Exit Lucentio.*]

BIONDELLO
I pray the gods she may with all my heart!

TRANIO
Dally not with the gods, but get thee gone.
                    Exit [*Biondello*].
Signor Baptista, shall I lead the way?
Welcome! One mess is like to be your cheer.   70
Come, sir, we will better it in Pisa.

BAPTISTA   I follow you.   72
                    Exeunt [*Tranio, Pedant, and Baptista*].

Enter Lucentio [*as Cambio*] *and Biondello.*

BIONDELLO   Cambio!
LUCENTIO   What say'st thou, Biondello?
BIONDELLO   You saw my master wink and laugh upon
you?
LUCENTIO   Biondello, what of that?
BIONDELLO   Faith, nothing; but he's left me here behind
to expound the meaning or moral of his signs and to-   79
kens.
LUCENTIO   I pray thee, moralize them.   81
BIONDELLO   Then thus. Baptista is safe, talking with   82
the deceiving father of a deceitful son.
LUCENTIO   And what of him?
BIONDELLO   His daughter is to be brought by you to
the supper.
LUCENTIO   And then?
BIONDELLO   The old priest at Saint Luke's church is at
your command at all hours.
LUCENTIO   And what of all this?

BIONDELLO   I cannot tell, except they are busied about a   91
counterfeit assurance. Take you assurance of her   92
cum privilegio ad imprimendum solum. To th'   93
church take the priest, clerk, and some sufficient hon-   94
est witnesses.
If this be not that you look for, I have no more to say,   96
But bid Bianca farewell forever and a day.
                    [*Biondello starts to leave.*]
LUCENTIO   Hear'st thou, Biondello?
BIONDELLO   I cannot tarry. I knew a wench married in
an afternoon as she went to the garden for parsley to
stuff a rabbit, and so may you, sir. And so, adieu, sir.
My master hath appointed me to go to Saint Luke's, to
bid the priest be ready to come against you come with   103
your appendix.   *Exit.*   104
LUCENTIO
I may, and will, if she be so contented.
She will be pleased; then wherefore should I doubt?
Hap what hap may, I'll roundly go about her.   107
It shall go hard if Cambio go without her.   *Exit.*   108

❧

[4.5]

Enter Petruchio, Kate, [*and*] *Hortensio.*

PETRUCHIO
Come on, i'God's name, once more toward our father's.   1
Good Lord, how bright and goodly shines the moon!
KATHARINA
The moon? The sun. It is not moonlight now.
PETRUCHIO
I say it is the moon that shines so bright.
KATHARINA
I know it is the sun that shines so bright.
PETRUCHIO
Now, by my mother's son, and that's myself,
It shall be moon, or star, or what I list   7
Or ere I journey to your father's house.—   8
Go on, and fetch our horses back again—
Evermore crossed and crossed, nothing but crossed!
HORTENSIO [*to Katharina*]
Say as he says, or we shall never go.
KATHARINA
Forward, I pray, since we have come so far,
And be it moon, or sun, or what you please;
An if you please to call it a rush candle,   14

---

53 **hearkening still** continually listening   54 **happily** haply   55 **an it like** if it please   56 **lie** lodge   57 **pass** transact   59 **scrivener** notary, one to draw up contracts.   **presently** at once.   61 **like** likely.   **slender pittance** i.e., scanty banquet.   70 **mess** dish.   **cheer** entertainment.   72.1 *Exeunt* (Technically, the cleared stage may mark a new scene, but the conversation of Lucentio and Biondello suggests that they come creeping back on stage as the others leave rather than doing the errands Baptista and Tranio bid them.)   79 **moral** hidden meaning   81 **moralize** elucidate   82 **safe** i.e., safely out of the way

91 **except** unless   92 **counterfeit assurance** pretended betrothal agreement.   **Take . . . of her** Legalize your claim to her (by marriage)   93 *cum . . . solum* with exclusive printing rights. (A copyright formula often appearing on the title pages of books, here jokingly applied to the marriage and to procreation as an act of imprinting.)   94 **sufficient** meeting the legal requirement in number and social standing   96 **that you look for** what you are looking for   103 **against you come** in anticipation of your arrival   104 **appendix** something appended, i.e., the bride. (Continuing the metaphor of printing.)   107 **roundly . . . her** set about marrying her in no uncertain terms.   108 **It . . . her** i.e., I'm determined to have her. (With pun about erection.)
4.5. Location: A road on the way to Padua.
1 **our father's** our father's house.   7 **list** please   8 **Or ere** before   14 **a rush candle** a rush dipped into tallow; hence a very feeble light

Henceforth I vow it shall be so for me.

PETRUCHIO
I say it is the moon.

KATHARINA   I know it is the moon.

PETRUCHIO
Nay, then you lie. It is the blessèd sun.

KATHARINA
Then, God be blessèd, it is the blessèd sun.
But sun it is not, when you say it is not,
And the moon changes even as your mind.
What you will have it named, even that it is,
And so it shall be so for Katharine.

HORTENSIO
Petruchio, go thy ways. The field is won.   23

PETRUCHIO
Well, forward, forward. Thus the bowl should run,
And not unluckily against the bias.   25
But soft! Company is coming here.

        Enter Vincentio.

[*To Vincentio*] Good morrow, gentle mistress. Where
        away?—   27
Tell me, sweet Kate, and tell me truly too,
Hast thou beheld a fresher gentlewoman?
Such war of white and red within her cheeks!
What stars do spangle heaven with such beauty
As those two eyes become that heavenly face?—
Fair lovely maid, once more good day to thee.—
Sweet Kate, embrace her for her beauty's sake.

HORTENSIO [*aside*]
'A will make the man mad, to make a woman of him.   35

KATHARINA [*embracing Vincentio*]
Young budding virgin, fair, and fresh, and sweet,
Whither away, or where is thy abode?
Happy the parents of so fair a child!
Happier the man whom favorable stars
Allots thee for his lovely bedfellow!   40

PETRUCHIO
Why, how now, Kate? I hope thou art not mad.
This is a man, old, wrinkled, faded, withered,
And not a maiden, as thou say'st he is.

KATHARINA
Pardon, old father, my mistaking eyes,
That have been so bedazzled with the sun
That everything I look on seemeth green.   46
Now I perceive thou art a reverend father.
Pardon, I pray thee, for my mad mistaking.

PETRUCHIO
Do, good old grandsire, and withal make known
Which way thou travelest—if along with us,
We shall be joyful of thy company.

VINCENTIO
Fair sir, and you, my merry mistress,
That with your strange encounter much amazed me,

My name is called Vincentio, my dwelling Pisa,
And bound I am to Padua, there to visit
A son of mine, which long I have not seen.

PETRUCHIO
What is his name?

VINCENTIO   Lucentio, gentle sir.

PETRUCHIO
Happily met, the happier for thy son.
And now by law as well as reverend age
I may entitle thee my loving father.
The sister to my wife, this gentlewoman,
Thy son by this hath married. Wonder not,   62
Nor be not grieved. She is of good esteem,   63
Her dowry wealthy, and of worthy birth;
Besides, so qualified as may beseem   65
The spouse of any noble gentleman.
Let me embrace with old Vincentio,
And wander we to see thy honest son,   68
Who will of thy arrival be full joyous.
                                    [*He embraces Vincentio.*]

VINCENTIO
But is this true? Or is it else your pleasure,
Like pleasant travelers, to break a jest   71
Upon the company you overtake?

HORTENSIO
I do assure thee, father, so it is.

PETRUCHIO
Come, go along, and see the truth hereof,
For our first merriment hath made thee jealous.   75
                            Exeunt [*all but Hortensio*].

HORTENSIO
Well, Petruchio, this has put me in heart.   76
Have to my widow! And if she be froward,   77
Then hast thou taught Hortensio to be untoward.   78
                                                        Exit.

                            ❧

[5.1]

        Enter Biondello, Lucentio [*no longer disguised*],
        and Bianca. Gremio is out before [*and stands
        aside*].

BIONDELLO   Softly and swiftly, sir, for the priest is
ready.

LUCENTIO   I fly, Biondello. But they may chance to need
thee at home; therefore leave us.

BIONDELLO   Nay, faith, I'll see the church a' your back,   5
and then come back to my master's as soon as I can.
                    [*Exeunt Lucentio, Bianca, and Biondello.*]

---

62 by this by this time   **63 esteem** reputation   **65 so qualified** having
such qualities.   **beseem** befit   **68 wander** go (having changed plans)
71 pleasant humorous, jocular.   **break a jest** play a practical joke
75 jealous suspicious.   **76 put me in heart** encouraged me.   **77 Have
to** i.e., Now for.   **froward** perverse   **78 untoward** unmannerly.
5.1. Location: Padua. Before Lucentio's house.
0.2 out before i.e., onstage first. (Gremio does not see Biondello,
Lucentio, and Bianca as they steal to church, or else he does not
recognize Lucentio in his own person.)   **5 a' your back** at your
back, behind you. (Biondello first wants to see them in church
and safely married.)

---

23 go thy ways i.e., well done, carry on.   **25 against the bias** off its
proper course. (The *bias* is an off-center weight in a bowling ball
enabling the bowler to roll the ball in an oblique or curving path.)
27 Where away? Where are you going?   **35 'A** He   **40 Allots** allot
46 green young and fresh.

GREMIO
I marvel Cambio comes not all this while.

Enter Petruchio, Kate, Vincentio, Grumio, with attendants.

PETRUCHIO
Sir, here's the door. This is Lucentio's house.
My father's bears more toward the marketplace;   9
Thither must I, and here I leave you, sir.
VINCENTIO
You shall not choose but drink before you go.   11
I think I shall command your welcome here,
And by all likelihood some cheer is toward.   *Knock.*   13
GREMIO [*advancing*] They're busy within. You were
best knock louder.   15

Pedant looks out of the window.

PEDANT   What's he that knocks as he would beat down
the gate?
VINCENTIO   Is Signor Lucentio within, sir?
PEDANT   He's within, sir, but not to be spoken withal.   19
VINCENTIO   What if a man bring him a hundred pound
or two to make merry withal?
PEDANT   Keep your hundred pounds to yourself. He
shall need none, so long as I live.
PETRUCHIO [*to Vincentio*]   Nay, I told you your son was
well beloved in Padua.—Do you hear, sir? To leave
frivolous circumstances, I pray you, tell Signor Lucen-   26
tio that his father is come from Pisa and is here at the
door to speak with him.
PEDANT   Thou liest. His father is come from Padua and   29
here looking out at the window.
VINCENTIO   Art thou his father?
PEDANT   Ay, sir, so his mother says, if I may believe
her.
PETRUCHIO [*to Vincentio*]   Why, how now, gentleman!
Why, this is flat knavery, to take upon you another   35
man's name.
PEDANT   Lay hands on the villain. I believe 'a means to
cozen somebody in this city under my countenance.   38

Enter Biondello.

BIONDELLO [*aside*]   I have seen them in the church
together, God send 'em good shipping! But who is   40
here? Mine old master Vincentio! Now we are undone
and brought to nothing.
VINCENTIO [*seeing Biondello*]   Come hither, crackhemp.   43
BIONDELLO   I hope I may choose, sir.   44

VINCENTIO   Come hither, you rogue. What, have you
forgot me?
BIONDELLO   Forgot you? No, sir. I could not forget you,
for I never saw you before in all my life.
VINCENTIO   What, you notorious villain, didst thou
never see thy master's father, Vincentio?
BIONDELLO   What, my old worshipful old master? Yes,
marry, sir, see where he looks out of the window.
VINCENTIO   Is't so, indeed?   *He beats Biondello.*
BIONDELLO   Help, help, help! Here's a madman will
murder me.   [*Exit.*]
PEDANT   Help, son! Help, Signor Baptista!
    [*Exit from the window.*]
PETRUCHIO   Prithee, Kate, let's stand aside and see the
end of this controversy.   [*They stand aside.*]

*Enter [below] Pedant with servants, Baptista,
[and] Tranio [as Lucentio].*

TRANIO   Sir, what are you that offer to beat my servant?   59
VINCENTIO   What am I, sir? Nay, what are you, sir? O
immortal gods! Oh, fine villain! A silken doublet, a vel-
vet hose, a scarlet cloak, and a copintank hat! Oh, I am   62
undone, I am undone! While I play the good husband   63
at home, my son and my servant spend all at the uni-
versity.
TRANIO   How now, what's the matter?
BAPTISTA   What, is the man lunatic?
TRANIO   Sir, you seem a sober ancient gentleman by
your habit, but your words show you a madman.   69
Why, sir, what 'cerns it you if I wear pearl and gold?   70
I thank my good father, I am able to maintain it.   71
VINCENTIO   Thy father! Oh, villain, he is a sailmaker in
Bergamo.
BAPTISTA   You mistake, sir, you mistake, sir. Pray, what
do you think is his name?
VINCENTIO   His name! As if I knew not his name! I have
brought him up ever since he was three years old, and
his name is Tranio.
PEDANT   Away, away, mad ass! His name is Lucentio,
and he is mine only son, and heir to the lands of me,
Signor Vincentio.
VINCENTIO   Lucentio! Oh, he hath murdered his master!
Lay hold on him, I charge you, in the Duke's name.
Oh, my son, my son! Tell me, thou villain, where is my
son Lucentio?
TRANIO   Call forth an officer.

[*Enter an Officer.*]

Carry this mad knave to the jail. Father Baptista, I
charge you see that he be forthcoming.   88
VINCENTIO   Carry me to the jail?
GREMIO   Stay, officer, he shall not go to prison.
BAPTISTA   Talk not, Signor Gremio. I say he shall go to
prison.

---

9 father's i.e., father-in-law's, Baptista's.   **bears** lies. (A nautical term.)   **11 You . . . but** i.e., I insist that   **13 cheer is toward** entertainment is in prospect.   **15.1 window** i.e., probably the gallery to the rear, over the stage.   **19 withal** with.   **26 circumstances** matters   **29 from Padua** i.e., from Padua, where we are right now. (Often emended to "from Mantua," "from Pisa," "to Padua," etc.)   **35 flat** downright   **38 cozen** cheat.   **under my countenance** by pretending to be me.   **40 good shipping** bon voyage, good fortune.   **43 crackhemp** i.e., rogue likely to end up being hanged.   **44 choose** do as I choose

59 offer dare, presume   **62 copintank** high-crowned, sugar-loaf shape   **63 good husband** careful provider, manager   **69 habit** clothing   **70 'cerns** concerns   **71 maintain** afford   **88 forthcoming** ready to stand trial when required.

GREMIO   Take heed, Signor Baptista, lest you be coney-   93
catched in this business. I dare swear this is the right   94
Vincentio.

PEDANT   Swear, if thou dar'st.

GREMIO   Nay, I dare not swear it.

TRANIO   Then thou wert best say that I am not Lucentio.   98

GREMIO   Yes, I know thee to be Signor Lucentio.

BAPTISTA   Away with the dotard! To the jail with him!

Enter Biondello, Lucentio, and Bianca.

VINCENTIO   Thus strangers may be haled and abused.   101
—Oh, monstrous villain!

BIONDELLO   Oh! We are spoiled and—yonder he is.   103
Deny him, forswear him, or else we are all undone.
*Exeunt Biondello, Tranio, and Pedant as fast as
may be. [Lucentio and Bianca] kneel.*

LUCENTIO
Pardon, sweet father.

VINCENTIO   Lives my sweet son?

BIANCA
Pardon, dear father.

BAPTISTA   How hast thou offended?
Where is Lucentio?

LUCENTIO   Here's Lucentio,
Right son to the right Vincentio,
That have by marriage made thy daughter mine,
While counterfeit supposes bleared thine eyne.   110

GREMIO
Here's packing, with a witness, to deceive us all!   111

VINCENTIO
Where is that damnèd villain Tranio,
That faced and braved me in this matter so?   113

BAPTISTA
Why, tell me, is not this my Cambio?

BIANCA
Cambio is changed into Lucentio.   115

LUCENTIO
Love wrought these miracles. Bianca's love
Made me exchange my state with Tranio,   117
While he did bear my countenance in the town,   118
And happily I have arrivèd at the last
Unto the wishèd haven of my bliss.
What Tranio did, myself enforced him to;
Then pardon him, sweet father, for my sake.

VINCENTIO   I'll slit the villain's nose, that would have
sent me to the jail.

BAPTISTA [*to Lucentio*]   But do you hear, sir? Have you
married my daughter without asking my good will?

VINCENTIO   Fear not, Baptista, we will content you. Go   127
to. But I will in, to be revenged for this villainy.   128
Exit.

BAPTISTA   And I, to sound the depth of this knavery.
Exit.

LUCENTIO   Look not pale, Bianca. Thy father will not
frown.   *Exeunt [Lucentio and Bianca].*

GREMIO
My cake is dough, but I'll in among the rest,   132
Out of hope of all but my share of the feast.   [*Exit.*]   133

KATHARINA   Husband, let's follow, to see the end of
this ado.

PETRUCHIO   First kiss me, Kate, and we will.

KATHARINA   What, in the midst of the street?

PETRUCHIO   What, art thou ashamed of me?

KATHARINA   No, sir, God forbid, but ashamed to kiss.

PETRUCHIO
Why, then let's home again. [*To Grumio*] Come, sirrah,
let's away.

KATHARINA
Nay, I will give thee a kiss. [*She kisses him.*] Now pray
thee, love, stay.

PETRUCHIO
Is not this well? Come, my sweet Kate.
Better once than never, for never too late.   *Exeunt.* 143

❖

5.[2]

*Enter Baptista, Vincentio, Gremio, the Pedant,
Lucentio, and Bianca; [Petruchio, Kate, Hortensio,] Tranio, Biondello, Grumio, and [the]
Widow; the servingmen with Tranio bringing
in a banquet.*

LUCENTIO
At last, though long, our jarring notes agree,   1
And time it is, when raging war is done,
To smile at scapes and perils overblown.   3
My fair Bianca, bid my father welcome,
While I with selfsame kindness welcome thine.
Brother Petruchio, sister Katharina,
And thou, Hortensio, with thy loving widow,
Feast with the best, and welcome to my house.
My banquet is to close our stomachs up   9
After our great good cheer. Pray you, sit down,   10
For now we sit to chat as well as eat.   [*They sit.*]

PETRUCHIO
Nothing but sit and sit, and eat and eat!

BAPTISTA
Padua affords this kindness, son Petruchio.

PETRUCHIO
Padua affords nothing but what is kind.

93–4 coney-catched tricked   **98 wert best** might as well
101 haled hauled about, maltreated   **103 spoiled** ruined   **110 supposes** suppositions, false appearances. (With an allusion to Gascoigne's *Supposes*, an adaptation of *I Suppositi* by Ariosto, from
which Shakespeare took the Lucentio-Bianca plot of intrigue.)
eyne eyes.   **111 Here's . . . all!** Here's evidence of a conspiracy, no
mistake about it!   **113 faced and braved** stood up to and defied
115 Cambio is changed (A pun. *Cambio* in Italian means "change"
or "exchange.")   **117 state** social station   **118 countenance** appearance, identity

127–8 Go to i.e., Don't worry. (An expression of impatience or annoyance.)   **132 My . . . dough** i.e., I'm out of luck, I failed
133 Out . . . but having hope for nothing other than   **143 once** at
some time. (Compare with "better late than never.")
5.2. Location: Padua. Lucentio's house.
1 long after long time   **3 scapes** close calls   **9 stomachs** (1) appetites
(2) quarrels   **10 cheer** i.e., wedding feast.

HORTENSIO
For both our sakes, I would that word were true.
PETRUCHIO
Now, for my life, Hortensio fears his widow.   16
WIDOW
Then never trust me if I be afeard.   17
PETRUCHIO
You are very sensible, and yet you miss my sense:
I mean Hortensio is afeard of you.
WIDOW
He that is giddy thinks the world turns round.
PETRUCHIO
Roundly replied.
KATHARINA   Mistress, how mean you that?   21
WIDOW   Thus I conceive by him.   22
PETRUCHIO
Conceives by me! How likes Hortensio that?
HORTENSIO
My widow says, thus she conceives her tale.   24
PETRUCHIO
Very well mended. Kiss him for that, good widow.
KATHARINA
"He that is giddy thinks the world turns round":
I pray you, tell me what you meant by that.
WIDOW
Your husband, being troubled with a shrew,
Measures my husband's sorrow by his woe.
And now you know my meaning.   29
KATHARINA
A very mean meaning.
WIDOW   Right, I mean you.   31
KATHARINA
And I am mean indeed, respecting you.   32
PETRUCHIO   To her, Kate!   33
HORTENSIO   To her, widow!
PETRUCHIO
A hundred marks, my Kate does put her down.   35
HORTENSIO   That's my office.
PETRUCHIO
Spoke like an officer. Ha' to thee, lad!   37
                    [He] drinks to Hortensio.
BAPTISTA
How likes Gremio these quick-witted folks?
GREMIO
Believe me, sir, they butt together well.   39
BIANCA
Head, and butt! An hasty-witted body   40
Would say your head and butt were head and horn.   41

VINCENTIO
Ay, mistress bride, hath that awakened you?
BIANCA
Ay, but not frighted me. Therefore I'll sleep again.
PETRUCHIO
Nay, that you shall not. Since you have begun,
Have at you for a bitter jest or two!   45
BIANCA
Am I your bird? I mean to shift my bush;   46
And then pursue me as you draw your bow.
You are welcome all.
                Exit Bianca [with Katharina and the Widow].
PETRUCHIO
She hath prevented me. Here, Signor Tranio,   49
This bird you aimed at, though you hit her not.   50
Therefore a health to all that shot and missed.   51
                          [He offers a toast.]
TRANIO
Oh, sir, Lucentio slipped me like his greyhound,   52
Which runs himself and catches for his master.
PETRUCHIO
A good swift simile, but something currish.   54
TRANIO
'Tis well, sir, that you hunted for yourself.
'Tis thought your deer does hold you at a bay.   56
BAPTISTA
Oho, Petruchio! Tranio hits you now.
LUCENTIO
I thank thee for that gird, good Tranio.   58
HORTENSIO
Confess, confess, hath he not hit you here?
PETRUCHIO
'A has has a little galled me, I confess;   60
And as the jest did glance away from me,
'Tis ten to one it maimed you two outright.
BAPTISTA
Now, in good sadness, son Petruchio,   63
I think thou hast the veriest shrew of all.
PETRUCHIO
Well, I say no. And therefore for assurance   65
Let's each one send unto his wife;
And he whose wife is most obedient
To come at first when he doth send for her
Shall win the wager which we will propose.
HORTENSIO
Content. What's the wager?
LUCENTIO   Twenty crowns.
PETRUCHIO   Twenty crowns!
I'll venture so much of my hawk or hound,   72
But twenty times so much upon my wife.

---

16 for my life upon my life.   **fears** is afraid of   **17 afeard** frightened (by Hortensio)   **21 Roundly** Boldly, bluntly   **22 Thus . . . him** i.e., That's what I think of him, Petruchio. (But Petruchio takes up *conceives* in the sense of "is made pregnant.")   **24 conceives** intends, interprets. (With a possible pun on *tale* and "tail.")   **29 his** his own   **31 very mean** contemptible. (But the Widow takes up *mean* in the sense of "have in mind," and Kate replies in the sense of "moderate in shrewishness.")   **32 respecting** compared to   **33 To her** (A cry used to egg on fighting roosters.)   **35 marks** coins worth thirteen shillings four pence.   **put her down** overcome her. (But Hortensio takes up the phrase in a bawdy sense.)   **37 officer** (playing on Hortensio's speaking of his *office* or function.)   **Ha'** Have, i.e., Here's   **39 butt** butt heads   **40 An hasty-witted body** A quick-witted person   **41 head and horn** (Alluding to the familiar joke about cuckolds' horns.)

45 Have at you for Here comes   **46 Am . . . bush** i.e., If you mean to shoot your barbs at me, I intend to move out of the way, as a bird would fly to another bush. (With a possible bawdy double meaning; *bush* can suggest pubic hair.)   **49 prevented** forestalled   **50 This bird** i.e., Bianca, whom Tranio courted (*aimed at*) in his disguise as Lucentio   **51 a health** a toast   **52 slipped** unleashed   **54 swift** (1) quick-witted (2) concerning swiftness.   **currish** (1) ignoble (2) concerning dogs.   **56 deer** (Punning on "dear.")   **does . . . bay** turns on you like a cornered animal and holds you at a distance.   **58 gird** sharp, biting jest   **60 galled** scratched, chafed   **63 sadness** seriousness   **65 assurance** proof   **72 of** on

LUCENTIO   A hundred then.
HORTENSIO   Content.
PETRUCHIO   A match. 'Tis done.
HORTENSIO   Who shall begin?
LUCENTIO   That will I.
    Go, Biondello, bid your mistress come to me.
BIONDELLO   I go.   *Exit.*
BAPTISTA
    Son, I'll be your half Bianca comes.   81
LUCENTIO
    I'll have no halves; I'll bear it all myself.

        Enter Biondello.

    How now, what news?
BIONDELLO
    Sir, my mistress sends you word
    That she is busy and she cannot come.
PETRUCHIO
    How? She's busy and she cannot come?
    Is that an answer?
GREMIO   Ay, and a kind one too.
    Pray God, sir, your wife send you not a worse.
PETRUCHIO   I hope better.
HORTENSIO
    Sirrah Biondello, go and entreat my wife
    To come to me forthwith.   *Exit Biondello.*
PETRUCHIO   Oho, entreat her!
    Nay, then she must needs come.
HORTENSIO   I am afraid, sir,
    Do what you can, yours will not be entreated.

        Enter Biondello.

    Now, where's my wife?
BIONDELLO
    She says you have some goodly jest in hand.
    She will not come. She bids you come to her.
PETRUCHIO
    Worse and worse. She will not come!
    Oh, vile, intolerable, not to be endured!—
    Sirrah Grumio, go to your mistress.
    Say I command her come to me.   *Exit* [*Grumio*].
HORTENSIO
    I know her answer.
PETRUCHIO   What?
HORTENSIO   She will not.
PETRUCHIO
    The fouler fortune mine, and there an end.   102

        Enter Katharina.

BAPTISTA
    Now, by my halidom, here comes Katharina!   103
KATHARINA
    What is your will, sir, that you send for me?
PETRUCHIO
    Where is your sister, and Hortensio's wife?

KATHARINA
    They sit conferring by the parlor fire.
PETRUCHIO
    Go fetch them hither. If they deny to come,
    Swinge me them soundly forth unto their husbands.   108
    Away, I say, and bring them hither straight.
                                    [*Exit Katharina.*]
LUCENTIO
    Here is a wonder, if you talk of a wonder.
HORTENSIO
    And so it is. I wonder what it bodes.
PETRUCHIO
    Marry, peace it bodes, and love, and quiet life,
    An awful rule, and right supremacy,   113
    And, to be short, what not that's sweet and happy.
BAPTISTA
    Now, fair befall thee, good Petruchio!   115
    The wager thou hast won, and I will add
    Unto their losses twenty thousand crowns,
    Another dowry to another daughter,
    For she is changed, as she had never been.   119
PETRUCHIO
    Nay, I will win my wager better yet,
    And show more sign of her obedience,
    Her new-built virtue and obedience.

        Enter Kate, Bianca, and [*the*] *Widow.*

    See where she comes and brings your froward wives
    As prisoners to her womanly persuasion.—
    Katharine, that cap of yours becomes you not.
    Off with that bauble. Throw it underfoot.
                                    [*She obeys.*]
WIDOW
    Lord, let me never have a cause to sigh
    Till I be brought to such a silly pass!   128
BIANCA
    Fie, what a foolish duty call you this?
LUCENTIO
    I would your duty were as foolish, too.
    The wisdom of your duty, fair Bianca,
    Hath cost me a hundred crowns since suppertime.
BIANCA
    The more fool you, for laying on my duty.   133
PETRUCHIO
    Katharine, I charge thee tell these headstrong women
    What duty they do owe their lords and husbands.
WIDOW
    Come, come, you're mocking. We will have no telling.
PETRUCHIO
    Come on, I say, and first begin with her.
WIDOW   She shall not.
PETRUCHIO
    I say she shall—and first begin with her.

---

81 **be your half** take half your bet   102 **there an end** that's that.
103 **by my halidom** (Originally an oath by the holy relics, but confused with an oath to the Virgin Mary.)

108 **Swinge** thrash.   **me** i.e., at my behest. (*Me* is used colloquially.)
113 **awful rule** authority commanding awe or respect   115 **fair befall
thee** good luck to you, and congratulations   119 **as . . . been** as if she
had never existed, i.e., she is totally changed.   128 **pass** state of
affairs.   133 **laying** wagering

KATHARINA

    Fie, fie! Unknit that threatening, unkind brow,
    And dart not scornful glances from those eyes
    To wound thy lord, thy king, thy governor.
    It blots thy beauty as frosts do bite the meads,   143
    Confounds thy fame as whirlwinds shake fair buds,   144
    And in no sense is meet or amiable.
    A woman moved is like a fountain troubled,   146
    Muddy, ill-seeming, thick, bereft of beauty;
    And while it is so, none so dry or thirsty   148
    Will deign to sip or touch one drop of it.
    Thy husband is thy lord, thy life, thy keeper,
    Thy head, thy sovereign; one that cares for thee,
    And for thy maintenance commits his body
    To painful labor both by sea and land,   153
    To watch the night in storms, the day in cold,   154
    Whilst thou liest warm at home, secure and safe;
    And craves no other tribute at thy hands
    But love, fair looks, and true obedience—
    Too little payment for so great a debt.
    Such duty as the subject owes the prince,
    Even such a woman oweth to her husband;
    And when she is froward, peevish, sullen, sour,   161
    And not obedient to his honest will,   162
    What is she but a foul contending rebel
    And graceless traitor to her loving lord?
    I am ashamed that women are so simple   165
    To offer war where they should kneel for peace,
    Or seek for rule, supremacy, and sway,
    When they are bound to serve, love, and obey.
    Why are our bodies soft, and weak, and smooth,
    Unapt to toil and trouble in the world,   170
    But that our soft conditions and our hearts   171
    Should well agree with our external parts?

143 meads meadows   **144 Confounds thy fame** ruins your reputation   **146 moved** angry   **148 none . . . thirsty** there is no one so thirsty that he   **153 painful** onerous   **154 watch** stay awake throughout   **161 peevish** obstinate   **162 to his honest will** (Kate may suggest that she will be obedient when his will is decent and virtuous, not that his will is always so.)   **165 simple** foolish   **170 Unapt to** unfit for   **171 conditions** qualities

    Come, come, you froward and unable worms!   173
    My mind hath been as big as one of yours,   174
    My heart as great, my reason haply more,
    To bandy word for word and frown for frown;
    But now I see our lances are but straws,
    Our strength as weak, our weakness past compare,   178
    That seeming to be most which we indeed least are.   179
    Then vail your stomachs, for it is no boot,   180
    And place your hands below your husband's foot,
    In token of which duty, if he please,
    My hand is ready; may it do him ease.   183

PETRUCHIO

    Why, there's a wench! Come on, and kiss me, Kate.
                          [They kiss.]

LUCENTIO

    Well, go thy ways, old lad, for thou shalt ha 't.   185

VINCENTIO

    'Tis a good hearing when children are toward.   186

LUCENTIO

    But a harsh hearing when women are froward.

PETRUCHIO   Come, Kate, we'll to bed.
    We three are married, but you two are sped.   189
    [To Lucentio] 'Twas I won the wager, though you hit
      the white,   190
    And, being a winner, God give you good night!   191
                Exit Petruchio [with Katharina].

HORTENSIO

    Now go thy ways. Thou hast tamed a curst shrew.   192

LUCENTIO

    'Tis a wonder, by your leave, she will be tamed so.
                            [Exeunt.]

173 unable worms i.e., poor feeble creatures.   **174 big** haughty   **178 as weak** i.e., as weak as straws   **179 That seeming to be** seeming to be that   **180 Then . . . boot** Then lower your pride, for it is no use striving   **183 do him ease** give him pleasure.   **185 go thy ways** well done.   **ha 't** have it, the prize.   **186 'Tis . . . toward** i.e., One likes to hear when children are obedient.   **189 We . . . sped** i.e., All we three men have taken wives, but you two are done for (*sped*) through disobedient wives.   **190 the white** the center of the target. (With quibble on the name of Bianca, which in Italian means "white.")   **191 being** since I am   **192 shrew** pronounced "shrow" (and thus spelled in the Folio). See also 4.1.198 and 5.2.28.

A Midsummer Night's Dream

One of the many astonishing achievements in *A Midsummer Night's Dream* (c. 1594–1595) is its development of the motif of love as an imaginative journey from a world of social conflict into a fantasy world created by the artist, ending in a return to a reality that has itself been partly transformed by the experience of the journey. As the lovers in this play flee from the Athenian law to lose themselves in the forest, they reveal and discover in themselves the simultaneously hilarious and horrifying effects of sexual desire. Moreover, their journey suggests the extent to which love or desire is itself an act of imagination, not unlike the imagination that underlies the creation of art. The fifth act especially invites us to see theatrical experience as like a dream, at times nightmarish but at its best an emancipating foray into an imagined space wholly beyond the realm of ordinary human happenings. Shakespeare gives us an earlier hint of an imaginary sylvan landscape in *The Two Gentlemen of Verona*, but not until *A Midsummer Night's Dream* is the idea fully realized. The motif of contrasting worlds, one of social convention and the other of visionary fantasy, will remain an enduring preoccupation of Shakespeare to the very last. This visionary world haunts the imagination with some of the most poetic passages of the entire Shakespeare canon, from Titania's evocation of her bond of affection with her votaress "in the spicèd Indian air by night" (2.1.123–37) to Oberon's memory of a mermaid singing on a dolphin's back (2.1.150–4). Containing the highest percentage of rhymed verse in all of Shakespeare's plays, *A Midsummer Night's Dream* calls attention to the seemingly magical capacity of words to weave spells not only on the characters but on the audience as well.

In construction, *A Midsummer Night's Dream* is a skillful interweaving of four plots involving four groups of characters: the court party of Theseus, the four young lovers, the fairies, and the "rude mechanicals" or would-be actors. Felix Mendelssohn's incidental music for the play evokes the contrasting textures of the various groups: Theseus's hunting horns and ceremonial wedding marches, the lovers' soaring and throbbing melodies, the fairies' pianissimo staccato, the tradesmen's clownish bassoon. Moreover, each plot is derived from its own set of source materials. The action involving Theseus and Hippolyta, for example, owes several details to Thomas North's translation (1579) of Plutarch's *Lives of the Noble Grecians and Romans*, to Chaucer's *Knight's Tale* and perhaps to his *Legend of Good Women*, and to Ovid's *Meta-morphoses* (in the Latin text or in Arthur Golding's popular Elizabethan translation). The lovers' story, meanwhile, is Italianate and Ovidian in tone and also, in the broadest sense, follows the conventions of plot in Plautus's and Terence's Roman comedies, although no particular source is known. Shakespeare's rich fairy lore, by contrast, is part folk tradition and part learned. For some of his material he seems to have turned to written sources, such as the French romance *Huon of Bordeaux* (translated into English by 1540), Robert Greene's play *James IV* (c. 1591), and Edmund Spenser's *The Faerie Queene*, II.i.8 (1590). Similarly, he may have taken Titania's name from the *Metamorphoses*, where it is used as an epithet for both Diana and Circe. At the same time, in his creation of Mustardseed, Cobweb, Mote, and Peaseblossom, Shakespeare also pays homage to a rich body of unwritten sources that are, for the most part, no longer accessible. Changeling children, mortals kidnapped by fairy queens, men transformed to beasts by evil spells: these were the stuff of oral tales circulated by firesides on winter nights. Finally, for Bottom the weaver and company, Shakespeare's primary inspiration was doubtless his own theatrical experience, although even here he is indebted to Ovid for the story of Pyramus and Thisbe, and probably to Apuleius's *Golden Ass* (translated by William Adlington, 1566) for Bottom's transformation.

Each of the four main plots in *A Midsummer Night's Dream* contains one or more pairs of lovers whose happiness has been frustrated by misunderstanding or parental opposition. Theseus and Hippolyta, once enemies in battle, become husband and wife; their court marriage, constituting the overplot of the play, provides a framework for other dramatic actions that similarly oscillate between conflict and harmony. In fact, Theseus's actions are instrumental in setting in motion and finally resolving the tribulations of the other characters. In the beginning of the play, for example, the lovers flee from Theseus's Athenian law; at the end, they are awakened by him from their dream. As the king and queen of fairies come to Athens to celebrate Theseus's wedding, they exchange jealous accusations: Oberon accuses his queen of being overly partial to Theseus, while she is critical of Oberon's attentions to Hippolyta. These plots of the Athenian and the fairy monarchs are drawn even more closely together by the common practice in today's theater of doubling the parts of Theseus and Oberon, Hippolyta and Titania (also, frequently, Philostrate and Puck). The broadly comic action of Bottom the Weaver and his companions is drawn into the overall design by means of their deciding to use the forest of Athens as the place where they will rehearse their performance of "Pyramus and Thisbe" in anticipation of the wedding festivities.

The tragic love story of Pyramus and Thisbe, although it seems absurdly ill suited to a wedding, reminds us of the discord and potentially fatal misunderstandings that threaten even the best of relationships between men and women. For all his graceful bearing and princely authority, Theseus is a conquering male who freely admits that he has won the love of Hippolyta with his sword, doing her "injuries" (1.1.17). He never questions that the accord between them should now be stated in terms of male ascendancy over the female. The Amazonian Hippolyta may accept with good grace the marriage she previously resisted with all her might, like Kate in *The Taming of the Shrew*, and yet, in many recent stage productions, the actress playing Hippolyta has found it easy to cast doubt on the presumed tranquility of this forthcoming marriage by a display of feminist impatience at Theseus's urbanely patriarchal ways. The reconciliation of Oberon and Titania, meanwhile, reinforces the hierarchy of male over female in no uncertain terms. Having taught Titania a lesson for trying to keep a changeling boy from him, Oberon relents and eventually frees Titania from her debasing enchantment. She does not reproach him with so much as a word when she is awakened from her "vision." Even so, the very existence of the abundantly female space of Titania's bower where, surrounded by her attendants, she has acted out desires that she thought were her own, poses an alternative to patriarchy. The four young lovers end up happily paired, but only after they have experienced rejection, rivalry, hatred, and the desire to kill; the final resolution of this plot would not be possible if Demetrius were not left under the spell of the fairy love-juice. Thus, Theseus's wedding provides a ceremonial occasion of harmony and reconciliation but in such a way as to highlight the difficulties that have beset the drama's various couples.

Despite Theseus's cheerful preoccupation with marriage, his court embodies at first a stern attitude toward young love. As administrator of the law, Theseus must accede to the remorseless demands of Hermia's father, Egeus. The inflexible Athenian law sides with parentage, age, male dominance, wealth, and position against youth and romantic choice in love. The penalties are harsh: death or perpetual virginity—and virginity is presented in this comedy (despite the nobly chaste examples of Christ, St. Paul, and Queen Elizabeth) as a fate worse than death. Egeus is a familiar type, the interfering parent found in the Roman comedy of Plautus and Terence (and in Shakespeare's *Romeo and Juliet*). Indeed, the lovers' story is distantly derived from Roman comedy, which conventionally celebrated the triumph of young love over the machinations of age and wealth. Lysander reminds us that "the course of true love never did run smooth," and he sees its enemies as being chiefly external: the conflicting interests of parents or friends; mismating with respect to years and blood; war; death; or sickness (1.1.134–42). This description clearly applies to "Pyramus and Thisbe," and it is tested by the action of *A Midsummer Night's Dream* as a whole (as well as by other early Shakespearean plays, such as *Romeo and Juliet*). The archetypal story, whether ending happily or sadly, is an evocation of love's difficulties in the face of social hostility and indifference.

While Shakespeare uses several elements of Roman comedy in setting up the basic conflicts of his drama, he also introduces important modifications from the beginning. For example, he discards one conventional confrontation of classical and neoclassical comedy, in which the heroine must choose between an old, wealthy suitor supported by her family and the young but impecunious darling of her heart. Lysander is equal to his rival in social position, income, and attractiveness. Egeus's demand, therefore—that Hermia marry Demetrius rather than Lysander—seems simply arbitrary and unjust. Shakespeare emphasizes in this way the irrationality of Egeus's harsh insistence on being obeyed and of Theseus's rather complacent acceptance of the law's inequity. Spurned by an unfeeling social order, Lysander and Hermia are compelled to elope. To be sure, in the end Egeus proves to be no formidable threat; even he must admit the logic of permitting the lovers to couple as they ultimately desire. Thus, the obstacles to love are seen from the start as fundamentally superficial and indeed almost whimsical. Egeus is as heavy a villain as we are likely to find in this *jeu d'esprit*. Moreover, the very irrationality of his position prepares the way for an ultimate resolution of the conflict. Nevertheless, by the end of the first act, the supposedly rational world of conformity and duty, by its customary insensitivity to youthful happiness, has set in motion a temporary escape to a fantasy world where the law cannot reach.

In the forest, all the lovers—including Titania and Bottom—undergo a transforming experience engineered by the mischievous Puck. This experience demonstrates the universal power of love, which can overcome the queen of fairies as readily as the lowliest of humans. It also suggests the irrational nature of love and its affinity to enchantment, witchcraft, and even madness. Love is seen as an affliction taken in through the frail senses, particularly the eyes. When it strikes, the victim cannot choose but to embrace the object of his or her infatuation. By his amusing miscalculations, Puck shuffles the four lovers through various permutations with mathematical predictability. First, two gentlemen compete for one lady, leaving the second lady sadly unrequited in love; then everything is at cross-purposes, with each gentleman pursuing the lady who is in love with the other man; then the two gentlemen compete for the lady they both previously ignored. Finally, of course, Jack shall have his Jill—whom else should he have? The couples are properly united, as they evidently were at some time prior to the commencement of the play, when Demetrius had been romantically attached to Helena and Lysander to Hermia.

Their experience in the forest is an unsettling one for the four young lovers. Although some of them seek out the forest as a refuge from the Athenian law, the place rapidly takes on the darker aspect of a nightmare. Hermia awakens from sleep to find Lysander gone and soon discovers that her dream of a serpent eating her heart away while Lysander watches smiling (2.2.155–6) is all too prophetically true. The forest is a place of testing of the lovers, and the test appears at first to show how they are all their own worst enemies. Helena, having been rejected by Demetrius, can only suppose that she is being mocked, with Lysander and Demetrius both paying court to her. Next, it occurs to her that Hermia must be part of their conspiracy, too. Even though Hermia and Helena recall to each other the selfless devotion they have known as young friends, they become hated rivals in their present mood of self-pity and injured self-regard. The threshold of sexual awakening, it would seem, confronts them with a hazardous rite of passage—one that is especially threatening to the nonsexual friendship of their adolescent years. The two young men respond to similar conflicts by turning on one another in characteristically aggressive male ways. Puck allows them to playact their intended mayhem in a way that cannot harm them and then brings all four lovers together where they can awaken from their nightmare of imagined persecution. How much do they remember? Have they been changed by their journey in the forest? The lovers convey a sense of confusion, of an unreconciled dissonance of perspective in which "everything seems double" (4.1.189). As the

lovers return to the daylight world of Athens and the court, their experiences assume the unreality of a remembered dream, like "far-off mountains turnèd into clouds" (4.1.187). When they thus awaken and return to the daylight world of Athens and the court, their renewed love and friendship are presumably deepened by their perception of how narrowly they have escaped from their own self-destructive imaginings. Their new happiness, they see, is better than they have deserved.

We sense that Puck is by no means unhappy about his knavish errors and manipulations: "Lord, what fools these mortals be!" Along with the other fairies in this play, Puck takes his being and his complex motivation from many denizens of the invisible world. As the agent of all-powerful love, Puck compares himself to Cupid. The love juice he administers comes from Cupid's flower, "love-in-idleness." Like Cupid, Puck acts at the behest of the gods, and yet he wields a power that the chiefest of the gods themselves cannot resist. Essentially, however, Puck is less a classical love deity than a prankish folk spirit, such as we find in every folklore: gremlin, leprechaun, hobgoblin, and the like. Titania's fairies recognize Puck as the folk figure Robin Goodfellow, able to deprive a beer barrel of its yeast so that it spoils rather than ferments. Puck characterizes himself as a practical joker, pulling stools out from under old ladies.

Folk wisdom imagines the inexplicable and unaccountable events in life to be caused by invisible spirits who laugh at mortals' discomfiture and mock them for mere sport. Puck is related to these mysterious spirits dwelling in nature, who must be placated with gifts and ceremonies. Although Shakespeare restricts Puck to a benign sportive role in dealing with the lovers or with Titania, the actual folk legends about Puck mentioned in this play are frequently disquieting. Puck is known to "mislead night wanderers, laughing at their harm"; indeed, he demonstrates as much with Demetrius and Lysander, leading them on through the forest to the point of exhaustion, even though we perceive the sportful intent. At the play's end, Puck links himself and his fellows with the ghoulish apparitions of death and night: wolves howling at the moon, screech owls, shrouds, gaping graves. Associations of this sort go beyond mere sportiveness to the witchcraft and demonology involving spirits rising from the dead. Even Oberon's assurance that the fairies will bless all the marriages of this play, shielding their progeny against mole, harelip, or other birth defects, carries the implication that such misfortunes can be caused by offended spirits. The magic of this play is thus explicitly related to deep irrational powers and forces capable of doing great harm, although, to be sure, the spirit of comedy keeps such veiled threats safely at a distance in A Midsummer Night's Dream.

Oberon and Titania, in their view of the relationship between gods and humans, reflect yet another aspect of the fairies' spiritual ancestry. The king and queen of fairies assert that, because they are immortal, their regal quarrels in love must inevitably have dire consequences on earth, either in the love relationship of Theseus and Hippolyta or in the management of the weather. Floods, storms, diseases, and sterility abound, "And this same progeny of evils comes / From our debate, from our dissension. / We are their parents and original" (2.1.115–17). This motif of the gods' quarreling over human affairs reminds us of Homer and Virgil. At the same time, in this lighthearted play the motif is more nearly mock-epic than truly epic. The consequences of the gods' anger are simply mirth-provoking, most of all in Titania's love affair with Bottom the weaver.

The story of Bottom and Titania is simultaneously classical and folk in nature. In a playfully classical mode, this love affair between a god and an earthy creature underscores humanity's double nature. Bottom himself becomes half man and half beast, even if he is more ludicrously comic than the centaurs, satyrs, griffins, sphinxes, and other amphibious beings of classical mythology. Some ballads of the early modern period tell of humans transformed into beasts, or of mortals kidnapped by a fairy queen; see, for example, "Tam Lin" and "Thomas Rhymer." Bottom is an especially comic example of metamorphosis because he reverses the usual pattern of a human head and an animal body: instead, his head is animal, his body human. His very name suggests the solid nature of his fleshly being (*bottom* is appropriately also a weaving term). He and Titania represent the opposites of flesh and spirit, miraculously yoked for a time in a twofold vision of humankind's absurd and ethereal nature.

A play bringing together fairies and mortals inevitably raises questions of illusion and reality. These questions reach their greatest intensity in the presentation of "Pyramus and Thisbe." This play within a play focuses our attention on the familiarly Shakespearean metaphor of art as illusion and of the world itself as a stage on which men and women are merely players. As Theseus observes, apologizing for the ineptness of the tradesmen's performance, "the best in this kind are but shadows" (5.1.210); that is, Shakespeare's own play is of the same order of reality as Bottom's play. Puck too, in his epilogue, invites any spectator offended by Shakespeare's play to dismiss it as a mere dream—as, indeed, the play's very title suggests. Theseus goes even further, linking dream to the essence of imaginative art, although he does so in a clearly critical and rather patronizing way. The artist, he says, is like the maniac or the lover in his or her frenzy of inspiration, giving "to airy nothing / A local habitation and a name" (5.1.16–17). Artistic achievements are too unsubstantial for Theseus; from his point of view they are the products of mere fantasy and irrationality, mere myths or fairy stories or old wives' tales. Behind this critical persona defending the "real" world of his court, how-

ever, we can hear Shakespeare's characteristically self-effacing defense of "dreaming."

"Pyramus and Thisbe," like the larger play surrounding it, attempts to body forth "the forms of things unknown." The play within the play gives us personified moonshine, a speaking wall, and an apologetic lion. Of course, it is an absurdly bad play, full of lame epithets, bombastic alliteration, and bathos. In part, Shakespeare here is satirizing the abuses of a theater he had helped reform. The players' chosen method of portraying imaginative matters is ridiculous and calls forth deliciously wry comments from the courtly spectators on stage: "Would you desire lime and hair to speak better?" (5.1.164–5). At the same time, those spectators on stage are actors in our play. Their sarcasms render them less sympathetic in our eyes; we see that their kind of sophistication is as restrictive as it is illuminating. Bottom and his friends have conceived moonshine and lion as they did because these simple men are so responsive to the terrifying power of art. A lion might frighten the ladies and get the men hanged. Theirs is a primitive faith, naive but strong, and in this sense it contrasts favorably with the jaded rationality of the court party. Theseus's valuable reminder that all art is only "illusion" is thus juxtaposed with Bottom's insistence that imaginative art has a reality of its own.

Theseus above all embodies the sophistication of the court in his description of art as a frenzy of seething brains. Ironically, Theseus's genial scoffing at "These antique fables" and "these fairy toys" (5.1.3) would seem to efface his own identity as the figure of legend. Limited by his own skepticism, Theseus seems to have forgotten his own forest wanderings, led by Titania through the "glimmering night" (2.1.77). Bottom, contrastingly, has experienced "a most rare vision," such a dream as is "past the wit of man to say what dream it was" (4.1.203–5). He alone can claim to have been the lover of the queen of fairies; and, although his language cannot adequately describe the experience, Bottom will see it made into a ballad called "Bottom's Dream." Shakespeare leaves the status of his fantasy world deliberately complex; Theseus's lofty denial of dreaming is too abrupt. Even if the Athenian forest world can be made only momentarily substantial in the artifact of Shakespeare's play, we as audience respond to its tantalizing vision. We emerge back into our lives wondering if the fairies were "real"; that is, we are puzzled by the relationship of these artistic symbols to the tangible concreteness of our daily existence. Unless our perceptions have been thus enlarged by sharing in the author's dream, we have not surrendered to the imaginative experience.

Recent performances of this enduringly popular play suggest how open it is to varying interpretation and especially to postmodern views of love and politics as thoroughly unsettling in their irrationality. Nineteenth-century staging generally preferred to see the play as a gossamer delight of diminutive gilded-winged fairies and prankish hobgoblins, all underscored by the romantic strains of Mendelssohn's incidental music. More recently, and especially after World War II, theater and film versions have responded to a darker view. Inspired by Jan Kott's *Shakespeare Our Contemporary* (1964), a book written from the perspective of Soviet-dominated eastern Europe of the Cold War, Peter Brook's brilliantly revisionary stage version for the Royal Shakespeare Theater in 1970 set the play in a brightly lit white box peopled with jugglers and athletic trapeze artists who tumbled and dashed about after one another with abandon. A clenched fist thrust between the legs of the button-nosed Bottom the Weaver, as he was carried offstage from his rendezvous with Queen Titania, affirmed the triumph of his phallic success.

Brook's avowed aim of freeing the play from what he saw as an oppressive tradition has proved to be immensely influential. Ever since, the young lovers have learned to express their sexual energies through vigorous pursuit and physical contact. Feminist insights have enriched the role of Queen Hippolyta: formerly a captive queen resigned to her marriage to Theseus, she has become in many productions a champion of Hermia's right to resist her father's patriarchal insistence on his will. Puck, in many a recent production, is the denizen of a drug culture, with the love potion as the weed he gleefully distributes. The experience of the forest becomes a drug-induced "high," for audiences as for the actors. The fairies, sometimes played by adult and hairy males, can exhibit a steak of cruelty. The doubling of some central roles, notably Theseus/Oberon, Hippolyta/Titania, and Philostrate/Puck, has given ironic emphasis to parallels between human society and fairyland. Throughout, modern productions have tended to exploit disenchantment with traditional social structures and the surging energy of sexual self-discovery. These modern interpretations are arguably neither more nor less "true" to Shakespeare's text than earlier or more "traditional" versions. What they do demonstrate is the play's remarkable permeability and openness to differing views.

A Midsummer Night's Dream

[*Dramatis Personae*

THESEUS, *Duke of Athens*

HIPPOLYTA, *Queen of the Amazons, betrothed to Theseus*
PHILOSTRATE, *Master of the Revels*
EGEUS, *father of Hermia*

HERMIA, *daughter of Egeus, in love with Lysander*
LYSANDER, *in love with Hermia*
DEMETRIUS, *in love with Hermia and favored by Egeus*
HELENA, *in love with Demetrius*

OBERON, *King of the Fairies*
TITANIA, *Queen of the Fairies*
PUCK, *or* ROBIN GOODFELLOW

PEASEBLOSSOM,
COBWEB,
MOTE,   } *fairies attending Titania*
MUSTARDSEED,
Other FAIRIES *attending*

PETER QUINCE, *a carpenter,*		PROLOGUE
NICK BOTTOM, *a weaver,*		PYRAMUS
FRANCIS FLUTE, *a bellows mender,*	*repre-senting*	THISBE
TOM SNOUT, *a tinker,*		WALL
SNUG, *a joiner,*		LION
ROBIN STARVELING, *a tailor,*		MOONSHINE

Lords and Attendants on Theseus and Hippolyta

SCENE: *Athens, and a wood near it*]

[1.1]

Enter Theseus, Hippolyta, [and Philostrate,]
with others.

THESEUS
Now, fair Hippolyta, our nuptial hour
Draws on apace. Four happy days bring in
Another moon; but, oh, methinks, how slow
This old moon wanes! She lingers my desires,   4
Like to a stepdame or a dowager   5
Long withering out a young man's revenue.   6

HIPPOLYTA
Four days will quickly steep themselves in night;   7
Four nights will quickly dream away the time;
And then the moon, like to a silver bow
New bent in heaven, shall behold the night
Of our solemnities.

THESEUS   Go, Philostrate,   11
Stir up the Athenian youth to merriments.
Awake the pert and nimble spirit of mirth.
Turn melancholy forth to funerals;
The pale companion is not for our pomp.   15
                              [*Exit Philostrate.*]
Hippolyta, I wooed thee with my sword   16
And won thy love doing thee injuries;
But I will wed thee in another key,
With pomp, with triumph, and with reveling.   19

Enter Egeus and his daughter Hermia, and
Lysander, and Demetrius.

EGEUS
Happy be Theseus, our renownèd duke!

THESEUS
Thanks, good Egeus. What's the news with thee?

EGEUS
Full of vexation come I, with complaint
Against my child, my daughter Hermia.—
Stand forth, Demetrius.—My noble lord,
This man hath my consent to marry her.—
Stand forth, Lysander.—And, my gracious Duke,
This man hath bewitched the bosom of my child.—
Thou, thou Lysander, thou hast given her rhymes
And interchanged love tokens with my child.
Thou hast by moonlight at her window sung
With feigning voice verses of feigning love,   31
And stol'n the impression of her fantasy   32
With bracelets of thy hair, rings, gauds, conceits,   33

Knacks, trifles, nosegays, sweetmeats—messengers   34
Of strong prevailment in unhardened youth.   35
With cunning hast thou filched my daughter's heart,
Turned her obedience, which is due to me,
To stubborn harshness. And, my gracious Duke,
Be it so she will not here before Your Grace   39
Consent to marry with Demetrius,
I beg the ancient privilege of Athens:
As she is mine, I may dispose of her,
Which shall be either to this gentleman
Or to her death, according to our law
Immediately provided in that case.   45

THESEUS
What say you, Hermia? Be advised, fair maid.
To you your father should be as a god—
One that composed your beauties, yea, and one
To whom you are but as a form in wax
By him imprinted, and within his power
To leave the figure or disfigure it.   51
Demetrius is a worthy gentleman.

HERMIA
So is Lysander.

THESEUS   In himself he is;
But in this kind, wanting your father's voice,   54
The other must be held the worthier.

HERMIA
I would my father looked but with my eyes.

THESEUS
Rather your eyes must with his judgment look.

HERMIA
I do entreat Your Grace to pardon me.
I know not by what power I am made bold,
Nor how it may concern my modesty
In such a presence here to plead my thoughts;
But I beseech Your Grace that I may know
The worst that may befall me in this case
If I refuse to wed Demetrius.

THESEUS
Either to die the death or to abjure   65
Forever the society of men.
Therefore, fair Hermia, question your desires,
Know of your youth, examine well your blood,   68
Whether, if you yield not to your father's choice,
You can endure the livery of a nun,   70
For aye to be in shady cloister mewed,   71
To live a barren sister all your life,
Chanting faint hymns to the cold fruitless moon.
Thrice blessèd they that master so their blood
To undergo such maiden pilgrimage;
But earthlier happy is the rose distilled   76
Than that which, withering on the virgin thorn,
Grows, lives, and dies in single blessedness.

1.1. Location: Athens. Theseus's court.
4 lingers frustrates   **5 stepdame** stepmother.   **a dowager** i.e., a
widow (whose right of inheritance from her dead husband is eating
into her son's estate)   **6 withering out** causing to dwindle
7 Four . . . night (The image is of the day sinking into the ocean as
night comes on.)   **11 solemnities** festive ceremonies of marriage.
15 companion fellow. (A pale complexion is linked to melancholy.)
pomp ceremonial magnificence.   **16 with my sword** i.e., in a military
engagement against the Amazons, when Hippolyta was taken captive   **19 triumph** public festivity   **31 feigning** (1) counterfeiting
(2) faining, desirous   **32 And . . . fantasy** and made her fall in love
with you (imprinting your image on her imagination) by stealthy and
dishonest means   **33 gauds, conceits** playthings, fanciful trifles

34 Knacks . . . sweetmeats knicknacks, trinkets, bouquets, candies
35 prevailment in influence on   **39 Be it so** if   **45 Immediately**
directly, with nothing intervening   **51 leave** i.e., leave unaltered
54 kind respect.   **wanting** lacking.   **voice** approval   **65 die the
death** be executed by legal process   **68 blood** passions   **70 livery**
habit, costume   **71 aye** ever.   **mewed** shut in. (Said of a hawk, poultry, etc.)   **76 earthlier happy** happier as respects this world.
distilled i.e., to make perfume

HERMIA
So will I grow, so live, so die, my lord,
Ere I will yield my virgin patent up   80
Unto His Lordship, whose unwishèd yoke
My soul consents not to give sovereignty.

THESEUS
Take time to pause, and by the next new moon—
The sealing day betwixt my love and me
For everlasting bond of fellowship—
Upon that day either prepare to die
For disobedience to your father's will,
Or else to wed Demetrius, as he would,
Or on Diana's altar to protest   89
For aye austerity and single life.

DEMETRIUS
Relent, sweet Hermia, and, Lysander, yield
Thy crazèd title to my certain right.   92

LYSANDER
You have her father's love, Demetrius;
Let me have Hermia's. Do you marry him.

EGEUS
Scornful Lysander! True, he hath my love,
And what is mine my love shall render him.
And she is mine, and all my right of her
I do estate unto Demetrius.   98

LYSANDER
I am, my lord, as well derived as he,   99
As well possessed; my love is more than his;   100
My fortunes every way as fairly ranked,   101
If not with vantage, as Demetrius';   102
And, which is more than all these boasts can be,
I am beloved of beauteous Hermia.
Why should not I then prosecute my right?
Demetrius, I'll avouch it to his head,   106
Made love to Nedar's daughter, Helena,
And won her soul; and she, sweet lady, dotes,
Devoutly dotes, dotes in idolatry
Upon this spotted and inconstant man.   110

THESEUS
I must confess that I have heard so much,
And with Demetrius thought to have spoke thereof;
But, being overfull of self-affairs,   113
My mind did lose it. But, Demetrius, come,
And come, Egeus, you shall go with me;
I have some private schooling for you both.   116
For you, fair Hermia, look you arm yourself   117
To fit your fancies to your father's will,   118
Or else the law of Athens yields you up—
Which by no means we may extenuate—   120
To death or to a vow of single life.
Come, my Hippolyta. What cheer, my love?
Demetrius and Egeus, go along.   123

I must employ you in some business
Against our nuptial, and confer with you   125
Of something nearly that concerns yourselves.   126

EGEUS
With duty and desire we follow you.
                    Exeunt [all but Lysander and Hermia].

LYSANDER
How now, my love, why is your cheek so pale?
How chance the roses there do fade so fast?

HERMIA
Belike for want of rain, which I could well   130
Beteem them from the tempest of my eyes.   131

LYSANDER
Ay me! For aught that I could ever read,
Could ever hear by tale or history,
The course of true love never did run smooth;
But either it was different in blood—   135

HERMIA
Oh, cross! Too high to be enthralled to low.   136

LYSANDER
Or else misgrafted in respect of years—   137

HERMIA
Oh, spite! Too old to be engaged to young.

LYSANDER
Or else it stood upon the choice of friends—   139

HERMIA
Oh, hell, to choose love by another's eyes!

LYSANDER
Or if there were a sympathy in choice,   141
War, death, or sickness did lay siege to it,
Making it momentany as a sound,   143
Swift as a shadow, short as any dream,
Brief as the lightning in the collied night   145
That in a spleen unfolds both heaven and earth,   146
And ere a man hath power to say "Behold!"
The jaws of darkness do devour it up.
So quick bright things come to confusion.   149

HERMIA
If then true lovers have been ever crossed,   150
It stands as an edict in destiny.
Then let us teach our trial patience,   152
Because it is a customary cross,
As due to love as thoughts, and dreams, and sighs,
Wishes, and tears, poor fancy's followers.   155

LYSANDER
A good persuasion. Therefore, hear me, Hermia: 156
I have a widow aunt, a dowager
Of great revenue, and she hath no child.
From Athens is her house remote seven leagues;   159
And she respects me as her only son.   160

---

80 **patent** privilege   89 **protest** vow   92 **crazèd** cracked, unsound
98 **estate unto** settle or bestow upon   99 **as well derived** as well born
and descended   100 **possessed** endowed with wealth   101 **fairly**
handsomely   102 **vantage** superiority   106 **head** i.e., face   110 **spotted** i.e., morally stained   113 **self-affairs** my own concerns
116 **schooling** admonition   117 **look you arm** take care you prepare
118 **fancies** likings, thoughts of love   120 **extenuate** mitigate, relax
123 **go** i.e., come

125 **Against** in preparation for   126 **nearly that** that closely
130 **Belike** Very likely   131 **Beteem** grant, afford   135 **blood** hereditary rank   136 **cross** vexation.   137 **misgrafted** ill grafted, badly
matched   139 **friends** relatives   141 **sympathy** agreement
143 **momentany** lasting but a moment   145 **collied** blackened (as
with coal dust), darkened   146 **in a spleen** in a swift impulse, in a
violent flash.   **unfolds** reveals   149 **confusion** ruin.   150 **ever
crossed** always thwarted   152 **teach . . . patience** i.e., teach ourselves
patience in this trial   155 **fancy's** amorous passion's   156 **persuasion** doctrine.   159 **seven leagues** about 21 miles   160 **respects**
regards

There, gentle Hermia, may I marry thee,
And to that place the sharp Athenian law
Cannot pursue us. If thou lovest me, then,
Steal forth thy father's house tomorrow night;
And in the wood, a league without the town, 165
Where I did meet thee once with Helena
To do observance to a morn of May, 167
There will I stay for thee.

HERMIA   My good Lysander!
I swear to thee, by Cupid's strongest bow,
By his best arrow with the golden head, 170
By the simplicity of Venus' doves, 171
By that which knitteth souls and prospers loves,
And by that fire which burned the Carthage queen 173
When the false Trojan under sail was seen, 174
By all the vows that ever men have broke,
In number more than ever women spoke,
In that same place thou hast appointed me
Tomorrow truly will I meet with thee.

LYSANDER
Keep promise, love. Look, here comes Helena.

Enter Helena.

HERMIA
God speed, fair Helena! Whither away? 180

HELENA
Call you me fair? That "fair" again unsay.
Demetrius loves your fair. Oh, happy fair! 182
Your eyes are lodestars, and your tongue's sweet air 183
More tunable than lark to shepherd's ear 184
When wheat is green, when hawthorn buds appear.
Sickness is catching. Oh, were favor so, 186
Yours would I catch, fair Hermia, ere I go;
My ear should catch your voice, my eye your eye,
My tongue should catch your tongue's sweet melody.
Were the world mine, Demetrius being bated, 190
The rest I'd give to be to you translated. 191
Oh, teach me how you look and with what art
You sway the motion of Demetrius' heart. 193

HERMIA
I frown upon him, yet he loves me still.

HELENA
Oh, that your frowns would teach my smiles such
   skill!

HERMIA
I give him curses, yet he gives me love.

HELENA
Oh, that my prayers could such affection move! 197

HERMIA
The more I hate, the more he follows me.

HELENA
The more I love, the more he hateth me.

HERMIA
His folly, Helena, is no fault of mine.

HELENA
None, but your beauty. Would that fault were mine!

HERMIA
Take comfort. He no more shall see my face.
Lysander and myself will fly this place.
Before the time I did Lysander see 204
Seemed Athens as a paradise to me. 205
Oh, then, what graces in my love do dwell,
That he hath turned a heaven unto a hell?

LYSANDER
Helen, to you our minds we will unfold.
Tomorrow night, when Phoebe doth behold 209
Her silver visage in the watery glass, 210
Decking with liquid pearl the bladed grass, 211
A time that lovers' flights doth still conceal, 212
Through Athens' gates have we devised to steal.

HERMIA
And in the wood, where often you and I
Upon faint primrose beds were wont to lie, 215
Emptying our bosoms of their counsel sweet, 216
There my Lysander and myself shall meet,
And thence from Athens turn away our eyes
To seek new friends and stranger companies. 219
Farewell, sweet playfellow. Pray thou for us,
And good luck grant thee thy Demetrius!
Keep word, Lysander. We must starve our sight
From lovers' food till morrow deep midnight.

LYSANDER
I will, my Hermia.   *Exit Hermia.*
             Helena, adieu!
As you on him, Demetrius dote on you!

                                    Exit Lysander.

HELENA
How happy some o'er other some can be! 226
Through Athens I am thought as fair as she.
But what of that? Demetrius thinks not so;
He will not know what all but he do know.
And as he errs, doting on Hermia's eyes,
So I, admiring of his qualities.
Things base and vile, holding no quantity, 232
Love can transpose to form and dignity.
Love looks not with the eyes, but with the mind,
And therefore is winged Cupid painted blind.

---

165 without outside   **167 To do . . . May** to perform the ceremonies of May Day   **170 best arrow** (Cupid's best gold-pointed arrows were supposed to induce love; his blunt leaden arrows, aversion.) **171 simplicity** innocence.   **doves** i.e., those that drew Venus's chariot **173, 174 Carthage queen, false Trojan** (Dido, Queen of Carthage, immolated herself on a funeral pyre after having been deserted by the Trojan hero Aeneas.)   **180 fair** fair-complexioned. (Generally regarded by the Elizabethans as more beautiful than a dark complexion.)   **182 your fair** your beauty (even though Hermia is dark complexioned).   **happy fair** lucky fair one.   **183 lodestars** guiding stars. **air** music   **184 tunable** tuneful, melodious   **186 favor** appearance, looks   **190 bated** excepted   **191 translated** transformed.   **193 sway the motion** control the impulses

197 Oh, that . . . move! Would that my prayers could arouse such desire!   **204–5 Before . . . to me** (Love has led to complications and jealousies, making Athens hell for Hermia.)   **209 Phoebe** Diana, the moon   **210 glass** reflecting surface (of a lake, etc.)   **211 liquid pearl** i.e., dew   **212 still** always   **215 faint** pale   **216 counsel** secret thought   **219 stranger companies** the company of strangers. **226 o'er . . . can be** can be in comparison to some others.   **232 holding no quantity** i.e., unsubstantial, unshapely

Nor hath Love's mind of any judgment taste; 236
Wings and no eyes figure unheedy haste. 237
And therefore is Love said to be a child,
Because in choice he is so oft beguiled. 239
As waggish boys in game themselves forswear, 240
So the boy Love is perjured everywhere.
For ere Demetrius looked on Hermia's eyne, 242
He hailed down oaths that he was only mine;
And when this hail some heat from Hermia felt,
So he dissolved, and showers of oaths did melt.
I will go tell him of fair Hermia's flight.
Then to the wood will he tomorrow night
Pursue her; and for this intelligence 248
If I have thanks, it is a dear expense. 249
But herein mean I to enrich my pain,
To have his sight thither and back again. *Exit.*

❖

[1.2]

Enter Quince the carpenter, and Snug the joiner, and Bottom the weaver, and Flute the bellows mender, and Snout the tinker, and Starveling the tailor.

QUINCE   Is all our company here?
BOTTOM   You were best to call them generally, man by 2
man, according to the scrip. 3
QUINCE   Here is the scroll of every man's name which
is thought fit, through all Athens, to play in our inter- 5
lude before the Duke and the Duchess on his wedding 6
day at night.
BOTTOM   First, good Peter Quince, say what the play
treats on, then read the names of the actors, and so
grow to a point. 10
QUINCE   Marry, our play is "The most lamentable com- 11
edy and most cruel death of Pyramus and Thisbe."
BOTTOM   A very good piece of work, I assure you, and
a merry. Now, good Peter Quince, call forth your
actors by the scroll. Masters, spread yourselves.
QUINCE   Answer as I call you. Nick Bottom, the weaver. 16
BOTTOM   Ready. Name what part I am for, and proceed.
QUINCE   You, Nick Bottom, are set down for Pyramus.
BOTTOM   What is Pyramus? A lover or a tyrant?
QUINCE   A lover, that kills himself most gallant for love.
BOTTOM   That will ask some tears in the true performing
of it. If I do it, let the audience look to their eyes. I will
move storms; I will condole in some measure. To the 23
rest—yet my chief humor is for a tyrant. I could play 24

Ercles rarely, or a part to tear a cat in, to make all split. 25
  "The raging rocks
  And shivering shocks
  Shall break the locks
    Of prison gates;
  And Phibbus' car 30
  Shall shine from far
  And make and mar
    The foolish Fates."
This was lofty! Now name the rest of the players. This is
Ercles' vein, a tyrant's vein. A lover is more condoling.
QUINCE   Francis Flute, the bellows mender.
FLUTE   Here, Peter Quince.
QUINCE   Flute, you must take Thisbe on you.
FLUTE   What is Thisbe? A wandering knight?
QUINCE   It is the lady that Pyramus must love.
FLUTE   Nay, faith, let not me play a woman. I have a
beard coming.
QUINCE   That's all one. You shall play it in a mask, and 43
you may speak as small as you will. 44
BOTTOM   An I may hide my face, let me play Thisbe too. 45
I'll speak in a monstrous little voice: "Thisne, Thisne!"
"Ah, Pyramus, my lover dear! Thy Thisbe dear, and
lady dear!"
QUINCE   No, no, you must play Pyramus, and Flute, you
Thisbe.
BOTTOM   Well, proceed.
QUINCE   Robin Starveling, the tailor.
STARVELING   Here, Peter Quince.
QUINCE   Robin Starveling, you must play Thisbe's
mother. Tom Snout, the tinker.
SNOUT   Here, Peter Quince.
QUINCE   You, Pyramus' father; myself, Thisbe's father;
Snug, the joiner, you, the lion's part; and I hope here is
a play fitted.
SNUG   Have you the lion's part written? Pray you, if it
be, give it me, for I am slow of study.
QUINCE   You may do it extempore, for it is nothing but
roaring.
BOTTOM   Let me play the lion too. I will roar that I will
do any man's heart good to hear me. I will roar that I
will make the Duke say, "Let him roar again, let him
roar again."
QUINCE   An you should do it too terribly, you would
fright the Duchess and the ladies, that they would
shriek; and that were enough to hang us all.
ALL   That would hang us, every mother's son.
BOTTOM   I grant you, friends, if you should fright the
ladies out of their wits, they would have no more discretion but to hang us; but I will aggravate my voice 74
so that I will roar you as gently as any sucking dove; I 75
will roar you an 'twere any nightingale. 76

---

236 Nor . . . taste i.e., Nor has Love, which dwells in the fancy or imagination, any least bit of judgment or reason   **237 figure** signify **239 in choice** in choosing.   **beguiled** self-deluded, making unaccountable choices.   **240 waggish** playful, mischievous.   **game** sport, jest   **242 eyne** eyes. (Old form of plural.)   **248 intelligence** information   **249 a dear expense** i.e., a trouble worth taking on my part.
1.2. Location: Athens.
2 generally (Bottom's blunder for "individually.")   **3 scrip** script. **5–6 interlude** play   **10 grow to** come to   **11 Marry** (A mild oath; originally the name of the Virgin Mary.)   **16 Bottom** (As a weaver's term, a *bottom* was an object around which thread was wound.) **23 condole** lament, arouse pity   **24 humor** inclination

---

25 Ercles Hercules. (The tradition of ranting came from Seneca's *Hercules Furens*.)   **tear a cat** i.e., rant.   **make all split** i.e., cause a stir, bring the house down.   **30 Phibbus' car** Phoebus's, the sun god's chariot   **43 That's all one** It makes no difference.   **44 small** high-pitched   **45 An** If. (Also at line 68.)   **74 aggravate** (Bottom's blunder for "moderate.")   **75 roar you** i.e., roar for you. **sucking dove** (Bottom conflates *sitting dove* and *sucking lamb*, two proverbial images of innocence.)   **76 an 'twere** as if it were

QUINCE   You can play no part but Pyramus; for Pyramus is a sweet-faced man, a proper man as one shall   78
see in a summer's day, a most lovely gentlemanlike
man. Therefore you must needs play Pyramus.

BOTTOM   Well, I will undertake it. What beard were I
best to play it in?

QUINCE   Why, what you will.

BOTTOM   I will discharge it in either your straw-color   84
beard, your orange-tawny beard, your purple-in-grain   85
beard, or your French-crown-color beard, your perfect   86
yellow.

QUINCE   Some of your French crowns have no hair at all,   88
and then you will play barefaced. But, masters, here
are your parts. [*He distributes parts.*] And I am to
entreat you, request you, and desire you to con them   91
by tomorrow night, and meet me in the palace wood,
a mile without the town, by moonlight. There will we
rehearse; for if we meet in the city, we shall be dogged
with company, and our devices known. In the mean-   95
time I will draw a bill of properties, such as our play   96
wants. I pray you, fail me not.

BOTTOM   We will meet, and there we may rehearse most
obscenely and courageously. Take pains, be perfect.   99
Adieu.

QUINCE   At the Duke's oak we meet.

BOTTOM   Enough. Hold, or cut bowstrings.   *Exeunt.*   102

[2.1]

*Enter a Fairy at one door, and Robin Goodfellow
[Puck] at another.*

PUCK
    How now, spirit, whither wander you?

FAIRY
        Over hill, over dale,
            Thorough bush, thorough brier,   3
        Over park, over pale,   4
            Thorough flood, thorough fire,
        I do wander everywhere,
        Swifter than the moon's sphere;   7
        And I serve the Fairy Queen,
        To dew her orbs upon the green.   9
        The cowslips tall her pensioners be.   10
        In their gold coats spots you see;

        Those be rubies, fairy favors;   12
            In those freckles live their savors.   13
    I must go seek some dewdrops here
    And hang a pearl in every cowslip's ear.
    Farewell, thou lob of spirits; I'll be gone.   16
    Our Queen and all her elves come here anon.   17

PUCK
    The King doth keep his revels here tonight.
    Take heed the Queen come not within his sight.
    For Oberon is passing fell and wrath,   20
    Because that she as her attendant hath
    A lovely boy, stolen from an Indian king;
    She never had so sweet a changeling.   23
    And jealous Oberon would have the child
    Knight of his train, to trace the forests wild.   25
    But she perforce withholds the lovèd boy,   26
    Crowns him with flowers, and makes him all her joy.
    And now they never meet in grove or green,
    By fountain clear, or spangled starlight sheen,   29
    But they do square, that all their elves for fear   30
    Creep into acorn cups and hide them there.

FAIRY
    Either I mistake your shape and making quite,
    Or else you are that shrewd and knavish sprite   33
    Called Robin Goodfellow. Are not you he
    That frights the maidens of the villagery,   35
    Skim milk, and sometimes labor in the quern,   36
    And bootless make the breathless huswife churn,   37
    And sometimes make the drink to bear no barm,   38
    Mislead night wanderers, laughing at their harm?   39
    Those that "Hobgoblin" call you, and "Sweet Puck,"   40
    You do their work, and they shall have good luck.
    Are you not he?

PUCK   Thou speakest aright;
    I am that merry wanderer of the night.
    I jest to Oberon and make him smile
    When I a fat and bean-fed horse beguile,   45
    Neighing in likeness of a filly foal;   46
    And sometimes lurk I in a gossip's bowl   47
    In very likeness of a roasted crab,   48
    And when she drinks, against her lips I bob
    And on her withered dewlap pour the ale.   50
    The wisest aunt, telling the saddest tale,   51

12 favors love tokens   **13 savors** sweet smells.   **16 lob** country
bumpkin   **17 anon** at once.   **20 passing fell** exceedingly angry.
wrath wrathful   **23 changeling** child exchanged for another by the
fairies.   **25 trace** range through   **26 perforce** forcibly   **29 fountain**
spring.   **starlight sheen** shining starlight   **30 square** quarrel
33 shrewd mischievous.   **sprite** spirit   **35 villagery** village population   **36 Skim milk** i.e., steal the cream.   **quern** hand mill (where
Puck presumably hampers the grinding of grain)   **37 bootless** in
vain. (Puck prevents the cream from turning to butter.)   **huswife**
housewife   **38 barm** head on the ale. (Puck prevents the barm or
yeast from producing fermentation.)   **39 Mislead night wanderers**
i.e., mislead with false fire those who walk abroad at night (hence
earning Puck his other names of Jack o' Lantern and Will o' the Wisp)
40 Those . . . Puck i.e., Those who call you by the names you favor
rather than those denoting the mischief you do   **45 bean-fed** full of
beans   **46 a filly foal** a mare (in heat)   **47 gossip's** old woman's
48 crab crab apple   **50 dewlap** loose skin on neck   **51 aunt** old
woman.   **saddest** most serious

78 proper handsome   **84 discharge** perform.   **your** i.e., you know
the kind I mean   **85 purple-in-grain** dyed a very deep red. (From
grain, the name applied to the dried insect used to make the dye.)
86 French-crown-color i.e., color of a French crown, a gold coin
88 crowns heads bald from syphilis, the "French disease"   **91 con**
memorize   **95 devices** plans   **96 draw a bill** draw up a list
99 obscenely (An unintentionally funny blunder, whatever Bottom
meant to say.)   **perfect** i.e., letter-perfect in memorizing your parts.
102 Hold . . . bowstrings (An archers' expression, not definitely
explained, but probably meaning here "keep your promises, or give
up the play.")
2.1. Location: A wood near Athens.
3 Thorough through   **4 pale** enclosure   **7 sphere** orbit   **9 dew**
sprinkle with dew.   **orbs** circles, i.e., fairy rings (circular bands of
grass, darker than the surrounding area, caused by fungi enriching
the soil)   **10 pensioners** retainers, members of the royal bodyguard

Sometime for three-foot stool mistaketh me;
Then slip I from her bum, down topples she,
And "Tailor" cries, and falls into a cough; 54
And then the whole choir hold their hips and laugh, 55
And waxen in their mirth, and neeze, and swear 56
A merrier hour was never wasted there. 57
But, room, fairy! Here comes Oberon. 58

FAIRY
And here my mistress. Would that he were gone!

Enter [Oberon] the King of Fairies at one door,
with his train, and [Titania] the Queen at
another, with hers.

OBERON
Ill met by moonlight, proud Titania.

TITANIA
What, jealous Oberon? Fairies, skip hence.
I have forsworn his bed and company.

OBERON
Tarry, rash wanton. Am not I thy lord? 63

TITANIA
Then I must be thy lady; but I know
When thou hast stolen away from Fairyland
And in the shape of Corin sat all day, 66
Playing on pipes of corn and versing love 67
To amorous Phillida. Why art thou here 68
Come from the farthest step of India, 69
But that, forsooth, the bouncing Amazon,
Your buskined mistress and your warrior love, 71
To Theseus must be wedded, and you come
To give their bed joy and prosperity.

OBERON
How canst thou thus for shame, Titania,
Glance at my credit with Hippolyta, 75
Knowing I know thy love to Theseus?
Didst not thou lead him through the glimmering night
From Perigenia, whom he ravishèd? 78
And make him with fair Aegles break his faith, 79
With Ariadne and Antiopa? 80

TITANIA
These are the forgeries of jealousy;
And never, since the middle summer's spring, 82
Met we on hill, in dale, forest, or mead, 83

By pavèd fountain or by rushy brook, 84
Or in the beachèd margent of the sea, 85
To dance our ringlets to the whistling wind, 86
But with thy brawls thou hast disturbed our sport.
Therefore the winds, piping to us in vain,
As in revenge, have sucked up from the sea
Contagious fogs which, falling in the land, 90
Hath every pelting river made so proud 91
That they have overborne their continents. 92
The ox hath therefore stretched his yoke in vain, 93
The plowman lost his sweat, and the green corn 94
Hath rotted ere his youth attained a beard;
The fold stands empty in the drownèd field, 96
And crows are fatted with the murrain flock; 97
The nine-men's morris is filled up with mud, 98
And the quaint mazes in the wanton green 99
For lack of tread are undistinguishable.
The human mortals want their winter here; 101
No night is now with hymn or carol blessed.
Therefore the moon, the governess of floods, 103
Pale in her anger, washes all the air, 104
That rheumatic diseases do abound. 105
And thorough this distemperature we see 106
The seasons alter: hoary-headed frosts
Fall in the fresh lap of the crimson rose,
And on old Hiems' thin and icy crown 109
An odorous chaplet of sweet summer buds
Is, as in mockery, set. The spring, the summer,
The childing autumn, angry winter, change 112
Their wonted liveries, and the mazèd world 113
By their increase now knows not which is which. 114
And this same progeny of evils comes
From our debate, from our dissension. 116
We are their parents and original. 117

OBERON
Do you amend it, then. It lies in you.
Why should Titania cross her Oberon?
I do but beg a little changeling boy
To be my henchman.

TITANIA　　　　　　　　Set your heart at rest. 121
The fairy land buys not the child of me.
His mother was a vot'ress of my order, 123

---

54 **"Tailor"** (Seemingly a cry of distress or embarrassment.) **55 choir** company **56 waxen** increase. **neeze** sneeze **57 wasted** spent **58 room** stand aside, make room **63 wanton** headstrong creature. **66, 68 Corin, Phillida** (Conventional names of pastoral lovers.) **67 corn** (Here, oat stalks.) **versing love** writing love verses **69 step** farthest limit of travel, or, perhaps, *steep*, "mountain range" **71 buskined** wearing half-boots called buskins **75 Glance . . . Hippolyta** make insinuations about my favored relationship with Hippolyta **78 Perigenia** i.e., Perigouna, one of Theseus's conquests. (This and the following women are named in Thomas North's translation of Plutarch's "Life of Theseus.") **79 Aegles** i.e., Aegle, for whom Theseus deserted Ariadne according to some accounts **80 Ariadne** the daughter of Minos, King of Crete, who helped Theseus to escape the labyrinth after killing the Minotaur; later she was abandoned by Theseus. **Antiopa** Queen of the Amazons and wife of Theseus; elsewhere identified with Hippolyta, but here thought of as a separate woman. **82 middle summer's spring** beginning of midsummer **83 mead** meadow

84 **pavèd** with pebbled bottom. **rushy** bordered with rushes **85 in** on. **margent** edge, border **86 ringlets** dances in a ring. (See *orbs* in line 9.) **to** to the sound of **90 Contagious** noxious **91 pelting** paltry **92 continents** banks that contain them. **93 stretched his yoke** i.e., pulled at his yoke in plowing **94 corn** grain of any kind **96 fold** pen for sheep or cattle **97 murrain** having died of the plague **98 nine-men's morris** i.e., portion of the village green marked out in a square for a game played with nine pebbles or pegs **99 quaint mazes** i.e., intricate paths marked out on the village green to be followed rapidly on foot as a kind of contest. **wanton** luxuriant **101 want** lack. **winter** i.e., regular winter season; or, proper observances of winter, such as the *hymn* or *carol* in the next line (?) **103 Therefore** i.e., As a result of our quarrel **104 washes** saturates with moisture **105 rheumatic diseases** colds, flu, and other respiratory infections **106 distemperature** disturbance in nature **109 Hiems'** the winter god's **112 childing** fruitful, pregnant **113 wonted liveries** usual apparel. **mazèd** bewildered **114 their increase** the increasing pace of change; or, their produce **116 debate** quarrel **117 original** origin. **121 henchman** attendant, page. **123 was . . . order** had taken a vow to serve me

And in the spicèd Indian air by night
Full often hath she gossiped by my side
And sat with me on Neptune's yellow sands,
Marking th'embarkèd traders on the flood,   127
When we have laughed to see the sails conceive
And grow big-bellied with the wanton wind;   129
Which she, with pretty and with swimming gait,   130
Following—her womb then rich with my young
    squire—
Would imitate, and sail upon the land
To fetch me trifles, and return again
As from a voyage, rich with merchandise.
But she, being mortal, of that boy did die;
And for her sake do I rear up her boy,
And for her sake I will not part with him.

OBERON
How long within this wood intend you stay?

TITANIA
Perchance till after Theseus' wedding day.
If you will patiently dance in our round   140
And see our moonlight revels, go with us;
If not, shun me, and I will spare your haunts.   142

OBERON
Give me that boy, and I will go with thee.

TITANIA
Not for thy fairy kingdom. Fairies, away!
We shall chide downright, if I longer stay.
                  Exeunt [Titania with her train].

OBERON
Well, go thy way. Thou shalt not from this grove   146
Till I torment thee for this injury.
My gentle Puck, come hither. Thou rememb'rest
Since once I sat upon a promontory,   149
And heard a mermaid on a dolphin's back
Uttering such dulcet and harmonious breath   151
That the rude sea grew civil at her song,   152
And certain stars shot madly from their spheres
To hear the sea-maid's music?

PUCK   I remember.

OBERON
That very time I saw, but thou couldst not,
Flying between the cold moon and the earth
Cupid, all armed. A certain aim he took   157
At a fair vestal thronèd by the west,   158
And loosed his love shaft smartly from his bow   159
As it should pierce a hundred thousand hearts;   160
But I might see young Cupid's fiery shaft   161
Quenched in the chaste beams of the wat'ry moon,
And the imperial vot'ress passèd on,
In maiden meditation, fancy-free.   164
Yet marked I where the bolt of Cupid fell: 165

It fell upon a little western flower,
Before milk-white, now purple with love's wound,
And maidens call it love-in-idleness.   168
Fetch me that flower; the herb I showed thee once.
The juice of it on sleeping eyelids laid
Will make or man or woman madly dote   171
Upon the next live creature that it sees.
Fetch me this herb, and be thou here again
Ere the leviathan can swim a league.   174

PUCK
I'll put a girdle round about the earth
In forty minutes.   [Exit.]

OBERON   Having once this juice,
I'll watch Titania when she is asleep
And drop the liquor of it in her eyes.
The next thing then she waking looks upon,
Be it on lion, bear, or wolf, or bull,
On meddling monkey, or on busy ape,
She shall pursue it with the soul of love.
And ere I take this charm from off her sight,
As I can take it with another herb,
I'll make her render up her page to me.
But who comes here? I am invisible,
And I will overhear their conference.

                              [He stands aside.]

        Enter Demetrius, Helena following him.

DEMETRIUS
I love thee not; therefore pursue me not.
Where is Lysander and fair Hermia?
The one I'll slay; the other slayeth me.
Thou toldst me they were stol'n unto this wood;
And here am I, and wood within this wood   192
Because I cannot meet my Hermia.
Hence, get thee gone, and follow me no more.

HELENA
You draw me, you hardhearted adamant!   195
But yet you draw not iron, for my heart
Is true as steel. Leave you your power to draw,   197
And I shall have no power to follow you.

DEMETRIUS
Do I entice you? Do I speak you fair?   199
Or rather do I not in plainest truth
Tell you I do not nor I cannot love you?

HELENA
And even for that do I love you the more.
I am your spaniel; and, Demetrius,
The more you beat me I will fawn on you.
Use me but as your spaniel, spurn me, strike me,
Neglect me, lose me; only give me leave,
Unworthy as I am, to follow you.
What worser place can I beg in your love—
And yet a place of high respect with me—
Than to be usèd as you use your dog?

---

127 **traders** trading vessels. **flood** flood tide **129 wanton** (1) playful (2) amorous **130 swimming** smooth, gliding **140 round** circular
dance **142 spare** shun **146 from** go from **149 Since** when
151 dulcet sweet. **breath** voice, song **152 rude** rough **157 all**
fully. **certain** sure **158 vestal** vestal virgin. (Contains a complimentary allusion to Queen Elizabeth as a votaress of Diana and probably
refers to an actual entertainment in her honor at Elvetham in 1591.)
by in the region of **159 loosed** released **160 As** as if **161 might**
could **164 fancy-free** free of love's spell. **165 bolt** arrow

168 **love-in-idleness** pansy, heartsease. **171 or man** either man
174 leviathan sea monster, whale **192 wood** mad, frantic. (With an
obvious wordplay on *wood*, meaning "woods.") **195 adamant** lode-
stone, magnet. (With pun on *hardhearted*, since adamant was also
thought to be the hardest of all stones and was confused with the diamond.) **197 Leave you** Give up **199 speak you fair** speak courteously to you.

DEMETRIUS

Tempt not too much the hatred of my spirit,
For I am sick when I do look on thee.

HELENA

And I am sick when I look not on you.

DEMETRIUS

You do impeach your modesty too much   214
To leave the city and commit yourself   215
Into the hands of one that loves you not,
To trust the opportunity of night
And the ill counsel of a desert place   218
With the rich worth of your virginity.

HELENA

Your virtue is my privilege. For that   220
It is not night when I do see your face,
Therefore I think I am not in the night;
Nor doth this wood lack worlds of company,
For you, in my respect, are all the world.   224
Then how can it be said I am alone
When all the world is here to look on me?

DEMETRIUS

I'll run from thee and hide me in the brakes,   227
And leave thee to the mercy of wild beasts.

HELENA

The wildest hath not such a heart as you.
Run when you will. The story shall be changed:
Apollo flies and Daphne holds the chase,   231
The dove pursues the griffin, the mild hind   232
Makes speed to catch the tiger—bootless speed,   233
When cowardice pursues and valor flies!

DEMETRIUS

I will not stay thy questions. Let me go!   235
Or if thou follow me, do not believe
But I shall do thee mischief in the wood.

HELENA

Ay, in the temple, in the town, the field,
You do me mischief. Fie, Demetrius!
Your wrongs do set a scandal on my sex.   240
We cannot fight for love, as men may do;
We should be wooed and were not made to woo.
                                    [Exit Demetrius.]
I'll follow thee and make a heaven of hell,
To die upon the hand I love so well.   [Exit.] 244

OBERON

Fare thee well, nymph. Ere he do leave this grove
Thou shalt fly him, and he shall seek thy love.

                    Enter Puck.

Hast thou the flower there? Welcome, wanderer.

PUCK

Ay, there it is.   [He offers the flower.]

OBERON   I pray thee, give it me.
I know a bank where the wild thyme blows,   249
Where oxlips and the nodding violet grows,   250
Quite overcanopied with luscious woodbine,   251
With sweet muskroses and with eglantine.   252
There sleeps Titania sometime of the night,   253
Lulled in these flowers with dances and delight;
And there the snake throws her enameled skin,   255
Weed wide enough to wrap a fairy in.   256
And with the juice of this I'll streak her eyes   257
And make her full of hateful fantasies.
Take thou some of it, and seek through this grove.
                    [He gives some love juice.]
A sweet Athenian lady is in love
With a disdainful youth. Anoint his eyes,
But do it when the next thing he espies
May be the lady. Thou shalt know the man
By the Athenian garments he hath on.
Effect it with some care, that he may prove
More fond on her than she upon her love;   266
And look thou meet me ere the first cock crow.

PUCK

Fear not, my lord, your servant shall do so.
                    Exeunt [separately].

                    ♣

[2.2]

        Enter Titania, Queen of Fairies, with her train.

TITANIA

Come, now a roundel and a fairy song;   1
Then, for the third part of a minute, hence—
Some to kill cankers in the muskrose buds,   3
Some war with reremice for their leathern wings   4
To make my small elves coats, and some keep back
The clamorous owl, that nightly hoots and wonders
At our quaint spirits. Sing me now asleep.   7
Then to your offices, and let me rest.

        Fairies sing.

FIRST FAIRY

You spotted snakes with double tongue,   9
    Thorny hedgehogs, be not seen;
Newts and blindworms, do no wrong;   11
    Come not near our Fairy Queen.

---

214 **impeach** call into question   215 **To leave** by leaving   218 **desert** deserted   220 **privilege** safeguard, warrant.   **For that** Because
224 **in my respect** as far as I am concerned, in my esteem
227 **brakes** thickets   231 **Apollo . . . chase** (In the ancient myth, Daphne fled from Apollo and was saved from rape by being transformed into a laurel tree; here it is the female who *holds the chase*, or pursues, instead of the male.)   232 **griffin** a fabulous monster with the head and wings of an eagle and the body of a lion.   **hind** female deer   233 **bootless** fruitless   235 **stay** wait for, put up with. **questions** talk or argument.   240 **Your . . . sex** i.e., The wrongs that you do me cause me to act in a manner that disgraces my sex.
244 **upon** by

---

249 **blows** blooms   250 **oxlips** flowers resembling cowslip and primrose   251 **woodbine** honeysuckle   252 **muskroses** a kind of large, sweet-scented rose.   **eglantine** sweetbrier, another kind of rose.
253 **sometime of** for part of   255 **throws** sloughs off, sheds
256 **Weed** garment   257 **streak** anoint, touch gently   266 **fond on** doting on
2.2. Location: The wood.
1 **roundel** dance in a ring   3 **cankers** cankerworms (i.e., caterpillars or grubs)   4 **reremice** bats   7 **quaint** dainty   9 **double** forked
11 **Newts** water lizards. (Considered poisonous, as were *blindworms*— small snakes with tiny eyes—and spiders.)

CHORUS [*dancing*]
Philomel, with melody   13
Sing in our sweet lullaby;
Lulla, lulla, lullaby, lulla, lulla, lullaby.
Never harm
Nor spell nor charm
Come our lovely lady nigh.
So good night, with lullaby.

FIRST FAIRY
Weaving spiders, come not here;
Hence, you long-legged spinners, hence!
Beetles black, approach not near;
Worm nor snail, do no offense.   23

CHORUS [*dancing*]
Philomel, with melody
Sing in our sweet lullaby;
Lulla, lulla, lullaby, lulla, lulla, lullaby.
Never harm
Nor spell nor charm
Come our lovely lady nigh.
So good night, with lullaby.   [*Titania sleeps.*]

SECOND FAIRY
Hence, away! Now all is well.
One aloof stand sentinel.   32
          [*Exeunt Fairies, leaving one sentinel.*]

Enter Oberon [and squeezes the flower on
Titania's eyelids].

OBERON
What thou see'st when thou dost wake,
Do it for thy true love take;
Love and languish for his sake.
Be it ounce, or cat, or bear,   36
Pard, or boar with bristled hair,   37
In thy eye that shall appear
When thou wak'st, it is thy dear.
Wake when some vile thing is near.   [*Exit.*]

Enter Lysander and Hermia.

LYSANDER
Fair love, you faint with wand'ring in the wood;
And to speak truth, I have forgot our way.
We'll rest us, Hermia, if you think it good,
And tarry for the comfort of the day.

HERMIA
Be it so, Lysander. Find you out a bed,
For I upon this bank will rest my head.

LYSANDER
One turf shall serve as pillow for us both;
One heart, one bed, two bosoms, and one troth.   48

HERMIA
Nay, good Lysander, for my sake, my dear,
Lie further off yet. Do not lie so near.

LYSANDER
Oh, take the sense, sweet, of my innocence!   51
Love takes the meaning in love's conference.   52
I mean that my heart unto yours is knit,
So that but one heart we can make of it;
Two bosoms interchainèd with an oath—
So then two bosoms and a single troth.
Then by your side no bed-room me deny,
For lying so, Hermia, I do not lie.   58

HERMIA
Lysander riddles very prettily.
Now much beshrew my manners and my pride   60
If Hermia meant to say Lysander lied.
But, gentle friend, for love and courtesy
Lie further off, in human modesty.
Such separation as may well be said
Becomes a virtuous bachelor and a maid,
So far be distant; and, good night, sweet friend.
Thy love ne'er alter till thy sweet life end!

LYSANDER
Amen, amen, to that fair prayer, say I,
And then end life when I end loyalty!
Here is my bed. Sleep give thee all his rest!

HERMIA
With half that wish the wisher's eyes be pressed!   71
          [*They sleep, separated by a short distance.*]

Enter Puck.

PUCK
Through the forest have I gone,
But Athenian found I none
On whose eyes I might approve   74
This flower's force in stirring love.
Night and silence.—Who is here?
Weeds of Athens he doth wear.
This is he, my master said,
Despisèd the Athenian maid;
And here the maiden, sleeping sound,
On the dank and dirty ground.
Pretty soul, she durst not lie
Near this lack-love, this kill-courtesy.
Churl, upon thy eyes I throw
All the power this charm doth owe.   85
          [*He applies the love juice.*]
When thou wak'st, let love forbid   86
Sleep his seat on thy eyelid.   87
So awake when I am gone,
For I must now to Oberon.   *Exit.*

Enter Demetrius and Helena, running.

HELENA
Stay, though thou kill me, sweet Demetrius!

---

13 Philomel the nightingale. (Philomela, daughter of King Pandion, was transformed into a nightingale, according to Ovid's *Metamorphoses* 6, after she had been raped by her sister Procne's husband, Tereus.)   **23 offense** harm.   **32 sentinel** (Presumably Oberon is able to outwit or intimidate this guard.)   **36 ounce** lynx   **37 Pard** leopard   **48 troth** faith, trothplight.

51–2 take … conference take my meaning in an innocent sense, with generosity and sympathy! True lovers do so when they converse.   **58 lie** tell a falsehood. (With a riddling pun on *lie,* "recline.")   **60 beshrew** (A mild oath.)   **71 With … pressed!** i.e., I return half that wish, so that you, the wisher, may sleep well too (instead of Sleep giving all his rest to me)!   **74 approve** test   **85 owe** own.   **86–7 let … eyelid** may love, heretofore denied, be enthroned in your eyes.

DEMETRIUS
    I charge thee, hence, and do not haunt me thus.
HELENA
    Oh, wilt thou darkling leave me? Do not so.   92
DEMETRIUS
    Stay, on thy peril! I alone will go.   [*Exit.*] 93
HELENA
    Oh, I am out of breath in this fond chase!   94
    The more my prayer, the lesser is my grace.   95
    Happy is Hermia, wheresoe'er she lies,   96
    For she hath blessèd and attractive eyes.
    How came her eyes so bright? Not with salt tears;
    If so, my eyes are oft'ner washed than hers.
    No, no, I am as ugly as a bear,
    For beasts that meet me run away for fear.
    Therefore no marvel though Demetrius   102
    Do, as a monster, fly my presence thus.   103
    What wicked and dissembling glass of mine   104
    Made me compare with Hermia's sphery eyne?   105
    But who is here? Lysander, on the ground?
    Dead, or asleep? I see no blood, no wound.
    Lysander, if you live, good sir, awake.
LYSANDER [*awaking*]
    And run through fire I will for thy sweet sake.
    Transparent Helena! Nature shows art,   110
    That through thy bosom makes me see thy heart.
    Where is Demetrius? Oh, how fit a word
    Is that vile name to perish on my sword!
HELENA
    Do not say so, Lysander; say not so.
    What though he love your Hermia? Lord, what
      though?
    Yet Hermia still loves you. Then be content.
LYSANDER
    Content with Hermia? No! I do repent
    The tedious minutes I with her have spent.
    Not Hermia but Helena I love.
    Who will not change a raven for a dove?
    The will of man is by his reason swayed,   121
    And reason says you are the worthier maid.
    Things growing are not ripe until their season;
    So I, being young, till now ripe not to reason.   124
    And, touching now the point of human skill,   125
    Reason becomes the marshal to my will
    And leads me to your eyes, where I o'erlook   127
    Love's stories written in love's richest book.
HELENA
    Wherefore was I to this keen mockery born?   129
    When at your hands did I deserve this scorn?
    Is't not enough, is't not enough, young man,
    That I did never—no, nor never can—
    Deserve a sweet look from Demetrius' eye,

    But you must flout my insufficiency?
    Good troth, you do me wrong, good sooth, you do,   135
    In such disdainful manner me to woo.
    But fare you well. Perforce I must confess
    I thought you lord of more true gentleness.   138
    Oh, that a lady, of one man refused,   139
    Should of another therefore be abused!   *Exit.* 140
LYSANDER
    She sees not Hermia. Hermia, sleep thou there,
    And never mayst thou come Lysander near!
    For as a surfeit of the sweetest things
    The deepest loathing to the stomach brings,
    Or as the heresies that men do leave   145
    Are hated most of those they did deceive,   146
    So thou, my surfeit and my heresy,
    Of all be hated, but the most of me!   148
    And, all my powers, address your love and might   149
    To honor Helen and to be her knight!   *Exit.*
HERMIA [*awaking*]
    Help me, Lysander, help me! Do thy best
    To pluck this crawling serpent from my breast!
    Ay me, for pity! What a dream was here!
    Lysander, look how I do quake with fear.
    Methought a serpent ate my heart away,
    And you sat smiling at his cruel prey.   156
    Lysander! What, removed? Lysander! Lord!
    What, out of hearing? Gone? No sound, no word?
    Alack, where are you? Speak, an if you hear;   159
    Speak, of all loves! I swoon almost with fear.   160
    No? Then I well perceive you are not nigh.
    Either death, or you, I'll find immediately.
        Exit. [*The sleeping Titania remains.*]

♣

3.1

Enter the clowns [*Quince, Snug, Bottom, Flute, Snout, and Starveling*].

BOTTOM   Are we all met?
QUINCE   Pat, pat; and here's a marvelous convenient   2
    place for our rehearsal. This green plot shall be our
    stage, this hawthorn brake our tiring-house, and we   4
    will do it in action as we will do it before the Duke.
BOTTOM   Peter Quince?
QUINCE   What sayest thou, bully Bottom?   7
BOTTOM   There are things in this comedy of Pyramus
    and Thisbe that will never please. First, Pyramus must
    draw a sword to kill himself, which the ladies cannot
    abide. How answer you that?
SNOUT   By'r lakin, a parlous fear.   12

---

92 darkling in the dark   **93 on thy peril** i.e., on pain of reprisal if you don't obey me and stay.   **94 fond** doting   **95 my grace** the favor I obtain.   **96 lies** dwells   **102–3 no marvel . . . thus** i.e., no wonder that Demetrius flies from me as from a monster.   **104 glass** mirror **105 compare** compare myself.   **sphery eyne** eyes as bright as stars in their spheres.   **110 Transparent** Radiant, pure.   **art** skill, magic power   **121 will** desire   **124 ripe not** have not ripened   **125 touching . . . skill** reaching now the age of mature judgment   **127 o'erlook** read over   **129 Wherefore** Why

135 Good troth, good sooth i.e., Indeed, truly   **138 lord of** i.e., possessor of.   **gentleness** courtesy.   **139 of** by   **140 abused** ill treated. **145–6 as . . . deceive** as renounced heresies are hated most by those persons who formerly were deceived by them   **148 Of . . . of** by . . . by   **149 address** direct, apply   **156 prey** act of preying.   **159 an if** if **160 of all loves** for love's sake. **3.1. Location: The action is continuous.** **0.1** *clowns* rustics   **2 Pat** On the dot, punctually   **4 brake** thicket. **tiring-house** attiring area, hence backstage   **7 bully** i.e., worthy, jolly, fine fellow   **12 By'r lakin** By our ladykin, i.e., the Virgin Mary. **parlous** perilous, alarming

STARVELING   I believe we must leave the killing out,
when all is done.   14

BOTTOM   Not a whit. I have a device to make all well.
Write me a prologue, and let the prologue seem to say,   16
we will do no harm with our swords, and that Pyramus is not killed indeed; and for the more better assurance, tell them that I, Pyramus, am not Pyramus but
Bottom the weaver. This will put them out of fear.

QUINCE   Well, we will have such a prologue, and it shall
be written in eight and six.   22

BOTTOM   No, make it two more: let it be written in eight
and eight.

SNOUT   Will not the ladies be afeard of the lion?

STARVELING   I fear it, I promise you.

BOTTOM   Masters, you ought to consider with yourself,
to bring in—God shield us!—a lion among ladies is a   28
most dreadful thing. For there is not a more fearful   29
wildfowl than your lion living, and we ought to look
to 't.

SNOUT   Therefore another prologue must tell he is not a
lion.

BOTTOM   Nay, you must name his name, and half his
face must be seen through the lion's neck, and he himself must speak through, saying thus or to the same
defect: "Ladies," or "Fair ladies, I would wish you," or   37
"I would request you," or "I would entreat you, not to
fear, not to tremble; my life for yours. If you think I   39
come hither as a lion, it were pity of my life. No, I am   40
no such thing; I am a man as other men are." And
there indeed let him name his name, and tell them
plainly he is Snug the joiner.

QUINCE   Well, it shall be so. But there is two hard things:
that is, to bring the moonlight into a chamber; for, you
know, Pyramus and Thisbe meet by moonlight.

SNOUT   Doth the moon shine that night we play our
play?

BOTTOM   A calendar, a calendar! Look in the almanac.
Find out moonshine, find out moonshine.

                                      [*They consult an almanac.*]

QUINCE   Yes, it doth shine that night.

BOTTOM   Why then may you leave a casement of the
great chamber window where we play open, and the
moon may shine in at the casement.

QUINCE   Ay; or else one must come in with a bush of   55
thorns and a lantern and say he comes to disfigure, or   56
to present, the person of Moonshine. Then there is
another thing: we must have a wall in the great cham-

ber; for Pyramus and Thisbe, says the story, did talk
through the chink of a wall.

SNOUT   You can never bring in a wall. What say you,
Bottom?

BOTTOM   Some man or other must present Wall. And let
him have some plaster, or some loam, or some rough-   64
cast about him, to signify wall; or let him hold his   65
fingers thus, and through that cranny shall Pyramus
and Thisbe whisper.

QUINCE   If that may be, then all is well. Come, sit down,
every mother's son, and rehearse your parts. Pyramus,
you begin. When you have spoken your speech, enter
into that brake, and so everyone according to his cue.

                          Enter Robin [Puck].

PUCK   [*aside*]
What hempen homespuns have we swagg'ring here   72
So near the cradle of the Fairy Queen?   73
What, a play toward? I'll be an auditor;   74
An actor, too, perhaps, if I see cause.

QUINCE   Speak, Pyramus. Thisbe, stand forth.

BOTTOM   [*as Pyramus*]
"Thisbe, the flowers of odious savors sweet—"

QUINCE   Odors, odors.

BOTTOM   "—Odors savors sweet;
   So hath thy breath, my dearest Thisbe dear.
But hark, a voice! Stay thou but here awhile,
   And by and by I will to thee appear."   *Exit.*

PUCK   A stranger Pyramus than e'er played here. [*Exit.*]   83

FLUTE   Must I speak now?

QUINCE   Ay, marry, must you; for you must understand
he goes but to see a noise that he heard, and is to come
again.

FLUTE   [*as Thisbe*]
"Most radiant Pyramus, most lily-white of hue,
   Of color like the red rose on triumphant brier,   89
Most brisky juvenal and eke most lovely Jew,   90
   As true as truest horse that yet would never tire.
I'll meet thee, Pyramus, at Ninny's tomb."

QUINCE   "Ninus' tomb," man. Why, you must not speak   93
that yet. That you answer to Pyramus. You speak all
your part at once, cues and all. Pyramus, enter. Your   95
cue is past; it is "never tire."

FLUTE
Oh—"As true as truest horse that yet would never
   tire."   97

                 [*Enter Puck, and Bottom as Pyramus with the
                 ass head.*]

---

14 **when all is done** i.e., when all is said and done.   16 **Write me** i.e.,
Write at my suggestion. (*Me* is used colloquially.)   22 **eight and six**
alternate lines of eight and six syllables, a common ballad measure.
28 **lion among ladies** (A contemporary pamphlet tells how, at the
christening in 1594 of Prince Henry, eldest son of King James VI of
Scotland, later James I of England, a "blackamoor" instead of a lion
drew the triumphal chariot, since the lion's presence might have
"brought some fear to the nearest.")   29 **fearful** fear-inspiring
37 **defect** (Bottom's blunder for "effect.")   39 **my life for yours** i.e., I
pledge my life to make your lives safe.   40 **it were . . . life** i.e., I
should be sorry, by my life; or, my life would be endangered.
55–6 **bush of thorns** bundle of thornbush fagots. (Part of the accoutrements of the man in the moon, according to the popular notions of
the time, along with his lantern and his dog.)   56 **disfigure** (Quince's
blunder for "figure," "represent.")

64–5 **roughcast** a mixture of lime and gravel used to plaster the outside of buildings   72 **hempen homespuns** i.e., rustics dressed in
homespun fabric made from hemp   73 **cradle** i.e., Titania's bower
74 **toward** about to take place.   83 **A stranger . . . here** The strangest
Pyramus you ever saw.   89 **triumphant** magnificent   90 **brisky
juvenal** lively youth.   **eke** also.   **Jew** (A desperate attempt to rhyme
with *hue*, inspired perhaps by the first syllable of *juvenal*.)   93 **Ninus**
mythical founder of Nineveh (whose wife, Semiramis, was supposed
to have built the walls of Babylon where the story of Pyramus and
Thisbe takes place)   95 **part** (An actor's *part* was a script consisting
only of his speeches and their cues.)   97.1–2 *with the ass head* (This
stage direction, taken from the Folio, presumably refers to a standard
stage property.)

BOTTOM
"If I were fair, Thisbe, I were only thine."   98
QUINCE   Oh, monstrous! Oh, strange! We are haunted.
Pray, masters! Fly, masters! Help!
*[Exeunt Quince, Snug, Flute,
Snout, and Starveling.]*

PUCK
I'll follow you: I'll lead you about a round,   101
    Through bog, through bush, through brake,
        through brier.
Sometimes a horse I'll be, sometimes a hound,
    A hog, a headless bear, sometimes a fire;   104
And neigh, and bark, and grunt, and roar, and burn,
Like horse, hound, hog, bear, fire, at every turn. *Exit.*

BOTTOM   Why do they run away? This is a knavery of
them to make me afeard.

Enter Snout.

SNOUT   Oh, Bottom, thou art changed! What do I see on
thee?
BOTTOM   What do you see? You see an ass head of your
own, do you?   *[Exit Snout.]*

Enter Quince.

QUINCE   Bless thee, Bottom, bless thee! Thou art trans-   113
lated.   *Exit.* 114
BOTTOM   I see their knavery. This is to make an ass of
me, to fright me, if they could. But I will not stir from
this place, do what they can. I will walk up and down
here, and I will sing, that they shall hear I am not
afraid.   *[He sings.]*
    The ouzel cock so black of hue,   120
        With orange-tawny bill,
    The throstle with his note so true,   122
        The wren with little quill—   123
TITANIA *[awaking]*
What angel wakes me from my flow'ry bed?
BOTTOM *[sings]*
    The finch, the sparrow, and the lark,
        The plainsong cuckoo gray,   126
    Whose note full many a man doth mark,
        And dares not answer nay—   128
For indeed, who would set his wit to so foolish a bird?   129
Who would give a bird the lie, though he cry "cuckoo"   130
never so?   131
TITANIA
I pray thee, gentle mortal, sing again.
Mine ear is much enamored of thy note;
So is mine eye enthrallèd to thy shape;
And thy fair virtue's force perforce doth move me   135
On the first view to say, to swear, I love thee.

BOTTOM   Methinks, mistress, you should have little reason for that. And yet, to say the truth, reason and love
keep little company together nowadays—the more the
pity that some honest neighbors will not make them
friends. Nay, I can gleek upon occasion.   141
TITANIA
Thou art as wise as thou art beautiful.
BOTTOM   Not so, neither. But if I had wit enough to get
out of this wood, I have enough to serve mine own   144
turn.   145
TITANIA
Out of this wood do not desire to go.
Thou shalt remain here, whether thou wilt or no.
I am a spirit of no common rate.   148
The summer still doth tend upon my state,   149
And I do love thee. Therefore, go with me.
I'll give thee fairies to attend on thee,
And they shall fetch thee jewels from the deep,
And sing while thou on pressèd flowers dost sleep.
And I will purge thy mortal grossness so
That thou shalt like an airy spirit go.—
Peaseblossom, Cobweb, Mote, and Mustardseed!   156

*Enter four Fairies [Peaseblossom, Cobweb,
Mote, and Mustardseed].*

PEASEBLOSSOM   Ready.
COBWEB
And I.
MOTE   And I.
MUSTARDSEED   And I.
ALL   Where shall we go?
TITANIA
Be kind and courteous to this gentleman.
Hop in his walks and gambol in his eyes;   160
Feed him with apricots and dewberries,   161
With purple grapes, green figs, and mulberries;
The honey bags steal from the humble-bees,
And for night tapers crop their waxen thighs,   164
And light them at the fiery glowworms' eyes,   165
To have my love to bed and to arise;
And pluck the wings from painted butterflies
To fan the moonbeams from his sleeping eyes.
Nod to him, elves, and do him courtesies.
PEASEBLOSSOM   Hail, mortal!
COBWEB   Hail!
MOTE   Hail!
MUSTARDSEED   Hail!
BOTTOM   I cry Your Worships mercy, heartily. I beseech 174
Your Worship's name.
COBWEB   Cobweb.

---

98 If Even if. fair handsome. were would be 101 about a round
roundabout 104 fire will-o'-the-wisp 113–14 translated transformed. 120 ouzel cock male blackbird 122 throstle song thrush
123 with little quill with small pipe, i.e., high-pitched note; or else
with small feathers 126 plainsong singing a melody without variations 128 dares . . . nay i.e., cannot deny that he is a cuckold
129 set his wit to employ his intelligence to answer 130 give . . . lie
call the bird a liar 131 never so ever so much. 135 thy . . . force the
power of your unblemished excellence

141 gleek jest 144–5 serve . . . turn answer my purpose. 148 rate
rank, value. 149 still . . . state always waits upon me as a part of my
royal retinue 156 Mote i.e., speck. (The two words *moth* and *mote*
were pronounced alike, and both meanings may be present.) 160 in
his eyes in his sight (i.e., before him) 161 dewberries blackberries
164 night . . . thighs (The waxen thighs of the bumble-bee are to be
fashioned into wax candles to light Bottom's way in the dark.) 165
eyes (In fact, the light is emitted by the abdomen. *Eyes* may be
metaphorical.) 174 I cry . . . mercy I beg pardon of Your Worships
(for presuming to ask a question)

BOTTOM   I shall desire you of more acquaintance, good 177
    Master Cobweb. If I cut my finger, I shall make bold 178
    with you.—Your name, honest gentleman? 179
PEASEBLOSSOM   Peaseblossom.
BOTTOM   I pray you, commend me to Mistress Squash, 181
    your mother, and to Master Peascod, your father. 182
    Good Master Peaseblossom, I shall desire you of more
    acquaintance too.—Your name, I beseech you, sir?
MUSTARDSEED   Mustardseed.
BOTTOM   Good Master Mustardseed, I know your 186
    patience well. That same cowardly, giantlike ox-beef 187
    hath devoured many a gentleman of your house. I
    promise you, your kindred hath made my eyes water 189
    ere now. I desire you of more acquaintance, good
    Master Mustardseed.
TITANIA
    Come wait upon him; lead him to my bower.
      The moon methinks looks with a wat'ry eye;
    And when she weeps, weeps every little flower, 194
    Lamenting some enforcèd chastity. 195
    Tie up my lover's tongue; bring him silently. 196

                                Exeunt.

❖

[3.2]

Enter [Oberon,] King of Fairies.

OBERON
    I wonder if Titania be awaked;
    Then, what it was that next came in her eye,
    Which she must dote on in extremity.

    [Enter] Robin Goodfellow [Puck].

    Here comes my messenger. How now, mad spirit?
    What night-rule now about this haunted grove? 5
PUCK
    My mistress with a monster is in love.
    Near to her close and consecrated bower, 7
    While she was in her dull and sleeping hour, 8
    A crew of patches, rude mechanicals, 9
    That work for bread upon Athenian stalls, 10
    Were met together to rehearse a play
    Intended for great Theseus' nuptial day.
    The shallowest thickskin of that barren sort, 13
    Who Pyramus presented, in their sport 14
    Forsook his scene and entered in a brake. 15
    When I did him at this advantage take,

    An ass's noll I fixèd on his head. 17
    Anon his Thisbe must be answerèd,
    And forth my mimic comes. When they him spy, 19
    As wild geese that the creeping fowler eye, 20
    Or russet-pated choughs, many in sort, 21
    Rising and cawing at the gun's report,
    Sever themselves and madly sweep the sky, 23
    So, at his sight, away his fellows fly;
    And, at our stamp, here o'er and o'er one falls;
    He "Murder!" cries and help from Athens calls.
    Their sense thus weak, lost with their fears thus
      strong, 27
    Made senseless things begin to do them wrong, 28
    For briers and thorns at their apparel snatch;
    Some, sleeves—some, hats; from yielders all things
      catch. 30
    I led them on in this distracted fear
    And left sweet Pyramus translated there,
    When in that moment, so it came to pass,
    Titania waked and straightway loved an ass.
OBERON
    This falls out better than I could devise.
    But hast thou yet latched the Athenian's eyes 36
    With the love juice, as I did bid thee do?
PUCK
    I took him sleeping—that is finished too—
    And the Athenian woman by his side,
    That, when he waked, of force she must be eyed. 40

    Enter Demetrius and Hermia.

OBERON
    Stand close. This is the same Athenian.
PUCK
    This is the woman, but not this the man.
                          [They stand aside.]
DEMETRIUS
    Oh, why rebuke you him that loves you so?
    Lay breath so bitter on your bitter foe.
HERMIA
    Now I but chide; but I should use thee worse,
    For thou, I fear, hast given me cause to curse.
    If thou hast slain Lysander in his sleep,
    Being o'er shoes in blood, plunge in the deep, 48
    And kill me too.
    The sun was not so true unto the day
    As he to me. Would he have stolen away
    From sleeping Hermia? I'll believe as soon
    This whole earth may be bored, and that the moon 53
    May through the center creep, and so displease
    Her brother's noontide with th'Antipodes. 55

---

177 I . . . acquaintance I crave to be better acquainted with you
178–9 If . . . you (Cobwebs were used to stanch bleeding.)
181 Squash unripe pea pod   **182 Peascod** ripe pea pod   **186–7 your patience** what you have endured. (Mustard is eaten with beef.)
189 water (1) weep for sympathy (2) smart, sting   **194 And . . . flower** (Dew was thought to fall from the heavens in greater proportion as the moon shown fully.)   **195 enforcèd** violated. (The moon is associated throughout the play with the goddess Diana and chastity.)
196 Tie . . . tongue (Presumably Bottom is braying like an ass.)
3.2. Location: The wood.
5 night-rule diversion or misrule for the night   **7 close** secret   **8 dull** drowsy   **9 patches** clowns, fools.   **rude mechanicals** ignorant artisans   **10 stalls** market booths   **13 barren sort** stupid company or crew   **14 presented** acted   **15 scene** playing area

17 noll noddle, head   **19 mimic** actor   **20 fowler** hunter of game birds   **21 russet-pated choughs** reddish brown or gray-headed jackdaws.   **in sort** in a flock   **23 Sever themselves** i.e., scatter
27–8 Their . . . wrong Their weakened physical senses, disabled by their strong fears, made it seem to them as though inanimate things in the forest were attacking them   **30 from . . . catch** the forest snatches away everything from those who yield to it.   **36 latched** snared, taken prisoner   **40 of force** perforce   **48 Being o'er shoes** having waded in so far   **53 whole** solid   **55 Her . . . Antipodes** i.e., the sun's noontime on the opposite side of the earth, among the people who live there, the Antipodes.

It cannot be but thou hast murdered him;
So should a murderer look, so dead, so grim.   57

DEMETRIUS
So should the murdered look, and so should I,
Pierced through the heart with your stern cruelty.
Yet you, the murderer, look as bright, as clear
As yonder Venus in her glimmering sphere.

HERMIA
What's this to my Lysander? Where is he?   62
Ah, good Demetrius, wilt thou give him me?

DEMETRIUS
I had rather give his carcass to my hounds.

HERMIA
Out, dog! Out, cur! Thou driv'st me past the bounds
Of maiden's patience. Hast thou slain him, then?
Henceforth be never numbered among men.
Oh, once tell true, tell true, even for my sake: 68
Durst thou have looked upon him being awake?   69
And hast thou killed him sleeping? Oh, brave touch!   70
Could not a worm, an adder, do so much?   71
An adder did it; for with doubler tongue   72
Than thine, thou serpent, never adder stung.

DEMETRIUS
You spend your passion on a misprised mood.   74
I am not guilty of Lysander's blood,
Nor is he dead, for aught that I can tell.

HERMIA
I pray thee, tell me then that he is well.

DEMETRIUS
And if I could, what should I get therefor?   78

HERMIA
A privilege never to see me more.
And from thy hated presence part I so.
See me no more, whether he be dead or no.   Exit.

DEMETRIUS
There is no following her in this fierce vein.
Here therefore for a while I will remain.
So sorrow's heaviness doth heavier grow   84
For debt that bankrupt sleep doth sorrow owe,   85
Which now in some slight measure it will pay,   86
If for his tender here I make some stay.   87
                    [He] lie[s] down [and sleeps].

OBERON
What hast thou done? Thou hast mistaken quite
And laid the love juice on some true love's sight.
Of thy misprision must perforce ensue   90
Some true love turned, and not a false turned true.

PUCK
Then fate o'errules, that, one man holding troth,   92
A million fail, confounding oath on oath.   93

OBERON
About the wood go swifter than the wind,
And Helena of Athens look thou find.
All fancy-sick she is and pale of cheer   96
With sighs of love, that cost the fresh blood dear.   97
By some illusion see thou bring her here.
I'll charm his eyes against she do appear.   99

PUCK
I go, I go, look how I go,
Swifter than arrow from the Tartar's bow.   [Exit.] 101

OBERON [applying love juice to Demetrius's eyes]
Flower of this purple dye,
Hit with Cupid's archery,
Sink in apple of his eye.   104
When his love he doth espy,
Let her shine as gloriously
As the Venus of the sky.
When thou wak'st, if she be by,
Beg of her for remedy.

          Enter Puck.

PUCK
Captain of our fairy band,
Helena is here at hand,
And the youth, mistook by me,
Pleading for a lover's fee.   113
Shall we their fond pageant see?   114
Lord, what fools these mortals be!

OBERON
Stand aside. The noise they make
Will cause Demetrius to awake.

PUCK
Then will two at once woo one;
That must needs be sport alone.   119
And those things do best please me
That befall preposterously.   121
                    [They stand aside.]

          Enter Lysander and Helena.

LYSANDER
Why should you think that I should woo in scorn?
Scorn and derision never come in tears.
Look when I vow, I weep; and vows so born,   124
In their nativity all truth appears.   125
How can these things in me seem scorn to you,
Bearing the badge of faith to prove them true?

HELENA
You do advance your cunning more and more.   128
When truth kills truth, oh, devilish-holy fray!   129
These vows are Hermia's. Will you give her o'er?
Weigh oath with oath, and you will nothing weigh;

57 dead deadly, or deathly pale   62 to to do with   68 once once and
for all   69 being awake when he was awake.   70 brave touch! fine
stroke! (Said ironically.)   71 worm serpent   72 doubler (1) more
forked (2) more deceitful   74 You . . . mood Your anger is misdirected.   78 therefor in return for that.   84–7 So . . . stay The heaviness of sorrow grows still heavier when sleepiness adds to the
weariness caused by sorrow, which debt to sleepiness I will now
repay in part if I can stop here and accept what sleep has to offer.
90 misprision mistake   92–3 Then . . . oath If so, then fate prevails;
for each male who is able to keep true faith in love, a million will fail,
breaking oath on oath.

96 fancy-sick lovesick.   cheer face   97 sighs . . . dear (Each sigh was
supposed to cost the heart a drop of blood.)   99 against . . . appear
in anticipation of her coming.   101 Tartar's bow (Tartars were
famed for their skill with the bow.)   104 apple pupil   113 fee privilege, reward.   114 fond pageant foolish spectacle   119 alone
unequaled.   121 preposterously out of the natural order.   124 Look
when Whenever   124–5 vows . . . appears i.e., vows, made by one
who is weeping give evidence thereby of their sincerity.
128 advance carry forward, display   129 When . . . truth i.e., When
one of your vows cancels the other

Your vows to her and me, put in two scales,
Will even weigh, and both as light as tales.

LYSANDER   133
I had no judgment when to her I swore.

HELENA
Nor none, in my mind, now you give her o'er.

LYSANDER
Demetrius loves her, and he loves not you.

DEMETRIUS [*awaking*]
O Helen, goddess, nymph, perfect, divine!
To what, my love, shall I compare thine eyne?
Crystal is muddy. Oh, how ripe in show
Thy lips, those kissing cherries, tempting grow!   139
That pure congealèd white, high Taurus' snow,
Fanned with the eastern wind, turns to a crow   141
When thou hold'st up thy hand. Oh, let me kiss   142
This princess of pure white, this seal of bliss!

HELENA   144
Oh, spite! Oh, hell! I see you all are bent
To set against me for your merriment.
If you were civil and knew courtesy,   146
You would not do me thus much injury.
Can you not hate me, as I know you do,
But you must join in souls to mock me too?
If you were men, as men you are in show,   150
You would not use a gentle lady so—
To vow, and swear, and superpraise my parts,
When I am sure you hate me with your hearts.   153
You both are rivals, and love Hermia,
And now both rivals to mock Helena.
A trim exploit, a manly enterprise,
To conjure tears up in a poor maid's eyes   157
With your derision! None of noble sort
Would so offend a virgin and extort   159
A poor soul's patience, all to make you sport.   160

LYSANDER
You are unkind, Demetrius. Be not so.
For you love Hermia; this you know I know.
And here, with all good will, with all my heart,
In Hermia's love I yield you up my part;
And yours of Helena to me bequeath,
Whom I do love, and will do till my death.

HELENA
Never did mockers waste more idle breath.

DEMETRIUS
Lysander, keep thy Hermia; I will none.
If e'er I loved her, all that love is gone.   169
My heart to her but as guestwise sojourned,
And now to Helen is it home returned,   171
There to remain.

LYSANDER   Helen, it is not so.

DEMETRIUS
Disparage not the faith thou dost not know,
Lest, to thy peril, thou aby it dear.   175
Look where thy love comes; yonder is thy dear.

Enter Hermia.

HERMIA
Dark night, that from the eye his function takes,   177
The ear more quick of apprehension makes;
Wherein it doth impair the seeing sense,
It pays the hearing double recompense.
Thou art not by mine eye, Lysander, found;
Mine ear, I thank it, brought me to thy sound.
But why unkindly didst thou leave me so?

LYSANDER
Why should he stay, whom love doth press to go?

HERMIA
What love could press Lysander from my side?

LYSANDER
Lysander's love, that would not let him bide—
Fair Helena, who more engilds the night
Than all yon fiery oes and eyes of light.   188
Why seek'st thou me? Could not this make thee
          know
The hate I bear thee made me leave thee so?

HERMIA
You speak not as you think. It cannot be.

HELENA
Lo, she is one of this confederacy!
Now I perceive they have conjoined all three
To fashion this false sport, in spite of me.   194
Injurious Hermia, most ungrateful maid!
Have you conspired, have you with these contrived
To bait me with this foul derision?   197
Is all the counsel that we two have shared—   198
The sisters' vows, the hours that we have spent
When we have chid the hasty-footed time
For parting us—oh, is all forgot?
All schooldays' friendship, childhood innocence?
We, Hermia, like two artificial gods   203
Have with our needles created both one flower,
Both on one sampler, sitting on one cushion,
Both warbling of one song, both in one key,
As if our hands, our sides, voices, and minds
Had been incorporate. So we grew together,   208
Like to a double cherry, seeming parted,
But yet an union in partition,
Two lovely berries molded on one stem;
So, with two seeming bodies but one heart,
Two of the first, like coats in heraldry,   213
Due but to one and crownèd with one crest.   214
And will you rend our ancient love asunder,
To join with men in scorning your poor friend?
It is not friendly, 'tis not maidenly.

---

133 **tales** lies.   139 **show** appearance   141 **Taurus** a lofty mountain range in Asia Minor   142 **turns to a crow** i.e., seems black by contrast   144 **seal** pledge   146 **set against** attack   150 **in souls** i.e., heart and soul   153 **superpraise** overpraise.   **parts** qualities   157 **trim** pretty, fine. (Said ironically.)   **sort** character, quality   160 **extort** twist, torture   169 **will none** i.e., want no part of her   171 **to . . . sojourned** only visited with her.

175 **aby** pay for   177 **his** its   188 **oes** spangles (here, stars)   194 **in spite of me** to vex me.   197 **bait** torment, as one sets on dogs to bait a bear   198 **counsel** confidential talk   203 **artificial** skilled in art or creation   208 **incorporate** of one body.   213–14 **Two . . . crest** i.e., we have two separate bodies, just as a coat of arms in heraldry can be represented twice on a shield but surmounted by a single crest.

Our sex, as well as I, may chide you for it,
Though I alone do feel the injury.

HERMIA
I am amazèd at your passionate words.
I scorn you not. It seems that you scorn me.

HELENA
Have you not set Lysander, as in scorn,
To follow me and praise my eyes and face?
And made your other love, Demetrius,
Who even but now did spurn me with his foot,
To call me goddess, nymph, divine, and rare,
Precious, celestial? Wherefore speaks he this
To her he hates? And wherefore doth Lysander
Deny your love, so rich within his soul,
And tender me, forsooth, affection,   230
But by your setting on, by your consent?
What though I be not so in grace as you,   232
So hung upon with love, so fortunate,
But miserable most, to love unloved?
This you should pity rather than despise.

HERMIA
I understand not what you mean by this.

HELENA
Ay, do! Persever, counterfeit sad looks,   237
Make mouths upon me when I turn my back,   238
Wink each at other, hold the sweet jest up.   239
This sport, well carried, shall be chronicled.   240
If you have any pity, grace, or manners,
You would not make me such an argument.   242
But fare ye well. 'Tis partly my own fault,
Which death, or absence, soon shall remedy.

LYSANDER
Stay, gentle Helena; hear my excuse,
My love, my life, my soul, fair Helena!

HELENA
Oh, excellent!

HERMIA [to Lysander]   Sweet, do not scorn her so.

DEMETRIUS [to Lysander]
If she cannot entreat, I can compel.   248

LYSANDER
Thou canst compel no more than she entreat.
Thy threats have no more strength than her weak
    prayers.—
Helen, I love thee, by my life, I do!
I swear by that which I will lose for thee,
To prove him false that says I love thee not.

DEMETRIUS [to Helena]
I say I love thee more than he can do.

LYSANDER
If thou say so, withdraw, and prove it too.   255

DEMETRIUS
Quick, come!

HERMIA   Lysander, whereto tends all this?

LYSANDER
Away, you Ethiope!

        [He tries to break away from Hermia.]

DEMETRIUS   No, no; he'll   257
Seem to break loose; take on as you would follow,   258
But yet come not. You are a tame man. Go!

LYSANDER [to Hermia]
Hang off, thou cat, thou burr! Vile thing, let loose,   260
Or I will shake thee from me like a serpent!

HERMIA
Why are you grown so rude? What change is this,
Sweet love?

LYSANDER   Thy love? Out, tawny Tartar, out!
Out, loathèd med'cine! O hated potion, hence!   264

HERMIA
Do you not jest?

HELENA   Yes, sooth, and so do you.   265

LYSANDER
Demetrius, I will keep my word with thee.

DEMETRIUS
I would I had your bond, for I perceive
A weak bond holds you. I'll not trust your word.   268

LYSANDER
What, should I hurt her, strike her, kill her dead?
Although I hate her, I'll not harm her so.

HERMIA
What, can you do me greater harm than hate?
Hate me? Wherefore? Oh, me, what news, my love?   272
Am not I Hermia? Are not you Lysander?
I am as fair now as I was erewhile.   274
Since night you loved me; yet since night you left me.
Why, then you left me—oh, the gods forbid!—
In earnest, shall I say?

LYSANDER   Ay, by my life!
And never did desire to see thee more.
Therefore be out of hope, of question, of doubt;
Be certain, nothing truer. 'Tis no jest
That I do hate thee and love Helena.

HERMIA [to Helena]
Oh, me! You juggler! You cankerblossom!   282
You thief of love! What, have you come by night
And stol'n my love's heart from him?

HELENA   Fine, i'faith!
Have you no modesty, no maiden shame,
No touch of bashfulness? What, will you tear
Impatient answers from my gentle tongue?
Fie, fie! You counterfeit, you puppet, you!   288

HERMIA
"Puppet"? Why, so! Ay, that way goes the game.
Now I perceive that she hath made compare
Between our statures; she hath urged her height,
And with her personage, her tall personage,

---

230 **tender** offer   232 **grace** favor   237 **sad** grave, serious
238 **mouths** i.e., mows, faces, grimaces. **upon** at   239 **hold . . . up**
keep up the joke.   240 **carried** carried out, brought off   242 **argument** subject for a jest.   248 **entreat** i.e., succeed by entreaty
255 **withdraw . . . too** i.e., withdraw with me and prove your claim
in a duel. (The two gentlemen are armed.)

257 **Ethiope** (Referring to Hermia's relatively dark hair and complexion; see also *tawny Tartar* six lines later.)   258 **take on as** act as if,
make a fuss as if   260 **Hang off** Let go   264 **med'cine** i.e., poison
265 **sooth** truly   268 **weak bond** i.e., Hermia's arm. (With a pun on
bond, "oath," in the previous line.)   272 **what news** what is the matter   274 **erewhile** just now.   282 **cankerblossom** worm that destroys
the flower bud, or wild rose.   288 **puppet** (1) counterfeit (2) dwarfish
woman (in reference to Hermia's smaller stature)

Her height, forsooth, she hath prevailed with him.
And are you grown so high in his esteem
Because I am so dwarfish and so low?
How low am I, thou painted maypole? Speak!
How low am I? I am not yet so low
But that my nails can reach unto thine eyes.

[She flails at Helena but is restrained.]

HELENA
I pray you, though you mock me, gentlemen,
Let her not hurt me. I was never curst;   300
I have no gift at all in shrewishness;
I am a right maid for my cowardice.   302
Let her not strike me. You perhaps may think,
Because she is something lower than myself,   304
That I can match her.

HERMIA   Lower? Hark, again!

HELENA
Good Hermia, do not be so bitter with me.
I evermore did love you, Hermia,
Did ever keep your counsels, never wronged you,
Save that, in love unto Demetrius,
I told him of your stealth unto this wood.   310
He followed you; for love I followed him.
But he hath chid me hence and threatened me   312
To strike me, spurn me, nay, to kill me too.   313
And now, so you will let me quiet go,   314
To Athens will I bear my folly back
And follow you no further. Let me go.
You see how simple and how fond I am.   317

HERMIA
Why, get you gone. Who is't that hinders you?

HELENA
A foolish heart, that I leave here behind.

HERMIA
What, with Lysander?

HELENA   With Demetrius.

LYSANDER
Be not afraid; she shall not harm thee, Helena.

DEMETRIUS
No, sir, she shall not, though you take her part.

HELENA
Oh, when she is angry, she is keen and shrewd.   323
She was a vixen when she went to school;
And though she be but little, she is fierce.

HERMIA
"Little" again? Nothing but "low" and "little"?—
Why will you suffer her to flout me thus?
Let me come to her.

LYSANDER   Get you gone, you dwarf!
You minimus, of hind'ring knotgrass made!   329
You bead, you acorn!

DEMETRIUS   You are too officious
In her behalf that scorns your services.
Let her alone. Speak not of Helena;

Take not her part. For, if thou dost intend   333
Never so little show of love to her,
Thou shalt aby it.

LYSANDER   Now she holds me not.   335
Now follow, if thou dar'st, to try whose right,
Of thine or mine, is most in Helena.   *[Exit.]*

DEMETRIUS
Follow? Nay, I'll go with thee, cheek by jowl.   338

[Exit, following Lysander.]

HERMIA
You, mistress, all this coil is 'long of you.   339
Nay, go not back.

HELENA   I will not trust you, I,   340
Nor longer stay in your curst company.
Your hands than mine are quicker for a fray;
My legs are longer, though, to run away.   *[Exit.]*

HERMIA
I am amazed and know not what to say.   *Exit.*

[Oberon and Puck come forward.]

OBERON
This is thy negligence. Still thou mistak'st,
Or else commit'st thy knaveries willfully.

PUCK
Believe me, king of shadows, I mistook.
Did not you tell me I should know the man
By the Athenian garments he had on?
And so far blameless proves my enterprise
That I have 'nointed an Athenian's eyes;
And so far am I glad it so did sort,   352
As this their jangling I esteem a sport.   353

OBERON
Thou see'st these lovers seek a place to fight.
Hie therefore, Robin, overcast the night;   355
The starry welkin cover thou anon   356
With drooping fog as black as Acheron,   357
And lead these testy rivals so astray
As one come not within another's way.   359
Like to Lysander sometimes frame thy tongue,   360
Then stir Demetrius up with bitter wrong;   361
And sometimes rail thou like Demetrius.
And from each other look thou lead them thus,
Till o'er their brows death-counterfeiting sleep
With leaden legs and batty wings doth creep.   365
Then crush this herb into Lysander's eye,   366

[giving herb]

Whose liquor hath this virtuous property,   367
To take from thence all error with his might   368
And make his eyeballs roll with wonted sight.   369
When they next wake, all this derision   370
Shall seem a dream and fruitless vision,

---

300 **curst** shrewish   302 **right** true   304 **something** somewhat
310 **stealth** stealing away   312 **chid me hence** driven me away with
his scolding   313 **spurn** kick   314 **so** if only   317 **fond** foolish
323 **keen and shrewd** fierce and shrewish.   329 **minimus** diminutive
creature.   **knotgrass** a weed, an infusion of which was thought to
stunt the growth

333 **intend** give sign of   335 **aby** pay for   338 **cheek by jowl** i.e.,
side by side.   339 **coil** turmoil, dissension.   **'long of** on account of
340 **go not back** i.e., don't retreat. (Hermia is again proposing a fight.)
352 **so far** at least to this extent.   **sort** turn out   353 **As** in that
355 **Hie** Hasten   356 **welkin** sky   357 **Acheron** river of Hades (here
representing Hades itself)   359 **As** that   360 **frame thy tongue** fashion your speech   361 **wrong** insults   365 **batty** batlike   366 **this
herb** i.e., the antidote (mentioned in 2.1.184) to love-in-idleness
367 **virtuous** efficacious   368 **his** its   369 **wonted** accustomed
370 **derision** laughable business

And back to Athens shall the lovers wend
With league whose date till death shall never end.   373
Whiles I in this affair do thee employ,
I'll to my queen and beg her Indian boy;
And then I will her charmèd eye release
From monster's view, and all things shall be peace.

PUCK
My fairy lord, this must be done with haste,
For night's swift dragons cut the clouds full fast,   379
And yonder shines Aurora's harbinger,   380
At whose approach ghosts, wand'ring here and there,
Troop home to churchyards. Damnèd spirits all,
That in crossways and floods have burial,   383
Already to their wormy beds are gone.
For fear lest day should look their shames upon,
They willfully themselves exile from light
And must for aye consort with black-browed night.   387

OBERON
But we are spirits of another sort.
I with the Morning's love have oft made sport,   389
And, like a forester, the groves may tread   390
Even till the eastern gate, all fiery red,
Opening on Neptune with fair blessèd beams,
Turns into yellow gold his salt green streams.
But notwithstanding, haste, make no delay.
We may effect this business yet ere day.   [Exit.]

PUCK
          Up and down, up and down,
          I will lead them up and down.
          I am feared in field and town.
          Goblin, lead them up and down.   399
Here comes one.

          Enter Lysander.

LYSANDER
Where art thou, proud Demetrius? Speak thou now.
PUCK [mimicking Demetrius]
Here, villain, drawn and ready. Where art thou?   402
LYSANDER
I will be with thee straight.
PUCK   Follow me, then,   403
To plainer ground.
          [Lysander wanders about, following the voice.]

          Enter Demetrius.

DEMETRIUS   Lysander! Speak again!   404
Thou runaway, thou coward, art thou fled?
Speak! In some bush? Where dost thou hide thy head?

PUCK [mimicking Lysander]
Thou coward, art thou bragging to the stars,
Telling the bushes that thou look'st for wars,
And wilt not come? Come, recreant; come, thou child,   409
I'll whip thee with a rod. He is defiled
That draws a sword on thee.
DEMETRIUS   Yea, art thou there?
PUCK
Follow my voice. We'll try no manhood here.   412
                    Exeunt.

          [Lysander returns.]

LYSANDER
He goes before me and still dares me on.
When I come where he calls, then he is gone.
The villain is much lighter-heeled than I.
I followed fast, but faster he did fly,
That fallen am I in dark uneven way,
And here will rest me. [He lies down.] Come, thou
     gentle day!
For if but once thou show me thy gray light,
I'll find Demetrius and revenge this spite. [He sleeps.]

          [Enter] Robin [Puck] and Demetrius.

PUCK
Ho, ho, ho! Coward, why com'st thou not?
DEMETRIUS
Abide me, if thou dar'st; for well I wot   422
Thou runn'st before me, shifting every place,
And dar'st not stand nor look me in the face.
Where art thou now?
PUCK   Come hither. I am here.
DEMETRIUS
Nay, then, thou mock'st me. Thou shalt buy this dear,   426
If ever I thy face by daylight see.
Now go thy way. Faintness constraineth me
To measure out my length on this cold bed.
By day's approach look to be visited.
                    [He lies down and sleeps.]

          Enter Helena.

HELENA
O weary night, O long and tedious night,
     Abate thy hours! Shine comforts from the east,   432
That I may back to Athens by daylight
     From these that my poor company detest;
And sleep, that sometimes shuts up sorrow's eye,
Steal me awhile from mine own company!
                    [She lies down and] sleep[s].

PUCK
          Yet but three? Come one more;
          Two of both kinds makes up four.
          Here she comes, curst and sad.   439
          Cupid is a knavish lad,
          Thus to make poor females mad.

          [Enter Hermia.]

373 date term of existence   379 dragons (Supposed here to be yoked to the car of the goddess of night or the moon.)   380 Aurora's harbinger the morning star, precursor of dawn   383 crossways . . . burial (Those who had committed suicide were buried at crossways, with a stake driven through them; those who intentionally or accidentally drowned [in floods or deep water] would be condemned to wander disconsolately for lack of burial rites.)   387 for aye forever   389 the Morning's love Cephalus, a beautiful youth beloved by Aurora; or perhaps the goddess of the dawn herself   390 forester keeper of a royal forest   399 Goblin Hobgoblin. (Puck refers to himself.)   402 drawn with drawn sword   403 straight immediately.   404 plainer more open. s.d. Lysander wanders about (Lysander may exit here, but perhaps not; neither exit nor reentrance is indicated in the early texts.)

HERMIA
Never so weary, never so in woe,
    Bedabbled with the dew and torn with briers,
I can no further crawl, no further go;
    My legs can keep no pace with my desires.
Here will I rest me till the break of day.
Heavens shield Lysander, if they mean a fray!
                    [*She lies down and sleeps.*]

PUCK
            On the ground
            Sleep sound.
            I'll apply
            To your eye,
        Gentle lover, remedy.
                [*He squeezes the juice on Lysander's eyes.*]
            When thou wak'st,
            Thou tak'st
            True delight
            In the sight
        Of thy former lady's eye;
        And the country proverb known,
        That every man should take his own,
        In your waking shall be shown:
            Jack shall have Jill;   461
            Naught shall go ill;
        The man shall have his mare again, and all shall
            be well. [*Exit. The four sleeping lovers remain.*]

❖

[4.1]

*Enter [Titania,] Queen of Fairies, and [Bottom
the] clown, and Fairies; and [Oberon,] the King,
behind them.*

TITANIA
Come, sit thee down upon this flow'ry bed,
    While I thy amiable cheeks do coy,   2
And stick muskroses in thy sleek smooth head,
    And kiss thy fair large ears, my gentle joy.
                            [*They recline.*]
BOTTOM   Where's Peaseblossom?
PEASEBLOSSOM   Ready.
BOTTOM   Scratch my head, Peaseblossom. Where's
Monsieur Cobweb?
COBWEB   Ready.
BOTTOM   Monsieur Cobweb, good monsieur, get you
your weapons in your hand, and kill me a red-hipped
humble-bee on the top of a thistle; and, good mon-
sieur, bring me the honey bag. Do not fret yourself too
much in the action, monsieur; and, good monsieur,
have a care the honey bag break not. I would be loath
to have you overflown with a honey bag, signor.
                            [*Exit Cobweb.*]
Where's Monsieur Mustardseed?
MUSTARDSEED   Ready.

BOTTOM   Give me your neaf, Monsieur Mustardseed.   19
Pray you, leave your courtesy, good monsieur.   20
MUSTARDSEED   What's your will?
BOTTOM   Nothing, good monsieur, but to help Cavalery   22
Cobweb to scratch. I must to the barber's, monsieur,   23
for methinks I am marvelous hairy about the face; and
I am such a tender ass, if my hair do but tickle me I
must scratch.
TITANIA
What, wilt thou hear some music, my sweet love?
BOTTOM   I have a reasonable good ear in music. Let's
have the tongs and the bones.   29
                    [*Music: tongs, rural music.*]
TITANIA
Or say, sweet love, what thou desirest to eat.
BOTTOM   Truly, a peck of provender. I could munch   31
your good dry oats. Methinks I have a great desire to
a bottle of hay. Good hay, sweet hay, hath no fellow.   33
TITANIA
I have a venturous fairy that shall seek
The squirrel's hoard, and fetch thee new nuts.
BOTTOM   I had rather have a handful or two of dried
peas. But, I pray you, let none of your people stir me.   37
I have an exposition of sleep come upon me.   38
TITANIA
Sleep thou, and I will wind thee in my arms.—
Fairies, begone, and be all ways away.   40
                    [*Exeunt Fairies.*]
So doth the woodbine the sweet honeysuckle   41
Gently entwist; the female ivy so
Enrings the barky fingers of the elm.
Oh, how I love thee! How I dote on thee!
                    [*They sleep.*]

Enter Robin Goodfellow [Puck].

OBERON [*coming forward*]
Welcome, good Robin. See'st thou this sweet sight?
Her dotage now I do begin to pity.
For, meeting her of late behind the wood
Seeking sweet favors for this hateful fool,   48
I did upbraid her and fall out with her.
For she his hairy temples then had rounded
With coronet of fresh and fragrant flowers;
And that same dew, which sometime on the buds   52
Was wont to swell like round and orient pearls,   53
Stood now within the pretty flowerets' eyes
Like tears that did their own disgrace bewail.
When I had at my pleasure taunted her,

---

19 **neaf** fist   20 **leave your courtesy** i.e., stop bowing, or put on your
hat   22 **Cavalery** Cavalier. (Form of address for a gentleman.)
23 **Cobweb** (Seemingly an error, since Cobweb has been sent to bring
honey, while Peaseblossom has been asked to scratch.)   29 **tongs . . .
bones** instruments for rustic music. (The tongs were played like a triangle, whereas the bones were held between the fingers and used as
clappers.)   29.1 *Music . . . music* (This stage direction is added from
the Folio.)   31 **peck of provender** one-quarter bushel of grain.
33 **bottle** bundle. **fellow** equal.   37 **stir** disturb   38 **exposition of**
(Bottom's phrase for "disposition to.")   40 **all ways** in all directions
41 **woodbine** bindweed, a climbing plant   48 **favors** i.e., gifts of
flowers   52 **sometime** formerly   53 **orient** lustrous

461 **Jack shall have Jill** (Proverbial for "boy gets girl.")
4.1. Location: The action is continuous. The four lovers are still
asleep onstage. (Compare with the Folio stage direction: "*They sleep
all the act.*")
2 **amiable** lovely. **coy** caress

And she in mild terms begged my patience,
I then did ask of her her changeling child,
Which straight she gave me, and her fairy sent
To bear him to my bower in Fairyland.
And, now I have the boy, I will undo
This hateful imperfection of her eyes.
And, gentle Puck, take this transformèd scalp
From off the head of this Athenian swain,
That he, awaking when the other do,   65
May all to Athens back again repair,   66
And think no more of this night's accidents
But as the fierce vexation of a dream.
But first I will release the Fairy Queen.
                    [*He squeezes an herb on her eyes.*]
          Be as thou wast wont to be;
          See as thou wast wont to see.
          Dian's bud o'er Cupid's flower   72
          Hath such force and blessèd power.
Now, my Titania, wake you, my sweet queen.

TITANIA [*awaking*]
     My Oberon! What visions have I seen!
     Methought I was enamored of an ass.

OBERON
     There lies your love.

TITANIA   How came these things to pass?
     Oh, how mine eyes do loathe his visage now!

OBERON
     Silence awhile. Robin, take off this head.
     Titania, music call, and strike more dead
     Than common sleep of all these five the sense.   81

TITANIA
     Music, ho! Music, such as charmeth sleep!   [*Music.*]   82

PUCK [*removing the ass head*]
     Now, when thou wak'st, with thine own fool's eyes
        peep.

OBERON
     Sound, music! Come, my queen, take hands with me,
     And rock the ground whereon these sleepers be.
                                            [*They dance.*]
     Now thou and I are new in amity,
     And will tomorrow midnight solemnly   87
     Dance in Duke Theseus' house triumphantly,
     And bless it to all fair prosperity.
     There shall the pairs of faithful lovers be
     Wedded, with Theseus, all in jollity.

PUCK
     Fairy King, attend, and mark:
     I do hear the morning lark.

OBERON
     Then, my queen, in silence sad,   94
     Trip we after night's shade.
     We the globe can compass soon,
     Swifter than the wand'ring moon.

TITANIA
     Come, my lord, and in our flight
     Tell me how it came this night
     That I sleeping here was found
     With these mortals on the ground.
               Exeunt [*Oberon, Titania, and Puck*].
                          Wind horn [*within*].

     Enter Theseus and all his train; [*Hippolyta,
     Egeus*].

THESEUS
     Go, one of you, find out the forester,
     For now our observation is performed;   103
     And since we have the vaward of the day,   104
     My love shall hear the music of my hounds.
     Uncouple in the western valley; let them go.   106
     Dispatch, I say, and find the forester.
                              [*Exit an Attendant.*]
     We will, fair queen, up to the mountain's top
     And mark the musical confusion
     Of hounds and echo in conjunction.

HIPPOLYTA
     I was with Hercules and Cadmus once   111
     When in a wood of Crete they bayed the bear   112
     With hounds of Sparta. Never did I hear   113
     Such gallant chiding; for, besides the groves,   114
     The skies, the fountains, every region near
     Seemed all one mutual cry. I never heard
     So musical a discord, such sweet thunder.

THESEUS
     My hounds are bred out of the Spartan kind,   118
     So flewed, so sanded; and their heads are hung   119
     With ears that sweep away the morning dew;
     Crook-kneed, and dewlapped like Thessalian bulls;   121
     Slow in pursuit, but matched in mouth like bells,   122
     Each under each. A cry more tunable   123
     Was never holloed to nor cheered with horn   124
     In Crete, in Sparta, nor in Thessaly.
     Judge when you hear. [*He sees the sleepers.*] But soft!
        What nymphs are these?   126

EGEUS
     My lord, this is my daughter here asleep,
     And this Lysander; this Demetrius is;
     This Helena, old Nedar's Helena.
     I wonder of their being here together.   130

THESEUS
     No doubt they rose up early to observe
     The rite of May, and hearing our intent,

---

65 other others   **66 repair** return   **72 Dian's bud** (Perhaps the flower of the *agnus castus* or chaste-tree, supposed to preserve chastity; or perhaps referring simply to Oberon's herb by which he can undo the effects of "Cupid's flower," the love-in-idleness of 2.1.166–8.) **81 these five** i.e., the four lovers and Bottom   **82 charmeth** brings about, as though by a charm   **87 solemnly** ceremoniously **94 sad** solemn

103 observation i.e., observance to a morn of May (1.1.167) **104 vaward** vanguard, i.e., earliest part   **106 Uncouple** Set free for the hunt   **111 Cadmus** mythical founder of Thebes. (This story about him is unknown.)   **112 bayed** brought to bay   **113 hounds of Sparta** (A breed famous in antiquity for their hunting skill.)   **114 chiding** i.e., yelping   **118 kind** strain, breed   **119 So flewed** similarly having large hanging chaps or fleshy covering of the jaw.   **sanded** of sandy color   **121 dewlapped** having pendulous folds of skin under the neck.   **Thessalian** from Thessaly, in Greece   **122–3 matched . . . each** i.e., harmoniously matched in their various cries like a set of bells, from treble down to bass.   **123 cry** pack of hounds.   **tunable** well tuned, melodious   **124 cheered** encouraged   **126 soft** i.e., gently, wait a minute.   **130 of** at

Came here in grace of our solemnity.   133
But speak, Egeus. Is not this the day
That Hermia should give answer of her choice?

EGEUS   It is, my lord.

THESEUS
Go bid the huntsmen wake them with their horns.

                     [*Exit an Attendant.*]

     Shout within. Wind horns. They all start up.

Good morrow, friends. Saint Valentine is past.   138
Begin these woodbirds but to couple now?

LYSANDER
Pardon, my lord.   [*They kneel.*]

THESEUS   I pray you all, stand up.

                       [*They stand.*]

I know you two are rival enemies;
How comes this gentle concord in the world,
That hatred is so far from jealousy
To sleep by hate and fear no enmity?

LYSANDER
My lord, I shall reply amazedly,
Half sleep, half waking; but as yet, I swear,
I cannot truly say how I came here.
But, as I think—for truly would I speak,
And now I do bethink me, so it is—
I came with Hermia hither. Our intent
Was to be gone from Athens, where we might,
Without the peril of the Athenian law—

EGEUS
Enough, enough, my lord; you have enough.
I beg the law, the law, upon his head.
They would have stol'n away; they would, Demetrius,
Thereby to have defeated you and me,
You of your wife and me of my consent,
Of my consent that she should be your wife.

DEMETRIUS
My lord, fair Helen told me of their stealth,
Of this their purpose hither to this wood,
And I in fury hither followed them,
Fair Helena in fancy following me.   162
But, my good lord, I wot not by what power—
But by some power it is—my love to Hermia,
Melted as the snow, seems to me now
As the remembrance of an idle gaud   166
Which in my childhood I did dote upon;
And all the faith, the virtue of my heart,
The object and the pleasure of mine eye,
Is only Helena. To her, my lord,
Was I betrothed ere I saw Hermia,
But like a sickness did I loathe this food;
But, as in health, come to my natural taste,
Now I do wish it, love it, long for it,
And will forevermore be true to it.

THESEUS
Fair lovers, you are fortunately met.
Of this discourse we more will hear anon.

Egeus, I will overbear your will;
For in the temple, by and by, with us
These couples shall eternally be knit.
And, for the morning now is something worn,   181
Our purposed hunting shall be set aside.
Away with us to Athens. Three and three,
We'll hold a feast in great solemnity.   184
Come, Hippolyta.

     [*Exeunt Theseus, Hippolyta, Egeus, and train.*]

DEMETRIUS
These things seem small and undistinguishable,
Like far-off mountains turnèd into clouds.

HERMIA
Methinks I see these things with parted eye,   188
When everything seems double.

HELENA   So methinks;
And I have found Demetrius like a jewel,   190
Mine own, and not mine own.

DEMETRIUS   Are you sure   191
That we are awake? It seems to me
That yet we sleep, we dream. Do not you think
The Duke was here, and bid us follow him?

HERMIA
Yea, and my father.

HELENA   And Hippolyta.

LYSANDER
And he did bid us follow to the temple.

DEMETRIUS
Why, then, we are awake. Let's follow him,
And by the way let us recount our dreams.

                 [*Exeunt the lovers.*]

BOTTOM [*awaking*]   When my cue comes, call me, and I
will answer. My next is "Most fair Pyramus." Heigh-
ho! Peter Quince! Flute, the bellows mender! Snout,
the tinker! Starveling! God's my life, stolen hence and   202
left me asleep! I have had a most rare vision. I have
had a dream, past the wit of man to say what dream
it was. Man is but an ass if he go about to expound this   205
dream. Methought I was—there is no man can tell
what. Methought I was—and methought I had—but
man is but a patched fool if he will offer to say what   208
methought I had. The eye of man hath not heard, the   209
ear of man hath not seen, man's hand is not able to   210
taste, his tongue to conceive, nor his heart to report,   211
what my dream was. I will get Peter Quince to write
a ballad of this dream. It shall be called "Bottom's   213
Dream," because it hath no bottom; and I will sing it   214
in the latter end of a play, before the Duke. Peradventure, to make it the more gracious, I shall sing it at her   216
death.   [*Exit.*]

❖

---

133 in . . . solemnity in honor of our wedding ceremony.   **138 Saint Valentine** (Birds were supposed to choose their mates on Saint Valentine's Day.)   **162 in fancy** driven by love   **166 idle gaud** worthless trinket

181 for since.   **something** somewhat   **184 in great solemnity** with great ceremony.   **188 parted** i.e., improperly focused   **190–1 like . . . own** i.e., something precious that seems mine and yet so mysteriously found that I can hardly believe it is mine.   **202 God's** May God save   **205 go about** attempt   **208 patched** wearing motley, i.e., a dress of various colors.   **offer** venture   **209–11 The eye . . . report** (Bottom garbles 1 Corinthians 2:9.)   **213 ballad** (The proper medium for relating sensational stories and preposterous events.)   **214 hath no bottom** is unfathomable   **216 her** Thisbe's (?)

[4.2]

Enter Quince, Flute, [Snout, and Starveling].

QUINCE   Have you sent to Bottom's house? Is he come home yet?

STARVELING   He cannot be heard of. Out of doubt he is transported. 4

FLUTE   If he come not, then the play is marred. It goes not forward. Doth it?

QUINCE   It is not possible. You have not a man in all Athens able to discharge Pyramus but he. 8

FLUTE   No, he hath simply the best wit of any handicraft 9 man in Athens.

QUINCE   Yea, and the best person too, and he is a very 11 paramour for a sweet voice.

FLUTE   You must say "paragon." A paramour is, God bless us, a thing of naught. 14

Enter Snug the joiner.

SNUG   Masters, the Duke is coming from the temple, and there is two or three lords and ladies more married. If our sport had gone forward, we had all 17 been made men. 18

FLUTE   Oh, sweet bully Bottom! Thus hath he lost sixpence a day during his life; he could not have 20 scaped sixpence a day. An the Duke had not given him sixpence a day for playing Pyramus, I'll be hanged. He would have deserved it. Sixpence a day in Pyramus, or nothing.

Enter Bottom.

BOTTOM   Where are these lads? Where are these hearts? 25

QUINCE   Bottom! Oh, most courageous day! Oh, most happy hour!

BOTTOM   Masters, I am to discourse wonders. But ask 28 me not what; for if I tell you, I am no true Athenian. I will tell you everything, right as it fell out.

QUINCE   Let us hear, sweet Bottom.

BOTTOM   Not a word of me. All that I will tell you is that 32 the Duke hath dined. Get your apparel together, good strings to your beards, new ribbons to your 34 pumps; meet presently at the palace; every man look 35 o'er his part; for the short and the long is, our play is preferred. In any case, let Thisbe have clean linen; and 37 let not him that plays the lion pare his nails, for they shall hang out for the lion's claws. And, most dear actors, eat no onions nor garlic, for we are to utter sweet breath; and I do not doubt but to hear them say it is a sweet comedy. No more words. Away! Go, away!

[*Exeunt.*]

❦

[5.1]

Enter Theseus, Hippolyta, and Philostrate, [lords, and attendants].

HIPPOLYTA
'Tis strange, my Theseus, that these lovers speak of. 1

THESEUS
More strange than true. I never may believe 2
These antique fables nor these fairy toys. 3
Lovers and madmen have such seething brains,
Such shaping fantasies, that apprehend 5
More than cool reason ever comprehends. 6
The lunatic, the lover, and the poet
Are of imagination all compact. 8
One sees more devils than vast hell can hold;
That is the madman. The lover, all as frantic,
Sees Helen's beauty in a brow of Egypt. 11
The poet's eye, in a fine frenzy rolling,
Doth glance from heaven to earth, from earth to heaven;
And as imagination bodies forth
The forms of things unknown, the poet's pen
Turns them to shapes and gives to airy nothing
A local habitation and a name.
Such tricks hath strong imagination
That, if it would but apprehend some joy,
It comprehends some bringer of that joy; 20
Or in the night, imagining some fear, 21
How easy is a bush supposed a bear!

HIPPOLYTA
But all the story of the night told over,
And all their minds transfigured so together,
More witnesseth than fancy's images 25
And grows to something of great constancy; 26
But, howsoever, strange and admirable. 27

Enter lovers: Lysander, Demetrius, Hermia, and Helena.

THESEUS
Here come the lovers, full of joy and mirth.
Joy, gentle friends! Joy and fresh days of love
Accompany your hearts!

LYSANDER   More than to us
Wait in your royal walks, your board, your bed!

THESEUS
Come now, what masques, what dances shall we have, 32
To wear away this long age of three hours
Between our after-supper and bedtime?
Where is our usual manager of mirth?

4.2. Location: Athens.
4 transported carried off by fairies; or, transformed. **8 discharge** perform **9 wit** intellect **11 person** appearance **14 a . . . naught** a shameful thing **17–18 we . . . men** i.e., we would have had our fortunes made. **20 sixpence a day** i.e., as a royal pension **25 hearts** good fellows. **28 am . . . wonders** have wonders to relate. **32 of** out of **34 strings** (to attach the beards) **35 pumps** light shoes or slippers **37 preferred** selected for consideration.

5.1. Location: Athens. The palace of Theseus.
1 that that which **2 may** can **3 antique** old-fashioned. (Punning, too, on *antic*, "strange," "grotesque.") **fairy toys** trifling stories about fairies. **5 fantasies** imaginations. **apprehend** conceive, imagine **6 comprehends** understands. **8 compact** formed, composed. **11 Helen's** i.e., of Helen of Troy, pattern of beauty. **brow of Egypt** i.e., face of a gypsy. **20 bringer** i.e., source **21 fear** object of fear **25 More . . . images** testifies to something more substantial than mere imaginings **26 constancy** certainty **27 howsoever** in any case. **admirable** a source of wonder. **32 masques** courtly entertainments

What revels are in hand? Is there no play
To ease the anguish of a torturing hour?
Call Philostrate.
PHILOSTRATE   Here, mighty Theseus.
THESEUS
Say, what abridgment have you for this evening?   39
What masque? What music? How shall we beguile
The lazy time, if not with some delight?
PHILOSTRATE [*giving him a paper*]
There is a brief how many sports are ripe.   42
Make choice of which Your Highness will see first.
THESEUS [*reads*]
"The battle with the Centaurs, to be sung   44
By an Athenian eunuch to the harp"?
We'll none of that. That have I told my love,
In glory of my kinsman Hercules.   47
[*He reads.*] "The riot of the tipsy Bacchanals,   48
Tearing the Thracian singer in their rage"?   49
That is an old device; and it was played   50
When I from Thebes came last a conqueror.
[*He reads.*] "The thrice three Muses mourning for the
     death   52
Of Learning, late deceased in beggary"?   53
That is some satire, keen and critical,
Not sorting with a nuptial ceremony.   55
[*He reads.*] "A tedious brief scene of young Pyramus
And his love Thisbe; very tragical mirth"?
Merry and tragical? Tedious and brief?
That is, hot ice and wondrous strange snow.   59
How shall we find the concord of this discord?
PHILOSTRATE
A play there is, my lord, some ten words long,
Which is as brief as I have known a play;
But by ten words, my lord, it is too long,
Which makes it tedious. For in all the play
There is not one word apt, one player fitted.
And tragical, my noble lord, it is,
For Pyramus therein doth kill himself.
Which, when I saw rehearsed, I must confess,
Made mine eyes water; but more merry tears
The passion of loud laughter never shed.
THESEUS   What are they that do play it?
PHILOSTRATE
Hardhanded men that work in Athens here,
Which never labored in their minds till now,
And now have toiled their unbreathed memories   74

With this same play, against your nuptial.   75
THESEUS
And we will hear it.
PHILOSTRATE   No, my noble lord,
It is not for you. I have heard it over,
And it is nothing, nothing in the world;
Unless you can find sport in their intents,
Extremely stretched and conned with cruel pain   80
To do you service.
THESEUS   I will hear that play;
For never anything can be amiss
When simpleness and duty tender it.
Go, bring them in; and take your places, ladies.
     [*Philostrate goes to summon the players.*]
HIPPOLYTA
I love not to see wretchedness o'ercharged,   85
And duty in his service perishing.   86
THESEUS
Why, gentle sweet, you shall see no such thing.
HIPPOLYTA
He says they can do nothing in this kind.   88
THESEUS
The kinder we, to give them thanks for nothing.
Our sport shall be to take what they mistake;
And what poor duty cannot do, noble respect   91
Takes it in might, not merit.   92
Where I have come, great clerks have purposèd   93
To greet me with premeditated welcomes;
Where I have seen them shiver and look pale,
Make periods in the midst of sentences,
Throttle their practiced accent in their fears,   97
And in conclusion dumbly have broke off,
Not paying me a welcome. Trust me, sweet,
Out of this silence yet I picked a welcome;
And in the modesty of fearful duty
I read as much as from the rattling tongue
Of saucy and audacious eloquence.
Love, therefore, and tongue-tied simplicity
In least speak most, to my capacity.   105

     [*Philostrate returns.*]

PHILOSTRATE
So please Your Grace, the Prologue is addressed.   106
THESEUS   Let him approach.   [*A flourish of trumpets.*]

     Enter the Prologue [*Quince*].

PROLOGUE
If we offend, it is with our good will.
     That you should think, we come not to offend,
But with good will. To show our simple skill,
     That is the true beginning of our end.

---

39 abridgment pastime (to abridge or shorten the evening)
42 brief summary   **44 battle . . . Centaurs** (Probably refers to the battle of the Centaurs and the Lapithae, when the Centaurs attempted to
carry off Hippodamia, bride of Theseus's friend Pirothous. The story
is told in Ovid's *Metamorphoses* 12.)   **47 kinsman** (Plutarch's "Life of
Theseus" states that Hercules and Theseus were near kinsmen. Theseus is referring to a version of the battle of the Centaurs in which
Hercules was said to be present.)   **48–9 The riot . . . rage** (This was
the story of the death of Orpheus, as told in *Metamorphoses* 11.)
50 device show, performance   **52–3 The thrice . . . beggary** (Possibly
an allusion to Spenser's *Teares of the Muses*, 1591, though "satires"
deploring the neglect of learning and the creative arts were commonplace.)   **55 sorting with** befitting   **59 strange** (Sometimes emended
to an adjective that would contrast with *snow*, just as *hot* contrasts
with *ice*.)   **74 toiled** taxed.   **unbreathed** unexercised

75 against in preparation for   **80 conned** memorized   **85 wretchedness o'ercharged** social or intellectual inferiority overburdened
86 his service its attempt to serve   **88 kind** kind of thing.
91–2 noble . . . merit noble consideration values it for the effort made
rather than for the actual worth.   **93 clerks** learned men   **97 practiced accent** i.e., rehearsed speech; or, usual way of speaking
105 least i.e., saying least.   **to my capacity** in my judgment and
understanding.   **106 Prologue** speaker of the prologue.   **addressed**
ready.

Consider, then, we come but in despite.
   We do not come, as minding to content you,   113
Our true intent is. All for your delight
   We are not here. That you should here repent you,
The actors are at hand; and, by their show,
You shall know all that you are like to know.

THESEUS   This fellow doth not stand upon points.   118

LYSANDER   He hath rid his prologue like a rough colt; he   119
knows not the stop. A good moral, my lord: it is not   120
enough to speak, but to speak true.

HIPPOLYTA   Indeed, he hath played on his prologue like
a child on a recorder: a sound, but not in government.   123

THESEUS   His speech was like a tangled chain: nothing   124
impaired, but all disordered. Who is next?

   Enter Pyramus [Bottom], and Thisbe [Flute],
   and Wall [Snout], and Moonshine [Starveling],
   and Lion [Snug].

PROLOGUE
Gentles, perchance you wonder at this show;
   But wonder on, till truth make all things plain.
This man is Pyramus, if you would know;
   This beauteous lady Thisbe is, certain.
This man with lime and roughcast doth present
   Wall, that vile wall which did these lovers sunder;
And through Wall's chink, poor souls, they are content
   To whisper. At the which let no man wonder.
This man, with lantern, dog, and bush of thorn,
   Presenteth Moonshine; for, if you will know,
By moonshine did these lovers think no scorn   136
   To meet at Ninus' tomb, there, there to woo.
This grisly beast, which Lion hight by name,   138
The trusty Thisbe coming first by night
Did scare away, or rather did affright;
And as she fled, her mantle she did fall,   141
   Which Lion vile with bloody mouth did stain.
Anon comes Pyramus, sweet youth and tall,   143
   And finds his trusty Thisbe's mantle slain;
Whereat, with blade, with bloody, blameful blade,
   He bravely broached his boiling bloody breast.   146
And Thisbe, tarrying in mulberry shade,
   His dagger drew, and died. For all the rest,
Let Lion, Moonshine, Wall, and lovers twain
At large discourse, while here they do remain.   150

   Exeunt Lion, Thisbe, and Moonshine.

THESEUS   I wonder if the lion be to speak.

DEMETRIUS   No wonder, my lord. One lion may, when
many asses do.

WALL
In this same interlude it doth befall   154
That I, one Snout by name, present a wall;
And such a wall as I would have you think

That had in it a crannied hole or chink,
Through which the lovers, Pyramus and Thisbe,
Did whisper often, very secretly.
This loam, this roughcast, and this stone doth show
That I am that same wall; the truth is so.
And this the cranny is, right and sinister,   162
Through which the fearful lovers are to whisper.

THESEUS   Would you desire lime and hair to speak
better?

DEMETRIUS   It is the wittiest partition that ever I heard   166
discourse, my lord.

   [Pyramus comes forward.]

THESEUS   Pyramus draws near the wall. Silence!

PYRAMUS
O grim-looked night! O night with hue so black!   169
   O night, which ever art when day is not!
O night, O night! Alack, alack, alack,
   I fear my Thisbe's promise is forgot.
And thou, O wall, O sweet, O lovely wall,
   That stand'st between her father's ground and
     mine,
Thou wall, O wall, O sweet and lovely wall,
   Show me thy chink, to blink through with mine
     eyne.   *[Wall makes a chink with his fingers.]*
Thanks, courteous wall. Jove shield thee well for
   this.
   But what see I? No Thisbe do I see.
O wicked wall, through whom I see no bliss!
   Cursed be thy stones for thus deceiving me!

THESEUS   The wall, methinks, being sensible, should   181
curse again.   182

PYRAMUS   No, in truth, sir, he should not. "Deceiving
me" is Thisbe's cue: she is to enter now, and I am to
spy her through the wall. You shall see, it will fall pat   185
as I told you. Yonder she comes.

   Enter Thisbe.

THISBE
O wall, full often hast thou heard my moans
   For parting my fair Pyramus and me.
My cherry lips have often kissed thy stones,
   Thy stones with lime and hair knit up in thee.

PYRAMUS
I see a voice. Now will I to the chink,
   To spy an I can hear my Thisbe's face.   192
Thisbe!

THISBE   My love! Thou art my love, I think.

PYRAMUS
   Think what thou wilt, I am thy lover's grace,   194
And like Limander am I trusty still.   195

THISBE
And I like Helen, till the Fates me kill.   196

---

113 minding intending   **118 stand upon points** (1) heed niceties or
small points (2) pay attention to punctuation in his reading. (The
humor of Quince's speech is in the blunders of its punctuation.)
119 rid ridden.   **rough** unbroken   **120 stop** (1) stopping of a colt by
reining it in (2) punctuation mark.   **123 recorder** wind instrument
like a flute.   **government** control.   **124 nothing** not at all   **136 think
no scorn** think it no disgraceful matter   **138 hight** is called   **141 fall**
let fall   **143 tall** courageous   **146 broached** stabbed   **150 At large** in
full, at length   **154 interlude** play

162 right and sinister from right to left   **166 partition** (1) wall (2) section of a learned treatise or oration   **169 grim-looked** grim-looking
181 sensible capable of feeling   **182 again** in return.   **185 pat** exactly
192 an if   **194 lover's grace** i.e., gracious lover   **195, 196 Limander,
Helen** (Blunders for "Leander" and "Hero.")

PYRAMUS
Not Shafalus to Procrus was so true.   197
THISBE
As Shafalus to Procrus, I to you.
PYRAMUS
Oh, kiss me through the hole of this vile wall!
THISBE
I kiss the wall's hole, not your lips at all.
PYRAMUS
Wilt thou at Ninny's tomb meet me straightway?
THISBE
'Tide life, 'tide death, I come without delay.   202
                    [*Exeunt Pyramus and Thisbe.*]
WALL
Thus have I, Wall, my part dischargèd so;
And, being done, thus Wall away doth go.   [*Exit.*]
THESEUS   Now is the mural down between the two
neighbors.
DEMETRIUS   No remedy, my lord, when walls are so
willful to hear without warning.   208
HIPPOLYTA   This is the silliest stuff that ever I heard.
THESEUS   The best in this kind are but shadows; and the 210
worst are no worse, if imagination amend them.
HIPPOLYTA   It must be your imagination then, and not
theirs.
THESEUS   If we imagine no worse of them than they of
themselves, they may pass for excellent men. Here
come two noble beasts in, a man and a lion.

Enter Lion and Moonshine.

LION
You, ladies, you, whose gentle hearts do fear
    The smallest monstrous mouse that creeps on
        floor,
May now perchance both quake and tremble here,
    When lion rough in wildest rage doth roar.
Then know that I, as Snug the joiner, am   221
A lion fell, nor else no lion's dam;   222
For, if I should as lion come in strife
Into this place, 'twere pity on my life.
THESEUS   A very gentle beast, and of a good conscience.
DEMETRIUS   The very best at a beast, my lord, that e'er I
saw.
LYSANDER   This lion is a very fox for his valor.   228
THESEUS   True; and a goose for his discretion.   229
DEMETRIUS   Not so, my lord, for his valor cannot carry
his discretion, and the fox carries the goose.
THESEUS   His discretion, I am sure, cannot carry his
valor; for the goose carries not the fox. It is well. Leave
it to his discretion, and let us listen to the moon.

MOON
This lanthorn doth the hornèd moon present—   235
DEMETRIUS   He should have worn the horns on his   236
head.   237
THESEUS   He is no crescent, and his horns are invisible 238
within the circumference.
MOON
This lanthorn doth the hornèd moon present;
Myself the man i'th' moon do seem to be.
THESEUS   This is the greatest error of all the rest. The
man should be put into the lanthorn. How is it else the
man i'th' moon?
DEMETRIUS   He dares not come there for the candle, for 245
you see it is already in snuff.   246
HIPPOLYTA   I am aweary of this moon. Would he would
change!
THESEUS   It appears, by his small light of discretion, that
he is in the wane; but yet, in courtesy, in all reason, we
must stay the time.
LYSANDER   Proceed, Moon.
MOON   All that I have to say is to tell you that the lanthorn is the moon, I, the man i'th' moon, this thornbush my thornbush, and this dog my dog.
DEMETRIUS   Why, all these should be in the lanthorn,
for all these are in the moon. But silence! Here comes
Thisbe.

Enter Thisbe.

THISBE
This is old Ninny's tomb. Where is my love?
LION [*roaring*]   Oh!
DEMETRIUS   Well roared, Lion.
                    [*Thisbe runs off, dropping her mantle.*]
THESEUS   Well run, Thisbe.
HIPPOLYTA   Well shone, Moon. Truly, the moon shines
with a good grace.
                    [*The Lion worries Thisbe's mantle.*]
THESEUS   Well moused, Lion.   265

Enter Pyramus.   [*Exit Lion.*]

DEMETRIUS   And then came Pyramus.
LYSANDER   And so the lion vanished.
PYRAMUS
Sweet Moon, I thank thee for thy sunny beams;
    I thank thee, Moon, for shining now so bright;
For, by thy gracious, golden, glittering gleams,
    I trust to take of truest Thisbe sight.
        But stay, oh, spite!
        But mark, poor knight,
    What dreadful dole is here?   274
        Eyes, do you see?
        How can it be?

---

197 Shafalus, Procrus (Blunders for "Cephalus" and "Procris," also
famous lovers.)   **202 'Tide** Betide, come   **208 willful** willing.   **without warning** i.e., without warning the parents. (Demetrius makes a
joke on the proverb "Walls have ears.")   **210 in this kind** of this sort.
shadows likenesses, representations   **221–2 am . . . dam** enact the
part of a fierce lion, but otherwise am not really a lion. (*Dam* means
"mother"; in Shakespeare's source the beast is a lioness.)
228 is . . . valor i.e., his valor consists of craftiness and discretion.
229 a goose . . . discretion i.e., as discreet as a goose, that is, more
foolish than discreet.

235 lanthorn (This original spelling, "lanthorne," may suggest a play
on the *horn* of which lanterns were made and also on a cuckold's
horns; however, the spelling "lanthorne" is not used consistently for
comic effect in this play or elsewhere. At 5.1.134, for example, the
word is "lanterne" in the original.)   **236–7 on his head** (As a sign of
cuckoldry.)   **238 crescent** a waxing moon   **245 for** because of, for
fear of   **246 in snuff** (1) offended (2) in need of snuffing or trimming.
265 moused shaken, torn, bitten   **274 dole** grievous event

Oh, dainty duck! Oh, dear!
 Thy mantle good,
 What, stained with blood?
Approach, ye Furies fell!   280
 O Fates, come, come,   281
 Cut thread and thrum;   282
Quail, crush, conclude, and quell!   283

THESEUS   This passion, and the death of a dear friend, 284
would go near to make a man look sad.   285

HIPPOLYTA   Beshrew my heart, but I pity the man.   286

PYRAMUS
Oh, wherefore, Nature, didst thou lions frame?   287
Since lion vile hath here deflowered my dear,
Which is—no, no, which was—the fairest dame
That lived, that loved, that liked, that looked with
 cheer.   290
 Come, tears, confound,
 Out, sword, and wound
The pap of Pyramus;   293
 Ay, that left pap,
 Where heart doth hop.   [*He stabs himself.*]
Thus die I, thus, thus, thus.
 Now am I dead,
 Now am I fled;
My soul is in the sky.
 Tongue, lose thy light;
 Moon, take thy flight.   [*Exit Moonshine.*]
Now die, die, die, die, die.   [*Pyramus dies.*]

DEMETRIUS   No die, but an ace, for him; for he is 303
but one.   304

LYSANDER   Less than an ace, man; for he is dead, he is
nothing.

THESEUS   With the help of a surgeon he might yet
recover, and yet prove an ass.   308

HIPPOLYTA   How chance Moonshine is gone before
Thisbe comes back and finds her lover?

THESEUS   She will find him by starlight.

[*Enter Thisbe.*]

Here she comes; and her passion ends the play.

HIPPOLYTA   Methinks she should not use a long one for
such a Pyramus. I hope she will be brief.

DEMETRIUS   A mote will turn the balance, which Pyra- 315
mus which Thisbe, is the better: he for a man, God 316
warrant us; she for a woman, God bless us.

LYSANDER   She hath spied him already with those sweet
eyes.

DEMETRIUS   And thus she means, videlicet: 320

THISBE
 Asleep, my love?
 What, dead, my dove?
O Pyramus, arise!
 Speak, speak. Quite dumb?
 Dead, dead? A tomb
Must cover thy sweet eyes.
 These lily lips,
 This cherry nose,
These yellow cowslip cheeks,
 Are gone, are gone!
 Lovers, make moan.
His eyes were green as leeks.
 O Sisters Three,   333
 Come, come to me,
With hands as pale as milk;
 Lay them in gore,
 Since you have shore   337
With shears his thread of silk.
 Tongue, not a word.
 Come, trusty sword,
Come, blade, my breast imbrue!   341
       [*She stabs herself.*]
 And farewell, friends.
 Thus Thisbe ends.
Adieu, adieu, adieu.   [*She dies.*]

THESEUS   Moonshine and Lion are left to bury the dead.

DEMETRIUS   Ay, and Wall too.

BOTTOM [*starting up, as Flute does also*]   No, I assure you,
the wall is down that parted their fathers. Will it please
you to see the epilogue, or to hear a Bergomask dance 349
between two of our company?

[*The other players enter.*]

THESEUS   No epilogue, I pray you; for your play needs
no excuse. Never excuse; for when the players are all
dead, there need none to be blamed. Marry, if he that
writ it had played Pyramus and hanged himself in
Thisbe's garter, it would have been a fine tragedy; and
so it is, truly, and very notably discharged. But, come,
your Bergomask. Let your epilogue alone. [*A dance.*]
The iron tongue of midnight hath told twelve.   358
Lovers, to bed, 'tis almost fairy time.
I fear we shall outsleep the coming morn
As much as we this night have overwatched.   361
This palpable-gross play hath well beguiled   362
The heavy gait of night. Sweet friends, to bed.   363
A fortnight hold we this solemnity,
In nightly revels and new jollity.   [*Exeunt.*]

Enter Puck [*carrying a broom*].

---

280 **Furies fell** fierce avenging goddesses of Greek myth.   281 **Fates** the three goddesses (Clotho, Lachesis, Atropos) of Greek myth who spun, drew, and cut the thread of human life   282 **thread and thrum** i.e., everything—the good and bad alike; literally, the warp in weaving and the loose end of the warp   283 **Quail** overpower.   **quell** kill, destroy.   284–5 **This . . . sad** i.e., If one had other reason to grieve, one might be sad, but not from this absurd portrayal of passion. 286 **Beshrew** Curse. (A mild curse.)   287 **frame** create.   290 **cheer** countenance.   293 **pap** breast   303 **ace** the side of the die featuring the single pip, or spot. (The pun is on *die* as a singular of *dice*; Bottom's performance is not worth a whole *die* but rather one single face of it, one small portion.)   304 **one** (1) an individual person (2) unique.   308 **ass** (With a pun on *ace*.)   315 **mote** small particle 315–16 **which . . . which** whether . . . or

320 **means** moans, laments. (With a pun on the meaning, "lodge a formal complaint.")   **videlicet** to wit   333 **Sisters Three** the Fates 337 **shore** shorn   341 **imbrue** stain with blood.   349 **Bergomask dance** a rustic dance named from Bergamo, a province in the state of Venice   358 **iron tongue** i.e., of a bell.   **told** counted, struck ("tolled")   361 **overwatched** stayed up too late.   362 **palpable-gross** palpably gross, obviously crude   363 **heavy** drowsy, dull

PUCK

 Now the hungry lion roars,
  And the wolf behowls the moon,
 Whilst the heavy plowman snores, 368
  All with weary task fordone. 369
 Now the wasted brands do glow, 370
  Whilst the screech owl, screeching loud,
 Puts the wretch that lies in woe
  In remembrance of a shroud.
 Now it is the time of night
  That the graves, all gaping wide,
 Every one lets forth his sprite, 376
  In the churchway paths to glide.
 And we fairies, that do run
  By the triple Hecate's team. 379
 From the presence of the sun,
  Following darkness like a dream,
 Now are frolic. Not a mouse 382
  Shall disturb this hallowed house.
 I am sent with broom before,
 To sweep the dust behind the door. 385

 Enter [Oberon and Titania,] King and Queen of
 Fairies, with all their train.

OBERON

 Through the house give glimmering light,
  By the dead and drowsy fire;
 Every elf and fairy sprite
  Hop as light as bird from brier;
 And this ditty, after me,
 Sing, and dance it trippingly.

TITANIA

 First, rehearse your song by rote, 392
 To each word a warbling note.
 Hand in hand, with fairy grace,
 Will we sing, and bless this place.
       [Song and dance.]

OBERON

 Now, until the break of day,
 Through this house each fairy stray.
 To the best bride-bed will we,
 Which by us shall blessèd be;
 And the issue there create 400
 Ever shall be fortunate.
 So shall all the couples three
 Ever true in loving be;
 And the blots of Nature's hand
 Shall not in their issue stand;
 Never mole, harelip, nor scar,
 Nor mark prodigious, such as are 407
 Despisèd in nativity,
 Shall upon their children be.
 With this field dew consecrate, 410
 Every fairy take his gait, 411
 And each several chamber bless, 412
 Through this palace, with sweet peace;
 And the owner of it blest
 Ever shall in safety rest.
 Trip away; make no stay;
 Meet me all by break of day.
     Exeunt [Oberon, Titania, and train].

PUCK *[to the audience]*

 If we shadows have offended,
 Think but this, and all is mended,
 That you have but slumbered here 420
 While these visions did appear.
 And this weak and idle theme,
 No more yielding but a dream, 423
 Gentles, do not reprehend.
 If you pardon, we will mend. 425
 And, as I am an honest Puck,
 If we have unearnèd luck
 Now to scape the serpent's tongue, 428
 We will make amends ere long;
 Else the Puck a liar call.
 So, good night unto you all.
 Give me your hands, if we be friends, 432
 And Robin shall restore amends. *[Exit.]* 433

368 **heavy** tired 369 **fordone** exhausted. **370 wasted brands** burned-out logs **376 Every . . . sprite** every grave lets forth its ghost **379 triple Hecate's** (Hecate ruled in three capacities: as Luna or Cynthia in heaven, as Diana on earth, and as Proserpina in hell.) **382 frolic** merry. **385 behind** from behind, or else like sweeping the dirt under the carpet. (Robin Goodfellow was a household spirit who helped good housemaids and punished lazy ones, but he could, of course, be mischievous.) **392 rehearse** recite

400 issue offspring. **create** created **407 prodigious** monstrous, unnatural **410 consecrate** consecrated **411 take his gait** go his way **412 several** separate **420 That . . . here** i.e., that it is a "midsummer night's dream" **423 No . . . but** yielding no more than **425 mend** improve. **428 serpent's tongue** i.e., hissing **432 Give . . . hands** Applaud **433 restore amends** give satisfaction in return.

The Merchant of Venice

Although Shylock is the most prominent character in *The Merchant of Venice*, he takes part in neither the beginning nor the ending of the play. And, although the play's title might seem to suggest that he is the "merchant" of Venice, Shylock is, strictly speaking, a moneylender whose usury is portrayed as the very opposite of true commerce. His vengeful struggle to obtain a pound of flesh from Antonio contrasts with the various romantic episodes woven together in this play: Bassanio's choosing of Portia by means of the caskets, Gratiano's wooing of Nerissa, Jessica's elopement with Lorenzo, Lancelot Gobbo's changing of masters, and the episode of the rings. In all these stories, a Christian ethic of generosity, love, and risk-taking friendship is set in pointed contrast with a non-Christian ethic that is seen, from a Christian point of view, as grudging, resentful, and self-calculating. Yet this contrasting vision is made problematic by the deplorable behavior of some Christians. In stage productions today, Belmont and its inhabitants are apt to seem frivolous, pleasure-loving, hedonistic, and above all racist in their insular preference for their own economically and culturally privileged position. The play invites us to question the motives of Shylock's enemies. It makes us (today, at least, after the terrors of the German Holocaust) uncomfortable at the insularity of a Venetian ethic that has no genuine place for non-Christians or cultural outsiders. The most painful question of all, for us, is to wonder whether the play assumes for its own dramatic purposes a Christian point of view, however much it sees a genuine and understandable motive in Shylock's desire for revenge. The problem of divided sympathies is exacerbated because Shylock's structural function in the play is essentially that of the villain in a love comedy. His remorseless pursuit of Antonio darkens the mood of the play, and his overthrow signals the providential triumph of love and friendship, even though that triumph is not without its undercurrent of wry melancholy. Before we examine the painful issue of anti-Semitism more closely,

we need to establish the structural context of this love comedy as a whole.

Like many of Shakespeare's philosophical and festive comedies, *The Merchant of Venice* presents two contrasting worlds—one fantasy-like and the other marked by conflict and anxiety. To an extent, these contrasting worlds can be identified with the locations of Belmont and Venice. Belmont, to which the various happy lovers and their friends eventually retire, is a place of magic and romance. As its name implies, it is on a mountain, and it is reached by a journey across water. As often happens in fairy stories, on this mountain dwells a princess who must be won by means of a riddling contest. We usually see Belmont at night. Music surrounds it, and women preside over it. Even its caskets, houses, and rings are essentially feminine symbols. Venice, on the other hand, is a place of bustle and economic competition, seen most characteristically in the heat of the day. It lies low and flat, at a point where rivers reach the sea. Men preside over its contentious marketplace and its haggling law courts. Actually, the opposition of Venice and Belmont is not quite so clear-cut: Venice contains much compassionate friendship, whereas Belmont is subject to the arbitrary command of Portia's dead father. (Portia somewhat resembles Jessica in being imprisoned by her father's will.) Even though Portia descends to Venice in the angelic role of mercy giver, she also remains very human: sharp-tongued and even venomous in caricaturing her unwelcome wooers, crafty in her legal maneuvering, saucily prankish in her torturing of Bassanio about the rings. For all its warmth and generosity, Belmont is also the embodiment of an insular Christian culture that makes room for outsiders only when they convert to Christian mores. The traits that Shylock carries to an unpleasant extreme are needed in moderation by the Venetians, notably thrift, promise-keeping, and prudent self-interest; only when the Christians temper their penchant for reckless extravagance, legal sophistry or even theft, and risk-taking is a happy resolution possible. Nevertheless, the polarity of two contrasting localities and two groups of characters is vividly real in this play.

The play's opening scene, from which Shylock is excluded, sets forth the interrelated themes of friendship, romantic love, and risk or "hazard." The merchant who seemingly fulfills the title role, Antonio, is the victim of a mysterious melancholy. He is wealthy enough and surrounded by friends, but something is missing from his life. He assures his solicitous companions that he has no financial worries, for he has been too careful to trust all his cargoes to one sea vessel. Antonio, in fact, has no idea why he is so sad. The question is haunting. What is the matter? Perhaps the answer is to be found in a paradox: those who strive to prosper in the world's terms are doomed to frustration, not because prosperity will necessarily elude them, but because it will not satisfy the spirit. "You have too much respect upon the world," argues the carefree Gratiano. "They lose it that do buy it with much care" (1.1.74–5). Portia and Jessica, too, are at first afflicted by a melancholy that stems from the incompleteness of living isolated lives, with insufficient opportunities for love and sacrifice. They must learn, as Antonio learns with the help of his dear friend Bassanio, to seek happiness by daring to risk everything for friendship. Antonio's risk is most extreme: only when he has thrown away concern for his life can he discover what there is to live for.

At first, Bassanio's request for assistance seems just as materialistic as the worldliness from which Antonio suffers. Bassanio proposes to marry a rich young lady, Portia, in order to recoup his fortune lost through prodigality, and he needs money from Antonio so that he may woo Portia in proper fashion. She is "richly left," the heiress of a dead father, a golden fleece for whom this new Jason will make a quest. Bassanio's adventure is partly commercial. Yet his pilgrimage for Portia is magnanimous as well. The occasional modern practice of playing Bassanio and Portia as cynical antiheroes of a "black" comedy points up the problematic character of their materialism and calculation, but it gives only one aspect of the portrayal. Bassanio has lost his previous fortune through the amiable faults of reckless generosity and a lack of concern for financial prudence. The money he must now borrow, and the fortune he hopes to acquire, are to him no more than a means to carefree happiness. Although Portia's rich dowry is a strong consideration, he describes her also as "fair and, fairer than that word,/Of wondrous virtues" (1.1.162–3). Moreover, he enjoys the element of risk in wooing her. It is like shooting a second arrow in order to recover one that has been lost—double or nothing. This gamble, or "hazard," involves risk for Antonio as well as for Bassanio, and it ultimately brings a double reward to them both—spiritual as well as financial. Unless one recognizes these aspects of Bassanio's quest, as well as the clear fairy-tale quality with which Shakespeare deliberately invests this part of the plot, one cannot properly assess Bassanio's role in this romantic comedy.

Bassanio's quest for Portia can, in fact, never succeed until he disavows the very financial considerations that brought him to Belmont in the first place. This is the paradox of the riddle of the three caskets, an ancient parable stressing the need for choosing by true substance rather than by outward show. To choose "what many men desire," as the Prince of Morocco does, is to pin one's hopes on worldly wealth; to believe that one "deserves" good fortune, as the Prince of Aragon does, is to reveal a fatal pride in one's own merit. Bassanio perceives that, in order to win true love, he must "give and hazard all he hath" (2.7.9). He is not "deceived with ornament" (3.2.74). Just as Antonio must risk all for friendship, and just as Bassanio himself must later be willing to risk losing Portia for the sake of true friendship (in the episode of the rings), Bassanio must renounce worldly ambition and beauty before he can be rewarded with success. Paradoxically, only those who learn to subdue such worldly desires may then legitimately enjoy the world's pleasures. Only they have acknowledged the hierarchical subservience of the flesh to the spirit. These are the philosophical truisms of Renaissance Neoplatonism, depicting love as a chain or ladder from the basest carnality to the supreme love of God for humanity. On this ladder, perfect friendship and spiritual union are more sublimely Godlike than sexual fulfillment. This idealism may seem a strange doctrine for Bassanio the fortune hunter, but, actually, its conventional wisdom simply confirms his role as romantic hero. He and Portia are not denied worldly happiness or erotic pleasure; they are merely asked to give first thought to their Christian duty in marriage.

For Portia, marriage represents both a gain and a loss. She can choose only by her dead father's will; the patriarchal system, according to which a woman is given in marriage by her father to a younger man, is seemingly able to extend its control even beyond the grave. The prospect of marrying the Prince of Morocco or the Prince of Aragon dismays her, and yet she persists in her vow of obedience and is eventually rewarded by the man of her choice. It is as though the benign father knew how to set the terms of choice in such a way that the "lottery" of the caskets would turn out right for her. When she accepts Bassanio, too, she must make a difficult choice, for in legal terms she makes Bassanio master over everything she owns. Portia is at once spirited and submissive, able to straighten out Venice's legal tangles when all the men have failed and yet ready to call Bassanio her lord. Her teasing him about the ring is a sign that she will make demands of him in marriage, but it is a testing that cannot produce lasting disharmony so long as Bassanio is truly loyal. Portia is, from Bassanio's male point of view, the perfect woman: humanly attainable and yet never seriously threatening. Guided by her, Bassanio makes the potentially hazardous transition from the male-oriented friendships of Venice (especially with Antonio) to heterosexual union. Portia is more fortunate than Jessica, who must break with her faith and her father in order to find marital happiness. The two women are alike, however, in that they experience the play's central paradox of losing the world in order to gain the world. Through them, we see that this paradox illuminates the casket episode, the struggle for the pound of flesh, the elopement of Jessica, the ring episode, and even the comic foolery of Lancelot Gobbo.

Shylock, in his quest for the pound of flesh, represents, as seen from a Christian point of view, a denial of all the paradoxical truths just described. As a usurer, he refuses to lend money interest-free in the name of friendship. Instead of taking risks, he insists on his bond. He spurns mercy and demands strict justice. By calculating all his chances too craftily, he appears to win at first but must eventually lose all. He has "too much respect upon the world" (1.1.74). His God is the Old Testament God of Moses, the God of wrath, the God of the Ten Commandments, with their forbidding emphasis on "Thou shalt not." (This oversimplified contrast between Judaism and Christianity was commonplace in Shakespeare's time.) Shylock abhors stealing but admires equivocation as a means of out-maneuvering a competitor; he approvingly cites Jacob's ruse to deprive Laban of his sheep (1.3.69–88). Any tactic is permissible so long as it falls within the realm of legality and contract.

Shylock's ethical outlook, then, justifies both usury and the old dispensation of the Jewish law. The two are philosophically combined, just as usury and Judaism had become equated in the popular imagination of Renaissance Europe. Even though lending at interest was becoming increasingly necessary and common, old prejudices against it still persisted. Angry moralists pointed out that the New Testament had condemned usury and that Aristotle had described money as barren. To breed money was therefore regarded as unnatural. Usury was considered sinful because it did not involve the usual risks of commerce; the lender was assured against loss of his principal by the posting of collateral and, at the same time, was sure to earn a handsome interest. The usurer seemed to be getting something for nothing. For these reasons, usury was sometimes declared illegal. Its practitioners were viewed as corrupt and grasping, hated as misers. In some European countries, Jews were permitted to practice this un-Christian living (and permitted to do very little else) and then, hypocritically, were detested for performing un-Christian deeds. Ironically, the moneylenders of England were Christians, and few Jews were to be found in any professions. Nominally excluded since Edward I's reign, the Jews had returned in small numbers to London but did not practice their Judaism openly.

They attended Anglican services as required by law and then worshiped in private, relatively undisturbed by the authorities. Shylock may not be based on observation from London life. He is derived from continental tradition and reflects a widespread conviction that Jews and usurers were alike in being un-Christian and sinister.

Shylock is unquestionably sinister, even if he also invites sympathy. He bears an "ancient grudge" against Antonio simply because Antonio is "a Christian." We recognize in Shylock the archetype of the supposed Jew who wishes to kill a Christian and obtain his flesh. In early medieval anti-Semitic legends of this sort, the flesh thus obtained was imagined to be eaten ritually during Passover. Because some Jews had once persecuted Christ, all were unfairly presumed to be implacable enemies of all Christians. These anti-Semitic superstitions were likely to erupt into hysteria at any time, as in 1594 when Dr. Roderigo Lopez, a Portuguese Jewish physician, was accused of having plotted against the life of Queen Elizabeth and of Don Antonio, pretender to the Portuguese throne. Christopher Marlowe's *The Jew of Malta* was revived for this occasion, enjoying an unusually successful run of fifteen performances, and scholars have often wondered if Shakespeare's play was not written under the same impetus. On this score, the evidence is inconclusive, and the play might have been written any time between 1594 and 1598 (when it is mentioned by Francis Meres), but, in any case, Shakespeare has made no attempt to avoid the anti-Semitic nature of his story.

To offset the portrayal of Jewish villainy, however, the play also dramatizes the possibility of conversion to Christianity, suggesting that Judaism is more a matter of benighted faith than of ethnic origin. Converted Jews were not new on the stage: they had appeared in medieval cycle drama, in the Croxton *Play of the Sacrament* (late fifteenth century), and more recently in *The Jew of Malta*, in which Barabas' daughter Abigail falls in love with a Christian and eventually becomes a nun. Shylock's daughter Jessica similarly embraces Christianity as Lorenzo's wife and is received into the happy comradeship of Belmont. Shylock is forced to accept Christianity, presumably for the benefit of his eternal soul (though today we find this deeply offensive, and it is sometimes cut from stage productions). Earlier in the play, Antonio repeatedly indicates his willingness to befriend Shylock if the latter will only give up usury, and he is even cautiously hopeful when Shylock offers him an interest-free loan: "The Hebrew will turn Christian; he grows kind" (1.3.177). To be sure, Antonio's denunciation of Shylock's usurious Judaism has been vehement and personal; we learn that he has spat on Shylock's gaberdine and kicked him as one would kick a dog. This violent disapproval offers no opportunity for the toleration of cultural and religious differences that we expect today from people of good will, but at least Antonio is prepared to accept Shylock if Shylock will embrace the Christian faith and its ethical responsibilities. Whether the play itself endorses Antonio's Christian point of view as normative or insists on a darker reading by making us uneasy with intolerance is a matter of unceasing critical debate. Quite possibly, the play's power to disturb emanates—at least in part—from the dramatic conflict of irreconcilable sets of values.

To Antonio, then, as well as to other Venetians, true Christianity is both an absolute good from which no deviation is possible without evil and a state of faith to which aliens may turn by abjuring the benighted creeds of their ancestors. By this token, the Prince of Morocco is condemned to failure in his quest for Portia, not so much because he is black as because he is an infidel, one who worships "blind fortune" and therefore chooses a worldly rather than a spiritual reward. Although Portia pertly dismisses him with "Let all of his complexion choose me so" (2.7.79), she professes earlier to find him handsome and agrees that he should not be judged by his complexion (2.1.13–22). Unless she is merely being hypocritical, she means by her later remark that black-skinned people are generally infidels, just as Jews are as a group un-Christian. Such pejorative thinking about persons as types is no doubt distressing and suggests—at least to a modern audience—the cultural limitation of Portia's view, but, in any case, it shows her to be no less well disposed toward black suitors than toward others who are also alien. She is glad not to be won by the Prince of Aragon because he, too, though nominally a Christian, is too self-satisfied and proud. All persons, therefore, may aspire to truly virtuous conduct, and those who choose virtue are equally blessed; however, the terms of defining that ideal in this play are essentially Christian. Jews and Blacks may rise spiritually only by abandoning their pagan creeds for the new dispensation of charity and forgiveness.

The superiority of Christian teaching to the older Jewish dispensation was, of course, a widely accepted notion of Shakespeare's time. After all, these were the years when people fought and died to maintain their religious beliefs. Today, the notion of a single true church is less widely held, and we have difficulty understanding why anyone would wish to force conversion on Shylock. Modern productions find it tempting to portray Shylock as a victim of bigotry and to put great stress on his heartrending assertions of his humanity: "Hath not a Jew eyes? . . . If you prick us, do we not bleed?" (3.1.56–62). Shylock does indeed suffer from his enemies, and his sufferings add a tortured complexity to this play—even, one suspects, for an Elizabethan audience. Those who profess Christianity must surely examine their own motives and conduct. Is it right to steal treasure from Shylock's house along with his eloped daughter? Is it considerate of Jessica and Lorenzo to squander Shylock's turquoise ring, the gift of his wife Leah, on a monkey? Does Shylock's vengeful insistence on law justify the quibbling counter-measures devised by Portia even as she piously declaims about mercy? Do Shylock's misfortunes deserve the mirthful parodies of Solanio ("My daughter! Oh, my ducats!") or the hostile jeering of Gratiano at the conclusion of the trial? Because he stands outside Christian faith, Shylock can provide a perspective whereby we see the hypocrisies of those who profess a higher ethical code. Nevertheless, Shylock's compulsive desire for vengeance according to an Old Testament code of an eye for an eye cannot be justified by the wrongdoings of any particular Christian. In the play's control of an ethical point of view, such deeds condemn the doer rather than undermine the Christian standards of true virtue as ideally expressed. Shakespeare humanizes Shylock by portraying him as a believable and sensitive man, and he shows much that is to be regretted in Shylock's Christian antagonists, but he also allows Shylock to place himself in the wrong by his refusal to forgive his enemies.

Shylock thus loses everything through his effort to win everything on his own terms. His daughter, Jessica, by her elopement, follows an opposite course. She characterizes her father's home as "hell," and she resents being locked up behind closed windows. Shylock detests music and the sounds of merriment; Jessica's new life in Belmont is immersed in music. He is old, suspicious, miserly; she is young, loving, adventurous. Most important, she seems to be at least part Christian when we first see her. As Lancelot jests half in earnest, "If a Christian did not play the knave and get thee, I am much deceived" (2.3.11–12). Her removal from Shylock's house involves theft, and her running from Venice is, she confesses, an "unthrift love." Paradoxically, however, she sees this recklessness as of more blessed effect than her father's legalistic caution. As she says, "I shall be saved by my husband. He hath made me a Christian" (3.5.17–18).

Lancelot Gobbo's clowning offers a similarly paradoxical comment on the tragedy of Shylock. Lancelot debates whether or not to leave Shylock's service in terms of a soul struggle between his conscience and the devil (2.2.1–29). Conscience bids him stay, for service is a debt, a bond, an obligation, whereas abandonment of one's indenture is a kind of rebellion or stealing away. Yet Shylock's house is "hell" to Lancelot as it is to Jessica. Comparing his new master with his old, Lancelot observes to Bassanio, "You have the grace of God, sir, and he hath enough." Service with Bassanio involves imprudent risks, since Bassanio is a spendthrift. The miserly Shylock rejoices to see the ever hungry Lancelot, this "huge feeder," wasting the substance of a hated Christian. Once again, however, Shylock will lose everything in his grasping quest for security. Another spiritual renewal occurs when Lancelot encounters his old and nearly blind father (2.2). In a scene echoing the biblical stories of the Prodigal Son and of Jacob and Esau, Lancelot teases the old man with false rumors of Lancelot's own death in order to make their reunion seem all the more unexpected and precious. The illusion of loss gives way to joy: Lancelot is, in language adapted from the liturgy, "your boy that was, your son that is, your child that shall be."

In the episode of the rings, we encounter a final playful variation on the paradox of winning through losing. Portia and Nerissa cleverly present their new husbands with a cruel choice: disguised as a doctor of law and his clerk, who have just saved the life of Antonio from Shylock's wrath, the two wives ask nothing more for their services than the rings they see on the fingers of Bassanio and Gratiano. The two husbands, who have vowed never to part with these wedding rings, must therefore choose between love and friendship. Portia knows well enough that Bassanio's obedience to the Neoplatonic ideal of disinterested friendship is an essential part of his virtue. Just as he previously renounced beauty and riches before he could deserve Portia, he must now risk losing her for friendship's sake. The testing of the husbands' constancy does border at times on gratuitous harshness and exercise of power, for it deals with the oldest of masculine nightmares: cuckoldry. Wives are not without weapons in the struggle for control in marriage, and Portia and Nerissa enjoy trapping their new husbands in a no-win situation. Still, the threat is easily resolved by the dispelling of farcically mistaken identities. The young men have been tricked into bestowing their rings on their wives for a second time in the name of perfect friendship, thereby confirming a relationship that is both platonic and fleshly. As Gratiano bawdily points out in the play's last line, the ring is both a spiritual and a sexual symbol of marriage. The resolution of this illusory quarrel also brings to an end the merry battle of the sexes between wives and husbands. Having hinted at the sorts of misunderstandings that afflict even the best of human relationships and having proved themselves wittily able to torture and deceive their husbands, Portia and Nerissa submit at last to the patriarchal norms of their age and to the authority of Bassanio and Gratiano.

Bassanio's marriage to Portia represents a heterosexual fulfillment of their courtship that leaves Antonio without a partner at the play's end. He is, to be sure, included in the camaraderie of Belmont, but a part of the sacrifice he has made for Bassanio is to give that young man the freedom and means to marry as he chooses. Antonio's attachment for Bassanio is a deeply loving one, and is sometimes portrayed as homosexual in modern productions. The force of Antonio's attachment to Bassanio should not be underestimated. At the same time, he does appear to be truly willing for the young man to marry. In this sense, the marriage represents a completion in which friendship and love are fully complementary. Heterosexual union is, in this play and in Shakespearean comedy generally, a dominant and theatrically conventional resolution; but it is so without denying that there are other forms of human happiness. Whether or not Antonio is entirely content with his final role as a kind of benign older friend we cannot be sure, but his pronouncements in the final act are all aimed at encouraging the harmony between husband and wife that he has risked his life to enable.

As defined by the accepted notions of gender relations in Shakespeare's time, then, all appears to be in harmony in Belmont. The disorders of Venice have been left far behind, however imperfectly they may have been resolved. Jessica and Lorenzo contrast their present happiness with the sufferings of less fortunate lovers of long ago: Troilus and Cressida, Pyramus and Thisbe, Aeneas and Dido, Jason and Medea. The tranquil joy found in Belmont is attuned to the music of the spheres, the singing of the "young-eyed cherubins" (5.1.62), although with a proper Christian humility the lovers also realize that the harmony of immortal souls is infinitely beyond their comprehension. Bound in by the grossness of the flesh, "this muddy vesture of decay" (5.1.64), they can only reach toward the bliss of eternity through music and the perfect friendship of true love. Even in their final joy, accordingly, the lovers find an incompleteness that lends a wistful and slightly melancholy reflective tone to the play's ending. That sense of imperfection is accentuated for us by our awareness that the play's serious problems of gender relations, friendship, and anti-Semitism have by no means been fully resolved; the final concord is one that arises out of discord. Even so, this concluding sense of the unavoidable incompleteness of all human life is of a very different order from that earlier melancholy of isolation and lack of commitment experienced by Portia, Jessica, Antonio, and others.

In performance, the play has prompted both hostile and genuinely sympathetic responses for Shylock. The traditional anti-Semitic interpretation in early stage history manifested itself, for instance, in the performance of George Frederick Cooke in 1803–1804, "bent with age and ugly with mental deformity, grinning with deadly malice, with the venom of his heart congealed in the expression of his countenance, sullen, morose, gloomy, inflexible" (these are William Hazlitt's words). Still other renditions made use of the red wig and hooked nose of the stereotypical stage Jew that associated Shylock with Judas Iscariot. Conversely, Edmund Kean, in 1814, evoked such sympathy as to make the Christians in the play seem hypocrites by comparison. Henry Irving in 1879, and Beerbohm Tree in 1908, combined a kind of ancient dignity with pathos. George C. Scott, at the New York Shakespeare Festival in 1962, acted Shylock as a persecuted and desperate man surrounded by powerful enemies. Laurence Olivier's anguished Shylock (1970, subsequently televised) showed up the Christians as complacent members of a bigoted Venetian social world of privilege and exclusivity. A production in Weimar, Germany, in 1995, commemorating the fiftieth anniversary of the liberation of the concentration camp at nearby Buchenwald, captured what is so horrendously problematic in the play by imagining what it would be like if enacted by German officers and guards amusing themselves with amateur theatricals during wartime and assigning three Jewish inmates to the roles of Shylock, Tubal, and Jessica. Perhaps no Shakespeare play raises more painful issues today for us to think hard about than *The Merchant of Venice*.

The Merchant of Venice

[*Dramatis Personae*

THE DUKE OF VENICE
ANTONIO, *a merchant of Venice*
BASSANIO, *his friend, suitor to Portia*
GRATIANO, *a follower of Bassanio, in love with Nerissa*
SOLANIO, ⎱ *friends to Antonio*
SALERIO, ⎰ *and Bassanio*
LORENZO, *in love with Jessica*
LEONARDO, *servant to Bassanio*

PORTIA, *a rich heiress of Belmont*
NERISSA, *her waiting-gentlewoman*
BALTHASAR, *servant to Portia*
STEPHANO, *servant to Portia*

THE PRINCE OF MOROCCO, *suitor to Portia*
THE PRINCE OF ARAGON, *suitor to Portia*
A MESSENGER *to Portia*

SHYLOCK, *a rich Jew*
JESSICA, *his daughter*
TUBAL, *a Jew, Shylock's friend*
LANCELOT GOBBO, *a clown, servant to Shylock and then to Bassanio*
OLD GOBBO, *Lancelot's father*

Magnificoes of Venice, Officers of the Court of Justice, Jailor, Servants to Portia, and other Attendants

SCENE: *Partly at Venice and partly at Belmont, the seat of Portia*]

[1.1]

Enter Antonio, Salerio, and Solanio.

ANTONIO
In sooth, I know not why I am so sad.   1
It wearies me, you say it wearies you;
But how I caught it, found it, or came by it,
What stuff 'tis made of, whereof it is born,
I am to learn;   5
And such a want-wit sadness makes of me   6
That I have much ado to know myself.

SALERIO
Your mind is tossing on the ocean,
There where your argosies with portly sail,   9
Like signors and rich burghers on the flood,   10
Or as it were the pageants of the sea,   11
Do overpeer the petty traffickers   12
That curtsy to them, do them reverence,   13
As they fly by them with their woven wings.   14
SOLANIO
Believe me, sir, had I such venture forth,   15
The better part of my affections would

1.1. Location: A street in Venice.
1 In sooth Truly.   sad morose, dismal-looking.   5 am to learn have yet to learn   6 such . . . of me such sadness makes me so distracted, lacking in good sense

9 argosies large merchant ships. (So named from *Ragusa*, the modern city of Dubrovnik.)   portly majestic   10 signors gentlemen.   flood sea   11 pageants mobile stages used in plays or processions   12 overpeer look down upon   13 curtsy i.e., bob up and down, or lower topsails in token of respect (*reverence*)   14 woven wings canvas sails.   15 venture forth investment at risk

Be with my hopes abroad. I should be still
Plucking the grass to know where sits the wind,
Peering in maps for ports and piers and roads;   19
And every object that might make me fear
Misfortune to my ventures, out of doubt
Would make me sad.

SALERIO   My wind cooling my broth
Would blow me to an ague when I thought   23
What harm a wind too great might do at sea.
I should not see the sandy hourglass run
But I should think of shallows and of flats,   26
And see my wealthy *Andrew* docked in sand,   27
Vailing her high-top lower than her ribs   28
To kiss her burial. Should I go to church   29
And see the holy edifice of stone
And not bethink me straight of dangerous rocks   31
Which, touching but my gentle vessel's side,
Would scatter all her spices on the stream,
Enrobe the roaring waters with my silks,
And, in a word, but even now worth this,   35
And now worth nothing? Shall I have the thought
To think on this, and shall I lack the thought
That such a thing bechanced would make me sad?   38
But tell not me. I know Antonio
Is sad to think upon his merchandise.

ANTONIO
Believe me, no. I thank my fortune for it,
My ventures are not in one bottom trusted,   42
Nor to one place; nor is my whole estate
Upon the fortune of this present year.   44
Therefore my merchandise makes me not sad.

SOLANIO
Why then, you are in love.

ANTONIO   Fie, fie!

SOLANIO
Not in love neither? Then let us say you are sad
Because you are not merry; and 'twere as easy
For you to laugh and leap, and say you are merry
Because you are not sad. Now, by two-headed
    Janus,   50
Nature hath framed strange fellows in her time: 51
Some that will evermore peep through their eyes   52
And laugh like parrots at a bagpiper,   53
And other of such vinegar aspect   54
That they'll not show their teeth in way of smile
Though Nestor swear the jest be laughable.   56

Enter Bassanio, Lorenzo, and Gratiano.

Here comes Bassanio, your most noble kinsman,
Gratiano, and Lorenzo. Fare ye well.
We leave you now with better company.

SALERIO
I would have stayed till I had made you merry,
If worthier friends had not prevented me.   61

ANTONIO
Your worth is very dear in my regard.
I take it your own business calls on you,
And you embrace th'occasion to depart.   64

SALERIO   Good morrow, my good lords.

BASSANIO
Good signors both, when shall we laugh? Say,
    when?   66
You grow exceeding strange. Must it be so?   67

SALERIO
We'll make our leisures to attend on yours.   68
                    Exeunt Salerio and Solanio.

LORENZO
My lord Bassanio, since you have found Antonio,
We two will leave you, but at dinnertime,
I pray you, have in mind where we must meet.

BASSANIO   I will not fail you.

GRATIANO
You look not well, Signor Antonio.
You have too much respect upon the world.   74
They lose it that do buy it with much care.
Believe me, you are marvelously changed.

ANTONIO
I hold the world but as the world, Gratiano—
A stage where every man must play a part,
And mine a sad one.

GRATIANO   Let me play the fool.
With mirth and laughter let old wrinkles come,
And let my liver rather heat with wine   81
Than my heart cool with mortifying groans.   82
Why should a man whose blood is warm within
Sit like his grandsire cut in alabaster?   84
Sleep when he wakes, and creep into the jaundice   85
By being peevish? I tell thee what, Antonio—
I love thee, and 'tis my love that speaks—
There are a sort of men whose visages
Do cream and mantle like a standing pond,   89
And do a willful stillness entertain   90
With purpose to be dressed in an opinion   91
Of wisdom, gravity, profound conceit,   92
As who should say, "I am Sir Oracle,   93

---

17 **still** continually   19 **roads** anchorages, open harbors   23 **blow . . . ague** i.e., start me shivering   26 **flats** shoals   27 *Andrew* name of a ship. (Perhaps after the *St. Andrew*, a Spanish galleon captured at Cadiz in 1596.)   28 **Vailing** lowering. (Usually as a sign of submission.)   **high-top** topmast   29 **burial** burial place.   31 **bethink me straight** be put in mind immediately   35 **even now** a short while ago.   **this** i.e., the cargo of spices and silks   38 **bechanced** having happened   42 **bottom** ship's hold   44 **Upon . . . year** i.e., risked upon the chance of the present year.   50 **two-headed Janus** a Roman god of all beginnings, represented by a figure with two faces   51 **framed** fashioned   52 **peep . . . eyes** i.e., look with eyes narrowed by laughter   53 **at a bagpiper** i.e., even at a bagpiper, whose music was regarded as melancholic   54 **other** others.   **vinegar aspect** sour, sullen looks   56 **Nestor** venerable senior officer in the *Iliad*, noted for gravity

61 **prevented** forestalled   64 **th'occasion** the opportunity   66 **laugh** i.e., be merry together.   67 **strange** distant.   **Must it be so**? Must you go? or, Must you show reserve?   68 **We'll . . . yours** We'll adjust our spare time to accommodate your schedule.   74 **respect . . . world** concern for worldly affairs of business.   81 **heat with wine** (The liver was regarded as the seat of the passions and wine as an agency for inflaming them.)   82 **mortifying** penitential and deadly. (Sighs were thought to cost the heart a drop of blood.)   84 **in alabaster** i.e., in a stone effigy upon a tomb.   85 **jaundice** (Regarded as arising from the effects of too much choler or yellow bile, one of the four humors, in the blood.)   89 **cream and mantle** become covered with scum, i.e., acquire a lifeless, stiff expression.   **standing** stagnant   90–2 **And . . . conceit** and who maintain a willful silence in order to acquire a reputation for gravity and deep thought   93 **As . . . say** as if to say

And when I ope my lips let no dog bark!"   94
Oh, my Antonio, I do know of these
That therefore only are reputed wise
For saying nothing, when, I am very sure,
If they should speak, would almost damn those ears   98
Which, hearing them, would call their brothers
     fools.   99
I'll tell thee more of this another time.
But fish not with this melancholy bait   101
For this fool gudgeon, this opinion.—   102
Come, good Lorenzo.—Fare ye well awhile.
I'll end my exhortation after dinner.

LORENZO [*to Antonio and Bassanio*]
Well, we will leave you then till dinnertime.
I must be one of these same dumb wise men,   106
For Gratiano never lets me speak.

GRATIANO
Well, keep me company but two years more,   108
Thou shalt not know the sound of thine own
     tongue.

ANTONIO
Fare you well. I'll grow a talker for this gear.   110

GRATIANO
Thanks, i'faith, for silence is only commendable
In a neat's tongue dried and a maid not vendible.   112
               Exeunt [*Gratiano and Lorenzo*].

ANTONIO   Is that anything now?   113

BASSANIO   Gratiano speaks an infinite deal of nothing,
more than any man in all Venice. His reasons are as   115
two grains of wheat hid in two bushels of chaff; you
shall seek all day ere you find them, and when you
have them they are not worth the search.

ANTONIO
Well, tell me now what lady is the same   119
To whom you swore a secret pilgrimage,
That you today promised to tell me of.

BASSANIO
'Tis not unknown to you, Antonio,
How much I have disabled mine estate
By something showing a more swelling port   124
Than my faint means would grant continuance.   125
Nor do I now make moan to be abridged   126
From such a noble rate; but my chief care   127
Is to come fairly off from the great debts   128
Wherein my time, something too prodigal,   129
Hath left me gaged. To you, Antonio,   130
I owe the most, in money and in love,

And from your love I have a warranty   132
To unburden all my plots and purposes   133
How to get clear of all the debts I owe.

ANTONIO
I pray you, good Bassanio, let me know it;
And if it stand, as you yourself still do,   136
Within the eye of honor, be assured   137
My purse, my person, my extremest means
Lie all unlocked to your occasions.

BASSANIO
In my schooldays, when I had lost one shaft,   140
I shot his fellow of the selfsame flight   141
The selfsame way with more advisèd watch   142
To find the other forth, and by adventuring both   143
I oft found both. I urge this childhood proof
Because what follows is pure innocence.   145
I owe you much, and, like a willful youth,
That which I owe is lost; but if you please
To shoot another arrow that self way   148
Which you did shoot the first, I do not doubt,
As I will watch the aim, or to find both   150
Or bring your latter hazard back again   151
And thankfully rest debtor for the first.   152

ANTONIO
You know me well, and herein spend but time   153
To wind about my love with circumstance;   154
And out of doubt you do me now more wrong
In making question of my uttermost   156
Than if you had made waste of all I have.
Then do but say to me what I should do
That in your knowledge may by me be done,
And I am prest unto it. Therefore speak.   160

BASSANIO
In Belmont is a lady richly left;   161
And she is fair and, fairer than that word,
Of wondrous virtues. Sometimes from her eyes   163
I did receive fair speechless messages.
Her name is Portia, nothing undervalued   165
To Cato's daughter, Brutus' Portia.   166
Nor is the wide world ignorant of her worth,
For the four winds blow in from every coast
Renownèd suitors, and her sunny locks
Hang on her temples like a golden fleece,
Which makes her seat of Belmont Colchis' strand,   171
And many Jasons come in quest of her.
Oh, my Antonio, had I but the means
To hold a rival place with one of them,

---

94 let . . . bark i.e., let no creature dare to interrupt me.   **98–9 would
. . . fools** i.e., would virtually condemn their hearers into calling them
fools. (Compare Matthew 5:22, in which anyone calling another a fool
is threatened with damnation.)   **101–2 fish . . . opinion** i.e., don't go
fishing for a reputation of being wise, using your melancholy silence as
the bait to fool people. (*Gudgeon*, a small fish, was thought of as a type
of gullibility.)   **106 dumb** mute, speechless   **108 keep** if you keep
110 for this gear in view of what you say.   **112 neat's** ox's.   **not
vendible** i.e., not yet salable in the marriage market.   **113 Is . . . now?**
i.e., Was all that talk about anything?   **115 reasons** reasonable ideas
119 the same i.e., the one   **124 By . . . port** by showing a somewhat
more lavish style of living   **125 grant continuance** allow to continue.
126–7 make . . . rate complain at being cut back from such a high style
of living   **128 to . . . off** honorably to extricate myself   **129 time** youthful lifetime   **130 gaged** pledged, in pawn.

132 warranty authorization   **133 unburden** disclose   **136–7 if . . .
honor** if it looks honorable, as your conduct has always done
140 shaft arrow   **141 his** its.   **selfsame flight** same kind and range
142 advisèd careful   **143 forth** out.   **adventuring** risking   **145 innocence** ingenuousness, sincerity.   **148 self** same   **150 or** either
151 hazard that which was risked   **152 rest** remain   **153 spend but
time** only waste time   **154 To . . . circumstance** i.e., in not asking
plainly what you want. (*Circumstance* here means "circumlocution.")
156 In . . . uttermost in showing any doubt of my intention to do all I
can   **160 prest** ready   **161 richly left** left a large fortune (by her
father's will)   **163 Sometimes** Once   **165–6 nothing undervalued To**
of no less worth than   **166 Portia** (The same Portia as in Shakespeare's *Julius Caesar*.)   **171 Colchis'** (Jason adventured for the
golden fleece in the land of Colchis, on the Black Sea.)   **strand** shore

I have a mind presages me such thrift 175
That I should questionless be fortunate.

ANTONIO
Thou know'st that all my fortunes are at sea;
Neither have I money nor commodity 178
To raise a present sum. Therefore go forth. 179
Try what my credit can in Venice do;
That shall be racked even to the uttermost 181
To furnish thee to Belmont, to fair Portia.
Go presently inquire, and so will I, 183
Where money is, and I no question make 184
To have it of my trust or for my sake.   *Exeunt.* 185

❧

[1.2]

Enter Portia with her waiting woman, Nerissa.

PORTIA   By my troth, Nerissa, my little body is aweary 1
of this great world.

NERISSA   You would be, sweet madam, if your miseries 3
were in the same abundance as your good fortunes
are; and yet, for aught I see, they are as sick that surfeit 5
with too much as they that starve with nothing. It is
no mean happiness, therefore, to be seated in the 7
mean. Superfluity comes sooner by white hairs, but 8
competency lives longer. 9

PORTIA   Good sentences, and well pronounced. 10

NERISSA   They would be better if well followed.

PORTIA   If to do were as easy as to know what were
good to do, chapels had been churches and poor
men's cottages princes' palaces. It is a good divine that 14
follows his own instructions. I can easier teach twenty
what were good to be done than to be one of the
twenty to follow mine own teaching. The brain may
devise laws for the blood, but a hot temper leaps o'er 18
a cold decree; such a hare is madness, the youth, to
skip o'er the meshes of good counsel, the cripple. But 20
this reasoning is not in the fashion to choose me a 21
husband. Oh, me, the word "choose"! I may neither 22
choose who I would nor refuse who I dislike; so is the
will of a living daughter curbed by the will of a dead 24
father. Is it not hard, Nerissa, that I cannot choose one
nor refuse none?

NERISSA   Your father was ever virtuous, and holy men
at their death have good inspirations; therefore the

lottery that he hath devised in these three chests of
gold, silver, and lead, whereof who chooses his mean- 30
ing chooses you, will no doubt never be chosen by
any rightly but one who you shall rightly love. But 32
what warmth is there in your affection towards any of
these princely suitors that are already come?

PORTIA   I pray thee, overname them, and as thou nam- 35
est them I will describe them; and according to my
description level at my affection. 37

NERISSA   First, there is the Neapolitan prince.

PORTIA   Ay, that's a colt indeed, for he doth nothing but 39
talk of his horse, and he makes it a great appropriation 40
to his own good parts that he can shoe him him- 41
self. I am much afeard my lady his mother played false
with a smith.

NERISSA   Then is there the County Palatine. 44

PORTIA   He doth nothing but frown, as who should say, 45
"An you will not have me, choose." He hears merry 46
tales and smiles not. I fear he will prove the weeping 47
philosopher when he grows old, being so full of un- 48
mannerly sadness in his youth. I had rather be mar- 49
ried to a death's-head with a bone in his mouth than
to either of these. God defend me from these two!

NERISSA   How say you by the French lord, Monsieur 52
Le Bon?

PORTIA   God made him, and therefore let him pass for a
man. In truth, I know it is a sin to be a mocker, but
he! Why, he hath a horse better than the Neapolitan's,
a better bad habit of frowning than the Count Palatine;
he is every man in no man. If a throstle sing, he 58
falls straight a-capering. He will fence with his own 59
shadow. If I should marry him, I should marry twenty
husbands. If he would despise me, I would forgive
him, for if he love me to madness, I shall never re- 62
quite him.

NERISSA   What say you, then, to Falconbridge, the 64
young baron of England?

PORTIA   You know I say nothing to him, for he understands not me, nor I him. He hath neither Latin,
French, nor Italian, and you will come into the court 68
and swear that I have a poor pennyworth in the Eng- 69
lish. He is a proper man's picture, but alas, who can 70
converse with a dumb show? How oddly he is suited! 71
I think he bought his doublet in Italy, his round hose 72

175 **presages** i.e., that presages.   **thrift** profit and good fortune
178 **commodity** merchandise   179 **a present sum** ready money.
181 **racked** stretched   183 **presently** immediately   184 **no question
make** have no doubt   185 **of my trust** on the basis of my credit as a
merchant.   **sake** i.e., personal sake.
1.2. Location: Belmont. Portia's house.
1 **troth** faith   3 **would be** would have reason to be (weary)
5 **surfeit** overindulge   7 **mean** small. (With a pun; see next note.)
7–8 **in the mean** having neither too much nor too little.   8 **comes
sooner by** acquires sooner   9 **competency** modest means   10 **sentences** maxims.   **pronounced** delivered.   14 **divine** clergyman
18 **blood** (Thought of as a chief agent of the passions, which in turn
were regarded as the enemies of reason.)   20 **meshes** nets. (Used
here for hunting hares.)   **good counsel, the cripple** (Wisdom is portrayed as old and no longer agile.)   20–2 **But . . . husband** But this
talk is not the way to help me choose a husband.   24 **will . . . will**
volition . . . testament

30 **who** whoever.   **his** i.e., the father's   32 **rightly . . . rightly** correctly . . . truly   35 **overname them** name them over   37 **level** aim,
guess   39 **colt** i.e., wanton and foolish young man. (With a punning
appropriateness to his interest in horses.)   40 **appropriation** addition
41 **good parts** accomplishments   44 **County Palatine** a count entitled
to supreme jurisdiction in his province.   45 **as who should say** as
one might say   46 **An** If.   **choose** i.e., do as you please.   47–8 **the
weeping philosopher** i.e., Heraclitus of Ephesus, a melancholic and
retiring philosopher of about 500 B.C., often contrasted with Democri-
tus, the "laughing philosopher"   49 **sadness** melancholy   52 **How
. . . by** What do you have to say about   58 **he is . . . no man** i.e., he
borrows aspects from everyone but has no character of his own.
throstle thrush   59 **straight** at once   62 **if** even if   64 **say you . . . to**
do you say about. (But Portia wittily puns, in her reply, on the literal
sense of "speak to.")   68–70 **come . . . English** i.e., bear witness that I
can speak very little English.   70 **He . . . picture** i.e., He looks handsome   71 **dumb show** pantomime.   **suited** dressed.   72 **doublet**
upper garment corresponding to a jacket.   **round hose** short, puffed-
out breeches

in France, his bonnet in Germany, and his behavior 73
everywhere.

NERISSA   What think you of the Scottish lord, his
neighbor?

PORTIA   That he hath a neighborly charity in him, for he
borrowed a box of the ear of the Englishman and swore 78
he would pay him again when he was able. I think the
Frenchman became his surety and sealed under for an- 80
other. 81

NERISSA   How like you the young German, the Duke of
Saxony's nephew?

PORTIA   Very vilely in the morning, when he is sober,
and most vilely in the afternoon, when he is drunk.
When he is best he is a little worse than a man, and
when he is worst he is little better than a beast. An 87
the worst fall that ever fell, I hope I shall make shift to 88
go without him.

NERISSA   If he should offer to choose, and choose the 90
right casket, you should refuse to perform your father's
will if you should refuse to accept him.

PORTIA   Therefore, for fear of the worst, I pray thee, set
a deep glass of Rhenish wine on the contrary casket, 94
for if the devil be within and that temptation without, 95
I know he will choose it. I will do anything, Nerissa, 96
ere I will be married to a sponge.

NERISSA   You need not fear, lady, the having any of
these lords. They have acquainted me with their de-
terminations, which is indeed to return to their home
and to trouble you with no more suit, unless you may
be won by some other sort than your father's imposi- 102
tion depending on the caskets. 103

PORTIA   If I live to be as old as Sibylla, I will die as chaste 104
as Diana, unless I be obtained by the manner of my 105
father's will. I am glad this parcel of wooers are so rea- 106
sonable, for there is not one among them but I dote on
his very absence, and I pray God grant them a fair
departure.

NERISSA   Do you not remember, lady, in your father's
time, a Venetian, a scholar and a soldier, that came
hither in company of the Marquess of Montferrat?

PORTIA   Yes, yes, it was Bassanio—as I think, so was
he called.

NERISSA   True, madam. He, of all the men that ever my
foolish eyes looked upon was the best deserving a fair
lady.

PORTIA   I remember him well, and I remember him
worthy of thy praise.

Enter a Servingman.

How now, what news?

SERVINGMAN   The four strangers seek for you, madam, 121
to take their leave; and there is a forerunner come from 122
a fifth, the Prince of Morocco, who brings word the
Prince his master will be here tonight.

PORTIA   If I could bid the fifth welcome with so good
heart as I can bid the other four farewell, I should be
glad of his approach. If he have the condition of a saint 127
and the complexion of a devil, I had rather he should 128
shrive me than wive me. 129
Come, Nerissa. [*To Servingman*] Sirrah, go before. 130
Whiles we shut the gate upon one wooer, another
knocks at the door.   *Exeunt.*

❀

[1.3]

Enter Bassanio with Shylock the Jew.

SHYLOCK   Three thousand ducats, well. 1

BASSANIO   Ay, sir, for three months.

SHYLOCK   For three months, well.

BASSANIO   For the which, as I told you, Antonio shall
be bound.

SHYLOCK   Antonio shall become bound, well.

BASSANIO   May you stead me? Will you pleasure me? 7
Shall I know your answer?

SHYLOCK   Three thousand ducats for three months and
Antonio bound.

BASSANIO   Your answer to that.

SHYLOCK   Antonio is a good man. 12

BASSANIO   Have you heard any imputation to the
contrary?

SHYLOCK   Ho, no, no, no, no! My meaning in saying he
is a good man is to have you understand me that he is
sufficient. Yet his means are in supposition. He hath an 17
argosy bound to Tripolis, another to the Indies. I understand, moreover, upon the Rialto, he hath a third 19
at Mexico, a fourth for England, and other ventures he
hath squandered abroad. But ships are but boards, 21
sailors but men. There be land rats and water rats,
water thieves and land thieves—I mean pirates—and
then there is the peril of waters, winds, and rocks. The
man is, notwithstanding, sufficient. Three thousand
ducats. I think I may take his bond.

BASSANIO   Be assured you may. 27

SHYLOCK   I will be assured I may; and that I may be 28
assured, I will bethink me. May I speak with Antonio?

---

73 bonnet hat   **78 borrowed** received. (But with a play on the idea of
something that must be repaid.)   **80–1 became . . . another** offered to
back up the Scottish lord and promised (with as solemn a vow as if
he were signing and sealing a document) to add a blow of his own.
(An allusion to the age-old alliance of the French and the Scots
against the English.)   **87 An** If   **88 fall** befall.   **make shift** manage
90 offer undertake   **94 Rhenish wine** a German white wine from the
Rhine Valley.   **contrary** i.e., wrong   **95 if** even if   **96 it** i.e., the
tempting red wine.   **102 sort** means. (With perhaps a suggestion too
of "casting or drawing of lots.")   **102–3 imposition** command,
charge   **104 Sibylla** the Cumaean Sibyl, to whom Apollo gave as
many years as there were grains in her handful of sand   **105 Diana**
goddess of chastity and of the hunt   **106 parcel** assembly, group

121 four (Nerissa actually names six suitors; possibly a sign of revision or the author's early draft.)   **122 forerunner** herald   **127 condition** disposition, character   **128 complexion of a devil** (Devils were
thought to be black; but *complexion* can also mean "temperament,"
"disposition.")   **129 shrive me** pardon me, excuse me from having to
be wooed. (Literally, act as my confessor and give absolution.)
130 Sirrah (Form of address to social inferior.)
1.3. Location: Venice. A public place.
1 ducats gold coins   **7 stead** supply, assist.   **pleasure** oblige
12 good (Shylock means "solvent," a good credit risk; Bassanio interprets it in the moral sense.)   **17 sufficient** i.e., a good security.   **in
supposition** doubtful, uncertain.   **19 the Rialto** the merchants'
exchange in Venice and the center of commercial activity   **21 squandered** scattered   **27, 28 assured** (Bassanio means that Shylock may
trust Antonio, whereas Shylock means that he will obtain legal assurances.)

BASSANIO   If it please you to dine with us.

SHYLOCK   Yes, to smell pork, to eat of the habitation
which your prophet the Nazarite conjured the devil   32
into. I will buy with you, sell with you, talk with you,
walk with you, and so following, but I will not eat   34
with you, drink with you, nor pray with you. What
news on the Rialto? Who is he comes here?

Enter Antonio.

BASSANIO   This is Signor Antonio.

SHYLOCK [*aside*]
How like a fawning publican he looks!   38
I hate him for he is a Christian,   39
But more for that in low simplicity   40
He lends out money gratis and brings down   41
The rate of usance here with us in Venice.   42
If I can catch him once upon the hip,   43
I will feed fat the ancient grudge I bear him.   44
He hates our sacred nation, and he rails,   45
Even there where merchants most do congregate,
On me, my bargains, and my well-won thrift,
Which he calls interest. Cursèd be my tribe
If I forgive him!

BASSANIO   Shylock, do you hear?

SHYLOCK   I am debating of my present store,   50
And, by the near guess of my memory,
I cannot instantly raise up the gross   52
Of full three thousand ducats. What of that?
Tubal, a wealthy Hebrew of my tribe,
Will furnish me. But soft, how many months   55
Do you desire? [*To Antonio*] Rest you fair, good
signor!
Your Worship was the last man in our mouths.   57

ANTONIO
Shylock, albeit I neither lend nor borrow
By taking nor by giving of excess,   59
Yet, to supply the ripe wants of my friend,   60
I'll break a custom. [*To Bassanio*] Is he yet possessed   61
How much ye would?   62

SHYLOCK   Ay, ay, three thousand ducats.

ANTONIO   And for three months.

SHYLOCK
I had forgot—three months, you told me so.
Well then, your bond. And let me see—but hear
you,
Methought you said you neither lend nor borrow
Upon advantage.

ANTONIO   I do never use it.   68

SHYLOCK
When Jacob grazed his uncle Laban's sheep—   69
This Jacob from our holy Abram was,   70
As his wise mother wrought in his behalf,
The third possessor; ay, he was the third—   72

ANTONIO
And what of him? Did he take interest?

SHYLOCK
No, not take interest, not as you would say
Directly interest. Mark what Jacob did.
When Laban and himself were compromised   76
That all the eanlings which were streaked and pied   77
Should fall as Jacob's hire, the ewes, being rank,   78
In end of autumn turnèd to the rams,
And when the work of generation was   80
Between these woolly breeders in the act,
The skillful shepherd peeled me certain wands,   82
And in the doing of the deed of kind   83
He stuck them up before the fulsome ewes,   84
Who then conceiving did in eaning time   85
Fall parti-colored lambs, and those were Jacob's.   86
This was a way to thrive, and he was blest;
And thrift is blessing, if men steal it not.   88

ANTONIO
This was a venture, sir, that Jacob served for,   89
A thing not in his power to bring to pass,
But swayed and fashioned by the hand of heaven.
Was this inserted to make interest good?   92
Or is your gold and silver ewes and rams?

SHYLOCK
I cannot tell. I make it breed as fast.   94
But note me, signor—

ANTONIO   Mark you this, Bassanio,
The devil can cite Scripture for his purpose.   96
An evil soul producing holy witness
Is like a villain with a smiling cheek,
A goodly apple rotten at the heart.
Oh, what a goodly outside falsehood hath!

SHYLOCK
Three thousand ducats. 'Tis a good round sum.
Three months from twelve, then let me see, the rate—

ANTONIO
Well, Shylock, shall we be beholding to you?   103

SHYLOCK
Signor Antonio, many a time and oft
In the Rialto you have rated me   105
About my moneys and my usances.
Still have I borne it with a patient shrug,

---

32 Nazarite Nazarene. (For the reference to Christ's casting evil spirits into a herd of swine, see Matthew 8:30–2, Mark 5:1–13, and Luke 8:32–3.)   **34 so following** so forth   **38 publican** Roman tax gatherer (a term of opprobrium; see Luke 18:9–14); or, innkeeper   **39 for** because   **40 low simplicity** humble foolishness   **41 gratis** without charging interest   **42 usance** usury, interest   **43 upon the hip** i.e., at my mercy. (A figure of speech from wrestling; see Genesis 32:24–9.)   **44 fat** until fatted for the kill   **45 our sacred nation** i.e., the Hebrew people   **50 I am . . . store** I am considering my current supply of money   **52 gross** total   **55 soft** i.e., wait a minute   **57 Your . . . mouths** i.e., We were just speaking of you. (But with ominous connotation of devouring; compare line 44.)   **59 excess** interest   **60 ripe wants** pressing needs   **61 possessed** informed   **62 ye would** you want.   **68 advantage** interest.

69 Jacob (See Genesis 27, 30:25–43.)   **70 Abram** Abraham   **72 third** i.e., after Abraham and Isaac.   **possessor** i.e., of the birthright of which, with the help of Rebecca, he was able to cheat Esau, his elder brother   **76 compromised** agreed   **77 eanlings** young lambs or kids.   **pied** spotted   **78 hire** wages, share.   **rank** in heat   **80 work of generation** mating   **82 peeled . . . wands** i.e., partly stripped the bark of some sticks. (*Me* is used colloquially.)   **83 deed of kind** i.e., copulation   **84 fulsome** lustful, well-fed   **85 eaning** lambing   **86 Fall** give birth to   **88 thrift** thriving, profit   **89 venture . . . for** uncertain commercial venture on which Jacob risked his wages   **92 inserted . . . good** brought in to justify the practice of usury.   **94 I cannot tell** i.e., I don't know about that.   **96 devil . . . Scripture** (See Matthew 4:6.)   **103 beholding** beholden, indebted   **105 rated** berated, rebuked

For sufferance is the badge of all our tribe.   108
You call me misbeliever, cutthroat dog,
And spit upon my Jewish gaberdine,   110
And all for use of that which is mine own.
Well then, it now appears you need my help.
Go to, then. You come to me and you say,   113
"Shylock, we would have moneys"—you say so,
You, that did void your rheum upon my beard   115
And foot me as you spurn a stranger cur   116
Over your threshold. Moneys is your suit.   117
What should I say to you? Should I not say,
"Hath a dog money? Is it possible
A cur can lend three thousand ducats?" Or
Shall I bend low, and in a bondman's key,   121
With bated breath and whispering humbleness,   122
Say this:
"Fair sir, you spit on me on Wednesday last,
You spurned me such a day, another time
You called me dog, and for these courtesies
I'll lend you thus much moneys"?

ANTONIO
I am as like to call thee so again,   128
To spit on thee again, to spurn thee too.
If thou wilt lend this money, lend it not
As to thy friends, for when did friendship take
A breed for barren metal of his friend?   132
But lend it rather to thine enemy,   133
Who, if he break, thou mayst with better face   134
Exact the penalty.

SHYLOCK   Why, look you how you storm!
I would be friends with you and have your love,
Forget the shames that you have stained me with,
Supply your present wants, and take no doit
Of usance for my moneys, and you'll not hear me.   138
This is kind I offer.   140

BASSANIO   This were kindness.   141

SHYLOCK   This kindness will I show.
Go with me to a notary, seal me there
Your single bond; and, in a merry sport,   144
If you repay me not on such a day,
In such a place, such sum or sums as are
Expressed in the condition, let the forfeit
Be nominated for an equal pound   148
Of your fair flesh, to be cut off and taken
In what part of your body pleaseth me.

ANTONIO
Content, in faith. I'll seal to such a bond
And say there is much kindness in the Jew.

BASSANIO
You shall not seal to such a bond for me!
I'll rather dwell in my necessity.   154

ANTONIO
Why, fear not, man, I will not forfeit it.
Within these two months—that's a month before
This bond expires—I do expect return
Of thrice three times the value of this bond.

SHYLOCK
O father Abram, what these Christians are,
Whose own hard dealings teaches them suspect
The thoughts of others! Pray you, tell me this:
If he should break his day, what should I gain
By the exaction of the forfeiture?
A pound of man's flesh taken from a man
Is not so estimable, profitable neither,   165
As flesh of muttons, beefs, or goats. I say
To buy his favor I extend this friendship.
If he will take it, so; if not, adieu.   168
And for my love, I pray you, wrong me not.   169

ANTONIO
Yes, Shylock, I will seal unto this bond.

SHYLOCK
Then meet me forthwith at the notary's.
Give him direction for this merry bond,
And I will go and purse the ducats straight,
See to my house, left in the fearful guard   174
Of an unthrifty knave, and presently
I'll be with you.   *Exit.*
ANTONIO   Hie thee, gentle Jew.—   176
The Hebrew will turn Christian; he grows kind.

BASSANIO
I like not fair terms and a villain's mind.

ANTONIO
Come on. In this there can be no dismay;
My ships come home a month before the day.
                                              [*Exeunt.*]

[2.1]

[*Flourish of cornets.*] *Enter* [*the Prince of*]
*Morocco, a tawny Moor all in white, and three
or four followers accordingly, with Portia, Nerissa, and their train.*

MOROCCO
Mislike me not for my complexion,
The shadowed livery of the burnished sun,   2
To whom I am a neighbor and near bred.   3
Bring me the fairest creature northward born,
Where Phoebus' fire scarce thaws the icicles,   5
And let us make incision for your love

---

108 **sufferance** endurance   110 **gaberdine** loose outer garment like a cape or mantle   113 **Go to** (An exclamation of impatience or annoyance.)   115 **rheum** spittle   116 **spurn** kick   117 **suit** request.
121 **bondman's key** serf's tone of voice   122 **bated** subdued
128 **like** likely   132 **A breed . . . metal** offspring from money, which cannot naturally breed. (One of the oldest arguments against usury was that it was thereby "unnatural.")   **of** from   133 **to** as if to
134 **Who** from whom.   **break** fail to pay on time   138 **doit** a Dutch coin of very small value   140 **kind** kindly   141 **were** would be (if seriously offered)   144 **single bond** bond signed alone without other security; unconditional. (Shylock pretends the *condition,* line 147, is only a joke.)   148 **nominated for** named, specified as.   **equal** exact

154 **dwell** remain   165 **estimable** valuable   168 **so** well and good
169 **wrong me not** do not think evil of me.   174 **fearful** to be mistrusted   176 **gentle** gracious, courteous. (With a play on "gentile.")
2.1. Location: Belmont. Portia's house.
0.3 *accordingly* similarly (i.e., dressed in white and dark-skinned like Morocco)   2 **shadowed livery** i.e., dark complexion, worn as though it were a costume of the sun's servants   3 **near bred** closely related
5 **Phoebus'** i.e., the sun's

To prove whose blood is reddest, his or mine.   7
I tell thee, lady, this aspect of mine   8
Hath feared the valiant. By my love I swear,   9
The best-regarded virgins of our clime
Have loved it too. I would not change this hue,
Except to steal your thoughts, my gentle queen.

PORTIA
In terms of choice I am not solely led
By nice direction of a maiden's eyes;   14
Besides, the lott'ry of my destiny
Bars me the right of voluntary choosing.
But if my father had not scanted me,   17
And hedged me by his wit to yield myself   18
His wife who wins me by that means I told you,   19
Yourself, renownèd prince, then stood as fair   20
As any comer I have looked on yet
For my affection.

MOROCCO   Even for that I thank you.   22
Therefore, I pray you, lead me to the caskets
To try my fortune. By this scimitar
That slew the Sophy and a Persian prince,   25
That won three fields of Sultan Solyman,   26
I would o'erstare the sternest eyes that look,   27
Outbrave the heart most daring on the earth,
Pluck the young sucking cubs from the she-bear,
Yea, mock the lion when 'a roars for prey,   30
To win thee, lady. But alas the while!
If Hercules and Lichas play at dice   32
Which is the better man, the greater throw
May turn by fortune from the weaker hand.
So is Alcides beaten by his page,
And so may I, blind Fortune leading me,
Miss that which one unworthier may attain,
And die with grieving.

PORTIA   You must take your chance,
And either not attempt to choose at all
Or swear before you choose, if you choose wrong
Never to speak to lady afterward
In way of marriage. Therefore be advised.   42

MOROCCO
Nor will not. Come, bring me unto my chance.   43

PORTIA
First, forward to the temple. After dinner   44
Your hazard shall be made.

MOROCCO   Good fortune then!
To make me blest or cursed'st among men.
                              [Cornets, and] exeunt.

❖

[2.2]

Enter [Lancelot] the clown, alone.

LANCELOT   Certainly my conscience will serve me to   1
run from this Jew my master. The fiend is at mine
elbow and tempts me, saying to me, "Gobbo, Lancelot
Gobbo, good Lancelot," or "Good Gobbo," or "Good
Lancelot Gobbo, use your legs, take the start, run
away." My conscience says, "No, take heed, honest
Lancelot, take heed, honest Gobbo," or, as aforesaid,
"Honest Lancelot Gobbo, do not run; scorn running
with thy heels." Well, the most courageous fiend bids   9
me pack. "Fia!" says the fiend. "Away!" says the fiend. 10
"For the heavens, rouse up a brave mind," says the   11
fiend, "and run." Well, my conscience, hanging about   12
the neck of my heart, says very wisely to me, "My hon-   13
est friend Lancelot, being an honest man's son," or
rather an honest woman's son—for indeed my father
did something smack, something grow to, he had a   16
kind of taste—well, my conscience says, "Lancelot,   17
budge not." "Budge," says the fiend "Budge not," says
my conscience. "Conscience," say I, "you counsel
well." "Fiend," say I, "you counsel well." To be ruled by
my conscience, I should stay with the Jew my master,
who, God bless the mark, is a kind of devil; and to run 22
away from the Jew, I should be ruled by the fiend, who,
saving your reverence, is the devil himself. Certainly
the Jew is the very devil incarnation; and, in my con-   25
science, my conscience is but a kind of hard conscience
to offer to counsel me to stay with the Jew. The fiend
gives the more friendly counsel. I will run, fiend. My
heels are at your commandment. I will run.

Enter Old Gobbo, with a basket.

GOBBO   Master young man, you, I pray you, which is   30
the way to master Jew's?

LANCELOT   [*aside*] Oh, heavens, this is my true-
begotten father, who, being more than sand-blind,   33
high-gravel-blind, knows me not. I will try confusions   34
with him.

GOBBO   Master young gentleman, I pray you, which is
the way to master Jew's?

LANCELOT   Turn up on your right hand at the next
turning, but at the next turning of all on your left;
marry, at the very next turning, turn of no hand, but   40
turn down indirectly to the Jew's house.

---

7 reddest (Red blood was regarded as a sign of courage.)   **8 aspect**
visage   **9 feared** frightened   **14 nice direction** careful guidance
17 scanted limited   **18 wit** wisdom   **18–19 yield . . . who** give
myself to be the wife of him who   **20 then . . . fair** would then have
looked as attractive and stood as fair a chance. (With a play on "fair-
skinned.")   **22 For my** of gaining my   **25 Sophy** Shah of Persia
26 fields battles.   **Solyman** a Turkish sultan ruling from 1520 to 1566
27 o'erstare outstare   **30 'a** he   **32 Lichas** a page of Hercules
(Alcides). See the note for 3.2.55.   **42 be advised** take warning, consider.   **43 Nor will not** i.e., Nor indeed will I violate the oath.   **44 to
the temple** i.e., in order to take the oaths.

2.2. Location: Venice. A street.
0.1 clown (1) country bumpkin (2) comic type in an Elizabethan acting company   **1 serve** permit   **9 with thy heels** i.e., emphatically.
(With a pun on the literal sense.)   **Fia!** i.e., Via,
away!   **11 For the heavens** i.e., In heaven's name   **12–13 hanging . . .
heart** i.e., timidly   **16–17 something smack . . . taste** i.e., had a tendency to lechery   **22 God . . . mark** (An expression by way of apology for introducing something potentially offensive, as also in *saving
your reverence* in line 24.)   **25 incarnation** (Lancelot means "incarnate.")   **30 you** (Gobbo uses the formal *you* but switches to the familiar *thou*, line 88, when he accepts Lancelot as his son.)   **33 sand-blind**
dim-sighted   **34 high-gravel-blind** blinder than sand-blind. (A term
seemingly invented by Lancelot.)   **try confusions** (Lancelot's blunder for "try conclusions," i.e., experiment, though his error is comically apt.)   **40 marry** i.e., by the Virgin Mary, indeed. (A mild
interjection.)   **of no hand** neither right nor left

GOBBO   By God's sonties, 'twill be a hard way to hit. 42
Can you tell me whether one Lancelot, that dwells
with him, dwell with him or no?

LANCELOT   Talk you of young Master Lancelot? [*Aside*]
Mark me now; now will I raise the waters.—Talk you 46
of young Master Lancelot?

GOBBO   No master, sir, but a poor man's son. His father, 48
though I say't, is an honest exceeding poor man and,
God be thanked, well to live. 50

LANCELOT   Well, let his father be what 'a will, we talk 51
of young Master Lancelot.

GOBBO   Your Worship's friend, and Lancelot, sir. 53

LANCELOT   But I pray you, ergo, old man, ergo, I be- 54
seech you, talk you of young Master Lancelot?

GOBBO   Of Lancelot, an't please Your Mastership.

LANCELOT   Ergo, Master Lancelot. Talk not of Master
Lancelot, father, for the young gentleman, according 58
to Fates and Destinies and such odd sayings, the Sis- 59
ters Three and such branches of learning, is indeed 60
deceased, or, as you would say in plain terms, gone to
heaven.

GOBBO   Marry, God forbid! The boy was the very staff
of my age, my very prop.

LANCELOT   Do I look like a cudgel or a hovel post, a 65
staff, or a prop? Do you know me, father?

GOBBO   Alack the day, I know you not, young gentleman. But I pray you, tell me, is my boy, God rest his
soul, alive or dead?

LANCELOT   Do you not know me, father?

GOBBO   Alack, sir, I am sand-blind. I know you not.

LANCELOT   Nay, indeed, if you had your eyes you
might fail of the knowing me; it is a wise father that 73
knows his own child. Well, old man, I will tell you 74
news of your son. [*He kneels.*] Give me your blessing.
Truth will come to light; murder cannot be hid long; a
man's son may, but in the end truth will out.

GOBBO   Pray you, sir, stand up. I am sure you are not
Lancelot, my boy.

LANCELOT   Pray you, let's have no more fooling about
it, but give me your blessing. I am Lancelot, your 81
boy that was, your son that is, your child that shall be. 82

GOBBO   I cannot think you are my son.

LANCELOT   I know not what I shall think of that; but I
am Lancelot, the Jew's man, and I am sure Margery
your wife is my mother.

GOBBO   Her name is Margery indeed. I'll be sworn, if
thou be Lancelot, thou art mine own flesh and blood.
Lord worshiped might he be, what a beard hast thou 89
got! Thou hast got more hair on thy chin than Dobbin
my fill horse has on his tail. 91

LANCELOT   [*rising*]   It should seem then that Dobbin's
tail grows backward. I am sure he had more hair of 93
his tail than I have of my face when I last saw him. 94

GOBBO   Lord, how art thou changed! How dost thou and
thy master agree? I have brought him a present. How
'gree you now?

LANCELOT   Well, well; but for mine own part, as I have
set up my rest to run away, so I will not rest till 99
I have run some ground. My master's a very Jew. Give 100
him a present? Give him a halter! I am famished in his 101
service; you may tell every finger I have with my ribs. 102
Father, I am glad you are come. Give me your present 103
to one Master Bassanio, who indeed gives rare new 104
liveries. If I serve not him, I will run as far as God has 105
any ground. Oh, rare fortune! Here comes the man. To
him, father, for I am a Jew if I serve the Jew any longer. 107

Enter Bassanio, with [*Leonardo and*] *a follower
or two.*

BASSANIO   You may do so, but let it be so hasted that 108
supper be ready at the farthest by five of the clock. See 109
these letters delivered, put the liveries to making, and
desire Gratiano to come anon to my lodging.

[*Exit a Servant.*]

LANCELOT   To him, father.

GOBBO   [*advancing*]   God bless Your Worship!

BASSANIO   Gramercy. Wouldst thou aught with me? 114

GOBBO   Here's my son, sir, a poor boy— 115

LANCELOT   Not a poor boy, sir, but the rich Jew's man,
that would, sir, as my father shall specify—

GOBBO   He hath a great infection, sir, as one would say, 118
to serve—

LANCELOT   Indeed, the short and the long is, I serve the
Jew, and have a desire, as my father shall specify—

GOBBO   His master and he, saving Your Worship's
reverence, are scarce cater-cousins— 123

LANCELOT   To be brief, the very truth is that the Jew,
having done me wrong, doth cause me, as my father,
being, I hope, an old man, shall frutify unto you— 126

GOBBO   I have here a dish of doves that I would bestow
upon Your Worship, and my suit is—

LANCELOT   In very brief, the suit is impertinent to 129
myself, as Your Worship shall know by this honest old
man, and, though I say it, though old man, yet poor
man, my father.

---

42 **sonties** little saints   46 **raise the waters** i.e., start tears.   48 **master** (The title was applied to gentlefolk only.)   50 **well to live** prospering, in good health.   51 **'a** he   53 **Your . . . Lancelot** (Again, Old Gobbo denies that Lancelot is entitled to be called "Master.")   54 **ergo** therefore. (But Lancelot may use this Latin word with no particular meaning in mind.)   58 **father** (1) old man (2) father   59–60 **the Sisters Three** the three Fates   65 **hovel post** post holding up a hovel or open shed   73–4 **it is . . . child** (Reverses the proverb "It is a wise child that knows his own father.")   81–2 **your . . . shall be** (Echoes the *Gloria* from the Book of Common Prayer: "As it was in the beginning, is now, and ever shall be.")   89 **beard** (Stage tradition has Old Gobbo mistaking Lancelot's long hair for a beard.)   91 **fill horse** cart horse

93 **grows backward** grows at the wrong end.   94 **of** on   99 **set up my rest** determined, risked all. (A metaphor from the card game *primero*, in which a final wager is made, with a pun also on *rest* as "place of residence.")   **not rest** i.e., not stop running. (More punning on *rest*.)   100 **very** veritable.   **Jew** (1) Hebrew (2) grasping old usurer   101 **halter** hangman's noose.   102 **tell** count.   **tell . . . ribs** (Comically reverses the usual saying of counting one's ribs with one's fingers.)   103 **Give me** Give. (*Me* suggests "on my behalf.")   104 **rare** splendid   105 **liveries** uniforms or costumes for servants.   107 **a Jew** i.e., a villain. (Punning on the literal sense in *the Jew*. Compare with line 100.)   108 **hasted** hastened, hurried   109 **farthest** latest   114 **Gramercy** Many thanks.   **aught** anything   115 **poor** (1) unfortunate (2) penniless (contrasted with *rich* in the next line)   118 **infection** (Blunder for "affection" or "inclination.")   123 **cater-cousins** good friends   126 **frutify** (Lancelot may be trying to say "fructify," but he means "certify" or "notify.")   129 **impertinent** (Blunder for "pertinent.")

BASSANIO   One speak for both. What would you?

LANCELOT   Serve you, sir.

GOBBO   That is the very defect of the matter, sir.   135

BASSANIO
I know thee well; thou hast obtained thy suit.
Shylock thy master spoke with me this day,
And hath preferred thee, if it be preferment   138
To leave a rich Jew's service to become
The follower of so poor a gentleman.

LANCELOT   The old proverb is very well parted be-   141
tween my master Shylock and you, sir: you have the
grace of God, sir, and he hath enough.

BASSANIO
Thou speak'st it well. Go, father, with thy son.
Take leave of thy old master, and inquire
My lodging out. [*To a Servant*] Give him a livery
More guarded than his fellows'. See it done.   147

LANCELOT   Father, in. I cannot get a service, no! I have
ne'er a tongue in my head, well! [*He looks at his palm.*]
If any man in Italy have a fairer table which doth offer   150
to swear upon a book, I shall have good fortune. Go   151
to, here's a simple line of life. Here's a small trifle of   152
wives! Alas, fifteen wives is nothing. Eleven widows
and nine maids is a simple coming-in for one man.   154
And then to scape drowning thrice, and to be in peril
of my life with the edge of a feather bed! Here are   156
simple scapes. Well, if Fortune be a woman, she's a   157
good wench for this gear. Father, come. I'll take my   158
leave of the Jew in the twinkling.
                              Exit clown [*Lancelot, with Old Gobbo*].

BASSANIO [*giving Leonardo a list*]
I pray thee, good Leonardo, think on this:
These things being bought and orderly bestowed,   161
Return in haste, for I do feast tonight   162
My best-esteemed acquaintance. Hie thee, go.

LEONARDO
My best endeavors shall be done herein.
                              [*He starts to leave.*]

           Enter Gratiano.

GRATIANO [*to Leonardo*]
Where's your master?

LEONARDO   Yonder, sir, he walks.
                              Exit Leonardo.

GRATIANO   Signor Bassanio!

BASSANIO   Gratiano!

GRATIANO
I have a suit to you.

BASSANIO   You have obtained it.

GRATIANO   You must not deny me. I must go with you
to Belmont.

BASSANIO
Why, then you must. But hear thee, Gratiano;
Thou art too wild, too rude and bold of voice—
Parts that become thee happily enough,   173
And in such eyes as ours appear not faults,
But where thou art not known, why, there they show
Something too liberal. Pray thee, take pain   176
To allay with some cold drops of modesty   177
Thy skipping spirit, lest through thy wild behavior
I be misconstered in the place I go to   179
And lose my hopes.

GRATIANO   Signor Bassanio, hear me:
If I do not put on a sober habit,   181
Talk with respect and swear but now and then,
Wear prayer books in my pocket, look demurely,
Nay more, while grace is saying, hood mine eyes   184
Thus with my hat, and sigh and say "amen,"
Use all the observance of civility,
Like one well studied in a sad ostent   187
To please his grandam, never trust me more.   188

BASSANIO   Well, we shall see your bearing.

GRATIANO
Nay, but I bar tonight. You shall not gauge me
By what we do tonight.

BASSANIO   No, that were pity.
I would entreat you rather to put on
Your boldest suit of mirth, for we have friends
That purpose merriment. But fare you well;
I have some business.

GRATIANO
And I must to Lorenzo and the rest,
But we will visit you at suppertime.   *Exeunt.*

                              ❖

[2.3]

           Enter Jessica and [*Lancelot*] *the clown.*

JESSICA
I am sorry thou wilt leave my father so.
Our house is hell, and thou, a merry devil,
Didst rob it of some taste of tediousness.
But fare thee well. There is a ducat for thee.
                              [*Giving money.*]
And, Lancelot, soon at supper shalt thou see
Lorenzo, who is thy new master's guest.
Give him this letter; do it secretly.   [*Giving a letter.*]
And so farewell. I would not have my father
See me in talk with thee.

---

135 **defect** (Blunder for "effect," i.e., "purport.")   138 **preferred** recommended   141 **proverb** i.e., "He who has the grace of God has enough."   **parted** divided   147 **guarded** trimmed with braided ornament   150 **table** palm of the hand. (Lancelot now reads the lines of his palm.)   151 **book** i.e., Bible. (The image is of a hand being laid on the Bible to take an oath.)   151–2 **Go to** (An expression of impatience. Said ironically.)   152 **simple** unremarkable.   **line of life** curved line at the base of the thumb.   154 **simple coming-in** modest beginning or income. (With sexual suggestion.)   156 **feather bed** (Suggesting marriage bed or love bed; Lancelot sees sexual adventure and the dangers of marriage in his palm reading.)   157 **scapes** 1) adventures (2) transgressions.   **Fortune . . . woman** (Fortune was personified as a goddess.)   158 **gear** matter.   161 **bestowed** i.e., stowed on board ship   162 **feast** give a feast for

173 **Parts** qualities   176 **liberal** free of manner. (Often with sexual connotation.)   177 **allay** temper, moderate.   **modesty** decorum   179 **misconstered** misconstrued   181 **habit** demeanor. (With a suggestion of "clothes.")   184 **saying** being said   187 **sad ostent** grave appearance   188 **grandam** grandmother
2.3. Location: Venice. Shylock's house.

LANCELOT   Adieu! Tears exhibit my tongue. Most   10
beautiful pagan, most sweet Jew! If a Christian did not
play the knave and get thee, I am much deceived. But,   12
adieu! These foolish drops do something drown my
manly spirit. Adieu!

JESSICA   Farewell, good Lancelot.   [*Exit Lancelot.*]
Alack, what heinous sin is it in me
To be ashamed to be my father's child!
But though I am a daughter to his blood,
I am not to his manners. O Lorenzo,
If thou keep promise, I shall end this strife,
Become a Christian and thy loving wife.   *Exit.*

❖

[2.4]

Enter Gratiano, Lorenzo, Salerio, and Solanio.

LORENZO
Nay, we will slink away in suppertime,   1
Disguise us at my lodging, and return
All in an hour.

GRATIANO
We have not made good preparation.

SALERIO
We have not spoke us yet of torchbearers.   5

SOLANIO
'Tis vile, unless it may be quaintly ordered,   6
And better in my mind not undertook.

LORENZO
'Tis now but four o'clock. We have two hours
To furnish us.

Enter Lancelot [with a letter].

Friend Lancelot, what's the news?

LANCELOT   An it shall please you to break up this, it   10
shall seem to signify.   [*Giving the letter.*]

LORENZO
I know the hand. In faith, 'tis a fair hand,
And whiter than the paper it writ on
Is the fair hand that writ.

GRATIANO   Love news, in faith.

LANCELOT   By your leave, sir.   [*He starts to leave.*]

LORENZO   Whither goest thou?

LANCELOT   Marry, sir, to bid my old master the Jew to
sup tonight with my new master the Christian.

LORENZO
Hold here, take this. [*He gives money.*] Tell gentle
Jessica
I will not fail her. Speak it privately.
    Exit clown [Lancelot].
Go, gentlemen,
Will you prepare you for this masque tonight?
I am provided of a torchbearer.

SALERIO
Ay, marry, I'll be gone about it straight.   24

SOLANIO
And so will I.

LORENZO   Meet me and Gratiano.
At Gratiano's lodging some hour hence.   26

SALERIO   'Tis good we do so.   *Exit [with Solanio].*

GRATIANO
Was not that letter from fair Jessica?

LORENZO
I must needs tell thee all. She hath directed   29
How I shall take her from her father's house,
What gold and jewels she is furnished with,
What page's suit she hath in readiness.
If e'er the Jew her father come to heaven,
It will be for his gentle daughter's sake;   34
And never dare misfortune cross her foot,   35
Unless she do it under this excuse,   36
That she is issue to a faithless Jew.   37
Come, go with me. Peruse this as thou goest.
    [*He gives Gratiano the letter.*]
Fair Jessica shall be my torchbearer.   *Exeunt.*

❖

[2.5]

*Enter [Shylock the] Jew and [Lancelot,] his man
that was, the clown.*

SHYLOCK
Well, thou shalt see, thy eyes shall be thy judge,
The difference of old Shylock and Bassanio.—   2
What, Jessica!—Thou shalt not gormandize,   3
As thou hast done with me—What, Jessica!—
And sleep and snore, and rend apparel out—   5
Why, Jessica, I say!

LANCELOT   Why, Jessica!

SHYLOCK
Who bids thee call? I do not bid thee call.

LANCELOT   Your Worship was wont to tell me I could
do nothing without bidding.

Enter Jessica.

JESSICA   Call you? What is your will?

SHYLOCK
I am bid forth to supper, Jessica.
There are my keys. But wherefore should I go?   13
I am not bid for love—they flatter me—
But yet I'll go in hate, to feed upon
The prodigal Christian. Jessica, my girl,
Look to my house. I am right loath to go.   17
There is some ill a-brewing towards my rest,
For I did dream of moneybags tonight.   19

LANCELOT   I beseech you, sir, go. My young master
doth expect your reproach.   21

---

10 **exhibit** (Blunder for "inhibit," "restrain.")   12 **get** beget
2.4. Location: Venice. A street.
1 **in** during   5 **spoke . . . of** yet bespoken, ordered   6 **quaintly
ordered** skillfully and tastefully managed   10 **An** If.   **break up this**
unseal the letter   24 **straight** at once.

26 **some hour** about an hour   29 **must needs** must   34 **gentle** (With
pun on "gentile"?)   35 **foot** footpath   36 **she** i.e., Misfortune   37 **she
is issue** i.e., Jessica is daughter.   **faithless** pagan
2.5. Location: Venice. Before Shylock's house.
2 **of** between   3 **gormandize** eat gluttonously   5 **rend apparel out**
i.e., wear out your clothes   13 **wherefore** why   17 **right loath** reluctant   19 **tonight** last night.   21 **reproach** (Lancelot's blunder for
"approach." Shylock takes it in grim humor.)

SHYLOCK   So do I his.

LANCELOT   And they have conspired together. I will not say you shall see a masque, but if you do, then it was not for nothing that my nose fell a-bleeding on Black Monday last at six o'clock i'th' morning, falling   26
out that year on Ash Wednesday was four year in th'afternoon.

SHYLOCK
What, are there masques? Hear you me, Jessica:
Lock up my doors, and when you hear the drum
And the vile squealing of the wry-necked fife,   31
Clamber not you up to the casements then,
Nor thrust your head into the public street
To gaze on Christian fools with varnished faces,   34
But stop my house's ears—I mean my casements.
Let not the sound of shallow fopp'ry enter
My sober house. By Jacob's staff I swear   37
I have no mind of feasting forth tonight.
But I will go.—Go you before me, sirrah.
Say I will come.

LANCELOT   I will go before, sir. [Aside to Jessica] Mistress, look out at window, for all this;
There will come a Christian by,
Will be worth a Jewess' eye.   [Exit.]

SHYLOCK
What says that fool of Hagar's offspring, ha?   45

JESSICA
His words were "Farewell, mistress," nothing else.

SHYLOCK
The patch is kind enough, but a huge feeder,   47
Snail-slow in profit, and he sleeps by day   48
More than the wildcat. Drones hive not with me;
Therefore I part with him, and part with him
To one that I would have him help to waste
His borrowed purse. Well, Jessica, go in.
Perhaps I will return immediately.
Do as I bid you. Shut doors after you.
Fast bind, fast find—   55
A proverb never stale in thrifty mind.   Exit.

JESSICA
Farewell, and if my fortune be not crossed,
I have a father, you a daughter, lost.   Exit.

❖

[2.6]

Enter the masquers, Gratiano and Salerio.

GRATIANO
This is the penthouse under which Lorenzo   1

Desired us to make stand.

SALERIO   His hour is almost past.

GRATIANO
And it is marvel he outdwells his hour,   4
For lovers ever run before the clock.

SALERIO
Oh, ten times faster Venus' pigeons fly   6
To seal love's bonds new-made than they are wont
To keep obligèd faith unforfeited.   8

GRATIANO
That ever holds. Who riseth from a feast   9
With that keen appetite that he sits down?
Where is the horse that doth untread again   11
His tedious measures with the unbated fire   12
That he did pace them first? All things that are
Are with more spirit chasèd than enjoyed.
How like a younger or a prodigal   15
The scarfèd bark puts from her native bay,   16
Hugged and embracèd by the strumpet wind!   17
How like the prodigal doth she return,
With overweathered ribs and ragged sails,   19
Lean, rent, and beggared by the strumpet wind!   20

Enter Lorenzo.

SALERIO
Here comes Lorenzo. More of this hereafter.

LORENZO
Sweet friends, your patience for my long abode;   22
Not I, but my affairs, have made you wait.
When you shall please to play the thieves for wives,
I'll watch as long for you then. Approach;   25
Here dwells my father Jew.—Ho! Who's within?   26

[Enter] Jessica, above [in boy's clothes].

JESSICA
Who are you? Tell me for more certainty,
Albeit I'll swear that I do know your tongue.

LORENZO   Lorenzo, and thy love.

JESSICA
Lorenzo, certain, and my love indeed,
For who love I so much? And now who knows
But you, Lorenzo, whether I am yours?   31

LORENZO
Heaven and thy thoughts are witness that thou art.

JESSICA [*throwing down a casket*]
Here, catch this casket. It is worth the pains.
I am glad 'tis night, you do not look on me,

---

26 Black Monday Easter Monday. (Lancelot's talk of omens is perhaps intentional gibberish, a parody of Shylock's fears.)   **31 wry-necked** i.e., played with the musician's head awry; or possibly comparing the fife's *vile squealing* to the call of the wryneck, a bird with a high-pitched call and a writhing movement of head and neck   **34 varnished faces** i.e., painted masks   **37 Jacob's staff** (See Genesis 32:10 and Hebrews 11:21.)   **45 Hagar's offspring** (Hagar, a gentile and Abraham's servant, gave birth to Ishmael; both mother and son were cast out after the birth of Isaac.)   **47 patch** fool   **48 profit** profitable labor   **55 Fast . . . find** i.e., Keep your property secure and you will always know where it is. (Proverbial.)
2.6. Location: Before Shylock's house, as in 2.5.
1 penthouse projecting roof or upper story of a house

4 it . . . hour i.e., it is surprising that he is late   **6–8 Oh, ten . . . unforfeited** i.e., Oh, lovers are ten times more alacritous in their first pledge of love than in keeping faith in a long-term commitment. (*Venus' pigeons* are the doves that draw her chariot.)   **9 ever holds** always holds true.   **11 untread** retrace   **12 measures** paces   **15 younger** i.e., younger son, as in the parable of the Prodigal Son (Luke 15). (Often emended to *younker*, youth.)   **16 scarfèd bark** sailing vessel festooned with flags or streamers   **17 strumpet** i.e., inconsistent, variable. (Likened metaphorically to the harlots with whom the Prodigal Son wasted his fortune.)   **19 overweathered ribs** i.e., weather-beaten and leaking timbers   **20 rent** torn   **22 your patience** i.e., I beg your patience.   **abode** delay   **25 watch** keep watch   **26 father** i.e., father-in-law   **31 But you** better than you

For I am much ashamed of my exchange.   36
But love is blind, and lovers cannot see
The pretty follies that themselves commit,   38
For if they could, Cupid himself would blush
To see me thus transformèd to a boy.

LORENZO
Descend, for you must be my torchbearer.

JESSICA
What, must I hold a candle to my shames?   42
They in themselves, good sooth, are too too light.   43
Why, 'tis an office of discovery, love,   44
And I should be obscured.

LORENZO   So are you, sweet,
Even in the lovely garnish of a boy.   46
But come at once,
For the close night doth play the runaway,   48
And we are stayed for at Bassanio's feast.   49

JESSICA
I will make fast the doors, and gild myself   50
With some more ducats, and be with you straight.
                                        [Exit above.]

GRATIANO
Now, by my hood, a gentle and no Jew.   52

LORENZO
Beshrew me but I love her heartily,   53
For she is wise, if I can judge of her,
And fair she is, if that mine eyes be true,
And true she is, as she hath proved herself;
And therefore, like herself, wise, fair, and true,
Shall she be placèd in my constant soul.

              Enter Jessica [below].

What, art thou come? On, gentlemen, away!
Our masquing mates by this time for us stay.   60
                    Exit [with Jessica and Salerio;
                    Gratiano is about to follow them].

              Enter Antonio.

ANTONIO   Who's there?
GRATIANO   Signor Antonio?
ANTONIO
Fie, fie, Gratiano! Where are all the rest?
'Tis nine o'clock; our friends all stay for you.
No masque tonight. The wind is come about;
Bassanio presently will go aboard.
I have sent twenty out to seek for you.

GRATIANO
I am glad on 't. I desire no more delight
Than to be under sail and gone tonight.   *Exeunt.*

                        ❧

[2.7]

[Flourish of cornets.] Enter Portia, with [the Prince of] Morocco, and both their trains.

PORTIA
Go, draw aside the curtains and discover   1
The several caskets to this noble prince.   2
Now make your choice.   *[The curtains are drawn.]*
MOROCCO
The first, of gold, who this inscription bears,   4
"Who chooseth me shall gain what many men desire";
The second, silver, which this promise carries,
"Who chooseth me shall get as much as he deserves";
This third, dull lead, with warning all as blunt,   8
"Who chooseth me must give and hazard all he hath."
How shall I know if I do choose the right?
PORTIA
The one of them contains my picture, Prince.
If you choose that, then I am yours withal.   12
MOROCCO
Some god direct my judgment! Let me see,
I will survey th'inscriptions back again.
What says this leaden casket?
"Who chooseth me must give and hazard all he hath."
Must give—for what? For lead? Hazard for lead?
This casket threatens. Men that hazard all
Do it in hope of fair advantages.
A golden mind stoops not to shows of dross.   20
I'll then nor give nor hazard aught for lead.   21
What says the silver with her virgin hue?
"Who chooseth me shall get as much as he deserves."
As much as he deserves! Pause there, Morocco,
And weigh thy value with an even hand.   25
If thou be'st rated by thy estimation,   26
Thou dost deserve enough; and yet enough
May not extend so far as to the lady;
And yet to be afeard of my deserving
Were but a weak disabling of myself.   30
As much as I deserve? Why, that's the lady.
I do in birth deserve her, and in fortunes,
In graces, and in qualities of breeding;
But more than these, in love I do deserve.
What if I strayed no farther, but chose here?
Let's see once more this saying graved in gold: 36
"Who chooseth me shall gain what many men desire."
Why, that's the lady; all the world desires her.
From the four corners of the earth they come
To kiss this shrine, this mortal breathing saint.   40
The Hyrcanian deserts and the vasty wilds   41
Of wide Arabia are as throughfares now
For princes to come view fair Portia.

---

36 exchange change of clothes.   **38 pretty** ingenious, artful   **42 hold a candle** i.e., stand by and witness. (With a play on the idea of acting as torchbearer.)   **43 light** (1) immodest (2) illuminated.   **44 'tis ... discovery** i.e., torchbearing is intended to shed light on matters   **46 garnish** outfit, trimmings   **48 close** dark, secretive.   **doth ... runaway** i.e., is quickly passing   **49 stayed** waited   **50 gild** adorn. (Literally, cover with gold.)   **52 by my hood** (An asseveration.)   **gentle** gracious person. (With pun on "gentile," as at 2.4.34.)   **53 Beshrew** i.e., A mischief on. (A mild oath.)   **60 stay** wait. (Also in line 64.)

2.7. Location: Belmont. Portia's house.
0.2 trains followers   **1 discover** reveal   **2 several** different, various   **4 who** which   **8 dull** (1) dull-colored (2) blunt.   **all as blunt** as blunt as lead   **12 withal** with it.   **20 dross** worthless matter. (Literally, the impurities cast off in the melting down of metals.)   **21 nor give** neither give   **25 even** impartial   **26 estimation** worth   **30 disabling** underrating   **36 graved** engraved   **40 mortal breathing** living   **41 Hyrcanian** (Hyrcania was the country south of the Caspian Sea celebrated for its wildness.)   **vasty** vast

The watery kingdom, whose ambitious head
Spits in the face of heaven, is no bar   45
To stop the foreign spirits, but they come,   46
As o'er a brook, to see fair Portia.
One of these three contains her heavenly picture.
Is't like that lead contains her? 'Twere damnation   49
To think so base a thought; it were too gross   50
To rib her cerecloth in the obscure grave.   51
Or shall I think in silver she's immured,   52
Being ten times undervalued to tried gold?   53
Oh, sinful thought! Never so rich a gem
Was set in worse than gold. They have in England   55
A coin that bears the figure of an angel   56
Stamped in gold, but that's insculped upon;   57
But here an angel in a golden bed
Lies all within. Deliver me the key.
Here do I choose, and thrive I as I may!

PORTIA
There, take it, Prince; and if my form lie there,   61
Then I am yours.
                                        [*He unlocks the golden casket.*]
MOROCCO   Oh, hell! What have we here?
A carrion Death, within whose empty eye   63
There is a written scroll! I'll read the writing.
[*He reads.*]
        "All that glisters is not gold;
        Often have you heard that told.
        Many a man his life hath sold
        But my outside to behold.   68
        Gilded tombs do worms infold.
        Had you been as wise as bold,
        Young in limbs, in judgment old,
        Your answer had not been inscrolled.   72
        Fare you well; your suit is cold."
    Cold, indeed, and labor lost.
    Then, farewell, heat, and welcome, frost!
Portia, adieu. I have too grieved a heart
To take a tedious leave. Thus losers part.   77
                        Exit [*with his train. Flourish of cornets.*]

PORTIA
A gentle riddance. Draw the curtains, go.
Let all of his complexion choose me so.   79
                        [*The curtains are closed, and*] *exeunt.*

❖

45 **Spits** (The image is of huge waves breaking at sea.)   46 **spirits** i.e.,
men of courage   49 **like** likely   50 **base** (1) ignoble (2) low in the
natural scale, as with lead, a *base* metal   50–1 **it were . . . grave** i.e., it
would be too gross an insult to inter her, as it were, wrapped in a
waxed cloth, in a lead casket.   52 **immured** enclosed, confined
53 **Being . . . gold** which has only one-tenth the value of assayed and
purified gold.   55 **set** fixed, as a precious stone, in a border of metal
56 **coin** i.e., the gold coin known as the *angel*, which bore the device
of the archangel Michael treading on the dragon   57 **insculped upon**
merely engraved upon the surface   61 **form** image   63 **carrion**
Death death's-head   68 **But** only   72 **inscrolled** i.e., written on this
scroll.   77 **part** depart.   79 **complexion** temperament (not merely
skin color)

[2.8]

Enter Salerio and Solanio.

SALERIO
Why, man, I saw Bassanio under sail.
With him is Gratiano gone along,
And in their ship I am sure Lorenzo is not.
SOLANIO
The villain Jew with outcries raised the Duke,   4
Who went with him to search Bassanio's ship.
SALERIO
He came too late. The ship was under sail.
But there the Duke was given to understand
That in a gondola were seen together
Lorenzo and his amorous Jessica.
Besides, Antonio certified the Duke
They were not with Bassanio in his ship.
SOLANIO
I never heard a passion so confused,   12
So strange, outrageous, and so variable
As the dog Jew did utter in the streets:
"My daughter! Oh, my ducats! Oh, my daughter!
Fled with a Christian! Oh, my Christian ducats!
Justice! The law! My ducats, and my daughter!
A sealèd bag, two sealèd bags of ducats,
Of double ducats, stol'n from me by my daughter!
And jewels, two stones, two rich and precious
        stones,
Stol'n by my daughter! Justice! Find the girl!
She hath the stones upon her, and the ducats."
SALERIO
Why, all the boys in Venice follow him,
Crying his stones, his daughter, and his ducats.   24
SOLANIO
Let good Antonio look he keep his day,   25
Or he shall pay for this.
SALERIO   Marry, well remembered.
I reasoned with a Frenchman yesterday,   27
Who told me, in the narrow seas that part   28
The French and English, there miscarrièd
A vessel of our country richly fraught.   30
I thought upon Antonio when he told me,
And wished in silence that it were not his.
SOLANIO
You were best to tell Antonio what you hear.
Yet do not suddenly, for it may grieve him.
SALERIO
A kinder gentleman treads not the earth.
I saw Bassanio and Antonio part.
Bassanio told him he would make some speed
Of his return; he answered, "Do not so.
Slubber not business for my sake, Bassanio,   39
But stay the very riping of the time;   40

2.8. Location: Venice. A street.
4 **raised** roused   12 **passion** passionate outburst   24 **stones** (In the
boys' jeering cry, the *two stones* suggest testicles; see line 20.)   25 **look . . .**
day see to it that he repays his loan on time   27 **reasoned** talked
28 **narrow seas** English Channel   30 **fraught** freighted.   39 **Slubber**
not business Don't do the business hastily and badly   40 **But . . . time**
i.e., Pursue your business at Belmont until it is brought to completion

And for the Jew's bond which he hath of me,   41
Let it not enter in your mind of love.   42
Be merry, and employ your chiefest thoughts
To courtship and such fair ostents of love   44
As shall conveniently become you there."
And even there, his eye being big with tears,   46
Turning his face, he put his hand behind him,   47
And with affection wondrous sensible   48
He wrung Bassanio's hand; and so they parted.

SOLANIO
I think he only loves the world for him.   50
I pray thee, let us go and find him out
And quicken his embracèd heaviness   52
With some delight or other.

SALERIO   Do we so.   *Exeunt.*

❖

[2.9]

Enter Nerissa and a Servitor.

NERISSA
Quick, quick, I pray thee, draw the curtain straight.   1
The Prince of Aragon hath ta'en his oath,
And comes to his election presently.   3
                              [The curtains are drawn back.]

[Flourish of cornets.] Enter [the Prince of]
Aragon, his train, and Portia.

PORTIA
Behold, there stand the caskets, noble Prince.
If you choose that wherein I am contained,
Straight shall our nuptial rites be solemnized;
But if you fail, without more speech, my lord,
You must be gone from hence immediately.

ARAGON
I am enjoined by oath to observe three things:
First, never to unfold to anyone   10
Which casket 'twas I chose; next, if I fail
Of the right casket, never in my life
To woo a maid in way of marriage;
Lastly,
If I do fail in fortune of my choice,
Immediately to leave you and be gone.

PORTIA
To these injunctions everyone doth swear
That comes to hazard for my worthless self.

ARAGON
And so have I addressed me. Fortune now   19
To my heart's hope! Gold, silver, and base lead.
"Who chooseth me must give and hazard all he hath."

You shall look fairer ere I give or hazard.
What says the golden chest? Ha, let me see:
"Who chooseth me shall gain what many men desire."
What many men desire! That "many" may be meant
By the fool multitude, that choose by show,   26
Not learning more than the fond eye doth teach,   27
Which pries not to th'interior, but like the martlet   28
Builds in the weather on the outward wall,   29
Even in the force and road of casualty.   30
I will not choose what many men desire,
Because I will not jump with common spirits   32
And rank me with the barbarous multitudes.
Why then, to thee, thou silver treasure-house!
Tell me once more what title thou dost bear:
"Who chooseth me shall get as much as he deserves."
And well said too; for who shall go about
To cozen fortune, and be honorable   38
Without the stamp of merit? Let none presume   39
To wear an undeservèd dignity.
Oh, that estates, degrees, and offices   41
Were not derived corruptly, and that clear honor
Were purchased by the merit of the wearer!
How many then should cover that stand bare?   44
How many be commanded that command?   45
How much low peasantry would then be gleaned   46
From the true seed of honor, and how much honor   47
Picked from the chaff and ruin of the times
To be new-varnished? Well, but to my choice: 49
"Who chooseth me shall get as much as he deserves."
I will assume desert. Give me a key for this,
And instantly unlock my fortunes here.
                              [He opens the silver casket.]

PORTIA
Too long a pause for that which you find there.

ARAGON
What's here? The portrait of a blinking idiot,
Presenting me a schedule! I will read it.   55
How much unlike art thou to Portia!
How much unlike my hopes and my deservings!
"Who chooseth me shall have as much as he
      deserves."
Did I deserve no more than a fool's head?
Is that my prize? Are my deserts no better?

PORTIA
To offend and judge are distinct offices   61
And of opposèd natures.

ARAGON   What is here?   62

---

41 **for** as for   42 **of** preoccupied with   44 **ostents** expressions, shows
46 **there** thereupon, then   47 **behind him** (Antonio turns away in
tears while extending his hand back to Bassanio.)   48 **affection wondrous sensible** wondrously sensitive and keen emotion   50 **he . . .
him** i.e., Bassanio is all he lives for   52 **quicken . . . heaviness** lighten
the sorrow he has embraced
2.9. Location: Belmont. Portia's house.
0.1 *Servitor* servant   1 **straight** at once.   3 **election presently** choice
immediately   10 **unfold** disclose   19 **addressed me** prepared myself
(by this swearing).

26 **By** for, to signify   27 **fond** foolish   28 **martlet** swift   29 **in**
exposed to   30 **force . . . casualty** power and path of mischance.
32 **jump** agree   38 **cozen** cheat   39 **stamp** seal of approval
41 **estates, degrees** status, social rank   44 **cover . . . bare** i.e., wear
hats (of authority) who now stand bareheaded.   45 **How . . . command?** How many then should be servants that are now masters?
46 **gleaned** culled out and discarded   47 **the true seed of honor** i.e.,
persons of noble descent   49 **new-varnished** i.e., having the luster of
their true nobility restored to them.   55 **schedule** written paper.
61–2 **To offend . . . natures** i.e., You have no right, having submitted
your case to judgment, to attempt to judge your own case; or, it is not
for me to say, since I've been the indirect cause of your discomfiture.

[*He reads.*]"The fire seven times tried this; 63
    Seven times tried that judgment is
    That did never choose amiss.
    Some there be that shadows kiss; 66
    Such have but a shadow's bliss.
    There be fools alive, iwis, 68
    Silvered o'er, and so was this. 69
    Take what wife you will to bed;
    I will ever be your head. 71
    So begone; you are sped." 72

Still more fool I shall appear 73
By the time I linger here. 74
With one fool's head I came to woo,
But I go away with two.
Sweet, adieu. I'll keep my oath,
Patiently to bear my wroth. 78

        [*Exeunt Aragon and train.*]

PORTIA
Thus hath the candle singed the moth.
Oh, these deliberate fools! When they do choose, 80
They have the wisdom by their wit to lose.

NERISSA
The ancient saying is no heresy:
Hanging and wiving goes by destiny.

PORTIA   Come, draw the curtain, Nerissa.
        [*The curtains are closed.*]

    Enter Messenger.

MESSENGER
Where is my lady?

PORTIA   Here. What would my lord? 85

MESSENGER
Madam, there is alighted at your gate
A young Venetian, one that comes before
To signify th'approaching of his lord,
From whom he bringeth sensible regreets, 89
To wit, besides commends and courteous breath, 90
Gifts of rich value. Yet I have not seen 91
So likely an ambassador of love.
A day in April never came so sweet,
To show how costly summer was at hand, 94
As this fore-spurrer comes before his lord. 95

PORTIA
No more, I pray thee. I am half afeard
Thou wilt say anon he is some kin to thee,
Thou spend'st such high-day wit in praising him. 98
Come, come, Nerissa, for I long to see
Quick Cupid's post that comes so mannerly. 100

NERISSA
Bassanio, Lord Love, if thy will it be!   *Exeunt.*

        ❖

[3.1]

    [*Enter*] *Solanio and Salerio.*

SOLANIO   Now, what news on the Rialto?

SALERIO   Why, yet it lives there unchecked that Anto- 2
nio hath a ship of rich lading wrecked on the narrow 3
seas—the Goodwins, I think they call the place, a 4
very dangerous flat, and fatal, where the carcasses of 5
many a tall ship lie buried, as they say, if my gossip 6
Report be an honest woman of her word. 7

SOLANIO   I would she were as lying a gossip in that as
ever knapped ginger or made her neighbors believe 9
she wept for the death of a third husband. But it is
true, without any slips of prolixity or crossing the 11
plain highway of talk, that the good Antonio, the 12
honest Antonio—oh, that I had a title good enough to
keep his name company!—

SALERIO   Come, the full stop. 15

SOLANIO   Ha, what sayest thou? Why, the end is, he
hath lost a ship.

SALERIO   I would it might prove the end of his losses.

SOLANIO   Let me say "amen" betimes, lest the devil 19
cross my prayer, for here he comes in the likeness of 20
a Jew.

    Enter Shylock.

How now, Shylock, what news among the merchants?

SHYLOCK   You knew, none so well, none so well as
you, of my daughter's flight.

SALERIO   That's certain. I for my part knew the tailor
that made the wings she flew withal. 26

SOLANIO   And Shylock for his own part knew the bird
was fledge, and then it is the complexion of them all 28
to leave the dam. 29

SHYLOCK   She is damned for it.

SALERIO   That's certain, if the devil may be her judge.

SHYLOCK   My own flesh and blood to rebel!

SOLANIO   Out upon it, old carrion! Rebels it at these 33
years? 34

SHYLOCK   I say my daughter is my flesh and my blood.

---

63 The fire . . . this This silver has been seven times tested and purified **66 shadows** illusions **68 iwis** certainly **69 Silvered o'er** i.e.,
with silver hair and so apparently wise **71 I . . . head** i.e., you will
always have a fool's head, be a fool. **72 sped** done for. **73–4 Still . . .
here** i.e., I shall seem all the greater fool for wasting any more time
here. **78 wroth** sorrow, unhappy lot (a variant of *ruth*); or, anger.
80 deliberate reasoning, calculating **85 my lord** (A jesting response
to "my lady.") **89 sensible regreets** tangible gifts, greetings
90 commends greetings. **breath** speech **91 Yet** Heretofore
94 costly lavish, rich **95 fore-spurrer** herald, harbinger
98 high-day holiday (i.e., extravagant) **100 post** messenger

3.1. Location: Venice. A street.
2 yet . . . unchecked i.e., a rumor is spreading undenied **3–4 the narrow seas** the English Channel, as at 2.8.28. **4 Goodwins** Goodwin
Sands, off the Kentish coast near the Thames estuary **5 flat** shoal,
sandbank **6 tall** gallant **6–7 gossip Report** i.e., Dame Rumor
9 knapped nibbled **11 slips of prolixity** lapses into long-winded-
ness; or, long-winded lies. *Slips* may be the cuttings or offshoots of
tediousness. **11–12 crossing . . . talk** deviating from honest, plain
speech **15 Come . . . stop** Finish your sentence; rein in your tongue
as a horse is checked in its manage. **19 betimes** while there is yet
time **20 cross** thwart; make the sign of the cross following
26 the wings . . . withal i.e., the disguise she escaped in. (With a play
on *wings* or ornamented shoulder flaps sewn on garments.)
28 fledge ready to fly. **complexion** natural disposition, as at 2.7.79
29 dam mother. **33–4 Rebels . . . years?** (Solanio pretends to interpret Shylock's cry about the rebellion of his own flesh and blood as
referring to his own carnal desires, his own erection.)

SALERIO   There is more difference between thy flesh and
hers than between jet and ivory, more between your 37
bloods than there is between red wine and Rhenish. 38
But tell us, do you hear whether Antonio have had
any loss at sea or no?

SHYLOCK   There I have another bad match! A bankrupt, 41
a prodigal, who dare scarce show his head on the
Rialto; a beggar, that was used to come so smug upon
the mart! Let him look to his bond. He was wont to 44
call me usurer. Let him look to his bond. He was wont
to lend money for a Christian courtesy. Let him look to
his bond.

SALERIO   Why, I am sure, if he forfeit, thou wilt not take
his flesh. What's that good for?

SHYLOCK   To bait fish withal. If it will feed nothing else,
it will feed my revenge. He hath disgraced me, and
hindered me half a million, laughed at my losses,
mocked at my gains, scorned my nation, thwarted my
bargains, cooled my friends, heated mine enemies;
and what's his reason? I am a Jew. Hath not a Jew
eyes? Hath not a Jew hands, organs, dimensions, senses, affections, passions? Fed with the same food, hurt
with the same weapons, subject to the same diseases,
healed by the same means, warmed and cooled by the
same winter and summer, as a Christian is? If you
prick us, do we not bleed? If you tickle us, do we not
laugh? If you poison us, do we not die? And if you
wrong us, shall we not revenge? If we are like you in
the rest, we will resemble you in that. If a Jew wrong
a Christian, what is his humility? Revenge. If a 65
Christian wrong a Jew, what should his sufferance be 66
by Christian example? Why, revenge. The villainy you
teach me I will execute, and it shall go hard but I will 68
better the instruction.

Enter a Man from Antonio.

MAN   Gentlemen, my master Antonio is at his house
and desires to speak with you both.

SALERIO   We have been up and down to seek him. 72

Enter Tubal.

SOLANIO   Here comes another of the tribe. A third
cannot be matched, unless the devil himself turn Jew. 74
     Exeunt gentlemen [Solanio, Salerio, with Man].

SHYLOCK   How now, Tubal, what news from Genoa?
Hast thou found my daughter?

TUBAL   I often came where I did hear of her, but cannot
find her.

SHYLOCK   Why, there, there, there, there! A diamond
gone, cost me two thousand ducats in Frankfort! The 80
curse never fell upon our nation till now; I never felt it 81

till now. Two thousand ducats in that, and other
precious, precious jewels. I would my daughter were
dead at my foot, and the jewels in her ear! Would she
were hearsed at my foot, and the ducats in her coffin! 85
No news of them? Why, so—and I know not what's
spent in the search. Why, thou loss upon loss! The
thief gone with so much, and so much to find the
thief, and no satisfaction, no revenge! Nor no ill luck
stirring but what lights o' my shoulders, no sighs but
o' my breathing, no tears but o' my shedding.

TUBAL   Yes, other men have ill luck too. Antonio, as I
heard in Genoa—

SHYLOCK   What, what, what? Ill luck, ill luck?

TUBAL   Hath an argosy cast away, coming from Tripolis. 95

SHYLCOK   I thank God, I thank God. Is it true, is it true?

TUBAL   I spoke with some of the sailors that escaped the
wreck.

SHYLOCK   I thank thee, good Tubal. Good news, good
news! Ha, ha! Heard in Genoa?

TUBAL   Your daughter spent in Genoa, as I heard, one
night fourscore ducats.

SHYLOCK   Thou stick'st a dagger in me. I shall never see
my gold again. Fourscore ducats at a sitting? Fourscore ducats?

TUBAL   There came divers of Antonio's creditors in my
company to Venice that swear he cannot choose but
break. 108

SHYLOCK   I am very glad of it. I'll plague him, I'll torture
him. I am glad of it.

TUBAL   One of them showed me a ring that he had of
your daughter for a monkey.

SHYLOCK   Out upon her! Thou torturest me, Tubal. It
was my turquoise; I had it of Leah when I was a 114
bachelor. I would not have given it for a wilderness of
monkeys.

TUBAL   But Antonio is certainly undone.

SHYLOCK   Nay, that's true, that's very true. Go, Tubal,
fee me an officer; bespeak him a fortnight before. I will 119
have the heart of him if he forfeit, for were he out of
Venice I can make what merchandise I will. Go, Tubal, 121
and meet me at our synagogue. Go, good Tubal; at our
synagogue, Tubal.   *Exeunt [separately].*

❖

[3.2]

*Enter Bassanio, Portia, Gratiano, [Nerissa,]
and all their trains.*

PORTIA
I pray you, tarry. Pause a day or two
Before you hazard, for in choosing wrong 2
I lose your company. Therefore forbear awhile.
There's something tells me—but it is not love—
I would not lose you; and you know yourself
Hate counsels not in such a quality. 6

---

37 jet a black, hard mineral, here contrasted with the whiteness of
ivory and Jessica's fair complexion   **38 Rhenish** i.e., a German white
wine from the Rhine valley. (Salerio seems to prefer the white wine as
more refined than the red.)   **41 match** bargain.   **44 mart** marketplace, Rialto.   **65 what . . . Revenge** i.e., in what spirit does the Christian receive the injury, that of Christian humility? No, he seeks
revenge.   **66 his sufferance** the Jew's patient endurance   **68 it shall
. . . but** i.e., assuredly; unless difficulties intervene   **72 up and down**
i.e., everywhere   **74 matched** i.e., found to match them   **80–1 The
curse** God's curse (such as the plagues visited upon Egypt in Exodus
7–12)

85 hearsed coffined   **95 cast away** shipwrecked   **108 break** go bankrupt.   **114 Leah** Shylock's wife   **119 fee** hire.   **officer** bailiff.
bespeak engage   **121 make . . . I will** drive whatever bargains I
please
3.2. Location: Belmont. Portia's house.
2 in choosing if you choose   **6 quality** way, manner.

But lest you should not understand me well—
And yet a maiden hath no tongue but thought—
I would detain you here some month or two
Before you venture for me. I could teach you
How to choose right, but then I am forsworn.
So will I never be. So may you miss me.   12
But if you do, you'll make me wish a sin,
That I had been forsworn. Beshrew your eyes,
They have o'erlooked me and divided me!   15
One half of me is yours, the other half yours—
Mine own, I would say; but if mine, then yours,
And so all yours. Oh, these naughty times   18
Puts bars between the owners and their rights!   19
And so, though yours, not yours. Prove it so,   20
Let Fortune go to hell for it, not I.   21
I speak too long, but 'tis to peise the time,   22
To eke it and to draw it out in length,   23
To stay you from election.
BASSANIO   Let me choose,   24
For as I am, I live upon the rack.
PORTIA
Upon the rack, Bassanio? Then confess   26
What treason there is mingled with your love.   27
BASSANIO
None but that ugly treason of mistrust,   28
Which makes me fear th'enjoying of my love.   29
There may as well be amity and life
'Tween snow and fire, as treason and my love.   31
PORTIA
Ay, but I fear you speak upon the rack,
Where men enforcèd do speak anything.
BASSANIO
Promise me life, and I'll confess the truth.
PORTIA
Well then, confess and live.
BASSANIO   "Confess and love"
Had been the very sum of my confession.
Oh, happy torment, when my torturer
Doth teach me answers for deliverance!
But let me to my fortune and the caskets.   39
PORTIA
Away, then! I am locked in one of them.
If you do love me, you will find me out.
Nerissa and the rest, stand all aloof.   42
Let music sound while he doth make his choice;
Then, if he lose, he makes a swanlike end,   44
Fading in music. That the comparison
May stand more proper, my eye shall be the stream

And wat'ry deathbed for him. He may win;
And what is music then? Then music is
Even as the flourish when true subjects bow   49
To a new-crownèd monarch. Such it is
As are those dulcet sounds in break of day
That creep into the dreaming bridegroom's ear
And summon him to marriage. Now he goes,
With no less presence, but with much more love,   54
Than young Alcides when he did redeem   55
The virgin tribute paid by howling Troy   56
To the sea monster. I stand for sacrifice;   57
The rest aloof are the Dardanian wives,   58
With blearèd visages, come forth to view   59
The issue of th'exploit. Go, Hercules!   60
Live thou, I live. With much, much more dismay   61
I view the fight than thou that mak'st the fray.

   A song, the whilst Bassanio comments on the
   caskets to himself.

Tell me where is fancy bred,   63
Or in the heart or in the head?   64
How begot, how nourishèd?
      Reply, reply.
It is engendered in the eyes,   67
With gazing fed, and fancy dies
In the cradle where it lies.   69
      Let us all ring fancy's knell.
      I'll begin it—Ding, dong, bell.
ALL   Ding, dong, bell.
BASSANIO
So may the outward shows be least themselves;   73
The world is still deceived with ornament.   74
In law, what plea so tainted and corrupt
But, being seasoned with a gracious voice,
Obscures the show of evil? In religion,
What damnèd error but some sober brow   78
Will bless it and approve it with a text,   79
Hiding the grossness with fair ornament?
There is no vice so simple but assumes   81
Some mark of virtue on his outward parts.   82
How many cowards, whose hearts are all as false
As stairs of sand, wear yet upon their chins   84
The beards of Hercules and frowning Mars,
Who, inward searched, have livers white as milk?   86
And these assume but valor's excrement   87

---

12 So i.e., Forsworn.   **So may . . . me** That being the case, you may
fail to win me.   **15 o'erlooked** bewitched   **18 naughty** wicked
19 bars barriers   **20 though yours, not yours** (I am) yours by right but
not by actual possession.   **20–1 Prove . . . not I** i.e., If it turn out thus
(that you are cheated of what is justly yours, i.e., of me), let Fortune be
blamed for it, not I, for I will not be forsworn.   **22 peise** retard (by
hanging on of weights)   **23 eke it** stretch it out, make it last   **24 election** choice.   **26–7 confess What treason** (The rack was used to force
traitors to confess.)   **28 mistrust** misapprehension   **29 fear** fearful
about   **31 as** as between   **39 fortune . . . caskets** (Presumably the curtains are drawn at about this point, as in the previous "casket" scenes,
revealing the three caskets.)   **42 aloof** apart, at a distance.   **44 swanlike** (Swans were believed to sing when they came to die.)

49 flourish sounding of trumpets   **54 presence** noble bearing
55 Alcides Hercules (called *Alcides*, as at 2.1.32–5, because he was the
grandson of Alcaeus) rescued Hesione, daughter of the Trojan king
Laomedon, from a monster to which, by command of Neptune, she
was about to be sacrificed. Hercules was rewarded, however, not
with the lady's love, but with a famous pair of horses.   **56 howling**
lamenting   **57 stand for sacrifice** represent the sacrificial victim
58 Dardanian Trojan   **59 blearèd** tear-stained   **60 issue** outcome
61 Live thou If you live   **63 fancy** love   **64 Or** either   **67 eyes** (Love
entered the heart especially through the eyes.)   **69 In the cradle** i.e.,
in its infancy, in the eyes   **73 be least themselves** least represent the
inner reality   **74 still** ever   **78 sober brow** i.e., solemn-faced clergyman   **79 approve** confirm   **81 simple** unadulterated   **82 his** its
84 stairs steps   **86 searched** surgically probed.   **livers** (The liver was
thought to be the seat of courage; for it to be deserted by the blood
would be the condition of cowardice.)   **87 excrement** outgrowth,
here a beard

To render them redoubted. Look on beauty,   88
And you shall see 'tis purchased by the weight,   89
Which therein works a miracle in nature,
Making them lightest that wear most of it.   91
So are those crispèd, snaky, golden locks,   92
Which maketh such wanton gambols with the wind
Upon supposèd fairness, often known   94
To be the dowry of a second head,   95
The skull that bred them in the sepulcher.   96
Thus ornament is but the guilèd shore   97
To a most dangerous sea, the beauteous scarf
Veiling an Indian beauty; in a word,   99
The seeming truth which cunning times put on
To entrap the wisest. Therefore, thou gaudy gold,
Hard food for Midas, I will none of thee;   102
Nor none of thee, thou pale and common drudge   103
'Tween man and man. But thou, thou meager lead,   104
Which rather threaten'st than dost promise aught,
Thy paleness moves me more than eloquence;
And here choose I. Joy be the consequence!

PORTIA [*aside*]
How all the other passions fleet to air,
As doubtful thoughts, and rash-embraced despair,   109
And shuddering fear, and green-eyed jealousy!
O love, be moderate, allay thy ecstasy,
In measure rain thy joy, scant this excess!   112
I feel too much thy blessing. Make it less,
For fear I surfeit.

BASSANIO [*opening the leaden casket*]
                 What find I here?
Fair Portia's counterfeit! What demigod   115
Hath come so near creation? Move these eyes?
Or whether, riding on the balls of mine,
Seem they in motion? Here are severed lips,
Parted with sugar breath; so sweet a bar   119
Should sunder such sweet friends. Here in her hairs   120
The painter plays the spider, and hath woven
A golden mesh t'entrap the hearts of men
Faster than gnats in cobwebs. But her eyes—   123
How could he see to do them? Having made one,
Methinks it should have power to steal both his
And leave itself unfurnished. Yet look how far   126
The substance of my praise doth wrong this shadow   127
In underprizing it, so far this shadow   128
Doth limp behind the substance. Here's the scroll,   129

The continent and summary of my fortune.   130
[*He reads.*] "You that choose not by the view
          Chance as fair, and choose as true.   132
          Since this fortune falls to you,
          Be content and seek no new.
          If you be well pleased with this,
          And hold your fortune for your bliss,
          Turn you where your lady is
          And claim her with a loving kiss."
A gentle scroll. Fair lady, by your leave,
I come by note, to give and to receive.   140
Like one of two contending in a prize,   141
That thinks he hath done well in people's eyes,
Hearing applause and universal shout,
Giddy in spirit, still gazing in a doubt
Whether those peals of praise be his or no,   145
So, thrice-fair lady, stand I, even so,
As doubtful whether what I see be true,
Until confirmed, signed, ratified by you.

PORTIA
You see me, Lord Bassanio, where I stand,
Such as I am. Though for myself alone
I would not be ambitious in my wish
To wish myself much better, yet for you
I would be trebled twenty times myself,
A thousand times more fair, ten thousand times
      more rich,
That only to stand high in your account   155
I might in virtues, beauties, livings, friends,   156
Exceed account. But the full sum of me   157
Is sum of something, which, to term in gross,   158
Is an unlessoned girl, unschooled, unpracticèd;
Happy in this, she is not yet so old
But she may learn; happier than this,
She is not bred so dull but she can learn;
Happiest of all is that her gentle spirit
Commits itself to yours to be directed
As from her lord, her governor, her king.
Myself and what is mine to you and yours
Is now converted. But now I was the lord   167
Of this fair mansion, master of my servants,
Queen o'er myself; and even now, but now,
This house, these servants, and this same myself
Are yours, my lord's. I give them with this ring,
Which when you part from, lose, or give away,
Let it presage the ruin of your love
And be my vantage to exclaim on you.   174
                     [*She puts a ring on his finger.*]

BASSANIO
Madam, you have bereft me of all words.
Only my blood speaks to you in my veins,

---

88 redoubted feared.   **89 purchased by the weight** bought (as cosmetics) at so much per ounce   **91 lightest** most frivolous or lascivious. (With pun on the sense of "least heavy.")   **92 crispèd** curly   **94 Upon supposèd fairness** i.e., on a woman supposed beautiful and fair-haired   **95–6 To . . . sepulcher** i.e., to be a wig of hair taken from a woman now dead.   **97 guilèd** treacherous   **99 Indian** i.e., swarthy, not fair   **102 Midas** the Phrygian king whose touch turned everything to gold, including his food   **103–4 pale . . . man** i.e., silver, used in commerce.   **104 meager** wanting in richness   **109 As** such as   **112 rain** rain down, or perhaps "rein."   **scant** lessen   **115 counterfeit** portrait.   **demigod** i.e., the painter as creator   **119–20 so . . . friends** i.e., only so sweet a barrier as her mouth and breath should be allowed to part such sweet friends as her two lips.   **123 Faster** (1) more tightly (2) quicker   **126 unfurnished** i.e., without a companion.   **look how far** however far   **127 shadow** painting, semblance   **128 underprizing it** failing to do it justice.   **so far** to a similar extent   **129 the substance** the subject, i.e., Portia.

130 continent container   **132 Chance as fair** take your chances fortunately   **140 by note** by a bill of dues (i.e., the scroll). The commercial metaphor continues in *confirmed, signed, ratified* (line 148), *account* (155), *sum* (157), *term in gross* (158), etc.   **141 prize** competition   **145 his** for him   **155 account** estimation   **156 livings** possessions   **157 account** calculation. (Playing on *account*, estimation, in line 155.)   **157–8 But . . . something** i.e., But the full sum of my worth can only be the sum of whatever I am   **158 term in gross** denote in full   **167 But now** A moment ago   **174 vantage to exclaim on** opportunity to reproach

And there is such confusion in my powers
As, after some oration fairly spoke
By a belovèd prince, there doth appear
Among the buzzing pleasèd multitude,
Where every something being blent together   181
Turns to a wild of nothing save of joy   182
Expressed and not expressed. But when this ring 183
Parts from this finger, then parts life from hence.
Oh, then be bold to say Bassanio's dead!

NERISSA
My lord and lady, it is now our time,
That have stood by and seen our wishes prosper, 187
To cry, "good joy." Good joy, my lord and lady!

GRATIANO
My lord Bassanio and my gentle lady,
I wish you all the joy that you can wish—
For I am sure you can wish none from me.   191
And when Your Honors mean to solemnize
The bargain of your faith, I do beseech you
Even at that time I may be married too.

BASSANIO
With all my heart, so thou canst get a wife.   195

GRATIANO
I thank Your Lordship, you have got me one.
My eyes, my lord, can look as swift as yours.
You saw the mistress, I beheld the maid;   198
You loved, I loved; for intermission   199
No more pertains to me, my lord, than you.
Your fortune stood upon the caskets there,
And so did mine too, as the matter falls;   202
For wooing here until I sweat again,   203
And swearing till my very roof was dry   204
With oaths of love, at last, if promise last,   205
I got a promise of this fair one here
To have her love, provided that your fortune
Achieved her mistress.

PORTIA   Is this true, Nerissa?

NERISSA
Madam, it is, so you stand pleased withal.   209

BASSANIO
And do you, Gratiano, mean good faith?

GRATIANO   Yes, faith, my lord.

BASSANIO
Our feast shall be much honored in your marriage.

GRATIANO   We'll play with them the first boy for a thou- 213
sand ducats.

NERISSA   What, and stake down?   215

GRATIANO   No, we shall ne'er win at that sport, and 177
stake down.

Enter Lorenzo, Jessica, and Salerio, a messenger
from Venice.

But who comes here? Lorenzo and his infidel?
What, and my old Venetian friend Salerio?

BASSANIO
Lorenzo and Salerio, welcome hither,
If that the youth of my new interest here   221
Have power to bid you welcome.—By your leave,
I bid my very friends and countrymen,   223
Sweet Portia, welcome.

PORTIA   So do I, my lord.
They are entirely welcome.

LORENZO
I thank Your Honor. For my part, my lord,
My purpose was not to have seen you here,
But, meeting with Salerio by the way,
He did entreat me, past all saying nay,
To come with him along.

SALERIO   I did, my lord,
And I have reason for it. Signor Antonio
Commends him to you.   [*He gives Bassanio a letter.*]

BASSANIO   Ere I ope his letter,   232
I pray you tell me how my good friend doth.

SALERIO
Not sick, my lord, unless it be in mind,
Nor well, unless in mind. His letter there
Will show you his estate.   [*Bassanio*] *open*[*s*] *the letter.* 236

GRATIANO [*indicating Jessica*]
Nerissa, cheer yond stranger, bid her welcome.   237
Your hand, Salerio. What's the news from Venice?
How doth that royal merchant, good Antonio?   239
I know he will be glad of our success.
We are the Jasons; we have won the fleece.   241

SALERIO
I would you had won the fleece that he hath lost.

PORTIA
There are some shrewd contents in yond same paper 243
That steals the color from Bassanio's cheek—
Some dear friend dead, else nothing in the world
Could turn so much the constitution
Of any constant man. What, worse and worse?   247
With leave, Bassanio; I am half yourself,   248
And I must freely have the half of anything
That this same paper brings you.

BASSANIO   O sweet Portia,
Here are a few of the unpleasant'st words
That ever blotted paper! Gentle lady,
When I did first impart my love to you,
I freely told you all the wealth I had
Ran in my veins, I was a gentleman;
And then I told you true. And yet, dear lady,

---

177 **powers** faculties   181–3 **Where . . . expressed** i.e., in which every individual utterance, being blended and confused, turns into a hub-bub of joy.   187 **That** we who   191 **For . . . me** i.e., I'm sure I can't wish you any more joy than you could wish for yourselves, or, I'm sure your wishes for happiness cannot take away from my happiness. 195 **so** provided   198 **maid** (Nerissa is a lady-in-waiting, not a house servant.)   199 **intermission** delay (in loving)   202 **falls** falls out, happens   203 **sweat again** sweated repeatedly   204 **roof** roof of my mouth   205 **if promise last** i.e., if Nerissa's promise should last, hold out. (With a play on *last* and *at last*, "finally.")   209 **so** provided 213 **We'll . . . boy** We'll wager with them to see who has the first male heir   215 **stake down** cash placed in advance. (But Gratiano, in his reply, turns the phrase into a bawdy joke; *stake down* to him suggests a non-erect phallus.)

221 **youth . . . interest** i.e., newness of my household authority 223 **very** true   232 **Commends him** desires to be remembered 236 **estate** situation.   237 **stranger** alien   239 **royal merchant** i.e., chief among merchants   241 **Jasons . . . fleece** (Compare with 1.1.170–2.)   243 **shrewd** cursed, grievous   247 **constant** settled, not swayed by passion   248 **With leave** With your permission

Rating myself at nothing, you shall see
How much I was a braggart. When I told you
My state was nothing, I should then have told you   259
That I was worse than nothing; for indeed
I have engaged myself to a dear friend,
Engaged my friend to his mere enemy,   262
To feed my means. Here is a letter, lady,
The paper as the body of my friend,
And every word in it a gaping wound
Issuing lifeblood. But is it true, Salerio?
Hath all his ventures failed? What, not one hit?   267
From Tripolis, from Mexico, and England,
From Lisbon, Barbary, and India,
And not one vessel scape the dreadful touch
Of merchant-marring rocks?

SALERIO   Not one, my lord.   271
Besides, it should appear that if he had
The present money to discharge the Jew   273
He would not take it. Never did I know   274
A creature that did bear the shape of man
So keen and greedy to confound a man.   276
He plies the Duke at morning and at night,
And doth impeach the freedom of the state   278
If they deny him justice. Twenty merchants,
The Duke himself, and the magnificoes   280
Of greatest port have all persuaded with him,   281
But none can drive him from the envious plea   282
Of forfeiture, of justice, and his bond.

JESSICA
When I was with him I have heard him swear
To Tubal and to Chus, his countrymen,   285
That he would rather have Antonio's flesh
Than twenty times the value of the sum
That he did owe him; and I know, my lord,
If law, authority, and power deny not,
It will go hard with poor Antonio.

PORTIA [to Bassanio]
Is it your dear friend that is thus in trouble?

BASSANIO
The dearest friend to me, the kindest man,
The best-conditioned and unwearied spirit   293
In doing courtesies, and one in whom
The ancient Roman honor more appears
Than any that draws breath in Italy.

PORTIA   What sum owes he the Jew?

BASSANIO
For me, three thousand ducats.

PORTIA   What, no more?
Pay him six thousand, and deface the bond;   299
Double six thousand, and then treble that,
Before a friend of this description

Shall lose a hair through Bassanio's fault.
First go with me to church and call me wife,
And then away to Venice to your friend;
For never shall you lie by Portia's side
With an unquiet soul. You shall have gold
To pay the petty debt twenty times over.
When it is paid, bring your true friend along.
My maid Nerissa and myself meantime
Will live as maids and widows. Come, away!
For you shall hence upon your wedding day.
Bid your friends welcome, show a merry cheer;   312
Since you are dear bought, I will love you dear.   313
But let me hear the letter of your friend.

BASSANIO [reads]   "Sweet Bassanio, my ships have all
miscarried, my creditors grow cruel, my estate is
very low, my bond to the Jew is forfeit; and since in
paying it, it is impossible I should live, all debts are
cleared between you and I if I might but see you at
my death. Notwithstanding, use your pleasure. If
your love do not persuade you to come, let not my
letter."

PORTIA
O love, dispatch all business, and begone!

BASSANIO
Since I have your good leave to go away,
I will make haste; but till I come again
No bed shall e'er be guilty of my stay,
Nor rest be interposer twixt us twain.   Exeunt.

❖

[3.3]

*Enter [Shylock] the Jew and Solanio and Antonio
and the Jailer.*

SHYLOCK
Jailer, look to him. Tell not me of mercy.
This is the fool that lent out money gratis.   2
Jailer, look to him.

ANTONIO   Hear me yet, good Shylock.

SHYLOCK
I'll have my bond. Speak not against my bond.
I have sworn an oath that I will have my bond.
Thou called'st me dog before thou hadst a cause,
But since I am a dog, beware my fangs.
The Duke shall grant me justice. I do wonder,
Thou naughty jailer, that thou art so fond   9
To come abroad with him at his request.   10

ANTONIO   I pray thee, hear me speak.

SHYLOCK
I'll have my bond. I will not hear thee speak.
I'll have my bond, and therefore speak no more.
I'll not be made a soft and dull-eyed fool,   14
To shake the head, relent, and sigh, and yield
To Christian intercessors. Follow not.
I'll have no speaking. I will have my bond.   *Exit Jew.*

---

259 **state** estate   262 **mere** absolute   267 **hit** success.   271 **merchant-marring** capable of damaging a merchant ship   273 **present** available. **discharge** pay off   274 **He** i.e., Shylock   276 **confound** destroy   278 **doth . . . state** i.e., calls in question the ability of Venice to defend legally the freedom of commerce of its citizens   280 **magnificoes** chief men of Venice   281 **port** dignity.   **persuaded** argued   282 **envious** malicious   285 **Chus** the Bishops' Bible spelling of *Cush*, son of Ham and grandson of Noah. *Tubal* was son of Japheth and grandson of Noah (Genesis 10:2, 6).   293 **best-conditioned** best-natured   299 **deface** erase

312 **cheer** countenance   313 **dear . . . dear** at great cost . . . dearly.
3.3. Location: Venice. A street.
2 **gratis** free (of interest).   9 **naughty** worthless, wicked.   **fond** foolish   10 **abroad** outside   14 **dull-eyed** easily duped

SOLANIO
　　It is the most impenetrable cur
　　That ever kept with men.

ANTONIO　　　　　　　　　　Let him alone.　　　　19
　　I'll follow him no more with bootless prayers.　　20
　　He seeks my life. His reason well I know:
　　I oft delivered from his forfeitures
　　Many that have at times made moan to me;
　　Therefore he hates me.

SOLANIO　　　　　　　　　I am sure the Duke
　　Will never grant this forfeiture to hold.

ANTONIO
　　The Duke cannot deny the course of law;
　　For the commodity that strangers have　　　　27
　　With us in Venice, if it be denied,
　　Will much impeach the justice of the state,
　　Since that the trade and profit of the city　　30
　　Consisteth of all nations. Therefore go.
　　These griefs and losses have so bated me　　32
　　That I shall hardly spare a pound of flesh
　　Tomorrow to my bloody creditor.—
　　Well, jailer, on. Pray God Bassanio come
　　To see me pay his debt, and then I care not.　　*Exeunt.*

❧

[3.4]

*Enter Portia, Nerissa, Lorenzo, Jessica, and
[Balthasar,] a man of Portia's.*

LORENZO
　　Madam, although I speak it in your presence,
　　You have a noble and a true conceit　　　　2
　　Of godlike amity, which appears most strongly　　3
　　In bearing thus the absence of your lord.
　　But if you knew to whom you show this honor,　　5
　　How true a gentleman you send relief,
　　How dear a lover of my lord your husband,　　7
　　I know you would be prouder of the work
　　Than customary bounty can enforce you.　　　　9

PORTIA
　　I never did repent for doing good,
　　Nor shall not now; for in companions
　　That do converse and waste the time together,　　12
　　Whose souls do bear an equal yoke of love,
　　There must be needs a like proportion　　　　14
　　Of lineaments, of manners, and of spirit;　　15
　　Which makes me think that this Antonio,
　　Being the bosom lover of my lord,　　　　17
　　Must needs be like my lord. If it be so,
　　How little is the cost I have bestowed
　　In purchasing the semblance of my soul　　20

From out the state of hellish cruelty!　　　　21
This comes too near the praising of myself;
Therefore no more of it. Hear other things:
Lorenzo, I commit into your hands
The husbandry and manage of my house　　25
Until my lord's return. For mine own part,
I have toward heaven breathed a secret vow
To live in prayer and contemplation,
Only attended by Nerissa here,
Until her husband and my lord's return.
There is a monastery two miles off,
And there we will abide. I do desire you
Not to deny this imposition,　　　　33
The which my love and some necessity
Now lays upon you.

LORENZO　　　　　　Madam, with all my heart,
　　I shall obey you in all fair commands.

PORTIA
　　My people do already know my mind,　　37
　　And will acknowledge you and Jessica
　　In place of Lord Bassanio and myself.
　　So fare you well till we shall meet again.

LORENZO
　　Fair thoughts and happy hours attend on you!

JESSICA
　　I wish Your Ladyship all heart's content.

PORTIA
　　I thank you for your wish and am well pleased
　　To wish it back on you. Fare you well, Jessica.
　　　　　　　　　　　　Exeunt [Jessica and Lorenzo].
　　Now, Balthasar,
　　As I have ever found thee honest-true,
　　So let me find thee still. Take this same letter,
　　　　　　　　　　　　　　　　[giving a letter]
　　And use thou all th'endeavor of a man
　　In speed to Padua. See thou render this
　　Into my cousin's hands, Doctor Bellario;
　　And look what notes and garments he doth give thee,　51
　　Bring them, I pray thee, with imagined speed　　52
　　Unto the traject, to the common ferry　　53
　　Which trades to Venice. Waste no time in words,　54
　　But get thee gone. I shall be there before thee.

BALTHASAR
　　Madam, I go with all convenient speed.　　*[Exit.]*

PORTIA
　　Come on, Nerissa, I have work in hand
　　That you yet know not of. We'll see our husbands
　　Before they think of us.

NERISSA　　　　　　　　Shall they see us?

PORTIA
　　They shall, Nerissa, but in such a habit　　60
　　That they shall think we are accomplishèd　　61
　　With that we lack. I'll hold thee any wager,　　62

---

19 kept associated, dwelt　**20 bootless** unavailing　**27 commodity** facilities or privileges for trading.　**strangers** noncitizens, including Jews　**30 Since that** since　**32 bated** reduced
3.4. Location: Belmont. Portia's house.
2 conceit understanding　**3 amity** friendship and love　**5 to whom . . . honor** i.e., Antonio, who you honor by sending money to relieve him　**7 lover** friend　**9 Than . . . you** than ordinary benevolence can make you.　**12 waste** spend　**14 must be needs** must be　**15 lineaments** physical features　**17 bosom lover** dear friend　**20 the semblance of my soul** i.e., Antonio, so like my Bassanio.

---

21 From . . . cruelty from the cruel state in which he presently stands.
25 husbandry and manage care and management　**33 deny this imposition** refuse this charge imposed　**37 people** servants　**51 look what** whatever　**52 imagined** all imaginable　**53 traject** ferry. (Italian *traghetto*.)　**common** public　**54 trades** plies back and forth　**60 habit** apparel, garb　**61 accomplishèd** supplied　**62 that** that which. (With a bawdy suggestion.)

When we are both accoutered like young men
I'll prove the prettier fellow of the two,
And wear my dagger with the braver grace,
And speak between the change of man and boy
With a reed voice, and turn two mincing steps
Into a manly stride, and speak of frays
Like a fine bragging youth, and tell quaint lies,   69
How honorable ladies sought my love,
Which I denying, they fell sick and died—
I could not do withal! Then I'll repent,   72
And wish, for all that, that I had not killed them;
And twenty of these puny lies I'll tell,   74
That men shall swear I have discontinued school   75
Above a twelvemonth. I have within my mind   76
A thousand raw tricks of these bragging Jacks,   77
Which I will practice.
NERISSA   Why, shall we turn to men?   78
PORTIA   Fie, what a question's that,
If thou wert near a lewd interpreter!
But come, I'll tell thee all my whole device   81
When I am in my coach, which stays for us
At the park gate; and therefore haste away,
For we must measure twenty miles today.   *Exeunt.*   84

❖

[3.5]

Enter [Lancelot the] clown and Jessica.

LANCELOT   Yes, truly, for look you, the sins of the father are to be laid upon the children; therefore, I prom-   2
ise you, I fear you. I was always plain with you, and   3
so now I speak my agitation of the matter. Therefore   4
be o' good cheer, for truly I think you are damned.
There is but one hope in it that can do you any good,
and that is but a kind of bastard hope, neither.   7
JESSICA   And what hope is that, I pray thee?
LANCELOT   Marry, you may partly hope that your father got you not, that you are not the Jew's daughter.   10
JESSICA   That were a kind of bastard hope, indeed! So
the sins of my mother should be visited upon me.
LANCELOT   Truly, then, I fear you are damned both by
father and mother. Thus when I shun Scylla, your   14
father, I fall into Charybdis, your mother. Well, you   15
are gone both ways.   16
JESSICA   I shall be saved by my husband. He hath made   17
me a Christian.

LANCELOT   Truly, the more to blame he! We were   19
Christians enough before, e'en as many as could well   20
live one by another. This making of Christians will   21
raise the price of hogs. If we grow all to be pork eaters,
we shall not shortly have a rasher on the coals for   23
money.   24

Enter Lorenzo.

JESSICA   I'll tell my husband, Lancelot, what you say.
Here he comes.
LORENZO   I shall grow jealous of you shortly, Lancelot,
if you thus get my wife into corners.
JESSICA   Nay, you need not fear us, Lorenzo. Lancelot
and I are out. He tells me flatly there's no mercy for me   30
in heaven because I am a Jew's daughter; and he says
you are no good member of the commonwealth, for in
converting Jews to Christians you raise the price of
pork.
LORENZO [*to Lancelot*]   I shall answer that better to the
commonwealth than you can the getting up of the
Negro's belly. The Moor is with child by you, Lancelot.   37
LANCELOT   It is much that the Moor should be more   38
than reason; but if she be less than an honest woman,   39
she is indeed more than I took her for.   40
LORENZO   How every fool can play upon the word! I
think the best grace of wit will shortly turn into   42
silence, and discourse grow commendable in none
only but parrots. Go in, sirrah, bid them prepare for
dinner.
LANCELOT   That is done, sir. They have all stomachs.   46
LORENZO   Goodly Lord, what a wit-snapper are you!
Then bid them prepare dinner.
LANCELOT   That is done too, sir, only "cover" is the   49
word.
LORENZO   Will you cover then, sir?   51
LANCELOT   Not so, sir, neither. I know my duty.   52
LORENZO   Yet more quarreling with occasion! Wilt thou 53
show the whole wealth of thy wit in an instant? I pray
thee, understand a plain man in his plain meaning: go
to thy fellows, bid them cover the table, serve in the
meat, and we will come in to dinner.   57
LANCELOT   For the table, sir, it shall be served in; for the   58
meat, sir, it shall be covered; for your coming in to   59

---

69 **quaint** elaborate, clever   72 **do withal** help it.   74 **puny** childish
75–6 **I . . . twelvemonth** i.e., that I am no mere schoolboy.   76 **Above**
more than   77 **Jacks** fellows   78 **turn to** turn into. (But Portia sees
the occasion for a bawdy quibble on the idea of "turning toward,
lying next to.")   81 **device** plan   84 **measure** traverse
3.5. Location: Belmont. Outside Portia's house.
2–3 **promise** assure   3 **fear you** fear for you.   4 **my agitation of** my
sense of agitation about   7 **bastard** i.e., unfounded. (But also anticipating the usual meaning in lines 9–10.)   **neither** i.e., to be sure.
10 **got** begot   14, 15 **Scylla, Charybdis** twin dangers of the *Odyssey*,
12.255, a monster and a whirlpool guarding the straits presumably
between Italy and Sicily. (*Fall into* plays on the idea of entering the
female sexual anatomy.)   16 **gone** done for   17 **I . . . husband**
(Compare 1 Corinthians 7:14: "the unbelieving wife is sanctified by
the husband.")

19–20 **We . . . enough** There were enough of us Christians   21 **one by**
another (1) as neighbors (2) off one another.   23 **rasher** i.e., of bacon
23–4 **for money** even for ready money, at any price.   30 **are out** have
fallen out.   37 **The Moor** (Lancelot has evidently impregnated some
woman of the household, who, being of African heritage, is referred
to as both "Negro" and "Moor.")   38–40 **It is . . . for** i.e., It is a matter
of concern that the Moor is larger (being pregnant) than usual, larger
than she should be; but if it turns out that she is less than perfectly
chaste, she is something more than I originally supposed. (Lancelot
professes to be surprised by what has happened. With wordplay on
less/more and *more/Moor*.)   42 **the best . . . wit** true wittiness   46 **They**
. . . stomachs The guests all have appetites, and are prepared in that
sense. (Lancelot quibbles with Lorenzo's meaning that the cooks and
servants should be told to get dinner ready.)   49, 51 **cover** spread the
table for the meal. (But in line 52 Lancelot uses the word to mean
"put on one's hat.")   52 **my duty** i.e., my duty to remain bareheaded.
53 **Yet . . . occasion!** i.e., Still quibbling at every opportunity!
57 **meat** food   58 **For** As for.   **table** (Here Lancelot quibblingly uses
the word to mean the food itself.)   59 **covered** (Here used in the
sense of providing a cover for each separate dish.)

dinner, sir, why, let it be as humors and conceits shall   60
govern.   *Exit [Lancelot the] clown.*

LORENZO
Oh, dear discretion, how his words are suited!   62
The fool hath planted in his memory
An army of good words; and I do know
A many fools, that stand in better place,   65
Garnished like him, that for a tricksy word   66
Defy the matter. How cheer'st thou, Jessica?   67
And now, good sweet, say thy opinion:
How dost thou like the Lord Bassanio's wife?

JESSICA
Past all expressing. It is very meet   70
The Lord Bassanio live an upright life,
For, having such a blessing in his lady,
He finds the joys of heaven here on earth;
And if on earth he do not merit it,
In reason he should never come to heaven.   75
Why, if two gods should play some heavenly match
And on the wager lay two earthly women,   77
And Portia one, there must be something else   78
Pawned with the other, for the poor rude world   79
Hath not her fellow.

LORENZO   Even such a husband   80
Hast thou of me as she is for a wife.

JESSICA
Nay, but ask my opinion too of that!

LORENZO
I will anon. First let us go to dinner.

JESSICA
Nay, let me praise you while I have a stomach.   84

LORENZO
No, pray thee, let it serve for table talk;
Then, howsome'er thou speak'st, 'mong other things
I shall digest it.

JESSICA   Well, I'll set you forth.   *Exeunt.*   87

✤

[4.1]

Enter the Duke, the Magnificoes, Antonio, Bas-sanio, [Salerio,] and Gratiano [with others. The judges take their places.]

DUKE   What, is Antonio here?
ANTONIO   Ready, so please Your Grace.

DUKE
I am sorry for thee. Thou art come to answer   3
A stony adversary, an inhuman wretch
Uncapable of pity, void and empty
From any dram of mercy.

ANTONIO   I have heard   6
Your Grace hath ta'en great pains to qualify   7
His rigorous course; but since he stands obdurate
And that no lawful means can carry me
Out of his envy's reach, I do oppose   10
My patience to his fury and am armed
To suffer with a quietness of spirit
The very tyranny and rage of his.   13

DUKE
Go one, and call the Jew into the court.

SALERIO
He is ready at the door. He comes, my lord.

Enter Shylock.

DUKE
Make room, and let him stand before our face.—   16
Shylock, the world thinks, and I think so too,
That thou but leadest this fashion of thy malice   18
To the last hour of act, and then 'tis thought   19
Thou'lt show thy mercy and remorse more strange   20
Than is thy strange apparent cruelty;   21
And where thou now exacts the penalty,
Which is a pound of this poor merchant's flesh,
Thou wilt not only loose the forfeiture,   24
But, touched with human gentleness and love,
Forgive a moiety of the principal,   26
Glancing an eye of pity on his losses
That have of late so huddled on his back—
Enough to press a royal merchant down
And pluck commiseration of his state   30
From brassy bosoms and rough hearts of flint,   31
From stubborn Turks and Tartars never trained
To offices of tender courtesy.
We all expect a gentle answer, Jew.

SHYLOCK
I have possessed Your Grace of what I purpose,   35
And by our holy Sabbath have I sworn
To have the due and forfeit of my bond.
If you deny it, let the danger light   38
Upon your charter and your city's freedom!   39
You'll ask me why I rather choose to have
A weight of carrion flesh than to receive
Three thousand ducats. I'll not answer that,
But say it is my humor. Is it answered?   43
What if my house be troubled with a rat
And I be pleased to give ten thousand ducats

---

60 **humors and conceits** whims and fancies   62 **Oh, dear discretion** Oh, what precious discrimination.   **suited** suited to the occasion   65 **A many** many.   **better place** higher social station   66 **Garnished** i.e., furnished with words, or with garments   66–7 **that . . . matter** who for the sake of ingenious wordplay torture the plain meaning.   67 **How cheer'st thou** i.e., What cheer, how are you doing   70 **meet** fitting   75 **In reason** It stands to reason. (Jessica jokes that for Bassanio to receive unmerited bliss on earth—unmerited because no person can earn bliss through his or her own deserving—is to run the risk of eternal damnation.)   77 **lay** stake   78 **else** more   79 **Pawned** staked, wagered   80 **fellow** equal.   84 **stomach** (1) appetite (2) inclination.   87 **digest** (1) ponder, analyze (2) "swallow," put up with. (With a play also on the gastronomic sense.)   **set you forth** (1) serve you up, as at a feast (2) set forth your praises.
4.1. Location: Venice. A court of justice. Benches, etc., are provided for the justices.

3 **answer** defend yourself against. (A legal term.)   6 **dram** sixty grains apothecaries' weight, a tiny quantity   7 **qualify** moderate   10 **envy's** malice's   13 **tyranny** cruelty   16 **our** (The royal plural.)   18 **That . . . fashion** that you only maintain this pretense or form   19 **the last . . . act** the brink of action   20 **remorse** pity.   **strange** remarkable   21 **strange** unnatural, foreign.   **apparent** (1) manifest, overt (2) seeming   24 **loose** release, waive   26 **moiety** part, portion   30 **of** for   31 **brassy** unfeeling, hard like brass   35 **possessed** informed   38 **danger** injury   39 **Upon . . . freedom** (See 3.2.278.)   43 **humor** whim.

To have it baned? What, are you answered yet?   46
Some men there are love not a gaping pig,   47
Some that are mad if they behold a cat,
And others, when the bagpipe sings i'th' nose,
Cannot contain their urine; for affection,   50
Mistress of passion, sways it to the mood
Of what it likes or loathes. Now, for your answer:
As there is no firm reason to be rendered
Why he cannot abide a gaping pig,   54
Why he a harmless necessary cat,   55
Why he a woolen bagpipe, but of force   56
Must yield to such inevitable shame
As to offend, himself being offended,
So can I give no reason, nor I will not,
More than a lodged hate and a certain loathing   60
I bear Antonio, that I follow thus
A losing suit against him. Are you answered?   62

BASSANIO
This is no answer, thou unfeeling man,
To excuse the current of thy cruelty.   64

SHYLOCK
I am not bound to please thee with my answers.

BASSANIO
Do all men kill the things they do not love?

SHYLOCK
Hates any man the thing he would not kill?

BASSANIO
Every offense is not a hate at first.

SHYLOCK
What, wouldst thou have a serpent sting thee twice?

ANTONIO
I pray you, think you question with the Jew.   70
You may as well go stand upon the beach
And bid the main flood bate his usual height;   72
You may as well use question with the wolf   73
Why he hath made the ewe bleat for the lamb;
You may as well forbid the mountain pines
To wag their high tops and to make no noise
When they are fretten with the gusts of heaven;   77
You may as well do anything most hard
As seek to soften that—than which what's harder?—
His Jewish heart. Therefore, I do beseech you,
Make no more offers, use no farther means,
But with all brief and plain conveniency
Let me have judgment, and the Jew his will.

BASSANIO [to Shylock]
For thy three thousand ducats here is six.

SHYLOCK
If every ducat in six thousand ducats
Were in six parts, and every part a ducat,
I would not draw them. I would have my bond.   87

DUKE
How shalt thou hope for mercy, rendering none?

SHYLOCK
What judgment shall I dread, doing no wrong?   89
You have among you many a purchased slave,
Which, like your asses and your dogs and mules,
You use in abject and in slavish parts,   92
Because you bought them. Shall I say to you,
"Let them be free, marry them to your heirs!
Why sweat they under burdens? Let their beds
Be made as soft as yours, and let their palates
Be seasoned with such viands"? You will answer   97
"The slaves are ours." So do I answer you:
The pound of flesh which I demand of him
Is dearly bought, is mine, and I will have it.
If you deny me, fie upon your law!
There is no force in the decrees of Venice.
I stand for judgment. Answer: shall I have it?

DUKE
Upon my power I may dismiss this court,   104
Unless Bellario, a learnèd doctor,   105
Whom I have sent for to determine this,   106
Come here today.

SALERIO   My lord, here stays without   107
A messenger with letters from the doctor,
New come from Padua.

DUKE
Bring us the letters. Call the messenger.   [Exit one.]

BASSANIO
Good cheer, Antonio. What, man, courage yet!
The Jew shall have my flesh, blood, bones, and all,
Ere thou shalt lose for me one drop of blood.

ANTONIO
I am a tainted wether of the flock,   114
Meetest for death. The weakest kind of fruit   115
Drops earliest to the ground, and so let me.
You cannot better be employed, Bassanio,
Than to live still and write mine epitaph.

Enter Nerissa [dressed like a lawyer's clerk].

DUKE
Came you from Padua, from Bellario?

NERISSA
From both, my lord. Bellario greets Your Grace.
[She presents a letter. Shylock whets his knife on his shoe.]

BASSANIO
Why dost thou whet thy knife so earnestly?

SHYLOCK
To cut the forfeiture from that bankrupt there.

GRATIANO
Not on thy sole, but on thy soul, harsh Jew,
Thou mak'st thy knife keen; but no metal can,
No, not the hangman's ax, bear half the keenness   125
Of thy sharp envy. Can no prayers pierce thee?   126

---

46 baned poisoned   **47 love** who love.   **gaping pig** pig roasted whole with its mouth open   **50 affection** feeling, desire   **54, 55, 56 he, he, he** one person, another, yet another   **55 necessary** i.e., useful for catching rats and mice   **56 woolen** i.e., with flannel-covered bag   **60 lodged** settled, steadfast.   **certain** unwavering, fixed   **62 losing** unprofitable   **64 current** flow, tendency   **70 think** bear in mind. **question** argue   **72 And . . . height** and bid the ocean put an end to its usual high tide   **73 use question with** interrogate   **77 fretten** fretted, i.e., disturbed, ruffled   **87 draw** receive

89 wrong legal wrong.   **92 parts** duties, capacities   **97 such viands** food such as you eat.   **104 Upon** In accordance with   **105 doctor** person of learning. (Here, of law.)   **106 determine this** resolve this legal dispute   **107 stays without** waits outside   **114 wether** ram, especially a castrated ram   **115 Meetest** fittest   **125 hangman's** executioner's.   **keenness** (1) sharpness (2) savagery   **126 envy** malice.

SHYLOCK
No, none that thou hast wit enough to make.

GRATIANO
Oh, be thou damned, inexecrable dog,   128
And for thy life let Justice be accused!   129
Thou almost mak'st me waver in my faith
To hold opinion with Pythagoras   131
That souls of animals infuse themselves
Into the trunks of men. Thy currish spirit
Governed a wolf who, hanged for human slaughter,   134
Even from the gallows did his fell soul fleet,   135
And, whilst thou layest in thy unhallowed dam,   136
Infused itself in thee; for thy desires
Are wolvish, bloody, starved, and ravenous.

SHYLOCK
Till thou canst rail the seal from off my bond,   139
Thou but offend'st thy lungs to speak so loud.   140
Repair thy wit, good youth, or it will fall
To cureless ruin. I stand here for law.   142

DUKE
This letter from Bellario doth commend
A young and learnèd doctor to our court.
Where is he?

NERISSA   He attendeth here hard by
To know your answer, whether you'll admit him.

DUKE
With all my heart. Some three or four of you
Go give him courteous conduct to this place.
                              [*Exeunt some.*]
Meantime the court shall hear Bellario's letter.
[*He reads.*] "Your Grace shall understand that at the   150
receipt of your letter I am very sick; but in the instant
that your messenger came, in loving visitation was
with me a young doctor of Rome. His name is Balthasar. I acquainted him with the cause in controversy
between the Jew and Antonio the merchant. We
turned o'er many books together. He is furnished with
my opinion, which, bettered with his own learning,
the greatness whereof I cannot enough commend,
comes with him, at my importunity, to fill up Your   159
Grace's request in my stead. I beseech you, let his lack
of years be no impediment to let him lack a reverend   161
estimation, for I never knew so young a body with so
old a head. I leave him to your gracious acceptance,
whose trial shall better publish his commendation."   164

     Enter Portia for Balthasar [*dressed like a doctor
     of laws, escorted*].

128 **inexecrable** thoroughly execrable   **129 And . . . accused!** and may
Justice herself be accused for allowing you to live!   **131 Pythagoras**
ancient Greek philosopher who argued for the transmigration of souls
134 hanged for human slaughter (A possible allusion to the Elizabethan practice of trying and punishing animals for various crimes.)
135 fell fierce, cruel.   **fleet** flit, i.e., pass from the body   **136 dam**
mother. (Usually used of animals.)   **139 rail** remove by your abusive
language   **140 Thou but offend'st** you merely injure   **142 cureless**
incurable   **150 [He reads.]** (In many modern editions, the reading of
the letter is assigned to a clerk, but the original text gives no such indication.)   **159 comes with him** accompanies him in the form of my
learned opinion.   **importunity** insistence   **161 to let him lack** such as
would deprive him of   **164 whose . . . commendation** the demonstration of whose excellence will proclaim what is commendable in him
better than my letter can.   **164.1 for** i.e., disguised as

You hear the learn'd Bellario, what he writes;
And here, I take it, is the doctor come.—
Give me your hand. Come you from old Bellario?

PORTIA
I did, my lord.

DUKE   You are welcome. Take your place.
                              [*Portia takes her place.*]
Are you acquainted with the difference   169
That holds this present question in the court?

PORTIA
I am informèd throughly of the cause.   171
Which is the merchant here, and which the Jew?

DUKE
Antonio and old Shylock, both stand forth.
             [*Antonio and Shylock stand forth.*]

PORTIA
Is your name Shylock?

SHYLOCK   Shylock is my name.

PORTIA
Of a strange nature is the suit you follow,
Yet in such rule that the Venetian law   176
Cannot impugn you as you do proceed.—   177
You stand within his danger, do you not?

ANTONIO
Ay, so he says.

PORTIA   Do you confess the bond?

ANTONIO
I do.

PORTIA   Then must the Jew be merciful.

SHYLOCK
On what compulsion must I? Tell me that.

PORTIA
The quality of mercy is not strained.   182
It droppeth as the gentle rain from heaven
Upon the place beneath. It is twice blest: 184
It blesseth him that gives and him that takes.
'Tis mightiest in the mightiest; it becomes
The thronèd monarch better than his crown.
His scepter shows the force of temporal power,   188
The attribute to awe and majesty,   189
Wherein doth sit the dread and fear of kings.
But mercy is above this sceptered sway;
It is enthronèd in the hearts of kings;
It is an attribute to God himself;
And earthly power doth then show likest God's
When mercy seasons justice. Therefore, Jew,
Though justice be thy plea, consider this,
That in the course of justice none of us   197
Should see salvation. We do pray for mercy,
And that same prayer doth teach us all to render
The deeds of mercy. I have spoke thus much
To mitigate the justice of thy plea,   201
Which if thou follow, this strict court of Venice
Must needs give sentence 'gainst the merchant there.

169 **difference** argument   **171 throughly** thoroughly.   **cause** case.
176 rule order   **177 impugn** find fault with   **182 strained** forced,
constrained.   **184 is twice blest** grants a double blessing   **188 His**
i.e., The monarch's   **189 attribute to** symbol of   **197 justice** divine
justice   **201 To . . . plea** i.e., to show the way in which your call for
justice needs to be mitigated or reduced in severity

SHYLOCK
My deeds upon my head! I crave the law,   204
The penalty and forfeit of my bond.
PORTIA
Is he not able to discharge the money?
BASSANIO
Yes, here I tender it for him in the court,
Yea, twice the sum. If that will not suffice,
I will be bound to pay it ten times o'er,
On forfeit of my hands, my head, my heart.
If this will not suffice, it must appear
That malice bears down truth. And I beseech you,   212
Wrest once the law to your authority.   213
To do a great right, do a little wrong,
And curb this cruel devil of his will.
PORTIA
It must not be. There is no power in Venice
Can alter a decree establishèd.
'Twill be recorded for a precedent,
And many an error by the same example
Will rush into the state. It cannot be.
SHYLOCK
A Daniel come to judgment! Yea, a Daniel!   221
O wise young judge, how I do honor thee!
PORTIA
I pray you, let me look upon the bond.
SHYLOCK [giving the bond]
Here 'tis, most reverend doctor, here it is.
PORTIA
Shylock, there's thrice thy money offered thee.
SHYLOCK
An oath, an oath! I have an oath in heaven.
Shall I lay perjury upon my soul?
No, not for Venice.
PORTIA   Why, this bond is forfeit,
And lawfully by this the Jew may claim
A pound of flesh, to be by him cut off
Nearest the merchant's heart.—Be merciful.
Take thrice thy money; bid me tear the bond.
SHYLOCK
When it is paid according to the tenor.   233
It doth appear you are a worthy judge.
You know the law. Your exposition
Hath been most sound. I charge you by the law,
Whereof you are a well-deserving pillar,
Proceed to judgment. By my soul I swear
There is no power in the tongue of man
To alter me. I stay here on my bond.   240
ANTONIO
Most heartily I do beseech the court
To give the judgment.
PORTIA   Why then, thus it is:
You must prepare your bosom for his knife.

SHYLOCK
O noble judge! O excellent young man!
PORTIA
For the intent and purpose of the law
Hath full relation to the penalty   246
Which here appeareth due upon the bond.
SHYLOCK
'Tis very true. O wise and upright judge!
How much more elder art thou than thy looks!
PORTIA
Therefore lay bare your bosom.
SHYLOCK   Ay, his breast.
So says the bond, doth it not, noble judge?
"Nearest his heart," those are the very words.
PORTIA
It is so. Are there balance here   253
To weigh the flesh?
SHYLOCK   I have them ready.
PORTIA
Have by some surgeon, Shylock, on your charge,   255
To stop his wounds, lest he do bleed to death.
SHYLOCK
Is it so nominated in the bond?
PORTIA
It is not so expressed, but what of that?
'Twere good you do so much for charity.
SHYLOCK
I cannot find it. 'Tis not in the bond.
PORTIA
You, merchant, have you anything to say?
ANTONIO
But little. I am armed and well prepared.—   262
Give me your hand, Bassanio; fare you well!
Grieve not that I am fall'n to this for you,
For herein Fortune shows herself more kind
Than is her custom. It is still her use   266
To let the wretched man outlive his wealth
To view with hollow eye and wrinkled brow
An age of poverty; from which ling'ring penance
Of such misery doth she cut me off.
Commend me to your honorable wife.
Tell her the process of Antonio's end,   272
Say how I loved you, speak me fair in death;   273
And, when the tale is told, bid her be judge
Whether Bassanio had not once a love.   275
Repent but you that you shall lose your friend,   276
And he repents not that he pays your debt.
For if the Jew do cut but deep enough,
I'll pay it instantly with all my heart.   279
BASSANIO
Antonio, I am married to a wife,
Which is as dear to me as life itself;
But life itself, my wife, and all the world

---

204 My . . . head! (Compare the cry of the crowd at Jesus' crucifixion: "His blood be on us, and on our children," Matthew 27:25.)
212 bears down truth overwhelms righteousness.   213 Wrest once for once, forcibly subject   221 Daniel (In the Apocrypha's story of Susannah and the Elders, Daniel is the young man who rescues Susannah from her false accusers.)   233 tenor conditions.   240 stay stand, insist

246 Hath . . . to is fully in accord with   253 balance scales   255 Have by Have ready at hand.   on your charge at your personal expense 262 armed i.e., fortified in spirit   266 still her use i.e., commonly Fortune's practice   272 process story, manner   273 speak me fair speak well of me   275 a love a friend's love.   276 Repent but you Grieve only   279 with . . . heart (1) wholeheartedly (2) literally, with my heart's blood.

Are not with me esteemed above thy life.
I would lose all, ay, sacrifice them all
Here to this devil, to deliver you.

PORTIA
Your wife would give you little thanks for that,
If she were by to hear you make the offer.   287

GRATIANO
I have a wife who, I protest, I love;
I would she were in heaven, so she could
Entreat some power to change this currish Jew.

NERISSA
'Tis well you offer it behind her back;
The wish would make else an unquiet house.

SHYLOCK
These be the Christian husbands. I have a daughter;
Would any of the stock of Barabbas   294
Had been her husband rather than a Christian!—
We trifle time. I pray thee, pursue sentence.   296

PORTIA
A pound of that same merchant's flesh is thine.
The court awards it, and the law doth give it.

SHYLOCK   Most rightful judge!

PORTIA
And you must cut this flesh from off his breast.
The law allows it, and the court awards it.

SHYLOCK
Most learnèd judge! A sentence!—Come, prepare.

PORTIA
Tarry a little; there is something else.
This bond doth give thee here no jot of blood;
The words expressly are "a pound of flesh."
Take then thy bond, take thou thy pound of flesh,
But in the cutting it if thou dost shed
One drop of Christian blood, thy lands and goods
Are by the laws of Venice confiscate
Unto the state of Venice.

GRATIANO
O upright judge! Mark, Jew. O learnèd judge!

SHYLOCK
Is that the law?

PORTIA   Thyself shalt see the act;
For, as thou urgest justice, be assured
Thou shalt have justice, more than thou desir'st.

GRATIANO
O learnèd judge! Mark, Jew, a learnèd judge!

SHYLOCK
I take this offer, then. Pay the bond thrice
And let the Christian go.

BASSANIO   Here is the money.

PORTIA   Soft!   318
The Jew shall have all justice. Soft, no haste.   319
He shall have nothing but the penalty.

GRATIANO
O Jew! An upright judge, a learnèd judge!

PORTIA
Therefore prepare thee to cut off the flesh.
Shed thou no blood, nor cut thou less nor more
But just a pound of flesh. If thou tak'st more
Or less than a just pound, be it but so much
As makes it light or heavy in the substance   326
Or the division of the twentieth part   327
Of one poor scruple, nay, if the scale do turn   328
But in the estimation of a hair,
Thou diest, and all thy goods are confiscate.

GRATIANO
A second Daniel, a Daniel, Jew!   331
Now, infidel, I have you on the hip.   332

PORTIA
Why doth the Jew pause? Take thy forfeiture.

SHYLOCK
Give me my principal, and let me go.

BASSANIO
I have it ready for thee. Here it is.

PORTIA
He hath refused it in the open court.
He shall have merely justice and his bond.

GRATIANO
A Daniel, still say I, a second Daniel!
I thank thee, Jew, for teaching me that word.

SHYLOCK
Shall I not have barely my principal?

PORTIA
Thou shalt have nothing but the forfeiture,
To be so taken at thy peril, Jew.

SHYLOCK
Why, then the devil give him good of it!
I'll stay no longer question.   [*He starts to go.*]

PORTIA   Tarry, Jew!   344
The law hath yet another hold on you.
It is enacted in the laws of Venice,
If it be proved against an alien
That by direct or indirect attempts
He seek the life of any citizen,
The party 'gainst the which he doth contrive
Shall seize one half his goods; the other half
Comes to the privy coffer of the state,   352
And the offender's life lies in the mercy   353
Of the Duke only, 'gainst all other voice.   354
In which predicament, I say, thou stand'st;
For it appears, by manifest proceeding,
That indirectly and directly too
Thou hast contrived against the very life
Of the defendant; and thou hast incurred
The danger formerly by me rehearsed.   360
Down therefore, and beg mercy of the Duke.   361

---

287 by nearby   294 Barabbas a thief whom Pontius Pilate set free instead of Christ in response to the people's demand (see Mark 15); also, the villainous protagonist of Marlowe's *The Jew of Malta* 296 trifle waste.   pursue proceed with   318 Soft! i.e., Not so fast! 319 all justice precisely what the law provides.

326 substance mass or gross weight   327 division fraction 328 scruple twenty grains apothecaries' weight, a small quantity 331 Daniel (See line 221 above and note.)   332 on the hip i.e., at a disadvantage. (A phrase from wrestling.)   344 I'll . . . question I'll stay no further pursuing of the case.   352 privy coffer private treasury   353 lies in lies at   354 'gainst . . . voice without appeal 360 The danger . . . rehearsed the penalty already cited by me. 361 Down Down on your knees

GRATIANO
    Beg that thou mayst have leave to hang thyself!
    And yet, thy wealth being forfeit to the state,
    Thou hast not left the value of a cord;
    Therefore thou must be hanged at the state's charge.   365
DUKE
    That thou shalt see the difference of our spirit,
    I pardon thee thy life before thou ask it.
    For half thy wealth, it is Antonio's;   368
    The other half comes to the general state,
    Which humbleness may drive unto a fine.   370
PORTIA
    Ay, for the state, not for Antonio.   371
SHYLOCK
    Nay, take my life and all! Pardon not that!
    You take my house when you do take the prop
    That doth sustain my house. You take my life
    When you do take the means whereby I live.
PORTIA
    What mercy can you render him, Antonio?
GRATIANO
    A halter gratis! Nothing else, for God's sake.   377
ANTONIO
    So please my lord the Duke and all the court
    To quit the fine for one half of his goods,   379
    I am content, so he will let me have   380
    The other half in use, to render it,   381
    Upon his death, unto the gentleman
    That lately stole his daughter.
    Two things provided more: that for this favor
    He presently become a Christian;   385
    The other, that he do record a gift
    Here in the court of all he dies possessed   387
    Unto his son Lorenzo and his daughter.
DUKE
    He shall do this, or else I do recant
    The pardon that I late pronouncèd here.   389
PORTIA
    Art thou contented, Jew? What dost thou say?
SHYLOCK
    I am content.
PORTIA   Clerk, draw a deed of gift.
SHYLOCK
    I pray you, give me leave to go from hence;
    I am not well. Send the deed after me,
    And I will sign it.
DUKE   Get thee gone, but do it.
GRATIANO
    In christening shalt thou have two godfathers.
    Had I been judge, thou shouldst have had ten more,   397

To bring thee to the gallows, not the font.
                                    Exit [Shylock].
DUKE [to Portia]
    Sir, I entreat you home with me to dinner.
PORTIA
    I humbly do desire Your Grace of pardon.
    I must away this night toward Padua,
    And it is meet I presently set forth.   402
DUKE
    I am sorry that your leisure serves you not.
    Antonio, gratify this gentleman,   404
    For in my mind you are much bound to him.
                            Exeunt Duke and his train.
BASSANIO [to Portia]
    Most worthy gentleman, I and my friend
    Have by your wisdom been this day acquitted
    Of grievous penalties, in lieu whereof,   408
    Three thousand ducats due unto the Jew
    We freely cope your courteous pains withal.   410
                                [He offers money.]
ANTONIO
    And stand indebted over and above
    In love and service to you evermore.
PORTIA
    He is well paid that is well satisfied,
    And I, delivering you, am satisfied,
    And therein do account myself well paid.
    My mind was never yet more mercenary.
    I pray you, know me when we meet again.   417
    I wish you well, and so I take my leave.
                                [She starts to leave.]
BASSANIO
    Dear sir, of force I must attempt you further.   419
    Take some remembrance of us as a tribute,
    Not as fee. Grant me two things, I pray you:
    Not to deny me, and to pardon me.   422
PORTIA
    You press me far, and therefore I will yield.
    Give me your gloves, I'll wear them for your sake.   424
    And, for your love, I'll take this ring from you.   425
    Do not draw back your hand; I'll take no more,
    And you in love shall not deny me this.
BASSANIO
    This ring, good sir? Alas, it is a trifle!
    I will not shame myself to give you this.
PORTIA
    I will have nothing else but only this;
    And now, methinks, I have a mind to it.
BASSANIO
    There's more depends on this than on the value.

---

365 charge expense.   368 For As for   370 which . . . fine i.e., which
penitence on your part may persuade me to reduce it to a fine.
371 Ay . . . Antonio i.e., Yes, the state's half may be reduced to a fine,
but not Antonio's half.   377 halter hangman's noose   379 To . . .
goods i.e., to cancel the fine of one-half of Shylock's estate owed to
the state of Venice (line 352)   380 so provided that   381 in use in
trust (until Shylock's death)   385 presently at once   387 of . . . possessed i.e., what remains of the portion not placed under Antonio's
trust (which will also go to Lorenzo and Jessica)   389 late lately
397 ten more i.e., to make up a jury of twelve. (Jurors were colloquially termed godfathers.)

402 meet necessary, suitable   404 gratify reward   408 in lieu
whereof in return for which   410 cope requite   417 know . . . again
i.e., consider our acquaintance well established. (But punning on
know in the sense of "recognize" and "have sexual relations with"—
meanings that are hidden from Bassanio by Portia's disguise.)
419 of force of necessity.   attempt urge   422 pardon me i.e., pardon
my presumption in pressing the matter.   424 gloves (Perhaps Bassanio
removes his gloves, thereby revealing the ring that "Balthasar" asks of
him.)   425 for your love i.e., for friendship's sake—a polite phrase, but
with ironic double meaning as applied to husband and wife

The dearest ring in Venice will I give you,   433
And find it out by proclamation.
Only for this, I pray you, pardon me.

PORTIA
I see, sir, you are liberal in offers.   436
You taught me first to beg, and now, methinks,
You teach me how a beggar should be answered.

BASSANIO
Good sir, this ring was given me by my wife,
And when she put it on she made me vow
That I should neither sell nor give nor lose it.

PORTIA
That 'scuse serves many men to save their gifts.
An if your wife be not a madwoman,   443
And know how well I have deserved this ring,
She would not hold out enemy forever
For giving it to me. Well, peace be with you!
                    Exeunt [*Portia and Nerissa*].

ANTONIO
My lord Bassanio, let him have the ring.
Let his deservings and my love withal
Be valued 'gainst your wife's commandement.   449

BASSANIO
Go, Gratiano, run and overtake him;
Give him the ring, and bring him, if thou canst,
Unto Antonio's house. Away, make haste!
                    Exit Gratiano [*with the ring*].
Come, you and I will thither presently,
And in the morning early will we both
Fly toward Belmont. Come, Antonio.   *Exeunt.*

❧

[4.2]

Enter [*Portia and*] *Nerissa* [*still disguised*].

PORTIA [*giving a deed to Nerissa*]
Inquire the Jew's house out; give him this deed   1
And let him sign it. We'll away tonight
And be a day before our husbands home.
This deed will be well welcome to Lorenzo.

Enter Gratiano.

GRATIANO   Fair sir, you are well o'erta'en.   5
My lord Bassanio upon more advice   6
Hath sent you here this ring and doth entreat
Your company at dinner.   [*He gives a ring.*]
PORTIA   That cannot be.
His ring I do accept most thankfully,
And so, I pray you, tell him. Furthermore,
I pray you, show my youth old Shylock's house.
GRATIANO
That will I do.
NERISSA   Sir, I would speak with you.
[*Aside to Portia*] I'll see if I can get my husband's
     ring,
Which I did make him swear to keep forever.

PORTIA [*aside to Nerissa*]
Thou mayst, I warrant. We shall have old swearing   15
That they did give the rings away to men;
But we'll outface them, and outswear them too.—   17
Away, make haste! Thou know'st where I will tarry.
NERISSA [*to Gratiano*]
Come, good sir, will you show me to this house?
                    [*Exeunt, Portia separately from the others.*]

❧

[5.1]

Enter Lorenzo and Jessica.

LORENZO
The moon shines bright. In such a night as this,
When the sweet wind did gently kiss the trees
And they did make no noise, in such a night
Troilus methinks mounted the Trojan walls   4
And sighed his soul toward the Grecian tents
Where Cressid lay that night.
JESSICA   In such a night
Did Thisbe fearfully o'ertrip the dew,   7
And saw the lion's shadow ere himself,
And ran dismayed away.
LORENZO   In such a night
Stood Dido with a willow in her hand   10
Upon the wild sea banks, and waft her love   11
To come again to Carthage.
JESSICA   In such a night
Medea gathered the enchanted herbs   13
That did renew old Aeson.
LORENZO   In such a night
Did Jessica steal from the wealthy Jew   15
And with an unthrift love did run from Venice   16
As far as Belmont.
JESSICA   In such a night
Did young Lorenzo swear he loved her well,
Stealing her soul with many vows of faith,
And ne'er a true one.
LORENZO   In such a night
Did pretty Jessica, like a little shrew,
Slander her love, and he forgave it her.
JESSICA
I would out-night you, did nobody come.   23
But hark, I hear the footing of a man.   24

Enter [*Stephano,*] *a messenger.*

LORENZO
Who comes so fast in silence of the night?

---

433 **dearest** most expensive   436 **liberal** generous   443 **An if** If
449 **commandement** (Pronounced in four syllables.)
4.2. Location: Venice. A street.
1 **this deed** i.e., the deed of gift   5 **you . . . o'erta'en** I'm happy to
have caught up with you.   6 **advice** consideration

15 **old** plenty of   17 **outface** boldly contradict
5.1. Location: Belmont. Outside Portia's house.
4 **Troilus** Trojan prince deserted by his beloved, Cressida, after she had
been transferred to the Greek camp   7 **Thisbe** beloved of Pyramus
who, arranging to meet him by night, was frightened by a lion and fled;
the tragic misunderstanding of her absence led to the suicides of both
lovers. (See *A Midsummer Night's Dream*, Act 5.)   10 **Dido** Queen of
Carthage, deserted by Aeneas.   **willow** (A symbol of forsaken love.)
11 **waft** wafted, beckoned   13 **Medea** famous sorceress of Colchis who,
after falling in love with Jason and helping him to gain the Golden
Fleece, used her magic to restore youth to Aeson, Jason's father
15 **steal** (1) escape (2) rob   16 **unthrift** prodigal   23 **out-night** i.e.,
outdo in the verbal games we've been playing   24 **footing** footsteps

STEPHANO   A friend.

LORENZO

A friend? What friend? Your name, I pray you,
   friend?

STEPHANO

Stephano is my name, and I bring word
My mistress will before the break of day
Be here at Belmont. She doth stray about
By holy crosses, where she kneels and prays   31
For happy wedlock hours.

LORENZO   Who comes with her?

STEPHANO

None but a holy hermit and her maid.
I pray you, is my master yet returned?

LORENZO

He is not, nor we have not heard from him.
But go we in, I pray thee, Jessica,
And ceremoniously let us prepare
Some welcome for the mistress of the house.

            Enter [Lancelot, the] clown.

LANCELOT   Sola, sola! Wo ha, ho! Sola, sola!   39
LORENZO   Who calls?
LANCELOT   Sola! Did you see Master Lorenzo? Master
Lorenzo, sola, sola!
LORENZO   Leave holloing, man! Here.
LANCELOT   Sola! Where, where?
LORENZO   Here.
LANCELOT   Tell him there's a post come from my mas-   46
ter, with his horn full of good news: my master will be   47
here ere morning.   [*Exit.*]

LORENZO

Sweet soul, let's in, and there expect their coming.   49
And yet no matter. Why should we go in?
My friend Stephano, signify, I pray you,   51
Within the house, your mistress is at hand,
And bring your music forth into the air.
                                  [*Exit Stephano.*]
How sweet the moonlight sleeps upon this bank!
Here will we sit and let the sounds of music
Creep in our ears. Soft stillness and the night
Become the touches of sweet harmony.   57
Sit, Jessica. [*They sit.*] Look how the floor of heaven
Is thick inlaid with patens of bright gold.   59
There's not the smallest orb which thou behold'st
But in his motion like an angel sings,
Still choiring to the young-eyed cherubins.   62
Such harmony is in immortal souls,
But whilst this muddy vesture of decay   64
Doth grossly close it in, we cannot hear it.   65

            [*Enter musicians.*]

Come, ho, and wake Diana with a hymn!   66
With sweetest touches pierce your mistress' ear
And draw her home with music.   *Play music.*

JESSICA

I am never merry when I hear sweet music.

LORENZO

The reason is, your spirits are attentive.   70
For do but note a wild and wanton herd,
Or race of youthful and unhandled colts,   72
Fetching mad bounds, bellowing and neighing loud,
Which is the hot condition of their blood;
If they but hear perchance a trumpet sound,
Or any air of music touch their ears,
You shall perceive them make a mutual stand,   77
Their savage eyes turned to a modest gaze
By the sweet power of music. Therefore the poet   79
Did feign that Orpheus drew trees, stones, and
   floods,   80
Since naught so stockish, hard, and full of rage   81
But music for the time doth change his nature.   82
The man that hath no music in himself,
Nor is not moved with concord of sweet sounds,
Is fit for treasons, stratagems, and spoils;   85
The motions of his spirit are dull as night
And his affections dark as Erebus.   87
Let no such man be trusted. Mark the music.

            Enter Portia and Nerissa.

PORTIA

That light we see is burning in my hall.
How far that little candle throws his beams!
So shines a good deed in a naughty world.   91

NERISSA

When the moon shone, we did not see the candle.

PORTIA

So doth the greater glory dim the less.
A substitute shines brightly as a king
Until a king be by, and then his state   95
Empties itself, as doth an inland brook
Into the main of waters. Music! Hark!   97

NERISSA

It is your music, madam, of the house.

PORTIA

Nothing is good, I see, without respect.   99
Methinks it sounds much sweeter than by day.

NERISSA

Silence bestows that virtue on it, madam.

PORTIA

The crow doth sing as sweetly as the lark
When neither is attended; and I think   103
The nightingale, if she should sing by day,

---

31 **holy crosses** wayside shrines   39 **Sola** (Imitation of a post horn.)
46 **post** courier   47 **horn** (Lancelot jestingly compares the courier's
post horn to a cornucopia; perhaps too with a glance at the frayed jest
about cuckolds' horns.)   49 **expect** await   51 **signify** make known
57 **Become** suit.   **touches** strains, notes (produced by the fingering of
an instrument)   59 **patens** thin, circular plates of metal   62 **Still
choiring** continually singing.   **young-eyed** eternally clear-sighted.
(In Ezekiel 10:12, the bodies and wings of cherubim are "full of eyes
round about.")   64 **muddy . . . decay** i.e., mortal flesh   65 **close it in**
i.e., enclose the soul.   **hear it** i.e., hear the music of the spheres.

66 **Diana** (Here, goddess of the moon; compare with 1.2.105.)
70 **spirits are attentive** (The spirits would be in motion within the
body in merriment, whereas in sadness they would be drawn to the
heart and, as it were, busy listening.)   72 **race** herd   77 **mutual** common or simultaneous   79 **poet** perhaps Ovid, with whom the story of
Orpheus was a favorite theme   80 **Orpheus** legendary musician.
drew attracted, charmed.   **floods** rivers   81 **stockish** unfeeling
82 **his** its (a tree, a stone, etc.)   85 **spoils** acts of pillage   87 **Erebus** a
place of primeval darkness on the way to Hades.   91 **naughty**
wicked   95 **his** i.e., the substitute's   97 **main of waters** sea.
99 **respect** comparison, context.   103 **attended** listened to

When every goose is cackling, would be thought
No better a musician than the wren.
How many things by season seasoned are　　　　107
To their right praise and true perfection!
Peace, ho! The moon sleeps with Endymion　　　109
And would not be awaked.　　　　　[*The music ceases.*]

LORENZO　　　　　　　　　That is the voice,
Or I am much deceived, of Portia.

PORTIA
He knows me as the blind man knows the cuckoo,
By the bad voice.

LORENZO　　　　　　　Dear lady, welcome home.

PORTIA
We have been praying for our husbands' welfare,
Which speed, we hope, the better for our words.　　115
Are they returned?

LORENZO　　　　　　　Madam, they are not yet;
But there is come a messenger before,
To signify their coming.

PORTIA　　　　　　　　Go in, Nerissa.
Give order to my servants that they take
No note at all of our being absent hence;
Nor you, Lorenzo; Jessica, nor you. [*A tucket sounds.*] 121

LORENZO
Your husband is at hand. I hear his trumpet.
We are no telltales, madam, fear you not.

PORTIA
This night, methinks, is but the daylight sick;　　124
It looks a little paler. 'Tis a day
Such as the day is when the sun is hid.

Enter Bassanio, Antonio, Gratiano, and their
followers.

BASSANIO
We should hold day with the Antipodes,　　127
If you would walk in absence of the sun.　　128

PORTIA
Let me give light, but let me not be light;　　129
For a light wife doth make a heavy husband,　　130
And never be Bassanio so for me.
But God sort all! You are welcome home, my lord.　132

BASSANIO
I thank you, madam. Give welcome to my friend.
This is the man, this is Antonio,
To whom I am so infinitely bound.

PORTIA
You should in all sense be much bound to him,　136
For, as I hear, he was much bound for you.　　137

ANTONIO
No more than I am well acquitted of.　　138

PORTIA
Sir, you are very welcome to our house.
It must appear in other ways than words;
Therefore I scant this breathing courtesy.　　141

GRATIANO [*to Nerissa*]
By yonder moon I swear you do me wrong!
In faith, I gave it to the judge's clerk.
Would he were gelt that had it, for my part,　　144
Since you do take it, love, so much at heart.

PORTIA
A quarrel, ho, already? What's the matter?

GRATIANO
About a hoop of gold, a paltry ring
That she did give me, whose posy was　　148
For all the world like cutler's poetry
Upon a knife, "Love me, and leave me not."

NERISSA
What talk you of the posy or the value?
You swore to me, when I did give it you,
That you would wear it till your hour of death
And that it should lie with you in your grave.
Though not for me, yet for your vehement oaths
You should have been respective and have kept it.　156
Gave it a judge's clerk! No, God's my judge,
The clerk will ne'er wear hair on 's face that had it.

GRATIANO
He will, an if he live to be a man.　　159

NERISSA
Ay, if a woman live to be a man.

GRATIANO
Now, by this hand, I gave it to a youth,
A kind of boy, a little scrubbèd boy　　162
No higher than thyself, the judge's clerk,
A prating boy, that begged it as a fee.　　164
I could not for my heart deny it him.

PORTIA
You were to blame—I must be plain with you—
To part so slightly with your wife's first gift,
A thing stuck on with oaths upon your finger,
And so riveted with faith unto your flesh.
I gave my love a ring and made him swear
Never to part with it; and here he stands.
I dare be sworn for him he would not leave it,
Nor pluck it from his finger, for the wealth
That the world masters. Now, in faith, Gratiano,　174
You give your wife too unkind a cause of grief.
An 'twere to me, I should be mad at it.　　176

BASSANIO [*aside*]
Why, I were best to cut my left hand off
And swear I lost the ring defending it.

GRATIANO
My lord Bassanio gave his ring away

---

107 season fit occasion. (But playing on the idea of seasoning, spices.)
109 Endymion a shepherd loved by the moon goddess, who caused him to sleep a perennial sleep in a cave on Mount Latmos where she could visit him　**115 Which . . . words** who prosper and return speedily, we hope, because we prayed for them.　**121 s.d.** *tucket* flourish on a trumpet　**124 sick** i.e., made pale by the approach of dawn　**127–8 We . . . sun** i.e., If you, Portia, like a second sun, would always walk about during the sun's absence, we should never have night but would enjoy daylight even when the Antipodes, those who dwell on the opposite side of the globe, enjoy daylight.　**129 be light** be wanton, unchaste　**130 heavy** sad. (With wordplay on the antithesis of *light* and *heavy*.)　**132 sort** decide, dispose　**136 in all sense** in every way, with every reason　**136–7 bound . . . bound** Portia plays on (1) obligated (2) indebted and imprisoned.

138 acquitted of freed from and amply repaid (by thanks and love).
141 scant . . . courtesy make brief these empty (i.e., merely verbal) compliments.　**144 gelt** gelded, castrated.　**for my part** as far as I'm concerned　**148 posy** a motto on a ring　**156 respective** mindful, careful　**159 an if** if　**162 scrubbèd** diminutive　**164 prating** chattering　**174 masters** owns.　**176 An** If.　**mad** beside myself

Unto the judge that begged it and indeed
Deserved it too; and then the boy, his clerk,
That took some pains in writing, he begged mine;
And neither man nor master would take aught   183
But the two rings.

PORTIA *[to Bassanio]*   What ring gave you, my lord?
Not that, I hope, which you received of me.

BASSANIO
If I could add a lie unto a fault,
I would deny it; but you see my finger
Hath not the ring upon it. It is gone.

PORTIA
Even so void is your false heart of truth.
By heaven, I will ne'er come in your bed
Until I see the ring!

NERISSA *[to Gratiano]*   Nor I in yours
Till I again see mine.

BASSANIO   Sweet Portia,
If you did know to whom I gave the ring,
If you did know for whom I gave the ring,
And would conceive for what I gave the ring,
And how unwillingly I left the ring,
When naught would be accepted but the ring,
You would abate the strength of your displeasure.

PORTIA
If you had known the virtue of the ring,   199
Or half her worthiness that gave the ring,
Or your own honor to contain the ring,   201
You would not then have parted with the ring.
What man is there so much unreasonable,
If you had pleased to have defended it
With any terms of zeal, wanted the modesty   205
To urge the thing held as a ceremony?   206
Nerissa teaches me what to believe:
I'll die for't but some woman had the ring.

BASSANIO
No, by my honor, madam! By my soul,
No woman had it, but a civil doctor,   210
Which did refuse three thousand ducats of me
And begged the ring, the which I did deny him
And suffered him to go displeased away—   213
Even he that had held up the very life
Of my dear friend. What should I say, sweet lady?
I was enforced to send it after him.
I was beset with shame and courtesy.
My honor would not let ingratitude
So much besmear it. Pardon me, good lady!   219
For by these blessèd candles of the night,   220
Had you been there, I think you would have begged
The ring of me to give the worthy doctor.

PORTIA
Let not that doctor e'er come near my house.
Since he hath got the jewel that I loved,
And that which you did swear to keep for me,
I will become as liberal as you:

I'll not deny him anything I have,   226
No, not my body nor my husband's bed.
Know him I shall, I am well sure of it.
Lie not a night from home. Watch me like Argus;   229
If you do not, if I be left alone,   230
Now, by mine honor, which is yet mine own,
I'll have that doctor for my bedfellow.   232

NERISSA
And I his clerk; therefore be well advised
How you do leave me to mine own protection.   234

GRATIANO
Well, do you so. Let not me take him, then!
For if I do, I'll mar the young clerk's pen.   236

ANTONIO   237
I am th'unhappy subject of these quarrels.

PORTIA
Sir, grieve not you; you are welcome notwithstanding.

BASSANIO
Portia, forgive me this enforcèd wrong,
And in the hearing of these many friends
I swear to thee, even by thine own fair eyes
Wherein I see myself—

PORTIA   Mark you but that!
In both my eyes he doubly sees himself;
In each eye, one. Swear by your double self,
And there's an oath of credit.   245

BASSANIO   Nay, but hear me.
Pardon this fault, and by my soul I swear   246
I never more will break an oath with thee.

ANTONIO
I once did lend my body for his wealth,
Which, but for him that had your husband's ring,   249
Had quite miscarried. I dare be bound again,
My soul upon the forfeit, that your lord
Will nevermore break faith advisedly.   252

PORTIA   253
Then you shall be his surety. Give him this,
And bid him keep it better than the other.   254
     [She gives the ring to Antonio, who gives it to Bassanio.]

ANTONIO
Here, Lord Bassanio. Swear to keep this ring.

BASSANIO
By heaven, it is the same I gave the doctor!

PORTIA
I had it of him. Pardon me, Bassanio,
For by this ring the doctor lay with me.

NERISSA
And pardon me, my gentle Gratiano,
For that same scrubbèd boy, the doctor's clerk,
In lieu of this last night did lie with me.
                              [Presenting her ring.] 262

---

226 liberal generous (sexually as well as otherwise)   **229 Know**
(With the suggestion of carnal knowledge.)   **230 from** away from.
Argus mythological monster with a hundred eyes   **232 honor**
(1) honorable name (2) chastity   **234 be well advised** take care
236 take apprehend   **237 pen** (With sexual double meaning.)
245 double i.e., deceitful   **246 of credit** worthy to be believed. (Said
ironically.)   **249 wealth** welfare   **252 My . . . forfeit** at the risk of
eternal damnation   **253 advisedly** intentionally.   **254 surety** guarantor.   **262 In lieu of** in return for

---

183 aught anything   **199 virtue** moral efficacy   **201 contain** keep
safe   **205 wanted the modesty** who would have been so lacking in
consideration as   **206 urge** insist upon receiving.   **ceremony** something sacred.   **210 civil doctor** i.e., doctor of civil law   **213 suffered**
allowed   **219 it** i.e., my honor.   **220 blessèd . . . night** i.e., stars

GRATIANO
      Why, this is like the mending of highways
      In summer, where the ways are fair enough.   264
      What, are we cuckolds ere we have deserved it?   265
PORTIA
      Speak not so grossly. You are all amazed.
      Here is a letter; read it at your leisure.
                                    [*She gives a letter.*]
      It comes from Padua, from Bellario.
      There you shall find that Portia was the doctor,
      Nerissa there her clerk. Lorenzo here
      Shall witness I set forth as soon as you,
      And even but now returned; I have not yet
      Entered my house. Antonio, you are welcome,
      And I have better news in store for you
      Than you expect. Unseal this letter soon.
                                    [*She gives him a letter.*]
      There you shall find three of your argosies
      Are richly come to harbor suddenly.
      You shall not know by what strange accident
      I chancèd on this letter.
ANTONIO   I am dumb.   279
BASSANIO [*to Portia*]
      Were you the doctor and I knew you not?
GRATIANO [*to Nerissa*]
      Were you the clerk that is to make me cuckold?
NERISSA
      Ay, but the clerk that never means to do it,
      Unless he live until he be a man.
BASSANIO
      Sweet doctor, you shall be my bedfellow.

      When I am absent, then lie with my wife.
ANTONIO
      Sweet lady, you have given me life and living;
      For here I read for certain that my ships
      Are safely come to road.
PORTIA   How now, Lorenzo?   288
      My clerk hath some good comforts too for you.
NERISSA
      Ay, and I'll give them him without a fee.
                                    [*She gives a deed.*]
      There do I give to you and Jessica,
      From the rich Jew, a special deed of gift,
      After his death, of all he dies possessed of.
LORENZO
      Fair ladies, you drop manna in the way   294
      Of starved people.
PORTIA   It is almost morning,
      And yet I am sure you are not satisfied
      Of these events at full. Let us go in;
      And charge us there upon inter'gatories,   298
      And we will answer all things faithfully.
GRATIANO
      Let it be so. The first inter'gatory
      That my Nerissa shall be sworn on is
      Whether till the next night she had rather stay   302
      Or go to bed now, being two hours to day.
      But were the day come, I should wish it dark
      Till I were couching with the doctor's clerk.   305
      Well, while I live I'll fear no other thing
      So sore as keeping safe Nerissa's ring.   *Exeunt.* 307

---

264 **are fair enough** i.e., are not in need of repair.   265 **cuckolds** husbands whose wives are unfaithful   279 **dumb** at a loss for words.

288 **road** anchorage.   294 **manna** the food from heaven that was miraculously supplied to the Israelites in the wilderness (Exodus 16)
298 **And . . . inter'gatories** and put questions to us (as in a court of law)   302 **stay** wait   305 **couching** going to bed   307 **ring** (With sexual suggestion.)

Much Ado About Nothing

Much Ado About Nothing belongs to a group of Shakespeare's most mature romantic comedies, linked by similar titles, that also includes *As You Like It* and *Twelfth Night* (subtitled *what You will*). All date from the period 1598 to 1600. These plays are the culmination of Shakespeare's exuberant, philosophical, and festive vein in comedy, with only an occasional anticipation of the darker problem comedies of the early 1600s. They also parallel the culmination of Shakespeare's writing of history plays, in *Henry IV* and *V*.

Much Ado excels in combative wit and in swift, colloquial prose. It differs, too, from several other comedies (including *A Midsummer Night's Dream* and *The Merchant of Venice*) in that it features no journey of the lovers, no heroine disguised as a man, no envious court or city contrasted with an idealized landscape of the artist's imagination. Instead, the prevailing motif is that of the mask. Prominent scenes include a masked ball (2.1), a charade offstage in which the villainous Borachio misrepresents himself as the lover of Hero (actually Margaret in disguise), and a marriage ceremony with the supposedly dead bride masking as her own cousin (5.3). The word *Nothing* in the play's title, pronounced rather like *noting* in the English of Elizabethan London and vicinity, suggests a pun on the idea of overhearing as well as of musical notation; it also has a bawdy connotation, as when Hamlet wryly suggests to Ophelia that "Nothing" is "a fair thought to lie between maids' legs" (*Hamlet*, 3.2.116–18; see also *Othello*, 3.3.317, where Iago responds to his wife's "I have a thing for you" with a degrading sexual insult). Overhearings are constant and are essential to the process of both misunderstanding (as in the false rumor of Don Pedro's wooing Hero for himself) and clarification (as in the discovery by the night watch of the slander done to Hero's reputation, or in the revelation to Beatrice and Benedick of each other's true state of mind). The masks, or roles, that the characters incessantly assume are, for the most part, defensive and inimical to mutual understanding. How can they be dispelled? It is the search for candor and self-awareness in relationships with others, the quest for honesty and respect beneath conventional outward appearances, that provides the journey in this play.

Structurally, the play contrasts two pairs of lovers. The ladies, Beatrice and Hero, are cousins and close friends. The gentlemen, Benedick and Claudio, Italian gentlemen and fellow officers under the command of Don Pedro, have returned from the war, in which they have fought bravely. These similarities chiefly serve, however, to accentuate the differences between the two couples. Hero is modest, retiring, usually silent, and obedient to her father's will. Claudio appears ideally suited to her, since he is also respectful and decorous. They are conventional lovers in the roles of romantic hero and naive heroine. Beatrice and Benedick, on the other hand, are renowned for "a kind of merry war" between them. Although obviously destined to come together, they are seemingly too independent and skeptical of convention to be tolerant and accepting in love. They scoff so at romantic sentimentality that they cannot permit themselves to drop their satirical masks. Yet, paradoxically, their relationship is ultimately more surefooted because of their refusal to settle for the illusory clichés of many young wooers.

As in some of his other comic double plots (*The Taming of the Shrew*, for example), Shakespeare has linked together two stories of diverse origins and contrasting tones in order to set off one against the other. The Hero-Claudio plot is Italianate in flavor and origin, sensational, melodramatic, and potentially tragic. In fact, the often told story of the maiden falsely slandered did frequently end in disaster—as, for example, in Edmund Spenser's *Faerie Queene*, 2.4 (1590). Spenser was apparently indebted to Ariosto's *Orlando Furioso* (translated into English by Sir John Harington, 1591), as were Peter Beverly in *The Historie of Ariodanto and Ieneura* (1566) and Richard Mulcaster in his play *Ariodante and Genevora* (1583).

Shakespeare seems to have relied more on the Italian version by Matteo Bandello (Lucca, 1554) and its French translation by Belleforest, *Histoires Tragiques* (1569). Still other versions have been discovered, both nondramatic and dramatic, although it cannot be established that Shakespeare was reworking an old play. Various factual inconsistencies in Shakespeare's text (such as Leonato's wife Imogen and a "kinsman" who are named briefly in both Quarto and Folio but have no roles in the play) can perhaps be explained by Shakespeare's having worked quickly from more than one source.

Shakespeare's other plot, of Benedick and Beatrice, is much more English and his own. The battle of the sexes is a staple of English medieval humor (Chaucer's Wife of Bath, the Wakefield play of *Noah*) and of Shakespeare's own early comedy: Berowne and Rosaline in *Love's Labor's Lost*, Petruchio and Katharina in *The Taming of the Shrew*. The merry war of Benedick and Beatrice is Shakespeare's finest achievement in this vein and was to become a rich legacy in the later English comedy of William Congreve, Oscar Wilde, and George Bernard Shaw. The tone is lighthearted, bantering, and reassuring, in contrast with the Italianate mood of vengeance and duplicity in the Claudio-Hero plot. No less English are the clownish antics of Dogberry and his crew, representing still another group of characters although not a separate plot. Like Constable Dull in *Love's Labor's Lost* or the tradesmen of *A Midsummer Night's Dream*, the buffoons of *Much Ado* function in a nominally Mediterranean setting but are nonetheless recognizable London types. Their preposterous antics not only puncture the ominous mood threatening our enjoyment of the main plot but also, absurdly enough, even help to abort a potential crime. When Dogberry comes, laughter cannot be far behind.

The two plots provide contrasting perspectives on the nature of love. Because it is sensational and melodramatic, the Claudio-Hero plot stresses situation at the expense of character. The conspiracy that nearly overwhelms the lovers is an engrossing story, but they themselves remain one-dimensional. They interest us more as conventional types, and hence as foils to Benedick and Beatrice, than as lovers in their own right. Benedick and Beatrice, on the other hand, are psychologically complex. Clearly, they are fascinated with each other. Beatrice's questions in the first scene, although abusive in tone, betray her concern for Benedick's welfare. Has he safely returned from the wars? How did he bear himself in battle? Who are his companions? She tests his moral character by high standards, suspecting that he will fail because she demands so much. We are not surprised when she lectures her docile cousin, Hero, on the folly of submitting to parental choice in marriage: "It is my cousin's duty to make curtsy and say, 'Father, as it please you.' But yet for all that, cousin, let him be a handsome fellow, or else

make another curtsy and say, 'Father, as it please me' " (2.1.49–52). Beatrice remains single not from love of spinsterhood but from insistence on a nearly perfect mate. Paradoxically, she who is the inveterate scoffer is the true idealist. And we know from her unceasing fascination with Benedick that he, of all the men in her acquaintance, comes closest to her mark. The only fear preventing the revelation of her love—a not unnatural fear, in view of the insults she and Benedick exchange—is that he will prove faithless and jest at her weakness.

Benedick is similarly hemmed in by his posturing as "a professed tyrant to their sex." Despite his reputation as a perennial bachelor and his wry amusement at Claudio's newfound passion, Benedick confesses in soliloquy (2.3.8–34) that he could be won to affection by the ideal woman. Again, his criteria are chiefly those of temperament and moral character, although he by no means spurns wealth, beauty, and social position; the happiest couples are those well matched in fortune's gifts. "Rich she shall be, that's certain; wise, or I'll none; virtuous, or I'll never cheapen her; fair, or I'll never look on her; mild, or come not near me; noble, or not I for an angel; of good discourse, an excellent musician, and her hair shall be of what color it please God." This last self-mocking concession indicates that Benedick is aware of how impossibly much he is asking. Still, there is one woman, Beatrice, who may well possess all of these qualities except mildness. Even her sharp wit is part of her admirable intelligence. She is a match for Benedick, and he is a man who would never tolerate the submissive conventionality of someone like Hero. All that appears to be lacking, in fact, is any sign of fondness on Beatrice's part. For him to make overtures would be to invite her withering scorn—not to mention the I-told-you-so mockery of his friends.

Benedick and Beatrice have been playing the game of verbal abuse for so long that they scarcely remember how it started—perhaps as a squaring-off between the only two intelligences worthy of contending with each other, perhaps as a more profoundly defensive reaction of two sensitive persons not willing to part lightly with their independence. They seem to have had a prior relationsip with each other that ended unhappily. They know that intimate involvement with another person is a complex matter—one that can cause heartache. Yet the masks they wear with each other are scarcely satisfactory. At the masked ball (2.1), we see how hurtful the "merry war" has become. Benedick, attempting to pass himself off as a stranger in a mask, abuses Beatrice by telling her of her reputation for disdain; but she, perceiving who he is, retaliates by telling him as a purported stranger what she "really" thinks of Benedick. These devices cut deeply and confirm the worst fears of each. Ironically, these fears can be dispelled only by the virtuous deceptions practiced on them by their friends. Once Benedick is assured that Beatrice secretly loves him, masking her affection with scorn, he acquires the confidence he needs to make a commitment, and vice versa in her case. The beauty of the virtuous deceptions, moreover, is that they are so plausible—because, indeed, they are essentially true. Benedick overhears himself described as a person so satirical that Beatrice dare not reveal her affection, for fear of being repulsed (2.3). Beatrice learns that she is indeed called disdainful by her friends (3.1). Both lovers respond generously to these revelations, accepting the accusations as richly deserved and placing no blame on the other. As Beatrice proclaims to herself, "Contempt, farewell, and maiden pride, adieu!" The relief afforded by this honesty is genuine and lasting.

Because Claudio knows so little about Hero and is content with superficial expectations, he is vulnerable to a far uglier sort of deception. Claudio's first questions about Hero betray his romantically stereotyped attitudes and his willingness to let Don Pedro and Hero's father, Leonato, arrange a financially advantageous match. Claudio treasures Hero's outward reputation for modesty, an appearance easily besmirched. When a false rumor suggests that Don Pedro is wooing the lady for himself, Claudio's response is predictably cliché-ridden: all's fair in love and war, you can't trust friends in an affair of the heart, and so farewell Hero. The rumor has a superficial plausibility about it, especially when the villainous Don John steps into the situation. Motivated in part by pure malice and the sport of ruining others' happiness, Don John speaks to the masked Claudio at the ball (2.1) as though he were speaking to Benedick and, in this guise, pretends to reveal the secret "fact" of Don Pedro's duplicity in love. (The device is precisely that used by Beatrice to put down Benedick in the same scene.) With this specious confirmation, Claudio leaps to a wrong conclusion, thereby judging both his friend and mistress to be false. He gives them no chance to speak in their own defense. To be sure, Hero's father and uncle have also believed in the false report and have welcomed the prospect of Don Pedro as Hero's husband. She herself raises no objection to the prospect of marriage with the older man. Don Pedro is, after all, a prince of presumably enormous wealth, power, and social status, well above that of Leonato and his well-to-do but bourgeois family; when he asks (perhaps as a pleasantry) if Beatrice will have him as her husband, her polite refusal seems tinged with a note of regret (2.1.303–21). These attractive features in Don Pedro tend to excuse the general willingness to accept the idea of him as a splendidly suitable husband for Hero. Even so, Claudio has revealed a lack of faith resulting from his slender knowledge of Hero and of himself.

The nearly tragic "demonstration" of Hero's infidelity follows the same course, because Claudio has not learned from his first experience. Once again, the villainous Don John first implants the insidious suggestion in Claudio's mind, then creates an illusion entirely plausible to the senses, and finally confirms it with Borachio's testimony. What Claudio and Don Pedro have actually seen is Margaret wooed at Hero's window, shrouded in the dark of night and seen from "afar off in the orchard." The power of suggestion is enough to do the rest. Don John's method, and his pleasure in evil, are much like those of his later counterparts, Iago in *Othello* and Edmund in *King Lear*. Indeed, John is compared with the devil, who has power over mortals' frail senses but must rely on their complicity and acquiescence in evil. Claudio is once again led to denounce faithlessly the virtuous woman whose loyalty he no longer deserves. Yet his fault is typically human and is shared by Don Pedro. Providence gives him a second chance, through the ludicrous and bumbling intervention of Dogberry's night watch. These men overhear the plot of Don John as soon as it is announced to us, so that we know justice will eventually prevail, even though it will also be farcically delayed. Once again, misunderstanding has become "much ado about nothing," an escalating of recriminations based on a purely chimerical assumption that must eventually be deflated. The painful experience is not without value, for it tests the characters' spiritual worth in a crisis. Beatrice, like Friar Francis, shows herself to be a person of unshakable faith in goodness. Benedick, though puzzled and torn in his loyalties, also passes the test and proves himself worthy of Beatrice. Claudio is found wanting, and indeed is judged by many modern readers and audiences to be wholly inadequate, but Hero forgives and accepts him anyway. In her role as the granter of a merciful second chance, she foreshadows the beatifically symbolic nature of many of Shakespeare's later heroines.

Much Ado comes perhaps closer to potentially tragic action than Shakespeare's other festive comedies, though *The Merchant of Venice* is another, and so are late romances like *Cymbeline* and *The Winter's Tale* that *Much Ado* can be said to anticipate in the serious matter of slander against a virtuous heroine. Most strikingly, Claudio's failure is unnervingly like that of Othello. The fact that both men are too easily persuaded to reject and humiliate the innocent women they love suggests a deep inadequacy in each. The tempters (Don John, Iago) cannot alone be blamed; the male lovers themselves are too prone to believe the worst of women. In Claudio we can see a vulnerability in the very way he looks at courtship and marriage. As Benedick jests, Claudio talks almost as though he wants to buy Hero (1.1.172). Certainly his attitude is acquisitive and superficial; as the conquering hero returned from the wars, he is ready to settle down into married respectability, and he needs a socially eligible wife. He desires Hero for her beauty, for her wealth and family connections, and above all for her modesty and her reputation for virginal purity. These are attributes easily impugned by false apearances, and in his too-quick rejection of Hero we see in Claudio a deep cynicism about women. He fears the betrayal and loss of masculine self-esteem that a woman can inflict on him by sexual infidelity. To Claudio, Hero is a saint one moment and a whore the next.

Nor is he the only man to demean her (and women) thus. Don Pedro, his patron and older friend, is no less ready to believe Don John's lies, even though Don Pedro has been deceived by his brother before and should know better. Hero's father collapses in shame when he hears his daughter publicly accused of promiscuity, for Leonato's own reputation is on the line: as a father in a patriarchal society, his responsibility is to guarantee the chastity of his daughter to the younger man who proposes to receive her. Leonato's first assumption is that she must be guilty if other men say so; even he is altogether ready to believe the worst of women. Virtually the whole male world of Messina is victimized by its own fear of womanly perfidy—a fear that seems to arise from male lack of self-assurance and a deep inner conviction of being unloved. Benedick is much to be commended for his skepticism about the slanderous attacks on Hero; in no way does he better prove his worthiness of being Beatrice's husband than in his defense of a traduced and innocent woman. Yet Benedick, too, suffers to such a degree from his own male insecurity that he nearly gives up Beatrice at the very end of the play, even as she is nearly ready to give up him. Despite their self-awareness, these lovers must be rescued from their autonomous self-defensiveness by one more intervention on the part of their friends. Benedick and Beatrice are not wholly unlike Claudio and Hero after all. Both pairs of lovers are saved from their own worst selves by a harmonizing force that works its will through strange and improbable means—even through Constable Dogberry and his watch.

Performance history has abundantly illustrated the durable quality of this remarkable play. Perhaps no other comedy by Shakespeare has been as influential as *Much Ado*, providing as it does a model for wit combat and comedy of manners in William Congreve's *The Way of the World*, Oscar Wilde's *The Importance of Being Earnest*, George Bernard Shaw's *Man and Superman*, Noel Coward's *Private Lives*, Tom Stoppard's *The Real Thing*, and many others. Onstage the play has always been a favorite in the repertory, featuring such couples as Hannah Pritchard and David Garrick, Ellen Terry and Henry Irving, Peggy Ashcroft and John Gielgud, Diana Wynyard and Anthony Quayle, Janet Suzman and Alan Howard, Maggie Smith and Robert Stephens, Judi Dench and Donald Sinden, Sinead Cusack and Derek Jacobi, and many more. A commercial television production by A. J. Antoon, originating in New York's Delacorte Theater in 1972, was witnessed by more viewers on that occasion than had seen the play in its entire stage history. Kenneth Branagh's 1993 film, with Emma Thompson and Branagh in the leading roles, along with Denzel Washington as Don Pedro and Michael Keaton as Dogberry, capitalized on a gorgeous Italian villa and its star-laden cast to produce one of the most popular of Shakespeare cinemas. Emma Thompson shows us a Beatrice who is strong, independent, not easily fooled, undaunted by men, and willing to marry Benedick (Branagh) only after she has tested him and made clear the mutuality of respect that she demands. In recent years the play has been located in a wide variety of updated settings: frontier Texas, small-town America right after the Spanish-American War, Victorian India of the British Raj, Regency England, the Edwardian era, mafiosa Sicily, and still more. The incessant updating testifies paradoxically to the play's engaging timelessness; it works anywhere and any time. The play continues to succeed because it is so genuinely open to such interpretations.

Much Ado About Nothing

[*Dramatis Personae*

DON PEDRO, *Prince of Aragon*
LEONATO, *Governor of Messina*
ANTONIO, *his brother*

BENEDICK, *a young lord of Padua*
BEATRICE, *Leonato's niece*
CLAUDIO, *a young lord of Florence*
HERO, *Leonato's daughter*
MARGARET, }
URSULA, } *gentlewomen attending Hero*

DON JOHN, *Don Pedro's bastard brother*
BORACHIO, }
CONRADE, } *followers of Don John*

DOGBERRY, *Constable in charge of the Watch*
VERGES, *the Headborough, or parish constable, Dogberry's partner*
A SEXTON (FRANCIS SEACOAL)
FIRST WATCHMAN
SECOND WATCHMAN (GEORGE SEACOAL)

BALTHASAR, *a singer attending Don Pedro*
FRIAR FRANCIS
A BOY
MESSENGER *to Leonato*
Another MESSENGER

Attendants, Musicians, Members of the Watch, Antonio's Son and other Kinsmen

SCENE: *Messina*]

[1.1]

Enter Leonato, Governor of Messina, Hero his daughter, and Beatrice his niece, with a Messenger.

LEONATO [*holding a letter*]   I learn in this letter that Don Pedro of Aragon comes this night to Messina.
MESSENGER   He is very near by this. He was not three leagues off when I left him. 4
LEONATO   How many gentlemen have you lost in this action? 6
MESSENGER   But few of any sort and none of name. 7
LEONATO   A victory is twice itself when the achiever brings home full numbers. I find here that Don Pedro hath bestowed much honor on a young Florentine called Claudio.
MESSENGER   Much deserved on his part and equally remembered by Don Pedro. He hath borne himself 13 beyond the promise of his age, doing in the figure of a lamb the feats of a lion. He hath indeed better bettered expectation than you must expect of me to tell 16 you how.
LEONATO   He hath an uncle here in Messina will be 18 very much glad of it.
MESSENGER   I have already delivered him letters, and there appears much joy in him, even so much that joy 21 could not show itself modest enough without a badge 22 of bitterness. 23
LEONATO   Did he break out into tears?
MESSENGER   In great measure.
LEONATO   A kind overflow of kindness. There are no 26 faces truer than those that are so washed. How much better is it to weep at joy than to joy at weeping!
BEATRICE   I pray you, is Signor Mountanto returned 29 from the wars or no?
MESSENGER   I know none of that name, lady. There was none such in the army of any sort.
LEONATO   What is he that you ask for, niece?

1.1. Location: Messina. Before Leonato's house.
4 leagues units of about three miles   **6 action** battle   **7 sort** rank
name reputation, or noble name   **13 remembered** rewarded

16 bettered surpassed   **18 will** who will   **21–3 joy . . . bitterness** joy could not show a decorous moderation only by weeping at the same time.   **26 kind** natural   **29 Mountanto** montanto, an upward blow or thrust in fencing

117

HERO   My cousin means Signor Benedick of Padua.

MESSENGER   Oh, he's returned, and as pleasant as ever 35
he was.

BEATRICE   He set up his bills here in Messina and chal- 37
lenged Cupid at the flight; and my uncle's fool, reading 38
the challenge, subscribed for Cupid and challenged 39
him at the bird-bolt. I pray you, how many hath he 40
killed and eaten in these wars? But how many hath he
killed? For indeed I promised to eat all of his killing.

LEONATO   Faith, niece, you tax Signor Benedick too 43
much, but he'll be meet with you, I doubt it not. 44

MESSENGER   He hath done good service, lady, in these
wars.

BEATRICE   You had musty victual, and he hath holp to 47
eat it. He is a very valiant trencherman; he hath an 48
excellent stomach. 49

MESSENGER   And a good soldier too, lady.

BEATRICE   And a good soldier to a lady, but what is he 51
to a lord? 52

MESSENGER   A lord to a lord, a man to a man, stuffed 53
with all honorable virtues.

BEATRICE   It is so, indeed, he is no less than a stuffed 55
man. But for the stuffing—well, we are all mortal. 56

LEONATO   You must not, sir, mistake my niece. There is
a kind of merry war betwixt Signor Benedick and her.
They never meet but there's a skirmish of wit between
them.

BEATRICE   Alas! He gets nothing by that. In our last
conflict, four of his five wits went halting off, and now 62
is the whole man governed with one; so that if he have
wit enough to keep himself warm, let him bear it for a
difference between himself and his horse, for it is all 65
the wealth that he hath left to be known a reasonable 66
creature. Who is his companion now? He hath every 67
month a new sworn brother. 68

MESSENGER   Is't possible?

BEATRICE   Very easily possible. He wears his faith but as 70
the fashion of his hat; it ever changes with the next
block. 72

MESSENGER   I see, lady, the gentleman is not in your 73
books. 74

BEATRICE   No. An he were, I would burn my study. But 75
I pray you, who is his companion? Is there no young
squarer now that will make a voyage with him to the 77
devil?

MESSENGER   He is most in the company of the right
noble Claudio.

BEATRICE   Oh, Lord, he will hang upon him like a 81
disease! He is sooner caught than the pestilence, and
the taker runs presently mad. God help the noble 83
Claudio! If he have caught the Benedick, it will cost 84
him a thousand pound ere 'a be cured. 85

MESSENGER   I will hold friends with you, lady. 86

BEATRICE   Do, good friend.

LEONATO   You will never run mad, niece. 88

BEATRICE   No, not till a hot January. 89

MESSENGER   Don Pedro is approached.

Enter Don Pedro, Claudio, Benedick, Balthasar,
and [Don] John the Bastard.

DON PEDRO   Good Signor Leonato, are you come to
meet your trouble? The fashion of the world is to 92
avoid cost, and you encounter it. 93

LEONATO   Never came trouble to my house in the
likeness of Your Grace. For trouble being gone,
comfort should remain; but when you depart from
me, sorrow abides and happiness takes his leave.

DON PEDRO   You embrace your charge too willingly.—I 98
think this is your daughter.

[Presenting himself to Hero.]

LEONATO   Her mother hath many times told me so.

BENEDICK   Were you in doubt, sir, that you asked her?

LEONATO   Signor Benedick, no; for then were you a
child.

DON PEDRO   You have it full, Benedick. We may guess 104
by this what you are, being a man. Truly, the lady
fathers herself. Be happy, lady, for you are like an 106
honorable father.

BENEDICK   If Signor Leonato be her father, she would
not have his head on her shoulders for all Messina, as 109
like him as she is.   *[Don Pedro and Leonato talk aside.]*

BEATRICE   I wonder that you will still be talking, Signor
Benedick. Nobody marks you.

BENEDICK   What, my dear Lady Disdain! Are you yet
living?

BEATRICE   Is it possible disdain should die while she
hath such meet food to feed it as Signor Benedick? 116

35 **pleasant** jocular   37 **bills** placards, advertisements   38 **at the flight** to a long-distance archery contest. (Beatrice mocks Benedick's pretentions as a lady killer.)   **my uncle's fool** (Perhaps a professional fool in her uncle's service.)   39 **subscribed for** accepted on behalf of   40 **bird-bolt** a blunt-headed arrow used for fowling. (Sometimes used by children because of its relative harmlessness and thus conventionally appropriate to Cupid.)   43 **tax** disparage   44 **meet** even, quits   47 **musty victual** stale food.   **holp** helped   48 **valiant trencherman** great eater   49 **stomach** appetite. (With a mocking suggestion also of "courage.")   51 **soldier to a lady** lady killer. (With a play on *to/too*.)   52 **to** compared to   53 **stuffed** amply supplied   55–6 **a stuffed man** i.e., a figure stuffed to resemble a man   56 **the stuffing** i.e., what he's truly made of.   **well . . . mortal** i.e., well, we all have our faults.   62 **five wits** i.e., not the five senses, but the five faculties: memory, imagination, judgment, fantasy, common sense.   **halting** limping   65 **difference** heraldic feature distinguishing a junior member or branch of a family. (With a play on the usual sense.)   65–7 **it is . . . creature** i.e., his feeble wit is all he has left to identify him as rationally human.   68 **sworn brother** brother in arms (*frater juratus,* an allusion to the ancient practice of swearing brotherhood).   70 **faith** allegiance, or fidelity   72 **block** mold for shaping hats.

73–4 **in your books** in favor with you, in your good books. (But Beatrice, in her reply, takes *books* in the literal sense of something to be found in a library.)   75 **An** If. (Also in line 131.)   77 **squarer** quarreler   81 **he** i.e., Benedick   83 **presently** immediately   84 **the Benedick** i.e., as if this were a disease   85 **'a** he   86 **hold friends** keep on friendly terms (so as not to earn your enmity)   88 **run mad** i.e., "catch the Benedick"   89 **not . . . January** i.e., not any time soon.   92 **your trouble** i.e., the expense of entertaining me and my retinue.   93 **encounter** go to meet   98 **charge** social responsibility and expense.   104 **have it full** are well answered   106 **fathers herself** shows by appearance who her father is.   109 **his head** i.e., with Leonato's white beard and signs of age   116 **meet** suitable. (With a pun on "meat.")

Courtesy itself must convert to disdain, if you come in 117
her presence.

BENEDICK   Then is courtesy a turncoat. But it is certain
I am loved of all ladies, only you excepted; and I
would I could find in my heart that I had not a hard
heart, for truly I love none.

BEATRICE   A dear happiness to women! They would 123
else have been troubled with a pernicious suitor. I
thank God and my cold blood I am of your humor for 125
that. I had rather hear my dog bark at a crow than a 126
man swear he loves me.

BENEDICK   God keep Your Ladyship still in that mind!
So some gentleman or other shall scape a predestinate 129
scratched face.

BEATRICE   Scratching could not make it worse, an 'twere
such a face as yours were.   132

BENEDICK   Well, you are a rare parrot-teacher.   133

BEATRICE   A bird of my tongue is better than a beast of 134
yours.   135

BENEDICK   I would my horse had the speed of your
tongue and so good a continuer. But keep your way, 137
i'God's name; I have done.

BEATRICE   You always end with a jade's trick. I know 139
you of old.

DON PEDRO   That is the sum of all, Leonato. Signor 141
Claudio and Signor Benedick, my dear friend Leonato
hath invited you all. I tell him we shall stay here at the
least a month, and he heartily prays some occasion
may detain us longer. I dare swear he is no hypocrite,
but prays from his heart.

LEONATO   If you swear, my lord, you shall not be forsworn. [*To Don John*] Let me bid you welcome, my
lord, being reconciled to the Prince your brother. I owe 149
you all duty.

DON JOHN   I thank you. I am not of many words, but I
thank you.

LEONATO   Please it Your Grace lead on?   153

DON PEDRO   Your hand, Leonato. We will go together. 154
Exeunt. Manent Benedick and Claudio.

CLAUDIO   Benedick, didst thou note the daughter of
Signor Leonato?

BENEDICK   I noted her not, but I looked on her.   157

CLAUDIO   Is she not a modest young lady?

BENEDICK   Do you question me as an honest man
should do, for my simple true judgment? Or would

you have me speak after my custom, as being a
professed tyrant to their sex?   162

CLAUDIO   No, I pray thee, speak in sober judgment.

BENEDICK   Why, i'faith, methinks she's too low for a 164
high praise, too brown for a fair praise, and too little
for a great praise. Only this commendation I can afford
her, that were she other than she is, she were unhandsome, and being no other but as she is, I do not like
her.

CLAUDIO   Thou thinkest I am in sport. I pray thee, tell
me truly how thou lik'st her.

BENEDICK   Would you buy her, that you inquire after
her?

CLAUDIO   Can the world buy such a jewel?

BENEDICK   Yea, and a case to put it into. But speak you 175
this with a sad brow? Or do you play the flouting Jack, 176
to tell us Cupid is a good hare-finder and Vulcan a rare 177
carpenter? Come, in what key shall a man take you, to 178
go in the song?   179

CLAUDIO   In mine eye she is the sweetest lady that ever
I looked on.

BENEDICK   I can see yet without spectacles, and I see no
such matter. There's her cousin, an she were not possessed with a fury, exceeds her as much in beauty as the 184
first of May doth the last of December. But I hope you
have no intent to turn husband, have you?

CLAUDIO   I would scarce trust myself, though I had
sworn the contrary, if Hero would be my wife.

BENEDICK   Is't come to this? In faith, hath not the world 189
one man but he will wear his cap with suspicion? Shall 190
I never see a bachelor of threescore again? Go to, 191
i'faith; an thou wilt needs thrust thy neck into a yoke,
wear the print of it and sigh away Sundays. Look, Don 193
Pedro is returned to seek you.

Enter Don Pedro.

DON PEDRO   What secret hath held you here, that you
followed not to Leonato's?

BENEDICK   I would Your Grace would constrain me to 197
tell.

DON PEDRO   I charge thee on thy allegiance.

BENEDICK   You hear, Count Claudio. I can be secret as a
dumb man—I would have you think so—but on my
allegiance, mark you this, on my allegiance! He is in
love. With who? Now that is Your Grace's part. Mark 203
how short his answer is: with Hero, Leonato's short
daughter.

---

117 **convert** change   123 **dear happiness** precious piece of luck
125–6 **I am . . . that** I am of the same disposition in that matter, i.e., of
loving no one.   129 **scape** escape.   **predestinate** inevitable (for any
man who should woo Beatrice)   132 **were** i.e., is.   133 **rare** outstanding.   **parrot-teacher** i.e., one who would teach a parrot well, because
you merely "parrot" my lines.   134 **of my tongue** taught to speak
like me, i.e., incessantly   134–5 **of yours** taught to speak like you.
137 **and . . . continuer** i.e., and as much staying power in running as
you have in talking.   139 **a jade's trick** i.e., an ill-tempered horse's
habit of slipping its head out of the collar or stopping suddenly (just
as Benedick proposes to abandon this exchange of witticisms when
he thinks he has had the last word).   141 **sum of all** (Don Pedro and
Leonato have been conversing apart on other matters.)   149 **being**
since you are   153 **Please it** May it please   154 **go together** i.e., go
arm in arm (thus avoiding the question of precedence in order of
leaving).   154.1 *Manent* They remain onstage   157 **noted her not**
gave her no special attention

162 **tyrant** one cruel or pitiless in attitude   164 **low** short   175 **case**
(1) jewel case (2) clothing, outer garments. (There is also a bawdy
play on the meaning "female pudenda.")   176 **sad** serious.   **flouting
Jack** i.e., mocking rascal   177–8 **to tell . . . carpenter**? i.e., are you
mocking us with nonsense? (Cupid was blind, not sharp-eyed like a
hunter, and Vulcan was a blacksmith, not a carpenter.)   178–9 **to . . .
song** as the song expresses it. (Alluding perhaps to some popular
song.)   184 **with a fury** by an avenging, infernal spirit   189–90 **hath
. . . suspicion?** i.e., isn't there a man left alive who will regard marriage with a jaundiced eye? (A cap might be used, unsuccessfully perhaps, in an attempt to hide a cuckold's horns.)   191 **Go to** (An
expression of impatience.)   193 **wear . . . Sundays** i.e., display the
marks of your domestic enslavement resignedly.   197 **constrain**
order   203 **part** speaking part. (I.e., to say, "With who?")

CLAUDIO   If this were so, so were it uttered.   206

BENEDICK   Like the old tale, my lord: "It is not so, nor   207
'twas not so, but indeed, God forbid it should be so."

CLAUDIO   If my passion change not shortly, God forbid
it should be otherwise.

DON PEDRO   Amen, if you love her, for the lady is very
well worthy.

CLAUDIO   You speak this to fetch me in, my lord.   213

DON PEDRO   By my troth, I speak my thought.   214

CLAUDIO   And in faith, my lord, I spoke mine.

BENEDICK   And by my two faiths and troths, my lord, I   216
spoke mine.

CLAUDIO   That I love her, I feel.

DON PEDRO   That she is worthy, I know.

BENEDICK   That I neither feel how she should be loved
nor know how she should be worthy is the opinion
that fire cannot melt out of me. I will die in it at the
stake.

DON PEDRO   Thou wast ever an obstinate heretic in the
despite of beauty.   225

CLAUDIO   And never could maintain his part but in the   226
force of his will.   227

BENEDICK   That a woman conceived me, I thank her;
that she brought me up, I likewise give her most humble thanks. But that I will have a recheat winded in my   230
forehead or hang my bugle in an invisible baldrick, all   231
women shall pardon me. Because I will not do them   232
the wrong to mistrust any, I will do myself the right to
trust none; and the fine is, for the which I may go the   234
finer, I will live a bachelor.   235

DON PEDRO   I shall see thee, ere I die, look pale with
love.

BENEDICK   With anger, with sickness, or with hunger,
my lord, not with love. Prove that ever I lose more   239
blood with love than I will get again with drinking,   240
pick out mine eyes with a ballad-maker's pen and   241
hang me up at the door of a brothel house for the sign   242
of blind Cupid.

DON PEDRO   Well, if ever thou dost fall from this faith,
thou wilt prove a notable argument.   245

BENEDICK   If I do, hang me in a bottle like a cat and   246
shoot at me, and he that hits me, let him be clapped on
the shoulder and called Adam.   248

DON PEDRO   Well, as time shall try:
"In time the savage bull doth bear the yoke."   250

BENEDICK   The savage bull may; but if ever the sensible
Benedick bear it, pluck off the bull's horns and set
them in my forehead, and let me be vilely painted, and
in such great letters as they write, "Here is good horse
to hire," let them signify under my sign, "Here you
may see Benedick the married man."

CLAUDIO   If this should ever happen, thou wouldst be
horn-mad.   258

DON PEDRO   Nay, if Cupid have not spent all his quiver
in Venice, thou wilt quake for this shortly.   260

BENEDICK   I look for an earthquake too, then.   261

DON PEDRO   Well, you will temporize with the hours. In   262
the meantime, good Signor Benedick, repair to
Leonato's. Commend me to him, and tell him I will
not fail him at supper, for indeed he hath made great
preparation.

BENEDICK   I have almost matter enough in me for such   267
an embassage; and so I commit you—   268

CLAUDIO   To the tuition of God. From my house, if I had   269
it—

DON PEDRO   The sixth of July. Your loving friend,
Benedick.

BENEDICK   Nay, mock not, mock not. The body of your
discourse is sometime guarded with fragments, and   274
the guards are but slightly basted on neither. Ere you   275
flout old ends any further, examine your conscience.   276
And so I leave you.   *Exit.*

CLAUDIO
My liege, Your Highness now may do me good.   278

DON PEDRO
My love is thine to teach. Teach it but how,
And thou shalt see how apt it is to learn
Any hard lesson that may do thee good.

CLAUDIO
Hath Leonato any son, my lord?

DON PEDRO
No child but Hero; she's his only heir.
Dost thou affect her, Claudio?

CLAUDIO   O my lord,   284

206 If . . . uttered If this were true, it might be told in words to this
effect.   **207 old tale** (In the English fairy tale known as "Mr. Fox," a
murderous wooer, discovered in his crimes by the lady he seeks to
marry and victimize, repeatedly disclaims her recital of what she has
seen by the refrain here set in quotations. The story is a variant of the
theme known as "the Robber Bridegroom." Benedick uses it mockingly here to characterize Claudio's reluctance to admit his "crime" of
falling in love.)   **213 fetch me in** get me to confess   **214 By my troth**
By my faith, upon my word. (A mild oath.)   **216 by . . . troths** as it
were, by my loyalty to you both   **225 despite** contempt   **226–7 in . . .
will** by mere obstinacy (which, as defined by the Schoolmen, was the
state of the heretic).   **230–2 But that . . . me** i.e., Women must pardon
me for refusing to have a horn placed on my head as if I were a cuckold. (A *recheat* is a hunting call sounded [*winded*] on a horn to assemble the hounds; a *baldrick* is a strap that supports the horn, here
invisible because the horn is the metaphorical one of cuckoldry.)
234 fine conclusion   **234–5 go the finer** be more finely dressed (since
without a wife I will have more money to spend on clothing)
239 Prove If you can prove   **239–40 lose . . . drinking** (According to
Elizabethan theory, each sigh cost the heart a drop of blood, whereas
blood was replenished by wine.)   **241 ballad-maker's pen** i.e., such
as would be used to write love ballads or satires   **242 sign** painted
sign, such as hung over inns and shops   **245 notable argument** notorious subject for conversation, example.

246 bottle wicker or leather basket (to hold the cat sometimes used as
an archery target)   **248 Adam** (Probably refers to Adam Bell, archer
outlaw of the ballads.)   **250 In . . . yoke** (Proverbial.)   **258 horn-mad**
stark mad. (From the fury of horned beasts; with allusion to cuckoldry.)   **259 Venice** (A city noted for licentiousness.)   **quake** (With a
pun on *quiver* in the previous line.)   **261 I . . . then** i.e., My falling in
love will be at least as rare as an earthquake.   **262 temporize . . .
hours** come to terms, or become milder, in time. (With perhaps a
bawdy pun on *hours*, "whores," pronounced something like "hoors.")
267 matter wit, intelligence   **268 embassage** mission.   **and so . . . you**
(A conventional close, which Claudio and Don Pedro mockingly play
with as though it were the complimentary close of a letter.)
269 tuition protection   **274 guarded** ornamented, trimmed
275 guards . . . neither trimmings are tenuously stitched on at best,
have only the flimsiest connection.   **276 flout old ends** quote or recite
mockingly proverbial tags of wisdom (as well as fragments of cloth, or
the *ends* of letters that Claudio and Don Pedro have been parodying).
examine your conscience look to your own behavior or speech.
278 do me good do me some good, help me.   **284 affect** love

When you went onward on this ended action,   285
I looked upon her with a soldier's eye,
That liked, but had a rougher task in hand
Than to drive liking to the name of love.
But now I am returned and that war thoughts   289
Have left their places vacant, in their rooms
Come thronging soft and delicate desires,
All prompting me how fair young Hero is,
Saying, I liked her ere I went to wars.

DON PEDRO
Thou wilt be like a lover presently
And tire the hearer with a book of words.
If thou dost love fair Hero, cherish it,
And I will break with her and with her father,   297
And thou shalt have her. Was't not to this end
That thou began'st to twist so fine a story?   299

CLAUDIO
How sweetly you do minister to love,
That know love's grief by his complexion!   301
But lest my liking might too sudden seem,
I would have salved it with a longer treatise.   303

DON PEDRO
What need the bridge much broader than the flood?   304
The fairest grant is the necessity.   305
Look what will serve is fit. 'Tis once: thou lovest, 306
And I will fit thee with the remedy.
I know we shall have reveling tonight;
I will assume thy part in some disguise
And tell fair Hero I am Claudio,
And in her bosom I'll unclasp my heart
And take her hearing prisoner with the force
And strong encounter of my amorous tale.
Then after to her father will I break,
And the conclusion is, she shall be thine.
In practice let us put it presently.   *Exeunt.*

❖

[1.2]

*Enter Leonato and an old man [Antonio],
brother to Leonato, [meeting].*

LEONATO   How now, brother, where is my cousin,   1
your son? Hath he provided this music?

ANTONIO   He is very busy about it. But brother, I can
tell you strange news that you yet dreamt not of.

LEONATO   Are they good?   5

ANTONIO   As the event stamps them, but they have a   6
good cover; they show well outward. The Prince and   7

Count Claudio, walking in a thick-pleached alley in   8
mine orchard, were thus much overheard by a man of   9
mine: the Prince discovered to Claudio that he loved   10
my niece your daughter and meant to acknowledge it
this night in a dance, and if he found her accordant, he 12
meant to take the present time by the top and instantly   13
break with you of it.

LEONATO   Hath the fellow any wit that told you this?   15

ANTONIO   A good sharp fellow. I will send for him, and
question him yourself.

LEONATO   No, no; we will hold it as a dream till it
appear itself. But I will acquaint my daughter withal,
that she may be the better prepared for an answer, if
peradventure this be true. Go you and tell her of it.

[*Enter Antonio's Son, with a musician and
others.*]

Cousins, you know what you have to do.—Oh, I cry   22
you mercy, friend; go you with me, and I will use your   23
skill.—Good cousin, have a care this busy time.
                                            Exeunt.

❖

[1.3]

*Enter Sir [Don] John the Bastard and Conrade,
his companion.*

CONRADE   What the goodyear, my lord! Why are you   1
thus out of measure sad?   2

DON JOHN   There is no measure in the occasion that
breeds; therefore the sadness is without limit.

CONRADE   You should hear reason.   5

DON JOHN   And when I have heard it, what blessing
brings it?

CONRADE   If not a present remedy, at least a patient
sufferance.   9

DON JOHN   I wonder that thou, being, as thou say'st
thou art, born under Saturn, goest about to apply a   11
moral medicine to a mortifying mischief. I cannot hide 12
what I am: I must be sad when I have cause and smile
at no man's jests, eat when I have stomach and wait   14
for no man's leisure, sleep when I am drowsy and
tend on no man's business, laugh when I am merry   16
and claw no man in his humor.   17

CONRADE   Yea, but you must not make the full show of
this till you may do it without controlment. You have   19
of late stood out against your brother, and he hath   20
ta'en you newly into his grace, where it is impossible 21
you should take true root but by the fair weather that

---

285 **ended action** military action now ended   289 **now** now that
297 **break** open the subject. (As also in line 314.)   299 **twist** draw out
the thread of   301 **his complexion** its outward appearance.
303 **salved** soothed, eased the way for   304 **What need** Why need be.
flood river.   305 **The fairest . . . necessity** The best thing to do is simply what is necessary.   306 **Look what** Whatever.   **'Tis once** In
short, once and for all. (This speech of Don Pedro's is overheard by a
servant of Antonio's, as we learn in the next scene.)
1.2 Location: Leonato's house.
1 **cousin** kinsman   5 **they** i.e., the news. (Often treated as a plural
noun, as at 2.1.167.)   6 **event** outcome   6–7 **they . . . cover** (The
image is of a printed book, promising well by its cover.)

8 **thick-pleached alley** walk lined with dense hedges of intertwined
shrubs   9 **orchard** garden.   **man** servant   10 **discovered** disclosed
12 **accordant** agreeing, consenting   13 **take . . . top** i.e., seize the
opportunity. (Proverbially, Occasion was imagined bald in the back of
the head but with a forelock hair in the front that opportunistically
could be grabbed.)   15 **wit** sense, intelligence   22–3 **cry you mercy**
beg your pardon   23 **friend** (Addressed perhaps to the musician.)
1.3. Location: Leonato's house.
1 **What the goodyear** i.e., What the deuce   2 **out of measure** immoderately   5 **hear** listen to   9 **sufferance** endurance.   11 **under Saturn**
(Hence, of a morose disposition.)   11–12 **goest . . . mischief** endeavor
to cure with moral commonplaces a deadly disease.   14 **stomach**
appetite   16 **tend on** attend to   17 **claw** flatter.   **humor** whim.
19 **controlment** restraint.   20 **stood out** rebelled   21 **grace** favor

you make yourself. It is needful that you frame the 23
season for your own harvest.

DON JOHN   I had rather be a canker in a hedge than a 25
rose in his grace, and it better fits my blood to be dis- 26
dained of all than to fashion a carriage to rob love from 27
any. In this, though I cannot be said to be a flattering
honest man, it must not be denied but I am a plain-
dealing villain. I am trusted with a muzzle and 30
enfranchised with a clog; therefore I have decreed not 31
to sing in my cage. If I had my mouth, I would bite; if
I had my liberty, I would do my liking. In the
meantime let me be that I am, and seek not to alter me.

CONRADE   Can you make no use of your discontent?

DON JOHN   I make all use of it, for I use it only. Who 36
comes here?

Enter Borachio.

What news, Borachio?

BORACHIO   I came yonder from a great supper. The
Prince your brother is royally entertained by Leonato,
and I can give you intelligence of an intended mar- 41
riage.

DON JOHN   Will it serve for any model to build mischief
on? What is he for a fool that betroths himself to 44
unquietness?

BORACHIO   Marry, it is your brother's right hand. 46

DON JOHN   Who, the most exquisite Claudio?

BORACHIO   Even he.

DON JOHN   A proper squire! And who, and who? Which 49
way looks he?

BORACHIO   Marry, one Hero, the daughter and heir of
Leonato.

DON JOHN   A very forward March chick! How came 53
you to this?

BORACHIO   Being entertained for a perfumer, as I was 55
smoking a musty room, comes me the Prince and 56
Claudio, hand in hand, in sad conference. I whipped 57
me behind the arras, and there heard it agreed upon 58
that the Prince should woo Hero for himself and,
having obtained her, give her to Count Claudio.

DON JOHN   Come, come, let us thither. This may prove
food to my displeasure. That young start-up hath all 62
the glory of my overthrow. If I can cross him any way, 63
I bless myself every way. You are both sure, and will 64
assist me?

CONRADE   To the death, my lord.

DON JOHN   Let us to the great supper. Their cheer is the
greater that I am subdued. Would the cook were o' my 68
mind! Shall we go prove what's to be done? 69

BORACHIO   We'll wait upon Your Lordship.   *Exeunt.*

[2.1]

*Enter Leonato, his brother [Antonio], Hero his
daughter, and Beatrice his niece [with Margaret
and Ursula].*

LEONATO   Was not Count John here at supper?

ANTONIO   I saw him not.

BEATRICE   How tartly that gentleman looks! I never can 3
see him but I am heartburned an hour after. 4

HERO   He is of a very melancholy disposition.

BEATRICE   He were an excellent man that were made 6
just in the midway between him and Benedick. The
one is too like an image and says nothing, and the 8
other too like my lady's eldest son, evermore tattling. 9

LEONATO   Then half Signor Benedick's tongue in Count
John's mouth, and half Count John's melancholy in
Signor Benedick's face—

BEATRICE   With a good leg and a good foot, uncle, and
money enough in his purse, such a man would win
any woman in the world, if 'a could get her good will. 15

LEONATO   By my troth, niece, thou wilt never get thee a
husband if thou be so shrewd of thy tongue. 17

ANTONIO   In faith, she's too curst. 18

BEATRICE   Too curst is more than curst. I shall lessen
God's sending that way; for it is said, "God sends a 20
curst cow short horns," but to a cow too curst he sends 21
none.

LEONATO   So, by being too curst, God will send you no
horns.

BEATRICE   Just, if he send me no husband, for the which 25
blessing I am at him upon my knees every morning
and evening. Lord, I could not endure a husband with
a beard on his face! I had rather lie in the woolen. 28

LEONATO   You may light on a husband that hath no
beard.

BEATRICE   What should I do with him? Dress him in my
apparel and make him my waiting-gentlewoman? He
that hath a beard is more than a youth, and he that
hath no beard is less than a man; and he that is more
than a youth is not for me, and he that is less than a
man, I am not for him. Therefore I will even take

---

23 **frame** fashion   25 **canker** dog rose, one that grows wild rather
than being cultivated in formal gardens   26 **blood** mood, disposition
27 **fashion . . . love** counterfeit a behavior to gain undeserved attention   30–1 **I . . . clog** I am trusted only with my muzzle on and am
allowed freedom only to the extent of being hampered by a heavy
wooden block   31 **decreed** determined   36 **I . . . only** Discontent is
my only resource, and I cultivate it alone.   41 **intelligence** news
44 **What . . . fool** What kind of fool is he   46 **Marry** By the Virgin
Mary, i.e., indeed   49 **proper squire** fine young man. (Said contemptuously.)   53 **forward March chick** precocious young thing (like a
chick hatched early).   55 **entertained for** hired as   56 **smoking**
sweetening the air of (with aromatic smoke).   **comes me** comes. (*Me*
is used colloquially, as also in line 58.)   57 **sad** serious   58 **arras**
tapestry, wall hanging   62 **start-up** upstart   63 **cross** thwart
64 **sure** trustworthy

68–9 **o' my mind** i.e., of a mind to poison the food.   69 **prove** try out
2.1. Location: Leonato's house.
3 **tartly** sour of disposition   4 **heartburned** afflicted with heartburn or
indigestion   6 **He were** A man would be   8 **image** statue   9 **my . . .
son** i.e., a spoiled child.   **tattling** chattering.   15 **'a** he   17 **shrewd**
sharp   18 **curst** shrewish   20 **that way** in that respect   21 **curst** i.e.,
savage, vicious. (God proverbially takes care that vicious are limited
in their ability to do harm.)   25 **Just** Right, exactly so.   **no husband**
If Beatrice has no husband, there can be no prospect of cuckold's
horns. (She may also be jesting about a short penis here and in lines
20–2.)   28 **in the woolen** between blankets, without sheets.

sixpence in earnest of the bearward, and lead his apes 37
into hell. 38

LEONATO   Well, then, go you into hell?

BEATRICE   No, but to the gate; and there will the devil
meet me, like an old cuckold, with horns on his head,
and say, "Get you to heaven, Beatrice, get you to
heaven, here's no place for you maids." So deliver I up
my apes, and away to Saint Peter, for the heavens; he 44
shows me where the bachelors sit, and there live we 45
as merry as the day is long.

ANTONIO [to Hero]   Well, niece, I trust you will be ruled
by your father.

BEATRICE   Yes, faith, it is my cousin's duty to make
curtsy and say, "Father, as it please you." But yet for
all that, cousin, let him be a handsome fellow, or else
make another curtsy and say, "Father, as it please me."

LEONATO   Well, niece, I hope to see you one day fitted
with a husband.

BEATRICE   Not till God make men of some other metal 55
than earth. Would it not grieve a woman to be over-
mastered with a piece of valiant dust? To make an
account of her life to a clod of wayward marl? No, 58
uncle, I'll none. Adam's sons are my brethren, and 59
truly I hold it a sin to match in my kindred. 60

LEONATO [to Hero]   Daughter, remember what I told
you. If the Prince do solicit you in that kind, you know 62
your answer.

BEATRICE   The fault will be in the music, cousin, if you
be not wooed in good time. If the Prince be too 65
important, tell him there is measure in everything, 66
and so dance out the answer. For, hear me, Hero:
wooing, wedding, and repenting is as a Scotch jig, a 68
measure, and a cinquepace. The first suit is hot and 69
hasty, like a Scotch jig, and full as fantastical; the
wedding, mannerly-modest, as a measure, full of state 71
and ancientry; and then comes Repentance, and with 72
his bad legs falls into the cinquepace faster and faster
till he sink into his grave.

LEONATO   Cousin, you apprehend passing shrewdly. 75

BEATRICE   I have a good eye, uncle; I can see a church by 76
daylight. 77

LEONATO   The revelers are entering, brother. Make good
room.   [The men put on their masks.]

*Enter [as maskers] Prince [Don] Pedro, Clau-
dio, and Benedick, and Balthasar, [Borachio,]
and Don John.*

DON PEDRO   Lady, will you walk a bout with your 80
friend?   [The couples pair off for the dance.] 81

HERO   So you walk softly and look sweetly and say
nothing, I am yours for the walk, and especially when
I walk away.

DON PEDRO   With me in your company?

HERO   I may say so, when I please.

DON PEDRO   And when please you to say so?

HERO   When I like your favor, for God defend the lute 88
should be like the case! 89

DON PEDRO   My visor is Philemon's roof; within the 90
house is Jove.

HERO   Why, then, your visor should be thatched. 92

DON PEDRO   Speak low, if you speak love. 93
                              [They dance to one side.]

BALTHASAR   Well, I would you did like me. 94

MARGARET   So would not I for your own sake, for I have
many ill qualities.

BALTHASAR   Which is one?

MARGARET   I say my prayers aloud.

BALTHASAR   I love you the better. The hearers may cry
Amen.

MARGARET   God match me with a good dancer!

BALTHASAR   Amen.

MARGARET   And God keep him out of my sight when
the dance is done! Answer, clerk. 104

BALTHASAR   No more words. The clerk is answered. 105
                              [They dance to one side.]

URSULA   I know you well enough. You are Signor
Antonio.

ANTONIO   At a word, I am not. 108

URSULA   I know you by the waggling of your head.

ANTONIO   To tell you true, I counterfeit him.

URSULA   You could never do him so ill-well unless you 111
were the very man. Here's his dry hand up and down. 112
You are he, you are he.

ANTONIO   At a word, I am not.

URSULA   Come, come, do you think I do not know you
by your excellent wit? Can virtue hide itself? Go to,
mum, you are he. Graces will appear, and there's an 117
end.   [They dance to one side.] 118

---

37 in earnest in token advance payment for. **bearward** one who
keeps and exhibits a bear (and sometimes apes) **37–8 lead . . . hell**
(An ancient proverb says, "Such as die maids do all lead apes in
hell.") **44 for the heavens** (A common interjection, like "Good heavens!" but here also carrying its literal meaning, i.e., bound for
heaven.) **45 bachelors** unmarried persons of either sex **55 metal**
substance. (With play on "mettle.") **58 marl** clay, earth (such as was
used by God to make Adam in Genesis 2). **59–60 Adam's . . . kindred** (Beatrice jests that since men and women are all descended from
Adam, it would be incestuous for her to marry a man.) **62 in that
kind** to that effect (i.e., to marriage) **65 in good time** (1) soon (2) in
time to the music, rhythmically. **66 important** importunate, urgent.
measure (1) moderation (2) rhythm, dance **68–9 a measure** a formal
dance **69 cinquepace** five-step lively dance, galliard. (The pun on
"sink apace," as it was pronounced, is evident in lines 72–4: repentance will *sink faster and faster,* with a suggestion of detumescence.)
71–2 state and ancientry dignity and traditional stateliness
75 apprehend passing shrewdly understand with unusual perspicac-
ity. **76–7 see . . . daylight** i.e., see something as plain as the nose on
your face.

80 walk a bout take a turn, join in a section of a dance. (Here probably a slow, stately pavane.) **81 friend** wooer. **88 favor** face
88–9 God . . . case! i.e., God forbid the face within should be as
unhandsome as its cover, your visor! **90 Philemon's roof** i.e., the
humble cottage in which the peasants Philemon and Baucis entertained Jove, or Jupiter, unawares. (See Ovid, *Metamorphoses,* 8.)
90–3 My . . . love (A fourteen-syllable rhymed couplet, the verse form
of Arthur Golding's translation of the *Metamorphoses,* 1567.) **92 visor**
mask. **thatched** i.e., whiskered, to resemble the thatch of a humble
cottage. **94–105 BALTHASAR** (The speech prefixes in the Quarto text
for Balthasar's lines read *Bene.* and *Balth.* Some editors speculate that
Borachio is intended.) **104 clerk** (So addressed because of Balthasar's
repeatedly answering "Amen" like the parish clerk saying the
responses.) **108 At a word** In short **111 do . . . ill-well** imitate his
imperfections so perfectly **112 dry hand** (A sign of age.) **up and
down** up exactly. **117 mum** be silent **117–18 an end** no more to
be said.

BEATRICE   Will you not tell me who told you so?

BENEDICK   No, you shall pardon me.

BEATRICE   Nor will you not tell me who you are?

BENEDICK   Not now.

BEATRICE   That I was disdainful and that I had my good
wit out of the *Hundred Merry Tales*—well, this was 124
Signor Benedick that said so.

BENEDICK   What's he?

BEATRICE   I am sure you know him well enough.

BENEDICK   Not I, believe me.

BEATRICE   Did he never make you laugh?

BENEDICK   I pray you, what is he?

BEATRICE   Why, he is the Prince's jester, a very dull fool.
Only his gift is in devising impossible slanders. None 132
but libertines delight in him, and the commendation 133
is not in his wit but in his villainy, for he both pleases 134
men and angers them, and then they laugh at him and 135
beat him. I am sure he is in the fleet. I would he had 136
boarded me. 137

BENEDICK   When I know the gentleman, I'll tell him 138
what you say.

BEATRICE   Do, do. He'll but break a comparison or two 140
on me, which peradventure not marked or not laughed 141
at strikes him into melancholy; and then there's a partridge wing saved, for the fool will eat no supper that
night. [*Music.*] We must follow the leaders. 144

BENEDICK   In every good thing.

BEATRICE   Nay, if they lead to any ill, I will leave them
at the next turning. 147

*Dance. Exeunt [all except Don John, Borachio, and
Claudio. Don John and Borachio are unmasked.]*

DON JOHN [*to Borachio*]   Sure my brother is amorous on
Hero and hath withdrawn her father to break with
him about it. The ladies follow her, and but one visor
remains.

BORACHIO   And that is Claudio. I know him by his
bearing.

DON JOHN [*advancing to Claudio*]   Are not you Signor
Benedick?

CLAUDIO   You know me well. I am he.

DON JOHN   Signor, you are very near my brother in his 157
love. He is enamored on Hero. I pray you, dissuade 158
him from her; she is no equal for his birth. You may do 159
the part of an honest man in it.

CLAUDIO   How know you he loves her?

DON JOHN   I heard him swear his affection.

BORACHIO   So did I, too, and he swore he would marry
her tonight.

DON JOHN   Come, let us to the banquet. 165

Exeunt. Manet Claudio.

CLAUDIO
Thus answer I in name of Benedick,
But hear these ill news with the ears of Claudio.
'Tis certain so. The Prince woos for himself.
Friendship is constant in all other things
Save in the office and affairs of love;
Therefore all hearts in love use their own tongues.
Let every eye negotiate for itself
And trust no agent; for beauty is a witch
Against whose charms faith melteth into blood. 174
This is an accident of hourly proof, 175
Which I mistrusted not. Farewell therefore Hero! 176

Enter Benedick [unmasked].

BENEDICK   Count Claudio?

CLAUDIO   Yea, the same.

BENEDICK   Come, will you go with me?

CLAUDIO   Whither?

BENEDICK   Even to the next willow, about your own 181
business, County. What fashion will you wear the gar- 182
land of? About your neck, like an usurer's chain? Or 183
under your arm, like a lieutenant's scarf? You must 184
wear it one way, for the Prince hath got your Hero. 185

CLAUDIO   I wish him joy of her.

BENEDICK   Why, that's spoken like an honest drover; so 187
they sell bullocks. But did you think the Prince would 188
have served you thus?

CLAUDIO   I pray you, leave me.

BENEDICK   Ho, now you strike like the blind man. 'Twas 191
the boy that stole your meat, and you'll beat the post. 192

CLAUDIO   If it will not be, I'll leave you.   *Exit.* 193

BENEDICK   Alas, poor hurt fowl! Now will he creep into 194
sedges. But that my Lady Beatrice should know me, 195
and not know me! The Prince's fool! Ha? It may be I 196
go under that title because I am merry. Yea, but so I am
apt to do myself wrong. I am not so reputed. It is the 198
base, though bitter, disposition of Beatrice that puts the 199
world into her person and so gives me out. Well, I'll be 200
revenged as I may.

*Enter the Prince [Don Pedro], Hero, [and]
Leonato. [All are unmasked.]*

124 Hundred Merry Tales (A popular collection of anecdotes first published by John Rastell in 1526.)   **132 Only his gift** His only talent.
impossible incredible   **133 libertines** i.e., those who disregard conventional moral laws   **134 villainy** i.e., mocking, raillery; also,
clownishness   **134–5 pleases . . . angers them** i.e., amuses some
with his rudeness and angers others with his slanders   **136 fleet** i.e.,
crowd, company sailing past in the dance.   **137 boarded** i.e.,
accosted. (Continuing the nautical metaphor begun in *fleet*.)
138 know become acquainted with   **140 break a comparison** i.e.,
make a scornful simile (as in a tilting or breaking of lances)   **141 peradventure** if it is   **144 leaders** i.e., of the dance.   **147 turning** turning
figure in the dance.   **157–8 near . . . love** close to my brother.
159 birth aristocratic rank.

165 banquet light repast of fruit, wine, and dessert.   **165.1** *Manet*
He remains onstage   **174 faith . . . blood** loyalty gives way to passion.   **175 accident** occurrence   **176 mistrusted** suspected   **181 willow** (An emblem of disappointed love.)   **182 County** count.
182–3 garland i.e., of willow   **183 usurer's chain** heavy gold chain,
worn by rich men as if it were a badge of office.   **184 scarf** sling.
185 one way one way or the other   **187 drover** cattle dealer
188 bullocks oxen.   **191 strike . . . man** lash out blindly in every
direction.   **191–2 'Twas . . . post** i.e., You're ready to blame anything
but the true cause of your distress. (Benedick seemingly alludes to
some fable about a boy and an innocent postman that demonstrates
this object lesson.)   **193 If . . . be** i.e., If you won't leave me as I asked
194–5 creep into sedges i.e., hide himself away, as wounded fowl
creep into rushes along the river.   **195–6 know me, and not know
me** i.e., be of my long acquaintance, and yet misjudge me so cruelly.
198–200 It is . . . out It is Beatrice's low and harsh disposition to assume
that she speaks for everyone when she characterizes me this way.

DON PEDRO Now, signor, where's the Count? Did you see him?

BENEDICK Troth, my lord, I have played the part of Lady 204 Fame. I found him here as melancholy as a lodge in a 205 warren. I told him, and I think I told him true, that 206 Your Grace had got the good will of this young lady, and I offered him my company to a willow tree, either 208 to make him a garland, as being forsaken, or to bind 209 him up a rod, as being worthy to be whipped. 210

DON PEDRO To be whipped! What's his fault?

BENEDICK The flat transgression of a schoolboy, who, 212 being overjoyed with finding a bird's nest, shows it his companion, and he steals it.

DON PEDRO Wilt thou make a trust a transgression? The 215 transgression is in the stealer.

BENEDICK Yet it had not been amiss the rod had been made, and the garland too; for the garland he might have worn himself, and the rod he might have bestowed on you, who, as I take it, have stolen his bird's nest.

DON PEDRO I will but teach them to sing and restore 222 them to the owner.

BENEDICK If their singing answer your saying, by my 224 faith, you say honestly.

DON PEDRO The Lady Beatrice hath a quarrel to you. 226 The gentleman that danced with her told her she is much wronged by you.

BENEDICK Oh, she misused me past the endurance of a block! An oak but with one green leaf on it would have 230 answered her. My very visor began to assume life and scold with her. She told me, not thinking I had been myself, that I was the Prince's jester, that I was duller than a great thaw; huddling jest upon jest with such 234 impossible conveyance upon me that I stood like a 235 man at a mark, with a whole army shooting at me. She 236 speaks poniards, and every word stabs. If her breath 237 were as terrible as her terminations, there were no liv- 238 ing near her; she would infect to the North Star. I 239 would not marry her, though she were endowed with all that Adam had left him before he transgressed. She 241 would have made Hercules have turned spit, yea, and 242 have cleft his club to make the fire, too. Come, talk not 243 of her. You shall find her the infernal Ate in good 244 apparel. I would to God some scholar would conjure 245 her, for certainly, while she is here, a man may live as 246 quiet in hell as in a sanctuary, and people sin upon purpose because they would go thither; so indeed all disquiet, horror, and perturbation follows her.

Enter Claudio and Beatrice.

DON PEDRO Look, here she comes.

BENEDICK Will Your Grace command me any service to the world's end? I will go on the slightest errand now to the Antipodes that you can devise to send me on; I 253 will fetch you a toothpicker now from the furthest inch 254 of Asia, bring you the length of Prester John's foot, 255 fetch you a hair off the great Cham's beard, do you any 256 embassage to the Pygmies, rather than hold three 257 words' conference with this harpy. You have no 258 employment for me?

DON PEDRO None but to desire your good company.

BENEDICK Oh, God, sir, here's a dish I love not! I cannot endure my Lady Tongue.   *Exit.*

DON PEDRO Come, lady, come, you have lost the heart of Signor Benedick.

BEATRICE Indeed, my lord, he lent it me awhile, and I 265 gave him use for it, a double heart for his single one. 266 Marry, once before he won it of me with false dice; 267 therefore Your Grace may well say I have lost it.

DON PEDRO You have put him down, lady, you have 269 put him down.

BEATRICE So I would not he should do me, my lord, lest I should prove the mother of fools. I have brought Count Claudio, whom you sent me to seek.

DON PEDRO Why, how now, Count? Wherefore are you sad?

CLAUDIO Not sad, my lord.

DON PEDRO How then? Sick?

CLAUDIO Neither, my lord.

BEATRICE The Count is neither sad, nor sick, nor merry, nor well; but civil count, civil as an orange, and some- 280 thing of that jealous complexion. 281

DON PEDRO I'faith, lady, I think your blazon to be true, 282 though I'll be sworn, if he be so, his conceit is false. 283 Here, Claudio, I have wooed in thy name, and fair

---

204 Troth By my faith   **204–5 Lady Fame** Dame Rumor
205–6 lodge in a warren isolated gamekeeper's hut in a large game preserve.   **208 offered . . . to** offered to accompany him to **209–10 bind . . . rod** tie several willow switches into a scourge for him   **212 flat** plain   **215 a trust** a trusted assignment (here, the Prince's having taken in trust the wooing of Hero for Claudio, not himself)   **222 them** i.e., the young birds in the nest   **224 answer your saying** correspond to what you say   **226 to** with   **230 block** (of wood).   **234 great thaw** i.e., time when roads are muddy and impassable, obliging one to stay dully at home. **huddling** piling, heaping up   **235 impossible conveyance** incredible dexterity **236 at a mark** at the target, marking where the arrows hit **237 poniards** daggers   **238 terminations** terms, expressions **239 North Star** (Popularly supposed to be the most remote of stars.) **241 all . . . him** i.e., Paradise before the fall of man   **242 Hercules . . . spit** (The Amazon Omphale forced the captive Hercules to wear women's clothing and spin; turning the spit would be an even more menial kitchen duty.)   **243 cleft** split   **244 Ate** goddess of discord

245 scholar . . . conjure (Scholars were supposed to be able to conjure evil spirits back into hell by addressing them in Latin.)   **246 here** i.e., on earth. (As long as Beatrice is on earth, hell will seem like a place of refuge.)   **253 Antipodes** people and region on the opposite side of the earth   **254 toothpicker** toothpick   **255 Prester John** a legendary Christian king of the Far East   **256 great Cham** the Khan of Tartary, ruler of the Mongols   **257 Pygmies** legendary small race thought to live in India   **258 harpy** legendary creature with a woman's face and body and a bird's wings and claws.   **265–7 he . . . dice** (Beatrice refers seemingly to a previous courtship in which she feels that Benedick prevailed over her unfairly, in return for which she now has paid him back with *use* or interest, two to one.)   **269 put him down** got the better of him. (But Beatrice plays with the phrase in its literal and sexual sense.)   **280 civil** serious, grave. (Punning on *Seville* for the city in Spain whence came bitter-tasting oranges.)   **280–1 something** somewhat   **281 jealous complexion** i.e., yellow, associated with melancholy and symbolic of jealousy.   **282 blazon** description. (A heraldic term.)   **283 conceit** (1) notion, idea (2) heraldic device. (Continuing the metaphor of *blazon*.)

Hero is won. I have broke with her father and his good 285
will obtained. Name the day of marriage, and God
give thee joy!

LEONATO   Count, take of me my daughter and with her
my fortunes. His Grace hath made the match, and all 289
grace say Amen to it.   290

BEATRICE   Speak, Count, 'tis your cue.

CLAUDIO   Silence is the perfectest herald of joy. I were
but little happy if I could say how much!—Lady, as
you are mine, I am yours. I give away myself for you
and dote upon the exchange.

BEATRICE   Speak, cousin, or if you cannot, stop his
mouth with a kiss, and let not him speak neither.
                           [Claudio and Hero kiss.]

DON PEDRO   In faith, lady, you have a merry heart.

BEATRICE   Yea, my lord; I thank it, poor fool, it keeps on
the windy side of care. My cousin tells him in his ear 300
that he is in her heart.

CLAUDIO   And so she doth, cousin.

BEATRICE   Good Lord, for alliance! Thus goes everyone 303
to the world but I, and I am sunburnt. I may sit in a 304
corner and cry, "Heigh-ho for a husband!"   305

DON PEDRO   Lady Beatrice, I will get you one.

BEATRICE   I would rather have one of your father's
getting. Hath Your Grace ne'er a brother like you? 308
Your father got excellent husbands, if a maid could come
by them.

DON PEDRO   Will you have me, lady?

BEATRICE   No, my lord, unless I might have another for
working days. Your Grace is too costly to wear every
day. But I beseech Your Grace, pardon me. I was born
to speak all mirth and no matter.   315

DON PEDRO   Your silence most offends me, and to be
merry best becomes you, for out o' question you were
born in a merry hour.

BEATRICE   No, sure, my lord, my mother cried; but then
there was a star danced, and under that was I born.
Cousins, God give you joy!

LEONATO   Niece, will you look to those things I told you
of?

BEATRICE   I cry you mercy, uncle. [To Don Pedro] By Your 324
Grace's pardon.   Exit Beatrice. 325

DON PEDRO   By my troth, a pleasant-spirited lady.

LEONATO   There's little of the melancholy element in 327
her, my lord. She is never sad but when she sleeps, and
not ever sad then; for I have heard my daughter say 329
she hath often dreamt of unhappiness and waked 330
herself with laughing.

DON PEDRO   She cannot endure to hear tell of a husband.

LEONATO   Oh, by no means. She mocks all her wooers 333
out of suit.   334

DON PEDRO   She were an excellent wife for Benedick.

LEONATO   Oh, Lord, my lord, if they were but a week
married they would talk themselves mad.

DON PEDRO   County Claudio, when mean you to go to
church?

CLAUDIO   Tomorrow, my lord. Time goes on crutches till
Love have all his rites.

LEONATO   Not till Monday, my dear son, which is hence
a just sevennight and a time too brief, too, to have all 343
things answer my mind.   344

DON PEDRO   Come, you shake the head at so long a
breathing, but I warrant thee, Claudio, the time shall 346
not go dully by us. I will in the interim undertake one
of Hercules' labors, which is to bring Signor Benedick
and the Lady Beatrice into a mountain of affection
th'one with th'other. I would fain have it a match, and 350
I doubt not but to fashion it, if you three will but
minister such assistance as I shall give you direction. 352

LEONATO   My lord, I am for you, though it cost me ten
nights' watchings.   354

CLAUDIO   And I, my lord.

DON PEDRO   And you too, gentle Hero?

HERO   I will do any modest office, my lord, to help my 357
cousin to a good husband.

DON PEDRO   And Benedick is not the unhopefullest hus- 359
band that I know. Thus far can I praise him: he is of a
noble strain, of approved valor and confirmed honesty. 361
I will teach you how to humor your cousin, that she
shall fall in love with Benedick; and I, with your two
helps, will so practice on Benedick that, in despite of
his quick wit and his queasy stomach, he shall fall in 365
love with Beatrice. If we can do this, Cupid is no longer
an archer; his glory shall be ours, for we are the
only love gods. Go in with me, and I will tell you my
drift.   Exeunt. 369

✤

[2.2]

Enter [Don] John and Borachio.

DON JOHN   It is so. The Count Claudio shall marry the 1
daughter of Leonato.

BORACHIO   Yea, my lord, but I can cross it.   3

DON JOHN   Any bar, any cross, any impediment will be 4
medicinable to me. I am sick in displeasure to him, 5

---

285 broke spoken   **289–90 all . . . to it** i.e., we thank God for this
union.   **300 windy** windward, safe. (In sailing, the ship to windward
has the advantage.)   **303 alliance** relationship by marriage. (Claudio
has just called her "cousin.")   **303–4 goes . . . world** i.e., everyone
gets married   **304 sunburnt** (The Renaissance considered dark complexions unattractive.)   **305 Heigh-ho . . . husband!** (The title of a
ballad.)   **308 getting** begetting. (Playing on *get*, "procure," in the previous speech.)   **315 matter** substance.   **324 cry you mercy** beg your
pardon (for not having obeyed earlier)   **324–5 By . . . pardon** i.e., I
beg you to excuse my departure.   **327 melancholy element** i.e.,
earth, associated with the humor of melancholy in the old physiology
329 ever always   **330 unhappiness** misfortune

333–4 She . . . suit She discomfits and discourages all her wooers.
343 a just sevennight exactly a week   **344 answer my mind** suit my
wishes.   **346 breathing** pause, interval   **350 fain** gladly   **352 minister** furnish, supply   **354 watchings** staying awake.   **357 do . . . office**
play any seemly role   **359 unhopefullest** most unpromising
361 strain ancestry.   **approved** tested.   **honesty** honor.   **365 queasy**
squeamish, delicate (about marriage)   **369 drift** purpose.
2.2. Location: Leonato's house.
1 shall is going to   **3 cross** thwart. (Also in line 7.)   **4 bar** obstacle
5 medicinable medicinal.   **in displeasure to** with dislike of

and whatsoever comes athwart his affection ranges 6
evenly with mine. How canst thou cross this mar- 7
riage?

BORACHIO Not honestly, my lord, but so covertly that
no dishonesty shall appear in me.

DON JOHN Show me briefly how.

BORACHIO I think I told Your Lordship, a year since, 12
how much I am in the favor of Margaret, the waiting
gentlewoman to Hero.

DON JOHN I remember.

BORACHIO I can, at any unseasonable instant of the 16
night, appoint her to look out at her lady's chamber
window.

DON JOHN What life is in that, to be the death of this
marriage?

BORACHIO The poison of that lies in you to temper. Go 21
you to the Prince your brother; spare not to tell him
that he hath wronged his honor in marrying the renowned Claudio—whose estimation do you mightily 24
hold up—to a contaminated stale, such a one as Hero. 25

DON JOHN What proof shall I make of that?

BORACHIO Proof enough to misuse the Prince, to vex 27
Claudio, to undo Hero, and kill Leonato. Look you for
any other issue? 29

DON JOHN Only to despite them I will endeavor any- 30
thing.

BORACHIO Go, then, find me a meet hour to draw Don 32
Pedro and the Count Claudio alone. Tell them that you
know that Hero loves me. Intend a kind of zeal both to 34
the Prince and Claudio, as—in love of your brother's 35
honor, who hath made this match, and his friend's
reputation, who is thus like to be cozened with the 37
semblance of a maid—that you have discovered thus. 38
They will scarcely believe this without trial. Offer
them instances, which shall bear no less likelihood 40
than to see me at her chamber window, hear me call
Margaret Hero, hear Margaret term me Claudio; and 42
bring them to see this the very night before the
intended wedding—for in the meantime I will so
fashion the matter that Hero shall be absent—and
there shall appear such seeming truth of Hero's
disloyalty that jealousy shall be called assurance and 47
all the preparation overthrown. 48

DON JOHN Grow this to what adverse issue it can, I will 49
put it in practice. Be cunning in the working this, and
thy fee is a thousand ducats. 51

BORACHIO Be you constant in the accusation, and my
cunning shall not shame me.

DON JOHN I will presently go learn their day of mar- 54
riage.   *Exit* [*with Borachio*].

❧

[2.3]

Enter Benedick alone.

BENEDICK Boy!

[*Enter Boy.*]

BOY Signor?

BENEDICK In my chamber window lies a book. Bring it
hither to me in the orchard. 4

BOY I am here already, sir. 5

BENEDICK I know that, but I would have thee hence and
here again.   *Exit* [*Boy*].
I do much wonder that one man, seeing how much
another man is a fool when he dedicates his behaviors
to love, will, after he hath laughed at such shallow follies in others, become the argument of his own scorn 11
by falling in love; and such a man is Claudio. I have
known when there was no music with him but the 13
drum and the fife, and now had he rather hear the 14
tabor and the pipe. I have known when he would have 15
walked ten mile afoot to see a good armor, and now 16
will he lie ten nights awake carving the fashion of a 17
new doublet. He was wont to speak plain and to the 18
purpose, like an honest man and a soldier, and now is
he turned orthography—his words are a very fantas- 20
tical banquet, just so many strange dishes. May I be so
converted and see with these eyes? I cannot tell; I think
not. I will not be sworn but Love may transform me to
an oyster, but I'll take my oath on it, till he have made
an oyster of me, he shall never make me such a fool.
One woman is fair, yet I am well; another is wise, yet
I am well; another virtuous, yet I am well; but till all
graces be in one woman, one woman shall not come
in my grace. Rich she shall be, that's certain; wise, or
I'll none; virtuous, or I'll never cheapen her; fair, or I'll 30
never look on her; mild, or come not near me; noble, 31
or not I for an angel; of good discourse, an excellent 32
musician, and her hair shall be of what color it please
God. Ha! The Prince and Monsieur Love. I will hide
me in the arbor.   [*He hides.*]

Enter Prince [*Don Pedro*], *Leonato, Claudio.*

DON PEDRO Come, shall we hear this music?

6–7 whatsoever . . . mine whatever crosses his inclination runs parallel with mine. **12 since** ago **16 unseasonable** unsuitable, unseemly **21 lies in** rests with. **temper** mix, compound. **24–5 whose . . . up** and emphasize how much you admire his reputation **25 stale** prostitute **27 misuse** abuse, deceive **29 issue** outcome. (With a pun on children as the product of marriage; cf. 4.1.132.) **30 despite** torture, injure **32 meet** suitable **34 Intend** Pretend **35 as** i.e., saying as follows. (The words between the dashes are to be understood as instructions to Don John as to what he is to say.) **37 like** likely. **cozened** deceived, cheated **38 semblance** semblance only, outward appearance. **discovered** revealed **40 instances** proofs **42 hear . . . Claudio** (Many editors read *Borachio* for *Claudio.* The present reading may be defended if one imagines that, by arrangement with Margaret, Borachio is playing the part of Claudio, but the reading may also be an inconsistency.) **47 jealousy** suspicion. **assurance** certainty **48 preparation** i.e., for marriage **49 Grow this** Let this ripen **51 ducats** gold coins.

54 presently immediately
2.3. Location: Leonato's garden.
4 orchard garden **5 I . . . already** i.e., I will be so quick as to use no time at all. (But Benedick quibbles on the literal sense.) **11 argument** subject **13-14 there was . . . fife** i.e., his only commitment was to soldiering **15 tabor . . . pipe** (Symbols of peaceful merriment and wooing.) **16 armor** suit of armor **17 carving** planning **18 doublet** jacket. **20 turned orthography** become fastidious and fashionable in his choice of language **30 I'll none** I'll have none of her. **30 cheapen** make a bid for. (The idea of lessening her value by using her may also be suggested, though historically it is a later meaning.) **31, 32 noble, angel** (Each of these words involves a pun on the meaning "a coin," a noble being worth six shillings eightpence and an angel, ten shillings.)

CLAUDIO
  Yea, my good lord. How still the evening is,
  As hushed on purpose to grace harmony!   38
DON PEDRO [*apart to them*]
  See you where Benedick hath hid himself?
CLAUDIO [*apart in reply*]
  Oh, very well, my lord. The music ended,   40
  We'll fit the kid-fox with a pennyworth.   41

          Enter Balthasar with music.

DON PEDRO
  Come, Balthasar, we'll hear that song again.
BALTHASAR
  Oh, good my lord, tax not so bad a voice   43
  To slander music any more than once.
DON PEDRO
  It is the witness still of excellency   45
  To put a strange face on his own perfection.   46
  I pray thee, sing, and let me woo no more.   47
BALTHASAR
  Because you talk of wooing, I will sing,   48
  Since many a wooer doth commence his suit   49
  To her he thinks not worthy, yet he woos,   50
  Yet will he swear he loves.
DON PEDRO   Nay, pray thee, come,   51
  Or if thou wilt hold longer argument,
  Do it in notes.
BALTHASAR   Note this before my notes: 53
  There's not a note of mine that's worth the noting.
DON PEDRO
  Why, these are very crotchets that he speaks!   55
  Note, notes, forsooth, and nothing.   [*Music.*]   56
BENEDICK [*aside*]   Now, divine air! Now is his soul rav- 57
  ished! Is it not strange that sheeps' guts should hale   58
  souls out of men's bodies? Well, a horn for my money,   59
  when all's done.

          The Song.

BALTHASAR
  Sigh no more, ladies, sigh no more.
    Men were deceivers ever,
  One foot in sea and one on shore,
    To one thing constant never.

Then sigh not so, but let them go,
  And be you blithe and bonny,   66
Converting all your sounds of woe
  Into Hey nonny, nonny.   68

Sing no more ditties, sing no moe,   69
  Of dumps so dull and heavy;   70
The fraud of men was ever so,
  Since summer first was leavy.   72
Then sigh not so, but let them go,
  And be you blithe and bonny,
Converting all your sounds of woe
  Into Hey nonny, nonny.

DON PEDRO   By my troth, a good song.
BALTHASAR   And an ill singer, my lord.
DON PEDRO   Ha, no, no, faith, thou sing'st well enough
  for a shift.   80
BENEDICK [*aside*]   An he had been a dog that should   81
  have howled thus, they would have hanged him, and
  I pray God his bad voice bode no mischief. I has as
  lief have heard the night raven, come what plague   84
  could have come after it.
DON PEDRO   Yea, marry, dost thou hear, Balthasar? I   86
  pray thee, get us some excellent music, for tomorrow
  night we would have it at the Lady Hero's chamber
  window.
BALTHASAR   The best I can, my lord.
DON PEDRO   Do so. Farewell.   *Exit Balthasar.*
  Come hither, Leonato. What was it you told me of
  today, that your niece Beatrice was in love with Signor
  Benedick?
CLAUDIO   Oh, ay! [*Aside to Pedro*] Stalk on, stalk on; the 95
  fowl sits.—I did never think that lady would have   96
  loved any man.
LEONATO   No, nor I neither, but most wonderful that she
  should so dote on Signor Benedick, whom she hath in
  all outward behaviors seemed ever to abhor.
BENEDICK [*aside*]   Is't possible? Sits the wind in that 101
  corner?   102
LEONATO   By my troth, my lord, I cannot tell what to
  think of it but that she loves him with an enraged   104
  affection; it is past the infinite of thought.   105
DON PEDRO   Maybe she doth but counterfeit.
CLAUDIO   Faith, like enough.   107
LEONATO   Oh, God, counterfeit? There was never coun-
  terfeit of passion came so near the life of passion as she
  discovers it.   110
DON PEDRO   Why, what effects of passion shows she?
CLAUDIO [*aside to them*]   Bait the hook well; this fish will
  bite.

---

38 As as if.   **grace harmony** do honor to music.   **40 The music ended**
When the music is over   **41 We'll . . . pennyworth** i.e., we'll give
our sly victim more than he bargained for. (A *kid-fox* is presumably a
young fox, as in beast fable; *kid*, i.e., young goat, also suggests one
whom they are stalking as their quarry. Claudio may be referring to
some children's game.)   **43 tax** task   **45–6 It . . . perfection** It is
always characteristic of excellence to pretend not to know its own
skill.   **47 woo** entreat   **48–51 Because . . . he loves** (Balthasar modestly claims to be unworthy of being *wooed,* i.e., entreated, but will
comply, since he knows Don Pedro speaks with the hyperbole all wooers use in addressing women they actually consider unworthy.)
53 notes music.   **55 crotchets** (1) whims, fancies (2) musical notes of
brief duration   **56 nothing** (With a pun on *noting;* the two words were
pronounced alike. Compare the same pun in the title of the play,
where *Nothing* suggests "noting," or eavesdropping.)   **57 air** melody.
58 sheeps' guts strings on musical instruments.   **hale** draw
59 a horn a hunting horn, a more masculine instrument than a lute.
(But with a perhaps unconscious allusion to a cuckold's horns.)

66 blithe and bonny cheerful and carefree   **68 Hey nonny, nonny** (A
nonsense refrain.)   **69 moe** more   **70 dumps** mournful songs; also,
dances   **72 leavy** leafy.   **80 for a shift** in a pinch.   **81 An** If. (Also in
line 161.)   **84 lief** willingly.   **night raven** a bird of night, portending
disaster   **86 Yea, marry** (A continuation of Don Pedro's speech preceding Benedick's aside.)   **95–6 Stalk . . . sits** i.e., Proceed stealthily;
the hunted bird is hiding in the bush.   **101–2 Sits . . . corner?** Is that
the way the wind is blowing?   **104 enraged** maddened with passion
105 infinite farthest reach. (It's unbelievable but true.)   **107 like**
likely   **110 discovers** betrays

LEONATO   What effects, my lord? She will sit you—you ¹¹⁴ heard my daughter tell you how.

CLAUDIO   She did indeed.

DON PEDRO   How, how, I pray you? You amaze me. I would have thought her spirit had been invincible against all assaults of affection.

LEONATO   I would have sworn it had, my lord—especially against Benedick.

BENEDICK [*aside*]   I should think this a gull but that the ¹²² white-bearded fellow speaks it. Knavery cannot, sure, hide himself in such reverence.

CLAUDIO [*apart to them*]   He hath ta'en th'infection. Hold it up.   ¹²⁶

DON PEDRO   Hath she made her affection known to Benedick?

LEONATO   No, and swears she never will. That's her torment.

CLAUDIO   'Tis true, indeed. So your daughter says. "Shall I," says she, "that have so oft encountered him ¹³² with scorn, write to him that I love him?"

LEONATO   This says she now when she is beginning to write to him, for she'll be up twenty times a night, and there will she sit in her smock till she have writ a sheet ¹³⁶ of paper. My daughter tells us all.

CLAUDIO   Now you talk of a sheet of paper, I remember a pretty jest your daughter told us of.

LEONATO   Oh, when she had writ it and was reading it over, she found "Benedick" and "Beatrice" between the sheet?

CLAUDIO   That.   ¹⁴³

LEONATO   Oh, she tore the letter into a thousand half- ¹⁴⁴ pence; railed at herself, that she should be so immod- ¹⁴⁵ est to write to one that she knew would flout her. "I ¹⁴⁶ measure him," says she, "by my own spirit, for I should flout him if he writ to me. Yea, though I love him, I should."

CLAUDIO   Then down upon her knees she falls, weeps, sobs, beats her heart, tears her hair, prays, curses: "O sweet Benedick! God give me patience!"

LEONATO   She doth indeed; my daughter says so. And the ecstasy hath so much overborne her that my ¹⁵⁴ daughter is sometime afeard she will do a desperate outrage to herself. It is very true.

DON PEDRO   It were good that Benedick knew of it by some other, if she will not discover it.   ¹⁵⁸

CLAUDIO   To what end? He would make but a sport of it and torment the poor lady worse.

DON PEDRO   An he should, it were an alms to hang him. ¹⁶¹ She's an excellent sweet lady, and, out of all suspicion, ¹⁶² she is virtuous.

CLAUDIO   And she is exceeding wise.

DON PEDRO   In everything but in loving Benedick.

LEONATO   O my lord, wisdom and blood combating in ¹⁶⁶ so tender a body, we have ten proofs to one that blood hath the victory. I am sorry for her, as I have just cause, being her uncle and her guardian.

DON PEDRO   I would she had bestowed this dotage on ¹⁷⁰ me. I would have doffed all other respects and made ¹⁷¹ her half myself. I pray you, tell Benedick of it, and hear ¹⁷² what 'a will say.

LEONATO   Were it good, think you?

CLAUDIO   Hero thinks surely she will die; for she says she will die if he love her not, and she will die ere she make her love known, and she will die if he woo her, rather than she will bate one breath of her accustomed ¹⁷⁸ crossness.   ¹⁷⁹

DON PEDRO   She doth well. If she should make tender ¹⁸⁰ of her love, 'tis very possible he'll scorn it; for the man, as you know all, hath a contemptible spirit.   ¹⁸²

CLAUDIO   He is a very proper man.   ¹⁸³

DON PEDRO   He hath indeed a good outward happiness. ¹⁸⁴

CLAUDIO   Before God, and in my mind, very wise.   ¹⁸⁵

DON PEDRO   He doth indeed show some sparks that are like wit.

CLAUDIO   And I take him to be valiant.

DON PEDRO   As Hector, I assure you; and in the manag- ¹⁸⁹ ing of quarrels you may say he is wise, for either he avoids them with great discretion or undertakes them with a most Christian-like fear.

LEONATO   If he do fear God, 'a must necessarily keep peace. If he break the peace, he ought to enter into a quarrel with fear and trembling.

DON PEDRO   And so will he do, for the man doth fear God, howsoever it seems not in him by some large ¹⁹⁷ jests he will make. Well, I am sorry for your niece. Shall we go seek Benedick and tell him of her love?

CLAUDIO   Never tell him, my lord. Let her wear it out ²⁰⁰ with good counsel.   ²⁰¹

LEONATO   Nay, that's impossible. She may wear her heart out first.

DON PEDRO   Well, we will hear further of it by your daughter. Let it cool the while. I love Benedick well, and I could wish he would modestly examine himself, to see how much he is unworthy so good a lady.

LEONATO   My lord, will you walk? Dinner is ready.

[*They walk aside.*]

CLAUDIO   If he do not dote on her upon this, I will never ²⁰⁹ trust my expectation.

DON PEDRO   Let there be the same net spread for her; and that must your daughter and her gentlewomen carry. The sport will be when they hold one an opinion ²¹³ of another's dotage, and no such matter; that's the ²¹⁴

---

114 **sit you** i.e., sit. (*You* is used idiomatically.)   122 **gull** trick, deception.   **but** except for the fact   126 **Hold it up** Keep up the jest.
132 **she** i.e., Beatrice   136 **smock** chemise   143 **That** i.e., That's it.
144–5 **halfpence** i.e., small pieces   146 **flout** mock   154 **overborne** overwhelmed   158 **discover** reveal   161 **alms** good deed. (Hanging would be too good for him.)   162 **out of** beyond   166 **blood** natural feeling

170 **dotage** doting affection   171 **doffed** put or turned aside. **respects** considerations   172 **half myself** i.e., my wife.   178 **bate** abate   179 **crossness** perversity, contrariety.   180 **tender** offer 182 **contemptible** contemptuous   183 **proper** handsome   184 **outward happiness** fortune in his good looks.   185 **Before God** i.e., By God, you're absolutely right   189 **Hector** the mightiest of the Trojans   197 **by** to judge by.   **large** broad, indelicate   200 **wear it out** eradicate it   201 **counsel** reflection, deliberation.   209 **upon** as a result of, after   213 **carry** carry out.   213–14 **they . . . dotage** each believes the other to be in love   214 **no such matter** the reality is quite otherwise

scene that I would see, which will be merely a dumb 215
show. Let us send her to call him in to dinner. 216

       [Exeunt Don Pedro, Claudio, and Leonato.]

BENEDICK *[coming forward]*   This can be no trick. The
conference was sadly borne. They have the truth of 218
this from Hero. They seem to pity the lady. It seems
her affections have their full bent. Love me? Why, it 220
must be requited. I hear how I am censured. They say
I will bear myself proudly if I perceive the love come
from her; they say too that she will rather die than give
any sign of affection. I did never think to marry. I must
not seem proud; happy are they that hear their detrac- 225
tions and can put them to mending. They say the lady 226
is fair; 'tis a truth, I can bear them witness; and virtuous; 'tis so, I cannot reprove it; and wise but for loving 228
me; by my troth, it is no addition to her wit, nor no
great argument of her folly, for I will be horribly in
love with her. I may chance have some odd quirks and 231
remnants of wit broken on me, because I have railed
so long against marriage. But doth not the appetite
alter? A man loves the meat in his youth that he cannot endure in his age. Shall quips and sentences and 235
these paper bullets of the brain awe a man from the 236
career of his humor? No, the world must be peopled. 237
When I said I would die a bachelor, I did not think I
should live till I were married. Here comes Beatrice.
By this day, she's a fair lady! I do spy some marks of
love in her.

     Enter Beatrice.

BEATRICE   Against my will I am sent to bid you come in
to dinner.
BENEDICK   Fair Beatrice, I thank you for your pains.
BEATRICE   I took no more pains for those thanks than
you take pains to thank me. If it had been painful I
would not have come.
BENEDICK   You take pleasure then in the message?
BEATRICE   Yea, just so much as you may take upon a 249
knife's point and choke a daw withal. You have no 250
stomach, signor. Fare you well.   *Exit.* 251
BENEDICK   Ha! "Against my will I am sent to bid you
come in to dinner." There's a double meaning in that.
"I took no more pains for those thanks than you took
pains to thank me." That's as much as to say, "Any
pains that I take for you is as easy as thanks." If I do
not take pity of her, I am a villain; if I do not love her,
I am a Jew. I will go get her picture.   *Exit.*

215–16 dumb show pantomime (lacking their usual banter)
218 sadly borne soberly conducted.   **220 have . . . bent** i.e., are fully
engaged. (The image is of a bow pulled taut.)   **225–6 that . . . mending** that can hear themselves criticized and undertake to remedy the
defect.   **228 reprove** refute   **231 quirks** witty conceits or jokes
235 sentences saws, maxims   **236 paper bullets** i.e., words
237 career of his humor pursuit of his inclination. (In horsemanship,
a *career* is a short gallop.)   **249–50 just . . . withal** i.e., very little. (A
daw or jackdaw is a common blackbird, smaller than a crow.)
251 stomach appetite

[3.1]

*Enter Hero and two gentlewomen, Margaret
and Ursula.*

HERO
  Good Margaret, run thee to the parlor.
  There shalt thou find my cousin Beatrice
  Proposing with the Prince and Claudio.   3
  Whisper her ear and tell her I and Ursley   4
  Walk in the orchard, and our whole discourse
  Is all of her. Say that thou overheard'st us,
  And bid her steal into the pleachèd bower,   7
  Where honeysuckles, ripened by the sun,
  Forbid the sun to enter, like favorites,
  Made proud by princes, that advance their pride   10
  Against that power that bred it. There will she hide
    her,   11
  To listen our propose. This is thy office.   12
  Bear thee well in it and leave us alone.   13
MARGARET
  I'll make her come, I warrant you, presently.   *[Exit.]* 14
HERO
  Now, Ursula, when Beatrice doth come,
  As we do trace this alley up and down,   16
  Our talk must only be of Benedick.
  When I do name him, let it be thy part
  To praise him more than ever man did merit.
  My talk to thee must be how Benedick
  Is sick in love with Beatrice. Of this matter
  Is little Cupid's crafty arrow made,
  That only wounds by hearsay.

     Enter Beatrice [behind].

                      Now begin,   23
  For look where Beatrice, like a lapwing, runs   24
  Close by the ground, to hear our conference.
URSULA *[to Hero]*
  The pleasant'st angling is to see the fish
  Cut with her golden oars the silver stream   27
  And greedily devour the treacherous bait.
  So angle we for Beatrice, who even now
  Is couchèd in the woodbine coverture.   30
  Fear you not my part of the dialogue.   31
HERO *[to Ursula]*
  Then go we near her, that her ear lose nothing
  Of the false sweet bait that we lay for it.
                 [They approach the bower.]
  No, truly, Ursula, she is too disdainful;
  I know her spirits are as coy and wild   35
  As haggards of the rock.
URSULA   But are you sure   36

3.1 Location: Leonato's garden.
3 Proposing conversing   **4 Ursley** (A nickname for *Ursula*)
7 pleachèd formed by densely interwoven branches   **10–11 that . . . it**
i.e., who dare set themselves up against the very princes who advanced
them.   **12 listen our propose** listen to our conversation.   **office** responsibility.   **13 leave us alone** leave the rest to us.   **14 presently** immediately.   **16 trace** walk   **23 only . . . hearsay** wounds by mere report.
24 lapwing bird of the plover family   **27 oars** i.e., fins   **30 Is . . . coverture** is hid in the honeysuckle bower.   **31 Fear . . . dialogue** Don't worry
about my not holding up my part in the conversation.   **35 coy** disdainful   **36 As . . . rock** as untamed female hawks in mountainous terrain.

That Benedick loves Beatrice so entirely?

HERO
So says the Prince and my new-trothèd lord.

URSULA
And did they bid you tell her of it, madam?

HERO
They did entreat me to acquaint her of it;
But I persuaded them, if they loved Benedick,
To wish him wrestle with affection
And never to let Beatrice know of it.

URSULA
Why did you so? Doth not the gentleman
Deserve as full as fortunate a bed   45
As ever Beatrice shall couch upon?   46

HERO
O god of love! I know he doth deserve
As much as may be yielded to a man;
But Nature never framed a woman's heart
Of prouder stuff than that of Beatrice.
Disdain and scorn ride sparkling in her eyes,
Misprizing what they look on, and her wit   52
Values itself so highly that to her
All matter else seems weak. She cannot love,   54
Nor take no shape nor project of affection,   55
She is so self-endearèd.

URSULA   Sure I think so,   56
And therefore certainly it were not good
She knew his love, lest she'll make sport at it.

HERO
Why, you speak truth. I never yet saw man,
How wise, how noble, young, how rarely featured,   60
But she would spell him backward. If fair-faced,   61
She would swear the gentleman should be her
    sister;
If black, why, Nature, drawing of an antic,   63
Made a foul blot; if tall, a lance ill-headed;
If low, an agate very vilely cut;   65
If speaking, why, a vane blown with all winds;
If silent, why, a block movèd with none.
So turns she every man the wrong side out
And never gives to truth and virtue that
Which simpleness and merit purchaseth.   70

URSULA
Sure, sure, such carping is not commendable.

HERO
No, not to be so odd and from all fashions   72
As Beatrice is cannot be commendable.
But who dare tell her so? If I should speak,
She would mock me into air; oh, she would laugh me   75
Out of myself, press me to death with wit.   76

Therefore let Benedick, like covered fire,
Consume away in sighs, waste inwardly.   78
It were a better death than die with mocks,
Which is as bad as die with tickling.

URSULA
Yet tell her of it. Hear what she will say.

HERO
No, rather I will go to Benedick
And counsel him to fight against his passion.
And truly, I'll devise some honest slanders   84
To stain my cousin with. One doth not know
How much an ill word may empoison liking.

URSULA
Oh, do not do your cousin such a wrong!
She cannot be so much without true judgment—
Having so swift and excellent a wit
As she is prized to have—as to refuse   90
So rare a gentleman as Signor Benedick.

HERO
He is the only man of Italy,
Always excepted my dear Claudio.

URSULA
I pray you, be not angry with me, madam,
Speaking my fancy: Signor Benedick,
For shape, for bearing, argument, and valor,   96
Goes foremost in report through Italy.

HERO
Indeed, he hath an excellent good name.

URSULA
His excellence did earn it ere he had it.
When are you married, madam?

HERO
Why, every day, tomorrow. Come, go in.   101
I'll show thee some attires and have thy counsel
Which is the best to furnish me tomorrow.
                                    [They walk away.]

URSULA [to Hero]
She's limed, I warrant you. We have caught her,
    madam.   104

HERO [to Ursula]
If it prove so, then loving goes by haps;   105
Some Cupid kills with arrows, some with traps.   106
                            [Exeunt Hero and Ursula.]

BEATRICE [coming forward]
What fire is in mine ears? Can this be true?   107
    Stand I condemned for pride and scorn so much?
Contempt, farewell, and maiden pride, adieu!
    No glory lives behind the back of such.   110
And Benedick, love on; I will requite thee,
    Taming my wild heart to thy loving hand.   112

If thou dost love, my kindness shall incite thee
　To bind our loves up in a holy band;　　　　　　　114
For others say thou dost deserve, and I
Believe it better than reportingly.　　　　　　　*Exit.* 116

❧

[3.2]

*Enter Prince [Don Pedro], Claudio, Benedick,
and Leonato.*

DON PEDRO　I do but stay till your marriage be con-　1
summate, and then go I toward Aragon.　　　　　　2

CLAUDIO　I'll bring you thither, my lord, if you'll　3
vouchsafe me.　　　　　　　　　　　　　　　　　4

DON PEDRO　Nay, that would be as great a soil in the　5
new gloss of your marriage as to show a child his new
coat and forbid him to wear it. I will only be bold with　7
Benedick for his company, for from the crown of his
head to the sole of his foot he is all mirth. He hath
twice or thrice cut Cupid's bowstring, and the little
hangman dare not shoot at him. He hath a heart as　11
sound as a bell, and his tongue is the clapper, for what
his heart thinks his tongue speaks.

BENEDICK　Gallants, I am not as I have been.

LEONATO　So say I. Methinks you are sadder.　　　15

CLAUDIO　I hope he be in love.

DON PEDRO　Hang him, truant! There's no true drop of　17
blood in him, to be truly touched with love. If he be
sad, he wants money.　　　　　　　　　　　　　19

BENEDICK　I have the toothache.　　　　　　　　20

DON PEDRO　Draw it.　　　　　　　　　　　　　21

BENEDICK　Hang it!　　　　　　　　　　　　　22

CLAUDIO　You must hang it first and draw it afterwards.

DON PEDRO　What, sigh for the toothache?

LEONATO　Where is but a humor or a worm.　　　26

BENEDICK　Well, everyone can master a grief but he that　27
has it.

CLAUDIO　Yet say I, he is in love.

DON PEDRO　There is no appearance of fancy in him,　30
unless it be a fancy that he hath to strange disguises;　31
as, to be a Dutchman today, a Frenchman tomorrow,
or in the shape of two countries at once, as, a German
from the waist downward, all slops, and a Spaniard　34
from the hip upward, no doublet. Unless he have a　35

fancy to this foolery, as it appears he hath, he is no fool　36
for fancy, as you would have it appear he is.　　　37

CLAUDIO　If he be not in love with some woman, there
is no believing old signs. 'A brushes his hat o'
mornings. What should that bode?

DON PEDRO　Hath any man seen him at the barber's?

CLAUDIO　No, but the barber's man hath been seen with
him, and the old ornament of his cheek hath already　43
stuffed tennis balls.　　　　　　　　　　　　　44

LEONATO　Indeed he looks younger than he did by the
loss of a beard.

DON PEDRO　Nay, 'a rubs himself with civet. Can you　47
smell him out by that?　　　　　　　　　　　　48

CLAUDIO　That's as much as to say the sweet youth's in
love.

DON PEDRO　The greatest note of it is his melancholy.　51

CLAUDIO　And when was he wont to wash his face?　52

DON PEDRO　Yea, or to paint himself? For the which I　53
hear what they say of him.　　　　　　　　　　　54

CLAUDIO　Nay, but his jesting spirit, which is now crept
into a lute string and now governed by stops.　　　56

DON PEDRO　Indeed, that tells a heavy tale for him.
Conclude, conclude he is in love.

CLAUDIO　Nay, but I know who loves him.

DON PEDRO　That would I know too. I warrant, one that
knows him not.

CLAUDIO　Yes, and his ill conditions; and, in despite of　62
all, dies for him.

DON PEDRO　She shall be buried with her face upwards.　64

BENEDICK　Yet is this no charm for the toothache. Old
signor, walk aside with me. I have studied eight or
nine wise words to speak to you, which these hobby-　67
horses must not hear. 　*[Exeunt Benedick and Leonato.]*　68

DON PEDRO　For my life, to break with him about　69
Beatrice.

CLAUDIO　'Tis even so. Hero and Margaret have by this　71
played their parts with Beatrice, and then the two
bears will not bite one another when they meet.

Enter [Don] John the Bastard.

DON JOHN　My lord and brother, God save you!

DON PEDRO　Good e'en, brother.　　　　　　　　75

DON JOHN　If your leisure served, I would speak with
you.

DON PEDRO　In private?

---

114 band bond　**116 better than reportingly** on better evidence than mere report
3.2. Location: Leonato's house.
1–2 consummate consummated　**3 bring** escort　**4 vouchsafe** allow
5 soil stain　**7 be bold with** ask　**11 hangman** executioner; rogue. (Playfully applied to Cupid.)　**15 sadder** more serious.　**17 truant** i.e., from love.　**19 wants** lacks　**20 toothache** (Thought to be a common ailment of lovers.)　**21 Draw** Extract. (But Claudio jokes on the method of executing traitors, who were hanged first and then cut down alive and drawn, i.e., disemboweled, and finally quartered.)
22 Hang it! Confound it!　**26 Where** Where there.　**humor or a worm** (A toothache was ascribed to "humors," or unhealthy secretions, and to actual worms in the teeth.)　**27 grief** pain.　**but** except
30 fancy love　**31 fancy** whim, liking　**34 slops** loose breeches
35 no doublet i.e., with a hip-length cloak in place of, or covering, the close-fitting doublet.

36–7 fool for fancy i.e., lover　**43–4 the old . . . tennis balls** i.e., Benedick's beard has gone to stuff tennis balls. (He appears onstage beardless in this scene for the first time.)　**47 civet** perfume derived from the civet cat.　**48 smell him out** (1) discern his secret (2) smell him coming　**51 note** mark　**52 wont** accustomed.　**wash** i.e., with cosmetics; similarly with *paint* in the next line　**53–4 For . . . him** That's what I hear people saying about him.　**56 stops** (1) frets on the fingerboard (2) restraints.　**62 ill conditions** bad qualities　**64 buried . . . upwards** i.e., as the faithful, not as a suicide, who were sometimes buried face downwards (?). (There is also a sexual suggestion of her being smothered under Benedick, continuing the joke on *dies for him,* meaning to have an orgasm.)　**67–8 hobbyhorses** i.e., buffoons. (Originally, figures in a morris dance made to resemble a horse and rider.)　**69 For** Upon.　**break** speak　**71 Margaret** (Ursula joined Hero in playing the trick on Beatrice, but Margaret has been in on it.)
75 e'en evening, i.e., afternoon

DON JOHN   If it please you. Yet Count Claudio may hear, for what I would speak of concerns him.

DON PEDRO   What's the matter?

DON JOHN   [to Claudio]   Means Your Lordship to be married tomorrow?

DON PEDRO   You know he does.

DON JOHN   I know not that, when he knows what I know.

CLAUDIO   If there be any impediment, I pray you discover it.   88

DON JOHN   You may think I love you not. Let that appear hereafter, and aim better at me by that I now   90
will manifest. For my brother, I think he holds you   91
well and in dearness of heart hath holp to effect your   92
ensuing marriage—surely suit ill spent and labor ill bestowed.

DON PEDRO   Why, what's the matter?

DON JOHN   I came hither to tell you, and, circumstances   96
shortened—for she has been too long a-talking of—   97
the lady is disloyal.   98

CLAUDIO   Who, Hero?

DON JOHN   Even she—Leonato's Hero, your Hero, every man's Hero.

CLAUDIO   Disloyal?

DON JOHN   The word is too good to paint out her   103
wickedness. I could say she were worse; think you of
a worse title, and I will fit her to it. Wonder not till fur-   105
ther warrant. Go but with me tonight, you shall see her   106
chamber window entered, even the night before her
wedding day. If you love her then, tomorrow wed her;
but it would better fit your honor to change your mind.

CLAUDIO   May this be so?

DON PEDRO   I will not think it.

DON JOHN   If you dare not trust that you see, confess not   113
that you know. If you will follow me, I will show you   114
enough; and when you have seen more and heard
more, proceed accordingly.

CLAUDIO   If I see anything tonight why I should not
marry her, tomorrow in the congregation, where I
should wed, there will I shame her.

DON PEDRO   And, as I wooed for thee to obtain her, I
will join with thee to disgrace her.

DON JOHN   I will disparage her no farther till you are my
witnesses. Bear it coldly but till midnight, and let the   123
issue show itself.   124

DON PEDRO   O day untowardly turned!   125

CLAUDIO   O mischief strangely thwarting!

DON JOHN   O plague right well prevented! So will you
say when you have seen the sequel.   [Exeunt.]

❧

[3.3]

*Enter Dogberry and his compartner [Verges]
with the Watch.*

DOGBERRY   Are you good men and true?

VERGES   Yea, or else it were pity but they should suffer
salvation, body and soul.   3

DOGBERRY   Nay, that were a punishment too good for
them, if they should have any allegiance in them,   5
being chosen for the Prince's watch.

VERGES   Well, give them their charge, neighbor Dog-   7
berry.

DOGBERRY   First, who think you the most desartless   9
man to be constable?

FIRST WATCH   Hugh Oatcake, sir, or George Seacoal, for
they can write and read.

DOGBERRY   Come hither, neighbor Seacoal. [Seacoal, or
Second Watch, steps forward.] God hath blessed you
with a good name. To be a well-favored man is the gift   15
of fortune, but to write and read comes by nature.

SEACOAL   Both which, Master Constable—

DOGBERRY   You have. I knew it would be your answer.
Well, for your favor, sir, why, give God thanks, and
make no boast of it; and for your writing and reading,
let that appear when there is no need of such vanity.
You are thought here to be the most senseless and fit   22
man for the constable of the watch; therefore bear you
the lantern. This is your charge: you shall comprehend   24
all vagrom men; you are to bid any man stand, in the   25
Prince's name.

SEACOAL   How if 'a will not stand?

DOGBERRY   Why, then, take no note of him, but let him
go, and presently call the rest of the watch together
and thank God you are rid of a knave.

VERGES   If he will not stand when he is bidden, he is
none of the Prince's subjects.

DOGBERRY   True, and they are to meddle with none but
the Prince's subjects. You shall also make no noise in
the streets; for, for the watch to babble and to talk is
most tolerable and not to be endured.   36

WATCH   We will rather sleep than talk. We know what
belongs to a watch.   38

DOGBERRY   Why, you speak like an ancient and most   39
quiet watchman, for I cannot see how sleeping should
offend. Only have a care that your bills be not stolen.   41
Well, you are to call at all the alehouses and bid those
that are drunk get them to bed.

WATCH   How if they will not?

3.3. Location: A street.
3 salvation (A blunder for "damnation.")   **5 allegiance** (For "treachery.")   **7 charge** instructions   **9 desartless** (For "deserving.")
15 a good name (Sea coal was high-grade coal shipped from Newcastle, not the charcoal usually sold by London colliers.)   **well-favored** good-looking   **22 senseless** (For "sensible.")   **24 comprehend** (For "apprehend.")   **25 vagrom** vagrant.   **stand** stand still, stop   **36 tolerable** (For "intolerable.")   **37 WATCH** (Here and at lines 44, 48, 53, and 66 Shakespeare's text does not specify which watchman speaks. These lines are sometimes assigned to the Second Watch, Seacoal, but could be spoken by others of the watch.)   **38 belongs to** are the duties of   **39 ancient** venerable, experienced   **41 bills** pikes, with axes fixed to long poles

---

88 **discover** reveal   90 **aim better at** judge better of.   **that** that which
91–2 **holds you well** thinks well of you   92 **holp** helped   96–7 **circumstances shortened** without unnecessary details   97 **a-talking of** under discussion (by us)   98 **disloyal** unfaithful.   103 **paint out** portray in full   105–6 **till further warrant** till further proof appears.
113–14 **If . . . know** i.e., If you are unwilling to believe what you see, then don't claim to know the truth.   123 **coldly** calmly   124 **issue** outcome   125 **untowardly turned** wretchedly altered

DOGBERRY   Why, then, let them alone till they are sober. If they make you not then the better answer, you may say they are not the men you took them for.

WATCH   Well, sir.

DOGBERRY   If you meet a thief, you may suspect him, by virtue of your office, to be no true man; and for such 50 kind of men, the less you meddle or make with them, 51 why, the more is for your honesty. 52

WATCH   If we know him to be a thief, shall we not lay hands on him?

DOGBERRY   Truly, by your office you may, but I think they that touch pitch will be defiled. The most 56 peaceable way for you, if you do take a thief, is to let him show himself what he is and steal out of your company.

VERGES   You have been always called a merciful man, partner.

DOGBERRY   Truly, I would not hang a dog by my will, much more a man who hath any honesty in him.

VERGES   If you hear a child cry in the night, you must call to the nurse and bid her still it.

WATCH   How if the nurse be asleep and will not hear us?

DOGBERRY   Why, then, depart in peace and let the child wake her with crying, for the ewe that will not hear her lamb when it baas will never answer a calf when he bleats.

VERGES   'Tis very true.

DOGBERRY   This is the end of the charge: you, Constable, are to present the Prince's own person. If you meet 74 the Prince in the night, you may stay him.

VERGES   Nay, by'r Lady, that I think 'a cannot. 76

DOGBERRY   Five shillings to one on't, with any man that knows the statutes, he may stay him; marry, not without the Prince be willing, for indeed the watch ought to offend no man, and it is an offense to stay a man against his will.

VERGES   By'r Lady, I think it be so.

DOGBERRY   Ha, ah ha! Well, masters, good night. An there be any matter of weight chances, call up me. Keep your fellows' counsels and your own, and good night. Come, neighbor. [*He starts to leave with Verges.*]

SEACOAL   Well, masters, we hear our charge. Let us go sit here upon the church bench till two, and then all to bed.

DOGBERRY   One word more, honest neighbors. I pray you, watch about Signor Leonato's door, for the wedding being there tomorrow, there is a great coil 92 tonight. Adieu. Be vigitant, I beseech you. 93

                    Exeunt [Dogberry and Verges].

Enter Borachio and Conrade.

BORACHIO   What, Conrade!

SEACOAL   [*aside*]   Peace! Stir not.

BORACHIO   Conrade, I say!

CONRADE   Here, man. I am at thy elbow.

BORACHIO   Mass, and my elbow itched; I thought there 98 would a scab follow. 99

CONRADE   I will owe thee an answer for that. And now, 100 forward with thy tale.

BORACHIO   Stand thee close, then, under this penthouse, 102 for it drizzles rain, and I will, like a true drunkard, 103 utter all to thee.

SEACOAL   [*aside*]   Some treason, masters. Yet stand 105 close. 106

BORACHIO   Therefore know I have earned of Don John a thousand ducats.

CONRADE   Is it possible that any villainy should be so dear? 110

BORACHIO   Thou shouldst rather ask if it were possible any villainy should be so rich; for when rich villains 112 have need of poor ones, poor ones may make what price they will.

CONRADE   I wonder at it.

BORACHIO   That shows thou art unconfirmed. Thou 116 knowest that the fashion of a doublet, or a hat, or a cloak, is nothing to a man. 118

CONRADE   Yes, it is apparel.

BORACHIO   I mean, the fashion. 120

CONRADE   Yes, the fashion is the fashion.

BORACHIO   Tush, I may as well say the fool's the fool. But see'st thou not what a deformed thief this fashion 123 is?

SEACOAL   [*aside*]   I know that Deformed. 'A has been a vile thief this seven year; 'a goes up and down like a 126 gentleman. I remember his name.

BORACHIO   Didst thou not hear somebody?

CONRADE   No, 'twas the vane on the house.

BORACHIO   See'st thou not, I say, what a deformed thief this fashion is, how giddily 'a turns about all the hot bloods between fourteen and five-and-thirty, sometimes fashioning them like Pharaoh's soldiers in the reechy painting, sometime like god Bel's priests in the 134 old church-window, sometime like the shaven 135 Hercules in the smirched worm-eaten tapestry, where 136 his codpiece seems as massy as his club? 137

---

98 Mass i.e., By the Mass.   **my elbow itched** (Proverbially, a warning against questionable companions.)   **99 scab** i.e., scoundrel. (With play on literal meaning.)   **100 owe thee an answer** answer later **102 penthouse** overhanging structure   **103 true drunkard** (Alludes to the commonplace that the drunkard tells all; Borachio's name in Spanish means "drunkard.")   **105–6 stand close** stay hidden. **110 dear** expensive.   **112 rich** well-paid   **116 unconfirmed** inexperienced.   **118 is . . . man** does not make the man. (But Conrade plays on the phrase in the sense of "means nothing to a man.")   **120 I . . . fashion** i.e., My emphasis was on the mere fashion, not on the apparel itself. (But Conrade wittily refuses to allow the difference.) **123 deformed thief** i.e., so called because fashion takes such varied and extreme shapes and because it impoverishes those who follow fashion   **126 up and down** about, here and there   **134 reechy** dirty, grimy. (Perhaps this painting is of the Israelites passing through the Red Sea.)   **god Bel's priests** (Probably alludes to the story of Bel and the Dragon, from the apocryphal Book of Daniel, depicted in a stained-glass window.)   **135–6 shaven Hercules** (A reference either to young Hercules at the crossroads, choosing between virtue and vice, or in the service of Omphale—see 2.1.242, note—or, confusedly, to the story of Samson.)   **137 codpiece** decorative pouch at the front of a man's breeches (indelicately conspicuous in this tapestry)

---

50 true honest   **51 meddle or make** have to do   **52 is** it is   **56 they . . . defiled** (A commonplace, derived from Ecclesiasticus 13:1.) **74 present** represent   **76 by'r Lady** i.e., by Our Lady. (A mild oath.) **92 coil** to-do   **93 vigitant** (For "vigilant.")

CONRADE   All this I see, and I see that the fashion wears 138
out more apparel than the man. But art not thou 139
thyself giddy with the fashion, too, that thou hast
shifted out of thy tale into telling me of the fashion?

BORACHIO   Not so, neither. But know that I have tonight
wooed Margaret, the Lady Hero's gentlewoman, by
the name of Hero. She leans me out at her mistress' 144
chamber window, bids me a thousand times good
night—I tell this tale vilely; I should first tell thee how
the Prince, Claudio, and my master, planted and
placed and possessed by my master Don John, saw 148
afar off in the orchard this amiable encounter. 149

CONRADE   And thought they Margaret was Hero?

BORACHIO   Two of them did, the Prince and Claudio,
but the devil my master knew she was Margaret; and
partly by his oaths, which first possessed them, partly
by the dark night, which did deceive them, but chiefly
by my villainy, which did confirm any slander that
Don John had made, away went Claudio enraged;
swore he would meet her, as he was appointed, next
morning at the temple, and there, before the whole
congregation, shame her with what he saw o'ernight
and send her home again without a husband.

SEACOAL   We charge you, in the Prince's name, stand!

FIRST WATCH   Call up the Right Master Constable. We 162
have here recovered the most dangerous piece of 163
lechery that ever was known in the commonwealth. 164

SEACOAL   And one Deformed is one of them. I know
him; 'a wears a lock. 166

CONRADE   Masters, masters—

FIRST WATCH   You'll be made bring Deformed forth, I
warrant you.

CONRADE   Masters—

SEACOAL   Never speak, we charge you. Let us obey you 171
to go with us.

BORACHIO   We are like to prove a goodly commodity, 173
being taken up of these men's bills. 174

CONRADE   A commodity in question, I warrant you. 175
Come, we'll obey you.   *Exeunt.*

❖

[3.4]

Enter Hero, and Margaret and Ursula.

HERO   Good Ursula, wake my cousin Beatrice, and
desire her to rise.

URSULA   I will, lady.

HERO   And bid her come hither.

URSULA   Well.   [*Exit.*]   5

MARGARET   Troth, I think your other rabato were better.   6

HERO   No, pray thee, good Meg, I'll wear this.

MARGARET   By my troth, 's not so good, and I warrant   8
your cousin will say so.

HERO   My cousin's a fool, and thou art another. I'll wear
none but this.

MARGARET   I like the new tire within excellently, if the   12
hair were a thought browner; and your gown's a most   13
rare fashion, i'faith. I saw the Duchess of Milan's gown
that they praise so.

HERO   Oh, that exceeds, they say.   16

MARGARET   By my troth, 's but a nightgown in respect   17
of yours: cloth o' gold, and cuts, and laced with silver,   18
set with pearls, down sleeves, side sleeves, and skirts,   19
round underborne with a bluish tinsel. But for a fine,   20
quaint, graceful, and excellent fashion, yours is worth   21
ten on't.   22

HERO   God give me joy to wear it! For my heart is
exceeding heavy.

MARGARET   'Twill be heavier soon by the weight of a
man.

HERO   Fie upon thee! Art not ashamed?

MARGARET   Of what, lady? Of speaking honorably? Is
not marriage honorable in a beggar? Is not your lord   29
honorable without marriage? I think you would have
me say, "saving your reverence, a husband." An bad   31
thinking do not wrest true speaking, I'll offend   32
nobody. Is there any harm in "the heavier for a husband"? None, I think, an it be the right husband and
the right wife; otherwise 'tis light, and not heavy. Ask   35
my Lady Beatrice else. Here she comes.

Enter Beatrice.

HERO   Good morrow, coz.

BEATRICE   Good morrow, sweet Hero.

HERO   Why, how now? Do you speak in the sick tune?   39

BEATRICE   I am out of all other tune, methinks.

MARGARET   Clap 's into "Light o 'love." That goes   41
without a burden; do you sing it, and I'll dance it.   42

BEATRICE   Ye light o' love with your heels! Then, if your   43
husband have stables enough, you'll see he shall lack
no barns.   45

MARGARET   Oh, illegitimate construction! I scorn that   46
with my heels.   47

138–9 fashion . . . man i.e., fashion prompts the discarding of clothes faster than honest use.   **144 leans me** leans. (*Me* is an emphatic marker.)   **148 possessed** (misleadingly) informed; also, perhaps, possessed, as by the devil   **149 amiable** amorous   **162 Right Master Constable** (A comic title on the pattern of "Right Worshipful," etc.)   **163 recovered** (For "discovered.")   **164 lechery** (For "treachery.")   **166 lock** lock of hair hanging down on the left shoulder; the lovelock.   **171 obey** (For "oblige," "command.")   **173 commodity** goods acquired   **174 taken up** (1) arrested (2) obtained on credit.   **bills** (1) pikes (2) bonds given as security.   **175 in question** (1) subject to judicial examination (2) of doubtful value
3.4. Location: Leonato's house.
5 Well Very well, as you wish.

6 rabato tall collar supporting a ruff, stiffened with wire or starch
8 troth, 's faith, it is   **12 tire within** headdress in the inner room
13 hair hairpiece attached to the *tire* (line 12)   **16 exceeds** i.e., exceeds comparison   **17 nightgown** dressing gown   **17–18 in respect of** compared to   **18 cuts . . . silver** slashes in a garment revealing the underlying fabic, and laced with silver thread   **19 down sleeves** tight-fitting sleeves to the wrist.   **side sleeves** secondary ornamental sleeves hanging from the shoulder   **20 round underborne** with a lining around the edge of the skirt.   **tinsel** cloth, usually silk, interwoven with threads of silver or gold.   **21 quaint** elegant   **22 on't** of it.   **29 in** even in   **31 saving . . . husband** (By this apologetic formula, Margaret suggests that Hero is too prudish even to hear the word *husband* mentioned.)   **An bad** If bawdy   **32 wrest** misinterpret   **35 light** harmless. (With a play on the meaning "wanton.")   **39 tune** i.e., mood.   **41 Clap 's** Let's shift.   **Light o' love** (A popular song.)   **42 burden** bass accompaniment. (With play on the idea of "the weight of a man.")   **43 Ye . . . heels!** i.e., You're light-heeled, wanton!   **45 barns** (With pun on "bairns," children.)   **46 illegitimate construction** false inference. (But with a play on the idea of bastard "bairns.")   **47 with my heels** (A proverbial expression of scorn.)

BEATRICE 'Tis almost five o'clock, cousin; 'tis time you were ready. By my troth, I am exceeding ill. Heigh-ho!

MARGARET For a hawk, a horse, or a husband?   50

BEATRICE For the letter that begins them all, H.   51

MARGARET Well, an you be not turned Turk, there's no   52 more sailing by the star.   53

BEATRICE What means the fool, trow?   54

MARGARET Nothing, I; but God send everyone their heart's desire!

HERO These gloves the Count sent me, they are an excellent perfume.   58

BEATRICE I am stuffed, cousin. I cannot smell.   59

MARGARET A maid, and stuffed! There's goodly catching of cold.

BEATRICE Oh, God help me, God help me! How long have you professed apprehension?   63

MARGARET Ever since you left it. Doth not my wit   64 become me rarely?

BEATRICE It is not seen enough; you should wear it in   66 your cap. By my troth, I am sick.   67

MARGARET Get you some of this distilled *carduus bene-*   68 *dictus*, and lay it to your heart. It is the only thing for a   69 qualm.   70

HERO There thou prick'st her with a thistle.

BEATRICE *Benedictus!* Why *benedictus?* You have some moral in this *benedictus.*   73

MARGARET Moral? No, by my troth, I have no moral meaning, I meant plain holy thistle. You may think   75 perchance that I think you are in love. Nay, by'r Lady, I am not such a fool to think what I list, nor I list not to   77 think what I can, nor indeed I cannot think, if I would think my heart out of thinking, that you are in love or   79 that you will be in love or that you can be in love. Yet Benedick was such another, and now is he become a   81 man. He swore he would ever marry, and yet now, in   82 despite of his heart, he eats his meat without grudg-   83 ing; and how you may be converted I know not, but   84 methinks you look with your eyes as other women do.

BEATRICE What pace is this that thy tongue keeps?

MARGARET Not a false gallop.   87

Enter Ursula.

URSULA Madam, withdraw. The Prince, the Count, Signor Benedick, Don John, and all the gallants of the town are come to fetch you to church.

HERO Help to dress me, good coz, good Meg, good Ursula.   [*Exeunt.*]

❧

[3.5]

Enter Leonato and the Constable [Dogberry] and the Headborough [Verges].

LEONATO What would you with me, honest neighbor?

DOGBERRY Marry, sir, I would have some confidence   2 with you that decerns you nearly.   3

LEONATO Brief, I pray you, for you see it is a busy time with me.

DOGBERRY Marry, this it is, sir.

VERGES Yes, in truth it is, sir.

LEONATO What is it, my good friends?

DOGBERRY Goodman Verges, sir, speaks a little off the   9 matter—an old man, sir, and his wits are not so blunt   10 as, God help, I would desire they were, but, in faith, honest as the skin between his brows.   12

VERGES Yes, I thank God I am as honest as any man living that is an old man and no honester than I.

DOGBERRY Comparisons are odorous. *Palabras*, neigh-   15 bor Verges.

LEONATO Neighbors, you are tedious.

DOGBERRY It pleases Your Worship to say so, but we are the poor Duke's officers. But truly, for mine own part,   19 if I were as tedious as a king, I could find in my heart   20 to bestow it all of Your Worship.   21

LEONATO All thy tediousness on me, ah?

DOGBERRY Yea, an 'twere a thousand pound more than 'tis; for I hear as good exclamation on Your Worship as   24 of any man in the city, and though I be but a poor man, I am glad to hear it.

VERGES And so am I.

LEONATO I would fain know what you have to say.

VERGES Marry, sir, our watch tonight, excepting Your   29 Worship's presence, ha' ta'en a couple of as arrant   30 knaves as any in Messina.

DOGBERRY A good old man, sir; he will be talking. As they say, when the age is in, the wit is out. God help   33 us, it is a world to see! Well said, i'faith, neighbor   34

Verges. Well, God's a good man. An two men ride 35
of a horse, one must ride behind. An honest soul, 36
i'faith, sir, by my troth he is, as ever broke bread. But, God
is to be worshiped, all men are not alike, alas, good
neighbor!

LEONATO   Indeed, neighbor, he comes too short of you.

DOGBERRY   Gifts that God gives.

LEONATO   I must leave you.

DOGBERRY   One word, sir. Our watch, sir, have indeed
comprehended two aspicious persons, and we would 44
have them this morning examined before Your Worship.

LEONATO   Take their examination yourself and bring
it me. I am now in great haste, as it may appear
unto you.

DOGBERRY   It shall be suffigance. 50

LEONATO   Drink some wine ere you go. Fare you well.

[Enter a Messenger.]

MESSENGER   My lord, they stay for you to give your
daughter to her husband.

LEONATO   I'll wait upon them. I am ready. 54

                    [Exeunt Leonato and Messenger.]

DOGBERRY   Go, good partner, go, get you to Francis Sea- 55
coal. Bid him bring his pen and inkhorn to the jail. We 56
are now to examination these men. 57

VERGES   And we must do it wisely.

DOGBERRY   We will spare for no wit, I warrant you.
Here's that shall drive some of them to a noncome. 60
Only get the learned writer to set down our excom- 61
munication, and meet me at the jail.   *[Exeunt.]* 62

❖

[4.1]

*Enter Prince [Don Pedro], [Don John the]
Bastard, Leonato, Friar [Francis], Claudio,
Benedick, Hero, and Beatrice [with attendants].*

LEONATO   Come, Friar Francis, be brief—only to the
plain form of marriage, and you shall recount their
particular duties afterwards.

FRIAR   You come hither, my lord, to marry this lady?

CLAUDIO   No.

LEONATO   To be married to her. Friar, you come to
marry her.

FRIAR   Lady, you come hither to be married to this
Count?

HERO   I do.

FRIAR   If either of you know any inward impediment 11

why you should not be conjoined, I charge you on
your souls to utter it.

CLAUDIO   Know you any, Hero?

HERO   None, my lord.

FRIAR   Know you any, Count?

LEONATO   I dare make his answer: none.

CLAUDIO   Oh, what men dare do! What men may do!
What men daily do, not knowing what they do!

BENEDICK   How now? Interjections? Why, then, some be 20
of laughing, as, ah, ha, he! 21

CLAUDIO
Stand thee by, Friar.—Father, by your leave, 22
Will you with free and unconstrainèd soul
Give me this maid, your daughter?

LEONATO
As freely, son, as God did give her me.

CLAUDIO
And what have I to give you back, whose worth
May counterpoise this rich and precious gift? 27

DON PEDRO
Nothing, unless you render her again.

CLAUDIO
Sweet Prince, you learn me noble thankfulness. 29
                    [He hands Hero to Leonato.]
There, Leonato, take her back again.
Give not this rotten orange to your friend;
She's but the sign and semblance of her honor. 32
Behold how like a maid she blushes here!
Oh, what authority and show of truth
Can cunning sin cover itself withal!
Comes not that blood as modest evidence 36
To witness simple virtue? Would you not swear, 37
All you that see her, that she were a maid,
By these exterior shows? But she is none:
She knows the heat of a luxurious bed. 40
Her blush is guiltiness, not modesty.

LEONATO
What do you mean, my lord?

CLAUDIO   Not to be married, 42
Not to knit my soul to an approvèd wanton. 43

LEONATO
Dear my lord, if you, in your own proof, 44
Have vanquished the resistance of her youth,
And made defeat of her virginity—

CLAUDIO
I know what you would say: if I have known her, 47
You will say, she did embrace me as a husband,
And so extenuate the forehand sin. 49
No, Leonato,
I never tempted her with word too large, 51

---

35 God's . . . man i.e., God is good. (A proverbial saying.)   **36 of** on
44 comprehended (For "apprehended.")   **aspicious** (For "suspicious.")   **50 suffigance** (For "sufficient.")   **54 wait upon** attend
55–6 Francis Seacoal i.e., the Sexton of 4.2, not George, the member of
the watch in 3.3.   **57 examination** (For "examine.")   **60 noncome**
(Probably an unintended contraction for *non compos mentis*, "not of
sound mind," but Dogberry may have intended "nonplus.")
61–2 excommunication (For "examination" or "communication.")
4.1. Location: A church.
11 inward secret

20–1 some . . . he (Benedick quotes from Lilly's Latin grammar on the
subject of interjections; according to Lilly, these are to be classified as
laughing interjections.)   **22 Stand thee by** Stand aside   **27 counterpoise** balance, be equivalent to   **29 learn** teach   **32 sign and semblance** pretense and outward show   **36 blood** i.e., blush.   **modest
evidence** evidence of modesty   **37 witness** bear witness to   **40 luxurious** lascivious, lustful   **42 mean** imply, suggest. (But Claudio bitterly replies in the sense of "intend.")   **43 approvèd** proved   **44 in . . .
proof** in making trial of her yourself   **47 known her** i.e., known her
sexually   **49 extenuate** excuse, lessen.   **forehand sin** sin of anticipating (marriage).   **51 large** broad, immodest

But, as a brother to his sister, showed
Bashful sincerity and comely love.

HERO
And seemed I ever otherwise to you?

CLAUDIO
Out on thee, seeming! I will write against it.   55
You seem to me as Dian in her orb,   56
As chaste as is the bud ere it be blown;   57
But you are more intemperate in your blood
Than Venus, or those pampered animals
That rage in savage sensuality.

HERO
Is my lord well, that he doth speak so wide?   61

LEONATO
Sweet Prince, why speak not you?

DON PEDRO   What should I speak?
I stand dishonored, that have gone about   63
To link my dear friend to a common stale.   64

LEONATO
Are these things spoken, or do I but dream?

DON JOHN
Sir, they are spoken, and these things are true.

BENEDICK   This looks not like a nuptial.

HERO   "True"! Oh, God!   68

CLAUDIO   Leonato, stand I here?
Is this the Prince? Is this the Prince's brother?
Is this face Hero's? Are our eyes our own?

LEONATO
All this is so. But what of this, my lord?

CLAUDIO
Let me but move one question to your daughter,   73
And by that fatherly and kindly power   74
That you have in her, bid her answer truly.

LEONATO [to Hero]
I charge thee do so, as thou art my child.

HERO
Oh, God defend me, how am I beset!
What kind of catechizing call you this?   78

CLAUDIO
To make you answer truly to your name.

HERO
Is it not Hero? Who can blot that name
With any just reproach?

CLAUDIO   Marry, that can Hero!
Hero itself can blot out Hero's virtue.   82
What man was he talked with you yesternight
Out at your window betwixt twelve and one?
Now, if you are a maid, answer to this.

HERO
I talked with no man at that hour, my lord.

DON PEDRO
Why, then are you no maiden. Leonato,
I am sorry you must hear. Upon mine honor,
Myself, my brother, and this grievèd Count   89
Did see her, hear her, at that hour last night
Talk with a ruffian at her chamber window,
Who hath indeed, most like a liberal villain,   92
Confessed the vile encounters they have had
A thousand times in secret.

DON JOHN
Fie, fie, they are not to be named, my lord,
Not to be spoke of!
There is not chastity enough in language
Without offense to utter them. Thus, pretty lady,
I am sorry for thy much misgovernment.   99

CLAUDIO
O Hero, what a Hero hadst thou been
If half thy outward graces had been placed
About thy thoughts and counsels of thy heart!
But fare thee well, most foul, most fair! Farewell,
Thou pure impiety and impious purity!
For thee I'll lock up all the gates of love,   105
And on my eyelids shall conjecture hang,   106
To turn all beauty into thoughts of harm,
And never shall it more be gracious.   108

LEONATO
Hath no man's dagger here a point for me?
                                              [Hero swoons.]

BEATRICE
Why, how now, cousin, wherefore sink you down?

DON JOHN
Come, let us go. These things, come thus to light,
Smother her spirits up.
                   [Exeunt Don Pedro, Don John, and Claudio.]

BENEDICK
How doth the lady?

BEATRICE   Dead, I think. Help, uncle!
Hero, why, Hero! Uncle! Signor Benedick! Friar!

LEONATO
O Fate, take not away thy heavy hand!
Death is the fairest cover for her shame
That may be wished for.

BEATRICE   How now, cousin Hero?

FRIAR   Have comfort, lady.

LEONATO
Dost thou look up?

FRIAR   Yea, wherefore should she not?   119

LEONATO
Wherefore? Why, doth not every earthly thing
Cry shame upon her? Could she here deny
The story that is printed in her blood?   122
Do not live, Hero, do not ope thine eyes;
For, did I think thou wouldst not quickly die,
Thought I thy spirits were stronger than thy shames,   125

---

55 Out . . . seeming! i.e., Shame on you, a mere semblance of good!
56 Dian . . . orb i.e., Diana, goddess of chastity, enthroned in the
moon   **57 be blown** open, flower   **61 wide** wide of the mark.
63 gone about undertaken   **64 stale** whore.   **68 True** (A response
to Don John's use of the term.)   **73 move** put   **74 kindly** natural
78 catechizing formal questioning used by the Church to teach the
principles of faith. The first question in the Church of England's
catechism is, "What is your name?"   **82 Hero itself** The very name
of Hero (who, in the story of Hero and Leander, is the faithful
tragic heroine)

89 grievèd (1) aggrieved, wronged (2) struck with grief   **92 liberal**
licentious   **99 much misgovernment** gross misconduct.   **105 For
thee** Because of you   **106 conjecture** evil suspicion   **108 be gracious**
seem attractive, graceful.   **119 wherefore** why   **122 blood** i.e.,
blushes.   **125 spirits** life-giving energies, vital powers

Myself would, on the rearward of reproaches,   126
Strike at thy life. Grieved I I had but one?
Chid I for that at frugal nature's frame?   128
Oh, one too much by thee! Why had I one?
Why ever wast thou lovely in my eyes?
Why had I not with charitable hand
Took up a beggar's issue at my gates,   132
Who, smirchèd thus and mired with infamy,
I might have said, "No part of it is mine;
This shame derives itself from unknown loins"?
But mine, and mine I loved, and mine I praised,   136
And mine that I was proud on, mine so much
That I myself was to myself not mine,   138
Valuing of her—why, she, oh, she, is fallen   139
Into a pit of ink, that the wide sea   140
Hath drops too few to wash her clean again
And salt too little which may season give   142
To her foul-tainted flesh!
BENEDICK   Sir, sir, be patient.
For my part, I am so attired in wonder,
I know not what to say.
BEATRICE
Oh, on my soul, my cousin is belied!
BENEDICK
Lady, were you her bedfellow last night?
BEATRICE
No, truly, not; although, until last night,
I have this twelvemonth been her bedfellow.
LEONATO
Confirmed, confirmed! Oh, that is stronger made
Which was before barred up with ribs of iron!   151
Would the two princes lie and Claudio lie,
Who loved her so that, speaking of her foulness,
Washed it with tears? Hence from her! Let her die.
FRIAR   Hear me a little;
For I have only been silent so long
And given way unto this course of fortune   157
By noting of the lady. I have marked
A thousand blushing apparitions
To start into her face, a thousand innocent shames
In angel whiteness beat away those blushes,
And in her eye there hath appeared a fire
To burn the errors that these princes hold
Against her maiden truth. Call me a fool;
Trust not my reading nor my observations,
Which with experimental seal doth warrant   166
The tenor of my book; trust not my age,   167
My reverence, calling, nor divinity,
If this sweet lady lie not guiltless here
Under some biting error.
LEONATO   Friar, it cannot be.
Thou see'st that all the grace that she hath left
Is that she will not add to her damnation

A sin of perjury; she not denies it.
Why seek'st thou then to cover with excuse
That which appears in proper nakedness?   175
FRIAR
Lady, what man is he you are accused of?
HERO
They know that do accuse me; I know none.
If I know more of any man alive
Than that which maiden modesty doth warrant,   179
Let all my sins lack mercy! O my father,
Prove you that any man with me conversed   181
At hours unmeet or that I yesternight   182
Maintained the change of words with any creature,   183
Refuse me, hate me, torture me to death!   184
FRIAR
There is some strange misprision in the princes.   185
BENEDICK
Two of them have the very bent of honor;   186
And if their wisdoms be misled in this,
The practice of it lives in John the Bastard,   188
Whose spirits toil in frame of villainies.   189
LEONATO
I know not. If they speak but truth of her,
These hands shall tear her; if they wrong her honor,
The proudest of them shall well hear of it.
Time hath not yet so dried this blood of mine,
Nor age so eat up my invention,   194
Nor fortune made such havoc of my means,
Nor my bad life reft me so much of friends,   196
But they shall find, awaked in such a kind,   197
Both strength of limb and policy of mind,   198
Ability in means, and choice of friends,
To quit me of them throughly.
FRIAR   Pause awhile,   200
And let my counsel sway you in this case.
Your daughter here the princes left for dead,   202
Let her awhile be secretly kept in,   203
And publish it that she is dead indeed.
Maintain a mourning ostentation,   205
And on your family's old monument   206
Hang mournful epitaphs, and do all rites
That appertain unto a burial.
LEONATO
What shall become of this? What will this do?   209
FRIAR
Marry, this, well carried, shall on her behalf   210
Change slander to remorse. That is some good.
But not for that dream I on this strange course,   212

126 on . . . reproaches following this public disgrace   128 Chid
Chided.   frame plan, order.   132 Took . . . issue taken up a beggar's
child   136 mine i.e., my own daughter   138–9 That . . . her i.e., that I
set no value on myself in caring so much for her   140 that such that
142 season preservative   151 before already   157 given . . . fortune
yielded to this turn of events   166–7 Which . . . book i.e., by means
of which observations and experience I have confirmed what I
learned from books

175 proper true   179 warrant sanction, permit   181 Prove you if you
prove   182 unmeet improper   183 Maintained the change held
exchange   184 Refuse disown   185 misprision mistake, misunderstanding   186 Two . . . honor i.e., Don Pedro and Claudio are wholly
honorable   188 practice scheming   189 frame contriving   194 eat
eaten. (Pronounced "et.")   invention power to plan (vengeance)
196 reft robbed   197 kind manner   198 policy shrewdness
200 quit . . . throughly settle accounts with them thoroughly.
202 the princes i.e., (whom) Don Pedro and Claudio   203 in in hiding, at home   205 Maintain . . . ostentation Perform all the outward
signs of mourning   206 monument burial vault   209 become of
result from   210 carried managed   212 not for that not for that
reason alone

But on this travail look for greater birth.   213
She—dying, as it must be so maintained,
Upon the instant that she was accused—
Shall be lamented, pitied, and excused
Of every hearer; for it so falls out
That what we have we prize not to the worth   218
Whiles we enjoy it, but, being lacked and lost,
Why then we rack the value, then we find   220
The virtue that possession would not show us
Whiles it was ours. So will it fare with Claudio.
When he shall hear she died upon his words,   223
Th'idea of her life shall sweetly creep
Into his study of imagination,   225
And every lovely organ of her life   226
Shall come appareled in more precious habit,   227
More moving-delicate, and full of life,
Into the eye and prospect of his soul,   229
Than when she lived indeed. Then shall he mourn,
If ever love had interest in his liver,   231
And wish he had not so accusèd her,
No, though he thought his accusation true.
Let this be so, and doubt not but success   234
Will fashion the event in better shape   235
Than I can lay it down in likelihood.   236
But if all aim but this be leveled false,   237
The supposition of the lady's death
Will quench the wonder of her infamy.
And if it sort not well, you may conceal her,   240
As best befits her wounded reputation,
In some reclusive and religious life,   242
Out of all eyes, tongues, minds, and injuries.   243

BENEDICK
Signor Leonato, let the Friar advise you.
And though you know my inwardness and love   245
Is very much unto the Prince and Claudio,
Yet, by mine honor, I will deal in this
As secretly and justly as your soul
Should with your body.

LEONATO   Being that I flow in grief,   249
The smallest twine may lead me.

FRIAR
'Tis well consented. Presently away;   251
    For to strange sores strangely they strain the cure.   252
Come, lady, die to live. This wedding day
    Perhaps is but prolonged. Have patience, and
    endure.   254

                Exit [with all but Benedick and Beatrice].
BENDICK   Lady Beatrice, have you wept all this while?

BEATRICE   Yea, and I will weep a while longer.
BENEDICK   I will not desire that.
BEATRICE   You have no reason. I do it freely.   258
BENEDICK   Surely I do believe your fair cousin is
    wronged.
BEATRICE   Ah, how much might the man deserve of me
    that would right her!
BENEDICK   Is there any way to show such friendship?
BEATRICE   A very even way, but no such friend.   264
BENEDICK   May a man do it?
BEATRICE   It is a man's office, but not yours.   266
BENEDICK   I do love nothing in the world so well as you.
    Is not that strange?
BEATRICE   As strange as the thing I know not. It were as
    possible for me to say I loved nothing so well as you.
    But believe me not; and yet I lie not. I confess nothing,
    nor I deny nothing. I am sorry for my cousin.
BENEDICK   By my sword, Beatrice, thou lovest me.
BEATRICE   Do not swear and eat it.   274
BENEDICK   I will swear by it that you love me, and I will
    make him eat it that says I love not you.   276
BEATRICE   Will you not eat your word?
BENEDICK   With no sauce that can be devised to it. I
    protest I love thee.   279
BEATRICE   Why, then, God forgive me!
BENEDICK   What offense, sweet Beatrice?
BEATRICE   You have stayed me in a happy hour. I was 282
    about to protest I loved you.
BENEDICK   And do it with all thy heart.
BEATRICE   I love you with so much of my heart that
    none is left to protest.   286
BENEDICK   Come, bid me do anything for thee.
BEATRICE   Kill Claudio.
BENEDICK   Ha! Not for the wide world.
BEATRICE   You kill me to deny it. Farewell.   [Going.]
BENEDICK   Tarry, sweet Beatrice.
BEATRICE   I am gone, though I am here. There is no love 292
    in you. Nay, I pray you, let me go.
BENEDICK   Beatrice—
BEATRICE   In faith, I will go.
BENEDICK   We'll be friends first.
BEATRICE   You dare easier be friends with me than fight
    with mine enemy.
BENEDICK   Is Claudio thine enemy?
BEATRICE   Is 'a not approved in the height a villain, that 300
    hath slandered, scorned, dishonored my kinswoman?
    Oh, that I were a man! What, bear her in hand until 302
    they come to take hands, and then, with public accus-
    ation, uncovered slander, unmitigated rancor—Oh, 304
    God, that I were a man! I would eat his heart in the
    marketplace.

---

213 on this travail from this effort (which is metaphorically like the *travail*, or labor, of childbirth)   **218 to the worth** as fully as it deserves
220 rack stretch, extend   **223 upon** in consequence of   **225 Into . . . imagination** into his thoughts   **226 organ . . . life** aspect of her when she was alive   **227 habit** apparel   **229 prospect** range of vision
231 interest in claim upon.   **liver** (The supposed seat of the passion of love.)   **234 success** i.e., what succeeds or happens in time as my plan unfolds   **235 event** outcome   **236 lay . . . likelihood** anticipate its probable course.   **237 if . . . false** i.e., if every other aim miscarry
240 sort turn out   **242 reclusive** cloistered   **243 injuries** insults.
245 inwardness and love close friendship   **249 Being . . . grief** Since I overflow in grief   **251 Presently** Immediately   **252 For . . . cure** for strange diseases require strange and desperate cures.   **254 prolonged** deferred.

---

258 You . . . reason (Beatrice twists Benedick's "I wish you weren't so unhappy," line 257, into "There's no need for you to bid me stop weeping.")   **264 even** direct, straightforward   **266 office** duty
274 eat it i.e., eat your words.   **276 eat it** i.e., eat my sword, be stabbed by it   **279 protest** affirm. (Also in line 283.)   **282 stayed** stopped.   **in . . . hour** at an appropriate moment.   **286 protest** object. (With a play on the sense of "affirm" in 279 and 283.)   **292 gone** i.e., in spirit   **300 approved in the height** proved in the highest degree
302 bear her in hand delude Hero with false hopes   **304 uncovered** open, unconcealed

BENEDICK   Hear me, Beatrice—

BEATRICE   Talk with a man out at a window! A proper 308
saying! 309

BENEDICK   Nay, but Beatrice—

BEATRICE   Sweet Hero! She is wronged, she is slandered,
she is undone.

BENEDICK   Beat—

BEATRICE   Princes and counties! Surely, a princely testi- 314
mony, a goodly count, Count Comfect; a sweet gallant, 315
surely! Oh, that I were a man for his sake! Or that I had
any friend would be a man for my sake! But manhood
is melted into curtsies, valor into compliment, and
men are only turned into tongue, and trim ones too. 319
He is now as valiant as Hercules that only tells a lie 320
and swears it. I cannot be a man with wishing, there- 321
fore I will die a woman with grieving.

BENEDICK   Tarry, good Beatrice. By this hand, I love
thee.

BEATRICE   Use it for my love some other way than
swearing by it.

BENEDICK   Think you in your soul the Count Claudio
hath wronged Hero?

BEATRICE   Yea, as sure as I have a thought or a soul.

BENEDICK   Enough, I am engaged. I will challenge him. 330
I will kiss your hand, and so I leave you. By this hand,
Claudio shall render me a dear account. As you hear 332
of me, so think of me. Go comfort your cousin. I must
say she is dead. And so, farewell. [*Exeunt separately.*]

❧

[4.2]

*Enter the Constables [Dogberry and Verges]
and the Town Clerk [Sexton] in gowns, Borachio, [Conrade, and Watch].*

DOGBERRY   Is our whole dissembly appeared? 1

VERGES   Oh, a stool and a cushion for the sexton.
[*Stool and cushion are brought. The Sexton sits.*]

SEXTON   Which be the malefactors?

DOGBERRY   Marry, that am I and my partner. 4

VERGES   Nay, that's certain; we have the exhibition to 5
examine.

SEXTON   But which are the offenders that are to be
examined? Let them come before Master Constable.

DOGBERRY   Yea, marry, let them come before me. [*The
prisoners are brought forward.*] What is your name,
friend?

BORACHIO   Borachio.

DOGBERRY   Pray, write down Borachio.—Yours, sirrah? 13

CONRADE   I am a gentleman, sir, and my name is
Conrade.

DOGBERRY   Write down Master Gentleman Conrade.
Masters, do you serve God?

CONRADE, BORACHIO   Yea, sir, we hope.

DOGBERRY   Write down that they hope they serve God;
and write God first, for God defend but God should 20
go before such villains! Masters, it is proved already
that you are little better than false knaves, and it will
go near to be thought so shortly. How answer you for
yourselves?

CONRADE   Marry, sir, we say we are none.

DOGBERRY   A marvelous witty fellow, I assure you, but 26
I will go about with him. [*To Borachio*] Come you 27
hither, sirrah. A word in your ear. Sir, I say to you, it is
thought you are false knaves.

BORACHIO   Sir, I say to you we are none.

DOGBERRY   Well, stand aside. 'Fore God, they are both
in a tale. Have you writ down that they are none? 32

SEXTON   Master Constable, you go not the way to
examine. You must call forth the watch that are their
accusers.

DOGBERRY   Yea, marry, that's the eftest way. Let the 36
watch come forth.—Masters, I charge you in the
Prince's name accuse these men.

SEACOAL   This man said, sir, that Don John, the Prince's
brother, was a villain.

DOGBERRY   Write down Prince John a villain. Why, this
is flat perjury, to call a prince's brother villain. 42

BORACHIO   Master Constable—

DOGBERRY   Pray thee, fellow, peace. I do not like thy
look, I promise thee.

SEXTON   What heard you him say else?

FIRST WATCH   Marry, that he had received a thousand
ducats of Don John for accusing the Lady Hero
wrongfully.

DOGBERRY   Flat burglary as ever was committed.

VERGES   Yea, by Mass, that it is. 51

SEXTON   What else, fellow?

SEACOAL   And that Count Claudio did mean, upon his 53
words, to disgrace Hero before the whole assembly, 54
and not marry her.

DOGBERRY   Oh, villain! Thou wilt be condemned into
everlasting redemption for this. 57

SEXTON   What else?

WATCH   This is all. 59

SEXTON   And this is more, masters, than you can deny:
Prince John is this morning secretly stolen away. Hero
was in this manner accused, in this very manner
refused, and upon the grief of this suddenly died.—
Master Constable, let these men be bound and
brought to Leonato's. I will go before and show him
their examination. [*Exit.*]

308–9 proper saying likely story.   **314 counties** counts.   **315 count**
(1) the title (2) declaration of complaint in an indictment (3) account.
Comfect candy or sweetmeat   **319 are . . . tongue** have become mere
(flattering) voices.   **trim** nice, elegant, fine. (Used ironically.)
320–1 He . . . swears it A man need only tell lies and swear they are
true to gain a reputation for bravery nowadays.   **330 I am engaged** I
pledge myself.   **332 dear** costly
4.2. Location: The jail.
1 dissembly (A blunder for "assembly.")   **4 that am I** (Dogberry evidently understands *malefactors* to mean "factors," agents.)   **5 exhibition** (Possibly for "commission.")   **13 sirrah** (Used to address
inferiors; Conrade objects.)

20 defend forbid   **26 witty** clever, cunning   **27 go about with** get
the better of, deal with   **32 in a tale** in agreement.   **36 eftest** (Some
sort of invention for "easiest" or "deftest.")   **42 perjury** (Dogberry
means "slander.")   **51 by Mass** by the Mass   **53–4 upon his words**
on the basis of Borachio's testimony   **57 redemption** (Dogberry
means "damnation.")   **59 WATCH** (Perhaps both Seacoal and his partner speak.)

DOGBERRY   Come, let them be opinioned.   67
VERGES   Let them be in the hands—
CONRADE   Off, coxcomb!
DOGBERRY   God's my life, where's the sexton? Let him   70
    write down the Prince's officer coxcomb. Come, bind
    them. Thou naughty varlet!   72
CONRADE   Away! You are an ass, you are an ass.
DOGBERRY   Dost thou not suspect my place? Dost thou   74
    not suspect my years? Oh, that he were here to write   75
    me down an ass! But masters, remember that I am an
    ass; though it be not written down, yet forget not that
    I am an ass. No, thou villain, thou art full of piety, as   78
    shall be proved upon thee by good witness. I am a
    wise fellow, and, which is more, an officer, and, which
    is more, a householder, and, which is more, as pretty
    a piece of flesh as any is in Messina, and one that
    knows the law, go to, and a rich fellow enough, go to,
    and a fellow that hath had losses, and one that hath
    two gowns and everything handsome about him.—
    Bring him away. Oh, that I had been writ down an ass!
                            Exeunt.

❖

5.1

Enter Leonato and his brother [Antonio].

ANTONIO
    If you go on thus, you will kill yourself;
    And 'tis not wisdom thus to second grief   2
    Against yourself.
LEONATO   I pray thee, cease thy counsel,
    Which falls into mine ears as profitless
    As water in a sieve. Give not me counsel,
    Nor let no comforter delight mine ear
    But such a one whose wrongs do suit with mine.   7
    Bring me a father that so loved his child,
    Whose joy of her is overwhelmed like mine,
    And bid him speak of patience;
    Measure his woe the length and breadth of mine,   11
    And let it answer every strain for strain,   12
    As thus for thus, and such a grief for such,
    In every lineament, branch, shape, and form;
    If such a one will smile and stroke his beard,
    Bid sorrow wag, cry "hem!" when he should groan,   16
    Patch grief with proverbs, make misfortune drunk   17
    With candle wasters, bring him yet to me,   18
    And I of him will gather patience.
    But there is no such man. For, brother, men
    Can counsel and speak comfort to that grief
    Which they themselves not feel; but tasting it,

Their counsel turns to passion, which before
Would give preceptial medicine to rage,   24
Fetter strong madness in a silken thread,
Charm ache with air and agony with words.   26
No, no, 'tis all men's office to speak patience   27
To those that wring under the load of sorrow,   28
But no man's virtue nor sufficiency   29
To be so moral when he shall endure   30
The like himself. Therefore give me no counsel.
My griefs cry louder than advertisement.   32
ANTONIO
    Therein do men from children nothing differ.   33
LEONATO
    I pray thee, peace. I will be flesh and blood;
    For there was never yet philosopher
    That could endure the toothache patiently,
    However they have writ the style of gods   37
    And made a push at chance and sufferance.   38
ANTONIO
    Yet bend not all the harm upon yourself.
    Make those that do offend you suffer, too.
LEONATO
    There thou speak'st reason. Nay, I will do so.
    My soul doth tell me Hero is belied,
    And that shall Claudio know; so shall the Prince
    And all of them that thus dishonor her.

Enter Prince [Don Pedro] and Claudio.

ANTONIO
    Here comes the Prince and Claudio hastily.
DON PEDRO
    Good e'en, good e'en.
CLAUDIO   Good day to both of you.
LEONATO
    Hear you, my lords—
DON PEDRO   We have some haste, Leonato.
LEONATO
    Some haste, my lord! Well, fare you well, my lord.
    Are you so hasty now? Well, all is one.   49
DON PEDRO
    Nay, do not quarrel with us, good old man.
ANTONIO
    If he could right himself with quarreling,   51
    Some of us would lie low.
CLAUDIO   Who wrongs him?   52
LEONATO
    Marry, thou dost wrong me, thou dissembler, thou!   53
    Nay, never lay thy hand upon thy sword;
    I fear thee not.
CLAUDIO   Marry, beshrew my hand   55
    If it should give your age such cause of fear.
    In faith, my hand meant nothing to my sword.   57

---

67 opinioned (For "pinioned.")   **70 God's** May God save
72 naughty wicked   **74 suspect** (For "respect.")   **75 my years** (With
an unconscious suggestion of "my ears," i.e., ass's ears.)   **78 piety**
(For "impiety.")
5.1. Location: Near Leonato's house.
2 second assist, encourage   **7 suit with** match   **11 Measure his woe**
let his woe equal in scope   **12 answer . . . for strain** correspond, pang
for pang. (With a musical sense also of echoing a refrain.)   **16 wag** be
off.   **cry "hem"** i.e., clear the throat as before some wordy speech
17 drunk i.e., insensible to pain   **18 candle wasters** those who waste
candles by late study, bookworms, moral philosophers

24 preceptial consisting of precepts   **26 air** mere breath, words
27 office duty   **28 wring** writhe   **29 sufficiency** ability, power
30 moral prone to moralizing   **32 advertisement** advice, counsel.
33 Therein . . . differ i.e., It is childish to be so inconsolable.   **37 writ . . .
gods** uttered godlike wisdom   **38 made . . . sufferance** scoffed at misfortune and suffering.   **49 all is one** it makes no difference.   **51 he** i.e.,
Leonato   **52 Some of us** i.e., Don Pedro and Claudio   **53 thou** (Used
contemptuously instead of the more polite *you*.)   **55 beshrew** curse
57 my . . . sword I had no intention of using my sword.

LEONATO
Tush, tush, man, never fleer and jest at me.   58
I speak not like a dotard nor a fool,
As under privilege of age to brag
What I have done being young or what would do
Were I not old. Know, Claudio, to thy head,   62
Thou hast so wronged mine innocent child and me
That I am forced to lay my reverence by,   64
And with gray hairs and bruise of many days
Do challenge thee to trial of a man.   66
I say thou hast belied mine innocent child.
Thy slander hath gone through and through her
heart,
And she lies buried with her ancestors—
Oh, in a tomb where never scandal slept,
Save this of hers, framed by thy villainy!   71

CLAUDIO
My villainy?

LEONATO   Thine, Claudio, thine, I say.

DON PEDRO
You say not right, old man.

LEONATO   My lord, my lord,
I'll prove it on his body if he dare,
Despite his nice fence and his active practice,   75
His May of youth and bloom of lustihood.   76

CLAUDIO
Away! I will not have to do with you.

LEONATO
Canst thou so daff me? Thou hast killed my child.   78
If thou kill'st me, boy, thou shalt kill a man.

ANTONIO
He shall kill two of us, and men indeed.
But that's no matter; let him kill one first.
Win me and wear me! Let him answer me.   82
Come follow me, boy. Come, sir boy, come follow me,
Sir boy, I'll whip you from your foining fence!   84
Nay, as I am a gentleman, I will.

LEONATO   Brother—

ANTONIO
Content yourself. God knows I loved my niece,   87
And she is dead, slandered to death by villains
That dare as well answer a man indeed
As I dare take a serpent by the tongue.
Boys, apes, braggarts, jacks, milksops!

LEONATO   Brother Antony—

ANTONIO
Hold you content. What, man! I know them, yea,
And what they weigh, even to the utmost scruple—   94
Scambling, outfacing, fashionmonging boys,   95
That lie and cog and flout, deprave and slander,   96

Go anticly, show outward hideousness,   97
And speak off half a dozen dangerous words   98
How they might hurt their enemies, if they durst,
And this is all.

LEONATO
But brother Antony—

ANTONIO   Come, 'tis no matter.
Do not you meddle; let me deal in this.

DON PEDRO
Gentlemen both, we will not wake your patience.   103
My heart is sorry for your daughter's death;
But, on my honor, she was charged with nothing
But what was true and very full of proof.

LEONATO   My lord, my lord—

DON PEDRO   I will not hear you.

LEONATO
No? Come, brother, away! I will be heard.

ANTONIO
And shall, or some of us will smart for it.   110

Exeunt ambo [Leonato and Antonio].

Enter Benedick.

DON PEDRO
See, see, here comes the man we went to seek.

CLAUDIO   Now, signor, what news?

BENEDICK   Good day, my lord.

DON PEDRO   Welcome, signor. You are almost come to
part almost a fray.

CLAUDIO   We had like to have had our two noses   116
snapped off with two old men without teeth.   117

DON PEDRO   Leonato and his brother. What think'st
thou? Had we fought, I doubt we should have been   119
too young for them.

BENEDICK   In a false quarrel there is no true valor. I came
to seek you both.

CLAUDIO   We have been up and down to seek thee, for
we are high-proof melancholy and would fain have it   124
beaten away. Wilt thou use thy wit?

BENEDICK   It is in my scabbard. Shall I draw it?

DON PEDRO   Dost thou wear thy wit by thy side?

CLAUDIO   Never any did so, though very many have
been beside their wit. I will bid thee draw as we do the   129
minstrels, draw to pleasure us.   130

DON PEDRO   As I am an honest man, he looks pale. Art
thou sick, or angry?

CLAUDIO   What, courage, man! What though care killed
a cat, thou hast mettle enough in thee to kill care.

BENEDICK   Sir, I shall meet your wit in the career, an you   135
charge it against me. I pray you, choose another sub-   136
ject.

---

58 **fleer** sneer, jeer   62 **head** i.e., face   64 **my reverence** i.e., the reverence due old age   66 **trial of a man** manly contest, i.e., duel.
71 **framed** devised   75 **nice fence** dexterous swordsmanship. (Said
contemptuously.)   76 **lustihood** bodily vigor   78 **daff** doff, brush
aside   82 **Win . . . me!** (A proverbial expression, used as a challenge,
meaning he'll have to overcome me before he can claim me as a
prize.)   **answer me** i.e., in a duel.   84 **foining** thrusting   87 **Content
yourself** i.e., Don't try to stop me.   94 **scruple** small measure of
weight   95 **Scambling . . . boys** contentious, swaggering, dandified
boys   96 **cog** cheat.   **deprave** defame, traduce

97 **anticly** fantastically dressed.   **hideousness** frightening appearance   98 **dangerous** threatening, haughty   103 **wake your patience**
put your patience to any further test.   110.1 *ambo* both   116 **We had
. . . had** We almost had   117 **with** by   119 **doubt** fear, suspect. (Said
ironically.)   124 **high-proof** to the highest degree.   **fain** gladly
129 **beside their wit** out of their wits. (Playing on *by thy side* in line
127.)   130 **draw** (1) draw your weapon (2) draw a bow across a musical instrument   135 **career** short gallop at full speed (as in a tourney).
an if   136 **charge** level (as a weapon)

CLAUDIO   Nay, then, give him another staff. This last 138
was broke cross. 139

DON PEDRO   By this light, he changes more and more. I
think he be angry indeed.

CLAUDIO   If he be, he knows how to turn his girdle. 142

BENEDICK   Shall I speak a word in your ear?

CLAUDIO   God bless me from a challenge!

BENEDICK [aside to Claudio]   You are a villain. I jest not. I
will make it good how you dare, with what you dare,
and when you dare. Do me right, or I will protest your 147
cowardice. You have killed a sweet lady, and her death
shall fall heavy on you. Let me hear from you.

CLAUDIO   Well, I will meet you, so I may have good
cheer. 151

DON PEDRO   What, a feast, a feast?

CLAUDIO   I'faith, I thank him, he hath bid me to a calf's 153
head and a capon, the which if I do not carve most 154
curiously, say my knife's naught. Shall I not find a 155
woodcock too? 156

BENEDICK   Sir, your wit ambles well; it goes easily. 157

DON PEDRO   I'll tell thee how Beatrice praised thy wit
the other day. I said thou hadst a fine wit. "True," said
she, "a fine little one." "No," said I, "a great wit."
"Right," says she, "a great gross one." "Nay," said I, "a
good wit." "Just," said she, "it hurts nobody." "Nay," 162
said I, "the gentleman is wise." "Certain," said she,
"a wise gentleman." "Nay," said I, "he hath the 164
tongues." "That I believe," said she, "for he swore a 165
thing to me on Monday night which he forswore on
Tuesday morning. There's a double tongue; there's
two tongues." Thus did she, an hour together, trans- 168
shape thy particular virtues. Yet at last she concluded 169
with a sigh, thou wast the proper'st man in Italy. 170

CLAUDIO   For the which she wept heartily and said she
cared not.

DON PEDRO   Yea, that she did. But yet for all that, an if
she did not hate him deadly, she would love him
dearly. The old man's daughter told us all. 175

CLAUDIO   All, all. And, moreover, God saw him when 176
he was hid in the garden. 177

DON PEDRO   But when shall we set the savage bull's
horns on the sensible Benedick's head?

CLAUDIO   Yea, and text underneath, "Here dwells 180
Benedick, the married man"?

BENEDICK   Fare you well, boy. You know my mind. I
will leave you now to your gossiplike humor. You
break jests as braggarts do their blades, which, God be 184
thanked, hurt not.—My lord, for your many courtesies I thank you. I must discontinue your company.
Your brother the bastard is fled from Messina. You
have among you killed a sweet and innocent lady. For
my Lord Lackbeard there, he and I shall meet, and till
then peace be with him.   [Exit.]

DON PEDRO   He is in earnest.

CLAUDIO   In most profound earnest, and, I'll warrant
you, for the love of Beatrice.

DON PEDRO   And hath challenged thee?

CLAUDIO   Most sincerely.

DON PEDRO   What a pretty thing man is when he goes 196
in his doublet and hose and leaves off his wit! 197

CLAUDIO   He is then a giant to an ape; but then is an ape 198
a doctor to such a man. 199

DON PEDRO   But, soft you, let me be. Pluck up, my heart, 200
and be sad. Did he not say my brother was fled? 201

*Enter Constables, [Dogberry and Verges, and
the Watch, with] Conrade and Borachio.*

DOGBERRY   Come you, sir. If Justice cannot tame you,
she shall ne'er weigh more reasons in her balance. 203
Nay, an you be a cursing hypocrite once, you must be 204
looked to.

DON PEDRO   How now, two of my brother's men
bound? Borachio one!

CLAUDIO   Hearken after their offense, my lord. 208

DON PEDRO   Officers, what offense have these men
done?

DOGBERRY   Marry, sir, they have committed false report;
moreover, they have spoken untruths; secondarily,
they are slanders; sixth and lastly, they have belied a 213
lady; thirdly, they have verified unjust things; and to
conclude, they are lying knaves.

DON PEDRO   First, I ask thee what they have done;
thirdly, I ask thee what's their offense; sixth and lastly,
why they are committed; and to conclude, what you
lay to their charge.

CLAUDIO   Rightly reasoned, and in his own division; 220
and, by my troth, there's one meaning well suited. 221

DON PEDRO   Who have you offended, masters, that you
are thus bound to your answer? This learned consta- 223
ble is too cunning to be understood. What's your
offense?

138 staff spear shaft.   139 broke cross i.e., broken by clumsily allowing the spear to break crosswise against the opponent's shield. (In
other words, Claudio accuses Benedick of having failed in his sally of
wit.)   142 turn his girdle i.e., turn his sword belt around so that he's
ready to fight. (A proverbial expression of uncertain meaning.)
147 Do me right Give me satisfaction.   protest proclaim before witnesses   151 cheer entertainment. (Claudio is ready to fight, he says,
for the pleasant diversion it should offer.)   153–6 calf's head, capon,
woodcock (In the proposed feast of dueling, Claudio plans to carve
various dishes connoting foolishness, effeminate cowardice, and stupidity.)   155 curiously daintily.   naught good for nothing.
157 ambles i.e., minces along   162 good (1) keen (2) harmless.   Just
Exactly   164 a wise gentleman i.e., an old fool.   164–5 hath the
tongues masters several languages   168–9 trans-shape distort, turn
the wrong side out   170 proper'st handsomest   175 old man's
daughter i.e., Hero   176–7 God . . . garden (Alluding to the trick
played on Benedick to love Beatrice, and also to Genesis 3:8.)
180 text (In 1.1.251–6, Benedick vowed that, if he were ever to fall in
love, his friends might set a bull's horns on his head and label him
"Benedick the married man.")

184 as . . . blades i.e., as braggarts furtively damage their blades to
make it appear they have been fighting fiercely   196–7 goes . . . wit
goes about fully dressed like a rational creature but forgets to equip
himself with good sense.   198–9 He . . . man i.e., Such a man looks
like a hero in a fool's eyes, but actually the fool is a wise man compared to him.   200–1 soft . . . be sad wait a minute, not so fast; let me
think. Rouse yourself, my heart, and be serious.   201.1–2 (The Quarto
placement of this stage direction after line 197 suggests that Dogberry
is visible, strutting and fussing with his prisoners, before he speaks.)
203 ne'er . . . balance never again weigh arguments of reason in her
scales. (But the pronunciation of reason as "raisin" invokes the comic
image of a shopkeeper weighing produce.)   204 cursing accursed.
once in a word   208 Hearken after Inquire into   213 slanders (For
"slanderers.")   220 his own division its own partition in a logical
arrangement. (Said ironically.)   221 well suited nicely dressed up in
the trappings of language.   223 bound (Playing on the meanings
"pinioned" and "headed for a destination.")   answer trial, account.

BORACHIO   Sweet Prince, let me go no farther to mine answer. Do you hear me, and let this count kill me. I have deceived even your very eyes. What your wisdoms could not discover, these shallow fools have brought to light, who in the night overheard me confessing to this man how Don John your brother incensed me to slander the Lady Hero, how you were 231 brought into the orchard and saw me court Margaret in Hero's garments, how you disgraced her when you should marry her. My villainy they have upon record, which I had rather seal with my death than repeat over to my shame. The lady is dead upon mine and 236 my master's false accusation; and, briefly, I desire nothing but the reward of a villain.

DON PEDRO   [to Claudio]
Runs not this speech like iron through your blood?

CLAUDIO
I have drunk poison whiles he uttered it.

DON PEDRO   [to Borachio]
But did my brother set thee on to this?

BORACHIO   Yea, and paid me richly for the practice of it. 242

DON PEDRO
He is composed and framed of treachery,
And fled he is upon this villainy.   244

CLAUDIO
Sweet Hero! Now thy image doth appear
In the rare semblance that I loved it first.   246

DOGBERRY   Come, bring away the plaintiffs. By this time 247 our sexton hath reformed Signor Leonato of the 248 matter. And masters, do not forget to specify, when 249 time and place shall serve, that I am an ass.

VERGES   Here, here comes Master Signor Leonato, and the sexton, too.

Enter Leonato, his brother [Antonio], and the Sexton.

LEONATO
Which is the villain? Let me see his eyes,
That when I note another man like him,
I may avoid him. Which of these is he?

BORACHIO
If you would know your wronger, look on me.

LEONATO
Art thou the slave that with thy breath hast killed
Mine innocent child?

BORACHIO   Yea, even I alone.

LEONATO
No, not so, villain, thou beliest thyself.
Here stand a pair of honorable men—   260
A third is fled—that had a hand in it.
I thank you, princes, for my daughter's death.
Record it with your high and worthy deeds.
'Twas bravely done, if you bethink you of it.

CLAUDIO
I know not how to pray your patience,
Yet I must speak. Choose your revenge yourself;

Impose me to what penance your invention   267
Can lay upon my sin. Yet sinned I not
But in mistaking.

DON PEDRO   By my soul, nor I.
And yet, to satisfy this good old man,
I would bend under any heavy weight
That he'll enjoin me to.

LEONATO
I cannot bid you bid my daughter live—
That were impossible—but, I pray you both,
Possess the people in Messina here   275
How innocent she died; and if your love
Can labor aught in sad invention,   277
Hang her an epitaph upon her tomb,
And sing it to her bones; sing it tonight.
Tomorrow morning come you to my house,
And since you could not be my son-in-law,
Be yet my nephew. My brother hath a daughter,
Almost the copy of my child that's dead,
And she alone is heir to both of us.   284
Give her the right you should have giv'n her cousin, 285
And so dies my revenge.

CLAUDIO   O noble sir,
Your overkindness doth wring tears from me!
I do embrace your offer; and dispose   288
For henceforth of poor Claudio.   289

LEONATO
Tomorrow then I will expect your coming;
Tonight I take my leave. This naughty man   291
Shall face to face be brought to Margaret,
Who I believe was packed in all this wrong,   293
Hired it to by your brother.

BORACHIO   No, by my soul, she was not,
Nor knew not what she did when she spoke to me,
But always hath been just and virtuous
In anything that I do know by her.   298

DOGBERRY   Moreover, sir, which indeed is not under 299 white and black, this plaintiff here, the offender, did 300 call me ass. I beseech you, let it be remembered in his punishment. And also the watch heard them talk of one Deformed. They say he wears a key in his ear and 303 a lock hanging by it and borrows money in God's 304 name, the which he hath used so long and never paid 305 that now men grow hardhearted and will lend nothing for God's sake. Pray you, examine him upon that point.

LEONATO   I thank thee for thy care and honest pains.

DOGBERRY   Your Worship speaks like a most thankful and reverend youth, and I praise God for you.

LEONATO   There's for thy pains.   [*He gives money.*]

DOGBERRY   God save the foundation!   313

---

267 **Impose me to** Impose on me   275 **Possess** inform   277 **aught** to any extent   284 **heir to both** (Leonato overlooks Antonio's son mentioned in 1.2.2.)   285 **right** equitable treatment. (Quibbling on "rite," "ceremony.")   288 **dispose** you may dispose   289 **For henceforth** for the future   291 **naughty** wicked   293 **packed** involved as an accomplice   298 **by** concerning   299–300 **under . . . black** written down in black and white   303–4 **key . . . by it** (This is what Dogberry has made out of the lovelock mentioned in 3.3.166.)   304–5 **in God's name** (A phrase of the professional beggar.)   313 **God . . . foundation!** (A formula of those who received alms at religious houses or charitable foundations.)

---

231 **incensed** incited   236 **upon** in consequence of   242 **practice** cunning execution   244 **upon** i.e., having committed   246 **rare semblance** splendid likeness   247 **plaintiffs** (For "defendants.") 248 **reformed** (For "informed.")   249 **specify** (For "testify"?) 260 **honorable men** i.e., Don Pedro and Claudio, men of rank

LEONATO   Go, I discharge thee of thy prisoner, and I thank thee.

DOGBERRY   I leave an arrant knave with Your Worship, which I beseech Your Worship to correct yourself, for the example of others. God keep Your Worship! I wish Your Worship well. God restore you to health! I humbly give you leave to depart; and if a merry meet- 320 ing may be wished, God prohibit it! Come, neighbor. 321
                                        [*Exeunt Dogberry and Verges.*]

LEONATO

Until tomorrow morning, lords, farewell.

ANTONIO

Farewell, my lords. We look for you tomorrow.

DON PEDRO

We will not fail.

CLAUDIO   Tonight I'll mourn with Hero.

LEONATO [*to the Watch*]

Bring you these fellows on.—We'll talk with Margaret,
How her acquaintance grew with this lewd fellow. 326
                                        Exeunt [*separately*].

[5.2]

Enter Benedick and Margaret, [meeting].

BENEDICK   Pray thee, sweet Mistress Margaret, deserve well at my hands by helping me to the speech of 2 Beatrice.

MARGARET   Will you then write me a sonnet in praise of my beauty?

BENEDICK   In so high a style, Margaret, that no man 6 living shall come over it, for in most comely truth thou 7 deservest it.

MARGARET   To have no man come over me! Why, shall I always keep below stairs? 10

BENEDICK   Thy wit is as quick as the greyhound's mouth; it catches.

MARGARET   And yours as blunt as the fencer's foils, which hit but hurt not.

BENEDICK   A most manly wit, Margaret; it will not hurt a woman. And so, I pray thee, call Beatrice. I give thee 16 the bucklers. 17

MARGARET   Give us the swords. We have bucklers of our own.

BENEDICK   If you use them, Margaret, you must put in the pikes with a vice, and they are dangerous weapons 21 for maids.

MARGARET   Well, I will call Beatrice to you, who I think hath legs.   *Exit Margaret.*

BENEDICK   And therefore will come.
[*He sings.*] "The god of love,   26
              That sits above,
              And knows me, and knows me,
              How pitiful I deserve—"   29
I mean in singing; but in loving, Leander the good 30 swimmer, Troilus the first employer of panders, and a 31 whole bookful of these quondam carpetmongers, 32 whose names yet run smoothly in the even road of a blank verse, why, they were never so truly turned over 34 and over as my poor self in love. Marry, I cannot show 35 it in rhyme. I have tried. I can find out no rhyme to "lady" but "baby," an innocent rhyme; for "scorn," 37 "horn," a hard rhyme; for "school," "fool," a babbling 38 rhyme; very ominous endings. No, I was not born under a rhyming planet, nor I cannot woo in festival terms.

Enter Beatrice.

Sweet Beatrice, wouldst thou come when I called thee?

BEATRICE   Yea, signor, and depart when you bid me.

BENEDICK   Oh, stay but till then!   [*She starts to leave.*]

BEATRICE   "Then" is spoken; fare you well now. And yet, ere I go, let me go with that I came, which is, with 46 knowing what hath passed between you and Claudio.

BENEDICK   Only foul words; and thereupon I will kiss thee.

BEATRICE   Foul words is but foul wind, and foul wind is but foul breath, and foul breath is noisome; there- 51 fore I will depart unkissed.

BENEDICK   Thou hast frighted the word out of his right 53 sense, so forcible is thy wit. But I must tell thee plainly, Claudio undergoes my challenge; and either I must shortly hear from him, or I will subscribe him a 56 coward. And I pray thee now tell me, for which of my bad parts didst thou first fall in love with me?

BEATRICE   For them all together, which maintained so politic a state of evil that they will not admit any good 60 part to intermingle with them. But for which of my good parts did you first suffer love for me? 62

BENEDICK   Suffer love! A good epithet. I do suffer love 63 indeed, for I love thee against my will.

BEATRICE   In spite of your heart, I think. Alas, poor heart, if you spite it for my sake I will spite it for yours, for I will never love that which my friend hates.

BENEDICK   Thou and I are too wise to woo peaceably.

---

320 give you leave (For "ask your leave.")   **321 prohibit** (For "per-mit.")   **326 lewd** wicked, worthless
5.2. Location: Leonato's garden (? At the scene's end, Leonato's house is some distance away.)
2 to the speech of to speak with   **6 style** (1) poetic style (2) stile, stairs over a fence   **7 come over** (1) excel beyond (2) traverse, as one would cross a stile (3) in Margaret's next speech, the phrase is taken to mean "mount sexually."   **comely** good. (With an allusion to Margaret's beauty.)   **10 keep below stairs** dwell in the servants' quarters. **16–17 I . . . bucklers** i.e., I acknowledge myself beaten (in repartee). (Bucklers are shields with spikes [pikes] in their centers. Margaret uses the word in a bawdy sense in her reply.)   **21 pikes** spikes in the center of a shield.   **vice** screw. (Benedick's bawdy sense continues Margaret's jest.)

26–9 The god . . . deserve (The beginning of an old song by William Elderton.)   **29 How . . . deserve** how I deserve pity. (But Benedick uses the phrase to mean "how little I deserve.")   **30 Leander** lover of Hero of Sestos; he swam the Hellespont nightly to see her until he drowned   **31 Troilus** lover of Cressida, whose affair was assisted by her uncle Pandarus   **32 quondam carpetmongers** ladies' men of old, such as one might find in the carpeted boudoirs of the women they woo   **34–5 over and over** i.e., head over heels   **37 innocent** childish   **38 hard** (1) exact (2) unpleasant, because of the association with cuck-old's horns   **46 that I came** what I came for   **51 noisome** noxious **53 his** its   **56 subscribe** formally proclaim in writing   **60 politic** pru-dently governed   **62 suffer** (1) experience (2) feel the pain of **63 epithet** expression.

BEATRICE   It appears not in this confession. There's not 69
one wise man among twenty that will praise himself.

BENEDICK   An old, an old instance, Beatrice, that lived 71
in the time of good neighbors. If a man do not erect in 72
this age his own tomb ere he dies, he shall live no 73
longer in monument than the bell rings and the 74
widow weeps. 75

BEATRICE   And how long is that, think you?

BENEDICK   Question: why, an hour in clamor and a 77
quarter in rheum. Therefore is it most expedient for 78
the wise, if Don Worm, his conscience, find no imped- 79
iment to the contrary, to be the trumpet of his own
virtues, as I am to myself. So much for praising myself,
who, I myself will bear witness, is praiseworthy. And
now tell me, how doth your cousin?

BEATRICE   Very ill.

BENEDICK   And how do you?

BEATRICE   Very ill too.

BENEDICK   Serve God, love me, and mend. There will I
leave you too, for here comes one in haste.

Enter Ursula.

URSULA   Madam, you must come to your uncle. Yonder's old coil at home. It is proved my lady Hero hath 90
been falsely accused, the Prince and Claudio mightily
abused, and Don John is the author of all, who is fled 92
and gone. Will you come presently? 93

BEATRICE   Will you go hear this news, signor?

BENEDICK   I will live in thy heart, die in thy lap, and be 95
buried in thy eyes; and moreover I will go with thee to
thy uncle's. *Exeunt.*

❧

[5.3]

*Enter Claudio, Prince [Don Pedro, Balthasar],
and three or four with tapers.*

CLAUDIO   Is this the monument of Leonato?

A LORD   It is, my lord.

CLAUDIO   *[reading from a scroll]*

Epitaph.

"Done to death by slanderous tongues
    Was the Hero that here lies.
Death, in guerdon of her wrongs, 5
    Gives her fame which never dies.
So the life that died with shame
Lives in death with glorious fame."

Hang thou there upon the tomb,
Praising her when I am dumb.

            [He hangs up the scroll.]

Now, music, sound, and sing your solemn hymn.

        Song.

BALTHASAR
    Pardon, goddess of the night, 12
    Those that slew thy virgin knight; 13
    For the which, with songs of woe,
    Round about her tomb they go.
      Midnight, assist our moan;
      Help us to sigh and groan,
        Heavily, heavily.
      Graves, yawn and yield your dead,
      Till death be utterèd, 20
        Heavily, heavily.

CLAUDIO
Now, unto thy bones good night!
Yearly will I do this rite.

DON PEDRO
Good morrow, masters. Put your torches out.
    The wolves have preyed; and look, the gentle day, 25
Before the wheels of Phoebus, round about 26
    Dapples the drowsy east with spots of gray.
Thanks to you all, and leave us. Fare you well.

CLAUDIO
Good morrow, masters. Each his several way. 29

DON PEDRO
Come, let us hence, and put on other weeds, 30
    And then to Leonato's we will go.

CLAUDIO
And Hymen now with luckier issue speed's 32
    Than this for whom we rendered up this woe.

              Exeunt.

❧

[5.4]

*Enter Leonato, Benedick, [Beatrice], Margaret,
Ursula, old man [Antonio], Friar [Francis, and]
Hero.*

FRIAR
Did I not tell you she was innocent?

LEONATO
So are the Prince and Claudio, who accused her
Upon the error that you heard debated. 3
But Margaret was in some fault for this,
Although against her will, as it appears 5
In the true course of all the question. 6

---

69 **It . . . confession** i.e., You don't show your wisdom in praising
yourself for being wise. **71 instance** proverb (i.e., "He has ill neighbors that is fain to praise himself"). **72 time . . . neighbors** good old
times (when one's neighbors spoke well of one). **73–5 he shall . . .
weeps** i.e., he will be memorialized only during the (brief) time of the
funeral service and the official mourning. **77 Question** i.e., An easy
question, which I will answer as follows. **clamor** noise (of the bell)
78 rheum tears (of the widow). **79 Don . . . conscience** (The action
of the conscience was traditionally described as the gnawing of a
worm; compare with Mark 9:44–8.) **90 old coil** great confusion
92 abused deceived **93 presently** immediately. **95 die** (With the
common connotation of "experience sexual climax.")
5.3. Location: A churchyard.
5 guerdon recompense

12 goddess of the night i.e., Diana, moon goddess, patroness of
chastity **13 knight** i.e., follower **20 utterèd** fully expressed
25 have preyed i.e., have done their preying **26 wheels of Phoebus**
i.e., chariot of the sun god **29 several** separate **30 weeds** garments
32 And . . . speed's And may the god of marriage favor us with better
fortune
5.4. Location: Leonato's house.
3 Upon on the basis of **5 against her will** unintentionally **6 question** investigation.

ANTONIO
   Well, I am glad that all things sorts so well.   7
BENEDICK
   And so am I, being else by faith enforced   8
   To call young Claudio to a reckoning for it.
LEONATO
   Well, daughter, and you gentlewomen all,
   Withdraw into a chamber by yourselves,
   And when I send for you, come hither masked.
   The Prince and Claudio promised by this hour
   To visit me. You know your office, brother:
   You must be father to your brother's daughter,
   And give her to young Claudio.   *Exeunt ladies.*
ANTONIO
   Which I will do with confirmed countenance.   17
BENEDICK
   Friar, I must entreat your pains, I think.   18
FRIAR   To do what, signor?
BENEDICK
   To bind me or undo me—one of them.   20
   Signor Leonato, truth it is, good signor,
   Your niece regards me with an eye of favor.
LEONATO
   That eye my daughter lent her. 'Tis most true.   23
BENEDICK
   And I do with an eye of love requite her.
LEONATO
   The sight whereof I think you had from me,   25
   From Claudio, and the Prince. But what's your will?   26
BENEDICK
   Your answer, sir, is enigmatical.
   But, for my will, my will is your good will   28
   May stand with ours, this day to be conjoined
   In the state of honorable marriage,
   In which, good Friar, I shall desire your help.
LEONATO
   My heart is with your liking.
FRIAR   And my help.
   Here comes the Prince and Claudio.

      Enter Prince [Don Pedro] and Claudio, and
      two or three other.

DON PEDRO
   Good morrow to this fair assembly.
LEONATO
   Good morrow, Prince. Good morrow, Claudio.
   We here attend you. Are you yet determined   35
   Today to marry with my brother's daughter?
CLAUDIO
   I'll hold my mind, were she an Ethiope.
LEONATO
   Call her forth, brother. Here's the Friar ready.
                        [Exit Antonio.]

DON PEDRO
   Good morrow, Benedick. Why, what's the matter,
   That you have such a February face,
   So full of frost, of storm, and cloudiness?
CLAUDIO
   I think he thinks upon the savage bull.   42
   Tush, fear not, man! We'll tip thy horns with gold,
   And all Europa shall rejoice at thee,   44
   As once Europa did at lusty Jove   45
   When he would play the noble beast in love.
BENEDICK
   Bull Jove, sir, had an amiable low,
   And some such strange bull leapt your father's cow
   And got a calf in that same noble feat
   Much like to you, for you have just his bleat.

      Enter [Leonato's] brother [Antonio], Hero,
      Beatrice, Margaret, [and] Ursula, [the ladies
      masked].

CLAUDIO
   For this I owe you. Here comes other reckonings.   51
   Which is the lady I must seize upon?
ANTONIO
   This same is she, and I do give you her.
CLAUDIO
   Why then, she's mine. Sweet, let me see your face.
LEONATO
   No, that you shall not, till you take her hand
   Before this friar and swear to marry her.
CLAUDIO
   Give me your hand before this holy friar.
   I am your husband, if you like of me.   58
HERO *[unmasking]*
   And when I lived, I was your other wife;
   And when you loved, you were my other husband.
CLAUDIO
   Another Hero!
HERO   Nothing certainer.
   One Hero died defiled, but I do live,
   And surely as I live, I am a maid.
DON PEDRO
   The former Hero! Hero that is dead!
LEONATO
   She died, my lord, but whiles her slander lived.   65
FRIAR
   All this amazement can I qualify,   66
   When, after that the holy rites are ended,
   I'll tell you largely of fair Hero's death.   68
   Meantime let wonder seem familiar,   69
   And to the chapel let us presently.   70
BENEDICK
   Soft and fair, Friar. Which is Beatrice?   71

---

7 sorts turn out   **8 being . . . enforced** since otherwise I would be enforced by my promise to Beatrice   **17 confirmed countenance** straight face.   **18 entreat your pains** beg your help   **20 undo** (1) ruin (2) untie, unbind   **23 That . . . her** (Alludes to Hero's role in tricking Beatrice into confessing her love for Benedick.)   **25–6 The sight . . . Prince** (Alludes to their role in tricking Benedick into confessing his love for Beatrice.)   **28 for** as for.   **is** is that   **35 yet** still

42 I . . . bull (A jocular reminiscence of the conversation in 1.1.250 ff.) **44 Europa** Europe   **45 Europa** a princess whom Jove approached in the form of a white bull and bore on his back through the sea to Crete **51 I owe you** i.e., I'll pay you back later (for calling me a calf and a bastard).   **other reckonings** i.e., other matters to be settled first. **58 like of** care for   **65 but whiles** only while   **66 qualify** moderate **68 largely** at large, in full   **69 let . . . familiar** treat these marvels as ordinary matters   **70 let us presently** let us go at once.   **71 Soft and fair** i.e., Wait a minute

BEATRICE [*unmasking*]
I answer to that name. What is your will?

BENEDICK
Do not you love me?

BEATRICE   Why, no, no more than reason.

BENEDICK
Why, then your uncle and the Prince and Claudio
Have been deceived. They swore you did.

BEATRICE
Do not you love me?

BENEDICK   Troth, no, no more than reason.

BEATRICE
Why, then my cousin, Margaret, and Ursula   77
Are much deceived, for they did swear you did.

BENEDICK
They swore that you were almost sick for me.

BEATRICE
They swore that you were well-nigh dead for me.

BENEDICK
'Tis no such matter. Then you do not love me?

BEATRICE
No, truly, but in friendly recompense.

LEONATO
Come, cousin, I am sure you love the gentleman.   83

CLAUDIO
And I'll be sworn upon't that he loves her;
For here's a paper written in his hand,
A halting sonnet of his own pure brain,   86
Fashioned to Beatrice.   [*He shows a paper.*]

HERO   And here's another
Writ in my cousin's hand, stol'n from her pocket,
Containing her affection unto Benedick.
                          [*She shows another paper.*]

BENEDICK   A miracle! Here's our own hands against our   90
hearts. Come, I will have thee, but by this light I take 91
thee for pity.

BEATRICE   I would not deny you, but by this good day,
I yield upon great persuasion, and partly to save your
life, for I was told you were in a consumption.   95

---

77 my cousin i.e., Hero **83 cousin** i.e., niece **86 halting** limping.
his own pure purely his own **90–1 against our hearts** i.e., to prove
our hearts guilty as charged. **95 in a consumption** i.e., wasting
away in sighs.

BENEDICK   Peace! I will stop your mouth. [*Kissing her.*]

DON PEDRO   How dost thou, Benedick, the married
man?

BENEDICK   I'll tell thee what, Prince: a college of wit-   99
crackers cannot flout me out of my humor. Dost thou
think I care for a satire or an epigram? No. If a man   101
will be beaten with brains, 'a shall wear nothing hand-   102
some about him. In brief, since I do purpose to marry,   103
I will think nothing to any purpose that the world can
say against it; and therefore never flout at me for what   105
I have said against it; for man is a giddy thing, and this
is my conclusion. For thy part, Claudio, I did think to
have beaten thee, but in that thou art like to be my   108
kinsman, live unbruised, and love my cousin.

CLAUDIO   I had well hoped thou wouldst have denied
Beatrice, that I might have cudgeled thee out of thy
single life, to make thee a double-dealer, which out of   112
question thou wilt be, if my cousin do not look   113
exceeding narrowly to thee.   114

BENEDICK   Come, come, we are friends. Let's have a
dance ere we are married, that we may lighten our
own hearts and our wives' heels.

LEONATO   We'll have dancing afterward.

BENEDICK   First, of my word! Therefore play, music.   119
Prince, thou art sad. Get thee a wife, get thee a wife.
There is no staff more reverend than one tipped with   121
horn.   122

        Enter Messenger.

MESSENGER
My lord, your brother John is ta'en in flight
And brought with armèd men back to Messina.

BENEDICK   Think not on him till tomorrow. I'll devise
thee brave punishments for him. Strike up, pipers!   126
                          Dance. [*Exeunt.*]

---

99 college assembly **101–3 If . . . him** i.e., If a man allows himself to
be cowed by ridicule, he'll never dare dress handsomely or do anything conspicuous that will draw attention. **105 flout** mock **108 in
that** in view of the fact that. **like** likely **112 a double-dealer** (1) a
married man (2) a deceiver, adulterer **113–14 look . . . narrowly to**
keep close watch over **119 of** on **121–2 tipped with horn** (Alludes
to the usual joke about cuckolds, as at line 43). **126 brave** fine

As You Like It

As You Like It represents, together with *Much Ado About Nothing* and *Twelfth Night,* the summation of Shakespeare's achievement in festive, happy comedy during the years 1598–1601. *As You Like It* contains several motifs found in other Shakespearean comedies: the journey from a jaded court into a transforming sylvan environment and back to a revitalized court (as in *A Midsummer Night's Dream*); hence, a contrasting of two worlds in the play—one presided over by a virtuous but exiled older brother and the other, by a usurping younger brother (as in *The Tempest*); the heroine disguised as a man (as in *The Merchant of Venice, The Two Gentlemen of Verona, Cymbeline,* and *Twelfth Night*); and a structure of multiple plotting in which numerous groups of characters are thematically played off against one another (as in several of Shakespeare's comedies). What chiefly distinguishes this play from the others, however, is the nature and function of its pastoral setting—the Forest of Arden.

The Forest of Arden is seen in many perspectives. As a natural wilderness, it is probably most like the real forest Shakespeare knew near Stratford-upon-Avon in Warwickshire—a place capable of producing the vulgarity of an Audrey or the bumptuous clowning of a William. The forest bears the name of Shakespeare's mother, Mary Arden, the daughter of a prosperous Warwickshire farmer. Its name also owes something to the forest in Shakespeare's source, *Rosalynde,* based in turn on the forest of Ardennes in France. No less vividly, the place recalls for us Nottinghamshire and the Sherwood Forest of Robin Hood, where persons in retreat from a society seemingly beyond repair find refuge in a mythic folk world purged of social injustice. As the "golden world" (1.1.114), the forest evokes an even deeper longing for a mythological past age of innocence and plenty, when humans shared some attributes of the giants and the gods. This myth has its parallel in the biblical Garden of Eden, before the human race experienced "the penalty of

Adam" (2.1.5). Finally, in another of its aspects, the forest is Arcadia, a pastoral landscape embodied in an ancient and sophisticated literary tradition and peopled by the likes of Corin, Silvius, and Phoebe.

All but the first of these Ardens, compared and contrasted with one another, involve some idealization, not only of nature and the natural landscape, but also of the human condition. These various Ardens place our real life in a complex perspective and force us to a fresh appraisal of our own ordinary existence. Duke Senior, for example, describes the forest environment as a corrective for the evils of society. He addresses his followers in the forest as "my co-mates and brothers in exile" (2.1.1), suggesting a kind of social equality that he could never know in the cramped formality of his previous official existence. The banished Duke Senior and his followers have had to leave behind their lands and revenues in the grip of the usurping Duke Frederick. No longer rich, though adequately provided with life's necessities, the Duke and his "merry men" live "like the old Robin Hood of England" and "fleet the time carelessly as they did in the golden world" (1.1.111–14). In this friendly society, a strong communal sense replaces the necessity for individual proprietorship. All comers are welcome, with food for all.

There are no luxuries in the forest, to be sure, but even this spare existence affords relief from the decadence of courtly life. "Sweet are the uses of adversity" (2.1.12), insists Duke Senior. He welcomes the cold of winter because it teaches him the true condition of humanity and of himself. The forest is serenely impartial: neither malicious nor compassionate. Death, and even killing for food, are an inevitable part of forest existence. The Duke concedes that his presence in the forest means the slaughter of deer, who were the original inhabitants; Orlando and Adam find that death through starvation in the forest is all too real a possibility. The forest is never guilty of the degrading perversity of humans at their worst, but it is also incapable of charity and forgiveness.

Shakespeare's sources reflect the complexity of his vision of Arden. The original of the Orlando story, which Shakespeare may not have used directly, is *The Cook's Tale of Gamelyn,* found in a number of manuscripts of *The Canterbury Tales* and wrongly attributed to Chaucer. This hearty English romance glorifies the rebellious and even violent spirit of its Robin Hood hero, the neglected youngest son Gamelyn, who, aided by faithful old Adam the Spencer, evades his wicked eldest brother in a cunning and bloody escape. As king of the outlaws in Sherwood Forest, Gamelyn eventually triumphs over his eldest brother (now the sheriff) and sees him hanged. Here, then, originates the motif of refuge from social injustice in Arden, even though most of the actual violence has been omitted from Shakespeare's version. (A trio of Robin Hood plays on a similar theme, beginning in 1598 with Anthony Munday's *The Downfall of Robert Earl of Huntingdon After Called Robin Hood,* was being performed with great success by the Admiral's company, chief rivals of the Lord Chamberlain's company to which Shakespeare belonged.)

As You Like It is clearly indebted to Thomas Lodge's *Rosalynde: Euphues' Golden Legacy* (published in 1590), a prose narrative version of the Gamelyn story in the ornate Euphuistic style of the 1580s. (Lodge's Epistle to the Gentleman Readers, casually inviting them to be pleased with this story if they are so inclined—"*If you like it, so*"—probably gave Shakespeare a hint for the name of his play.) Lodge accentuated the love story with its courtship in masquerade, provided some charming songs, and introduced the pastoral love motif involving Corin, Silvius, Phoebe, and Ganymede. Shakespeare's ordering of episode is generally close to that of Lodge. Pastoral literature, which had become a literary rage in the 1580s and early 1590s, owing particularly to Edmund Spenser's *Shepheardes Calendar* (1579) and Philip Sidney's *Arcadia* (1590), traced its ancestry through such Renaissance continental writers as Jorge de Montemayor, Jacopo Sannazaro, and Giovanni Battista Guarini to the so-called Greek romances, and finally back to the eclogues of Virgil, Theocritus, and Bion. A literary mode that had begun originally as a realistic evocation of difficult country life had become, in the Renaissance, an elegant vehicle for the loftiest and most patrician sentiments in love, for philosophic debate, and even for extensive political analysis and satire of the clergy.

Shakespeare's alterations and additions give us insight into his method of construction and his thematic focus. Whereas Lodge cheerfully accepts the pastoral conventions of his day, Shakespeare exposes those conventions to some criticism and considerable irony. Alongside the mannered and literary Silvius and Phoebe, he places William and Audrey, as peasantlike a couple as ever drew milk from a cow's teat. The juxtaposition holds up to critical perspective the rival claims of the literary and natural worlds by examining the defects of each in relation to the strengths of the other. William and Audrey are Shakespeare's own creation, based presumably on observation and also on the dramatic convention of the rustic clown and wench, as exemplified earlier in his Costard and Jaquenetta *(Love's Labor's Lost).*

Equally original, and essential to the many-sided debate concerning the virtues of the court versus those of the country, are Touchstone and Jaques. Touchstone is a professional court fool, dressed in motley, a new comic type in Shakespeare, created apparently in response to the recent addition to the Lord Chamberlain's company of the brilliant actor Robert Armin. Jaques is also a new type, the malcontent satirist, reflecting the very latest literary vogue in the nondramatic poetry and in drama of George Chapman, John Marston, and Ben Jonson. (The so-called private theaters, featuring boy actors, reopened in 1598–1599 after nearly a decade of enforced silence and proceeded at once to specialize in satirical drama; the public theaters like the Globe, the Rose, and the Swan sometimes joined in.) Touchstone and Jaques complement one another as critics and observers—one laughing at human folly with quizzical comic detachment and the other satirizing it with self-righteous scorn. Once we have been exposed to this assortment of newly created characters, we can no longer view either pastoral life or pastoral love as simply as Lodge and some other writers of the period portray them.

When *As You Like It* is compared with its chief source, Shakespeare can also be seen to have altered and considerably softened the characters of the wicked brothers Oliver and Frederick. Whereas Lodge's Saladyne is motivated by a greedy desire to seize his younger brother Rosader's property, Shakespeare's Oliver is envious of Orlando's natural goodness and popularity. As he confesses in soliloquy, Orlando is "so much in the heart of the world and especially of my own people . . . that I am altogether misprized" (1.1.159–61). In his warped way, Oliver desires to be more like Orlando, and in the enchanted forest of Arden he eventually becomes so. Duke Frederick, too, is plainly envious of goodness. Trying to persuade his daughter Celia of the need for banishing Rosalind, he argues, "thou wilt show more bright and seem more virtuous / When she is gone" (1.3.79–80). In spite of his obsession with the mere "seeming" of virtue, Duke Frederick acknowledges the power of a goodness that will eventually convert him along with the rest. Penitence and conciliation replace the vengeful conclusion of Lodge's novel, in which the nobles of France finally overthrow and execute the usurping king. Although Shakespeare's resolutions are sudden, like all miracles they attest to the inexplicable power of goodness.

The court of Duke Frederick is "the envious court," identified by this fixed epithet. In it, brothers turn unnaturally against brothers: the younger Frederick usurps his older brother's throne, whereas the older Oliver denies the younger Orlando his birthright of education. In still another parallel, both Rosalind and Orlando find themselves mistrusted as the children of Frederick's political enemies, Duke Senior and Sir Rowland de Boys. A daughter and a son are held to be guilty by association. "Thou art thy father's daughter. There's enough" (1.3.56), Frederick curtly retorts in explaining Rosalind's exile. And to Orlando, triumphant in wrestling with Charles, Frederick asserts, "I would thou hadst been son to some man else" (1.2.214). Here again, Frederick plaintively reveals his envy of goodness, even if at present any potential for goodness in him is thwarted by tyrannous whim. Many of Frederick's entourage might also be better persons if they only knew how to escape the insincerities of their courtly life. Charles the wrestler, for example, places himself at Oliver's service, and yet he would happily avoid breaking Orlando's neck if to do so were consistent with self-interest. Even Le Beau, the giddy fop so delighted at first with the cruel sport of wrestling, takes Orlando aside at some personal risk to warn him of Duke Frederick's foul humor. Ideally, Le Beau would prefer to be a companion of Orlando's "in a better world than this" (1.2.275). The vision of a regenerative Utopia secretly abides in the heart of this courtly creature.

It is easier to anatomize the defects of a social order than to propound solutions. As have other creators of visionary landscapes (including Thomas More in his *Utopia*), Shakespeare uses playful debate to elicit complicated responses on the part of his audience. Which is preferable, the court or the country? Jaques and Touchstone are adept gadflies, incessantly pointing out contradictions and ironies. Jaques, the malcontent railer derived from literary satire, takes delight in being out of step with everyone. Seemingly, his chief reason for having joined the others in the forest is to jibe at their motives for being there. To their song about the rejection of courtly ambition he mockingly supplies another verse, charging them with having left their wealth and ease out of mere willfulness (2.5.46–54). With ironic appropriateness, Jaques eventually decides to remain in the forest in the company of Frederick; Jaques cannot thrive on resolution and harmony. His humor is "melancholy," from which, as he observes, he draws consolation as a weasel sucks eggs (2.5.11–12). The others treat him as a sort of profane jester whose soured conceits add relish to their enjoyment of the forest life.

Despite his affectation, however, Jaques is serious and even excited in his defense of satire as a curative form of laughter (2.7.47–87). The appearance of Touchstone in the forest has reaffirmed in Jaques his profound commitment to a view of life as an absurd process of decay governed by inexorable time. His function in such a life is to be mordant, unsparing. As literary satirist, he must be free to awaken people's minds to their own folly. To Duke Senior's protestation that the satirist is merely self-indulgent and licentious, Jaques counters with a thoughtful and classically Horatian defense of satire as an art form devoted not to libelous attacks on individuals but to exposing types of folly. Any observer who feels individually portrayed merely condemns himself or herself by confessing his or her resemblance to the type. This particular debate between Duke Senior and Jaques ends, appropriately, in a draw. The Duke's point is well taken, for Jaques's famous "Seven Ages of Man" speech, so often read out of context, occurs in a scene that also witnesses the sacrifices and brave deeds that Orlando and Adam are prepared to undertake for each other. The feeling bond between the generations that they share refutes Jaques's wry narrative of isolated self-interest. As though in answer to Jaques's acid depiction of covetous old age, we see old Adam's self-sacrifice and trust in Providence. Instead of "mere oblivion," we see charitable compassion prompting Duke Senior to aid Orlando and Orlando to aid Adam. Perhaps this vision seems of a higher spiritual order than that of Jaques. Nonetheless, without him the forest would lack a satirical perspective that continually requires us to reexamine our romantic assumptions about human happiness.

Touchstone's name suggests that he similarly offers a multiplicity of viewpoints. (A touchstone is a kind of stone used to test for gold and silver.) He shares with Jaques a skeptical view of life, but for Touchstone the inconsistency and absurdity of life are occasions for wit and humor rather than melancholy and cynicism. As a professional fool, he observes that many supposedly sane men are more foolish than he—as, for example, in their elaborate dueling code of the Retort Courteous and the Reply Churlish, leading finally to the Lie Circumstantial and the Lie Direct. He is fascinated by the games people make of their lives and is amused by their inability to be content with what they already have. Of the shepherd's life, he comments, "In respect that it is solitary, I like it very well; but in respect that it is private, it is a very vile life" (3.2.15–16). This paradox, though nonsensical, captures the restlessness of human striving for a life that can somehow combine the peaceful solitude of nature with the convenience and excitement of city life. Although Touchstone marries, even his marriage is a spoof of the institution rather than a serious attempt at commitment. Like all fools, who in Renaissance times were regarded as a breed apart, Touchstone exists outside the realm of ordinary human responses. There he can comment disinterestedly on human folly. He is prevented, however, from sharing fully in the human love and conciliation with which the play ends. He and Jaques are not touched by the play's regenerative magic; Jaques will remain in the forest, and Touchstone will remain forever a childlike entertainer.

The regenerative power of Arden, as we have seen, is not the forest's alone. What saves Orlando is the human charity practiced by him and by Duke Senior, who, for all his love of the forest, longs to rejoin that human society where he has "with holy bell been knolled to church" (2.7.120). Civilization at its best is no less necessary to the human spirit than is the natural order of the forest. In love, also, perception and wisdom must be combined with nature's gifts. Orlando, when we first see him, is a young man of the finest natural qualities but admittedly lacking experience in the nuances of complex human relationships. Nowhere does his lack of sophistication betray him more unhappily than in his first encounter with Rosalind, following the wrestling match. In response to her unmistakable hints of favor, he stands ox-like, tongue-tied. Later, in the forest, his first attempts at self-education in love lead him into an opposite danger: an excess of platitudinous manners parading in the guise of Petrarchism. (The Italian sonneteer Francis Petrarch has given to the language a name for the stereotypical literary mannerisms we associate with courtly love: the sighing and self-abasement of the young man, the chaste denial of love by the woman whom he worships, and the like.) Orlando's newfound self-abasement and idealization of his absent mistress are as unsatisfactory as his former naiveté. The sonnets he hangs on trees are too deserving of the delicious parody they get from Touchstone. Orlando must learn from Rosalind that a quest for true understanding in love avoids the extreme of pretentious mannerism as well as that of mere artlessness. Orlando as Petrarchan lover too much resembles Silvius, the lovesick young man, cowering before the imperious will of his coy mistress Phoebe. This stereotyped relationship, taken from the pages of fashionable pastoral romance, represents a posturing that Rosalind hopes to cure in Silvius and Phoebe even as she will also cure Orlando.

Rosalind is, above all, the realistic one, the plucky Shakespearean heroine showing her mettle in the world of men, emotionally more mature than her lover. Her concern is with a working and clear-sighted relationship in love, and to that end she daringly insists that Orlando learn something of woman's changeable mood. Above all, she must disabuse him of the dangerously misleading clichés of the Petrarchan love myth. When he protests he would die for love of Rosalind, she lectures him mockingly in her guise of Ganymede: "No, faith, die by attorney. The poor world is almost six thousand years old, and in all this time there was not any man died in his own person, videlicet, in a love cause." She debunks the legends of Troilus and Leander, youths supposed to have died for love who, if they had ever really existed, would no doubt have met with more prosaic ends. "But these are all lies. Men have died from time to time, and worms have eaten them, but not for love" (4.1.89–102). Rosalind wants Orlando to know that women are not goddesses but frail human beings who can be giddy, jealous, infatuated with novelty, irritatingly talkative, peremptory, and hysterical (4.1.142–9), though she is circumspect as to whether women can also be unfaithful. Orlando must be taught that love is a madness (3.2.390), and he must be cured, not of loving Rosalind, but of worshiping her with unrealistic expectations that can lead only to disillusionment. Rosalind teaches him, as Portia does Bassanio in *The Merchant of Venice,* but she does not seriously threaten him with wantonness. Her disguise as Ganymede provides for her the perfect role in Orlando's approach to sexual manhood: he can learn to love "Ganymede" as a friend and then make the transition to heterosexual union in his blessed discovery that the friend is also the lover. Rosalind's own rite of passage is easier; for all her reliance on her loving friendship with Celia, or "Aliena," she is ready to exclaim, "But what talk we of fathers, when there is such a man as Orlando?" (3.4.36–7). She is spiritedly independent, even more so than Portia; whereas Portia's choice of husband is controlled by her father from his grave, Rosalind picks for herself. To be sure, Duke Senior is certainly happy that she marries Orlando, and she is glad to be reunited with her father, but her choice in marriage is very much her own. The forest is indeed a place where she can encounter her father "man to man," as it were, and be liberated from him while coming to terms with a patriarchal world. She is ready to give herself to Orlando, but she must educate him first. When Orlando has been sufficiently tested as to patience, loyalty, and understanding, she unmasks herself to him and simultaneously unravels the plot of ridiculous love we have come to associate with Silvius and Phoebe.

Rosalind's disguise name, Ganymede, has connotations that suggest ways in which human sexuality can be partly understood as socially constructed. If Rosalind in disguise as Ganymede wins the affection and eventually the love of Orlando, while her father and the other forest dwellers are equally taken in by the disguise, are maleness and femaleness chiefly matters of sartorial convention and superficial appearance? When Phoebe falls in love with Ganymede, is not her infatuation a way of showing that the roles of the sexes can be put on and off? Theatrically, the device of having a young male actor play Rosalind who then disguises him/herself as a young man adds to the witty confusion of sexual identities by introducing homoerotic possibilities. Not only can the roles of the sexes be put on and off, sexual desire itself is unstable, attaching itself to effeminate or sexually indeterminate young men like Ganymede, who is described as being "Of female favor" and "Like a ripe sister" (4.3.87–8; compare *Twelfth Night*, 1.4.31–4, where Orsino says of "Cesario" that "all is semblative a woman's part"). Both Phoebe and Orlando are in some ways attracted to Ganymede; when Rosalind says of Orlando that "his kissing is as full of sanctity as the touch of holy bread" (3.4.13–14), she seems to suggest that Orlando has kissed her in her male disguise. Mythologically Ganymede is Zeus's or Jupiter's young male lover as well as cupbearer. The very role of boy actors in an all-male acting company must have struck some viewers as homoerotically suggestive.

At the same time, the motif of disguise enables the play to pursue a serious point about love and friendship. Orlando can speak frankly and personally to "Ganymede" as a perfect friend, one who can enable him as a young man still faced with the uncertainties and hazards of courtship to traverse the potentially difficult transition from male-to-male friendship into adult heterosexuality. The relationship closely anticipates that of "Cesario" and Orsino in *Twelfth Night*, where once again a powerful and loving attraction to a sexually ambiguous young man/woman ripens into mature love when the older man has been educated by the experience of loving friendship. Both plays depict heterosexual courtship as full of dangers for the male. In *As You Like It*, Rosalind is at pains to coach Orlando in what to expect from unruly women; and indeed, Rosalind's very readiness to wear male apparel bespeaks her daring intrusion into a man's world, even if Shakespeare carefully hedges this threat by insisting on Rosalind's hesitancy in being so bold. Rosalind is thus, like Portia in *The Merchant of Venice*, both spirited and eventually ready to comply with the mores of a male-dominated world.

By becoming Orlando's teacher, Rosalind is able to claim a strong position in their friendship and in our estimate of her remarkable worthiness. Posing as Ganymede, Rosalind can observe and test Orlando and thereby learn the truth about his capability for lifelong fidelity as only another man would have the opportunity to do. Once a loving friendship has grown strong between them, the unmasking of Rosalind's sexual identity makes possible a physical union between them to confirm and express the spiritual. In these terms, the play's happy ending affirms marriage as an institution, not simply as the expected denouement. The procession to the altar is synchronous with the return to civilization's other institutions, made whole again not solely by the forest but by the power of goodness embodied in Rosalind, Orlando, Duke Senior, and the others who persevere.

As You Like It

[*Dramatis Personae*

DUKE SENIOR, *a banished duke*
DUKE FREDERICK, *his usurping brother*
ROSALIND, *daughter of Duke Senior, later disguised as* GANYMEDE
CELIA, *daughter of Duke Frederick, later disguised as* ALIENA

OLIVER,
JAQUES,   } *sons of Sir Rowland de Boys*
ORLANDO,

AMIENS,
JAQUES,   } *lords attending Duke Senior*

LE BEAU, *a courtier attending Duke Frederick*
CHARLES, *a wrestler in the court of Duke Frederick*

ADAM, *an aged servant of Oliver and then Orlando*
DENNIS, *a servant of Oliver*

TOUCHSTONE, *the* CLOWN *or* FOOL

CORIN, *an old shepherd*
SILVIUS, *a young shepherd, in love with Phoebe*
PHOEBE, *a shepherdess*
WILLIAM, *a country youth, in love with Audrey*
AUDREY, *a country wench*
SIR OLIVER MAR-TEXT, *a country vicar*

HYMEN, *god of marriage*

Lords and Attendants waiting on Duke Frederick and Duke Senior

SCENE: *Oliver's house; Duke Frederick's court; and the Forest of Arden*]

1.1

Enter Orlando and Adam.

ORLANDO   As I remember, Adam, it was upon this fash- 1
ion bequeathed me by will but poor a thousand 2
crowns and, as thou say'st, charged my brother on his 3
blessing to breed me well; and there begins my 4
sadness. My brother Jaques he keeps at school, and 5
report speaks goldenly of his profit. For my part, he 6
keeps me rustically at home—or, to speak more
properly, stays me here at home unkept; for call you 8
that "keeping" for a gentleman of my birth, that
differs not from the stalling of an ox? His horses are
bred better, for besides that they are fair with their 11
feeding, they are taught their manage, and to that end 12

riders dearly hired. But I, his brother, gain nothing 13
under him but growth, for the which his animals on
his dunghills are as much bound to him as I. Besides
this nothing that he so plentifully gives me, the
something that nature gave me his countenance 17
seems to take from me. He lets me feed with his
hinds, bars me the place of a brother, and as much as 19
in him lies, mines my gentility with my education. 20
This is it, Adam, that grieves me; and the spirit of my
father, which I think is within me, begins to mutiny
against this servitude. I will no longer endure it,
though yet I know no wise remedy how to avoid it.

Enter Oliver.

ADAM   Yonder comes my master, your brother.
ORLANDO   Go apart, Adam, and thou shalt hear how 26
he will shake me up.   [*Adam stands aside.*] 27
OLIVER   Now, sir, what make you here? 28

1.1 Location: The garden of Oliver's house.
1–3 it was . . . crowns it was in this way that I was left, by the terms of my father's will, a mere thousand crowns or £250   **3 crowns** coins worth five shillings.   **3–4 charged . . . well** my brother was instructed as a condition of my father's blessing to educate me well   **5 My . . . school** My oldest brother Oliver maintains my other brother, Jaques, at university   **6 profit** progress.   **8 stays** detains.   **unkept** poorly supported   **11–12 fair . . . feeding** kept well groomed with good diet   **12 manage** manège, paces and maneuvers in the art of horsemanship

13 riders trainers.   **dearly** expensively   **17 countenance** behavior; (neglectful) patronage   **19 hinds** farm hands.   **bars me** excludes me from   **19–20 as much . . . education** with all the power at his disposal, undermines my right to be educated as a gentleman.   **26 Go apart** Stand aside   **27 shake me up** abuse me.   **28 make** do. (But Orlando takes it in the more usual sense.)

ORLANDO   Nothing. I am not taught to make anything.

OLIVER   What mar you then, sir?   30

ORLANDO   Marry, sir, I am helping you to mar that   31
which God made, a poor unworthy brother of yours,
with idleness.

OLIVER   Marry, sir, be better employed, and be naught   34
awhile.   35

ORLANDO   Shall I keep your hogs and eat husks with   36
them? What prodigal portion have I spent, that I   37
should come to such penury?   38

OLIVER   Know you where you are, sir?   39

ORLANDO   Oh, sir, very well: here in your orchard.   40

OLIVER   Know you before whom, sir?

ORLANDO   Ay, better than him I am before knows me.
I know you are my eldest brother, and in the gentle   43
condition of blood you should so know me. The cour-   44
tesy of nations allows you my better, in that you are   45
the firstborn, but the same tradition takes not away
my blood, were there twenty brothers betwixt us. I   47
have as much of my father in me as you, albeit I confess your coming before me is nearer to his reverence.   49

OLIVER   What, boy!   [He strikes Orlando.]

ORLANDO   Come, come, elder brother, you are too
young in this.   [He seizes Oliver by the throat.]   52

OLIVER   Wilt thou lay hands on me, villain?   53

ORLANDO   I am no villain. I am the youngest son of Sir
Rowland de Boys. He was my father, and he is thrice   55
a villain that says such a father begot villains. Wert
thou not my brother, I would not take this hand from
thy throat till this other had pulled out thy tongue for
saying so. Thou hast railed on thyself.   59

ADAM   Sweet masters, be patient! For your father's   60
remembrance, be at accord.   61

OLIVER   Let me go, I say.

ORLANDO   I will not till I please. You shall hear me. My
father charged you in his will to give me good education. You have trained me like a peasant, obscuring
and hiding from me all gentlemanlike qualities. The   66
spirit of my father grows strong in me, and I will no
longer endure it; therefore allow me such exercises as   68
may become a gentleman, or give me the poor allotery   69
my father left me by testament. With that I will go buy
my fortunes.   [He releases Oliver.]

OLIVER   And what wilt thou do? Beg when that is
spent? Well, sir, get you in. I will not long be troubled
with you; you shall have some part of your will. I pray   74
you, leave me.

ORLANDO   I will no further offend you than becomes me
for my good.

OLIVER [to Adam]   Get you with him, you old dog.

ADAM   Is "old dog" my reward? Most true, I have lost
my teeth in your service. God be with my old master!
He would not have spoke such a word.
    Exeunt Orlando [and] Adam.

OLIVER   Is it even so? Begin you to grow upon me? I will   82
physic your rankness and yet give no thousand   83
crowns neither.—Holla, Dennis!   84

    Enter Dennis.

DENNIS   Calls Your Worship?

OLIVER   Was not Charles, the Duke's wrestler, here to
speak with me?

DENNIS   So please you, he is here at the door and   88
importunes access to you.

OLIVER   Call him in.   [Exit Dennis.]
'Twill be a good way; and tomorrow the wrestling is.

    Enter Charles.

CHARLES   Good morrow to Your Worship.   92

OLIVER   Good Monsieur Charles, what's the new news
at the new court?

CHARLES   There's no news at the court, sir, but the old
news: that is, the old Duke is banished by his younger
brother the new Duke, and three or four loving lords
have put themselves into voluntary exile with him,
whose lands and revenues enrich the new Duke;   99
therefore he gives them good leave to wander.   100

OLIVER   Can you tell if Rosalind, the Duke's daughter,
be banished with her father?

CHARLES   Oh, no; for the Duke's daughter, her cousin, so
loves her, being ever from their cradles bred together,   104
that she would have followed her exile or have died to   105
stay behind her. She is at the court and no less beloved   106
of her uncle than his own daughter, and never
two ladies loved as they do.

OLIVER   Where will the old Duke live?

CHARLES   They say he is already in the Forest of Arden,
and a many merry men with him; and there they live
like the old Robin Hood of England. They say many
young gentlemen flock to him every day and fleet the   113
time carelessly as they did in the golden world.   114

OLIVER   What, you wrestle tomorrow before the new
Duke?

---

30 mar ("To make or mar" is a commonplace antithesis.)   **31 Marry**
i.e., Indeed. (Originally an oath by the Virgin Mary.)   **34–5 be
naught awhile** i.e., stay in your place, don't grumble.   **36–8 Shall . . .
penury?** (Alluding to the story of the Prodigal Son, in Matthew
25:14–30 and Luke 15:11–32, who, having wasted his "portion" or
inheritance, had to tend swine and eat with them.)   **39 where** in
whose presence. (But Orlando sarcastically takes the more literal
meaning.)   **40 orchard** garden.   **43–4 in . . . blood** acknowledging
the bond of our being of gentle birth   **44–5 courtesy of nations** recognized custom (of primogeniture, whereby the eldest son inherits all
the land)   **47 blood** (1) gentlemanly lineage (2) spirit   **49 is nearer . . .
reverence** is closer to his position of authority (as head of family).
52 young inexperienced (at fighting)   **53 villain** i.e., wicked fellow.
(But Orlando plays on the literal meaning of "bondman" or "serf," as
well as Oliver's meaning.)   **55 he** anyone   **59 railed on thyself**
insulted your own blood.   **60–1 your father's remembrance** the sake
of your father's memory   **66 qualities** (1) characteristics (2) accomplishments.   **68 exercises** employments   **69 allottery** portion

---

74 will (1) desire (2) portion from your father's will (3) willfulness
(i.e., you'll get what is coming to you).   **82 grow upon me** take liberties with me; grow too big for your breeches.   **83 physic your rankness** apply medicine to your overweening   **84 neither** either.
88 So please you If you please   **92 Good morrow** Good morning
99 whose all of whose   **100 good leave** full permission   **104 being**
they being   **105–6 died to stay** died from being forced to stay
113 fleet pass   **114 carelessly** free from care.   **golden world** the primal age of innocence and ease from which humankind was thought
to have degenerated. (See Ovid, *Metamorphoses* 1.)

CHARLES   Marry, do I, sir; and I came to acquaint you with a matter. I am given, sir, secretly to understand that your younger brother Orlando hath a disposition to come in disguised against me to try a fall. Tomor-120 row, sir, I wrestle for my credit, and he that escapes 121 me without some broken limb shall acquit him well. 122 Your brother is but young and tender, and for your love I would be loath to foil him, as I must for my 124 own honor if he come in. Therefore, out of my love to you, I came hither to acquaint you withal, that either 126 you might stay him from his intendment or brook 127 such disgrace well as he shall run into, in that it is a thing of his own search and altogether against my will. 129

OLIVER   Charles, I thank thee for thy love to me, which thou shalt find I will most kindly requite. I had myself notice of my brother's purpose herein and have by underhand means labored to dissuade him from it, but 133 he is resolute. I'll tell thee, Charles, it is the stubbornest young fellow of France, full of ambition, an envious emulator of every man's good parts, a secret and 136 villainous contriver against me his natural brother. 137 Therefore use thy discretion. I had as lief thou didst 138 break his neck as his finger. And thou wert best look 139 to't; for if thou dost him any slight disgrace, or if he 140 do not mightily grace himself on thee, he will practice 141 against thee by poison, entrap thee by some treacherous device, and never leave thee till he hath ta'en thy life by some indirect means or other; for I assure thee, and almost with tears I speak it, there is not one so young and so villainous this day living. I speak but brotherly of him, but should I anatomize him to thee as 147 he is, I must blush and weep, and thou must look pale and wonder.

CHARLES   I am heartily glad I came hither to you. If he come tomorrow, I'll give him his payment. If ever he go alone again, I'll never wrestle for prize more. And 152 so God keep Your Worship!

OLIVER   Farewell, good Charles.   *Exit* [*Charles*]. Now will I stir this gamester. I hope I shall see an end of 155 him; for my soul, yet I know not why, hates nothing more than he. Yet he's gentle, never schooled and yet 157 learned, full of noble device, of all sorts enchantingly 158 beloved, and indeed so much in the heart of the world and especially of my own people, who best know him, 160 that I am altogether misprized. But it shall not be so 161

long; this wrestler shall clear all. Nothing remains but 162 that I kindle the boy thither, which now I'll go about. 163
                                                                        Exit.

❖

1.2

Enter Rosalind and Celia.

CELIA   I pray thee, Rosalind, sweet my coz, be merry.   1

ROSALIND   Dear Celia, I show more mirth than I am mistress of, and would you yet I were merrier? Unless you could teach me to forget a banished father, you must not learn me how to remember any extraordi-   5 nary pleasure.

CELIA   Herein I see thou lov'st me not with the full weight that I love thee. If my uncle, thy banished   8 father, had banished thy uncle, the Duke my father, so thou hadst been still with me, I could have taught   10 my love to take thy father for mine. So wouldst thou, if the truth of thy love to me were so righteously   12 tempered as mine is to thee.   13

ROSALIND   Well, I will forget the condition of my estate   14 to rejoice in yours.

CELIA   You know my father hath no child but I, nor none is like to have. And truly, when he dies thou   17 shalt be his heir, for what he hath taken away from thy father perforce I will render thee again in affection. By   19 mine honor, I will, and when I break that oath, let me turn monster. Therefore, my sweet Rose, my dear Rose, be merry.

ROSALIND   From henceforth I will, coz, and devise sports. Let me see, what think you of falling in love?

CELIA   Marry, I prithee, do, to make sport withal. But   25 love no man in good earnest, nor no further in sport neither than with safety of a pure blush thou mayst in   27 honor come off again.   28

ROSALIND   What shall be our sport, then?

CELIA   Let us sit and mock the good huswife Fortune   30 from her wheel, that her gifts may henceforth be bestowed equally.

ROSALIND   I would we could do so, for her benefits are mightily misplaced, and the bountiful blind woman   34 doth most mistake in her gifts to women.

CELIA   'Tis true, for those that she makes fair she scarce   36 makes honest, and those that she makes honest she   37 makes very ill-favoredly.   38

---

120 a fall a bout of wrestling.   **121 credit** reputation   **122 shall . . . well** (1) must exert himself very skillfully (2) will be lucky indeed. **124 foil** defeat   **126 withal** with this   **127 stay . . . intendment** restrain him from his intent.   **brook** endure   **129 search** seeking **133 underhand** unobtrusive   **136 envious emulator** malicious disparager.   **parts** qualities   **137 contriver** plotter.   **natural** blood **138 lief** willingly   **139–40 thou . . . to't** you'd better beware   **140–1 if he . . . on thee** if he fails to distinguish himself at your expense **141 practice** plot   **147 brotherly** as a brother should.   **anatomize** analyze   **152 go alone** walk unassisted   **155 gamester** sportsman. (Said sardonically.)   **157 gentle** gentlemanly   **158 noble device** lofty aspiration.   **sorts** classes of people.   **enchantingly** as if they were under his spell   **160 people** servants   **161 misprized** undervalued, scorned

162 clear all solve everything.   **163 kindle . . . thither** inflame Orlando with desire to go to the wrestling match **1.2 Location: Duke Frederick's court. A place suitable for wrestling. 1 sweet my coz** my sweet cousin   **5 learn** teach   **8 that** with which **10 so** provided that   **12–13 righteously tempered** harmoniously composed   **14 condition of my estate** state of my fortunes   **17 like** likely   **19 perforce** by force   **25 sport** pastimes   **27 pure** (1) mere (2) innocent   **28 come off** retire, leave   **30 huswife** one who manages household affairs and operates the spinning wheel. (Shakespeare conflates this wheel with the commonplace wheel of Fortune.) *Huswife* is used derogatorily here, with a suggestion of "hussy." **34 bountiful blind woman** i.e., Fortune   **36 scarce** rarely   **37 honest** chaste   **38 ill-favoredly** ugly

ROSALIND   Nay, now thou goest from Fortune's office to
Nature's. Fortune reigns in gifts of the world, not in   40
the lineaments of Nature.   41

Enter [Touchstone the] Clown.

CELIA   No; when Nature hath made a fair creature, may
she not by Fortune fall into the fire? Though Nature   43
hath given us wit to flout at Fortune, hath not Fortune   44
sent in this fool to cut off the argument?

ROSALIND   Indeed, there is Fortune too hard for Nature,   46
when Fortune makes Nature's natural the cutter-off of   47
Nature's wit.   48

CELIA   Peradventure this is not Fortune's work neither   49
but Nature's, who perceiveth our natural wits too dull
to reason of such goddesses and hath sent this natural   51
for our whetstone; for always the dullness of the fool   52
is the whetstone of the wits.—How now, wit, whither   53
wander you?   54

TOUCHSTONE   Mistress, you must come away to your
father.

CELIA   Were you made the messenger?

TOUCHSTONE   No, by mine honor, but I was bid to
come for you.

ROSALIND   Where learned you that oath, Fool?

TOUCHSTONE   Of a certain knight that swore by his
honor they were good pancakes and swore by his   62
honor the mustard was naught. Now I'll stand to it the   63
pancakes were naught and the mustard was good,
and yet was not the knight forsworn.   65

CELIA   How prove you that in the great heap of your
knowledge?

ROSALIND   Ay, marry, now unmuzzle your wisdom.

TOUCHSTONE   Stand you both forth now. Stroke your
chins, and swear by your beards that I am a knave.

CELIA   By our beards, if we had them, thou art.

TOUCHSTONE   By my knavery, if I had it, then I were;
but if you swear by that that is not, you are not
forsworn. No more was this knight, swearing by his
honor, for he never had any; or if he had, he had
sworn it away before ever he saw those pancakes or
that mustard.

CELIA   Prithee, who is't that thou mean'st?

TOUCHSTONE   One that old Frederick, your father, loves.

CELIA   My father's love is enough to honor him enough.
Speak no more of him; you'll be whipped for taxation   81
one of these days.

TOUCHSTONE   The more pity that fools may not speak
wisely what wise men do foolishly.

CELIA   By my troth, thou sayest true; for since the little   85
wit that fools have was silenced, the little foolery that   86
wise men have makes a great show. Here comes
Monsieur Le Beau.

Enter Le Beau.

ROSALIND   With his mouth full of news.

CELIA   Which he will put on us as pigeons feed their   90
young.

ROSALIND   Then shall we be news-crammed.

CELIA   All the better; we shall be the more mar-   93
ketable.—*Bonjour,* Monsieur Le Beau. What's the   94
news?

LE BEAU   Fair princess, you have lost much good sport.

CELIA   Sport? Of what color?   97

LE BEAU   What color, madam? How shall I answer you?

ROSALIND   As wit and fortune will.

TOUCHSTONE   Or as the Destinies decrees.

CELIA   Well said. That was laid on with a trowel.   101

TOUCHSTONE   Nay, if I keep not my rank—   102

ROSALIND   Thou loosest thy old smell.

LE BEAU   You amaze me, ladies. I would have told you   104
of good wrestling, which you have lost the sight of.

ROSALIND   Yet tell us the manner of the wrestling.

LE BEAU   I will tell you the beginning, and if it please
Your Ladyships you may see the end, for the best is yet   108
to do, and here, where you are, they are coming to   109
perform it.

CELIA   Well, the beginning, that is dead and buried.   111

LE BEAU   There comes an old man and his three sons—

CELIA   I could match this beginning with an old tale.

LE BEAU   Three proper young men, of excellent growth   114
and presence—

ROSALIND   With bills on their necks, "Be it known unto   116
all men by these presents."   117

LE BEAU   The eldest of the three wrestled with Charles,
the Duke's wrestler, which Charles in a moment threw
him and broke three of his ribs, that there is little hope
of life in him. So he served the second, and so the   121
third. Yonder they lie, the poor old man their father
making such pitiful dole over them that all the behold-   123
ers take his part with weeping.

ROSALIND   Alas!

TOUCHSTONE   But what is the sport, monsieur, that the
ladies have lost?

LE BEAU   Why, this that I speak of.

---

40 gifts of the world e.g., riches and power   **41 the lineaments of
Nature** the features that Nature provides (like beauty or ugliness).
41.1 *Touchstone* a stone used to test for gold and silver   **43 she** the
woman whom Nature has made beautiful   **44 flout** scoff   **46 there**
in that instance   **47–8 when . . . wit** i.e., when Fortune makes this
natural half-wit (Touchstone) the cutter-off of witty dialogue that our
natural gifts enable us to engage in. (A *natural* here means a born
idiot; also in line 51.)   **49 Peradventure** Perhaps   **51 to reason . . .
goddesses** to engage in debate about Reason and Nature   **52 whetstone** grinding stone against which to sharpen things (in this case,
wit)   **52–3 the dullness . . . wits** i.e., the mindless things said by an
idiot serve as material on which to sharpen our wits.   **53–4 whither
wander you** (An allusion to the expression "wandering wits.")
62 pancakes fritters (which might be made of meat and so require
mustard)   **63 naught** worthless.   **stand to it** maintain, argue
65 forsworn perjured.   **81 taxation** censure, slander

85–6 since . . . silenced (Perhaps refers specifically to the Bishops'
order of June 1599 banning satirical books.)   **90 put on** force upon
93–4 marketable i.e., like animals that have been crammed with food
before being sent to market.   **97 color** kind.   **101 with a trowel** i.e.,
thick.   **102 rank** i.e., status as a wit. (But Rosalind plays on the sense
of "stench.")   **104 amaze** bewilder   **108–9 yet to do** still to come
111 the beginning tell us what has already occurred   **114 proper**
handsome   **116 bills** proclamations   **117 these presents** the present
document. (Rosalind uses this legal phrase to pun on *presence* in line
115.)   **121 So** Similarly   **123 dole** lamentation

TOUCHSTONE   Thus men may grow wiser every day. It is the first time that ever I heard breaking of ribs was sport for ladies.

CELIA   Or I, I promise thee.   132

ROSALIND   But is there any else longs to see this broken 133 music in his sides? Is there yet another dotes upon rib 134 breaking?—Shall we see this wrestling, cousin?

LE BEAU   You must if you stay here, for here is the place appointed for the wrestling, and they are ready to perform it.

CELIA   Yonder, sure, they are coming. Let us now stay and see it.

Flourish. Enter Duke [Frederick], Lords, Orlando, Charles, and attendants.

DUKE FREDERICK   Come on. Since the youth will not be entreated, his own peril on his forwardness.   142

ROSALIND   [*to Le Beau*]   Is yonder the man?

LE BEAU   Even he, madam.

CELIA   Alas, he is too young! Yet he looks successfully.   145

DUKE FREDERICK   How now, daughter and cousin? Are 146 you crept hither to see the wrestling?

ROSALIND   Ay, my liege, so please you give us leave.   148

DUKE FREDERICK   You will take little delight in it, I can tell you, there is such odds in the man. In pity of the 150 challenger's youth I would fain dissuade him, but he 151 will not be entreated. Speak to him, ladies; see if you can move him.

CELIA   Call him hither, good Monsieur Le Beau.

DUKE FREDERICK   Do so. I'll not be by.   [*He steps aside.*]

LE BEAU   [*to Orlando*]   Monsieur the challenger, the princess calls for you.

ORLANDO   [*approaching the ladies*]   I attend them with all respect and duty.

ROSALIND   Young man, have you challenged Charles the wrestler?

ORLANDO   No, fair princess. He is the general chal- 162 lenger. I come but in, as others do, to try with him the 163 strength of my youth.

CELIA   Young gentleman, your spirits are too bold for your years. You have seen cruel proof of this man's strength. If you saw yourself with your eyes or knew 167 yourself with your judgment, the fear of your adven- 168 ture would counsel you to a more equal enterprise. We 169 pray you, for your own sake, to embrace your own safety and give over this attempt.

ROSALIND   Do, young sir. Your reputation shall not therefore be misprized. We will make it our suit to the 173 Duke that the wrestling might not go forward.

ORLANDO   I beseech you, punish me not with your hard thoughts, wherein I confess me much guilty to deny 176 so fair and excellent ladies anything. But let your fair eyes and gentle wishes go with me to my trial, wherein if I be foiled, there is but one shamed that was never gracious, if killed, but one dead that is willing to 180 be so. I shall do my friends no wrong, for I have none to lament me; the world no injury, for in it I have nothing. Only in the world I fill up a place which may 183 be better supplied when I have made it empty.

ROSALIND   The little strength that I have, I would it were with you.

CELIA   And mine, to eke out hers.

ROSALIND   Fare you well. Pray heaven I be deceived 188 in you!   189

CELIA   Your heart's desires be with you!

CHARLES   Come, where is this young gallant that is so desirous to lie with his mother earth?

ORLANDO   Ready, sir, but his will hath in it a more modest working.   194

DUKE FREDERICK   You shall try but one fall.

CHARLES   No, I warrant Your Grace, you shall not entreat him to a second, that have so mightily persuaded him from a first.

ORLANDO   You mean to mock me after; you should not have mocked me before. But come your ways.   200

ROSALIND   Now Hercules be thy speed, young man!   201

CELIA   I would I were invisible, to catch the strong fellow by the leg.   [*Orlando and Charles*] *wrestle.*

ROSALIND   Oh, excellent young man!

CELIA   If I had a thunderbolt in mine eye, I can tell who 205 should down.   *Shout.* [*Charles is thrown.*]   206

DUKE FREDERICK   No more, no more.

ORLANDO   Yes, I beseech Your Grace. I am not yet well 208 breathed.   209

DUKE FREDERICK
How dost thou, Charles?

LE BEAU   He cannot speak, my lord.

DUKE FREDERICK
Bear him away.—What is thy name, young man?
                                    [*Charles is borne out.*]

ORLANDO   Orlando, my liege, the youngest son of Sir Rowland de Boys.

DUKE FREDERICK
I would thou hadst been son to some man else.
The world esteemed thy father honorable,
But I did find him still mine enemy.
Thou shouldst have better pleased me with this deed
Hadst thou descended from another house.
But fare thee well; thou art a gallant youth.
I would thou hadst told me of another father.
                Exit Duke [with train, and others. Rosalind and Celia remain; Orlando stands apart from them.]

---

132 **promise** assure   133 **any else** anyone else who   133–4 **broken music** literally, music arranged in parts for different instruments; here applied to the breaking of ribs   134 **another** another who 142 **entreated . . . forwardness** i.e., entreated to desist, let the risk be blamed upon his own rashness.   145 **successfully** i.e., as if he would be successful.   146 **cousin** i.e., niece   148 **so . . . leave** if you will permit us.   150 **there . . . man** Charles is such an odds-on favorite to win.   151 **fain** willingly   162–3 **the general challenger** the one who is ready to take on all comers. (Orlando is the challenger in a more limited sense.)   167–8 **If . . . judgment** If you saw yourself objectively   169 **equal** i.e., where the odds are more equal   173 **misprized** despised, undervalued.

176 **wherein** though.   **to deny** in denying   180 **gracious** looked upon with favor   183 **Only . . . I** In the world I merely 188–9 **deceived in you** i.e., mistaken in fearing you will lose. 194 **modest working** decorous endeavor (than to lie with one's mother earth. For a man to lie with his mother is to commit incest.) 200 **come your ways** come on.   201 **Hercules be thy speed** may Hercules help you   205 **If . . . eye** i.e., If I were Zeus or Jupiter 206 **down** fall.   208–9 **well breathed** warmed up.

CELIA [*to Rosalind*]
  Were I my father, coz, would I do this?
ORLANDO [*to no one in particular*]
  I am more proud to be Sir Rowland's son,
  His youngest son, and would not change that calling 223
  To be adopted heir to Frederick.
ROSALIND [*to Celia*]
  My father loved Sir Rowland as his soul,
  And all the world was of my father's mind.
  Had I before known this young man his son,
  I should have given him tears unto entreaties 228
  Ere he should thus have ventured.
CELIA [*to Rosalind*]   Gentle cousin,
  Let us go thank him and encourage him.
  My father's rough and envious disposition
  Sticks me at heart.—Sir, you have well deserved. 232
  If you do keep your promises in love
  But justly as you have exceeded all promise, 234
  Your mistress shall be happy.
ROSALIND [*giving him a chain from her neck*] Gentleman, 235
  Wear this for me, one out of suits with fortune, 236
  That could give more, but that her hand lacks means. 237
  [*To Celia*] Shall we go, coz?
CELIA   Ay.—Fare you well, fair gentleman.
                [*Rosalind and Celia start to leave.*]
ORLANDO [*aside*]
  Can I not say, "I thank you"? My better parts
  Are all thrown down, and that which here stands up
  Is but a quintain, a mere lifeless block. 241
ROSALIND [*to Celia*]
  He calls us back. My pride fell with my fortunes;
  I'll ask him what he would.—Did you call, sir? 243
  Sir, you have wrestled well and overthrown
  More than your enemies.
CELIA   Will you go, coz?
ROSALIND   Have with you.—Fare you well. 247
                    Exit [*with Celia*].
ORLANDO
  What passion hangs these weights upon my tongue?
  I cannot speak to her, yet she urged conference. 249
  O poor Orlando, thou art overthrown!
  Or Charles or something weaker masters thee. 251

        Enter Le Beau.

LE BEAU
  Good sir, I do in friendship counsel you
  To leave this place. Albeit you have deserved
  High commendation, true applause, and love,
  Yet such is now the Duke's condition 255
  That he misconsters all that you have done. 256
  The Duke is humorous. What he is indeed 257
  More suits you to conceive than I to speak of. 258

ORLANDO
  I thank you, sir. And, pray you, tell me this:
  Which of the two was daughter of the Duke
  That here was at the wrestling?
LE BEAU
  Neither his daughter, if we judge by manners,
  But yet indeed the taller is his daughter. 263
  The other is daughter to the banished Duke,
  And here detained by her usurping uncle
  To keep his daughter company, whose loves
  Are dearer than the natural bond of sisters.
  But I can tell you that of late this Duke
  Hath ta'en displeasure gainst his gentle niece,
  Grounded upon no other argument 270
  But that the people praise her for her virtues
  And pity her for her good father's sake;
  And, on my life, his malice gainst the lady
  Will suddenly break forth. Sir, fare you well. 274
  Hereafter, in a better world than this, 275
  I shall desire more love and knowledge of you.
ORLANDO
  I rest much bounden to you. Fare you well. 277
                    [*Exit Le Beau.*]
  Thus must I from the smoke into the smother, 278
  From tyrant Duke unto a tyrant brother.
  But heavenly Rosalind!   *Exit.*

                    ❧

1.3

        Enter Celia and Rosalind.

CELIA   Why, cousin, why, Rosalind! Cupid have mercy!
  Not a word?
ROSALIND   Not one to throw at a dog.
CELIA   No, thy words are too precious to be cast away
  upon curs. Throw some of them at me. Come, lame 5
  me with reasons. 6
ROSALIND   Then there were two cousins laid up, when
  the one should be lamed with reasons and the other
  mad without any.
CELIA   But is all this for your father?
ROSALIND   No, some of it is for my child's father. Oh, 11
  how full of briers is this working-day world!
CELIA   They are but burs, cousin, thrown upon thee in 13
  holiday foolery. If we walk not in the trodden paths, 14
  our very petticoats will catch them. 15
ROSALIND   I could shake them off my coat. These burs
  are in my heart.

---

223 change that calling exchange that name and vocation   **228 unto** in addition to   **232 Sticks** stabs   **234 But justly** exactly   **235 s.d. chain** (See 3.2.178, where Celia speaks of a chain given to Orlando by Rosalind.)   **236 out . . . fortune** (1) whose petitions to Fortune are rejected (2) not wearing the livery of Fortune, not in her service   **237 could** would   **241 quintain** wooden figure used as a target in tilting   **243 would** wants.   **247 Have with you** I'll go with you.   **249 urged conference** invited conversation.   **251 Or** Either   **255 condition** disposition   **256 misconsters** misconstrues   **257 humorous** capricious.   **258 conceive** imagine, understand

263 taller (Perhaps a textual error for *smaller* or *lesser,* or else an inconsistency on Shakespeare's part; at 1.3.113, Rosalind is shown to be the taller.)   **270 argument** reason   **274 suddenly** very soon   **275 in . . . world** in better times   **277 bounden** indebted   **278 from . . . smother** i.e., out of the frying pan into the fire. (*Smother* means "a dense suffocating smoke.")
1.3 Location: Duke Frederick's court.
5–6 lame . . . reasons throw some explanations (for your silence) at me.   **11 my child's father** one who might father my children, i.e., Orlando.   **13–15 They . . . them** i.e., You are making too much of minor difficulties; one catches such burs on one's clothes constantly if one strays from the path of propriety (by falling into the folly of love). (*Holiday* and *working-day,* lines 12 and 14, form a crucial comic binary in this play.)

CELIA   Hem them away.   18

ROSALIND   I would try, if I could cry "hem" and have   19
him.

CELIA   Come, come, wrestle with thy affections.

ROSALIND   Oh, they take the part of a better wrestler than
myself.

CELIA   Oh, a good wish upon you! You will try in time,   24
in despite of a fall. But, turning these jests out of   25
service, let us talk in good earnest. Is it possible, on   26
such a sudden, you should fall into so strong a liking
with old Sir Rowland's youngest son?

ROSALIND   The Duke my father loved his father dearly.

CELIA   Doth it therefore ensue that you should love his
son dearly? By this kind of chase, I should hate him,   31
for my father hated his father dearly; yet I hate not   32
Orlando.

ROSALIND   No, faith, hate him not, for my sake.   34

CELIA   Why should I not? Doth he not deserve well?   35

Enter Duke [Frederick], with Lords.

ROSALIND   Let me love him for that, and do you love
him because I do.—Look, here comes the Duke.

CELIA   With his eyes full of anger.

DUKE FREDERICK *[to Rosalind]*
Mistress, dispatch you with your safest haste
And get you from our court.

ROSALIND   Me, uncle?

DUKE FREDERICK   You, cousin.   40
Within these ten days if that thou be'st found
So near our public court as twenty miles,
Thou diest for it.

ROSALIND   I do beseech Your Grace
Let me the knowledge of my fault bear with me.
If with myself I hold intelligence   45
Or have acquaintance with mine own desires,
If that I do not dream or be not frantic—   47
As I do trust I am not—then, dear uncle,
Never so much as in a thought unborn
Did I offend Your Highness.

DUKE FREDERICK   Thus do all traitors.
If their purgation did consist in words,   51
They are as innocent as grace itself.
Let it suffice thee that I trust thee not.

ROSALIND
Yet your mistrust cannot make me a traitor.
Tell me whereon the likelihood depends.

DUKE FREDERICK
Thou art thy father's daughter. There's enough.   56

ROSALIND
So was I when Your Highness took his dukedom;
So was I when Your Highness banished him.
Treason is not inherited, my lord;
Or, if we did derive it from our friends,   60
What's that to me? My father was no traitor.
Then, good my liege, mistake me not so much
To think my poverty is treacherous.   63

CELIA   Dear sovereign, hear me speak.

DUKE FREDERICK
Ay, Celia, we stayed her for your sake,   65
Else had she with her father ranged along.   66

CELIA
I did not then entreat to have her stay;
It was your pleasure and your own remorse.   68
I was too young that time to value her,   69
But now I know her. If she be a traitor,
Why, so am I. We still have slept together,   71
Rose at an instant, learned, played, eat together,   72
And wheresoe'er we went, like Juno's swans   73
Still we went coupled and inseparable.

DUKE FREDERICK
She is too subtle for thee; and her smoothness,
Her very silence, and her patience
Speak to the people, and they pity her.
Thou art a fool. She robs thee of thy name,   78
And thou wilt show more bright and seem more
      virtuous
When she is gone. Then open not thy lips.
Firm and irrevocable is my doom   81
Which I have passed upon her; she is banished.

CELIA
Pronounce that sentence then on me, my liege!
I cannot live out of her company.

DUKE FREDERICK
You are a fool.—You, niece, provide yourself.   85
If you outstay the time, upon mine honor,
And in the greatness of my word, you die.   87
           Exit Duke [with Lords].

CELIA
O my poor Rosalind, whither wilt thou go?
Wilt thou change fathers? I will give thee mine.   89
I charge thee, be not thou more grieved than I am.

ROSALIND
I have more cause.

CELIA   Thou hast not, cousin.
Prithee, be cheerful. Know'st thou not the Duke
Hath banished me, his daughter?

ROSALIND   That he hath not.

---

18 Hem (1) Tuck (2) Cough (since you say they are in the chest.) A *bur* can be something that sticks in the throat.   **19 cry "hem"** attract Orlando's attention by coughing. (But with the suggestion too of a bawd's warning cry to the lovers whose secrecy is being guarded. With a pun on "*hem*" and *him*.)   **24–5 Oh . . . fall** i.e., Good luck to you; you'll undertake to wrestle with Orlando sooner or later, despite the danger of your being thrown down. (With sexual suggestion.) **25–6 turning . . . service** i.e., dismissing this banter   **31 By . . . chase** To pursue this line of reasoning   **32 dearly** intensely   **34 faith** in truth   **35 Why . . . not?** Why shouldn't I hate him, i.e., love him? (Celia has just argued by chop-logic, in lines 30-2, that to love is to hate and vice versa.)   **40 cousin** i.e., niece.   **45 If . . . intelligence** If I understand my own feelings   **47 If that** If.   **frantic** insane   **51 purgation** clearing of guilt. (A medical, legal, and theological metaphor.)

56 There's enough That's reason enough.   **60 friends** relatives **63 To think** as to think   **65 stayed** kept   **66 ranged** roamed **68 remorse** compassion.   **69 that time** at that time   **71 still** continually   **72 at an instant** at the same time.   **eat** ate   **73 Juno's swans** i.e., yoked together. (Though according to Ovid it was Venus, not Juno, who used swans to draw her chariot.)   **78 name** reputation **81 doom** sentence   **85 provide yourself** get ready   **87 in . . . word** upon my authority as Duke   **89 change** exchange

CELIA

No, hath not? Rosalind lacks then the love
Which teacheth thee that thou and I am one.
Shall we be sundered? Shall we part, sweet girl?
No, let my father seek another heir.
Therefore devise with me how we may fly,
Whither to go, and what to bear with us.
And do not seek to take your change upon you,   100
To bear your griefs yourself and leave me out;
For, by this heaven, now at our sorrows pale,   102
Say what thou canst, I'll go along with thee.

ROSALIND   Why, whither shall we go?

CELIA

To seek my uncle in the Forest of Arden.

ROSALIND

Alas, what danger will it be to us,
Maids as we are, to travel forth so far!
Beauty provoketh thieves sooner than gold.

CELIA

I'll put myself in poor and mean attire   109
And with a kind of umber smirch my face;   110
The like do you. So shall we pass along
And never stir assailants.

ROSALIND   Were it not better,
Because that I am more than common tall,
That I did suit me all points like a man?   114
A gallant curtal ax upon my thigh,   115
A boar spear in my hand, and—in my heart
Lie there what hidden woman's fear there will—
We'll have a swashing and a martial outside,   118
As many other mannish cowards have
That do outface it with their semblances.   120

CELIA

What shall I call thee when thou art a man?

ROSALIND

I'll have no worse a name than Jove's own page,
And therefore look you call me Ganymede.
But what will you be called?   123

CELIA

Something that hath a reference to my state:
No longer Celia, but Aliena.   126

ROSALIND

But, cousin, what if we assayed to steal   127
The clownish fool out of your father's court?
Would he not be a comfort to our travel?   129

CELIA

He'll go along o'er the wide world with me.
Leave me alone to woo him. Let's away,   131
And get our jewels and our wealth together,
Devise the fittest time and safest way
To hide us from pursuit that will be made

After my flight. Now go we in content   135
To liberty, and not to banishment.   *Exeunt.*

❖

2.1

*Enter Duke Senior, Amiens, and two or three
Lords, [dressed] like foresters.*

DUKE SENIOR

Now, my co-mates and brothers in exile,
Hath not old custom made this life more sweet   2
Than that of painted pomp? Are not these woods
More free from peril than the envious court?
Here feel we not the penalty of Adam,   5
The seasons' difference, as the icy fang   6
And churlish chiding of the winter's wind,
Which when it bites and blows upon my body
Even till I shrink with cold, I smile and say
"This is no flattery; these are counselors
That feelingly persuade me what I am."
Sweet are the uses of adversity,
Which, like the toad, ugly and venomous,   13
Wears yet a precious jewel in his head;   14
And this our life, exempt from public haunt,   15
Finds tongues in trees, books in the running brooks,
Sermons in stones, and good in everything.

AMIENS

I would not change it. Happy is Your Grace
That can translate the stubbornness of fortune
Into so quiet and so sweet a style.

DUKE SENIOR

Come, shall we go and kill us venison?
And yet it irks me the poor dappled fools,   22
Being native burghers of this desert city,   23
Should in their own confines with forkèd heads   24
Have their round haunches gored.

FIRST LORD   Indeed, my lord,
The melancholy Jaques grieves at that,
And in that kind swears you do more usurp   27
Than doth your brother that hath banished you.
Today my lord of Amiens and myself
Did steal behind him as he lay along   30
Under an oak whose antique root peeps out   31
Upon the brook that brawls along this wood,   32
To the which place a poor sequestered stag   33
That from the hunter's aim had ta'en a hurt
Did come to languish. And indeed, my lord,
The wretched animal heaved forth such groans

100 change change of fortune   **102 pale** (Heaven is pale in sympathy with their plight.)   **109 mean** lowly   **110 umber** yellow-brown pigment (to give a tanned appearance appropriate to countrywomen)
114 suit me all points outfit myself in all ways   **115 curtal ax** broad cutting sword   **118 swashing** swaggering   **120 outface . . . semblances** bluff their way through with mere appearances.   **123 Ganymede** Jupiter's cupbearer. (The name used for disguise also in Lodge's *Rosalynde.*)   **126 Aliena** the estranged one.   **127 assayed** tried   **129 travel** (1) movement from place to place (2) labor, hardship (*travail*)   **131 Leave . . . him** Leave it to me to persuade him.

135 content contentment
2.1 Location: The Forest of Arden.
2 old custom long experience   **5–6 feel . . . difference** we don't mind the consequences of Adam's original sin—the hardship of the seasons. (*Not* is often emended to *but.*)   **6 as** such as   **13–14 like . . . head** (Alludes to the widespread belief that the toad was a poisonous creature but with a jewel embedded in its head that worked as an antidote.)   **15 exempt** cut off.   **haunt** society   **22 fools** innocents   **23 burghers** citizens.   **desert city** uninhabited place   **24 forkèd heads** barbed hunting arrows, but also suggesting antlers   **27 kind** regard   **30 along** stretched out   **31 antique** (1) ancient or (2) *antic,* "gnarled"   **32 brawls** noisily flows   **33 sequestered** separated (from the herd)

That their discharge did stretch his leathern coat
Almost to bursting, and the big round tears
Coursed one another down his innocent nose   39
In piteous chase. And thus the hairy fool,
Much markèd of the melancholy Jaques,   41
Stood on th'extremest verge of the swift brook,   42
Augmenting it with tears.

DUKE SENIOR   But what said Jaques?
Did he not moralize this spectacle?   44

FIRST LORD
Oh, yes, into a thousand similes.
First, for his weeping into the needless stream: 46
"Poor deer," quoth he, "thou mak'st a testament   47
As worldings do, giving thy sum of more   48
To that which had too much." Then, being there alone,   49
Left and abandoned of his velvet friends: 50
"'Tis right," quoth he, "thus misery doth part   51
The flux of company." Anon a careless herd,   52
Full of the pasture, jumps along by him   53
And never stays to greet him. "Ay," quoth Jaques,
"Sweep on, you fat and greasy citizens;   55
'Tis just the fashion. Wherefore do you look   56
Upon that poor and broken bankrupt there?"   57
Thus most invectively he pierceth through   58
The body of the country, city, court,
Yea, and of this our life, swearing that we
Are mere usurpers, tyrants, and what's worse,   61
To fright the animals and to kill them up   62
In their assigned and native dwelling place.

DUKE SENIOR
And did you leave him in this contemplation?

SECOND LORD
We did, my lord, weeping and commenting
Upon the sobbing deer.

DUKE SENIOR   Show me the place.
I love to cope him in these sullen fits,   67
For then he's full of matter.   68

FIRST LORD   I'll bring you to him straight.   *Exeunt.*   69

❧

2.2

Enter Duke [Frederick], with Lords.

DUKE FREDERICK
Can it be possible that no man saw them?
It cannot be. Some villains of my court
Are of consent and sufferance in this.   3

FIRST LORD
I cannot hear of any that did see her.   4
The ladies, her attendants of her chamber,
Saw her abed, and in the morning early
They found the bed untreasured of their mistress.

SECOND LORD
My lord, the roynish clown, at whom so oft   8
Your Grace was wont to laugh, is also missing.
Hisperia, the princess' gentlewoman,
Confesses that she secretly o'erheard
Your daughter and her cousin much commend
The parts and graces of the wrestler   13
That did but lately foil the sinewy Charles,
And she believes wherever they are gone
That youth is surely in their company.

DUKE FREDERICK
Send to his brother. Fetch that gallant hither.   17
If he be absent, bring his brother to me;   18
I'll make him find him. Do this suddenly,   19
And let not search and inquisition quail   20
To bring again these foolish runaways.   *Exeunt.*   21

❧

2.3

Enter Orlando and Adam, [meeting].

ORLANDO   Who's there?

ADAM
What, my young master? Oh, my gentle master,
Oh, my sweet master, oh, you memory   3
Of old Sir Rowland! Why, what make you here?   4
Why are you virtuous? Why do people love you?
And wherefore are you gentle, strong, and valiant?
Why would you be so fond to overcome   7
The bonny prizer of the humorous Duke?   8
Your praise is come too swiftly home before you.
Know you not, master, to some kind of men
Their graces serve them but as enemies?
No more do yours. Your virtues, gentle master,   12
Are sanctified and holy traitors to you.

Oh, what a world is this, when what is comely
Envenoms him that bears it!

ORLANDO

Why, what's the matter?

ADAM   O unhappy youth,
Come not within these doors! Within this roof
The enemy of all your graces lives.
Your brother—no, no brother; yet the son—
Yet not the son, I will not call him son
Of him I was about to call his father—
Hath heard your praises, and this night he means   22
To burn the lodging where you use to lie   23
And you within it. If he fail of that,
He will have other means to cut you off.
I overheard him and his practices.   26
This is no place, this house is but a butchery.   27
Abhor it, fear it, do not enter it.

ORLANDO

Why, whither, Adam, wouldst thou have me go?

ADAM

No matter whither, so you come not here.   30

ORLANDO

What, wouldst thou have me go and beg my food?
Or with a base and boist'rous sword enforce   32
A thievish living on the common road?
This I must do or know not what to do;
Yet this I will not do, do how I can.
I rather will subject me to the malice
Of a diverted blood and bloody brother.   37

ADAM

But do not so. I have five hundred crowns,
The thrifty hire I saved under your father,   39
Which I did store to be my foster nurse
When service should in my old limbs lie lame   41
And unregarded age in corners thrown.   42
Take that, and He that doth the ravens feed,   43
Yea, providently caters for the sparrow,   44
Be comfort to my age! Here is the gold; [offering gold]
All this I give you. Let me be your servant.
Though I look old, yet I am strong and lusty,   47
For in my youth I never did apply
Hot and rebellious liquors in my blood,
Nor did not with unbashful forehead woo   50
The means of weakness and debility;   51
Therefore my age is as a lusty winter,
Frosty but kindly. Let me go with you.   53
I'll do the service of a younger man
In all your business and necessities.

ORLANDO

Oh, good old man, how well in thee appears
The constant service of the antique world,   57
When service sweat for duty, not for meed!   58
Thou art not for the fashion of these times,
Where none will sweat but for promotion,
And having that do choke their service up   61
Even with the having. It is not so with thee.   62
But, poor old man, thou prun'st a rotten tree,
That cannot so much as a blossom yield
In lieu of all thy pains and husbandry.   65
But come thy ways. We'll go along together,
And ere we have thy youthful wages spent,
We'll light upon some settled low content.   68

ADAM

Master, go on, and I will follow thee
To the last gasp, with truth and loyalty.
From seventeen years till now almost fourscore
Here livèd I, but now live here no more.
At seventeen years many their fortunes seek,
But at fourscore it is too late a week;   74
Yet fortune cannot recompense me better
Than to die well and not my master's debtor.

Exeunt.

❖

2.4

*Enter Rosalind for Ganymede, Celia for Aliena,
and Clown, alias Touchstone.*

ROSALIND   Oh, Jupiter, how weary are my spirits!

TOUCHSTONE   I care not for my spirits, if my legs were
not weary.

ROSALIND   I could find in my heart to disgrace my man's
apparel and to cry like a woman; but I must comfort   5
the weaker vessel, as doublet and hose ought to show   6
itself courageous to petticoat. Therefore courage, good
Aliena!

CELIA   I pray you, bear with me. I cannot go no further.

TOUCHSTONE   For my part, I had rather bear with you
than bear you; yet I should bear no cross if I did bear   11
you, for I think you have no money in your purse.

ROSALIND   Well, this is the Forest of Arden.

TOUCHSTONE   Ay, now am I in Arden; the more fool I.
When I was at home I was in a better place, but
travelers must be content.

Enter Corin and Silvius.

22 **your praises** people's praise of you   23 **use** are accustomed
26 **practices** plots.   27 **place** place for you   30 **so** provided that
32 **boist'rous** rough   37 **diverted blood** kinship diverted from the
natural source   39 **thrifty . . . saved** wages I thriftily saved   41 **lie
lame** i.e., be performed only lamely   42 **And . . . thrown** and when I
will be neglected and thrown aside because of my old age.   43–4 **and
He . . . sparrow** i.e., and may God, who guards over all His creatures
(see Luke 12:6, 22-4, Psalms 147.9, etc.)   47 **lusty** vigorous   50–1 **Nor
. . . debility** nor did I with shameless countenance chase after pleasures that would have weakened and disabled me   53 **Frosty** i.e.,
white-haired

57 **constant** faithful.   **antique** ancient (as in the Golden Age)
58 **sweat** sweated.   **meed** reward.   61–2 **do choke . . . having** i.e.,
cease serving once they have gained promotion.   65 **lieu of** return
for   68 **low content** lowly contented state.   74 **too . . . week** i.e., too
late in life
2.4 Location: The Forest of Arden.
0.1. *for* i.e., disguised as   5–6 **comfort the weaker vessel** (Saint Paul,
in 1 Peter 3:7, bids husbands give honor to their wives "as unto the
weaker vessel.")   6 **doublet and hose** close-fitting jacket and
breeches; typical male attire   11 **cross** (1) burden (2) coin having on it
a figure of a cross

ROSALIND　　Ay, be so, good Touchstone.—Look you
who comes here, a young man and an old in solemn
talk.　　　　　　　　　　　　*[They stand aside and listen.]*

CORIN
That is the way to make her scorn you still.

SILVIUS
Oh, Corin, that thou knew'st how I do love her!

CORIN
I partly guess, for I have loved ere now.

SILVIUS
No, Corin, being old, thou canst not guess,
Though in thy youth thou wast as true a lover
As ever sighed upon a midnight pillow.
But if thy love were ever like to mine—
As sure I think did never man love so—
How many actions most ridiculous
Hast thou been drawn to by thy fantasy?　　　　　　29

CORIN
Into a thousand that I have forgotten.

SILVIUS
Oh, thou didst then never love so heartily!
If thou remember'st not the slightest folly
That ever love did make thee run into,
Thou hast not loved.
Or if thou hast not sat as I do now,
Wearing thy hearer in thy mistress' praise,　　　　36
Thou hast not loved.
Or if thou hast not broke from company
Abruptly, as my passion now makes me,
Thou has not loved.
O Phoebe, Phoebe, Phoebe!　　　　　　　　*Exit.*

ROSALIND
Alas, poor shepherd! Searching of thy wound,　　42
I have by hard adventure found mine own.　　　　43

TOUCHSTONE　　And I mine. I remember, when I was in
love I broke my sword upon a stone and bid him take　45
that for coming a-night to Jane Smile; and I remember　46
the kissing of her batler and the cow's dugs that her　47
pretty chapped hands had milked; and I remember　48
the wooing of a peascod instead of her, from whom I　49
took two cods and, giving her them again, said with　50
weeping tears, "Wear these for my sake." We that are　51
true lovers run into strange capers; but as all is mortal　52
in nature, so is all nature in love mortal in folly.　　53

ROSALIND　　Thou speak'st wiser than thou art ware of.　54

TOUCHSTONE　　Nay, I shall ne'er be ware of mine own　55
wit till I break my shins against it.　　　　　　　　56

ROSALIND
Jove, Jove! This shepherd's passion
Is much upon my fashion.　　　　　　　　　　　　58

TOUCHSTONE
And mine, but it grows something stale with me.　59

CELIA
I pray you, one of you question yond man
If he for gold will give us any food.
I faint almost to death.

TOUCHSTONE *[to Corin]*　　Holla: you, clown!　　62

ROSALIND
Peace, Fool! He's not thy kinsman.

CORIN　　　　　　　　　　　Who calls?

TOUCHSTONE
Your betters, sir.

CORIN　　　　　　　　Else are they very wretched.

ROSALIND
Peace, I say.—Good even to you, friend.　　　　65

CORIN
And to you, gentle sir, and to you all.

ROSALIND
I prithee, shepherd, if that love or gold　　　　　67
Can in this desert place buy entertainment,　　　68
Bring us where we may rest ourselves and feed.
Here's a young maid with travel much oppressed,
And faints for succor.

CORIN　　　　　　　　Fair sir, I pity her　　　　71
And wish, for her sake more than for mine own,
My fortunes were more able to relieve her;
But I am shepherd to another man
And do not shear the fleeces that I graze.　　　　75
My master is of churlish disposition,　　　　　　76
And little recks to find the way to heaven　　　　77
By doing deeds of hospitality.
Besides, his cote, his flocks, and bounds of feed　79
Are now on sale, and at our sheepcote now,
By reason of his absence, there is nothing
That you will feed on. But what is, come see,　　82
And in my voice most welcome shall you be.　　83

ROSALIND
What is he that shall buy his flock and pasture?　84

CORIN
That young swain that you saw here but erewhile,　85
That little cares for buying anything.

ROSALIND
I pray thee, if it stand with honesty,　　　　　　87
Buy thou the cottage, pasture, and the flock,
And thou shalt have to pay for it of us.　　　　　89

---

29 **fantasy** love imaginings.　**36 Wearing** wearing out　**42 Searching of** Probing　**43 hard adventure** painful experience　**45–6 I broke . . . Smile** (In his parody of a distraught lover, Touchstone imagines himself attacking a stone as if it were his rival for a country maiden named Jane Smile. *A-night* means "by night.")　**47 batler** club for beating clothes in process of washing.　**dugs** udder　**48–51 and I . . . sake** (Touchstone absurdly imagines himself courting a pea plant as though it were Jane Smile and exchanging pea pods with her by way of love tokens.)　**52 mortal** subject to death　**53 mortal** typically human, frail　**54 ware** aware　**55–6 Nay . . . against it** (Touchstone, as a professional fool, laughs at the idea of stumbling on or discovering his own capacity for saying something wise. His use of *ware* plays on [1] aware [2] wary.)

58 **upon** after, according to　**59 something** somewhat　**62 clown** yokel. (But Rosalind then alludes to the word as it applies to Touchstone as a court fool or clown.)　**65 even** evening, i.e., afternoon　**67 if that** if　**68 desert** uninhabited.　**entertainment** hospitality, provision　**71 for succor** for lack of food.　**75 do . . . fleeces** i.e., do not obtain the profits from the flock　**76 churlish** miserly　**77 recks** reckons　**79 cote** cottage.　**bounds of feed** range of pasture　**82 That . . . feed on** suitable for your refined tastes.　**83 in my voice** insofar as I have authority to speak　**84 What** Who　**85 but erewhile** just now　**87 stand** be consistent　**89 have to pay** have the money

CELIA
　　And we will mend thy wages. I like this place　　　　90
　　And willingly could waste my time in it.　　　　　　91
CORIN
　　Assuredly the thing is to be sold.
　　Go with me. If you like upon report
　　The soil, the profit, and this kind of life,
　　I will your very faithful feeder be　　　　　　　　95
　　And buy it with your gold right suddenly.　　*Exeunt.*　96

❧

2.5

　　　*Enter Amiens, Jaques, and others. [A table is
　　　set out.]*

　　　　　Song.

AMIENS [*sings*]
　　　　Under the greenwood tree
　　　　Who loves to lie with me,　　　　　　　　　2
　　　　And turn his merry note　　　　　　　　　3
　　　　Unto the sweet bird's throat,　　　　　　　4
　　Come hither, come hither, come hither,
　　　　Here shall he see
　　　　No enemy
　　But winter and rough weather.

JAQUES　　More, more, I prithee, more.
AMIENS　　It will make you melancholy, Monsieur Jaques.
JAQUES　　I thank it. More, I prithee, more. I can suck mel-
　　ancholy out of a song as a weasel sucks eggs. More, I
　　prithee, more.
AMIENS　　My voice is ragged. I know I cannot please you.　14
JAQUES　　I do not desire you to please me, I do desire
　　you to sing. Come, more, another stanzo. Call you　16
　　'em "stanzos"?
AMIENS　　What you will, Monsieur Jaques.
JAQUES　　Nay, I care not for their names; they owe me　19
　　nothing. Will you sing?　　　　　　　　　　　20
AMIENS　　More at your request than to please myself.
JAQUES　　Well then, if ever I thank any man, I'll thank
　　you; but that they call "compliment" is like th'en-　23
　　counter of two dog-apes, and when a man thanks　24
　　me heartily, methinks I have given him a penny and
　　he renders me the beggarly thanks. Come, sing; and　26
　　you that will not, hold your tongues.
AMIENS　　Well, I'll end the song.—Sirs, cover the while;　28
　　the Duke will drink under this tree.—He hath been all
　　this day to look you.　　　　[*Food and drink are set out.*]　30

JAQUES　　And I have been all this day to avoid him. He
　　is too disputable for my company. I think of as many　32
　　matters as he, but I give heaven thanks and make no
　　boast of them. Come, warble, come.

　　　　　Song.

AMIENS [*sings*]
　　　　Who doth ambition shun
　　　　And loves to live i'th' sun,　　　　　　　36
　　　　Seeking the food he eats　　　　　　　　37
　　　　And pleased with what he gets,
　　　　　　　　　　　All together here.
　　Come hither, come hither, come hither.
　　　　Here shall he see
　　　　No enemy
　　But winter and rough weather.

JAQUES　　I'll give you a verse to this note that I made　43
　　yesterday in despite of my invention.　　　　　44
AMIENS　　And I'll sing it.
JAQUES　　Thus it goes:

　　　　If it do come to pass
　　　　That any man turn ass,
　　　　Leaving his wealth and ease,
　　　　A stubborn will to please,
　　Ducdame, ducdame, ducdame.　　　　　　　51
　　　　Here shall he see
　　　　Gross fools as he,
　　An if he will come to me.

AMIENS　　What's that "ducdame"?
JAQUES　　'Tis a Greek invocation, to call fools into a circle.
　　I'll go sleep, if I can; if I cannot, I'll rail against all the
　　firstborn of Egypt.　　　　　　　　　　　58
AMIENS　　And I'll go seek the Duke. His banquet is pre-　59
　　pared.　　　　　　　　　*Exeunt [separately].*

❧

2.6

　　　Enter Orlando and Adam.

ADAM　　Dear master, I can go no further. Oh, I die for
　　food! Here lie I down and measure out my grave.
　　Farewell, kind master.　　　　　　[*He lies down.*]

---

90 mend improve　**91 waste** spend　**95 feeder** dependent, servant
96 right suddenly without delay.
2.5 Location: The forest.
2 Who anyone who.　**lie** dwell　**3–4 And . . . throat** and tune his
song to the bird's voice　**14 ragged** hoarse.　**16 stanzo** (The word
stanza, variously spelled, was newfangled and therefore of ironic
interest to Jaques.)　**19–20 they owe me nothing** (Jaques speaks of
names as of something valuable only when written as signatures to a
bond of indebtedness.)　**23 that** what.　**"compliment"** courtesy
24 dog-apes dog-faced baboons　**26 beggarly** effusive, like the
thanks of a beggar　**28 cover the while** set the table for a meal
meanwhile　**30 to look** looking for

32 disputable inclined to dispute　**36 live i'th' sun** dwell in the open
air, without the cares of the court　**37 Seeking** hunting for　**43 note**
tune　**44 in . . . invention** i.e., without needing to make use of my
powerful rhetorical skills. (The nonsense that follows will make a
mockery of true invention.)　**51 Ducdame** (Probably a nonsense term
devised to puzzle Jaques's hearers, although with intriguing resemblances to phrases in Romany, *dukrà me,* "I foretell," or Welsh *Dewch
da mi,* "Come with (or to) me," or dog-Latin *Duc ad me,* "Lead him to
me," or simply "Duke damn me.")　**58 firstborn of Egypt** (In Exodus
12:28–33, the firstborn of Egypt are slain by the Lord as the enemies
of Moses and the Israelites, who, like the Duke and his followers, are
in exile.)　**59 banquet** wine and dessert after dinner. (This repast,
now prepared on stage, seemingly is to remain there during the short
following scene.)
**2.6. Location: The forest. The scene is continuous. By convention
we understand that Adam and Orlando are in a different part of the
forest and do not "see" the table remaining onstage.**

ORLANDO   Why, how now, Adam? No greater heart in
thee? Live a little, comfort a little, cheer thyself a little.   5
If this uncouth forest yield anything savage, I will   6
either be food for it or bring it for food to thee. Thy   7
conceit is nearer death than thy powers. For my sake   8
be comfortable; hold death awhile at the arm's end. I   9
will here be with thee presently, and if I bring thee not
something to eat, I will give thee leave to die; but if
thou diest before I come, thou art a mocker of my
labor. Well said! Thou look'st cheerly, and I'll be with   13
thee quickly. Yet thou liest in the bleak air. Come, I   14
will bear thee to some shelter; and thou shalt not die
for lack of a dinner, if there live anything in this desert.
[*He picks up Adam.*] Cheerly, good Adam!   *Exeunt.*

2.7

Enter Duke Senior and Lords, like outlaws.

DUKE SENIOR
I think he be transformed into a beast,
For I can nowhere find him like a man.
FIRST LORD
My lord, he is but even now gone hence.
Here was he merry, hearing of a song.
DUKE SENIOR
If he, compact of jars, grow musical,   5
We shall have shortly discord in the spheres.   6
Go seek him. Tell him I would speak with him.

Enter Jaques.

FIRST LORD
He saves my labor by his own approach.
DUKE SENIOR
Why, how now, monsieur, what a life is this,
That your poor friends must woo your company!
What, you look merrily.
JAQUES
A fool, a fool! I met a fool i'th' forest,
A motley fool. A miserable world!   13
As I do live by food, I met a fool,
Who laid him down and basked him in the sun,
And railed on Lady Fortune in good terms,
In good set terms, and yet a motley fool.   17
"Good morrow, Fool," quoth I. "No, sir," quoth he,
"Call me not fool till heaven hath sent me fortune."   19
And then he drew a dial from his poke   20
And, looking on it with lackluster eye,
Says very wisely, "It is ten o'clock.

Thus we may see," quoth he, "how the world wags.   23
'Tis but an hour ago since it was nine,
And after one hour more 'twill be eleven;
And so from hour to hour we ripe and ripe,
And then from hour to hour we rot and rot,
And thereby hangs a tale." When I did hear
The motley fool thus moral on the time,   29
My lungs began to crow like Chanticleer,   30
That fools should be so deep-contemplative,
And I did laugh sans intermission   32
An hour by his dial. Oh, noble fool!
A worthy fool! Motley's the only wear.   34
DUKE SENIOR   What fool is this?
JAQUES
Oh, worthy fool! One that hath been a courtier,
And says, if ladies be but young and fair,
They have the gift to know it. And in his brain,   38
Which is as dry as the remainder biscuit   39
After a voyage, he hath strange places crammed   40
With observation, the which he vents   41
In mangled forms. Oh, that I were a fool!
I am ambitious for a motley coat.
DUKE SENIOR
Thou shalt have one.
JAQUES   It is my only suit,   44
Provided that you weed your better judgments
Of all opinion that grows rank in them   46
That I am wise. I must have liberty
Withal, as large a charter as the wind,   48
To blow on whom I please, for so fools have.
And they that are most gallèd with my folly,   50
They most must laugh. And why, sir, must they so?
The "why" is plain as way to parish church:
He that a fool doth very wisely hit   53
Doth very foolishly, although he smart,   54
Not to seem senseless of the bob. If not,   55
The wise man's folly is anatomized   56
Even by the squand'ring glances of the fool.   57
Invest me in my motley; give me leave   58
To speak my mind, and I will through and through
Cleanse the foul body of th'infected world,   60
If they will patiently receive my medicine.
DUKE SENIOR
Fie on thee! I can tell what thou wouldst do.
JAQUES
What, for a counter, would I do but good?   63

---

5 comfort comfort yourself   **6 uncouth** strange, wild   **7–8 Thy conceit . . . powers** You imagine you are nearer death than you really are.
9 comfortable comforted   **13 Well said!** Well done!   **14 Yet** Still
2.7. Location: The forest; the scene is continuous. (A repast, set out
for the Duke in 2.5, has remained onstage during 2.6.)
5 compact of jars composed of discords   **6 the spheres** the concentric spheres of the old Ptolemaic solar system (which, by their movement, were thought to produce harmonious music)   **13 motley**
wearing motley, the parti-colored dress of the professional jester
17 set carefully composed   **19 Call . . . fortune** (An allusion to the
proverb "Fortune favors fools.")   **20 dial** pocket sundial or watch.
poke pouch or pocket

23 wags goes.   **29 moral** moralize   **30 crow** i.e., laugh merrily.
Chanticleer a rooster   **32 sans** without   **34 only wear** only thing
worth wearing.   **38 know it** i.e., put their beauty to advantage.
39 dry (According to Elizabethan physiology, a dry brain was marked
by a strong memory but a slowness of apprehension.)   **remainder**
left over   **40 places** (1) nooks and corners (2) rhetorical topics
41 vents utters   **44 suit** (1) request (2) suit of clothes   **46 rank** wildly,
coarsely   **48 Withal** in addition.   **charter** license, privilege   **50 gallèd** rubbed sore   **53–5 He . . . bob** He whom a fool wittily attacks
behaves very foolishly, no matter how much he feels the sting, unless
he pretends to be unaware of the taunt.   **55–7 If not . . . fool** Otherwise, the folly of even a wise person is dissected and laid open even
by the variously directed shots of wit made by the fool.   **58 Invest**
Array   **60 Cleanse** purge. (A medical metaphor.)   **63 counter**
(1) thing of no intrinsic value, a metal disk used in counting (2) parry

DUKE SENIOR
Most mischievous foul sin, in chiding sin.
For thou thyself hast been a libertine,
As sensual as the brutish sting itself; 66
And all th'embossèd sores and headed evils 67
That thou with license of free foot hast caught 68
Wouldst thou disgorge into the general world. 69
JAQUES   Why, who cries out on pride 70
That can therein tax any private party? 71
Doth it not flow as hugely as the sea, 72
Till that the weary very means do ebb? 73
What woman in the city do I name,
When that I say the city woman bears 75
The cost of princes on unworthy shoulders? 76
Who can come in and say that I mean her, 77
When such a one as she, such is her neighbor?
Or what is he of basest function 79
That says his bravery is not on my cost, 80
Thinking that I mean him, but therein suits 81
His folly to the mettle of my speech? 82
There then, how then? What then? Let me see
    wherein
My tongue hath wronged him. If it do him right, 84
Then he hath wronged himself. If he be free, 85
Why then my taxing like a wild goose flies, 86
Unclaimed of any man.—But who comes here? 87

Enter Orlando [with his sword drawn].

ORLANDO
Forbear, and eat no more!
JAQUES   Why, I have eat none yet. 88
ORLANDO
Nor shalt not, till necessity be served.
JAQUES
Of what kind should this cock come of? 90
DUKE SENIOR
Art thou thus boldened, man, by thy distress,
Or else a rude despiser of good manners,
That in civility thou seem'st so empty?
ORLANDO
You touched my vein at first. The thorny point 94
Of bare distress hath ta'en from me the show
Of smooth civility; yet am I inland bred 96

66 **brutish sting** carnal impulse   67 **th'embossèd** the swollen.
headed evils sores that have come to a head   68 **license . . . foot** the
licentious freedom of a libertine   69 **disgorge** vomit   70–1 **who . . .
party?** what true satirist inveighs against extravagance in dress with
only some private individual in mind?   72–3 **Doth . . . ebb?** Is not
pride as universal as the sea, overflowing everywhere until it finally
ebbs like the tide, having exhausted what it fed upon?   75–6 **when . . .
shoulders?** when I characterize the typical citizen's wife as dressing
herself in finery that is costly enough to adorn a prince?   77 **come in**
i.e., come into court as a complainant   79–82 **Or . . . speech?** Or who
is he of even the lowest social standing that does not object to my
saying that sartorial finery is a fit subject for my satirical spleen,
thinking I am satirizing him when his own folly shows how well he
fits the contents of my speech?   84–7 **If . . . man** If my satirical sketch
fits him, then he condemns himself by resembling my portrait of
folly. If he does not resemble my sketch, my criticism does him no
harm.   88 **have eat** have eaten. (Pronounced "et.")   90 **Of . . . of?**
What sort of fighting cock is this?   94 **You . . . first** Your first supposition is correct.   96 **inland bred** i.e., raised in the center of civilization rather than on the outskirts

And know some nurture. But forbear, I say. 97
He dies that touches any of this fruit
Till I and my affairs are answerèd. 99
JAQUES
An you will not be answered with reason, I must die. 100
DUKE SENIOR
What would you have? Your gentleness shall force
More than your force move us to gentleness.
ORLANDO
I almost die for food, and let me have it!
DUKE SENIOR
Sit down and feed, and welcome to our table.
ORLANDO
Speak you so gently? Pardon me, I pray you.
I thought that all things had been savage here,
And therefore put I on the countenance
Of stern commandment. But whate'er you are
That in this desert inaccessible,
Under the shade of melancholy boughs, 110
Lose and neglect the creeping hours of time;
If ever you have looked on better days,
If ever been where bells have knolled to church, 113
If ever sat at any good man's feast,
If ever from your eyelids wiped a tear
And know what 'tis to pity and be pitied,
Let gentleness my strong enforcement be,
In the which hope I blush and hide my sword.
                                    [He sheathes his sword.]
DUKE SENIOR
True is it that we have seen better days,
And have with holy bell been knolled to church,
And sat at good men's feasts, and wiped our eyes
Of drops that sacred pity hath engendered.
And therefore sit you down in gentleness,
And take upon command what help we have 124
That to your wanting may be ministered. 125
ORLANDO
Then but forbear your food a little while,
Whiles, like a doe, I go to find my fawn
And give it food. There is an old poor man
Who after me hath many a weary step
Limped in pure love. Till he be first sufficed,
Oppressed with two weak evils, age and hunger, 131
I will not touch a bit.
DUKE SENIOR   Go find him out,
And we will nothing waste till you return. 133
ORLANDO
I thank ye; and be blest for your good comfort!
                                    [Exit.]
DUKE SENIOR
Thou see'st we are not all alone unhappy.
This wide and universal theater
Presents more woeful pageants than the scene
Wherein we play in.
JAQUES   All the world's a stage,

97 **nurture** education, training.   99 **answerèd** satisfied.   100 **An** If.
reason (A pun on "raisin" plays upon *fruit* in line 98.)   110 **melancholy** dark, shadowy   113 **knolled** knelled, rung   124 **upon command** for the asking   125 **wanting** need   131 **weak evils** disabilities
causing weakness   133 **waste** consume

And all the men and women merely players.
They have their exits and their entrances,
And one man in his time plays many parts,
His acts being seven ages. At first the infant, 143
Mewling and puking in the nurse's arms.
Then the whining schoolboy, with his satchel
And shining morning face, creeping like snail
Unwillingly to school. And then the lover,
Sighing like furnace, with a woeful ballad
Made to his mistress' eyebrow. Then a soldier,
Full of strange oaths and bearded like the pard, 149
Jealous in honor, sudden, and quick in quarrel, 150
Seeking the bubble reputation
Even in the cannon's mouth. And then the justice,
In fair round belly with good capon lined, 153
With eyes severe and beard of formal cut,
Full of wise saws and modern instances; 155
And so he plays his part. The sixth age shifts
Into the lean and slippered pantaloon, 157
With spectacles on nose and pouch on side,
His youthful hose, well saved, a world too wide
For his shrunk shank; and his big manly voice, 160
Turning again toward childish treble, pipes
And whistles in his sound. Last scene of all, 162
That ends this strange, eventful history,
Is second childishness and mere oblivion, 164
Sans teeth, sans eyes, sans taste, sans everything. 165

Enter Orlando, with Adam.

DUKE SENIOR
Welcome. Set down your venerable burden
And let him feed.
ORLANDO   I thank you most for him.
                    [*He sets down Adam.*]
ADAM   So had you need.
I scarce can speak to thank you for myself.
DUKE SENIOR
Welcome. Fall to. I will not trouble you
As yet to question you about your fortunes.—
Give us some music, and, good cousin, sing. 173
                    [*They eat, while Orlando and Duke Senior
                                    converse apart.*]

                    Song.

AMIENS [*sings*]
            Blow, blow, thou winter wind.
            Thou art not so unkind
                    As man's ingratitude.
            Thy tooth is not so keen,
            Because thou art not seen,
                    Although thy breath be rude. 180

Heigh-ho, sing heigh-ho, unto the green holly. 181
Most friendship is feigning, most loving mere
        folly.
            Then heigh-ho, the holly!
                This life is most jolly.
        Freeze, freeze, thou bitter sky,
        That dost not bite so nigh 186
            As benefits forgot.
        Though thou the waters warp, 188
        Thy sting is not so sharp
            As friend remembered not.
Heigh-ho, sing heigh-ho, unto the green holly.
Most friendship is feigning, most loving mere
        folly.
            Then heigh-ho, the holly!
                This life is most jolly.

DUKE SENIOR [*to Orlando*]
If that you were the good Sir Rowland's son, 195
As you have whispered faithfully you were, 196
And as mine eye doth his effigies witness 197
Most truly limned and living in your face, 198
Be truly welcome hither. I am the Duke
That loved your father. The residue of your fortune, 200
Go to my cave and tell me.—Good old man,
Thou art right welcome as thy master is.—
Support him by the arm. Give me your hand,
And let me all your fortunes understand.   *Exeunt.* 204

                    ❧

3.1

Enter Duke [Frederick], Lords, and Oliver.

DUKE FREDERICK
Not see him since? Sir, sir, that cannot be. 1
But were I not the better part made mercy, 2
I should not seek an absent argument 3
Of my revenge, thou present. But look to it: 4
Find out thy brother, wheresoe'er he is.
Seek him with candle. Bring him dead or living 6
Within this twelvemonth, or turn thou no more 7
To seek a living in our territory.
Thy lands and all things that thou dost call thine
Worth seizure do we seize into our hands, 10
Till thou canst quit thee by thy brother's mouth 11
Of what we think against thee.

---

143 Mewling crying with a catlike noise   **149 bearded ... pard** having bristling mustaches like the leopard's   **150 Jealous in honor** quick to anger in matters of honor   **153 capon** rooster castrated to make the flesh more tender for eating (and often presented to judges as a bribe)   **155 saws** sayings.   **modern instances** commonplace illustrations   **157 pantaloon** ridiculous, enfeebled old man. (A stock type in Italian *commedia dell'arte*.)   **160 shank** calf   **162 his** its   **164 mere oblivion** total forgetfulness   **165 Sans** without   **173 cousin** (A term used by sovereigns to address their nobility.)   **180 rude** rough

181 holly (An emblem of Christmastime and holiday cheer, as in "the holly and the ivy.")   **186 nigh** deeply, near (to the heart)   **188 warp** freeze so that the surface of the ice cracks and forces up ridges   **195 If that** If   **196 faithfully** persuasively and honestly   **197 doth ... witness** witnesses the likeness of the dead Sir Rowland   **198 limned** painted   **200 The ... fortune** The rest of your adventure   **204 s.d. *Exeunt*** (The table must be removed at this point.)
3.1. Location: Duke Frederick's court.
1 Not ... since? i.e., You mean to tell me you claim not to have seen Orlando since the disappearance of Celia and Rosalind?   **2 were ... mercy** i.e., if I were not a merciful man. (Literally, if I were not composed mostly of mercy.)   **3–4 I ... present** i.e., I would seek revenge not on the absent Orlando, but on you, who are right here.   **6 Seek ... candle** i.e., Look for him everywhere, even in the darkest corners. (See Luke 15:8.)   **7 turn** return   **10 we ... our** (The royal plural.)   **11 quit ... mouth** acquit yourself by the direct testimony of Orlando. (The Duke suspects that Oliver has murdered Orlando.)

OLIVER
Oh, that Your Highness knew my heart in this!
I never loved my brother in my life.

DUKE FREDERICK
More villain thou.—Well, push him out of doors,
And let my officers of such a nature   16
Make an extent upon his house and lands.   17
Do this expediently, and turn him going.   *Exeunt.*   18

❖

3.2

Enter Orlando [with a paper].

ORLANDO
Hang there, my verse, in witness of my love;
    And thou, thrice-crownèd queen of night, survey   2
With thy chaste eye, from thy pale sphere above,
    Thy huntress' name that my full life doth sway.   4
O Rosalind! These trees shall be my books,
    And in their barks my thoughts I'll character,   6
That every eye which in this forest looks
    Shall see thy virtue witnessed everywhere.
Run, run, Orlando, carve on every tree
The fair, the chaste, and unexpressive she.   *Exit.* 10

Enter Corin and [Touchstone the] Clown.

CORIN   And how like you this shepherd's life, Master
Touchstone?

TOUCHSTONE   Truly, shepherd, in respect of itself, it is a   13
good life; but in respect that it is a shepherd's life, it is
naught. In respect that it is solitary, I like it very well;   15
but in respect that it is private, it is a very vile life.
Now in respect it is in the fields, it pleaseth me well;
but in respect it is not in the court, it is tedious. As it
is a spare life, look you, it fits my humor well; but as   19
there is no more plenty in it, it goes much against my
stomach. Hast any philosophy in thee, shepherd?

CORIN   No more but that I know the more one sickens
the worse at ease he is; and that he that wants money,   23
means, and content is without three good friends; that
the property of rain is to wet and fire to burn; that
good pasture makes fat sheep and that a great cause
of the night is lack of the sun; that he that hath learned
no wit by nature nor art may complain of good   28
breeding or comes of a very dull kindred.

TOUCHSTONE   Such a one is a natural philosopher.
Wast ever in court, shepherd?

CORIN   No, truly.

TOUCHSTONE   Then thou art damned.

CORIN   Nay, I hope.   34

TOUCHSTONE   Truly, thou art damned, like an ill-
roasted egg, all on one side.

CORIN   For not being at court? Your reason.

TOUCHSTONE   Why, if thou never wast at court, thou
never saw'st good manners; if thou never saw'st good   39
manners, then thy manners must be wicked; and   40
wickedness is sin, and sin is damnation. Thou art in
a parlous state, shepherd.   42

CORIN   Not a whit, Touchstone. Those that are good
manners at the court are as ridiculous in the country as
the behavior of the country is most mockable at the
court. You told me you salute not at the court but you   46
kiss your hands; that courtesy would be uncleanly, if   47
courtiers were shepherds.

TOUCHSTONE   Instance, briefly; come, instance.   49

CORIN   Why, we are still handling our ewes, and their   50
fells you know are greasy.   51

TOUCHSTONE   Why, do not your courtier's hands sweat?   52
And is not the grease of a mutton as wholesome as the   53
sweat of a man? Shallow, shallow. A better instance, I   54
say. Come.

CORIN   Besides, our hands are hard.

TOUCHSTONE   Your lips will feel them the sooner.
Shallow again. A more sounder instance. Come.

CORIN   And they are often tarred over with the surgery   59
of our sheep; and would you have us kiss tar? The
courtier's hands are perfumed with civet.   61

TOUCHSTONE   Most shallow man! Thou worms' meat, in   62
respect of a good piece of flesh indeed! Learn of the   63
wise, and perpend: civet is of a baser birth than tar,   64
the very uncleanly flux of a cat. Mend the instance,   65
shepherd.

CORIN   You have too courtly a wit for me. I'll rest.

TOUCHSTONE   Wilt thou rest damned? God help thee,
shallow man! God make incision in thee! Thou art   69
raw.   70

CORIN   Sir, I am a true laborer: I earn that I eat, get that   71
I wear, owe no man hate, envy no man's happiness,
glad of other men's good, content with my harm, and   73
the greatest of my pride is to see my ewes graze and
my lambs suck.

TOUCHSTONE   That is another simple sin in you, to bring   76
the ewes and the rams together and to offer to get your   77

---

34 hope i.e., hope not.   **39 manners** etiquette   **40 manners** morals
42 parlous perilous   **46 salute** greet   **46–7 but . . . hands** without
kissing the other person's hands   **49 Instance** Proof   **50 still** constantly   **51 fells** skins with the wool, or fleeces   **52 your courtier's**
your typical courtier's   **53–4 And . . . man?** (Human sweat was
thought to be fat oozing from the pores.)   **59 tarred over** anointed
with tar on their cuts and sores   **61 civet** a musky perfume derived
from glands in the anal pouch of the civet cat. (As Touchstone points
out.)   **62–3 Thou . . . indeed!** You miserable creature (literally, you
food for worms, subject to the decay of death), if we compare you
with any worthy sample of humankind!   **64 perpend** consider
65 flux secretion.   **Mend** Improve   **69 incision** a cut, perhaps for the
purpose of letting blood (here, to let out folly); or for seasoning as
raw meat is scored and salted before cooking   **70 raw** (1) wet behind
the ears (2) uncooked (3) afflicted with a raw wound.   **71 earn . . . eat**
earn my living   **73 content . . . harm** patient with my ill fortune
76 simple sin sin arising from simplicity   **77 offer** undertake

---

16 of such a nature who attend to such duties   **17 extent** writ of
seizure   **18 expediently** expeditiously.   **turn him going** send him
packing.
3.2. Location: The forest.
2 thrice-crownèd . . . night i.e., Diana in the three aspects of her
divinity: as Luna or Cynthia, goddess of the moon; as Diana, goddess
on earth; and as Hecate or Proserpina, goddess in the lower world
4 Thy huntress' i.e., Rosalind's, who is here thought of as accompanying Diana, patroness of the hunt and of chastity.   **sway** control.
6 character inscribe   **10 unexpressive** inexpressible   **13 in respect of
itself** considered in and for itself   **15 naught** vile, of no social consequence.   **19 spare** frugal.   **humor** temperament   **23 wants** lacks
28 wit wisdom.   **art** study.   **complain of** lament the lack of

living by the copulation of cattle; to be bawd to a bell- 78
wether, and to betray a she-lamb of a twelvemonth to 79
a crooked-pated old cuckoldly ram, out of all reasonable 80
match. If thou be'st not damned for this, the devil him- 81
self will have no shepherds; I cannot see else how thou 82
shouldst scape. 83

CORIN   Here comes young Master Ganymede, my new
mistress's brother.

Enter Rosalind [with a paper, reading].

ROSALIND
    "From the east to western Ind, 86
    No jewel is like Rosalind.
    Her worth, being mounted on the wind,
    Through all the world bears Rosalind.
    All the pictures fairest lined 90
    Are but black to Rosalind. 91
    Let no face be kept in mind
    But the fair of Rosalind." 93

TOUCHSTONE   I'll rhyme you so eight years together, 94
dinners and suppers and sleeping hours excepted. It 95
is the right butter-women's rank to market. 96

ROSALIND   Out, fool! 97

TOUCHSTONE   For a taste:
    If a hart do lack a hind,
    Let him seek out Rosalind. 99
    If the cat will after kind,
    So, be sure, will Rosalind. 101
    Wintered garments must be lined,
    So must slender Rosalind. 103
    They that reap must sheaf and bind; 105
    Then to cart with Rosalind. 106
    Sweetest nut hath sourest rind;
    Such a nut is Rosalind.
    He that sweetest rose will find
    Must find love's prick and Rosalind. 110

This is the very false gallop of verses. Why do you 111
infect yourself with them?

ROSALIND   Peace, you dull fool! I found them on a tree.

TOUCHSTONE   Truly, the tree yields bad fruit.

ROSALIND   I'll graft it with you, and then I shall graft it 115
with a medlar. Then it will be the earliest fruit i'th' 116
country; for you'll be rotten ere you be half ripe, and
that's the right virtue of the medlar. 118

TOUCHSTONE   You have said; but whether wisely or no,
let the forest judge.

Enter Celia, with a writing.

ROSALIND   Peace! Here comes my sister, reading. Stand
aside.

CELIA [*reads*]
    "Why should this a desert be?
      For it is unpeopled? No. 124
    Tongues I'll hang on every tree,
      That shall civil sayings show: 126
    Some, how brief the life of man
      Runs his erring pilgrimage, 128
    That the stretching of a span 129
      Buckles in his sum of age; 130
    Some, of violated vows
      Twixt the souls of friend and friend;
    But upon the fairest boughs,
      Or at every sentence end,
    Will I 'Rosalinda' write,
      Teaching all that read to know
    The quintessence of every sprite 137
      Heaven would in little show. 138
    Therefore heaven Nature charged 139
      That one body should be filled
    With all graces wide-enlarged. 141
      Nature presently distilled
    Helen's cheek, but not her heart, 143
      Cleopatra's majesty,
    Atalanta's better part, 145
      Sad Lucretia's modesty. 146
    Thus Rosalind of many parts
      By heavenly synod was devised 148
    Of many faces, eyes, and hearts
      To have the touches dearest prized. 150
    Heaven would that she these gifts should have, 151
    And I to live and die her slave." 152

---

78 cattle livestock   **78–9 bellwether** the leading male sheep of a flock, wearing a bell   **80 crooked-pated** with crooked horns. **cuckoldly** i.e., horned like a cuckold (husband of an unfaithful wife). **out of** contrary to   **81–2 If . . . shepherds** i.e., Your only possible escape from damnation would be if the devil should find shepherds too objectionable to have in hell under any circumstances   **83 scape** escape.   **86 Ind** Indies   **90 lined** drawn   **91 black to** dark-complectioned and hence ugly compared to   **93 fair** beauty   **94 together** without stop   **95–6 It is . . . market** i.e., The rhymes, all alike, follow each other precisely like a line of butter women or dairy women jogging along to market.   **97 Out** (An exclamation here denoting comic indignation.)   **99 If . . . hind** If a male deer longs for a female deer. (Touchstone wryly suggests in his verses that Rosalind is the responsive object of male desire.)   **101 after kind** follow its natural instinct   **103 Wintered** Old, worn; used in winter.   **lined** (1) given a winter lining (2) stuffed. (The term was sometimes used for the copulating of dogs.)   **105 sheaf and bind** tie in a bundle   **106 to cart** (1) onto the harvest cart (2) onto the cart used to carry prostitutes through the streets, exposing them to public ridicule   **110 prick** thorn. (With bawdy suggestion.)   **111 false gallop** canter

115 you (With a pun on "yew.")   **116 medlar** a fruit like a small brown-skinned apple that is eaten when it starts to decay. (With a pun on "meddler.")   **118 right virtue** true quality   **124 For** Because   **126 civil sayings** maxims of civilized life   **128 his erring** its wandering   **129–30 That . . . age** i.e., so that a very brief span encompasses his whole life. (A *span* is a handbreadth. See Psalm 39:5.)   **137 quintessence** highest perfection. (Literally, the fifth essence or element of the medieval alchemists, purer even than fire.)   **sprite** spirit **138 Heaven . . . show** that heaven wishes to show in one small person, Rosalind (who, in microcosm, embodies the supreme essence of the heavens, or macrocosm).   **139 heaven . . . charged** heaven commanded Nature   **141 wide-enlarged** all-encompassing.   **143 Helen's . . . heart** i.e., the beauty of Helen of Troy but not her false heart **145 Atalanta's better part** i.e., her beauty or her fleetness of foot, not her scornfulness and greed. (She refused to marry any man who was unable to defeat her in a foot race and, when challenged by Hippomenes, lost to him because Hippomenes dropped in her way three golden apples of the Hesperides.)   **146 Lucretia** an honorable Roman lady raped by Tarquin (whose story Shakespeare tells in *The Rape of Lucrece*).   **148 synod** assembly   **150 touches** traits   **151 would** decree   **152 And I to** and that I should

ROSALIND   Oh, most gentle Jupiter, what tedious homily 153
of love have you wearied your parishioners withal,
and never cried, "Have patience, good people!"

CELIA   How now? Back, friends. Shepherd, go off a 156
little. [*To Touchstone*] Go with him, sirrah. 157

TOUCHSTONE   Come, shepherd, let us make an honorable retreat, though not with bag and baggage, yet 159
with scrip and scrippage.   *Exit* [*with Corin*]. 160

CELIA   Didst thou hear these verses?

ROSALIND   Oh, yes, I heard them all, and more, too, for
some of them had in them more feet than the verses
would bear.

CELIA   That's no matter. The feet might bear the verses.

ROSALIND   Ay, but the feet were lame and could not
bear themselves without the verse and therefore stood 167
lamely in the verse.

CELIA   But didst thou hear without wondering how thy
name should be hanged and carved upon these trees?

ROSALIND   I was seven of the nine days out of the 171
wonder before you came; for look here what I found 172
on a palm tree. I was never so berhymed since
Pythagoras' time, that I was an Irish rat, which I can 174
hardly remember.

CELIA   Trow you who hath done this? 176

ROSALIND   Is it a man?

CELIA   And a chain that you once wore about his neck. 178
Change you color?

ROSALIND   I prithee, who?

CELIA   Oh, Lord, Lord, it is a hard matter for friends to 181
meet; but mountains may be removed with earth- 182
quakes and so encounter. 183

ROSALIND   Nay, but who is it?

CELIA   Is it possible? 185

ROSALIND   Nay, I prithee now with most petitionary
vehemence, tell me who it is.

CELIA   Oh, wonderful, wonderful, and most wonderful,
wonderful! And yet again wonderful, and after that,
out of all whooping! 190

ROSALIND   Good my complexion! Dost thou think, 191
though I am caparisoned like a man, I have a doublet 192
and hose in my disposition? One inch of delay more 193
is a South Sea of discovery. I prithee, tell me who is it 194
quickly, and speak apace. I would thou couldst stam-

mer, that thou mightst pour this concealed man out of
thy mouth as wine comes out of a narrow-mouthed
bottle, either too much at once or none at all. I prithee,
take the cork out of thy mouth that I may drink thy
tidings.

CELIA   So you may put a man in your belly. 201

ROSALIND   Is he of God's making? What manner of 202
man? Is his head worth a hat, or his chin worth a
beard?

CELIA   Nay, he hath but a little beard.

ROSALIND   Why, God will send more, if the man will be
thankful. Let me stay the growth of his beard, if thou 207
delay me not the knowledge of his chin.

CELIA   It is young Orlando, that tripped up the wrestler's heels and your heart both in an instant.

ROSALIND   Nay, but the devil take mocking. Speak sad 211
brow and true maid. 212

CELIA   I'faith, coz, 'tis he.

ROSALIND   Orlando?

CELIA   Orlando.

ROSALIND   Alas the day, what shall I do with my
doublet and hose? What did he when thou saw'st him?
What said he? How looked he? Wherein went he? 218
What makes he here? Did he ask for me? Where 219
remains he? How parted he with thee? And when 220
shalt thou see him again? Answer me in one word.

CELIA   You must borrow me Gargantua's mouth first; 222
'tis a word too great for any mouth of this age's size.
To say ay and no to these particulars is more than to 224
answer in a catechism. 225

ROSALIND   But doth he know that I am in this forest
and in man's apparel? Looks he as freshly as he did
the day he wrestled?

CELIA   It is as easy to count atomies as to resolve the 229
propositions of a lover. But take a taste of my finding 230
him, and relish it with good observance. I found him 231
under a tree, like a dropped acorn.

ROSALIND   It may well be called Jove's tree, when it 233
drops forth such fruit.

CELIA   Give me audience, good madam. 235

ROSALIND   Proceed.

CELIA   There lay he, stretched along, like a wounded
knight.

ROSALIND   Though it be pity to see such a sight, it well
becomes the ground. 240

CELIA   Cry "holla" to thy tongue, I prithee; it curvets 241
unseasonably. He was furnished like a hunter. 242

---

153 Jupiter (Often emended to "pulpiter.")   **156 Back** i.e., Move back,
away. (Addressed to Corin and Touchstone.)   **157 sirrah** a form of
address to inferiors (here, Touchstone).   **159 bag and baggage** i.e.,
equipment appropriate to a retreating army   **160 scrip and scrippage**
shepherd's pouch and its contents.   **167 without** (1) without the help
of (2) outside   **171–2 seven . . . wonder** (A reference to the common
phrase "a nine days' wonder.")   **174 Pythagoras** Greek philosopher
credited with the doctrine of the transmigration of souls.   **that** when.
Irish rat (Refers to a current belief that Irish enchanters could rhyme
rats and other animals to death.)   **which** a thing which   **176 Trow
you** Have you any idea   **178 And a chain** And with a chain   **181–3 it
is . . . encounter** (A playful inversion of the proverb, "Friends may
meet, but mountains never greet." Celia appears to be teasing Rosalind's eagerness to meet Orlando.)   **removed with** moved by
185 possible i.e., possible you don't know   **190 out . . . whooping**
beyond all power to utter.   **191 Good my complexion!** Oh, my (feminine) temperament, my woman's curiosity!   **192 caparisoned**
bedecked. (Usually said of a horse.)   **192–3 I have . . . disposition?**
i.e., that I have a man's patience?   **194 a South Sea of discovery** i.e.,
as tedious as a long exploratory voyage to the South Pacific Ocean.

201 belly (1) stomach (2) womb.   **202 of God's making** i.e., a real
man, not of a tailor's making.   **207 stay** wait for   **211–12 sad . . .
maid** i.e., seriously and truthfully.   **218 Wherein went he?** In what
clothes was he dressed?   **219 makes** does   **220 remains** dwells
222 Gargantua's mouth (Gargantua is the giant of popular literature
who, in Rabelais' novel, swallowed five pilgrims in a salad.)
224–5 To . . . catechism To give even yes and no answers to these
questions would take longer than to go through the catechism (i.e.,
the formal questioning used in the Church to teach the principles of
faith).   **229 atomies** motes, specks of dirt   **230 propositions** questions   **231 relish it** heighten its pleasant taste.   **observance** attention.   **233 Jove's tree** the oak   **235 Give me audience** Listen to me
240 becomes adorns   **241 holla** stop.   **curvets** prances   **242 furnished** equipped, dressed

ROSALIND   Oh, ominous! He comes to kill my heart.   243

CELIA   I would sing my song without a burden. Thou 244
bring'st me out of tune.   245

ROSALIND   Do you not know I am a woman? When I
think, I must speak. Sweet, say on.

Enter Orlando and Jaques.

CELIA   You bring me out.—Soft, comes he not here?   248

ROSALIND   'Tis he. Slink by, and note him.
[*They stand aside and listen.*]

JAQUES   [*to Orlando*]   I thank you for your company,
but, good faith, I had as lief have been myself alone.

ORLANDO   And so had I; but yet, for fashion sake, I 252
thank you too for your society.

JAQUES   God b'wi'you. Let's meet as little as we can.   254

ORLANDO   I do desire we may be better strangers.

JAQUES   I pray you, mar no more trees with writing
love songs in their barks.

ORLANDO   I pray you, mar no more of my verses with
reading them ill-favoredly.   259

JAQUES   Rosalind is your love's name?

ORLANDO   Yes, just.   261

JAQUES   I do not like her name.

ORLANDO   There was no thought of pleasing you when
she was christened.

JAQUES   What stature is she of?

ORLANDO   Just as high as my heart.

JAQUES   You are full of pretty answers. Have you not
been acquainted with goldsmiths' wives, and conned 268
them out of rings?   269

ORLANDO   Not so; but I answer you right painted cloth, 270
from whence you have studied your questions.

JAQUES   You have a nimble wit; I think 'twas made of
Atalanta's heels. Will you sit down with me? And we 273
two will rail against our mistress the world and all our
misery.

ORLANDO   I will chide no breather in the world but 276
myself, against whom I know most faults.

JAQUES   The worst fault you have is to be in love.

ORLANDO   'Tis a fault I will not change for your best
virtue. I am weary of you.

JAQUES   By my troth, I was seeking for a fool when I
found you.

ORLANDO   He is drowned in the brook. Look but in,
and you shall see him.

JAQUES   There I shall see mine own figure.   285

ORLANDO   Which I take to be either a fool or a cipher.   286

JAQUES   I'll tarry no longer with you. Farewell, good
Seigneur Love.

ORLANDO   I am glad of your departure. Adieu, good
Monsieur Melancholy.   [*Exit Jaques.*]

ROSALIND   [*aside to Celia*]   I will speak to him like a
saucy lackey and under that habit play the knave 292
with him.—Do you hear, forester?

ORLANDO   Very well. What would you?

ROSALIND   I pray you, what is't o'clock?

ORLANDO   You should ask me what time o' day.
There's no clock in the forest.

ROSALIND   Then there is no true lover in the forest, else
sighing every minute and groaning every hour would
detect the lazy foot of Time as well as a clock.   300

ORLANDO   And why not the swift foot of Time? Had
not that been as proper?

ROSALIND   By no means, sir. Time travels in divers
paces with divers persons. I'll tell you who Time
ambles withal, who Time trots withal, who Time 305
gallops withal, and who he stands still withal.

ORLANDO   I prithee, who doth he trot withal?

ROSALIND   Marry, he trots hard with a young maid
between the contract of her marriage and the day it is
solemnized. If the interim be but a se'nnight, Time's 310
pace is so hard that it seems the length of seven year.

ORLANDO   Who ambles Time withal?

ROSALIND   With a priest that lacks Latin and a rich man
that hath not the gout, for the one sleeps easily
because he cannot study and the other lives merrily
because he feels no pain, the one lacking the burden of
lean and wasteful learning, the other knowing no 317
burden of heavy tedious penury. These Time ambles
withal.

ORLANDO   Who doth he gallop withal?

ROSALIND   With a thief to the gallows, for though he go
as softly as foot can fall, he thinks himself too soon
there.

ORLANDO   Who stays it still withal?

ROSALIND   With lawyers in the vacation; for they sleep
between term and term, and then they perceive not 326
how Time moves.

ORLANDO   Where dwell you, pretty youth?

ROSALIND   With this shepherdess, my sister, here in the
skirts of the forest, like fringe upon a petticoat.

ORLANDO   Are you native of this place?

ROSALIND   As the coney that you see dwell where she is 332
kindled.   333

ORLANDO   Your accent is something finer than you 334
could purchase in so removed a dwelling.   334

ROSALIND   I have been told so of many. But indeed an
old religious uncle of mine taught me to speak, who 337
was in his youth an inland man, one that knew 338
courtship too well, for there he fell in love. I have 339

---

243 **heart** (With pun on "hart.")   244 **burden** refrain, or bass part.
244–5 **Thou bring'st** You put   248 **Soft** i.e., Wait a minute, or, stop
talking   252 **fashion** fashion's   254 **God b'wi'you** God be with you,
good-bye   259 **ill-favoredly** unsympathetically.   261 **just** just so.
268 **conned** memorized   269 **rings** (Verses or "posies" were often
inscribed in rings.)   270 **right painted cloth** in the true spirit of a
painted cloth decorated with commonplace pictures and cliché mot-
toes (frequently mythological or scriptural)   273 **Atalanta's heels**
(See above, the note for line 145.)   276 **breather** living being
285 **figure** reflection. (Narcissus fell in love with his own reflection in
a pool.)   286 **cipher** nonentity, zero.

292 **and under . . . knave** and in that disguise (1) pose as a boy
(2) deal mischievously   300 **detect** reveal   305 **withal** with
310 **se'nnight** week   317 **lean** unremunerative.   **wasteful** making
one waste away   326 **term** court session   332 **coney** rabbit   333 **kindled** littered, born.   334 **something** somewhat   335 **purchase**
acquire.   **removed** remote   337 **religious** i.e., belonging to a religious order   338 **inland** from a center of civilization   339 **courtship**
(1) wooing (2) knowledge of courtly manners

heard him read many lectures against it, and I thank 340
God I am not a woman, to be touched with so many 341
giddy offences as he hath generally taxed their whole
sex withal.

ORLANDO   Can you remember any of the principal evils
that he laid to the charge of women?

ROSALIND   There were none principal; they were all like
one another as halfpence are, every one fault seeming
monstrous till his fellow fault came to match it.   348

ORLANDO   I prithee, recount some of them.

ROSALIND   No, I will not cast away my physic but on 350
those that are sick. There is a man haunts the forest
that abuses our young plants with carving "Rosalind"
on their barks, hangs odes upon hawthorns and
elegies on brambles, all, forsooth, deifying the name of
Rosalind. If I could meet that fancy-monger, I would 355
give him some good counsel, for he seems to have the
quotidian of love upon him.   357

ORLANDO   I am he that is so love-shaked. I pray you,
tell me your remedy.

ROSALIND   There is none of my uncle's marks upon you.
He taught me how to know a man in love, in which
cage of rushes I am sure you are not prisoner.   362

ORLANDO   What were his marks?

ROSALIND   A lean cheek, which you have not; a blue eye 364
and sunken, which you have not; an unquestionable 365
spirit, which you have not; a beard neglected, which
you have not—but I pardon you for that, for simply 367
your having in beard is a younger brother's revenue. 368
Then your hose should be ungartered, your bonnet un- 369
banded, your sleeve unbuttoned, your shoe untied, 370
and everything about you demonstrating a careless
desolation. But you are no such man. You are rather
point-device in your accoutrements, as loving your- 373
self, than seeming the lover of any other.

ORLANDO   Fair youth, I would I could make thee believe
I love.

ROSALIND   Me believe it? You may as soon make her
that you love believe it, which I warrant she is apter to
do than to confess she does. That is one of the points
in the which women still give the lie to their con- 380
sciences. But in good sooth, are you he that hangs the 381
verses on the trees, wherein Rosalind is so
admired?

ORLANDO   I swear to thee, youth, by the white hand of
Rosalind, I am that he, that unfortunate he.

ROSALIND   But are you so much in love as your rhymes
speak?

ORLANDO   Neither rhyme nor reason can express how
much.

ROSALIND   Love is merely a madness and, I tell you, 390
deserves as well a dark house and a whip as madmen 391
do; and the reason why they are not so punished and
cured is that the lunacy is so ordinary that the
whippers are in love too. Yet I profess curing it by 394
counsel.

ORLANDO   Did you ever cure any so?

ROSALIND   Yes, one, and in this manner. He was to
imagine me his love, his mistress; and I set him every
day to woo me. At which time would I, being but a
moonish youth, grieve, be effeminate, changeable, 399
longing and liking, proud, fantastical, apish, shallow,
inconstant, full of tears, full of smiles; for every passion
something and for no passion truly anything, as boys
and women are for the most part cattle of this color;
would now like him, now loathe him; then entertain 404
him, then forswear him; now weep for him, then spit
at him; that I drave my suitor from his mad humor of 406
love to a living humor of madness, which was to for- 407
swear the full stream of the world and to live in a nook
merely monastic. And thus I cured him; and this way 409
will I take upon me to wash your liver as clean as a 410
sound sheep's heart, that there shall not be one spot of
love in't.

ORLANDO   I would not be cured, youth.

ROSALIND   I would cure you, if you would but call me
Rosalind and come every day to my cote and woo me. 415

ORLANDO   Now by the faith of my love, I will. Tell me
where it is.

ROSALIND   Go with me to it, and I'll show it you; and
by the way you shall tell me where in the forest you 419
live. Will you go?

ORLANDO   With all my heart, good youth.

ROSALIND   Nay, you must call me Rosalind.—Come,
sister, will you go?   *Exeunt.*

❖

3.3

*Enter [Touchstone the] Clown, Audrey; and Jaques
[apart].*

TOUCHSTONE   Come apace, good Audrey. I will fetch up 1
your goats, Audrey. And how, Audrey, am I the man 2
yet? Doth my simple feature content you?   3

AUDREY   Your features, Lord warrant us! What features? 4

TOUCHSTONE   I am here with thee and thy goats, as the
most capricious poet, honest Ovid, was among the 6
Goths.   7

---

340 **read many lectures** deliver many admonitory speeches
341 **touched** tainted   348 **his** its   350 **physic** medicine   355 **fancy-
monger** love peddler   357 **quotidian** fever recurring daily. (See *love-
shaked,* line 358).   362 **cage of rushes** i.e., flimsy prison   364 **blue eye**
i.e., having dark circles   365 **unquestionable** unwilling to be conversed with   367–8 **simply . . . revenue** what beard you have is like a
younger brother's inheritance (i.e., small)   369–70 **bonnet unbanded**
hat lacking a band around the crown   373 **point-device** faultless
380 **still** continually   381 **good sooth** honest truth

390 **merely** utterly   391 **dark . . . whip** (The common treatment of
lunatics.)   394 **profess** am expert in   399 **moonish** changeable
404 **entertain** receive cordially   406 **that** with the result that.   **drave**
drove   406–7 **mad . . . madness** mad fancy of love to a real madness
409 **merely** utterly   410 **liver** (Supposed seat of the emotions, especially love.)   415 **cote** cottage   419 **by** on
3.3 Location: The forest.
1 **apace** quickly   2 **And how** i.e., What do you say   3 **simple feature**
plain appearance. (But Audrey, in her answer, may have her mind on
features as "parts of the body.")   4 **warrant** protect   6 **capricious**
witty, fanciful. (Derived from the Latin *caper,* "male goat"; hence,
"goatish, lascivious.")   7 **Goths** (With pun on "goats"; the two words
were pronounced alike.)

JAQUES [*aside*]   Oh, knowledge ill-inhabited, worse than Jove in a thatched house!   8 / 9

TOUCHSTONE   When a man's verses cannot be understood, nor a man's good wit seconded with the forward child, understanding, it strikes a man more dead than a great reckoning in a little room. Truly, I would the gods had made thee poetical.   10–13

AUDREY   I do not know what "poetical" is. Is it honest in deed and word? Is it a true thing?

TOUCHSTONE   No, truly; for the truest poetry is the most feigning, and lovers are given to poetry, and what they swear in poetry may be said as lovers they do feign.   18–20

AUDREY   Do you wish then that the gods had made me poetical?

TOUCHSTONE   I do, truly; for thou swear'st to me thou art honest. Now, if thou wert a poet, I might have some hope thou didst feign.   24 / 25

AUDREY   Would you not have me honest?

TOUCHSTONE   No, truly, unless thou wert hard-favored; for honesty coupled to beauty is to have honey a sauce to sugar.   27 / 28

JAQUES [*aside*]   A material fool!   30

AUDREY   Well, I am not fair, and therefore I pray the gods make me honest.

TOUCHSTONE   Truly, and to cast away honesty upon a foul slut were to put good meat into an unclean dish.   34

AUDREY   I am not a slut, though I thank the gods I am foul.   35 / 36

TOUCHSTONE   Well, praised be the gods for thy foulness! Sluttishness may come hereafter. But be it as it may be, I will marry thee, and to that end I have been with Sir Oliver Mar-text, the vicar of the next village, who hath promised to meet me in this place of the forest and to couple us.   40

JAQUES [*aside*]   I would fain see this meeting.   43

AUDREY   Well, the gods give us joy!

TOUCHSTONE   Amen. A man may, if he were of a fearful heart, stagger in this attempt; for here we have no temple but the wood, no assembly but horn-beasts.   46 / 47

But what though? Courage! As horns are odious, they are necessary. It is said, "Many a man knows no end of his goods." Right! Many a man has good horns and knows no end of them. Well, that is the dowry of his wife; 'tis none of his own getting. Horns? Even so. Poor men alone? No, no, the noblest deer hath them as huge as the rascal. Is the single man therefore blessed? No. As a walled town is more worthier than a village, so is the forehead of a married man more honorable than the bare brow of a bachelor; and by how much defense is better than no skill, by so much is a horn more precious than to want.   48–59

Enter Sir Oliver Mar-text.

Here comes Sir Oliver.—Sir Oliver Mar-text, you are well met. Will you dispatch us here under this tree, or shall we go with you to your chapel?   61

SIR OLIVER   Is there none here to give the woman?   63

TOUCHSTONE   I will not take her on gift of any man.

SIR OLIVER   Truly, she must be given, or the marriage is not lawful.

JAQUES [*advancing*]   Proceed, proceed. I'll give her.

TOUCHSTONE   Good even, good Master What-ye-call-'t. How do you, sir? You are very well met. God 'ild you for your last company. I am very glad to see you. Even a toy in hand here, sir.—Nay, pray be covered.   68–71

JAQUES   Will you be married, motley?

TOUCHSTONE   As the ox hath his bow, sir, the horse his curb, and the falcon her bells, so man hath his desires; and as pigeons bill, so wedlock would be nibbling.   73–75

JAQUES   And will you, being a man of your breeding, be married under a bush like a beggar? Get you to church, and have a good priest that can tell you what marriage is. This fellow will but join you together as they join wainscot; then one of you will prove a shrunk panel and, like green timber, warp, warp.   77–81

---

8 ill-inhabited ill-lodged   **9 Jove . . . house!** (An allusion to Ovid's *Metamorphoses* 8, containing the story of Jupiter and Mercury lodging disguised in the humble cottage of Baucis and Philemon.) **10–11 verses . . . understood** (Ovid's verses were misunderstood by the barbaric Goths, among whom he lived in exile, just as Touchstone's wit is misunderstood by Audrey.)   **11–12 nor . . . understanding** (Wisdom, understanding, and memory were thought to occupy three main ventricles in the brain, and to be interconnected in the process of thought. *Forward* means "precocious.")   **13 great . . . room** exorbitant charge for refreshment or lodging in a cramped tavern room. (Some scholars see in this passage an allusion to the death of Christopher Marlowe, who was stabbed by Ingram Frysar at an inn in Deptford in a quarrel over a tavern reckoning, May 30, 1593.) **18 feigning** inventive, imaginative. (But Touchstone plays on the sense of "false, lying.")   **19 may be said** i.e., it may be said   **20 feign** (With a further play on "desire.")   **24 honest** chaste.   **25 feign** (1) pretend (2) desire.   **27–8 hard-favored** ugly   **28 honesty** chastity   **30 material** full of pithy matter   **34 foul** ugly   **35–6 I thank . . . foul** i.e., my unattractive looks are what destiny has allotted to me. **40 Sir** (Courtesy title for a clergyman.)   **43 fain** gladly   **46 stagger** hesitate   **47 horn-beasts** antlered animals like deer and cattle, and therefore resembling cuckolded men with their cuckolds' horns.

48 what though what though it be so.   **As** Though   **49 necessary** (1) useful to horned animals (2) unavoidable to cuckolds. **49–50 knows . . . goods** is endlessly well provided.   **51 knows . . . them** i.e., is endlessly supplied with cuckold's horns. (A sardonic interpretation of the proverb in lines 49–50.)   **dowry** marriage gift **52 getting** (1) obtaining (2) begetting (in the sense that his wife's children will not be his).   **Even so** That's just how it is.   **53 deer** (1) horned animal (2) dear husband   **54 rascal** (1) young deer that are lean and out of season (2) poor ordinary husband.   **single** unmarried **58 defense** (1) fortifications (including a type known as "hornwork") (2) the art of self-defense   **59 than to want** i.e., than to be without a horn. (Recalling the "horn of plenty," which is indeed precious.) **61 dispatch us** finish off our business   **63 give the woman** give away the bride; conventionally, the bride's father answered the question, "Who giveth this woman to be married to this man?"   **68 What-ye-call-'t** (Probably joking on *Jakes* as "outhouse.")   **69 'ild you** yield you, reward you   **70 last** most recent   **71 a toy in hand** a trifle to be attended to, or literally by the hand.   **be covered** put on your hat, i.e., no need to show respect; or, cover up your bosom. (Said to Audrey, or perhaps to Jaques, who may have removed his hat in sardonic deference to the ceremony.)   **73 bow** yoke   **74 curb** chain or strap attached to the horse's bit and used to control it.   **bells** (Attached to a falcon's leg during training.)   **75 bill** stroke bill with bill   **77 under a bush** i.e., by a "hedge-priest," an uneducated clergyman   **78–9 tell . . . is** expound the obligations of marriage   **81 warp** (1) shrivel and fit badly together (2) stray from the true path.

TOUCHSTONE   I am not in the mind but I were better 82
to be married of him than of another, for he is not 83
like to marry me well; and not being well married, 84
it will be a good excuse for me hereafter to leave my
wife.

JAQUES   Go thou with me, and let me counsel thee.

TOUCHSTONE
Come, sweet Audrey.
We must be married, or we must live in bawdry. 89
Farewell, good Master Oliver; not 91
    "O sweet Oliver, 91
    O brave Oliver, 92
  Leave me not behind thee";
but
    "Wind away, 95
    Begone, I say,
I will not to wedding with thee." 97
        [*Exeunt Jaques, Touchstone, and Audrey.*]

SIR OLIVER   'Tis no matter. Ne'er a fantastical knave of 98
them all shall flout me out of my calling.   *Exit.*

❧

3.4

Enter Rosalind and Celia.

ROSALIND   Never talk to me. I will weep.

CELIA   Do, I prithee, but yet have the grace to consider
that tears do not become a man.

ROSALIND   But have I not cause to weep?

CELIA   As good cause as one would desire; therefore
weep.

ROSALIND   His very hair is of the dissembling color. 7

CELIA   Something browner than Judas's. Marry, his 8
kisses are Judas's own children. 9

ROSALIND   I'faith, his hair is of a good color.

CELIA   An excellent color. Your chestnut was ever the 11
only color. 12

ROSALIND   And his kissing is as full of sanctity as the
touch of holy bread. 14

CELIA   He hath bought a pair of cast lips of Diana. A 15
nun of winter's sisterhood kisses not more religiously; 16
the very ice of chastity is in them.

ROSALIND   But why did he swear he would come this
morning, and comes not?

CELIA   Nay, certainly, there is no truth in him.

ROSALIND   Do you think so?

CELIA   Yes. I think he is not a pickpurse nor a horse-
stealer, but for his verity in love, I do think him as
concave as a covered goblet or a worm-eaten nut. 24

ROSALIND   Not true in love?

CELIA   Yes, when he is in, but I think he is not in.

ROSALIND   You have heard him swear downright he
was.

CELIA   "Was" is not "is." Besides, the oath of a lover is
no stronger than the word of a tapster; they are both
the confirmer of false reckonings. He attends here in 31
the forest on the Duke your father.

ROSALIND   I met the Duke yesterday and had much
question with him. He asked me of what parentage I 34
was. I told him, of as good as he; so he laughed and let
me go. But what talk we of fathers, when there is such 36
a man as Orlando?

CELIA   Oh, that's a brave man! He writes brave verses, 38
speaks brave words, swears brave oaths, and breaks
them bravely, quite traverse, athwart the heart of his 40
lover, as a puny tilter, that spurs his horse but on 41
one side, breaks his staff like a noble goose. But all's 42
brave that youth mounts and folly guides. Who comes 43
here?

Enter Corin.

CORIN
Mistress and master, you have oft inquired
After the shepherd that complained of love, 46
Who you saw sitting by me on the turf,
Praising the proud disdainful shepherdess
That was his mistress.

CELIA   Well, and what of him?

CORIN
If you will see a pageant truly played
Between the pale complexion of true love 51
And the red glow of scorn and proud disdain,
Go hence a little, and I shall conduct you,
If you will mark it.

ROSALIND   Oh, come, let us remove! 54
The sight of lovers feedeth those in love.
Bring us to this sight, and you shall say
I'll prove a busy actor in their play.   *Exeunt.*

❧

---

82 **I am . . . better** I do not know but that it would be better for me.
(Touchstone may be speaking aside here.)   **83 of** by   **84 like** likely.
well (1) suitably (2) legally   **89 married** i.e., properly married, as
Jaques suggests, not by a hedge-priest. (Having been found out,
Touchstone wryly defers matters for the present.)   **91–7 "O . . . thee."**
(Phrases from a current ballad.)   **92 brave** worthy   **95 Wind** Wend,
go   **98 fantastical** affected
3.4 Location: The forest.
7 the dissembling color i.e., reddish, traditionally the color of Judas's
hair.   **8 Something** Somewhat   **9 Judas's own children** i.e., as false
and betraying as the kiss given by Judas to Jesus when he betrayed
him to the high priests.   **11 Your chestnut** i.e., This chestnut color
that people talk about   **12 only** only fashionable   **14 holy bread**
either the unleavened bread of the Eucharist or ordinary leavened
bread that was blessed after the Eucharist and distributed to those
who had not received communion.   **15 cast** (1) chaste, cold
(2) molded, or (3) cast off.   **Diana** goddess of chastity.   **16 of winter's sisterhood** i.e., devoted to barrenness and cold

24 concave hollow, i.e., insincere   **31 false reckonings** (Tapsters, or
barkeeps, were notorious for inflating bills.)   **34 question** conversation   **36 what** why   **38 brave** fine, excellent   **40 traverse** across,
awry. (A term from medieval jousting or tilting; hence *tilters*, line 41.)
41 puny inexperienced. (Literally, junior.)   **but** only   **42 a noble
goose** i.e., a goose-headed young gallant.   **42–3 But . . . guides** But
everything is admirable that youth undertakes under the influence
of folly. (Said sardonically.)   **46 complained of** uttered a lament
against   **51 pale complexion** (Sighing was believed to draw the
blood from the heart.)   **54 will mark** wish to observe.   **remove**
leave here and go.

3.5

Enter Silvius and Phoebe.

SILVIUS
Sweet Phoebe, do not scorn me, do not, Phoebe!
Say that you love me not, but say not so
In bitterness. The common executioner,
Whose heart th'accustomed sight of death makes
    hard,
Falls not the ax upon the humbled neck   5
But first begs pardon. Will you sterner be   6
Than he that dies and lives by bloody drops?   7

Enter Rosalind, Celia, and Corin [behind].

PHOEBE
I would not be thy executioner;
I fly thee, for I would not injure thee.
Thou tell'st me there is murder in mine eye.
'Tis pretty, sure, and very probable,   11
That eyes, that are the frail'st and softest things,
Who shut their coward gates on atomies,   13
Should be called tyrants, butchers, murderers!
Now I do frown on thee with all my heart,
And if mine eyes can wound, now let them kill thee.
Now counterfeit to swoon; why, now fall down,
Or if thou canst not, oh, for shame, for shame,
Lie not, to say mine eyes are murderers!   19
Now show the wound mine eye hath made in thee.
Scratch thee but with a pin, and there remains
Some scar of it; lean upon a rush,   22
The cicatrice and capable impressure   23
Thy palm some moment keeps; but now mine eyes,   24
Which I have darted at thee, hurt thee not,
Nor, I am sure, there is no force in eyes
That can do hurt.
SILVIUS   O dear Phoebe,
If ever—as that "ever" may be near—
You meet in some fresh cheek the power of fancy,   29
Then shall you know the wounds invisible
That love's keen arrows make.
PHOEBE   But till that time
Come not thou near me; and when that time comes,
Afflict me with thy mocks; pity me not,
As till that time I shall not pity thee.   34
ROSALIND *[advancing]*
And why, I pray you? Who might be your mother,   35
That you insult, exult, and all at once,   36

Over the wretched? What though you have no
    beauty—   37
As, by my faith, I see no more in you   38
Than without candle may go dark to bed—   39
Must you be therefore proud and pitiless?
Why, what means this? Why do you look on me?
I see no more in you than in the ordinary   42
Of nature's sale-work. 'Od's my little life,   43
I think she means to tangle my eyes too!   44
No, faith, proud mistress, hope not after it.
'Tis not your inky brows, your black silk hair,
Your bugle eyeballs, nor your cheek of cream   47
That can entame my spirits to your worship.   48
[To Silvius] You foolish shepherd, wherefore do you
    follow her,
Like foggy south, puffing with wind and rain?   50
You are a thousand times a properer man   51
Than she a woman. 'Tis such fools as you
That makes the world full of ill-favored children.   53
'Tis not her glass, but you, that flatters her,   54
And out of you she sees herself more proper   55
Than any of her lineaments can show her.—   56
But, mistress, know yourself. Down on your knees,
And thank heaven, fasting, for a good man's love!
For I must tell you friendly in your ear,
Sell when you can. You are not for all markets.
Cry the man mercy, love him, take his offer;   61
Foul is most foul, being foul to be a scoffer.—   62
So take her to thee, shepherd. Fare you well.
PHOEBE
Sweet youth, I pray you, chide a year together.   64
I had rather hear you chide than this man woo.
ROSALIND *[to Phoebe]* He's fallen in love with your foul-
ness, *[to Silvius]* and she'll fall in love with my
anger. If it be so, as fast as she answers thee with
frowning looks, I'll sauce her with bitter words. *[To* 69
Phoebe] Why look you so upon me?
PHOEBE   For no ill will I bear you.
ROSALIND
I pray you, do not fall in love with me,
For I am falser than vows made in wine.   73
Besides, I like you not. *[To Silvius]* If you will know
    my house,
'Tis at the tuft of olives here hard by.—
Will you go, sister?—Shepherd, ply her hard.—

3.5 Location: The forest.
5 Falls lets fall **6 But first begs pardon** without first begging pardon
(as executioners did in Elizabethan times). **7 dies . . . drops** makes
his living by the deaths of others. (Stated as an oxymoron.) **11 sure**
to be sure **13 coward gates on atomies** i.e., sensitive eyelids to protect against specks of dirt **19 to say** by saying **22 a rush** a reed
23–4 The cicatrice . . . keeps the scarlike and perceptible impression
is retained by one's palm for a moment **29 You . . . fancy** you yourself feel the powerful spell of love for some new face **34 As** since
35 Who . . . mother (1) What human mother could have produced so
inhuman a daughter (2) From what sort of a mother did you learn
such scorn **36 insult** exult scornfully.   **all at once** all at the same
time

37 have no beauty are not particularly beautiful **38–9 I see . . . bed**
i.e., I see nothing in your beauty that might not go entirely unnoticed,
nothing to distinguish you from other young women **42 ordinary**
common run **43 sale-work** ready-made products, not of the best
quality, not distinctive.   **'Od's** May God save **44 tangle** ensnare
47 bugle beadlike, black and glassy **48 to your worship** (1) to the
worship of you (2) to adore Your Worship (as such beauty deserved
an honorific title). **50 south** south wind (from which came fog and
rain; hence, Silvius's sighs and tears) **51 properer** better-looking
(since handsome is as handsome does) **53 ill-favored** ugly
54 glass mirror **55 out of you** i.e., with you as her mirror **56 lineaments** features **61 Cry . . . mercy** Beg the man's pardon **62 Foul . . .
scoffer** i.e., unattractive behavior like yours is at its most foul when it
consists of scoffing. (Plays on two meanings of *foul*.) **64 together**
without intermission. **69 sauce** rebuke **73 in wine** while drunk.

Come, sister.—Shepherdess, look on him better,   76
And be not proud. Though all the world could see,
None could be so abused in sight as he.—   78
Come, to our flock.   *Exit [with Celia and Corin].*   79

PHOEBE
Dead shepherd, now I find thy saw of might,
"Who ever loved that loved not at first sight?"   81

SILVIUS   82
Sweet Phoebe—

PHOEBE   Ha, what say'st thou, Silvius?

SILVIUS   Sweet Phoebe, pity me.

PHOEBE
Why, I am sorry for thee, gentle Silvius.

SILVIUS
Wherever sorrow is, relief would be.
If you do sorrow at my grief in love,   86
By giving love, your sorrow and my grief
Were both extermined.

PHOEBE   89
Thou hast my love. Is not that neighborly?

SILVIUS   90
I would have you.

PHOEBE   Why, that were covetousness.
Silvius, the time was that I hated thee,   91
And yet it is not that I bear thee love;
But since that thou canst talk of love so well,   93
Thy company, which erst was irksome to me,   94
I will endure, and I'll employ thee too.   95
But do not look for further recompense
Than thine own gladness that thou art employed.

SILVIUS
So holy and so perfect is my love,
And I in such a poverty of grace,
That I shall think it a most plenteous crop   100
To glean the broken ears after the man
That the main harvest reaps. Loose now and then
A scattered smile, and that I'll live upon.

PHOEBE   104
Know'st thou the youth that spoke to me erewhile?

SILVIUS   105
Not very well, but I have met him oft,
And he hath bought the cottage and the bounds
That the old carlot once was master of.   107

PHOEBE   108
Think not I love him, though I ask for him.
'Tis but a peevish boy—yet he talks well—
But what care I for words? Yet words do well

When he that speaks them pleases those that hear.
It is a pretty youth—not very pretty—
But sure he's proud—and yet his pride becomes him.
He'll make a proper man. The best thing in him
Is his complexion; and faster than his tongue   115
Did make offense, his eye did heal it up.
He is not very tall—yet for his years he's tall.
His leg is but so-so—and yet 'tis well.
There was a pretty redness in his lip,
A little riper and more lusty red
Than that mixed in his cheek; 'twas just the difference
Betwixt the constant red and mingled damask.
There be some women, Silvius, had they marked him   123
In parcels as I did, would have gone near
To fall in love with him; but for my part,   125
I love him not nor hate him not; and yet   126
I have more cause to hate him than to love him.
For what had he to do to chide at me?
He said mine eyes were black and my hair black,   129
And, now I am remembered, scorned at me.
I marvel why I answered not again.   131
But that's all one; omittance is no quittance.   132
I'll write to him a very taunting letter,   133
And thou shalt bear it. Wilt thou, Silvius?

SILVIUS
Phoebe, with all my heart.

PHOEBE   I'll write it straight;
The matter's in my head and in my heart.   136
I will be bitter with him and passing short.
Go with me, Silvius.   *Exeunt.*   138

❖

4.1

Enter Rosalind and Celia, and Jaques.

JAQUES   I prithee, pretty youth, let me be better acquainted with thee.

ROSALIND   They say you are a melancholy fellow.

JAQUES   I am so. I do love it better than laughing.

ROSALIND   Those that are in extremity of either are
abominable fellows and betray themselves to every   5
modern censure worse than drunkards.

JAQUES   Why, 'tis good to be sad and say nothing.   7

ROSALIND   Why then, 'tis good to be a post.

JAQUES   I have neither the scholar's melancholy, which
is emulation, nor the musician's, which is fantastical,
nor the courtier's, which is proud, nor the soldier's, 11
which is ambitious, nor the lawyer's, which is politic,
nor the lady's, which is nice, nor the lover's, which is 13

---

76 ply her hard woo her energetically.   **78 could see** could look at
you   **79 abused in sight** deceived through the eyes   **81 Dead shepherd** i.e., Christopher Marlowe, who died in 1593.   **saw** saying.   **of
might** forceful, convincing   **82 Who . . . sight?** (From Marlowe's *Hero
and Leander*, Sestiad 1, 176, first published in 1598.)   **86 Wherever . . .
be** Sorrow cries out for relief.   **89 Were both extermined** would both
be exterminated, ended.   **90 Is . . . neighborly?** i.e., May not I love
you in the sense of loving one's neighbor as oneself?   **91 covetousness** (The tenth commandment forbids coveting anything that is
one's neighbor's.)   **93 yet it is not** the time has not yet come
94 since that since   **95 erst** formerly   **100 poverty of grace** lack of
reciprocated affection   **104 scattered** thrown negligently, as in the
gleanings of the harvest   **105 erewhile** just now.   **107 bounds** pastures   **108 carlot** churl, countryman. (Perhaps a proper name.)

115 proper handsome   **123 mingled damask** mingled red and white,
the color of the damask rose.   **125 In parcels** bit by bit   **125–6 gone . . .
fall** been on the point of falling   **129 what . . . do** what business had
he   **131 am remembered** remember   **132 again** back.   **133 But . . .
quittance** i.e., But just the same, my failure to answer him doesn't
mean I won't do so later.   **136 straight** immediately   **138 passing
short** exceedingly curt.
4.1. Location: The forest.
5 are . . . of go to extremes in   **7 modern censure** common judgment
11 emulation envy (of the fellow scholar).   **fantastical** extravagantly
fanciful   **13 politic** grave and diplomatic, calculated

all these; but it is a melancholy of mine own, com- 14
pounded of many simples, extracted from many 15
objects, and indeed the sundry contemplation of my 16
travels, in which my often rumination wraps me in a 17
most humorous sadness. 18

ROSALIND   A traveler! By my faith, you have great 19
reason to be sad. I fear you have sold your own lands
to see other men's. Then to have seen much and to
have nothing is to have rich eyes and poor hands.

JAQUES   Yes, I have gained my experience.

Enter Orlando.

ROSALIND   And your experience makes you sad. I had
rather have a fool to make me merry than experience
to make me sad—and to travel for it too!

ORLANDO   Good day and happiness, dear Rosalind! 27

JAQUES   Nay, then, God b'wi'you, an you talk in blank
verse. 29

ROSALIND   Farewell, Monsieur Traveler. Look you lisp
and wear strange suits, disable all the benefits of your 31
own country, be out of love with your nativity, and 32
almost chide God for making you that countenance 33
you are, or I will scarce think you have swam in a
gondola.   [*Exit Jaques.*] 35
Why, how now, Orlando, where have you been all this 36
while? You a lover? An you serve me such another
trick, never come in my sight more.

ORLANDO   My fair Rosalind, I come within an hour of
my promise.

ROSALIND   Break an hour's promise in love? He that will
divide a minute into a thousand parts and break but
a part of the thousandth part of a minute in the affairs
of love, it may be said of him that Cupid hath clapped
him o'th' shoulder, but I'll warrant him heart-whole. 45

ORLANDO   Pardon me, dear Rosalind. 46

ROSALIND   Nay, an you be so tardy, come no more in
my sight. I had as lief be wooed of a snail.

ORLANDO   Of a snail? 49

ROSALIND   Ay, of a snail; for though he comes slowly,
he carries his house on his head—a better jointure, I
think, than you make a woman. Besides, he brings his 52
destiny with him. 53

ORLANDO   What's that?

ROSALIND   Why, horns, which such as you are fain to
be beholding to your wives for. But he comes armed in 56

his fortune and prevents the slander of his wife. 57

ORLANDO   Virtue is no horn-maker, and my Rosalind is 58
virtuous.

ROSALIND   And I am your Rosalind.

CELIA   It pleases him to call you so; but he hath a Rosalind of a better leer than you.

ROSALIND   Come, woo me, woo me, for now I am in a 63
holiday humor and like enough to consent. What
would you say to me now, an I were your very, very
Rosalind?

ORLANDO   I would kiss before I spoke.

ROSALIND   Nay, you were better speak first, and when
you were graveled for lack of matter, you might take
occasion to kiss. Very good orators, when they are out, 70
they will spit; and for lovers lacking—God warrant 71
us!—matter, the cleanliest shift is to kiss. 72

ORLANDO   How if the kiss be denied? 73

ROSALIND   Then she puts you to entreaty, and there
begins new matter.

ORLANDO   Who could be out, being before his beloved
mistress?

ROSALIND   Marry, that should you, if I were your
mistress, or I should think my honesty ranker than
my wit. 80

ORLANDO   What, of my suit?

ROSALIND   Not out of your apparel, and yet out of your 82
suit. Am not I your Rosalind?

ORLANDO   I take some joy to say you are, because I
would be talking of her.

ROSALIND   Well, in her person I say I will not have you.

ORLANDO   Then in mine own person, I die.

ROSALIND   No, faith, die by attorney. The poor world is
almost six thousand years old, and in all this time 89
there was not any man died in his own person, 90
videlicet, in a love cause. Troilus had his brains 91
dashed out with a Grecian club, yet he did what he 92
could to die before, and he is one of the patterns of 93
love. Leander, he would have lived many a fair year
though Hero had turned nun, if it had not been for a 95
hot midsummer night; for, good youth, he went but
forth to wash him in the Hellespont and being taken
with the cramp was drowned; and the foolish chron-

---

57 beholding beholden, indebted   **57–8 But . . . fortune** The snail
comes already provided with the horns that are his nature and his
destiny, thereby forestalling the scandal that would otherwise attach
to his wife. (Since a snail is naturally horned, no scandal can be
adduced from them.)   **63 leer** appearance, color   **70 graveled** stuck.
(Literally, run aground on a shoal.)   **71 out** at a loss through forgetfulness or confusion   **72 warrant** defend   **73 shift** tactic   **80 honesty ranker** chastity more corrupt. (Rosalind would rely on her wit to
keep her lover off balance and thus defend her chastity. She may use
Orlando's *out*, line 77, in a sexual sense of not being admitted.)   **82 of
my suit** (Orlando means "out of my suit," at a loss for words in my
wooing; but Rosalind puns on the meaning "suit of clothes"; to be out
of apparel would be to be undressed.)   **89 attorney** proxy.   **90 six . . .
old** (A common figure in biblical calculation.)   **91 died** who died
92 videlicet namely.   **Troilus** hero of the story of Troilus and Cressida, in which he remains faithful to her, but she is faithless to him
92–3 had . . . club (Troilus was slain by Achilles with sword or spear
in more traditional accounts. Rosalind's version is calculatedly unro-
mantic.)   **95 Leander** the hero of the story of Hero and Leander, who
lost his life swimming the Hellespont to visit his sweetheart. (Rosalind's account of the cramp again undercuts romantic idealism.)

---

14 nice fastidious   **15–19 compounded . . . sadness** made up of
many ingredients, extracted from the many objects of my observation
and, indeed, from the diversified considerations of my travels, my
frequent rumination upon which wraps me in a most whimsical and
moody sadness.   **27 travel** (Meaning also "travail," labor.)   **29 an** if
31 Look Be sure. (Said ironically.)   **lisp** i.e., affect a foreign accent
32 disable disparage   **33 nativity** country of birth   **35 are** i.e., have
35–6 swam . . . gondola floated in a gondola, i.e., been in Venice,
where almost all travelers go.   **45–6 Cupid . . . heart-whole** Cupid
may have tried to arrest him, but I'm sure his heart remains unen-
gaged. (Arresting officers customarily grasped the culprit by the
shoulder.)   **49 lief** willingly.   **of** by   **52 jointure** marriage settlement   **53 than . . . woman** than you, Orlando, are able to settle on
your prospective wife.   **56 horns** (1) snails' horns (2) cuckold's
horns, signs of an unfaithful wife.   **fain** obliged

iclers of that age found it was—Hero of Sestos. But these are all lies. Men have died from time to time, 100 and worms have eaten them, but not for love.

ORLANDO   I would not have my right Rosalind of this mind, for I protest her frown might kill me.   103

ROSALIND   By this hand, it will not kill a fly. But come, 104 now I will be your Rosalind in a more coming-on disposition; and ask me what you will, I will grant it. 106

ORLANDO   Then love me, Rosalind.

ROSALIND   Yes, faith, will I, Fridays and Saturdays and all.

ORLANDO   And wilt thou have me?

ROSALIND   Ay, and twenty such.

ORLANDO   What sayest thou?

ROSALIND   Are you not good?

ORLANDO   I hope so.

ROSALIND   Why then, can one desire too much of a good thing?—Come, sister, you shall be the priest and marry us.—Give me your hand, Orlando.— What do you say, sister?

ORLANDO   Pray thee, marry us.

CELIA   I cannot say the words.

ROSALIND   You must begin, "Will you,Orlando—"

CELIA   Go to. Will you, Orlando, have to wife this Rosalind?   123

ORLANDO   I will.

ROSALIND   Ay, but when?

ORLANDO   Why now, as fast as she can marry us.

ROSALIND   Then you must say, "I take thee, Rosalind, for wife."

ORLANDO   I take thee, Rosalind, for wife.

ROSALIND   I might ask you for your commission; but I do take thee, Orlando, for my husband. There's a girl 131 goes before the priest, and certainly a woman's thought runs before her actions.   133

ORLANDO   So do all thoughts; they are winged.   134

ROSALIND   Now tell me how long you would have her after you have possessed her.

ORLANDO   For ever and a day.

ROSALIND   Say "a day," without the "ever." No, no, Or- lando, men are April when they woo, December when they wed. Maids are May when they are maids, but the sky changes when they are wives. I will be more jealous of thee than a Barbary cock-pigeon over his hen, more clamorous than a parrot against rain, more 143 newfangled than an ape, more giddy in my desires 144 than a monkey. I will weep for nothing, like Diana in 145

the fountain, and I will do that when you are disposed 146 to be merry; I will laugh like a hyena, and that when 147 thou art inclined to sleep.

ORLANDO   But will my Rosalind do so?

ROSALIND   By my life, she will do as I do.

ORLANDO   Oh, but she is wise.

ROSALIND   Or else she could not have the wit to do this. The wiser, the waywarder. Make the doors upon a woman's wit, and it will out at the casement; shut 154 that, and 'twill out at the keyhole; stop that, 'twill fly 155 with the smoke out at the chimney.

ORLANDO   A man that had a wife with such a wit, he might say, "Wit, whither wilt?"

ROSALIND   Nay, you might keep that check for it till 159 you met your wife's wit going to your neighbor's bed. 160

ORLANDO   And what wit could wit have to excuse that?

ROSALIND   Marry, to say she came to seek you there. You shall never take her without her answer unless you take her without her tongue. Oh, that woman that cannot make her fault her husband's occasion, let her never nurse her child herself, for she will breed it like 166 a fool!   167

ORLANDO   For these two hours, Rosalind, I will leave thee.

ROSALIND   Alas, dear love, I cannot lack thee two hours!

ORLANDO   I must attend the Duke at dinner. By two o'clock I will be with thee again.

ROSALIND   Ay, go your ways, go your ways. I knew what you would prove. My friends told me as much, and I thought no less. That flattering tongue of yours won me. 'Tis but one cast away, and so, come, death! Two o'clock is your hour?   177

ORLANDO   Ay, sweet Rosalind.

ROSALIND   By my troth, and in good earnest, and so God mend me, and by all pretty oaths that are not dangerous, if you break one jot of your promise or come one minute behind your hour, I will think you 182 the most pathetical break-promise, and the most hollow lover, and the most unworthy of her you call 184 Rosalind, that may be chosen out of the gross band of the unfaithful. Therefore beware my censure, and 186 keep your promise.

ORLANDO   With no less religion than if thou wert indeed my Rosalind. So adieu.   189

---

100 found it was arrived at the verdict that the cause (of his death) was   **103 right** real   **104 protest** insist, proclaim   **106 coming-on** compliant   **123 Go to** (An exclamation of mild impatience.)   **131 ask . . . commission** ask you what authority you have for taking her (since no one is here to give the bride away and since she herself has not yet consented)   **133 goes . . . priest** who anticipates before the "priest" has even asked the question   **134 runs . . . actions** i.e., goes flightily on, outstripping sane conduct.   **143 Barbary cock-pigeon** an ornamental pigeon actually from the orient, not the Barbary (north) coast of Africa. (Following Pliny, the cock-pigeon's jealousy was often contrasted with the mildness of the hen.)   **144 against** in expectation of   **145 newfangled** infatuated with novelty

146 for nothing for no apparent reason   **146–7 Diana in the fountain** (Diana frequently appeared as the centerpiece of fountains. Stow's *Survey of London* describes the setting up of a fountain with a Diana in green marble in the year 1596.)   **154 The wiser, the waywarder** i.e., The more experienced in the war of the sexes, the more insisting on her own way.   **Make** Make fast, shut   **155 casement** hinged window **159 Wit, whither wilt?** Wit, where are you going? (A common Eliza- bethan expression implying that one is talking fantastically, with a wildly wandering wit.)   **160 check** retort   **166 make . . . occasion** i.e., turn a defense of her own conduct into an accusation against her husband   **167 breed it** bring it up   **177 but one cast away** only one woman jilted   **182 dangerous** i.e., blasphemous. (Rosalind's oaths are decorous.)   **184 pathetical** awful, miserable   **186 gross band** whole troop   **189 religion** strict fidelity

ROSALIND   Well, Time is the old justice that examines
all such offenders, and let Time try. Adieu.   192

Exit [Orlando].

CELIA   You have simply misused our sex in your love   193
prate. We must have your doublet and hose plucked   194
over your head and show the world what the bird   195
hath done to her own nest.   196

ROSALIND   Oh, coz, coz, coz, my pretty little coz, that thou
didst know how many fathom deep I am in love! But
it cannot be sounded; my affection hath an unknown   199
bottom, like the Bay of Portugal.

CELIA   Or rather, bottomless, that as fast as you pour   201
affection in, it runs out.

ROSALIND   No, that same wicked bastard of Venus, that 203
was begot of thought, conceived of spleen, and born of   204
madness, that blind rascally boy that abuses every-   205
one's eyes because his own are out, let him be judge   206
how deep I am in love. I'll tell thee, Aliena, I cannot be
out of the sight of Orlando. I'll go find a shadow and   208
sigh till he come.

CELIA   And I'll sleep.   *Exeunt.*

❖

4.2

Enter Jaques and Lords [dressed as] foresters.

JAQUES   Which is he that killed the deer?

FIRST LORD   Sir, it was I.

JAQUES   Let's present him to the Duke, like a Roman
conqueror, and it would do well to set the deer's horns
upon his head for a branch of victory. Have you no   5
song, Forester, for this purpose?

SECOND LORD   Yes, sir.

JAQUES   Sing it. 'Tis no matter how it be in tune, so it 8
make noise enough.   *Music.*

Song.

SECOND LORD *[sings]*
    What shall he have that killed the deer?
    His leather skin and horns to wear.
    Then sing him home; the rest shall bear   12
        This burden.   13
    Take thou no scorn to wear the horn;   14
    It was a crest ere thou wast born.
        Thy father's father wore it,
        And thy father bore it.
    The horn, the horn, the lusty horn
    Is not a thing to laugh to scorn.   *Exeunt.*

❖

4.3

Enter Rosalind and Celia.

ROSALIND   How say you now? Is it not past two o'clock?
And here much Orlando!   2

CELIA   I warrant you, with pure love and troubled brain   3
he hath ta'en his bow and arrows and is gone
forth—to sleep.

Enter Silvius [with a letter].

Look who comes here.

SILVIUS *[to Rosalind]*
My errand is to you, fair youth.
My gentle Phoebe bid me give you this.
                                   [He gives the letter.]
I know not the contents, but as I guess,
By the stern brow and waspish action
Which she did use as she was writing of it,
It bears an angry tenor. Pardon me;
I am but as a guiltless messenger.

ROSALIND *[examining the letter]*
Patience herself would startle at this letter   14
And play the swaggerer. Bear this, bear all!   15
She says I am not fair, that I lack manners;
She calls me proud, and that she could not love me
Were man as rare as phoenix. 'Od's my will!   18
Her love is not the hare that I do hunt.
Why writes she so to me? Well, shepherd, well,
This is a letter of your own device.

SILVIUS
No, I protest, I know not the contents.
Phoebe did write it.

ROSALIND   Come, come, you are a fool,
And turned into the extremity of love.   24
I saw her hand; she has a leathern hand,   25
A freestone-colored hand. I verily did think   26
That her old gloves were on, but 'twas her hands;
She has a huswife's hand—but that's no matter.   28
I say she never did invent this letter;
This is a man's invention and his hand.

SILVIUS   Sure it is hers.

ROSALIND
Why, 'tis a boisterous and a cruel style,
A style for challengers. Why, she defies me,
Like Turk to Christian. Women's gentle brain
Could not drop forth such giant-rude invention,

---

192 **try** determine, judge.   193 **simply misused** absolutely slandered
194–6 We . . . nest i.e., We must expose you for what you are, a
woman, and show everyone how a woman has defamed her own
kind just as a foul bird proverbially fouls its own nest.   199 **sounded**
measured for depth   201 **that** so that   203 **bastard of Venus** i.e.,
Cupid, son of Venus and Mercury (or Zeus) rather than Vulcan,
Venus's husband   204 **thought** fancy.   **spleen** i.e., impulse
205 **abuses** deceives   206 **out** blinded   208 **shadow** shady spot
4.2 Location: The forest.
5 **branch** wreath   8 **so** provided that   12–13 **bear This burden** (1) sing
this refrain (2) wear the horns that all cuckolds must wear.   14 **Take . . .**
scorn Be not ashamed. (Alludes to joke about cuckold's horns.)

4.3 Location: The forest.
2 **much** (Said ironically: A fat lot we see of Orlando!)   3 **warrant**
assure   **14–15 Patience . . . all!** Patience herself would be startled into
a violent display by this letter. If one were to put up with such a missive, one would have to accept any insult!   15 **play the swaggerer**
(Patience herself would bluster and rant at such a letter.)
18 **phoenix** a fabulous bird of Arabia, the only one of its kind, which
lived five hundred years, died in flames, and was reborn of its own
ashes.   **'Od's my will!** (An oath: "May God's will be done!")
24 **turned** transformed   25 **leathern** leathery   26 **freestone-colored**
sandstone-colored, brownish-yellow   28 **hand** handwriting. (With
play on "dishpan hands.")

Such Ethiop words, blacker in their effect   36
Than in their countenance. Will you hear the letter?   37

SILVIUS
So please you, for I never heard it yet;
Yet, heard too much of Phoebe's cruelty.

ROSALIND
She Phoebes me. Mark how the tyrant writes.   40
    (*Read*) "Art thou god to shepherd turned,
    That a maiden's heart hath burned?"
Can a woman rail thus?

SILVIUS   Call you this railing?

ROSALIND
    (*Read*) "Why, thy godhead laid apart,   45
    War'st thou with a woman's heart?"
Did you ever hear such railing?
    "Whiles the eye of man did woo me,
    That could do no vengeance to me."—   49
Meaning me a beast.   50
    "If the scorn of your bright eyne   51
    Have power to raise such love in mine,
    Alack, in me what strange effect
    Would they work in mild aspect!   54
    Whiles you chid me, I did love;   55
    How then might your prayers move!
    He that brings this love to thee
    Little knows this love in me;
    And by him seal up thy mind,   59
    Whether that thy youth and kind   60
    Will the faithful offer take
    Of me and all that I can make,   62
    Or else by him my love deny,
    And then I'll study how to die."

SILVIUS   Call you this chiding?

CELIA   Alas, poor shepherd!

ROSALIND   Do you pity him? No, he deserves no pity.—
Wilt thou love such a woman? What, to make thee an   68
instrument and play false strains upon thee? Not to be   69
endured! Well, go your way to her, for I see love hath
made thee a tame snake, and say this to her: that if she   71
love me, I charge her to love thee; if she will not, I will
never have her unless thou entreat for her. If you be a
true lover, hence, and not a word; for here comes
more company.   *Exit Silvius.*

    Enter Oliver.

OLIVER
Good morrow, fair ones. Pray you, if you know,

Where in the purlieus of this forest stands   77
A sheepcote fenced about with olive trees?

CELIA
West of this place, down in the neighbor bottom;   79
The rank of osiers by the murmuring stream   80
Left on your right hand brings you to the place.   81
But at this hour the house doth keep itself;
There's none within.

OLIVER
If that an eye may profit by a tongue,
Then should I know you by description,
Such garments and such years: "The boy is fair,
Of female favor, and bestows himself   87
Like a ripe sister; the woman, low   88
And browner than her brother." Are not you
The owner of the house I did inquire for?

CELIA
It is no boast, being asked, to say we are.

OLIVER
Orlando doth commend him to you both,   92
And to that youth he calls his Rosalind
He sends this bloody napkin. Are you he?   94
    [*He produces a bloody handkerchief.*]

ROSALIND
I am. What must we understand by this?

OLIVER
Some of my shame, if you will know of me
What man I am, and how, and why, and where
This handkerchief was stained.

CELIA   I pray you, tell it.

OLIVER
When last the young Orlando parted from you
He left a promise to return again
Within an hour, and, pacing through the forest,
Chewing the food of sweet and bitter fancy,   102
Lo, what befell! He threw his eye aside,
And mark what object did present itself:
Under an old oak, whose boughs were mossed with
    age
And high top bald with dry antiquity,
A wretched, ragged man, o'ergrown with hair,
Lay sleeping on his back. About his neck
A green and gilded snake had wreathed itself,
Who with her head, nimble in threats, approached
The opening of his mouth; but suddenly,
Seeing Orlando, it unlinked itself   112
And with indented glides did slip away   113
Into a bush, under which bush's shade
A lioness, with udders all drawn dry,   115
Lay couching, head on ground, with catlike watch,
When that the sleeping man should stir; for 'tis   117

---

36 Ethiop i.e., black   **36–7 blacker . . . countenance** even blacker in
what they say than in their black appearance on the page.
40 Phoebes me i.e., addresses me in her cruel style.   **45 thy . . . apart**
having laid aside your godhead (for human shape)   **49 vengeance**
mischief, harm   **50 Meaning me** i.e., Implying that I am   **51 eyne**
eyes   **54 in mild aspect** i.e., if they looked on me mildly. (Suggests
also astrological influence.)   **55 chid** chided   **59 by . . . mind** i.e.,
send your thoughts in a letter via Silvius   **60 Whether . . . kind** if
your youthful nature   **62 make** make offer of   **68–9 to make . . .
instrument** to make an instrument (i.e., messenger) of you. (With a
suggestion of making a person into a musical instrument; cf. *Hamlet*,
3.2.363, "You would play upon me," etc.)   **69 strains** parts of a piece
of music   **71 tame snake** i.e., pathetic wretch

77 purlieus borders, boundaries   **79 neighbor bottom** neighboring
dell   **80 rank of osiers** row of willows   **81 Left** left behind, passed
87 favor features.   **bestows** comports   **88 ripe** mature or elder
92 doth commend him sends his greetings   **94 napkin** handkerchief.
102 Chewing . . . fancy ruminating on the bittersweet nature of love
112 unlinked uncoiled   **113 indented** zigzag   **115 with . . . dry** (It
would therefore be fierce with hunger.)   **117 When** for the moment

The royal disposition of that beast
To prey on nothing that doth seem as dead.
This seen, Orlando did approach the man
And found it was his brother, his elder brother.

CELIA
Oh, I have heard him speak of that same brother,
And he did render him the most unnatural   123
That lived amongst men.

OLIVER   And well he might so do,
For well I know he was unnatural.

ROSALIND
But to Orlando: did he leave him there,
Food to the sucked and hungry lioness?

OLIVER
Twice did he turn his back and purposed so;
But kindness, nobler ever than revenge,
And nature, stronger than his just occasion,   130
Made him give battle to the lioness,
Who quickly fell before him; in which hurtling   132
From miserable slumber I awaked.

CELIA
Are you his brother?

ROSALIND   Was't you he rescued?

CELIA
Was't you that did so oft contrive to kill him?

OLIVER
'Twas I, but 'tis not I. I do not shame   136
To tell you what I was, since my conversion
So sweetly tastes, being the thing I am.

ROSALIND
But for the bloody napkin?

OLIVER   By and by.   139
When from the first to last betwixt us two
Tears our recountments had most kindly bathed,   141
As how I came into that desert place,
In brief, he led me to the gentle Duke,
Who gave me fresh array and entertainment,   144
Committing me unto my brother's love;
Who led me instantly unto his cave,
There stripped himself, and here upon his arm
The lioness had torn some flesh away,
Which all this while had bled; and now he fainted
And cried, in fainting, upon Rosalind.
Brief, I recovered him, bound up his wound,   151
And after some small space, being strong at heart,
He sent me hither, stranger as I am,
To tell this story, that you might excuse
His broken promise, and to give this napkin
Dyed in his blood unto the shepherd youth
That he in sport doth call his Rosalind.
                                        [Rosalind swoons.]

CELIA
Why, how now, Ganymede, sweet Ganymede!

OLIVER
Many will swoon when they do look on blood.

CELIA
There is more in it.—Cousin Ganymede!

OLIVER   Look, he recovers.

ROSALIND   I would I were at home.

CELIA   We'll lead you thither.—
I pray you, will you take him by the arm?
                                        [They help Rosalind up.]

OLIVER   Be of good cheer, youth. You a man? You lack
a man's heart.

ROSALIND   I do so, I confess it. Ah, sirrah, a body would   167
think this was well counterfeited. I pray you, tell your
brother how well I counterfeited. Heigh-ho!

OLIVER   This was not counterfeit. There is too great testimony in your complexion that it was a passion of   171
earnest.   172

ROSALIND   Counterfeit, I assure you.

OLIVER   Well then, take a good heart and counterfeit to
be a man.

ROSALIND   So I do; but, i'faith, I should have been a
woman by right.

CELIA   Come, you look paler and paler. Pray you, draw
homewards.—Good sir, go with us.

OLIVER
That will I, for I must bear answer back
How you excuse my brother, Rosalind.

ROSALIND   I shall devise something. But, I pray you,
commend my counterfeiting to him. Will you go?
                                        Exeunt.

❧

5.1

Enter [Touchstone the] Clown and Audrey.

TOUCHSTONE   We shall find a time, Audrey. Patience,
gentle Audrey.

AUDREY   Faith, the priest was good enough, for all the   3
old gentleman's saying.   4

TOUCHSTONE   A most wicked Sir Oliver, Audrey, a most
vile Mar-text. But Audrey, there is a youth here in the
forest lays claim to you.

AUDREY   Ay, I know who 'tis. He hath no interest in me   8
in the world. Here comes the man you mean.

Enter William.

TOUCHSTONE   It is meat and drink to me to see a clown.   10
By my troth, we that have good wits have much to   11
answer for. We shall be flouting; we cannot hold.   12

WILLIAM   Good even, Audrey.

AUDREY   God gi' good even, William.   14

WILLIAM   And good even to you, sir.
                                        [He removes his hat.]

---

123 **render him** describe him as   130 **just occasion** just opportunity
and motive (for revenge)   132 **hurtling** conflict, tumult   136 **do not
shame** am not ashamed   139 **for** as regards   141 **recountments**
relating of events (to one another)   144 **array** attire.   **entertainment**
hospitality, provision   151 **Brief** In brief.   **recovered** revived

167 **a body** anybody   171–2 **a passion of earnest** a genuine swoon.
5.1 Location: The forest.
3–4 **the old gentleman's** i.e., Jaques's   8 **interest in** claim to
10 **clown** i.e., country yokel.   11–12 **we . . . hold** i.e., we professional
fools have much to answer for in providing a model of folly that
yokels like William are too apt to imitate. We fools are always scoffing; we can't restrain ourselves.   14 **God gi' good even** God give you
good evening. (Here, afternoon.)

TOUCHSTONE   Good even, gentle friend. Cover thy head, cover thy head. Nay, prithee be covered. How old are you, friend?

WILLIAM   Five-and-twenty, sir.

TOUCHSTONE   A ripe age. Is thy name William?

WILLIAM   William, sir.

TOUCHSTONE   A fair name. Wast born i'th' forest here?

WILLIAM   Ay, sir, I thank God.

TOUCHSTONE   "Thank God"—a good answer. Art rich?

WILLIAM   Faith, sir, so-so.

TOUCHSTONE   "So-so" is good, very good, very excellent good; and yet it is not, it is but so-so. Art thou wise?

WILLIAM   Ay, sir, I have a pretty wit.

TOUCHSTONE   Why, thou say'st well. I do now remember a saying, "The fool doth think he is wise, but the wise man knows himself to be a fool." The heathen 31 philosopher, when he had a desire to eat a grape, 32 would open his lips when he put it into his mouth, 33 meaning thereby that grapes were made to eat and 34 lips to open. You do love this maid? 35

WILLIAM   I do, sir.

TOUCHSTONE   Give me your hand. Art thou learned?

WILLIAM   No, sir.

TOUCHSTONE   Then learn this of me: to have is to have. For it is a figure in rhetoric that drink, being poured 40 out of a cup into a glass, by filling the one doth empty 41 the other. For all your writers do consent that *ipse* is 42 he. Now, you are not *ipse*, for I am he. 43

WILLIAM   Which he, sir?

TOUCHSTONE   He, sir, that must marry this woman. Therefore, you clown, abandon—which is in the vulgar "leave"—the society—which in the boorish is "company"—of this female—which in the common is "woman"; which together is, abandon the society of this female, or, clown, thou perishest; or, to thy better understanding, diest; or, to wit, I kill thee, make thee away, translate thy life into death, thy liberty into bondage. I will deal in poison with thee, or in basti- 53 nado, or in steel; I will bandy with thee in faction, I 54 will o'errun thee with policy; I will kill thee a hundred 55 and fifty ways. Therefore tremble, and depart.

AUDREY   Do, good William.

WILLIAM   God rest you merry, sir.   *Exit.* 58

Enter Corin.

CORIN   Our master and mistress seeks you. Come, away, away!

TOUCHSTONE   Trip, Audrey, trip, Audrey!—I attend, I 61 attend.   *Exeunt.*

❖

5.2

Enter Orlando [with his wounded arm in a sling] and Oliver.

ORLANDO   Is't possible that on so little acquaintance you should like her? That but seeing, you should love her? And loving, woo? And, wooing, she should grant? And will you persevere to enjoy her?

OLIVER   Neither call the giddiness of it in question, the 5 poverty of her, the small acquaintance, my sudden wooing, nor her sudden consenting; but say with me, "I love Aliena"; say with her that she loves me; consent with both that we may enjoy each other. It shall be to your good; for my father's house and all the revenue that was old Sir Rowland's will I estate upon 11 you, and here live and die a shepherd.

Enter Rosalind.

ORLANDO   You have my consent. Let your wedding be tomorrow. Thither will I invite the Duke and all 's 14 contented followers. Go you and prepare Aliena; for look you, here comes my Rosalind.

ROSALIND   God save you, brother. 17

OLIVER   And you, fair sister.   [*Exit.*] 18

ROSALIND   O my dear Orlando, how it grieves me to see thee wear thy heart in a scarf! 20

ORLANDO   It is my arm.

ROSALIND   I thought thy heart had been wounded with the claws of a lion.

ORLANDO   Wounded it is, but with the eyes of a lady.

ROSALIND   Did your brother tell you how I countefeited to swoon when he showed me your handkerchief?

ORLANDO   Ay, and greater wonders than that.

ROSALIND   Oh, I know where you are. Nay, 'tis true. 28 There was never anything so sudden but the fight of two rams and Caesar's thrasonical brag of "I came, 30 saw, and overcame." For your brother and my sister 31 no sooner met but they looked, no sooner looked but they loved, no sooner loved but they sighed, no sooner sighed but they asked one another the reason, no sooner knew the reason but they sought the remedy; and in these degrees have they made a pair of 36

31–5 **The heathen . . . open** (This bit of fatuously self-evident wisdom parodies the logical proofs of the ancient philosophers. William, whose mouth is no doubt gaping like a rustic's, is invited to consider the consequences of his desire.)   40 **figure** figure of speech, trope   40–2 **drink . . . other** i.e., both Touchstone and William cannot possess Audrey.   42–3 **For . . . am he** For all the ancient authorities concur that the word *ipse* in Latin means "he." But you are not *ipse*, i.e., the man of the hour, the one destined to win Audrey, for I am that man.   53–4 **bastinado** beating with a cudgel   54 **bandy** contend.   **in faction** factiously   55 **o'errun . . . policy** overwhelm you with craft, cunning   58 **God . . . merry** (A common salutation at parting.)

61 **Trip** Go nimbly
5.2 Location: The forest.
5 **giddiness** sudden speed   11 **estate** settle as an estate, bestow   14 **all 's** all his   17 **brother** i.e., brother-in-law to be.   18 **sister** (Rosalind is still dressed as a man, but Oliver evidently adopts the fiction that "Ganymede" is Orlando's Rosalind. See 4.3.92 ff.)   20 **scarf** sling.   28 **where you are** i.e., what you mean.   30 **thrasonical** boastful. (From Thraso, the boaster in Terence's *Eunuchus*.)   30–1 **"I came . . . overcame"** (Julius Caesar's famous pronouncement, *Veni, vidi, vici*, on the occasion of his victory over Pharnaces at Zela in 47 B.C.)   36 **degrees** (Plays on the original meaning, "steps," and also on the rhetorical figure of climax illustrated by Rosalind's sentence as it moves from one step to the next by linked words, *looked, loved, sighed,* etc.)   **pair** flight

stairs to marriage which they will climb incontinent, or 37
else be incontinent before marriage. They are in the
very wrath of love, and they will together. Clubs 39
cannot part them.

ORLANDO They shall be married tomorrow, and I will
bid the Duke to the nuptial. But oh, how bitter a thing
it is to look into happiness through another man's
eyes! By so much the more shall I tomorrow be at the
height of heart-heaviness, by how much I shall think
my brother happy in having what he wishes for.

ROSALIND Why, then, tomorrow I cannot serve your
turn for Rosalind?

ORLANDO I can live no longer by thinking.

ROSALIND I will weary you then no longer with idle
talking. Know of me then—for now I speak to some
purpose—that I know you are a gentleman of good con- 52
ceit. I speak not this that you should bear a good opin- 53
ion of my knowledge, insomuch I say I know you are; 54
neither do I labor for a greater esteem than may in 55
some little measure draw a belief from you to do 56
yourself good, and not to grace me. Believe then, if you 57
please, that I can do strange things. I have, since I was
three year old, conversed with a magician, most 59
profound in his art and yet not damnable. If you do 60
love Rosalind so near the heart as your gesture cries it 61
out, when your brother marries Aliena shall you 62
marry her. I know into what straits of fortune she is 63
driven; and it is not impossible to me, if it appear not
inconvenient to you, to set her before your eyes 65
tomorrow, human as she is, and without any danger. 66

ORLANDO Speak'st thou in sober meanings? 67

ROSALIND By my life, I do, which I tender dearly, 68
though I say I am a magician. Therefore, put you in 69
your best array; bid your friends; for if you will be 70
married tomorrow, you shall, and to Rosalind, if you
will.

Enter Silvius and Phoebe.

Look, here comes a lover of mine and a lover of hers.

PHOEBE [*to Rosalind*]
Youth, you have done me much ungentleness, 74
To show the letter that I writ to you.

ROSALIND
I care not if I have. It is my study 76
To seem despiteful and ungentle to you.
You are there followed by a faithful shepherd.
Look upon him; love him. He worships you.

PHOEBE [*to Silvius*]
Good shepherd, tell this youth what 'tis to love.

SILVIUS
It is to be all made of sighs and tears;
And so am I for Phoebe.

PHOEBE And I for Ganymede.

ORLANDO And I for Rosalind.

ROSALIND And I for no woman.

SILVIUS
It is to be all made of faith and service;
And so am I for Phoebe.

PHOEBE And I for Ganymede.

ORLANDO And I for Rosalind.

ROSALIND And I for no woman.

SILVIUS
It is to be all made of fantasy, 91
All made of passion and all made of wishes,
All adoration, duty, and observance, 93
All humbleness, all patience and impatience,
All purity, all trial, all observance; 95
And so am I for Phoebe.

PHOEBE And so am I for Ganymede.

ORLANDO And so am I for Rosalind.

ROSALIND And so am I for no woman.

PHOEBE [*to Rosalind*]
If this be so, why blame you me to love you? 100

SILVIUS [*to Phoebe*]
If this be so, why blame you me to love you?

ORLANDO
If this be so, why blame you me to love you?

ROSALIND Why do you speak too, "Why blame you me
to love you?"

ORLANDO To her that is not here, nor doth not hear.

ROSALIND Pray you, no more of this; 'tis like the
howling of Irish wolves against the moon. [*To Silvius*]
I will help you, if I can. [*To Phoebe*] I would love you, if
I could.—Tomorrow meet me all together. [*To Phoebe*] I
will marry you, if ever I marry woman, and I'll be
married tomorrow. [*To Orlando*] I will satisfy you, if
ever I satisfied man, and you shall be married
tomorrow. [*To Silvius*] I will content you, if what
pleases you contents you, and you shall be married
tomorrow. [*To Orlando*] As you love Rosalind, meet.
[*To Silvius*] As you love Phoebe, meet. And as I love
no woman, I'll meet. So fare you well. I have left you
commands.

SILVIUS I'll not fail, if I live.

PHOEBE Nor I.

ORLANDO Nor I.   *Exeunt* [*separately*].

---

37 incontinent immediately. (Followed by a pun on the meaning "unchaste or sexually unrestrained.") **39 wrath** impetuosity, ardor. **Clubs** i.e., Physical force, such as that employed by nightwatchmen armed with clubs **52–3 conceit** intelligence, understanding. **53 that** in order that **54 insomuch . . . are** from my saying I know you to be intelligent **55–7 neither . . . grace me** nor am I interested in winning approval except insofar as it may, by inspiring your confidence in my ability, prompt you to do something for your own benefit; it is not intended to bring favor on myself. **59 conversed** associated **60 not damnable** not a practicer of forbidden or black magic, worthy of execution and damnation. **61 gesture** bearing **61–2 cries it out** proclaims **63 she** Rosalind **65 inconvenient** inappropriate **66 human** i.e., the real Rosalind, not a phantom. **danger** i.e., the danger to the soul from one's involvement in magic or witchcraft. **67 in sober meanings** seriously. **68 tender dearly** value highly **69 though . . . magician** (According to Elizabethan antiwitchcraft statutes, some forms of witchcraft were punishable by death; Rosalind thus endangers her life by what she has said.) **70 bid** invite. **friends** family and friends **74 ungentleness** discourtesy

76 study conscious endeavor **91 fantasy** fancy, imagination **93 observance** devotion, respect **95 observance** (Perhaps a compositor's error, repeated from two lines previous; many editors emend it to *obedience*.) **100 to love you** for loving you.

5.3

Enter [Touchstone the] Clown and Audrey.

TOUCHSTONE   Tomorrow is the joyful day, Audrey;
tomorrow will we be married.

AUDREY   I do desire it with all my heart; and I hope it is
no dishonest desire to desire to be a woman of the   4
world. Here come two of the banished Duke's pages.   5

Enter two Pages.

FIRST PAGE   Well met, honest gentleman.   6

TOUCHSTONE   By my troth, well met. Come, sit, sit,
and a song.   [*They sit.*]

SECOND PAGE   We are for you. Sit i'th' middle.   9

FIRST PAGE   Shall we clap into't roundly, without hawk-   10
ing or spitting or saying we are hoarse, which are the   11
only prologues to a bad voice?   12

SECOND PAGE   I'faith, i'faith, and both in a tune, like   13
two gypsies on a horse.   14

Song.

BOTH PAGES

It was a lover and his lass,
    With a hey, and a ho, and a hey-nonny-no,
That o'er the green cornfield did pass   17
    In springtime, the only pretty ring time,   18
When birds do sing, hey ding a ding, ding,
Sweet lovers love the spring.

Between the acres of the rye,   21
    With a hey, and a ho, and a hey-nonny-no,
These pretty country folks would lie
    In springtime, the only pretty ring time,
When birds do sing, hey ding a ding, ding,
Sweet lovers love the spring.

This carol they began that hour,
    With a hey, and a ho, and hey-nonny-no,
How that a life was but a flower
    In springtime, the only pretty ring time,
When birds do sing, hey ding a ding, ding,
Sweet lovers love the spring.

And therefore take the present time,
    With a hey, and a ho, and a hey-nonny-no,
For love is crownèd with the prime   35
    In springtime, the only pretty ring time,
When birds do sing, hey ding a ding, ding,
Sweet lovers love the spring.

TOUCHSTONE   Truly, young gentlemen, though there
was no great matter in the ditty, yet the note was very   40
untunable.   41

FIRST PAGE   You are deceived, sir. We kept time, we lost   42
not our time.

TOUCHSTONE   By my troth, yes; I count it but time lost
to hear such a foolish song. God b'wi'you, and God
mend your voices! Come, Audrey. *Exeunt [separately].*

❖

5.4

*Enter Duke Senior, Amiens, Jaques, Orlando,
Oliver, [and] Celia.*

DUKE SENIOR

Dost thou believe, Orlando, that the boy
Can do all this that he hath promisèd?

ORLANDO

I sometimes do believe, and sometimes do not,
As those that fear they hope and know they fear.   4

Enter Rosalind, Silvius, and Phoebe.

ROSALIND

Patience once more, whiles our compact is urged.   5
[*To the Duke*] You say, if I bring in your Rosalind
You will bestow her on Orlando here?

DUKE SENIOR

That would I, had I kingdoms to give with her.

ROSALIND [*to Orlando*]

And you say you will have her when I bring her?

ORLANDO

That would I, were I of all kingdoms king.

ROSALIND [*to Phoebe*]

You say you'll marry me if I be willing?

PHOEBE

That will I, should I die the hour after.

ROSALIND

But if you do refuse to marry me
You'll give yourself to this most faithful shepherd?

PHOEBE   So is the bargain.

ROSALIND [*to Silvius*]

You say that you'll have Phoebe if she will?

SILVIUS

Though to have her and death were both one thing.

ROSALIND

I have promised to make all this matter even.   18
Keep you your word, O Duke, to give your daughter;
You yours, Orlando, to receive his daughter;
Keep you your word, Phoebe, that you'll marry me,
Or else, refusing me, to wed this shepherd;
Keep your word, Silvius, that you'll marry her
If she refuse me; and from hence I go,
To make these doubts all even.

Exeunt Rosalind and Celia.

DUKE SENIOR

I do remember in this shepherd boy
Some lively touches of my daughter's favor.   27

5.3 Location: The forest.
4 dishonest immodest   **4–5 woman of the world** married woman;
also, one who advances herself socially.   **6 honest** worthy   **9 We are
for you** i.e., Fine, we're ready.   **10 clap . . . roundly** begin briskly and
with spirit   **10–11 hawking** clearing the throat   **12 only** customary
13 in a tune (1) in unison (2) keeping time   **14 on a** on one   **17 cornfield** field of grain   **18 ring time** time most apt for marriage
21 Between the acres On unplowed strips between the fields
35 prime (1) height of perfection (2) spring   **40 matter** sense, meaning.   **note** music   **41 untunable** discordant.

42 deceived mistaken
5.4 Location: The forest.
4 they hope i.e., that they merely hope   **5 urged** put forward.
18 make . . . even set all this to rights, square accounts.   **27 lively**
lifelike.   **favor** appearance.

ORLANDO

My lord, the first time that I ever saw him
Methought he was a brother to your daughter.
But, my good lord, this boy is forest-born
And hath been tutored in the rudiments
Of many desperate studies by his uncle,   32
Whom he reports to be a great magician,
Obscurèd in the circle of this forest.   34

Enter [Touchstone the] Clown and Audrey.

JAQUES   There is, sure, another flood toward, and these   35
couples are coming to the ark. Here comes a pair of   36
very strange beasts, which in all tongues are called
fools.

TOUCHSTONE   Salutation and greeting to you all!

JAQUES   [*to the Duke*]   Good my lord, bid him welcome.
This is the motley-minded gentleman that I have so often
met in the forest. He hath been a courtier, he swears.

TOUCHSTONE   If any man doubt that, let him put me to
my purgation. I have trod a measure; I have flattered a   44
lady; I have been politic with my friend, smooth with   45
mine enemy; I have undone three tailors; I have had   46
four quarrels and like to have fought one.   47

JAQUES   And how was that ta'en up?   48

TOUCHSTONE   Faith, we met and found the quarrel was
upon the seventh cause.

JAQUES   How seventh cause?—Good my lord, like this
fellow.

DUKE SENIOR   I like him very well.

TOUCHSTONE   God 'ild you, sir, I desire you of the like.   54
I press in here, sir, amongst the rest of the country   55
copulatives, to swear and to forswear, according as   56
marriage binds and blood breaks. A poor virgin, sir,   57
an ill-favored thing, sir, but mine own; a poor humor   58
of mine, sir, to take that that no man else will. Rich
honesty dwells like a miser, sir, in a poor house, as   60
your pearl in your foul oyster.   61

DUKE SENIOR   By my faith, he is very swift and senten-   62
tious.   63

TOUCHSTONE   According to the fool's bolt, sir, and such   64
dulcet diseases.   65

JAQUES   But for the seventh cause. How did you find
the quarrel on the seventh cause?

TOUCHSTONE   Upon a lie seven times removed—bear
your body more seeming, Audrey—as thus, sir. I did   69
dislike the cut of a certain courtier's beard. He sent me   70
word if I said his beard was not cut well, he was in
the mind it was: this is called the Retort Courteous. If I
sent him word again it was not well cut, he would
send me word he cut it to please himself: this is called
the Quip Modest. If again it was not well cut, he dis-   75
abled my judgment: this is called the Reply Churlish. If   76
again it was not well cut, he would answer I spoke
not true: this is called the Reproof Valiant. If again it
was not well cut, he would say I lie: this is called the
Countercheck Quarrelsome. And so to the Lie Cir-   80
cumstantial and the Lie Direct.

JAQUES   And how oft did you say his beard was not well
cut?

TOUCHSTONE   I durst go no further than the Lie Circumstantial, nor he durst not give me the Lie Direct;
and so we measured swords and parted.   86

JAQUES   Can you nominate in order now the degrees of
the lie?

TOUCHSTONE   Oh, sir, we quarrel in print, by the book, as   89
you have books for good manners. I will name you the
degrees. The first, the Retort Courteous; the second,
the Quip Modest; the third, the Reply Churlish; the
fourth, the Reproof Valiant; the fifth, the Countercheck
Quarrelsome; the sixth, the Lie with Circumstance;
the seventh, the Lie Direct. All these you may
avoid but the Lie Direct; and you may avoid that, too,
with an If. I knew when seven justices could not take   97
up a quarrel, but when the parties were met them-   98
selves, one of them thought but of an If, as, "If you
said so, then I said so"; and they shook hands and
swore brothers. Your If is the only peacemaker; much   101
virtue in If.

JAQUES   Is not this a rare fellow, my lord? He's as good
at anything and yet a fool.

DUKE SENIOR   He uses his folly like a stalking-horse,   105
and under the presentation of that he shoots his wit.   106

Enter Hymen, Rosalind, and Celia. Still music.
[Rosalind and Celia are no longer disguised.]

HYMEN

Then is there mirth in heaven,   107
When earthly things made even   108
Atone together.   109
Good Duke, receive thy daughter;
Hymen from heaven brought her,
Yea, brought her hither,

---

32 desperate dangerous   **34 Obscurèd** hidden.   **circle** compass, boundaries. (With a possible allusion to the magic circle that protected the magician from the devil during incantation.)   **35 toward** coming on   **36 a pair** (In Genesis 7:2, God commands Noah to take on board every "clean" beast by sevens, but those that are not clean, by twos.)   **44 purgation** proof, trial.   **measure** slow, stately dance   **45 politic** cunning, Machiavellian.   **smooth** insinuating   **46 undone** bankrupted (by refusing to pay debts owed them)   **47 like** came close   **48 ta'en up** settled, made up.   **54 'ild** yield, reward.   **I . . . like** I wish the same to you. (A polite phrase used to reply to a compliment.)   **55–6 country copulatives** country couples about to marry and with sex on their minds   **57 blood breaks** as desire bursts forth.   **58 humor** whim   **60 honesty** chastity   **61 your pearl** i.e., the pearl that one hears about   **62–3 swift and sententious** quick-witted and good at aphorisms.   **64 fool's bolt** (Alluding to the proverb "A fool's bolt [arrow] is soon shot.")   **65 dulcet diseases** pleasant afflictions, entertaining yet sharp. (Touchstone wryly agrees with the Duke's assessment of the Fool as swift and sententious.)

69 seeming seemly   **70 dislike** express dislike of   **75–6 disabled** disparaged   **80 Countercheck** Rebuff   **86 measured swords** i.e., as in the mere preliminary to a duel   **89 in . . . book** in a precise way. (Touchstone is travestying books on the general subject of honor and arms, which dealt with occasions and circumstances of the duel.)   **97–8 take up** settle   **101 swore brothers** became sworn brothers.   **105 stalking-horse** a real or artificial horse under cover of which the hunter approached his game   **106 presentation** semblance   **106.1 *Hymen*** Roman god of faithful marriage.   ***Still*** Soft   **107 mirth** joy   **108 made even** set straight   **109 Atone** are at one

That thou mightst join her hand with his
Whose heart within his bosom is.   114

ROSALIND [to the Duke]
To you I give myself, for I am yours.
[To Orlando] To you I give myself, for I am yours.
DUKE SENIOR
If there be truth in sight, you are my daughter.
ORLANDO
If there be truth in sight, you are my Rosalind.
PHOEBE
If sight and shape be true,
Why then, my love adieu!
ROSALIND [to the Duke]
I'll have no father, if you be not he.
[To Orlando] I'll have no husband, if you be not he.
[To Phoebe] Nor ne'er wed woman, if you be not she.
HYMEN
Peace, ho! I bar confusion.
'Tis I must make conclusion
     Of these most strange events.
Here's eight that must take hands
To join in Hymen's bands,
     If truth holds true contents.   129
[To Orlando and Rosalind]
You and you no cross shall part.   130
[To Oliver and Celia]
You and you are heart in heart.
[To Phoebe]
You to his love must accord   132
Or have a woman to your lord.   133
[To Touchstone and Audrey]
You and you are sure together,   134
As the winter to foul weather.
[To all]
Whiles a wedlock hymn we sing,
Feed yourselves with questioning,   137
That reason wonder may diminish   138
How thus we met, and these things finish.

                          Song.

Wedding is great Juno's crown,   140
     O blessèd bond of board and bed!   141
'Tis Hymen peoples every town;
     High wedlock then be honorèd.   143
Honor, high honor and renown
     To Hymen, god of every town!

DUKE SENIOR [to Celia]
O my dear niece, welcome thou art to me!
Even daughter, welcome, in no less degree.   147

PHOEBE [to Silvius]
I will not eat my word, now thou art mine;
Thy faith my fancy to thee doth combine.   149

          Enter Second Brother [Jaques de Boys].

JAQUES DE BOYS
Let me have audience for a word or two.
I am the second son of old Sir Rowland,
That bring these tidings to this fair assembly.
Duke Frederick, hearing how that every day
Men of great worth resorted to this forest,
Addressed a mighty power, which were on foot   155
In his own conduct, purposely to take   156
His brother here and put him to the sword;
And to the skirts of this wild wood he came,
Where, meeting with an old religious man,
After some question with him, was converted   160
Both from his enterprise and from the world,
His crown bequeathing to his banished brother,
And all their lands restored to them again
That were with him exiled. This to be true
I do engage my life.
DUKE SENIOR   Welcome, young man.   165
Thou offer'st fairly to thy brothers' wedding: 166
To one his lands withheld and to the other   167
A land itself at large, a potent dukedom.   168
First, in this forest let us do those ends   169
That here were well begun and well begot;   170
And after, every of this happy number   171
That have endured shrewd days and nights with us   172
Shall share the good of our returnèd fortune
According to the measure of their states.   174
Meantime, forget this new-fall'n dignity,   175
And fall into our rustic revelry.
Play, music! And you, brides and bridegrooms all,
With measure heaped in joy, to th' measures fall.   178
JAQUES
Sir, by your patience.—If I heard you rightly,   179
The Duke hath put on a religious life
And thrown into neglect the pompous court.   181
JAQUES DE BOYS   He hath.
JAQUES
To him will I. Out of these convertites   183
There is much matter to be heard and learned.   184
[To the Duke] You to your former honor I bequeath;
Your patience and your virtue well deserves it.
[To Orlando] You to a love that your true faith doth
     merit;

114 Whose (Refers to Rosalind.)   129 If . . . contents if the newly revealed truths are indeed true and bring true contentment.
130 cross vexation, mischance   132 his i.e., Silvius's   accord agree
133 to your lord for your husband.   134 sure closely united
137 Feed satisfy   138 That . . . diminish that understanding may lessen your wonder   140 Juno's (Juno was the Roman queen of the gods, presiding, in the Renaissance view, over faithful wedlock.)
141 board and bed sustenance and lodging; the household.
143 High solemn   147 Even . . . degree You are as welcome as a daughter.

149 Thy faith . . . combine your faithful love for me ties my love to you.   155 Addressed prepared.   power army   156 In . . . conduct under his own command   160 question conversation   165 engage pledge   166 Thou offer'st fairly You contribute handsomely   167 To one to Duke Senior   167–8 to the other . . . large to Orlando an entire dukedom (since, as husband of Rosalind, Orlando will eventually inherit as duke).   169 do those ends accomplish those purposes   170 begot conceived   171 every every one   172 shrewd hard, trying   174 According . . . states according to their degrees.   175 new-fall'n newly acquired   178 With . . . fall with an overflowing measure of joy, fall to dancing. (With wordplay on *measure* and *measures*, "dances.")   179 by your patience by your leave, i.e., let the music wait a moment.   181 pompous ceremonious   183 convertites converts   184 matter sound sense

[*To Oliver*] You to your land and love and great allies;   188
[*To Silvius*] You to a long and well-deservèd bed;
[*To Touchstone*] And you to wrangling, for thy loving
    voyage
Is but for two months victualed. So, to your pleasures.   191
I am for other than for dancing measures.

DUKE SENIOR   Stay, Jaques, stay.

JAQUES
To see no pastime I. What you would have
I'll stay to know at your abandoned cave.   *Exit.*

DUKE SENIOR
Proceed, proceed. We'll begin these rites,
As we do trust they'll end, in true delights.
          [*They dance.*] *Exeunt* [*all but Rosalind*].

[Epilogue]

ROSALIND
It is not the fashion to see the lady the epilogue;
but it is no more unhandsome than to see the   2

lord the prologue. If it be true that good wine needs   3
no bush, 'tis true that a good play needs no epilogue.   4
Yet to good wine they do use good bushes, and good
plays prove the better by the help of good epilogues.
What a case am I in then, that am neither a good epilogue nor cannot insinuate with you in the behalf of a   8
good play! I am not furnished like a beggar; therefore   9
to beg will not become me. My way is to conjure you,   10
and I'll begin with the women. I charge you, O
women, for the love you bear to men, to like as much
of this play as please you; and I charge you, O men,
for the love you bear to women—as I perceive by your
simpering, none of you hates them—that between
you and the women the play may please. If I were a   16
woman I would kiss as many of you as had beards   17
that pleased me, complexions that liked me, and   18
breaths that I defied not; and I am sure as many as   19
have good beards or good faces or sweet breaths will,
for my kind offer, when I make curtsy, bid me fare-   21
well.   *Exit.*   22

---

188 allies kinfolk   **191 victualed** provisioned.
Epilogue
2 unhandsome in bad taste

3–4 good . . . bush (A proverb derived from the custom of displaying a piece of ivy or holly at the tavern door to denote that wine was for sale there.)   **8 insinuate** ingratiate myself   **9 furnished** equipped, decked out   **10 conjure** adjure, earnestly charge   **16–17 If . . . woman** (Womens's parts on the Elizabethan stage were played by boys in feminine costume.)   **18 liked** pleased   **19 defied** rejected, disdained   **21–2 bid me farewell** i.e., applaud me.

Twelfth Night; or, What You Will

welfth Night is possibly the latest of the three festive comedies, including *Much Ado About Nothing* and *As You Like It*, with which Shakespeare climaxed his distinctively philosophical and joyous vein of comic writing. Performed on February 2, 1602, at the Middle Temple and written possibly as early as 1599, *Twelfth Night* is usually dated 1600 or 1601. This play is indeed the most festive of the lot. Its keynote is Saturnalian release and the carnival pursuit of love and mirth. Along with such familiar motifs as the plucky heroine disguised as a man (found earlier in *The Two Gentlemen of Verona, As You Like It,* and *The Merchant of Venice*), *Twelfth Night* also returns to the more farcical routines of mistaken identity found in Shakespeare's early comedy. As a witness of the 1602 performance, John Manningham, observes, the play is "much like the *Comedy of Errors*, or *Menaechmi* in Plautus, but most like and near to that in Italian called *Inganni.*"

The carnival atmosphere is appropriate to the season designated in the play's title: the twelfth night of Christmas, January 6, the Feast of Epiphany. (The prologue to *Gl'Ingannati,* perhaps the Italian play referred to by Manningham, speaks of "La Notte di Beffania," Epiphany night.) Along with its primary Christian significance as the Feast of the Magi, Epiphany was also in Renaissance times the last day of the Christmas revels. Over a twelve-day period, from Christmas until January 6, noble households sponsored numerous performances of plays, masks, banquets, and every kind of festivity. (Leslie Hotson argues, in fact, that *Twelfth Night* was first performed on twelfth night in early 1601, in the presence of Queen Elizabeth.) Students left schools for vacations, celebrating release from study with plays and revels of their own. The stern rigors of a rule-bound society gave way temporarily to playful inversions of authority. The reign of the Boy Bishop and the Feast of Fools, for example, gave choristers and minor church functionaries the cherished opportunity to boss the hierarchy around, mock the

liturgy with outrageous lampooning, and generally let off steam. Although such customs occasionally got out of hand, the idea was to channel potentially destructive insubordination into playacting and thereby promote harmony. Behind these Elizabethan midwinter customs lies the Roman Saturnalia, with its pagan spirit of gift giving, sensual indulgence, and satirical hostility to those who would curb merriment. Shakespeare's play captures the medieval and Renaissance spirit of Epiphany by its often playful allusions to religious practice: Feste's disguise as "Sir Topas," the priest, Feste's joke about living by the church (3.1.3–7), Sir Toby's defense of "cakes and ale," Feste's swearing by Saint Anne, mother of the Virgin Mary (2.3.115–16), Feste's joking about "clerestories" (4.2.38), and the like. Shakespeare lovingly evokes a tradition of festivals and ceremonies that incorporates self-mockery into its celebration of renewal at Christmas time.

Shakespeare's choice of sources for *Twelfth Night* underscores his commitment to mirth. Renaissance literature offered numerous instances of mistaken identity among twins and of the disguised heroine serving as page to her beloved. Among those in English were the anonymous play *Sir Clyomon and Sir Clamydes* (c. 1570–1583), Sir Philip Sidney's *Arcadia* (1590), and the prose romance *Parismus* by Emmanuel Forde (1598), featuring both a shipwreck and two characters with the names of Olivia and Violetta. Of particular significance, though partly for negative reasons, is Barnabe Riche's tale of "Apollonius and Silla" in *Riche His Farewell to Military Profession* (1581), which was based on François de Belleforest's 1571 French version of Matteo Bandello's *Novelle* (1554). Here we find most of the requisite plot elements: the shipwreck; Silla's disguise as a page in Duke Apollonius' court; her office as ambassador of love from Apollonius to the lady Julina, who thereupon falls in love with Silla; and the arrival of Silla's twin brother Silvio and his consequent success in winning Julina's affection. To Riche, however, this tale is merely a long warning against the enervating power of infatuation. Silvio gets Julina with child and disappears forthwith, making his belated reappearance almost too late to save the wrongly accused Silla. Riche's moralizing puts the blame on the gross and drunken appetite of carnal love. The total mismatching of affection with which the story begins, and the sudden realignments of desire based on mere outward resemblances, are seen as proofs of love's unreasonableness. Shakespeare, of course, retains and capitalizes on the irrational quality of love, as in *A Midsummer Night's Dream,* but in doing so he minimizes the harm done (Olivia is not made pregnant) and repudiates any negative moral judgments. The added subplot, with its rebuking of Malvolio's censoriousness, may have been conceived as a further answer to Riche, Fenton, and their sober school.

Shakespeare's festive spirit owes much, as Manningham observed, to Plautus and the neoclassical Italian comic writers. At least three Italian comedies called *Gl'Inganni* ("The Frauds") employ the motif of mistaken identity, and one of them, by Curzio Gonzaga (1592), supplies Viola's assumed name of "Cesare," or Cesario. Another play with the same title appeared in 1562. More useful is *Gl'Ingannati* ("The Deceived"), performed in 1531 and translated into French in 1543. Besides a plot line generally similar to *Twelfth Night* and the reference to La Notte di Beffania (Epiphany), this play offers the suggestive name *Malevolti,* "evil-faced," and *Fabio* (which resembles "Fabian"). It also contains possible hints for Malvolio, Sir Toby, and company, although the plot of the counterfeit letter is original with Shakespeare. Essentially, Shakespeare combines his own plot with an Italianate novella plot, as he did in *The Taming of the Shrew* and *Much Ado About Nothing.* And it is in the Malvolio story that Shakespeare most pointedly defends merriment. Feste the professional fool, an original stage type for Shakespeare in *Twelfth Night* and in *As You Like It,* also reinforces the theme of seizing the moment of mirth.

This great lesson, of savoring life's pleasures while one is still young, is something that Orsino and Olivia have not yet learned when the play commences. Although suited to one another in rank, wealth, and attractiveness, they are unable to overcome their own willful posturing in the elaborate charade of courtship. Like Silvius in *As You Like It,* Orsino is the conventional wooer trapped in the courtly artifice of love's rules. He opens the play on a cloying note of self-pity. He is fascinated with his own degradation as a rejected suitor and bores his listeners with his changeable moods and fondness for poetical "conceits." He sees himself as a hart pursued by his desires "like fell and cruel hounds," reminding us that enervating lovesickness has, in fact, robbed him of his manly occupation, hunting. He sends ornately contrived messages to Olivia but has not seen her in so long that his passion has become unreal and fantastical, feeding on itself.

Olivia plays the opposite role of chaste, denying womanhood. She explains her retirement from the world as mourning for a dead brother (whose name we never learn), but this withdrawal from life is another unreal vision. Olivia's practice of mourning, whereby she will "water once a day her chamber round / With eye-offending brine" (1.1.28–9), is a lifeless ritual. As others view the matter, she is senselessly wasting her beauty and affection on the dead. "What a plague means my niece to take the death of her brother thus?" Sir Toby expostulates (1.3.1–2). Viola, though she, too, has seemingly lost a brother, is an important foil in this regard, for she continues to hope for her brother's safety, trusts his soul is in heaven if he is dead, and refuses to give up her commitment to life in any case. We suspect that Olivia takes a willful pleasure in self-denial not unlike Orsino's self-congratulatory suffering. She appears to derive satisfaction from the power she holds over Orsino, a power of refusal. And she must know that she looks stunning in black.

Olivia's household reflects, in part, her mood of self-denial. She keeps Malvolio as steward because he, too, dresses somberly, insists on quiet as befits a house in mourning, and maintains order. Yet Olivia also retains a fool, Feste, who is Malvolio's opposite in every way. Hard-pressed to defend his mirthful function in a household so given over to melancholy, Feste must find some way of persuading his mistress that her very gravity is itself the essence of folly. This is a paradox, because sobriety and order appeal to the conventional wisdom of the world. Malvolio, sensing that his devotion to propriety is being challenged by the fool's prating, chides Olivia for taking "delight in such a barren rascal" (1.5.80–1).

Feste must argue for an inversion of appearance and reality whereby many of the world's ordinary pursuits can be seen to be ridiculous. As he observes, in his habitually elliptical manner of speech, "*Cucullus non facit monachum* [the cowl doesn't make the monk]; that's as much to say as I wear not motley in my brain" (1.5.52–4). Feste wins his case by making Olivia laugh at her own illogic in grieving for a brother whose soul she assumes to be in heaven. By extension, Olivia has indeed been a fool for allowing herself to be deprived of happiness in love by her brother's death ("there is no true cuckold but calamity") and for failing to consider the brevity of youth ("beauty's a flower"). Yet, paradoxically, only one who professes to be a fool can point this out, enabled by his detachment and innocence to perceive simple but profound truths denied to supposedly rational persons. This vision of the fool as naturally wise, and of society as self-indulgently insane, fascinated Renaissance writers, from Erasmus's *In Praise of Folly* and Cervantes's *Don Quixote* to Shakespeare's *King Lear.*

Viola, although not dressed in motley, aligns herself with Feste's rejection of self-denial. Refreshingly, even comically, she challenges the staid artifice of Orsino's and Olivia's lives. She is an ocean traveler, like many of Shakespeare's later heroines (Marina in *Pericles*, Perdita in *The Winter's Tale*), arriving on Illyria's shore plucky and determined. On her first embassy to Olivia from Orsino, she exposes with disarming candor the willfully ritualistic quality of Olivia's existence. Viola discards the flowery set speech she had prepared and memorized at Orsino's behest; despite her charmingly conceited assertion that the speech has been "excellently well penned," she senses that its elegant but empty rhetoric is all too familiar to the disdainful Olivia. Instead, Viola departs from her text to urge seizing the moment of happiness. "You do usurp yourself," she lectures Olivia, "for what is yours to bestow is not yours to reserve" (1.5.183–4). Beauty is a gift of nature, and failure to use it is a sin against nature. Or, again, "Lady, you are the cruel'st she alive / If you will lead these graces [Olivia's beauty] to the grave / And leave the world no copy" (lines 236–8). An essential argument in favor of love, as in Shakespeare's sonnets, is the necessity of marriage and childbearing in order to perpetuate beauty. This approach is new to Olivia and catches her wholly by surprise. In part, she reacts, like Phoebe in *As You Like It,* with perverse logic, rejecting a too-willing wooer for one who is hard to get. Yet Olivia is also attracted by a new note of sincerity, prompting her to reenter life and accept maturely both the risks and rewards of romantic involvement. Her longing for "Cesario" is, of course, sexually misdirected, but the appearance of Viola's identical twin, Sebastian, soon puts all to rights.

The motifs of Olivia's attraction for another woman (both actors would have been boys) and of Orsino's deep fondness for a seeming young man ("Cesario"), which matures into sexual love, raise delicate suggestions of love between members of the same sex, as in *As You Like It*. Once again, the ambiguities of disguise point toward the socially constructed nature of sexual difference. Viola as "Cesario" strikes those who meet her as almost sexually indeterminate. Orsino puts the matter well, in conversing with "Cesario," when he observes, "they shall yet belie thy happy years / That say thou art a man. Diana's lip / Is not more smooth and rubious; thy small pipe / Is as the maiden's organ, shrill and sound, / And all is semblative a woman's part" (1.4.30–4). Male adolescence and femininity are seen as virtually indistinguishable—a point that is wittily reinforced in the theater by the fact that a boy actor is playing Viola disguised as "Cesario."

At the same time, this playful confusion of sexual difference becomes the vehicle for a serious exploration of love and friendship. Like Rosalind in *As You Like It*, Viola uses her male attire to win Orsino's pure affection in a friendship nominally devoid of sexual interest, since both seemingly are men. Friendship must come first; the Renaissance generally accorded a higher value to friendship than to erotic passion. Yet Shakespeare also insists, as did many of his contemporaries (including Montaigne), that friendship is not only possible between men and women but also that such a relationship, formalized in marriage, offers the best of all worlds; hence, the importance of Viola's male disguise. As "Cesario," she can teach Orsino about the conventions of love in relaxed and frank conversations that would not be possible if she were known to be a woman. She teaches him to avoid the beguiling but misleading myths of Petrarchan love (named after the Italian sonneteer Francis Petrarch, whose poems embody the idealization of courtly love) and so prepares him for the realities of marriage. Comparing men and women in love, she confides, "We men may say more, swear more, but indeed / Our shows are more than will; for still we prove / Much in our vows, but little in our love" (2.4.116–18). Once she and Orsino have achieved an instinctive rapport—all the more remarkable for their talking so often at cross-purposes—Viola's unmasking can make possible a physical communion as well. Orsino, no longer trapped in the futile worship of a seemingly unapproachable goddess, can come to terms with his sexuality as part of a unified and loving human relationship.

The friendship of Sebastian and Antonio, meanwhile, sorely tested by the mix-ups of the mistaken identity plot, similarly places Sebastian in a love-and-friendship triangle like that involving Bassanio, Portia, and Antonio in *The Merchant of Venice*. Sebastian and Antonio are loving friends, so much so that Antonio willingly risks his life to be with Sebastian in a country where Antonio has many enemies. Antonio's expressions of fondness for Sebastian are extraordinarily warm. "If you will not murder me for my love, let me be your servant," he pleads. "I do adore thee so / That danger shall seem sport, and I will go" (2.1.33–4, 45–6). A desire "More sharp than filèd steel" spurs Antonio to seek out his friend, despite the manifest danger (3.3.4–5). "A witchcraft" draws him to Sebastian (5.1.72). Whether the attachment is homosexual, as it is often played on the modern stage, is debatable; expressions of warmth between men seem to have been more common in Elizabethan times than today, and centuries of intervening time have no doubt altered our understanding of same-sex relationships; the term *homosexual* is of much later date. What remains true for the play is that this portrayal of emotional and loving closeness between two men gives way to the marriage of one of them to a woman (as in *The Merchant of Venice*). The depiction of love and friendship between two men is a repeated motif in the play, embodied most of all in the loving relationship of Orsino and "Cesario." Shakespeare chooses to resolve his plot by defining heterosexual marriage as the completion of relationships begun in friendship and incorporating that friendship in a union that finally offers heterosexual fulfillment as well.

The below-stairs characters of the subplot, Sir Toby and the rest, share with Feste and Viola a commitment to joy. As Sir Toby proclaims in his first speech, "care's an enemy to life" (1.3.2–3). Even the simpleton Sir Andrew, although gulled by Sir Toby into spending his money on a hopeless pursuit of Olivia, seems none the worse for his treatment; he loves to drink in Sir Toby's company and can afford to pay for his entertainment. Sir Toby gives us some of the richly inventive humor of Falstaff, another lovable fat roguish knight. In this subplot, however, the confrontations between merriment and sobriety are more harshly drawn than in the main plot. Whereas the gracious Olivia is won away from her folly, the obdurate Malvolio can only be exposed to ridicule. He is chiefly to blame for the polarization of attitudes, for he insists on rebuking the mirth of others. His name (*Mal-volio*, the "ill-wisher") implies a self-satisfied determination to impose his rigid moral code on others. As Sir Toby taunts him, "Dost thou think, because thou art virtuous, there shall be no more cakes and ale?" (2.3.114–15). Malvolio's inflexible hostility provokes a desire for comic vengeance. The method is satiric: the clever manipulators, Maria and Sir Toby, invent a scheme to entrap Malvolio in his own self-deceit. The punishment fits the crime, for he has long dreamed of himself as "Count Malvolio," rich, powerful, and in a position to demolish Sir Toby and the rest. Without Malvolio's infatuated predisposition to believe that Olivia could actually love him and write such a letter as he finds, Maria's scheme would have no hope of success. He tortures the text to make it yield a suitable meaning, much in the style of Puritan theologizing. His conviction that Jove is

with him (2.5.169) reminds us of the Puritan belief that prosperity of the "elect" is a sign of God's grace.

Indeed, Malvolio in some ways does resemble a Puritan, as Maria observes (2.3.139–47), even though she qualifies the assertion by saying that he is not a religious fanatic but a "time-pleaser." She directs her observation not at a religious group but at all who would be killjoys; if the Puritans are like that, she intimates, so much the worse for them. This uncharacteristic lack of charity gives a sharp tone to the vengeance practiced on Malvolio, evoking from Olivia a protest that "he hath been most notoriously abused" (5.1.379). The belated attempt to make a reconciliation with him seems, however, doomed to failure, in light of his grim resolve to "be revenged on the whole pack of you." At the height of his discomfiture, he has been tricked into doing the two things he hates most: smiling affably and wearing sportive attire. The appearance of merriment is so grossly unsuited to him that he is declared mad and put into safekeeping. The apostle of sobriety in this play thus comes before us as a declared madman, while the fool Feste offers him sage comment in the guise of a priest. Wisdom and folly have changed places. The upside-down character of the play is epitomized in Malvolio's plaintive remark to Feste (no longer posing as the priest): "I am as well in my wits, Fool, as thou art" (4.2.88). Malvolio's comeuppance is richly deserved, but the severity of vengeance and countervengeance suggests that the triumph of festival will not last long. This brevity is, of course, inherent in the nature of such holiday release from responsibility. As Feste sings, "What's to come is still unsure. / In delay there lies no plenty."

Twelfth Night; or, What You Will

[*Dramatis Personae*

ORSINO, *Duke (sometimes called Count) of Illyria*
VALENTINE, *gentleman attending on Orsino*
CURIO, *gentleman attending on Orsino*

VIOLA, *a shipwrecked lady, later disguised as Cesario*
SEBASTIAN, *twin brother of Viola*
ANTONIO, *a sea captain, friend to Sebastian*
CAPTAIN *of the shipwrecked vessel*

OLIVIA, *a rich countess of Illyria*
MARIA, *gentlewoman in Olivia's household*

    SCENE: *Illyria*]

SIR TOBY BELCH, *Olivia's uncle*
SIR ANDREW AGUECHEEK, *a companion of Sir Toby*
MALVOLIO, *steward of Olivia's household*
FABIAN, *a member of Olivia's household*
FESTE, *a clown, also called* FOOL, *Olivia's jester*

A PRIEST
FIRST OFFICER
SECOND OFFICER

Lords, Sailors, Musicians, and other Attendants

1.1

*Enter Orsino Duke of Illyria, Curio, and other
lords [with musicians].*

ORSINO
If music be the food of love, play on;
Give me excess of it, that surfeiting,
The appetite may sicken and so die.
That strain again! It had a dying fall!   4
Oh, it came o'er my ear like the sweet sound
That breathes upon a bank of violets,
Stealing and giving odor. Enough, no more.
'Tis not so sweet now as it was before.
O spirit of love, how quick and fresh art thou,   9
That, notwithstanding thy capacity
Receiveth as the sea, naught enters there,
Of what validity and pitch soe'er,   12
But falls into abatement and low price   13
Even in a minute! So full of shapes is fancy   14
That it alone is high fantastical.   15

CURIO
Will you go hunt, my lord?
ORSINO   What, Curio?
CURIO   The hart.
ORSINO
Why, so I do, the noblest that I have.   17
Oh, when mine eyes did see Olivia first,
Methought she purged the air of pestilence.
That instant was I turned into a hart,
And my desires, like fell and cruel hounds,   21
E'er since pursue me.

Enter Valentine.

            How now, what news from her?   22
VALENTINE
So please my lord, I might not be admitted,
But from her handmaid do return this answer:
The element itself, till seven years' heat,   25
Shall not behold her face at ample view;
But like a cloistress she will veilèd walk,   27
And water once a day her chamber round
With eye-offending brine—all this to season   29

1.1 Location: Orsino's court.
0.1 *Illyria* Nominally on the east coast of the Adriatic Sea, but with a suggestion also of "illusion" and "delirium." **4 fall** cadence **9 quick and fresh** keen and hungry **12 validity** value. **pitch** superiority. (Literally, the highest point of a falcon's flight.) **13 abatement** depreciation. (The lover's brain entertains innumerable fantasies but soon tires of them all.) **14 shapes** imagined forms. **fancy** love **15 it . . . fantastical** it surpasses everything else in imaginative power.

17 the noblest . . . have i.e., my noblest part, my heart. (Punning on *hart*.) **21 fell** fierce **22 pursue me** (Alludes to the story in Ovid of Actaeon, who, having seen Diana bathing, was transformed into a stag and killed by his own hounds.) **25 element** sky. **seven years' heat** seven summers **27 cloistress** nun secluded in a religious community **29 season** keep fresh. (Playing on the idea of the salt in her tears.)

A brother's dead love, which she would keep fresh 30
And lasting in her sad remembrance.

ORSINO

Oh, she that hath a heart of that fine frame 32
To pay this debt of love but to a brother,
How will she love, when the rich golden shaft 34
Hath killed the flock of all affections else 35
That live in her; when liver, brain, and heart, 36
These sovereign thrones, are all supplied, and filled 37
Her sweet perfections, with one self king! 38
Away before me to sweet beds of flowers.
Love-thoughts lie rich when canopied with bowers.
Exeunt.

✤

1.2

Enter Viola, a Captain, and sailors.

VIOLA   What country, friends, is this?

CAPTAIN   This is Illyria, lady.

VIOLA

And what should I do in Illyria?
My brother he is in Elysium. 4
Perchance he is not drowned. What think you, sailors? 5

CAPTAIN

It is perchance that you yourself were saved. 6

VIOLA

Oh, my poor brother! And so perchance may he be.

CAPTAIN

True, madam, and to comfort you with chance, 8
Assure yourself, after our ship did split,
When you and those poor number saved with you
Hung on our driving boat, I saw your brother, 11
Most provident in peril, bind himself,
Courage and hope both teaching him the practice,
To a strong mast that lived upon the sea; 14
Where, like Arion on the dolphin's back, 15
I saw him hold acquaintance with the waves
So long as I could see.

VIOLA   For saying so, there's gold.   [*She gives money.*]
Mine own escape unfoldeth to my hope, 19
Whereto thy speech serves for authority, 20
The like of him. Know'st thou this country? 21

CAPTAIN

Ay, madam, well, for I was bred and born
Not three hours' travel from this very place.

VIOLA   Who governs here?

CAPTAIN   A noble duke, in nature as in name.

VIOLA   What is his name?

CAPTAIN   Orsino.

VIOLA

Orsino! I have heard my father name him.
He was a bachelor then.

CAPTAIN

And so is now, or was so very late; 30
For but a month ago I went from hence,
And then 'twas fresh in murmur—as, you know, 32
What great ones do the less will prattle of— 33
That he did seek the love of fair Olivia.

VIOLA   What's she?

CAPTAIN

A virtuous maid, the daughter of a count
That died some twelvemonth since, then leaving her
In the protection of his son, her brother,
Who shortly also died; for whose dear love,
They say, she hath abjured the sight
And company of men.

VIOLA   Oh, that I served that lady,
And might not be delivered to the world 42
Till I had made mine own occasion mellow, 43
What my estate is!

CAPTAIN   That were hard to compass, 44
Because she will admit no kind of suit,
No, not the Duke's. 46

VIOLA

There is a fair behavior in thee, Captain,
And though that nature with a beauteous wall 48
Doth oft close in pollution, yet of thee
I will believe thou hast a mind that suits
With this thy fair and outward character. 51
I prithee, and I'll pay thee bounteously,
Conceal me what I am, and be my aid
For such disguise as haply shall become 54
The form of my intent. I'll serve this duke. 55
Thou shalt present me as an eunuch to him. 56
It may be worth thy pains, for I can sing
And speak to him in many sorts of music
That will allow me very worth his service. 59
What else may hap, to time I will commit;
Only shape thou thy silence to my wit. 61

CAPTAIN

Be you his eunuch, and your mute I'll be; 62
When my tongue blabs, then let mine eyes not see.

VIOLA   I thank thee. Lead me on.   *Exeunt.*

✤

---

30 A brother's dead love her love for her dead brother and the memory of his love for her   **32 frame** construction   **34 golden shaft** Cupid's golden-tipped arrow, causing love. (His lead-tipped arrow causes aversion.)   **35 affections else** other feelings   **36–8 when . . . king** i.e., when passion, thought, and feeling all sit in majesty in their proper thrones (liver, brain, and heart), and her sweet perfections are brought to completion by her union with a single lord and husband.
1.2 Location: The seacoast.
4 Elysium classical abode of the blessed dead   **5-6 Perchance . . . perchance** Perhaps . . . by mere chance   **8 chance** i.e., what one may hope that chance will bring about   **11 driving** drifting, driven by the seas   **14 lived** i.e., kept afloat   **15 Arion** a Greek poet who so charmed the dolphins with his lyre that they saved him when he leaped into the sea to escape murderous sailors   **19-21 unfoldeth . . . him** offers a hopeful example that he may have escaped similarly, to which hope your speech provides support.

30 late lately   **32 murmur** rumor   **33 less** social inferiors   **42 delivered** revealed, made known. (With suggestion of "born.")   **43 Till . . . mellow** until the time is ripe for my purpose   **44 estate** social rank. **compass** encompass, bring about   **46 not** not even   **48 though that** though   **51 character** face or features as indicating moral qualities. **54–5 as haply . . . intent** as may suit the nature of my purpose. **56 eunuch** castrato, high-voiced singer   **59 allow** prove   **61 wit** plan, invention.   **62 mute** silent attendant. (Sometimes used of nonspeaking actors.)

1.3

Enter Sir Toby [Belch] and Maria.

SIR TOBY   What a plague means my niece to take the
death of her brother thus? I am sure care's an enemy
to life.

MARIA   By my troth, Sir Toby, you must come in earlier
o'nights. Your cousin, my lady, takes great exceptions   5
to your ill hours.

SIR TOBY   Why, let her except before excepted.   7

MARIA   Ay, but you must confine yourself within the
modest limits of order.   9

SIR TOBY   Confine? I'll confine myself no finer than I am.   10
These clothes are good enough to drink in, and so be
these boots too. An they be not, let them hang them-   12
selves in their own straps.

MARIA   That quaffing and drinking will undo you. I
heard my lady talk of it yesterday, and of a foolish
knight that you brought in one night here to be her
wooer.

SIR TOBY   Who, Sir Andrew Aguecheek?

MARIA   Ay, he.

SIR TOBY   He's as tall a man as any's in Illyria.   20

MARIA   What's that to the purpose?

SIR TOBY   Why, he has three thousand ducats a year.   22

MARIA   Ay, but he'll have but a year in all these ducats.   23
He's a very fool and a prodigal.

SIR TOBY   Fie, that you'll say so! He plays o'th' viol-de-   25
gamboys, and speaks three or four languages word   26
for word without book, and hath all the good gifts of   27
nature.

MARIA   He hath indeed, almost natural, for, besides that   29
he's a fool, he's a great quarreler, and but that he hath
the gift of a coward to allay the gust he hath in quar-   31
reling, 'tis thought among the prudent he would
quickly have the gift of a grave.

SIR TOBY   By this hand, they are scoundrels and sub-   34
stractors that say so of him. Who are they?   35

MARIA   They that add, moreover, he's drunk nightly in
your company.

SIR TOBY   With drinking healths to my niece. I'll drink
to her as long as there is a passage in my throat and
drink in Illyria. He's a coward and a coistrel that will   40
not drink to my niece till his brains turn o'th' toe like

a parish top. What, wench? *Castiliano vulgo!* For here   42
comes Sir Andrew Agueface.   43

Enter Sir Andrew [Aguecheek].

SIR ANDREW   Sir Toby Belch! How now, Sir Toby Belch?

SIR TOBY   Sweet Sir Andrew!

SIR ANDREW   [*to Maria*]   Bless you, fair shrew.   46

MARIA   And you too, sir.

SIR TOBY   Accost, Sir Andrew, accost.   48

SIR ANDREW   What's that?

SIR TOBY   My niece's chambermaid.   50

SIR ANDREW   Good Mistress Accost, I desire better
acquaintance.

MARIA   My name is Mary, sir.

SIR ANDREW   Good Mistress Mary Accost—

SIR TOBY   You mistake, knight. "Accost" is front her,   55
board her, woo her, assail her.   56

SIR ANDREW   By my troth, I would not undertake her in   57
this company. Is that the meaning of "accost"?

MARIA   Fare you well, gentlemen.   [*Going.*]

SIR TOBY   An thou let part so, Sir Andrew, would thou   60
mightst never draw sword again.

SIR ANDREW   An you part so, mistress, I would I might
never draw sword again. Fair lady, do you think you
have fools in hand?   64

MARIA   Sir, I have not you by the hand.

SIR ANDREW   Marry, but you shall have, and here's my   66
hand.   [*He gives her his hand.*]

MARIA   Now, sir, thought is free. I pray you, bring your   68
hand to th' buttery-bar, and let it drink.   69

SIR ANDREW   Wherefore, sweetheart? What's your
metaphor?

MARIA   It's dry, sir.   72

SIR ANDREW   Why, I think so. I am not such an ass but
I can keep my hand dry. But what's your jest?

MARIA   A dry jest, sir.   75

SIR ANDREW   Are you full of them?

MARIA   Ay, sir, I have them at my fingers' ends. Marry,   77
now I let go your hand, I am barren.   78

[*She lets go his hand.*] *Exit Maria.*

1.3 Location: Olivia's house.
5 cousin kinswoman   **7 let . . . excepted** i.e., let her take exception to
my conduct all she wants; I don't care. (Plays on the legal phrase
exceptis excipiendis, "with the exceptions before named.")   **9 modest**
moderate   **10 I'll . . . finer** (1) I'll constrain myself no more rigorously (2) I'll dress myself no more finely   **12 An** If   **20 tall** brave.
(But Maria pretends to take the word in the common sense.)
22 ducats coins worth about four or five shillings   **23 he'll . . . ducats**
he'll spend all his money within a year.   **25–6 viol-de-gamboys** viola
da gamba, leg-viol, bass viol   **27 without book** by heart
29 natural (With a play on the sense "born idiot.")   **31 gift** natural
ability. (But shifted to mean "present" in line 33.)   **allay the gust**
moderate the taste   **34–5 substractors** detractors   **40 coistrel** horse-
groom, base fellow

42 parish top a large top provided by the parish to be spun by whipping, apparently for exercise.   **Castiliano vulgo!** (Of uncertain meaning. Possibly Sir Toby is saying "Speak of the devil!" Castiliano is the
name adopted by a devil in Haughton's *Grim the Collier of Croydon.*)
43 Agueface (Like *Aguecheek,* this name betokens the thin, pale countenance of one suffering from an ague or fever.)   **46 shrew** i.e.,
diminutive creature. (But with probably unintended suggestion of
shrewishness.)   **48 Accost** Go alongside (a nautical term), i.e., greet
her, address her   **50 chambermaid** lady-in-waiting (a gentlewoman,
not one who would do menial tasks).   **55 front** confront, come alongside   **56 board** greet, approach (as though preparing to board in a
naval encounter)   **57 undertake** have to do with. (Here with unintended sexual suggestion, to which Maria mirthfully replies with her
jokes about *dry jests, barren* and *buttery-bar.*)   **60 An . . . part** If you let
her leave   **64 have . . . hand** i.e., have to deal with fools. (But Maria
puns on the literal sense.)   **66 Marry** i.e., Indeed. (Originally, "By the
Virgin Mary.")   **68 thought is free** i.e., I may think what I like.
(Proverbial; replying to *do you think . . . in hand,* above.)   **buttery-
bar** ledge on top of the half-door to the buttery or the wine cellar.
(Maria's language is sexually suggestive, though Sir Andrew seems
oblivious to that.)   **72 dry** thirsty; also dried up, a sign of age and
sexual debility   **75 dry** (1) ironic (2) dull, barren. (Referring to Sir
Andrew.)   **77 at my fingers' ends** (1) at the ready (2) by the hand.
78 barren i.e., empty of jests and of Sir Andrew's hand.

SIR TOBY   Oh, knight, thou lack'st a cup of canary! When 79
did I see thee so put down?

SIR ANDREW   Never in your life, I think, unless you see
canary put me down. Methinks sometimes I have no 82
more wit than a Christian or an ordinary man has. But
I am a great eater of beef, and I believe that does harm
to my wit.

SIR TOBY   No question.

SIR ANDREW   An I thought that, I'd forswear it. I'll ride
home tomorrow, Sir Toby.

SIR TOBY   *Pourquoi,* my dear knight? 89

SIR ANDREW   What is *"pourquoi"*? Do or not do? I would
I had bestowed that time in the tongues that I 91
have in fencing, dancing, and bearbaiting. Oh, had I 92
but followed the arts! 93

SIR TOBY   Then hadst thou had an excellent head of hair.

SIR ANDREW   Why, would that have mended my hair? 95

SIR TOBY   Past question, for thou see'st it will not curl by
nature.

SIR ANDREW   But it becomes me well enough, does't
not?

SIR TOBY   Excellent. It hangs like flax on a distaff; and I 100
hope to see a huswife take thee between her legs and
spin it off. 102

SIR ANDREW   Faith, I'll home tomorrow, Sir Toby. Your
niece will not be seen, or if she be, it's four to one
she'll none of me. The Count himself here hard by 105
woos her.

SIR TOBY   She'll none o'th' Count. She'll not match
above her degree, neither in estate, years, nor wit; I 108
have heard her swear't. Tut, there's life in't, man. 109

SIR ANDREW   I'll stay a month longer. I am a fellow o'th'
strangest mind i'th' world; I delight in masques and
revels sometimes altogether.

SIR TOBY   Art thou good at these kickshawses, knight? 113

SIR ANDREW   As any man in Illyria, whatsoever he be,
under the degree of my betters, and yet I will not 115
compare with an old man. 116

SIR TOBY   What is thy excellence in a galliard, knight? 117

SIR ANDREW   Faith, I can cut a caper. 118

SIR TOBY   And I can cut the mutton to't.

SIR ANDREW   And I think I have the back-trick simply 120
as strong as any man in Illyria.

SIR TOBY   Wherefore are these things hid? Wherefore
have these gifts a curtain before 'em? Are they like to 123
take dust, like Mistress Mall's picture? Why dost thou 124
not go to church in a galliard and come home in a
coranto? My very walk should be a jig; I would not so 126
much as make water but in a sink-a-pace. What dost 127
thou mean? Is it a world to hide virtues in? I did think, 128
by the excellent constitution of thy leg, it was formed
under the star of a galliard. 130

SIR ANDREW   Ay, 'tis strong, and it does indifferent well 131
in a dun-colored stock. Shall we set about some 132
revels?

SIR TOBY   What shall we do else? Were we not born
under Taurus? 135

SIR ANDREW   Taurus? That's sides and heart.

SIR TOBY   No, sir, it is legs and thighs. Let me see thee
caper. [*Sir Andrew capers.*] Ha, higher! Ha, ha, excel-
lent!   *Exeunt.*

✣

1.4

Enter Valentine, and Viola in man's attire.

VALENTINE   If the Duke continue these favors towards
you, Cesario, you are like to be much advanced. He 2
hath known you but three days, and already you are
no stranger.

VIOLA   You either fear his humor or my negligence, 5
that you call in question the continuance of his love. Is
he inconstant, sir, in his favors?

VALENTINE   No, believe me.

Enter Duke [Orsino], Curio, and attendants.

VIOLA   I thank you. Here comes the Count.

ORSINO   Who saw Cesario, ho?

VIOLA   On your attendance, my lord, here. 11

ORSINO
Stand you awhile aloof. [*The others stand aside.*]
    Cesario, 12
Thou know'st no less but all. I have unclasped
To thee the book even of my secret soul.
Therefore, good youth, address thy gait unto her; 15
Be not denied access, stand at her doors,

---

79 thou . . . canary i.e., you look as if you need a drink. (*Canary* is a
sweet wine from the Canary Islands.)   **82 put me down** (1) baffle my
wits (2) lay me out flat.   **89 *Pourquoi*** Why   **91 tongues** languages.
(Sir Toby then puns on "tongs," curling irons.)   **92 bearbaiting** the
sport of setting dogs on a chained bear.   **93 the arts** the liberal arts,
learning. (But Sir Toby plays on the phrase as meaning "artifice," the
antithesis of *nature*.)   **95 mended** improved   **100 distaff** a staff for
holding the flax, tow, or wool in spinning   **102 spin it off** i.e.,
(1) treat your flaxen hair as though it were flax on a distaff to be spun
(2) cause you to lose hair as a result of venereal disease (3) make you
ejaculate. (*Huswife* suggests "hussy," "whore.")   **105 Count** i.e., Duke
Orsino, sometimes referred to as Count.   **hard** near   **108 degree**
social position.   **estate** fortune, social position   **109 there's life in't**
i.e., while there's life there's hope   **113 kickshawses** delicacies, fancy
trifles. (From the French, *quelque chose*.)   **115 under . . . betters**
excepting those who are above me   **116 old man** i.e., one experienced through age.   **117 galliard** lively dance in triple time   **118 cut
a caper** make a lively leap. (But Sir Toby puns on the *caper* used to
make a sauce served with mutton. *Mutton,* in turn, suggests
"whore.")

120 back-trick backward step in the galliard. (With sexual innuendo;
the back was associated with sexual vigor.)   **123–4 like to take** likely
to collect   **124 Mistress Mall's picture** i.e., perhaps the portrait of
some woman protected from light and dust, as many pictures were,
by curtains. (*Mall* is a diminutive of *Mary.*)   **126 coranto** lively running dance.   **127 sink-a-pace** dance like the galliard. (French
cinquepace. Sink also suggests a cesspool into which one might uri-
nate.)   **128 virtues** talents   **130 under . . . galliard** i.e., under a star
favorable to dancing.   **131 indifferent** well enough. (Said complacently.)   **132 dun-colored stock** mouse-colored stocking.
135 Taurus zodiacal sign. (Sir Andrew is mistaken, since Leo governed sides and hearts in medical astrology. Taurus governed legs
and thighs, or, more commonly, neck and throat.)
1.4 Location: Orsino's court.
2 like likely   **5 humor** changeableness   **11 On your attendance**
Ready to do you service   **12 aloof** aside.   **15 address thy gait** go

And tell them, there thy fixèd foot shall grow 17
Till thou have audience.

VIOLA   Sure, my noble lord,
If she be so abandoned to her sorrow
As it is spoke, she never will admit me.

ORSINO
Be clamorous and leap all civil bounds 21
Rather than make unprofited return.

VIOLA
Say I do speak with her, my lord, what then?

ORSINO
Oh, then unfold the passion of my love;
Surprise her with discourse of my dear faith. 25
It shall become thee well to act my woes; 26
She will attend it better in thy youth
Than in a nuncio's of more grave aspect. 28

VIOLA
I think not so, my lord.

ORSINO   Dear lad, believe it;
For they shall yet belie thy happy years
That say thou art a man. Diana's lip
Is not more smooth and rubious; thy small pipe 32
Is as the maiden's organ, shrill and sound, 33
And all is semblative a woman's part. 34
I know thy constellation is right apt 35
For this affair.—Some four or five attend him.
All, if you will, for I myself am best
When least in company.—Prosper well in this,
And thou shalt live as freely as thy lord,
To call his fortunes thine.

VIOLA   I'll do my best
To woo your lady. [*Aside*] Yet a barful strife! 41
Whoe'er I woo, myself would be his wife.   *Exeunt.*

❖

1.5

Enter Maria and Clown [Feste].

MARIA   Nay, either tell me where thou hast been, or I
will not open my lips so wide as a bristle may enter in
way of thy excuse. My lady will hang thee for thy
absence.

FESTE   Let her hang me. He that is well hanged in this
world needs to fear no colors. 6

MARIA   Make that good. 7

FESTE   He shall see none to fear. 8

MARIA   A good Lenten answer. I can tell thee where
that saying was born, of "I fear no colors." 9

FESTE   Where, good Mistress Mary?

MARIA   In the wars, and that may you be bold to say in 12
your foolery. 13

FESTE   Well, God give them wisdom that have it; and
those that are fools, let them use their talents. 15

MARIA   Yet you will be hanged for being so long absent;
or to be turned away, is not that as good as a hanging 17
to you?

FESTE   Many a good hanging prevents a bad marriage; 19
and for turning away, let summer bear it out. 20

MARIA   You are resolute, then?

FESTE   Not so, neither, but I am resolved on two
points. 23

MARIA   That if one break, the other will hold; or if both
break, your gaskins fall. 25

FESTE   Apt, in good faith, very apt. Well, go thy way. If
Sir Toby would leave drinking, thou wert as witty a 27
piece of Eve's flesh as any in Illyria. 28

MARIA   Peace, you rogue, no more o' that. Here comes
my lady. Make your excuse wisely, you were best. 30
                                      [*Exit.*]

*Enter Lady Olivia with Malvolio, [and
attendants].*

FESTE   [*aside*] Wit, an't be thy will, put me into good 31
fooling! Those wits that think they have thee do very
oft prove fools, and I that am sure I lack thee may pass
for a wise man. For what says Quinapalus? "Better a 34
witty fool than a foolish wit."—God bless thee, lady!

OLIVIA   [*to attendants*] Take the fool away.

FESTE   Do you not hear, fellows? Take away the lady.

OLIVIA   Go to, you're a dry fool. I'll no more of you. 38
Besides, you grow dishonest.

FESTE   Two faults, madonna, that drink and good 40
counsel will amend. For give the dry fool drink, then
is the fool not dry. Bid the dishonest man mend
himself; if he mend, he is no longer dishonest; if he
cannot, let the botcher mend him. Anything that's 44
mended is but patched; virtue that transgresses is but 45
patched with sin, and sin that amends is but patched
with virtue. If that this simple syllogism will serve, so; 47
if it will not, what remedy? As there is no true cuckold 48
but calamity, so beauty's a flower. The lady bade take 49

---

17 them i.e., Olivia's servants   **21 civil bounds** bounds of civility
25 Surprise Take by storm. (A military term.)   **dear** heartfelt
26 become suit   **28 nuncio's** messenger's   **32 rubious** ruby red.
pipe voice, throat   **33 shrill and sound** high and clear, uncracked
34 semblative resembling, like   **35 constellation** i.e., nature as determined by your horoscope   **41 barful strife** endeavor full of impediments.
1.5 Location: Olivia's house.
6 fear no colors i.e., fear no foe, fear nothing. (With pun on *colors*,
worldly deceptions, and "collars," halters or nooses.)   **7 Make that
good** Explain that.   **8 He . . . fear** i.e., The hanged man will be dead
and unable to see anything.   **9 Lenten** meager, scanty (like Lenten
fare), and morbid

12 In the wars (Where *colors* would mean "military standards, enemy
flags"—the literal meaning of the proverb.)   **12–13 that . . . foolery**
that's an answer you may be bold to use in your fool's conundrums.
(*Colors* here refer to military banners and insignia used to align rows
of fighting men in battle.)   **15 talents** abilities. (Also alluding to the
parable of the talents, Matthew 25:14–29, and to "talons," claws.)
17 turned away dismissed. (Possibly also meaning "turned off,"
"hanged.")   **19 good hanging** (With possible bawdy pun on "being
well hung.")   **20 for** as for.   **let . . . out** i.e., let mild weather make
dismissal endurable.   **23 points** (Maria plays on the meaning "laces
used to hold up hose or breeches.")   **25 gaskins** wide breeches
27–8 thou . . . Illyria (Feste may be hinting ironically that Maria
would be a suitable mate for Sir Toby.)   **30 you were best** it would be
best for you.   **31 an't** if it   **34 Quinapalus** (Feste's invented authority.)   **38 Go to** (An expression of annoyance or expostulation.)   **dry**
dull   **40 madonna** my lady   **44 botcher** mender of old clothes and
shoes. (Playing on two senses of *mend*: "reform" and "repair.")
44–5 Anything . . . patched i.e., Life is patched or parti-colored like
the Fool's garment, a mix of good and bad   **47 so** well and good
48–9 As . . . flower (Nonsense, yet with a suggestion that Olivia has
wedded calamity but should not be faithful to it, for the natural
course is to seize the moment of youth and beauty before we lose it.)

away the fool; therefore I say again, take her away.

OLIVIA   Sir, I bade them take away you.

FESTE   Misprision in the highest degree! Lady, *cucullus* 52
non facit monachum; that's as much to say as I wear not 53
motley in my brain. Good madonna, give me leave to 54
prove you a fool.

OLIVIA   Can you do it?

FESTE   Dexteriously, good madonna.

OLIVIA   Make your proof.

FESTE   I must catechize you for it, madonna. Good my 59
mouse of virtue, answer me. 60

OLIVIA   Well, sir, for want of other idleness, I'll bide 61
your proof.

FESTE   Good madonna, why mourn'st thou?

OLIVIA   Good fool, for my brother's death.

FESTE   I think his soul is in hell, madonna.

OLIVIA   I know his soul is in heaven, fool.

FESTE   The more fool, madonna, to mourn for your
brother's soul, being in heaven.—Take away the fool,
gentlemen.

OLIVIA   What think you of this fool, Malvolio? Doth he
not mend? 71

MALVOLIO   Yes, and shall do till the pangs of death
shake him. Infirmity, that decays the wise, doth ever
make the better fool.

FESTE   God send you, sir, a speedy infirmity for the
better increasing your folly! Sir Toby will be sworn
that I am no fox, but he will not pass his word for 77
twopence that you are no fool.

OLIVIA   How say you to that, Malvolio?

MALVOLIO   I marvel Your Ladyship takes delight in such
a barren rascal. I saw him put down the other day
with an ordinary fool that has no more brain than a 82
stone. Look you now, he's out of his guard already. 83
Unless you laugh and minister occasion to him, he is 84
gagged. I protest I take these wise men that crow so at 85
these set kind of fools no better than the fools' zanies. 86

OLIVIA   Oh, you are sick of self-love, Malvolio, and taste
with a distempered appetite. To be generous, guiltless, 88
and of free disposition is to take those things for bird- 89
bolts that you deem cannon bullets. There is no slan- 90
der in an allowed fool, though he do nothing but rail; 91
nor no railing in a known discreet man, though he do 92
nothing but reprove. 93

FESTE   Now Mercury endue thee with leasing, for thou 94
speak'st well of fools!

Enter Maria.

MARIA   Madam, there is at the gate a young gentleman
much desires to speak with you.

OLIVIA   From the Count Orsino, is it?

MARIA   I know not, madam. 'Tis a fair young man, and
well attended.

OLIVIA   Who of my people hold him in delay?

MARIA   Sir Toby, madam, your kinsman.

OLIVIA   Fetch him off, I pray you. He speaks nothing
but madman. Fie on him!   [*Exit Maria.*] 104
Go you, Malvolio. If it be a suit from the Count, I am
sick or not at home; what you will, to dismiss it.
                                                Exit Malvolio.
Now you see, sir, how your fooling grows old, and 107
people dislike it.

FESTE   Thou hast spoke for us, madonna, as if thy eldest
son should be a fool; whose skull Jove cram with
brains, for—here he comes—

Enter Sir Toby.

one of thy kin has a most weak *pia mater*. 112

OLIVIA   By mine honor, half drunk.—What is he at the
gate, cousin?

SIR TOBY   A gentleman.

OLIVIA   A gentleman? What gentleman?

SIR TOBY   'Tis a gentleman here—[*He belches.*] A plague
o' these pickle-herring! [*To Feste*] How now, sot? 118

FESTE   Good Sir Toby.

OLIVIA   Cousin, cousin, how have you come so early by 120
this lethargy?

SIR TOBY   Lechery? I defy lechery. There's one at the
gate.

OLIVIA   Ay, marry, what is he?

SIR TOBY   Let him be the devil an he will, I care not.
Give me faith, say I. Well, it's all one.   *Exit.* 126

OLIVIA   What's a drunken man like, Fool?

FESTE   Like a drowned man, a fool, and a madman.
One draft above heat makes him a fool, the second 129
mads him, and a third drowns him.

OLIVIA   Go thou and seek the crowner, and let him sit 131
o' my coz; for he's in the third degree of drink, he's 132
drowned. Go, look after him.

FESTE   He is but mad yet, madonna; and the fool shall
look to the madman.   [*Exit.*]

Enter Malvolio.

MALVOLIO   Madam, yond young fellow swears he will
speak with you. I told him you were sick; he takes on
him to understand so much, and therefore comes to
speak with you. I told him you were asleep; he seems

52 **Misprision** Mistake, misunderstanding. (A legal term meaning a wrongful action or misdemeanor.)   **52–3 cucullus . . . monachum** the cowl does not make the monk   **54 motley** the many-colored garment of jesters   **59–60 Good . . . virtue** My good, virtuous mouse. (A term of endearment.)   **61 idleness** pastime.   **bide** endure   **71 mend** i.e., improve, grow more amusing. (But Malvolio uses the word to mean "grow more like a fool.")   **77 pass** give   **82 with** by   **83 out of his guard** defenseless, unprovided with a witty answer   **84 minister occasion** provide opportunity (for his fooling)   **85 protest** avow, declare.   **crow** laugh stridently   **86 set** artificial, stereotyped.   **zanies** assistants, aping attendants.   **88 distempered** diseased.   **generous** noble-minded   **89 free** magnanimous   **89–90 bird-bolts** blunt arrows for shooting small birds   **91 allowed** licensed (to speak freely)   **90–3 There . . . reprove** Both a licensed fool and a man known for discretion can criticize freely without being accused of slander in the first instance or railing in the second. (In rebuking Malvolio here, Olivia implies that he is not behaving like a "known discreet man.")

94 **Now . . . leasing** i.e., May Mercury, the god of deception, make you a skillful liar   **104 madman** i.e., the words of madness.   **107 old** stale   **112 pia mater** i.e., brain. (Actually the soft membrane enclosing the brain.)   **118 sot** (1) fool (2) drunkard.   **120 Cousin** Kinsman. (Here, uncle.)   **126 Give me faith** i.e., to resist the devil.   **it's all one** it doesn't matter.   **129 draft above heat** helping of drink raising his temperature above normal bodily warmth   **131 crowner** coroner   **131–2 sit o' my coz** hold an inquest on my kinsman (Sir Toby)

to have a foreknowledge of that too, and therefore comes to speak with you. What is to be said to him, lady? He's fortified against any denial.

OLIVIA Tell him he shall not speak with me.

MALVOLIO He's been told so; and he says he'll stand at your door like a sheriff's post, and be the supporter to 145 a bench, but he'll speak with you.

OLIVIA What kind o' man is he?

MALVOLIO Why, of mankind.

OLIVIA What manner of man?

MALVOLIO Of very ill manner. He'll speak with you, will you or no.

OLIVIA Of what personage and years is he?

MALVOLIO Not yet old enough for a man, nor young enough for a boy; as a squash is before 'tis a peascod, 154 or a codling when 'tis almost an apple. 'Tis with him in 155 standing water between boy and man. He is very 156 well-favored, and he speaks very shrewishly. One 157 would think his mother's milk were scarce out of him.

OLIVIA Let him approach. Call in my gentlewoman.

MALVOLIO Gentlewoman, my lady calls.   *Exit.*

Enter Maria.

OLIVIA
Give me my veil. Come, throw it o'er my face.
We'll once more hear Orsino's embassy. [*Olivia veils.*]

Enter Viola.

VIOLA The honorable lady of the house, which is she?

OLIVIA Speak to me; I shall answer for her. Your will?

VIOLA Most radiant, exquisite, and unmatchable beauty—I pray you, tell me if this be the lady of the house, for I never saw her. I would be loath to cast away my speech; for besides that it is excellently well penned, I have taken great pains to con it. Good 170 beauties, let me sustain no scorn; I am very comptible, 171 even to the least sinister usage. 172

OLIVIA Whence came you, sir?

VIOLA I can say little more than I have studied, and that question's out of my part. Good gentle one, give me modest assurance if you be the lady of the house, 176 that I may proceed in my speech.

OLIVIA Are you a comedian? 178

VIOLA No, my profound heart; and yet, by the very 179 fangs of malice, I swear I am not that I play. Are you 180 the lady of the house?

OLIVIA If I do not usurp myself, I am. 182

VIOLA Most certain, if you are she, you do usurp your- 183 self; for what is yours to bestow is not yours to reserve. 184

But this is from my commission. I will on with my 185 speech in your praise, and then show you the heart of my message.

OLIVIA Come to what is important in't. I forgive you 188 the praise.

VIOLA Alas, I took great pains to study it, and 'tis poetical.

OLIVIA It is the more like to be feigned. I pray you, keep it in. I heard you were saucy at my gates, and allowed your approach rather to wonder at you than to hear you. If you be not mad, begone; if you have 195 reason, be brief. 'Tis not that time of moon with me to 196 make one in so skipping a dialogue. 197

MARIA Will you hoist sail, sir? Here lies your way.

VIOLA No, good swabber, I am to hull here a little 199 longer.—Some mollification for your giant, sweet 200 lady. Tell me your mind; I am a messenger.

OLIVIA Sure you have some hideous matter to deliver, when the courtesy of it is so fearful. Speak your office. 203

VIOLA It alone concerns your ear. I bring no overture of 204 war, no taxation of homage. I hold the olive in my 205 hand; my words are as full of peace as matter.

OLIVIA Yet you began rudely. What are you? What 207 would you?

VIOLA The rudeness that hath appeared in me have I learned from my entertainment. What I am and what 210 I would are as secret as maidenhead—to your ears, 211 divinity; to any other's, profanation. 212

OLIVIA [*to the others*] Give us the place here alone. We will hear this divinity.   [*Exeunt Maria and attendants.*] Now, sir, what is your text?

VIOLA Most sweet lady—

OLIVIA A comfortable doctrine, and much may be said 217 of it. Where lies your text?

VIOLA In Orsino's bosom.

OLIVIA In his bosom? In what chapter of his bosom?

VIOLA To answer by the method, in the first of his 221 heart.

OLIVIA Oh, I have read it. It is heresy. Have you no more to say?

VIOLA Good madam, let me see your face.

OLIVIA Have you any commission from your lord to negotiate with my face? You are now out of your text. 227 But we will draw the curtain and show you the

---

145 **sheriff's post** post before the sheriff's door to mark a residence of authority, often elaborately carved and decorated. **supporter** prop 154 **squash** unripe pea pod. **peascod** ripe pea pod. (The image suggests that the boy's testicles have not yet dropped.) 155 **codling** unripe apple 155–6 **in standing water** at the turn of the tide 157 **well-favored** good-looking. **shrewishly** sharply. 170 **con** memorize 171 **comptible** susceptible, sensitive 172 **least sinister** slightest discourteous 176 **modest** reasonable 178 **comedian** actor. 179 **my profound heart** my most wise lady; or, in all sincerity 179–80 **by . . . I play** (Viola hints at her true identity, with a touch of malice against her rival.) 182 **do . . . myself** am not an impostor 183–4 **usurp yourself** i.e., misappropriate yourself, by withholding yourself from love and marriage

185 **from** outside of 188 **forgive you** excuse you from repeating 195 **not mad** i.e., not altogether mad 196 **reason** sanity. **moon** (The moon was thought to affect lunatics according to its changing phases.) 197 **make one** take part 199 **swabber** one in charge of washing the decks. (A nautical retort to *hoist sail.*) **hull** lie with sails furled 200 **Some . . . for** i.e., Please mollify, pacify. **giant** i.e., the diminutive Maria, who, like many giants in medieval romances, is guarding the lady 203 **courtesy** i.e., complimentary, "poetical" introduction. (Or Olivia may refer to Cesario's importunate manner at her gate, as reported by Malvolio.) **office** commission, business. 204 **overture** declaration. (Literally, opening.) 205 **taxation of homage** demand for tribute. **olive** olive-branch (signifying peace) 207 **Yet . . . rudely** i.e., Yet you were saucy at my gates. 210 **entertainment** reception. 211 **maidenhead** virginity 212 **divinity** sacred discourse 217 **comfortable** comforting 221 **To . . . method** i.e., To continue the metaphor of delivering a sermon, begun with *divinity* and *what is your text* and continued in *doctrine, heresy,* etc. 227 **out of** straying from

picture. [*Unveiling.*] Look you, sir, such a one I was   229
this present. Is't not well done?   230

VIOLA   Excellently done, if God did all.

OLIVIA   'Tis in grain, sir; 'twill endure wind and   232
weather.

VIOLA
'Tis beauty truly blent, whose red and white   234
Nature's own sweet and cunning hand laid on.   235
Lady, you are the cruel'st she alive
If you will lead these graces to the grave
And leave the world no copy.   238

OLIVIA   Oh, sir, I will not be so hardhearted. I will give
out divers schedules of my beauty. It shall be invento-   240
ried, and every particle and utensil labeled to my   241
will: as, item, two lips, indifferent red; item, two gray   242
eyes, with lids to them; item, one neck, one chin, and
so forth. Were you sent hither to praise me?   244

VIOLA
I see you what you are: you are too proud.
But, if you were the devil, you are fair.   246
My lord and master loves you. Oh, such love   247
Could be but recompensed, though you were
    crowned   248
The nonpareil of beauty!

OLIVIA   How does he love me?   249

VIOLA
With adorations, fertile tears,   250
With groans that thunder love, with sighs of fire.

OLIVIA
Your lord does know my mind; I cannot love him.
Yet I suppose him virtuous, know him noble,
Of great estate, of fresh and stainless youth,
In voices well divulged, free, learned, and valiant,   255
And in dimension and the shape of nature   256
A gracious person. But yet I cannot love him.   257
He might have took his answer long ago.

VIOLA
If I did love you in my master's flame,   259
With such a suff'ring, such a deadly life,   260
In your denial I would find no sense;
I would not understand it.

OLIVIA   Why, what would you?

VIOLA
Make me a willow cabin at your gate   263
And call upon my soul within the house;   264
Write loyal cantons of contemnèd love   265

And sing them loud even in the dead of night;
Hallow your name to the reverberate hills,   267
And make the babbling gossip of the air   268
Cry out "Olivia!" Oh, you should not rest
Between the elements of air and earth   270
But you should pity me!

OLIVIA   You might do much.
What is your parentage?

VIOLA
Above my fortunes, yet my state is well: 273
I am a gentleman.

OLIVIA   Get you to your lord.
I cannot love him. Let him send no more—
Unless, perchance, you come to me again
To tell me how he takes it. Fare you well.
I thank you for your pains. Spend this for me.
                    [*She offers a purse.*]

VIOLA
I am no fee'd post, lady. Keep your purse.   279
My master, not myself, lacks recompense.
Love make his heart of flint that you shall love,   281
And let your fervor, like my master's, be
Placed in contempt! Farewell, fair cruelty.   *Exit.*

OLIVIA   "What is your parentage?"
"Above my fortunes, yet my state is well:
I am a gentleman." I'll be sworn thou art!
Thy tongue, thy face, thy limbs, actions, and spirit
Do give thee fivefold blazon. Not too fast! Soft, soft!   288
Unless the master were the man. How now?   289
Even so quickly may one catch the plague?
Methinks I feel this youth's perfections
With an invisible and subtle stealth
To creep in at mine eyes. Well, let it be.—
What ho, Malvolio!

            Enter Malvolio.

MALVOLIO   Here, madam, at your service.

OLIVIA
Run after that same peevish messenger,
The County's man. He left this ring behind him,   296
                    [*giving a ring*]
Would I or not. Tell him I'll none of it.   297
Desire him not to flatter with his lord,   298
Nor hold him up with hopes; I am not for him.
If that the youth will come this way tomorrow,
I'll give him reasons for't. Hie thee, Malvolio.   301

MALVOLIO   Madam, I will.   *Exit.*

OLIVIA
I do I know not what, and fear to find
Mine eye too great a flatterer for my mind.   304

229–30 such . . . present this is a recent portrait of me. (Since it was customary to hang curtains in front of pictures, Olivia in unveiling speaks as if she were displaying a picture of herself.)   **232 in grain** fast dyed   **234 blent** blended   **235 cunning** skillful   **238 copy** i.e., a child. (But Olivia uses the word to mean "transcript.")   **240 sched-ules** inventories   **241 utensil** article, item.   **labeled** added as a codicil   **242 indifferent** somewhat   **244 praise** (With pun on "appraise.")   **246 if** even if   **247–9 Oh . . . beauty!** i.e., Even if you were the most beautiful woman alive, that beauty could do no more than repay my master's love for you!   **250 fertile** copious   **255 In . . . divulged** well spoken of.   **free** generous   **256 in . . . nature** in his physical form   **257 gracious** graceful, attractive   **259 flame** passion   **260 deadly** deathlike   **263 willow cabin** shelter, hut. (Willow was a symbol of unrequited love.)   **264 my soul** i.e., Olivia   **265 cantons** songs.   **contemnèd** rejected

267 Hallow (1) halloo (2) bless   **268 babbling . . . air** echo   **270 Between . . . air** i.e., anywhere   **273 state** social standing   **279 fee'd post** messenger to be tipped   **281 Love . . . love** May Cupid make the heart of the man you love as hard as flint   **288 blazon** heraldic description.   **Soft** Wait a minute   **289 Unless . . . man** i.e., Unless Cesario and Orsino changed places.   **296 County's** Count's, i.e., Duke's   **297 Would I or not** whether I wanted it or not.   **298 flatter with** encourage   **301 Hie thee** Hasten   **304 Mine . . . mind** i.e., that my eyes (through which love enters the soul) have deceived my reason.

Fate, show thy force. Ourselves we do not owe.   305
What is decreed must be; and be this so.   [*Exit.*]

❖

2.1

Enter Antonio and Sebastian.

ANTONIO   Will you stay no longer? Nor will you not   1
that I go with you?

SEBASTIAN   By your patience, no. My stars shine darkly   3
over me. The malignancy of my fate might perhaps   4
distemper yours; therefore I shall crave of you your   5
leave that I may bear my evils alone. It were a bad
recompense for your love to lay any of them on you.

ANTONIO   Let me yet know of you whither you are
bound.

SEBASTIAN   No, sooth, sir; my determinate voyage is   10
mere extravagancy. But I perceive in you so excellent   11
a touch of modesty that you will not extort from me
what I am willing to keep in; therefore it charges me in   13
manners the rather to express myself. You must know   14
of me then, Antonio, my name is Sebastian, which I
called Roderigo. My father was that Sebastian of
Messaline whom I know you have heard of. He left   17
behind him myself and a sister, both born in an hour.   18
If the heavens had been pleased, would we had so
ended! But you, sir, altered that, for some hour before   20
you took me from the breach of the sea was my sister   21
drowned.

ANTONIO   Alas the day!

SEBASTIAN   A lady, sir, though it was said she much resembled me, was yet of many accounted beautiful. But
though I could not with such estimable wonder over-   26
far believe that, yet thus far I will boldly publish her: 27
she bore a mind that envy could not but call fair. She   28
is drowned already, sir, with salt water, though I seem
to drown her remembrance again with more.

ANTONIO   Pardon me, sir, your bad entertainment.   31

SEBASTIAN   O good Antonio, forgive me your trouble.   32

ANTONIO   If you will not murder me for my love, let me   33
be your servant.

SEBASTIAN   If you will not undo what you have done,
that is, kill him whom you have recovered, desire it   36
not. Fare ye well at once. My bosom is full of

kindness, and I am yet so near the manners of my   38
mother that upon the least occasion more mine eyes   39
will tell tales of me. I am bound to the Count Orsino's
court. Farewell.   *Exit.*

ANTONIO
The gentleness of all the gods go with thee!
I have many enemies in Orsino's court,
Else would I very shortly see thee there.
But come what may, I do adore thee so
That danger shall seem sport, and I will go.   *Exit.*

❖

2.2

Enter Viola and Malvolio, at several doors.

MALVOLIO   Were not you even now with the Countess
Olivia?

VIOLA   Even now, sir. On a moderate pace I have since
arrived but hither.

MALVOLIO   She returns this ring to you, sir. You might
have saved me my pains, to have taken it away   6
yourself. She adds, moreover, that you should put
your lord into a desperate assurance she will none of   8
him. And one thing more: that you be never so hardy   9
to come again in his affairs, unless it be to report your   10
lord's taking of this. Receive it so.

VIOLA   She took the ring of me. I'll none of it.   12

MALVOLIO   Come, sir, you peevishly threw it to her,
and her will is it should be so returned. [*He throws
down the ring.*] If it be worth stooping for, there it lies,
in your eye; if not, be it his that finds it.   *Exit.*   16

VIOLA [*picking up the ring*]
I left no ring with her. What means this lady?
Fortune forbid my outside have not charmed her!   18
She made good view of me, indeed so much
That sure methought her eyes had lost her tongue,   20
For she did speak in starts, distractedly.
She loves me, sure! The cunning of her passion
Invites me in this churlish messenger.   23
None of my lord's ring? Why, he sent her none.
I am the man. If it be so—as 'tis—   25
Poor lady, she were better love a dream.
Disguise, I see, thou art a wickedness
Wherein the pregnant enemy does much.   28
How easy is it for the proper false   29
In women's waxen hearts to set their forms!   30
Alas, our frailty is the cause, not we,   31
For such as we are made of, such we be.   32

305 owe own, control
2.1 Location: Somewhere in Illyria.
1 Nor will you not Do you not wish   **3 patience** leave   **4 malignancy** malevolence (of the stars; also in a medical sense)   **5 distemper** infect   **10 sooth** truly.   **determinate** intended, determined upon
11 extravagancy aimless wandering   **13 am willing . . . in** wish to
keep secret   **13–14 it . . . manners** it is incumbent upon me in all
courtesy   **14 express** reveal   **17 Messaline** possibly Messina, or,
more likely, Massila (the modern Marseilles). In Plautus's *Menaechmi*,
Massilians and Illyrians are mentioned together.   **18 in an hour** in
the same hour   **20 some hour** about an hour   **21 breach of the sea**
surf   **26 estimable wonder** admiring judgment   **27 publish** proclaim   **28 envy** even malice   **31 Pardon . . . entertainment** i.e., I'm
sorry I cannot offer you better hospitality and comfort.   **32 your
trouble** the trouble I put you to   **33 murder . . . love** i.e., cause me to
die from lacking your love   **36 recovered** rescued, restored

38 kindness emotion, affection   **38–9 manners of my mother** i.e.,
womanly inclination to weep
2.2 Location: Near Olivia's house.
0.1 *several* different   **6 to have taken** by taking   **8 desperate** without hope   **9–10 so hardy to come** so bold as to come   **12 She . . . it**
(Viola tells a quick and friendly lie to shield Olivia.)   **16 in your eye**
in plain sight   **18 charmed** enchanted   **20 her eyes . . . tongue** i.e.,
the sight of me had deprived her of speech   **23 in** in the person of
25 the man the man of her choice.   **28 the pregnant enemy** the
resourceful enemy (either Satan or Cupid)   **29 the proper false**
deceptively handsome men   **30 waxen** i.e., malleable, impressionable.   **set their forms** stamp their images (as of a seal).   **31–2 our . . .
be** i.e., the fault lies not in us as individuals, but in the frailty of
female nature.

How will this fadge? My master loves her dearly,   33
And I, poor monster, fond as much on him;   34
And she, mistaken, seems to dote on me.
What will become of this? As I am man,
My state is desperate for my master's love;
As I am woman—now, alas the day!—
What thriftless sighs shall poor Olivia breathe!   39
O Time, thou must untangle this, not I;
It is too hard a knot for me t'untie.   [*Exit.*]

❧

2.3

Enter Sir Toby and Sir Andrew.

SIR TOBY   Approach, Sir Andrew. Not to be abed after
midnight is to be up betimes; and *diluculo surgere*, thou   2
know'st—

SIR ANDREW   Nay, by my troth, I know not, but I know
to be up late is to be up late.

SIR TOBY   A false conclusion. I hate it as an unfilled can.   6
To be up after midnight and to go to bed then, is early;
so that to go to bed after midnight is to go to bed
betimes. Does not our lives consist of the four   9
elements?   10

SIR ANDREW   Faith, so they say, but I think it rather
consists of eating and drinking.

SIR TOBY   Thou'rt a scholar; let us therefore eat and
drink.—Marian, I say, a stoup of wine!   14

Enter Clown [Feste].

SIR ANDREW   Here comes the Fool, i'faith.

FESTE   How now, my hearts! Did you never see the
picture of "we three"?   17

SIR TOBY   Welcome, ass. Now let's have a catch.   18

SIR ANDREW   By my troth, the Fool has an excellent
breast. I had rather than forty shillings I had such a   20
leg, and so sweet a breath to sing, as the Fool has. In   21
sooth, thou wast in very gracious fooling last night,
when thou spok'st of Pigrogromitus, of the Vapians   23
passing the equinoctial of Queubus. 'Twas very good,   24
i'faith. I sent thee sixpence for thy leman. Hadst it?   25

FESTE   I did impeticos thy gratillity; for Malvolio's nose   26
is no whipstock. My lady has a white hand, and the   27
Myrmidons are no bottle-ale houses.   28

SIR ANDREW   Excellent! Why, this is the best fooling,
when all is done. Now, a song.

SIR TOBY   Come on, there is sixpence for you. [*He gives
money.*] Let's have a song.

SIR ANDREW   There's a testril of me too. [*He gives money.*]   33
If one knight give a—

FESTE   Would you have a love song, or a song of good   35
life?   36

SIR TOBY   A love song, a love song.

SIR ANDREW   Ay, ay, I care not for good life.

FESTE (*sings*)
O mistress mine, where are you roaming?
Oh, stay and hear, your true love 's coming,
That can sing both high and low.
Trip no further, pretty sweeting;
Journeys end in lovers' meeting,
Every wise man's son doth know.

SIR ANDREW   Excellent good, i'faith.

SIR TOBY   Good, good.

FESTE [*sings*]
What is love? 'tis not hereafter;
Present mirth hath present laughter;
What's to come is still unsure.   49
In delay there lies no plenty.
Then come kiss me, sweet and twenty;   51
Youth's a stuff will not endure.

SIR ANDREW   A mellifluous voice, as I am true knight.

SIR TOBY   A contagious breath.   54

SIR ANDREW   Very sweet and contagious, i'faith.

SIR TOBY   To hear by the nose, it is dulcet in contagion.   56
But shall we make the welkin dance indeed? Shall we   57
rouse the night owl in a catch that will draw three   58
souls out of one weaver? Shall we do that?   59

SIR ANDREW   An you love me, let's do't. I am dog at a   60
catch.   61

FESTE   By'r Lady, sir, and some dogs will catch well.   62

SIR ANDREW   Most certain. Let our catch be "Thou   63
knave."   64

FESTE   "Hold thy peace, thou knave," knight? I shall be   65
constrained in't to call thee knave, knight.   66

SIR ANDREW   'Tis not the first time I have constrained
one to call me knave. Begin, Fool. It begins, "Hold thy
peace."

---

33 fadge turn out   **34 monster** i.e., being both man and woman.
fond dote   **39 thriftless** unprofitable
2.3. Location: Olivia's house.
2 betimes early. *diluculo surgere* (*saluberrimum est*) to rise early is
most healthful. (A sentence from Lilly's *Latin Grammar*.)   **6 can**
tankard.   **9-10 four elements** i.e., fire, air, water, and earth, the elements that were thought to make up all matter.   **14 stoup** drinking
vessel   **17 picture of "we three"** picture of two fools or asses
inscribed "we three," the spectator being the third.   **18 catch** round.
20 breast voice.   **21 leg** (for dancing)   **23-4 Pigrogromitus . . .
Queubus** (Feste's mock erudition.)   **25 leman** sweetheart.
26 impeticos thy gratillity (Suggests "impetticoat, or pocket up, thy
gratuity.")   **27 is no whipstock** is no whip-handle. (More nonsense,
but perhaps suggesting that Malvolio's nose for smelling out faults
does not give him the right to punish, so that he need not be feared.)
has a white hand i.e., is lady-like. (But Feste's speech may be mere
nonsense.)   **28 Myrmidons** followers of Achilles.   **bottle-ale houses**
(Used contemptuously of taverns because they sold low-class drink.)

33 testril tester, a coin worth sixpence   **35-6 good life** virtuous living. (Or perhaps Feste means simply "life's pleasures," but is misunderstood by Sir Andrew to mean "virtuous living.")   **49 still** always
51 sweet and twenty i.e., sweet and twenty times sweet, or twenty
years old   **54 contagious** infectiously delightful   **56 To . . . contagion** i.e., If we were to describe hearing in olfactory terms, we could
say it is sweet in stench.   **57 make . . . dance** i.e., drink till the sky
seems to turn around   **58-9 draw three souls** (Refers to the threefold
nature of the soul—vegetal, sensible, and intellectual—or to the three
singers of the three-part catch; or, just a comic exaggeration.)
59 weaver (Weavers were often associated with psalm singing.)
60 dog at very clever at. (But Feste uses the word literally.)   **61 catch**
round. (But Feste uses it to mean "seize.")   **62 By 'r Lady** (An oath,
originally, "by the Virgin Mary.")   **63-4 "Thou knave"** (This popular
round is arranged so that the three singers repeatedly accost one
another with "Thou knave.")   **65-6 "Hold . . . knight** ("Knight and
knave" is a common antithesis, like "rich and poor.")

FESTE   I shall never begin if I hold my peace.

SIR ANDREW   Good, i'faith. Come, begin.   *Catch sung.*

Enter Maria.

MARIA   What a caterwauling do you keep here! If my   72
lady have not called up her steward Malvolio and bid
him turn you out of doors, never trust me.

SIR TOBY   My lady's a Cataian, we are politicians,   75
Malvolio's a Peg-o'-Ramsey, and [*he sings*] "Three   76
merry men be we." Am not I consanguineous? Am I   77
not of her blood? Tillyvally! Lady! [*He sings.*] "There   78
dwelt a man in Babylon, lady, lady."   79

FESTE   Beshrew me, the knight's in admirable fooling.   80

SIR ANDREW   Ay, he does well enough if he be disposed,
and so do I too. He does it with a better grace,
but I do it more natural.   83

SIR TOBY [*sings*]
"O' the twelfth day of December"—   84

MARIA   For the love o' God, peace!

Enter Malvolio.

MALVOLIO   My masters, are you mad? Or what are you?
Have you no wit, manners, nor honesty but to gabble   87
like tinkers at this time of night? Do ye make an alehouse of my lady's house, that ye squeak out your coz-   89
iers' catches without any mitigation or remorse of   90
voice? Is there no respect of place, persons, nor time in
you?

SIR TOBY   We did keep time, sir, in our catches. Sneck   93
up!   94

MALVOLIO   Sir Toby, I must be round with you. My   95
lady bade me tell you that though she harbors you as
her kinsman, she's nothing allied to your disorders. If
you can separate yourself and your misdemeanors,
you are welcome to the house; if not, an it would
please you to take leave of her, she is very willing to
bid you farewell.

SIR TOBY [*sings*]
"Farewell, dear heart, since I must needs be gone."   102

MARIA   Nay, good Sir Toby.

FESTE [*sings*]
"His eyes do show his days are almost done."

MALVOLIO   Is't even so?

SIR TOBY [*sings*]
"But I will never die."

FESTE
"Sir Toby, there you lie."

MALVOLIO   This is much credit to you.

SIR TOBY [*sings*]
"Shall I bid him go?"

FESTE [*sings*]
"What an if you do?"

SIR TOBY [*sings*]
"Shall I bid him go, and spare not?"

FESTE [*sings*]
"Oh, no, no, no, no, you dare not."

SIR TOBY   Out o' tune, sir? Ye lie. Art any more than a   113
steward? Dost thou think, because thou art virtuous,
there shall be no more cakes and ale?

FESTE   Yes, by Saint Anne, and ginger shall be hot i'th'   116
mouth, too.

SIR TOBY   Thou'rt i'the right.—Go, sir, rub your chain   118
with crumbs.—A stoup of wine, Maria!   119

MALVOLIO   Mistress Mary, if you prized my lady's
favor at anything more than contempt, you would not
give means for this uncivil rule. She shall know of it,   122
by this hand.   *Exit.*

MARIA   Go shake your ears.   124

SIR ANDREW   'Twere as good a deed as to drink when a
man's a-hungry to challenge him the field and then to   126
break promise with him and make a fool of him.

SIR TOBY   Do't, knight. I'll write thee a challenge, or I'll
deliver thy indignation to him by word of mouth.

MARIA   Sweet Sir Toby, be patient for tonight. Since the
youth of the Count's was today with my lady, she is
much out of quiet. For Monsieur Malvolio, let me   132
alone with him. If I do not gull him into a nayword   133
and make him a common recreation, do not think I   134
have wit enough to lie straight in my bed. I know I can
do it.

SIR TOBY   Possess us, possess us. Tell us something of   137
him.

MARIA   Marry, sir, sometimes he is a kind of puritan.   139

SIR ANDREW   Oh, if I thought that, I'd beat him like a
dog.

SIR TOBY   What, for being a puritan? Thy exquisite
reason, dear knight?

SIR ANDREW   I have no exquisite reason for't, but I
have reason good enough.

---

72 keep keep up   **75 Cataian** Cathayan, i.e., Chinese, a trickster or inscrutable; or, just nonsense.   **politicians** schemers, intriguers   **76 Peg-o'-Ramsey** character in a popular song. (Used here contemptuously.)   **76–7 "Three . . . we"** (A snatch of an old song.)   **77 consanguineous** i.e., a blood relative of Olivia.   **78 Tillyvally!** Nonsense, fiddle-faddle!   **78–9 "There . . . lady"** (The first line of a ballad, "The Constancy of Susanna," together with the refrain, "Lady, lady.")   **80 Beshrew** i.e., The devil take. (A mild curse.)   **83 natural** naturally. (But unconsciously suggesting idiocy.)   **84 "O' . . . December"** (Possibly part of a ballad about the Battle of Musselburgh Field, or Toby's error for the "twelfth day of Christmas," i.e., Twelfth Night.)   **87 wit** common sense.   **honesty** decency   **89–90 coziers'** cobblers'   **90 mitigation or remorse** i.e., considerate lowering   **93–4 Sneck up!** Go hang!   **95 round** blunt   **102 "Farewell . . . gone"** (From the ballad "Corydon's Farewell to Phyllis.")

113 Out o' tune (Perhaps a quibbling reply—"We did too keep time in our tune"—to Malvolio's accusation of having no respect for place or time, line 91. Often emended to *Out o' time,* easily misread in secretary hand.)   **116 Saint Anne** mother of the Virgin Mary. (Her cult was derided in the Reformation, much as Puritan reformers also derided the tradition of *cakes and ale* at church feasts.)   **ginger** (Commonly used to spice ale.)   **118–19 rub . . . crumbs** i.e., scour or polish your steward's chain; attend to your own business and remember your station   **122 give means** i.e., supply drink.   **rule** conduct.   **124 your ears** i.e., your ass's ears.   **126 the field** i.e., to a duel   **132 For** As for   **132–3 let . . . him** leave him to me.   **133 gull** trick.   **nayword** byword. (His name will be synonymous with "dupe.")   **134 recreation** sport   **137 Possess** Inform   **139 puritan** (Maria's point is that Malvolio is sometimes a *kind* of puritan, insofar as he is precise about moral conduct and censorious of others for immoral conduct, but that he is nothing consistently except a time-server. He is not, then, simply a satirical type of the Puritan sect. The extent of the resemblance is left unstated.)

MARIA   The devil a puritan that he is, or anything con- 146
stantly, but a time-pleaser; an affectioned ass, that cons 147
state without book and utters it by great swaths; the 148
best persuaded of himself, so crammed, as he thinks, 149
with excellencies, that it is his grounds of faith that all 150
that look on him love him; and on that vice in him
will my revenge find notable cause to work.

SIR TOBY   What wilt thou do?

MARIA   I will drop in his way some obscure epistles of 154
love, wherein by the color of his beard, the shape of
his leg, the manner of his gait, the expressure of his 156
eye, forehead, and complexion, he shall find himself
most feelingly personated. I can write very like my 158
lady your niece; on a forgotten matter we can hardly 159
make distinction of our hands. 160

SIR TOBY   Excellent! I smell a device.

SIR ANDREW   I have't in my nose too.

SIR TOBY   He shall think, by the letters that thou wilt
drop, that they come from my niece, and that she's in
love with him.

MARIA   My purpose is indeed a horse of that color.

SIR ANDREW   And your horse now would make him an
ass.

MARIA   Ass, I doubt not. 169

SIR ANDREW   Oh, 'twill be admirable!

MARIA   Sport royal, I warrant you. I know my physic 171
will work with him. I will plant you two, and let the
Fool make a third, where he shall find the letter. Observe his construction of it. For this night, to bed, 174
and dream on the event. Farewell.   *Exit.* 175

SIR TOBY   Good night, Penthesilea. 176

SIR ANDREW   Before me, she's a good wench. 177

SIR TOBY   She's a beagle true-bred and one that adores 178
me. What o'that?

SIR ANDREW   I was adored once, too.

SIR TOBY   Let's to bed, knight. Thou hadst need send
for more money.

SIR ANDREW   If I cannot recover your niece, I am a foul 183
way out. 184

SIR TOBY   Send for money, knight. If thou hast her not
i'th' end, call me cut. 186

SIR ANDREW   If I do not, never trust me, take it how
you will.

SIR TOBY   Come, come, I'll go burn some sack. 'Tis too 189
late to go to bed now. Come, knight; come, knight. 190
                                              Exeunt.

❖

2.4

Enter Duke [Orsino], Viola, Curio, and others.

ORSINO
Give me some music. Now, good morrow, friends.   1
Now, good Cesario, but that piece of song,   2
That old and antique song we heard last night.   3
Methought it did relieve my passion much,
More than light airs and recollected terms   5
Of these most brisk and giddy-pacèd times.
Come, but one verse.

CURIO   He is not here, so please Your Lordship, that
should sing it.

ORSINO   Who was it?

CURIO   Feste the jester, my lord, a fool that the Lady
Olivia's father took much delight in. He is about the
house.

ORSINO
Seek him out, and play the tune the while.
                          [Exit Curio.] Music plays.
[*To Viola*] Come hither, boy. If ever thou shalt love,
In the sweet pangs of it remember me;
For such as I am, all true lovers are,
Unstaid and skittish in all motions else   18
Save in the constant image of the creature
That is beloved. How dost thou like this tune?

VIOLA
It gives a very echo to the seat   21
Where Love is throned.

ORSINO   Thou dost speak masterly.
My life upon't, young though thou art, thine eye
Hath stayed upon some favor that it loves.   24
Hath it not, boy?

VIOLA   A little, by your favor.   25

ORSINO
What kind of woman is't?

VIOLA   Of your complexion.

ORSINO
She is not worth thee, then. What years, i'faith?

VIOLA   About your years, my lord.

ORSINO
Too old, by heaven. Let still the woman take   29
An elder than herself. So wears she to him;   30
So sways she level in her husband's heart.   31
For, boy, however we do praise ourselves,

146–7 **constantly** consistently   147 **time-pleaser** time-server, syco-
phant.   **affectioned** affected   147–8 **cons . . . book** learns by heart
the phrases and mannerisms of the great   148 **by great swaths** in
great sweeps, like rows of mown grain   148–9 **the best persuaded**
having the best opinion   150 **grounds of faith** creed, belief
154 **some obscure epistles** an ambiguously worded letter
156 **expressure** expression   158 **personated** represented.   159 **on a
forgotten matter** when we've forgotten which of us wrote something
or what it was about   160 **hands** handwriting.   169 **Ass, I** (With a
pun on "as I.")   171 **physic** medicine   174 **construction** interpretation   175 **event** outcome   176 **Penthesilea** Queen of the Amazons.
(Another ironical allusion to Maria's diminutive stature.)
177 **Before me** i.e., On my soul. (A mild oath.)   178 **beagle** a small,
intelligent hunting dog   183 **recover** win   183–4 **foul way out** i.e.,
miserably out of pocket. (Literally, out of my way and in the mire.)
186 **cut** a proverbial term of abuse: literally, a horse with a docked
tail; also, a gelding, or the female genital organ.

189 **burn some sack** warm some Spanish wine.   **190.1 *Exeunt*** (Feste
may have left earlier; he says nothing after line 117 and is perhaps
referred to without his being present at 172–3.)
2.4 Location: Orsino's court.
1 **morrow** morning   2 **but** i.e., I ask only   3 **antique** old, quaint, fantastic   5 **recollected terms** studied and artificial expressions   18 **all
motions else** all other thoughts and emotions   21 **the seat** i.e., the
heart   24 **stayed . . . favor** rested upon some face   25 **by your favor**
if you please. (But also hinting at "like you in feature.")   29 **still**
always   30 **wears she** she adapts herself   31 **sways she level** she
keeps a perfect equipoise and steady affection

Our fancies are more giddy and unfirm,
More longing, wavering, sooner lost and worn,   34
Than women's are.

VIOLA   I think it well, my lord.

ORSINO
Then let thy love be younger than thyself,
Or thy affection cannot hold the bent;   37
For women are as roses, whose fair flower
Being once displayed, doth fall that very hour.   39

VIOLA
And so they are. Alas that they are so,
To die even when they to perfection grow!   41

Enter Curio and Clown [Feste].

ORSINO
Oh, fellow, come, the song we had last night.
Mark it, Cesario, it is old and plain;
The spinsters and the knitters in the sun,   44
And the free maids that weave their thread with
    bones,   45
Do use to chant it. It is silly sooth,   46
And dallies with the innocence of love,   47
Like the old age.   48

FESTE   Are you ready, sir?

ORSINO   Ay, prithee, sing.   *Music.*

The Song.

FESTE *[sings]*
    Come away, come away, death,   51
        And in sad cypress let me be laid.   52
    Fly away, fly away, breath;
        I am slain by a fair cruel maid.
    My shroud of white, stuck all with yew,   55
        Oh, prepare it!
    My part of death, no one so true   57
        Did share it.   58

    Not a flower, not a flower sweet
        On my black coffin let there be strown;   60
    Not a friend, not a friend greet
        My poor corpse, where my bones shall be
            thrown.
    A thousand thousand sighs to save,
        Lay me, oh, where
    Sad true lover never find my grave,
        To weep there!

ORSINO   *[offering money]*   There's for thy pains.
FESTE   No pains, sir. I take pleasure in singing, sir.
ORSINO   I'll pay thy pleasure then.

FESTE   Truly, sir, and pleasure will be paid, one time   70
    or another.   71
ORSINO   Give me now leave to leave thee.   72
FESTE   Now, the melancholy god protect thee, and the   73
    tailor make thy doublet of changeable taffeta, for thy   74
    mind is a very opal. I would have men of such con-   75
    stancy put to sea, that their business might be every-   76
    thing and their intent everywhere, for that's it that   77
    always makes a good voyage of nothing. Farewell.   78
                                                        Exit.

ORSINO
Let all the rest give place.
                    [Curio and attendants withdraw.]
                    Once more, Cesario,   79
Get thee to yond same sovereign cruelty.
Tell her, my love, more noble than the world,
Prizes not quantity of dirty lands;
The parts that fortune hath bestowed upon her,   83
Tell her, I hold as giddily as fortune;   84
But 'tis that miracle and queen of gems   85
That nature pranks her in attracts my soul.   86

VIOLA   But if she cannot love you, sir?

ORSINO
I cannot be so answered.

VIOLA   Sooth, but you must.   88
Say that some lady—as perhaps there is—
Hath for your love as great a pang of heart
As you have for Olivia. You cannot love her;
You tell her so. Must she not then be answered?   92

ORSINO   There is no woman's sides
Can bide the beating of so strong a passion   94
As love doth give my heart; no woman's heart
So big, to hold so much. They lack retention.   96
Alas, their love may be called appetite,
No motion of the liver, but the palate,   98
That suffer surfeit, cloyment, and revolt;   99
But mine is all as hungry as the sea,
And can digest as much. Make no compare   101
Between that love a woman can bear me
And that I owe Olivia.

VIOLA   Ay, but I know—   103

ORSINO   What dost thou know?

70–1 pleasure . . . another sooner or later one must pay for indulgence.   **72 leave to leave** permission to take leave of, dismiss   **73 the
melancholy god** i.e., Saturn, whose planet was thought to control the
melancholy temperament   **74 doublet** close-fitting jacket.
changeable taffeta a silk so woven of various-colored threads that its
color shifts with changing perspective   **75 opal** an iridescent precious stone that changes color when seen from various angles or in
different lights.   **76–7 that . . . everywhere** i.e., so that in the changeableness of the sea their inconstancy could always be exercised
77–8 for . . . nothing because that's the quality that is satisfied with
an aimless voyage.   **79 give place** withdraw.   **83 parts** attributes
such as wealth or rank   **84 I . . . fortune** I esteem as carelessly as I do
fortune, that fickle goddess   **85 that miracle . . . gems** i.e., her beauty
86 pranks adorns.   **attracts** that attracts   **88 Sooth** In truth   **92 be
answered** be satisfied with your answer.   **94 bide** withstand   **96 to
hold** as to contain.   **retention** constancy, the power of retaining
98 motion impulse.   **liver . . . palate** (Real love is a passion of the
liver, whereas fancy, light love, is born in the eye and nourished in
the palate.)   **99 cloyment** satiety.   **revolt** revulsion   **101 compare**
comparison   **103 owe** have for

---

34 worn exhausted. (Sometimes emended to *won*.)   **37 hold the bent**
hold steady, keep the intensity (like the tension of a bow)   **39 displayed** full blown   **41 even when** just as   **44 spinsters** spinners
45 free carefree, innocent.   **bones** bobbins on which bone-lace was
made   **46 Do use** are accustomed.   **silly sooth** simple truth   **47 dallies with** dwells lovingly on, sports with   **48 Like . . . age** as in the
good old times.   **51 Come away** Come hither   **52 cypress** i.e., a coffin of cypress wood, or bier strewn with sprigs of cypress   **55 yew**
yew sprigs. (Emblematic of mourning, like cypress.)   **57–8 My . . . it**
No one died for love so true to love as I.   **60 strown** strewn

VIOLA
Too well what love women to men may owe.
In faith, they are as true of heart as we.
My father had a daughter loved a man
As it might be, perhaps, were I a woman,
I should Your Lordship.

ORSINO   And what's her history?

VIOLA
A blank, my lord. She never told her love,
But let concealment, like a worm i'th' bud,
Feed on her damask cheek. She pined in thought,   112
And with a green and yellow melancholy;   113
She sat like Patience on a monument,   114
Smiling at grief. Was not this love indeed?
We men may say more, swear more, but indeed
Our shows are more than will; for still we prove   117
Much in our vows, but little in our love.

ORSINO
But died thy sister of her love, my boy?

VIOLA
I am all the daughters of my father's house,
And all the brothers too—and yet I know not.
Sir, shall I to this lady?

ORSINO   Ay, that's the theme.
To her in haste; give her this jewel. [*He gives a jewel.*]
    Say
My love can give no place, bide no denay.   124
                            Exeunt [*separately*].

❧

2.5

Enter Sir Toby, Sir Andrew, and Fabian.

SIR TOBY   Come thy ways, Signor Fabian.   1

FABIAN   Nay, I'll come. If I lose a scruple of this sport,   2
let me be boiled to death with melancholy.   3

SIR TOBY   Wouldst thou not be glad to have the niggardly rascally sheep-biter come by some notable   5
shame?

FABIAN   I would exult, man. You know he brought me
out o'favor with my lady about a bearbaiting here.   8

SIR TOBY   To anger him we'll have the bear again, and
we will fool him black and blue. Shall we not, Sir An- 10
drew?

SIR ANDREW   An we do not, it is pity of our lives.   12

Enter Maria [*with a letter*].

SIR TOBY   Here comes the little villain.—How now, my   13
metal of India!   14

MARIA   Get ye all three into the boxtree. Malvolio's   15
coming down this walk. He has been yonder i'the sun
practicing behavior to his own shadow this half hour.
Observe him, for the love of mockery, for I know this
letter will make a contemplative idiot of him. Close, in   19
the name of jesting! [*The others hide.*] Lie thou there
[*throwing down a letter*]; for here comes the trout that
must be caught with tickling.   *Exit.*   22

Enter Malvolio.

MALVOLIO   'Tis but fortune; all is fortune. Maria once
told me she did affect me; and I have heard herself   24
come thus near, that should she fancy, it should be   25
one of my complexion. Besides, she uses me with a
more exalted respect than anyone else that follows   27
her. What should I think on't?

SIR TOBY   Here's an overweening rogue!

FABIAN   Oh, peace! Contemplation makes a rare turkey-   30
cock of him. How he jets under his advanced plumes!   31

SIR ANDREW   'Slight, I could so beat the rogue!   32

SIR TOBY   Peace, I say.

MALVOLIO   To be Count Malvolio.

SIR TOBY   Ah, rogue!

SIR ANDREW   Pistol him, pistol him.

SIR TOBY   Peace, peace!

MALVOLIO   There is example for't. The lady of the Stra-   38
chy married the yeoman of the wardrobe.   39

SIR ANDREW   Fie on him, Jezebel!   40

FABIAN   Oh, peace! Now he's deeply in. Look how imagination blows him.   42

MALVOLIO   Having been three months married to her,
sitting in my state—   44

SIR TOBY   Oh, for a stone-bow, to hit him in the eye!   45

MALVOLIO   Calling my officers about me, in my
branched velvet gown; having come from a daybed,   47
where I have left Olivia sleeping—

SIR TOBY   Fire and brimstone!

FABIAN   Oh, peace, peace!

MALVOLIO   And then to have the humor of state; and   51
after a demure travel of regard, telling them I know   52
my place as I would they should do theirs, to ask for
my kinsman Toby.   54

SIR TOBY   Bolts and shackles!

FABIAN   Oh, peace, peace, peace! Now, now.

---

112 damask pink and white like the damask rose   **113 green and yellow** pale and sallow   **114 on a monument** carved in statuary on a
tomb   **117 shows** displays of passion.   **more than will** greater than
our determination.   **still** always   **124 can . . . denay** cannot yield or
endure denial.
2.5 Location: Olivia's garden.
1 Come thy ways Come along   **2 a scruple** the least bit   **3 boiled**
(With a pun on "biled"; black bile was the "humor" of melancholy
and was thought to be a cold humor.)   **5 sheep-biter** a dog that bites
sheep, i.e., a scoundrel   **8 bearbaiting** (A special target of Puritan
disapproval.)   **10 fool . . . blue** mock him until he is figuratively
black and blue.   **12 An** If.   **pity of our lives** a pity we should live.

13 villain (Here, a term of endearment.)   **14 metal** gold, i.e., priceless
one   **15 boxtree** an evergreen shrub.   **19 contemplative** i.e., from
his musings.   **Close** i.e., Keep close, stay hidden   **22 tickling**
(1) stroking gently about the gills—an actual method of fishing
(2) deception.   **24 she** Olivia.   **affect** have fondness for   **25 fancy**
fall in love   **27 follows** serves   **30 rare** extraordinary   **31 jets** struts.
advanced prominent   **32 'Slight** By His (God's) light   **38 example**
precedent   **38–9 lady of the Strachy** (Apparently a lady who had
married below her station; no certain identification.)   **40 Jezebel** the
proud queen of Ahab, King of Israel.   **42 blows** puffs up   **44 state**
chair of state   **45 stone-bow** crossbow that shoots stones
47 branched adorned with a figured pattern suggesting branched
leaves or flowers.   **daybed** sofa, couch   **51 have . . . state** adopt the
imperious manner of authority   **52 demure . . . regard** grave survey
of the company.   **54 Toby** (Malvolio omits the title *Sir*.)

MALVOLIO   Seven of my people, with an obedient start, make out for him. I frown the while, and perchance wind up my watch, or play with my—some rich 59 jewel. Toby approaches; curtsies there to me— 60

SIR TOBY   Shall this fellow live?

FABIAN   Though our silence be drawn from us with 62 cars, yet peace. 63

MALVOLIO   I extend my hand to him thus, quenching my familiar smile with an austere regard of control— 65

SIR TOBY   And does not Toby take you a blow o'the lips 66 then?

MALVOLIO   Saying, "Cousin Toby, my fortunes having cast me on your niece give me this prerogative of speech—"

SIR TOBY   What, what?

MALVOLIO   "You must amend your drunkenness."

SIR TOBY   Out, scab! 73

FABIAN   Nay, patience, or we break the sinews of our 74 plot.

MALVOLIO   "Besides, you waste the treasure of your time with a foolish knight—"

SIR ANDREW   That's me, I warrant you.

MALVOLIO   "One Sir Andrew."

SIR ANDREW   I knew 'twas I, for many do call me fool.

MALVOLIO   What employment have we here? 81
                                                [Taking up the letter.]

FABIAN   Now is the woodcock near the gin. 82

SIR TOBY   Oh, peace, and the spirit of humors intimate 83 reading aloud to him!

MALVOLIO   By my life, this is my lady's hand. These be her very c's, her u's, and her t's; and thus makes she 86 her great P's. It is in contempt of question her hand. 87

SIR ANDREW   Her c's, her u's, and her t's. Why that?

MALVOLIO   [reads]   "To the unknown beloved, this, and my good wishes."—Her very phrases! By your 90 leave, wax. Soft! And the impressure her Lucrece, 91 with which she uses to seal. 'Tis my lady. To whom 92 should this be?   [He opens the letter.]

FABIAN   This wins him, liver and all. 94

MALVOLIO   [reads]

    "Jove knows I love,
        But who?
    Lips, do not move;
        No man must know."

"No man must know." What follows? The numbers 99 altered! "No man must know." If this should be thee, 100 Malvolio?

SIR TOBY   Marry, hang thee, brock! 102

MALVOLIO   [reads]
    "I may command where I adore,
        But silence, like a Lucrece knife,
    With bloodless stroke my heart doth gore;
        M.O.A.I. doth sway my life."

FABIAN   A fustian riddle! 107

SIR TOBY   Excellent wench, say I.

MALVOLIO   "M.O.A.I. doth sway my life." Nay, but first, let me see, let me see, let me see.

FABIAN   What dish o'poison has she dressed him! 111

SIR TOBY   And with what wing the staniel checks 112 at it! 113

MALVOLIO   "I may command where I adore." Why, she may command me; I serve her, she is my lady. Why, this is evident to any formal capacity. There is no 116 obstruction in this. And the end—what should that alphabetical position portend? If I could make that 118 resemble something in me! Softly! "M.O.A.I."—

SIR TOBY   Oh, ay, make up that. He is now at a cold scent. 120

FABIAN   Sowter will cry upon't for all this, though it be 121 as rank as a fox. 122

MALVOLIO   "M"—Malvolio. "M"! Why, that begins my name!

FABIAN   Did not I say he would work it out? The cur is excellent at faults. 126

MALVOLIO   "M"—But then there is no consonancy in the 127 sequel that suffers under probation: "A" should fol- 128 low, but "O" does.

FABIAN   And "O" shall end, I hope. 130

SIR TOBY   Ay, or I'll cudgel him, and make him cry "Oh!"

MALVOLIO   And then "I" comes behind.

FABIAN   Ay, an you had any eye behind you, you 133 might see more detraction at your heels than fortunes 134 before you.

MALVOLIO   "M.O.A.I." This simulation is not as the 136 former. And yet, to crush this a little, it would bow to me, for every one of these letters are in my name. Soft! Here follows prose.

---

59 play with my (Malvolio perhaps means his steward's chain but checks himself in time; as "Count Malvolio," he would not be wearing it. A bawdy meaning of playing with himself is also suggested.) 60 curtsies bows   62–3 with cars with chariots, i.e., pulling apart by force   65 familiar (1) customary (2) friendly.   regard of control look of authority   66 take deliver   73 scab scurvy fellow.   74 break . . . of hamstring, disable   81 employment business   82 woodcock (A bird proverbial for its stupidity.)   gin snare.   83 humors whim, caprice   86 c's . . . t's i.e., cut, slang for the female pudenda   87 great (1) uppercase (2) copious. (P suggests "pee.")   in contempt of beyond   90–1 By . . . wax (Addressed to the seal on the letter.) 91 Soft Softly, not so fast.   impressure device imprinted on the seal. Lucrece Lucretia, chaste matron who, ravished by Tarquin, committed suicide   92 uses is accustomed   94 liver i.e., the seat of passion 99–100 The numbers altered! More verses, in a different meter!

102 brock badger. (Used contemptuously.)   107 fustian bombastic, ridiculously pompous   111 What What a.   dressed prepared for 112 wing speed.   staniel kestrel, a sparrow hawk. (The word is used contemptuously because of the uselessness of the staniel for falconry.) 112–13 checks at it turns to fly at it.   116 formal capacity normal understanding.   118 position arrangement   120 Oh, ay (Playing on O.I. of M.O.A.I.)   make up work out   121–2 Sowter . . . fox The hound Sowter (literally, "Cobbler") will bay triumphantly at picking up this false scent, even though the smell is as rank as a fox. ("M.O.A.I." is a false lead that reeks.)   126 at faults i.e., at maneuvering his way past breaks in the line of scent—in this case, on a false trail.   127–8 no consonancy . . . probation no pattern in the following letters that stands up under examination. (In fact, the letters "M.O.A.I." represent the first, last, second, and next to last letters of Malvolio's name.)   130 "O" shall end (1) "O" ends Malvolio's name (2) omega ends the Greek alphabet and is thus a symbol for the ending of the world, alpha to omega (3) Malvolio's cry of pain will end the matter, as Sir Toby suggests in the next line.   133 eye (punning on the "I" of "Oh, ay" and "M.O.A.I.")   134 detraction . . . heels defamation pursuing you   136 simulation disguise, puzzle

[*He reads.*] "If this fall into thy hand, revolve. In my 140
stars I am above thee, but be not afraid of greatness. 141
Some are born great, some achieve greatness, and
some have greatness thrust upon 'em. Thy Fates open 143
their hands; let thy blood and spirit embrace them; 144
and, to inure thyself to what thou art like to be, cast 145
thy humble slough and appear fresh. Be opposite with 146
a kinsman, surly with servants. Let thy tongue tang 147
arguments of state; put thyself into the trick of 148
singularity. She thus advises thee that sighs for thee. 149
Remember who commended thy yellow stockings,
and wished to see thee ever cross-gartered. I say, 151
remember. Go to, thou art made, if thou desir'st to be 152
so. If not, let me see thee a steward still, the fellow of
servants, and not worthy to touch Fortune's fingers.
Farewell. She that would alter services with thee, 155
                    The Fortunate-Unhappy."
Daylight and champaign discovers not more! This is 157
open. I will be proud, I will read politic authors, I will 158
baffle Sir Toby, I will wash off gross acquaintance, I 159
will be point-devise the very man. I do not now fool 160
myself, to let imagination jade me; for every reason 161
excites to this, that my lady loves me. She did com- 162
mend my yellow stockings of late, she did praise my
leg being cross-gartered; and in this she manifests her- 164
self to my love, and with a kind of injunction drives
me to these habits of her liking. I thank my stars, I am 166
happy. I will be strange, stout, in yellow stockings 167
and cross-gartered, even with the swiftness of putting
on. Jove and my stars be praised! Here is yet a postscript. [*He reads.*] "Thou canst not choose but know who
I am. If thou entertain'st my love, let it appear in thy 171
smiling; thy smiles become thee well. Therefore in my
presence still smile, dear my sweet, I prithee." 173
Jove, I thank thee. I will smile; I will do everything that
thou wilt have me.   *Exit.*

[*Sir Toby, Sir Andrew, and Fabian come from hiding.*]

FABIAN   I will not give my part of this sport for a
pension of thousands to be paid from the Sophy. 177
SIR TOBY   I could marry this wench for this device.
SIR ANDREW   So could I too.
SIR TOBY   And ask no other dowry with her but such
another jest.

Enter Maria.

SIR ANDREW   Nor I neither.
FABIAN   Here comes my noble gull-catcher. 183
SIR TOBY   Wilt thou set thy foot o' my neck?
SIR ANDREW   Or o' mine either?
SIR TOBY   Shall I play my freedom at tray-trip, and 186
become thy bondslave?
SIR ANDREW   I'faith, or I either?
SIR TOBY   Why, thou hast put him in such a dream that
when the image of it leaves him he must run mad.
MARIA   Nay, but say true, does it work upon him?
SIR TOBY   Like aqua vitae with a midwife. 192
MARIA   If you will then see the fruits of the sport, mark
his first approach before my lady. He will come to her
in yellow stockings, and 'tis a color she abhors, and
cross-gartered, a fashion she detests; and he will smile
upon her, which will now be so unsuitable to her
disposition, being addicted to a melancholy as she is,
that it cannot but turn him into a notable contempt. If 199
you will see it, follow me.
SIR TOBY   To the gates of Tartar, thou most excellent 201
devil of wit!
SIR ANDREW   I'll make one too.   *Exeunt.* 203

♣

3.1

*Enter Viola, and Clown [Feste, playing his pipe
and tabor].*

VIOLA   Save thee, friend, and thy music. Dost thou live 1
by thy tabor? 2
FESTE   No, sir, I live by the church.
VIOLA   Art thou a churchman?
FESTE   No such matter, sir. I do live by the church, for
I do live at my house, and my house doth stand by the
church.
VIOLA   So thou mayst say the king lies by a beggar if 8
a beggar dwell near him, or the church stands by thy 9
tabor if thy tabor stand by the church. 10
FESTE   You have said, sir. To see this age! A sentence is 11
but a cheveril glove to a good wit. How quickly the 12
wrong side may be turned outward!
VIOLA   Nay, that's certain. They that dally nicely with 14
words may quickly make them wanton. 15
FESTE   I would therefore my sister had had no name,
sir.
VIOLA   Why, man?

---

140 **revolve** consider.   141 **stars** fortune   143–4 **open their hands**
offer their bounty   145 **inure** accustom.   **like** likely.   **cast** cast off
146 **slough** skin of a snake; hence, former demeanor of humbleness.
opposite contradictory   147 **tang** sound loud with   148 **state** politics, statecraft   148–9 **trick of singularity** eccentricity of manner.
151 **cross-gartered** wearing garters above and below the knee so as to
cross behind it.   152 **Go to** (An expression of remonstrance.)
155 **alter services** i.e., exchange place of mistress and servant
157 **champaign** open country.   **discovers** discloses   158 **politic** dealing with state affairs   159 **baffle** deride, degrade. (A technical chivalric term used to describe the disgrace of a perjured knight.)   **gross**
base   160 **point-devise** correct to the letter   161 **to let** by letting.
jade me trick me, make me look ridiculous (as an unruly horse might
do)   162 **excites to this** prompts this conclusion   164 **this** this letter
166 **these habits** this attire   167 **happy** fortunate.   **strange, stout**
aloof, haughty   171 **thou entertain'st** you accept   173 **still** continually   177 **Sophy** Shah of Persia.

183 **gull-catcher** tricker of *gulls* or dupes.   186 **play** gamble.   **tray-
trip** a game of dice, success in which depended on throwing a three
(*tray*)   192 **aqua vitae** brandy or other distilled liquor   199 **notable
contempt** notorious object of contempt.   201 **Tartar** Tartarus, the
infernal regions   203 **make one** i.e., tag along
3.1 Location: Olivia's garden.
1 **Save** God save   1–2 **live by** earn your living with. (But Feste uses
the phrase to mean "dwell near.")   2 **tabor** small drum.   8 **lies by**
(1) lies sexually with (2) dwells near   9–10 **stands by . . . stand by**
(1) is maintained by (2) is placed near   11 **You have said** You've
expressed your opinion.   **sentence** maxim, judgment, opinion
12 **cheveril** kidskin   14 **dally nicely** (1) play subtly (2) toy amorously
15 **wanton** (1) equivocal (2) licentious, unchaste. (Feste then "dallies"
with the word in its sexual sense; see line 20.)

FESTE   Why, sir, her name's a word, and to dally with that word might make my sister wanton. But indeed, words are very rascals since bonds disgraced them.   21

VIOLA   Thy reason, man?

FESTE   Troth, sir, I can yield you none without words, and words are grown so false I am loath to prove reason with them.

VIOLA   I warrant thou art a merry fellow and car'st for nothing.   26 27

FESTE   Not so, sir, I do care for something; but in my conscience, sir, I do not care for you. If that be to care for nothing, sir, I would it would make you invisible.   30

VIOLA   Art not thou the Lady Olivia's fool?

FESTE   No indeed, sir. The Lady Olivia has no folly. She will keep no fool, sir, till she be married, and fools are as like husbands as pilchers are to herrings—the husband's the bigger. I am indeed not her fool but her corrupter of words.   34 35

VIOLA   I saw thee late at the Count Orsino's.   37

FESTE   Foolery, sir, does walk about the orb like the sun; it shines everywhere. I would be sorry, sir, but the fool should be as oft with your master as with my mistress. I think I saw Your Wisdom there.   38 39 40 41

VIOLA   Nay, an thou pass upon me, I'll no more with thee. Hold, there's expenses for thee.   42

[She gives a coin.]

FESTE   Now Jove, in his next commodity of hair, send thee a beard!   44

VIOLA   By my troth, I'll tell thee, I am almost sick for one—*[aside]* though I would not have it grow on my chin.—Is thy lady within?   46 47

FESTE   Would not a pair of these have bred, sir?

VIOLA   Yes, being kept together and put to use.   50

FESTE   I would play Lord Pandarus of Phrygia, sir, to bring a Cressida to this Troilus.   51

VIOLA   I understand you, sir. 'Tis well begged.

[She gives another coin.]

FESTE   The matter, I hope, is not great, sir, begging but a beggar; Cressida was a beggar. My lady is within, sir. I will conster to them whence you come. Who you are and what you would are out of my welkin—I might say "element," but the word is overworn.   54 55 56 58

Exit.

VIOLA
This fellow is wise enough to play the fool,
And to do that well craves a kind of wit.
He must observe their mood on whom he jests,
The quality of persons, and the time,   63
Not, like the haggard, check at every feather   64
That comes before his eye. This is a practice   65
As full of labor as a wise man's art;
For folly that he wisely shows is fit,   67
But wise men, folly-fall'n, quite taint their wit.   68

Enter Sir Toby and [Sir] Andrew.

SIR TOBY   Save you, gentleman.

VIOLA   And you, sir.

SIR ANDREW   *Dieu vous garde, monsieur.*   71

VIOLA   *Et vous aussi; votre serviteur.*   72

SIR ANDREW   I hope, sir, you are, and I am yours.

SIR TOBY   Will you encounter the house? My niece is desirous you should enter, if your trade be to her.   74 75

VIOLA   I am bound to your niece, sir; I mean, she is the list of my voyage.   76 77

SIR TOBY   Taste your legs, sir. Put them to motion.   78

VIOLA   My legs do better understand me, sir, than I understand what you mean by bidding me taste my legs.   79

SIR TOBY   I mean, to go, sir, to enter.

VIOLA   I will answer you with gait and entrance.—But we are prevented.   82 83

Enter Olivia and gentlewoman [Maria].

Most excellent accomplished lady, the heavens rain odors on you!

SIR ANDREW   *[to Sir Toby]* That youth's a rare courtier. "Rain odors"—well.

VIOLA   *[to Sir Toby]* My matter hath no voice, lady, but to your own most pregnant and vouchsafed ear.   88 89

SIR ANDREW   *[to Sir Toby]* "Odors," "pregnant," and "vouchsafed." I'll get 'em all three all ready.   91

OLIVIA   Let the garden door be shut, and leave me to my hearing. *[Exeunt Sir Toby, Sir Andrew, and Maria.]* Give me your hand, sir.

VIOLA
My duty, madam, and most humble service.

OLIVIA   What is your name?

VIOLA
Cesario is your servant's name, fair princess.

---

21 since . . . them i.e., since bonds have been needed to make sworn statements good. (Words cannot be relied on since not even contractual promises are reliable.)   **26–7 car'st for nothing** are without any worries. (But Feste puns on *care for* in lines 29–30 in the sense of "like.") **30 invisible** i.e., nothing; absent.   **34 pilchers** pilchards, fish resembling herring but smaller   **35 the bigger** (1) the larger (2) the bigger fool.   **37 late** recently   **38 orb** earth   **39–41 I would . . . mistress** (1) I should be sorry not to visit Orsino's house often (2) It would be a shame if folly were no less common there than in Olivia's household. **41 Your Wisdom** i.e., you. (A title of mock courtesy.)   **42 an . . . me** if you fence (verbally) with me, pass judgment on me   **44 commodity** supply   **46–7 sick for one** (1) eager to have a beard (2) in love with a bearded man   **50 put to use** put out at interest.   **51 Pandarus** the go-between in the love story of Troilus and Cressida; uncle to Cressida **54–5 begging . . . was a beggar** (A reference to Henryson's *Testament of Cresseid* in which Cressida became a leper and a beggar. Feste desires another coin to be the mate of the one he has, just as Cressida, the beggar, was mate to Troilus.)   **56 conster** construe, explain   **58 welkin** sky. **element** (The word can be synonymous with *welkin*, but the common phrase *out of my element* means "beyond my scope.")

63 quality character, rank   **64 haggard** untrained adult hawk, hence unmanageable   **64–5 check . . . eye** strike at every bird it sees, i.e., dart from subject to subject.   **65 practice** exercise of skill   **67–8 For . . . wit** for the folly he judiciously displays is appropriate and clever, whereas when wise men fall into folly they utterly infect their own intelligence.   **71 *Dieu . . . monsieur*** God keep you, sir.   **72 *Et . . . serviteur*** And you, too; (I am) your servant. (Sir Andrew is not quite up to a reply in French.)   **74 encounter** (High-sounding word to express "approach.")   **75 trade** business. (Suggesting also a commercial venture.)   **76 I am bound** (1) I am on a journey. (Continuing Sir Toby's metaphor in *trade*.) (2) I am confined, obligated   **77 list** limit, destination   **78 Taste** Try   **79 understand** stand under, support **82 gait and entrance** going and entering. (With a pun on *gate:* [1] stride [2] entryway.)   **83 prevented** anticipated.   **88 hath no voice** cannot be uttered   **89 pregnant and vouchsafed** receptive and attentive   **91 all ready** committed to memory for future use.

OLIVIA

My servant, sir? 'Twas never merry world   98
Since lowly feigning was called compliment.   99
You're servant to the Count Orsino, youth.

VIOLA

And he is yours, and his must needs be yours;   101
Your servant's servant is your servant, madam.

OLIVIA

For him, I think not on him. For his thoughts,   103
Would they were blanks, rather than filled with me!   104

VIOLA

Madam, I come to whet your gentle thoughts
On his behalf.

OLIVIA   Oh, by your leave, I pray you.   106
I bade you never speak again of him.
But, would you undertake another suit,
I had rather hear you to solicit that
Than music from the spheres.

VIOLA   Dear lady—   110

OLIVIA

Give me leave, beseech you. I did send,
After the last enchantment you did here,
A ring in chase of you; so did I abuse   113
Myself, my servant, and, I fear me, you.
Under your hard construction must I sit,   115
To force that on you in a shameful cunning   116
Which you knew none of yours. What might you
    think?
Have you not set mine honor at the stake   118
And baited it with all th'unmuzzled thoughts   119
That tyrannous heart can think? To one of your
    receiving   120
Enough is shown; a cypress, not a bosom,   121
Hides my heart. So, let me hear you speak.   122

VIOLA

I pity you.

OLIVIA   That's a degree to love.

VIOLA

No, not a grece; for 'tis a vulgar proof   124
That very oft we pity enemies.

OLIVIA

Why then, methinks 'tis time to smile again.   126
Oh, world, how apt the poor are to be proud!   127
If one should be a prey, how much the better

To fall before the lion than the wolf!   *Clock strikes.* 129
The clock upbraids me with the waste of time.
Be not afraid, good youth, I will not have you;
And yet, when wit and youth is come to harvest
Your wife is like to reap a proper man.   133
There lies your way, due west.

VIOLA   Then westward ho!   134
Grace and good disposition attend Your Ladyship.   135
You'll nothing, madam, to my lord by me?

OLIVIA   Stay.
I prithee, tell me what thou think'st of me.

VIOLA

That you do think you are not what you are.   139

OLIVIA

If I think so, I think the same of you.   140

VIOLA

Then think you right. I am not what I am.

OLIVIA

I would you were as I would have you be!

VIOLA

Would it be better, madam, than I am?
I wish it might, for now I am your fool.   144

OLIVIA [*aside*]
Oh, what a deal of scorn looks beautiful
In the contempt and anger of his lip!
A murderous guilt shows not itself more soon
Than love that would seem hid; love's night is noon.— 148
Cesario, by the roses of the spring,
By maidhood, honor, truth, and everything,
I love thee so that, maugre all thy pride,   151
Nor wit nor reason can my passion hide.   152
Do not extort thy reasons from this clause,   153
For that I woo, thou therefore hast no cause.   154
But rather reason thus with reason fetter: 155
Love sought is good, but given unsought is better.

VIOLA

By innocence I swear, and by my youth,
I have one heart, one bosom, and one truth,
And that no woman has, nor never none
Shall mistress be of it save I alone.
And so adieu, good madam. Nevermore
Will I my master's tears to you deplore.   162

OLIVIA

Yet come again, for thou perhaps mayst move
That heart, which now abhors, to like his love.
                          Exeunt [separately].

❖

98–9 'Twas . . . compliment Things have never been the same since affected humility (like calling oneself another's servant) began to be mistaken for courtesy.   **101 yours** your servant.   **his** those belonging to him   **103 For** As for   **104 blanks** blank coins ready to be stamped or empty sheets of paper   **106 by your leave** i.e., allow me to interrupt   **110 music from the spheres** (The heavenly bodies were thought to be fixed in hollow concentric spheres that revolved one about the other, producing a harmony too exquisite to be heard by human ears.)   **113 abuse** wrong, mislead   **115 hard construction** harsh interpretation   **116 To force** for forcing the ring   **118 at the stake** (The figure is from bearbaiting.)   **119 baited** harassed. (Literally, set the unmuzzled dogs on to bite the bear.)   **120 receiving** capacity, intelligence   **121–2 a cypress . . . heart** i.e., I have shown my heart to you, veiled only with thin, gauzelike cypress cloth rather than the opaque flesh of my bosom.   **124 grece** step. (Synonymous with *degree* in the preceding line.)   **vulgar proof** common experience   **126 smile** i.e., cast off love's melancholy   **127 how . . . proud!** how ready the unfortunate and rejected (like myself) are to find something to be proud of in their distress! Or, how apt are persons of comparatively low social station like yourself to show pride in rejecting love!

129 To fall . . . wolf! i.e., to fall before a noble adversary rather than to a person like you who attacks me thus!   **133 like** likely.   **proper** handsome, worthy   **134 westward ho** (The cry of Thames watermen to attract westward-bound passengers.)   **135 Grace . . . Ladyship** May you enjoy God's blessing and a happy frame of mind.   **139 That . . . are** i.e., That you think you are in love with a man, and you are mistaken.   **140 If . . . you** (Olivia may interpret Viola's cryptic statement as suggesting that Olivia "does not know herself," i.e., is distracted with passion; she may also hint at her suspicion that "Cesario" is higher born than he admits.)   **144 fool** butt.   **148 love's . . . noon** i.e., love, despite its attempt to be secret, reveals itself as plain as day.   **151 maugre** in spite of   **152 Nor** neither   **153–4 Do . . . cause** Do not rationalize your indifference along these lines, that because I am the wooer you have no cause to reciprocate.   **155 But . . . fetter** But instead control your reasoning with the following reason   **162 deplore** beweep.

3.2

Enter Sir Toby, Sir Andrew, and Fabian.

SIR ANDREW   No, faith, I'll not stay a jot longer.

SIR TOBY   Thy reason, dear venom, give thy reason. 2

FABIAN   You must needs yield your reason, Sir Andrew.

SIR ANDREW   Marry, I saw your niece do more favors to the Count's servingman than ever she bestowed upon me. I saw't i'th' orchard. 6

SIR TOBY   Did she see thee the while, old boy? Tell me that.

SIR ANDREW   As plain as I see you now.

FABIAN   This was a great argument of love in her toward 10 you.

SIR ANDREW   'Slight, will you make an ass o'me? 12

FABIAN   I will prove it legitimate, sir, upon the oaths of 13 judgment and reason.

SIR TOBY   And they have been grand-jurymen since before Noah was a sailor.

FABIAN   She did show favor to the youth in your sight only to exasperate you, to awake your dormouse valor, 18 to put fire in your heart and brimstone in your liver. You should then have accosted her, and with some excellent jests, fire-new from the mint, you should 21 have banged the youth into dumbness. This was 22 looked for at your hand, and this was balked. The dou- 23 ble gilt of this opportunity you let time wash off, and 24 you are now sailed into the north of my lady's opinion, 25 where you will hang like an icicle on a Dutchman's 26 beard unless you do redeem it by some laudable at- 27 tempt either of valor or policy. 28

SIR ANDREW   An't be any way, it must be with valor, for policy I hate. I had as lief be a Brownist as a poli- 30 tician. 31

SIR TOBY   Why, then, build thy fortunes upon the 32 basis of valor. Challenge me the Count's youth to fight 33 with him; hurt him in eleven places. My niece shall take note of it; and assure thyself, there is no love-broker in the world can more prevail in man's 36 commendation with woman than report of valor.

FABIAN   There is no way but this, Sir Andrew.

SIR ANDREW   Will either of you bear me a challenge to him?

SIR TOBY   Go, write it in a martial hand. Be curst and 41 brief; it is no matter how witty, so it be eloquent and full of invention. Taunt him with the license of ink. If 43

thou "thou"-est him some thrice, it shall not be amiss; 44 and as many lies as will lie in thy sheet of paper, 45 although the sheet were big enough for the bed of 46 Ware in England, set 'em down. Go, about it. Let 47 there be gall enough in thy ink, though thou write 48 with a goose pen, no matter. About it. 49

SIR ANDREW   Where shall I find you?

SIR TOBY   We'll call thee at the cubiculo. Go. 51

Exit Sir Andrew.

FABIAN   This is a dear manikin to you, Sir Toby. 52

SIR TOBY   I have been dear to him, lad, some two 53 thousand strong or so.

FABIAN   We shall have a rare letter from him; but you'll 55 not deliver't?

SIR TOBY   Never trust me, then; and by all means stir on the youth to an answer. I think oxen and wainropes 58 cannot hale them together. For Andrew, if he were 59 opened and you find so much blood in his liver as will 60 clog the foot of a flea, I'll eat the rest of th'anatomy. 61

FABIAN   And his opposite, the youth, bears in his 62 visage no great presage of cruelty.

Enter Maria.

SIR TOBY   Look where the youngest wren of nine 64 comes.

MARIA   If you desire the spleen, and will laugh your- 66 selves into stitches, follow me. Yond gull Malvolio is turned heathen, a very renegado; for there is no 68 Christian that means to be saved by believing rightly can ever believe such impossible passages of gross- 70 ness. He's in yellow stockings. 71

SIR TOBY   And cross-gartered?

MARIA   Most villainously, like a pedant that keeps a 73 school i'th' church. I have dogged him like his murderer. He does obey every point of the letter that I dropped to betray him. He does smile his face into more lines than is in the new map with the augmen- 77 tation of the Indies. You have not seen such a thing as 78 'tis. I can hardly forbear hurling things at him. I know my lady will strike him. If she do, he'll smile and take't for a great favor.

SIR TOBY   Come, bring us, bring us where he is.

Exeunt omnes.

44 "thou"-est ("Thou" was used only between friends or to inferiors.) **45 lies** charges of lying   **46–7 bed of Ware** a famous bedstead capable of holding twelve persons, about eleven feet square, said to have been at the Stag Inn in Ware, Hertfordshire   **48 gall** (1) bitterness, rancor (2) a growth found on certain oaks, used as an ingredient of ink **49 goose pen** (1) goose quill (2) foolish style   **51 call thee** call for you. **cubiculo** little chamber, bedchamber.   **52 manikin** puppet   **53 dear** expensive. (Playing on *dear,* "fond," in the previous speech.)   **55 rare** extraordinary   **58 wainropes** wagon ropes   **59 hale** haul.   **For** As for   **60 liver** (A pale and bloodless liver was a sign of cowardice.) **61 th'anatomy** the cadaver   **62 opposite** adversary   **64 youngest . . . nine** the last hatched and smallest of a nest of wrens   **66 the spleen** a laughing fit. (The spleen was thought to be the seat of immoderate laughter.)   **68 renegado** renegade, deserter of his religion **70–1 impossible . . . grossness** gross impossibilities (i.e., in the letter). **73 villainously** i.e., abominably.   **pedant** schoolmaster   **77–8 the new . . . Indies** (Probably a reference to a map made by Emmeric Mollineux in 1599–1600 to be printed in Hakluyt's *Voyages,* showing more of the East indies, including Japan, than had ever been mapped before.)

3.2. Location: Olivia's house.
2 venom i.e., person filled with venomous anger   **6 orchard** garden. **10 argument** proof   **12 'Slight** By his (God's) light   **13 it** my con- tention.   **oaths** i.e., testimony under oath   **18 dormouse** i.e., sleepy and timid   **21 fire-new . . . mint** newly coined   **22 banged** struck **23 balked** missed, neglected.   **23–4 double gilt** thick layer of gold, i.e., rare worth   **25 into . . . opinion** i.e., out of the warmth and sun- shine of Olivia's favor   **26–7 icicle . . . beard** (Alludes to the arctic voyage of William Barents in 1596–1597.)   **28 policy** stratagem. **28 policy** stratagem.   **30 Brownist** (An early name of the Congrega- tionalists, from the name of the founder, Robert Browne.) **30–1 politician** intriguer. (Sir Andrew misinterprets Sir Toby's more neutral use of *policy,* "clever stratagem.")   **32–3 build me . . . Chal- lenge me** build . . . Challenge. ("Me" is idiomatic.)   **36 love-broker** agent between lovers   **41 curst** fierce   **43 with . . . ink** i.e., with the freedom that may be risked in writing but not in conversation.

3.3

Enter Sebastian and Antonio.

SEBASTIAN
I would not by my will have troubled you,
But since you make your pleasure of your pains,
I will no further chide you.

ANTONIO
I could not stay behind you. My desire,
More sharp than filèd steel, did spur me forth,
And not all love to see you—though so much   6
As might have drawn one to a longer voyage—
But jealousy what might befall your travel,   8
Being skilless in these parts, which to a stranger,   9
Unguided and unfriended, often prove
Rough and unhospitable. My willing love,
The rather by these arguments of fear,   12
Set forth in your pursuit.

SEBASTIAN   My kind Antonio,
I can no other answer make but thanks,
And thanks; and ever oft good turns   15
Are shuffled off with such uncurrent pay.   16
But were my worth, as is my conscience, firm,   17
You should find better dealing. What's to do?   18
Shall we go see the relics of this town?   19

ANTONIO
Tomorrow, sir. Best first go see your lodging.

SEBASTIAN
I am not weary, and 'tis long to night.
I pray you, let us satisfy our eyes
With the memorials and the things of fame
That do renown this city.

ANTONIO   Would you'd pardon me.   24
I do not without danger walk these streets.
Once in a sea fight 'gainst the Count his galleys   26
I did some service, of such note indeed
That were I ta'en here it would scarce be answered.   28

SEBASTIAN
Belike you slew great number of his people?   29

ANTONIO
Th'offense is not of such a bloody nature,
Albeit the quality of the time and quarrel
Might well have given us bloody argument.   32
It might have since been answered in repaying   33
What we took from them, which for traffic's sake   34
Most of our city did. Only myself stood out,
For which, if I be lapsèd in this place,   36
I shall pay dear.

SEBASTIAN   Do not then walk too open.

ANTONIO
It doth not fit me. Hold, sir, here's my purse.
                                        [*He gives his purse.*]
In the south suburbs, at the Elephant,   39
Is best to lodge. I will bespeak our diet,   40
Whiles you beguile the time and feed your knowl-
edge
With viewing of the town. There shall you have me.   42

SEBASTIAN   Why I your purse?

ANTONIO
Haply your eye shall light upon some toy   44
You have desire to purchase; and your store   45
I think is not for idle markets, sir.   46

SEBASTIAN
I'll be your purse-bearer and leave you
For an hour.

ANTONIO   To th'Elephant.

SEBASTIAN   I do remember.
                                Exeunt [*separately*].

❧

3.4

Enter Olivia and Maria.

OLIVIA [*aside*]
I have sent after him; he says he'll come.   1
How shall I feast him? What bestow of him?   2
For youth is bought more oft than begged or
borrowed.
I speak too loud.—
Where's Malvolio? He is sad and civil,   5
And suits well for a servant with my fortunes.
Where is Malvolio?

MARIA   He's coming, madam, but in very strange
manner. He is, sure, possessed, madam.   9

OLIVIA   Why, what's the matter? Does he rave?

MARIA   No, madam, he does nothing but smile. Your
Ladyship were best to have some guard about you if he
come, for sure the man is tainted in's wits.   13

OLIVIA
Go call him hither. [*Maria summons Malvolio.*] I am as
mad as he,
If sad and merry madness equal be.   15

        Enter Malvolio, [*cross-gartered and in yellow
        stockings*].

How now, Malvolio?

MALVOLIO   Sweet lady, ho, ho!

OLIVIA   Smil'st thou? I sent for thee upon a sad   18
occasion.

3.3. **Location: A Street.**
6 all only, merely.   **so much** i.e., that was great enough   **8 jealousy**
anxiety   **9 skilless in** unacquainted with   **12 The rather** made all the
more willing   **15 And . . . turns** (this probably corrupt line is usually
made to read, "And thanks and ever thanks; and oft good turns.")
16 shuffled off turned aside.   **uncurrent** worthless (such as mere
thanks)   **17 worth** wealth.   **conscience** i.e., moral inclination to assist
18 dealing treatment, payment.   **19 relics** antiquities   **24 renown**
make famous   **26 Count his** Count's, i.e., Duke's   **28 it . . . answered**
I'd be hard put to offer a defense.   **29 Belike** Perhaps   **32 bloody**
argument cause for bloodshed.   **33 answered** compensated   **34 traffic's** trade's   **36 lapsèd** caught off guard, surprised

39 Elephant the name of an inn   **40 bespeak our diet** order our food
42 have find   **44 Haply** Perhaps.   **toy** trifle   **45 store** store of money
46 is not . . . markets cannot afford luxuries
3.4. **Location: Olivia's garden.**
1 he . . . come i.e., suppose he says he'll come.   **2 of** on   **5 sad and
civil** sober and decorous   **9 possessed** (1) possessed with an evil
spirit (2) mad   **13 in's** in his   **15 If . . . equal be** i.e., if love melancholy and smiling madness are essentially alike. (Love melancholy
was regarded as a kind of madness.)   **18 sad** serious

MALVOLIO   Sad, lady? I could be sad. This does make 20
some obstruction in the blood, this cross-gartering,
but what of that? If it please the eye of one, it is with
me as the very true sonnet is, "Please one and please 23
all."   24

OLIVIA   Why, how dost thou, man? What is the matter
with thee?

MALVOLIO   Not black in my mind, though yellow in my 27
legs. It did come to his hands, and commands shall be 28
executed. I think we do know the sweet roman hand. 29

OLIVIA   Wilt thou go to bed, Malvolio? 30

MALVOLIO   To bed! "Ay, sweetheart, and I'll come to 31
thee." 32

OLIVIA   God comfort thee! Why dost thou smile so and
kiss thy hand so oft?

MARIA   How do you, Malvolio?

MALVOLIO   At your request? Yes, nightingales answer 36
daws. 37

MARIA   Why appear you with this ridiculous boldness
before my lady?

MALVOLIO   "Be not afraid of greatness." 'Twas well writ.

OLIVIA   What mean'st thou by that, Malvolio?

MALVOLIO   "Some are born great—"

OLIVIA   Ha?

MALVOLIO   "Some achieve greatness—"

OLIVIA   What say'st thou?

MALVOLIO   "And some have greatness thrust upon them."

OLIVIA   Heaven restore thee!

MALVOLIO   "Remember who commended thy yellow
stockings—"

OLIVIA   Thy yellow stockings?

MALVOLIO   "And wished to see thee cross-gartered."

OLIVIA   Cross-gartered?

MALVOLIO   "Go to, thou art made, if thou desir'st to
be so—"

OLIVIA   Am I made?

MALVOLIO   "If not, let me see thee a servant still."

OLIVIA   Why, this is very midsummer madness. 57

Enter Servant.

SERVANT   Madam, the young gentleman of the Count
Orsino's is returned. I could hardly entreat him back.
He attends Your Ladyship's pleasure.

OLIVIA   I'll come to him.   [*Exit Servant.*]
Good Maria, let this fellow be looked to. Where's my
cousin Toby? Let some of my people have a special

care of him. I would not have him miscarry for the half 64
of my dowry.

Exeunt [Olivia and Maria, different ways].

MALVOLIO   Oho, do you come near me now? No worse 66
man than Sir Toby to look to me! This concurs directly
with the letter. She sends him on purpose that I may
appear stubborn to him, for she incites me to that in
the letter. "Cast thy humble slough," says she; "be opposite with a kinsman, surly with servants; let thy
tongue tang with arguments of state; put thyself into
the trick of singularity." And consequently sets down 73
the manner how: as, a sad face, a reverend carriage, a 74
slow tongue, in the habit of some sir of note, and so 75
forth. I have limed her, but it is Jove's doing, and Jove 76
make me thankful! And when she went away now,
"Let this fellow be looked to." "Fellow!" Not "Malvo- 78
lio," nor after my degree, but "fellow." Why, every- 79
thing adheres together, that no dram of a scruple, no 80
scruple of a scruple, no obstacle, no incredulous or un- 81
safe circumstance—what can be said?—nothing that 82
can be can come between me and the full prospect of
my hopes. Well, Jove, not I, is the doer of this, and he
is to be thanked.

Enter [Sir] Toby, Fabian, and Maria.

SIR TOBY   Which way is he, in the name of sanctity? If
all the devils of hell be drawn in little, and Legion him- 87
self possessed him, yet I'll speak to him.

FABIAN   Here he is, here he is.—How is't with you,
sir? How is't with you, man?

MALVOLIO   Go off. I discard you. Let me enjoy my
private. Go off. 92

MARIA   Lo, how hollow the fiend speaks within him!
Did not I tell you? Sir Toby, my lady prays you to have
a care of him.

MALVOLIO   Aha, does she so?

SIR TOBY   Go to, go to! Peace, peace, we must deal
gently with him. Let me alone.—How do you, 98
Malvolio? How is't with you? What, man, defy the 99
devil! Consider, he's an enemy to mankind.

MALVOLIO   Do you know what you say?

MARIA   La you, an you speak ill of the devil, how he 102
takes it at heart! Pray God he be not bewitched!

FABIAN   Carry his water to th' wisewoman. 104

MARIA   Marry, and it shall be done tomorrow morning,
if I live. My lady would not lose him for more than
I'll say.

MALVOLIO   How now, mistress?

---

20 sad (1) serious (2) melancholy.   **23 sonnet** song, ballad
23–4 "Please . . . all" "To please one special person is as good as to
please everybody." (The refrain of a ballad.)   **27 black** i.e., melancholic
28 It i.e., The letter.   **his** Malvolio's   **29 roman hand** fashionable italic
or Italian style of handwriting rather than English "secretary" handwriting.   **30 go to bed** i.e., try to sleep off your mental distress. (But
Malvolio misinterprets as a sexual invitation.)   **31–2 "Ay . . . thee"**
(Malvolio quotes from a popular song of the day.)   **36–7 nightingales
answer daws** i.e. (to Maria), do you suppose a fine fellow like me
would answer a lowly creature (a *daw*, a "jackdaw") like you?
57 midsummer madness (A proverbial phrase; the midsummer
moon was supposed to cause madness.)

64 miscarry come to harm   **66 come near** understand, appreciate
73 consequently thereafter   **74 sad** serious   **75 habit . . . note** attire
suited to a man of distinction   **76 limed** caught like a bird with
birdlime (a sticky substance spread on branches)   **78 Fellow** (Malvolio takes the basic meaning, "companion.")   **79 after my degree**
according to my position   **80 dram** (Literally, one-eighth of a fluid
ounce.)   **scruple** (Literally, one-third of a dram.)   **81 incredulous**
incredible   **81–2 unsafe** uncertain, unreliable   **87 drawn in little**
(1) portrayed in miniature (2) gathered into a small space.   **Legion**
an unclean spirit. ("My name is Legion, for we are many," Mark 5:9.)
92 private privacy.   **98 Let me alone** Leave him to me.   **99 defy**
renounce   **102 La you** Look you   **104 water** urine (for medical
analysis)

MARIA   Oh, Lord!

SIR TOBY   Prithee, hold thy peace; this is not the way. Do you not see you move him? Let me alone with him. [111]

FABIAN   No way but gentleness, gently, gently. The fiend is rough, and will not be roughly used.

SIR TOBY   Why, how now, my bawcock! How dost [115] thou, chuck? [116]

MALVOLIO   Sir!

SIR TOBY   Ay, biddy, come with me. What, man, 'tis [118] not for gravity to play at cherry-pit with Satan. Hang [119] him, foul collier! [120]

MARIA   Get him to say his prayers, good Sir Toby, get him to pray.

MALVOLIO   My prayers, minx?

MARIA   No, I warrant you, he will not hear of godliness.

MALVOLIO   Go hang yourselves all! You are idle, shal- [125] low things; I am not of your element. You shall know [126] more hereafter.   *Exit.* [127]

SIR TOBY   Is't possible?

FABIAN   If this were played upon a stage, now, I could condemn it as an improbable fiction.

SIR TOBY   His very genius hath taken the infection of [131] the device, man.

MARIA   Nay, pursue him now, lest the device take air [133] and taint. [134]

FABIAN   Why, we shall make him mad indeed.

MARIA   The house will be the quieter.

SIR TOBY   Come, we'll have him in a dark room and [137] bound. My niece is already in the belief that he's mad. [138] We may carry it thus for our pleasure and his penance [139] till our very pastime, tired out of breath, prompt us to have mercy on him, at which time we will bring the device to the bar and crown thee for a finder of [142] madmen. But see, but see! [143]

Enter Sir Andrew [with a letter].

FABIAN   More matter for a May morning. [144]

SIR ANDREW   Here's the challenge. Read it. I warrant there's vinegar and pepper in't.

FABIAN   Is't so saucy? [147]

SIR ANDREW   Ay, is't, I warrant him. Do but read. [148]

SIR TOBY   Give me. [*He reads.*] "Youth, whatsoever thou art, thou art but a scurvy fellow."

FABIAN   Good, and valiant.

SIR TOBY [*reads*]   "Wonder not, nor admire not in thy [152] mind, why I do call thee so, for I will show thee no reason for't."

FABIAN   A good note, that keeps you from the blow of [155] the law.

SIR TOBY [*reads*]   "Thou com'st to the Lady Olivia, and in my sight she uses thee kindly. But thou liest in thy throat; that is not the matter I challenge thee for."

FABIAN   Very brief, and to exceeding good sense—less.

SIR TOBY [*reads*]   "I will waylay thee going home, where if it be thy chance to kill me—"

FABIAN   Good.

SIR TOBY [*reads*]   "Thou kill'st me like a rogue and a villain."

FABIAN   Still you keep o' th' windy side of the law. [166] Good.

SIR TOBY [*reads*]   "Fare thee well, and God have mercy upon one of our souls! He may have mercy upon mine, but my hope is better, and so look to thyself. [170] Thy friend, as thou usest him, and thy sworn enemy, Andrew Aguecheek."

If this letter move him not, his legs cannot. I'll give't [173] him.

MARIA   You may have very fit occasion for't. He is now in some commerce with my lady, and will by and by [176] depart.

SIR TOBY   Go, Sir Andrew. Scout me for him at the [178] corner of the orchard like a bum-baily. So soon as ever [179] thou see'st him, draw, and as thou draw'st, swear hor- [180] rible; for it comes to pass oft that a terrible oath, with [181] a swaggering accent sharply twanged off, gives man-hood more approbation than ever proof itself would [183] have earned him. Away!

SIR ANDREW   Nay, let me alone for swearing.   *Exit.* [185]

SIR TOBY   Now will not I deliver his letter, for the behav-ior of the young gentleman gives him out to be of good capacity and breeding; his employment between his lord and my niece confirms no less. Therefore this letter, being so excellently ignorant, will breed no ter-ror in the youth. He will find it comes from a clodpoll. [191] But, sir, I will deliver his challenge by word of mouth, set upon Aguecheek a notable report of valor, and drive the gentleman—as I know his youth will aptly [194] receive it—into a most hideous opinion of his rage, [195] skill, fury, and impetuosity. This will so fright them both that they will kill one another by the look, like cockatrices. [198]

Enter Olivia and Viola.

FABIAN   Here he comes with your niece. Give them way [199] till he take leave, and presently after him. [200]

---

111 move upset, excite   **115 bawcock** fine fellow. (From the French *beau-coq*.)   **116 chuck** (A form of "chick," term of endearment.)   **118 biddy** chicken   **119 for gravity** suitable for a man of your dig-nity.   **cherry-pit** a children's game consisting of throwing cherry stones into a little hole   **120 collier** i.e., Satan. (Literally, a coal ven-dor.)   **125 idle** foolish   **126 element** sphere.   **126–7 know more** i.e. hear about this   **131 genius** i.e., soul, spirit   **133–4 take . . . taint** become exposed to air (i.e., become known) and thus spoil.   **137–8 have . . . bound** (The standard treatment for insanity at this time.)   **139 carry** manage   **142 bar** i.e., bar of judgment   **142–3 finder of madmen** member of a jury changed with "finding" if the accused is insane.   **144 matter . . . morning** sport for Mayday plays or games.   **147 saucy** (1) spicy (2) insolent.   **148 him** it.   **152 admire** marvel

155 note observation, remark   **166 windy** windward, i.e., safe, where one is less likely to be driven onto legal rocks and shoals   **170 my hope is better** (Sir Andrew's comically inept way of saying he hopes to be the survivor; instead, he seems to say, "May I be damned.")   **173 move** (1) stir up (2) set in motion   **176 commerce** transaction   **178 Scout me** Keep watch   **179 bum-baily** minor sheriff's officer employed in making arrests.   **180–1 horrible** horribly   **183 approba-tion** reputation (for courage;   **proof** performance   **185 let . . . swearing** don't worry about my ability in swearing.   **191 clodpoll** blockhead.   **194–5 his . . . it** his inexperience will make him all the more ready to believe it   **198 cockatrices** basilisks, fabulous serpents reputed to be able to kill by a mere look.   **199 Give them way** Stay out of their way   **200 presently** immediately

SIR TOBY   I will meditate the while upon some horrid 201
message for a challenge.

[*Exeunt Sir Toby, Fabian, and Maria.*]

OLIVIA
I have said too much unto a heart of stone
And laid mine honor too unchary on't.   204
There's something in me that reproves my fault,
But such a headstrong potent fault it is
That it but mocks reproof.

VIOLA
With the same havior that your passion bears   208
Goes on my master's griefs.   209

OLIVIA [*giving a locket*]
Here, wear this jewel for me. 'Tis my picture.
Refuse it not; it hath no tongue to vex you.
And I beseech you come again tomorrow.
What shall you ask of me that I'll deny,
That honor, saved, may upon asking give?   214

VIOLA
Nothing but this: your true love for my master.

OLIVIA
How with mine honor may I give him that
Which I have given to you?

VIOLA   I will acquit you.   217

OLIVIA
Well, come again tomorrow. Fare thee well.
A fiend like thee might bear my soul to hell.   [*Exit.*] 219

Enter [Sir] Toby and Fabian.

SIR TOBY   Gentleman, God save thee.
VIOLA   And you, sir.
SIR TOBY   That defense thou hast, betake thee to't. Of 222
what nature the wrongs are thou hast done him, I
know not, but thy intercepter, full of despite, bloody 224
as the hunter, attends thee at the orchard end. 225
Dismount thy tuck, be yare in thy preparation, for thy 226
assailant is quick, skillful, and deadly.
VIOLA   You mistake sir. I am sure no man hath any
quarrel to me. My remembrance is very free and clear 229
from any image of offense done to any man.
SIR TOBY   You'll find it otherwise, I assure you. Therefore, if you hold your life at any price, betake you to
your guard, for your opposite hath in him what youth, 233
strength, skill, and wrath can furnish man withal.   234
VIOLA   I pray you, sir, what is he?
SIR TOBY   He is knight, dubbed with unhatched rapier 236

and on carpet consideration, but he is a devil in 237
private brawl. Souls and bodies hath he divorced
three, and his incensement at this moment is so implacable that satisfaction can be none but by pangs of
death and sepulchre. Hob, nob is his word; give't or 241
take't.
VIOLA   I will return again into the house and desire
some conduct of the lady. I am no fighter. I have 244
heard of some kind of men that put quarrels purposely
on others, to taste their valor. Belike this is a 246
man of that quirk.   247
SIR TOBY   Sir, no. His indignation derives itself out of a
very competent injury; therefore, get you on and give 249
him his desire. Back you shall not to the house unless
you undertake that with me which with as much
safety you might answer him. Therefore, on, or strip 252
your sword stark naked; for meddle you must, that's 253
certain, or forswear to wear iron about you.   254
VIOLA   This is as uncivil as strange. I beseech you, do
me this courteous office as to know of the knight what 256
my offense to him is. It is something of my negligence, 257
nothing of my purpose.   258
SIR TOBY   I will do so.—Signor Fabian, stay you by this
gentleman till my return.   *Exit [Sir] Toby.*
VIOLA   Pray you, sir, do you know of this matter?
FABIAN   I know the knight is incensed against you,
even to a mortal arbitrament, but nothing of the 263
circumstance more.
VIOLA   I beseech you, what manner of man is he?
FABIAN   Nothing of that wonderful promise, to read 266
him by his form, as you are like to find him in the 267
proof of his valor. He is, indeed, sir, the most skillful,
bloody, and fatal opposite that you could possibly
have found in any part of Illyria. Will you walk 270
towards him, I will make your peace with him if I can.
VIOLA   I shall be much bound to you for't. I am one
that had rather go with Sir Priest than Sir Knight. I 273
care not who knows so much of my mettle.   *Exeunt.*

Enter [Sir] Toby and [Sir] Andrew.

SIR TOBY   Why, man, he's a very devil; I have not seen
such a firago. I had a pass with him, rapier, scabbard, 276
and all, and he gives me the stuck-in with such a 277
mortal motion that it is inevitable; and on the answer, 278
he pays you as surely as your feet hits the ground they
step on. They say he has been fencer to the Sophy. 280
SIR ANDREW   Pox on't, I'll not meddle with him.

---

201 horrid terrifying. (Literally, "bristling.")   **204 laid** hazarded.
unchary on't recklessly on it.   **208–9 With . . . griefs** i.e., Orsino's sufferings in love are as reckless and uncontrollable as your feelings.
214 That . . . give? that can be granted without compromising my
honor?   **217 acquit you** release you of your promise.   **219 A fiend . . .
hell** i.e., You are my torment. (*Like thee* means "in your likeness.")
222 That . . . to't Get ready to deploy whatever skill you have in fencing.   **224 intercepter** he who lies in wait.   **despite** defiance, ill will
224–5 bloody as the hunter bloodthirsty as a hunting dog   **226 Dismount thy tuck** Draw your rapier.   **yare** ready, nimble   **229 to** with
233 opposite opponent.   **what** whatsoever   **234 withal** with.
236 unhatched unhacked, unused in battle

237 carpet consideration (A carpet knight was one whose title was
obtained, not in battle, but through connections at court.)   **241 Hob,
nob** Have or have not, i.e., give it or take it, kill or be killed.   **word**
motto   **244 conduct** safe-conduct, escort   **246 taste** test, prove
Belike Probably   **247 quirk** peculiar humor.   **249 competent** sufficient   **252–3 strip . . . naked** draw your sword from its sheath
253 meddle engage (in conflict)   **254 forswear . . . iron** give up your
right to wear a sword   **256 know of** inquire from   **257–8 It is . . .
purpose** It is the result of some oversight, not anything I intended.
263 mortal arbitrament trial to the death   **266–7 read . . . form** judge
him by his appearance   **270 Will you** If you will
273 go with associate with.   **Sir Priest** (*Sir* was a courtesy title for
priests.)   **276 firago** virago.   **pass** bout   **277 stuck-in** stoccado, a
thrust in fencing   **278 answer** return hit   **280 to** in the service of

SIR TOBY   Ay, but he will not now be pacified. Fabian can scarce hold him yonder.

SIR ANDREW   Plague on't, an I thought he had been valiant and so cunning in fence, I'd have seen him damned ere I'd have challenged him. Let him let the matter slip and I'll give him my horse, gray Capilet.   287

SIR TOBY   I'll make the motion. Stand here, make a 288 good show on't. This shall end without the perdition 289 of souls. [*Aside, as he crosses to meet Fabian*] Marry, I'll 290 ride your horse as well as I ride you.

Enter Fabian and Viola.

[*Aside to Fabian*] I have his horse to take up the 292 quarrel. I have persuaded him the youth's a devil.

FABIAN   He is as horribly conceited of him, and pants 294 and looks pale as if a bear were at his heels.

SIR TOBY [*to Viola*]   There's no remedy, sir, he will fight with you for's oath's sake. Marry, he hath better bethought him of his quarrel, and he finds that now scarce to be worth talking of. Therefore draw, for the supportance of his vow; he protests he 300 will not hurt you.

VIOLA [*aside*]   Pray God defend me! A little thing 302 would make me tell them how much I lack of a man. 303

FABIAN   Give ground, if you see him furious.

SIR TOBY [*crossing to Sir Andrew*]   Come, Sir Andrew, there's no remedy. The gentleman will, for his honor's sake, have one bout with you. He cannot by the *duello* avoid it. But he has promised me, as he is 308 a gentleman and a soldier, he will not hurt you. Come on, to't.

SIR ANDREW   Pray God he keep his oath!

Enter Antonio.

VIOLA [*to Fabian*]   I do assure you, 'tis against my will.
                                      [*They draw.*]

ANTONIO [*drawing, to Sir Andrew*]
   Put up your sword. If this young gentleman
   Have done offense, I take the fault on me;
   If you offend him, I for him defy you.

SIR TOBY   You, sir? Why, what are you?

ANTONIO
   One, sir, that for his love dares yet do more
   Than you have heard him brag to you he will.

SIR TOBY [*drawing*]
   Nay, if you be an undertaker, I am for you.   319

Enter Officers.

FABIAN   Oh, good Sir Toby, hold! Here come the officers.

SIR TOBY [*to Antonio*]   I'll be with you anon.

VIOLA [*to Sir Andrew*]   Pray, sir, put your sword up, if you please.

SIR ANDREW   Marry, will I, sir; and for that I promised 324 you, I'll be as good as my word. He will bear you 325 easily, and reins well.

FIRST OFFICER   This is the man. Do thy office.

SECOND OFFICER
   Antonio, I arrest thee at the suit
   Of Count Orsino.

ANTONIO   You do mistake me, sir.

FIRST OFFICER
   No, sir, no jot. I know your favor well,   330
   Though now you have no sea-cap on your head.—
   Take him away. He knows I know him well.

ANTONIO
   I must obey. [*To Viola*] This comes with seeking you.
   But there's no remedy; I shall answer it.   334
   What will you do, now my necessity
   Makes me to ask you for my purse? It grieves me
   Much more for what I cannot do for you
   Than what befalls myself. You stand amazed,
   But be of comfort.

SECOND OFFICER   Come, sir, away.

ANTONIO [*to Viola*]
   I must entreat of you some of that money.

VIOLA   What money, sir?
   For the fair kindness you have showed me here,
   And part being prompted by your present trouble,   343
   Out of my lean and low ability
   I'll lend you something. My having is not much;   345
   I'll make division of my present with you.   346
   Hold, there's half my coffer.   [*She offers money.*] 347

ANTONIO   Will you deny me now?
   Is't possible that my deserts to you   349
   Can lack persuasion? Do not tempt my misery,   350
   Lest that it make me so unsound a man   351
   As to upbraid you with those kindnesses
   That I have done for you.

VIOLA   I know of none,
   Nor know I you by voice or any feature.
   I hate ingratitude more in a man
   Than lying, vainness, babbling drunkenness,   356
   Or any taint of vice whose strong corruption
   Inhabits our frail blood.

ANTONIO   Oh, heavens themselves!

SECOND OFFICER   Come, sir, I pray you, go.

ANTONIO
   Let me speak a little. This youth that you see here
   I snatched one half out of the jaws of death,
   Relieved him with such sanctity of love,   363
   And to his image, which methought did promise   364
   Most venerable worth, did I devotion.   365

---

287 **Capilet** i.e., "little horse." (From "capel," a nag.)   288 **motion** offer.   289–90 **perdition of souls** i.e., loss of lives.   292 **take up** settle, make up   294 **He . . . him** i.e., Cesario has as horrible a conception of Sir Andrew   300 **supportance** upholding   302–3 **A little . . . man** (With bawdy suggestion of the penis.)   308 *duello* dueling code   319 **undertaker** one who takes upon himself a task or business; here, a challenger.   **for you** ready for you.

324 **for that** as for what   325 **He** i.e., The horse   330 **favor** face   334 **answer it** stand trial and make reparation for it.   343 **part** partly   345 **having** wealth   346 **present** present store   347 **coffer** purse. (Literally, strongbox.)   349–50 **deserts . . . persuasion** claims on you can fail to persuade you to help me.   350 **tempt** try too severely   351 **unsound** morally weak, lacking in self-control   356 **vainness** vaingloriousness   363 **such . . . love** i.e., such veneration as is due to a sacred relic   364 **image** what he appeared to be. (Playing on the idea of a religious icon to be venerated.)   365 **venerable worth** worthiness of being venerated

FIRST OFFICER
What's that to us? The time goes by. Away!

ANTONIO
But, Oh, how vile an idol proves this god!
Thou hast, Sebastian, done good feature shame.   368
In nature there's no blemish but the mind;
None can be called deformed but the unkind.   370
Virtue is beauty, but the beauteous evil   371
Are empty trunks o'erflourished by the devil.   372

FIRST OFFICER
The man grows mad. Away with him! Come, come,
sir.

ANTONIO   Lead me on.   Exit [with Officers].

VIOLA [aside]
Methinks his words do from such passion fly
That he believes himself. So do not I.   376
Prove true, imagination, oh, prove true,
That I, dear brother, be now ta'en for you!

SIR TOBY   Come hither, knight. Come hither, Fabian.
We'll whisper o'er a couplet or two of most sage saws. 380
                [They gather apart from Viola.]

VIOLA
He named Sebastian. I my brother know   381
Yet living in my glass; even such and so   382
In favor was my brother, and he went   383
Still in this fashion, color, ornament,   384
For him I imitate. Oh, if it prove,   385
Tempests are kind, and salt waves fresh in love!
                                      [Exit.]

SIR TOBY   A very dishonest paltry boy, and more a 387
coward than a hare. His dishonesty appears in leaving 388
his friend here in necessity and denying him; and for 389
his cowardship, ask Fabian.

FABIAN   A coward, a most devout coward, religious in it. 391

SIR ANDREW   'Slid, I'll after him again and beat him. 392

SIR TOBY   Do, cuff him soundly, but never draw thy
sword.

SIR ANDREW   An I do not—   [Exit.]

FABIAN   Come, let's see the event.   396

SIR TOBY   I dare lay any money 'twill be nothing yet. 397
                                      Exeunt.

♣

4.1

Enter Sebastian and Clown [Feste].

FESTE   Will you make me believe that I am not sent for
you?

SEBASTIAN   Go to, go to, thou art a foolish fellow. Let
me be clear of thee.

FESTE   Well held out, i'faith! No, I do not know you, 5
nor I am not sent to you by my lady to bid you come
speak with her, nor your name is not Master Cesario,
nor this is not my nose, neither. Nothing that is so is so.

SEBASTIAN   I prithee, vent thy folly somewhere else.   9
Thou know'st not me.

FESTE   Vent my folly! He has heard that word of some 11
great man, and now applies it to a fool. Vent my folly!
I am afraid this great lubber, the world, will prove a 13
cockney. I prithee now, ungird thy strangeness and   14
tell me what I shall vent to my lady. Shall I vent to her
that thou art coming?

SEBASTIAN   I prithee, foolish Greek, depart from me.   17
There's money for thee. [He gives money.] If you tarry
longer, I shall give worse payment.

FESTE   By my troth, thou hast an open hand. These   20
wise men that give fools money get themselves a good
report—after fourteen years' purchase.   22

Enter [Sir] Andrew, [Sir] Toby, and Fabian.

SIR ANDREW   Now, sir, have I met you again? There's
for you!   [He strikes Sebastian.]

SEBASTIAN   Why, there's for thee, and there, and there!
        [He beats Sir Andrew with the hilt of his dagger.]
Are all the people mad?

SIR TOBY   Hold, sir, or I'll throw your dagger o'er the
house.

FESTE   This will I tell my lady straight. I would not be in 29
some of your coats for twopence.   [Exit.]   30

SIR TOBY   Come on, sir, hold!   [He grips Sebastian.]

SIR ANDREW   Nay, let him alone. I'll go another way to
work with him. I'll have an action of battery against 33
him, if there be any law in Illyria. Though I struck him
first, yet it's no matter for that.

SEBASTIAN   Let go thy hand!

SIR TOBY   Come, sir, I will not let you go. Come, my
young soldier, put up your iron. You are well fleshed. 38
Come on.

SEBASTIAN
I will be free from thee. [He breaks free and draws his
        sword.] What wouldst thou now?
If thou dar'st tempt me further, draw thy sword.   41

SIR TOBY   What, what? Nay, then I must have an ounce
or two of this malapert blood from you.   [He draws.] 43

Enter Olivia.

---

368 **Thou . . . shame** i.e., You have shamed physical beauty by showing that it does not always reflect inner beauty.   **370 unkind** ungrateful, unnatural.   **371 beauteous evil** those who are outwardly beautiful but evil within   **372 trunks** (1) chests (2) bodies. **o'erflourished** (1) covered with ornamental carvings (2) made outwardly beautiful   **376 So . . . I** i.e., I do not believe myself (in the hope that he has arisen in me).   **380 We'll . . . saws** i.e., Let's converse privately. (*Saws* are sayings.)   **381–2 I . . . glass** i.e., I know that my brother's likeness lives in me   **383 favor** appearance   **384 Still** always   **385 prove** prove true   **387 dishonest** dishonorable **388 dishonesty** dishonor   **389 denying** refusing to acknowledge **391 religious in it** making a religion of cowardice.   **392 'Slid** By his (God's) eyelid   **396 event** outcome.   **397 lay** wager.   **yet** nevertheless, after all.
4.1. Location: Before Olivia's house.

5 held out kept up   **9 vent** (1) utter (2) void, excrete, get rid of   **11 of** from, suited to the diction of; or, with reference to   **13 lubber** lout **14 cockney** effeminate or foppish fellow. (Feste comically despairs of finding common sense anywhere if people start using affected phrases like those Sebastian uses.)   **ungird thy strangeness** put off your affectation of being a stranger. (Feste apes the kind of high-flown speech he has just deplored.)   **17 Greek** (1) one who speaks gibberish (as in "It's all Greek to me") (2) buffoon (as in "merry Greek")   **20 open** generous. (With money or with blows.)   **22 report** reputation.   **after . . . purchase** i.e., at great cost and after long delays. (Land was ordinarily valued at the price of twelve years' rental; the Fool adds two years to this figure.)   **29 straight** at once. **29–30 in . . . coats** i.e., in your shoes   **33 action of battery** lawsuit for physical assault   **38 fleshed** initiated into battle.   **41 tempt** make trial of   **43 malapert** saucy, impudent

OLIVIA

Hold, Toby! On thy life I charge thee, hold!

SIR TOBY   Madam—

OLIVIA

Will it be ever thus? Ungracious wretch,
Fit for the mountains and the barbarous caves,
Where manners ne'er were preached! Out of my
    sight!—
Be not offended, dear Cesario.—
Rudesby, begone!
                [*Exeunt Sir Toby, Sir Andrew, and Fabian.*]
                    I prithee, gentle friend,   50
Let thy fair wisdom, not thy passion, sway
In this uncivil and unjust extent   52
Against thy peace. Go with me to my house,
And hear thou there how many fruitless pranks
This ruffian hath botched up, that thou thereby   55
Mayst smile at this. Thou shalt not choose but go.   56
Do not deny. Beshrew his soul for me!   57
He started one poor heart of mine, in thee.   58

SEBASTIAN [*aside*]

What relish is in this? How runs the stream?   59
Or I am mad, or else this is a dream.   60
Let fancy still my sense in Lethe steep;   61
If it be thus to dream, still let me sleep!

OLIVIA

Nay, come, I prithee. Would thou'dst be ruled by me!

SEBASTIAN

Madam, I will.

OLIVIA   Oh, say so, and so be!   *Exeunt.*

❧

4.2

*Enter Maria [carrying a gown and a false
beard], and Clown [Feste].*

MARIA   Nay, I prithee, put on this gown and this beard;
make him believe thou art Sir Topas the curate. Do it   2
quickly. I'll call Sir Toby the whilst.   [*Exit.*]   3

FESTE   Well, I'll put it on, and I will dissemble myself   4
in't, and I would I were the first that ever dissembled
in such a gown. [*He disguises himself in gown and
beard.*] I am not tall enough to become the function   7
well, nor lean enough to be thought a good student;   8

but to be said an honest man and a good housekeeper   9
goes as fairly as to say a careful man and a great   10
scholar. The competitors enter.   11

Enter [Sir] Toby [and Maria].

SIR TOBY   Jove bless thee, Master Parson.

FESTE   *Bonos dies*, Sir Toby. For, as the old hermit of   13
Prague, that never saw pen and ink, very wittily said   14
to a niece of King Gorboduc, "That that is, is"; so I,   15
being Master Parson, am Master Parson; for what is
"that" but "that," and "is" but "is"?

SIR TOBY   To him, Sir Topas.

FESTE   What, ho, I say! Peace in this prison!
                [*He approaches the door
                behind which Malvolio is confined.*]

SIR TOBY   The knave counterfeits well; a good knave.

MALVOLIO (*within*)   Who calls there?

FESTE   Sir Topas the curate, who comes to visit Malvolio
the lunatic.

MALVOLIO   Sir Topas, Sir Topas, good Sir Topas, go to
my lady—

FESTE   Out, hyperbolical fiend! How vexest thou this   26
man! Talkest thou nothing but of ladies?

SIR TOBY   Well said, Master Parson.

MALVOLIO   Sir Topas, never was man thus wronged.
Good Sir Topas, do not think I am mad. They have
laid me here in hideous darkness.

FESTE   Fie, thou dishonest Satan! I call thee by the most
modest terms, for I am one of those gentle ones that   33
will use the devil himself with courtesy. Say'st thou
that house is dark?   35

MALVOLIO   As hell, Sir Topas.

FESTE   Why, it hath bay windows transparent as barri-   37
cadoes, and the clerestories toward the south north   38
are as lustrous as ebony; and yet complainest thou of
obstruction?

MALVOLIO   I am not mad, Sir Topas. I say to you this
house is dark.

FESTE   Madman, thou errest. I say there is no darkness
but ignorance, in which thou art more puzzled than
the Egyptians in their fog.   45

MALVOLIO   I say this house is as dark as ignorance,
though ignorance were as dark as hell; and I say there
was never man thus abused. I am no more mad than
you are. Make the trial of it in any constant question.   49

---

50 **Rudesby** Ruffian   52 **extent** attack   55 **botched up** clumsily contrived   56 **Thou . . . go** I insist on your going with me.   57 **deny**
refuse.   **Beshrew** Curse. (A mild oath.)   **for me** for my part.
58 **He . . . thee** i.e., He alarmed that part of my heart which lies in
your bosom. (To *start* is also to drive an animal such as a *hart* [*heart*]
from its cover.)   59 **What . . . this?** i.e., What am I to make of this?
(*Relish* means "taste.")   60 **Or** Either   61 **Let . . . steep** i.e., Let this
fantasy continue to steep my senses in forgetfulness. (*Lethe* is the river
of forgetfulness in the underworld.)
4.2. Location: Olivia's house.
2 **Sir** (An honorific title for priests.)   **Topas** (A name perhaps derived
from Chaucer's comic knight in the "Rime of Sir Thopas" or from a
similar character in Lyly's *Endymion*. Topaz, a semiprecious stone,
was believed to be a cure for lunacy.)   **3 the whilst** in the meantime.
4 **dissemble** disguise. (With a play on "feign.")   7 **become the function** adorn the priestly office   8 **lean** (Scholars were proverbially
sparing of diet.)   **student** scholar (in divinity)

9–11 **to be . . . scholar** to be accounted honest and hospitable is as
good as being known as a painstaking scholar. (Feste suggests that
honesty and charity are found as often in ordinary men as in clerics.)
11 **competitors** associates, partners (in this plot)   13 *Bonos dies* Good
day   13–14 **hermit of Prague** (Probably another invented authority.)
15 **King Gorboduc** a legendary king of ancient Britain, protagonist in
the English tragedy *Gorboduc* (1562)   26 **hyperbolical** vehement,
boisterous.   **fiend** i.e., the devil supposedly possessing Malvolio.
33 **modest** moderate   35 **house** i.e., room   37–8 **barricadoes** barri-
cades. (Which are opaque. Feste speaks comically in impossible paradoxes, but Malvolio seems not to notice.)   38 **clerestories** windows
in an upper wall   45 **Egyptians . . . fog** (Alluding to the darkness
brought upon Egypt by Moses; see Exodus 10:21–3.)   49 **constant
question** problem that requires consecutive reasoning.

FESTE   What is the opinion of Pythagoras concerning   50
wildfowl?   51

MALVOLIO   That the soul of our grandam might haply   52
inhabit a bird.

FESTE   What think'st thou of his opinion?

MALVOLIO   I think nobly of the soul, and no way
approve his opinion.

FESTE   Fare thee well. Remain thou still in darkness.
Thou shalt hold th'opinion of Pythagoras ere I will
allow of thy wits, and fear to kill a woodcock lest thou   59
dispossess the soul of thy grandam. Fare thee well.
[He moves away from Malvolio's prison.]

MALVOLIO   Sir Topas, Sir Topas!

SIR TOBY   My most exquisite Sir Topas!

FESTE   Nay, I am for all waters.   63

MARIA   Thou mightst have done this without thy beard
and gown. He sees thee not.

SIR TOBY   To him in thine own voice, and bring me
word how thou find'st him.—I would we were well rid
of this knavery. If he may be conveniently delivered, I   68
would he were, for I am now so far in offense with
my niece that I cannot pursue with any safety this
sport to the upshot. Come by and by to my chamber.   71
Exit [with Maria].

FESTE   *[singing as he approaches Malvolio's prison]*
"Hey, Robin, jolly Robin,   72
Tell me how thy lady does."   73

MALVOLIO   Fool!

FESTE   "My lady is unkind, pardie."   75

MALVOLIO   Fool!

FESTE   "Alas, why is she so?"

MALVOLIO   Fool, I say!

FESTE   "She loves another—" Who calls, ha?

MALVOLIO   Good Fool, as ever thou wilt deserve well at
my hand, help me to a candle, and pen, ink, and
paper. As I am a gentleman, I will live to be thankful
to thee for't.

FESTE   Master Malvolio?

MALVOLIO   Ay, good Fool.

FESTE   Alas, sir, how fell you besides your five wits?   86

MALVOLIO   Fool, there was never man so notoriously   87
abused. I am as well in my wits, Fool, as thou art.   88

FESTE   But as well? Then you are mad indeed, if you be   89
no better in your wits than a fool.

MALVOLIO   They have here propertied me, keep me in   91
darkness, send ministers to me—asses—and do all
they can to face me out of my wits.   93

FESTE   Advise you what you say. The minister is here.   94
[He speaks as Sir Topas.] Malvolio, Malvolio, thy wits
the heavens restore! Endeavor thyself to sleep, and
leave thy vain bibble-babble.

MALVOLIO   Sir Topas!

FESTE   *[in Sir Topas's voice]* Maintain no words with
him, good fellow. *[In his own voice]* Who, I, sir? Not
I, sir. God b'wi'you, good Sir Topas. *[In Sir Topas's
voice]* Marry, amen. *[In his own voice]* I will, sir, I will.

MALVOLIO   Fool! Fool! Fool, I say!

FESTE   Alas, sir, be patient. What say you, sir? I am
shent for speaking to you.   105

MALVOLIO   Good Fool, help me to some light and some
paper. I tell thee I am as well in my wits as any man in
Illyria.

FESTE   Welladay that you were, sir!   109

MALVOLIO   By this hand, I am. Good Fool, some ink,
paper, and light; and convey what I will set down to
my lady. It shall advantage thee more than ever the
bearing of letter did.

FESTE   I will help you to't. But tell me true, are you
not mad indeed, or do you but counterfeit?

MALVOLIO   Believe me, I am not. I tell thee true.

FESTE   Nay, I'll ne'er believe a madman till I see his
brains. I will fetch you light and paper and ink.

MALVOLIO   Fool, I'll requite it in the highest degree. I
prithee, begone.

FESTE   *[sings]*
I am gone, sir,
And anon, sir,
I'll be with you again,
In a trice,
Like to the old Vice,   125
Your need to sustain;

Who, with dagger of lath,   127
In his rage and his wrath,
Cries, "Aha!" to the devil;
Like a mad lad,
"Pare thy nails, dad?   131
Adieu, goodman devil!"   *Exit.*   132

❧

4.3

Enter Sebastian [with a pearl].

SEBASTIAN
This is the air; that is the glorious sun;

50–1 **Pythagoras . . . wildfowl** (An opening for the discussion of
transmigration of souls, a doctrine held by Pythagoras.)   **52 haply**
perhaps   **59 allow of thy wits** certify your sanity.   **woodcock** (A
proverbially stupid bird, easily caught.)   **63 Nay . . . waters** i.e.,
Indeed, I can turn my hand to anything.   **68 delivered** i.e., delivered
from prison   **71 upshot** conclusion.   **72–3 "Hey, Robin . . . does"**
(Another fragment of an old song, a version of which is attributed to
Sir Thomas Wyatt.)   **75 pardie** i.e., by God, certainly.   **86 besides**
out of.   **five wits** The intellectual faculties, usually listed as common
wit, imagination, fantasy, judgment, and memory.   **87–8 notoriously
abused** egregiously ill treated.   **89 But** Only   **91 propertied me** i.e.,
treated me as property and thrown me into the lumber-room
93 face . . . wits brazenly represent me as having lost my wits.

---

94 Advise you Take care   **105 shent** scolded, rebuked   **109 Welladay** Alas, would that   **125 Vice** comic tempter of the "old" morality
plays   **127 dagger of lath** comic weapon of the Vice in at least some
morality plays   **131 Pare thy nails** (This may allude to the belief that
evil spirits could use nail parings to get control of their victims; cf.
Dromio of Syracuse in *The Comedy of Errors*, 4.3.69, "Some devils ask
but the parings of one's nail," and the Boy's characterization of Pistol
in *Henry V*, 4.4.72–3, as "this roaring devil i'th' old play, that everyone
may pare his nails with a wooden dagger.")   **132 goodman** title for a
person of substance but not of gentle birth. (This line could be Feste's
farewell to Malvolio and his "devil.")
4.3. Location: Olivia's garden.

This pearl she gave me, I do feel't and see't;
And though 'tis wonder that enwraps me thus,
Yet 'tis not madness. Where's Antonio, then?
I could not find him at the Elephant;
Yet there he was, and there I found this credit,   6
That he did range the town to seek me out.
His counsel now might do me golden service;
For though my soul disputes well with my sense   9
That this may be some error, but no madness,
Yet doth this accident and flood of fortune   11
So far exceed all instance, all discourse,   12
That I am ready to distrust mine eyes
And wrangle with my reason that persuades me
To any other trust but that I am mad,   15
Or else the lady's mad. Yet if 'twere so,
She could not sway her house, command her
    followers,   17
Take and give back affairs and their dispatch   18
With such a smooth, discreet, and stable bearing
As I perceive she does. There's something in't
That is deceivable. But here the lady comes.   21

Enter Olivia and Priest.

OLIVIA
Blame not this haste of mine. If you mean well,
Now go with me and with this holy man
Into the chantry by. There, before him,   24
And underneath that consecrated roof,
Plight me the full assurance of your faith,
That my most jealous and too doubtful soul   27
May live at peace. He shall conceal it
Whiles you are willing it shall come to note,   29
What time we will our celebration keep   30
According to my birth. What do you say?   31

SEBASTIAN
I'll follow this good man, and go with you,
And having sworn truth, ever will be true.

OLIVIA
Then lead the way, good father, and heavens so shine
That they may fairly note this act of mine!   *Exeunt.* 35

❖

5.1

Enter Clown [Feste] and Fabian.

FABIAN   Now, as thou lov'st me, let me see his letter.
FESTE   Good Master Fabian, grant me another request.
FABIAN   Anything.

FESTE   Do not desire to see this letter.
FABIAN   This is to give a dog and in recompense desire   5
my dog again.   6

Enter Duke [Orsino], Viola, Curio, and lords.

ORSINO   Belong you to the Lady Olivia, friends?
FESTE   Ay, sir, we are some of her trappings.   8
ORSINO   I know thee well. How dost thou, my good fellow?
FESTE   Truly, sir, the better for my foes and the worse 10
for my friends.
ORSINO   Just the contrary—the better for thy friends.
FESTE   No, sir, the worse.
ORSINO   How can that be?
FESTE   Marry, sir, they praise me, and make an ass of   15
me. Now my foes tell me plainly I am an ass, so that   16
by my foes, sir, I profit in the knowledge of myself,
and by my friends I am abused; so that, conclusions to   18
be as kisses, if your four negatives make your two   19
affirmatives, why then the worse for my friends and   20
the better for my foes.
ORSINO   Why, this is excellent.
FESTE   By my troth, sir, no, though it please you to be 23
one of my friends.   24
ORSINO   Thou shalt not be the worse for me. There's gold.
                                          [He gives a coin.]
FESTE   But that it would be double-dealing, sir, I would 26
you could make it another.
ORSINO   Oh, you give me ill counsel.
FESTE   Put your grace in your pocket, sir, for this once, 29
and let your flesh and blood obey it.   30
ORSINO   Well, I will be so much a sinner to be a   31
double-dealer. There's another. *[He gives another coin.]*
FESTE   *Primo, secundo, tertio,* is a good play, and the old 33
saying is, the third pays for all. The triplex, sir, is a 34
good tripping measure; or the bells of Saint Bennet,   35
sir, may put you in mind—one, two, three.
ORSINO   You can fool no more money out of me at this
throw. If you will let your lady know I am here to   38
speak with her, and bring her along with you, it may
awake my bounty further.
FESTE   Marry, sir, lullaby to your bounty till I come
again. I go, sir, but I would not have you to think that

5–6 This . . . again (Apparently a reference to a well-known reply of Dr. Bulleyn when Queen Elizabeth asked for his dog and promised a gift of his choosing in return; he asked to have his dog back.)   **8 trappings** ornaments, decorations.   **10 for** because of   **15–16 make an ass of me** i.e., flatter me into foolishly thinking well of myself.   **18 abused** flatteringly deceived   **18–20 conclusions . . . affirmatives** i.e., as when a young lady, asked for a kiss, says "no, no" really meaning "yes"; or, as in grammar, two negatives make an affirmative   **23 though** even though   **24 friends** i.e., those who, according to Feste's syllogism, flatter him.   **26 But** Except for the fact.   **double-dealing** (1) giving twice (2) deceit, duplicity   **29 Put . . . pocket** (1) Pay no attention to your honor, put it away (2) Reach in your pocket or purse and show your customary grace or munificence. (*Your Grace* is also the formal way of addressing a duke.)   **30 it** i.e., my "ill counsel."   **31 to be** as to be   **33 *Primo . . . tertio*** Latin ordinals: first, second, third.   **play** (Perhaps a mathematical game or game of dice.)   **34 the third . . . all** the third time is lucky. (Proverbial.)   **triplex** triple time in music   **35 Saint Bennet** church of St. Benedict   **38 throw** (1) time (2) throw of the dice.

my desire of having is the sin of covetousness. But as
you say, sir, let your bounty take a nap. I will awake
it anon.   *Exit.*

Enter Antonio and Officers.

VIOLA
Here comes the man, sir, that did rescue me.
ORSINO
That face of his I do remember well,
Yet when I saw it last it was besmeared
As black as Vulcan in the smoke of war.   49
A baubling vessel was he captain of,   50
For shallow draft and bulk unprizable,   51
With which such scatheful grapple did he make   52
With the most noble bottom of our fleet   53
That very envy and the tongue of loss   54
Cried fame and honor on him. What's the matter?
FIRST OFFICER
Orsino, this is that Antonio
That took the *Phoenix* and her freight from Candy, 57
And this is he that did the *Tiger* board
When your young nephew Titus lost his leg.
Here in the streets, desperate of shame and state, 60
In private brabble did we apprehend him.   61
VIOLA
He did me kindness, sir, drew on my side,
But in conclusion put strange speech upon me.   63
I know not what 'twas but distraction.   64
ORSINO
Notable pirate, thou saltwater thief,   65
What foolish boldness brought thee to their mercies
Whom thou in terms so bloody and so dear   67
Hast made thine enemies?
ANTONIO   Orsino, noble sir,
Be pleased that I shake off these names you give me. 69
Antonio never yet was thief or pirate,
Though, I confess, on base and ground enough   71
Orsino's enemy. A witchcraft drew me hither.
That most ingrateful boy there by your side
From the rude sea's enraged and foamy mouth
Did I redeem; a wreck past hope he was.   75
His life I gave him, and did thereto add
My love, without retention or restraint,   77
All his in dedication. For his sake   78
Did I expose myself—pure for his love—   79
Into the danger of this adverse town,   80
Drew to defend him when he was beset;

Where being apprehended, his false cunning,
Not meaning to partake with me in danger,
Taught him to face me out of his acquaintance   84
And grew a twenty years' removèd thing   85
While one would wink; denied me mine own purse,   86
Which I had recommended to his use   87
Not half an hour before.
VIOLA   How can this be?
ORSINO   When came he to this town?
ANTONIO
Today, my lord; and for three months before,
No interim, not a minute's vacancy,
Both day and night did we keep company.

Enter Olivia and attendants.

ORSINO
Here comes the Countess. Now heaven walks on
    earth.
But for thee, fellow—fellow, thy words are madness. 95
Three months this youth hath tended upon me;
But more of that anon.—Take him aside.
OLIVIA [*to Orsino*]
What would my lord—but that he may not have—   98
Wherein Olivia may seem serviceable?—
Cesario, you do not keep promise with me.
VIOLA   Madam?
ORSINO   Gracious Olivia—
OLIVIA
What do you say, Cesario?—Good my lord—   103
VIOLA
My lord would speak. My duty hushes me.
OLIVIA
If it be aught to the old tune, my lord,
It is as fat and fulsome to mine ear   106
As howling after music.
ORSINO   Still so cruel?
OLIVIA   Still so constant, lord.
ORSINO
What, to perverseness? You uncivil lady,
To whose ingrate and unauspicious altars   111
My soul the faithfull'st off'rings have breathed out
That e'er devotion tendered! What shall I do?
OLIVIA
Even what it please my lord that shall become him. 114
ORSINO
Why should I not, had I the heart to do it,
Like to th'Egyptian thief at point of death   116
Kill what I love?—a savage jealousy
That sometime savors nobly. But hear me this: 118

---

49 **Vulcan** Roman god of fire and smith to the other gods; his face
was blackened by the fire   50 **baubling** insignificant, trifling   51 **For**
because of.   **draft** depth of water a ship draws.   **unprizable** of value
too slight to be estimated, not worth taking as a "prize"   52 **scatheful** destructive   53 **bottom** ship   54 **very envy** i.e., even those who
had most reason to hate him, his enemies.   **loss** i.e., the losers
57 **from Candy** on her return from Candia, or Crete   60 **desperate . . .
state** recklessly disregarding the disgrace and danger to himself
61 **brabble** brawl   63 **put . . . me** spoke to me strangely.   64 **but distraction** unless (it was) madness.   65 **Notable** Notorious   67 in
terms . . . dear in so bloodthirsty and costly a manner   69 **Be pleased
that I** Allow me to   71 **base and ground** solid grounds   75 **wreck**
shipwrecked person   77 **retention** reservation   78 **All . . . dedication**
devoted wholly to him.   79 **pure** entirely, purely   80 **Into** unto.
adverse hostile

84 **face . . . acquaintance** brazenly deny he knew me   85–6 **grew . . .
wink** in the twinkling of an eye acted as though we had been
estranged for twenty years   87 **recommended** consigned   95 **for** as
for   98 **but . . . have** except that which he may not have—i.e., my
love   103 **Good my lord** (Olivia urges Orsino to listen to Cesario.)
106 **fat and fulsome** gross and offensive   111 **ingrate and unauspicious** thankless and unpropitious   114 **become** suit   116 **th'Egyptian thief** (An allusion to the story of Theagenes and Chariclea in the
Ethiopica, a Greek romance by Heliodorus. The robber chief, Thyamis
of Memphis, having captured Chariclea and fallen in love with her, is
attacked by a larger band of robbers; threatened with death, he
attempts to slay her first.)   118 **savors nobly** is not without nobility

Since you to nonregardance cast my faith,   119
And that I partly know the instrument   120
That screws me from my true place in your favor,   121
Live you the marble-breasted tyrant still.
But this your minion, whom I know you love,   123
And whom, by heaven I swear, I tender dearly,   124
Him will I tear out of that cruel eye   125
Where he sits crownèd in his master's spite.—   126
Come, boy, with me. My thoughts are ripe in
    mischief.
I'll sacrifice the lamb that I do love,   128
To spite a raven's heart within a dove.   [*Going.*] 129

VIOLA
And I, most jocund, apt, and willingly,   130
To do you rest, a thousand deaths would die.   131
                                                  [*Going.*]

OLIVIA
Where goes Cesario?

VIOLA   After him I love
More than I love these eyes, more than my life,
More by all mores than e'er I shall love wife.   134
If I do feign, you witnesses above
Punish my life for tainting of my love!   136

OLIVIA
Ay me, detested! How am I beguiled!   137

VIOLA
Who does beguile you? Who does do you wrong?

OLIVIA
Hast thou forgot thyself? Is it so long?
Call forth the holy father.   [*Exit an attendant.*]

ORSINO [*to Viola*]   Come, away!

OLIVIA
Whither, my lord?—Cesario, husband, stay.

ORSINO
Husband?

OLIVIA   Ay, husband. Can he that deny?

ORSINO [*to Viola*]
Her husband, sirrah?

VIOLA   No, my lord, not I.   143

OLIVIA
Alas, it is the baseness of thy fear
That makes thee strangle thy propriety.   145
Fear not, Cesario, take thy fortunes up;
Be that thou know'st thou art, and then thou art   147
As great as that thou fear'st.

    Enter Priest.

                      Oh, welcome, father!   148
Father, I charge thee by thy reverence

Here to unfold—though lately we intended
To keep in darkness what occasion now   151
Reveals before 'tis ripe—what thou dost know
Hath newly passed between this youth and me.

PRIEST
A contract of eternal bond of love,
Confirmed by mutual joinder of your hands,   155
Attested by the holy close of lips,   156
Strengthened by interchangement of your rings,
And all the ceremony of this compact
Sealed in my function, by my testimony;   159
Since when, my watch hath told me, toward my
    grave
I have traveled but two hours.

ORSINO [*to Viola*]
Oh, thou dissembling cub! What wilt thou be
When time hath sowed a grizzle on thy case?   163
Or will not else thy craft so quickly grow
That thine own trip shall be thine overthrow?   165
Farewell, and take her, but direct thy feet
Where thou and I henceforth may never meet.

VIOLA
My Lord, I do protest—

OLIVIA   Oh, do not swear!
Hold little faith, though thou hast too much fear.   169

    Enter Sir Andrew.

SIR ANDREW   For the love of God, a surgeon! Send one
presently to Sir Toby.   171

OLIVIA   What's the matter?

SIR ANDREW   He's broke my head across, and has given   173
Sir Toby a bloody coxcomb too. For the love of God,   174
your help! I had rather than forty pound I were at
home.

OLIVIA   Who has done this, Sir Andrew?

SIR ANDREW   The Count's gentleman, one Cesario. We
took him for a coward, but he's the very devil
incardinate.   180

ORSINO   My gentleman, Cesario?

SIR ANDREW   'Od's lifelings, here he is!—You broke my   182
head for nothing, and that that I did I was set on to
do't by Sir Toby.

VIOLA
Why do you speak to me? I never hurt you.
You drew your sword upon me without cause,
But I bespake you fair, and hurt you not.   187

SIR ANDREW   If a bloody coxcomb be a hurt, you have
hurt me. I think you set nothing by a bloody cox-   189
comb.

    Enter [Sir] Toby and Clown [Feste].

---

119 nonregardance neglect   **120 that** since   **121 screws** pries, forces
123 minion darling, favorite   **124 tender** regard   **125–6 Him . . . spite**
I will tear Cesario away from Olivia, in whose cruel eye he sits like a
king to spite me, his true master.   **128–9 I'll . . . dove** i.e., I'll kill
Cesario, whom I love, to revenge myself on this seemingly gracious
but black-hearted lady.   **130 apt** readily   **131 do you rest** give you
ease   **134 by all mores** by all such comparisons   **136 Punish . . . love!**
Punish me with death for being disloyal to the love I feel!
137 detested hated and denounced by another.   **143 sirrah** (The normal way of addressing an inferior.)   **145 strangle thy propriety** i.e.,
deny what is properly yours, disavow your marriage to me.   **147 that**
that which   **148 as that thou fear'st** as him you fear, i.e., Orsino.

151 occasion necessity   **155 joinder** joining   **156 close** meeting
159 Sealed . . . function ratified through my carrying out of my
priestly office   **163 a grizzle** scattering of gray hair.   **case** skin.
165 trip wrestling trick used to throw an opponent. (You'll get over-
clever and trip yourself up.)   **169 Hold . . . fear** Keep to your oath as
well as you can, even if you are frightened by Orsino's threats.
171 presently immediately   **173 broke** broken the skin, cut   **174 coxcomb** fool's cap resembling the crest of a cock; here, head   **180 incardinate** (For "incarnate.")   **182 'Od's lifelings** By God's little lives
187 bespake you fair addressed you courteously   **189 set nothing by**
regard as insignificant

Here comes Sir Toby, halting. You shall hear more. 191
But if he had not been in drink, he would have tickled
you othergates than he did. 193

ORSINO How now, gentleman? How is't with you?

SIR TOBY That's all one. He's hurt me, and there's 195
th'end on't.—Sot, didst see Dick surgeon, sot? 196

FESTE Oh, he's drunk, Sir Toby, an hour agone; his eyes 197
were set at eight i'th' morning. 198

SIR TOBY Then he's a rogue, and a passy measures 199
pavane. I hate a drunken rogue. 200

OLIVIA Away with him! Who hath made this havoc
with them?

SIR ANDREW I'll help you, Sir Toby, because we'll be 203
dressed together. 204

SIR TOBY Will you help? An ass-head and a coxcomb
and a knave, a thin-faced knave, a gull!

OLIVIA
Get him to bed, and let his hurt be looked to.
    [*Exeunt Feste, Fabian, Sir Toby, and Sir Andrew.*]

    Enter Sebastian.

SEBASTIAN
I am sorry, madam, I have hurt your kinsman;
But, had it been the brother of my blood, 209
I must have done no less with wit and safety.— 210
You throw a strange regard upon me, and by that 211
I do perceive it hath offended you.
Pardon me, sweet one, even for the vows
We made each other but so late ago.

ORSINO
One face, one voice, one habit, and two persons, 215
A natural perspective, that is and is not! 216

SEBASTIAN
Antonio, O my dear Antonio!
How have the hours racked and tortured me 218
Since I have lost thee!

ANTONIO Sebastian are you?

SEBASTIAN Fear'st thou that, Antonio? 221

ANTONIO
How have you made division of yourself?
An apple cleft in two is not more twin
Than these two creatures. Which is Sebastian?

OLIVIA Most wonderful!

SEBASTIAN [*seeing Viola*]
Do I stand there? I never had a brother;
Nor can there be that deity in my nature
Of here and everywhere. I had a sister, 228
Whom the blind waves and surges have devoured. 229
Of charity, what kin are you to me?

What countryman? What name? What parentage? 230

VIOLA
Of Messaline. Sebastian was my father.
Such a Sebastian was my brother, too.
So went he suited to his watery tomb. 234
If spirits can assume both form and suit, 235
You come to fright us.

SEBASTIAN   A spirit I am indeed,
But am in that dimension grossly clad 237
Which from the womb I did participate. 238
Were you a woman, as the rest goes even, 239
I should my tears let fall upon your cheek
And say, "Thrice welcome, drownèd Viola!"

VIOLA
My father had a mole upon his brow.

SEBASTIAN And so had mine.

VIOLA
And died that day when Viola from her birth
Had numbered thirteen years.

SEBASTIAN
Oh, that record is lively in my soul! 246
He finishèd indeed his mortal act
That day that made my sister thirteen years.

VIOLA
If nothing lets to make us happy both 249
But this my masculine usurped attire,
Do not embrace me till each circumstance
Of place, time, fortune, do cohere and jump 252
That I am Viola—which to confirm
I'll bring you to a captain in this town
Where lie my maiden weeds, by whose gentle help 255
I was preserved to serve this noble count.
All the occurrence of my fortune since
Hath been between this lady and this lord.

SEBASTIAN [*to Olivia*]
So comes it, lady, you have been mistook.
But nature to her bias drew in that. 260
You would have been contracted to a maid,
Nor are you therein, by my life, deceived.
You are betrothed both to a maid and man. 263

ORSINO [*to Olivia*]
Be not amazed; right noble is his blood.
If this be so, as yet the glass seems true, 265
I shall have share in this most happy wreck. 266
[*To Viola*] Boy, thou hast said to me a thousand times
Thou never shouldst love woman like to me. 268

VIOLA
And all those sayings will I over swear, 269
And all those swearings keep as true in soul

---

191 **halting** limping. 193 **othergates** otherwise 195 **That's all one**
It doesn't matter; never mind. 195–6 **there's . . . on't** that's all there
is to it. 196 **Sot** (1) Fool (2) Drunkard 197 **agone** ago 198 **set** fixed
or closed 199–200 **passy measures pavane** passe-measure pavane, a
slow-moving, stately dance. (Suggesting Sir Toby's impatience to
have his wounds dressed.) 203–4 **be dressed** have our wounds surgically dressed 209 **the brother . . . blood** my own brother
210 **with wit and safety** with intelligent concern for my own safety.
211 **You . . . me** You look strangely at me 215 **habit** dress 216 **A**
natural perspective an optical device or illusion created in this
instance by nature 218 **racked** tortured 221 **Fear'st thou that** Do
you doubt that 228 **here and everywhere** omnipresence.
229 **blind** heedless, indiscriminate

230 **Of charity** (Tell me) in kindness 234 **suited** dressed; clad in
human form 235 **form and suit** physical appearance and dress
237 **in . . . clad** clothed in that fleshly shape 238 **participate** possess
in common with all humanity. 239 **as . . . even** since everything else
agrees 246 **record** recollection 249 **lets** hinders 252 **jump** coincide, fit exactly 255 **weeds** clothes 260 **nature . . . that** nature followed her bent in that. (The metaphor is from the game of bowls.)
263 **a maid** i.e., a virgin man 265 **the glass** i.e., the *natural perspective*
of line 216 266 **wreck** shipwreck, accident. 268 **like to me** as well
as you love me. 269 **over swear** swear again

As doth that orbèd continent the fire   271
That severs day from night.
ORSINO   Give me thy hand,
And let me see thee in thy woman's weeds.
VIOLA
The captain that did bring me first on shore
Hath my maid's garments. He upon some action   275
Is now in durance, at Malvolio's suit,   276
A gentleman and follower of my lady's.
OLIVIA
He shall enlarge him. Fetch Malvolio hither.   278
And yet, alas, now I remember me,
They say, poor gentleman, he's much distract.

Enter Clown [Feste] with a letter, and Fabian.

A most extracting frenzy of mine own   281
From my remembrance clearly banished his.   282
How does he, sirrah?
FESTE   Truly, madam, he holds Beelzebub at the stave's 284
end as well as a man in his case may do. He's here 285
writ a letter to you; I should have given't you today
morning. But as a madman's epistles are no gospels, 287
so it skills not much when they are delivered.   288
OLIVIA   Open't and read it.
FESTE   Look then to be well edified when the fool
delivers the madman. [*He reads loudly.*] "By the Lord, 291
madam—"
OLIVIA   How now, art thou mad?
FESTE   No, madam, I do but read madness. An Your
Ladyship will have it as it ought to be, you must allow
vox.   296
OLIVIA   Prithee, read i'thy right wits.
FESTE   So I do, madonna; but to read his right wits is to 298
read thus. Therefore perpend, my princess, and give 299
ear.
OLIVIA [*to Fabian*]   Read it you, sirrah.
FABIAN (*reads*)   "By the Lord, madam, you wrong me,
and the world shall know it. Though you have put me
into darkness and given your drunken cousin rule
over me, yet have I the benefit of my senses as well
as Your Ladyship. I have your own letter that induced
me to the semblance I put on, with the which I 307
doubt not but to do myself much right or you much
shame. Think of me as you please. I leave my duty 309
a little unthought of, and speak out of my injury. 310
                         The madly used Malvolio."

OLIVIA   Did he write this?
FESTE   Ay, madam.
ORSINO   This savors not much of distraction.
OLIVIA
See him delivered, Fabian. Bring him hither.   315
                         [*Exit Fabian.*]
My lord, so please you, these things further thought
on,   316
To think me as well a sister as a wife,   317
One day shall crown th'alliance on't, so please you,   318
Here at my house and at my proper cost.   319
ORSINO
Madam, I am most apt t'embrace your offer.   320
[*To Viola*] Your master quits you; and for your
service done him,   321
So much against the mettle of your sex,   322
So far beneath your soft and tender breeding,
And since you called me master for so long,
Here is my hand. You shall from this time be
Your master's mistress.
OLIVIA   A sister! You are she.

Enter [Fabian, with] Malvolio.

ORSINO
Is this the madman?
OLIVIA   Ay, my lord, this same.
How now, Malvolio?
MALVOLIO   Madam, you have done me wrong,
Notorious wrong.
OLIVIA   Have I, Malvolio? No.
MALVOLIO [*showing a letter*]
Lady, you have. Pray you, peruse that letter.
You must not now deny it is your hand.
Write from it, if you can, in hand or phrase,   332
Or say 'tis not your seal, not your invention.   333
You can say none of this. Well, grant it then,
And tell me, in the modesty of honor,   335
Why you have given me such clear lights of favor,   336
Bade me come smiling and cross-gartered to you,
To put on yellow stockings, and to frown
Upon Sir Toby and the lighter people?   339
And, acting this in an obedient hope,   340
Why have you suffered me to be imprisoned,
Kept in a dark house, visited by the priest,   342
And made the most notorious geck and gull   343
That e'er invention played on? Tell me why?   344
OLIVIA
Alas, Malvolio, this is not my writing,
Though, I confess, much like the character;   346

271 **As . . . fire** i.e., as the sphere of the sun keeps the fire   275 **action**
legal charge   276 **in durance** imprisoned   278 **enlarge** release
281 **extracting** i.e., that obsessed me and drew all thoughts except of
Cesario from my mind   282 **his** i.e., his madness.   284–5 **holds . . .
end** i.e., keeps the devil at a safe distance. (The metaphor is of fighting with quarterstaffs or long poles.)   287 **a madman's . . . gospels**
i.e., there is no truth in a madman's letters. (An allusion to readings
in the church service of selected passages from the epistles and the
gospels.)   288 **skills** matters.   **delivered** (1) delivered to their recipient (2) read aloud.   291 **delivers** speaks the words of   296 *vox* voice,
i.e., an appropriately loud voice.   298 **to read . . . wits** to express his
true state of mind   299 **perpend** consider, attend. (A deliberately
lofty word.)   307 **the which** i.e., the letter   309–10 **I leave . . . injury**
I leave unsaid the expressions of duty with which I would normally
conclude, and convey instead my sense of having been wronged.

315 **delivered** released.   316 **so . . . on** if you are pleased on further
consideration of all that has happened   317 **To . . . wife** to regard me
as favorably as a sister-in-law as you had hoped to regard me as a
wife   318 **crown . . . on't** i.e., serve as occasion for two marriages
confirming our new relationships   319 **proper** own   320 **apt** ready
321 **quits** releases   322 **mettle** natural disposition   332 **from it** differently   333 **invention** composition.   335 **in . . . honor** in the name
of all that is decent and honorable   336 **clear lights** evident signs
339 **lighter** lesser   340 **acting . . . hope** when I acted thus out of obedience to you and in hope of your favor   342 **priest** i.e., Feste
343 **geck** dupe   344 **invention played on** contrivance sported with.
346 **the character** my handwriting

But out of question 'tis Maria's hand.   347
And now I do bethink me, it was she
First told me thou wast mad; then cam'st in smiling,   349
And in such forms which here were presupposed   350
Upon thee in the letter. Prithee, be content.
This practice hath most shrewdly passed upon thee;   352
But when we know the grounds and authors of it,
Thou shalt be both the plaintiff and the judge
Of thine own cause.
FABIAN   Good madam, hear me speak,
And let no quarrel nor no brawl to come   356
Taint the condition of this present hour,   357
Which I have wondered at. In hope it shall not,
Most freely I confess, myself and Toby
Set this device against Malvolio here,
Upon some stubborn and uncourteous parts   361
We had conceived against him. Maria writ   362
The letter at Sir Toby's great importance,   363
In recompense whereof he hath married her.
How with a sportful malice it was followed   365
May rather pluck on laughter than revenge,   366
If that the injuries be justly weighed   367
That have on both sides passed.
OLIVIA [to Malvolio]
Alas, poor fool, how have they baffled thee!   369
FESTE   Why, "Some are born great, some achieve
greatness, and some have greatness thrown upon
them." I was one, sir, in this interlude, one Sir Topas,   372
sir, but that's all one. "By the Lord, fool, I am not   373
mad." But do you remember? "Madam, why laugh
you at such a barren rascal? An you smile not, he's
gagged." And thus the whirligig of time brings in his   376
revenges.
MALVOLIO   I'll be revenged on the whole pack of you!
[Exit.]

OLIVIA
He hath been most notoriously abused.
ORSINO
Pursue him, and entreat him to a peace.
He hath not told us of the captain yet.
When that is known, and golden time convents,   382
A solemn combination shall be made
Of our dear souls. Meantime, sweet sister,
We will not part from hence. Cesario, come—
For so you shall be, while you are a man;
But when in other habits you are seen,   387
Orsino's mistress and his fancy's queen.   388
                                    Exeunt [all, except Feste].
FESTE (sings)
When that I was and a little tiny boy,   389
    With hey, ho, the wind and the rain,
A foolish thing was but a toy,   391
    For the rain it raineth every day.

But when I came to man's estate,
    With hey, ho, the wind and the rain,
'Gainst knaves and thieves men shut their gate,
    For the rain it raineth every day.

But when I came, alas, to wive,
    With hey, ho, the wind and the rain,
By swaggering could I never thrive,
    For the rain it raineth every day.

But when I came unto my beds,   401
    With hey, ho, the wind and the rain,
With tosspots still had drunken heads,   403
    For the rain it raineth every day.

A great while ago the world begun,
    With hey, ho, the wind and the rain,
But that's all one, our play is done,
    And we'll strive to please you every day.
                                            [Exit.]

---

347 **out of** beyond   349 **cam'st** you came   350 **presupposed** specified beforehand   352 **practice** plot.   **shrewdly passed** mischievously
been perpetrated   356 **to come** in the future   357 **condition** (happy)
nature   361 **Upon** on account of.   **parts** qualities, deeds   362 **conceived against him** seen and resented in him.   363 **importance**
importunity   365 **followed** carried out   366 **pluck on** induce
367 **If that** if   369 **baffled** disgraced, quelled   372 **interlude** little play
373 **that's all one** no matter for that.   376 **whirligig** spinning top

382 **convents** (1) summons, calls together (2) suits   387 **habits** attire
388 **fancy's** love's   389 **and a little** a little   391 **toy** trifle   401 **unto**
my beds i.e., (1) drunk to bed, or, perhaps, (2) in the evening of life
403 **tosspots** drunkards

Measure for Measure

"A play Caled Mesur for Mesur" by "Shaxberd" was performed at court, for the new King James I, by "his Maiesties plaiers" on December 26, 1604. Probably it had been composed that same year or in late 1603. The play dates from the very height of Shakespeare's tragic period, three years or so after *Hamlet*, contemporary with *Othello*, shortly before *King Lear* and *Macbeth*. This period includes very little comedy of any sort, and what there is differs markedly from the festive comedy of the 1590s. *Troilus and Cressida* (c. 1601–1602), hovering between satire and tragedy, bleakly portrays a hopeless love affair caught in the toils of a pointless and stalemated war. *All's Well That Ends Well* (c. 1601–1604) resembles *Measure for Measure* in its portrayal of an undeserving protagonist who must be deceived into marriage by the ethically ambiguous trick of substituting one woman for another in the protagonist's bed. *Measure for Measure*, perhaps the last such comedy from the tragic period, illustrates most clearly of all what critics usually mean by "problem comedy" or "problem play."

Its chief concern is not with the triumphs of love, as in the happy comedies, but with moral and social problems: "filthy vices" arising from sexual desire and the abuses of judicial authority. Images of disease abound in this play. We see corruption in Vienna "boil and bubble / Till it o'errun the stew" (5.1.326–7). The protagonist, Angelo, is for most of the play a deeply torn character, abhorring his own perverse sinfulness, compulsively driven to an attempted murder in order to cover up his lust for the heroine, Isabella. His soliloquies are introspective, tortured, focused on the psychological horror of an intelligent mind succumbing to criminal desire. The disguised Duke Vincentio, witnessing this fall into depravity and despair, can offer Angelo's intended victims no better philosophical counsel than Christian renunciation of the world and all its vain hopes. Tragedy is averted only by providential intervention and by the harsh trickery of "Craft against vice" (3.2.270), in which the Duke becomes involved as chief manipulator and stage manager. Of the concluding marriages, two are foisted on the bridegrooms (Angelo and Lucio) against their wills, whereas that of the Duke and Isabella jars oddly with his stoical teachings and with her previous determination to be a nun. The ending thus seems arbitrary; both justice and romantic happiness are so perilously achieved in this play that they seem inconsistent with the injustice and lechery that have prevailed until the last.

Yet the very improbability of the ending and the sense of tragedy narrowly averted are perhaps intentional. These features are appropriate, not only for problem comedy, but also for tragicomedy or comedy of forgiveness, overlapping genres toward which Shakespeare gravitated in his late romances. Angelo is, like Leontes in *The Winter's Tale* (or like Bertram in *All's Well That Ends Well* and Claudio in *Much Ado About Nothing*), an erring protagonist forgiven in excess of his deserving, spared by a benign, overseeing providence from destroying that which is most precious to him.

That providence is partly ascribed to divine intervention, as when the disguised Duke, at a loss for a means of saving Claudio from imminent death, and learning that a prisoner named Ragozine has just died and is enough like Claudio physically that his head can be substituted for that of Claudio as proof that an execution has taken place, exclaims, "Oh, 'tis an accident that heaven provides!" (4.3.77). Yet most of the "providential" oversight in this play is essentially theatrical and humanly devised. It is engineered by "the old fantastical duke of dark corners" (4.3.156–7), the resourceful Vincentio. Indeed, this mysterious Duke becomes a kind of embodiment of the manipulations and sleights of hand through which this dark comedy achieves its improbable ends.

The play's title, *Measure for Measure*, introduces a paradox of human justice which this "problem" play cannot wholly resolve. How are fallible humans to judge the sins of their fellow mortals and still obey Christ's injunction

227

of the Sermon on the Mount: "Judge not that ye be not judged"? Three positions emerge from the debate: absolute justice at one extreme, mercy at the other, and equity as a middle ground. Isabella speaks for mercy, and her words ring with biblical authority. Since all humanity would be condemned to eternal darkness were God not merciful as well as just, should not humans also be merciful? The difficulty, however, is that Vienna shows all too clearly the effects of leniency under the indulgent Duke. Vice is rampant; stern measures are needed. Though he has not wished to crack the whip himself, the Duke firmly endorses "strict statutes and most biting laws, / The needful bits and curbs to headstrong steeds" (1.3.19–20). To carry out necessary reform, the Duke has chosen Angelo, spokesman for absolute justice, to represent him. Angelo's position is cold but consistent. Only by a literal and impartial administering of the statutes, he maintains, can the law deter potential offenders. If the judge is found guilty, he must pay the penalty as well. One difficulty here, however, is that literal enforcement of the statute on fornication seems ironically to catch the wrong culprits. Claudio and Juliet, who are about to be married and are already joined by a "true contract" of betrothal, are sentenced to the severest limit of the law, whereas the pimps and whores of Vienna's suburbs manage at first to evade punishment entirely. Angelo's deputy, Escalus, can only shake his head in dismay at this unjust result of strict justice. Angelo has not remembered fully the terms of his commission from the Duke: to practice both "Mortality and mercy" in Vienna, to "enforce or qualify the laws / As to your soul seems good." The attributes of a ruler, like those of God, must include "terror" but also "love" (1.1.20–67).

Escalus's compassionate and pragmatic approach to law illustrates equity or the flexible application of the law to particular cases. Because Claudio is only technically guilty (though still guilty), Escalus would pronounce for him a light sentence. Pompey and Mistress Overdone, on the other hand, require vigorous prosecution. The problem of policing vice is compounded by the law's inefficiency, as well as by erring human nature, which will never be wholly tamed. Constable Elbow, like Dogberry in *Much Ado*, is a pompous user of malapropisms, less clever by far than the criminals he would arrest. His evidence against Pompey is so absurdly circumstantial that Escalus is first obliged to let off this engaging pimp with a stern warning. Yet Escalus patiently and tenaciously attends to such proceedings, unlike Angelo, whose interest in the law is too theoretical. Escalus deals with day-to-day problems effectively. He orders reforms of the system by which constables are selected, instructs Elbow in the rudiments of his office, and so proceeds, ultimately, to an effective arrest. Vice is not eliminated; as Pompey defiantly points out, unless someone plans to "geld and splay all the youth of the city," they "will to't then" (2.1.229–33). Still, vice is held in check. Law can shape the outer person and hope for some inner reform. Even Pompey is taught a trade, albeit a grisly one, as an apprentice hangman. The law must use both "correction" and "instruction."

The solutions arrived at in the comic subplot do not fit the case of Angelo, for he is powerful enough to be above the Viennese law. Indeed, he tries finally to brazen it out, pitting his authority against that of the seemingly friendless Isabella, much like the biblical Elders when justly accused of immorality by the innocent Susannah. Society is on Angelo's side—even the well-meaning Escalus; only a seeming providence can rescue the defenseless. The Duke of Vienna, hovering in the background and seeing all that happens, intervenes just at those points when tragedy threatens to become irreversible. Moreover, the Duke is testing those he observes. As he says to Friar Thomas, explaining why he has delegated his power to Angelo: "Hence shall we see, / If power change purpose, what our seemers be" (1.3.53–4). The Duke obviously expects Angelo to fall. Indeed, he has known all along that Angelo had dishonorably repudiated his solemn contract to Mariana when her marriage dowry disappeared at sea (3.1.215–25). Like an all-seeing deity who keeps a reckoning of humanity's good and evil deeds, the Duke has found out Angelo's great weakness. As Angelo confesses, "I perceive Your Grace, like power divine, / Hath looked upon my passes" (5.1.377–8). Paradoxically, this seemingly tragic story of temptation and fall yields precious benefits of remorse and humility. Angelo is rescued from his self-made nightmare of seduction, murder, and tyranny. Knowing now that he is prone like other mortals to fleshly weakness, he knows also that he needs spiritual assistance and that, as judge, he ought to use mercy. Seen in retrospect, his panic, despair, and humiliation are curative.

The Duke is no less a problematic character than Angelo, Isabella, and the rest. Vienna's deep corruption is, in part, the result of his unwillingness to bear down on vice, and yet, rather than undertake to remedy the failure himself, this strange monarch elects to leave the business to one he suspects will make matters worse. The Duke has a great deal to learn about his own dislike of crowds, his complacent tolerance of human weakness, and his naive supposition that all his subjects speak well of him. He is a highly manipulative character, the one most responsible in the play for the ethically dubious solutions through which craft must be employed against vice. The comforting words of spiritual counsel he offers Claudio, Juliet, and the rest are spoken by a secular ruler fraudulently disguised as a friar. Certainly, the Duke is no allegorized god-figure, for all his omniscience and final role as both punisher and forgiver. As *deux ex machina* of this problem comedy, the Duke is human, frail, and vulnerable—as indeed he ought to be in a play that explores with such rich complexity the ironic distance between divine and human justice.

Yet, for all his manifest and even comic weaknesses, the Duke is finally the authority figure who must attempt to bring order to the imperfect world of Vienna. The devices he employs, including the bed trick, seem morally questionable and yet are palpable comic fictions that unmistakably notify us what genre we are watching. If the Duke's role is more that of artist than ruler or diety, his being so is appropriate to the artistically contrived and theatrical world that Shakespeare presents to us. Within the world of this play, the disguised Duke's chief function is to test the other characters and to mislead them intentionally into expecting the worst, in order to try their resolve. On a comic level, he exposes the amiable but loose-tongued Lucio as a slanderer against the Duke himself and devises for Lucio a suitably satirical exposure and witty punishment. More seriously, as confessor to Juliet, he assures her that her beloved Claudio must die on the morrow. As she ought, she penitentially accepts "shame with joy" and so is cleansed (2.3.37). Because the Duke is not really a friar, he does not have the spiritual authority to do this, and the ruse strikes us as theatrical, employing devices of illusion that actors and dramatists use. Even so, it provides real comfort for Juliet. The very theatricality of the illusion, by reminding us that we are in the theater, enables us to see the Duke as a kind of morally persuasive playwright who can change the lives of his characters for the better.

Similarly, the counsel of Christian renunciation offered to Claudio by the bogus friar (3.1) is at once illusory and comforting. The Duke's poignant reflection on the vanity of human striving is made ironic but not invalid by our awareness that we are viewing a deception with a seemingly benign purpose—that of persuading Claudio to see matters in their true perspective. The Duke characterizes life as a breath, a dreamlike "after-dinner's sleep," a fever of inconstancy in which timorous humans long fretfully for what they do not have and spurn those things they have. Claudio responds as he ought, resolving to "find life" by "seeking death" (3.1.5–43). He achieves this calm, however, in the face of certain execution; ironically, what he must then learn to overmaster is the desperate hope of living by means of his sister's dishonor. Claudio is broken by this test and perversely begs for a few years of guilty life at the cost of eternal shame for himself and Isabella. From this harrowing experience, he emerges at length with a better understanding of his own weakness and a greater compassion toward the weakness of others.

The searing encounter between Claudio and Isabella puts her to the test as well, and her response seems hysterical and no doubt prudish to modern audiences. She has much to learn about the complexities of human behavior. Although she is sincere in protesting that she would lay down her life for her brother and is correct, in the play's terms, to prefer virtue to mere existence, her tone is too strident. Like other major characters, she must be humbled before she can rise. She and Claudio must heed the Duke's essential admonition: "Do not satisfy your resolution with hopes that are fallible" (3.1.170–1). Only then, paradoxically, can Isabella and Claudio go on to achieve earthly happiness.

Isabella and Angelo are paradoxically alike. Both have retreated from the world of carnal pleasure into havens they regard as safe but that turn out not to work in the way they had hoped. Isabella longs for the restraints of the sisterhood into which she is about to enter. Her suspicions about human frailty can be seen in her testing of her brother; she fears he will fail her by begging life at the cost of her eternal shame, and when he does just that, she reacts with shrill condemnation and even hatred. This is a dark moment for Isabella, and she needs the spiritual counsel of the disguised Duke to enable her to forgive not only her brother but also herself. Angelo, meanwhile, has attempted to put down the rebellion of the flesh by suppressing and denying all such feeling in himself. We see him at first as the workaholic official who is not hesitant to condemn in others what he believes he is free of personally. He cherishes restraint as much as Isabella does, and that is why he is so terrified when the apparent absence of his only superior, the Duke, opens up to him the abyss of his own licentiousness. Once his word is law, Angelo perceives that he can play the tyrant and seducer without check. He is horrified to discover not only that he has ungovernable sexual longings within him but also that they perversely direct themselves toward a woman who is virginal and saintly. Why does he yearn to "raze the sanctuary" thus (2.2.178)? The revelation to him of his own innate evil is virtually tragic in the intensity of his self-loathing, and yet, in this strange comedy, this revelation is a first step toward coming to terms with his reprobate self. Until Angelo acknowledges the carnal within, he cannot begin looking for a way to understand and accept this frailty. The Duke's test provides the means of self-discovery that Angelo cannot fashion on his own.

In her final testing, Isabella shows greatness of spirit. Here, Shakespeare significantly alters his chief sources, George Whetstone's *Promos and Cassandra* (1578), Giovanni Baptista Giraldi Cinthio's *Hecatommithi*, and Whetstone's *Heptameron of Civil Discourses*. In all these versions, the character corresponding to Angelo does actually ravish the heroine, and in the *Hecatommithi* he also murders her brother. Shakespeare, by withholding these irreversible acts, not only gives to Angelo a technical innocence, but also allows the Duke, as *deus ex machina*, to practice virtuous deception on Isabella one more time. Can she forgive the supposed murderer of her brother? Her affirmative answer confutes the Old Testament ethic of "An Angelo for Claudio, death for death" whereby "Like doth quit like, and measure still for measure"

(5.1.417–19). Although Angelo concedes that he deserves to die for what he intended, the forfeit need not be paid so long as humanity can reveal itself capable of Isabella's godlike mercy.

With its apparently unsuitable marriages and its improbable plotting, *Measure for Measure* does end by dealing directly with the problems of human nature confronted in the earlier scenes. The bed trick (switching Mariana for Isabella) may seem a legalistic and contrived way to bring Angelo to terms with his own carnality, but it is instructive not only to him but also to Isabella; she, like Angelo, must learn to accept the realities of the human condition. By helping Mariana to achieve her legitimate desire to couple and marry, Isabella sees into her own need. Her begging for Angelo's life is not merely an act of forgiveness to an enemy; it is a gift of continued marriage to Mariana. This realization helps to prepare Isabella herself for a marriage that, although dramatically surprising on stage (and even rejected by her in some modern productions), may be intended to demonstrate her having given up the cloistered life for all that marriage signifies. *Measure for Measure* is thus essentially comic (unlike *Troilus and Cressida*), despite its harrowing scenes of conflict and its awareness of vice everywhere in human nature. The play celebrates the *felix culpa* of human nature, the fall from grace that is an integral part of humanity's rise to happiness and self-knowledge. Throughout, in the play's finest scenes, poignancy is tempered by a wit and humor that are ultimately gracious. The formal and substantive emphasis on marriage stresses not just the benefits of remorse and humility but also the real possibility of psychic and spiritual growth: Isabella can acknowledge that she is a woman, Angelo can be genuinely freed from repression, and Claudio can value life more intensely because he has confronted death. All these recognitions affirm the acceptance and proper use of the physical and sexual side of human nature, and yet they are achieved only through charity and forgiveness. Humanity can learn, however slowly and painfully, that the talents entrusted to it by providence are to be used wisely.

The guardedly hopeful reading of the play offered here is, to be sure, not the only way in which it can be understood. The stage history of *Measure for Measure* highlights much that is problematic and troubling about it. For virtually all of the seventeenth, eighteenth, and nineteenth centuries, after its initial production, the play disappeared from the theater, other than in a heavily rewritten adaptation of the Restoration period and an even more radically recast nineteenth-century operatic version by Richard Wagner called *Das Liebesverbot* ("Forbidden Love"). The play was, it seems, too disagreeable for audiences in those centuries, too given over to vice and moral ambiguity. Readers were sometimes warned away from it. The twentieth and twenty-first centuries, conversely, have found in *Measure for Measure* a persuasive and even devastating dramatization of human imperfection. In an age that has learned to distrust authority figures, Duke Vincentio can come across as officious and sadistic in his manipulation of human lives, rather than ultimately benign. The director Keith Hack, at Stratford-upon-Avon in 1974, saw the Duke as devious, hypocritical, deeply implicated in the corruption of his city, and bitterly resented by the characters whose lives are intrusively managed by him. Some productions have asked if Lucio is justified in his suspicions that the Duke is really a fleshmonger after all. Isabella's longing for the cloistered life of the convent is sometimes seen today as psychologically driven by a fear of sexuality more than by religious faith. Some stage productions revel in the tawdriness of the bordello world of a corrupted Vienna, as for example in Michael Bogdanov's production at Stratford, Canada, in 1985. To Keith Hack, in 1974, the play was as fable of social impression in the vein of Bertolt Brecht. The marriages with which the play ends are often held up to skeptical scrutiny. Is Angelo chastised by his searing experience into resolving to be a good husband to Mariana, or does he snarl at her when he is led off with her to be married? Most significantly, perhaps, does Isabella accept the surprising offer of marriage from the Duke who has protected her but also deceived her into believing that her brother was dead? Today, beginning with Estelle Kohler in John Barton's production at Stratford-upon-Avon in 1970, actresses and directors get to choose; since Isabella is given no lines indicating her acceptance, the actress may simply be bewildered or may decide, with a gesture of defiance or indifference, to have nothing to do with men. The range of options is extraordinary, and helps demonstrate the way in which Shakespeare provides such an unsettling challenge to actors, directors, and audiences alike.

Measure for Measure

The Names of All the Actors

VINCENTIO, *the Duke*
ANGELO, *the deputy*
ESCALUS, *an ancient lord*
CLAUDIO, *a young gentleman*
LUCIO, *a fantastic*
Two other like GENTLEMEN
PROVOST
THOMAS, } *two friars*
PETER,
[A JUSTICE]
[VARRIUS, *a friend of the Duke*]

ELBOW, *a simple constable*
FROTH, *a foolish gentleman*
CLOWN [POMPEY, *a servant to Mistress Overdone*]

THE SCENE: *Vienna*

ABHORSON, *an executioner*
BARNARDINE, *a dissolute prisoner*

ISABELLA, *sister to Claudio*
MARIANA, *betrothed to Angelo*
JULIET, *beloved of Claudio*
FRANCISCA, *a nun*
MISTRESS OVERDONE, *a bawd*

[A SERVANT *of Angelo*
BOY *singer*
A MESSENGER *from Angelo*

Lords, Officers, Citizens, Servants, and other Attendants]

1.1

Enter Duke, Escalus, lords, [and attendants].

DUKE Escalus.
ESCALUS   My lord.
DUKE
  Of government the properties to unfold   3
  Would seem in me t'affect speech and discourse,   4
  Since I am put to know that your own science   5
  Exceeds, in that, the lists of all advice   6
  My strength can give you. Then no more remains   7
  But that to your sufficiency   8
  . . . . as your worth is able,   9
  And let them work. The nature of our people,

Our city's institutions, and the terms   11
For common justice, you're as pregnant in   12
As art and practice hath enrichèd any   13
That we remember. There is our commission,
                          [*giving a paper*]
From which we would not have you warp.—Call
    hither,   15
I say, bid come before us Angelo.   [*Exit one.*]
What figure of us think you he will bear?   17
For you must know, we have with special soul   18
Elected him our absence to supply,   19
Lent him our terror, dressed him with our love,   20
And given his deputation all the organs   21
Of our own power. What think you of it?
ESCALUS
  If any in Vienna be of worth
  To undergo such ample grace and honor,   24

1.1 Location: Vienna. The court of Duke Vincentio.
3–4 Of . . . discourse For me to deliver an oration on the qualities needed in governing well would make me seem enamored of my own pomposity **5 put to know** obliged to admit. **science** knowledge **6 that** i.e., properties of government (line 3). **lists** limits **7 strength** power of mind **8–9 But . . . able** (The passage appears in the Folio as a single line. Several attempts at emendation have been made, but the most plausible explanation is that something has been deleted or inadvertently omitted.)

11 terms terms of court; or, modes of procedure **12 pregnant** well-informed **13 art** learning, theory **15 warp** deviate. **17 What . . . bear?** i.e., How do you think he will do as my substitute? **18 special soul** all the powers of the mind; whole heart **19 Elected** chosen. **supply** fill, make up for **20 terror** power to inspire awe and fear **21 his deputation** him as deputy. **organs** instruments **24 undergo** bear the weight of

It is Lord Angelo.

Enter Angelo.

DUKE   Look where he comes.

ANGELO
Always obedient to Your Grace's will,
I come to know your pleasure.

DUKE   Angelo,
There is a kind of character in thy life
That to th'observer doth thy history
Fully unfold. Thyself and thy belongings   30
Are not thine own so proper as to waste   31
Thyself upon thy virtues, they on thee.   32
Heaven doth with us as we with torches do,   33
Not light them for themselves; for if our virtues
Did not go forth of us, 'twere all alike   35
As if we had them not. Spirits are not finely touched   36
But to fine issues, nor Nature never lends   37
The smallest scruple of her excellence   38
But, like a thrifty goddess, she determines   39
Herself the glory of a creditor,   40
Both thanks and use. But I do bend my speech   41
To one that can my part in him advertise.   42
Hold, therefore, Angelo:
In our remove be thou at full ourself.   44
Mortality and mercy in Vienna   45
Live in thy tongue and heart. Old Escalus,
Though first in question, is thy secondary.   47
Take thy commission.   [*He gives a paper.*]

ANGELO   Now, good my lord,
Let there be some more test made of my mettle   49
Before so noble and so great a figure
Be stamped upon it.

DUKE   No more evasion.
We have with a leavened and preparèd choice   52
Proceeded to you; therefore take your honors.
Our haste from hence is of so quick condition   54
That it prefers itself and leaves unquestioned   55
Matters of needful value. We shall write to you,
As time and our concernings shall importune,   57
How it goes with us, and do look to know   58

What doth befall you here. So, fare you well.
To th' hopeful execution do I leave you   60
Of your commissions.

ANGELO   Yet give leave, my lord,   61
That we may bring you something on the way.   62

DUKE   My haste may not admit it;   63
Nor need you, on mine honor, have to do   64
With any scruple. Your scope is as mine own,   65
So to enforce or qualify the laws
As to your soul seems good. Give me your hand.
I'll privily away. I love the people   68
But do not like to stage me to their eyes;   69
Though it do well, I do not relish well   70
Their loud applause and "aves" vehement,   71
Nor do I think the man of safe discretion   72
That does affect it. Once more, fare you well.   73

ANGELO
The heavens give safety to your purposes!

ESCALUS
Lead forth and bring you back in happiness!   75

DUKE   I thank you. Fare you well.   *Exit.*

ESCALUS
I shall desire you, sir, to give me leave
To have free speech with you; and it concerns me   78
To look into the bottom of my place.   79
A power I have, but of what strength and nature
I am not yet instructed.

ANGELO
'Tis so with me. Let us withdraw together,
And we may soon our satisfaction have
Touching that point.

ESCALUS   I'll wait upon Your Honor.
                                        Exeunt.

❖

1.2

Enter Lucio and two other Gentlemen.

LUCIO   If the Duke with the other dukes come not to
composition with the King of Hungary, why then all   2
the dukes fall upon the King.   3

FIRST GENTLEMAN   Heaven grant us its peace, but not
the King of Hungary's!

SECOND GENTLEMAN   Amen.

LUCIO   Thou conclud'st like the sanctimonious pirate
that went to sea with the Ten Commandments but
scraped one out of the table.   9

SECOND GENTLEMAN   "Thou shalt not steal"?

LUCIO   Ay, that he razed.   11

---

30 belongings attributes, endowments   **31 proper** exclusively
31–2 as to . . . thee that you can expend all your efforts developing
your own talents or use them solely for your own advantage.
33 torches (Compare Jesus' command that we not hide our light
under a bushel, Matthew 5:14–16.)   **35 forth of us** out of us and into
the world.   **'twere all alike** it would be exactly the same   **36–7 Spirits . . . issues** Souls are not deeply moved unless for noble purposes
38 scruple bit. (Literally, a small weight.)   **39–41 But . . . use** unless,
like a thrifty goddess, she gathers to herself the glory due to a creditor, gaining both thanks from her debtor and interest on the loan.
41 bend direct   **42 that . . . advertise** who can instruct my role as
duke now vested in him, i.e., who knows already more about governing in my absence than I can tell him.   **44 In . . . ourself** During my
absence be in every respect my deputy. (The royal plural.)   **45 Mortality** The full rigor of the law, the death sentence   **47 first in question** senior and first appointed   **49 mettle** substance, quality. (With
play on "metal," a common variant spelling, continued in the coining
imagery of lines 50–1.)   **52 leavened** i.e., carefully considered (just as
yeast is given time to leaven dough)   **54–5 Our . . . itself** The cause
for my hasty departure is so urgent that it takes precedence over all
other matters   **55 unquestioned** not yet considered   **57 concernings**
affairs.   **importune** urge   **58 look to know** expect to be informed

60 th' hopeful exciting hopes of success.   **execution** carrying out
61 leave permission   **62 bring you something** accompany you for a
short distance   **63 admit** permit   **64–5 have . . . scruple** have the
least doubt or hesitation about what is to be done.   **68 I'll privily
away** I'll go away secretly.   **69 stage me** make a show of myself
70 do well i.e., serves a political purpose   **71 aves** hails of acclama-
tion   **72 safe** sound   **73 affect** desire, court   **75 Lead** May the heavens conduct you   **78 free** frank   **79 the bottom of my place** the
extent of my commission.
1.2. Location: A public place.
2 composition agreement   **3 fall upon** attack   **9 table** tablet.
11 razed scraped out. (The word may also suggest *rased*, "erased.")

FIRST GENTLEMAN   Why, 'twas a commandment to command the captain and all the rest from their function; they put forth to steal. There's not a soldier of us all that, in the thanksgiving before meat, do relish the petition well that prays for peace. 14 15

SECOND GENTLEMAN   I never heard any soldier dislike it.

LUCIO   I believe thee, for I think thou never wast where grace was said.

SECOND GENTLEMAN   No? A dozen times at least.

FIRST GENTLEMAN   What, in meter?

LUCIO   In any proportion or in any language. 22

FIRST GENTLEMAN   I think, or in any religion.

LUCIO   Ay, why not? Grace is grace, despite of all controversy; as, for example, thou thyself art a wicked villain, despite of all grace. 24 25

FIRST GENTLEMAN   Well, there went but a pair of shears between us. 27 28

LUCIO   I grant; as there may between the lists and the velvet. Thou art the list. 29 30

FIRST GENTLEMAN   And thou the velvet. Thou art good velvet; thou'rt a three-piled piece, I warrant thee. I had as lief be a list of an English kersey as be piled, as thou art piled, for a French velvet. Do I speak feelingly now? 32 33 34

LUCIO   I think thou dost, and indeed with most painful feeling of thy speech. I will, out of thine own confession, learn to begin thy health, but, whilst I live, forget to drink after thee. 37 38

FIRST GENTLEMAN   I think I have done myself wrong, have I not? 39

SECOND GENTLEMAN   Yes, that thou hast, whether thou art tainted or free. 42

Enter bawd [Mistress Overdone].

LUCIO   Behold, behold, where Madam Mitigation comes! I have purchased as many diseases under her roof as come to— 43

SECOND GENTLEMAN   To what, I pray?

LUCIO   Judge. 47

SECOND GENTLEMAN   To three thousand dolors a year. 48

FIRST GENTLEMAN   Ay, and more.

LUCIO   A French crown more. 50

FIRST GENTLEMAN   Thou art always figuring diseases in me, but thou art full of error. I am sound. 51

LUCIO   Nay, not, as one would say, healthy, but so sound as things that are hollow. Thy bones are hollow; impiety has made a feast of thee. 54 55

FIRST GENTLEMAN [*to Mistress Overdone*]   How now, which of your hips has the most profound sciatica? 57

MISTRESS OVERDONE   Well, well; there's one yonder arrested and carried to prison was worth five thousand of you all.

SECOND GENTLEMAN   Who's that, I pray thee?

MISTRESS OVERDONE   Marry, sir, that's Claudio, Signor Claudio. 62

FIRST GENTLEMAN   Claudio to prison? 'Tis not so.

MISTRESS OVERDONE   Nay, but I know 'tis so. I saw him arrested, saw him carried away; and, which is more, within these three days his head to be chopped off. 66

LUCIO   But, after all this fooling, I would not have it so. Art thou sure of this? 68

MISTRESS OVERDONE   I am too sure of it; and it is for getting Madam Julietta with child.

LUCIO   Believe me, this may be. He promised to meet me two hours since, and he was ever precise in promise-keeping. 73

SECOND GENTLEMAN   Besides, you know, it draws something near to the speech we had to such a purpose. 75 76 77

FIRST GENTLEMAN   But most of all agreeing with the proclamation.

LUCIO   Away! Let's go learn the truth of it.

Exit [Lucio with the Gentlemen].

MISTRESS OVERDONE   Thus, what with the war, what with the sweat, what with the gallows, and what with poverty, I am custom-shrunk. 82 83

Enter Clown [Pompey].

How now, what's the news with you?

POMPEY   Yonder man is carried to prison.

MISTRESS OVERDONE   Well, what has he done? 86

POMPEY   A woman.

MISTRESS OVERDONE   But what's his offense?

POMPEY   Groping for trouts in a peculiar river. 89

---

14 put forth set out to sea   **15 thanksgiving before meat** saying of grace before a meal. (As in line 19.)   **22 proportion** form   **24–5 Grace . . . controversy** (Refers to the Catholic-Protestant *controversy*, line 25, as to whether humanity can be saved by works or by grace alone; with punning on *grace* as "thanks for a meal," line 19, and "gracefulness" or "becomingness," line 26.)   **27–8 there . . . between us** i.e., we're cut from the same cloth.   **29–30 as . . . list** (Lucio jokes that the shears might also cut between, i.e., distinguish between, the mere *lists* or selvages, edges of a woven fabric, and the *velvet* betokening a true gentlemen. Lucio wittily asserts himself to be a true gentleman; the other speaker, not.)   **32 three-piled** having a threefold pile or nap, the best grade. (Velvet patches might be used to conceal syphilitic sores or scars.)   **33 as lief** as soon, rather.   **kersey** a coarse woolen fabric. (The First Gentleman turns the joke on Lucio by saying he would rather be a plain, homespun Englishman than a Frenchified velvet gentleman in decay and threadbare. *Velvet* suggests prostitutes and venereal disease, as in the following notes.)   **be piled** (1) have a cloth nap (2) suffer from hemorrhoids (3) be pilled or peeled, i.e., hairless, bald, as a result of mercury treatment for syphilis (known as the "French disease"; see *French velvet* in the next line and *French crown,* line 50)   **34 feelingly** to the purpose, so as to hit home. (But Lucio's reply quibbles on "painfully," meaning the Gentleman's mouth is affected by the French disease; hence, Lucio will not drink from the same cup after him.)   **37 begin thy health** drink to your health   **37–8 forget . . . thee** take care not to drink from your cup.   **39 done myself wrong** i.e., asked for that   **42 tainted** infected   **43 Mitigation** (So called because her function is to relieve desire.)

47 Judge Guess.   **48 dolors** (Quibbling on *dollars;* spelled "Dollours" in the Folio.)   **50 French crown** (1) gold coin (2) bald head incurred through syphilis, the "French disease"   **51 figuring** (1) imagining (2) reckoning. (Recalling the monetary puns of lines 48 and 50.)   **54 sound** (1) healthy (2) resounding (because of hollow bones caused by syphilis)   **55 impiety** wickedness   **57 sciatica** a disease affecting the sciatic nerve in the hip and thigh, thought to be a symptom of syphilis.   **62 Marry** i.e., By the Virgin Mary   **66 which** what   **68 after** notwithstanding   **73 ever** always   **75–6 draws . . . near to** approaches, sounds somewhat like   **76–7 to . . . purpose** on that topic.   **82 sweat** sweating sickness (often fatal), or the plague; also, the sweating tub, a treatment for syphilis   **83 custom-shrunk** having fewer customers.   **86 done** (Pompey quibbles in line 87 on a sexual sense of the word, present also in Mistress Overdone's name.)   **89 peculiar** privately owned. (With bawdy suggestion.)

MISTRESS OVERDONE   What? Is there a maid with child
by him?

POMPEY   No, but there's a woman with maid by him.   92
You have not heard of the proclamation, have you?

MISTRESS OVERDONE   What proclamation, man?

POMPEY   All houses in the suburbs of Vienna must be   95
plucked down.

MISTRESS OVERDONE   And what shall become of those
in the city?

POMPEY   They shall stand for seed. They had gone   99
down too, but that a wise burgher put in for them.   100

MISTRESS OVERDONE   But shall all our houses of resort
in the suburbs be pulled down?

POMPEY   To the ground, mistress.

MISTRESS OVERDONE   Why, here's a change indeed in
the commonwealth! What shall become of me?

POMPEY   Come, fear not you. Good counselors lack no   106
clients. Though you change your place, you need not   107
change your trade; I'll be your tapster still. Courage!   108
There will be pity taken on you. You that have worn   109
your eyes almost out in the service, you will be con-   110
sidered.

MISTRESS OVERDONE   What's to do here, Thomas Tapster? Let's withdraw.

POMPEY   Here comes Signor Claudio, led by the Pro-   114
vost to prison; and there's Madam Juliet.   *Exeunt.*   115

Enter Provost, Claudio, Juliet, Officers; Lucio
and two Gentlemen [follow].

CLAUDIO   *[to the Provost]*
Fellow, why dost thou show me thus to the world?
Bear me to prison, where I am committed.

PROVOST
I do it not in evil disposition
But from Lord Angelo by special charge.

CLAUDIO
Thus can the demigod Authority
Make us pay down for our offense, by weight,   121
The words of heaven. On whom it will, it will;   122
On whom it will not, so; yet still 'tis just.   123

LUCIO
Why, how now, Claudio? Whence comes this
restraint?

CLAUDIO
From too much liberty, my Lucio, liberty.

As surfeit is the father of much fast,   126
So every scope, by the immoderate use,   127
Turns to restraint. Our natures do pursue,
Like rats that ravin down their proper bane,   129
A thirsty evil, and when we drink we die.

LUCIO   If I could speak so wisely under an arrest, I   131
would send for certain of my creditors. And yet, to say   132
the truth, I had as lief have the foppery of freedom as   133
the morality of imprisonment. What's thy offense,
Claudio?

CLAUDIO
What but to speak of would offend again.

LUCIO
What, is't murder?

CLAUDIO   No.

LUCIO   Lechery?

CLAUDIO
Call it so.

PROVOST   Away, sir, you must go.

CLAUDIO
One word, good friend.—Lucio, a word with you.

LUCIO
A hundred, if they'll do you any good.
Is lechery so looked after?   141

CLAUDIO
Thus stands it with me: upon a true contract   142
I got possession of Julietta's bed.
You know the lady; she is fast my wife,   144
Save that we do the denunciation lack   145
Of outward order. This we came not to,   146
Only for propagation of a dower   147
Remaining in the coffer of her friends,   148
From whom we thought it meet to hide our love   149
Till time had made them for us. But it chances   150
The stealth of our most mutual entertainment
With character too gross is writ on Juliet.   152

LUCIO
With child, perhaps?

CLAUDIO   Unhappily, even so.
And the new deputy now for the Duke—
Whether it be the fault and glimpse of newness,   155
Or whether that the body public be
A horse whereon the governor doth ride,
Who, newly in the seat, that it may know
He can command, lets it straight feel the spur;   159

---

92 woman with maid (Pompey playfully corrects Mistress Overdone's use of the word "maid," joking that a pregnant woman cannot
be a virgin [*maid*] though the child she carries is one.)   **95 houses** i.e.,
brothels.   **suburbs** (Location of the brothels in Shakespeare's London, as in other walled cities.)   **99 for seed** to preserve the species.
(With ribald pun.)   **100 burgher** citizen.   **put . . . them** interceded on
their behalf, offered to acquire them.   **106–7 Good . . . clients** Good
lawyers (and, by implication, pimps and bawds) are never at a loss
for clients.   **108 tapster** one who draws beer in an alehouse
109–10 worn . . . out i.e., worked so hard. (Perhaps with an ironic reference to the traditional image of the blind Cupid, often depicted on
signs hung at the doors of brothels.)   **114–15 Provost** officer charged
with apprehension, custody, and punishment of offenders
121–2 Make . . . heaven make us pay the full penalty for our offenses
called for in the Bible.   **122–3 On whom . . . 'tis just** (Compare
Romans 9:18: "Therefore hath he [God] mercy on whom he will have
mercy, and whom he will he hardeneth.")

126 As . . . fast Just as excessive indulgence inevitably leads to revulsion and abstinence   **127 scope** liberty, license   **129 ravin . . . bane**
greedily devour what is poisonous to them   **131–2 If . . . creditors** If
imprisonment would gain me such wisdom, I would send for those
to whom I owe money and thus be arrested for debt.   **133 lief** willingly.   **foppery** folly   **141 looked after** kept under observation.
142 a true contract i.e., one made in the presence of witnesses, though
without a religious ceremony. (Such a precontract was binding but, in
the eyes of the Church, did not confer the right of sexual consummation before the nuptials.)   **144 fast my wife** i.e., firmly bound by precontract   **145 denunciation** formal declaration   **146 outward order**
public ceremony.   **147 propagation** increase, begetting   **148 friends**
relatives   **149 meet** fitting, necessary   **150 made . . . us** disposed
them in our favor.   **152 character too gross** writing too evident
155 the fault . . . newness the faulty flashiness of novelty
159 straight at once

Whether the tyranny be in his place,   160
Or in his eminence that fills it up,   161
I stagger in—but this new governor   162
Awakes me all the enrollèd penalties   163
Which have, like unscoured armor, hung by the wall
So long that nineteen zodiacs have gone round   165
And none of them been worn; and for a name   166
Now puts the drowsy and neglected act
Freshly on me. 'Tis surely for a name.
LUCIO   I warrant it is, and thy head stands so tickle on 169
thy shoulders that a milkmaid, if she be in love, may
sigh it off. Send after the Duke and appeal to him.

CLAUDIO
I have done so, but he's not to be found.
I prithee, Lucio, do me this kind service:
This day my sister should the cloister enter   174
And there receive her approbation.   175
Acquaint her with the danger of my state;
Implore her, in my voice, that she make friends
To the strict deputy; bid herself assay him.   178
I have great hope in that, for in her youth
There is a prone and speechless dialect   180
Such as move men; beside, she hath prosperous art   181
When she will play with reason and discourse,
And well she can persuade.
LUCIO   I pray she may, as well for the encouragement of 184
the like, which else would stand under grievous impo-   185
sition, as for the enjoying of thy life, who I would   186
be sorry should be thus foolishly lost at a game of tick- 187
tack. I'll to her.   188
CLAUDIO   I thank you, good friend Lucio.
LUCIO   Within two hours.
CLAUDIO   Come, officer, away!   *Exeunt.*

❧

1.[3]

Enter Duke and Friar Thomas.

DUKE
No, holy Father, throw away that thought;
Believe not that the dribbling dart of love
Can pierce a complete bosom. Why I desire thee   3
To give me secret harbor hath a purpose   4
More grave and wrinkled than the aims and ends   5
Of burning youth.
FRIAR THOMAS   May Your Grace speak of it?

DUKE
My holy sir, none better knows than you
How I have ever loved the life removed   8
And held in idle price to haunt assemblies   9
Where youth and cost witless bravery keeps.   10
I have delivered to Lord Angelo,
A man of stricture and firm abstinence,   12
My absolute power and place here in Vienna,
And he supposes me traveled to Poland;
For so I have strewed it in the common ear,
And so it is received. Now, pious sir,
You will demand of me why I do this.
FRIAR THOMAS   Gladly, my lord.
DUKE
We have strict statutes and most biting laws,
The needful bits and curbs to headstrong steeds,   20
Which for this fourteen years we have let slip,   21
Even like an o'ergrown lion in a cave   22
That goes not out to prey. Now, as fond fathers,   23
Having bound up the threat'ning twigs of birch
Only to stick it in their children's sight
For terror, not to use, in time the rod
Becomes more mocked than feared, so our decrees,
Dead to infliction, to themselves are dead;   28
And liberty plucks justice by the nose,   29
The baby beats the nurse, and quite athwart   30
Goes all decorum.
FRIAR THOMAS   It rested in Your Grace   31
To unloose this tied-up justice when you pleased;
And it in you more dreadful would have seemed
Than in Lord Angelo.
DUKE   I do fear, too dreadful.
Sith 'twas my fault to give the people scope,   35
'Twould be my tyranny to strike and gall them   36
For what I bid them do; for we bid this be done   37
When evil deeds have their permissive pass   38
And not the punishment. Therefore indeed, my father,
I have on Angelo imposed the office,   40
Who may in th'ambush of my name strike home,   41
And yet my nature never in the fight   42
To do in slander. And to behold his sway   43
I will, as 'twere a brother of your order,
Visit both prince and people. Therefore, I prithee,
Supply me with the habit, and instruct me   46
How I may formally in person bear   47

160 **in his place** inherent in the office   161 **his eminence** the emi-nence of him   162 **I stagger in** I am uncertain   163 **Awakes me** i.e., awakes, activates. (*Me* is used colloquially.)   **enrollèd** written on a roll or deed   165 **zodiacs** i.e., years   166 **for a name** for reputation's sake   169 **tickle** uncertain, unstable   174 **cloister** i.e., convent   175 **approbation** novitiate, period of probation.   178 **To** with.   **assay** try, test   180 **prone** eager, apt, supplicating.   **dialect** language   181 **prosperous art** skill or ability to gain favorable results   184–6 **as well . . . life** both for the encouragement of similar sexual activity, which otherwise would be subject to grave charges or accusations, and for you to continue to live   187–8 **tick-tack** a form of backgam-mon in which pegs were fitted into holes. (Here applied bawdily.)   **1.3. Location: A friary.**
2 **dribbling** falling short or wide of the mark   3 **complete** perfect, whole, strong   4 **harbor** shelter   5 **wrinkled** i.e., mature

8 **removed** retired   9 **in idle price** as little worth. *Idle* means "unprofitable."   10 **Where . . . keeps** where youth and costly expen-diture put themselves foolishly on display.   12 **stricture** strictness   20 **steeds** (The Folio reading, "weedes," is possible in the sense of "lawless and uncontrolled impulses.")   21 **fourteen** (Claudio men-tions nineteen years at 1.2.165; possibly the compositor confused *xiv* and *xix*.)   22 **o'ergrown** too old and large   23 **fond** doting   28 **Dead to infliction** dead in that they are not executed   29 **liberty** license   30 **athwart** wrongly, awry   31 **decorum** social order.   **It rested . . . Grace** It lay in your ducal authority, was incumbent on you   35 **Sith** Since   36 **gall** chafe, injure   37 **we . . . done** i.e., we virtually order a crime to be committed   38 **pass** sanction   40 **office** duty   41 **Who . . . home** who may, under cover of my ducal authority, strike to the heart of the matter   42 **nature** i.e., personal identity (as distinguished from official capacity)   43 **do in slander** act so as to invite slander (for being too repressive).   **sway** rule   46 **habit** garment (of a friar)   47 **formally** in outward appearance.   **bear** bear myself

Like a true friar. More reasons for this action
At our more leisure shall I render you.   49
Only this one: Lord Angelo is precise,   50
Stands at a guard with envy, scarce confesses   51
That his blood flows or that his appetite   52
Is more to bread than stone. Hence shall we see,   53
If power change purpose, what our seemers be.
                                                                Exeunt.

❧

1.[4]

Enter Isabella and Francisca, a nun.

ISABELLA
And have you nuns no farther privileges?
FRANCISCA   Are not these large enough?
ISABELLA
Yes, truly. I speak not as desiring more,
But rather wishing a more strict restraint
Upon the sisterhood, the votarists of Saint Clare.   5
LUCIO   (*within*)
Ho! Peace be in this place!
ISABELLA   Who's that which calls?
FRANCISCA
It is a man's voice. Gentle Isabella,
Turn you the key, and know his business of him.
You may, I may not; you are yet unsworn.   9
When you have vowed, you must not speak with men
But in the presence of the prioress;
Then if you speak you must not show your face,
Or if you show your face you must not speak.
He calls again. I pray you, answer him.   [*Exit.*]
ISABELLA
Peace and prosperity! Who is 't that calls?

[*She opens the door. Enter Lucio.*]

LUCIO
Hail, virgin, if you be, as those cheek roses   16
Proclaim you are no less. Can you so stead me   17
As bring me to the sight of Isabella,   18
A novice of this place, and the fair sister
To her unhappy brother Claudio?   20
ISABELLA
Why "her unhappy brother"? Let me ask,
The rather for I now must make you know   22
I am that Isabella, and his sister.
LUCIO
Gentle and fair, your brother kindly greets you.
Not to be weary with you, he's in prison.   25

ISABELLA   Woe me! For what?
LUCIO
For that which, if myself might be his judge,
He should receive his punishment in thanks:
He hath got his friend with child.
ISABELLA
Sir, make me not your story.
LUCIO   'Tis true.   30
I would not—though 'tis my familiar sin   31
With maids to seem the lapwing, and to jest,   32
Tongue far from heart—play with all virgins so.
I hold you as a thing enskied and sainted   34
By your renouncement, an immortal spirit
And to be talked with in sincerity
As with a saint.
ISABELLA
You do blaspheme the good in mocking me.   38
LUCIO
Do not believe it. Fewness and truth, 'tis thus: 39
Your brother and his lover have embraced.
As those that feed grow full, as blossoming time   41
That from the seedness the bare fallow brings   42
To teeming foison, even so her plenteous womb   43
Expresseth his full tilth and husbandry.   44
ISABELLA
Someone with child by him? My cousin Juliet?
LUCIO   Is she your cousin?
ISABELLA
Adoptedly, as schoolmaids change their names   47
By vain though apt affection.
LUCIO   She it is.   48
ISABELLA
Oh, let him marry her.
LUCIO   This is the point.
The Duke is very strangely gone from hence;
Bore many gentlemen, myself being one,   51
In hand and hope of action; but we do learn,   52
By those that know the very nerves of state,
His givings-out were of an infinite distance   54
From his true-meant design. Upon his place,   55
And with full line of his authority,   56
Governs Lord Angelo, a man whose blood
Is very snow broth; one who never feels   58
The wanton stings and motions of the sense,   59
But doth rebate and blunt his natural edge   60

---

49 more greater   **50 precise** strict, puritanical   **51 Stands . . . envy**
guards himself severely against calumny   **52–3 or . . . stone** or that
he has an appetite for bread (i.e., food or physical pleasure) any more
than if it were stone. (See Matthew 4.3, where the devil tempts Jesus
to turn stone into bread.)
1.4. Location: A convent.
5 votarists of Saint Clare An order founded in 1212 by Saint Francis
of Assisi and Saint Clare; its members were enjoined to a life of
poverty, service, and contemplation.   **9 you . . . unsworn** i.e., you
have not yet taken your formal vows to enter the convent.   **16 cheek
roses** i.e., blushes   **17 stead** help   **18 As** as to   **20 unhappy** unfortunate   **22 The rather for** the more so because   **25 weary** wearisome

30 story subject for mirth.   **31 familiar** customary   **32 lapwing** pee-
wit or plover. (The lapwing runs away from its nest in order to draw
away enemies from its young, much as Lucio throws up smoke-
screens in his seductive talk with young women.)   **34 enskied** placed
in heaven   **38 You . . . me** You blaspheme goodness itself when you
mockingly praise me, unworthy as I am, for saintliness.   **39 it** i.e.,
that I am mocking.   **Fewness and truth** In few words and truly
41–3 As . . . foison Just as the season of blossoming brings the sowing
of the bare untilled land to teeming fruitfulness   **44 Expresseth . . .
husbandry** makes plainly visible Claudio's tilling of the crop, i.e., his
plowing and fertilizing Juliet's body.   **47 change** exchange   **48 vain
though apt** girlish though natural and suitable   **51–2 Bore . . . action**
i.e., he misleadingly kept us in expectation of some military action
54 givings-out public statements   **55 Upon** In   **56 line** extent
58 snow broth melted snow (i.e., ice water)   **59 motions . . . sense**
promptings of sexual desire   **60 But . . . edge** but dulls and blunts
the sharp desire of sexuality

With profits of the mind, study, and fast.
He—to give fear to use and liberty,   62
Which have for long run by the hideous law
As mice by lions—hath picked out an act,
Under whose heavy sense your brother's life   65
Falls into forfeit. He arrests him on it
And follows close the rigor of the statute
To make him an example. All hope is gone,
Unless you have the grace by your fair prayer
To soften Angelo. And that's my pith of business   70
Twixt you and your poor brother.

ISABELLA   Doth he so
Seek his life?

LUCIO   He's censured him already,   72
And, as I hear, the Provost hath a warrant
For 's execution.

ISABELLA   Alas, what poor
Ability's in me to do him good?

LUCIO   Assay the power you have.   76

ISABELLA
My power? Alas, I doubt.

LUCIO   Our doubts are traitors,
And makes us lose the good we oft might win,   78
By fearing to attempt. Go to Lord Angelo,
And let him learn to know, when maidens sue
Men give like gods, but when they weep and kneel,
All their petitions are as freely theirs   82
As they themselves would owe them.   83

ISABELLA   I'll see what I can do.

LUCIO   But speedily.

ISABELLA   I will about it straight,
No longer staying but to give the Mother   87
Notice of my affair. I humbly thank you.
Commend me to my brother. Soon at night   89
I'll send him certain word of my success.   90

LUCIO
I take my leave of you.

ISABELLA   Good sir, adieu.

Exeunt [separately].

❧

2.1

Enter Angelo, Escalus, and servants, [a] Justice.

ANGELO
We must not make a scarecrow of the law,
Setting it up to fear the birds of prey,   2
And let it keep one shape till custom make it
Their perch and not their terror.

ESCALUS   Ay, but yet
Let us be keen and rather cut a little   5

Than fall and bruise to death. Alas, this gentleman   6
Whom I would save had a most noble father!
Let but Your Honor know,   8
Whom I believe to be most strait in virtue,   9
That, in the working of your own affections,   10
Had time cohered with place, or place with wishing,
Or that the resolute acting of your blood   12
Could have attained th'effect of your own purpose,   13
Whether you had not sometime in your life   14
Erred in this point which now you censure him,   15
And pulled the law upon you.

ANGELO
'Tis one thing to be tempted, Escalus,
Another thing to fall. I not deny
The jury, passing on the prisoner's life,
May in the sworn twelve have a thief or two
Guiltier than him they try. What's open made to
    justice,
That justice seizes. What knows the laws   22
That thieves do pass on thieves? 'Tis very pregnant,   23
The jewel that we find, we stoop and take't
Because we see it; but what we do not see
We tread upon and never think of it.
You may not so extenuate his offense
For I have had such faults; but rather tell me,   28
When I that censure him do so offend,
Let mine own judgment pattern out my death   30
And nothing come in partial. Sir, he must die.   31

Enter Provost.

ESCALUS
Be it as your wisdom will.

ANGELO   Where is the Provost?

PROVOST
Here, if it like Your Honor.

ANGELO   See that Claudio   33
Be executed by nine tomorrow morning.
Bring him his confessor; let him be prepared.
For that's the utmost of his pilgrimage.   36

[Exit Provost.]

ESCALUS
Well, heaven forgive him, and forgive us all!
Some rise by sin, and some by virtue fall;
Some run from breaks of ice and answer none,   39
And some condemnèd for a fault alone.   40

Enter Elbow, Froth, Clown [Pompey], officers.

---

62 **use and liberty** habitual licentiousness   65 **heavy sense** severe
interpretation   70 **my pith of business** the essence of my business
72 **censured** sentenced   76 **Assay** Try   78 **makes** make   82 **their
petitions** i.e., the things the maidens ask for   83 **As . . . them** as they
themselves would wish to have them.   87 **but** than.   **Mother**
Mother Superior, prioress   89 **Soon at night** Early tonight   90 **my
success** how I have succeeded.
2.1 Location: A court of justice.
2 **fear** frighten   5 **keen** sharp

6 **fall** let fall heavily.   **bruise** i.e., crush   8 **know** consider   9 **strait**
strict   10 **affections** desires   12 **blood** passion   13 **effect** realization
14 **had** would have.   **sometime** on some occasion   15 **censure him**
sentence him for   22–3 **What . . . on thieves?** Who knows what laws
thieves apply to their fellow thieves?   23 **pregnant** clear   28 **For**
because   30–1 **Let . . . partial** let the sentence I have imposed serve as
a model in sentencing me if I commit a crime, no partiality or extenu-
ating circumstances being admitted.   33 **like** please   36 **that's . . .
pilgrimage** that's the furthest point of his life's journey.   39 **Some . . .
none** some break the ice repeatedly (i.e., commit serious infractions of
the law) and yet escape punishment. (A famous crux; the Folio reads
"brakes of Ice.")   40 **a fault alone** one single infraction.

ELBOW   Come, bring them away. If these be good 41
people in a commonweal that do nothing but use their 42
abuses in common houses, I know no law. Bring them 43
away.

ANGELO   How now, sir, what's your name? And what's
the matter?

ELBOW   If it please Your Honor, I am the poor Duke's 47
constable, and my name is Elbow. I do lean upon 48
justice, sir, and do bring in here before Your good Honor
two notorious benefactors.

ANGELO   Benefactors? Well, what benefactors are they?
Are they not malefactors?

ELBOW   If it please Your Honor, I know not well what
they are; but precise villains they are, that I am sure of, 54
and void of all profanation in the world that good 55
Christians ought to have.

ESCALUS   [to Angelo]   This comes off well. Here's a
wise officer.

ANGELO   Go to. What quality are they of?—Elbow is 59
your name? Why dost thou not speak, Elbow?

POMPEY   He cannot, sir; he's out at elbow. 61

ANGELO   What are you, sir?

ELBOW   He, sir? A tapster, sir, parcel-bawd, one that 63
serves a bad woman, whose house, sir, was, as they
say, plucked down in the suburbs; and now she
professes a hothouse, which I think is a very ill house 66
too.

ESCALUS   How know you that?

ELBOW   My wife, sir, whom I detest before heaven and 69
Your Honor—

ESCALUS   How? Thy wife?

ELBOW   Ay, sir; whom I thank heaven is an honest
woman—

ESCALUS   Dost thou detest her therefore?

ELBOW   I say, sir, I will detest myself also, as well as
she, that this house, if it be not a bawd's house, it is
pity of her life, for it is a naughty house. 77

ESCALUS   How dost thou know that, Constable?

ELBOW   Marry, sir, by my wife, who, if she had been a
woman cardinally given, might have been accused in 80
fornication, adultery, and all uncleanliness there.

ESCALUS   By the woman's means?

ELBOW   Ay, sir, by Mistress Overdone's means; but as
she spit in his face, so she defied him. 84

POMPEY   Sir, if it please Your Honor, this is not so.

ELBOW   Prove it before these varlets here, thou honor- 86
able man, prove it. 87

ESCALUS   [to Angelo]   Do you hear how he misplaces?

POMPEY   Sir, she came in great with child, and longing,
saving Your Honor's reverence, for stewed prunes. Sir, 90
we had but two in the house, which at that very
distant time stood, as it were, in a fruit dish, a 92
dish of some threepence. Your Honors have seen such
dishes; they are not China dishes, but very good
dishes—

ESCALUS   Go to, go to. No matter for the dish, sir.

POMPEY   No, indeed, sir, not of a pin; you are therein 97
in the right. But to the point. As I say, this Mistress
Elbow, being, as I say, with child, and being great-
bellied, and longing, as I said, for prunes; and having
but two in the dish, as I said, Master Froth here, this
very man, having eaten the rest, as I said, and, as I
say, paying for them very honestly—for, as you
know, Master Froth, I could not give you threepence
again. 105

FROTH   No, indeed.

POMPEY   Very well. You being then, if you be
remembered, cracking the stones of the foresaid 108
prunes—

FROTH   Ay, so I did indeed.

POMPEY   Why, very well; I telling you then, if you be
remembered, that such a one and such a one were
past cure of the thing you wot of, unless they kept 113
very good diet, as I told you— 114

FROTH   All this is true.

POMPEY   Why, very well, then—

ESCALUS   Come, you are a tedious fool. To the purpose.
What was done to Elbow's wife, that he hath cause to
complain of? Come me to what was done to her. 119

POMPEY   Sir, Your Honor cannot come to that yet.

ESCALUS   No, sir, nor I mean it not.

POMPEY   Sir, but you shall come to it, by Your Honor's
leave. And, I beseech you, look into Master Froth here,
sir, a man of fourscore pound a year, whose father 124
died at Hallowmas.—Was 't not at Hallowmas, Mas- 125
ter Froth?

FROTH   All-hallond eve. 127

POMPEY   Why, very well. I hope here be truths. He, sir,
sitting, as I say, in a lower chair, sir—'twas in the 129
Bunch of Grapes, where indeed you have a delight to 130
sit, have you not?

41 **away** onward.   42–3 **use . . . houses** practice their vices in bawdy
houses   47 **poor Duke's** i.e., Duke's poor   48 **lean upon** rely on,
appeal to. (With an unintended comic reference to the idea of leaning
on one's elbow.)   54 **precise** complete. (Or perhaps a blunder for "precious." *Precise* unintentionally recalls the description of Angelo as
precise, i.e., strict or puritanical, at 1.3.50.)   55 **profanation** (A blunder
for "profession," or a word meaning "irreverence" where Elbow
intends "reverence." Elbow already has used several malapropisms,
including *lean upon, benefactors,* and *precise.*)   59 **Go to** An expression
of impatience or reproof.   **quality** social standing, occupation   61 **out
at elbow** (1) impoverished, threadbare, hence without any ideas (2)
missing his cue, i.e., at a loss for words after being called by his name.
63 **parcel-bawd** part-time bawd (and part-time tapster)   66 **professes
a hothouse** professes to run a bathhouse   69 **detest** (For "protest.")
77 **pity of her life** a great pity.   **naughty** wicked   80 **cardinally** (For
"carnally.")   **given** inclined   84 **she spit . . . face** Elbow's wife spit in
the face of Pompey (who, as pimp, was acting as Mistress Overdone's
means, line 83).

86–7 **varlets . . . honorable** (Elbow reverses or *misplaces* these epithets.)   90 **saving . . . reverence** i.e., begging your pardon for what
I'm about to say.   **stewed prunes** (Commonly served in houses of
prostitution, or *stews*, and therefore suggesting prostitutes. The dialogue throughout is sexually suggestive.)   92 **distant** (Blunder for
"instant"?)   97 **a pin** i.e., an insignificant trifle   105 **again** back.
108 **stones** pits. (With suggestion also of "testicles.")   113 **the thing . . .
of** you know what I mean (i.e., venereal disease)   114 **diet** strict regimen prescribed for medical treatment   119 **Come me** i.e., Come. (*Me*
is used colloquially. Pompey makes a vulgar joke on the words *come*
and *done*; see note at line 140.)   124 **of . . . year** i.e., well off   125 **Hallowmas** All Saints' Day, November 1   127 **All-hallond eve** Hal-
loween, October 31.   129 **a lower chair** i.e., an easy chair (?)
130 **Bunch of Grapes** (It was not uncommon to designate particular
rooms in inns by such names.)

FROTH   I have so, because it is an open room and good 132
for winter.

POMPEY   Why, very well, then. I hope here be truths.

ANGELO
This will last out a night in Russia,
When nights are longest there. I'll take my leave
And leave you to the hearing of the cause, 137
Hoping you'll find good cause to whip them all.

ESCALUS
I think no less. Good morrow to Your Lordship. 139

                                    Exit [Angelo].
Now, sir, come on. What was done to Elbow's wife, 140
once more?

POMPEY   Once, sir? There was nothing done to her
once. 143

ELBOW   I beseech you, sir, ask him what this man did
to my wife.

POMPEY   I beseech Your Honor, ask me.

ESCALUS   Well, sir, what did this gentleman to her?

POMPEY   I beseech you, sir, look in this gentleman's
face. Good Master Froth, look upon His Honor; 'tis for
a good purpose. Doth Your Honor mark his face? 150

ESCALUS   Ay, sir, very well.

POMPEY   Nay, I beseech you, mark it well.

ESCALUS   Well, I do so.

POMPEY   Doth Your Honor see any harm in his face?

ESCALUS   Why, no.

POMPEY   I'll be supposed upon a book, his face is the 156
worst thing about him. Good, then; if his face be the
worst thing about him, how could Master Froth do the
Constable's wife any harm? I would know that of Your
Honor.

ESCALUS   He's in the right, Constable. What say you
to it?

ELBOW   First, an it like you, the house is a respected 163
house; next, this is a respected fellow; and his mistress
is a respected woman.

POMPEY   By this hand, sir, his wife is a more respected
person than any of us all.

ELBOW   Varlet, thou liest! Thou liest, wicked varlet! The
time is yet to come that she was ever respected with
man, woman, or child.

POMPEY   Sir, she was respected with him before he
married with her.

ESCALUS   Which is the wiser here, Justice or Iniquity?— 173
Is this true?

ELBOW   O thou caitiff! O thou varlet! O thou wicked 175
Hannibal! I respected with her before I was married to 176
her?—If ever I was respected with her, or she with
me, let not Your Worship think me the poor Duke's

officer.—Prove this, thou wicked Hannibal, or I'll
have mine action of battery on thee. 180

ESCALUS   If he took you a box o'th'ear, you might have 181
your action of slander too.

ELBOW   Marry, I thank Your good Worship for it. What
is't Your Worship's pleasure I shall do with this
wicked caitiff?

ESCALUS   Truly, officer, because he hath some offenses
in him that thou wouldst discover if thou couldst, let 187
him continue in his courses till thou know'st what 188
they are.

ELBOW   Marry, I thank Your Worship for it.—Thou see'st,
thou wicked varlet, now, what's come upon thee: thou
art to continue now, thou varlet, thou art to continue. 192

ESCALUS   [to Froth]   Where were you born, friend?

FROTH   Here in Vienna, sir.

ESCALUS   Are you of fourscore pounds a year? 195

FROTH   Yes, an't please you, sir.

ESCALUS   So. [To Pompey] What trade are you of, sir?

POMPEY   A tapster, a poor widow's tapster.

ESCALUS   Your mistress' name?

POMPEY   Mistress Overdone.

ESCALUS   Hath she had any more than one husband?

POMPEY   Nine, sir. Overdone by the last. 202

ESCALUS   Nine?—Come hither to me, Master Froth.
Master Froth, I would not have you acquainted with
tapsters. They will draw you, Master Froth, and you 205
will hang them. Get you gone, and let me hear no 206
more of you.

FROTH   I thank Your Worship. For mine own part, I
never come into any room in a taphouse but I am 209
drawn in. 210

ESCALUS   Well, no more of it, Master Froth. Farewell.

                                    [Exit Froth.]
Come you hither to me, Master Tapster. What's your
name, Master Tapster?

POMPEY   Pompey.

ESCALUS   What else?

POMPEY   Bum, sir.

ESCALUS   Troth, and your bum is the greatest thing
about you, so that in the beastliest sense you are Pompey the Great. Pompey, you are partly a bawd, Pompey, howsoever you color it in being a tapster, are you 220
not? Come, tell me true. It shall be the better for you.

POMPEY   Truly, sir, I am a poor fellow that would live.

ESCALUS   How would you live, Pompey? By being a 223
bawd? What do you think of the trade, Pompey? Is it
a lawful trade?

POMPEY   If the law would allow it, sir.

---

132 **open** public   137 **cause** case. (With word play on *cause*, "reason,"
in the next line. See also the play on *leave* in 136–7.)   139 **I . . . less** I
think so, too.   140 **done** (Pompey, in his answer, uses *done* in a sexual
sense.)   143 **once** only once. (Pompey replies wittily to Escalus's *once
more* in 141, meaning "once again.")   150 **mark** observe   156 **supposed** (A malapropism for "deposed," i.e., sworn.)   **book** i.e., Bible
163 **an it like** if it please.   **respected** (For "suspected.")   173 **Justice
or Iniquity** (Personified characters in a morality play.)   175 **caitiff**
knave, villain.   176 **Hannibal** (A blunder for "cannibal," perhaps
also suggested by the fact that Hannibal and Pompey were both
famous generals in the classical world.)

180 **battery** (An error for "slander," as Escalus amusedly points
out.)   181 **took** gave.   **o'** on   187 **discover** (1) detect (2) reveal
188 **courses** courses of action   192 **continue** (Elbow may confuse the
word with its opposite.)   195 **of** possessed of   202 **Overdone . . . last**
(1) Her name, Overdone, was given her by her last husband (2) She
has been worn out (*overdone*) by the last one.   205 **draw** (1) cheat,
take in (2) empty, deplete. (With a pun on the tapster's trade of drawing liquor from a barrel, and on Froth's name.) (3) disembowel, or
drag to execution   206 **will hang them** will be the cause of their
hanging   209 **taphouse** alehouse   210 **drawn in** enticed. (Still
another meaning of *draw*, line 205.)   220 **color** disguise   223 **live**
make a living

ESCALUS   But the law will not allow it, Pompey; nor it
shall not be allowed in Vienna.

POMPEY   Does Your Worship mean to geld and splay all   229
the youth of the city?

ESCALUS   No, Pompey.

POMPEY   Truly, sir, in my poor opinion they will to't
then. If Your Worship will take order for the drabs and   233
the knaves, you need not to fear the bawds.

ESCALUS   There is pretty orders beginning, I can tell
you. It is but heading and hanging.   236

POMPEY   If you head and hang all that offend that way
but for ten year together, you'll be glad to give out a   238
commission for more heads. If this law hold in Vienna   239
ten year, I'll rent the fairest house in it after threepence   240
a bay. If you live to see this come to pass, say Pompey   241
told you so.

ESCALUS   Thank you, good Pompey. And, in requital of   243
your prophecy, hark you: I advise you let me not find
you before me again upon any complaint whatsoever;
no, not for dwelling where you do. If I do, Pompey, I
shall beat you to your tent and prove a shrewd Caesar   247
to you; in plain dealing, Pompey, I shall have you
whipped. So for this time, Pompey, fare you well.

POMPEY   I thank Your Worship for your good counsel.
[Aside] But I shall follow it as the flesh and fortune
shall better determine.
Whip me? No, no, let carman whip his jade.   253
The valiant heart's not whipped out of his trade.
                                                           Exit.

ESCALUS   Come hither to me, Master Elbow; come
hither, Master Constable. How long have you been in
this place of constable?

ELBOW   Seven year and a half, sir.

ESCALUS   I thought, by the readiness in the office, you   259
had continued in it some time. You say, seven years
together?

ELBOW   And a half, sir.

ESCALUS   Alas, it hath been great pains to you. They do
you wrong to put you so oft upon't. Are there not
men in your ward sufficient to serve it?   265

ELBOW   Faith, sir, few of any wit in such matters. As
they are chosen, they are glad to choose me for them.   267
I do it for some piece of money and go through with   268
all.   269

ESCALUS   Look you bring me in the names of some six   270
or seven, the most sufficient of your parish.

ELBOW   To Your Worship's house, sir?

ESCALUS   To my house. Fare you well.   [Exit Elbow.]
What's o'clock, think you?

JUSTICE   Eleven, sir.

ESCALUS
I pray you home to dinner with me.   276

JUSTICE   I humbly thank you.

ESCALUS
It grieves me for the death of Claudio;
But there's no remedy.

JUSTICE   Lord Angelo is severe.

ESCALUS   It is but needful.
Mercy is not itself, that oft looks so;   281
Pardon is still the nurse of second woe.   282
But yet—poor Claudio! There is no remedy.
Come, sir.   Exeunt.

❖

2.2

Enter Provost [and a] Servant.

SERVANT
He's hearing of a cause; he will come straight.   1
I'll tell him of you.

PROVOST   Pray you, do.   [Exit Servant.]
                                                       I'll know
His pleasure; maybe he will relent. Alas,
He hath but as offended in a dream!   4
All sects, all ages smack of this vice—and he   5
To die for't!

         Enter Angelo.

ANGELO   Now, what's the matter, Provost?

PROVOST
Is it your will Claudio shall die tomorrow?

ANGELO
Did not I tell thee yea? Hadst thou not order?
Why dost thou ask again?

PROVOST   Lest I might be too rash.
Under your good correction, I have seen   11
When, after execution, judgment hath
Repented o'er his doom.   13

ANGELO   Go to; let that be mine.   14
Do you your office, or give up your place,
And you shall well be spared.   16

PROVOST   I crave Your Honor's pardon.
What shall be done, sir, with the groaning Juliet?   18
She's very near her hour.   19

ANGELO   Dispose of her
To some more fitter place, and that with speed.

         [Enter a Servant.]

---

229 **splay** spay   233 **take order** take measures.   **drabs** prostitutes
236 **It . . . hanging** Beheading and hanging are the order of the day.
238 **year together** years at a stretch   239 **commission** order.   **hold**
remain in force   240 **after** at the rate of   241 **bay** division of a house
included under one gable.   243 **requital of** return for   247 **shrewd**
harsh, severe.   **Caesar** (Julius Caesar defeated Pompey at Pharsalia
in 48 B.C.)   253 **carman** cart driver.   **jade** broken-down horse.
259 **readiness** proficiency, alacrity   265 **sufficient** able   267 **for them**
i.e., to take their place.   268–9 **go . . . all** i.e., perform my duties thoroughly.   270 **Look** See to it that

276 **dinner** (Dinner was customarily eaten just before midday.)
281 **Mercy . . . so** i.e., What seems merciful may not really be so (since
it may encourage crime and hence lead to more punishment)
282 **Pardon . . . woe** i.e., pardon continually nurtures and encourages
a repetition of offenses and hence of punishment.
2.2 **Location: Adjacent to the court of justice, perhaps at Angelo's
official residence.**
1 **hearing . . . cause** listening to a case.   **straight** immediately.   4 **He . . .
dream** i.e., Claudio offended without conscious intent.   5 **All sects . . .
smack** All classes of people of all ages (and in all past history) partake   11 **Under . . . correction** i.e., Allow me to say   13 **doom** sentence.   14 **mine** my business.   16 **well be spared** easily be done
without.   18 **groaning** (with labor pains)   19 **hour** time of delivery.

SERVANT
  Here is the sister of the man condemned
  Desires access to you.

ANGELO   Hath he a sister?   22

PROVOST
  Ay, my good lord, a very virtuous maid,
  And to be shortly of a sisterhood,
  If not already.

ANGELO   Well, let her be admitted.

                            [Exit Servant.]

  See you the fornicatress be removed.
  Let her have needful but not lavish means.
  There shall be order for't.

        Enter Lucio and Isabella.

PROVOST   Save Your Honor!   28

ANGELO *[to Provost]*
  Stay a little while. *[To Isabella]* You're welcome.
    What's your will?

ISABELLA
  I am a woeful suitor to Your Honor,
  Please but Your Honor hear me.

ANGELO   Well, what's your suit? 31

ISABELLA
  There is a vice that most I do abhor,
  And most desire should meet the blow of justice,
  For which I would not plead, but that I must;
  For which I must not plead, but that I am
  At war twixt will and will not.

ANGELO   Well, the matter?

ISABELLA
  I have a brother is condemned to die.
  I do beseech you, let it be his fault,   38
  And not my brother.

PROVOST *[aside]*   Heaven give thee moving graces!

ANGELO
  Condemn the fault, and not the actor of it?
  Why, every fault's condemned ere it be done.
  Mine were the very cipher of a function,
  To fine the faults, whose fine stands in record, 43
  And let go by the actor.

ISABELLA   Oh, just but severe law!
  I had a brother, then. Heaven keep your honor!

LUCIO *[aside to Isabella]*
  Give't not o'er so. To him again, entreat him! 47
  Kneel down before him; hang upon his gown.
  You are too cold. If you should need a pin, 49
  You could not with more tame a tongue desire it.
  To him, I say!

ISABELLA *[to Angelo]*
  Must he needs die?

ANGELO   Maiden, no remedy.

ISABELLA
  Yes, I do think that you might pardon him,
  And neither heaven nor man grieve at the mercy.

ANGELO
  I will not do't.

ISABELLA   But can you, if you would?

ANGELO
  Look what I will not, that I cannot do. 56

ISABELLA
  But might you do't, and do the world no wrong,
  If so your heart were touched with that remorse 58
  As mine is to him?

ANGELO   He's sentenced. 'Tis too late.

LUCIO *[aside to Isabella]*   You are too cold.

ISABELLA
  Too late? Why, no; I that do speak a word
  May call it back again. Well, believe this:
  No ceremony that to great ones 'longs, 64
  Not the king's crown, nor the deputed sword, 65
  The marshal's truncheon, nor the judge's robe 66
  Become them with one half so good a grace
  As mercy does.
  If he had been as you, and you as he,
  You would have slipped like him; but he, like you, 70
  Would not have been so stern.

ANGELO   Pray you, begone.

ISABELLA
  I would to heaven I had your potency,
  And you were Isabel. Should it then be thus?
  No, I would tell what 'twere to be a judge 74
  And what a prisoner.

LUCIO *[aside to Isabella]*   Ay, touch him; there's the vein. 75

ANGELO
  Your brother is a forfeit of the law, 76
  And you but waste your words.

ISABELLA   Alas, alas!
  Why, all the souls that were were forfeit once, 78
  And He that might the vantage best have took 79
  Found out the remedy. How would you be, 80
  If He, which is the top of judgment, should 81
  But judge you as you are? Oh, think on that,
  And mercy then will breathe within your lips,
  Like man new-made.

ANGELO   Be you content, fair maid. 84
  It is the law, not I, condemn your brother.
  Were he my kinsman, brother, or my son,
  It should be thus with him. He must die tomorrow.

ISABELLA
  Tomorrow! Oh, that's sudden! Spare him, spare him!
  He's not prepared for death. Even for our kitchens
  We kill the fowl of season. Shall we serve heaven 90
  With less respect than we do minister

---

22 **Desires** who desires 28 **Save** May God save 31 **Please . . . me** if Your Honor will please hear me. 38 **let . . . fault** i.e., let the fault die, be condemned 43 **To fine . . . record** to punish only the faults, for which the penalty stands in the statute books 47 **Give't . . . so** Don't give up so soon. 49 **need a pin** i.e., ask for the smallest trifle

56 **Look what** Whatever 58 **remorse** pity 64 **'longs** is fitting, belongs 65 **deputed sword** sword of justice entrusted to the ruler 66 **truncheon** staff borne by military officers 70 **like you** in your situation 74 **tell** make known 75 **there's the vein** i.e., that's the right approach. (*Vein* means "lode to be profitably mined," or perhaps "vein for bloodletting.") 76 **a forfeit** one who must incur the penalty 78–80 **Why . . . remedy** (A reference to God's redemption of sinful humanity when He would have been justified in destroying humankind.) 81 **top of judgment** supreme judge 84 **new-made** i.e., created new by salvation, born again. 90 **of season** that is in season and properly mature.

To our gross selves? Good, good my lord, bethink
  you:
Who is it that hath died for this offense?
There's many have committed it.

LUCIO [*aside to Isabella*]   Ay, well said.

ANGELO
The law hath not been dead, though it hath slept.
Those many had not dared to do that evil
If the first that did th'edict infringe
Had answered for his deed. Now 'tis awake,
Takes note of what is done, and like a prophet
Looks in a glass that shows what future evils,   100
Either now, or by remissness new-conceived   101
And so in progress to be hatched and born,   102
Are now to have no successive degrees,   103
But ere they live, to end.

ISABELLA   Yet show some pity.   104

ANGELO
I show it most of all when I show justice;
For then I pity those I do not know,
Which a dismissed offense would after gall,   107
And do him right that, answering one foul wrong,   108
Lives not to act another. Be satisfied;
Your brother dies tomorrow. Be content.

ISABELLA
So you must be the first that gives this sentence,
And he that suffers. Oh, it is excellent
To have a giant's strength, but it is tyrannous
To use it like a giant.

LUCIO [*aside to Isabella*]   That's well said.

ISABELLA   Could great men thunder
As Jove himself does, Jove would never be quiet,   116
For every pelting, petty officer   117
Would use his heaven for thunder,
Nothing but thunder. Merciful heaven,
Thou rather with thy sharp and sulfurous bolt   120
Splits the unwedgeable and gnarlèd oak   121
Than the soft myrtle; but man, proud man,
Dressed in a little brief authority,
Most ignorant of what he's most assured,   124
His glassy essence, like an angry ape   125
Plays such fantastic tricks before high heaven
As makes the angels weep; who, with our spleens,   127
Would all themselves laugh mortal.   128

LUCIO [*aside to Isabella*]
Oh, to him, to him, wench! He will relent.
He's coming, I perceive't.

PROVOST [*aside*]   Pray heaven she win him!   130

ISABELLA
We cannot weigh our brother with ourself.   131
Great men may jest with saints; 'tis wit in them,   132
But in the less, foul profanation.   133

LUCIO [*aside to Isabella*]
Thou'rt i'th' right, girl. More o' that.

ISABELLA
That in the captain's but a choleric word   135
Which in the soldier is flat blasphemy.

LUCIO [*aside to Isabella*]   Art advised o' that? More on't. 137

ANGELO
Why do you put these sayings upon me?   138

ISABELLA
Because authority, though it err like others,   139
Hath yet a kind of medicine in itself   140
That skins the vice o'th' top. Go to your bosom;   141
Knock there, and ask your heart what it doth know
That's like my brother's fault. If it confess
A natural guiltiness such as is his,
Let it not sound a thought upon your tongue
Against my brother's life.

ANGELO [*aside*]   She speaks, and 'tis such sense   147
That my sense breeds with it.—Fare you well.   148
                    [*He starts to go.*]

ISABELLA   Gentle my lord, turn back.   149

ANGELO
I will bethink me. Come again tomorrow.   150

ISABELLA
Hark how I'll bribe you. Good my lord, turn back.

ANGELO   How? Bribe me?

ISABELLA
Ay, with such gifts that heaven shall share with you.   153

LUCIO [*aside to Isabella*]   You had marred all else.   154

ISABELLA
Not with fond sicles of the tested gold,   155
Or stones whose rate are either rich or poor   156
As fancy values them, but with true prayers   157
That shall be up at heaven and enter there
Ere sunrise—prayers from preservèd souls,   159

---

100 glass magic crystal **101 Either . . . new-conceived** i.e., both evils already hatched and those that would be encouraged by continued laxity of enforcement **102 in progress** in the course of time **103 successive degrees** successors or future stages. (Future evils are to be aborted before they are born and propagate.) **104 ere they live** i.e., before they can be committed **107 Which . . . gall** whom a forgiven offense would give trouble to later on **108 do . . . answering** do justice to that person who, by paying the penalty for **116 be quiet** have any quiet **117 pelting** paltry **120 bolt** thunderbolt **121 unwedgeable** unsplittable **124–5 Most . . . essence** i.e., most ignorant of what should give him best comfort and assurance, his immortal soul. (*Glassy* suggests the reflective qualities of the soul as a mirror of God.) **125 angry ape** i.e., ludicrous buffoon **127–8 who . . . mortal** who, if they had the organs of laughter that we have, would laugh themselves mortal, becoming like us. (The *spleen* was thought to be the seat of laughter.)

130 coming coming around **131–3 We . . . profanation** We cannot judge our fellow mortals by the same standards we use in judging ourselves. Persons of great authority are allowed liberties that in lesser persons would be condemned as blasphemies. (Lines 135–6 make much the same point.) **135 That . . . word** i.e., We treat the abusive language a commanding officer uses in anger merely as an outburst; we are indulgent toward the failings of *great men*. (As in lines 131–3, Isabella's point seems to be that our judgments are biased by our inordinate regard for authority.) **137 advised** informed, aware. **on't** of it. **138 put . . . me** apply these sayings to me. **139–41 Because . . . top** Because authority, though prone to sinfulness like all of humankind, has a way of seeming to heal itself by covering over the boil with a film of skin, leaving the sore unhealed. **147–8 sense . . . sense** import . . . sensuality **149 Gentle my lord** My noble lord **150 bethink me** think it over. **153 that** as **154 else** otherwise. **155 Not . . . gold** Not with foolishly valued shekels of pure gold. (*Shekels* are Hebrew coins.) **156–7 Or . . . them** or jewels the value of which is merely subjective and transitory **159 preservèd souls** devout religious who have withdrawn from the world

From fasting maids whose minds are dedicate   160
To nothing temporal.

ANGELO   Well, come to me tomorrow.

LUCIO [*aside to Isabella*]   Go to, 'tis well. Away!

ISABELLA
Heaven keep Your Honor safe!

ANGELO [*aside*]   Amen!
For I am that way going to temptation,
Where prayers cross.

ISABELLA   At what hour tomorrow   165
Shall I attend Your Lordship?

ANGELO   At any time 'fore noon.

ISABELLA   Save Your Honor!   168

                    [*Exeunt Isabella, Lucio, and Provost.*]

ANGELO   From thee, even from thy virtue!
What's this, what's this? Is this her fault or mine?
The tempter or the tempted, who sins most, ha?
Not she, nor doth she tempt; but it is I
That, lying by the violet in the sun,
Do, as the carrion does, not as the flower,   174
Corrupt with virtuous season. Can it be   175
That modesty may more betray our sense   176
Than woman's lightness? Having waste ground
    enough,   177
Shall we desire to raze the sanctuary
And pitch our evils there? Oh, fie, fie, fie!   179
What dost thou, or what art thou, Angelo?
Dost thou desire her foully for those things
That make her good? Oh, let her brother live!
Thieves for their robbery have authority
When judges steal themselves. What, do I love her,
That I desire to hear her speak again
And feast upon her eyes? What is't I dream on?
Oh, cunning enemy that, to catch a saint,   187
With saints dost bait thy hook! Most dangerous
Is that temptation that doth goad us on
To sin in loving virtue. Never could the strumpet,
With all her double vigor—art and nature—   191
Once stir my temper; but this virtuous maid   192
Subdues me quite. Ever till now,
When men were fond, I smiled and wondered how.   194

                                              Exit.

❖

2.3

*Enter, [meeting,] Duke [disguised as a friar]
and Provost.*

DUKE
Hail to you, Provost—so I think you are.

---

160 fasting maids i.e., nuns. **dedicate** dedicated   **165 cross** are at cross purposes.   **168 Save** May God save   **174 carrion** decaying flesh   **175 Corrupt . . . season** i.e., putrefy while all else flourishes. (The warmth of flowering time causes the violet, Isabella, to blossom but causes the carrion lying beside it, Angelo, to rot.)   **176 modesty** virtue, chastity.   **sense** sensual nature   **177 lightness** immodesty, lust.   **179 pitch our evils there** i.e., erect a privy, not on *waste ground* (line 177), but on sanctified ground. (*Evils* also has the more common meaning of "wickedness.")   **187 enemy** i.e., Satan   **191 double . . . nature** twofold power (of alluring men) through artifice and a sensuous nature   **192 temper** temperament   **194 fond** foolishly in love   **2.3 Location: A prison.**

PROVOST
I am the Provost. What's your will, good Friar?

DUKE
Bound by my charity and my blest order,
I come to visit the afflicted spirits
Here in the prison. Do me the common right   5
To let me see them and to make me know
The nature of their crimes, that I may minister
To them accordingly.

PROVOST
I would do more than that, if more were needful.

            Enter Juliet.

Look, here comes one: a gentlewoman of mine,
Who, falling in the flaws of her own youth,   11
Hath blistered her report. She is with child,   12
And he that got it, sentenced—a young man   13
More fit to do another such offense
Than die for this.

DUKE
When must he die?

PROVOST   As I do think, tomorrow.
[*To Juliet*] I have provided for you. Stay awhile,   17
And you shall be conducted.   18

DUKE
Repent you, fair one, of the sin you carry?

JULIET
I do, and bear the shame most patiently.

DUKE
I'll teach you how you shall arraign your conscience,   21
And try your penitence, if it be sound   22
Or hollowly put on.   23

JULIET   I'll gladly learn.

DUKE   Love you the man that wronged you?

JULIET
Yes, as I love the woman that wronged him.

DUKE
So then it seems your most offenseful act
Was mutually committed?

JULIET   Mutually.

DUKE
Then was your sin of heavier kind than his.

JULIET
I do confess it and repent it, Father.

DUKE
'Tis meet so, daughter. But lest you do repent   31
As that the sin hath brought you to this shame,   32
Which sorrow is always toward ourselves, not heaven,   33
Showing we would not spare heaven as we love it, 34
But as we stand in fear—

JULIET
I do repent me as it is an evil,

---

5 common right i.e., right of all clerics   **11 flaws** (1) weaknesses, fissures (2) sudden gusts (of passion)   **12 blistered her report** marred her reputation.   **13 got** begot   **17 provided** provided a place to stay   **18 conducted** taken there.   **21 arraign** accuse   **22 try** test   **23 hollowly** falsely   **31 'Tis meet so** It is fitting that you do so   **32 As that** merely because   **33 toward ourselves** i.e., narrowly self-concerned rather than loving virtue for its own sake   **34 Showing . . . it** showing that we wish to avoid offending heaven not out of sheer love of goodness

And take the shame with joy.

DUKE   There rest.   37
Your partner, as I hear, must die tomorrow,
And I am going with instruction to him.
Grace go with you. *Benedicite!*   *Exit.* 40

JULIET
Must die tomorrow? O injurious love,   41
That respites me a life whose very comfort   42
Is still a dying horror!

PROVOST   'Tis pity of him.   *Exeunt.* 43

❖

2.4

Enter Angelo.

ANGELO
When I would pray and think, I think and pray
To several subjects. Heaven hath my empty words,   2
Whilst my invention, hearing not my tongue,   3
Anchors on Isabel; Heaven in my mouth,
As if I did but only chew His name,   5
And in my heart the strong and swelling evil
Of my conception. The state, whereon I studied,   7
Is like a good thing, being often read,
Grown sere and tedious. Yea, my gravity,   9
Wherein—let no man hear me—I take pride,
Could I with boot change for an idle plume,   11
Which the air beats for vain. O place, O form,   12
How often dost thou with thy case, thy habit,   13
Wrench awe from fools and tie the wiser souls   14
To thy false seeming! Blood, thou art blood.   15
Let's write "good angel" on the devil's horn,   16
'Tis not the devil's crest.

Enter Servant.
                              How now? Who's there?   17

SERVANT
One Isabel, a sister, desires access to you.

ANGELO   Teach her the way.   [*Exit Servant.*]
                              Oh, heavens!   19
Why does my blood thus muster to my heart,   20

Making both it unable for itself   21
And dispossessing all my other parts
Of necessary fitness?
So play the foolish throngs with one that swoons,   24
Come all to help him, and so stop the air
By which he should revive; and even so
The general subject to a well-wished king   27
Quit their own part and in obsequious fondness   28
Crowd to his presence, where their untaught love   29
Must needs appear offense.

Enter Isabella.
                              How now, fair maid?   30

ISABELLA   I am come to know your pleasure.

ANGELO
That you might know it would much better please me   32
Than to demand what 'tis. Your brother cannot live. 33

ISABELLA
Even so. Heaven keep Your Honor!   34
                              [*She turns to leave.*]

ANGELO
Yet may he live awhile; and, it may be,
As long as you or I. Yet he must die.

ISABELLA   Under your sentence?

ANGELO   Yea.

ISABELLA
When, I beseech you? That in his reprieve,
Longer or shorter, he may be so fitted   40
That his soul sicken not.

ANGELO
Ha? Fie, these filthy vices! It were as good   42
To pardon him that hath from nature stolen   43
A man already made, as to remit   44
Their saucy sweetness that do coin heaven's image   45
In stamps that are forbid. 'Tis all as easy   46
Falsely to take away a life true made
As to put metal in restrainèd means   48
To make a false one.

ISABELLA
'Tis set down so in heaven, but not in earth.   50

ANGELO
Say you so? Then I shall pose you quickly: 51
Which had you rather, that the most just law
Now took your brother's life, or, to redeem him,
Give up your body to such sweet uncleanness

---

37 There rest. Hold fast to that truth.   **40** *Benedicite!* Blessings on
you!   **41–3 O . . . horror!** i.e., O sinful pregnancy, that prolongs a life
whose greatest comfort will always be a deadly horror! (Pregnancy
could save a woman from being executed. However, *love* is sometimes emended to *law*.)   **43 pity of** a pity about
2.4 Location: Angelo's official residence.
2 several separate   **3 invention** imagination   **5 His** i.e., heaven's,
God's   **7 conception** thought.   **The state** Statecraft   **9 sere** withered,
old   **11–12 Could . . . vain** I would willingly exchange (my gravity)
for the frivolity of a pleasure-loving gallant, sporting a feather that
seems to beat the air in its vanity (or, perhaps, is beaten by the air in
reproof of its vanity).   **12 O place, O form** O authority of high position, O ceremonial dignity of office   **13 thy case . . . habit** your mere
outward appearance and garb   **14–15 Wrench . . . seeming** intimidate
ordinary foolish men and subjugate even the wise to the seeming
virtue of authority.   **15 Blood . . . blood** i.e., No position of authority
or birth, no matter how lofty, can protect a person from the instinctual
power of desire.   **16–17 Let's . . . crest** i.e., No matter how hard we try
to disguise evil under the semblance of good, it remains recognizably
evil still. (In heraldic terms, the devil is known by his baleful horns;
the heraldic crest on his coat of arms does not alter his true identity.)
19 Teach Show   **20 muster to** assemble like soldiers in

21 unable ineffectual   **24 play** behave   **27 general subject** i.e., commoners, subjects.   **well-wished** attended by good wishes   **28 Quit . . .
part** abandon their proper function and (politely distant) place
29 untaught ignorant, unmannerly   **30 Must needs** will necessarily
32–3 That . . . 'tis i.e., I wish you could know the nature of my desire
without your asking and my having to be explicit. (*Know* suggests
carnal knowledge.)   **34 Even so** So be it.   **40 fitted** prepared
42–6 It were . . . forbid One might as well pardon the murderer of a
man already alive as pardon the wanton pleasures of those persons
who produce illegitimate offspring, like counterfeit coiners.
(*Heaven's image* is humankind, made in God's likeness; Genesis 1:27.)
48 metal i.e., the metal used in coining (lines 45–6), with a play on
mettle, natural vigor or spirit.   **restrainèd** prohibited, illicit (both in
counterfeiting coinage and in begetting illegitimate children)
50 'Tis . . . earth i.e., Equating murder and bastardizing accords with
divine law but not with human law, according to which murder is
more heinous.   **51 pose you** put a perplexing question to you

As she that he hath stained?

ISABELLA   Sir, believe this,
I had rather give my body than my soul.   56

ANGELO
I talk not of your soul. Our compelled sins   57
Stand more for number than for account.

ISABELLA   How say you?   58

ANGELO
Nay, I'll not warrant that, for I can speak   59
Against the thing I say. Answer to this:
I, now the voice of the recorded law,
Pronounce a sentence on your brother's life;
Might there not be a charity in sin
To save this brother's life?

ISABELLA   Please you to do't,   64
I'll take it as a peril to my soul;   65
It is no sin at all, but charity.

ANGELO
Pleased you to do't at peril of your soul   67
Were equal poise of sin and charity.   68

ISABELLA
That I do beg his life, if it be sin,
Heaven let me bear it! You granting of my suit,
If that be sin, I'll make it my morn prayer
To have it added to the faults of mine,
And nothing of your answer.

ANGELO   Nay, but hear me.   73
Your sense pursues not mine. Either you are ignorant
Or seem so craftily; and that's not good.

ISABELLA
Let me be ignorant, and in nothing good,
But graciously to know I am no better.   77

ANGELO
Thus wisdom wishes to appear most bright
When it doth tax itself, as these black masks   79
Proclaim an enshield beauty ten times louder   80
Than beauty could, displayed. But mark me.
To be receivèd plain, I'll speak more gross: 82
Your brother is to die.

ISABELLA   So.

ANGELO
And his offense is so, as it appears,
Accountant to the law upon that pain.   86

ISABELLA   True.

ANGELO
Admit no other way to save his life—   88
As I subscribe not that, nor any other,   89
But in the loss of question—that you, his sister,   90

Finding yourself desired of such a person   91
Whose credit with the judge, or own great place,
Could fetch your brother from the manacles
Of the all-binding law; and that there were
No earthly means to save him, but that either
You must lay down the treasures of your body
To this supposed, or else to let him suffer.   97
What would you do?

ISABELLA
As much for my poor brother as myself:
That is, were I under the terms of death,   100
Th'impression of keen whips I'd wear as rubies,
And strip myself to death as to a bed
That longing have been sick for, ere I'd yield   103
My body up to shame.

ANGELO   Then must your brother die.

ISABELLA   And 'twere the cheaper way.
Better it were a brother died at once   107
Than that a sister, by redeeming him,
Should die forever.

ANGELO
Were not you then as cruel as the sentence
That you have slandered so?

ISABELLA
Ignomy in ransom and free pardon   112
Are of two houses. Lawful mercy   113
Is nothing kin to foul redemption.   114

ANGELO
You seemed of late to make the law a tyrant,
And rather proved the sliding of your brother   116
A merriment than a vice.

ISABELLA
Oh, pardon me, my lord. It oft falls out,
To have what we would have, we speak not what
    we mean.
I something do excuse the thing I hate   120
For his advantage that I dearly love.

ANGELO
We are all frail.

ISABELLA   Else let my brother die,
If not a fedary but only he   123
Owe and succeed thy weakness.   124

ANGELO   Nay, women are frail too.

ISABELLA
Ay, as the glasses where they view themselves,   126
Which are as easy broke as they make forms.   127

---

56 give i.e., give to death or punishment. (Isabella avoids or does not understand the drift of the question.)   **57–8 Our ... account** Our sins committed under compulsion are recorded but not charged to our spiritual account.   **59 I'll ... that** i.e., I'm not necessarily endorsing the view I just expressed   **64 Please you** If you please   **65 take** accept   **67 Pleased** If it pleased   **68 Were equal poise** there would be equal balance   **73 of your answer** to which you will have to answer.   **77 graciously** through divine grace   **79 tax itself** accuse itself (of ignorance).   **these** (Generically referring to any.)   **80 enshield** shielded, protected from view behind the black masks   **82 receivèd plain** plainly understood.   **gross** (1) openly (2) offensively   **86 Accountant** accountable.   **pain** penalty.   **88 Admit** Suppose   **89–90 As ... question** since I will admit no alternative possibility in our discussion. (*Loss of question* means "forfeiting the terms of our debate.")

91 of by   **97 supposed** hypothetical person.   **him** i.e., Claudio   **100 terms** sentence   **103 That ... for** i.e., that I have been sick with longing for. (Isabella's images are of love, death, and flagellation.)   **107 died at once** should die once for all, rather than *die forever* (line 109) in the death of the soul through sin   **112–14 Ignomy ... redemption** Being ransomed under ignominious circumstances and being released without conditions are two entirely different things. Mercy under law bears no relation to being spared under foul stipulations.   **116 proved** argued   **120 something** to some extent   **123 fedary** confederate, companion who is equally guilty   **124 Owe ... weakness** possess and inherit the weakness you speak of, or the weakness to which all men as a class are prone. (Isabella argues that Claudio should die only if he is the only man who is frail.)   **126 glasses** mirrors   **127 forms** (1) images (2) copies of themselves, i.e., children

Women? Help, heaven! Men their creation mar 128
In profiting by them. Nay, call us ten times frail, 129
For we are soft as our complexions are, 130
And credulous to false prints.

ANGELO   I think it well. 131
And from this testimony of your own sex— 132
Since I suppose we are made to be no stronger 133
Than faults may shake our frames—let me be bold. 134
I do arrest your words. Be that you are, 135
That is, a woman; if you be more, you're none. 136
If you be one, as you are well expressed 137
By all external warrants, show it now 138
By putting on the destined livery. 139

ISABELLA
I have no tongue but one. Gentle my lord, 140
Let me entreat you speak the former language. 141

ANGELO   Plainly conceive, I love you.

ISABELLA   My brother did love Juliet,
And you tell me that he shall die for't.

ANGELO
He shall not, Isabel, if you give me love.

ISABELLA
I know your virtue hath a license in't, 146
Which seems a little fouler than it is 147
To pluck on others.

ANGELO   Believe me, on mine honor, 148
My words express my purpose.

ISABELLA
Ha! Little honor to be much believed,
And most pernicious purpose! Seeming, seeming!
I will proclaim thee, Angelo, look for't!
Sign me a present pardon for my brother, 153
Or with an outstretched throat I'll tell the world
    aloud
What man thou art.

ANGELO   Who will believe thee, Isabel?
My unsoiled name, th'austereness of my life,
My vouch against you, and my place i'th' state 157
Will so your accusation overweigh
That you shall stifle in your own report
And smell of calumny. I have begun, 160
And now I give my sensual race the rein. 161
Fit thy consent to my sharp appetite;
Lay by all nicety and prolixious blushes 163
That banish what they sue for. Redeem thy brother 164

By yielding up thy body to my will,
Or else he must not only die the death, 166
But thy unkindness shall his death draw out
To ling'ring sufferance. Answer me tomorrow, 168
Or, by the affection that now guides me most, 169
I'll prove a tyrant to him. As for you,
Say what you can, my false o'erweighs your true.
                                                    Exit.

ISABELLA
To whom should I complain? Did I tell this, 172
Who would believe me? O perilous mouths, 173
That bear in them one and the selfsame tongue, 174
Either of condemnation or approof, 175
Bidding the law make curtsy to their will, 176
Hooking both right and wrong to th'appetite, 177
To follow as it draws! I'll to my brother. 178
Though he hath fall'n by prompture of the blood, 179
Yet hath he in him such a mind of honor
That, had he twenty heads to tender down 181
On twenty bloody blocks, he'd yield them up
Before his sister should her body stoop
To such abhorred pollution.
Then, Isabel, live chaste, and, brother, die;
More than our brother is our chastity.
I'll tell him yet of Angelo's request,
And fit his mind to death, for his soul's rest.   Exit.

❖

3.1

*Enter Duke [disguised as before], Claudio, and
Provost.*

DUKE
So then you hope of pardon from Lord Angelo?

CLAUDIO
The miserable have no other medicine
But only hope.
I have hope to live and am prepared to die.

DUKE
Be absolute for death. Either death or life
Shall thereby be the sweeter. Reason thus with life:
If I do lose thee, I do lose a thing
That none but fools would keep. A breath thou art,
Servile to all the skyey influences 9
That dost this habitation where thou keep'st 10
Hourly afflict. Merely, thou art death's fool, 11
For him thou labor'st by thy flight to shun,
And yet run'st toward him still. Thou art not noble, 13

128–9 Men . . . them Men mar their creation in God's likeness by taking advantage of women.   130 complexions constitutions, appearance   131 credulous . . . prints susceptible to false impressions. (The metaphor is from the stamping of coins and other metal.)   132 of about   133 we i.e., men and women   134 than than that   135 arrest your words take what you have said and hold you to it.   that what   136 if . . . none i.e., if you insist on remaining a virgin and free of fleshly desire, you are no woman as we have defined the term—that is, frail and susceptible.   137–8 expressed . . . warrants shown to be by your physical beauty   139 putting . . . livery i.e., assuming the characteristic frailty that all women possess.   140 tongue language   141 speak . . . language speak to be understood, in the language I understand.   146–8 I know . . . others i.e., I am sure that you, out of virtuous motives, are speaking licentiously (and with the license of authority) in order to put me to the test.   153 present immediate   157 vouch testimony   160 calumny slander.   161 I give . . . rein I give free rein to my sensual desires to gallop as they please.   163–4 Lay . . . sue for Set aside all the coyness and time-wasting blushes that make a pretense of repulsing the embrace they actually beg for.

166 die the death be put to death   168 sufferance torture.   169 affection passion   172 Did I tell If I told   173–8 O perilous . . . draws! O dangerous voices of authority, able with one tongue either to condemn or approve, forcing both right and wrong to obey the willful appetite!   179 prompture prompting, suggestion   181 tender down lay down in payment
3.1 Location: The prison.
9 skyey influences influence of the stars   10 this habitation i.e., the earth (and the body as well).   keep'st dwell   11 Merely Utterly, only   13 still always.

For all th'accommodations that thou bear'st   14
Are nursed by baseness. Thou'rt by no means valiant,   15
For thou dost fear the soft and tender fork   16
Of a poor worm. Thy best of rest is sleep,   17
And that thou oft provok'st, yet grossly fear'st   18
Thy death, which is no more. Thou art not thyself,
For thou exists on many a thousand grains
That issue out of dust. Happy thou art not,
For what thou hast not, still thou striv'st to get,
And what thou hast, forget'st. Thou art not certain,   23
For thy complexion shifts to strange effects,   24
After the moon. If thou art rich, thou'rt poor,   25
For, like an ass whose back with ingots bows,
Thou bear'st thy heavy riches but a journey,
And death unloads thee. Friend hast thou none,
For thine own bowels which do call thee sire,   29
The mere effusion of thy proper loins,   30
Do curse the gout, serpigo, and the rheum   31
For ending thee no sooner. Thou hast nor youth
          nor age,   32
But as it were an after-dinner's sleep   33
Dreaming on both, for all thy blessèd youth   34
Becomes as agèd and doth beg the alms   35
Of palsied eld; and, when thou art old and rich,   36
Thou hast neither heat, affection, limb, nor beauty   37
To make thy riches pleasant. What's yet in this
That bears the name of life? Yet in this life
Lie hid more thousand deaths; yet death we fear,
That makes these odds all even.
CLAUDIO   I humbly thank you.   41
To sue to live, I find I seek to die,   42
And, seeking death, find life. Let it come on.

          Enter Isabella.

ISABELLA
What, ho! Peace here; grace and good company!   44
PROVOST
Who's there? Come in. The wish deserves a welcome.
                              [*He goes to greet her.*]
DUKE [*to Claudio*]
Dear sir, ere long I'll visit you again.
CLAUDIO   Most holy sir, I thank you.
ISABELLA
My business is a word or two with Claudio.
PROVOST
And very welcome.—Look, signor, here's your sister.
DUKE [*aside to the Provost*]   Provost, a word with you.

PROVOST   As many as you please.
DUKE
Bring me to hear them speak, where I may be
Concealed.   [*The Duke and the Provost withdraw.*]
CLAUDIO   Now, sister, what's the comfort?
ISABELLA   Why,
As all comforts are: most good, most good indeed.
Lord Angelo, having affairs to heaven,
Intends you for his swift ambassador,
Where you shall be an everlasting leiger.   57
Therefore your best appointment make with speed;   58
Tomorrow you set on.
CLAUDIO   Is there no remedy?   59
ISABELLA
None but such remedy as, to save a head,
To cleave a heart in twain.
CLAUDIO   But is there any?
ISABELLA   Yes, brother, you may live.
There is a devilish mercy in the judge,
If you'll implore it, that will free your life
But fetter you till death.
CLAUDIO   Perpetual durance?   66
ISABELLA
Ay, just; perpetual durance, a restraint,   67
Though all the world's vastidity you had,   68
To a determined scope.
CLAUDIO   But in what nature?   69
ISABELLA
In such a one as, you consenting to't,
Would bark your honor from that trunk you bear   71
And leave you naked.
CLAUDIO   Let me know the point.
ISABELLA
Oh, I do fear thee, Claudio, and I quake   73
Lest thou a feverous life shouldst entertain,   74
And six or seven winters more respect   75
Than a perpetual honor. Dar'st thou die?
The sense of death is most in apprehension,   77
And the poor beetle that we tread upon
In corporal sufferance finds a pang as great
As when a giant dies.
CLAUDIO   Why give you me this shame?
Think you I can a resolution fetch   82
From flow'ry tenderness? If I must die,   83
I will encounter darkness as a bride
And hug it in mine arms.
ISABELLA
There spake my brother! There my father's grave
Did utter forth a voice. Yes, thou must die.
Thou art too noble to conserve a life

---

14 accommodations conveniences, civilized comforts   **15 nursed by baseness** nurtured by ignoble means.   **16 fork** forked tongue   **17 worm** (1) snake (2) grave worm.   **18 thou oft provok'st** you often invoke, summon   **23 certain** steadfast   **24 complexion** constitution. **strange effects** new appearances, manifestations   **25 After** in obedience to, under the influence of   **29 bowels** i.e., offspring   **30 mere** very.   **proper** own   **31 serpigo** a skin eruption.   **rheum** catarrh **32 nor youth** neither youth   **33 after-dinner's** i.e., afternoon's **34–6 all . . . eld** your happy youth must decline all too soon into old age and become like a beggar, pleading for the little comfort that palsied infirmity can provide. (Youth is penniless and dependent on the aged, whereas the old lack the physical capacity of youth.) **37 heat, affection** vigor, passion   **41 makes . . . even** makes all equal. **42 To sue** Suing, petitioning   **44 grace** God's grace

57 leiger resident ambassador.   **58 appointment** preparation   **59 set on** set forward.   **66 durance** imprisonment.   **67 just** just so   **67–9 a restraint . . . scope** a confinement to fixed limits or bounds (i.e., to inescapable guilt and perpetual remorse for the sinful bargain you had struck), even if you had the entire vastness of the world to wander in.   **71 bark** strip off (as one strips bark from a tree *trunk*) **73 fear** fear for   **74 feverous** feverish.   **entertain** maintain, desire **75 respect** value   **77 apprehension** anticipation   **82–3 Think . . . tenderness?** Do you think I can find the courage to face death in flowery figures of speech?

In base appliances. This outward-sainted deputy,   89
Whose settled visage and deliberate word   90
Nips youth i'th' head, and follies doth enew   91
As falcon doth the fowl, is yet a devil;   92
His filth within being cast, he would appear   93
A pond as deep as hell.

CLAUDIO   The prenzie Angelo?   94

ISABELLA
Oh, 'tis the cunning livery of hell,   95
The damned'st body to invest and cover   96
In prenzie guards! Dost thou think, Claudio: 97
If I would yield him my virginity,
Thou mightst be freed!

CLAUDIO   Oh, heavens, it cannot be.

ISABELLA
Yes, he would give't thee, from this rank offense,   100
So to offend him still. This night's the time   101
That I should do what I abhor to name,
Or else thou diest tomorrow.

CLAUDIO   Thou shalt not do't.

ISABELLA   Oh, were it but my life,
I'd throw it down for your deliverance
As frankly as a pin.

CLAUDIO   Thanks, dear Isabel.   107

ISABELLA
Be ready, Claudio, for your death tomorrow.

CLAUDIO
Yes. Has he affections in him,   109
That thus can make him bite the law by th' nose   110
When he would force it? Sure it is no sin,   111
Or of the deadly seven it is the least.

ISABELLA   Which is the least?

CLAUDIO
If it were damnable, he being so wise,
Why would he for the momentary trick   115
Be perdurably fined? Oh, Isabel!   116

ISABELLA
What says my brother?

CLAUDIO   Death is a fearful thing.

ISABELLA   And shamèd life a hateful.

CLAUDIO
Ay, but to die, and go we know not where,
To lie in cold obstruction and to rot,   120
This sensible warm motion to become   121

A kneaded clod, and the delighted spirit   122
To bathe in fiery floods, or to reside
In thrilling region of thick-ribbèd ice;   124
To be imprisoned in the viewless winds   125
And blown with restless violence round about
The pendent world; or to be worse than worst   127
Of those that lawless and incertain thought   128
Imagine howling—'tis too horrible!
The weariest and most loathèd worldly life
That age, ache, penury, and imprisonment
Can lay on nature is a paradise
To what we fear of death.   133

ISABELLA   Alas, alas!

CLAUDIO   Sweet sister, let me live.
What sin you do to save a brother's life,
Nature dispenses with the deed so far   137
That it becomes a virtue.

ISABELLA   Oh, you beast!
Oh, faithless coward! Oh, dishonest wretch!   139
Wilt thou be made a man out of my vice?
Is't not a kind of incest, to take life
From thine own sister's shame? What should I think?
Heaven shield my mother played my father fair!   143
For such a warpèd slip of wilderness   144
Ne'er issued from his blood. Take my defiance,
Die, perish! Might but my bending down   146
Reprieve thee from thy fate, it should proceed.
I'll pray a thousand prayers for thy death,
No word to save thee.

CLAUDIO
Nay, hear me, Isabel.

ISABELLA   Oh, fie, fie, fie!
Thy sin's not accidental, but a trade.   151
Mercy to thee would prove itself a bawd;   152
'Tis best that thou diest quickly.

CLAUDIO   Oh, hear me, Isabella!

[The Duke comes forward.]

DUKE
Vouchsafe a word, young sister, but one word.   155

ISABELLA   What is your will?

DUKE   Might you dispense with your leisure, I would
by and by have some speech with you. The satisfaction I would require is likewise your own benefit.   159

ISABELLA   I have no superfluous leisure—my stay
must be stolen out of other affairs—but I will attend   161
you awhile.   *[She walks apart.]*

DUKE   Son, I have overheard what hath passed between
you and your sister. Angelo had never the purpose to

---

89 In base appliances by means of ignoble devices, remedies.
89–92 This . . . fowl This outwardly holy deputy, who with composed
features and judiciously chosen words swoops down on youth like a
falcon and drives his prey into covert. (To *enew* is to drive prey down
into the water or into hiding.)   **93 cast** dug out; diagnosed, sounded;
vomited (?)   **94, 97 prenzie** (A word unknown elsewhere, perhaps
meaning "princely" or "precise.")   **95–7 'tis . . . guards** it is the cunning ruse of the devil to clothe and conceal the wickedest man imaginable in decorously proper trimmings   **97 Dost thou think** i.e.,
Would you believe   **100–1 he would . . . still** he would grant you
license, in return for your committing this foul crime, to continue
with your fornication.   **107 frankly** freely   **109 affections** passions
110 bite . . . nose i.e., flout the law   **111 force** enforce. (Claudio wonders that lust can drive Angelo to make a mockery of the law even
while seeking to enforce it.)   **115 trick** trifle   **116 perdurably fined**
everlastingly punished.   **120 obstruction** cessation of vital functions
121 sensible endowed with feeling.   **motion** organism

122 kneaded clod shapeless lump of earth.   **delighted spirit** spirit
that is now attended with delight, or capable of being so
124 thrilling piercingly cold   **125 viewless** invisible   **127 pendent**
hanging in space. (A Ptolemaic concept.)   **128 lawless . . . thought**
i.e., wild conjecture   **133 To** compared to   **137 dispenses with**
grants a dispensation for, excuses   **139 dishonest** dishonorable
143 shield forfend, forbid   **144 warpèd . . . wilderness** perverse,
licentious scion, one that reverts to the original wild stock   **146 but**
merely   **151 accidental** casual.   **trade** established habit.   **152 prove . . .
bawd** i.e., provide opportunity for sexual license   **155 Vouchsafe**
Allow   **159 require** ask   **161 attend** await; listen to

corrupt her; only he hath made an assay of her virtue 165
to practice his judgment with the disposition of na- 166
tures. She, having the truth of honor in her, hath made 167
him that gracious denial which he is most glad to re- 168
ceive. I am confessor to Angelo, and I know this to be
true; therefore prepare yourself to death. Do not satisfy
your resolution with hopes that are fallible. Tomorrow
you must die. Go to your knees and make ready.

CLAUDIO   Let me ask my sister pardon. I am so out of
love with life that I will sue to be rid of it.

DUKE   Hold you there. Farewell.   [*Claudio retires.*] 175
Provost, a word with you.

[*The Provost comes forward.*]

PROVOST   What's your will, Father?

DUKE   That now you are come, you will be gone. Leave
me awhile with the maid. My mind promises with my 179
habit no loss shall touch her by my company. 180

PROVOST   In good time.   *Exit* [*Provost with Claudio*]. 181

[*Isabella comes forward.*]

DUKE   The hand that hath made you fair hath made you
good. The goodness that is cheap in beauty makes 183
beauty brief in goodness; but grace, being the soul of 184
your complexion, shall keep the body of it ever fair. 185
The assault that Angelo hath made to you, fortune
hath conveyed to my understanding; and, but that 187
frailty hath examples for his falling, I should wonder 188
at Angelo. How will you do to content this substitute 189
and to save your brother?

ISABELLA   I am now going to resolve him. I had rather 191
my brother die by the law than my son should be
unlawfully born. But, oh, how much is the good Duke
deceived in Angelo! If ever he return and I can speak
to him, I will open my lips in vain, or discover his 195
government. 196

DUKE   That shall not be much amiss. Yet, as the matter
now stands, he will avoid your accusation; he made 198
trial of you only. Therefore fasten your ear on my
advisings. To the love I have in doing good a remedy
presents itself. I do make myself believe that you may
most uprighteously do a poor wronged lady a merited
benefit, redeem your brother from the angry law, do
no stain to your own gracious person, and much
please the absent Duke, if peradventure he shall ever
return to have hearing of this business.

ISABELLA   Let me hear you speak farther. I have spirit 207
to do anything that appears not foul in the truth of my 208
spirit. 209

DUKE   Virtue is bold, and goodness never fearful. Have
you not heard speak of Mariana, the sister of Frederick, the great soldier who miscarried at sea?

ISABELLA   I have heard of the lady, and good words
went with her name.

DUKE   She should this Angelo have married, was 215
affianced to her by oath, and the nuptial appointed;
between which time of the contract and limit of the 217
solemnity, her brother Frederick was wrecked at sea, 218
having in that perished vessel the dowry of his sister.
But mark how heavily this befell to the poor gentlewoman. There she lost a noble and renowned brother,
in his love toward her ever most kind and natural;
with him, the portion and sinew of her fortune, her 223
marriage dowry; with both, her combinate husband, 224
this well-seeming Angelo.

ISABELLA   Can this be so? Did Angelo so leave her?

DUKE   Left her in her tears, and dried not one of them
with his comfort; swallowed his vows whole, pretend- 228
ing in her discoveries of dishonor; in few, bestowed 229
her on her own lamentation, which she yet wears for 230
his sake; and he, a marble to her tears, is washed with 231
them but relents not.

ISABELLA   What a merit were it in death to take this
poor maid from the world! What corruption in this
life, that it will let this man live! But how out of this can
she avail? 236

DUKE   It is a rupture that you may easily heal, and the
cure of it not only saves your brother but keeps you
from dishonor in doing it.

ISABELLA   Show me how, good Father.

DUKE   This forenamed maid hath yet in her the continuance of her first affection; his unjust unkindness, that
in all reason should have quenched her love, hath, like
an impediment in the current, made it more violent
and unruly. Go you to Angelo; answer his requiring
with a plausible obedience; agree with his demands to 246
the point. Only refer yourself to this advantage: first, 247
that your stay with him may not be long, that the time
may have all shadow and silence in it, and the place 249
answer to convenience. This being granted in
course—and now follows all—we shall advise this
wronged maid to stead up your appointment, go in 252
your place. If the encounter acknowledge itself here- 253
after, it may compel him to her recompense. And here, 254
by this, is your brother saved, your honor untainted,
the poor Mariana advantaged, and the corrupt deputy
scaled. The maid will I frame and make fit for his at- 257

---

165 only he hath he has only.   **assay** test   **166–7 his judgment . . .
natures** his ability to judge people's characters.   **168 gracious** virtuous   **175 Hold you there** Hold fast to that resolution.
179–80 with my habit as well as my priestly garb (that)   **181 In good
time** i.e., Very well.   **183–84 The goodness . . . in goodness** i.e., The
physical attractions that come easily with beauty make beauty soon
cease to be morally good   **185 complexion** character and appearance
187 but that were it not that   **188 examples** precedents   **189 this
substitute** i.e., the deputy, Angelo   **191 resolve him** set his mind at
rest.   **195–6 discover his government** expose Angelo's misconduct.
198 avoid evade, refute.   **he made** i.e., he will say that he made
207 spirit courage   **208 truth** righteousness   **209 spirit** soul.

215 She . . . married Angelo was supposed to have married her.
was i.e., he was   **217–18 limit . . . solemnity** date set for the ceremony   **223 the portion and sinew** i.e., the mainstay   **224 combinate
husband** i.e., betrothed   **228–9 pretending . . . dishonor** falsely alleg-
ing to have found evidence of unchastity in her   **229–30 in few . . .
lamentation** in short, left her to her grief. (With quibble on *bestowed*,
meaning "gave in marriage.")   **230 wears** i.e., carries in her heart
231 a marble to i.e., unmoved by   **236 avail** benefit.   **246–7 to the
point** precisely.   **247 refer . . . advantage** obtain these conditions
249 shadow darkness, secrecy   **252 stead . . . appointment** go in your
stead   **253–4 If the . . . hereafter** i.e., If she should become pregnant
257 scaled weighed in the scales of justice (and found wanting).
frame prepare

tempt. If you think well to carry this as you may, the
doubleness of the benefit defends the deceit from reproof. What think you of it?

ISABELLA   The image of it gives me content already,
and I trust it will grow to a most prosperous perfection.

DUKE   It lies much in your holding up. Haste you speed- 264
ily to Angelo. If for this night he entreat you to his
bed, give him promise of satisfaction. I will presently
to Saint Luke's; there, at the moated grange, resides 267
this dejected Mariana. At that place call upon me; and
dispatch with Angelo, that it may be quickly.   269

ISABELLA   I thank you for this comfort. Fare you well,
good Father.   *Exit. [The Duke remains.]*

[3.2]

*Enter [to the Duke] Elbow, Clown [Pompey, and]
officers.*

ELBOW   Nay, if there be no remedy for it but that you
will needs buy and sell men and women like beasts,
we shall have all the world drink brown and white
bastard.   4

DUKE *[aside]*   Oh, heavens, what stuff is here?

POMPEY   'Twas never merry world since, of two usur- 6
ies, the merriest was put down, and the worser al-   7
lowed by order of law a furred gown to keep him   8
warm, and furred with fox on lambskins too, to signify that craft, being richer than innocency, stands 10
for the facing.   11

ELBOW   Come your way, sir.—Bless you, good Father
Friar.

DUKE   And you, good Brother Father. What offense hath 14
this man made you, sir?

ELBOW   Marry, sir, he hath offended the law; and, sir,
we take him to be a thief too, sir, for we have found
upon him, sir, a strange picklock, which we have sent 18
to the deputy.

DUKE *[to Pompey]*
Fie, sirrah, a bawd, a wicked bawd!
The evil that thou causest to be done,
That is thy means to live. Do thou but think
What 'tis to cram a maw or clothe a back   23
From such a filthy vice; say to thyself,
From their abominable and beastly touches   25
I drink, I eat, array myself, and live.

Canst thou believe thy living is a life,
So stinkingly depending? Go mend, go mend.   28

POMPEY   Indeed, it does stink in some sort, sir. But yet,
sir, I would prove—   30

DUKE
Nay, if the devil have given thee proofs for sin,   31
Thou wilt prove his.—Take him to prison, officer.   32
Correction and instruction must both work
Ere this rude beast will profit.

ELBOW   He must before the deputy, sir; he has given 35
him warning. The deputy cannot abide a whoremaster. If he be a whoremonger and comes before him, he 37
were as good go a mile on his errand.   38

DUKE
That we were all, as some would seem to be,   39
From our faults, as faults from seeming, free!   40

Enter Lucio.

ELBOW   His neck will come to your waist—a cord, sir. 41

POMPEY   I spy comfort, I cry bail. Here's a gentleman
and a friend of mine.

LUCIO   How now, noble Pompey? What, at the wheels
of Caesar? Art thou led in triumph? What, is there   45
none of Pygmalion's images, newly made woman, to   46
be had now, for putting the hand in the pocket and
extracting it clutched? What reply, ha? What say'st thou 48
to this tune, matter, and method? Is 't not drowned i' th' 49
last rain, ha? What say'st thou, trot? Is the world   50
as it was, man? Which is the way? Is it sad, and few 51
words? Or how? The trick of it?   52

DUKE   Still thus, and thus; still worse!

LUCIO   How doth my dear morsel, thy mistress? Procures she still, ha?

POMPEY   Troth, sir, she hath eaten up all her beef, and 56
she is herself in the tub.   57

LUCIO   Why, 'tis good. It is the right of it, it must be so.
Ever your fresh whore and your powdered bawd; an   59
unshunned consequence, it must be so. Art going to   60
prison, Pompey?

---

264 holding up ability to carry it off.   **267 moated grange** country
house surrounded by a ditch   **269 dispatch** settle, conclude business
3.2 Location: Scene continues. The Duke remains onstage.
4 bastard sweet Spanish wine. (Used quibblingly.)   **6–7 two usuries**
i.e., moneylending (the *worser*) and procuring for fornication (the
merriest), both of which yield increase   **8 furred gown** (Characteristic
attire of usurers.)   **10–11 stands . . . facing** represents the outer covering. (Fox symbolizes *craft* or craftiness, lambskin, *innocency*.)
14 Brother Father (The Duke's retort to Elbow's *Father Friar*, i.e.,
Father Brother.)   **18 picklock** skeleton key, or perhaps a chastity belt
in Pompey's possession as pimp; it might seem *strange* to the innocent Elbow   **23 cram . . . back** fill a stomach or provide clothing
25 touches sexual encounters

28 depending supported.   **30 prove** i.e., argue, demonstrate
31 proofs for arguments in defense of   **32 prove** turn out to be
35 must must go.   **deputy** i.e., Angelo. (Though Escalus gave Pompey
the warning.)   **37–8 he . . . errand** i.e., he will have a hard road to
travel.   **39 That** Would that   **40 From . . . free** i.e., free from faults, and
our faults free from dissembling.   **41 His . . . cord** i.e., He is likely to
hang by a cord like that around your waist. (The Duke is habited as a
friar.)   **45 Caesar** (Who defeated Pompey at Pharsalia and led his sons
in triumph after defeating them at Munda.)   **46 Pygmalion's images**
i.e., prostitutes, so called because they "painted" with cosmetics like a
painted statue. (Pygmalion was a sculptor, according to legend, whose
female statue came to life "newly made.")   **48 clutched** i.e., with
money in it. (But also with sexual suggestion.)   **48–50 What say'st . . .
rain** i.e., What do you say now to this latest turn of events? Are our
prospects a little dampened?   **50 trot** old bawd.   **51–2 Which . . .
words?** i.e., What is the latest fashion? Is melancholy now in vogue? (A
wry comment on Pompey's silence.)   **52 trick** fashion   **56 eaten . . .
beef** (1) consumed all her salt beef, which had been prepared in a
powder-tub like that also used to treat venereal disease (2) run through
all her prostitutes   **57 in the tub** being treated for venereal disease by
the sweating-tub treatment (much as beef was salted down in a tub to
preserve it).   **59 Ever . . . bawd** i.e., It is always thus with young
whores and old bawds, *powdered* like beef in a tub and caked with cosmetics   **60 unshunned** unshunnable, unavoidable

POMPEY   Yes, faith, sir.
LUCIO   Why, 'tis not amiss, Pompey. Farewell. Go, say
I sent thee thither. For debt, Pompey? Or how?
ELBOW   For being a bawd, for being a bawd.
LUCIO   Well, then, imprison him. If imprisonment be
the due of a bawd, why, 'tis his right. Bawd is he
doubtless, and of antiquity too; bawd-born. Farewell, 68
good Pompey. Commend me to the prison, Pompey.
You will turn good husband now, Pompey; you will 70
keep the house. 71
POMPEY   I hope, sir, Your good Worship will be my bail.
LUCIO   No, indeed, will I not, Pompey; it is not the
wear. I will pray, Pompey, to increase your bondage. 74
If you take it not patiently, why, your mettle is the 75
more. Adieu, trusty Pompey.—Bless you, Friar. 76
DUKE   And you.
LUCIO   Does Bridget paint still, Pompey, ha? 78
ELBOW   [to Pompey]   Come your ways, sir, come. 79
POMPEY   [to Lucio]   You will not bail me, then, sir?
LUCIO   Then, Pompey, nor now.—What news abroad, 81
Friar? What news?
ELBOW   Come your ways, sir, come.
LUCIO   Go to kennel, Pompey, go.
                [Exeunt Elbow, Pompey, and Officers.]
What news, Friar, of the Duke?
DUKE   I know none. Can you tell me of any?
LUCIO   Some say he is with the Emperor of Russia; other 87
some, he is in Rome. But where is he, think you? 88
DUKE   I know not where; but wheresoever, I wish him
well.
LUCIO   It was a mad fantastical trick of him to steal from 91
the state and usurp the beggary he was never born to. 92
Lord Angelo dukes it well in his absence; he puts 93
transgression to't. 94
DUKE   He does well in't.
LUCIO   A little more lenity to lechery would do no harm
in him. Something too crabbed that way, Friar. 97
DUKE   It is too general a vice, and severity must cure it.
LUCIO   Yes, in good sooth, the vice is of a great kindred; 99
it is well allied. But it is impossible to extirp it quite, 100
Friar, till eating and drinking be put down. They say
this Angelo was not made by man and woman after 102
this downright way of creation. Is it true, think you? 103
DUKE   How should he be made, then?
LUCIO   Some report a sea maid spawned him; some, 105
that he was begot between two stockfishes. But it is 106

certain that when he makes water his urine is congealed ice; that I know to be true. And he is a motion 108
ungenerative; that's infallible. 109
DUKE   You are pleasant, sir, and speak apace. 110
LUCIO   Why, what a ruthless thing is this in him, for the
rebellion of a codpiece to take away the life of a man! 112
Would the Duke that is absent have done this? Ere he
would have hanged a man for the getting a hundred
bastards, he would have paid for the nursing a
thousand. He had some feeling of the sport; he knew
the service, and that instructed him to mercy. 117
DUKE   I never heard the absent Duke much detected for 118
women. He was not inclined that way.
LUCIO   Oh, sir, you are deceived.
DUKE   'Tis not possible.
LUCIO   Who, not the Duke? Yes, your beggar of fifty;
and his use was to put a ducat in her clack-dish. The 123
Duke had crotchets in him. He would be drunk too,
that let me inform you.
DUKE   You do him wrong, surely.
LUCIO   Sir, I was an inward of his. A shy fellow was the 127
Duke, and I believe I know the cause of his with-
drawing.
DUKE   What, I prithee, might be the cause?
LUCIO   No, pardon. 'Tis a secret must be locked within
the teeth and the lips. But this I can let you understand:
the greater file of the subject held the Duke to 133
be wise.
DUKE   Wise? Why, no question but he was.
LUCIO   A very superficial, ignorant, unweighing fellow. 136
DUKE   Either this is envy in you, folly, or mistaking. The 137
very stream of his life and the business he hath helmed 138
must, upon a warranted need, give him a better proc- 139
lamation. Let him be but testimonied in his own 140
bringings-forth, and he shall appear to the envious a 141
scholar, a statesman, and a soldier. Therefore you
speak unskillfully; or, if your knowledge be more, it is 143
much darkened in your malice.
LUCIO   Sir, I know him, and I love him.
DUKE   Love talks with better knowledge, and knowledge with dearer love.
LUCIO   Come, sir, I know what I know.
DUKE   I can hardly believe that, since you know not
what you speak. But if ever the Duke return, as our
prayers are he may, let me desire you to make your
answer before him. If it be honest you have spoke,
you have courage to maintain it. I am bound to call
upon you; and, I pray you, your name?

68 antiquity long continuance.   bawd-born a born bawd and born of a bawd.   70 good husband thrifty manager   71 keep the house stay indoors. (With pun on the pimp's function as doorkeeper.)   74 wear fashion.   75–6 your . . . more (1) your spirit is revealed all the more (2) your shackles will be made heavier. (Playing on mettle/metal.)   78 paint use cosmetics   79 Come your ways Come along   81 Then Neither then.   abroad about town   87–8 other some some others   91 steal steal away   92 beggary i.e., status of a wanderer or traveler. (With unconscious ironic appropriateness; Lucio clearly does not see through the Duke's disguise as a mendicant friar.)   93–4 puts . . . to't puts lawbreaking under severe restraint.   97 Something too crabbed Somewhat too harsh   99 kindred i.e., family, numerous and well connected   100 extirp eradicate   102 after in accordance with   103 downright straightforward, usual   105 sea maid mermaid   106 stockfishes dried codfish.

108–9 motion ungenerative masculine puppet, without sexual potency   110 pleasant jocose.   apace fast and idly.   112 codpiece an appendage to the front of close-fitting hose or breeches worn by men, often ornamented and indelicately conspicuous; hence, slang for "penis"   117 the service i.e., prostitution   118 detected accused   123 his . . . clack-dish his custom was to put a coin in her wooden beggar's bowl, with its lid that was "clacked" to attract attention. (Lucio hints that the Duke had sex with her.)   127 inward intimate   133 the greater . . . subject most of his subjects   136 unweighing injudicious   137 envy malice   138 helmed steered   139 upon . . . need if a warrant were needed   139–40 give . . . proclamation proclaim him better (than you assert)   140–1 in . . . bringings-forth by his own public actions   141 to the envious even to the malicious   143 unskillfully in ignorance

LUCIO   Sir, my name is Lucio, well known to the Duke.

DUKE   He shall know you better, sir, if I may live to report you.

LUCIO   I fear you not.

DUKE   Oh, you hope the Duke will return no more, or you imagine me too unhurtful an opposite. But indeed 160 I can do you little harm; you'll forswear this again. 161

LUCIO   I'll be hanged first. Thou art deceived in me, Friar. But no more of this. Canst thou tell if Claudio die tomorrow or no?

DUKE   Why should he die, sir?

LUCIO   Why? For filling a bottle with a tundish. I would 166 the Duke we talk of were returned again. This ungen- 167 itured agent will unpeople the province with conti- 168 nency. Sparrows must not build in his house eaves, 169 because they are lecherous. The Duke yet would have dark deeds darkly answered; he would never bring 171 them to light. Would he were returned! Marry, this Claudio is condemned for untrussing. Farewell, good 173 Friar. I prithee, pray for me. The Duke, I say to thee again, would eat mutton on Fridays. He's now past it, 175 yet, and I say to thee, he would mouth with a beggar, 176 though she smelt brown bread and garlic. Say that I 177 said so. Farewell.   *Exit.*

DUKE

No might nor greatness in mortality   179
Can censure scape; back-wounding calumny   180
The whitest virtue strikes. What king so strong   181
Can tie the gall up in the slanderous tongue?
But who comes here?

Enter Escalus, Provost, and [officers with] bawd
[Mistress Overdone].

ESCALUS   Go, away with her to prison.

MISTRESS OVERDONE   Good my lord, be good to me. Your Honor is accounted a merciful man. Good my lord.

ESCALUS   Double and treble admonition, and still forfeit 188 in the same kind! This would make mercy swear and 189 play the tyrant.

PROVOST   A bawd of eleven years' continuance, may it please Your Honor.

MISTRESS OVERDONE   My lord, this is one Lucio's infor- 193 mation against me. Mistress Kate Keepdown was with 194 child by him in the Duke's time; he promised her mar-

riage. His child is a year and a quarter old, come Philip 196 and Jacob. I have kept it myself; and see how he goes 197 about to abuse me!   198

ESCALUS   That fellow is a fellow of much license. Let him be called before us. Away with her to prison! Go to, no more words.   [*Exeunt Officers with Mistress Overdone.*]

Provost, my brother Angelo will not be al- 202 tered; Claudio must die tomorrow. Let him be fur- nished with divines and have all charitable 204 preparation. If my brother wrought by my pity, it 205 should not be so with him.

PROVOST   So please you, this friar hath been with him, and advised him for th'entertainment of death.   208

ESCALUS   Good even, good Father.

DUKE   Bliss and goodness on you!

ESCALUS   Of whence are you?

DUKE

Not of this country, though my chance is now
To use it for my time. I am a brother   213
Of gracious order, late come from the See   214
In special business from His Holiness.

ESCALUS   What news abroad i'th' world?

DUKE   None but that there is so great a fever on good- ness that the dissolution of it must cure it. Novelty is 218 only in request, and, as it is, as dangerous to be aged 219 in any kind of course as it is virtuous to be constant 220 in any undertaking. There is scarce truth enough alive 221 to make societies secure, but security enough to make 222 fellowships accursed. Much upon this riddle runs the 223 wisdom of the world. This news is old enough, yet it is every day's news. I pray you, sir, of what disposi- tion was the Duke?

ESCALUS   One that, above all other strifes, contended 227 especially to know himself.

DUKE   What pleasure was he given to?

ESCALUS   Rather rejoicing to see another merry than merry at anything which professed to make him re- 231 joice—a gentleman of all temperance. But leave we him to his events, with a prayer they may prove pros- 233 perous, and let me desire to know how you find Clau- dio prepared. I am made to understand that you have lent him visitation.   236

---

160 **too . . . opposite** too harmless an adversary.   161 **forswear this again** deny another time what you have said under oath.
166 **tundish** funnel. (Here representing the penis.)   167–8 **ungeni- tured agent** sexless deputy   169 **Sparrows** (Proverbially lecherous birds.)   171 **darkly** secretly   173 **untrussing** undressing. (Specifi- cally, untying the points used to fasten hose to doublet.)   175 **eat . . . Fridays** i.e., frequent loose women in flagrant disregard of the law. (Literally, violate religious observance by eating meat on fast days.) **past it** beyond the age for sex   176 **mouth** kiss   177 **smelt brown bread** smelled of coarse bran bread   179 **mortality** humankind; human life   180–1 **Can . . . strikes** can escape censure; backbiting slander strikes even the purest of virtues.   181 **so** be he never so 188–9 **forfeit . . . kind** guilty of the same offense.   189 **mercy** i.e., even mercy   193–4 **information** accusation

196–7 **Philip and Jacob** the Feast of Saint Philip and Saint James (*Jacobus* in Latin), May 1.   197–8 **goes about** busies himself 202 **brother** i.e., fellow officer of state   204 **divines** clergymen 205 **wrought . . . pity** acted in accord with my impulses of pity 208 **th'entertainment** the reception, acceptance   213 **To . . . time** to dwell here for my present purposes.   214 **the See** Rome   218 **the dissolution . . . cure it** i.e., only by dying can goodness be rid of the disease.   218–19 **is only in request** is the only thing people seek 219–21 **as it . . . undertaking** as things currently stand, (it is) as dan- gerous to be constant in any undertaking as it is virtuous to be thus constant.   221–3 **There . . . accursed** i.e., There is hardly enough integrity extant to establish secure and trusting associations among men, but binding contractual obligations enough to be the curse of friendship. (The Duke thus puns on *security* [1] a sense of trust [2] financial pledge required to borrow money, and on *fellowship* [1] friendship [2] corporations formed for trading ventures.) 223 **upon this riddle** in this riddling fashion   227 **strifes** endeavors 231 **professed** attempted   233 **his events** the outcome of his affairs 236 **lent him visitation** paid him a visit.

DUKE   He professes to have received no sinister measure 237
from his judge, but most willingly humbles himself to
the determination of justice; yet had he framed to him- 239
self, by the instruction of his frailty, many deceiving 240
promises of life, which I, by my good leisure, have
discredited to him, and now is he resolved to die.

ESCALUS   You have paid the heavens your function, and
the prisoner the very debt of your calling. I have la- 244
bored for the poor gentleman to the extremest shore of 245
my modesty, but my brother justice have I found so 246
severe that he hath forced me to tell him he is indeed
Justice.

DUKE   If his own life answer the straitness of his 249
proceeding, it shall become him well; wherein if he
chance to fail, he hath sentenced himself.

ESCALUS   I am going to visit the prisoner. Fare you well.

DUKE   Peace be with you!

                     [Exeunt Escalus and Provost.]

He who the sword of heaven will bear
Should be as holy as severe;
Pattern in himself to know,   256
Grace to stand, and virtue go;   257
More nor less to others paying   258
Than by self-offenses weighing.   259
Shame to him whose cruel striking
Kills for faults of his own liking!
Twice treble shame on Angelo,
To weed my vice and let his grow!   263
Oh, what may man within him hide,
Though angel on the outward side!
How may likeness made in crimes,   266
Making practice on the times,   267
To draw with idle spiders' strings   268
Most ponderous and substantial things!   269
Craft against vice I must apply.
With Angelo tonight shall lie
His old betrothèd but despised;
So disguise shall, by the disguisèd,   273
Pay with falsehood false exacting   274
And perform an old contracting.   *Exit.* 275

4.1

Enter Mariana, and Boy singing.

Song.

BOY

Take, oh, take those lips away,
    That so sweetly were forsworn,
And those eyes, the break of day,
    Lights that do mislead the morn;   4
But my kisses bring again, bring again,   5
Seals of love, but sealed in vain, sealed in vain.   6

Enter Duke [disguised as before].

MARIANA

Break off thy song, and haste thee quick away.
Here comes a man of comfort, whose advice
Hath often stilled my brawling discontent. *[Exit Boy.]* 9
I cry you mercy, sir, and well could wish   10
You had not found me here so musical.
Let me excuse me, and believe me so,
My mirth it much displeased, but pleased my woe. 13

DUKE

'Tis good; though music oft hath such a charm
To make bad good, and good provoke to harm.   15
I pray you, tell me, hath anybody inquired for me here
today? Much upon this time have I promised here 17
to meet.

MARIANA   You have not been inquired after. I have sat
here all day.

Enter Isabella.

DUKE   I do constantly believe you. The time is come 21
even now. I shall crave your forbearance a little. May- 22
be I will call upon you anon, for some advantage to 23
yourself.

MARIANA   I am always bound to you.   *Exit.*

DUKE   Very well met, and welcome.
What is the news from this good deputy?

ISABELLA

He hath a garden circummured with brick,   28
Whose western side is with a vineyard backed;
And to that vineyard is a planchèd gate,   30
That makes his opening with this bigger key.   31

                         [She shows keys.]

---

237 sinister measure unfair treatment meted out to him
239–40 framed to himself formulated in his mind   **240 by . . . frailty**
at the prompting of his natural human weakness   **244 the
prisoner . . . calling** what your calling as a friar obliges you to give
the prisoner, i.e., the comforts of spiritual counsel.   **245–6 shore . . .
modesty** limit of propriety   **249 straitness** strictness   **256–9 Pattern . . . weighing** he must know himself and be a pattern for others
to emulate, with the grace to stand firm and the virtue to guide himself in the straight path, judging and punishing others with neither
more nor less severity than he applies to his own offenses.   **263 my
vice** i.e., vice in everyone except Angelo. (The Duke speaks chorically
on behalf of everyone generally.)   **266–9 How . . . things!** How may
false seeming of a criminal sort, practicing deception on the world,
make weighty and substantial matters seem as illusory and unsubstantial as spider webs!   **273–5 So . . . contracting** so shall disguise,
employed by those in disguise (i.e., Mariana and the Duke himself),
use a kind of (virtuous) falsehood to pay back what was exacted
through deception (by Angelo), and thereby fulfill an old contract.

4.1 Location: The moated grange at Saint Luke's.
4 Lights . . . morn eyes that mislead the morning (the goddess of
dawn, Eos or Aurora) into taking them for the rising sun   **5 again**
back   **6 Seals** confirmations, pledges   **9 brawling** clamorous
10 cry you mercy beg your pardon   **13 My . . . woe** i.e., it suited not a
merry but a melancholy mood.   **15 bad good** i.e., bad seem good,
attractive. (The Duke, echoing Renaissance conceptions of the psychological effects of music, warns that music may soothe melancholy
at times but may also produce unvirtuous effects on the mind.)
17 Much upon Pretty nearly about   **21 constantly** confidently
22 crave . . . little i.e., ask you to withdraw briefly.   **23 anon**
presently   **28 circummured** walled about   **30 planchèd** made of
boards, planks   **31 his** its

This other doth command a little door
Which from the vineyard to the garden leads;
There have I made my promise, upon the 34
Heavy middle of the night, to call upon him.

DUKE
But shall you on your knowledge find this way?

ISABELLA
I have ta'en a due and wary note upon't.
With whispering and most guilty diligence,
In action all of precept, he did show me 39
The way twice o'er.

DUKE   Are there no other tokens
Between you 'greed concerning her observance? 41

ISABELLA
No, none, but only a repair i'th' dark, 42
And that I have possessed him my most stay 43
Can be but brief; for I have made him know
I have a servant comes with me along,
That stays upon me, whose persuasion is 46
I come about my brother.

DUKE   'Tis well borne up. 47
I have not yet made known to Mariana
A word of this.—What, ho, within! Come forth!

Enter Mariana.

I pray you, be acquainted with this maid;
She comes to do you good.

ISABELLA   I do desire the like.

DUKE
Do you persuade yourself that I respect you? 52

MARIANA
Good Friar, I know you do, and have found it. 53

DUKE
Take then this your companion by the hand,
Who hath a story ready for your ear.
I shall attend your leisure. But make haste;
The vaporous night approaches.

MARIANA   Will't please you walk aside?

                                Exit [with Isabella].

DUKE
O place and greatness! Millions of false eyes
Are stuck upon thee. Volumes of report 60
Run with these false and most contrarious quests 61
Upon thy doings; thousand escapes of wit 62
Make thee the father of their idle dream 63
And rack thee in their fancies.

Enter Mariana and Isabella.

                        Welcome. How agreed? 64

ISABELLA
She'll take the enterprise upon her, Father,
If you advise it.

DUKE   It is not my consent, 66
But my entreaty too.

ISABELLA   Little have you to say 67
When you depart from him but, soft and low,
"Remember now my brother."

MARIANA   Fear me not. 69

DUKE
Nor, gentle daughter, fear you not at all.
He is your husband on a precontract; 71
To bring you thus together, 'tis no sin,
Sith that the justice of your title to him 73
Doth flourish the deceit. Come, let us go. 74
Our corn's to reap, for yet our tithe's to sow. *Exeunt.* 75

❧

4.2

Enter Provost and Clown [Pompey].

PROVOST   Come hither, sirrah. Can you cut off a man's head?

POMPEY   If the man be a bachelor, sir, I can; but if he be a married man, he's his wife's head, and I can never 4 cut off a woman's head. 5

PROVOST   Come, sir, leave me your snatches, and yield 6 me a direct answer. Tomorrow morning are to die Claudio and Barnardine. Here is in our prison a com- 8 mon executioner, who in his office lacks a helper. If 9 you will take it on you to assist him, it shall redeem you from your gyves; if not, you shall have your full 11 time of imprisonment and your deliverance with an unpitied whipping, for you have been a notorious bawd.

POMPEY   Sir, I have been an unlawful bawd time out of mind, but yet I will be content to be a lawful hangman. I would be glad to receive some instruction from my fellow partner.

PROVOST   What, ho, Abhorson! Where's Abhorson, there?

Enter Abhorson.

ABHORSON   Do you call, sir?

PROVOST   Sirrah, here's a fellow will help you tomorrow in your execution. If you think it meet, compound 23 with him by the year, and let him abide here with you; if not, use him for the present and dismiss him.

---

34 **upon** during, at   39 **In action . . . precept** i.e., teaching by demonstration   41 **her observance** what she is supposed to do.   42 **repair** act of going or coming to a place   43 **possessed** informed.   **my most stay** my stay at the longest   46 **stays upon** waits for.   **persuasion** belief   47 **borne up** sustained, carried out.   52 **respect you** are concerned for your welfare.   53 **found it** found it to be true.   60 **stuck** fastened   60–2 **Volumes . . . doings** Innumerable rumors follow a false scent and hunt counter in pursuing your activities   62 **escapes** sallies   63 **Make . . . dream** credit you with being the source of their fantasies   64 **rack** stretch as on the rack, distort

66 **not** not only   67 **Little . . . say** Say little   69 **Fear me not** i.e., Don't worry about my carrying out my part.   71 **precontract** legally binding agreement entered into before any church ceremony. (Compare Claudio's and Juliet's *true contract* at 1.2.142.)   73 **Sith that** since   74 **flourish** adorn, make fair   75 **Our corn's . . . sow** We must first sow grain before we can expect to reap a harvest; i.e., we must get started.   **tithe** grain sown for tithe dues; or, an error for "tilth"
4.2 Location: The prison.
4 **he's . . . head** (Compare Ephesians 5:23: "The husband is the head of the wife.")   5 **head** (With wordplay on "maidenhead.")   6 **leave . . . snatches** leave off your quibbles   8–9 **common** public   11 **gyves** fetters, shackles   23 **compound** make an agreement

He cannot plead his estimation with you; he hath 26
been a bawd.

ABHORSON   A bawd, sir? Fie upon him! He will discredit our mystery.   29

PROVOST   Go to, sir, you weigh equally; a feather will
turn the scale.   *Exit.*

POMPEY   Pray, sir, by your good favor—for surely, sir, 32
a good favor you have, but that you have a hanging 33
look—do you call, sir, your occupation a mystery? 34

ABHORSON   Ay, sir, a mystery.

POMPEY   Painting, sir, I have heard say, is a mystery, 36
and your whores, sir, being members of my occupation, using painting, do prove my occupation a
mystery. But what mystery there should be in hanging, if I should be hanged, I cannot imagine.

ABHORSON   Sir, it is a mystery.

POMPEY   Proof?

ABHORSON   Every true man's apparel fits your thief. If it 43
be too little for your thief, your true man thinks it big 44
enough; if it be too big for your thief, your thief thinks 45
it little enough. So every true man's apparel fits your 46
thief.   47

Enter Provost.

PROVOST   Are you agreed?

POMPEY   Sir, I will serve him, for I do find your hangman is a more penitent trade than your bawd: he doth 50
oftener ask forgiveness.   51

PROVOST   You, sirrah, provide your block and your ax
tomorrow four o'clock.

ABHORSON   Come on, bawd. I will instruct thee in my
trade. Follow!

POMPEY   I do desire to learn, sir; and I hope, if you have
occasion to use me for your own turn, you shall find 57
me yare. For truly, sir, for your kindness I owe you a 58
good turn.

PROVOST
Call hither Barnardine and Claudio.
                            Exit [Pompey, with Abhorson].
Th'one has my pity; not a jot the other,
Being a murderer, though he were my brother.

Enter Claudio.

Look, here's the warrant, Claudio, for thy death.
'Tis now dead midnight, and by eight tomorrow
Thou must be made immortal. Where's Barnardine? 65

CLAUDIO
As fast locked up in sleep as guiltless labor   66
When it lies starkly in the traveler's bones.   67
He will not wake.

PROVOST   Who can do good on him?
Well, go, prepare yourself. [*Knocking within.*] But hark,
what noise?
Heaven give your spirits comfort!   [*Exit Claudio.*]
                        [*calling*] By and by.—
I hope it is some pardon or reprieve
For the most gentle Claudio.

        Enter Duke [disguised as before].

                        Welcome, Father.
DUKE
The best and wholesom'st spirits of the night
Envelop you, good Provost! Who called here of late?
PROVOST   None since the curfew rung.
DUKE
Not Isabel?
PROVOST   No.
DUKE   They will, then, ere't be long.
PROVOST   What comfort is for Claudio?
DUKE
There's some in hope.
PROVOST   It is a bitter deputy.
DUKE
Not so, not so. His life is paralleled   79
Even with the stroke and line of his great justice. 80
He doth with holy abstinence subdue
That in himself which he spurs on his power   82
To qualify in others. Were he mealed with that   83
Which he corrects, then were he tyrannous;
But this being so, he's just. [*Knocking within.*] Now
are they come.   [*The Provost goes to the door.*]
This is a gentle provost; seldom when   86
The steelèd jailer is the friend of men.   87
                            [*Knocking within.*]
How now? What noise? That spirit's possessed with
haste
That wounds th'unsisting postern with these strokes. 89
PROVOST [*speaking at the door*]
There he must stay until the officer
Arise to let him in. He is called up.
                            [*He returns to the Duke.*]
DUKE
Have you no countermand for Claudio yet,
But he must die tomorrow?
PROVOST   None, sir, none.
DUKE
As near the dawning, Provost, as it is,

---

26 **plead his estimation** claim any respect on account of his reputation   29 **mystery** craft, occupation.   32 **favor** leave, permission
33 **favor** face   33–4 **hanging look** (1) downcast look (2) look of a
hangman   36 **Painting** (1) Painting of pictures (2) Applying cosmetics   43–7 **Every . . . thief** (Abhorson alludes to the custom of giving
to the hangman the garments of the executed criminal. Whether the
clothes are too little or too big, the hangman has to make do with
what he gets, just as the thief must make do with what he steals.)
44–5 **big enough** i.e., enough of a loss   46 **little enough** little enough
for his efforts.   50–1 **he doth . . . forgiveness** (The executioner per-
functorily asked forgiveness of those whose lives he was about to
take.)   57 **for . . . turn** (1) as a pimp to provide for your sexual needs
(2) as your hangman when it is your turn to be hanged or "turned
off" the ladder   58 **yare** ready, alacritous.   65 **made immortal** i.e.,
executed.

66 **fast** firmly, soundly.   **guiltless labor** (A personification of the
well-earned weariness that tires the innocent laborer.)   67 **starkly**
stiffly.   **traveler's bones** bones of one who travails or labors or journeys.   79–80 **His . . . justice** His life runs parallel and in exact conformity with the stroke of his pen as he carries out justice.   82 **spurs on**
encourages, urges   83 **qualify** mitigate.   **mealed** spotted, stained
86 **seldom when** i.e., it is seldom that   87 **steelèd** hardened
89 **unsisting** unassisting, unresting, or unresisting (?).   **postern**
small door

You shall hear more ere morning.
PROVOST   Happily   95
You something know, yet I believe there comes
No countermand. No such example have we;   97
Besides, upon the very siege of justice   98
Lord Angelo hath to the public ear
Professed the contrary.

Enter a Messenger.

                              This is His Lordship's man.
DUKE
And here comes Claudio's pardon.
MESSENGER [*giving a paper*] My lord hath sent you
this note, and by me this further charge, that you
swerve not from the smallest article of it, neither in
time, matter, or other circumstance. Good morrow;
for, as I take it, it is almost day.
PROVOST   I shall obey him.   [*Exit Messenger.*]
DUKE [*aside*]
This is his pardon, purchased by such sin
For which the pardoner himself is in.   109
Hence hath offense his quick celerity,   110
When it is borne in high authority,   111
When vice makes mercy, mercy's so extended   112
That for the fault's love is th'offender friended.— 113
Now, sir, what news?
PROVOST   I told you. Lord Angelo, belike thinking me 115
remiss in mine office, awakens me with this un- 116
wonted putting-on—methinks strangely, for he hath 117
not used it before.
DUKE   Pray you, let's hear.
PROVOST [*reads*] *the letter* "Whatsoever you may hear
to the contrary, let Claudio be executed by four of
the clock, and in the afternoon Barnardine. For my
better satisfaction, let me have Claudio's head sent 123
me by five. Let this be duly performed, with a
thought that more depends on it than we must yet
deliver. Thus fail not to do your office, as you will 126
answer it at your peril." What say you to this, sir?
DUKE   What is that Barnardine who is to be executed in
th'afternoon?
PROVOST   A Bohemian born, but here nursed up and 131
bred; one that is a prisoner nine years old.   132
DUKE   How came it that the absent Duke had not either
delivered him to his liberty or executed him? I have
heard it was ever his manner to do so.
PROVOST   His friends still wrought reprieves for him;
and indeed his fact, till now in the government of Lord 137
Angelo, came not to an undoubtful proof.
DUKE   It is now apparent?

PROVOST   Most manifest, and not denied by himself.
DUKE   Hath he borne himself penitently in prison? How
seems he to be touched?   142
PROVOST   A man that apprehends death no more dread- 143
fully but as a drunken sleep—careless, reckless, and 144
fearless of what's past, present, or to come; insensible 145
of mortality, and desperately mortal.   146
DUKE   He wants advice.   147
PROVOST   He will hear none. He hath evermore had the 148
liberty of the prison; give him leave to escape hence, 149
he would not. Drunk many times a day, if not many
days entirely drunk. We have very oft awaked him, as
if to carry him to execution, and showed him a
seeming warrant for it; it hath not moved him at all.
DUKE   More of him anon. There is written in your brow,
Provost, honesty and constancy; if I read it not truly,
my ancient skill beguiles me, but, in the boldness of 156
my cunning, I will lay myself in hazard. Claudio, 157
whom here you have warrant to execute, is no greater
forfeit to the law than Angelo who hath sentenced him.
To make you understand this in a manifested effect, I 160
crave but four days' respite, for the which you are to
do me both a present and a dangerous courtesy.   162
PROVOST   Pray, sir, in what?
DUKE   In the delaying death.
PROVOST   Alack, how may I do it, having the hour
limited, and an express command, under penalty, to 166
deliver his head in the view of Angelo? I may make
my case as Claudio's, to cross this in the smallest.
DUKE   By the vow of mine order I warrant you, if my
instructions may be your guide. Let this Barnardine
be this morning executed, and his head borne to
Angelo.
PROVOST   Angelo hath seen them both and will discover 173
the favor.   174
DUKE   Oh, death's a great disguiser, and you may add to
it. Shave the head, and tie the beard, and say it was 176
the desire of the penitent to be so bared before his
death. You know the course is common. If anything 178
fall to you upon this more than thanks and good 179
fortune, by the saint whom I profess, I will plead 180
against it with my life.
PROVOST   Pardon me, good Father, it is against my oath.
DUKE   Were you sworn to the Duke or to the deputy?
PROVOST   To him, and to his substitutes.
DUKE   You will think you have made no offense if the
Duke avouch the justice of your dealing?   186
PROVOST   But what likelihood is in that?
DUKE   Not a resemblance, but a certainty. Yet since I see
you fearful, that neither my coat, integrity, nor

---

95 Happily Haply, perhaps   **97 example** precedent   **98 siege** seat
109 in engaged.   **110–11 Hence . . . authority** Hence it is that criminal
behavior in high places has its (*his*) own quick way of covering its
tracks.   **112–13 When . . . friended** When criminality acts to save a
life, as in this case, mercy is so strangely broadened in definition that
the offender (here, Claudio) is spared for the fault committed by the
person in authority.   **115 belike** perchance   **116–17 unwonted
putting-on** unaccustomed urging   **123 better satisfaction** greater
assurance   **126 deliver** make known.   **131 here** i.e., in Vienna
132 a prisoner . . . old nine years a prisoner.   **137 fact** crime

142 touched affected, touched by remorse.   **143–4 no more dreadfully but** with no more dread than   **145–6 insensible . . . mortal**
incapable of comprehending the meaning of death, and incorrigible.
147 wants advice needs spiritual counsel.   **148 evermore** constantly
148–9 the liberty . . . prison freedom to go anywhere within the
prison   **156–7 in the . . . hazard** confident in my knowledge (of
human character), I will put myself at risk.   **160 in . . . effect** by
means of concrete proof   **162 present** immediate   **166 limited** fixed,
set   **173–4 discover the favor** recognize the face.   **176 tie** tie up, tidy
up   **178 course** practice   **179 fall** to befall   **180 the saint . . . profess**
i.e., St. Benedict, whose example I follow   **186 avouch** confirm

persuasion can with ease attempt you, I will go further 190
than I meant, to pluck all fears out of you. Look you,
sir, here is the hand and seal of the Duke. [*He shows a
letter.*] You know the character, I doubt not, and the 193
signet is not strange to you. 194

PROVOST   I know them both.

DUKE   The contents of this is the return of the Duke.
You shall anon overread it at your pleasure, where
you shall find within these two days he will be here.
This is a thing that Angelo knows not, for he this very
day receives letters of strange tenor, perchance of the
Duke's death, perchance entering into some monas- 201
tery, but by chance nothing of what is writ. Look, th'un- 202
folding star calls up the shepherd. Put not yourself 203
into amazement how these things should be; all difficulties are but easy when they are known. Call your
executioner, and off with Barnardine's head. I will
give him a present shrift and advise him for a better 207
place. Yet you are amazed, but this shall absolutely 208
resolve you. Come away; it is almost clear dawn. 209

Exit [*with Provost*].

❧

4.3

Enter Clown [*Pompey*].

POMPEY   I am as well acquainted here as I was in our 1
house of profession. One would think it were Mistress
Overdone's own house, for here be many of her old
customers. First, here's young Master Rash; he's in for 4
a commodity of brown paper and old ginger, nine- 5
score and seventeen pounds, of which he made five 6
marks, ready money. Marry, then ginger was not 7
much in request, for the old women were all dead. 8
Then is there here one Master Caper, at the suit of 9
Master Three-pile the mercer, for some four suits of 10
peach-colored satin, which now peaches him a beggar. 11
Then have we here young Dizzy, and young 12
Master Deep-vow, and Master Copper-spur, and 13

Master Starve-lackey the rapier and dagger man, and 14
young Drop-heir that killed lusty Pudding, and Mas- 15
ter Forthlight the tilter, and brave Master Shoe-tie the 16
great traveler, and wild Half-can that stabbed Pots, 17
and I think forty more, all great doers in our trade, and
are now "for the Lord's sake." 19

Enter Abhorson.

ABHORSON   Sirrah, bring Barnardine hither.

POMPEY   [*calling*] Master Barnardine! You must rise and 21
be hanged, Master Barnardine! 22

ABHORSON   What, ho, Barnardine!

BARNARDINE   (*within*)   A pox o' your throats! Who
makes that noise there? What are you?

POMPEY   Your friends, sir, the hangman. You must be
so good, sir, to rise and be put to death.

BARNARDINE   [*within*]   Away, you rogue, away! I am
sleepy.

ABHORSON   Tell him he must awake, and that quickly,
too.

POMPEY   Pray, Master Barnardine, awake till you are executed, and sleep afterwards.

ABHORSON   Go in to him, and fetch him out.

POMPEY   He is coming, sir, he is coming. I hear his
straw rustle.

Enter Barnardine.

ABHORSON   Is the ax upon the block, sirrah?

POMPEY   Very ready, sir.

BARNARDINE   How now, Abhorson? What's the news
with you?

ABHORSON   Truly, sir, I would desire you to clap into 41
your prayers; for, look you, the warrant's come.

BARNARDINE   You rogue, I have been drinking all night.
I am not fitted for't.

POMPEY   Oh, the better, sir, for he that drinks all night
and is hanged betimes in the morning may sleep the 46
sounder all the next day.

Enter Duke [*disguised as before*].

ABHORSON   Look you, sir, here comes your ghostly 48
father. Do we jest now, think you?

DUKE   Sir, induced by my charity, and hearing how
hastily you are to depart, I am come to advise you,
comfort you, and pray with you.

BARNARDINE   Friar, not I. I have been drinking hard all
night, and I will have more time to prepare me, or

190 **attempt** win, tempt   193 **character** handwriting   194 **strange**
unknown   201 **entering** of his entering   202 **writ** i.e., written here.
202-3 **unfolding star** i.e., morning star, Venus, which bids the shepherd lead his sheep from the fold   207 **present shrift** immediate
absolution for sins (after confession)   207–8 **advise . . . place** counsel
him on the comforts of heaven.   208 **Yet** Still   209 **resolve you** dispel
your uncertainties.
4.3 Location: The prison.
1 **well** widely   4 **Rash** (All the names mentioned by Pompey apparently glance at contemporary social affectations and defects. *Rash*
means "reckless.")   5–8 **a commodity . . . dead** (To circumvent the
laws against excessive rates of interest, moneylenders often advanced
cheap commodities to gullible borrowers in lieu of cash. Master Rash,
having agreed to a valuation of 197 pounds for such merchandise,
has been able to resell it for only five marks, each mark worth about
two-thirds of a pound, and has been thrown into prison for debt. The
ginger has not fetched a good price, owing to lack of customers, since
the old women who are proverbially fond of ginger are no longer
alive.)   9 **Caper** (To *caper* was to dance or leap gracefully.)
10 **Three-pile** the thickest nap and most expensive grade of velvet.
mercer cloth merchant.   **suits** (With a play on *suit*, line 9.)
11 **peaches him** denounces him as. (With a play on *peach*.)   12 **Dizzy**
i.e., giddy, foolish   13 **Deep-vow** one who swears earnestly and
often.   **Copper-spur** (Copper was often used fraudulently to simu-
late gold.)

14 **Starve-lackey** (Spendthrift gallants often virtually starved their
pages.)   15 **Drop-heir** (Perhaps referring to those who disinherited
or preyed on unsuspecting heirs; or else *Drop-hair*, losing hair from
syphilis.)   **lusty** vigorous.   **Pudding** i.e., sausage   16 **Forthlight**
(Unexplained; perhaps an error for *Forthright*, referring to a style of
tilting.)   **tilter** jouster.   **brave** showy, splendidly dressed.   **Shoe-tie**
(Evidently a nickname for travelers and others who affected the foreign fashion of elaborate rosettes on the tie of the shoe.)   17 **Half-can**
i.e., a small drinking tankard.   **Pots** i.e., ale pots   19 **"for . . . sake"**
(The cry of prisoners from jail grates to passers-by to give them food
or alms.)   22 **be hanged** (With a play on the imprecation; compare
"go to the devil.")   41 **clap into** quickly begin   46 **betimes** early
48 **ghostly** spiritual

they shall beat out my brains with billets. I will not 55
consent to die this day, that's certain.
DUKE
  Oh, sir, you must, and therefore I beseech you
  Look forward on the journey you shall go.
BARNARDINE I swear I will not die today for any man's
persuasion.
DUKE But hear you—
BARNARDINE Not a word. If you have anything to say
to me, come to my ward, for thence will not I today. 63
                                                         Exit.

        Enter Provost.

DUKE
  Unfit to live or die. Oh, gravel heart! 64
  After him, fellows. Bring him to the block.
                    [*Exeunt Abhorson and Pompey.*]
PROVOST
  Now, sir, how do you find the prisoner?
DUKE
  A creature unprepared, unmeet for death; 67
  And to transport him in the mind he is 68
  Were damnable.
PROVOST   Here in the prison, Father,
  There died this morning of a cruel fever
  One Ragozine, a most notorious pirate,
  A man of Claudio's years, his beard and head
  Just of his color. What if we do omit 73
  This reprobate till he were well inclined,
  And satisfy the deputy with the visage
  Of Ragozine, more like to Claudio?
DUKE
  Oh, 'tis an accident that heaven provides!
  Dispatch it presently; the hour draws on 78
  Prefixed by Angelo. See this be done, 79
  And sent according to command, whiles I
  Persuade this rude wretch willingly to die. 81
PROVOST
  This shall be done, good Father, presently.
  But Barnardine must die this afternoon.
  And how shall we continue Claudio, 84
  To save me from the danger that might come
  If he were known alive?
DUKE   Let this be done:
  Put them in secret holds, both Barnardine and
    Claudio. 87
  Ere twice the sun hath made his journal greeting 88
  To yond generation, you shall find 89
  Your safety manifested.
PROVOST I am your free dependent. 91

DUKE
  Quick, dispatch, and send the head to Angelo.
                                 Exit [*Provost*].
  Now will I write letters to Varrius— 93
  The Provost, he shall bear them—whose contents
  Shall witness to him I am near at home,
  And that, by great injunctions, I am bound 96
  To enter publicly. Him I'll desire
  To meet me at the consecrated fount 98
  A league below the city; and from thence, 99
  By cold gradation and well-balanced form, 100
  We shall proceed with Angelo.

        Enter Provost [*with Ragozine's head*].

PROVOST
  Here is the head. I'll carry it myself.
DUKE
  Convenient is it. Make a swift return, 103
  For I would commune with you of such things 104
  That want no ear but yours.
PROVOST   I'll make all speed. *Exit.* 105
ISABELLA (*within*) Peace, ho, be here!
DUKE
  The tongue of Isabel. She's come to know
  If yet her brother's pardon be come hither.
  But I will keep her ignorant of her good,
  To make her heavenly comforts of despair 110
  When it is least expected.

        Enter Isabella.

ISABELLA   Ho, by your leave!
DUKE
  Good morning to you, fair and gracious daughter.
ISABELLA
  The better, given me by so holy a man.
  Hath yet the deputy sent my brother's pardon?
DUKE
  He hath released him, Isabel, from the world.
  His head is off and sent to Angelo.
ISABELLA
  Nay, but it is not so!
DUKE   It is no other.
  Show your wisdom, daughter, in your close patience. 118
ISABELLA
  Oh, I will to him and pluck out his eyes!
DUKE
  You shall not be admitted to his sight.
ISABELLA
  Unhappy Claudio! Wretched Isabel!
  Injurious world! Most damnèd Angelo!

---

55 billets cudgels, blocks of wood. **63 ward** cell **64 gravel** stony
67 unmeet unready, unfit **68 transport him** i.e., send him to his
doom. **he is** he is in **73 omit** ignore, overlook **78 presently**
immediately. (As also in line 82.) **79 Prefixed** appointed beforehand,
stipulated **81 rude** uncivilized **84 continue** preserve
87 holds cells, dungeons **88 journal** daily **89 yond** i.e., beyond
these walls, outside the perpetually dark prison (?). Sometimes it is
emended to *th' under*, the people of the Antipodes, on the opposite
side of the earth, or, people under the sun, the human race. **91 free
dependent** willing servant.

93 to Varrius (The Folio reads "to Angelo," but see line 99 below and
4.5.12–14; evidently, the Duke's plan is to meet Varrius "a league
below the city" and then proceed to the rendezvous with Angelo.)
96 by great injunctions by powerful precedent or for compelling reasons **98 fount** spring **99 league** (A measure of varying length but
usually about three miles.) **100 cold . . . form** i.e., moving deliberately and with proper observance of all formalities **103 Convenient**
Timely, fitting **104 commune** converse **105 want** require **110 of**
from, transformed out of **118 close patience** silent enduring.

DUKE

This nor hurts him nor profits you a jot.   123
Forbear it therefore; give your cause to heaven.
Mark what I say, which you shall find
By every syllable a faithful verity.   126
The Duke comes home tomorrow. Nay, dry your eyes;
One of our convent, and his confessor,
Gives me this instance. Already he hath carried   129
Notice to Escalus and Angelo,
Who do prepare to meet him at the gates,
There to give up their pow'r. If you can, pace your
　　wisdom   132
In that good path that I would wish it go,
And you shall have your bosom on this wretch,   134
Grace of the Duke, revenges to your heart,   135
And general honor.

ISABELLA　　　　　　I am directed by you.

DUKE

This letter, then, to Friar Peter give.
　　　　　　　　　　　　[*He gives her a letter.*]
'Tis that he sent me of the Duke's return.   138
Say, by this token, I desire his company
At Mariana's house tonight. Her cause and yours
I'll perfect him withal, and he shall bring you   141
Before the Duke, and to the head of Angelo   142
Accuse him home and home. For my poor self,   143
I am combinèd by a sacred vow,   144
And shall be absent. Wend you with this letter.
Command these fretting waters from your eyes   146
With a light heart. Trust not my holy order
If I pervert your course. Who's here?

Enter Lucio.

LUCIO　Good even. Friar, where's the Provost?

DUKE　Not within, sir.

LUCIO　Oh, pretty Isabella, I am pale at mine heart to see 151
thine eyes so red. Thou must be patient. I am fain to   152
dine and sup with water and bran; I dare not for my   153
head fill my belly; one fruitful meal would set me   154
to't. But they say the Duke will be here tomorrow.   155
By my troth, Isabel, I loved thy brother. If the old fantastical Duke of dark corners had been at home, he
had lived.　　　　　　　　　　　　[*Exit Isabella.*]

DUKE　Sir, the Duke is marvelous little beholding to   159
your reports; but the best is, he lives not in them.   160

LUCIO　Friar, thou knowest not the Duke so well as I
do. He's a better woodman than thou tak'st him for.   162

DUKE　Well, you'll answer this one day. Fare ye well.
　　　　　　　　　　　　　　　[*He starts to go.*]

LUCIO　Nay, tarry, I'll go along with thee. I can tell thee
pretty tales of the Duke.

DUKE　You have told me too many of him already, sir, if
they be true; if not true, none were enough.

LUCIO　I was once before him for getting a wench with
child.

DUKE　Did you such a thing?

LUCIO　Yes, marry, did I, but I was fain to forswear it.
They would else have married me to the rotten medlar.   172

DUKE　Sir, your company is fairer than honest. Rest you
well.

LUCIO　By my troth, I'll go with thee to the lane's end.
If bawdy talk offend you, we'll have very little of it.
Nay, Friar, I am a kind of burr; I shall stick.　　*Exeunt.*

4.4

Enter Angelo and Escalus, [reading letters].

ESCALUS　Every letter he hath writ hath disvouched   1
other.

ANGELO　In most uneven and distracted manner. His
actions show much like to madness. Pray heaven his
wisdom be not tainted! And why meet him at the   5
gates and redeliver our authorities there?

ESCALUS　I guess not.   7

ANGELO　And why should we proclaim it in an hour be-   8
fore his entering, that if any crave redress of injustice,
they should exhibit their petitions in the street?   10

ESCALUS　He shows his reason for that: to have a
dispatch of complaints, and to deliver us from devices   12
hereafter, which shall then have no power to stand
against us.

ANGELO　Well, I beseech you, let it be proclaimed.
Betimes i'th' morn I'll call you at your house. Give   16
notice to such men of sort and suit as are to meet him. 17

ESCALUS　I shall, sir. Fare you well.

ANGELO　Good night.　　　　　　　*Exit [Escalus].*
This deed unshapes me quite, makes me unpregnant   20
And dull to all proceedings. A deflowered maid,
And by an eminent body that enforced   22
The law against it! But that her tender shame   23
Will not proclaim against her maiden loss,
How might she tongue me! Yet reason dares her no,   25
For my authority bears of a credent bulk   26
That no particular scandal once can touch
But it confounds the breather. He should have lived,   28

123 nor hurts neither hurts　**126 By** with respect to　**129 instance**
proof.　**132 pace** teach to move in response to your will, as with a
horse　**134 bosom** heart's desire　**135 Grace of** manifestation of
favor from.　**to your heart** to your heart's content　**138 that** that
which.　**of** concerning　**141 perfect** acquaint completely.　**withal**
with　**142 head** i.e., face　**143 home and home** thoroughly.
144 combinèd bound　**146 fretting** corroding　**151 pale . . . heart** i.e.,
pale from sighing (since sighs cost the heart loss of blood)　**152 fain**
compelled. (As also in line 171.)　**153–4 for my head** i.e., on my life
154 fruitful abundant　**154–5 set me to't** i.e., awaken my lust and
thus place me in danger of Angelo's edict.　**159 marvelous** marvelously.　**beholding** beholden　**160 he . . . them** i.e., he is not accurately described by them.　**162 woodman** i.e., hunter (of women)

172 medlar a fruit that was eaten after it had begun to rot; here, signifying a prostitute.　**4.4. Location: In Vienna.**
1 disvouched contradicted　**5 tainted** diseased.　**7 guess not** cannot
guess.　**8 in an hour** i.e., a full hour　**10 exhibit** present
12 dispatch prompt settlement.　**devices** contrived complaints
16 Betimes Early　**17 men . . . suit** men of rank with a retinue
20 unpregnant unapt　**22 body** person　**23 But that** Were it not that
25 tongue i.e., reproach, accuse.　**dares her no** i.e., frightens her to
say nothing　**26 bears . . . bulk** bears such a huge credibility　**28 But
. . . breather** without its confuting the person who speaks.

Save that his riotous youth, with dangerous sense,   29
Might in the times to come have ta'en revenge
By so receiving a dishonored life   31
With ransom of such shame. Would yet he had lived!
Alack, when once our grace we have forgot,
Nothing goes right; we would, and we would not.

Exit.

❧

4.5

Enter Duke [in his own habit] and Friar Peter.

DUKE
These letters at fit time deliver me.   [*Giving letters.*]   1
The Provost knows our purpose and our plot.
The matter being afoot, keep your instruction,   3
And hold you ever to our special drift,   4
Though sometimes you do blench from this to that   5
As cause doth minister. Go call at Flavius' house,   6
And tell him where I stay. Give the like notice
To Valencius, Rowland, and to Crassus,
And bid them bring the trumpets to the gate;   9
But send me Flavius first.
FRIAR PETER   It shall be speeded well.   [*Exit.*]   11

Enter Varrius.

DUKE
I thank thee, Varrius. Thou hast made good haste.
Come, we will walk. There's other of our friends
Will greet us here anon. My gentle Varrius!   *Exeunt.*

❧

4.6

Enter Isabella and Mariana.

ISABELLA
To speak so indirectly I am loath.
I would say the truth, but to accuse him so,
That is your part. Yet I am advised to do it,
He says, to veil full purpose.
MARIANA   Be ruled by him.
ISABELLA
Besides, he tells me that if peradventure   5
He speak against me on the adverse side,
I should not think it strange, for 'tis a physic   7
That's bitter to sweet end.

Enter [Friar] Peter.

MARIANA
I would Friar Peter—
ISABELLA   Oh, peace, the Friar is come.

FRIAR PETER
Come, I have found you out a stand most fit,   10
Where you may have such vantage on the Duke
He shall not pass you. Twice have the trumpets
    sounded.
The generous and gravest citizens   13
Have hent the gates, and very near upon   14
The Duke is entering. Therefore hence, away!

Exeunt.

❧

5.1

*Enter Duke, Varrius, lords, Angelo, Escalus,
Lucio, [Provost, officers, and] citizens at several
doors.*

DUKE
My very worthy cousin, fairly met!   1
Our old and faithful friend, we are glad to see you.   2
ANGELO, ESCALUS
Happy return be to Your Royal Grace!
DUKE
Many and hearty thankings to you both.
We have made inquiry of you, and we hear
Such goodness of your justice that our soul
Cannot but yield you forth to public thanks,   7
Forerunning more requital.   8
ANGELO   You make my bonds still greater.   9
DUKE
Oh, your desert speaks loud, and I should wrong it
To lock it in the wards of covert bosom,   11
When it deserves with characters of brass   12
A forted residence 'gainst the tooth of time   13
And razure of oblivion. Give me your hand,   14
And let the subject see, to make them know   15
That outward courtesies would fain proclaim   16
Favors that keep within. Come, Escalus,   17
You must walk by us on our other hand,
And good supporters are you.

Enter [Friar] Peter and Isabella.

FRIAR PETER [*to Isabella*]
Now is your time. Speak loud, and kneel before him.
ISABELLA [*kneeling*]
Justice, O royal Duke! Vail your regard   21
Upon a wronged—I would fain have said a maid.
O worthy prince, dishonor not your eye
By throwing it on any other object
Till you have heard me in my true complaint
And given me justice, justice, justice, justice!

---

29 **sense** passion, intention   31 **By** for, because of
4.5. Location: Outside the city.
1 **me** for me   3 **keep** keep to   4 **drift** plot   5 **blench . . . that** swerve
from one expedient to another   6 **minister** prompt, provide occasion.
9 **trumpets** trumpeters   11 **speeded** accomplished, expedited
4.6. Location: Near the city gate.
5 **peradventure** perhaps   7 **physic** remedy

10 **stand** place to stand   13 **generous** highborn   14 **hent** reached,
occupied.   **very near upon** almost immediately now
5.1 Location: The city gate.
0.2 *several* separate   1 **cousin** fellow nobleman. (Addressed to
Angelo.)   2 **friend** i.e., Escalus   7 **yield . . . to** call you forth to give
you   8 **more requital** further reward.   9 **bonds** obligations   11 **To
lock . . . bosom** i.e., to keep it locked up in my heart   12 **characters**
writing, letters   13 **forted** fortified   14 **razure** effacement   15 **the
subject** those who are subjects   16–17 **That . . . within** that public
ceremonies serve as outward manifestations of the approval my heart
feels for you.   21 **Vail your regard** Look down

DUKE
Relate your wrongs. In what? By whom? Be brief.
Here is Lord Angelo shall give you justice.   28
Reveal yourself to him.

ISABELLA   O worthy Duke,
You bid me seek redemption of the devil.
Hear me yourself; for that which I must speak
Must either punish me, not being believed,   32
Or wring redress from you.
Hear me, oh, hear me, hear!

ANGELO
My lord, her wits, I fear me, are not firm.
She hath been a suitor to me for her brother
Cut off by course of justice.

ISABELLA [standing]   By course of justice!

ANGELO
And she will speak most bitterly and strange.   38

ISABELLA
Most strange, but yet most truly, will I speak.
That Angelo's forsworn, is it not strange?
That Angelo's a murderer, is 't not strange?
That Angelo is an adulterous thief,
An hypocrite, a virgin-violator,
Is it not strange, and strange?

DUKE   Nay, it is ten times strange.

ISABELLA
It is not truer he is Angelo
Than this is all as true as it is strange.   47
Nay, it is ten times true, for truth is truth
To th'end of reck'ning.

DUKE   Away with her! Poor soul,   49
She speaks this in th'infirmity of sense.   50

ISABELLA
O prince, I conjure thee, as thou believ'st
There is another comfort than this world,
That thou neglect me not with that opinion   53
That I am touched with madness. Make not
    impossible   54
That which but seems unlike. 'Tis not impossible   55
But one, the wicked'st caitiff on the ground,   56
May seem as shy, as grave, as just, as absolute   57
As Angelo; even so may Angelo,
In all his dressings, characts, titles, forms,   59
Be an archvillain. Believe it, royal prince,
If he be less, he's nothing; but he's more,   61
Had I more name for badness.

DUKE   By mine honesty,
If she be mad—as I believe no other—
Her madness hath the oddest frame of sense,   64
Such a dependency of thing on thing,   65

As e'er I heard in madness.

ISABELLA   O gracious Duke,
Harp not on that, nor do not banish reason   67
For inequality, but let your reason serve   68
To make the truth appear where it seems hid,
And hide the false seems true.   70

DUKE   Many that are not mad
Have, sure, more lack of reason. What would
    you say?

ISABELLA
I am the sister of one Claudio,
Condemned upon the act of fornication
To lose his head, condemned by Angelo.
I, in probation of a sisterhood,   76
Was sent to by my brother; one Lucio
As then the messenger—

LUCIO   That's I, an't like Your Grace.   78
I came to her from Claudio and desired her
To try her gracious fortune with Lord Angelo
For her poor brother's pardon.

ISABELLA   That's he indeed.

DUKE [to Lucio]
You were not bid to speak.

LUCIO   No, my good lord,
Nor wished to hold my peace.

DUKE   I wish you now, then.
Pray you, take note of it. And when you have
A business for yourself, pray heaven you then
Be perfect.   86

LUCIO   I warrant Your Honor.   87

DUKE
The warrant's for yourself. Take heed to 't.

ISABELLA
This gentleman told somewhat of my tale—

LUCIO   Right.

DUKE
It may be right, but you are i'the wrong
To speak before your time.—Proceed.

ISABELLA   I went
To this pernicious caitiff deputy—

DUKE
That's somewhat madly spoken.

ISABELLA   Pardon it;
The phrase is to the matter.   95

DUKE   Mended again. The matter; proceed.   96

ISABELLA
In brief, to set the needless process by,   97
How I persuaded, how I prayed and kneeled,
How he refelled me, and how I replied—   99
For this was of much length—the vile conclusion

I now begin with grief and shame to utter.
He would not, but by gift of my chaste body
To his concupiscible intemperate lust,   103
Release my brother; and after much debatement   104
My sisterly remorse confutes mine honor,   105
And I did yield to him. But the next morn betimes,   106
His purpose surfeiting, he sends a warrant   107
For my poor brother's head.

DUKE   This is most likely!

ISABELLA
Oh, that it were as like as it is true!   109

DUKE
By heaven, fond wretch, thou know'st not what thou
    speak'st,   110
Or else thou art suborned against his honor   111
In hateful practice. First, his integrity   112
Stands without blemish. Next, it imports no reason   113
That with such vehemency he should pursue
Faults proper to himself. If he had so offended,   115
He would have weighed thy brother by himself   116
And not have cut him off. Someone hath set you on.
Confess the truth, and say by whose advice
Thou cam'st here to complain.

ISABELLA   And is this all?
Then, O you blessèd ministers above,
Keep me in patience, and with ripened time
Unfold the evil which is here wrapped up   122
In countenance! Heaven shield Your Grace from woe,   123
As I thus wrongèd hence unbelievèd go!
                              [She starts to leave.]

DUKE
I know you'd fain be gone.—An officer!
To prison with her. Shall we thus permit
A blasting and a scandalous breath to fall   127
On him so near us? This needs must be a practice.
Who knew of your intent and coming hither?

ISABELLA
One that I would were here, Friar Lodowick.

DUKE
A ghostly father, belike. Who knows that Lodowick?   131

LUCIO
My lord, I know him; 'tis a meddling friar.
I do not like the man. Had he been lay, my lord,   133
For certain words he spake against Your Grace
In your retirement, I had swinged him soundly.   135

DUKE
Words against me? This' a good friar, belike!   136
And to set on this wretched woman here

Against our substitute! Let this friar be found.
                    [Exit one or more attendants.]

LUCIO
But yesternight, my lord, she and that friar,
I saw them at the prison. A saucy friar,
A very scurvy fellow.

FRIAR PETER   Blessed be Your Royal Grace!
I have stood by, my lord, and I have heard
Your royal ear abused. First, hath this woman
Most wrongfully accused your substitute,
Who is as free from touch or soil with her
As she from one ungot.   147

DUKE   We did believe no less.
Know you that Friar Lodowick that she speaks of?

FRIAR PETER
I know him for a man divine and holy,
Not scurvy, nor a temporary meddler,   151
As he's reported by this gentleman;
And, on my trust, a man that never yet
Did, as he vouches, misreport Your Grace.

LUCIO
My lord, most villainously, believe it.

FRIAR PETER
Well, he in time may come to clear himself;
But at this instant he is sick, my lord,
Of a strange fever. Upon his mere request,   158
Being come to knowledge that there was complaint   159
Intended 'gainst Lord Angelo, came I hither,
To speak, as from his mouth, what he doth know
Is true and false, and what he with his oath
And all probation will make up full clear,   163
Whensoever he's convented. First, for this woman,   164
To justify this worthy nobleman,
So vulgarly and personally accused,   166
Her shall you hear disprovèd to her eyes,   167
Till she herself confess it.   [Exit Isabella, guarded.]

DUKE   Good Friar, let's hear it.
                [Friar Peter goes to bring in Mariana.]
Do you not smile at this, Lord Angelo?
Oh, heaven, the vanity of wretched fools!   170
Give us some seats.   [Seats are provided.]
                        Come, cousin Angelo,
In this I'll be impartial. Be you judge
Of your own cause.   [The Duke and Angelo sit.]

        Enter Mariana, [veiled, with Friar Peter].

                          Is this the witness, Friar?
First, let her show her face, and after speak.

MARIANA
Pardon, my lord, I will not show my face
Until my husband bid me.

---

103 **concupiscible** lustful 104 **debatement** argument, debate
105 **remorse** pity. **confutes** confounds, silences 106 **betimes** early
107 **surfeiting** being satiated 109 **like** likely 110 **fond** foolish
111 **suborned** induced to give false testimony 112 **practice** machination, conspiracy. 113 **imports no reason** i.e., makes no sense
115 **proper to himself** of which he himself is guilty. 116 **weighed**
judged 122 **Unfold** disclose 122–3 **wrapped . . . countenance** concealed by the privilege of authority. 127 **blasting** blighting 131 **A
ghostly . . . belike** A cleric, apparently. 133 **lay** not a cleric 135 **In
your retirement** during your absence. **had swinged** would have
beaten 136 **This'** This is

147 **ungot** unbegotten. 151 **temporary meddler** meddler in temporal
affairs. 158 **Upon . . . request** Solely at his request 159 **Being . . .
knowledge** he having learned 163 **probation** proof 164 **convented**
summoned. 166 **vulgarly** publicly 167 **to her eyes** i.e., to her face
168 s.d. **Exit Isbella, guarded** (Isabella seemingly must leave the stage
here or soon afterwards. She is described as "gone" at line 250, and is
summoned at line 278. The phrase "to her eyes" in line 167 may mean
"incontrovertibly.") 170 **vanity** folly

DUKE   What, are you married?

MARIANA   No, my lord.

DUKE   Are you a maid?

MARIANA   No, my lord.

DUKE   A widow, then?

MARIANA   Neither, my lord.

DUKE   Why, you are nothing then, neither maid, widow, nor wife?

LUCIO   My lord, she may be a punk, for many of them   185
are neither maid, widow, nor wife.

DUKE
Silence that fellow. I would he had some cause
To prattle for himself.   188

LUCIO   Well, my lord.

MARIANA
My lord, I do confess I ne'er was married,
And I confess besides I am no maid.
I have known my husband, yet my husband   192
Knows not that ever he knew me.

LUCIO   He was drunk then, my lord; it can be no better.

DUKE   For the benefit of silence, would thou wert so too!

LUCIO   Well, my lord.

DUKE
This is no witness for Lord Angelo.

MARIANA   Now I come to 't, my lord.
She that accuses him of fornication
In selfsame manner doth accuse my husband,
And charges him, my lord, with such a time   201
When, I'll depose, I had him in mine arms   202
With all th'effect of love.   203

ANGELO   Charges she more than me?   204

MARIANA   Not that I know.

DUKE   No? You say your husband?

MARIANA
Why, just, my lord, and that is Angelo,   207
Who thinks he knows that he ne'er knew my body,
But knows he thinks that he knows Isabel's.

ANGELO
This is a strange abuse. Let's see thy face.   210

MARIANA
My husband bids me. Now I will unmask.
                                        [She unveils.]
This is that face, thou cruel Angelo,
Which once thou swor'st was worth the looking on;
This is the hand which, with a vowed contract,
Was fast belocked in thine; this is the body   215
That took away the match from Isabel,   216
And did supply thee at thy garden house
In her imagined person.

DUKE [to Angelo]   Know you this woman?

LUCIO   Carnally, she says.

DUKE   Sirrah, no more!

LUCIO   Enough, my lord.

ANGELO
My lord, I must confess I know this woman,
And five years since there was some speech of
    marriage
Betwixt myself and her, which was broke off,
Partly for that her promisèd proportions   226
Came short of composition, but in chief   227
For that her reputation was disvalued   228
In levity. Since which time of five years   229
I never spake with her, saw her, nor heard from her,
Upon my faith and honor.

MARIANA [kneeling]   Noble prince,
As there comes light from heaven and words from
    breath,
As there is sense in truth and truth in virtue,
I am affianced this man's wife as strongly
As words could make up vows; and, my good lord,
But Tuesday night last gone in's garden house
He knew me as a wife. As this is true,
Let me in safety raise me from my knees,
Or else forever be confixèd here,   239
A marble monument!

ANGELO   I did but smile till now.
Now, good my lord, give me the scope of justice. 242
My patience here is touched. I do perceive   243
These poor informal women are no more   244
But instruments of some more mightier member   245
That sets them on. Let me have way, my lord,
To find this practice out.

DUKE   Ay, with my heart,
And punish them to your height of pleasure.—
Thou foolish friar, and thou pernicious woman,
Compact with her that's gone, think'st thou thy oaths, 250
Though they would swear down each particular saint, 251
Were testimonies against his worth and credit
That's sealed in approbation?—You, Lord Escalus,   253
Sit with my cousin; lend him your kind pains
To find out this abuse, whence 'tis derived.
There is another friar that set them on;
Let him be sent for.
                    [The Duke rises; Escalus takes his chair.]

FRIAR PETER
Would he were here, my lord! For he indeed
Hath set the women on to this complaint.
Your Provost knows the place where he abides,
And he may fetch him.

DUKE   Go do it instantly.
                                        [Exit Provost.]
And you, my noble and well-warranted cousin,
Whom it concerns to hear this matter forth,   263
Do with your injuries as seems you best,   264

---

185 punk harlot   188 To . . . himself to speak in his own defense. (The Duke hints that there might well be charges pending against Lucio.)   192 known had sexual intercourse with   201 with . . . time with doing the deed at just the same time   202 depose testify under oath   203 With . . . love i.e., with sexual fulfillment.   204 Charges . . . me? Does she (Isabella) bring charges against persons besides myself?   207 just just so   210 abuse deception.   215 fast belocked firmly locked   216 match assignation

226 for that because.   proportions dowry   227 composition agreement   228–9 disvalued In levity discredited for lightness.   239 confixèd firmly fixed   242 scope full authority   243 touched injured, affected.   244 informal rash, distracted   245 But than   250 Compact . . . gone i.e., in collusion with Isabella   251 swear . . . saint call down to witness every single saint   253 sealed in approbation ratified by proof, like weights and measures being given a stamp or seal to attest to their genuineness.   263 forth through   264 Do . . . best respond to the wrongs done you as seems best to you

In any chastisement. I for a while
Will leave you; but stir not you till you have
Well determined upon these slanderers.   267

ESCALUS   My lord, we'll do it throughly.   *Exit [Duke].* 268
Signor Lucio, did not you say you knew that Friar
Lodowick to be a dishonest person?

LUCIO   *Cucullus non facit monachum*; honest in nothing 271
but in his clothes, and one that hath spoke most
villainous speeches of the Duke.

ESCALUS   We shall entreat you to abide here till he come,
and enforce them against him. We shall find this friar 275
a notable fellow.   276

LUCIO   As any in Vienna, on my word.

ESCALUS   Call that same Isabel here once again. I would
speak with her.   *[Exit an Attendant.]*
Pray you, my lord, give me leave to question. You shall
see how I'll handle her.

LUCIO   Not better than he, by her own report.   282

ESCALUS   Say you?

LUCIO   Marry, sir, I think, if you handled her privately, 284
she would sooner confess; perchance publicly she'll
be ashamed.

ESCALUS   I will go darkly to work with her.   287

LUCIO   That's the way, for women are light at midnight. 288

Enter Duke [disguised as a friar], Provost, Isabella,
[and officers].

ESCALUS   Come on, mistress. Here's a gentlewoman
denies all that you have said.

LUCIO   My lord, here comes the rascal I spoke of, here
with the Provost.

ESCALUS   In very good time. Speak not you to him till
we call upon you.

LUCIO   Mum.

ESCALUS   Come, sir, did you set these women on to
slander Lord Angelo? They have confessed you did.

DUKE   'Tis false.

ESCALUS   How? Know you where you are?

DUKE
Respect to your great place! And let the devil   300
Be sometime honored for his burning throne!   301
Where is the Duke? 'Tis he should hear me speak.

ESCALUS
The Duke's in us, and we will hear you speak.
Look you speak justly.

DUKE
Boldly, at least. But oh, poor souls,
Come you to seek the lamb here of the fox?
Good night to your redress! Is the Duke gone?
Then is your cause gone too. The Duke's unjust,
Thus to retort your manifest appeal,   309

And put your trial in the villain's mouth
Which here you come to accuse.

LUCIO
This is the rascal. This is he I spoke of.

ESCALUS
Why, thou unreverend and unhallowed friar,
Is't not enough thou hast suborned these women
To accuse this worthy man, but, in foul mouth
And in the witness of his proper ear,   316
To call him villain? And then to glance from him
To th'Duke himself, to tax him with injustice?—   318
Take him hence. To th' rack with him!—We'll touse
you   319
Joint by joint, but we will know his purpose.   320
What, "unjust"?

DUKE   Be not so hot. The Duke
Dare no more stretch this finger of mine than he
Dare rack his own. His subject am I not,
Nor here provincial. My business in this state   324
Made me a looker-on here in Vienna,
Where I have seen corruption boil and bubble
Till it o'errun the stew; laws for all faults,   327
But faults so countenanced that the strong statutes   328
Stand like the forfeits in a barber's shop,   329
As much in mock as mark.

ESCALUS   Slander to th' state!   330
Away with him to prison.

ANGELO
What can you vouch against him, Signor Lucio?
Is this the man that you did tell us of?

LUCIO   'Tis he, my lord.—Come hither, Goodman 334
Baldpate. Do you know me?   335

DUKE   I remember you, sir, by the sound of your voice.
I met you at the prison, in the absence of the Duke.

LUCIO   Oh, did you so? And do you remember what you
said of the Duke?

DUKE   Most notedly, sir.   340

LUCIO   Do you so, sir? And was the Duke a fleshmonger, a fool, and a coward, as you then reported him to be?

DUKE   You must, sir, change persons with me ere you 344
make that my report. You indeed spoke so of him, and
much more, much worse.

LUCIO   Oh, thou damnable fellow! Did not I pluck thee by
the nose for thy speeches?

DUKE   I protest I love the Duke as I love myself.

ANGELO   Hark how the villain would close now, after 350
his treasonable abuses!

---

267 **determined** reached judgment   268 **throughly** thoroughly.
271 *Cucullus . . . monachum* A cowl doesn't make a monk
275 **enforce them** forcefully urge your charges   276 **notable** notorious   282 **Not . . . report** (Lucio salaciously turns Escalus's *handle her*
into a sexual slur: You, Escalus, will do no better at "handling"
Isabella than did Angelo, according to Isabella's testimony.)   284 **if
. . . privately** (Lucio continues his sexual joke about "handling.")
287 **darkly** subtly, slyly   288 **light** wanton, unchaste   300–1 **let . . .
throne** i.e., may all authority be respected, even the devil's. (Said
sardonically.)   309 **retort** turn back.   **manifest** obviously just

316 **in . . . ear** within his own hearing   318 **tax him with** accuse him
of   319 **touse** tear   320 **but we will** i.e., if necessary to; until we
324 **provincial** subject to the religious authority of this province or
state.   327 **stew** (1) stewpot (2) brothel   328 **countenanced** tolerated
and protected by corrupt authority   329 **forfeits** cautionary displays,
or lists of rules and fines for handling razors, etc., which barbers
(who also acted as dentists and surgeons) hung in their shops
330 **As . . . mark** as often flouted as observed.   334–5 **Goodman
Baldpate** (Lucio refers to the tonsure that he assumes the Duke must
have under his hood, though the Duke is clearly hooded at this
point.)   340 **notedly** particularly   344 **change** exchange   350 **close**
come to terms, compromise

ESCALUS   Such a fellow is not to be talked withal. Away
with him to prison! Where is the Provost? Away with
him to prison! Lay bolts enough upon him. Let him   354
speak no more. Away with those giglots too, and with   355
the other confederate companion!   356
                        [*The Provost lays hands on the Duke.*]

DUKE [*to Provost*]   Stay, sir, stay awhile.

ANGELO   What, resists he? Help him, Lucio.

LUCIO   Come, sir, come, sir, come, sir; foh, sir! Why,
you bald-pated, lying rascal, you must be hooded,
must you? Show your knave's visage, with a pox to
you! Show your sheep-biting face, and be hanged an   362
hour! Will't not off?   363
                [*He pulls off the friar's hood, and discovers
                    the Duke. Angelo and Escalus rise.*]

DUKE
Thou art the first knave that e'er mad'st a duke.
First, Provost, let me bail these gentle three.   365
[*To Lucio*] Sneak not away, sir, for the Friar and you
Must have a word anon.—Lay hold on him.

LUCIO   This may prove worse than hanging.

DUKE [*to Escalus*]
What you have spoke I pardon. Sit you down.
We'll borrow place of him. [*To Angelo*] Sir, by your
    leave.   [*He takes Angelo's seat. Escalus also sits.*]
Hast thou or word, or wit, or impudence,   371
That yet can do thee office? If thou hast,   372
Rely upon it till my tale be heard,
And hold no longer out.

ANGELO [*kneeling*]   O my dread lord,   374
I should be guiltier than my guiltiness
To think I can be undiscernible,
When I perceive Your Grace, like power divine,
Hath looked upon my passes. Then, good prince,   378
No longer session hold upon my shame,
But let my trial be mine own confession.
Immediate sentence then and sequent death   381
Is all the grace I beg.

DUKE   Come hither, Mariana.—
Say, wast thou e'er contracted to this woman?

ANGELO   I was, my lord.

DUKE
Go take her hence and marry her instantly.
Do you the office, Friar, which consummate,   386
Return him here again. Go with him, Provost.
                Exit [*Angelo, with Mariana, Friar Peter, and
                                            Provost*].

ESCALUS
My lord, I am more amazed at his dishonor
Than at the strangeness of it.

DUKE   Come hither, Isabel.
Your friar is now your prince. As I was then

Advertising and holy to your business,   391
Not changing heart with habit, I am still
Attorneyed at your service.

ISABELLA   Oh, give me pardon,   393
That I, your vassal, have employed and pained   394
Your unknown sovereignty!

DUKE   You are pardoned, Isabel.
And now, dear maid, be you as free to us.   396
Your brother's death, I know, sits at your heart;
And you may marvel why I obscured myself,
Laboring to save his life, and would not rather
Make rash remonstrance of my hidden power   400
Than let him so be lost. O most kind maid,
It was the swift celerity of his death,
Which I did think with slower foot came on,
That brained my purpose. But peace be with him!   404
That life is better life past fearing death
Than that which lives to fear. Make it your comfort,
So happy is your brother.

        *Enter Angelo, Mariana, [Friar] Peter, [and]
        Provost.*

ISABELLA   I do, my lord.   407

DUKE
For this new-married man approaching here,
Whose salt imagination yet hath wronged   409
Your well-defended honor, you must pardon
For Mariana's sake. But as he adjudged your
    brother—
Being criminal, in double violation
Of sacred chastity and of promise-breach   413
Thereon dependent, for your brother's life—   414
The very mercy of the law cries out   415
Most audible, even from his proper tongue,   416
"An Angelo for Claudio, death for death!"
Haste still pays haste, and leisure answers leisure; 418
Like doth quit like, and measure still for measure.   419
Then, Angelo, thy fault's thus manifested,
Which, though thou wouldst deny, denies thee
    vantage.   421
We do condemn thee to the very block
Where Claudio stooped to death, and with like haste.
Away with him!

MARIANA   O my most gracious lord,
I hope you will not mock me with a husband!

DUKE
It is your husband mocked you with a husband.
Consenting to the safeguard of your honor,
I thought your marriage fit; else imputation,   428
For that he knew you, might reproach your life   429

---

354 bolts iron fetters   **355 giglots** wanton women   **356 confederate
companion** i.e., Friar Peter.   **362 sheep-biting** knavish. (From the
action of wolves or dogs that prey on sheep.)   **362–3 hanged an hour**
(A sardonic way of saying "hanged.")   **365 gentle three** i.e., Mariana,
Isabella, and Friar Peter.   **371 or word** either word   **372 office** service.   **374 hold . . . out** then persist no longer.   **378 passes** actions,
trespasses.   **381 sequent** subsequent   **386 Do . . . office** Please perform the service.   **consummate** being completed

391 Advertising and holy attentive and wholly dedicated (in my
priestly role)   **393 Attorneyed at** serving as agent in   **394 pained** put
to trouble   **396 as free to us** i.e., as generous in pardoning me
400 rash remonstrance sudden manifestation   **404 brained** dashed,
defeated   **407 So thus**   **409 salt** lecherous   **413–14 promise-breach . . .
dependent** i.e., breaking his promise made in return for the yielding up
of chastity   **415 The very . . . law** i.e., even mercy itself   **416 his proper**
its own   **418 still** always   **419 quit** requite   **421 though** even if.
vantage i.e., any advantage. (Angelo must suffer the same penalty as
Claudio.)   **428 fit** appropriate.   **imputation** accusation, slander
429 For that he knew you since he knew you sexually

And choke your good to come. For his possessions,   430
Although by confiscation they are ours,
We do instate and widow you withal,   432
To buy you a better husband.
MARIANA   O my dear lord,
I crave no other, nor no better man.
DUKE
Never crave him; we are definitive.   435
MARIANA [*kneeling*]
Gentle my liege—
DUKE   You do but lose your labor.—
Away with him to death! [*To Lucio*] Now, sir, to you.
MARIANA
O my good lord!—Sweet Isabel, take my part!
Lend me your knees, and all my life to come
I'll lend you all my life to do you service.
DUKE
Against all sense you do importune her.
Should she kneel down in mercy of this fact,   442
Her brother's ghost his pavèd bed would break,   443
And take her hence in horror.
MARIANA   Isabel,
Sweet Isabel, do yet but kneel by me!
Hold up your hands, say nothing; I'll speak all.
They say best men are molded out of faults,   447
And, for the most, become much more the better   448
For being a little bad. So may my husband.
O Isabel, will you not lend a knee?
DUKE
He dies for Claudio's death.
ISABELLA [*kneeling*]   Most bounteous sir,
Look, if it please you, on this man condemned
As if my brother lived. I partly think
A due sincerity governed his deeds,
Till he did look on me. Since it is so,
Let him not die. My brother had but justice,
In that he did the thing for which he died.
For Angelo,
His act did not o'ertake his bad intent,
And must be buried but as an intent   460
That perished by the way. Thoughts are no subjects,   461
Intents but merely thoughts.
MARIANA   Merely, my lord.
DUKE
Your suit's unprofitable. Stand up, I say.
                                    [*They stand.*]
I have bethought me of another fault.
Provost, how came it Claudio was beheaded
At an unusual hour?
PROVOST   It was commanded so.
DUKE
Had you a special warrant for the deed?
PROVOST
No, my good lord, it was by private message.

DUKE
For which I do discharge you of your office.
Give up your keys.
PROVOST   Pardon me, noble lord.
I thought it was a fault, but knew it not,   472
Yet did repent me after more advice;   473
For testimony whereof, one in the prison,
That should by private order else have died,
I have reserved alive.
DUKE   What's he?
PROVOST   His name is Barnardine.
DUKE
I would thou hadst done so by Claudio.
Go fetch him hither. Let me look upon him.
                                    [*Exit Provost.*]
ESCALUS
I am sorry one so learnèd and so wise
As you, Lord Angelo, have still appeared,   482
Should slip so grossly, both in the heat of blood
And lack of tempered judgment afterward.
ANGELO
I am sorry that such sorrow I procure,   485
And so deep sticks it in my penitent heart
That I crave death more willingly than mercy.
'Tis my deserving, and I do entreat it.   488

         Enter Barnardine and Provost, Claudio [muffled],
         [and] Juliet.

DUKE
Which is that Barnardine?
PROVOST   This, my lord.
DUKE
There was a friar told me of this man.—
Sirrah, thou art said to have a stubborn soul
That apprehends no further than this world,
And squar'st thy life according. Thou'rt condemned;   493
But, for those earthly faults, I quit them all,   494
And pray thee take this mercy to provide
For better times to come.—Friar, advise him;
I leave him to your hand.—What muffled fellow's
    that?
PROVOST
This is another prisoner that I saved,
Who should have died when Claudio lost his head,
As like almost to Claudio as himself.
                                    [*He unmuffles Claudio.*]
DUKE [*to Isabella*]
If he be like your brother, for his sake
Is he pardoned, and for your lovely sake,
Give me your hand and say you will be mine;
He is my brother too. But fitter time for that.
By this Lord Angelo perceives he's safe;
Methinks I see a quick'ning in his eye.
Well, Angelo, your evil quits you well.   507
Look that you love your wife, her worth worth yours.   508

---

430 **For** As for   432 **widow** endow with a widow's rights
435 **definitive** firmly resolved.   442 **in . . . fact** pleading mercy for
this crime   443 **pavèd bed** grave covered with a stone slab   447 **best
men** even the best of men   448 **most** most part   460 **buried** i.e., forgotten   461 **no subjects** i.e., not subject to the state's authority

472 **knew it not** was not sure   473 **advice** consideration   482 **still** always   485 **procure** cause, prompt   488.1 *muffled* wrapped up so as to
conceal identity. (As also in line 497.)   493 **squar'st** regulates   494 **for**
as for.   **quit** pardon   507 **quits** rewards, requites   508 **her . . . yours**
her worthiness richly deserving your love and worthy of your estate.

I find an apt remission in myself;   509
And yet here's one in place I cannot pardon.   510
[*To Lucio*] You, sirrah, that knew me for a fool, a
    coward,
One all of luxury, an ass, a madman—   512
Wherein have I so deserved of you
That you extol me thus?

LUCIO   Faith, my lord, I spoke it but according to the
trick. If you will hang me for it, you may; but I had   516
rather it would please you I might be whipped.

DUKE
Whipped first, sir, and hanged after.—
Proclaim it, Provost, round about the city,
If any woman wronged by this lewd fellow—
As I have heard him swear himself there's one
Whom he begot with child—let her appear,
And he shall marry her. The nuptial finished,
Let him be whipped and hanged.

LUCIO   I beseech Your Highness, do not marry me to a
whore. Your Highness said even now I made you a   526
duke; good my lord, do not recompense me in mak-
ing me a cuckold.

DUKE
Upon mine honor, thou shalt marry her.
Thy slanders I forgive and therewithal   530
Remit thy other forfeits.—Take him to prison,   531

And see our pleasure herein executed.   532

LUCIO   Marrying a punk, my lord, is pressing to death,   533
whipping, and hanging.

DUKE
Slandering a prince deserves it.
                    [*Exeunt officers with Lucio.*]
She, Claudio, that you wronged, look you restore.   536
Joy to you, Mariana! Love her, Angelo.
I have confessed her, and I know her virtue.
Thanks, good friend Escalus, for thy much goodness;
There's more behind that is more gratulate.   540
Thanks, Provost, for thy care and secrecy;
We shall employ thee in a worthier place.
Forgive him, Angelo, that brought you home
The head of Ragozine for Claudio's;
Th'offense pardons itself. Dear Isabel,
I have a motion much imports your good,   546
Whereto if you'll a willing ear incline,
What's mine is yours, and what is yours is mine.—
So, bring us to our palace, where we'll show   549
What's yet behind, that's meet you all should know.   550
                                        [*Exeunt.*]

---

509 apt remission readiness to show mercy   **510 in place** present
512 luxury lechery   **516 trick** fashion.   **526 even** just   **530–1 and
therewithal . . . forfeits** i.e., and therefore will not have you whipped
and hanged.

532 see . . . executed i.e., see that my order be carried out that Lucio
marry Kate Keepdown (see 3.2.194–6).   **533 pressing to death** i.e., by
having heavy weights placed on the chest. (A standard form of executing those who refused to plead to a felony charge.) Lucio wryly
complains that marrying a whore is as bad as death by torture.
536 She . . . restore i.e., See to it that you marry Juliet.   **540 behind** in
store, to come.   **gratulate** gratifying.   **546 motion** proposal (which)
549 bring escort   **550 What's yet behind** what is still to be told

The Histories

The Tragedy of King Richard the Third

The fascinating evil ruler for whom *Richard III* is named has already made his appearance in the third part of *Henry VI*, in the four-play sequence that makes up Shakespeare's first foray into English history. In the final installment in this tetralogy, Richard, Duke of Gloucester, stands fully revealed as the evil genius of England's prolonged crisis of civil war. With a bold stroke, Shakespeare opens *Richard III* with his arresting soliloquy; Richard takes over the stage in a way that has held audiences spellbound ever since Richard Burbage first performed the role. Richard announces his determination to "prove a villain," both defying and fulfilling Nature, which made his body deformed. In fact, he has already begun his treacherous course, and we see at once how his plot against Clarence, founded on something so trivial as the letter G, has manipulated the King and has ensnared Clarence. Then, with outrageous hypocrisy, he "comforts" Clarence. Within less than a hundred lines, Shakespeare makes us feel how brilliant, cynical, charming, and dangerous Richard of Gloucester is. Richard proceeds to dominate the other characters—and the whole play—to an extraordinary degree.

By organizing this play firmly around Richard, Shakespeare solved the problems of giving form to his drama and of concluding the series of plays about the dynastic rivalry of York and Lancaster. *Richard III* begins and ends with a peace, yet the recent peace of the Yorkist King Edward is scorned and sabotaged by Richard as soon as it is introduced. It is vulnerable to factions at court and is bitterly denounced by that living embodiment of the cruel and violent past, Queen Margaret. There can be no peace in England while Richard lives to undermine it. Still, as the plot moves through Richard's exhilarating rise to the throne and the events of his tragic fall—when his conscience, the spirits of those he murdered, and the Earl of Richmond punish and defeat him—we see that his career is part of a larger order, a seemingly providential plan of retribution for wickedness and injustice and for reconciling England's divisions. For all its specific reminders of past warfare and atrocity on both Yorkist and Lancastrian sides, *Richard III* dramatizes an archetypal struggle between good and evil, personified in Richard the villain-hero and Richmond his opponent, who plays the role of the righteous agent of divine and poetic justice.

Dramatically, Richmond, like Queen Margaret, is more a symbol than a fully developed character. It is Richard who is the exciting figure as he deceives and manipulates others and finally faces the chillingly isolated condition into which he has brought himself by being so truly a villain. He climbs to power by deceit, and so he is constantly acting a part. Richard's ability as an actor is seemingly limitless. He has already boasted, in *3 Henry VI*, that he can deceive more slyly than Ulysses, Sinon, or Machiavelli and can put on more false shapes than Proteus. To us as audience, he is cynically candid and boastful, setting us up in advance to watch his unbelievable performances. In an instant, before our eyes, he is the concerned younger brother of Clarence, sharing a hatred of Queen Elizabeth and her kindred; he is the jocular uncle of the little princes; or he is the pious recluse studying divinity with his clerical teachers, reluctant to accept the responsibilities of state that are thrust upon him by his importunate subjects (i.e., by Catesby and Buckingham, who are also actors in this staged scene).

None of these bravura performances, however, matches the wooing of Lady Anne. Richard himself sees it as the great test of his powers and is suitably impressed by his victory. The wooing scene, to some critics, challenges credibility. One key to credibility must lie in superb acting. The actor who plays Richard must transform himself from the gloating villain we know in soliloquy to the grief-stricken lover. Richard's argument is, after all, speciously plausible: that he has killed Anne's husband and father-in-law out of desperate love for her. The argument appeals to vanity, that most fatal of human weaknesses.

What power Anne suddenly appears to have over Richard! She can kill him or spare his life. Richard shrewdly judges her as one who is not able to kill, and so he risks offering her his sword. As stage manager, he has altered her role from that of sincere mourner to the stereotype of the proud woman worshiped by her groveling servant in love. With superb irony, Richard has inverted the appearance and the reality of control in this struggle between man and woman, winning mastery by flattering Anne that she has such power over his emotions and his life. From his amazing success, Richard concludes that ordinary men and women can be made to believe anything and to betray their own instincts by "the plain devil and dissembling looks" (1.2.239). Richard is indeed devil-like; his role as actor stems in part from that of the Vice in the morality play, brilliantly comic and sinister. Yet even the devil can prevail over his victims only when they acquiesce in evil. The devil can deceive the senses, but acceptance of evil is still an act of the perverted will. Anne is guilty, however much we can appreciate the mesmerizing power of Richard's personality. By the end of the scene, she has violated everything she holds sacred.

The image of Richard as devil or Vice raises questions of motivation and of symbolic meaning, and suggests two seemingly disparate ways of reading the play, one psychological and the other providential. Is Richard a human character, propelled toward the throne by his insatiable ambition, like Macbeth? Is there a clue to his behavior in his ugliness and misanthropy? One might argue that he compensates for his ugliness and unlovability by resolving to domineer. Feeling unwanted, he despises all humans and undertakes to prove them weak and corrupt in order to affirm himself. He expresses a universal human penchant for cruelty and senseless domination. Yet the proposition that Richard is evil *because* he was born ugly logically can be reversed as well: he was born ugly *because* he is evil. In providential terms, Richard can be seen as the result of a divine plan in which evil ironically has a place in a larger scheme of things that is ultimately benign.

This latter concept, owing much to Renaissance notions of platonic correspondence between outer appearances and inner qualities, is grounded on the idea of a vast struggle in the cosmos between the forces of absolute good and the forces of absolute evil, one in which every event in human life has divine meaning and cause. Richard's birth is, according to this theory, a physical manifestation of that divine meaning. Providential destiny, having determined the need for a genius of evil at this point in English history, decrees that Richard shall be born. The teeth and hunched back merely give evidence of what is already predetermined. In the apt words of the choric Queen Margaret, Richard was "sealed in thy nativity / The slave of nature and the son of hell" (1.3.229–30). Though he devotes himself to selfish ambition and evil-doing, Richard ultimately serves the righteous purpose of divine Providence in human affairs. He functions, in this interpretation, as a scourge of God, whose plots or tyranny are permitted in order to bring just retribution upon offenders of the moral law. He is fundamentally unlike Shakespeare's more human villains, such as Macbeth or Claudius, but belongs, instead, to a special group of villains, including Iago in *Othello* and Edmund in *King Lear*. Like them, Richard is driven both by human motivation and by his preexistent evil genius; he displays the "motiveless malignity" ascribed by Coleridge to Iago.

Such a reading is only one approach to an understanding of Richard's character and function; he is also a human being involved in a struggle for power, motivated by ambition and hatred. The two readings, one psychological and the other providential, are complementary and need not contradict each other. The psychological reading seems more intelligible to us today, based as it is on character and motivation. The providential reading, more traditional in its ideology, helps explain not only Richard's delight in evil but also the necessity for so much evil and suffering in England's civil wars. This theory of history owes much to Edward Hall's *Union of the Two Noble and Illustre Families of Lancaster and York* (1542), Shakespeare's chief source, along with Raphael Holinshed's *Chronicles* (1578), for his *Henry VI* plays. Shakespeare's treatment of Richard is ultimately indebted to Polydore Vergil's *Anglica Historia* (1534) and especially to *The History of King Richard the Third*, attributed to Sir Thomas More (published 1557). This latter work, adopted in turn by Edward Hall, Richard Grafton, and Raphael Holinshed, purposefully blackens Richard's character. He becomes a study in the nature of tyranny, an object lesson to future rulers and their subjects. He is, moreover, a result of the curse placed by God on the English people for their sinful disobedience.

Richmond, in this Tudor explanation, becomes God's minister, chosen to destroy the scourge and thereafter to fulfill a new and happy covenant between God and humanity as King Henry VII. Thus, the play hardly touches on the sensitive matter of his somewhat remote Lancastrian claim to the crown. His victory at Bosworth is not one more turn of Fortune's wheel raising or deposing Lancastrian or Yorkist kings, but the end of a long cycle of unnatural violence, and his marriage to the Yorkist Princess Elizabeth is the restoration and the symbol of unity and peace in England's fair land. Although modern historians more impartially regard the defeat of Richard III at Bosworth Field in 1485 as a political overthrow not unlike Henry IV's overthrow of Richard II and stress that Richard III was a talented administrator guilty of no worse political crimes than those of his more fortunate successor, Elizabethan audiences (under constant promptings of the Tudor state) could not have found sufficient meaning in such a neutral interpretation. They were taught to see history as revealing God's intention and to view Henry VII's accession not as a parallel to the deposing of Richard II by Henry IV but, instead, as a divinely sanctioned deliverance of the English nation, to which Elizabeth's subjects were the happy heirs. Accordingly, the Tudor myth stressed the tyrannical nature of Richard III's seizure of power and conversely minimized the political and Machiavellian elements in Henry VII's takeover. Bosworth Field was seen as an act of God, a rising up of some irresistible force, and under no circumstances as a precedent for future rebellion.

In the *Henry VI* plays, Shakespeare puts considerable distance between himself and the Tudor orthodox reading of history, allowing the grim realities of civil war to speak for themselves. In *Richard III*, however, the pattern shown in the chronicles provides Shakespeare with an essential structural device. Viewing the civil wars in retrospect, *Richard III* potentially manifests a cohesive sense in which England's suffering has fulfilled a necessary plan of fall from innocence, leading through sin and penitence to regeneration. Evil is seen at last as something through which good triumphs, in English history, as in the story of humankind's fall and a restoration by divine grace.

This providential scheme imposes a double irony on *Richard III*. In the short run, Richard appears to be complete master over his victims. "Your imprisonment shall not be long," Richard assures his brother Clarence. "I will deliver you, or else lie for you" (1.1.114–15). The audience, already let in on the secret, can shiver at the grisly humor of these double entendres. Clarence will indeed soon be delivered—to his death. Richard's henchmen are fond of such jokes, too. When Lord Hastings is on his way to the Tower, where he plans to stay for midday dinner, Buckingham observes aside, "And supper too, although thou know'st it not" (3.2.122). Buckingham, knowing that Hastings is about to be arrested in the Tower and executed for treason, chillingly suggests that Hastings will soon be a feast for worms. Shortly before, Catesby has assured Hastings of Richard's and Buckingham's favor: "The princes both make high account of you—/[Aside] For they account his head upon the Bridge" (3.2.69–70). That is to say, Hastings's severed head will soon be raised on a pole on London Bridge as a grim warning to those who run afoul of the new regime. Richard has a phrase for such wit: "Thus, like the formal Vice, Iniquity, /I moralize two meanings in one word" (3.1.82–3). The point of such ironies is always the same: the scheming villain is cleverer than his victims, deceiving them through equivocation and triumphing in their spriritual blindness.

The delayed irony of the play, however, ultimately offers another possible explanation for the seemingly nihilistic conclusions of the early scenes; that is, there may be a larger plan at work, of which Richard is unconscious and in which he plays a role quite unlike the one he creates for himself. In this interpretive view, Shakespeare's Richard fulfills a plan of which he is unaware, as in the chronicles of Edward Hall and others, even in the process of what he gloatingly regards as his own self-aggrandizement.

Providential plans are always complex, inscrutable to the minds of mortals, and understood least by those who unwittingly execute them. In attempting to prove his own contention that human nature is bestial and that a Machiavellian man of utter self-confidence can force his way to the top, flouting all conventions of morality, Richard succeeds in demonstrating the opposite. From the moment he takes the throne, he feels it insecure beneath him; opposition and betrayal spring up from every quarter, and, in his last moments, a mere horse is worth his whole kingdom. With sardonic comedy and poetic justice, Richard becomes the proverbial beguiler who is beguiled.

Even if this is not the only way to interpret Richard's character, the play does offer for our consideration a theory of divine causality in which virtually all of Richard's victims deserve their fate because they have offended God. Prophecies and dreams give structure to the sequence of retributive actions and keep grim score. As the choric Margaret observes, a York must pay for a Lancaster, eye for an eye: Edward IV for Henry VI, young Edward V for Henry VI's son Edward. Thus, the Yorkist princes, though guiltless, die for their family's sins. The Yorkist Queen Elizabeth, like the Lancastrian Margaret, must outlive her husband into impotent old age, bewailing her children's cruel deaths. Clarence sees his death as punishment for breaking his oath at the battle of Tewkesbury and for his part in murdering Henry VI's son, Prince Edward. The Queen's kindred have been guilty of ambition, and Lord Hastings, in turn, is vulnerable because he has been willing to plot with Richard against the Queen's kindred. Margaret's curses serve both to warn the characters of their fates (a warning they blindly ignore) and to invite each person to curse himself or herself unwittingly but with ironic appropriateness. Lady Anne wishes unhappiness on any woman so insane as to marry Richard. Buckingham protests in a most sacred oath that whenever he turns again on the Queen's kindred, he will deserve to be punished by the treachery of his dearest friend (i.e., Richard). Dreams serve the same purpose of divine warning, giving Clarence a grotesque intimation of his death by drowning (in a butt of malmsey wine) and warning Hastings (through Stanley's dream) that the boar, Richard, will cut off his head. Thus, the English court punishes itself through Richard. He is the essence of the courtiers' factionalism, able to succeed as he does only because they forswear their most holy vows and conspire to destroy one another. They deserve to be outwitted at their own dismal game. Yet their falls are curative as well; Richard's victims acknowledge the justice of their undoings and penitently implore divine forgiveness. Richard contrastingly finds conscience a torment, rather than a voice of comfort and wisdom.

Richard III is not without its ironies and historical anxieties. Richard's own successful career of evil through much of the play demonstrates how rhetoric and theater can be used to dupe and to corrupt. The political process seems endlessly prone to cynical manipulation, and triumph comes chiefly to those who know how to use rhetoric to calculated effect. The Lord Mayor and his London associates are as pliable as the aristocracy. For all the belated assurances of providential meaning in Richard's rise to power and overthrow, we are allowed to speculate uncomfortably about the pragmatic action of history and its seeming ability to thrust forward into prominence an evil king or a good one, as individual temperament happens to dictate. Finally, there is the question of how Richard is supplanted. Whatever the reasons for Richard's baleful emergence, the process of his overthrow requires human agency and a rebellion against established (even if tyrannical) royal authority. To thoughtful observers in the sixteenth century, including Queen Elizabeth, any such rebellion, no matter how seemingly necessary, established a disturbing precedent and a threat to Tudor monarchical stability. If *Richard III* finds reassuring answers in the victory of Henry Tudor, Earl of Richmond, it does so in the face of pressing and troublesome circumstances.

The pattern of reciprocity and retaliation is much more than a way of demonstrating an ultimate divine purpose in human affairs; it is also a theatrically effective way of structuring a drama so as to make it coherent and entertaining. Shakespeare strikes us as above all a man of the theater, an artist and entertainer who senses masterfully what his audiences want. The shape of *Richard III*, as it moves through the anxieties of Richard's seemingly unstoppable rise to power to an eventual affirmation that brings closure not only to this play but to the entire four-play cycle of the three parts of *Henry VI* and *Richard III*, is immensely satisfying as theatrical experience. Modern audiences, with no ideological commitment to the propagandistic view that God chose Henry VII as the savior of England, can respond warmly to the play's artistic and theatrical depiction of coherence and pattern. That pattern allows us to enjoy Richard's villainies as theatrical performance while perceiving that those villainies are contained and disarmed by a larger structure.

Good eventually triumphs over evil in *Richard III*, if only because some Englishmen have the patience and common sense to endure a presumably deserved punishment and wait for deliverance. As in *3 Henry VI*, the common people have little to do with the action of the play. They are choric spokesmen and bystanders, virtuous in their attitude (except for the two suborned murderers of Clarence). In their plain folk wisdom, they see the folly and evil their betters ignore: "Oh, full of danger is the Duke of Gloucester,/And the Queen's sons and brothers haught and proud" (2.3.28–9). And, although they accept Richard as ruler, they do so most reluctantly; Buckingham's first attempt to persuade the people to this course meets with apathy and silence. Their wisdom is to "leave it all to God" (line 46). In the fullness of time, this faith in goodness brings its just reward.

Richard III compresses historical time. It begins where *3 Henry VI* has left off, with the return of Edward IV to the throne in 1471, and ends with the defeat of Richard III, the last Yorkist king, at the battle of Bosworth (1485). Because of its close relation in subject to passages in *3 Henry VI* and its similar Senecan style, the play appears to have been written soon after its predecessors, sometime between 1591 and 1594. It greatly condenses events of fourteen years, particularly at the beginning, when King Henry VI's funeral rites (1471), Richard's courtship of Lady Anne (1472), Clarence's murder in the Tower (1478), and Edward's death (1483) are made to take place at the same time. Similarly, Buckingham's rebellion (1483), Richmond's thwarted sailing (1483), and his landing at Milford Haven (1485) are also compressed. Queen Margaret's role is a nonhistorical addition to the play, for the widowed Queen never left France after her ransom in 1475 by Louis XI.

Richard III is irresistible in performance. However much Richard reveals himself to be a conscienceless villain, his versatility as a performer and his taking us into his confidence invite a kind of complicity between actor and audience that is the stuff of dramatic excitement. These qualities are brilliantly on display in two film versions, that of Laurence Olivier in 1955 and that of Ian McKellan in 1995. The first shows Richard's protean skills in deception as he soliloquizes candidly to us as his confidants, then transforms himself into the devoted brother of George Clarence (John Gielgud) and then the heartstricken wooer of the Lady Anne (Claire Bloom), seemingly at the mercy of the lady he worships. Ian McKellan transfers the play to the era of an imagined English civil war in the 1930s in which the ruthless, Nazi-like Richard claws his way to the top. His thirst for mayhem is psychotic, but is not without its esthetic dimension as well; he murders with artistry and style, and savors the results by examining photographs of his dead victims. His teamwork with Buckingham (Jim Broadbent) in bamboozling the citizens of London is a thing of beauty. Closeups focus on McKellan's creased visage as he contemplates his next move. Al Pacino's *Looking for Richard* (1996) explores the play in rehearsal with an all-star cast including Winona Ryder, Kevin Spacey, Alec Baldwin, and Aidan Quinn. Many other great actors have excelled in the quintessentially theatrical role of Richard, including Marius Goring, Brian Bedford, Ian Holm, Antony Sher, Kevin Kline, and Simon Russell Beale.

The Tragedy of King Richard the Third

[*Dramatis Personae*

KING EDWARD THE FOURTH
QUEEN ELIZABETH, *wife of King Edward*
EDWARD, PRINCE OF WALES, } *sons of Edward and*
RICHARD, DUKE OF YORK, } *Elizabeth*
GEORGE, DUKE OF CLARENCE,
RICHARD, DUKE OF GLOUCESTER, } *brothers of the King*
    later King Richard III,
DUCHESS OF YORK, *mother of Edward IV,*
    Clarence, and Richard, Duke of Gloucester
LADY ANNE, *widow of Edward, Prince of Wales*
    (son of Henry VI); later wife of Richard, Duke of
    Gloucester
MARGARET, *widow of King Henry VI*
BOY, *son of Clarence (Edward Plantagenet, Earl of*
    Warwick)
GIRL, *daughter of Clarence (Margaret Plantagenet,*
    Countess of Salisbury)

ANTHONY WOODVILLE, EARL RIVERS, *brother of*
    Queen Elizabeth
MARQUESS OF DORSET, } *sons of Queen*
LORD GREY, } *Elizabeth*
SIR THOMAS VAUGHAN, *executed with Rivers and*
    Grey

WILLIAM, LORD HASTINGS, *the Lord Chamberlain*
DUKE OF BUCKINGHAM, *Richard's supporter, later*
    in opposition
SIR WILLIAM CATESBY, }
SIR RICHARD RATCLIFFE, } *Richard's supporters*
LORD LOVELL, } *and henchmen*
SIR JAMES TYRREL, }
DUKE OF NORFOLK, } *Richard's generals*
EARL OF SURREY, }

HENRY, EARL OF RICHMOND, *later King Henry VII*

SCENE: *England.*]

LORD STANLEY, EARL OF DERBY,
EARL OF OXFORD,
SIR JAMES BLUNT, } *supporters of*
SIR WALTER HERBERT, } *Richmond*
SIR WILLIAM BRANDON,
CHRISTOPHER URSWICK, *a priest,*

CARDINAL BOURCHIER, *Archbishop of Canterbury*
ARCHBISHOP OF YORK (*Thomas Rotherham*)
BISHOP OF ELY (*John Morton*)
GHOSTS *of King Henry VI, Edward Prince of*
    Wales, and others murdered by Richard
    (Clarence, Rivers, Grey, Vaughan, Hastings, the
    two young princes, Anne, and Buckingham)
SIR ROBERT BRACKENBURY, *Lieutenant of the Tower*
TRESSEL,
BERKELEY, } *attending the*
HALBERDIER, } *Lady Anne*
GENTLEMAN,
Two MURDERERS
KEEPER *in the Tower*
Three CITIZENS
MESSENGER *to Queen Elizabeth*
LORD MAYOR OF LONDON
MESSENGER *to Lord Hastings*
PURSUIVANT
PRIEST
SCRIVENER
Two BISHOPS
PAGE *to Richard III*
Four MESSENGERS *to Richard III*
SHERIFF OF WILTSHIRE

Lords, Attendants, Aldermen, Citizens, Councilors,
Soldiers

1.1

Enter Richard, Duke of Gloucester, solus.

RICHARD
Now is the winter of our discontent
Made glorious summer by this son of York,　　2
And all the clouds that loured upon our house　　3
In the deep bosom of the ocean buried.
Now are our brows bound with victorious wreaths,　　5
Our bruisèd arms hung up for monuments,　　6
Our stern alarums changed to merry meetings,　　7
Our dreadful marches to delightful measures.　　8
Grim-visaged War hath smoothed his wrinkled
　front;　　9
And now, instead of mounting barbèd steeds　　10
To fright the souls of fearful adversaries,　　11
He capers nimbly in a lady's chamber
To the lascivious pleasing of a lute.
But I, that am not shaped for sportive tricks,　　14
Nor made to court an amorous looking glass;
I, that am rudely stamped, and want love's majesty　　16
To strut before a wanton ambling nymph;　　17
I, that am curtailed of this fair proportion,　　18
Cheated of feature by dissembling Nature,　　19
Deformed, unfinished, sent before my time
Into this breathing world scarce half made up,
And that so lamely and unfashionable　　22
That dogs bark at me as I halt by them—　　23
Why, I, in this weak piping time of peace,　　24
Have no delight to pass away the time,
Unless to see my shadow in the sun
And descant on mine own deformity.　　27
And therefore, since I cannot prove a lover
To entertain these fair well-spoken days,　　29
I am determinèd to prove a villain
And hate the idle pleasures of these days.
Plots have I laid, inductions dangerous,　　32
By drunken prophecies, libels, and dreams,
To set my brother Clarence and the King
In deadly hate the one against the other;
And if King Edward be as true and just

As I am subtle, false, and treacherous,
This day should Clarence closely be mewed up　　38
About a prophecy, which says that G　　39
Of Edward's heirs the murderer shall be.
Dive, thoughts, down to my soul; here Clarence
　comes.

*Enter Clarence, guarded, and Brackenbury,
[Lieutenant of the Tower].*

Brother, good day. What means this armèd guard
That waits upon Your Grace?
CLARENCE　　　　　　　　　His Majesty,　　43
Tend'ring my person's safety, hath appointed　　44
This conduct to convey me to the Tower.　　45
RICHARD
Upon what cause?
CLARENCE　　　　　　　　Because my name is George.
RICHARD
Alack, my lord, that fault is none of yours.
He should, for that, commit your godfathers.
Oh, belike His Majesty hath some intent　　49
That you should be new christened in the Tower.　　50
But what's the matter, Clarence, may I know?　　51
CLARENCE
Yea, Richard, when I know; for I protest
As yet I do not. But, as I can learn,
He hearkens after prophecies and dreams,
And from the crossrow plucks the letter G,　　55
And says a wizard told him that by G
His issue disinherited should be;　　57
And, for my name of George begins with G,　　58
It follows in his thought that I am he.
These, as I learn, and suchlike toys as these　　60
Hath moved His Highness to commit me now.　　61
RICHARD
Why, this it is when men are ruled by women.
'Tis not the King that sends you to the Tower;
My Lady Grey his wife, Clarence, 'tis she　　64
That tempers him to this extremity.　　65
Was it not she, and that good man of worship,　　66
Anthony Woodville, her brother there,　　67

1.1. Location: London. Near the Tower.
0.1 solus alone.　**2 son** Edward IV was the son of Richard, Duke of York. (With a pun on "sun"; Edward IV used the sun on his badge.)
3 loured looked threateningly　**5 brows** foreheads　**6 arms** armor.
monuments trophies　**7 alarums** calls to arms, or assaults　**8 dreadful** formidable, awe-inspiring.　**measures** stately dances.　**9 wrinkled front** furrowed forehead　**10 barbèd** armored　**11 fearful** frightened
14 sportive amorous　**16 rudely stamped** roughly fashioned, coined.
want lack　**17 ambling** walking affectedly, i.e., wantonly　**18 curtailed** cut short, denied.　**proportion** shape　**19 feature** shapeliness of body　**22 unfashionable** badly fashioned　**23 halt** limp　**24 piping time** i.e., a time when the music heard is that of pipes and not fifes and drums　**27 descant** compose variations, comment on　**29 entertain** pass away pleasurably.　**well-spoken** refined, elegant　**32 inductions** preparations

38 mewed up confined (like a hawk)　**39 prophecy . . . G** (The prophecy is mentioned in the chronicles; the quibble is that *G* stands for *Gloucester* and not for *George*, the given name of the Duke of Clarence.)
43 waits attends　**44 Tend'ring** having care for　**45 conduct** escort
49 belike probably　**50 new christened** (Anticipates, ironically, Clarence's death by drowning in 1.4.)　**51 matter** reason, cause
55 crossrow Christ-crossrow, or alphabet (so called from the cross printed before the alphabet in the hornbook)　**57 issue** offspring
58 for because　**60 toys** trifles　**61 commit** arrest　**64 My Lady Grey** (A disrespectful reference to the Queen, whose maiden name was Elizabeth Woodville and who, when the King married her, was the widow of Sir John Grey.)　**65 tempers** governs, directs　**66 worship** honor. (Said ironically.)　**67 Woodville** i.e., Earl Rivers (whom Richard also disrespectfully refers to by his family name rather than by his recently acquired title)

That made him send Lord Hastings to the Tower,
From whence this present day he is delivered?
We are not safe, Clarence, we are not safe.

CLARENCE

By heaven, I think there is no man secure
But the Queen's kindred and night-walking heralds   72
That trudge betwixt the King and Mistress Shore.   73
Heard you not what an humble suppliant
Lord Hastings was to her for his delivery?   75

RICHARD

Humbly complaining to Her Deity   76
Got my Lord Chamberlain his liberty.   77
I'll tell you what: I think it is our way,   78
If we will keep in favor with the King,
To be her men and wear her livery.   80
The jealous, o'erworn widow and herself,   81
Since that our brother dubbed them gentlewomen,   82
Are mighty gossips in our monarchy.   83

BRACKENBURY

I beseech Your Graces both to pardon me:
His Majesty hath straitly given in charge   85
That no man shall have private conference,
Of what degree soever, with your brother.   87

RICHARD

Even so? An't please Your Worship, Brackenbury,   88
You may partake of anything we say.
We speak no treason, man. We say the King
Is wise and virtuous, and his noble queen
Well struck in years, fair, and not jealous.   92
We say that Shore's wife hath a pretty foot,
A cherry lip, a bonny eye, a passing pleasing tongue;   94
And that the Queen's kindred are made gentlefolks.
How say you, sir? Can you deny all this?

BRACKENBURY

With this, my lord, myself have naught to do.

RICHARD

Naught to do with Mistress Shore? I tell thee, fellow,   98
He that doth naught with her, excepting one,
Were best to do it secretly, alone.

BRACKENBURY   What one, my lord?

RICHARD

Her husband, knave. Wouldst thou betray me?   102

BRACKENBURY

I beseech Your Grace to pardon me, and withal   103
Forbear your conference with the noble Duke.

CLARENCE

We know thy charge, Brackenbury, and will obey.

RICHARD

We are the Queen's abjects, and must obey.   106
Brother, farewell. I will unto the King;
And whatsoe'er you will employ me in,
Were it to call King Edward's widow sister,   109
I will perform it to enfranchise you.   110
Meantime, this deep disgrace in brotherhood
Touches me deeper than you can imagine.   112

CLARENCE

I know it pleaseth neither of us well.

RICHARD

Well, your imprisonment shall not be long;
I will deliver you, or else lie for you.   115
Meantime, have patience.

CLARENCE   I must perforce. Farewell.   116

Exit Clarence [with Brackenbury and guard].

RICHARD

Go tread the path that thou shalt ne'er return.
Simple, plain Clarence, I do love thee so
That I will shortly send thy soul to heaven,
If heaven will take the present at our hands.
But who comes here? The new-delivered Hastings?   121

Enter Lord Hastings.

HASTINGS

Good time of day unto my gracious lord.

RICHARD

As much unto my good Lord Chamberlain.
Well are you welcome to the open air.
How hath Your Lordship brooked imprisonment?   125

HASTINGS

With patience, noble lord, as prisoners must.
But I shall live, my lord, to give them thanks   127
That were the cause of my imprisonment.

RICHARD

No doubt, no doubt; and so shall Clarence too,
For they that were your enemies are his,
And have prevailed as much on him as you.

HASTINGS

More pity that the eagles should be mewed,
Whiles kites and buzzards prey at liberty.   133

RICHARD   What news abroad?   134

HASTINGS

No news so bad abroad as this at home:

---

72 **night-walking heralds** i.e., secret messengers for an assignation
73 **Mistress Shore** Jane Shore, the King's mistress, and wife of a gold-smith in Lombard Street. (The title *Mistress* is a respectful form of address for any woman, married or unmarried.)   75 **her** i.e., Jane Shore   76 **Her Deity** (A mock title for Jane Shore, suggesting she is even more elevated than "Her Grace" or "Her Majesty.")   77 **Lord Chamberlain** i.e., Lord Hastings   78 **our way** i.e., our only way (to succeed)   80 **men** servants   81 **widow** i.e., Queen Elizabeth. (See the note for line 64.)   **herself** i.e., Jane Shore   82 **Since that** since.   **gent-lewomen** (A sneer at the Queen's family, which was gentle but not noble until after her marriage with the King; Jane Shore was, of course, neither gentle nor noble.)   83 **mighty gossips** i.e., influential busybodies   85 **straitly . . . charge** strictly ordered   87 **degree** rank   88 **An't** If it   92 **Well struck** i.e., well along.   **not jealous** (Implies there are things she might be jealous about.)   94 **passing** surpassingly   98 **Naught** (Richard quibbles on the meanings "nothing" and "naughtiness," "the sexual act.")   102 **betray me** i.e., into naming the King as a person who does "naught" with Mistress Shore.

103 **withal** furthermore   106 **abjects** abjectly servile subjects
109 **King Edward's widow** i.e., the widow whom Edward has made queen   110 **enfranchise** release from imprisonment   112 **Touches . . . imagine** (1) distresses me more than can be imagined (2) concerns me (in my personal ambition) more than you could possibly guess.
115 **lie for you** (1) take your place in prison (2) tell lies about you.
116 **perforce** necessarily.   121 **new-delivered** recently released
125 **brooked** endured   127 **give them thanks** i.e., pay them back. (Said ironically.)   133 **kites** scavengers of the hawk family
134 **abroad** at large, circulating.

The King is sickly, weak, and melancholy,
And his physicians fear him mightily.   137

RICHARD
Now, by Saint John, that news is bad indeed!
Oh, he hath kept an evil diet long   139
And overmuch consumed his royal person.
'Tis very grievous to be thought upon.
Where is he, in his bed?

HASTINGS   He is.

RICHARD
Go you before, and I will follow you.   *Exit Hastings.*
He cannot live, I hope, and must not die
Till George be packed with post-horse up to heaven.   146
I'll in, to urge his hatred more to Clarence
With lies well steeled with weighty arguments;   148
And, if I fail not in my deep intent,
Clarence hath not another day to live.
Which done, God take King Edward to his mercy
And leave the world for me to bustle in!
For then I'll marry Warwick's youngest daughter.   153
What though I killed her husband and her father?   154
The readiest way to make the wench amends
Is to become her husband and her father,
The which will I; not all so much for love
As for another secret close intent   158
By marrying her which I must reach unto.
But yet I run before my horse to market.
Clarence still breathes, Edward still lives and reigns;
When they are gone, then must I count my gains.
                                                  Exit.

❖

1.2

*Enter the corpse of [King] Henry the Sixth, with
Halberds to guard it; Lady Anne being the
mourner [attended by Tressel and Berkeley].*

ANNE
Set down, set down your honorable load—
If honor may be shrouded in a hearse—   2
Whilst I awhile obsequiously lament   3
Th'untimely fall of virtuous Lancaster.
              [The bearers set down the coffin.]
Poor key-cold figure of a holy king,   5
Pale ashes of the house of Lancaster,
Thou bloodless remnant of that royal blood,
Be it lawful that I invocate thy ghost   8
To hear the lamentations of poor Anne,

Wife to thy Edward, to thy slaughtered son,
Stabbed by the selfsame hand that made these wounds!
Lo, in these windows that let forth thy life   12
I pour the helpless balm of my poor eyes.   13
Oh, cursèd be the hand that made these holes!
Cursèd the heart that had the heart to do it!
Cursèd the blood that let this blood from hence!
More direful hap betide that hated wretch   17
That makes us wretched by the death of thee
Than I can wish to wolves, to spiders, toads,
Or any creeping venomed thing that lives!
If ever he have child, abortive be it,   21
Prodigious, and untimely brought to light,   22
Whose ugly and unnatural aspect   23
May fright the hopeful mother at the view,
And that be heir to his unhappiness!   25
If ever he have wife, let her be made
More miserable by the life of him
Than I am made by my young lord and thee!—   28
Come now towards Chertsey with your holy load,   29
Taken from Paul's to be interrèd there.   30
              [The bearers take up the hearse.]
And still as you are weary of this weight,   31
Rest you, whiles I lament King Henry's corpse.

Enter Richard, Duke of Gloucester.

RICHARD
Stay, you that bear the corpse, and set it down.

ANNE
What black magician conjures up this fiend
To stop devoted charitable deeds?   35

RICHARD
Villains, set down the corpse, or, by Saint Paul,
I'll make a corpse of him that disobeys.

HALBERDIER *[advancing with his halberd lowered]*
My lord, stand back, and let the coffin pass.

RICHARD
Unmannered dog, stand thou when I command!   39
Advance thy halberd higher than my breast,   40
Or, by Saint Paul, I'll strike thee to my foot
And spurn upon thee, beggar, for thy boldness.   42
              [The bearers set down the hearse.]

ANNE
What do you tremble? Are you all afraid?   43
Alas, I blame you not, for you are mortal,
And mortal eyes cannot endure the devil.—
Avaunt, thou dreadful minister of hell!   46
Thou hadst but power over his mortal body;
His soul thou canst not have. Therefore, begone.

---

137 **fear** fear for   139 **diet** course of life, regimen   146 **with post-horse** by post-horses, i.e., by swiftest possible means   148 **steeled** reinforced   153 **Warwick's youngest daughter** the Lady Anne Neville, widow of Edward, Prince of Wales, son of King Henry VI. 154 **father** i.e., father-in-law (Henry VI).   158 **intent** design (i.e., Richard hopes to ally himself with the house of Lancaster to bolster his claim to the throne).
1.2. Location: London. A street.
0.2 *Halberds* halberdiers, guards with halberds, or long poleaxes 2 **hearse** (Probably here an open coffin on a bier.)   3 **obsequiously** as befits a funeral, mournfully   5 **key-cold** extremely cold, cold as a metal key. (Proverbial.)   8 **Be it** Let it be.   **invocate** invoke

12 **windows** i.e., wounds   13 **helpless** useless, unavailing 17 **hap betide** fortune befall   21 **abortive** misshapen, premature 22 **Prodigious** monstrous, unnatural   23 **aspect** appearance 25 **unhappiness** evil nature, bad luck.   28 **by . . . thee** i.e., by the deaths of Prince Edward and King Henry VI.   29 **Chertsey** monastery in Surrey, near London, where King Henry's body is to be buried   30 **Paul's** Saint Paul's Cathedral in London   31 **still as** often as   35 **devoted** holy   39 **stand** halt   40 **Advance . . . breast** Raise your halberd upright   42 **spurn** trample   43 **What** Why 46 **Avaunt** Begone

RICHARD
  Sweet saint, for charity, be not so curst.   49
ANNE
  Foul devil, for God's sake hence and trouble us not,   50
  For thou hast made the happy earth thy hell,
  Filled it with cursing cries and deep exclaims.   52
  If thou delight to view thy heinous deeds,
  Behold this pattern of thy butcheries.   54
                              [She uncovers the corpse.]
  Oh, gentlemen, see, see dead Henry's wounds
  Open their congealed mouths and bleed afresh!   56
  Blush, blush, thou lump of foul deformity!
  For 'tis thy presence that exhales this blood   58
  From cold and empty veins where no blood dwells.
  Thy deeds inhuman and unnatural
  Provokes this deluge most unnatural.
  O God, which this blood mad'st, revenge his death!
  O earth, which this blood drink'st, revenge his death!
  Either heav'n with lightning strike the murd'rer dead,
  Or earth gape open wide and eat him quick,   65
  As thou dost swallow up this good king's blood,
  Which his hell-governed arm hath butcherèd!
RICHARD
  Lady, you know no rules of charity,
  Which renders good for bad, blessings for curses.
ANNE
  Villain, thou know'st nor law of God nor man.   70
  No beast so fierce but knows some touch of pity.   71
RICHARD
  But I know none, and therefore am no beast.
ANNE
  Oh, wonderful, when devils tell the truth!   73
RICHARD
  More wonderful, when angels are so angry.
  Vouchsafe, divine perfection of a woman,   75
  Of these supposèd crimes to give me leave
  By circumstance but to acquit myself.   77
ANNE
  Vouchsafe, defused infection of a man,   78
  Of these known evils but to give me leave
  By circumstance t'accuse thy cursèd self.
RICHARD
  Fairer than tongue can name thee, let me have
  Some patient leisure to excuse myself.
ANNE
  Fouler than heart can think thee, thou canst make
  No excuse current but to hang thyself.   84
RICHARD
  By such despair I should accuse myself.

ANNE
  And by despairing shalt thou stand excused
  For doing worthy vengeance on thyself
  That didst unworthy slaughter upon others.
RICHARD   Say that I slew them not?
ANNE   Then say they were not slain.
  But dead they are, and, devilish slave, by thee.
RICHARD   I did not kill your husband.
ANNE   Why, then he is alive.
RICHARD
  Nay, he is dead, and slain by Edward's hand.
ANNE
  In thy foul throat thou liest! Queen Margaret saw
  Thy murd'rous falchion smoking in his blood,   96
  The which thou once didst bend against her breast,   97
  But that thy brothers beat aside the point.
RICHARD
  I was provokèd by her sland'rous tongue,
  That laid their guilt upon my guiltless shoulders.   100
ANNE
  Thou wast provokèd by thy bloody mind,
  That never dream'st on aught but butcheries.   102
  Didst thou not kill this king?
RICHARD   I grant ye.
ANNE
  Dost grant me, hedgehog? Then God grant me too   104
  Thou mayst be damnèd for that wicked deed!
  Oh, he was gentle, mild, and virtuous!
RICHARD
  The better for the King of Heaven that hath him.
ANNE
  He is in heaven, where thou shalt never come.
RICHARD
  Let him thank me that holp to send him thither;   109
  For he was fitter for that place than earth.
ANNE
  And thou unfit for any place but hell.
RICHARD
  Yes, one place else, if you will hear me name it.
ANNE   Some dungeon.
RICHARD   Your bedchamber.
ANNE
  Ill rest betide the chamber where thou liest!   115
RICHARD
  So will it, madam, till I lie with you.
ANNE
  I hope so.
RICHARD   I know so. But, gentle Lady Anne,
  To leave this keen encounter of our wits
  And fall something into a slower method,   119
  Is not the causer of the timeless deaths   120
  Of these Plantagenets, Henry and Edward,
  As blameful as the executioner?

---

49 curst spiteful, shrewish.   **50 hence** go hence, depart   **52 exclaims** exclamations.   **54 pattern** example   **56 bleed afresh** (A phenomenon popularly supposed to occur in the presence of the murderer.)   **58 exhales** draws out   **65 quick** alive   **70 nor . . . nor** neither . . . nor   **71 so fierce but knows** is so savage that it has not   **73 Oh . . . truth** (Anne bitterly reinterprets Richard's *am no beast,* "am not beastly," to mean that he is neither man nor beast, but devil.)   **75 Vouchsafe** Deign, consent   **77 circumstance** detailed argument   **78 defused** diffused, disordered, shapeless; *defused infection* means "spreading plague"   **84 current** genuine, acceptable (as in coinage)

96 falchion curved sword   **97 bend** direct, aim   **100 their** my brothers'   **102 aught** anything   **104 hedgehog** (Richard's heraldic emblem featured a boar or wild hog.)   **109 holp** helped   **115 betide** befall   **119 something into a** into a somewhat   **120 timeless** untimely

ANNE
    Thou wast the cause and most accurst effect.   123
RICHARD
    Your beauty was the cause of that effect—   124
    Your beauty, that did haunt me in my sleep
    To undertake the death of all the world,
    So I might live one hour in your sweet bosom.
ANNE
    If I thought that, I tell thee, homicide,   128
    These nails should rend that beauty from my cheeks.   129
RICHARD
    These eyes could not endure that beauty's wrack;   130
    You should not blemish it, if I stood by.
    As all the world is cheerèd by the sun,
    So I by that. It is my day, my life.
ANNE
    Black night o'ershade thy day, and death thy life!
RICHARD
    Curse not thyself, fair creature—thou art both.
ANNE
    I would I were, to be revenged on thee.   136
RICHARD
    It is a quarrel most unnatural
    To be revenged on him that loveth thee.
ANNE
    It is a quarrel just and reasonable
    To be revenged on him that killed my husband.
RICHARD
    He that bereft thee, lady, of thy husband
    Did it to help thee to a better husband.
ANNE
    His better doth not breathe upon the earth.
RICHARD
    He lives that loves thee better than he could.   144
ANNE
    Name him.
RICHARD   Plantagenet.
ANNE   Why, that was he.   145
RICHARD
    The selfsame name, but one of better nature.
ANNE
    Where is he?
RICHARD   Here.   [She] spits at him.
            Why dost thou spit at me?
ANNE
    Would it were mortal poison for thy sake!
RICHARD
    Never came poison from so sweet a place.
ANNE
    Never hung poison on a fouler toad.   150

    Out of my sight! Thou dost infect mine eyes.
RICHARD
    Thine eyes, sweet lady, have infected mine.   152
ANNE
    Would they were basilisks, to strike thee dead!   153
RICHARD
    I would they were, that I might die at once;
    For now they kill me with a living death.
    Those eyes of thine from mine have drawn salt tears,
    Shamed their aspects with store of childish drops;   157
    These eyes, which never shed remorseful tear—
    No, when my father York and Edward wept
    To hear the piteous moan that Rutland made   160
    When black-faced Clifford shook his sword at him;   161
    Nor when thy warlike father, like a child,   162
    Told the sad story of my father's death
    And twenty times made pause to sob and weep,
    That all the standers-by had wet their cheeks   165
    Like trees bedashed with rain—in that sad time
    My manly eyes did scorn an humble tear;
    And what these sorrows could not thence exhale,   168
    Thy beauty hath, and made them blind with weeping.
    I never sued to friend nor enemy;   170
    My tongue could never learn sweet smoothing words;   171
    But now thy beauty is proposed my fee,   172
    My proud heart sues and prompts my tongue to speak.
                        She looks scornfully at him.
    Teach not thy lip such scorn, for it was made
    For kissing, lady, not for such contempt.
    If thy revengeful heart cannot forgive,
    Lo, here I lend thee this sharp-pointed sword,
    Which if thou please to hide in this true breast
    And let the soul forth that adoreth thee,
    I lay it naked to the deadly stroke
    And humbly beg the death upon my knee.   181
        He [kneels and] lays his breast open; she offers at [it]
                        with his sword.
    Nay, do not pause; for I did kill King Henry—
    But 'twas thy beauty that provokèd me.
    Nay, now dispatch; 'twas I that stabbed young Edward—
    But 'twas thy heavenly face that set me on.   185
                        She falls the sword.
    Take up the sword again, or take up me.
ANNE
    Arise, dissembler. Though I wish thy death,
    I will not be thy executioner.
RICHARD [*rising*]
    Then bid me kill myself, and I will do it.

---

123 **effect** fulfillment.   124 **effect** result   128 **homicide** murderer
129 **rend** tear   130 **wrack** destruction   136 **I would I were** (If Anne
were truly both Richard's day and his life, she could terminate both.)
144 **He lives** i.e., There is a man.   **he** i.e., Prince Edward   145 **Plantagenet** (Richard's father, the Duke of York, adopted this name when
he made his claim to the English throne—see *1 Henry VI*, 2.4.36—but
the name had been in the family of England's Angevin rulers since
the time of Henry II and thus could also be claimed by Henry VI and
his son, Prince Edward.)   150 **poison . . . toad** (Toads were popularly
regarded as poisonous.)

152 **infected** i.e., with love (since love was thought to enter through
the eyes)   153 **basilisks** mythical reptiles reputed to kill by their
looks   157 **aspects** appearance   160 **Rutland** second son of Richard,
Duke of York. (See *3 Henry VI*, 1.3, for his death scene.)   161 **black-
faced** i.e., foreboding in appearance   162 **thy warlike father** i.e., the
Earl of Warwick   165 **That** so that   168 **exhale** draw out   170 **sued**
supplicated, appealed   171 **smoothing** flattering   172 **now** now
that.   **proposed my fee** proposed as my reward   181 **the death**
death after sentencing.   181.1 *offers* aims   185.1 *falls* lets fall

ANNE
I have already.

RICHARD   That was in thy rage.
Speak it again, and even with the word
This hand, which for thy love did kill thy love,
Shall for thy love kill a far truer love.
To both their deaths shalt thou be accessory.

ANNE   I would I knew thy heart.   195

RICHARD   'Tis figured in my tongue.   196

ANNE   I fear me both are false.

RICHARD   Then never man was true.

ANNE   Well, well, put up your sword.

RICHARD   Say, then, my peace is made.

ANNE   That shalt thou know hereafter.

RICHARD   But shall I live in hope?

ANNE   All men, I hope, live so.

RICHARD   Vouchsafe to wear this ring.   204

ANNE   To take is not to give.   205

                 [*He slips the ring on her finger.*]

RICHARD
Look how my ring encompasseth thy finger,   206
Even so thy breast encloseth my poor heart;
Wear both of them, for both of them are thine.
And if thy poor devoted servant may   209
But beg one favor at thy gracious hand,
Thou dost confirm his happiness forever.

ANNE   What is it?

RICHARD
That it may please you leave these sad designs
To him that hath most cause to be a mourner,
And presently repair to Crosby House,   215
Where, after I have solemnly interred
At Chertsey monast'ry this noble king
And wet his grave with my repentant tears,
I will with all expedient duty see you.   219
For divers unknown reasons, I beseech you,   220
Grant me this boon.

ANNE
With all my heart, and much it joys me, too,
To see you are become so penitent.—
Tressel and Berkeley, go along with me.

RICHARD
Bid me farewell.

ANNE   'Tis more than you deserve;
But since you teach me how to flatter you,
Imagine I have said farewell already.
               Exeunt two [Tressel and Berkeley] with Anne.

RICHARD
Sirs, take up the corpse.

GENTLEMAN   Towards Chertsey, noble lord?

RICHARD
No, to Whitefriars. There attend my coming.   229
               Exeunt [bearers with] corpse.

Was ever woman in this humor wooed?
Was ever woman in this humor won?
I'll have her, but I will not keep her long.
What? I, that killed her husband and his father,
To take her in her heart's extremest hate,
With curses in her mouth, tears in her eyes,
The bleeding witness of my hatred by,
Having God, her conscience, and these bars against me, 237
And I no friends to back my suit withal
But the plain devil and dissembling looks?
And yet to win her! All the world to nothing!   240
Ha!
Hath she forgot already that brave prince,
Edward, her lord, whom I, some three months since,
Stabbed in my angry mood at Tewkesbury?
A sweeter and a lovelier gentleman,
Framed in the prodigality of nature,   246
Young, valiant, wise, and, no doubt, right royal,
The spacious world cannot again afford.   248
And will she yet abase her eyes on me,   249
That cropped the golden prime of this sweet prince   250
And made her widow to a woeful bed?
On me, whose all not equals Edward's moiety?   252
On me, that halts and am misshapen thus?   253
My dukedom to a beggarly denier,   254
I do mistake my person all this while.
Upon my life, she finds, although I cannot,
Myself to be a marv'lous proper man.   257
I'll be at charges for a looking glass,   258
And entertain a score or two of tailors   259
To study fashions to adorn my body.
Since I am crept in favor with myself,
I will maintain it with some little cost.
But first I'll turn yon fellow in his grave,   263
And then return lamenting to my love.
Shine out, fair sun, till I have bought a glass,   265
That I may see my shadow as I pass.   *Exit.*

                              ❖

1.3

Enter the Queen Mother [Elizabeth], Lord Rivers,
[Marquess of Dorset,] and Lord Grey.

RIVERS
Have patience, madam. There's no doubt His Majesty
Will soon recover his accustomed health.

GREY
In that you brook it ill, it makes him worse.   3
Therefore, for God's sake, entertain good comfort,   4
And cheer His Grace with quick and merry eyes.

---

195 **would** wish   196 **figured** portrayed   204 **Vouchsafe** Consent
205 **To take . . . give** i.e., I accept the ring but I make no promises.
206 **Look how** Just as   209 **servant** i.e., male admirer, one whom she
may command   215 **presently repair** go right away.   **Crosby House**
(One of Richard's London dwellings; built originally by Sir John Crosby.)
219 **expedient** expeditious   220 **unknown** secret   229 **Whitefriars**
the Carmelite priory in London.   **attend** await

237 **bars** obstacles   240 **All . . . nothing** i.e., Against infinite odds.
246 **Framed . . . nature** i.e., formed in nature's most lavish mood
248 **afford** (because Nature was so lavish).   249 **abase her eyes** degrade
herself by looking favorably   250 **cropped** cut short.   **prime** springtime, early manhood   252 **Edward's moiety** half of Edward's worth.
253 **halts** limps   254 **denier** small copper coin, the twelfth part of a sou
257 **proper** handsome   258 **be . . . for** undertake the expense of
259 **entertain** retain, employ   263 **in** into   265 **glass** mirror
1.3. **Location:** London. The royal court.
3 **brook** endure   4 **entertain . . . comfort** cheer up

QUEEN ELIZABETH
    If he were dead, what would betide on me?   6

GREY
    No other harm but loss of such a lord.

QUEEN ELIZABETH
    The loss of such a lord includes all harms.

GREY
    The heavens have blessed you with a goodly son
    To be your comforter when he is gone.

QUEEN ELIZABETH
    Ah, he is young, and his minority
    Is put unto the trust of Richard Gloucester,
    A man that loves not me, nor none of you.

RIVERS
    Is it concluded he shall be Protector?

QUEEN ELIZABETH
    It is determined, not concluded yet;   15
    But so it must be, if the King miscarry.   16

    Enter Buckingham and [Lord Stanley Earl of]
    Derby.

GREY
    Here come the lords of Buckingham and Derby.

BUCKINGHAM
    Good time of day unto Your Royal Grace!

STANLEY
    God make Your Majesty joyful, as you have been!

QUEEN ELIZABETH
    The Countess Richmond, good my lord of Derby,   20
    To your good prayer will scarcely say amen.
    Yet, Derby, notwithstanding she's your wife
    And loves not me, be you, good lord, assured
    I hate not you for her proud arrogance.   24

STANLEY
    I do beseech you, either not believe
    The envious slanders of her false accusers,   26
    Or, if she be accused on true report,
    Bear with her weakness, which I think proceeds
    From wayward sickness and no grounded malice.   29

QUEEN ELIZABETH
    Saw you the King today, my lord of Derby?

STANLEY
    But now the Duke of Buckingham and I   31
    Are come from visiting His Majesty.

QUEEN ELIZABETH
    What likelihood of his amendment, lords?   33

BUCKINGHAM
    Madam, good hope; His Grace speaks cheerfully.

QUEEN ELIZABETH
    God grant him health! Did you confer with him?

BUCKINGHAM
    Ay, madam. He desires to make atonement   36
    Between the Duke of Gloucester and your brothers,   37
    And between them and my Lord Chamberlain,   38
    And sent to warn them to his royal presence.   39

QUEEN ELIZABETH
    Would all were well! But that will never be.
    I fear our happiness is at the height.

    Enter Richard [Duke of Gloucester, and Lord
    Hastings].

RICHARD
    They do me wrong, and I will not endure it!
    Who is it that complains unto the King
    That I, forsooth, am stern and love them not?
    By holy Paul, they love His Grace but lightly
    That fill his ears with such dissentious rumors.   46
    Because I cannot flatter and look fair,   47
    Smile in men's faces, smooth, deceive, and cog,   48
    Duck with French nods and apish courtesy,   49
    I must be held a rancorous enemy.
    Cannot a plain man live and think no harm,
    But thus his simple truth must be abused
    With silken, sly, insinuating Jacks?   53

GREY
    To whom in all this presence speaks Your Grace?   54

RICHARD
    To thee, that hast nor honesty nor grace.   55
    When have I injured thee? When done thee wrong?
    Or thee? Or thee? Or any of your faction?
    A plague upon you all! His Royal Grace—
    Whom God preserve better than you would wish!—
    Cannot be quiet scarce a breathing while   60
    But you must trouble him with lewd complaints.   61

QUEEN ELIZABETH
    Brother of Gloucester, you mistake the matter.
    The King, on his own royal disposition,   63
    And not provoked by any suitor else,
    Aiming, belike, at your interior hatred,   65
    That in your outward action shows itself
    Against my children, brothers, and myself,
    Makes him to send, that he may learn the ground   68
    Of your ill will, and thereby to remove it.

RICHARD
    I cannot tell. The world is grown so bad   70
    That wrens make prey where eagles dare not perch.

---

6 **betide on** become of   15 **determined, not concluded** i.e., decided though not officially passed   16 **miscarry** perish.   20 **The Countess Richmond** i.e., Margaret Beaufort (1443–1509), who married, successively, Edmund Tudor (Earl of Richmond), Lord Henry Stafford, and Thomas Lord Stanley (here called the Earl of Derby), to whom she is currently married. By the Earl of Richmond, she was mother of the future Henry VII.   24 **arrogance** i.e., ambition for her son.   26 **envious** malicious   29 **wayward** not yielding readily to treatment. **grounded** firmly fixed   31 **But now** Just now   33 **amendment** recovery

36 **atonement** reconciliation   37 **brothers** (Only one brother, Earl Rivers, is mentioned in the play, though historically Elizabeth had others; Shakespeare may be thinking of other kinsmen, including her sons, whom she helped to advance.)   38 **Lord Chamberlain** Hastings   39 **warn** summon   46 **dissentious** quarrelsome, discordant   47 **look fair** put on a pleasing appearance   48 **smooth** flatter. **cog** deceive   49 **Duck . . . nods** i.e., bow affectedly   53 **With silken** by smooth. **Jacks** lowbred persons.   54 **presence** company   55 **grace** sense of duty or propriety. (Playing upon *Your Grace* in the preceding line.)   60 **breathing while** i.e., brief time   61 **lewd** vile, base   63 **disposition** inclination   65 **Aiming** guessing. **belike** probably   68 **Makes him** causes him. (The implied subject is "The king's own disposition.") **ground** cause   70 **I cannot tell** i.e., I don't know what to think. (Richard plays the role of the exasperated moralist.)

Since every Jack became a gentleman,
There's many a gentle person made a Jack.

QUEEN ELIZABETH
Come, come, we know your meaning, brother Gloucester;
You envy my advancement and my friends'.   75
God grant we never may have need of you!

RICHARD
Meantime, God grants that I have need of you.
Our brother is imprisoned by your means,   78
Myself disgraced, and the nobility
Held in contempt, while great promotions
Are daily given to ennoble those
That scarce some two days since were worth a noble.   82

QUEEN ELIZABETH
By Him that raised me to this careful height   83
From that contented hap which I enjoyed,   84
I never did incense His Majesty
Against the Duke of Clarence, but have been
An earnest advocate to plead for him.
My lord, you do me shameful injury
Falsely to draw me in these vile suspects.   89

RICHARD
You may deny that you were not the mean   90
Of my Lord Hastings' late imprisonment.

RIVERS   She may, my lord, for—

RICHARD
She may, Lord Rivers! Why, who knows not so?
She may do more, sir, than denying that:
She may help you to many fair preferments,   95
And then deny her aiding hand therein,
And lay those honors on your high desert.   97
What may she not? She may, ay, marry, may she—   98

RIVERS   What, marry, may she?

RICHARD
What, marry, may she? Marry with a king,   100
A bachelor, and a handsome stripling too!   101
Iwis your grandam had a worser match.   102

QUEEN ELIZABETH
My lord of Gloucester, I have too long borne
Your blunt upbraidings and your bitter scoffs.
By heaven, I will acquaint His Majesty
Of those gross taunts that oft I have endured.
I had rather be a country servant maid
Than a great queen with this condition,
To be so baited, scorned, and stormèd at.   109

Enter old Queen Margaret [behind].

Small joy have I in being England's queen.

QUEEN MARGARET *[aside]*
And lessened be that small, God I beseech him!
Thy honor, state, and seat is due to me.   112

RICHARD
What? Threat you me with telling of the King?   113
Tell him, and spare not. Look what I have said   114
I will avouch 't in presence of the King.
I dare adventure to be sent to the Tower.   116
'Tis time to speak; my pains are quite forgot.   117

QUEEN MARGARET *[aside]*
Out, devil! I do remember them too well: 118
Thou killed'st my husband Henry in the Tower,
And Edward, my poor son, at Tewkesbury.

RICHARD
Ere you were queen, ay, or your husband king,
I was a packhorse in his great affairs,   122
A weeder-out of his proud adversaries,
A liberal rewarder of his friends.
To royalize his blood I spent mine own.

QUEEN MARGARET *[aside]*
Ay, and much better blood than his or thine.

RICHARD
In all which time you and your husband Grey
Were factious for the house of Lancaster;   128
And, Rivers, so were you. Was not your husband   129
In Margaret's battle at Saint Albans slain?
Let me put in your minds, if you forget,
What you have been ere this, and what you are;
Withal, what I have been, and what I am.   133

QUEEN MARGARET *[aside]*
A murd'rous villain, and so still thou art.

RICHARD
Poor Clarence did forsake his father, Warwick,   135
Ay, and forswore himself—which Jesu pardon!—

QUEEN MARGARET *[aside]*   Which God revenge!

RICHARD
To fight on Edward's party for the crown;
And for his meed, poor lord, he is mewed up.   139
I would to God my heart were flint, like Edward's,
Or Edward's soft and pitiful, like mine.
I am too childish-foolish for this world.

QUEEN MARGARET *[aside]*
Hie thee to hell for shame, and leave this world,   143
Thou cacodemon! There thy kingdom is.   144

RIVERS
My lord of Gloucester, in those busy days
Which here you urge to prove us enemies,   146

75 **friends'** i.e., kinsmen's.   78 **Our brother** i.e., Clarence   82 **noble** (1) gold coin worth six shillings eight pence (2) nobleman.   83 **careful** full of cares   84 **hap** fortune   89 **in** into.   **suspects** suspicions.   90 **mean** means   95 **preferments** advantages, promotions   97 **lay . . . desert** attribute these high honors to your rich deservings.   98 **marry** i.e., indeed. (A mild oath, literally, "by the Virgin Mary.")   100 **Marry with** Wed. (Punning on *marry*, indeed, in line 98.)   101 **stripling** young man   102 **Iwis** (1) Certainly (2) *I wis*, I know   109 **baited** harassed, as in bearbaiting   109.1 *Queen Margaret* (Historically, the widow of Henry VI was held prisoner in England for five years following the battle of Tewkesbury in 1471 and then was sent to France; see the note to line 167 below.)

112 **state** degree, high rank.   **seat** throne   113 **Threat** Threaten   114 **Look what** Whatever   116 **adventure to be** risk being   117 **pains** efforts (in King Edward's behalf)   118 **Out** (An exclamation of anger.)   122 **packhorse** workhorse, beast of burden   128 **Were factious for** fought factiously on the side of   129 **husband** (Queen Elizabeth's first husband, Sir John Grey, fell fighting on the Lancastrian side at Saint Albans.)   133 **Withal** in addition   135 **father** i.e., father-in-law. (See *3 Henry VI*, 4.1, when Clarence deserted his brothers to marry Warwick's daughter Isabella and supported the Lancastrian cause for a time; thereafter, he forswore his oath to Warwick by returning to fight on Edward's *party* [line 138] or side.)   139 **meed** reward.   **mewed** caged (like a hawk)   143 **Hie** Hasten   144 **cacodemon** evil spirit.   146 **urge** cite

We followed then our lord, our sovereign king.
So should we you, if you should be our king.

RICHARD

If I should be? I had rather be a peddler.
Far be it from my heart, the thought thereof!

QUEEN ELIZABETH

As little joy, my lord, as you suppose
You should enjoy were you this country's king,
As little joy you may suppose in me
That I enjoy, being the queen thereof.

QUEEN MARGARET [aside]

Ah, little joy enjoys the queen thereof,
For I am she, and altogether joyless.
I can no longer hold me patient.   [Advancing.]
Hear me, you wrangling pirates, that fall out
In sharing that which you have pilled from me!   159
Which of you trembles not that looks on me?
If not, that I am queen, you bow like subjects,   161
Yet that, by you deposed, you quake like rebels?   162
[To Richard] Ah, gentle villain, do not turn away! 163

RICHARD

Foul wrinkled witch, what mak'st thou in my sight? 164

QUEEN MARGARET

But repetition of what thou hast marred;   165
That will I make before I let thee go.   166

RICHARD

Wert thou not banishèd on pain of death?   167

QUEEN MARGARET

I was; but I do find more pain in banishment
Than death can yield me here by my abode.
A husband and a son you ow'st to me,   170
And thou a kingdom; all of you allegiance.   171
This sorrow that I have by right is yours,
And all the pleasures you usurp are mine.

RICHARD

The curse my noble father laid on thee   174
When thou didst crown his warlike brows with paper
And with thy scorns drew'st rivers from his eyes,
And then, to dry them, gav'st the Duke a clout   177
Steeped in the faultless blood of pretty Rutland—   178
His curses then, from bitterness of soul
Denounced against thee, are all fall'n upon thee;   180
And God, not we, hath plagued thy bloody deed.

QUEEN ELIZABETH

So just is God, to right the innocent.

HASTINGS

Oh, 'twas the foulest deed to slay that babe,   183
And the most merciless, that e'er was heard of!

RIVERS

Tyrants themselves wept when it was reported.   185

DORSET

No man but prophesied revenge for it.   186

BUCKINGHAM

Northumberland, then present, wept to see it.

QUEEN MARGARET

What? Were you snarling all before I came,
Ready to catch each other by the throat,
And turn you all your hatred now on me?
Did York's dread curse prevail so much with heaven
That Henry's death, my lovely Edward's death,
Their kingdom's loss, my woeful banishment,
Should all but answer for that peevish brat?   194
Can curses pierce the clouds and enter heaven?
Why, then, give way, dull clouds, to my quick curses! 196
Though not by war, by surfeit die your king,   197
As ours by murder, to make him a king!
Edward thy son, that now is Prince of Wales,
For Edward our son, that was Prince of Wales,
Die in his youth by like untimely violence!
Thyself a queen, for me that was a queen,
Outlive thy glory, like my wretched self!
Long mayst thou live to wail thy children's death
And see another, as I see thee now,
Decked in thy rights, as thou art stalled in mine! 206
Long die thy happy days before thy death,
And, after many lengthened hours of grief,
Die neither mother, wife, nor England's queen!
Rivers and Dorset, you were standers-by,   210
And so wast thou, Lord Hastings, when my son   211
Was stabbed with bloody daggers: God, I pray him,
That none of you may live his natural age,   213
But by some unlooked accident cut off!   214

RICHARD

Have done thy charm, thou hateful withered hag!   215

QUEEN MARGARET

And leave out thee? Stay, dog, for thou shalt hear me.
If heaven have any grievous plague in store
Exceeding those that I can wish upon thee,
Oh, let them keep it till thy sins be ripe,   219
And then hurl down their indignation
On thee, the troubler of the poor world's peace!
The worm of conscience still begnaw thy soul!   222
Thy friends suspect for traitors while thou liv'st,
And take deep traitors for thy dearest friends!
No sleep close up that deadly eye of thine,
Unless it be while some tormenting dream
Affrights thee with a hell of ugly devils!
Thou elvish-marked, abortive, rooting hog,   228

---

159 **pilled** pillaged, robbed   161–2 **If . . . rebels** i.e., Even if you do not bow low to me as your queen, you quake as rebels who have deposed me.   163 **gentle** nobly born. *Gentle villain* is an oxymoron, since *villain* can mean "one ignobly born."   164 **mak'st thou** are you doing   165 **But . . . marred** Only reciting your crimes   166 **That** that repetition or recital   167 **banishèd** (Margaret was banished in 1464, returned to England in 1471, and after the Battle of Tewkesbury was confined in the Tower until 1476, when she returned to France, dying there in 1482, one year before the historical time of this scene.)   170 **thou** i.e., Richard   171 **thou** i.e., Elizabeth   174 **The curse** (See *3 Henry VI*, 1.4.164–6.)   177 **clout** cloth, handkerchief   178 **faultless** innocent   180 **Denounced** proclaimed vengefully   183 **that babe** i.e., Rutland (who historically was an older brother of Richard)

185 **Tyrants** Even pitiless men   186 **No . . . prophesied** There was no one who did not prophesy   194 **but answer for** merely atone for, equal.   **peevish** silly, senseless   196 **quick** lively, piercing   197 **surfeit** dissipated living   206 **Decked** dressed.   **stalled** installed   210–11 **Rivers, Dorset, Hastings** (Not present in Shakespeare's dramatization of the event in *3 Henry VI*, 5.5, but named in the chronicles as having been present.)   213 **natural age** full course of life   214 **unlooked** unexpected   215 **charm** magic curse, pronounced by a witch   219 **them** i.e., the heavens, heaven   222 **still begnaw** continually gnaw   228 **elvish-marked** marked by elves at birth.   **hog** (Alludes to Richard's badge, the wild boar.)

Thou that wast sealed in thy nativity   229
The slave of nature and the son of hell!   230
Thou slander of thy heavy mother's womb,   231
Thou loathèd issue of thy father's loins,
Thou rag of honor, thou detested—   233

RICHARD
  Margaret.

QUEEN MARGARET   Richard!

RICHARD   Ha?

QUEEN MARGARET   I call thee not.

RICHARD
  I cry thee mercy then, for I did think   235
  That thou hadst called me all these bitter names.

QUEEN MARGARET
  Why, so I did, but looked for no reply.
  Oh, let me make the period to my curse!   238

RICHARD
  'Tis done by me, and ends in "Margaret."

QUEEN ELIZABETH [to Queen Margaret]
  Thus have you breathed your curse against yourself.

QUEEN MARGARET
  Poor painted queen, vain flourish of my fortune!   241
  Why strew'st thou sugar on that bottled spider,   242
  Whose deadly web ensnareth thee about?
  Fool, fool, thou whet'st a knife to kill thyself.
  The day will come that thou shalt wish for me
  To help thee curse this poisonous bunch-backed toad. 246

HASTINGS
  False-boding woman, end thy frantic curse,   247
  Lest to thy harm thou move our patience.

QUEEN MARGARET
  Foul shame upon you! You have all moved mine.

RIVERS
  Were you well served, you would be taught your duty. 250

QUEEN MARGARET
  To serve me well, you all should do me duty,   251
  Teach me to be your queen, and you my subjects.   252
  Oh, serve me well, and teach yourselves that duty!

DORSET
  Dispute not with her. She is lunatic.

QUEEN MARGARET
  Peace, Master Marquess, you are malapert.   255
  Your fire-new stamp of honor is scarce current.   256
  Oh, that your young nobility could judge
  What 'twere to lose it and be miserable!
  They that stand high have many blasts to shake them, 259
  And if they fall, they dash themselves to pieces.

RICHARD
  Good counsel, marry! Learn it, learn it, Marquess.

DORSET
  It touches you, my lord, as much as me.

RICHARD
  Ay, and much more; but I was born so high.   263
  Our aerie buildeth in the cedar's top,   264
  And dallies with the wind and scorns the sun.

QUEEN MARGARET
  And turns the sun to shade; alas, alas!   266
  Witness my son, now in the shade of death,
  Whose bright outshining beams thy cloudy wrath
  Hath in eternal darkness folded up.
  Your aerie buildeth in our aerie's nest.
  O God, that see'st it, do not suffer it!
  As it is won with blood, lost be it so!

BUCKINGHAM
  Peace, peace, for shame, if not for charity!

QUEEN MARGARET
  Urge neither charity nor shame to me.
                          [Turning to the others.]
  Uncharitably with me have you dealt,
  And shamefully my hopes by you are butchered.
  My charity is outrage, life my shame,   277
  And in that shame still live my sorrow's rage!

BUCKINGHAM   Have done, have done.

QUEEN MARGARET
  O princely Buckingham, I'll kiss thy hand
  In sign of league and amity with thee.
  Now fair befall thee and thy noble house!   282
  Thy garments are not spotted with our blood,
  Nor thou within the compass of my curse.   284

BUCKINGHAM
  Nor no one here; for curses never pass   285
  The lips of those that breathe them in the air.

QUEEN MARGARET
  I will not think but they ascend the sky   287
  And there awake God's gentle-sleeping peace.
  O Buckingham, take heed of yonder dog!
  Look when he fawns, he bites; and when he bites,   290
  His venom tooth will rankle to the death.   291
  Have not to do with him, beware of him;
  Sin, death, and hell have set their marks on him,
  And all their ministers attend on him.

RICHARD
  What doth she say, my lord of Buckingham?

BUCKINGHAM
  Nothing that I respect, my gracious lord.   296

QUEEN MARGARET
  What, dost thou scorn me for my gentle counsel?

---

229 **sealed** stamped   230 **slave of nature** i.e., wretch made by the malignancy of nature (as seen in his deformity)   231 **heavy** (1) sorrowful (2) weighted down in pregnancy   233 **rag** tattered remnant   235 **cry thee mercy** beg your pardon. (Said sarcastically.)   238 **period** conclusion   241 **painted** counterfeit.   **vain . . . fortune** i.e., mere ornament of a position that is mine by right.   242 **bottled** bottle-shaped, swollen   246 **bunch-backed** hunch-backed   247 **False-boding** Falsely prophesying   250 **well served** treated as you deserve. (But Margaret turns the phrase around to mean "served as befitting one of royal rank.")   **your duty** your place (i.e., to be obedient).   251 **duty** reverence   252 **Teach me** i.e., show by your obedience what is my role   255 **Master** (A title for a boy of good family, used insultingly here.)   **malapert** impudent.   256 **fire-new** newly coined.   **current** genuine as legal tender.   259 **blasts** strong gusts of wind

263 **born so high** i.e., born noble—unlike you.   264 **aerie** eagle's brood   266 **sun** (With a play on *son* in the next line.)   277 **My . . . shame** i.e., Instead of charity I receive outrage, and the only life given me is one of shame; or, outrage is all the charity I feel, and shame is my only life   282 **fair befall** good luck to   284 **compass** scope, boundary   285 **pass** get any further than   287 **I . . . but** I must believe that   290 **Look when** (1) Whenever (2) Expect that when   291 **venom** envenomed.   **rankle** cause a festering wound   296 **respect** heed

And soothe the devil that I warn thee from?   298
Oh, but remember this another day,
When he shall split thy very heart with sorrow,
And say poor Margaret was a prophetess!
Live each of you the subjects to his hate,   302
And he to yours, and all of you to God's!   *Exit.*

BUCKINGHAM
My hair doth stand on end to hear her curses.

RIVERS
And so doth mine. I muse why she's at liberty.   305

RICHARD
I cannot blame her. By God's holy mother,
She hath had too much wrong, and I repent
My part thereof that I have done to her.

QUEEN ELIZABETH
I never did her any, to my knowledge.

RICHARD
Yet you have all the vantage of her wrong.   310
I was too hot to do somebody good   311
That is too cold in thinking of it now.   312
Marry, as for Clarence, he is well repaid;
He is franked up to fatting for his pains—   314
God pardon them that are the cause thereof!

RIVERS
A virtuous and a Christian-like conclusion,
To pray for them that have done scathe to us.   317

RICHARD
So do I ever—(*speaks to himself*) being well advised.   318
For had I cursed now, I had cursed myself.

Enter Catesby.

CATESBY
Madam, His Majesty doth call for you,
And for Your Grace, and yours, my gracious lord.

QUEEN ELIZABETH
Catesby, I come.—Lords, will you go with me?

RIVERS
We wait upon Your Grace.   323
             Exeunt all but [Richard Duke of] Gloucester.

RICHARD
I do the wrong, and first begin to brawl.
The secret mischiefs that I set abroach   325
I lay unto the grievous charge of others.   326
Clarence, who I indeed have cast in darkness,
I do beweep to many simple gulls—   328
Namely, to Derby, Hastings, Buckingham—
And tell them 'tis the Queen and her allies
That stir the King against the Duke my brother.
Now they believe it, and withal whet me   332
To be revenged on Rivers, Dorset, Grey.
But then I sigh and, with a piece of Scripture,

Tell them that God bids us do good for evil.   335
And thus I clothe my naked villainy
With odd old ends stol'n forth of Holy Writ,   337
And seem a saint when most I play the devil.

Enter two Murderers.

But soft! Here come my executioners.—   339
How now, my hardy, stout, resolvèd mates,   340
Are you now going to dispatch this thing?

FIRST MURDERER
We are, my lord, and come to have the warrant
That we may be admitted where he is.

RICHARD
Well thought upon. I have it here about me.
                              [He gives the warrant.]
When you have done, repair to Crosby Place.   345
But sirs, be sudden in the execution,
Withal obdurate; do not hear him plead;   347
For Clarence is well-spoken, and perhaps
May move your hearts to pity if you mark him.   349

FIRST MURDERER
Tut, tut, my lord, we will not stand to prate;   350
Talkers are no good doers. Be assured
We go to use our hands and not our tongues.

RICHARD
Your eyes drop millstones when fools' eyes fall tears.   353
I like you, lads. About your business straight.
Go, go, dispatch.

FIRST MURDERER   We will, my noble lord.   *[Exeunt.]*

❖

1.4

Enter Clarence and Keeper.

KEEPER
Why looks Your Grace so heavily today?   1

CLARENCE
Oh, I have passed a miserable night,
So full of fearful dreams, of ugly sights,
That, as I am a Christian faithful man,
I would not spend another such a night
Though 'twere to buy a world of happy days,
So full of dismal terror was the time!

KEEPER
What was your dream, my lord? I pray you, tell me.

CLARENCE
Methoughts that I had broken from the Tower   9
And was embarked to cross to Burgundy,   10
And in my company my brother Gloucester,
Who from my cabin tempted me to walk

---

298 soothe flatter   **302 the subjects to** subjugated to   **305 muse**
wonder   **310 vantage of her wrong** benefits derived from the
wrongs she has suffered.   **311 too hot . . . good** i.e., too eager in
helping Edward to the throne   **312 That . . . cold** who is too ungrateful   **314 franked . . . fatting** shut up in a frank or sty to be fattened
for slaughter   **317 scathe** harm   **318 well advised** cautious.
323 wait upon attend   **325 set abroach** set flowing   **326 lay . . . of**
impute as a serious accusation against   **328 gulls** credulous persons
332 withal furthermore.   **whet** urge, incite

335 for in return for   **337 ends** fragments, tags   **339 soft** gently; wait
a minute.   **340 stout . . . mates** bold, resolute fellows   **345 repair**
betake yourselves   **347 Withal** at the same time   **349 mark** pay
attention to   **350 prate** prattle   **353 millstones** heavy stone disks
used for grinding. (To *drop millstones* was proverbially to show signs
of hardheartedness.)   **fall** let fall
1.4. Location: London. The Tower.
1 heavily sad   **9 Methoughts** It seemed to me   **10 Burgundy**
(Clarence and Richard, according to the chronicles, had been sent to
Burgundy for protection following their father's death.)

Upon the hatches. Thence we looked toward England   13
And cited up a thousand heavy times,   14
During the wars of York and Lancaster,
That had befall'n us. As we paced along
Upon the giddy footing of the hatches,   17
Methought that Gloucester stumbled, and in falling
Struck me, that thought to stay him, overboard   19
Into the tumbling billows of the main.   20
Oh, Lord, methought what pain it was to drown!
What dreadful noise of waters in my ears!
What sights of ugly death within my eyes!
Methought I saw a thousand fearful wracks;   24
Ten thousand men that fishes gnawed upon;
Wedges of gold, great anchors, heaps of pearl,   26
Inestimable stones, unvalued jewels,   27
All scattered in the bottom of the sea.
Some lay in dead men's skulls, and in the holes
Where eyes did once inhabit there were crept,
As 'twere in scorn of eyes, reflecting gems,
That wooed the slimy bottom of the deep   32
And mocked the dead bones that lay scattered by.

KEEPER
Had you such leisure in the time of death
To gaze upon these secrets of the deep?

CLARENCE
Methought I had, and often did I strive
To yield the ghost; but still the envious flood   37
Stopped in my soul and would not let it forth   38
To seek the empty, vast, and wand'ring air,
But smothered it within my panting bulk,   40
Which almost burst to belch it in the sea.

KEEPER
Awaked you not in this sore agony?

CLARENCE
No, no, my dream was lengthened after life.
Oh, then began the tempest to my soul!
I passed, methought, the melancholy flood,   45
With that sour ferryman which poets write of,   46
Unto the kingdom of perpetual night.
The first that there did greet my stranger soul   48
Was my great father-in-law, renownèd Warwick,
Who spake aloud, "What scourge for perjury
Can this dark monarchy afford false Clarence?"
And so he vanished. Then came wand'ring by
A shadow like an angel, with bright hair   53
Dabbled in blood, and he shrieked out aloud,
"Clarence is come—false, fleeting, perjured Clarence,   55
That stabbed me in the field by Tewkesbury.
Seize on him, Furies, take him unto torment!"
With that, methought, a legion of foul fiends

Environed me and howlèd in mine ears
Such hideous cries that with the very noise
I trembling waked, and for a season after   61
Could not believe but that I was in hell,
Such terrible impression made my dream.

KEEPER
No marvel, my lord, though it affrighted you.
I am afraid, methinks, to hear you tell it.

CLARENCE
Ah, keeper, keeper, I have done these things,
That now give evidence against my soul,
For Edward's sake, and see how he requites me!   68
O God! If my deep prayers cannot appease thee,
But thou wilt be avenged on my misdeeds,
Yet execute thy wrath in me alone!
Oh, spare my guiltless wife and my poor children!
Keeper, I prithee, sit by me awhile.
My soul is heavy, and I fain would sleep.   74

KEEPER
I will, my lord. God give Your Grace good rest!
                    [Clarence sleeps.]

Enter Brackenbury, the Lieutenant.

BRACKENBURY
Sorrow breaks seasons and reposing hours,   76
Makes the night morning and the noontide night.
Princes have but their titles for their glories,
An outward honor for an inward toil,
And, for unfelt imaginations,   80
They often feel a world of restless cares;
So that between their titles and low name   82
There's nothing differs but the outward fame.   83

Enter two Murderers.

FIRST MURDERER   Ho! Who's here?
BRACKENBURY
What would'st thou, fellow, and how cam'st thou hither?
SECOND MURDERER   I would speak with Clarence, and I
came hither on my legs.
BRACKENBURY   What, so brief?
FIRST MURDERER   'Tis better, sir, than to be tedious.—
Let him see our commission, and talk no more.
                    [*Brackenbury*] reads [*it*].
BRACKENBURY
I am in this commanded to deliver
The noble Duke of Clarence to your hands.
I will not reason what is meant hereby,
Because I will be guiltless from the meaning.   94
There lies the Duke asleep, and there the keys.
                    [*He gives keys.*]
I'll to the King and signify to him
That thus I have resigned to you my charge.

---

13 **hatches** movable planks forming a deck.   14 **cited up** recalled.
heavy difficult   17 **giddy** unsteady   19 **stay** hold, steady   20 **main**
ocean.   24 **wracks** shipwrecked vessels   26 **Wedges** ingots
27 **Inestimable** precious and innumerable.   **unvalued** priceless
32 **wooed** (These lifeless eyes have nothing to flirt with but the
murky depths.)   37 **envious flood** malicious water   38 **Stopped**
held   40 **bulk** body   45 **melancholy flood** i.e., River Styx   46 **ferry-**
man i.e., Charon, who ferried souls to Hades, *the kingdom of perpetual*
night (line 47)   48 **stranger** i.e., newly arrived   53 **shadow** i.e., ghost of
Edward, Prince of Wales, son of Henry VI   55 **fleeting** fickle, deceitful

61 **season** time   68 **requites** repays   74 **fain** willingly   76 **breaks . . .**
hours disrupts the normal rhythms of life and hours properly
devoted to sleep   80 **for unfelt imaginations** in return for glories
that are merely illusory   82 **low name** i.e., the lowly position of ordinary men   83 **fame** reputation.   94 **will be** wish to be

FIRST MURDERER   You may, sir; 'tis a point of wisdom.
Fare you well.   *Exit [Brackenbury with Keeper]*.

SECOND MURDERER   What, shall I stab him as he
sleeps?

FIRST MURDERER   No. He'll say 'twas done cowardly,
when he wakes.

SECOND MURDERER   Why, he shall never wake until the
great Judgment Day.

FIRST MURDERER   Why, then he'll say we stabbed him
sleeping.

SECOND MURDERER   The urging of that word "judgment" hath bred a kind of remorse in me.

FIRST MURDERER   What, art thou afraid?

SECOND MURDERER   Not to kill him, having a warrant,
but to be damned for killing him, from the which no
warrant can defend me.

FIRST MURDERER   I thought thou hadst been resolute.

SECOND MURDERER   So I am—to let him live.

FIRST MURDERER   I'll back to the Duke of Gloucester
and tell him so.

SECOND MURDERER   Nay, I prithee, stay a little. I hope
this passionate humor of mine will change. It was   119
wont to hold me but while one tells twenty.   120

FIRST MURDERER   How dost thou feel thyself now?

SECOND MURDERER   Faith, some certain dregs of conscience are yet within me.

FIRST MURDERER   Remember our reward when the
deed 's done.

SECOND MURDERER   Zounds, he dies! I had forgot the   126
reward.

FIRST MURDERER   Where's thy conscience now?

SECOND MURDERER   Oh, in the Duke of Gloucester's
purse.

FIRST MURDERER   When he opens his purse to give us
our reward, thy conscience flies out.

SECOND MURDERER   'Tis no matter; let it go. There's few
or none will entertain it.   134

FIRST MURDERER   What if it come to thee again?

SECOND MURDERER   I'll not meddle with it; it makes a
man a coward. A man cannot steal but it accuseth him;
a man cannot swear but it checks him; a man cannot   138
lie with his neighbor's wife but it detects him. 'Tis a
blushing, shamefaced spirit that mutinies in a man's
bosom. It fills a man full of obstacles. It made me once
restore a purse of gold that by chance I found. It
beggars any man that keeps it. It is turned out of
towns and cities for a dangerous thing, and every man
that means to live well endeavors to trust to himself
and live without it.

FIRST MURDERER   Zounds, 'tis even now at my elbow,
persuading me not to kill the Duke.

SECOND MURDERER   Take the devil in thy mind, and   149
believe him not. He would insinuate with thee but to   150
make thee sigh.   151

FIRST MURDERER   Tut, I am strong-framed; he cannot
prevail with me.

SECOND MURDERER   Spoke like a tall man that respects   154
thy reputation. Come, shall we fall to work?

FIRST MURDERER   Take him on the costard with the hilts   156
of thy sword, and then throw him into the malmsey   157
butt in the next room.   158

SECOND MURDERER   Oh, excellent device! And make a sop   159
of him.

FIRST MURDERER   Soft, he wakes.

SECOND MURDERER   Strike!

FIRST MURDERER   No, we'll reason with him.   163

CLARENCE [*waking*]
Where art thou, keeper? Give me a cup of wine.

SECOND MURDERER
You shall have wine enough, my lord, anon.

CLARENCE   In God's name, what art thou?

FIRST MURDERER   A man, as you are.

CLARENCE   But not, as I am, royal.

FIRST MURDERER   Nor you, as we are, loyal.

CLARENCE
Thy voice is thunder, but thy looks are humble.

FIRST MURDERER
My voice is now the King's, my looks mine own.

CLARENCE
How darkly and how deadly dost thou speak!   172
Your eyes do menace me. Why look you pale?
Who sent you hither? Wherefore do you come?

SECOND MURDERER   To, to, to—

CLARENCE   To murder me?

BOTH   Ay, ay.

CLARENCE
You scarcely have the hearts to tell me so,
And therefore cannot have the hearts to do it.
Wherein, my friends, have I offended you?

FIRST MURDERER
Offended us you have not, but the King.

CLARENCE
I shall be reconciled to him again.

SECOND MURDERER
Never, my lord; therefore prepare to die.

CLARENCE
Are you drawn forth among a world of men   184
To slay the innocent? What is my offense?
Where is the evidence that doth accuse me?
What lawful quest have given their verdict up   187
Unto the frowning judge? Or who pronounced
The bitter sentence of poor Clarence' death
Before I be convict by course of law?   190
To threaten me with death is most unlawful.
I charge you, as you hope to have redemption
By Christ's dear blood shed for our grievous sins,
That you depart and lay no hands on me.
The deed you undertake is damnable.

---

119 **passionate humor** compassionate mood   120 **wont** accustomed.
tells counts   126 **Zounds** i.e., By God's (Christ's) wounds   134 **entertain** it receive it, give it welcome.   138 **checks** reproves, stops
149–50 **Take . . . not** i.e., Listen to the devil and pay no heed to conscience.
150–1 **He . . . sigh** Your conscience would ingratiate itself with you merely
for the purpose of making you unhappy.

154 **tall** brave   156 **Take** Strike.   **costard** head. (Literally, a kind of
apple.)   157–8 **malmsey butt** wine barrel. (Malmsey is a sweet wine.)
159 **sop** bread or cake soaked in wine   163 **reason** talk   172 **darkly**
ominously   184 **drawn . . . men** especially selected from the whole
human race   187 **quest** inquest, i.e., jury   190 **convict** convicted

FIRST MURDERER
    What we will do, we do upon command.
SECOND MURDERER
    And he that hath commanded is our king.
CLARENCE
    Erroneous vassals! The great King of kings   198
    Hath in the table of His law commanded   199
    That thou shalt do no murder. Will you then
    Spurn at His edict and fulfill a man's?
    Take heed; for He holds vengeance in His hand
    To hurl upon their heads that break His law.
SECOND MURDERER
    And that same vengeance doth He hurl on thee
    For false forswearing and for murder, too.
    Thou didst receive the Sacrament to fight   206
    In quarrel of the house of Lancaster.
FIRST MURDERER
    And, like a traitor to the name of God,
    Didst break that vow, and with thy treacherous blade
    Unripped'st the bowels of thy sovereign's son.   210
SECOND MURDERER
    Whom thou wast sworn to cherish and defend.
FIRST MURDERER
    How canst thou urge God's dreadful law to us
    When thou hast broke it in such dear degree?   213
CLARENCE
    Alas! For whose sake did I that ill deed?
    For Edward, for my brother, for his sake.
    He sends you not to murder me for this,
    For in that sin he is as deep as I.
    If God will be avengèd for the deed,
    Oh, know you yet he doth it publicly!
    Take not the quarrel from His powerful arm.
    He needs no indirect or lawless course
    To cut off those that have offended Him.
FIRST MURDERER
    Who made thee, then, a bloody minister   223
    When gallant-springing brave Plantagenet,   224
    That princely novice, was struck dead by thee?   225
CLARENCE
    My brother's love, the devil, and my rage.   226
FIRST MURDERER
    Thy brother's love, our duty, and thy faults
    Provoke us hither now to slaughter thee.
CLARENCE
    If you do love my brother, hate not me!
    I am his brother, and I love him well.
    If you are hired for meed, go back again,   231
    And I will send you to my brother Gloucester,
    Who shall reward you better for my life
    Than Edward will for tidings of my death.

SECOND MURDERER
    You are deceived. Your brother Gloucester hates you.
CLARENCE
    Oh, no, he loves me, and he holds me dear.
    Go you to him from me.
FIRST MURDERER   Ay, so we will.
CLARENCE
    Tell him, when that our princely father York
    Blessed his three sons with his victorious arm
    And charged us from his soul to love each other,
    He little thought of this divided friendship.
    Bid Gloucester think of this, and he will weep.
FIRST MURDERER
    Ay, millstones, as he lessoned us to weep.   243
CLARENCE
    Oh, do not slander him, for he is kind.
FIRST MURDERER
    Right, as snow in harvest. Come, you deceive
        yourself.   245
    'Tis he that sends us to destroy you here.
CLARENCE
    It cannot be, for he bewept my fortune,
    And hugged me in his arms, and swore with sobs
    That he would labor my delivery.   249
FIRST MURDERER
    Why, so he doth, when he delivers you
    From this earth's thralldom to the joys of heaven. 251
SECOND MURDERER
    Make peace with God, for you must die, my lord.
CLARENCE
    Have you that holy feeling in your souls
    To counsel me to make my peace with God,
    And are you yet to your own souls so blind
    That you will war with God by murd'ring me?
    Oh, sirs, consider, they that set you on
    To do this deed will hate you for the deed.
SECOND MURDERER [to First Murderer]
    What shall we do?
CLARENCE   Relent, and save your souls.
    Which of you, if you were a prince's son,
    Being pent from liberty, as I am now,   261
    If two such murderers as yourselves came to you,
    Would not entreat for life?
FIRST MURDERER
    Relent? No. 'Tis cowardly and womanish.
CLARENCE
    Not to relent is beastly, savage, devilish.
    [To Second Murderer] My friend, I spy some pity in thy looks..
    Oh, if thine eye be not a flatterer,
    Come thou on my side, and entreat for me,
    As you would beg, were you in my distress.
    A begging prince what beggar pities not?
SECOND MURDERER   Look behind you, my lord.

198 Erroneous vassals! Sinful and mistaken wretches!   199 table
tablet (the Ten Commandments)   206 receive the Sacrament i.e.,
swear upon the Sacrament   210 sovereign's son i.e., Prince Edward,
son of Henry VI.   213 dear grievous, costly   223 minister agent of
God   224 gallant-springing i.e., gallant and sprightly, aspiring.
Plantagenet i.e., the Lancastrian Prince Edward, killed in 3 Henry VI,
5.5. (See the note at 1.2.145 on Edward's claim to this name.)
225 novice youth   226 My brother's love i.e., My love for my brother
231 meed financial reward

243 lessoned taught   245 Right . . . harvest i.e., He's just as kind and
natural—that is, both affectionate and with the natural feelings of a
brother—as is snow at harvest time.   249 labor my delivery work for
my release.   251 thralldom bondage, captivity   261 pent shut up

FIRST MURDERER
Take that, and that! (*Stabs him.*) If all this will not do,
I'll drown you in the malmsey butt within.
                                    Exit [with the body].

SECOND MURDERER
A bloody deed, and desperately dispatched!
How fain, like Pilate, would I wash my hands   275
Of this most grievous murder!

            Enter First Murderer.

FIRST MURDERER
How now? What mean'st thou that thou help'st me not?
By heaven, the Duke shall know how slack you
        have been.

SECOND MURDERER
I would he knew that I had saved his brother!
Take thou the fee, and tell him what I say,
For I repent me that the Duke is slain.   *Exit.*

FIRST MURDERER
So do not I. Go, coward as thou art.—
Well, I'll go hide his body in some hole
Till that the Duke give order for his burial;
And when I have my meed, I will away,
For this will out, and then I must not stay.   *Exit.* 286

2.1

Flourish. Enter the King [Edward], sick, the
Queen [Elizabeth], Lord Marquess Dorset, [Grey,]
Rivers, Hastings, Catesby, Buckingham, [and
others].

KING EDWARD
Why, so. Now have I done a good day's work.
You peers, continue this united league.
I every day expect an embassage
From my Redeemer to redeem me hence;
And more in peace my soul shall part to heaven,
Since I have made my friends at peace on earth.
Rivers and Hastings, take each other's hand;
Dissemble not your hatred, swear your love.   8

RIVERS [*taking Hastings' hand*]
By heaven, my soul is purged from grudging hate,
And with my hand I seal my true heart's love.

HASTINGS
So thrive I, as I truly swear the like!

KING EDWARD
Take heed you dally not before your king,   12
Lest he that is the supreme King of kings
Confound your hidden falsehood, and award   14
Either of you to be the other's end.   15

HASTINGS
So prosper I, as I swear perfect love!

RIVERS
And I, as I love Hastings with my heart!

KING EDWARD
Madam, yourself is not exempt from this,
Nor you, son Dorset, Buckingham, nor you;   19
You have been factious one against the other.   20
Wife, love Lord Hastings; let him kiss your hand;
And what you do, do it unfeignedly.

QUEEN ELIZABETH
There, Hastings, I will never more remember
Our former hatred, so thrive I and mine!   24
            [*Hastings kisses her hand.*]

KING EDWARD
Dorset, embrace him. Hastings, love Lord Marquess.

DORSET
This interchange of love, I here protest,   26
Upon my part shall be inviolable.

HASTINGS   And so swear I.   [*They embrace.*]

KING EDWARD
Now, princely Buckingham, seal thou this league
With thy embracements to my wife's allies,
And make me happy in your unity.

BUCKINGHAM [*to the Queen*]
Whenever Buckingham doth turn his hate
Upon Your Grace, but with all duteous love   33
Doth cherish you and yours, God punish me
With hate in those where I expect most love!
When I have most need to employ a friend,
And most assurèd that he is a friend,
Deep, hollow, treacherous, and full of guile   38
Be he unto me! This do I beg of God,
When I am cold in love to you or yours.
                            [*They*] embrace.

KING EDWARD
A pleasing cordial, princely Buckingham,   41
Is this thy vow unto my sickly heart.
There wanteth now our brother Gloucester here   43
To make the blessèd period of this peace.   44

BUCKINGHAM   And, in good time,
Here comes Sir Richard Ratcliffe and the Duke.

            Enter Ratcliffe and [Richard Duke of] Gloucester.

RICHARD
Good morrow to my sovereign king and queen;
And, princely peers, a happy time of day!

KING EDWARD
Happy, indeed, as we have spent the day.
Gloucester, we have done deeds of charity,
Made peace of enmity, fair love of hate,
Between these swelling wrong-incensèd peers.   52

RICHARD
    A blessèd labor, my most sovereign lord.
    Among this princely heap, if any here,   54
    By false intelligence, or wrong surmise,   55
    Hold me a foe;
    If I unwittingly, or in my rage,
    Have aught committed that is hardly borne   58
    By any in this presence, I desire
    To reconcile me to his friendly peace.
    'Tis death to me to be at enmity;
    I hate it, and desire all good men's love.
    First, madam, I entreat true peace of you,
    Which I will purchase with my duteous service;
    Of you, my noble cousin Buckingham,
    If ever any grudge were lodged between us;
    Of you and you, Lord Rivers, and of Dorset,
    That all without desert have frowned on me;   68
    Dukes, earls, lords, gentlemen—indeed, of all.
    I do not know that Englishman alive
    With whom my soul is any jot at odds
    More than the infant that is born tonight.   72
    I thank my God for my humility.
QUEEN ELIZABETH
    A holy day shall this be kept hereafter.
    I would to God all strifes were well compounded.   75
    My sovereign lord, I do beseech Your Highness
    To take our brother Clarence to your grace.
RICHARD
    Why, madam, have I offered love for this,
    To be so flouted in this royal presence?   79
    Who knows not that the gentle Duke is dead?   80
                                          They all start.
    You do him injury to scorn his corpse.
KING EDWARD
    Who knows not he is dead? Who knows he is?
QUEEN ELIZABETH
    All-seeing heaven, what a world is this!
BUCKINGHAM
    Look I so pale, Lord Dorset, as the rest?
DORSET
    Ay, my good lord, and no man in the presence   85
    But his red color hath forsook his cheeks.
KING EDWARD
    Is Clarence dead? The order was reversed.
RICHARD
    But he, poor man, by your first order died,
    And that a wingèd Mercury did bear;   89
    Some tardy cripple bare the countermand,   90
    That came too lag to see him buried.   91

God grant that some, less noble and less loyal,   92
Nearer in bloody thoughts but not in blood,   93
Deserve not worse than wretched Clarence did,   94
And yet go current from suspicion!   95

                    Enter [Lord Stanley] Earl of Derby.

STANLEY [*kneeling*]
    A boon, my sovereign, for my service done!   96
KING EDWARD
    I prithee, peace. My soul is full of sorrow.
STANLEY
    I will not rise unless Your Highness hear me.
KING EDWARD
    Then say at once what is it thou requests.
STANLEY
    The forfeit, sovereign, of my servant's life,   100
    Who slew today a riotous gentleman
    Lately attendant on the Duke of Norfolk.
KING EDWARD
    Have I a tongue to doom my brother's death,   103
    And shall that tongue give pardon to a slave?   104
    My brother killed no man; his fault was thought,
    And yet his punishment was bitter death.
    Who sued to me for him? Who, in my wrath,
    Kneeled at my feet, and bid me be advised?   108
    Who spoke of brotherhood? Who spoke of love?
    Who told me how the poor soul did forsake
    The mighty Warwick and did fight for me?
    Who told me, in the field at Tewkesbury,
    When Oxford had me down, he rescued me   113
    And said, "Dear brother, live, and be a king"?
    Who told me, when we both lay in the field
    Frozen almost to death, how he did lap me   116
    Even in his garments, and did give himself,
    All thin and naked, to the numb-cold night?   118
    All this from my remembrance brutish wrath
    Sinfully plucked, and not a man of you
    Had so much grace to put it in my mind.
    But when your carters or your waiting vassals   122
    Have done a drunken slaughter and defaced   123
    The precious image of our dear Redeemer,   124
    You straight are on your knees for pardon, pardon;   125
    And I, unjustly too, must grant it you.
                                          [*Stanley rises.*]
    But for my brother not a man would speak,
    Nor I, ungracious, speak unto myself
    For him, poor soul. The proudest of you all
    Have been beholding to him in his life;   130

---

54 heap assembly   **55 false intelligence** being misinformed
58 hardly borne taken amiss, deeply resented   **68 all without desert**
wholly without my having deserved it   **72 More than the infant** i.e.,
more than is that infant's soul   **75 compounded** settled.   **79 flouted**
mocked   **80 gentle** noble   **85 presence** i.e., royal presence   **89 Mercury** messenger of the classical gods   **90 tardy cripple** (Richard privately shares with the audience a jest on his own role in this.)   **bare**
bore   **91 lag** late

92–5 God . . . suspicion! i.e., (ironically) Pray God there be not persons
who deserve worse than Clarence got, persons less noble or related by
blood to the King than he, although closely involved in bloody plots,
who yet go undetected! (Richard means the Queen and her kindred.)
95 go current are accepted at face value (like legal currency).   **from**
free from   **96 A boon** (I crave) a favor   **100 The forfeit** i.e., The
remission of the forfeit   **103 doom** decree   **104 slave** servant, wretch.
108 advised cautious.   **113 Oxford** (See *3 Henry VI*, 5.5.2; this episode
has no historical basis.)   **116 lap** wrap   **118 thin** thinly clad   **122 your
carters . . . vassals** your cart drivers or your attendants   **123–4 defaced
. . . Redeemer** i.e., killed a man. (God made humanity in his own
image; Genesis 1:27.)   **125 straight** at once   **130 beholding** beholden

Yet none of you would once beg for his life.
O God, I fear thy justice will take hold
On me and you, and mine and yours, for this!
Come, Hastings, help me to my closet. Ah, poor Clarence! 134
              Exeunt some with King and Queen.

RICHARD
This is the fruits of rashness. Marked you not
How that the guilty kindred of the Queen
Looked pale when they did hear of Clarence' death?
Oh, they did urge it still unto the King.   138
God will revenge it. Come, lords, will you go
To comfort Edward with our company?

BUCKINGHAM   We wait upon Your Grace.   *Exeunt.*

                 ❖

2.2

        Enter the old Duchess of York, with the two
        children of Clarence, [Edward and Margaret
        Plantagenet].

BOY
Good grandam, tell us, is our father dead?
DUCHESS   No, boy.
GIRL
Why do you weep so oft, and beat your breast,
And cry, "O Clarence, my unhappy son"?
BOY
Why do you look on us, and shake your head,
And call us orphans, wretches, castaways,
If that our noble father were alive?   7
DUCHESS
My pretty cousins, you mistake me both.   8
I do lament the sickness of the King,
As loath to lose him, not your father's death;
It were lost sorrow to wail one that's lost.
BOY
Then, you conclude, my grandam, he is dead.
The King mine uncle is to blame for it.
God will revenge it, whom I will importune   14
With earnest prayers all to that effect.
GIRL   And so will I.
DUCHESS
Peace, children, peace! The King doth love you well.
Incapable and shallow innocents,   18
You cannot guess who caused your father's death.
BOY
Grandam, we can; for my good uncle Gloucester
Told me the King, provoked to it by the Queen,
Devised impeachments to imprison him;   22
And when my uncle told me so, he wept,
And pitied me, and kindly kissed my cheek;
Bade me rely on him as on my father,
And he would love me dearly as his child.

DUCHESS
Ah, that deceit should steal such gentle shape,
And with a virtuous visor hide deep vice!   28
He is my son—ay, and therein my shame;
Yet from my dugs he drew not this deceit.   30
BOY
Think you my uncle did dissemble, grandam?
DUCHESS   Ay, boy.
BOY
I cannot think it. Hark, what noise is this?   33

        Enter the Queen [Elizabeth], with her hair about
        her ears; Rivers and Dorset after her.

QUEEN ELIZABETH
Ah, who shall hinder me to wail and weep,
To chide my fortune and torment myself?
I'll join with black despair against my soul,
And to myself become an enemy.
DUCHESS
What means this scene of rude impatience?   38
QUEEN ELIZABETH
To make an act of tragic violence.   39
Edward, my lord, thy son, our king, is dead!   40
Why grow the branches when the root is gone?
Why wither not the leaves that want their sap?
If you will live, lament; if die, be brief,   43
That our swift-wingèd souls may catch the King's
Or, like obedient subjects, follow him
To his new kingdom of ne'er-changing night.
DUCHESS
Ah, so much interest have I in thy sorrow
As I had title in thy noble husband!   48
I have bewept a worthy husband's death
And lived with looking on his images;   50
But now two mirrors of his princely semblance   51
Are cracked in pieces by malignant death,
And I for comfort have but one false glass,   53
That grieves me when I see my shame in him.   54
Thou art a widow; yet thou art a mother,
And hast the comfort of thy children left;
But death hath snatched my husband from mine arms
And plucked two crutches from my feeble hands,
Clarence and Edward. Oh, what cause have I,   59
Thine being but a moiety of my moan,   60
To overgo thy woes and drown thy cries!   61
BOY
Ah, aunt! You wept not for our father's death.
How can we aid you with our kindred tears?   63

---

28 **visor** mask   30 **dugs** breasts   33.1–2 *with her . . . ears* (A conventional sign of grief.)   38 **rude impatience** violent unwillingness to accept misfortune.   39 **make** perform. (Continues the theatrical metaphor in the previous line.)   40 **Edward . . . dead** (Clarence's death, February 1478, and Edward IV's death, April 1483, are treated as if they had occurred nearly together.)   43 **brief** quick   48 **title** i.e., as mother of the King   50 **images** likenesses; here, children   51 **two mirrors** i.e., Edward and Clarence. (The Duchess does not count Rutland.)   53 **false glass** i.e., Richard   54 **my . . . him** a son of whom to be ashamed.   59 **what . . . I** what a cause I have   60 **moiety of my moan** half (the cause) of my grief   61 **overgo** exceed   63 **kindred tears** i.e., tears of kinfolks.

---

134 **closet** private chambers.   138 **still** continually
2.2. Location: London. The royal court.
7 **If that** if   8 **cousins** kinfolks   14 **importune** solicit, beg
18 **Incapable** Unable to understand   22 **impeachments** accusations

GIRL
    Our fatherless distress was left unmoaned;
    Your widow-dolor likewise be unwept!   65

QUEEN ELIZABETH
    Give me no help in lamentation;
    I am not barren to bring forth complaints.   67
    All springs reduce their currents to mine eyes, 68
    That I, being governed by the watery moon,   69
    May send forth plenteous tears to drown the world!
    Ah for my husband, for my dear lord Edward!

CHILDREN
    Ah for our father, for our dear lord Clarence!

DUCHESS
    Alas for both, both mine, Edward and Clarence!

QUEEN ELIZABETH
    What stay had I but Edward? And he's gone.   74

CHILDREN
    What stay had we but Clarence? And he's gone.

DUCHESS
    What stays had I but they? And they are gone.

QUEEN ELIZABETH
    Was never widow had so dear a loss!   77

CHILDREN
    Were never orphans had so dear a loss!

DUCHESS
    Was never mother had so dear a loss!
    Alas, I am the mother of these griefs;
    Their woes are parceled, mine is general.   81
    She for an Edward weeps, and so do I;
    I for a Clarence weep, so doth not she.
    These babes for Clarence weep, and so do I;
    I for an Edward weep, so do not they.
    Alas, you three, on me, threefold distressed,
    Pour all your tears! I am your sorrow's nurse, 87
    And I will pamper it with lamentation.   88

DORSET [to Queen Elizabeth]
    Comfort, dear mother. God is much displeased
    That you take with unthankfulness his doing.
    In common worldly things 'tis called ungrateful
    With dull unwillingness to repay a debt   92
    Which with a bounteous hand was kindly lent;
    Much more to be thus opposite with heaven 94
    For it requires the royal debt it lent you.   95

RIVERS
    Madam, bethink you like a careful mother
    Of the young Prince your son. Send straight for him;
    Let him be crowned. In him your comfort lives.
    Drown desperate sorrow in dead Edward's grave

    And plant your joys in living Edward's throne.

    Enter Richard [Duke of Gloucester], Buckingham,
    [Lord Stanley Earl of] Derby, Hastings, and
    Ratcliffe.

RICHARD [to Queen Elizabeth]
    Sister, have comfort. All of us have cause
    To wail the dimming of our shining star,
    But none can help our harms by wailing them.—
    Madam, my mother, I do cry you mercy;   104
    I did not see Your Grace. Humbly on my knee
    I crave your blessing.   [He kneels.]

DUCHESS
    God bless thee, and put meekness in thy breast,
    Love, charity, obedience, and true duty!

RICHARD
    Amen! [Aside] And make me die a good old man!
    That is the butt end of a mother's blessing;   110
    I marvel that Her Grace did leave it out.

BUCKINGHAM
    You cloudy princes and heart-sorrowing peers, 112
    That bear this heavy mutual load of moan, 113
    Now cheer each other in each other's love.
    Though we have spent our harvest of this king,
    We are to reap the harvest of his son.
    The broken rancor of your high-swoll'n hates,
    But lately splintered, knit, and joined together, 118
    Must gently be preserved, cherished, and kept. 119
    Me seemeth good that with some little train   120
    Forthwith from Ludlow the young Prince be fet 121
    Hither to London, to be crowned our king.

RIVERS
    Why with some little train, my lord of Buckingham?

BUCKINGHAM
    Marry, my lord, lest by a multitude   124
    The new-healed wound of malice should break out,
    Which would be so much the more dangerous
    By how much the estate is green and yet ungoverned. 127
    Where every horse bears his commanding rein 128
    And may direct his course as please himself, 129
    As well the fear of harm, as harm apparent, 130
    In my opinion, ought to be prevented.

RICHARD
    I hope the King made peace with all of us;
    And the compact is firm and true in me.

RIVERS
    And so in me, and so, I think, in all.
    Yet since it is but green, it should be put
    To no apparent likelihood of breach,

---

65 **widow-dolor** widow's grief   67 **barren to** i.e., unable to. (She is pregnant with grief.)   68 **All . . . eyes** Let all springs be concentrated in my eyes   69 **I . . . moon** (Her grief is now a sea, fed by springs and her tides governed by the moon.)   74 **stay** support   77 **dear** costly, grievous   81 **Their . . . general** the woes of Queen Elizabeth and these children are particular to each of them, mine is all-embracing.   87 **nurse** source of sustenance   88 **pamper** feed luxuriously, nourish   92 **dull** sluggish   94 **opposite with** contrary toward   95 **For it requires** because it calls back

104 **cry you mercy** beg your pardon   110 **butt end** concluding portion. (The *butt* is the end of a spear shaft.)   112 **cloudy** clouded with grief   113 **moan** lamentation   118 **But lately splintered** only recently bound together (as with a splint)   119 **Must . . . preserved** i.e., the recent mending of differences must be preserved   120 **Me seemeth** It seems to me. **train** entourage   121 **Ludlow** royal castle in Shropshire, near the Welsh border. **fet** fetched   124 **multitude** i.e., large train or entourage   127 **estate** state, government. **green** unripe, i.e., newly established   128 **bears . . . rein** controls the reins that ought to control him   129 **as please** as it pleases   130 **As . . . apparent** both the fear of trouble and the actual manifestation of it

Which haply by much company might be urged.   137
Therefore I say with noble Buckingham
That it is meet so few should fetch the Prince.   139

HASTINGS   And so say I.

RICHARD
Then be it so; and go we to determine
Who they shall be that straight shall post to Ludlow.   142
Madam, and you, my sister, will you go
To give your censures in this business?   144

QUEEN ELIZABETH, DUCHESS   With all our hearts.   145

Exeunt. Manent Buckingham and Richard.

BUCKINGHAM
My lord, whoever journeys to the Prince,
For God's sake let not us two stay at home;
For by the way I'll sort occasion,   148
As index to the story we late talked of,   149
To part the Queen's proud kindred from the Prince.

RICHARD
My other self, my counsel's consistory,   151
My oracle, my prophet! My dear cousin,
I, as a child, will go by thy direction.
Toward Ludlow then, for we'll not stay behind.

Exeunt.

❖

2.3

Enter one Citizen at one door, and another at the other.

FIRST CITIZEN
Good morrow, neighbor. Whither away so fast?

SECOND CITIZEN
I promise you, I scarcely know myself.   2
Hear you the news abroad?

FIRST CITIZEN   Yes, that the King is dead.

SECOND CITIZEN
Ill news, by'r Lady; seldom comes the better.   5
I fear, I fear 'twill prove a giddy world.   6

Enter another Citizen.

THIRD CITIZEN
Neighbors, God speed!

FIRST CITIZEN   Give you good morrow, sir.

THIRD CITIZEN
Doth the news hold of good King Edward's death?   8

SECOND CITIZEN
Ay, sir, it is too true, God help the while!

THIRD CITIZEN
Then, masters, look to see a troublous world.   10

FIRST CITIZEN
No, no; by God's good grace his son shall reign.

THIRD CITIZEN
Woe to that land that's governed by a child!   12

SECOND CITIZEN
In him there is a hope of government,
Which in his nonage, council under him,   14
And in his full and ripened years, himself,
No doubt shall then, and till then, govern well.

FIRST CITIZEN
So stood the state when Henry the Sixth
Was crowned in Paris but at nine months old.

THIRD CITIZEN
Stood the state so? No, no, good friends, God wot,   19
For then this land was famously enriched
With politic, grave counsel; then the King   21
Had virtuous uncles to protect His Grace.

FIRST CITIZEN
Why, so hath this, both by his father and mother.

THIRD CITIZEN
Better it were they all came by his father,
Or by his father there were none at all;
For emulation who shall now be nearest   26
Will touch us all too near, if God prevent not.
Oh, full of danger is the Duke of Gloucester,
And the Queen's sons and brothers haught and proud!   29
And were they to be ruled, and not to rule,
This sickly land might solace as before.   31

FIRST CITIZEN
Come, come, we fear the worst. All will be well.

THIRD CITIZEN
When clouds are seen, wise men put on their cloaks;
When great leaves fall, then winter is at hand;
When the sun sets, who doth not look for night?
Untimely storms makes men expect a dearth.
All may be well; but if God sort it so,   37
'Tis more than we deserve or I expect.

SECOND CITIZEN
Truly, the hearts of men are full of fear.
You cannot reason almost with a man   40
That looks not heavily and full of dread.   41

THIRD CITIZEN
Before the days of change, still is it so.   42
By a divine instinct men's minds mistrust   43
Ensuing danger; as, by proof, we see   44
The water swell before a boist'rous storm.
But leave it all to God. Whither away?

SECOND CITIZEN
Marry, we were sent for to the justices.

THIRD CITIZEN
And so was I. I'll bear you company.   *Exeunt.*

❖

---

137 haply perhaps.   **urged** encouraged, provoked.   **139 meet** fitting
142 post hasten   **144 censures** judgments   **145.1** *Manent* They
remain onstage   **148 by** on.   **sort** find, contrive   **149 index** prologue.   **late** lately   **151 consistory** council chamber
2.3. Location: London. A street.
2 promise assure   **5 Ill . . . better** Ill news, by Our Lady. Good news
comes seldom; most news is bad news.   **6 giddy** mad   **8 Doth the
news hold** Is the news true   **10 masters** good sirs.   **troublous** troubled, disorderly

12 Woe . . . child! (Compare with Ecclesiastes 10:16: "Woe to thee, O
land, when thy king is a child.")   **14 nonage** minority.   **council
under him** i.e., with the Privy Council governing in his name
19 wot knows   **21 politic** sagacious   **26 emulation** ambitious rivalry
29 haught haughty   **31 solace** be happy, have comfort   **37 sort** dispose   **40 You . . . man** There is scarcely anyone with whom you can
talk   **41 heavily** sad   **42 still** ever   **43 mistrust** suspect, fear
44 proof experience

2.4

*Enter [the] Archbishop [of York], [the] young
[Duke of] York, the Queen [Elizabeth], and the
Duchess [of York].*

ARCHBISHOP
Last night, I hear, they lay at Stony Stratford,   1
And at Northampton they do rest tonight.   2
Tomorrow, or next day, they will be here.
DUCHESS
I long with all my heart to see the Prince.
I hope he is much grown since last I saw him.
QUEEN ELIZABETH
But I hear, no; they say my son of York
Has almost overta'en him in his growth.
YORK
Ay, mother, but I would not have it so.
DUCHESS
Why, my young cousin? It is good to grow.
YORK
Grandam, one night as we did sit at supper,
My uncle Rivers talked how I did grow
More than my brother. "Ay," quoth my uncle Gloucester,
"Small herbs have grace; great weeds do grow apace."   13
And since, methinks, I would not grow so fast,   14
Because sweet flow'rs are slow and weeds make haste.
DUCHESS
Good faith, good faith, the saying did not hold   16
In him that did object the same to thee.   17
He was the wretched'st thing when he was young,
So long a-growing and so leisurely,
That, if his rule were true, he should be gracious.
ARCHBISHOP
And so no doubt he is, my gracious madam.
DUCHESS
I hope he is, but yet let mothers doubt.
YORK
Now, by my troth, if I had been remembered,   23
I could have given my uncle's Grace a flout   24
To touch his growth nearer than he touched mine.   25
DUCHESS
How, my young York? I prithee, let me hear it.
YORK
Marry, they say my uncle grew so fast
That he could gnaw a crust at two hours old;
'Twas full two years ere I could get a tooth.
Grandam, this would have been a biting jest.   30

DUCHESS
I prithee, pretty York, who told thee this?
YORK   Grandam, his nurse.
DUCHESS
His nurse? Why, she was dead ere thou wast born.
YORK
If 'twere not she, I cannot tell who told me.
QUEEN ELIZABETH
A parlous boy! Go to, you are too shrewd.   35
DUCHESS
Good madam, be not angry with the child.
QUEEN ELIZABETH   Pitchers have ears.   37

Enter a Messenger.

ARCHBISHOP
Here comes a messenger.—What news?
MESSENGER
Such news, my lord, as grieves me to report.
QUEEN ELIZABETH
How doth the Prince?
MESSENGER   Well, madam, and in health.
DUCHESS   What is thy news?
MESSENGER
Lord Rivers and Lord Grey are sent to Pomfret,   42
And with them Sir Thomas Vaughan, prisoners.
DUCHESS
Who hath committed them?
MESSENGER   The mighty dukes
Gloucester and Buckingham.
ARCHBISHOP   For what offense?
MESSENGER
The sum of all I can, I have disclosed.
Why or for what the nobles were committed
Is all unknown to me, my gracious lord.
QUEEN ELIZABETH
Ay me, I see the ruin of my house!
The tiger now hath seized the gentle hind;   50
Insulting tyranny begins to jut   51
Upon the innocent and aweless throne.   52
Welcome, destruction, blood, and massacre!
I see, as in a map, the end of all.   54
DUCHESS
Accursèd and unquiet wrangling days,
How many of you have mine eyes beheld!
My husband lost his life to get the crown,
And often up and down my sons were tossed   58
For me to joy and weep their gain and loss;
And being seated, and domestic broils   60
Clean overblown, themselves the conquerors   61
Make war upon themselves, brother to brother,
Blood to blood, self against self. O preposterous   63

2.4. Location: London. The royal court.
1 Stony Stratford village in Buckinghamshire   **2 Northampton** town
in Northamptonshire and hence farther from London than Stony
Stratford. The Prince was taken back to Northampton after the arrest
of Rivers, Grey, and Vaughan. The Archbishop does not yet know of
that arrest, but the Folio version of his speech, followed here, is based
misleadingly on historical information of subsequent events. (The quartos reverse the order in which the two towns are named.)   **13 grace**
virtuous qualities.   **apace** rapidly.   **14 since** ever since   **16–17 the
saying . . . thee** the saying did not at all apply to the person who
applied it to you, i.e., Richard.   **23 troth** truth, faith.   **had been
remembered** had recollected   **24 my . . . flout** His Grace, my uncle, a
mocking gibe   **25 touch . . . nearer** i.e., taunt him about his growth
more tellingly   **30 biting** (With a play on the idea of teething.)

35 parlous cunning, precocious.   **Go to** (An expression of remonstrance.)   **shrewd** sharp-tongued.   **37 Pitchers have ears** Little
pitchers have large ears. (Proverbial.)   **42 Pomfret** the castle at Pontefract in Yorkshire   **50 hind** doe   **51 Insulting** scornfully triumphing.   **jut** encroach   **52 aweless** inspiring no awe (because of the
youth of the King)   **54 map** i.e., of future events   **58 up . . . tossed**
i.e., my sons were raised and then lowered on fortune's wheel
60 seated i.e., on the throne   **61 Clean overblown** entirely finished
63 preposterous monstrous, perverse

And frantic outrage, end thy damnèd spleen,   64
Or let me die, to look on death no more!

QUEEN ELIZABETH
Come, come, my boy, we will to sanctuary.   66
Madam, farewell.

DUCHESS   Stay, I will go with you.

QUEEN ELIZABETH
You have no cause.

ARCHBISHOP [to the Queen]   My gracious lady, go,
And thither bear your treasure and your goods.
For my part, I'll resign unto Your Grace
The seal I keep; and so betide to me   71
As well I tender you and all of yours!   72
Go, I'll conduct you to the sanctuary.   Exeunt.

❧

3.1

The trumpets sound. Enter [the] young Prince
[Edward], the Dukes of Gloucester and
Buckingham, [Lord] Cardinal [Bourchier, Catesby],
etc.

BUCKINGHAM
Welcome, sweet Prince, to London, to your chamber.   1

RICHARD
Welcome, dear cousin, my thoughts' sovereign!
The weary way hath made you melancholy.

PRINCE EDWARD
No, uncle, but our crosses on the way   4
Have made it tedious, wearisome, and heavy.
I want more uncles here to welcome me.   6

RICHARD
Sweet Prince, the untainted virtue of your years
Hath not yet dived into the world's deceit.
Nor more can you distinguish of a man
Than of his outward show—which, God he knows,
Seldom or never jumpeth with the heart.   11
Those uncles which you want were dangerous.
Your Grace attended to their sugared words
But looked not on the poison of their hearts.
God keep you from them, and from such false
    friends!

PRINCE EDWARD
God keep me from false friends! But they were none.

RICHARD
My lord, the Mayor of London comes to greet you.

Enter [the] Lord Mayor [and his train].

MAYOR
God bless Your Grace with health and happy days!

PRINCE EDWARD
I thank you, good my lord, and thank you all.
        [The Mayor and his train stand aside.]
I thought my mother and my brother York
Would long ere this have met us on the way.
Fie, what a slug is Hastings, that he comes not   22
To tell us whether they will come or no!

Enter Lord Hastings.

BUCKINGHAM
And, in good time, here comes the sweating lord.

PRINCE EDWARD
Welcome, my lord. What, will our mother come?

HASTINGS
On what occasion God he knows, not I,   26
The Queen your mother and your brother York
Have taken sanctuary. The tender Prince
Would fain have come with me to meet Your Grace,
But by his mother was perforce withheld.   30

BUCKINGHAM
Fie, what an indirect and peevish course   31
Is this of hers!—Lord Cardinal, will Your Grace
Persuade the Queen to send the Duke of York
Unto his princely brother presently?   34
If she deny, Lord Hastings, go with him,
And from her jealous arms pluck him perforce.   36

CARDINAL
My lord of Buckingham, if my weak oratory
Can from his mother win the Duke of York,
Anon expect him here; but if she be obdurate   39
To mild entreaties, God in heaven forbid
We should infringe the holy privilege
Of blessèd sanctuary! Not for all this land
Would I be guilty of so deep a sin.

BUCKINGHAM
You are too senseless-obstinate, my lord,
Too ceremonious and traditional.   45
Weigh it but with the grossness of this age,   46
You break not sanctuary in seizing him.
The benefit thereof is always granted
To those whose dealings have deserved the place
And those who have the wit to claim the place.
This prince hath neither claimed it nor deserved it,
And therefore, in mine opinion, cannot have it.
Then, taking him from thence that is not there,   53
You break no privilege nor charter there.
Oft have I heard of sanctuary men,
But sanctuary children never till now.

CARDINAL
My lord, you shall o'errule my mind for once.
Come on, Lord Hastings, will you go with me?

64 spleen i.e., malice, hatred   66 sanctuary (Queen Elizabeth, with
her son, daughters, and kinsmen, lodged in the precincts of Westminster Abbey, which served as a legal refuge for criminals and persons
in danger of their lives.)   71 seal seal of office i.e., the Great Seal of
England. (The Archbishop's giving the Great Seal to Elizabeth is an
unusual and extralegal action.)   71–2 so . . . you may my fortunes be
measured by the care I take of you
3.1. Location: London. A street.
1 chamber (London was called the camera regis, or King's chamber.)
4 crosses vexations (i.e., the arrests of the Queen's kindred)   6 want
(1) lack (2) wish   11 jumpeth agrees

22 slug sluggard   26 On what occasion For what reason   30 perforce by force   31 peevish perverse   34 presently at once.   36 jealous suspicious   39 Anon shortly   45 ceremonious bound by
formalities   46 grossness lack of moral refinement   53 taking . . .
there i.e., taking the Prince from a place that cannot properly be
called a sanctuary in his case

HASTINGS   I go, my lord.

PRINCE EDWARD
Good lords, make all the speedy haste you may.
                [*Exeunt Cardinal and Hastings.*]
Say, uncle Gloucester, if our brother come,
Where shall we sojourn till our coronation?   62

RICHARD
Where it seems best unto your royal self.
If I may counsel you, some day or two
Your Highness shall repose you at the Tower;   65
Then where you please, and shall be thought most fit
For your best health and recreation.

PRINCE EDWARD
I do not like the Tower, of any place.   68
Did Julius Caesar build that place, my lord?

BUCKINGHAM
He did, my gracious lord, begin that place,
Which, since, succeeding ages have re-edified.   71

PRINCE EDWARD
Is it upon record, or else reported   72
Successively from age to age, he built it?

BUCKINGHAM   Upon record, my gracious lord.

PRINCE EDWARD
But say, my lord, it were not registered,   75
Methinks the truth should live from age to age,
As 'twere retailed to all posterity,   77
Even to the general all-ending day.   78

RICHARD [*aside*]
So wise so young, they say, do never live long.

PRINCE EDWARD   What say you, uncle?

RICHARD
I say, without characters fame lives long.   81
[*Aside*] Thus, like the formal Vice, Iniquity,   82
I moralize two meanings in one word.   83

PRINCE EDWARD
That Julius Caesar was a famous man;
With what his valor did enrich his wit,   85
His wit set down to make his valor live.   86
Death makes no conquest of this conqueror,
For now he lives in fame, though not in life.
I'll tell you what, my cousin Buckingham—

BUCKINGHAM   What, my gracious lord?

PRINCE EDWARD
An if I live until I be a man,   91
I'll win our ancient right in France again
Or die a soldier, as I lived a king.

RICHARD [*aside*]
Short summers lightly have a forward spring.   94

     Enter young York, Hastings, [and the] Cardinal.

BUCKINGHAM
Now, in good time, here comes the Duke of York.

PRINCE EDWARD
Richard of York, how fares our loving brother?   96

YORK
Well, my dread lord—so must I call you now.   97

PRINCE EDWARD
Ay, brother, to our grief, as it is yours.
Too late he died that might have kept that title,   99
Which by his death hath lost much majesty.

RICHARD
How fares our cousin, noble lord of York?

YORK
I thank you, gentle uncle. Oh, my lord,   102
You said that idle weeds are fast in growth;   103
The Prince my brother hath outgrown me far.

RICHARD
He hath, my lord.

YORK   And therefore is he idle?

RICHARD
Oh, my fair cousin, I must not say so.

YORK
Then he is more beholding to you than I.   107

RICHARD
He may command me as my sovereign,
But you have power in me as in a kinsman.

YORK
I pray you, uncle, give me this dagger.

RICHARD
My dagger, little cousin? With all my heart.   111

PRINCE EDWARD   A beggar, brother?

YORK
Of my kind uncle, that I know will give;   113
And being but a toy, which is no grief to give.   114

RICHARD
A greater gift than that I'll give my cousin.

YORK
A greater gift? Oh, that's the sword to it.

RICHARD
Ay, gentle cousin, were it light enough.

YORK
Oh, then I see you will part but with light gifts.   118
In weightier things you'll say a beggar nay.

RICHARD
It is too heavy for Your Grace to wear.

YORK
I weigh it lightly, were it heavier.   121

---

62 sojourn reside   **65 Tower** (Although in the fifteenth century—the historical time this play represents—the Tower of London was a royal palace, by Shakespeare's day it had acquired a sinister reputation.) **68 of any place** of all places.   **71 re-edified** rebuilt.   **72 upon record** in the written record.   **reported** i.e., by oral tradition   **75 say** suppose.   **registered** written down   **77 retailed** repeated, handed down from one to another   **78 general . . . day** Day of Judgment.   **81 without characters** even lacking written records   **82 formal Vice** i.e., the conventional Vice figure of the morality play, a comic tempter to evil, who would habitually *moralize two meanings in one word*, that is, play on double meanings in a single phrase, as Richard does in the phrase *live long*   **83 moralize** interpret, illustrate   **85–6 With . . . live** having improved his understanding through his military achievements, he used his understanding to set down in writing an account (the *Gallic Wars*) that would make his valor immortal.   **91 An if** If

94 lightly commonly, often.   **forward** early. (Alludes to Edward's precociousness.)   **96 our** i.e., my. (The royal "we.")   **97 dread** inspiring reverential fear (as King)   **99 late** lately   **102 gentle** noble   **103 idle** worthless   **107 beholding** beholden   **111 With . . . heart** Willingly. (Richard combines in one phrase an overt generosity and a hidden threat.)   **113 that** who   **114 toy** trifle   **118 light** trivial   **121 I weigh . . . heavier** I consider it a trifle (playing on the literal meanings of "light" and "heavy") and would do so even if it were heavier.

RICHARD
What, would you have my weapon, little lord?

YORK
I would, that I might thank you as you call me.

RICHARD How?

YORK Little. 125

PRINCE EDWARD
My lord of York will still be cross in talk. 126
Uncle, Your Grace knows how to bear with him.

YORK
You mean, to bear me, not to bear with me.
Uncle, my brother mocks both you and me:
Because that I am little, like an ape,
He thinks that you should bear me on your shoulders. 131

BUCKINGHAM [aside to Hastings]
With what a sharp-provided wit he reasons! 132
To mitigate the scorn he gives his uncle,
He prettily and aptly taunts himself.
So cunning and so young is wonderful.

RICHARD [to the Prince]
My lord, will't please you pass along?
Myself and my good cousin Buckingham
Will to your mother, to entreat of her
To meet you at the Tower and welcome you.

YORK [to the Prince]
What, will you go unto the Tower, my lord?

PRINCE EDWARD
My Lord Protector needs will have it so.

YORK
I shall not sleep in quiet at the Tower.

RICHARD Why, what should you fear?

YORK
Marry, my uncle Clarence' angry ghost.
My grandam told me he was murdered there.

PRINCE EDWARD I fear no uncles dead.

RICHARD Nor none that live, I hope.

PRINCE EDWARD
An if they live, I hope I need not fear. 148
But come, my lord; with a heavy heart,
Thinking on them, go I unto the Tower. 150

[A sennet.] Exeunt Prince, York,
Hastings, [Cardinal, and others]. Manent
Richard, Buckingham, [and Catesby].

BUCKINGHAM
Think you, my lord, this little prating York 151
Was not incensèd by his subtle mother 152
To taunt and scorn you thus opprobriously?

RICHARD
No doubt, no doubt. Oh, 'tis a parlous boy, 154
Bold, quick, ingenious, forward, capable.
He is all the mother's, from the top to toe.

BUCKINGHAM
Well, let them rest.—Come hither, Catesby. 157
Thou art sworn as deeply to effect what we intend
As closely to conceal what we impart.
Thou know'st our reasons urged upon the way. 160
What think'st thou? Is it not an easy matter
To make William Lord Hastings of our mind
For the installment of this noble Duke
In the seat royal of this famous isle?

CATESBY
He for his father's sake so loves the Prince 165
That he will not be won to aught against him.

BUCKINGHAM
What think'st thou, then, of Stanley? Will not he?

CATESBY
He will do all in all as Hastings doth.

BUCKINGHAM
Well, then, no more but this: go, gentle Catesby,
And, as it were far off, sound thou Lord Hastings 170
How he doth stand affected to our purpose, 171
And summon him tomorrow to the Tower
To sit about the coronation. 173
If thou dost find him tractable to us,
Encourage him, and tell him all our reasons.
If he be leaden, icy, cold, unwilling,
Be thou so too; and so break off the talk,
And give us notice of his inclination.
For we tomorrow hold divided councils, 179
Wherein thyself shalt highly be employed.

RICHARD
Commend me to Lord William. Tell him, Catesby, 181
His ancient knot of dangerous adversaries 182
Tomorrow are let blood at Pomfret Castle; 183
And bid my lord, for joy of this good news,
Give Mistress Shore one gentle kiss the more. 185

BUCKINGHAM
Good Catesby, go, effect this business soundly. 186

CATESBY
My good lords both, with all the heed I can. 187

RICHARD
Shall we hear from you, Catesby, ere we sleep?

CATESBY You shall, my lord.

RICHARD
At Crosby House, there shall you find us both.
Exit Catesby.

---

125 **Little** (York saucily suggests that he would give little thanks for such a "light" gift.) 126 **My . . . talk** i.e., My younger brother is always twisting words in his wittily perverse but annoying way. 131 **bear me . . . shoulders** (At fairs, the bear commonly carried an ape on his back. The speech is doubtless an allusion to Richard's hump and puns triply on *bear with*, "put up with," *bear*, "carry," and *bear*, "an animal.") 132 **sharp-provided** nimble and ready 148 **An if** If. **they** i.e., Rivers and Grey. (Grey was, in fact, Edward's stepbrother, not his uncle. See the note to 1.3.37.) 150.1 **sennet** trumpet call to announce the approach or departure of processions. 150.2 *Manent* They remain onstage 151 **prating** chattering, prattling 152 **incensèd** incited

154 **parlous** clever, but also dangerous 157 **let them rest** leave them for the moment. 160 **the way** i.e., the journey to London from Ludlow. 165 **He . . . sake** i.e., Hastings for King Edward IV's sake 170 **sound** sound out 171 **doth stand affected** is disposed 173 **sit** sit in council 179 **divided councils** (While the regular Council meets about the coronation, Richard plans also to have his own private consultation at Crosby House.) 181 **Lord William** i.e., Hastings. 182 **knot** group 183 **are let blood** will be bled, i.e., executed 185 **Mistress Shore** (According to Thomas More, Jane Shore had become the mistress of Hastings after the death of Edward IV.) 186 **soundly** thoroughly. 187 **heed** attention, care

BUCKINGHAM
Now, my lord, what shall we do if we perceive
Lord Hastings will not yield to our complots?   192
RICHARD
Chop off his head. Something we will determine.
And look when I am king, claim thou of me   194
The earldom of Hereford and all the movables   195
Whereof the King my brother was possessed.
BUCKINGHAM
I'll claim that promise at Your Grace's hand.
RICHARD
And look to have it yielded with all kindness.
Come, let us sup betimes, that afterwards   199
We may digest our complots in some form.   *Exeunt.*   200

❖

3.2

Enter a Messenger to the door of Hastings.

MESSENGER   My lord! My lord!
HASTINGS [*within*]   Who knocks?
MESSENGER   One from the Lord Stanley.
HASTINGS [*within*]   What is't o'clock?   4
MESSENGER   Upon the stroke of four.

Enter Lord Hastings.

HASTINGS
Cannot my Lord Stanley sleep these tedious nights?
MESSENGER
So it appears by that I have to say.
First, he commends him to your noble self.
HASTINGS   What then?
MESSENGER
Then certifies Your Lordship that this night   10
He dreamt the boar had razèd off his helm.   11
Besides, he says there are two councils kept,
And that may be determined at the one
Which may make you and him to rue at th'other.   14
Therefore he sends to know Your Lordship's pleasure,
If you will presently take horse with him   16
And with all speed post with him toward the north,
To shun the danger that his soul divines.
HASTINGS
Go, fellow, go, return unto thy lord.
Bid him not fear the separated councils.
His Honor and myself are at the one,   21
And at the other is my good friend Catesby,
Where nothing can proceed that toucheth us
Whereof I shall not have intelligence.   24
Tell him his fears are shallow, without instance.   25

And for his dreams, I wonder he's so simple   26
To trust the mock'ry of unquiet slumbers.
To fly the boar before the boar pursues   28
Were to incense the boar to follow us,
And make pursuit where he did mean no chase.
Go, bid thy master rise and come to me,
And we will both together to the Tower,
Where he shall see the boar will use us kindly.
MESSENGER
I'll go, my lord, and tell him what you say.   *Exit.*

Enter Catesby.

CATESBY
Many good morrows to my noble lord!
HASTINGS
Good morrow, Catesby. You are early stirring.
What news, what news, in this our tott'ring state?
CATESBY
It is a reeling world, indeed, my lord,
And I believe will never stand upright
Till Richard wear the garland of the realm.
HASTINGS
How? Wear the garland? Dost thou mean the crown?
CATESBY   Ay, my good lord.
HASTINGS
I'll have this crown of mine cut from my shoulders   43
Before I'll see the crown so foul misplaced.
But canst thou guess that he doth aim at it?
CATESBY
Ay, on my life, and hopes to find you forward   46
Upon his party for the gain thereof;   47
And thereupon he sends you this good news,
That this same very day your enemies,
The kindred of the Queen, must die at Pomfret.
HASTINGS
Indeed, I am no mourner for that news,
Because they have been still my adversaries.   52
But that I'll give my voice on Richard's side
To bar my master's heirs in true descent,
God knows I will not do it, to the death.   55
CATESBY
God keep Your Lordship in that gracious mind!
HASTINGS
But I shall laugh at this a twelvemonth hence,
That they which brought me in my master's hate,   58
I live to look upon their tragedy.   59
Well, Catesby, ere a fortnight make me older,
I'll send some packing that yet think not on't.
CATESBY
'Tis a vile thing to die, my gracious lord,
When men are unprepared and look not for it.

---

192 complots conspiracies.   **194 look when** as soon as   **195 movables**
personal property, other than real estate   **199 betimes** early, soon
200 digest arrange, perfect.   **form** good order.
3.2. Location: Before Lord Hastings' house.
4 What is't o'clock? What time is it?   **10 certifies** informs   **11 boar**
i.e., Richard.   **razèd** torn, slashed   **14 th'other** i.e., the regular Council meeting in the Tower, in which Hastings and Stanley will participate.   **16 presently** immediately   **21 His Honor** Lord Stanley
24 intelligence information.   **25 instance** grounds.

26 for as for.   **simple** simpleminded (as)   **28 fly** flee   **43 crown** i.e.,
head. (Recalls Stanley's dream in line 11 and anticipates Hastings'
execution by beheading.)   **46 forward** inclined   **47 Upon his party**
on his side   **52 still** always   **55 to the death** i.e., though I lose my
life. (A common asseveration, but here with ironic meaning.)
58–9 That . . . tragedy that I will live to see the fatal end of those who
brought me out of favor with King Edward IV.

HASTINGS
Oh, monstrous, monstrous! And so falls it out   64
With Rivers, Vaughan, Grey; and so 'twill do
With some men else, that think themselves as safe
As thou and I—who, as thou know'st, are dear
To princely Richard and to Buckingham.

CATESBY
The princes both make high account of you—   69
[*Aside*] For they account his head upon the Bridge.   70

HASTINGS
I know they do, and I have well deserved it.

       Enter Lord Stanley [*Earl of Derby*].

Come on, come on, where is your boar spear, man?
Fear you the boar, and go so unprovided?

STANLEY
My lord, good morrow. Good morrow, Catesby.
You may jest on, but, by the Holy Rood,   75
I do not like these several councils, I.   76

HASTINGS   My lord,
I hold my life as dear as you do yours,
And never in my days, I do protest,
Was it so precious to me as 'tis now.
Think you, but that I know our state secure,   81
I would be so triumphant as I am?

STANLEY
The lords at Pomfret, when they rode from London,   83
Were jocund and supposed their states were sure,   84
And they indeed had no cause to mistrust;
But yet you see how soon the day o'ercast.   86
This sudden stab of rancor I misdoubt.   87
Pray God, I say, I prove a needless coward!
What, shall we toward the Tower? The day is spent.   89

HASTINGS
Come, come, have with you. Wot you what, my lord?   90
Today the lords you talk of are beheaded.

STANLEY
They, for their truth, might better wear their heads   92
Than some that have accused them wear their hats.   93
But come, my lord, let's away.   94

       Enter a Pursuivant.

HASTINGS
Go on before. I'll talk with this good fellow.
     Exit Lord Stanley [*Earl of Derby*] *and Catesby.*

How now, sirrah? How goes the world with thee?   96

PURSUIVANT
The better that Your Lordship please to ask.

HASTINGS
I tell thee, man, 'tis better with me now
Than when thou met'st me last where now we meet.
Then was I going prisoner to the Tower,
By the suggestion of the Queen's allies;   101
But now, I tell thee—keep it to thyself—
This day those enemies are put to death,
And I in better state than e'er I was.

PURSUIVANT
God hold it, to Your Honor's good content!   105

HASTINGS
Gramercy, fellow. There, drink that for me.   106
       Throws him his purse.

PURSUIVANT   I thank Your Honor.   *Exit Pursuivant.*

     Enter a Priest.

PRIEST
Well met, my lord. I am glad to see Your Honor.

HASTINGS
I thank thee, good Sir John, with all my heart.   109
I am in your debt for your last exercise;   110
Come the next Sabbath, and I will content you.   111
       [*He whispers in his ear.*]

PRIEST   I'll wait upon Your Lordship.

     Enter Buckingham.

BUCKINGHAM
What, talking with a priest, Lord Chamberlain?
Your friends at Pomfret, they do need the priest;
Your Honor hath no shriving work in hand.   115

HASTINGS
Good faith, and when I met this holy man,
The men you talk of came into my mind.
What, go you toward the Tower?

BUCKINGHAM
I do, my lord, but long I cannot stay there.
I shall return before Your Lordship thence.

HASTINGS
Nay, like enough, for I stay dinner there.   121

BUCKINGHAM [*aside*]
And supper too, although thou know'st it not.—   122
Come, will you go?

HASTINGS   I'll wait upon Your Lordship.
       Exeunt.

       ❧

---

64 so . . . out so it has happened   **69 high account** great estimation.
(The quibble on *high* appears in the next line.)   **70 account** expect,
reckon. (Punning on *account* in the previous line.)   **the Bridge** London Bridge, on a tower of which the heads of traitors were exposed.
75 Rood cross   **76 several** separate   **81 our state** the positions we
(Stanley and Hastings) occupy   **83 London** (An error for "Ludlow"?)
84 jocund merry   **86 o'ercast** became overcast.   **87 This . . . misdoubt**
This sudden rancorous vengeance (against Rivers, Vaughan, and Grey)
makes me uneasy.   **89 spent** i.e., well advanced (although the scene
began at 4:00 A.M.).   **90 have with you** let's go together.   **Wot** Know
92-3 They . . . hats They, for their honest loyalty (to King Edward and
now his son), might more justly be allowed to keep their heads than
some of their accusers wear their hats of office.   **94.1 *Pursuivant***
attendant on a herald with authority to serve warrants.

96 sirrah (Form of address to inferiors.)   **101 suggestion** instigation
105 hold it continue it (i.e., the better state)   **106 Gramercy** Many
thanks   **109 Sir** (Common title for addressing any priest.)
110 exercise sermon or devotional exercise   **111 content** compensate
115 shriving work confession and absolution   **121 stay** stay for
122 And supper . . . not i.e., You won't be leaving as soon as you
think. (Also suggesting that Hastings will be a feast for worms.)

3.3

Enter Sir Richard Ratcliffe, with Halberds, carrying the nobles [Rivers, Grey, and Vaughan] to death at Pomfret.

RATCLIFFE   Come, bring forth the prisoners.

RIVERS
Sir Richard Ratcliffe, let me tell thee this:
Today shalt thou behold a subject die
For truth, for duty, and for loyalty.

GREY
God bless the Prince from all the pack of you!   5
A knot you are of damnèd bloodsuckers.   6

VAUGHAN
You live that shall cry woe for this hereafter.

RATCLIFFE
Dispatch. The limit of your lives is out.   8

RIVERS
O Pomfret, Pomfret! O thou bloody prison,
Fatal and ominous to noble peers!
Within the guilty closure of thy walls   11
Richard the Second here was hacked to death;
And, for more slander to thy dismal seat,   13
We give to thee our guiltless blood to drink.

GREY
Now Margaret's curse is fall'n upon our heads,
When she exclaimed on Hastings, you, and I,
For standing by when Richard stabbed her son.

RIVERS
Then cursed she Richard, then cursed she Buckingham,
Then cursed she Hastings. Oh, remember, God,
To hear her prayer for them, as now for us!
And for my sister and her princely sons,
Be satisfied, dear God, with our true blood,
Which, as thou know'st, unjustly must be spilt.

RATCLIFFE
Make haste. The hour of death is expiate.   24

RIVERS
Come, Grey, come, Vaughan, let us here embrace.
                                        [*They embrace.*]
Farewell, until we meet again in heaven.   *Exeunt.*

❧

3.4

Enter Buckingham, [Lord Stanley Earl of] Derby, Hastings, Bishop of Ely, Norfolk, Ratcliffe, Lovell, with others, at a table.

HASTINGS
Now, noble peers, the cause why we are met
Is to determine of the coronation.   2
In God's name, speak. When is the royal day?

BUCKINGHAM
Is all things ready for the royal time?

STANLEY
It is, and wants but nomination.   5

ELY
Tomorrow, then, I judge a happy day.   6

BUCKINGHAM
Who knows the Lord Protector's mind herein?
Who is most inward with the noble Duke?   8

ELY
Your Grace, methinks, should soonest know his mind.

BUCKINGHAM
We know each other's faces; for our hearts,   10
He knows no more of mine than I of yours,
Or I of his, my lord, than you of mine.
Lord Hastings, you and he are near in love.

HASTINGS
I thank His Grace, I know he loves me well;
But, for his purpose in the coronation,
I have not sounded him, nor he delivered
His gracious pleasure any way therein.
But you, my honorable lords, may name the time,
And in the Duke's behalf I'll give my voice,   19
Which I presume he'll take in gentle part.   20

Enter [Richard Duke of] Gloucester.

ELY
In happy time, here comes the Duke himself.

RICHARD
My noble lords and cousins all, good morrow.   22
I have been long a sleeper; but I trust
My absence doth neglect no great design   24
Which by my presence might have been concluded.

BUCKINGHAM
Had you not come upon your cue, my lord,
William Lord Hastings had pronounced your part,
I mean your voice for crowning of the King.

RICHARD
Than my Lord Hastings no man might be bolder.
His Lordship knows me well, and loves me well.—
My lord of Ely, when I was last in Holborn,   31
I saw good strawberries in your garden there.
I do beseech you send for some of them.

ELY
Marry, and will, my lord, with all my heart.
                                        Exit Bishop.

RICHARD
Cousin of Buckingham, a word with you.
                                        [*Drawing him aside.*]
Catesby hath sounded Hastings in our business,
And finds the testy gentleman so hot
That he will lose his head ere give consent
His master's child, as worshipfully he terms it,   39
Shall lose the royalty of England's throne.

3.3. Location: Pomfret (Pontefract) Castle.
5 pack gang   **6 knot** group   **8 Dispatch** Hurry.   **is out** has been reached.   **11 closure** enclosure   **13 for . . . seat** i.e., to add further to the evil reputation of this place   **24 expiate** fully come.
3.4. Location: London. The Tower.
2 determine of decide upon

5 wants but nomination lacks only naming of the day.   **6 happy** favorable   **8 inward** intimate   **10 for** as for   **19 voice** vote   **20 in gentle part** with gracious acceptance.   **22 cousins** i.e., peers   **24 neglect** cause the neglect of   **31 Holborn** (location of the Bishop's London palace)   **39 worshipfully** reverently. (Said contemptuously.)

BUCKINGHAM

Withdraw yourself awhile. I'll go with you.
Exeunt [Richard and Buckingham].

STANLEY

We have not yet set down this day of triumph.
Tomorrow, in my judgment, is too sudden,
For I myself am not so well provided   44
As else I would be, were the day prolonged.   45

Enter the Bishop of Ely.

ELY

Where is my lord the Duke of Gloucester?
I have sent for these strawberries.

HASTINGS

His Grace looks cheerfully and smooth this morning;   48
There's some conceit or other likes him well   49
When that he bids good morrow with such spirit.
I think there's never a man in Christendom
Can lesser hide his love or hate than he,
For by his face straight shall you know his heart.

STANLEY

What of his heart perceive you in his face
By any likelihood he showed today?

HASTINGS

Marry, that with no man here he is offended;
For, were he, he had shown it in his looks.

STANLEY   I pray God he be not, I say.

Enter Richard and Buckingham.

RICHARD

I pray you all, tell me what they deserve
That do conspire my death with devilish plots
Of damnèd witchcraft, and that have prevailed
Upon my body with their hellish charms?

HASTINGS

The tender love I bear Your Grace, my lord,   63
Makes me most forward in this princely presence
To doom th'offenders, whosoe'er they be:
I say, my lord, they have deservèd death.

RICHARD

Then be your eyes the witness of their evil.
[He bares his arm.]
Look how I am bewitched! Behold, mine arm
Is like a blasted sapling withered up.   69
And this is Edward's wife, that monstrous witch,
Consorted with that harlot strumpet Shore,   71
That by their witchcraft thus have markèd me.

HASTINGS

If they have done this deed, my noble lord—

RICHARD

If? Thou protector of this damnèd strumpet,
Talk'st thou to me of "ifs"? Thou art a traitor.—
Off with his head! Now, by Saint Paul I swear,
I will not dine until I see the same.
Lovell and Ratcliffe, look that it be done.   78

The rest that love me, rise and follow me.   79
*Exeunt. Manent Lovell and Ratcliffe, with the Lord
Hastings.*

HASTINGS

Woe, woe for England! Not a whit for me,
For I, too fond, might have prevented this.   81
Stanley did dream the boar did raze our helms,
And I did scorn it and disdain to fly.
Three times today my footcloth horse did stumble,   84
And started, when he looked upon the Tower,
As loath to bear me to the slaughterhouse.
Oh, now I need the priest that spake to me!
I now repent I told the pursuivant,
As too triumphing, how mine enemies
Today at Pomfret bloodily were butchered,
And I myself secure in grace and favor.
O Margaret, Margaret, now thy heavy curse
Is lighted on poor Hastings' wretched head!

RATCLIFFE

Come, come, dispatch. The Duke would be at
dinner.
Make a short shrift. He longs to see your head.   95

HASTINGS

Oh, momentary grace of mortal men,   96
Which we more hunt for than the grace of God!
Who builds his hope in air of your good looks   98
Lives like a drunken sailor on a mast,
Ready with every nod to tumble down
Into the fatal bowels of the deep.

LOVELL

Come, come, dispatch. 'Tis bootless to exclaim.   102

HASTINGS

Oh, bloody Richard! Miserable England!
I prophesy the fearful'st time to thee
That ever wretched age hath looked upon.
Come, lead me to the block; bear him my head.
They smile at me who shortly shall be dead.
Exeunt.

❖

[3.5]

*Enter Richard [Duke of Gloucester] and
Buckingham in rotten armor, marvelous
ill-favored.*

RICHARD

Come, cousin, canst thou quake and change thy color,
Murder thy breath in middle of a word,   2
And then again begin, and stop again,
As if thou wert distraught and mad with terror?

79.1 Manent They remain onstage   **81 fond** foolish   **84 footcloth**
large, richly ornamented cloth laid over the back of a horse and hanging to the ground on each side.   **stumble** (An omen of misfortune.)
95 shrift confession.   **96 grace** favor, fortune   **98 Who** Anyone who.
in . . . looks on the insubstantial foundation of your favor   **102 bootless** useless
3.5. Location: London. The Tower.
0.2 rotten rusty   **0.2–3 marvelous ill-favored** remarkably unattractive.   **2 Murder** i.e., stop, catch

---

44 provided equipped   **45 prolonged** postponed.   **48 smooth** pleasant   **49 conceit** fancy, idea.   **likes** pleases   **63 tender** dear
69 blasted shriveled   **71 Consorted** associated   **78 look** see to it

BUCKINGHAM

   Tut, I can counterfeit the deep tragedian,

   Speak and look back, and pry on every side,   6

   Tremble and start at wagging of a straw;

   Intending deep suspicion, ghastly looks   8

   Are at my service, like enforcèd smiles;

   And both are ready in their offices,   10

   At any time, to grace my stratagems.

   But what, is Catesby gone?

RICHARD

   He is; and, see, he brings the Mayor along.

Enter the Mayor and Catesby.

BUCKINGHAM   Lord Mayor—

RICHARD   Look to the drawbridge there!

BUCKINGHAM   Hark, a drum!

RICHARD   Catesby, o'erlook the walls.   *[Exit Catesby.]*   17

BUCKINGHAM

   Lord Mayor, the reason we have sent—

RICHARD

   Look back, defend thee, here are enemies!

BUCKINGHAM

   God and our innocence defend and guard us!

Enter Lovell and Ratcliffe, with Hastings' head.

RICHARD

   Be patient. They are friends, Ratcliffe and Lovell.

LOVELL

   Here is the head of that ignoble traitor,

   The dangerous and unsuspected Hastings.

RICHARD

   So dear I loved the man that I must weep.

   I took him for the plainest harmless creature

   That breathed upon the earth a Christian,

   Made him my book wherein my soul recorded   27

   The history of all her secret thoughts.

   So smooth he daubed his vice with show of virtue

   That, his apparent open guilt omitted—   30

   I mean, his conversation with Shore's wife—   31

   He lived from all attainder of suspects.   32

BUCKINGHAM

   Well, well, he was the covert'st sheltered traitor   33

   That ever lived. Look ye, my Lord Mayor,

   Would you imagine, or almost believe,   35

   Were't not that by great preservation   36

   We live to tell it, that the subtle traitor

   This day had plotted, in the Council House,

   To murder me and my good lord of Gloucester?

MAYOR   Had he done so?   39

RICHARD

   What, think you we are Turks or infidels?

   Or that we would, against the form of law,

Proceed thus rashly in the villain's death,

But that the extreme peril of the case,

The peace of England, and our persons' safety,

Enforced us to this execution?

MAYOR

   Now fair befall you! He deserved his death,   47

   And Your good Graces both have well proceeded   48

   To warn false traitors from the like attempts.

BUCKINGHAM

   I never looked for better at his hands

   After he once fell in with Mistress Shore.

   Yet had we not determined he should die   52

   Until Your Lordship came to see his end,

   Which now the loving haste of these our friends,

   Something against our meanings, have prevented;   55

   Because, my lord, we would have had you hear   56

   The traitor speak and timorously confess

   The manner and the purpose of his treasons,

   That you might well have signified the same

   Unto the citizens, who haply may   60

   Misconster us in him and wail his death.   61

MAYOR

   But, my good lord, Your Grace's words shall serve

   As well as I had seen and heard him speak.   63

   And do not doubt, right noble princes both,

   But I'll acquaint our duteous citizens

   With all your just proceedings in this cause.

RICHARD

   And to that end we wished Your Lordship here,

   T'avoid the censures of the carping world.

BUCKINGHAM

   Which, since you come too late of our intent,   69

   Yet witness what you hear we did intend.   70

   And so, my good Lord Mayor, we bid farewell.

Exit Mayor.

RICHARD

   Go, after, after, cousin Buckingham.

   The Mayor towards Guildhall hies him in all post.   73

   There, at your meet'st advantage of the time,   74

   Infer the bastardy of Edward's children.   75

   Tell them how Edward put to death a citizen

   Only for saying he would make his son

   Heir to the Crown—meaning indeed his house,   78

   Which, by the sign thereof, was termèd so.   79

   Moreover, urge his hateful luxury   80

---

6 back over my shoulder.   **pry** peer   **8 Intending** pretending **10 offices** uses, functions   **17 o'erlook** inspect   **27 book** i.e., table book or diary   **30 his . . . omitted** apart from his manifest open guilt **31 conversation** sexual intimacy   **32 from . . . suspects** free from all stain of suspicion   **33 covert'st sheltered** most secret, hidden **35 almost** even   **36 great preservation** providential protection **39 Had he** Would he have

47 fair good fortune   **48 Your . . . proceeded** Your Graces (the Dukes of Gloucester and Buckingham) have done well   **52 had we . . . die** we had determined he should not die   **55 Something . . . meanings** somewhat contrary to our intent   **56 we . . . heard** we would have wished you to have heard   **60 haply** perhaps   **61 Misconster . . . him** i.e., misconstrue our intentions regarding him   **63 as** as if   **69 of** to accord with   **70 witness** bear witness to   **73 Guildhall** central hall for municipal affairs.   **hies . . . post** hurries with all possible speed. **74 meet'st advantage** most suitable opportunity   **75 Infer** allege, adduce   **78 the Crown** i.e., a tavern in Cheapside identified by the sign of the Crown. (King Edward is portrayed as having been so sensitive to possible rivals that he put to death a man merely for naming his son heir to "the Crown," even though the poor fellow innocently meant nothing more than his own tavern. The story is from Sir Thomas More's *History of King Richard III*.)   **79 sign** tavern or shop sign displayed over the door   **80 luxury** lechery

And bestial appetite in change of lust,   81
Which stretched unto their servants, daughters, wives,   82
Even where his raging eye or savage heart,
Without control, lusted to make a prey.
Nay, for a need, thus far come near my person: 85
Tell them, when that my mother went with child   86
Of that insatiate Edward, noble York   87
My princely father then had wars in France,
And by true computation of the time
Found that the issue was not his begot—
Which well appearèd in his lineaments,   91
Being nothing like the noble duke my father.
Yet touch this sparingly, as 'twere far off,
Because, my lord, you know my mother lives.

BUCKINGHAM
Doubt not, my lord, I'll play the orator
As if the golden fee for which I plead   96
Were for myself. And so, my lord, adieu.

RICHARD
If you thrive well, bring them to Baynard's Castle,   98
Where you shall find me well accompanied
With reverend fathers and well-learnèd bishops.

BUCKINGHAM
I go; and towards three or four o'clock
Look for the news that the Guildhall affords.
                                    Exit Buckingham.

RICHARD
Go, Lovell, with all speed to Doctor Shaw.   103
[*To Ratcliffe*] Go thou to Friar Penker. Bid them both 104
Meet me within this hour at Baynard's Castle.
                              Exeunt [all but Richard].
Now will I go to take some privy order   106
To draw the brats of Clarence out of sight,
And to give order that no manner person   108
Have any time recourse unto the princes.   *Exit.* 109

❧

[3.6]

Enter a Scrivener [with a paper in his hand].

SCRIVENER
Here is the indictment of the good Lord Hastings,
Which in a set hand fairly is engrossed   2
That it may be today read o'er in Paul's.   3
And mark how well the sequel hangs together: 4

Eleven hours I have spent to write it over,
For yesternight by Catesby was it sent me;
The precedent was full as long a-doing.   7
And yet within these five hours Hastings lived,
Untainted, unexamined, free, at liberty.   9
Here's a good world the while! Who is so gross   10
That cannot see this palpable device?
Yet who so bold but says he sees it not?
Bad is the world, and all will come to naught
When such ill dealing must be seen in thought.   14
                                              Exit.

❧

[3.7]

*Enter Richard [Duke of Gloucester] and
Buckingham, at several doors.*

RICHARD
How now, how now, what say the citizens?

BUCKINGHAM
Now, by the holy mother of our Lord,
The citizens are mum, say not a word.

RICHARD
Touched you the bastardy of Edward's children?   4

BUCKINGHAM
I did; with his contract with Lady Lucy   5
And his contract by deputy in France;   6
Th'insatiate greediness of his desire   7
And his enforcement of the city wives;   8
His tyranny for trifles; his own bastardy,   9
As being got, your father then in France,   10
And his resemblance, being not like the Duke.
Withal I did infer your lineaments,   12
Being the right idea of your father   13
Both in your form and nobleness of mind;
Laid open all your victories in Scotland;   15
Your discipline in war, wisdom in peace,   16
Your bounty, virtue, fair humility;
Indeed, left nothing fitting for your purpose
Untouched or slightly handled in discourse.
And when mine oratory drew toward end,
I bid them that did love their country's good
Cry, "God save Richard, England's royal king!"

RICHARD   And did they so?

---

7 precedent prepared indictment serving as a first draft   **9 Untainted, unexamined** not yet accused or interrogated   **10 Here's . . . while!** Here's a fine state of affairs!   **gross** dull, stupid   **14 seen in thought** i.e., perceived in silence.
3.7. Location: The courtyard of Baynard's Castle.
0.2 *several* separate   **4 Touched you** Did you deal with, touch upon, discuss   **5 contract** betrothal.   **Lady Lucy** Elizabeth Lucy (by whom Edward had a child, though there was no formal contract of betrothal)   **6 deputy** (See *3 Henry VI*, 3.3.49 ff., where Warwick, as deputy, contracts with Louis XI of France for the marriage of King Edward to Lady Bona, sister of the French queen.)   **7 Th'insatiate** the insatiable   **8 enforcement** forcible seduction   **9 tyranny for trifles** harsh punishment of minor offenses, or cruel behavior over trifles   **10 got** begot   **12 Withal . . . lineaments** Besides that, I pointed to your features   **13 right idea** true image   **15 Laid . . . Scotland** I elaborated on your successful expedition against Scotland in 1482   **16 discipline** skill, training

81 in . . . lust i.e., constantly desiring new mistresses   **82 their** i.e., the citizens'   **85 for a need** if necessary   **86–7 when . . . Of** when my mother was pregnant with   **91 his lineaments** Edward's features   **96 golden fee** i.e., crown   **98 Baynard's Castle** Richard's residence on the north bank of the Thames. It was founded by Baynard, a nobleman in the time of the Conquest, and had belonged to Richard's father.   **103, 104 Doctor Shaw, Friar Penker** (Well-known divines who delivered sermons in Richard's favor.)   **106 take . . . order** give some secret instruction   **108 no manner person** no one at all   **109 Have . . . recourse** have access at any time
3.6. Location: London. A street.
2 in . . . engrossed is written out in a style of script used for legal documents   **3 read . . . Paul's** posted and read publicly in St. Paul's Cathedral.   **4 the sequel** what follows

BUCKINGHAM
No, so God help me, they spake not a word,
But, like dumb statues or breathing stones,
Stared each on other and looked deadly pale.
Which when I saw, I reprehended them,
And asked the Mayor what meant this willful silence.
His answer was, the people were not used
To be spoke to but by the Recorder.   30
Then he was urged to tell my tale again:
"Thus saith the Duke, thus hath the Duke inferred"—   32
But nothing spake in warrant from himself.   33
When he had done, some followers of mine own,
At lower end of the hall, hurled up their caps,
And some ten voices cried, "God save King Richard!"
And thus I took the vantage of those few: 37
"Thanks, gentle citizens and friends," quoth I,
"This general applause and cheerful shout
Argues your wisdoms and your love to Richard"—
And even here brake off and came away.   41
RICHARD
What tongueless blocks were they! Would they not speak?
BUCKINGHAM   No, by my troth, my lord.
RICHARD
Will not the Mayor, then, and his brethren come?   44
BUCKINGHAM
The Mayor is here at hand. Intend some fear;   45
Be not you spoke with but by mighty suit.   46
And look you get a prayer book in your hand,
And stand between two churchmen, good my lord,
For on that ground I'll make a holy descant;   49
And be not easily won to our requests.
Play the maid's part: still answer nay and take it.
RICHARD
I go; and if you plead as well for them
As I can say nay to thee for myself,
No doubt we'll bring it to a happy issue.   54
BUCKINGHAM
Go, go, up to the leads. The Lord Mayor knocks.   55
                                        [Exit Richard.]

            Enter the Mayor, [aldermen,] and citizens.

Welcome, my lord. I dance attendance here;   56
I think the Duke will not be spoke withal.   57

            Enter Catesby.

Now, Catesby, what says your lord to my request?
CATESBY
He doth entreat Your Grace, my noble lord,
To visit him tomorrow or next day.
He is within, with two right reverend fathers,
Divinely bent to meditation,

And in no worldly suits would he be moved
To draw him from his holy exercise.
BUCKINGHAM
Return, good Catesby, to the gracious Duke.
Tell him myself, the Mayor and aldermen,
In deep designs, in matter of great moment,
No less importing than our general good,   68
Are come to have some conference with His Grace.
CATESBY
I'll signify so much unto him straight.   Exit.
BUCKINGHAM
Aha, my lord, this prince is not an Edward!
He is not lolling on a lewd love bed
But on his knees at meditation;
Not dallying with a brace of courtesans   74
But meditating with two deep divines;   75
Not sleeping, to engross his idle body,   76
But praying, to enrich his watchful soul.
Happy were England, would this virtuous prince
Take on His Grace the sovereignty thereof;
But sure I fear we shall not win him to it.
MAYOR
Marry, God defend His Grace should say us nay!   81
BUCKINGHAM
I fear he will.—Here Catesby comes again.

            Enter Catesby.

Now, Catesby, what says His Grace?
CATESBY   My lord,
He wonders to what end you have assembled
Such troops of citizens to come to him,
His Grace not being warned thereof before.
He fears, my lord, you mean no good to him.
BUCKINGHAM
Sorry I am my noble cousin should
Suspect me that I mean no good to him.
By heaven, we come to him in perfect love,
And so once more return and tell His Grace.
                                        Exit [Catesby].
When holy and devout religious men
Are at their beads, 'tis much to draw them thence,   93
So sweet is zealous contemplation.   94

            Enter Richard aloft, between two bishops. [Catesby
            returns to the main stage.]

MAYOR
See where His Grace stands, 'tween two clergymen!
BUCKINGHAM
Two props of virtue for a Christian prince,
To stay him from the fall of vanity.   97
And, see, a book of prayer in his hand,
True ornaments to know a holy man.—   99
Famous Plantagenet, most gracious prince,

---

30 the Recorder London's chief legal officer.   32 inferred alleged,
asserted   33 in . . . himself on his own authority.   37 vantage
advantage   41 brake broke   44 brethren fellow aldermen
45 Intend Pretend   46 mighty suit importunate entreaty.
49 ground the plainsong or melody on which a *descant* or melodious
accompaniment is raised   54 issue outcome.   55 leads flat lead cov-
erings for roof; hence, the roof itself.   56 dance attendance i.e., am
kept waiting   57 withal with.

68 No less importing concerned with nothing less   74 brace pair
75 deep learned   76 engross fatten   81 defend forbid   93 beads i.e.,
prayers beads.   much hard   94.1 aloft i.e., on the gallery above the
stage, rear. (The tiring-house facade in this scene is imagined to be the
facade of Baynard's Castle.)   97 stay steady or keep   99 ornaments
i.e., the bishops as well as the prayer book

Lend favorable ear to our requests,
And pardon us the interruption
Of thy devotion and right Christian zeal.

RICHARD
My lord, there needs no such apology.
I do beseech Your Grace to pardon me,
Who, earnest in the service of my God,
Deferred the visitation of my friends.
But, leaving this, what is Your Grace's pleasure?

BUCKINGHAM
Even that, I hope, which pleaseth God above,
And all good men of this ungoverned isle.

RICHARD
I do suspect I have done some offense
That seems disgracious in the city's eye,   112
And that you come to reprehend my ignorance.

BUCKINGHAM
You have, my lord. Would it might please Your Grace,
On our entreaties, to amend your fault!

RICHARD
Else wherefore breathe I in a Christian land?   116

BUCKINGHAM
Know then, it is your fault that you resign
The supreme seat, the throne majestical,
The sceptered office of your ancestors,
Your state of fortune and your due of birth,   120
The lineal glory of your royal house,
To the corruption of a blemished stock;   122
While, in the mildness of your sleepy thoughts,   123
Which here we waken to our country's good,
The noble isle doth want her proper limbs;   125
Her face defaced with scars of infamy,
Her royal stock graft with ignoble plants,   127
And almost shouldered in the swallowing gulf   128
Of dark forgetfulness and deep oblivion.
Which to recure, we heartily solicit   130
Your gracious self to take on you the charge
And kingly government of this your land—
Not as protector, steward, substitute,
Or lowly factor for another's gain,   134
But as successively from blood to blood,   135
Your right of birth, your empery, your own.   136
For this, consorted with the citizens,   137
Your very worshipful and loving friends,   138
And by their vehement instigation,
In this just cause come I to move Your Grace.

RICHARD
I cannot tell if to depart in silence
Or bitterly to speak in your reproof

Best fitteth my degree or your condition.   143
If not to answer, you might haply think   144
Tongue-tied ambition, not replying, yielded   145
To bear the golden yoke of sovereignty,
Which fondly you would here impose on me.   147
If to reprove you for this suit of yours,
So seasoned with your faithful love to me,   149
Then on the other side I checked my friends.   150
Therefore, to speak, and to avoid the first,
And then, in speaking, not to incur the last,
Definitively thus I answer you.   153
Your love deserves my thanks, but my desert   154
Unmeritable shuns your high request.   155
First, if all obstacles were cut away,
And that my path were even to the crown   157
As the ripe revenue and due of birth,   158
Yet so much is my poverty of spirit,
So mighty and so many my defects,
That I would rather hide me from my greatness—   161
Being a bark to brook no mighty sea—   162
Than in my greatness covet to be hid   163
And in the vapor of my glory smothered.
But, God be thanked, there is no need of me,
And much I need to help you, were there need.   166
The royal tree hath left us royal fruit,
Which, mellowed by the stealing hours of time,   168
Will well become the seat of majesty
And make, no doubt, us happy by his reign.
On him I lay that you would lay on me,   171
The right and fortune of his happy stars,
Which God defend that I should wring from him!   173

BUCKINGHAM
My lord, this argues conscience in Your Grace;
But the respects thereof are nice and trivial,   175
All circumstances well considerèd.
You say that Edward is your brother's son.
So say we too, but not by Edward's wife;
For first was he contract to Lady Lucy—   179
Your mother lives a witness to his vow—   180
And afterward by substitute betrothed   181
To Bona, sister to the King of France.   182
These both put off, a poor petitioner,
A care-crazed mother to a many sons,

---

112 **disgracious** unbecoming, displeasing   116 **Else . . . land?** i.e.,
How could I call myself a Christian if I am not prepared to amend my
faults?   120 **state of fortune** position to which fortune entitles you
122 **blemished** i.e., through bastardy; see lines 177–91 below
123 **sleepy** passive   125 **want her proper limbs** lack its own limbs, is
crippled   127 **graft** engrafted   128 **shouldered in** jostled into, or
immersed up to the shoulders in   130 **recure** restore, make whole
134 **factor** agent   135 **successively** in order of succession   136 **empery**
empire   137 **consorted** associated, leagued   138 **worshipful** respectful

143 **degree** rank.   **condition** social status.   144 **haply** perhaps
145 **Tongue-tied** silent. (Silence gives consent.)   **yielded** consented
147 **fondly** foolishly   149 **seasoned** i.e., made agreeable or palatable
150 **checked** rebuked, i.e., would have rebuked   153 **Definitively**
once and for all   154–5 **my desert Unmeritable** my unworthiness
157 **even** smooth   158 **ripe revenue** possession ready to be inherited
161 **my greatness** i.e., my claim to the throne   162 **bark** ship.   **brook**
endure   163 **Than . . . hid** than wish to be enveloped in and overwhelmed by my greatness, i.e., the throne.   166 **I need** I lack the requisite ability   168 **stealing** stealthily moving   171 **that** what
173 **defend** forbid   175 **respects thereof** considerations by which
you support your argument.   **nice** overscrupulous   179 **contract**
contracted   180 **Your . . . vow** (According to the chronicles, Richard's
mother, in opposing Edward's intention of marrying Lady Grey because
it was interfering with the negotiations for his marriage to Lady Bona
of Savoy, asserted that Lady Elizabeth Lucy was already Edward's
trothplight wife. Compare with 3.5.75 and 3.7.6.)   181 **substitute**
proxy   182 **sister** i.e., sister-in-law, the Queen's sister

A beauty-waning and distressèd widow,
Even in the afternoon of her best days,
Made prize and purchase of his wanton eye,   187
Seduced the pitch and height of his degree   188
To base declension and loathed bigamy.   189
By her, in his unlawful bed, he got
This Edward, whom our manners call the Prince.   191
More bitterly could I expostulate,   192
Save that, for reverence to some alive,   193
I give a sparing limit to my tongue.
Then, good my lord, take to your royal self   195
This proffered benefit of dignity,
If not to bless us and the land withal,
Yet to draw forth your noble ancestry   198
From the corruption of abusing times
Unto a lineal true-derivèd course.

MAYOR
Do, good my lord. Your citizens entreat you.

BUCKINGHAM
Refuse not, mighty lord, this proffered love.

CATESBY
Oh, make them joyful. Grant their lawful suit!

RICHARD
Alas, why would you heap this care on me?
I am unfit for state and majesty.
I do beseech you, take it not amiss;
I cannot nor I will not yield to you.

BUCKINGHAM
If you refuse it—as, in love and zeal,   208
Loath to depose the child, your brother's son,
As well we know your tenderness of heart   210
And gentle, kind, effeminate remorse,   211
Which we have noted in you to your kindred
And equally indeed to all estates—   213
Yet know, whe'er you accept our suit or no,   214
Your brother's son shall never reign our king,
But we will plant some other in the throne
To the disgrace and downfall of your house.
And in this resolution here we leave you.—
Come, citizens. Zounds! I'll entreat no more.   219

RICHARD
Oh, do not swear, my lord of Buckingham.
                              Exeunt [Buckingham,
                     Mayor, aldermen, and the citizens].

CATESBY
Call him again, sweet prince. Accept their suit.
If you deny them, all the land will rue it.

RICHARD
Will you enforce me to a world of cares?
Call them again. I am not made of stone,
But penetrable to your kind entreaties,
Albeit against my conscience and my soul.

          Enter Buckingham and the rest.

Cousin of Buckingham, and sage, grave men,
Since you will buckle fortune on my back,
To bear her burden, whe'er I will or no,
I must have patience to endure the load.
But if black scandal or foul-faced reproach
Attend the sequel of your imposition,   232
Your mere enforcement shall acquittance me   233
From all the impure blots and stains thereof;
For God doth know, and you may partly see,
How far I am from the desire of this.

MAYOR
God bless Your Grace! We see it and will say it.

RICHARD
In saying so, you shall but say the truth.

BUCKINGHAM
Then I salute you with this royal title:
Long live Richard, England's worthy king!

MAYOR AND CITIZENS   Amen.

BUCKINGHAM
Tomorrow may it please you to be crowned?

RICHARD
Even when you please, for you will have it so.

BUCKINGHAM
Tomorrow, then, we will attend Your Grace.
And so most joyfully we take our leave.

RICHARD [*to the Bishops*]
Come, let us to our holy work again.—
Farewell, my cousin. Farewell, gentle friends. *Exeunt.*

                         ❦

4.1

          *Enter [at one door] the Queen [Elizabeth], the
          Duchess of York, and Marquess [of] Dorset; [at
          another door] Anne, Duchess of Gloucester,
          [leading Lady Margaret Plantagenet, Clarence's
          young daughter].*

DUCHESS
Who meets us here? My niece Plantagenet   1
Led in the hand of her kind aunt of Gloucester?
Now, for my life, she's wand'ring to the Tower,   3
On pure heart's love to greet the tender Prince.   4
Daughter, well met.

ANNE   God give Your Graces both   5
A happy and a joyful time of day!

QUEEN ELIZABETH
As much to you, good sister. Whither away?   7

---

187 **purchase** booty   188–9 **Seduced . . . declension** i.e., seduced him
away from his high rank to ignoble decline. (*Pitch* is the highest point
in a falcon's flight.)   189 **bigamy** (Edward was not only bound by
previous contracts, as indicated in lines 178–82 above, but also, by
marrying a widow, entered into a union that was widely regarded as
bigamous.)   191 **manners** sense of politeness   192 **expostulate** discuss, dilate   193 **some alive** i.e., the Duchess of York. (See 3.5.93–4.)
195 **good my lord** my good lord   198 **draw forth** rescue, extract
208 **as** from being   210 **As . . . know** since we know well   211 **kind,
effeminate remorse** natural, tender pity   213 **estates** ranks. (Buckingham argues that this virtue of pity is found in Richard's treatment
of everyone.)   214 **whe'er** whether   219 **Zounds!** By His (God's)
wounds!

232 **your imposition** the duty that you lay upon me   233 **Your . . .
acquittance me** the mere fact of your insistence will exonerate me
4.1. Location: London. Before the Tower.
1 **niece** i.e., granddaughter   3 **for** on   4 **On** out of.   **tender** young
5 **Daughter** i.e., Daughter-in-law   7 **sister** i.e., sister-in-law.

ANNE
No farther than the Tower, and, as I guess,
Upon the like devotion as yourselves,   9
To gratulate the gentle princes there.   10

QUEEN ELIZABETH
Kind sister, thanks. We'll enter all together.

Enter [Brackenbury] the Lieutenant.

And, in good time, here the Lieutenant comes.—
Master Lieutenant, pray you, by your leave,
How doth the Prince and my young son of York?

BRACKENBURY
Right well, dear madam. By your patience,
I may not suffer you to visit them;   16
The King hath strictly charged the contrary.

QUEEN ELIZABETH
The King! Who's that?

BRACKENBURY   I mean the Lord Protector.

QUEEN ELIZABETH
The Lord protect him from that kingly title!
Hath he set bounds between their love and me?   20
I am their mother; who shall bar me from them?

DUCHESS
I am their father's mother; I will see them.

ANNE
Their aunt I am in law, in love their mother;
Then bring me to their sights. I'll bear thy blame
And take thy office from thee, on my peril.   25

BRACKENBURY
No, madam, no; I may not leave it so.
I am bound by oath, and therefore pardon me.
                         Exit Lieutenant.

Enter [Lord] Stanley [Earl of Derby].

STANLEY
Let me but meet you, ladies, one hour hence,
And I'll salute Your Grace of York as mother,   29
And reverend looker-on, of two fair queens.   30
[*To Anne*] Come, madam, you must straight to
     Westminster,
There to be crownèd Richard's royal queen.

QUEEN ELIZABETH   Ah, cut my lace asunder,   33
That my pent heart may have some scope to beat,
Or else I swoon with this dead-killing news!

ANNE
Despiteful tidings! Oh, unpleasing news!

DORSET
Be of good cheer. Mother, how fares Your Grace?

QUEEN ELIZABETH
Oh, Dorset, speak not to me. Get thee gone!
Death and destruction dogs thee at thy heels;
Thy mother's name is ominous to children.
If thou wilt outstrip death, go cross the seas

And live with Richmond, from the reach of hell.   42
Go, hie thee, hie thee from this slaughterhouse,   43
Lest thou increase the number of the dead
And make me die the thrall of Margaret's curse,   45
Nor mother, wife, nor England's counted queen.   46

STANLEY
Full of wise care is this your counsel, madam.
[*To Dorset*] Take all the swift advantage of the hours.
You shall have letters from me to my son   49
In your behalf, to meet you on the way.   50
Be not ta'en tardy by unwise delay.   51

DUCHESS
Oh, ill-dispersing wind of misery!   52
Oh, my accursèd womb, the bed of death!
A cockatrice hast thou hatched to the world,   54
Whose unavoided eye is murderous.

STANLEY [*to Anne*]
Come, madam, come. I in all haste was sent.

ANNE
And I with all unwillingness will go.
Oh, would to God that the inclusive verge   58
Of golden metal that must round my brow
Were red-hot steel, to sear me to the brains!
Anointed let me be with deadly venom   61
And die ere men can say, "God save the Queen!"

QUEEN ELIZABETH
Go, go, poor soul. I envy not thy glory.
To feed my humor, wish thyself no harm.   64

ANNE
No? Why? When he that is my husband now
Came to me, as I followed Henry's corpse,
When scarce the blood was well washed from his hands
Which issued from my other angel husband   68
And that dear saint which then I weeping followed—   69
Oh, when, I say, I looked on Richard's face,
This was my wish: "Be thou," quoth I, "accurst
For making me, so young, so old a widow!   72
And, when thou wed'st, let sorrow haunt thy bed;
And be thy wife—if any be so mad—
More miserable by the life of thee
Than thou hast made me by my dear lord's death!"
Lo, ere I can repeat this curse again,
Within so small a time, my woman's heart
Grossly grew captive to his honey words   79
And proved the subject of mine own soul's curse,

---

9 **like devotion** same devout errand   10 **gratulate** greet, salute
16 **suffer** permit   20 **bounds** barriers   25 **take . . . thee** i.e., relieve
you of the responsibility   29 **mother** i.e., mother-in-law (of Elizabeth
as widow of Edward and of Anne as wife of King Richard)
30 **looker-on** beholder.   **two fair queens** i.e., Elizabeth and Anne,
since Anne's husband, Richard, is about to be crowned.   33 **lace** cord
used to lace the bodice

42 **with Richmond** i.e., with Henry Tudor, Earl of Richmond, at this
time in Brittany   43 **hie** hasten   45 **thrall** subject, victim   46 **Nor**
neither.   **counted** accepted, esteemed   49–50 **You . . . way** i.e., I will
arrange to have a letter catch up with you on your journey, recom-
mending you to my stepson, the Earl of Richmond. (Lord Stanley's
own son, George Stanley, may also be involved in this rapid negotiation; see 4.4.494–6 ff. below.)   51 **ta'en** taken, caught   52 **ill-dispersing**
evil-spreading   54 **cockatrice** basilisk. (See the note for 1.2.153.)
58 **inclusive verge** enclosing circle, i.e., the crown, here likened to an
instrument of torture used to punish regicides or other criminals
61 **Anointed** (Anne desires to be anointed with poison rather than
with holy oil, as in the ceremony of coronation.)   64 **To . . . harm** Do
not curse yourself (or, possibly, I do not wish you harm) just to satisfy
my vengeful mood.   68 **angel husband** Edward, son of Henry VI
69 **saint** Henry VI   72 **so old a widow** i.e., destined to live so long as
a widow.   79 **Grossly** stupidly

Which hitherto hath held mine eyes from rest;   81
For never yet one hour in his bed
Did I enjoy the golden dew of sleep,
But with his timorous dreams was still awaked.   84
Besides, he hates me for my father Warwick,
And will, no doubt, shortly be rid of me.

QUEEN ELIZABETH
Poor heart, adieu! I pity thy complaining.

ANNE
No more than with my soul I mourn for yours.

DORSET
Farewell, thou woeful welcomer of glory!   89

ANNE
Adieu, poor soul, that tak'st thy leave of it!

DUCHESS [to Dorset]
Go thou to Richmond, and good fortune guide thee!
[To Anne] Go thou to Richard, and good angels tend thee!
[To Queen Elizabeth] Go thou to sanctuary, and good
    thoughts possess thee!
I to my grave, where peace and rest lie with me!
Eighty-odd years of sorrow have I seen,
And each hour's joy wracked with a week of teen.   96
                                [They start to go.]

QUEEN ELIZABETH
Stay, yet look back with me unto the Tower.
Pity, you ancient stones, those tender babes
Whom envy hath immured within your walls—   99
Rough cradle for such little pretty ones!
Rude ragged nurse, old sullen playfellow   101
For tender princes, use my babies well!
So foolish sorrows bids your stones farewell.   Exeunt.

4.2

Sound a sennet. Enter Richard, in pomp;
Buckingham, Catesby, Ratcliffe, Lovell, [a Page,
and others].

KING RICHARD
Stand all apart. Cousin of Buckingham!   1
                [The others stand aside, out of earshot.]

BUCKINGHAM   My gracious sovereign?

KING RICHARD
Give me thy hand.
                Sound [trumpets. Here he ascends the throne.]
                Thus high, by thy advice
And thy assistance, is King Richard seated.
But shall we wear these glories for a day?
Or shall they last, and we rejoice in them?

BUCKINGHAM
Still live they, and forever let them last!

KING RICHARD
Ah, Buckingham, now do I play the touch,   8
To try if thou be current gold indeed: 9
Young Edward lives. Think now what I would speak.

BUCKINGHAM   Say on, my loving lord.

KING RICHARD
Why, Buckingham, I say I would be king.

BUCKINGHAM
Why, so you are, my thrice-renownèd lord.

KING RICHARD
Ha! Am I king? 'Tis so. But Edward lives.

BUCKINGHAM
True, noble prince.

KING RICHARD   Oh, bitter consequence,   15
That Edward still should live "true, noble prince"!   16
Cousin, thou wast not wont to be so dull.   17
Shall I be plain? I wish the bastards dead,
And I would have it suddenly performed.   19
What say'st thou now? Speak suddenly; be brief.

BUCKINGHAM   Your Grace may do your pleasure.

KING RICHARD
Tut, tut, thou art all ice; thy kindness freezes.
Say, have I thy consent that they shall die?

BUCKINGHAM
Give me some little breath, some pause, dear lord,
Before I positively speak in this.
I will resolve you herein presently.   *Exit Buckingham.*   26

CATESBY [to those standing aside]
The King is angry. See, he gnaws his lip.

KING RICHARD [aside]
I will converse with iron-witted fools   28
And unrespective boys. None are for me   29
That look into me with considerate eyes.   30
High-reaching Buckingham grows circumspect.—   31
    Boy!

PAGE [approaching]   My lord?

KING RICHARD
Know'st thou not any whom corrupting gold
Will tempt unto a close exploit of death?   35

PAGE
My lord, I know a discontented gentleman
Whose humble means match not his haughty spirit.
Gold were as good as twenty orators,
And will, no doubt, tempt him to anything.

KING RICHARD
What is his name?

PAGE   His name, my lord, is Tyrrel.

KING RICHARD
I partly know the man. Go call him hither, boy.
                                        Exit [Page].

81 hitherto until now   **84 timorous** full of fears.   **still** continually
89 glory i.e., the rank of queen—*woeful* because it involves marriage
to Richard.   **96 wracked** destroyed, or, *racked*, tortured.   **teen** woe.
99 envy malice.   **immured** walled up   **101 Rude** Rough
4.2. Location: London. The royal court.
1 apart aside.

8 play the touch play the part of a touchstone (to test the quality of
gold)   **9 current** sterling, genuine   **15 bitter consequence** i.e., intolerable answer to my words, and an intolerable fact   **16 "true, noble
prince"** (Richard mockingly repeats Buckingham's evasive reply in
line 15 and applies it to the irritating fact that young Edward still
lives and is a noble prince.)   **17 wast not wont** used not   **19 suddenly** swiftly   **26 resolve** answer   **28–31 I will . . . circumspect** i.e.,
Apparently I have no choice but to communicate my intentions to
dim-witted fools and inattentive boys. I will have nothing more to do
with men who look into my thoughts too searchingly. Ambitious
Buckingham grows wary.   **35 close** secret

[*Aside*] The deep-revolving, witty Buckingham　　42
No more shall be the neighbor to my counsels.
Hath he so long held out with me untired,
And stops he now for breath? Well, be it so.

Enter [*Lord*] *Stanley* [*Earl of Derby*].

How now, Lord Stanley? What's the news?
STANLEY　　Know, my loving lord,
The Marquess Dorset, as I hear, is fled
To Richmond, in the parts where he abides.
　　　　　　　　　　　　　　　　[*He stands apart.*]
KING RICHARD
Come hither, Catesby. Rumor it abroad
That Anne my wife is very grievous sick;
I will take order for her keeping close.　　52
Inquire me out some mean poor gentleman,　　53
Whom I will marry straight to Clarence' daughter.
The boy is foolish, and I fear not him.　　55
Look how thou dream'st! I say again, give out
That Anne my queen is sick and like to die.　　57
About it, for it stands me much upon　　58
To stop all hopes whose growth may damage me.
　　　　　　　　　　　　　　　　[*Exit Catesby.*]
I must be married to my brother's daughter,　　60
Or else my kingdom stands on brittle glass.
Murder her brothers, and then marry her—
Uncertain way of gain! But I am in
So far in blood that sin will pluck on sin.　　64
Tear-falling pity dwells not in this eye.　　65

Enter [*Page, with*] *Tyrrel*.

Is thy name Tyrrel?
TYRREL
James Tyrrel, and your most obedient subject.
KING RICHARD
Art thou, indeed?
TYRREL　　　　　　　　Prove me, my gracious lord.　　68
KING RICHARD
Dar'st thou resolve to kill a friend of mine?
TYRREL　　Please you;　　70
But I had rather kill two enemies.
KING RICHARD
Why, there thou hast it: two deep enemies,
Foes to my rest and my sweet sleep's disturbers
Are they that I would have thee deal upon—　　74
Tyrrel, I mean those bastards in the Tower.
TYRREL
Let me have open means to come to them,　　76
And soon I'll rid you from the fear of them.

KING RICHARD
Thou sing'st sweet music. Hark, come hither, Tyrrel.
Go, by this token. [*He gives him a token.*] Rise, and lend
　thine ear.　　　　　　　　　　　　　*Whispers.*
There is no more but so. Say it is done,
And I will love thee and prefer thee for it.　　81
TYRREL　　I will dispatch it straight.　　　　*Exit.*

Enter Buckingham.

BUCKINGHAM
My lord, I have considered in my mind
The late request that you did sound me in.　　84
KING RICHARD
Well, let that rest. Dorset is fled to Richmond.
BUCKINGHAM　　I hear the news, my lord.
KING RICHARD
Stanley, he is your wife's son. Well, look to it.　　87
BUCKINGHAM
My lord, I claim the gift, my due by promise,
For which your honor and your faith is pawned:　　89
Th'earldom of Hereford and the movables
Which you have promisèd I shall possess.
KING RICHARD
Stanley, look to your wife. If she convey
Letters to Richmond, you shall answer it.　　93
BUCKINGHAM
What says Your Highness to my just request?
KING RICHARD
I do remember me, Henry the Sixth
Did prophesy that Richmond should be king,
When Richmond was a little peevish boy.
A king! Perhaps, perhaps—
BUCKINGHAM　　My lord!
KING RICHARD
How chance the prophet could not at that time　　100
Have told me, I being by, that I should kill him?　　101
BUCKINGHAM
My lord, your promise for the earldom!
KING RICHARD
Richmond! When last I was at Exeter,
The Mayor in courtesy showed me the castle
And called it Rougemont, at which name I started,　　105
Because a bard of Ireland told me once
I should not live long after I saw Richmond.
BUCKINGHAM　　My lord!
KING RICHARD　　Ay, what's o'clock?　　109
BUCKINGHAM
I am thus bold to put Your Grace in mind
Of what you promised me.
KING RICHARD　　Well, but what's o'clock?
BUCKINGHAM　　Upon the stroke of ten.
KING RICHARD　　Well, let it strike.
BUCKINGHAM　　Why let it strike?

---

42 deep-revolving deeply scheming.　**witty** cunning　**52 I will . . .
close** I will give orders for her close confinement.　**53 mean** of humble station　**55 boy** i.e., Clarence's eldest son, Edward Plantagenet,
Earl of Warwick　**57 like** likely　**58 stands . . . upon** is a matter of the
utmost importance to me　**60 brother's daughter** i.e., Elizabeth of
York, daughter to Edward IV, who will, in fact, later become the
queen of Henry VII; see 4.5.7–9 and 5.5.29–31　**64 pluck on** draw on
65 Tear-falling Tear-dropping　**68 Prove** Test　**70 Please** If it please
74 deal upon proceed against　**76 open** unhampered

81 prefer promote, advance　**84 late** recent.　**sound me in** ask me
about.　**87 he** i.e., Richmond　**89 pawned** pledged　**93 it** for it.
100 the prophet i.e., Henry VI　**101 by** nearby.　**him** (The word
applies to Richmond and Henry VI.)　**105 Rougemont** i.e., Red Hill.
(With a play on "Richmond.")　**109 what's o'clock?** what time is it?

KING RICHARD
Because that, like a jack, thou keep'st the stroke 116
Betwixt thy begging and my meditation.
I am not in the giving vein today. 118

BUCKINGHAM
May it please you to resolve me in my suit. 119

KING RICHARD
Thou troublest me. I am not in the vein.
Exit [with all but Buckingham].

BUCKINGHAM
And is it thus? Repays he my deep service
With such contempt? Made I him king for this?
O, let me think on Hastings, and be gone
To Brecknock, while my fearful head is on! *Exit.* 124

❖

[4.3]

Enter Tyrrel.

TYRREL
The tyrannous and bloody act is done,
The most arch deed of piteous massacre 2
That ever yet this land was guilty of.
Dighton and Forrest, whom I did suborn 4
To do this piece of ruthless butchery,
Albeit they were fleshed villains, bloody dogs, 6
Melted with tenderness and mild compassion,
Wept like to children in their deaths' sad story. 8
"Oh, thus," quoth Dighton, "lay the gentle babes."
"Thus, thus," quoth Forrest, "girdling one another
Within their alabaster innocent arms.
Their lips were four red roses on a stalk,
Which in their summer beauty kissed each other.
A book of prayers on their pillow lay,
Which once," quoth Forrest, "almost changed my mind;
But oh, the devil!"—there the villain stopped;
When Dighton thus told on: "We smotherèd
The most replenishèd sweet work of Nature 18
That from the prime creation e'er she framed." 19
Hence both are gone; with conscience and remorse 20
They could not speak; and so I left them both,
To bear this tidings to the bloody king.

Enter [King] Richard.

And here he comes.—All health, my sovereign lord!

KING RICHARD
Kind Tyrrel, am I happy in thy news?

TYRREL
If to have done the thing you gave in charge 25
Beget your happiness, be happy then,
For it is done.

KING RICHARD   But didst thou see them dead?

TYRREL
I did, my lord.

KING RICHARD   And buried, gentle Tyrrel?

TYRREL
The chaplain of the Tower hath buried them;
But where, to say the truth, I do not know.

KING RICHARD
Come to me, Tyrrel, soon at after-supper, 31
When thou shalt tell the process of their death. 32
Meantime, but think how I may do thee good,
And be inheritor of thy desire. 34
Farewell till then.

TYRREL   I humbly take my leave. [*Exit.*]

KING RICHARD
The son of Clarence have I pent up close, 36
His daughter meanly have I matched in marriage, 37
The sons of Edward sleep in Abraham's bosom, 38
And Anne my wife hath bid this world good night.
Now, for I know the Breton Richmond aims 40
At young Elizabeth, my brother's daughter, 41
And by that knot looks proudly on the crown, 42
To her go I, a jolly thriving wooer.

Enter Ratcliffe.

RATCLIFFE   My lord!

KING RICHARD
Good or bad news, that thou com'st in so bluntly?

RATCLIFFE
Bad news, my lord. Morton is fled to Richmond, 46
And Buckingham, backed with the hardy Welshmen,
Is in the field, and still his power increaseth. 48

KING RICHARD
Ely with Richmond troubles me more near 49
Than Buckingham and his rash-levied strength. 50
Come, I have learned that fearful commenting 51
Is leaden servitor to dull delay; 52
Delay leads impotent and snail-paced beggary. 53
Then fiery expedition be my wing, 54
Jove's Mercury, and herald for a king! 55

---

116 **jack** the figure of a man that strikes the bell on the outside of a clock. (With a play on the meaning "lowbred fellow." Richard's complaint is that Buckingham, like the jack of a clock, being on the point of striking the hour—i.e., speaking his request—breaks the continuity of Richard's reflections.)   118 **vein** mood   119 **resolve me** give me a final answer   124 **Brecknock** i.e., Brecon, Buckingham's family seat in Wales.   **fearful** full of fears
4.3. Location: London. The royal court.
2 **arch deed** i.e., chief or notorious act   4 **suborn** bribe   6 **fleshed** experienced in bloodshed   8 **in their . . . story** in telling the story of their deaths.   18 **replenishèd** complete, perfect   19 **prime** first
20 **gone** undone, unnerved

25 **gave in charge** ordered, commanded   31 **after-supper** dessert after supper   32 **process** story   34 **be . . . desire** expect to get what you ask.   36 **pent up close** strictly confined   37 **His . . . marriage** (Margaret Plantagenet was about twelve years old when Richard died. Shakespeare may have confused her with Lady Cicely, a daughter of Edward IV, whom Richard, according to Holinshed, intended to marry to "a man found in a cloud, and of an unknown lineage and family.")   38 **Abraham's bosom** (See Luke 16:22.)   40 **for** because. **Breton** located in Brittany   41 **my brother's** Edward's   42 **by that knot** by virtue of that alliance   46 **Morton** i.e., John Morton, Bishop of Ely, who had been kept prisoner at Brecknock (or Brecon) Castle; he is the Ely of 3.4   48 **power** army   49 **near** deeply   50 **rash-levied** hastily recruited   51 **fearful commenting** timorous talk   52 **leaden servitor** sluggish attendant   53 **leads** leads to. **beggary** ruin. 54 **expedition** speed   55 **Mercury** messenger of the gods

Go muster men. My counsel is my shield;   56
We must be brief when traitors brave the field.   57

Exeunt.

❖

4.[4]

Enter old Queen Margaret.

QUEEN MARGARET
So now prosperity begins to mellow   1
And drop into the rotten mouth of death.
Here in these confines slyly have I lurked   3
To watch the waning of mine enemies.
A dire induction am I witness to,   5
And will to France, hoping the consequence   6
Will prove as bitter, black, and tragical.
Withdraw thee, wretched Margaret. Who comes here?

[She steps aside.]

Enter Duchess [of York] and Queen [Elizabeth].

QUEEN ELIZABETH
Ah, my poor princes! Ah, my tender babes!
My unblown flowers, new-appearing sweets!   10
If yet your gentle souls fly in the air
And be not fixed in doom perpetual,   12
Hover about me with your airy wings
And hear your mother's lamentation!

QUEEN MARGARET *[aside]*
Hover about her; say that right for right   15
Hath dimmed your infant morn to agèd night.   16

DUCHESS
So many miseries have crazed my voice   17
That my woe-wearied tongue is still and mute.
Edward Plantagenet, why art thou dead?   19

QUEEN MARGARET *[aside]*
Plantagenet doth quit Plantagenet.   20
Edward for Edward pays a dying debt.   21

QUEEN ELIZABETH
Wilt thou, O God, fly from such gentle lambs   22
And throw them in the entrails of the wolf?
When didst thou sleep when such a deed was done?   24

QUEEN MARGARET *[aside]*
When holy Harry died, and my sweet son.   25

DUCHESS
Dead life, blind sight, poor mortal-living ghost,   26

Woe's scene, world's shame, grave's due by life usurped,   27
Brief abstract and record of tedious days,   28
Rest thy unrest on England's lawful earth,

[sitting down]

Unlawfully made drunk with innocent blood!   30

QUEEN ELIZABETH
Ah, that thou wouldst as soon afford a grave   31
As thou canst yield a melancholy seat!
Then would I hide my bones, not rest them here.
Ah, who hath any cause to mourn but we?

[Sitting down by her.]

QUEEN MARGARET *[coming forward]*
If ancient sorrow be most reverend,   35
Give mine the benefit of seniory   36
And let my griefs frown on the upper hand.   37
If sorrow can admit society,   *[sitting down with them]*
Tell o'er your woes again by viewing mine:
I had an Edward, till a Richard killed him;   40
I had a Harry, till a Richard killed him: 41
Thou hadst an Edward, till a Richard killed him;   42
Thou hadst a Richard, till a Richard killed him.   43

DUCHESS
I had a Richard too, and thou didst kill him;   44
I had a Rutland too, thou holp'st to kill him.   45

QUEEN MARGARET
Thou hadst a Clarence too, and Richard killed him.
From forth the kennel of thy womb hath crept
A hellhound that doth hunt us all to death.
That dog, that had his teeth before his eyes   49
To worry lambs and lap their gentle blood,   50
That foul defacer of God's handiwork,
That excellent grand tyrant of the earth   52
That reigns in gallèd eyes of weeping souls,   53
Thy womb let loose, to chase us to our graves.
O upright, just, and true-disposing God,
How do I thank thee that this carnal cur   56
Preys on the issue of his mother's body   57
And makes her pew-fellow with others' moan!   58

DUCHESS
O Harry's wife, triumph not in my woes!
God witness with me, I have wept for thine.

QUEEN MARGARET
Bear with me. I am hungry for revenge,
And now I cloy me with beholding it.   62

---

56 My . . . shield i.e., I will take counsel by arming myself and trust no adviser other than my own weapons   **57 brave** challenge
4.4. Location: London. Near the royal court.
1 mellow mature   **3 confines** regions.   **slyly** stealthily   **5 induction** beginning (as of a play)   **6 will** will go.   **the consequence** what follows, the sequel and conclusion (as in a play)   **10 unblown** unopened.   **sweets** flowers.   **12 doom perpetual** eternal destiny
15 right for right i.e., a just punishment for an offense against justice
16 dimmed . . . night i.e., brought the youthful promise of your children to ruin and death.   **17 crazed** cracked   **19 Edward Plantagenet** the Duchess's son, the dead King Edward IV; or, his son Edward V
20 quit requite   **21 Edward . . . debt** Edward IV (or else Edward V) for Edward, the son of Margaret and Henry VI.   **dying debt** debt paid through death.   **22 fly . . . lambs** i.e., abandon my two sons
24 When i.e., Whenever till now   **25 Harry** i.e., Henry VI   **26 mortal-living ghost** i.e., a dead person still among the living

27 grave's . . . usurped i.e., one who, by living too long, deprives the grave of its due   **28 abstract** epitome   **30 Unlawfully . . . drunk** i.e., England's earth, which is unlawfully made drunk   **31 that thou** would that you, England's earth   **35 reverend** worthy of respect
36 seniory seniority of claim   **37 on . . . hand** i.e., from a place of precedence.   **40 Edward** i.e., my son, the former Prince of Wales
41 Harry i.e., my husband, King Henry VI   **42 Thou** i.e., Queen Elizabeth.   **Edward** i.e., Edward V   **43 Thou . . . Richard** You, Queen Elizabeth, had a son, the young Duke of York   **44 Richard** i.e., Duke of York, the Duchess's husband and father of Richard III, killed by Margaret's army at the Battle of Wakefield in 1460   **45 Rutland** i.e., Edmund, son of the Duke of York, also killed at Wakefield   **49 teeth** (Richard was supposedly born with teeth.)   **50 worry** bite on the throat, tear to pieces   **52 excellent** unparalleled   **53 gallèd** sore with weeping   **56 carnal** flesh-eating   **57 issue** offspring   **58 pew-fellow** i.e., intimate associate   **62 cloy me** gorge myself

Thy Edward he is dead that killed my Edward;   63
Thy other Edward dead, to quit my Edward;   64
Young York he is but boot, because both they   65
Matched not the high perfection of my loss.
Thy Clarence he is dead that stabbed my Edward;
And the beholders of this frantic play,   68
Th'adulterate Hastings, Rivers, Vaughan, Grey,   69
Untimely smothered in their dusky graves.   70
Richard yet lives, hell's black intelligencer,   71
Only reserved their factor to buy souls   72
And send them thither; but at hand, at hand
Ensues his piteous and unpitied end.   74
Earth gapes, hell burns, fiends roar, saints pray,
To have him suddenly conveyed from hence.
Cancel his bond of life, dear God, I pray,
That I may live and say, "The dog is dead!"

QUEEN ELIZABETH
Oh, thou didst prophesy the time would come
That I should wish for thee to help me curse
That bottled spider, that foul bunch-backed toad!   81

QUEEN MARGARET
I called thee then vain flourish of my fortune;   82
I called thee then poor shadow, painted queen,
The presentation of but what I was,   84
The flattering index of a direful pageant,   85
One heaved a-high to be hurled down below,
A mother only mocked with two fair babes,
A dream of what thou wast, a garish flag   88
To be the aim of every dangerous shot;   89
A sign of dignity, a breath, a bubble,   90
A queen in jest, only to fill the scene.
Where is thy husband now? Where be thy brothers?
Where be thy two sons? Wherein dost thou joy?
Who sues and kneels and says, "God save the Queen"
Where be the bending peers that flattered thee?   95
Where be the thronging troops that followed thee?   96
Decline all this, and see what now thou art: 97
For happy wife, a most distressèd widow;
For joyful mother, one that wails the name;
For one being sued to, one that humbly sues;
For queen, a very caitiff crowned with care;   101
For she that scorned at me, now scorned of me;   102
For she being feared of all, now fearing one;
For she commanding all, obeyed of none.
Thus hath the course of justice whirled about

And left thee but a very prey to time,
Having no more but thought of what thou wast   107
To torture thee the more, being what thou art.
Thou didst usurp my place, and dost thou not
Usurp the just proportion of my sorrow?
Now thy proud neck bears half my burdened yoke,   111
From which even here I slip my weary head
And leave the burden of it all on thee.
Farewell, York's wife, and queen of sad mischance!
These English woes shall make me smile in France.
                                        [She starts to leave.]

QUEEN ELIZABETH
O thou well skilled in curses, stay awhile,
And teach me how to curse mine enemies!

QUEEN MARGARET
Forbear to sleep the nights, and fast the days;
Compare dead happiness with living woe;
Think that thy babes were sweeter than they were
And he that slew them fouler than he is.
Bett'ring thy loss makes the bad causer worse;   122
Revolving this will teach thee how to curse.   123

QUEEN ELIZABETH
My words are dull. Oh, quicken them with thine!   124

QUEEN MARGARET
Thy woes will make them sharp, and pierce like mine.
                                          Exit Margaret.

DUCHESS
Why should calamity be full of words?

QUEEN ELIZABETH
Windy attorneys to their client's woes,   127
Airy succeeders of intestate joys,   128
Poor breathing orators of miseries,   129
Let them have scope! Though what they will impart
Help nothing else, yet do they ease the heart.

DUCHESS
If so, then be not tongue-tied. Go with me,
And in the breath of bitter words let's smother
My damnèd son that thy two sweet sons smothered.
                                        [Sound trumpet.]
The trumpet sounds. Be copious in exclaims.   135

    Enter King Richard and his train [marching, with
    drums and trumpets].

KING RICHARD
Who intercepts me in my expedition?   136

DUCHESS
Oh, she that might have intercepted thee,
By strangling thee in her accursèd womb,
From all the slaughters, wretch, that thou hast done!

QUEEN ELIZABETH
Hid'st thou that forehead with a golden crown
Where should be branded, if that right were right,

63 Thy Edward Edward IV.   my Edward the son of Henry VI   64 other
Edward Edward V.   quit requite   65 Young York Richard, Duke of
York, the younger of the princes murdered in the Tower.   but boot
merely into the bargain   68 frantic frenzied, insane   69 Th'adulterate the adulterous   70 smothered buried   71 intelligencer agent,
go-between, spy   72 Only . . . factor chosen above all others as their
(hell's) agent, and sent to earth for no other purpose   74 piteous
deplorable   81 bottled bottle-shaped, swollen (as at 1.3.242).
bunch-backed hunchbacked   82 flourish mere ornament, embellish-
ment. (See 1.3.241.)   84 presentation representation, semblance
85 index argument, preface, prologue.   pageant spectacular entertainment   88–9 garish . . . shot i.e., standard-bearer, conspicuous in
appearance, and thus the target of enemy fire   90 sign mere token
95 bending bowing   96 troops supporters, followers   97 Decline
Go through in order. (A grammatical metaphor.)   101 caitiff wretch,
slave   102 of by. (Also in lines 103 and 104.)

107 no . . . thought only the memory   111 burdened burdensome
122 Bett'ring Magnifying   123 Revolving meditating on   124 quicken
put life into   127 Windy . . . woes i.e., Words, which are airy pleaders
on behalf of one who is suffering   128 Airy . . . joys insubstantial
words, all that is left of joys that died unfulfilled. (Literally, having
died without anything to bequeath.)   129 breathing speaking
135 exclaims exclamations.   136 expedition (1) haste (2) military
undertaking.

The slaughter of the prince that owed that crown   142
And the dire death of my poor sons and brothers?
Tell me, thou villain slave, where are my children?

DUCHESS
Thou toad, thou toad, where is thy brother Clarence?
And little Ned Plantagenet, his son?   146

QUEEN ELIZABETH
Where is the gentle Rivers, Vaughan, Grey?

DUCHESS   Where is kind Hastings?

KING RICHARD
A flourish, trumpets! Strike alarum, drums!   149
Let not the heavens hear these telltale women   150
Rail on the Lord's anointed. Strike, I say!
                                    Flourish. Alarums.
Either be patient and entreat me fair,   152
Or with the clamorous report of war   153
Thus will I drown your exclamations.

DUCHESS   Art thou my son?

KING RICHARD
Ay, I thank God, my father, and yourself.

DUCHESS
Then patiently hear my impatience.

KING RICHARD
Madam, I have a touch of your condition,   158
That cannot brook the accent of reproof.

DUCHESS
Oh, let me speak!

KING RICHARD   Do then, but I'll not hear.

DUCHESS
I will be mild and gentle in my words.

KING RICHARD
And brief, good mother, for I am in haste.

DUCHESS
Art thou so hasty? I have stayed for thee,   163
God knows, in torment and in agony.   164

KING RICHARD
And came I not at last to comfort you?

DUCHESS
No, by the Holy Rood, thou know'st it well,   166
Thou cam'st on earth to make the earth my hell.
A grievous burden was thy birth to me;
Tetchy and wayward was thy infancy;   169
Thy schooldays frightful, desp'rate, wild, and furious;
Thy prime of manhood daring, bold, and venturous;
Thy age confirmed, proud, subtle, sly, and bloody,   172
More mild, but yet more harmful—kind in hatred.   173
What comfortable hour canst thou name
That ever graced me with thy company?

KING RICHARD
Faith, none, but Humphrey Hour, that called Your Grace   176

To breakfast once forth of my company.   177
If I be so disgracious in your eye,   178
Let me march on and not offend you, madam.—
Strike up the drum.

DUCHESS   I prithee, hear me speak.

KING RICHARD
You speak too bitterly.

DUCHESS   Hear me a word,
For I shall never speak to thee again.

KING RICHARD   So.

DUCHESS
Either thou wilt die by God's just ordinance
Ere from this war thou turn a conqueror,   185
Or I with grief and extreme age shall perish
And nevermore behold thy face again.
Therefore take with thee my most grievous curse,
Which in the day of battle tire thee more
Than all the complete armor that thou wear'st!
My prayers on the adverse party fight,   191
And there the little souls of Edward's children
Whisper the spirits of thine enemies   193
And promise them success and victory!
Bloody thou art, bloody will be thy end;
Shame serves thy life and doth thy death attend.   196
                                                Exit.

QUEEN ELIZABETH
Though far more cause, yet much less spirit to curse
Abides in me; I say amen to her.

KING RICHARD
Stay, madam. I must talk a word with you.

QUEEN ELIZABETH
I have no more sons of the royal blood
For thee to slaughter. For my daughters, Richard,   201
They shall be praying nuns, not weeping queens,
And therefore level not to hit their lives.   203

KING RICHARD
You have a daughter called Elizabeth,
Virtuous and fair, royal and gracious.

QUEEN ELIZABETH
And must she die for this? Oh, let her live,
And I'll corrupt her manners, stain her beauty,   207
Slander myself as false to Edward's bed,
Throw over her the veil of infamy;
So she may live unscarred of bleeding slaughter,   210
I will confess she was not Edward's daughter.

KING RICHARD
Wrong not her birth. She is a royal princess.

QUEEN ELIZABETH
To save her life, I'll say she is not so.

KING RICHARD
Her life is safest only in her birth.   214

QUEEN ELIZABETH
And only in that safety died her brothers.

---

142 **owed** owned   146 **Ned Plantagenet** (See 4.3.36.)   149 **flourish** fanfare.   **alarum** call to arms   150 **telltale** tattling, gabbling   152 **entreat me fair** treat me with courtesy   153 **report** noise   158 **condition** disposition   163 **stayed** waited   164 **in agony** i.e., in childbirth.
166 **Holy Rood** Christ's cross   169 **Tetchy** fretful, peevish   172 **age confirmed** riper manhood   173 **kind in hatred** concealing hatred under pretense of kindness.   176 **Humphrey Hour** (To "dine with Duke Humphrey" was to go hungry; hence, Richard flippantly suggests, he was saved from a spare breakfast. The passage is obscure.)

177 **forth of** away from   178 **disgracious** unpleasing, disliked   185 **turn** return   191 **party** side   193 **Whisper** whisper to   196 **serves** accompanies   201 **For my** As for my   203 **level** aim   207 **manners** morals   210 **So** provided.   **of** by   214 **Her . . . birth** Her best guarantee of personal safety is her high birth.

KING RICHARD
Lo, at their birth good stars were opposite.   216

QUEEN ELIZABETH
No, to their lives ill friends were contrary.   217

KING RICHARD
All unavoided is the doom of destiny.   218

QUEEN ELIZABETH
True, when avoided grace makes destiny.   219
My babes were destined to a fairer death,
If grace had blessed thee with a fairer life.

KING RICHARD
You speak as if that I had slain my cousins.   222

QUEEN ELIZABETH
Cousins, indeed, and by their uncle cozened   223
Of comfort, kingdom, kindred, freedom, life.
Whose hand soever lanced their tender hearts,   225
Thy head, all indirectly, gave direction.   226
No doubt the murd'rous knife was dull and blunt
Till it was whetted on thy stone-hard heart,
To revel in the entrails of my lambs.
But that still use of grief makes wild grief tame,
My tongue should to thy ears not name my boys   230
Till that my nails were anchored in thine eyes;
And I, in such a desp'rate bay of death,   233
Like a poor bark of sails and tackling reft,   234
Rush all to pieces on thy rocky bosom.

KING RICHARD
Madam, so thrive I in my enterprise   236
And dangerous success of bloody wars   237
As I intend more good to you and yours
Than ever you or yours by me were harmed!

QUEEN ELIZABETH
What good is covered with the face of heaven,   240
To be discovered, that can do me good?

KING RICHARD
Th'advancement of your children, gentle lady.

QUEEN ELIZABETH
Up to some scaffold, there to lose their heads.

KING RICHARD
Unto the dignity and height of fortune,
The high imperial type of this earth's glory.   245

QUEEN ELIZABETH
Flatter my sorrow with report of it;
Tell me what state, what dignity, what honor,
Canst thou demise to any child of mine?   248

KING RICHARD
Even all I have—ay, and myself and all—
Will I withal endow a child of thine,
So in the Lethe of thy angry soul   251

Thou drown the sad remembrance of those wrongs
Which thou supposest I have done to thee.

QUEEN ELIZABETH
Be brief, lest that the process of thy kindness   254
Last longer telling than thy kindness' date.   255

KING RICHARD
Then know that from my soul I love thy daughter.   256

QUEEN ELIZABETH
My daughter's mother thinks it with her soul.

KING RICHARD   What do you think?

QUEEN ELIZABETH
That thou dost love my daughter from thy soul.
So from thy soul's love didst thou love her brothers,   260
And from my heart's love I do thank thee for it.

KING RICHARD
Be not so hasty to confound my meaning.   262
I mean that with my soul I love thy daughter
And do intend to make her Queen of England.

QUEEN ELIZABETH
Well then, who dost thou mean shall be her king?

KING RICHARD
Even he that makes her queen. Who else should be?

QUEEN ELIZABETH
What, thou?

KING RICHARD   Even so. How think you of it?

QUEEN ELIZABETH
How canst thou woo her?

KING RICHARD   That would I learn of you,
As one being best acquainted with her humor.   269

QUEEN ELIZABETH
And wilt thou learn of me?

KING RICHARD   Madam, with all my heart.

QUEEN ELIZABETH
Send to her, by the man that slew her brothers,
A pair of bleeding hearts; thereon engrave
"Edward" and "York"; then haply will she weep.   273
Therefore present to her—as sometime Margaret   274
Did to thy father, steeped in Rutland's blood—   275
A handkerchief, which, say to her, did drain
The purple sap from her sweet brother's body;
And bid her wipe her weeping eyes withal.
If this inducement move her not to love,
Send her a letter of thy noble deeds.
Tell her thou mad'st away her uncle Clarence,
Her uncle Rivers, ay, and for her sake
Mad'st quick conveyance with her good aunt Anne.   283

KING RICHARD
You mock me, madam. This is not the way
To win your daughter.

QUEEN ELIZABETH   There is no other way,
Unless thou couldst put on some other shape
And not be Richard that hath done all this.

216 opposite hostile. **217 contrary** opposed. **218 unavoided** unavoidable **219 avoided grace** i.e., Richard, in whom grace is void or lacking **222 as if that** as if **223 cozened** cheated **225 Whose hand soever** Whoever it was whose hand **226 all indirectly** by indirect means, and wrongly **230 But . . . grief** Were it not that constant grieving **233 bay** (1) inlet (2) position of a hunted animal turning to face the hounds **234 bark** sailing vessel. **reft** bereft **236 so thrive I may** I so thrive **237 success** sequel, result **240 covered with** hidden by (and therefore not yet revealed to humanity) **245 imperial type** symbol of rule **248 demise** convey, transmit, lease **251 So** provided that. **Lethe** river in the underworld, the waters of which produce forgetfulness

254 process story **255 date** duration. **256 from** with. (But Queen Elizabeth, in lines 259–61, sarcastically uses the word in the sense "apart from," "at variance with.") **260 So** Just so. (Said ironically.) **262 confound** deliberately misconstrue **269 humor** temperament. **273 haply** perhaps **274 sometime** once **275 Rutland's** (See *3 Henry VI*, 1.4.79–83.) **283 conveyance** with disposal of

KING RICHARD
Say that I did all this for love of her.

QUEEN ELIZABETH
Nay, then indeed she cannot choose but hate thee,
Having bought love with such a bloody spoil.   290

KING RICHARD
Look what is done cannot be now amended.   291
Men shall deal unadvisedly sometimes,   292
Which after-hours gives leisure to repent.
If I did take the kingdom from your sons,
To make amends I'll give it to your daughter.
If I have killed the issue of your womb,
To quicken your increase I will beget   297
Mine issue of your blood upon your daughter.
A grandam's name is little less in love
Than is the doting title of a mother;
They are as children but one step below,
Even of your metal, of your very blood,   302
Of all one pain, save for a night of groans   303
Endured of her for whom you bid like sorrow.   304
Your children were vexation to your youth,
But mine shall be a comfort to your age.
The loss you have is but a son being king,
And by that loss your daughter is made queen.
I cannot make you what amends I would;
Therefore accept such kindness as I can.   310
Dorset your son, that with a fearful soul
Leads discontented steps in foreign soil,
This fair alliance quickly shall call home
To high promotions and great dignity.
The king that calls your beauteous daughter wife
Familiarly shall call thy Dorset brother;   316
Again shall you be mother to a king,
And all the ruins of distressful times
Repaired with double riches of content.
What? We have many goodly days to see.
The liquid drops of tears that you have shed
Shall come again, transformed to orient pearl,   322
Advantaging their love with interest   323
Of ten times double gain of happiness.
Go then, my mother, to thy daughter go.
Make bold her bashful years with your experience;
Prepare her ears to hear a wooer's tale;
Put in her tender heart th'aspiring flame
Of golden sovereignty; acquaint the Princess
With the sweet silent hours of marriage joys.
And when this arm of mine hath chastisèd
The petty rebel, dull-brained Buckingham,
Bound with triumphant garlands will I come
And lead thy daughter to a conqueror's bed;
To whom I will retail my conquest won,   335
And she shall be sole victoress, Caesar's Caesar.

QUEEN ELIZABETH
What were I best to say? Her father's brother
Would be her lord? Or shall I say her uncle?
Or, he that slew her brothers and her uncles?
Under what title shall I woo for thee
That God, the law, my honor, and her love
Can make seem pleasing to her tender years?

KING RICHARD
Infer fair England's peace by this alliance.   343

QUEEN ELIZABETH
Which she shall purchase with still-lasting war.   344

KING RICHARD
Tell her the King, that may command, entreats.

QUEEN ELIZABETH
That at her hands which the King's King forbids.   346

KING RICHARD
Say she shall be a high and mighty queen.

QUEEN ELIZABETH
To vail the title, as her mother doth.   348

KING RICHARD
Say I will love her everlastingly.

QUEEN ELIZABETH
But how long shall that title "ever" last?

KING RICHARD
Sweetly in force unto her fair life's end.

QUEEN ELIZABETH
But how long fairly shall her sweet life last?   352

KING RICHARD
As long as heaven and nature lengthens it.

QUEEN ELIZABETH
As long as hell and Richard likes of it.

KING RICHARD
Say I, her sovereign, am her subject low.

QUEEN ELIZABETH
But she, your subject, loathes such sovereignty.

KING RICHARD
Be eloquent in my behalf to her.

QUEEN ELIZABETH
An honest tale speeds best being plainly told.   358

KING RICHARD
Then plainly to her tell my loving tale.

QUEEN ELIZABETH
Plain and not honest is too harsh a style.

KING RICHARD
Your reasons are too shallow and too quick.   361

QUEEN ELIZABETH
Oh, no, my reasons are too deep and dead—
Too deep and dead, poor infants, in their graves.

KING RICHARD
Harp not on that string, madam. That is past.

QUEEN ELIZABETH
Harp on it still shall I till heartstrings break.

---

290 spoil slaughter. (A hunting term.)   **291 Look what** Whatever
292 shall deal cannot but act   **297 quicken your increase** give new
life to your progeny   **302 metal** substance. (With a suggestion also of
mettle, "spirit." The Folio reads "mettall.")   **303 pain** labor, effort   **304**
of by.   **bid** endured, bided   **310 can** am able (to give).   **316 Famil-**
iarly familially   **322 orient** bright, shining   **323 Advantaging their**
love augmenting the love that prompted tears   **335 retail** relate

343 Infer Allege, adduce (as a reason)   **344 still-lasting war** i.e., perpetual domestic strife.   **346 forbids** (*The Book of Common Prayer*,
echoing the injunctions of Leviticus 18, prohibits the marriage of a
man with his brother's daughter.)   **348 vail** yield; lower or abase as a
sign of submission   **352 fairly** without foul play   **358 speeds** succeeds   **361 quick** hasty. (With a pun on the meaning "alive," contrasted with *dead* in the next line, just as *shallow* is punningly
contrasted with *deep*.)

KING RICHARD
    Now, by my George, my Garter, and my crown—   366
QUEEN ELIZABETH
    Profaned, dishonored, and the third usurped.
KING RICHARD
    I swear—
QUEEN ELIZABETH   By nothing, for this is no oath.
    Thy George, profaned, hath lost his lordly honor;   369
    Thy Garter, blemished, pawned his knightly virtue;
    Thy crown, usurped, disgraced his kingly glory.
    If something thou wouldst swear to be believed,
    Swear then by something that thou hast not wronged.
KING RICHARD
    Then, by myself—
QUEEN ELIZABETH   Thyself is self-misused.
KING RICHARD
    Now, by the world—
QUEEN ELIZABETH   'Tis full of thy foul wrongs.
KING RICHARD
    My father's death—
QUEEN ELIZABETH   Thy life hath it dishonored.
KING RICHARD
    Why then, by God—
QUEEN ELIZABETH   God's wrong is most of all.
    If thou didst fear to break an oath with Him,
    The unity the King my husband made   379
    Thou hadst not broken, nor my brothers died.
    If thou hadst feared to break an oath by Him,
    Th'imperial metal circling now thy head
    Had graced the tender temples of my child,
    And both the princes had been breathing here,
    Which now, two tender bedfellows for dust,
    Thy broken faith hath made the prey for worms.
    What canst thou swear by now?
KING RICHARD   The time to come.
QUEEN ELIZABETH
    That thou hast wrongèd in the time o'erpast;
    For I myself have many tears to wash
    Hereafter time, for time past wronged by thee.   390
    The children live whose fathers thou hast slaughtered,
    Ungoverned youth, to wail it in their age;   392
    The parents live whose children thou hast butchered,
    Old barren plants, to wail it with their age.
    Swear not by time to come, for that thou hast
    Misused ere used, by times ill-used o'erpast.   396
KING RICHARD
    As I intend to prosper and repent,   397
    So thrive I in my dangerous affairs
    Of hostile arms! Myself myself confound!   399

Heaven and fortune bar me happy hours!
Day, yield me not thy light, nor, night, thy rest!
Be opposite all planets of good luck   402
To my proceeding if, with dear heart's love,
Immaculate devotion, holy thoughts,
I tender not thy beauteous, princely daughter!   405
In her consists my happiness and thine;
Without her follows to myself and thee,
Herself, the land, and many a Christian soul,
Death, desolation, ruin, and decay.
It cannot be avoided but by this;
It will not be avoided but by this.
Therefore, dear mother—I must call you so—
Be the attorney of my love to her.
Plead what I will be, not what I have been,
Not my deserts, but what I will deserve.
Urge the necessity and state of times,   416
And be not peevish-fond in great designs.   417
QUEEN ELIZABETH
    Shall I be tempted of the devil thus?
KING RICHARD
    Ay, if the devil tempt you to do good.
QUEEN ELIZABETH
    Shall I forget myself to be myself?   420
KING RICHARD
    Ay, if yourself's remembrance wrong yourself.   421
QUEEN ELIZABETH
    Yet thou didst kill my children.
KING RICHARD
    But in your daughter's womb I bury them,
    Where in that nest of spicery they will breed   424
    Selves of themselves, to your recomforture.   425
QUEEN ELIZABETH
    Shall I go win my daughter to thy will?
KING RICHARD
    And be a happy mother by the deed.
QUEEN ELIZABETH
    I go. Write to me very shortly,
    And you shall understand from me her mind.
KING RICHARD
    Bear her my true love's kiss; and so, farewell.
                    Exit Queen [Elizabeth].
    Relenting fool, and shallow, changing woman!

        Enter Ratcliffe; [Catesby following].

    How now, what news?
RATCLIFFE
    Most mighty sovereign, on the western coast
    Rideth a puissant navy; to our shores   434
    Throng many doubtful, hollow-hearted friends,   435

---

366 George . . . Garter (The George, a badge showing Saint George slaying the dragon, was not added to the insignia of the Order of the Garter until the reign of Henry VII or Henry VIII.)   **369 his** its (as also in lines 370, 371)   **379 The unity** i.e., the reconciliation between Queen Elizabeth and her enemies   **390 Hereafter time** in the future   **392 Ungoverned** i.e., without a father's guidance or rule   **396 Misused . . . o'erpast** misused even before it came time to be used, by your ill use of past times.   **397 As . . . repent** i.e., I swear that as I hope to thrive and intend to repent   **399 Myself . . . confound!** May I destroy myself!

402 opposite opposed, adverse   **405 I tender not** I fail to show a tender regard for   **416 state of times** urgent political need   **417 And . . . designs** and do not stand by, childishly foolish as great plans are afoot.   **420 Shall . . . myself?** i.e., Shall I, in order to be queen mother, forget that I am the person you have wronged?   **421 wrong yourself** i.e., interferes with what is to your advantage.   **424 nest of spicery** (The fabled phoenix arose anew from the nest of spices, its funeral pyre.)   **425 recomforture** comfort, consolation.   **434 puissant** powerful   **435 doubtful** apprehensive

Unarmed and unresolved to beat them back.
'Tis thought that Richmond is their admiral;   437
And there they hull, expecting but the aid   438
Of Buckingham to welcome them ashore.

KING RICHARD
Some light-foot friend post to the Duke of Norfolk: 440
Ratcliffe, thyself, or Catesby; where is he?

CATESBY
Here, my good lord.

KING RICHARD   Catesby, fly to the Duke.

CATESBY
I will, my lord, with all convenient haste.   443

KING RICHARD
Ratcliffe, come hither. Post to Salisbury.
When thou com'st thither—[*To Catesby*] Dull, unmindful
    villain,
Why stay'st thou here, and go'st not to the Duke?

CATESBY
First, mighty liege, tell me Your Highness' pleasure,
What from Your Grace I shall deliver to him.

KING RICHARD
Oh, true, good Catesby. Bid him levy straight
The greatest strength and power that he can make,   450
And meet me suddenly at Salisbury.   451

CATESBY   I go.   *Exit.*

RATCLIFFE
What, may it please you, shall I do at Salisbury?

KING RICHARD
Why, what wouldst thou do there before I go?

RATCLIFFE
Your Highness told me I should post before.   455

KING RICHARD
My mind is changed.

    Enter Lord Stanley [*Earl of Derby*].

                    Stanley, what news with you?

STANLEY
None good, my liege, to please you with the hearing,
Nor none so bad but well may be reported.

KING RICHARD
Hoyday, a riddle! Neither good nor bad!   459
What need'st thou run so many miles about,
When thou mayst tell thy tale the nearest way?   461
Once more, what news?

STANLEY   Richmond is on the seas.

KING RICHARD
There let him sink, and be the seas on him!
White-livered runagate, what doth he there?   464

STANLEY
I know not, mighty sovereign, but by guess.

KING RICHARD   Well, as you guess?

STANLEY
Stirred up by Dorset, Buckingham, and Morton,

He makes for England, here to claim the crown.

KING RICHARD
Is the chair empty? Is the sword unswayed?   469
Is the King dead? The empire unpossessed?   470
What heir of York is there alive but we?
And who is England's king but great York's heir?
Then tell me, what makes he upon the seas?   473

STANLEY
Unless for that, my liege, I cannot guess.

KING RICHARD
Unless for that he comes to be your liege,
You cannot guess wherefore the Welshman comes.   476
Thou wilt revolt and fly to him, I fear.

STANLEY
No, my good lord; therefore mistrust me not.

KING RICHARD
Where is thy power, then, to beat him back?   479
Where be thy tenants and thy followers?
Are they not now upon the western shore,
Safe-conducting the rebels from their ships?

STANLEY
No, my good lord, my friends are in the north.

KING RICHARD
Cold friends to me! What do they in the north
When they should serve their sovereign in the west?

STANLEY
They have not been commanded, mighty King.
Pleaseth Your Majesty to give me leave,   487
I'll muster up my friends and meet Your Grace
Where and what time Your Majesty shall please.

KING RICHARD
Ay, thou wouldst be gone to join with Richmond.
But I'll not trust thee.

STANLEY   Most mighty sovereign,
You have no cause to hold my friendship doubtful.
I never was nor never will be false.

KING RICHARD
Go then and muster men, but leave behind
Your son, George Stanley. Look your heart be firm,
Or else his head's assurance is but frail.   496

STANLEY
So deal with him as I prove true to you.

                    Exit Stanley [*Earl of Derby*].

            Enter a Messenger.

FIRST MESSENGER
My gracious sovereign, now in Devonshire,
As I by friends am well advertisèd,   499
Sir Edward Courtney and the haughty prelate,
Bishop of Exeter, his elder brother,   501
With many more confederates, are in arms.

            Enter another Messenger.

---

437 **their admiral** i.e., of the *puissant navy* named three lines earlier
438 **hull** drift with the sails furled   440 **light-foot** swift-footed.   **post**
hasten   443 **convenient** appropriate, suitable   450 **make** raise
451 **suddenly** swiftly   455 **post** hasten   459 **Hoyday** Heyday.
(Expressing mock wonderment.)   461 **the nearest way** directly, simply.   464 **White-livered runagate** Cowardly renegade, vagabond

469 **chair** throne   470 **empire** kingdom   473 **makes he** is he doing
476 **Welshman** (Richmond was the grandson of Owen Tudor, a
Welshman of Anglesea, who fathered three sons and a daughter by
Katharine of Valois, widow of Henry V.)   479 **power** army
487 **Pleaseth** May it please   496 **assurance** safety   499 **advertisèd**
informed   501 **brother** (Actually, a cousin.)

SECOND MESSENGER
In Kent, my liege, the Guildfords are in arms,
And every hour more competitors 504
Flock to the rebels, and their power grows strong.

Enter another Messenger.

THIRD MESSENGER
My lord, the army of great Buckingham—
KING RICHARD
Out on ye, owls! Nothing but songs of death? 507
He striketh him.
There, take thou that, till thou bring better news.
THIRD MESSENGER
The news I have to tell Your Majesty
Is that by sudden floods and fall of waters
Buckingham's army is dispersed and scattered,
And he himself wandered away alone,
No man knows whither.
KING RICHARD　　　　　　I cry thee mercy. 513
There is my purse to cure that blow of thine.
[*He gives money.*]
Hath any well-advisèd friend proclaimed 515
Reward to him that brings the traitor in?
THIRD MESSENGER
Such proclamation hath been made, my lord.

Enter another Messenger.

FOURTH MESSENGER
Sir Thomas Lovell and Lord Marquess Dorset,
'Tis said, my liege, in Yorkshire are in arms, 518
But this good comfort bring I to Your Highness:
The Breton navy is dispersed by tempest.
Richmond, in Dorsetshire, sent out a boat
Unto the shore, to ask those on the banks
If they were his assistants, yea or no,
Who answered him they came from Buckingham
Upon his party. He, mistrusting them,
Hoised sail and made his course again for Brittany. 527
KING RICHARD
March on, march on, since we are up in arms,
If not to fight with foreign enemies,
Yet to beat down these rebels here at home.

Enter Catesby.

CATESBY
My liege, the Duke of Buckingham is taken!
That is the best news. That the Earl of Richmond
Is with a mighty power landed at Milford 533
Is colder tidings, yet they must be told.
KING RICHARD
Away towards Salisbury! While we reason here, 535

A royal battle might be won and lost.
Someone take order Buckingham be brought
To Salisbury. The rest march on with me.
Flourish. Exeunt.

❧

4.[5]

*Enter [Lord Stanley Earl of] Derby and Sir
Christopher [Urswick, a priest].*

STANLEY
Sir Christopher, tell Richmond this from me:
That in the sty of the most deadly boar
My son George Stanley is franked up in hold. 3
If I revolt, off goes young George's head;
The fear of that holds off my present aid.
So get thee gone; commend me to thy lord.
Withal say that the Queen hath heartily consented 7
He should espouse Elizabeth her daughter.
But tell me, where is princely Richmond now?
CHRISTOPHER
At Pembroke, or at Ha'rfordwest, in Wales. 10
STANLEY　　What men of name resort to him? 11
CHRISTOPHER
Sir Walter Herbert, a renownèd soldier,
Sir Gilbert Talbot, Sir William Stanley,
Oxford, redoubted Pembroke, Sir James Blunt, 14
And Rice ap Thomas, with a valiant crew,
And many other of great name and worth;
And towards London do they bend their power, 17
If by the way they be not fought withal.
STANLEY
Well, hie thee to thy lord; I kiss his hand. 19
My letter will resolve him of my mind. 20
[*He gives a letter.*]
Farewell.　　　　　　　　　　　　*Exeunt.*

❧

5.1

*Enter Buckingham, with [Sheriff and] halberds, led
to execution.*

BUCKINGHAM
Will not King Richard let me speak with him?
SHERIFF
No, my good lord. Therefore be patient.
BUCKINGHAM
Hastings, and Edward's children, Grey, and Rivers,
Holy King Henry, and thy fair son Edward, 4
Vaughan, and all that have miscarrièd 5

---

504 **competitors** confederates　507 **owls** (The cry of the owl was
thought to portend death.)　513 **I cry thee mercy** I beg your pardon.
515 **well-advisèd** judicious　518 **Sir Thomas Lovell** (Not the Lovell
of 3.4 and 3.5, who was historically Sir Francis Lovell, Richard's Lord
Chamberlain, but perhaps related to him.)　527 **Hoised** hoisted
533 **Milford** Milford Haven on the coast of Wales in the county of
Pembroke. (A gap of two years is bridged here. Richmond's first
fruitless expedition was in October 1483; his landing at Milford was
in August 1485.)　535 **reason** talk

4.5. Location: London. The house of Lord Stanley, Earl of Derby.
0.1 *Sir* (Honorific title for a clergyman.)　**3 franked up in hold** shut
up in custody, as in a pigpen.　**7 Withal** In addition　**10 Ha'rfordwest** Haverfordwest, in Wales　**11 name** rank　**14 redoubted Pembroke** awe-inspiring Jasper Tudor, Earl of Pembroke (uncle to
Richmond)　**17 bend their power** direct their forces　**19 hie** hasten
20 resolve him of inform him concerning
5.1. Location: Salisbury. An open place.
4 thy i.e., Henry VI's　**5 miscarrièd** perished

By underhand corrupted foul injustice:
If that your moody, discontented souls   7
Do through the clouds behold this present hour,
Even for revenge mock my destruction!
This is All Souls' Day, fellow, is it not?   10

SHERIFF   It is, my lord.

BUCKINGHAM
Why, then All Souls' Day is my body's doomsday.
This is the day which, in King Edward's time,
I wished might fall on me when I was found
False to his children and his wife's allies;
This is the day wherein I wished to fall
By the false faith of him whom most I trusted;
This, this All Souls' Day to my fearful soul
Is the determined respite of my wrongs.   19
That high All-Seer which I dallied with
Hath turned my feignèd prayer on my head
And given in earnest what I begged in jest.
Thus doth he force the swords of wicked men
To turn their own points in their masters' bosoms.
Thus Margaret's curse falls heavy on my neck:
"When he," quoth she, "shall split thy heart with sorrow,   26
Remember Margaret was a prophetess."
Come lead me, officers, to the block of shame.
Wrong hath but wrong, and blame the due of blame.
                    Exeunt Buckingham with officers.

❧

5.2

*Enter Richmond, Oxford, [Sir James] Blunt, [Sir
Walter] Herbert, and others, with drum and
colors.*

RICHMOND
Fellows in arms, and my most loving friends
Bruised underneath the yoke of tyranny,
Thus far into the bowels of the land   3
Have we marched on without impediment;
And here receive we from our father Stanley   5
Lines of fair comfort and encouragement.
The wretched, bloody, and usurping boar,
That spoiled your summer fields and fruitful vines,   8
Swills your warm blood like wash, and makes his trough   9
In your emboweled bosoms, this foul swine   10
Is now even in the center of this isle,
Near to the town of Leicester, as we learn.
From Tamworth thither is but one day's march.
In God's name, cheerly on, courageous friends,   14
To reap the harvest of perpetual peace
By this one bloody trial of sharp war.

OXFORD
Every man's conscience is a thousand swords
To fight against this guilty homicide.

HERBERT
I doubt not but his friends will turn to us.

BLUNT
He hath no friends but what are friends for fear,   20
Which in his dearest need will fly from him.   21

RICHMOND
All for our vantage. Then, in God's name, march!
True hope is swift and flies with swallow's wings;
Kings it makes gods and meaner creatures kings.   24
                                    Exeunt omnes.

❧

[5.3]

*Enter King Richard in arms, with Norfolk,
Ratcliffe, and the Earl of Surrey [and others].*

KING RICHARD
Here pitch our tent, even here in Bosworth Field.
My lord of Surrey, why look you so sad?

SURREY
My heart is ten times lighter than my looks.

KING RICHARD
My lord of Norfolk—

NORFOLK   Here, most gracious liege.

KING RICHARD
Norfolk, we must have knocks; ha! Must we not?   5

NORFOLK
We must both give and take, my loving lord.

KING RICHARD
Up with my tent! Here will I lie tonight.
        [*Soldiers begin to set up King Richard's tent.*]
But where tomorrow? Well, all's one for that.   8
Who hath descried the number of the traitors?   9

NORFOLK
Six or seven thousand is their utmost power.

KING RICHARD
Why, our battalia trebles that account.   11
Besides, the King's name is a tower of strength,
Which they upon the adverse faction want.   13
Up with the tent! Come, noble gentlemen,
Let us survey the vantage of the ground.   15
Call for some men of sound direction.   16
Let's lack no discipline, make no delay,
For, lords, tomorrow is a busy day.   *Exeunt.*

*Enter [on the other side of the stage] Richmond,
Sir William Brandon, Oxford, and Dorset, [Blunt,
Herbert, and others. Some of the soldiers pitch
Richmond's tent.]*

---

7 **moody, discontented** angry, vengeance-seeking   **10 All Souls' Day**
November 2, the day on which the Church intercedes for all Christian
souls   **19 the determined . . . wrongs** the ordained date to which
the punishment of my evil practices was respited or postponed.
26 he Richard
5.2. Location: A camp near Tamworth.
3 bowels interior   **5 father** stepfather, Lord Stanley, Earl of Derby
8 spoiled despoiled   **9 Swills** gulps.   **wash** hogwash, swill
10 emboweled disemboweled   **14 cheerly** cheerily, heartily

20 for fear i.e., out of fearing Richard   **21 dearest** direst   **24 meaner**
of lower degree.   **24.1 omnes** all.
5.3. Location: Bosworth Field.
5 knocks blows   **8 all's . . . that** be that as it may.   **9 descried** recon-
noitred   **11 battalia** army   **13 want** lack.   **15 vantage of the ground**
i.e., way in which the field can best be used for tactical advantage.
16 direction judgment, military skill.

RICHMOND
  The weary sun hath made a golden set,
  And, by the bright track of his fiery car,   20
  Gives token of a goodly day tomorrow.
  Sir William Brandon, you shall bear my standard.   22
  Give me some ink and paper in my tent.
  I'll draw the form and model of our battle,
  Limit each leader to his several charge,   25
  And part in just proportion our small power.   26
  My lord of Oxford, you, Sir William Brandon,
  And you, Sir Walter Herbert, stay with me.
  The Earl of Pembroke keeps his regiment;   29
  Good Captain Blunt, bear my good-night to him,
  And by the second hour in the morning
  Desire the Earl to see me in my tent.
  Yet one thing more, good Captain, do for me:
  Where is Lord Stanley quartered, do you know?
BLUNT
  Unless I have mista'en his colors much,
  Which well I am assured I have not done,
  His regiment lies half a mile at least
  South from the mighty power of the King.   38
RICHMOND
  If without peril it be possible,
  Sweet Blunt, make some good means to speak with him,
  And give him from me this most needful note.
                                        [He gives a letter.]
BLUNT
  Upon my life, my lord, I'll undertake it.
  And so, God give you quiet rest tonight!
RICHMOND
  Good night, good Captain Blunt.   [Exit Blunt.]
                                  Come, gentlemen,
  Let us consult upon tomorrow's business.
  Into my tent; the dew is raw and cold.
                              They withdraw into the tent.

      Enter [to his tent, King] Richard, Ratcliffe,
      Norfolk, and Catesby.

KING RICHARD
  What is't o'clock?
CATESBY   It's suppertime, my lord;
  It's nine o'clock.
KING RICHARD   I will not sup tonight.
  Give me some ink and paper.
  What, is my beaver easier than it was,   50
  And all my armor laid into my tent?
CATESBY
  It is, my liege, and all things are in readiness.
KING RICHARD
  Good Norfolk, hie thee to thy charge.
  Use careful watch; choose trusty sentinels.
NORFOLK   I go, my lord.

KING RICHARD
  Stir with the lark tomorrow, gentle Norfolk.
NORFOLK   I warrant you, my lord.   [Exit.]   57
KING RICHARD   Catesby!
CATESBY
  My lord?
KING RICHARD   Send out a pursuivant at arms   59
  To Stanley's regiment. Bid him bring his power   60
  Before sunrising, lest his son George fall
  Into the blind cave of eternal night.   [Exit Catesby.]
  Fill me a bowl of wine. Give me a watch.   63
  Saddle white Surrey for the field tomorrow.   64
  Look that my staves be sound and not too heavy.   65
  Ratcliffe!
RATCLIFFE   My lord?
KING RICHARD
  Saw'st thou the melancholy Lord Northumberland?
RATCLIFFE
  Thomas the Earl of Surrey and himself,
  Much about cockshut time, from troop to troop   70
  Went through the army, cheering up the soldiers.
KING RICHARD
  So, I am satisfied. Give me a bowl of wine.
  I have not that alacrity of spirit
  Nor cheer of mind that I was wont to have.   74
                              [Wine is brought.]
  Set it down. Is ink and paper ready?
RATCLIFFE
  It is, my lord.
KING RICHARD   Bid my guard watch. Leave me.
  Ratcliffe, about the mid of night come to my tent
  And help to arm me. Leave me, I say.
                        Exit Ratcliffe. [Richard sleeps.]

      Enter [Lord Stanley Earl of] Derby, to Richmond
      in his tent, [lords and others attending].

STANLEY
  Fortune and victory sit on thy helm!   79
RICHMOND
  All comfort that the dark night can afford
  Be to thy person, noble father-in-law!   81
  Tell me, how fares our loving mother?
STANLEY
  I, by attorney, bless thee from thy mother,   83
  Who prays continually for Richmond's good.
  So much for that. The silent hours steal on,
  And flaky darkness breaks within the east.   86
  In brief—for so the season bids us be—   87
  Prepare thy battle early in the morning,   88
  And put thy fortune to the arbitrament   89

---

57 **warrant** guarantee   59 **pursuivant at arms** junior officer acting as
messenger   60 **power** forces   63 **watch** watch light, candle marked
into equal divisions to show time; or, perhaps, sentinel.   64 **white
Surrey** (The name seems to be Shakespeare's invention. The chroni-
clers say that Richard was mounted on a "great white courser.")
65 **staves** lance shafts   70 **cockshut time** evening twilight; possibly,
the time at which the poultry are shut up   74 **was wont** used   79 **helm**
helmet.   81 **father-in-law** stepfather.   83 **by attorney** as proxy
86 **flaky** streaked with light   87 **season** time   88 **battle** troops
89 **arbitrament** arbitration

---

20 **car** chariot (of Phoebus)   22 **standard** flag.   25 **Limit** appoint.
several charge individual command   26 **And . . . power** and divide
proportionally our small army.   29 **keeps** i.e., is with   38 **power**
army   50 **beaver** face-guard or visor of helmet.   **easier** looser, better
fitting

Of bloody strokes and mortal-staring war.   90
I, as I may—that which I would I cannot—   91
With best advantage will deceive the time   92
And aid thee in this doubtful shock of arms.   93
But on thy side I may not be too forward,   94
Lest, being seen, thy brother, tender George,   95
Be executed in his father's sight.
Farewell. The leisure and the fearful time   97
Cuts off the ceremonious vows of love
And ample interchange of sweet discourse
Which so long sundered friends should dwell upon.
God give us leisure for these rites of love!
Once more, adieu. Be valiant, and speed well!   102

RICHMOND
Good lords, conduct him to his regiment.
I'll strive with troubled thoughts to take a nap,
Lest leaden slumber peise me down tomorrow,   105
When I should mount with wings of victory.
Once more, good night, kind lords and gentlemen.
                                        Exeunt. [Richmond remains.]
O Thou whose captain I account myself,
Look on my forces with a gracious eye;
Put in their hands thy bruising irons of wrath,
That they may crush down with a heavy fall
The usurping helmets of our adversaries!
Make us thy ministers of chastisement,
That we may praise thee in the victory!
To thee I do commend my watchful soul
Ere I let fall the windows of mine eyes.   116
Sleeping and waking, oh, defend me still!   117
                                        [He sleeps.]

            Enter the Ghost of young Prince Edward, son [of]
            Harry the Sixth, to Richard.

GHOST *(to Richard)*
Let me sit heavy on thy soul tomorrow!   118
Think, how thou stabbed'st me in my prime of youth
At Tewkesbury. Despair therefore and die!
(To Richmond) Be cheerful, Richmond, for the wrongèd souls
Of butchered princes fight in thy behalf.
King Henry's issue, Richmond, comforts thee. *[Exit.]*

            Enter the Ghost of Henry the Sixth.

GHOST *(to Richard)*
When I was mortal, my anointed body   124
By thee was punchèd full of deadly holes.
Think on the Tower and me. Despair and die!   126
Harry the Sixth bids thee despair and die!
(To Richmond) Virtuous and holy, be thou conqueror!

Harry, that prophesied thou shouldst be king,   129
Doth comfort thee in thy sleep. Live and flourish!
                                        [Exit.]

            Enter the Ghost of Clarence.

GHOST *[to Richard]*
Let me sit heavy in thy soul tomorrow,
I, that was washed to death with fulsome wine,   132
Poor Clarence, by thy guile betrayed to death!
Tomorrow in the battle think on me,
And fall thy edgeless sword. Despair and die!   135
(To Richmond) Thou offspring of the house of Lancaster,
The wrongèd heirs of York do pray for thee.
Good angels guard thy battle! Live and flourish!   138
                                        [Exit.]

            Enter the Ghosts of Rivers, Grey, [and] Vaughan.

GHOST OF RIVERS *[to Richard]*
Let me sit heavy in thy soul tomorrow,
Rivers that died at Pomfret! Despair and die!
GHOST OF GREY *[to Richard]*
Think upon Grey, and let thy soul despair!
GHOST OF VAUGHAN *[to Richard]*
Think upon Vaughan, and, with guilty fear,
Let fall thy lance. Despair and die!
ALL *(to Richmond)*
Awake, and think our wrongs in Richard's bosom
Will conquer him! Awake, and win the day!
                                        [Exeunt Ghosts.]

            Enter the Ghost of Hastings.

GHOST *[to Richard]*
Bloody and guilty, guiltily awake
And in a bloody battle end thy days!
Think on Lord Hastings. Despair and die!
(To Richmond) Quiet untroubled soul, awake, awake!
Arm, fight, and conquer for fair England's sake!
                                        [Exit.]

            Enter the Ghosts of the two young Princes.

GHOSTS *(to Richard)*
Dream on thy cousins smothered in the Tower.   151
Let us be lead within thy bosom, Richard,
And weigh thee down to ruin, shame, and death!
Thy nephews' souls bid thee despair and die!
(To Richmond) Sleep, Richmond, sleep in peace, and
    wake in joy.
Good angels guard thee from the boar's annoy!   156
Live, and beget a happy race of kings!
Edward's unhappy sons do bid thee flourish.
                                        [Exeunt Ghosts.]

            Enter the Ghost of Lady Anne, his wife.

GHOST *[to Richard]*
Richard, thy wife, that wretched Anne thy wife,
That never slept a quiet hour with thee,

---

90 mortal-staring fatal-visaged   **91 that . . . cannot** i.e., I cannot fight openly on your side, though I want to   **92 With . . . time** as best I can I will work for your side without seeming to do so   **93 shock** encounter   **94 forward** zealous   **95 brother** i.e., stepbrother.   **tender** young, of tender years   **97 leisure** i.e., brief time allowed   **102 speed well** may you succeed.   **105 peise** weigh   **116 windows** i.e., eyelids   **117 still** continually.   **118 sit heavy on** be oppressive to   **124 anointed** i.e., with the sacred oil used in the coronation ceremony; compare with 4.4.151   **126 Tower** (Where Henry VI was supposed to have been murdered.)

129 prophesied (See *3 Henry VI*, 4.6.68 ff.)   **132 washed to death** i.e., drowned in a butt of malmsey.   **fulsome** cloying   **135 fall** let fall.   **edgeless** blunt, useless   **138 battle** troops.   **151 cousins** i.e., nephews   **156 the boar's annoy** i.e., Richard's attack.

Now fills thy sleep with perturbations.
Tomorrow in the battle think on me,
And fall thy edgeless sword. Despair and die!
(*To Richmond*) Thou quiet soul, sleep thou a quiet sleep;
Dream of success and happy victory!
Thy adversary's wife doth pray for thee.   [*Exit.*]

Enter the Ghost of Buckingham.

GHOST [*to Richard*]
The first was I that helped thee to the crown;
The last was I that felt thy tyranny.
Oh, in the battle think on Buckingham,
And die in terror of thy guiltiness!
Dream on, dream on of bloody deeds and death;
Fainting, despair; despairing, yield thy breath!   172
(*To Richmond*) I died for hope ere I could lend thee aid,   173
But cheer thy heart, and be thou not dismayed.
God and good angels fight on Richmond's side,
And Richard fall in height of all his pride!   [*Exit.*] 176
              Richard starteth up out of a dream.

KING RICHARD
Give me another horse! Bind up my wounds!
Have mercy, Jesu!—Soft, I did but dream.
O coward conscience, how dost thou afflict me!
The lights burn blue. It is now dead midnight.   180
Cold fearful drops stand on my trembling flesh.
What do I fear? Myself? There's none else by.
Richard loves Richard; that is, I am I.   183
Is there a murderer here? No. Yes, I am.
Then fly. What, from myself? Great reason why: 185
Lest I revenge. What, myself upon myself?
Alack, I love myself. Wherefore? For any good   187
That I myself have done unto myself?
Oh, no! Alas, I rather hate myself
For hateful deeds committed by myself!
I am a villain. Yet I lie, I am not.
Fool, of thyself speak well. Fool, do not flatter.
My conscience hath a thousand several tongues,   193
And every tongue brings in a several tale,
And every tale condemns me for a villain.
Perjury, perjury, in the highest degree,
Murder, stern murder, in the direst degree,
All several sins, all used in each degree,   198
Throng to the bar, crying all, "Guilty! Guilty!"   199
I shall despair. There is no creature loves me,   200
And if I die no soul will pity me.
And wherefore should they, since that I myself
Find in myself no pity to myself?
Methought the souls of all that I had murdered

Came to my tent, and every one did threat
Tomorrow's vengeance on the head of Richard.

Enter Ratcliffe.

RATCLIFFE   My lord!
KING RICHARD   Zounds! Who is there?
RATCLIFFE
My lord, 'tis I. The early village cock
Hath twice done salutation to the morn.
Your friends are up and buckle on their armor.
KING RICHARD
Oh, Ratcliffe, I have dreamed a fearful dream!
What think'st thou, will our friends prove all true?
RATCLIFFE
No doubt, my lord.
KING RICHARD   Oh, Ratcliffe, I fear, I fear!
RATCLIFFE
Nay, good my lord, be not afraid of shadows.
KING RICHARD
By the apostle Paul, shadows tonight
Have struck more terror to the soul of Richard
Than can the substance of ten thousand soldiers
Armèd in proof and led by shallow Richmond.   219
'Tis not yet near day. Come, go with me;
Under our tents I'll play the eavesdropper,
To see if any mean to shrink from me.
              Exeunt [Richard and Ratcliffe].

Enter the Lords to Richmond, [sitting in his tent].

LORDS   Good morrow, Richmond!
RICHMOND
Cry mercy, lords and watchful gentlemen,   224
That you have ta'en a tardy sluggard here.
A LORD   How have you slept, my lord?
RICHMOND
The sweetest sleep and fairest-boding dreams
That ever entered in a drowsy head
Have I since your departure had, my lords.
Methought their souls whose bodies Richard murdered
Came to my tent and cried on victory.   231
I promise you, my soul is very jocund   232
In the remembrance of so fair a dream.
How far into the morning is it, lords?
A LORD   Upon the stroke of four.
RICHMOND
Why, then 'tis time to arm and give direction.

His oration to his soldiers.

More than I have said, loving countrymen,   237
The leisure and enforcement of the time   238
Forbids to dwell upon. Yet remember this:
God and our good cause fight upon our side.
The prayers of holy saints and wrongèd souls,
Like high-reared bulwarks, stand before our faces.

---

172 Fainting losing heart   **173 for hope** i.e., for hoping to support you, or for want of hope, hoping in vain to help   **176 Richard fall** may Richard fall   **180 lights burn blue** (Superstitiously regarded as evidence of the presence of ghosts.)   **183 I am I** (A blasphemy of God's "*ego sum.*")   **185 fly** flee.   **187 Wherefore?** Why?   **193 several** different, separate   **198 used . . . degree** committed in every degree of infamy, from bad to worst   **199 bar** i.e., bar of justice   **200 despair** (Considered the only unforgivable sin.)

219 proof armor   **224 Cry mercy** I beg your pardon   **231 cried on victory** invoked victory, cried out to it.   **232 promise** assure. **jocund** cheerful   **237 have said** have already said before **238 leisure** i.e., brief time allowed

Richard except, those whom we fight against   243
Had rather have us win than him they follow.
For what is he they follow? Truly, gentlemen,
A bloody tyrant and a homicide;
One raised in blood, and one in blood established;   247
One that made means to come by what he hath,   248
And slaughtered those that were the means to help him;
A base, foul stone, made precious by the foil   250
Of England's chair, where he is falsely set;   251
One that hath ever been God's enemy.
Then if you fight against God's enemy,
God will in justice ward you as his soldiers;   254
If you do sweat to put a tyrant down,
You sleep in peace, the tyrant being slain;
If you do fight against your country's foes,
Your country's fat shall pay your pains the hire;   258
If you do fight in safeguard of your wives,
Your wives shall welcome home the conquerors;
If you do free your children from the sword,
Your children's children quits it in your age.   262
Then, in the name of God and all these rights,
Advance your standards! Draw your willing swords!   264
For me, the ransom of my bold attempt   265
Shall be this cold corpse on the earth's cold face;   266
But if I thrive, the gain of my attempt
The least of you shall share his part thereof.
Sound drums and trumpets boldly and cheerfully;
God and Saint George! Richmond and victory!
                                        [*Exeunt.*]

*Enter King Richard, Ratcliffe, [attendants and
forces].*

KING RICHARD
What said Northumberland as touching Richmond?
RATCLIFFE
That he was never trainèd up in arms.
KING RICHARD
He said the truth. And what said Surrey then?
RATCLIFFE
He smiled and said, "The better for our purpose."
KING RICHARD
He was in the right, and so indeed it is.
                                The clock striketh.
Tell the clock there. Give me a calendar.   276
Who saw the sun today?   [*He takes an almanac.*]
RATCLIFFE   Not I, my lord.
KING RICHARD
Then he disdains to shine, for by the book   278
He should have braved the east an hour ago.   279
A black day will it be to somebody.

Ratcliffe!
RATCLIFFE
My lord?
KING RICHARD   The sun will not be seen today;
The sky doth frown and lour upon our army.   283
I would these dewy tears were from the ground.
Not shine today? Why, what is that to me
More than to Richmond? For the selfsame heaven
That frowns on me looks sadly upon him.

Enter Norfolk.

NORFOLK
Arm, arm, my lord, the foe vaunts in the field!   288
KING RICHARD
Come, bustle, bustle! Caparison my horse.   289
Call up Lord Stanley; bid him bring his power.
I will lead forth my soldiers to the plain,
And thus my battle shall be orderèd: 292
My foreward shall be drawn out all in length,   293
Consisting equally of horse and foot;
Our archers shall be placèd in the midst.
John Duke of Norfolk, Thomas Earl of Surrey,
Shall have the leading of this foot and horse.
They thus directed, we will follow   298
In the main battle, whose puissance on either side   299
Shall be well wingèd with our chiefest horse.   300
This, and Saint George to boot! What think'st thou,
Norfolk?   301
NORFOLK
A good direction, warlike sovereign.
This found I on my tent this morning.
                                He showeth him a paper.
KING RICHARD [*reads*]
"Jockey of Norfolk, be not so bold,   304
For Dickon thy master is bought and sold."   305
A thing devisèd by the enemy.
Go, gentlemen, every man unto his charge.
Let not our babbling dreams affright our souls;
Conscience is but a word that cowards use,
Devised at first to keep the strong in awe.
Our strong arms be our conscience, swords our law!
March on, join bravely! Let us to it pell-mell;   312
If not to heaven, then hand in hand to hell.

His oration to his army.

What shall I say more than I have inferred?   314
Remember whom you are to cope withal:
A sort of vagabonds, rascals, and runaways,   316
A scum of Bretons and base lackey peasants,   317
Whom their o'ercloyèd country vomits forth   318
To desperate adventures and assured destruction.

---

243 except excepted   **247 in blood** by bloodshed   **248 made means**
i.e., has taken advantage, created opportunity   **250 foil** a thin leaf of
metal placed under a gem to set it off to advantage   **251 chair** throne.
set (1) seated (2) set like a jewel   **254 ward** protect   **258 Your . . . hire**
England's prosperity will reward your efforts   **262 Your . . . age** your
grandchildren will requite it when you are old.   **264 Advance** raise
265–6 the ransom . . . face i.e., if I fail, there will be no question of
ransom, but only death   **276 Tell** Count the strokes of.   **calendar**
almanac.   **278 the book** i.e., the almanac   **279 braved** made splendid

283 lour look threateningly   **288 vaunts** boasts his strength
289 Caparison Put on the battle trappings of   **292 battle** troops
293 foreward vanguard   **298 directed** deployed   **299 main battle**
main body of troops.   **puissance** strength   **300 wingèd** flanked.
horse cavalry.   **301 to boot** i.e., to give us aid in addition.   **304 Jockey**
i.e., Jack, John   **305 Dickon** i.e., Dick, Richard.   **bought and sold**
done for, finished.   **312 join** join battle.   **pell-mell** headlong, hand
to hand   **314 inferred** alleged.   **316 sort** gang   **317 lackey** servile
318 o'ercloyèd satiated, glutted

You sleeping safe, they bring to you unrest;
You having lands, and blest with beauteous wives,
They would restrain the one, distain the other.   322
And who doth lead them but a paltry fellow,
Long kept in Brittany at our mother's cost?   324
A milksop, one that never in his life
Felt so much cold as over shoes in snow?   326
Let's whip these stragglers o'er the seas again.
Lash hence these overweening rags of France,   328
These famished beggars, weary of their lives,
Who, but for dreaming on this fond exploit,   330
For want of means, poor rats, had hanged themselves.   331
If we be conquered, let men conquer us,
And not these bastard Bretons, whom our fathers
Have in their own land beaten, bobbed, and thumped,   334
And in record left them the heirs of shame.   335
Shall these enjoy our lands? Lie with our wives?
Ravish our daughters? [*Drum afar off.*] Hark! I hear
    their drum.
Fight, gentlemen of England! Fight, bold yeomen!
Draw, archers, draw your arrows to the head!   339
Spur your proud horses hard, and ride in blood;
Amaze the welkin with your broken staves!   341

[*Enter a Messenger.*]

What says Lord Stanley? Will he bring his power?
MESSENGER   My lord, he doth deny to come.
KING RICHARD   Off with his son George's head!
NORFOLK
My lord, the enemy is past the marsh.
After the battle let George Stanley die.
KING RICHARD
A thousand hearts are great within my bosom.
Advance our standards! Set upon our foes!   348
Our ancient word of courage, fair Saint George,   349
Inspire us with the spleen of fiery dragons!   350
Upon them! Victory sits on our helms!   *Exeunt.*

♣

[5.4]

*Alarum. Excursions. [Norfolk and forces continue
to make forays, entering and exiting.] Enter [in the
melee] Catesby.*

CATESBY
Rescue, my lord of Norfolk, rescue, rescue!
The King enacts more wonders than a man,   2
Daring an opposite to every danger.   3
His horse is slain, and all on foot he fights,
Seeking for Richmond in the throat of death.
Rescue, fair lord, or else the day is lost!

[*Alarums.*] Enter [*King*] Richard.

KING RICHARD
A horse! A horse! My kingdom for a horse!
CATESBY
Withdraw, my lord. I'll help you to a horse.
KING RICHARD
Slave, I have set my life upon a cast,   9
And I will stand the hazard of the die.   10
I think there be six Richmonds in the field;   11
Five have I slain today instead of him.
A horse! A horse! My kingdom for a horse!   [*Exeunt.*]

♣

[5.5]

*Alarum. Enter Richard and Richmond; they fight.
Richard is slain. [Exit Richmond.] Then, retreat
being sounded, [flourish, and] enter Richmond,
[Lord Stanley Earl of] Derby bearing the crown,
with other lords, etc.*

RICHMOND
God and your arms be praised, victorious friends!
The day is ours; the bloody dog is dead.
STANLEY [*offering him the crown*]
Courageous Richmond, well hast thou acquit thee.
Lo, here this long-usurpèd royalty
From the dead temples of this bloody wretch
Have I plucked off, to grace thy brows withal.   6
Wear it, enjoy it, and make much of it.
RICHMOND
Great God of heaven, say amen to all!
But, tell me, is young George Stanley living?
STANLEY
He is, my lord, and safe in Leicester town,
Whither, if it please you, we may now withdraw us.
RICHMOND
What men of name are slain on either side?   12
STANLEY
John Duke of Norfolk, Walter Lord Ferrers,
Sir Robert Brackenbury, and Sir William Brandon.
RICHMOND
Inter their bodies as becomes their births.
Proclaim a pardon to the soldiers fled

---

322 **restrain** deprive you of.   **distain** defile, sully   324 **our mother's**
(Richmond's mother was not Richard's. This error occurs in the second
edition of Holinshed's *Chronicles*. The first edition reads "brothers," the
reference being to the fact that Richmond had been supported at the
court of the Duke of Brittany at the cost of Charles, Duke of Burgundy,
Richard's brother-in-law.)   326 **over shoes** i.e., over his shoe-tops
328 **rags** ragged fellows   330 **fond** foolish   331 **want of means** poverty
334 **bobbed** thrashed   335 **And . . . shame** and left them with nothing but the promise of a shameful record in history.   339 **to the head**
to the head of the arrow.   341 **Amaze the welkin** Frighten the skies
348 **Advance our standards!** Raise our flags!   349 **word of courage**
battle cry   350 **dragons** (Richard ironically identifies with the dragon
slain by Saint George.)
5.4. Location: Bosworth Field, as before; the action is continuous.
0.1 *Excursions* Sorties

2 **than a man** than seems possible for a human being   3 **Daring . . .
danger** boldly facing every danger in battle.   9 **cast** throw of the dice
10 **stand the hazard** accept the fortune.   **die** (Singular of *dice*.)
11 **six Richmonds** i.e., Richmond himself and five men dressed like
him as a safety precaution.
5.5. Location: Action continues at Bosworth Field.
0.2 *retreat* trumpet signal to withdraw, cease the attack   6 **withal**
with.   12 **of name** of title

That in submission will return to us,
And then, as we have ta'en the Sacrament,   18
We will unite the white rose and the red.
Smile heaven upon this fair conjunction,   20
That long have frowned upon their enmity!
What traitor hears me and says not amen?
England hath long been mad, and scarred herself;
The brother blindly shed the brother's blood,
The father rashly slaughtered his own son,
The son, compelled, been butcher to the sire.
All this divided York and Lancaster,
Divided in their dire division.

Oh, now let Richmond and Elizabeth,
The true succeeders of each royal house,
By God's fair ordinance conjoin together!   31
And let their heirs, God, if thy will be so,
Enrich the time to come with smooth-faced peace,
With smiling plenty, and fair prosperous days!
Abate the edge of traitors, gracious Lord,   35
That would reduce these bloody days again   36
And make poor England weep in streams of blood!
Let them not live to taste this land's increase
That would with treason wound this fair land's peace!
Now civil wounds are stopped, peace lives again.   40
That she may long live here, God say amen! [*Exeunt.*]

---

18 ta'en the Sacrament sworn a sacred oath on the Sacrament (to marry Princess Elizabeth, daughter of Edward IV, thereby uniting the houses of York and of Lancaster, white rose and red rose) **20 conjunction** union. (An astrological metaphor.)

31 ordinance decree **35 Abate** Blunt, render ineffective **36 reduce** bring back **40 stopped** closed up

The Tragedy of King Richard the Second

❧

Richard II (c. 1595–1596) is the first play in Shakespeare's great four-play historical saga, or tetralogy, that continues with the two parts of *Henry IV* (c. 1596–1598) and concludes with *Henry V* (1599). In this, his second, tetralogy, Shakespeare dramatizes the beginnings of the great conflict called the Wars of the Roses, having already dramatized the conclusion of that civil war in his earlier tetralogy on Henry VI and Richard III (c. 1589–1594). Both sequences move from an outbreak of civil faction to the eventual triumph of political stability. Together, they comprise the story of England's long century of political turmoil from the 1390s until Henry Tudor's victory over Richard III in 1485. Yet Shakespeare chose to tell the two halves of this chronicle in reverse order. His culminating statement about kingship in *Henry V* focuses on the earlier historical period, on the education and kingly success of Prince Hal.

With *Richard II,* then, Shakespeare turns to the events that had launched England's century of crisis. These events were still fresh and relevant to Elizabethan minds. Richard and Bolingbroke's contest for the English crown provided a sobering example of political wrongdoing and, at least by implication, a rule for political right conduct. One prominent reason for studying history, to an Elizabethan, was to avoid the errors of the past. The relevance of such historical analogy was, in fact, vividly underscored some six years after Shakespeare wrote the play: in 1601, followers of the Earl of Essex commissioned Shakespeare's acting company to perform a revived play about Richard II on the eve of what was to be an abortive rebellion, perhaps with the intention of inciting a riot. Whether the play was Shakespeare's is not certain, but it seems likely. The acting company was ultimately exonerated, but not before Queen Elizabeth concluded that she was being compared to Richard II. When he wrote the play, Shakespeare presumably did not know that it would be used for such a purpose, but he must have known that the overthrow of Richard II was, in any case,

a controversial subject because of its potential use as a precedent for rebellion. The scene of Richard's deposition (4.1) was considered so provocative by Elizabeth's government that it was censored in the printed quartos of Shakespeare's play during the Queen's lifetime.

In view of the startling relevance of this piece of history to Shakespeare's own times, then, what are the rights and wrongs of Richard's deposition, and to what extent can political lessons be drawn from Shakespeare's presentation?

To begin with, we should not underestimate Richard's attractive qualities, as a man and even as a king. Throughout the play, Richard is consistently more impressive and majestic in appearance than his rival, Bolingbroke. Richard fascinates us with his verbal sensitivity, his poetic insight, and his dramatic self-consciousness. He eloquently expounds a sacramental view of kingship, according to which "Not all the water in the rough rude sea / Can wash the balm off from an anointed king" (3.2.54–5). Bolingbroke can depose Richard but can never capture the aura of majesty Richard possesses; Bolingbroke may succeed politically but only at the expense of desecrating an idea. Richard is much more interesting to us as a man than Bolingbroke, more capable of grief, more tender in his personal relationships, and more in need of being understood. Indeed, a major factor in Richard's tragedy is the conflict between his public role (wherein he sees himself as divinely appointed, almost superhuman) and his private role (wherein he is emotionally dependent and easily hurt). He confuses what the medieval and Renaissance world knew as the king's "two bodies," the sacramental body of kingship, which is eternal, and the human body of a single occupant of the throne, whose frail mortal condition is subject to time and fortune. Richard's failure to perceive and to act wisely on this difference is part of his tragic predicament, but his increasing insight, through suffering, into the truth of the distinction is also part of his spiritual growth. His dilemma, however poignantly individual, lies at the heart of kingship. Richard is thus very much a king. Although he sometimes indulges in childish sentimentality, at his best he is superbly refined, perceptive, and poetic.

These qualities notwithstanding, Richard is an incompetent ruler, compared with the man who supplants him. Richard himself confesses to the prodigal expense of "too great a court." In order to raise funds, he has been obliged to "farm our royal realm"; that is, to sell for ready cash the right of collecting taxes to individual courtiers, who are then free to extort what the market will bear (1.4.43–5). Similarly, Richard proposes to issue "blank charters" (line 48) to his minions, who will then be authorized to fill in the amount of tax to be paid by any hapless subject. These abuses were infamous to Elizabethan audiences as symbols of autocratic misgovernment. No less heinous is Richard's seizure of the dukedom of Lancaster from his cousin Bolingbroke. Although Richard does receive the consent of his Council to banish Bolingbroke because of the divisiveness of the quarrel between him and Mowbray, the King violates the very idea of inheritance of property when he takes away Bolingbroke's title and lands. And, as his uncle the Duke of York remonstrates, Richard's own right to the throne depends on that idea of due inheritance. By offending against the most sacred concepts of order and degree, he teaches others to rebel.

Richard's behavior even prior to the commencement of the play arouses suspicion. The nature of his complicity in the death of his uncle Thomas of Woodstock, Duke of Gloucester, is perhaps never entirely clear, and Gloucester may have given provocation. Indeed, one can sympathize with the predicament of a young ruler prematurely thrust into the center of power by the untimely death of his father, the crown prince, now having to cope with an array of worldly-wise, advice-giving uncles. Nevertheless, Richard is unambiguously guilty of murder in the eyes of Gloucester's widow, while her brother-in-law John of Gaunt, Duke of Lancaster, assumes that Richard has caused Gloucester's death, "the which if wrongfully / Let heaven revenge" (1.2.39–40). Apparently, too, Gaunt's son Bolingbroke believes Richard to be a murderer, and he brings accusation against Thomas Mowbray, Duke of Norfolk, partly as a means of embarrassing the King, whom he cannot accuse directly. Mowbray's lot is an unenviable one: he was in command at Calais when Gloucester was executed there, and he hints that Richard ordered the execution (even though Mowbray alleges that he himself did not carry out the order). For his part, Richard is only too glad to banish the man suspected of having been his agent in murder. Mowbray is a convenient scapegoat.

The polished, ceremonial tone of the play's opening is vitiated, then, by our growing awareness of hidden violence and factionalism going on behind the scene. Our first impression of Richard is of a king devoted to the public display of conciliatory even-handedness. He listens to the rival claims of Bolingbroke and Mowbray, and, when he cannot reconcile them peacefully, he orders a trial by combat. This trial (1.3) is replete with ceremonial repetition and ritual. The combatants are duly sworn in the justice of their cause, and God is to decide the quarrel by awarding victory to the champion who speaks the truth. Richard, the presiding officer, assumes the role of God's anointed deputy on earth. Yet it becomes evident in due course that Richard is a major perpetrator of injustice rather than an impartial judge, that Bolingbroke is after greater objectives than he acknowledges even to himself, and that Richard's refusal to let the trial by combat take place and his banishment of the two contenders are his desperate ways of burying a problem he cannot deal with forthrightly. His uncles reluctantly consent to the banishment only because they, too, see that disaffection has reached alarming proportions.

Bolingbroke's motivation in these opening scenes is perhaps even more obscure than Richard's. Our first impression of Bolingbroke is of forthrightness, moral indignation, and patriotic zeal. In fact, we never really question the earnestness of his outrage at Richard's misgovernance, his longing to avenge a family murder (for Gloucester was his uncle, too), or his bitter disappointment at being banished. Yet we are prompted to ask further: what is the essential cause of the enmity between Bolingbroke and Richard? If Mowbray is only a stalking-horse, is not Gloucester's death also the excuse for pursuing a preexistent animosity? Richard, for one, appears to think so. His portrayal of Bolingbroke as a scheming politician, who curries favor with the populace in order to build a widely based alliance against the King himself, is telling and prophetic. Bolingbroke, says Richard, acts "As were our England in reversion his, / And he our subjects' next degree in hope" (1.4.35–6). This unflattering appraisal might be ascribed to malicious envy on Richard's part, were it not proved by subsequent events to be wholly accurate.

Paradoxically, Richard is far the more prescient of the two contenders for the English throne. It is he, in fact, who perceives from the start that the conflict between them is irreconcilable. He banishes Bolingbroke as his chief rival and does not doubt what motives will call Bolingbroke home again. Meanwhile, Bolingbroke disclaims any motive for his return other than love of country and hatred of injustice. Although born with a political canniness that Richard lacks, Bolingbroke does not reflect (out loud, at least) upon the consequences of his own acts. As a man of action, he lives in the present. Richard, conversely, a person of exquisite contemplative powers and poetic imagination, does not deign to cope with the practical. He both envies and despises Bolingbroke's easy way with the commoners. Richard cherishes kingship for the majesty and the royal prerogative it confers, not for the power to govern wisely. Thus it is that, despite his perception of what will follow, Richard habitually indulges his worst instincts, buying a moment of giddy pleasure at the expense of future disaster.

Granted Richard's incompetence as a ruler, is Bolingbroke justified in armed rebellion against him? According to Bolingbroke's uncle, the Duke of York (who later, to be sure, shifts his allegiance), and to the Bishop of Carlisle, Bolingbroke is not justified in the rebellion. The attitude of these men can be summed up by the phrase "passive obedience." And, although Bolingbroke's own father, John of Gaunt, dies before his son returns to England to seize power, Gaunt, too, is opposed to such human defiances of the sacred institution of kingship. "God's is the quarrel," he insists (1.2.37). Because Richard is God's anointed deputy on earth, as Gaunt sees the matter, only God may punish the King's wrongdoing. Gaunt may not question Richard's guilt, but neither does he question God's ability to avenge. Gaunt sees human intervention in God's affair as blasphemous: "for I may never lift / An angry arm against His minister" (1.2.40–1). To be sure, Gaunt does acknowledge a solemn duty to offer frank advice to extremists of both sides, and he does so unsparingly. He consents to the banishment of his son, and he rebukes Richard with his dying breath.

This doctrine of passive obedience was familiar to Elizabethans, for they heard it in church periodically in official homilies against rebellion. It was the Tudor state's answer to those who asserted a right to overthrow reputedly evil kings. The argument was logically ingenious. Why are evil rulers permitted to govern from time to time? Presumably, because God wishes to test a people or to punish them for waywardness. Any king performing such chastisement is a divine scourge. Accordingly, the worst thing a people can do is to rebel against God's scourge, thereby manifesting more waywardness. Instead, they must attempt to remedy the insolence in their hearts, advise the King to mend his ways, and patiently await God's pardon. If they do so, they will not long be disappointed. The doctrine is essentially conservative, defending the status quo. It is reinforced in this play by the Bishop of Carlisle's prophecy that God will avenge through civil war the deposition of his anointed (4.1.126–50); an Elizabethan audience would have appreciated the irony of the prophecy's having come true and having been the subject of Shakespeare's first historical tetralogy. Moreover, in *Richard II* the doctrine of passive obedience is a moderate position between the extremes of tyranny and rebellion, and is expressed by thoughtful, selfless characters. We might be tempted to label it Shakespeare's view if we did not also perceive that the doctrine is continually placed in ironic conflict with harsh political realities. The character who most reflects

the ironies and even ludicrous incongruities of the position is the Duke of York.

York is to an extent a choric character, that is, one who helps direct our viewpoint, because his transfer of loyalties from Richard to Bolingbroke structurally delineates the decline of Richard's fortunes and the concurrent rise of Bolingbroke's. At first York shares his brother Gaunt's unwillingness to act, despite their dismay at Richard's willfulness. It is only when Richard seizes the dukedom of Lancaster that York can no longer hold his tongue. His condemnation is as bitter as that of Gaunt, hinting even at loss of allegiance (2.1.200–8). Still, he accepts the responsibility, so cavalierly bestowed by Richard, of governing England in the King's absence. He musters what force he can to oppose Bolingbroke's advance and lectures against this rebellion with the same vehemence he had used against Richard's despotism. Yet, when faced with Bolingbroke's overwhelming military superiority, he accedes rather than fights in behalf of a lost cause. However much this may resemble cowardice or mere expediency, it also displays a pragmatic logic. Once Bolingbroke has become de facto king, in York's view, he must be acknowledged and obeyed. By a kind of analogy to the doctrine of passive obedience (which more rigorous theorists would never allow), York accepts the status quo as inevitable. He is vigorously ready to defend the new regime, just as he earlier defended Richard's de jure rule. York's inconsistent loyalty helps define the structure of the play.

When, however, this conclusion brings York to the point of turning in his own son, Aumerle, for a traitor and quarreling with his wife as to whether their son shall live, the ironic absurdity is apparent. Bolingbroke, now King Henry, himself is amused, in one of the play's rare lighthearted moments (5.3.79–80). At the same time, the comedy deals with serious issues, especially the conflict between public responsibility urged by York and private or emotional satisfaction urged by his Duchess—a conflict seen earlier, for example, in the debate between Gaunt and his sister-in-law, the widowed Duchess of Gloucester (1.2). When a family and a kingdom are divided against one another, there can be no really satisfactory resolution.

We are never entirely convinced that all the fine old medieval theories surrounding kingship—divine right, passive obedience, trial by combat, and the like—can ever wholly explain or remedy the complex and nasty political situation afflicting England. The one man capable of decisive action, in fact, is he who never theorizes at all: Bolingbroke. As we have seen, his avowed motive for opposing Mowbray—simple patriotic indignation—is uttered with such earnestness that we wonder if indeed Bolingbroke has examined those political ambitions in himself that are so plainly visible to Richard and others. This same discrepancy between surface and depth applies to Bolingbroke's motives in returning to England. We cannot be sure at what time he begins to plot that return; the conspiracy announced by Northumberland (2.1.224–300) follows so closely after Richard's violation of Bolingbroke's hereditary rights and is already so well advanced that we gain the impression of an already existing plot, though some of this impression may be simply owing to Shakespeare's characteristic compression of historic time. When Bolingbroke arrives in England, in any case, he protests to York with seemingly passionate sincerity that he comes only for his dukedom of Lancaster (2.3.113–36). If so, why does he set about executing Richard's followers without legal authority and otherwise establishing his own claim to power? Why does he indulge in homophobic slurs against Richard, insinuating that Richard's favorites have "Broke the possession of a royal bed" (3.1.13), when, as far as we can see from the devotion Richard shows to his queen, the charges are trumped up and untrue? Does Bolingbroke seriously think he can reclaim his dukedom by force and then yield to Richard without either maintaining Richard as a puppet king or placing himself in intolerable jeopardy? And can he suppose that his allies, Northumberland and the rest, who have now openly defied the King, will countenance the return to power of one who would never trust them again? It is in this context that York protests, "Well, well, I see the issue of these arms" (2.3.152). The deposition of Richard and then Richard's death are unavoidable conclusions once Bolingbroke has succeeded in an armed rebellion. There can be no turning back. Yet Bolingbroke simply will not think in these terms. He permits Northumberland to proceed with almost sadistic harshness in the arrest and impeachment of Richard and then admonishes Northumberland in public for acting so harshly; the dirty work goes forward, with Northumberland taking the blame, while Bolingbroke assumes a statesmanlike pose. When the new King Henry discovers—to his surprise, evidently—that Richard's life is now a burden to the state, he ponders aloud, "Have I no friend will rid me of this living fear?" (5.4.2) and then rebukes Exton for proceeding on cue.

Bolingbroke's pragmatic spirit and new mode of governing are the embodiment of de facto rule. Ultimately, the justification for his authority is the very fact of its existence, its functioning. Bolingbroke is the man of the hour. To apply William Butler Yeats's striking contrast, the Lancastrian usurpers, Bolingbroke and his son, are vessels of clay, whereas Richard is a vessel of porcelain. One is durable and utilitarian, yet unattractive; the other is exquisite, fragile, and impractical. The comparison does not force us to prefer one to the other, even though Yeats himself characteristically sided with beauty against politics. Rather, Shakespeare gives us our choice, allowing us to see in ourselves an inclination toward political and social stability or toward artistic temperament.

The paradox may suggest that the qualities of a good administrator are not those of a sensitive, thoughtful man. However hopeless as a king, Richard stands before us increasingly as an introspective and fascinating person. The contradictions of his character are aptly focused in the business of breaking a mirror during his deposition: it is at once symbolic of a narcissistic, shallow concern for appearances and a quest for a deeper, inward truth, so that the smashing of the mirror is an act both of self-destruction and of self-discovery. When Richard's power crumbles, his spirit is enhanced, as though loss of power and royal identity were necessary for the discovery of true values.

In this there is a faint anticipation of King Lear's self-learning, fearfully and preciously bought. The trace is only slight here, because in good part Richard II is a political history play rather than a tragedy and because Richard's self-realization is imperfect. Nevertheless, when Richard faces deposition and separation from his queen, and especially when he is alone in prison expecting to die, he strives to understand his life and through it the general condition of humanity. He gains our sympathy in the wonderfully humane interchange between this deposed king and the poor groom of his stable, who once took care of Richard's horse, roan Barbary, now the possession of the new monarch (5.5.67–94). Richard perceives a contradiction in heaven's assurances about salvation: Christ promises to receive all God's children, and yet He also warns that it is as hard for a rich man to enter heaven as for a camel to be thread through a needle's eye (5.5.16–17). The paradox echoes the Beatitudes: the last shall be first, the meek shall inherit the earth. Richard, now one of the downtrodden, gropes for an understanding of the vanity of human achievement whereby he can aspire to the victory Christ promised. At his death, that victory seems to him assured: his soul will mount to its seat on high "Whilst my gross flesh sinks downward, here to die" (line 112).

In this triumph of spirit over flesh, the long downward motion of Richard's worldly fortune is crucially reversed. By the same token, the worldly success of Bolingbroke is shown to be no more than that: worldly success. His archetype is Cain, the primal murderer of a brother. To the extent that the play is a history, Bolingbroke's de facto success is a matter of political relevance; but, in the belated movement toward Richard's personal tragedy, we experience a profound countermovement that partly achieves a purgative sense of atonement and reassurance. Whatever Richard may have lost, his gain is also great.

Balance and symmetry are unusually important in *Richard II*. The play begins and ends with elaborate ritual obeisance to the concept of social and monarchic order, and yet, in both cases, a note of personal disorder refuses to be subdued by the public ceremonial. Shakespeare keeps our response to both Richard and Bolingbroke ambivalent by clouding their respective responsibilities for murder. Just as Richard's role in Gloucester's death remains unclear, so Bolingbroke's role in the assassination of Richard remains equally unclear. Mowbray and Exton, as scapegoats, are in some respects parallel. Because Richard and Bolingbroke are both implicated in the deaths of near kinsmen, both are associated with Cain's murder of Abel. As Bolingbroke rises in worldly fortune, Richard falls; as Richard finds insight and release through suffering, Bolingbroke finds guilt and remorse through distasteful political necessity. Verbally and structurally, the play explores the rhetorical figure of chiasmus, or the pairing of opposites in an inverted and diagonal pattern whereby one goes down as the other goes up and vice versa. Again and again, the ritual effects of staging and style draw our attention to the balanced conflicts between the two men and within Richard. Symmetry helps to focus these conflicts in visual and aural ways. In particular, the deposition scene, with its spectacle of a coronation in reverse, brings the sacramental and human sides of the central figure into poignant dramatic relationship.

Women play a subsidiary role in this play about male struggles for power, and yet the brief scenes in which women take part—the Duchess of Gloucester with Gaunt (1.2), Richard's queen with his courtiers and gardeners and then with Richard himself (2.2, 3.4, 5.1), the Duchess of York with her husband and son and King Henry (5.2–5.3)—highlight for us important thematic contrasts between the public and private spheres, power and powerlessness, political struggle and humane sensitivity, the state and the family. The women, excluded from roles of practical authority, offer, nonetheless, an invaluable critical perspective on the fateful and often self-consuming political games that men play among themselves. As in *Julius Caesar* and *Troilus and Cressida*, the men of *Richard II* ignore women's warnings and insights to their own peril and to the discomfiting of the body politic.

The imagery of *Richard II* reinforces structure and meaning. The play is unlike the history plays that follow in its extensive use of blank verse and rhyme and in its interwoven sets of recurring images; *Richard II* is, in this respect, more typical of the so-called lyric period (c. 1594–1596) that also produced *Romeo and Juliet* and *A Midsummer Night's Dream*. Image patterns locate the play

in our imaginations as a kind of lost Eden. England is a garden mismanaged by her royal gardener, so that weeds and caterpillars (e.g., Bushy, Bagot, and Green) flourish. The "garden" scene (3.4), located near the center of the play, offering a momentary haven of allegorical reflection on the play's hectic events, is central in the development of the garden metaphor. England is also a sick body, ill-tended by her royal physician, and a family divided against itself, yielding abortive and sterile progeny. Her political ills are attested to by disorders in the cosmos: comets, shooting stars, withered bay trees, and weeping rains. Night owls, associated with death, prevail over the larks of morning. The sun, royally associated at first with Richard, deserts him for Bolingbroke and leaves Richard as the Phaëthon who has mishandled the sun-god's chariot and so scorched the earth. Linked to the sun image is the prevalent leitmotif of ascent and descent. And, touching on all these, a cluster of Biblical images sees England as a despoiled garden of Eden witnessing a second fall of humanity. Richard repeatedly brands his enemies and deserters as Judases and Pilates—not always fairly; nonetheless, in his last agony, he finds genuine consolation in Christ's example. For a man so self-absorbed in the drama of his existence, this poetic method is intensely suitable. Language and stage action have combined perfectly to express the conflict between a sensitive but flawed king and his efficient but unlovable successor.

In performance, the play belongs to Richard. However much he ends up the loser, his role calls for a kind of royal charisma that Bolingbroke never achieves. Such was the effect, at any rate, in Brian Bedford's enactment of the role at Stratford, Canada, in 1983; his appearance on the walls of Flint Castle in 3.3, splendidly attired in white robes with gold trim, embodied a regal image of kingship that was then forced to humble itself before Bolingbroke's brute might. John Gielgud, Alec Guinness, Michael Redgrave, Paul Scofield, John Neville, Ian McKellan, Ian Richardson, Richard Pasco, Ian Richardson, Derek Jacobi, Alan Howard, Jeremy Irons, Ralph Fiennes, the actress Fiona Shaw, and still other leading performers of their day have found the role one in which they could enthrall audiences with the nuanced cadences of Richard's speeches. The role has also afforded a wide range of interpretations; Guinness saw him as unhappily neurotic, Gielgud as kindly, Redgrave as effeminate, Scofield as cerebral and remote, McKellan as one who is convinced of his semi-divine nature. The play has also become a vehicle for spectacle and striking visual effects emphasizing the symmetries of the text's attention to poetic symbolism and social ritual; glittering pageantry and fading splendor vie for our interest and our loyalties.

The Tragedy of King Richard the Second

[*Dramatis Personae*

KING RICHARD THE SECOND
QUEEN, *Richard's wife*
JOHN OF GAUNT, *Duke of Lancaster, King Richard's uncle*
HENRY BOLINGBROKE, *John of Gaunt's son, Duke of Hereford and claimant to his father's dukedom of Lancaster, later King Henry IV*
DUKE OF YORK, *Edmund of Langley, King Richard's uncle*
DUCHESS OF YORK
DUKE OF AUMERLE, *York's son and the Earl of Rutland*
DUCHESS OF GLOUCESTER, *widow of Thomas of Woodstock, Duke of Gloucester (King Richard's uncle)*

THOMAS MOWBRAY, *Duke of Norfolk,*
EARL OF SALISBURY,
LORD BERKELEY,
DUKE OF SURREY,
BISHOP OF CARLISLE,
SIR STEPHEN SCROOP,
ABBOT OF WESTMINSTER,
BUSHY,
BAGOT, } *favorites of King Richard,*
GREEN,
CAPTAIN *of the Welsh Army,*

} *supporters of King Richard*

EARL OF NORTHUMBERLAND,
HARRY PERCY, *Northumberland's son,*
LORD ROSS,
LORD WILLOUGHBY,
LORD FITZWATER,
SIR PIERCE OF EXTON,
Another LORD,

} *supporters of Bolingbroke*

LORD MARSHAL
Two HERALDS
GARDENER
GARDENER'S MAN
LADY *attending the Queen*
KEEPER *of the prison*
A MAN *attending Exton*

SERVINGMAN *to York*
GROOM *of the stable*

Lords, Officers, Soldiers, Attendants, Ladies attending the Queen

scene: *England and Wales*]

[1.1]

Enter King Richard, John of Gaunt, with other nobles and attendants.

KING RICHARD
Old John of Gaunt, time-honored Lancaster,   1
Hast thou according to thy oath and bond
Brought hither Henry Hereford, thy bold son,
Here to make good the boist'rous late appeal,   4
Which then our leisure would not let us hear,   5
Against the Duke of Norfolk, Thomas Mowbray?
GAUNT   I have, my liege.   7
KING RICHARD
Tell me, moreover, hast thou sounded him   8

1.1 **Location: A room of state. (Holinshed's** *Chronicles* **places this scene at Windsor, in 1398.)**
1 **Old John of Gaunt** (Born in 1340 at Ghent; hence the surname *Gaunt.* In 1398 he was fifty-eight years old.)

4 **late** recent.   **appeal** accusation, formal challenge or impeachment that the accuser was obliged to maintain in combat   5 **our, us** (The royal plural.)   **leisure** i.e., lack of leisure   7 **liege** i.e., sovereign.   8 **sounded** inquired of

If he appeal the Duke on ancient malice,   9
Or worthily, as a good subject should,
On some known ground of treachery in him?

GAUNT
As near as I could sift him on that argument,   12
On some apparent danger seen in him   13
Aimed at Your Highness, no inveterate malice.

KING RICHARD
Then call them to our presence.   [*Exit an attendant.*]
                                   Face to face,
And frowning brow to brow, ourselves will hear   16
The accuser and the accusèd freely speak.
High-stomached are they both, and full of ire;   18
In rage, deaf as the sea, hasty as fire.

Enter Bolingbroke and Mowbray.

BOLINGBROKE
Many years of happy days befall
My gracious sovereign, my most loving liege!

MOWBRAY
Each day still better others' happiness,   22
Until the heavens, envying earth's good hap,   23
Add an immortal title to your crown!

KING RICHARD
We thank you both. Yet one but flatters us,
As well appeareth by the cause you come: 26
Namely, to appeal each other of high treason.
Cousin of Hereford, what dost thou object   38
Against the Duke of Norfolk, Thomas Mowbray?

BOLINGBROKE
First—heaven be the record to my speech!—   30
In the devotion of a subject's love,
Tend'ring the precious safety of my prince,   32
And free from other misbegotten hate,
Come I appellant to this princely presence.   34
Now, Thomas Mowbray, do I turn to thee;
And mark my greeting well, for what I speak
My body shall make good upon this earth
Or my divine soul answer it in heaven.   38
Thou art a traitor and a miscreant,   39
Too good to be so and too bad to live,   40
Since the more fair and crystal is the sky,   41
The uglier seem the clouds that in it fly.
Once more, the more to aggravate the note,   43
With a foul traitor's name stuff I thy throat,
And wish, so please my sovereign, ere I move,   45
What my tongue speaks my right-drawn sword may prove.   46

MOWBRAY
Let not my cold words here accuse my zeal.   47
'Tis not the trial of a woman's war,   48
The bitter clamor of two eager tongues,   49
Can arbitrate this cause betwixt us twain;   50
The blood is hot that must be cooled for this.
Yet can I not of such tame patience boast
As to be hushed and naught at all to say.
First, the fair reverence of Your Highness curbs me
From giving reins and spurs to my free speech,
Which else would post until it had returned   56
These terms of treason doubled down his throat.
Setting aside his high blood's royalty,   58
And let him be no kinsman to my liege,   59
I do defy him, and I spit at him,
Call him a slanderous coward and a villain;
Which to maintain I would allow him odds
And meet him, were I tied to run afoot   63
Even to the frozen ridges of the Alps
Or any other ground inhabitable   65
Wherever Englishman durst set his foot.
Meantime, let this defend my loyalty:
By all my hopes, most falsely doth he lie.

BOLINGBROKE [*throwing down his gage*]
Pale trembling coward, there I throw my gage,   69
Disclaiming here the kindred of the King,   70
And lay aside my high blood's royalty,
Which fear, not reverence, makes thee to except.   72
If guilty dread have left thee so much strength
As to take up mine honor's pawn, then stoop.   74
By that, and all the rites of knighthood else,
Will I make good against thee, arm to arm,
What I have spoke or thou canst worse devise.   77

MOWBRAY [*taking up the gage*]
I take it up; and by that sword I swear
Which gently laid my knighthood on my shoulder,
I'll answer thee in any fair degree
Or chivalrous design of knightly trial;
And when I mount, alive may I not light   82
If I be traitor or unjustly fight!

KING RICHARD
What doth our cousin lay to Mowbray's charge?
It must be great that can inherit us   85
So much as of a thought of ill in him.

BOLINGBROKE
Look what I speak, my life shall prove it true: 87
That Mowbray hath received eight thousand nobles   88
In name of lendings for Your Highness' soldiers,   89

---

9 **appeal** accuse.   **on . . . malice** on the grounds of a long-standing enmity   12 **sift** discover by questioning.   **argument** subject   13 **apparent** obvious, manifest   16 **ourselves** I myself. (The royal plural.)   18 **High-stomached** Haughty   22 **Each . . . happiness** May each day improve on the happiness of other past days   23 **hap** fortune   26 **you come** for which you come   28 **what . . . object** what accusation do you bring   30 **record** witness   32 **Tend'ring** watching over, holding dear   34 **appellant** as the accuser   38 **answer** answer for   39 **miscreant** irreligious villain   40 **good** i.e., noble, high-born   41 **crystal** clear. (The image alludes to the crystal spheres in which, according to the Ptolemaic conception of the universe, the heavenly bodies were fixed.)   43 **aggravate the note** emphasize the stigma, i.e., the charge of treason   45 **so please** if it please   46 **right-drawn** justly drawn

47 **accuse my zeal** cast doubt on my zeal or loyalty.   48 **woman's war** i.e., war of words   49 **eager** sharp, biting   50 **Can** that can   56 **post** ride at high speed (like a messenger riding relays of horses)   58 **Setting . . . royalty** Disregarding Bolingbroke's royal blood (as grandson of Edward III)   59 **let him be** suppose him to be   63 **tied** obliged   65 **inhabitable** uninhabitable   69 **gage** a pledge to combat (usually a glove or gauntlet, i.e., a mailed or armored glove)   70 **Disclaiming** relinquishing.   **kindred** kinship   72 **except** exempt, set aside.   74 **pawn** i.e., the gage   77 **or . . . devise** or anything worse you can imagine to have been said about you.   82 **light** alight, dismount   85 **inherit us** put me in possession of, make me have   87 **Look what** Whatever   88 **nobles** gold coins worth six shillings eight pence   89 **lendings** advances on pay

The which he hath detained for lewd employments,   90
Like a false traitor and injurious villain.
Besides I say, and will in battle prove
Or here or elsewhere to the furthest verge   93
That ever was surveyed by English eye,
That all the treasons for these eighteen years   95
Complotted and contrivèd in this land   96
Fetch from false Mowbray their first head and
    spring.   97
Further I say, and further will maintain
Upon his bad life to make all this good,
That he did plot the Duke of Gloucester's death,   100
Suggest his soon-believing adversaries,   101
And consequently, like a traitor coward,   102
Sluiced out his innocent soul through streams of
    blood—   103
Which blood, like sacrificing Abel's, cries   104
Even from the tongueless caverns of the earth   105
To me for justice and rough chastisement.
And, by the glorious worth of my descent,
This arm shall do it or this life be spent.

KING RICHARD
How high a pitch his resolution soars!   109
Thomas of Norfolk, what say'st thou to this?

MOWBRAY
Oh, let my sovereign turn away his face
And bid his ears a little while be deaf,
Till I have told this slander of his blood   113
How God and good men hate so foul a liar!

KING RICHARD
Mowbray, impartial are our eyes and ears.
Were he my brother, nay, my kingdom's heir,
As he is but my father's brother's son,
Now, by my scepter's awe I make a vow,   118
Such neighbor nearness to our sacred blood
Should nothing privilege him nor partialize   120
The unstooping firmness of my upright soul.
He is our subject, Mowbray; so art thou.
Free speech and fearless I to thee allow.

MOWBRAY
Then, Bolingbroke, as low as to thy heart
Through the false passage of thy throat thou liest!
Three parts of that receipt I had for Calais   126
Disbursed I duly to His Highness' soldiers;

The other part reserved I by consent,
For that my sovereign liege was in my debt   129
Upon remainder of a dear account   130
Since last I went to France to fetch his queen.   131
Now swallow down that lie. For Gloucester's death,   132
I slew him not, but to my own disgrace   133
Neglected my sworn duty in that case.   134
[To Gaunt] For you, my noble lord of Lancaster,
The honorable father to my foe,
Once did I lay an ambush for your life,
A trespass that doth vex my grievèd soul;
But ere I last received the Sacrament
I did confess it, and exactly begged   140
Your Grace's pardon, and I hope I had it.
This is my fault. As for the rest appealed,   142
It issues from the rancor of a villain,
A recreant and most degenerate traitor,   144
Which in myself I boldly will defend,   145
And interchangeably hurl down my gage   146
Upon this overweening traitor's foot,   147
To prove myself a loyal gentleman
Even in the best blood chambered in his bosom.   149
    [He throws down his gage. Bolingbroke picks it up.]
In haste whereof most heartily I pray   150
Your Highness to assign our trial day.

KING RICHARD
Wrath-kindled gentlemen, be ruled by me;
Let's purge this choler without letting blood.   153
This we prescribe, though no physician;
Deep malice makes too deep incision.
Forget, forgive; conclude and be agreed;   156
Our doctors say this is no month to bleed.—   157
Good uncle, let this end where it begun;
We'll calm the Duke of Norfolk, you your son.

GAUNT
To be a make-peace shall become my age.
Throw down, my son, the Duke of Norfolk's gage.

KING RICHARD
And Norfolk, throw down his.

GAUNT   When, Harry, when?
Obedience bids I should not bid again.

KING RICHARD
Norfolk, throw down, we bid; there is no boot.   164

---

90 lewd vile, base   **93 Or** either   **95 these eighteen years** i.e., ever since the Peasants' Revolt of 1381   **96 Complotted** plotted in a conspiracy   **97 Fetch** derive.   **head and spring** (Synonymous words meaning "origin.")   **100 Duke of Gloucester's death** (Thomas of Woodstock, Duke of Gloucester, a younger son of Edward III and brother of John of Gaunt, was murdered at Calais in September 1397, while in Mowbray's custody.)   **101 Suggest . . . adversaries** did prompt Gloucester's easily persuaded enemies (to believe him guilty of treason)   **102 consequently** afterward   **103 Sluiced out** let flow (as by the opening of a sluice, or valve)   **104 Abel's** (For the story of Cain's murder of his brother Abel, the first such murder on earth and the archetype of the killing of a kinsman, see Genesis 4:3–12.)   **105 tongueless** resonant but without articulate speech; echoing   **109 pitch** highest reach of a falcon's flight   **113 this slander . . . blood** this disgrace to the royal family   **118 my scepter's awe** the reverence due my scepter   **120 nothing** not at all.   **partialize** make partial, bias   **126 receipt** money received

129 For that because   **130 Upon . . . account** for the balance of a heavy debt   **131 Since . . . queen** (Mowbray went in 1395 to France to negotiate the King's marriage to Isabella, daughter of the French King Charles VI, but Richard himself escorted her to England.)   **132 For** As for   **132–4 For . . . case** (Mowbray speaks guardedly but seems to imply that he postponed the execution of Gloucester that he was ordered by Richard to carry out.)   **140 exactly** (1) explicitly (2) fully   **142 appealed** of which I am charged   **144 recreant** cowardly; or, coward (used as a noun)   **145 Which** which charge.   **in myself** in my own person   **146 interchangeably** in exchange, reciprocally   **147 overweening** arrogant, proud   **149 Even in** by shedding   **150 In haste whereof** To hasten which proof of my innocence   **153 Let's . . . blood** let's treat this wrath (caused by an excess of bile or choler) by purging (vomiting or evacuation) rather than by medical bloodletting. (With a play on "bloodshed in combat.")   **156 conclude** come to a final agreement   **157 no month to bleed** (Learned authorities often differed as to which months or seasons were best for medicinal bloodletting.)   **164 boot** help for it.

MOWBRAY [*kneeling*]

Myself I throw, dread sovereign, at thy foot. 165
My life thou shalt command, but not my shame.
The one my duty owes; but my fair name,
Despite of death that lives upon my grave, 168
To dark dishonor's use thou shalt not have.
I am disgraced, impeached, and baffled here, 170
Pierced to the soul with slander's venomed spear,
The which no balm can cure but his heart-blood
Which breathed this poison.

KING RICHARD   Rage must be withstood. 173
Give me his gage. Lions make leopards tame. 174

MOWBRAY

Yea, but not change his spots. Take but my shame, 175
And I resign my gage. My dear dear lord,
The purest treasure mortal times afford 177
Is spotless reputation; that away,
Men are but gilded loam or painted clay.
A jewel in a ten-times-barred-up chest
Is a bold spirit in a loyal breast.
Mine honor is my life; both grow in one; 182
Take honor from me, and my life is done.
Then, dear my liege, mine honor let me try; 184
In that I live, and for that will I die.

KING RICHARD [*to Bolingbroke*]

Cousin, throw up your gage; do you begin. 186

BOLINGBROKE

Oh, God defend my soul from such deep sin!
Shall I seem crestfallen in my father's sight?
Or with pale beggar-fear impeach my height 189
Before this out-dared dastard? Ere my tongue 190
Shall wound my honor with such feeble wrong, 191
Or sound so base a parle, my teeth shall tear 192
The slavish motive of recanting fear 193
And spit it bleeding in his high disgrace, 194
Where shame doth harbor, even in Mowbray's face. 195

[*Exit Gaunt.*]

KING RICHARD

We were not born to sue but to command;
Which since we cannot do to make you friends,
Be ready, as your lives shall answer it,
At Coventry upon Saint Lambert's day. 199

There shall your swords and lances arbitrate
The swelling difference of your settled hate.
Since we cannot atone you, we shall see 202
Justice design the victor's chivalry. 203
Lord Marshal, command our officers at arms
Be ready to direct these home alarms. 205

Exeunt.

❖

[1.2]

Enter John of Gaunt with the Duchess of Gloucester.

GAUNT

Alas, the part I had in Woodstock's blood 1
Doth more solicit me than your exclaims 2
To stir against the butchers of his life! 3
But since correction lieth in those hands 4
Which made the fault that we cannot correct,
Put we our quarrel to the will of heaven,
Who, when they see the hours ripe on earth,
Will rain hot vengeance on offenders' heads.

DUCHESS

Finds brotherhood in thee no sharper spur?
Hath love in thy old blood no living fire?
Edward's seven sons, whereof thyself art one, 11
Were as seven vials of his sacred blood
Or seven fair branches springing from one root.
Some of those seven are dried by nature's course,
Some of those branches by the Destinies cut;
But Thomas, my dear lord, my life, my Gloucester,
One vial full of Edward's sacred blood,
One flourishing branch of his most royal root,
Is cracked, and all the precious liquor spilt,
Is hacked down, and his summer leaves all faded,
By envy's hand and murder's bloody ax. 21
Ah, Gaunt, his blood was thine! That bed, that womb,
That metal, that self mold that fashioned thee, 23
Made him a man; and though thou livest and breathest,
Yet art thou slain in him. Thou dost consent 25
In some large measure to thy father's death
In that thou see'st thy wretched brother die,
Who was the model of thy father's life. 28
Call it not patience, Gaunt; it is despair.
In suff'ring thus thy brother to be slaughtered,
Thou showest the naked pathway to thy life, 31

---

165 **Myself I throw** i.e., I throw myself, instead of my gage
168 **Despite . . . grave** that will live in the epitaph on my grave in
spite of devouring Death   170 **impeached** accused.   **baffled** publicly dishonored   173 **Which . . . poison** of him who uttered this slander.   174 **Lions . . . tame.** (The royal arms showed a lion rampant;
Mowbray's emblem was a leopard.)   175 **spots** (1) leopard spots
(2) stains of dishonor.   177 **mortal times** our earthly lives   182 **in
one** inseparably   184 **try** put to the test   186 **throw . . . gage** i.e., surrender your gage up to me, thereby ending the quarrel. (Richard is
probably seated on a raised throne, as in scene 3.)   189 **impeach my
height** discredit my high rank   190 **out-dared** dared down, cowed.
dastard coward.   191 **feeble wrong** dishonorable submission
192 **sound . . . parle** trumpet so shameful a negotiation, i.e., consent
to ask a truce   192–5 **my teeth . . . face** my teeth will bite off my
tongue as a craven instrument of cowardly capitulation and spit it
out bleeding, to its (the tongue's) great disgrace, into Mowbray's face,
where shame abides perpetually.   195.1 *Exit Gaunt* (A stage direction from the Folio, adopted by most editors so that Gaunt will not be
required to exit at the end of scene 1 and then immediately reenter.)
199 **Saint Lambert's day** September 17.

---

202 **atone** reconcile   203 **design . . . chivalry** designate who is the
true chivalric victor.   205 **home alarms** domestic conflicts.
1.2. Location: John of Gaunt's house (? No place is specified, and
the scene is not in Holinshed.)
1 **the part . . . blood** my kinship with Thomas of Woodstock, the
Duke of Gloucester (i.e., as his older brother)   2 **exclaims** exclamations   3 **stir** take action   4 **those hands** i.e., Richard's (whom Gaunt
charges with responsibility for Gloucester's death)   11 **Edward's**
Edward III's   21 **envy's** malice's   23 **metal** substance out of which a
person or a thing is made. (With a sense too of *mettle,* "temperament,
disposition.")   **self** selfsame   25 **consent** acquiesce   28 **model** likeness, copy   31 **naked** i.e., undefended

Teaching stern murder how to butcher thee.
That which in mean men we entitle patience   33
Is pale cold cowardice in noble breasts.
What shall I say? To safeguard thine own life
The best way is to venge my Gloucester's death.

GAUNT
God's is the quarrel; for God's substitute,   37
His deputy anointed in His sight,
Hath caused his death; the which if wrongfully   39
Let heaven revenge, for I may never lift
An angry arm against His minister.

DUCHESS
Where then, alas, may I complain myself?   42

GAUNT
To God, the widow's champion and defense.

DUCHESS
Why, then, I will. Farewell, old Gaunt.
Thou goest to Coventry, there to behold
Our cousin Hereford and fell Mowbray fight.   46
Oh, sit my husband's wrongs on Hereford's spear,   47
That it may enter butcher Mowbray's breast!
Or if misfortune miss the first career,   49
Be Mowbray's sins so heavy in his bosom
That they may break his foaming courser's back
And throw the rider headlong in the lists,   52
A caitiff recreant to my cousin Hereford!   53
Farewell, old Gaunt. Thy sometimes brother's wife   54
With her companion, Grief, must end her life.

GAUNT
Sister, farewell. I must to Coventry.
As much good stay with thee as go with me!

DUCHESS
Yet one word more. Grief boundeth where it falls,   58
Not with the empty hollowness, but weight.   59
I take my leave before I have begun,   60
For sorrow ends not when it seemeth done.
Commend me to thy brother, Edmund York.   62
Lo, this is all. Nay, yet depart not so!
Though this be all, do not so quickly go;
I shall remember more. Bid him—ah, what?—
With all good speed at Pleshey visit me.   66
Alack, and what shall good old York there see
But empty lodgings and unfurnished walls,   68
Unpeopled offices, untrodden stones,   69
And what hear there for welcome but my groans?
Therefore commend me; let him not come there

To seek out sorrow that dwells everywhere.
Desolate, desolate, will I hence and die.
The last leave of thee takes my weeping eye.   *Exeunt.*

[1.3]

Enter Lord Marshal and the Duke [of] Aumerle.

MARSHAL
My Lord Aumerle, is Harry Hereford armed?

AUMERLE
Yea, at all points, and longs to enter in.   2

MARSHAL
The Duke of Norfolk, sprightfully and bold,   3
Stays but the summons of the appellant's trumpet.   4

AUMERLE
Why then the champions are prepared, and stay
For nothing but His Majesty's approach.

*The trumpets sound, and the King enters with his
nobles [Gaunt, Bushy, Bagot, Green, and others].
When they are set, enter [Mowbray] the Duke of
Norfolk in arms, defendant, [with a herald].*

KING RICHARD
Marshal, demand of yonder champion
The cause of his arrival here in arms.
Ask him his name, and orderly proceed   9
To swear him in the justice of his cause.

MARSHAL [*to Mowbray*]
In God's name and the King's, say who thou art
And why thou comest thus knightly clad in arms,
Against what man thou com'st, and what thy quarrel. 13
Speak truly on thy knighthood and thy oath,
As so defend thee heaven and thy valor!

MOWBRAY
My name is Thomas Mowbray, Duke of Norfolk,
Who hither come engagèd by my oath—
Which God defend a knight should violate!—   18
Both to defend my loyalty and truth
To God, my king, and my succeeding issue
Against the Duke of Hereford that appeals me,   21
And by the grace of God and this mine arm
To prove him, in defending of myself,
A traitor to my God, my king, and me;
And as I truly fight, defend me heaven!

*The trumpets sound. Enter [Bolingbroke,] Duke of
Hereford, appellant, in armor, [with a herald].*

KING RICHARD
Marshal, ask yonder knight in arms

33 **mean** lowly   37 **God's substitute** i.e., the King, God's deputy on
earth   39 **his** i.e., Gloucester's   42 **complain myself** lodge a complaint on my own behalf.   46 **cousin** kinsman. **fell** fierce   47 **sit . . .
wrongs** may my husband's wrongs sit   49 **misfortune** i.e., Mowbray's downfall.   **career** charge of the horse in a tourney or combat
52 **lists** barriers enclosing the tournament area   53 **caitiff** base, cowardly   54 **sometimes** late   58 **boundeth** bounces, rebounds, returns.
(The Duchess apologizes for speaking yet again; her grief, she says,
continues on and on, like a bouncing tennis ball.)   59 **Not . . . weight**
(Grief is not hollow, like a tennis ball, but continues to move because
of its heaviness.)   60 **begun** i.e., begun to grieve   62 **Edmund York**
Edmund of Langley, fifth son of Edward III.   66 **Pleshey** Gloucester's country seat, in Essex   68 **unfurnished** bare   69 **offices** service
quarters, workrooms

1.3. Location: The lists at Coventry. Scaffolds or raised seats are provided for the King and his nobles, and chairs are provided for the
combatants.
2 **at all points** completely.   **in** i.e., into the lists, the space designed
for combat.   3 **sprightfully** with high spirit   4 **Stays** awaits
9 **orderly** according to the rules   13 **quarrel** complaint.   18 **defend**
forbid   21 **appeals** accuses

Both who he is and why he cometh hither
Thus plated in habiliments of war;   28
And formally, according to our law,
Depose him in the justice of his cause.   30

MARSHAL [to Bolingbroke]
What is thy name? And wherefore com'st thou hither,
Before King Richard in his royal lists?
Against whom comest thou? And what's thy quarrel?
Speak like a true knight, so defend thee heaven!

BOLINGBROKE
Harry of Hereford, Lancaster, and Derby
Am I, who ready here do stand in arms
To prove, by God's grace and my body's valor,
In lists, on Thomas Mowbray, Duke of Norfolk,
That he is a traitor foul and dangerous
To God of heaven, King Richard, and to me;
And as I truly fight, defend me heaven!

MARSHAL
On pain of death, no person be so bold
Or daring-hardy as to touch the lists,   43
Except the Marshal and such officers
Appointed to direct these fair designs.

BOLINGBROKE
Lord Marshal, let me kiss my sovereign's hand
And bow my knee before His Majesty;   47
For Mowbray and myself are like two men
That vow a long and weary pilgrimage.
Then let us take a ceremonious leave
And loving farewell of our several friends.   51

MARSHAL [to King Richard]
The appellant in all duty greets Your Highness
And craves to kiss your hand and take his leave.

KING RICHARD [coming down]
We will descend and fold him in our arms.
                        [He embraces Bolingbroke.]
Cousin of Hereford, as thy cause is right,   55
So be thy fortune in this royal fight!   56
Farewell, my blood—which if today thou shed,
Lament we may, but not revenge thee dead.

BOLINGBROKE
Oh, let no noble eye profane a tear   59
For me if I be gored with Mowbray's spear.   60
As confident as is the falcon's flight
Against a bird do I with Mowbray fight.
[To the King] My loving lord, I take my leave of you;
[To Aumerle] Of you, my noble cousin, Lord Aumerle;
Not sick, although I have to do with death,
But lusty, young, and cheerly drawing breath.   66
Lo, as at English feasts, so I regreet   67
The daintiest last, to make the end most sweet.   68

[To Gaunt] O thou, the earthly author of my blood,
Whose youthful spirit, in me regenerate,   70
Doth with a twofold vigor lift me up   71
To reach at victory above my head,
Add proof unto mine armor with thy prayers,   73
And with thy blessings steel my lance's point
That it may enter Mowbray's waxen coat   75
And furbish new the name of John o' Gaunt   76
Even in the lusty havior of his son.   77

GAUNT
God in thy good cause make thee prosperous!
Be swift like lightning in the execution,
And let thy blows, doubly redoubled,
Fall like amazing thunder on the casque   81
Of thy adverse pernicious enemy.
Rouse up thy youthful blood, be valiant, and live.

BOLINGBROKE
Mine innocence and Saint George to thrive!   84

MOWBRAY
However God or fortune cast my lot,
There lives or dies, true to King Richard's throne,
A loyal, just, and upright gentleman.
Never did captive with a freer heart
Cast off his chains of bondage and embrace
His golden uncontrolled enfranchisement   90
More than my dancing soul doth celebrate
This feast of battle with mine adversary.
Most mighty liege, and my companion peers,
Take from my mouth the wish of happy years.   94
As gentle and as jocund as to jest   95
Go I to fight. Truth hath a quiet breast.   96

KING RICHARD
Farewell, my lord. Securely I espy   97
Virtue with valor couchèd in thine eye.—   98
Order the trial, Marshal, and begin.

MARSHAL
Harry of Hereford, Lancaster, and Derby,
Receive thy lance; and God defend the right!
                        [A lance is given to Bolingbroke.]

BOLINGBROKE
Strong as a tower in hope, I cry "Amen!"   102

MARSHAL [to an officer]
Go bear this lance to Thomas, Duke of Norfolk.
                        [A lance is given to Norfolk.]

FIRST HERALD
Harry of Hereford, Lancaster, and Derby
Stands here for God, his sovereign, and himself,
On pain to be found false and recreant,
To prove the Duke of Norfolk, Thomas Mowbray,

---

28 **plated** armored.   **habiliments** the attire   **30 Depose him** take his sworn deposition   **43 daring-hardy** daringly bold, reckless.   **touch** i.e., interfere in   **47 bow my knee** (Presumably Bolingbroke kneels to Richard and, at about line 69, to Gaunt.)   **51 several** various   **55 as** insofar as   **56 royal fight** i.e., a fight taking place in the presence of the King.   **59–60 profane . . . For me** misuse tears by weeping for me   **66 lusty** full of vigor.   **cheerly** cheerfully   **67 regreet** greet, salute   **68 The daintiest** i.e., the most tasty, the finest. (Bolingbroke refers to the custom of ending banquets with a sweet dessert.)

70 **regenerate** born anew   **71 twofold** i.e., of father and son   **73 proof** invulnerability   **75 enter . . . coat** pierce Mowbray's armor as though it were made of wax   **76 furbish** polish   **77 lusty havior** vigorous behavior, deportment   **81 amazing** bewildering.   **casque** helmet   **84 Mine . . . thrive!** May my innocence and the protectorship of Saint George bring me victory!   **90 enfranchisement** freedom   **94 Take . . . years** take from me the wish that you may enjoy many happy years.   **95 gentle** unperturbed in spirit.   **to jest** i.e., to a play or entertainment   **96 quiet** calm   **97 Securely** Confidently   **98 couchèd** lodged, expressed, leveled in readiness (as with a lance)   **102 Strong . . . hope** (Alludes to Psalm 61:3: "for thou hast been my hope, and a strong tower for me against the face of the enemy.")

A traitor to his God, his king, and him,   108
And dares him to set forward to the fight.

SECOND HERALD
Here standeth Thomas Mowbray, Duke of Norfolk,
On pain to be found false and recreant,
Both to defend himself and to approve   112
Henry of Hereford, Lancaster, and Derby,
To God, his sovereign, and to him disloyal,   114
Courageously and with a free desire
Attending but the signal to begin.   116

MARSHAL
Sound, trumpets, and set forward, combatants!
[A charge is sounded. Richard throws
down his baton.]
Stay! The King hath thrown his warder down.   118

KING RICHARD
Let them lay by their helmets and their spears,
And both return back to their chairs again.
[To his counselors] Withdraw with us, and let the trumpets
sound
While we return these dukes what we decree.   122
[A long flourish. Richard consults apart with
Gaunt and others.]
Draw near,
And list what with our council we have done.   124
For that our kingdom's earth should not be soiled   125
With that dear blood which it hath fosterèd;
And for our eyes do hate the dire aspect   127
Of civil wounds plowed up with neighbors' sword;
And for we think the eagle-wingèd pride
Of sky-aspiring and ambitious thoughts,
With rival-hating envy, set on you   131
To wake our peace, which in our country's cradle
Draws the sweet infant breath of gentle sleep,
Which, so roused up with boist'rous untuned drums,   134
With harsh-resounding trumpets' dreadful bray
And grating shock of wrathful iron arms,
Might from our quiet confines fright fair peace
And make us wade even in our kindred's blood:
Therefore we banish you our territories.
You, cousin Hereford, upon pain of life,   140
Till twice five summers have enriched our fields,
Shall not regreet our fair dominions,
But tread the stranger paths of banishment.   143

BOLINGBROKE
Your will be done. This must my comfort be:
That sun that warms you here shall shine on me,
And those his golden beams to you here lent
Shall point on me and gild my banishment.

KING RICHARD
Norfolk, for thee remains a heavier doom,

Which I with some unwillingness pronounce:
The sly slow hours shall not determine   150
The dateless limit of thy dear exile.   151
The hopeless word of "never to return"
Breathe I against thee, upon pain of life.

MOWBRAY
A heavy sentence, my most sovereign liege,
And all unlooked-for from Your Highness' mouth.
A dearer merit, not so deep a maim   156
As to be cast forth in the common air,
Have I deservèd at Your Highness' hands.
The language I have learned these forty years,
My native English, now I must forgo;
And now my tongue's use is to me no more
Than an unstringèd viol or a harp,   162
Or like a cunning instrument cased up,   163
Or, being open, put into his hands   164
That knows no touch to tune the harmony.
Within my mouth you have enjailed my tongue,
Doubly portcullised with my teeth and lips,   167
And dull unfeeling barren ignorance
Is made my jailer to attend on me.
I am too old to fawn upon a nurse,
Too far in years to be a pupil now.
What is thy sentence then but speechless death,
Which robs my tongue from breathing native breath?   173

KING RICHARD
It boots thee not to be compassionate.   174
After our sentence plaining comes too late.   175

MOWBRAY
Then thus I turn me from my country's light,
To dwell in solemn shades of endless night.
[He starts to leave.]

KING RICHARD
Return again, and take an oath with thee.
Lay on our royal sword your banished hands.
[They place their hands on Richard's sword.]
Swear by the duty that you owe to God—
Our part therein we banish with yourselves—   181
To keep the oath that we administer:
You never shall, so help you truth and God,
Embrace each other's love in banishment,
Nor never look upon each other's face,
Nor never write, regreet, nor reconcile
This louring tempest of your homebred hate;   187
Nor never by advisèd purpose meet   188
To plot, contrive, or complot any ill   189
'Gainst us, our state, our subjects, or our land.

BOLINGBROKE   I swear.

---

108 **him** himself, Bolingbroke. (See line 40.)   112 **approve** prove
114 **him** i.e., Mowbray. (See line 24.)   116 **Attending** awaiting
118 **warder** staff or truncheon borne by the King when presiding over
a trial by combat   122 **While we return** until I inform   122.1 *flourish*
fanfare.   124 **list** hear   125 **For that** In order that   127 **for** because
(also in line 129)   131 **envy** enmity.   **set on you** set you on
134 **Which** i.e., which enmity, disturbance of the peace. (Although, in
literal terms, the antecedent of *Which* is *peace* in line 132.)   140 **life**
i.e., loss of life   143 **stranger** alien

150 **sly** stealthy.   **determine** put to an end   151 **dateless limit**
unlimited term.   **dear** grievous   156 **dearer merit** better reward.
maim injury   162 **viol** a six-stringed instrument, related to the modern violin, played with a curved bow   163 **cunning** skillfully made
164 **open** taken from its case.   **his** that person's   167 **portcullised**
shut in by a portcullis, an iron grating over a gateway that can be
raised and lowered   173 **breathing . . . breath** speaking English.
174 **boots** avails.   **compassionate** full of laments.   175 **plaining**
complaining   181 **Our part therein** i.e., the duty you owe me as King
187 **louring** threatening, scowling   188 **advisèd** deliberate, premeditated   189 **complot** plot together

MOWBRAY And I, to keep all this.

BOLINGBROKE
Norfolk, so far as to mine enemy: 193
By this time, had the King permitted us,
One of our souls had wandered in the air,
Banished this frail sepulchre of our flesh,   196
As now our flesh is banished from this land.
Confess thy treasons ere thou fly the realm.
Since thou hast far to go, bear not along
The clogging burden of a guilty soul.   200

MOWBRAY
No, Bolingbroke. If ever I were traitor,
My name be blotted from the book of life,
And I from heaven banished as from hence!
But what thou art, God, thou, and I do know,
And all too soon, I fear, the King shall rue.—
Farewell, my liege. Now no way can I stray;   206
Save back to England, all the world's my way.   *Exit.*

KING RICHARD *[to Gaunt]*
Uncle, even in the glasses of thine eyes   208
I see thy grievèd heart. Thy sad aspect
Hath from the number of his banished years
Plucked four away. [*To Bolingbroke*] Six frozen winters
    spent,
Return with welcome home from banishment.

BOLINGBROKE
How long a time lies in one little word!
Four lagging winters and four wanton springs   214
End in a word; such is the breath of kings.

GAUNT
I thank my liege that in regard of me
He shortens four years of my son's exile.
But little vantage shall I reap thereby;
For, ere the six years that he hath to spend
Can change their moons and bring their times about,
My oil-dried lamp and time-bewasted light   221
Shall be extinct with age and endless night;
My inch of taper will be burnt and done,   223
And blindfold Death not let me see my son.   224

KING RICHARD
Why, uncle, thou hast many years to live.

GAUNT
But not a minute, King, that thou canst give.
Shorten my days thou canst with sullen sorrow,
And pluck nights from me, but not lend a morrow;
Thou canst help Time to furrow me with age,
But stop no wrinkle in his pilgrimage;   230
Thy word is current with him for my death,   231
But dead, thy kingdom cannot buy my breath.   232

KING RICHARD
Thy son is banished upon good advice,
Whereto thy tongue a party verdict gave.   234
Why at our justice seem'st thou then to lour?

GAUNT
Things sweet to taste prove in digestion sour.
You urged me as a judge, but I had rather
You would have bid me argue like a father.
Oh, had it been a stranger, not my child,
To smooth his fault I should have been more mild.   240
A partial slander sought I to avoid   241
And in the sentence my own life destroyed.
Alas, I looked when some of you should say   243
I was too strict, to make mine own away;   244
But you gave leave to my unwilling tongue
Against my will to do myself this wrong.

KING RICHARD
Cousin, farewell; and, uncle, bid him so.
Six years we banish him, and he shall go.
          [*Flourish. Exit King Richard with his train.*]

AUMERLE *[to Bolingbroke]*
Cousin, farewell. What presence must not know,   249
From where you do remain let paper show.   [*Exit.*] 250

MARSHAL *[to Bolingbroke]*
My lord, no leave take I, for I will ride,   251
As far as land will let me, by your side.
          [*Bolingbroke makes no answer. The Lord Marshal
                                        stands aside.*]

GAUNT *[to Bolingbroke]*
Oh, to what purpose dost thou hoard thy words,
That thou returnest no greeting to thy friends?

BOLINGBROKE
I have too few to take my leave of you,
When the tongue's office should be prodigal   256
To breathe the abundant dolor of the heart.   257

GAUNT
Thy grief is but thy absence for a time.   258

BOLINGBROKE
Joy absent, grief is present for that time.   259

GAUNT
What is six winters? They are quickly gone.

BOLINGBROKE
To men in joy; but grief makes one hour ten.

GAUNT
Call it a travel that thou tak'st for pleasure.   262

BOLINGBROKE
My heart will sigh when I miscall it so,
Which finds it an enforcèd pilgrimage.

GAUNT
The sullen passage of thy weary steps   265

---

193 **so far** let me say this much   196 **sepulchre of our flesh** i.e., body, the temple or tomb of the soul   200 **clogging** (A clog was a wooden block attached to the leg to hinder movement.)   206 **stray** take the wrong road   208 **glasses** mirrors (here glistening with tears) 214 **wanton** luxuriant   221 **oil-dried** empty of oil   223 **taper** candle 224 **blindfold Death** i.e., *blindfold* because *Death* deprives its victims of their sight and because it is often pictured as an eyeless skull 230 **in his pilgrimage** brought about in time's journey   231 **current** i.e., as good as current coin, valid   232 **dead** i.e., once I am dead. **buy** i.e., restore with a payment

234 **a party verdict** one person's share in a joint verdict   240 **smooth** extenuate   241 **partial slander** accusation of partiality (on behalf of my son)   243 **looked when** expected that, awaited the point at which 244 **to . . . away** in making away with my own (son)   249 **What . . . know** What I cannot learn from you in person   250 **s.d.** *Exit* (The exit is uncertain; see 1.4.1–4.)   251 **no leave take I** i.e., I will not take my leave of you, my lord; I will not say good-bye   256 **office** function. **prodigal** lavish   257 **To breathe** in uttering   258 **grief** grievance 259 **grief** unhappiness   262 **travel** (The Quarto spelling, "trauaile," suggests an interchangeable meaning of "travel" and "labor.") 265 **sullen** (1) melancholy (2) dull

Esteem as foil wherein thou art to set   266
The precious jewel of thy home return.

BOLINGBROKE

Nay, rather every tedious stride I make
Will but remember me what a deal of world   269
I wander from the jewels that I love.
Must I not serve a long apprenticehood
To foreign passages, and in the end,   272
Having my freedom, boast of nothing else   273
But that I was a journeyman to grief?   274

GAUNT

All places that the eye of heaven visits   275
Are to a wise man ports and happy havens.
Teach thy necessity to reason thus:
There is no virtue like necessity.
Think not the King did banish thee,
But thou the King. Woe doth the heavier sit   280
Where it perceives it is but faintly borne.   281
Go, say I sent thee forth to purchase honor,   282
And not the King exiled thee; or suppose
Devouring pestilence hangs in our air
And thou art flying to a fresher clime.
Look what thy soul holds dear, imagine it   286
To lie that way thou goest, not whence thou com'st.
Suppose the singing birds musicians,
The grass whereon thou tread'st the presence strewed,   289
The flowers fair ladies, and thy steps no more
Than a delightful measure or a dance;   291
For gnarling sorrow hath less power to bite   292
The man that mocks at it and sets it light.   293

BOLINGBROKE

Oh, who can hold a fire in his hand
By thinking on the frosty Caucasus?   295
Or cloy the hungry edge of appetite
By bare imagination of a feast?
Or wallow naked in December snow
By thinking on fantastic summer's heat?   299
Oh, no, the apprehension of the good
Gives but the greater feeling to the worse.
Fell Sorrow's tooth doth never rankle more   302
Than when he bites but lanceth not the sore.   303

GAUNT

Come, come, my son, I'll bring thee on thy way.   304
Had I thy youth and cause, I would not stay.   305

BOLINGBROKE

Then, England's ground, farewell. Sweet soil, adieu,
My mother and my nurse that bears me yet!
Where'er I wander, boast of this I can:
Though banished, yet a trueborn Englishman.
                                                      Exeunt.

❖

[1.4]

*Enter the King, with Bagot, [Green,] etc. at one
door, and the Lord Aumerle at another.*

KING RICHARD

We did observe.—Cousin Aumerle,   1
How far brought you high Hereford on his way?

AUMERLE

I brought high Hereford, if you call him so,
But to the next highway, and there I left him.   4

KING RICHARD

And say, what store of parting tears were shed?

AUMERLE

Faith, none for me, except the northeast wind,   6
Which then blew bitterly against our faces,
Awaked the sleeping rheum and so by chance   8
Did grace our hollow parting with a tear.   9

KING RICHARD

What said our cousin when you parted with him?

AUMERLE   "Farewell!"
And, for my heart disdainèd that my tongue   12
Should so profane the word, that taught me craft   13
To counterfeit oppression of such grief
That words seemed buried in my sorrow's grave.
Marry, would the word "farewell" have lengthened   16
  hours
And added years to his short banishment,
He should have had a volume of farewells;
But since it would not, he had none of me.   19

KING RICHARD

He is our cousin, cousin; but 'tis doubt,
When time shall call him home from banishment,
Whether our kinsman come to see his friends.   22
Ourself and Bushy, Bagot here, and Green
Observed his courtship to the common people,
How he did seem to dive into their hearts
With humble and familiar courtesy,
What reverence he did throw away on slaves,
Wooing poor craftsmen with the craft of smiles

And patient underbearing of his fortune,   29
As 'twere to banish their affects with him.   30
Off goes his bonnet to an oyster wench;
A brace of draymen bid God speed him well   32
And had the tribute of his supple knee,
With "Thanks, my countrymen, my loving friends,"
As were our England in reversion his,   35
And he our subjects' next degree in hope.   36

GREEN
Well, he is gone, and with him go these thoughts.   37
Now for the rebels which stand out in Ireland,   38
Expedient manage must be made, my liege,   39
Ere further leisure yield them further means
For their advantage and Your Highness' loss.

KING RICHARD
We will ourself in person to this war.
And, for our coffers with too great a court   43
And liberal largess are grown somewhat light,   44
We are enforced to farm our royal realm,   45
The revenue whereof shall furnish us
For our affairs in hand. If that come short,
Our substitutes at home shall have blank charters,   48
Whereto, when they shall know what men are rich,
They shall subscribe them for large sums of gold   50
And send them after to supply our wants;   51
For we will make for Ireland presently.   52

Enter Bushy.

Bushy, what news?

BUSHY
Old John of Gaunt is grievous sick, my lord,
Suddenly taken, and hath sent posthaste
To entreat Your Majesty to visit him.

KING RICHARD   Where lies he?

BUSHY   At Ely House.   58

KING RICHARD
Now put it, God, in the physician's mind
To help him to his grave immediately!
The lining of his coffers shall make coats   61
To deck our soldiers for these Irish wars.
Come, gentlemen, let's all go visit him.
Pray God we may make haste and come too late!

ALL   Amen.   *Exeunt.*

[2.1]

Enter John of Gaunt sick, with the Duke of York, etc.

GAUNT
Will the King come, that I may breathe my last
In wholesome counsel to his unstaid youth?   2

YORK
Vex not yourself, nor strive not with your breath,   3
For all in vain comes counsel to his ear.

GAUNT
Oh, but they say the tongues of dying men
Enforce attention like deep harmony.
Where words are scarce, they are seldom spent in vain,
For they breathe truth that breathe their words in pain.   8
He that no more must say is listened more   9
   Than they whom youth and ease have taught to glose.   10
More are men's ends marked than their lives before.   11
   The setting sun, and music at the close,
As the last taste of sweets, is sweetest last,   13
Writ in remembrance more than things long past.   14
Though Richard my life's counsel would not hear,   15
My death's sad tale may yet undeaf his ear.   16

YORK
No, it is stopped with other, flattering sounds,
As praises, of whose taste the wise are fond;   18
Lascivious meters, to whose venom sound   19
The open ear of youth doth always listen;
Report of fashions in proud Italy,   21
Whose manners still our tardy-apish nation   22
Limps after in base imitation.
Where doth the world thrust forth a vanity—
So it be new, there's no respect how vile—   25
That is not quickly buzzed into his ears?
Then all too late comes counsel to be heard
Where will doth mutiny with wit's regard.   28
Direct not him whose way himself will choose.   29
'Tis breath thou lack'st, and that breath wilt thou lose.

GAUNT
Methinks I am a prophet new inspired,
And thus expiring do foretell of him:
His rash fierce blaze of riot cannot last,   33
For violent fires soon burn out themselves;
Small showers last long, but sudden storms are short;

---

29 underbearing bearing, endurance   **30 banish . . . him** take their affections with him into banishment.   **32 brace of draymen** pair of cart drivers   **35 As . . . his** i.e., as if my England were to revert to him as true owner after my death   **36 our . . . hope** i.e., the heir presumptive to the throne and favorite choice of the people.   **37 go** let go   **38 for** as for.   **stand out** hold out, resist   **39 Expedient manage** speedy arrangements   **43 for** because.   **too great a court** i.e., too great an extravagance at court   **44 liberal largess** extravagant generosity (to courtiers)   **45 farm** lease the right of collecting taxes, for a present cash payment, to the highest bidder   **48 substitutes** deputies. **blank charters** writs authorizing the collection of revenues or forced loans to the crown, blank spaces being left for the names of the parties and the sums they were to provide   **50 subscribe them** put down their names   **51 them** i.e., the sums collected   **52 presently** at once.   **58 Ely House** (Palace of the Bishop of Ely in Holborn, a London district.)   **61 lining** contents. (With pun on lining for coats.) **coats** coats of mail, armor

2.1 Location: Ely House.
0.1 Enter John of Gaunt sick (Presumably he is carried in by servants in a chair.)   **2 unstaid** uncontrolled   **3 strive . . . breath** i.e., don't waste your breath   **8 they** those persons   **9 He . . . listened more** He who will soon be silenced by death is listened to more   **10 glose** flatter, deceive in speech.   **11 marked** noticed   **13 is sweetest last** is longest remembered as sweet   **14 Writ in remembrance** written down in the memory   **15 my life's counsel** my advice while I lived   **16 My . . . tale** my grave dying speech   **18 As . . . fond** such as praises, which even wise men are foolishly inclined to hear   **19 meters** verses. **venom** poisonous   **21 proud Italy** (Roger Ascham, John Lyly, and other sixteenth-century writers complained of the growing influence of Italian luxury.)   **22 still** always.   **tardy-apish** imitative but behind the times   **25 So** so long as.   **there's no respect** it makes no difference   **28 Where . . . regard** where natural inclination rebels against what reason esteems.   **29 Direct . . . choose** Don't try to offer advice to one who insists on going his own way.   **33 riot** profligacy

He tires betimes that spurs too fast betimes;   36
With eager feeding food doth choke the feeder;
Light vanity, insatiate cormorant,   38
Consuming means, soon preys upon itself.   39
This royal throne of kings, this sceptered isle,
This earth of majesty, this seat of Mars,   41
This other Eden, demi-paradise,
This fortress built by Nature for herself
Against infection and the hand of war,   44
This happy breed of men, this little world,   45
This precious stone set in the silver sea,
Which serves it in the office of a wall   47
Or as a moat defensive to a house,
Against the envy of less happier lands,
This blessed plot, this earth, this realm, this England,
This nurse, this teeming womb of royal kings,   51
Feared by their breed and famous by their birth,   52
Renownèd for their deeds as far from home
For Christian service and true chivalry
As is the sepulcher in stubborn Jewry   55
Of the world's ransom, blessèd Mary's son,
This land of such dear souls, this dear dear land,
Dear for her reputation through the world,
Is now leased out—I die pronouncing it—
Like to a tenement or pelting farm.   60
England, bound in with the triumphant sea,   61
Whose rocky shore beats back the envious siege
Of wat'ry Neptune, is now bound in with shame,   63
With inky blots and rotten parchment bonds.   64
That England that was wont to conquer others
Hath made a shameful conquest of itself.
Ah, would the scandal vanish with my life,
How happy then were my ensuing death!   68

*Enter King [Richard] and Queen, [Aumerle,
Bushy, Green, Bagot, Ross, and Willoughby,] etc.*

YORK
   The King is come. Deal mildly with his youth,
   For young hot colts being reined do rage the more.
QUEEN
   How fares our noble uncle Lancaster?
KING RICHARD
   What comfort, man? How is't with agèd Gaunt?
GAUNT
   Oh, how that name befits my composition!   73
   Old Gaunt indeed, and gaunt in being old.
   Within me grief hath kept a tedious fast,
   And who abstains from meat that is not gaunt?   76
   For sleeping England long time have I watched;   77

Watching breeds leanness, leanness is all gaunt.
The pleasure that some fathers feed upon
Is my strict fast—I mean, my children's looks—   80
And, therein fasting, hast thou made me gaunt.   81
Gaunt am I for the grave, gaunt as a grave,
Whose hollow womb inherits naught but bones.   83
KING RICHARD
   Can sick men play so nicely with their names?   84
GAUNT
   No, misery makes sport to mock itself.   85
   Since thou dost seek to kill my name in me,   86
   I mock my name, great King, to flatter thee.   87
KING RICHARD
   Should dying men flatter with those that live?   88
GAUNT
   No, no, men living flatter those that die.   89
KING RICHARD
   Thou, now a-dying, sayest thou flatterest me.
GAUNT
   Oh, no, thou diest, though I the sicker be.
KING RICHARD
   I am in health, I breathe, and see thee ill.
GAUNT
   Now He that made me knows I see thee ill;
   Ill in myself to see, and in thee seeing ill.   94
   Thy deathbed is no lesser than thy land,
   Wherein thou liest in reputation sick;
   And thou, too careless patient as thou art,
   Commit'st thy anointed body to the cure
   Of those physicians that first wounded thee.   99
   A thousand flatterers sit within thy crown,
   Whose compass is no bigger than thy head,   101
   And yet, encagèd in so small a verge,   102
   The waste is no whit lesser than thy land.   103
   Oh, had thy grandsire with a prophet's eye   104
   Seen how his son's son should destroy his sons,   105
   From forth thy reach he would have laid thy shame,   106
   Deposing thee before thou wert possessed,   107
   Which art possessed now to depose thyself.   108
   Why, cousin, wert thou regent of the world,   109
   It were a shame to let this land by lease;

---

36 **betimes** soon, early   38 **Light vanity** frivolous dissipation.
cormorant glutton. (Literally, a voracious seabird.)   39 **means** i.e.,
means of sustenance   41 **earth of majesty** land fit for kings.   **seat of
Mars** residence of the god of war   44 **infection** (1) plague (2) moral
pollution   45 **happy breed** fortunate race   47 **office** function
51 **teeming** fruitful   52 **by their breed** for their ancestral reputation
for prowess   55 **stubborn Jewry** i.e., Judea, called stubborn because
it resisted Christianity   60 **tenement** land or property held by a tenant.   **pelting** paltry   61 **bound in** bordered, surrounded   63 **bound
in** legally constrained   64 **blots . . . bonds** i.e., the blank charters.
68 **ensuing** approaching   73 **composition** constitution.   76 **meat**
food   77 **watched** kept watch at night, been vigilant

80 **Is . . . fast** is something I must forgo   81 **therein fasting** i.e., since I
am starved of that pleasure   83 **inherits** possesses, will receive
84 **nicely** (1) ingeniously (2) triflingly   85 **to mock** of mocking
86–7 **Since . . . thee** Since you seek to destroy my family name (by
banishing my son), I mock my name to please you and flatter your
greatness.   88 **flatter with** try to please   89 **flatter** i.e., are attentive
to, offer comfort to   94 **Ill . . . ill** seeing myself to be physically ill,
and seeing the illness in you of abusing your royal authority.
99 **physicians** i.e., the King's favorites   101 **compass** circle, circumference   102 **verge** (1) circle, ring (2) the compass about the King's
court, which extended for twelve miles   103 **waste** (1) waist, circumference (2) that which is destroyed. (With a quibble on the legal
meaning of *waste*, "damage done to property by a tenant.")   **whit** bit,
speck   104 **grandsire** i.e., Edward III   105 **destroy his sons** (1) destroy
Edward III's sons, Richard's uncles (2) destroy Richard's own heritage   106 **From . . . shame** he would have put the matter you have
shamefully handled out of your reach   107 **Deposing** dispossessing.
possessed put in possession of the crown   108 **Which . . . thyself**
you who are now seized with an obsessive desire to give away your
authority (by leasing the realm to favorites).   109 **cousin** kinsman,
nephew.   **regent** ruler

But, for thy world enjoying but this land,   111
Is it not more than shame to shame it so?
Landlord of England art thou now, not king.   113
Thy state of law is bondslave to the law,   114
And thou—

KING RICHARD   A lunatic lean-witted fool,
Presuming on an ague's privilege,   116
Darest with thy frozen admonition   117
Make pale our cheek, chasing the royal blood
With fury from his native residence.   119
Now, by my seat's right royal majesty,   120
Wert thou not brother to great Edward's son,   121
This tongue that runs so roundly in thy head   122
Should run thy head from thy unreverent shoulders.   123

GAUNT
Oh, spare me not, my brother Edward's son,
For that I was his father Edward's son!   125
That blood already, like the pelican,   126
Hast thou tapped out and drunkenly caroused.   127
My brother Gloucester, plain well-meaning soul—
Whom fair befall in heaven 'mongst happy souls!—   129
May be a precedent and witness good
That thou respect'st not spilling Edward's blood.   131
Join with the present sickness that I have,   132
And thy unkindness be like crooked age   133
To crop at once a too-long-withered flower!—   134
Live in thy shame, but die not shame with thee!   135
These words hereafter thy tormentors be!—
Convey me to my bed, then to my grave.
Love they to live that love and honor have.   138

Exit [*borne off by his attendants*].

KING RICHARD
And let them die that age and sullens have,   139
For both hast thou, and both become the grave.   140

YORK
I do beseech Your Majesty, impute his words
To wayward sickliness and age in him.
He loves you, on my life, and holds you dear
As Harry Duke of Hereford, were he here.   144

KING RICHARD
Right, you say true. As Hereford's love, so his;   145
As theirs, so mine; and all be as it is.

[*Enter Northumberland.*]

NORTHUMBERLAND
My liege, old Gaunt commends him to Your Majesty.

KING RICHARD
What says he?

NORTHUMBERLAND   Nay, nothing, all is said.
His tongue is now a stringless instrument;
Words, life, and all, old Lancaster hath spent.

YORK
Be York the next that must be bankrupt so!
Though death be poor, it ends a mortal woe.   152

KING RICHARD
The ripest fruit first falls, and so doth he;
His time is spent, our pilgrimage must be.   154
So much for that. Now for our Irish wars:
We must supplant those rough rug-headed kerns,   156
Which live like venom where no venom else   157
But only they have privilege to live.   158
And, for these great affairs do ask some charge,   159
Towards our assistance we do seize to us
The plate, coin, revenues, and movables   161
Whereof our uncle Gaunt did stand possessed.

YORK
How long shall I be patient? Ah, how long
Shall tender duty make me suffer wrong?
Not Gloucester's death, nor Hereford's banishment,
Nor Gaunt's rebukes, nor England's private wrongs,   166
Nor the prevention of poor Bolingbroke   167
About his marriage, nor my own disgrace,   168
Have ever made me sour my patient cheek
Or bend one wrinkle on my sovereign's face.   170
I am the last of noble Edward's sons,
Of whom thy father, Prince of Wales, was first.
In war was never lion raged more fierce,   173
In peace was never gentle lamb more mild,
Than was that young and princely gentleman.
His face thou hast, for even so looked he,
Accomplished with the number of thy hours;   177
But when he frowned, it was against the French
And not against his friends. His noble hand

---

111 **But . . . land** i.e., but since you enjoy as your domain only this land of England (rather than the whole world)   113 **Landlord** i.e., One who leases out property   114 **Thy . . . the law** i.e., Your legal status as King is now subservient to and at the mercy of the law governing contracts, such as blank charters   116 **an ague's privilege** i.e., a sick person's right to be testy   117 **frozen** (1) chilly (2) caused by a chill   119 **his** its   120 **seat's** throne's   121 **great Edward's son** Edward the Black Prince, Richard's father   122–3 **runs . . . run** runs on, talks . . . drive, chase   122 **roundly** unceremoniously, bluntly   123 **unreverent** irreverent, disrespectful   125 **For that** simply because   126 **pelican** (The pelican was thought to feed its ingrateful and murderous young with its own blood.)   127 **tapped out** drawn as from a tapped barrel.   **caroused** gulped, quaffed.   129 **Whom fair befall** to whom may good come   131 **thou respect'st not** you care nothing about   132–4 **Join . . . flower!** May your unnatural behavior act in concert with my present illness and my advanced years to cut down my life like a too-long-withered flower! (*Unkindness* means both cruelty and behavior contrary to the natural bond that should exist in blood ties.)   135 **die . . . thee** i.e., may your shame live after you.   138 **Love they** Let them desire   139 **sullens** sullenness, melancholy   140 **become** suit   144 **As** i.e., as he would love. (But see the next note.)

145 **Right . . . his** (Richard deliberately takes the opposite of what York had intended to say; Richard gibes that Gaunt is as little fond of the King as is Hereford.)   152 **Though . . . woe** Though death is the privation of life, it does end the misery of human existence which is itself a kind of death in life.   154 **our . . . be** i.e., our journey through life is yet to be completed but will also end.   156–8 **We . . . live** We must expel these shaggy-haired light-armed Irish foot soldiers, who live there like poisonous snakes where no others are allowed to exist. (Richard alludes to the freedom of Ireland from snakes, traditionally ascribed to Saint Patrick.)   159 **for** because.   **ask some charge** require some expenditure   161 **movables** personal property   166 **Nor . . . wrongs** nor the rebukes given to Gaunt, nor wrongs inflicted on private English subjects   167–8 **prevention . . . marriage** (Holinshed's *Chronicles* report that Richard had forestalled Bolingbroke's intended marriage with the Duke de Berri's daughter.)   170 **bend . . . on** once frown at   173 **was . . . fierce** never was there a lion more fiercely enraged   177 **Accomplished . . . hours** i.e., when he was your age

Did win what he did spend, and spent not that
Which his triumphant father's hand had won.
His hands were guilty of no kindred blood,   182
But bloody with the enemies of his kin.
Oh, Richard! York is too far gone with grief,
Or else he never would compare between.   185

KING RICHARD
Why, uncle, what's the matter?

YORK   O my liege,
Pardon me, if you please; if not, I, pleased   187
Not to be pardoned, am content withal.   188
Seek you to seize and grip into your hands
The royalties and rights of banished Hereford?   190
Is not Gaunt dead? And doth not Hereford live?
Was not Gaunt just? And is not Harry true?
Did not the one deserve to have an heir?
Is not his heir a well-deserving son?
Take Hereford's rights away, and take from Time   195
His charters and his customary rights;   196
Let not tomorrow then ensue today;   197
Be not thyself; for how art thou a king
But by fair sequence and succession?
Now, afore God—God forbid I say true!—
If you do wrongfully seize Hereford's rights,
Call in the letters patents that he hath   202
By his attorneys general to sue   203
His livery, and deny his offered homage,   204
You pluck a thousand dangers on your head,
You lose a thousand well-disposèd hearts,
And prick my tender patience to those thoughts   207
Which honor and allegiance cannot think.

KING RICHARD
Think what you will, we seize into our hands
His plate, his goods, his money, and his lands.

YORK
I'll not be by the while. My liege, farewell.   211
What will ensue hereof there's none can tell;
But by bad courses may be understood   213
That their events can never fall out good.   Exit. 214

KING RICHARD
Go, Bushy, to the Earl of Wiltshire straight.   215
Bid him repair to us to Ely House   216
To see this business. Tomorrow next   217
We will for Ireland, and 'tis time, I trow.   218
And we create, in absence of ourself,
Our uncle York Lord Governor of England,
For he is just and always loved us well.—

Come on, our queen. Tomorrow must we part.
Be merry, for our time of stay is short.   223
        [*Flourish.*] *Exeunt King and Queen* [*with attendants*].
        Manet Northumberland [*with Willoughby and Ross*].

NORTHUMBERLAND
Well, lords, the Duke of Lancaster is dead.

ROSS
And living too, for now his son is duke.

WILLOUGHBY
Barely in title, not in revenues.

NORTHUMBERLAND
Richly in both, if justice had her right.

ROSS
My heart is great, but it must break with silence,   228
Ere 't be disburdened with a liberal tongue.   229

NORTHUMBERLAND
Nay, speak thy mind; and let him ne'er speak more   230
That speaks thy words again to do thee harm!

WILLOUGHBY
Tends that thou wouldst speak to the Duke of
    Hereford?   232
If it be so, out with it boldly, man.
Quick is mine ear to hear of good towards him.

ROSS
No good at all that I can do for him,
Unless you call it good to pity him,
Bereft and gelded of his patrimony.   237

NORTHUMBERLAND
Now, afore God, 'tis shame such wrongs are borne
In him, a royal prince, and many more   239
Of noble blood in this declining land.
The King is not himself, but basely led
By flatterers; and what they will inform   242
Merely in hate 'gainst any of us all,   243
That will the King severely prosecute
'Gainst us, our lives, our children, and our heirs.

ROSS
The commons hath he pilled with grievous taxes,   246
And quite lost their hearts; the nobles hath he fined
For ancient quarrels, and quite lost their hearts.

WILLOUGHBY
And daily new exactions are devised,
As blanks, benevolences, and I wot not what.   250
But what i' God's name doth become of this?   251

NORTHUMBERLAND
Wars hath not wasted it, for warred he hath not,
But basely yielded upon compromise
That which his noble ancestors achieved with blows.
More hath he spent in peace than they in wars.

ROSS
The Earl of Wiltshire hath the realm in farm.   256

---

182 kindred blood blood of one's relatives   **185 compare between** draw comparisons.   **187 pleased** satisfied   **188 withal** with that, nonetheless.   **190 royalties** privileges granted through the King and belonging, in this case, to a member of the royal family   **195 Take . . . and take** i.e., If you take . . . you take   **196 His** Time's   **197 ensue** follow   **202–4 Call . . . livery** i.e., revoke the royal grant giving him the privilege to sue through his attorneys for possession of his inheritance   **204 deny** refuse.   **homage** avowal of allegiance (by which ceremony Bolingbroke would be able legally to secure his inheritance)   **207 prick** i.e., incite   **211 by** nearby, present   **213 by** concerning.   **may** it may   **214 events** outcomes   **215 Earl of Wiltshire** (The King's Lord Treasurer and one of his notorious favorites.)   **216 repair** come   **217 see** see to.   **Tomorrow next** Tomorrow   **218 trow** believe.

223.2 Manet He remains onstage   **228 great** i.e., great with sorrow   **229 liberal** unrestrained, freely speaking   **230 ne'er speak more** i.e., die   **232 Tends . . . to** Does what you wish to say concern   **237 gelded** i.e., deprived. (Literally, castrated.)   **239 In him** in his case, or, by him   **242 inform** charge, report as spies   **243 Merely in hate** out of pure hatred   **246 pilled** plundered   **250 blanks** blank charters.   **benevolences** forced loans to the crown (not actually employed until considerably later, in 1473).   **wot** know   **251 this** i.e., this unjustly collected revenue.   **256 in farm** on lease.

WILLOUGHBY
The King's grown bankrupt, like a broken man.   257

NORTHUMBERLAND
Reproach and dissolution hangeth over him.

ROSS
He hath not money for these Irish wars,
His burdenous taxations notwithstanding,
But by the robbing of the banished Duke.

NORTHUMBERLAND
His noble kinsman. Most degenerate king!
But, lords, we hear this fearful tempest sing,
Yet seek no shelter to avoid the storm;
We see the wind sit sore upon our sails,   265
And yet we strike not, but securely perish.   266

ROSS
We see the very wrack that we must suffer,   267
And unavoided is the danger now   268
For suffering so the causes of our wrack.   269

NORTHUMBERLAND
Not so. Even through the hollow eyes of death   270
I spy life peering; but I dare not say
How near the tidings of our comfort is.

WILLOUGHBY
Nay, let us share thy thoughts, as thou dost ours.

ROSS
Be confident to speak, Northumberland.
We three are but thyself, and speaking so
Thy words are but as thoughts. Therefore be bold.

NORTHUMBERLAND
Then thus: I have from Port le Blanc,
A bay in Brittany, received intelligence
That Harry Duke of Hereford, Rainold Lord Cobham,
. . . .   280
That late broke from the Duke of Exeter,   281
His brother, Archbishop late of Canterbury,   282
Sir Thomas Erpingham, Sir John Ramston,
Sir John Norbery, Sir Robert Waterton, and Francis
    Coint,
All these well furnished by the Duke of Brittany
With eight tall ships, three thousand men of war,   286
Are making hither with all due expedience   287
And shortly mean to touch our northern shore.
Perhaps they had ere this, but that they stay   289
The first departing of the King for Ireland.   290
If then we shall shake off our slavish yoke,

Imp out our drooping country's broken wing,   292
Redeem from broking pawn the blemished crown,   293
Wipe off the dust that hides our scepter's gilt,   294
And make high majesty look like itself,
Away with me in post to Ravenspurgh;   296
But if you faint, as fearing to do so,   297
Stay and be secret, and myself will go.

ROSS
To horse, to horse! Urge doubts to them that fear.

WILLOUGHBY
Hold out my horse, and I will first be there.   *Exeunt.* 300

❖

[2.2]

Enter the Queen, Bushy, [and] Bagot.

BUSHY
Madam, Your Majesty is too much sad.
You promised, when you parted with the King,   2
To lay aside life-harming heaviness   3
And entertain a cheerful disposition.   4

QUEEN
To please the King I did; to please myself
I cannot do it. Yet I know no cause
Why I should welcome such a guest as grief,
Save bidding farewell to so sweet a guest
As my sweet Richard. Yet again methinks
Some unborn sorrow ripe in Fortune's womb
Is coming towards me, and my inward soul
With nothing trembles. At something it grieves
More than with parting from my lord the King.

BUSHY
Each substance of a grief hath twenty shadows,   14
Which shows like grief itself but is not so;
For sorrow's eyes, glazèd with blinding tears,
Divides one thing entire to many objects,   17
Like perspectives, which rightly gazed upon   18
Show nothing but confusion, eyed awry   19
Distinguish form. So your sweet Majesty,   20
Looking awry upon your lord's departure,   21
Find shapes of grief more than himself to wail,   22
Which, looked on as it is, is naught but shadows
Of what it is not. Then, thrice-gracious Queen,

---

257 **broken** financially ruined   265 **sore** sorely, grievously   266 **strike** (1) furl the sails (2) strike blows.   **securely** heedlessly, overconfidently   267 **wrack** ruin   268 **unavoided** unavoidable   269 **suffering** permitting   270 **eyes** eye sockets   280 . . . (A line is probably missing here, perhaps because of censorship. From information contained in Holinshed, it may have read something like "Thomas, son and heir to the Earl of Arundel" or "The son of Richard, Earl of Arundel.")   281 **late broke from** lately escaped from the custody of. (Holinshed records that "the Earl of Arundel's son, named Thomas, which was kept in the Duke of Exeter's house, escaped out of the realm . . . and went to his uncle Thomas Arundel, late Archbishop of Canterbury.")   282 **His** i.e., the Earl of Arundel's.   **late** until recently   286 **tall** stately.   **men of war** troops   287 **expedience** expedition, speed   289–90 **stay . . . King** wait until the King departs

292 **Imp out** piece out. (A term from falconry, meaning to attach new feathers to a disabled wing of a bird.)   293 **from broking pawn** from being pledged to pawnbrokers   294 **gilt** gold (with pun on *guilt*)   296 **past** haste.   **Ravenspurgh** on the Yorkshire coast, at the mouth of the Humber River   297 **faint** are fainthearted   300 **Hold . . . and** If my horse holds out
2.2 **Location: The court. According to Holinshed, the Queen remained at Windsor Castle when Richard left for Ireland.**
2 **with** from   3 **heaviness** melancholy   4 **entertain** put on   14 **Each . . . shadows** i.e., For every real grief there exist twenty imagined ones   17 **thing entire to** complete thing into   18 **perspectives** (In lines 16–17, Bushy seems to have in mind a glass with a multifaceted lens, multiplying images of the object being viewed; in lines 18–20, *perspectives* are pictures of figures made to appear distorted or confused, except when viewed obliquely, *eyed awry*.)   **rightly** directly, straight   19 **awry** obliquely   20 **Distinguish form** make the form distinct and normal.   21 **awry** i.e., mistakenly, distortedly   22 **himself** i.e., the grief itself.   **wail** bewail

More than your lord's departure weep not. More is not
   seen,
Or if it be, 'tis with false sorrow's eye,
Which for things true weeps things imaginary.   27

QUEEN
It may be so, but yet my inward soul
Persuades me it is otherwise. Howe'er it be,
I cannot but be sad—so heavy sad
As, though on thinking on no thought I think,   31
Makes me with heavy nothing faint and shrink.   32

BUSHY
'Tis nothing but conceit, my gracious lady.   33

QUEEN
'Tis nothing less. Conceit is still derived   34
From some forefather grief. Mine is not so,
For nothing hath begot my something grief,   36
Or something hath the nothing that I grieve.   37
'Tis in reversion that I do possess;   38
But what it is, that is not yet known what,   39
I cannot name. 'Tis nameless woe, I wot.   40

      [Enter Green.]

GREEN
God save Your Majesty! And well met, gentlemen.
I hope the King is not yet shipped for Ireland.

QUEEN
Why hopest thou so? 'Tis better hope he is,
For his designs crave haste, his haste good hope.   44
Then wherefore dost thou hope he is not shipped?

GREEN
That he, our hope, might have retired his power,   46
And driven into despair an enemy's hope,
Who strongly hath set footing in this land.
The banished Bolingbroke repeals himself   49
And with uplifted arms is safe arrived   50
At Ravenspurgh.

QUEEN   Now God in heaven forbid!

GREEN
Ah, madam, 'tis too true; and that is worse,   52
The lord Northumberland, his son young Harry
   Percy,
The lords of Ross, Beaumont, and Willoughby,
With all their powerful friends, are fled to him.

BUSHY
Why have you not proclaimed Northumberland
And all the rest revolted faction traitors?   57

GREEN
We have, whereupon the Earl of Worcester
Hath broken his staff, resigned his stewardship,   59
And all the household servants fled with him
To Bolingbroke.

QUEEN
So, Green, thou art the midwife to my woe,
And Bolingbroke my sorrow's dismal heir.   63
Now hath my soul brought forth her prodigy,   64
And I, a gasping new-delivered mother,
Have woe to woe, sorrow to sorrow joined.

BUSHY
Despair not, madam.

QUEEN   Who shall hinder me?
I will despair, and be at enmity
With cozening hope. He is a flatterer,   69
A parasite, a keeper-back of death
Who gently would dissolve the bonds of life   71
Which false hope lingers in extremity.   72

      [Enter York.]

GREEN   Here comes the Duke of York.

QUEEN
With signs of war about his agèd neck.   74
Oh, full of careful business are his looks!   75
Uncle, for God's sake, speak comfortable words.   76

YORK
Should I do so, I should belie my thoughts.
Comfort's in heaven, and we are on the earth,
Where nothing lives but crosses, cares, and grief.   79
Your husband, he is gone to save far off,   80
Whilst others come to make him lose at home.
Here am I left to underprop his land,   82
Who, weak with age, cannot support myself.
Now comes the sick hour that his surfeit made;
Now shall he try his friends that flattered him.   85

      [Enter a Servingman.]

SERVINGMAN
My lord, your son was gone before I came.   86

YORK
He was? Why, so. Go all which way it will!
The nobles they are fled, the commons they are cold,
And will, I fear, revolt on Hereford's side.
Sirrah, get thee to Pleshey, to my sister Gloucester;   90
Bid her send me presently a thousand pound.   91
Hold, take my ring.   92

---

27 for in place of. **weeps** weeps for **31–2 As . . . shrink** that, though I seem to be thinking of nothing, my "nothing" is so *heavy* or saddening that I faint and fall back under the weight. **33 conceit** fancy **34 'Tis nothing less** i.e., It is anything but that. **still** always **36 something** i.e., substantial **37 something . . . grieve** the unsubstantial grief, the nothing, that I grieve about has something to it, some substance. **38–40 'Tis . . . name** i.e., My grief is like a legacy that will come to me at some future time, but I cannot tell its nature yet. **40 wot** know, assume. **44 For . . . hope** for his plans require that he proceed expeditiously to Ireland, and with our hopes that his haste bring success. **46 retired his power** held back his army (in order to be able to repulse Bolingbroke's landing) **49 repeals** recalls (from exile) **50 uplifted arms** brandished weapons **52 that** what **57 rest** rest of the

59 broken his staff broken his badge of office (in token of resignation as Lord High Steward. Worcester is brother of the Earl of Northumberland.) **63 dismal heir** ill-omened offspring. **64 prodigy** monstrous birth **69 cozening** cheating. **He** i.e., False hope **71 Who** i.e., death **72 lingers** causes to linger **74 signs of war** i.e., a piece of armor called the gorget, an iron collar that could be worn with ordinary clothes **75 careful business** worried preoccupation **76 comfortable** affording comfort **79 crosses** obstacles, obstructions **80 save far off** i.e., defend his rule in Ireland **82 underprop** prop up, support **85 try** test **86 your son** i.e., the Duke of Aumerle **90 Sirrah** (Said to inferiors.) **sister** sister-in-law **91 presently** immediately **92 ring** (By which the Duchess will know that the request is sent by York himself.)

SERVINGMAN
My lord, I had forgot to tell Your Lordship:
Today, as I came by, I callèd there—
But I shall grieve you to report the rest.
YORK What is't, knave?   96
SERVINGMAN
An hour before I came, the Duchess died.
YORK
God for his mercy, what a tide of woes
Comes rushing on this woeful land at once!
I know not what to do. I would to God,
So my untruth had not provoked him to it,   101
The King had cut off my head with my brother's.   102
What, are there no posts dispatched for Ireland?
How shall we do for money for these wars?
Come, sister—cousin, I would say—pray pardon
     me.—
Go, fellow, get thee home. Provide some carts
And bring away the armor that is there.
                              [Exit Servingman.]
Gentlemen, will you go muster men?
If I know how or which way to order these affairs
Thus disorderly thrust into my hands,
Never believe me. Both are my kinsmen:
Th'one is my sovereign, whom both my oath
And duty bids defend; t'other again
Is my kinsman, whom the King hath wronged,
Whom conscience and my kindred bids to right.   115
Well, somewhat we must do.—Come, cousin,   116
I'll dispose of you.—Gentlemen,   117
Go, muster up your men, and meet me presently
At Berkeley. I should to Pleshey too,   119
But time will not permit. All is uneven,
And everything is left at six and seven.   121
                    Exeunt Duke [of York], Queen.
                    Manent Bushy, [Bagot,] Green.

BUSHY
The wind sits fair for news to go to Ireland,
But none returns. For us to levy power
Proportionable to the enemy
Is all unpossible.
GREEN
Besides, our nearness to the King in love
Is near the hate of those love not the King.   127
BAGOT
And that is the wavering commons, for their love
Lies in their purses, and whoso empties them
By so much fills their hearts with deadly hate.
BUSHY
Wherein the King stands generally condemned.

BAGOT
If judgment lie in them, then so do we,   132
Because we ever have been near the King.   133
GREEN
Well, I will for refuge straight to Bristol Castle.
The Earl of Wiltshire is already there.
BUSHY
Thither will I with you, for little office   136
Will the hateful commons perform for us,   137
Except like curs to tear us all to pieces.
[To Bagot] Will you go along with us?
BAGOT
No, I will to Ireland to His Majesty.
Farewell. If heart's presages be not vain,   141
We three here part that ne'er shall meet again.
BUSHY
That's as York thrives to beat back Bolingbroke.   143
GREEN
Alas, poor duke! The task he undertakes
Is numbering sands and drinking oceans dry.
Where one on his side fights, thousands will fly.
Farewell at once, for once, for all, and ever.
BUSHY
Well, we may meet again.
BAGOT   I fear me, never.
                                   [Exeunt.]

❦

[2.3]

Enter [Bolingbroke, Duke of] Hereford, [and]
Northumberland [with forces].

BOLINGBROKE
How far is it, my lord, to Berkeley now?
NORTHUMBERLAND Believe me, noble lord,
I am a stranger here in Gloucestershire.
These high wild hills and rough uneven ways
Draws out our miles and makes them wearisome;
And yet your fair discourse hath been as sugar,
Making the hard way sweet and delectable.
But I bethink me what a weary way
From Ravenspurgh to Cotswold will be found   9
In Ross and Willoughby, wanting your company,   10
Which, I protest, hath very much beguiled   11
The tediousness and process of my travel.   12
But theirs is sweetened with the hope to have
The present benefit which I possess;
And hope to joy is little less in joy   15
Than hope enjoyed. By this the weary lords   16

132 If . . . we i.e., If the power to pass judgment is given to the wavering commons, then we, too, stand condemned   133 ever always
136 office service   137 hateful full of hate, angry   141 vain in
vain   143 That's . . . thrives i.e., That depends upon York's efforts
and success
2.3 Location: In Gloucestershire, near Berkeley Castle.
9 Cotswold hilly district in Gloucestershire   10 In by. wanting
lacking   11 protest declare   12 tediousness and process tedious
process   15–16 And hope . . . enjoyed and the hope of future happiness is only slightly less joyous than happiness already enjoyed.
16 this this expectation

96 knave i.e., fellow.   101 So my untruth provided that my disloyalty   102 brother's i.e., the Duke of Gloucester's.   115 my . . . right
my kinship to him bids that I right his wrong.   116 somewhat something.   cousin i.e., the Queen   117 dispose of make arrangements
for   119 Berkeley a castle near Bristol.   121 at six and seven i.e., in
confusion.   121.2 Manent They remain onstage   127 Is . . . King
makes us enemies of those who oppose the King.

Shall make their way seem short, as mine hath done
By sight of what I have: your noble company.

BOLINGBROKE
Of much less value is my company
Than your good words. But who comes here?

Enter Harry Percy.

NORTHUMBERLAND
It is my son, young Harry Percy,
Sent from my brother Worcester whencesoever.—   22
Harry, how fares your uncle?   23

PERCY
I had thought, my lord, to have learned his health of
   you.

NORTHUMBERLAND   Why, is he not with the Queen?

PERCY
No, my good lord. He hath forsook the court,
Broken his staff of office, and dispersed
The household of the King.

NORTHUMBERLAND   What was his reason?
He was not so resolved when last we spake together.

PERCY
Because Your Lordship was proclaimèd traitor.
But he, my lord, is gone to Ravenspurgh
To offer service to the Duke of Hereford,
And sent me over by Berkeley to discover
What power the Duke of York had levied there,   34
Then with directions to repair to Ravenspurgh.   35

NORTHUMBERLAND
Have you forgot the Duke of Hereford, boy?   36

PERCY
No, my good lord, for that is not forgot
Which ne'er I did remember. To my knowledge
I never in my life did look on him.

NORTHUMBERLAND
Then learn to know him now. This is the Duke.

PERCY
My gracious lord, I tender you my service,   41
Such as it is, being tender, raw, and young,
Which elder days shall ripen and confirm
To more approvèd service and desert.   44

BOLINGBROKE
I thank thee, gentle Percy, and be sure
I count myself in nothing else so happy
As in a soul rememb'ring my good friends;   47
And as my fortune ripens with thy love,   48
It shall be still thy true love's recompense.   49
My heart this covenant makes, my hand thus seals it.
                [*He offers Percy his hand.*]

NORTHUMBERLAND
How far is it to Berkeley? And what stir   51
Keeps good old York there with his men of war?

PERCY
There stands the castle by yon tuft of trees,
Manned with three hundred men, as I have heard,
And in it are the lords of York, Berkeley, and Seymour,
None else of name and noble estimate.   56

[*Enter Ross and Willoughby.*]

NORTHUMBERLAND
Here come the lords of Ross and Willoughby,
Bloody with spurring, fiery red with haste.   58

BOLINGBROKE
Welcome, my lords. I wot your love pursues   59
A banished traitor. All my treasury
Is yet but unfelt thanks, which, more enriched,   61
Shall be your love and labor's recompense.

ROSS
Your presence makes us rich, most noble lord.

WILLOUGHBY
And far surmounts our labor to attain it.

BOLINGBROKE
Evermore thank's the exchequer of the poor,   65
Which, till my infant fortune comes to years,   66
Stands for my bounty. But who comes here?   67

[*Enter Berkeley.*]

NORTHUMBERLAND
It is my lord of Berkeley, as I guess.

BERKELEY
My lord of Hereford, my message is to you.

BOLINGBROKE
My lord, my answer is—to "Lancaster";   70
And I am come to seek that name in England,
And I must find that title in your tongue
Before I make reply to aught you say.

BERKELEY
Mistake me not, my lord, 'tis not my meaning
To raze one title of your honor out.   75
To you, my lord, I come, what lord you will,   76
From the most gracious regent of this land,
The Duke of York, to know what pricks you on   78
To take advantage of the absent time   79
And fright our native peace with self-borne arms.   80

[*Enter York.*]

---

22 whencesoever from wherever he is.   **23 your uncle** i.e., the Earl of Worcester.   **34 power** troops   **35 directions** instructions.   **repair** go **36 boy** (A rebuke for not respectfully greeting Bolingbroke, though historically Percy was two years Bolingbroke's senior.)   **41 tender** offer. (With a pun in the next line on the meaning "inexperienced.") **my service** (Presumably Percy kneels to Bolingbroke, and so do Ross and Willoughby when they enter.)   **44 approvèd** proven, demonstrated   **47 in a** in my   **48–9 And . . . recompense** and as my fortunes improve, assisted by your loyalty to me, I will be increasingly enabled to reward you for that loyalty.

51 stir action   **56 estimate** rank.   **58 spurring** i.e., hard riding **59 wot** am aware that. (Bolingbroke graciously indicates his awareness of the risk they are taking in supporting him.)   **61 unfelt** impalpable, expressed in words, not gifts.   **which** i.e., which treasury. **more enriched** i.e., with still more thanks added, or, with substantial gifts at a later date   **65 Evermore . . . poor** "Thank you" is always the exchequer of the poor, i.e., the only means they have to repay favors **66 comes to years** reaches maturity   **67 Stands for** serves in place of **70 "Lancaster"** (Bolingbroke will enter into no negotiations unless his proper title, taken away by Richard, is given him.)   **75 raze** scrape (or perhaps *rase*, "erase")   **76 what . . . will** whatever title you prefer to be addressed by. (Said sardonically.)   **78 pricks** spurs   **79 the absent time** i.e., the time of the King's absence   **80 self-borne** borne in your own private cause, not the country's welfare. (Also suggesting *self-born*, "originating in the self.")

BOLINGBROKE
I shall not need transport my words by you;
Here comes His Grace in person.—My noble uncle!

[*He kneels.*]

YORK
Show me thy humble heart, and not thy knee,
Whose duty is deceivable and false.   84

BOLINGBROKE   My gracious uncle—

YORK   Tut, tut!
Grace me no grace, nor uncle me no uncle.
I am no traitor's uncle; and that word "grace"
In an ungracious mouth is but profane.
Why have those banished and forbidden legs
Dared once to touch a dust of England's ground?   91
But then more "why?" Why have they dared to march
So many miles upon her peaceful bosom,
Frighting her pale-faced villages with war
And ostentation of despisèd arms?   95
Com'st thou because the anointed King is hence?
Why, foolish boy, the King is left behind,
And in my loyal bosom lies his power.
Were I but now the lord of such hot youth
As when brave Gaunt, thy father, and myself
Rescued the Black Prince, that young Mars of men,   101
From forth the ranks of many thousand French,
Oh, then how quickly should this arm of mine,
Now prisoner to the palsy, chastise thee
And minister correction to thy fault!   105

BOLINGBROKE
My gracious uncle, let me know my fault.
On what condition stands it and wherein?   107

YORK
Even in condition of the worst degree:
In gross rebellion and detested treason.
Thou art a banished man, and here art come
Before the expiration of thy time
In braving arms against thy sovereign.   112

BOLINGBROKE [*standing*]
As I was banished, I was banished Hereford;
But as I come, I come for Lancaster.   114
And, noble uncle, I beseech Your Grace
Look on my wrongs with an indifferent eye.   116
You are my father, for methinks in you
I see old Gaunt alive. Oh, then, my father,
Will you permit that I shall stand condemned   119
A wandering vagabond, my rights and royalties   120
Plucked from my arms perforce and given away
To upstart unthrifts? Wherefore was I born?   122
If that my cousin king be King in England,
It must be granted I am Duke of Lancaster.
You have a son, Aumerle, my noble cousin;

Had you first died, and he been thus trod down,   126
He should have found his uncle Gaunt a father
To rouse his wrongs and chase them to the bay.   128
I am denied to sue my livery here,   129
And yet my letters patents give me leave.   130
My father's goods are all distrained and sold,   131
And these, and all, are all amiss employed.
What would you have me do? I am a subject,
And I challenge law. Attorneys are denied me,   134
And therefore personally I lay my claim
To my inheritance of free descent.   136

NORTHUMBERLAND
The noble Duke hath been too much abused.

ROSS
It stands Your Grace upon to do him right.   138

WILLOUGHBY
Base men by his endowments are made great.   139

YORK
My lords of England, let me tell you this:
I have had feeling of my cousin's wrongs   141
And labored all I could to do him right;
But in this kind to come, in braving arms,   143
Be his own carver, and cut out his way   144
To find out right with wrong—it may not be;
And you that do abet him in this kind
Cherish rebellion and are rebels all.

NORTHUMBERLAND
The noble Duke hath sworn his coming is
But for his own, and for the right of that
We all have strongly sworn to give him aid;
And let him never see joy that breaks that oath!   151

YORK
Well, well, I see the issue of these arms.   152
I cannot mend it, I must needs confess,
Because my power is weak and all ill-left;   154
But if I could, by Him that gave me life,
I would attach you all and make you stoop   156
Unto the sovereign mercy of the King.
But since I cannot, be it known unto you
I do remain as neuter. So fare you well—   159
Unless you please to enter in the castle
And there repose you for this night.

BOLINGBROKE
An offer, uncle, that we will accept.
But we must win Your Grace to go with us   163
To Bristol Castle, which they say is held
By Bushy, Bagot, and their complices,   165

---

84 **duty** gesture of obeisance.   **deceivable** deceitful, deceptive
91 **dust** particle of dust   95 **ostentation** display.   **despisèd** despicable   101 **the Black Prince** i.e., Edward, the eldest son of Edward III and King Richard's father   105 **minister** administer   107 **condition** defect in me, or provision of the law.   **wherein** in what does it consist.   112 **braving** defiant (also at line 143)   114 **for Lancaster** i.e., under the title of Lancaster and in order to claim it.   116 **indifferent** impartial   119 **condemned** condemned as   120 **royalties** privileges granted by the King   122 **unthrifts** spendthrifts.

126 **first** i.e., before Gaunt   128 **rouse** chase from cover, expose.   **the bay** the extremity where the hunted animal turns on its pursuers.
129 **I am . . . here** I am denied the right to sue for possession of hereditary rights in England. (See 2.1.202–4 and note.)   130 **letters patents** i.e., letters from the King indicating a subject's legal rights
131 **distrained** seized officially   134 **challenge law** claim my legal rights.   136 **of free descent** by legal succession.   138 **stands . . . upon** is incumbent upon Your Grace   139 **his endowments** i.e., the properties that rightly belong to Bolingbroke   141 **cousin's** nephew's   143 **kind** fashion   144 **Be . . . carver** i.e., act on his own authority, help himself   151 **joy** i.e., the joy of heaven   152 **issue** outcome   154 **power** army.   **ill-left** left in dismay and with inadequate means   156 **attach** arrest   159 **as neuter** neutral.   163 **win** persuade   165 **Bagot** (According to 2.2.140, Bagot had gone to Ireland.)

The caterpillars of the commonwealth,
Which I have sworn to weed and pluck away.

YORK
It may be I will go with you; but yet I'll pause,
For I am loath to break our country's laws.
Nor friends nor foes, to me welcome you are.   170
Things past redress are now with me past care.
                                                    Exeunt.

❧

[2.4]

Enter Earl of Salisbury and a Welsh Captain.

WELSH CAPTAIN
My lord of Salisbury, we have stayed ten days   1
And hardly kept our countrymen together,   2
And yet we hear no tidings from the King.   3
Therefore we will disperse ourselves. Farewell.

SALISBURY
Stay yet another day, thou trusty Welshman.
The King reposeth all his confidence in thee.

WELSH CAPTAIN
'Tis thought the King is dead. We will not stay.
The bay trees in our country are all withered,
And meteors fright the fixèd stars of heaven;
The pale-faced moon looks bloody on the earth,
And lean-looked prophets whisper fearful change;   11
Rich men look sad, and ruffians dance and leap,
The one in fear to lose what they enjoy,
The other to enjoy by rage and war.   14
These signs forerun the death or fall of kings.   15
Farewell. Our countrymen are gone and fled,
As well assured Richard their king is dead. [*Exit.*] 17

SALISBURY
Ah, Richard! With the eyes of heavy mind
I see thy glory like a shooting star
Fall to the base earth from the firmament.
Thy sun sets weeping in the lowly west,
Witnessing storms to come, woe, and unrest.   22
Thy friends are fled to wait upon thy foes,   23
And crossly to thy good all fortune goes.   [*Exit.*]   24

❧

[3.1]

*Enter [Bolingbroke,] Duke of Hereford, York,
Northumberland, [with] Bushy and Green,
prisoners.*

BOLINGBROKE   Bring forth these men.
Bushy and Green, I will not vex your souls—
Since presently your souls must part your bodies—   3
With too much urging your pernicious lives,   4

For 'twere no charity; yet, to wash your blood
From off my hands, here in the view of men
I will unfold some causes of your deaths.   7
You have misled a prince, a royal king,
A happy gentleman in blood and lineaments,   9
By you unhappied and disfigured clean.   10
You have in manner with your sinful hours   11
Made a divorce betwixt his queen and him,
Broke the possession of a royal bed,
And stained the beauty of a fair queen's cheeks
With tears drawn from her eyes by your foul wrongs.
Myself—a prince by fortune of my birth,
Near to the King in blood, and near in love
Till you did make him misinterpret me—
Have stooped my neck under your injuries
And sighed my English breath in foreign clouds,   20
Eating the bitter bread of banishment,
Whilst you have fed upon my seigniories,   22
Disparked my parks and felled my forest woods,   23
From my own windows torn my household coat,   24
Razed my imprese, leaving me no sign,   25
Save men's opinions and my living blood,
To show the world I am a gentleman.
This and much more, much more than twice all this,
Condemns you to the death.—See them delivered
    over
To execution and the hand of death.

BUSHY
More welcome is the stroke of death to me
Than Bolingbroke to England. Lords, farewell.

GREEN
My comfort is that heaven will take our souls
And plague injustice with the pains of hell.

BOLINGBROKE
My lord Northumberland, see them dispatched.
    [*Exeunt Northumberland with the prisoners, guarded.*]
Uncle, you say the Queen is at your house.
For God's sake, fairly let her be entreated.   37
Tell her I send to her my kind commends.   38
Take special care my greetings be delivered.

YORK
A gentleman of mine I have dispatched
With letters of your love to her at large.   41

BOLINGBROKE
Thanks, gentle uncle. Come, lords, away,
To fight with Glendower and his complices.   43
Awhile to work, and after holiday.   *Exeunt.*   44

❧

170 **Nor** Neither as
2.4 Location: A camp in Wales.
1 **stayed** waited 2 **hardly** with difficulty 3 **yet** still 11 **lean-looked**
lean-looking 14 **to . . . rage** in hopes of possessing by violence
15 **forerun** anticipate 17 **As** as being 22 **Witnessing** betokening
23 **wait upon** attend, offer allegiance to 24 **crossly** adversely
3.1 Location: Bristol. The castle.
3 **presently** immediately 4 **urging** emphasizing as reasons (for your
executions)

7 **unfold** reveal 9 **happy** fortunate. **blood and lineaments** birth
and natural characteristics 10 **By . . . clean** by you made wretched
and wholly marred in reputation. 11 **in manner** as it were 20 **foreign clouds** i.e., the air of foreign lands (and adding to the clouds
with sighs) 22 **seigniories** estates 23 **Disparked** thrown open to
uses other than hunting and forestry 24 **household coat** coat of
arms (frequently emblazoned on stained or painted windows)
25 **Razed** scraped (or perhaps *rased,* "erased"). **imprese** heraldic
device, emblematic design 37 **entreated** treated. 38 **commends**
regards, compliments 41 **at large** conveyed in full. 43 **Glendower**
(Owen Glendower was not, according to Holinshed's *Chronicles,* at this
time in arms against Bolingbroke. Possibly he is to be identified here
with the Welsh captain of the preceding scene.) 44 **after** afterwards

[3.2]

[Drums. Flourish and colors.] Enter the King,
Aumerle, [the Bishop of] Carlisle, etc. [with
soldiers].

KING RICHARD
Barkloughly Castle call they this at hand?   1
AUMERLE
Yea, my lord. How brooks Your Grace the air   2
After your late tossing on the breaking seas?   3
KING RICHARD
Needs must I like it well. I weep for joy   4
To stand upon my kingdom once again.
Dear earth, I do salute thee with my hand,
        [He bends and touches the ground.]
Though rebels wound thee with their horses' hoofs.
As a long-parted mother with her child   8
Plays fondly with her tears and smiles in meeting,
So, weeping, smiling, greet I thee, my earth,
And do thee favors with my royal hands.
Feed not thy sovereign's foe, my gentle earth,
Nor with thy sweets comfort his ravenous sense,   13
But let thy spiders, that suck up thy venom,   14
And heavy-gaited toads lie in their way,   15
Doing annoyance to the treacherous feet
Which with usurping steps do trample thee.
Yield stinging nettles to mine enemies;
And when they from thy bosom pluck a flower,
Guard it, I pray thee, with a lurking adder,
Whose double tongue may with a mortal touch   21
Throw death upon thy sovereign's enemies.—
Mock not my senseless conjuration, lords.   23
This earth shall have a feeling, and these stones
Prove armèd soldiers, ere her native king   25
Shall falter under foul rebellion's arms.
CARLISLE
Fear not, my lord. That Power that made you king
Hath power to keep you king in spite of all.
The means that heavens yield must be embraced
And not neglected; else heaven would,   30
And we will not. Heaven's offer we refuse,   31
The proffered means of succor and redress.   32
AUMERLE
He means, my lord, that we are too remiss,
Whilst Bolingbroke through our security   34
Grows strong and great in substance and in power.
KING RICHARD
Discomfortable cousin, know'st thou not   36

That when the searching eye of heaven is hid   37
Behind the globe that lights the lower world,   38
Then thieves and robbers range abroad unseen
In murders and in outrage boldly here;
But when from under this terrestrial ball   41
He fires the proud tops of the eastern pines   42
And darts his light through every guilty hole,
Then murders, treasons, and detested sins,
The cloak of night being plucked from off their backs,
Stand bare and naked, trembling at themselves?   46
So when this thief, this traitor, Bolingbroke,
Who all this while hath reveled in the night
Whilst we were wand'ring with the Antipodes,   49
Shall see us rising in our throne, the east,
His treasons will sit blushing in his face,
Not able to endure the sight of day,
But, self-affrighted, tremble at his sin.
Not all the water in the rough rude sea
Can wash the balm off from an anointed king;   55
The breath of worldly men cannot depose   56
The deputy elected by the Lord.   57
For every man that Bolingbroke hath pressed   58
To lift shrewd steel against our golden crown,   59
God for his Richard hath in heavenly pay
A glorious angel. Then, if angels fight,
Weak men must fall, for heaven still guards the right.   62

    Enter Salisbury.

Welcome, my lord. How far off lies your power?
SALISBURY
Nor near nor farther off, my gracious lord,   64
Than this weak arm. Discomfort guides my tongue   65
And bids me speak of nothing but despair.
One day too late, I fear me, noble lord,
Hath clouded all thy happy days on earth.
Oh, call back yesterday, bid time return,
And thou shalt have twelve thousand fighting men!
Today, today, unhappy day too late,
O'erthrows thy joys, friends, fortune, and thy state;   72
For all the Welshmen, hearing thou wert dead,
Are gone to Bolingbroke, dispersed, and fled.
AUMERLE
Comfort, my liege. Why looks Your Grace so pale?
KING RICHARD
But now the blood of twenty thousand men   76
   Did triumph in my face, and they are fled;   77
And till so much blood thither come again,
   Have I not reason to look pale and dead?   79

3.2. Location: The coast of Wales, near Harlech Castle.
1 Barkloughly i.e., Harlech **2 brooks** enjoys **3 late** recent **4 Needs
must** Necessarily **8 a long-parted mother with** a mother long
parted from **13 sweets** i.e., bounty. **sense** appetite **14 suck . . .
venom** (Alludes to the belief that spiders drew their poison from the
earth.) **15 heavy-gaited** lumbering, clumsy **21 double** forked.
mortal deadly **23 senseless conjuration** solemn entreaty of senseless things; or, one that makes no sense to you, being so fanciful
25 native entitled (to the crown) by birth, rightful. (Richard was born
at Bordeaux.) **30–1 else . . . not** i.e., otherwise, we spurn heaven's
will. **32 succor and redress** help and remedy. **34 security** overconfidence **36 Discomfortable** Disheartening, discouraging

37–8 when . . . world i.e., when the sun is hid behind the earth, lighting its lower side **41 this terrestrial ball** the earth **42 He fires** the
sun lights up. (Literally, "sets on fire.") **46 at themselves** i.e., at
being caught in their crimes. **49 Antipodes** people on the other side
of the world; here, the Irish. (A geographical hyperbole.) **55 balm**
consecrated oil used in anointing a king **56 worldly** earthly
57 elected chosen **58 pressed** impressed, forced into the ranks
59 shrewd keen, biting **62 still** always **64 Nor near** Neither nearer
65 Discomfort Discouragement **72 state** royal power **76 But now**
Even now. **twenty** (A seeming discrepancy with *twelve* in line 70;
perhaps the result of Richard's hyperbole.) **77 triumph** i.e., shine
forth **79 pale and dead** deathly pale.

All souls that will be safe, fly from my side,
For time hath set a blot upon my pride.   81

AUMERLE

Comfort, my liege. Remember who you are.

KING RICHARD

I had forgot myself. Am I not king?
Awake, thou coward majesty, thou sleepest!
Is not the king's name twenty thousand names?
Arm, arm, my name! A puny subject strikes
At thy great glory. Look not to the ground,
Ye favorites of a king. Are we not high?
High be our thoughts. I know my uncle York
Hath power enough to serve our turn. But who comes
here?

Enter Scroop.

SCROOP

More health and happiness betide my liege   91
Than can my care-tuned tongue deliver him!   92

KING RICHARD

Mine ear is open and my heart prepared.
The worst is worldly loss thou canst unfold.   94
Say, is my kingdom lost? Why, 'twas my care,   95
And what loss is it to be rid of care?
Strives Bolingbroke to be as great as we?
Greater he shall not be; if he serve God,
We'll serve Him too, and be his fellow so.   99
Revolt our subjects? That we cannot mend;
They break their faith to God as well as us.
Cry woe, destruction, ruin, and decay;
The worst is death, and death will have his day.

SCROOP

Glad am I that Your Highness is so armed   104
To bear the tidings of calamity.
Like an unseasonable stormy day,
Which makes the silver rivers drown their shores
As if the world were all dissolved to tears,
So high above his limits swells the rage   109
Of Bolingbroke, covering your fearful land   110
With hard bright steel and hearts harder than steel.
Whitebeards have armed their thin and hairless scalps 112
Against Thy Majesty; boys with women's voices
Strive to speak big, and clap their female joints   114
In stiff unwieldy arms against thy crown.   115
Thy very beadsmen learn to bend their bows   116
Of double-fatal yew against thy state;   117

Yea, distaff-women manage rusty bills   118
Against thy seat. Both young and old rebel,   119
And all goes worse than I have power to tell.

KING RICHARD

Too well, too well thou tell'st a tale so ill.
Where is the Earl of Wiltshire? Where is Bagot?   122
What is become of Bushy? Where is Green,
That they have let the dangerous enemy
Measure our confines with such peaceful steps?   125
If we prevail, their heads shall pay for it.
I warrant they have made peace with Bolingbroke.

SCROOP

Peace have they made with him indeed, my lord.

KING RICHARD

Oh, villains, vipers, damned without redemption!
Dogs easily won to fawn on any man!
Snakes in my heart-blood warmed, that sting my
heart!
Three Judases, each one thrice worse than Judas!
Would they make peace? Terrible hell
Make war upon their spotted souls for this!   134

SCROOP

Sweet love, I see, changing his property,   135
Turns to the sourest and most deadly hate.
Again uncurse their souls. Their peace is made
With heads and not with hands. Those whom you
curse   138
Have felt the worst of death's destroying wound
And lie full low, graved in the hollow ground.   140

AUMERLE

Is Bushy, Green, and the Earl of Wiltshire dead?

SCROOP

Ay, all of them at Bristol lost their heads.

AUMERLE

Where is the Duke my father with his power?

KING RICHARD

No matter where. Of comfort no man speak!
Let's talk of graves, of worms, and epitaphs,
Make dust our paper, and with rainy eyes
Write sorrow on the bosom of the earth.
Let's choose executors and talk of wills.
And yet not so, for what can we bequeath
Save our deposèd bodies to the ground?   150
Our lands, our lives, and all are Bolingbroke's,
And nothing can we call our own but death
And that small model of the barren earth   153
Which serves as paste and cover to our bones.   154
For God's sake, let us sit upon the ground

---

81 blot stain **91 More . . . betide** May more health and happiness befall **92 care-tuned** i.e., tuned by sorrow and to the key of sorrow. **deliver** deliver to **94 unfold** reveal. **95 care** trouble **99 his fellow** his (Bolingbroke's) equal **104 armed** prepared **109 his limits** (1) its banks (2) the limits properly allowed to Bolingbroke's rage **110 fearful** full of fears **112 Whitebeards** Old men. **thin** sparsely haired **114 Strive . . . joints** strive to speak with deep manlike voices, and thrust their adolescent limbs **115 arms** armor **116 beadsmen** old almsmen or pensioners whose duty it was to pray for a benefactor; here, for the King **117 double-fatal** doubly fatal (since the wood of the yew was used for bows and since its foliage and berries are poisonous; yews were also commonly planted in graveyards)

118–19 distaff-women . . . seat spinning women wield unused and hence rusty pikes (long-handled ax-like weapons) against your throne. **122 Bagot** (Although the King names Bagot here, he mentions only *three Judases* in line 132 and Aumerle does not ask about Bagot in line 141; in 3.4 we learn that Bagot is not executed along with the other three but reappears instead in 4.1.) **125 Measure our confines** travel over my kingdom. **peaceful** unopposed **134 spotted** stained with treason **135 his property** its distinctive quality **138 hands** (Used in swearing oaths, surrendering, etc.) **140 graved** buried **150 deposèd** (1) dethroned, as in 4.1 (2) deprived of those functions carried out by the body in this transitory life (3) deposited **153 model** microcosm or mold, i.e., the body **154 paste** pastry, pie crust

And tell sad stories of the death of kings—
How some have been deposed, some slain in war,
Some haunted by the ghosts they have deposed,   158
Some poisoned by their wives, some sleeping killed,
All murdered. For within the hollow crown
That rounds the mortal temples of a king   161
Keeps Death his court, and there the antic sits,   162
Scoffing his state and grinning at his pomp,   163
Allowing him a breath, a little scene,   164
To monarchize, be feared, and kill with looks,   165
Infusing him with self and vain conceit,   166
As if this flesh which walls about our life
Were brass impregnable; and humored thus,   168
Comes at the last and with a little pin
Bores through his castle wall, and—farewell, king!
Cover your heads, and mock not flesh and blood   171
With solemn reverence. Throw away respect,
Tradition, form, and ceremonious duty,
For you have but mistook me all this while.
I live with bread like you, feel want,
Taste grief, need friends. Subjected thus,   176
How can you say to me I am a king?

CARLISLE
My lord, wise men ne'er sit and wail their woes,
But presently prevent the ways to wail.   179
To fear the foe, since fear oppresseth strength,   180
Gives in your weakness strength unto your foe,   181
And so your follies fight against yourself.
Fear, and be slain. No worse can come to fight;   183
And fight and die is death destroying death,   184
Where fearing dying pays death servile breath.   185

AUMERLE
My father hath a power. Inquire of him,   186
And learn to make a body of a limb.   187

KING RICHARD
Thou chid'st me well. Proud Bolingbroke, I come
To change blows with thee for our day of doom.   189
This ague fit of fear is overblown;   190
An easy task it is to win our own.   191

Say, Scroop, where lies our uncle with his power?
Speak sweetly, man, although thy looks be sour.

SCROOP
Men judge by the complexion of the sky   194
    The state and inclination of the day.
So may you by my dull and heavy eye;
    My tongue hath but a heavier tale to say.
I play the torturer, by small and small   198
To lengthen out the worst that must be spoken:
Your uncle York is joined with Bolingbroke,
And all your northern castles yielded up,
And all your southern gentlemen in arms   202
Upon his party.

KING RICHARD   Thou hast said enough.   203
[To Aumerle] Beshrew thee, cousin, which didst lead
    me forth   204
Of that sweet way I was in to despair.
What say you now? What comfort have we now?
By heaven, I'll hate him everlastingly
That bids me be of comfort any more.
Go to Flint Castle. There I'll pine away;   209
A king, woe's slave, shall kingly woe obey.
That power I have, discharge, and let them go
To ear the land that hath some hope to grow,   212
For I have none. Let no man speak again
To alter this, for counsel is but vain.

AUMERLE
My liege, one word.

KING RICHARD   He does me double wrong   215
That wounds me with the flatteries of his tongue.
Discharge my followers. Let them hence away,
From Richard's night to Bolingbroke's fair day.
                                                    [Exeunt.]

❖

[3.3]

Enter [with drum and colors] Bolingbroke, York,
Northumberland, [attendants, and forces].

BOLINGBROKE
So that by this intelligence we learn   1
The Welshmen are dispersed, and Salisbury
Is gone to meet the King, who lately landed
With some few private friends upon this coast.

NORTHUMBERLAND
The news is very fair and good, my lord:
Richard not far from hence hath hid his head.

YORK
It would beseem the Lord Northumberland   7
To say "King Richard." Alack the heavy day
When such a sacred king should hide his head!

---

158 deposed deprived of life   **161 rounds** encircles   **162 antic**
grotesque figure, jester   **163 Scoffing his state** scoffing at the King's
regality   **164 breath** breathing space, moment   **165 monarchize** play
the monarch.   **kill with looks** i.e., order someone's death with a mere
glance   **166 self and vain conceit** vain conceit of himself   **168 and
humored thus** and Death, having amused himself at the King's
expense, having led the King on in this humor   **171 Cover your heads**
Replace your hats (which have been removed out of respect for the
King)   **176 Subjected** Made subject to grief, want, etc. (With pun on
"being treated like a subject.")   **179 But . . . wail** but promptly
anticipate and thus prevent the courses that result in lamentation.
180–1 To fear . . . foe i.e., To be afraid of the foe is merely a weakness
that, by oppressing your own resolve, gives advantage to the foe
183 Fear . . . fight i.e., If you fear, you are sure to be slain, and no
worse fate can come to you if you fight   **184–5 fight . . . breath** to
die fighting is to conquer death in the very act of dying, whereas to
die fearfully pays to death the tribute of servility.   **186 power** army
(as also in line 192).   **of** about, or from   **187 learn . . . limb** i.e., discover how to make a partial force substitute for a complete one.
189 change exchange.   **for . . . doom** i.e., in order to settle our fates,
which of us is to die now.   **190 This ague . . . overblown** This parox-
ysm of shivering in fear has blown over   **191 our own** i.e., my own
kingdom.

194 complexion appearance   **198 by small and small** little by little
202–3 And . . . party and all your men of rank in southern England
are also in arms on Bolingbroke's side.   **204 Beshrew** Confound. (Literally, *curse.*)   **forth** out   **209 Flint Castle** (Near Chester.)   **212 ear**
plow   **215 double wrong** i.e., in deceiving me and in leading me into
false hope once again
3.3 Location: Wales. Before Flint Castle.
1 intelligence information   **7 beseem** be appropriate for, be seemly
behavior in

NORTHUMBERLAND
    Your Grace mistakes. Only to be brief
    Left I his title out.
YORK   The time hath been,
    Would you have been so brief with him, he would
    Have been so brief with you to shorten you,   13
    For taking so the head, your whole head's length.   14
BOLINGBROKE
    Mistake not, uncle, further than you should.
YORK
    Take not, good cousin, further than you should,
    Lest you mistake the heavens are over our heads.   17
BOLINGBROKE
    I know it, uncle, and oppose not myself
    Against their will. But who comes here?

        Enter Percy.

    Welcome, Harry. What, will not this castle yield?
PERCY
    The castle royally is manned, my lord,
    Against thy entrance.
BOLINGBROKE
    Royally? Why, it contains no king?
PERCY   Yes, my good lord,
    It doth contain a king. King Richard lies   25
    Within the limits of yon lime and stone,
    And with him are the Lord Aumerle, Lord Salisbury,
    Sir Stephen Scroop, besides a clergyman
    Of holy reverence—who, I cannot learn.
NORTHUMBERLAND
    Oh, belike it is the Bishop of Carlisle.   30
BOLINGBROKE [*to Northumberland*]   Noble lord,
    Go to the rude ribs of that ancient castle;   32
    Through brazen trumpet send the breath of parley   33
    Into his ruined ears, and thus deliver: 34
    Henry Bolingbroke
    On both his knees doth kiss King Richard's hand
    And sends allegiance and true faith of heart
    To his most royal person, hither come
    Even at his feet to lay my arms and power,
    Provided that my banishment repealed   40
    And lands restored again be freely granted.   41
    If not, I'll use the advantage of my power,   42
    And lay the summer's dust with showers of blood
    Rained from the wounds of slaughtered Englishmen—
    The which how far off from the mind of Bolingbroke
    It is such crimson tempest should bedrench   46
    The fresh green lap of fair King Richard's land,
    My stooping duty tenderly shall show.   48

    Go, signify as much while here we march
    Upon the grassy carpet of this plain.
        [*Northumberland and attendants advance to the castle.*]
    Let's march without the noise of threat'ning drum,
    That from this castle's tottered battlements   52
    Our fair appointments may be well perused.   53
    Methinks King Richard and myself should meet
    With no less terror than the elements
    Of fire and water, when their thund'ring shock   56
    At meeting tears the cloudy cheeks of heaven.
    Be he the fire, I'll be the yielding water;
    The rage be his, whilst on the earth I rain   59
    My waters—on the earth, and not on him.   60
    March on, and mark King Richard how he looks.   61

        [*Bolingbroke's forces march about the stage.*] *The*
        trumpets sound [*a parley without and answer*
        within, then a flourish. King] *Richard appeareth*
        on the walls [*with the Bishop of Carlisle, Aumerle,*
        Scroop, and Salisbury].

    See, see, King Richard doth himself appear,
    As doth the blushing discontented sun   63
    From out the fiery portal of the east
    When he perceives the envious clouds are bent   65
    To dim his glory and to stain the track
    Of his bright passage to the occident.   67
YORK
    Yet looks he like a king. Behold, his eye,   68
    As bright as is the eagle's, lightens forth   69
    Controlling majesty. Alack, alack, for woe,
    That any harm should stain so fair a show!
KING RICHARD [*to Northumberland*]
    We are amazed; and thus long have we stood
    To watch the fearful bending of thy knee,   73
    Because we thought ourself thy lawful king.
    And if we be, how dare thy joints forget
    To pay their awful duty to our presence?   76
    If we be not, show us the hand of God   77
    That hath dismissed us from our stewardship;
    For well we know, no hand of blood and bone   79
    Can grip the sacred handle of our scepter,
    Unless he do profane, steal, or usurp.   81
    And though you think that all, as you have done,
    Have torn their souls by turning them from us,   83
    And we are barren and bereft of friends,   84
    Yet know, my master, God omnipotent,   85
    Is mustering in his clouds on our behalf

---

13 to as to   **14 taking so the head** i.e., (1) presumptuously omitting thus his title (2) being headstrong   **17 mistake** fail to perceive that. (Plays on Bolingbroke's use of *mistake*, just as York has punned on *brief* and *head*.)   **25 lies** resides   **30 belike** probably   **32 rude ribs** i.e., rugged walls   **33 brazen** (1) brass (2) bold.   **breath of parley** i.e., call for a conference   **34 his ruined ears** i.e., its (the castle's) ancient and battered loopholes   **40 my banishment repealed** the revocation of my banishment   **41 lands restored again** the restoration of my lands   **42 advantage of my power** superiority of my army   **46 is** is that   **48 stooping duty** submissive kneeling

52 tottered in tottering condition, or dilapidated   **53 fair appointments** handsome show of military preparedness   **56 fire and water** i.e., lightning and rain   **59–60 whilst . . . waters** while I moisten the earth with my tears   **61.2 parley** trumpet summons to a negotiation. **61.4 on the walls** i.e., in the gallery of the tiring-house, above, to the rear of the stage   **63 blushing** i.e., turning red with anger   **65 he** i.e., the sun.   **envious** hostile   **67 occident** west.   **68 Yet** Still, or nevertheless.   **he** i.e., King Richard   **69 lightens forth** flashes out, like lightning   **73 watch** wait for   **76 awful** reverential, full of awe **77 hand** signature   **79 no . . . bone** no human hand   **81 Unless he do profane** without committing sacrilege   **83 Have . . . us** have imperiled their souls by turning traitor to me   **84 And** and that **85 know** know that

Armies of pestilence; and they shall strike
Your children yet unborn and unbegot,
That lift your vassal hands against my head 89
And threat the glory of my precious crown. 90
Tell Bolingbroke—for yon methinks he stands—
That every stride he makes upon my land
Is dangerous treason. He is come to open 93
The purple testament of bleeding war; 94
But ere the crown he looks for live in peace,
Ten thousand bloody crowns of mothers' sons 96
Shall ill become the flower of England's face, 97
Change the complexion of her maid-pale peace 98
To scarlet indignation, and bedew
Her pastures' grass with faithful English blood.

NORTHUMBERLAND
The King of heaven forbid our lord the King
Should so with civil and uncivil arms 102
Be rushed upon! Thy thrice-noble cousin
Harry Bolingbroke doth humbly kiss thy hand;
And by the honorable tomb he swears
That stands upon your royal grandsire's bones,
And by the royalties of both your bloods,
Currents that spring from one most gracious head, 108
And by the buried hand of warlike Gaunt,
And by the worth and honor of himself,
Comprising all that may be sworn or said,
His coming hither hath no further scope 112
Than for his lineal royalties, and to beg 113
Enfranchisement immediate on his knees; 114
Which on thy royal party granted once, 115
His glittering arms he will commend to rust, 116
His barbèd steeds to stables, and his heart 117
To faithful service of Your Majesty.
This swears he, as he is a prince and just,
And as I am a gentleman I credit him.

KING RICHARD
Northumberland, say thus the King returns: 121
His noble cousin is right welcome hither,
And all the number of his fair demands
Shall be accomplished without contradiction. 124
With all the gracious utterance thou hast
Speak to his gentle hearing kind commends. 126
    [*Northumberland and attendants retire to Bolingbroke and York.*]
[*To Aumerle*] We do debase ourself, cousin, do we not,
To look so poorly and to speak so fair? 128
Shall we call back Northumberland, and send
Defiance to the traitor, and so die?

AUMERLE
No, good my lord. Let's fight with gentle words
Till time lend friends, and friends their helpful swords.
KING RICHARD
Oh, God, oh, God, that e'er this tongue of mine,
That laid the sentence of dread banishment
On yon proud man, should take it off again
With words of sooth! Oh, that I were as great 136
As is my grief, or lesser than my name!
Or that I could forget what I have been,
Or not remember what I must be now!
Swell'st thou, proud heart? I'll give thee scope to beat, 140
Since foes have scope to beat both thee and me. 141
    [*Northumberland returns to the castle walls.*]
AUMERLE
Northumberland comes back from Bolingbroke.
KING RICHARD
What must the King do now? Must he submit?
The King shall do it. Must he be deposed?
The King shall be contented. Must he lose
The name of king? I' God's name, let it go.
I'll give my jewels for a set of beads, 147
My gorgeous palace for a hermitage,
My gay apparel for an almsman's gown, 149
My figured goblets for a dish of wood, 150
My scepter for a palmer's walking-staff, 151
My subjects for a pair of carvèd saints,
And my large kingdom for a little grave,
A little, little grave, an obscure grave;
Or I'll be buried in the King's highway,
Some way of common trade, where subjects' feet 156
May hourly trample on their sovereign's head;
For on my heart they tread now whilst I live,
And, buried once, why not upon my head? 159
Aumerle, thou weep'st, my tenderhearted cousin.
We'll make foul weather with despisèd tears;
Our sighs and they shall lodge the summer corn 162
And make a dearth in this revolting land. 163
Or shall we play the wantons with our woes 164
And make some pretty match with shedding tears? 165
As thus, to drop them still upon one place, 166
Till they have fretted us a pair of graves 167
Within the earth; and, therein laid, there lies
Two kinsmen digged their graves with weeping eyes. 169
Would not this ill do well? Well, well, I see
I talk but idly, and you laugh at me.—
Most mighty prince, my lord Northumberland,
What says King Bolingbroke? Will His Majesty
Give Richard leave to live till Richard die?
You make a leg, and Bolingbroke says ay. 175

---

89 **That** of you that. **vassal** subject   90 **threat** threaten   93–4 **open . . . testament** initiate a bloodstained legacy. (Blood was often said to be purple.)   96–7 **Ten . . . face** the bloody heads of 10,000 young men (the flower of England) will disfigure the blossoming face of our country   98 **maid-pale** i.e., pale like the complexion of a young English maid   102 **civil** used in civil strife.   **uncivil** barbarous, violent   108 **head** source   112 **scope** purpose, aim   113 **lineal royalties** hereditary rights as one of royal blood   114 **Enfranchisement** freedom (from banishment)   115 **party** part   116 **commend** give over   117 **barbèd** armored   121 **returns** answers   124 **accomplished** fulfilled   126 **commends** regards.   128 **poorly** abject.   **fair** courteously.

136 **sooth** cajolery, flattery.   140 **scope** freedom, space   141 **scope** capacity, opportunity   147 **set of beads** rosary   149 **almsman's gown** plain attire of one who lives on alms or charity   150 **figured** ornamented, embossed   151 **palmer's** pilgrim's   156 **trade** passage   159 **buried once** once I am buried   162 **Our . . . corn** our sighs and tears will beat down the summer grain fields   163 **revolting** rebelling   164 **play the wantons** sport, frolic   165 **match** game, contest   166 **still** continually   167 **fretted us** eaten away for us, worn. (With a play on "complained.")   169 **digged** who dug   175 **a leg** an obeisance

NORTHUMBERLAND
My lord, in the base court he doth attend   176
To speak with you, may it please you to come down.   177

KING RICHARD
Down, down I come, like glistering Phaëthon,   178
Wanting the manage of unruly jades.   179
In the base court? Base court, where kings grow base,
To come at traitors' calls and do them grace.   181
In the base court? Come down? Down, court! Down,
      king!
For night owls shriek where mounting larks should
      sing.   [*Exeunt from above.*]

[*Northumberland rejoins Bolingbroke.*]

BOLINGBROKE
What says His Majesty?

NORTHUMBERLAND   Sorrow and grief of heart
Makes him speak fondly, like a frantic man.   185
Yet he is come.

[*Enter King Richard and his attendants below.*]

BOLINGBROKE   Stand all apart,   187
And show fair duty to His Majesty.   *He kneels down.* 188
My gracious lord!

KING RICHARD
Fair cousin, you debase your princely knee   190
To make the base earth proud with kissing it.   191
Me rather had my heart might feel your love   192
Than my unpleased eye see your courtesy.
Up, cousin, up. Your heart is up, I know,
Thus high at least [*touching his crown*], although your
      knee be low.

BOLINGBROKE [*rising*]
My gracious lord, I come but for mine own.

KING RICHARD
Your own is yours, and I am yours, and all.

BOLINGBROKE
So far be mine, my most redoubted lord,   198
As my true service shall deserve your love.

KING RICHARD
Well you deserve. They well deserve to have
That know the strong'st and surest way to get.
[*To York, who weeps*] Uncle, give me your hands. Nay,
      dry your eyes;
Tears show their love, but want their remedies.   203
[*To Bolingbroke*] Cousin, I am too young to be your
      father,   204

Though you are old enough to be my heir.
What you will have, I'll give, and willing too,
For do we must what force will have us do.
Set on towards London, cousin, is it so?

BOLINGBROKE
Yea, my good lord.

KING RICHARD   Then I must not say no.
                                        [*Flourish. Exeunt.*]

❖

[3.4]

Enter the Queen with [two Ladies,] her attendants.

QUEEN
What sport shall we devise here in this garden,
To drive away the heavy thought of care?

LADY   Madam, we'll play at bowls.   3

QUEEN
'Twill make me think the world is full of rubs,   4
And that my fortune runs against the bias.   5

LADY   Madam, we'll dance.

QUEEN
My legs can keep no measure in delight   7
When my poor heart no measure keeps in grief.   8
Therefore, no dancing, girl; some other sport.

LADY   Madam, we'll tell tales.

QUEEN
Of sorrow or of joy?

LADY   Of either, madam.

QUEEN   Of neither, girl;
For if of joy, being altogether wanting,   13
It doth remember me the more of sorrow;   14
Or if of grief, being altogether had,
It adds more sorrow to my want of joy.
For what I have I need not to repeat,
And what I want it boots not to complain.   18

LADY
Madam, I'll sing.

QUEEN   'Tis well that thou hast cause,
But thou shouldst please me better wouldst thou
      weep.   20

LADY
I could weep, madam, would it do you good.

QUEEN
And I could sing, would weeping do me good,   22
And never borrow any tear of thee.   23

Enter Gardeners [a Master and two Men].

But stay, here come the gardeners.
Let's step into the shadow of these trees.

---

176 **base court** outer or lower court of a castle   177 **may it please you**
if you please   178 **glistering** glistening, glittering.   **Phaëthon** son of
the sun-god, whose chariot he attempted to steer across the sky;
unable to control the horses of the sun, he was hurled from the chariot by Jupiter   179 **Wanting . . . jades** lacking the skill in horsemanship to control unruly nags.   181 **do them grace** (1) bow to them
(2) treat them graciously.   185 **fondly** foolishly.   **frantic** mad
187 **apart** aside   188 **fair duty** respect   190–91 **debase . . . base** (Continues the wordplay on *base* in line 180.)   192 **Me rather had** I had
rather   198 **mine** i.e., my loved lord (changing Richard's meaning of
yours in the previous line).   **redoubted** dread   203 **want their remedies** lack remedies for what caused them.   204 **too young** (Historically, Richard and Bolingbroke were both thirty-three.)

3.4 Location: The Duke of York's garden.
3 **bowls**, lawn bowling. (A common Elizabethan game.)   4 **rubs**
impediments (in the game of bowls)   5 **against the bias** i.e., contrary,
athwart. (Literally, not following the naturally curved path of a bowl,
which was weighted on one side.)   7 **measure** a stately slow dance
8 **measure** moderation   13 **wanting** lacking   14 **remember** remind
18 **boots** helps   20 **wouldst thou** if you would   22 **would . . . good**
i.e., if weeping would make me any less unhappy   23 **never borrow**
never need to borrow

My wretchedness unto a row of pins,   26
They will talk of state, for everyone doth so   27
Against a change; woe is forerun with woe.   28
[*The Queen and Ladies stand apart.*]

GARDENER [*to one Man*]
Go bind thou up young dangling apricots
Which, like unruly children, make their sire
Stoop with oppression of their prodigal weight.   31
Give some supportance to the bending twigs.
[*To the other*] Go thou, and like an executioner
Cut off the heads of too-fast-growing sprays
That look too lofty in our commonwealth.
All must be even in our government.   36
You thus employed, I will go root away
The noisome weeds which without profit suck   38
The soil's fertility from wholesome flowers.

MAN
Why should we in the compass of a pale   40
Keep law and form and due proportion,
Showing as in a model our firm estate,   42
When our sea-wallèd garden, the whole land,
Is full of weeds, her fairest flowers choked up,
Her fruit trees all unpruned, her hedges ruined,
Her knots disordered, and her wholesome herbs   46
Swarming with caterpillars?

GARDENER   Hold thy peace.
He that hath suffered this disordered spring   48
Hath now himself met with the fall of leaf.   49
The weeds which his broad-spreading leaves did
    shelter,
That seemed in eating him to hold him up,   51
Are plucked up root and all by Bolingbroke:
I mean the Earl of Wiltshire, Bushy, Green.

MAN
What, are they dead?

GARDENER   They are; and Bolingbroke
Hath seized the wasteful King. Oh, what pity is it
That he had not so trimmed and dressed his land   56
As we this garden! We at time of year   57
Do wound the bark, the skin of our fruit trees,
Lest being overproud in sap and blood   59
With too much riches it confound itself;
Had he done so to great and growing men,
They might have lived to bear and he to taste
Their fruits of duty. Superfluous branches
We lop away, that bearing boughs may live;   64
Had he done so, himself had borne the crown   65
Which waste of idle hours hath quite thrown down.

MAN
What, think you the King shall be deposed?

GARDENER
Depressed he is already, and deposed   68
'Tis doubt he will be. Letters came last night   69
To a dear friend of the good Duke of York's,
That tell black tidings.

QUEEN [*coming forward*]   Oh, I am pressed to death   71
Through want of speaking! Thou, old Adam's likeness,   72
Set to dress this garden, how dares   73
Thy harsh rude tongue sound this unpleasing news?
What Eve, what serpent, hath suggested thee   75
To make a second fall of cursèd man?
Why dost thou say King Richard is deposed?
Dar'st thou, thou little better thing than earth,
Divine his downfall? Say where, when, and how   79
Cam'st thou by this ill tidings? Speak, thou wretch.

GARDENER
Pardon me, madam. Little joy have I
To breathe this news, yet what I say is true.
King Richard, he is in the mighty hold
Of Bolingbroke. Their fortunes both are weighed:
In your lord's scale is nothing but himself
And some few vanities that make him light;
But in the balance of great Bolingbroke,
Besides himself, are all the English peers,
And with that odds he weighs King Richard down.
Post you to London and you will find it so;   90
I speak no more than everyone doth know.

QUEEN
Nimble mischance, that art so light of foot,
Doth not thy embassage belong to me,   93
And am I last that knows it? Oh, thou thinkest
To serve me last, that I may longest keep
Thy sorrow in my breast.—Come, ladies, go   96
To meet at London London's king in woe.
What, was I born to this, that my sad look
Should grace the triumph of great Bolingbroke?   99
Gard'ner, for telling me these news of woe,
Pray God the plants thou graft'st may never grow.
                    Exit [*with Ladies*].

GARDENER
Poor queen! So that thy state might be no worse,   102
I would my skill were subject to thy curse.
Here did she fall a tear; here in this place   104
I'll set a bank of rue, sour herb of grace.   105
Rue even for ruth here shortly shall be seen,   106
In the remembrance of a weeping queen.   *Exeunt.*

❧

26 My . . . pins i.e., I'd bet my immeasurable grief against the merest trifle   27 state statecraft, politics   28 Against . . . woe when change is imminent; sad times are heralded by gloomy predictions. 31 prodigal excessive   36 even equal   38 noisome harmful   40 pale enclosure, enclosed garden   42 firm stable   46 knots flower beds laid out in intricate designs   48 suffered allowed   49 fall of leaf i.e., autumn.   51 in eating him i.e., while they were really eating his sustenance   56 dressed put in order   57 at . . . year in the appropriate season   59 overproud in swollen with   64 bearing fruit-bearing 65 crown (1) royal crown (2) crown of a tree

68 Depressed Brought low   69 'Tis doubt there is fear   71 pressed to death (Allusion to the *peine forte et dure,* inflicted by pressure of heavy weights upon the chests of indicted persons who refused to plead and remained silent.)   72 old Adam (In his role as the first gardener.)   73 dress cultivate   75 suggested tempted   79 Divine prophesy   90 Post Hasten. (See the note at 1.1.56.)   93 embassage message.   belong to concern   96 Thy sorrow the sorrow that you (mischance) report   99 triumph triumphal procession.   Bolingbroke (The original spelling, "Bullingbrooke," indicates the rhyme with *look* in the previous line, pronounced something like "bruke" and "luke.")   102 So that Provided that   104 fall let fall   105 rue "herb of grace," a plant symbolical of repentance, ruth, or sorrow for another's misery   106 ruth pity

[4.1]

Enter Bolingbroke with the Lords [Aumerle,
Northumberland, Harry Percy, Fitzwater, Surrey,
the Bishop of Carlisle, the Abbot of Westminster,
and another Lord, Herald, officers] to Parliament.
[The throne is provided on stage.]

BOLINGBROKE
Call forth Bagot.

Enter [officers with] Bagot.

Now, Bagot, freely speak thy mind,
What thou dost know of noble Gloucester's death,
Who wrought it with the King, and who performed　　4
The bloody office of his timeless end.　　5

BAGOT
Then set before my face the Lord Aumerle.

BOLINGBROKE *[to Aumerle]*
Cousin, stand forth, and look upon that man.
　　　　　　　　　　　[Aumerle comes forward.]

BAGOT
My lord Aumerle, I know your daring tongue
Scorns to unsay what once it hath delivered.　　9
In that dead time when Gloucester's death was plotted,　　10
I heard you say, "Is not my arm of length,　　11
That reacheth from the restful English court　　12
As far as Calais, to mine uncle's head?"
Amongst much other talk that very time　　14
I heard you say that you had rather refuse
The offer of an hundred thousand crowns
Than Bolingbroke's return to England—　　17
Adding withal how blest this land would be　　18
In this your cousin's death.

AUMERLE　　Princes and noble lords,
What answer shall I make to this base man?
Shall I so much dishonor my fair stars　　22
On equal terms to give him chastisement?　　23
Either I must, or have mine honor soiled
With the attainder of his slanderous lips.　　25
　　　　　　　　[He throws down his gage.]
There is my gage, the manual seal of death,　　26
That marks thee out for hell. I say thou liest,
And will maintain what thou hast said is false
In thy heart-blood, though being all too base
To stain the temper of my knightly sword.

BOLINGBROKE
Bagot, forbear. Thou shalt not take it up.

AUMERLE
Excepting one, I would he were the best　　32
In all this presence that hath moved me so.

FITZWATER *[throwing down a gage]*
If that thy valor stand on sympathy,　　34
There is my gage, Aumerle, in gage to thine.　　35
By that fair sun which shows me where thou stand'st,
I heard thee say, and vauntingly thou spak'st it,　　37
That thou wert cause of noble Gloucester's death.
If thou deny'st it twenty times, thou liest,
And I will turn thy falsehood to thy heart,　　40
Where it was forgèd, with my rapier's point.

AUMERLE *[taking up the gage]*
Thou dar'st not, coward, live to see that day.

FITZWATER
Now, by my soul, I would it were this hour.

AUMERLE
Fitzwater, thou art damned to hell for this.

PERCY
Aumerle, thou liest. His honor is as true
In this appeal as thou art all unjust;　　46
And that thou art so, there I throw my gage
　　　　　　　　　[throwing down a gage]
To prove it on thee to the extremest point　　48
Of mortal breathing. Seize it if thou dar'st.　　49

AUMERLE *[taking up the gage]*
An if I do not, may my hands rot off　　50
And never brandish more revengeful steel　　51
Over the glittering helmet of my foe!

ANOTHER LORD *[throwing down a gage]*
I task the earth to the like, forsworn Aumerle,　　53
And spur thee on with full as many lies　　54
As may be holloed in thy treacherous ear
From sun to sun. There is my honor's pawn;　　56
Engage it to the trial, if thou darest.　　57

AUMERLE *[taking up the gage]*
Who sets me else? By heaven, I'll throw at all!　　58
I have a thousand spirits in one breast
To answer twenty thousand such as you.

SURREY
My lord Fitzwater, I do remember well
The very time Aumerle and you did talk.

FITZWATER
'Tis very true. You were in presence then,　　63
And you can witness with me this is true.

SURREY　　As false, by heaven, as heaven itself is true.

FITZWATER
Surrey, thou liest.

SURREY　　　　　　　Dishonorable boy!
That lie shall lie so heavy on my sword

4.1 Location: Westminster Hall.
4 Who . . . King who prevailed upon the King to have the murder performed　5 office function.　timeless untimely　9 unsay deny, take back.　delivered reported.　10 dead (1) deadly (2) dark, silent　11 of length long　12 restful i.e., untroubled by Gloucester　14 that very time (An inconsistency; Gloucester's death occurred before Bolingbroke left England.)　17 Than . . . return than have Bolingbroke return　18 withal in addition　22 stars i.e., fortune, rank　23 On . . . chastisement as to challenge him as my equal.　25 attainder dishonoring accusation　25.1 gage usually a glove or a gauntlet (a mailed or armored glove), as at 1.1.69 ff.　26 manual . . . death death warrant sealed by my hand

32 one i.e., Bolingbroke.　best highest in rank　34 stand on sympathy i.e., insists on correspondence of rank in your opponent　35 in gage engaged　37 vauntingly boastfully　40 turn turn back　46 appeal accusation. (As also in line 80.)　all unjust totally false　48–9 to . . . breathing to the point of death.　50 An if If　51 more any more, ever again　53 I . . . like I burden the ground in the same way　54 lies accusations of lying　56 sun to sun sunrise to sunset.　honor's pawn pledge of honor. (Also in line 71.)　57 Engage . . . trial take it up as a pledge to combat　58 Who . . . else? Who else puts up stakes against me or challenges me to a game?　throw (1) throw dice (2) throw down gages　63 in presence present

That it shall render vengeance and revenge,   68
Till thou the lie-giver and that lie do lie
In earth as quiet as thy father's skull.
In proof whereof, there is my honor's pawn.
                        [He throws down a gage.]
Engage it to the trial if thou dar'st.

FITZWATER *[taking up the gage]*
How fondly dost thou spur a forward horse!   73
If I dare eat, or drink, or breathe, or live,
I dare meet Surrey in a wilderness   75
And spit upon him whilst I say he lies,
And lies, and lies. There is my bond of faith,
To tie thee to my strong correction.
                        [He throws down a gage.]
As I intend to thrive in this new world,   79
Aumerle is guilty of my true appeal.   80
Besides, I heard the banished Norfolk say
That thou, Aumerle, didst send two of thy men
To execute the noble Duke at Calais.

AUMERLE
Some honest Christian trust me with a gage.
          [He borrows a gage and throws it down.]
That Norfolk lies, here do I throw down this,
If he may be repealed, to try his honor.   86

BOLINGBROKE
These differences shall all rest under gage   87
Till Norfolk be repealed. Repealed he shall be,
And, though mine enemy, restored again
To all his lands and seigniories. When he is returned,
Against Aumerle we will enforce his trial.

CARLISLE
That honorable day shall never be seen.
Many a time hath banished Norfolk fought
For Jesu Christ in glorious Christian field,
Streaming the ensign of the Christian cross   95
Against black pagans, Turks, and Saracens;
And, toiled with works of war, retired himself   97
To Italy, and there at Venice gave
His body to that pleasant country's earth
And his pure soul unto his captain, Christ,
Under whose colors he had fought so long.

BOLINGBROKE   Why, Bishop, is Norfolk dead?

CARLISLE   As surely as I live, my lord.

BOLINGBROKE
Sweet peace conduct his sweet soul to the bosom   104
Of good old Abraham! Lords appellants,   105
Your differences shall all rest under gage
Till we assign you to your days of trial.   107

    Enter York.

YORK
Great Duke of Lancaster, I come to thee
From plume-plucked Richard, who with willing soul
Adopts thee heir, and his high scepter yields
To the possession of thy royal hand.
Ascend his throne, descending now from him,
And long live Henry, fourth of that name!

BOLINGBROKE
In God's name, I'll ascend the regal throne.

CARLISLE   Marry, God forbid!
Worst in this royal presence may I speak,   116
Yet best beseeming me to speak the truth.   117
Would God that any in this noble presence
Were enough noble to be upright judge
Of noble Richard! Then true noblesse would   120
Learn him forbearance from so foul a wrong.   121
What subject can give sentence on his king?
And who sits here that is not Richard's subject?
Thieves are not judged but they are by to hear,   124
Although apparent guilt be seen in them;   125
And shall the figure of God's majesty,   126
His captain, steward, deputy elect,
Anointed, crownèd, planted many years,
Be judged by subject and inferior breath,
And he himself not present? Oh, forfend it God   130
That in a Christian climate souls refined   131
Should show so heinous, black, obscene a deed!   132
I speak to subjects, and a subject speaks,
Stirred up by God thus boldly for his king.
My lord of Hereford here, whom you call king,   135
Is a foul traitor to proud Hereford's king.
And if you crown him, let me prophesy:
The blood of English shall manure the ground
And future ages groan for this foul act;
Peace shall go sleep with Turks and infidels,
And in this seat of peace tumultuous wars
Shall kin with kin and kind with kind confound;   142
Disorder, horror, fear, and mutiny
Shall here inhabit, and this land be called
The field of Golgotha and dead men's skulls.   145
Oh, if you raise this house against this house,   146
It will the woefullest division prove
That ever fell upon this cursèd earth.
Prevent it, resist it, let it not be so,
Lest child, child's children, cry against you woe!

NORTHUMBERLAND
Well have you argued, sir, and for your pains
Of capital treason we arrest you here.—   152

---

68 **it** i.e., my sword   73 **fondly** foolishly. **forward** willing   75 **in a wilderness** i.e., where fighting might go on uninterrupted to the death   79 **in . . . world** i.e., under the new king   80 **appeal** accusation.   86 **repealed** recalled from exile.   **try** test   87 **under gage** as challenges   95 **Streaming** flying   97 **toiled** wearied   104–5 **bosom . . . Abraham** i.e., heaven. (See Luke 16:22.)   105 **Lords appellants** Lords who appear as formal accusers   107.1 **Enter York** (Probably Richard's scepter, etc., are brought in at line 162, but York here invites Bolingbroke to ascend the throne with the surrendered scepter, and so perhaps the regalia are brought on here.)

116 **Worst** Least in rank   117 **best beseeming me** i.e., most befitting to me as a clergyman   120 **noblesse** nobleness   121 **Learn him forbearance** teach him to forbear   124 **judged . . . by** condemned unless they are present   125 **apparent** manifest   126 **figure** image   130 **forfend** forbid   131 **souls refined** civilized people   132 **obscene** odious, repulsive   135 **My . . . Hereford** (Carlisle refuses to refer to Bolingbroke as king or even as Duke of Lancaster, since he lost the latter title at the time of his banishment.)   142 **Shall . . . confound** shall destroy kinsmen by means of kinsmen and fellow countrymen by means of fellow countrymen   145 **Golgotha** Calvary, the hill outside of Jerusalem called "the place of dead men's skulls" (see Mark 15:22 and John 19:17) where Jesus was crucified   146 **this house . . . this house** i.e., Lancaster against York. (See Mark 3:25.)   152 **Of** on a charge of

My lord of Westminster, be it your charge
To keep him safely till his day of trial.
                    [*Carlisle is taken into custody.*]
May it please you, lords, to grant the commons' suit? 155

BOLINGBROKE
Fetch hither Richard, that in common view
He may surrender; so we shall proceed   157
Without suspicion.

YORK   I will be his conduct.   *Exit.* 158

BOLINGBROKE
Lords, you that here are under our arrest,
Procure your sureties for your days of answer.   160
Little are we beholding to your love,   161
And little looked for at your helping hands.   162

        Enter Richard and York [with Officers bearing
        the crown and regalia].

KING RICHARD
Alack, why am I sent for to a king,
Before I have shook off the regal thoughts
Wherewith I reigned? I hardly yet have learned
To insinuate, flatter, bow, and bend my knee.
Give sorrow leave awhile to tutor me
To this submission. Yet I well remember
The favors of these men. Were they not mine?   169
Did they not sometime cry, "All hail!" to me?
So Judas did to Christ. But he, in twelve,
Found truth in all but one; I, in twelve thousand, none.
God save the King! Will no man say amen?
Am I both priest and clerk? Well then, amen.   174
God save the King, although I be not he;
And yet, amen, if heaven do think him me.
To do what service am I sent for hither?

YORK
To do that office of thine own good will
Which tired majesty did make thee offer:
The resignation of thy state and crown
To Henry Bolingbroke.

KING RICHARD
Give me the crown. [*He takes the crown.*] Here, cousin,
    seize the crown.
Here, cousin,
On this side my hand, and on that side thine.
Now is this golden crown like a deep well
That owes two buckets, filling one another,   186
The emptier ever dancing in the air,
The other down, unseen, and full of water.

That bucket down and full of tears am I,
Drinking my griefs, whilst you mount up on high.

BOLINGBROKE
I thought you had been willing to resign.

KING RICHARD
My crown I am, but still my griefs are mine.
You may my glories and my state depose,
But not my griefs; still am I king of those.

BOLINGBROKE
Part of your cares you give me with your crown.

KING RICHARD
Your cares set up do not pluck my cares down.   196
My care is loss of care, by old care done;   197
Your care is gain of care, by new care won.   198
The cares I give I have, though given away;   199
They 'tend the crown, yet still with me they stay.   200

BOLINGBROKE
Are you contented to resign the crown?

KING RICHARD
Ay, no; no, ay; for I must nothing be;   202
Therefore no, no, for I resign to thee.   203
Now mark me how I will undo myself: 204
        [*He yields his crown and scepter.*]
I give this heavy weight from off my head
And this unwieldy scepter from my hand,
The pride of kingly sway from out my heart;
With mine own tears I wash away my balm,
With mine own hands I give away my crown,
With mine own tongue deny my sacred state,
With mine own breath release all duteous oaths.   211
All pomp and majesty I do forswear;
My manors, rents, revenues I forgo;
My acts, decrees, and statutes I deny.
God pardon all oaths that are broke to me!
God keep all vows unbroke are made to thee!   216
Make me, that nothing have, with nothing grieved,   217
And thou with all pleased, that hast all achieved!
Long mayst thou live in Richard's seat to sit,
And soon lie Richard in an earthy pit!
God save King Henry, unkinged Richard says,
And send him many years of sunshine days!—
What more remains?

NORTHUMBERLAND [*presenting a paper*]
                    No more but that you read   223
These accusations and these grievous crimes
Committed by your person and your followers
Against the state and profit of this land;

---

155 the commons' suit request of the commons (i.e., that Richard be formally tried and the causes of his deposition made public. This line begins the abdication passage omitted in early quartos of the play.) **157 surrender** i.e., surrender the crown, abdicate **158 conduct** escort. **160 sureties** persons who will guarantee your appearance. **your days of answer** the time when you must appear to stand trial. **161 beholding** beholden, indebted **162 little . . . hands** i.e., I did not expect this from you, thinking you were on our side. **169 favors** (1) faces (2) support, good will **174 priest and clerk** (In religious services, the clerk or assistant would say "Amen" to the priest's prayers.) **186 owes** owns, has. **filling one another** (The raising of the full bucket lowers the other to be filled in turn.)

196–200 Your . . . stay i.e., Your assuming the cares of office does not assuage my griefs. My grief is loss of kingly responsibility, destroyed by a failure in diligence; your concern is gaining of kingly responsibility, won by zealous effort. The anxieties I transfer to you I also keep for myself, despite my giving them to you; they accompany the crown and yet still remain with me. **202 Ay** (1) Yes (2) I. (But, says Richard, I am nothing, and therefore "Ay" is "I" or "nothing," that is, "no.") **203 no, no . . . thee** (Richard plays on the logic that a double negative equals a positive; with an aural pun on *no/know*.) **204 undo** (1) divest (2) unmake **211 release . . . oaths** release my subjects from their oaths of duty. **216 are** that are **217 Make** i.e., May God make. **with nothing grieved** (1) grieved at nothing (2) grieved at having nothing **223 read** i.e., read aloud

That, by confessing them, the souls of men
May deem that you are worthily deposed.
KING RICHARD
    Must I do so? And must I ravel out   229
    My weaved-up follies? Gentle Northumberland,
    If thy offenses were upon record,
    Would it not shame thee in so fair a troop   232
    To read a lecture of them? If thou wouldst,   233
    There shouldst thou find one heinous article
    Containing the deposing of a king
    And cracking the strong warrant of an oath,
    Marked with a blot, damned in the book of heaven.   237
    Nay, all of you that stand and look upon me,
    Whilst that my wretchedness doth bait myself,   239
    Though some of you, with Pilate, wash your hands,   240
    Showing an outward pity, yet you Pilates
    Have here delivered me to my sour cross,   242
    And water cannot wash away your sin.
NORTHUMBERLAND
    My lord, dispatch. Read o'er these articles.   244
KING RICHARD
    Mine eyes are full of tears; I cannot see.
    And yet salt water blinds them not so much
    But they can see a sort of traitors here.   247
    Nay, if I turn mine eyes upon myself,
    I find myself a traitor with the rest;
    For I have given here my soul's consent
    T'undeck the pompous body of a king,   251
    Made glory base and sovereignty a slave,
    Proud majesty a subject, state a peasant.   253
NORTHUMBERLAND   My lord—
KING RICHARD
    No lord of thine, thou haught insulting man,   255
    Nor no man's lord. I have no name, no title,
    No, not that name was given me at the font,
    But 'tis usurped. Alack the heavy day,
    That I have worn so many winters out
    And know not now what name to call myself!
    Oh, that I were a mockery king of snow,
    Standing before the sun of Bolingbroke,
    To melt myself away in water drops!
    Good king, great king, and yet not greatly good,
    An if my word be sterling yet in England,   265
    Let it command a mirror hither straight,   266
    That it may show me what a face I have,
    Since it is bankrupt of his majesty.   268
BOLINGBROKE
    Go some of you and fetch a looking glass.   269
                              [Exit an Attendant.]
NORTHUMBERLAND
    Read o'er this paper while the glass doth come.

KING RICHARD
    Fiend, thou torments me ere I come to hell!
BOLINGBROKE
    Urge it no more, my lord Northumberland.
NORTHUMBERLAND
    The commons will not then be satisfied.
KING RICHARD
    They shall be satisfied. I'll read enough
    When I do see the very book indeed
    Where all my sins are writ, and that's myself.   276

        Enter one with a glass.

    Give me that glass, and therein will I read.
                              [He takes the mirror.]
    No deeper wrinkles yet? Hath sorrow struck
    So many blows upon this face of mine,
    And made no deeper wounds? O flattering glass,
    Like to my followers in prosperity,   281
    Thou dost beguile me! Was this face the face   282
    That every day under his household roof
    Did keep ten thousand men? Was this the face
    That, like the sun, did make beholders wink?   285
    Is this the face which faced so many follies,   286
    That was at last outfaced by Bolingbroke?   287
    A brittle glory shineth in this face—
    As brittle as the glory is the face,
                        [He throws down the mirror.]
    For there it is, cracked in an hundred shivers.
    Mark, silent king, the moral of this sport:
    How soon my sorrow hath destroyed my face.
BOLINGBROKE
    The shadow of your sorrow hath destroyed   293
    The shadow of your face.
KING RICHARD   Say that again.   294
    The shadow of my sorrow? Ha! Let's see.
    'Tis very true, my grief lies all within;
    And these external manners of laments   297
    Are merely shadows to the unseen grief   298
    That swells with silence in the tortured soul.
    There lies the substance; and I thank thee, King,   300
    For thy great bounty, that not only giv'st   301
    Me cause to wail, but teachest me the way
    How to lament the cause. I'll beg one boon,   303
    And then be gone and trouble you no more.
    Shall I obtain it?
BOLINGBROKE   Name it, fair cousin.
KING RICHARD
    "Fair cousin"? I am greater than a king.
    For when I was a king, my flatterers
    Were then but subjects; being now a subject,

---

229 **ravel out** unravel   232 **troop** company   233 **read a lecture** give a
public reading (as a warning)   237 **Marked . . . damned** (Modifying
article in line 234)   239 **bait** torment, harass (as in bearbaiting)
240 **wash your hands** (See Matthew 27:24. Richard persistently compares himself to Christ; see also 3.2.132; 4.1.171.)   242 **sour** bitter
244 **dispatch** conclude, be done.   247 **sort** gang   251 **pompous**
stately, splendid   253 **state** high rank, stateliness   255 **haught**
haughty   265 **An if** if.   **sterling** valid currency   266 **straight** immediately   268 **his** its   269 **some** i.e., someone

276.1 *glass* mirror.   281 **in prosperity** i.e., in my prosperity   282 **Was
this face** (An echo of Christopher Marlowe's *Doctor Faustus*, 5.1, in
which the protagonist addresses Helen of Troy.)   285 **wink** close the
eyes, blink.   286 **faced** countenanced   287 **outfaced** stared down,
discountenanced   293 **shadow** outward show, or, overshadowing
nature   294 **shadow** reflection (in the mirror)   297 **manners** forms,
manifestations   298 **shadows to** shadowings forth or embodiments
of   300 **There** i.e., In my soul   301 **that** you who   303 **boon** favor

I have a king here to my flatterer.   309
Being so great, I have no need to beg.
BOLINGBROKE   Yet ask.
KING RICHARD   And shall I have?
BOLINGBROKE   You shall.
KING RICHARD   Then give me leave to go.
BOLINGBROKE   Whither?
KING RICHARD
Whither you will, so I were from your sights.
BOLINGBROKE
Go some of you, convey him to the Tower.   317
KING RICHARD
Oh, good! "Convey"? Conveyers are you all,   318
That rise thus nimbly by a true king's fall.
        [Exeunt King Richard, some lords, and a guard.]
BOLINGBROKE
On Wednesday next we solemnly set down
Our coronation. Lords, prepare yourselves.   321
    Exeunt. Manent [the Abbot of] Westminster, [the
              Bishop of] Carlisle, Aumerle.
ABBOT
A woeful pageant have we here beheld.
CARLISLE
The woe's to come, the children yet unborn
Shall feel this day as sharp to them as thorn.   324
AUMERLE
You holy clergymen, is there no plot
To rid the realm of this pernicious blot?
ABBOT   My lord,
Before I freely speak my mind herein,
You shall not only take the Sacrament
To bury mine intents, but also to effect   330
Whatever I shall happen to devise.
I see your brows are full of discontent,
Your hearts of sorrow, and your eyes of tears.
Come home with me to supper; I'll lay
A plot shall show us all a merry day.   Exeunt. 335

❧

[5.1]

    Enter the Queen with [Ladies,] her attendants.

QUEEN
This way the King will come. This is the way
To Julius Caesar's ill-erected tower,   2
To whose flint bosom my condemnèd lord
Is doomed a prisoner by proud Bolingbroke.
Here let us rest, if this rebellious earth
Have any resting for her true king's queen.

    Enter Richard [and guard].

But soft, but see, or rather do not see
My fair rose wither. Yet look up, behold,

That you in pity may dissolve to dew,
And wash him fresh again with true-love tears.—
Ah, thou, the model where old Troy did stand,   11
Thou map of honor, thou King Richard's tomb,   12
And not King Richard! Thou most beauteous inn,   13
Why should hard-favored grief be lodged in thee   14
When triumph is become an alehouse guest?   15
KING RICHARD
Join not with grief, fair woman, do not so,
To make my end too sudden. Learn, good soul,   17
To think our former state a happy dream,
From which awaked, the truth of what we are
Shows us but this. I am sworn brother, sweet,
To grim Necessity, and he and I
Will keep a league till death. Hie thee to France,   22
And cloister thee in some religious house.   23
Our holy lives must win a new world's crown,   24
Which our profane hours here have thrown down.
QUEEN
What, is my Richard both in shape and mind
Transformed and weakened? Hath Bolingbroke
Deposed thine intellect? Hath he been in thy heart?
The lion dying thrusteth forth his paw
And wounds the earth, if nothing else, with rage
To be o'erpowered; and wilt thou, pupil-like,   31
Take the correction, mildly kiss the rod,
And fawn on rage with base humility,
Which art a lion and the king of beasts?   34
KING RICHARD
A king of beasts, indeed! If aught but beasts,   35
I had been still a happy king of men.
Good sometimes queen, prepare thee hence for France.   37
Think I am dead and that even here thou takest,
As from my deathbed, thy last living leave.
In winter's tedious nights sit by the fire
With good old folks, and let them tell thee tales
Of woeful ages long ago betid;   42
And ere thou bid good night, to quit their griefs   43
Tell thou the lamentable tale of me
And send the hearers weeping to their beds;
Forwhy the senseless brands will sympathize   46
The heavy accent of thy moving tongue,   47
And in compassion weep the fire out;
And some will mourn in ashes, some coal-black,   49
For the deposing of a rightful king.

    Enter Northumberland [attended].

---

309 to as   **317 convey** escort   **318 Convey** Steal.   **321.1 Manent**
They remain onstage   **324 Shall** who will   **330 To . . . intents** to conceal my plans   **335 shall** that shall
5.1 Location: London. A street leading to the Tower.
2 Julius . . . tower (The Tower of London, ascribed by tradition to
Julius Caesar, was built by William the Conqueror to hold the city in
subordination.)   **ill-erected** erected for evil ends or with evil results

11 thou . . . stand i.e., you ruined majesty, pattern of fallen greatness
like the desolate waste where Troy once stood   **12 map of honor** i.e.,
the mere outline of a once-glorious honor   **13 inn** residence, house
14 hard-favored unpleasant-looking   **15 is . . . guest** lodges in such a
vulgar tavern (i.e., in Bolingbroke).   **17 To . . . sudden** to kill me
quickly with grief.   **22 Hie** Hasten   **23 religious house** convent.
24 new world's heaven's   **31 To be** at being   **34 Which art** you who
are   **35 king of beasts** (1) lion (2) ruler over beastly men   **37 sometimes** former   **42 Of . . . betid** of woe that happened ages ago
43 quit their griefs requite their tales of woe   **46–7 Forwhy . . .
tongue** because even the inanimate and unfeeling firebrands will
respond to the doleful tone of your affecting tale   **49 And . . . coal-
black** and some of the brands will heap ashes on themselves like
grieving mourners and turn black with charring as though dressing
themselves in the black of mourning

NORTHUMBERLAND
My lord, the mind of Bolingbroke is changed;
You must to Pomfret, not unto the Tower.   52
And, madam, there is order ta'en for you: 53
With all swift speed you must away to France.

KING RICHARD
Northumberland, thou ladder wherewithal
The mounting Bolingbroke ascends my throne,
The time shall not be many hours of age
More than it is ere foul sin, gathering head,   58
Shall break into corruption. Thou shalt think,   59
Though he divide the realm and give thee half,
It is too little, helping him to all;   61
He shall think that thou, which knowest the way
To plant unrightful kings, wilt know again,
Being ne'er so little urged another way,   64
To pluck him headlong from the usurpèd throne.   65
The love of wicked men converts to fear,   66
That fear to hate, and hate turns one or both   67
To worthy danger and deservèd death.   68

NORTHUMBERLAND
My guilt be on my head, and there an end.   69
Take leave and part, for you must part forthwith.   70

KING RICHARD
Doubly divorced! Bad men, you violate
A twofold marriage, twixt my crown and me,
And then betwixt me and my married wife.
[To Queen] Let me unkiss the oath twixt thee and me;   74
And yet not so, for with a kiss 'twas made.—
Part us, Northumberland: I towards the north,
Where shivering cold and sickness pines the clime;   77
My wife to France, from whence, set forth in pomp,
She came adornèd hither like sweet May,
Sent back like Hallowmas or short'st of day.   80

QUEEN
And must we be divided? Must we part?

KING RICHARD
Ay, hand from hand, my love, and heart from heart.

QUEEN [to Northumberland]
Banish us both and send the King with me.

NORTHUMBERLAND
That were some love, but little policy.   84

QUEEN
Then whither he goes, thither let me go.

KING RICHARD
So two, together weeping, make one woe.
Weep thou for me in France, I for thee here;
Better far off than, near, be ne'er the near.   88

Go count thy way with sighs, I mine with groans.

QUEEN
So longest way shall have the longest moans.   90

KING RICHARD
Twice for one step I'll groan, the way being short,
And piece the way out with a heavy heart.   92
Come, come, in wooing sorrow let's be brief,
Since, wedding it, there is such length in grief.   94
One kiss shall stop our mouths, and dumbly part;   95
Thus give I mine, and thus take I thy heart.
                                        [They kiss.]

QUEEN
Give me mine own again. 'Twere no good part   97
To take on me to keep and kill thy heart.   [They kiss.]   98
So, now I have mine own again, begone,
That I may strive to kill it with a groan.

KING RICHARD
We make woe wanton with this fond delay.   101
Once more, adieu! The rest let sorrow say.
                    Exeunt [in two separate groups].

[5.2]

Enter Duke of York and the Duchess.

DUCHESS
My lord, you told me you would tell the rest,
When weeping made you break the story off,
Of our two cousins coming into London.   3

YORK
Where did I leave?

DUCHESS   At that sad stop, my lord,   4
Where rude misgoverned hands from windows' tops   5
Threw dust and rubbish on King Richard's head.

YORK
Then, as I said, the Duke, great Bolingbroke,
Mounted upon a hot and fiery steed
Which his aspiring rider seemed to know,   9
With slow but stately pace kept on his course,
Whilst all tongues cried, "God save thee, Bolingbroke!"
You would have thought the very windows spake,
So many greedy looks of young and old
Through casements darted their desiring eyes
Upon his visage, and that all the walls
With painted imagery had said at once,   16
"Jesu preserve thee! Welcome, Bolingbroke!"

---

52 **Pomfret** Pontefract Castle in Yorkshire   53 **order ta'en** arrangement made   58 **gathering head** gathering to a head   59 **corruption** putrid matter, pus.   61 **helping** since you helped   64 **Being . . . way** though scarcely urged at all   65 **To** how to   66 **converts** changes   67 **That fear** i.e., that fear changes.   **one or both** i.e., the new king or his partner, or both   68 **worthy** well-merited   69 **and . . . end** and let the topic be closed on that note.   70 **part . . . part** separate . . . depart   74 **unkiss** annul with a kiss (regarded as the seal of a ceremonial bond)   77 **pines the clime** afflicts the climate   80 **Hallowmas** All Saints' Day (November 1), regarded as the beginning of winter.   **short'st of day** the winter solstice.   84 **policy** political practicality.   88 **better . . . the near** i.e., better to be far apart than near and yet unable to meet. (The second *near* means "nearer.")

90 **So . . . moans** i.e., Then I will have to sigh and groan more than you, since my journey is longer.   92 **piece . . . out** make the journey seem longer   94 **Since . . . grief** i.e., since wedding ourselves to grief, we embark on a sadness that is only beginning. (A wry joke on the commonplace that a brief and romantic courtship is often the prelude to an interminable marriage.)   95 **and dumbly part** and then let us part in silence   97–8 **'Twere . . . me** It would not be wise of me to take it upon myself   101 **We . . . wanton** We sport with our grief. **fond** (1) loving (2) pointless, foolish
5.2 Location: The Duke of York's house.
3 **cousins** kinsmen, i.e., nephews (Richard and Bolingbroke)   4 **leave** leave off.   5 **misgoverned** unruly.   **windows' tops** upper windows   9 **Which . . . know** which seemed to know its ambitious rider   16 **With painted imagery** i.e., showing crowds of people, as on a tapestry or painted cloth, depicting a procession.   **at once** all together

Whilst he, from the one side to the other turning,
Bareheaded, lower than his proud steed's neck, 19
Bespake them thus: "I thank you, countrymen." 20
And thus still doing, thus he passed along. 21

DUCHESS
Alack, poor Richard! Where rode he the whilst?

YORK
As in a theater the eyes of men,
After a well-graced actor leaves the stage,
Are idly bent on him that enters next, 25
Thinking his prattle to be tedious,
Even so, or with much more contempt, men's eyes
Did scowl on gentle Richard. No man cried, "God
 save him!"
No joyful tongue gave him his welcome home,
But dust was thrown upon his sacred head—
Which with such gentle sorrow he shook off,
His face still combating with tears and smiles,
The badges of his grief and patience, 33
That had not God for some strong purpose steeled
The hearts of men, they must perforce have melted, 35
And barbarism itself have pitied him.
But heaven hath a hand in these events,
To whose high will we bound our calm contents. 38
To Bolingbroke are we sworn subjects now,
Whose state and honor I for aye allow. 40

 [Enter Aumerle.]

DUCHESS
Here comes my son Aumerle.
YORK   Aumerle that was; 41
But that is lost for being Richard's friend,
And, madam, you must call him Rutland now.
I am in Parliament pledge for his truth 44
And lasting fealty to the new-made king.

DUCHESS
Welcome, my son. Who are the violets now 46
That strew the green lap of the new-come spring? 47

AUMERLE
Madam, I know not, nor I greatly care not.
God knows I had as lief be none as one. 49

YORK
Well, bear you well in this new spring of time, 50
Lest you be cropped before you come to prime. 51
What news from Oxford? Do these jousts and triumphs
 hold? 52

AUMERLE   For aught I know, my lord, they do.
YORK   You will be there, I know.
AUMERLE
If God prevent not, I purpose so.
YORK
What seal is that, that hangs without thy bosom? 56
Yea, look'st thou pale? Let me see the writing.
AUMERLE
My lord, 'tis nothing.
YORK   No matter, then, who see it.
I will be satisfied. Let me see the writing.
AUMERLE
I do beseech Your Grace to pardon me. 60
It is a matter of small consequence,
Which for some reasons I would not have seen. 62
YORK
Which for some reasons, sir, I mean to see.
I fear, I fear—
DUCHESS   What should you fear?
'Tis nothing but some bond that he is entered into
For gay apparel 'gainst the triumph day. 66
YORK
Bound to himself? What doth he with a bond 67
That he is bound to? Wife, thou art a fool.— 68
Boy, let me see the writing.
AUMERLE
I do beseech you, pardon me. I may not show it.
YORK
I will be satisfied. Let me see it, I say.
        He plucks it out of his bosom and reads it.
Treason! Foul treason! Villain! Traitor! Slave!
DUCHESS   What is the matter, my lord?
YORK [calling offstage]   Ho! Who is within there?

        [Enter a Servingman.]

                    Saddle my horse!—
God for his mercy, what treachery is here? 75
DUCHESS   Why, what is it, my lord?
YORK [to the Servingman]
Give me my boots, I say! Saddle my horse!—
                    [Exit Servingman.]
Now, by mine honor, by my life, my troth, 78
I will appeach the villain.
DUCHESS   What is the matter? 79
YORK
Peace, foolish woman.
DUCHESS
I will not peace. What is the matter, Aumerle?
AUMERLE
Good mother, be content. It is no more
Than my poor life must answer.
DUCHESS   Thy life answer?

---

19 lower bowing lower   20 Bespake addressed   21 still continually
25 idly indifferently   33 badges insignia, outward signs   35 perforce necessarily   38 we . . . contents i.e., we bind ourselves to be
calmly content.   40 state i.e., royal title.   allow acknowledge.
41 Aumerle that was (Aumerle, as a member of Richard's party, lost
his dukedom, though he remained Earl of Rutland.)   44 pledge the
guarantor.   truth loyalty   46–7 Who . . . spring i.e., Who are the
favorites of the new king?   49 I had . . . one I'd be just as glad to be
left out as to be a favorite at court.   50 bear you bear yourself
51 cropped plucked, i.e., beheaded   52 Do . . . hold? Are those tourneys and pageants going forward? (According to Holinshed, these
tourneys at Oxford were part of a conspiracy against Bolingbroke by
the Abbot of Westminster and others; the new king was to be invited
to attend and there be assassinated.)

56 seal i.e., seal attached to the border of a document   60 pardon me
i.e., excuse me if I don't comply.   62 have seen wish to be seen.
66 'gainst in anticipation of   67–8 What . . . bound to? i.e., Why
should he have the bond instead of the creditor to whom the debt is
owed?   75 God i.e., I pray God   78 troth faith, allegiance
79 appeach inform against, publicly accuse

YORK [*calling*]
 Bring me my boots! I will unto the King.

His [Serving]man enters with his boots.

DUCHESS
 Strike him, Aumerle. Poor boy, thou art amazed.   85
 [*To the Servingman*] Hence, villain! Never more come
 in my sight.
YORK   Give me my boots, I say.

[*The Servingman helps him on with his boots, and exit.*]

DUCHESS   Why, York, what wilt thou do?
 Wilt thou not hide the trespass of thine own?
 Have we more sons? Or are we like to have?   90
 Is not my teeming date drunk up with time?   91
 And wilt thou pluck my fair son from mine age
 And rob me of a happy mother's name?
 Is he not like thee? Is he not thine own?
YORK   Thou fond mad woman,   95
 Wilt thou conceal this dark conspiracy?
 A dozen of them here have ta'en the Sacrament,   97
 And interchangeably set down their hands,   98
 To kill the King at Oxford.
DUCHESS   He shall be none;   99
 We'll keep him here. Then what is that to him?   100
YORK
 Away, fond woman! Were he twenty times my son
 I would appeach him.
DUCHESS   Hadst thou groaned for him   102
 As I have done, thou wouldst be more pitiful.   103
 But now I know thy mind. Thou dost suspect
 That I have been disloyal to thy bed,
 And that he is a bastard, not thy son.
 Sweet York, sweet husband, be not of that mind!
 He is as like thee as a man may be,
 Not like to me, or any of my kin,
 And yet I love him.
YORK   Make way, unruly woman!   *Exit.*
DUCHESS
 After, Aumerle! Mount thee upon his horse,   111
 Spur post, and get before him to the King,   112
 And beg thy pardon ere he do accuse thee.
 I'll not be long behind. Though I be old,
 I doubt not but to ride as fast as York.
 And never will I rise up from the ground
 Till Bolingbroke have pardoned thee. Away, begone!

[*Exeunt separately.*]

❧

85 Strike him i.e., Strike the servant.   **amazed** confused, bewildered.
90 Have we more sons? (Historically, this Duchess of York was the
Duke's second wife and was not Aumerle's mother; she was, however, the mother of another son, Richard, subsequently Earl of Cambridge.)   **91 teeming date** period of childbearing   **95 fond** foolish
97–9 A dozen . . . Oxford ("Hereupon was an indenture sextipartite
made, sealed with their seals and signed with their hands, in the
which each stood bound to other, to do their whole endeavor for the
accomplishing of their purposed exploit." [Holinshed])
100 that i.e., the plot   **102 groaned for** i.e., given birth to. (But see
note, line 90.)   **103 pitiful** pitying.   **111 After** Go after him.   **his
horse** i.e., one of York's horses   **112 Spur post** ride as fast as possible

[5.3]

*Enter [Bolingbroke, now] King [Henry], with his
nobles [Harry Percy and others].*

KING HENRY
 Can no man tell me of my unthrifty son?   1
 'Tis full three months since I did see him last.
 If any plague hang over us, 'tis he.
 I would to God, my lords, he might be found.
 Inquire at London, 'mongst the taverns there,
 For there, they say, he daily doth frequent
 With unrestrainèd loose companions,
 Even such, they say, as stand in narrow lanes
 And beat our watch, and rob our passengers—   9
 While he, young wanton and effeminate boy,   10
 Takes on the point of honor to support   11
 So dissolute a crew.
PERCY
 My lord, some two days since I saw the Prince,
 And told him of those triumphs held at Oxford.   14
KING HENRY   And what said the gallant?
PERCY
 His answer was, he would unto the stews,   16
 And from the common'st creature pluck a glove,   17
 And wear it as a favor, and with that   18
 He would unhorse the lustiest challenger.   19
KING HENRY
 As dissolute as desperate! Yet through both
 I see some sparks of better hope, which elder years
 May happily bring forth. But who comes here?   22

Enter Aumerle, amazed.

AUMERLE   Where is the King?
KING HENRY
 What means our cousin, that he stares and looks
 So wildly?
AUMERLE
 God save Your Grace! I do beseech Your Majesty
 To have some conference with Your Grace alone.
KING HENRY [*to his nobles*]
 Withdraw yourselves, and leave us here alone.
                   [*Exeunt Percy and lords.*]
 What is the matter with our cousin now?
AUMERLE [*kneeling*]
 Forever may my knees grow to the earth,
 My tongue cleave to the roof within my mouth,   31
 Unless a pardon ere I rise or speak.
KING HENRY
 Intended or committed was this fault?
 If on the first, how heinous e'er it be,   34

5.3 Location: The court (i.e., Windsor Castle).
1 unthrifty profligate   **9 watch** night watchmen.   **passengers**
passers-by, wayfarers   **10 wanton** pampered youth.   **effeminate**
self-indulgent   **11 Takes on the** i.e., makes it a   **14 held** i.e., to be
held   **16 stews** brothels   **17 common'st** most promiscuous   **18 with
that** i.e., wearing that as a favor   **19 lustiest** most vigorous and brave
22 happily with good fortune.   **22.1 amazed** distraught.   **31 My . . .
mouth** (See Psalm 137:6: "If I do not remember thee, let my tongue
cleave to the roof of my mouth.")   **34 If on the first** i.e., If intended
only

To win thy after-love I pardon thee.

AUMERLE [*rising*]

Then give me leave that I may turn the key,
That no man enter till my tale be done.

KING HENRY Have thy desire.

[*Aumerle locks the door.*] *The Duke of York*
knocks at the door and crieth.

YORK [*within*]

My liege, beware! Look to thyself.
Thou hast a traitor in thy presence there.

KING HENRY [*drawing*] Villain, I'll make thee safe. 41

AUMERLE

Stay thy revengeful hand. Thou hast no cause to fear.

YORK [*within*]

Open the door, secure, foolhardy King! 43
Shall I for love speak treason to thy face? 44
Open the door, or I will break it open.

[*King Henry unlocks the door.*]

[*Enter York.*]

KING HENRY

What is the matter, uncle? Speak.
Recover breath; tell us how near is danger,
That we may arm us to encounter it.

YORK [*giving letter*]

Peruse this writing here, and thou shalt know
The treason that my haste forbids me show. 50

AUMERLE

Remember, as thou read'st, thy promise passed.
I do repent me. Read not my name there;
My heart is not confederate with my hand. 53

YORK

It was, villain, ere thy hand did set it down.
I tore it from the traitor's bosom, King;
Fear, and not love, begets his penitence.
Forget to pity him, lest thy pity prove 57
A serpent that will sting thee to the heart.

KING HENRY

Oh, heinous, strong, and bold conspiracy!
O loyal father of a treacherous son,
Thou sheer, immaculate, and silver fountain, 61
From whence this stream through muddy passages
Hath held his current and defiled himself, 63
Thy overflow of good converts to bad, 64
And thy abundant goodness shall excuse
This deadly blot in thy digressing son. 66

YORK

So shall my virtue be his vice's bawd,
And he shall spend mine honor with his shame,
As thriftless sons their scraping fathers' gold. 69

Mine honor lives when his dishonor dies,
Or my shamed life in his dishonor lies. 71
Thou kill'st me in his life; giving him breath, 72
The traitor lives, the true man's put to death.

DUCHESS [*within*]

What ho, my liege! For God's sake, let me in.

KING HENRY

What shrill-voiced suppliant makes this eager cry?

DUCHESS [*within*]

A woman, and thy aunt, great King. 'Tis I.
Speak with me, pity me, open the door!
A beggar begs that never begged before.

KING HENRY

Our scene is altered from a serious thing,
And now changed to "The Beggar and the King." 80
My dangerous cousin, let your mother in.
I know she is come to pray for your foul sin.

[*Aumerle opens the door. Enter the Duchess. She*
kneels.]

YORK

If thou do pardon whosoever pray, 83
More sins for this forgiveness prosper may. 84
This festered joint cut off, the rest rest sound;
This let alone will all the rest confound. 86

DUCHESS

O King, believe not this hardhearted man.
Love loving not itself, none other can. 88

YORK

Thou frantic woman, what dost thou make here? 89
Shall thy old dugs once more a traitor rear? 90

DUCHESS

Sweet York, be patient.—Hear me, gentle liege.

KING HENRY

Rise up, good aunt.

DUCHESS   Not yet, I thee beseech.
Forever will I walk upon my knees,
And never see day that the happy sees, 94
Till thou give joy, until thou bid me joy,
By pardoning Rutland, my transgressing boy.

AUMERLE [*kneeling*]

Unto my mother's prayers I bend my knee. 97

YORK [*kneeling*]

Against them both my true joints bended be.
Ill mayst thou thrive, if thou grant any grace!

DUCHESS

Pleads he in earnest? Look upon his face.
His eyes do drop no tears, his prayers are in jest;
His words come from his mouth, ours from our breast.
He prays but faintly and would be denied;

---

41 I'll . . . safe I'll make you harmless (by running you through).
43 secure unsuspecting, heedless **44 speak . . . face** i.e., speak so disrespectfully as to call you *secure* and *foolhardy*. **50 haste . . . show** i.e., breathlessness prevents me from revealing. **53 hand** signature.
57 Forget Forget your promise **61 sheer** clear, pure **63 himself** (1) itself (2) himself, Aumerle **64 Thy . . . bad** your excess of goodness changes to bad (in Aumerle) **66 digressing** deviating from his proper course, transgressing **69 scraping** parsimonious

71 in . . . lies will be hostage to his dishonorable conduct. **72 in his life** if you permit him to live **80 "The Beggar . . . King"** (Probably one of Shakespeare's many allusions to the ballad of King Cophetua and the Beggar Maid.) **83 whosoever pray** anyone who presents a petition **84 for** because of **86 alone** untreated. **confound** ruin.
88 Love . . . can i.e., He who does not love himself in his own son can love no one else, not even the King. **89 make** do **90 once . . . rear** i.e., give life again to a traitor by now redeeming Aumerle from death. **94 And . . . sees** and never enjoy the happiness that those who are happy experience **97 Unto** In support of

We pray with heart and soul and all beside.   104
His weary joints would gladly rise, I know;
Our knees still kneel till to the ground they grow.   106
His prayers are full of false hypocrisy,
Ours of true zeal and deep integrity.
Our prayers do outpray his; then let them have
That mercy which true prayer ought to have.

KING HENRY
Good aunt, stand up.

DUCHESS   Nay, do not say "stand up."
Say "pardon" first, and afterwards "stand up."
An if I were thy nurse, thy tongue to teach,   113
"Pardon" should be the first word of thy speech.
I never longed to hear a word till now;
Say "pardon," King; let pity teach thee how.
The word is short, but not so short as sweet;
No word like "pardon" for kings' mouths so meet.

YORK
Speak it in French, King: say "pardonne moy."   119

DUCHESS
Dost thou teach pardon pardon to destroy?
Ah, my sour husband, my hardhearted lord,
That sets the word itself against the word!
Speak "pardon" as 'tis current in our land;
The chopping French we do not understand.   124
Thine eye begins to speak; set thy tongue there,
Or in thy piteous heart plant thou thine ear,
That hearing how our plaints and prayers do pierce,
Pity may move thee "pardon" to rehearse.   128

KING HENRY
Good aunt, stand up.

DUCHESS   I do not sue to stand.
Pardon is all the suit I have in hand.

KING HENRY
I pardon him, as God shall pardon me.

DUCHESS
Oh, happy vantage of a kneeling knee!   132
Yet am I sick for fear. Speak it again;
Twice saying "pardon" doth not pardon twain
But makes one pardon strong.

KING HENRY   With all my heart
I pardon him.   [All rise.]

DUCHESS   A god on earth thou art.

KING HENRY
But for our trusty brother-in-law and the Abbot,   137
With all the rest of that consorted crew,   138
Destruction straight shall dog them at the heels.
Good uncle, help to order several powers   140
To Oxford, or where'er these traitors are.
They shall not live within this world, I swear,
But I will have them, if I once know where.
Uncle, farewell, and, cousin, adieu.

Your mother well hath prayed; and prove you true.   145
DUCHESS
Come, my old son. I pray God make thee new.   146
Exeunt [in two groups].

❧

[5.4]

Enter Sir Pierce [of] Exton [and his Men].

EXTON
Didst thou not mark the King, what words he spake,
"Have I no friend will rid me of this living fear?"   2
Was it not so?

MAN   These were his very words.

EXTON
"Have I no friend?" quoth he. He spake it twice,
And urged it twice together, did he not?

MAN   He did.

EXTON
And speaking it, he wishtly looked on me,   7
As who should say, "I would thou wert the man   8
That would divorce this terror from my heart"—
Meaning the King at Pomfret. Come, let's go.
I am the King's friend, and will rid his foe.   11
[Exeunt.]

❧

[5.5]

Enter Richard alone.

KING RICHARD
I have been studying how I may compare
This prison where I live unto the world;
And, for because the world is populous,   3
And here is not a creature but myself,
I cannot do it. Yet I'll hammer it out.   5
My brain I'll prove the female to my soul,
My soul the father, and these two beget
A generation of still-breeding thoughts;   8
And these same thoughts people this little world,   9
In humors like the people of this world,   10
For no thought is contented. The better sort,
As thoughts of things divine, are intermixed   12
With scruples and do set the word itself   13
Against the word, as thus, "Come, little ones,"   14
And then again,
"It is as hard to come as for a camel
To thread the postern of a small needle's eye."   17

---

104 **beside** besides.   **106 still** continually   **113 An if** If   **119 pardonne moy** *pardonnez-moi,* excuse me. (An affectedly polite refusal.)
124 chopping logic chopping, changing the sense   **128 rehearse** pronounce.   **132 happy vantage** fortunate gain   **137 But for** But as for.
brother-in-law i.e., John Holland, Earl of Huntingdon and Duke of
Exeter, who had married Bolingbroke's sister (see 2.1.281 and note).
Abbot Abbot of Westminster; see 4.1.321–34   **138 consorted** conspiring, confederate   **140 powers** forces

145 **prove you true** may you prove loyal.   **146 old** unregenerate
**5.4 Location: The court. The opening stage direction in the Quarto
reads** *Manet Sir Pierce Exton, etc.,* **suggesting continuity of action
with the preceding scene.**
2 **will** who will   **7 wishtly** intently   **8 As . . . say** as if to say   **11 rid**
rid him of
5.5 Location: Pomfret Castle. A dungeon.
3 **for because** because   **5 hammer** i.e., work, puzzle   **8 still-breeding**
constantly breeding   **9 this little world** myself and this prison as a
microcosm of the world   **10 humors** temperaments, peculiar fancies
12 As such as   **13 scruples** doubts   **13–14 do set . . . word** i.e., oppose
one scriptural passage against its apparent opposite   **14–17 Come . . .
eye** (See Matthew 19:14, 24.)   **17 postern** narrow gate

Thoughts tending to ambition, they do plot
Unlikely wonders—how these vain weak nails
May tear a passage through the flinty ribs
Of this hard world, my ragged prison walls,   21
And, for they cannot, die in their own pride.   22
Thoughts tending to content flatter themselves   23
That they are not the first of fortune's slaves,
Nor shall not be the last—like seely beggars   25
Who, sitting in the stocks, refuge their shame   26
That many have and others must sit there;
And in this thought they find a kind of ease,
Bearing their own misfortunes on the back
Of such as have before endured the like.
Thus play I in one person many people,
And none contented. Sometimes am I king;
Then treason makes me wish myself a beggar,   33
And so I am. Then crushing penury   34
Persuades me I was better when a king;
Then am I kinged again, and by and by
Think that I am unkinged by Bolingbroke,
And straight am nothing. But whate'er I be,
Nor I, nor any man that but man is,   39
With nothing shall be pleased till he be eased   40
With being nothing. (*The music plays.*) Music do I   41
    hear?
Ha, ha, keep time! How sour sweet music is,
When time is broke and no proportion kept!
So is it in the music of men's lives.
And here have I the daintiness of ear
To check time broke in a disordered string,   46
But for the concord of my state and time
Had not an ear to hear my true time broke.
I wasted time, and now doth time waste me;
For now hath Time made me his numb'ring clock.   50
My thoughts are minutes, and with sighs they jar   51
Their watches on unto mine eyes, the outward watch   52
Whereto my finger, like a dial's point,   53
Is pointing still in cleansing them from tears.
Now sir, the sounds that tell what hour it is
Are clamorous groans that strike upon my heart,
Which is the bell. So sighs and tears and groans
Show minutes, hours, and times. But my time   58
Runs posting on in Bolingbroke's proud joy,   59
While I stand fooling here, his jack of the clock.   60
This music mads me. Let it sound no more,   61
For though it have holp madmen to their wits,   62

In me it seems it will make wise men mad.
                                [*The music ceases.*]
Yet blessing on his heart that gives it me!
For 'tis a sign of love; and love to Richard
Is a strange brooch in this all-hating world.   66

            Enter a Groom of the stable.

GROOM
    Hail, royal prince!
KING RICHARD   Thanks, noble peer.
    The cheapest of us is ten groats too dear.   68
    What art thou, and how comest thou hither,
    Where no man never comes but that sad dog
    That brings me food to make misfortune live?
GROOM
    I was a poor groom of thy stable, King,
    When thou wert king; who, traveling towards York,
    With much ado at length have gotten leave
    To look upon my sometimes royal master's face.   75
    Oh, how it earned my heart when I beheld   76
    In London streets, that coronation day,
    When Bolingbroke rode on roan Barbary,
    That horse that thou so often hast bestrid,
    That horse that I so carefully have dressed!   80
KING RICHARD
    Rode he on Barbary? Tell me, gentle friend,
    How went he under him?
GROOM
    So proudly as if he disdained the ground.
KING RICHARD
    So proud that Bolingbroke was on his back!
    That jade hath eat bread from my royal hand;   85
    This hand hath made him proud with clapping him.   86
    Would he not stumble? Would he not fall down,
    Since pride must have a fall, and break the neck
    Of that proud man that did usurp his back?
    Forgiveness, horse! Why do I rail on thee,
    Since thou, created to be awed by man,
    Wast born to bear? I was not made a horse,
    And yet I bear a burden like an ass,
    Spurred, galled, and tired by jauncing Bolingbroke.   94

        Enter one [a Keeper] to Richard with meat.

KEEPER [*to Groom*]
    Fellow, give place. Here is no longer stay.
KING RICHARD [*to Groom*]
    If thou love me, 'tis time thou wert away.
GROOM
    What my tongue dares not, that my heart shall say.
                                        Exit Groom.

---

21 **ragged** rugged   22 **for** because.   **pride** prime.   23 **content** contentment   25 **seely** simpleminded   26 **refuge their shame** i.e., seek refuge from their disgrace by reflecting   33 **treason** i.e., the thought of treason   34 **penury** poverty   39–41 **Nor . . . nothing** neither I nor any person alive can be fully satisfied with the things of this life until he or she is released by death.   46 **check** rebuke.   **string** stringed instrument   50 **numb'ring clock** i.e., a clock that numbers hours and minutes (not an hourglass).   51–2 **My . . . watch** My sad thoughts, occurring every minute, are parts of an inner clock that, by means of the sighs they provoke, transfer their cares to my eyes, the face of the clock   53 **dial's point** clock hand   58 **times** quarters and halves.   59 **posting** hastening   60 **jack of the clock** manikin that struck the bell on a clock.   61 **mads** maddens   62 **holp** helped

66 **strange brooch** rare jewel   68 **ten groats too dear** (There is a pun on *royal* and *noble* in the preceding lines. A royal (ten shillings) is worth ten groats (ten times four pence) more than a noble (six shillings, eight pence) is; hence, Richard is saying that he, "the cheapest of us" because he is a prisoner, is worth no more than the groom, whom he greets as his "noble peer.")   75 **sometimes** former   76 **earned** grieved   80 **dressed** tended, groomed.   85 **eat** eaten. (Pronounced "et.")   86 **clapping** patting, stroking   94 **galled** made sore. **jauncing** prancing, hard-riding.   94.1 *meat* food.

KEEPER
My lord, will't please you to fall to?

KING RICHARD
Taste of it first, as thou art wont to do.   99

KEEPER
My lord, I dare not. Sir Pierce of Exton, who
Lately came from the King, commands the contrary.

KING RICHARD
The devil take Henry of Lancaster and thee!
Patience is stale, and I am weary of it.
                              [*He beats the Keeper.*]

KEEPER Help, help, help!

The murderers [Exton and his men] rush in.

KING RICHARD
How now, what means death in this rude assault?
Villain, thy own hand yields thy death's instrument.
     [*He snatches a weapon from a man and kills him.*]
Go thou, and fill another room in hell.   107
          [*He kills another.*] *Here Exton strikes him down.*
That hand shall burn in never-quenching fire
That staggers thus my person. Exton, thy fierce hand 109
Hath with the King's blood stained the King's own
     land.
Mount, mount, my soul! Thy seat is up on high,
Whilst my gross flesh sinks downward, here to die.
                                        [*He dies.*]

EXTON
As full of valor as of royal blood.
Both have I spilled. Oh, would the deed were good!
For now the devil, that told me I did well,
Says that this deed is chronicled in hell.
This dead king to the living king I'll bear.
Take hence the rest, and give them burial here.
                           [*Exeunt, with the bodies.*]

[5.6]

*[Flourish.] Enter Bolingbroke [as King], with the
Duke of York, [other lords, and attendants].*

KING HENRY
Kind uncle York, the latest news we hear
Is that the rebels have consumed with fire
Our town of Ci'cester in Gloucestershire,   3
But whether they be ta'en or slain we hear not.

Enter Northumberland.

Wecome, my lord. What is the news?

NORTHUMBERLAND
First, to thy sacred state wish I all happiness.
The next news is, I have to London sent

The heads of Salisbury, Spencer, Blunt, and Kent.
The manner of their taking may appear   9
At large discoursèd in this paper here.   10
                           [*He gives a paper.*]

KING HENRY
We thank thee, gentle Percy, for thy pains,
And to thy worth will add right worthy gains.   12

Enter Lord Fitzwater.

FITZWATER
My lord, I have from Oxford sent to London
The heads of Brocas and Sir Bennet Seely,
Two of the dangerous consorted traitors   15
That sought at Oxford thy dire overthrow.

KING HENRY
Thy pains, Fitzwater, shall not be forgot;
Right noble is thy merit, well I wot.   18

*Enter Henry Percy [with the Bishop of Carlisle,
guarded].*

PERCY
The grand conspirator, Abbot of Westminster,   19
With clog of conscience and sour melancholy   20
Hath yielded up his body to the grave;
But here is Carlisle living, to abide   22
Thy kingly doom and sentence of his pride.   23

KING HENRY Carlisle, this is your doom:
Choose out some secret place, some reverent room, 25
More than thou hast, and with it joy thy life.   26
So as thou liv'st in peace, die free from strife; 27
For though mine enemy thou hast ever been,
High sparks of honor in thee have I seen.

Enter Exton, with [attendants bearing] the coffin.

EXTON
Great King, within this coffin I present
Thy buried fear. Herein all breathless lies
The mightiest of thy greatest enemies,
Richard of Bordeaux, by me hither brought.

KING HENRY
Exton, I thank thee not, for thou hast wrought
A deed of slander with thy fatal hand   35
Upon my head and all this famous land.

EXTON
From your own mouth, my lord, did I this deed.

KING HENRY
They love not poison that do poison need,
Nor do I thee. Though I did wish him dead,
I hate the murderer, love him murderèd.

---

99 **Taste . . . first** i.e., to ensure that it isn't poisoned   107 **room** place
109 **staggers** causes to stagger
5.6 **Location:** The court.
3 **Ci'cester** Cirencester

9 **taking** capture   10 **At large discoursèd** related in full   12 **worth**
(1) deserving (2) present wealth   15 **consorted** conspiring   18 **wot**
know.   19 **grand** chief   20 **clog** burden   22 **abide** await   23 **doom**
judgment   25 **reverent room** place suitable for religious retirement
26 **More than thou hast** i.e., larger than your present cell, or more
worthy of reverence.   **joy** enjoy, have the benefit of   27 **So as** Provided that   35 **deed of slander** i.e., a deed sure to arouse slanderous
talk about the new King

The guilt of conscience take thou for thy labor,
But neither my good word nor princely favor.
With Cain go wander through the shades of night,   43
And never show thy head by day nor light.
                              [*Exeunt Exton and attendants.*]
Lords, I protest my soul is full of woe
That blood should sprinkle me to make me grow.

Come mourn with me for what I do lament,
And put on sullen black incontinent.   48
I'll make a voyage to the Holy Land
To wash this blood off from my guilty hand.
March sadly after. Grace my mournings here   51
In weeping after this untimely bier.
                    [*Exeunt in procession, following the coffin.*]

43 Cain murderer of his brother Abel; see 1.1.104

48 incontinent immediately.   **51 Grace** Dignify

The First Part of King Henry the Fourth

The opening of *1 Henry IV* is taut and grave in tone. England is "shaken" and "wan with care." The troubles of *Richard II,* to which this play (c. 1596–1597) is a close sequel, have not been left behind. However much King Henry would prefer to unite his countrymen against a common foreign enemy in a crusade to the Holy Lands, he is prevented from doing so by continuing civil war. The impassioned rhetoric of his opening speech can only end in anticlimax, for the actual purpose of this meeting in council is to receive and assess reports of military action against the throne.

Henry's current troubles are in the far reaches of his kingdom: Scots in the north, Welsh in the west. Fighting for Henry on these two fronts are the nobles of the Percy family who helped him to power: Harry Percy ("Hotspur"), his father (Henry Percy) the Earl of Northumberland, his uncle the Earl of Worcester, and his brother-in-law Edmund Mortimer, the Earl of March. Apparently, they have fought bravely. Yet we soon sense that all is not well between the new King and those who rebelled with him against Richard II. A quarrel breaks out because Hotspur refuses to deliver to Henry some prisoners as required by feudal obedience. The matter of the ransom money is only a technicality; what is really at issue? In part, it is Henry's insistence on being obeyed on principle. Admiring Hotspur inordinately, the King feels he must discipline affectionately this fine young warrior as a father would discipline his son. Even more deeply, however, the issue of the prisoners galls Henry because of the proviso that he ransom Mortimer, captured by the Welsh. Henry does not forget that Mortimer is his chief rival for the English crown, being descended from the Duke of Clarence (elder brother to Henry's father, Gaunt) and having been proclaimed by Richard as heir to the throne. (Shakespeare accentuates the dynastic threat by combining two Edmund Mortimers from his historical sources: one who married Glendower's daughter and another who claimed the English throne; see 1.3.80–5 and

note.) Mortimer is the last person Henry would wish ransomed. Moreover, the King suspects Mortimer of having fought with something less than total zeal against the Welsh Glendower. Mortimer's marriage to Glendower's daughter confirms the King's worst fears. Henry knows Northumberland and Worcester to be expert in treasonous plotting, since they conspired with him to overthrow Richard. Now, Henry believes, these Percys are extending their alliance by a series of calculated marriages in order to seize power once again. This time their claimant is Mortimer.

Shakespeare's sympathies are many sided. The Percy clan is, in fact, organizing against Henry, but not without cause. As they see it, the man they helped to the throne has done little for them since. His manner of disciplining them sounds too much like hostility and ingratitude. Other counselors attend the King constantly while Worcester is banished from court. In such an atmosphere of distrust, suspicion breeds still more suspicion. The situation has deteriorated, surely more than either party originally intended.

Hotspur is the most attractive of the rebels—to us as well as to King Henry. He is outspoken, courageous, witty, and domineering in conversation. Above all, he is a disciple of manliness, loyalty, chivalry, bravery in battle—the attributes of an upstanding and somewhat old-fashioned sense of honor. Yet a fatal defect dwells even in these attractive qualities. Hotspur is impatient, proud, unwilling to tolerate a rival—be it Glendower or Prince Hal (Henry, Prince of Wales). In his first speech, purporting to explain his refusal to deliver the prisoners, he brilliantly satirizes an effete courtier who had come to him from King Henry in the midst of a battle. The satire betrays many harsh qualities in Hotspur: the self-indulgent wrath that returns fully to him even in recollection of the encounter, the pride in his own stoical indifference to suffering, and especially the obsessive nature (revealed in the repetitive pattern of the rhetoric) of his contempt for courtiers generally. Surely his scorn for stay-at-home politicians is directed in part at King Henry himself. To Hotspur, all courtiers are effeminate, perfume-wearing, affected in mannerism and speech, and scarcely masculine. This preoccupation of Hotspur's makes him extraordinarily prone to one-sided judgments. Like most excessive devotees of chivalry, he divides humanity into two categories: those who are gentlemen, like himself, and those who are beneath contempt. The "vile politician" Bolingbroke and his son, the "sword-and-buckler Prince of Wales" (1.3.240, 229) fall into the latter category.

Prone as he is to such an overly simple view of political behavior, Hotspur can see no good in the King's cause and no evil in his own. He is a poor listener because of his obsession and yet an easy prey to his uncle and father, who require his leadership for their cause. They need only implant the suggestion that King Henry is acting from a political motive in his refusal to ransom Mortimer, and Hotspur is ready to leap incautiously to the defense of their cause. The great irony is that Hotspur fails to see political motives in the machinations of his own relatives. While he fights for bright honor, they maneuver cautiously for position and prove to be uncertain allies when the hour of battle approaches. Most crucially, they betray Hotspur in the prebattle negotiations, at which he is not present. As Worcester explains to Vernon during their return to rebel headquarters (5.2.3–25), they cannot let Hotspur know of the King's offer to settle matters by a general pardon. Although, as they realize, the King could pardon Hotspur's youth, there can be no turning back for themselves. Thus, the honor for which Hotspur fights is at bottom a lie, and the mutual esteem that might have grown between him and a much-reformed Prince of Wales is thwarted by the polarization of attitudes in the two camps. Hotspur's brand of honor is the victim of its own excess and lends some credence to Falstaff's wry conclusion that honor "is a mere scutcheon" (5.1.139–40).

The contrasting of Falstaff and Hotspur on the theme of honor suggests that they are dramatic foils for each other, representing extremes between which Hal must choose. Shakespeare uses this foil device structurally and consciously; for example, he has considerably reduced the age of the Hotspur he found in Raphael Holinshed's *Chronicles* (1578) in order to stress the similarity between Hotspur and Prince Hal. Conversely, to emphasize the contrast between Falstaff and Hotspur, Shakespeare envisages Falstaff as old (nearly sixty, by his own admission), fat, humorous, and without honor. Falstaff's vices are Hotspur's virtues, and the reverse. Whereas Hotspur offers to Hal a model of chivalric striving and attention to duty, Falstaff is a highwayman and a liar. On the other hand, Hotspur is a fanatic, unbending and self-absorbed even in the company of his sprightly wife, Kate, and irritated by music and poetry; Falstaff is the epitome of merriment and joie de vivre. We excuse much in him because

he lusts after life with such an appetite and ingratiates himself to others by inviting them to laugh at his expense.

Despite the nearly irresistible attractiveness of Falstaff as a jolly companion and butt of humorous joking, he and Prince Hal are perennially caught up in witty debate as to the importance of Falstaff in Hal's life and whether the young man will have to get rid of Falstaff once Hal is king. The bantering raillery of their first scene (1.2) seems designed to provide diverting entertainment for the Prince and for us, and yet, beneath the word games and oneupmanship, we perceive that Hal and Falstaff are talking about the hanging of thieves and the question of whether or not Hal should give in to sinful temptation. Can the relationship of Hal and Falstaff continue unchanged into the reign of Henry V? Will there be gallows standing and justice for highwaymen? Will "Monsieur Remorse," as Poins calls Falstaff, ever sincerely repent? Will the Prince, for that matter? To allay our fears, Hal soliloquizes at scene's end, vowing his determination to use these scapegrace companions as mere foils for his triumphal reformation at the appropriate time. But this explanation raises an opposite danger in our sympathies: is he callously using his companions merely to create a self-serving myth of Prince Hal, the Politician with the Common Touch? Is Francis the drawer no more to Hal than a butt for his raillery? Since the rejection of Falstaff is, by Hal's own words, already determined, can we credit him with a serious friendship? Where do Shakespeare's sympathies lie—with the need for political order or with the hedonistic spirit of youth? One possible interpretation is that he recognizes the validity of both, and accordingly shows us a prince who is genuinely fond of Falstaff's exuberant company but who also knows that he is a king's son and must sooner or later accept the consequences of that unsought role. Falstaff's gift to him is youthful irresponsibility, which must be cherished (by all of us), even though it cannot last.

This compassionate interpretation is, to be sure, only one of many possibilities. Recent theater history has demonstrated how supple the play is, allowing directors and actors to choose among an array of possibilities. At one extreme, Hal can be played as a matter-of-fact and even cynical young man who knows from the very start exactly where he is going and what use he can make of Falstaff and company—as played, for example, by Richard Burton at Stratford-upon-Avon in 1951 (directed by Anthony Quayle and John Kidd). At the opposite extreme, Hal can be seen as a defiant rebel whose hatred for his unsympathetically cold father makes him reluctant to grow up and accept adult responsibility; this was the line taken, for example, by Gerard Murphy in Trevor Nunn's 1982 production for the Royal Shakespeare Company. Murphy's Hal was an unruly child for whom Falstaff was a nurturing substitute parent. Between these polarities, Hal can be variously seen as an alcoholic or a prudish snob or a playboy or simply a young man who wants to enjoy life. Correspondingly, the role of Falstaff offers widely varying possibilities as a kind of jolly scapegrace older friend, a calculating con artist and jokester who knows how to play for sympathy through self-effacing humor, or a dangerously irresponsible hedonist. King Henry as father can be seen as a sorely tested father burdened with heavy responsibilities and an ungrateful son, a guilt-ridden monarch who fears remorsefully that Hal's waywardness is heaven's punishment for the King's sins, or a hard-bitten politician engaged in a life-and-death struggle for power with aristocrats as Machiavellian as he. An important reason for the play's great success is its openness to interpretation.

In the Gad's Hill robbery, Falstaff reveals that his "cowardice" differs from the natural craven fear of Bardolph and Peto. He fights no longer than he sees "reason," that is, not against unfair odds such as two athletic young men in the dark (or later, at Shrewsbury, against the burly Scots giant, the Douglas). A man could get killed that way. Falstaff's cowardice, then, is philosophic, seen by himself in a humorous perspective. The same is true of his lying about the robbery. However much Hal exults in exposing Falstaff as a fraud, we cannot dismiss the possibility that Falstaff may see through the Prince's scheme, and may then feed Hal the expectedly outlandish lie (two men in buckram become eleven men) as a means of begging for affection. Falstaff's only way of pleading his cause is to tickle the Prince's fancy, in his role as a kind of court fool. What Falstaff most wants is to be loved and retained for what he is, and that, poignantly enough, is the one thing the mature Henry V cannot grant.

Throughout *1 Henry IV,* Shakespeare seems interested in the relationships between fathers and sons. These relationships help structure the comparisons and contrasts among foil characters. Falstaff is a foil, not only for Hotspur, but also for Henry IV; that is, despite all his insistence on youthful irresponsibility, Falstaff acts as a kind of parental figure to Hal. In the tavern scene (2.4), Falstaff and Hal take turns playing king and crown prince, and in both roles Falstaff wittily argues his case as companion and guide to the heir to the throne. Is it better to be old and merry, fat and loved, or to be hated like Pharaoh's lean kine? Falstaff argues against the gravity of council meetings with the same amused fervor that he later directs at the grinning honor of a dead hero. Hal, in his turn as king, questions the propriety of a "devil" haunting the crown prince "in the likeness of an old fat man," a "reverend Vice," a "gray Iniquity," a "father ruffian" (2.4.442–9). For all the good humor in this exchange, both men are asking whether Falstaff or King Henry serves Hal as the better model. Hal anticipates some of the very arguments his father will use against him next day at court, and, indeed, the insistent presence of that sober adult world makes itself felt even in the tavern. When, under the pressure of that looming responsibility, Falstaff's merrymaking turns to something like urgent self-

justification in his moving litany of appeals that Hal "banish not him thy Harry's company—banish plump Jack, and banish all the world," the Prince seems aware that he must face the consequences of his destiny. "I do, I will," he answers (lines 472–6), in a tone that can vary onstage (depending on the actor) from sober resolution to fond regret to awakening as from a dream.

Hotspur, too, is regarded as a son by more than one father. King Henry only half-jokingly wishes it could be proved that some night-tripping fairy had exchanged his Harry in the cradle for Harry Percy (1.1.85–9). Paradoxically, the King admires Hotspur all the more for standing up to him, just as another imperious father figure, Owen Glendower, bestows grudging but real admiration on Hotspur for his outspokenness (3.1.1–185). Hotspur's rebellious ways are cherished because they seem to promise manliness and fame; Hal's rebellious ways are feared and despised because they seem to reject the values of duty and leadership on which King Henry bases his self-respect. In these terms, the play must resolve Hal's coming of age, his acceptance of his role as true son of the King, and his proving his worth to the King. Hal must find his adult self—a self that differs greatly from that of King Henry—but must do so in a way that preserves the integrity of their relationship and the real debt he owes his father.

Prince Hal's uncertain journey toward maturity does not involve him in any significant relationships with women. His task is to fulfill what is expected of him as his father's son in a world of political and military conflict. Women stand on the periphery of affairs, as in *Richard II,* and yet the scenes in which they appear offer important perspectives on male competitiveness and ambition. Hotspur's wife, Kate, must put up with being condescended to and told little about men's doings; yet Hotspur's genuine fondness for her shows the best side of his personality, and her worries about his obsessive ways indicate that she understands him better than he understands himself. Morton's Welsh wife, too, introduces into this play an element of tenderness and anxious concern that is notably lacking in the earlier part of 3.1, when Hotspur cannot stop himself from quarreling pointlessly with his senior ally, Glendower. Hotspur's insensitivity to the Welsh lady's beautiful song is perhaps a key to his impending tragedy, for he is never a good listener. On a lower social scale, Mistress Quickly devotedly looks after Falstaff, only to be repaid with misogynistic insults that she does not appear to understand and with mooching that she recognizes all too well. Prince Hal, meantime, plays the role of intelligent observer of the battle of the sexes, even while he postpones his own engagement in that merry war. He must first sort out who he is in terms of male goals of career and success.

These conflicts surrounding Hal reach their climax and resolution at the field of Shrewsbury in Act 5. Hal's worth must be proven at Hotspur's expense. The rivalry between the two has been intense throughout the play, as seen for example in Hal's brilliant mimicking of Hotspur's devotion to bloodshed (2.4.101–8). Aware that his tarnished reputation puts him at a disadvantage, Hal speaks nobly of his rival and impresses even the adversarial camp with his regal bearing (5.1.83–100, 5.2.51–68). He rescues his father in the battle, thereby proving to King Henry that his son does not wish to supplant him, as he had feared. After the battle, Hal frees his Scottish adversary the Douglas in a display of princely magnificence, doing so with a more generous motive than Hotspur had displayed in his earlier release of the Douglas as his prisoner (1.3.259–62). Meantime, Hal has put considerable distance between himself and Falstaff, though sensitive still to the warmth of old memories. When he sees Hotspur and Fal-

staff on the ground together, both seemingly dead, Hal views as in a tableau the contrasting models between which he has shaped his own identity. Yet Falstaff is not dead. He rises to mutilate Hotspur's body and to claim the honor due Hal for Hotspur's death. For all Falstaff's witty commentary at the expense of honor, his own opposite course is unsuited to a time of war or to Hal's new public role. Falstaff's abuse of military conscription, his carrying a bottle of sack in place of a pistol, show him at his wittiest still, but in a world that may not tolerate such pranks. The merry games are out of place and childish. With characteristic generosity and imprudence, Hal gives the credit for Hotspur's death to Falstaff, who claims it so cravenly. Even so, the magic of their association has vanished. The time of adulthood is upon Hal.

The First Part of King Henry The Fourth

[*Dramatis Personae*

KING HENRY THE FOURTH
PRINCE HENRY, *Prince of Wales*, } *sons of the King*
PRINCE JOHN OF LANCASTER,
EARL OF WESTMORLAND
SIR WALTER BLUNT

EARL OF NORTHUMBERLAND, *Henry Percy,*
HARRY PERCY (HOTSPUR), *his son,*
EARL OF WORCESTER, *Northumberland's younger brother,*
LORD MORTIMER, *Edmund Mortimer also referred to as the Earl of March,*   } *rebels against the King*
OWEN GLENDOWER,
EARL OF DOUGLAS, *Archibald Douglas,*
SIR RICHARD VERNON,
ARCHBISHOP OF YORK, *Richard Scroop,*
SIR MICHAEL, *a member of the Archbishop's household,*

LADY PERCY, *Hotspur's wife and Mortimer's sister*
LADY MORTIMER, *Mortimer's wife and Glendower's daughter*

SIR JOHN FALSTAFF
NED POINS
BARDOLPH
PETO
GADSHILL, *arranger of the highway robbery*
HOSTESS OF THE TAVERN, *Mistress Quickly*
FRANCIS, *a drawer, or tapster*
VINTNER, *or tavern keeper*

FIRST CARRIER
SECOND CARRIER
HOSTLER
CHAMBERLAIN
FIRST TRAVELER
SHERIFF
SERVANT *to Hotspur*
MESSENGER
SECOND MESSENGER

Soldiers, Travelers, Lords, Attendants

SCENE: *England and Wales*]

[1.1]

*Enter the King, Lord John of Lancaster, [the] Earl
of Westmorland, [Sir Walter Blunt,] with others.*

KING
So shaken as we are, so wan with care,
Find we a time for frighted peace to pant,   2
And breathe short-winded accents of new broils   3
To be commenced in strands afar remote.   4
No more the thirsty entrance of this soil   5
Shall daub her lips with her own children's blood;   6
No more shall trenching war channel her fields   7
Nor bruise her flowerets with the armèd hoofs
Of hostile paces. Those opposèd eyes,   9
Which, like the meteors of a troubled heaven,
All of one nature, of one substance bred,
Did lately meet in the intestine shock   12
And furious close of civil butchery,   13
Shall now in mutual well-beseeming ranks
March all one way and be no more opposed
Against acquaintance, kindred, and allies.
The edge of war, like an ill-sheathèd knife,
No more shall cut his master. Therefore, friends,   18
As far as to the sepulcher of Christ—
Whose soldier now, under whose blessèd cross
We are impressèd and engaged to fight—   21
Forthwith a power of English shall we levy,   22
Whose arms were molded in their mothers' womb   23
To chase these pagans in those holy fields
Over whose acres walked those blessèd feet
Which fourteen hundred years ago were nailed
For our advantage on the bitter cross.
But this our purpose now is twelve month old,
And bootless 'tis to tell you we will go.   29
Therefore we meet not now. Then let me hear   30
Of you, my gentle cousin Westmorland,   31
What yesternight our council did decree
In forwarding this dear expedience.   33

WESTMORLAND
My liege, this haste was hot in question,   34
And many limits of the charge set down   35
But yesternight, when all athwart there came   36
A post from Wales loaden with heavy news,   37
Whose worst was that the noble Mortimer,
Leading the men of Herefordshire to fight
Against the irregular and wild Glendower,

Was by the rude hands of that Welshman taken,
A thousand of his people butcherèd—
Upon whose dead corpse there was such misuse,   43
Such beastly shameless transformation,   44
By those Welshwomen done as may not be
Without much shame retold or spoken of.

KING
It seems then that the tidings of this broil
Brake off our business for the Holy Land.

WESTMORLAND
This matched with other did, my gracious lord;   49
For more uneven and unwelcome news   50
Came from the north, and thus it did import:
On Holy Rood Day, the gallant Hotspur there,   52
Young Harry Percy, and brave Archibald,
That ever-valiant and approvèd Scot,   54
At Holmedon met, where they did spend   55
A sad and bloody hour,
As by discharge of their artillery   57
And shape of likelihood the news was told;   58
For he that brought them, in the very heat   59
And pride of their contention did take horse,   60
Uncertain of the issue any way.

KING
Here is a dear, a true industrious friend,   62
Sir Walter Blunt, new lighted from his horse,   63
Stained with the variation of each soil
Betwixt that Holmedon and this seat of ours;
And he hath brought us smooth and welcome news.   66
The Earl of Douglas is discomfited;   67
Ten thousand bold Scots, two-and-twenty knights,
Balked in their own blood, did Sir Walter see   69
On Holmedon's plains. Of prisoners, Hotspur took
Mordake, Earl of Fife and eldest son   71
To beaten Douglas, and the Earl of Atholl,
Of Murray, Angus, and Menteith.
And is not this an honorable spoil?
A gallant prize? Ha, cousin, is it not?

WESTMORLAND
In faith, it is a conquest for a prince to boast of.

KING
Yea, there thou mak'st me sad, and mak'st me sin
In envy that my lord Northumberland
Should be the father to so blest a son—
A son who is the theme of honor's tongue,
Amongst a grove the very straightest plant,   81
Who is sweet Fortune's minion and her pride,   82
Whilst I, by looking on the praise of him,
See riot and dishonor stain the brow   84
Of my young Harry. Oh, that it could be proved

1.1. Location: The royal court.
2 Find we let us find.   **frighted** frightened   **3 breathe short-winded
accents** speak, even though we are out of breath.   **accents** words.
broils battles   **4 strands afar remote** far-off shores, i.e., of the Holy
Land (to which, at the end of *Richard II*, Henry has pledged himself
to a crusade).   **5 thirsty entrance** i.e., parched mouth   **6 daub** coat,
smear   **7 trenching** cutting, plowing   **9 paces** horses' tread.
12 intestine internal   **13 close** hand-to-hand encounter.   **civil** (as in
"civil war")   **18 his** its   **21 impressèd** conscripted   **22 power** army
23 their mother's i.e., England's, but also suggesting *their mothers'*
29 bootless useless   **30 Therefore . . . now** That is not the reason for
our present meeting.   **31 Of** from.   **gentle cousin** noble kinsman
33 dear expedience urgent expedition.   **34 hot in question** being
hotly debated   **35 limits . . . charge** particulars of military responsibility   **36 athwart** at cross purposes, contrarily   **37 post** messenger.
loaden laden

43 corpse corpses   **44 transformation** mutilation   **49 other** other
news   **50 uneven** disconcerting, distressing   **52 Holy Rood Day**
September 14   **54 approvèd** proved by experience   **55 Holmedon**
Humbleton in Northumberland   **57 by** judging from   **58 shape of
likelihood** likely outcome   **59 them** the news   **60 pride** height
62–3 Here . . . Blunt (Whether Blunt enters at the start of the scene,
or now, or possibly not at all, is not certain in the original text.)
66 smooth pleasant   **67 discomfited** defeated   **69 Balked** heaped up
in balks, or ridges   **71 Mordake** i.e., Murdoch, son of the Earl of
Albany   **81 plant** young tree   **82 minion** favorite   **84 riot** debauchery

That some night-tripping fairy had exchanged 86
In cradle clothes our children where they lay,
And called mine Percy, his Plantagenet! 88
Then would I have his Harry, and he mine.
But let him from my thoughts. What think you, coz, 90
Of this young Percy's pride? The prisoners
Which he in this adventure hath surprised 92
To his own use he keeps, and sends me word 93
I shall have none but Mordake, Earl of Fife. 94

WESTMORLAND
This is his uncle's teaching. This is Worcester,
Malevolent to you in all aspects, 96
Which makes him prune himself and bristle up 97
The crest of youth against your dignity.

KING
But I have sent for him to answer this;
And for this cause awhile we must neglect
Our holy purpose to Jerusalem.
Cousin, on Wednesday next our council we
Will hold at Windsor. So inform the lords.
But come yourself with speed to us again,
For more is to be said and to be done
Than out of anger can be utterèd.

WESTMORLAND   I will, my liege.   *Exeunt.*

[1.2]

Enter Prince of Wales and Sir John Falstaff.

FALSTAFF
Now, Hal, what time of day is it, lad?
PRINCE   Thou art so fat-witted with drinking of old sack, 2
and unbuttoning thee after supper, and sleeping upon
benches after noon, that thou hast forgotten to de- 4
mand that truly which thou wouldst truly know. What
a devil hast thou to do with the time of the day? Unless 6
hours were cups of sack, and minutes capons, and
clocks the tongues of bawds, and dials the signs of 8
leaping houses, and the blessèd sun himself a fair hot 9
wench in flame-colored taffeta, I see no reason why 10
thou shouldst be so superfluous to demand the time 11
of the day.
FALSTAFF   Indeed, you come near me now, Hal, for we 13
that take purses go by the moon and the seven stars, 14

and not by Phoebus, "he, that wandering knight so 15
fair." And I prithee, sweet wag, when thou art king, 16
as, God save Thy Grace—Majesty I should say, for 17
grace thou wilt have none—
PRINCE   What, none?
FALSTAFF   No, by my troth, not so much as will serve to 20
be prologue to an egg and butter. 21
PRINCE   Well, how then? Come, roundly, roundly. 22
FALSTAFF   Marry, then, sweet wag, when thou art 23
king, let not us that are squires of the night's body be 24
called thieves of the day's beauty. Let us be Diana' for- 25
esters, gentlemen of the shade, minions of the moon; 26
and let men say we be men of good government, 27
being governed, as the sea is, by our noble and chaste
mistress the moon, under whose countenance we steal. 29
PRINCE   Thou sayest well, and it holds well too, for the 30
fortune of us that are the moon's men doth ebb and
flow like the sea, being governed, as the sea is, by the
moon. As, for proof, now: a purse of gold most
resolutely snatched on Monday night and most disso-
lutely spent on Tuesday morning, got with swearing
"Lay by" and spent with crying "Bring in," now in as 36
low an ebb as the foot of the ladder and by and by in 37
as high a flow as the ridge of the gallows. 38
FALSTAFF   By the Lord, thou say'st true, lad. And is not
my hostess of the tavern a most sweet wench?
PRINCE   As the honey of Hybla, my old lad of the castle. 41
And is not a buff jerkin a most sweet robe of durance? 42
FALSTAFF   How now, how now, mad wag, what, in thy
quips and thy quiddities? What a plague have I to do 44
with a buff jerkin?
PRINCE   Why, what a pox have I to do with my hostess 46
of the tavern?
FALSTAFF   Well, thou hast called her to a reckoning many 48
a time and oft.
PRINCE   Did I ever call for thee to pay thy part?
FALSTAFF   No, I'll give thee thy due, thou hast paid all
there.
PRINCE   Yea, and elsewhere, so far as my coin would
stretch, and where it would not I have used my credit.

15–16 Phoebus . . . fair (Phoebus, god of the sun, is here equated with the wandering knight of a ballad or popular romance.)   **17 Grace** royal highness. (With pun on spiritual *grace* and also on the *grace* or blessing before a meal.)   **20 troth** faith   **21 prologue . . . butter** i.e., grace before a brief meal.   **22 roundly** i.e., out with it.   **23 Marry** Indeed. (Literally, "by the Virgin Mary.")   **wag** joker   **24–5 let . . . beauty** i.e., let not us who are attendants on the goddess of night, members of her household, be blamed for stealing daylight by sleeping in the daytime.   **25–6 Diana's foresters** (An elegant name for thieves by night; Diana is goddess of the moon and the hunt.)   **26 minions** favorites   **27 government** (1) conduct (2) commonwealth   **29 countenance** (1) face (2) patronage, approval.   **steal** (1) move stealthily (2) rob.   **30 it holds well** the comparison is apt   **36 Lay by** (A cry of highwaymen, like "Hands up!")   **Bring in** (An order given to a waiter in a tavern.)   **37 ladder** (1) pier ladder (2) gallows ladder   **38 ridge** crossbar   **41 Hybla** (A town, famed for its honey, in Sicily near Syracuse.)   **old . . . castle** (1) a roisterer (2) the name, Sir John Oldcastle, borne by Falstaff in an earlier version of this play.   **42 buff jerkin** a leather jacket worn by officers of the law.   **durance** (1) imprisonment (2) durability, durable cloth.   **44 quiddities** subtleties of speech.   **46 pox** syphilis. (Here, *what a pox* is used as an expletive, like "what the devil.")   **48 reckoning** settlement of the bill. (With bawdy suggestion that is continued in *pay thy part* and *my coin would stretch.*)

86 night-tripping i.e., moving nimbly in the night   **88 Plantagenet** (Family name of English royalty since Henry II.)   **90 let him** let him go.   **coz** cousin, i.e., kinsman   **92 surprised** ambushed, captured   **93 To . . . use** i.e., to collect ransom for them   **94 none but Mordake** (Since Mordake was of royal blood, being grandson to Robert II of Scotland, Hotspur could not claim him as his prisoner according to the law of arms.)   **96 Malevolent . . . aspects** (1) implacably hostile to you (2) in astrological terms, a planet in a disobedient orbit, ominous as seen from every angle   **97 Which . . . himself** i.e., which teaching makes Hotspur preen himself (as a falcon preens its feathers)   **1.2. Location: London, perhaps in an apartment of the Prince's.**   **2 sack** a Spanish white wine   **4 forgotten** forgotten how   **6 a devil** in the devil   **8 dials** clocks   **9 leaping houses** houses of prostitution   **10 taffeta** (Commonly worn by prostitutes.)   **11 superfluous** (1) unnecessarily concerned (2) self-indulgent   **13 you . . . now** i.e., you've scored a point on me   **14 go by** (1) travel by the light of (2) tell time by.   **the seven stars** the Pleiades

FALSTAFF   Yea, and so used it that, were it not here apparent that thou art heir apparent—But I prithee, sweet wag, shall there be gallows standing in England when thou art king? And resolution thus fubbed as it 58 is with the rusty curb of old father Antic the law? Do 59 not thou, when thou art king, hang a thief.

PRINCE   No, thou shalt.

FALSTAFF   Shall I? Oh, rare! By the Lord, I'll be a brave 62 judge.

PRINCE   Thou judgest false already. I mean, thou shalt have the hanging of the thieves, and so become a rare 65 hangman.

FALSTAFF   Well, Hal, well; and in some sort it jumps 67 with my humor as well as waiting in the court, I can 68 tell you.

PRINCE   For obtaining of suits? 70

FALSTAFF   Yea, for obtaining of suits, whereof the hangman hath no lean wardrobe. 'Sblood, I am as 72 melancholy as a gib cat or a lugged bear. 73

PRINCE   Or an old lion, or a lover's lute.

FALSTAFF   Yea, or the drone of a Lincolnshire bagpipe.

PRINCE   What sayest thou to a hare, or the melancholy 76 of Moorditch? 77

FALSTAFF   Thou hast the most unsavory similes, and art indeed the most comparative, rascalliest, sweet young 79 prince. But Hal, I prithee, trouble me no more with vanity. I would to God thou and I knew where a com- 81 modity of good names were to be bought. An old lord 82 of the council rated me the other day in the street 83 about you, sir, but I marked him not; and yet he talked very wisely, but I regarded him not; and yet he talked wisely, and in the street too.

PRINCE   Thou didst well, for wisdom cries out in the 87 streets and no man regards it. 88

FALSTAFF   Oh, thou hast damnable iteration, and art 89 indeed able to corrupt a saint. Thou hast done much harm upon me, Hal, God forgive thee for it. Before I knew thee, Hal, I knew nothing; and now am I, if a 92 man should speak truly, little better than one of the wicked. I must give over this life, and I will give it over. By the Lord, an I do not I am a villain. I'll be 95 damned for never a king's son in Christendom.

PRINCE   Where shall we take a purse tomorrow, Jack?

FALSTAFF   Zounds, where thou wilt, lad, I'll make one. 98 An I do not, call me villain and baffle me. 99

PRINCE   I see a good amendment of life in thee—from praying to purse taking.

FALSTAFF   Why, Hal, 'tis my vocation, Hal. 'Tis no sin for a man to labor in his vocation. 102

Enter Poins.

Poins! Now shall we know if Gadshill have set a 104 match. Oh, if men were to be saved by merit, what 105 hole in hell were hot enough for him? This is the most omnipotent villain that ever cried "Stand!" to a 107 true man. 108

PRINCE   Good morrow, Ned.

POINS   Good morrow, sweet Hal.—What says Monsieur Remorse? What says Sir John, Sack-and-Sugar Jack? How agrees the devil and thee about thy soul that thou soldest him on Good Friday last for a cup of Madeira and a cold capon's leg?

PRINCE   Sir John stands to his word; the devil shall have 115 his bargain, for he was never yet a breaker of proverbs. He will give the devil his due.

POINS   Then art thou damned for keeping thy word with the devil.

PRINCE   Else he had been damned for cozening the 120 devil.

POINS   But my lads, my lads, tomorrow morning, by four o'clock early, at Gad's Hill, there are pilgrims 123 going to Canterbury with rich offerings and traders riding to London with fat purses. I have vizards for 125 you all; you have horses for yourselves. Gadshill lies 126 tonight in Rochester. I have bespoke supper tomorrow 127 night in Eastcheap. We may do it as secure as sleep. If 128 you will go, I will stuff your purses full of crowns; if 129 you will not, tarry at home and be hanged.

FALSTAFF   Hear ye, Yedward, if I tarry at home and go 131 not, I'll hang you for going. 132

POINS   You will, chops? 133

FALSTAFF   Hal, wilt thou make one?

PRINCE   Who, I rob? I a thief? Not I, by my faith.

FALSTAFF   There's neither honesty, manhood, nor good fellowship in thee, nor thou cam'st not of the blood royal, if thou darest not stand for ten shillings. 138

---

58 resolution courage (of a highwayman).   **fubbed** cheated
59 Antic buffoon   **62 rare** splendid.   **brave** excellent   **65 have . . . thieves** (1) be in charge of hanging thieves (or protecting them from hanging) (2) hang like other thieves.   **rare** (1) rarely used (2) excellent   **67–8 jumps . . . humor** suits my temperament   **68 waiting in the court** being in attendance at the royal court   **70 suits** petitions. (But Falstaff uses the word to mean suits of clothes; clothes belonging to an executed man were given to the executioner.)   **72 'Sblood** By his (Christ's) blood   **73 gib cat** tomcat.   **lugged bear** bear led by a chain and baited by dogs.   **76 hare** (A proverbially melancholy animal.)   **77 Moorditch** (A foul ditch draining Moorfields, outside London walls.)   **79 comparative** given to abusive comparisons   **81 vanity** worldliness.   **81–2 commodity** supply   **82 names** reputations   **83 rated** chastised   **87–8 wisdom . . . regards it** (Hal paraphrases Proverbs 1:20–4, "Wisdom crieth without, and putteth forth her voice in the streets . . . and no man regarded," in jocose reply to Falstaff's mock sanctimoniousness.)   **89 iteration** repetition (of biblical texts, with a neat twist)   **92 nothing** i.e., no evil   **95 an** if

98 Zounds By his (Christ's) wounds.   **make one** be one of the party.
99 baffle publicly disgrace   **102 vocation** (A favorite term of the reforming Protestant ministers to describe the function or station to which one is called by God. Falstaff comically misapplies it to justify highway robbing.)   **104 Gadshill** (The name of one of the highwaymen.)   **104–5 set a match** arranged a robbery.   **105 by merit** i.e., according to their deservings rather than by God's grace   **107 omnipotent** unparalleled, utter.   **"Stand!"** "Stand and deliver!" i.e., Hand over your money.   **108 true man** honest citizen.   **115 stands to** keeps   **120 Else** Otherwise.   **cozening** cheating   **123 Gad's Hill** (Location near Rochester on the road from London to Canterbury; one of the highwaymen is called Gadshill.)   **125 vizards** masks   **126 lies** lodges   **127 bespoke** ordered   **128 Eastcheap** market district in London, with many taverns.   **129 crowns** gold coins   **131 Yedward** (Nickname for *Edward*, Poins's first name.)   **131–2 if I . . . going** i.e., there's no chance of my not going; sooner than that, I'd see you hanged instead for going in my place.   **133 chops** i.e., fat jaws or cheeks.   **138 stand . . . shillings** (1) stand up and fight for booty (2) be worth ten shillings, the value of the *royal*, the gold coin alluded to in *blood royal* (line 138).

PRINCE   Well then, once in my days I'll be a madcap.

FALSTAFF   Why, that's well said.

PRINCE   Well, come what will, I'll tarry at home.

FALSTAFF   By the Lord, I'll be a traitor then, when thou art king.

PRINCE   I care not.

POINS   Sir John, I prithee leave the Prince and me alone. I will lay him down such reasons for this adventure that he shall go.

FALSTAFF   Well, God give thee the spirit of persuasion and him the ears of profiting, that what thou speakest may move and what he hears may be believed, that the true prince may, for recreation sake, prove a false thief; for the poor abuses of the time want counte- 152
nance. Farewell. You shall find me in Eastcheap. 153

PRINCE   Farewell, thou latter spring! Farewell, All- 154
hallown summer!   [*Exit Falstaff.*] 155

POINS   Now, my good sweet honey lord, ride with us tomorrow. I have a jest to execute that I cannot manage alone. Falstaff, Peto, Bardolph, and Gadshill shall rob those men that we have already waylaid— 159
yourself and I will not be there—and when they have the booty, if you and I do not rob them, cut this head off from my shoulders.

PRINCE   How shall we part with them in setting forth?

POINS   Why, we will set forth before or after them and appoint them a place of meeting, wherein it is at our pleasure to fail; and then will they adventure upon the 166
exploit themselves, which they shall have no sooner achieved but we'll set upon them.

PRINCE   Yea, but 'tis like that they will know us by our 169
horses, by our habits, and by every other appoint- 170
ment, to be ourselves. 171

POINS   Tut, our horses they shall not see—I'll tie them in the wood; our vizards we will change after we leave them; and, sirrah, I have cases of buckram for the 174
nonce, to immask our noted outward garments. 175

PRINCE   Yea, but I doubt they will be too hard for us. 176

POINS   Well, for two of them, I know them to be as 178
true-bred cowards as ever turned back; and for the third, if he fight longer than he sees reason, I'll for- 180
swear arms. The virtue of this jest will be the incompre- 181
hensible lies that this same fat rogue will tell us when we meet at supper—how thirty at least he fought with, what wards, what blows, what extremities he 183
endured; and in the reproof of this lives the jest. 184

PRINCE   Well, I'll go with thee. Provide us all things necessary and meet me tomorrow night in Eastcheap. There I'll sup. Farewell.

POINS   Farewell, my lord.   *Exit Poins.*

PRINCE
I know you all, and will awhile uphold
The unyoked humor of your idleness. 190
Yet herein will I imitate the sun,
Who doth permit the base contagious clouds 192
To smother up his beauty from the world,
That when he please again to be himself, 194
Being wanted he may be more wondered at 195
By breaking through the foul and ugly mists
Of vapors that did seem to strangle him.
If all the year were playing holidays,
To sport would be as tedious as to work;
But when they seldom come, they wished-for come,
And nothing pleaseth but rare accidents. 201
So when this loose behavior I throw off
And pay the debt I never promisèd,
By how much better than my word I am,
By so much shall I falsify men's hopes; 205
And like bright metal on a sullen ground, 206
My reformation, glitt'ring o'er my fault,
Shall show more goodly and attract more eyes
Than that which hath no foil to set it off. 209
I'll so offend to make offense a skill, 210
Redeeming time when men think least I will.   *Exit.* 211

[1.3]

Enter the King, Northumberland, Worcester,
Hotspur, Sir Walter Blunt, with others.

KING
My blood hath been too cold and temperate,
Unapt to stir at these indignities,
And you have found me, for accordingly 3
You tread upon my patience. But be sure
I will from henceforth rather be myself, 5
Mighty and to be feared, than my condition, 6
Which hath been smooth as oil, soft as young down,
And therefore lost that title of respect
Which the proud soul ne'er pays but to the proud.

WORCESTER
Our house, my sovereign liege, little deserves 10
The scourge of greatness to be used on it—
And that same greatness too which our own hands
Have holp to make so portly. 13

NORTHUMBERLAND [*to the King*]   My lord—

KING
Worcester, get thee gone, for I do see

152–3 want countenance lack sponsorship (from men of rank).
154–5 All-hallown summer a season of clement weather around All Saints' Day, November 1; the *latter spring* or "Indian summer" of Falstaff's old age.   **159 waylaid** set an ambush for   **166 pleasure** choice, discretion   **169 like** likely   **170 habits** garments   **170–1 appointment** accoutrement   **174 sirrah** (Usually addressed to an inferior; here, a sign of intimacy.)   **174–5 cases . . . nonce** suits of buckram, a stiff-finished heavily sized fabric, for the purpose   **175 immask** hide, disguise.   **noted** known   **176 doubt** fear.   **too hard** too formidable   **178 turned back** turned their backs and ran away   **180–1 incomprehensible** boundless   **183 wards** parries   **184 reproof** disproof

190 unyoked . . . idleness unbridled inclination of your frivolity.
192 contagious noxious   **194 That** so that   **195 wanted** missed, lacked   **201 accidents** events.   **205 hopes** expectations   **206 sullen ground** dark background, like a *foil*. (See line 209.)   **209 foil** metal sheet laid contrastingly behind a jewel to set off its luster   **210 to** as to.   **skill** i.e., clever tactic, piece of good policy   **211 Redeeming time** i.e., making amends for lost time
1.3. Location: London. The court (historically at Windsor).
3 found me found me so   **5 myself** i.e., my royal self   **6 my condition** my natural (mild) disposition   **10 Our house** i.e., The Percy family   **13 holp** helped.   **portly** majestic, prosperous.

Danger and disobedience in thine eye.
Oh, sir, your presence is too bold and peremptory,
And majesty might never yet endure
The moody frontier of a servant brow.   19
You have good leave to leave us. When we need   20
Your use and counsel, we shall send for you.
                         Exit Worcester.
[*To Northumberland*] You were about to speak.
NORTHUMBERLAND   Yea, my good lord.
Those prisoners in Your Highness' name demanded,
Which Harry Percy here at Holmedon took,
Were, as he says, not with such strength denied
As is delivered to Your Majesty.   26
Either envy, therefore, or misprision   27
Is guilty of this fault, and not my son.
HOTSPUR [*to the King*]
My liege, I did deny no prisoners,
But I remember when the fight was done,
When I was dry with rage and extreme toil,
Breathless and faint, leaning upon my sword,
Came there a certain lord, neat and trimly dressed,
Fresh as a bridegroom, and his chin new reaped   34
Showed like a stubble land at harvest home.   35
He was perfumèd like a milliner,   36
And twixt his finger and his thumb he held
A pouncet box, which ever and anon   38
He gave his nose and took't away again,
Who therewith angry, when it next came there,   40
Took it in snuff; and still he smiled and talked,   41
And as the soldiers bore dead bodies by
He called them untaught knaves, unmannerly,
To bring a slovenly unhandsome corpse
Betwixt the wind and his nobility.
With many holiday and lady terms   46
He questioned me, amongst the rest demanded
My prisoners in Your Majesty's behalf.
I then, all smarting with my wounds being cold,
To be so pestered with a popinjay,   50
Out of my grief and my impatience   51
Answered neglectingly I know not what,
He should, or he should not; for he made me mad
To see him shine so brisk, and smell so sweet,
And talk so like a waiting-gentlewoman
Of guns and drums and wounds—God save the
    mark!—   56
And telling me the sovereignest thing on earth   57
Was parmacety for an inward bruise,   58

And that it was great pity, so it was,
This villainous saltpeter should be digged   60
Out of the bowels of the harmless earth,
Which many a good tall fellow had destroyed   62
So cowardly, and but for these vile guns
He would himself have been a soldier.
This bald unjointed chat of his, my lord,   65
I answered indirectly, as I said,   66
And I beseech you, let not his report
Come current for an accusation   68
Betwixt my love and your high majesty.
BLUNT [*to the King*]
The circumstance considered, good my lord,
Whate'er Lord Harry Percy then had said
To such a person and in such a place,
At such a time, with all the rest retold,
May reasonably die, and never rise
To do him wrong or any way impeach   75
What then he said, so he unsay it now.   76
KING
Why, yet he doth deny his prisoners,   77
But with proviso and exception   78
That we at our own charge shall ransom straight   79
His brother-in-law, the foolish Mortimer,   80
Who, on my soul, hath willfully betrayed
The lives of those that he did lead to fight
Against that great magician, damned Glendower,
Whose daughter, as we hear, that Earl of March   84
Hath lately married. Shall our coffers then
Be emptied to redeem a traitor home?
Shall we buy treason and indent with fears   87
When they have lost and forfeited themselves?
No, on the barren mountains let him starve!
For I shall never hold that man my friend
Whose tongue shall ask me for one penny cost
To ransom home revolted Mortimer.   92
HOTSPUR   Revolted Mortimer?
He never did fall off, my sovereign liege,   94
But by the chance of war. To prove that true
Needs no more but one tongue for all those wounds,
Those mouthèd wounds, which valiantly he took,   97
When on the gentle Severn's sedgy bank,   98
In single opposition, hand to hand,

---

60 saltpeter potassium nitrate, used to make gunpowder and also used medicinally **62 tall** brave **65 bald** trivial **66 indirectly** inattentively, offhandedly **68 Come current** (1) be taken at face value (2) come rushing in **75 impeach** discredit **76 so** provided that **77 yet** (emphatic) i.e., even now. **deny** refuse to surrender **78 proviso and exception** (synonymous terms) **79 straight** straightway, at once **80 Mortimer** (There were two Edmund Mortimers; Shakespeare confuses them and combines their stories. It was the uncle [1376–1409?] who was captured by Glendower and married Glendower's daughter; it was the nephew [1391–1425], fifth Earl of March, who was proclaimed heir presumptive to King Richard II after the death of his father, the fourth earl, whom Richard had named as his heir. The uncle was brother to the fourth earl and to Hotspur's wife, Elizabeth, called Kate in this play.) **84 Earl of March** (The "Mortimer" of line 80; see note there.) **87 indent with fears** i.e., make a bargain or come to terms with traitors whom we have reason to fear **92 revolted** rebellious **94 fall off** change his allegiance **97 mouthèd** gaping and eloquent **98 Severn's** (The Severn River flows from northern Wales and western England into the Bristol Channel.) **sedgy** bordered with reeds

---

19 moody frontier i.e., angry brow, frown. (*Frontier* literally means "outwork" or "fortification.") **20 good leave** full permission **26 delivered** reported **27 envy** malice. **misprision** misunderstanding **34 chin new reaped** i.e., with beard freshly barbered according to the latest fashion, not like a soldier's beard **35 Showed** looked. **harvest home** end of harvest, fields being cut back to stubble. **36 milliner** dealer in fancy articles, such as gloves and hats **38 pouncet box** perfume box with perforated lid **40 Who** i.e., his nose **41 Took it in snuff** (1) inhaled it (2) took offense. **still** continually **46 holiday and lady** dainty and effeminate **50 popinjay** parrot **51 grief** pain **56 God . . . mark** (Probably originally a formula to avert evil omen; here, an expression of impatience.) **57 sovereignest** most efficacious **58 parmacety** spermaceti, a fatty substance taken from the head of the sperm whale, used as a medicinal ointment

He did confound the best part of an hour   100
In changing hardiment with great Glendower.   101
Three times they breathed, and three times did they
    drink,   102
Upon agreement, of swift Severn's flood,   103
Who then, affrighted with their bloody looks,   104
Ran fearfully among the trembling reeds
And hid his crisp head in the hollow bank,   106
Bloodstainèd with these valiant combatants.
Never did bare and rotten policy   108
Color her working with such deadly wounds,   109
Nor never could the noble Mortimer
Receive so many, and all willingly.
Then let not him be slandered with revolt.   112

KING
Thou dost belie him, Percy, thou dost belie him.
He never did encounter with Glendower.
I tell thee,
He durst as well have met the devil alone
As Owen Glendower for an enemy.
Art thou not ashamed? But, sirrah, henceforth
Let me not hear you speak of Mortimer.
Send me your prisoners with the speediest means,
Or you shall hear in such a kind from me   121
As will displease you.—My lord Northumberland,
We license your departure with your son.
Send us your prisoners, or you will hear of it.
        Exit King [with Blunt, and train].

HOTSPUR
An if the devil come and roar for them   125
I will not send them. I will after straight   126
And tell him so, for I will ease my heart,
Albeit I make a hazard of my head.   128

NORTHUMBERLAND
What, drunk with choler? Stay and pause awhile.   129
Here comes your uncle.

        Enter Worcester.

HOTSPUR   Speak of Mortimer?
Zounds, I will speak of him, and let my soul
Want mercy if I do not join with him!   132
Yea, on his part I'll empty all these veins,   133
And shed my dear blood drop by drop in the dust,
But I will lift the downtrod Mortimer
As high in the air as this unthankful king,
As this ingrate and cankered Bolingbroke.   137

NORTHUMBERLAND
Brother, the King hath made your nephew mad.

WORCESTER
Who struck this heat up after I was gone?

HOTSPUR
He will forsooth have all my prisoners;
And when I urged the ransom once again
Of my wife's brother, then his cheek looked pale,
And on my face he turned an eye of death,   143
Trembling even at the name of Mortimer.

WORCESTER
I cannot blame him. Was not he proclaimed   145
By Richard, that dead is, the next of blood?   146

NORTHUMBERLAND
He was; I heard the proclamation.
And then it was when the unhappy king—   148
Whose wrongs in us God pardon!—did set forth   149
Upon his Irish expedition;   150
From whence he, intercepted, did return   151
To be deposed and shortly murderèd.

WORCESTER
And for whose death we in the world's wide mouth
Live scandalized and foully spoken of.

HOTSPUR
But, soft, I pray you, did King Richard then   155
Proclaim my brother Edmund Mortimer   156
Heir to the crown?

NORTHUMBERLAND   He did; myself did hear it.

HOTSPUR
Nay, then I cannot blame his cousin king,   158
That wished him on the barren mountains starve.
But shall it be that you set the crown
Upon the head of this forgetful man,
And for his sake wear the detested blot
Of murderous subornation—shall it be   163
That you a world of curses undergo,
Being the agents, or base second means,   165
The cords, the ladder, or the hangman rather?
Oh, pardon me that I descend so low
To show the line and the predicament   168
Wherein you range under this subtle king!   169
Shall it for shame be spoken in these days,
Or fill up chronicles in time to come,
That men of your nobility and power
Did gage them both in an unjust behalf,   173
As both of you—God pardon it!—have done,
To put down Richard, that sweet lovely rose,
And plant this thorn, this canker, Bolingbroke?   176
And shall it in more shame be further spoken
That you are fooled, discarded, and shook off
By him for whom these shames ye underwent?
No! Yet time serves wherein you may redeem   180
Your banished honors and restore yourselves

---

100 confound consume   **101 changing hardiment** exchanging blows, matching valor   **102 breathed** paused for breath   **103 flood** river   **104 Who** i.e., the river   **106 crisp** curly, i.e., rippled   **108 bare** paltry. **policy** cunning   **109 Color** disguise   **112 revolt** i.e., the accusation of rebellion.   **121 kind** manner   **125 An if** If   **126 will after straight** will go after him immediately   **128 Albeit . . . head** even if I risk being beheaded.   **129 choler** anger.   **132 Want mercy** lack mercy, be damned   **133 on his part** i.e., fighting on Mortimer's side **137 cankered** spoiled, malignant.   **Bolingbroke** i.e., King Henry IV. (Hotspur pointedly refuses to acknowledge his royalty.)

143 an eye of death a fearful look   **145 he** i.e., Mortimer   **146 next of blood** heir to the throne.   **148 unhappy** unfortunate   **149 in us** caused by our doings   **150 Irish expedition** (Richard II was putting down a rebellion in Ireland when Bolingbroke returned to England from exile.)   **151 intercepted** interrupted   **155 soft** i.e., wait a minute   **156 brother** brother-in-law   **158 cousin** (With a pun on cozen, "cheat.")   **163 murderous subornation** the suborning of, or inciting to, murder   **165 second means** agents   **168 To . . . predicament** to show the direction things are moving and the danger to you **169 range** (1) are ranked; (2) stray   **173 gage them** engage, pledge themselves   **176 canker** (1) canker rose or dog rose, wild and unfragrant (2) ulcer   **180 Yet** Still

Into the good thoughts of the world again;
Revenge the jeering and disdained contempt   183
Of this proud king, who studies day and night
To answer all the debt he owes to you   185
Even with the bloody payment of your deaths.
Therefore, I say—

WORCESTER   Peace, cousin, say no more.   187
And now I will unclasp a secret book,
And to your quick-conceiving discontents   189
I'll read you matter deep and dangerous,
As full of peril and adventurous spirit
As to o'erwalk a current roaring loud
On the unsteadfast footing of a spear.   193

HOTSPUR
If he fall in, good night, or sink or swim!   194
Send danger from the east unto the west,
So honor cross it from the north to south,   196
And let them grapple. Oh, the blood more stirs
To rouse a lion than to start a hare!

NORTHUMBERLAND [to Worcester]
Imagination of some great exploit
Drives him beyond the bounds of patience.

HOTSPUR
By heaven, methinks it were an easy leap
To pluck bright honor from the pale-faced moon,
Or dive into the bottom of the deep,
Where fathom line could never touch the ground,   204
And pluck up drownèd honor by the locks,
So he that doth redeem her thence might wear
Without corrival all her dignities;   207
But out upon this half-faced fellowship!   208

WORCESTER [to Northumberland]
He apprehends a world of figures here,   209
But not the form of what he should attend.—   210
Good cousin, give me audience for a while.

HOTSPUR
I cry you mercy.

WORCESTER   Those same noble Scots   212
That are your prisoners—

HOTSPUR   I'll keep them all.
By God, he shall not have a Scot of them,   214
No, if a scot would save his soul, he shall not!   215
I'll keep them, by this hand.

WORCESTER   You start away
And lend no ear unto my purposes.
Those prisoners you shall keep.

HOTSPUR   Nay, I will, that's flat.   218

He said he would not ransom Mortimer,
Forbade my tongue to speak of Mortimer,
But I will find him when he lies asleep,
And in his ear I'll holler "Mortimer!"
Nay, I'll have a starling shall be taught to speak
Nothing but "Mortimer," and give it him
To keep his anger still in motion.   225

WORCESTER   Hear you, cousin, a word.

HOTSPUR
All studies here I solemnly defy,   227
Save how to gall and pinch this Bolingbroke,
And that same sword-and-buckler Prince of Wales.   229
But that I think his father loves him not
And would be glad he met with some mischance,
I would have him poisoned with a pot of ale.

WORCESTER
Farewell, kinsman. I'll talk to you
When you are better tempered to attend.

NORTHUMBERLAND [to Hotspur]
Why, what a wasp-stung and impatient fool
Art thou to break into this woman's mood,
Tying thine ear to no tongue but thine own!

HOTSPUR
Why, look you, I am whipped and scourged with rods,
Nettled and stung with pismires, when I hear   239
Of this vile politician, Bolingbroke.   240
In Richard's time—what do you call the place?—
A plague upon it, it is in Gloucestershire;
'Twas where the madcap duke his uncle kept,   243
His uncle York; where I first bowed my knee
Unto this king of smiles, this Bolingbroke—
'Sblood, when you and he came back from
Ravenspurgh.   246

NORTHUMBERLAND   At Berkeley Castle.   247

HOTSPUR   You say true.
Why, what a candy deal of courtesy   249
This fawning greyhound then did proffer me!
"Look when his infant fortune came to age,"   251
And "gentle Harry Percy," and "kind cousin"—
Oh, the devil take such cozeners!—God forgive me!   253
Good uncle, tell your tale; I have done.

WORCESTER
Nay, if you have not, to it again;
We will stay your leisure.

HOTSPUR   I have done, i'faith.   256

WORCESTER
Then once more to your Scottish prisoners.
Deliver them up without their ransom straight,   258
And make the Douglas' son your only mean   259

---

183 Revenge and wherein you may revenge yourself against.
disdained disdainful   **185 answer** satisfy, discharge   **187 cousin**
nephew   **189 quick-conceiving** comprehending quickly   **193 spear**
i.e., spear laid across a stream as a narrow bridge.   **194 If . . . swim** i.e.,
Anyone daring such a thing will face a life-or-death challenge. (Hotspur's imagination is fired by the thought of risking everything on such
an attempt.)   **196 So** provided that. (Also at line 206.)   **204 fathom
line** a weighted line marked at fathom intervals (six feet), used for
measuring the depth of water   **207 corrival** rival, competitor
208 out . . . fellowship! down with this paltry business of sharing glory
with others!   **209 apprehends** snatches at.   **figures** figures of the
imagination, or figures of speech   **210 form** essential nature.   **attend**
give attention to.   **212 cry you mercy** beg your pardon.   **214–15 Scot
. . . scot** Scotsman . . . trifling amount   **218 that's flat** that's for sure.

225 still continually   **227 studies** pursuits.   **defy** renounce
229 sword-and-buckler swashbuckling. (Gentlemen generally preferred
to wear the rapier and the dagger.)   **239 Nettled** stung with nettles.
pismires ants. (From the urinous smell of an anthill.)   **240 politician**
deceitful schemer   **243 kept** dwelled   **246 Ravenspurgh** on the
Yorkshire coast, at the mouth of the Humber River, where Bolingbroke
landed on his return from exile (*Richard II*, 2.1.296).   **247 Berkeley
Castle** castle near Bristol.   **249 candy** sugared, flattering   **251 Look
when** When, as soon as   **253 cozeners** cheats. (With pun on *cousins*.)
256 stay await   **258 Deliver them up** Free them   **259 the Douglas' son**
i.e., Mordake. (See 1.1.71 and note.)   **mean** i.e., agent

For powers in Scotland, which, for divers reasons   260
Which I shall send you written, be assured
Will easily be granted. [*To Northumberland*] You, my
    lord,
Your son in Scotland being thus employed,
Shall secretly into the bosom creep   264
Of that same noble prelate well beloved,
The Archbishop.

HOTSPUR   Of York, is it not?

WORCESTER   True, who bears hard   268
His brother's death at Bristol, the Lord Scroop.
I speak not this in estimation,   270
As what I think might be, but what I know
Is ruminated, plotted, and set down,
And only stays but to behold the face
Of that occasion that shall bring it on.

HOTSPUR
I smell it. Upon my life, it will do well.

NORTHUMBERLAND
Before the game is afoot thou still let'st slip.   276

HOTSPUR
Why, it cannot choose but be a noble plot.   277
And then the power of Scotland and of York   278
To join with Mortimer, ha?

WORCESTER   And so they shall.

HOTSPUR
In faith, it is exceedingly well aimed.   280

WORCESTER
And 'tis no little reason bids us speed,
To save our heads by raising of a head;   282
For, bear ourselves as even as we can,   283
The King will always think him in our debt,   284
And think we think ourselves unsatisfied
Till he hath found a time to pay us home.   286
And see already how he doth begin
To make us strangers to his looks of love.

HOTSPUR
He does, he does. We'll be revenged on him.

WORCESTER
Cousin, farewell. No further go in this
Than I by letters shall direct your course.
When time is ripe, which will be suddenly,   292
I'll steal to Glendower and Lord Mortimer,
Where you and Douglas and our powers at once,   294
As I will fashion it, shall happily meet   295
To bear our fortunes in our own strong arms,   296
Which now we hold at much uncertainty.

NORTHUMBERLAND
Farewell, good brother. We shall thrive, I trust.

HOTSPUR
Uncle, adieu. Oh, let the hours be short
Till fields and blows and groans applaud our sport!   300
                Exeunt [in separate groups].

❧

260 **For powers** for raising an army   264 **secretly . . . creep** win the confidence   268 **bears hard** resents   270 **estimation** guesswork   276 **still let'st slip** always let loose the dogs.   277 **cannot choose but be** cannot help being   278 **power** army   280 **aimed** designed.   282 **head** army   283 **even** carefully   284 **him** himself   286 **home** (1) fully (2) with a thrust to the heart.   292 **suddenly** soon   294 **at once** all together   295 **happily** fortunately   296 **arms** (1) limbs (2) military might   300 **fields** battlefields

[2.1]

Enter a Carrier with a lantern in his hand.

FIRST CARRIER   Heigh-ho! An it be not four by the day,   1
I'll be hanged. Charles's Wain is over the new   2
chimney, and yet our horse not packed. What, hostler!   3

HOSTLER [*within*]   Anon, anon.   4

FIRST CARRIER   I prithee, Tom, beat Cut's saddle, put a   5
few flocks in the point. Poor jade is wrung in the   6
withers out of all cess.   7

Enter another Carrier.

SECOND CARRIER   Peas and beans are as dank here as a   8
dog, and that is the next way to give poor jades the   9
bots. This house is turned upside down since Robin   10
Hostler died.

FIRST CARRIER   Poor fellow never joyed since the price
of oats rose. It was the death of him.

SECOND CARRIER   I think this be the most villainous
house in all London road for fleas. I am stung like a
tench.   16

FIRST CARRIER   Like a tench? By the Mass, there is ne'er
a king Christian could be better bit than I have been   18
since the first cock.   19

SECOND CARRIER   Why, they will allow us ne'er a jordan,   20
and then we leak in your chimney, and your chamber-   21
lye breeds fleas like a loach.   22

FIRST CARRIER [*calling*]   What, Hostler! Come away and   23
be hanged! Come away.

SECOND CARRIER   I have a gammon of bacon and two   25
races of ginger, to be delivered as far as Charing Cross.   26

FIRST CARRIER   God's body, the turkeys in my pannier   27
are quite starved. What, hostler! A plague on thee!
Hast thou never an eye in thy head? Canst not hear?
An 'twere not as good deed as drink to break the pate   30
on thee, I am a very villain. Come, and be hanged!   31
Hast no faith in thee?   32

Enter Gadshill.

2.1. Location: An innyard on the London-Canterbury road.
0.1 Carrier one whose trade was conveying goods, usually by packhorses   **1 An** If.   **by the day** in the morning   **2 Charles's Wain** i.e., Charlemagne's wagon; the constellation Ursa Major (the Big Dipper)   **3 horse** horses.   **hostler** groom.   **4 Anon** Right away, coming   **5 beat** soften.   **Cut's saddle** packsaddle of the horse named *Cut*, meaning "bobtailed"   **6 flocks** tufts of wool.   **point** pommel of the saddle.   **jade** nag   **6–7 wrung . . . withers** chafed (by his saddle) on the ridge between his shoulder-blades   **7 cess** measure, estimate.   **8 Peas and beans** i.e., Horse fodder   **8–9 dank . . . dog** i.e., damp as can be   **9 next** nearest, quickest   **10 bots** intestinal maggots.   **house** inn   **16 tench** a spotted fish, whose spots may have been likened to flea bites.   **18 king Christian** Christian king, accustomed to have the best of everything   **19 first cock** i.e., midnight.   **20 jordan** chamberpot   **21 chimney** fireplace   **21–2 chamber-lye** urine   **22 loach** a small freshwater fish, thought to harbor parasites.   **23 Come away** Come along   **25 gammon of bacon** ham   **26 races** roots.   **Charing Cross** a market town lying between London and Westminster.   **27 pannier** basket   **30 An** If   **30–1 An . . . hanged!** i.e., I'll be hanged if it wouldn't be a good idea to smack you on the head. Come along, damn you!   **32 faith** trustworthiness

GADSHILL   Good morrow, carriers. What's o'clock?

FIRST CARRIER   I think it be two o'clock.   34

GADSHILL   I prithee, lend me thy lantern to see my
gelding in the stable.   36

FIRST CARRIER   Nay, by God, soft, I know a trick worth   37
two of that, i'faith.

GADSHILL   [to the Second Carrier]   I pray thee, lend me thine.

SECOND CARRIER   Ay, when, canst tell? Lend me thy   40
lantern, quoth he! Marry, I'll see thee hanged first.   41

GADSHILL   Sirrah carrier, what time do you mean to
come to London?

SECOND CARRIER   Time enough to go to bed with a   44
candle, I warrant thee.—Come, neighbor Mugs, we'll   45
call up the gentlemen. They will along with company,   46
for they have great charge.   Exeunt [Carriers].   47

GADSHILL   What, ho! Chamberlain!   48

Enter Chamberlain.

CHAMBERLAIN   At hand, quoth pickpurse.   49

GADSHILL   That's even as fair as—at hand, quoth the   50
chamberlain; for thou variest no more from picking of   51
purses than giving direction doth from laboring; thou   52
layest the plot how.   53

CHAMBERLAIN   Good morrow, Master Gadshill. It holds   54
current that I told you yesternight: there's a franklin in   55
the Weald of Kent hath brought three hundred marks   56
with him in gold. I heard him tell it to one of his company last night at supper—a kind of auditor, one that
hath abundance of charge too, God knows what. They
are up already, and call for eggs and butter. They will
away presently.   61

GADSHILL   Sirrah, if they meet not with Saint Nicholas'   62
clerks, I'll give thee this neck.   63

CHAMBERLAIN   No, I'll none of it. I pray thee, keep that   64
for the hangman, for I know thou worshipest Saint
Nicholas as truly as a man of falsehood may.

GADSHILL   What talkest thou to me of the hangman? If   67
I hang, I'll make a fat pair of gallows; for if I hang, old
Sir John hangs with me, and thou knowest he is no
starveling. Tut, there are other Trojans that thou   70
dream'st not of, the which for sport sake are content
to do the profession some grace, that would, if matters   72

should be looked into, for their own credit sake   73
make all whole. I am joined with no foot-landrakers,   74
no long-staff sixpenny strikers, none of these mad   75
mustachio purple-hued malt-worms, but with nobility   76
and tranquillity, burgomasters and great oneyers, such   77
as can hold in, such as will strike sooner than speak,   78
and speak sooner than drink, and drink sooner than
pray. And yet, zounds, I lie, for they pray continually
to their saint, the commonwealth, or rather not pray to
her but prey on her, for they ride up and down on her
and make her their boots.   83

CHAMBERLAIN   What, the commonwealth their boots?
Will she hold out water in foul way?   85

GADSHILL   She will, she will. Justice hath liquored her.   86
We steal as in a castle, cocksure. We have the receipt   87
of fern seed; we walk invisible.   88

CHAMBERLAIN   Nay, by my faith, I think you are more
beholding to the night than to fern seed for your   90
walking invisible.

GADSHILL   Give me thy hand. Thou shalt have a share
in our purchase, as I am a true man.   93

CHAMBERLAIN   Nay, rather let me have it as you are a
false thief.

GADSHILL   Go to; *homo* is a common name to all men.   96
Bid the hostler bring my gelding out of the stable. Farewell, you muddy knave.   [Exeunt separately.]   98

❦

[2.2]

Enter Prince, Poins, Peto, and [Bardolph].

POINS   Come, shelter, shelter! I have removed Falstaff's
horse, and he frets like a gummed velvet.   2

PRINCE   Stand close.   [They step aside.]   3

Enter Falstaff.

FALSTAFF   Poins! Poins, and be hanged! Poins!

PRINCE   [coming forward]   Peace, ye fat-kidneyed rascal!
What a brawling dost thou keep!   6

FALSTAFF   Where's Poins, Hal?

---

34 two o'clock (An evasive answer; the First Carrier knows that it is at least four o'clock; see line 1.)   36 gelding castrated male horse   37 soft i.e., wait a minute   40 Ay . . . tell? i.e., You must be joking.   41 quoth he forsooth, indeed.   44–5 Time . . . candle i.e., Soon enough. (Another evasive answer.)   46–7 They . . . charge i.e., They wish to travel in company, because they have lots of valuable cargo.   48 Chamberlain (Male equivalent of a chambermaid. His entrance in the Quarto at line 47 may suggest that he is visible before Gadshill calls for him, giving point to his remark about being "At hand.")   49 At . . . pickpurse i.e., I am right beside you, as the pickpurse said.   50 fair good, apt   51–3 thou variest . . . how i.e., you don't actually do the stealing, but you give directions, like a master workman to his apprentices.   54–5 holds current that holds true what   55 a franklin a yeoman owning his own land   56 Weald wooded region.   marks coins of the value of thirteen shillings four pence   61 presently immediately.   62–3 Saint Nicholas' clerks highwaymen. (Saint Nicholas was popularly supposed to be the patron of thieves.)   64 I'll none I want none   67 What Why   70 Trojans i.e., jolly fellows, roisterers   72 profession i.e., robbery.   grace credit, favor

73–4 for . . . whole for the sake of their own reputation will make sure that all goes well. (Gadshill hints that they may be joined by some persons of social importance, such as the Prince.)   74 foot-landrakers thieves who travel on foot   75 long-staff six-penny strikers robbers with long staves who would knock down their victims for sixpence   76 mustachio . . . malt-worms purple-faced drunkards with huge mustaches   77 tranquillity those who lead easy lives.   oneyers ones, persons (?)   78 hold in keep a secret; hold fast   83 boots booty. (With pun on boots, "shoes.")   85 Will . . . way? Will she let you go dry in muddy roads? i.e., Will she protect you in tight places?   86 liquored (1) made waterproof by oiling (2) bribed (3) made drunk   87 as in a castle i.e., in complete security.   receipt recipe, formula   88 of fern seed i.e., of becoming invisible (since fern seed, almost invisible itself, was popularly supposed to render its possessor invisible)   90 beholding beholden   93 purchase booty.   96 Go to (An expression of impatience.   homo . . . men the Latin name for man applies to all types; the phrase "true man" applies to me as well as the next man.   98 muddy stupid
2.2. Location: The highway, near Gad's Hill.
2 frets (1) is vexed (2) rubs and frays like gummed velvet, velvet made glossy with a stiffening gum   3 close concealed.   6 keep keep up.

PRINCE   He is walked up to the top of the hill. I'll go
   seek him.   [*He steps aside.*]
FALSTAFF   I am accursed to rob in that thief's company.
   The rascal hath removed my horse and tied him I
   know not where. If I travel but four foot by the square   12
   further afoot, I shall break my wind. Well, I doubt not
   but to die a fair death for all this, if I scape hanging for   14
   killing that rogue. I have forsworn his company hourly
   any time this two-and-twenty years, and yet I am bewitched with the rogue's company. If the rascal have
   not given me medicines to make me love him, I'll be   18
   hanged; it could not be else—I have drunk medicines.
   Poins! Hal! A plague upon you both! Bardolph! Peto!
   I'll starve ere I'll rob a foot further. An 'twere not as   21
   good a deed as drink to turn true man and to leave   22
   these rogues, I am the veriest varlet that ever chewed   23
   with a tooth. Eight yards of uneven ground is three-   24
   score-and-ten miles afoot with me, and the stony-
   hearted villains know it well enough. A plague upon
   it when thieves cannot be true one to another! (*They*
   whistle.) Whew! A plague upon you all! Give me my   28
   horse, you rogues, give me my horse, and be hanged!
PRINCE [*coming forward*]   Peace, ye fat-guts! Lie down.
   Lay thine ear close to the ground and list if thou   31
   canst hear the tread of travelers.
FALSTAFF   Have you any levers to lift me up again, being
   down? 'Sblood, I'll not bear mine own flesh so far
   afoot again for all the coin in thy father's Exchequer.
   What a plague mean ye to colt me thus?   36
PRINCE   Thou liest. Thou art not colted, thou art
   uncolted.
FALSTAFF   I prithee, good Prince Hal, help me to my   39
   horse, good king's son.   40
PRINCE   Out, ye rogue! Shall I be your hostler?
FALSTAFF   Go hang thyself in thine own heir-apparent
   garters! If I be ta'en, I'll peach for this. An I have not   43
   ballads made on you all and sung to filthy tunes, let a
   cup of sack be my poison. When a jest is so forward,   45
   and afoot too! I hate it.   46

   Enter Gadshill.

GADSHILL   Stand!   47
FALSTAFF   So I do, against my will.
POINS [*coming forward with Bardolph and Peto*]   Oh, 'tis our
   setter. I know his voice.   50
BARDOLPH   What news?
GADSHILL   Case ye, case ye, on with your vizards!   52

There's money of the King's coming down the hill; 'tis
   going to the King's Exchequer.
FALSTAFF   You lie, ye rogue, 'tis going to the King's
   Tavern.
GADSHILL   There's enough to make us all.   57
FALSTAFF   To be hanged.
PRINCE   Sirs, you four shall front them in the narrow   59
   lane; Ned Poins and I will walk lower. If they scape   60
   from your encounter, then they light on us.
PETO   How many be there of them?
GADSHILL   Some eight or ten.
FALSTAFF   Zounds, will they not rob us?
PRINCE   What, a coward, Sir John Paunch?
FALSTAFF   Indeed, I am not John of Gaunt, your   66
   grandfather, but yet no coward, Hal.
PRINCE   Well, we leave that to the proof.   68
POINS   Sirrah Jack, thy horse stands behind the hedge.
   When thou need'st him, there thou shalt find him.
   Farewell, and stand fast.
FALSTAFF   Now cannot I strike him, if I should be   72
   hanged.   73
PRINCE [*to Poins*]   Ned, where are our disguises?
POINS [*to Prince*]   Here, hard by. Stand close.
                              [*Exeunt Prince and Poins.*]
FALSTAFF   Now, my masters, happy man be his dole,   76
   say I. Every man to his business.   [*They stand aside.*]

   Enter the Travelers.

FIRST TRAVELER   Come, neighbor. The boy shall lead
   our horses down the hill; we'll walk afoot awhile, and
   ease our legs.
THIEVES [*coming forward*]   Stand!
TRAVELERS   Jesus bless us!
FALSTAFF   Strike! Down with them! Cut the villains'
   throats! Ah, whoreson caterpillars, bacon-fed knaves!   84
   They hate us youth. Down with them, fleece them!
TRAVELERS   Oh, we are undone, both we and ours for-
   ever!
FALSTAFF   Hang ye, gorbellied knaves, are ye undone?   88
   No, ye fat chuffs; I would your store were here. On,   89
   bacons, on! What, ye knaves, young men must live.   90
   You are grandjurors, are ye? We'll jure ye, 'faith.   91
      Here they rob them and bind them. Exeunt.

   Enter the Prince and Poins [*in buckram*].

PRINCE   The thieves have bound the true men. Now
   could thou and I rob the thieves and go merrily to
   London, it would be argument for a week, laughter   94
   for a month, and a good jest forever.

---

12 square a measuring tool   **14 fair** exemplary.   **for all** despite all
18 medicines love potions   **21–4 An . . . tooth** i.e., If it don't think it's a
good idea to reform and turn informer, I'm the damnedest scoundrel
that ever lived. (Cf. 2.1.30–1 and n.)   **28 Whew** (Perhaps Falstaff tries
to answer the whistling he hears or mocks it.)   **31 list** listen   **36 colt**
trick, cheat. (In lines 37–8, Prince Hal puns on the common meaning.)
39–40 help . . . horse help me to find my horse. (But in line 41, the
Prince comically retorts as though having been asked to hold the stirrup while Falstaff mounted, as a hostler would do.)   **43 peach** inform
on you   **45 so forward** so far advanced   **46 afoot** (1) in progress (2)
on foot, i.e., not on horseback   **47 Stand!** Don't move! (But Falstaff
answers in the sense of "stand on one's feet.")   **50 setter** arranger of
the robbery. (See 1.2.104–5 and note.)   **52 Case ye** Put on your masks

57 make us all make our fortunes (or, as Falstaff sees it, make us be
hanged).   **59 front** confront   **60 lower** further downhill.   **66 John of
Gaunt** Henry IV's father, born at Ghent (and hence giving Falstaff a
chance to pun on *gaunt* as the opposite of his fatness)   **68 proof** test.
72–3 Now . . . hanged (Falstaff wishes he could hit Poins, who is too
quick for him.)   **76 happy . . . dole** may happiness be every man's
portion or lot   **84 Ah . . . knaves!** i.e., Ah, you abominable parasites,
you over-fed rascals!   **88 gorbellied** big-bellied   **89 chuffs** churls,
rich but miserly.   **store** total wealth   **90 bacons** fat men   **91 grandjurors** i.e., men of wealth, able to serve on juries   **94 argument** a subject for conversation

POINS   Stand close. I hear them coming.

           [*They stand aside.*]

       Enter the thieves again.

FALSTAFF   Come, my masters, let us share, and then to   97
horse before day. An the Prince and Poins be not two
arrant cowards, there's no equity stirring. There's no   99
more valor in that Poins than in a wild duck.

       [*The thieves begin to share the booty.*]

PRINCE   Your money!

POINS   Villains!

      As they are sharing, the Prince and Poins set upon
      them. They all run away, and Falstaff, after a blow
      or two, runs away too, leaving the booty behind
                           them.

PRINCE

Got with much ease. Now merrily to horse.
The thieves are all scattered and possessed with fear
So strongly that they dare not meet each other;
Each takes his fellow for an officer.
Away, good Ned. Falstaff sweats to death
And lards the lean earth as he walks along.   108
Were't not for laughing, I should pity him.

POINS   How the fat rogue roared!   *Exeunt.*

❖

[2.3]

       Enter Hotspur, solus, reading a letter.

HOTSPUR   "But, for mine own part, my lord, I could be
well contented to be there, in respect of the love I bear
your house." He could be contented; why is he not,   3
then? In respect of the love he bears our house! He
shows in this he loves his own barn better than he
loves our house. Let me see some more. "The purpose
you undertake is dangerous"—why, that's certain.
'Tis dangerous to take a cold, to sleep, to drink; but I
tell you, my lord fool, out of this nettle, danger, we
pluck this flower, safety. "The purpose you undertake
is dangerous, the friends you have named uncertain,
the time itself unsorted, and your whole plot too light   12
for the counterpoise of so great an opposition." Say   13
you so, say you so? I say unto you again, you are a
shallow, cowardly hind, and you lie. What a lack-brain   15
is this! By the Lord, our plot is a good plot as
ever was laid, our friends true and constant; a good
plot, good friends, and full of expectation; an excellent   18
plot, very good friends. What a frosty-spirited rogue is
this! Why, my lord of York commends the plot and   20

the general course of the action. Zounds, an I were   21
now by this rascal, I could brain him with his lady's   22
fan. Is there not my father, my uncle, and myself? Lord   23
Edmund Mortimer, my lord of York, and Owen Glendower? Is there not besides the Douglas? Have I not all
their letters to meet me in arms by the ninth of the next
month, and are they not some of them set forward
already? What a pagan rascal is this, an infidel! Ha,   28
you shall see now in very sincerity of fear and
cold heart will he to the King and lay open all our
proceedings. Oh, I could divide myself and go to buf-   31
fets for moving such a dish of skim milk with so hon-   32
orable an action! Hang him, let him tell the King, we
are prepared. I will set forward tonight.

       Enter his Lady.

How now, Kate? I must leave you within these two
hours.

LADY PERCY

Oh, my good lord, why are you thus alone?
For what offense have I this fortnight been
A banished woman from my Harry's bed?
Tell me, sweet lord, what is't that takes from thee
Thy stomach, pleasure, and thy golden sleep?   41
Why dost thou bend thine eyes upon the earth
And start so often when thou sit'st alone?
Why hast thou lost the fresh blood in thy cheeks
And given my treasures and my rights of thee   45
To thick-eyed musing and curst melancholy?   46
In thy faint slumbers I by thee have watched   47
And heard thee murmur tales of iron wars,
Speak terms of manage to thy bounding steed,   49
Cry, "Courage! To the field!" And thou hast talked
Of sallies and retires, of trenches, tents,   51
Of palisadoes, frontiers, parapets,   52
Of basilisks, of cannon, culverin,   53
Of prisoners' ransom, and of soldiers slain,
And all the currents of a heady fight.   55
Thy spirit within thee hath been so at war,
And thus hath so bestirred thee in thy sleep,
That beads of sweat have stood upon thy brow
Like bubbles in a late-disturbèd stream,   59
And in thy face strange motions have appeared,
Such as we see when men restrain their breath
On some great sudden hest. Oh, what portents are
    these?   62
Some heavy business hath my lord in hand,
And I must know it, else he loves me not.

---

97 **masters** good sirs   99 **arrant** notorious, unmitigated.   **equity**
judgment, discernment   108 **lards** drips fat on, bastes
**2.3. Location: Hotspur's estate (identified historically as Warkworth
Castle in Northumberland).**
0.1 *solus* alone   3 **house** family. (But Hotspur replies derisively in
lines 4–6 as though to the literal sense of a building that one might
compare to a barn.)   12 **unsorted** unsuitable   13 **for . . . of** to counterbalance   15 **hind** menial, peasant   18 **expectation** promise
20 **lord of York** i.e., Archbishop Scroop. (Also in line 24.)

21–2 **an . . . rascal** if I were face to face with this rascal, instead of
reading his letter   22–3 **his lady's fan** his wife's fan—a suitable light
weapon with which to chastise such a milktoast.   28 **pagan** unbelieving   31–2 **divide . . . buffets** i.e., fight with myself   32 **moving** urging   41 **stomach** appetite   45 **And . . . thee** and given the precious
right I have as wife to share your thoughts   46 **thick-eyed** dull-
sighted, vacant, abstracted.   **curst** ill-tempered.   47 **faint** restless.
watched lain awake   49 **manage** horsemanship   51 **retires** retreats
52–3 **Of . . . culverin** of stakes set in the ground for defense, of ram-
parts, protective walls, of large and smaller cannon   55 **heady** headlong   59 **late-disturbèd** recently stirred up   62 **hest** command;
endeavor.

HOTSPUR [*calling*]
What, ho!

[*Enter a Servant.*]

Is Gilliams with the packet gone?
SERVANT   He is, my lord, an hour ago.
HOTSPUR
Hath Butler brought those horses from the sheriff?   67
SERVANT
One horse, my lord, he brought even now.   68
HOTSPUR
What horse? A roan, a crop-ear, is it not?   69
SERVANT
It is, my lord.
HOTSPUR   That roan shall be my throne.
Well, I will back him straight. Oh, *Esperance!*   71
Bid Butler lead him forth into the park.

[*Exit Servant.*]

LADY PERCY   But hear you, my lord.
HOTSPUR   What say'st thou, my lady?
LADY PERCY   What is it carries you away?   75
HOTSPUR   Why, my horse, my love, my horse.
LADY PERCY   Out, you mad-headed ape!   77
A weasel hath not such a deal of spleen   78
As you are tossed with. In faith,   79
I'll know your business, Harry, that I will.
I fear my brother Mortimer doth stir
About his title, and hath sent for you   82
To line his enterprise; but if you go—   83
HOTSPUR
So far afoot, I shall be weary, love.
LADY PERCY
Come, come, you paraquito, answer me   85
Directly unto this question that I ask.
In faith, I'll break thy little finger, Harry,
An if thou wilt not tell me all things true.   88
HOTSPUR   Away,
Away, you trifler! Love? I love thee not;
I care not for thee, Kate. This is no world
To play with mammets and to tilt with lips.   92
We must have bloody noses and cracked crowns,   93
And pass them current too. Gods me, my horse!   94
What say'st thou, Kate? What wouldst thou have with
me?
LADY PERCY
Do you not love me? Do you not, indeed?
Well, do not, then, for since you love me not

I will not love myself. Do you not love me?
Nay, tell me if you speak in jest or no.
HOTSPUR   Come, wilt thou see me ride?
And when I am a-horseback I will swear
I love thee infinitely. But hark you, Kate,
I must not have you henceforth question me
Whither I go, nor reason whereabout.   104
Whither I must, I must; and, to conclude,
This evening must I leave you, gentle Kate.
I know you wise, but yet no farther wise
Than Harry Percy's wife; constant you are,
But yet a woman; and for secrecy,
No lady closer, for I well believe   110
Thou wilt not utter what thou dost not know,
And so far will I trust thee, gentle Kate.
LADY PERCY   How, so far?
HOTSPUR
Not an inch further. But hark you, Kate:
Whither I go, thither shall you go too.
Today will I set forth, tomorrow you.
Will this content you, Kate?
LADY PERCY   It must, of force.   *Exeunt.*   117

❧

[2.4]

Enter Prince and Poins.

PRINCE   Ned, prithee, come out of that fat room, and   1
lend me thy hand to laugh a little.
POINS   Where hast been, Hal?
PRINCE   With three or four loggerheads amongst three   4
or four score hogsheads. I have sounded the very bass   5
string of humility. Sirrah, I am sworn brother to a
leash of drawers, and can call them all by their Christian   7
names, as Tom, Dick, and Francis. They take it already   8
upon their salvation that, though I be but Prince of   9
Wales, yet I am the king of courtesy, and tell me flatly
I am no proud Jack like Falstaff, but a Corinthian, a lad   11
of mettle, a good boy—by the Lord, so they call me!—
and when I am King of England I shall command all
the good lads in Eastcheap. They call drinking deep   14
"dyeing scarlet"; and when you breathe in your water-   15
ing they cry "hem!" and bid you "play it off." To con-   16
clude, I am so good a proficient in one quarter of an
hour that I can drink with any tinker in his own language during my life. I tell thee, Ned, thou hast lost
much honor that thou wert not with me in this action.

---

67 **sheriff** i.e., bailiff.   68 **even** just   69 **roan** roan-colored, i.e., with white or grey interspersed in the overall color of the coat   71 **back** mount.   *Esperance* Hope. (The motto of the Percy family.)   75 **carries you away** carries you beyond the bounds of reason and judgment. (But Hotspur puns on the literal meaning.)   77 **Out** (An expression of impatience.)   78 **spleen** (The spleen was thought to be the source of impulsive and irritable behavior.)   79 **tossed** tossed about, agitated   82 **title** claim to the throne   83 **line** strengthen   85 **paraquito** little parrot. (A term of endearment.)   88 **An if** if   92 **mammets** dolls. (With a quibble on the Latin *mamma* meaning "breast.")   93 **crowns** (1) heads (2) coins worth five shillings. (Cracked coins would not "pass current," as Hotspur jokes in the next line.)   94 **Gods me** God save me

104 **reason whereabout** ask about what.   110 **closer** more close-mouthed   117 **of force** perforce, of necessity.
2.4. Location: A tavern in Eastcheap, London, usually identified as the Boar's Head. Some tavern furniture, including stools, is provided onstage.
1 **fat** stuffy, or, a vat room   4 **loggerheads** blockheads   5 **hogsheads** wine barrels.   **bass** (With a pun on *base*.)   7 **leash of drawers** three waiters   8–9 **take ... salvation** already maintain it as they hope to be saved   11 **Jack** (1) Jack Falstaff (2) fellow.   **Corinthian** i.e., gay blade, good sport. (Corinth was reputed to be licentious.)
14–15 **They ... scarlet** (Either because excessive drinking causes a red complexion or because urine, produced by *drinking deep*, was sometimes used for fixing dyes.)   15–16 **breathe ... watering** pause for breath in your drinking   16 **play it off** drink it up.

But, sweet Ned—to sweeten which name of Ned, I give thee this pennyworth of sugar, clapped even now 22 into my hand by an underskinker, one that never 23 spake other English in his life than "Eight shillings and sixpence," and "You are welcome," with this shrill addition, "Anon, anon, sir! Score a pint of bas- 26 tard in the Half-Moon," or so. But, Ned, to drive away 27 the time till Falstaff come, I prithee do thou stand in some by-room while I question my puny drawer to 29 what end he gave me the sugar; and do thou never leave calling "Francis," that his tale to me may be nothing but "Anon." Step aside, and I'll show thee a precedent.   [Exit Poins.] 33

POINS [within]   Francis!
PRINCE   Thou art perfect.
POINS [within]   Francis!

Enter [Francis, a] drawer.

FRANCIS   Anon, anon, sir.—Look down into the Pom- 37
garnet, Ralph.   38
PRINCE   Come hither, Francis.
FRANCIS   My lord?
PRINCE   How long hast thou to serve, Francis?   41
FRANCIS   Forsooth, five years, and as much as to—
POINS [within]   Francis!
FRANCIS [calling]   Anon, anon, sir.
PRINCE   Five year! By'r Lady, a long lease for the 45
clinking of pewter. But Francis, darest thou be so valiant as to play the coward with thy indenture and 47 show it a fair pair of heels and run from it?
FRANCIS   Oh, Lord, sir, I'll be sworn upon all the books in 49
England, I could find in my heart—
POINS [within]   Francis!
FRANCIS [calling]   Anon, sir.
PRINCE   How old art thou, Francis?
FRANCIS   Let me see, about Michaelmas next I shall 54
be—
POINS [within]   Francis!
FRANCIS [calling]   Anon, sir. Pray, stay a little, my lord.
PRINCE   Nay, but hark you, Francis: for the sugar thou gavest me, 'twas a pennyworth, was 't not?
FRANCIS   Oh, Lord, I would it had been two!
PRINCE   I will give thee for it a thousand pound. Ask me when thou wilt, and thou shalt have it.
POINS [within]   Francis!
FRANCIS [calling]   Anon, anon.
PRINCE   Anon, Francis? No, Francis; but tomorrow, Francis, or, Francis, o'Thursday, or indeed, Francis, when thou wilt. But, Francis—
FRANCIS   My lord?

PRINCE   Wilt thou rob this leathern-jerkin, crystal- button, not-pated, agate-ring, puke-stocking, caddis- 69 garter, smooth-tongue, Spanish-pouch—   70
FRANCIS   Oh, Lord, sir, who do you mean?   71
PRINCE   Why, then, your brown bastard is your only drink; for look you, Francis, your white canvas 73 doublet will sully. In Barbary, sir, it cannot come to so 74 much.   75
FRANCIS   What, sir?   76
POINS [within]   Francis!
PRINCE   Away, you rogue! Dost thou not hear them call?
Here they both call him; the drawer stands 79
amazed, not knowing which way to go.

Enter Vintner.

VINTNER   What stand'st thou still and hear'st such a calling? Look to the guests within.   [Exit Francis.] 80
My lord, old Sir John, with half a dozen more, are at the door. Shall I let them in?
PRINCE   Let them alone awhile, and then open the door.
[Exit Vintner.]
[Calling]   Poins!

Enter Poins.

POINS   Anon, anon, sir.
PRINCE   Sirrah, Falstaff and the rest of the thieves are at the door. Shall we be merry?
POINS   As merry as crickets, my lad. But hark ye, what cunning match have you made with this jest of the drawer? Come, what's the issue?   90
PRINCE   I am now of all humors that have showed 91
themselves humors since the old days of Goodman 92
Adam to the pupil age of this present twelve o'clock at 93
midnight.   94
95

[*Enter Francis, hurrying across the stage with wine.*]

What's o'clock, Francis?
FRANCIS   Anon, anon, sir.   [Exit.]
PRINCE   That ever this fellow should have fewer words than a parrot, and yet the son of a woman! His indus- try is upstairs and downstairs, his eloquence the parcel of a reckoning. I am not yet of Percy's mind, the Hot- 100
spur of the north, he that kills me some six or seven 101
dozen of Scots at a breakfast, washes his hands, and 102
says to his wife, "Fie upon this quiet life! I want work." "Oh, my sweet Harry," says she, "how many

22 sugar (Used to sweeten wine.)   23 underskinker assistant to a waiter or bartender   26–7 Anon . . . Half-Moon Coming, sir!— Charge a pint of a sweet Spanish wine to the customers in the room of the inn called "the Half-Moon."   29 by-room side-room.   puny drawer inexperienced tapster or bartender   33 precedent example. 37–8 Pomgarnet Pomegranate. (Another room in the inn.)   41 serve i.e., serve out your apprenticeship   45 By'r Lady By Our Lady 47 indenture contract of apprenticeship   49 books i.e., Bibles 54 Michaelmas September 29

69–71 Wilt . . . Spanish-pouch i.e., Will you rob your master of your services by running away, this man with his leather jacket, transpar- ent buttons, cropped hair, a ring with small figures in an agate stone for a seal, dark woolen stockings, worsted garters, an ingratiating flattering manner of speech, wallet of Spanish leather   73–6 Why . . . much (The Prince talks seeming nonsense in order to bewilder Fran- cis, but he also implies that Francis should stick to his trade, since he will not cut much of a figure in the world.)   75 it i.e., sugar 79.3 Vintner i.e., Innkeeper.   80 What Why   90 match game, contest 91 issue outcome, point.   92–5 I . . . midnight i.e., I'm now in a mood for anything that has happened in the whole history of the world.   93 Goodman (Title for a yeoman.)   94 pupil youthful 100–1 parcel . . . reckoning items of a bill.   102 kills me i.e., kills. (Me is used colloquially.)

hast thou killed today?" "Give my roan horse a
drench," says he, and answers, "Some fourteen," an
hour after, "a trifle, a trifle." I prithee, call in Falstaff. 107
I'll play Percy, and that damned brawn shall play Dame
Mortimer his wife. "Rivo!" says the drunkard. Call in 109
ribs, call in tallow.   110

> Enter Falstaff, [Gadshill, Bardolph, and Peto;   111
> Francis following with wine].

POINS Welcome, Jack. Where hast thou been?

FALSTAFF A plague of all cowards, I say, and a
vengeance too! Marry and amen! Give me a cup of 113
sack, boy. Ere I lead this life long, I'll sew netherstocks, and mend them and foot them too. A plague 115
of all cowards! Give me a cup of sack, rogue. Is there 116
no virtue extant?   *He drinketh.*

PRINCE Didst thou never see Titan kiss a dish of butter,
pitiful-hearted Titan, that melted at the sweet tale of 119
the sun's? If thou didst, then behold that compound. 120

FALSTAFF You rogue, here's lime in this sack too. There 121
is nothing but roguery to be found in villainous man, 122
yet a coward is worse than a cup of sack with lime in
it. A villainous coward! Go thy ways, old Jack, die
when thou wilt. If manhood, good manhood, be not
forgot upon the face of the earth, then am I a shotten
herring. There lives not three good men unhanged in 127
England, and one of them is fat and grows old, God 128
help the while! A bad world, I say. I would I were a
weaver; I could sing psalms or anything. A plague of 130
all cowards, I say still.   131

PRINCE How now, woolsack, what mutter you?

FALSTAFF A king's son! If I do not beat thee out of thy 133
kingdom with a dagger of lath, and drive all thy
subjects afore thee like a flock of wild geese, I'll never 135
wear hair on my face more. You, Prince of Wales!

PRINCE Why, you whoreson round man, what's the
matter?

FALSTAFF Are not you a coward? Answer me to that.
And Poins there?

POINS Zounds, ye fat paunch, an ye call me coward, by
the Lord, I'll stab thee.

FALSTAFF I call thee coward? I'll see thee damned ere I
call thee coward, but I would give a thousand pound
I could run as fast as thou canst. You are straight
enough in the shoulders; you care not who sees your
back. Call you that backing of your friends? A plague
upon such backing! Give me them that will face me.

Give me a cup of sack. I am a rogue if I drunk today.

PRINCE Oh, villain, thy lips are scarce wiped since thou
drunk'st last.

FALSTAFF All is one for that. (*He drinketh.*) A plague of 153
all cowards, still say I.

PRINCE What's the matter?

FALSTAFF What's the matter? There be four of us here
have ta'en a thousand pound this day morning.   157

PRINCE Where is it, Jack, where is it?

FALSTAFF Where is it? Taken from us it is. A hundred
upon poor four of us.

PRINCE What, a hundred, man?

FALSTAFF I am a rogue if I were not at half-sword with 162
a dozen of them two hours together. I have scaped by 163
miracle. I am eight times thrust through the doublet, 164
four through the hose, my buckler cut through and 165
through, my sword hacked like a handsaw—*ecce* 166
signum! I never dealt better since I was a man. All 167
would not do. A plague of all cowards! Let them 168
speak. If they speak more or less than truth, they are
villains and the sons of darkness.

PRINCE Speak, sirs, how was it?

GADSHILL We four set upon some dozen—

FALSTAFF Sixteen at least, my lord.

GADSHILL And bound them.

PETO No, no, they were not bound.

FALSTAFF You rogue, they were bound, every man of
them, or I am a Jew else, an Hebrew Jew.

GADSHILL As we were sharing, some six or seven fresh
men set upon us—

FALSTAFF And unbound the rest, and then come in the
other.   181

PRINCE What, fought you with them all?

FALSTAFF All? I know not what you call all, but if I
fought not with fifty of them, I am a bunch of radish.
If there were not two- or three-and-fifty upon poor old
Jack, then am I no two-legged creature.

PRINCE Pray God you have not murdered some of them.

FALSTAFF Nay, that's past praying for. I have peppered
two of them. Two I am sure I have paid, two rogues
in buckram suits. I tell thee what, Hal, if I tell thee a
lie, spit in my face, call me horse. Thou knowest my
old ward. Here I lay, and thus I bore my point. [*He* 192
demonstrates his stance.] Four rogues in buckram let
drive at me—

PRINCE What, four? Thou said'st but two even now.   195

FALSTAFF Four, Hal, I told thee four.

POINS Ay, ay, he said four.

FALSTAFF These four came all afront, and mainly thrust 198
at me. I made me no more ado but took all their seven 199
points in my target, thus.   200

---

107 **drench** draft (sometimes of medicine). **says he** i.e., he tells a servant 109 **brawn** fat boar 110 **Rivo** (An exclamation of uncertain meaning, but related to drinking.) 111 **ribs** rib roast. **tallow** fat drippings. 113 **of** on 115–16 **netherstocks** stockings (the sewing or mending of which is a menial occupation) 116 **foot** make a new foot for 119 **Titan** i.e., the sun 120 **that** i.e., the butter 121 **compound** melting butter, i.e., Falstaff. 122 **lime in this sack** i.e., lime added to make the wine sparkle 127–8 **a shotten herring** a herring that has cast its roe and is consequently thin. 130 **the while** i.e., in these bad times. 131 **weaver** (Many psalm-singing Protestant immigrants from the Low Countries were weavers.) 133 **woolsack** bale of wool 135 **dagger of lath** (The Vice, a stock comic figure in morality plays, was so armed.)

153 **All . . . that** No matter. 157 **this day morning** this morning. 162 **at half-sword** fighting at close quarters 163 **scaped** escaped 164 **doublet** Elizabethan upper garment like a jacket 165 **hose** close-fitting breeches. **buckler** shield 166–7 **ecce signum** behold the proof. (Familiar words from the Mass.) 167–8 **All . . . do** All that I did was of no use. 181 **other** others. 192 **ward** defensive stance, parry. **lay** stood 195 **even** just 198 **afront** abreast. **mainly** powerfully 199 **made me** made. (*Me* is used colloquially.) 200 **target** shield

PRINCE Seven? Why, there were but four even now.

FALSTAFF In buckram?

POINS Ay, four, in buckram suits.

FALSTAFF Seven, by these hilts, or I am a villain else.   204

PRINCE [aside to Poins] Prithee, let him alone. We shall have more anon.

FALSTAFF Dost thou hear me, Hal?

PRINCE Ay, and mark thee too, Jack.   208

FALSTAFF Do so, for it is worth the listening to. These nine in buckram that I told thee of—

PRINCE So, two more already.

FALSTAFF Their points being broken—   212

POINS Down fell their hose.

FALSTAFF Began to give me ground; but I followed me   214
close, came in foot and hand; and with a thought   215
seven of the eleven I paid.

PRINCE Oh, monstrous! Eleven buckram men grown out of two!

FALSTAFF But, as the devil would have it, three misbegotten knaves in Kendal green came at my back   220
and let drive at me; for it was so dark, Hal, that thou couldst not see thy hand.

PRINCE These lies are like their father that begets them,   223
gross as a mountain, open, palpable. Why, thou claybrained guts, thou knotty-pated fool, thou whore-   225
son, obscene, greasy tallow-keech—   226

FALSTAFF What, art thou mad? Art thou mad? Is not the truth the truth?

PRINCE Why, how couldst thou know these men in Kendal green when it was so dark thou couldst not see thy hand? Come, tell us your reason. What sayest thou to this?

POINS Come, your reason, Jack, your reason.

FALSTAFF What, upon compulsion? Zounds, an I were at the strappado, or all the racks in the world, I would   235
not tell you on compulsion. Give you a reason on compulsion? If reasons were as plentiful as blackberries,   237
I would give no man a reason upon compulsion, I.

PRINCE I'll be no longer guilty of this sin. This sanguine   239
coward, this bed-presser, this horse-backbreaker, this huge hill of flesh—

FALSTAFF 'Sblood, you starveling, you eel-skin, you dried neat's tongue, you bull's pizzle, you stockfish!   243
Oh, for breath to utter what is like thee! You tailor's yard, you sheath, you bowcase, you vile standing   245
tuck—   246

PRINCE Well, breathe awhile, and then to it again, and when thou hast tired thyself in base comparisons, hear me speak but this.

POINS Mark, Jack.

PRINCE We two saw you four set on four and bound them, and were masters of their wealth. Mark now how a plain tale shall put you down. Then did we two set on you four, and, with a word, outfaced you from   254
your prize, and have it, yea, and can show it you here in the house. And, Falstaff, you carried your guts away as nimbly, with as quick dexterity, and roared for mercy, and still run and roared, as ever I heard bull calf. What a slave art thou, to hack thy sword as thou hast done, and then say it was in fight! What trick, what device, what starting-hole canst thou now find   261
out to hide thee from this open and apparent shame?

POINS Come, let's hear, Jack. What trick hast thou now?

FALSTAFF By the Lord, I knew ye as well as he that made ye. Why, hear you, my masters, was it for me to kill the heir apparent? Should I turn upon the true prince? Why, thou knowest I am as valiant as Hercules, but beware instinct. The lion will not touch the true prince. Instinct is a great matter; I was now a coward on instinct. I shall think the better of myself and thee during my life—I for a valiant lion, and thou for a true prince. But by the Lord, lads, I am glad you have the money. Hostess, clap to the doors! Watch   273
tonight, pray tomorrow. Gallants, lads, boys, hearts   274
of gold, all the titles of good fellowship come to you! What, shall we be merry? Shall we have a play extempore?

PRINCE Content; and the argument shall be thy running away.   278

FALSTAFF Ah, no more of that, Hal, an thou lovest me!

Enter Hostess.

HOSTESS Oh, Jesu, my lord the Prince!

PRINCE How now, my lady the hostess, what say'st thou to me?

HOSTESS Marry, my lord, there is a nobleman of the court at door would speak with you. He says he comes from your father.

PRINCE Give him as much as will make him a royal   287
man, and send him back again to my mother.   288

FALSTAFF What manner of man is he?

HOSTESS An old man.

FALSTAFF What doth Gravity out of his bed at mid-   291
night? Shall I give him his answer?

PRINCE Prithee, do, Jack.

FALSTAFF Faith, and I'll send him packing.   *Exit.*

PRINCE Now, sirs. By'r Lady, you fought fair; so did you, Peto; so did you, Bardolph. You are lions too, you ran away upon instinct, you will not touch the true prince; no, fie!

BARDOLPH Faith, I ran when I saw others run.

---

204 **by these hilts** by my sword hilt.   208 **mark** (1) pay heed (2) keep count   212 **points** sword points. (But Poins puns on the sense of laces, by which the hose were attached to the doublet.)   214 **followed me** followed   215 **with a thought** quick as a thought   220 **Kendal** a town known for its textiles   223 **their father** (1) Falstaff (2) the devil, proverbially the father of lies   225 **knotty-pated** thickheaded   226 **tallow-keech** lump of tallow   235 **strappado** a kind of torture   237 **reasons . . . blackberries** (Falstaff puns on *raisins*, pronounced nearly like *reasons*.)   239 **sanguine** ruddy   243 **neat's** ox's.   **pizzle** penis.   **stockfish** dried cod.   245 **yard** yardstick   245–6 **standing tuck** rapier standing on its point, or no longer pliant

254 **with a word** (1) in a word (2) with a minimum of speech.   **outfaced** frightened   261 **starting-hole** point of shelter (like a rabbit's hole)   273 **Watch** (1) Keep watchful vigil. (See Matthew 26:41.) (2) Carouse   274 **pray** (1) pray to God (2) prey   278 **argument** plot of the play   287–8 **Give . . . man** (Prince Hal puns on the value of coins: a *noble* was worth six shillings eight pence; a *royal* was worth ten shillings.)   291 **What doth** Why is

PRINCE   Faith, tell me now in earnest, how came Falstaff's sword so hacked?

PETO   Why, he hacked it with his dagger, and said he would swear truth out of England but he would make 303 you believe it was done in fight, and persuaded us to do the like.

BARDOLPH   Yea, and to tickle our noses with spear grass to make them bleed, and then to beslubber our gar- 307 ments with it and swear it was the blood of true men. I did that I did not this seven year before: I blushed to 309 hear his monstrous devices.

PRINCE   Oh, villain, thou stolest a cup of sack eighteen years ago and wert taken with the manner, and ever 312 since thou hast blushed extempore. Thou hadst fire 313 and sword on thy side, and yet thou ran'st away. What instinct hadst thou for it?

BARDOLPH   My lord, do you see these meteors? Do you 316 behold these exhalations?   *[Pointing to his own face.]* 317

PRINCE   I do.

BARDOLPH   What think you they portend? 319

PRINCE   Hot livers and cold purses. 320

BARDOLPH   Choler, my lord, if rightly taken. 321

PRINCE   No, if rightly taken, halter. 322

Enter Falstaff.

Here comes lean Jack, here comes bare-bone.—How now, my sweet creature of bombast? How long is't 324 ago, Jack, since thou sawest thine own knee?

FALSTAFF   My own knee? When I was about thy years, Hal, I was not an eagle's talon in the waist; I could have crept into any alderman's thumb ring. A plague of sighing and grief! It blows a man up like a bladder. There's villainous news abroad. Here was Sir John Bracy from your father. You must to the court in the morning. That same mad fellow of the north, Percy, and he of Wales that gave Amamon the bastinado and 333 made Lucifer cuckold and swore the devil his true 334 liegeman upon the cross of a Welsh hook—what a 335 plague call you him?

POINS   Owen Glendower.

FALSTAFF   Owen, Owen, the same; and his son-in-law Mortimer, and old Northumberland, and that sprightly Scot of Scots, Douglas, that runs a-horseback up a hill perpendicular—

PRINCE   He that rides at high speed, and with his pistol kills a sparrow flying.

FALSTAFF   You have hit it. 344

PRINCE   So did he never the sparrow.

FALSTAFF   Well, that rascal hath good mettle in him; he will not run. 347

PRINCE   Why, what a rascal art thou then to praise him so for running!

FALSTAFF   A-horseback, ye cuckoo; but afoot he will not budge a foot.

PRINCE   Yes, Jack, upon instinct.

FALSTAFF   I grant ye, upon instinct. Well, he is there too, and one Mordake, and a thousand blue-caps more. 354 Worcester is stolen away tonight. Thy father's beard is turned white with the news. You may buy land now as cheap as stinking mackerel.

PRINCE   Why, then, it is like, if there come a hot June 358 and this civil buffeting hold, we shall buy maiden- 359 heads as they buy hobnails, by the hundreds.

FALSTAFF   By the mass, lad, thou sayest true; it is like we shall have good trading that way. But tell me, Hal, art not thou horrible afeard? Thou being heir appar- ent, could the world pick thee out three such enemies again as that fiend Douglas, that spirit Percy, and that devil Glendower? Art thou not horribly afraid? Doth not thy blood thrill at it?

PRINCE   Not a whit, i'faith. I lack some of thy instinct.

FALSTAFF   Well, thou wilt be horribly chid tomorrow 369 when thou comest to thy father. If thou love me, practice an answer.

PRINCE   Do thou stand for my father, and examine me upon the particulars of my life.

FALSTAFF   Shall I? Content. This chair shall be my state, 374 this dagger my scepter, and this cushion my crown.

[Falstaff establishes himself on his "throne."]

PRINCE   Thy state is taken for a joint stool, thy golden 376 scepter for a leaden dagger, and thy precious rich 377 crown for a pitiful bald crown.

FALSTAFF   Well, an the fire of grace be not quite out of thee, now shalt thou be moved. Give me a cup of sack to make my eyes look red, that it may be thought I have wept; for I must speak in passion, and I will do it in King Cambyses' vein. 383

PRINCE   Well, here is my leg.   *[He bows.]*

FALSTAFF   And here is my speech. Stand aside, nobil- ity.

HOSTESS   Oh, Jesu, this is excellent sport, i'faith!

FALSTAFF

Weep not, sweet queen, for trickling tears are vain.

HOSTESS   Oh, the Father, how he holds his countenance! 389

---

303 **swear . . . would** swear oaths until they go out of fashion if he did not   307 **beslubber** smear, cover   309 **that** something   312 **taken . . . manner** caught with the goods   313 **extempore** without needing any occasion. (Bardolph is red-faced whether he blushes or not.) **fire** i.e., a red nose and complexion caused by heavy drinking 316, 317 **meteors, exhalations** i.e., the red blotches on Bardolph's face. 319 **portend** signify. (Meteors, comets, and other meteorological phe- nomena were widely regarded as omens of disaster.)   320 **Hot . . . purses** i.e., Livers inflamed by drink and purses made empty by spending.   321 **Choler** A choleric or combative temperament.   **taken** understood. (But the Prince, in his next speech, uses the word to mean "arrested.")   322 **halter** hangman's noose. (The Prince plays on Bardolph's *choler,* which he takes as *collar.*)   322.1 (Falstaff's entry in the Quarto after line 321 suggests he is visible to the audience while the Prince talks of a hangman's halter.)   324 **bombast** (1) cotton padding (2) fustian speech.   333 **Amamon** (The name of a demon.) **bastinado** beating on the soles of the feet   334 **made . . . cuckold** i.e., gave Lucifer his horns, the sign of cuckoldry   334–5 **and swore . . . liegeman** and made the devil take an oath of allegiance as a true sub- ject   335 **Welsh hook** curved-bladed pike lacking the cross shape of the sword on which such oaths were usually sworn

344 **hit it** described it exactly. (But the Prince takes *hit* literally in the next line.)   347 **run** flee. (But the Prince answers punningly in the sense of "ride at high speed.")   354 **blue-caps** Scottish soldiers 358 **like** likely   359 **hold** continues   369 **chid** chided   374 **state** chair of state, throne   376 **joint stool** a stool made by a joiner or furniture maker   377 **leaden** of soft metal, hence inferior   383 **in . . . vein** i.e., in the ranting and (by Shakespeare's time) old-fashioned style of Thomas Preston's *Cambyses,* an early Elizabethan tragedy.   389 **the Father** i.e., in God's name.   **holds his countenance** keeps a straight face.

FALSTAFF
For God's sake, lords, convey my tristful queen,   390
For tears do stop the floodgates of her eyes.   391
HOSTESS   Oh, Jesu, he doth it as like one of these harlotry   392
players as ever I see!   393
FALSTAFF
Peace, good pint pot; peace, good tickle-brain.—   394
Harry, I do not only marvel where thou spendest thy
time, but also how thou art accompanied; for though   396
the camomile, the more it is trodden on the faster it   397
grows, yet youth, the more it is wasted the sooner it   398
wears. That thou art my son I have partly thy mother's   399
word, partly my own opinion, but chiefly a villainous
trick of thine eye and a foolish hanging of thy nether   401
lip that doth warrant me. If then thou be son to me,   402
here lies the point: why, being son to me, art thou so
pointed at? Shall the blessed sun of heaven prove a
micher and eat blackberries? A question not to be   405
asked. Shall the son of England prove a thief and take
purses? A question to be asked. There is a thing, Harry,
which thou hast often heard of, and it is known
to many in our land by the name of pitch. This pitch,   409
as ancient writers do report, doth defile; so doth the   410
company thou keepest. For, Harry, now I do not speak
to thee in drink but in tears, not in pleasure but in
passion, not in words only but in woes also. And yet   413
there is a virtuous man whom I have often noted in
thy company, but I know not his name.
PRINCE   What manner of man, an it like Your Majesty?   416
FALSTAFF   A goodly portly man, i'faith, and a corpulent;   417
of a cheerful look, a pleasing eye, and a most noble
carriage; and, as I think, his age some fifty, or, by'r
Lady, inclining to threescore; and now I remember me,
his name is Falstaff. If that man should be lewdly   421
given, he deceiveth me; for, Harry, I see virtue in his
looks. If then the tree may be known by the fruit, as the   423
fruit by the tree, then peremptorily I speak it, there is   424
virtue in that Falstaff. Him keep with, the rest banish.
And tell me now, thou naughty varlet, tell me, where
hast thou been this month?
PRINCE   Dost thou speak like a king? Do thou stand for
me, and I'll play my father.
FALSTAFF   Depose me? If thou dost it half so gravely, so
majestically, both in word and matter, hang me up by
the heels for a rabbit-sucker or a poulter's hare.   432
[Hal takes Falstaff's place on the "throne."]

PRINCE   Well, here I am set.   433
FALSTAFF   And here I stand. Judge, my masters.
PRINCE   Now, Harry, whence come you?
FALSTAFF   My noble lord, from Eastcheap.
PRINCE   The complaints I hear of thee are grievous.
FALSTAFF   'Sblood, my lord, they are false.—Nay, I'll   438
tickle ye for a young prince, i'faith.   439
PRINCE   Swearest thou, ungracious boy? Henceforth
ne'er look on me. Thou art violently carried away from
grace. There is a devil haunts thee in the likeness of an
old fat man; a tun of man is thy companion. Why dost   443
thou converse with that trunk of humors, that bolting-   444
hutch of beastliness, that swollen parcel of dropsies,   445
that huge bombard of sack, that stuffed cloak-bag of   446
guts, that roasted Manningtree ox with the pudding in   447
his belly, that reverend Vice, that gray Iniquity, that   448
father ruffian, that vanity in years? Wherein is he good   449
but to taste sack and drink it? Wherein neat and
cleanly but to carve a capon and eat it? Wherein   451
cunning but in craft? Wherein crafty but in villainy?   452
Wherein villainous but in all things? Wherein worthy
but in nothing?
FALSTAFF   I would Your Grace would take me with   455
you. Whom means Your Grace?   456
PRINCE   That villainous abominable misleader of youth,
Falstaff, that old white-bearded Satan.
FALSTAFF   My lord, the man I know.
PRINCE   I know thou dost.
FALSTAFF   But to say I know more harm in him than in
myself were to say more than I know. That he is old,
the more the pity, his white hairs do witness it; but
that he is, saving your reverence, a whoremaster, that   464
I utterly deny. If sack and sugar be a fault, God help
the wicked! If to be old and merry be a sin, then many
an old host that I know is damned. If to be fat be to be   467
hated, then Pharaoh's lean kine are to be loved. No,   468
my good lord, banish Peto, banish Bardolph, banish
Poins; but for sweet Jack Falstaff, kind Jack Falstaff,
true Jack Falstaff, valiant Jack Falstaff, and therefore
more valiant being as he is old Jack Falstaff, banish not
him thy Harry's company, banish not him thy Harry's
company—banish plump Jack, and banish all the
world.

390 convey escort away.   tristful sorrowing   391 stop fill   392 harlotry scurvy, vagabond   393 players actors   394 tickle-brain (A slang
term for strong liquor, here applied as a nickname for the tavern hostess.)   396–9 for though . . . wears (Falstaff parodies the style of John
Lyly's Euphues, with its elaborate balanced antitheses, alliterative
effects, and illustrations drawn from fanciful natural history. Camomile
is an aromatic creeping herb whose flowers and leaves are used medicinally.)   401 trick trait   402 warrant assure   405 micher truant
409–10 This . . . defile (An allusion to the familiar proverb from
Ecclesiasticus 13:1 about the defilement of touching pitch.)   pitch a
sticky, black residue from the distillation of tar, used to seal wood
from moisture   413 passion sorrow   416 an it like if it please
417 portly (1) stately (2) corpulent   421 lewdly wickedly   423 If . . .
by the fruit (See Matthew 12:33.)   424 peremptorily decisively
432 rabbit-sucker unweaned rabbit.   poulter's poulterer's

433 set seated.   438 'Sblood i.e., By Christ's blood   439 tickle ye for
amuse you in the role of   443 tun (1) large barrel (2) ton   444 converse associate.   humors body fluids, diseases   444–5 bolting-hutch
large bin   445 dropsies accumulations of fluids causing swelling
446 bombard leathern drinking vessel.   cloak-bag portmanteau
447 Manningtree ox (Manningtree, a town in Essex, had noted fairs
where, no doubt, oxen were roasted whole.)   pudding sausage-like
entrails   448 Vice, Iniquity (Allegorical names for the chief comic
character and tempter in morality plays.)   449 vanity person given
to worldly desires   451 cleanly (1) pure (2) deft.   a capon a castrated
rooster for the table   452 cunning (1) skillful (2) crafty   455–6 take
me with you let me catch up with your meaning   464 saving your
reverence i.e., with my apology for using offensive language
467 host innkeeper   468 Pharaoh's lean kine (See Genesis 41, where
Pharaoh's dream of seven well-fattened cattle being devoured by
seven lean ones is interpreted by Joseph as a prophecy of seven years'
famine to come.)

PRINCE I do, I will.   [*A knocking.*
                              Exeunt Hostess, Francis, and Bardolph.]

Enter Bardolph, running.

BARDOLPH Oh, my lord, my lord! The sheriff with a
most monstrous watch is at the door.   478
FALSTAFF Out, ye rogue! Play out the play. I have
much to say in the behalf of that Falstaff.

Enter the Hostess.

HOSTESS Oh, Jesu, my lord, my lord!
PRINCE Heigh, heigh! The devil rides upon a fiddle-   482
stick. What's the matter?   483
HOSTESS The sheriff and all the watch are at the door.
They are come to search the house. Shall I let them in?
FALSTAFF Dost thou hear, Hal? Never call a true piece   486
of gold a counterfeit. Thou art essentially made   487
without seeming so.   488
PRINCE And thou a natural coward without instinct.
FALSTAFF I deny your major. If you will deny the   490
sheriff, so; if not, let him enter. If I become not a cart 491
as well as another man, a plague on my bringing up!   492
I hope I shall as soon be strangled with a halter as
another.
PRINCE Go hide thee behind the arras. The rest walk   495
up above. Now, my masters, for a true face and good   496
conscience.
FALSTAFF Both which I have had, but their date is out, 498
and therefore I'll hide me.   [*He hides behind the arras.*]
PRINCE Call in the sheriff.
                         [*Exeunt all except the Prince and Peto.*]

Enter Sheriff and the Carrier.

Now, Master Sheriff, what is your will with me?
SHERIFF
First, pardon me, my lord. A hue and cry   502
Hath followed certain men unto this house.
PRINCE What men?
SHERIFF
One of them is well known, my gracious lord,
A gross, fat man.
CARRIER   As fat as butter.
PRINCE
The man, I do assure you, is not here,
For I myself at this time have employed him.
And, Sheriff, I will engage my word to thee   509
That I will, by tomorrow dinnertime,   510
Send him to answer thee, or any man,

For anything he shall be charged withal;
And so let me entreat you leave the house.
SHERIFF
I will, my lord. There are two gentlemen
Have in this robbery lost three hundred marks.
PRINCE
It may be so. If he have robbed these men,
He shall be answerable; and so farewell.
SHERIFF Good night, my noble lord.
PRINCE
I think it is good morrow, is it not?   519
SHERIFF
Indeed, my lord, I think it be two o'clock.
                              Exit [*with Carrier*].
PRINCE This oily rascal is known as well as Paul's. Go 521
call him forth.
PETO [*discovering Falstaff*] Falstaff—Fast asleep behind
the arras, and snorting like a horse.
PRINCE Hark, how hard he fetches breath. Search his
pockets. (*He searcheth his pockets, and findeth certain
papers.*) What hast thou found?
PETO Nothing but papers, my lord.
PRINCE Let's see what they be. Read them.
PETO [*reads*]
        Item, A capon, ...2s. 2d.
        Item, Sauce, ...4d.
        Item, Sack, two gallons, ...5s. 8d.
        Item, Anchovies and sack after
            supper, ...2s. 6d.
        Item, Bread, ...ob. 534
PRINCE Oh, monstrous! But one halfpennyworth of
bread to this intolerable deal of sack? What there is
else, keep close; we'll read it at more advantage. There 537
let him sleep till day. I'll to the court in the morning.
We must all to the wars, and thy place shall be
honorable. I'll procure this fat rogue a charge of foot, 540
and I know his death will be a march of twelve score.   541
The money shall be paid back again with advantage.   542
Be with me betimes in the morning; and so, good   543
morrow, Peto.
PETO Good morrow, good my lord.   545
                    Exeunt [*separately. Falstaff is concealed
                              once more behind the arras.*]

❖

[3.1]

*Enter Hotspur, Worcester, Lord Mortimer,
[and] Owen Glendower.*

---

478 **watch** posse of constables   482–3 **The . . . fiddlestick** i.e., Here's
much ado about nothing.   486–8 **Dost . . . seeming so** (In this difficult passage, Falstaff seems to suggest that he is true gold, not counterfeit, and so should not be betrayed to the watch by the Prince,
who, he hopes, is not merely playacting at the tavern but is truly one
of its madcap members.)   490 **deny your major** reject your major
premise.   **deny** refuse entrance to   491 **become** befit, adorn.   **cart**
i.e., hangman's cart   492 **bringing up** (1) upbringing (2) being
brought before the authorities to be hanged.   495 **arras** wall hanging
or tapestry.   496 **up above** upstairs.   498 **date is out** lease has run
out   502 **hue and cry** outcry calling for the pursuit of a felon   509
engage pledge   510 **dinnertime** i.e., about noon

519 **morrow** morning   521 **Paul's** Saint Paul's Cathedral.   534 **ob.**
obolus, i.e., halfpenny   537 **close** hidden.   **advantage** favorable
opportunity.   540 **charge of foot** command of a company of infantry
541 **twelve score** i.e., two hundred and forty yards.   542 **advantage**
interest.   543 **betimes** early   545.1–2 *Exeunt . . . arras* (Onstage, the
arras is evidently arranged so that Falstaff can exit behind it once the
scene is over.)
**3.1 Location: Wales. Glendower's residence. (Holinshed places a
meeting of the rebel deputies at Bangor in the Archdeacon's house,
but in this present "unhistorical" scene, as invented by Shakespeare, Glendower is host throughout.) Seats are provided onstage.**

MORTIMER
These promises are fair, the parties sure,
And our induction full of prosperous hope.   2

HOTSPUR
Lord Mortimer, and cousin Glendower,
Will you sit down? And uncle Worcester—
A plague upon it, I have forgot the map.

GLENDOWER [*producing a map*]
No, here it is. Sit, cousin Percy,
Sit, good cousin Hotspur—for by that name
As oft as Lancaster doth speak of you   8
His cheek looks pale, and with a rising sigh
He wisheth you in heaven.

HOTSPUR   And you in hell,
As oft as he hears Owen Glendower spoke of.

GLENDOWER
I cannot blame him. At my nativity
The front of heaven was full of fiery shapes,   13
Of burning cressets, and at my birth   14
The frame and huge foundation of the earth
Shaked like a coward.

HOTSPUR   Why, so it would have done
At the same season, if your mother's cat
Had but kittened, though yourself had never been
    born.

GLENDOWER
I say the earth did shake when I was born.

HOTSPUR
And I say the earth was not of my mind,
If you suppose as fearing you it shook.

GLENDOWER
The heavens were all on fire; the earth did tremble.

HOTSPUR
Oh, then the earth shook to see the heavens on fire,
And not in fear of your nativity.
Diseasèd nature oftentimes breaks forth
In strange eruptions; oft the teeming earth
Is with a kind of colic pinched and vexed
By the imprisoning of unruly wind
Within her womb, which, for enlargement striving,   29
Shakes the old beldam earth and topples down   30
Steeples and moss-grown towers. At your birth
Our grandam earth, having this distemp'rature,   32
In passion shook.

GLENDOWER   Cousin, of many men   33
I do not bear these crossings. Give me leave   34
To tell you once again that at my birth
The front of heaven was full of fiery shapes,
The goats ran from the mountains, and the herds
Were strangely clamorous to the frighted fields.
These signs have marked me extraordinary,
And all the courses of my life do show
I am not in the roll of common men.

Where is he living, clipped in with the sea   42
That chides the banks of England, Scotland, Wales,   43
Which calls me pupil or hath read to me?   44
And bring him out that is but woman's son   45
Can trace me in the tedious ways of art   46
And hold me pace in deep experiments.   47

HOTSPUR
I think there's no man speaks better Welsh.   48
I'll to dinner.

MORTIMER
Peace, cousin Percy; you will make him mad.

GLENDOWER
I can call spirits from the vasty deep.   51

HOTSPUR
Why, so can I, or so can any man;
But will they come when you do call for them?

GLENDOWER
Why, I can teach you, cousin, to command the devil.

HOTSPUR
And I can teach thee, coz, to shame the devil
By telling truth. Tell truth and shame the devil.
If thou have power to raise him, bring him hither,
And I'll be sworn I have power to shame him hence.
Oh, while you live, tell truth and shame the devil!

MORTIMER
Come, come, no more of this unprofitable chat.

GLENDOWER
Three times hath Henry Bolingbroke made head   61
Against my power; thrice from the banks of Wye   62
And sandy-bottomed Severn have I sent him
Bootless home and weather-beaten back.   64

HOTSPUR
Home without boots, and in foul weather too!
How scapes he agues, in the devil's name?   66

GLENDOWER
Come, here is the map. Shall we divide our right
According to our threefold order ta'en?   68

MORTIMER
The Archdeacon hath divided it   69
Into three limits very equally: 70
England, from Trent and Severn hitherto,   71
By south and east is to my part assigned;
All westward, Wales beyond the Severn shore,
And all the fertile land within that bound,
To Owen Glendower; and, dear coz, to you   75
The remnant northward, lying off from Trent.

---

2 **induction** beginning.   **prosperous hope** hope of prospering.
8 **Lancaster** i.e., King Henry, here demoted to Duke of Lancaster
13 **front** brow, face. (As also at line 36.)   14 **cressets** lights burning in
metal baskets suspended from the ends of long poles or ceilings;
hence, meteors   29 **enlargement** release   30 **beldam** grandmother
32 **distemp'rature** disorder   33 **passion** suffering.   **of** from
34 **crossings** contradictions.

42–4 **Where . . . to me?** i.e., Where is there anyone in all of sea-walled
Great Britain who can claim to have been my instructor?   45–7 **And . . .
experiments** And I challenge you to produce a single human being
who can follow my tracks in the arcane craft of magic or keep up with
me in occult experiments.   48 **speaks better Welsh** (Hotspur hides
an insult behind the literal meaning, since "to speak Welsh" meant
colloquially both "to boast" and "to speak nonsense.")   51 **call** summon. (but Hotspur sardonically replies in the sense of "call out to,"
whether or not there is any response.)   **vasty deep** lower world.
61 **made head** raised a force   62 **power** army   64 **Bootless** without
advantage. (But Hotspur quibbles on the sense of "barefoot.")
66 **agues** fevers   68 **order ta'en** arrangements made.   69 **Archdeacon** i.e., the Archdeacon of Bangor, in whose house, according to
Holinshed, a meeting took place between deputies of the rebel leaders   70 **limits** regions   71 **hitherto** to this point   75 **coz** cousin, i.e.,
brother-in-law

And our indentures tripartite are drawn,   77
Which being sealèd interchangeably—
A business that this night may execute—   79
Tomorrow, cousin Percy, you and I
And my good lord of Worcester will set forth
To meet your father and the Scottish power,
As is appointed us, at Shrewsbury.
My father Glendower is not ready yet,   84
Nor shall we need his help these fourteen days.
[*To Glendower*] Within that space you may have drawn together   86
Your tenants, friends, and neighboring gentlemen.

GLENDOWER
A shorter time shall send me to you, lords;
And in my conduct shall your ladies come,   89
From whom you now must steal and take no leave,
For there will be a world of water shed
Upon the parting of your wives and you.

HOTSPUR [*consulting the map*]
Methinks my moiety, north from Burton here,   93
In quantity equals not one of yours.
See how this river comes me cranking in   95
And cuts me from the best of all my land
A huge half-moon, a monstrous cantle, out.   97
I'll have the current in this place dammed up,
And here the smug and silver Trent shall run   99
In a new channel, fair and evenly.
It shall not wind with such a deep indent
To rob me of so rich a bottom here.   102

GLENDOWER
Not wind? It shall, it must. You see it doth.

MORTIMER
Yea, but mark how he bears his course and runs me up   104
With like advantage on the other side,
Gelding the opposèd continent as much   106
As on the other side it takes from you.

WORCESTER
Yea, but a little charge will trench him here   108
And on this north side win this cape of land;
And then he runs straight and even.

HOTSPUR
I'll have it so. A little charge will do it.

GLENDOWER   I'll not have it altered.

HOTSPUR   Will not you?

GLENDOWER   No, nor you shall not.

HOTSPUR   Who shall say me nay?

GLENDOWER   Why, that will I.

HOTSPUR
Let me not understand you, then; speak it in Welsh.

GLENDOWER
I can speak English, lord, as well as you;
For I was trained up in the English court,
Where, being but young, I framèd to the harp   120
Many an English ditty lovely well,
And gave the tongue a helpful ornament—   122
A virtue that was never seen in you.

HOTSPUR
Marry, and I am glad of it with all my heart!
I had rather be a kitten and cry "mew"
Than one of these same meter balladmongers.
I had rather hear a brazen can'stick turned   127
Or a dry wheel grate on the axletree,   128
And that would set my teeth nothing on edge,   129
Nothing so much as mincing poetry.
'Tis like the forced gait of a shuffling nag.   131

GLENDOWER   Come, you shall have Trent turned.

HOTSPUR
I do not care. I'll give thrice so much land
To any well-deserving friend;
But in the way of bargain, mark ye me,
I'll cavil on the ninth part of a hair.   136
Are the indentures drawn? Shall we be gone?   137

GLENDOWER
The moon shines fair; you may away by night.
I'll haste the writer and withal   139
Break with your wives of your departure hence.   140
I am afraid my daughter will run mad,
So much she doteth on her Mortimer.   *Exit.*

MORTIMER
Fie, cousin Percy, how you cross my father!

HOTSPUR
I cannot choose. Sometimes he angers me
With telling me of the moldwarp and the ant,   145
Of the dreamer Merlin and his prophecies,   146
And of a dragon and a finless fish,
A clip-winged griffin and a moulten raven,   148
A couching lion and a ramping cat,   149
And such a deal of skimble-skamble stuff   150
As puts me from my faith. I tell you what: 151
He held me last night at least nine hours
In reckoning up the several devils' names   153

---

77 tripartite i.e., drawn up in triplicate, each document *sealèd interchangeably* (line 78) with the seal of all signatories.   **drawn** drawn up **79 this night may execute** may be carried out tonight   **84 father** father-in-law   **86 may** will be able to   **89 conduct** escort   **93 moiety** share   **95 comes me cranking in** comes bending in on my share. (The Trent, by turning northward to the North Sea instead of continuing eastward into the Wash, cuts Hotspur off from rich land in Lincolnshire and its vicinity.)   **97 cantle** piece   **99 smug** smooth   **102 bottom** valley   **104 runs me** runs. (*Me* is used colloquially.)   **106 Gelding ... continent** cutting off from the land which it bounds on the opposite side. (The Trent's southerly loop from Stoke to Burton deprives Mortimer of a piece of land, just as its later northerly course deprives Hotspur.)   **108 charge** expenditure.   **trench** provide a new channel

120 framèd to the harp set to harp accompaniment   **122 gave ... ornament** i.e., added to the words a pleasing ornament of music; also, gave to the English tongue the ornament of music and poetry   **127 can'stick turned** candlestick turned on a lathe   **128 axletree** axle   **129 nothing** not at all   **131 shuffling** hobbled   **136 cavil ... hair** i.e., argue about the most trivial detail.   **137 drawn** drawn up.   **139 writer** i.e., scrivener who would be drawing the indentures.   **withal** also   **140 Break with** inform   **145 moldwarp** mole. (Holinshed tells us that the division was arranged because of a prophecy that represented King Henry as the mole and the others as the dragon, the lion, and the wolf, who should divide the land among them.)   **146 Merlin** the bard, prophet, and magician of Arthurian story, Welsh in origin   **148 griffin** a fabulous beast, half lion, half eagle.   **moulten** having molted   **149 couching** couchant, crouching. (Heraldic term.)   **ramping** rampant, advancing on its hind legs. (Hotspur is ridiculing the heraldic emblems that Glendower holds so dear.)   **150 skimble-skamble** foolish, nonsensical   **151 puts ... faith** drives me from my (Christian) faith.   **153 several** various

That were his lackeys. I cried "Hum," and "Well, go to," 154
But marked him not a word. Oh, he is as tedious
As a tirèd horse, a railing wife,
Worse than a smoky house. I had rather live
With cheese and garlic in a windmill, far,
Than feed on cates and have him talk to me 159
In any summer house in Christendom.

MORTIMER
In faith, he is a worthy gentleman,
Exceedingly well read, and profited 162
In strange concealments, valiant as a lion 163
And wondrous affable, and as bountiful
As mines of India. Shall I tell you, cousin?
He holds your temper in a high respect 166
And curbs himself even of his natural scope 167
When you come 'cross his humor. Faith, he does. 168
I warrant you that man is not alive
Might so have tempted him as you have done 170
Without the taste of danger and reproof.
But do not use it oft, let me entreat you.

WORCESTER [to Hotspur]
In faith, my lord, you are too willful-blame, 173
And since your coming hither have done enough
To put him quite besides his patience. 175
You must needs learn, lord, to amend this fault.
Though sometimes it show greatness, courage,
    blood— 177
And that's the dearest grace it renders you— 178
Yet oftentimes it doth present harsh rage, 179
Defect of manners, want of government, 180
Pride, haughtiness, opinion, and disdain, 181
The least of which haunting a nobleman
Loseth men's hearts and leaves behind a stain
Upon the beauty of all parts besides, 184
Beguiling them of commendation. 185

HOTSPUR
Well, I am schooled. Good manners be your speed! 186
Here come our wives, and let us take our leave.

Enter Glendower with the ladies.

MORTIMER
This is the deadly spite that angers me: 188
My wife can speak no English, I no Welsh.

GLENDOWER
My daughter weeps she'll not part with you;
She'll be a soldier too, she'll to the wars.

MORTIMER
Good father, tell her that she and my aunt Percy 192

Shall follow in your conduct speedily. 193
*Glendower speaks to her in Welsh, and she answers
                                            him in the same.*
GLENDOWER
She is desperate here; a peevish self-willed harlotry, 194
One that no persuasion can do good upon.
                            The lady speaks in Welsh.
MORTIMER [to her]
I understand thy looks. That pretty Welsh 196
Which thou pourest down from these swelling heavens 197
I am too perfect in; and, but for shame, 198
In such a parley should I answer thee. 199
                            The lady again in Welsh.
I understand thy kisses and thou mine,
And that's a feeling disputation. 201
But I will never be a truant, love,
Till I have learned thy language; for thy tongue
Makes Welsh as sweet as ditties highly penned, 204
Sung by a fair queen in a summer's bower,
With ravishing division, to her lute. 206
GLENDOWER
Nay, if you melt, then will she run mad. 207
                        The lady speaks again in Welsh.
MORTIMER
Oh, I am ignorance itself in this!
GLENDOWER
She bids you on the wanton rushes lay you down 209
And rest your gentle head upon her lap,
And she will sing the song that pleaseth you
And on your eyelids crown the god of sleep, 212
Charming your blood with pleasing heaviness, 213
Making such difference twixt wake and sleep 214
As is the difference betwixt day and night
The hour before the heavenly-harnessed team 216
Begins his golden progress in the east.
MORTIMER
With all my heart I'll sit and hear her sing.
By that time will our book, I think, be drawn. 219
GLENDOWER   Do so;
And those musicians that shall play to you
Hang in the air a thousand leagues from hence,
And straight they shall be here. Sit, and attend.
                        *[Mortimer reclines with his head
                                            in his wife's lap.]*
HOTSPUR   Come, Kate, thou art perfect in lying down;
    come, quick, quick, that I may lay my head in thy lap.
LADY PERCY   Go, ye giddy goose.
                        *[Hotspur lies with his head
                            in Kate's lap.] The music plays.*

---

154 **go to** i.e., you don't say   159 **cates** delicacies   162 **profited** proficient   163 **concealments** occult practices   166 **temper** temperament   167 **scope** freedom of speech   168 **come 'cross** contradict   170 **Might** who could   173 **too willful-blame** blameworthy for too much self-will   175 **besides** out of   177 **blood** spirit   178 **dearest grace** best (and costliest) credit   179 **present** represent   180 **want of government** lack of self-control   181 **opinion** vanity, arrogance   184 **all parts besides** all other abilities   185 **Beguiling** depriving   186 **Good . . . speed!** i.e., May these good manners you praise so bring you success! (Said wryly; Hotspur doubts that good manners count for much in a time of war.)   188 **spite** vexation   192 **aunt** (Percy's wife, here called Kate, was aunt of Edmund Mortimer, the fifth Earl of March, but was sister-in-law to the Sir Edward Mortimer who married Glendower's daughter.)

193 **conduct** safe-conduct, escort   194 **desperate here** adamant on this point (i.e., her decision to accompany Mortimer).   **peevish self-willed harlotry** childish, willful, silly wench   196 **That pretty Welsh** i.e., Your eloquent tears   197 **heavens** i.e., eyes   198 **perfect** proficient   199 **such a parley** i.e., the same language (of weeping)   201 **disputation** conversation, debate.   204 **highly penned** eloquently composed, in high style   206 **division** variation, passage in which rapid short notes vary a theme   207 **melt** i.e., weep   209 **wanton rushes** i.e., soft floor covering   212 **crown . . . sleep** make sleep supreme ruler   213 **heaviness** drowsiness   214 **difference** nearly indistinguishable difference   216 **the heavenly-harnessed team** i.e., the team of horses drawing the chariot of the sun   219 **book** document, indentures

HOTSPUR
Now I perceive the devil understands Welsh;
And 'tis no marvel he is so humorous.   228
By'r Lady, he is a good musician.

LADY PERCY   Then should you be nothing but musical,
for you are altogether governed by humors. Lie still,
ye thief, and hear the lady sing in Welsh.   232

HOTSPUR   I had rather hear Lady, my brach, howl in   233
Irish.

LADY PERCY   Wouldst thou have thy head broken?   235

HOTSPUR   No.

LADY PERCY   Then be still.

HOTSPUR   Neither, 'tis a woman's fault.   238

LADY PERCY   Now God help thee!   239

HOTSPUR   To the Welsh lady's bed.

LADY PERCY   What's that?

HOTSPUR   Peace, she sings.

                    Here the lady sings a Welsh song.

HOTSPUR
Come, Kate, I'll have your song too.

LADY PERCY
Not mine, in good sooth.

HOTSPUR   Not yours, in good sooth! Heart, you swear   245
like a comfit maker's wife. "Not you, in good sooth,"   246
and "as true as I live," and "as God shall mend me,"
and "as sure as day,"
And givest such sarcenet surety for thy oaths   249
As if thou never walk'st further than Finsbury.   250
Swear me, Kate, like a lady as thou art,
A good mouth-filling oath, and leave "in sooth,"
And such protest of pepper-gingerbread,   253
To velvet-guards and Sunday citizens.   254
Come, sing.

LADY PERCY   I will not sing.

HOTSPUR   'Tis the next way to turn tailor, or be redbreast   257
teacher. An the indentures be drawn, I'll away within   258
these two hours; and so, come in when ye will.   *Exit.*

GLENDOWER
Come, come, Lord Mortimer. You are as slow
As hot Lord Percy is on fire to go.
By this our book is drawn; we'll but seal,   262
And then to horse immediately.

MORTIMER   With all my heart.   *Exeunt.*

228 **humorous** whimsical, capricious.   232 **thief** i.e., rascal
233 **brach** bitch hound   235 **broken** i.e., struck so as to break the
skin.   238 **Neither . . . fault** i.e., I won't do that either; it's womanish
to be submissive.   239 **help** amend. (But Hotspur answers in the
sense of "assist with an amour.")   245 **Heart** i.e., By Christ's heart
246 **comfit maker's** confectioner's   249 **sarcenet** soft, flimsy. (From
the soft silken material known as *sarcenet*.)   250 **Finsbury** a field just
outside London frequented by the London citizenry. (Hotspur jokes
with Kate as though she were a citizen's wife, using the pious and
modest oaths of such people.)   253 **protest . . . gingerbread** i.e.,
mealy-mouthed protestations   254 **velvet-guards** i.e., wives who
wear velvet trimming   257–8 **'Tis . . . teacher** i.e., The only use one
might put singing to is to become a tailor (since tailors were noted for
effeminacy and singing at their work) or an instructor to caged song-
birds before they are sold. (Hotspur airily dismisses singing, as he
does poetry.)   262 **By this** By this time.   **but** just

    Enter the King, Prince of Wales, and others.

KING
Lords, give us leave. The Prince of Wales and I
Must have some private conference; but be near at
    hand,
For we shall presently have need of you.
                                    Exeunt Lords.
I know not whether God will have it so
For some displeasing service I have done,
That in his secret doom out of my blood   6
He'll breed revengement and a scourge for me;
But thou dost in thy passages of life   8
Make me believe that thou art only marked   9
For the hot vengeance and the rod of heaven   10
To punish my mistreadings. Tell me else,   11
Could such inordinate and low desires,   12
Such poor, such bare, such lewd, such mean attempts,   13
Such barren pleasures, rude society,
As thou art matched withal and grafted to,   15
Accompany the greatness of thy blood
And hold their level with thy princely heart?   17

PRINCE
So please Your Majesty, I would I could
Quit all offenses with as clear excuse   19
As well as I am doubtless I can purge   20
Myself of many I am charged withal.
Yet such extenuation let me beg
As, in reproof of many tales devised,   23
Which oft the ear of greatness needs must hear
By smiling pickthanks and base newsmongers,   25
I may, for some things true, wherein my youth
Hath faulty wandered and irregular,
Find pardon on my true submission.

KING
God pardon thee! Yet let me wonder, Harry,
At thy affections, which do hold a wing   30
Quite from the flight of all thy ancestors.   31
Thy place in Council thou hast rudely lost,   32
Which by thy younger brother is supplied,
And art almost an alien to the hearts
Of all the court and princes of my blood.
The hope and expectation of thy time   36
Is ruined, and the soul of every man
Prophetically do forethink thy fall.

3.2 **Location:** The royal court (historically, Westminster).
6 **doom** judgment.   **blood** offspring   8 **passages** course, conduct
9–11 **thou . . . mistreadings** (1) you are marked as the means of heaven's
vengeance against me, or (2) you are marked to suffer heaven's
vengeance because of my sins.   11 **else** how otherwise   12 **inordinate** (1) immoderate (2) unworthy of your rank   13 **lewd** low, base.
attempts undertakings   15 **withal** with   17 **hold their level** claim
equality   19 **Quit** acquit myself of   20 **doubtless** certain   23 **in
reproof** upon disproof   25 **By . . . newsmongers** from smiling flatterers and ignoble talebearers   30 **affections** inclinations.   **hold a wing**
fly a course   31 **from** at variance with   32 **rudely** by violence.
(According to an apocryphal story, Prince Hal boxed the ears of the
Lord Chief Justice and was sent to prison for it; see *2 Henry IV*,
1.2.54–5, 192, and 5.2.70–1.)   36 **The hope . . . time** The hopes that
people had for you

Had I so lavish of my presence been,
So common-hackneyed in the eyes of men,   40
So stale and cheap to vulgar company,
Opinion, that did help me to the crown,   42
Had still kept loyal to possession   43
And left me in reputeless banishment,
A fellow of no mark nor likelihood.   45
By being seldom seen, I could not stir
But like a comet I was wondered at,
That men would tell their children, "This is he!"
Others would say, "Where, which is Bolingbroke?"
And then I stole all courtesy from heaven,   50
And dressed myself in such humility
That I did pluck allegiance from men's hearts,
Loud shouts and salutations from their mouths,
Even in the presence of the crownèd King.
Thus did I keep my person fresh and new,
My presence, like a robe pontifical,   56
Ne'er seen but wondered at; and so my state,   57
Seldom but sumptuous, showed like a feast   58
And won by rareness such solemnity.   59
The skipping King, he ambled up and down
With shallow jesters and rash bavin wits,   61
Soon kindled and soon burnt; carded his state,   62
Mingled his royalty with cap'ring fools,
Had his great name profanèd with their scorns,   64
And gave his countenance, against his name,   65
To laugh at gibing boys and stand the push   66
Of every beardless vain comparative;   67
Grew a companion to the common streets,
Enfeoffed himself to popularity,   69
That, being daily swallowed by men's eyes,
They surfeited with honey and began
To loathe the taste of sweetness, whereof a little
More than a little is by much too much.
So when he had occasion to be seen,
He was but as the cuckoo is in June,
Heard, not regarded—seen, but with such eyes
As, sick and blunted with community,   77
Afford no extraordinary gaze,
Such as is bent on sunlike majesty
When it shines seldom in admiring eyes;
But rather drowsed and hung their eyelids down,
Slept in his face, and rendered such aspect   82
As cloudy men use to their adversaries,   83

Being with his presence glutted, gorged, and full.
And in that very line, Harry, standest thou;   85
For thou hast lost thy princely privilege
With vile participation. Not an eye   87
But is aweary of thy common sight,
Save mine, which hath desired to see thee more—
Which now doth that I would not have it do,   90
Make blind itself with foolish tenderness.   91

PRINCE
I shall hereafter, my thrice gracious lord,
Be more myself.

KING   For all the world   93
As thou art to this hour was Richard then
When I from France set foot at Ravenspurgh,
And even as I was then is Percy now.
Now, by my scepter, and my soul to boot,   97
He hath more worthy interest to the state   98
Than thou the shadow of succession.   99
For of no right, nor color like to right,   100
He doth fill fields with harness in the realm,   101
Turns head against the lion's armèd jaws,   102
And, being no more in debt to years than thou,   103
Leads ancient lords and reverend bishops on
To bloody battles and to bruising arms.
What never-dying honor hath he got
Against renownèd Douglas! Whose high deeds,   107
Whose hot incursions and great name in arms
Holds from all soldiers chief majority   109
And military title capital   110
Through all the kingdoms that acknowledge Christ.
Thrice hath this Hotspur, Mars in swaddling clothes,
This infant warrior, in his enterprises
Discomfited great Douglas, ta'en him once,   114
Enlargèd him and made a friend of him,   115
To fill the mouth of deep defiance up   116
And shake the peace and safety of our throne.
And what say you to this? Percy, Northumberland,
The Archbishop's Grace of York, Douglas, Mortimer,   119
Capitulate against us and are up.   120
But wherefore do I tell these news to thee?
Why, Harry, do I tell thee of my foes,
Which art my nearest and dearest enemy?   123
Thou that art like enough, through vassal fear,   124
Base inclination, and the start of spleen,   125
To fight against me under Percy's pay,

---

40 common-hackneyed cheapened, vulgarized   **42 Opinion** public opinion   **43 to possession** i.e., to Richard II's sovereignty   **45 mark nor likelihood** importance or likeliness to succeed.   **50 I . . . heaven** i.e., I assumed a bearing of the utmost meekness   **56 pontifical** like that of a pope or archbishop   **57–9 and so . . . solemnity** and so my magnificence on public occasions, infrequent but always sumptuous, looked festive and achieved by this rarity a suitable formal impressiveness.   **61 bavin** brushwood, soon burnt out   **62 carded his state** debased his royal dignity. (To *card* is to stir or mix, hence to adulterate.)   **64 with their scorns** by his favorites' scornful and contemptuous behavior   **65–7 And gave . . . comparative** and lent his authority, to the detriment of his royal dignity and reputation, to find amusement in young scoffers and submit himself to the insolence of every frivolous witcracker   **69 Enfeoffed himself** gave himself up   **77 community** commonness   **82–3 Slept . . . adversaries** dozed off right before his eyes, and looked at the King in the way sullen men look at their adversaries

85 line degree, category   **87 vile participation** base association or companionship.   **90 that** that which   **91 tenderness** i.e., tears. **93 For all the world** In every way   **97 to boot** in addition   **98–9 He . . . succession** i.e., this rebel Hotspur has a better claim to the throne than your merely hereditary claim unsupported by deeds.   **100 of . . . to right** having no rightful claim or even the pretext of one   **101 harness** armor, i.e., men in armor   **102 Turns head** leads an armed insurrection. **lion's** i.e., King's   **103 being . . . thou** i.e., being no older than you. (Though historically Hotspur was twenty-three years older than the prince.)   **107 Whose** i.e., Hotspur's   **109 majority** preeminence   **110 capital** chief, principal   **114 Discomfited** defeated **115 Enlargèd** freed   **116 To . . . up** to swell the roar of deep defiance **119 The Archbishop's Grace** His Grace the Archbishop   **120 Capitulate** form a league, draw up articles.   **up** up in arms.   **123 dearest** (1) most precious (2) direst   **124 like** likely.   **vassal** slavish **125 Base . . . spleen** inclination for baseness, and sudden bursts of capricious irascibility

To dog his heels and curtsy at his frowns,
To show how much thou art degenerate.

PRINCE
Do not think so. You shall not find it so.
And God forgive them that so much have swayed
Your Majesty's good thoughts away from me!
I will redeem all this on Percy's head
And in the closing of some glorious day
Be bold to tell you that I am your son,
When I will wear a garment all of blood
And stain my favors in a bloody mask,   136
Which, washed away, shall scour my shame with it.
And that shall be the day, whene'er it lights,   138
That this same child of honor and renown,
This gallant Hotspur, this all-praisèd knight,
And your unthought-of Harry chance to meet.   141
For every honor sitting on his helm,   142
Would they were multitudes, and on my head
My shames redoubled! For the time will come
That I shall make this northern youth exchange
His glorious deeds for my indignities.
Percy is but my factor, good my lord,   147
To engross up glorious deeds on my behalf;   148
And I will call him to so strict account
That he shall render every glory up,
Yea, even the slightest worship of his time,   151
Or I will tear the reckoning from his heart.
This in the name of God I promise here,
The which if He be pleased I shall perform,
I do beseech Your Majesty may salve   155
The long-grown wounds of my intemperance.   156
If not, the end of life cancels all bonds,
And I will die a hundred thousand deaths
Ere break the smallest parcel of this vow.

KING
A hundred thousand rebels die in this!
Thou shalt have charge and sovereign trust herein.   161

Enter Blunt.

How now, good Blunt? Thy looks are full of speed.

BLUNT
So hath the business that I come to speak of.
Lord Mortimer of Scotland hath sent word   164
That Douglas and the English rebels met
The eleventh of this month at Shrewsbury.
A mighty and a fearful head they are,   167
If promises be kept on every hand,
As ever offered foul play in a state.

KING
The Earl of Westmorland set forth today,
With him my son, Lord John of Lancaster;
For this advertisement is five days old.   172
On Wednesday next, Harry, you shall set forward;

On Thursday we ourselves will march. Our meeting   174
Is Bridgnorth. And, Harry, you shall march   175
Through Gloucestershire; by which account,
Our business valuèd, some twelve days hence   177
Our general forces at Bridgnorth shall meet.
Our hands are full of business. Let's away!
Advantage feeds him fat while men delay.   *Exeunt.* 180

[3.3]

Enter Falstaff and Bardolph.

FALSTAFF   Bardolph, am I not fallen away vilely since   1
this last action? Do I not bate? Do I not dwindle? Why, 2
my skin hangs about me like an old lady's loose gown;
I am withered like an old applejohn. Well, I'll repent, 4
and that suddenly, while I am in some liking. I shall be 5
out of heart shortly, and then I shall have no strength   6
to repent. An I have not forgotten what the inside of a
church is made of, I am a peppercorn, a brewer's   8
horse. The inside of a church! Company, villainous   9
company, hath been the spoil of me.
BARDOLPH   Sir John, you are so fretful you cannot live   11
long.
FALSTAFF   Why, there is it. Come sing me a bawdy
song; make me merry. I was as virtuously given as a   14
gentleman need to be, virtuous enough: swore little,
diced not above seven times—a week, went to a
bawdy house not above once in a quarter—of an
hour, paid money that I borrowed—three or four
times, lived well and in good compass; and now I live   19
out of all order, out of all compass.
BARDOLPH   Why, you are so fat, Sir John, that you must
needs be out of all compass, out of all reasonable
compass, Sir John.
FALSTAFF   Do thou amend thy face, and I'll amend my
life. Thou art our admiral, thou bearest the lantern in 25
the poop, but 'tis in the nose of thee. Thou art the
Knight of the Burning Lamp.   27
BARDOLPH   Why, Sir John, my face does you no harm.
FALSTAFF   No, I'll be sworn, I make as good use of it as
many a man doth of a death's-head or a *memento mori.*   30
I never see thy face but I think upon hellfire and

136 **favors** features   138 **lights** dawns   141 **unthought-of** lightly valued, disregarded   142 **For** As for   147 **factor** agent   148 **engross up**
amass, buy up   151 **even . . . time** every smallest honor he has ever
won   155 **salve** soothe, heal   156 **intemperance** dissolute living.
161 **charge** command (of troops)   164 **Lord Mortimer of Scotland** (A
Scottish nobleman, unrelated to Glendower's son-in-law.)   167 **head**
armed force   172 **advertisement** tidings, news

174 **meeting** place of rendezvous   175 **Bridgnorth** a town near
Shrewsbury.   177 **Our business valuèd** estimating how long our
business will take   180 **Advantage . . . fat** Opportunity (for rebellion)
prospers.   **him** himself
3.3. Location: A tavern in Eastcheap, as in 2.4.
1 **fallen away** shrunk   2 **action** i.e., the robbery at Gad's Hill.   **bate**
lose weight.   4 **applejohn** a kind of apple still in good eating condition when shriveled.   5 **liking** (1) good bodily condition (2) inclination.   6 **out of heart** (1) disinclined, disheartened (2) out of condition   8 **peppercorn** unground dried pepper berry   8–9 **brewer's horse** i.e.,
one that is old, withered, and decrepit.   11 **fretful** (1) anxious (2) fretted, frayed   14 **given** inclined   19 **good compass** reasonable limits;
also, in Bardolph's speech, girth, circumference   25 **admiral** flagship.
lantern i.e., a light for the rest of the fleet to follow; here applied to
Bardolph's inflamed nose, red from overdrinking   27 **Knight . . .
Lamp** Falstaff parodies the names of heroes in popular chivalric
romances.   30 *memento mori* reminder of death, such as a death's
head or a skull engraved on a seal ring.

Dives that lived in purple; for there he is in his robes, 32
burning, burning. If thou wert any way given to
virtue, I would swear by thy face; my oath should be
"By this fire, that's God's angel." But thou art 35
altogether given over, and wert indeed, but for the 36
light in thy face, the son of utter darkness. When thou
ran'st up Gad's Hill in the night to catch my horse, if
I did not think thou hadst been an *ignis fatuus* or a ball 39
of wildfire, there's no purchase in money. Oh, thou art 40
a perpetual triumph, an everlasting bonfire light! 41
Thou hast saved me a thousand marks in links and 42
torches, walking with thee in the night betwixt tavern
and tavern; but the sack that thou hast drunk me
would have bought me lights as good cheap at the 45
dearest chandler's in Europe. I have maintained that 46
salamander of yours with fire any time this two-and- 47
thirty years. God reward me for it!

BARDOLPH   'Sblood, I would my face were in your belly! 49

FALSTAFF   God-a-mercy! So should I be sure to be
heartburned.

Enter Hostess.

How now, Dame Partlet the hen? Have you inquired 52
yet who picked my pocket?

HOSTESS   Why, Sir John, what do you think, Sir John?
Do you think I keep thieves in my house? I have
searched, I have inquired, so has my husband, man
by man, boy by boy, servant by servant. The tithe of a 57
hair was never lost in my house before.

FALSTAFF   Ye lie, hostess. Bardolph was shaved and 59
lost many a hair; and I'll be sworn my pocket was 60
picked. Go to, you are a woman, go.

HOSTESS   Who, I? No, I defy thee! God's light, I was 62
never called so in mine own house before.

FALSTAFF   Go to, I know you well enough.

HOSTESS   No, Sir John, you do not know me, Sir John.
I know you, Sir John. You owe me money, Sir John,
and now you pick a quarrel to beguile me of it. I
bought you a dozen of shirts to your back.

FALSTAFF   Dowlas, filthy dowlas. I have given them 69
away to bakers' wives; they have made bolters of 70
them.

HOSTESS   Now, as I am a true woman, holland of eight 72
shillings an ell. You owe money here besides, Sir 73
John, for your diet and by-drinkings, and money lent 74
you, four-and-twenty pound.

FALSTAFF   He had his part of it. Let him pay. 76

HOSTESS   He? Alas, he is poor, he hath nothing.

FALSTAFF   How, poor? Look upon his face. What call
you rich? Let them coin his nose, let them coin his
cheeks. I'll not pay a denier. What, will you make a 80
younker of me? Shall I not take mine ease in mine inn 81
but I shall have my pocket picked? I have lost a seal
ring of my grandfather's worth forty mark.

HOSTESS   Oh, Jesu, I have heard the Prince tell him, I
know not how oft, that that ring was copper.

FALSTAFF   How? The Prince is a Jack, a sneak-up. 86
'Sblood, an he were here, I would cudgel him like a
dog if he would say so. 88

*Enter the Prince [with Peto], marching, and
Falstaff meets him playing upon his truncheon like
a fife.*

How now, lad, is the wind in that door, i'faith? Must 89
we all march?

BARDOLPH   Yea, two and two, Newgate fashion. 91

HOSTESS   My lord, I pray you, hear me.

PRINCE   What say'st thou, Mistress Quickly? How doth
thy husband? I love him well; he is an honest man.

HOSTESS   Good my lord, hear me.

FALSTAFF   Prithee, let her alone and list to me.

PRINCE   What say'st thou, Jack?

FALSTAFF   The other night I fell asleep here behind the
arras and had my pocket picked. This house is turned 99
bawdy house; they pick pockets.

PRINCE   What didst thou lose, Jack?

FALSTAFF   Wilt thou believe me, Hal? Three or four
bonds of forty pound apiece and a seal ring of my
grandfather's.

PRINCE   A trifle, some eightpenny matter.

HOSTESS   So I told him, my lord, and I said I heard Your
Grace say so; and, my lord, he speaks most vilely of
you, like a foulmouthed man as he is, and said he
would cudgel you.

PRINCE   What, he did not!

HOSTESS   There's neither faith, truth, nor womanhood
in me else.

FALSTAFF   There's no more faith in thee than in a stewed 113
prune, nor no more truth in thee than in a drawn fox; 114
and for womanhood, Maid Marian may be the dep- 115
uty's wife of the ward to thee. Go, you thing, go. 116

HOSTESS   Say, what thing, what thing?

FALSTAFF   What thing? Why, a thing to thank God on. 118

HOSTESS   I am no thing to thank God on, I would thou 119
shouldst know it! I am an honest man's wife, and,

32 **Dives** the rich man who went to hell, referred to in Luke 16:19–31
35 **"By . . . angel"** (Psalms 104:4, Hebrews 1:7, and Exodus 3:2
describe angels that appear in flames of fire.)   36 **given over** abandoned to wickedness   39 *ignis fatuus* will-o'-the-wisp   40 **wildfire**
fireworks; lightning; will-o'-the-wisp   41 **triumph** procession led by
torches   42 **links** torches, flares   45 **good cheap** cheap   46 **dearest
chandler's** most expensive candle maker's   47 **salamander** lizard
reputed to be able to live in fire   49 **I . . . belly** (A colloquial way of
objecting to an insult. Falstaff responds in the literal sense: A face like
yours would give me massive indigestion.)   52 **Partlet** (Traditional
name of a hen.)   57 **tithe** tenth part   59 **was shaved** (1) had his
beard cut (2) was cheated and robbed   60 **lost many a hair** (1) was
shaved (2) was made bald by syphilis   62 **God's light** (A mild oath.)
69 **Dowlas** a coarse kind of linen   70 **bolters** cloths for sifting flour
72 **holland** fine linen   73 **an ell** a measure of forty-five inches.
74 **diet** meals.   **by-drinkings** drinks between meals

76 **He** Bardolph   80 **denier** one-twelfth of a French sou; type of very
small coin.   81 **younker** greenhorn   86 **Jack** knave, rascal.   **sneak-
up** sneak.   88.2 *truncheon* officer's staff   89 **is . . . door** i.e., is that the
way the wind is blowing   91 **Newgate** a famous city prison in London.
(Prisoners marched two by two.)   99 **arras** curtain   113–14 **stewed
prune** (Customarily associated with bawdy houses.)   114 **drawn fox**
fox driven from cover and wily in getting back   115–16 **Maid . . .
thee** i.e., Maid Marian, a disreputable woman in Robin Hood ballads,
morris dances, and the like, was a model of respectability compared
with you.   118–19 **What thing . . . no thing** (With sexual quibbles.)

setting thy knighthood aside, thou art a knave to call 121
me so.

FALSTAFF   Setting thy womanhood aside, thou art a
beast to say otherwise.

HOSTESS   Say, what beast, thou knave, thou?

FALSTAFF   What beast? Why, an otter.

PRINCE   An otter, Sir John! Why an otter?

FALSTAFF   Why? She's neither fish nor flesh; a man
knows not where to have her.   129

HOSTESS   Thou art an unjust man in saying so. Thou or
any man knows where to have me, thou knave, thou.

PRINCE   Thou sayst true, hostess, and he slanders thee
most grossly.

HOSTESS   So he doth you, my lord, and said this other
day you owed him a thousand pound.

PRINCE   Sirrah, do I owe you a thousand pound?

FALSTAFF   A thousand pound, Hal? A million. Thy love
is worth a million; thou owest me thy love.

HOSTESS   Nay, my lord, he called you Jack and said he
would cudgel you.

FALSTAFF   Did I, Bardolph?

BARDOLPH   Indeed, Sir John, you said so.

FALSTAFF   Yea, if he said my ring was copper.

PRINCE   I say 'tis copper. Darest thou be as good as thy
word now?

FALSTAFF   Why, Hal, thou knowest, as thou art but
man, I dare; but as thou art prince, I fear thee as I fear
the roaring of the lion's whelp.   148

PRINCE   And why not as the lion?

FALSTAFF   The King himself is to be feared as the lion.
Dost thou think I'll fear thee as I fear thy father? Nay,
an I do, I pray God my girdle break.

PRINCE   Oh, if it should, how would thy guts fall about
thy knees! But, sirrah, there's no room for faith, truth,
nor honesty in this bosom of thine; it is all filled up
with guts and midriff. Charge an honest woman with
picking thy pocket? Why, thou whoreson, impudent,
embossed rascal, if there were anything in thy pocket 158
but tavern reckonings, memorandums of bawdy 159
houses, and one poor pennyworth of sugar candy to
make thee long-winded, if thy pocket were enriched
with any other injuries but these, I am a villain. And 162
yet you will stand to it; you will not pocket up wrong! 163
Art thou not ashamed?

FALSTAFF   Dost thou hear, Hal? Thou knowest in the
state of innocency Adam fell; and what should poor
Jack Falstaff do in the days of villainy? Thou see'st I
have more flesh than another man, and therefore
more frailty. You confess then you picked my pocket.

PRINCE   It appears so by the story.

FALSTAFF   Hostess, I forgive thee. Go make ready breakfast. Love thy husband, look to thy servants, cherish
thy guests. Thou shalt find me tractable to any honest
reason; thou see'st I am pacified still. Nay, prithee, 174
begone.   *Exit Hostess.*

Now, Hal, to the news at court: for the robbery, lad,
how is that answered?

PRINCE   Oh, my sweet beef, I must still be good angel to
thee. The money is paid back again.

FALSTAFF   Oh, I do not like that paying back. 'Tis a
double labor.   180

PRINCE   I am good friends with my father and may do
anything.

FALSTAFF   Rob me the exchequer the first thing thou
dost, and do it with unwashed hands too.   184

BARDOLPH   Do, my lord.

PRINCE   I have procured thee, Jack, a charge of foot.   186

FALSTAFF   I would it had been of horse. Where shall I
find one that can steal well? Oh, for a fine thief, of the 188
age of two-and-twenty or thereabouts! I am heinously
unprovided. Well, God be thanked for these rebels; 190
they offend none but the virtuous. I laud them, I 191
praise them.

PRINCE   Bardolph!

BARDOLPH   My lord?

PRINCE [*giving letters*]
Go bear this letter to Lord John of Lancaster,
To my brother John; this to my lord of Westmorland.
                                          [*Exit Bardolph.*]
Go, Peto, to horse, to horse, for thou and I
Have thirty miles to ride yet ere dinnertime.
                                             [*Exit Peto.*]
Jack, meet me tomorrow in the Temple Hall   199
At two o'clock in the afternoon.
There shalt thou know thy charge, and there receive
Money and order for their furniture.   202
The land is burning. Percy stands on high,
And either we or they must lower lie.   [*Exit.*]

FALSTAFF
Rare words! Brave world! Hostess, my breakfast, come! 205
Oh, I could wish this tavern were my drum!   [*Exit.*] 206

❖

[4.1]

[*Enter Hotspur, Worcester, and Douglas.*]

HOTSPUR
Well said, my noble Scot. If speaking truth

---

121 setting . . . aside (Mistress Quickly means, "without wishing to
offend your rank of knighthood," but Falstaff replies in line 123 with
the meaning, "setting aside your womanhood as of no value or perti-
nence.")   129 have understand. (With a sly suggestion of sexual possession—a meaning that eludes Mistress Quickly.)   148 whelp cub.
158 embossed (1) swollen with fat (2) foaming at the mouth and
exhausted, like a hunted animal.   rascal (1) scoundrel (2) immature
and inferior deer   159 memorandums souvenirs   162 injuries i.e.,
those things you claim to have lost, thereby suffering harm   163 stand
to it make a stand, insist on your supposed rights.   pocket up
endure silently

174 still always.   180 double labor i.e., the taking and the returning.
184 with unwashed hands without further ado   186 charge of foot
command of a company of infantry.   188 one i.e., a companion in
thievery. (Falstaff sees war as the opportunity for stealing and con-
ning.)   190 unprovided ill-equipped.   191 they . . . virtuous i.e., the
rebels, by providing the occasion of war, give dishonest men a chance
to profiteer and hence offend only those who are honest.   199 Temple Hall i.e., at the Inner Temple, one of the Inns of Court   202 furniture equipment, furnishing.   205 Brave Splendid   206 drum
(Possibly Falstaff means that he wishes he could continue to enjoy
this tavern instead of risking his life in battle. He may also be punning on *tavern/taborn*, i.e., *taborin*, a kind of drum.)
4.1. Location: The rebel camp near Shrewsbury.

In this fine age were not thought flattery,
Such attribution should the Douglas have 3
As not a soldier of this season's stamp 4
Should go so general current through the world. 5
By God, I cannot flatter; I do defy 6
The tongues of soothers! But a braver place 7
In my heart's love hath no man than yourself.
Nay, task me to my word; approve me, lord. 9
DOUGLAS   Thou art the king of honor.
No man so potent breathes upon the ground 11
But I will beard him.

Enter one [a Messenger] with letters.

HOTSPUR   Do so, and 'tis well.— 12
What letters hast thou there?—I can but thank you. 13
MESSENGER
These letters come from your father.
HOTSPUR
Letters from him? Why comes he not himself?
MESSENGER
He cannot come, my lord. He is grievous sick.
HOTSPUR
Zounds, how has he the leisure to be sick
In such a jostling time? Who leads his power? 18
Under whose government come they along? 19
MESSENGER
His letters bears his mind, not I, my lord.
[Hotspur reads the letter.]
WORCESTER
I prithee, tell me, doth he keep his bed? 21
MESSENGER
He did, my lord, four days ere I set forth,
And at the time of my departure thence
He was much feared by his physicians. 24
WORCESTER
I would the state of time had first been whole 25
Ere he by sickness had been visited.
His health was never better worth than now.
HOTSPUR
Sick now? Droop now? This sickness doth infect
The very life-blood of our enterprise;
'Tis catching hither, even to our camp.
He writes me here that inward sickness—
And that his friends by deputation 32
Could not so soon be drawn, nor did he think it meet 33
To lay so dangerous and dear a trust
On any soul removed but on his own. 35
Yet doth he give us bold advertisement 36

That with our small conjunction we should on, 37
To see how fortune is disposed to us;
For, as he writes, there is no quailing now, 39
Because the King is certainly possessed 40
Of all our purposes. What say you to it?
WORCESTER
Your father's sickness is a maim to us. 42
HOTSPUR
A perilous gash, a very limb lopped off.
And yet, in faith, it is not! His present want 44
Seems more than we shall find it. Were it good 45
To set the exact wealth of all our states 46
All at one cast? To set so rich a main 47
On the nice hazard of one doubtful hour? 48
It were not good, for therein should we read 49
The very bottom and the soul of hope, 50
The very list, the very utmost bound 51
Of all our fortunes.
DOUGLAS   Faith, and so we should;
Where now remains a sweet reversion, 53
We may boldly spend upon the hope
Of what is to come in.
A comfort of retirement lives in this. 56
HOTSPUR
A rendezvous, a home to fly unto,
If that the devil and mischance look big 58
Upon the maidenhead of our affairs. 59
WORCESTER
But yet I would your father had been here.
The quality and hair of our attempt 61
Brooks no division. It will be thought 62
By some that know not why he is away
That wisdom, loyalty, and mere dislike 64
Of our proceedings kept the Earl from hence.
And think how such an apprehension 66
May turn the tide of fearful faction 67
And breed a kind of question in our cause.
For well you know we of the off'ring side 69
Must keep aloof from strict arbitrament, 70
And stop all sight-holes, every loop from whence 71
The eye of reason may pry in upon us.
This absence of your father's draws a curtain 73
That shows the ignorant a kind of fear
Before not dreamt of.
HOTSPUR   You strain too far. 75
I rather of his absence make this use:

3 **attribution** praise, tribute   4–5 **As . . . world** that no one coined as a soldier in this current campaign should enjoy such a current reputation. (To *go . . . current* is to be put into circulation, continuing the image of coining in line 4.)   6 **defy** proclaim against   7 **soothers** flatterers.   **braver** better, dearer   9 **task . . . word** challenge me to make good my word.   **approve** test   11–12 **No . . . him** i.e., I am ready to defy anyone alive.   13 **I can . . . you** (Said to Douglas.)   18 **jostling** contending, clashing   19 **government** command   21 **keep** keep to   24 **feared** feared for   25 **time** the times   32–3 **And that . . . drawn** and that his allies could not so soon be assembled by anyone other than himself, any deputy   33 **meet** appropriate   35 **On . . . own** on anyone other than himself.   36 **advertisement** counsel, advice

37 **conjunction** joint force.   **on** go on   39 **quailing** losing heart   40 **possessed** informed   42 **maim** injury   44 **want** absence   45 **more** more serious   46 **To . . . states** to stake the absolute total of our resources   47 **cast** throw of the dice.   **main** stake in gambling; also, an army   48 **nice** precarious, delicate.   **hazard** (1) game at dice (2) venture   49–50 **should . . . hope** we should discover the utmost foundation and basis of our hopes, the most we could rely on   51 **list** limit   53 **Where . . . reversion** since as things stand we can expect reinforcements. (A *reversion* is literally part of an estate yet to be inherited.)   56 **retirement** something to fall back on   58 **big** threatening   59 **maidenhead** i.e., commencement   61 **hair** kind, nature   62 **Brooks** tolerates   64 **loyalty** i.e., to the crown   66 **apprehension** (1) perception (2) apprehensiveness   67 **fearful faction** timid support   69 **off'ring side** side that attacks   70 **strict arbitrament** just inquiry or investigation   71 **sight-holes** peep-holes. (*Loop* or *loophole* has the same meaning.)   73 **draws** draws aside, opens   75 **strain too far** exaggerate.

It lends a luster and more great opinion,   77
A larger dare to our great enterprise,   78
Than if the Earl were here; for men must think,
If we without his help can make a head   80
To push against a kingdom, with his help
We shall o'erturn it topsy-turvy down.
Yet all goes well, yet all our joints are whole.   83

DOUGLAS
As heart can think. There is not such a word
Spoke of in Scotland as this term of fear.

Enter Sir Richard Vernon.

HOTSPUR
My cousin Vernon, welcome, by my soul.

VERNON
Pray God my news be worth a welcome, lord.
The Earl of Westmorland, seven thousand strong,
Is marching hitherwards; with him Prince John.

HOTSPUR
No harm. What more?

VERNON   And further I have learned
The King himself in person is set forth,
Or hitherwards intended speedily,   92
With strong and mighty preparation.

HOTSPUR
He shall be welcome too. Where is his son,
The nimble-footed madcap Prince of Wales,
And his comrades, that doffed the world aside   96
And bid it pass?

VERNON   All furnished, all in arms   97
All plumed like estridges, that with the wind   98
Bated like eagles having lately bathed,   99
Glittering in golden coats, like images,   100
As full of spirit as the month of May
And gorgeous as the sun at midsummer,
Wanton as youthful goats, wild as young bulls.   103
I saw young Harry, with his beaver on,   104
His cuisses on his thighs, gallantly armed,   105
Rise from the ground like feathered Mercury,
And vaulted with such ease into his seat   107
As if an angel dropped down from the clouds
To turn and wind a fiery Pegasus   109
And witch the world with noble horsemanship.   110

HOTSPUR
No more, no more! Worse than the sun in March   111
This praise doth nourish agues. Let them come.   112
They come like sacrifices in their trim,   113

And to the fire-eyed maid of smoky war   114
All hot and bleeding will we offer them.
The mailèd Mars shall on his altar sit   116
Up to the ears in blood. I am on fire
To hear this rich reprisal is so nigh,   118
And yet not ours. Come, let me taste my horse,   119
Who is to bear me like a thunderbolt
Against the bosom of the Prince of Wales.
Harry to Harry shall, hot horse to horse,
Meet and ne'er part till one drop down a corse.   123
Oh, that Glendower were come!

VERNON   There is more news:
I learned in Worcester, as I rode along,
He cannot draw his power this fourteen days.   126

DOUGLAS
That's the worst tidings that I hear of yet.

WORCESTER
Ay, by my faith, that bears a frosty sound.

HOTSPUR
What may the King's whole battle reach unto?   129

VERNON
To thirty thousand.

HOTSPUR   Forty let it be!
My father and Glendower being both away,
The powers of us may serve so great a day.   132
Come, let us take a muster speedily.
Doomsday is near; die all, die merrily.

DOUGLAS
Talk not of dying. I am out of fear   135
Of death or death's hand for this one half year.

                                              Exeunt.

❧

[4.2]

Enter Falstaff, [and] Bardolph.

FALSTAFF   Bardolph, get thee before to Coventry; fill me
a bottle of sack. Our soldiers shall march through; we'll
to Sutton Coldfield tonight.   3

BARDOLPH   Will you give me money, Captain?

FALSTAFF   Lay out, lay out.   5

BARDOLPH   This bottle makes an angel.   6

FALSTAFF   An if it do, take it for thy labor; an if it make
twenty, take them all; I'll answer the coinage. Bid my   8
lieutenant Peto meet me at town's end.

BARDOLPH   I will, Captain. Farewell.   *Exit.*

FALSTAFF   If I be not ashamed of my soldiers, I am a
soused gurnet. I have misused the King's press dam-   12
nably. I have got, in exchange of a hundred and fifty

---

77 opinion renown   **78 dare** daring   **80 make a head** raise an armed
force   **83 Yet** Still.   **joints** limbs   **92 intended** on the verge of departure   **96–7 that doffed . . . pass?** i.e., that thumbed their noses at
responsibilities, telling the world to mind its own business?   **97 furnished** equipped   **98–9 All . . . bathed** i.e., all plumed with ostrich
feathers, fluttering their wings in the wind like eagles having just
bathed. (The text may be defective.)   **100 coats** (1) coats of mail
(2) heraldic coats of arms.   **images** gilded statues   **103 Wanton**
sportive, frolicsome   **104 beaver** visor; hence, helmet   **105 cuisses**
armor for the thighs   **107 seat** saddle   **109 wind** wheel about.
Pegasus winged horse of Greek mythology   **110 witch** bewitch
111–12 Worse . . . agues (The spring sun was believed to give impetus
to chills and fevers, by drawing up vapors. Vernon's speech, says
Hotspur, gives one the shudders.)   **113 sacrifices** beasts for sacrifice.
trim fine apparel, trappings

114 maid i.e., Bellona, goddess of war   **116 mailèd** dressed in mail,
armor   **118 reprisal** prize   **119 taste** try, feel under me   **123 corse**
corpse.   **126 draw his power** muster his army   **129 battle** army
132 The . . . us our forces   **135 out of** free from
4.2. Location: A public road near Coventry.
3 Sutton Coldfield (In Warwickshire near Coventry.)   **5 Lay out** Pay
for it yourself   **6 makes an angel** i.e., makes ten shillings I've spent
for you. (But Falstaff answers as though *makes* means "produces,"
implying that Bardolph can profit from the transaction.)   **8 I'll . . .
coinage** I'll take responsibility for any proceeds.   **12 soused gurnet** a
kind of pickled fish.   **King's press** royal warrant for the impressment of troops

soldiers, three hundred and odd pounds. I press me 14
none but good householders, yeomen's sons, inquire 15
me out contracted bachelors, such as had been asked 16
twice on the banns—such a commodity of warm 17
slaves as had as lief hear the devil as a drum, such as 18
fear the report of a caliver worse than a struck fowl or 19
a hurt wild duck. I pressed me none but such toasts- 20
and-butter, with hearts in their bellies no bigger than 21
pins' heads, and they have bought out their services; 22
and now my whole charge consists of ancients, cor- 23
porals, lieutenants, gentlemen of companies—slaves 24
as ragged as Lazarus in the painted cloth, where the 25
glutton's dogs licked his sores, and such as indeed
were never soldiers, but discarded unjust servingmen, 27
younger sons to younger brothers, revolted tapsters, 28
and hostlers trade-fallen, the cankers of a calm world 29
and a long peace, ten times more dishonorable-ragged
than an old feazed ancient. And such have I, to fill up 31
the rooms of them as have bought out their services,
that you would think that I had a hundred and fifty tattered prodigals lately come from swine keeping, from 34
eating draff and husks. A mad fellow met me on the way 35
and told me I had unloaded all the gibbets and pressed 36
the dead bodies. No eye hath seen such scarecrows. I'll
not march through Coventry with them, that's flat. 38
Nay, and the villains march wide betwixt the legs as if
they had gyves on, for indeed I had the most of them 40
out of prison. There's not a shirt and a half in all my
company, and the half shirt is two napkins tacked together and thrown over the shoulders like a herald's
coat without sleeves; and the shirt, to say the truth,
stolen from my host at Saint Albans, or the red-nose 45
innkeeper of Daventry. But that's all one; they'll find 46
linen enough on every hedge. 47

Enter the Prince [and the] Lord of Westmorland.

PRINCE   How now, blown Jack? How now, quilt? 48
FALSTAFF   What, Hal? How now, mad wag? What a
devil dost thou in Warwickshire?—My good lord of

Westmorland, I cry you mercy. I thought Your Honor 51
had already been at Shrewsbury.
WESTMORLAND   Faith, Sir John, 'tis more than time that
I were there, and you too; but my powers are there 54
already. The King, I can tell you, looks for us all. We
must away all night. 56
FALSTAFF   Tut, never fear me. I am as vigilant as a cat to 57
steal cream.
PRINCE   I think, to steal cream indeed, for thy theft hath 59
already made thee butter. But tell me, Jack, whose 60
fellows are these that come after?
FALSTAFF   Mine, Hal, mine.
PRINCE   I did never see such pitiful rascals.
FALSTAFF   Tut, tut, good enough to toss; food for 64
powder, food for powder. They'll fill a pit as well as 65
better. Tush, man, mortal men, mortal men.
WESTMORLAND   Ay, but, Sir John, methinks they are
exceeding poor and bare, too beggarly. 68
FALSTAFF   Faith, for their poverty, I know not where 69
they had that, and for their bareness, I am sure they
never learned that of me.
PRINCE   No, I'll be sworn, unless you call three fingers 72
in the ribs bare. But, sirrah, make haste. Percy is 73
already in the field.   *Exit.*
FALSTAFF   What, is the King encamped?
WESTMORLAND   He is, Sir John. I fear we shall stay too
long.   [*Exit.*]
FALSTAFF   Well,
To the latter end of a fray and the beginning of a feast 79
Fits a dull fighter and a keen guest.   *Exit.* 80

❖

[4.3]

*Enter Hotspur, Worcester, Douglas, [and]
Vernon.*

HOTSPUR
We'll fight with him tonight.
WORCESTER   It may not be.
DOUGLAS
You give him then advantage.
VERNON   Not a whit. 2
HOTSPUR
Why say you so? Looks he not for supply? 3
VERNON
So do we.
HOTSPUR   His is certain; ours is doubtful.

14 press me draft, conscript   15 good i.e., wealthy.   yeomen's small freeholders'   16 contracted engaged to be married   17 banns public announcements, declared on three Sundays in succession, of an intent to marry.   warm i.e., loving their comfort   18 lief willingly   19 caliver musket.   struck wounded   20–1 toasts-and-butter weaklings   22 bought . . . services i.e., paid, bribed, to be released from military duty   23 charge company, troop.   ancients ensigns, standard-bearers. (By appointing a disproportionate number of junior officers, Falstaff has made it possible to collect for himself their more substantial pay.)   24 gentlemen of companies a kind of junior officer   25 painted cloth cheap hangings for a room. (For the story of Lazarus the beggar and Dives the rich man, see Luke 16:19–31.)   27 unjust dishonest   28 younger . . . brothers (i.e., with no possibility of inheritance).   revolted runaway   29 trade-fallen whose business has fallen away.   cankers cankerworms that destroy leaves and buds. (Used figuratively.)   31 feazed ancient frayed flag.   34 prodigals spendthrifts (See Luke 15:15–16.)   35 draff hogwash.   mad madcap   36 gibbets gallows   38 that's flat that's for sure.   40 gyves fetters   45 my host the innkeeper   45, 46 Saint Albans, Daventry (Towns north and west of London, on the road to Coventry.)   46 that's all one no matter   47 hedge (where wet linen was spread out to dry and could be easily stolen.)   48 blown swollen, inflated; also, short of wind.   quilt thickly padded.

51 cry you mercy beg your pardon.   54 powers soldiers   56 must away must march   57 fear worry about   59–60 thy . . . butter i.e., all the cream (rich things) you have stolen has been churned into butter-fat in your barrel-like belly.   64 toss toss on a pike   64–5 food for powder cannon fodder   68 poor and bare inferior and threadbare. (But Falstaff puns on the sense of "financially strapped and lean.")   69 for as for   72–3 three . . . ribs i.e., Falstaff's fat-covered ribs. (A *finger* was a measure of three-fourths of an inch.)   79–80 To . . . guest i.e., Better to be late to a battle and early to a feast. (*Keen* means "with keen appetite.")
4.3. Location: The rebel camp near Shrewsbury.
2 then i.e., if you wait. (Addressed to Worcester, not Hotspur.)   3 supply reinforcements.

WORCESTER
Good cousin, be advised, stir not tonight.

VERNON
Do not, my lord.

DOUGLAS   You do not counsel well.
You speak it out of fear and cold heart.

VERNON
Do me no slander, Douglas. By my life,
And I dare well maintain it with my life,
If well-respected honor bid me on,   10
I hold as little counsel with weak fear   11
As you, my lord, or any Scot that this day lives.
Let it be seen tomorrow in the battle
Which of us fears.

DOUGLAS   Yea, or tonight.

VERNON   Content.

HOTSPUR   Tonight, say I.

VERNON
Come, come, it may not be. I wonder much,
Being men of such great leading as you are,   19
That you foresee not what impediments
Drag back our expedition. Certain horse   21
Of my cousin Vernon's are not yet come up.
Your uncle Worcester's horse came but today,
And now their pride and mettle is asleep,   24
Their courage with hard labor tame and dull,
That not a horse is half the half of himself.

HOTSPUR
So are the horses of the enemy
In general journey-bated and brought low.   28
The better part of ours are full of rest.

WORCESTER
The number of the King exceedeth our.
For God's sake, cousin, stay till all come in.   31
                    The trumpet sounds a parley.

                    Enter Sir Walter Blunt.

BLUNT
I come with gracious offers from the King,
If you vouchsafe me hearing and respect.   33

HOTSPUR
Welcome, Sir Walter Blunt; and would to God
You were of our determination!   35
Some of us love you well; and even those some   36
Envy your great deservings and good name
Because you are not of our quality   38
But stand against us like an enemy.

BLUNT
And God defend but still I should stand so,   40
So long as out of limit and true rule   41
You stand against anointed majesty.
But to my charge. The King hath sent to know   43

The nature of your griefs and whereupon   44
You conjure from the breast of civil peace
Such bold hostility, teaching his duteous land
Audacious cruelty. If that the King   47
Have any way your good deserts forgot,
Which he confesseth to be manifold,
He bids you name your griefs, and with all speed
You shall have your desires with interest
And pardon absolute for yourself and these
Herein misled by your suggestion.   53

HOTSPUR
The King is kind; and well we know the King
Knows at what time to promise, when to pay.
My father and my uncle and myself
Did give him that same royalty he wears,
And when he was not six-and-twenty strong,
Sick in the world's regard, wretched and low,
A poor unminded outlaw sneaking home,   60
My father gave him welcome to the shore;
And when he heard him swear and vow to God
He came but to be Duke of Lancaster,
To sue his livery and beg his peace   64
With tears of innocency and terms of zeal,
My father, in kind heart and pity moved,
Swore him assistance, and performed it too.
Now when the lords and barons of the realm
Perceived Northumberland did lean to him,
The more and less came in with cap and knee,   70
Met him in boroughs, cities, villages,
Attended him on bridges, stood in lanes,   72
Laid gifts before him, proffered him their oaths,
Gave him their heirs as pages, followed him   74
Even at the heels in golden multitudes.   75
He presently, as greatness knows itself,   76
Steps me a little higher than his vow   77
Made to my father while his blood was poor   78
Upon the naked shore at Ravenspurgh,
And now, forsooth, takes on him to reform
Some certain edicts and some strait decrees   81
That lie too heavy on the commonwealth,
Cries out upon abuses, seems to weep
Over his country's wrongs; and by this face,   84
This seeming brow of justice, did he win
The hearts of all that he did angle for;
Proceeded further—cut me off the heads   87
Of all the favorites that the absent King
In deputation left behind him here
When he was personal in the Irish war.   90

---

10 **well-respected** well weighed or considered   **11 I hold . . . counsel** I have as little to do   **19 leading** leadership   **21 expedition** speedy progress.   **horse** cavalry. (As also at line 23.)   **24 pride and mettle** spirit   **28 journey-bated** tired from the journey   **31.1 *parley*** trumpet summons to a conference.   **33 respect** attention.   **35 determination** persuasion (in the fight).   **36 even those some** those same persons   **38 Because** only because.   **quality** party   **40 defend** forbid.   **still** always   **41 limit** bounds of allegiance   **43 charge** commission.

44 **griefs** grievances   **47 If that** If   **53 suggestion** instigation.   **60 unminded** disregarded   **64 To sue . . . peace** to petition to take possession of his rightful inheritance and be reconciled with King Richard II   **70 The more . . . knee** persons of all ranks came to him with cap in hand and with bended knee   **72 Attended** waited for.   **stood in lanes** stood row-deep along the roads   **74 Gave . . . pages** i.e., brought him their heirs to serve as pages and also as hostages to the fathers' loyalty   **75 golden** (1) auspicious, celebrating (2) majestically attired   **76 knows itself** perceives its own strength   **77 Steps me** i.e., steps. (*Me* is used colloquially.)   **vow** i.e., Bolingbroke's vow to seek no more than his inheritance   **78 while . . . poor** i.e., while Bolingbroke's spirits were still humbled and his dynastic claim in question   **81 strait** strict   **84 face** show, pretense   **87 cut me** i.e., cut   **90 personal** in person

BLUNT
   Tut, I came not to hear this.

HOTSPUR   Then to the point.
   In short time after, he deposed the King,
   Soon after that, deprived him of his life,
   And in the neck of that tasked the whole state;   94
   To make that worse, suffered his kinsman March—
   Who is, if every owner were well placed,   96
   Indeed his king—to be engaged in Wales,   97
   There without ransom to lie forfeited;   98
   Disgraced me in my happy victories,   99
   Sought to entrap me by intelligence;   100
   Rated mine uncle from the Council board;   101
   In rage dismissed my father from the court;
   Broke oath on oath, committed wrong on wrong,
   And in conclusion drove us to seek out
   This head of safety, and withal to pry   105
   Into his title, the which we find
   Too indirect for long continuance.

BLUNT
   Shall I return this answer to the King?

HOTSPUR
   Not so, Sir Walter. We'll withdraw awhile.
   Go to the King; and let there be impawned   110
   Some surety for a safe return again,
   And in the morning early shall mine uncle
   Bring him our purposes. And so farewell.   113

BLUNT
   I would you would accept of grace and love.

HOTSPUR
   And maybe so we shall.

BLUNT
                     Pray God you do. [*Exeunt.*]

❧

[4.4]

Enter [the] Archbishop of York, [and] Sir Michael.

ARCHBISHOP [*giving letters*]
   Hie, good Sir Michael, bear this sealèd brief   1
   With wingèd haste to the Lord Marshal,   2
   This to my cousin Scroop, and all the rest   3
   To whom they are directed. If you knew
   How much they do import, you would make haste.

SIR MICHAEL   My good lord, I guess their tenor.

ARCHBISHOP   Like enough you do.   7
   Tomorrow, good Sir Michael, is a day

   Wherein the fortune of ten thousand men
   Must bide the touch; for, sir, at Shrewsbury,   10
   As I am truly given to understand,
   The King with mighty and quick-raisèd power
   Meets with Lord Harry. And I fear, Sir Michael,
   What with the sickness of Northumberland,
   Whose power was in the first proportion,   15
   And what with Owen Glendower's absence thence,
   Who with them was a rated sinew too   17
   And comes not in, o'erruled by prophecies,
   I fear the power of Percy is too weak
   To wage an instant trial with the King.   20

SIR MICHAEL
   Why, my good lord, you need not fear;
   There is Douglas and Lord Mortimer.

ARCHBISHOP   No, Mortimer is not there.

SIR MICHAEL
   But there is Mordake, Vernon, Lord Harry Percy,
   And there is my lord of Worcester, and a head   25
   Of gallant warriors, noble gentlemen.

ARCHBISHOP
   And so there is. But yet the King hath drawn
   The special head of all the land together: 28
   The Prince of Wales, Lord John of Lancaster,
   The noble Westmorland, and warlike Blunt,
   And many more corrivals and dear men   31
   Of estimation and command in arms.   32

SIR MICHAEL
   Doubt not, my lord, they shall be well opposed.

ARCHBISHOP
   I hope no less, yet needful 'tis to fear;
   And, to prevent the worst, Sir Michael, speed.
   For if Lord Percy thrive not, ere the King
   Dismiss his power he means to visit us,   37
   For he hath heard of our confederacy,
   And 'tis but wisdom to make strong against him.
   Therefore make haste. I must go write again
   To other friends; and so farewell, Sir Michael.
                     Exeunt [separately].

❧

[5.1]

Enter the King, Prince of Wales, Lord John of Lancaster, Sir Walter Blunt, [and] Falstaff.

KING
   How bloodily the sun begins to peer
   Above yon bosky hill! The day looks pale   2
   At his distemperature.

PRINCE   The southern wind   3
   Doth play the trumpet to his purposes,   4

---

94 in . . . that next, immediately after.   **tasked** laid taxes upon   **96 if . . . placed** if every claimant were given his proper place   **97 engaged** held as hostage   **98 lie forfeited** remain prisoner, unreclaimed **99 Disgraced me** (by demanding the prisoners; see 1.3.23 ff.)   **happy** fortunate   **100 intelligence** secret information, i.e., from spies **101 Rated** scolded   **105 head of safety** armed force for our protection. **withal** also   **110 impawned** pledged   **113 purposes** proposals. **4.4. Location: York. The Archbishop's palace.**
1 brief letter, dispatch   **2 Lord Marshal** i.e., Thomas Mowbray, son of the Duke of Norfolk who is exiled in *Richard II*, and a longtime enemy of the new King   **3 Scroop** i.e., perhaps Sir Stephen Scroop of *Richard II*, 3.2.91–218, or Lord Scroop of Masham of *Henry* V, 2.2 **7 Like** Likely

10 bide the touch be put to the test (like gold)   **15 in . . . proportion** of the largest size   **17 rated sinew** main strength or support reckoned upon   **20 instant** immediate   **25 head** troop   **28 special head** notable leaders   **31 corrivals** partners in the enterprise   **32 estimation** reputation, importance   **37 he** i.e., the King **5.1. Location: The King's camp near Shrewsbury.**
2 bosky bushy   **3 his distemperature** i.e., the sun's unhealthy appearance.   **4 trumpet** trumpeter.   **his** its, the sun's

And by his hollow whistling in the leaves
Foretells a tempest and a blust'ring day.

KING

Then with the losers let it sympathize,
For nothing can seem foul to those that win.

The trumpet sounds.

Enter Worcester [and Vernon].

How now, my lord of Worcester? 'Tis not well
That you and I should meet upon such terms
As now we meet. You have deceived our trust
And made us doff our easy robes of peace   12
To crush our old limbs in ungentle steel.
This is not well, my lord, this is not well.
What say you to it? Will you again unknit
This churlish knot of all-abhorrèd war
And move in that obedient orb again   17
Where you did give a fair and natural light,
And be no more an exhaled meteor,   19
A prodigy of fear, and a portent   20
Of broachèd mischief to the unborn times?   21

WORCESTER   Hear me, my liege:
For mine own part, I could be well content
To entertain the lag end of my life   24
With quiet hours, for I protest
I have not sought the day of this dislike.   26

KING

You have not sought it? How comes it, then?

FALSTAFF   Rebellion lay in his way, and he found it.

PRINCE   Peace, chewet, peace!   29

WORCESTER

It pleased Your Majesty to turn your looks
Of favor from myself and all our house;
And yet I must remember you, my lord,   32
We were the first and dearest of your friends.
For you my staff of office did I break
In Richard's time, and posted day and night   35
To meet you on the way, and kiss your hand,
When yet you were in place and in account
Nothing so strong and fortunate as I.   38
It was myself, my brother, and his son
That brought you home and boldly did outdare   40
The dangers of the time. You swore to us,
And you did swear that oath at Doncaster,
That you did nothing purpose 'gainst the state,
Nor claim no further than your new-fall'n right, 44
The seat of Gaunt, dukedom of Lancaster.
To this we swore our aid. But in short space
It rained down fortune show'ring on your head,
And such a flood of greatness fell on you—

What with our help, what with the absent King,
What with the injuries of a wanton time,   50
The seeming sufferances that you had borne,   51
And the contrarious winds that held the King
So long in his unlucky Irish wars
That all in England did repute him dead—
And from this swarm of fair advantages
You took occasion to be quickly wooed   56
To grip the general sway into your hand;
Forgot your oath to us at Doncaster;
And being fed by us, you used us so
As that ungentle gull, the cuckoo's bird,   60
Useth the sparrow; did oppress our nest,
Grew by our feeding to so great a bulk
That even our love durst not come near your sight 63
For fear of swallowing; but with nimble wing
We were enforced, for safety sake, to fly
Out of your sight and raise this present head,   66
Whereby we stand opposèd by such means   67
As you yourself have forged against yourself
By unkind usage, dangerous countenance,   69
And violation of all faith and troth
Sworn to us in your younger enterprise.

KING

These things indeed you have articulate,   72
Proclaimed at market crosses, read in churches,   73
To face the garment of rebellion   74
With some fine color that may please the eye   75
Of fickle changelings and poor discontents,   76
Which gape and rub the elbow at the news   77
Of hurly-burly innovation.   78
And never yet did insurrection want   79
Such water-colors to impaint his cause,   80
Nor moody beggars, starving for a time   81
Of pell-mell havoc and confusion.   82

PRINCE

In both your armies there is many a soul   83
Shall pay full dearly for this encounter,
If once they join in trial. Tell your nephew
The Prince of Wales doth join with all the world
In praise of Henry Percy. By my hopes—   87
This present enterprise set off his head—   88
I do not think a braver gentleman,
More active-valiant or more valiant-young,
More daring or more bold, is now alive
To grace this latter age with noble deeds.

---

12 **easy** comfortable   17 **orb** orbit, sphere of action. (The King's subjects, like planets and stars in the Ptolemaic cosmos, were supposed
to revolve around the kingly center, comparable to the earth, in fixed
courses.)   19 **exhaled meteor** (Meteors were believed to be vapors
drawn up or *exhaled* by the sun and visible as streaks of light; they
were regarded as ill omens.)   20 **prodigy of fear** fearful omen
21 **broachèd** set flowing, already begun   24 **entertain** occupy
26 **the . . . dislike** this time of discord.   29 **chewet** chough, jackdaw.
(Here, a chatterer.)   32 **remember** remind   35 **posted** rode swiftly
38 **Nothing** not at all   40 **home** back to England from exile   44 **new-
fall'n** recently inherited (by the death of John of Gaunt)

50 **injuries** abuses.   **wanton** ill-managed   51 **sufferances** suffering,
distress   56 **occasion** the opportunity   60 **ungentle . . . bird** rude
nestling, the cuckoo's young offspring. (The cuckoo lays its eggs in
other birds' nests.)   63 **our love** we who loved you   66 **head** armed
force   67 **opposèd . . . means** goaded into opposition by such factors
69 **dangerous countenance** threatening behavior   72 **articulate** set
forth, specified   73 **market crosses** (Christian crosses were often
erected in the centers of marketplaces—a good place for public
announcements.)   74 **face** trim, adorn   75 **color** (1) hue (2) specious
appearance   76 **changelings** turncoats   77 **rub the elbow** i.e., hug
themselves with delight   78 **innovation** rebellion.   79 **want** lack
80 **water-colors** i.e., thin excuses. (See *color*, line 75.)   **his** its
81 **moody** sullen, angry   82 **havoc** plundering   83 **both your** i.e., your
and our   87 **hopes** i.e., hopes of salvation   88 **This . . . head** i.e., if
this present rebellion is taken from his account, not held against him

For my part, I may speak it to my shame,
I have a truant been to chivalry;
And so I hear he doth account me too.
Yet this before my father's majesty:
I am content that he shall take the odds
Of his great name and estimation,   98
And will, to save the blood on either side,
Try fortune with him in a single fight.

KING
And, Prince of Wales, so dare we venture thee,   101
Albeit considerations infinite   102
Do make against it.—No, good Worcester, no.
We love our people well; even those we love
That are misled upon your cousin's part;   105
And, will they take the offer of our grace,   106
Both he and they and you, yea, every man
Shall be my friend again, and I'll be his.
So tell your cousin, and bring me word
What he will do. But if he will not yield,
Rebuke and dread correction wait on us,   111
And they shall do their office. So, begone.
We will not now be troubled with reply.
We offer fair; take it advisedly.
                          Exit Worcester [with Vernon].

PRINCE
It will not be accepted, on my life.
The Douglas and the Hotspur both together
Are confident against the world in arms.

KING
Hence, therefore, every leader to his charge;
For on their answer will we set on them,
And God befriend us as our cause is just!   120
                    Exeunt. Manent Prince, Falstaff.

FALSTAFF   Hal, if thou see me down in the battle and
bestride me, so; 'tis a point of friendship.   122

PRINCE   Nothing but a colossus can do thee that friendship. Say thy prayers, and farewell.

FALSTAFF   I would 'twere bedtime, Hal, and all well.

PRINCE   Why, thou owest God a death.   [*Exit.*] 126

FALSTAFF   'Tis not due yet; I would be loath to pay him
before his day. What need I be so forward with him
that calls not on me? Well, 'tis no matter; honor pricks   129
me on. Yea, but how if honor prick me off when I   130
come on? How then? Can honor set to a leg? No. Or   131
an arm? No. Or take away the grief of a wound? No.   132
Honor hath no skill in surgery, then? No. What is
honor? A word. What is in that word "honor"? What is
that "honor"? Air. A trim reckoning! Who hath it? He
that died o' Wednesday. Doth he feel it? No. Doth he
hear it? No. 'Tis insensible, then? Yea, to the dead. But
will it not live with the living? No. Why? Detraction   138

will not suffer it. Therefore I'll none of it. Honor is a   139
mere scutcheon. And so ends my catechism.   140
                                              Exit.

❖

[5.2]

Enter Worcester [and] Sir Richard Vernon.

WORCESTER
Oh, no, my nephew must not know, Sir Richard,
The liberal and kind offer of the King.

VERNON
'Twere best he did.

WORCESTER   Then are we all undone.
It is not possible, it cannot be,
The King should keep his word in loving us;
He will suspect us still and find a time
To punish this offense in other faults.   7
Suspicion all our lives shall be stuck full of eyes;   8
For treason is but trusted like the fox,
Who, never so tame, so cherished, and locked up,   10
Will have a wild trick of his ancestors.   11
Look how we can, or sad or merrily,   12
Interpretation will misquote our looks,
And we shall feed like oxen at a stall,
The better cherished still the nearer death.
My nephew's trespass may be well forgot;
It hath the excuse of youth and heat of blood,
And an adopted name of privilege—   18
A harebrained Hotspur, governed by a spleen.   19
All his offenses live upon my head
And on his father's. We did train him on,   21
And, his corruption being ta'en from us,   22
We as the spring of all shall pay for all.   23
Therefore, good cousin, let not Harry know
In any case the offer of the King.

Enter Hotspur [and Douglas, with soldiers].

VERNON
Deliver what you will; I'll say 'tis so.   26
Here comes your cousin.

HOTSPUR   My uncle is returned.
Deliver up my lord of Westmorland.   28
Uncle, what news?

WORCESTER
The King will bid you battle presently.

DOUGLAS
Defy him by the lord of Westmorland.   31

98 estimation reputation   **101 venture** hazard, risk   **102 Albeit**
although it be that. (The subjunctive has the force of "were it not
that.")   **105 cousin's** i.e., nephew's   **106 will they** if they will.
grace pardon   **111 wait on us** are awaiting my royal command
120.1 *Manent* They remain onstage   **122 bestride** stand over in order
to defend.   **so** well and good   **126 thou . . . death** (Proverbial, with a
pun on *debt*.)   **129 pricks** spurs   **130 prick me off** mark me off (as
one dead)   **131 set to** rejoin or set   **132 grief** pain   **138 Detraction**
Slander

139 suffer allow   **140 scutcheon** heraldic emblem carried in funerals,
displayed on coaches, etc.; it was the lowest form of symbol, having
no pennon or other insignia.   **catechism** the principles of faith given
in the form of question and answer.
5.2. Location: Near the rebel camp.
7 To . . . faults to find other faults in us to punish (as a way of getting
back at us for defying him militarily).   **8 stuck . . . eyes** i.e., provided
with many eyes, suspiciously inquisitive   **10 never so** be he never so
11 trick trait   **12 or sad** either sad   **18 an adopted . . . privilege** i.e., a
nickname, "Hotspur," to justify his rashness   **19 spleen** intemperate
impulse.   **21 train** incite, draw   **22 his . . . us** i.e., since his guilt originated in us   **23 spring** source   **26 Deliver** Report   **28 Deliver up**
Release (as hostage; see 4.3.110–11)   **31 Defy him by** Send back your
defiance with

HOTSPUR
Lord Douglas, go you and tell him so.

DOUGLAS
Marry, and shall, and very willingly.   *Exit Douglas.*

WORCESTER
There is no seeming mercy in the King.

HOTSPUR
Did you beg any? God forbid!

WORCESTER
I told him gently of our grievances,
Of his oathbreaking, which he mended thus,
By now forswearing that he is forsworn.
He calls us rebels, traitors, and will scourge
With haughty arms this hateful name in us.

Enter Douglas.

DOUGLAS
Arm, gentlemen, to arms! For I have thrown
A brave defiance in King Henry's teeth,   42
And Westmorland, that was engaged, did bear it;   43
Which cannot choose but bring him quickly on.

WORCESTER
The Prince of Wales stepped forth before the King,
And, nephew, challenged you to single fight.

HOTSPUR
Oh, would the quarrel lay upon our heads,
And that no man might draw short breath today
But I and Harry Monmouth! Tell me, tell me,   49
How showed his tasking? Seemed it in contempt?   50

VERNON
No, by my soul. I never in my life
Did hear a challenge urged more modestly,   52
Unless a brother should a brother dare
To gentle exercise and proof of arms.   54
He gave you all the duties of a man,   55
Trimmed up your praises with a princely tongue,   56
Spoke your deservings like a chronicle,
Making you ever better than his praise
By still dispraising praise valued with you;   59
And, which became him like a prince indeed,
He made a blushing cital of himself,   61
And chid his truant youth with such a grace
As if he mastered there a double spirit
Of teaching and of learning instantly.   64
There did he pause. But let me tell the world,
If he outlive the envy of this day,   66
England did never owe so sweet a hope,   67
So much misconstrued in his wantonness.   68

HOTSPUR
Cousin, I think thou art enamorèd
On his follies. Never did I hear
Of any prince so wild a liberty.   71

But be he as he will, yet once ere night
I will embrace him with a soldier's arm,
That he shall shrink under my courtesy.   74
Arm, arm with speed! And, fellows, soldiers, friends,
Better consider what you have to do
Than I, that have not well the gift of tongue,
Can lift your blood up with persuasion.

Enter a Messenger.

FIRST MESSENGER   My lord, here are letters for you.

HOTSPUR   I cannot read them now.
Oh, gentlemen, the time of life is short!
To spend that shortness basely were too long   82
If life did ride upon a dial's point,   83
Still ending at the arrival of an hour.   84
An if we live, we live to tread on kings;
If die, brave death, when princes die with us!   86
Now, for our consciences, the arms are fair   87
When the intent of bearing them is just.

Enter another [Messenger].

SECOND MESSENGER
My lord, prepare. The King comes on apace.

HOTSPUR
I thank him that he cuts me from my tale,
For I profess not talking. Only this—   91
Let each man do his best. And here draw I
A sword, whose temper I intend to stain
With the best blood that I can meet withal
In the adventure of this perilous day.
Now, *Esperance!* Percy! And set on.   96
Sound all the lofty instruments of war,
And by that music let us all embrace;
For, heaven to earth, some of us never shall   99
A second time do such a courtesy.
    Here they embrace. The trumpets sound. [*Exeunt.*]

❖

[5.3]

*The King enters with his power [and passes over
the stage]. Alarum to the battle. Then enter
Douglas, and Sir Walter Blunt [dressed like King
Henry].*

BLUNT
What is thy name, that in the battle thus
Thou crossest me? What honor dost thou seek
Upon my head?

DOUGLAS   Know then my name is Douglas,
And I do haunt thee in the battle thus
Because some tell me that thou art a king.

---

42 **brave** proud   43 **engaged** held as hostage   49 **Monmouth** (A name for the Prince, taken from the Welsh town where he was born.) 50 **showed his tasking** appeared his giving the challenge.   52 **urged** put forward   54 **gentle** befitting noble birth.   **proof of arms** test of martial skill.   55 **duties** due merits   56 **Trimmed . . . praises** adorned his praise of you   59 **By . . . you** by consistently disparaging praise itself as not sufficient to measure your true worth   61 **cital** account, recital   64 **instantly** simultaneously.   66 **envy** hostility   67 **owe** own   68 **wantonness** playful sportiveness.   71 **liberty** licentiousness.

74 **shrink under my courtesy** (1) be daunted by my greater courtesy (2) fall back before my attack.   82–4 **To . . . hour** Life is too short to spend it basely, even if life were to last only the time needed for the dial (or sundial) to advance a single hour, ending when that hour is up.   86 **brave** glorious   87 **for** as for.   **fair** just   91 **I . . . talking** I have no calling as an orator.   96 **Esperance** (The motto of the Percy family.)   99 **heaven to earth** i.e., I'll wager heaven against earth 5.3. **Location: Shrewsbury field. The scene is virtually continuous.** 0.1 *power* army.   0.2 *Alarum* Trumpet signal to advance

BLUNT   They tell thee true.

DOUGLAS
The lord of Stafford dear today hath bought   7
Thy likeness, for instead of thee, King Harry,   8
This sword hath ended him. So shall it thee,
Unless thou yield thee as my prisoner.

BLUNT
I was not born a yielder, thou proud Scot,
And thou shalt find a king that will revenge
Lord Stafford's death.   *They fight. Douglas kills Blunt.*

            Then enter Hotspur.

HOTSPUR
Oh, Douglas, hadst thou fought at Holmedon thus,
I never had triumphed upon a Scot.

DOUGLAS
All's done, all's won; here breathless lies the King.   16

HOTSPUR   Where?

DOUGLAS   Here.

HOTSPUR
This, Douglas? No. I know this face full well.
A gallant knight he was; his name was Blunt,
Semblably furnished like the King himself.   21

DOUGLAS
A fool go with thy soul, whither it goes!   22
A borrowed title hast thou bought too dear.
Why didst thou tell me that thou wert a king?

HOTSPUR
The King hath many marching in his coats.   25

DOUGLAS
Now, by my sword, I will kill all his coats!
I'll murder all his wardrobe, piece by piece,
Until I meet the King.

HOTSPUR   Up, and away!
Our soldiers stand full fairly for the day.   *[Exeunt.]*   29

            Alarum. Enter Falstaff, solus.

FALSTAFF   Though I could scape shot-free at London, I   30
fear the shot here; here's no scoring but upon the pate.   31
Soft, who are you? Sir Walter Blunt. There's honor for
you. Here's no vanity! I am as hot as molten lead, and   33
as heavy too. God keep lead out of me! I need no more
weight than mine own bowels. I have led my ragamuffins where they are peppered. There's not three of
my hundred and fifty left alive, and they are for the
town's end, to beg during life. But who comes here?   38

            Enter the Prince.

PRINCE
What, stands thou idle here? Lend me thy sword.

Many a nobleman lies stark and stiff
Under the hoofs of vaunting enemies,
Whose deaths are yet unrevenged. I prithee,
Lend me thy sword.

FALSTAFF   Oh, Hal, I prithee, give me leave to breathe
awhile. Turk Gregory never did such deeds in arms as   45
I have done this day. I have paid Percy, I have made   46
him sure.   47

PRINCE
He is, indeed, and living to kill thee.
I prithee, lend me thy sword.

FALSTAFF   Nay, before God, Hal, if Percy be alive, thou
gets not my sword; but take my pistol, if thou wilt.

PRINCE
Give it me. What, is it in the case?

FALSTAFF   Ay, Hal, 'tis hot, 'tis hot. There's that will   53
sack a city.
            *The Prince draws it out and finds it to be a bottle
                                                    of sack.*

PRINCE
What, is it a time to jest and dally now?
                        He throws the bottle at him. Exit.

FALSTAFF   Well, if Percy be alive, I'll pierce him. If he do   56
come in my way, so; if he do not, if I come in his   57
willingly, let him make a carbonado of me. I like not in   58
such grinning honor as Sir Walter hath. Give me life,
which if I can save, so; if not, honor comes unlooked
for, and there's an end.   *[Exit.]*   61

                        ❖

[5.4]

            *Alarum. Excursions. Enter the King, the Prince,
            Lord John of Lancaster, [and the] Earl of
            Westmorland.*

KING   I prithee,
Harry, withdraw thyself; thou bleedest too much.
Lord John of Lancaster, go you with him.

LANCASTER
Not I, my lord, unless I did bleed too.

PRINCE
I beseech Your Majesty, make up,   5
Lest your retirement do amaze your friends.   6

KING
I will do so. My lord of Westmorland,
Lead him to his tent.

---

7 dear dearly   **7–8 bought Thy likeness** paid for his resemblance to you   **16 breathless** i.e., dead   **21 Semblably furnished** similarly accoutered   **22 A . . . soul** i.e., May the stigma of "fool" accompany your soul (for having dressed as a decoy of King Henry)   **25 coats** vests worn over armor embroidered with a coat of arms.   **29 stand . . . day** i.e., seem in an auspicious position, likely to win the victory.   **30 shot-free** without paying the tavern bill   **31 scoring** (1) cutting (2) marking up of charges, by notches on a stick or on the inn door   **33 Here's no vanity!** i.e. (ironically), If this doesn't show what I was saying about honor, then nothing does!   **38 town's end** i.e., city gate, frequented by beggars

45 Turk Gregory (*Turk* is an abusive term signifying a tyrant, and Gregory refers probably to Pope Gregory XIII, who was assumed to have encouraged the Massacre of Saint Bartholomew [1572], in which many French Protestants were slain, and to have encouraged plots against Elizabeth.)   **46–7 made him sure** made sure of him. (But Prince Hal takes *sure* in a different sense, meaning "safe.")   **53 hot** (Falstaff implies he has been firing at the enemy.)   **56 Percy . . . pierce** (Elizabethan pronunciation rendered the pun more obvious than it is now.)   **57 so** well and good   **58 carbonado** meat scored across for broiling   **61 there's an end** (1) that concludes the subject of my catechism (see 5.1.129–40) (2) thus life ends.   **5.4 Location: Scene continues at Shrewsbury field.**   **0.1 Excursions** Sorties. (The fallen body of Blunt may be removed at some point or may be onstage still at 5.4.77 when Hal kills Hotspur.)   **5 make up** go forward   **6 retirement** retreat.   **amaze** alarm

WESTMORLAND
  Come, my lord, I'll lead you to your tent.
PRINCE
  Lead me, my lord? I do not need your help.
  And God forbid a shallow scratch should drive
  The Prince of Wales from such a field as this,
  Where stained nobility lies trodden on
  And rebels' arms triumph in massacres!
LANCASTER
  We breathe too long. Come, cousin Westmorland,   15
  Our duty this way lies. For God's sake, come.
                    [*Exeunt Prince John and Westmorland.*]
PRINCE
  By God, thou hast deceived me, Lancaster!
  I did not think thee lord of such a spirit.
  Before, I loved thee as a brother, John,
  But now I do respect thee as my soul.
KING
  I saw him hold Lord Percy at the point   21
  With lustier maintenance than I did look for   22
  Of such an ungrown warrior.
PRINCE
  Oh, this boy lends mettle to us all!   *Exit.*

            [*Enter Douglas.*]

DOUGLAS
  Another king? They grow like Hydra's heads.   25
  I am the Douglas, fatal to all those
  That wear those colors on them. What art thou   27
  That counterfeit'st the person of a king?
KING
  The King himself, who, Douglas, grieves at heart
  So many of his shadows thou hast met   30
  And not the very King. I have two boys
  Seek Percy and thyself about the field;   32
  But, seeing thou fall'st on me so luckily,
  I will assay thee; and defend thyself.   34
DOUGLAS
  I fear thou art another counterfeit;
  And yet, in faith, thou bearest thee like a king.
  But mine I am sure thou art, whoe'er thou be,
  And thus I win thee.
              They fight; the King being in danger,
                    enter Prince of Wales.
PRINCE
  Hold up thy head, vile Scot, or thou art like   39
  Never to hold it up again! The spirits
  Of valiant Shirley, Stafford, Blunt, are in my arms.
  It is the Prince of Wales that threatens thee,
  Who never promiseth but he means to pay.   43
                    They fight. Douglas flieth.
  Cheerly, my lord. How fares Your Grace?

  Sir Nicholas Gawsey hath for succor sent,
  And so hath Clifton. I'll to Clifton straight.
KING   Stay and breathe awhile.
  Thou hast redeemed thy lost opinion,   48
  And showed thou mak'st some tender of my life   49
  In this fair rescue thou hast brought to me.
PRINCE
  Oh, God, they did me too much injury
  That ever said I hearkened for your death.   52
  If it were so, I might have let alone
  The insulting hand of Douglas over you,   54
  Which would have been as speedy in your end
  As all the poisonous potions in the world,
  And saved the treacherous labor of your son.
KING
  Make up to Clifton; I'll to Sir Nicholas Gawsey.   58
                          Exit King.

        Enter Hotspur.

HOTSPUR
  If I mistake not, thou art Harry Monmouth.
PRINCE
  Thou speak'st as if I would deny my name.
HOTSPUR
  My name is Harry Percy.
PRINCE   Why then, I see
  A very valiant rebel of the name.
  I am the Prince of Wales; and think not, Percy,
  To share with me in glory any more.
  Two stars keep not their motion in one sphere,
  Nor can one England brook a double reign   66
  Of Harry Percy and the Prince of Wales.
HOTSPUR
  Nor shall it, Harry, for the hour is come
  To end the one of us; and would to God
  Thy name in arms were now as great as mine!
PRINCE
  I'll make it greater ere I part from thee,
  And all the budding honors on thy crest
  I'll crop to make a garland for my head.   73
HOTSPUR
  I can no longer brook thy vanities.   *They fight.*   74

        Enter Falstaff.

FALSTAFF   Well said, Hal! To it, Hal! Nay, you shall find 75
  no boy's play here, I can tell you.   76

        Enter Douglas. He fighteth with Falstaff, who falls
        down as if he were dead.   [*Exit Douglas.*]
        The Prince killeth Percy.

HOTSPUR
  Oh, Harry, thou hast robbed me of my youth!
  I better brook the loss of brittle life
  Than those proud titles thou hast won of me;

---

15 breathe rest, pause for breath (as also at line 47)   **21 at the point**
at sword's point   **22 lustier maintenance** more vigorous bearing
25 Hydra's heads (The heads of the Lernaean Hydra grew again as
fast as they were cut off.)   **27 colors** i.e., the colors of the King's
insignia   **30 shadows** having form without substance   **32 Seek** who
seek   **34 assay thee** put you to the test   **39 like** likely   **43 pay**
(1) settle a debt (2) kill.

48 opinion reputation   **49 thou . . . of** you have some care for
52 hearkened listened (as for welcome news)   **54 insulting** exulting
58 Make up Advance   **66 brook** endure   **73 crop** pluck   **74 vanities**
empty boasts.   **75 Well said** Well done   **76.3 killeth** mortally
wounds

They wound my thoughts worse than thy sword my
  flesh.
But thoughts, the slaves of life, and life, time's fool,   81
And time, that takes survey of all the world,
Must have a stop. Oh, I could prophesy,
But that the earthy and cold hand of death
Lies on my tongue. No, Percy, thou art dust,
And food for—   [*He dies.*]
PRINCE
  For worms, brave Percy. Fare thee well, great heart.
Ill-weaved ambition, how much art thou shrunk!
When that this body did contain a spirit,
A kingdom for it was too small a bound;
But now two paces of the vilest earth
Is room enough. This earth that bears thee dead
Bears not alive so stout a gentleman.   93
If thou wert sensible of courtesy,   94
I should not make so dear a show of zeal;   95
But let my favors hide thy mangled face,   96
And, even in thy behalf, I'll thank myself
For doing these fair rites of tenderness.
                    [*He covers Hotspur's face with a scarf
                                     or other favor.*]
Adieu, and take thy praise with thee to heaven!
Thy ignominy sleep with thee in the grave,
But not remembered in thy epitaph!
                    He spieth Falstaff on the ground.
What, old acquaintance, could not all this flesh
Keep in a little life? Poor Jack, farewell!
I could have better spared a better man.
Oh, I should have a heavy miss of thee   105
If I were much in love with vanity.   106
Death hath not struck so fat a deer today,
Though many dearer, in this bloody fray.
Emboweled will I see thee by and by.   109
Till then in blood by noble Percy lie.   *Exit.*
                              Falstaff riseth up.
FALSTAFF   Emboweled? If thou embowel me today, I'll
give you leave to powder me and eat me too tomor-   112
row. 'Sblood, 'twas time to counterfeit, or that hot ter- 113
magant Scot had paid me, scot and lot too. Counterfeit?   114
I lie, I am no counterfeit. To die is to be a counterfeit,
for he is but the counterfeit of a man who hath not the
life of a man; but to counterfeit dying, when a man
thereby liveth, is to be no counterfeit but the true and
perfect image of life indeed. The better part of valor is 119
discretion, in the which better part I have saved my
life. Zounds, I am afraid of this gunpowder Percy,
though he be dead. How if he should counterfeit too
and rise? By my faith, I am afraid he would prove the

better counterfeit. Therefore I'll make him sure; yea,
and I'll swear I killed him. Why may not he rise as well
as I? Nothing confutes me but eyes, and nobody sees   126
me. Therefore, sirrah [*stabbing him*], with a new
wound in your thigh, come you along with me.
                    He takes up Hotspur on his back.

        Enter Prince [*and*] *John of Lancaster.*
PRINCE
  Come, brother John; full bravely hast thou fleshed   129
Thy maiden sword.
LANCASTER   But soft, whom have we here?
Did you not tell me this fat man was dead?
PRINCE   I did; I saw him dead,
Breathless and bleeding on the ground.—Art thou
  alive?
Or is it fantasy that plays upon our eyesight?
I prithee, speak. We will not trust our eyes
Without our ears. Thou art not what thou seem'st.
FALSTAFF   No, that's certain, I am not a double man; but   137
if I be not Jack Falstaff, then am I a Jack. There is Percy 138
[*throwing the body down*]. If your father will do me
any honor, so; if not, let him kill the next Percy himself. I look to be either earl or duke, I can assure you.
PRINCE
  Why, Percy I killed myself and saw thee dead.
FALSTAFF   Didst thou? Lord, Lord, how this world is
given to lying! I grant you I was down and out of
breath, and so was he; but we rose both at an instant   145
and fought a long hour by Shrewsbury clock. If I may
be believed, so; if not, let them that should reward
valor bear the sin upon their own heads. I'll take it   148
upon my death I gave him this wound in the thigh.   149
If the man were alive and would deny it, zounds, I
would make him eat a piece of my sword.
LANCASTER
  This is the strangest tale that ever I heard.
PRINCE
  This is the strangest fellow, brother John.—
Come, bring your luggage nobly on your back.
For my part, if a lie may do thee grace,   155
I'll gild it with the happiest terms I have.   156
                    A retreat is sounded.
The trumpet sounds retreat; the day is our.
Come, brother, let us to the highest of the field,   158
To see what friends are living, who are dead.
                    Exeunt [*Prince of Wales and Lancaster*].
FALSTAFF   I'll follow, as they say, for reward. He that re-
wards me, God reward him! If I do grow great, I'll
grow less; for I'll purge, and leave sack, and live   162
cleanly as a nobleman should do.
                    Exit [*bearing off the body*].

---

81 **thoughts . . . fool** i.e., our mental consciousness, which is dependent on physical existence, and our life itself, which is subject to time
93 **stout** valiant   94 **sensible of courtesy** able to hear my praise
95 **dear** handsome, heartfelt.   **zeal** admiration   96 **favors** plume,
scarf, glove, or similar article   105 **heavy** (1) serious (2) corpulent
106 **vanity** frivolity.   109 **Emboweled** Disemboweled, i.e., for
embalming and burial   112 **powder** salt   113–14 **termagant** violent
and blustering, like the heathen god of the Saracens in medieval and
Renaissance lore   114 **paid** i.e., killed.   **scot and lot** i.e., in full.
(Originally the phrase was the term for a parish tax.)   119 **part** con-
stituent part, quality, role

126 **Nothing . . . eyes** i.e., Nothing can contradict me but an eyewitness   129 **fleshed** initiated (in battle)   137 **double man** (1) specter
(2) two men   138 **Jack** knave.   145 **at an instant** simultaneously
148–9 **take . . . death** i.e., swear with my eternal soul at risk   155 **a lie**
i.e., this lie of yours.   **grace** credit   156 **happiest** most felicitous
158 **highest** highest vantage point   162 **purge** (1) reduce in weight,
using laxatives (2) repent

[5.5]

*The trumpets sound. Enter the King, Prince of
Wales, Lord John of Lancaster, Earl of
Westmorland, with Worcester and Vernon
prisoners.*

KING
Thus ever did rebellion find rebuke.
Ill-spirited Worcester! Did not we send grace,
Pardon, and terms of love to all of you?
And wouldst thou turn our offers contrary?
Misuse the tenor of thy kinsman's trust?   5
Three knights upon our party slain today,
A noble earl, and many a creature else
Had been alive this hour,
If like a Christian thou hadst truly borne
Betwixt our armies true intelligence.   10

WORCESTER
What I have done my safety urged me to;
And I embrace this fortune patiently,
Since not to be avoided it falls on me.

KING
Bear Worcester to the death, and Vernon too.
Other offenders we will pause upon.
           [*Exeunt Worcester and Vernon, guarded.*]
How goes the field?

PRINCE
The noble Scot, Lord Douglas, when he saw
The fortune of the day quite turned from him,
The noble Percy slain, and all his men

Upon the foot of fear, fled with the rest;   20
And falling from a hill, he was so bruised
That the pursuers took him. At my tent
The Douglas is; and I beseech Your Grace
I may dispose of him.

KING   With all my heart.

PRINCE
Then, brother John of Lancaster,
To you this honorable bounty shall belong.   26
Go to the Douglas, and deliver him
Up to his pleasure, ransomless and free.
His valors shown upon our crests today   29
Have taught us how to cherish such high deeds
Even in the bosom of our adversaries.

LANCASTER
I thank Your Grace for this high courtesy,
Which I shall give away immediately.   33

KING
Then this remains, that we divide our power.
You, son John, and my cousin Westmorland
Towards York shall bend you with your dearest speed   36
To meet Northumberland and the prelate Scroop,
Who, as we hear, are busily in arms.
Myself and you, son Harry, will towards Wales,
To fight with Glendower and the Earl of March.
Rebellion in this land shall lose his sway,   41
Meeting the check of such another day;   42
And since this business so fair is done,   43
Let us not leave till all our own be won.   *Exeunt.*   44

5.5 Location: The battlefield.
5 Misuse . . . trust? i.e., Would you abuse Hotspur's confidence in
you (by concealing the generosity of my offer, in your role as emissary)?   **10 intelligence** information, report.

20 Upon . . . fear fleeing in panic   **26 this honorable bounty** the
honor of this bounteous act   **29 crests** i.e., helmets   **33 give away**
pass along, confer on Douglas   **36 bend you** direct your course.
dearest most urgent   **41 his** its   **42 Meeting . . . day** i.e., when the
rebellion is entirely repulsed at one more battlefield   **43 fair** successfully   **44 leave** leave off

The Life of King Henry the Fifth

Henry V (1599) is Shakespeare's culminating statement in the genre of the English history play. Unlike the late and atypical *Henry VIII* (1613), which is separated from the rest of Shakespeare's history plays by some fourteen years, *Henry V* sums up the historical themes with which Shakespeare had been fascinated for an entire decade. The play, first published in a memorially reconstructed and abridged quarto in 1600, must have been written not long after *2 Henry IV*, perhaps as an opening production for the Chamberlain's Men's new Bankside theater, the Globe, in 1599. To be sure, the play does not entirely fulfill the promise made in *2 Henry IV* to "continue the story, with Sir John in it, and make you merry with fair Katharine of France." Falstaff is missing. As before, Shakespeare apparently saw a grand design to his four-play sequence (which had started with *Richard II*) but improvised when he came to the writing of each part. Despite these minor adjustments in the overall plan, however, *Henry V* is clearly intended to bring to fulfillment the education of a politician-prince and to illustrate the arts of political kingship that Prince Hal had derived from his experiences in the earlier plays.

In a sense, too, *Henry V* sums up the achievement of the English history play, not only for Shakespeare, but also for other popular playwrights. The patriotic history play, born in the excitement of the Armada era immediately after 1588, had nearly run its course by 1599 and was soon to be supplanted by other dramatic genres, such as satire and revenge tragedy. Dark and complex political realities were already changing the buoyant mood in which the history play had been born: the aging Queen Elizabeth was near death and without a Protestant heir, while fear of another invasion threatened. In *Henry V*, we sense the approaching end of an era, for the play both celebrates the achievements of the English monarchy and examines its limits.

Henry V has become a controversial play, chiefly because our recent experiences with war have led us to be wary of political leaders who, in the name of patriotism, lay claim to and invade another country. George Bernard Shaw is prominent among those who have deplored Henry as a priggish and complacent warmonger and imperialist. Many historically minded critics, on the other hand, warn of the dangers of reading anachronistically from a modern perspective, and they argue that Henry is an admirable model of conduct according to Renaissance notions of statecraft and military leadership. What is Shakespeare's attitude toward his war hero? Does he sympathize with Henry's condescension toward the French and his order to every soldier to kill his French prisoners? Or is Shakespeare's admiration qualified by ironic reservations? As is usual in Shakespeare's work, the perspective is complex and balanced. The play pulls us in two directions. Although the Chorus, which interprets the play for us, approves of Henry's military posture, the grandiose rhetoric of war is consistently undercut by matter-of-fact revelations of people's self-interested motives. This contrast between rhetorical illusion and political reality extends from the justification of Henry's French campaign to his state marriage with Katharine of France. On the ethical issue of killing the French prisoners, for example, the play offers us contradictory and seemingly irreconcilable impressions. At the end of 4.6, Henry orders that "every soldier" is to "kill his prisoners," evidently because the English are under attack and cannot spare men to guard those who have been captured. In 4.7 (lines 1–10 and 54–5), however, we are told by Gower that the King gave the order in retaliation for the massacre by the cowardly French of the boys guarding the English luggage. Similarly, on the eve of the battle of Agincourt, we are left to draw our own conclusions about King Henry's conversation with his soldiers (4.1. 98–227). Is he evading the question of whether his cause is just by turning to a really very different matter of responsibility for someone else's sins, or is he simply testing his men with hard questions to prepare them for battle? Ironic puzzles such as these probably never amount to open disillusionment in this play, although some modern critics and directors would argue otherwise; the ironies are perhaps, instead, the acknowledgment of a special kind of morality pertaining to kingship.

Skill in rhetoric is a key to Henry's success—in defying the French Dauphin, in preparing troops for battle, or in wooing the French princess for his queen. As the Archbishop of Canterbury notes approvingly, King Henry's versatility as a rhetorician applies to all the vital disciplines of kingship: Henry can "reason in divinity," "debate of commonwealth affairs," "discourse of war," handle "any cause of policy," and in all such matters speak in "sweet and honeyed sentences" (1.1.39–51). Through the arts of language, Henry displays piety, learning, administrative sagacity, political cunning, and military intrepidity. Like the contemporary play *Julius Caesar* (1599), *Henry V* is concerned with techniques of persuasion. (The earlier *Richard III* is also a highly rhetorical play, though chiefly through the negative example of tyrannical behavior.) Yet, however much we may be swayed emotionally by the rhetoric, we realize that the public figure of Henry V is a mask behind which we can perceive little. Only rarely do we glimpse the affable young companion of the *Henry IV* plays. King Henry has accepted the responsibility of playing a political role. It denies him a private and separate identity, even—or especially—in choosing a wife. And it complicates our task of assessing the sincerity of his utterances. Is he genuinely pious, or has he merely learned the usefulness of pious utterance in swaying people's hearts? What especially are his motives for going to war against France?

Shakespeare could have begun this play with the stirring scene (1.2) in which Henry, urged on by his advisers, issues a defiant challenge to the French ambassadors. Instead, Shakespeare treats us to a prior glimpse beneath the patriotic surface. It seems that the Archbishop of Canterbury, threatened with a bill in Parliament designed to take away the better half of the Church's possessions, has resolved to parry with a counterproposal, whereby the Church will give Henry a very substantial sum for his French campaign, provided the offensive tax bill can be conveniently forgotten. The Archbishop has already been negotiating with Henry and surmises that the plan will work. This revelation is not shocking to us; it merely reveals the political process at work. The faint undercurrent of anticlericalism suggests that Henry is to be admired for putting pressure on his clergy with such success; they are rich and can afford to support the war. In any case, the dramatic effect is to show how men's practical motives affect their rhetoric. When, in the subsequent scene, the Archbishop delivers a public lecture on the English claim to France, we know that this learned prelate has a prior and self-interested commitment to the war. His intricate dynastic argument, which he proclaims

to be "as clear as is the summer's sun" (1.2.86), gives to the war a much-needed public justification. Henry's questions indicate not only his genuine concern about the legitimacy of his claim but also his political need for the Church's endorsement of his cause; he has already claimed certain French dukedoms and must have the Church's official approval of those claims before he can proceed. He similarly needs the backing of his nobles, who also have their own reasons for approving the campaign. Henry skillfully orchestrates the scene to produce the desired effect of unanimous and patriotic consent.

Although never directly stated, Henry's own motives for going to war must also combine sincere zeal with calculated self-interest. As king, he longs to recover the French territory that England governed in the great days of Poitiers and Crécy. As a man, he bristles at the contemptuous challenge of the Dauphin; Henry must still strive to overcome his reputation as a wastrel and must prove himself worthy of honorable comparison with his great ancestors. Politically (and this motive remains most hidden), Henry has absorbed his father's sage advice to "busy giddy minds / With foreign quarrels" (2 *Henry IV,* 4.5.213–14), to blunt political opposition at home by uniting English resentment against a foreign scapegoat.

The exigencies of war do indeed provide Henry with an opportunity for proceeding against his political enemies. He arrests the Earl of Cambridge, Lord Scroop, and Sir Thomas Grey at Southampton on charges of conspiring with France. The scene (2.2) is, for Shakespeare, uncharacteristically one-sided. We are never even told that Cambridge is the chief pretender to the English throne, son of the Duke of York, married to Anne Mortimer, and founder of the Yorkist claim in the York-Lancastrian wars—the sort of rival whom Shakespeare elsewhere portrays with understanding. Instead, the rhetoric of the Chorus to Act 2 blatantly warns us to expect "hell and treason" (line 29). These three conspirators, like Judases, says the Chorus, have bargained away their king for gold. (In fact, Cambridge insists that his motive was not financial, though he is not permitted to say what it was.) The playwright does not give them complex motives; they are sinners, so horrified by their own intents that they are actually grateful to be caught. The scene serves, by such rhetorical devices, to strengthen Henry's claim to the English throne as well as to the territories in France. Opposition to his rule during wartime is, in the view of the Chorus, simply treasonous; all persuasive evidences of dynastic rival claims are hidden from our view.

Comedy also contributes to the rhetorical image-making of the hero in *Henry V*. The tavern crew is on hand, though deprived of the now-deceased Falstaff's beguiling company and more distant from Henry than in the earlier history plays. Only briefly and in disguise, on the night before the battle, does the King encounter Pistol. The name of Bardolph comes to Henry as though in recollection of a distant past, when he hears that Bardolph is about to be executed for stealing from French churches. Henry confirms the sentence: "We would have all such offenders so cut off" (3.6.107). Whatever momentary pang Henry may feel, he remains constant to his banishment of Falstaff. And, although Shakespeare pleads for our sympathies in the seriocomic account of Falstaff's death, seen through the childlike naiveté of Mistress Quickly, there is no hope of reconciliation between Henry and his former mates. Pistol, despite his ornamental language, is little more than a boaster, coward, and thief. The tavern revelers are now the opportunists of war, troublemakers such as are found in every army, engaging rascals deserving to be cudgeled by more honorable men.

Pistol gets his comeuppance from Captain Fluellen, who replaces Falstaff as the chief comic figure, both in prominence (his role is second in length to that of Henry) and in proximity to the King. Fluellen is a Welshman, like King Henry, who was born at Monmouth in what was then Wales (hence the appropriateness of his former title as Prince of Wales). Fluellen is proud of this kinship. Because he is loyal and valiant, he is a person worthy to be seen in Henry's company. Yet there is none of the brilliant duel of wits previously linking Henry and Falstaff. Fluellen is a humorous character, identified at once by such comically exaggerated features as his Welsh accent and mannerisms of speech, his old-fashioned and somewhat fanatical sense of military propriety, and his devotion to the ancient rules of military discipline. Fluellen is a caricature, subject to mild satirical laughter, and there is a note of condescension in Henry's habit of playing practical jokes on the captain. We tend to laugh at, rather than with, him. (Henry makes practical jokes at others' expense as well, such as the soldier named Williams, with whom he exchanges gloves.) Unlike Falstaff, Fluellen lacks perspective on his own pomposity. He is a zealot for duty, and one feels Henry is taking unfair advantage when he picks on one who is such an easy mark for laughter. We suspect that Henry is using people again, bolstering his public image as the king with the common touch, borrowing a little Welsh color for myth-making purposes. At the same time, Fluellen is steadfast, upright, and a credit to his countryman Henry. With his fellow captains from Scotland, Ireland, and England, he demonstrates that Britishers can fight together, even if they do antagonize one another with their proud regional customs. Those customs are to be cherished as part of the British character; because Pistol offers gratuitous insult to the Welsh tradition of wearing a leek in the cap on Saint Davy's Day, he must be thrashed.

As with the comic characters and Henry's political enemies, *Henry V* is rhetorically one-sided in its presentation of the French. Patriotism is a raw emotion, and Henry cannot appeal to it without awakening hostility toward the enemy. (Ironically enough, the great film version of *Henry*

V by Laurence Olivier was created in 1944 during World War II to arouse national feelings against the Germans rather than against the French, and with complete success. Any enemy will do in such patriotic moods.) The French are portrayed as haughty, vastly superior in numbers, envious of one another, contemptuous of their own leadership (especially the Dauphin), treacherous (attacking the boys with the luggage), and craven. Even their joking is characterized by an unattractively bestial kind of bawdry (3.7.48–68). The British—"we few, we happy few" (4.3.60)—are tired and outnumbered but invincible and seemingly protected by God. Henry's order to kill the French prisoners and his description of the rapes and pillages his soldiers will commit if Harfleur fails to surrender (3.3.1–27) do, to be sure, raise serious questions about the morality of war under the best of kings; the play may be caustic toward the French nobility but does not necessarily exonerate the English. Even here, however, we are led to believe that, because the French are so execrably governed, France will suffer less under English rule. Henry takes care that his soldiers will not despoil the French countryside except under conditions of military "necessity." Only in Montjoy, the Duke of Burgundy, and Katharine of France does Shakespeare offer redeeming portraits of the French character, and in these instances the terms of hierarchical ascendancy seem clear: masculine English dominance, gentle French submissiveness. Katharine becomes "la belle France," depicted in Burgundy's eloquent peacemaking speech as being so much in need of competent management.

Women exist only on the margins of this war play, as in Shakespeare's other historical plays. Mistress Quickly's role is chiefly as a reminder to us that men fight with one another for the possession of women; the ludicrous quarrel of Pistol and Nym over Mistress Quickly anticipates the way in which Katharine of France will be one of the chief spoils of the war itself. Women also wait patiently at home while their men fight, and tend them when they are sick. Mistress Quickly's recollection of the death of Falstaff (2.3.9–25) is masterful in its evocation of tender solicitude, illiterate piety, and unwitting eroticism. Later, in France, Pistol pauses with momentary regret over news of the death of his wife from venereal disease (5.1.80–1). Katharine of France, though vastly better born, finds her role as a woman no less circumscribed. We first see her learning English from Alice, her lady in waiting (3.4). Why is she learning English? The obvious political reason, never explicitly stated, emerges with a kind of violence: the scene of the English lesson follows immediately after King Henry's ultimatum to the citizens of Harfleur to surrender or see their women raped and their children impaled by English weapons (3.3.27–41). Katharine accepts her lot with good grace, as though she had any other choice but to do so. We gather from her scene with Alice that she is a woman of spirit who can be imperious, vain, and curious about sex. Because she also is very French, the wooing scene in Act 5 can play comically on the differences of temperament between her and Henry, who is as English as she is French. These differences make Henry and Katharine potentially compatible through complementarity—male and female, soldier and lady, English and French—but the compact is patently a hierarchical one of conqueror and conquered. (Emma Thompson, in Kenneth Branagh's film version of 1989, brings to the role of Katharine a gracefully and persuasively feminist interpretation of an independent-minded woman who is decidedly skeptical about the courtship to which she is subjected, but even she discovers that she has no choice other than to capitulate to Henry's—i.e., Branagh's—charm and the imperatives of international diplomacy.) Historically, we know that the product of their sexual union, Henry VI, will bring to a dismal end the harmony of discords that presides uncertainly over the end of *Henry V.*

Henry woos Katharine with real flair, despite their unstated mutual recognition that their courtship is, above all, a matter of state, in which they must play predetermined roles. The individual within Henry V gives way to the public personality, but he never loses his style. He manages always to be true to himself, as a wooer or as a soldier. We see him in disguise, hobnobbing with common soldiers of his camp on the eve of battle, earnestly discussing with them the morality of war. We see him, with endearing human inconsistency, coveting all the glory of victory over the French and then adjuring his soldiers to give credit for that victory to God alone. Even if we are at times less attracted to this successful warrior and politician than to the carefree young man of *1 Henry IV,* we can still honor Henry's choice of responsible maturity and see that it is even compassionately self-denying. A king cannot be like other men, and Henry is willing to accept this price of leadership.

The Chorus presents *Henry V* to us as if it were an epic poem as well as a drama. Henry is an epic hero, defined in terms of mythic allusions and abstractions. He is compared to Mars, the god of war, with Famine, Sword, and Fire leashed at his heels, crouched and ready for employment. He is the "mirror of all Christian kings," and his followers are "English Mercurys" (2.0.6–7) with winged heels. Personified Expectation sits in the air, promising crowns and crownets to Henry and his followers. Henry's fleet of ships in the English Channel becomes "A city on th'inconstant billows dancing" (3.0.15). On the eve of battle, amidst his brothers, friends, and countrymen, Henry warms every heart with "cheerful semblance and sweet majesty" and with his "largess universal like the sun" (4.0.40–3). He forbids vainglorious pride and gives credit for his victory "Quite from himself to God" (5.0.22).

The action the Chorus describes is comparably epic, as it moves from England to France and back again, leaping over time, surveying all levels of society in the English nation, portraying famous military encounters seemingly more suited to epic narration (or to film, as both Laurence Olivier's 1944 film and Kenneth Branagh's more recent film version brilliantly demonstrate) than to the stage. The stage's limitation forms, indeed, a major burden of the Chorus's argument. He apologizes to the spectators for the "flat unraisèd spirits" that have dared to bring forth so vast an object "On this unworthy scaffold," in this "cockpit" or "wooden O" (Prologue). The play confines "mighty men" "In little room," "Mangling by starts the full course of their glory" (Epilogue).

This apology sounds like becoming modesty on Shakespeare's part, in conceding the truth of Ben Jonson's objection that a few hired actors with rusty swords can scarcely do justice to England's great wars of the past. *Henry V* is not a Jonsonian neoclassical play. Paradoxically, however, Shakespeare's acknowledgment of the limited means at his disposal to create mimetic spectacle amounts to a defense of his own theater of the imagination. Through the Chorus's repeated urgings that we use our "imaginary forces" to supply what the actors and the theater necessarily lack, Shakespeare invites us as spectators and partners into his world of art. The play becomes a journey of thought, of making "imaginary puissance." When Shakespeare and his acting company talk of horses, we are to "see them / Printing their proud hoofs i'th' receiving earth" (Prologue). This is not to minimize the importance of the theatrical experience but, indeed, quite the opposite, since we are instructed to liberate ourselves through that theatrical experience and to re-create by means of Shakespeare's script an epic vision. Shakespeare's stage, bare of scenery, relying on good actors and the words they speak, becomes through its very flexibility more versatile in creating that vision than the most ornate and mechanically sophisticated illusionistic theater.

Nothing illustrates better the controversial and timely nature of this play than the history of recent productions, on stage and in film and television. Once viewed as a stalwart defense of England's national greatness, so much so that Winston Churchill could invoke Henry's famous speech before the Battle of Agincourt ("We few, we happy few") in celebration of Britain's "finest hour" of defending England against Nazi Germany, *Henry V* was destined to become, in the years of disillusionment following World War II and especially during the Vietnam era, a vehicle for a satirical and dismaying view of war. Directors have sometimes chosen to have the Boy who accompanies Pistol, Bardolph, and Nym to France brutally killed in open view of the audience by French soldiers. (The script does not specify such action.) A production by the Royal Shakespeare Company in 1964, directed by Peter Hall, showed the influence of Bertolt Brecht and Jan Kott (author of *Shakespeare Our Contemporary*) by staging the Battle of Agincourt in terrifying darkness, with reminiscences of the Guernica atrocity of the Spanish Civil War celebrated by Pablo Picasso's famous painting on the subject. In a number of productions, King Henry has been presented as a brazen devotee of imperialistic war, or a calculating politician for whom even the business of wooing is a matter of wearisome diplomatic necessity (as in Ian Holm's portrayal at Stratford-upon-Avon in 1964).

Alternatively, Henry has sometimes been seen as a self-doubting hero, keenly attuned to the absurdity of what it is that destiny has thrust upon him. Some of these remarkable contrasts can be discerned in the differences between Olivier's World War II film production and that of Branagh in 1989, in the wake of Vietnam and the Falklands episode.

The Life of King Henry the Fifth

[*Dramatis Personae*

CHORUS

KING HENRY THE FIFTH
HUMPHREY, DUKE OF GLOUCESTER,
JOHN, DUKE OF BEDFORD,
DUKE OF CLARENCE, } *the King's brothers*
DUKE OF EXETER, *the King's uncle*
DUKE OF YORK, *the King's cousin*
EARL OF SALISBURY
EARL OF WESTMORLAND
EARL OF WARWICK
EARL OF HUNTINGDON

ARCHBISHOP OF CANTERBURY
BISHOP OF ELY

RICHARD, EARL OF CAMBRIDGE, } *conspirators*
HENRY, LORD SCROOP OF MASHAM, } *against the King*
SIR THOMAS GREY,

SIR THOMAS ERPINGHAM,
CAPTAIN GOWER,
CAPTAIN FLUELLEN, } *officers in the King's army*
CAPTAIN MACMORRIS,
CAPTAIN JAMY,
JOHN BATES,
ALEXANDER COURT, } *soldiers in the King's army*
MICHAEL WILLIAMS,
An English HERALD

PISTOL,
NYM, } *Falstaff's former tavern-mates*
BARDOLPH,
BOY, *formerly Falstaff's page*
HOSTESS, *formerly Mistress Quickly, now married to Pistol*

DUKE OF BURGUNDY

FRENCH KING, *Charles the Sixth*
QUEEN ISABEL *of France*
DAUPHIN, *Lewis*
KATHARINE, *Princess of France*
ALICE, *a lady attending Katharine*
DUKE OF ORLEANS
DUKE OF BERRI
DUKE OF BOURBON
DUKE OF BRITTANY
CONSTABLE OF FRANCE
LORD RAMBURES
LORD GRANDPRÉ
GOVERNOR OF HARFLEUR
MONSIEUR LE FER, *a French soldier*
MONTJOY, *the French herald*
French AMBASSADORS *to England*

Lords, Ladies, Officers, Soldiers, Citizens, Messengers, and Attendants

SCENE: *England, afterwards France*]

Prologue

Enter [Chorus as] Prologue.

CHORUS

Oh, for a Muse of fire, that would ascend   1
The brightest heaven of invention!   2
A kingdom for a stage, princes to act,
And monarchs to behold the swelling scene!   4
Then should the warlike Harry, like himself,   5
Assume the port of Mars; and at his heels,   6
Leashed in like hounds, should famine, sword, and
    fire
Crouch for employment. But pardon, gentles all,   8
The flat unraisèd spirits that hath dared   9
On this unworthy scaffold to bring forth   10
So great an object. Can this cockpit hold   11
The vasty fields of France? Or may we cram   12
Within this wooden O the very casques   13
That did affright the air at Agincourt?
Oh, pardon! Since a crooked figure may   15
Attest in little place a million;   16
And let us, ciphers to this great account,   17
On your imaginary forces work.   18
Suppose within the girdle of these walls
Are now confined two mighty monarchies,
Whose high uprearèd and abutting fronts   21
The perilous narrow ocean parts asunder.   22
Piece out our imperfections with your thoughts:
Into a thousand parts divide one man,
And make imaginary puissance.   25
Think, when we talk of horses, that you see them
Printing their proud hoofs i'th' receiving earth.
For 'tis your thoughts that now must deck our kings,   28
Carry them here and there, jumping o'er times,
Turning th'accomplishment of many years
Into an hourglass—for the which supply,   31
Admit me Chorus to this history,
Who, Prologue-like, your humble patience pray
Gently to hear, kindly to judge, our play.   *Exit.*

❖

Prologue.
1 Muse of fire (Of the four elements—earth, air, fire, and water—fire is the most sublime and mounting.)   **2 invention** poetic imagination. **4 swelling** splendid, magnificent   **5 like himself** i.e., presented in a fashion worthy of so great a king.   **6 port** bearing   **8 gentles** gentlemen and gentlewomen   **9 flat unraisèd** uninspired, lifeless.   **spirits** i.e., actors and playwright.   **hath** (Elizabethan usage often pairs a plural subject with a singular verb.)   **10 scaffold** stage   **11 cockpit** (Elizabethan theaters were shaped rather like arenas for animal fighting.)   **12 vasty** vast, spacious   **13 O** (Refers to a round theater such as the Globe; the play may have been performed at the Curtain Theater.)   **casques** helmets   **15 crooked figure** cipher or zero (which, added to a number, will multiply its value tenfold)   **16 Attest** stand for   **17 account** (1) sum total (continuing the metaphor of *crooked figure*) (2) story   **18 imaginary forces** forces of imagination   **21 abutting** touching, bordering.   **fronts** (1) frontiers, i.e., the cliffs of Dover and Calais (2) foreheads   **22 perilous . . . ocean** i.e., English Channel   **25 puissance** armed might, army.   **28 deck** dress, adorn   **31 the which supply** which service

1.1

Enter the two bishops, [the Archbishop] of Canterbury and [the Bishop of] Ely.

CANTERBURY

My lord, I'll tell you. That self bill is urged   1
Which in th'eleventh year of the last king's reign
Was like, and had indeed against us passed,   3
But that the scambling and unquiet time   4
Did push it out of farther question.   5

ELY

But how, my lord, shall we resist it now?

CANTERBURY

It must be thought on. If it pass against us,
We lose the better half of our possession.
For all the temporal lands which men devout   9
By testament have given to the Church
Would they strip from us, being valued thus:
As much as would maintain, to the King's honor,
Full fifteen earls and fifteen hundred knights,
Six thousand and two hundred good esquires,   14
And, to relief of lazars and weak age   15
Of indigent faint souls past corporal toil,   16
A hundred almshouses right well supplied;
And to the coffers of the King beside
A thousand pounds by th' year. Thus runs the bill.

ELY   This would drink deep.

CANTERBURY   'Twould drink the cup and all.

ELY   But what prevention?

CANTERBURY

The King is full of grace and fair regard.

ELY

And a true lover of the holy Church.

CANTERBURY

The courses of his youth promised it not.
The breath no sooner left his father's body
But that his wildness, mortified in him,   27
Seemed to die too; yea, at that very moment
Consideration like an angel came   29
And whipped th'offending Adam out of him,   30
Leaving his body as a paradise
T'envelop and contain celestial spirits.
Never was such a sudden scholar made;
Never came reformation in a flood
With such a heady currance, scouring faults;   35
Nor never Hydra-headed willfulness   36
So soon did lose his seat, and all at once,   37
    As in this king.

ELY   We are blessed in the change.

CANTERBURY

Hear him but reason in divinity,

1.1. Location: England. The royal court.
1 self same   **3 like** likely (to have passed)   **4 scambling** unsettled   **5 question** consideration.   **9 temporal** used for secular purposes   **14 esquires** members of the gentry, ranking just below knights   **15 lazars** lepers   **16 corporal** physical   **27 mortified** killed   **29 Consideration** meditation, reflection   **30 offending Adam** original sin   **35 heady currance** headlong current   **36 Hydra-headed** i.e., many-headed. (Alludes to the Lernaean Hydra, a monster of many heads overcome by Hercules.)   **37 his seat** its throne

And, all-admiring, with an inward wish
You would desire the King were made a prelate.
Hear him debate of commonwealth affairs,
You would say it hath been all in all his study.
List his discourse of war, and you shall hear   44
A fearful battle rendered you in music.   45
Turn him to any cause of policy,   46
The Gordian knot of it he will unloose,   47
Familiar as his garter, that, when he speaks,   48
The air, a chartered libertine, is still,   49
And the mute wonder lurketh in men's ears   50
To steal his sweet and honeyed sentences;   51
So that the art and practic part of life   52
Must be the mistress to this theoric.   53
Which is a wonder how His Grace should glean it,
Since his addiction was to courses vain,   55
His companies unlettered, rude, and shallow,   56
His hours filled up with riots, banquets, sports,   57
And never noted in him any study,
Any retirement, any sequestration
From open haunts and popularity.   60

ELY
The strawberry grows underneath the nettle,
And wholesome berries thrive and ripen best
Neighbored by fruit of baser quality;
And so the Prince obscured his contemplation
Under the veil of wildness, which, no doubt,
Grew like the summer grass, fastest by night,
Unseen, yet crescive in his faculty.   67

CANTERBURY
It must be so, for miracles are ceased.   68
And therefore we must needs admit the means   69
How things are perfected.

ELY   But, my good lord,
How now for mitigation of this bill
Urged by the Commons? Doth His Majesty
Incline to it, or no?

CANTERBURY   He seems indifferent,   73
Or rather swaying more upon our part
Than cherishing th'exhibiters against us;   75
For I have made an offer to His Majesty,
Upon our spiritual convocation   77
And in regard of causes now in hand,   78
Which I have opened to His Grace at large,   79

---

44 **List** Listen to   45 **rendered . . . music** i.e., eloquently narrated.
46 cause of policy matter of statecraft   **47 Gordian knot** i.e., great
difficulty resolved forcefully. (It was foretold that whoever should
untie the Gordian knot would rule Asia. Alexander solved the problem by cutting the knot.)   48 **Familiar** as offhandedly or routinely.
that so that   **49 chartered libertine** free spirit, licensed to roam at
will   **50–1 the mute . . . sentences** i.e., wonder makes men silent,
eagerly listening to hear more of his sweetly profitable wise sayings
52–3 So . . . theoric so that experience in practical life must have been
the teacher by which he acquired his theoretical conception.
55 addiction inclination   **56 companies** companions.   **rude** coarse
57 riots reveling.   **sports** amusements   **60 open . . . popularity**
places of public resort and low company.   **67 crescive . . . faculty** naturally inclined to grow.   **68 miracles are ceased** (Protestants generally believed that no miracles occurred after the revelation of Christ.)
69 means i.e., natural causes   **73 indifferent** impartial   **75 exhibiters** those who introduce bills in Parliament   **77 Upon** on behalf of.
convocation formal assembly of the clergy   **78 in hand** under consideration   **79 opened** expounded.   **at large** in full

---

As touching France, to give a greater sum
Than ever at one time the clergy yet
Did to his predecessors part withal.   82

ELY
How did this offer seem received, my lord?

CANTERBURY
With good acceptance of His Majesty,
Save that there was not time enough to hear,
As I perceived His Grace would fain have done,   86
The severals and unhidden passages   87
Of his true titles to some certain dukedoms,
And generally to the crown and seat of France,   89
Derived from Edward, his great-grandfather.   90

ELY
What was th'impediment that broke this off?

CANTERBURY
The French ambassador upon that instant
Craved audience; and the hour I think is come
To give him hearing. Is it four o'clock?

ELY   It is.

CANTERBURY
Then go we in to know his embassy,   96
Which I could with a ready guess declare
Before the Frenchman speak a word of it.

ELY
I'll wait upon you, and I long to hear it.   *Exeunt.*

❧

[1.2]

*Enter the King, Humphrey [Duke of Gloucester],
Bedford, Clarence, Warwick, Westmorland, and
Exeter [with attendants].*

KING
Where is my gracious lord of Canterbury?

EXETER
Not here in presence.

KING   Send for him, good uncle.

WESTMORLAND
Shall we call in th'ambassador, my liege?

KING
Not yet, my cousin. We would be resolved,   4
Before we hear him, of some things of weight
That task our thoughts, concerning us and France.   6

*Enter two bishops, [the Archbishop of Canter-
bury and the Bishop of Ely].*

CANTERBURY
God and his angels guard your sacred throne,
And make you long become it!

KING   Sure we thank you.   8
My learnèd lord, we pray we to proceed,

---

82 **withal** with.   86 **fain** gladly   87 **severals** details.   **unhidden passages** clear lines of descent   89 **seat** throne   90 **Edward** Edward III
96 **embassy** message
1.2. Location: England. The royal court.
4 **cousin** (A form of address customarily used by royalty in addressing their nobles. In this case, Westmorland is in fact related to the
King by marriage.)   **be resolved** come to a decision   6 **task** engage,
occupy   8 **become** adorn, grace

And justly and religiously unfold
Why the law Salic that they have in France   11
Or should or should not bar us in our claim.   12
And God forbid, my dear and faithful lord,
That you should fashion, wrest, or bow your reading,
Or nicely charge your understanding soul   15
With opening titles miscreate, whose right   16
Suits not in native colors with the truth;   17
For God doth know how many now in health
Shall drop their blood in approbation   19
Of what your reverence shall incite us to.   20
Therefore take heed how you impawn our person,   21
How you awake our sleeping sword of war.
We charge you in the name of God take heed;
For never two such kingdoms did contend
Without much fall of blood, whose guiltless drops
Are every one a woe, a sore complaint   26
'Gainst him whose wrongs gives edge unto the
     swords   27
That makes such waste in brief mortality.   28
Under this conjuration speak, my lord;   29
For we will hear, note, and believe in heart
That what you speak is in your conscience washed
As pure as sin with baptism.

CANTERBURY
Then hear me, gracious sovereign, and you peers,
That owe yourselves, your lives, and services
To this imperial throne. There is no bar
To make against Your Highness' claim to France
But this, which they produce from Pharamond: 37
"In terram Salicam mulieres ne succedant,"
"No woman shall succeed in Salic land."
Which Salic land the French unjustly gloze   40
To be the realm of France, and Pharamond
The founder of this law and female bar.
Yet their own authors faithfully affirm
That the land Salic is in Germany,
Between the floods of Saale and of Elbe;   45
Where, Charles the Great having subdued the Saxons,   46
There left behind and settled certain French,
Who, holding in disdain the German women
For some dishonest manners of their life,   49
Established then this law: to wit, no female
Should be inheritrix in Salic land—
Which Salic, as I said, twixt Elbe and Saale,
Is at this day in Germany called Meissen.
Then doth it well appear the Salic law
Was not devisèd for the realm of France;
Nor did the French possess the Salic land

Until four hundred one-and-twenty years
After defunction of King Pharamond,   58
Idly supposed the founder of this law,   59
Who died within the year of our redemption
Four hundred twenty-six; and Charles the Great
Subdued the Saxons, and did seat the French
Beyond the River Saale, in the year
Eight hundred five. Besides, their writers say,
King Pepin, which deposèd Childeric,   65
Did, as heir general, being descended   66
Of Blithild, which was daughter to King Clothair,
Make claim and title to the crown of France.
Hugh Capet also, who usurped the crown
Of Charles the Duke of Lorraine, sole heir male
Of the true line and stock of Charles the Great,
To find his title with some shows of truth,   72
Though, in pure truth, it was corrupt and naught,
Conveyed himself as th'heir to th' Lady Lingard,   74
Daughter to Charlemagne, who was the son   75
To Lewis the Emperor, and Lewis the son
Of Charles the Great. Also King Lewis the Tenth,   77
Who was sole heir to the usurper Capet,
Could not keep quiet in his conscience,
Wearing the crown of France, till satisfied
That fair Queen Isabel, his grandmother,
Was lineal of the Lady Ermengard,   82
Daughter to Charles the foresaid Duke of Lorraine;
By the which marriage the line of Charles the Great
Was reunited to the crown of France.
So that, as clear as is the summer's sun,
King Pepin's title and Hugh Capet's claim,
King Lewis his satisfaction, all appear   88
To hold in right and title of the female;
So do the kings of France unto this day,
Howbeit they would hold up this Salic law   91
To bar Your Highness claiming from the female,
And rather choose to hide them in a net   93
Than amply to imbar their crooked titles   94
Usurped from you and your progenitors.

KING
May I with right and conscience make this claim?
CANTERBURY
The sin upon my head, dread sovereign!
For in the Book of Numbers is it writ,
When the man dies, let the inheritance   99
Descend unto the daughter. Gracious lord,   100
Stand for your own; unwind your bloody flag!   101
Look back into your mighty ancestors:

---

11 Salic (See explanation at lines 39–45.)   **12 Or** either   **15 nicely charge** subtly and foolishly burden   **16 opening titles miscreate** expounding spurious claims   **17 Suits . . . colors** i.e., does not naturally harmonize   **19 approbation** support, proof   **20 your reverence** (1) an honorific title for an archbishop, Your Reverence (2) your sacred authority   **21 impawn** put under an obligation   **26 woe** grievance.   **sore** severe, grievous   **27 wrongs** wrongdoings   **28 in brief mortality** i.e., among mortal, short-lived men.   **29 conjuration** solemn adjuration   **37 Pharamond** legendary Frankish king   **40 gloze** gloss   **45 floods** rivers   **46 Charles the Great** Charlemagne   **49 dishonest** unchaste

58 defunction death   **59 Idly** foolishly   **65 which** who. (As also in line 67.)   **66 heir general** heir through male or female line   **72 find** provide   **74 Conveyed himself** passed himself off   **75 Charlemagne** (Holinshed's and Hall's error, followed by Shakespeare, for Charles the Bald or Charles II, emperor of the West; Luitgard [Shakespeare's Lingard] became Charlemagne's wife after the death of Fastrada in 794.)   **77 Lewis the Tenth** (Actually, Louis IX; an error copied from Holinshed.)   **82 lineal of** descended from   **88 Lewis his satisfaction** Lewis's conviction   **91 Howbeit** notwithstanding   **93 hide . . . net** i.e., conceal the weakness of their case in a tangle of contradictions   **94 amply to imbar** frankly to bar claim to   **99–100 When . . . daughter** (This paraphrase leaves out an important phrase. Numbers 27:8 reads, "When a man dies leaving no son, his patrimony shall pass to his daughter.")   **101 unwind** unfurl

Go, my dread lord, to your great-grandsire's tomb,   103
From whom you claim! Invoke his warlike spirit,
And your great-uncle's, Edward the Black Prince,
Who on the French ground played a tragedy,   106
Making defeat on the full power of France,   107
Whiles his most mighty father on a hill
Stood smiling to behold his lion's whelp
Forage in blood of French nobility.
O noble English, that could entertain   111
With half their forces the full pride of France
And let another half stand laughing by,
All out of work and cold for action!   114

ELY
Awake remembrance of these valiant dead,
And with your puissant arm renew their feats!
You are their heir; you sit upon their throne;
The blood and courage that renownèd them   118
Runs in your veins; and my thrice-puissant liege
Is in the very May morn of his youth,
Ripe for exploits and mighty enterprises.

EXETER
Your brother kings and monarchs of the earth
Do all expect that you should rouse yourself
As did the former lions of your blood.

WESTMORLAND
They know Your Grace hath cause, and means, and might;
So hath Your Highness. Never king of England   126
Had nobles richer and more loyal subjects,
Whose hearts have left their bodies here in England
And lie pavilioned in the fields of France.   129

CANTERBURY
Oh, let their bodies follow, my dear liege,
With blood, and sword, and fire to win your right!
In aid whereof we of the spirituality   132
Will raise Your Highness such a mighty sum
As never did the clergy at one time
Bring in to any of your ancestors.

KING
We must not only arm t'invade the French,
But lay down our proportions to defend   137
Against the Scot, who will make road upon us   138
With all advantages.   139

CANTERBURY
They of those marches, gracious sovereign,   140
Shall be a wall sufficient to defend
Our inland from the pilfering borderers.

KING
We do not mean the coursing snatchers only,   143

But fear the main intendment of the Scot,   144
Who hath been still a giddy neighbor to us.   145
For you shall read that my great-grandfather
Never went with his forces into France
But that the Scot on his unfurnished kingdom   148
Came pouring like the tide into a breach
With ample and brim fullness of his force,   150
Galling the gleanèd land with hot assays,   151
Girding with grievous siege castles and towns;
That England, being empty of defense,
Hath shook and trembled at th'ill neighborhood.   154

CANTERBURY
She hath been then more feared than harmed, my
liege.   155
For hear her but exampled by herself: 156
When all her chivalry hath been in France   157
And she a mourning widow of her nobles,   158
She hath herself not only well defended
But taken and impounded as a stray   160
The King of Scots, whom she did send to France   161
To fill King Edward's fame with prisoner kings
And make her chronicle as rich with praise
As is the ooze and bottom of the sea
With sunken wrack and sumless treasuries.   165

A LORD
But there's a saying very old and true:
"If that you will France win,
Then with Scotland first begin."
For once the eagle England being in prey,   169
To her unguarded nest the weasel Scot
Comes sneaking, and so sucks her princely eggs,
Playing the mouse in absence of the cat,
To 'tame and havoc more than she can eat.   173

EXETER
It follows then the cat must stay at home;
Yet that is but a crushed necessity,   175
Since we have locks to safeguard necessaries
And pretty traps to catch the petty thieves.   177
While that the armèd hand doth fight abroad,   178
Th'advisèd head defends itself at home;   179
For government, though high, and low, and lower,   180
Put into parts, doth keep in one consent,   181

---

103 **great-grandsire's** i.e., Edward III's. His descent through his mother Isabella from the French King Philip IV is the basis of English claims to the French kingdom—a claim through female inheritance. Hence the importance of lines 39–55.   106 **tragedy** i.e., the Battle of Crécy, 1346, a major defeat for the French   107 **power** army   111 **entertain** engage, encounter   114 **for action** for want of action.   118 **renownèd** brought renown to   126 **So** so indeed   129 **pavilioned** tented, encamped   132 **spiritualty** clergy   137 **lay . . . proportions** allocate our forces   138 **road** inroad, raid   139 **With all advantages** whenever a good opportunity presents itself.   140 **They . . . marches** Our English forces in the territories bordering Scotland   143 **coursing snatchers** hit-and-run Scottish raiders on fast-galloping horses

144 **intendment** plan, hostile intent   145 **still** always.   **giddy** unstable, fickle   148 **unfurnished** unprovided with defense   150 **brim** absolute, complete   151 **Galling . . . assays** harassing the land stripped of defenders with hot attacks   154 **th'ill neighborhood** the unneighborliness.   155 **feared** frightened   156 **hear . . . herself** i.e., only listen how England can be instructed by an example from her own history   157 **chivalry** knights   158 **And she . . . nobles** and she, England, widowlike in being deprived of her nobility while they fight in France   160–1 **impounded . . . Scots** (King David II of Scotland was captured and imprisoned in 1346 while Edward III was in France.)   161 **to France** (Historically, David II was imprisoned in London, not sent to France.)   165 **wrack** wreckage.   **sumless** inestimable   169 **in prey** absent in search of prey   173 **to 'tame and havoc** to attame (i.e., break into) and ravage   175 **crushed necessity** distorted conclusion   177 **pretty** ingenious   178 **While that** While   179 **advisèd** wise, prudent   180 **though . . . lower** i.e., though composed of three broad social ranks (corresponding also to three singing voices from treble to bass)   181 **Put into parts** separated into different functions (and into different parts in part-music).   **one consent** mutual harmony

Congreeing in a full and natural close, 182
Like music.

CANTERBURY   Therefore doth heaven divide
The state of man in divers functions,
Setting endeavor in continual motion,
To which is fixèd, as an aim or butt, 186
Obedience; for so work the honeybees,
Creatures that by a rule in nature teach
The act of order to a peopled kingdom.
They have a king, and officers of sorts, 190
Where some, like magistrates, correct at home; 191
Others, like merchants, venture trade abroad;
Others, like soldiers, armèd in their stings,
Make boot upon the summer's velvet buds, 194
Which pillage they with merry march bring home
To the tent royal of their emperor,
Who, busied in his majesty, surveys
The singing masons building roofs of gold,
The civil citizens kneading up the honey,
The poor mechanic porters crowding in 200
Their heavy burdens at his narrow gate,
The sad-eyed justice with his surly hum 202
Delivering o'er to executors pale 203
The lazy yawning drone. I this infer,
That many things, having full reference 205
To one consent, may work contrariously. 206
As many arrows loosèd several ways 207
Come to one mark, as many ways meet in one town, 208
As many fresh streams meet in one salt sea,
As many lines close in the dial's center, 210
So may a thousand actions once afoot
End in one purpose, and be all well borne 212
Without defeat. Therefore to France, my liege!
Divide your happy England into four,
Whereof take you one quarter into France,
And you withal shall make all Gallia shake. 216
If we with thrice such powers left at home
Cannot defend our own doors from the dog,
Let us be worried, and our nation lose 219
The name of hardiness and policy. 220

KING
Call in the messengers sent from the Dauphin. 221
                [Exeunt some.]
Now are we well resolved, and by God's help
And yours, the noble sinews of our power,
France being ours, we'll bend it to our awe, 224

Or break it all to pieces. Or there we'll sit, 225
Ruling in large and ample empery 226
O'er France and all her almost kingly dukedoms,
Or lay these bones in an unworthy urn,
Tombless, with no remembrance over them.
Either our history shall with full mouth
Speak freely of our acts, or else our grave,
Like Turkish mute, shall have a tongueless mouth,
Not worshiped with a waxen epitaph. 233

Enter Ambassadors of France.

Now are we well prepared to know the pleasure
Of our fair cousin Dauphin; for we hear 235
Your greeting is from him, not from the King.
FIRST AMBASSADOR
May't please Your Majesty to give us leave
Freely to render what we have in charge,
Or shall we sparingly show you far off
The Dauphin's meaning and our embassy?
KING
We are no tyrant, but a Christian king,
Unto whose grace our passion is as subject
As is our wretches fettered in our prisons.
Therefore with frank and with uncurbèd plainness
Tell us the Dauphin's mind.
FIRST AMBASSADOR   Thus, then, in few:
Your Highness, lately sending into France,
Did claim some certain dukedoms, in the right
Of your great predecessor, King Edward the Third.
In answer of which claim, the Prince our master
Says that you savor too much of your youth,
And bids you be advised there's naught in France
That can be with a nimble galliard won; 252
You cannot revel into dukedoms there.
He therefore sends you, meeter for your spirit, 254
This tun of treasure, and in lieu of this 255
Desires you let the dukedoms that you claim
Hear no more of you. This the Dauphin speaks.
           [*A casket is presented;*
           Exeter examines its contents.]

KING
What treasure, uncle?
EXETER   Tennis balls, my liege.
KING
We are glad the Dauphin is so pleasant with us. 259
His present and your pains we thank you for.
When we have matched our rackets to these balls, 261
We will in France, by God's grace, play a set
Shall strike his father's crown into the hazard. 263

---

182 **Congreeing** agreeing together. **close** musical cadence   186 **aim or butt** target. (All endeavor is to direct itself toward obedience.) 190 **They . . . king** (A common error of early natural history, derived from Aristotle. The simile of the bees appears in Virgil, Sir Thomas Elyot, John Lyly, and others.) **of sorts** various kinds   191 **correct** administer justice   194 **Make boot** prey   200 **mechanic** engaged in manual labor   202 **sad-eyed** grave-eyed   203 **executors pale** executioners, pale in their terrible sternness   205–6 **having . . . consent** united by a common understanding   207 **As** Just as. **loosèd several ways** shot from different directions   208 **ways** roads   210 **close** come together. **dial's** sundial's   212 **borne** carried out, sustained   216 **Gallia** France. (Latin name.)   219 **worried** (1) torn apart or harried, as by dogs (2) made anxious   220 **hardiness and policy** bravery and statesmanship.   221 **Dauphin** heir apparent to the French throne.   224 **ours** i.e., ours by right. **our awe** submission to us

225 **Or there** Either there   226 **empery** dominion   233 **Not . . . epitaph** i.e., with not even so much as a wax (as opposed to bronze) epitaph; one easily effaced.   235 **cousin** fellow prince (though Henry does also claim a line of descent in the French royal family)   252 **galliard** a lively dance   254 **meeter** more fitting   255 **tun** cask   259 **pleasant** jocular. (Also in line 281.)   261 **rackets** (1) tennis rackets (2) noisy military assaults   263 **crown** (1) royal crown (2) final point scored, or a coin (worth five shillings in English coinage) staked in the game.   **hazard** (1) in "royal" tennis, an opening in one of the high walls enclosing the court; hitting the ball into such a "hazard" scored a winning point (2) jeopardy.

Tell him he hath made a match with such a wrangler 264
That all the courts of France will be disturbed 265
With chases. And we understand him well, 266
How he comes o'er us with our wilder days, 267
Not measuring what use we made of them.
We never valued this poor seat of England, 269
And therefore, living hence, did give ourself 270
To barbarous license—as 'tis ever common
That men are merriest when they are from home. 272
But tell the Dauphin I will keep my state, 273
Be like a king, and show my sail of greatness 274
When I do rouse me in my throne of France.
For that I have laid by my majesty 276
And plodded like a man for working days, 277
But I will rise there with so full a glory
That I will dazzle all the eyes of France,
Yea, strike the Dauphin blind to look on us.
And tell the pleasant Prince this mock of his
Hath turned his balls to gunstones, and his soul 282
Shall stand sore chargèd for the wasteful vengeance 283
That shall fly with them; for many a thousand
    widows
Shall this his mock mock out of their dear husbands,
Mock mothers from their sons, mock castles down,
And some are yet ungotten and unborn 287
That shall have cause to curse the Dauphin's scorn.
But this lies all within the will of God,
To whom I do appeal, and in whose name
Tell you the Dauphin I am coming on
To venge me as I may, and to put forth
My rightful hand in a well-hallowed cause.
So get you hence in peace; and tell the Dauphin
His jest will savor but of shallow wit
When thousands weep more than did laugh at it.—
Convey them with safe conduct.—Fare you well. 297

Exeunt Ambassadors.

EXETER   This was a merry message.
KING
We hope to make the sender blush at it.
Therefore, my lords, omit no happy hour 300
That may give furth'rance to our expedition; 301
For we have now no thought in us but France,
Save those to God, that run before our business. 303
Therefore let our proportions for these wars 304
Be soon collected, and all things thought upon
That may with reasonable swiftness add
More feathers to our wings; for, God before, 307

We'll chide this Dauphin at his father's door.
Therefore let every man now task his thought, 309
That this fair action may on foot be brought.

Flourish. Exeunt.

❧

2.0

Enter Chorus.

CHORUS
Now all the youth of England are on fire,
And silken dalliance in the wardrobe lies. 2
Now thrive the armorers, and honor's thought
Reigns solely in the breast of every man.
They sell the pasture now to buy the horse,
Following the mirror of all Christian kings, 6
With wingèd heels, as English Mercurys. 7
For now sits Expectation in the air
And hides a sword from hilts unto the point 9
With crowns imperial, crowns and coronets, 10
Promised to Harry and his followers.
The French, advised by good intelligence 12
Of this most dreadful preparation,
Shake in their fear, and with pale policy 14
Seek to divert the English purposes.
O England! Model to thy inward greatness, 16
Like little body with a mighty heart,
What mightst thou do, that honor would thee do, 18
Were all thy children kind and natural?
But see, thy fault France hath in thee found out,
A nest of hollow bosoms, which he fills
With treacherous crowns; and three corrupted men, 22
One, Richard Earl of Cambridge, and the second,
Henry Lord Scroop of Masham, and the third,
Sir Thomas Grey, knight, of Northumberland,
Have, for the gilt of France—oh, guilt indeed!— 26
Confirmed conspiracy with fearful France, 27
And by their hands this grace of kings must die,
If hell and treason hold their promises,
Ere he take ship for France, and in Southampton.
Linger your patience on, and we'll digest 31
Th'abuse of distance, force a play. 32
The sum is paid, the traitors are agreed,
The King is set from London, and the scene
Is now transported, gentles, to Southampton.
There is the playhouse now, there must you sit,
And thence to France shall we convey you safe,

---

264 **wrangler** adversary, disputant   265 **courts** (1) tennis courts (2)
royal courts   266 **chases** (1) returns of the ball (2) chasing after game
(3) chasing the enemy   267 **comes o'er us** taunts me. (*Us* is the royal
plural.)   269 **seat** throne   270 **living hence** not frequenting the royal
court   272 **from** away from   273 **keep my state** i.e., fulfill the role of
king   274 **sail** full swell. (Henry says he has not yet revealed his full
majesty in laying claim to France.)   276 **For that** i.e., In anticipation
of that great event   277 **for** suited and ready for   282 **gunstones**
cannonballs   283 **sore chargèd** sorely burdened with responsibility.
wasteful destructive   287 **yet ungotten** not yet conceived   297 **Convey** Escort   300 **omit . . . hour** lose no favorable opportunity
301 **expedition** (1) invasion of France (2) haste   303 **that . . . business**
that properly come first.   304 **proportions** levies of men   307 **God
before** with God leading, helping

309 **task** tax, exercise
2.0 Chorus.
2 **silken . . . lies** i.e., silken apparel and idle pleasure are packed
away.   6 **the mirror . . . kings** i.e., the ideal or model to which all
other kings should compare themselves   7 **Mercurys** (Mercury, classical messenger of the gods, always wears wingèd heels.)   9 **hides a
sword** i.e., holds up a sword completely impaled with the prizes of
war   10 **With . . . coronets** with the crowns of emperors, kings, and
nobles   12 **intelligence** information gathering   14 **pale policy** fainthearted stratagems   16 **Model to** Outward manifestation of
18 **would** would have   22 **crowns** coins, money (as a bribe)   26 **gilt**
gold   27 **fearful** frightened, cowardly   31–2 **digest . . . play** com-
press long distance (and time) into what can be encompassed in a
play, an *abuse* of the unities of time and place.

And bring you back, charming the narrow seas
To give you gentle pass; for, if we may, 39
We'll not offend one stomach with our play. 40
But, when the King come forth, and not till then, 41
Unto Southampton do we shift our scene. *Exit.* 42

❖

2.1

Enter Corporal Nym and Lieutenant Bardolph.

BARDOLPH Well met, Corporal Nym.

NYM Good morrow, Lieutenant Bardolph.

BARDOLPH What, are Ancient Pistol and you friends 3
yet?

NYM For my part, I care not. I say little; but when time
shall serve, there shall be smiles—but that shall be as
it may. I dare not fight, but I will wink and hold out 7
mine iron. It is a simple one, but what though? It will 8
toast cheese, and it will endure cold as another man's 9
sword will—and there's an end. 10

BARDOLPH I will bestow a breakfast to make you
friends, and we'll be all three sworn brothers to
France. Let 't be so, good Corporal Nym.

NYM Faith, I will live so long as I may, that's the certain
of it; and when I cannot live any longer, I will do as I
may. That is my rest; that is the rendezvous of it. 16

BARDOLPH It is certain, Corporal, that he is married to
Nell Quickly, and certainly she did you wrong, for
you were trothplight to her. 19

NYM I cannot tell. Things must be as they may. Men
may sleep, and they may have their throats about
them at that time, and some say knives have edges. It
must be as it may. Though Patience be a tired mare, 23
yet she will plod. There must be conclusions. Well, I 24
cannot tell.

Enter Pistol and [Hostess] Quickly.

BARDOLPH Here comes Ancient Pistol and his wife.
Good Corporal, be patient here.

NYM How now, mine host Pistol?

PISTOL
Base tike, call'st thou me host? 29
Now, by this hand, I swear, I scorn the term!
Nor shall my Nell keep lodgers.

HOSTESS No, by my troth, not long; for we cannot lodge
and board a dozen or fourteen gentlewomen that live

honestly by the prick of their needles, but it will be 34
thought we keep a bawdy house straight. [*Nym and
Pistol draw.*] Oh, welladay, Lady! If he be not hewn 36
now, we shall see willful adultery and murder com- 37
itted.

BARDOLPH Good Lieutenant! Good Corporal! Offer 39
nothing here. 40

NYM Pish!

PISTOL
Pish for thee, Iceland dog! 42
Thou prick-eared cur of Iceland!

HOSTESS Good Corporal Nym, show thy valor, and 44
put up your sword.   [*They sheathe their swords.*]

NYM Will you shog off? I would have you solus. 46

PISTOL
Solus, egregious dog? O viper vile!
The solus in thy most mervailous face! 48
The solus in thy teeth, and in thy throat, 49
And in thy hateful lungs, yea, in thy maw, pardie, 50
And, which is worse, within thy nasty mouth!
I do retort the solus in thy bowels;
For I can take, and Pistol's cock is up, 53
And flashing fire will follow.

NYM I am not Barbason; you cannot conjure me. I have 55
an humor to knock you indifferently well. If you grow 56
foul with me, Pistol, I will scour you with my rapier, as 57
I may, in fair terms. If you would walk off, I would 58
prick your guts a little, in good terms, as I may, and
that's the humor of it. 60

PISTOL
O braggart vile and damnèd furious wight! 61
The grave doth gape, and doting death is near.
Therefore exhale!   [*They draw their swords.*] 63

BARDOLPH [*drawing his sword*] Hear me, hear me what
I say. He that strikes the first stroke, I'll run him up to
the hilts, as I am a soldier.

PISTOL
An oath of mickle might, and fury shall abate. 67
    [*Pistol and Nym sheathe their swords.*]
[*To Nym*] Give me thy fist, thy forefoot to me give.
Thy spirits are most tall. 69

---

34 prick (With a bawdy double meaning, probably unintended, as also in *Pistol's cock*, line 53.) **36 welladay** wellaway, alas. **Lady** i.e., by Our Lady. (An oath.) **hewn** struck down **37 adultery** (Blunder for "battery"?) **39–40 Offer nothing** Attempt no violence **42 Iceland dog** a small, shaggy dog often kept as a house pet. (Pistol's humor is to use extravagant epithets, like this one, tags from current plays, and scraps of foreign languages.) **44 valor** (She means "calm," "forbearance.") **46 shog off** move along. **solus** alone. (Nym proposes a duel; see *walk off* in line 58.) **48 mervailous** marvelous, astonishing **49–50 The solus . . . thy lungs** (Nym mocks Pistol's hyperbolic rant as though it were a conjuration.) **55–6 I have an humor** I'm in the mood. (*Humor* is a favorite word with Nym, as in lines 60, 71, 97, 116, 121, and 126.) **57 foul** (1) foulmouthed (2) fouled from firing and in need of scouring **58 in fair terms** i.e., make no mistake about it. (*In good terms* at line 59 means the same.) **walk off** walk aside (to fight) **60 that's . . . it** that's my mood. **61 wight** person. **63 exhale** draw (sword, much as the sun draws forth vapors). **67 mickle** great **69 tall** valiant.

---

39 pass passage **40 offend one stomach** (1) offend anyone's taste by sudden shifts in scene (2) make anyone seasick **41–2 But . . . scene** i.e., The scene will be shifted to Southampton after a scene in London. (These lines sound as though they were added as an afterthought, to accommodate the inclusion of the comic scene in 2.1.)
2.1. Location: London. A street.
3 Ancient ensign, standard-bearer **7 wink** shut the eyes **8 iron** sword. **though** of that. **9 endure cold** i.e., doesn't mind being drawn from its sheath **10 there's an end** that's all there is to it.
16 rest last stake (in the gambling game of primero). **rendezvous** last resort **19 trothplight** betrothed **23–4 Though . . . plod** i.e., Patient persistence will ultimately achieve its goal. (Nym hints, as he does elsewhere, at violence toward Pistol.) **24 conclusions** an end to matters. (Nym hints darkly that the end must come soon.)
29 tike cur

NYM   I will cut thy throat, one time or other, in fair
terms. That is the humor of it.
PISTOL   *Couple a gorge!*   72
That is the word. I thee defy again.
O hound of Crete, think'st thou my spouse to get?   74
No, to the spital go,   75
And from the powdering tub of infamy   76
Fetch forth the lazar kite of Cressid's kind,   77
Doll Tearsheet she by name, and her espouse.
I have, and I will hold, the quondam Quickly   79
For the only she; and—*pauca!* There's enough.   80
Go to.

Enter the Boy.

BOY   Mine host Pistol, you must come to my master,
and you, hostess. He is very sick and would to bed.
Good Bardolph, put thy face between his sheets, and   84
do the office of a warming pan. Faith, he's very ill.
BARDOLPH   Away, you rogue!
HOSTESS   By my troth, he'll yield the crow a pudding   87
one of these days. The King has killed his heart. Good   88
husband, come home presently.   *Exit* [*with Boy*].   89
BARDOLPH   Come, shall I make you two friends? We
must to France together. Why the devil should we
keep knives to cut one another's throats?
PISTOL
Let floods o'erswell, and fiends for food howl on!
NYM   You'll pay me the eight shillings I won of you at
betting?
PISTOL   Base is the slave that pays.
NYM   That now I will have. That's the humor of it.
PISTOL   As manhood shall compound. Push home.   98
                                                          [*They*] *draw.*
BARDOLPH   [*drawing*]   By this sword, he that makes
the first thrust, I'll kill him! By this sword, I will.
PISTOL
Sword is an oath, and oaths must have their course.   101
                                           [*He sheathes his sword.*]
BARDOLPH   Corporal Nym, an thou wilt be friends, be   102
friends; an thou wilt not, why, then, be enemies with
me too. Prithee, put up.   104
NYM   I shall have my eight shillings I won of you at
betting?
PISTOL
A noble shalt thou have, and present pay;   107
And liquor likewise will I give to thee,

And friendship shall combine, and brotherhood.
I'll live by Nym, and Nym shall live by me.   110
Is not this just? For I shall sutler be   111
Unto the camp, and profits will accrue.
Give me thy hand.
NYM   I shall have my noble?
PISTOL   In cash most justly paid.
NYM   Well, then, that's the humor of't.
                    [*Nym and Bardolph sheathe their swords.*]

Enter Hostess.

HOSTESS   As ever you come of women, come in quickly 117
to Sir John. Ah, poor heart, he is so shaked of a burn-
ing quotidian tertian that it is most lamentable to be-   119
hold. Sweet men, come to him.   [*Exit.*]
NYM   The King hath run bad humors on the knight,   121
that's the even of it.   122
PISTOL   Nym, thou hast spoke the right.
His heart is fracted and corroborate.   124
NYM   The King is a good king, but it must be as it may;
he passes some humors and careers.   126
PISTOL
Let us condole the knight, for, lambkins, we will live. 127
                                                                   [*Exeunt.*]

❖

[2.2]

Enter Exeter, Bedford, and Westmorland.

BEDFORD
'Fore God, His Grace is bold to trust these traitors.
EXETER
They shall be apprehended by and by.
WESTMORLAND
How smooth and even they do bear themselves!   3
As if allegiance in their bosoms sat,
Crownèd with faith and constant loyalty.
BEDFORD
The King hath note of all that they intend,
By interception which they dream not of.
EXETER
Nay, but the man that was his bedfellow,   8
Whom he hath dulled and cloyed with gracious
   favors—   9

---

72 *Couple a gorge! Couper la gorge!,* "Cut the throat!"   74 hound of
Crete (Parallel to *Iceland dog,* line 42.)   75 spital hospital   76 powdering tub (Originally a tub used for salting beef; here, alluding to a
method of curing venereal disease by sweating.)   77 lazar . . . kind
i.e., diseased, leprous whore (a *kite* is a bird of prey) like Cressida,
the fallen woman, who, in Robert Henryson's *Testament of Cresseid,* is
shown as being rejected by Diomede and infected with leprosy
79 quondam former   80 only she i.e., only woman in the world.
pauca i.e., in brief   84 face (Bardolph's face is fiery with drinking.)
87 he'll (Refers to the Boy or Falstaff.)   yield . . . pudding i.e., be
hanged on the gallows and eaten by carrion birds   88 his i.e., Falstaff's   89 presently immediately.   98 As . . . compound As valor
shall settle the matter (in fight).   101 Sword is an oath (Quibbling on
sword as *'s word,* i.e., "God's word.")   102 an if   104 put up i.e., put
up your sword.   107 A noble . . . pay i.e., I'll settle for paying you six
shillings eight pence ready money

110 Nym (Quibbles on *nim,* meaning "thief.")   111 sutler seller of
liquor and provisions to the soldiers   117 come of were born of
119 quotidian tertian (A *quotidian* fever was one that came daily; a
tertian fever, one that came on alternate days, though some authorities believed that different fevers might mix and intensify their
effects.)   121 run bad humors i.e., vented his displeasure   122 even
level truth   124 fracted broken.   corroborate (Blunder for "broken
to pieces" or "corrupted"? The word means "strengthened, confirmed.")   126 passes . . . careers lets pass (i.e., indulges in) some
idiosyncrasies and capers. (A *career* is a full gallop.)   127 condole
express our commiseration of or sympathy with.   lambkins (A term
of endearment.)
2.2. Location: Southampton, a seaport on England's southern coast.
3 smooth and even pleasant and calm   8 bedfellow i.e., constant
companion. (Refers to Scroop.)   9 dulled dulled the appetite of

That he should, for a foreign purse, so sell
His sovereign's life to death and treachery!

Sound trumpets. Enter the King, Scroop, Cam-
bridge, and Grey, [and attendants].

KING
Now sits the wind fair, and we will aboard.   12
My lord of Cambridge, and my kind lord of Masham,
And you, my gentle knight, give me your thoughts.
Think you not that the pow'rs we bear with us   15
Will cut their passage through the force of France,
Doing the execution and the act
For which we have in head assembled them?   18
SCROOP
No doubt, my liege, if each man do his best.
KING
I doubt not that, since we are well persuaded
We carry not a heart with us from hence
That grows not in a fair consent with ours,   22
Nor leave not one behind that doth not wish
Success and conquest to attend on us.
CAMBRIDGE
Never was monarch better feared and loved
Than is Your Majesty. There's not, I think, a subject
That sits in heart-grief and uneasiness
Under the sweet shade of your government.
GREY
True. Those that were your father's enemies
Have steeped their galls in honey, and do serve you   30
With hearts create of duty and of zeal.   31
KING
We therefore have great cause of thankfulness,
And shall forget the office of our hand   33
Sooner than quittance of desert and merit   34
According to the weight and worthiness.
SCROOP
So service shall with steelèd sinews toil,
And labor shall refresh itself with hope,
To do Your Grace incessant services.
KING
We judge no less.—Uncle of Exeter,
Enlarge the man committed yesterday   40
That railed against our person. We consider
It was excess of wine that set him on,
And on his more advice we pardon him.   43
SCROOP
That's mercy, but too much security.   44
Let him be punished, sovereign, lest example
Breed, by his sufferance, more of such a kind.   46
KING   Oh, let us yet be merciful.
CAMBRIDGE
So may Your Highness, and yet punish too.

GREY
Sir, you show great mercy if you give him life   50
After the taste of much correction.   51
KING
Alas, your too much love and care of me
Are heavy orisons 'gainst this poor wretch!   53
If little faults proceeding on distemper   54
Shall not be winked at, how shall we stretch our eye 55
When capital crimes, chewed, swallowed, and
    digested,   56
Appear before us? We'll yet enlarge that man,   57
Though Cambridge, Scroop, and Grey, in their dear
    care
And tender preservation of our person,
Would have him punished. And now to our French
    causes.
Who are the late commissioners?   61
CAMBRIDGE   I one, my lord.
Your Highness bade me ask for it today.   63
SCROOP   So did you me, my liege.
GREY   And I, my royal sovereign.
KING [*giving them papers*]
Then, Richard Earl of Cambridge, there is yours;
There yours, Lord Scroop of Masham; and sir knight,
Grey of Northumberland, this same is yours.
Read them, and know I know your worthiness.—
My lord of Westmorland, and uncle Exeter,
We will aboard tonight.—Why, how now, gentlemen?
What see you in those papers, that you lose
So much complexion?—Look ye how they change! 73
Their cheeks are paper.—Why, what read you there   74
That have so cowarded and chased your blood
Out of appearance?
CAMBRIDGE   I do confess my fault,   76
And do submit me to Your Highness' mercy.
GREY, SCROOP   To which we all appeal.
KING
The mercy that was quick in us but late   79
By your own counsel is suppressed and killed.
You must not dare, for shame, to talk of mercy,
For your own reasons turn into your bosoms,
As dogs upon their masters, worrying you.—   83
See you, my princes and my noble peers,
These English monsters! My lord of Cambridge here,
You know how apt our love was to accord   86
To furnish him with all appurtenants   87
Belonging to his honor; and this man
Hath for a few light crowns lightly conspired   89
And sworn unto the practices of France   90

---

50 give him life allow him to live   **51 correction** punishment.
53 heavy orisons weighty prayers, pleas   **54 proceeding on distemper** resulting from unstable condition (caused by excessive drinking)
55 stretch open wide, not wink   **56 capital** punishable by death.
chewed . . . digested i.e., premeditated   **57 yet** in spite of what you say   **61 late** recently appointed (to serve while Henry is in France)
63 it i.e., my commission   **73 complexion** color.   **74 paper** i.e., white as a sheet.   **76 appearance** (1) sight (2) your faces. (Presumably the traitors kneel at this point.)   **79 quick** alive   **83 worrying you** tearing at your throat.   **86 accord** consent   **87 appurtenants** appurtenances   **89 light** insignificant.   **lightly** readily, casually
90 practices plots

---

12 sits . . . fair the wind blows from a favorable quarter   **15 pow'rs** armed forces   **18 in head** as an army   **22 grows . . . consent** does not act in harmony   **30 galls** i.e., resentment   **31 create** composed
33 office use, function   **34 quittance** requital   **40 Enlarge** set free
43 more advice explaining and apologizing for what happened
44 security overconfidence.   **46 sufferance** being pardoned

To kill us here in Hampton. To the which
This knight, no less for bounty bound to us   92
Than Cambridge is, hath likewise sworn. But oh,
What shall I say to thee, Lord Scroop, thou cruel,
Ingrateful, savage, and inhuman creature?
Thou that didst bear the key of all my counsels,
That knew'st the very bottom of my soul,
That almost mightst have coined me into gold,
Wouldst thou have practiced on me for thy use?   99
May it be possible that foreign hire
Could out of thee extract one spark of evil
That might annoy my finger? 'Tis so strange   102
That though the truth of it stands off as gross   103
As black and white, my eye will scarcely see it.
Treason and murder ever kept together,
As two yoke-devils sworn to either's purpose,   106
Working so grossly in a natural cause   107
That admiration did not whoop at them.   108
But thou, 'gainst all proportion, didst bring in   109
Wonder to wait on treason and on murder;   110
And whatsoever cunning fiend it was
That wrought upon thee so preposterously   112
Hath got the voice in hell for excellence.   113
All other devils that suggest by treasons   114
Do botch and bungle up damnation   115
With patches, colors, and with forms being fetched   116
From glist'ring semblances of piety;   117
But he that tempered thee bade thee stand up,   118
Gave thee no instance why thou shouldst do treason,   119
Unless to dub thee with the name of traitor.   120
If that same demon that hath gulled thee thus
Should with his lion gait walk the whole world,   122
He might return to vasty Tartar back   123
And tell the legions, "I can never win
A soul so easy as that Englishman's."
Oh, how hast thou with jealousy infected   126
The sweetness of affiance! Show men dutiful?   127
Why, so didst thou. Seem they grave and learnèd?
Why, so didst thou. Come they of noble family?
Why, so didst thou. Seem they religious?
Why, so didst thou. Or are they spare in diet,
Free from gross passion or of mirth or anger,   132
Constant in spirit, not swerving with the blood,   133

Garnished and decked in modest complement,   134
Not working with the eye without the ear,   135
And but in purgèd judgment trusting neither?   136
Such and so finely bolted didst thou seem.   137
And thus thy fall hath left a kind of blot   138
To mark the full-fraught man and best endued   139
With some suspicion. I will weep for thee;   140
For this revolt of thine, methinks, is like
Another fall of man.—Their faults are open.   142
Arrest them to the answer of the law;   143
And God acquit them of their practices!

EXETER   I arrest thee of high treason, by the name of
Richard Earl of Cambridge.
I arrest thee of high treason, by the name of Henry Lord
Scroop of Masham.
I arrest thee of high treason, by the name of Thomas
Grey, knight, of Northumberland.

SCROOP
Our purposes God justly hath discovered,   151
And I repent my fault more than my death,
Which I beseech Your Highness to forgive,
Although my body pay the price of it.

CAMBRIDGE
For me, the gold of France did not seduce,
Although I did admit it as a motive   156
The sooner to effect what I intended.   157
But God be thankèd for prevention,
Which I in sufferance heartily will rejoice,   159
Beseeching God and you to pardon me.

GREY
Never did faithful subject more rejoice
At the discovery of most dangerous treason
Than I do at this hour joy o'er myself,
Prevented from a damnèd enterprise.
My fault, but not my body, pardon, sovereign.

KING
God quit you in his mercy! Hear your sentence.   166
You have conspired against our royal person,
Joined with an enemy proclaimed, and from his
    coffers
Received the golden earnest of our death,   169
Wherein you would have sold your king to slaughter,
His princes and his peers to servitude,
His subjects to oppression and contempt,
And his whole kingdom into desolation.
Touching our person seek we no revenge,   174

---

92 **This knight** i.e., Grey   99 **practiced on** plotted against.   **use** profit.
(With play on the meaning "interest derived from usury"; Scroop had
served as Lord Treasurer.)   102 **annoy** injure   103 **stands . . . gross**
appears as obvious   106 **yoke-devils** partners in a diabolical cause
107–8 **Working . . . them** working together so manifestly toward a
purpose suited to their evil natures that they provoked no outcry of
wonder.   109 **proportion** fitness of things   110 **Wonder** astonishment (that Scroop should be a murderer).   **wait on** attend, accompany   112 **wrought** worked.   **preposterously** unnaturally   113 **voice**
vote   114–17 **All . . . piety** All other devils that tempt make at least
some effort to dress damnation up in a plausible semblance of piety
118–20 **But . . . traitor** but the devil that tempted you to treason simply ordered you to stand up an unabashed rebel, and gave you no
specious justification to do treason other than for the sheer sake of
having the name of traitor.   122 **lion gait** (The devil, according to 1
Peter 5:8, strides about the world like a roaring lion, "seeking whom
he may devour.")   123 **vasty** vast.   **Tartar** Tartarus, the hell of classical mythology   126 **jealousy** suspicion   127 **affiance** trust.   **Show**
Appear   132 **or of** either of   133 **swerving with the blood** sinning
through passion

134 **decked . . . complement** wearing the look of modesty   135–6 **Not
. . . neither** trusting neither eye nor ear alone, and not trusting either
one except when refined by wisdom and judgment.   138–40 **And . . .
suspicion** And thus your fall into sin has been such as to cast some
suspicion on even those who seem fully and richly endowed with virtuous qualities.   142 **fall of man** humankind's original disobedience
to God in the Garden of Eden.   **open** apparent, obvious.   143 **to the
answer of** so that they will be answerable to   151 **discovered**
revealed   156 **did . . . motive** i.e., accepted money from France as a
means   157 **The . . . intended** (Cambridge's real motive, barely
hinted at here, was to assist his brother-in-law Edmund Mortimer,
fifth Earl of March, to the throne as the standard-bearer of the Yorkist
claim against the Lancastrian Henry.)   159 **sufferance** my suffering
and patient endurance   166 **quit** (1) pardon (2) requite, punish
169 **golden earnest** advance payment   174 **Touching our person** As
regards my own personal safety

But we our kingdom's safety must so tender, 175
Whose ruin you have sought, that to her laws
We do deliver you. Get you therefore hence,
Poor miserable wretches, to your death,
The taste whereof God of his mercy give
You patience to endure, and true repentance
Of all your dear offenses!—Bear them hence. 181
Exeunt [Cambridge, Scroop, and Grey, guarded].
Now, lords, for France, the enterprise whereof
Shall be to you, as us, like glorious. 183
We doubt not of a fair and lucky war,
Since God so graciously hath brought to light
This dangerous treason lurking in our way
To hinder our beginnings. We doubt not now
But every rub is smoothèd on our way. 188
Then forth, dear countrymen! Let us deliver
Our puissance into the hand of God, 190
Putting it straight in expedition. 191
Cheerly to sea! The signs of war advance! 192
No king of England, if not king of France!
Flourish. [Exeunt.]

❖

[2.3]

Enter Pistol, Nym, Bardolph, Boy, and Hostess.

HOSTESS Prithee, honey-sweet husband, let me bring
thee to Staines. 2
PISTOL No, for my manly heart doth earn. Bardolph, be 3
blithe; Nym, rouse thy vaunting veins; Boy, bristle thy
courage up; for Falstaff he is dead, and we must earn
therefore.
BARDOLPH Would I were with him, wheresome'er he is,
either in heaven or in hell!
HOSTESS Nay, sure he's not in hell. He's in Arthur's 9
bosom, if ever man went to Arthur's bosom. 'A made 10
a finer end, and went away an it had been any 11
christom child. 'A parted ev'n just between twelve 12
and one, ev'n at the turning o'th' tide. For after I saw
him fumble with the sheets, and play with flowers,
and smile upon his finger's end, I knew there was but
one way; for his nose was as sharp as a pen, and 'a 16
babbled of green fields. "How now, Sir John?" quoth I. 17
"What, man? Be o' good cheer." So 'a cried out, "God,
God, God!" three or four times. Now I, to comfort him,
bid him 'a should not think of God; I hoped there was

no need to trouble himself with any such thoughts yet.
So 'a bade me lay more clothes on his feet. I put my
hand into the bed and felt them, and they were as cold
as any stone; then I felt to his knees, and so upward 24
and upward, and all was as cold as any stone. 25
NYM They say he cried out of sack. 26
HOSTESS Ay, that 'a did.
BARDOLPH And of women.
HOSTESS Nay, that 'a did not.
BOY Yes, that 'a did, and said they were devils incarnate.
HOSTESS 'A could never abide carnation; 'twas a color
he never liked.
BOY 'A said once the devil would have him about
women.
HOSTESS 'A did in some sort, indeed, handle women; 36
but then he was rheumatic, and talked of the Whore of 37
Babylon.
BOY Do you not remember, 'a saw a flea stick upon
Bardolph's nose, and 'a said it was a black soul
burning in hell?
BARDOLPH Well, the fuel is gone that maintained that 42
fire. That's all the riches I got in his service.
NYM Shall we shog? The King will be gone from South- 44
ampton.
PISTOL
Come, let's away.—My love, give me thy lips.
[He kisses the Hostess.]
Look to my chattels and my movables. 47
Let senses rule. The word is "Pitch and pay." 48
Trust none,
For oaths are straws, men's faiths are wafer cakes, 50
And Holdfast is the only dog, my duck. 51
Therefore, *caveto* be thy counselor. 52
Go, clear thy crystals.—Yokefellows in arms, 53
Let us to France, like horseleeches, my boys,
To suck, to suck, the very blood to suck!
BOY And that's but unwholesome food, they say.
PISTOL Touch her soft mouth, and march.
BARDOLPH Farewell, hostess. *[Kissing her.]*
NYM I cannot kiss, that is the humor of it; but adieu.
PISTOL
Let huswifery appear. Keep close, I thee command. 60
HOSTESS Farewell! Adieu! *Exeunt [separately].*

❖

175 **tender** regard, hold dear   181 **dear** grievous, dire   183 **like** alike, equally   188 **But** but that.   **rub** obstacle. (A bowling term.) 190 **puissance** armed might   191 **straight in expedition** immediately in action.   192 **The signs . . . advance!** Lift high our banners!
2.3. London. A street.
2 **Staines** town on the road from London to Southampton.   3 **earn** grieve. (But in line 5 there may also be a play on the sense of "find other employment," since Pistol and the others are now on their own.)   9–10 **Arthur's bosom** (Malapropism for "Abraham's bosom"; see Luke 16:22.)   10 **'A** He   11 **an** as if   12 **christom** (Mistress Quickly means "new christened." A *chrisom* is a white robe put on a child at baptism to betoken innocence. Christenings were performed soon after birth because of the high rate of infant mortality.)   16–17 **'a babbled of green fields** (This line contains Theobald's famous emendation. The Folio has "and a Table of greene fields." Mistress Quickly seems unaware that Falstaff was reciting the Twenty-third Psalm.)

24–5 **upward . . . stone** (The Hostess seems unaware of the sexual implications of her speech. *Stone* can mean "testicle.")   26 **of sack** against sack (a Spanish wine).   36 **handle** discuss. (Though an unintended literal sense is also comically present.)   37 **rheumatic** feverish, or perhaps an error for "lunatic." (Because "Rome" was pronounced "room," *rheumatic* also prepares for the allusion to the Whore of Babylon, i.e., the Church of Rome. See also Revelation 17:4–5.)   42 **fuel** i.e., liquor, supplied by Falstaff, that has given Bardolph his red face   44 **shog** be off. 47 **chattels . . . movables** personal property.   48 **Let . . . pay** i.e., Keep your eyes and ears open, and let your motto as hostess be "cash down." 50 **wafer cakes** i.e., easily broken   51 **Holdfast . . . dog** i.e., a large clamp or *holdfast* is best at holding things tight, like a tenacious dog. (Compare the proverb, "Brag is a good dog, but Holdfast is better.") Mistress Quickly is bidden to keep a tight hold on things.   52 **caveto** beware. (The correct imperative plural of the Latin is *cavete*.)   53 **clear thy crystals** wipe your eyes.   **Yokefellows** Companions   60 **Let . . . close** i.e., Be a thrifty housekeeper and stay at home

2.4

Flourish. Enter the French King, the Dauphin, the Dukes of Berri and Brittany, [the Constable, and others].

FRENCH KING
Thus comes the English with full power upon us,
And more than carefully it us concerns
To answer royally in our defenses.
Therefore the Dukes of Berri and of Brittany,
Of Brabant and of Orleans, shall make forth,   5
And you, Prince Dauphin, with all swift dispatch,
To line and new-repair our towns of war   7
With men of courage and with means defendant;   8
For England his approaches makes as fierce   9
As waters to the sucking of a gulf.   10
It fits us then to be as provident
As fear may teach us, out of late examples   12
Left by the fatal and neglected English   13
Upon our fields.
DAUPHIN   My most redoubted father,   14
It is most meet we arm us 'gainst the foe;   15
For peace itself should not so dull a kingdom,
Though war nor no known quarrel were in question,
But that defenses, musters, preparations,
Should be maintained, assembled, and collected
As were a war in expectation.   20
Therefore, I say 'tis meet we all go forth
To view the sick and feeble parts of France.
And let us do it with no show of fear—
No, with no more than if we heard that England
Were busied with a Whitsun morris dance.   25
For, my good liege, she is so idly kinged,   26
Her scepter so fantastically borne
By a vain, giddy, shallow, humorous youth,   28
That fear attends her not.
CONSTABLE   Oh, peace, Prince Dauphin!
You are too much mistaken in this king.
Question Your Grace the late ambassadors,
With what great state he heard their embassy,   32
How well supplied with noble counselors,
How modest in exception, and withal   34
How terrible in constant resolution,   35
And you shall find his vanities forespent   36
Were but the outside of the Roman Brutus,   37
Covering discretion with a coat of folly,
As gardeners do with ordure hide those roots   39

That shall first spring and be most delicate.
DAUPHIN
Well, 'tis not so, my Lord High Constable;
But though we think it so, it is no matter.
In cases of defense 'tis best to weigh
The enemy more mighty than he seems.
So the proportions of defense are filled,   45
Which of a weak and niggardly projection   46
Doth, like a miser, spoil his coat with scanting
A little cloth.
FRENCH KING   Think we King Harry strong;
And, princes, look you strongly arm to meet him.   49
The kindred of him hath been fleshed upon us;   50
And he is bred out of that bloody strain
That haunted us in our familiar paths.
Witness our too-much-memorable shame
When Crécy battle fatally was struck,   54
And all our princes captived by the hand
Of that black name, Edward, Black Prince of Wales;
Whiles that his mountain sire, on mountain standing,   57
Up in the air, crowned with the golden sun,
Saw his heroical seed and smiled to see him   59
Mangle the work of nature and deface   60
The patterns that by God and by French fathers   61
Had twenty years been made. This is a stem   62
Of that victorious stock; and let us fear
The native mightiness and fate of him.   64

Enter a Messenger.

MESSENGER
Ambassadors from Harry King of England
Do crave admittance to Your Majesty.
FRENCH KING
We'll give them present audience. Go and bring them.
            [Exit Messenger.]
You see this chase is hotly followed, friends.
DAUPHIN
Turn head and stop pursuit; for coward dogs   69
Most spend their mouths when what they seem to
    threaten   70
Runs far before them. Good my sovereign,
Take up the English short, and let them know
Of what a monarchy you are the head.
Self-love, my liege, is not so vile a sin
As self-neglecting.

Enter Exeter [and others].

FRENCH KING   From our brother of England?   75

2.4. Location: France. The royal court.
5 make forth set forth   **7 line** reinforce   **8 defendant** defensive
9 England the King of England   **10 gulf** whirlpool.   **12 late** recent
13 fatal and neglected fatally underestimated   **14 redoubted** reverenced   **15 meet** appropriate   **20 As were** as if there were   **25 Whitsun morris dance** folk dance often performed during Whitsuntide, in early summer, by persons in fancy costumes and decked with bells.
26 idly frivolously   **28 humorous** capricious   **32 state** dignity
34 exception making objections.   **withal** in addition   **35 terrible** awesome, terrifying   **36 vanities forespent** follies used up and now a thing of the past   **37 Brutus** i.e., the elder Brutus, Lucius Junius Brutus, who pretended to be stupid (*brutus*) as a ruse to allay the suspicions of the tyrant Tarquin until the time for overthrow was ripe
39 ordure manure, mulch

45 So . . . filled In that way an adequate and full defense is provided
46 Which . . . projection which defense, if designed on too small and miserly a scale   **49 look** be sure   **50 kindred** i.e., his great-grandfather Edward III and great-uncle Edward the Black Prince.   **fleshed** initiated in the shedding of blood, with foretaste of further success
54 Crécy French defeat in 1346.   **struck** waged   **57 mountain sire** i.e., Edward III, born in mountainous Wales, and of sturdy proportions   **59–62 Saw . . . made** Beheld his heroical son (the Black Prince) and smiled to see him mangle Nature's handiwork in the shape of young Frenchmen, whom, some twenty or so years earlier, God and their French fathers had created and begotten.   **64 fate** what he is destined to do   **69 Turn . . . pursuit** Turn and face the pursuing hounds. (Hunting terms.)   **70 Most . . . mouths** bay the loudest
75 brother fellow monarch

EXETER
From him, and thus he greets Your Majesty:
He wills you, in the name of God Almighty,
That you divest yourself and lay apart　　　　　　　78
The borrowed glories that by gift of heaven,
By law of nature and of nations, 'longs　　　　　　　80
To him and to his heirs, namely, the crown
And all wide-strechèd honors that pertain　　　　　82
By custom and the ordinance of times　　　　　　　83
Unto the crown of France. That you may know
'Tis no sinister nor no awkward claim,　　　　　　　85
Picked from the wormholes of long-vanished days,
Nor from the dust of old oblivion raked,
He sends you this most memorable line,　　　　　　88
　　　　　　　　　　　　[*giving a paper*]
In every branch truly demonstrative,
Willing you overlook this pedigree.　　　　　　　　90
And when you find him evenly derived　　　　　　91
From his most famed of famous ancestors,
Edward the Third, he bids you then resign
Your crown and kingdom, indirectly held　　　　　94
From him the native and true challenger.　　　　　95

FRENCH KING　Or else what follows?

EXETER
Bloody constraint; for if you hide the crown　　　97
Even in your hearts, there will he rake for it.
Therefore in fierce tempest is he coming,
In thunder and in earthquake, like a Jove,
That if requiring fail, he will compel;　　　　　　101
And bids you, in the bowels of the Lord,　　　　　102
Deliver up the crown, and to take mercy
On the poor souls for whom this hungry war
Opens his vasty jaws, and on your head　　　　　105
Turning the widows' tears, the orphans' cries,　　106
The dead men's blood, the privèd maidens' groans,　107
For husbands, fathers, and betrothèd lovers
That shall be swallowed in this controversy.
This is his claim, his threat'ning, and my message—
Unless the Dauphin be in presence here,
To whom expressly I bring greeting too.

FRENCH KING
For us, we will consider of this further.
Tomorrow shall you bear our full intent
Back to our brother of England.

DAUPHIN　　　　　　　　　　For the Dauphin,
I stand here for him. What to him from England?

EXETER
Scorn and defiance, slight regard, contempt,
And anything that may not misbecome　　　　　　118
The mighty sender, doth he prize you at.　　　　　119

Thus says my king, and if your father's Highness
Do not, in grant of all demands at large,　　　　　121
Sweeten the bitter mock you sent His Majesty,
He'll call you to so hot an answer of it　　　　　　123
That caves and womby vaultages of France　　　124
Shall chide your trespass and return your mock
In second accent of his ordinance.　　　　　　　126

DAUPHIN
Say if my father render fair return　　　　　　　127
It is against my will, for I desire
Nothing but odds with England. To that end,　　129
As matching to his youth and vanity,
I did present him with the Paris balls.　　　　　　131

EXETER
He'll make your Paris Louvre shake for it,　　　　132
Were it the mistress court of mighty Europe.
And be assured, you'll find a diff'rence,
As we his subjects have in wonder found,
Between the promise of his greener days　　　　136
And these his masters now. Now he weighs time
Even to the utmost grain. That you shall read　　138
In your own losses, if he stay in France.

FRENCH KING
Tomorrow shall you know our mind at full.　　　140
　　　　　　　　　　　　　　　　Flourish.

EXETER
Dispatch us with all speed, lest that our king
Come here himself to question our delay;
For he is footed in this land already.

FRENCH KING
You shall be soon dispatched with fair conditions.
A night is but small breath and little pause
To answer matters of this consequence.
　　　　　　　　　　　　　　Flourish. Exeunt.

❧

[3.0]

Enter Chorus.

CHORUS
Thus with imagined wing our swift scene flies　　1
In motion of no less celerity
Than that of thought. Suppose that you have seen
The well-appointed King at Dover pier　　　　　4
Embark his royalty, and his brave fleet　　　　　5
With silken streamers the young Phoebus fanning.　6
Play with your fancies, and in them behold

---

78 apart aside　**80 'longs** belongs　**82 wide-strechèd** stretching far and wide　**83 ordinance of times** decrees of tradition　**85 sinister** illegitimate.　**awkward** oblique　**88 line** pedigree　**90 Willing you overlook** desiring that you look over　**91 evenly** directly　**94 indirectly** wrongfully　**95 native** natural (by birthright).　**challenger** claimant.　**97 constraint** coercion, compulsion　**101 requiring** requesting　**102 in . . . Lord** in the name of God's compassion. (See Philippians 1:8.)　**105–6 and on . . . tears** and who, pour souls, are pouring on your head their widows' tears　**107 privèd** deprived (by loss of loved ones)　**118 misbecome** be inappropriate for　**119 prize** value, appraise

121 in grant of in assenting to.　**at large** in full　**123 of it** for it
124 womby vaultages hollow recesses　**126 In . . . ordinance** in loud echoing of the sound of King Henry's ordnance (cannon).　**127 fair return** courteous reply　**129 odds** (1) strife (2) betting odds, as in tennis　**131 Paris balls** tennis balls.　**132 Louvre** the French royal palace
136 greener younger　**138 grain** grain of sand (in an hourglass).
That . . . read i.e., You will see this new seriousness manifested
140.1 Flourish (This trumpet call is sounded as the French King arises from his throne, thereby dismissing the embassy, but Exeter boldly insists on speaking further.)
3.0. Chorus.
1 imagined wing wings of imagination　**4 well-appointed** well-equipped.　**Dover** (Seemingly an error for Hampton, i.e., Southampton.)　**5 brave** handsome　**6 the . . . fanning** i.e., fluttering in the rising sun.

Upon the hempen tackle shipboys climbing;   8
Hear the shrill whistle, which doth order give
To sounds confused; behold the threaden sails,   10
Borne with th'invisible and creeping wind,
Draw the huge bottoms through the furrowed sea,   12
Breasting the lofty surge. Oh, do but think   13
You stand upon the rivage and behold   14
A city on th'inconstant billows dancing;
For so appears this fleet majestical,
Holding due course to Harfleur. Follow, follow!
Grapple your minds to sternage of this navy,   18
And leave your England as dead midnight still,
Guarded with grandsires, babies, and old women,
Either past or not arrived to pith and puissance;   21
For who is he whose chin is but enriched
With one appearing hair that will not follow
These culled and choice-drawn cavaliers to France?   24
Work, work your thoughts, and therein see a siege;
Behold the ordnance on their carriages,
With fatal mouths gaping on girded Harfleur.   27
Suppose th'ambassador from the French comes back,
Tells Harry that the King doth offer him
Katharine his daughter, and with her, to dowry,
Some petty and unprofitable dukedoms.
The offer likes not; and the nimble gunner   32
With linstock now the devilish cannon touches,   33
           Alarum, and chambers go off.
And down goes all before them. Still be kind,
And eke out our performance with your mind.
           Exit.

❖

[3.1]

Enter the King, Exeter, Bedford, and Gloucester.
Alarum, [with soldiers carrying] scaling ladders at
Harfleur.

KING
Once more unto the breach, dear friends, once more,
Or close the wall up with our English dead!
In peace there's nothing so becomes a man
As modest stillness and humility.
But when the blast of war blows in our ears,
Then imitate the action of the tiger:
Stiffen the sinews, conjure up the blood,
Disguise fair nature with hard-favored rage.   8
Then lend the eye a terrible aspect: 9
Let it pry through the portage of the head   10
Like the brass cannon; let the brow o'erwhelm it   11

As fearfully as doth a gallèd rock   12
O'erhang and jutty his confounded base,   13
Swilled with the wild and wasteful ocean.   14
Now set the teeth and stretch the nostril wide,
Hold hard the breath, and bend up every spirit
To his full height. On, on, you noblest English,
Whose blood is fet from fathers of war-proof,   18
Fathers that, like so many Alexanders,   19
Have in these parts from morn till even fought,   20
And sheathed their swords for lack of argument.   21
Dishonor not your mothers; now attest
That those whom you called fathers did beget you.
Be copy now to men of grosser blood,   24
And teach them how to war. And you, good yeomen,
Whose limbs were made in England, show us here
The mettle of your pasture. Let us swear   27
That you are worth your breeding, which I doubt not,
For there is none of you so mean and base
That hath not noble luster in your eyes.
I see you stand like greyhounds in the slips,   31
Straining upon the start. The game's afoot.   32
Follow your spirit, and upon this charge   33
Cry, "God for Harry! England and Saint George!"   34
        Alarum, and chambers go off. [*Exeunt.*]

❖

[3.2]

Enter Nym, Bardolph, Pistol, and Boy.

BARDOLPH   On, on, on, on, on! To the breach, to the
breach!
NYM   Pray thee, Corporal, stay. The knocks are too hot,
and for mine own part I have not a case of lives. The   4
humor of it is too hot, that is the very plainsong of it.   5
PISTOL
"The plainsong" is most just; for humors do abound.
Knocks go and come; God's vassals drop and die;   7
[*He sings*] "And sword and shield
     In bloody field
   Doth win immortal fame."
BOY   Would I were in an alehouse in London! I would
give all my fame for a pot of ale and safety.
PISTOL   And I:
[*He sings*] "If wishes would prevail with me,   14
   My purpose should not fail with me,
     But thither would I hie."   16

---

8 **hempen** rope   10 **threaden** stitched   12 **bottoms** hulls of ships
13 **surge** swell of the sea.   14 **rivage** shore   18 **Grapple** Attach, hook.
to sternage to the sterns   21 **pith** strength   24 **choice-drawn** carefully
selected   27 **fatal** deadly.   **girded** besieged   32 **likes** pleases
33 **linstock** staff holding a gunner's match.   33.1 ***Alarum*** Call to arms.
chambers small cannon (fired off backstage, or "within")
3.1. Location: France. Before Harfleur.
0.2 *scaling ladders* (Presumably these are set up against the facade
of the tiring-house, upstage, which is perceived to be the walls of
Harfleur.)   8 **hard-favored** unsightly, ugly   9 **terrible aspect** terrifying appearance   10 **portage** portholes, eyes   11 **o'erwhelm** project
over

12 **fearfully** frighteningly.   **gallèd** washed away, eroded   13 **O'er-**
hang . . . base hang and project over its worn-away base   14 **Swilled**
washed.   **wasteful** destructive   18 **fet** fetched, derived.   **of war-**
proof tested in war   19 **Alexanders** (Alexander grieved that there
were no new worlds for him to conquer.)   20 **even** evening
21 **argument** opposition.   24 **copy** models   27 **mettle . . . pasture**
quality of your breeding. (Literally, *pasture* means "feeding.")
31 **slips** leashes   32 **The game's afoot** The quarry is out of its lair and
running.   33 **Follow your spirit** i.e., Obey the impulse of your vital
powers   34 **Saint George** patron saint of England.
3.2. Location: Before Harfleur, as in the previous scene; the action is
essentially continuous.
4 **case** set   5 **plainsong** simple melody, simple truth   7 **God's vas-**
sals i.e., mortal men   14 **with me** in my case   16 **hie** hasten.

BOY [*sings*]
  "As duly, but not as truly,
    As bird doth sing on bough."

Enter Fluellen.

FLUELLEN   Up to the breach, you dogs! Avaunt, you cul- 19
lions!   [*Driving them forward.*] 20

PISTOL
  Be merciful, great duke, to men of mold. 21
  Abate thy rage, abate thy manly rage,
  Abate thy rage, great duke!
  Good bawcock, bate thy rage! Use lenity, sweet chuck! 24

NYM   These be good humors! Your Honor runs bad 25
humors.   *Exit* [*with all but Boy*]. 26

BOY   As young as I am, I have observed these three
swashers. I am boy to them all three, but all they three, 28
though they would serve me, could not be man to me; 29
for indeed three such antics do not amount to a man. 30
For Bardolph, he is white-livered and red-faced, by the 31
means whereof 'a faces it out but fights not. For Pistol, 32
he hath a killing tongue and a quiet sword, by the
means whereof 'a breaks words and keeps whole 34
weapons. For Nym, he hath heard that men of few
words are the best men, and therefore he scorns to say
his prayers, lest 'a should be thought a coward; but
his few bad words are matched with as few good
deeds, for 'a never broke any man's head but his own,
and that was against a post when he was drunk. They
will steal anything and call it purchase. Bardolph 41
stole a lute case, bore it twelve leagues, and sold it for 42
three halfpence. Nym and Bardolph are sworn brothers in filching, and in Calais they stole a fire shovel. I
knew by that piece of service the men would carry 45
coals. They would have me as familiar with men's 46
pockets as their gloves or their handkerchiefs, which
makes much against my manhood, if I should take 48
from another's pocket to put into mine, for it is plain
pocketing up of wrongs. I must leave them and seek 50
some better service. Their villainy goes against my 51
weak stomach, and therefore I must cast it up.   *Exit.* 52

Enter Gower [*and Fluellen, meeting*].

GOWER   Captain Fluellen, you must come presently to
the mines. The Duke of Gloucester would speak with 54
you.

FLUELLEN   To the mines? Tell you the Duke it is not so
good to come to the mines; for look you, the mines is
not according to the disciplines of the war. The 58
concavities of it is not sufficient. For look you, th'athver- 59
sary, you may discuss unto the Duke, look you, 60
is digt himself four yard under the countermines. By 61
Cheshu, I think 'a will plow up all, if there is not better 62
directions.

GOWER   The Duke of Gloucester, to whom the order of
the siege is given, is altogether directed by an Irish-
man, a very valiant gentleman, i'faith.

FLUELLEN   It is Captain Macmorris, is it not?

GOWER   I think it be.

FLUELLEN   By Cheshu, he is an ass, as in the world! I
will verify as much in his beard. He has no more di- 70
rections in the true disciplines of the wars, look you,
of the Roman disciplines, than is a puppy dog.

Enter Macmorris and Captain Jamy.

GOWER   Here 'a comes, and the Scots captain, Captain
Jamy, with him.

FLUELLEN   Captain Jamy is a marvelous falorous gentleman, that is certain, and of great expedition and 76
knowledge in th'aunchient wars, upon my particular
knowledge of his directions. By Cheshu, he will
maintain his argument as well as any military man in
the world, in the disciplines of the pristine wars of the 80
Romans.

JAMY   I say gud day, Captain Fluellen.

FLUELLEN   Good e'en to Your Worship, good Captain 83
James.

GOWER   How now, Captain Macmorris, have you quit
the mines? Have the pioneers given o'er? 86

MACMORRIS   By Chrish, la, 'tish ill done! The work ish
give over, the trompet sound the retreat. By my hand
I swear, and my father's soul, the work ish ill done; it
ish give over. I would have blowed up the town, so
Chrish save me, la, in an hour. Oh, 'tish ill done, 'tish
ill done! By my hand, 'tish ill done!

FLUELLEN   Captain Macmorris, I beseech you now, will
you voutsafe me, look you, a few disputations with 94
you, as partly touching or concerning the disciplines
of the war, the Roman wars, in the way of argument,

---

19 Avaunt Begone   **19–20 cullions** rascals. (The original meaning
was "testicles.")   **21 duke** leader, commander. (Latin *dux*.) A flattering title for a captain.   **men of mold** mere mortals.   **24 bawcock**
fine fellow. (French *beau coq*.)   **chuck** (A term of endearment.)
25–6 Your . . . humors i.e., (1) You are behaving very idiosyncratically,
Your Honor (2) Your fury is out of control. (Addressed to Fluellen,
who is doubtless threatening or beating Nym, Bardolph, and Pistol to
make them go forward.)   **28 swashers** swashbucklers.   **29 man**
(1) servant (2) a manly, brave person   **30 antics** buffoons, zanies
31 For As for. (Also in lines 32 and 35.)   **white-livered** i.e., cowardly.
(In extreme fear, the blood was thought to sink below the liver, leaving it bloodless.)   **32 'a faces it out** he has the martial-looking face
for it, puts on a brave front   **34 breaks words** (1) misuses language
and fails to keep his word (2) uses words as weapons   **41 purchase**
(1) something paid for (2) thieves' cant for stolen goods.   **42 leagues**
(about three miles each)   **45–6 carry coals** (1) do dirty, hard work,
such as hauling coal (2) put up with insults   **48 makes** goes
50 pocketing . . . wrongs (1) putting up with insults (2) receiving
stolen goods.   **51–2 goes . . . stomach** (1) goes against my inclination
(2) makes me sick   **52 cast it up** (1) cast it aside (2) vomit it.   **s.d.**
Exit (A scene break may occur here, though it is not marked as such
in most editions. Possibly Fluellen did not leave the stage at line 26.)

54 mines tunnels dug under the walls of the beseiged city to plant
explosives.   **58 disciplines of the war** science of warfare (about
which there were many books from Greek and Roman times down to
the Renaissance; Fluellen's humor involves an obsession with this
study and a preference for traditional methods).   **59 concavities** i.e.,
depth   **59–60 athversary** (Fluellen's pronunciation of *adversary*.)
60 discuss explain   **61 is digt . . . countermines** has dug himself
countermines four yards beneath our mines.   **62 Cheshu** Jesu, Jesus.
plow blow. (In Fluellen's Welsh dialect, *p* is regularly substituted for *b*
and *f* for *v*.)   **70 in his beard** i.e., to his face.   **76 expedition** readiness of argument, quickness of wit   **80 pristine** ancient   **83 Good**
e'en Good afternoon or evening   **86 pioneers** sappers, diggers
94 voutsafe vouchsafe, permit

look you, and friendly communication—partly to satisfy my opinion, and partly for the satisfaction, look you, of my mind, as touching the direction of the military discipline, that is the point.

JAMY   It sall be vary gud, gud feith, gud captens bath, 101
and I sall quite you with gud leve, as I may pick 102
occasion. That sall I, marry. 103

MACMORRIS   It is no time to discourse, so Chrish save me! The day is hot, and the weather, and the wars, and the King, and the dukes. It is no time to discourse. The town is beseeched, and the trumpet call us to the 107
breach, and we talk, and, be Chrish, do nothing. 'Tis 108
shame for us all. So God sa' me, 'tis shame to stand still, it is shame, by my hand! And there is throats to be cut, and works to be done, and there ish nothing done, so Chrish sa' me, la! 112

JAMY   By the Mess, ere theise eyes of mine take 113
themselves to slomber, ay'll de gud service, or I'll lig i'th' 114
grund for it, ay, or go to death! And I'll pay't as valorously as I may, that sall I suerly do, that is the breff and the long. Marry, I wad full fain heard some 117
question 'tween you twae. 118

FLUELLEN   Captain Macmorris, I think, look you, under your correction, there is not many of your nation—

MACMORRIS   Of my nation? What ish my nation? Ish a 121
villain, and a bastard, and a knave, and a rascal? What 122
ish my nation? Who talks of my nation?

FLUELLEN   Look you, if you take the matter otherwise than is meant, Captain Macmorris, peradventure I shall think you do not use me with that affability as in discretion you ought to use me, look you, being as good a man as yourself, both in the disciplines of war and in the derivation of my birth, and in other particularities.

MACMORRIS   I do not know you so good a man as myself. So Chrish save me, I will cut off your head!

GOWER   Gentlemen both, you will mistake each other. 133

JAMY   Ah, that's a foul fault!   *A parley [is sounded].* 134

GOWER   The town sounds a parley.

FLUELLEN   Captain Macmorris, when there is more better opportunity to be required, look you, I will be so 137
bold as to tell you I know the disciplines of war; and there is an end.   *Exit [with others].*

❧

[3.3]

[Enter the Governor and some citizens on the walls.] Enter the King [Henry] and all his train before the gates.

KING
How yet resolves the Governor of the town?
This is the latest parle we will admit.   2
Therefore to our best mercy give yourselves,
Or, like to men proud of destruction,   4
Defy us to our worst; for as I am a soldier,
A name that in my thoughts becomes me best,
If I begin the batt'ry once again   7
I will not leave the half-achievèd Harfleur
Till in her ashes she lie buried.
The gates of mercy shall be all shut up,
And the fleshed soldier, rough and hard of heart,   11
In liberty of bloody hand shall range   12
With conscience wide as hell, mowing like grass   13
Your fresh fair virgins and your flow'ring infants.
What is it then to me if impious War,
Arrayed in flames like to the prince of fiends,
Do with his smirched complexion all fell feats   17
Enlinked to waste and desolation?
What is't to me, when you yourselves are cause,
If your pure maidens fall into the hand
Of hot and forcing violation?
What rein can hold licentious Wickedness
When down the hill he holds his fierce career?   23
We may as bootless spend our vain command   24
Upon th'enragèd soldiers in their spoil
As send precepts to the leviathan   26
To come ashore. Therefore, you men of Harfleur,
Take pity of your town and of your people
Whiles yet my soldiers are in my command,
Whiles yet the cool and temperate wind of grace   30
O'erblows the filthy and contagious clouds   31
Of heady murder, spoil, and villainy.   32
If not, why, in a moment look to see   33
The blind and bloody soldier with foul hand   34
Defile the locks of your shrill-shrieking daughters;
Your fathers taken by the silver beards,
And their most reverend heads dashed to the walls;
Your naked infants spitted upon pikes,

---

101 **bath** both   102 **quite** requite, answer.   **with gud leve** with good leave, with your kind permission   103 **marry** indeed. (Originally, "by the Virgin Mary.")   107 **beseeched** besieged   108 **be** by   112 **Chrish sa' me** Christ save me   113 **Mess** Mass   114 **ay'll de** I'll do.   **lig** lie   117 **breff** brief.   **wad full fain heard** would very willingly have heard   118 **question** discussion   121 **What ish** i.e., What about   121–2 **Ish a villain** i.e., Is my nation a villain (etc.)?, or Macmorris may be making a declarative statement, saying that anyone who says anything against my nation is a villain, etc.   133 **will mistake** (Two possible meanings: [1] insist on misunderstanding [2] are going to misunderstand.)   134 **s.d. parley** trumpet summons to a negotiation   137 **required** found

3.3. **Location: Before the gates of Harfleur, as in the previous scene. The action is essentially continuous, as it is usually in battle sequences; possibly some of the captains in 3.2 do not need to exit here. The gates are represented by the tiring-house facade. Those who appear** *on the walls* **are seen in the gallery backstage.**
2 **latest parle** last parley   4 **like . . . destruction** i.e., like men elated at the prospect of slaughter and glorying in destruction   7 **batt'ry** attack   11 **fleshed** made fierce with the taste of blood   12–13 **In liberty . . . as hell** will range with free license to shed blood and with a conscience wide and loose enough to sanction anything that hell itself would justify   17 **smirched** blackened, covered with grime.   **fell** savage   23 **career** gallop.   24 **bootless** fruitlessly   26 **precepts** written summons.   **leviathan** whale   30 **grace** mercy   31 **O'er blows** blows away. (Contagion was thought to reside in clouds and mists.)   32 **heady** violent; headstrong   33 **look** expect   34 **blind** i.e., blinded with lust and rage

Whiles the mad mothers with their howls confused
Do break the clouds, as did the wives of Jewry   40
At Herod's bloody-hunting slaughtermen.   41
What say you? Will you yield, and this avoid,
Or, guilty in defense, be thus destroyed?   43

GOVERNOR
Our expectation hath this day an end.
The Dauphin, whom of succors we entreated,   45
Returns us that his powers are yet not ready   46
To raise so great a siege. Therefore, great King,
We yield our town and lives to thy soft mercy.
Enter our gates, dispose of us and ours,
For we no longer are defensible.

KING
Open your gates.   [*Exit Governor.*]
          Come, uncle Exeter,
Go you and enter Harfleur; there remain,
And fortify it strongly 'gainst the French.
Use mercy to them all. For us, dear uncle,   54
The winter coming on and sickness growing
Upon our soldiers, we will retire to Calais.
Tonight in Harfleur will we be your guest;
Tomorrow for the march are we addressed.   58

                      Flourish, and enter the town.

                              ❖

[3.4]

Enter Katharine and [Alice,] an old gentlewoman.

KATHARINE   Alice, tu as été en Angleterre, et tu bien   1
parles le langage.
ALICE   Un peu, madame.
KATHARINE   Je te prie, m'enseignez; il faut que
j'apprenne à parler. Comment appelez-vous la main
en anglais?
ALICE   La main? Elle est appelée de hand.
KATHARINE   De hand. Et les doigts?
ALICE   Les doigts? Ma foi, j'oublie les doigts; mais je me
souviendrai. Les doigts? Je pense qu'ils sont appelés   10
de fingres; oui, de fingres.
KATHARINE   La main, de hand; les doigts, de fingres. Je
pense que je suis le bon écolier; j'ai gagné deux
mots d'anglais vîtement. Comment appelez-vous les
ongles?

40 Jewry Judaea   **41 Herod's . . . slaughtermen** (For the account of
Herod's slaughter of the innocent children in his attempt to murder
the infant Jesus, see Matthew 2:16–18.)   **43 in defense** i.e., by not surrendering   **45 of succors** for help   **46 Returns** replies to   **54 For** As
for   **58 addressed** prepared.
3.4. Location: The French court at Rouen.

Translation:
KATHARINE   Alice, you have been in England and speak the language
well.
ALICE   A little, my lady.
KATHARINE I pray you teach me; I have to learn to speak it. What do
you call *la main* in English?
ALICE   *La main?* It is called de hand.
KATHARINE   De hand. And *les doigts?*
ALICE   *Les doigts?* Dear me, I forget *les doigts;* but I shall remember. I
think that they are called de fingres; yes, de fingres.
KATHARINE   *La main,* de hand; *les doigts,* de fingres. I think that I am a
clever scholar; I have learned two English words in no time. What
do you call *les ongles?*

ALICE   Les ongles? Nous les appelons de nailes.
KATHARINE   De nailes. Écoutez, dites-moi si je parle
bien: de hand, de fingres, et de nailes.
ALICE   C'est bien dit, madame; il est fort bon anglais.
KATHARINE   Dites-moi l'anglais pour le bras.   20
ALICE   De arm, madame.
KATHARINE   Et le coude?
ALICE   D' elbow.
KATHARINE   D' elbow. Je m'en fais la répétition de tous
les mots que vous m'avez appris dès à présent.
ALICE   Il est trop difficile, madame, comme je pense.
KATHARINE   Excusez-moi, Alice; écoutez: d' hand, de
fingre, de nailes, d' arma, de bilbow.
ALICE   D' elbow, madame.
KATHARINE   Oh, Seigneur Dieu, je m'en oublie! D' elbow.   30
Comment appelez-vous le col?
ALICE   De nick, madame.
KATHARINE   De nick. Et le menton?
ALICE   De chin.
KATHARINE   De sin. Le col, de nick; le menton, de sin.
ALICE   Oui. Sauf votre honneur, en vérité, vous pro-
noncez les mots aussi droit que les natifs d'Angleterre.
KATHARINE   Je ne doute point d'apprendre, par la grâce
de Dieu, et en peu de temps.
ALICE   N'avez-vous pas déjà oublié ce que je vous ai   40
enseigné?
KATHARINE   Non, je réciterai à vous promptement: d'
hand, de fingre, de mailes—
ALICE   De nailes, madame.
KATHARINE   De nailes, de arm, de ilbow.
ALICE   Sauf votre honneur, d' elbow.
KATHARINE   Ainsi dis-je; d' elbow, de nick, et de sin.
Comment appelez-vous le pied et la robe?

ALICE   *Les ongles?* We call them de nailes.
KATHARINE   De nailes. Listen; tell me whether or not I speak correctly:
de hand, de fingres, and de nailes.
ALICE   That is correct, my lady; it is very good English.
KATHARINE   Tell me the English for *le bras.*
ALICE   De arm, my lady.
KATHARINE   And *le coude?*
ALICE   D' elbow.
KATHARINE   D' elbow. I am going to repeat all the words you have
taught me so far.
ALICE   It is too hard, my lady, I fear.
KATHARINE   Pardon me, Alice; listen: d' hand, de fingre, de nailes, d'
arma, de bilbow.
ALICE   D' elbow, my lady.
KATHARINE   Oh, Lord, I can't remember! D' elbow. What do you call *le
col?*
ALICE   De nick, my lady.
KATHARINE   De nick. And *le menton?*
ALICE   De chin.
KATHARINE   De sin. *Le col,* de nick; *le menton,* de sin.
ALICE   Yes. If I may say so, really you pronounce the words just as cor-
rectly as native Englishmen.
KATHARINE   I have no doubt that I shall learn, with God's help, in a
very short time.
ALICE   Haven't you already forgotten what I have taught you?
KATHARINE   No. I shall recite to you at once: d' hand, de fingre, de
mailes—
ALICE   De nailes, my lady.
KATHARINE   De nailes, de arm, de ilbow.
ALICE   By your leave, d' elbow.
KATHARINE   That's what I said; d' elbow, de nick, and de sin. What do
you call *le pied* and *la robe?*

ALICE   Le foot, madame, et le count.

KATHARINE   Le foot et le count! Oh, Seigneur Dieu! Ils 50
sont les mots de son mauvais, corruptible, gros, et
impudique, et non pour les dames d'honneur d'user.
Je ne voudrais prononcer ces mots devant les seig-
neurs de France pour tout le monde. Foh! Le foot et le
count! Néanmoins, je réciterai une autre fois ma leçon
ensemble: d' hand, de fingre, de nailes, de arm,
d' elbow, de nick, de sin, de foot, le count.

ALICE   Excellent, madame!

KATHARINE   C'est assez pour une fois. Allons-nous à
dîner.   *Exit* [*with Alice*].

[3.5]

Enter the King of France, the Dauphin, [the Duke
of Brittany,] the Constable of France, and others.

FRENCH KING
'Tis certain he hath passed the River Somme.

CONSTABLE
And if he be not fought withal, my lord,   2
Let us not live in France; let us quit all
And give our vineyards to a barbarous people.

DAUPHIN
O Dieu vivant! Shall a few sprays of us,   5
The emptying of our fathers' luxury,   6
Our scions, put in wild and savage stock,   7
Spurt up so suddenly into the clouds   8
And overlook their grafters?   9

BRITTANY
Normans, but bastard Normans, Norman bastards!
Mort de ma vie, if they march along   11
Unfought withal, but I will sell my dukedom   12
To buy a slobbery and a dirty farm   13
In that nook-shotten isle of Albion.   14

CONSTABLE
Dieu de batailles, where have they this mettle?   15
Is not their climate foggy, raw, and dull,

On whom as in despite the sun looks pale,   17
Killing their fruit with frowns? Can sodden water,   18
A drench for sur-reined jades, their barley broth,   19
Decoct their cold blood to such valiant heat?   20
And shall our quick blood, spirited with wine,   21
Seem frosty? Oh, for honor of our land,
Let us not hang like roping icicles   23
Upon our houses' thatch, whiles a more frosty people
Sweat drops of gallant youth in our rich fields!
"Poor" may we call them in their native lords.   26

DAUPHIN   By faith and honor,
Our madams mock at us and plainly say   28
Our mettle is bred out, and they will give   29
Their bodies to the lust of English youth
To new-store France with bastard warriors.   31

BRITTANY
They bid us to the English dancing schools   32
And teach lavoltas high and swift corantos,   33
Saying our grace is only in our heels   34
And that we are most lofty runaways.   35

FRENCH KING
Where is Montjoy the herald? Speed him hence.   36
Let him greet England with our sharp defiance.
Up, princes, and with spirit of honor edged   38
More sharper than your swords, hie to the field!   39
Charles Delabreth, High Constable of France,
You Dukes of Orleans, Bourbon, and of Berri,
Alençon, Brabant, Bar, and Burgundy,
Jaques Chatillion, Rambures, Vaudemont,
Beaumont, Grandpré, Roussi, and Faulconbridge,
Foix, Lestrelles, Boucicault, and Charolais,
High dukes, great princes, barons, lords, and knights,
For your great seats now quit you of great shames.   47
Bar Harry England, that sweeps through our land   48
With pennons painted in the blood of Harfleur.   49
Rush on his host, as doth the melted snow   50
Upon the valleys, whose low vassal seat
The Alps doth spit and void his rheum upon.   52
Go down upon him—you have power enough—
And in a captive chariot into Rouen
Bring him our prisoner.

CONSTABLE   This becomes the great.   55
Sorry am I his numbers are so few,
His soldiers sick and famished in their march,
For I am sure, when he shall see our army,

ALICE   Le foot, my lady, and le count. [As she pronounces them, *foot*
sounds to Katharine like *foutre,* fornicate, and *count* (for *gown*) sounds
like French for the female sexual organ, *cunt* in English.]
KATHARINE   Le foot and le count! Oh, Lord! Those are naughty words,
wicked, coarse, and immodest, and are not fit to be used by ladies. I
wouldn't say those words before French gentlemen for the whole
world. Bah! Le foot and le count! Nevertheless, I shall recite my
whole lesson once more: d' hand, de fingre, de nailes, de arm, d'
elbow, de nick, de sin, de foot, le count.
ALICE   Excellent, my lady.
KATHARINE   That's enough for one time. Let's go to dinner.
3.5. Location: The French court at Rouen.
2 withal with. (As also in line 12).   **5–9 O . . . grafters?** O living God,
shall a few sprigs derived from native French stock, from the pouring
out of our forefathers' lust (during and after the Norman Conquest)
being grafted onto the wild and savage stock (of English Saxons),
sprout up suddenly to lofty heights and domineer over the plants or
trees from which the grafts were taken, i.e., us native French?
11 *Mort de ma vie* Death to my life   **12 but I will** i.e., if I do not
13 slobbery wet and slimy   **14 nook-shotten** full of nooks and
angles. (Refers to the coastline.)   **isle of Albion** island of England,
Scotland, and Wales.   **15** *Dieu de batailles* God of battles.   **where**
from where

17 as in despite as if despising them, the English   **18 sodden water**
boiled water   **19 A drench . . . jades** i.e., stuff no better than what
they give their overridden horses to drink.   **barley broth** ale
20 Decoct warm up   **21 quick** lively   **23 roping** hanging down
like a rope   **26 "Poor" . . . lords** i.e., Our fields, though rich in themselves, may be called poor in that they are owned by a spiritless
aristocracy.   **28 madams** wives, ladies   **29 bred out** exhausted by
breeding   **31 new-store** newly supply   **32 bid us** bid us go
33 lavoltas, corantos fashionable dances   **34 in our heels** (1) in dancing gracefully (2) in running away   **35 lofty** (1) noble (2) leaping.
runaways cowards. (But referring also to the movements of the
dances.)   **36 Montjoy** title of the chief herald of France   **38 edged**
given a sharp edge   **39 hie** hasten   **47 For** in the name of, in defense
of.   **seats** positions.   **quit you** rid, free yourselves   **48 Bar** Stop; bar
the claim of   **49 pennons** banners, streamers   **50 host** army
52 rheum watery discharge, i.e., streams or avalanches   **55 becomes**
the great befits greatness.

He'll drop his heart into the sink of fear   59
And for achievement offer us his ransom.   60

FRENCH KING
Therefore, Lord Constable, haste on Montjoy,
And let him say to England that we send
To know what willing ransom he will give.
Prince Dauphin, you shall stay with us in Rouen.

DAUPHIN
Not so, I do beseech Your Majesty.

FRENCH KING
Be patient, for you shall remain with us.
Now forth, Lord Constable and princes all,
And quickly bring us word of England's fall. *Exeunt.*

❖

[3.6]

Enter Captains, English and Welsh: Gower and
Fluellen, [meeting].

GOWER   How now, Captain Fluellen? Come you from
the bridge?   2
FLUELLEN   I assure you, there is very excellent services   3
committed at the bridge.
GOWER   Is the Duke of Exeter safe?
FLUELLEN   The Duke of Exeter is as magnanimous as
Agamemnon, and a man that I love and honor with   7
my soul, and my heart, and my duty, and my live,   8
and my living, and my uttermost power. He is not—
God be praised and blessed!—any hurt in the world,
but keeps the bridge most valiantly, with excellent discipline. There is an aunchient lieutenant there at the   12
pridge, I think in my very conscience he is as valiant
a man as Mark Antony, and he is a man of no esti-   14
mation in the world, but I did see him do as gallant   15
service.
GOWER   What do you call him?
FLUELLEN   He is called Aunchient Pistol.
GOWER   I know him not.

Enter Pistol.

FLUELLEN   Here is the man.
PISTOL
Captain, I thee beseech to do me favors.
The Duke of Exeter doth love thee well.
FLUELLEN   Ay, I praise God, and I have merited some
love at his hands.
PISTOL
Bardolph, a soldier, firm and sound of heart,
And of buxom valor, hath, by cruel fate   26
And giddy Fortune's furious fickle wheel,

That goddess blind
That stands upon the rolling restless stone—
FLUELLEN   By your patience, Aunchient Pistol. Fortune
is painted blind, with a muffler afore her eyes, to sig-   31
nify to you that Fortune is blind; and she is painted
also with a wheel, to signify to you, which is the moral
of it, that she is turning, and inconstant, and mutabil-
ity, and variation; and her foot, look you, is fixed upon
a spherical stone, which rolls, and rolls, and rolls. In
good truth, the poet is make a most excellent descrip-   37
tion of it. Fortune is an excellent moral.   38
PISTOL
Fortune is Bardolph's foe, and frowns on him;   39
For he hath stol'n a pax,   40
And hangèd must 'a be—a damnèd death!
Let gallows gape for dog; let man go free,
And let not hemp his windpipe suffocate.
But Exeter hath given the doom of death   44
For pax of little price.
Therefore, go speak—the Duke will hear thy voice—
And let not Bardolph's vital thread be cut
With edge of penny cord and vile reproach.   48
Speak, Captain, for his life, and I will thee requite.   49
FLUELLEN   Aunchient Pistol, I do partly understand
your meaning.
PISTOL   Why then rejoice therefor.
FLUELLEN   Certainly, Aunchient, it is not a thing to re-
joice at. For if, look you, he were my brother, I would
desire the Duke to use his good pleasure and put him
to execution; for discipline ought to be used.
PISTOL
Die and be damned! And *figo* for thy friendship!   57
FLUELLEN   It is well.
PISTOL   The fig of Spain!   *Exit.*
FLUELLEN   Very good.
GOWER   Why, this is an arrant counterfeit rascal! I
remember him now; a bawd, a cutpurse.
FLUELLEN   I'll assure you, 'a uttered as prave words at
the pridge as you shall see in a summer's day. But it is
very well. What he has spoke to me, that is well, I
warrant you, when time is serve.
GOWER   Why, 'tis a gull, a fool, a rogue, that now and   67
then goes to the wars, to grace himself at his return
into London under the form of a soldier. And such
fellows are perfect in the great commanders' names,   70
and they will learn you by rote where services were   71
done—at such and such a sconce, at such a breach, at   72
such a convoy; who came off bravely, who was shot,
who disgraced, what terms the enemy stood on—and   74
this they con perfectly in the phrase of war, which   75

---

59 **sink** pit   60 **for achievement** instead of achieving victory, as his
sole accomplishment
3.6 Location: The English camp in northern France.
2 bridge (According to Holinshed, the French were beaten in their
attempt to break down the bridge over the Ternoise. The audience is
not told this, however, and might assume the river to be the Somme,
mentioned in 3.5.1.)   **3 services** exploits. (As also in line 71.)
7 Agamemnon leader of the Greeks against Troy   **8 live** life
12 aunchient lieutenant (Pistol is elsewhere given the rank of
ancient, or ensign.)   **14–15 estimation** fame   **26 buxom** (1) vigorous
(2) compliant, meek

31 muffler blindfold   **37 is make** has made   **38 moral** emblem.
39 Fortune . . . foe (Probably alludes to the ballad "Fortune, my foe!")
40 pax metal disk with a crucifix stamped on it, kissed by the priest
and communicants during Mass. (But Holinshed describes an incident in which the object stolen is a *pyx*, the vessel containing the consecrated host.)   **44 doom** judgment, sentence   **48 cord** rope
49 requite repay.   **57 *figo*** gesture of contempt made by thrusting the
thumb between the index and middle fingers   **67 gull** simpleton
70 are perfect in i.e., can recite perfectly   **71 learn** teach, recite
72 sconce fortification   **74 terms . . . stood on** conditions the enemy
insisted on   **75 con** learn by heart

they trick up with new-tuned oaths. And what a 76
beard of the General's cut and a horrid suit of the 77
camp will do among foaming bottles and ale-washed 78
wits is wonderful to be thought on. But you must
learn to know such slanders of the age, or else you 80
may be marvelously mistook. 81

FLUELLEN   I tell you what, Captain Gower, I do perceive
he is not the man that he would gladly make show
to the world he is. If I find a hole in his coat, I will tell 84
him my mind. [*Drum heard.*] Hark you, the King is
coming, and I must speak with him from the pridge. 86

Drum and colors. Enter the King and his poor
soldiers [and Gloucester].

God pless Your Majesty!
KING   How now, Fluellen, cam'st thou from the bridge?
FLUELLEN   Ay, so please Your Majesty. The Duke of
Exeter has very gallantly maintained the pridge. The
French is gone off, look you, and there is gallant and
most prave passages. Marry, th'athversary was have 93
possession of the pridge, but he is enforced to retire,
and the Duke of Exeter is master of the pridge. I can
tell Your Majesty, the Duke is a prave man.
KING   What men have you lost, Fluellen?
FLUELLEN   The perdition of th'athversary hath been very 98
great, reasonable great. Marry, for my part, I think the
Duke hath lost never a man, but one that is like to be ex- 100
ecuted for robbing a church, one Bardolph, if Your Majesty know the man. His face is all bubukles, and whelks, 102
and knobs, and flames o' fire, and his lips blows at his
nose, and it is like a coal of fire, sometimes plue and
sometimes red; but his nose is executed, and his fire's
out.
KING   We would have all such offenders so cut off. And we
give express charge that, in our marches through the 108
country, there be nothing compelled from the villages,
nothing taken but paid for, none of the French up-
braided or abused in disdainful language; for when lenity and cruelty play for a kingdom, the gentler gamester 112
is the soonest winner. 113

Tucket. Enter Montjoy.

MONTJOY   You know me by my habit. 114
KING   Well then, I know thee. What shall I know of thee?
MONTJOY   My master's mind.
KING   Unfold it.
MONTJOY   Thus says my King: "Say thou to Harry of
England, though we seemed dead, we did but sleep.
Advantage is a better soldier than rashness. Tell him 120
we could have rebuked him at Harfleur, but that we

thought not good to bruise an injury till it were full 122
ripe. Now we speak upon our cue, and our voice is
imperial. England shall repent his folly, see his 124
weakness, and admire our sufferance. Bid him there- 125
fore consider of his ransom, which must proportion 126
the losses we have borne, the subjects we have lost,
the disgrace we have digested; which in weight to re- 128
answer, his pettiness would bow under. For our losses, 129
his exchequer is too poor; for th'effusion of our blood, 130
the muster of his kingdom too faint a number; and for 131
our disgrace, his own person kneeling at our feet but
a weak and worthless satisfaction. To this add defiance; and tell him, for conclusion, he hath betrayed his
followers, whose condemnation is pronounced." So far 135
my King and master; so much my office.
KING
What is thy name? I know thy quality. 137
MONTJOY   Montjoy.
KING
Thou dost thy office fairly. Turn thee back
And tell thy King I do not seek him now,
But could be willing to march on to Calais
Without impeachment. For, to say the sooth, 142
Though 'tis no wisdom to confess so much
Unto an enemy of craft and vantage, 144
My people are with sickness much enfeebled,
My numbers lessened, and those few I have
Almost no better than so many French,
Who when they were in health, I tell thee, herald,
I thought upon one pair of English legs 149
Did march three Frenchmen. Yet, forgive me, God, 150
That I do brag thus! This your air of France
Hath blown that vice in me. I must repent. 152
Go, therefore, tell thy master here I am;
My ransom is this frail and worthless trunk, 154
My army but a weak and sickly guard.
Yet, God before, tell him we will come on,
Though France himself and such another neighbor
Stand in our way. There's for thy labor, Montjoy.
[He gives a purse.]
Go bid thy master well advise himself. 159
If we may pass, we will; if we be hindered,
We shall your tawny ground with your red blood
Discolor. And so, Montjoy, fare you well.
The sum of all our answer is but this:
We would not seek a battle as we are,
Nor, as we are, we say we will not shun it. 165
So tell your master.

76 **trick** dress.   **new-tuned** i.e., of the latest fashion   **77–8 horrid . . .
camp** fierce battle outfit   80 **slanders of the age** persons who are a
disgrace to the times   81 **mistook** mistaken, deluded.   84 **a hole . . .
coat** i.e., a weak spot in him. (Proverbial.)   86 **from the pridge** with
news concerning the bridge.   86.1 *poor* bedraggled   93 **passages**
deeds of arms.   **was** did   98 **perdition** losses   100 **like** likely
102 **bubukles** carbuncles.   **whelks** boils, pimples   108 **express
charge** explicit orders   112 **gamester** player   113.1 *Tucket* Trumpet
signal, fanfare.   114 **habit** i.e., tabard, herald's coat.   120 **Advantage**
Knowing how to wait for favorable circumstance and position

122 **bruise an injury** squeeze a boil or pimple   124 **England** i.e.,
King Henry   125 **admire our sufferance** wonder at our patience.
126 **proportion** be proportional to   128–9 **which . . . under** i.e., to
compensate for which his means are too slender.   130 **exchequer**
treasury   131 **muster** roll call   135 **condemnation** death sentence
137 **quality** rank and profession; ability.   142 **impeachment** impediment.   **sooth** truth   144 **vantage** superiority in resources
149–50 **upon . . . Frenchman** i.e., an English soldier is worth three
Frenchmen.   152 **blown** swelled; caused to blossom   154 **trunk**
body   159 **advise himself** consider.   165 **as we are** being who we
are. (Playing on the meaning "in the condition we are" in the previous line.)

MONTJOY
I shall deliver so. Thanks to Your Highness.   [*Exit.*]

GLOUCESTER
I hope they will not come upon us now.

KING
We are in God's hand, brother, not in theirs.
March to the bridge. It now draws toward night.
Beyond the river we'll encamp ourselves,
And on tomorrow bid them march away.   *Exeunt.* 172

[3.7]

Enter the Constable of France, the Lord Rambures,
Orleans, Dauphin, with others.

CONSTABLE   Tut, I have the best armor of the world.
Would it were day!

ORLEANS   You have an excellent armor; but let my
horse have his due.

CONSTABLE   It is the best horse of Europe.

ORLEANS   Will it never be morning?

DAUPHIN   My lord of Orleans and my Lord High
Constable, you talk of horse and armor?

ORLEANS   You are as well provided of both as any
prince in the world.

DAUPHIN   What a long night is this! I will not change
my horse with any that treads but on four pasterns. 12
Ça, ha! He bounds from the earth as if his entrails 13
were hairs; *le cheval volant*, the Pegasus, *qui a les narines* 14
de feu! When I bestride him, I soar, I am a hawk. He 15
trots the air. The earth sings when he touches it. The
basest horn of his hoof is more musical than the pipe 17
of Hermes. 18

ORLEANS   He's of the color of the nutmeg.

DAUPHIN   And of the heat of the ginger. It is a beast for
Perseus. He is pure air and fire; and the dull elements 21
of earth and water never appear in him, but only in 22
patient stillness while his rider mounts him. He is indeed a horse, and all other jades you may call beasts.

CONSTABLE   Indeed, my lord, it is a most absolute and 25
excellent horse.

DAUPHIN   It is the prince of palfreys. His neigh is like 27
the bidding of a monarch, and his countenance
enforces homage.

ORLEANS   No more, cousin.

DAUPHIN   Nay, the man hath no wit that cannot, from
the rising of the lark to the lodging of the lamb, vary 32

deserved praise on my palfrey. It is a theme as fluent
as the sea; turn the sands into eloquent tongues, and
my horse is argument for them all. 'Tis a subject for a 35
sovereign to reason on, and for a sovereign's sovereign 36
to ride on, and for the world, familiar to us and un- 37
known, to lay apart their particular functions and 38
wonder at him. I once writ a sonnet in his praise, and 39
began thus: "Wonder of nature—"

ORLEANS   I have heard a sonnet begin so to one's
mistress.

DAUPHIN   Then did they imitate that which I composed
to my courser, for my horse is my mistress. 44

ORLEANS   Your mistress bears well.

DAUPHIN   Me well, which is the prescript praise and 46
perfection of a good and particular mistress. 47

CONSTABLE   Nay, for methought yesterday your mistress shrewdly shook your back. 49

DAUPHIN   So perhaps did yours.

CONSTABLE   Mine was not bridled. 51

DAUPHIN   Oh, then belike she was old and gentle, and 52
you rode like a kern of Ireland, your French hose off, 53
and in your strait strossers. 54

CONSTABLE   You have good judgment in horsemanship.

DAUPHIN   Be warned by me, then: they that ride so,
and ride not warily, fall into foul bogs. I had rather
have my horse to my mistress. 58

CONSTABLE   I had as lief have my mistress a jade. 59

DAUPHIN   I tell thee, Constable, my mistress wears his 60
own hair. 61

CONSTABLE   I could make as true a boast as that, if I had
a sow to my mistress.

DAUPHIN   "*Le chien est retourné à son propre vomissement,* 64
et la truie lavée au bourbier." Thou mak'st use of 65
anything.

CONSTABLE   Yet do I not use my horse for my mistress,
or any such proverb so little kin to the purpose. 68

RAMBURES   My Lord Constable, the armor that I saw in
your tent tonight, are those stars or suns upon it?

CONSTABLE   Stars, my lord.

DAUPHIN   Some of them will fall tomorrow, I hope.

CONSTABLE   And yet my sky shall not want. 73

DAUPHIN   That may be, for you bear a many superflu- 74
ously, and 'twere more honor some were away. 75

---

172 bid . . . away bid our army march toward Calais.
3.7. Location: The French camp, near Agincourt.
12 pasterns i.e., hooves. (The *pastern* literally is the part of the horse's
leg just above the hoof.)   **13–14 as . . . hairs** i.e., as if he were a tennis
ball. (Tennis balls were stuffed with hair. Or perhaps *hairs* should
read *hares.*)   **14–15 le cheval . . . feu** the flying horse, Pegasus, with
nostrils breathing fire.   **17 basest horn** (1) lowest part (2) hoofbeat
17–18 pipe of Hermes (Hermes, messenger of the gods, charmed
Argus of the hundred eyes asleep with playing on his pipe.)
21 Perseus (According to some Greek legends and to Ovid, Perseus
rode Pegasus when he rescued Andromeda from the dragon.)
21–2 air . . . water (Of the four elements supposed to make up all matter, water and earth are the heavier, while fire and air ascend.)
25 absolute perfect   **27 palfreys** saddle horses   **32 lodging** lying
down.   **vary** produce variations of

35 argument subject   **36 reason** discourse   **37–9 for . . . him** for both
the known and unknown worlds to put aside their differences and
join in wondering at him.   **44 horse is my mistress** (Here begins a
series of bawdy double entendres involving human and animal sexuality: *bears, shook your back, rode, foul bogs, doing,* etc.)   **46 prescript**
prescribed   **47 particular** acknowledging only one master
49 shrewdly viciously   **51 Mine . . . bridled** i.e., At least my mistress
was not a horse.   **52 belike** probably   **53 kern** Irish foot soldier.
(Here it is used to mean "rustic" or "boor.")   **French hose** wide
breeches   **54 strait strossers** tight trousers, i.e., bare-legged.   **58 to** as
59 lief happily.   **jade** (1) worn-out horse (2) slut.   **60–1 wears . . .
hair** i.e., is not artificially wigged, like an elegant court lady, and perhaps bald from syphilis.   **64–5 "Le chien . . . bourbier"** The dog is
returned to his own vomit, and the washed sow to the mire. (See 2
Peter 2:22.)   **68 kin** related   **73 sky** i.e., sky of honor.   **want** be lacking (in honor).   **74 a many** many. (Parallel to "a few.")   **75 'twere . . .
away** i.e., it would be more honest and proper if some of your stars
were done away with.

CONSTABLE   Even as your horse bears your praises, who would trot as well, were some of your brags dismounted.

DAUPHIN   Would I were able to load him with his desert! Will it never be day? I will trot tomorrow a mile, and my way shall be paved with English faces.   79 80

CONSTABLE   I will not say so, for fear I should be faced out of my way. But I would it were morning, for I would fain be about the ears of the English.   82 83 84

RAMBURES   Who will go to hazard with me for twenty prisoners?   85

CONSTABLE   You must first go yourself to hazard, ere you have them.

DAUPHIN   'Tis midnight. I'll go arm myself.   *Exit.*

ORLEANS   The Dauphin longs for morning.

RAMBURES   He longs to eat the English.

CONSTABLE   I think he will eat all he kills.

ORLEANS   By the white hand of my lady, he's a gallant prince.

CONSTABLE   Swear by her foot, that she may tread out the oath.   95 96

ORLEANS   He is simply the most active gentleman of France.

CONSTABLE   Doing is activity, and he will still be doing.   99

ORLEANS   He never did harm, that I heard of.   100

CONSTABLE   Nor will do none tomorrow. He will keep that good name still.

ORLEANS   I know him to be valiant.

CONSTABLE   I was told that by one that knows him better than you.

ORLEANS   What's he?

CONSTABLE   Marry, he told me so himself, and he said he cared not who knew it.

ORLEANS   He needs not; it is no hidden virtue in him.   109

CONSTABLE   By my faith, sir, but it is. Never anybody saw it but his lackey. 'Tis a hooded valor, and when it appears it will bate.   110 111 112

ORLEANS   Ill will never said well.

CONSTABLE   I will cap that proverb with "There is flattery in friendship."

ORLEANS   And I will take up that with "Give the devil his due."   116 117

CONSTABLE   Well placed. There stands your friend for the devil. Have at the very eye of that proverb with "A pox of the devil."   118 119

ORLEANS   You are the better at proverbs by how much "A fool's bolt is soon shot."   122

CONSTABLE   You have shot over.   123

ORLEANS   'Tis not the first time you were overshot.   124

Enter a Messenger.

MESSENGER   My Lord High Constable, the English lie within fifteen hundred paces of your tents.

CONSTABLE   Who hath measured the ground?

MESSENGER   The Lord Grandpré.

CONSTABLE   A valiant and most expert gentleman.
                 [*Exit Messenger.*]
Would it were day! Alas, poor Harry of England! He longs not for the dawning as we do.

ORLEANS   What a wretched and peevish fellow is this King of England, to mope with his fat-brained followers so far out of his knowledge!   133

CONSTABLE   If the English had any apprehension, they would run away.   135

ORLEANS   That they lack; for if their heads had any intellectual armor, they could never wear such heavy headpieces.

RAMBURES   That island of England breeds very valiant creatures; their mastiffs are of unmatchable courage.

ORLEANS   Foolish curs, that run winking into the mouth of a Russian bear and have their heads crushed like rotten apples. You may as well say "That's a valiant flea that dare eat his breakfast on the lip of a lion."   142

CONSTABLE   Just, just! And the men do sympathize with the mastiffs in robustious and rough coming on, leaving their wits with their wives; and then give them great meals of beef and iron and steel, they will eat like wolves and fight like devils.   146 147

ORLEANS   Ay, but these English are shrewdly out of beef.   151

CONSTABLE   Then shall we find tomorrow they have only stomachs to eat and none to fight. Now is it time to arm. Come, shall we about it?   154

ORLEANS
It is now two o'clock; but let me see, by ten
We shall have each a hundred Englishmen.   *Exeunt.*

❦

[4.0]

[Enter] Chorus.

CHORUS
Now entertain conjecture of a time   1
When creeping murmur and the poring dark   2
Fills the wide vessel of the universe.
From camp to camp, through the foul womb of night,
The hum of either army stilly sounds,   5

79–80 Would . . . desert! I wish I could find words to equal his deserving!   **82–3 faced . . . way** braved out of my way, put to shame.   **84 fain** gladly.   **about the ears** buffeting the heads   **85 go to hazard** bet, play at dice. (But the Constable replies in the sense of "encounter danger.") **95–6 tread . . . oath** (1) fulfill the oath by dancing (2) stamp on, spurn the oath.   **99 Doing** (1) Acting, pretending (2) Copulating.   **still** continually   **100 did harm** i.e., offended. (But the Constable uses it to mean "hurt any enemy.")   **109 He needs not** i.e., There is no need for him to proclaim it himself.   **it** i.e., valor   **110–11 Never . . . lackey** i.e., He shows "valor" only in beating his servant.   **111 hooded valor** (The hawk was kept hooded to prevent it from beating its wings, or "bating.")   **112 bate** (1) beat its wings (2) abate, be downcast.   **116–17 Give . . . due** Give even the devil his due; everyone deserves some praise. (But the Constable turns this proverb against the Dauphin by likening him to the devil.)   **118–19 There . . . devil** i.e., You just called the Dauphin the devil.   **119 Have . . . eye** Shoot straight at the mark. (A sporting term appropriate to this verbal contest of "capping proverbs.")

122 bolt short, blunt arrow   **123 shot over** i.e., shot over the mark.   **124 overshot** i.e., outshot, defeated.   **133 mope** (1) wander about (2) be downcast   **135 apprehension** (1) sense (2) sense of danger   **142 winking** shutting their eyes   **146 Just** Exactly.   **sympathize with** resemble   **147 robustious** violent, boisterous   **151 shrewdly out of** devilishly short of   **154 stomachs** appetites   **4.0. Chorus.**
1 entertain conjecture of imagine   **2 poring** in which one must strain the eyes to see   **5 stilly** softly

That the fixed sentinels almost receive
The secret whispers of each other's watch.
Fire answers fire, and through their paly flames   8
Each battle sees the other's umbered face.   9
Steed threatens steed, in high and boastful neighs
Piercing the night's dull ear; and from the tents
The armorers, accomplishing the knights,   12
With busy hammers closing rivets up,
Give dreadful note of preparation.
The country cocks do crow, the clocks do toll,
And the third hour of drowsy morning name.
Proud of their numbers and secure in soul,   17
The confident and overlusty French   18
Do the low-rated English play at dice,   19
And chide the cripple tardy-gaited night,
Who like a foul and ugly witch doth limp
So tediously away. The poor condemnèd English,
Like sacrifices, by their watchful fires
Sit patiently and inly ruminate   24
The morning's danger; and their gesture sad,   25
Investing lank-lean cheeks and war-worn coats,   26
Presenteth them unto the gazing moon
So many horrid ghosts. Oh, now, who will behold
The royal captain of this ruined band
Walking from watch to watch, from tent to tent,
Let him cry, "Praise and glory on his head!"
For forth he goes and visits all his host,   32
Bids them good morrow with a modest smile,
And calls them brothers, friends, and countrymen.
Upon his royal face there is no note
How dread an army hath enrounded him.   36
Nor doth he dedicate one jot of color   37
Unto the weary and all-watchèd night,   38
But freshly looks and overbears attaint   39
With cheerful semblance and sweet majesty;
That every wretch, pining and pale before,
Beholding him, plucks comfort from his looks.
A largess universal like the sun
His liberal eye doth give to everyone,
Thawing cold fear, that mean and gentle all   45
Behold, as may unworthiness define,   46
A little touch of Harry in the night.
And so our scene must to the battle fly;
Where—oh, for pity!—we shall much disgrace
With four or five most vile and ragged foils,   50
Right ill-disposed in brawl ridiculous,
The name of Agincourt. Yet sit and see,
Minding true things by what their mockeries be.   53

Exit.

❖

8 **paly** pale   9 **battle** army.   **umbered** shadowed   12 **accomplishing**
equipping   17 **secure** overconfident   18 **overlusty** overly merry
19 **play** gamble for   24 **inly** inwardly   25 **gesture sad** serious bearing
26 **Investing** clothing   32 **host** army   36 **enrounded** surrounded
37 **dedicate** yield up.   **color** i.e., bright color of complexion   38 **all-
watchèd** spent entirely in wakefulness and waiting   39 **overbears
attaint** overcomes the effects of weariness and depression   45 **mean
and gentle** those of low and of high birth   46 **unworthiness** I, who am
unworthy of praising so great an object   50 **foils** blunted fencing swords
53 **Minding** bearing in mind.   **mockeries** inadequate imitations

[4.1]

Enter the King, Bedford, and Gloucester.

KING
Gloucester, 'tis true that we are in great danger;
The greater therefore should our courage be.
Good morrow, brother Bedford. God Almighty!
There is some soul of goodness in things evil,
Would men observingly distill it out;   5
For our bad neighbor makes us early stirrers,
Which is both healthful and good husbandry.   7
Besides, they are our outward consciences,
And preachers to us all, admonishing
That we should dress us fairly for our end.   10
Thus may we gather honey from the weed
And make a moral of the devil himself.

Enter Erpingham.

Good morrow, old Sir Thomas Erpingham.
A good soft pillow for that good white head
Were better than a churlish turf of France.   15
ERPINGHAM
Not so, my liege. This lodging likes me better,   16
Since I may say, "Now lie I like a king."
KING
'Tis good for men to love their present pains
Upon example; so the spirit is eased.   19
And when the mind is quickened, out of doubt
The organs, though defunct and dead before,
Break up their drowsy grave and newly move   22
With casted slough and fresh legerity.   23
Lend me thy cloak, Sir Thomas. [*The King puts on
Erpingham's cloak.*] Brothers both,   24
Commend me to the princes in our camp;   25
Do my good morrow to them, and anon
Desire them all to my pavilion.
GLOUCESTER   We shall, my liege.
ERPINGHAM   Shall I attend Your Grace?
KING   No, my good knight,
Go with my brothers to my lords of England.
I and my bosom must debate awhile,
And then I would no other company.
ERPINGHAM
The Lord in heaven bless thee, noble Harry!
Exeunt [all but the King].
KING
God-a-mercy, old heart! Thou speak'st cheerfully.

Enter Pistol.

PISTOL   *Che vous là?*   36

4.1. Location: The English camp at Agincourt.
5 **Would men** if one could   7 **husbandry** economy, thrift.   10 **dress
us fairly** prepare ourselves well   15 **churlish** rough, hard   16 **likes**
pleases   19 **Upon example** i.e., following or considering the example
of persons such as King Henry and Erpingham   22–3 **Break . . . legerity** break out of their lethargy and move nimbly, like a snake having cast off its old skin.   24 **Brothers both** i.e., Bedford and
Gloucester   25 **Commend me** convey my greetings   36 **Che vous là?**
i.e., *Qui va là?* ("Who goes there?") or *Qui vous là?* ("Who are you
there?"). (Pistol's imperfect French.)

KING   A friend.

PISTOL
Discuss unto me: art thou officer,   38
Or art thou base, common, and popular?   39

KING   I am a gentleman of a company.   40

PISTOL   Trail'st thou the puissant pike?   41

KING   Even so. What are you?

PISTOL
As good a gentleman as the Emperor.

KING   Then you are a better than the King.

PISTOL
The King's a bawcock and a heart of gold,   45
A lad of life, an imp of fame,   46
Of parents good, of fist most valiant.
I kiss his dirty shoe, and from heartstring
I love the lovely bully. What is thy name?   49

KING   Harry le Roy.

PISTOL
Le Roy? A Cornish name. Art thou of Cornish crew?

KING   No, I am a Welshman.   52

PISTOL   Know'st thou Fluellen?

KING   Yes.

PISTOL
Tell him I'll knock his leek about his pate   55
Upon Saint Davy's Day.   56

KING   Do not you wear your dagger in your cap that
day, lest he knock that about yours.

PISTOL   Art thou his friend?

KING   And his kinsman too.

PISTOL   The *figo* for thee, then!   61

KING   I thank you. God be with you!

PISTOL   My name is Pistol called.   *Exit.*

KING   It sorts well with your fierceness.   64
                                    Manet King [*standing apart*].

                        Enter Fluellen and Gower [*meeting*].

GOWER   Captain Fluellen!

FLUELLEN   So, in the name of Jesu Christ, speak fewer.   66
It is the greatest admiration in the universal world,   67
when the true and aunchient prerogatifes and laws of
the wars is not kept. If you would take the pains but
to examine the wars of Pompey the Great, you shall   70
find, I warrant you, that there is no tiddle-taddle nor   71
pibble-pabble in Pompey's camp. I warrant you, you   72
shall find the ceremonies of the wars, and the cares of
it, and the forms of it, and the sobriety of it, and the   74
modesty of it, to be otherwise.   75

38 Discuss Declare   39 popular of low birth.   40 gentleman of a
company gentleman serving as a volunteer.   41 Trail'st . . . pike? i.e.,
Are you in the infantry?   45 bawcock fine fellow. (From the French
beau coq.)   46 imp of fame child or scion of renown   49 bully (A term
of endearment meaning "fine fellow.")   52 Welshman (Henry was
born at Monmouth, then considered part of Wales.)   55–6 leek . . . Day
(On Saint David's Day, March 1, the leek was worn in memory of a
Welsh victory over the Saxons in 540 A.D., since Saint David, the
Welsh leader, had commanded his followers to wear leeks in their
caps on that occasion.)   61 figo (A provoking gesture of contempt;
see the note for 3.6.57.)   64 sorts fits, agrees   64.1 *Manet King* The
King remains.   66 fewer i.e., calmly, more quietly.   67 admiration
wonder   70 Pompey the Great Roman general defeated by Julius
Caesar   71–2 tiddle-taddle nor pibble-pabble tittle-tattle nor bibble-
babble   74 sobriety orderliness, decorum   75 modesty propriety

GOWER   Why, the enemy is loud; you hear him all
night.

FLUELLEN   If the enemy is an ass and a fool and a prating   78
coxcomb, is it meet, think you, that we should also,   79
look you, be an ass and a fool and a prating coxcomb?
In your own conscience, now?

GOWER   I will speak lower.

FLUELLEN   I pray you and beseech you that you will.
                                    Exit [*with Gower*].

KING
Though it appear a little out of fashion,
There is much care and valor in this Welshman.

        *Enter three soldiers, John Bates, Alexander Court,
        and Michael Williams.*

COURT   Brother John Bates, is not that the morning
which breaks yonder?

BATES   I think it be. But we have no great cause to
desire the approach of day.

WILLIAMS   We see yonder the beginning of the day, but
I think we shall never see the end of it.—Who goes
there?

KING   A friend.

WILLIAMS   Under what captain serve you?

KING   Under Sir Thomas Erpingham.

WILLIAMS   A good old commander and a most kind
gentleman. I pray you, what thinks he of our estate?   97

KING   Even as men wrecked upon a sand, that look to   98
be washed off the next tide.

BATES   He hath not told his thought to the King?

KING   No, nor it is not meet he should. For, though I   101
speak it to you, I think the King is but a man, as I am.
The violet smells to him as it doth to me; the element   103
shows to him as it doth to me; all his senses have but   104
human conditions. His ceremonies laid by, in his   105
nakedness he appears but a man; and though his
affections are higher mounted than ours, yet when   107
they stoop, they stoop with the like wing. Therefore
when he sees reason of fears, as we do, his fears, out
of doubt, be of the same relish as ours are. Yet, in   110
reason, no man should possess him with any appear-   111
ance of fear, lest he, by showing it, should dishearten
his army.

BATES   He may show what outward courage he will; but
I believe, as cold a night as 'tis, he could wish himself
in Thames up to the neck; and so I would he were,
and I by him, at all adventures, so we were quit here.   117

KING   By my troth, I will speak my conscience of the
King: I think he would not wish himself anywhere but
where he is.

78–9 prating coxcomb chattering fool   97 estate situation.
98 wrecked shipwrecked   101 meet fitting   103–4 element shows
sky appears   105 ceremonies symbols of royalty   107 affections . . .
mounted desires soar higher. (A falcony metaphor continued in
stoop, "descend," "swoop down," and *with the like wing*, "similarly.")
110 relish taste   111 possess him with induce in him   117 at all
adventures at all events (since the Thames would be less risky
under any circumstances than the impending battle).   quit here
out of this situation.

BATES　　Then I would he were here alone. So should he be sure to be ransomed, and a many poor men's lives saved.

KING　　I dare say you love him not so ill to wish him here alone, howsoever you speak this to feel other men's minds. Methinks I could not die anywhere so contented as in the King's company, his cause being just and his quarrel honorable.

WILLIAMS　　That's more than we know.

BATES　　Ay, or more than we should seek after; for we know enough if we know we are the King's subjects. If his cause be wrong, our obedience to the King wipes the crime of it out of us.

WILLIAMS　　But if the cause be not good, the King himself hath a heavy reckoning to make, when all those legs and arms and heads, chopped off in a battle, shall join together at the Latter Day and cry all, "We died at such a place"—some swearing, some crying for a surgeon, some upon their wives left poor behind them, some upon the debts they owe, some upon their children rawly left. I am afeard there are few die well that die in a battle; for how can they charitably dispose of anything, when blood is their argument? Now, if these men do not die well, it will be a black matter for the King that led them to it; who to disobey were against all proportion of subjection.

KING　　So, if a son that is by his father sent about merchandise do sinfully miscarry upon the sea, the imputation of his wickedness, by your rule, should be imposed upon his father that sent him; or if a servant, under his master's command transporting a sum of money, be assailed by robbers and die in many irreconciled iniquities, you may call the business of the master the author of the servant's damnation. But this is not so. The King is not bound to answer the particular endings of his soldiers, the father of his son, nor the master of his servant; for they purpose not their deaths when they propose their services. Besides, there is no king, be his cause never so spotless, if it come to the arbitrament of swords, can try it out with all unspotted soldiers. Some, peradventure, have on them the guilt of premeditated and contrived murder; some, of beguiling virgins with the broken seals of perjury; some, making the wars their bulwark, that have before gored the gentle bosom of peace with pillage and robbery. Now, if these men have defeated the law and outrun native punishment, though they can outstrip men, they have no wings to fly from God. War is his beadle, war is his vengeance; so that here

men are punished for before-breach of the King's laws in now the King's quarrel. Where they feared the death, they have borne life away; and where they would be safe, they perish. Then if they die unprovided, no more is the King guilty of their damnation than he was before guilty of those impieties for the which they are now visited. Every subject's duty is the King's; but every subject's soul is his own. Therefore should every soldier in the wars do as every sick man in his bed, wash every mote out of his conscience; and dying so, death is to him advantage, or not dying, the time was blessedly lost wherein such preparation was gained. And in him that escapes, it were not sin to think that, making God so free an offer, He let him outlive that day to see His greatness and to teach others how they should prepare.

WILLIAMS　　'Tis certain, every man that dies ill, the ill upon his own head, the King is not to answer it.

BATES　　I do not desire he should answer for me, and yet I determine to fight lustily for him.

KING　　I myself heard the King say he would not be ransomed.

WILLIAMS　　Ay, he said so, to make us fight cheerfully; but when our throats are cut, he may be ransomed and we ne'er the wiser.

KING　　If I live to see it, I will never trust his word after.

WILLIAMS　　You pay him then! That's a perilous shot out of an elder-gun, that a poor and a private displeasure can do against a monarch. You may as well go about to turn the sun to ice with fanning in his face with a peacock's feather. You'll never trust his word after! Come, 'tis a foolish saying.

KING　　Your reproof is something too round. I should be angry with you, if the time were convenient.

WILLIAMS　　Let it be a quarrel between us, if you live.

KING　　I embrace it.

WILLIAMS　　How shall I know thee again?

KING　　Give me any gage of thine, and I will wear it in my bonnet. Then if ever thou dar'st acknowledge it, I will make it my quarrel.

WILLIAMS　　Here's my glove. Give me another of thine.

KING　　There.　　　　　　　　　　[They exchange gloves.]

WILLIAMS　　This will I also wear in my cap. If ever thou come to me and say, after tomorrow, "This is my glove," by this hand, I will take thee a box on the ear.

KING　　If ever I live to see it, I will challenge it.

WILLIAMS　　Thou dar'st as well be hanged.

KING　　Well, I will do it, though I take thee in the King's company.

WILLIAMS　　Keep thy word. Fare thee well.

---

125 **feel** feel out　137 **Latter Day** last day, Christian Day of Judgment　141 **rawly** without provision　145 **who** whom　146 **proportion of subjection** proper duty of a subject.　148 **sinfully miscarry** die in his sins　149 **imputation . . . wickedness** wickedness imputed to him　152–3 **in . . . iniquities** with his wicked deeds unabsolved　155 **answer** answer for　157 **purpose** intend　159–60 **if . . . swords** if a dispute can be settled only by swords　161 **unspotted** innocent　163 **broken seals** (1) broken promises (2) violated maidenheads　164 **bulwark** refuge from punishment (for offenses committed)　166 **defeated** broken　167 **native** at home　169 **beadle** parish officer responsible for punishing petty offenders

170 **before-breach** prior violation　171–3 **Where . . . perish** i.e., Whereas before they feared execution but escaped punishment, here where they look for safety they die in battle.　173–4 **unprovided** spiritually unprepared　176 **visited** i.e., by punishment.　179 **mote** small impurity　186 **dies ill** dies in sin　196 **You pay him then!** i.e., That will really pay him back for his perfidy, won't it? (Said sarcastically.)　197 **elder-gun** popgun made from a branch of elder with the pith hollowed out　202 **round** direct, brusque.　207 **gage** pledge　214 **take** give, strike

BATES Be friends, you English fools, be friends. We
have French quarrels enough, if you could tell how to 221
reckon.

KING Indeed, the French may lay twenty French crowns 223
to one they will beat us, for they bear them on their
shoulders; but it is no English treason to cut French 225
crowns, and tomorrow the King himself will be a
clipper.   *Exeunt soldiers.*
Upon the King! Let us our lives, our souls,
Our debts, our careful wives,   229
Our children, and our sins lay on the King!
We must bear all. Oh, hard condition,
Twin-born with greatness, subject to the breath   232
Of every fool, whose sense no more can feel   233
But his own wringing! What infinite heartsease   234
Must kings neglect that private men enjoy!
And what have kings that privates have not too,   236
Save ceremony, save general ceremony?
And what art thou, thou idol ceremony?
What kind of god art thou, that suffer'st more
Of mortal griefs than do thy worshipers?
What are thy rents? What are thy comings-in?   241
O ceremony, show me but thy worth!
What is thy soul of adoration?   243
Art thou aught else but place, degree, and form,   244
Creating awe and fear in other men?
Wherein thou art less happy, being feared,
Than they in fearing.
What drink'st thou oft, instead of homage sweet,
But poisoned flattery? Oh, be sick, great greatness,   249
And bid thy ceremony give thee cure!   250
Thinks thou the fiery fever will go out   251
With titles blown from adulation?   252
Will it give place to flexure and low bending?   253
Canst thou, when thou command'st the beggar's
   knee,
Command the health of it? No, thou proud dream,
That play'st so subtly with a king's repose.
I am a king that find thee, and I know   257
'Tis not the balm, the scepter, and the ball,   258
The sword, the mace, the crown imperial,   259

The intertissued robe of gold and pearl,   260
The farcèd title running 'fore the king,   261
The throne he sits on, nor the tide of pomp
That beats upon the high shore of this world—
No, not all these, thrice-gorgeous ceremony,
Not all these, laid in bed majestical,
Can sleep so soundly as the wretched slave
Who, with a body filled and vacant mind,
Gets him to rest, crammed with distressful bread;   268
Never sees horrid night, the child of hell,
But like a lackey from the rise to set   270
Sweats in the eye of Phoebus, and all night   271
Sleeps in Elysium; next day after dawn   272
Doth rise and help Hyperion to his horse,   273
And follows so the ever-running year
With profitable labor to his grave.
And but for ceremony, such a wretch,
Winding up days with toil and nights with sleep,
Had the forehand and vantage of a king.   278
The slave, a member of the country's peace,   279
Enjoys it, but in gross brain little wots   280
What watch the King keeps to maintain the peace,   281
Whose hours the peasant best advantages.   282

   Enter Erpingham.

ERPINGHAM
My lord, your nobles, jealous of your absence,   283
Seek through your camp to find you.
KING   Good old knight,
Collect them all together at my tent.
I'll be before thee.
ERPINGHAM   I shall do't, my lord.   *Exit.* 286
KING
O God of battles, steel my soldiers' hearts;
Possess them not with fear! Take from them now
The sense of reck'ning, ere th'opposèd numbers   289
Pluck their hearts from them. Not today, O Lord,
Oh, not today, think not upon the fault   291
My father made in compassing the crown!   292
I Richard's body have interrèd new,   293
And on it have bestowed more contrite tears
Than from it issued forcèd drops of blood.
Five hundred poor I have in yearly pay
Who twice a day their withered hands hold up
Toward heaven, to pardon blood; and I have built
Two chantries, where the sad and solemn priests   299
Sing still for Richard's soul. More will I do;   300

---

221 could tell knew   **223 lay** bet. (But also anticipating the meaning
"lay down or lose in battle.")   **crowns** (1) coins (2) heads   **225 English treason** (It was a treasonable offense to clip or "cut" English coins;
it obviously is no offense to slash French heads, and even King Henry
will be such a "clipper.")   **229 careful** full of cares   **232–4 Twin-born
. . . wringing** i.e., inseparable from the condition of being born of
royal rank, a condition that makes a king the subject of the idle gossip
of every fool, even those whose sensibilities pay attention to nothing
other than the rumbling of their own stomachs.   **236 privates** private
persons   **241 comings-in** revenues.   **243 thy soul of adoration** the
essential quality that makes you so much admired.   **244 place** rank
249–50 Oh . . . cure! Learn to cure yourself by being sick, by treating
poisoned flattery and ceremoniousness as a medicine that will purge
you of being in love with your own great greatness.   **251–2 Thinks . . .
adulation?** Do you really think that the fever of vain pride will be
extinguished by speeches breathed by flatterers? (*Blown* also suggests
"inflated.")   **253 Will . . . bending?** i.e., Will the sickness yield to
bowing and scraping?   **257 find thee** i.e., experience greatness and
am able to appraise its worth and limitations   **258 balm** consecrating
oil used to anoint a king in his coronation.   **ball** orb of sovereignty
259 mace ceremonial staff

260 intertissued interwoven   **261 farcèd** stuffed (with pompous
phrases)   **268 distressful** earned by hard work   **270 lackey** (1) footman running alongside the chariot of the sun (2) peasant.   **rise to set**
sunrise to sunset   **271 Phoebus** the sun god   **272 Elysium** in Greek
mythology, the abode of the blessed   **273 Hyperion** the father of the
sun, or the sun itself. (The peasant is up before the sun.)   **278 Had**
would have.   **forehand** upper hand   **279 member** sharer   **280 it** i.e.,
peace.   **wots** knows   **281 watch** wakeful guard   **282 the peasant
best advantages** most benefit the peasant.   **283 jealous of** apprehensive because of   **286 be** be there   **289 sense of reck'ning** ability to
reckon up the odds   **291 the fault** i.e., the deposition and murder of
Richard II   **292 compassing** obtaining   **293 new** anew   **299 chantries**
chapels in which masses for the dead were celebrated.   **sad** grave
300 still continually

Though all that I can do is nothing worth,
Since that my penitence comes after all,   302
Imploring pardon.

Enter Gloucester.

GLOUCESTER   My liege!
KING   My brother Gloucester's voice? Ay;
I know thy errand. I will go with thee.
The day, my friends, and all things stay for me.

Exeunt.

❖

[4.2]

*Enter the Dauphin, Orleans, Rambures, and
Beaumont.*

ORLEANS
The sun doth gild our armor. Up, my lords!
DAUPHIN   *Monte à cheval!* My horse! *Varlet! Lacquais!* Ha!   2
ORLEANS   Oh, brave spirit!
DAUPHIN   *Via, les eaux et terre!*   4
ORLEANS   *Rien puis? L'air et feu?*   5
DAUPHIN   *Cieux,* cousin Orleans.   6

Enter Constable.

Now, my Lord Constable?
CONSTABLE
Hark, how our steeds for present service neigh!   8
DAUPHIN
Mount them, and make incision in their hides,   9
That their hot blood may spin in English eyes   10
And dout them with superfluous courage. Ha!   11
RAMBURES
What, will you have them weep our horses' blood?
How shall we then behold their natural tears?

Enter Messenger.

MESSENGER
The English are embattled, you French peers.   14
CONSTABLE
To horse, you gallant princes, straight to horse!
Do but behold yond poor and starvèd band,
And your fair show shall suck away their souls,   17
Leaving them but the shales and husks of men.   18
There is not work enough for all our hands,
Scarce blood enough in all their sickly veins
To give each naked curtal ax a stain   21

That our French gallants shall today draw out
And sheathe for lack of sport. Let us but blow on
them,
The vapor of our valor will o'erturn them.
'Tis positive against all exceptions, lords,   25
That our superfluous lackeys and our peasants,
Who in unnecessary action swarm
About our squares of battle, were enough   28
To purge this field of such a hilding foe,   29
Though we upon this mountain's basis by   30
Took stand for idle speculation—   31
But that our honors must not. What's to say?   32
A very little little let us do
And all is done. Then let the trumpets sound
The tucket sonance and the note to mount;   35
For our approach shall so much dare the field   36
That England shall couch down in fear and yield.

Enter Grandpré.

GRANDPRÉ
Why do you stay so long, my lords of France?
Yond island carrions, desperate of their bones,   39
Ill-favoredly become the morning field.   40
Their ragged curtains poorly are let loose,   41
And our air shakes them passing scornfully.   42
Big Mars seems bankrupt in their beggared host   43
And faintly through a rusty beaver peeps.   44
The horsemen sit like fixèd candlesticks,
With torch staves in their hand, and their poor jades   46
Lob down their heads, drooping the hides and hips, 47
The gum down-roping from their pale-dead eyes,   48
And in their pale dull mouths the gimmaled bit   49
Lies foul with chewed grass, still and motionless;
And their executors, the knavish crows,   51
Fly o'er them all impatient for their hour.
Description cannot suit itself in words
To demonstrate the life of such a battle   54
In life so lifeless as it shows itself.
CONSTABLE
They have said their prayers, and they stay for death.   56
DAUPHIN
Shall we go send them dinners and fresh suits,
And give their fasting horses provender,   58
And after fight with them?
CONSTABLE
I stay but for my guard. On to the field!   60
I will the banner from a trumpet take,   61

---

302 Since that necessitating that
4.2. Location: The French camp.
0.2 Beaumont (The Folio text mentions Lord Beaumont but does not
give him a speaking part.)   **2 Monte à cheval!** To horse!   **4 Via . . .
terre!** Begone, waters and earth! (The Dauphin imagines himself riding through and over rivers and solid ground.)   **5 Rien . . . feu?**
Nothing more? What about air and fire? (i.e., Why not soar above all
four elements, not just water and earth?)   **6 Cieux** The heavens. (The
Dauphin carries the metaphor one step further to its ultimate height.)
8 present service immediate action   **9 incision** i.e., with spurs
10 spin gush, spatter   **11 And . . . courage** i.e., and put out the English eyes with the horses' superfluous blood, the proof of their excessive courage.   **dout** put out   **14 embattled** arranged in battle order
17 fair show impressive appearance   **18 shales** shells   **21 curtal ax**
cutlass, short sword

25 exceptions objections   **28 squares of battle** four-sided military
formations   **29 hilding** worthless, base   **30 basis** foot.   **by** nearby
31 speculation looking on   **32 But that** except for the fact that
35 tucket sonance trumpet call.   **mount** mount our horses   **36 dare**
(1) defy (2) stupify with fear   **39 carrions** cadavers for the scavenger
birds.   **desperate of** without hope of saving   **40 Ill-favoredly**
become i.e., are an eyesore to   **41 curtains** colors, banners   **42 passing** exceedingly   **43 Mars** the god of war   **44 beaver** visor   **46 torch
staves** i.e., tapers in place of lances. (The horsemen themselves look
like carved candleholders.)   **47 Lob down** hang down.   **drooping**
letting droop   **48 gum** watery discharge.   **down-roping** hanging
down ropelike   **49 gimmaled** jointed   **51 their executors** the dis-
posers of their remains   **54 battle** army   **56 stay for** await
58 provender fodder   **60 guard** (Including a standard-bearer.)
61 trumpet trumpeter

And use it for my haste. Come, come, away!
The sun is high, and we outwear the day.   *Exeunt.*   63

❖

[4.3]

Enter Gloucester, Bedford, Exeter, Erpingham,
with all his host, Salisbury, and Westmorland.

GLOUCESTER   Where is the King?

BEDFORD
The King himself is rode to view their battle.   2

WESTMORLAND
Of fighting men they have full threescore thousand.

EXETER
There's five to one. Besides, they all are fresh.

SALISBURY
God's arm strike with us! 'Tis a fearful odds.
God b'wi' you, princes all; I'll to my charge.   6
If we no more meet till we meet in heaven,
Then, joyfully, my noble lord of Bedford,
My dear lord Gloucester, and my good lord Exeter,
And my kind kinsman, warriors all, adieu!   10

BEDFORD
Farewell, good Salisbury, and good luck go with thee!

EXETER
Farewell, kind lord. Fight valiantly today!
And yet I do thee wrong to mind thee of it,   13
For thou art framed of the firm truth of valor.   14
                                        [*Exit Salisbury.*]

BEDFORD
He is as full of valor as of kindness,
Princely in both.

                Enter the King.

WESTMORLAND   Oh, that we now had here
But one ten thousand of those men in England
That do no work today!

KING   What's he that wishes so?   18
My cousin Westmorland? No, my fair cousin.
If we are marked to die, we are enough   20
To do our country loss; and if to live,   21
The fewer men, the greater share of honor.
God's will, I pray thee, wish not one man more.
By Jove, I am not covetous for gold,
Nor care I who doth feed upon my cost;   25
It yearns me not if men my garments wear;   26
Such outward things dwell not in my desires.
But if it be a sin to covet honor
I am the most offending soul alive.
No, faith, my coz, wish not a man from England.   30
God's peace, I would not lose so great an honor
As one man more, methinks, would share from me   32
For the best hope I have. Oh, do not wish one more!   33

Rather proclaim it, Westmorland, through my host   34
That he which hath no stomach to this fight,   35
Let him depart; his passport shall be made
And crowns for convoy put into his purse.   37
We would not die in that man's company
That fears his fellowship to die with us.   39
This day is called the Feast of Crispian.   40
He that outlives this day and comes safe home
Will stand a-tiptoe when this day is named
And rouse him at the name of Crispian.
He that shall see this day and live old age   44
Will yearly on the vigil feast his neighbors   45
And say, "Tomorrow is Saint Crispian."
Then will he strip his sleeve and show his scars,
And say, "These wounds I had on Crispin's Day."
Old men forget; yet all shall be forgot,   49
But he'll remember with advantages   50
What feats he did that day. Then shall our names,
Familiar in his mouth as household words—
Harry the King, Bedford and Exeter,
Warwick and Talbot, Salisbury and Gloucester—
Be in their flowing cups freshly remembered.
This story shall the good man teach his son;
And Crispin Crispian shall ne'er go by,
From this day to the ending of the world,
But we in it shall be rememberèd—
We few, we happy few, we band of brothers.
For he today that sheds his blood with me
Shall be my brother; be he ne'er so vile,   62
This day shall gentle his condition.   63
And gentlemen in England now abed
Shall think themselves accurst they were not here,
And hold their manhoods cheap whiles any speaks
That fought with us upon Saint Crispin's Day.

                Enter Salisbury.

SALISBURY
My sovereign lord, bestow yourself with speed.   68
The French are bravely in their battles set,   69
And will with all expedience charge on us.   70

KING
All things are ready, if our minds be so.

WESTMORLAND
Perish the man whose mind is backward now!   72

KING
Thou dost not wish more help from England, coz?

WESTMORLAND
God's will, my liege, would you and I alone,
Without more help, could fight this royal battle!

---

63 **outwear** waste
4.3. Location: The English camp.
2 battle army.   **6 charge** post, command.   **10 kinsman** i.e., Westmorland, whose son had married Salisbury's daughter   **13 mind** remind   **14 framed** made, built   **18 What's** Who is   **20–1 enough . . . loss** enough loss for our country to suffer   **25 upon my cost** at my expense   **26 yearns** grieves   **30 coz** cousin, kinsman   **32 share from me** take from me as his share   **33 For . . . have** i.e., in exchange for my hope of eternal life.

34 host army   **35 stomach to** appetite for   **37 crowns for convoy** travel money   **39 That . . . us** who is afraid to risk his life in my company.   **40 Feast of Crispian** Saint Crispin's Day, October 25. (Crispinus and Crispianus were martyrs who fled from Rome in the third century; according to legend, they disguised themselves as shoemakers and afterward became the patron saints of that craft.)   **44 live** live to see   **45 vigil** evening before a feast day   **49 yet** in time   **50 advantages** additions of his own   **62 vile** lowly   **63 gentle his condition** i.e., raise his social status to the equivalent of gentleman in that he is my "brother."   **68 bestow yourself** take up your battle position   **69 bravely . . . set** finely arrayed in their battalions   **70 expedience** speed   **72 backward** reluctant

KING

Why, now thou hast unwished five thousand men,
Which likes me better than to wish us one.—
You know your places. God be with you all! 77

Tucket. Enter Montjoy.

MONTJOY

Once more I come to know of thee, King Harry,
If for thy ransom thou wilt now compound 80
Before thy most assurèd overthrow;
For certainly thou art so near the gulf 82
Thou needs must be englutted. Besides, in mercy 83
The Constable desires thee thou wilt mind 84
Thy followers of repentance, that their souls
May make a peaceful and a sweet retire 86
From off these fields where, wretches, their poor
bodies
Must lie and fester.

KING   Who hath sent thee now?
MONTJOY   The Constable of France.
KING

I pray thee, bear my former answer back:
Bid them achieve me, and then sell my bones. 91
Good God, why should they mock poor fellows thus?
The man that once did sell the lion's skin
While the beast lived was killed with hunting him.
A many of our bodies shall no doubt 95
Find native graves, upon the which, I trust, 96
Shall witness live in brass of this day's work.
And those that leave their valiant bones in France,
Dying like men, though buried in your dunghills,
They shall be famed; for there the sun shall greet them
And draw their honors reeking up to heaven, 101
Leaving their earthly parts to choke your clime,
The smell whereof shall breed a plague in France.
Mark then abounding valor in our English, 104
That, being dead, like to the bullets crazing 105
Break out into a second course of mischief,
Killing in relapse of mortality. 107
Let me speak proudly. Tell the Constable
We are but warriors for the working day. 109
Our gayness and our gilt are all besmirched
With rainy marching in the painful field.
There's not a piece of feather in our host—
Good argument, I hope, we will not fly—
And time hath worn us into slovenry. 114
But, by the Mass, our hearts are in the trim! 115
And my poor soldiers tell me, yet ere night

They'll be in fresher robes, or they will pluck 117
The gay new coats o'er the French soldiers' heads 118
And turn them out of service. If they do this— 119
As, if God please, they shall—my ransom then
Will soon be levied. Herald, save thou thy labor. 121
Come thou no more for ransom, gentle herald. 122
They shall have none, I swear, but these my joints,
Which if they have as I will leave 'em them,
Shall yield them little, tell the Constable.
MONTJOY

I shall, King Harry. And so fare thee well.
Thou never shalt hear herald any more.   *Exit.*
KING

I fear thou wilt once more come again for a ransom.

Enter York [and kneels].

YORK

My lord, most humbly on my knee I beg
The leading of the vaward. 130
KING

Take it, brave York. Now, soldiers, march away.
And how thou pleasest, God, dispose the day!
Exeunt.

❖

[4.4]

*Alarum. Excursions. Enter Pistol, French Soldier,
[and] Boy.*

PISTOL   Yield, cur!
FRENCH SOLDIER   *Je pense que vous êtes le gentilhomme de* 2
bonne qualité. 3
PISTOL

Qualtitie calmie custure me! 4
Art thou a gentleman? What is thy name? Discuss. 5
FRENCH SOLDIER   *O Seigneur Dieu!* 6
PISTOL

Oh, Signieur Dew should be a gentleman.
Perpend my words, O Signieur Dew, and mark: 8
O Signieur Dew, thou diest on point of fox, 9
Except, O signieur, thou do give to me 10
Egregious ransom.   [*He threatens him with his sword.*] 11
FRENCH SOLDIER   *Oh, prenez miséricorde! Ayez pitié de* 12
moi! 13
PISTOL

"Moy" shall not serve. I will have forty moys, 14
Or I will fetch thy rim out at thy throat 15

117–19 They'll . . . service they will be more freshly dressed by nightfall, if no other way than by defrocking the French soldiers like incapable servants being dismissed and stripped of their livery. (Soldiers
got to keep such spoils of war from their victims.)   **121 levied** collected.   **122 gentle** noble   **130 vaward** vanguard.
4.4. Location: The field of battle.
0.1 *Excursions* Sorties.   **2–3** *Je . . . qualité* I think that you are a gentleman of high rank.   **4** *calmie custure me* (These words are perhaps
derived from the refrain of a popular song, supposed to be Irish, "Calen
o custure me.")   **5 Discuss** Speak.   **6** *O Seigneur Dieu!* O Lord God!
8 Perpend Attend to, consider   **9 fox** sword   **10 Except** unless
11 Egregious huge   **12–13 Oh . . . moi!** Oh, have mercy! Take pity on me!
14 Moy (Pistol, not understanding, takes *moi* for the name of a coin or
a sum of money, a moiety or half.)   **15 rim** midriff, diaphragm

77 likes pleases   **80 compound** make terms   **82 gulf** whirlpool
83 englutted swallowed up.   **84 mind** remind   **86 retire** retreat
91 achieve capture   **95 A many** Many. (The phrase is an exact parallel to "a few.")   **96 native** in our own land (i.e., England)   **101 reeking** (1) breathing (2) smelling   **104 abounding** overflowing,
abundant   **105 crazing** shattering, with a suggestion also of *grazing*,
"ricocheting"   **107 Killing . . . mortality** killing (their foes) as they
(the English) fall back (decompose) into their elements; also, like the
bullet, with a deadly ricochet.   **109 for the working day** to do serious work, not take a holiday.   **114 slovenry** slovenliness, untidiness.
115 in the trim fully rigged, ready for action.

In drops of crimson blood.

FRENCH SOLDIER　*Est-il impossible d'échapper la force de ton* 17
bras? 18

PISTOL　Brass, cur?
Thou damnèd and luxurious mountain goat, 20
Offer'st me brass?

FRENCH SOLDIER　*Oh, pardonnez-moi!*

PISTOL
Say'st thou me so? Is that a ton of moys?— 23
Come hither, boy. Ask me this slave in French
What is his name.

BOY　*Écoutez: comment êtes-vous appelé?* 26

FRENCH SOLDIER　*Monsieur Le Fer.*

BOY　He says his name is Master Fer.

PISTOL　Master Fer? I'll fer him, and firk him, and ferret 29
him. Discuss the same in French unto him.

BOY　I do not know the French for fer, and ferret, and
firk.

PISTOL
Bid him prepare, for I will cut his throat.

FRENCH SOLDIER　*Que dit-il, monsieur?* 34

BOY　*Il me commande à vous dire que vous faites vous* 35
prêt; car ce soldat ici est disposé tout à cette heure de 36
couper votre gorge. 37

PISTOL
Owy, cuppele gorge, permafoy, 38
Peasant, unless thou give me crowns, brave crowns,
Or mangled shalt thou be by this my sword.

FRENCH SOLDIER　*Oh, je vous supplie, pour l'amour de* 41
Dieu, me pardonner! Je suis le gentilhomme de bonne 42
maison. Gardez ma vie, et je vous donnerai deux cents 43
écus. 44

PISTOL　What are his words?

BOY　He prays you to save his life. He is a gentleman of
a good house, and for his ransom he will give you two 47
hundred crowns.

PISTOL
Tell him my fury shall abate, and I
The crowns will take.

FRENCH SOLDIER　*Petit monsieur, que dit-il?* 51

BOY　*Encore qu'il est contre son jurement de pardonner* 52
aucun prisonnier, néanmoins, pour les écus que vous 53
l'avez promis, il est content à vous donner la liberté, 54
le franchisement. 55

FRENCH SOLDIER　[*kneeling*]　*Sur mes genoux je vous* 56
donne mille remercîments; et je m'estime heureux que 57
j'ai tombé entre les mains d'un chevalier, je pense, 58
le plus brave, vaillant, et très-distingué seigneur 59
d'Angleterre. 60

PISTOL　Expound unto me, boy.

BOY　He gives you, upon his knees, a thousand thanks,
and he esteems himself happy that he hath fallen into
the hands of one, as he thinks, the most brave, valor-
ous, and thrice-worthy signieur of England.

PISTOL
As I suck blood, I will some mercy show.
Follow me!

BOY　*Suivez-vous le grand capitaine.* 68

　　　　　[*Exeunt Pistol and French Soldier.*]
I did never know so full a voice issue
from so empty a heart! But the saying is true, "The
empty vessel makes the greatest sound." Bardolph and
Nym had ten times more valor than this roaring devil 72
i'th'old play, that everyone may pare his nails with 73
a wooden dagger, and they are both hanged; and so 74
would this be, if he durst steal anything adventur-
ously. I must stay with the lackeys, with the luggage
of our camp. The French might have a good prey of 77
us, if he knew of it, for there is none to guard it but
boys.　　　　　　　　　　　　　　　　　*Exit.*

❧

[4.5]

Enter Constable, Orleans, Bourbon, Dauphin, and
Rambures.

CONSTABLE　*Oh, diable!* 1

ORLEANS　*Oh, Seigneur! Le jour est perdu, tout est perdu!* 2

DAUPHIN
Mort de ma vie! All is confounded, all. 3
Reproach and everlasting shame
Sits mocking in our plumes.　　　*A short alarum.*
Oh, méchante fortune! Do not run away. 6

CONSTABLE　Why, all our ranks are broke.

DAUPHIN
Oh, perdurable shame! Let's stab ourselves. 8
Be these the wretches that we played at dice for?

ORLEANS
Is this the king we sent to for his ransom?

BOURBON
Shame and eternal shame, nothing but shame!
Let us die! In once more! Back again!

17–18 *Est-il . . . bras?* Is it impossible to escape the strength of your
arm? (But Pistol takes *bras,* "arm," for *brass.*)　20 **luxurious** lecherous
23 **a ton of moys** (This is what Pistol phonetically makes out of
pardonnez-moi.)　26 *Écoutez . . . appelé*? Listen: what is your name?
29 **firk** trounce.　**ferret** worry (like a ferret)　34–7 *Que . . . gorge*
What does he say, sir? BOY He bids me tell you that you must prepare
yourself, because this soldier intends to cut your throat immediately.
38 *Owy Oui,* "yes."　*permafoy per ma foi,* by my faith　41–4 *Oh . . .*
écus Oh, I pray you, for the love of God, to pardon me! I am a gentleman of a good house; preserve my life, and I shall give you two hundred crowns.　47 **house** family　51–5 *Petit . . . franchisement* What
does he say, little sir? BOY Although it is against his oath to pardon
any prisoner, nevertheless, for the sake of the crowns you have
promised, he is willing to give you your liberty, your freedom.

56–60 *Sur . . . d'Angleterre* On my knees, I give you a thousand
thanks, and I consider myself happy that I have fallen into the hands
of a knight, as I think, the bravest, most valiant, and very distinguished gentleman in England.　68 *Suivez-vous . . . capitaine* Follow
the great captain.　72–4 **this roaring . . . dagger** Shakespeare refers
several times to the devil in the morality play with his dagger of lath;
see *2H6,* 4.2.2 and *Twelfth Night,* 4.2.126. The paring of the devil's nails
was a proverbial act of bravado.　77 **a good prey** i.e., easy pickings
4.5. Location: The field of battle still.
1 *Oh, diable!* Oh, the devil!　2 *Oh . . . perdu!* Oh, Lord, the day is lost,
all is lost!　3 *Mort . . . vie!* Death to my life!　**confounded** lost
6 *Oh, méchante fortune!* Oh, malicious fortune!　8 **perdurable** everlasting

And he that will not follow Bourbon now,
Let him go hence, and with his cap in hand,
Like a base pander, hold the chamber door
Whilst by a slave, no gentler than my dog,   16
His fairest daughter is contaminated.

CONSTABLE
Disorder, that hath spoiled us, friend us now!   18
Let us on heaps go offer up our lives.   19

ORLEANS
We are enough yet living in the field
To smother up the English in our throngs,
If any order might be thought upon.

BOURBON
The devil take order now! I'll to the throng.
Let life be short, else shame will be too long.
                                                                    Exeunt.

[4.6]

*Alarum. Enter the King and his train, [Exeter,
and others,] with prisoners.*

KING
Well have we done, thrice valiant countrymen!
But all's not done; yet keep the French the field.   2

EXETER
The Duke of York commends him to Your Majesty.

KING
Lives he, good uncle? Thrice within this hour
I saw him down, thrice up again and fighting.
From helmet to the spur all blood he was.

EXETER
In which array, brave soldier, doth he lie,
Larding the plain; and by his bloody side,   8
Yokefellow to his honor-owing wounds,   9
The noble Earl of Suffolk also lies.
Suffolk first died; and York, all haggled over,   11
Comes to him, where in gore he lay insteeped,   12
And takes him by the beard, kisses the gashes
That bloodily did yawn upon his face.   14
He cries aloud, "Tarry, my cousin Suffolk!
My soul shall thine keep company to heaven;
Tarry, sweet soul, for mine, then fly abreast,
As in this glorious and well-foughten field
We kept together in our chivalry!"
Upon these words I came and cheered him up.
He smiled me in the face, raught me his hand,   21
And with a feeble grip says, "Dear my lord,
Commend my service to my sovereign."
So did he turn, and over Suffolk's neck
He threw his wounded arm, and kissed his lips,
And so, espoused to death, with blood he sealed

A testament of noble-ending love.
The pretty and sweet manner of it forced
Those waters from me which I would have stopped;   29
But I had not so much of man in me,
And all my mother came into mine eyes   31
And gave me up to tears.

KING   I blame you not;
For, hearing this, I must perforce compound   33
With mistful eyes, or they will issue too.   *Alarum.*   34
But, hark, what new alarum is this same?
The French have reinforced their scattered men.
Then every soldier kill his prisoners!   37
Give the word through.   *Exeunt.*

❖

[4.7]

Enter Fluellen and Gower.

FLUELLEN   Kill the poys and the luggage? 'Tis expressly   1
against the law of arms. 'Tis as arrant a piece of
knavery, mark you now, as can be offert; in your
conscience, now, is it not?

GOWER   'Tis certain there's not a boy left alive; and the
cowardly rascals that ran from the battle ha' done this
slaughter. Besides, they have burned and carried
away all that was in the King's tent, wherefore the
King most worthily hath caused every soldier to cut
his prisoner's throat. Oh, 'tis a gallant king!

FLUELLEN   Ay, he was porn at Monmouth, Captain   11
Gower. What call you the town's name where Alexander the Pig was born?

GOWER   Alexander the Great.

FLUELLEN   Why, I pray you, is not "pig" great? The pig,
or the great, or the mighty, or the huge, or the
magnanimous, are all one reckonings, save the phrase   17
is a little variations.

GOWER   I think Alexander the Great was born in
Macedon. His father was called Philip of Macedon, as
I take it.

FLUELLEN   I think it is e'en Macedon where Alexander is
born. I tell you, Captain, if you look in the maps of the
'orld, I warrant you sall find, in the comparisons between Macedon and Monmouth, that the situations,
look you, is both alike. There is a river in Macedon,
and there is also moreover a river at Monmouth. It is
called Wye at Monmouth, but it is out of my prains
what is the name of the other river; but 'tis all one, 'tis
alike as my fingers is to my fingers, and there is sal-
mons in both. If you mark Alexander's life well, Harry
of Monmouth's life is come after it indifferent well, for 32
there is figures in all things. Alexander, God knows,   33

---

16 **gentler** (1) more nobly born (2) tenderer   18 **friend** befriend
19 **on** in
4.6. Location: The field of battle still.
2 **yet . . . field** the French are in the field of battle still.   8 **Larding**
fattening, enriching (with his blood)   9 **honor-owing** honor-owning,
honorable   11 **haggled over** mangled, hacked   12 **insteeped**
steeped, soaked   14 **yawn** gape   21 **me in the** in my.   **raught**
reached

29 **waters** i.e., tears   31 **my mother** i.e., the tenderer part of me
33 **perforce** necessarily.   **compound** come to terms   34 **issue** issue
forth tears   37 **kill his prisoners** (This follows Holinshed, who says
that Henry, alarmed by the outcry of the lackeys and boys of the
camp, feared a new attack and ordered the prisoners killed as a precaution. Gower, 4.7.8–10, attributes the King's action to revenge.)
4.7. Location: The field of battle still.
1 **luggage** i.e., lackeys guarding the luggage.   11 **Monmouth** (i.e., in
Wales)   17 **are . . . reckonings** come to the same thing   32 **is . . . well**
resembles it fairly well   33 **figures** comparisons, similes

and you know, in his rages, and his furies, and his
wraths, and his cholers, and his moods, and his dis-
pleasures, and his indignations, and also being a little
intoxicates in his prains, did, in his ales and his angers, 37
look you, kill his best friend, Cleitus. 38

GOWER   Our King is not like him in that. He never killed
any of his friends.

FLUELLEN   It is not well done, mark you now, to take
the tales out of my mouth ere it is made and finished.
I speak but in the figures and comparisons of it. As
Alexander killed his friend Cleitus, being in his ales
and his cups, so also Harry Monmouth, being in his
right wits and his good judgments, turned away the
fat knight with the great-belly doublet. He was full of 47
jests, and gipes, and knaveries, and mocks. I have 48
forgot his name.

GOWER   Sir John Falstaff.

FLUELLEN   That is he. I'll tell you there is good men
porn at Monmouth.

GOWER   Here comes His Majesty.

Alarum. Enter King Harry, [Warwick, Gloucester,
Exeter, and others,] and Bourbon, with [other]
prisoners. Flourish.

KING
I was not angry since I came to France
Until this instant. Take a trumpet, herald; 55
Ride thou unto the horsemen on yond hill.
If they will fight with us, bid them come down,
Or void the field. They do offend our sight. 58
If they'll do neither, we will come to them,
And make them skirr away as swift as stones 60
Enforcèd from the old Assyrian slings. 61
Besides, we'll cut the throats of those we have,
And not a man of them that we shall take
Shall taste our mercy. Go and tell them so.

Enter Montjoy.

EXETER
Here comes the herald of the French, my liege.

GLOUCESTER
His eyes are humbler than they used to be.

KING
How now, what means this, herald? Know'st thou
not
That I have fined these bones of mine for ransom? 68
Com'st thou again for ransom?

MONTJOY   No, great King.
I come to thee for charitable license,
That we may wander o'er this bloody field
To book our dead and then to bury them, 72
To sort our nobles from our common men.

For many of our princes—woe the while!—
Lie drowned and soaked in mercenary blood; 75
So do our vulgar drench their peasant limbs 76
In blood of princes; and the wounded steeds
Fret fetlock-deep in gore and with wild rage 78
Yerk out their armèd heels at their dead masters, 79
Killing them twice. Oh, give us leave, great King,
To view the field in safety, and dispose
Of their dead bodies!

KING   I tell thee truly, herald,
I know not if the day be ours or no,
For yet a many of your horsemen peer 84
And gallop o'er the field.

MONTJOY   The day is yours.

KING
Praisèd be God, and not our strength, for it!
What is this castle called that stands hard by?

MONTJOY   They call it Agincourt.

KING
Then call we this the field of Agincourt,
Fought on the day of Crispin Crispianus.

FLUELLEN   Your grandfather of famous memory, an't 91
please Your Majesty, and your great-uncle Edward the
Plack Prince of Wales, as I have read in the chronicles,
fought a most prave pattle here in France.

KING   They did, Fluellen.

FLUELLEN   Your Majesty says very true. If Your Majesties is remembered of it, the Welshmen did good
service in a garden where leeks did grow, wearing
leeks in their Monmouth caps, which, Your Majesty 99
know, to this hour is an honorable badge of the
service; and I do believe Your Majesty takes no scorn
to wear the leek upon Saint Tavy's Day. 102

KING
I wear it for a memorable honor,
For I am Welsh, you know, good countryman.

FLUELLEN   All the water in Wye cannot wash Your
Majesty's Welsh plood out of your pody, I can tell you
that. God pless it and preserve it, as long as it pleases
His Grace, and His Majesty too!

KING   Thanks, good my countryman.

FLUELLEN   By Jeshu, I am Your Majesty's countryman.
I care not who know it. I will confess it to all the 'orld.
I need not to be ashamed of Your Majesty, praised be
God, so long as Your Majesty is an honest man.

KING
God keep me so!

Enter Williams [with a glove in his cap].

Our heralds go with him.
Bring me just notice of the numbers dead 115

---

37 in his ales i.e., under the influence of ale   **38 Cleitus** a general
and close associate of Alexander, whom Alexander killed in a drinking bout.   **47 great-belly doublet** a man's close-fitting jacket, in
which the lower part was stuffed out with bombast or padding.
48 gipes gibes, jokes   **55 trumpet** trumpeter   **58 void** leave
60 skirr scurry   **61 Enforcèd** discharged   **68 fined . . . ransom** i.e.,
agreed to pay as a fine or ransom only these bones of mine and no
more.   **72 book** record

75 mercenary i.e., of common soldiers, who fought for pay   **76 vulgar** commoners   **78 fetlock-deep** (The *fetlock* is above the hoof, at the
back of the leg.)   **79 Yerk** kick   **84 peer** (1) look bout anxiously
(2) appear   **91 grandfather** i.e., great-grandfather, Edward III.   **an't**
if it   **99 Monmouth caps** round and rimless caps with a tapering
crown, commonly worn by the Welsh   **102 Saint Tavy's Day** the festival of Saint David, patron saint of Wales, March 1—an occasion for
the celebration of Welsh traditions, though the wearing of leeks to
commemorate the great victory in 540 against the Saxons did not
begin until well after the setting of this play.   **115 just** exact

On both our parts.
        [Exeunt Heralds and Gower with Montjoy.]
        Call yonder fellow hither.

EXETER *[to Williams]*   Soldier, you must come to the King.

KING   Soldier, why wear'st thou that glove in thy cap?

WILLIAMS   An't please Your Majesty, 'tis the gage of one that I should fight withal, if he be alive.

KING   An Englishman?

WILLIAMS   An't please Your Majesty, a rascal that swaggered with me last night, who, if 'a live and ever dare to challenge this glove, I have sworn to take him a box o'th'ear; or if I can see my glove in his cap, which he swore, as he was a soldier, he would wear if 'a lived, I will strike it out soundly.

KING   What think you, Captain Fluellen, is it fit this soldier keep his oath?

FLUELLEN   He is a craven and a villain else, an't please 130 Your Majesty, in my conscience.

KING   It may be his enemy is a gentleman of great sort, 132 quite from the answer of his degree. 133

FLUELLEN   Though he be as good a gentleman as the devil is, as Lucifer and Beelzebub himself, it is necessary, look Your Grace, that he keep his vow and his oath. If he be perjured, see you now, his reputation is as arrant a villain and a Jack-sauce as ever his 138 black shoe trod upon God's ground and His earth, in my conscience, la!

KING *[to Williams]*   Then keep thy vow, sirrah, when thou meet'st the fellow.

WILLIAMS   So I will, my liege, as I live.

KING   Who serv'st thou under?

WILLIAMS   Under Captain Gower, my liege.

FLUELLEN   Gower is a good captain, and is good knowledge and literatured in the wars. 147

KING   Call him hither to me, soldier.

WILLIAMS   I will, my liege.   *Exit.*

KING   Here, Fluellen, wear thou this favor for me and stick it in thy cap. *[He gives Fluellen Williams' glove.]* When Alençon and myself were down together, I plucked this glove from his helm. If any man challenge 153 this, he is a friend to Alençon and an enemy to our person. If thou encounter any such, apprehend him, an thou dost me love. 156

FLUELLEN *[putting the glove in his cap]*   Your Grace doo's 157 me as great honors as can be desired in the hearts of his subjects. I would fain see the man that 159 has but two legs that shall find himself aggriefed at this glove, that is all. But I would fain see it once, an't 161 please God of his grace that I might see.

KING   Know'st thou Gower?

FLUELLEN   He is my dear friend, an't please you.

KING   Pray thee, go seek him and bring him to my tent.

FLUELLEN   I will fetch him.   *Exit.*

KING
My lord of Warwick, and my brother Gloucester,
Follow Fluellen closely at the heels.
The glove which I have given him for a favor
May haply purchase him a box o'th'ear. 170
It is the soldier's; I by bargain should
Wear it myself. Follow, good cousin Warwick.
If that the soldier strike him, as I judge
By his blunt bearing he will keep his word,
Some sudden mischief may arise of it;
For I do know Fluellen valiant
And touched with choler, hot as gunpowder, 177
And quickly will return an injury. 178
Follow, and see there be no harm between them.
Go you with me, uncle of Exeter.   *Exeunt [separately].*

[4.8]

Enter Gower and Williams.

WILLIAMS   I warrant it is to knight you, Captain.

Enter Fluellen.

FLUELLEN   God's will and his pleasure, Captain, I beseech you now, come apace to the King. There is more good toward you, peradventure, than is in your knowledge to dream of.

WILLIAMS   Sir, know you this glove?

FLUELLEN   Know the glove? I know the glove is a glove.

WILLIAMS   I know this, and thus I challenge it.
                      Strikes him.

FLUELLEN   'Sblood, an arrant traitor as any 's in the 9 universal world, or in France, or in England!

GOWER *[to Williams]*   How now, sir? You villain!

WILLIAMS   Do you think I'll be forsworn?

FLUELLEN   Stand away, Captain Gower. I will give treason his payment into plows, I warrant you. 14

WILLIAMS   I am no traitor.

FLUELLEN   That's a lie in thy throat.—I charge you in His 16 Majesty's name, apprehend him. He's a friend of the Duke Alençon's.

Enter Warwick and Gloucester.

WARWICK   How now, how now, what's the matter?

FLUELLEN   My lord of Warwick, here is—praised be God for it!—a most contagious treason come to light, 21 look you, as you shall desire in a summer's day.— Here is His Majesty.

Enter King [Henry] and Exeter.

KING   How now, what's the matter?

FLUELLEN   My liege, here is a villain and a traitor that, look Your Grace, has struck the glove which Your Majesty is take out of the helmet of Alençon.

---

130 **craven** coward   132 **sort** rank   133 **quite . . . degree** i.e., too high in rank to answer the challenge of one so low.   138 **Jack-sauce** saucy knave   147 **literatured** well read   153 **helm** helmet.   156 **an** if 157 **doo's** does   159 **fain** willingly   161 **an't** if it. (Also in line 164.)

170 **haply** perhaps   177 **touched with choler** hot-tempered
178 **return an injury** repay an insult.
4.8. Location: The English camp.
9 **'Sblood** By His (Christ's) blood   14 **his** its.   **into plows** in blows
16 **lie in thy throat** i.e., inexcusable lie.   21 **contagious** noxious

WILLIAMS   My liege, this was my glove; here is the fellow of it. [*Showing his other glove.*] And he that I gave it
to in change promised to wear it in his cap. I promised   30
to strike him, if he did. I met this man with my glove
in his cap, and I have been as good as my word.

FLUELLEN   Your Majesty hear now, saving Your Majesty's manhood, what an arrant, rascally, beggarly,
lousy knave it is. I hope Your Majesty is pear me   35
testimony and witness, and will avouchment, that this   36
is the glove of Alençon that Your Majesty is give me,
in your conscience, now.

KING   Give me thy glove, soldier. Look, here is the
fellow of it.   [*He shows his other glove.*]
'Twas I indeed thou promisèd'st to strike,
And thou hast given me most bitter terms.   42

FLUELLEN   An't please Your Majesty, let his neck
answer for it, if there is any martial law in the world.

KING
How canst thou make me satisfaction?

WILLIAMS   All offenses, my lord, come from the heart.
Never came any from mine that might offend Your
Majesty.

KING   It was ourself thou didst abuse.

WILLIAMS   Your Majesty came not like yourself. You
appeared to me but as a common man—witness the
night, your garments, your lowliness. And what Your   52
Highness suffered under that shape, I beseech you take
it for your own fault and not mine; for had you been
as I took you for, I made no offense. Therefore I beseech Your Highness pardon me.

KING
Here, uncle Exeter, fill this glove with crowns,
And give it to this fellow.—Keep it, fellow,
And wear it for an honor in thy cap
Till I do challenge it.—Give him the crowns.
                    [*Exeter gives the glove and gold to Williams.*]
And Captain, you must needs be friends with him.

FLUELLEN   By this day and this light, the fellow has
mettle enough in his belly.—Hold, there is twelve-
pence for you. [*He offers Williams a coin.*] And I pray you
to serve God, and keep you out of prawls, and
prabbles, and quarrels, and dissensions, and I warrant   66
you it is the better for you.

WILLIAMS   I will none of your money.

FLUELLEN   It is with a good will. I can tell you, it will
serve you to mend your shoes. Come, wherefore
should you be so pashful? Your shoes is not so good.
'Tis a good silling, I warrant you, or I will change it.

          Enter [an English] Herald.

KING   Now, herald, are the dead numbered?

HERALD [*giving a paper*]
Here is the number of the slaughtered French.

KING
What prisoners of good sort are taken, uncle?   75

EXETER [*reading*]
Charles Duke of Orleans, nephew to the King;   76
John Duke of Bourbon, and Lord Boucicault;
Of other lords and barons, knights and squires,
Full fifteen hundred, besides common men.

KING
This note doth tell me of ten thousand French
That in the field lie slain. Of princes, in this number,
And nobles bearing banners, there lie dead   82
One hundred twenty-six; added to these,
Of knights, esquires, and gallant gentlemen,
Eight thousand and four hundred, of the which
Five hundred were but yesterday dubbed knights.
So that in these ten thousand they have lost
There are but sixteen hundred mercenaries;
The rest are princes, barons, lords, knights, squires,
And gentlemen of blood and quality.
The names of those their nobles that lie dead:
Charles Delabreth, High Constable of France;
Jaques of Chatillion, Admiral of France;
The Master of the Crossbows, Lord Rambures;
Great-Master of France, the brave Sir Guichard
     Dauphin   95
John, Duke of Alençon; Anthony, Duke of Brabant,
The brother to the Duke of Burgundy;
And Edward, Duke of Bar; of lusty earls,   98
Grandpré and Roussi, Faulconbridge and Foix,
Beaumont and Marle, Vaudemont and Lestrelles.
Here was a royal fellowship of death!
Where is the number of our English dead?
                    [*He is given another paper.*]
Edward the Duke of York, the Earl of Suffolk,
Sir Richard Keighley, Davy Gam, esquire;
None else of name, and of all other men   105
But five-and-twenty. O God, thy arm was here!
And not to us, but to thy arm alone,
Ascribe we all. When, without stratagem,
But in plain shock and even play of battle,   109
Was ever known so great and little loss
On one part and on th'other? Take it, God,
For it is none but thine.

EXETER   'Tis wonderful.   112

KING
Come, go we in procession to the village.
And be it death proclaimèd through our host
To boast of this or take that praise from God
Which is his only.

FLUELLEN   Is it not lawful, an't please Your Majesty, to
tell how many is killed?

KING
Yes, Captain, but with this acknowledgment,
That God fought for us.

---

30 **change** exchange   35 **is pear** will bear   36 **avouchment** avouch
42 **terms** words.   52 **lowliness** humble mien.
66 **prabbles** i.e., brabbles, scuffles   75 **good sort** high rank

76–112 **Charles . . . thine** (The catalogue of the captured and slain is
from Holinshed.)   82 **bearing banners** i.e., with coats of arms
95 **Great-Master** grandmaster, i.e., the chief officer of the royal household   98 **lusty** vigorous   105 **name** rank, social importance
109 **even** equal

FLUELLEN Yes, in my conscience, he did us great good.
KING Do we all holy rites.
    Let there be sung *Non nobis* and *Te Deum*,   123
    The dead with charity enclosed in clay;
    And then to Calais, and to England then,
    Where ne'er from France arrived more happy men.   126
                                Exeunt.

❧

5.0

Enter Chorus.

CHORUS
    Vouchsafe to those that have not read the story   1
    That I may prompt them; and of such as have,
    I humbly pray them to admit th'excuse   3
    Of time, of numbers, and due course of things,
    Which cannot in their huge and proper life
    Be here presented. Now we bear the King
    Toward Calais. Grant him there. There seen,
    Heave him away upon your wingèd thoughts
    Athwart the sea. Behold, the English beach   9
    Pales in the flood with men, wives, and boys,   10
    Whose shouts and claps outvoice the deep-mouthed
        sea,
    Which like a mighty whiffler 'fore the King   12
    Seems to prepare his way. So let him land,
    And solemnly see him set on to London.
    So swift a pace hath thought that even now
    You may imagine him upon Blackheath,   16
    Where that his lords desire him to have borne   17
    His bruisèd helmet and his bended sword
    Before him through the city. He forbids it,
    Being free from vainness and self-glorious pride,
    Giving full trophy, signal, and ostent   21
    Quite from himself to God. But now behold,
    In the quick forge and working-house of thought,
    How London doth pour out her citizens!
    The Mayor and all his brethren, in best sort,   25
    Like to the senators of th'antique Rome
    With the plebeians swarming at their heels,
    Go forth and fetch their conquering Caesar in;

    As by a lower but loving likelihood,   29
    Were now the General of our gracious Empress,   30
    As in good time he may, from Ireland coming,
    Bringing rebellion broachèd on his sword,   32
    How many would the peaceful city quit
    To welcome him! Much more, and much more cause,   34
    Did they this Harry. Now in London place him;
    As yet the lamentation of the French   36
    Invites the King of England's stay at home;   37
    The Emperor's coming in behalf of France,   38
    To order peace between them . . . and omit   39
    All the occurrences, whatever chanced,
    Till Harry's back-return again to France.   41
    There must we bring him; and myself have played
    The interim by rememb'ring you 'tis past.   43
    Then brook abridgment, and your eyes advance,   44
    After your thoughts, straight back again to France.
                                 Exit.

❧

[5.1]

*Enter Fluellen [with a leek in his cap, and a
cudgel], and Gower.*

GOWER Nay, that's right. But why wear you your leek
today? Saint Davy's Day is past.
FLUELLEN There is occasions and causes why and
wherefore in all things. I will tell you asse my friend,   4
Captain Gower. The rascally, scald, beggarly, lousy,   5
pragging knave, Pistol, which you and yourself and all
the world know to be no petter than a fellow, look you
now, of no merits, he is come to me and prings me
pread and salt yesterday, look you, and bid me eat my
leek. It was in a place where I could not breed no contention with him; but I will be so bold as to wear it in
my cap till I see him once again, and then I will tell
him a little piece of my desires.

Enter Pistol.

GOWER Why, here he comes, swelling like a turkey-
cock.
FLUELLEN 'Tis no matter for his swellings nor his
turkey-cocks.—God pless you, Aunchient Pistol! You
scurvy, lousy knave, God pless you!
PISTOL
    Ha, art thou bedlam? Dost thou thirst, base Trojan,   19

---

123 Non nobis i.e., Psalm 115, beginning, "Not unto us, O Lord,
not unto us, but unto thy name give glory." **Te Deum** a hymn
of thanksgiving, beginning, "We praise thee O God" **126 happy**
fortunate
**5.0. (Between Acts 4 and 5, there is historically an interval of about
five years during which Henry made a second campaign in France
that brought the French to terms in the Treaty of Troyes, with which
the play ends.)**
1 Vouchsafe Permit it   **3 admit th'excuse** excuse our handling
9 Athwart across   **10 Pales in** hems in, surrounds.   **flood** sea
12 whiffler an usher heading the procession to clear the way
16 Blackheath open area just outside London, to the southeast
17 Where that where   **21 Giving . . . ostent** giving every memorial,
token, and display of victory   **25 sort** array

29–34 As . . . him (Seemingly, an allusion to the Earl of Essex, who left
London on his Irish expedition on March 27, 1599, in an attempt to
put down Tyrone's rebellion; he returned unsuccessful and under a
cloud on September 28 of the same year. These lines, therefore, were
probably written between the dates mentioned.)   **29 a . . . likelihood**
a less exalted comparison but one that shows much love   **30 Empress**
i.e., Elizabeth   **32 broachèd** transfixed, spitted   **36–7 As . . . home**
i.e., the French are so dejected that Henry can stay in England without fear of loss in France   **38 Emperor's coming** (The Holy Roman
Emperor, Sigismund, came to England on behalf of France in May
1416.)   **39 them . . . and omit** (Something appears to be left out here.
Possibly it should read, "them, and the death / O' the Dauphin, leap
we over, and omit . . .")   **41 Harry's back-return** i.e., Henry's second
campaign, commencing in 1417   **43 rememb'ring** reminding
44 brook tolerate, excuse
5.1. Location: France. The English camp.
4 asse as   **5 scald** scurvy   **19 bedlam** crazy.   **Trojan** i.e., rascal

To have me fold up Parca's fatal web?   20
Hence, I am qualmish at the smell of leek.   21
FLUELLEN   I peseech you heartily, scurvy, lousy knave,
at my desires, and my requests, and my petitions, to
eat, look you, this leek. [*He offers the leek.*] Because,
look you, you do not love it, nor your affections and
your appetites and your disgestions doo's not agree
with it, I would desire you to eat it.
PISTOL
Not for Cadwallader and all his goats.   28
FLUELLEN   There is one goat for you. (*Strikes him.*) Will
you be so good, scald knave, as eat it?
PISTOL   Base Trojan, thou shalt die.
FLUELLEN   You say very true, scald knave, when God's
will is. I will desire you to live in the meantime and
eat your victuals. Come, there is sauce for it. [*He strikes
him.*] You called me yesterday mountain squire, but I   35
will make you today a squire of low degree. I pray   36
you, fall to. If you can mock a leek, you can eat a leek.
GOWER   Enough, Captain, you have astonished him.   38
FLUELLEN   By Jesu, I will make him eat some part of my
leek, or I will peat his pate four days. Bite, I pray you;   40
it is good for your green wound and your ploody   41
coxcomb.   42
PISTOL   Must I bite?
FLUELLEN   Yes, certainly, and out of doubt and out of
question too, and ambiguities.
PISTOL
By this leek, I will most horribly revenge—
                        [*Fluellen threatens him.*]
I eat and eat—I swear—
FLUELLEN   Eat, I pray you. Will you have some more
sauce to your leek? There is not enough leek to
swear by.
PISTOL
Quiet thy cudgel; thou dost see I eat.
FLUELLEN   Much good do you, scald knave, heartily.
Nay, pray you, throw none away; the skin is good for
your broken coxcomb. When you take occasions to see   54
leeks hereafter, I pray you, mock at 'em, that is all.
PISTOL   Good.
FLUELLEN   Ay, leeks is good. Hold you, there is a groat   57
to heal your pate.   [*He offers a coin.*]
PISTOL   Me, a groat?
FLUELLEN   Yes, verily, and in truth you shall take it, or
I have another leek in my pocket which you shall eat.
PISTOL
I take thy groat in earnest of revenge.   62

FLUELLEN   If I owe you anything, I will pay you in
cudgels. You shall be a woodmonger and buy nothing
of me but cudgels. God b'wi'you, and keep you, and
heal your pate.   *Exit.*
PISTOL   All hell shall stir for this.
GOWER   Go, go, you are a counterfeit cowardly knave.
Will you mock at an ancient tradition, begun upon an
honorable respect and worn as a memorable trophy of   70
predeceased valor, and dare not avouch in your deeds   71
any of your words? I have seen you gleeking and   72
galling at this gentleman twice or thrice. You thought   73
because he could not speak English in the native garb
he could not therefore handle an English cudgel. You
find it otherwise; and henceforth let a Welsh cor-
rection teach you a good English condition. Fare
ye well.   *Exit.*
PISTOL
Doth Fortune play the huswife with me now?   79
News have I that my Doll is dead   80
I'th' spital of a malady of France,   81
And there my rendezvous is quite cut off.
Old I do wax, and from my weary limbs   83
Honor is cudgeled. Well, bawd I'll turn,
And something lean to cutpurse of quick hand.   85
To England will I steal, and there I'll steal;
And patches will I get unto these cudgeled scars,
And swear I got them in the Gallia wars.   *Exit.* 88

❖

[5.2]

*Enter, at one door, King Henry, Exeter, Bedford,
[Gloucester, Clarence,] Warwick, [Westmorland,]
and other lords; at another, Queen Isabel, the
[French] King, the Duke of Burgundy, [the
Princess Katharine, Alice,] and other French.*

KING HENRY
Peace to this meeting, wherefor we are met!
Unto our brother France and to our sister,
Health and fair time of day; joy and good wishes
To our most fair and princely cousin Katharine;
And, as a branch and member of this royalty,   5
By whom this great assembly is contrived,
We do salute you, Duke of Burgundy;
And princes French, and peers, health to you all!
FRENCH KING
Right joyous are we to behold your face,
Most worthy brother England. Fairly met!
So are you, princes English, every one.

QUEEN ISABEL

So happy be the issue, brother England,   12
Of this good day and of this gracious meeting,
As we are now glad to behold your eyes—
Your eyes, which hitherto have borne in them
Against the French that met them in their bent   16
The fatal balls of murdering basilisks.   17
The venom of such looks, we fairly hope,
Have lost their quality, and that this day
Shall change all griefs and quarrels into love.   20

KING HENRY

To cry amen to that, thus we appear.

QUEEN ISABEL

You English princes all, I do salute you.

BURGUNDY

My duty to you both, on equal love,
Great Kings of France and England! That I have
    labored
With all my wits, my pains, and strong endeavors
To bring your most imperial Majesties
Unto this bar and royal interview,   27
Your mightiness on both parts best can witness.
Since, then, my office hath so far prevailed
That, face to face and royal eye to eye,
You have congreeted, let it not disgrace me   31
If I demand, before this royal view,   32
What rub or what impediment there is   33
Why that the naked, poor, and mangled Peace,
Dear nurse of arts, plenties, and joyful births,
Should not in this best garden of the world,
Our fertile France, put up her lovely visage?   37
Alas, she hath from France too long been chased,
And all her husbandry doth lie on heaps,   39
Corrupting in it own fertility.   40
Her vine, the merry cheerer of the heart,
Unprunèd dies; her hedges even-pleached,   42
Like prisoners wildly overgrown with hair,
Put forth disordered twigs; her fallow leas   44
The darnel, hemlock, and rank fumitory   45
Doth root upon, while that the coulter rusts   46
That should deracinate such savagery.   47
The even mead, that erst brought sweetly forth   48
The freckled cowslip, burnet, and green clover,   49
Wanting the scythe, all uncorrected, rank,   50
Conceives by idleness, and nothing teems   51
But hateful docks, rough thistles, kecksies, burrs,   52
Losing both beauty and utility.
And all our vineyards, fallows, meads, and hedges,   54

Defective in their natures, grow to wildness;   55
Even so our houses and ourselves and children   56
Have lost, or do not learn for want of time,
The sciences that should become our country,   58
But grow like savages—as soldiers will
That nothing do but meditate on blood—
To swearing and stern looks, diffused attire,   61
And everything that seems unnatural.
Which to reduce into our former favor   63
You are assembled, and my speech entreats
That I may know the let why gentle Peace   65
Should not expel these inconveniences
And bless us with her former qualities.

KING HENRY

If, Duke of Burgundy, you would the peace,   68
Whose want gives growth to th'imperfections   69
Which you have cited, you must buy that peace
With full accord to all our just demands,
Whose tenors and particular effects   72
You have enscheduled briefly in your hands.   73

BURGUNDY

The King hath heard them, to the which as yet
There is no answer made.

KING HENRY   Well then, the peace,
Which you before so urged, lies in his answer.

FRENCH KING

I have but with a cursitory eye   77
O'erglanced the articles. Pleaseth Your Grace   78
To appoint some of your council presently
To sit with us once more, with better heed
To re-survey them, we will suddenly   81
Pass our accept and peremptory answer.   82

KING HENRY

Brother, we shall.—Go, uncle Exeter,
And brother Clarence, and you, brother Gloucester,
Warwick, and Huntingdon, go with the King,
And take with you free power to ratify,
Augment, or alter, as your wisdoms best
Shall see advantageable for our dignity,   88
Anything in or out of our demands,
And we'll consign thereto.—Will you, fair sister,   90
Go with the princes, or stay here with us?

QUEEN ISABEL

Our gracious brother, I will go with them.
Haply a woman's voice may do some good   93
When articles too nicely urged be stood on.   94

KING HENRY

Yet leave our cousin Katharine here with us.
She is our capital demand, comprised   96
Within the fore-rank of our articles.   97

---

12 issue outcome   **16 in their bent** (1) as they were directed (2) in their glance   **17 fatal balls** (1) cannonballs (2) eyeballs.   **basilisks** (1) large cannon (2) monsters supposed to kill with their gaze. **20 griefs** grievances   **27 bar** tribunal   **31 congreeted** greeted each other   **32 demand** ask   **33 rub** obstacle. (A term from bowls.) **37 put up** show, lift up   **39 husbandry** harvest, foison   **40 it** its **42 even-pleached** smoothly intertwined   **44 fallow leas** uncultivated open fields   **45 darnel . . . fumitory** i.e., weeds that grow in cultivated land   **46 coulter** plow blade   **47 deracinate** root out   **48 even mead** level meadow.   **erst** formerly   **49 burnet** a herb   **50 Wanting** lacking   **51 Conceives** gives birth (to weeds).   **teems** flourishes **52 kecksies** dry stalks   **54 fallows** land plowed and left lying

55 Defective . . . natures naturally inclined to wildness   **56 houses** households   **58 sciences** skills   **61 diffused** disordered   **63 reduce . . . favor** return to our former good appearance and good graces **65 let** hindrance   **68 would** wish   **69 want** lack   **72 tenors . . . effects** general purport and specific details   **73 enscheduled** drawn up in writing   **77 cursitory** cursory, hasty   **78 Pleaseth** May it please **81 suddenly** speedily   **82 Pass . . . answer** deliver our agreed-to and final answer.   **88 advantageable** advantageous   **90 consign** agree, subscribe   **93 Haply** Perhaps   **94 nicely** punctiliously, with insistence on detail.   **stood on** insisted on.   **96 capital** chief   **97 forerank** first row

QUEEN ISABEL
She hath good leave.

Exeunt omnes. Manent King [Henry]
and Katharine [with Alice].

KING HENRY   Fair Katharine, and most fair,   98
Will you vouchsafe to teach a soldier terms
Such as will enter at a lady's ear
And plead his love suit to her gentle heart?

KATHARINE   Your Majesty shall mock at me. I cannot
speak your England.

KING HENRY   O fair Katharine, if you will love me
soundly with your French heart, I will be glad to hear
you confess it brokenly with your English tongue. Do
you like me, Kate?

KATHARINE   *Pardonnez-moi,* I cannot tell wat is "like
me."

KING HENRY   An angel is like you, Kate, and you are
like an angel.

KATHARINE   [*to Alice*]   *Que dit-il? Que je suis semblable à*   112
les anges?   113

ALICE   *Oui, vraiment, sauf Votre Grâce, ainsi dit-il.*   114

KING HENRY   I said so, dear Katharine, and I must not
blush to affirm it.

KATHARINE   *Oh, bon Dieu! Les langues des hommes sont*
pleines de tromperies.

KING HENRY   What says she, fair one? That the tongues
of men are full of deceits?

ALICE   *Oui,* dat de tongues of de mans is be full of
deceits. Dat is de Princess.

KING HENRY   The Princess is the better Englishwoman.   123
I'faith, Kate, my wooing is fit for thy understanding.
I am glad thou canst speak no better English, for if
thou couldst, thou wouldst find me such a plain king
that thou wouldst think I had sold my farm to buy my
crown. I know no ways to mince it in love, but directly   128
to say, "I love you." Then if you urge me farther than
to say, "Do you, in faith?" I wear out my suit. Give me   130
your answer, i'faith, do, and so clap hands and a   131
bargain. How say you, lady?

KATHARINE   *Sauf votre honneur,* me understand well.

KING HENRY   Marry, if you would put me to verses or
to dance for your sake, Kate, why, you undid me. For
the one I have neither words nor measure, and for the   136
other I have no strength in measure, yet a reasonable   137
measure in strength. If I could win a lady at leapfrog,   138
or by vaulting into my saddle with my armor on my
back, under the correction of bragging be it spoken, I
should quickly leap into a wife. Or if I might buffet for   141
my love, or bound my horse for her favors, I could lay   142
on like a butcher and sit like a jackanapes, never off.   143
But before God, Kate, I cannot look greenly, nor gasp   144
out my eloquence, nor I have no cunning in protesta-

tion—only downright oaths, which I never use till   146
urged, nor never break for urging. If thou canst love a
fellow of this temper, Kate, whose face is not worth   148
sunburning, that never looks in his glass for love of   149
anything he sees there, let thine eye be thy cook. I   150
speak to thee plain soldier. If thou canst love me for
this, take me. If not, to say to thee that I shall die is
true; but for thy love, by the Lord, no. Yet I love thee
too. And while thou liv'st, dear Kate, take a fellow of
plain and uncoined constancy, for he perforce must   155
do thee right, because he hath not the gift to woo in
other places. For these fellows of infinite tongue that
can rhyme themselves into ladies' favors, they do
always reason themselves out again. What? A speaker
is but a prater, a rhyme is but a ballad. A good leg will
fall, a straight back will stoop, a black beard will turn   161
white, a curled pate will grow bald, a fair face will
wither, a full eye will wax hollow; but a good heart,
Kate, is the sun and the moon—or rather the sun and
not the moon, for it shines bright and never changes,
but keeps his course truly. If thou would have such a
one, take me. And take me, take a soldier; take a
soldier, take a king. And what say'st thou then to my
love? Speak, my fair, and fairly, I pray thee.

KATHARINE   Is it possible dat I sould love de *ennemi* of
France?

KING HENRY   No, it is not possible you should love the
enemy of France, Kate; but in loving me you should
love the friend of France, for I love France so well that
I will not part with a village of it. I will have it all mine.
And, Kate, when France is mine and I am yours, then
yours is France and you are mine.

KATHARINE   I cannot tell wat is dat.

KING HENRY   No, Kate? I will tell thee in French, which
I am sure will hang upon my tongue like a new-
married wife about her husband's neck, hardly to be
shook off. *Je quand sur le possession de France, et quand*   182
vous avez le possession de moi—let me see, what ?   183
Saint Denis be my speed!—*donc vôtre est France et vous*   184
êtes mienne. It is as easy for me, Kate, to conquer the   185
kingdom as to speak so much more French. I shall
never move thee in French, unless it be to laugh at
me.

KATHARINE   *Sauf votre honneur, le français que vous parlez,*   189
il est meilleur que l' anglais lequel je parle.   190

KING HENRY   No, faith, is't not, Kate. But thy speaking
of my tongue, and I thine, most truly-falsely, must   192
needs be granted to be much at one. But, Kate, dost   193
thou understand thus much English: Canst thou
love me?

---

98 s.d. *omnes* all.   ***Manent*** They remain onstage   **112–14 *Que . . .***
***ainsi dit-il*?** What does he say? That I am like the angels? ALICE Yes,
truly, save Your Grace, he says so.   **123 is . . . Englishwoman** i.e., is
the better for preferring honesty.   **128 mince it** speak coyly
130 wear out my suit expend all my resources as a wooer.   **131 clap**
clasp   **136 measure** (skill in) meter   **137 measure** dance
138 measure amount, aptitude   **141 buffet** box   **142 bound** make
prance   **143 jackanapes** ape, monkey   **144 greenly** like a lovesick
youth

146 downright straightforward   **148–9 not . . . sunburning** i.e.,
already so tanned that more sun could make it worse. (Tanned and
dark complexions were generally considered unhandsome.)
149 glass mirror   **150 be thy cook** dress up and garnish my plain
looks.   **155 uncoined** (1) not put into circulation (2) unalloyed, fixed,
steady   **161 fall** shrink, lose its shapeliness   **182–5 *Je . . . mienne***
(Henry haltingly translates into French the last sentence of his previous speech.)   **184 Saint Denis** patron saint of France.   **be my speed**
help me.   **189–90 *Sauf . . . parle*** Saving your honor, the French that
you speak is better than the English that I speak.   **192 truly-falsely**
true-heartedly but incorrectly   **193 at one** alike.

KATHARINE   I cannot tell.

KING HENRY   Can any of your neighbors tell, Kate? I'll ask them. Come, I know thou lovest me. And at night, when you come into your closet, you'll question this gentlewoman about me; and I know, Kate, you will to her dispraise those parts in me that you love with your heart. But, good Kate, mock me mercifully, the rather, gentle Princess, because I love thee cruelly. If ever thou be'st mine, Kate, as I have a saving faith within me tells me thou shalt, I get thee with scambling, and thou must therefore needs prove a good soldier-breeder. Shall not thou and I, between Saint Denis and Saint George, compound a boy, half French, half English, that shall go to Constantinople and take the Turk by the beard? Shall we not? What say'st thou, my fair flower-de-luce? 211

KATHARINE   I do not know dat.

KING HENRY   No; 'tis hereafter to know, but now to promise. Do but now promise, Kate, you will endeavor for your French part of such a boy, and for my English moiety take the word of a king and a bachelor. 216 How answer you, *la plus belle Katharine du monde, mon* 217 *très cher et devin déesse?* 218

KATHARINE   Your Majestee 'ave *fausse* French enough 219 to deceive de most *sage demoiselle* dat is *en France.*

KING HENRY   Now, fie upon my false French! By mine honor, in true English, I love thee, Kate; by which honor I dare not swear thou lovest me, yet my blood begins to flatter me that thou dost, notwithstanding the poor and untempering effect of my visage. Now 225 beshrew my father's ambition! He was thinking of civil 226 wars when he got me; therefore was I created with a stubborn outside, with an aspect of iron, that when I 228 come to woo ladies I fright them. But in faith, Kate, the elder I wax the better I shall appear. My comfort is that old age, that ill layer-up of beauty, can do no more spoil upon my face. Thou hast me, if thou hast me, at the worst; and thou shalt wear me, if thou wear me, better and better. And therefore tell me, most fair Katharine, will you have me? Put off your maiden blushes; avouch the thoughts of your heart with the 236 looks of an empress; take me by the hand, and say, "Harry of England, I am thine." Which word thou shalt no sooner bless mine ear withal, but I will tell thee aloud, "England is thine, Ireland is thine, France is thine, and Henry Plantagenet is thine"—who, though I speak it before his face, if he be not fellow with the best king, thou shalt find the best king 243 of good fellows. Come, your answer in broken music! 244 For thy voice is music, and thy English broken. Therefore, queen of all, Katharine, break thy mind to 246 me in broken English. Wilt thou have me?

KATHARINE   Dat is as it shall please de *roi mon père.* 248

KING HENRY   Nay, it will please him well, Kate. It shall please him, Kate.

KATHARINE   Den it sall also content me.

KING HENRY   Upon that I kiss your hand, and I call you my queen.   [*He attempts to kiss her hand.*]

KATHARINE   *Laissez, mon seigneur, laissez, laissez! Ma* 254 *foi, je ne veux point que vous abaissiez votre grandeur* 255 *en baisant la main d'une—Notre Seigneur!—indigne* 256 *serviteur. Excusez-moi, je vous supplie, mon très-puissant* 257 *seigneur.* 258

KING HENRY   Then I will kiss your lips, Kate.

KATHARINE   *Les dames et demoiselles pour être baisées* 260 *devant leur noces, il n'est pas la coutume de France.* 261

KING HENRY   [*to Alice*]   Madam my interpreter, what says she?

ALICE   Dat it is not be de fashion *pour les* ladies of France—I cannot tell wat is *baiser* en Anglish.

KING HENRY   To kiss.

ALICE   Your Majestee *entend* bettre *que moi.* 267

KING HENRY   It is not a fashion for the maids in France to kiss before they are married, would she say?

ALICE   *Oui, vraiment.* 270

KING HENRY   O Kate, nice customs curtsy to great kings. 271 Dear Kate, you and I cannot be confined within the weak list of a country's fashion. We are the makers of 273 manners, Kate; and the liberty that follows our places 274 stops the mouth of all find-faults, as I will do yours, for upholding the nice fashion of your country in denying me a kiss. Therefore, patiently and yielding. [*He kisses her.*] You have witchcraft in your lips, Kate. There is more eloquence in a sugar touch of them than in the tongues of the French council, and they should sooner persuade Harry of England than a general petition of monarchs.—Here comes your father.

Enter the French power and the English lords.

BURGUNDY   God save Your Majesty! My royal cousin, teach you our princess English?

KING HENRY   I would have her learn, my fair cousin, how perfectly I love her, and that is good English.

BURGUNDY   Is she not apt?

KING HENRY   Our tongue is rough, coz, and my condi- 288 tion is not smooth; so that, having neither the voice 289 nor the heart of flattery about me, I cannot so conjure up the spirit of love in her that he will appear in his true likeness.

---

199 **closet** private chamber   206 **scambling** the scuffles of war 211 **flower-de-luce** fleur-de-lis, the emblem of France.   216 **moiety** half   217–18 *la plus . . . déesse* the most beautiful Katharine in the world, my very dear and divine goddess.   219 *fausse* i.e., false (both "incorrect" and "deceptive")   225 **untempering** unsettling, unsoftening   226 **beshrew** curses on   228 **aspect** appearance   236 **avouch** vouch for, confirm   243 **fellow with** on equal terms with   244 **broken music** (Henry quibbles on the term for music composed in parts for different instruments.)   246 **break** open

248 *de roi mon père* the King my father.   254–8 *Laissez . . . seigneur* Don't, my lord, don't, don't! By my faith, I do not wish you to lower your greatness by kissing the hand of an—our dear Lord!— unworthy servant; excuse me, I beg you, my most powerful lord. (*Serviteur* is masculine and not appropriately applied to a lady, but the error may be Shakespeare's.)   260–1 *Les dames . . . France* It is not customary in France for ladies and young girls to be kissed before their marriage.   267 *entend . . . moi* understands better than I. 270 *Oui, vraiment* Yes, truly.   271 **nice** fastidious   273 **list** limit, barrier   274 **follows our places** attends our (high) rank   288 **Our tongue** (1) Our English language (2) My soldierly speech   288–9 **condition** soldierly manner

BURGUNDY   Pardon the frankness of my mirth, if I
answer you for that. If you would conjure in her, you 294
must make a circle; if conjure up love in her in his true
likeness, he must appear naked and blind. Can you 296
blame her then, being a maid yet rosed over with the 297
virgin crimson of modesty, if she deny the appearance 298
of a naked blind boy in her naked seeing self? It were, 299
my lord, a hard condition for a maid to consign to. 300

KING HENRY   Yet they do wink and yield, as love is 301
blind and enforces. 302

BURGUNDY   They are then excused, my lord, when they
see not what they do.

KING HENRY   Then, good my lord, teach your cousin to
consent winking.

BURGUNDY   I will wink on her to consent, my lord, if 307
you will teach her to know my meaning; for maids,
well summered and warm kept, are like flies at Bar- 309
tholomew-tide: blind, though they have their eyes, 310
and then they will endure handling, which before 311
would not abide looking on.

KING HENRY   This moral ties me over to time and a hot 313
summer; and so I shall catch the fly, your cousin, in 314
the latter end, and she must be blind too.

BURGUNDY   As love is, my lord, before it loves. 316

KING HENRY   It is so; and you may, some of you, thank
love for my blindness, who cannot see many a fair 318
French city for one fair French maid that stands in 319
my way. 320

FRENCH KING   Yes, my lord, you see them perspectively, 321
the cities turned into a maid; for they are all girdled
with maiden walls that war hath never entered. 323

KING HENRY   Shall Kate be my wife?

FRENCH KING   So please you.

KING HENRY   I am content, so the maiden cities you talk 326
of may wait on her. So the maid that stood in the way 327
for my wish shall show me the way to my will. 328

FRENCH KING
We have consented to all terms of reason.

KING HENRY   Is't so, my lords of England?

WESTMORLAND
The King hath granted every article:
His daughter first, and then in sequel all
According to their firm proposèd natures. 333

EXETER
Only he hath not yet subscribèd this: 334
Where Your Majesty demands that the King of France,
having any occasion to write for matter of grant, shall 336
name Your Highness in this form and with this ad- 337
dition, in French, *Notre très cher fils Henri, Roi* 338
d'Angleterre, Héritier de France; and thus in Latin, 339
Praeclarissimus filius noster Henricus, Rex Angliae et 340
Haeres Franciae.

FRENCH KING
Nor this I have not, brother, so denied 342
But your request shall make me let it pass. 343

KING HENRY
I pray you then, in love and dear alliance,
Let that one article rank with the rest,
And thereupon give me your daughter.

FRENCH KING
Take her, fair son, and from her blood raise up
Issue to me, that the contending kingdoms
Of France and England, whose very shores look pale
With envy of each other's happiness,
May cease their hatred, and this dear conjunction
Plant neighborhood and Christian-like accord
In their sweet bosoms, that never war advance
His bleeding sword twixt England and fair France.

LORDS   Amen!

KING HENRY
Now, welcome, Kate; and bear me witness all,
That here I kiss her as my sovereign queen.
[He kisses her.] Flourish.

QUEEN ISABEL
God, the best maker of all marriages,
Combine your hearts in one, your realms in one!
As man and wife, being two, are one in love,
So be there twixt your kingdoms such a spousal 361
That never may ill office, or fell jealousy, 362
Which troubles oft the bed of blessèd marriage,
Thrust in between the paction of these kingdoms 364
To make divorce of their incorporate league;
That English may as French, French Englishmen,
Receive each other. God speak this "Amen"!

ALL   Amen!

KING HENRY
Prepare we for our marriage, on which day,
My lord of Burgundy, we'll take your oath,
And all the peers', for surety of our leagues.
Then shall I swear to Kate, and you to me;

---

294 conjure in her (with bawdy double meaning of raising up something within her *circle*, line 295)   **296 naked and blind** (as Cupid is
conventionally portrayed)   **297 yet rosed over** still blushing
298–9 if . . . self if she refuses to admit the entry of a naked boy in her
sight, or herself being naked?   **300 a hard condition** (Suggesting
erection.)   **consign** agree   **301–2 Yet . . . enforces** Yet young maidens
do close their eyes and say yes, prompted to do so by their own bashfulness and male importunity.   **307 wink on her** give her an encouraging wink   **309 summered** nurtured   **309–10 Bartholomew-tide**
August 24 (when flies, bees, etc., are sluggish)   **311 handling**
(1) handling of the beehive (2) sexual handling   **313–14 This moral
. . . summer** The lesson of your fable would oblige me to wait for the
heat of summer   **316 As . . . loves** (Love is blind before it loves,
because it cannot yet see the beloved and because love has not yet
opened the lover's eyes.)   **318–20 who . . . my way** i.e., since I am so
preoccupied with Katharine that I have forgotten for the moment
about all those French towns I want. (He is joking; he gets the French
towns, along with her.)   **321 perspectively** i.e., as in an optical device
that presents different images when viewed from different angles
323 maiden unbreached. (With a sexual metaphor, continued in
entered.)   **326 so** provided that   **327 wait on her** attend her, go along
with her (as part of her dowry).   **328 will** (1) intention of ruling
France (2) sexual desire.

333 According . . . natures exactly as specified in the proposals.
334 subscribèd agreed to, signed to   **336 for . . . grant** in official
deeds, granting title to land and the like   **337–8 addition** title
338–9 Notre . . . France i.e., Our very dear son Henry, King of England, Heir of France.   **340 Praeclarissimus** most famous. (Presumably an error for "Praecharissimus" or "Praeclarissimus," "most dear."
Shakespeare is following Holinshed, who took the error from Hall.)
342 so so firmly   **343 But** but that   **361 spousal** marriage   **362 ill
office** unfriendly dealings.   **fell** cruel   **364 paction** alliance, compact

And may our oaths well kept and prosperous be!

Sennet.   *Exeunt.*

❖

[Epilogue]

Enter Chorus.

CHORUS

Thus far, with rough and all-unable pen,
    Our bending author hath pursued the story,   2
In little room confining mighty men,
    Mangling by starts the full course of their glory.   4

Small time, but in that small most greatly lived   5
    This star of England. Fortune made his sword,
By which the world's best garden he achieved,   7
    And of it left his son imperial lord.
Henry the Sixth, in infant bands crowned King   9
    Of France and England, did this king succeed;
Whose state so many had the managing,
    That they lost France and made his England bleed,
Which oft our stage hath shown; and, for their sake,   13
In your fair minds let this acceptance take.   *[Exit.]*   14

Epilogue.
2 bending i.e., under the weight of his task   **4 by starts** in fits and starts, in fragments

5 Small time (Henry V ruled for only nine years, dying at the age of thirty-five.)   **7 best garden** i.e., France   **9 infant bands** swaddling clothes   **13 Which . . . shown** (Refers to the three parts of *King Henry VI.*)   **their** i.e., the actors and the author, the presenters on *our stage* (line 13)   **14 let . . . take** let this play meet with your approval.

The Tragedies

Romeo and Juliet

Though a tragedy, *Romeo and Juliet* is, in some ways, more closely comparable to Shakespeare's romantic comedies and early writings than to his later tragedies. Stylistically belonging to the years 1594–1596, it is in the lyric vein of the sonnets, *A Midsummer Night's Dream*, *The Merchant of Venice*, and *Richard II*, all of which are from the mid 1590s. Like them, it uses a variety of rhyme schemes (couplets, quatrains, octets, and even sonnets) and revels in punning, metaphor, and wit combat. It is separated in tone and in time from the earliest of the great tragedies, *Julius Caesar* and *Hamlet*, by almost half a decade, and, except for the experimental *Titus Andronicus*, it is the only tragedy (that is not also a history) that Shakespeare wrote in the first decade of his career—a period devoted otherwise to romantic comedy and English history.

Like many comedies, *Romeo and Juliet* is a love story, celebrating the exquisite, brief joy of youthful passion. Even its tragic ending stresses the poignancy of that brief beauty, not the bitter futility of love, as in *Troilus and Cressida* or *Othello*. The tragic ending of *Romeo and Juliet* underscores the observation made by a vexed lover in *A Midsummer Night's Dream* that "The course of true love never did run smooth" (1.1.134). True love in *Romeo and Juliet*, as in *A Midsummer Night's Dream*, is destined to be crossed by differences in blood or family background, differences in age, arbitrary choices of family or friends, or uncontrollable catastrophes, such as war, death, and sickness. Love is thus, as in *A Midsummer Night's Dream*, "momentary as a sound, / Swift as a shadow, short as any dream," swallowed up by darkness; "So quick bright things come to confusion" (1.1.143–9). A dominant pattern of imagery in *Romeo and Juliet* evokes a corresponding sense of suddenness and violence: fire, gunpowder, hot blood, lightning, the inconstant wind, the storm-tossed or shipwrecked vessel. The beauty of a love that is so threatened and so fragile is intensified by the brevity of the experience. A tragic outcome therefore affirms the uniqueness and pristine quality of youthful ecstasy. The flowering and fading of a joy "too rich for use, for earth too dear" (1.5.48), does not so much condemn the unfeeling world as welcome the martyrdom of literally dying for love.

As protagonists, Romeo and Juliet lack tragic stature by any classical definition or in terms of the medieval convention of the Fall of Princes. The lovers are not extraordinary except in their passionate attachment to one another. They belong to prominent merchant families rather than to the nobility. They (especially Juliet) are very young, more so than any other of Shakespeare's tragic protagonists, and are indeed younger than most couples marrying in England at the time the play was written; Juliet is not yet fourteen (1.2.9, 1.3.13). Romeo and Juliet's dilemma of parental opposition is of the domestic sort often found in comedy. In fact, several characters in the play partly resemble the conventional character types of the Latin comic playwright Plautus or of Italian neoclassical comedy: the domineering father who insists that his daughter marry according to his choice, the unwelcome rival wooer, the garrulous and bawdy nurse, and, of course, the lovers. The Italian *novella*, to which Shakespeare often turned for his plots, made use of these same types and paid little attention to the classical precept that protagonists in a tragic story ought to be persons of high rank who are humbled through some inner flaw, or hamartia.

The story of Romeo and Juliet goes back ultimately to the fifth-century A.D. Greek romance of *Ephesiaca*, in which we find the motif of the sleeping potion as a means of escaping an unwelcome marriage. Masuccio of Salerno, in his *Il Novellino*, in 1476, combined the narrative of the heroine's deathlike trance and seeming burial alive with that of the hero's tragic failure to receive news from the friar that she is still alive. Luigi da Porto, in his *novella* (c. 1530), set the scene at Verona, provided the names of Romeo and Giulietta for the hero and heroine, added the account of their feuding families, the Montecchi and Cappelletti, introduced the killing of Tybalt (Theobaldo), and provided other important details. Luigi's version was followed by Matteo Bandello's famous *Novelle* of 1554, which was translated into French by Pierre Boaistuau (1559). The French version became the source for Arthur Brooke's long narrative poem in English, *The Tragical History of Romeus and Juliet* (1562). Brooke mentions having seen a play on the subject, but it is doubtful that Shakespeare knew this old play or, if he did know it, made use of it. Brooke's poem was his chief and probably only source. Shakespeare has condensed Brooke's action from nine months to less than a week, has greatly expanded the role of Mercutio, and has given to the Nurse a warmth and humorous richness not found in the usual Italian duenna, or *balia*. He has also tidied up the Friar's immorality and deleted the antipapal tone. Inheriting from Brooke a cautionary narrative against unruly yielding to sexual passion, in the homiletic vein of Puritan preachers, Shakespeare instead sympathizes with the perils of young lovers whose desires are unappreciated by an unfeeling world. Throughout all these changes, Shakespeare retains Brooke's romantic (rather than classically tragic) conception of love overwhelmed by external obstacles.

Like the romantic comedies, *Romeo and Juliet* is often funny and bawdy. Samson and Gregory in the first scene are slapstick cowards, hiding behind the law and daring to quarrel only when reinforcements arrive. The Nurse delights us with her earthy recollections of the day she weaned Juliet: the child tasting "the wormwood on the nipple / Of my dug" (1.3.31–2), the warm Italian sun, an earthquake, the Nurse's husband telling his lame but often-repeated bawdy joke about women falling on their backs. Mercutio employs his inventive and sardonic humor to twit Romeo for lovesickness and the Nurse for her pomposity. She, in turn, scolds Peter and plagues Juliet (who is breathlessly awaiting news from Romeo) with a history of her back ailments. Mercutio and the Nurse are among Shakespeare's bawdiest characters. Their wry and salacious view of love contrasts with the nobly innocent and yet physically passionate love of Romeo and Juliet. Mercutio and the Nurse cannot take part in the play's denouement; one dies, misinterpreting Romeo's appeasement of Tybalt, and the other proves insensitive to Juliet's depth of feeling. Yet the disappearance of these engaging companions takes from the play some of its vitality and most of its funniness. The death of Tybalt turns the play from comedy to tragedy.

The lovers, too, are at first well suited to Shakespearean romantic comedy. When we meet Romeo, he is not in love with Juliet at all, despite the play's title, but is mooning over a "hardhearted wench" (in Mercutio's words) named Rosaline. This "goddess" appropriately never appears in the play; she is almost a disembodied idea in Romeo's mind, a scornful beauty like Phoebe in *As You Like It*. Romeo's love for her is tedious and self-pitying, like that of the conventional wooer in a sonnet sequence by Francesco Petrarch or one of his imitators. Juliet, although not yet fourteen, must change all this by teaching Romeo the nature of true love. She will have none of his shopworn clichés learned in the service of Rosaline, his flowery protestations and swearing by the moon, lest they prove to be love's perjuries. With her innocent candor, she insists (like many heroines of the romantic comedies) on dispelling the mask of pretense that lovers too often show one another. "Capulet" and "Montague" are mere labels, not the inner self. Although Juliet would have been more coy, she confesses, had she known that Romeo was overhearing her, she will now "prove more true / Than those that have more cunning to be strange" (2.2.100–1). She is more practical than he in assessing danger and making plans. Later she also proves herself remarkably able to bear misfortune.

The comedy of the play's first half is, to be sure, overshadowed by the certainty of disaster. The opening chorus plainly warns us that the lovers will die. They are "star-crossed," and they speak of themselves as such. Romeo fears "Some consequence yet hanging in the stars" when he reluctantly goes to the Capulets' feast (1.4.107); after he has slain Tybalt, he cries "Oh, I am fortune's fool!" (3.1.135); and, at the news of Juliet's supposed death, he proclaims "Then I defy you, stars!" (5.1.24). Yet in what sense are Romeo and Juliet "star-crossed"? The concept is deliberately broad in this play, encompassing many factors, such as hatred, bumbling, bad luck, and simple lack of awareness.

The first scene presents feuding as a major cause in the tragedy. The quarrel between the two families is so ancient that the original motives are no longer even discussed. Inspired by the "fiery" Tybalt, factionalism pursues its mindless course, despite the efforts of the Prince to end it. Although the elders of both families talk of peace, they call for their swords quickly enough when a fray begins. Still, this senseless hatred does not lead to tragedy until its effects are fatally complicated through misunderstanding. With poignant irony, good intentions are repeatedly undermined by lack of knowledge. We can see why Juliet does not tell her family of her secret marriage with a presumably hated Montague, but, in fact, Capulet has accepted Romeo as a guest in his house under the terms of chivalric hospitality, praising him as a "virtuous and well governed youth" (1.5.69). For all his dictatorial ways, and the manifest advantages he may see in marrying his daughter to an aristocrat like Paris, Capulet would, of course, never propose the match if he knew his daughter to be married already. Not knowing of Juliet's marriage, he and his wife can only interpret her refusal to marry Paris as caprice. Count Paris himself is victim of this tragedy of unawareness. He is an eminently suitable wooer for Juliet, rich and nobly born, considerate, peace-loving, and deeply fond of Juliet (as he shows by his private and sincere grief at her tomb). Certainly, he would never intentionally woo a married woman. Not knowing, he plays the unattractive role of the rival wooer and dies for it. Similarly, Mercutio cannot understand Romeo's seemingly craven behavior toward Tybalt and so begins the duel that leads to Romeo's banishment. The final scene, with Friar Laurence's retelling of the story, allows us to see the survivors confronted with what they have all unknowingly done.

Chance, or accident, plays a role of importance equal to that of hatred and unawareness. An outbreak of the plague prevents Friar John from conveying Friar Laurence's letter to Romeo at Mantua. Friar Laurence, going hurriedly to the Capulets' tomb, arrives in time for Juliet's awakening but some minutes after Romeo has killed Paris and taken poison. Juliet awakens only moments later. The Watch comes just too late to prevent her suicide. Friar Laurence expresses well the sense of frustration at plans gone awry by such narrow margins: "what an unkind hour / Is guilty of this lamentable chance!" (5.3.145–6). Earlier, Capulet's decision to move the wedding date up one day has crucially affected the timing. Human miscalculation contributes also to the catastrophe: Mercutio is killed under Romeo's arm, and Friar Laurence wonders unhappily if any of his complicated plans "Miscarried by my fault" (5.3.267). Character and human decision play a part in this tragedy, for Romeo should not have dueled with Tybalt, no matter what the provocation. In choosing to kill Tybalt, he has deliberately cast aside as "effeminate" the gentle and forgiving qualities he has learned from his love of Juliet (3.1.113) and thus is guilty of a rash and self-destructive action. To ascribe the cause of the tragedy in Aristotelian fashion to his and Juliet's impulsiveness is, however, to ignore much of the rest of the play.

Instead, the ending of the play brings a pattern out of the seeming welter of mistakes and animosities. "A greater power than we can contradict / Hath thwarted our intents," says Friar Laurence, suggesting that the seeming bad luck of the delayed letter was, in fact, the intent of a mysterious higher intelligence (5.3.153–4). Prince Escalus, too, finds a necessary meaning in the tragic event. "See what a scourge is laid upon your hate," he admonishes the Montagues and Capulets, "That heaven finds means to kill your joys with love." Romeo and Juliet are "Poor sacrifices of our enmity" (lines 292–304). As the Prologue had foretold, their deaths will "bury their parents' strife"; the families' feud is a stub-

born evil force "Which, but their children's end, naught could remove." Order is preciously restored; the price is great, but the sacrifice nonetheless confirms a sense of a larger intention in what had appeared to be simply hatred and misfortune. Throughout the play, love and hate are interrelated opposites, yoked through the rhetorical device of oxymoron, or inherent contradiction. Romeo apostrophizes "O brawling love, O loving hate" (1.1.176), and Juliet later echoes his words: "My only love sprung from my only hate" (1.5.139). This paradox expresses a conflict in humankind, as in the universe itself. "Two such opposèd kings encamp them still / In man as well as herbs," says Friar Laurence, "grace and rude will" (2.3.27–8). Hatred is a condition of our corrupted wills, of our fall from grace, and it attempts to destroy what is gracious in human beings. In this cosmic strife, love must pay the sacrifice, as Romeo and Juliet do with their lives, but, because their deaths are finally perceived as the cost of so much hatred, the two families come to terms with their collective guilt and resolve henceforth to be worthy of the sacrifice.

Structurally, *Romeo and Juliet* gives considerable prominence to the feuding of the two families. Public scenes occur at key points—at beginning, middle, and end (1.1, 3.1, and 5.3)—and each such scene concerns violence and its consequences. The play begins with a brawl. Tybalt is a baleful presence in 1.1 and 3.1, implacably bent on vengeance. The three public scenes are alike, too, in that they bring into confrontation the entire families of Capulets and Montagues, who call for swords and demand reprisal from the state for what they themselves have set in motion. Prince Escalus dominates these three public scenes. He must offer judgment in each, giving the families fair warning, then exiling Romeo for Tybalt's death, and finally counseling the families on the meaning of their collective tragedy. He is a spokesman for public order and security ("Mercy but murders, pardoning those that kill," 3.1.196), even though he is also unable to prevent the tragedy. He stands above the conflict and yet is affected by it; his own kinsman, Mercutio, is one of the casualties. For all his dignity and impartiality, Escalus's official function is somehow tangential to the central emotional experience of the play. The law does not provide a remedy. Still, it can preside and arbitrate. To Escalus is given the final speech promising both punishment and pardon, and it is he who sums up the paradoxical interdependence of love and hate. Although the morning after the catastrophe brings with it sorrow, it also brings peace, however "glooming." Escalus is master of ceremonies for a restored order through which the families and we are reconciled to what has occurred.

In good part, the public scenes of the play serve to frame the love plot and the increasing isolation of the separated lovers, but these public scenes have a function of their own to the extent that the tragedy has touched and altered everyone. The final tableau is not the kiss of the dying lovers but the handclasp of the reconciled fathers. The long, last public ceremonial is important because, although the private catastrophe of the lovers is unalterably complete, recognition occurs only when the Friar recounts at great length to all the community the story we already know. As we watch the bereaved families responding with shock to the story of Romeo and Juliet's tragedy, we understand the reason for its length: only when it is too late do the families begin to comprehend their own complicity in the disaster that has occurred. This recognition is not that of the protagonists, as in the Aristotelian conception of recognition, nor does it accompany a reversal in the love tragedy; that reversal already has taken place in Romeo's banishment and the lovers' deaths. This lack of correspondence with an Aristotelian definition of tragedy is not, however, a structural flaw; rather, it is a manifestation of the dual focus of the tragedy on the lovers and on all Verona. The city itself is a kind of protagonist, suffering through its own violence and coming at last to the sad comfort that wisdom brings.

The timeless nature of a tragic story about young lovers has resulted in its being an irresistible vehicle for modern updatings in the theater and in film, many of them highly successful in bringing the play into the lives of modern and young audiences. Productions in this vein have raised important questions about the protagonists' attitudes toward love and the nature of the social environment in which their tragedy occurs. The play's vivid bawdry invites an atmosphere of hedonism that can be understood, implicitly at least, in terms of the sexual revolution of the 1960s and afterwards. The boy actor who originally played Juliet on Shakespeare's stage has been replaced by Olivia Hussey, for example, in Franco Zeffirelli's popular film of 1968; Hussey is so gorgeously appealing in her first long night-time conversation with Romeo that his insistent "Oh, wilt thou leave me so unsatisfied?" takes on new urgency. Subsequently, the film briefly shows the lovers in bed, unclothed. Mercutio is sometimes portrayed as homosexual: mutedly so in the Zeffirelli film, aggressively so in Terry Hands's 1973 production at Stratford-upon-Avon, and flamboyantly so in Baz Luhrmann's immensely successful film, *Romeo + Juliet*, of 1996. In this last version, Mercutio is an African American drag queen, while Friar Laurence is a New Age priest. Juliet's mother in this same film is hilarious as a pill-popping, chain-smoking, and hard-drinking society dame slithering her ectomorphically slim body into a Cleopatra outfit for the huge masked ball that she and her nouveau riche husband are putting on in their tastelessly expensive block-long mansion—just the sort of parents whom one can count on not to understand their daughter. Luhrmann's Nurse is an Hispanic woman bellowing "Huliet! Huliet!" to remind us that the film is set in a southern United States city like Los Angeles or Miami. (It was actually filmed in Mexico City.) The street violence is also Hispanic, with rival gangs setting fire to gas stations and shooting automatic weapons during high-speed car chases. This updating of the violence with which the play begins owes some of its inspiration, presumably, to Leonard Bernstein's *West Side Story* (1957), set in Spanish Harlem.

Such innovations are at their best when they point to the play's insistent dramatization of violence and love in conflict. What responsibility does society bear for youthful tragedy when the models for behavior available to young people are what they are in today's world? How can a young man like Romeo escape the peer pressures of gang loyalties and macho stereotypes? Romeo struggles against these pressures in his crucial moment of decision; knowing that Juliet has taught him a better way, he yet succumbs to the mores of his tribe and to his own need to revenge on Tybalt the death of Mercutio. In these modern productions, as in the play itself, the violent response is too believable. As Friar Laurence says, "grace and rude will" do battle within the human psyche, too often with tragic outcome, and young love must pay the price.

Romeo and Juliet

[*Dramatis Personae*

CHORUS

ESCALUS, *Prince of Verona*
MERCUTIO, *the Prince's kinsman and Romeo's friend*
PARIS, *a young count and kinsman of the Prince*
PAGE *to Count Paris*

MONTAGUE
MONTAGUE'S WIFE
ROMEO, *son of the Montagues*
BENVOLIO, *Montague's nephew and Romeo's friend*
ABRAHAM, *a servant of the Montague household*
BALTHASAR, *a servant of the Montague household*
   attending Romeo

CAPULET
CAPULET'S WIFE
JULIET, *daughter of the Capulets*
NURSE
TYBALT, *nephew of Capulet's Wife*

    SCENE: *Verona; Mantua*]

PETRUCHIO, *Capulet's kinsman*
SECOND CAPULET, *an old man, Capulet's kinsman*
PETER, *a servant of the Capulet household attending the*
   Nurse
SAMSON
GREGORY
ANTHONY   } *servants of the Capulet household*
POTPAN
CLOWN *or* SERVANT
Other SERVANTS

FRIAR LAURENCE } *Franciscan friars*
FRIAR JOHN

APOTHECARY
Three MUSICIANS (*Simon Catling, Hugh Rebeck, and James*
   Soundpost)
Three WATCHMEN

Citizens, Maskers, Torchbearers, Guards, Servants, and
   Attendants

The Prologue

[*Enter Chorus.*]

CHORUS
Two households, both alike in dignity,   1
   In fair Verona, where we lay our scene,
From ancient grudge break to new mutiny,   3
   Where civil blood makes civil hands unclean.   4
From forth the fatal loins of these two foes.
   A pair of star-crossed lovers take their life;   6
Whose misadventured piteous overthrows   7
Doth with their death bury their parents' strife.
The fearful passage of their death-marked love,   9
   And the continuance of their parents' rage,
Which, but their children's end, naught could remove,
   Is now the two hours' traffic of our stage;   12
The which if you with patient ears attend,
What here shall miss, our toil shall strive to mend.   14
       [*Exit.*]

❦

Prologue.
1–14 (The Prologue is in the form of a sonnet.)
1 dignity rank, status   **3 mutiny** strife, discord   **4 Where . . .**
unclean where citizens' hands uncivilly are stained in civil strife with
their fellow citizens' blood.   **6 star-crossed** thwarted by destiny, by
adverse stars   **7 misadventured** unlucky

9 passage progress   **12 two hours' traffic** A conventional way of
referring to the length of stage performances in the early modern
period, not to be taken too literally, but indicative of a brisk pace
14 What . . . mend what is defective or inadequate in the short summary I have given you here, the actors' efforts in the following two
hours will amply and fully make clear.

[1.1]

*Enter Samson and Gregory, with swords
and bucklers, of the house of Capulet.*

SAMSON Gregory, on my word, we'll not carry coals. 1

GREGORY No, for then we should be colliers. 2

SAMSON I mean, an we be in choler, we'll draw. 3

GREGORY Ay, while you live, draw your neck out of 4
collar. 5

SAMSON I strike quickly, being moved. 6

GREGORY But thou art not quickly moved to strike.

SAMSON A dog of the house of Montague moves me. 8

GREGORY To move is to stir, and to be valiant is to
stand. Therefore, if thou art moved, thou run'st away. 10

SAMSON A dog of that house shall move me to stand. I
will take the wall of any man or maid of Montague's. 12

GREGORY That shows thee a weak slave, for the 13
weakest goes to the wall. 14

SAMSON 'Tis true, and therefore women, being the
weaker vessels, are ever thrust to the wall. Therefore I 16
will push Montague's men from the wall and thrust
his maids to the wall.

GREGORY The quarrel is between our masters and us 19
their men. 20

SAMSON 'Tis all one. I will show myself a tyrant: when 21
I have fought with the men, I will be civil with the
maids—I will cut off their heads.

GREGORY The heads of the maids?

SAMSON Ay, the heads of the maids, or their maidenheads. Take it in what sense thou wilt. 26

GREGORY They must take it in sense that feel it. 27

SAMSON Me they shall feel while I am able to stand, 28
and 'tis known I am a pretty piece of flesh. 29

GREGORY 'Tis well thou art not fish; if thou hadst, thou 30
hadst been Poor John. Draw thy tool. Here comes of 31
the house of Montagues.

*Enter two other Servingmen
[Abraham and another].*

1.1. Location: Verona. A public place.
0.2 bucklers small shields **1 carry coals** i.e., endure insults. **2 colliers**
(Coal carriers were regarded as dirty and of evil repute.) **3 an** if.
choler anger (produced by one of the four humors). **draw** draw
swords. **5 collar** i.e., hangman's noose. (With pun on *colliers* and
choler.) **6 moved** i.e., to anger. (With pun in next line.) **8 moves**
incites **10 stand** i.e., stand one's ground. **12 take the wall** take the
cleaner side of the walk nearest the wall, thus forcing others out into
the gutter **13–14 the weakest . . . wall** (A proverb expressing the
idea that the weakest are always forced to give way.) **16 weaker
vessels** (Saint Paul bids husbands give honor to their wives "as unto
the weaker vessel," 1 Peter 3:7.) **thrust to the wall** (With suggestion
of amorous assault.) **19–20 between . . . men** i.e., between the males
of one household and the males of the other household; we have no
quarrel with the women. **21 one** the same. **26 what sense** whatever meaning **27 They . . . feel it** i.e., It is the maids who must
receive by way of physical sensation (*sense*) what I have to offer,
because they are the ones who can feel it. **28 stand** (With suggestion
of "have an erection," continued in the next few lines in *draw thy tool*
and *my naked weapon is out*.) **29–30 flesh . . . fish** (Refers to the
proverbial phrase, "neither fish nor flesh.") **31 Poor John** hake
salted and dried—a poor Lenten kind of food. (Probably with a
bawdy suggestion of sexual insufficiency.). **comes of** i.e., come
members of

SAMSON My naked weapon is out. Quarrel, I will back
thee.

GREGORY How, turn thy back and run?

SAMSON Fear me not. 36

GREGORY No, marry. I fear thee! 37

SAMSON Let us take the law of our side. Let them 38
begin.

GREGORY I will frown as I pass by, and let them take it
as they list. 41

SAMSON Nay, as they dare. I will bite my thumb at 42
them, which is disgrace to them if they bear it.
[Samson makes taunting gestures.]

ABRAHAM Do you bite your thumb at us, sir?

SAMSON I do bite my thumb, sir.

ABRAHAM Do you bite your thumb at us, sir?

SAMSON *[aside to Gregory]* Is the law of our side if I
say ay?

GREGORY *[aside to Samson]* No.

SAMSON *[to Abraham]* No, sir, I do not bite my thumb
at you, sir, but I bite my thumb, sir.

GREGORY Do you quarrel, sir?

ABRAHAM Quarrel, sir? No, sir.

SAMSON But if you do, sir, I am for you. I serve as good
a man as you.

ABRAHAM No better.

SAMSON Well, sir.

Enter Benvolio.

GREGORY *[to Samson]* Say "better." Here comes one of 58
my master's kinsmen. 59

SAMSON *[to Abraham]* Yes, better, sir.

ABRAHAM You lie.

SAMSON Draw, if you be men. Gregory, remember thy
washing blow.   *They fight.* 63

BENVOLIO Part, fools!
Put up your swords. You know not what you do.

Enter Tybalt [with sword drawn].

TYBALT
What, art thou drawn among these heartless hinds? 66
Turn thee, Benvolio. Look upon thy death.

BENVOLIO
I do but keep the peace. Put up thy sword,
Or manage it to part these men with me. 69

TYBALT
What, drawn and talk of peace? I hate the word
As I hate hell, all Montagues, and thee.
Have at thee, coward!   *[They fight.]* 72

*Enter three or four Citizens with clubs
or partisans.*

---

36 Fear Mistrust. (But Gregory deliberately misunderstands in the
next line, saying, in effect, "No indeed, do you think I'd be afraid of
you?") **37 marry** i.e., indeed. (Originally an oath, "by the Virgin
Mary.") **38 take the law of** have the law on **41 list** please. **42 bite
my thumb** i.e., make an insulting and probably obscene gesture
58–9 one . . . kinsmen i.e., Tybalt, who is approaching. (Not Benvolio,
who has just entered unobserved by the servingmen.) **63 washing**
slashing with great force **66 heartless hinds** cowardly menials.
69 manage use **72 Have at thee** i.e., On guard, here I come
72.2 partisans long-handled spears.

CITIZENS
Clubs, bills, and partisans! Strike! Beat them down!   73
Down with the Capulets! Down with the Montagues!   74

Enter old Capulet in his gown, and his Wife.

CAPULET
What noise is this? Give me my long sword, ho!   75
CAPULET'S WIFE
A crutch, a crutch! Why call you for a sword?
CAPULET
My sword, I say! Old Montague is come
And flourishes his blade in spite of me.   78

Enter old Montague and his Wife.

MONTAGUE
Thou villain Capulet!—Hold me not; let me go.
MONTAGUE'S WIFE
Thou shalt not stir one foot to seek a foe.   80

Enter Prince Escalus, with his train.

PRINCE
Rebellious subjects, enemies to peace,
Profaners of this neighbor-stainèd steel—   82
Will they not hear? What, ho! You men, you beasts,
That quench the fire of your pernicious rage
With purple fountains issuing from your veins,   85
On pain of torture, from those bloody hands
Throw your mistempered weapons to the ground   87
And hear the sentence of your movèd prince.   88
Three civil brawls, bred of an airy word,   89
By thee, old Capulet, and Montague,
Have thrice disturbed the quiet of our streets
And made Verona's ancient citizens
Cast by their grave-beseeming ornaments   93
To wield old partisans in hands as old,
Cankered with peace, to part your cankered hate.   95
If ever you disturb our streets again
Your lives shall pay the forfeit of the peace.   97
For this time all the rest depart away.
You, Capulet, shall go along with me,
And Montague, come you this afternoon,
To know our farther pleasure in this case,
To old Freetown, our common judgment-place.   102
Once more, on pain of death, all men depart.

Exeunt [all but Montague, Montague's Wife,
and Benvolio].

MONTAGUE
Who set this ancient quarrel new abroach?   104
Speak, nephew, were you by when it began?   105
BENVOLIO
Here were the servants of your adversary,
And yours, close fighting ere I did approach.
I drew to part them. In the instant came
The fiery Tybalt with his sword prepared,   109
Which, as he breathed defiance to my ears,
He swung about his head and cut the winds
Who, nothing hurt withal, hissed him in scorn.   112
While we were interchanging thrusts and blows,
Came more and more, and fought on part and part   114
Till the Prince came, who parted either part.   115
MONTAGUE'S WIFE
Oh, where is Romeo? Saw you him today?
Right glad I am he was not at this fray.
BENVOLIO
Madam, an hour before the worshiped sun
Peered forth the golden window of the east,   119
A troubled mind drave me to walk abroad,   120
Where, underneath the grove of sycamore
That westward rooteth from this city side,   122
So early walking did I see your son.
Towards him I made, but he was ware of me   124
And stole into the covert of the wood.   125
I, measuring his affections by my own,   126
Which then most sought where most might not be
found,   127
Being one too many by my weary self,
Pursued my humor, not pursuing his,   129
And gladly shunned who gladly fled from me.   130
MONTAGUE
Many a morning hath he there been seen,
With tears augmenting the fresh morning's dew,
Adding to clouds more clouds with his deep sighs;
But all so soon as the all-cheering sun
Should in the farthest east begin to draw
The shady curtains from Aurora's bed,   136
Away from light steals home my heavy son   137
And private in his chamber pens himself,
Shuts up his windows, locks fair daylight out,
And makes himself an artificial night.
Black and portentous must this humor prove
Unless good counsel may the cause remove.
BENVOLIO
My noble uncle, do you know the cause?
MONTAGUE
I neither know it nor can learn of him.

---

73 **Clubs** rallying cry, summoning apprentices with their clubs.
bills long-handled spears with hooked blades   **74.1** *gown* nightgown, dressing gown   **75 long sword** heavy, old-fashioned sword
78 spite defiance, despite   **80.1 train** retinue.   **82 Profaners . . . steel**
you who profane your weapons by staining them with neighbors'
blood   **85 purple** bloody, dark red   **87 mistempered** (1) having been
tempered, or hardened, in hot blood rather than cold water (2) malignant, ill-tempered   **88 movèd** angry   **89 airy** flippant, saucy
93 grave-beseeming ornaments i.e., staffs and other appurtenances
suited to wise old age   **95 Cankered . . . cankered** corroded (from
disuse) . . . malignant   **97 Your . . . peace** death will be the penalty for
breaking the peace.   **102 Freetown** (Brooke's translation, in his poem
Romeus and Juliet, of *Villa Franca,* as found in the Italian story.)
common public

104 **set . . . abroach** reopened this old quarrel, set it flowing.   **105 by**
near   **109 prepared** drawn, ready   **112 Who . . . withal** which winds,
not at all injured thereby   **114 on part and part** on one side and the
other   **115 either part** both parties.   **119 forth** from forth   **120 drave
. . . abroad** drove me to take a walk   **122 That . . . side** that grows on
the west side of this city   **124 made** moved.   **ware** wary, aware
125 covert cover, hiding place   **126 affections** wishes, inclination
127 Which . . . found which then chiefly desired a place where I
might be alone   **129 humor** mood   **130 who** him who   **136 Aurora**
goddess of dawn   **137 heavy** (1) sad (2) the opposite of *light.*   **son**
(punning on *sun,* line 134)

BENVOLIO
Have you importuned him by any means?   145
MONTAGUE
Both by myself and many other friends.
But he, his own affections' counselor,
Is to himself—I will not say how true,   148
But to himself so secret and so close,   149
So far from sounding and discovery,   150
As is the bud bit with an envious worm   151
Ere he can spread his sweet leaves to the air
Or dedicate his beauty to the sun.
Could we but learn from whence his sorrows grow,
We would as willingly give cure as know.

                    Enter Romeo.

BENVOLIO
See where he comes. So please you, step aside.   156
I'll know his grievance or be much denied.
MONTAGUE
I would thou wert so happy by thy stay   158
To hear true shrift.—Come, madam, let's away.   159
                    Exeunt [Montague and his Wife].
BENVOLIO
Good morrow, cousin.
ROMEO   Is the day so young?   160
BENVOLIO
But new struck nine.
ROMEO   Ay me! Sad hours seem long.
Was that my father that went hence so fast?
BENVOLIO
It was. What sadness lengthens Romeo's hours?
ROMEO
Not having that which, having, makes them short.
BENVOLIO
In love?
ROMEO   Out—
BENVOLIO   Of love?
ROMEO
Out of her favor where I am in love.
BENVOLIO
Alas, that Love, so gentle in his view,   169
Should be so tyrannous and rough in proof!   170
ROMEO
Alas, that Love, whose view is muffled still,   171
Should without eyes see pathways to his will!   172
Where shall we dine?—Oh, me! What fray was here?
Yet tell me not, for I have heard it all.
Here's much to do with hate, but more with love.
Why, then, O brawling love, O loving hate,
O anything of nothing first create,   177
O heavy lightness, serious vanity,
Misshapen chaos of well-seeming forms,
Feather of lead, bright smoke, cold fire, sick health,

Still-waking sleep, that is not what it is!   181
This love feel I, that feel no love in this.
Dost thou not laugh?
BENVOLIO   No, coz, I rather weep.   183
ROMEO
Good heart, at what?
BENVOLIO   At thy good heart's oppression.
ROMEO
Why, such is love's transgression.
Griefs of mine own lie heavy in my breast,
Which thou wilt propagate, to have it pressed   187
With more of thine. This love that thou hast shown   188
Doth add more grief to too much of mine own.
Love is a smoke made with the fume of sighs;
Being purged, a fire sparkling in lovers' eyes;   191
Being vexed, a sea nourished with lovers' tears.
What is it else? A madness most discreet,   193
A choking gall, and a preserving sweet.
Farewell, my coz.
BENVOLIO   Soft! I will go along.   195
An if you leave me so, you do me wrong.   196
ROMEO
Tut, I have lost myself. I am not here.
This is not Romeo; he's some other where.
BENVOLIO
Tell me in sadness, who is that you love?   199
ROMEO   What, shall I groan and tell thee?
BENVOLIO
Groan? Why, no, but sadly tell me who.   201
ROMEO
Bid a sick man in sadness make his will—
A word ill urged to one that is so ill!   203
In sadness, cousin, I do love a woman.
BENVOLIO
I aimed so near when I supposed you loved.
ROMEO
A right good markman! And she's fair I love.   206
BENVOLIO
A right fair mark, fair coz, is soonest hit.   207
ROMEO
Well, in that hit you miss. She'll not be hit
With Cupid's arrow. She hath Dian's wit,   209
And, in strong proof of chastity well armed,   210
From love's weak childish bow she lives unharmed.
She will not stay the siege of loving terms,   212
Nor bide th'encounter of assailing eyes,   213
Nor ope her lap to saint-seducing gold.
Oh, she is rich in beauty, only poor
That when she dies, with beauty dies her store.   216

---

181 Still-waking continually awake   **183 coz** cousin, kinsman
187–8 propagate . . . thine increase by having it, i.e., my own grief,
oppressed or made still heavier with your grief on my account.
(The image of propagating and pressing is appropriately sexual.)
191 purged i.e., of smoke   **193 discreet** judicious, prudent   **195 Soft!**
i.e., Wait a moment!   **196 An if** If   **199 sadness** seriousness.   **is that**
is it that   **201 sadly** seriously. (But Romeo plays on the word, and
on *in sadness,* in the sense of "sorrowfully.")   **203 A word** i.e., *sadly*
or *in sadness*—too sad a word, says Romeo, for a melancholy lover
206 fair beautiful   **207 fair mark** clear, distinct target   **209 Dian**
Diana, huntress and goddess of chastity   **210 proof** armor   **212 stay**
submit to   **213 bide** abide, endure   **216 store** wealth. (She will die
without children, and therefore her beauty will die with her.)

---

145 any means every means possible.   **148 true** i.e., wise in counseling himself   **149 close** secretive   **150 sounding** being fathomed (to
discover deep or inner secrets)   **151 envious** malicious   **156 So
please you** If you please   **158 happy** fortunate, successful   **159 To** as
to.   **shrift** confession.   **160 cousin** kinsman.   **169 Love** Cupid.
view appearance   **170 in proof** in reality, in experience.   **171 view . . .
still** sight is blindfolded always. (Love is blind.)   **172 to his will** to
what he wants.   **177 create** created

BENVOLIO
Then she hath sworn that she will still live chaste? 217
ROMEO
She hath, and in that sparing makes huge waste, 218
For beauty starved with her severity 219
Cuts beauty off from all posterity.
She is too fair, too wise, wisely too fair,
To merit bliss by making me despair. 222
She hath forsworn to love, and in that vow 223
Do I live dead, that live to tell it now.
BENVOLIO
Be ruled by me. Forget to think of her.
ROMEO
Oh, teach me how I should forget to think!
BENVOLIO
By giving liberty unto thine eyes:
Examine other beauties.
ROMEO   'Tis the way
To call hers, exquisite, in question more. 229
These happy masks that kiss fair ladies' brows,
Being black, puts us in mind they hide the fair.
He that is strucken blind cannot forget
The precious treasure of his eyesight lost.
Show me a mistress that is passing fair: 234
What doth her beauty serve but as a note
Where I may read who passed that passing fair? 236
Farewell. Thou canst not teach me to forget.
BENVOLIO
I'll pay that doctrine, or else die in debt. Exeunt. 238

❖

[1.2]

Enter Capulet, County Paris, and the Clown
[a Servingman].

CAPULET
But Montague is bound as well as I, 1
In penalty alike, and 'tis not hard, I think,
For men so old as we to keep the peace.
PARIS
Of honorable reckoning are you both, 4
And pity 'tis you lived at odds so long.
But now, my lord, what say you to my suit?
CAPULET
But saying o'er what I have said before: 7
My child is yet a stranger in the world;
She hath not seen the change of fourteen years.
Let two more summers wither in their pride
Ere we may think her ripe to be a bride.

PARIS
Younger than she are happy mothers made.
CAPULET
And too soon marred are those so early made.
The earth hath swallowed all my hopes but she;
She is the hopeful lady of my earth. 15
But woo her, gentle Paris, get her heart;
My will to her consent is but a part;
And, she agreed, within her scope of choice 18
Lies my consent and fair-according voice. 19
This night I hold an old accustomed feast, 20
Whereto I have invited many a guest
Such as I love; and you among the store, 22
One more, most welcome, makes my number more.
At my poor house look to behold this night
Earth-treading stars that make dark heaven light.
Such comfort as do lusty young men feel 26
When well-appareled April on the heel 27
Of limping winter treads, even such delight
Among fresh fennel buds shall you this night 29
Inherit at my house. Hear all, all see, 30
And like her most whose merit most shall be;
Which on more view of many, mine, being one, 32
May stand in number, though in reck'ning none. 33
Come, go with me. [*To the Servingman, giving a paper*]
Go, sirrah, trudge about 34
Through fair Verona; find those persons out
Whose names are written there, and to them say,
My house and welcome on their pleasure stay. 37
Exit [with Paris].
SERVINGMAN   Find them out whose names are written
here! It is written that the shoemaker should meddle 39
with his yard and the tailor with his last, the fisher 40
with his pencil, and the painter with his nets; but I am 41
sent to find those persons whose names are here writ, 42
and can never find what names the writing person 43
hath here writ. I must to the learned.—In good time! 44

Enter Benvolio and Romeo.

217 still always   218 sparing miserliness   219 starved with killed by
222 To . . . despair to achieve her own salvation through chaste living
while driving me to the spiritually dangerous state of despair.
223 forsworn to renounced, repudiated   229 in question more even
more keenly to mind, into consideration.   234 mistress i.e., eligible
young woman.   passing surpassingly   236 passed surpassed
238 I'll . . . debt i.e., I'll fulfill my obligation to do that, or feel I have
failed as a friend.
1.2. Location: Verona.
0.1 County Count   1 bound legally obligated (to keep the peace)
4 reckoning estimation, repute   7 o'er again

15 the hopeful . . . earth i.e., my heir and hope for posterity. (Earth
includes property and lands.)   18 she if she be   19 according agreeing   20 old accustomed traditional   22 store group   26 lusty lively
27 well-appareled newly clothed in green   29 fennel flowering herb
thought to have the power of awakening passion   30 Inherit possess
32–3 Which . . . none i.e., when you have looked over many ladies,
my daughter, being one of them, may be numerically counted among
the lot, but you will not think her worth your notice. (Capulet refers
to the proverbial saying, "one is no number.")   34 sirrah (Customary
form of address to servants.)   37 on . . . stay wait to serve their pleasure.   39–41 It is . . . nets i.e., If a shoemaker cannot be expected to
have any skill with a yard (a tailor's yardstick) and conversely a tailor
with a last (a shoemaker's form), and similarly with a painter's pencil
(a paintbrush) in a fisherman's hands or a net in a painter's hands,
why should I, an illiterate servant, be expected to be able to read a
written note of invitation? (Meddle, yard, and pencil are often slang
expressions for sexual activity and the male sexual organ, but since
last and nets don't seem to convey sexual meaning here, the humor is
more directed at comic inappropriateness.)   42 find locate   43 find
figure out   44 In good time i.e., Here comes help.

BENVOLIO
    Tut, man, one fire burns out another's burning,
    One pain is lessened by another's anguish;   46
    Turn giddy, and be holp by backward turning;   47
    One desperate grief cures with another's languish.   48
    Take thou some new infection to thy eye,
    And the rank poison of the old will die.   50

ROMEO
    Your plaintain leaf is excellent for that.   51

BENVOLIO
    For what, I pray thee?

ROMEO   For your broken shin.

BENVOLIO   Why, Romeo, art thou mad?

ROMEO
    Not mad, but bound more than a madman is;   54
    Shut up in prison, kept without my food,
    Whipped and tormented and—Good e'en, good
      fellow.   56

SERVINGMAN   God gi' good e'en. I pray, sir, can you read?   57

ROMEO
    Ay, mine own fortune in my misery.

SERVINGMAN   Perhaps you have learned it without   59
book. But, I pray, can you read anything you see?   60

ROMEO
    Ay, if I know the letters and the language.

SERVINGMAN   Ye say honestly. Rest you merry!   62
                                    [Going.]

ROMEO   Stay, fellow, I can read.   *He reads the letter.*
    "Signor Martino and his wife and daughters,
    County Anselme and his beauteous sisters,
    The lady widow of Vitruvio,
    Signor Placentio and his lovely nieces,
    Mercutio and his brother Valentine,
    Mine uncle Capulet, his wife, and daughters,
    My fair niece Rosaline, and Livia,
    Signor Valentio and his cousin Tybalt,
    Lucio and the lively Helena."
    A fair assembly. Whither should they come?

SERVINGMAN   Up.

ROMEO   Whither? To supper?

SERVINGMAN   To our house.

ROMEO   Whose house?

SERVINGMAN   My master's.

ROMEO
    Indeed, I should have asked thee that before.

SERVINGMAN   Now I'll tell you without asking. My
master is the great rich Capulet; and if you be not of
the house of Montagues, I pray, come and crush a cup   82
of wine. Rest you merry!   *[Exit.]*

BENVOLIO
    At this same ancient feast of Capulet's   84
    Sups the fair Rosaline whom thou so loves,
    With all the admirèd beauties of Verona.
    Go thither, and with unattainted eye   87
    Compare her face with some that I shall show,
    And I will make thee think thy swan a crow.

ROMEO
    When the devout religion of mine eye   90
      Maintains such falsehood, then turn tears to fires;   91
    And these who, often drowned, could never die,   92
      Transparent heretics, be burnt for liars!   93
    One fairer than my love? The all-seeing sun
    Ne'er saw her match since first the world begun.

BENVOLIO
    Tut, you saw her fair, none else being by,
    Herself poised with herself in either eye;   97
    But in that crystal scales let there be weighed   98
    Your lady's love against some other maid
    That I will show you shining at this feast,
    And she shall scant show well that now seems best.   101

ROMEO
    I'll go along, no such sight to be shown,
    But to rejoice in splendor of mine own.   *[Exeunt.]* 103

❖

[1.3]

Enter Capulet's Wife and Nurse.

WIFE
    Nurse, where's my daughter? Call her forth to me.

NURSE
    Now, by my maidenhead at twelve year old,
    I bade her come. What, lamb! What, ladybird!   3
    God forbid, where's this girl? What, Juliet!   4

Enter Juliet.

JULIET   How now? Who calls?

NURSE   Your mother.

JULIET
    Madam, I am here. What is your will?

WIFE
    This is the matter.—Nurse, give leave awhile,   8
    We must talk in secret.—Nurse, come back again;
    I have remembered me, thou's hear our counsel.   10
    Thou knowest my daughter's of a pretty age.

---

46 another's anguish the anguish of another pain   **47 holp . . . turning** helped by turning in the reverse direction   **48 cures . . . languish** is cured by the suffering of a second *grief* or pain.   **50 rank** foul **51 Your . . . that** i.e., (sardonically) Your proverbial nostrums are about as useful in curing my real grief as is a folk remedy for minor abrasions such as a *broken shin* (line 52) or surface wound on the leg— that is, no use at all.   **54 bound** (The usual treatment for madness.) **56 Good e'en** Good evening. (Used after noon.)   **57 gi'** give you **59–60 Perhaps . . . book** (1) Perhaps that's some sort of book that you've committed to memory (2) Misery is something one can learn without knowing how to read.   **62 Rest you merry** i.e., Farewell. (The servingman can see he is getting nowhere.)   **82 crush** i.e., drink

84 ancient customary   **87 unattainted** unbiased   **90–3 When . . . liars!** (Romeo, recalling that persons suspected of witchcraft were sometimes thrown into water to see if they would drown or float, and that those who did not drown were declared witches and burned at the stake, protests that whenever he is a heretic in love by looking at some woman other than Rosaline he should be similarly burned by having his own tears turn into flames, since he will have shown that his flood of tears could not drown him, i.e., was insufficient. *Transparent* means "manifest," "clear.")   **97 poised** weighed, balanced   **98 crystal scales** i.e., Romeo's eyes   **101 scant** scarcely **103 mine own** i.e., the sight of my own Rosaline.
1.3. Location: Verona. Capulet's house.
3 ladybird (A term of affection.)   **4 God forbid** (A mild oath.)
8 give leave leave us   **10 thou's** thou shalt

NURSE
Faith, I can tell her age unto an hour.

WIFE
She's not fourteen.

NURSE   I'll lay fourteen of my teeth—
And yet, to my teen be it spoken, I have but four—   14
She's not fourteen. How long is it now
To Lammastide?

WIFE   A fortnight and odd days.   16

NURSE
Even or odd, of all days in the year,
Come Lammas Eve at night shall she be fourteen.
Susan and she—God rest all Christian souls!—   19
Were of an age. Well, Susan is with God;
She was too good for me. But, as I said,
On Lammas Eve at night shall she be fourteen,
That shall she, marry, I remember it well.   23
'Tis since the earthquake now eleven years,
And she was weaned—I never shall forget it—
Of all the days of the year, upon that day;
For I had then laid wormwood to my dug,   27
Sitting in the sun under the dovehouse wall.
My lord and you were then at Mantua—
Nay, I do bear a brain! But, as I said,   30
When it did taste the wormwood on the nipple
Of my dug and felt it bitter, pretty fool,   32
To see it tetchy and fall out wi'th' dug!   33
"Shake" quoth the dovehouse. 'Twas no need, I trow,   34
To bid me trudge!   35
And since that time it is eleven years,
For then she could stand high-lone; nay, by the rood,   37
She could have run and waddled all about.
For even the day before, she broke her brow,   39
And then my husband—God be with his soul!
'A was a merry man—took up the child.   41
"Yea," quoth he, "dost thou fall upon thy face?
Thou wilt fall backward when thou hast more wit,   43
Wilt thou not, Jule?" and, by my halidom,   44
The pretty wretch left crying and said "Ay."
To see now how a jest shall come about!   46
I warrant, an I should live a thousand years,
I never should forget it. "Wilt thou not, Jule?" quoth
    he,
And, pretty fool, it stinted and said "Ay."   49

WIFE
Enough of this. I pray thee, hold thy peace.

NURSE
Yes, madam. Yet I cannot choose but laugh
To think it should leave crying and say "Ay."
And yet, I warrant, it had upon it brow   53
A bump as big as a young cockerel's stone—   54
A perilous knock—and it cried bitterly.
"Yea," quoth my husband, "fall'st upon thy face?
Thou wilt fall backward when thou comest to age,
Wilt thou not, Jule?" It stinted and said "Ay."

JULIET
And stint thou too, I pray thee, Nurse, say I.   59

NURSE
Peace, I have done. God mark thee to his grace!
Thou wast the prettiest babe that e'er I nursed.
An I might live to see thee married once,   62
I have my wish.

WIFE
Marry, that "marry" is the very theme
I came to talk of. Tell me, daughter Juliet,
How stands your disposition to be married?   66

JULIET
It is an honor that I dream not of.

NURSE
An honor? Were not I thine only nurse,
I would say thou hadst sucked wisdom from thy teat.   69

WIFE
Well, think of marriage now. Younger than you
Here in Verona, ladies of esteem,
Are made already mothers. By my count
I was your mother much upon these years   73
That you are now a maid. Thus then in brief:
The valiant Paris seeks you for his love.

NURSE
A man, young lady! Lady, such a man
As all the world—why, he's a man of wax.   77

WIFE
Verona's summer hath not such a flower.

NURSE
Nay, he's a flower, in faith, a very flower.   79

WIFE
What say you? Can you love the gentleman?
This night you shall behold him at our feast.
Read o'er the volume of young Paris' face,
And find delight writ there with beauty's pen;
Examine every married lineament,   84
And see how one another lends content;   85
And what obscured in this fair volume lies   86
Find written in the margent of his eyes.   87
This precious book of love, this unbound lover,   88

---

14 **teen** sorrow. (Playing on *teen* and *four* in *fourteen*.) **16 Lammastide** the days near August 1. **19 Susan** the Nurse's own child, who has evidently died **23 marry** i.e., by the Virgin Mary. (A mild oath.) **27 wormwood** (A bitter-tasting plant used to wean the child from the *dug* or "teat.") **30 bear a brain** maintain a keen memory. **32 fool** (A term of endearment here.) **33 tetchy** peevish, irritable **34 "Shake" . . . dovehouse** i.e., The dovehouse shook. **trow** believe, assure you **35 trudge** be off quickly. **37 high-lone** on her feet, without help. **rood** cross **39 broke her brow** bruised her forehead (by falling) **41 'A** He **43 wit** understanding **44 by my halidom** (A mild oath: "by all things holy," but popularly confused with "by my Holy Dame.") **46 come about** come true. **49 stinted** ceased

53 **it** its **54 cockerel's stone** young rooster's testicle **59 say I** (With a pun on *said "Ay"* of previous line.) **62 An** If. **once** someday **66 disposition** inclination **69 thy teat** the teat that nourished you. **73 much . . . years** at much the same age **77 a man of wax** as handsome as a figure modeled in wax. **79 Nay** Indeed **84 married lineament** harmonized feature **85 And . . . content** and see how his handsome features enhance one another **86–7 And what . . . eyes** and whatever you don't fully grasp by seeing his handsome features, find explained in his eyes, as though they were a kind of marginal gloss or commentary found in books. **88 unbound** i.e., because not bound in marriage. (With a double meaning in the continuing metaphor of an unbound book.)

To beautify him, only lacks a cover.   89
The fish lives in the sea, and 'tis much pride   90
For fair without the fair within to hide.   91
That book in many's eyes doth share the glory,   92
That in gold clasps locks in the golden story;   93
So shall you share all that he doth possess
By having him, making yourself no less.

NURSE
No less? Nay, bigger. Women grow by men.   96

WIFE
Speak briefly, can you like of Paris' love?   97

JULIET
I'll look to like, if looking liking move;   98
But no more deep will I endart mine eye
Than your consent gives strength to make it fly.

Enter Servingman.

SERVINGMAN   Madam, the guests are come, supper
served up, you called, my young lady asked for, the
Nurse cursed in the pantry, and everything in extremity. I must hence to wait. I beseech you, follow straight.   104

WIFE   We follow thee.   [*Exit Servingman.*]
                           Juliet, the County stays.   105

NURSE
Go, girl, seek happy nights to happy days.   *Exeunt.*

❖

[1.4]

*Enter Romeo, Mercutio, Benvolio, with five or
six other masquers; torchbearers.*

ROMEO
What, shall this speech be spoke for our excuse?   1
Or shall we on without apology?   2

BENVOLIO
The date is out of such prolixity.   3
We'll have no Cupid hoodwinked with a scarf,   4
Bearing a Tartar's painted bow of lath,   5
Scaring the ladies like a crowkeeper,   6
Nor no without-book prologue, faintly spoke
After the prompter, for our entrance;   7
But let them measure us by what they will,   9
We'll measure them a measure, and be gone.   10

ROMEO
Give me a torch. I am not for this ambling.
Being but heavy, I will bear the light.   12

MERCUTIO
Nay, gentle Romeo, we must have you dance.

ROMEO
Not I, believe me. You have dancing shoes
With nimble soles; I have a soul of lead   15
So stakes me to the ground I cannot move.

MERCUTIO
You are a lover; borrow Cupid's wings,
And soar with them above a common bound.   18

ROMEO
I am too sore enpiercèd with his shaft   19
To soar with his light feathers, and so bound
I cannot bound a pitch above dull woe.   21
Under love's heavy burden do I sink.

MERCUTIO
And, to sink in it, should you burden love—   23
Too great oppression for a tender thing.

ROMEO
Is love a tender thing? It is too rough,
Too rude, too boisterous, and it pricks like thorn.

MERCUTIO
If love be rough with you, be rough with love;
Prick love for pricking, and you beat love down.   28
Give me a case to put my visage in.   29
                              [*He puts on a mask.*]
A visor for a visor! What care I   30
What curious eye doth quote deformities?   31
Here are the beetle brows shall blush for me.

BENVOLIO
Come, knock and enter, and no sooner in
But every man betake him to his legs.   34

ROMEO
A torch for me. Let wantons light of heart
Tickle the senseless rushes with their heels,   36
For I am proverbed with a grandsire phrase: 37
I'll be a candle-holder and look on.   38
The game was ne'er so fair, and I am done.   39

---

89 **a cover** i.e., marriage, an embracing wife.   **90–1 The fish . . . hide**
i.e., The fish has its own suitable environment, and similarly in marriage the fair Juliet (here imagined as a beautiful book cover "binding" Paris) would suitably enhance Paris's worth.   **92–3 That book
. . . story** i.e., In many persons' eyes, a good story is all the more
admirable for being handsomely bound. (*Clasps* means [1] book fas-
tenings [2] embraces.)   **96 bigger** i.e., by pregnancy.   **97 like of** be
pleased with   **98 liking move** may provoke affection   **104 straight**
at once.   **105 County stays** Count (Paris) waits for you.
1.4. Location: Verona. A street.
1 speech (Masquers were customarily preceded by a messenger or
"presenter" with a set speech of compliment.)   **2 on** go on, approach
3 The date . . . prolixity Such windy rhetoric is out of fashion.
4 Cupid i.e., messenger or "presenter," probably a boy, disguised as
Cupid.   **hoodwinked** blindfolded   **5 Tartar's . . . bow** (Tartars'
bows, shorter and more curved than the English longbow, were
thought to have resembled the old Roman bow with which Cupid
was pictured.)   **lath** flimsy wood   **6 crowkeeper** scarecrow
7 without-book memorized   **9 measure** judge   **10 measure . . .
measure** tread a dance for them

12 **heavy** (1) sad (2) the opposite of *light* (as at 1.1.137)   **15 soul** (Punning on *sole*.)   **18 common bound** (1) ordinary limit (2) normal
dance leap.   **19 sore** sorely. (With pun on *soar*.)   **21 bound** leap.
(With wordplay on *bound*, "confined," in the previous line.)   **pitch**
height. (A term from falconry for the highest point of a hawk's flight.)
23 And . . . love i.e., You wouldn't just sink *under* love's heavy burden, you'd sink *into* it and burden it. (Suggesting sexual penetration.)
28 Prick . . . down i.e., If love gets rough, fight back. (But with bawdy
suggestion of *pricking* as a way to satisfy desire and cause detumescence.)   **29 case** mask   **30 A visor . . . visor** i.e., A mask for an ugly
masklike face.   **31 quote** take notice of   **34 to his legs** to dancing.
36 senseless rushes reeds used as floor covering, or insensate green
rushes   **37 proverbed . . . phrase** furnished with an old proverb
38 candle-holder i.e., bystander. (Referring to the proverbial idea that
one who lacks ability himself can hold the candle and thus provide
light for one who is able to act.)   **39 The game . . . done** (Another
proverbial truism, that it is best to quit when one is ahead.)

MERCUTIO
Tut, dun's the mouse, the constable's own word.   40
If thou art dun, we'll draw thee from the mire   41
Of—save your reverence—love, wherein thou stickest   42
Up to the ears. Come, we burn daylight, ho!   43
ROMEO
Nay, that's not so.
MERCUTIO   I mean, sir, in delay
We waste our lights in vain, like lamps by day.
Take our good meaning, for our judgment sits   46
Five times in that ere once in our five wits.   47
ROMEO
And we mean well in going to this masque,
But 'tis no wit to go.
MERCUTIO   Why, may one ask?   49
ROMEO
I dreamt a dream tonight.
MERCUTIO   And so did I.   50
ROMEO
Well, what was yours?
MERCUTIO   That dreamers often lie.   51
ROMEO
In bed asleep, while they do dream things true.
MERCUTIO
Oh, then, I see Queen Mab hath been with you.   53
She is the fairies' midwife, and she comes
In shape no bigger than an agate stone   55
On the forefinger of an alderman,   56
Drawn with a team of little atomi   57
Over men's noses as they lie asleep.
Her chariot is an empty hazelnut,
Made by the joiner squirrel or old grub,   60
Time out o' mind the fairies' coachmakers.
Her wagon spokes made of long spinners' legs,   62
The cover of the wings of grasshoppers,
Her traces of the smallest spider web,
Her collars of the moonshine's wat'ry beams,
Her whip of cricket's bone, the lash of film,   66
Her wagoner a small gray-coated gnat,   67

Not half so big as a round little worm   68
Pricked from the lazy finger of a maid.   69
And in this state she gallops night by night
Through lovers' brains, and then they dream of love;
O'er courtiers' knees, that dream on curtsies straight; 72
O'er lawyers' fingers, who straight dream on fees;
O'er ladies' lips, who straight on kisses dream,
Which oft the angry Mab with blisters plagues
Because their breaths with sweetmeats tainted are.   76
Sometime she gallops o'er a courtier's nose,
And then dreams he of smelling out a suit.   78
And sometime comes she with a tithe-pig's tail   79
Tickling a parson's nose as 'a lies asleep;
Then dreams he of another benefice.   81
Sometime she driveth o'er a soldier's neck,
And then dreams he of cutting foreign throats,
Of breaches, ambuscadoes, Spanish blades,   84
Of healths five fathom deep, and then anon   85
Drums in his ear, at which he starts and wakes,
And being thus frighted swears a prayer or two
And sleeps again. This is that very Mab
That plats the manes of horses in the night,   89
And bakes the elflocks in foul sluttish hairs,   90
Which once untangled much misfortune bodes.   91
This is the hag, when maids lie on their backs,
That presses them and learns them first to bear,   93
Making them women of good carriage.   94
This is she—
ROMEO   Peace, peace, Mercutio, peace!
Thou talk'st of nothing.
MERCUTIO   True, I talk of dreams,
Which are the children of an idle brain,
Begot of nothing but vain fantasy,   98
Which is as thin of substance as the air,
And more inconstant than the wind, who woos
Even now the frozen bosom of the north,
And being angered, puffs away from thence,
Turning his side to the dew-dropping south.
BENVOLIO
This wind you talk of blows us from ourselves.   104
Supper is done, and we shall come too late.
ROMEO
I fear, too early; for my mind misgives   106
Some consequence yet hanging in the stars

40 dun's . . . word i.e., "keep still"—just the sort of thing a constable might say. (Matching proverb with proverb, Mercutio answers Romeo's "I am done" by twitting him for being mousy. Constables were much laughed at for inappropriately pompous speech.) **41–3 If . . . ears** (To Mercutio, Romeo's love melancholy recalls the Christmas game called "Dun is in the mire," in which a heavy log, representing a horse named Dun, was hauled out of an imaginary mire by the players. *Save your reverence* is Mercutio's mock apology for speaking of so improper an expression as being mired up to the ears in love.) **43 burn daylight** i.e., waste time. (But Romeo quibbles, protesting that it is not literally daytime.) **46–7 Take . . . wits** Try to understand what I am trying to say (rather than quibbling with phrases like "burn daylight"), for wise judgment is five times more pleased with good meaning than with the ingenious wit of our frail senses. **49 wit** wisdom (playing on *wits* in line 47; *mean* in line 48 plays on *meaning* in line 46) **50 tonight** last night. **51 lie** tell falsehoods. (But Mercutio answers in the sense of "lie down in bed.") **53 Queen Mab** (Possibly a name of Celtic origin for the Fairy Queen.) **55 agate stone** (Precious stone often carved with diminutive figures and set in a ring.) **56 alderman** member of the municipal council **57 atomi** tiny creatures (atoms) **60 joiner** furniture maker. **grub** insect larva (which bores holes in nuts) **62 spinners'** spiders' **66 film** gossamer thread **67 wagoner** chariot driver

68–9 a round . . . maid (Worms proverbially breed in the fingers of the idle.) **72 curtsies** bows, obeisances. **straight** immediately **76 sweetmeats** candies or candied preserves **78 smelling . . . suit** i.e., finding a petitioner who will pay for the use of his influence at court. **79 tithe-pig** pig given to the parson in lieu of money as the parishioner's tithing, or granting of a tenth **81 benefice** ecclesiastical living. **84 Of breaches . . . blades** of opening up gaps in fortifications, of ambushes, of swords from Toledo in Spain, where the best swords were made **85 Of healths . . . deep** of toasts drunk deep **89 That plats . . . night** (According to popular superstition, the tangles that persistently turn up in the manes of horses were "witches' stirrups," i.e., footholds for witches as they rode.) **90–1 And bakes . . . bodes** (*Elflocks* or clumps of matted hair were so named because they were imagined to be the work of elves, who would torment anyone so presumptuous as to untangle the elflocks.) **93 learns** teaches **94 good carriage** (1) commendable deportment (2) skill in bearing the weight of men in sexual intercourse (3) able subsequently to carry a child. **98 vain fantasy** delusive imagination **104 from ourselves** from our plans. **106 misgives** fears

Shall bitterly begin his fearful date   108
With this night's revels, and expire the term   109
Of a despisèd life closed in my breast
By some vile forfeit of untimely death.
But He that hath the steerage of my course
Direct my suit! On, lusty gentlemen.   113
BENVOLIO   Strike, drum.   *They march about the stage,* 114
                           and [retire to one side].

❧

[1.5]

Servingmen come forth with napkins.

FIRST SERVINGMAN   Where's Potpan, that he helps not
to take away? He shift a trencher? He scrape a trencher?   2
SECOND SERVINGMAN   When good manners shall lie all
in one or two men's hands, and they unwashed too,
'tis a foul thing.
FIRST SERVINGMAN   Away with the joint stools, remove   6
the court cupboard, look to the plate. Good thou, save   7
me a piece of marchpane, and, as thou loves me, let   8
the porter let in Susan Grindstone and Nell.
                        [Exit Second Servingman.]
Anthony and Potpan!

           [Enter two more Servingmen.]

THIRD SERVINGMAN   Ay, boy, ready.
FIRST SERVINGMAN   You are looked for and called for,
asked for and sought for, in the great chamber.
FOURTH SERVINGMAN   We cannot be here and there
too. Cheerly, boys! Be brisk awhile, and the longest   15
liver take all.   *Exeunt.*   16

      Enter [Capulet and family and] all the guests
      and gentlewomen to the masquers.

CAPULET *[to the masquers]*
Welcome, gentlemen! Ladies that have their toes
Unplagued with corns will walk a bout with you.   18
Ah, my mistresses, which of you all
Will now deny to dance? She that makes dainty,   20
She, I'll swear, hath corns. Am I come near ye now? 21
Welcome, gentlemen! I have seen the day
That I have worn a visor and could tell
A whispering tale in a fair lady's ear
Such as would please. 'Tis gone, 'tis gone, 'tis gone.
You are welcome, gentlemen! Come, musicians, play.
               Music plays, and they dance.

A hall, a hall! Give room! And foot it, girls.   27
[To Servingmen]   More light, you knaves, and turn the
   tables up,   28
And quench the fire; the room is grown too hot.
[To his cousin]   Ah, sirrah, this unlooked-for sport
   comes well.   30
Nay, sit, nay, sit, good cousin Capulet,   31
For you and I are past our dancing days.
How long is't now since last yourself and I
Were in a mask?
SECOND CAPULET   By'r Lady, thirty years.
CAPULET
What, man? 'Tis not so much, 'tis not so much;
'Tis since the nuptial of Lucentio,
Come Pentecost as quickly as it will,   37
Some five-and-twenty years, and then we masked.
SECOND CAPULET
'Tis more, 'tis more. His son is elder, sir;
His son is thirty.
CAPULET   Will you tell me that?
His son was but a ward two years ago.   41
ROMEO *[to a Servingman]*
What lady's that which doth enrich the hand
Of yonder knight?
SERVINGMAN   I know not, sir.
ROMEO
Oh, she doth teach the torches to burn bright!
It seems she hangs upon the cheek of night
As a rich jewel in an Ethiop's ear—
Beauty too rich for use, for earth too dear!   48
So shows a snowy dove trooping with crows   49
As yonder lady o'er her fellows shows.
The measure done, I'll watch her place of stand,   51
And, touching hers, make blessèd my rude hand.   52
Did my heart love till now? Forswear it, sight!   53
For I ne'er saw true beauty till this night.
TYBALT
This, by his voice, should be a Montague.
Fetch me my rapier, boy. What dares the slave   56
Come hither, covered with an antic face,   57
To fleer and scorn at our solemnity?   58
Now, by the stock and honor of my kin,
To strike him dead I hold it not a sin.
CAPULET
Why, how now, kinsman? Wherefore storm you so?

27 **A hall** i.e., Clear the hall for dancing   28 **turn . . . up** move the tables out of the way for the dancing (by taking up the boards and then removing the supporting trestles)   30 **sirrah** (Normally used in addressing social inferiors. Perhaps Capulet uses a jesting tone toward his kinsman or possibly addresses himself.)   **unlooked-for sport** i.e., arrival of the masquers, providing more men for the dancing   31 **cousin** (*Cousin* often means "kinsman"; at 1.2.69, "Mine uncle Capulet" is named on the invitation list.)   37 **Pentecost** seventh Sunday after Easter (and never as late as mid-July, two weeks before Lammas or August 1, when according to 1.3.16, the play takes place; a seeming inconsistency).   41 **a ward** a minor under guardianship   48 **dear** precious.   49 **shows** appears   51 **The measure done** When this dance is over.   **her place of stand** where she stands   52 **hers** her hand.   **rude** rough   53 **Forswear it** Deny any previous oath   56 **What** How   57 **antic face** grotesque mask   58 **fleer** jeer. **solemnity** time-honored festivity.

108 **date** appointed time   109 **expire** bring to an end   113 **lusty** lively   114 **drum** drummer.
1.5. Location: The action, continuous from the previous scene, is now imaginatively transferred to a hall in Capulet's house.
2 **take away** clear the table.   **trencher** wooden dish or plate.   6 **joint stools** stools of which the parts are fitted by a joiner or furniture maker   7 **court cupboard** sideboard.   **plate** silverware.   8 **marchpane** cake made from sugar and almonds, marzipan   15–16 **the longest . . . all** (A proverb in defense of merriment.)   18 **walk a bout** dance a turn   20 **makes dainty** seems coyly reluctant (to dance)   21 **Am . . . now?** Have I hit a sensitive point, struck home?

TYBALT
Uncle, this is a Montague, our foe,
A villain that is hither come in spite   63
To scorn at our solemnity this night.
CAPULET
Young Romeo is it?
TYBALT   'Tis he, that villain Romeo.
CAPULET
Content thee, gentle coz, let him alone.
'A bears him like a portly gentleman,   67
And, to say truth, Verona brags of him
To be a virtuous and well governed youth.
I would not for the wealth of all this town
Here in my house do him disparagement.
Therefore be patient; take no note of him.
It is my will, the which if thou respect,
Show a fair presence and put off these frowns,   74
An ill-beseeming semblance for a feast.   75
TYBALT
It fits when such a villain is a guest.
I'll not endure him.
CAPULET   He shall be endured.
What, goodman boy? I say he shall. Go to!   78
Am I the master here, or you? Go to.
You'll not endure him! God shall mend my soul,
You'll make a mutiny among my guests!   81
You will set cock-a-hoop! You'll be the man!   82
TYBALT
Why, uncle, 'tis a shame.
CAPULET   Go to, go to,
You are a saucy boy. Is't so, indeed?
This trick may chance to scathe you. I know what,   85
You must contrary me. Marry, 'tis time.—   86
Well said, my hearts!—You are a princox, go.   87
Be quiet, or—More light, more light!—For shame!
I'll make you quiet.—What, cheerly, my hearts!
TYBALT
Patience perforce with willful choler meeting   90
Makes my flesh tremble in their different greeting.   91
I will withdraw. But this intrusion shall,
Now seeming sweet, convert to bitt'rest gall.   Exit.
ROMEO [to Juliet]
If I profane with my unworthiest hand   94
This holy shrine, the gentle sin is this: 95
My lips, two blushing pilgrims, ready stand
To smooth that rough touch with a tender kiss.
JULIET
Good pilgrim, you do wrong your hand too much,

Which mannerly devotion shows in this;
For saints have hands that pilgrims' hands do touch,   100
And palm to palm is holy palmers' kiss.   101
ROMEO
Have not saints lips, and holy palmers too?
JULIET
Ay, pilgrim, lips that they must use in prayer.
ROMEO
Oh, then, dear saint, let lips do what hands do.   104
They pray; grant thou, lest faith turn to despair.
JULIET
Saints do not move, though grant for prayers' sake.   106
ROMEO
Then move not, while my prayer's effect I take.   107
                                    [He kisses her.]
Thus from my lips, by thine, my sin is purged.
JULIET
Then have my lips the sin that they have took.
ROMEO
Sin from my lips? Oh, trespass sweetly urged!
Give me my sin again.   [He kisses her.]
JULIET   You kiss by th' book.   111
NURSE [approaching]
Madam, your mother craves a word with you.
                                    [Juliet retires.]
ROMEO
What is her mother?
NURSE   Marry, bachelor,   113
Her mother is the lady of the house,
And a good lady, and a wise and virtuous.
I nursed her daughter that you talked withal.   116
I tell you, he that can lay hold of her
Shall have the chinks.
ROMEO [aside]   Is she a Capulet?   118
Oh, dear account! My life is my foe's debt.   119
BENVOLIO [approaching]
Away, begone! The sport is at the best.   120
ROMEO
Ay, so I fear; the more is my unrest.
                          [The masquers prepare to leave.]
CAPULET
Nay, gentlemen, prepare not to be gone.
We have a trifling foolish banquet towards.   123
                          [One whispers in his ear.]
Is it e'en so? Why, then, I thank you all.
I thank you, honest gentlemen. Good night.   125

---

63 spite malice   **67 portly** of good deportment   **74 presence**
demeanor   **75 semblance** facial expression   **78 goodman boy** (A
belittling term for Tybalt; *Goodman* applied to one below the rank of
gentleman but still of some substance, like a wealthy farmer.)   **Go to**
(An expression of irritation.)   **81 mutiny** disturbance   **82 You . . .
man!** i.e., You'll set mischief abroach (literally, turn the tap and let the
liquor flow)! You'll be the big shot!   **85 scathe** harm   **86 contrary**
oppose, thwart.   **'tis time** i.e., it's time you were taught a lesson.
87 Well said Well done. (Said to the dancers.)   **princox** saucy boy
90–1 Patience . . . greeting The attempt to be patient under duress
when I am so angry causes me to tremble at the contrary meeting of
these two opposite impulses.   **94–107** (These lines are in the form of
a Shakespearean sonnet; they are followed by a quatrain.)   **95 shrine**
i.e., Juliet's hand

100 saints i.e., images of saints that are venerated by pilgrims
101 palmers pilgrims who have been to the Holy Land and have
brought back a palm. (With a pun on the palm of the hand.)   **104 let . . .
do** let lips touch, just as hands touch.   **106 Saints . . . sake** Venerated
images and statues of saints remain motionless but nonetheless inter-
cede on behalf of praying pilgrims.   **107 move** (Romeo quibbles on
Juliet's metaphorical use of the word *move* to urge that she remain
motionless while he kisses her.)   **111 by th' book** by the rules, like
an expert.   **113 What** Who   **116 withal** with.   **118 the chinks** plenty
of coins, money. (A slang expression.)   **119 dear account** heavy reckoning.   **my foe's debt** due to my foe, at his mercy.   **120 The sport . . .
best** i.e., It is time to leave. (Refers to the proverb, "When play is at
the best, it is time to leave"; compare at 1.4.39.)   **123 foolish banquet
towards** insignificant light refreshment just ready.   **125 honest**
honorable

More torches here! Come on then, let's to bed.   126
[*To his cousin*] Ah, sirrah, by my fay, it waxes late.   127
I'll to my rest.
        [*All proceed to leave but Juliet and the Nurse.*]

JULIET
Come hither, Nurse. What is yond gentleman?

NURSE
The son and heir of old Tiberio.

JULIET
What's he that now is going out of door?

NURSE
Marry, that, I think, be young Petruchio.

JULIET
What's he that follows here, that would not dance?

NURSE   I know not.

JULIET
Go ask his name. [*The Nurse goes.*] If he be married,
My grave is like to be my wedding bed.   136

NURSE [*returning*]
His name is Romeo, and a Montague,
The only son of your great enemy.

JULIET
My only love sprung from my only hate!
Too early seen unknown, and known too late!
Prodigious birth of love it is to me   141
That I must love a loathèd enemy.

NURSE
What's tis? What's tis?

JULIET   A rhyme I learned even now   143
Of one I danced withal.   *One calls within* "Juliet."

NURSE   Anon, anon!   144
Come, let's away. The strangers all are gone.   *Exeunt.*

❖

[2.0]

        [*Enter*] *Chorus.*

CHORUS
Now old desire doth in his deathbed lie,   1
  And young affection gapes to be his heir;   2
That fair for which love groaned for and would die,   3
  With tender Juliet matched, is now not fair.   4
Now Romeo is beloved and loves again,
  Alike bewitchèd by the charm of looks;   6
But to his foe supposed he must complain,   7
  And she steal love's sweet bait from fearful hooks.   8
Being held a foe, he may not have access
  To breathe such vows as lovers use to swear;   10
And she as much in love, her means much less
  To meet her new-belovèd anywhere.

---

126 torches i.e., to light the guests as they leave   **127 fay** faith
136 like likely   **141 Prodigious** Ominous   **143 tis** this. (Dialect pronunciation.)   **144 Anon** i.e., We're coming
2.0. Chorus.
1–14 (This chorus is a sonnet.)   **2 gapes** waits open-mouthed   **3 fair** beauty, i.e., Rosaline   **4 matched** compared   **6 Alike** i.e., equally with Juliet   **7 foe supposed** i.e., Juliet, a Capulet; also, his opposite number in the war of love.   **complain** offer his love plaint   **8 And she . . . hooks** and she must steal moments of happy love from frightening circumstances designed to catch her unawares.   **10 use** are accustomed

---

But passion lends them power, time means, to meet,   13
Temp'ring extremities with extreme sweet.   [*Exit.*] 14

❖

[2.1]

    Enter Romeo alone.

ROMEO
Can I go forward when my heart is here?   1
Turn back, dull earth, and find thy center out.   2
            [*Romeo retires.*]

    Enter Benvolio with Mercutio.

BENVOLIO
Romeo! My cousin Romeo! Romeo!

MERCUTIO   He is wise
And, on my life, hath stol'n him home to bed.

BENVOLIO
He ran this way and leapt this orchard wall.
Call, good Mercutio.

MERCUTIO   Nay, I'll conjure too. 7
Romeo! Humors! Madman! Passion! Lover!   8
Appear thou in the likeness of a sigh.
Speak but one rhyme, and I am satisfied;
Cry but "Ay me!" Pronounce but "love" and "dove."
Speak to my gossip Venus one fair word,   12
One nickname for her purblind son and heir,   13
Young Abraham Cupid, he that shot so trim   14
When King Cophetua loved the beggar maid.—   15
He heareth not, he stirreth not, he moveth not;
The ape is dead, and I must conjure him.—   17
I conjure thee by Rosaline's bright eyes,
By her high forehead and her scarlet lip,
By her fine foot, straight leg, and quivering thigh,
And the demesnes that there adjacent lie,   21
That in thy likeness thou appear to us.

BENVOLIO
An if he hear thee, thou wilt anger him.   23

MERCUTIO
This cannot anger him. 'Twould anger him
To raise a spirit in his mistress' circle   25
Of some strange nature, letting it there stand   26

---

13 time means time lends them means   **14 Temp'ring extremities** mitigating the hardships.   **sweet** sweetness, pleasure.
2.1. Location: Verona. Outside of Capulet's walled orchard.
1 forward i.e., away   **2 Turn . . . out** (Romeo bids his own earthbound body find out its *center*, its soul or heart (i.e., Juliet), much as in the Ptolemaic system all earthly things seek out their center, the earth, standing at the center of the universe. His body is *dull* in that, like earth, it is the lowest and heaviest of the four elements, associated with melancholy.)   **7 conjure** raise him with magical incantation   **8 Humors** Moods.   **12 gossip** crony   **13 purblind** dim-sighted   **14 Young Abraham** i.e., one who is young and yet, like the Biblical Abraham, old; Cupid was paradoxically the youngest and the oldest of the gods   **15 King Cophetua** (In an old ballad, the King falls in love with a beggar maid and makes her his queen.)   **17 ape** (Used as a term of endearment.)   **21 demesnes** regions. (With bawdy suggestion as to what is adjacent to the thighs; bawdy puns on terms of conjuration continue in *raise, spirit,* i.e., "phallus" or "semen," *circle, stand, laid it, raise up.*)   **23 An if** If   **25 circle** (1) conjuring circle (2) vagina   **26 strange** belonging to another person. (With suggestion of a rival possessing Rosaline sexually.)

Till she had laid it and conjured it down;   27
That were some spite. My invocation   28
Is fair and honest; in his mistress' name
I conjure only but to raise up him.

BENVOLIO
Come, he hath hid himself among these trees
To be consorted with the humorous night.   32
Blind is his love, and best befits the dark.

MERCUTIO
If love be blind, love cannot hit the mark.
Now will he sit under a medlar tree   35
And wish his mistress were that kind of fruit
As maids call medlars when they laugh alone.
Oh, Romeo, that she were, oh, that she were
An open-arse, and thou a pop'ring pear!   39
Romeo, good night. I'll to my truckle bed;   40
This field bed is too cold for me to sleep.   41
Come, shall we go?

BENVOLIO   Go, then, for 'tis in vain
To seek him here that means not to be found.
                                        Exit [with Mercutio].

                              ❧

[2.2]

ROMEO [*coming forward*]
He jests at scars that never felt a wound.   1
                 [*A light appears above, as at Juliet's window.*]
But soft, what light through yonder window breaks?
It is the east, and Juliet is the sun.
Arise, fair sun, and kill the envious moon,
Who is already sick and pale with grief
That thou her maid art far more fair than she.   6
Be not her maid, since she is envious;   7
Her vestal livery is but sick and green   8
And none but fools do wear it. Cast it off.
                 [*Juliet appears aloft as at her window.*]
It is my lady, oh, it is my love.
Oh, that she knew she were!
She speaks, yet she says nothing. What of that?

Her eye discourses. I will answer it.
I am too bold. 'Tis not to me she speaks.
Two of the fairest stars in all the heaven,
Having some business, do entreat her eyes
To twinkle in their spheres till they return.   17
What if her eyes were there, they in her head?   18
The brightness of her cheek would shame those stars
As daylight doth a lamp; her eyes in heaven
Would through the airy region stream so bright   21
That birds would sing and think it were not night.
See how she leans her cheek upon her hand!
Oh, that I were a glove upon that hand,
That I might touch that cheek!

JULIET   Ay me!

ROMEO [*aside*]   She speaks.
Oh, speak again, bright angel, for thou art
As glorious to this night, being o'er my head,
As is a wingèd messenger of heaven
Unto the white-upturnèd wond'ring eyes   29
Of mortals that fall back to gaze on him
When he bestrides the lazy puffing clouds
And sails upon the bosom of the air.

JULIET [*to herself*]
Oh, Romeo, Romeo, wherefore art thou Romeo?   33
Deny thy father and refuse thy name!
Or, if thou wilt not, be but sworn my love,
And I'll no longer be a Capulet.

ROMEO [*aside*]
Shall I hear more, or shall I speak at this?

JULIET
'Tis but thy name that is my enemy;
Thou art thyself, though not a Montague.   39
What's Montague? It is nor hand, nor foot,   40
Nor arm, nor face, nor any other part
Belonging to a man. Oh, be some other name!
What's in a name? That which we call a rose
By any other word would smell as sweet;
So Romeo would, were he not Romeo called,
Retain that dear perfection which he owes   46
Without that title. Romeo, doff thy name,   47
And for thy name, which is no part of thee,   48
Take all myself.

ROMEO   I take thee at thy word!
Call me but love, and I'll be new baptized;
Henceforth I never will be Romeo.

JULIET
What man art thou that, thus bescreened in night,   52
So stumblest on my counsel?

ROMEO   By a name   53
I know not how to tell thee who I am.
My name, dear saint, is hateful to myself,
Because it is an enemy to thee;
Had I it written, I would tear the word.

---

27 laid it (1) laid the spirit to rest (2) provided sexual satisfaction leading to detumescence   **28 were some spite** would be vexing.
32 consorted associated.   **humorous** (1) moist, damp (2) well suited to the *humor* of melancholy   **35 medlar** a fruit that was edible only when partly decayed, used as a slang term for women's sexual organs   **39 open-arse** (Another name for the *medlar*, making explicit the sexual metaphor.)   **pop'ring pear** poppering pear (named after Poperinghe in Flanders). A fruit with phallic associations because of its shape and its suggestive name ("pop 'er in").   **40 truckle bed** a bed on casters to be rolled under a standing bed when not in use
41 field bed i.e., the ground
2.2. Location: The action, continuous from the previous scene, is now imaginatively transferred to inside Capulet's orchard. A rhymed couplet links the two scenes. Romeo has been hiding from his friends as though concealed by the orchard wall. He speaks at once and then turns to observe Juliet's window, which is probably in the gallery above, rearstage.
1.1 *A light appears* (Some editors assume that Juliet is visible at line 1.)
6 maid i.e., votary of Diana, goddess of the moon and patroness of virgins   **7 her** the moon's, Diana's, as the goddess of chastity. (Addressed to Juliet as the sun; Romeo hopes that she will not be a devotee of chastity.)   **8 Her vestal livery** the uniform of Diana's chaste votaries.
sick and green (Suggesting the pallor of moonlight, as well as anemia or *greensickness* [see 3.5.156], to which teenage girls were susceptible.)

17 spheres transparent concentric shells supposed to carry the heavenly bodies with them in their revolution around the earth   **18 there** i.e., in the spheres   **21 stream** shine   **29 white-upturnèd** looking upward so that the whites of the eyes are visible   **33 wherefore** why   **39 though not** (1) even if you were not (2) though not in anything essential   **40 nor hand** neither hand   **46 owes** owns   **47 doff** cast off   **48 for** in exchange for   **52 bescreened** concealed   **53 counsel** secret thought.

JULIET

My ears have yet not drunk a hundred words
Of thy tongue's uttering, yet I know the sound:
Art thou not Romeo and a Montague?

ROMEO

Neither, fair maid, if either thee dislike.   61

JULIET

How camest thou hither, tell me, and wherefore?
The orchard walls are high and hard to climb,
And the place death, considering who thou art,
If any of my kinsmen find thee here.

ROMEO

With love's light wings did I o'erperch these walls,   66
For stony limits cannot hold love out,
And what love can do, that dares love attempt;
Therefore thy kinsmen are no stop to me.

JULIET

If they do see thee, they will murder thee.

ROMEO

Alack, there lies more peril in thine eye
Than twenty of their swords. Look thou but sweet,
And I am proof against their enmity.   73

JULIET

I would not for the world they saw thee here.

ROMEO

I have night's cloak to hide me from their eyes;
And but thou love me, let them find me here.   76
My life were better ended by their hate
Than death prorogued, wanting of thy love.   78

JULIET

By whose direction found'st thou out this place?

ROMEO

By love, that first did prompt me to inquire.
He lent me counsel, and I lent him eyes.
I am no pilot; yet, wert thou as far
As that vast shore washed with the farthest sea,
I should adventure for such merchandise.

JULIET

Thou knowest the mask of night is on my face,
Else would a maiden blush bepaint my cheek
For that which thou hast heard me speak tonight.
Fain would I dwell on form—fain, fain deny   88
What I have spoke; but farewell compliment!   89
Dost thou love me? I know thou wilt say "Ay,"
And I will take thy word. Yet if thou swear'st
Thou mayst prove false. At lovers' perjuries,
They say, Jove laughs. O gentle Romeo,
If thou dost love, pronounce it faithfully.
Or if thou thinkest I am too quickly won,
I'll frown and be perverse and say thee nay,
So thou wilt woo, but else not for the world.
In truth, fair Montague, I am too fond,   98
And therefore thou mayst think my havior light.   99
But trust me, gentleman, I'll prove more true
Than those that have more cunning to be strange.   101

I should have been more strange, I must confess,
But that thou overheard'st, ere I was ware,   103
My true-love passion. Therefore pardon me,
And not impute this yielding to light love,
Which the dark night hath so discovered.   106

ROMEO

Lady, by yonder blessèd moon I vow,
That tips with silver all these fruit-tree tops—

JULIET

Oh, swear not by the moon, th'inconstant moon,
That monthly changes in her circled orb,   110
Lest that thy love prove likewise variable.

ROMEO

What shall I swear by?

JULIET   Do not swear at all;
Or, if thou wilt, swear by thy gracious self,
Which is the god of my idolatry,
And I'll believe thee.

ROMEO   If my heart's dear love—

JULIET

Well, do not swear. Although I joy in thee,
I have no joy of this contract tonight.   117
It is too rash, too unadvised, too sudden,   118
Too like the lightning, which doth cease to be
Ere one can say it lightens. Sweet, good night!
This bud of love, by summer's ripening breath,
May prove a beauteous flower when next we meet.
Good night, good night! As sweet repose and rest   123
Come to thy heart as that within my breast!

ROMEO

Oh, wilt thou leave me so unsatisfied?

JULIET

What satisfaction canst thou have tonight?

ROMEO

Th'exchange of thy love's faithful vow for mine.

JULIET

I gave thee mine before thou didst request it;
And yet I would it were to give again.

ROMEO

Wouldst thou withdraw it? For what purpose, love?

JULIET

But to be frank and give it thee again.   131
And yet I wish but for the thing I have.
My bounty is as boundless as the sea,
My love as deep; the more I give to thee,
The more I have, for both are infinite.

                               [The Nurse calls within.]
I hear some noise within. Dear love, adieu!—
Anon, good Nurse!—Sweet Montague, be true.
Stay but a little; I will come again.   [Exit, above.]

ROMEO

Oh, blessèd, blessèd night! I am afeard,
Being in night, all this is but a dream,
Too flattering-sweet to be substantial.

    [Enter Juliet, above.]

---

61 thee dislike displeases you.   66 o'erperch fly over   73 proof protected   76 but unless   78 proroguèd postponed.   wanting of lacking   88 Fain Gladly.   dwell on form preserve the proper formalities
89 compliment etiquette, convention.   98 fond infatuated   99 havior light behavior frivolous.   101 strange reserved, aloof, modest.

103 ware aware   106 Which i.e., which yielding.   discoverèd
revealed.   110 orb orbit, sphere   117 contract exchanging of vows
118 unadvised unconsidered   123 As May just as   131 frank liberal,
bounteous

JULIET

    Three words, dear Romeo, and good night indeed.
    If that thy bent of love be honorable,   143
    Thy purpose marriage, send me word tomorrow,
    By one that I'll procure to come to thee,
    Where and what time thou wilt perform the rite,
    And all my fortunes at thy foot I'll lay
    And follow thee my lord throughout the world.

NURSE [*within*]   Madam!

JULIET

    I come, anon.—But if thou meanest not well,
    I do beseech thee—

NURSE [*within*]   Madam!

JULIET   By and by, I come—   151
    To cease thy strife and leave me to my grief.   152
    Tomorrow will I send.

ROMEO   So thrive my soul—

JULIET   A thousand times good night!   [*Exit, above.*]

ROMEO

    A thousand times the worse, to want thy light.
    Love goes toward love as schoolboys from their
        books,
    But love from love, toward school with heavy looks.
                   [*He starts to leave.*]

       Enter Juliet [above] again.

JULIET

    Hist! Romeo, hist! Oh, for a falconer's voice,
    To lure this tassel-gentle back again!   160
    Bondage is hoarse and may not speak aloud,   161
    Else would I tear the cave where Echo lies   162
    And make her airy tongue more hoarse than mine
    With repetition of "My Romeo!"

ROMEO

    It is my soul that calls upon my name.
    How silver-sweet sound lovers' tongues by night,
    Like softest music to attending ears!

JULIET

    Romeo!

ROMEO   My nyas?

JULIET   What o'clock tomorrow   168
    Shall I send to thee?

ROMEO   By the hour of nine.

JULIET

    I will not fail. 'Tis twenty year till then.—
    I have forgot why I did call thee back.

ROMEO

    Let me stand here till thou remember it.

JULIET

    I shall forget, to have thee still stand there,   173
    Remembering how I love thy company.

ROMEO

    And I'll still stay, to have thee still forget,
    Forgetting any other home but this.

JULIET

    'Tis almost morning. I would have thee gone—
    And yet no farther than a wanton's bird,   178
    That lets it hop a little from his hand,
    Like a poor prisoner in his twisted gyves,   180
    And with a silken thread plucks it back again,
    So loving-jealous of his liberty.   182

ROMEO

    I would I were thy bird.

JULIET   Sweet, so would I.
    Yet I should kill thee with much cherishing.
    Good night, good night! Parting is such sweet sorrow
    That I shall say good night till it be morrow.
                   [*Exit, above.*]

ROMEO

    Sleep dwell upon thine eyes, peace in thy breast!
    Would I were sleep and peace, so sweet to rest!
    Hence will I to my ghostly friar's close cell,   189
    His help to crave, and my dear hap to tell.   *Exit.* 190

                     ❖

[2.3]

    Enter Friar [Laurence] alone, with a basket.

FRIAR LAURENCE

    The gray-eyed morn smiles on the frowning night,
    Check'ring the eastern clouds with streaks of light,
    And fleckled darkness like a drunkard reels   3
    From forth day's path and Titan's fiery wheels.   4
    Now, ere the sun advance his burning eye,   5
    The day to cheer and night's dank dew to dry,
    I must up-fill this osier cage of ours   7
    With baleful weeds and precious-juicèd flowers.   8
    The earth that's nature's mother is her tomb;
    What is her burying grave, that is her womb;
    And from her womb children of divers kind
    We sucking on her natural bosom find,
    Many for many virtues excellent,
    None but for some, and yet all different.   14
    Oh, mickle is the powerful grace that lies   15
    In plants, herbs, stones, and their true qualities.   16
    For naught so vile that on the earth doth live   17
    But to the earth some special good doth give;
    Nor aught so good but, strained from that fair use,   19
    Revolts from true birth, stumbling on abuse.
    Virtue itself turns vice, being misapplied,
    And vice sometime by action dignified.

       Enter Romeo.

---

143 bent purpose, inclination   **151 By and by** Immediately
152 strife striving   **160 tassel-gentle** tercel gentle, the male of the
goshawk   **161 Bondage is hoarse** i.e., In confinement one can speak
only in a loud whisper   **162 tear** pierce (with noise).   **Echo** (In Book
3 of Ovid's *Metamorphoses*, Echo, rejected by Narcissus, pines away in
lonely caves until only her voice is left.)   **168 nyas** eyas, fledgling
173 still always

178 wanton's spoiled child's   **180 gyves** fetters   **182 his** its
189 ghostly spiritual.   **close** narrow   **190 dear hap** good fortune
2.3. Location: Verona. Friar Laurence's monastery garden.
3 fleckled dappled   **4 From forth** out of the way of.   **Titan's** (Helios,
the sun god, was a descendant of the race of Titans.)   **5 advance** raise
7 osier cage willow basket   **8 baleful** harmful   **14 None but for some**
there are none that are not useful for something   **15 mickle** great.
grace beneficent virtue   **16 true** proper, inherent   **17 For naught so
vile** For there is nothing so vile   **19 strained** forced, perverted

Within the infant rind of this weak flower
Poison hath residence and medicine power:
For this, being smelt, with that part cheers each part;   25
Being tasted, stays all senses with the heart.   26
Two such opposèd kings encamp them still   27
In man as well as herbs—grace and rude will;
And where the worser is predominant,
Full soon the canker death eats up that plant.   30

ROMEO
Good morrow, Father.

FRIAR LAURENCE   Benedicite!   31
What early tongue so sweet saluteth me?
Young son, it argues a distempered head   33
So soon to bid good morrow to thy bed.
Care keeps his watch in every old man's eye,
And where care lodges sleep will never lie;
But where unbruisèd youth with unstuffed brain   37
Doth couch his limbs, there golden sleep doth reign.
Therefore thy earliness doth me assure
Thou art uproused with some distemp'rature;
Or if not so, then here I hit it right:
Our Romeo hath not been in bed tonight.

ROMEO
That last is true. The sweeter rest was mine.

FRIAR LAURENCE
God pardon sin! Wast thou with Rosaline?

ROMEO
With Rosaline, my ghostly father? No.
I have forgot that name, and that name's woe.

FRIAR LAURENCE
That's my good son. But where hast thou been, then?

ROMEO
I'll tell thee ere thou ask it me again.
I have been feasting with mine enemy,
Where on a sudden one hath wounded me
That's by me wounded. Both our remedies   51
Within thy help and holy physic lies.   52
I bear no hatred, blessèd man, for, lo,
My intercession likewise steads my foe.   54

FRIAR LAURENCE
Be plain, good son, and homely in thy drift.   55
Riddling confession finds but riddling shrift.   56

ROMEO
Then plainly know my heart's dear love is set
On the fair daughter of rich Capulet.
As mine on hers, so hers is set on mine,
And all combined, save what thou must combine
By holy marriage. When and where and how
We met, we wooed, and made exchange of vow
I'll tell thee as we pass; but this I pray,
That thou consent to marry us today.

FRIAR LAURENCE
Holy Saint Francis, what a change is here!
Is Rosaline, that thou didst love so dear,

So soon forsaken? Young men's love then lies
Not truly in their hearts, but in their eyes.
Jesu Maria, what a deal of brine
Hath washed thy sallow cheeks for Rosaline!
How much salt water thrown away in waste
To season love, that of it doth not taste!
The sun not yet thy sighs from heaven clears,
Thy old groans yet ringing in mine ancient ears.
Lo, here upon thy cheek the stain doth sit
Of an old tear that is not washed off yet.
If e'er thou wast thyself and these woes thine,   77
Thou and these woes were all for Rosaline.
And art thou changed? Pronounce this sentence then: 79
Women may fall, when there's no strength in men.

ROMEO
Thou chid'st me oft for loving Rosaline.

FRIAR LAURENCE
For doting, not for loving, pupil mine.

ROMEO
And bad'st me bury love.

FRIAR LAURENCE   Not in a grave
To lay one in, another out to have.

ROMEO
I pray thee, chide not. She whom I love now
Doth grace for grace and love for love allow.   86
The other did not so.

FRIAR LAURENCE   Oh, she knew well
Thy love did read by rote, that could not spell.   88
But come, young waverer, come, go with me,
In one respect I'll thy assistant be;   90
For this alliance may so happy prove
To turn your households' rancor to pure love.   92

ROMEO
Oh, let us hence! I stand on sudden haste.   93

FRIAR LAURENCE
Wisely and slow. They stumble that run fast.

                                             Exeunt.

                        ❈

[2.4]

Enter Benvolio and Mercutio.

MERCUTIO
Where the devil should this Romeo be?   1
Came he not home tonight?   2

BENVOLIO
Not to his father's. I spoke with his man.

MERCUTIO
Why, that same pale hardhearted wench, that
    Rosaline,
Torments him so that he will sure run mad.

BENVOLIO
Tybalt, the kinsman to old Capulet,
Hath sent a letter to his father's house.

---

25 **that part** i.e., the odor   26 **stays** halts.   **with** together with   27 **them still** themselves always   30 **canker** cankerworm   31 **Benedicite!** A blessing on you!   33 **argues** demonstrates, provides evidence of.   **distempered** disturbed, disordered   37 **unstuffed** not overcharged, carefree   51 **Both our remedies** The remedy for both of us   52 **physic** medicine, healing property   54 **intercession** petition.   **steads** helps   55 **homely** simple   56 **shrift** absolution.

77 **If . . . thine** If ever you had any proper sense of self and understanding of your love sorrows   79 **sentence** maxim   86 **grace** favor,   88 **did read . . . spell** i.e., was like a schoolboy's exercise, repeating words without understanding.   90 **In one respect** for one reason (at least)   92 **To** as to   93 **stand on** am in need of, insist on   2.4. Location: Verona. A street.   1 **should** can   2 **tonight** last night.

MERCUTIO   A challenge, on my life.

BENVOLIO   Romeo will answer it.   9

MERCUTIO   Any man that can write may answer a letter.

BENVOLIO   Nay, he will answer the letter's master, how he dares, being dared.

MERCUTIO   Alas poor Romeo! He is already dead, stabbed with a white wench's black eye, run through the ear with a love song, the very pin of his heart cleft   15 with the blind bow-boy's butt shaft. And is he a man   16 to encounter Tybalt?

BENVOLIO   Why, what is Tybalt?

MERCUTIO   More than prince of cats. Oh, he's the   19 courageous captain of compliments. He fights as you   20 sing prick song, keeps time, distance, and proportion;   21 he rests his minim rests, one, two, and the third in   22 your bosom. The very butcher of a silk button, a   23 duellist, a duellist, a gentleman of the very first house,   24 of the first and second cause. Ah, the immortal   25 *passado!* The *punto reverso!* The *hay!*   26

BENVOLIO   The what?

MERCUTIO   The pox of such antic, lisping, affecting phan-   28 tasimes, these new tuners of accent! "By Jesu, a very   29 good blade! A very tall man! A very good whore!"   30 Why, is not this a lamentable thing, grandsire, that we   31 should be thus afflicted with these strange flies, these   32 fashionmongers, these pardon-me's, who stand so   33 much on the new form that they cannot sit at ease on   34 the old bench? Oh, their bones, their bones!   35

> *Enter Romeo.*

BENVOLIO   Here comes Romeo, here comes Romeo.

MERCUTIO   Without his roe, like a dried herring. Oh,   37 flesh, flesh, how art thou fishified! Now is he for the numbers that Petrarch flowed in. Laura to his lady   39 was but a kitchen wench—marry, she had a better

love to berhyme her—Dido a dowdy, Cleopatra a   41 gypsy, Helen and Hero hildings and harlots, Thisbe a   42 gray eye or so, but not to the purpose. Signor Romeo,   43 *bonjour!* There's a French salutation to your French   44 slop. You gave us the counterfeit fairly last night.   45

ROMEO   Good morrow to you both. What counterfeit did I give you?

MERCUTIO   The slip, sir, the slip. Can you not conceive?   48

ROMEO   Pardon, good Mercutio. My business was great, and in such a case as mine a man may strain courtesy.

MERCUTIO   That's as much as to say, such a case as yours   51 constrains a man to bow in the hams.   52

ROMEO   Meaning, to curtsy.   53

MERCUTIO   Thou hast most kindly hit it.   54

ROMEO   A most courteous exposition.

MERCUTIO   Nay, I am the very pink of courtesy.   56

ROMEO   Pink for flower.

MERCUTIO   Right.

ROMEO   Why then is my pump well flowered.   59

MERCUTIO   Sure wit, follow me this jest now till thou hast worn out thy pump, that when the single sole of it is worn, the jest may remain, after the wearing, solely singular.   63

ROMEO   Oh, single-soled jest, solely singular for the   64 singleness!   65

MERCUTIO   Come between us, good Benvolio. My wits faints.

ROMEO   Switch and spurs, switch and spurs! Or I'll cry   68 a match.   69

MERCUTIO   Nay, if our wits run the wild-goose chase, I   70 am done, for thou hast more of the wild goose in one of thy wits than, I am sure, I have in my whole five. Was I with you there for the goose?   73

ROMEO   Thou wast never with me for anything when thou wast not there for the goose.   75

MERCUTIO   I will bite thee by the ear for that jest.   76

ROMEO   Nay, good goose, bite not.

MERCUTIO   Thy wit is a very bitter sweeting; it is a most   78 sharp sauce.   79

ROMEO   And is it not, then, well served in to a sweet goose?

---

9 answer it accept the challenge. (But Mercutio replies in the sense of "write in reply.")   **15 pin** peg in the center of a target   **16 butt shaft** unbarbed arrow, allotted to children and thus to Cupid.   **19 prince of cats** (The name of the king of cats in *Reynard the Fox* was Tybalt or Tybert.)   **20 captain of compliments** master of ceremony and dueling etiquette.   **21 prick song** music written out.   **proportion** rhythm   **22 minim rests** short rests in musical notation   **23 butcher . . . button** i.e., one able to strike a specific button on his adversary's person   **24 first house** best school of fencing   **25 first and second cause** causes according to the code of dueling that would oblige one to seek the satisfaction of one's honor.   **26 passado** forward thrust.   ***punto reverso*** backhanded stroke.   **hay** thrust through. (From the Italian *hai*, meaning "you have [it].")   **28 The pox of** Plague take.   **antic** grotesque   **28–9 phantasimes** coxcombs, fantastically dressed or mannered   **29 new tuners of accent** those who introduce new foreign words and slang phrases into their speech.   **30 tall** valiant   **31 grandsire** i.e., one who disapproves of the new fashion and prefers old custom   **32 flies** parasites   **33 pardon-me's** i.e., those who affect overly polite manners.   **stand** (1) insist (2) the opposite of *sit*, line 34   **34–5 form . . . bench** (*Form* means both "fashion" or "code of manners" and "bench.")   **35 bones** French *bon*, "good" (with play on English *bone*)   **37 Without his roe** i.e., Looking thin and emaciated, sexually spent. (With a pun on the first syllable of Romeo's name; the remaining syllables, *me-oh*, sound like the expression of a melancholy lover. *Roe* also suggests a female deer or "dear.")   **39 numbers** verses.   **Laura** the lady to whom the Italian Renaissance poet Petrarch addressed his love poems. (Other romantic heroines are named in the following passage: Dido, Queen of Carthage; Cleopatra; Helen of Troy; Hero, beloved of Leander; and Thisbe, beloved of Pyramus.)   **to** in comparison with

41 dowdy homely woman   **42 gypsy** Egyptian; whore.   **hildings** good-for-nothings   **43 not** i.e., that is not   **44 to** to match   **44–5 French slop** loose trousers of French fashion.   **45 fairly** handsomely, effectively   **48 slip** (Counterfeit coins were called "slips.")   **conceive** i.e., get the joke.   **51 case** (1) situation (2) physical condition. (Mercutio also bawdily suggests that Romeo has been in a *case*, i.e., the female genitalia.)   **52 bow in the hams** (1) make a low bow (2) show the effects of venereal disease.   **53 curtsy** bow, make obeisance.   **54 kindly** graciously. (But also suggesting natural and physical explanations.)   **56 pink** embodied perfection. (But suggesting also the flower called *pink*, the color, and *pinking* of a shoe; see next note.)   **59 pump well flowered** shoe expertly pinked or perforated in ornamental figures suggesting flowers.   **63 solely singular** unique.   **64 single-soled** i.e., thin, contemptible   **65 singleness** feebleness.   **68 Switch and spurs** i.e., Keep up the rapid pace of the hunt (in the game of wits)   **68–9 cry a match** claim the victory.   **70 wild-goose chase** a horse race in which the leading rider dares his competitors to follow him wherever he goes   **73 Was . . . goose?** Did I score a point in calling you a goose?   **75 for the goose** (1) behaving like a goose (2) looking for a prostitute.   **76 bite . . . ear** i.e., give you an affectionate nibble on the ear. (Said ironically, however, and Romeo parries.)   **78 sweeting** sweet-flavored variety of apple   **79 sharp sauce** (1) "biting" retort (2) tart sauce, of the sort that should be served with cooked goose (as Romeo points out).

MERCUTIO Oh, here's a wit of cheveril, that stretches 82
from an inch narrow to an ell broad! 83

ROMEO I stretch it out for that word "broad," which,
added to the goose, proves thee far and wide a broad 85
goose.

MERCUTIO Why, is not this better now than groaning for
love? Now art thou sociable, now art thou Romeo;
now art thou what thou art, by art as well as by nature.
For this driveling love is like a great natural that runs 90
lolling up and down to hide his bauble in a hole. 91

BENVOLIO Stop there, stop there.

MERCUTIO Thou desirest me to stop in my tale against 93
the hair. 94

BENVOLIO Thou wouldst else have made thy tale large.

MERCUTIO Oh, thou art deceived; I would have made it
short, for I was come to the whole depth of my tale
and meant indeed to occupy the argument no longer.

ROMEO Here's goodly gear! 99

Enter Nurse and her man [Peter].

A sail, a sail! 100

MERCUTIO Two, two: a shirt and a smock. 101

NURSE Peter!

PETER Anon!

NURSE My fan, Peter.

MERCUTIO Good Peter, to hide her face, for her fan's
the fairer face.

NURSE God gi' good morrow, gentlemen.

MERCUTIO God gi' good e'en, fair gentlewoman.

NURSE Is it good e'en? 109

MERCUTIO 'Tis no less, I tell ye, for the bawdy hand of
the dial is now upon the prick of noon. 111

NURSE Out upon you! What a man are you? 112

ROMEO One, gentlewoman, that God hath made for
himself to mar. 114

NURSE By my troth, it is well said. "For himself to mar," 115
quoth 'a? Gentlemen, can any of you tell me where I 116
may find the young Romeo?

ROMEO I can tell you; but young Romeo will be older
when you have found him than he was when you
sought him. I am the youngest of that name, for fault 120
of a worse.

NURSE You say well.

MERCUTIO Yea, is the worst well? Very well took, i'faith, 123
wisely, wisely.

NURSE If you be he, sir, I desire some confidence with 125
you.

BENVOLIO She will indite him to some supper. 127

MERCUTIO A bawd, a bawd, a bawd! So ho! 128

ROMEO What hast thou found?

MERCUTIO No hare, sir, unless a hare, sir, in a lenten 130
pie, that is something stale and hoar ere it be spent. 131
[He sings.]

An old hare hoar,
And an old hare hoar,
Is very good meat in Lent.
But a hare that is hoar
Is too much for a score, 136
When it hoars ere it be spent.

Romeo, will you come to your father's? We'll to dinner thither.

ROMEO I will follow you.

MERCUTIO Farewell, ancient lady. Farewell,   *[singing]*
"Lady, lady, lady."   *Exeunt [Mercutio and Benvolio].* 142

NURSE I pray you, sir, what saucy merchant was this 143
that was so full of his ropery? 144

ROMEO A gentleman, Nurse, that loves to hear himself
talk, and will speak more in a minute than he will
stand to in a month. 147

NURSE An 'a speak anything against me, I'll take him 148
down, an 'a were lustier than he is, and twenty such 149
Jacks; and if I cannot, I'll find those that shall. Scurvy 150
knave! I am none of his flirt-gills. I am none of his 151
skains-mates. *[To Peter]* And thou must stand by, too, 152
and suffer every knave to use me at his pleasure!

PETER I saw no man use you at his pleasure. If I had,
my weapon should quickly have been out; I warrant 155
you, I dare draw as soon as another man, if I see
occasion in a good quarrel, and the law on my side.

NURSE Now, afore God, I am so vexed that every part 158
about me quivers. Scurvy knave! Pray you, sir, a 159
word; and as I told you, my young lady bid me
inquire you out. What she bid me say, I will keep to
myself. But first let me tell ye, if ye should lead her
in a fool's paradise, as they say, it were a very gross
kind of behavior, as they say. For the gentlewoman
is young; and therefore if you should deal double

---

82 **cheveril** kid leather, easily stretched   83 **ell** (forty-five inches)
85 **broad** large, complete; perhaps also wanton   90 **natural** idiot
91 **lolling** with his tongue (or bauble) hanging out.   **bauble** (1) jester's
wand (2) phallus   93 **stop in my tale** (1) stop short in my story (2) stuff
in my penis   93–4 **against the hair** against the grain, against my wish.
(With bawdy suggestion of pubic hair. The sexual punning continues
in *large* [erect], *short* [detumescent], *come to the depth of my tale, occupy,*
etc.)   99 **goodly gear** matter for mockery. (With suggestion of "ample
sexual apparatus.")   100 **A sail** (To Romeo, the Nurse is an imposing
galleon in full sail.)   101 **a shirt and a smock** i.e., a man and a woman.
109 **Is it good e'en?** Is it afternoon already?   111 **prick** point on the
dial of a clock. (With bawdy suggestion.)   112 **Out upon you** (Expression of indignation.)   **What** What kind of   114 **mar** i.e., disfigure
morally through sin. (Humankind, made in God's image, mars that
image sinfully.)   115 **troth** faith   116 **quoth 'a** said he. (A sarcastic
interjection, meaning "forsooth" or "indeed.")   120 **fault** lack

123 **took** understood   125 **confidence** (The Nurse's mistake for "conference.")   127 **indite** (Benvolio's deliberate malapropism for
"invite.")   128 **So ho** (Cry of hunter sighting game.)   130 **hare**
(Slang word for "prostitute"; similarly, with *stale* and *meat* in the following lines.)   130–1 **a lenten pie** a pie that should contain no meat,
in observance of Lent   131 **hoar** moldy. (With pun on "whore"; *stale*
also can mean "whore.")   **spent** consumed.   136 **for a score** for a
reckoning, to pay good money for   142 **"Lady, lady, lady"** (Refrain
from the ballad *Chaste Susanna.*)   143 **merchant** i.e., fellow   144 **ropery** vulgar humor, knavery.   147 **stand to** carry out, stand in support
of   148 **An 'a** If he   148–9 **take him down** cut him down to size.
(With unintended bawdy suggestion.)   150 **Jacks** knaves   151 **flirt-
gills** loose women.   152 **skains-mates** (Perhaps daggermates, outlaws, or gangster molls.)   155 **weapon** (With bawdy suggestion,
perhaps unrecognized by the speaker, as also in *at his pleasure.*)
158–9 **every part . . . quivers** (More bawdy suggestion, unrecognized
by the Nurse.)

with her, truly it were an ill thing to be offered to any
gentlewoman, and very weak dealing.   167
ROMEO   Nurse, commend me to thy lady and mistress.
I protest unto thee—   169
NURSE   Good heart, and i'faith I will tell her as much.
Lord, Lord, she will be a joyful woman.
ROMEO   What wilt thou tell her, Nurse? Thou dost not
mark me.   173
NURSE   I will tell her, sir, that you do protest, which, as
I take it, is a gentlemanlike offer.
ROMEO   Bid her devise
Some means to come to shrift this afternoon,   177
And there she shall at Friar Laurence' cell
Be shrived and married. Here is for thy pains.   179
                                        [*He offers money.*]
NURSE   No, truly, sir, not a penny.
ROMEO   Go to, I say you shall.
NURSE
This afternoon, sir? Well, she shall be there.
ROMEO
And stay, good Nurse, behind the abbey wall.
Within this hour my man shall be with thee
And bring thee cords made like a tackled stair,   185
Which to the high topgallant of my joy   186
Must be my convoy in the secret night.   187
Farewell. Be trusty, and I'll quit thy pains.   188
Farewell. Commend me to thy mistress.
                                        [*Romeo starts to leave.*]
NURSE
Now God in heaven bless thee! Hark you, sir.
ROMEO   What say'st thou, my dear Nurse?
NURSE
Is your man secret? Did you ne'er hear say,   192
"Two may keep counsel, putting one away"?   193
ROMEO
'Warrant thee, my man's as true as steel.
NURSE   Well, sir, my mistress is the sweetest lady—
Lord, Lord! When 'twas a little prating thing—Oh,
there is a nobleman in town, one Paris, that would
fain lay knife aboard; but she, good soul, had as lief   198
see a toad, a very toad, as see him. I anger her
sometimes and tell her that Paris is the properer man,   200
but I'll warrant you, when I say so, she looks as pale
as any clout in the versal world. Doth not rosemary   202
and Romeo begin both with a letter?   203
ROMEO   Ay, Nurse, what of that? Both with an R.

NURSE   Ah, mocker! That's the dog's name; R is for   205
the—No; I know it begins with some other letter; and   206
she hath the prettiest sententious of it, of you and   207
rosemary, that it would do you good to hear it.
ROMEO   Commend me to thy lady.
NURSE   Ay, a thousand times.   [*Exit Romeo.*]
Peter!
PETER   Anon!
NURSE   Before, and apace.   *Exeunt.* 212

                              ❧

[2.5]

                    Enter Juliet.

JULIET
The clock struck nine when I did send the Nurse;
In half an hour she promised to return.
Perchance she cannot meet him. That's not so.
Oh, she is lame! Love's heralds should be thoughts,
Which ten times faster glides than the sun's beams
Driving back shadows over louring hills.   6
Therefore do nimble-pinioned doves draw Love,   7
And therefore hath the wind-swift Cupid wings.
Now is the sun upon the highmost hill
Of this day's journey, and from nine till twelve
Is three long hours, yet she is not come.
Had she affections and warm youthful blood,   12
She would be as swift in motion as a ball;
My words would bandy her to my sweet love,   14
And his to me.
But old folks, many feign as they were dead—   16
Unwieldy, slow, heavy, and pale as lead.

                    Enter Nurse [and Peter].

Oh, God, she comes!—O honey Nurse, what news?
Hast thou met with him? Send thy man away.
NURSE   Peter, stay at the gate.   [*Exit Peter.*]
JULIET
Now, good sweet Nurse—Oh, Lord, why lookest thou
sad?
Though news be sad, yet tell them merrily;
If good, thou shamest the music of sweet news
By playing it to me with so sour a face.
NURSE
I am aweary. Give me leave awhile.   25
Fie, how my bones ache! What a jaunce have I had!   26
JULIET
I would thou hadst my bones and I thy news.
Nay, come, I pray thee, speak. Good, good Nurse,
speak.

167 weak contemptible   **169 protest** vow. (Romeo may intend only
to protest his good intentions, but the Nurse seemingly takes the
word to mean "propose," as if Romeo is making a *gentlemanlike offer*
[line 175] of marriage that would ensure against Juliet's being led into
a *fool's paradise* [line 163]—i.e., being seduced.)   **173 mark** attend to
177 shrift confession and absolution   **179 shrived** absolved
185 tackled stair rope ladder   **186 topgallant** highest mast and sail of
a ship, the summit   **187 convoy** conveyance, means of passage
188 quit reward, requite   **192 secret** trustworthy.   **193 keep counsel**
keep a secret   **198 fain lay knife aboard** like to assert his claim (just
as a guest at an inn did by bringing his knife to the dinner table; with
sexual suggestion also).   **lief** willingly   **200 properer** handsomer
202 clout faded rag.   **versal** universal.   **rosemary** (Associated with
weddings and funerals.)   **203 a letter** one and the same letter.

205 the dog's name (The letter *R* was thought to resemble the dog's
growl.)   **205–6 R is for . . . letter** (Perhaps the Nurse is about to say
"arse," but has a notion that it begins with some other letter. In any case,
she decides against saying such an indelicate word.)   **207 sententious**
(The Nurse probably means "sentences," maxims.)   **212 Before, and
apace** Go before me quickly.
2.5. Location: Verona. Outside Capulet's house, perhaps in the
orchard or garden.
6 louring dark, threatening   **7 Love** i.e., Venus, whose chariot was
drawn by swift-winged doves   **12 affections** desires   **14 bandy** toss
to and fro, as in tennis   **16 feign as** act as though   **25 Give me leave**
Let me alone   **26 jaunce** jouncing, jolting

NURSE
Jesu, what haste! Can you not stay awhile?   29
Do you not see that I am out of breath?

JULIET
How art thou out of breath, when thou hast breath
To say to me that thou art out of breath?
The excuse that thou dost make in this delay
Is longer than the tale thou dost excuse.   34
Is thy news good or bad? Answer to that;
Say either, and I'll stay the circumstance.   36
Let me be satisfied: is't good or bad?

NURSE   Well, you have made a simple choice. You know   38
not how to choose a man. Romeo? No, not he. Though
his face be better than any man's, yet his leg excels all
men's; and for a hand, and a foot, and a body, though
they be not to be talked on, yet they are past compare.   42
He is not the flower of courtesy, but, I'll warrant him,
as gentle as a lamb. Go thy ways, wench. Serve God.
What, have you dined at home?

JULIET
No, no; but all this did I know before.
What says he of our marriage? What of that?

NURSE
Lord, how my head aches! What a head have I!
It beats as it would fall in twenty pieces.
My back o' t'other side—ah, my back, my back!   50
Beshrew your heart for sending me about   51
To catch my death with jauncing up and down!

JULIET
I'faith, I am sorry that thou art not well.
Sweet, sweet, sweet Nurse, tell me, what says my
    love?

NURSE
Your love says, like an honest gentleman,
And a courteous, and a kind, and a handsome,
And, I warrant, a virtuous—Where is your mother?

JULIET
Where is my mother? Why, she is within,
Where should she be? How oddly thou repliest!
"Your love says, like an honest gentleman,   60
'Where is your mother?' "

NURSE   O God's Lady dear!
Are you so hot? Marry, come up, I trow.   62
Is this the poultice for my aching bones?
Henceforward do your messages yourself.

JULIET
Here's such a coil! Come, what says Romeo?   65

NURSE
Have you got leave to go to shrift today?

JULIET   I have.

NURSE
Then hie you hence to Friar Laurence' cell;   68
There stays a husband to make you a wife.

Now comes the wanton blood up in your cheeks;
They'll be in scarlet straight at any news.   71
Hie you to church. I must another way,
To fetch a ladder, by the which your love
Must climb a bird's nest soon when it is dark.   74
I am the drudge, and toil in your delight,
But you shall bear the burden soon at night.
Go. I'll to dinner. Hie you to the cell.

JULIET
Hie to high fortune! Honest Nurse, farewell.
    Exeunt [separately].

❖

[2.6]

Enter Friar [Laurence] and Romeo.

FRIAR LAURENCE
So smile the heavens upon this holy act   1
That after-hours with sorrow chide us not!

ROMEO
Amen, amen! But come what sorrow can,
It cannot countervail the exchange of joy   4
That one short minute gives me in her sight.
Do thou but close our hands with holy words,   6
Then love-devouring death do what he dare;
It is enough I may but call her mine.

FRIAR LAURENCE
These violent delights have violent ends
And in their triumph die, like fire and powder,   10
Which as they kiss consume. The sweetest honey
Is loathsome in his own deliciousness,   12
And in the taste confounds the appetite.   13
Therefore love moderately. Long love doth so;
Too swift arrives as tardy as too slow.

Enter Juliet.

Here comes the lady. Oh, so light a foot
Will ne'er wear out the everlasting flint.
A lover may bestride the gossamers   18
That idles in the wanton summer air,   19
And yet not fall, so light is vanity.   20

JULIET
Good even to my ghostly confessor.   21

FRIAR LAURENCE
Romeo shall thank thee, daughter, for us both.   22

JULIET
As much to him, else is his thanks too much.   23

---

71 **in scarlet straight** i.e., blushing immediately   74 **bird's nest** i.e.,
Juliet's room. (Continues the association of Juliet as a bird, as at 1.3.3,
2.2.168–82, with erotic suggestion. The bawdry is continued in *bear
the burden* two lines later.)
2.6. Location: Verona. Friar Laurence's cell.
1 **So . . . heavens** May the heavens so smile   4 **countervail** outweigh,
counterbalance   6 **close** join   10 **powder** gunpowder   12 **his** its
13 **confounds** destroys   18 **gossamers** filmy cobwebs   19 **wanton**
playful   20 **vanity** transitory human joy.   21 **ghostly** spiritual
22 **thank thee** i.e., give a kiss in thanks for your greeting   23 **As . . .
too much** either (1) Then I must repay him with a kiss, lest I be over-
paid, or (2) My greeting is to Romeo as much as to you; otherwise, his
greeting would exceed mine.

---

29 **stay** wait   34 **excuse** excuse yourself from telling.   36 **stay the circumstance** wait patiently for the details.   38 **simple** foolish   42 **be
not to be talked on** are beneath mention (especially in refined lady-
like company)   50 **o' t'other** on the other   51 **Beshrew** A curse on.
(Used as a mild oath.)   60 **honest** honorable   62 **hot** impatient.
Marry, come up (An expression of impatient reproof.)   65 **coil** turmoil, fuss.   68 **hie** hasten

ROMEO
Ah, Juliet, if the measure of thy joy
Be heaped like mine, and that thy skill be more   25
To blazon it, then sweeten with thy breath   26
This neighbor air, and let rich music's tongue
Unfold the imagined happiness that both   28
Receive in either by this dear encounter.   29

JULIET
Conceit, more rich in matter than in words,   30
Brags of his substance, not of ornament.   31
They are but beggars that can count their worth.
But my true love is grown to such excess
I cannot sum up sum of half my wealth.   34

FRIAR LAURENCE
Come, come with me, and we will make short work;
For, by your leaves, you shall not stay alone
Till Holy Church incorporate two in one.   [*Exeunt.*]

❖

[3.1]

Enter Mercutio, Benvolio, and men.

BENVOLIO
I pray thee, good Mercutio, let's retire.
The day is hot, the Capels are abroad,   2
And if we meet we shall not scape a brawl,
For now, these hot days, is the mad blood stirring.

MERCUTIO   Thou art like one of these fellows that when
he enters the confines of a tavern, claps me his sword   6
upon the table and says, "God send me no need of
thee!" and by the operation of the second cup draws   8
him on the drawer, when indeed there is no need.   9

BENVOLIO   Am I like such a fellow?

MERCUTIO   Come, come, thou art as hot a Jack in thy   11
mood as any in Italy, and as soon moved to be moody,   12
and as soon moody to be moved.   13

BENVOLIO   And what to?

MERCUTIO   Nay, an there were two such, we should   15
have none shortly, for one would kill the other. Thou!
Why, thou wilt quarrel with a man that hath a hair
more or a hair less in his beard than thou hast. Thou
wilt quarrel with a man for cracking nuts, having no
other reason but because thou hast hazel eyes. What
eye but such an eye would spy out such a quarrel? Thy
head is as full of quarrels as an egg is full of meat, and 22
yet thy head hath been beaten as addle as an egg for   23
quarreling. Thou hast quarreled with a man for coughing in the street, because he hath wakened thy dog that

hath lain asleep in the sun. Didst thou not fall out
with a tailor for wearing his new doublet before   27
Easter? With another, for tying his new shoes with old
ribbon? And yet thou wilt tutor me from quarreling!

BENVOLIO   An I were so apt to quarrel as thou art, any
man should buy the fee simple of my life for an hour   31
and a quarter.   32

MERCUTIO   The fee simple! Oh, simple!   33

Enter Tybalt, Petruchio, and others.

BENVOLIO   By my head, here comes the Capulets.
MERCUTIO   By my heel, I care not.
TYBALT   [*to his companions*]
Follow me close, for I will speak to them.—
Gentlemen, good e'en. A word with one of you.

MERCUTIO   And but one word with one of us? Couple it
with something: make it a word and a blow.

TYBALT   You shall find me apt enough to that, sir, an
you will give me occasion.

MERCUTIO   Could you not take some occasion without
giving?

TYBALT   Mercutio, thou consortest with Romeo.   44

MERCUTIO   "Consort"? What, dost thou make us minstrels? An thou make minstrels of us, look to hear
nothing but discords. Here's my fiddlestick; here's   47
that shall make you dance. Zounds, "consort"!   48

BENVOLIO
We talk here in the public haunt of men.
Either withdraw unto some private place,
Or reason coldly of your grievances,   51
Or else depart; here all eyes gaze on us.   52

MERCUTIO
Men's eyes were made to look, and let them gaze.
I will not budge for no man's pleasure, I.

Enter Romeo.

TYBALT
Well, peace be with you, sir. Here comes my man.

MERCUTIO
But I'll be hanged, sir, if he wear your livery.   56
Marry, go before to field, he'll be your follower;   57
Your Worship in that sense may call him "man."   58

TYBALT
Romeo, the love I bear thee can afford
No better term than this: thou art a villain.

ROMEO
Tybalt, the reason that I have to love thee
Doth much excuse the appertaining rage   62
To such a greeting. Villain am I none.

---

25 **that** if   26 **blazon** describe, set forth. (A heraldic term.)
28 **Unfold** make known.   **imagined** i.e., unexpressed   29 **in either**
from each other   30–1 **Conceit . . . ornament** True understanding,
more enriched by the actual reality (of love) than by mere words, finds
more worth in the substance of that reality than in outward show.
34 **sum up sum** add up the total
3.1. Location: Verona. A public place.
2 **Capels** Capulets   6 **claps me** claps. (*Me* is a now-archaic dative of
reference, used colloquially.)   8–9 **draws . . . drawer** draws his sword
against the tapster or waiter   9 **there is no need** i.e., of his sword.
11 **as hot a Jack** as hot-tempered a fellow   12 **moody** angry   13 **to be
moved** at being provoked.   15 **an** if   22 **meat** i.e., edible matter
23 **addle** addled, confused

27 **doublet** man's jacket   31 **fee simple** outright possession   31–2 **an
hour . . . quarter** i.e., my life would last no longer in such circumstances.
33 **Oh, simple!** Oh, how stupid!   44 **consortest** keep company with.
(But Mercutio quibbles on its musical sense of "accompany" or "play
together.")   47 **fiddlestick** (Mercutio means his sword.)   48 **that** that
which.   **Zounds** By God's (Christ's) wounds   51 **coldly** calmly
52 **depart** go away separately   56 **livery** servant's uniform. (Mercutio
deliberately mistakes Tybalt's phrase *my man* to mean "my servant.")
57 **field** field where a duel might occur   58 **Your Worship** (A title of
honor used here with mock politeness.)   62 **the appertaining rage** the
rage that would ordinarily be appropriate to

Therefore, farewell. I see thou knowest me not.

TYBALT

Boy, this shall not excuse the injuries   65
That thou hast done me. Therefore turn and draw.

ROMEO

I do protest I never injured thee,
But love thee better than thou canst devise   68
Till thou shalt know the reason of my love.
And so, good Capulet—which name I tender   70
As dearly as mine own—be satisfied.

MERCUTIO

Oh, calm, dishonorable, vile submission!
Alla stoccata carries it away.   [*He draws.*]   73
Tybalt, you ratcatcher, will you walk?   74

TYBALT   What wouldst thou have with me?

MERCUTIO   Good king of cats, nothing but one of your
nine lives, that I mean to make bold withal, and, as   77
you shall use me hereafter, dry-beat the rest of the   78
eight. Will you pluck your sword out of his pilcher by   79
the ears? Make haste, lest mine be about your ears ere   80
it be out.

TYBALT   I am for you.   [*He draws.*]

ROMEO

Gentle Mercutio, put thy rapier up.

MERCUTIO   Come, sir, your *passado.*   [*They fight.*]   84

ROMEO

Draw, Benvolio, beat down their weapons.
Gentlemen, for shame, forbear this outrage!
Tybalt, Mercutio, the Prince expressly hath
Forbid this bandying in Verona streets.
Hold, Tybalt! Good Mercutio!
         [*Tybalt under Romeo's arm stabs Mercutio.*] *Away*
                    Tybalt [*with his followers*].

MERCUTIO   I am hurt.   89
A plague o' both your houses! I am sped.   90
Is he gone, and hath nothing?

BENVOLIO   What, art thou hurt?

MERCUTIO

Ay, ay, a scratch, a scratch; marry, 'tis enough.
Where is my page? Go, villain, fetch a surgeon.
                                        [*Exit Page.*]

ROMEO

Courage, man, the hurt cannot be much.

MERCUTIO   No, 'tis not so deep as a well, nor so wide as
a church door, but 'tis enough, 'twill serve. Ask for me
tomorrow, and you shall find me a grave man. I am   97
peppered, I warrant, for this world. A plague o' both   98
your houses! Zounds, a dog, a rat, a mouse, a cat, to
scratch a man to death! A braggart, a rogue, a villain,
that fights by the book of arithmetic! Why the devil   101
came you between us? I was hurt under your arm.

ROMEO   I thought all for the best.

MERCUTIO

Help me into some house, Benvolio,
Or I shall faint. A plague o' both your houses!
They have made worm's meat of me. I have it,
And soundly too. Your houses!
                    Exit [*supported by Benvolio*].

ROMEO

This gentleman, the Prince's near ally,   108
My very friend, hath got this mortal hurt   109
In my behalf; my reputation stained
With Tybalt's slander—Tybalt, that an hour
Hath been my cousin! O sweet Juliet,   112
Thy beauty hath made me effeminate,   113
And in my temper softened valor's steel.   114

         Enter Benvolio.

BENVOLIO

O Romeo, Romeo, brave Mercutio is dead!
That gallant spirit hath aspired the clouds,   116
Which too untimely here did scorn the earth.

ROMEO

This day's black fate on more days doth depend;   118
This but begins the woe others must end.   119

         [*Enter Tybalt.*]

BENVOLIO

Here comes the furious Tybalt back again.

ROMEO

Alive in triumph, and Mercutio slain!
Away to heaven, respective lenity,   122
And fire-eyed fury be my conduct now!   123
Now, Tybalt, take the "villain" back again
That late thou gavest me, for Mercutio's soul
Is but a little way above our heads,
Staying for thine to keep him company.
Either thou or I, or both, must go with him.

TYBALT

Thou, wretched boy, that didst consort him here,
Shalt with him hence.

ROMEO   This shall determine that.
                    They fight. Tybalt falls.

BENVOLIO   Romeo, away, begone!
The citizens are up, and Tybalt slain.

65 **Boy** (A deliberate and grave insult when addressed to a grown man. Tybalt's use of *thee* and *thou* in lines 59–60 and following is similarly insulting; Romeo's use of this personal form in lines 61–4 and 67–9, on the other hand, is appropriate to a close family tie that he privately acknowledges but is of course misunderstood by Tybalt and the bystanders.)   68 **devise** imagine   70 **tender** value   73 *Alla stoccata . . .* **away** i.e. (scornfully), This elegant Italian way of fencing, and the fancy terminology to go with it, will win the day, I suppose. (*Alla stoccata* means "at the thrust.")   74 **ratcatcher** (An allusion to Tybalt as king of cats; see 2.4.19.)   77 **make bold withal** make free with   78 **dry-beat** beat soundly (without drawing blood)   79–80 **out . . . ears** out of its scabbard by the handle or hilt.   84 **passado** forward thrust. (Another fancy Italian fencing term of the sort Mercutio despises.)   89 s.d. *Away Tybalt* (Because the phrase is unusual for an exit stage direction, some editors plausibly assign this as a speech to Petruchio, who enters at line 33.1 and is otherwise silent.)   90 **sped** done for.

97 **grave** (Mercutio thus puns with his last breath.)   98 **peppered** finished, done for   101 **by . . . arithmetic** by the numbers, as in a textbook on fencing (as at 2.4.20–3).   108 **ally** kinsman   109 **very** true   112 **cousin** kinsman.   113 **effeminate** weak   114 **temper** disposition. (But with a play on the tempering of a steel sword.)   116 **aspired** ascended to   118 **This day's . . . depend** This day hangs threateningly over the time to come   119 **others** other days to come   122 **respective lenity** considerate gentleness   123 **conduct** guide

Stand not amazed. The Prince will doom thee death   133
If thou art taken. Hence, begone, away!

ROMEO
Oh, I am fortune's fool!

BENVOLIO   Why dost thou stay?   135
                              Exit Romeo.

Enter Citizens.

FIRST CITIZEN
Which way ran he that killed Mercutio?
Tybalt, that murderer, which way ran he?

BENVOLIO
There lies that Tybalt.

FIRST CITIZEN   Up, sir, go with me.
I charge thee in the Prince's name, obey.

*Enter Prince [attended], old Montague,
Capulet, their Wives, and all.*

PRINCE
Where are the vile beginners of this fray?

BENVOLIO
O noble Prince, I can discover all   141
The unlucky manage of this fatal brawl.   142
There lies the man, slain by young Romeo,
That slew thy kinsman, brave Mercutio.

CAPULET'S WIFE
Tybalt, my cousin! O my brother's child!
O Prince! O cousin! Husband! Oh, the blood is spilled
Of my dear kinsman! Prince, as thou art true,
For blood of ours shed blood of Montague.
O cousin, cousin!

PRINCE
Benvolio, who began this bloody fray?

BENVOLIO
Tybalt, here slain, whom Romeo's hand did slay.
Romeo, that spoke him fair, bid him bethink   152
How nice the quarrel was, and urged withal   153
Your high displeasure. All this—utterèd
With gentle breath, calm look, knees humbly bowed—
Could not take truce with the unruly spleen   156
Of Tybalt deaf to peace, but that he tilts
With piercing steel at bold Mercutio's breast,
Who, all as hot, turns deadly point to point,
And, with a martial scorn, with one hand beats
Cold death aside and with the other sends
It back to Tybalt, whose dexterity
Retorts it. Romeo he cries aloud,   163
"Hold, friends! Friends, part!" and swifter than his
    tongue
His agile arm beats down their fatal points,
And twixt them rushes; underneath whose arm
An envious thrust from Tybalt hit the life   167
Of stout Mercutio, and then Tybalt fled;   168
But by and by comes back to Romeo,
Who had but newly entertained revenge,   170

And to't they go like lightning, for, ere I
Could draw to part them was stout Tybalt slain,
And, as he fell, did Romeo turn and fly.
This is the truth, or let Benvolio die.

CAPULET'S WIFE
He is a kinsman to the Montague.
Affection makes him false; he speaks not true.   176
Some twenty of them fought in this black strife,
And all those twenty could but kill one life.
I beg for justice, which thou, Prince, must give.
Romeo slew Tybalt; Romeo must not live.

PRINCE
Romeo slew him, he slew Mercutio.
Who now the price of his dear blood doth owe?

MONTAGUE
Not Romeo, Prince, he was Mercutio's friend;
His fault concludes but what the law should end,   184
The life of Tybalt.

PRINCE   And for that offense
Immediately we do exile him hence.
I have an interest in your hate's proceeding;
My blood for your rude brawls doth lie a-bleeding;   188
But I'll amerce you with so strong a fine   189
That you shall all repent the loss of mine.
I will be deaf to pleading and excuses;
Nor tears nor prayers shall purchase out abuses.   192
Therefore use none. Let Romeo hence in haste,   193
Else, when he is found, that hour is his last.   194
Bear hence this body and attend our will.   195
Mercy but murders, pardoning those that kill.   196
        Exeunt, [some carrying Tybalt's body].

❧

[3.2]

Enter Juliet alone.

JULIET
Gallop apace, you fiery-footed steeds,   1
Towards Phoebus' lodging! Such a wagoner   2
As Phaëton would whip you to the west   3
And bring in cloudy night immediately.   4
Spread thy close curtain, love-performing night,   5

---

176 **Affection** Partiality   184 **concludes but** only finishes   188 **My blood** i.e., blood of my kinsman. (Here we learn that Mercutio is kin to the Prince.)   189 **amerce** penalize   192 **Nor** neither. **purchase out abuses** redeem misdeeds.   193 **hence** depart   194 **Else** Otherwise   195 **attend our will** be on hand to hear further judgment. 196 **but murders** merely encourages murder by excessive leniency
3.2. Location: Verona. Capulet's house.
1 **apace** quickly. **steeds** i.e., the horses of the sun god's chariot
2 **Phoebus** (Often equated with Helios, the sun god.) **lodging** i.e., in the west, below the horizon.   2–4 **Such . . . immediately** i.e., One who is impetuously young, as we are, would understand the need to make the day as short as possible and would quickly bring it to an end. (The mythical allusion is sadly ironic, for Phaëton drove the chariot of the sun so badly that he had to be destroyed by Zeus.)
5 **close** enclosing

---

133 **amazed** dazed.   **doom thee death** sentence you to death
135 **fool** dupe.   141 **discover** reveal   142 **manage** conduct   152 **fair** civilly.   **bethink** consider   153 **nice** trivial.   **withal** besides
156 **take truce** make peace   163 **Retorts** returns   167 **envious** malicious   168 **stout** brave   170 **entertained** harbored thoughts of

That runaways' eyes may wink, and Romeo   6
Leap to these arms, untalked of and unseen.   7
Lovers can see to do their amorous rites
By their own beauties; or, if love be blind,
It best agrees with night. Come, civil night,   10
Thou sober-suited matron all in black,
And learn me how to lose a winning match   12
Played for a pair of stainless maidenhoods.
Hood my unmanned blood, bating in my cheeks,   14
With thy black mantle till strange love grown bold   15
Think true love acted simple modesty.
Come, night. Come, Romeo. Come, thou day in night;
For thou wilt lie upon the wings of night
Whiter than new snow upon a raven's back.
Come, gentle night, come, loving, black-browed night,
Give me my Romeo, and when I shall die   21
Take him and cut him out in little stars,
And he will make the face of heaven so fine
That all the world will be in love with night
And pay no worship to the garish sun.   25
Oh, I have bought the mansion of a love
But not possessed it, and though I am sold,
Not yet enjoyed. So tedious is this day
As is the night before some festival
To an impatient child that hath new robes
And may not wear them. Oh, here comes my nurse,   31

Enter Nurse, with cords.

And she brings news, and every tongue that speaks
But Romeo's name speaks heavenly eloquence.
Now, Nurse, what news? What hast thou there? The
    cords
That Romeo bid thee fetch?

NURSE   Ay, ay, the cords.
    [She throws them down.]
JULIET
Ay me, what news? Why dost thou wring thy hands?
NURSE
Ah, weraday! He's dead, he's dead, he's dead!   37
We are undone, lady, we are undone!
Alack the day, he's gone, he's killed, he's dead!
JULIET
Can heaven be so envious?
NURSE   Romeo can,   40
Though heaven cannot. Oh, Romeo, Romeo!
Who ever would have thought it? Romeo!

JULIET
What devil art thou that dost torment me thus?
This torture should be roared in dismal hell.
Hath Romeo slain himself? Say thou but "Ay,"
And that bare vowel "I" shall poison more   46
Than the death-darting eye of cockatrice.   47
I am not I, if there be such an "Ay,"
Or those eyes shut, that makes thee answer "Ay."   49
If he be slain, say "Ay," or if not, "No."
Brief sounds determine of my weal or woe.   51
NURSE
I saw the wound. I saw it with mine eyes—
God save the mark!—here on his manly breast.   53
A piteous corpse, a bloody piteous corpse;
Pale, pale as ashes, all bedaubed in blood,
All in gore-blood. I swoonèd at the sight.   56
JULIET
Oh, break, my heart! Poor bankrupt, break at once!
To prison, eyes; ne'er look on liberty!
Vile earth, to earth resign; end motion here,   59
And thou and Romeo press one heavy bier!   60
NURSE
O Tybalt, Tybalt, the best friend I had!
O courteous Tybalt! Honest gentleman!   62
That ever I should live to see thee dead!
JULIET
What storm is this that blows so contrary?
Is Romeo slaughtered, and is Tybalt dead?
My dearest cousin, and my dearer lord?
Then, dreadful trumpet, sound the general doom!   67
For who is living, if those two are gone?
NURSE
Tybalt is gone, and Romeo banishèd;
Romeo that killed him, he is banishèd.
JULIET
Oh, God! Did Romeo's hand shed Tybalt's blood?
NURSE
It did, it did. Alas the day it did!
JULIET
O serpent heart, hid with a flow'ring face!   73
Did ever dragon keep so fair a cave?   74
Beautiful tyrant! Fiend angelical!
Dove-feathered raven! Wolvish-ravening lamb!
Despisèd substance of divinest show!   77
Just opposite to what thou justly seem'st,
A damnèd saint, an honorable villain!
O nature, what hadst thou to do in hell
When thou didst bower the spirit of a fiend   81
In mortal paradise of such sweet flesh?
Was ever book containing such vile matter

6–7 That runaways' . . . unseen (Perhaps Juliet is thinking of the elopement that will surely be necessary once she and Romeo secretly marry; they will embrace in the dark of *love-performing night*, untalked of and unseen by others and by each other. A difficult passage that is sometimes interpreted, uncertainly, as referring to the sun's horses as the *runaways*. *Wink* means "close, be shut.")   **10 civil** circumspect, somberly attired   **12 learn** teach   **14 Hood** Cover. (A term in falconry; the hawk's eyes were covered so that it would not *bate* or beat its wings.)   **unmanned** untamed (in falconry; with a pun on "not yet sexually possessed")   **15 strange** diffident   **21 I** (Often emended to *he*, following the Fourth Quarto, but Juliet may mean that when she is dead she will share Romeo's beauty with the world. Dying may also hint at sexual climax.)   **25 garish** dazzling   **31.1 cords** ropes (for the ladder).   **37 weraday!** welladay, alas!   **40 envious** malicious.

46 "I" (Pronounced identically with "Ay.")   **47 cockatrice** basilisk, a mythical serpent that could kill by its look.   **49 those eyes shut** if Romeo's eyes are shut (in death)   **51 weal** welfare, happiness   **53 God . . . mark** (An oath registering shock and horror.)   **56 gore-blood** clotted blood.   **59 Vile . . . here** May my vile body resign itself to burial, ending life itself   **60 press** weigh down.   **bier** litter for carrying corpses.   **62 Honest** Honorable   **67 trumpet** i.e., the last trumpet.   **general doom** Day of Judgment.   **73 hid . . . face** concealed beneath a beautiful face.   **74 keep** occupy, guard.   **cave** i.e., one with treasure in it.   **77 show** appearance.   **81 bower** give lodging to

So fairly bound? Oh, that deceit should dwell
In such a gorgeous palace!
NURSE   There's no trust,
No faith, no honesty in men; all perjured,
All forsworn, all naught, all dissemblers.   87
Ah, where's my man? Give me some aqua vitae.   88
These griefs, these woes, these sorrows make me old.
Shame come to Romeo!
JULIET   Blistered be thy tongue
For such a wish! He was not born to shame.
Upon his brow shame is ashamed to sit,
For 'tis a throne where honor may be crowned
Sole monarch of the universal earth.
Oh, what a beast was I to chide at him!
NURSE
Will you speak well of him that killed your cousin?
JULIET
Shall I speak ill of him that is my husband?
Ah, poor my lord, what tongue shall smooth thy name   98
When I, thy three-hours wife, have mangled it?
But wherefore, villain, didst thou kill my cousin?
That villain cousin would have killed my husband.
Back, foolish tears, back to your native spring!
Your tributary drops belong to woe,   103
Which you, mistaking, offer up to joy.
My husband lives, that Tybalt would have slain,   105
And Tybalt's dead, that would have slain my
    husband.
All this is comfort. Wherefore weep I then?
Some word there was, worser than Tybalt's death,
That murdered me. I would forget it fain,   109
But oh, it presses to my memory
Like damnèd guilty deeds to sinners' minds!
"Tybalt is dead, and Romeo—banishèd."
That "banishèd," that one word "banishèd"
Hath slain ten thousand Tybalts. Tybalt's death
Was woe enough, if it had ended there;
Or, if sour woe delights in fellowship
And needly will be ranked with other griefs,   117
Why followed not, when she said "Tybalt's dead,"
"Thy father," or "thy mother," nay, or both,
Which modern lamentation might have moved?   120
But with a rearward following Tybalt's death,   121
"Romeo is banishèd"—to speak that word
Is father, mother, Tybalt, Romeo, Juliet,
All slain, all dead. "Romeo is banishèd!"
There is no end, no limit, measure, bound,
In that word's death; no words can that woe sound.   126
Where is my father and my mother, Nurse?
NURSE
Weeping and wailing over Tybalt's corpse.
Will you go to them? I will bring you thither.

JULIET
Wash they his wounds with tears? Mine shall be spent,
When theirs are dry, for Romeo's banishment.
Take up those cords.—Poor ropes, you are beguiled,
Both you and I, for Romeo is exiled.
He made you for a highway to my bed,
But I, a maid, die maiden-widowèd.
Come, cords, come, Nurse. I'll to my wedding bed,
And death, not Romeo, take my maidenhead.
NURSE [taking up the cords]
Hie to your chamber. I'll find Romeo
To comfort you. I wot well where he is.   139
Hark ye, your Romeo will be here at night.
I'll to him. He is hid at Laurence' cell.
JULIET [giving a ring]
Oh, find him! Give this ring to my true knight,
And bid him come to take his last farewell.
                                   Exeunt [separately].

                              ❖

[3.3]

            Enter Friar [Laurence].

FRIAR LAURENCE
Romeo, come forth; come forth, thou fearful man.   1
Affliction is enamored of thy parts,   2
And thou art wedded to calamity.

            [Enter] Romeo.

ROMEO
Father, what news? What is the Prince's doom?   4
What sorrow craves acquaintance at my hand
That I yet know not?
FRIAR LAURENCE   Too familiar
Is my dear son with such sour company.
I bring thee tidings of the Prince's doom.
ROMEO
What less than doomsday is the Prince's doom?   9
FRIAR LAURENCE
A gentler judgment vanished from his lips: 10
Not body's death, but body's banishment.
ROMEO
Ha, banishment? Be merciful, say "death";
For exile hath more terror in his look,
Much more than death. Do not say "banishment."
FRIAR LAURENCE
Here from Verona art thou banishèd.
Be patient, for the world is broad and wide.
ROMEO
There is no world without Verona walls   17
But purgatory, torture, hell itself.
Hence "banishèd" is banished from the world,
And world's exile is death. Then "banishèd,"   20
Is death mistermed. Calling death "banishèd,"

---

87 **naught** worthless, evil   88 **man** servant.   **aqua vitae** alcoholic
spirits.   98 **poor my lord** my poor lord.   **smooth thy name** speak
your name kindly   103 **Your . . . woe** You should be shed, offered as
a tribute, on some occasion of real woe   105 **that** whom   109 **fain**
gladly   117 **needly** of necessity.   **ranked with** accompanied by
120 **Which . . . moved** which might have prompted a normal grief-
stricken response.   121 **rearward** rearguard, following afterward
126 **sound** (1) fathom (2) express.

139 **wot** know
3.3. **Location: Verona. Friar Laurence's cell.**
1 **fearful** full of fear   2 **parts** qualities   4 **doom** judgment.
9 **doomsday** the Day of judgment, i.e., end of the world
10 **vanished** issued (into air)   17 **without** outside of   20 **world's
exile** exile from the world

Thou cut'st my head off with a golden ax
And smilest upon the stroke that murders me.

FRIAR LAURENCE
Oh, deadly sin! Oh, rude unthankfulness!
Thy fault our law calls death, but the kind Prince,   25
Taking thy part, hath rushed aside the law   26
And turned that black word "death" to "banishment."
This is dear mercy, and thou see'st it not.

ROMEO
'Tis torture, and not mercy. Heaven is here
Where Juliet lives, and every cat and dog
And little mouse, every unworthy thing,
Live here in heaven and may look on her,
But Romeo may not. More validity,   33
More honorable state, more courtship lives   34
In carrion flies than Romeo. They may seize
On the white wonder of dear Juliet's hand
And steal immortal blessing from her lips,
Who even in pure and vestal modesty   38
Still blush, as thinking their own kisses sin;   39
But Romeo may not, he is banishèd.
Flies may do this, but I from this must fly.
They are free men, but I am banishèd.
And sayest thou yet that exile is not death?
Hadst thou no poison mixed, no sharp-ground knife,
No sudden mean of death, though ne'er so mean,   45
But "banishèd" to kill me? "Banishèd"?
Oh, Friar, the damnèd use that word in hell;
Howling attends it. How hast thou the heart,
Being a divine, a ghostly confessor,
A sin absolver, and my friend professed,
To mangle me with that word "banishèd"?

FRIAR LAURENCE
Thou fond mad man, hear me a little speak.   52

ROMEO
Oh, thou wilt speak again of banishment.

FRIAR LAURENCE
I'll give thee armor to keep off that word,
Adversity's sweet milk, philosophy,
To comfort thee, though thou art banishèd.

ROMEO
Yet "banishèd"? Hang up philosophy!   57
Unless philosophy can make a Juliet,
Displant a town, reverse a prince's doom,   59
It helps not, it prevails not. Talk no more.

FRIAR LAURENCE
Oh, then I see that madmen have no ears.

ROMEO
How should they, when that wise men have no eyes?

FRIAR LAURENCE
Let me dispute with thee of thy estate.   63

ROMEO
Thou canst not speak of that thou dost not feel.   64
Wert thou as young as I, Juliet thy love,
An hour but married, Tybalt murderèd,
Doting like me, and like me banishèd,
Then mightst thou speak, then mightst thou tear thy
    hair,
And fall upon the ground, as I do now,
Taking the measure of an unmade grave.
                [*He falls upon the ground.*] *Knock* [*within*].

FRIAR LAURENCE
Arise. One knocks. Good Romeo, hide thyself.

ROMEO
Not I, unless the breath of heartsick groans,
Mistlike, infold me from the search of eyes.   *Knock.*

FRIAR LAURENCE
Hark, how they knock!—Who's there?—Romeo, arise.
Thou wilt be taken.—Stay awhile!—Stand up.
                                                  Knock.
Run to my study.—By and by!—God's will,
What simpleness is this?—I come, I come!   *Knock.*   77
Who knocks so hard? Whence come you? What's your
    will?   [*Going to the door.*]

NURSE [*within*]
Let me come in, and you shall know my errand.
I come from Lady Juliet.

FRIAR LAURENCE   Welcome, then.
                                     [*He opens the door.*]

                    Enter Nurse.

NURSE
O holy Friar, oh, tell me, holy Friar,
Where's my lady's lord, where's Romeo?

FRIAR LAURENCE
There on the ground, with his own tears made drunk.

NURSE
Oh, he is even in my mistress' case,   84
Just in her case! Oh, woeful sympathy!   85
Piteous predicament! Even so lies she,
Blubb'ring and weeping, weeping and blubb'ring.—
Stand up, stand up! Stand, an you be a man.
For Juliet's sake, for her sake, rise and stand!
Why should you fall into so deep an O?   90

ROMEO   Nurse!   [*He rises.*]

NURSE
Ah sir, ah sir! Death's the end of all.

ROMEO
Spakest thou of Juliet? How is it with her?
Doth not she think me an old murderer,   94
Now I have stained the childhood of our joy
With blood removed but little from her own?
Where is she? And how doth she? And what says
My concealed lady to our canceled love?   98

---

25 **Thy fault . . . death** For your crime, the law demands a death sentence   26 **rushed** thrust   33 **validity** true worth   34 **courtship** (1) courtliness (2) occasion for wooing   38 **vestal** maidenly   39 **Still . . . sin** continually look red, as though blushing to think that their touching each other is sin   45 **mean . . . mean** means . . . base   52 **fond** foolish, frantic   57 **Yet** Still   59 **Displant** uproot   63 **dispute** reason. **estate** situation.

64 **that** that which   77 **simpleness** foolishness   84 **even** exactly. **case** situation   85 **woeful sympathy** mutuality of grief.   90 **an O** a fit of groaning. (A sexual meaning, unrecognized by the speaker, is suggested by *rise and stand* in the previous line.)   94 **old** hardened   98 **concealed** secret.   **canceled** nullified (by the impending exile)

NURSE
Oh, she says nothing, sir, but weeps and weeps,
And now falls on her bed, and then starts up,
And "Tybalt" calls, and then on Romeo cries,
And then down falls again.

ROMEO   As if that name,
Shot from the deadly level of a gun,   103
Did murder her, as that name's cursèd hand
Murdered her kinsman. Oh, tell me, Friar, tell me,
In what vile part of this anatomy
Doth my name lodge? Tell me, that I may sack   107
The hateful mansion.

[He draws a weapon, but is restrained.]

FRIAR LAURENCE   Hold thy desperate hand!
Art thou a man? Thy form cries out thou art;
Thy tears are womanish, thy wild acts denote
The unreasonable fury of a beast.
Unseemly woman in a seeming man,
And ill-beseeming beast in seeming both!
Thou hast amazed me. By my holy order,
I thought thy disposition better tempered.   115
Hast thou slain Tybalt? Wilt thou slay thyself,
And slay thy lady, that in thy life lives,
By doing damnèd hate upon thyself?
Why railest thou on thy birth, the heaven, and earth,
Since birth, and heaven, and earth, all three do meet   120
In thee at once, which thou at once wouldst lose?
Fie, fie, thou shamest thy shape, thy love, thy wit,   122
Which, like a usurer, abound'st in all,   123
And usest none in that true use indeed   124
Which should bedeck thy shape, thy love, thy wit.   125
Thy noble shape is but a form of wax,   126
Digressing from the valor of a man;
Thy dear love sworn but hollow perjury,
Killing that love which thou hast vowed to cherish;
Thy wit, that ornament to shape and love,
Misshapen in the conduct of them both,   131
Like powder in a skilless soldier's flask   132
Is set afire by thine own ignorance,
And thou dismembered with thine own defense.   134
What, rouse thee, man! Thy Juliet is alive,
For whose dear sake thou wast but lately dead;   136
There art thou happy. Tybalt would kill thee,   137
But thou slewest Tybalt; there art thou happy.
The law that threatened death becomes thy friend
And turns it to exile; there art thou happy.
A pack of blessings light upon thy back,
Happiness courts thee in her best array,
But like a mishavèd and sullen wench   143
Thou pout'st upon thy fortune and thy love.

Take heed, take heed, for such die miserable.
Go, get thee to thy love, as was decreed.   146
Ascend her chamber; hence and comfort her.
But look thou stay not till the watch be set,   148
For then thou canst not pass to Mantua,
Where thou shalt live till we can find a time
To blaze your marriage, reconcile your friends,   151
Beg pardon of the Prince, and call thee back
With twenty hundred thousand times more joy
Than thou went'st forth in lamentation.
Go before, Nurse. Commend me to thy lady,
And bid her hasten all the house to bed,
Which heavy sorrow makes them apt unto.
Romeo is coming.

NURSE
Oh, Lord, I could have stayed here all the night
To hear good counsel. Oh, what learning is!—
My lord, I'll tell my lady you will come.

ROMEO
Do so, and bid my sweet prepare to chide.

NURSE *[giving a ring]*
Here, sir, a ring she bid me give you, sir.
Hie you, make haste, for it grows very late.   *[Exit.]*

ROMEO
How well my comfort is revived by this!

FRIAR LAURENCE
Go hence. Good night. And here stands all your state: 166
Either be gone before the watch be set,
Or by the break of day disguised from hence.
Sojourn in Mantua. I'll find out your man,
And he shall signify from time to time
Every good hap to you that chances here.   171
Give me thy hand. 'Tis late. Farewell, good night.

ROMEO
But that a joy past joy calls out on me,
It were a grief so brief to part with thee.   174
Farewell.   *Exeunt [separately].*

❖

[3.4]

Enter old Capulet, his Wife, and Paris.

CAPULET
Things have fall'n out, sir, so unluckily,   1
That we have had no time to move our daughter.   2
Look you, she loved her kinsman Tybalt dearly,
And so did I. Well, we were born to die.
'Tis very late. She'll not come down tonight.
I promise you, but for your company   6
I would have been abed an hour ago.

PARIS
These times of woe afford no times to woo.
Madam, good night. Commend me to your daughter.

---

103 **level** aim   107 **sack** destroy   115 **tempered** harmonized, balanced.   120 **birth . . . earth** life, soul, and body   122–5 **thou shamest . . . wit** you shame your physical form, love, and mind (corresponding to life, soul, and body), all of which you have in abundance but which you misuse as a usurer misuses wealth, using improperly the treasure that you should put to proper use.   126 **form of wax** waxwork, mere outer form   131 **conduct** guidance   132 **powder** gunpowder.   **flask** powder horn   134 **dismembered . . . defense** blown to pieces by that which should defend you, i.e., your *wit*, or intellect.   136 **wast . . . dead** i.e., only recently were wishing yourself dead. (See line 70.)   137 **happy** fortunate.   143 **mishavèd** misbehaved

146 **decreed** (1) arranged earlier (2) decreed by heaven for those who have married.   148 **the watch be set** guards are posted (at the city gates)   151 **blaze** publish, divulge.   **friends** relations   166 **here . . . state** your fortune depends on what follows   171 **good hap** fortunate event   174 **brief** quickly
3.4. Location: Verona. Capulet's house.
1 **fall'n out** happened   2 **move** persuade   6 **promise** assure

WIFE

    I will, and know her mind early tomorrow.
    Tonight she's mewed up to her heaviness.   11

CAPULET

    Sir Paris, I will make a desperate tender   12
    Of my child's love. I think she will be ruled
    In all respects by me; nay, more, I doubt it not.
    Wife, go you to her ere you go to bed.
    Acquaint her here of my son Paris' love,
    And bid her, mark you me, on Wednesday next—   17
    But soft, what day is this?

PARIS   Monday, my lord.   18

CAPULET

    Monday! Ha, ha! Well, Wednesday is too soon;
    O' Thursday let it be. O' Thursday, tell her,
    She shall be married to this noble earl.
    Will you be ready? Do you like this haste?
    We'll keep no great ado—a friend or two;
    For hark you, Tybalt being slain so late,   24
    It may be thought we held him carelessly,   25
    Being our kinsman, if we revel much.
    Therefore we'll have some half a dozen friends,
    And there an end. But what say you to Thursday?

PARIS

    My lord, I would that Thursday were tomorrow.

CAPULET

    Well, get you gone. O' Thursday be it, then.
    [*To his Wife*] Go you to Juliet ere you go to bed;
    Prepare her, wife, against this wedding day.—   32
    Farewell, my lord.—Light to my chamber, ho!—
    Afore me, it is so very late   34
    That we may call it early by and by.
    Good night.   *Exeunt.*

❦

[3.5]

Enter Romeo and Juliet aloft [at the window].

JULIET

    Wilt thou be gone? It is not yet near day.
    It was the nightingale, and not the lark,
    That pierced the fearful hollow of thine ear;   3
    Nightly she sings on yond pomegranate tree.
    Believe me, love, it was the nightingale.

ROMEO

    It was the lark, the herald of the morn,
    No nightingale. Look, love, what envious streaks
    Do lace the severing clouds in yonder east.   8
    Night's candles are burnt out, and jocund day   9
    Stands tiptoe on the misty mountain tops.
    I must be gone and live, or stay and die.

JULIET

    Yond light is not daylight, I know it, I.
    It is some meteor that the sun exhaled   13
    To be to thee this night a torchbearer
    And light thee on thy way to Mantua.
    Therefore stay yet. Thou need'st not to be gone.

ROMEO

    Let me be ta'en; let me be put to death.
    I am content, so thou wilt have it so.   18
    I'll say yon gray is not the morning's eye;
    'Tis but the pale reflex of Cynthia's brow.   20
    Nor that is not the lark whose notes do beat
    The vaulty heaven so high above our heads.
    I have more care to stay than will to go.   23
    Come, death, and welcome! Juliet wills it so.
    How is't, my soul? Let's talk. It is not day.

JULIET

    It is, it is. Hie hence, begone, away!   26
    It is the lark that sings so out of tune,
    Straining harsh discords and unpleasing sharps.   28
    Some say the lark makes sweet division;   29
    This doth not so, for she divideth us.
    Some say the lark and loathèd toad changed eyes;   31
    Oh, now I would they had changed voices too,
    Since arm from arm that voice doth us affray,   33
    Hunting thee hence with hunt's-up to the day.   34
    Oh, now begone! More light and light it grows.

ROMEO

    More light and light, more dark and dark our woes!

Enter Nurse [hastily].

NURSE   Madam!

JULIET   Nurse?

NURSE

    Your lady mother is coming to your chamber.
    The day is broke; be wary, look about.   [*Exit.*]

JULIET

    Then window, let day in, and let life out.

ROMEO

    Farewell, farewell! One kiss, and I'll descend.
    [*They kiss. He climbs down from the window.*]

JULIET

    Art thou gone so? Love, lord, ay, husband, friend!   43
    I must hear from thee every day in the hour,
    For in a minute there are many days.
    Oh, by this count I shall be much in years   46
    Ere I again behold my Romeo!

ROMEO [*from below her window*]   Farewell!

---

11 mewed up to cooped up with. (A term from falconry, reminiscent of 2.2.159–68.) **heaviness** sorrow. **12 desperate tender** bold offer **17 mark you me** listen to this **18 soft** wait a minute **24 late** recently **25 held him carelessly** did not regard him highly **32 against** in anticipation of **34 Afore me** i.e., By my life. (A mild oath.)
3.5. Location: Verona. Capulet's orchard with Juliet's chamber window above, and, at lines 68 ff., the interior of Juliet's chamber.
3 fearful apprehensive, anxious **8 severing** separating **9 jocund** cheerful

13 exhaled i.e., has drawn out of the ground. (Meteors were thought to be vapors of luminous gas drawn up by the sun.) **18 so** as long as, since **20 reflex** reflection. **Cynthia's** the moon's **23 care** desire, concern **26 Hie hence** Hasten away **28 sharps** notes relatively high in pitch and hence discordant. **29 division** variations on a melody, made by dividing each note into notes of briefer duration **31 changed** exchanged. (A popular saying, to account for the observation that the lark has very ordinary eyes and the toad remarkable ones.) **33 arm from arm** from one another's arms. **affray** frighten **34 hunt's-up** a song or tune originally designed to awaken huntsmen; later, used also to serenade a newly married couple **43 friend** lover. **46 much in years** much older

I will omit no opportunity
That may convey my greetings, love, to thee.

JULIET
Oh, think'st thou we shall ever meet again?

ROMEO
I doubt it not, and all these woes shall serve
For sweet discourses in our times to come.

JULIET
Oh, God, I have an ill-divining soul!   54
Methinks I see thee, now thou art so low,
As one dead in the bottom of a tomb.
Either my eyesight fails or thou lookest pale.

ROMEO
And trust me, love, in my eye so do you.
Dry sorrow drinks our blood. Adieu, adieu!   *Exit.*   59

JULIET
O Fortune, Fortune! All men call thee fickle.
If thou art fickle, what dost thou with him
That is renowned for faith? Be fickle, Fortune.
For then, I hope, thou wilt not keep him long,
But send him back.

Enter Mother [Capulet's Wife].

WIFE   Ho, daughter, are you up?

JULIET
Who is't that calls? It is my lady mother.
Is she not down so late, or up so early?   66
What unaccustomed cause procures her hither?   67

[She goeth down from the window.]

WIFE
Why, how now, Juliet?

JULIET   Madam, I am not well.

WIFE
Evermore weeping for your cousin's death?
What, wilt thou wash him from his grave with tears?
An if thou couldst, thou couldst not make him live;
Therefore, have done. Some grief shows much of love,   72
But much of grief shows still some want of wit.   73

JULIET
Yet let me weep for such a feeling loss.   74

WIFE
So shall you feel the loss, but not the friend
Which you weep for.

JULIET   Feeling so the loss,
I cannot choose but ever weep the friend.   77

WIFE
Well, girl, thou weep'st not so much for his death
As that the villain lives which slaughtered him.

JULIET
What villain, madam?

WIFE   That same villain, Romeo.

JULIET *[aside]*
Villain and he be many miles asunder.—
God pardon him! I do, with all my heart;
And yet no man like he doth grieve my heart.   83

WIFE
That is because the traitor murderer lives.

JULIET
Ay, madam, from the reach of these my hands.
Would none but I might venge my cousin's death!

WIFE
We will have vengeance for it, fear thou not.
Then weep no more. I'll send to one in Mantua,
Where that same banished runagate doth live,   89
Shall give him such an unaccustomed dram   90
That he shall soon keep Tybalt company.
And then, I hope, thou wilt be satisfied.

JULIET
Indeed, I never shall be satisfied
With Romeo till I behold him—dead—
Is my poor heart so for a kinsman vexed.
Madam, if you could find out but a man
To bear a poison, I would temper it,   97
That Romeo should, upon receipt thereof,
Soon sleep in quiet. Oh, how my heart abhors
To hear him named, and cannot come to him
To wreak the love I bore my cousin   101
Upon his body that hath slaughtered him!   102

WIFE
Find thou the means, and I'll find such a man.
But now I'll tell thee joyful tidings, girl.

JULIET
And joy comes well in such a needy time.
What are they, beseech Your Ladyship?

WIFE
Well, well, thou hast a careful father, child,   107
One who, to put thee from thy heaviness,   108
Hath sorted out a sudden day of joy   109
That thou expects not, nor I looked not for.

JULIET
Madam, in happy time, what day is that?

WIFE
Marry, my child, early next Thursday morn,   112
The gallant, young, and noble gentleman,
The County Paris, at Saint Peter's Church
Shall happily make thee there a joyful bride.

JULIET
Now, by Saint Peter's Church, and Peter too,
He shall not make me there a joyful bride!

---

54 ill-divining prophesying of evil   **59 Dry sorrow** (The heat of the body in sorrow and despair was thought to descend into the bowels and dry up the blood.)   **66 down** in bed   **67 procures** induces to come.   **67.1** (As indicated by the bracketed stage direction, which is from the First Quarto, Juliet, who has appeared until now at her "window" above the stage, evidently descends quickly to the main stage and joins her mother for the remainder of the scene. The stage, which before was to have been imagined as Capulet's orchard, is now Juliet's chamber. Juliet's mother has entered onto the main stage four lines earlier.)   **72 have done** cease.   **73 want of wit** lack of intelligence.   **74 feeling** deeply felt   **77 the friend** (Juliet secretly means "my lover," as at line 43, but, of course, her mother hears it as "Tybalt.")

83 no man like he no man so much as he.   **grieve** (1) anger (2) grieve with longing. (Juliet speaks to her mother throughout in intentional ambiguities, at lines 85, 86, 99, 100–2, etc.)   **89 runagate** renegade, fugitive   **90 Shall** who will.   **dram** dose. (Literally, one-eighth of a fluid ounce.)   **97 temper** (1) mix, concoct (2) alloy, dilute. (In her intended double meanings about Romeo dead, poisoned, and sleeping in quiet, Juliet is, of course, unaware of an ironic anticipation of how these things will be fulfilled.)   **101 wreak** (1) avenge (2) bestow   **102 his body that** the body of him who   **107 careful** full of care (for you)   **108 heaviness** sorrow   **109 sorted** chosen   **112 Marry** i.e., By the Virgin Mary

I wonder at this haste, that I must wed
Ere he that should be husband comes to woo.
I pray you, tell my lord and father, madam,
I will not marry yet, and when I do I swear
It shall be Romeo, whom you know I hate,
Rather than Paris. These are news indeed!

WIFE
Here comes your father. Tell him so yourself,
And see how he will take it at your hands.

Enter Capulet and Nurse.

CAPULET
When the sun sets, the earth doth drizzle dew,
But for the sunset of my brother's son
It rains downright.—
How now, a conduit, girl? What, still in tears?   129
Evermore show'ring? In one little body
Thou counterfeits a bark, a sea, a wind;   131
For still thy eyes, which I may call the sea,
Do ebb and flow with tears; the bark thy body is,
Sailing in this salt flood; the winds, thy sighs,
Who, raging with thy tears, and they with them,
Without a sudden calm, will overset   136
Thy tempest-tossèd body.—How now, wife?
Have you delivered to her our decree?

WIFE
Ay, sir, but she will none, she gives you thanks.   139
I would the fool were married to her grave!

CAPULET
Soft, take me with you, take me with you, wife.   141
How? Will she none? Doth she not give us thanks?
Is she not proud? Doth she not count her blest,   143
Unworthy as she is, that we have wrought   144
So worthy a gentleman to be her bride?   145

JULIET
Not proud you have, but thankful that you have.
Proud can I never be of what I hate,
But thankful even for hate that is meant love.   148

CAPULET
How, how, how, how, chopped logic? What is this?
"Proud," and "I thank you," and "I thank you not,"
And yet "not proud"? Mistress minion, you,   151
Thank me no thankings, nor proud me no prouds,
But fettle your fine joints 'gainst Thursday next   153
To go with Paris to Saint Peter's Church,
Or I will drag thee on a hurdle thither.   155
Out, you greensickness carrion! Out, you baggage!   156
You tallow-face!

WIFE [*to Capulet*]   Fie, fie! What, are you mad?   157

JULIET [*kneeling*]
Good father, I beseech you on my knees,
Hear me with patience but to speak a word.

CAPULET
Hang thee, young baggage, disobedient wretch!
I tell thee what: get thee to church o' Thursday
Or never after look me in the face.
Speak not, reply not, do not answer me!
My fingers itch. Wife, we scarce thought us blest
That God had lent us but this only child;
But now I see this one is one too much,
And that we have a curse in having her.
Out on her, hilding!

NURSE   God in heaven bless her!   168
You are to blame, my lord, to rate her so.   169

CAPULET
And why, my Lady Wisdom? Hold your tongue,
Good Prudence. Smatter with your gossips, go.   171

NURSE
I speak no treason.

CAPULET   Oh, God-i'-good-e'en!   172

NURSE
May not one speak?

CAPULET   Peace, you mumbling fool!
Utter your gravity o'er a gossip's bowl,   174
For here we need it not.

WIFE   You are too hot.

CAPULET   God's bread, it makes me mad!   176
Day, night, hour, tide, time, work, play,   177
Alone, in company, still my care hath been
To have her matched. And having now provided
A gentleman of noble parentage,
Of fair demesnes, youthful, and nobly liened,   181
Stuffed, as they say, with honorable parts,   182
Proportioned as one's thought would wish a man—
And then to have a wretched puling fool,   184
A whining mammet, in her fortune's tender,   185
To answer, "I'll not wed, I cannot love,
I am too young; I pray you, pardon me."
But, an you will not wed, I'll pardon you.   188
Graze where you will, you shall not house with me.
Look to't, think on't. I do not use to jest.   190
Thursday is near. Lay hand on heart; advise.   191
An you be mine, I'll give you to my friend;
An you be not, hang, beg, starve, die in the streets,
For, by my soul, I'll ne'er acknowledge thee,
Nor what is mine shall never do thee good.
Trust to't, bethink you. I'll not be forsworn.   *Exit.* 196

JULIET
Is there no pity sitting in the clouds
That sees into the bottom of my grief?

---

129 **conduit** water pipe, fountain   131 **bark** sailing vessel   136 **Without** unless there is   139 **will . . . thanks** says "no thank you," she'll have no part of it.   141 **take . . . you** let me understand you   143 **count her** consider herself   144 **wrought** arranged for   145 **bride** bridegroom.   148 **hate . . . love** that which is hateful but which was meant lovingly.   151 **minion** spoiled darling, minx   153 **fettle** make ready. **'gainst** in anticipation of   155 **a hurdle** a conveyance on which criminals were dragged to execution   156 **greensickness** (An anemic ailment of young unmarried women; it suggests Juliet's paleness.) **baggage** hussy.   157 **tallow-face** paleface.

168 **hilding** jade, baggage.   169 **rate** berate, scold   171 **Smatter** Chatter. **gossips** gossiping women friends   172 **God-i'-good-e'en** i.e., For God's sake. (Literally, God give you good evening.)   174 **gravity** wisdom. (Said contemptuously.)   176 **God's bread** i.e., By God's (Christ's) Sacrament   177 **tide** season   181 **demesnes** estates. **liened** descended   182 **parts** qualities   184 **puling** whining   185 **mammet** doll. **in . . . tender** when an offer of good fortune is made to her   188 **pardon you** i.e., allow you to depart. (Said caustically.)   190 **do not use** am not accustomed   191 **advise** consider carefully.   196 **be forsworn** i.e., go back on my word.

O sweet my mother, cast me not away!
Delay this marriage for a month, a week;
Or if you do not, make the bridal bed
In that dim monument where Tybalt lies.

WIFE
Talk not to me, for I'll not speak a word.
Do as thou wilt, for I have done with thee.   *Exit.*

JULIET [*rising*]
Oh, God!—O Nurse, how shall this be prevented?
My husband is on earth, my faith in heaven.   206
How shall that faith return again to earth,   207
Unless that husband send it me from heaven   208
By leaving earth? Comfort me, counsel me.   209
Alack, alack, that heaven should practice stratagems
Upon so soft a subject as myself!
What say'st thou? Hast thou not a word of joy?
Some comfort, Nurse.

NURSE   Faith, here it is.
Romeo is banished, and all the world to nothing   214
That he dares ne'er come back to challenge you,   215
Or if he do, it needs must be by stealth.
Then, since the case so stands as now it doth,
I think it best you married with the County.
Oh, he's a lovely gentleman!
Romeo's a dishclout to him. An eagle, madam,   220
Hath not so green, so quick, so fair an eye
As Paris hath. Beshrew my very heart,   222
I think you are happy in this second match,
For it excels your first; or if it did not,
Your first is dead—or 'twere as good he were,
As living here and you no use of him.

JULIET   Speak'st thou from thy heart?

NURSE
And from my soul too. Else beshrew them both.

JULIET   Amen!   229

NURSE   What?

JULIET
Well, thou hast comforted me marvelous much.
Go in, and tell my lady I am gone,
Having displeased my father, to Laurence' cell
To make confession and to be absolved.

NURSE
Marry, I will; and this is wisely done.   [*Exit.*]

JULIET
Ancient damnation! Oh, most wicked fiend!   236
Is it more sin to wish me thus forsworn,   237
Or to dispraise my lord with that same tongue
Which she hath praised him with above compare
So many thousand times? Go, counselor,
Thou and my bosom henceforth shall be twain.   241

I'll to the Friar to know his remedy.
If all else fail, myself have power to die.   *Exit.*

❖

[4.1]

Enter Friar [Laurence] and County Paris.

FRIAR LAURENCE
On Thursday, sir? The time is very short.

PARIS
My father Capulet will have it so,
And I am nothing slow to slack his haste.   3

FRIAR LAURENCE
You say you do not know the lady's mind?
Uneven is the course. I like it not.

PARIS
Immoderately she weeps for Tybalt's death,
And therefore have I little talked of love,
For Venus smiles not in a house of tears.   8
Now, sir, her father counts it dangerous
That she do give her sorrow so much sway,
And in his wisdom hastes our marriage
To stop the inundation of her tears,
Which, too much minded by herself alone,   13
May be put from her by society.   14
Now do you know the reason of this haste.

FRIAR LAURENCE [*aside*]
I would I knew not why it should be slowed.—
Look, sir, here comes the lady toward my cell.

Enter Juliet.

PARIS
Happily met, my lady and my wife!

JULIET
That may be, sir, when I may be a wife.

PARIS
That "may be" must be, love, on Thursday next.

JULIET
What must be shall be.

FRIAR LAURENCE   That's a certain text.

PARIS
Come you to make confession to this father?

JULIET
To answer that, I should confess to you.

PARIS
Do not deny to him that you love me.

JULIET
I will confess to you that I love him.

PARIS
So will ye, I am sure, that you love me.

JULIET
If I do so, it will be of more price,   27
Being spoke behind your back, than to your face.

---

206 **my faith in heaven** i.e., I am married to Romeo in the sight of
heaven.   **207–9 How . . . leaving earth?** i.e., How can I remarry while
Romeo is still alive?   **214 all . . . nothing** the odds are overwhelming
215 challenge lay claim to   **220 dishclout** dishrag   **222 Beshrew** (A
mild oath. Also in line 228.)   **229 Amen** (Juliet says "Amen" as
though to answer the Nurse's prayer that her heart and soul be
cursed. The Nurse does not get the point.)   **236 Ancient damnation!**
Damnable old woman!   **237 forsworn** i.e., false to my marriage vows
241 bosom secret thoughts.   **twain** separated.

4.1. Location: Verona. Friar Laurence's cell.
3 nothing . . . haste not at all reluctant to lessen his haste, i.e., willing to
speed matters along.   **8 Venus . . . tears** (1) amorousness is not appropriate in a house of mourning (2) the planet Venus does not exert a
favorable influence when it is in an inauspicious *house* or constellation
of the zodiac.   **13 too . . . alone** too mind-consuming when she is alone
14 society companionship.   **27 more price** greater worth

PARIS

Poor soul, thy face is much abused with tears.

JULIET

The tears have got small victory by that,

For it was bad enough before their spite.   31

PARIS

Thou wrong'st it more than tears with that report.   32

JULIET

That is no slander, sir, which is a truth;

And what I spake, I spake it to my face.   34

PARIS

Thy face is mine, and thou hast slandered it.

JULIET

It may be so, for it is not mine own.—   36

Are you at leisure, holy Father, now,

Or shall I come to you at evening Mass?

FRIAR LAURENCE

My leisure serves me, pensive daughter, now.—   39

My lord, we must entreat the time alone.   40

PARIS

God shield I should disturb devotion!   41

Juliet, on Thursday early will I rouse ye.

Till then, adieu, and keep this holy kiss.   *Exit.*

JULIET

Oh, shut the door! And when thou hast done so,

Come weep with me—past hope, past cure, past help!

FRIAR LAURENCE

Ah, Juliet, I already know thy grief;

It strains me past the compass of my wits.   47

I hear thou must, and nothing may prorogue it,   48

On Thursday next be married to this county.

JULIET

Tell me not, Friar, that thou hearest of this,

Unless thou tell me how I may prevent it.

If in thy wisdom thou canst give no help,

Do thou but call my resolution wise

And with this knife I'll help it presently.   54

[She shows a knife.]

God joined my heart and Romeo's, thou our hands;

And ere this hand, by thee to Romeo sealed,

Shall be the label to another deed,   57

Or my true heart with treacherous revolt

Turn to another, this shall slay them both.   59

Therefore, out of thy long-experienced time,   60

Give me some present counsel, or, behold,

Twixt my extremes and me this bloody knife   62

Shall play the umpire, arbitrating that

Which the commission of thy years and art   64

Could to no issue of true honor bring.

Be not so long to speak; I long to die   66

If what thou speak'st speak not of remedy.

FRIAR LAURENCE

Hold, daughter. I do spy a kind of hope,

Which craves as desperate an execution

As that is desperate which we would prevent.

If, rather than to marry County Paris,

Thou hast the strength of will to slay thyself,

Then is it likely thou wilt undertake

A thing like death to chide away this shame,

That cop'st with Death himself to scape from it;   75

And if thou darest, I'll give thee remedy.

JULIET

Oh, bid me leap, rather than marry Paris,

From off the battlements of any tower,

Or walk in thievish ways, or bid me lurk   79

Where serpents are; chain me with roaring bears,

Or hide me nightly in a charnel house,   81

O'ercovered quite with dead men's rattling bones,

With reeky shanks and yellow chopless skulls;   83

Or bid me go into a new-made grave

And hide me with a dead man in his tomb—

Things that, to hear them told, have made me tremble—

And I will do it without fear or doubt,

To live an unstained wife to my sweet love.

FRIAR LAURENCE

Hold, then. Go home, be merry, give consent

To marry Paris. Wednesday is tomorrow.

Tomorrow night look that thou lie alone;

Let not the Nurse lie with thee in thy chamber.

Take thou this vial, being then in bed,

[showing her a vial]

And this distilling liquor drink thou off,   94

When presently through all thy veins shall run

A cold and drowsy humor; for no pulse   96

Shall keep his native progress, but surcease;   97

No warmth, no breath shall testify thou livest;

The roses in thy lips and cheeks shall fade

To wanny ashes, thy eyes' windows fall   100

Like death when he shuts up the day of life;

Each part, deprived of supple government,   102

Shall, stiff and stark and cold, appear like death.

And in this borrowed likeness of shrunk death

Thou shalt continue two-and-forty hours,

And then awake as from a pleasant sleep.

Now, when the bridegroom in the morning comes

To rouse thee from thy bed, there art thou dead.

Then, as the manner of our country is,

In thy best robes uncovered on the bier

Thou shalt be borne to that same ancient vault

Where all the kindred of the Capulets lie.

In the meantime, against thou shalt awake,   113

Shall Romeo by my letters know our drift,   114

31 spite malice.   **32 Thou . . . report** Your apology for your face slanders it more than your tears do.   **34 to my face** (1) openly (2) about my face.   **36 is not mine own** (1) is beyond my control, does not reveal me truly (2) belongs to Romeo.   **39 pensive** sorrowful   **40 entreat . . . alone** ask you to leave us alone.   **41 God shield** God forbid   **47 compass** bounds   **48 prorogue** delay   **54 presently** at once.   **57 label** strip attached to a deed to carry the seal; hence, confirmation, seal   **59 both** i.e., hand and heart.   **60 time** age   **62 extremes** extreme difficulties   **64 commission** authority.   **art** skill   **66 so long** so slow. (With wordplay on *long,* "yearn," later in this same line.)

75 That . . . himself either (1) you who are willing to encounter Death by killing yourself, or (2) that simulates Death itself.   **it** this shame   **79 thievish ways** roads frequented by thieves   **81 charnel house** vault for human bones   **83 reeky** reeking, malodorous.   **chopless** without the lower jaw   **94 distilling** infusing the body, or distilled   **96 humor** fluid   **97 his native** its natural.   **surcease** cease   **100 wanny** wan, pale   **102 supple government** control of motion   **113 against** anticipating when   **114 drift** plan

And hither shall he come; and he and I
Will watch thy waking, and that very night   116
Shall Romeo bear thee hence to Mantua.
And this shall free thee from this present shame,
If no inconstant toy nor womanish fear   119
Abate thy valor in the acting it.

JULIET [*taking the vial*]
Give me, give me! Oh, tell not me of fear!

FRIAR LAURENCE
Hold, get you gone. Be strong and prosperous   122
In this resolve. I'll send a friar with speed
To Mantua, with my letters to thy lord.

JULIET
Love give me strength, and strength shall help afford.   125
Farewell, dear Father!   *Exeunt* [*separately*].

❖

[4.2]

Enter Father Capulet, Mother [*Capulet's Wife*],
Nurse, and Servingmen, two or three.

CAPULET
So many guests invite as here are writ.
         [*Exit one or two servingmen.*]
Sirrah, go hire me twenty cunning cooks.   2

SERVINGMAN   You shall have none ill, sir, for I'll try if   3
they can lick their fingers.

CAPULET   How canst thou try them so?

SERVINGMAN   Marry, sir, 'tis an ill cook that cannot lick
his own fingers; therefore he that cannot lick his
fingers goes not with me.

CAPULET   Go, begone.   [*Exit Servingman.*]
We shall be much unfurnished for this time.   10
What, is my daughter gone to Friar Laurence?

NURSE   Ay, forsooth.

CAPULET
Well, he may chance to do some good on her.
A peevish self-willed harlotry it is.   14

Enter Juliet.

NURSE
See where she comes from shrift with merry look.

CAPULET
How now, my headstrong, where have you been
     gadding?

JULIET
Where I have learned me to repent the sin
Of disobedient opposition
To you and your behests, and am enjoined   19
By holy Laurence to fall prostrate here,   [*kneeling*]
To beg your pardon. Pardon, I beseech you!
Henceforward I am ever ruled by you.

CAPULET
Send for the County! Go tell him of this.
I'll have this knot knit up tomorrow morning.

JULIET
I met the youthful lord at Laurence' cell
And gave him what becomèd love I might,   26
Not stepping o'er the bounds of modesty.

CAPULET
Why, I am glad on't. This is well. Stand up.
         [*Juliet rises.*]
This is as 't should be. Let me see the County;
Ay, marry, go, I say, and fetch him hither.
Now, afore God, this reverend holy friar,
All our whole city is much bound to him.   32

JULIET
Nurse, will you go with me into my closet   33
To help me sort such needful ornaments   34
As you think fit to furnish me tomorrow?

WIFE
No, not till Thursday. There is time enough.

CAPULET
Go, Nurse, go with her. We'll to church tomorrow.
         Exeunt [*Juliet and Nurse*].

WIFE
We shall be short in our provision.
'Tis now near night.

CAPULET   Tush, I will stir about,
And all things shall be well, I warrant thee, wife.
Go thou to Juliet, help to deck up her.
I'll not to bed tonight. Let me alone.   42
I'll play the huswife for this once.—What, ho!—   43
They are all forth. Well, I will walk myself
To County Paris, to prepare up him
Against tomorrow. My heart is wondrous light,
Since this same wayward girl is so reclaimed.
         Exeunt.

❖

[4.3]

Enter Juliet and Nurse.

JULIET
Ay, those attires are best. But, gentle Nurse,
I pray thee, leave me to myself tonight;
For I have need of many orisons   3
To move the heavens to smile upon my state,
Which, well thou knowest, is cross and full of sin.   5

Enter Mother [*Capulet's Wife*].

WIFE
What, are you busy, ho? Need you my help?

JULIET
No, madam, we have culled such necessaries   7
As are behooveful for our state tomorrow.   8
So please you, let me now be left alone,
And let the Nurse this night sit up with you,

---

116 **watch** keep a watch over, be on hand for   119 **toy** idle fancy
122 **prosperous** successful   125 **help afford** provide help.
4.2. Location: Verona. Capulet's house.
2 **cunning** skilled   3 **none ill** no bad ones.   **try** test   10 **unfurnished** unprovided   14 **A peevish . . . is** i.e., She's a silly good-fornothing.   19 **behests** commands

26 **becomèd** befitting   32 **bound** indebted   33 **closet** chamber
34 **sort** choose   42 **Let me alone** Leave things to me.   43 **huswife**
housewife
**4.3. Location: Verona. Capulet's house; Juliet's bed, enclosed by
bedcurtains, is set up in the discovery space.**
3 **orisons** prayers   5 **cross** perverse   7 **culled** picked out
8 **behooveful** needful.   **state** ceremony

For I am sure you have your hands full all
In this so sudden business.

WIFE   Good night.
Get thee to bed and rest, for thou hast need.
                    Exeunt [Capulet's Wife and Nurse].

JULIET
Farewell! God knows when we shall meet again.
I have a faint cold fear thrills through my veins   15
That almost freezes up the heat of life.
I'll call them back again to comfort me.—
Nurse!—What should she do here?
My dismal scene I needs must act alone.
Come, vial.   *[She takes out the vial.]*
What if this mixture do not work at all?
Shall I be married then tomorrow morning?
No, no, this shall forbid it. Lie thou there.
                    [She lays down a dagger.]
What if it be a poison, which the Friar
Subtly hath ministered to have me dead,
Lest in this marriage he should be dishonored
Because he married me before to Romeo?
I fear it is; and yet methinks it should not,
For he hath still been tried a holy man.   29
How if, when I am laid into the tomb,
I wake before the time that Romeo
Come to redeem me? There's a fearful point!
Shall I not then be stifled in the vault,
To whose foul mouth no healthsome air breathes in,
And there die strangled ere my Romeo comes?
Or, if I live, is it not very like   36
The horrible conceit of death and night,   37
Together with the terror of the place—
As in a vault, an ancient receptacle,   39
Where for this many hundred years the bones
Of all my buried ancestors are packed;
Where bloody Tybalt, yet but green in earth,   42
Lies fest'ring in his shroud; where, as they say,
At some hours in the night spirits resort—
Alack, alack, is it not like that I,
So early waking, what with loathsome smells,
And shrieks like mandrakes torn out of the earth,   47
That living mortals, hearing them, run mad—   48
Oh, if I wake, shall I not be distraught,
Environèd with all these hideous fears,   50
And madly play with my forefathers' joints,
And pluck the mangled Tybalt from his shroud,
And in this rage, with some great kinsman's bone   53
As with a club dash out my desp'rate brains?
Oh, look! Methinks I see my cousin's ghost
Seeking out Romeo, that did spit his body   56

Upon a rapier's point. Stay, Tybalt, stay!   57
Romeo, Romeo, Romeo! Here's drink—I drink to thee.
                    [She drinks and falls upon her bed,
                            within the curtains.]

[4.4]

Enter Lady of the House [Capulet's Wife]
and Nurse.

WIFE
Hold, take these keys, and fetch more spices, Nurse.
NURSE
They call for dates and quinces in the pastry.   2

                    Enter old Capulet.

CAPULET
Come, stir, stir, stir! The second cock hath crowed.
The curfew bell hath rung; 'tis three o'clock.
Look to the baked meats, good Angelica.   5
Spare not for cost.
NURSE   Go, you cotquean, go,   6
Get you to bed. Faith, you'll be sick tomorrow
For this night's watching.   8
CAPULET
No, not a whit. What, I have watched ere now
All night for lesser cause, and ne'er been sick.
WIFE
Ay, you have been a mouse-hunt in your time,   11
But I will watch you from such watching now.   12
                    Exeunt Lady and Nurse.
CAPULET   A jealous hood, a jealous hood!   13

                    Enter three or four [Servingmen] with spits and
                    logs, and baskets.

Now, fellow, what is there?
FIRST SERVINGMAN
Things for the cook, sir, but I know not what.
CAPULET   Make haste, make haste. *[Exit First Servingman.]*
[To Second Servingman]   Sirrah, fetch drier logs.
Call Peter. He will show thee where they are.
SECOND SERVINGMAN
I have a head, sir, that will find out logs   18
And never trouble Peter for the matter.
CAPULET
Mass, and well said. A merry whoreson, ha!   20

57 **Stay** Stop, wait
4.4. Location: Scene continues. Juliet's bed remains visible.
2 **pastry** room in which pastry was made.   5 **baked meats** pies, pastry 6 **cotquean** i.e., a man who acts the housewife. (Literally, a cottage housewife.)   8 **watching** being awake.   11 **mouse-hunt** i.e.,
hunter of women. (Literally, a weasel.)   12 **watch . . . watching** i.e.,
keep an eye on you to prevent such nighttime activity. (Playing on
watching in line 8.)   13 **A jealous hood** i.e., You wear the cap of jealousy 18 **I . . . logs** i.e., (1) I have a good head for finding things (2)
My wooden head knows all about logs   20 **Mass** By the Mass.
whoreson i.e., fellow. (An abusive term used familiarly.)

15 **faint** producing faintness.   **thrills** that pierces, shivers 29 **still
been tried** always been tried and proven to be   36 **like** likely. (Also
at line 45.)   37 **conceit** idea 39 **As** namely   42 **green** new, freshly
47 **mandrakes** (The root of the mandragora or mandrake resembled
the human form; the plant was fabled to utter a shriek when torn
from the ground.)   48 **That** so that   50 **fears** objects of fear 53 **rage**
madness.   **great** i.e., of an earlier generation, as in *great*-grandfather
56 **spit** impale

Thou shalt be loggerhead.   [*Exit Servingman.*]
                 Good faith, 'tis day.   21
The County will be here with music straight,   22
For so he said he would.   *Play music* [*within*].
             I hear him near.
Nurse! Wife! What, ho! What, Nurse, I say!

    Enter Nurse.

Go waken Juliet, go and trim her up.
I'll go and chat with Paris. Hie, make haste,
Make haste. The bridegroom he is come already.
Make haste, I say.   [*Exit Capulet.*]

                   ❧

[4.5]

    [*The Nurse goes to the bed.*]

NURSE
Mistress! What, mistress! Juliet!—Fast, I warrant her,
    she.   1
Why, lamb, why, lady! Fie, you slugabed!
Why, love, I say! Madam! Sweetheart! Why, bride!
What, not a word? You take your pennyworths now.   4
Sleep for a week; for the next night, I warrant,
The County Paris hath set up his rest   6
That you shall rest but little. God forgive me,   7
Marry, and amen! How sound is she asleep!   8
I needs must wake her.—Madam, madam, madam!
Ay, let the County take you in your bed;   10
He'll fright you up, i'faith.—Will it not be?
           [*She opens the bedcurtains.*]
What, dressed, and in your clothes, and down again?
I must needs wake you. Lady, lady, lady!
Alas, alas! Help, help! My lady's dead!
Oh, weraday, that ever I was born!   15
Some aqua vitae, ho! My lord! My lady!   16

    [*Enter Capulet's Wife.*]

WIFE
What noise is here?
NURSE   Oh, lamentable day!
WIFE
What is the matter?
NURSE   Look, look! Oh, heavy day!   18
WIFE
Oh, me, oh, me! My child, my only life!
Revive, look up, or I will die with thee!
Help, help! Call help.

    Enter Father [*Capulet*].

CAPULET
For shame, bring Juliet forth. Her lord is come.

NURSE
She's dead, deceased. She's dead, alack the day!
WIFE
Alack the day, she's dead, she's dead, she's dead!
CAPULET
Ha! Let me see her. Out, alas! She's cold.
Her blood is settled, and her joints are stiff;   26
Life and these lips have long been separated.
Death lies on her like an untimely frost
Upon the sweetest flower of all the field.
NURSE
Oh, lamentable day!
WIFE   Oh, woeful time!
CAPULET
Death, that hath ta'en her hence to make me wail,
Ties up my tongue and will not let me speak.

    Enter Friar [*Laurence*] *and the County* [*Paris,
    with Musicians*].

FRIAR LAURENCE
Come, is the bride ready to go to church?
CAPULET
Ready to go, but never to return.
Oh, son, the night before thy wedding day
Hath Death lain with thy wife. There she lies,
Flower as she was, deflowered by him.
Death is my son-in-law, Death is my heir;
My daughter he hath wedded. I will die,
And leave him all; life, living, all is Death's.   40
PARIS
Have I thought long to see this morning's face,   41
And doth it give me such a sight as this?
WIFE
Accurst, unhappy, wretched, hateful day!
Most miserable hour that e'er time saw
In lasting labor of his pilgrimage!   45
But one, poor one, one poor and loving child,
But one thing to rejoice and solace in,
And cruel Death hath catched it from my sight!
NURSE
O woe! O woeful, woeful, woeful day!
Most lamentable day, most woeful day
That ever, ever I did yet behold!
O day, O day, O day! O hateful day!
Never was seen so black a day as this.
O woeful day, O woeful day!
PARIS
Beguiled, divorcèd, wrongèd, spited, slain!
Most detestable Death, by thee beguiled,
By cruel, cruel thee quite overthrown!
O love! O life! Not life, but love in death!
CAPULET
Despised, distressèd, hated, martyred, killed!
Uncomfortable time, why cam'st thou now   60

---

21 **loggerhead** (1) put in charge of getting logs (2) a blockhead.
22 **straight** straightway, immediately
4.5. Location: Scene continues. Juliet's bed remains visible.
1 **Fast** Fast asleep   4 **pennyworths** small portions (of sleep)   6 **set . . .
rest** staked his all, resolved to play all out. (From the card game of
primero, here with obviously bawdy meaning.)   7–8 **God . . . amen!**
(The Nurse apologizes amiably for her bawdy talk.)   10 **take . . . bed**
(1) find you still abed (2) possess you sexually   15 **weraday** wellaway,
alas   16 **aqua vitae** strong alcoholic spirits   18 **heavy** sorrowful

26 **settled** congealed   40 **living** means of living, property
41–64 Have . . . buried (A stage direction in the First Quarto, "*All at
once cry out and wring their hands,*" may suggest that the four mourners are to speak simultaneously, a possibility since all have six lines of
text.)   45 **lasting** unceasing   60 **Uncomfortable** Comfortless

To murder, murder our solemnity?   61
O child! O child! My soul, and not my child!
Dead art thou! Alack, my child is dead,
And with my child my joys are buried.   64

FRIAR LAURENCE
Peace, ho, for shame! Confusion's cure lives not   65
In these confusions. Heaven and yourself
Had part in this fair maid; now heaven hath all,
And all the better is it for the maid.
Your part in her you could not keep from death,   69
But heaven keeps his part in eternal life.
The most you sought was her promotion,   71
For 'twas your heaven she should be advanced;   72
And weep ye now, seeing she is advanced
Above the clouds, as high as heaven itself?
Oh, in this love you love your child so ill
That you run mad, seeing that she is well.
She's not well married that lives married long,
But she's best married that dies married young.
Dry up your tears, and stick your rosemary   79
On this fair corpse, and, as the custom is,
And in her best array, bear her to church;
For though fond nature bids us all lament,   82
Yet nature's tears are reason's merriment.   83

CAPULET
All things that we ordainèd festival   84
Turn from their office to black funeral: 85
Our instruments to melancholy bells,
Our wedding cheer to a sad burial feast,
Our solemn hymns to sullen dirges change,   88
Our bridal flowers serve for a buried corpse,
And all things change them to the contrary.   90

FRIAR LAURENCE
Sir, go you in, and, madam, go with him,
And go, Sir Paris. Everyone prepare
To follow this fair corpse unto her grave.
The heavens do lour upon you for some ill;   94
Move them no more by crossing their high will.   95

Exeunt. Manet [*Nurse with Musicians*].

FIRST MUSICIAN
Faith, we may put up our pipes and be gone.

NURSE
Honest good fellows, ah, put up, put up!
For well you know this is a pitiful case.   [*Exit.*]

FIRST MUSICIAN
Ay, by my troth, the case may be amended.   99

Enter Peter.

PETER   Musicians, oh, musicians, "Heart's ease,"   100
"Heart's ease." Oh, an you will have me live, play
"Heart's ease."

FIRST MUSICIAN   Why "Heart's ease"?

PETER   Oh, musicians, because my heart itself plays "My
heart is full." Oh, play me some merry dump to   105
comfort me.

FIRST MUSICIAN   Not a dump we! 'Tis no time to play
now.

PETER   You will not, then?

FIRST MUSICIAN   No.

PETER   I will then give it you soundly.

FIRST MUSICIAN   What will you give us?

PETER   No money, on my faith, but the gleek; I will give   113
you the minstrel.   114

FIRST MUSICIAN   Then will I give you the serving-   115
creature.   116

PETER   Then will I lay the serving-creature's dagger on   117
your pate. I will carry no crotchets. I'll re you, I'll fa   118
you. Do you note me?   119

FIRST MUSICIAN   An you re us and fa us, you note us.

SECOND MUSICIAN   Pray you, put up your dagger and   121
put out your wit.   122

PETER   Then have at you with my wit! I will dry-beat   123
you with an iron wit, and put up my iron dagger.
Answer me like men:
      "When griping griefs the heart doth wound,   126
            And doleful dumps the mind oppress,
      Then music with her silver sound—"   128
Why "silver sound"? Why "music with her silver
sound"? What say you, Simon Catling?   130

FIRST MUSICIAN   Marry, sir, because silver hath a sweet
sound.

PETER   Pretty! What say you, Hugh Rebeck?   133

SECOND MUSICIAN   I say "silver sound" because musi-
cians sound for silver.   135

PETER   Pretty too! What say you, James Soundpost?   136

THIRD MUSICIAN   Faith, I know not what to say.

---

61 solemnity ceremony, festivity.   **65 Confusion's** Calamity's   **69 Your part** i.e., The mortal part you begot   **71 promotion** social advancement   **72 your heaven** i.e., your idea of the greatest good   **79 rosemary** symbol of immortality and enduring love; therefore used at both funerals and weddings   **82 fond nature** foolish human nature   **83 nature's . . . merriment** that which causes human nature to weep is an occasion of joy to reason.   **84 ordainèd festival** intended to be festive   **85 office** function   **88 sullen** mournful   **90 them** themselves   **94 lour . . . ill** frown upon you because of some sinfulness   **95 Move** anger.   **95.1 Manet** She remains onstage   **99 the case . . . amended** things generally could be much better. (With a punning suggestion of an instrument case that is in need of repair.)   **99.1 Peter** (The Second Quarto has *Enter Will Kemp*, the actor for whom Shakespeare or perhaps the bookkeeper intended this role.)

100 "Heart's ease" (A popular ballad; so too with "My heart is full" in lines 104–5.)   **105 dump** mournful tune or dance   **113 gleek** scornful rebuke   **113–14 I will . . . minstrel** I will insult you by calling you what you are, a minstrel. (Minstrels were widely regarded as vagabonds.)   **115–16 Then . . . serving-creature** Then I'll insult you right back by calling you what you are, a servant.   **117–18 Then . . . crotchets** Then I'll knock you about the head with my dagger. I'll not put up with your whims. (*Crotchets* are also quarter notes, appropriate to the musicians' trade.)   **118–19 I'll re . . . me?** i.e., I'll give you a thrashing, do you hear? (Again using musical terms: *re* and *fa* are the names of notes, and *note* can mean "set to music.")   **121–2 put up . . . wit** sheathe your dagger and stop being a smart aleck. (But *put up* and *put out* can also mean "display." Peter chooses to answer to this meaning.)   **123 have at you** i.e., here I come.   **dry-beat** thrash (without drawing blood)   **126–8 "When . . . sound"** (From Richard Edwards's song, "In Commendation of Music," published in *The Paradise of Dainty Devices*, 1576.)   **130 Catling** (A catling was a small lute-string made of catgut.)   **133 Rebeck** (A rebeck was a fiddle with three strings.)   **135 sound** make music   **136 Soundpost** (A soundpost is the pillar or peg that supports the sounding board of a stringed instrument.)

PETER   Oh, I cry you mercy, you are the singer. I will say   138
for you. It is "music with her silver sound" because
musicians have no gold for sounding: 140
    "Then music with her silver sound
        With speedy help doth lend redress."   *Exit.*
FIRST MUSICIAN   What a pestilent knave is this same!
SECOND MUSICIAN   Hang him, Jack! Come, we'll in here,
tarry for the mourners, and stay dinner.   *Exeunt.*   145

❧

[5.1]

Enter Romeo.

ROMEO
If I may trust the flattering truth of sleep,   1
My dreams presage some joyful news at hand.
My bosom's lord sits lightly in his throne,   3
And all this day an unaccustomed spirit
Lifts me above the ground with cheerful thoughts.
I dreamt my lady came and found me dead—
Strange dream, that gives a dead man leave to
    think!—
And breathed such life with kisses in my lips
That I revived and was an emperor.
Ah me, how sweet is love itself possessed   10
When but love's shadows are so rich in joy!   11

Enter Romeo's man [Balthasar, booted].

News from Verona! How now, Balthasar,
Dost thou not bring me letters from the Friar?
How doth my lady? Is my father well?
How fares my Juliet? That I ask again,
For nothing can be ill if she be well.
BALTHASAR
Then she is well, and nothing can be ill.
Her body sleeps in Capels' monument,
And her immortal part with angels lives.
I saw her laid low in her kindred's vault,
And presently took post to tell it you.   21
Oh, pardon me for bringing these ill news,
Since you did leave it for my office, sir.   23
ROMEO
Is it e'en so? Then I defy you, stars!—
Thou knowest my lodging. Get me ink and paper,
And hire post-horses. I will hence tonight.
BALTHASAR
I do beseech you, sir, have patience.
Your looks are pale and wild, and do import   28
Some misadventure.
ROMEO   Tush, thou art deceived.
Leave me, and do the thing I bid thee do.
Hast thou no letters to me from the Friar?

BALTHASAR
No, my good lord.
ROMEO   No matter. Get thee gone,
And hire those horses. I'll be with thee straight.
                                  Exit [Balthasar].
Well, Juliet, I will lie with thee tonight.
Let's see for means. O mischief, thou art swift   35
To enter in the thoughts of desperate men!
I do remember an apothecary—   37
And hereabouts 'a dwells—which late I noted   38
In tattered weeds, with overwhelming brows,   39
Culling of simples. Meager were his looks;   40
Sharp misery had worn him to the bones;
And in his needy shop a tortoise hung,
An alligator stuffed, and other skins
Of ill-shaped fishes; and about his shelves
A beggarly account of empty boxes,   45
Green earthen pots, bladders, and musty seeds,
Remnants of packthread, and old cakes of roses   47
Were thinly scattered to make up a show.
Noting this penury, to myself I said,
"An if a man did need a poison now,   50
Whose sale is present death in Mantua,   51
Here lives a caitiff wretch would sell it him."   52
Oh, this same thought did but forerun my need,
And this same needy man must sell it me.
As I remember, this should be the house.
Being holiday, the beggar's shop is shut.—
What, ho! Apothecary!

[Enter Apothecary.]

APOTHECARY   Who calls so loud?
ROMEO
Come hither, man. I see that thou art poor.
Hold, there is forty ducats. [*He shows gold*.] Let me
    have   59
A dram of poison, such soon-speeding gear   60
As will disperse itself through all the veins
That the life-weary taker may fall dead,
And that the trunk may be discharged of breath   63
As violently as hasty powder fired
Doth hurry from the fatal cannon's womb.
APOTHECARY
Such mortal drugs I have, but Mantua's law   66
Is death to any he that utters them.   67
ROMEO
Art thou so bare and full of wretchedness,
And fearest to die? Famine is in thy cheeks,

---

138 **cry you mercy** beg your pardon   140 **have . . . sounding** i.e., (1) are paid only silver for playing (2) have no gold to jingle in their pockets   145 **stay** await
5.1. Location: Mantua. A street.
1 **flattering** i.e., telling me what I want to believe   3 **bosom's lord** i.e., heart   10 **itself possessed** actually enjoyed   11 **love's shadows** dreams of love   11.1 *booted* wearing riding boots—a conventional stage sign of traveling   21 **presently took post** at once started off with post-horses   23 **for my office** as my duty   28 **import** denote

35 **for means** by what means.   37 **apothecary** druggist   38 **which . . . noted** whom lately I noticed   39 **weeds** garments.   **overwhelming brows** forehead and eyebrows jutting out over his eyes   40 **simples** medicinal herbs.   **Meager** Impoverished   45 **beggarly account** poor array   47 **cakes of roses** petals pressed into cakes to be used as perfume   50 **An if** If   51 **present** immediate   52 **caitiff** miserable. **would** who would   59 **ducats** gold coins.   60 **soon-speeding gear** quickly effective stuff   63 **trunk** body   66 **mortal** deadly   67 **any he** anyone.   **utters** issues, sells

Need and oppression starveth in thy eyes,   70
Contempt and beggary hangs upon thy back.
The world is not thy friend, nor the world's law;
The world affords no law to make thee rich.
Then be not poor, but break it, and take this.

APOTHECARY
My poverty but not my will consents.

ROMEO
I pay thy poverty and not thy will.

APOTHECARY [*giving poison*]
Put this in any liquid thing you will
And drink it off, and if you had the strength
Of twenty men it would dispatch you straight.

ROMEO [*giving gold*]
There is thy gold—worse poison to men's souls,
Doing more murder in this loathsome world
Than these poor compounds that thou mayst not sell.
I sell thee poison; thou hast sold me none.
Farewell. Buy food, and get thyself in flesh.
                                   [*Exit Apothecary.*]
Come, cordial and not poison, go with me   85
To Juliet's grave, for there must I use thee.   *Exit.*

❧

[5.2]

Enter Friar John to Friar Laurence.

FRIAR JOHN
Holy Franciscan friar! Brother, ho!

Enter [Friar] Laurence.

FRIAR LAURENCE
This same should be the voice of Friar John.
Welcome from Mantua! What says Romeo?
Or if his mind be writ, give me his letter.

FRIAR JOHN
Going to find a barefoot brother out—
One of our order—to associate me   6
Here in this city visiting the sick,
And finding him, the searchers of the town,   8
Suspecting that we both were in a house
Where the infectious pestilence did reign,
Sealed up the doors and would not let us forth,
So that my speed to Mantua there was stayed.   12

FRIAR LAURENCE
Who bare my letter, then, to Romeo?

FRIAR JOHN
I could not send it—here it is again—
Nor get a messenger to bring it thee,
So fearful were they of infection.   [*He gives a letter.*]

FRIAR LAURENCE
Unhappy fortune! By my brotherhood,
The letter was not nice but full of charge,   18
Of dear import, and the neglecting it   19
May do much danger. Friar John, go hence.
Get me an iron crow and bring it straight   21
Unto my cell.

FRIAR JOHN   Brother, I'll go and bring it thee.   *Exit.*

FRIAR LAURENCE
Now must I to the monument alone.
Within this three hours will fair Juliet wake.
She will beshrew me much that Romeo   26
Hath had no notice of these accidents;   27
But I will write again to Mantua,
And keep her at my cell till Romeo come—
Poor living corpse, closed in a dead man's tomb!
                                            Exit.

❧

[5.3]

*Enter Paris, and his Page [bearing flowers, per-
fumed water, and a torch. Juliet, lying in seeming death atop her bier and perhaps concealed at
first from the audience's view, is understood to
be in the Capulets' burial vault, with Tybalt's
body also there.]*

PARIS
Give me thy torch, boy. Hence, and stand aloof.   1
Yet put it out, for I would not be seen.
Under yond yew trees lay thee all along,   3
Holding thy ear close to the hollow ground.
So shall no foot upon the churchyard tread,
Being loose, unfirm, with digging up of graves,   6
But thou shalt hear it. Whistle then to me
As signal that thou hearest something approach.
Give me those flowers. Do as I bid thee. Go.

PAGE [*aside*]
I am almost afraid to stand alone   10
Here in the churchyard, yet I will adventure.
                                      [*He retires.*]

PARIS [*strewing flowers and perfumed water*]
Sweet flower, with flowers thy bridal bed I strew—   12
  Oh, woe! Thy canopy is dust and stones—   13
Which with sweet water nightly I will dew,   14
  Or wanting that, with tears distilled by moans.   15
The obsequies that I for thee will keep   16
Nightly shall be to strew thy grave and weep.
                                   Whistle Boy.
The boy gives warning something doth approach.
What cursèd foot wanders this way tonight

---

18 **nice** trivial. **charge** importance 19 **dear** precious, urgent 21 **crow**
crowbar 26 **beshrew** i.e., reprove 27 **accidents** events
5.3. **Location: Verona.** A churchyard and the vault or tomb belonging to the Capulets. Juliet's bier may be thrust onstage from the
"discovery" space or may be concealed until the tomb is "opened"
by Romeo at 83.1, perhaps by the drawing back of curtains.
1 **aloof** to one side, at a distance. 3 **all along** at full length 6 **Being**
i.e., the soil being 10 **stand** stay 12 **Sweet flower** i.e., Juliet
13 **canopy** covering 14 **sweet** perfumed. **dew** moisten 15 **wanting** lacking 16 **obsequies** ceremonies in memory of the dead

---

70 **starveth** are revealed by the starving look   85 **cordial** restorative
for the heart
5.2. **Location: Verona. Friar Laurence's cell.**
6 **associate** accompany   8 **searchers of the town** town officials charged
with public health (and especially concerned about the *pestilence* or
plague)   12 **speed** successful journey, progress.   **stayed** stopped.

To cross my obsequies and true love's rite?   20
What, with a torch? Muffle me, night, awhile.   21
                                        [*He retires.*]

Enter Romeo and Balthasar, [with a torch, a
mattock, and a crowbar].

ROMEO
Give me that mattock and the wrenching iron.   22
                                    [*He takes the tools.*]
Hold, take this letter. Early in the morning
See thou deliver it to my lord and father.
                        [*He gives a letter and takes a torch.*]
Give me the light. Upon thy life I charge thee,
Whate'er thou hearest or see'st, stand all aloof
And do not interrupt me in my course.   27
Why I descend into this bed of death
Is partly to behold my lady's face,
But chiefly to take thence from her dead finger
A precious ring—a ring that I must use
In dear employment. Therefore hence, begone.   32
But if thou, jealous, dost return to pry   33
In what I farther shall intend to do,
By heaven, I will tear thee joint by joint
And strew this hungry churchyard with thy limbs.   36
The time and my intents are savage-wild,
More fierce and more inexorable far
Than empty tigers or the roaring sea.   39
BALTHASAR
I will be gone, sir, and not trouble ye.
ROMEO
So shalt thou show me friendship. Take thou that.
                                    [*He gives him money.*]
Live, and be prosperous; and farewell, good fellow.
BALTHASAR [*aside*]
For all this same, I'll hide me hereabout.   43
His looks I fear, and his intents I doubt.   [*He retires.*]   44
ROMEO
Thou detestable maw, thou womb of death,   45
Gorged with the dearest morsel of the earth,
Thus I enforce thy rotten jaws to open,
And in despite I'll cram thee with more food.   48
                            [*He begins to open the tomb.*]
PARIS
This is that banished haughty Montague
That murdered my love's cousin, with which grief
It is supposèd the fair creature died,
And here is come to do some villainous shame
To the dead bodies. I will apprehend him.
                                    [*He comes forward.*]
Stop thy unhallowed toil, vile Montague!
Can vengeance be pursued further than death?

Condemnèd villain, I do apprehend thee.
Obey and go with me, for thou must die.
ROMEO
I must indeed, and therefore came I hither.
Good gentle youth, tempt not a desperate man.
Fly hence and leave me. Think upon these gone;   60
Let them affright thee. I beseech thee, youth,
Put not another sin upon my head
By urging me to fury. Oh, begone!
By heaven, I love thee better than myself,
For I come hither armed against myself.
Stay not, begone. Live, and hereafter say
A madman's mercy bid thee run away.
PARIS
I do defy thy conjuration,   68
And apprehend thee for a felon here.
ROMEO
Wilt thou provoke me? Then have at thee, boy!
                                        [*They fight.*]
PAGE
Oh, Lord, they fight! I will go call the watch.   [*Exit.*]
PARIS
Oh, I am slain! [*He falls.*] If thou be merciful,
Open the tomb, lay me with Juliet.   [*He dies.*]
ROMEO
In faith, I will. Let me peruse this face.
Mercutio's kinsman, noble County Paris!
What said my man when my betossèd soul
Did not attend him as we rode? I think
He told me Paris should have married Juliet.   78
Said he not so? Or did I dream it so?
Or am I mad, hearing him talk of Juliet,
To think it was so? Oh, give me thy hand,
One writ with me in sour misfortune's book.
I'll bury thee in a triumphant grave.
                                    [*He opens the tomb.*]
A grave? Oh, no! A lantern, slaughtered youth,   84
For here lies Juliet, and her beauty makes
This vault a feasting presence full of light.   86
Death, lie thou there, by a dead man interred.
                                [*He lays Paris in the tomb.*]
How oft when men are at the point of death
Have they been merry, which their keepers call   89
A lightening before death! Oh, how may I   90
Call this a lightening? O my love, my wife!
Death, that hath sucked the honey of thy breath,
Hath had no power yet upon thy beauty.
Thou art not conquered; beauty's ensign yet   94
Is crimson in thy lips and in thy cheeks,
And death's pale flag is not advancèd there.   96
Tybalt, liest thou there in thy bloody sheet?   97
Oh, what more favor can I do to thee
Than with that hand that cut thy youth in twain
To sunder his that was thine enemy?   100

---

20 cross interrupt   **21 Muffle** Conceal.   **22 wrenching iron** crowbar.
27 course intended action.   **32 dear employment** important business.
33 jealous suspicious   **36 hungry** hungry for corpses   **39 empty**
hungry   **43 For all this same** All the same   **44 fear** distrust.   **doubt**
suspect.   **45 womb** belly   **48 in despite** defiantly   **48.1** *He . . . tomb*
Whether the tomb is represented by a bier thrust onstage or by a curtained recess (see indication of scene location above at the start of
5.3), Romeo may mime the action here and at line 83.1 of using tools
to open it.

60 gone dead   **68 conjuration** solemn entreaty   **78 should have** was
to have   **84 lantern** turret room full of windows   **86 feasting presence** reception chamber for feasting   **89 keepers** attendants, jailers
90 lightening exhilaration (supposed to occur just before death)
94 ensign banner   **96 advancèd** raised   **97 sheet** shroud.   **100 his**
i.e., my (Romeo's) own

Forgive me, cousin!—Ah, dear Juliet,
Why art thou yet so fair? Shall I believe
That unsubstantial Death is amorous,   103
And that the lean abhorrèd monster keeps
Thee here in dark to be his paramour?
For fear of that I still will stay with thee   106
And never from this palace of dim night
Depart again. Here, here will I remain
With worms that are thy chambermaids. Oh, here
Will I set up my everlasting rest   110
And shake the yoke of inauspicious stars
From this world-wearied flesh. Eyes, look your last!
Arms, take your last embrace! And lips, O you
The doors of breath, seal with a righteous kiss
A dateless bargain to engrossing death!   115
                                   [*He kisses Juliet.*]
Come, bitter conduct, come, unsavory guide,   116
Thou desperate pilot, now at once run on   117
The dashing rocks thy seasick weary bark!
Here's to my love. [*He drinks.*] O true apothecary!
Thy drugs are quick. Thus with a kiss I die. [*He dies.*]

Enter Friar [Laurence] with lantern, crow,
and spade.

FRIAR LAURENCE
Saint Francis be my speed! How oft tonight   121
Have my old feet stumbled at graves! Who's there?
BALTHASAR
Here's one, a friend, and one that knows you well.
FRIAR LAURENCE
Bliss be upon you. Tell me, good my friend,
What torch is yond that vainly lends his light   125
To grubs and eyeless skulls? As I discern,   126
It burneth in the Capels' monument.
BALTHASAR
It doth so, holy sir, and there's my master,
One that you love.
FRIAR LAURENCE   Who is it?
BALTHASAR   Romeo.
FRIAR LAURENCE
How long hath he been there?
BALTHASAR   Full half an hour.
FRIAR LAURENCE
Go with me to the vault.
BALTHASAR   I dare not, sir.
My master knows not but I am gone hence,
And fearfully did menace me with death
If I did stay to look on his intents.
FRIAR LAURENCE
Stay, then, I'll go alone. Fear comes upon me.
Oh, much I fear some ill unthrifty thing.   136

BALTHASAR
As I did sleep under this yew tree here
I dreamt my master and another fought,
And that my master slew him.
FRIAR LAURENCE [*advancing to the tomb*]   Romeo!
Alack, alack, what blood is this which stains
The stony entrance of this sepulcher?
What mean these masterless and gory swords
To lie discolored by this place of peace?   143
                           [*He looks in the tomb.*]
Romeo! Oh, pale! Who else? What, Paris too?
And steeped in blood? Ah, what an unkind hour   145
Is guilty of this lamentable chance!
The lady stirs.   [*Juliet wakes.*]
JULIET
O comfortable Friar, where is my lord?   148
I do remember well where I should be,
And there I am. Where is my Romeo?
                              [*A noise within.*]
FRIAR LAURENCE
I hear some noise. Lady, come from that nest
Of death, contagion, and unnatural sleep.
A greater power than we can contradict
Hath thwarted our intents. Come, come away.
Thy husband in thy bosom there lies dead,
And Paris, too. Come, I'll dispose of thee
Among a sisterhood of holy nuns.
Stay not to question, for the watch is coming.
Come, go, good Juliet. [*A noise again.*] I dare no longer
    stay.   *Exit [Friar Laurence].*
JULIET
Go, get thee hence, for I will not away.
What's here? A cup, closed in my true love's hand?
Poison, I see, hath been his timeless end.   162
O churl, drunk all, and left no friendly drop   163
To help me after? I will kiss thy lips;
Haply some poison yet doth hang on them,   165
To make me die with a restorative.   [*She kisses him.*]
Thy lips are warm.

Enter [Paris's] Boy and Watch.

FIRST WATCH   Lead, boy. Which way?
JULIET
Yea, noise? Then I'll be brief. O happy dagger!   169
                          [*She takes Romeo's dagger.*]
This is thy sheath. There rust, and let me die.
                          [*She stabs herself and dies.*]
PAGE
This is the place, there where the torch doth burn.
FIRST WATCH
The ground is bloody. Search about the churchyard.
Go, some of you, whoe'er you find attach.   173
                              [*Exeunt some.*]

Pitiful sight! Here lies the County slain,

103 **unsubstantial** lacking material existence   106 **still** always
110 **set . . . rest** (See 4.5.6. The meaning is, "make my final determination," with allusion to the idea of repose.)   115 **dateless bargain**
everlasting contract.   **engrossing** monopolizing, taking all; also,
drawing up the contract   116 **conduct** guide (i.e., the poison)
117 **desperate** reckless, despairing   121 **be my speed** prosper me and
let me arrive in time.   125 **vainly** uselessly   126 **grubs** insect larvae
136 **unthrifty** unfortunate.

143.1 *He looks . . . tomb* Whether the Friar is to enter the tomb
depends on staging arrangements.   145 **unkind** unnatural
148 **comfortable** comforting   162 **timeless** (1) untimely (2) everlasting   163 **churl** miser   165 **Haply** perhaps   169 **happy** opportune
173 **attach** arrest, detain.

And Juliet bleeding, warm, and newly dead,
Who here hath lain these two days burièd.
Go tell the Prince. Run to the Capulets.
Raise up the Montagues. Some others search.

[*Exeunt others.*]

We see the ground whereon these woes do lie,
But the true ground of all these piteous woes   180
We cannot without circumstance descry.   181

*Enter [some of the Watch, with] Romeo's
man [Balthasar].*

SECOND WATCH
Here's Romeo's man. We found him in the
churchyard.

FIRST WATCH
Hold him in safety till the Prince come hither.   183

*Enter Friar [Laurence], and another Watchman
[with tools].*

THIRD WATCH
Here is a friar, that trembles, sighs, and weeps.
We took this mattock and this spade from him
As he was coming from this churchyard's side.

FIRST WATCH
A great suspicion. Stay the Friar, too.   187

Enter the Prince [and attendants].

PRINCE
What misadventure is so early up
That calls our person from our morning rest?   189

Enter Capels [Capulet and his Wife].

CAPULET
What should it be that is so shrieked abroad?

CAPULET'S WIFE
Oh, the people in the street cry "Romeo,"
Some "Juliet," and some "Paris," and all run
With open outcry toward our monument.

PRINCE
What fear is this which startles in our ears?   194

FIRST WATCH
Sovereign, here lies the County Paris slain,
And Romeo dead, and Juliet, dead before,
Warm and new killed.

PRINCE
Search, seek, and know how this foul murder comes. 198

FIRST WATCH
Here is a friar, and slaughtered Romeo's man,
With instruments upon them fit to open   200
These dead men's tombs.

CAPULET
O heavens! O wife, look how our daughter bleeds!
This dagger hath mista'en, for lo, his house   203
Is empty on the back of Montague,
And it mis-sheathèd in my daughter's bosom!

CAPULET'S WIFE
Oh, me! This sight of death is as a bell
That warns my old age to a sepulcher.

Enter Montague.

PRINCE
Come, Montague, for thou art early up
To see thy son and heir more early down.

MONTAGUE
Alas, my liege, my wife is dead tonight;
Grief of my son's exile hath stopped her breath.
What further woe conspires against mine age?

PRINCE   Look, and thou shalt see.

MONTAGUE [*seeing Romeo's body*]
O thou untaught! What manners is in this,   214
To press before thy father to a grave?   215

PRINCE
Seal up the mouth of outrage for a while,   216
Till we can clear these ambiguities
And know their spring, their head, their true descent; 218
And then will I be general of your woes   219
And lead you even to death. Meantime, forbear,   220
And let mischance be slave to patience.   221
Bring forth the parties of suspicion.   222

FRIAR LAURENCE
I am the greatest, able to do least,
Yet most suspected, as the time and place
Doth make against me, of this direful murder;   225
And here I stand, both to impeach and purge   226
Myself condemnèd and myself excused.   227

PRINCE
Then say at once what thou dost know in this.

FRIAR LAURENCE
I will be brief, for my short date of breath   229
Is not so long as is a tedious tale.
Romeo, there dead, was husband to that Juliet,
And she, there dead, that Romeo's faithful wife.
I married them, and their stol'n marriage day
Was Tybalt's doomsday, whose untimely death
Banished the new-made bridegroom from this city,
For whom, and not for Tybalt, Juliet pined.
You, to remove that siege of grief from her,
Betrothed and would have married her perforce   238
To County Paris. Then comes she to me,
And with wild looks bid me devise some means
To rid her from this second marriage,
Or in my cell there would she kill herself.
Then gave I her—so tutored by my art—
A sleeping potion, which so took effect
As I intended, for it wrought on her   245
The form of death. Meantime I writ to Romeo   246

---

180 ground basis. (Playing on the meaning "earth" in line 179.)   **181
circumstance** details   **183 in safety** under guard   **187 Stay** Detain
189 our person (The royal "we.")   **194 startles** cries alarmingly
198 know learn   **200 instruments** tools   **203 his house** its scabbard

214 untaught ill-mannered youth. (Said with affectionate irony.)
215 press hasten, go   **216 mouth of outrage** (1) popular outcry (2)
entrance to the tomb   **218 spring, head** (Both words mean "source.")
219 be . . . woes be leader in lamentation   **220 even to death** in
lamentation for the dead.   **221 let . . . patience** i.e., let us bear our
misfortune patiently.   **222 of** under   **225 make** conspire, tell
226–7 to . . . excused to accuse myself of what is to be condemned in
me and to exonerate myself where I ought to be excused.   **229 date
of breath** time left to live   **238 perforce** by compulsion   **245 wrought**
fashioned   **246 form** appearance

That he should hither come as this dire night　247
To help to take her from her borrowed grave,
Being the time the potion's force should cease.
But he which bore my letter, Friar John,
Was stayed by accident, and yesternight　251
Returned my letter back. Then all alone
At the prefixèd hour of her waking
Came I to take her from her kindred's vault,
Meaning to keep her closely at my cell　255
Till I conveniently could send to Romeo.
But when I came, some minute ere the time
Of her awakening, here untimely lay
The noble Paris and true Romeo dead.
She wakes, and I entreated her come forth
And bear this work of heaven with patience.
But then a noise did scare me from the tomb,
And she, too desperate, would not go with me,
But, as it seems, did violence on herself.
All this I know, and to the marriage
Her nurse is privy; and if aught in this　266
Miscarried by my fault, let my old life
Be sacrificed some hour before his time　268
Unto the rigor of severest law.

PRINCE
We still have known thee for a holy man.　270
Where's Romeo's man? What can he say to this?

BALTHASAR
I brought my master news of Juliet's death,
And then in post he came from Mantua　273
To this same place, to this same monument.
This letter he early bid me give his father,　275
　　　　　　　　　　　　[showing a letter]
And threatened me with death, going in the vault,
If I departed not and left him there.

PRINCE [taking the letter]
Give me the letter. I will look on it.
Where is the County's page, that raised the watch?
Sirrah, what made your master in this place?　280

PAGE
He came with flowers to strew his lady's grave,
And bid me stand aloof, and so I did.
Anon comes one with light to ope the tomb,
And by and by my master drew on him,
And then I ran away to call the watch.

PRINCE
This letter doth make good the Friar's words,
Their course of love, the tidings of her death;
And here he writes that he did buy a poison
Of a poor 'pothecary, and therewithal　289
Came to this vault to die, and lie with Juliet.
Where be these enemies? Capulet, Montague,
See what a scourge is laid upon your hate,
That heaven finds means to kill your joys with love.　293
And I, for winking at your discords, too　294
Have lost a brace of kinsmen. All are punished.　295

CAPULET
O brother Montague, give me thy hand.
This is my daughter's jointure, for no more　297
Can I demand.

MONTAGUE　　　　But I can give thee more,
For I will raise her statue in pure gold,　299
That whiles Verona by that name is known
There shall no figure at such rate be set　301
As that of true and faithful Juliet.

CAPULET
As rich shall Romeo's by his lady's lie;
Poor sacrifices of our enmity!

PRINCE
A glooming peace this morning with it brings;
　　The sun, for sorrow, will not show his head.
Go hence to have more talk of these sad things.
　　Some shall be pardoned, and some punishèd;
For never was a story of more woe
Than this of Juliet and her Romeo.　　　　[Exeunt.]

247 **as this** this very　251 **stayed** stopped　255 **closely** secretly
266 **privy** in on the secret　268 **his** its　270 **still** always　273 **post**
haste　275 **This . . . father** He bade me give this letter to his father
early in the morning (5.3.23–4)　280 **made** did

289 **therewithal** with the poison　293 **kill your joys** (1) destroy your
happiness (2) kill your children. **with** by means of　294 **winking at**
shutting my eyes to　295 **a brace** of two　297 **jointure** marriage
settlement　299 **raise** (The Second Quarto reading, "raie," is defended
by some editors in the sense of "array," make ready.)　301 **rate** value

Julius Caesar

*J*ulius Caesar stands midway in Shakespeare's dramatic career, at a critical juncture. In some ways, it is an epilogue to his English history plays of the 1590s; in other ways, it introduces the period of the great tragedies. The play evidently was first performed at the new Globe playhouse in the fall of 1599, shortly after *Henry V* (the last of Shakespeare's history plays about medieval England) and around the time of *As You Like It* (one of the last of Shakespeare's happy romantic comedies). It shortly preceded *Hamlet*. It is placed among the tragedies in the Folio of 1623, where it was first published, and is entitled *The Tragedy of Julius Caesar,* but in the table of contents it is listed as *The Life and Death of Julius Caesar* as though it were a history.

Julius Caesar shares with Shakespeare's history plays an absorption in the problems of civil war and popular unrest. Rome, like England, suffers an internal division that is reflected in the perturbed state of the heavens themselves. The commoners, or plebeians, are easily swayed by demagogues. Opportunists prosper in this atmosphere of crisis, although fittingly even they are sometimes undone by their own scheming. Politics seems to require a morality quite apart from that of personal life, posing a tragic dilemma for Brutus, as it did for Richard II or Henry VI. The blending of history and tragedy in *Julius Caesar,* then, is not unlike that found in several English history plays. Rome was a natural subject to which Shakespeare might turn in his continuing depiction of political behavior. Roman culture had recently been elevated to new importance by the classical orientation of the Renaissance. As a model of political organization, it loomed larger in Elizabethan consciousness than it does in ours, because so few other models were available and because Greek culture was less accessible in language and tradition. According to a widely accepted mythology, Elizabethans considered themselves descended from the Romans through another Brutus, the great-grandson of Aeneas.

Yet the differences between Roman and English history are as important as the similarities. Rome's choice during her civil wars lay between a senatorial republican form of government and a strong single ruler. Although the monarchical English might be inclined to be suspicious of republicanism, they had no experience to compare with it—certainly not their various peasants' revolts, such as Jack Cade's rebellion (in *2 Henry VI*). On the other hand, Roman one-man rule as it flourished under Octavius Caesar lacked the English sanctions of divine right. Rome was, after all, a pagan culture, and Shakespeare carefully preserves this non-Christian frame of reference. The gods are frequently invoked and appear to respond with prophetic dreams and auguries, but their ultimate intentions are baffling. Human beings strive blindly; the will of the gods is inscrutable. The outcome of *Julius Caesar* is far different from the restoration of providentially ordained order at the end of *Richard III*. Calm is restored and political authority reestablished, but we are by no means sure that a divine morality has been served. Roman history for Shakespeare is history divested of its divine imperatives and located in a distant political setting, making dispassionate appraisal less difficult. In Plutarch's *Lives of the Noble Grecians and Romans,* as translated by Sir Thomas North, Shakespeare discovered a rich opportunity for pursuing the ironies of political life to which he had been increasingly attracted in the English histories. In fact, he was drawn throughout his career to Plutarch: to the portrait of Portia in "The Life of Marcus Brutus," not only for Portia in *Julius Caesar,* but also for Lucrece in *The Rape of Lucrece,* Kate in *1 Henry IV,* and Portia in *The Merchant of Venice;* to "The Life of Theseus" for the Duke of *A Midsummer Night's Dream;* and to various lives for *Julius Caesar, Coriolanus, Antony and Cleopatra,* and *Timon of Athens.* Freed from the orthodoxies of the Elizabethan worldview, Shakespeare turned in the Roman or classical plays toward irony or outright satire (as in *Troilus and Cressida*) and toward the personal tragedy of political dilemma (as in *Coriolanus* and *Julius Caesar*). These are to be the dominant motifs of the Roman or classical plays, as distinguished from both the English histories and the great tragedies of evil, in which politics plays a lesser part (*Hamlet, Othello, King Lear, Macbeth*).

Julius Caesar is an ambivalent study of civil conflict. As in *Richard II*, the play is structured around two protagonists rather than one. Caesar and Brutus, men of extraordinary abilities and debilitating weaknesses, are more like one another than either would care to admit. This antithetical balance reflects a dual tradition: the medieval view of Dante and of Geoffrey Chaucer, condemning Brutus and Cassius as conspirators, and the Renaissance view of Sir Philip Sidney and Ben Jonson, condemning Caesar as a tyrant. These opposing views still live on in various twentieth-century productions that seek to enlist the play on the side of conservatism or liberalism. In one famous production by Orson Welles for the Mercury Theatre in 1937, Caesar was made out to resemble Benito Mussolini, Italy's fascist dictator, with reference also to Franco's fascists in Spain when that civil war was at its peak. Welles's subtitle for his production, "Death of a Dictator," left no doubt as to the intended statement. The film version of 1953 by John Houseman and Joseph Maniewicz dyed its khaki military uniforms green to suggest the German Wehrmacht; the music adopted for the production deliberately aped the music that accompanied Nazi marching columns in newsreels in the 1930s. Trevor Nunn, at Stratford-upon-Avon in 1972, similarly drew overt parallels to German fascism. At Stratford, Connecticut, in 1979, director Gerald Freedman presented Caesar as a Latin American dictator; at Ashland, Oregon, in 1982, Jerry Turner likened Caesar to Che Guevara. Such interpretations reflect what the conspirators themselves believe, as they cry "Liberty! Freedom! Tyranny is dead!" but the play itself invites widely varying interpretations. Caesar has sometimes appeared as a great leader and a man of great natural authority despite his manifest weaknesses, involved in a struggle to the death with conspirators whose motives and personalities are as complex as his. Anthony Quayle and Michael Langham sought such a balance in their 1950 production at Stratford-upon-Avon; so did Glen Byam Shaw in 1957. The film version of 1953 by John Houseman and Joseph Maniewicz achieved a kind of balance, despite its antifascist leanings, by evenly distributing its major roles among various well-known actors and actresses—John Gielgud as Cassius, Marlon Brando as Antony, James Mason as Brutus, Louis Calhern as Caesar, Greer Garson as Calpurnia, Deborah Kerr as Portia—instead of allowing one actor to dominate the play. Most recent criticism similarly has abandoned the fruitless debate as to whether Brutus or Caesar is the tragic protagonist, and whether one or the other of them is to be seen as morally superior, in favor of a multiple perspective.

Caesar is a study in paradox. He is unquestionably a great general, astute in politics, decisive in his judgments, and sharp in his evaluation of men, as, for example, in his distrust of Cassius with his "lean and hungry look" (1.2.194). Yet this mightiest of men, who in Cassius's phrase bestrides the narrow world "like a Colossus" (line 136), is also deaf in one ear, prone to fevers and epilepsy, unable to compete with Cassius by swimming the Tiber fully armed, and afflicted with a sterile marriage. Physical limitations of this sort are common enough, but in Caesar they are constantly juxtaposed with his aspirations to be above mortal weakness. He dies boasting that he is like the "northern star," constant, unique, "Unshaked of motion" (3.1.61–71). He professes to fear nothing and yet is notoriously superstitious. He calmly reflects that "death, a necessary end, / Will come when it will come," and then arrogantly boasts in the next moment that "Danger knows full well / That Caesar is more dangerous than he" (2.2.36–45). As his wife puts it, Caesar's "wisdom is consumed in confidence" (line 49). He willfully betrays his own best instincts and ignores plain warnings through self-deception. He stops a procession to hear a soothsayer and then dismisses the man as "a dreamer" (1.2.24). He commissions his augurers to determine whether he should stay at home on the ides of March and then persuades himself that acting on their advice would be a sign of weakness. Most fatally, he thinks himself above flattery and so is especially vulnerable to it. So wise and powerful a man as this cannot stop the process of his own fate, because his fate and character are interwoven: he is the victim of his own hubris. His insatiable desire for the crown overbalances his judgment; no warnings of the gods can save him. Even his virtues conspire against him, for he regards himself as one who puts public interest ahead of personal affairs, and so he brushes aside the letter of Artemidorus that would have told him of the conspiracy.

Brutus, for all his opposition to Caesar, is also a paradoxical figure. His strengths are quite unlike those of Caesar, but his weaknesses are surprisingly similar. Brutus is a noble Roman from an ancient family whose glory it has been to defend the personal liberties of Rome, the republican tradition. Brutus's virtues are personal virtues. He enjoys an admirable rapport with his courageous and intelligent wife, and is genuinely kind to his servants. In friendship he is trustworthy. He deplores oaths in the conspiracy because his word is his bond. He finds Caesar's ambition for power distasteful and vulgar; his opposition to Caesar is both idealistic and patrician. Brutus's hubris is a pride of family, and on this score he is vulnerable to flattery. As Cassius reminds him, alluding to Brutus's ancestor Lucius Junius Brutus, who founded the Roman Republic in 509 B.C.: "There was a Brutus once that would have brooked / Th'eternal devil to keep his state in Rome / As easily as a king" (1.2.159–61). Should not Marcus Brutus be the savior of his country from a return to tyranny? Is not he a more fit leader for Rome than Caesar? " 'Brutus' and 'Caesar.' What should be in that 'Caesar'? / Why should that name be sounded more than yours?" (lines 142–3). Cassius's strategy is to present to Brutus numerous testimonials "all tending to the great opinion / That Rome holds of his name" (lines 318–19). Cassius plays the role of tempter here, but the notion he suggests is not new to Brutus.

The parallelism of Brutus's pride and Caesar's ambition is strongly underscored by the way in which these great figures appear to us in two adjoining scenes: 2.1 and 2.2. In these two scenes, the protagonists enter alone during the troubled night, call for a servant, receive the conspirators, and dispute the wise caution of their wives. Both men are predisposed to the temptations that are placed before them. Brutus has often thought of himself as the indispensable man for the preservation of Rome's liberties. Despite his good breeding and coolly rational manner, he is as dominating a personality as Caesar and as hard to move once his mind is made up. Indeed, the conspiracy founders on Brutus's repeated insistence on having his own way. He allows no oaths among the conspirators and will not kill Antony along with Caesar. He permits Antony to speak after him at Caesar's funeral. He vetoes Cicero as a fellow conspirator. In each instance, the other conspirators are unanimously opposed to Brutus's choice but yield to him. Brutus cuts off Cassius's objections before hearing them fully, being accustomed to having his way without dispute. His motives are in part noble and idealistic: Brutus wishes to have the conspirators behave generously and openly, as heroes rather than as henchmen. Yet there is something loftily patrician in his desire to have the fruits of conspiracy without any of the dirty work. His willingness to have Antony speak after him betrays a vain confidence in his own oratory and an unjustified faith in the plebeian mob. Moreover, when Brutus overrides Cassius once more in the decision to fight at Philippi and is proved wrong by the event, no idealistic motive can excuse Brutus's insistence on being obeyed; Cassius is the more experienced soldier. Still, Brutus's fatal limitations as leader of a coup d'état are inseparable from his virtues as a private man. The truth is that such a noble man is, by his very nature, unsuited for the stern exigencies of assassination and civil war. Brutus is strong-minded about his ideals, but he cannot be ruthless. The means and the end of revolution drift further and further apart. He cannot supply his troops at Philippi because he will not forage among the peasants of the countryside and will not countenance among his allies the routine corruptions of an army in time of war, though at the same time that he upbraids Cassius for not sending him gold he does not stop to ask where the gold would come from. Even suicide is distasteful for Brutus, obliging him to embarrass his friends by asking their help. Brutus is too high-minded and genteel a man for the troubled times in which he lives.

The times indeed seem to demand ruthless action of the sort Antony and Octavius are all too ready to provide. The greatest irony of Brutus's fall is that the coup he undertakes for Roman liberty yields only further diminutions of that liberty. The plebeians are not ready for the commonwealth Brutus envisages. From the first, they are portrayed as amiable but "saucy" (even in the opinion of their tribunes, Flavius and Marullus). They adulate Caesar at the expense of their previous idol, Pompey. When Brutus successfully appeals for a moment to their changeable loyalties, they cry "Let him be Caesar," and "Caesar's better parts / Shall be crowned in Brutus" (3.2.51–2). If Brutus were not swayed by this hero-worship, he would have good cause to be disillusioned. To his credit, he is not the demogogue the plebeians take him for and so cannot continue to bend them to his will. Cassius, too, for all his villainlike role as tempter to Brutus, his envious motive, and his Epicurean skepticism, reveals a finer nature as the play progresses. Inspired perhaps by Brutus's philosophic idealism, Cassius turns philosopher also and accepts defeat in a noble but ineffectual cause. Yet even his death is futile; Cassius is misinformed about the fate of his friend Titinius and so stabs himself just when the battle is going well for the conspirators.

The ultimate victors are Antony and Octavius. Antony, whatever finer nature he may possess, becomes under the stress of circumstance a cunning bargainer with the conspirators and a masterful rhetorician who characterizes himself to the plebeians as a "plain blunt man" (3.2.219). In sardonic soliloquy at the end of his funeral oration, he observes, "Now let it work. Mischief, thou art afoot. / Take thou what course thou wilt" (lines 261–2). He is, to be sure, stirred by loyalty to Caesar's memory, but to the end of avenging Caesar's death he is prepared to unleash violence at whatever risk to the state. He regards Lepidus contemptuously as a mere creature under his command. Antony is older than Octavius and teaches the younger man about political realities, but an Elizabethan audience would probably savor the irony that Octavius will subsequently beat Antony at his own game. At Philippi, Octavius's refusal to accept Antony's directions in the battle (5.1.16–20) gives us a glimpse of the peremptory manner for which he is to become famous, like his predecessor. Antony and Octavius together are, in any case, a fearsome pair, matter-of-factly noting down the names of those who must die, including their own kinsmen. They cut off the bequests left to the populace in Caesar's will, by which Antony had won the hearts of the plebeians (4.1). Many innocent persons are sacrificed in the new reign of terror, including Cicero and the poet unluckily named Cinna. In such deaths, art and civilization yield to expediency. Rationality gives way to frenzied rhetoric and to a struggle for power in which

Rome's republican tradition is buried forever. Such is the achievement of Brutus's noble revolution.

Appropriately for such a depiction of ambivalent political strife, *Julius Caesar* is written chiefly in the oratorical mode. It resembles its near contemporary, *Henry V*, in devoting so much attention to speeches of public persuasion. The famous orations following Caesar's assassination—one by Brutus in the so-called Laconic style (that is, concise and sententious) and one by Antony in the Asiatic style (that is, more florid, anecdotal, and literary)—are only the most prominent of many public utterances. In the first scene, Marullus rebukes the plebeians for their disloyalty to Pompey and for the moment dissuades them from idolizing Caesar. Decius Brutus changes Caesar's presumably unalterable mind about staying home on the ides of March (2.2). Caesar lectures the Senate on the virtues of constancy. Before Philippi, the contending armies clash with verbal taunts. Antony and Octavius end the play with tributes to the dead Brutus. In less public scenes as well, oratory serves to win Brutus over to the conspirators, to urge unavailingly that Brutus confide in his wife, or to warn the unheeding Caesar of his danger. The decline of the conspirators' cause shows in their descent from rational discourse to private bickering (4.3). The play gives us a range of rhetorical styles, from the deliberative (having to do with careful consideration of choices) to the forensic (analogous to pleading at law, maintaining one side or the other of a given question), to the epideictic (for display, as in set orations). The imagery, suitably public and rhetorical in its function, is of a fixed star in the firmament, a Colossus bestriding the petty world of humans, a tide of fortune in the affairs of humankind, a statue spouting fountains of blood. The city of Rome is a vivid presence in the play, conveyed at times through Elizabethan anachronisms, such as striking clocks, sweaty nightcaps, "towers and windows, yea, . . . chimney tops" (1.1.39), but in an eclectic fusion of native and classical traditions wherein anachronisms become functionally purposeful. Style affords us one more way of considering *Julius Caesar* as a Janus play, looking back to Shakespeare's history plays and forward to his tragedies.

Women are marginalized in *Julius Caesar*, much as in Shakespeare's English history plays. Portia and Calpurnia are alike, not only in their concern for their husbands' welfare, but also in their inability to do anything to ensure their husbands' safety and prosperity. Fittingly in such an unremittingly patriarchal play, Portia and Calpurnia are noble Roman matrons of the type we also see earlier in *The Rape of Lucrece* or *Titus Andronicus* and later in Octavia (*Antony and Cleopatra*) and Volumnia (*Coriolanus*): unassailably virtuous, descended from patrician stock, and submissive to the essentially male values of unflinching duty and stoical reserve. Portia, daughter of the great Cato of Utica who committed suicide rather than submit to Caesar's tyranny, emulates her father's example by taking her own life rather than outlive her husband's shame in defeat. Calpurnia expounds her prophetic dream of Caesar's bleeding statue (2.2.76–9) only to be rebuked for womanly cowardice. These women do what they can to offer their men an alternative perspective on political ambition—one in which caution and attentiveness to family values stand in opposition to the competitive mores of the male-dominated world—but the women are doomed, like Cassandra and Andromache (in *Troilus and Cressida*), to see their quiet wisdom ignored or misinterpreted. Most touching of all is the scene of marital mutuality between Portia and Brutus (2.1.234–310), in which we realize that Portia's concern and sympathy for her husband cannot save Brutus from himself.

A structural pattern to be found in *Julius Caesar*, as noted by John Velz (see bibliography), is the replicating action of rise and fall by which the great men of ancient Rome succeed one another. The process antedates the play itself, for Pompey's faded glory mentioned in Act 1 is a reminder—or should be a reminder—that good fortune lasts but a day. We behold Caesar at the point of his greatest triumph and his imminent decline to death. "O mighty Caesar! Dost thou lie so low?" asks Antony when he sees the prostrate body of the once most powerful man alive. "Are all thy conquests, glories, triumphs, spoils, / Shrunk to this little measure?" (3.1.150–2). Brutus and Cassius step forward into prominence only to be supplanted by Antony and Octavius. Antony is unaware, though presumably the audience is aware, that Antony is to fall at the hands of Octavius. The process of incessant change, reinforced by such metaphors as the tide in the affairs of humans (already noted), offering its mocking comment on Caesar's self-comparison to the fixed northern star, is not simply a meaningless descent on the grand staircase of history, for Octavius's *Pax Romana* lies at the end of the cycle from republic to empire. Still, that resting place is beyond the conclusion of this open-ended play. What we see here again and again is a human blindness to history, through which a succession of protagonists repeat one another's errors without intending to do so. Cassius, like Caesar, goes to his death in the face of unpropitious omens that he now partly believes to be true. The eagles that accompanied Cassius and his army to Philippi desert him as the moment of battle approaches. These omens suggest a balance between character and fate, for, though the leaders of Rome have one by one fallen through their own acts and choices, they have also, it seems, fulfilled a prearranged destiny. Brutus, confronted by the Ghost of Caesar and assured that he will see this spirit of Caesar at Philippi, answers resolutely, "Why, I will see thee at Philippi, then" (4.3.288). Defeated in battle, as he sensed he would be, Brutus takes his own life. Cassius dies on his birthday. *Sic transit gloria mundi.*

Julius Caesar

[*Dramatis Personae*

JULIUS CAESAR
CALPURNIA, *Caesar's wife*
MARK ANTONY,
OCTAVIUS CAESAR, } *triumvirs after Caesar's death*
LEPIDUS,

MARCUS BRUTUS
PORTIA, *Brutus's wife*
CAIUS CASSIUS,
CASCA,
DECIUS BRUTUS,
CINNA, } *conspirators with Brutus*
METELLUS CIMBER,
TREBONIUS,
CAIUS LIGARIUS,

CICERO,
PUBLIUS, } *senators*
POPILIUS LENA,
FLAVIUS,
MARULLUS, } *tribunes of the people*

SOOTHSAYER
ARTEMIDORUS, *a teacher of rhetoric*
CINNA, *a poet*
Another POET

LUCILIUS,
TITINIUS,
MESSALA,
YOUNG CATO,
VOLUMNIUS,
VARRO, } *officers and soldiers in the army*
CLAUDIUS,   *of Brutus and Cassius*
CLITUS,
DARDANIUS,
LABEO,
FLAVIUS,

PINDARUS, *Cassius's servant*
LUCIUS, } *Brutus's servants*
STRATO,
Caesar's SERVANT
Antony's SERVANT
Octavius's SERVANT

CARPENTER
COBBLER
Five PLEBEIANS
Three SOLDIERS *in Brutus' army*
Two SOLDIERS *in Antony's army*
MESSENGER

GHOST *of Caesar*

Senators, Plebeians, Officers, Soldiers, and Attendants

SCENE: *Rome; the neighborhood of Sardis; the neighborhood of Philippi*]

1.1

Enter Flavius, Marullus, and certain commoners
over the stage.

FLAVIUS
Hence! Home, you idle creatures, get you home!

Is this a holiday? What, know you not,
Being mechanical, you ought not walk   3
Upon a laboring day without the sign   4
Of your profession?—Speak, what trade art thou?
CARPENTER   Why, sir, a carpenter.
MARULLUS
Where is thy leather apron and thy rule?

1.1 Location: Rome. A street.

3 mechanical of the artisan class   **4 sign** garb and implements

What dost thou with thy best apparel on?—
You, sir, what trade are you?

COBBLER Truly, sir, in respect of a fine workman, I am   10
but, as you would say, a cobbler.   11

MARULLUS
But what trade art thou? Answer me directly.

COBBLER A trade, sir, that I hope I may use with a safe
conscience, which is indeed, sir, a mender of bad soles.   14

FLAVIUS
What trade, thou knave? Thou naughty knave, what
trade?   15

COBBLER Nay, I beseech you, sir, be not out with me.   16
Yet if you be out, sir, I can mend you.   17

FLAVIUS
What mean'st thou by that? Mend me, thou saucy
fellow?

COBBLER Why, sir, cobble you.   19

FLAVIUS Thou art a cobbler, art thou?

COBBLER Truly, sir, all that I live by is with the awl. I   21
meddle with no tradesman's matters nor women's   22
matters, but withal I am indeed, sir, a surgeon to old   23
shoes. When they are in great danger, I recover them.   24
As proper men as ever trod upon neat's leather have   25
gone upon my handiwork.

FLAVIUS
But wherefore art not in thy shop today?
Why dost thou lead these men about the streets?

COBBLER Truly, sir, to wear out their shoes, to get myself
into more work. But indeed, sir, we make holiday
to see Caesar and to rejoice in his triumph.   31

MARULLUS
Wherefore rejoice? What conquest brings he home?
What tributaries follow him to Rome   33
To grace in captive bonds his chariot wheels?
You blocks, you stones, you worse than senseless
things!   35
O you hard hearts, you cruel men of Rome,
Knew you not Pompey? Many a time and oft   37
Have you climbed up to walls and battlements,   38
To towers and windows, yea, to chimney tops,   39
Your infants in your arms, and there have sat
The livelong day, with patient expectation,

To see great Pompey pass the streets of Rome.   42
And when you saw his chariot but appear,
Have you not made an universal shout,
That Tiber trembled underneath her banks   45
To hear the replication of your sounds   46
Made in her concave shores?   47
And do you now put on your best attire?
And do you now cull out a holiday?   49
And do you now strew flowers in his way
That comes in triumph over Pompey's blood?   51
Begone!
Run to your houses, fall upon your knees,
Pray to the gods to intermit the plague   54
That needs must light on this ingratitude.   55

FLAVIUS
Go, go, good countrymen, and for this fault
Assemble all the poor men of your sort;   57
Draw them to Tiber banks, and weep your tears
Into the channel, till the lowest stream   59
Do kiss the most exalted shores of all.   60
                              Exeunt all the commoners.
See whe'er their basest mettle be not moved.   61
They vanish tongue-tied in their guiltiness.
Go you down that way towards the Capitol;
This way will I. Disrobe the images   64
If you do find them decked with ceremonies.   65

MARULLUS May we do so?
You know it is the Feast of Lupercal.   67

FLAVIUS
It is no matter. Let no images
Be hung with Caesar's trophies. I'll about   69
And drive away the vulgar from the streets;   70
So do you too, where you perceive them thick.
These growing feathers plucked from Caesar's wing
Will make him fly an ordinary pitch,   73
Who else would soar above the view of men   74
And keep us all in servile fearfulness.   *Exeunt.*

10 in . . . workman (1) as far as skilled work is concerned (2) compared with a skilled worker   11 cobbler (1) one who works with
shoes (2) bungler.   14 soles (With pun on "souls.")   15 naughty
good-for-nothing   16 out out of temper   17 out having worn-out
shoes.   mend you (1) cure your bad temper (2) repair your shoes.
19 cobble you mend your shoes. (The meaning "to pelt with stones"
also suggests itself here, though perhaps it was not in general use
until later in the seventeenth century.)   21 awl (Punning on *all*.)
22 meddle with (1) have to do with (2) have sexual intercourse with
23 withal yet. (With pun on *with awl*.)   24 recover (1) resole (2) cure
25 proper fine, handsome.   as . . . leather (Proverbial. *Neat's leather* is
cowhide.)   31 triumph triumphal procession. (Caesar had overthrown the sons of Pompey the Great in Spain at the Battle of Munda,
March 17, 45 B.C. The triumph was held that October.)   33 tributaries
captives who will pay ransom (tribute)   35 senseless insensible like
stone (hence, unfeeling)   37 Pompey (Caesar had overthrown the
great soldier and onetime triumvir at the Battle of Pharsalus in 48 B.C.
Pompey fled to Egypt, where he was murdered.)   38–9 battlements
. . . chimney tops (The details are appropriate to an Elizabethan
cityscape.)

42 great (Alludes to Pompey's epithet, *Magnus*, "great.")   pass pass
through   45 Tiber the Tiber River   46 replication echo   47 concave
hollowed out, overhanging   49 cull pick   51 Pompey's blood (1)
Pompey's offspring (2) the blood of the Pompeys.   54 intermit suspend   55 needs must must necessarily   57 sort rank   59–60 till . . .
all until even at its lowest reach the river is filled to the brim.   61 See
. . . moved See how even their ignoble natures can be appealed to.
(*Mettle* and *metal* are interchangeable, meaning both "temperament"
and the natural substance. A base *metal* is one that is easily changed
or *moved*, unlike gold; compare 1.2.308–10.)   64 images statues (of
Caesar in royal regalia, set up by his followers)   65 ceremonies ceremonial trappings.   67 Feast of Lupercal a feast of purification
(*Februa*, whence *February*) in honor of Pan, celebrated from ancient
times in Rome on February 15 of each year. (Historically, this celebration came some months after Caesar's triumph in October of 45 B.C.
The celebrants, called *Luperci*, raced around the Palatine Hill and the
Circus carrying thongs of goatskin, with which they lightly struck
those who came in their way. Women so touched were suppposed to
be cured of barrenness; hence Caesar's wish that Antony would
strike Calpurnia, 1.2.6–9.)   69 trophies spoils of war hung up as
memorials of victory.   about go around the other way   70 vulgar
commoners, plebeians   73 pitch highest point in flight. (A term from
falconry.)   74 else otherwise

[1.2]

Enter Caesar, Antony for the course, Calpurnia,
Portia, Decius, Cicero, Brutus, Cassius, Casca, a
Soothsayer; after them, Marullus and Flavius;
[citizens following].

CAESAR
    Calpurnia!
CASCA   Peace, ho! Caesar speaks.
CAESAR   Calpurnia!
CALPURNIA   Here, my lord.
CAESAR
    Stand you directly in Antonio's way   3
    When he doth run his course. Antonio!
ANTONY   Caesar, my lord?
CAESAR
    Forget not, in your speed, Antonio,
    To touch Calpurnia; for our elders say
    The barren, touchèd in this holy chase,
    Shake off their sterile curse.
ANTONY   I shall remember.   9
    When Caesar says "Do this," it is performed.
CAESAR
    Set on, and leave no ceremony out.   [*Flourish.*]   11
SOOTHSAYER   Caesar!
CAESAR   Ha? Who calls?
CASCA
    Bid every noise be still. Peace yet again!
                                    [*The music ceases.*]
CAESAR
    Who is it in the press that calls on me?   15
    I hear a tongue shriller than all the music
    Cry "Caesar!" Speak. Caesar is turned to hear.
SOOTHSAYER
    Beware the ides of March.
CAESAR   What man is that?   18
BRUTUS
    A soothsayer bids you beware the ides of March.
CAESAR
    Set him before me. Let me see his face.
CASSIUS
    Fellow, come from the throng. [*The Soothsayer comes*
    forward.] Look upon Caesar.
CAESAR
    What say'st thou to me now? Speak once again.
SOOTHSAYER   Beware the ides of March.
CAESAR
    He is a dreamer. Let us leave him. Pass.   24
            Sennet. Exeunt. Manent Brutus and Cassius.
CASSIUS
    Will you go see the order of the course?   25

BRUTUS   Not I.
CASSIUS   I pray you, do.
BRUTUS
    I am not gamesome. I do lack some part   28
    Of that quick spirit that is in Antony.
    Let me not hinder, Cassius, your desires;
    I'll leave you.
CASSIUS
    Brutus, I do observe you now of late.
    I have not from your eyes that gentleness
    And show of love as I was wont to have.   34
    You bear too stubborn and too strange a hand   35
    Over your friend that loves you.
BRUTUS   Cassius,
    Be not deceived. If I have veiled my look,   37
    I turn the trouble of my countenance
    Merely upon myself. Vexèd I am   39
    Of late with passions of some difference,   40
    Conceptions only proper to myself,   41
    Which give some soil, perhaps, to my behaviors.   42
    But let not therefore my good friends be grieved—
    Among which number, Cassius, be you one—
    Nor construe any further my neglect
    Than that poor Brutus, with himself at war,
    Forgets the shows of love to other men.
CASSIUS
    Then, Brutus, I have much mistook your passion,
    By means whereof this breast of mine hath buried   49
    Thoughts of great value, worthy cogitations.   50
    Tell me, good Brutus, can you see your face?
BRUTUS
    No, Cassius, for the eye sees not itself
    But by reflection, by some other things.
CASSIUS   'Tis just.   54
    And it is very much lamented, Brutus,
    That you have no such mirrors as will turn
    Your hidden worthiness into your eye,
    That you might see your shadow. I have heard   58
    Where many of the best respect in Rome,   59
    Except immortal Caesar, speaking of Brutus
    And groaning underneath this age's yoke,
    Have wished that noble Brutus had his eyes.   62
BRUTUS
    Into what dangers would you lead me, Cassius,
    That you would have me seek into myself
    For that which is not in me?
CASSIUS
    Therefore, good Brutus, be prepared to hear;
    And since you know you cannot see yourself

**1.2. Location: A public place or street, perhaps as in the previous
scene.**
0.1 *for the course* i.e., stripped for the race, carrying a goatskin thong
3 Antonio (Here and occasionally elsewhere Shakespeare employs
Italian forms of Latin proper names, perhaps for metrical reasons.)
9 sterile curse curse of barrenness.   **11 Set on** Proceed   **15 press**
throng   **18 ides of March** March 15.   **24.1** *Sennet* trumphet call signaling the arrival or departure of a dignitary   *Manent* They remain
onstage   **25 order of the course** ritual and progress of the race.

28 gamesome fond of sports, merry.   **34 wont** accustomed   **35 You
. . . hand** You behave too stubbornly and in too unfriendly a manner.
(The metaphor is from horsemanship.)   **37 veiled my look** i.e., been
introverted, seemed less friendly   **39 Merely** entirely   **40 passions
of some difference** conflicting emotions   **41 only proper to** relating
only to   **42 soil** blemish   **49–50 By . . . value** because of which misunderstanding (my assuming you were displeased with me) I have
kept to myself important thoughts   **54 just** true.   **58 shadow** image,
reflection.   **59 best respect** highest repute and station   **62 had his
eyes** (1) could see things from the perspective of Caesar's critics, or
(2) could see better with his own eyes.

So well as by reflection, I, your glass,   68
Will modestly discover to yourself   69
That of yourself which you yet know not of.
And be not jealous on me, gentle Brutus.   71
Were I a common laughter, or did use   72
To stale with ordinary oaths my love   73
To every new protester; if you know   74
That I do fawn on men and hug them hard
And after scandal them, or if you know   76
That I profess myself in banqueting   77
To all the rout, then hold me dangerous.   78
                                   Flourish, and shout.

BRUTUS
What means this shouting? I do fear the people
Choose Caesar for their king.

CASSIUS   Ay, do you fear it?
Then must I think you would not have it so.

BRUTUS
I would not, Cassius, yet I love him well.
But wherefore do you hold me here so long?
What is it that you would impart to me?
If it be aught toward the general good,
Set honor in one eye and death i'th'other
And I will look on both indifferently;   87
For let the gods so speed me as I love   88
The name of honor more than I fear death.

CASSIUS
I know that virtue to be in you, Brutus,
As well as I do know your outward favor.   91
Well, honor is the subject of my story.
I cannot tell what you and other men
Think of this life; but, for my single self,
I had as lief not be as live to be   95
In awe of such a thing as I myself.   96
I was born free as Caesar, so were you;
We both have fed as well, and we can both
Endure the winter's cold as well as he.
For once, upon a raw and gusty day,
The troubled Tiber chafing with her shores,
Caesar said to me, "Dar'st thou, Cassius, now
Leap in with me into this angry flood
And swim to yonder point?" Upon the word,
Accoutred as I was, I plungèd in   105
And bade him follow; so indeed he did.
The torrent roared, and we did buffet it
With lusty sinews, throwing it aside   108
And stemming it with hearts of controversy.   109

But ere we could arrive the point proposed,
Caesar cried, "Help me, Cassius, or I sink!"
Ay, as Aeneas, our great ancestor,   112
Did from the flames of Troy upon his shoulder
The old Anchises bear, so from the waves of Tiber
Did I the tirèd Caesar. And this man
Is now become a god, and Cassius is
A wretched creature and must bend his body   117
If Caesar carelessly but nod on him.
He had a fever when he was in Spain,
And when the fit was on him I did mark
How he did shake. 'Tis true, this god did shake.
His coward lips did from their color fly,   122
And that same eye whose bend doth awe the world   123
Did lose his luster. I did hear him groan.   124
Ay, and that tongue of his that bade the Romans
Mark him and write his speeches in their books,
Alas, it cried, "Give me some drink, Titinius,"
As a sick girl. Ye gods, it doth amaze me
A man of such a feeble temper should   129
So get the start of the majestic world   130
And bear the palm alone.   *Shout. Flourish.* 131

BRUTUS   Another general shout!
I do believe that these applauses are
For some new honors that are heaped on Caesar.

CASSIUS
Why, man, he doth bestride the narrow world
Like a Colossus, and we petty men   136
Walk under his huge legs and peep about
To find ourselves dishonorable graves.
Men at some time are masters of their fates.
The fault, dear Brutus, is not in our stars,
But in ourselves, that we are underlings.
"Brutus" and "Caesar." What should be in that
    "Caesar"?
Why should that name be sounded more than yours? 143
Write them together, yours is as fair a name;
Sound them, it doth become the mouth as well;
Weigh them, it is as heavy; conjure with 'em,
"Brutus" will start a spirit as soon as "Caesar."   147
Now, in the names of all the gods at once,
Upon what meat doth this our Caesar feed
That he is grown so great? Age, thou art shamed!
Rome, thou hast lost the breed of noble bloods!   151
When went there by an age since the great flood   152

---

68 **glass** mirror   69 **modestly discover** reveal without exaggeration
71 **jealous on** suspicious of.   **gentle** noble   72 **laughter** laughingstock, as at 4.3.114; or perhaps *laugher,* a shallow fellow who laughs at
every jest.   **did use** were accustomed   73 **stale** cheapen, make common.   **ordinary** (1) commonplace (2) customary (3) tavern   74 **protester** one who protests or declares friendship   76 **after scandal**
afterwards slander   77 **profess myself** make declarations of friendship   78 **rout** mob   78.1 *Flourish* Fanfare for a dignitary   87 **indifferently** impartially   88 **speed me** make me prosper   91 **favor**
appearance.   95 **as lief not be** just as soon not exist   96 **such . . .
myself** i.e., a fellow mortal.   105 **Accoutred** fully dressed in armor
108 **lusty sinews** vigorous might. (Literally, tendons.)   109 **stemming** making headway against.   **hearts of controversy** hearts fired
up by rivalry.

112 **Aeneas** hero of Virgil's *Aeneid,* the legendary founder of Rome
(hence *our great ancestor*), who bore his aged father Anchises out of
burning Troy as it was falling to the Greeks   117 **bend his body** bow
122 **color** (1) i.e., normal healthy hue (2) military colors, flag. (The lips
are personified as deserters.)   123 **bend** glance, gaze   124 **his** its
129 **temper** constitution   130 **get . . . of** gain ascendancy over
131 **palm** victor's prize   136 **Colossus** (A 100-foot-high bronze statue
of Helios, the sun god, one of the seven wonders of the ancient
world, was commonly supposed to have stood astride the entrance to
the harbor of Rhodes.)   143 **be sounded** (1) be spoken and celebrated
(2) resound   147 **start** raise. (Perhaps the crowd is heard to shout a
third time at this point, or somewhere else in this conversation. At
line 226 below, we are told that "They shouted thrice.")   151 **the
breed . . . bloods** the bloodline of men of noble stock and valiant
spirit.   152 **flood** i.e., the classical analogue of Noah's flood, in which
all humanity was destroyed except for Deucalion and his wife Pyrrha

But it was famed with more than with one man?   153
When could they say, till now, that talked of Rome,
That her wide walks encompassed but one man?
Now is it Rome indeed, and room enough,   156
When there is in it but one only man.
Oh, you and I have heard our fathers say
There was a Brutus once that would have brooked   159
Th'eternal devil to keep his state in Rome   160
As easily as a king.   161

BRUTUS
That you do love me, I am nothing jealous.   162
What you would work me to, I have some aim.   163
How I have thought of this and of these times
I shall recount hereafter. For this present,
I would not, so with love I might entreat you,   166
Be any further moved. What you have said   167
I will consider; what you have to say
I will with patience hear and find a time
Both meet to hear and answer such high things.   170
Till then, my noble friend, chew upon this:
Brutus had rather be a villager
Than to repute himself a son of Rome
Under these hard conditions as this time
Is like to lay upon us.   175

CASSIUS   I am glad that my weak words
Have struck but thus much show of fire from Brutus.   177

Enter Caesar and his train. [Brutus and
Cassius continue to confer privately.]

BRUTUS
The games are done, and Caesar is returning.

CASSIUS
As they pass by, pluck Casca by the sleeve,
And he will, after his sour fashion, tell you
What hath proceeded worthy note today.

BRUTUS
I will do so. But look you, Cassius,
The angry spot doth glow on Caesar's brow,
And all the rest look like a chidden train.   184
Calpurnia's cheek is pale, and Cicero
Looks with such ferret and such fiery eyes   186
As we have seen him in the Capitol,
Being crossed in conference by some senators.   188

CASSIUS
Casca will tell us what the matter is.

CAESAR   Antonio!

ANTONY   Caesar?

CAESAR
Let me have men about me that are fat,

Sleek-headed men, and such as sleep o' nights.
Yond Cassius has a lean and hungry look.
He thinks too much. Such men are dangerous.

ANTONY
Fear him not, Caesar, he's not dangerous.
He is a noble Roman, and well given.   197

CAESAR
Would he were fatter! But I fear him not.
Yet if my name were liable to fear,
I do not know the man I should avoid
So soon as that spare Cassius. He reads much,
He is a great observer, and he looks
Quite through the deeds of men. He loves no plays,   203
As thou dost, Antony; he hears no music.   204
Seldom he smiles, and smiles in such a sort   205
As if he mocked himself and scorned his spirit
That could be moved to smile at anything.
Such men as he be never at heart's ease
Whiles they behold a greater than themselves,
And therefore are they very dangerous.
I rather tell thee what is to be feared
Than what I fear, for always I am Caesar.
Come on my right hand, for this ear is deaf,
And tell me truly what thou think'st of him.
    Sennet. Exeunt Caesar and his train. [Casca remains
    with Brutus and Cassius.]

CASCA   You pulled me by the cloak. Would you speak   215
with me?

BRUTUS
Ay, Casca. Tell us what hath chanced today,   217
That Caesar looks so sad.   218

CASCA   Why, you were with him, were you not?

BRUTUS
I should not then ask Casca what had chanced.

CASCA   Why, there was a crown offered him; and, being
offered him, he put it by with the back of his hand,
thus, and then the people fell a-shouting.

BRUTUS   What was the second noise for?

CASCA   Why, for that too.

CASSIUS
They shouted thrice. What was the last cry for?   226

CASCA   Why, for that too.

BRUTUS   Was the crown offered him thrice?

CASCA   Ay, marry, was't, and he put it by thrice, every   229
time gentler than other, and at every putting-by mine
honest neighbors shouted.   231

CASSIUS   Who offered him the crown?

CASCA   Why, Antony.

BRUTUS
Tell us the manner of it, gentle Casca.   234

CASCA   I can as well be hanged as tell the manner of it.
It was mere foolery; I did not mark it. I saw Mark An-

---

153 **famed with** famous for   156 **Rome, room** (Pronounced alike.)
159 **Brutus** i.e., Lucius Junius Brutus, who expelled the Tarquins and
founded the Roman republic (c. 509 B.C.).   **brooked** tolerated
160 **keep his state** set himself up in majesty   161 **As . . . king** as readily as he would tolerate a king.   162 **nothing jealous** not at all doubtful.   163 **work** persuade.   **aim** inkling.   166 **so . . . you** if I might
entreat you in the name of friendship   167 **moved** urged.   170 **meet**
fitting   175 **like** likely   177.1 *train* retinue. (See 1.2.0.1–4 for the
names of those in the procession.)   184 **a chidden train** scolded followers.   186 **ferret** ferretlike, i.e., small and red   188 **crossed in conference** opposed in debate

197 **given** disposed.   203 **through** i.e., into the motives of   204 **hears
no music** (Regarded as a sign of a morose and treacherous character.)
205 **sort** manner   215 **cloak** (Elizabethan costume; see also *sleeve*, line
179, and *doublet*, line 265. The Roman toga was sleeveless.)
217 **chanced** happened   218 **sad** serious.   226 **thrice** (See note at
1.2.147.)   229 **marry** i.e., indeed. (Originally, "by the Virgin Mary.")
231 **honest** worthy. (Said contemptuously.)   234 **gentle** noble

tony offer him a crown—yet 'twas not a crown neither, 'twas one of these coronets—and, as I told you, 238 he put it by once; but for all that, to my thinking, he would fain have had it. Then he offered it to him again; 240 then he put it by again; but to my thinking he was very loath to lay his fingers off it. And then he offered it the third time. He put it the third time by, and still 243 as he refused it the rabblement hooted and clapped 244 their chapped hands, and threw up their sweaty night- 245 caps, and uttered such a deal of stinking breath be- 246 cause Caesar refused the crown that it had almost choked Caesar, for he swooned and fell down at it. And for mine own part I durst not laugh for fear of opening my lips and receiving the bad air.

CASSIUS
But soft, I pray you. What, did Caesar swoon? 251

CASCA　He fell down in the marketplace, and foamed at mouth, and was speechless.

BRUTUS
'Tis very like. He hath the falling sickness. 254

CASSIUS
No, Caesar hath it not, but you and I,
And honest Casca, we have the falling sickness.

CASCA　I know not what you mean by that, but I am sure Caesar fell down. If the tag-rag people did not 258 clap him and hiss him, according as he pleased and displeased them, as they use to do the players in the 260 theater, I am no true man. 261

BRUTUS
What said he when he came unto himself?

CASCA　Marry, before he fell down, when he perceived the common herd was glad he refused the crown, he plucked me ope his doublet and offered them his throat 265 to cut. An I had been a man of any occupation, if I 266 would not have taken him at a word, I would I might go to hell among the rogues. And so he fell. When he came to himself again, he said if he had done or said anything amiss, he desired Their Worships to think it was his infirmity. Three or four wenches where I stood cried, "Alas, good soul!" and forgave him with all their hearts. But there's no heed to be taken of them; if Caesar had stabbed their mothers they would have done no less.

BRUTUS
And after that, he came thus sad away? 276

CASCA　Ay.

CASSIUS　Did Cicero say anything?

CASCA　Ay, he spoke Greek.

CASSIUS　To what effect?

CASCA　Nay, an I tell you that, I'll ne'er look you i'th' face again. But those that understood him smiled at one another and shook their heads; but, for mine own part, it was Greek to me. I could tell you more news too. Marullus and Flavius, for pulling scarves off Cae- 285 sar's images, are put to silence. Fare you well. There 286 was more foolery yet, if I could remember it.

CASSIUS　Will you sup with me tonight, Casca?

CASCA　No, I am promised forth. 289

CASSIUS　Will you dine with me tomorrow?

CASCA　Ay, if I be alive, and your mind hold, and your dinner worth the eating.

CASSIUS　Good. I will expect you.

CASCA　Do so. Farewell both.　　　　　　　　　　　　*Exit.*

BRUTUS
What a blunt fellow is this grown to be!
He was quick mettle when he went to school. 296

CASSIUS
So is he now in execution
Of any bold or noble enterprise,
However he puts on this tardy form. 299
This rudeness is a sauce to his good wit, 300
Which gives men stomach to digest his words 301
With better appetite.

BRUTUS
And so it is. For this time I will leave you.
Tomorrow, if you please to speak with me,
I will come home to you; or, if you will,
Come home to me, and I will wait for you.

CASSIUS
I will do so. Till then, think of the world. 307
　　　　　　　　　　　　　　　　　　　Exit Brutus.

Well, Brutus, thou art noble. Yet I see
Thy honorable mettle may be wrought 309
From that it is disposed. Therefore it is meet 310
That noble minds keep ever with their likes;
For who so firm that cannot be seduced?
Caesar doth bear me hard, but he loves Brutus. 313
If I were Brutus now, and he were Cassius,
He should not humor me. I will this night 315
In several hands in at his windows throw, 316
As if they came from several citizens,
Writings, all tending to the great opinion

---

285 **scarves** decorations, festoons　286 **put to silence** dismissed from office. (So reported in Plutarch. Shakespeare's wording ominously suggests that they were executed.)　289 **promised forth** engaged to dine out.　296 **quick mettle** of a lively temperament　299 **However** however much.　**tardy form** air of ennui and disengagement. 300 **rudeness** rough manner.　**wit** intellect　301 **stomach** appetite, inclination　307 **the world** i.e., the state of the world.　309 **mettle** (As often, the word combines the senses of *mettle*, "temperament," and *metal*, "substance." The latter meaning continues here in the chemical metaphor of metal that is *wrought* or transmuted. As *honorable mettle* [or noble metal], gold cannot be transmuted into base substances, and yet Cassius proposes to do just that with Brutus. Compare this with 1.1.61.)　309–10 **wrought . . . disposed** turned away from its natural disposition.　310 **meet** fitting　313 **doth . . . hard** bears me a grudge and keeps me on a short rein.　315 **He . . . humor me** i.e., I wouldn't put up with being cajoled or humored. (*He* could refer to Caesar or Brutus.)　316 **several hands** different handwritings

---

238 **coronets** chaplets, garlands　240 **fain** gladly　243–4 **still as** whenever　245–6 **nightcaps** (Scornful allusion to the *pilleus*, a felt cap worn by the plebeians on festival days.)　251 **soft** i.e., wait a minute 254 **like** likely.　**falling sickness** epilepsy. (But Cassius takes it to mean "falling into servitude.")　258 **tag-rag** ragtag, riffraff　260 **use** are accustomed　261 **true** honest　265 **plucked me ope** pulled open. (*Me* is used colloquially.)　**doublet** Elizabethan upper garment, like a jacket　266 **An** If.　**man . . . occupation** (1) working man (2) man of action　276 **sad** somberly

That Rome holds of his name, wherein obscurely
Caesar's ambition shall be glancèd at.   320
And after this let Caesar seat him sure,   321
For we will shake him, or worse days endure.   *Exit.*

❖

[1.3]

*Thunder and lightning. Enter, [meeting,] Casca
[with his sword drawn] and Cicero.*

CICERO
Good even, Casca. Brought you Caesar home?   1
Why are you breathless? And why stare you so?

CASCA
Are not you moved, when all the sway of earth   3
Shakes like a thing unfirm? Oh, Cicero,
I have seen tempests when the scolding winds
Have rived the knotty oaks, and I have seen   6
Th'ambitious ocean swell and rage and foam
To be exalted with the threat'ning clouds;   8
But never till tonight, never till now,
Did I go through a tempest dropping fire.
Either there is a civil strife in heaven,
Or else the world, too saucy with the gods,   12
Incenses them to send destruction.

CICERO
Why, saw you anything more wonderful?   14

CASCA
A common slave—you know him well by sight—
Held up his left hand, which did flame and burn
Like twenty torches joined, and yet his hand,
Not sensible of fire, remained unscorched.   18
Besides—I ha' not since put up my sword—   19
Against the Capitol I met a lion,   20
Who glazed upon me and went surly by   21
Without annoying me. And there were drawn   22
Upon a heap a hundred ghastly women,   23
Transformèd with their fear, who swore they saw
Men all in fire walk up and down the streets.
And yesterday the bird of night did sit   26
Even at noonday upon the marketplace,
Hooting and shrieking. When these prodigies   28
Do so conjointly meet, let not men say,   29
"These are their reasons, they are natural,"
For I believe they are portentous things
Unto the climate that they point upon.   32

CICERO
Indeed, it is a strange-disposèd time.
But men may construe things after their fashion,   34

Clean from the purpose of the things themselves.   35
Comes Caesar to the Capitol tomorrow?

CASCA
He doth; for he did bid Antonio
Send word to you he would be there tomorrow.

CICERO
Good night then, Casca. This disturbèd sky
Is not to walk in.

CASCA   Farewell, Cicero.   *Exit Cicero.*

Enter Cassius.

CASSIUS
Who's there?

CASCA   A Roman.

CASSIUS   Casca, by your voice.

CASCA
Your ear is good. Cassius, what night is this!   42

CASSIUS
A very pleasing night to honest men.

CASCA
Who ever knew the heavens menace so?

CASSIUS
Those that have known the earth so full of faults.
For my part, I have walked about the streets,
Submitting me unto the perilous night,
And thus unbracèd, Casca, as you see,   48
Have bared my bosom to the thunder-stone;   49
And when the cross blue lightning seemed to open   50
The breast of heaven, I did present myself
Even in the aim and very flash of it.

CASCA
But wherefore did you so much tempt the heavens?
It is the part of men to fear and tremble   54
When the most mighty gods by tokens send   55
Such dreadful heralds to astonish us.   56

CASSIUS
You are dull, Casca, and those sparks of life
That should be in a Roman you do want,   58
Or else you use not. You look pale, and gaze,
And put on fear, and cast yourself in wonder,   60
To see the strange impatience of the heavens.
But if you would consider the true cause
Why all these fires, why all these gliding ghosts,
Why birds and beasts from quality and kind,   64
Why old men, fools, and children calculate,   65
Why all these things change from their ordinance,   66
Their natures, and preformèd faculties,   67
To monstrous quality—why, you shall find   68
That heaven hath infused them with these spirits
To make them instruments of fear and warning
Unto some monstrous state.   71

---

320 **glancèd** hinted   321 **seat him sure** seat himself securely in power (i.e., watch out)
1.3 Location: A street.
1 **Brought** Escorted   3 **sway** established order   6 **rived** split
8 **exalted with** raised to the level of   12 **saucy** insolent   14 **more wonderful** else that was wondrous.   18 **Not sensible of** not feeling
19 **put up** sheathed   20 **Against** in front of, opposite   21 **glazed** stared glassily   22 **annoying** harming   22–3 **drawn . . . heap** huddled together   23 **ghastly** pallid   26 **bird of night** owl, a bird of evil omen   28 **prodigies** abnormalities, wonders   29 **conjointly meet** coincide   32 **climate** region   34 **construe** interpret.   **after their fashion** in their own way

35 **Clean . . . purpose** contrary to the actual import or meaning
42 **what night** what a night   48 **unbracèd** with doublet unfastened
49 **thunder-stone** thunderbolt   50 **cross** forked, jagged   54 **part** appropriate role   55 **tokens** signs   56 **astonish** stun, terrify
58 **want** lack   60 **put on** adopt, show signs of.   **in wonder** into a state of wonder   64 **from . . . kind** (behaving) contrary to their true nature   65 **calculate** reckon, prophesy   66 **ordinance** established nature   67 **preformèd** innate, congenital   68 **monstrous** unnatural
71 **Unto . . . state** pointing to some disorder in the commonwealth or state of affairs.

Now could I, Casca, name to thee a man
Most like this dreadful night,
That thunders, lightens, opens graves, and roars
As doth the lion in the Capitol—
A man no mightier than thyself or me
In personal action, yet prodigious grown   77
And fearful, as these strange eruptions are.   78

CASCA
'Tis Caesar that you mean, is it not, Cassius?

CASSIUS
Let it be who it is. For Romans now
Have thews and limbs like to their ancestors';   81
But, woe the while, our fathers' minds are dead,   82
And we are governed with our mothers' spirits.
Our yoke and sufferance show us womanish.   84

CASCA
Indeed, they say the senators tomorrow
Mean to establish Caesar as a king,
And he shall wear his crown by sea and land
In every place save here in Italy.

CASSIUS
I know where I will wear this dagger then;
Cassius from bondage will deliver Cassius.
Therein, ye gods, you make the weak most strong;   91
Therein, ye gods, you tyrants do defeat.
Nor stony tower, nor walls of beaten brass,   93
Nor airless dungeon, nor strong links of iron,
Can be retentive to the strength of spirit;   95
But life, being weary of these worldly bars,   96
Never lacks power to dismiss itself.
If I know this, know all the world besides,   98
That part of tyranny that I do bear
I can shake off at pleasure.   *Thunder still.*   99

CASCA   So can I.
So every bondman in his own hand bears
The power to cancel his captivity.

CASSIUS
And why should Caesar be a tyrant then?
Poor man, I know he would not be a wolf
But that he sees the Romans are but sheep;
He were no lion, were not Romans hinds.   106
Those that with haste will make a mighty fire
Begin it with weak straws. What trash is Rome,
What rubbish and what offal, when it serves   109
For the base matter to illuminate   110
So vile a thing as Caesar! But, O grief,
Where hast thou led me? I perhaps speak this
Before a willing bondman; then I know
My answer must be made. But I am armed,   114
And dangers are to me indifferent.   115

CASCA
You speak to Casca, and to such a man
That is no fleering telltale. Hold. My hand.   117
Be factious for redress of all these griefs,   118
And I will set this foot of mine as far
As who goes farthest.   [*They shake hands.*]

CASSIUS   There's a bargain made.   120
Now know you, Casca, I have moved already   121
Some certain of the noblest-minded Romans
To undergo with me an enterprise
Of honorable dangerous consequence;
And I do know by this they stay for me   125
In Pompey's porch. For now, this fearful night,   126
There is no stir or walking in the streets,
And the complexion of the element   128
In favor 's like the work we have in hand,   129
Most bloody, fiery, and most terrible.

        Enter Cinna.

CASCA
Stand close awhile, for here comes one in haste.   131

CASSIUS
'Tis Cinna; I do know him by his gait.
He is a friend.—Cinna, where haste you so?

CINNA
To find out you. Who's that? Metellus Cimber?

CASSIUS
No, it is Casca, one incorporate   135
To our attempts. Am I not stayed for, Cinna?

CINNA
I am glad on't. What a fearful night is this!   137
There's two or three of us have seen strange sights.

CASSIUS   Am I not stayed for? Tell me.

CINNA
Yes, you are. Oh, Cassius, if you could
But win the noble Brutus to our party—

CASSIUS
Be you content. Good Cinna, take this paper,   142
          [*giving papers*]
And look you lay it in the praetor's chair,   143
Where Brutus may but find it. And throw this   144
In at his window. Set this up with wax
Upon old Brutus' statue. All this done,   146
Repair to Pompey's porch, where you shall find us. 147
Is Decius Brutus and Trebonius there?

CINNA
All but Metellus Cimber, and he's gone

---

77 **prodigious** ominous   78 **fearful** inspiring fear   81 **thews** sinews, muscles   82 **woe the while** alas for the age   84 **yoke and sufferance** patience under the yoke   91 **Therein** i.e., In the ability to commit suicide   93 **Nor** Neither   95 **Can . . . spirit** can confine a resolute spirit   96 **bars** (1) prison bars (2) burdens (such as tyranny)   98 **know . . . besides** let the rest of the world know   99 s.d. *Thunder still* Continuous thunder.   106 **were** would be.   **hinds** (1) female of the red deer (2) servants, menials.   109 **offal** refuse, wood shavings   110 **matter** i.e., fuel   114 **My answer . . . made** I will have to answer (to Caesar) for what I have said.   **armed** (1) provided with weapons (2) morally fortified   115 **indifferent** unimportant.

117 **fleering** fawning; scornful.   **Hold. My hand** Enough; here is my hand.   118 **factious** active as a partisan.   **griefs** grievances   120 **who** whoever   121 **moved** urged   125 **by this** by this time.   **stay** wait   126 **Pompey's porch** the colonnade of Pompey's great open theater, dedicated in 55 B.C. (Caesar was assassinated there, though Shakespeare has the assassination take place in the Capitol [i.e., the Senate chamber].)   128 **element** sky   129 **favor 's** appearance is   131 **close** concealed, still   135 **incorporate** admitted as a member   137 **on't** of it.   142 **Be you content** Set your mind at rest.   143 **praetor's chair** official seat of a praetor, Roman magistrate ranking next below the consul. (Brutus was praetor, one of sixteen.)   144 **Where . . . it** where Brutus cannot help finding it.   146 **old Brutus** (Lucius Junius Brutus; Brutus was reputed to be his descendant.)   147 **Repair** proceed. (Also in line 152.)

To seek you at your house. Well, I will hie,   150
And so bestow these papers as you bade me.

CASSIUS
    That done, repair to Pompey's theater.   *Exit Cinna.*
    Come, Casca, you and I will yet ere day
    See Brutus at his house. Three parts of him   154
    Is ours already, and the man entire
    Upon the next encounter yields him ours.

CASCA
    Oh, he sits high in all the people's hearts;
    And that which would appear offense in us,   158
    His countenance, like richest alchemy,   159
    Will change to virtue and to worthiness.   160

CASSIUS
    Him and his worth, and our great need of him,
    You have right well conceited. Let us go,   162
    For it is after midnight, and ere day
    We will awake him and be sure of him.   *Exeunt.*

❖

2.1

Enter Brutus in his orchard.

BRUTUS   What, Lucius, ho!—
    I cannot by the progress of the stars
    Give guess how near to day.—Lucius, I say!—
    I would it were my fault to sleep so soundly.—
    When, Lucius, when? Awake, I say! What, Lucius!   5

    Enter Lucius.

LUCIUS   Called you, my lord?
BRUTUS
    Get me a taper in my study, Lucius.   7
    When it is lighted, come and call me here.
LUCIUS   I will, my lord.   *Exit.*
BRUTUS
    It must be by his death. And for my part
    I know no personal cause to spurn at him,   11
    But for the general. He would be crowned.   12
    How that might change his nature, there's the
        question.
    It is the bright day that brings forth the adder,
    And that craves wary walking. Crown him—that—   15
    And then I grant we put a sting in him
    That at his will he may do danger with.
    Th'abuse of greatness is when it disjoins
    Remorse from power. And to speak truth of Caesar,   19

I have not known when his affections swayed   20
More than his reason. But 'tis a common proof   21
That lowliness is young ambition's ladder,   22
Whereto the climber-upward turns his face;
But when he once attains the upmost round   24
He then unto the ladder turns his back,
Looks in the clouds, scorning the base degrees   26
By which he did ascend. So Caesar may.
Then, lest he may, prevent. And since the quarrel
Will bear no color for the thing he is,   29
Fashion it thus: that what he is, augmented,   30
Would run to these and these extremities;
And therefore think him as a serpent's egg
Which, hatched, would, as his kind, grow
    mischievous;   33
And kill him in the shell.

    Enter Lucius.

LUCIUS
    The taper burneth in your closet, sir.   35
    Searching the window for a flint, I found
    This paper, thus sealed up, and I am sure
    It did not lie there when I went to bed.
                            Gives him the letter.
BRUTUS
    Get you to bed again. It is not day.
    Is not tomorrow, boy, the ides of March?   40
LUCIUS   I know not, sir.
BRUTUS
    Look in the calendar and bring me word.
LUCIUS   I will, sir.   *Exit.*
BRUTUS
    The exhalations whizzing in the air   44
    Give so much light that I may read by them.
                        Opens the letter and reads.
    "Brutus, thou sleep'st. Awake, and see thyself!
    Shall Rome, etc. Speak, strike, redress!"
    "Brutus, thou sleep'st. Awake!"
    Such instigations have been often dropped
    Where I have took them up.
    "Shall Rome, etc." Thus must I piece it out:
    Shall Rome stand under one man's awe? What, Rome?
    My ancestors did from the streets of Rome
    The Tarquin drive, when he was called a king.
    "Speak, strike, redress!" Am I entreated
    To speak and strike? O Rome, I make thee promise,
    If the redress will follow, thou receivest   57
    Thy full petition at the hand of Brutus.   58

    Enter Lucius.

LUCIUS   Sir, March is wasted fifteen days.

                            Knock within.

---

150 hie go quickly   **154 parts** i.e., quarters   **158–60 that which . . . worthiness** his endorsement and honorable name will convert into virtue and worthiness those things in our conspiracy that would otherwise seem offensive, just as alchemy is supposed to transform base metals into richest gold.   **162 conceited** (1) conceived, grasped (2) expressed in a figure.
2.1. Location: Rome. Brutus' orchard, or garden.
5 When (An exclamation of impatience.)   **7 Get . . . taper** Put a candle for me   **11 spurn** kick   **12 general** general cause, common good.
15 craves requires.   **that** that is the issue   **19 Remorse** scruple, compassion

20 affections swayed passions ruled   **21 proof** experience   **22 lowliness** pretended humbleness   **24 round** rung   **26 base degrees** (1) lower rungs (2) persons of lower social station   **29 Will . . . is** can carry no appearance of justice so far as his conduct to date is concerned   **30 Fashion** it put the matter   **33 as his kind** according to its nature.   **mischievous** harmful   **35 closet** private chamber, study
40 ides fifteenth day   **44 exhalations** meteors   **57 If . . . follow** i.e., if striking Caesar will lead to the reform of grievances   **58 at** from

BRUTUS

'Tis good. Go to the gate; somebody knocks.

[*Exit Lucius.*]

Since Cassius first did whet me against Caesar,
I have not slept.
Between the acting of a dreadful thing
And the first motion, all the interim is   64
Like a phantasma or a hideous dream.   65
The genius and the mortal instruments   66
Are then in council; and the state of man,   67
Like to a little kingdom, suffers then
The nature of an insurrection.   69

Enter Lucius.

LUCIUS

Sir, 'tis your brother Cassius at the door,   70
Who doth desire to see you.

BRUTUS   Is he alone?

LUCIUS

No, sir. There are more with him.

BRUTUS   Do you know them?

LUCIUS

No, sir. Their hats are plucked about their ears,
And half their faces buried in their cloaks,
That by no means I may discover them   75
By any mark of favor.

BRUTUS   Let 'em enter.   [*Exit Lucius.*]   76

They are the faction. O conspiracy,
Sham'st thou to show thy dangerous brow by night,
When evils are most free? Oh, then, by day   79
Where wilt thou find a cavern dark enough
To mask thy monstrous visage? Seek none,
    conspiracy!
Hide it in smiles and affability;
For if thou put thy native semblance on,
Not Erebus itself were dim enough   84
To hide thee from prevention.   85

Enter the conspirators, Cassius, Casca, Decius,
Cinna, Metellus [Cimber] , and Trebonius.

CASSIUS

I think we are too bold upon your rest.   86
Good morrow, Brutus. Do we trouble you?

BRUTUS

I have been up this hour, awake all night.
Know I these men that come along with you?

CASSIUS

Yes, every man of them, and no man here
But honors you; and every one doth wish
You had but that opinion of yourself

Which every noble Roman bears of you.
This is Trebonius.

BRUTUS   He is welcome hither.

CASSIUS

This, Decius Brutus.

BRUTUS   He is welcome too.

CASSIUS

This, Casca; this, Cinna; and this, Metellus Cimber.

BRUTUS   They are all welcome.

What watchful cares do interpose themselves   98
Betwixt your eyes and night?

CASSIUS   Shall I entreat a word?

They [Brutus and Cassius] whisper.

DECIUS

Here lies the east. Doth not the day break here?   101

CASCA   No.

CINNA

Oh, pardon, sir, it doth; and yon gray lines
That fret the clouds are messengers of day.   104

CASCA

You shall confess that you are both deceived.   105
Here, as I point my sword, the sun arises,
Which is a great way growing on the south,   107
Weighing the youthful season of the year.   108
Some two months hence, up higher toward the north
He first presents his fire; and the high east   110
Stands, as the Capitol, directly here.

BRUTUS [*coming forward*]

Give me your hands all over, one by one.   112

CASSIUS

And let us swear our resolution.

BRUTUS

No, not an oath. If not the face of men,   114
The sufferance of our souls, the time's abuse—   115
If these be motives weak, break off betimes,   116
And every man hence to his idle bed;   117
So let high-sighted tyranny range on   118
Till each man drop by lottery. But if these,   119
As I am sure they do, bear fire enough
To kindle cowards and to steel with valor   121
The melting spirits of women, then, countrymen,
What need we any spur but our own cause
To prick us to redress? What other bond   124
Than secret Romans that have spoke the word   125
And will not palter? And what other oath   126
Than honesty to honesty engaged   127
That this shall be or we will fall for it?

---

64 **motion** proposal or impulse   65 **phantasma** hallucination
66–7 **The genius . . . council** The tutelary god or attendant spirit allotted to every person at birth is then intensely at debate with the person's physical faculties and passionate nature   69 **The nature of an** a
kind of   70 **brother** i.e., brother-in-law. (Cassius had married a sister
of Brutus.)   75 **discover** identify   76 **favor** appearance.   79 **free** free
to roam at will.   84 **Erebus** primeval Darkness (sprung, according to
Hesiod, from Chaos and his sister Night)   85 **prevention** detection
and being forestalled.   86 **upon** in intruding upon

98 **watchful cares** sleep-preventing worries   101 **Here** (Decius points
eastward.)   104 **fret** mark with interlacing lines   105 **deceived** mistaken.   107 **growing** encroaching   108 **Weighing** considering, in
consequence of   110 **high** due   112 **all over** one and all   114–16 **If . . .**
betimes If the gravely serious faces of Romans, the suffering we feel,
the corruptions of the present day are insufficient to move us, we
should break off at once   117 **idle** (1) unused (2) in which men are
idle   118 **high-sighted** upward-gazing (compare with 2.1.26); or
haughty, looking down from on high   119 **by lottery** i.e., as the capricious tyrant chances to pick on him.   **these** i.e., these injustices just
cited   121 **cowards** even cowards.   **steel** harden   124 **prick** spur
125 **Than . . . word** than the word of Romans who, having given their
word of honor, will remain secret   126 **palter** shift position evasively.
127 **honesty** personal honor

Swear priests and cowards and men cautelous,	129
Old feeble carrions, and such suffering souls	130
That welcome wrongs; unto bad causes swear	131
Such creatures as men doubt. But do not stain	132
The even virtue of our enterprise,	133
Nor th'insuppressive mettle of our spirits,	134
To think that or our cause or our performance	135
Did need an oath, when every drop of blood	
That every Roman bears—and nobly bears—	
Is guilty of a several bastardy	138
If he do break the smallest particle	
Of any promise that hath passed from him.	

CASSIUS
But what of Cicero? Shall we sound him?   141
I think he will stand very strong with us.

CASCA
Let us not leave him out.

CINNA   No, by no means.

METELLUS
Oh, let us have him, for his silver hairs
Will purchase us a good opinion   145
And buy men's voices to commend our deeds.
It shall be said his judgment ruled our hands;
Our youths and wildness shall no whit appear,
But all be buried in his gravity.

BRUTUS
Oh, name him not. Let us not break with him,   150
For he will never follow anything
That other men begin.

CASSIUS   Then leave him out.

CASCA   Indeed he is not fit.

DECIUS
Shall no man else be touched but only Caesar?

CASSIUS
Decius, well urged. I think it is not meet   156
Mark Antony, so well beloved of Caesar,
Should outlive Caesar. We shall find of him   158
A shrewd contriver; and you know his means,   159
If he improve them, may well stretch so far   160
As to annoy us all. Which to prevent,   161
Let Antony and Caesar fall together.

BRUTUS
Our course will seem too bloody, Caius Cassius,
To cut the head off and then hack the limbs,
Like wrath in death and envy afterwards;   165
For Antony is but a limb of Caesar.
Let's be sacrificers, but not butchers, Caius.
We all stand up against the spirit of Caesar,
And in the spirit of men there is no blood.

Oh, that we then could come by Caesar's spirit	
And not dismember Caesar! But, alas,	
Caesar must bleed for it. And, gentle friends,	172
Let's kill him boldly, but not wrathfully;	
Let's carve him as a dish fit for the gods,	
Not hew him as a carcass fit for hounds.	
And let our hearts, as subtle masters do,	
Stir up their servants to an act of rage	177
And after seem to chide 'em. This shall make	
Our purpose necessary, and not envious;	179
Which so appearing to the common eyes,	
We shall be called purgers, not murderers.	181
And for Mark Antony, think not of him;	182
For he can do no more than Caesar's arm	
When Caesar's head is off.	

CASSIUS   Yet I fear him,
For in the engrafted love he bears to Caesar—   185

BRUTUS
Alas, good Cassius, do not think of him.
If he love Caesar, all that he can do
Is to himself—take thought and die for Caesar.   188
And that were much he should, for he is given   189
To sports, to wildness, and much company.

TREBONIUS
There is no fear in him. Let him not die,   191
For he will live, and laugh at this hereafter.   192
                                  Clock strikes.

BRUTUS
Peace! Count the clock.

CASSIUS   The clock hath stricken three.

TREBONIUS
'Tis time to part.

CASSIUS   But it is doubtful yet
Whether Caesar will come forth today or no;
For he is superstitious grown of late,
Quite from the main opinion he held once
Of fantasy, of dreams, and ceremonies.   198
It may be these apparent prodigies,   199
The unaccustomed terror of this night,
And the persuasion of his augurers   201
May hold him from the Capitol today.

DECIUS
Never fear that. If he be so resolved,
I can o'ersway him; for he loves to hear
That unicorns may be betrayed with trees,   205
And bears with glasses, elephants with holes,   206
Lions with toils, and men with flatterers;   207

129–32 Swear . . . doubt Let priests and cowards and shifty old men tottering on the brink of the grave swear oaths, and long-suffering souls that submit supinely to wrongs; it is contemptible, untrustworthy persons like these who swear oaths to bad causes. **133 even** steadfast, consistent   **134 insuppressive** indomitable   **135 or . . . or** either . . . or **138 a several bastardy** an individual act unworthy of his parentage **141 sound him** sound him out.   **145 purchase** procure. (Playing on the financial sense of *silver*, line 144.)   **150 break with** confide in **156 meet** fitting   **158 of** in   **159 shrewd** malicious; artful **160 improve** exploit, make good use of   **161 annoy** injure   **165 envy** malice

172 gentle noble   **177 their servants** i.e., our hands   **179 envious** malicious   **181 purgers** those who heal by bleeding the patient **182 for** as for   **185 engrafted** firmly implanted   **188 take thought** give way to melancholy   **189 much he should** more than is to be expected of him, hence unlikely; or, eminently desirable   **191 no fear** nothing to fear   **192.1 Clock strikes** (An anachronism much commented upon; the mechanical clock was not invented until c. 1300.) **198 fantasy** imaginings.   **ceremonies** omens drawn from the performance of some rite.   **199 apparent** manifest, both visible and obvious **201 augurers** augurs, official interpreters of omens   **205 unicorns . . . trees** i.e., by having the unicorn imprison itself by driving its horn into a tree as it charges at the hunter   **206 glasses** mirrors (enabling the hunter to approach the bear while it dazzles itself in the mirror). **holes** pitfalls   **207 toils** nets, snares

But when I tell him he hates flatterers,
He says he does, being then most flattered.
Let me work;
For I can give his humor the true bent,   211
And I will bring him to the Capitol.

CASSIUS
Nay, we will all of us be there to fetch him.

BRUTUS
By the eighth hour. Is that the uttermost?   214

CINNA
Be that the uttermost, and fail not then.

METELLUS
Caius Ligarius doth bear Caesar hard,   216
Who rated him for speaking well of Pompey.   217
I wonder none of you have thought of him.

BRUTUS
Now, good Metellus, go along by him.   219
He loves me well, and I have given him reasons;
Send him but hither, and I'll fashion him.   221

CASSIUS
The morning comes upon 's. We'll leave you, Brutus.
And, friends, disperse yourselves; but all remember
What you have said, and show yourselves true
    Romans.

BRUTUS
Good gentlemen, look fresh and merrily;
Let not our looks put on our purposes,   226
But bear it as our Roman actors do,
With untired spirits and formal constancy.   228
And so good morrow to you every one.   229
                          Exeunt. Manet Brutus.
Boy! Lucius!—Fast asleep? It is no matter.   230
Enjoy the honey-heavy dew of slumber.
Thou hast no figures nor no fantasies   232
Which busy care draws in the brains of men;   233
Therefore thou sleep'st so sound.

        Enter Portia.

PORTIA   Brutus, my lord!
BRUTUS
Portia, what mean you? Wherefore rise you now?
It is not for your health thus to commit
Your weak condition to the raw cold morning.

PORTIA
Nor for yours neither. You've ungently, Brutus,   238
Stole from my bed. And yesternight, at supper,
You suddenly arose, and walked about
Musing and sighing, with your arms across,   241

And when I asked you what the matter was,
You stared upon me with ungentle looks.
I urged you further; then you scratched your head
And too impatiently stamped with your foot.
Yet I insisted, yet you answered not,   246
But with an angry wafture of your hand   247
Gave sign for me to leave you. So I did,
Fearing to strengthen that impatience
Which seemed too much enkindled, and withal   250
Hoping it was but an effect of humor,   251
Which sometime hath his hour with every man.   252
It will not let you eat, nor talk, nor sleep,
And could it work so much upon your shape
As it hath much prevailed on your condition,   255
I should not know you, Brutus. Dear my lord,   256
Make me acquainted with your cause of grief.

BRUTUS
I am not well in health, and that is all.

PORTIA
Brutus is wise, and were he not in health
He would embrace the means to come by it.

BRUTUS
Why, so I do. Good Portia, go to bed.   261

PORTIA
Is Brutus sick? And is it physical   262
To walk unbracèd and suck up the humors   263
Of the dank morning? What, is Brutus sick,
And will he steal out of his wholesome bed
To dare the vile contagion of the night,
And tempt the rheumy and unpurgèd air   267
To add unto his sickness? No, my Brutus,
You have some sick offense within your mind,
Which by the right and virtue of my place
I ought to know of. [*She kneels.*] And upon my knees
I charm you, by my once-commended beauty,   272
By all your vows of love, and that great vow
Which did incorporate and make us one,
That you unfold to me, your self, your half,
Why you are heavy, and what men tonight   276
Have had resort to you; for here have been
Some six or seven, who did hide their faces
Even from darkness.

BRUTUS   Kneel not, gentle Portia.
                                    [*He raises her.*]
PORTIA
I should not need if you were gentle Brutus.
Within the bond of marriage, tell me, Brutus,
Is it excepted I should know no secrets   282
That appertain to you? Am I your self
But as it were in sort or limitation,   284

---

211 humor disposition   **214 the eighth hour** i.e., 8 A.M. (The Elizabethan way of reckoning time. By Roman reckoning, the day began at
6 A.M., so that *the eighth hour* would be 2 P.M.)   **uttermost** latest.
216 bear Caesar hard bear a grudge toward Caesar. (See 1.2.313n.)
217 rated rebuked   **219 by him** by way of his house.   **221 fashion**
shape (to our purposes)   **226 put on** display, wear in open view
228 formal constancy steadfast appearance, decorum.   **229.1 *Manet***
He remains onstage   **230 Lucius** (Brutus calls to his servant, who is
evidently within, asleep, after having admitted the conspirators at
line 85; later, at line 310, he is still within when Brutus calls to him.)
232 figures imaginings   **233 care** anxiety   **238 ungently** discourte-
ously, unkindly   **241 across** folded. (A sign of melancholy.)

246 Yet . . . yet Still . . . still   **247 wafture** waving   **250 withal** moreover   **251 humor** imbalance of temperament   **252 his** its   **255 condition** inner state of mind   **256 know you** recognize you as   **261 so I
do** (Said with a double meaning not perceived by Portia: I seek
through Caesar's death the means to better the health of the state.)
262 physical healthful   **263 unbracèd** with loosened clothing.
humors damps, mists   **267 rheumy and unpurgèd** conducive to illness and not cleansed of its impurities (which night air was thought to
contain)   **272 charm** conjure, entreat   **276 heavy** sad   **282 excepted**
made an exception that   **284 in . . . limitation** only up to a point. (A
legal phrase.)

To keep with you at meals, comfort your bed,　285
And talk to you sometimes? Dwell I but in the suburbs　286
Of your good pleasure? If it be no more,
Portia is Brutus' harlot, not his wife.

BRUTUS
You are my true and honorable wife,
As dear to me as are the ruddy drops
That visit my sad heart.

PORTIA
If this were true, then should I know this secret.
I grant I am a woman, but withal　293
A woman that Lord Brutus took to wife.
I grant I am a woman, but withal
A woman well reputed, Cato's daughter.　296
Think you I am no stronger than my sex,
Being so fathered and so husbanded?
Tell me your counsels, I will not disclose 'em.　299
I have made strong proof of my constancy,
Giving myself a voluntary wound
Here, in the thigh. Can I bear that with patience,
And not my husband's secrets?

BRUTUS　　　　　　　　　　　　O ye gods,
Render me worthy of this noble wife!

Knock [_within_].

Hark, hark, one knocks. Portia, go in awhile,
And by and by thy bosom shall partake
The secrets of my heart.
All my engagements I will construe to thee,　308
All the charactery of my sad brows.　309
Leave me with haste.　　　　　　　　　_Exit Portia._
　　[_Calling_]　　　　Lucius, who's that knocks?

Enter Lucius and [_Caius_] _Ligarius_ [_wearing a
kerchief_].

LUCIUS
Here is a sick man that would speak with you.　311

BRUTUS
Caius Ligarius, that Metellus spake of.
Boy, stand aside.　　　　　　　　[_Exit Lucius._]
　　　　　　　Caius Ligarius, how?　313

LIGARIUS
Vouchsafe good morrow from a feeble tongue.　314

BRUTUS
Oh, what a time have you chose out, brave Caius,　315
To wear a kerchief! Would you were not sick!

LIGARIUS
I am not sick, if Brutus have in hand
Any exploit worthy the name of honor.

BRUTUS
Such an exploit have I in hand, Ligarius,

Had you a healthful ear to hear of it.

LIGARIUS
By all the gods that Romans bow before,
I here discard my sickness! [_He throws off his kerchief._]
　　　　　　　　　　　　Soul of Rome!
Brave son, derived from honorable loins!
Thou like an exorcist hast conjured up
My mortifièd spirit. Now bid me run,　325
And I will strive with things impossible,
Yea, get the better of them. What's to do?

BRUTUS
A piece of work that will make sick men whole.　328

LIGARIUS
But are not some whole that we must make sick?

BRUTUS
That must we also. What it is, my Caius,
I shall unfold to thee as we are going
To whom it must be done.

LIGARIUS　　　　　　　　Set on your foot,　332
And with a heart new-fired I follow you
To do I know not what; but it sufficeth
That Brutus leads me on.　　　　　　_Thunder._

BRUTUS　　　　　　　　Follow me, then.　_Exeunt._

❧

[2.2]

_Thunder and lightning. Enter Julius Caesar, in his
nightgown._

CAESAR
Nor heaven nor earth have been at peace tonight.　1
Thrice hath Calpurnia in her sleep cried out,
"Help, ho, they murder Caesar!"—Who's within?

Enter a Servant.

SERVANT　　My lord?

CAESAR
Go bid the priests do present sacrifice　5
And bring me their opinions of success.　6

SERVANT　　I will, my lord.　　　　　　_Exit._

Enter Calpurnia.

CALPURNIA
What mean you, Caesar? Think you to walk forth?
You shall not stir out of your house today.

CAESAR
Caesar shall forth. The things that threatened me
Ne'er looked but on my back. When they shall see
The face of Caesar, they are vanishèd.

CALPURNIA
Caesar, I never stood on ceremonies,　13

---

285 **keep** stay, be　286 **suburbs** periphery. (In Elizabethan London, prostitutes frequented the suburbs.)　293 **withal** in addition
296 **Cato's daughter** (Cato the Younger of Utica was famous for his integrity; he sided with Pompey against Caesar in 48 B.C. and later killed himself rather than submit to Caesar's tyranny. He was Brutus's uncle as well as his father-in-law.)　299 **counsels** secrets　308 **construe** explain fully　309 **charactery** handwriting, i.e., what is figured there
311 **sick man** (In Elizabethan medicine, a poultice was often applied to the forehead of a patient and wrapped in a handkerchief; hence the kerchief in line 316.)　313 **how?** i.e., how are you?　314 **Vouchsafe** Deign (to accept)　315 **brave** noble

325 **mortifièd** deadened　328 **whole** healthy, i.e., free of the disease of tyranny.　332 **To whom** i.e., to him to whom
2.2 Location: Caesar's house.
0.2 _nightgown_ housecoat.　1 **Nor** Neither　5 **present sacrifice** immediate examination of the entrails of sacrificed animals for omens
6 **success** the result, what will follow.　13 **stood on ceremonies** attached importance to omens

Yet now they fright me. There is one within,
Besides the things that we have heard and seen,
Recounts most horrid sights seen by the watch.   16
A lioness hath whelpèd in the streets,   17
And graves have yawned and yielded up their dead.   18
Fierce fiery warriors fight upon the clouds
In ranks and squadrons and right form of war,   20
Which drizzled blood upon the Capitol.
The noise of battle hurtled in the air;   22
Horses did neigh, and dying men did groan,
And ghosts did shriek and squeal about the streets.
Oh, Caesar, these things are beyond all use,   25
And I do fear them.
CAESAR   What can be avoided
Whose end is purposed by the mighty gods?
Yet Caesar shall go forth; for these predictions
Are to the world in general as to Caesar.
CALPURNIA
When beggars die there are no comets seen;
The heavens themselves blaze forth the death of
    princes.   31
CAESAR
Cowards die many times before their deaths;
The valiant never taste of death but once.
Of all the wonders that I yet have heard,
It seems to me most strange that men should fear,
Seeing that death, a necessary end,
Will come when it will come.

            Enter a Servant.

                    What say the augurers?
SERVANT
They would not have you to stir forth today.
Plucking the entrails of an offering forth,
They could not find a heart within the beast.
CAESAR
The gods do this in shame of cowardice.
Caesar should be a beast without a heart
If he should stay at home today for fear.
No, Caesar shall not. Danger knows full well
That Caesar is more dangerous than he.
We are two lions littered in one day,
And I the elder and more terrible;
And Caesar shall go forth.
CALPURNIA   Alas, my lord,
Your wisdom is consumed in confidence.   49
Do not go forth today! Call it my fear
That keeps you in the house, and not your own.
We'll send Mark Antony to the Senate House,
And he shall say you are not well today.
Let me, upon my knee, prevail in this.   [*She kneels.*]
CAESAR
Mark Antony shall say I am not well,

And for thy humor I will stay at home.   56
                    [*He raises her.*]

            Enter Decius.

Here's Decius Brutus. He shall tell them so.
DECIUS
Caesar, all hail! Good morrow, worthy Caesar.
I come to fetch you to the Senate House.
CAESAR
And you are come in very happy time   60
To bear my greeting to the senators
And tell them that I will not come today.
Cannot is false, and that I dare not, falser;
I will not come today. Tell them so, Decius.
CALPURNIA
Say he is sick.
CAESAR   Shall Caesar send a lie?
Have I in conquest stretched mine arm so far
To be afeard to tell graybeards the truth?
Decius, go tell them Caesar will not come.
DECIUS
Most mighty Caesar, let me know some cause,
Lest I be laughed at when I tell them so.
CAESAR
The cause is in my will: I will not come.
That is enough to satisfy the Senate.
But for your private satisfaction,
Because I love you, I will let you know.
Calpurnia here, my wife, stays me at home.   75
She dreamt tonight she saw my statue,   76
Which like a fountain with an hundred spouts
Did run pure blood; and many lusty Romans   78
Came smiling and did bathe their hands in it.
And these does she apply for warnings and portents   80
Of evils imminent, and on her knee
Hath begged that I will stay at home today.
DECIUS
This dream is all amiss interpreted;
It was a vision fair and fortunate.
Your statue spouting blood in many pipes,
In which so many smiling Romans bathed,
Signifies that from you great Rome shall suck
Reviving blood, and that great men shall press   88
For tinctures, stains, relics, and cognizance.   89
This by Calpurnia's dream is signified.
CAESAR
And this way have you well expounded it.
DECIUS
I have, when you have heard what I can say;
And know it now. The Senate have concluded
To give this day a crown to mighty Caesar.
If you shall send them word you will not come,

---

16 **watch** (An anachronism, since there was no *watch,* or "body of night watchmen," in Caesar's Rome.) 17 **whelpèd** given birth 18 **yawned** gaped 20 **right form** regular formation 22 **hurtled** clashed 25 **use** normal experience 31 **blaze forth** proclaim (in a blaze of light) 49 **consumed in confidence** destroyed by overconfidence.

56 **humor** whim 60 **happy** opportune 75 **stays** detains 76 **tonight** last night 78 **lusty** lively, merry 80 **apply for** interpret as 88 **press** crowd around 89 **tinctures** handkerchiefs dipped in the blood of martyrs, with healing powers; or colors in a coat of arms. (*Tinctures, stains,* and *relics* are all venerated properties, as though Caesar were a saint.) **cognizance** heraldic emblems worn by a nobleman's followers.

Their minds may change. Besides, it were a mock 96
Apt to be rendered for someone to say 97
"Break up the Senate till another time
When Caesar's wife shall meet with better dreams."
If Caesar hide himself, shall they not whisper
"Lo, Caesar is afraid"?
Pardon me, Caesar, for my dear dear love
To your proceeding bids me tell you this, 103
And reason to my love is liable. 104

CAESAR
How foolish do your fears seem now, Calpurnia!
I am ashamèd I did yield to them.
Give me my robe, for I will go.

*Enter Brutus, Ligarius, Metellus, Casca,
Trebonius, Cinna, and Publius.*

And look where Publius is come to fetch me.

PUBLIUS
Good morrow, Caesar.

CAESAR   Welcome, Publius.
What, Brutus, are you stirred so early too?
Good morrow, Casca. Caius Ligarius,
Caesar was ne'er so much your enemy
As that same ague which hath made you lean. 113
What is't o'clock?

BRUTUS   Caesar, 'tis strucken eight. 114

CAESAR
I thank you for your pains and courtesy.

Enter Antony.

See, Antony, that revels long o' nights,
Is notwithstanding up. Good morrow, Antony.

ANTONY   So to most noble Caesar.

CAESAR [*to a Servant*]   Bid them prepare within. 119
                                        [*Exit Servant.*]
I am to blame to be thus waited for.
Now, Cinna. Now, Metellus. What, Trebonius,
I have an hour's talk in store for you;
Remember that you call on me today.
Be near me, that I may remember you.

TREBONIUS
Caesar, I will. [*Aside*] And so near will I be
That your best friends shall wish I had been further.

CAESAR
Good friends, go in and taste some wine with me,
And we, like friends, will straightway go together.

BRUTUS [*aside*]
That every like is not the same, O Caesar, 129
The heart of Brutus earns to think upon!   *Exeunt.* 130

❧

[2.3]

Enter Artemidorus [reading a paper].

ARTEMIDORUS   "Caesar, beware of Brutus; take heed of
Cassius; come not near Casca; have an eye to Cinna;
trust not Trebonius; mark well Metellus Cimber; De-
cius Brutus loves thee not; thou hast wronged Caius
Ligarius. There is but one mind in all these men, and
it is bent against Caesar. If thou be'st not immortal,
look about you. Security gives way to conspiracy. The 7
mighty gods defend thee! Thy lover, 8
                                        Artemidorus."
Here will I stand till Caesar pass along,
And as a suitor will I give him this.
My heart laments that virtue cannot live
Out of the teeth of emulation. 13
If thou read this, O Caesar, thou mayest live;
If not, the Fates with traitors do contrive.   *Exit.* 15

❧

[2.4]

Enter Portia and Lucius.

PORTIA
I prithee, boy, run to the Senate House.
Stay not to answer me, but get thee gone.—
Why dost thou stay?

LUCIUS   To know my errand, madam.

PORTIA
I would have had thee there and here again
Ere I can tell thee what thou shouldst do there.
[*Aside*] O constancy, be strong upon my side; 6
Set a huge mountain 'tween my heart and tongue!
I have a man's mind, but a woman's might.
How hard it is for women to keep counsel!— 9
Art thou here yet?

LUCIUS   Madam, what should I do?
Run to the Capitol, and nothing else?
And so return to you, and nothing else?

PORTIA
Yes, bring me word, boy, if thy lord look well,
For he went sickly forth; and take good note
What Caesar doth, what suitors press to him.
Hark, boy, what noise is that?

LUCIUS   I hear none, madam.

PORTIA   Prithee, listen well.
I heard a bustling rumor, like a fray, 19
And the wind brings it from the Capitol.

LUCIUS   Sooth, madam, I hear nothing. 21

Enter the Soothsayer.

96–7 **mock . . . rendered** sarcastic remark apt to be made   103 **proceeding** advantage   104 **reason . . . liable** my reasoning is swayed by
my affection.   113 **ague** fever   114 **eight** 8 A.M. (See 2.1.214n on
Roman time.)   119 **prepare within** i.e., set out wine in the other room
and prepare to leave. (Perhaps addressed to the servant who entered
at line 37, or to Calpurnia.) The ritual drinking of wine is a pledge of
friendship that should preclude violence; see lines 127–8.
129 **That . . . same** i.e., That not all those who behave "like friends"
(line 128) are actually so. (Proverbial.)   130 **earns** grieves

2.3 **Location:** A street near the Capitol.
7 **Security gives way** Overconfidence opens a path   8 **lover** friend
13 **Out . . . emulation** beyond the bite of grudging envy.   15 **contrive**
conspire.
2.4 **Location:** Before the house of Brutus.
6 **constancy** resolution   9 **counsel** a secret.   19 **bustling rumor** confused sound.   **fray** fight   21 **Sooth** Truly

PORTIA
Come hither, fellow. Which way hast thou been?

SOOTHSAYER At mine own house, good lady.

PORTIA
What is't o'clock?

SOOTHSAYER About the ninth hour, lady. 24

PORTIA
Is Caesar yet gone to the Capitol?

SOOTHSAYER
Madam, not yet. I go to take my stand,
To see him pass on to the Capitol.

PORTIA
Thou hast some suit to Caesar, hast thou not?

SOOTHSAYER
That I have, lady, if it will please Caesar
To be so good to Caesar as to hear me:
I shall beseech him to befriend himself.

PORTIA
Why, know'st thou any harm 's intended towards him?

SOOTHSAYER
None that I know will be, much that I fear may chance.
Good morrow to you. Here the street is narrow.
The throng that follows Caesar at the heels,
Of senators, of praetors, common suitors, 36
Will crowd a feeble man almost to death.
I'll get me to a place more void, and there 38
Speak to great Caesar as he comes along. *Exit.*

PORTIA
I must go in. Ay me, how weak a thing
The heart of woman is! O Brutus,
The heavens speed thee in thine enterprise!—
Sure, the boy heard me.—Brutus hath a suit
That Caesar will not grant.—Oh, I grow faint.—
Run, Lucius, and commend me to my lord;
Say I am merry. Come to me again 46
And bring me word what he doth say to thee.
Exeunt [separately].

❖

3.1

*Flourish. Enter Caesar, Brutus, Cassius, Casca,
Decius, Metellus [Cimber], Trebonius, Cinna,
Antony, Lepidus, Artemidorus, Publius, [Popilius
Lena], and the Soothsayer; [others following].*

CAESAR *[to the Soothsayer]* The ides of March are come.

SOOTHSAYER Ay, Caesar, but not gone.

ARTEMIDORUS Hail, Caesar! Read this schedule. 3

DECIUS
Trebonius doth desire you to o'erread,

At your best leisure, this his humble suit.

ARTEMIDORUS
O Caesar, read mine first, for mine's a suit
That touches Caesar nearer. Read it, great Caesar.

CAESAR
What touches us ourself shall be last served.

ARTEMIDORUS
Delay not, Caesar, read it instantly.

CAESAR
What, is the fellow mad?

PUBLIUS Sirrah, give place. 10

CASSIUS
What, urge you your petitions in the street?
Come to the Capitol.

*[Caesar goes to the Capitol and takes his place, the
rest following.]*

POPILIUS *[to Cassius]*
I wish your enterprise today may thrive.

CASSIUS What enterprise, Popilius?

POPILIUS *[to Cassius]* Fare you well.
[He advances to Caesar.]

BRUTUS What said Popilius Lena?

CASSIUS
He wished today our enterprise might thrive.
I fear our purpose is discoverèd.

BRUTUS
Look how he makes to Caesar. Mark him. 19
[Popilius speaks apart to Caesar.]

CASSIUS
Casca, be sudden, for we fear prevention.
Brutus, what shall be done? If this be known,
Cassius or Caesar never shall turn back, 22
For I will slay myself.

BRUTUS Cassius, be constant. 23
Popilius Lena speaks not of our purposes;
For look, he smiles, and Caesar doth not change. 25

CASSIUS
Trebonius knows his time, for look you, Brutus,
He draws Mark Antony out of the way.
[Exit Trebonius with Antony.]

DECIUS
Where is Metellus Cimber? Let him go
And presently prefer his suit to Caesar. 29

BRUTUS
He is addressed. Press near and second him. 30

CINNA
Casca, you are the first that rears your hand.
[They press near Caesar.]

CAESAR
Are we all ready? What is now amiss
That Caesar and his Senate must redress?

---

24 **the ninth hour** i.e., 9 A.M. (In Roman reckoning, the ninth hour
would be 3 P.M.) 36 **praetors** judges 38 **void** empty, uncrowded
46 **merry** cheerful. (Not "mirthful.")
**3.1 Location: Before the Capitol, and, following line 12, within the
Capitol.**
0.4. *others following* (Citizens may be present, though not certainly
so; see lines 83 and 93–4.) 3 **schedule** document.

10 **Sirrah** Fellow. (A form of address to a social inferior.) **place** way.
19 **makes to** advances toward **22–3 Cassius . . . myself** Either Cassius or Caesar will never return from the Capitol alive, for I will commit suicide if this attempt fails. 23 **be constant** hold steady.
25 **change** change expression. 29 **presently prefer** immediately urge
30 **addressed** ready.

METELLUS [*kneeling*]
Most high, most mighty, and most puissant Caesar,   34
Metellus Cimber throws before thy seat
An humble heart—
CAESAR   I must prevent thee, Cimber.   36
These couchings and these lowly courtesies   37
Might fire the blood of ordinary men,   38
And turn preordinance and first decree   39
Into the law of children. Be not fond   40
To think that Caesar bears such rebel blood   41
That will be thawed from the true quality   42
With that which melteth fools—I mean, sweet words,
Low-crookèd curtsies, and base spaniel fawning.   44
Thy brother by decree is banishèd.
If thou dost bend and pray and fawn for him,   46
I spurn thee like a cur out of my way.   47
Know, Caesar doth not wrong, nor without cause
Will he be satisfied.
METELLUS
Is there no voice more worthy than my own
To sound more sweetly in great Caesar's ear
For the repealing of my banished brother?   52
BRUTUS [*kneeling*]
I kiss thy hand, but not in flattery, Caesar,
Desiring thee that Publius Cimber may
Have an immediate freedom of repeal.   55
CAESAR
What, Brutus?
CASSIUS [*kneeling*]   Pardon, Caesar! Caesar, pardon!
As low as to thy foot doth Cassius fall,
To beg enfranchisement for Publius Cimber.   58
CAESAR
I could be well moved, if I were as you;
If I could pray to move, prayers would move me.   60
But I am constant as the northern star,   61
Of whose true-fixed and resting quality   62
There is no fellow in the firmament.   63
The skies are painted with unnumbered sparks;
They are all fire and every one doth shine;
But there's but one in all doth hold his place.
So in the world: 'tis furnished well with men,
And men are flesh and blood, and apprehensive;   68
Yet in the number I do know but one
That unassailable holds on his rank,   70
Unshaked of motion. And that I am he,   71
Let me a little show it even in this:

That I was constant Cimber should be banished,
And constant do remain to keep him so.
CINNA [*kneeling*]
O Caesar—
CAESAR   Hence! Wilt thou lift up Olympus?   75
DECIUS [*kneeling*]
Great Caesar—
CAESAR   Doth not Brutus bootless kneel?   76
CASCA   Speak hands for me!
          They stab Caesar, [Casca first, Brutus last].
CAESAR   *Et tu, Brutè?* Then fall, Caesar!   *Dies.*   78
CINNA
Liberty! Freedom! Tyranny is dead!
Run hence, proclaim, cry it about the streets.
CASSIUS
Some to the common pulpits, and cry out   81
"Liberty, freedom, and enfranchisement!"   82
BRUTUS
People and senators, be not affrighted.
Fly not; stand still. Ambition's debt is paid.   84
CASCA
Go to the pulpit, Brutus.
DECIUS   And Cassius too.
BRUTUS   Where's Publius?   86
CINNA
Here, quite confounded with this mutiny.   87
METELLUS
Stand fast together, lest some friend of Caesar's
Should chance—
BRUTUS
Talk not of standing. Publius, good cheer.   90
There is no harm intended to your person,
Nor to no Roman else. So tell them, Publius.
CASSIUS
And leave us, Publius, lest that the people,
Rushing on us, should do your age some mischief.
BRUTUS
Do so, and let no man abide this deed   95
But we the doers.   [*Exeunt all but the conspirators.*]

          Enter Trebonius.

CASSIUS
Where is Antony?
TREBONIUS   Fled to his house amazed.   97
Men, wives, and children stare, cry out, and run
As it were doomsday.
BRUTUS   Fates, we will know your pleasures.   99
That we shall die, we know; 'tis but the time,   100
And drawing days out, that men stand upon.   101

CASCA
  Why, he that cuts off twenty years of life
  Cuts off so many years of fearing death.
BRUTUS
  Grant that, and then is death a benefit.
  So are we Caesar's friends, that have abridged
  His time of fearing death. Stoop, Romans, stoop,
  And let us bathe our hands in Caesar's blood
  Up to the elbows and besmear our swords.
  Then walk we forth even to the marketplace,   109
  And, waving our red weapons o'er our heads,
  Let's all cry "Peace, freedom, and liberty!"
CASSIUS
  Stoop, then, and wash. [*They bathe their hands and
      weapons.*] How many ages hence
  Shall this our lofty scene be acted over
  In states unborn and accents yet unknown!   114
BRUTUS
  How many times shall Caesar bleed in sport,   115
  That now on Pompey's basis lies along   116
  No worthier than the dust!
CASSIUS   So oft as that shall be,
  So often shall the knot of us be called   119
  The men that gave their country liberty.
DECIUS
  What, shall we forth?
CASSIUS   Ay, every man away.
  Brutus shall lead, and we will grace his heels   122
  With the most boldest and best hearts of Rome.

          Enter a Servant.

BRUTUS
  Soft, who comes here? A friend of Antony's.
SERVANT [*kneeling*]
  Thus, Brutus, did my master bid me kneel;
  Thus did Mark Antony bid me fall down,
  And, being prostrate, thus he bade me say:
  "Brutus is noble, wise, valiant, and honest;   128
  Caesar was mighty, bold, royal, and loving.
  Say I love Brutus and I honor him;
  Say I feared Caesar, honored him, and loved him.
  If Brutus will vouchsafe that Antony
  May safely come to him and be resolved   133
  How Caesar hath deserved to lie in death,
  Mark Antony shall not love Caesar dead
  So well as Brutus living, but will follow
  The fortunes and affairs of noble Brutus
  Thorough the hazards of this untrod state   138
  With all true faith." So says my master Antony.
BRUTUS
  Thy master is a wise and valiant Roman;
  I never thought him worse.

Tell him, so please him come unto this place,   142
  He shall be satisfied and, by my honor,
  Depart untouched.
SERVANT   I'll fetch him presently.   144
                                Exit Servant.
BRUTUS
  I know that we shall have him well to friend.   145
CASSIUS
  I wish we may. But yet have I a mind
  That fears him much, and my misgiving still   147
  Falls shrewdly to the purpose.   148

          Enter Antony.

BRUTUS
  But here comes Antony.—Welcome, Mark Antony.
ANTONY
  O mighty Caesar! Dost thou lie so low?
  Are all thy conquests, glories, triumphs, spoils,
  Shrunk to this little measure? Fare thee well.—
  I know not, gentlemen, what you intend,
  Who else must be let blood, who else is rank;   154
  If I myself, there is no hour so fit
  As Caesar's death's hour, nor no instrument
  Of half that worth as those your swords, made rich
  With the most noble blood of all this world.
  I do beseech ye, if you bear me hard,   159
  Now, whilst your purpled hands do reek and smoke,   160
  Fulfill your pleasure. Live a thousand years,   161
  I shall not find myself so apt to die;   162
  No place will please me so, no mean of death,
  As here by Caesar, and by you cut off,
  The choice and master spirits of this age.
BRUTUS
  Oh, Antony, beg not your death of us.
  Though now we must appear bloody and cruel,
  As by our hands and this our present act
  You see we do, yet see you but our hands
  And this the bleeding business they have done.
  Our hearts you see not. They are pitiful;   171
  And pity to the general wrong of Rome—
  As fire drives out fire, so pity pity—   173
  Hath done this deed on Caesar. For your part,
  To you our swords have leaden points, Mark Antony.   175
  Our arms in strength of malice, and our hearts   176
  Of brothers' temper, do receive you in   177
  With all kind love, good thoughts, and reverence.
CASSIUS
  Your voice shall be as strong as any man's   179
  In the disposing of new dignities.   180

---

109 **the marketplace** i.e., the Forum   114 **accents** languages   115 **in sport** for entertainment   116 **on Pompey's . . . along** lies prostrate on the pedestal of Pompey's statue   119 **knot** group   122 **grace his heels** follow him close at heels (in a triumphal procession; cf. 1.1.34)   128 **honest** honorable   133 **be resolved** receive an explanation   138 **Thorough** through.   **untrod state** still unexplored state of affairs

142 **so** if it should   144 **presently** immediately.   145 **to friend** for a friend.   147 **fears** distrusts   148 **Falls . . . purpose** is intensely to the point.   154 **let blood** bled (a medical term), i.e., killed.   **rank** swollen, diseased (and hence in need of bleeding), i.e.,   159 **bear me hard** bear ill will to me   160 **purpled** bloody.   **reek** steam   161 **Live** If I should live   162 **apt** ready   171 **pitiful** full of pity   173 **pity pity** i.e., pity for the general wrong of Rome has driven out pity for Caesar   175 **leaden** i.e., blunt   176–7 **Our . . . temper** i.e., Both our arms, though seeming strong in enmity, and our hearts, full of brotherly feeling   179 **voice** vote, authority   180 **dignities** offices of state.

BRUTUS
　Only be patient till we have appeased
　The multitude, beside themselves with fear,
　And then we will deliver you the cause   183
　Why I, that did love Caesar when I struck him,
　Have thus proceeded.
ANTONY   I doubt not of your wisdom.
　Let each man render me his bloody hand.
　　　　　　[*He shakes hands with the conspirators.*]
　First, Marcus Brutus, will I shake with you;
　Next, Caius Cassius, do I take your hand;
　Now, Decius Brutus, yours; now yours, Metellus;
　Yours, Cinna; and, my valiant Casca, yours;
　Though last, not least in love, yours, good Trebonius.
　Gentlemen all—alas, what shall I say?
　My credit now stands on such slippery ground   193
　That one of two bad ways you must conceit me,   194
　Either a coward or a flatterer.
　That I did love thee, Caesar, oh, 'tis true!
　If then thy spirit look upon us now,
　Shall it not grieve thee dearer than thy death   198
　To see thy Antony making his peace,
　Shaking the bloody fingers of thy foes—
　Most noble—in the presence of thy corpse?
　Had I as many eyes as thou hast wounds,
　Weeping as fast as they stream forth thy blood,
　It would become me better than to close   204
　In terms of friendship with thine enemies.
　Pardon me, Julius! Here wast thou bayed, brave hart, 206
　Here didst thou fall, and here thy hunters stand,
　Signed in thy spoil and crimsoned in thy lethe.   208
　O world, thou wast the forest to this hart,
　And this indeed, O world, the heart of thee!
　How like a deer, strucken by many princes,
　Dost thou here lie!
CASSIUS
　Mark Antony—
ANTONY   Pardon me, Caius Cassius.
　The enemies of Caesar shall say this;   214
　Then in a friend it is cold modesty.   215
CASSIUS
　I blame you not for praising Caesar so,
　But what compact mean you to have with us?
　Will you be pricked in number of our friends,   218
　Or shall we on and not depend on you?
ANTONY
　Therefore I took your hands, but was indeed
　Swayed from the point by looking down on Caesar.
　Friends am I with you all, and love you all,

Upon this hope, that you shall give me reasons
Why and wherein Caesar was dangerous.
BRUTUS
　Or else were this a savage spectacle.   225
　Our reasons are so full of good regard   226
　That were you, Antony, the son of Caesar,
　You should be satisfied.
ANTONY   That's all I seek,
　And am moreover suitor that I may
　Produce his body to the marketplace,   230
　And in the pulpit, as becomes a friend,   231
　Speak in the order of his funeral.   232
BRUTUS
　You shall, Mark Antony.
CASSIUS   Brutus, a word with you.
　[*Aside to Brutus*] You know not what you do. Do not
　　consent
　That Antony speak in his funeral.
　Know you how much the people may be moved
　By that which he will utter?
BRUTUS [*aside to Cassius*]   By your pardon:
　I will myself into the pulpit first
　And show the reason of our Caesar's death.
　What Antony shall speak, I will protest   240
　He speaks by leave and by permission,
　And that we are contented Caesar shall
　Have all true rites and lawful ceremonies.
　It shall advantage more than do us wrong.
CASSIUS [*aside to Brutus*]
　I know not what may fall. I like it not.   245
BRUTUS
　Mark Antony, here, take you Caesar's body.
　You shall not in your funeral speech blame us,
　But speak all good you can devise of Caesar,
　And say you do't by our permission.
　Else shall you not have any hand at all
　About his funeral. And you shall speak
　In the same pulpit whereto I am going,
　After my speech is ended.
ANTONY   Be it so.
　I do desire no more.
BRUTUS
　Prepare the body then, and follow us.   255
　　　　　　　　　　　　　　Exeunt. Manet Antony.
ANTONY
　Oh, pardon me, thou bleeding piece of earth,
　That I am meek and gentle with these butchers!
　Thou art the ruins of the noblest man
　That ever livèd in the tide of times.   259
　Woe to the hand that shed this costly blood!   260
　Over thy wounds now do I prophesy—
　Which, like dumb mouths, do ope their ruby lips

---

183 deliver report to   **193 credit** credibility   **194 conceit** think, judge
198 dearer more deeply   **204 close** come to an agreement
206 bayed brought to bay.   **hart** stag. (With pun on *heart*.)
208 Signed . . . spoil marked with the tokens of your slaughter.
(The *spoil* in hunting is the cutting up of the quarry and distribution
of reward to the hounds.)   **lethe** river of oblivion in the underworld,
here associated with death and blood. (Perhaps fused with Cocytus,
river of blood in the underworld.)   **214 The enemies** Even the
enemies   **215 cold modesty** sober moderation.   **218 pricked** marked
down

225 else were this otherwise this would be   **226 regard** account, consideration   **230 Produce** bring forth.   **marketplace** Forum
231 pulpit public platform   **232 order** ceremony   **240 protest**
announce, insist   **245 fall** befall, happen.   **255.1 Manet** He remains
onstage   **259 tide of times** course of all history.   **260 costly** (1) valuable (2) fraught with dire consequences

To beg the voice and utterance of my tongue—
A curse shall light upon the limbs of men;
Domestic fury and fierce civil strife
Shall cumber all the parts of Italy;   266
Blood and destruction shall be so in use
And dreadful objects so familiar   268
That mothers shall but smile when they behold
Their infants quartered with the hands of war,   270
All pity choked with custom of fell deeds;   271
And Caesar's spirit, ranging for revenge,   272
With Ate by his side come hot from hell,   273
Shall in these confines with a monarch's voice   274
Cry havoc and let slip the dogs of war,   275
That this foul deed shall smell above the earth
With carrion men, groaning for burial.

Enter Octavius' Servant.

You serve Octavius Caesar, do you not?
SERVANT   I do, Mark Antony.
ANTONY
Caesar did write for him to come to Rome.
SERVANT
He did receive his letters, and is coming,   281
And bid me say to you by word of mouth—
O Caesar!—   [*Seeing the body.*]
ANTONY
Thy heart is big. Get thee apart and weep.
Passion, I see, is catching, for mine eyes,   285
Seeing those beads of sorrow stand in thine,
Began to water. Is thy master coming?
SERVANT
He lies tonight within seven leagues of Rome.   288
ANTONY
Post back with speed and tell him what hath chanced.   289
Here is a mourning Rome, a dangerous Rome,
No Rome of safety for Octavius yet;   291
Hie hence and tell him so. Yet stay awhile;
Thou shalt not back till I have borne this corpse
Into the marketplace. There shall I try,   294
In my oration, how the people take
The cruel issue of these bloody men,   296
According to the which thou shalt discourse   297
To young Octavius of the state of things.   298
Lend me your hand.   *Exeunt* [*with Caesar's body*].

---

266 **cumber** overwhelm; entangle, burden   268 **objects** sights
270 **quartered** cut to pieces   271 **custom . . . deeds** the familiarity of
cruel deeds   272 **ranging** roaming up and down in search of prey
273 **Ate** goddess of discord and moral chaos   274 **confines** regions.
monarch's i.e., authoritative   275 **Cry havoc** give the signal for sack,
pillage, and slaughter, taking no prisoners.   **let slip** unleash
281 **letters** (Not necessarily plural. The Latin word for letter, *litterae*,
has a plural form.)   285 **Passion** Sorrow   288 **lies** lodges.   **seven
leagues** about twenty miles   289 **Post** Ride.   **chanced** happened.
291 **Rome** (With pun on "room," as at 1.2.156.)   294 **try** test
296 **cruel issue** outcome of the cruelty   297 **the which** the outcome of which   298 **young Octavius** (He was eighteen in March
of 44 B.C.)

[3.2]

Enter Brutus and [*presently*] *goes into the pulpit,
and Cassius, with the Plebeians.*

PLEBEIANS
We will be satisfied! Let us be satisfied!   1
BRUTUS
Then follow me, and give me audience, friends.—
Cassius, go you into the other street
And part the numbers.   4
Those that will hear me speak, let 'em stay here;
Those that will follow Cassius, go with him;
And public reasons shall be renderèd
Of Caesar's death.
FIRST PLEBEIAN   I will hear Brutus speak.
SECOND PLEBEIAN
I will hear Cassius, and compare their reasons
When severally we hear them renderèd.   10
            [*Exit Cassius, with some of the Plebeians.*]
THIRD PLEBEIAN
The noble Brutus is ascended. Silence!
BRUTUS   Be patient till the last.
Romans, countrymen, and lovers, hear me for my   13
cause, and be silent that you may hear. Believe me for
mine honor, and have respect to mine honor, that you
may believe. Censure me in your wisdom, and awake   16
your senses, that you may the better judge. If there be 17
any in this assembly, any dear friend of Caesar's, to
him I say that Brutus' love to Caesar was no less than
his. If then that friend demand why Brutus rose
against Caesar, this is my answer: not that I loved Caesar less, but that I loved Rome more. Had you rather
Caesar were living and die all slaves, than that Caesar
were dead, to live all free men? As Caesar loved me, I
weep for him; as he was fortunate, I rejoice at it; as he
was valiant, I honor him; but, as he was ambitious, I
slew him. There is tears for his love; joy for his fortune;
honor for his valor; and death for his ambition.
Who is here so base that would be a bondman? If any,
speak, for him have I offended. Who is here so rude   30
that would not be a Roman? If any, speak, for him
have I offended. Who is here so vile that will not love
his country? If any, speak, for him have I offended. I
pause for a reply.
ALL   None, Brutus, none!
BRUTUS   Then none have I offended. I have done no
more to Caesar than you shall do to Brutus. The ques-   37
tion of his death is enrolled in the Capitol, his glory   38
not extenuated wherein he was worthy, nor his   39

3.2 Location: The Forum.
1 **be satisfied** have an explanation.   4 **part** divide   10 **severally** separately   13 **lovers** friends. (This speech by Brutus is in what Plutarch
calls the Lacedemonian or Spartan style, brief and sententious. Its
content is original with Shakespeare.)   16 **Censure** Judge   17 **senses**
intellectual powers   30 **rude** barbarous   37 **than . . . Brutus** (In lines
45–7 below, Brutus offers to die for Rome if his country should ask.)
37–8 **The question . . . enrolled** The considerations that necessitated
his death are recorded   39 **extenuated** minimized

offenses enforced for which he suffered death.   40

Enter Mark Antony [and others] with Caesar's body.

Here comes his body, mourned by Mark Antony, who, though he had no hand in his death, shall receive the benefit of his dying, a place in the commonwealth, as which of you shall not? With this I depart, that, as I slew my best lover for the good of Rome, I have the   45
same dagger for myself when it shall please my country to need my death.

ALL   Live, Brutus, live, live!   *[Brutus comes down.]*

FIRST PLEBEIAN
Bring him with triumph home unto his house.

SECOND PLEBEIAN
Give him a statue with his ancestors.   50

THIRD PLEBEIAN
Let him be Caesar.

FOURTH PLEBEIAN   Caesar's better parts
Shall be crowned in Brutus.

FIRST PLEBEIAN
We'll bring him to his house with shouts and clamors.

BRUTUS
My countrymen—

SECOND PLEBEIAN   Peace, silence! Brutus speaks.

FIRST PLEBEIAN   Peace, ho!

BRUTUS
Good countrymen, let me depart alone,
And, for my sake, stay here with Antony.
Do grace to Caesar's corpse, and grace his speech   58
Tending to Caesar's glories, which Mark Antony,   59
By our permission, is allowed to make.
I do entreat you, not a man depart,
Save I alone, till Antony have spoke.   *Exit.*

FIRST PLEBEIAN
Stay, ho, and let us hear Mark Antony.

THIRD PLEBEIAN
Let him go up into the public chair.
We'll hear him. Noble Antony, go up.

ANTONY
For Brutus' sake I am beholding to you.   66
    [He goes into the pulpit.]

FOURTH PLEBEIAN   What does he say of Brutus?

THIRD PLEBEIAN   He says, for Brutus' sake
He finds himself beholding to us all.

FOURTH PLEBEIAN
'Twere best he speak no harm of Brutus here.

FIRST PLEBEIAN
This Caesar was a tyrant.

THIRD PLEBEIAN   Nay, that's certain.
We are blest that Rome is rid of him.

SECOND PLEBEIAN
Peace! Let us hear what Antony can say.

ANTONY
You gentle Romans—

ALL   Peace, ho! Let us hear him.

ANTONY
Friends, Romans, countrymen, lend me your ears.   75
I come to bury Caesar, not to praise him.
The evil that men do lives after them;
The good is oft interrèd with their bones.
So let it be with Caesar. The noble Brutus
Hath told you Caesar was ambitious,
If it were so, it was a grievous fault,
And grievously hath Caesar answered it.   82
Here, under leave of Brutus and the rest—   83
For Brutus is an honorable man,
So are they all, all honorable men—
Come I to speak in Caesar's funeral.
He was my friend, faithful and just to me;
But Brutus says he was ambitious,
And Brutus is an honorable man.
He hath brought many captives home to Rome,
Whose ransoms did the general coffers fill.
Did this in Caesar seem ambitious?
When that the poor have cried, Caesar hath wept;   93
Ambition should be made of sterner stuff.
Yet Brutus says he was ambitious,
And Brutus is an honorable man.
You all did see that on the Lupercal   97
I thrice presented him a kingly crown,
Which he did thrice refuse. Was this ambition?
Yet Brutus says he was ambitious,
And sure he is an honorable man.
I speak not to disprove what Brutus spoke,
But here I am to speak what I do know.
You all did love him once, not without cause.
What cause withholds you then to mourn for him?
O judgment! Thou art fled to brutish beasts,
And men have lost their reason. Bear with me;
My heart is in the coffin there with Caesar,
And I must pause till it come back to me.

FIRST PLEBEIAN
Methinks there is much reason in his sayings.

SECOND PLEBEIAN
If thou consider rightly of the matter,
Caesar has had great wrong.

THIRD PLEBEIAN   Has he, masters?   112
I fear there will a worse come in his place.

FOURTH PLEBEIAN
Marked ye his words? He would not take the crown,
Therefore 'tis certain he was not ambitious.

FIRST PLEBEIAN
If it be found so, some will dear abide it.   116

---

40 **enforced** exaggerated, insisted upon   45 **lover** friend   50 SECOND PLEBEIAN (Not the same person who exited at line 10; the numbering here refers to those who stay to hear Brutus.)   58 **Do grace** Show respect.   **grace his speech** listen courteously to Antony's speech   59 **Tending to** relating to, dealing with   66 **beholding** beholden

75 **Friends** (This speech by Antony is thought to illustrate the Asiatic or "florid" style of speaking. In it Shakespeare gathers various hints from Plutarch ("Marcus Antonius" and "Dion") and Appian, but the speech is Shakespeare's invention.)   82 **answered** paid the penalty for   83 **under leave** by permission   93 **When that** When   97 **Lupercal** (See 1.1.67 and note.)   112 **masters** good sirs.   116 **dear abide it** pay a heavy penalty for it.

SECOND PLEBEIAN
Poor soul, his eyes are red as fire with weeping.
THIRD PLEBEIAN
There's not a nobler man in Rome than Antony.
FOURTH PLEBEIAN
Now mark him. He begins again to speak.
ANTONY
But yesterday the word of Caesar might
Have stood against the world. Now lies he there,
And none so poor to do him reverence.   122
Oh, masters, if I were disposed to stir
Your hearts and minds to mutiny and rage,   124
I should do Brutus wrong, and Cassius wrong,
Who, you all know, are honorable men.
I will not do them wrong; I rather choose
To wrong the dead, to wrong myself and you,
Than I will wrong such honorable men.
But here's a parchment with the seal of Caesar.
I found it in his closet; 'tis his will.   131
                                    [*He shows the will.*]
Let but the commons hear this testament—   132
Which, pardon me, I do not mean to read—
And they would go and kiss dead Caesar's wounds
And dip their napkins in his sacred blood,   135
Yea, beg a hair of him for memory,
And dying, mention it within their wills,
Bequeathing it as a rich legacy
Unto their issue.
FOURTH PLEBEIAN
We'll hear the will! Read it, Mark Antony.
ALL
The will, the will! We will hear Caesar's will.
ANTONY
Have patience, gentle friends: I must not read it.
It is not meet you know how Caesar loved you.   143
You are not wood, you are not stones, but men;
And being men, hearing the will of Caesar,
It will inflame you, it will make you mad.
'Tis good you know not that you are his heirs,
For if you should, oh, what would come of it?
FOURTH PLEBEIAN
Read the will! We'll hear it, Antony.
You shall read us the will, Caesar's will.
ANTONY
Will you be patient? Will you stay awhile?
I have o'ershot myself to tell you of it.   152
I fear I wrong the honorable men
Whose daggers have stabbed Caesar; I do fear it.
FOURTH PLEBEIAN
They were traitors. "Honorable men"!
ALL   The will! The testament!
SECOND PLEBEIAN
They were villains, murderers. The will! Read the will!

ANTONY
You will compel me then to read the will?
Then make a ring about the corpse of Caesar
And let me show you him that made the will.
Shall I descend? And will you give me leave?
ALL   Come down.
SECOND PLEBEIAN   Descend.
THIRD PLEBEIAN   You shall have leave.
            [*Antony comes down. They gather around Caesar.*]
FOURTH PLEBEIAN   A ring; stand round.
FIRST PLEBEIAN
Stand from the hearse. Stand from the body.   166
SECOND PLEBEIAN
Room for Antony, most noble Antony!
ANTONY
Nay, press not so upon me. Stand farre off.   168
ALL   Stand back! Room! Bear back!
ANTONY
If you have tears, prepare to shed them now.
You all do know this mantle. I remember   171
The first time ever Caesar put it on;
'Twas on a summer's evening in his tent,
That day he overcame the Nervii.   174
Look, in this place ran Cassius' dagger through.
See what a rent the envious Casca made.   176
Through this the well-belovèd Brutus stabbed,
And as he plucked his cursèd steel away,
Mark how the blood of Caesar followed it,
As rushing out of doors to be resolved   180
If Brutus so unkindly knocked or no;   181
For Brutus, as you know, was Caesar's angel.   182
Judge, O you gods, how dearly Caesar loved him!
This was the most unkindest cut of all;   184
For when the noble Caesar saw him stab,
Ingratitude, more strong than traitors' arms,
Quite vanquished him. Then burst his mighty heart,
And in his mantle muffling up his face,
Even at the base of Pompey's statue,
Which all the while ran blood, great Caesar fell.
Oh, what a fall was there, my countrymen!
Then I, and you, and all of us fell down,
Whilst bloody treason flourished over us.   193
Oh, now you weep, and I perceive you feel
The dint of pity. These are gracious drops.   195
Kind souls, what weep you when you but behold   196
Our Caesar's vesture wounded? Look you here,   197
Here is himself, marred as you see with traitors.
                                    [*He lifts Caesar's mantle.*]
FIRST PLEBEIAN   Oh, piteous spectacle!
SECOND PLEBEIAN   O noble Caesar!

---

166 hearse bier.   **168 farre** farther   **171 mantle** cloak, toga.   **174 the Nervii** the Belgian tribe whose defeat in 57 B.C. is described in Caesar's *Gallic Wars*, 2.15–28   **176 rent** tear, hole   **envious** malicious, spiteful   **180 be resolved** learn for certain   **181 unkindly** cruelly and unnaturally   **182 angel** (1) daimon or genius, guardian angel (2) best beloved.   **184 unkindest** (1) most cruel (2) most unnatural. (The double superlative was grammatically acceptable in Shakespeare's day.)   **193 flourished** (1) triumphed insolently (2) brandished its sword   **195 dint** impression   **196 what** why, or how much   **197 vesture** clothing

---

122 And none . . . reverence i.e., and yet no one is below him in fortune now, no one of even the lowest social station to look up to and revere him.   **124 mutiny** riot, tumult   **131 closet** private chamber, study   **132 commons** common people   **135 napkins** handkerchiefs   **143 meet** fitting that   **152 o'ershot myself** gone further than I should

THIRD PLEBEIAN   Oh, woeful day!

FOURTH PLEBEIAN   Oh, traitors, villains!

FIRST PLEBEIAN   Oh, most bloody sight!

SECOND PLEBEIAN   We will be revenged.

ALL   Revenge! About! Seek! Burn! Fire! Kill! Slay! Let 205
not a traitor live!

ANTONY   Stay, countrymen.

FIRST PLEBEIAN   Peace there! Hear the noble Antony.

SECOND PLEBEIAN   We'll hear him, we'll follow him,
we'll die with him!

ANTONY
Good friends, sweet friends, let me not stir you up
To such a sudden flood of mutiny.
They that have done this deed are honorable.
What private griefs they have, alas, I know not,   214
That made them do it. They are wise and honorable,
And will no doubt with reasons answer you.
I come not, friends, to steal away your hearts.
I am no orator, as Brutus is,
But, as you know me all, a plain blunt man
That love my friend, and that they know full well
That gave me public leave to speak of him.   221
For I have neither wit, nor words, nor worth,   222
Action, nor utterance, nor the power of speech   223
To stir men's blood. I only speak right on.
I tell you that which you yourselves do know,
Show you sweet Caesar's wounds, poor poor dumb
    mouths,
And bid them speak for me. But were I Brutus,
And Brutus Antony, there were an Antony
Would ruffle up your spirits and put a tongue   229
In every wound of Caesar that should move
The stones of Rome to rise and mutiny.

ALL
We'll mutiny!

FIRST PLEBEIAN   We'll burn the house of Brutus!

THIRD PLEBEIAN
Away, then! Come, seek the conspirators.

ANTONY
Yet hear me, countrymen. Yet hear me speak.

ALL
Peace, ho! Hear Antony, most noble Antony!

ANTONY
Why, friends, you go to do you know not what.
Wherein hath Caesar thus deserved your loves?
Alas, you know not. I must tell you then:
You have forgot the will I told you of.

ALL
Most true. The will! Let's stay and hear the will.

ANTONY
Here is the will, and under Caesar's seal.
To every Roman citizen he gives,
To every several man, seventy-five drachmas.   243

SECOND PLEBEIAN
Most noble Caesar! We'll revenge his death.

THIRD PLEBEIAN   O royal Caesar!

ANTONY   Hear me with patience.

ALL   Peace, ho!

ANTONY
Moreover, he hath left you all his walks,
His private arbors, and new-planted orchards,
On this side Tiber; he hath left them you,
And to your heirs forever—common pleasures,   251
To walk abroad and recreate yourselves.
Here was a Caesar! When comes such another?

FIRST PLEBEIAN
Never, never! Come, away, away!
We'll burn his body in the holy place
And with the brands fire the traitors' houses.
Take up the body.

SECOND PLEBEIAN   Go fetch fire!

THIRD PLEBEIAN   Pluck down benches!

FOURTH PLEBEIAN   Pluck down forms, windows, any- 259
thing!   Exeunt Plebeians [with the body].

ANTONY
Now let it work. Mischief, thou art afoot.
Take thou what course thou wilt.

Enter [Octavius'] Servant.

                                How now, fellow?

SERVANT
Sir, Octavius is already come to Rome.

ANTONY   Where is he?

SERVANT
He and Lepidus are at Caesar's house.

ANTONY
And thither will I straight to visit him.   266
He comes upon a wish. Fortune is merry,   267
And in this mood will give us anything.

SERVANT
I heard him say Brutus and Cassius
Are rid like madmen through the gates of Rome.   270

ANTONY
Belike they had some notice of the people,   271
How I had moved them. Bring me to Octavius.
                                Exeunt.

❦

[3.3]

Enter Cinna the poet, and after him the Ple-
beians.

CINNA
I dreamt tonight that I did feast with Caesar,   1

---

205 **About!** To work!   214 **griefs** grievances   221 **public leave** permission to speak publicly   222–3 **neither . . . speech** neither intelligence, vocabulary, moral authority, gesture, rhetorical skill, nor
polished delivery   229 **ruffle up** stir to anger   243 **several** individual.   **drachmas** coins. (This is a substantial bequest.)

251 **common pleasures** public pleasure gardens (in which)
259 **forms, windows** benches, window frames and shutters
266 **straight** straightway, at once   267 **upon a wish** just when
wanted.   **merry** favorably disposed   270 **Are rid** have ridden
271 **Belike** Likely enough.   **of** about; or, from
3.3. Location: A street.
1 **tonight** last night

And things unluckily charge my fantasy.
I have no will to wander forth of doors,
Yet something leads me forth.

FIRST PLEBEIAN   What is your name?

SECOND PLEBEIAN   Whither are you going?

THIRD PLEBEIAN   Where do you dwell?

FOURTH PLEBEIAN   Are you a married man or a
bachelor?

SECOND PLEBEIAN   Answer every man directly.

FIRST PLEBEIAN   Ay, and briefly.

FOURTH PLEBEIAN   Ay, and wisely.

THIRD PLEBEIAN   Ay, and truly, you were best.   13

CINNA   What is my name? Whither am I going? Where
do I dwell? Am I a married man or a bachelor? Then
to answer every man directly and briefly, wisely and
truly: wisely I say, I am a bachelor.

SECOND PLEBEIAN   That's as much as to say they are
fools that marry. You'll bear me a bang for that, I fear.   19
Proceed directly.   20

CINNA   Directly, I am going to Caesar's funeral.   21

FIRST PLEBEIAN   As a friend or an enemy?

CINNA   As a friend.

SECOND PLEBEIAN   That matter is answered directly.

FOURTH PLEBEIAN   For your dwelling—briefly.

CINNA   Briefly, I dwell by the Capitol.

THIRD PLEBEIAN   Your name, sir, truly.

CINNA   Truly, my name is Cinna.

FIRST PLEBEIAN   Tear him to pieces! He's a conspirator!

CINNA   I am Cinna the poet, I am Cinna the poet!

FOURTH PLEBEIAN   Tear him for his bad verses, tear him
for his bad verses!

CINNA   I am not Cinna the conspirator.

FOURTH PLEBEIAN   It is no matter, his name's Cinna.
Pluck but his name out of his heart, and turn him   35
going.   36

THIRD PLEBEIAN   Tear him, tear him! Come, brands, ho,
firebrands! To Brutus', to Cassius'; burn all! Some to
Decius' house, and some to Casca's; some to Ligarius'.
Away, go!

Exeunt all the Plebeians, [dragging off Cinna].

❖

4.1

Enter Antony [with a list], Octavius, and Lepidus.

ANTONY
These many, then, shall die. Their names are pricked.   1

OCTAVIUS
Your brother too must die. Consent you, Lepidus?

LEPIDUS
I do consent—

OCTAVIUS   Prick him down, Antony.

LEPIDUS
Upon condition Publius shall not live,
Who is your sister's son, Mark Antony.

ANTONY
He shall not live. Look, with a spot I damn him.   6
But Lepidus, go you to Caesar's house.
Fetch the will hither, and we shall determine   8
How to cut off some charge in legacies.   9

LEPIDUS   What, shall I find you here?

OCTAVIUS   Or here or at the Capitol.   *Exit Lepidus.*   11

ANTONY
This is a slight, unmeritable man,   12
Meet to be sent on errands. Is it fit,
The threefold world divided, he should stand   14
One of the three to share it?

OCTAVIUS   So you thought him,
And took his voice who should be pricked to die   16
In our black sentence and proscription.   17

ANTONY
Octavius, I have seen more days than you;
And though we lay these honors on this man,
To ease ourselves of divers sland'rous loads,   20
He shall but bear them as the ass bears gold,
To groan and sweat under the business,
Either led or driven as we point the way;
And having brought our treasure where we will,
Then take we down his load, and turn him off,
Like to the empty ass, to shake his ears   26
And graze in commons.

OCTAVIUS   You may do your will;   27
But he's a tried and valiant soldier.

ANTONY
So is my horse, Octavius, and for that
I do appoint him store of provender.   30
It is a creature that I teach to fight,
To wind, to stop, to run directly on,   32
His corporal motion governed by my spirit.   33
And in some taste is Lepidus but so.   34
He must be taught, and trained, and bid go forth—
A barren-spirited fellow, one that feeds
On objects, arts, and imitations,   37
Which, out of use and staled by other men,   38
Begin his fashion. Do not talk of him   39
But as a property. And now, Octavius,   40

---

2 unluckily . . . fantasy oppress my imagination with foreboding.
13 you were best you'd better.   **19 bear . . . bang** get a beating from
me   **20 directly** without evasion.   **21 Directly** (1) Straight there
(2) At once   **35–6 turn him going** send him packing.
4.1. Location: Rome. A table is perhaps set out.
1 pricked marked down on a list (with a stylus making an impression
on a wax tablet, or piercing a sheet of paper).

6 spot mark (on the list).   **damn** condemn   **8–9 determine . . . legacies** find a way to reduce the outlay of Caesar's estate, by altering the
will.   **11 Or** Either   **12 slight, unmeritable** insignificant and undeserving   **14 threefold** i.e., consisting of Europe, Africa, and Asia. The
Roman world was divided among the triumvirate, with most of Gaul
on both sides of the Alps to Antony, Spain and Old Gaul to Lepidus,
and Africa, Sardinia, and Sicily to Octavius.   **16 took his voice** acceded
to his opinion (i.e., about Publius)   **17 black sentence** death sentence.
proscription (Proscription branded a man as an outlaw, confiscated
his property, offered a reward for his murder, and prohibited his sons
and grandsons from holding public office.)   **20 sland'rous** giving
cause for slander   **26 empty** unloaded   **27 commons** public pasture.
30 appoint assign, provide.   **provender** fodder.   **32 wind** turn.
(Horse trainer's term.)   **directly on** straight ahead   **33 corporal**
bodily   **34 taste** degree, sense   **37 On . . . imitations** on curiosities,
artificial things, and the following of fashion—copied things merely,
taken up secondhand   **38 staled** made common or cheap
39 Begin his fashion are for him the ultimate in fashion.   **40 property** tool.

Listen great things. Brutus and Cassius   41
Are levying powers. We must straight make head.   42
Therefore let our alliance be combined,   43
Our best friends made, our means stretched;   44
And let us presently go sit in council
How covert matters may be best disclosed   46
And open perils surest answerèd.   47

OCTAVIUS
Let us do so, for we are at the stake   48
And bayed about with many enemies;   49
And some that smile have in their hearts, I fear,
Millions of mischiefs.   *Exeunt.*   51

❧

[4.2]

*Drum. Enter Brutus, Lucilius, [Lucius,] and the
army. Titinius and Pindarus meet them.*

BRUTUS   Stand, ho!   1
LUCILIUS   Give the word, ho, and stand!   2
BRUTUS
What now, Lucilius, is Cassius near?
LUCILIUS
He is at hand, and Pindarus is come
To do you salutation from his master.
BRUTUS
He greets me well. Your master, Pindarus,   6
In his own change, or by ill officers,   7
Hath given me some worthy cause to wish   8
Things done, undone; but if he be at hand
I shall be satisfied.
PINDARUS   I do not doubt   10
But that my noble master will appear
Such as he is, full of regard and honor.   12
BRUTUS
He is not doubted.—A word, Lucilius.
               [Brutus and Lucilius speak apart.]
How he received you let me be resolved.   14
LUCILIUS
With courtesy and with respect enough,
But not with such familiar instances   16
Nor with such free and friendly conference   17
As he hath used of old.
BRUTUS   Thou hast described

A hot friend cooling. Ever note, Lucilius:
When love begins to sicken and decay
It useth an enforcèd ceremony.   21
There are no tricks in plain and simple faith.
But hollow men, like horses hot at hand,   23
Make gallant show and promise of their mettle;   24
                          Low march within.
But when they should endure the bloody spur,
They fall their crests and like deceitful jades   26
Sink in the trial. Comes his army on?   27
LUCILIUS
They mean this night in Sardis to be quartered.   28
The greater part, the horse in general,   29
Are come with Cassius.

Enter Cassius and his powers.

BRUTUS   Hark, he is arrived.
March gently on to meet him.   31
CASSIUS   Stand, ho!
BRUTUS   Stand, ho! Speak the word along.
FIRST SOLDIER   Stand!
SECOND SOLDIER   Stand!
THIRD SOLDIER   Stand!
CASSIUS
Most noble brother, you have done me wrong.
BRUTUS
Judge me, you gods! Wrong I mine enemies?
And if not so, how should I wrong a brother?
CASSIUS
Brutus, this sober form of yours hides wrongs;   40
And when you do them—
BRUTUS   Cassius, be content;   41
Speak your griefs softly. I do know you well.   42
Before the eyes of both our armies here,
Which should perceive nothing but love from us,
Let us not wrangle. Bid them move away.
Then in my tent, Cassius, enlarge your griefs,   46
And I will give you audience.
CASSIUS   Pindarus,
Bid our commanders lead their charges off   48
A little from this ground.
BRUTUS
Lucius, do you the like, and let no man
Come to our tent till we have done our conference.
Let Lucilius and Titinius guard our door.   52
          Exeunt. Manent Brutus and Cassius.
   [Lucilius and Titinius stand guard at the door.]

❧

---

41 Listen hear   **42 powers** armies.   **straight make head** immediately raise an army.   **43 let . . . combined** let us work as one   **44 made** mustered, made certain.   **stretched** used to fullest advantage, extended to the utmost   **46 How . . . disclosed** (to determine) how hidden dangers may best be discovered   **47 surest answerèd** most safely met.   **48 at the stake** i.e., like a bear in the sport of bear-baiting   **49 bayed about** surrounded as by baying dogs   **51 mischiefs** harms, evils.
4.2. Location: Camp near Sardis, in Asia Minor. Before Brutus's tent.   **1–2 Stand . . . stand!** Halt! Pass the word!   **6 He . . . well** His greetings are welcome.   **7 In . . . officers** whether from an alteration in his feelings toward me or through the acts of unworthy subordinates   **8 worthy** justifiable   **10 be satisfied** have things explained to my satisfaction.   **12 full . . . honor** deserving all respect and honor.   **14 resolved** informed, put out of doubt.   **16 familiar instances** proofs of intimate friendship   **17 conference** conversation

21 enforcèd constrained   **23 hollow** insincere.   **hot at hand** restless and full of spirit when held in, at the start   **24 mettle** spirit   **26 fall their crests** lower their necks (literally, the ridge or mane of the neck), hang their heads.   **jades** worthless horses   **27 Sink** give way, fail   **28 Sardis** (The capital city of Lydia in Asia Minor.)   **29 the horse in general** all the cavalry   **31 gently** mildly, not hostilely   **40 sober form** dignified manner, appearance   **41 be content** keep calm   **42 griefs** grievances.   **I . . . well** i.e., We've known one another long and can proceed calmly.   **46 enlarge** speak freely   **48 charges** troops   **52 Lucilius** (The Folio reads *Lucius* here and *Lucillius* in line 50, but, when Shakespeare interpolated a passage in the next scene at lines 124–66, he evidently intended to have Lucilius guarding the door.)

[4.3]

CASSIUS
    That you have wronged me doth appear in this:
    You have condemned and noted Lucius Pella   2
    For taking bribes here of the Sardians,
    Wherein my letters, praying on his side,   4
    Because I knew the man, was slighted off.   5

BRUTUS
    You wronged yourself to write in such a case.

CASSIUS
    In such a time as this it is not meet   7
    That every nice offense should bear his comment.   8

BRUTUS
    Let me tell you, Cassius, you yourself
    Are much condemned to have an itching palm,   10
    To sell and mart your offices for gold   11
    To undeservers.

CASSIUS   I an itching palm?
    You know that you are Brutus that speaks this,
    Or, by the gods, this speech were else your last.   14

BRUTUS
    The name of Cassius honors this corruption,   15
    And chastisement doth therefore hide his head.   16

CASSIUS   Chastisement?

BRUTUS
    Remember March, the ides of March remember.
    Did not great Julius bleed for justice' sake?
    What villain touched his body that did stab   20
    And not for justice? What, shall one of us,   21
    That struck the foremost man of all this world
    But for supporting robbers, shall we now   23
    Contaminate our fingers with base bribes,
    And sell the mighty space of our large honors   25
    For so much trash as may be graspèd thus?   26
    I had rather be a dog and bay the moon   27
    Than such a Roman.

CASSIUS   Brutus, bait not me.   28
    I'll not endure it. You forget yourself
    To hedge me in. I am a soldier, I,   30
    Older in practice, abler than yourself
    To make conditions.   32

BRUTUS   Go to! You are not, Cassius.

CASSIUS   I am.

BRUTUS   I say you are not.

CASSIUS
    Urge me no more; I shall forget myself.   36
    Have mind upon your health. Tempt me no farther.   37

BRUTUS   Away, slight man!   38

CASSIUS
    Is't possible?

BRUTUS   Hear me, for I will speak.
    Must I give way and room to your rash choler?   40
    Shall I be frighted when a madman stares?   41

CASSIUS
    O ye gods, ye gods! Must I endure all this?

BRUTUS
    All this? Ay, more. Fret till your proud heart break.
    Go show your slaves how choleric you are,
    And make your bondmen tremble. Must I budge?   45
    Must I observe you? Must I stand and crouch   46
    Under your testy humor? By the gods,   47
    You shall digest the venom of your spleen   48
    Though it do split you; for, from this day forth,
    I'll use you for my mirth, yea, for my laughter,
    When you are waspish.

CASSIUS   Is it come to this?   51

BRUTUS
    You say you are a better soldier.
    Let it appear so; make your vaunting true,   53
    And it shall please me well. For mine own part,
    I shall be glad to learn of noble men.   55

CASSIUS
    You wrong me every way! You wrong me, Brutus.
    I said an elder soldier, not a better.
    Did I say "better"?

BRUTUS   If you did, I care not.

CASSIUS
    When Caesar lived he durst not thus have moved me.   59

BRUTUS
    Peace, peace! You durst not so have tempted him.   60

CASSIUS   I durst not?

BRUTUS   No.

CASSIUS
    What, durst not tempt him?

BRUTUS   For your life you durst not.

CASSIUS
    Do not presume too much upon my love.
    I may do that I shall be sorry for.

BRUTUS
    You have done that you should be sorry for.
    There is no terror, Cassius, in your threats,
    For I am armed so strong in honesty
    That they pass by me as the idle wind,

4.3. Location: The scene is continuous. Brutus and Cassius remain onstage, which now represents the interior of Brutus's tent.
2 noted publicly disgraced.   **Lucius Pella** a Roman praetor in Sardis
4 letters i.e., letter. (See 3.1.281n.)   **praying** entreating   **5 slighted off** slightingly dismissed.   **7 meet** fitting   **8 nice** trivial.   **bear his comment** be taken note of. (*His* means "its.")   **10 condemned to have** accused of having   **11 mart** traffic in   **14 else** otherwise   **15 honors** lends the appearance of honor to, countenances   **16 And . . . head** and for that reason those who might rebuke such corruption are reluctant to speak out.   **20–1 What . . . justice?** Which of us was villain enough to stab for any cause other than justice?   **23 But** only.   **robbers** (According to Plutarch, Caesar "was a favorer and suborner of all of them that did rob and spoil by his countenance and authority.")   **25 the mighty . . . honors** the greatness of our honorable reputations and the high offices we have power to confer   **26 trash** i.e., money (despised in Brutus's stoic philosophy)   **27 bay** howl at   **28 bait** harass   **30 hedge me in** crowd me, limit my authority.   **32 make conditions** i.e., manage affairs, make decisions about Lucius Pella and other officers.

36 Urge Provoke   **37 Tempt** Provoke   **38 slight** insignificant   **40 way and room** free course and scope.   **choler** wrathful temperament.   **41 stares** looks wildly at me.   **45 bondmen** (Probably not distinguished from "slaves" in line 44.)   **budge** flinch.   **46 observe** defer to.   **crouch** cringe   **47 humor** temperament.   **48 digest** swallow.   **spleen** i.e., irascibility   **51 waspish** hotheaded.   **53 vaunting** boasting   **55 I shall . . . men** (Said sarcastically: "Wouldn't it be a nice surprise to learn that some men can be noble after all?", or, "I am glad to be corrected by such a noble person as yourself.")   **59 moved** angered   **60 tempted** provoked

Which I respect not. I did send to you   70
For certain sums of gold, which you denied me;
For I can raise no money by vile means.   72
By heaven, I had rather coin my heart
And drop my blood for drachmas than to wring
From the hard hands of peasants their vile trash
By any indirection. I did send   76
To you for gold to pay my legions,
Which you denied me. Was that done like Cassius?
Should I have answered Caius Cassius so?
When Marcus Brutus grows so covetous
To lock such rascal counters from his friends,   81
Be ready, gods, with all your thunderbolts,
Dash him to pieces!

CASSIUS   I denied you not.

BRUTUS
You did.

CASSIUS   I did not. He was but a fool
That brought my answer back. Brutus hath rived my
    heart.   85
A friend should bear his friend's infirmities,
But Brutus makes mine greater than they are.

BRUTUS
I do not, till you practice them on me.

CASSIUS
You love me not.

BRUTUS   I do not like your faults.

CASSIUS
A friendly eye could never see such faults.

BRUTUS
A flatterer's would not, though they do appear
As huge as high Olympus.

CASSIUS
Come, Antony, and young Octavius, come,
Revenge yourselves alone on Cassius;
For Cassius is aweary of the world,
Hated by one he loves, braved by his brother,   96
Checked like a bondman, all his faults observed,   97
Set in a notebook, learned and conned by rote   98
To cast into my teeth. Oh, I could weep
My spirit from mine eyes! There is my dagger,
        [offering his unsheathed dagger]
And here my naked breast; within, a heart
Dearer than Pluto's mine, richer than gold.   102
If that thou be'st a Roman, take it forth.
I, that denied thee gold, will give my heart.   104
Strike, as thou didst at Caesar; for I know,
When thou didst hate him worst, thou loved'st him
    better
Than ever thou loved'st Cassius.

BRUTUS   Sheathe your dagger.
Be angry when you will, it shall have scope;   108

Do what you will, dishonor shall be humor.   109
Oh, Cassius, you are yokèd with a lamb   110
That carries anger as the flint bears fire,
Who, much enforcèd, shows a hasty spark   112
And straight is cold again.

CASSIUS   Hath Cassius lived   113
To be but mirth and laughter to his Brutus
When grief and blood ill-tempered vexeth him?   115

BRUTUS
When I spoke that, I was ill-tempered too.

CASSIUS
Do you confess so much? Give me your hand.

BRUTUS
And my heart too.   [They embrace.]

CASSIUS   Oh, Brutus!

BRUTUS   What's the matter?

CASSIUS
Have not you love enough to bear with me,
When that rash humor which my mother gave me   120
Makes me forgetful?

BRUTUS   Yes, Cassius, and from henceforth,
When you are overearnest with your Brutus,
He'll think your mother chides, and leave you so.   123

        Enter a Poet [followed by Lucilius and Titinius,
        who have been standing guard at the door].

POET
Let me go in to see the generals!
There is some grudge between 'em; 'tis not meet
They be alone.

LUCILIUS   You shall not come to them.

POET   Nothing but death shall stay me.

CASSIUS   How now? What's the matter?

POET
For shame, you generals! What do you mean?
Love and be friends, as two such men should be;
For I have seen more years, I'm sure, than ye.

CASSIUS
Ha, ha, how vilely doth this cynic rhyme!   132

BRUTUS
Get you hence, sirrah. Saucy fellow, hence!

CASSIUS
Bear with him, Brutus. 'Tis his fashion.

BRUTUS
I'll know his humor when he knows his time.   135
What should the wars do with these jigging fools?   136
Companion, hence!

CASSIUS   Away, away, begone!   Exit Poet.   137

BRUTUS
Lucilius and Titinius, bid the commanders

---

70 **respect not** pay no attention to. 72 **can raise no money** i.e., refuse to raise money 76 **indirection** devious or unjust means. 81 **rascal counters** i.e., paltry sums. (*Counters* were uncurrent coins or disks used by shopkeepers as tokens in making reckonings.) 85 **rived** cleft, split 96 **braved** defied 97 **Checked** rebuked 98 **conned by rote** memorized 102 **Dearer** richer. **Pluto** god of the underworld (fused with Plutus, god of riches) 104 **that denied** i.e., who you insist denied 108 **scope** free rein

109 **dishonor . . . humor** i.e., I'll regard your dishonorable conduct and self-righteous anger as the effects of temperament, something to be humored. 110 **yokèd with** allied with 112 **enforcèd** provoked, struck upon 113 **straight** at once 115 **blood ill-tempered** disposition imbalanced by the humors of the body 120 **that rash humor** i.e., choler, anger 123 **leave you so** let it go at that. 132 **cynic** i.e., rude fellow; also one claiming to be a Cynic philosopher, hence outspoken 135 **I'll . . . time** I'll indulge his eccentric behavior when he knows the proper time for it. 136 **jigging** rhyming in jerky doggerel 137 **Companion** Fellow

Prepare to lodge their companies tonight.

CASSIUS
And come yourselves, and bring Messala with you
Immediately to us.   [*Exeunt Lucilius and Titinius.*]

BRUTUS [*to Lucius within*]   Lucius, a bowl of wine.

CASSIUS
I did not think you could have been so angry.

BRUTUS
Oh, Cassius, I am sick of many griefs.

CASSIUS
Of your philosophy you make no use
If you give place to accidental evils.   145

BRUTUS
No man bears sorrow better. Portia is dead.

CASSIUS   Ha? Portia?

BRUTUS   She is dead.

CASSIUS
How scaped I killing when I crossed you so?   149
Oh, insupportable and touching loss!
Upon what sickness?

BRUTUS   Impatient of my absence,
And grief that young Octavius with Mark Antony
Have made themselves so strong—for with her death 153
That tidings came—with this she fell distract
And, her attendants absent, swallowed fire.   155

CASSIUS
And died so?

BRUTUS   Even so.

CASSIUS   O ye immortal gods!

Enter Boy [Lucius] with wine and tapers.

BRUTUS
Speak no more of her.—Give me a bowl of wine.—
In this I bury all unkindness, Cassius.   *Drinks.*

CASSIUS
My heart is thirsty for that noble pledge.
Fill, Lucius, till the wine o'erswell the cup;
I cannot drink too much of Brutus' love.   161
                          [*He drinks. Exit Lucius.*]

Enter Titinius and Messala.

BRUTUS
Come in, Titinius. Welcome, good Messala.
Now sit we close about this taper here
And call in question our necessities.   [*They sit.*] 164

CASSIUS
Portia, art thou gone?

BRUTUS   No more, I pray you.
Messala, I have here receivèd letters   166

That young Octavius and Mark Antony
Come down upon us with a mighty power,   168
Bending their expedition toward Philippi.   169
                          [*He shows a letter.*]

MESSALA
Myself have letters of the selfsame tenor.

BRUTUS   With what addition?

MESSALA
That by proscription and bills of outlawry   172
Octavius, Antony, and Lepidus
Have put to death an hundred senators.

BRUTUS
Therein our letters do not well agree;
Mine speak of seventy senators that died
By their proscriptions, Cicero being one.

CASSIUS
Cicero one?

MESSALA   Cicero is dead,
And by that order of proscription.
Had you your letters from your wife, my lord?   180

BRUTUS   No, Messala.

MESSALA
Nor nothing in your letters writ of her?   182

BRUTUS
Nothing, Messala.

MESSALA   That, methinks, is strange.

BRUTUS
Why ask you? Hear you aught of her in yours?

MESSALA   No, my lord.

BRUTUS
Now, as you are a Roman, tell me true.

MESSALA
Then like a Roman bear the truth I tell,
For certain she is dead, and by strange manner.

BRUTUS
Why, farewell, Portia. We must die, Messala.
With meditating that she must die once,   190
I have the patience to endure it now.

MESSALA
Even so great men great losses should endure.   192

CASSIUS
I have as much of this in art as you,   193
But yet my nature could not bear it so.   194

BRUTUS
Well, to our work alive. What do you think   195
Of marching to Philippi presently?

---

168 power army   **169 Bending** directing.   **expedition** rapid march;
warlike enterprise   **172 proscription** (See the note at 4.1.17.)
180–94 Had . . . so (This passage is sometimes regarded as contradictory to lines 142–65 and redundant. Perhaps it is the original account of
Portia's death, and lines 142–65 are part of a later interpolation, but it is
also possible that both are intended, the first being Brutus's intimate
revelation of the news to his friend and the second being Brutus's
recovery of his stoic reserve now on display for Messala and Titinius.)
182 nothing . . . her nothing written about her in the letter or letters
you've received.   **190 once** at some time   **192 Even so** In just such a
way   **193 art** i.e., the acquired theoretical wisdom of stoical fortitude
(as contrasted with the gifts of *nature* in line 194)   **195 alive** concerning
us who are alive and dealing with present and future realities.

---

145 place way.   **accidental evils** misfortunes caused by chance
(which should be a matter of indifference to a philosopher like Brutus).   **149 scaped I killing** did I escape being killed   **153 her death**
i.e., news of her death   **155 swallowed fire** (According to Plutarch,
as translated by Thomas North, Portia "took hot burning coals and
cast them in her mouth, and kept her mouth so close that she choked
herself.")   **161.2 *Titinius*** (Lucilius does not return with Titinius, as he
was ordered to do at lines 140–1, probably because he was not in Shakespeare's original version of this scene.)   **164 call in question** consider,
discuss   **166 letters** (Probably a single letter. See 3.1.281n and 4.3.4n.)

CASSIUS
  I do not think it good.
BRUTUS   Your reason?
CASSIUS   This it is:
  'Tis better that the enemy seek us.
  So shall he waste his means, weary his soldiers,
  Doing himself offense, whilst we, lying still,   200
  Are full of rest, defense, and nimbleness.
BRUTUS
  Good reasons must of force give place to better.   202
  The people twixt Philippi and this ground
  Do stand but in a forced affection,
  For they have grudged us contribution.
  The enemy, marching along by them,
  By them shall make a fuller number up,
  Come on refreshed, new-added, and encouraged;
  From which advantage shall we cut him off
  If at Philippi we do face him there,
  These people at our back.
CASSIUS   Hear me, good brother—   211
BRUTUS
  Under your pardon. You must note beside   212
  That we have tried the utmost of our friends;
  Our legions are brim full, our cause is ripe.
  The enemy increaseth every day;
  We, at the height, are ready to decline.
  There is a tide in the affairs of men
  Which, taken at the flood, leads on to fortune;
  Omitted, all the voyage of their life
  Is bound in shallows and in miseries.   220
  On such a full sea are we now afloat,
  And we must take the current when it serves
  Or lose our ventures.
CASSIUS   Then, with your will, go on.   223
  We'll along ourselves and meet them at Philippi.
BRUTUS
  The deep of night is crept upon our talk,
  And nature must obey necessity,
  Which we will niggard with a little rest.   227
  There is no more to say.
CASSIUS   No more. Good night.
  Early tomorrow will we rise and hence.   229
BRUTUS
  Lucius!

      Enter Lucius.

        My gown.   [*Exit Lucius.*]
                 Farewell, good Messala.   230
  Good night, Titinius. Noble, noble Cassius,
  Good night and good repose.
CASSIUS   Oh, my dear brother!

This was an ill beginning of the night.
Never come such division 'tween our souls!
Let it not, Brutus.

      Enter Lucius with the gown.

BRUTUS   Everything is well.
CASSIUS   Good night, my lord.   200
BRUTUS   Good night, good brother.
TITINIUS, MESSALA   Good night, Lord Brutus.
BRUTUS   Farewell, everyone.
                    Exeunt [all but Brutus and Lucius].
  Give me the gown. Where is thy instrument?   241
LUCIUS
  Here in the tent.
BRUTUS   What, thou speak'st drowsily!
  Poor knave, I blame thee not; thou art o'erwatched.   243
  Call Claudius and some other of my men;
  I'll have them sleep on cushions in my tent.
LUCIUS [*calling*]   Varro and Claudius!

      Enter Varro and Claudius.

VARRO   Calls my lord?
BRUTUS
  I pray you, sirs, lie in my tent and sleep.
  It may be I shall raise you by and by   249
  On business to my brother Cassius.
VARRO
  So please you, we will stand and watch your pleasure. 251
BRUTUS
  I will not have it so. Lie down, good sirs.
  It may be I shall otherwise bethink me.   253
              [*Varro and Claudius lie down.*]
  Look, Lucius, here's the book I sought for so;
  I put it in the pocket of my gown.
LUCIUS
  I was sure Your Lordship did not give it me.
BRUTUS
  Bear with me, good boy, I am much forgetful.
  Canst thou hold up thy heavy eyes awhile
  And touch thy instrument a strain or two?   259
LUCIUS
  Ay, my lord, an't please you.
BRUTUS   It does, my boy.   260
  I trouble thee too much, but thou art willing.
LUCIUS   It is my duty, sir.
BRUTUS
  I should not urge thy duty past thy might;
  I know young bloods look for a time of rest.   264
LUCIUS   I have slept, my lord, already.
BRUTUS
  It was well done, and thou shalt sleep again;
  I will not hold thee long. If I do live,

---

200 **offense** harm   202 **of force** necessarily   211 **These . . . back** i.e.,
with the people our enemy would otherwise recruit being instead in
territory we control.   212 **Under your pardon** i.e., Excuse me, let me
continue.   220 **bound in** confined to   223 **ventures** investments (of
enterprise at sea).   **with your will** as you wish   227 **niggard** stint
(by sleeping only briefly)   229 **hence** depart.   230 **gown** housecoat.

241 **instrument** i.e., perhaps a lute or cithern.   243 **knave** boy.
o'erwatched tired from lack of sleep.   249 **raise** rouse   251 **watch
your pleasure** wakefully await your commands.   253 **otherwise
bethink me** change my mind.   259 **touch** i.e., play on.   **strain**
tune, musical phrase   260 **an't** if it   264 **young bloods** youthful
constitutions

I will be good to thee.
              Music, and a song. [Lucius falls asleep.]
This is a sleepy tune. O murd'rous slumber,   269
Layest thou thy leaden mace upon my boy,   270
That plays thee music? Gentle knave, good night;
I will not do thee so much wrong to wake thee.
If thou dost nod, thou break'st thy instrument;
I'll take it from thee. And, good boy, good night.
            [He removes Lucius' instrument,
                    and begins to read.]
Let me see, let me see; is not the leaf turned down
Where I left reading? Here it is, I think.

    Enter the Ghost of Caesar.

How ill this taper burns! Ha! Who comes here?   277
I think it is the weakness of mine eyes
That shapes this monstrous apparition.
It comes upon me.—Art thou any thing?   280
Art thou some god, some angel, or some devil,
That mak'st my blood cold and my hair to stare?   282
Speak to me what thou art.
GHOST
  Thy evil spirit, Brutus.
BRUTUS   Why com'st thou?
GHOST
  To tell thee thou shalt see me at Philippi.
BRUTUS Well; then I shall see thee again?
GHOST   Ay, at Philippi.
BRUTUS
  Why, I will see thee at Philippi, then.   *[Exit Ghost.]*
Now I have taken heart, thou vanishest.
Ill spirit, I would hold more talk with thee.—
Boy, Lucius! Varro! Claudius! Sirs, awake!
Claudius!
LUCIUS   The strings, my lord, are false.   292
BRUTUS
  He thinks he still is at his instrument.—
Lucius, awake!
LUCIUS My lord?
BRUTUS
  Didst thou dream, Lucius, that thou so cried'st out?
LUCIUS
  My lord, I do not know that I did cry.
BRUTUS
  Yes, that thou didst. Didst thou see anything?
LUCIUS Nothing, my lord.
BRUTUS
  Sleep again, Lucius. Sirrah Claudius!
  [To Varro] Fellow thou, awake!
VARRO   My lord?
CLAUDIUS   My lord?
                  [They get up.]

BRUTUS
  Why did you so cry out, sirs, in your sleep?
VARRO, CLAUDIUS
  Did we, my lord?
BRUTUS   Ay. Saw you anything?
VARRO
  No, my lord, I saw nothing.
CLAUDIUS   Nor I, my lord.
BRUTUS
  Go and commend me to my brother Cassius.   305
Bid him set on his powers betimes before,   306
And we will follow.
VARRO, CLAUDIUS   It shall be done, my lord.
                    Exeunt.

❧

5.1

    Enter Octavius, Antony, and their army.

OCTAVIUS
  Now, Antony, our hopes are answerèd.
You said the enemy would not come down,
But keep the hills and upper regions.   3
It proves not so. Their battles are at hand;   4
They mean to warn us at Philippi here,   5
Answering before we do demand of them.
ANTONY
  Tut, I am in their bosoms, and I know   7
Wherefore they do it. They could be content
To visit other places, and come down   9
With fearful bravery, thinking by this face   10
To fasten in our thoughts that they have courage;
But 'tis not so.   12

    Enter a Messenger.

MESSENGER   Prepare you, generals.
The enemy comes on in gallant show.
Their bloody sign of battle is hung out,   14
And something to be done immediately.   15
ANTONY
  Octavius, lead your battle softly on   16
Upon the left hand of the even field.
OCTAVIUS
  Upon the right hand, I. Keep thou the left.
ANTONY
  Why do you cross me in this exigent?   19

---

305 commend me deliver my greetings   **306 set . . . before** march away with his troops early in the morning, before me
5.1 Location: The plains of Philippi, in Macedonia.
3 keep remain in **4 battles** armies **5 warm** challenge **7 bosoms** secret councils **9 visit other places** i.e., be elsewhere **10 fearful bravery** (1) awesome ostentation (2) a show of bravery to conceal their fear. **face** pretense (of courage) **12 'tis not so** (1) their plan cannot deceive us (2) they have no courage. **14 bloody sign** red flag or crimson coat of arms as battle signal **15 to be** is to be **16 softly** warily, with restraint **19 cross** contradict. **exigent** critical moment.

---

269 murd'rous producing the likeness of death **270 leaden mace** heavy staff of office (used by a sheriff to touch the shoulder of one being placed under arrest) **277 How . . . burns!** (Ghostly apparitions were thought to be accompanied by such effects as lights burning low and blue.) **280 upon** toward **282 stare** stand on end. **292 false** out of tune.

OCTAVIUS
    I do not cross you, but I will do so.   *March.*   20

    Drum. Enter Brutus, Cassius, and their army;
    [Lucilius, Titinius, Messala, and others].

BRUTUS   They stand and would have parley.
CASSIUS
    Stand fast, Titinius. We must out and talk.   22
OCTAVIUS
    Mark Antony, shall we give sign of battle?
ANTONY
    No, Caesar, we will answer on their charge.   24
    Make forth. The generals would have some words.   25
OCTAVIUS   [*to his officers*]   Stir not until the signal.
         [*The two sides advance toward one another.*]
BRUTUS
    Words before blows. Is it so, countrymen?
OCTAVIUS
    Not that we love words better, as you do.
BRUTUS
    Good words are better than bad strokes, Octavius.
ANTONY
    In your bad strokes, Brutus, you give good words.   30
    Witness the hole you made in Caesar's heart,
    Crying "Long live! Hail, Caesar!"
CASSIUS   Antony,
    The posture of your blows are yet unknown;   33
    But for your words, they rob the Hybla bees,   34
    And leave them honeyless.
ANTONY   Not stingless too?
BRUTUS   Oh, yes, and soundless too.
    For you have stol'n their buzzing, Antony,
    And very wisely threat before you sting.   39
ANTONY
    Villains! You did not so when your vile daggers   40
    Hacked one another in the sides of Caesar.
    You showed your teeth like apes, and fawned like
        hounds,   42
    And bowed like bondmen, kissing Caesar's feet,
    Whilst damnèd Casca, like a cur, behind,
    Struck Caesar on the neck. Oh, you flatterers!
CASSIUS
    Flatterers? Now, Brutus, thank yourself!
    This tongue had not offended so today
    If Cassius might have ruled.   48
OCTAVIUS
    Come, come, the cause. If arguing make us sweat,   49
    The proof of it will turn to redder drops.   50
    Look,   [*He draws.*]

    I draw a sword against conspirators.
    When think you that the sword goes up again?   53
    Never, till Caesar's three-and-thirty wounds   54
    Be well avenged, or till another Caesar   55
    Have added slaughter to the sword of traitors.   56
BRUTUS
    Caesar, thou canst not die by traitors' hands,   57
    Unless thou bring'st them with thee.
OCTAVIUS   So I hope.   58
    I was not born to die on Brutus' sword.   59
BRUTUS
    Oh, if thou wert the noblest of thy strain,   60
    Young man, thou couldst not die more honorable.
CASSIUS
    A peevish schoolboy, worthless of such honor,   62
    Joined with a masker and a reveler!   63
ANTONY
    Old Cassius still.
OCTAVIUS   Come, Antony, away!—   64
    Defiance, traitors, hurl we in your teeth.
    If you dare fight today, come to the field;
    If not, when you have stomachs.   67
         Exeunt Octavius, Antony, and army.
CASSIUS
    Why, now, blow wind, swell billow, and swim bark!   68
    The storm is up, and all is on the hazard.   69
BRUTUS
    Ho, Lucilius! Hark, a word with you.
LUCILIUS (*stands forth*)   My lord?
        [*Brutus and Lucilius converse apart.*]
CASSIUS   Messala!
MESSALA (*stands forth*)   What says my general?
CASSIUS   Messala,
    This is my birthday, as this very day   75
    Was Cassius born. Give me thy hand, Messala.
    Be thou my witness that against my will,
    As Pompey was, am I compelled to set   78
    Upon one battle all our liberties.
    You know that I held Epicurus strong   80
    And his opinion. Now I change my mind
    And partly credit things that do presage.   82
    Coming from Sardis, on our former ensign   83

---

20 cross you contradict you perversely.   **do so** do as I said.   **22 out** go out   **24 answer on their charge** respond when they attack. **25 Make forth** March forward.   **30 In . . . words** i.e., As you deliver cruel blows, Brutus, you use deceiving flattery.   **33 The posture . . . are** how you will strike your blows is   **34 for** as for.   **Hybla** a mountain and a town in ancient Sicily, famous for honey   **39 very wisely** (Said ironically; Brutus suggests that Antony is all bluster and no action.)   **threat** threaten   **40 so** i.e., give warning   **42 showed your teeth** i.e., in smiles   **48 ruled** prevailed (in urging that Antony be killed).   **49 the cause** to our business.   **50 proof** trial

53 up in its sheath   **54 three-and-thirty** (Plutarch has it three-and-twenty.)   **55 another Caesar** i.e., myself, Octavius   **56 Have . . . to** has also been slaughtered by   **57–8 thou . . . thee** i.e., the only traitors here are in your own army.   **58–9 So . . . sword** i.e. (sardonically), I'm glad to hear that, since you are the traitor I mean, and since you are not in my army, I cannot, according to your assertion, die at your hands.   **60 if** even if.   **strain** lineage   **62 peevish** silly, childish. **schoolboy** (Octavius was eighteen at the time of Caesar's assassination.)   **worthless** unworthy   **63 a masker . . . reveler** i.e., Antony, noted for his dissipation   **64 Old . . . still** i.e., Cassius, as envious and ill-willed as ever. (Said sardonically.)   **67 stomachs** appetites (for fighting), courage.   **68 billow** wave.   **swim bark** let the sailing vessel swim for its life.   **69 on the hazard** at stake.   **75 as** inasmuch as **78 Pompey** (The reference is to the battle of Pharsalus, where Pompey was persuaded to fight Caesar against his own judgment.)   **set** stake   **80 Epicurus** Greek philosopher (341–270 B.C.) who, because he held the gods to be indifferent to human affairs, spurned belief in omens or superstitions   **82 presage** foretell events.   **83 former ensign** foremost standard, the legion's *aquila,* a tall standard surmounted by the image of an eagle

Two mighty eagles fell, and there they perched,   84
Gorging and feeding from our soldiers' hands,
Who to Philippi here consorted us.   86
This morning are they fled away and gone,
And in their steads do ravens, crows, and kites   88
Fly o'er our heads and downward look on us
As we were sickly prey. Their shadows seem   90
A canopy most fatal, under which   91
Our army lies, ready to give up the ghost.

MESSALA
Believe not so.

CASSIUS   I but believe it partly,   93
For I am fresh of spirit and resolved
To meet all perils very constantly.   95

BRUTUS
Even so, Lucilius.   [*He rejoins Cassius.*]

CASSIUS   Now, most noble Brutus,   96
The gods today stand friendly, that we may,   97
Lovers in peace, lead on our days to age!   98
But since the affairs of men rest still incertain,   99
Let's reason with the worst that may befall.   100
If we do lose this battle, then is this
The very last time we shall speak together.
What are you then determinèd to do?

BRUTUS
Even by the rule of that philosophy
By which I did blame Cato for the death   105
Which he did give himself—I know not how,
But I do find it cowardly and vile,
For fear of what might fall, so to prevent   108
The time of life—arming myself with patience   109
To stay the providence of some high powers   110
That govern us below.

CASSIUS   Then, if we lose this battle,
You are contented to be led in triumph
Thorough the streets of Rome?   113

BRUTUS
No, Cassius, no. Think not, thou noble Roman,
That ever Brutus will go bound to Rome;
He bears too great a mind. But this same day
Must end that work the ides of March begun.
And whether we shall meet again I know not;
Therefore our everlasting farewell take.
Forever and forever farewell, Cassius!
If we do meet again, why, we shall smile;
If not, why then this parting was well made.

CASSIUS
Forever and forever farewell, Brutus!
If we do meet again, we'll smile indeed;
If not, 'tis true this parting was well made.

BRUTUS
Why, then, lead on. Oh, that a man might know
The end of this day's business ere it come!   127
But it sufficeth that the day will end,
And then the end is known.—Come, ho, away!
                                          Exeunt.

❧

[5.2]

Alarum. Enter Brutus and Messala.

BRUTUS
Ride, ride, Messala, ride, and give these bills   1
Unto the legions on the other side.   2
                    [*He hands him written orders.*]
                              Loud alarum.
Let them set on at once; for I perceive   3
But cold demeanor in Octavio's wing,   4
And sudden push gives them the overthrow.
Ride, ride, Messala! Let them all come down.   6
                              Exeunt [*separately*].

❧

[5.3]

Alarums. Enter Cassius [*carrying a standard*], *and
Titinius.*

CASSIUS
Oh, look, Titinius, look, the villains fly!   1
Myself have to mine own turned enemy.   2
This ensign here of mine was turning back;   3
I slew the coward and did take it from him.   4

TITINIUS
Oh, Cassius, Brutus gave the word too early,
Who, having some advantage on Octavius,
Took it too eagerly. His soldiers fell to spoil,   7
Whilst we by Antony are all enclosed.   8

Enter Pindarus.

---

84 **fell** swooped down   86 **consorted** accompanied   88 **kites** scavenger birds (also raptors)   90 **As** as if   91 **fatal** presaging death   93 **but** only   95 **constantly** resolutely.   96 **Even so, Lucilius** (This phrase marks the end of Brutus's private conversation apart with Lucilius.)   97 **The gods** May the gods   98 **Lovers** friends.   **age** old age.   99 **still** always   100 **reason** reckon   105 **Cato** i.e., Marcus Porcius Cato, Brutus' father-in-law, who killed himself to avoid submission to Caesar in 46 B.C. (See 2.1.296 and note.) Brutus's condemnation of Cato's suicide out of fear of failure can perhaps be reconciled with lines 114–17 below and with Brutus's own later suicide (5.5.50), since on that occasion Brutus is responding to certain defeat and disgrace. The seeming contradiction may also be owing to an ambiguity in North's Plutarch.   108 **fall** befall.   **prevent** anticipate the end, cut short   109 **time** term, extent   110 **stay** await   113 **Thorough** through

127 **ere** before
5.2 **Location: The plains of Philippi. The field of battle.**
0.1 *Alarum* (This is seemingly an anticipatory stage direction; the battle actually begins with the *Loud alarum* at line 2. An *alarum* is off stage sounds, signifying a battle.)   1 **bills** orders   2 **side** wing (i.e., Cassius's wing).   3 **set on** attack   4 **cold demeanor** faintheartedness   6 **come down** i.e., from the hills, where the Republican army has been awaiting the signal to attack. (See 5.1.2–3.)
5.3 **Location: The field of battle still.**
1 **the villains** i.e., my own troops   2 **mine own** my own men   3 **ensign** bearer of the standard. (A legion's *aquila*, or "eagle standard," had great significance and needed to be guarded.)   4 **it** i.e., the standard   7 **spoil** looting   8 **enclosed** surrounded.

PINDARUS
 Fly further off, my lord, fly further off!
 Mark Antony is in your tents, my lord.
 Fly therefore, noble Cassius, fly far off.
CASSIUS
 This hill is far enough. Look, look, Titinius:
 Are those my tents where I perceive the fire?
TITINIUS
 They are, my lord.
CASSIUS   Titinius, if thou lovest me,
 Mount thou my horse, and hide thy spurs in him
 Till he have brought thee up to yonder troops
 And here again, that I may rest assured
 Whether yond troops are friend or enemy.
TITINIUS
 I will be here again even with a thought. *Exit.* 19
CASSIUS
 Go, Pindarus, get higher on that hill.
 My sight was ever thick. Regard Titinius, 21
 And tell me what thou not'st about the field. 22
      [Pindarus goes up.]
 This day I breathèd first. Time is come round, 23
 And where I did begin, there shall I end.
 My life is run his compass.—Sirrah, what news? 25
PINDARUS *(above)* Oh, my lord!
CASSIUS What news?
PINDARUS *[above]*
 Titinius is enclosèd round about
 With horsemen, that make to him on the spur, 29
 Yet he spurs on. Now they are almost on him.
 Now, Titinius! Now some light. Oh, he 31
 Lights too. He's ta'en. *(Shout.)* And hark! They shout
  for joy.
CASSIUS Come down, behold no more.
 Oh, coward that I am, to live so long
 To see my best friend ta'en before my face! 35

   Enter Pindarus [from above].

 Come hither, sirrah.
 In Parthia did I take thee prisoner, 37
 And then I swore thee, saving of thy life, 38
 That whatsoever I did bid thee do
 Thou shouldst attempt it. Come now, keep thine oath;
 Now be a freeman, and with this good sword,
 That ran through Caesar's bowels, search this bosom. 42
 Stand not to answer. Here, take thou the hilts, 43
 And when my face is covered, as 'tis now,
 Guide thou the sword. *[Pindarus does so.]* Caesar, thou
  art revenged,
 Even with the sword that killed thee. *[He dies.]*

PINDARUS
 So, I am free, yet would not so have been, 47
 Durst I have done my will. Oh, Cassius! 48
 Far from this country Pindarus shall run,
 Where never Roman shall take note of him. *[Exit.]*

  Enter Titinius [wearing a garland of laurel] and
  Messala.

MESSALA
 It is but change, Titinius; for Octavius 51
 Is overthrown by noble Brutus' power,
 As Cassius' legions are by Antony.
TITINIUS
 These tidings will well comfort Cassius.
MESSALA
 Where did you leave him?
TITINIUS   All disconsolate,
 With Pindarus his bondman, on this hill.
MESSALA
 Is not that he that lies upon the ground?
TITINIUS
 He lies not like the living. Oh, my heart!
MESSALA
 Is not that he?
TITINIUS   No, this was he, Messala,
 But Cassius is no more. O setting sun,
 As in thy red rays thou dost sink to night,
 So in his red blood Cassius' day is set.
 The sun of Rome is set. Our day is gone; 63
 Clouds, dews, and dangers come; our deeds are done.
 Mistrust of my success hath done this deed. 65
MESSALA
 Mistrust of good success hath done this deed.
 O hateful Error, Melancholy's child, 67
 Why dost thou show to the apt thoughts of men 68
 The things that are not? O Error, soon conceived,
 Thou never com'st unto a happy birth,
 But kill'st the mother that engenderèd thee. 71
TITINIUS
 What, Pindarus! Where art thou, Pindarus?
MESSALA
 Seek him, Titinius, whilst I go to meet
 The noble Brutus, thrusting this report
 Into his ears. I may say "thrusting" it,
 For piercing steel and darts envenomèd
 Shall be as welcome to the ears of Brutus
 As tidings of this sight.
TITINIUS   Hie you, Messala,
 And I will seek for Pindarus the while.
      [Exit Messala.]
 Why didst thou send me forth, brave Cassius?
 Did I not meet thy friends? And did not they
 Put on my brows this wreath of victory

---

19 even . . . thought as quick as thought. **21 thick** imperfect, dim.
Regard Observe **22.1** *Pindarus goes up* (Pindarus may climb to the gallery, or may exit and ascend behind the scenes; see line 35.1 and note.) **23 I breathèd first** i.e., it is my birthday. **25 his compass** its circuit, circle (as drawn by a geometer's compass). **29 make . . . spur** approach him riding rapidly **31 light** alight, dismount. **35.1** *Enter* (Pindarus may descend in full view of the audience; see note at 22.1.)
37 Parthia (What is now northern Iran.) **38 swore . . . of** made you swear, when I spared **42 search** probe, penetrate **43 Stand** Delay.
hilts sword hilt

47 so in this manner **48 Durst . . . will** if I had dared do what I wished. **51 change** exchange of advantage, quid pro quo **63 sun** (With pun on *son.*) **65 Mistrust** i.e., Cassius's doubt **67 Melancholy's child** i.e., bred of pessimism **68 apt** impressionable **71 the mother** i.e., the melancholy person who too readily believes the worst

And bid me give it thee? Didst thou not hear their
   shouts?
Alas, thou hast misconstrued everything.
But, hold thee, take this garland on thy brow.   85
         [*He places the garland on Cassius's brow.*]
Thy Brutus bid me give it thee, and I
Will do his bidding. Brutus, come apace   87
And see how I regarded Caius Cassius.
By your leave, gods! This is a Roman's part.
Come, Cassius' sword, and find Titinius' heart.
         [*He stabs himself and*] *dies.*

      Alarum. Enter Brutus, Messala, young Cato,
      Strato, Volumnius, and Lucilius, [Labeo, and
      Flavius].

BRUTUS
Where, where, Messala, doth his body lie?
MESSALA
Lo, yonder, and Titinius mourning it.
BRUTUS
Titinius' face is upward.
CATO   He is slain.
BRUTUS
O Julius Caesar, thou art mighty yet!
Thy spirit walks abroad and turns our swords
In our own proper entrails.   *Low alarums.*
CATO   Brave Titinius!   96
Look whe'er he have not crowned dead Cassius.   97
BRUTUS
Are yet two Romans living such as these?
The last of all the Romans, fare thee well!
It is impossible that ever Rome
Should breed thy fellow. Friends, I owe more tears
To this dead man than you shall see me pay.—
I shall find time, Cassius, I shall find time.—
Come, therefore, and to Thasos send his body.   104
His funerals shall not be in our camp,   105
Lest it discomfort us. Lucilius, come,   106
And come, young Cato, let us to the field.
Labeo and Flavius, set our battles on.   108
'Tis three o'clock, and, Romans, yet ere night   109
We shall try fortune in a second fight.
           Exeunt [with the bodies].

❖

[5.4]

      Alarum. Enter Brutus, Messala, [young] Cato,
      Lucilius, and Flavius.

BRUTUS
Yet, countrymen, oh, yet hold up your heads!
        [*Exit, followed by Messala and Flavius.*]
CATO
What bastard doth not? Who will go with me?   2
I will proclaim my name about the field:
I am the son of Marcus Cato, ho!
A foe to tyrants, and my country's friend.
I am the son of Marcus Cato, ho!

      Enter soldiers, and fight.

LUCILIUS
And I am Brutus, Marcus Brutus I!
Brutus, my country's friend! Know me for Brutus!
       [*Young Cato is slain by Antony's men.*]
O young and noble Cato, art thou down?
Why, now thou diest as bravely as Titinius,
And mayst be honored, being Cato's son.
FIRST SOLDIER [*capturing Lucilius*]
Yield, or thou diest.
LUCILIUS [*offering money*]   Only I yield to die.   12
There is so much that thou wilt kill me straight;   13
Kill Brutus, and be honored in his death.
FIRST SOLDIER
We must not. A noble prisoner!
SECOND SOLDIER
Room, ho! Tell Antony, Brutus is ta'en.

      Enter Antony.

FIRST SOLDIER
I'll tell the news. Here comes the General.—
Brutus is ta'en, Brutus is ta'en, my lord.
ANTONY   Where is he?
LUCILIUS
Safe, Antony, Brutus is safe enough.
I dare assure thee that no enemy
Shall ever take alive the noble Brutus.
The gods defend him from so great a shame!
When you do find him, or alive or dead,   24
He will be found like Brutus, like himself.
ANTONY [*to First Soldier*]
This is not Brutus, friend, but, I assure you,
A prize no less in worth. Keep this man safe;
Give him all kindness. I had rather have
Such men my friends than enemies.—Go on,
And see whe'er Brutus be alive or dead;   30
And bring us word unto Octavius' tent
How everything is chanced.   32
        Exeunt [separately, some bearing Cato's body].

❖

85 hold thee wait   **87 apace** quickly   **96 own proper** very own
96 s.d. *Low alarums* Offstage sound effects suggesting the activity
of distant battle.   **97 whe'er** whether   **104 Thasos** an island off
the coast of Thrace, near Philippi   **105 funerals** funeral obsequies
106 discomfort us discourage our troops.   **108 battles** armies
109 yet ere might (The historical battles fought at Philippi were
actually weeks apart.)
5.4. Location: Scene continues at the field of battle.

2 What . . . not? Who is so base that he would not do so?   **12 Only . . .
die** I surrender only on condition that I die at your hands.   **13 There
. . . straight** Here is money if you will kill me at once   **24 or alive**
either alive   **30 whe'er** whether   **32 is chanced** has fallen out.

[5.5]

Enter Brutus, Dardanius, Clitus, Strato, and
Volumnius.

BRUTUS
Come, poor remains of friends, rest on this rock.
                                              [*He sits.*]

CLITUS
Statilius showed the torchlight, but, my lord,   2
He came not back. He is or ta'en or slain.   3

BRUTUS
Sit thee down, Clitus. Slaying is the word.
It is a deed in fashion. Hark thee, Clitus.
                                              [*He whispers.*]

CLITUS
What, I, my lord? No, not for all the world.

BRUTUS
Peace then. No words.

CLITUS   I'll rather kill myself.

BRUTUS
Hark thee, Dardanius.   [*He whispers.*]

DARDANIUS   Shall I do such a deed?
          [*Dardanius and Clitus move away from Brutus.*]

CLITUS   Oh, Dardanius!

DARDANIUS   Oh, Clitus!

CLITUS
What ill request did Brutus make to thee?

DARDANIUS
To kill him, Clitus. Look, he meditates.

CLITUS
Now is that noble vessel full of grief,
That it runs over even at his eyes.

BRUTUS
Come hither, good Volumnius. List a word.   15

VOLUMNIUS
What says my lord?

BRUTUS   Why, this, Volumnius:
The ghost of Caesar hath appeared to me
Two several times by night—at Sardis once,   18
And this last night here in Philippi fields.
I know my hour is come.

VOLUMNIUS   Not so, my lord.

BRUTUS
Nay, I am sure it is, Volumnius.
Thou see'st the world, Volumnius, how it goes;
Our enemies have beat us to the pit.   *Low alarums.*   23
It is more worthy to leap in ourselves
Than tarry till they push us. Good Volumnius,
Thou know'st that we two went to school together.
Even for that our love of old, I prithee,   27

Hold thou my sword hilts whilst I run on it.   28

VOLUMNIUS
That's not an office for a friend, my lord.
                                              Alarum still.

CLITUS
Fly, fly, my lord! There is no tarrying here.

BRUTUS
Farewell to you, and you, and you, Volumnius.
Strato, thou hast been all this while asleep;
Farewell to thee too, Strato. Countrymen,
My heart doth joy that yet in all my life
I found no man but he was true to me.
I shall have glory by this losing day
More than Octavius and Mark Antony
By this vile conquest shall attain unto.
So fare you well at once, for Brutus' tongue   39
Hath almost ended his life's history.
Night hangs upon mine eyes; my bones would rest,
That have but labored to attain this hour.   42
          Alarum. Cry within, "Fly, fly, fly!"

CLITUS
Fly, my lord, fly!

BRUTUS   Hence, I will follow.
          [*Exeunt Clitus, Dardanius, and Volumnius.*]
I prithee, Strato, stay thou by thy lord.
Thou art a fellow of a good respect;   45
Thy life hath had some smatch of honor in it.   46
Hold then my sword, and turn away thy face,
While I do run upon it. Wilt thou, Strato?

STRATO
Give me your hand first. Fare you well, my lord.

BRUTUS
Farewell, good Strato. [*He runs on his sword.*] Caesar,
     now be still.
I killed not thee with half so good a will.   *Dies.*   51

          Alarum. Retreat. Enter Antony, Octavius;
          Messala, Lucilius [as prisoners]; and the army.

OCTAVIUS   What man is that?

MESSALA
My master's man. Strato, where is thy master?

STRATO
Free from the bondage you are in, Messala.
The conquerors can but make a fire of him,
For Brutus only overcame himself,   56
And no man else hath honor by his death.

LUCILIUS
So Brutus should be found. I thank thee, Brutus,
That thou hast proved Lucilius' saying true.   59

OCTAVIUS
All that served Brutus, I will entertain them.   60

5.5. Location: The field of battle still.
2–3 Statilius . . . slain (According to Plutarch, a scout named Statilius
has gone through the enemy lines to reconnoitre and to hold up a
torch if all is well at Cassius's camp; he signals back but is then captured and slain.)   **3 or ta'en** either taken   **15 List** Listen to   **18 several** separate   **23 beat** driven.   **pit** trap for wild animals; also, a
grave.   **27 that our love** that friendship of ours

28 hilts hilt   **39 at once** all together, or without further ado   **42 That
. . . hour** that have striven all life long only to achieve this moment
of death.   **45 respect** reputation   **46 some smatch** some flavor, a
touch   **51.1 *Retreat*** signal to retire.   **56 Brutus . . . himself** only
Brutus conquered Brutus   **59 saying** (See 5.4.21–5.)   **60 entertain**
take into service

Fellow, wilt thou bestow thy time with me?

STRATO

Ay, if Messala will prefer me to you.   62

OCTAVIUS   Do so, good Messala.

MESSALA   How died my master, Strato?

STRATO

I held the sword, and he did run on it.

MESSALA

Octavius, then take him to follow thee,   66
That did the latest service to my master.   67

ANTONY

This was the noblest Roman of them all.
All the conspirators save only he
Did that they did in envy of great Caesar;
He only in a general honest thought   71
And common good to all made one of them.

His life was gentle, and the elements   73
So mixed in him that Nature might stand up
And say to all the world, "This was a man!"

OCTAVIUS

According to his virtue let us use him,
With all respect and rites of burial.
Within my tent his bones tonight shall lie,
Most like a soldier, ordered honorably.   79
So call the field to rest, and let's away   80
To part the glories of this happy day.   81

Exeunt omnes [with Brutus's body].

---

62 prefer recommend   **66 follow** serve   **67 latest** last   **71 general**
i.e., selfless. (Cf. 2.1.2 n.)

73 gentle noble.   **elements** (Humankind as a microcosm is made up
of earth, air, fire, and water, formed into the four humors of phlegm,
blood, yellow bile [or choler], and black bile [or melancholy], whose
qualities were mingled in Brutus in due proportions.)   **79 ordered**
treated, arranged for; accorded solemn rites. (Cf. 1.2.25 n.)   **80 field**
army in the field   **81 part** share.   **happy** fortunate   **81.1** *omnes* all

Hamlet, Prince of Denmark

A recurring motif in *Hamlet* is of a seemingly healthy exterior concealing an interior sickness. Mere pretense of virtue, as Hamlet warns his mother, "will but skin and film the ulcerous place, / Whiles rank corruption, mining all within, / Infects unseen" (3.4.154–6). Polonius confesses, when he is about to use his daughter as a decoy for Hamlet, that "with devotion's visage / And pious action we do sugar o'er / The devil himself"; and his observation elicits a more anguished mea culpa from Claudius in an aside: "How smart a lash that speech doth give my conscience! / The harlot's cheek, beautied with plast'ring art, / Is not more ugly to the thing that helps it / Than is my deed to my most painted word" (3.1.47–54).

This motif of concealed evil and disease continually reminds us that, in both a specific and a broader sense, "Something is rotten in the state of Denmark" (1.4.90). The specific source of contamination is a poison: the poison with which Claudius has killed Hamlet's father, the poison in the players' enactment of "The Murder of Gonzago," and the two poisons (envenomed sword and poisoned drink) with which Claudius and Laertes plot to rid themselves of young Hamlet. More generally, the poison is an evil nature seeking to destroy humanity's better self, as in the archetypal murder of Abel by Cain. "Oh, my offense is rank! It smells to heaven," laments Claudius, "It hath the primal eldest curse upon 't, / A brother's murder" (3.3.36–8). To Hamlet, his father and Claudius typify what is best and worst in humanity; one is the sun-god Hyperion and the other, a satyr. Claudius is a "serpent" and a "mildewed ear, / Blasting his wholesome brother" (1.5.40; 3.4.65–6). Many a person, in Hamlet's view, is tragically destined to behold his or her better qualities corrupted by "some vicious mole of nature" over which the individual seems to have no control. "His virtues else, be they as pure as grace, / As infinite as man may undergo, / Shall in the general censure take corruption / From that particular fault." The "dram of evil" pollutes "all the noble substance" (1.4.24–37). Thus, poison spreads outward to infect the whole individual, just as bad individuals can infect an entire court or nation.

Hamlet, his mind attuned to philosophical matters, is keenly and poetically aware of humanity's fallen condition. He is, moreover, a shrewd observer of the Danish court, familiar with its ways and at the same time newly returned from abroad, looking at Denmark with a stranger's eyes. What particularly darkens his view of humanity, however, is not the general fact of corrupted human nature but rather Hamlet's knowledge of a dreadful secret. Even before he learns of his father's murder, Hamlet senses that there is something more deeply amiss than his mother's overhasty marriage to her deceased husband's brother. This is serious enough, to be sure, for it violates a taboo (parallel to the marriage of a widower to his deceased wife's sister, long regarded as incestuous by the English) and is thus understandably referred to as "incest" by Hamlet and his father's ghost. The appalling spectacle of Gertrude's "wicked speed, to post / With such dexterity to incestuous sheets" (1.2.156–7) overwhelms Hamlet with revulsion at carnal appetite and intensifies the emotional crisis any son would go through when forced to contemplate his father's death and his mother's remarriage. Still, the Ghost's revelation is of something far worse, something Hamlet has subconsciously feared and suspected. "Oh, my prophetic soul! My uncle!" (1.5.42). Now Hamlet believes he has confirming evidence for his intuition that the world itself is "an unweeded garden / That grows to seed. Things rank and gross in nature / Possess it merely" (1.2.135–7).

Something is indeed rotten in the state of Denmark. The monarch on whom the health and safety of the kingdom depend is a murderer. Yet few persons know his secret: Hamlet, Horatio only belatedly, Claudius himself, and ourselves as audience. Many ironies and misunderstandings within the play cannot be understood without a proper awareness of this gap between Hamlet's knowledge and most others' ignorance of the murder. For, according to their own lights, Polonius and the rest behave as courtiers normally behave, obeying and flattering a king whom they acknowledge as their legitimate ruler who has been chosen by a constitutional process of "election" and is therefore their legitimate ruler. They do not know that he is a murderer. Hamlet, for his part, is so obsessed with the secret murder that he overreacts to those around him, rejecting overtures of friendship and becoming embittered, callous, brutal, and even violent. His antisocial behavior gives the others good reason to fear him as a menace to the state. Nevertheless, we share with Hamlet a knowledge of the truth and know that he is right, whereas the others are at best unhappily deceived by their own blind complicity in evil.

Rosencrantz and Guildenstern, for instance, are boyhood friends of Hamlet but are now dependent on the favor of King Claudius. Despite their seeming concern for their one-time comrade and Hamlet's initial pleasure in receiving them, they are faceless courtiers whose very names, like their personalities, are virtually interchangeable. "Thanks, Rosencrantz and gentle Guildenstern," says the King, and "Thanks, Guildenstern and gentle Rosencrantz," echoes the Queen (2.2.33–4). They cannot understand why Hamlet increasingly mocks their overtures of friendship, whereas Hamlet cannot stomach their subservience to the King. The secret murder divides Hamlet from them, since only he knows of it. As the confrontation between Hamlet and Claudius grows more deadly, Rosencrantz and Guildenstern, not knowing the true cause, can only interpret Hamlet's behavior as dangerous madness. The wild display he puts on during the performance of "The Murder of Gonzago" and then the killing of Polonius are evidence of a treasonous threat to the crown, eliciting from them staunch assertions of the divine right of kings. "Most holy and religious fear it is / To keep those many many bodies safe / That live and feed upon Your Majesty," professes Guildenstern, and Rosencrantz reiterates the theme: "The cess of majesty / Dies not alone, but like a gulf doth draw / What's near it with it" (3.3.8–17). These sentiments of Elizabethan orthodoxy, similar to ones frequently heard in Shakespeare's history plays, are here undercut by a devastating irony, since they are spoken unwittingly in defense of a murderer. This irony pursues Rosencrantz and Guildenstern to their graves, for they are killed performing what they see as their duty to convey Hamlet safely to England. They are as ignorant of Claudius's secret orders for the murder of Hamlet in England as they are of Claudius's real reason for wishing to be rid of his stepson. That Hamlet should ingeniously remove the secret commission from Rosencrantz and Guildenstern's packet and substitute an order for their execution is ironically fitting, even though they are guiltless of having plotted Hamlet's death. "Why, man, they did make love to this employment," says Hamlet to Horatio. "They are not

near my conscience. Their defeat / Does by their own insinuation grow" (5.2.57–9). They have condemned themselves, in Hamlet's eyes, by interceding officiously in deadly affairs of which they had no comprehension. Hamlet's judgment of them is harsh, and he himself appears hardened and pitiless in his role as agent in their deaths, but he is right that they have courted their own destiny.

Polonius, too, dies for meddling. It seems an unfair fate, since he wishes no physical harm to Hamlet and is only trying to ingratiate himself with Claudius. Yet Polonius's complicity in jaded court politics is deeper than his fatuous parental sententiousness might lead one to suppose. His famous advice to his son, often quoted out of context as though it were wise counsel, is, in fact, a worldly gospel of self-interest and concern for appearances. Like his son, Laertes, he cynically presumes that Hamlet's affection for Ophelia cannot be serious, since princes are not free to marry ladies of the court; accordingly, Polonius obliges his daughter to return the love letters she so cherishes. Polonius's spies are everywhere, seeking to entrap Polonius's own son in fleshly sin or to discover symptoms of Hamlet's presumed lovesickness. Polonius may cut a ridiculous figure as a prattling busybody, but he is wily and even menacing in his intent. He has actually helped Claudius to the throne and is an essential instrument of royal policy. His ineffectuality and ignorance of the murder do not really excuse his guilty involvement.

Ophelia is more innocent than her father and brother, and more truly affectionate toward Hamlet. She earns our sympathy because she is caught between the conflicting wills of the men who are supremely important to her— her lover, her father, and her brother. Obedient by instinct and training to patriarchal instruction, she is unprepared to cope with divided authority and so takes refuge in passivity. Nevertheless, her pitiable story suggests that weak-willed acquiescence is poisoned by the evil to which it surrenders. However passively, Ophelia becomes an instrument through which Claudius attempts to spy on Hamlet. She is much like Gertrude, for the Queen has yielded to Claudius's importunity without ever knowing fully what awful price Claudius has paid for her and for the throne. The resemblance between Ophelia and Gertrude confirms Hamlet's tendency to generalize about feminine weakness—"frailty, thy name is woman" (1.2.146)—and prompts his misogynistic outburst against Ophelia when he concludes she, too, is spying on him. His rejection of love and friendship (except for Horatio's) seems paranoid in character and yet is at least partially justified by the fact that so many of the court are in fact conspiring to learn what he is up to.

Their oversimplification of his dilemma and their facile analyses vex Hamlet as much as their meddling. When they presume to diagnose his malady, the courtiers actually reveal more about themselves than about Hamlet— something we as readers and viewers might well bear in mind. Rosencrantz and Guildenstern think in political terms, reflecting their own ambitious natures, and Hamlet takes mordant delight in leading them on. "Sir, I lack advancement," he mockingly answers Rosencrantz's questioning as to the cause of his distemper. Rosencrantz is immediately taken in: "How can that be, when you have the voice of the King himself for your succession in Denmark?" (3.2.338–41). Actually, Hamlet does hold a grudge against Claudius for having "Popped in between th'election and my hopes" (5.2.65), using the Danish custom of "election" by the chief lords of the realm to deprive young Hamlet of the succession that would normally have been his. Nevertheless, it is a gross oversimplification to suppose that political frustration is the key to Hamlet's sorrow, and to speculate thus is presumptuous. "Why, look you now, how unworthy a thing you make of me!" Hamlet protests to Rosencrantz and Guildenstern. "You would play upon me, you would seem to know my stops, you would pluck out the heart of my mystery" (3.2.362–5). An even worse offender in the distortion of complex truth is Polonius, whose facile diagnosis of lovesickness appears to have been inspired by recollections of Polonius's own far-off youth. ("Truly in my youth I suffered much extremity for love, very near this," 2.2.189–91). Polonius's fatuous complacency in his own powers of analysis—"If circumstances lead me, I will find / Where truth is hid, though it were hid indeed / Within the center" (2.2.157–9)—reads like a parody of Hamlet's struggle to discover what is true and what is not.

Thus, although Hamlet may seem to react with excessive bitterness toward those who are set to watch over him, the corruption he decries in Denmark is both real and universal. "The time is out of joint," he laments. "Oh, cursèd spite / That ever I was born to set it right!" (1.5.197–8). How is he to proceed in setting things right? Ever since the nineteenth century, it has been fashionable to discover reasons for Hamlet's delaying his revenge. The basic Romantic approach is to find a defect, or tragic flaw, in Hamlet himself. In Coleridge's words, Hamlet suffers from "an overbalance in the contemplative faculty" and is "one who vacillates from sensibility and procrastinates from thought, and loses the power of action in the energy of resolve." More recent psychological critics, such as Freud's disciple Ernest Jones, still seek answers to the Romantics' question by explaining Hamlet's failure of will. In Jones' interpretation, Hamlet is the victim of an Oedipal trauma: he has longed unconsciously to possess his mother and for that very reason cannot bring himself to punish the hated uncle who has supplanted him in his incestuous and forbidden desire. Such interpretations suggest, among other things, that Hamlet continues to serve as a mirror in which analysts who would pluck out the heart of his mystery see an image of their own concerns—just as Rosencrantz and Guildenstern read politics, and Polonius reads lovesickness, into Hamlet's distress.

We can ask, however, not only whether the explanations for Hamlet's supposed delay are valid but also whether the question they seek to answer is itself valid. Is the delay unnecessary or excessive? The question did not even arise until the nineteenth century. Earlier audiences were evidently satisfied that Hamlet must test the Ghost's credibility, since apparitions can tell half-truths to deceive people, and that, once Hamlet has confirmed the Ghost's word, he proceeds as resolutely as his canny adversary allows. More recent criticism, perhaps reflecting a modern absorption in existentialist philosophy, has proposed that Hamlet's dilemma is a matter, not of personal failure, but of the absurdity of action itself in a corrupt world. Does what Hamlet is asked to do make any sense, given the bestial nature of humanity and the impossibility of knowing what is right? In part, it is a matter of style: Claudius's Denmark is crassly vulgar, and to combat this vulgarity on its own terms seems to require the sort of bad histrionics Hamlet derides in actors who mouth their lines or tear a passion to tatters. Hamlet's dilemma of action can best be studied in the play by comparing him with various characters who are obliged to act in situations similar to his own and who respond in meaningfully different ways.

Three young men—Hamlet, Laertes, and Fortinbras—are called upon to avenge their fathers' violent deaths. Ophelia, too, has lost a father by violent means, and her madness and death are another kind of reaction to such a loss. The responses of Laertes and Fortinbras offer rich parallels to Hamlet, in both cases implying the futility of positive and forceful action. Laertes thinks he has received an unambiguous mandate to take revenge, since Hamlet has undoubtedly slain Polonius and helped to deprive Ophelia of her sanity. Accordingly, Laertes comes back to Denmark in a fury, stirring the rabble with his demagoguery and spouting Senecan rant about dismissing conscience "to the profoundest pit" in his quest for vengeance (4.5.135). When Claudius asks what Laertes would do to Hamlet "To show yourself in deed your father's son / More than in words," Laertes fires back: "To cut his throat i'th' church" (4.7.126–7). This resolution is understandable. The pity is, however, that Laertes has only superficially identified the murderer in the case. He is too easily deceived by Claudius, because he has jumped to easy and fallacious conclusions, and so is doomed to become a pawn in Claudius's sly maneuverings. Too late he sees his error and must die for it, begging and receiving Hamlet's forgiveness. Before we accuse Hamlet of thinking too deliberately before acting, we must consider that Laertes does not think enough.

Fortinbras of Norway, as his name implies ("strong in arms"), is one who believes in decisive action. At the beginning of the play, we learn that his father has been slain in battle by old Hamlet and that Fortinbras has collected an army to win back by force the territory fairly won by the Danes in that encounter. Like Hamlet, young Fortinbras does not succeed his father to the throne but must now contend with an uncle-king. When this uncle, at Claudius's instigation, forbids Fortinbras to march against the Danes and rewards him for his restraint with a huge annual income and a commission to fight the Poles instead, Fortinbras sagaciously welcomes the new opportunity. He pockets the money, marches against Poland, and waits for occasion to deliver Denmark as well into his hands. Clearly this is more of a success story than that of Laertes, and Hamlet does, after all, give his blessing to the "election" of Fortinbras to the Danish throne. Fortinbras is the man of the hour, the representative of a restored political stability. Yet Hamlet's admiration for this man on horseback is qualified by a profound reservation. Hamlet's dying prophecy that the election will light on Fortinbras (5.2.357–8) is suffused with ironies, so much so that the incongruity is sometimes made conscious and deliberate in performance. Earlier in the play, the spectacle of Fortinbras marching against Poland "to gain a little patch of ground / That hath in it no profit but the name" prompts Hamlet to berate himself for inaction, but he cannot ignore the absurdity of the effort. "Two thousand souls and twenty thousand ducats / Will not debate the question of this straw." The soldiers will risk their very lives "Even for an eggshell" (4.4.19–54). It is only one step from this view of the vanity of ambitious striving to the speculation that great Caesar or Alexander, dead and turned to dust, may one day produce the loam or clay with which to stop the bunghole of a beer barrel. Fortinbras epitomizes the ongoing political order after Hamlet's death, but is that order of any consequence to us after we have imagined with Hamlet the futility of most human endeavor?

To ask such a question is to seek passive or self-abnegating answers to the riddle of life, and Hamlet is attuned to such inquiries. Even before he learns of his father's murder, he contemplates suicide, wishing "that the Everlasting had not fixed / His canon 'gainst self-slaughter" (1.2.131–2). As with the alternative of action, other characters serve as foils to Hamlet, revealing both the attractions and perils of withdrawal. Ophelia is destroyed by meekly acquiescing in others' desires. Whether she commits suicide is uncertain, but the very possibility reminds us that Hamlet has twice considered and reluctantly rejected this despairing path as forbidden by Christian teaching—the second such occasion being his "To be, or not to be" soliloquy in 3.1. He has also playacted at the madness to which Ophelia succumbs. Gertrude identifies herself with Ophelia and like her has surrendered her will to male aggressiveness. We suspect she knows little of the actual murder (see 3.4.31) but dares not think how deeply she may be implicated. Although her death is evidently not a suicide (see 5.2.291–7), it is passive and expiatory.

A more attractive alternative to decisive action for Hamlet is acting in the theater, and he is full of exuberant advice to the visiting players. The play they perform before Claudius at Hamlet's request and with some lines added by him—a play consciously archaic in style—offers to the Danish court a kind of heightened reflection of itself, a homiletic artifact, rendering in conventional terms the taut anxieties and terrors of murder for the sake of noble passion. Structurally, the play within the play becomes not an escape for Hamlet into inaction but rather the point on which the whole drama pivots and the scene in which contemplation of past events is largely replaced with stirrings toward action. When Lucianus in the Mousetrap play turns out to be nephew rather than brother to the dead king, the audience finds itself face to face, not with history, but with prophecy. We are not surprised when, in his conversations with the players, Hamlet openly professes his admiration for the way in which art holds "the mirror up to nature, to show virtue her feature, scorn her own image, and the very age and body of the time his form and pressure" (3.2.22–4). Hamlet admires the dramatist's ability to transmute raw human feeling into tragic art, depicting and ordering reality as Shakespeare's play of *Hamlet* does for us. Yet playacting can also be, Hamlet recognizes, a self-indulgent escape for him, a way of unpacking his heart with words and of verbalizing his situation without doing something to remedy it. Acting and talking remind him too much of Polonius, who was an actor in his youth and who continues to be, like Hamlet, an inveterate punster.

Of the passive responses in the play, the stoicism of Hortatio is by far the most attractive to Hamlet. "More an antique Roman than a Dane" (5.2.343), Horatio is, as Hamlet praises him, immune to flattering or to opportunities for cheap self-advancement. He is "As one, in suffering all, that suffers nothing, / A man that Fortune's buffets and rewards / Hast ta'en with equal thanks" (3.2.65–7). Such a person has a sure defense against the worst that life can offer. Hamlet can trust and love Horatio as he can no one else. Yet even here there are limits, for Horatio's skeptical and Roman philosophy cuts him off from a Christian and metaphysical overview. "There are more things in heaven and earth, Horatio, / Than are dreamt of in your philosophy" (1.5.175–6). After they have beheld together the skulls of Yorick's graveyard, Horatio seemingly does not share with Hamlet the exulting Christian perception that, although human life is indeed vain, Providence will reveal a pattern transcending human sorrow.

Hamlet's path must lie somewhere between the rash suddenness of Laertes or the canny resoluteness of Fortinbras on the one hand, and the passivity of Ophelia or Gertrude and the stoic resignation of Horatio on the other. At first he alternates between action and inaction, finding neither satisfactory. The Ghost has commanded Hamlet to revenge but has not explained how this is to be done; indeed, Gertrude is to be left passively to heaven and her conscience. If this method will suffice for her (and Christian wisdom taught that such a purgation was as thorough as it was sure), why not for Claudius? If Claudius must be killed, should it be while he is at his sin rather than at his prayers? The play is full of questions, stemming chiefly from the enigmatic commands of the Ghost. "Say, why is this? Wherefore? What should we do?" (1.4.57). Hamlet is not incapable of action. He shows unusual strength and cunning on the pirate ship, in his duel with Laertes ("I shall win at the odds"; 5.2.209), and especially in his slaying of Polonius—an action hardly characterized by "thinking too precisely on th'event" (4.4.42). Here is forthright action of the sort Laertes espouses. Yet, when the corpse behind his mother's arras turns out to be Polonius rather than Claudius, Hamlet concludes from the mistake that he has offended heaven. Even if Polonius deserves what he got, Hamlet believes he has made himself into a cruel "scourge" of Providence who must himself suffer retribution as well as deal it out. Swift action has not accomplished what the Ghost commanded.

The Ghost does not appear to speak for Providence in any case. His message is of revenge, a pagan concept deeply embedded in most societies but at odds with Christian teaching. His wish that Claudius be sent to hell and that Gertrude be more gently treated might, in fact, be the judgment of an impartial deity but here comes wrapped in the passionate involvement of a murdered man's restless spirit. This is not to say that Hamlet is being tempted to perform a damnable act, as he fears is possible, but that the Ghost's command cannot readily be reconciled with a complex and balanced view of justice. If Hamlet were to spring on Claudius in the fullness of his vice and cut his throat, we would pronounce Hamlet a murderer. What Hamlet believes he has learned instead is that he must become the instrument of Providence according to *its* plans, not his own. After his return from England, he senses triumphantly that all will be for the best if he allows an unseen power to decide the time and place for his final act. Under these conditions, rash action will be right. "Rashly, / And praised be rashness for it— let us know / Our indiscretion sometime serves us well / When our deep plots do pall, and that should learn us / There's a divinity that shapes our ends, / Rough-hew them how we will" (5.2.6–11). Passivity, too, is now a proper course, for Hamlet puts himself wholly at the disposal of Providence. What had seemed so impossible when Hamlet tried to formulate his own design proves elementary once he trusts to a divine justice in which he now firmly believes. Rashness and passivity are perfectly fused. Hamlet is revenged without having to commit premeditated murder and is relieved of his painful existence without having to commit suicide.

The circumstances of *Hamlet'*s catastrophe do indeed seem to accomplish all that Hamlet desires, by a route so circuitous that no one could ever have foreseen or devised

it. Polonius's death, as it turns out, was instrumental after all, for it led to Laertes's angry return to Denmark and the challenge to a duel. Every seemingly unrelated event has its place; "There is special providence in the fall of a sparrow" (5.2.217–18). Repeatedly, the characters stress the role of seeming accident leading to just retribution. Even Horatio, for whom the events of the play suggest a pattern of randomness and violence, of "accidental judgments" and "casual slaughters," can see at last, "in this upshot, purposes mistook / Fall'n on th'inventors' heads" (5.2.384–7). In a similar vein, Laertes confesses himself "a woodcock to mine own springe" (line 309). As Hamlet had said earlier, of Rosencrantz and Guildenstern, " 'tis the sport to have the engineer / Hoist with his own petard" (3.4.213–14). Thus, too, Claudius's poisoned cup, intended for Hamlet, kills the Queen for whom Claudius had done such evil in order to acquire her and the throne. The destiny of evil in this play is to overreach itself.

In its final resolution, *Hamlet* incorporates a broader conception of justice than its revenge formula seemed at first to make possible. Yet, in its origins, *Hamlet* is a revenge story, and these traditions have left some residual savagery in the play. In the *Historia Danica* of Saxo Grammaticus, 1180–1208, and in the rather free translation of Saxo into French by François de Belleforest, *Histoires Tragiques* (1576), Hamlet is cunning and bloodily resolute throughout. He kills an eavesdropper without a qualm during the interview with his mother and exchanges letters on his way to England with characteristic shrewdness. Ultimately, he returns to Denmark, sets fire to his uncle's hall, slays its courtly inhabitants, and claims his rightful throne from a grateful people. The Ghost, absent in this account, may well have been supplied by Thomas Kyd, author of *The Spanish Tragedy* (c. 1587) and seemingly of a lost *Hamlet* play in existence by 1589. *The Spanish Tragedy* bears many resemblances to our *Hamlet* and suggests what the lost *Hamlet* may well have contained: a sensational murder, a Senecan Ghost demanding revenge, the avenger hampered by court intrigue, his resort to a feigned madness, and his difficulty in authenticating the ghostly vision. A German version of *Hamlet*, called *Der bestrafte Brudermord* (1710), based seemingly on the older *Hamlet*, includes such details as the play within the play, the sparing of the King at his prayers in order to damn his soul, Ophelia's madness, the fencing match with poisoned swords and poisoned drink, and the final catastrophe of vengeance and death. Similarly, the early unauthorized First Quarto of *Hamlet* (1603) offers some passages seemingly based on the older play by Kyd.

Although this evidence suggests that Shakespeare received most of the material for the plot intact, his transformation of that material was nonetheless immeasurable. To be sure, Kyd's *The Spanish Tragedy* contains many rhetorical passages on the inadequacy of human justice, but the overall effect is still sensational and the outcome is a triumph for the pagan spirit of revenge. So, too, with the many revenge plays of the 1590s and 1600s that Kyd's dramatic genius had inspired, including Shakespeare's own *Titus Andronicus* (c. 1589–1592). *Hamlet,* written in about 1599–1601 (it is not mentioned by Frances Meres in his *Palladis Tamia: Wit's Treasury,* in 1598, and was entered in the Stationers' Register, the official record book of the London Company of Stationers [booksellers and printers], in 1602), is unparalleled in its philosophical richness. Its ending is truly cathartic, for Hamlet dies, not as a bloodied avenger, but as one who has affirmed the tragic dignity of the human race. His courage and faith, maintained in the face of great odds, atone for the dismal corruption in which Denmark has festered. His resolutely honest inquiries have taken him beyond the revulsion and doubt that express so eloquently, among other matters, the fearful response of Shakespeare's own generation to a seeming breakdown of established political, theological, and cosmological beliefs. Hamlet finally perceives that "if it be not now, yet it will come," and that "The readiness is all" (5.2.219–20). This discovery, this revelation of necessity and meaning in Hamlet's great reversal of fortune, enables him to confront the tragic circumstance of his life with understanding and heroism and to demonstrate the triumph of the human spirit even in the moment of his catastrophe.

Such an assertion of the individual will does not lessen the tragic waste with which *Hamlet* ends. Hamlet is dead, and the great promise of his life is forever lost. Few others have survived. Justice has seemingly been fulfilled in the deaths of Claudius, Gertrude, Rosencrantz and Guildenstern, Polonius, Laertes, and perhaps even Ophelia, but in a wild and extravagant way, as though Justice herself, more vengeful than providential, were unceasingly hungry for victims. Hamlet, the minister of that justice, has likewise grown indifferent to the spilling of blood, even if he submits himself at last to the will of a force he recognizes as providential. Denmark faces the kind of political uncertainty with which the play began. However much Hamlet may admire Fortinbras's resolution, the prince of Norway seems an alien choice for Denmark—even an ironic one. Horatio sees so little point in outliving the catastrophe of this play that he would choose death, were it not that he must draw his breath in pain to ensure that Hamlet's story is truly told. Still, that truth has been rescued from oblivion. Amid the ruin of the final scene, we share the artist's vision, through which we struggle to interpret and give order to the tragedy that proves inseparable from human existence.

The performance history of *Hamlet* is extraordinarily rich. It also attests to a variety of interpetations that is equally textured. Eighteenth-century versions by David Garrick and others often took out or severely reduced the Fortinbras plot; indeed, the play is so long that it almost certainly was not acted in its entirety even in Shake-

speare's day. Garrick also deleted the Gravediggers' scene and much besides in Act 5. Pictorial scenery in the nineteenth century tended to favor opulent renditions of the play-within-the-play and Ophelia's mad scenes. Hamlet was portrayed in 1864, at the Lyceum Theater, as a Viking in a primitive medieval decor. Henry Irving, undertaking the role of Hamlet from 1864 to 1885, chose a decor of the fifth or sixth century, with castle battlements set among massive rocks glimmering under the soft light of the moon in the first act. John Gielgud became famous as a leading Hamlet of his day, beginning in 1930 at the Old Vic, emphasizing the pale, introspective, sonorous-voiced Hamlet that Coleridge had imagined. More recently, *Hamlet* has been seen from an existential vantage (by Tyrone Guthrie, 1938, at the Old Vic) in the modern-dress context of a Europe precariously trapped between the first World War and a second about to begin. Laurence Olivier, in his film version of 1948, explored the Freudian dimensions of "a man who could not make up his mind"; influenced by Ernest Jones's *Hamlet and Oedipus,* Olivier allowed the camera eye to linger on the Queen's bedchamber and its bed, where Hamlet encountered his mother in a scene (3.4) heavy with incestuous overtones.

Recent productions on stage, in film, and on television amply demonstrate how Shakespeare's best-known play can lend itself to other kinds of relevance to our modern world. Political interpretations sometimes focus on Claudius as a Machiavel in the school of modern spin-doctoring. At the Wisdom Bridge Theater's Chicago production in the 1970s, for example, directed by Robert Falls with Aiden Quinn as Hamlet, Claudius was the Great Communicator in the style of Ronald Reagan. His first scene (1.2) featured the new king on an array of television sets, blandly explaining to the Danish public the reasons for his rapid assumption of power and marriage with the widow of his dead brother. Claudius and Gertrude never appeared onstage in this scene; the audience saw the king on television, while the stage itself was given over to his zealous public relations team, nattily dressed, preparing a reception for the press representatives, making sure the event went smoothly. Fading posters of the dead king offered contrasting reminders of the regime which Claudius had so astutely supplanted.

More recently, in Michael Almereyda's low-budget film of 2000, the setting throughout is the New York world of privilege and high finance. Claudius (Kyle MacLachlan) is a chief executive officer of a superconglomerate financial empire. Gertrude (Diane Venora) is a suburban wife utterly seduced by the expensive privileges she now enjoys, of stretch limosines, private bathing pools in their high-rise empire, and the surroundings of obsequious flattery that immense wealth can command. Hamlet (Ethan Hawke), conversely, is a rebel with a cause, ostentatiously out of step in his moth-eaten ski cap, his scruffy clothes, his mania for the latest film and computer technology, and his disdain for corrupting privilege. The ghost of Hamlet's father (Sam Shepard) eerily appears on the swank penthouse battlements of New York's concrete skyscrapers, berattling the television monitors of up-to-date security systems. The overall effect is indeed strikingly modern and plausible. Another popular film version is that of Franco Zeffirelli (1990), with Mel Gibson as a matinee idol Hamlet, Alan Bates as a believably sexy Claudius, Glenn Close as a Gertrude who is erotically infatuated with her new husband, and some compellingly handsome scenery. Grigori Kozintsev's Russian film version of 1964, based on a script by Boris Pasternak, is visually eloquent in its recurring images of stone, iron, fire, sea, and earth. Kenneth Branagh's four-hour *Hamlet* (1996) is notable for its intrepedity in offering an essentially uncut version and for some superb performances, especially that of Derek Jacobi as Claudius. Jacobi had starred earlier as Hamlet onstage (Old Vic, 1979) and in the BBC television series of all the plays beginning in 1979. Richard Burton's memorable stage performance (1964, at New York's Lunt-Fontanne Theater) is available on video. This play is especially fortunate in a rich archive of filmed or televised versions that make possible a comparative study in production by some of the greatest Shakespearean actors of the twentieth and twenty-first centuries. These varied interpretations abundantly show how *Hamlet* and its fascinating protagonist can be satirical, rebellious, mordant, funny, disillusioned, melancholic, introspective, and much more. The play that puzzles and fascinates readers is also immensely disturbing in performance.

Hamlet, Prince of Denmark

[*Dramatis Personae*

GHOST *of Hamlet, the former King of Denmark*
CLAUDIUS, *King of Denmark, the former King's brother*
GERTRUDE, *Queen of Denmark, widow of the former King and now wife of Claudius*
HAMLET, *Prince of Denmark, son of the late King and of Gertrude*

POLONIUS, *councillor to the King*
LAERTES, *his son*
OPHELIA, *his daughter*
REYNALDO, *his servant*

HORATIO, *Hamlet's friend and fellow student*

VOLTIMAND,
CORNELIUS,
ROSENCRANTZ,
GUILDENSTERN, } *members of the Danish court*
OSRIC,
A GENTLEMAN,
A LORD,

BERNARDO,
FRANCISCO, } *officers and soldiers on watch*
MARCELLUS,

FORTINBRAS, *Prince of Norway*
CAPTAIN *in his army*

Three or Four PLAYERS, *taking the roles of* PROLOGUE, PLAYER KING, PLAYER QUEEN, *and* LUCIANUS
Two MESSENGERS
FIRST SAILOR
Two CLOWNS, *a gravedigger and his companion*
PRIEST
FIRST AMBASSADOR *from England*

Lords, Soldiers, Attendants, Guards, other Players, Followers of Laertes, other Sailors, another Ambassador or Ambassadors from England

SCENE: *Denmark*]

[1.1]

Enter Bernardo and Francisco, two sentinels,
[meeting].

BERNARDO   Who's there?

FRANCISCO
   Nay, answer me. Stand and unfold yourself.   2

BERNARDO   Long live the King!

FRANCISCO   Bernardo?

BERNARDO   He.

FRANCISCO
   You come most carefully upon your hour.

BERNARDO
   'Tis now struck twelve. Get thee to bed, Francisco.

FRANCISCO
   For this relief much thanks. 'Tis bitter cold,
   And I am sick at heart.

BERNARDO   Have you had quiet guard?

FRANCISCO   Not a mouse stirring.

BERNARDO   Well, good night.
   If you do meet Horatio and Marcellus,
   The rivals of my watch, bid them make haste.   14

Enter Horatio and Marcellus.

FRANCISCO
   I think I hear them.—Stand, ho! Who is there?

HORATIO   Friends to this ground.   16

MARCELLUS   And liegemen to the Dane.   17

FRANCISCO   Give you good night.   18

MARCELLUS
   Oh, farewell, honest soldier. Who hath relieved you?

FRANCISCO
   Bernardo hath my place. Give you good night.
                                        Exit Francisco.

MARCELLUS   Holla! Bernardo!

BERNARDO   Say, what, is Horatio there?

HORATIO   A piece of him.

BERNARDO
   Welcome, Horatio. Welcome, good Marcellus.

HORATIO
   What, has this thing appeared again tonight?

BERNARDO   I have seen nothing.

MARCELLUS
   Horatio says 'tis but our fantasy,   27
   And will not let belief take hold of him
   Touching this dreaded sight twice seen of us.
   Therefore I have entreated him along   30
   With us to watch the minutes of this night,   31
   That if again this apparition come
   He may approve our eyes and speak to it.   33

HORATIO
   Tush, tush, 'twill not appear.

BERNARDO   Sit down awhile

And let us once again assail your ears,
That are so fortified against our story,
What we have two nights seen.

HORATIO   Well, sit we down,
And let us hear Bernardo speak of this.

BERNARDO   Last night of all,   39
When yond same star that's westward from the pole   40
Had made his course t'illume that part of heaven   41
Where now it burns, Marcellus and myself,
The bell then beating one—

Enter Ghost.

MARCELLUS
Peace, break thee off! Look where it comes again!

BERNARDO
In the same figure like the King that's dead.

MARCELLUS
Thou art a scholar. Speak to it, Horatio.   46

BERNARDO
Looks 'a not like the King? Mark it, Horatio.   47

HORATIO
Most like. It harrows me with fear and wonder.

BERNARDO
It would be spoke to.

MARCELLUS   Speak to it, Horatio.   49

HORATIO
What art thou that usurp'st this time of night,   50
Together with that fair and warlike form
In which the majesty of buried Denmark   52
Did sometimes march? By heaven, I charge thee, speak!   53

MARCELLUS
It is offended.

BERNARDO   See, it stalks away.

HORATIO
Stay! Speak, speak! I charge thee, speak!   *Exit Ghost.*

MARCELLUS   'Tis gone and will not answer.

BERNARDO
How now, Horatio? You tremble and look pale.
Is not this something more than fantasy?
What think you on't?   59

HORATIO
Before my God, I might not this believe
Without the sensible and true avouch   61
Of mine own eyes.

MARCELLUS   Is it not like the King?

HORATIO   As thou art to thyself.
Such was the very armor he had on
When he the ambitious Norway combated.   65
So frowned he once when, in an angry parle,   66
He smote the sledded Polacks on the ice.   67
'Tis strange.

1.1 Location: Elsinore castle. A guard platform.
2 me (Francisco emphasizes that *he* is the sentry currently on watch.)
unfold yourself reveal your identity.   **14 rivals** partners   **16 ground**
country, land.   **17 liegemen to the Dane** men sworn to serve the
Danish king.   **18 Give** May God give   **27 fantasy** imagination
30 along to come along   **31 watch** keep watch during   **33 approve**
corroborate

39 Last . . . all i.e., This *very* last night. (Emphatic.)   **40 pole** polestar,
north star   **41 his** its.   **t'illume** to illuminate   **46 scholar** one
learned enough to know how to question a ghost properly.   **47 'a** he
49 It . . . to (It was commonly believed that a ghost could not speak
until spoken to.)   **50 usurp'st** wrongfully takes over   **52 buried**
Denmark the buried King of Denmark   **53 sometimes** formerly
59 on't of it.   **61 sensible** confirmed by the senses.   **avouch** warrant,
evidence   **65 Norway** King of Norway   **66 parle** parley   **67 sledded**
traveling on sleds.   **Polacks** Poles

MARCELLUS
Thus twice before, and jump at this dead hour,   69
With martial stalk hath he gone by our watch.   70

HORATIO
In what particular thought to work I know not,   71
But in the gross and scope of mine opinion   72
This bodes some strange eruption to our state.

MARCELLUS
Good now, sit down, and tell me, he that knows,   74
Why this same strict and most observant watch
So nightly toils the subject of the land,   76
And why such daily cast of brazen cannon   77
And foreign mart for implements of war,   78
Why such impress of shipwrights, whose sore task   79
Does not divide the Sunday from the week.
What might be toward, that this sweaty haste   81
Doth make the night joint-laborer with the day?
Who is't that can inform me?

HORATIO   That can I;
At least, the whisper goes so. Our last king,
Whose image even but now appeared to us,
Was, as you know, by Fortinbras of Norway,
Thereto pricked on by a most emulate pride,   87
Dared to the combat; in which our valiant Hamlet—
For so this side of our known world esteemed him—   89
Did slay this Fortinbras; who by a sealed compact   90
Well ratified by law and heraldry   91
Did forfeit, with his life, all those his lands
Which he stood seized of, to the conqueror;   93
Against the which a moiety competent   94
Was gagèd by our king, which had returned   95
To the inheritance of Fortinbras   96
Had he been vanquisher, as, by the same cov'nant   97
And carriage of the article designed,   98
His fell to Hamlet. Now, sir, young Fortinbras,
Of unimprovèd mettle hot and full,   100
Hath in the skirts of Norway here and there   101
Sharked up a list of lawless resolutes   102
For food and diet to some enterprise   103
That hath a stomach in't, which is no other—   104
As it doth well appear unto our state—
But to recover of us, by strong hand
And terms compulsatory, those foresaid lands
So by his father lost. And this, I take it,
Is the main motive of our preparations,

The source of this our watch, and the chief head   110
Of this posthaste and rummage in the land.   111

BERNARDO
I think it be no other but e'en so.
Well may it sort that this portentous figure   113
Comes armèd through our watch so like the King
That was and is the question of these wars.   115

HORATIO
A mote it is to trouble the mind's eye.   116
In the most high and palmy state of Rome,   117
A little ere the mightiest Julius fell,   118
The graves stood tenantless, and the sheeted dead   119
Did squeak and gibber in the Roman streets;
As stars with trains of fire and dews of blood,   121
Disasters in the sun; and the moist star   122
Upon whose influence Neptune's empire stands   123
Was sick almost to doomsday with eclipse.   124
And even the like precurse of feared events,   125
As harbingers preceding still the fates   126
And prologue to the omen coming on,   127
Have heaven and earth together demonstrated
Unto our climatures and countrymen.   129

        Enter Ghost.

But soft, behold! Lo, where it comes again!   130
I'll cross it, though it blast me. (*It spreads his arms.*) Stay,
    illusion!   131
If thou hast any sound or use of voice,
Speak to me!
If there be any good thing to be done
That may to thee do ease and grace to me,
Speak to me!
If thou art privy to thy country's fate,   137
Which, happily, foreknowing may avoid,   138
Oh, speak!
Or if thou hast uphoarded in thy life
Extorted treasure in the womb of earth,
For which, they say, you spirits oft walk in death,
Speak of it! (*The cock crows.*) Stay and speak!—Stop it,
    Marcellus.

MARCELLUS
Shall I strike at it with my partisan?   144
HORATIO   Do, if it will not stand.   [*They strike at it.*]
BERNARDO   'Tis here!   146
HORATIO   'Tis here!   [*Exit Ghost.*]   147

---

69 jump exactly   **70 stalk** stride   **71 to work** i.e., to collect my thoughts and try to understand this   **72 gross and scope** general drift   **74 Good now** (An expression denoting entreaty or expostulation.)   **76 toils** causes to toil.   **subject** subjects   **77 cast** casting   **78 mart** shopping   **79 impress** impressment, conscription   **81 toward** in preparation   **87 Thereto . . . pride** (Refers to old Fortinbras, not the Danish King.)   **emulate** emulous, ambitious   **89 this . . . world** i.e., all Europe, the Western world   **90 sealed** certified, confirmed   **91 heraldry** chivalry   **93 seized** possessed   **94 Against the** in return for.   **moiety competent** corresponding portion   **95 gagèd** engaged, pledged.   **had returned** would have passed   **96 inheritance** possession   **97 cov'nant** i.e., the *sealed compact* of line 90   **98 carriage . . . designed** purport of the article referred to   **100 unimprovèd mettle** untried, undisciplined spirits   **101 skirts** outlying regions, outskirts   **102–4 Sharked . . . in't** rounded up (as a shark scoops up fish) a troop of lawless desperadoes to feed and supply an enterprise of considerable daring

110 head source   **111 posthaste and rummage** frenetic activity and bustle   **113 Well . . . sort** That would explain why   **115 question** focus of contention   **116 mote** speck of dust   **117 palmy** flourishing   **118 Julius** Julius Caesar   **119 sheeted** shrouded   **121 As** (This abrupt transition suggests that matter is possibly omitted between lines 120 and 121.)   **trains** trails   **122 Disasters** unfavorable signs or aspects.   **moist star** i.e., moon, governing tides   **123 Neptune's . . . stands** the sea depends   **124 Was . . . eclipse** was eclipsed nearly to the cosmic darkness predicted for the second coming of Christ and the ending of the world. (See Matthew 24:29 and Revelation 6:12.)   **125 precurse** heralding, foreshadowing   **126 harbingers** forerunners.   **still** always   **127 omen** calamitous event   **129 climatures** climes, regions   **130 soft** i.e., enough, break off   **131 cross** stand in its path, confront.   **blast** wither, strike with a curse.   **131 s.d. his** its   **137 privy to** in on the secret of   **138 happily** haply, perchance   **144 partisan** long-handled spear.   **146–7 'Tis Here! / 'Tis here!** (Perhaps they attempt to strike at the Ghost, but are baffled by its seeming ability to be here and there and nowhere.)

MARCELLUS 'Tis gone.
We do it wrong, being so majestical,
To offer it the show of violence,
For it is as the air invulnerable,
And our vain blows malicious mockery.

BERNARDO

It was about to speak when the cock crew.

HORATIO

And then it started like a guilty thing
Upon a fearful summons. I have heard
The cock, that is the trumpet to the morn,   156
Doth with his lofty and shrill-sounding throat
Awake the god of day, and at his warning,
Whether in sea or fire, in earth or air,
Th'extravagant and erring spirit hies   160
To his confine; and of the truth herein
This present object made probation.   162

MARCELLUS

It faded on the crowing of the cock.
Some say that ever 'gainst that season comes   164
Wherein our Savior's birth is celebrated,
This bird of dawning singeth all night long,
And then, they say, no spirit dare stir abroad;
The nights are wholesome, then no planets strike,   168
No fairy takes, nor witch hath power to charm,   169
So hallowed and so gracious is that time.   170

HORATIO

So have I heard and do in part believe it.
But, look, the morn in russet mantle clad   172
Walks o'er the dew of yon high eastward hill.
Break we our watch up, and by my advice
Let us impart what we have seen tonight
Unto young Hamlet; for upon my life,
This spirit, dumb to us, will speak to him.
Do you consent we shall acquaint him with it,
As needful in our loves, fitting our duty?

MARCELLUS

Let's do't, I pray, and I this morning know
Where we shall find him most conveniently.

                              Exeunt.

                 ❧

[1.2]

     Flourish. Enter Claudius, King of Denmark,
     Gertrude the Queen, [the] Council, as Polonius
     and his son Laertes, Hamlet, cum aliis [including
     Voltimand and Cornelius].

KING

Though yet of Hamlet our dear brother's death   1
The memory be green, and that it us befitted
To bear our hearts in grief and our whole kingdom

To be contracted in one brow of woe,
Yet so far hath discretion fought with nature
That we with wisest sorrow think on him
Together with remembrance of ourselves.
Therefore our sometime sister, now our queen,   8
Th'imperial jointress to this warlike state,   9
Have we, as 'twere with a defeated joy—
With an auspicious and a dropping eye,   11
With mirth in funeral and with dirge in marriage,
In equal scale weighing delight and dole—   13
Taken to wife. Nor have we herein barred
Your better wisdoms, which have freely gone
With this affair along. For all, our thanks.
Now follows that you know young Fortinbras,   17
Holding a weak supposal of our worth,   18
Or thinking by our late dear brother's death
Our state to be disjoint and out of frame,   20
Co-leaguèd with this dream of his advantage,   21
He hath not failed to pester us with message
Importing the surrender of those lands   23
Lost by his father, with all bonds of law,   24
To our most valiant brother. So much for him.
Now for ourself and for this time of meeting.
Thus much the business is: we have here writ
To Norway, uncle of young Fortinbras—
Who, impotent and bed-rid, scarcely hears   29
Of this his nephew's purpose—to suppress
His further gait herein, in that the levies,   31
The lists, and full proportions are all made   32
Out of his subject; and we here dispatch   33
You, good Cornelius, and you, Voltimand,
For bearers of this greeting to old Norway,
Giving to you no further personal power
To business with the King more than the scope
Of these dilated articles allow.   [*He gives a paper.*]   38
Farewell, and let your haste commend your duty.   39

CORNELIUS, VOLTIMAND

In that, and all things, will we show our duty.

KING

We doubt it nothing. Heartily farewell.   41
           [*Exeunt Voltimand and Cornelius.*]
And now, Laertes, what's the news with you?
You told us of some suit; what is't, Laertes?
You cannot speak of reason to the Dane   44
And lose your voice. What wouldst thou beg, Laertes,   45
That shall not be my offer, not thy asking?
The head is not more native to the heart,   47

---

156 trumpet trumpeter   **160 extravagant and erring** wandering beyond bounds. (The words have similar meaning.)   **hies** hastens   **162 probation** proof.   **164 'gainst** just before   **168 strike** destroy by evil influence   **169 takes** bewitches.   **charm** cast a spell, control by enchantment   **170 gracious** full of grace   **172 russet** reddish brown **1.2 Location: The castle.**
0.2 *as* i.e., such as, including.   **0.3** *cum aliis* with others   **1 our** my. (The royal "we"; also in the following lines.)

8 sometime former   **9 jointress** woman possessing property with her husband   **11 With . . . eye** with one eye smiling and the other weeping   **13 dole** grief   **17 Now . . . know** Next, you need to be informed that   **18 weak supposal** low estimate   **20 disjoint . . . frame** in a state of total disorder   **21 Co-leaguèd . . . advantage** joined to his illusory sense of having the advantage over us and to his vision of future success   **23 Importing** having for its substance   **24 with . . . law** (See 1.1.91, "Well ratified by law and heraldry.")   **29 impotent** helpless   **31 His** i.e., Fortinbras'.   **gait** proceeding   **31–3 in that . . . subject** since the levying of troops and supplies is drawn entirely from the King of Norway's own subjects   **38 dilated** set out at length   **39 let . . . duty** let your swift obeying of orders, rather than mere words, express your dutifulness.   **41 nothing** not at all.   **44 the Dane** the Danish king   **45 lose your voice** waste your speech.   **47 native** closely connected, related

The hand more instrumental to the mouth,   48
Than is the throne of Denmark to thy father.
What wouldst thou have, Laertes?

LAERTES   My dread lord,
Your leave and favor to return to France,   51
From whence though willingly I came to Denmark
To show my duty in your coronation,
Yet now I must confess, that duty done,
My thoughts and wishes bend again toward France
And bow them to your gracious leave and pardon.   56

KING
Have you your father's leave? What says Polonius?

POLONIUS
H'ath, my lord, wrung from me my slow leave   58
By laborsome petition, and at last
Upon his will I sealed my hard consent.   60
I do beseech you, give him leave to go.

KING
Take thy fair hour, Laertes. Time be thine,   62
And thy best graces spend it at thy will.   63
But now, my cousin Hamlet, and my son—   64

HAMLET
A little more than kin, and less than kind.   65

KING
How is it that the clouds still hang on you?

HAMLET
Not so, my lord. I am too much in the sun.   67

QUEEN
Good Hamlet, cast thy nighted color off,   68
And let thine eye look like a friend on Denmark.   69
Do not forever with thy vailèd lids   70
Seek for thy noble father in the dust.
Thou know'st 'tis common, all that lives must die,   72
Passing through nature to eternity.

HAMLET
Ay, madam, it is common.

QUEEN   If it be,
Why seems it so particular with thee?   75

HAMLET
Seems, madam? Nay, it is. I know not "seems."
'Tis not alone my inky cloak, good mother,
Nor customary suits of solemn black,   78
Nor windy suspiration of forced breath,   79

No, nor the fruitful river in the eye,   80
Nor the dejected havior of the visage,   81
Together with all forms, moods, shapes of grief,   82
That can denote me truly. These indeed seem,
For they are actions that a man might play.
But I have that within which passes show;
These but the trappings and the suits of woe.

KING
'Tis sweet and commendable in your nature, Hamlet,
To give these mourning duties to your father.
But you must know your father lost a father,
That father lost, lost his, and the survivor bound
In filial obligation for some term
To do obsequious sorrow. But to persever   92
In obstinate condolement is a course   93
Of impious stubbornness. 'Tis unmanly grief.
It shows a will most incorrect to heaven,
A heart unfortified, a mind impatient,   96
An understanding simple and unschooled.   97
For what we know must be and is as common
As any the most vulgar thing to sense,   99
Why should we in our peevish opposition
Take it to heart? Fie, 'tis a fault to heaven,
A fault against the dead, a fault to nature,
To reason most absurd, whose common theme
Is death of fathers, and who still hath cried,   104
From the first corpse till he that died today,   105
"This must be so." We pray you, throw to earth
This unprevailing woe and think of us   107
As of a father; for let the world take note,
You are the most immediate to our throne,   109
And with no less nobility of love
Than that which dearest father bears his son
Do I impart toward you. For your intent   112
In going back to school in Wittenberg,   113
It is most retrograde to our desire,   114
And we beseech you bend you to remain   115
Here in the cheer and comfort of our eye,
Our chiefest courtier, cousin, and our son.

QUEEN
Let not thy mother lose her prayers, Hamlet.
I pray thee, stay with us, go not to Wittenberg.

HAMLET
I shall in all my best obey you, madam.   120

KING
Why, 'tis a loving and a fair reply.
Be as ourself in Denmark. Madam, come.
This gentle and unforced accord of Hamlet
Sits smiling to my heart, in grace whereof   124
No jocund health that Denmark drinks today   125

48 instrumental serviceable   **51 leave and favor** kind permission
56 bow . . . pardon entreatingly make a deep bow, asking your permission to depart.   **58 H'ath** He has   **60 sealed** (as if sealing a legal
document).   **hard** reluctant   **62 Take thy fair hour** Enjoy your time
of youth   **63 And . . . will** and may your time be spent in exercising
your best qualities.   **64 cousin** any kin not of the immediate family
65 A little . . . kind Too close a blood relation, and yet we are less
than kinsmen in that our relationship lacks affection and is indeed
unnatural. (Hamlet plays on *kind* as [1] kindly [2] belonging to
nature, suggesting that Claudius is not the same kind of being as the
rest of humanity. The line is often delivered as an aside, though it
need not be.)   **67 the sun** i.e., the sunshine of the King's royal favor.
(With pun on *son.*)   **68 nighted color** (1) mourning garments of black
(2) dark melancholy   **69 Denmark** the King of Denmark.   **70 vailèd
lids** lowered eyes   **72 common** of universal occurrence. (But Hamlet
plays on the sense of "vulgar" in line 74.)   **75 particular** personal
78 customary customary to mourning   **79 suspiration** sighing

80 fruitful abundant   **81 havior** expression   **82 moods** outward
expression of feeling   **92 obsequious** suited to obsequies or funerals.
93 condolement sorrowing   **96 unfortified** i.e., against adversity
97 simple ignorant   **99 As . . . sense** as the most ordinary experience
104 still always   **105 the first corpse** (Abel's)   **107 unprevailing**
unavailing, useless   **109 most immediate** next in succession
112 impart toward liberally bestow on.   **For** As for   **113 to school**
i.e., to your studies.   **Wittenberg** famous German university
founded in 1502   **114 retrograde** contrary   **115 bend you** incline
yourself   **120 in all my best** to the best of my ability   **124 to** i.e., at.
grace thanksgiving   **125 jocund** merry

But the great cannon to the clouds shall tell,
And the King's rouse the heaven shall bruit again,   127
Respeaking earthly thunder. Come away.   128

Flourish. Exeunt all but Hamlet.

HAMLET
Oh, that this too too sullied flesh would melt,   129
Thaw, and resolve itself into a dew!
Or that the Everlasting had not fixed
His canon 'gainst self-slaughter! Oh, God, God,   132
How weary, stale, flat, and unprofitable
Seem to me all the uses of this world!
Fie on't, ah fie! 'Tis an unweeded garden
That grows to seed. Things rank and gross in nature
Possess it merely. That it should come to this!   137
But two months dead—nay, not so much, not two.
So excellent a king, that was to this   139
Hyperion to a satyr, so loving to my mother   140
That he might not beteem the winds of heaven   141
Visit her face too roughly. Heaven and earth,
Must I remember? Why, she would hang on him
As if increase of appetite had grown
By what it fed on, and yet within a month—
Let me not think on't; frailty, thy name is woman!—
A little month, or ere those shoes were old   147
With which she followed my poor father's body,
Like Niobe, all tears, why she, even she—   149
Oh, God, a beast, that wants discourse of reason,   150
Would have mourned longer—married with my
    uncle,
My father's brother, but no more like my father
Than I to Hercules. Within a month,
Ere yet the salt of most unrighteous tears
Had left the flushing in her gallèd eyes,   155
She married. Oh, most wicked speed, to post   156
With such dexterity to incestuous sheets!   157
It is not, nor it cannot come to good.
But break, my heart, for I must hold my tongue.

Enter Horatio, Marcellus, and Bernardo.

HORATIO
Hail to Your Lordship!
HAMLET   I am glad to see you well.
Horatio!—or I do forget myself.
HORATIO
The same, my lord, and your poor servant ever.

HAMLET
Sir, my good friend; I'll change that name with you.   163
And what make you from Wittenberg, Horatio?—   164
Marcellus.
MARCELLUS   My good lord.
HAMLET
I am very glad to see you. [*To Bernardo*] Good even,
    sir.—
But what in faith make you from Wittenberg?
HORATIO
A truant disposition, good my lord.
HAMLET
I would not hear your enemy say so,
Nor shall you do my ear that violence
To make it truster of your own report   171
Against yourself. I know you are no truant.
But what is your affair in Elsinore?
We'll teach you to drink deep ere you depart.
HORATIO
My lord, I came to see your father's funeral.
HAMLET
I prithee, do not mock me, fellow student;
I think it was to see my mother's wedding.
HORATIO
Indeed, my lord, it followed hard upon.   179
HAMLET
Thrift, thrift, Horatio! The funeral baked meats   180
Did coldly furnish forth the marriage tables.   181
Would I had met my dearest foe in heaven   182
Or ever I had seen that day, Horatio!   183
My father!—Methinks I see my father.
HORATIO
Where, my lord?
HAMLET   In my mind's eye, Horatio.
HORATIO
I saw him once. 'A was a goodly king.   186
HAMLET
'A was a man. Take him for all in all,
I shall not look upon his like again.
HORATIO
My lord, I think I saw him yesternight.
HAMLET   Saw? Who?
HORATIO   My lord, the King your father.
HAMLET   The King my father?
HORATIO
Season your admiration for a while   193
With an attent ear till I may deliver,   194
Upon the witness of these gentlemen,
This marvel to you.
HAMLET   For God's love, let me hear!
HORATIO
Two nights together had these gentlemen,

---

127 rouse drinking of a draft of liquor.   **bruit again** loudly echo
128 thunder i.e., of trumpet and kettledrum, sounded when the King
drinks; see 1.4.8–12.   **129 sullied** defiled. (The early quartos read
"sallied"; the Folio, "solid.")   **132 canon** law   **137 merely** completely.   **139 to** in comparison to   **140 Hyperion** Titan sun-god,
father of Helios.   **satyr** a lecherous creature of classical mythology,
half-human but with a goat's legs, tail, ears, and horns   **141 beteem**
allow   **147 or ere** even before   **149 Niobes** Tantalus's daughter,
Queen of Thebes, who boasted that she had more sons and daughters
than Leto; for this, Apollo and Artemis, children of Leto, slew her
fourteen children. She was turned by Zeus into a stone that continually dropped tears.   **150 wants . . . reason** lacks the faculty of reason
155 gallèd irritated, inflamed   **156 post** hasten   **157 incestuous** (In
Shakespeare's day, the marriage of a man like Claudius to his
deceased brother's wife was considered incestuous.)

163 change that name i.e., give and receive reciprocally the name of
"friend" rather than talk of "servant." Or Hamlet may be saying,
"No, I am *your* servant."   **164 make you from** are you doing away
from   **171 To . . . of** to make it trust   **179 hard** close   **180 baked
meats** meat pies   **181 coldly** i.e., as cold leftovers   **182 dearest** closest (and therefore deadliest)   **183 Or ever** ere, before   **186 'A** He
193 Season your admiration Moderate your astonishment
194 attent attentive

Marcellus and Bernardo, on their watch,
In the dead waste and middle of the night,   199
Been thus encountered. A figure like your father,
Armèd at point exactly, cap-à-pie,   201
Appears before them, and with solemn march
Goes slow and stately by them. Thrice he walked
By their oppressed and fear-surprisèd eyes
Within his truncheon's length, whilst they, distilled   205
Almost to jelly with the act of fear,   206
Stand dumb and speak not to him. This to me
In dreadful secrecy impart they did,   208
And I with them the third night kept the watch,
Where, as they had delivered, both in time,
Form of the thing, each word made true and good,
The apparition comes. I knew your father;
These hands are not more like.

HAMLET   But where was this?

MARCELLUS
My lord, upon the platform where we watch.

HAMLET
Did you not speak to it?

HORATIO   My lord, I did,
But answer made it none. Yet once methought
It lifted up it head and did address   217
Itself to motion, like as it would speak;   218
But even then the morning cock crew loud,   219
And at the sound it shrunk in haste away
And vanished from our sight.

HAMLET   'Tis very strange.

HORATIO
As I do live, my honored lord, 'tis true,
And we did think it writ down in our duty
To let you know of it.

HAMLET
Indeed, indeed, sirs. But this troubles me.
Hold you the watch tonight?

ALL   We do, my lord.

HAMLET   Armed, say you?

ALL   Armed, my lord.

HAMLET   From top to toe?

ALL   My lord, from head to foot.

HAMLET   Then saw you not his face?

HORATIO
Oh, yes, my lord, he wore his beaver up.   232

HAMLET   What looked he, frowningly?   233

HORATIO
A countenance more in sorrow than in anger.

HAMLET   Pale or red?

HORATIO   Nay, very pale.

HAMLET   And fixed his eyes upon you?

HORATIO   Most constantly.

HAMLET   I would I had been there.

HORATIO   It would have much amazed you.

HAMLET   Very like, very like. Stayed it long?

HORATIO
While one with moderate haste might tell a hundred.   242

MARCELLUS, BERNARDO   Longer, longer.

HORATIO   Not when I saw't.

HAMLET   His beard was grizzled—no?

HORATIO
It was, as I have seen it in his life,
A sable silvered.

HAMLET   I will watch tonight.
Perchance 'twill walk again.

HORATIO   I warr'nt it will.

HAMLET
If it assume my noble father's person,
I'll speak to it though hell itself should gape
And bid me hold my peace. I pray you all,
If you have hitherto concealed this sight,
Let it be tenable in your silence still,   253
And whatsomever else shall hap tonight,
Give it an understanding but no tongue.
I will requite your loves. So, fare you well.
Upon the platform twixt eleven and twelve
I'll visit you.

ALL   Our duty to Your Honor.

HAMLET
Your loves, as mine to you. Farewell.   259
                              Exeunt [all but Hamlet].
My father's spirit in arms! All is not well.
I doubt some foul play. Would the night were come!   261
Till then sit still, my soul. Foul deeds will rise,
Though all the earth o'erwhelm them, to men's eyes.
                                                            Exit.

❧

[1.3]

Enter Laertes and Ophelia, his sister.

LAERTES
My necessaries are embarked. Farewell.
And, sister, as the winds give benefit
And convoy is assistant, do not sleep   3
But let me hear from you.

OPHELIA   Do you doubt that?

LAERTES
For Hamlet, and the trifling of his favor,   5
Hold it a fashion and a toy in blood,   6
A violet in the youth of primy nature,   7
Forward, not permanent, sweet, not lasting,   8
The perfume and suppliance of a minute—   9
No more.

OPHELIA   No more but so?

LAERTES   Think it no more.

---

199 **dead waste** desolate stillness   201 **at point** correctly in every detail.   **cap-à-pie** from head to foot   205 **truncheon** officer's staff.   **distilled** dissolved   206 **act** action, operation   208 **dreadful** full of dread   217 **it** its   217–18 **did . . . speak** prepared to move as though it was about to speak   219 **even then** at that very instant   232 **beaver** visor on the helmet   233 **What** How

242 **tell** count   253 **tenable** held   259 **Your loves** i.e., Say "Your loves" to me, not just your "duty."   261 **doubt** suspect
1.3. Location: Polonius's chambers.
3 **convoy is assistant** means of conveyance are available   5 **For** As for   6 **toy in blood** passing amorous fancy   7 **primy** in its prime, springtime   8 **Forward** precocious   9 **suppliance** pastime, something to fill the time

For nature crescent does not grow alone   11
In thews and bulk, but as this temple waxes   12
The inward service of the mind and soul
Grows wide withal. Perhaps he loves you now,   14
And now no soil nor cautel doth besmirch   15
The virtue of his will; but you must fear,   16
His greatness weighed, his will is not his own.   17
For he himself is subject to his birth.
He may not, as unvalued persons do,
Carve for himself, for on his choice depends   20
The safety and health of this whole state,
And therefore must his choice be circumscribed
Unto the voice and yielding of that body   23
Whereof he is the head. Then if he says he loves you,
It fits your wisdom so far to believe it
As he in his particular act and place   26
May give his saying deed, which is no further
Than the main voice of Denmark goes withal.   28
Then weigh what loss your honor may sustain
If with too credent ear you list his songs,   30
Or lose your heart, or your chaste treasure open
To his unmastered importunity.   32
Fear it, Ophelia, fear it, my dear sister,
And keep you in the rear of your affection,   34
Out of the shot and danger of desire.
The chariest maid is prodigal enough   36
If she unmask her beauty to the moon.   37
Virtue itself scapes not calumnious strokes.
The canker galls the infants of the spring   39
Too oft before their buttons be disclosed,   40
And in the morn and liquid dew of youth   41
Contagious blastments are most imminent.   42
Be wary then; best safety lies in fear.
Youth to itself rebels, though none else near.   44

OPHELIA
I shall the effect of this good lesson keep
As watchman to my heart. But, good my brother,
Do not, as some ungracious pastors do,   47
Show me the steep and thorny way to heaven,
Whiles like a puffed and reckless libertine   49
Himself the primrose path of dalliance treads,
And recks not his own rede.

Enter Polonius.

LAERTES   Oh, fear me not.   51

I stay too long. But here my father comes.
A double blessing is a double grace;   53
Occasion smiles upon a second leave.   54
POLONIUS
Yet here, Laertes? Aboard, aboard, for shame!
The wind sits in the shoulder of your sail,
And you are stayed for. There—my blessing with thee!
And these few precepts in thy memory
Look thou character. Give thy thoughts no tongue,   59
Nor any unproportioned thought his act.   60
Be thou familiar, but by no means vulgar.   61
Those friends thou hast, and their adoption tried,   62
Grapple them unto thy soul with hoops of steel,
But do not dull thy palm with entertainment   64
Of each new-hatched, unfledged courage. Beware   65
Of entrance to a quarrel, but being in,
Bear't that th'opposèd may beware of thee.   67
Give every man thy ear, but few thy voice;
Take each man's censure, but reserve thy judgment.   69
Costly thy habit as thy purse can buy,   70
But not expressed in fancy; rich, not gaudy,   71
For the apparel oft proclaims the man,
And they in France of the best rank and station
Are of a most select and generous chief in that.   74
Neither a borrower nor a lender be,
For loan oft loses both itself and friend,
And borrowing dulleth edge of husbandry.   77
This above all: to thine own self be true,
And it must follow, as the night the day,
Thou canst not then be false to any man.
Farewell. My blessing season this in thee!   81
LAERTES
Most humbly do I take my leave, my lord.
POLONIUS
The time invests you. Go, your servants tend.   83
LAERTES
Farewell, Ophelia, and remember well
What I have said to you.
OPHELIA   'Tis in my memory locked,
And you yourself shall keep the key of it.
LAERTES   Farewell.   *Exit Laertes.*
POLONIUS
What is't, Ophelia, he hath said to you?
OPHELIA
So please you, something touching the Lord Hamlet.
POLONIUS   Marry, well bethought.   91
'Tis told me he hath very oft of late
Given private time to you, and you yourself

11–14 For nature . . . withal For nature, as it ripens, does not grow only in physical strength, but as the body matures the inner qualities of mind and soul grow along with it. (Laertes warns Ophelia that the mature Hamlet may not cling to his youthful interests.) **15 soil nor cautel** blemish nor deceit **16 The . . . will** the purity of his desire **17 His greatness weighed** taking into account his high fortune **20 Carve** i.e., choose **23 voice and yielding** assent, approval **26 in . . . place** in his particular restricted circumstances **28 main voice** general assent. **withal** along with. **30 credent** credulous. **list** listen to **32 unmastered** uncontrolled **34 keep . . . affection** don't advance as far as your affection might lead you. (A military metaphor.) **36 chariest** most scrupulously modest **37 If she unmask** if she does no more than show her beauty. **moon** (Symbol of chastity.) **39 canker galls** cankerworm destroys **40 buttons be disclosed** buds be opened **41 liquid dew** i.e., time when dew is fresh and bright **42 blastments** blights **44 Youth . . . rebels** Youth yields to the rebellion of the flesh **47 ungracious** ungodly **49 puffed** bloated, or swollen with pride **51 recks** heeds. **rede** counsel.   **fear me not** don't worry on my account.

53–4 A double . . . leave The goddess Occasion or Opportunity smiles on the happy circumstance of being able to say good-bye twice and thus receive a second blessing. **59 Look thou character** see to it that you inscribe. **60 unproportioned** badly calculated, intemperate. **his** its **61 familiar** sociable. **vulgar** common. **62 and . . . tried** and their suitability to be your friends having been put to the test **64 dull thy palm** i.e., shake hands so often as to make the gesture meaningless **65 courage** swashbuckler. **67 Bear't that** manage it so that **69 censure** opinion, judgment **70 habit** clothing **71 fancy** excessive ornament, decadent fashion **74 Are . . . that** are of a most refined and well-bred preeminence in choosing what to wear. **77 husbandry** thrift. **81 season** mature **83 invests** besieges, presses upon. **tend** attend, wait. **91 Marry** i.e., By the Virgin Mary. (A mild oath.)

Have of your audience been most free and bounteous.
If it be so—as so 'tis put on me,   95
And that in way of caution—I must tell you
You do not understand yourself so clearly
As it behooves my daughter and your honor.   98
What is between you? Give me up the truth.

OPHELIA
He hath, my lord, of late made many tenders   100
Of his affection to me.

POLONIUS
Affection? Pooh! You speak like a green girl,
Unsifted in such perilous circumstance.   103
Do you believe his tenders, as you call them?

OPHELIA
I do not know, my lord, what I should think.

POLONIUS
Marry, I will teach you. Think yourself a baby
That you have ta'en these tenders for true pay
Which are not sterling. Tender yourself more dearly,   108
Or—not to crack the wind of the poor phrase,   109
Running it thus—you'll tender me a fool.   110

OPHELIA
My lord, he hath importuned me with love
In honorable fashion.

POLONIUS
Ay, fashion you may call it. Go to, go to.   113

OPHELIA
And hath given countenance to his speech, my lord,   114
With almost all the holy vows of heaven.

POLONIUS
Ay, springes to catch woodcocks. I do know,   116
When the blood burns, how prodigal the soul   117
Lends the tongue vows. These blazes, daughter,
Giving more light than heat, extinct in both
Even in their promise as it is a-making,   120
You must not take for fire. From this time
Be something scanter of your maiden presence.   122
Set your entreatments at a higher rate   123
Than a command to parle. For Lord Hamlet,   124
Believe so much in him that he is young,   125
And with a larger tether may he walk
Than may be given you. In few, Ophelia,   127
Do not believe his vows, for they are brokers,   128
Not of that dye which their investments show,   129
But mere implorators of unholy suits,   130

Breathing like sanctified and pious bawds,   131
The better to beguile. This is for all: 132
I would not, in plain terms, from this time forth
Have you so slander any moment leisure   134
As to give words or talk with the Lord Hamlet.
Look to't, I charge you. Come your ways.   136

OPHELIA   I shall obey, my lord.   Exeunt.

❧

[1.4]

Enter Hamlet, Horatio, and Marcellus.

HAMLET
The air bites shrewdly; it is very cold.   1

HORATIO
It is a nipping and an eager air.   2

HAMLET
What hour now?

HORATIO   I think it lacks of twelve.   3

MARCELLUS
No, it is struck.

HORATIO   Indeed? I heard it not.
It then draws near the season   5
Wherein the spirit held his wont to walk.   6
                        A flourish of trumpets, and two pieces go off
                                                                    [*within*].
What does this mean, my lord?

HAMLET
The King doth wake tonight and takes his rouse,   8
Keeps wassail, and the swagg'ring upspring reels;   9
And as he drains his drafts of Rhenish down,   10
The kettledrum and trumpet thus bray out
The triumph of his pledge.

HORATIO   Is it a custom?   12

HAMLET   Ay, marry, is't,
But to my mind, though I am native here
And to the manner born, it is a custom   15
More honored in the breach than the observance.   16
This heavy-headed revel east and west   17
Makes us traduced and taxed of other nations.   18
They clepe us drunkards, and with swinish phrase   19
Soil our addition; and indeed it takes   20
From our achievements, though performed at height,   21
The pith and marrow of our attribute.   22

---

95 **put on** impressed on, told to   98 **behooves** befits   100 **tenders** offers   103 **Unsifted** i.e., untried   108 **sterling** legal currency. **Tender . . . dearly** (1) Bargain for your favors at a higher rate—i.e., hold out for marriage (2) Show greater care of yourself   109 **crack the wind** i.e., run it until it is broken-winded   110 **tender . . . fool** (1) make a fool of me (2) present me with a *fool* or baby.   113 **fashion** mere form, pretense.   **Go to** (An expression of impatience.)   114 **countenance** credit, confirmation   116 **springes** snares. **woodcocks** birds easily caught; here used to connote gullibility.   117 **prodigal** prodigally   120 **it** i.e., the promise   122 **something** somewhat   123–4 **Set . . . parle** i.e., As defender of your chastity, negotiate for something better than a surrender simply because the besieger requests an interview.   124 **For** As for   125 **so . . . him** this much concerning him   127 **In few** Briefly   128 **brokers** go-betweens, procurers   129 **dye** color or sort.   **investments** clothes. (The vows are not what they seem.)   130 **mere implorators** out-and-out solicitors

131 **Breathing** speaking   132 **for all** once for all, in sum   134 **slander** abuse, misuse.   **moment** moment's   136 **Come your ways** Come along.
1.4 Location: The guard platform.
1 **shrewdly** keenly, sharply   2 **eager** biting   3 **lacks of** is just short of   5 **season** time   6 **held his wont** was accustomed.   6.1 *pieces* i.e., of ordnance, cannon   8 **wake** stay awake and hold revel.   **takes his rouse** carouses   9 **Keeps . . . reels** carouses, and riotously dances a German dance called the upspring   10 **Rhenish** Rhine wine   12 **The triumph . . . pledge** the celebration of his offering a toast.   15 **manner** custom (of drinking)   16 **More . . . observance** better neglected than followed.   17 **east and west** i.e., everywhere   18 **taxed of** censured by   19 **clepe** call.   **with swinish phrase** i.e., by calling us swine   20 **addition** reputation   21 **at height** outstandingly   22 **The pith . . . attribute** the most essential part of the esteem that should be attributed to us.

So, oft it chances in particular men,
That for some vicious mole of nature in them, 24
As in their birth—wherein they are not guilty,
Since nature cannot choose his origin— 26
By their o'ergrowth of some complexion, 27
Oft breaking down the pales and forts of reason, 28
Or by some habit that too much o'erleavens 29
The form of plausive manners, that these men, 30
Carrying, I say, the stamp of one defect,
Being nature's livery or fortune's star, 32
His virtues else, be they as pure as grace, 33
As infinite as man may undergo, 34
Shall in the general censure take corruption 35
From that particular fault. The dram of evil 36
Doth all the noble substance often dout 37
To his own scandal.

Enter Ghost.

HORATIO   Look, my lord, it comes! 38
HAMLET
Angels and ministers of grace defend us! 39
Be thou a spirit of health or goblin damned, 40
Bring with thee airs from heaven or blasts from hell, 41
Be thy intents wicked or charitable, 42
Thou com'st in such a questionable shape 43
That I will speak to thee. I'll call thee Hamlet,
King, father, royal Dane. Oh, answer me!
Let me not burst in ignorance, but tell
Why thy canonized bones, hearsèd in death, 47
Have burst their cerements; why the sepulcher 48
Wherein we saw thee quietly inurned 49
Hath oped his ponderous and marble jaws
To cast thee up again. What may this mean,
That thou, dead corpse, again in complete steel, 52
Revisits thus the glimpses of the moon, 53
Making night hideous, and we fools of nature 54
So horridly to shake our disposition 55
With thoughts beyond the reaches of our souls?
Say, why is this? Wherefore? What should we do?
                    [*The Ghost*] *beckons* [*Hamlet*].

HORATIO
It beckons you to go away with it,
As if it some impartment did desire 59
To you alone.
MARCELLUS   Look with what courteous action
It wafts you to a more removèd ground.
But do not go with it.
HORATIO   No, by no means.
HAMLET
It will not speak. Then I will follow it.
HORATIO
Do not, my lord!
HAMLET   Why, what should be the fear?
I do not set my life at a pin's fee, 65
And for my soul, what can it do to that, 66
Being a thing immortal as itself?
It waves me forth again. I'll follow it.
HORATIO
What if it tempt you toward the flood, my lord, 69
Or to the dreadful summit of the cliff
That beetles o'er his base into the sea, 71
And there assume some other horrible form
Which might deprive your sovereignty of reason 73
And draw you into madness? Think of it.
The very place puts toys of desperation, 75
Without more motive, into every brain
That looks so many fathoms to the sea
And hears it roar beneath.
HAMLET
It wafts me still.—Go on, I'll follow thee.
MARCELLUS
You shall not go, my lord.   [*They try to stop him.*]
HAMLET   Hold off your hands!
HORATIO
Be ruled. You shall not go.
HAMLET   My fate cries out, 81
And makes each petty artery in this body 82
As hardy as the Nemean lion's nerve. 83
Still am I called. Unhand me, gentlemen.
By heaven, I'll make a ghost of him that lets me! 85
I say, away!—Go on, I'll follow thee.
                    Exeunt Ghost and Hamlet.
HORATIO
He waxes desperate with imagination.
MARCELLUS
Let's follow. 'Tis not fit thus to obey him.
HORATIO
Have after. To what issue will this come? 89
MARCELLUS
Something is rotten in the state of Denmark.

---

24 for . . . mole on account of some natural defect in their constitutions   **26 his** its   **27 their o'ergrowth . . . complexion** the excessive growth in individuals of some natural trait   **28 pales** palings, fences (as of a fortification)   **29–30 o'erleavens . . . manners** i.e., infects the way we should behave (much as bad yeast spoils the dough). *Plausive* means "pleasing."   **32 Being . . . star** (that stamp of defect) being a sign identifying one as wearing the livery of, and hence being the servant to, nature (unfortunate inherited qualities) or fortune (mischance)   **33 His virtues else** i.e., the other qualities of *these men* (line 30)   **34 may undergo** can sustain   **35 in . . . censure** in overall appraisal, in people's opinion generally   **36-8 The dram . . . scandal** i.e., The small drop of evil blots out or works against the noble substance of the whole and brings it into disrepute. (To *dout* is to blot out. A famous crux.)   **39 ministers of grace** messengers of God   **40 Be . . . health** Whether you are a good angel   **41 Bring** whether you bring   **42 Be thy intents** whether your intentions are   **43 questionable** inviting question   **47 canonized** buried according to the canons of the church.   **hearsèd** coffined   **48 cerements** grave clothes   **49 inurned** entombed   **52 complete steel** full armor   **53 the glimpses . . . moon** i.e., the sublunary world, all that is beneath the moon   **54 fools of nature** mere mortals, limited to natural knowledge and subject to nature   **55 So . . . disposition** to distress our mental composure so violently

59 impartment communication   **65 fee** value   **66 for** as for   **69 flood** sea   **71 beetles o'er** overhangs threateningly (like bushy eyebrows).   **his** its   **73 deprive . . . reason** take away the rule of reason over your mind   **75 toys of desperation** fancies of desperate acts, i.e., suicide   **81 My fate cries out** My destiny summons me   **82 petty** weak.   **artery** blood vessel system through which the vital spirits were thought to have been conveyed   **83 Nemean lion's nerve** as a sinew of the huge lion slain by Hercules as the first of his twelve labors.   **85 lets** hinders   **89 Have after** Let's go after him.   **issue** outcome

HORATIO
Heaven will direct it.
MARCELLUS   Nay, let's follow him.   *Exeunt.*   91

❖

[1.5]

Enter Ghost and Hamlet.

HAMLET
Whither wilt thou lead me? Speak. I'll go no further.
GHOST
Mark me.
HAMLET   I will.
GHOST   My hour is almost come,
When I to sulf'rous and tormenting flames
Must render up myself.
HAMLET   Alas, poor ghost!
GHOST
Pity me not, but lend thy serious hearing
To what I shall unfold.
HAMLET   Speak. I am bound to hear.   7
GHOST
So art thou to revenge, when thou shalt hear.
HAMLET   What?
GHOST   I am thy father's spirit,
Doomed for a certain term to walk the night,
And for the day confined to fast in fires,   12
Till the foul crimes done in my days of nature   13
Are burnt and purged away. But that I am forbid   14
To tell the secrets of my prison house,
I could a tale unfold whose lightest word
Would harrow up thy soul, freeze thy young blood,   17
Make thy two eyes like stars start from their spheres,   18
Thy knotted and combinèd locks to part,   19
And each particular hair to stand on end
Like quills upon the fretful porcupine.
But this eternal blazon must not be   22
To ears of flesh and blood. List, list, oh, list!
If thou didst ever thy dear father love—
HAMLET   Oh, God!
GHOST
Revenge his foul and most unnatural murder.
HAMLET   Murder?
GHOST
Murder most foul, as in the best it is,   28
But this most foul, strange, and unnatural.
HAMLET
Haste me to know't, that I, with wings as swift
As meditation or the thoughts of love,
May sweep to my revenge.
GHOST   I find thee apt;

And duller shouldst thou be than the fat weed   33
That roots itself in ease on Lethe wharf,   34
Wouldst thou not stir in this. Now, Hamlet, hear.
'Tis given out that, sleeping in my orchard,   36
A serpent stung me. So the whole ear of Denmark
Is by a forgèd process of my death   38
Rankly abused. But know, thou noble youth,   39
The serpent that did sting thy father's life
Now wears his crown.
HAMLET   Oh, my prophetic soul! My uncle!
GHOST
Ay, that incestuous, that adulterate beast,   43
With witchcraft of his wit, with traitorous gifts—   44
Oh, wicked wit and gifts, that have the power
So to seduce!—won to his shameful lust
The will of my most seeming-virtuous queen.
Oh, Hamlet, what a falling off was there!
From me, whose love was of that dignity
That it went hand in hand even with the vow   50
I made to her in marriage, and to decline
Upon a wretch whose natural gifts were poor
To those of mine!   53
But virtue, as it never will be moved,   54
Though lewdness court it in a shape of heaven,   55
So lust, though to a radiant angel linked,
Will sate itself in a celestial bed   57
And prey on garbage.
But soft, methinks I scent the morning air.
Brief let me be. Sleeping within my orchard,
My custom always of the afternoon,
Upon my secure hour thy uncle stole,   62
With juice of cursèd hebona in a vial,   63
And in the porches of my ears did pour   64
The leprous distillment, whose effect   65
Holds such an enmity with blood of man
That swift as quicksilver it courses through
The natural gates and alleys of the body,   68
And with a sudden vigor it doth posset   69
And curd, like eager droppings into milk,   70
The thin and wholesome blood. So did it mine,
And a most instant tetter barked about,   72
Most lazar-like, with vile and loathsome crust,   73
All my smooth body.
Thus was I, sleeping, by a brother's hand
Of life, of crown, of queen at once dispatched,   76

---

91 **it** i.e., the outcome.
1.5 Location: The battlements of the castle.
7 bound (1) ready (2) obligated by duty and fate. (The Ghost, in line 8, answers in the second sense.)   **12 fast** do penance by fasting
13 crimes sins.   **of nature** as a mortal   **14 But that** Were it not that
17 harrow up lacerate, tear   **18 spheres** i.e., eye-sockets, here compared to the orbits or transparent revolving spheres in which, according to Ptolemaic astronomy, the heavenly bodies were fixed
19 knotted . . . locks hair neatly arranged and confined   **22 eternal blazon** revelation of the secrets of eternity   **28 in the best** even at best

33 shouldst thou be you would have to be.   **fat** torpid, lethargic
34 Lethe the river of forgetfulness in Hades   **36 orchard** garden
38 forgèd process falsified account   **39 abused** deceived.   **43 adulterate** adulterous   **44 gifts** (1) talents (2) presents   **50 even with the vow** with the very vow   **53 To** compared with   **54 virtue, as it** just as virtue   **55 shape of heaven** heavenly form   **57 sate . . . bed** gratify its lustful appetite to the point of revulsion or ennui, even in a virtuously lawful marriage   **62 secure hour** time of being free from worries   **63 hebona** a poison. (The word seems to be a form of *ebony*, though it is thought perhaps to be related to *henbane*, a poison, or to *ebenus*, "yew.")   **64 porches** gateways   **65 leprous distillment** distillation causing leprosylike disfigurement   **68 gates** entry ways
69–70 posset . . . curd coagulate and curdle   **70 eager** sour, acid
72 tetter eruption of scabs.   **barked** covered with a rough covering, like bark on a tree   **73 lazar-like** leperlike   **76 dispatched** suddenly deprived

Cut off even in the blossoms of my sin,
Unhouseled, disappointed, unaneled,   78
No reck'ning made, but sent to my account   79
With all my imperfections on my head.
Oh, horrible! Oh, horrible, most horrible!
If thou hast nature in thee, bear it not.   82
Let not the royal bed of Denmark be
A couch for luxury and damnèd incest.   84
But, howsomever thou pursues this act,
Taint not thy mind nor let thy soul contrive
Against thy mother aught. Leave her to heaven
And to those thorns that in her bosom lodge,
To prick and sting her. Fare thee well at once.
The glowworm shows the matin to be near,   90
And 'gins to pale his uneffectual fire.   91
Adieu, adieu, adieu! Remember me.   [*Exit.*]

HAMLET
O all you host of heaven! O earth! What else?
And shall I couple hell? Oh, fie! Hold, hold, my heart,   94
And you, my sinews, grow not instant old,   95
But bear me stiffly up. Remember thee?
Ay, thou poor ghost, whiles memory holds a seat
In this distracted globe. Remember thee?   98
Yea, from the table of my memory   99
I'll wipe away all trivial fond records,   100
All saws of books, all forms, all pressures past   101
That youth and observation copied there,
And thy commandment all alone shall live
Within the book and volume of my brain,
Unmixed with baser matter. Yes, by heaven!
Oh, most pernicious woman!
Oh, villain, villain, smiling, damnèd villain!
My tables—meet it is I set it down   108
That one may smile, and smile, and be a villain.
At least I am sure it may be so in Denmark.
So, uncle, there you are. Now to my word: 111
It is "Adieu, adieu! Remember me."
I have sworn't.

Enter Horatio and Marcellus.

HORATIO   My lord, my lord!
MARCELLUS   Lord Hamlet!
HORATIO   Heavens secure him!   116
HAMLET   So be it.
MARCELLUS   Hillo, ho, ho, my lord!
HAMLET   Hillo, ho, ho, boy! Come, bird, come.   119
MARCELLUS   How is't, my noble lord?

HORATIO   What news, my lord?
HAMLET   Oh, wonderful!
HORATIO   Good my lord, tell it.
HAMLET   No, you will reveal it.
HORATIO   Not I, my lord, by heaven.
MARCELLUS   Nor I, my lord
HAMLET
How say you, then, would heart of man once think it?   127
But you'll be secret?
HORATIO, MARCELLUS   Ay, by heaven, my lord.
HAMLET
There's never a villain dwelling in all Denmark
But he's an arrant knave.   130
HORATIO
There needs no ghost, my lord, come from the grave
To tell us this.
HAMLET   Why, right, you are in the right.
And so, without more circumstance at all,   133
I hold it fit that we shake hands and part,
You as your business and desire shall point you—
For every man hath business and desire,
Such as it is—and for my own poor part,
Look you, I'll go pray.
HORATIO
These are but wild and whirling words, my lord.
HAMLET
I am sorry they offend you, heartily;
Yes, faith, heartily.
HORATIO   There's no offense, my lord.
HAMLET
Yes, by Saint Patrick, but there is, Horatio,   142
And much offense too. Touching this vision here,   143
It is an honest ghost, that let me tell you.   144
For your desire to know what is between us,
O'ermaster't as you may. And now, good friends,
As you are friends, scholars, and soldiers,
Give me one poor request.
HORATIO   What is't, my lord? We will.
HAMLET
Never make known what you have seen tonight.
HORATIO, MARCELLUS   My lord, we will not.
HAMLET   Nay, but swear't.
HORATIO   In faith, my lord, not I.   153
MARCELLUS   Nor I, my lord, in faith.
HAMLET   Upon my sword.   [*He holds out his sword.*]   155
MARCELLUS   We have sworn, my lord, already.   156
HAMLET   Indeed, upon my sword, indeed.
GHOST (*cries under the stage*)   Swear.
HAMLET
Ha, ha, boy, say'st thou so? Art thou there, truepenny?   159

---

78 Unhouseled . . . unaneled without having received the Sacrament or other last rites including confession, absolution, and the holy oil of extreme unction   **79 reck'ning** settling of accounts   **82 nature** i.e., the promptings of a son   **84 luxury** lechery   **90 matin** morning   **91 his** its   **94 couple** add.   **Hold** Hold together   **95 instant** instantly   **98 globe** (1) head (2) world (3) Globe Theater.   **99 table** tablet, slate   **100 fond** foolish   **101 All . . . past** all wise sayings, all shapes or images imprinted on the tablets of my memory, all past impressions   **108 My tables . . . down** (Editors often specify that Hamlet makes a note in his writing tablet, but he may simply mean that he is making a mental observation of lasting impression.)   **111 there you are** i.e., there, I've noted that against you.   **116 secure him** keep him safe.   **119 Hillo . . . come** (A falconer's call to a hawk in air. Hamlet mocks the hallooing as though it were a part of hawking.)

127 once ever   **130 But . . . knave** (Hamlet jokingly gives a self-evident answer: every villain is a thoroughgoing knave.)   **133 circumstance** ceremony, elaboration   **142 Saint Patrick** the keeper of Purgatory   **143 offense** (Hamlet deliberately changes Horatio's "no offense taken" to "an offense against all decency.")   **144 honest** genuine   **153 In faith . . . I** i.e., I swear not to tell what I have seen. (Horatio is not refusing to swear.)   **155 sword** i.e., the hilt in the form of a cross.   **156 We . . . already** i.e., We swore *in faith*.   **159 truepenny** honest old fellow.

Come on, you hear this fellow in the cellarage.
Consent to swear.

HORATIO   Propose the oath, my lord.

HAMLET
Never to speak of this that you have seen,
Swear by my sword.

GHOST [*beneath*]   Swear.   [*They swear.*] 164

HAMLET
Hic et ubique? Then we'll shift our ground.   165
                    [*He moves to another spot.*]
Come hither, gentlemen,
And lay your hands again upon my sword.
Swear by my sword
Never to speak of this that you have heard.

GHOST [*beneath*]   Swear by his sword.   [*They swear.*]

HAMLET
Well said, old mole. Canst work i'th'earth so fast?
A worthy pioneer!—Once more remove, good friends. 172
                    [*He moves again.*]

HORATIO
Oh, day and night, but this is wondrous strange!

HAMLET
And therefore as a stranger give it welcome.   174
There are more things in heaven and earth, Horatio,
Than are dreamt of in your philosophy.   176
But come;
Here, as before, never, so help you mercy,   178
How strange or odd some'er I bear myself—
As I perchance hereafter shall think meet
To put an antic disposition on—   181
That you, at such times seeing me, never shall,
With arms encumbered thus, or this headshake,   183
Or by pronouncing of some doubtful phrase
As "Well, we know," or "We could, an if we would," 185
Or "If we list to speak," or "There be, an if they
  might,"   186
Or such ambiguous giving out, to note   187
That you know aught of me—this do swear,   188
So grace and mercy at your most need help you.

GHOST [*beneath*]   Swear.   [*They swear.*]

HAMLET
Rest, rest, perturbèd spirit!—So, gentlemen,
With all my love I do commend me to you;   192
And what so poor a man as Hamlet is
May do t'express his love and friending to you,   194
God willing, shall not lack. Let us go in together, 195
And still your fingers on your lips, I pray.   196

The time is out of joint. Oh, cursèd spite   197
That ever I was born to set it right!
                    [*They wait for him to leave first.*]
Nay, come, let's go together.   *Exeunt.* 199

❖

[2.1]

Enter old Polonius with his man [Reynaldo].

POLONIUS
Give him this money and these notes, Reynaldo.
                    [*He gives money and papers.*]

REYNALDO   I will, my lord.

POLONIUS
You shall do marvelous wisely, good Reynaldo,   3
Before you visit him, to make inquire   4
Of his behavior.

REYNALDO   My lord, I did intend it.

POLONIUS
Marry, well said, very well said. Look you, sir,
Inquire me first what Danskers are in Paris,   7
And how, and who, what means, and where they
  keep,   8
What company, at what expense; and finding
By this encompassment and drift of question   10
That they do know my son, come you more nearer   11
Than your particular demands will touch it.   12
Take you, as 'twere, some distant knowledge of him, 13
As thus, "I know his father and his friends,
And in part him." Do you mark this, Reynaldo?

REYNALDO   Ay, very well, my lord.

POLONIUS
"And in part him, but," you may say, "not well.
But if't be he I mean, he's very wild,
Addicted so and so," and there put on him   19
What forgeries you please—marry, none so rank   20
As may dishonor him, take heed of that,
But, sir, such wanton, wild, and usual slips   22
As are companions noted and most known
To youth and liberty.

REYNALDO   As gaming, my lord.

POLONIUS   Ay, or drinking, fencing, swearing,
Quarreling, drabbing—you may go so far.   27

REYNALDO   My lord, that would dishonor him.

POLONIUS
Faith, no, as you may season it in the charge.   29
You must not put another scandal on him
That he is open to incontinency;   31

---

164 s.d. *They swear* (Seemingly they swear here, and at lines 170 and
190, as they lay their hands on Hamlet's sword. Triple oaths would
have particular force; these three oaths deal with what they have
seen, what they have heard, and what they promise about Hamlet's
antic disposition.)   165 *Hic et ubique?* Here and everywhere? (Latin.)
172 **pioneer** foot soldier assigned to dig tunnels and excavations.
174 **as a stranger** i.e., needing your hospitality   176 **your philosophy**
this subject that is called "natural philosophy" or "science." (*Your* is
not personal.)   178 **so help you mercy** as you hope for God's mercy
when you are judged   181 **antic** grotesque, strange   183 **encumbered** folded   185 **an if** if   186 **list** wished.   **There . . . might** There
are those who could talk if they were at liberty to do so   187 **note**
indicate   188 **aught** anything   192 **commend . . . you** give you my
best wishes   194 **friending** friendliness   195 **lack** be lacking.
196 **still** always

197 **out of joint** in utter disorder.   199 **let's go together** (Probably
they wait for him to leave first, but he refuses this ceremoniousness.)
2.1 Location: Polonius's chambers.
3 **marvelous** marvelously   4 **inquire** inquiry   7 **Danskers** Danes
8 **what means** what wealth (they have).   **keep** dwell   10 **encompassment . . . question** roundabout way of questioning   11-12 **come . . .
it** you will find out more this way than by asking pointed questions
(*particular demands*).   13 **Take you** Assume, pretend   19 **put on**
impute to   20 **forgeries** invented tales.   **rank** gross   22 **wanton**
sportive, unrestrained   27 **drabbing** whoring   29 **season** temper,
soften   31 **incontinency** habitual sexual excess

That's not my meaning. But breathe his faults so
    quaintly   32
That they may seem the taints of liberty,   33
The flash and outbreak of a fiery mind,
A savageness in unreclaimèd blood,   35
Of general assault.   36

REYNALDO   But, my good lord—
POLONIUS   Wherefore should you do this?
REYNALDO   Ay, my lord, I would know that.
POLONIUS   Marry, sir, here's my drift,
And I believe it is a fetch of warrant.   41
You laying these slight sullies on my son,
As 'twere a thing a little soiled wi'th' working,   43
Mark you,
Your party in converse, him you would sound,   45
Having ever seen in the prenominate crimes   46
The youth you breathe of guilty, be assured   47
He closes with you in this consequence: 48
"Good sir," or so, or "friend," or "gentleman,"
According to the phrase or the addition   50
Of man and country.

REYNALDO   Very good, my lord.
POLONIUS   And then, sir, does 'a this—'a does—what
was I about to say? By the Mass, I was about to say
something. Where did I leave?
REYNALDO   At "closes in the consequence."
POLONIUS

At "closes in the consequence," ay, marry.
He closes thus: "I know the gentleman,
I saw him yesterday," or "th'other day,"
Or then, or then, with such or such, "and as you say,
There was 'a gaming," "there o'ertook in 's rouse,"   60
"There falling out at tennis," or perchance   61
"I saw him enter such a house of sale,"
Videlicet a brothel, or so forth. See you now,   63
Your bait of falsehood takes this carp of truth;   64
And thus do we of wisdom and of reach,   65
With windlasses and with assays of bias,   66
By indirections find directions out.   67
So by my former lecture and advice   68
Shall you my son. You have me, have you not?   69

REYNALDO
My lord, I have.
POLONIUS   God b'wi'ye; fare ye well.
REYNALDO   Good my lord.

POLONIUS
Observe his inclination in yourself.   72
REYNALDO   I shall, my lord.
POLONIUS   And let him ply his music.
REYNALDO   Well, my lord.
POLONIUS
Farewell.   *Exit Reynaldo.*

Enter Ophelia.

          How now, Ophelia, what's the matter?
OPHELIA
Oh, my lord, my lord, I have been so affrighted!
POLONIUS   With what, i'th' name of God?
OPHELIA
My lord, as I was sewing in my closet,   79
Lord Hamlet, with his doublet all unbraced,   80
No hat upon his head, his stockings fouled,
Ungartered, and down-gyvèd to his ankle,   82
Pale as his shirt, his knees knocking each other,
And with a look so piteous in purport   84
As if he had been loosèd out of hell
To speak of horrors—he comes before me.
POLONIUS
Mad for thy love?
OPHELIA   My lord, I do not know,
But truly I do fear it.
POLONIUS   What said he?
OPHELIA
He took me by the wrist and held me hard.
Then goes he to the length of all his arm,
And, with his other hand thus o'er his brow
He falls to such perusal of my face
As 'a would draw it. Long stayed he so.   93
At last, a little shaking of mine arm
And thrice his head thus waving up and down,
He raised a sigh so piteous and profound
As it did seem to shatter all his bulk   97
And end his being. That done, he lets me go,
And with his head over his shoulder turned
He seemed to find his way without his eyes,
For out o' doors he went without their helps,
And to the last bended their light on me.
POLONIUS
Come, go with me. I will go seek the King.
This is the very ecstasy of love,   104
Whose violent property fordoes itself   105
And leads the will to desperate undertakings
As oft as any passion under heaven
That does afflict our natures. I am sorry.
What, have you given him any hard words of late?
OPHELIA
No, my good lord, but as you did command
I did repel his letters and denied

---

32 **quaintly** artfully, subtly 33 **taints of liberty** faults resulting from free living **35-6 A savageness . . . assault** a wildness in untamed youth that assails all indiscriminately. **41 fetch of warrant** legitimate trick. **43 wi'th' working** in the process of being made, i.e., in everyday experience **45 Your . . . converse** the person you are conversing with. **sound** sound out **46 Having ever** if he has ever. **prenominate crimes** aforenamed offenses **47 breathe** speak **48 closes . . . consequence** takes you into his confidence as follows **50 addition** title **60 o'ertook in 's rouse** overcome by drink **61 falling out** quarreling **63 Videlicet** namely **64 carp** a fish **65 reach** capacity, ability **66 windlasses** i.e., circuitous paths. (Literally, circuits made to head off the game in hunting.) **assays of bias** attempts through indirection (like the curving path of the bowling ball, which is biased or weighted to one side) **67 directions** i.e., the way things really are **68 former lecture** just-ended set of instructions **69 have** understand

72 **in yourself** in your own person (as well as by asking questions of others). **79 closet** private chamber **80 doublet** close-fitting jacket. **unbraced** unfastened **82 down-gyvèd** fallen to the ankles (like gyves or fetters) **84 in purport** in what it expressed **93 As** as if **97 As** that. **bulk** body **104 ecstasy** madness **105 property fordoes** nature destroys

His access to me.
POLONIUS   That hath made him mad.
I am sorry that with better heed and judgment
I had not quoted him. I feared he did but trifle   114
And meant to wrack thee. But beshrew my jealousy!   115
By heaven, it is as proper to our age   116
To cast beyond ourselves in our opinions   117
As it is common for the younger sort
To lack discretion. Come, go we to the King.
This must be known, which, being kept close, might
    move   120
More grief to hide than hate to utter love.   121
Come.   *Exeunt.*

❧

[2.2]

*Flourish. Enter King and Queen, Rosencrantz,
and Guildenstern [with others].*

KING
Welcome, dear Rosencrantz and Guildenstern.
Moreover that we much did long to see you,   2
The need we have to use you did provoke
Our hasty sending. Something have you heard
Of Hamlet's transformation—so call it,
Sith nor th'exterior nor the inward man   6
Resembles that it was. What it should be,   7
More than his father's death, that thus hath put him
So much from th'understanding of himself,
I cannot dream of. I entreat you both
That, being of so young days brought up with him,   11
And sith so neighbored to his youth and havior,   12
That you vouchsafe your rest here in our court   13
Some little time, so by your companies
To draw him on to pleasures, and to gather
So much as from occasion you may glean,   16
Whether aught to us unknown afflicts him thus
That, opened, lies within our remedy.   18
QUEEN
Good gentlemen, he hath much talked of you,
And sure I am two men there is not living
To whom he more adheres. If it will please you
To show us so much gentry and good will   22
As to expend your time with us awhile
For the supply and profit of our hope,   24

Your visitation shall receive such thanks
As fits a kings's remembrance.
ROSENCRANTZ   Both Your Majesties   26
Might, by the sovereign power you have of us,   27
Put your dread pleasures more into command   28
Than to entreaty.
GUILDENSTERN   But we both obey,
And here give up ourselves in the full bent   30
To lay our service freely at your feet,
To be commanded.
KING
Thanks, Rosencrantz and gentle Guildenstern.
QUEEN
Thanks, Guildenstern and gentle Rosencrantz.
And I beseech you instantly to visit
My too much changèd son.—Go, some of you,
And bring these gentlemen where Hamlet is.
GUILDENSTERN
Heavens make our presence and our practices   38
Pleasant and helpful to him!
QUEEN   Ay, amen!
        *Exeunt Rosencrantz and Guildenstern [with some
                                        attendants].*

Enter Polonius.

POLONIUS
Th'ambassadors from Norway, my good lord,
Are joyfully returned.
KING
Thou still hast been the father of good news.   42
POLONIUS
Have I, my lord? I assure my good liege
I hold my duty, as I hold my soul,
Both to my God and to my gracious king;
And I do think, or else this brain of mine
Hunts not the trail of policy so sure   47
As it hath used to do, that I have found
The very cause of Hamlet's lunacy.
KING
Oh, speak of that! That do I long to hear.
POLONIUS
Give first admittance to th'ambassadors.
My news shall be the fruit to that great feast.   52
KING
Thyself do grace to them and bring them in.   53
                                        [Exit Polonius.]
He tells me, my dear Gertrude, he hath found
The head and source of all your son's distemper.
QUEEN
I doubt it is no other but the main,   56
His father's death and our o'erhasty marriage.

*Enter Ambassadors [Voltimand and Cornelius,
with Polonius].*

---

114 **quoted** observed   115 **wrack** ruin, seduce.   **beshrew my jealousy!** a plague upon my suspicious nature!   116 **proper . . . age** characteristic of us (old) men   117 **cast beyond** overshoot, miscalculate.
(A metaphor from hunting.)   120 **known** made known (to the King).
close secret   120–1 **might . . . love** i.e., might cause more grief
(because of what Hamlet might do) by hiding the knowledge of Hamlet's strange behavior to Ophelia than unpleasantness by telling it.
2.2 Location: The castle.
2 **Moreover that** Besides the fact that   6 **Sith nor** since neither   7 **that**
what   11–12 **That . . . havior** that, seeing as you were brought up
with him from early youth (see 3.4.209, where Hamlet refers to
Rosencrantz and Guildenstern as "my two schoolfellows"), and since
you have been intimately acquainted with his youthful ways
13 **vouchsafe your rest** consent to stay   16 **occasion** opportunity
18 **opened** being revealed   22 **gentry** courtesy   24 **supply . . . hope**
aid and furtherance of what we hope for

26 **As fits . . . remembrance** as would be a fitting gift of a king who
rewards true service.   27 **of** over   28 **dread** inspiring awe   30 **in . . .
bent** to the utmost degree of our capacity. (An archery metaphor.)
38 **practices** doings   42 **still** always   47 **policy** statecraft   52 **fruit**
dessert   53 **grace** honor. (Punning on *grace* said before a *feast*, line
52.)   56 **doubt** fear, suspect.

KING

Well, we shall sift him.—Welcome, my good friends!   58
Say, Voltimand, what from our brother Norway?   59

VOLTIMAND

Most fair return of greetings and desires.   60
Upon our first, he sent out to suppress   61
His nephew's levies, which to him appeared
To be a preparation 'gainst the Polack,
But, better looked into, he truly found
It was against Your Highness. Whereat grieved
That so his sickness, age, and impotence   66
Was falsely borne in hand, sends out arrests   67
On Fortinbras, which he, in brief, obeys,
Receives rebuke from Norway, and in fine   69
Makes vow before his uncle never more
To give th'assay of arms against Your Majesty.   71
Whereon old Norway, overcome with joy,
Gives him three thousand crowns in annual fee
And his commission to employ those soldiers,
So levied as before, against the Polack,
With an entreaty, herein further shown,
                                        [giving a paper]
That it might please you to give quiet pass
Through your dominions for this enterprise
On such regards of safety and allowance   79
As therein are set down.

KING   It likes us well,   80
And at our more considered time we'll read,   81
Answer, and think upon this business.
Meantime we thank you for your well-took labor.
Go to your rest; at night we'll feast together.
Most welcome home!   Exeunt Ambassadors.

POLONIUS   This business is well ended.
My liege, and madam, to expostulate   86
What majesty should be, what duty is,
Why day is day, night night, and time is time,
Were nothing but to waste night, day, and time.
Therefore, since brevity is the soul of wit,   90
And tediousness the limbs and outward flourishes,
I will be brief. Your noble son is mad.
Mad call I it, for, to define true madness,
What is't but to be nothing else but mad?
But let that go.

QUEEN   More matter, with less art.

POLONIUS

Madam, I swear I use no art at all.
That he's mad, 'tis true; 'tis true 'tis pity,
And pity 'tis 'tis true—a foolish figure,   98
But farewell it, for I will use no art.
Mad let us grant him, then, and now remains
That we find out the cause of this effect,

Or rather say, the cause of this defect,
For this effect defective comes by cause.   103
Thus it remains, and the remainder thus.
Perpend.   105
I have a daughter—have while she is mine—
Who, in her duty and obedience, mark,
Hath given me this. Now gather and surmise.   108
[He reads the letter.] "To the celestial and my soul's
idol, the most beautified Ophelia"—
That's an ill phrase, a vile phrase; "beautified" is a
vile phrase. But you shall hear. Thus: [He reads.]
"In her excellent white bosom, these, etc."   113

QUEEN   Came this from Hamlet to her?

POLONIUS

Good madam, stay awhile, I will be faithful.   115
                                        [He reads.]

        "Doubt thou the stars are fire,
            Doubt that the sun doth move,
        Doubt truth to be a liar,   118
            But never doubt I love.
O dear Ophelia, I am ill at these numbers. I have not   120
art to reckon my groans. But that I love thee best, O   121
most best, believe it. Adieu.
            Thine evermore, most dear lady, whilst this
                    machine is to him, Hamlet."   124
This in obedience hath my daughter shown me,
And, more above, hath his solicitings,   126
As they fell out by time, by means, and place,   127
All given to mine ear.

KING   But how hath she   128
Received his love?

POLONIUS   What do you think of me?

KING

As of a man faithful and honorable.

POLONIUS

I would fain prove so. But what might you think,   131
When I had seen this hot love on the wing—
As I perceived it, I must tell you that,
Before my daughter told me—what might you,
Or my dear Majesty your queen here, think,
If I had played the desk or table book,   136
Or given my heart a winking, mute and dumb,   137
Or looked upon this love with idle sight?   138
What might you think? No, I went round to work,   139
And my young mistress thus I did bespeak: 140
"Lord Hamlet is a prince out of thy star;   141
This must not be." And then I prescripts gave her,   142

---

58 **sift him** question Polonius (or Hamlet closely). 59 **brother** fellow king 60 **desires** good wishes. 61 **Upon our first** At our first words on the business 66 **impotence** weakness 67 **borne in hand** deluded, taken advantage of. **arrests** orders to desist 69 **in fine** in conclusion 71 **give th'assay** make trial of strength, challenge 79 **On . . . allowance** i.e., with such considerations for the safety of Denmark and permission for Fortinbras 80 **likes** pleases 81 **considered** suitable for deliberation 86 **expostulate** expound, inquire into 90 **wit** sense or judgment 98 **figure** figure of speech

103 **For . . . cause** i.e., for this defective behavior, this madness, must have a cause. 105 **Perpend** Consider. 108 **gather and surmise** draw your own conclusions. 113 **"In . . . etc."** (The letter is poetically addressed to her heart, where a letter would be kept by a young lady.) 115 **stay . . . faithful** i.e., hold on, I will do as you wish. 118 **Doubt** suspect 120 **ill . . . numbers** unskilled at writing verses. 121 **reckon** (1) count (2) number metrically, scan 124 **machine** i.e., body 126–8 **And . . . ear** and moreover she has told me when, how, and where his solicitings of her occurred. 131 **fain** gladly 136–7 **If . . . dumb** if I had acted as go-between, passing love notes, or if I had refused to let my heart acknowledge what my eyes could see 138 **with idle sight** complacently or incomprehendingly. 139 **round** roundly, plainly 140 **bespeak** address 141 **out of thy star** above your sphere, position 142 **prescripts** orders

That she should lock herself from his resort,
Admit no messengers, receive no tokens.
Which done, she took the fruits of my advice;
And he, repellèd—a short tale to make—
Fell into a sadness, then into a fast,
Thence to a watch, thence into a weakness,   148
Thence to a lightness, and by this declension   149
Into the madness wherein now he raves,
And all we mourn for.

KING [to the Queen]   Do you think 'tis this?

QUEEN   It may be, very like.

POLONIUS
Hath there been such a time—I would fain know
     that—
That I have positively said "'Tis so,"
When it proved otherwise?

KING   Not that I know.

POLONIUS
Take this from this, if this be otherwise.   156
If circumstances lead me, I will find
Where truth is hid, though it were hid indeed
Within the center.

KING   How may we try it further?   159

POLONIUS
You know sometimes he walks four hours together
Here in the lobby.

QUEEN   So he does indeed.

POLONIUS
At such a time I'll loose my daughter to him.   162
Be you and I behind an arras then.   163
Mark the encounter. If he love her not
And be not from his reason fall'n thereon,   165
Let me be no assistant for a state,
But keep a farm and carters.

KING   We will try it.   167

Enter Hamlet [reading on a book].

QUEEN
But look where sadly the poor wretch comes reading.

POLONIUS
Away, I do beseech you both, away.
I'll board him presently. Oh, give me leave.   170
          Exeunt King and Queen [with attendants].
How does my good Lord Hamlet?

HAMLET   Well, God-a-mercy.   172

POLONIUS   Do you know me, my lord?

HAMLET   Excellent well. You are a fishmonger.   174

POLONIUS   Not I, my lord.

HAMLET   Then I would you were so honest a man.

POLONIUS   Honest, my lord?

HAMLET   Ay, sir. To be honest, as this world goes, is to
be one man picked out of ten thousand.

POLONIUS   That's very true, my lord.

HAMLET   For if the sun breed maggots in a dead dog,
being a good kissing carrion—Have you a daughter?   182

POLONIUS   I have, my lord.

HAMLET   Let her not walk i'th' sun. Conception is a   184
blessing, but as your daughter may conceive, friend,
look to't.

POLONIUS [aside]   How say you by that? Still harping
on my daughter. Yet he knew me not at first; 'a said
I was a fishmonger. 'A is far gone. And truly in my
youth I suffered much extremity for love, very near
this. I'll speak to him again.—What do you read,
my lord?

HAMLET   Words, words, words.

POLONIUS   What is the matter, my lord?   194

HAMLET   Between who?

POLONIUS   I mean, the matter that you read, my lord.

HAMLET   Slanders, sir; for the satirical rogue says here
that old men have gray beards, that their faces are wrinkled, their eyes purging thick amber and plum-tree   199
gum, and that they have a plentiful lack of wit, to-   200
gether with most weak hams. All which, sir, though I
most powerfully and potently believe, yet I hold it not
honesty to have it thus set down, for yourself, sir, shall   203
grow old as I am, if like a crab you could go backward.   204

POLONIUS [aside]   Though this be madness, yet there is
method in't.—Will you walk out of the air, my lord?   206

HAMLET   Into my grave.

POLONIUS   Indeed, that's out of the air. [Aside] How
pregnant sometimes his replies are! A happiness that   209
often madness hits on, which reason and sanity could
not so prosperously be delivered of. I will leave him   211
and suddenly contrive the means of meeting between   212
him and my daughter.—My honorable lord, I will
most humbly take my leave of you.

HAMLET   You cannot, sir, take from me anything that I
will more willingly part withal—except my life, except   216
my life, except my life.

Enter Guildenstern and Rosencrantz.

POLONIUS   Fare you well, my lord.

HAMLET   These tedious old fools!

POLONIUS   You go to seek the Lord Hamlet. There he is.

ROSENCRANTZ [to Polonius]   God save you, sir!
                                   [Exit Polonius.]

GUILDENSTERN   My honored lord!

---

148 **watch** state of sleeplessness   149 **lightness** lightheadedness.
declension decline, deterioration. (With a pun on the grammatical
sense.)   156 **Take this from this** (The actor probably gestures, indicating that he means his head from his shoulders, or his staff of office
or chain from his hands or neck, or something similar.)   159 **center**
center of the earth, traditionally an extraordinarily inaccessible place.
try test   162 **loose** (As one might release an animal that is being
mated.)   163 **arras** hanging, tapestry   165 **thereon** on that account
167 **carters** wagon drivers.   170 **I'll . . . leave** I'll accost him at once.
Please leave us alone; leave him to me.   172 **God-a-mercy** God have
mercy, i.e., thank you.   174 **fishmonger** fish merchant.

182 **a good kissing carrion** i.e., a good piece of flesh for kissing, or for
the sun to kiss   184 **i'th' sun** in public. (With additional implication
of the sunshine of princely favors.)   **Conception** (1) Understanding
(2) Pregnancy   194 **matter** substance. (But Hamlet plays on the sense
of "basis for a dispute.")   199 **purging** discharging.   **amber** i.e.,
resin, like the resinous *plum-tree gum*   200 **wit** understanding
203 **honesty** decency, decorum   204 **old** as old   206 **out of the air**
(The open air was considered dangerous for sick people.)   209 **pregnant** quick-witted, full of meaning.   **happiness** felicity of expression
211 **prosperously** successfully   212 **suddenly** immediately
216 **withal** with

ROSENCRANTZ   My most dear lord!

HAMLET   My excellent good friends! How dost thou, Guildenstern? Ah, Rosencrantz! Good lads, how do you both?

ROSENCRANTZ
As the indifferent children of the earth.   227

GUILDENSTERN
Happy in that we are not overhappy.
On Fortune's cap we are not the very button.

HAMLET   Nor the soles of her shoe?

ROSENCRANTZ   Neither, my lord.

HAMLET   Then you live about her waist, or in the mid-   232
dle of her favors?   233

GUILDENSTERN   Faith, her privates we.   234

HAMLET   In the secret parts of Fortune? Oh, most true, she is a strumpet. What news?   236

ROSENCRANTZ   None, my lord, but the world's grown honest.

HAMLET   Then is doomsday near. But your news is not true. Let me question more in particular. What have you, my good friends, deserved at the hands of Fortune that she sends you to prison hither?

GUILDENSTERN   Prison, my lord?

HAMLET   Denmark's a prison.

ROSENCRANTZ   Then is the world one.

HAMLET   A goodly one, in which there are many confines, wards, and dungeons, Denmark being one   247
o'th' worst.

ROSENCRANTZ   We think not so, my lord.

HAMLET   Why then 'tis none to you, for there is nothing either good or bad but thinking makes it so. To me it is a prison.

ROSENCRANTZ   Why then, your ambition makes it one. 'Tis too narrow for your mind.

HAMLET   Oh, God, I could be bounded in a nutshell and count myself a king of infinite space, were it not that I have bad dreams.

GUILDENSTERN   Which dreams indeed are ambition, for the very substance of the ambitious is merely the   259
shadow of a dream.

HAMLET   A dream itself is but a shadow.

ROSENCRANTZ   Truly, and I hold ambition of so airy and light a quality that it is but a shadow's shadow.

HAMLET   Then are our beggars bodies, and our mon-   264
archs and outstretched heroes the beggars' shadows.   265
Shall we to th' court? For, by my fay, I cannot reason.   266

ROSENCRANTZ, GUILDENSTERN   We'll wait upon you.   267

HAMLET   No such matter. I will not sort you with the   268
rest of my servants, for, to speak to you like an honest man, I am most dreadfully attended. But, in the   270
beaten way of friendship, what make you at Elsinore?   271

ROSENCRANTZ   To visit you, my lord, no other occasion.

HAMLET   Beggar that I am, I am even poor in thanks; but I thank you, and sure, dear friends, my thanks are too dear a halfpenny. Were you not sent for? Is it your   275
own inclining? Is it a free visitation? Come, come, deal   276
justly with me. Come, come. Nay, speak.

GUILDENSTERN   What should we say, my lord?

HAMLET   Anything but to th' purpose. You were sent   279
for, and there is a kind of confession in your looks which your modesties have not craft enough to color.   281
I know the good King and Queen have sent for you.

ROSENCRANTZ   To what end, my lord?

HAMLET   That you must teach me. But let me conjure   284
you, by the rights of our fellowship, by the consonancy   285
of our youth, by the obligation of our ever-preserved   286
love, and by what more dear a better proposer   287
could charge you withal, be even and direct with me   288
whether you were sent for or no.

ROSENCRANTZ   [aside to Guildenstern]   What say you?

HAMLET   [aside]   Nay, then, I have an eye of you.—If   291
you love me, hold not off.   292

GUILDENSTERN   My lord, we were sent for.

HAMLET   I will tell you why; so shall my anticipation   294
prevent your discovery, and your secrecy to the King   295
and Queen molt no feather. I have of late—but   296
wherefore I know not—lost all my mirth, forgone all custom of exercises; and indeed it goes so heavily with my disposition that this goodly frame, the earth, seems to me a sterile promontory; this most excellent canopy, the air, look you, this brave o'erhanging   301
firmament, this majestical roof fretted with golden   302
fire, why, it appeareth nothing to me but a foul and pestilent congregation of vapors. What a piece of work   304
is a man! How noble in reason, how infinite in faculties, in form and moving how express and admirable, in   306
action how like an angel, in apprehension how like a   307
god! The beauty of the world, the paragon of animals! And yet, to me, what is this quintessence of dust?   309
Man delights not me—no, nor woman neither, though by your smiling you seem to say so.

---

227 **indifferent** ordinary, at neither extreme of fortune or misfortune 232–3 **the middle . . . favors** i.e., her genitals. 234 **her privates we** (1) we dwell in her privates, her genitals, in the middle of her favors (2) we are her ordinary footsoldiers. 236 **strumpet** (Fortune was proverbially thought of as fickle.) 247 **confines** places of confinement 259 **the very . . . ambitious** that seemingly very substantial thing that the ambitious pursue 264–5 **Then . . . shadows** (Hamlet pursues their argument about ambition to its absurd extreme: if ambition is only a shadow of a shadow, then beggars (who are presumably without ambition) must be real, whereas monarchs and heroes are only their shadows—*outstretched* like elongated shadows, made to look bigger than they are.) 266 **fay** faith 267 **wait upon** accompany, attend. (But Hamlet uses the phrase in the sense of providing menial service.)

268 **sort** class, categorize 270 **dreadfully attended** waited upon in slovenly fashion. 271 **beaten way** familiar path, tried-and-true course. **make** do 275 **too dear a halfpenny** (1) too expensive at even a halfpenny, i.e., of little worth (2) too expensive *by* a halfpenny in return for worthless kindness. 276 **free** voluntary 279 **Anything but to th' purpose** Anything except a straightforward answer. (Said ironically.) 281 **color** disguise. 284 **conjure** adjure, entreat 285–6 **the consonancy of our youth** our closeness in our younger days 287 **better** more skillful 288 **charge** urge. **even** straight, honest 291 **of** on 292 **hold not off** don't hold back. 294–5 **so . . . discovery** in that way my saying it first will spare you from having to reveal the truth 296 **molt no feather** i.e., not diminish in the least. 301 **brave** splendid 302 **fretted** adorned (with fretwork, as in a vaulted ceiling) 304 **congregation** mass. **piece of work** masterpiece 306 **express** well-framed, exact, expressive 307 **apprehension** power of comprehending 309 **quintessence** very essence. (Literally, the fifth essence beyond earth, water, air, and fire, supposed to be extractable from them.)

ROSENCRANTZ   My lord, there was no such stuff in my thoughts.

HAMLET   Why did you laugh, then, when I said man delights not me?

ROSENCRANTZ   To think, my lord, if you delight not in man, what Lenten entertainment the players shall 317 receive from you. We coted them on the way, and 318 hither are they coming to offer you service.

HAMLET   He that plays the king shall be welcome; His Majesty shall have tribute of me. The adventurous 321 knight shall use his foil and target, the lover shall not 322 sigh gratis, the humorous man shall end his part in 323 peace, the clown shall make those laugh whose lungs 324 are tickle o'th' sear, and the lady shall say her mind 325 freely, or the blank verse shall halt for't. What players 326 are they?

ROSENCRANTZ   Even those you were wont to take such delight in, the tragedians of the city. 329

HAMLET   How chances it they travel? Their residence, 330 both in reputation and profit, was better both ways.

ROSENCRANTZ   I think their inhibition comes by the 332 means of the late innovation. 333

HAMLET   Do they hold the same estimation they did when I was in the city? Are they so followed?

ROSENCRANTZ   No, indeed are they not.

HAMLET   How comes it? Do they grow rusty? 337

ROSENCRANTZ   Nay, their endeavor keeps in the wonted 338 pace. But there is, sir, an aerie of children, little eyases, 339 that cry out on the top of question and are most tyran- 340 nically clapped for't. These are now the fashion, and 341 so berattle the common stages—so they call them— 342 that many wearing rapiers are afraid of goose quills 343 and dare scarce come thither.

HAMLET   What, are they children? Who maintains 'em? How are they escotted? Will they pursue the quality no 346 longer than they can sing? Will they not say after- 347

wards, if they should grow themselves to common 348 players—as it is most like, if their means are no 349 better—their writers do them wrong to make them 350 exclaim against their own succession? 351

ROSENCRANTZ   Faith, there has been much to-do on 352 both sides, and the nation holds it no sin to tar them to 353 controversy. There was for a while no money bid for 354 argument unless the poet and the player went to cuffs 355 in the question. 356

HAMLET   Is't possible?

GUILDENSTERN   Oh, there has been much throwing about of brains.

HAMLET   Do the boys carry it away? 360

ROSENCRANTZ   Ay, that they do, my lord—Hercules 361 and his load too. 362

HAMLET   It is not very strange; for my uncle is King of Denmark, and those that would make mouths at him 364 while my father lived give twenty, forty, fifty, a hundred ducats apiece for his picture in little. 'Sblood, 366 there is something in this more than natural, if philos- ophy could find it out.

A flourish [*of trumpets within*].

GUILDENSTERN   There are the players.

HAMLET   Gentlemen, you are welcome to Elsinore. Your hands, come then. Th'appurtenance of welcome is 371 fashion and ceremony. Let me comply with you in this 372 garb, lest my extent to the players, which, I tell you, 373 must show fairly outwards, should more appear like 374 entertainment than yours. You are welcome. But my 375 uncle-father and aunt-mother are deceived.

GUILDENSTERN   In what, my dear lord?

HAMLET   I am but mad north-north-west. When the 378 wind is southerly I know a hawk from a handsaw. 379

Enter Polonius.

POLONIUS   Well be with you, gentlemen!

HAMLET   Hark you, Guildenstern, and you too; at each ear a hearer. That great baby you see there is not yet out of his swaddling clouts. 383

ROSENCRANTZ   Haply he is the second time come to 384 them, for they say an old man is twice a child.

---

317 Lenten entertainment meager reception (appropriate to Lent) **318 coted** overtook and passed by   **321 tribute** (1) applause (2) homage paid in money.   **of** from   **322 foil and target** sword and shield   **323 gratis** for nothing.   **humorous man** eccentric character, dominated by one trait or "humor"   **323–4 in peace** i.e., with full license   **325 tickle o'th' sear** hair trigger, ready to laugh easily. (A *sear* is part of a gun-lock.)   **326 halt** limp   **329 tragedians** actors **330 residence** remaining in their usual place, i.e., in the city **332 inhibition** formal prohibition (from acting plays in the city) **333 late innovation** i.e., recent new fashion in satirical plays per- formed by boy actors in the "private" theaters; or the Earl of Essex's abortive rebellion in 1601 against Elizabeth's government. (A much debated passage of seemingly topical reference.)   **337 How . . . rusty?** Have they lost their polish, gone out of fashion? (This passage, through line 362, alludes to the rivalry between the children's compa- nies and the adult actors, given strong impetus by the reopening of the Children of the Chapel at the Blackfriars Theater in late 1600.) **338 keeps . . . wonted** continues in the usual   **339 aerie** nest.   **eyases** young hawks   **340 cry . . . question** speak shrilly, dominating the controversy (in decrying the public theaters)   **340–1 tyrannically** vehemently   **342 berattle . . . stages** clamor against the public the- aters   **343 many wearing rapiers** i.e., many men of fashion, afraid to patronize the common players for fear of being satirized by the poets writing for the boy actors.   **goose quills** i.e., pens of satirists **346 escotted** maintained.   **quality** (acting) profession   **346–7 no longer . . . sing** i.e., only until their voices change.

348 common regular, adult   **349 like** likely   **349–50 if . . . better** if they find no better way to support themselves   **351 succession** i.e., future careers.   **352 to-do** ado   **353 tar** incite (as in inciting dogs to attack a chained bear)   **354–6 There . . . question** i.e., For a while, no money was offered by the acting companies to playwrights for the plot to a play unless the satirical poets who wrote for the boys and the adult actors came to blows in the play itself.   **360 carry it away** i.e., win the day.   **361–2 Hercules . . . load** (Thought to be an allusion to the sign of the Globe Theatre, which allegedly was Hercules bear- ing the world on his shoulders.)   **364 mouths** faces   **366 ducats** gold coins.   **in little** in miniature.   **'Sblood** By God's (Christ's) blood **371 Th'appurtenance** The proper accompaniment   **372 comply** observe the formalities of courtesy   **373 garb** i.e., manner.   **my extent** that which I extend, i.e., my polite behavior   **374 show fairly outwards** show every evidence of cordiality   **375 entertainment** a (warm) reception   **378 north-north-west** just off true north, only partly.   **379 I . . . handsaw** (Speaking in his mad guise, Hamlet per- haps suggests that he can tell true from false. A *handsaw* may be a *hernshaw* or heron. Still, a supposedly mad disposition might com- pare hawks and handsaws.)   **383 swaddling clouts** cloths in which to wrap a newborn baby.   **384 Haply** Perhaps

HAMLET   I will prophesy he comes to tell me of the
players. Mark it.—You say right, sir, o' Monday   387
morning, 'twas then indeed.   388

POLONIUS   My lord, I have news to tell you.

HAMLET   My lord, I have news to tell you. When Roscius   390
was an actor in Rome—

POLONIUS   The actors are come hither, my lord.

HAMLET   Buzz, buzz!   393

POLONIUS   Upon my honor—

HAMLET   Then came each actor on his ass.

POLONIUS   The best actors in the world, either for
tragedy, comedy, history, pastoral, pastoral-comical,
historical-pastoral, tragical-historical, tragical-comical-
historical-pastoral, scene individable, or poem unlim-   399
ited. Seneca cannot be too heavy, nor Plautus too   400
light. For the law of writ and the liberty, these are the   401
only men.

HAMLET   O Jephthah, judge of Israel, what a treasure   403
hadst thou!

POLONIUS   What a treasure had he, my lord?

HAMLET   Why,
"One fair daughter, and no more,
The which he lovèd passing well."   408

POLONIUS   [aside]   Still on my daughter.

HAMLET   Am I not i'th' right, old Jephthah?

POLONIUS   If you call me Jephthah, my lord, I have a
daughter that I love passing well.

HAMLET   Nay, that follows not.   413

POLONIUS   What follows then, my lord?   414

HAMLET   Why,
"As by lot, God wot,"   416
and then, you know,
"It came to pass, as most like it was"—   418
the first row of the pious chanson will show you more,   419
for look where my abridgement comes.   420

Enter the Players.

You are welcome, masters; welcome, all. I am glad to   421
see thee well. Welcome, good friends. Oh, old friend!
Why, thy face is valanced since I saw thee last. Com'st   423
thou to beard me in Denmark? What, my young lady   424

and mistress! By'r Lady, Your Ladyship is nearer to   425
heaven than when I saw you last, by the altitude of a   426
chopine. Pray God your voice, like a piece of uncur-   427
rent gold, be not cracked within the ring. Masters, you   428
are all welcome. We'll e'en to't like French falconers,   429
fly at anything we see. We'll have a speech straight.   430
Come, give us a taste of your quality. Come, a   431
passionate speech.

FIRST PLAYER   What speech, my good lord?

HAMLET   I heard thee speak me a speech once, but it
was never acted, or if it was, not above once, for the
play, I remember, pleased not the million; 'twas cav-   436
iar to the general. But it was—as I received it, and   437
others, whose judgments in such matters cried in the   438
top of mine—an excellent play, well digested in the   439
scenes, set down with as much modesty as cunning. I   440
remember one said there were no sallets in the lines to   441
make the matter savory, nor no matter in the phrase
that might indict the author of affectation, but called it   443
an honest method, as wholesome as sweet, and by very
much more handsome than fine. One speech in't I   445
chiefly loved: 'twas Aeneas' tale to Dido, and there-
about of it especially when he speaks of Priam's   447
slaughter. If it live in your memory, begin at this line: 448
let me see, let me see—
"The rugged Pyrrhus, like th' Hyrcanian beast"—   450
'Tis not so. It begins with Pyrrhus:
"The rugged Pyrrhus, he whose sable arms,   452
Black as his purpose, did the night resemble
When he lay couchèd in th' ominous horse,   454
Hath now this dread and black complexion
smeared
With heraldry more dismal. Head to foot   456
Now is he total gules, horridly tricked   457
With blood of fathers, mothers, daughters, sons,
Baked and impasted with the parching streets,   459
That lend a tyrannous and a damnèd light   460

387–8 You say . . . then indeed (Said to impress upon Polonius the idea
that Hamlet is in serious conversation with his friends.)   **390 Roscius** a
famous Roman actor who died in 62 B.C.   **393 Buzz** (An interjection
used to denote stale news.)   **399–400 scene . . . unlimited** plays that
are unclassifiable and all-inclusive. (An absurdly catchall conclusion to
Polonius's pompous list of categories.)   **400 Seneca** writer of Latin
tragedies.   **Plautus** writer of Latin comedies   **401 law . . . liberty** dramatic composition both according to the rules and disregarding the
rules.   **these** i.e., the actors   **403 Jephthah . . . Israel** (Jephthah had to
sacrifice his daughter; see Judges 11. Hamlet goes on to quote from a
ballad on the theme.)   **408 passing** surpassingly   **413 that follows not**
i.e., just because you resemble Jephthah in having a daughter does not
logically prove that you love her.   **414 What . . . lord?** What does follow logically? (But Hamlet, pretending madness, answers with a fragment of a ballad, as if Polonius had asked, "What comes next?" See
419n.)   **416 lot** chance.   **wot** knows   **418 like** likely, probable
419 the first . . . more the first stanza of this biblically based ballad will
satisfy your stated desire to know *what follows* (line 414).   **420 my
abridgment** something that cuts short my conversation; also, a diversion   **421 masters** good sirs   **423 valanced** fringed (with a beard)
424 beard confront, challenge. (With obvious pun.)   **young lady** i.e.,
boy playing women's parts

425 By'r Lady By Our Lady   **425–6 nearer to heaven** i.e., taller
427 chopine thick-soled shoe of Italian fashion.   **427–8 uncurrent** not
passable as lawful coinage   **428 cracked . . . ring** i.e., changed from
adolescent to male voice, no longer suitable for women's roles. (Coins
featured rings enclosing the sovereign's head; if the coin was sufficiently clipped to invade within this ring, it was unfit for currency.)
429 e'en to't go at it   **430 straight** at once.   **431 quality** professional
skill.   **436–7 caviar to the general** i.e., an expensive delicacy not generally palatable to uneducated tastes.   **438–9 cried in the top of** i.e.,
spoke with greater authority than   **439 digested** arranged, ordered
440 modesty moderation, restraint.   **cunning** skill.   **441 sallets** i.e.,
something savory, spicy improprieties   **443 indict** convict
445 handsome well-proportioned.   **fine** elaborately ornamented,
showy.   **447–8 Priam's slaughter** the slaying of the ruler of Troy,
when the Greeks finally took the city   **450 Pyrrhus** a Greek hero in
the Trojan War, also known as Neoptolemus, son of Achilles—another
avenging son.   **th' Hyrcanian beast** i.e., the tiger. (On the death of
Priam, see Virgil, *Aeneid*, 2.506 ff.; compare the whole speech with
Marlowe's *Dido Queen of Carthage*, 2.1.214 ff. On the *Hyrcanian* tiger,
see *Aeneid*, 4.366–7. Hyrcania is on the Caspian Sea.)   **452 rugged**
shaggy, savage.   **sable** black (for reasons of camouflage during the
episode of the Trojan horse)   **454 couchèd** concealed.   **ominous
horse** fateful Trojan horse, by which the Greeks gained access to Troy
456 dismal calamitous.   **457 total gules** entirely red. (A heraldic
term.)   **tricked** spotted and smeared. (Heraldic.)   **459 Baked . . .
streets** roasted and encrusted, like a thick paste, by the parching heat
of the streets (because of the fires everywhere)   **460 tyrannous** cruel

To their lord's murder. Roasted in wrath and fire, 461
And thus o'ersizèd with coagulate gore, 462
With eyes like carbuncles, the hellish Pyrrhus 463
Old grandsire Priam seeks."
So proceed you.
POLONIUS   'Fore God, my lord, well spoken, with good
accent and good discretion.
FIRST PLAYER   "Anon he finds him
Striking too short at Greeks. His antique sword, 469
Rebellious to his arm, lies where it falls,
Repugnant to command. Unequal matched, 471
Pyrrhus at Priam drives, in rage strikes wide,
But with the whiff and wind of his fell sword 473
Th'unnervèd father falls. Then senseless Ilium, 474
Seeming to feel this blow, with flaming top
Stoops to his base, and with a hideous crash 476
Takes prisoner Pyrrhus' ear. For, lo! His sword,
Which was declining on the milky head 478
Of reverend Priam, seemed i'th'air to stick.
So as a painted tyrant Pyrrhus stood, 480
And, like a neutral to his will and matter, 481
Did nothing.
But as we often see against some storm 483
A silence in the heavens, the rack stand still, 484
The bold winds speechless, and the orb below 485
As hush as death, anon the dreadful thunder
Doth rend the region, so, after Pyrrhus' pause, 487
A rousèd vengeance sets him new a-work,
And never did the Cyclops' hammers fall 489
On Mars's armor forged for proof eterne 490
With less remorse than Pyrrhus' bleeding sword 491
Now falls on Priam.
Out, out, thou strumpet Fortune! All you gods
In general synod take away her power! 494
Break all the spokes and fellies from her wheel, 495
And bowl the round nave down the hill of heaven 496
As low as to the fiends!"
POLONIUS   This is too long.
HAMLET   It shall to the barber's with your beard.—Pri-
thee, say on. He's for a jig or a tale of bawdry, or he 500
sleeps. Say on; come to Hecuba. 501
FIRST PLAYER
"But who, ah woe! had seen the moblèd queen"— 502
HAMLET   "The moblèd queen?"
POLONIUS   That's good. "Moblèd queen" is good.

FIRST PLAYER
"Run barefoot up and down, threat'ning the flames 505
With bisson rheum, a clout upon that head 506
Where late the diadem stood, and, for a robe, 507
About her lank and all o'erteemèd loins 508
A blanket, in the alarm of fear caught up—
Who this had seen, with tongue in venom steeped,
'Gainst Fortune's state would treason have
pronounced. 511
But if the gods themselves did see her then
When she saw Pyrrhus make malicious sport
In mincing with his sword her husband's limbs,
The instant burst of clamor that she made,
Unless things mortal move them not at all,
Would have made milch the burning eyes of heaven, 517
And passion in the gods." 518
POLONIUS   Look whe'er he has not turned his color and 519
has tears in 's eyes. Prithee, no more.
HAMLET   'Tis well; I'll have thee speak out the rest of
this soon.—Good my lord, will you see the players well
bestowed? Do you hear, let them be well used, for they 523
are the abstract and brief chronicles of the time. After 524
your death you were better have a bad epitaph than
their ill report while you live.
POLONIUS   My lord, I will use them according to their
desert.
HAMLET   God's bodikin, man, much better. Use every 529
man after his desert, and who shall scape whipping?
Use them after your own honor and dignity. The less 531
they deserve, the more merit is in your bounty. Take
them in.
POLONIUS   Come, sirs.   [Exit.]
HAMLET   Follow him, friends. We'll hear a play tomor-
row. [As they start to leave, Hamlet detains the First
Player.] Dost thou hear me, old friend? Can you play
The Murder of Gonzago?
FIRST PLAYER   Ay, my lord.
HAMLET   We'll ha 't tomorrow night. You could, for a 540
need, study a speech of some dozen or sixteen lines 541
which I would set down and insert in't, could you not?
FIRST PLAYER   Ay, my lord.
HAMLET   Very well. Follow that lord, and look you mock
him not.   Exeunt players.
My good friends, I'll leave you till night. You are wel-
come to Elsinore.
ROSENCRANTZ   Good my lord!
                        Exeunt [Rosencrantz and Guildenstern].
HAMLET
Ay, so, goodbye to you.—Now I am alone.
Oh, what a rogue and peasant slave am I!

---

461 their lord's i.e., Priam's   **462 o'ersizèd** covered as with size or glue   **463 carbuncles** large fiery-red precious stones thought to emit their own light   **469 antique** ancient, long-used   **471 Repugnant** disobedient, resistant   **473 fell** cruel   **474 Th' unnervèd** the strengthless.   **senseless Ilium** inanimate citadel of Troy   **476 his** its   **478 declining** descending.   **milky** white-haired   **480 painted** motionless, as in a painting   **481 like . . . matter** i.e., as though suspended between his intention and its fulfillment   **483 against** just before   **484 rack** mass of clouds   **485 orb** globe, earth   **487 region** sky   **489 Cyclops** giant armor makers in the smithy of Vulcan   **490 proof** proven or tested resistance to assault   **491 remorse** pity   **494 synod** assembly   **495 fellies** pieces of wood forming the rim of a wheel   **496 nave** hub.   **hill of heaven** Mount Olympus   **500 jig** comic song and dance often given at the end of a play   **501 Hecuba** wife of Priam.   **502 who . . . had** anyone who had. (Also in line 510.)   **moblèd** muffled

505 threat'ning the flames i.e., weeping hard enough to dampen the flames   **506 bisson rheum** blinding tears.   **clout** cloth   **507 late** lately   **508 all o'erteemèd** utterly worn out with bearing children   **511 state** rule, managing.   **pronounced** proclaimed.   **517 milch** milky, moist with tears.   **burning eyes of heaven** i.e., stars, heavenly bodies   **518 passion** overpowering emotion   **519 whe'er** whether   **523 bestowed** lodged.   **524 abstract** summary account   **529 God's bodikin** By God's (Christ's) little body, *bodykin*. (Not to be confused with *bodkin*, "dagger.")   **531 after** according to   **540 ha 't** have it   **541 study** memorize

Is it not monstrous that this player here,
But in a fiction, in a dream of passion,   552
Could force his soul so to his own conceit   553
That from her working all his visage wanned,   554
Tears in his eyes, distraction in his aspect,   555
A broken voice, and his whole function suiting   556
With forms to his conceit? And all for nothing!   557
For Hecuba!
What's Hecuba to him, or he to Hecuba,
That he should weep for her? What would he do
Had he the motive and the cue for passion
That I have? He would drown the stage with tears
And cleave the general ear with horrid speech,   563
Make mad the guilty and appall the free,   564
Confound the ignorant, and amaze indeed   565
The very faculties of eyes and ears. Yet I,
A dull and muddy-mettled rascal, peak   567
Like John-a-dreams, unpregnant of my cause,   568
And can say nothing—no, not for a king
Upon whose property and most dear life   570
A damned defeat was made. Am I a coward?   571
Who calls me villain? Breaks my pate across?   572
Plucks off my beard and blows it in my face?
Tweaks me by the nose? Gives me the lie i'th' throat   574
As deep as to the lungs? Who does me this?
Ha, 'swounds, I should take it; for it cannot be   576
But I am pigeon-livered and lack gall   577
To make oppression bitter, or ere this   578
I should ha' fatted all the region kites   579
With this slave's offal. Bloody, bawdy villain!   580
Remorseless, treacherous, lecherous, kindless villain!   581
Oh, vengeance!
Why, what an ass am I! This is most brave,   583
That I, the son of a dear father murdered,
Prompted to my revenge by heaven and hell,
Must like a whore unpack my heart with words
And fall a-cursing, like a very drab,   587
A scullion! Fie upon't, foh! About, my brains!   588
Hum, I have heard
That guilty creatures sitting at a play
Have by the very cunning of the scene   591
Been struck so to the soul that presently   592

They have proclaimed their malefactions;
For murder, though it have no tongue, will speak
With most miraculous organ. I'll have these players
Play something like the murder of my father
Before mine uncle. I'll observe his looks;
I'll tent him to the quick. If 'a do blench,   598
I know my course. The spirit that I have seen
May be the devil, and the devil hath power
T'assume a pleasing shape; yea, and perhaps,
Out of my weakness and my melancholy,
As he is very potent with such spirits,   603
Abuses me to damn me. I'll have grounds   604
More relative than this. The play's the thing   605
Wherein I'll catch the conscience of the King.   *Exit.*

❖

[3.1]

Enter King, Queen, Polonius, Ophelia,
Rosencrantz, Guildenstern, lords.

KING
And can you by no drift of conference   1
Get from him why he puts on this confusion,
Grating so harshly all his days of quiet
With turbulent and dangerous lunacy?

ROSENCRANTZ
He does confess he feels himself distracted,
But from what cause 'a will by no means speak.

GUILDENSTERN
Nor do we find him forward to be sounded,   7
But with a crafty madness keeps aloof
When we would bring him on to some confession
Of his true state.

QUEEN   Did he receive you well?

ROSENCRANTZ   Most like a gentleman.

GUILDENSTERN
But with much forcing of his disposition.   12

ROSENCRANTZ
Niggard of question, but of our demands   13
Most free in his reply.

QUEEN   Did you assay him   14
To any pastime?

ROSENCRANTZ
Madam, it so fell out that certain players
We o'erraught on the way. Of these we told him,   17
And there did seem in him a kind of joy
To hear of it. They are here about the court,
And, as I think, they have already order
This night to play before him.

POLONIUS   'Tis most true,
And he beseeched me to entreat Your Majesties
To hear and see the matter.

---

552 **But** merely   553 **force . . . conceit** bring his innermost being so entirely into accord with his conception (of the role)   554 **from her working** as a result of, or in response to, his soul's activity.   **wanned** grew pale   555 **aspect** look, glance   556–7 **his whole . . . conceit** all his bodily powers responding with actions to suit his thought.   563 **the general ear** everyone's ear.   **horrid** horrible   564 **appall** (Literally, make pale.)   **free** innocent   565 **Confound the ignorant** i.e., dumbfound those who know nothing of the crime that has been committed.   **amaze** stun   567 **muddy-mettled** dull-spirited   567–8 **peak . . . cause** mope, like a dreaming idler, not quickened by my cause   570 **property** person and function   571 **damned defeat** damnable act of destruction   572 **pate** head   574 **Gives . . . throat** Calls me an out-and-out liar   576 **'swounds** by his (Christ's) wounds   577 **pigeon-livered** (The pigeon or dove was popularly supposed to be mild because it secreted no gall.)   578 **To . . . bitter** to make things bitter for oppressors   579 **region kites** kites (birds of prey) of the air   580 **offal** entrails.   581 **Remorseless** Pitiless.   **kindless** unnatural   583 **brave** fine, admirable. (Said ironically.)   587 **drab** whore   588 **scullion** menial kitchen servant. (Apt to be foul-mouthed.)   **About** About it, to work   591 **cunning** art, skill.   **scene** dramatic presentation   592 **presently** at once

598 **tent** probe.   **the quick** the tender part of a wound, the core.   **blench** quail, flinch   603 **spirits** humors (of melancholy)   604 **Abuses** deludes   605 **relative** cogent, pertinent   3.1 Location: The castle.   1 **drift of conference** course of talk   7 **forward** willing.   **sounded** questioned   12 **disposition** inclination.   13 **Niggard of question** Laconic.   **demands** questions   14 **assay** try to win   17 **o'erraught** overtook

KING
> With all my heart, and it doth much content me
> To hear him so inclined.
> Good gentlemen, give him a further edge   26
> And drive his purpose into these delights.

ROSENCRANTZ
> We shall, my lord.
> > *Exeunt Rosencrantz and Guildenstern.*

KING   Sweet Gertrude, leave us too,
> For we have closely sent for Hamlet hither,   29
> That he, as 'twere by accident, may here
> Affront Ophelia.   31
> Her father and myself, lawful espials,   32
> Will so bestow ourselves that seeing, unseen,
> We may of their encounter frankly judge,
> And gather by him, as he is behaved,
> If 't be th'affliction of his love or no
> That thus he suffers for.

QUEEN   I shall obey you.
> And for your part, Ophelia, I do wish
> That your good beauties be the happy cause
> Of Hamlet's wildness. So shall I hope your virtues
> Will bring him to his wonted way again,
> To both your honors.

OPHELIA   Madam, I wish it may.
> > [*Exit Queen.*]

POLONIUS
> Ophelia, walk you here.—Gracious, so please you,   43
> We will bestow ourselves. [*To Ophelia*] Read on this
> book,   [*giving her a book*]   44
> That show of such an exercise may color   45
> Your loneliness. We are oft to blame in this—   46
> 'Tis too much proved—that with devotion's visage   47
> And pious action we do sugar o'er
> The devil himself.

KING [*aside*]   Oh, 'tis too true!
> How smart a lash that speech doth give my
> > conscience!
> The harlot's cheek, beautied with plast'ring art,
> Is not more ugly to the thing that helps it   53
> Than is my deed to my most painted word.   54
> Oh, heavy burden!

POLONIUS
> I hear him coming. Let's withdraw, my lord.   56
> > [*The King and Polonius withdraw.*]

> > *Enter Hamlet.* [*Ophelia pretends to read a book.*]

HAMLET
> To be, or not to be, that is the question:
> Whether 'tis nobler in the mind to suffer
> The slings and arrows of outrageous fortune,

> Or to take arms against a sea of troubles
> And by opposing end them. To die, to sleep—
> No more—and by a sleep to say we end
> The heartache and the thousand natural shocks
> That flesh is heir to. 'Tis a consummation
> Devoutly to be wished. To die, to sleep;
> To sleep, perchance to dream. Ay, there's the rub,   66
> For in that sleep of death what dreams may come,
> When we have shuffled off this mortal coil,   68
> Must give us pause. There's the respect   69
> That makes calamity of so long life.   70
> For who would bear the whips and scorns of time,
> Th'oppressor's wrong, the proud man's contumely,   72
> The pangs of disprized love, the law's delay,   73
> The insolence of office, and the spurns   74
> That patient merit of th'unworthy takes,   75
> When he himself might his quietus make   76
> With a bare bodkin? Who would fardels bear,   77
> To grunt and sweat under a weary life,
> But that the dread of something after death,
> The undiscovered country from whose bourn   80
> No traveler returns, puzzles the will,
> And makes us rather bear those ills we have
> Than fly to others that we know not of?
> Thus conscience does make cowards of us all;
> And thus the native hue of resolution   85
> Is sicklied o'er with the pale cast of thought,   86
> And enterprises of great pitch and moment   87
> With this regard their currents turn awry   88
> And lose the name of action.—Soft you now,   89
> The fair Ophelia.—Nymph, in thy orisons   90
> Be all my sins remembered.

OPHELIA   Good my lord,   91
> How does Your Honor for this many a day?

HAMLET
> I humbly thank you; well, well, well.

OPHELIA
> My lord, I have remembrances of yours,
> That I have longèd long to redeliver.
> I pray you, now receive them.   [*She offers tokens.*]

HAMLET
> No, not I, I never gave you aught.

OPHELIA
> My honored lord, you know right well you did,
> And with them words of so sweet breath composed
> As made the things more rich. Their perfume lost,
> Take these again, for to the noble mind

---

26 edge incitement   **29 closely** privately   **31 Affront** confront, meet **32 espials** spies   **43 Gracious** Your Grace (i.e., the King) **44 bestow** conceal   **45 exercise** religious exercise. (The book she reads is one of devotion.)   **color** give a plausible appearance to **46 loneliness** being alone.   **47 too much proved** too often shown to be true, too often practiced   **53 to . . . helps it** in comparison with the cosmetic that fashions the cheek's false beauty   **54 painted word** deceptive utterances.   **56.1** *withdraw* (The King and Polonius may retire behind an arras. The stage directions specify that they "enter" again near the end of the scene.)

66 rub (Literally, an obstacle in the game of bowls.)   **68 shuffled** sloughed, cast.   **coil** turmoil   **69 respect** consideration   **70 of . . . life** so long-lived, something we willingly endure for so long. (Also suggesting that long life is itself a calamity.)   **72 contumely** insolent abuse   **73 disprized** unvalued   **74 office** officialdom.   **spurns** insults   **75 of . . . takes** receives from unworthy persons   **76 quietus** acquittance; here, death   **77 a bare bodkin** a mere dagger, unsheathed.   **fardels** burdens   **80 bourn** frontier, boundary **85 native hue** natural color, complexion   **86 cast** tinge, shade of color **87 pitch** height (as of a falcon's flight).   **moment** importance **88 regard** respect, consideration.   **currents** courses   **89 Soft you** i.e., Wait a minute, gently   **90–1 in . . . remembered** i.e., pray for me, sinner that I am.

Rich gifts wax poor when givers prove unkind.
There, my lord.   [*She gives tokens.*]

HAMLET   Ha, ha! Are you honest?   104

OPHELIA   My lord?

HAMLET   Are you fair?   106

OPHELIA   What means Your Lordship?

HAMLET   That if you be honest and fair, your honesty   108
should admit no discourse to your beauty.   109

OPHELIA   Could beauty, my lord, have better commerce   110
than with honesty?

HAMLET   Ay, truly, for the power of beauty will sooner
transform honesty from what it is to a bawd than the
force of honesty can translate beauty into his likeness.   114
This was sometime a paradox, but now the time gives   115
it proof. I did love you once.   116

OPHELIA   Indeed, my lord, you made me believe so.

HAMLET   You should not have believed me, for virtue   118
cannot so inoculate our old stock but we shall relish of   119
it. I loved you not.   120

OPHELIA   I was the more deceived.

HAMLET   Get thee to a nunnery. Why wouldst thou be a   122
breeder of sinners? I am myself indifferent honest, but   123
yet I could accuse me of such things that it were better
my mother had not borne me: I am very proud,
revengeful, ambitious, with more offenses at my beck   126
than I have thoughts to put them in, imagination to
give them shape, or time to act them in. What should
such fellows as I do crawling between earth and
heaven? We are arrant knaves all; believe none of us.
Go thy ways to a nunnery. Where's your father?

OPHELIA   At home, my lord.

HAMLET   Let the doors be shut upon him, that he may
play the fool nowhere but in 's own house. Farewell.

OPHELIA   Oh, help him, you sweet heavens!

HAMLET   If thou dost marry, I'll give thee this plague for
thy dowry: be thou as chaste as ice, as pure as snow,
thou shalt not escape calumny. Get thee to a nunnery,
farewell. Or, if thou wilt needs marry, marry a fool, for
wise men know well enough what monsters you   140
make of them. To a nunnery, go, and quickly too.
Farewell.

OPHELIA   Heavenly powers, restore him!

HAMLET   I have heard of your paintings too, well   144
enough. God hath given you one face, and you make
yourselves another. You jig, you amble, and you   146
lisp, you nickname God's creatures, and make your   147
wantonness your ignorance. Go to, I'll no more on't;   148

it hath made me mad. I say we will have no more
marriage. Those that are married already—all but
one—shall live. The rest shall keep as they are. To a
nunnery, go.   *Exit.*

OPHELIA
Oh, what a noble mind is here o'erthrown!
The courtier's, soldier's, scholar's, eye, tongue, sword,
Th'expectancy and rose of the fair state,   155
The glass of fashion and the mold of form,   156
Th'observed of all observers, quite, quite down!   157
And I, of ladies most deject and wretched,
That sucked the honey of his music vows,   159
Now see that noble and most sovereign reason
Like sweet bells jangled out of tune and harsh,
That unmatched form and feature of blown youth   162
Blasted with ecstasy. Oh, woe is me,   163
T'have seen what I have seen, see what I see!

Enter King and Polonius.

KING
Love? His affections do not that way tend;   165
Nor what he spake, though it lacked form a little,
Was not like madness. There's something in his soul
O'er which his melancholy sits on brood,   168
And I do doubt the hatch and the disclose   169
Will be some danger; which for to prevent,
I have in quick determination
Thus set it down: he shall with speed to England   172
For the demand of our neglected tribute.
Haply the seas and countries different
With variable objects shall expel   175
This something-settled matter in his heart,   176
Whereon his brains still beating puts him thus   177
From fashion of himself. What think you on't?   178

POLONIUS
It shall do well. But yet do I believe
The origin and commencement of his grief
Sprung from neglected love.—How now, Ophelia?
You need not tell us what Lord Hamlet said;
We heard it all.—My lord, do as you please,
But, if you hold it fit, after the play
Let his queen-mother all alone entreat him
To show his grief. Let her be round with him;   186
And I'll be placed, so please you, in the ear
Of all their conference. If she find him not,   188
To England send him, or confine him where

---

104 **honest** (1) truthful (2) chaste.   106 **fair** (1) beautiful (2) just, honorable.   108 **your honesty** your chastity   109 **discourse to** familiar
dealings with   110 **commerce** dealings, intercourse   114 **his** its
115–16 **This . . . proof** This was formerly an unfashionable view, but
now the present age confirms how true it is.   118–20 **virtue . . . of it**
virtue cannot be grafted onto our sinful condition without our retaining some taste of the old stock.   122 **nunnery** convent. (With an
awareness that the word was also used derisively to denote a
brothel.)   123 **indifferent honest** reasonably virtuous   126 **beck**
command   140 **monsters** (An illusion to the horns of a cuckold.)
you i.e., you women   144 **paintings** use of cosmetics   146–8 **You jig
. . . ignorance** i.e., You prance about frivolously and speak with
affected coynesss, you put new labels on God's creatures (by your use
of cosmetics), and you excuse your affectations on the grounds of pretended ignorance.   148 **on't** of it

155 **Th'expectancy and rose** the hope and ornament   156 **The glass
. . . form** the mirror of true self-fashioning and the pattern of courtly
behavior   157 **Th'observed . . . observers** i.e., the center of attention
and honor in the court   159 **music** musical, sweetly uttered
162 **blown** blossoming   163 **Blasted with ecstasy** blighted with madness.   165 **affections** emotions, feelings   168 **sits on brood** sits like a
bird on a nest, about to *hatch* mischief (line 169)   169 **doubt** suspect,
fear.   **disclose** disclosure, hatching   172 **set it down** resolved
175 **variable objects** various sights and surroundings to divert him
176 **This something . . . heart** the strange matter settled in his heart
177 **still** continually   178 **From . . . himself** out of his natural manner.   186 **round** blunt   188 **find him not** fails to discover what is
troubling him

Your wisdom best shall think.

KING   It shall be so.
Madness in great ones must not unwatched go.

Exeunt.

❖

[3.2]

Enter Hamlet and three of the Players.

HAMLET   Speak the speech, I pray you, as I pronounced
it to you, trippingly on the tongue. But if you mouth
it, as many of our players do, I had as lief the town crier   3
spoke my lines. Nor do not saw the air too much with
your hand, thus, but use all gently; for in the very
torrent, tempest, and, as I may say, whirlwind of your
passion, you must acquire and beget a temperance
that may give it smoothness. Oh, it offends me to the
soul to hear a robustious periwig-pated fellow tear a   9
passion to tatters, to very rags, to split the ears of the
groundlings, who for the most part are capable of   11
nothing but inexplicable dumb shows and noise. I   12
would have such a fellow whipped for o'erdoing Ter-   13
magant. It out-Herods Herod. Pray you, avoid it.   14

FIRST PLAYER   I warrant Your Honor.

HAMLET   Be not too tame neither, but let your own
discretion be your tutor. Suit the action to the word,
the word to the action, with this special observance,
that you o'erstep not the modesty of nature. For   19
anything so o'erdone is from the purpose of playing,   20
whose end, both at the first and now, was and is to
hold as 'twere the mirror up to nature, to show virtue
her feature, scorn her own image, and the very age   23
and body of the time his form and pressure. Now this   24
overdone or come tardy off, though it makes the   25
unskillful laugh, cannot but make the judicious grieve,   26
the censure of the which one must in your allowance   27
o'erweigh a whole theater of others. Oh, there be players that I have seen play, and heard others praise, and
that highly, not to speak it profanely, that, neither   30
having th'accent of Christians nor the gait of Chris-   31
tian, pagan, nor man, have so strutted and bellowed   32
that I have thought some of nature's journeymen had   33

made men and not made them well, they imitated
humanity so abominably.   35

FIRST PLAYER   I hope we have reformed that indifferently   36
with us, sir.

HAMLET   Oh, reform it altogether. And let those that play
your clowns speak no more than is set down for them;
for there be of them that will themselves laugh, to set   40
on some quantity of barren spectators to laugh too,   41
though in the meantime some necessary question of
the play be then to be considered. That's villainous,
and shows a most pitiful ambition in the fool that uses
it. Go make you ready.   [*Exeunt Players.*]

Enter Polonius, Guildenstern, and Rosencrantz.

How now, my lord, will the King hear this piece of
work?

POLONIUS   And the Queen too, and that presently.   48

HAMLET   Bid the players make haste.   [*Exit Polonius.*]
Will you two help to hasten them?

ROSENCRANTZ
Ay, my lord.   *Exeunt they two.*

HAMLET   What ho, Horatio!

Enter Horatio.

HORATIO   Here, sweet lord, at your service.

HAMLET
Horatio, thou art e'en as just a man
As e'er my conversation coped withal.   54

HORATIO
Oh, my dear lord—

HAMLET   Nay, do not think I flatter,
For what advancement may I hope from thee
That no revenue hast but thy good spirits
To feed and clothe thee? Why should the poor be
     flattered?
No, let the candied tongue lick absurd pomp,   59
And crook the pregnant hinges of the knee   60
Where thrift may follow fawning. Dost thou hear?   61
Since my dear soul was mistress of her choice
And could of men distinguish her election,   63
Sh' hath sealed thee for herself, for thou hast been   64
As one, in suffering all, that suffers nothing,
A man that Fortune's buffets and rewards
Hast ta'en with equal thanks; and blest are those
Whose blood and judgment are so well commeddled   68
That they are not a pipe for Fortune's finger
To sound what stop she please. Give me that man   70
That is not passion's slave, and I will wear him
In my heart's core, ay, in my heart of heart,
As I do thee.—Something too much of this.—
There is a play tonight before the King.
One scene of it comes near the circumstance
Which I have told thee of my father's death.

3.2 **Location: The castle.**
3 **our players** players nowadays.   **I had as lief** I would just as soon
9 **robustious** violent, boisterous.   **periwig-pated** wearing a wig
11 **groundlings** spectators who paid least and stood in the yard of the
theater.   **capable of** able to understand   12 **dumb shows and noise**
noisy spectacle (rather than thoughtful drama)   13–14 **Termagant** a
supposed deity of the Mohammedans, not found in any English
medieval play but elsewhere portrayed as violent and blustering
14 **Herod** Herod of Jewry. (A character in *The Slaughter of the Innocents*
and other cycle plays. The part was played with great noise and fury.)
19 **modesty** restraint, moderation   20 **from** contrary to   23 **scorn** i.e.,
something foolish and deserving of scorn   23–4 **and the . . . pressure**
and the present state of affairs its likeness as seen in an impression,
such as wax.   25 **come tardy off** falling short   25–6 **the unskillful**
those lacking in judgment   27 **the censure . . . one** the judgment of
even one of whom.   **your allowance** your scale of values   30 **not . . .
profanely** (Hamlet anticipates his idea in lines 33–4 that some men
were not made by God at all.)   31-2 **Christians** i.e., ordinary decent
folk   32 **nor man** i.e., nor any human being at all   33 **journeymen**
common workmen

35 **abominably** (Shakespeare's usual spelling, "abhominably," suggests a literal though etymologically incorrect meaning, "removed
from human nature.")   36 **indifferently** tolerably   40 **of them** some
among them   41 **barren** i.e., of wit   48 **presently** at once.   54 **my . . .
withal** my dealings encountered.   59 **candied** sugared, flattering
60 **pregnant** compliant   61 **thrift** profit   63 **could . . . election** could
make distinguishing choices among persons   64 **sealed thee** (Literally, as one would seal a legal document to mark possession.)
68 **blood** passion.   **commeddled** commingled   70 **stop** hole in a
wind instrument for controlling the sound

I prithee, when thou see'st that act afoot,
Even with the very comment of thy soul   78
Observe my uncle. If his occulted guilt   79
Do not itself unkennel in one speech,   80
It is a damnèd ghost that we have seen,
And my imaginations are as foul
As Vulcan's stithy. Give him heedful note,   83
For I mine eyes will rivet to his face,
And after we will both our judgments join
In censure of his seeming.
HORATIO   Well, my lord.   86
If 'a steal aught the whilst this play is playing   87
And scape detecting, I will pay the theft.

[*Flourish.*] *Enter trumpets and kettledrums, King,
Queen, Polonius, Ophelia, [Rosencrantz,
Guildenstern, and other lords, with guards
carrying torches].*

HAMLET   They are coming to the play. I must be idle.   89
Get you a place.   [*The King, Queen, and courtiers sit.*]
KING   How fares our cousin Hamlet?   91
HAMLET   Excellent, i'faith, of the chameleon's dish: I eat   92
the air, promise-crammed. You cannot feed capons so.   93
KING   I have nothing with this answer, Hamlet. These   94
words are not mine.   95
HAMLET   No, nor mine now. [*To Polonius*] My lord, you   96
played once i'th'university, you say?
POLONIUS   That did I, my lord, and was accounted a
good actor.
HAMLET   What did you enact?
POLONIUS   I did enact Julius Caesar. I was killed i'th'   101
Capitol; Brutus killed me.   102
HAMLET   It was a brute part of him to kill so capital a   103
calf there.—Be the players ready?   104
ROSENCRANTZ   Ay, my lord. They stay upon your   105
patience.
QUEEN   Come hither, my dear Hamlet, sit by me.
HAMLET   No, good mother, here's metal more attractive.   108
POLONIUS [*to the King*]   Oho, do you mark that?
HAMLET   Lady, shall I lie in your lap?   110
[*Lying down at Ophelia's feet.*]

OPHELIA   No, my lord.
HAMLET   I mean, my head upon your lap?
OPHELIA   Ay, my lord.
HAMLET   Do you think I meant country matters?   114
OPHELIA   I think nothing, my lord.
HAMLET   That's a fair thought to lie between maids'
legs.
OPHELIA   What is, my lord?
HAMLET   Nothing.   119
OPHELIA   You are merry, my lord.
HAMLET   Who, I?
OPHELIA   Ay, my lord.
HAMLET   Oh, God, your only jig maker. What should a   123
man do but be merry? For look you how cheerfully my
mother looks, and my father died within 's two hours.   125
OPHELIA   Nay, 'tis twice two months, my lord.
HAMLET   So long? Nay then, let the devil wear black, for
I'll have a suit of sables. O heavens! Die two months   128
ago, and not forgotten yet? Then there's hope a great
man's memory may outlive his life half a year. But, by'r
Lady, 'a must build churches, then, or else shall 'a
suffer not thinking on, with the hobbyhorse, whose   132
epitaph is "For oh, for oh, the hobbyhorse is forgot."   133

The trumpets sound. Dumb show follows.

*Enter a King and a Queen [very lovingly]; the
Queen embracing him, and he her. [She kneels,
and makes show of protestation unto him.] He
takes her up, and declines his head upon her neck.
He lies him down upon a bank of flowers. She,
seeing him asleep, leaves him. Anon comes in
another man, takes off his crown, kisses it, pours
poison in the sleeper's ears, and leaves him. The
Queen returns, finds the King dead, makes
passionate action. The Poisoner with some three or
four come in again, seem to condole with her. The
dead body is carried away. The Poisoner woos the
Queen with gifts; she seems harsh awhile, but in
the end accepts love.*

[*Exeunt players.*]
OPHELIA   What means this, my lord?
HAMLET   Marry, this' miching mallico; it means mis-   135
chief.

---

78 very . . . soul your most penetrating observation and consideration
79 occulted hidden   **80 unkennel** (As one would say of a fox driven
from its lair.)   **83 Vulcan's stithy** the smithy, the place of stiths (anvils)
of the Roman god of fire and metalworking.   **86 censure of his seeming** judgment of his appearance or behavior.   **87 If 'a steal aught** If he
gets away with anything   **89 idle** (1) unoccupied (2) mad.   **91 cousin**
i.e., close relative   **92 chameleon's dish** (Chameleons were supposed
to feed on air. Hamlet deliberately misinterprets the King's *fares* as
"feeds." By his phrase *eat the air* he also plays on the idea of feeding
himself with the promise of succession, of being the *heir*.)   **93 capons**
roosters castrated and *crammed* with feed to make them succulent
94 have . . . with make nothing of, or gain nothing from   **95 are not
mine** do not respond to what I asked.   **96 nor mine now** (Once spoken, words are proverbially no longer the speaker's own—and hence
should be uttered warily.)   **101–2 i'th' Capitol** (where Caesar was
assassinated, according to *Julius Caesar*, 3.1, but see 1.3.126n in that
play)   **103 brute** (The Latin meaning of *brutus*, "stupid," was often
used punningly with the name Brutus.)   **part** (1) deed (2) role
104 calf fool   **105 stay upon** await   **108 metal** substance that is
attractive, i.e., magnetic, but with suggestion also of *mettle*, "disposition"   **110 Lady . . . lap?** Onstage, Hamlet often lies at Ophelia's feet,
but he could instead offer to do this and continue to stand.

114 country matters sexual intercourse. (With a bawdy pun on the
first syllable of *country*.)   **119 Nothing** The figure zero or naught,
suggesting the female sexual anatomy. (*Thing* not infrequently has a
bawdy connotation of male or female anatomy, and the reference here
could be male.)   **123 only jig maker** very best composer of jigs, i.e.,
pointless merriment. (Hamlet replies sardonically to Ophelia's observation that he is merry by saying, "If you're looking for someone who
is really merry, you've come to the right person.")   **125 within 's**
within this (i.e., these)   **128 suit of sables** garments trimmed with
the dark fur of the sable and hence suited for a person in mourning.
132 suffer . . . on undergo oblivion   **133 "For . . . forgot"** (Verse of a
song occurring also in *Love's Labor's Lost*, 3.1.27–8. The hobbyhorse
was a character made up to resemble a horse and rider, appearing in
the morris dance and such May-game sports. This song laments the
disappearance of such customs under pressure from the Puritans.)
133.12 condole with offer sympathy to   **135 this' miching mallico**
this is sneaking mischief

OPHELIA   Belike this show imports the argument of the   137
play.

Enter Prologue.

HAMLET   We shall know by this fellow. The players can-
not keep counsel; they'll tell all.   140
OPHELIA   Will 'a tell us what this show meant?
HAMLET   Ay, or any show that you will show him. Be   142
not you ashamed to show, he'll not shame to tell you   143
what it means.
OPHELIA   You are naught, you are naught. I'll mark the   145
play.
PROLOGUE
For us, and for our tragedy,
Here stooping to your clemency,   148
We beg your hearing patiently.   [*Exit.*]
HAMLET   Is this a prologue, or the posy of a ring?   150
OPHELIA   'Tis brief, my lord.
HAMLET   As woman's love.

Enter [two Players as] King and Queen.

PLAYER KING
Full thirty times hath Phoebus' cart gone round   153
Neptune's salt wash and Tellus' orbèd ground,   154
And thirty dozen moons with borrowed sheen   155
About the world have times twelve thirties been,
Since love our hearts and Hymen did our hands   157
Unite commutual in most sacred bands.   158
PLAYER QUEEN
So many journeys may the sun and moon
Make us again count o'er ere love be done!
But, woe is me, you are so sick of late,
So far from cheer and from your former state,
That I distrust you. Yet, though I distrust,   163
Discomfort you, my lord, it nothing must.   164
For women's fear and love hold quantity;   165
In neither aught, or in extremity.   166
Now, what my love is, proof hath made you know,   167
And as my love is sized, my fear is so.
Where love is great, the littlest doubts are fear;   169
Where little fears grow great, great love grows there.
PLAYER KING
Faith, I must leave thee, love, and shortly too;
My operant powers their functions leave to do.   172
And thou shalt live in this fair world behind,   173
Honored, beloved; and haply one as kind
For husband shalt thou—
PLAYER QUEEN   Oh, confound the rest!

Such love must needs be treason in my breast.
In second husband let me be accurst!
None wed the second but who killed the first.   178
HAMLET   Wormwood, wormwood.   179
PLAYER QUEEN
The instances that second marriage move   180
Are base respects of thrift, but none of love.   181
A second time I kill my husband dead
When second husband kisses me in bed.
PLAYER KING
I do believe you think what now you speak,
But what we do determine oft we break.
Purpose is but the slave to memory,   186
Of violent birth, but poor validity,   187
Which now, like fruit unripe, sticks on the tree,   188
But fall unshaken when they mellow be.
Most necessary 'tis that we forget   190
To pay ourselves what to ourselves is debt.   191
What to ourselves in passion we propose,
The passion ending, doth the purpose lose.
The violence of either grief or joy
Their own enactures with themselves destroy.   195
Where joy most revels, grief doth most lament;   196
Grief joys, joy grieves, on slender accident.   197
This world is not for aye, nor 'tis not strange   198
That even our loves should with our fortunes change;
For 'tis a question left us yet to prove,
Whether love lead fortune, or else fortune love.
The great man down, you mark his favorite flies;   202
The poor advanced makes friends of enemies.   203
And hitherto doth love on fortune tend;   204
For who not needs shall never lack a friend,   205
And who in want a hollow friend doth try   206
Directly seasons him his enemy.   207
But, orderly to end where I begun,
Our wills and fates do so contrary run   209
That our devices still are overthrown;   210
Our thoughts are ours, their ends none of our own.   211
So think thou wilt no second husband wed,
But die thy thoughts when thy first lord is dead.
PLAYER QUEEN
Nor earth to me give food, nor heaven light,   214
Sport and repose lock from me day and night,   215

137 **Belike** Probably.   **argument** plot   140 **counsel** secret   142–3 **Be not you** Provided you are not   145 **naught** indecent. (Ophelia is reacting to Hamlet's pointed remarks about not being ashamed to show us all.)   148 **stooping** bowing   150 **posy . . . ring** brief motto in verse inscribed in a ring.   153 **Phoebus' cart** the sun-god's chariot, making its yearly cycle   154 **salt wash** the sea.   **Tellus** goddess of the earth, of the *orbèd* ground   155 **borrowed** i.e., reflected   157 **Hymen** god of matrimony   158 **commutual** mutually.   **bands** bonds.   163 **distrust** am anxious about   164 **Discomfort . . . must it** must not distress you at all.   165 **hold quantity** keep proportion with one another   166 **In . . . extremity** (women feel) either no anxiety if they do not love or extreme anxiety if they do love.   167 **proof** experience   169 **the littlest** even the littlest   172 **My . . . to do** my vital functions are shutting down.   173 **behind** after I have gone

178 **None** (1) Let no woman; or (2) No woman does.   **but who** except the one who   179 **Wormwood** i.e., How bitter. (Literally, a bitter-tasting plant.)   180 **instances** motives.   **move** motivate   181 **base . . . thrift** ignoble considerations of material prosperity   186 **Purpose . . . memory** Our good intentions are subject to forgetfulness   187 **validity** strength, durability   188 **Which** i.e., purpose   190–1 **Most . . . debt** It's inevitable that in time we forget the obligations we have imposed on ourselves.   195 **enactures** fulfillments   196–7 **Where . . . accident** The capacity for extreme joy and grief go together, and often one extreme is instantly changed into its opposite on the slightest provocation.   198 **aye** ever   202 **down** fallen in fortune   203 **The poor . . . enemies** when one of humble station is promoted, you see his enemies suddenly becoming his friends.   204 **hitherto** up to this point in the argument, or, to this extent.   **tend** attend   205 **who not needs** he who is not in need (of wealth)   206 **who in want** he who, being in need.   **try** test (his generosity)   207 **seasons him** ripens him into   209 **Our . . . run** what we want and what we get go so contrarily   210 **devices** intentions.   **still** continually   211 **ends** results   214 **Nor** Let neither   215 **Sport . . . night** may day deny me its pastimes and night its repose

To desperation turn my trust and hope,
An anchor's cheer in prison be my scope!   217
Each opposite that blanks the face of joy   218
Meet what I would have well and it destroy!   219
Both here and hence pursue me lasting strife   220
If, once a widow, ever I be wife!

HAMLET   If she should break it now!

PLAYER KING
'Tis deeply sworn. Sweet, leave me here awhile;
My spirits grow dull, and fain I would beguile   224
The tedious day with sleep.

PLAYER QUEEN   Sleep rock thy brain,
And never come mischance between us twain!
                    [*He sleeps.*] *Exit* [*Player Queen*].

HAMLET   Madam, how like you this play?

QUEEN   The lady doth protest too much, methinks.   228

HAMLET   Oh, but she'll keep her word.

KING   Have you heard the argument? Is there no   230
offense in't?

HAMLET   No, no, they do but jest, poison in jest. No of-   232
fense i'th' world.   233

KING   What do you call the play?

HAMLET   *The Mousetrap*. Marry, how? Tropically.   235
This play is the image of a murder done in Vienna.
Gonzago is the Duke's name, his wife, Baptista. You   237
shall see anon. 'Tis a knavish piece of work, but what
of that? Your Majesty, and we that have free souls, it   239
touches us not. Let the galled jade wince, our withers   240
are unwrung.   241

Enter Lucianus.

This is one Lucianus, nephew to the King.

OPHELIA   You are as good as a chorus, my lord.   243

HAMLET   I could interpret between you and your love,   244
if I could see the puppets dallying   245

OPHELIA   You are keen, my lord, you are keen.   246

HAMLET   It would cost you a groaning to take off mine
edge.

OPHELIA   Still better, and worse   249

HAMLET   So you mis-take your husbands.—Begin, mur-   250
derer; leave thy damnable faces and begin. Come, the
croaking raven doth bellow for revenge.

LUCIANUS
Thoughts black, hands apt, drugs fit, and time
    agreeing,
Confederate season, else no creature seeing,   254
Thou mixture rank, of midnight weeds collected,
With Hecate's ban thrice blasted, thrice infected,   256
Thy natural magic and dire property   257
On wholesome life usurp immediately.
            [*He pours the poison into the sleeper's ear.*]

HAMLET   'A poisons him i'th' garden for his estate. His   259
name's Gonzago. The story is extant, and written in
very choice Italian. You shall see anon how the
murderer gets the love of Gonzago's wife.
                    [*Claudius rises.*]

OPHELIA   The King rises.

HAMLET   What, frighted with false fire?   264

QUEEN   How fares my lord?

POLONIUS   Give o'er the play.

KING   Give me some light. Away!

POLONIUS   Lights, lights, lights!
                    Exeunt all but Hamlet and Horatio.

HAMLET
    "Why, let the strucken deer go weep,   269
        The hart ungallèd play.   270
    For some must watch, while some must sleep;   271
        Thus runs the world away."   272
Would not this, sir, and a forest of feathers—if the   273
rest of my fortunes turn Turk with me—with two   274
Provincial roses on my razed shoes, get me a fellow-   275
ship in a cry of players?   276

HORATIO   Half a share.

HAMLET   A whole one, I.
    "For thou dost know, O Damon dear,   279
        This realm dismantled was   280
    Of Jove himself, and now reigns here   281
        A very, very—pajock."   282

---

217 **anchor's cheer** anchorite's or hermit's fare.   **my scope** the extent of my happiness.   218–19 Each . . . destroy! May every adverse thing that causes the face of joy to turn pale meet and destroy everything that I desire to see prosper!   220 **hence** in the life hereafter   224 **spirits** vital spirits   228 **doth . . . much** makes too many promises and protestations   230 **argument** plot.   232 **jest** make believe. 232–3 **offense** crime, injury. (Hamlet playfully alters the King's use of the word in line 231 to mean "cause for objection.")   235 **Tropically** Figuratively. (The First Quarto reading, "trapically," suggests a pun on *trap* in *Mousetrap*.)   237 **Duke's** i.e., King's. (An inconsistency that may be due to Shakespeare's possible acquaintance with a historical incident, the alleged murder of the Duke of Urbino by Luigi Gonzaga in 1538.)   239 **free** guiltless   240 **galled jade** horse whose hide is rubbed by saddle or harness.   **withers** the part between the horse's shoulder blades   241 **unwrung** not rubbed sore.   243 **chorus** (In many Elizabethan plays, the forthcoming action was explained by an actor known as the "chorus"; at a puppet show, the actor who spoke the dialogue was known as an "interpreter," as indicated by the lines following.)   244 **interpret** (1) ventriloquize the dialogue, as in puppet show (2) act as pander   245 **puppets dallying** (With suggestion of sexual play, continued in *keen*, "sexually aroused," *groaning*, "moaning in pregnancy," and *edge*, "sexual desire" or "impetuosity.") 246 **keen** sharp, bitter   249 **Still . . . worse** More keen, always *bettering* what other people say with witty wordplay, but at the same time more offensive.

250 **So** Even thus (in marriage).   **mis-take** take falseheartedly and cheat on. (The marriage vows say "for better, for worse.")   254 **Confederate . . . seeing** the time and occasion conspiring (to assist me), and also no one seeing me   256 **Hecate's ban** the curse of Hecate, the goddess of witchcraft   257 **dire property** baleful quality   259 **estate** i.e., the kingship.   **His** i.e., the King's   264 **false fire** the blank discharge of a gun loaded with powder but no shot.   269–72 **Why . . . away** (Perhaps from an old ballad, with allusion to the popular belief that a wounded deer retires to weep and die; compare with *As You Like It*, 2.1.33–66.)   270 **ungallèd** unafflicted   271 **watch** remain awake   272 **Thus . . . away** Thus the world goes.   273 **this** i.e., this success with the play I have just presented.   **feathers** (Allusion to the plumes that Elizabethan actors were fond of wearing.)   274 **turn Turk with** turn renegade against, go back on   275 **Provincial roses** rosettes of ribbon, named for roses grown in a part of France.   **razed** with ornamental slashing   275–6 **fellowship . . . players** partnership in a theatrical company.   276 **cry** pack (of hounds, etc.)   279 **Damon** the friend of Pythias, as Horatio is friend of Hamlet; or, a traditional pastoral name   280–2 **This realm . . . pajock** i.e., Jove, representing divine authority and justice, has abandoned this realm to its own devices, leaving in his stead only a peacock or vain pretender to virtue (though the rhyme-word expected in place of *pajock or* "peacock" suggests that the realm is now ruled over by an "ass"). 280 **dismantled** stripped, divested

HORATIO   You might have rhymed.

HAMLET   Oh, good Horatio, I'll take the ghost's word for a thousand pound. Didst perceive?

HORATIO   Very well, my lord.

HAMLET   Upon the talk of the poisoning?

HORATIO   I did very well note him.

Enter Rosencrantz and Guildenstern.

HAMLET   Aha! Come, some music! Come, the recorders.
  "For if the King like not the comedy,
  Why then, belike, he likes it not, perdy."   292
Come, some music.

GUILDENSTERN   Good my lord, vouchsafe me a word with you.

HAMLET   Sir, a whole history.

GUILDENSTERN   The King, sir—

HAMLET   Ay, sir, what of him?

GUILDENSTERN   Is in his retirement marvelous dis-   299
tempered.   300

HAMLET   With drink, sir?

GUILDENSTERN   No, my lord, with choler.   302

HAMLET   Your wisdom should show itself more richer to signify this to the doctor, for for me to put him to his purgation would perhaps plunge him into more 305
choler.

GUILDENSTERN   Good my lord, put your discourse into some frame and start not so wildly from my affair. 308

HAMLET   I am tame, sir. Pronounce.

GUILDENSTERN   The Queen, your mother, in most great affliction of spirit, hath sent me to you.

HAMLET   You are welcome.

GUILDENSTERN   Nay, good my lord, this courtesy is not of the right breed. If it shall please you to make me a 314
wholesome answer, I will do your mother's command-
ment; if not, your pardon and my return shall be the 316
end of my business.

HAMLET   Sir, I cannot.

ROSENCRANTZ   What, my lord?

HAMLET   Make you a wholesome answer; my wit's dis-
eased. But, sir, such answer as I can make, you shall command, or rather, as you say, my mother. Therefore no more, but to the matter. My mother, you say—

ROSENCRANTZ   Then thus she says: your behavior hath struck her into amazement and admiration.   325

HAMLET   Oh, wonderful son, that can so 'stonish a mother! But is there no sequel at the heels of this mother's admiration? Impart.

ROSENCRANTZ   She desires to speak with you in her closet ere you go to bed.   330

HAMLET   We shall obey, were she ten times our mother. Have you any further trade with us?

ROSENCRANTZ   My lord, you once did love me.

HAMLET   And do still, by these pickers and stealers.   334

ROSENCRANTZ   Good my lord, what is your cause of distemper? You do surely bar the door upon your own liberty if you deny your griefs to your friend.   337

HAMLET   Sir, I lack advancement.

ROSENCRANTZ   How can that be, when you have the voice of the King himself for your succession in Denmark?

HAMLET   Ay, sir, but "While the grass grows"—the   342
proverb is something musty.   343

Enter the Players with recorders.

Oh, the recorders. Let me see one. [*He takes a recorder.*]
To withdraw with you: why do you go about to recover 345
the wind of me, as if you would drive me into a toil? 346

GUILDENSTERN   Oh, my lord, if my duty be too bold, my 347
love is too unmannerly.   348

HAMLET   I do not well understand that. Will you play   349
upon this pipe?

GUILDENSTERN   My lord, I cannot.

HAMLET   I pray you.

GUILDENSTERN   Believe me, I cannot.

HAMLET   I do beseech you.

GUILDENSTERN   I know no touch of it, my lord.

HAMLET   It is as easy as lying. Govern these ventages   356
with your fingers and thumb, give it breath with your mouth, and it will discourse most eloquent music. Look you, these are the stops.

GUILDENSTERN   But these cannot I command to any utterance of harmony. I have not the skill.

HAMLET   Why, look you now, how unworthy a thing you make of me! You would play upon me, you would seem to know my stops, you would pluck out the heart of my mystery, you would sound me from my lowest 365
note to the top of my compass, and there is much   366
music, excellent voice, in this little organ, yet cannot 367
you make it speak. 'Sblood, do you think I am easier to be played on than a pipe? Call me what instrument you will, though you can fret me, you cannot play   370
upon me.

Enter Polonius.

God bless you, sir!

---

292 **perdy** (A corruption of the French *par dieu*, "by God.")
299 **retirement** withdrawal to his chambers 299–300 **distempered** out of humor. (But Hamlet deliberately plays on the wider applica-
tion to any illness of mind or body, as in lines 335–6, especially to drunkenness.) 302 **choler** anger. (But Hamlet takes the word in its more basic humoral sense of "bilious disorder.") 305 **purgation** (Hamlet hints at something going beyond medical treatment to bloodletting and the extraction of confession.) 308 **frame** order.
start shy or jump away (like a horse; the opposite of *tame* in line 309)
314 **breed** (1) kind (2) breeding, manners. 316 **pardon** permission to depart 325 **admiration** bewilderment. 330 **closet** private chamber

334 **pickers and stealers** i.e., hands. (So called from the catechism, "to keep my hands from picking and stealing.") 337 **liberty** i.e., being freed from *distemper*, line 336; but perhaps with a veiled threat as well.
deny refuse to share 342 **"While . . . grows"** (The rest of the proverb is "the silly horse starves"; Hamlet implies that his hopes of succession are distant in time at best.) 343 **something** somewhat 343.1 *Players* actors 345 **withdraw** speak privately 345–6 **recover the wind** get to the windward side (thus allowing the game to scent the hunter and thereby be driven in the opposite direction into the *toil* or net) 346 **toil** snare. 347–8 **if . . . unmannerly** if I am using an unmannerly boldness, it is my love that occasions it. 349 **I . . . that** i.e., I don't understand how genuine love can be unmannerly. 356 **ventages** finger-holes or *stops* (line 359) of the recorder 365 **sound** (1) fathom (2) produce sound in 366 **compass** range (of voice) 367 **organ** musical instrument
370 **fret** irritate. (With a quibble on the *frets* or ridges on the fingerboard of some stringed instruments to regulate the fingering.)

POLONIUS My lord, the Queen would speak with you,
and presently.　　　　　　　　　　　　　　374

HAMLET Do you see yonder cloud that's almost in
shape of a camel?

POLONIUS By th' Mass and 'tis, like a camel indeed.

HAMLET Methinks it is like a weasel.

POLONIUS It is backed like a weasel.

HAMLET Or like a whale.

POLONIUS Very like a whale.

HAMLET Then I will come to my mother by and by.
[Aside] They fool me to the top of my bent.—I will 383
come by and by.

POLONIUS I will say so.　　　　　　　　　　　[Exit.]

HAMLET "By and by" is easily said. Leave me, friends.
　　　　　　　　　　　　　[Exeunt all but Hamlet.]
'Tis now the very witching time of night,　　　　387
When churchyards yawn and hell itself breathes out
Contagion to this world. Now could I drink hot
　blood
And do such bitter business as the day
Would quake to look on. Soft, now to my mother.
O heart, lose not thy nature! Let not ever　　　392
The soul of Nero enter this firm bosom.　　　　393
Let me be cruel, not unnatural;
I will speak daggers to her, but use none.
My tongue and soul in this be hypocrites:
How in my words somever she be shent,　　　　397
To give them seals never my soul consent!　　Exit. 398

❧

[3.3]

Enter King, Rosencrantz, and Guildenstern.

KING
I like him not, nor stands it safe with us　　　　1
To let his madness range. Therefore prepare you.
I your commission will forthwith dispatch,　　　3
And he to England shall along with you.
The terms of our estate may not endure　　　　5
Hazard so near 's as doth hourly grow
Out of his brows.

GUILDENSTERN　　　　We will ourselves provide.　　7
Most holy and religious fear it is　　　　　　　　8
To keep those many many bodies safe
That live and feed upon Your Majesty.

ROSENCRANTZ
The single and peculiar life is bound　　　　　　11

With all the strength and armor of the mind
To keep itself from noyance, but much more　　　13
That spirit upon whose weal depends and rests　14
The lives of many. The cess of majesty　　　　　15
Dies not alone, but like a gulf doth draw　　　　16
What's near it with it; or it is a massy wheel　　17
Fixed on the summit of the highest mount,
To whose huge spokes ten thousand lesser things
Are mortised and adjoined, which, when it falls,　20
Each small annexment, petty consequence,　　　21
Attends the boist'rous ruin. Never alone　　　　22
Did the King sigh, but with a general groan.

KING
Arm you, I pray you, to this speedy voyage,　　24
For we will fetters put about this fear,
Which now goes too free-footed.

ROSENCRANTZ　　　　　　　　We will haste us.
　　Exeunt gentlemen [Rosencrantz and Guildenstern].

　　Enter Polonius.

POLONIUS
My lord, he's going to his mother's closet.
Behind the arras I'll convey myself　　　　　　28
To hear the process. I'll warrant she'll tax him home, 29
And, as you said—and wisely was it said—
'Tis meet that some more audience than a mother,　31
Since nature makes them partial, should o'erhear
The speech of vantage. Fare you well, my liege.　33
I'll call upon you ere you go to bed
And tell you what I know.

KING　　　　　　　　　　Thanks, dear my lord.
　　　　　　　　　　　　　　　　　Exit [Polonius].
Oh, my offense is rank! It smells to heaven.
It hath the primal eldest curse upon 't,　　　　37
A brother's murder. Pray can I not,
Though inclination be as sharp as will;　　　　39
My stronger guilt defeats my strong intent,
And like a man to double business bound　　　41
I stand in pause where I shall first begin,
And both neglect. What if this cursèd hand
Were thicker than itself with brother's blood,
Is there not rain enough in the sweet heavens
To wash it white as snow? Whereto serves mercy　46
But to confront the visage of offense?　　　　47
And what's in prayer but this twofold force,

---

13 noyance harm　**14 weal** well-being　**15 cess** decease, cessation
16 gulf whirlpool　**17 massy** massive　**20 mortised** fastened (as with
a fitted joint).　**when it falls** i.e., when it descends, like the wheel of
Fortune, bringing a king down with it　**21 Each . . . consequence** i.e.,
every hanger-on and unimportant person or thing connected with the
King　**22 Attends** participates in　**24 Arm** Provide, prepare
28 arras screen of tapestry placed around the walls of household
apartments. (On the Elizabethan stage, the arras was presumably
over a door or aperture in the tiring-house facade.)　**29 process** proceedings.　**tax him home** reprove him severely　**31 meet** fitting
33 of vantage from an advantageous place, or, in addition.　**37 the
primal eldest curse** the curse of Cain, the first murderer; he killed his
brother Abel　**39 Though . . . will** though my desire is as strong as
my determination　**41 bound** (1) destined (2) obliged. (The King
wants to repent and still enjoy what he has gained.)　**46–7 Whereto . . .
offense?** What function does mercy serve other than to meet sin face
to face?

---

374 presently at once.　**383 They fool . . . bent** They humor my odd
behavior to the limit of my ability or endurance. (Literally, the extent
to which a bow may be bent.)　**387 witching time** time when spells
are cast and evil is abroad　**392 nature** natural feeling.　**393 Nero**
(This infamous Roman emperor put to death his mother, Agrippina,
who had murdered her husband, Claudius.)　**397–8 How . . . consent!** however much she is to be rebuked by my words, may my soul
never consent to ratify those words with deeds of violence!
3.3. Location: The castle.
1 him i.e., his behavior　**3 dispatch** prepare, cause to be drawn up
5 terms of our estate circumstances of my royal position　**7 Out . . .
brows** i.e., from his brain, in the form of plots and threats.　**We . . .
provide** We'll put ourselves in readiness.　**8 religious fear** sacred
concern　**11 single and peculiar** individual and private

To be forestallèd ere we come to fall,   49
Or pardoned being down? Then I'll look up.
My fault is past. But oh, what form of prayer
Can serve my turn? "Forgive me my foul murder"?
That cannot be, since I am still possessed
Of those effects for which I did the murder:
My crown, mine own ambition, and my queen.
May one be pardoned and retain th'offense?   56
In the corrupted currents of this world   57
Offense's gilded hand may shove by justice,   58
And oft 'tis seen the wicked prize itself   59
Buys out the law. But 'tis not so above.
There is no shuffling, there the action lies   61
In his true nature, and we ourselves compelled,   62
Even to the teeth and forehead of our faults,   63
To give in evidence. What then? What rests?   64
Try what repentance can. What can it not?
Yet what can it, when one cannot repent?
O wretched state, O bosom black as death,
O limèd soul that, struggling to be free,   68
Art more engaged! Help, angels! Make assay.   69
Bow, stubborn knees, and heart with strings of steel,
Be soft as sinews of the newborn babe!
All may be well.   [He kneels.]

              Enter Hamlet.

HAMLET
Now might I do it pat, now 'a is a-praying;   73
And now I'll do't. [He draws his sword.] And so 'a goes
     to heaven,
And so am I revenged. That would be scanned: 75
A villain kills my father, and for that,
I, his sole son, do this same villain send
To heaven.
Why, this is hire and salary, not revenge.
'A took my father grossly, full of bread,   80
With all his crimes broad blown, as flush as May;   81
And how his audit stands who knows save heaven?   82
But in our circumstance and course of thought   83
'Tis heavy with him. And am I then revenged,
To take him in the purging of his soul,
When he is fit and seasoned for his passage?   86
No!
Up, sword, and know thou a more horrid hent.   88
                            [He puts up his sword.]

When he is drunk asleep, or in his rage,   89
Or in th'incestuous pleasure of his bed,
At game, a-swearing, or about some act   91
That has no relish of salvation in't—   92
Then trip him, that his heels may kick at heaven,
And that his soul may be as damned and black
As hell, whereto it goes. My mother stays.   95
This physic but prolongs thy sickly days.   *Exit.*   96
KING
My words fly up, my thoughts remain below.
Words without thoughts never to heaven go.   *Exit.*

❖

[3.4]

              Enter [Queen] Gertrude and Polonius.

POLONIUS
'A will come straight. Look you lay home to him.   1
Tell him his pranks have been too broad to bear with,   2
And that Your Grace hath screened and stood
     between
Much heat and him. I'll silence me even here.   4
Pray you, be round with him.   5
HAMLET (*within*)   Mother, mother, mother!
QUEEN   I'll warrant you, fear me not.
Withdraw, I hear him coming.
                    [*Polonius hides behind the arras.*]

              Enter Hamlet.

HAMLET   Now, mother, what's the matter?
QUEEN
Hamlet, thou hast thy father much offended.   10
HAMLET
Mother, you have my father much offended.
QUEEN
Come, come, you answer with an idle tongue.   12
HAMLET
Go, go, you question with a wicked tongue.
QUEEN
Why, how now, Hamlet?
HAMLET   What's the matter now?
QUEEN
Have you forgot me?
HAMLET   No, by the rood, not so: 15
You are the Queen, your husband's brother's wife,
And—would it were not so!—you are my mother.
QUEEN
Nay, then, I'll set those to you that can speak.   18

49 **forestallèd** prevented (from sinning)   56 **th'offense** the thing for
which one offended   57 **currents** courses of events   58 **gilded hand**
hand offering gold as a bribe.   **shove by** thrust aside   59 **wicked
prize** prize won by wickedness   61 **There . . . lies** There in heaven
can be no evasion, there the deed lies exposed to view   62 **his** its
63 **to the teeth and forehead** face to face, concealing nothing
64 **give in** provide.   **rests** remains.   68 **limèd** caught as with
birdlime, a sticky substance used to ensnare birds   69 **engaged**
entangled.   **assay** trial. (Said to himself, or to the angels to try him.)
73 **pat** opportunely   75 **would be scanned** needs to be looked into,
or, would be interpreted as follows   80 **grossly, full of bread** i.e.,
enjoying his worldly pleasures rather than fasting. (See Ezekiel 16:49.)
81 **crimes broad blown** sins in full bloom.   **flush** vigorous   82 **audit**
account.   **save** except for   83 **in . . . thought** as we see it from our
mortal perspective   86 **seasoned** matured, readied   88 **know . . .
hent** await to be grasped by me on a more horrid occasion. (*Hent*
means "act of seizing.")

89 **drunk . . . rage** dead drunk, or in a fit of sexual passion   91 **game**
gambling   92 **relish** trace, savor   95 **stays** awaits (me).   96 **physic**
purging (by prayer), or, Hamlet's postponement of the killing
3.4. Location: The Queen's private chamber.
1 **lay home** reprove him soundly   2 **broad** unrestrained   4 **Much
heat** i.e., the King's anger.   **I'll silence me** I'll quietly conceal myself.
(Ironic, since it is his crying out at line 24 that leads to his death.
Some editors emend *silence* to "sconce." The First Quarto's reading,
"shroud," is attractive.)   5 **round** blunt   10 **thy father** i.e., your stepfather, Claudius   12 **idle** foolish   15 **forgot me** i.e., forgotten that I
am your mother.   **rood** cross of Christ   18 **speak** i.e., speak to someone so rude.

HAMLET
Come, come, and sit you down; you shall not budge.
You go not till I set you up a glass
Where you may see the inmost part of you.

QUEEN
What wilt thou do? Thou wilt not murder me?
Help, ho!

POLONIUS [*behind the arras*]   What ho! Help!

HAMLET [*drawing*]
How now? A rat? Dead for a ducat, dead!   25
    [*He thrusts his rapier through the arras.*]

POLONIUS [*behind the arras*]
Oh, I am slain!   [*He falls and dies.*]

QUEEN   Oh, me, what hast thou done?

HAMLET   Nay, I know not. Is it the King?

QUEEN
Oh, what a rash and bloody deed is this!

HAMLET
A bloody deed—almost as bad, good mother,
As kill a king, and marry with his brother.

QUEEN
As kill a king!

HAMLET   Ay, lady, it was my word.
    [*He parts the arras and discovers Polonius.*]
Thou wretched, rash, intruding fool, farewell!
I took thee for thy better. Take thy fortune.
Thou find'st to be too busy is some danger.—   34
Leave wringing of your hands. Peace, sit you down,
And let me wring your heart, for so I shall,
If it be made of penetrable stuff,
If damnèd custom have not brazed it so   38
That it be proof and bulwark against sense.   39

QUEEN
What have I done, that thou dar'st wag thy tongue
In noise so rude against me?

HAMLET   Such an act
That blurs the grace and blush of modesty,
Calls virtue hypocrite, takes off the rose
From the fair forehead of an innocent love
And sets a blister there, makes marriage vows   45
As false as dicers' oaths. Oh, such a deed
As from the body of contraction plucks   47
The very soul, and sweet religion makes   48
A rhapsody of words. Heaven's face does glow   49
O'er this solidity and compound mass   50
With tristful visage, as against the doom,   51
Is thought-sick at the act.

QUEEN   Ay me, what act,   52
That roars so loud and thunders in the index?   53

HAMLET [*showing her two likenesses*]
Look here upon this picture, and on this,

The counterfeit presentment of two brothers.   55
See what a grace was seated on this brow:
Hyperion's curls, the front of Jove himself,   57
An eye like Mars to threaten and command,   58
A station like the herald Mercury   59
New-lighted on a heaven-kissing hill—   60
A combination and a form indeed
Where every god did seem to set his seal   62
To give the world assurance of a man.
This was your husband. Look you now what follows:
Here is your husband, like a mildewed ear,   65
Blasting his wholesome brother. Have you eyes?   66
Could you on this fair mountain leave to feed   67
And batten on this moor? Ha, have you eyes?   68
You cannot call it love, for at your age
The heyday in the blood is tame, it's humble,   70
And waits upon the judgment, and what judgment
Would step from this to this? Sense, sure, you have,   72
Else could you not have motion, but sure that sense
Is apoplexed, for madness would not err,   74
Nor sense to ecstasy was ne'er so thralled   75
But it reserved some quantity of choice   76
To serve in such a difference. What devil was't   77
That thus hath cozened you at hoodman-blind?   78
Eyes without feeling, feeling without sight,
Ears without hands or eyes, smelling sans all,   80
Or but a sickly part of one true sense
Could not so mope. O shame, where is thy blush?   82
Rebellious hell,
If thou canst mutine in a matron's bones,   84
To flaming youth let virtue be as wax   85
And melt in her own fire. Proclaim no shame   86
When the compulsive ardor gives the charge,   87
Since frost itself as actively doth burn,   88
And reason panders will.   89

QUEEN   Oh, Hamlet, speak no more!
Thou turn'st mine eyes into my very soul,
And there I see such black and grainèd spots   92

---

25 Dead for a ducat i.e., I bet a ducat he's dead; or, a ducat is his life's fee. **34 busy** nosey **38 damnèd custom** habitual wickedness. **brazed** brazened, hardened **39 proof** impenetrable, like *proof* or tested armor. **sense** feeling. **45 sets a blister** i.e., brands as a harlot **47 contraction** the marriage contract **48 sweet religion makes** i.e., makes marriage vows **49 rhapsody** senseless string **49–52 Heaven's . . . act** Heaven's face blushes at this solid world compounded of the various elements, with sorrowful face as though the day of doom were near, and is sick with horror at the deed (i.e., Gertrude's marriage). **53 index** table of contents, prelude or preface.

55 counterfeit presentment representation in portraiture **57 Hyperion's** the sun-god's. **front** brow **58 Mars** god of war **59 station** manner of standing. **Mercury** winged messenger of the gods **60 New-lighted** newly alighted. **heaven-kissing** reaching to the sky **62 set his seal** i.e., affix his approval **65 ear** i.e., of grain **66 Blasting** blighting **67 leave** cease **68 batten** gorge. **moor** barren or marshy ground. (Suggesting also "dark-skinned.") **70 The heyday . . . blood** (The blood was thought to be the source of sexual desire.) **72 Sense** Perception through the five senses (the functions of the middle or sensible soul) **74 apoplexed** paralyzed. **err** so err **75–7 Nor . . . difference** nor could your physical senses ever have been so enthralled to *ecstasy* or lunacy that they could not distinguish to some degree between Hamlet Senior and Claudius. **78 cozened** cheated. **hoodman-blind** blindman's buff. (In this game, says Hamlet, the devil must have pushed Claudius toward Gertrude while she was blindfolded.) **80 sans** without **82 mope** be dazed, act aimlessly. **84 mutine** mutiny **85–6 To . . . fire** when it comes to sexually passionate youth, let virtue melt like a candle or stick of sealing wax held over a candle flame. (There's no point in hoping for self-restraint among young people when matronly women set such a bad example.) **86–9 Proclaim . . . will** Call it no shameful business when the compelling ardor of youth delivers the attack, i.e., commits lechery, since the *frost* of advanced age burns with as active a fire of lust and reason perverts itself by fomenting lust rather than restraining it. **92 grainèd** ingrained, indelible

As will not leave their tinct.

HAMLET   Nay, but to live   93
In the rank sweat of an enseamèd bed,   94
Stewed in corruption, honeying and making love   95
Over the nasty sty!   96

QUEEN   Oh, speak to me no more!
These words like daggers enter in my ears.
No more, sweet Hamlet!

HAMLET   A murderer and a villain,
A slave that is not twentieth part the tithe   100
Of your precedent lord, a vice of kings,   101
A cutpurse of the empire and the rule,
That from a shelf the precious diadem stole
And put it in his pocket!

QUEEN   No more!   105

Enter Ghost [in his nightgown].

HAMLET   A king of shreds and patches—   106
Save me, and hover o'er me with your wings,
You heavenly guards! What would your gracious
    figure?

QUEEN   Alas, he's mad!

HAMLET
Do you not come your tardy son to chide,
That, lapsed in time and passion, lets go by   111
Th'important acting of your dread command?   112
Oh, say!

GHOST
Do not forget. This visitation
Is but to whet thy almost blunted purpose.   115
But look, amazement on thy mother sits.   116
Oh, step between her and her fighting soul!
Conceit in weakest bodies strongest works.   118
Speak to her, Hamlet.

HAMLET   How is it with you, lady?

QUEEN   Alas, how is't with you,
That you do bend your eye on vacancy,
And with th'incorporal air do hold discourse?   122
Forth at your eyes your spirits wildly peep,
And, as the sleeping soldiers in th'alarm,   124
Your bedded hair, like life in excrements,   125
Start up and stand on end. O gentle son,
Upon the heat and flame of thy distemper   127
Sprinkle cool patience. Whereon do you look?

HAMLET
On him, on him! Look you how pale he glares!
His form and cause conjoined, preaching to stones,   130
Would make them capable.—Do not look upon me,   131
Lest with this piteous action you convert   132
My stern effects. Then what I have to do   133
Will want true color—tears perchance for blood.   134

QUEEN   To whom do you speak this?

HAMLET   Do you see nothing there?

QUEEN
Nothing at all, yet all that is I see.

HAMLET   Nor did you nothing hear?

QUEEN   No, nothing but ourselves.

HAMLET
Why, look you there, look how it steals away!
My father, in his habit as he lived!   141
Look where he goes even now out at the portal!

Exit Ghost.

QUEEN
This is the very coinage of your brain.   143
This bodiless creation ecstasy   144
Is very cunning in.   145

HAMLET   Ecstasy?
My pulse as yours doth temperately keep time,
And makes as healthful music. It is not madness
That I have uttered. Bring me to the test,
And I the matter will reword, which madness   150
Would gambol from. Mother, for love of grace,   151
Lay not that flattering unction to your soul   152
That not your trespass but my madness speaks.
It will but skin and film the ulcerous place,   154
Whiles rank corruption, mining all within,   155
Infects unseen. Confess yourself to heaven,
Repent what's past, avoid what is to come,
And do not spread the compost on the weeds   158
To make them ranker. Forgive me this my virtue;   159
For in the fatness of these pursy times   160
Virtue itself of vice must pardon beg,
Yea, curb and woo for leave to do him good.   162

QUEEN
Oh, Hamlet, thou hast cleft my heart in twain.

HAMLET
Oh, throw away the worser part of it,
And live the purer with the other half.
Good night. But go not to my uncle's bed;
Assume a virtue, if you have it not.
That monster, custom, who all sense doth eat,   168
Of habits devil, is angel yet in this,   169

---

93 leave their tinct surrender their dark stain.   **94 enseamèd** saturated in the grease and filth of passionate lovemaking   **95 Stewed** soaked, bathed. (With a suggestion of "stew," brothel.)   **96 Over . . . sty** (Like barnyard animals.)   **100 tithe** tenth part   **101 precedent lord** former husband.   **vice** (From the morality plays, a model of iniquity and a buffoon.)   **105.1 nightgown** a robe for indoor wear   **106 A king . . . patches** i.e., a king whose splendor is all sham; a clown or fool dressed in motley   **111 lapsed . . . passion** having let time and passion slip away   **112 Th'important** the importunate, urgent   **115 whet** sharpen   **116 amazement** distraction   **118 Conceit** Imagination   **122 th'incorporal** the immaterial   **124 as . . . th'alarm** like soldiers called out of sleep by an alarum   **125 bedded** laid flat. **like life in excrements** i.e., as though hair, an outgrowth of the body, had a life of its own. (Hair was thought to be lifeless because it lacks sensation, and so its standing on end would be unnatural and ominous.)   **127 distemper** disorder

130 His . . . conjoined His appearance joined to his cause for speaking   **131 capable** capable of feeling, receptive.   **132–3 convert . . . effects** divert me from my stern duty.   **134 want . . . blood** lack plausibility so that (with a play on the normal sense of *color*) I shall shed colorless tears instead of blood.   **141 habit** clothes.   **as** as when   **143 very** mere   **144–5 This . . . in** Madness is skillful in creating this kind of hallucination.   **150 reword** repeat word for word   **151 gambol** skip away   **152 unction** ointment   **154 skin** grow a skin over   **155 mining** working under the surface   **158 compost** manure   **159 this my virtue** my virtuous talk in reproving you   **160 fatness** grossness. **pursy** flabby, out of shape   **162 curb** bow, bend the knee.   **leave** permission   **168 who . . . eat** which consumes and overwhelms the physical senses   **169 Of habits devil** devil-like in prompting evil habits

That to the use of actions fair and good
He likewise gives a frock or livery   171
That aptly is put on. Refrain tonight,   172
And that shall lend a kind of easiness
To the next abstinence; the next more easy;   175
For use almost can change the stamp of nature,
And either . . . the devil, or throw him out   176
With wondrous potency. Once more, good night;
And when you are desirous to be blest,   178
I'll blessing beg of you. For this same lord,   179
                    [*pointing to Polonius*]
I do repent; but heaven hath pleased it so
To punish me with this, and this with me,   181
That I must be their scourge and minister.   182
I will bestow him, and will answer well   183
The death I gave him. So, again, good night.
I must be cruel only to be kind.
This bad begins, and worse remains behind.   186
One word more, good lady.

QUEEN   What shall I do?

HAMLET
Not this by no means that I bid you do:
Let the bloat king tempt you again to bed,   189
Pinch wanton on your cheek, call you his mouse,   190
And let him, for a pair of reechy kisses,   191
Or paddling in your neck with his damned fingers,   192
Make you to ravel all this matter out   193
That I essentially am not in madness,
But mad in craft. 'Twere good you let him know,   195
For who that's but a queen, fair, sober, wise,
Would from a paddock, from a bat, a gib,   197
Such dear concernings hide? Who would do so?   198
No, in despite of sense and secrecy,   199
Unpeg the basket on the house's top,   200
Let the birds fly, and like the famous ape,   201
To try conclusions, in the basket creep   202
And break your own neck down.   203

QUEEN
Be thou assured, if words be made of breath,
And breath of life, I have no life to breathe
What thou hast said to me.

HAMLET
I must to England. You know that?

QUEEN   Alack,
I had forgot. 'Tis so concluded on.

HAMLET
There's letters sealed, and my two schoolfellows,
Whom I will trust as I will adders fanged,
They bear the mandate; they must sweep my way   211
And marshal me to knavery. Let it work.   212
For 'tis the sport to have the engineer   213
Hoist with his own petard, and 't shall go hard   214
But I will delve one yard below their mines   215
And blow them at the moon. Oh, 'tis most sweet
When in one line two crafts directly meet.   217
This man shall set me packing.   218
I'll lug the guts into the neighbor room.
Mother, good night indeed. This counselor
Is now most still, most secret, and most grave,
Who was in life a foolish prating knave.—
Come, sir, to draw toward an end with you.—   223
Good night, mother.
        Exeunt [separately, Hamlet dragging in Polonius].

[4.1]

*Enter King and Queen, with Rosencrantz and
Guildenstern.*

KING
There's matter in these sighs, these profound heaves.   1
You must translate; 'tis fit we understand them.
Where is your son?

QUEEN
Bestow this place on us a little while.
        [*Exeunt Rosencrantz and Guildenstern.*]
Ah, mine own lord, what have I seen tonight!

171 **livery** an outer appearance, a customary garb (and hence a predisposition easily assumed in time of stress)   172 **aptly** readily   175 **use** habit.   **the stamp of nature** our inborn traits   176 **And either** (A defective line, often emended by inserting the word "master" after *either*, following the Third Quarto and early editors, or some other word such as "shame," "lodge," "curb," or "house.")   178–9 **when . . . you** i.e., when you are ready to be penitent and seek God's blessing, I will ask your blessing as a dutiful son should.   181 **To punish . . . with me** to seek retribution from me for killing Polonius, and from him through my means   182 **their scourge and minister** i.e., agent of heavenly retribution.   183 **bestow** stow, dispose of.   **answer** account or pay for   186 **This** i.e., The killing of Polonius.   **behind** to come.   189 **bloat** bloated   190 **Pinch wanton** i.e., leave his love pinches on your cheeks, branding you as wanton   191 **reechy** dirty, filthy   192 **paddling** fingering amorously   193 **ravel . . . out** unravel, disclose   195 **in craft** by cunning.   **good** (Said sarcastically; also the following eight lines.)   197 **paddock** toad.   **gib** tomcat   198 **dear concernings** important affairs   199 **sense and secrecy** secrecy that common sense requires   200 **Unpeg the basket** open the cage, i.e., let out the secret   201 **famous ape** (In a story now lost.)   202 **try conclusions** test the outcome (in which the ape apparently enters a cage from which birds have been released and then tries to fly out of the cage as they have done, falling to its death)   203 **down** in the fall.

211–12 **sweep . . . knavery** sweep a path before me and conduct me to some *knavery* or treachery prepared for me.   212 **work** proceed.   213 **engineer** maker of *engines* of war   214 **Hoist with** blown up by.   **petard** an explosive used to blow in a door or make a breach   214–15 **'t shall . . . will** unless luck is against me, I will   215 **mines** tunnels used in warfare to undermine the enemy's emplacements; Hamlet will countermine by going under their mines   217 **in one line** i.e., mines and countermines on a collision course, or the countermines directly below the mines.   **crafts** acts of guile, plots   218 **set me packing** set me to making schemes, and set me to lugging (him) and, also, send me off in a hurry.   223 **draw . . . end** finish up. (With a pun on *draw*, "pull.")
4.1 Location: The castle.
0.1 *Enter . . . Queen (Some editors argue that Gertrude does not in fact exit at the end of 3.4 and that the scene is continuous here. It is true that the Folio ends 3.4 with "*Exit Hamlet tugging in Polonius*," not naming Gertrude, and opens 4.1 with "*Enter King.*" Yet the Second Quarto concludes 3.4 with a simple "*Exit*," which often stands ambiguously for a single exit or an exeunt in early modern texts, and then starts 4.1 with "*Enter King, and Queene, with Rosencraus and Guyldensterne.*" The King's opening lines in 4.1 suggest that he has had time, during a brief intervening pause, to become aware of Gertrude's highly wrought emotional state. In line 35, the King refers to Gertrude's *closet* as though it were elsewhere. The differences between the Second Quarto and the Folio offer an alternative staging. In either case, 4.1 follows swiftly upon 3.4.)   **1 matter** significance.   **heaves** heavy sighs.

KING
> What, Gertrude? How does Hamlet?

QUEEN
> Mad as the sea and wind when both contend
> Which is the mightier. In his lawless fit,
> Behind the arras hearing something stir,
> Whips out his rapier, cries, "A rat, a rat!"
> And in this brainish apprehension kills   11
> The unseen good old man.

KING   Oh, heavy deed!   12
> It had been so with us, had we been there.   13
> His liberty is full of threats to all—
> To you yourself, to us, to everyone.
> Alas, how shall this bloody deed be answered?   16
> It will be laid to us, whose providence   17
> Should have kept short, restrained, and out of haunt 18
> This mad young man. But so much was our love,
> We would not understand what was most fit,
> But, like the owner of a foul disease,
> To keep it from divulging, let it feed   22
> Even on the pith of life. Where is he gone?

QUEEN
> To draw apart the body he hath killed,
> O'er whom his very madness, like some ore   25
> Among a mineral of metals base,   26
> Shows itself pure: 'a weeps for what is done.

KING   Oh, Gertrude, come away!
> The sun no sooner shall the mountains touch
> But we will ship him hence, and this vile deed
> We must with all our majesty and skill
> Both countenance and excuse.—Ho, Guildenstern!   32

Enter Rosencrantz and Guildenstern.

> Friends both, go join you with some further aid.
> Hamlet in madness hath Polonius slain,
> And from his mother's closet hath he dragged him.
> Go seek him out, speak fair, and bring the body   36
> Into the chapel. I pray you, haste in this.
> > [*Exeunt Rosencrantz and Guildenstern.*]
> Come, Gertrude, we'll call up our wisest friends
> And let them know both what we mean to do
> And what's untimely done   40
> Whose whisper o'er the world's diameter,   41
> As level as the cannon to his blank,   42
> Transports his poisoned shot, may miss our name
> And hit the woundless air. Oh, come away!   44
> My soul is full of discord and dismay.   *Exeunt.*

11 **brainish apprehension** frenzied misapprehension   12 **heavy** grievous   13 **us** i.e., me. (The royal "we"; also in line 15.)   16 **answered** explained.   17 **providence** foresight   18 **short** i.e., on a short tether. **out of haunt** secluded   22 **from divulging** from becoming publicly known   25 **ore** vein of gold   26 **mineral** mine   32 **countenance** put the best face on   36 **fair** gently, courteously   40 **And . . . done** (A defective line; conjectures as to the missing words include "So, haply, slander" [Capell and others]; "For, haply, slander" [Theobald and others]; and "So envious slander" [Jenkins].)   41 **diameter** extent from side to side   42 **As level** with as direct aim. **his blank** its target at point-blank range   44 **woundless** invulnerable

---

[4.2]

Enter Hamlet.

HAMLET   Safely stowed.

ROSENCRANTZ, GUILDENSTERN (*within*)   Hamlet! Lord Hamlet!

HAMLET   But soft, what noise? Who calls on Hamlet? Oh, here they come.

Enter Rosencrantz and Guildenstern.

ROSENCRANTZ
> What have you done, my lord, with the dead body?

HAMLET
> Compounded it with dust, whereto 'tis kin.

ROSENCRANTZ
> Tell us where 'tis, that we may take it thence
> And bear it to the chapel.

HAMLET   Do not believe it.

ROSENCRANTZ   Believe what?

HAMLET   That I can keep your counsel and not mine   12
own. Besides, to be demanded of a sponge, what rep-   13
lication should be made by the son of a king?   14

ROSENCRANTZ   Take you me for a sponge, my lord?

HAMLET   Ay, sir, that soaks up the King's countenance,   16
his rewards, his authorities. But such officers do the   17
King best service in the end. He keeps them, like an
ape, an apple, in the corner of his jaw, first mouthed
to be last swallowed. When he needs what you have
gleaned, it is but squeezing you, and, sponge, you
shall be dry again.

ROSENCRANTZ   I understand you not, my lord.

HAMLET   I am glad of it. A knavish speech sleeps in a   24
foolish ear.

ROSENCRANTZ   My lord, you must tell us where the
body is and go with us to the King.

HAMLET   The body is with the King, but the King is not   28
with the body. The King is a thing—   29

GUILDENSTERN   A thing, my lord?

HAMLET   Of nothing. Bring me to him. Hide fox, and all   31
after!   *Exeunt [running].*   32

♣

[4.3]

Enter King, and two or three.

4.2 Location: The castle.
12–13 That . . . own i.e., Don't expect me to do as you bid me and not follow my own counsel.   **13 demanded of** questioned by **13–14 replication** reply   **16 countenance** favor   **17 authorities** delegated power, influence.   **24 sleeps in** has no meaning to   **28–9 The . . . body** (Perhaps alludes to the legal commonplace of "the king's two bodies," which drew a distinction between the sacred office of kingship and the particular mortal who possessed it at any given time. Hence, although Claudius's body is necessarily a part of him, true kingship is not contained in it. Similarly, Claudius will have Polonius's body when it is found, but there is no kingship in this business either.)   **31 Of nothing** (1) of no account (2) lacking the essence of kingship, as in lines 28–9 and note.   **31–2 Hide . . . after** (An old signal cry in the game of hide-and-seek, suggesting that Hamlet now runs away from them.)
4.3. Location: The castle.

KING

I have sent to seek him, and to find the body.
How dangerous is it that this man goes loose!
Yet must not we put the strong law on him.
He's loved of the distracted multitude,   4
Who like not in their judgment, but their eyes,   5
And where 'tis so, th'offender's scourge is weighed,   6
But never the offense. To bear all smooth and even,   7
This sudden sending him away must seem
Deliberate pause. Diseases desperate grown   9
By desperate appliance are relieved,   10
Or not at all.

Enter Rosencrantz, [Guildenstern,]
and all the rest.

How now, what hath befall'n?

ROSENCRANTZ

Where the dead body is bestowed, my lord,
We cannot get from him.

KING   But where is he?

ROSENCRANTZ

Without, my lord; guarded, to know your pleasure.   14

KING

Bring him before us.

ROSENCRANTZ *[calling]*   Ho! Bring in the lord.

They enter [with Hamlet].

KING   Now, Hamlet, where's Polonius?

HAMLET   At supper.

KING   At supper? Where?

HAMLET   Not where he eats, but where 'a is eaten. A
certain convocation of politic worms are e'en at him.   20
Your worm is your only emperor for diet. We fat all   21
creatures else to fat us, and we fat ourselves for maggots. Your fat king and your lean beggar is but
variable service—two dishes, but to one table. That's   24
the end.

KING   Alas, alas!

HAMLET   A man may fish with the worm that hath eat   27
of a king, and eat of the fish that hath fed of that
worm.

KING   What dost thou mean by this?

HAMLET   Nothing but to show you how a king may go
a progress through the guts of a beggar.   32

KING   Where is Polonius?

HAMLET   In heaven. Send thither to see. If your messenger find him not there, seek him i'th'other place yourself. But if indeed you find him not within this month,

you shall nose him as you go up the stairs into the   37
lobby.

KING *[to some attendants]*   Go seek him there.

HAMLET   'A will stay till you come. *[Exeunt attendants.]*

KING

Hamlet, this deed, for thine especial safety—
Which we do tender, as we dearly grieve   42
For that which thou hast done—must send thee hence
With fiery quickness. Therefore prepare thyself.
The bark is ready, and the wind at help,   45
Th'associates tend, and everything is bent   46
For England.

HAMLET   For England!

KING   Ay, Hamlet.

HAMLET   Good.

KING

So is it, if thou knew'st our purposes.

HAMLET   I see a cherub that sees them. But come, for   52
England! Farewell, dear mother.

KING   Thy loving father, Hamlet.

HAMLET   My mother. Father and mother is man and
wife, man and wife is one flesh, and so, my mother.
Come, for England!   *Exit.*

KING

Follow him at foot; tempt him with speed aboard.   58
Delay it not. I'll have him hence tonight.
Away! For everything is sealed and done
That else leans on th'affair. Pray you, make haste.   61
                              [Exeunt all but the King.]
And, England, if my love thou hold'st at aught—   62
As my great power thereof may give thee sense,   63
Since yet thy cicatrice looks raw and red   64
After the Danish sword, and thy free awe   65
Pays homage to us—thou mayst not coldly set   66
Our sovereign process, which imports at full,   67
By letters conguring to that effect,   68
The present death of Hamlet. Do it, England,   69
For like the hectic in my blood he rages,   70
And thou must cure me. Till I know 'tis done,
Howe'er my haps, my joys were ne'er begun.   *Exit.*   72

❖

[4.4]

Enter Fortinbras with his army over the stage.

FORTINBRAS

Go, Captain, from me greet the Danish king.

---

4 of by.   **distracted** fickle, unstable   **5 Who . . . eyes** who choose not
by judgment but by appearance   **6–7 th'offender's . . . offense** i.e.,
the populace often takes umbrage at the severity of a punishment
without taking into account the gravity of the crime.   **7 To . . . even**
To manage the business in an unprovocative way   **9 Deliberate
pause** carefully considered action.   **10 appliance** remedies   **14 Without** Outside   **20 politic worms** crafty worms (suited to a master spy
like Polonius).   **e'en** even now   **21 Your worm** Your average worm.
(Compare *your fat king and your lean beggar* in line 23.)   **diet** food, eating. (With a punning reference to the Diet of Worms, a famous
convocation held in 1521.)   **24 service** food served at table. (Worms
feed on kings and beggars alike.)   **27 eat** eaten. (Pronounced *et*.)
32 progress royal journey of state

37 nose smell   **42 tender** regard, hold dear.   **dearly** intensely
45 bark sailing vessel   **46 tend** wait.   **bent** in readiness   **52 cherub**
(Cherubim are angels of knowledge. Hamlet hints that both he and
heaven are onto Claudius's tricks.)   **58 at foot** close behind, at heel
61 leans on bears upon, is related to   **62 England** i.e., King of England.   **at aught** at any value   **63 As . . . sense** for so my great power
may give you a just appreciation of the importance of valuing my
love   **64 cicatrice** scar   **65 free awe** unconstrained show of respect
66 coldly set regard with indifference   **67 process** command.
imports at full conveys specific directions for   **68 conguring** agreeing   **69 present** immediate   **70 hectic** persistent fever   **72 Howe'er
. . . begun** whatever else happens, I cannot begin to be happy.
4.4 Location: The coast of Denmark.

Tell him that by his license Fortinbras   2
Craves the conveyance of a promised march   3
Over his kingdom. You know the rendezvous.
If that His Majesty would aught with us,
We shall express our duty in his eye;   6
And let him know so.
CAPTAIN   I will do't, my lord.
FORTINBRAS   Go softly on.   [*Exeunt all but the Captain.*]   9

Enter Hamlet, Rosencrantz, [Guildenstern,] etc.

HAMLET   Good sir, whose powers are these?   10
CAPTAIN   They are of Norway, sir.
HAMLET   How purposed, sir, I pray you?
CAPTAIN   Against some part of Poland.
HAMLET   Who commands them, sir?
CAPTAIN
   The nephew to old Norway, Fortinbras.
HAMLET
   Goes it against the main of Poland, sir,   16
   Or for some frontier?
CAPTAIN
   Truly to speak, and with no addition,   18
   We go to gain a little patch of ground
   That hath in it no profit but the name.
   To pay five ducats, five, I would not farm it;   21
   Nor will it yield to Norway or the Pole
   A ranker rate, should it be sold in fee.   23
HAMLET
   Why, then the Polack never will defend it.
CAPTAIN
   Yes, it is already garrisoned.
HAMLET
   Two thousand souls and twenty thousand ducats
   Will not debate the question of this straw.   27
   This is th'impostume of much wealth and peace,   28
   That inward breaks, and shows no cause without   29
   Why the man dies. I humbly thank you, sir.
CAPTAIN
   God b'wi'you, sir.   [*Exit.*]
ROSENCRANTZ   Will't please you go, my lord?
HAMLET
   I'll be with you straight. Go a little before.
                                        [*Exeunt all except Hamlet.*]
   How all occasions do inform against me   33
   And spur my dull revenge! What is a man,
   If his chief good and market of his time   35
   Be but to sleep and feed? A beast, no more.
   Sure he that made us with such large discourse,   37
   Looking before and after, gave us not   38
   That capability and godlike reason

To fust in us unused. Now, whether it be   40
Bestial oblivion, or some craven scruple   41
Of thinking too precisely on th'event—   42
A thought which, quartered, hath but one part
     wisdom
And ever three parts coward—I do not know
Why yet I live to say "This thing's to do,"
Sith I have cause, and will, and strength, and means   46
To do't. Examples gross as earth exhort me: 47
Witness this army of such mass and charge,   48
Led by a delicate and tender prince,   49
Whose spirit with divine ambition puffed
Makes mouths at the invisible event,   51
Exposing what is mortal and unsure
To all that fortune, death, and danger dare,   53
Even for an eggshell. Rightly to be great   54
Is not to stir without great argument,   55
But greatly to find quarrel in a straw   56
When honor's at the stake. How stand I, then,   57
That have a father killed, a mother stained,
Excitements of my reason and my blood,   59
And let all sleep, while to my shame I see
The imminent death of twenty thousand men
That for a fantasy and trick of fame   62
Go to their graves like beds, fight for a plot   63
Whereon the numbers cannot try the cause,   64
Which is not tomb enough and continent   65
To hide the slain? Oh, from this time forth
My thoughts be bloody or be nothing worth!   *Exit.*

❧

[4.5]

*Enter Horatio, [Queen] Gertrude, and a Gentle-
man.*

QUEEN
   I will not speak with her.
GENTLEMAN   She is importunate,
   Indeed distract. Her mood will needs be pitied.   2
QUEEN   What would she have?
GENTLEMAN
   She speaks much of her father, says she hears
   There's tricks i'th' world, and hems, and beats her
        heart,   5
   Spurns enviously at straws, speaks things in doubt   6

2 **license** permission   3 **conveyance** unhindered passage   6 **We . . .
eye** I will come pay my respects in person   9 **softly** slowly, circum-
spectly   10 **powers** forces   16 **main** main part   18 **addition** exaggeration   21 **To pay** i.e., For a yearly rental of.   **farm it** take a lease
of it   23 **ranker** higher.   **in fee** fee simple, outright.   27 **debate . . .
straw** argue about this trifling matter.   28 **th'impostume** the abscess
29 **inward breaks** festers within.   **without** externally   33 **inform
against** denounce; take shape against   35 **market of** profit of
37 **discourse** power of reasoning   38 **Looking before and after** able
to review past events and anticipate the future

40 **fust** grow moldy   41 **oblivion** forgetfulness.   **craven** cowardly
42 **precisely** scrupulously.   **th'event** the outcome   46 **Sith** since
47 **gross** obvious   48 **charge** expense   49 **delicate and tender** of fine
and youthful qualities   51 **Makes mouths** makes scornful faces.
invisible event unforeseeable outcome   53 **dare** could do (to him)
54–7 **Rightly . . . stake** True greatness is not a matter of being moved
to action solely by a great cause; rather, it is to respond greatly to an
apparently trivial cause when honor is at the stake.   59 **blood** (The
supposed seat of the passions.)   62 **fantasy** fanciful caprice, illusion.
trick trifle, deceit   63 **plot** plot of ground   64 **Whereon . . . cause** on
which there is insufficient room for the soldiers needed to fight for it
65 **continent** receptacle, container
4.5 Location: The castle.
2 **distract** out of her mind.   5 **tricks** deceptions.   **hems** clears her
throat, makes "hmm" sounds.   **heart** i.e., breast   6 **Spurns . . .
straws** kicks spitefully, takes offense at trifles.   **in doubt** of obscure
meaning

That carry but half sense. Her speech is nothing,
Yet the unshapèd use of it doth move   8
The hearers to collection; they yawn at it,   9
And botch the words up fit to their own thoughts,   10
Which, as her winks and nods and gestures yield
     them,   11
Indeed would make one think there might be thought,   12
Though nothing sure, yet much unhappily.   13

HORATIO
'Twere good she were spoken with, for she may strew
Dangerous conjectures in ill-breeding minds.   15
QUEEN   Let her come in.   [*Exit Gentleman.*]
   [*Aside*] To my sick soul, as sin's true nature is,
Each toy seems prologue to some great amiss.   18
So full of artless jealousy is guilt,   19
It spills itself in fearing to be spilt.   20

     Enter Ophelia [distracted].

OPHELIA
Where is the beauteous majesty of Denmark?
QUEEN   How now, Ophelia?
OPHELIA (*she sings*)
     "How should I your true love know
         From another one?
     By his cockle hat and staff,   25
         And his sandal shoon."   26
QUEEN   Alas, sweet lady, what imports this song?
OPHELIA   Say you? Nay, pray you, mark.
     "He is dead and gone, lady,   (*Song.*)
         He is dead and gone;
     At his head a grass-green turf,
         At his heels a stone."

   Oho!   33
QUEEN   Nay, but Ophelia—
OPHELIA   Pray you, mark.
   [*Sings*] "White his shroud as the mountain snow"—

     Enter King.

QUEEN   Alas, look here, my lord.
OPHELIA
     "Larded with sweet flowers;   (*Song.*)   38
     Which bewept to the ground did not go
         With true-love showers."   40
KING   How do you, pretty lady?
OPHELIA   Well, God 'ild you! They say the owl was a   42

baker's daughter. Lord, we know what we are, but
know not what we may be. God be at your table!
KING   Conceit upon her father.   45
OPHELIA   Pray let's have no words of this; but when
they ask you what it means, say you this:
     "Tomorrow is Saint Valentine's day,   (*Song.*)
         All in the morning betime,   49
     And I a maid at your window,
         To be your Valentine.
     Then up he rose, and donned his clothes,
         And dupped the chamber door,   53
     Let in the maid, that out a maid
         Never departed more."
KING   Pretty Ophelia—
OPHELIA   Indeed, la, without an oath, I'll make an end
on't:
   [*Sings*] "By Gis and by Saint Charity,   59
         Alack, and fie for shame!
     Young men will do't, if they come to't;
         By Cock, they are to blame.   62
     Quoth she, 'Before you tumbled me,
         You promised me to wed.'"
   He answers:
     "'So would I ha' done, by yonder sun,
         An thou hadst not come to my bed.'"   67
KING   How long hath she been thus?
OPHELIA   I hope all will be well. We must be patient,
but I cannot choose but weep to think they would lay
him i'th' cold ground. My brother shall know of it.
And so I thank you for your good counsel. Come, my
coach! Good night, ladies, good night, sweet ladies,
good night, good night.   [*Exit.*]
KING [*to Horatio*]
Follow her close. Give her good watch, I pray you.
         [*Exit Horatio.*]
Oh, this is the poison of deep grief; it springs
All from her father's death—and now behold!
Oh, Gertrude, Gertrude,
When sorrows come, they come not single spies,   79
But in battalions. First, her father slain;
Next, your son gone, and he most violent author
Of his own just remove; the people muddied,   82
Thick and unwholesome in their thoughts and
     whispers
For good Polonius' death—and we have done but
     greenly,   84
In hugger-mugger to inter him; poor Ophelia   85
Divided from herself and her fair judgment,
Without the which we are pictures or mere beasts;
Last, and as much containing as all these,   88
Her brother is in secret come from France,

---

8 unshapèd use incoherent manner   **9 collection** inference, a guess
at some sort of meaning.   **yawn** gape, wonder; grasp. (The Folio
reading, "aim," is possible.)   **10 botch** patch   **11 Which** which
words.   **yield** deliver, represent   **12–13 there might . . . unhappily**
that a great deal could be guessed at of a most unfortunate nature,
even if one couldn't be at all sure.   **15 ill-breeding** prone to suspect
the worst and to make mischief   **18 toy** trifle.   **amiss** calamity.
19–20 So . . . spilt Guilt is so burdened with conscience and guileless
fear of detection that it reveals itself through apprehension of disaster.   **20.1 *Enter Ophelia*** (In the First Quarto, Ophelia enters, "*playing
on a lute, and her hair down, singing.*")   **25 cockle hat** hat with cockleshell stuck in it as a sign that the wearer had been a pilgrim to the
shrine of Saint James of Compostella in Spain   **26 shoon** shoes.
33 Oho! (Perhaps a sigh.)   **38 Larded** strewn, bedecked   **40 showers**
i.e., tears   **42 God 'ild** God yield or reward.   **owl** (Refers to a legend
about a baker's daughter who was turned into an owl for being
ungenerous when Jesus begged a loaf of bread.)

45 Conceit Fancy, brooding   **49 betime** early   **53 dupped** did up,
opened   **59 Gis** Jesus   **62 Cock** (A perversion of "God" in oaths;
here also with a quibble on the slang word for penis.)   **67 An** if
79 spies scouts sent in advance of the main force   **82 remove**
removal.   **muddied** stirred up, confused   **84 greenly** foolishly
85 hugger-mugger secret haste   **88 as much containing** as full of
serious matter

Feeds on this wonder, keeps himself in clouds,   90
And wants not buzzers to infect his ear   91
With pestilent speeches of his father's death,
Wherein necessity, of matter beggared,   93
Will nothing stick our person to arraign   94
In ear and ear. Oh, my dear Gertrude, this,   95
Like to a murd'ring piece, in many places   96
Gives me superfluous death.   *A noise within.*   97

QUEEN   Alack, what noise is this?
KING   Attend!   99
Where is my Switzers? Let them guard the door.   100

Enter a Messenger.

What is the matter?
MESSENGER   Save yourself, my lord!
The ocean, overpeering of his list,   102
Eats not the flats with more impetuous haste   103
Than young Laertes, in a riotous head,   104
O'erbears your officers. The rabble call him lord,
And, as the world were now but to begin,   106
Antiquity forgot, custom not known,   107
The ratifiers and props of every word,   108
They cry, "Choose we! Laertes shall be king!"
Caps, hands, and tongues applaud it to the clouds,   110
"Laertes shall be king, Laertes king!"

QUEEN
How cheerfully on the false trail they cry!
                                    A noise within.
Oh, this is counter, you false Danish dogs!   113

Enter Laertes with others.

KING   The doors are broke.
LAERTES
Where is this King?—Sirs, stand you all without.
ALL   No, let's come in.
LAERTES   I pray you, give me leave.
ALL   We will, we will.
LAERTES   I thank you. Keep the door. [*Exeunt followers.*]
                                Oh, thou vile king,
Give me my father!
QUEEN [*restraining him*]   Calmly, good Laertes.
LAERTES
That drop of blood that's calm proclaims me bastard,

Cries cuckold to my father, brands the harlot
Even here between the chaste unsmirchèd brow   123
Of my true mother.
KING   What is the cause, Laertes,
That thy rebellion looks so giantlike?   125
Let him go, Gertrude. Do not fear our person.   126
There's such divinity doth hedge a king   127
That treason can but peep to what it would,   128
Acts little of his will. Tell me, Laertes,   129
Why thou art thus incensed. Let him go, Gertrude.
Speak, man.
LAERTES   Where is my father?
KING   Dead.
QUEEN
But not by him.
KING   Let him demand his fill.
LAERTES
How came he dead? I'll not be juggled with.   133
To hell, allegiance! Vows, to the blackest devil!
Conscience and grace, to the profoundest pit!
I dare damnation. To this point I stand,   136
That both the worlds I give to negligence,   137
Let come what comes, only I'll be revenged
Most throughly for my father.   139
KING   Who shall stay you?
LAERTES   My will, not all the world's.   141
And for my means, I'll husband them so well   142
They shall go far with little.
KING   Good Laertes,
If you desire to know the certainty
Of your dear father, is't writ in your revenge
That, swoopstake, you will draw both friend and foe, 146
Winner and loser?
LAERTES   None but his enemies.
KING   Will you know them, then?
LAERTES
To his good friends thus wide I'll ope my arms,
And like the kind life-rendering pelican   151
Repast them with my blood.
KING   Why, now you speak   152
Like a good child and a true gentleman.
That I am guiltless of your father's death,
And am most sensibly in grief for it,   155
It shall as level to your judgment 'pear   156
As day does to your eye.   *A noise within.*

90 **Feeds . . . clouds** feeds his resentment on this whole shocking turn of events, keeps himself aloof and mysterious   91 **wants** lacks. **buzzers** gossipers, informers   93 **necessity** i.e., the need to invent some plausible explanation.   **of matter beggared** unprovided with facts   94–5 **Will . . . ear** will not hesitate to accuse my (royal) person in everybody's ears.   96 **murd'ring piece** cannon loaded so as to scatter its shot   97 **Gives . . . death** kills me over and over.
99 **Attend!** Guard me!   100 **Switzers** Swiss guards, mercenaries
102 **overpeering of his list** overflowing its shore, boundary   103 **flats** i.e., flatlands near shore.   **impetuous** violent (perhaps also with the meaning of *impiteous* ["impitious," Q2], "pitiless")   104 **riotous head** insurrectionary advance   106–8 **And . . . word** and, as if the world were to be started all over afresh, utterly setting aside all ancient traditional customs that should confirm and underprop our every word and promise   110 **Caps** (The caps are thrown in the air.)
113 **counter** (A hunting term, meaning to follow the trail in a direction opposite to that which the game has taken.)

123 **between** amidst   125 **giantlike** (Recalling the rising of the giants of Greek mythology against Olympus.)   126 **fear our** fear for my   127 **hedge** protect, as with a surrounding barrier   128 **can . . . would** can only peep furtively, as through a barrier, at what it would intend   129 **Acts . . . will** (but) performs little of what it intends.   133 **juggled with** cheated, deceived.   136 **To . . . stand** I am resolved in this   137 **both . . . negligence** i.e., both this world and the next are of no consequence to me   139 **throughly** thoroughly   141 **My will . . . world's** I'll stop (*stay*) when my will is accomplished, not for anyone else's.   142 **for** as for   146 **swoopstake** i.e., indiscriminately. (Literally, taking all stakes on the gambling table at once. *Draw* is also a gambling term, meaning "take from.")   151 **pelican** (Refers to the belief that the female pelican fed its young with its own blood.)
152 **Repast** feed   155 **sensibly** feelingly   156 **level** plain

LAERTES

How now, what noise is that?

Enter Ophelia.

KING   Let her come in.

LAERTES

O heat, dry up my brains! Tears seven times salt
Burn out the sense and virtue of mine eye!   160
By heaven, thy madness shall be paid with weight   161
Till our scale turn the beam. O rose of May!   162
Dear maid, kind sister, sweet Ophelia!
O heavens, is't possible a young maid's wits
Should be as mortal as an old man's life?
Nature is fine in love, and where 'tis fine   166
It sends some precious instance of itself   167
After the thing it loves.   168

OPHELIA

"They bore him barefaced on the bier,   (*Song.*)
Hey non nonny, nonny, hey nonny,
And in his grave rained many a tear—"
Fare you well, my dove!

LAERTES

Hadst thou thy wits and didst persuade revenge,
It could not move thus.

OPHELIA   You must sing "A-down a-down," and you 175
"call him a-down-a." Oh, how the wheel becomes it! It 176
is the false steward that stole his master's daughter.   177

LAERTES   This nothing's more than matter.   178

OPHELIA   There's rosemary, that's for remembrance; 179
pray you, love, remember. And there is pansies; that's 180
for thoughts.

LAERTES   A document in madness, thoughts and re- 182
membrance fitted.

OPHELIA   There's fennel for you, and columbines. 184
There's rue for you, and here's some for me; we may 185
call it herb of grace o' Sundays. You must wear your
rue with a difference. There's a daisy. I would give 187
you some violets, but they withered all when my 188
father died. They say 'a made a good end—

[*Sings*] "For bonny sweet Robin is all my joy."

LAERTES

Thought and affliction, passion, hell itself,   191
She turns to favor and to prettiness.   192

OPHELIA

"And will 'a not come again?   (*Song.*)
And will 'a not come again?
No, no, he is dead.
Go to thy deathbed,
He never will come again.

"His beard was as white as snow,
All flaxen was his poll.   199
He is gone, he is gone,
And we cast away moan.
God ha' mercy on his soul!"
And of all Christian souls, I pray God. God b'wi'you.
[*Exit, followed by Gertrude.*]

LAERTES   Do you see this, O God?

KING

Laertes, I must commune with your grief,
Or you deny me right. Go but apart,
Make choice of whom your wisest friends you will,   207
And they shall hear and judge twixt you and me.
If by direct or by collateral hand   209
They find us touched, we will our kingdom give,   210
Our crown, our life, and all that we call ours
To you in satisfaction; but if not,
Be you content to lend your patience to us,
And we shall jointly labor with your soul
To give it due content.

LAERTES   Let this be so.
His means of death, his obscure funeral—
No trophy, sword, nor hatchment o'er his bones,   217
No noble rite, nor formal ostentation—   218
Cry to be heard, as 'twere from heaven to earth,
That I must call't in question.

KING   So you shall,   220
And where th'offense is, let the great ax fall.
I pray you, go with me.   *Exeunt.*

❧

[4.6]

Enter Horatio and others.

HORATIO

What are they that would speak with me?

GENTLEMAN   Seafaring men, sir. They say they have
letters for you.   3

HORATIO   Let them come in.   [*Exit Gentleman.*]
I do not know from what part of the world

---

160 **virtue** faculty, power   161 **paid with weight** repaid, avenged equally or more   162 **beam** crossbar of a balance.   166–8 **Nature . . . loves** Human nature is exquisitely sensitive in matters of love, and in cases of sudden loss it sends some precious part of itself after the lost object of that love. (In this case, Ophelia's sanity deserts her out of sorrow for her lost father and perhaps too out of her love for Hamlet.)   175–6 **You . . . a-down-a** (Ophelia assigns the singing of refrains, like her own "Hey non nonny," to others present.)   176 **wheel** spinning wheel as accompaniment to the song, or refrain   177 **false steward** (The story is unknown.)   178 **This . . . matter** This seeming nonsense is more eloquent than sane utterance.   179 **rosemary** (Used as a symbol of remembrance both at weddings and at funerals.)   180 **pansies** (Emblems of love and courtship; perhaps from French *pensèes*, "thoughts.")   182 **document** instruction, lesson   184 **There's fennel . . . columbines** (*Fennel* betokens flattery; *columbines*, unchastity or ingratitude. Throughout, Ophelia addresses her various listeners, giving one flower to one and another to another, perhaps with particular symbolic significance in each case.)   185 **rue** (Emblem of repentance—a signification that is evident in its popular name, *herb of grace*.)   187 **with a difference** (A device used in heraldry to distinguish one family from another on the coat of arms, here suggesting that Ophelia and the others have different causes of sorrow and repentance; perhaps with a play on *rue* in the sense of "ruth," "pity.")   **daisy** (Emblem of love's victims and of faithlessness.)   188 **violets** (Emblems of faithfulness.)

191 **Thought** Melancholy.   **passion** suffering   192 **favor** grace, beauty   199 **poll** head.   207 **whom** whichever of   209 **collateral hand** indirect agency   210 **us touched** me implicated   217 **trophy** memorial.   **hatchment** tablet displaying the armorial bearings of a deceased person   218 **ostentation** ceremony   220 **That** so that. **call't in question** demand an explanation.
4.6. Location: The castle.
3 letters a letter

I should be greeted, if not from Lord Hamlet.

Enter Sailors.

FIRST SAILOR   God bless you, sir.

HORATIO   Let him bless thee too.

FIRST SAILOR   'A shall, sir, an't please him. There's a   9
letter for you, sir—it came from th'ambassador that   10
was bound for England—if your name be Horatio, as
I am let to know it is.   [*He gives a letter.*]

HORATIO [*reads*]   "Horatio, when thou shalt have over-   13
looked this, give these fellows some means to the King;   14
they have letters for him. Ere we were two days old at
sea, a pirate of very warlike appointment gave us   16
chase. Finding ourselves too slow of sail, we put on a
compelled valor, and in the grapple I boarded them.
On the instant they got clear of our ship, so I alone
became their prisoner. They have dealt with me like
thieves of mercy, but they knew what they did: I am to   21
do a good turn for them. Let the King have the letters
I have sent, and repair thou to me with as much speed   23
as thou wouldest fly death. I have words to speak in
thine ear will make thee dumb, yet are they much too
light for the bore of the matter. These good fellows will   26
bring thee where I am. Rosencrantz and Guildenstern
hold their course for England. Of them I have much to
tell thee. Farewell.

     He that thou knowest thine, Hamlet."
Come, I will give you way for these your letters,   31
And do't the speedier that you may direct me
To him from whom you brought them.   *Exeunt.*

✿

[4.7]

Enter King and Laertes.

KING
Now must your conscience my acquittance seal,   1
And you must put me in your heart for friend,
Sith you have heard, and with a knowing ear,   3
That he which hath your noble father slain
Pursued my life.

LAERTES   It well appears. But tell me
Why you proceeded not against these feats   6
So crimeful and so capital in nature,   7
As by your safety, greatness, wisdom, all things else,
You mainly were stirred up.   9

KING   Oh, for two special reasons,
Which may to you perhaps seem much unsinewed,   11
But yet to me they're strong. The Queen his mother
Lives almost by his looks, and for myself—
My virtue or my plague, be it either which—

She is so conjunctive to my life and soul   15
That, as the star moves not but in his sphere,   16
I could not but by her. The other motive
Why to a public count I might not go   18
Is the great love the general gender bear him,   19
Who, dipping all his faults in their affection,
Work like the spring that turneth wood to stone,   21
Convert his gyves to graces, so that my arrows,   22
Too slightly timbered for so loud a wind,   23
Would have reverted to my bow again
But not where I had aimed them.

LAERTES
And so have I a noble father lost,
A sister driven into desp'rate terms,   27
Whose worth, if praises may go back again,   28
Stood challenger on mount of all the age   29
For her perfections. But my revenge will come.

KING
Break not your sleeps for that. You must not think
That we are made of stuff so flat and dull
That we can let our beard be shook with danger
And think it pastime. You shortly shall hear more.
I loved your father, and we love ourself;
And that, I hope, will teach you to imagine—

Enter a Messenger with letters.

How now? What news?

MESSENGER   Letters, my lord, from Hamlet:
This to Your Majesty, this to the Queen.
        [*He gives letters.*]

KING   From Hamlet? Who brought them?

MESSENGER
Sailors, my lord, they say. I saw them not.
They were given me by Claudio. He received them
Of him that brought them.

KING   Laertes, you shall hear them.—
Leave us.   [*Exit Messenger.*]
[*He reads.*] "High and mighty, you shall know I am set
naked on your kingdom. Tomorrow shall I beg leave   45
to see your kingly eyes, when I shall, first asking your
pardon, thereunto recount the occasion of my sudden   47
and more strange return.   Hamlet."
What should this mean? Are all the rest come back?
Or is it some abuse, and no such thing?   50

LAERTES
Know you the hand?

KING   'Tis Hamlet's character. "Naked!"   51
And in a postscript here he says "alone."

---

9 an't if it   **10 th'ambassador** (Hamlet's ostensible role; see 3.2.172-3.)
13–14 overlooked looked over   **14 means** means of access
16 appointment equipage   **21 thieves of mercy** merciful thieves
23 repair come   **26 bore** caliber, i.e., importance   **31 way** means of
access
4.7. Location: The castle.
1 my acquittance seal confirm or acknowledge my innocence   **3 Sith**
since   **6 feats** acts   **7 capital** punishable by death   **9 mainly** greatly
11 unsinewed weak

15 conjunctive closely united. (An astronomical metaphor.)   **16 his**
its.   **sphere** one of the hollow spheres in which, according to Ptolemaic astronomy, the planets were supposed to move   **18 count**
account, reckoning, indictment   **19 general gender** common people
21 Work operate, act.   **spring** i.e., a spring with such a concentration
of lime that it coats a piece of wood with limestone, in effect gilding
and petrifying it   **22 gyves** fetters (which, gilded by the people's
praise, would look like badges of honor)   **23 Too . . . wind** with too
light a shaft for so powerful a gust (of popular sentiment)   **27 terms**
state, condition   **28 go back** recall what she was   **29 on mount** set
up on high   **45 naked** destitute, unarmed, without following
47 pardon (for returning without authorization)   **50 abuse** deceit.
no such thing not what the letter says.   **51 character** handwriting.

Can you devise me?   53

LAERTES
I am lost in it, my lord. But let him come.
It warms the very sickness in my heart
That I shall live and tell him to his teeth,
"Thus didst thou."

KING   If it be so, Laertes—   57
As how should it be so? How otherwise?—   58
Will you be ruled by me?

LAERTES   Ay, my lord,
So you will not o'errule me to a peace.   60

KING
To thine own peace. If he be now returned,
As checking at his voyage, and that he means   62
No more to undertake it, I will work him
To an exploit, now ripe in my device,   64
Under the which he shall not choose but fall;
And for his death no wind of blame shall breathe,
But even his mother shall uncharge the practice   67
And call it accident.

LAERTES   My lord, I will be ruled,
The rather if you could devise it so
That I might be the organ.

KING   It falls right.   70
You have been talked of since your travel much,
And that in Hamlet's hearing, for a quality
Wherein they say you shine. Your sum of parts   73
Did not together pluck such envy from him
As did that one, and that, in my regard,
Of the unworthiest siege.   76

LAERTES   What part is that, my lord?

KING
A very ribbon in the cap of youth,
Yet needful too, for youth no less becomes   79
The light and careless livery that it wears
Than settled age his sables and his weeds   81
Importing health and graveness. Two months since   82
Here was a gentleman of Normandy.
I have seen myself, and served against, the French,
And they can well on horseback, but this gallant   85
Had witchcraft in't; he grew unto his seat,
And to such wondrous doing brought his horse
As had he been incorpsed and demi-natured   88
With the brave beast. So far he topped my thought   89
That I in forgery of shapes and tricks   90
Come short of what he did.

LAERTES   A Norman was't?

KING   A Norman.   53

LAERTES
Upon my life, Lamord.

KING   The very same.

LAERTES
I know him well. He is the brooch indeed   94
And gem of all the nation.

KING   He made confession of you,   96
And gave you such a masterly report
For art and exercise in your defense,   98
And for your rapier most especial,
That he cried out 'twould be a sight indeed
If one could match you. Th'escrimers of their nation,   101
He swore, had neither motion, guard, nor eye
If you opposed them. Sir, this report of his
Did Hamlet so envenom with his envy
That he could nothing do but wish and beg
Your sudden coming o'er, to play with you.   106
Now, out of this—

LAERTES   What out of this, my lord?

KING
Laertes, was your father dear to you?
Or are you like the painting of a sorrow,
A face without a heart?

LAERTES   Why ask you this?

KING
Not that I think you did not love your father,
But that I know love is begun by time,   112
And that I see, in passages of proof,   113
Time qualifies the spark and fire of it.   114
There lives within the very flame of love
A kind of wick or snuff that will abate it,   116
And nothing is at a like goodness still,   117
For goodness, growing to a pleurisy,   118
Dies in his own too much. That we would do,   119
We should do when we would; for this "would"
  changes
And hath abatements and delays as many   121
As there are tongues, are hands, are accidents,   122
And then this "should" is like a spendthrift sigh,   123
That hurts by easing. But, to the quick o'th'ulcer: 124
Hamlet comes back. What would you undertake
To show yourself in deed your father's son
More than in words?

LAERTES   To cut his throat i'th' church.

---

53 **devise** explain to   57 **Thus didst thou** i.e., Here's for what you did to my father.   58 **As . . . otherwise?** how can this (Hamlet's return) be true? Yet how otherwise than true (since we have the evidence of his letter)?   60 **So** provided that   62 **checking at** i.e., turning aside from (like a falcon leaving the quarry to fly at a chance bird).   **that** if   64 **device** devising, invention   67 **uncharge the practice** acquit the stratagem of being a plot   70 **organ** agent, instrument.   73 **Your . . . parts** All your other virtues   76 **unworthiest siege** least important rank.   79 **no less becomes** is no less adorned by   81–2 **his sables . . . graveness** its rich robes furred with sable and its garments denoting dignified well-being and seriousness.   85 **can well** are skilled   88–9 **As . . . beast** as if, centaurlike, he had been made into one body with the horse, possessing half its nature.   89 **topped** surpassed   90 **forgery** fabrication

94 **brooch** ornament   96 **confession** testimonial, admission of superiority   98 **For . . . defense** with respect to your skill and practice with your weapon   101 **Th'escrimers** The fencers   106 **sudden** immediate.   **play** fence   112 **begun by time** i.e., created by the right circumstance and hence subject to change   113 **passages of proof** actual well-attested instances   114 **qualifies** weakens, moderates   116 **snuff** the charred part of a candlewick   117 **nothing . . . still** nothing remains at a constant level of perfection   118 **pleurisy** excess, plethora. (Literally, a chest inflammation.)   119 **in . . . much** of its own excess.   **That That** which   121 **abatements** diminutions   122 **As . . . accidents** as there are tongues to dissuade, hands to prevent, and chance events to intervene   123 **spendthrift sigh** (An allusion to the belief that sighs draw blood from the heart.)   124 **hurts by easing** i.e., costs the heart blood and wastes precious opportunity even while it affords emotional relief.   **quick o'th'ulcer** i.e., heart of the matter

KING
    No place, indeed, should murder sanctuarize;   128
    Revenge should have no bounds. But good Laertes,
    Will you do this, keep close within your chamber.   130
    Hamlet returned shall know you are come home.
    We'll put on those shall praise your excellence   132
    And set a double varnish on the fame
    The Frenchman gave you, bring you in fine together,   134
    And wager on your heads. He, being remiss,   135
    Most generous, and free from all contriving,   136
    Will not peruse the foils, so that with ease,
    Or with a little shuffling, you may choose
    A sword unbated, and in a pass of practice   139
    Requite him for your father.
LAERTES   I will do't,
    And for that purpose I'll anoint my sword.
    I bought an unction of a mountebank   142
    So mortal that, but dip a knife in it,
    Where it draws blood no cataplasm so rare,   144
    Collected from all simples that have virtue   145
    Under the moon, can save the thing from death   146
    That is but scratched withal. I'll touch my point
    With this contagion, that if I gall him slightly,   148
    It may be death.
KING   Let's further think of this,
    Weigh what convenience both of time and means
    May fit us to our shape. If this should fail,   151
    And that our drift look through our bad performance,   152
    'Twere better not assayed. Therefore this project
    Should have a back or second, that might hold
    If this did blast in proof. Soft, let me see.   155
    We'll make a solemn wager on your cunnings—   156
    I ha 't!
    When in your motion you are hot and dry—
    As make your bouts more violent to that end—   159
    And that he calls for drink, I'll have prepared him
    A chalice for the nonce, whereon but sipping,   161
    If he by chance escape your venomed stuck,   162
    Our purpose may hold there. [*A cry within.*] But stay,
        what noise?

            Enter Queen.

QUEEN
    One woe doth tread upon another's heel,
    So fast they follow. Your sister's drowned, Laertes.
LAERTES   Drowned! Oh, where?

QUEEN
    There is a willow grows askant the brook,   167
    That shows his hoar leaves in the glassy stream;   168
    Therewith fantastic garlands did she make
    Of crowflowers, nettles, daisies, and long purples,   170
    That liberal shepherds give a grosser name,   171
    But our cold maids do dead men's fingers call them.   172
    There on the pendent boughs her crownet weeds   173
    Clamb'ring to hang, an envious sliver broke,   174
    When down her weedy trophies and herself   175
    Fell in the weeping brook. Her clothes spread wide,
    And mermaidlike awhile they bore her up,
    Which time she chanted snatches of old lauds,   178
    As one incapable of her own distress,   179
    Or like a creature native and endued   180
    Unto that element. But long it could not be
    Till that her garments, heavy with their drink,
    Pulled the poor wretch from her melodious lay   183
    To muddy death.
LAERTES   Alas, then she is drowned?
QUEEN   Drowned, drowned.
LAERTES
    Too much of water hast thou, poor Ophelia,
    And therefore I forbid my tears. But yet
    It is our trick; nature her custom holds,   188
    Let shame say what it will. [*He weeps.*] When these
        are gone,   189
    The woman will be out. Adieu, my lord.   190
    I have a speech of fire that fain would blaze,
    But that this folly douts it.   *Exit.*
KING   Let's follow, Gertrude.   192
    How much I had to do to calm his rage!
    Now fear I this will give it start again;
    Therefore let's follow.   *Exeunt.*

❖

[5.1]

    Enter two Clowns [with spades and mattocks].

FIRST CLOWN   Is she to be buried in Christian burial,
    when she willfully seeks her own salvation?   2

---

128 sanctuarize protect from punishment. (Alludes to the right of sanctuary with which certain religious places were invested.) **130 Will you do this** if you wish to do this   **132 put on those shall** arrange for some to   **134 in fine** finally   **135 remiss** negligently unsuspicious   **136 generous** noble-minded   **139 unbated** not blunted, having no button.   **pass of practice** treacherous thrust in an arranged bout   **142 unction** ointment.   **mountebank** quack doctor **144 cataplasm** plaster or poultice   **145 simples** herbs.   **virtue** potency   **146 Under the moon** i.e., anywhere (with reference perhaps to the belief that herbs gathered at night had a special power) **148 gall** graze, wound   **151 shape** part we propose to act.   **152 drift . . . performance** intention should be made visible by our bungling **155 blast in proof** come to grief when put to the test.   **156 cunnings** respective skills   **159 As** i.e., and you should   **161 nonce** occasion **162 stuck** thrust. (From *stoccado*, a fencing term.)

167 askant aslant   **168 hoar leaves** white or gray undersides of the leaves   **170 long purples** early purple orchids   **171 liberal** free-spoken.   **a grosser name** (The testicle-resembling tubers of the orchid, which also in some cases resemble *dead men's fingers*, have earned various slang names like "dogstones" and "cullions.")   **172 cold** chaste **173 pendent** overhanging.   **crownet** made into a chaplet or coronet **174 envious sliver** malicious branch   **175 weedy** i.e., of plants **178 lauds** hymns   **179 incapable of** lacking capacity to apprehend **180 endued** adapted by nature   **183 lay** ballad, song   **188 It is our trick** i.e., weeping is our natural way (when sad)   **189–90 When . . . out** When my tears are all shed, the woman in me will be expended, satisfied.   **192 douts** extinguishes. (The Second Quarto reads "drownes.")
5.1 Location: A churchyard.
0.1 *Clowns* rustics   **2 salvation** (A blunder for "damnation," or perhaps a suggestion that Ophelia was taking her own shortcut to heaven.)

SECOND CLOWN   I tell thee she is; therefore make her grave straight. The crowner hath sat on her, and finds it Christian burial. 4 5

FIRST CLOWN   How can that be, unless she drowned herself in her own defense?

SECOND CLOWN   Why, 'tis found so. 8

FIRST CLOWN   It must be *se offendendo*, it cannot be else. For here lies the point: if I drown myself wittingly, it argues an act, and an act hath three branches—it is to act, to do, and to perform. Argal, she drowned herself wittingly. 9 12

SECOND CLOWN   Nay, but hear you, goodman delve— 14

FIRST CLOWN   Give me leave. Here lies the water; good. Here stands the man; good. If the man go to this water and drown himself, it is, will he, nill he, he goes, mark you that. But if the water come to him and drown him, he drowns not himself. Argal, he that is not guilty of his own death shortens not his own life. 17

SECOND CLOWN   But is this law?

FIRST CLOWN   Ay, marry, is't—crowner's quest law. 22

SECOND CLOWN   Will you ha' the truth on't? If this had not been a gentlewoman, she should have been buried out o' Christian burial.

FIRST CLOWN   Why, there thou say'st. And the more pity that great folk should have countenance in this world to drown or hang themselves, more than their even-Christian. Come, my spade. There is no ancient gentlemen but gardeners, ditchers, and grave makers. They hold up Adam's profession. 26 27 29 31

SECOND CLOWN   Was he a gentleman?

FIRST CLOWN   'A was the first that ever bore arms. 33

SECOND CLOWN   Why, he had none.

FIRST CLOWN   What, art a heathen? How dost thou understand the Scripture? The Scripture says Adam digged. Could he dig without arms? I'll put another question to thee. If thou answerest me not to the purpose, confess thyself— 37 39

SECOND CLOWN   Go to.

FIRST CLOWN   What is he that builds stronger than either the mason, the shipwright, or the carpenter?

SECOND CLOWN   The gallows maker, for that frame outlives a thousand tenants. 43

FIRST CLOWN   I like thy wit well, in good faith. The gallows does well. But how does it well? It does well to those that do ill. Now thou dost ill to say the gallows 46

is built stronger than the church. Argal, the gallows may do well to thee. To't again, come.

SECOND CLOWN   "Who builds stronger than a mason, a shipwright, or a carpenter?"

FIRST CLOWN   Ay, tell me that, and unyoke. 52

SECOND CLOWN   Marry, now I can tell.

FIRST CLOWN   To't.

SECOND CLOWN   Mass, I cannot tell. 55

Enter Hamlet and Horatio [at a distance].

FIRST CLOWN   Cudgel thy brains no more about it, for your dull ass will not mend his pace with beating; and when you are asked this question next, say "a grave maker." The houses he makes lasts till doomsday. Go get thee in and fetch me a stoup of liquor. 60

[Exit Second Clown. First Clown digs.]
Song.

"In youth, when I did love, did love,
   Methought it was very sweet,
To contract—oh—the time for—a—my behove,
   Oh, methought there—a—was nothing—a—
      meet." 61 63 64

HAMLET   Has this fellow no feeling of his business, 'a sings in grave-making? 65

HORATIO   Custom hath made it in him a property of easiness. 67 68

HAMLET   'Tis e'en so. The hand of little employment hath the daintier sense. 70

FIRST CLOWN   *Song.*
"But age with his stealing steps
   Hath clawed me in his clutch,
And hath shipped me into the land,
   As if I had never been such." 73

[He throws up a skull.]

HAMLET   That skull had a tongue in it and could sing once. How the knave jowls it to the ground, as if 'twere Cain's jawbone, that did the first murder! This might be the pate of a politician, which this ass now o'erreaches, one that would circumvent God, might it not? 76 78 79

HORATIO   It might, my lord.

HAMLET   Or of a courtier, which could say, "Good morrow, sweet lord! How dost thou, sweet lord?" This might be my Lord Such-a-one, that praised my Lord Such-a-one's horse when 'a meant to beg it, might it not?

HORATIO   Ay, my lord.

---

4 straight straightway, immediately. (But with a pun on *strait*, "narrow.")   **crowner** coroner.   **sat on her** conducted an inquest on her case   **4–5 finds it** gives his official verdict that her means of death was consistent with   **8 found so** determined so in the coroner's verdict.   **9 se offendendo** (A comic mistake for *se defendendo*, a term used in verdicts of self-defense.)   **12 Argal** (Corruption of *ergo*, "therefore.")   **14 goodman** (An honorific title often used with the name of a profession or craft.)   **17 will he, nill he** whether he will or no, willy-nilly   **22 quest** inquest   **26 there thou say'st** i.e., that's right.   **27 countenance** privilege   **29 even-Christian** fellow Christians.   **ancient** going back to ancient times   **31 hold up** maintain   **33 bore arms** (To be entitled to bear a coat of arms would make Adam a gentleman, but as one who bore a spade, our common ancestor was an ordinary delver in the earth.)   **37 arms** i.e., the arms of the body.   **39 confess thyself** (The saying continues, "and be hanged.")   **43 frame** (1) gallows (2) structure   **46 does well** (1) is an apt answer (2) does a good turn.

52 unyoke i.e., after this great effort, you may unharness the team of your wits.   **55 Mass** By the Mass   **60 stoup** two-quart measure   **61 In . . . love** (This and the two following stanzas, with nonsensical variations, are from a poem attributed to Lord Vaux and printed in *Tottel's Miscellany*, 1557. The *oh* and *a* [for "ah"] seemingly are the grunts of the digger.)   **63 To contract . . . behove** i.e., to shorten the time for my own advantage. (Perhaps he means to *prolong* it.)   **64 meet** suitable, i.e., more suitable.   **65 'a** that he   **67–8 property of easiness** something he can do easily and indifferently.   **70 daintier sense** more delicate sense of feeling.   **73 into the land** i.e., toward my grave (?) (But note the lack of rhyme in *steps, land*.)   **76 jowls** dashes. (With a pun on *jowl*, "jawbone.")   **78 politician** schemer, plotter   **79 o'erreaches** circumvents, gets the better of

HAMLET   Why, e'en so, and now my Lady Worm's, chapless, and knocked about the mazard with a sexton's spade. Here's fine revolution, an we had the trick to see't. Did these bones cost no more the breeding but to play at loggets with them? Mine ache to think on't. 89 90 91 92

FIRST CLOWN   *Song.*
    "A pickax and a spade, a spade,
        For and a shrouding sheet;
    Oh, a pit of clay for to be made
        For such a guest is meet." 95

                              [*He throws up another skull.*]

HAMLET   There's another. Why may not that be the skull of a lawyer? Where be his quiddities now, his quillities, his cases, his tenures, and his tricks? Why does he suffer this mad knave now to knock him about the sconce with a dirty shovel, and will not tell him of his action of battery? Hum, this fellow might be in 's time a great buyer of land, with his statutes, his recognizances, his fines, his double vouchers, his recoveries. Is this the fine of his fines and the recovery of his recoveries, to have his fine pate full of fine dirt? Will his vouchers vouch him no more of his purchases, and double ones too, than the length and breadth of a pair of indentures? The very conveyances of his lands will scarcely lie in this box, and must th'inheritor himself have no more, ha? 99 100 102 103 104 105 106 107 108 109 110 111

HORATIO   Not a jot more, my lord.

HAMLET   Is not parchment made of sheepskins?

HORATIO   Ay, my lord, and of calves' skins too.

HAMLET   They are sheep and calves which seek out assurance in that. I will speak to this fellow.—Whose grave's this, sirrah? 116 117 118

FIRST CLOWN   Mine, sir.
    [*Sings*] "Oh, pit of clay for to be made
            For such a guest is meet."

HAMLET   I think it be thine, indeed, for thou liest in't.

FIRST CLOWN   You lie out on't, sir, and therefore 'tis not yours. For my part, I do not lie in't, yet it is mine.

HAMLET   Thou dost lie in't, to be in't and say it is thine. 'Tis for the dead, not for the quick; therefore thou liest. 126

FIRST CLOWN   'Tis a quick lie, sir; 'twill away again from me to you.

HAMLET   What man dost thou dig it for?

FIRST CLOWN   For no man, sir.

HAMLET   What woman, then?

FIRST CLOWN   For none, neither.

HAMLET   Who is to be buried in't?

FIRST CLOWN   One that was a woman, sir, but, rest her soul, she's dead.

HAMLET   How absolute the knave is! We must speak by the card, or equivocation will undo us. By the Lord, Horatio, this three years I have took note of it: the age is grown so picked that the toe of the peasant comes so near the heel of the courtier he galls his kibe.—How long hast thou been grave maker? 137 138 139 140 141

FIRST CLOWN   Of all the days i'th' year, I came to't that day that our last king Hamlet overcame Fortinbras.

HAMLET   How long is that since?

FIRST CLOWN   Cannot you tell that? Every fool can tell that. It was that very day that young Hamlet was born—he that is mad and sent into England.

HAMLET   Ay, marry, why was he sent into England?

FIRST CLOWN   Why, because 'a was mad. 'A shall recover his wits there, or if 'a do not, 'tis no great matter there.

HAMLET   Why?

FIRST CLOWN   'Twill not be seen in him there. There the men are as mad as he.

HAMLET   How came he mad?

FIRST CLOWN   Very strangely, they say.

HAMLET   How strangely?

FIRST CLOWN   Faith, e'en with losing his wits.

HAMLET   Upon what ground? 160

FIRST CLOWN   Why, here in Denmark. I have been sexton here, man and boy, thirty years.

HAMLET   How long will a man lie i'th'earth ere he rot?

FIRST CLOWN   Faith, if 'a be not rotten before 'a die—as we have many pocky corpses nowadays, that will scarce hold the laying in—'a will last you some eight year or nine year. A tanner will last you nine year. 165 166

HAMLET   Why he more than another?

FIRST CLOWN   Why, sir, his hide is so tanned with his trade that 'a will keep out water a great while, and

---

89 chapless having no lower jaw.   **mazard** i.e., head. (Literally, a drinking vessel.)   **90 revolution** turn of Fortune's wheel, change.   **trick** knack   **91–2 cost . . . but** involve so little expense and care in upbringing that we may   **92 loggets** a game in which pieces of hard wood shaped like Indian clubs or bowling pins are thrown to lie as near as possible to a stake   **95 For and** and moreover   **99–100 his quiddities . . . quillities** his subtleties, his legal niceties   **100 tenures** the holding of a piece of property or office, or the conditions or period of such holding   **102 sconce** head   **103 action of battery** lawsuit about physical assault.   **104 his statutes** his legal documents acknowledging obligation of a debt   **104–5 recognizances** bonds undertaking to repay debts   **105 fines** procedures for converting entailed estates into "fee simple" or freehold.   **double vouchers** vouchers signed by two signatories guaranteeing the legality of real estate titles.   **recoveries** suits to obtain the authority of a court judgment for the holding of land.   **106–7 Is this . . . dirt?** Is this the end of his legal maneuvers and profitable land deals, to have the skull of his elegant head filled full of minutely sifted dirt? (With multiple wordplay on *fine* and *fines*.)   **107–10 Will . . . indentures?** Will his vouchers, even double ones, guarantee him no more land than is needed to bury him in, being no bigger than the deed of conveyance? (An *indenture* is literally a legal document drawn up in duplicate on a single sheet and then cut apart on a zigzag line so that each pair was uniquely matched.)   **111 box** (1) deed box (2) coffin.   **th'inheritor** the acquirer, owner   **116–17 assurance in that** safety in legal parchments.   **118 sirrah** (A term of address to inferiors.)

126 quick living   **137 absolute** strict, precise   **137–8 by the card** i.e., with precision. (Literally, by the mariner's compass-card, on which the points of the compass were marked.)   **138 equivocation** ambiguity in the use of terms   **139 took** taken   **139–41 the age . . . kibe** i.e., the age has grown so finical and mannered that the lower classes ape their social betters, chafing at their heels. (*Kibes* are chilblains on the heels.)   **160 ground** cause. (But, in the next line, the gravedigger takes the word in the sense of "land," "country.")   **165 pocky** rotten, diseased. (Literally, with the pox, or syphilis.)   **166 hold the laying in** hold together long enough to be interred.   **last you** last. (*You* is used colloquially here and in the following lines.)

your water is a sore decayer of your whoreson dead 171
body. [*He picks up a skull.*] Here's a skull now hath
lien you i'th'earth three-and-twenty years. 173

HAMLET   Whose was it?

FIRST CLOWN   A whoreson mad fellow's it was. Whose
do you think it was?

HAMLET   Nay, I know not.

FIRST CLOWN   A pestilence on him for a mad rogue! 'A
poured a flagon of Rhenish on my head once. This 179
same skull, sir, was, sir, Yorick's skull, the King's jester.

HAMLET   This?

FIRST CLOWN   E'en that.

HAMLET   Let me see. [*He takes the skull.*] Alas, poor
Yorick! I knew him, Horatio, a fellow of infinite jest, of
most excellent fancy. He hath bore me on his back a 185
thousand times, and now how abhorred in my
imagination it is! My gorge rises at it. Here hung those 187
lips that I have kissed I know not how oft. Where be
your gibes now? Your gambols, your songs, your 189
flashes of merriment that were wont to set the table on
a roar? Not one now, to mock your own grinning?
Quite chopfallen? Now get you to my lady's chamber 192
and tell her, let her paint an inch thick, to this favor 193
she must come. Make her laugh at that. Prithee,
Horatio, tell me one thing.

HORATIO   What's that, my lord?

HAMLET   Dost thou think Alexander looked o' this
fashion i'th'earth?

HORATIO   E'en so.

HAMLET   And smelt so? Pah! [*He throws down the skull.*]

HORATIO   E'en so, my lord.

HAMLET   To what base uses we may return, Horatio!
Why may not imagination trace the noble dust of
Alexander till 'a find it stopping a bunghole? 204

HORATIO   'Twere to consider too curiously to consider 205
so.

HAMLET   No, faith, not a jot, but to follow him thither
with modesty enough, and likelihood to lead it. As 208
thus: Alexander died, Alexander was buried, Alexander returneth to dust, the dust is earth, of earth we
make loam, and why of that loam whereto he was 211
converted might they not stop a beer barrel?
Imperious Caesar, dead and turned to clay, 213
Might stop a hole to keep the wind away.
Oh, that that earth which kept the world in awe
Should patch a wall t'expel the winter's flaw! 216

*Enter King, Queen, Laertes, and the corpse [of
Ophelia, in procession, with Priest, lords, etc.].*

But soft, but soft awhile! Here comes the King, 217

The Queen, the courtiers. Who is this they follow?
And with such maimèd rites? This doth betoken 219
The corpse they follow did with desperate hand
Fordo it own life. 'Twas of some estate. 221
Couch we awhile and mark. 222

[*He and Horatio conceal themselves.
Ophelia's body is taken to the grave.*]

LAERTES   What ceremony else?

HAMLET   [*to Horatio*]
That is Laertes, a very noble youth. Mark.

LAERTES   What ceremony else?

PRIEST
Her obsequies have been as far enlarged
As we have warranty. Her death was doubtful, 227
And but that great command o'ersways the order 228
She should in ground unsanctified been lodged 229
Till the last trumpet. For charitable prayers, 230
Shards, flints, and pebbles should be thrown on her. 231
Yet here she is allowed her virgin crants, 232
Her maiden strewments, and the bringing home 233
Of bell and burial. 234

LAERTES
Must there no more be done?

PRIEST   No more be done.
We should profane the service of the dead
To sing a requiem and such rest to her 237
As to peace-parted souls.

LAERTES   Lay her i'th'earth, 238
And from her fair and unpolluted flesh
May violets spring! I tell thee, churlish priest, 240
A ministering angel shall my sister be
When thou liest howling.

HAMLET   [*to Horatio*]   What, the fair Ophelia! 242

QUEEN   [*scattering flowers*]   Sweets to the sweet! Farewell.
I hoped thou shouldst have been my Hamlet's wife.
I thought thy bride-bed to have decked, sweet maid,
And not t' have strewed thy grave.

LAERTES   Oh, treble woe
Fall ten times treble on that cursèd head
Whose wicked deed thy most ingenious sense 248
Deprived thee of! Hold off the earth awhile,
Till I have caught her once more in mine arms.

[*He leaps into the grave and embraces Ophelia.*]
Now pile your dust upon the quick and dead,
Till of this flat a mountain you have made
T' o'ertop old Pelion or the skyish head 253
Of blue Olympus.

---

171 **sore** keen, veritable. **whoreson** (An expression of contemptuous familiarity.) 173 **lien you** lain. (See the note at line 166.) 179 **Rhenish** Rhine wine 185 **bore** borne 187 **My gorge rises** i.e., I feel nauseated 189 **gibes** taunts 192 **chopfallen** (1) lacking the lower jaw (2) dejected. 193 **favor** aspect, appearance 204 **bunghole** hole for filling or emptying a cask. 205 **curiously** minutely 208 **with . . . lead it** with moderation and plausibility. 211 **loam** a mixture of clay, straw, sand, etc. used to mold bricks, or, in this case, bungs for a beer barrel 213 **Imperious** Imperial 216 **flaw** gust of wind. 217 **soft** i.e., wait, be careful

219 **maimèd** mutilated, incomplete 221 **Fordo it** destroy its. **estate** rank. 222 **Couch we** Let's hide, lie low 227 **warranty** i.e., ecclesiastical authority. 228 **order** (1) prescribed practice (2) religious order of clerics 229 **She should . . . lodged** she should have been buried in unsanctified ground 230 **For** In place of 231 **Shards** broken bits of pottery 232 **crants** garlands betokening maidenhood 233 **strewments** flowers strewn on a coffin 233–4 **bringing . . . burial** laying the body to rest, to the sound of the bell. 237 **such rest** i.e., to pray for such rest 238 **peace-parted souls** those who have died at peace with God. 240 **violets** (See 4.5.188 and note.) 242 **howling** i.e., in hell. 248 **ingenious sense** a mind that is quick, alert, of fine qualities 253 **Pelion** a mountain in northern Thessaly; compare *Olympus* and *Ossa* in lines 254 and 286. (In their rebellion against the Olympian gods, the giants attempted to heap Ossa on Pelion in order to scale Olympus.)

HAMLET [*coming forward*]   What is he whose grief
    Bears such an emphasis, whose phrase of sorrow   255
    Conjures the wandering stars and makes them stand   256
    Like wonder-wounded hearers? This is I,   257
    Hamlet the Dane.   258
LAERTES [*grappling with him*]   The devil take thy soul!   259
HAMLET   Thou pray'st not well.
    I prithee, take thy fingers from my throat,
    For though I am not splenitive and rash,   262
    Yet have I in me something dangerous,
    Which let thy wisdom fear. Hold off thy hand.
KING   Pluck them asunder.
QUEEN   Hamlet, Hamlet!
ALL   Gentlemen!
HORATIO   Good my lord, be quiet.
                 [*Hamlet and Laertes are parted.*]
HAMLET
    Why, I will fight with him upon this theme
    Until my eyelids will no longer wag.   270
QUEEN   Oh, my son, what theme?
HAMLET
    I loved Ophelia. Forty thousand brothers
    Could not with all their quantity of love
    Make up my sum. What wilt thou do for her?
KING   Oh, he is mad, Laertes.
QUEEN   For love of God, forbear him.   276
HAMLET
    'Swounds, show me what thou'lt do.   277
    Woo't weep? Woo't fight? Woo't fast? Woo't tear
      thyself?   278
    Woo't drink up eisel? Eat a crocodile?   279
    I'll do't. Dost come here to whine?
    To outface me with leaping in her grave?
    Be buried quick with her, and so will I.   282
    And if thou prate of mountains, let them throw
    Millions of acres on us, till our ground,
    Singeing his pate against the burning zone,   285
    Make Ossa like a wart! Nay, an thou'lt mouth,   286
    I'll rant as well as thou.
QUEEN   This is mere madness,   287
    And thus awhile the fit will work on him;
    Anon, as patient as the female dove

When that her golden couplets are disclosed,   290
    His silence will sit drooping.
HAMLET   Hear you, sir.
    What is the reason that you use me thus?
    I loved you ever. But it is no matter.
    Let Hercules himself do what he may,   294
    The cat will mew, and dog will have his day.   295
                       Exit Hamlet.
KING
    I pray thee, good Horatio, wait upon him.
                      [*Exit*] *Horatio.*
    [*To Laertes*] Strengthen your patience in our last
      night's speech;   297
    We'll put the matter to the present push.—   298
    Good Gertrude, set some watch over your son.—
    This grave shall have a living monument.   300
    An hour of quiet shortly shall we see;   301
    Till then, in patience our proceeding be.   *Exeunt.*

                       ❖

[5.2]

Enter Hamlet and Horatio.

HAMLET
    So much for this, sir; now shall you see the other.   1
    You do remember all the circumstance?
HORATIO   Remember it, my lord!
HAMLET
    Sir, in my heart there was a kind of fighting
    That would not let me sleep. Methought I lay
    Worse than the mutines in the bilboes. Rashly,   6
    And praised be rashness for it—let us know   7
    Our indiscretion sometime serves us well   8
    When our deep plots do pall, and that should learn us   9
    There's a divinity that shapes our ends,
    Rough-hew them how we will—
HORATIO   That is most certain.   11
HAMLET   Up from my cabin,
    My sea-gown scarfed about me, in the dark   13
    Groped I to find out them, had my desire,   14
    Fingered their packet, and in fine withdrew   15
    To mine own room again, making so bold,
    My fears forgetting manners, to unseal
    Their grand commission; where I found, Horatio—
    Ah, royal knavery!—an exact command,

---

255 **emphasis** i.e., rhetorical and florid emphasis. (*Phrase* has a similar rhetorical connotation.)   256 **wandering stars** planets   257 **wonder-wounded** struck with amazement   258 **the Dane** (This title normally signifies the King; see 1.1.17 and note.)   259 **s.d. *grappling with him*** The testimony of the First Quarto that *"Hamlet leaps in after Laertes"* and of the ballad "Elegy on Burbage," published in *Gentleman's Magazine* in 1825 ("Oft have I seen him leap into a grave") seem to indicate one way in which this fight was staged; however, the difficulty of fitting two contenders and Ophelia's body into a confined space (probably the trapdoor) suggests to many editors the alternative, that Laertes jumps out of the grave to attack Hamlet.)   262 **splenitive** quick-tempered   270 **wag** move. (A fluttering eyelid is a conventional sign that life has not yet gone.)   276 **forbear him** leave him alone.   277 **'Swounds** By His (Christ's) wounds   278 **Woo't** Wilt thou   279 **Woo't . . . eisel?** Will you drink up a whole draft of vinegar? (An extremely self-punishing task as a way of expressing grief.) **crocodile** (Crocodiles were tough and dangerous, and were supposed to shed crocodile tears.)   282 **quick** alive   285 **his pate** its head, i.e., top.   **burning zone** zone in the celestial sphere containing the sun's orbit, between the tropics of Cancer and Capricorn   286 **Ossa** (See 253n.)   **an thou'lt mouth** if you want to rant   287 **mere** utter

290 **golden couplets** two baby pigeons, covered with yellow down. **disclosed** hatched   294–5 **Let . . . day** i.e., (1) Even Hercules couldn't stop Laertes's theatrical rant (2) I, too, will have my turn; i.e., despite any blustering attempts at interference, every person will sooner or later do what he or she must do.   297 **in** i.e., by recalling   298 **present push** immediate test.   300 **living** lasting. (For Laertes's private understanding, Claudius also hints that Hamlet's death will serve as such a monument.)   301 **hour of quiet** time free of conflict
5.2 **Location: The castle.**
1 **see the other** hear the other news. (See 4.6.24–6.)   6 **mutines** mutineers.   **bilboes** shackles.   **Rashly** On impulse. (This adverb goes with lines 12 ff.)   7 **know** acknowledge   8 **indiscretion** lack of foresight and judgment (not an indiscreet act)   9 **pall** fail, falter, go stale. **learn** teach   11 **Rough-hew** shape roughly   13 **sea-gown** seaman's coat.   **scarfed** loosely wrapped   14 **them** i.e., Rosencrantz and Guildenstern   15 **Fingered** pilfered, pinched.   **in fine** finally, in conclusion

Larded with many several sorts of reasons   20
Importing Denmark's health and England's too,   21
With, ho! such bugs and goblins in my life,   22
That on the supervise, no leisure bated,   23
No, not to stay the grinding of the ax,   24
My head should be struck off.

HORATIO   Is't possible?

HAMLET *[giving a document]*
Here's the commission. Read it at more leisure.
But wilt thou hear now how I did proceed?

HORATIO   I beseech you.

HAMLET
Being thus benetted round with villainies—
Ere I could make a prologue to my brains,   30
They had begun the play—I sat me down,   31
Devised a new commission, wrote it fair.   32
I once did hold it, as our statists do,   33
A baseness to write fair, and labored much   34
How to forget that learning, but, sir, now
It did me yeoman's service. Wilt thou know
Th'effect of what I wrote?

HORATIO   Ay, good my lord.

HAMLET
An earnest conjuration from the King,   38
As England was his faithful tributary,
As love between them like the palm might flourish,   40
As peace should still her wheaten garland wear   41
And stand a comma 'tween their amities,   42
And many suchlike "as"es of great charge,   43
That on the view and knowing of these contents,
Without debatement further more or less,
He should those bearers put to sudden death,
Not shriving time allowed.

HORATIO   How was this sealed?   47

HAMLET
Why, even in that was heaven ordinant.   48
I had my father's signet in my purse,   49
Which was the model of that Danish seal;   50
Folded the writ up in the form of th'other,   51
Subscribed it, gave't th'impression, placed it safely,   52
The changeling never known. Now, the next day   53
Was our sea fight, and what to this was sequent   54
Thou knowest already.

HORATIO
So Guildenstern and Rosencrantz go to't.

HAMLET
Why, man, they did make love to this employment.
They are not near my conscience. Their defeat   58
Does by their own insinuation grow.   59
'Tis dangerous when the baser nature comes   60
Between the pass and fell incensèd points   61
Of mighty opposites.

HORATIO   Why, what a king is this!   62

HAMLET
Does it not, think thee, stand me now upon—   63
He that hath killed my king and whored my mother,
Popped in between th'election and my hopes,   65
Thrown out his angle for my proper life,   66
And with such coz'nage—is't not perfect conscience   67
To quit him with this arm? And is't not to be damned   68
To let this canker of our nature come   69
In further evil?   70

HORATIO
It must be shortly known to him from England
What is the issue of the business there.

HAMLET
It will be short. The interim is mine,
And a man's life's no more than to say "one."   74
But I am very sorry, good Horatio,
That to Laertes I forgot myself,
For by the image of my cause I see
The portraiture of his. I'll court his favors.
But, sure, the bravery of his grief did put me   79
Into a tow'ring passion.

HORATIO   Peace, who comes here?

Enter a Courtier [Osric].

OSRIC   Your Lordship is right welcome back to Denmark.

HAMLET   I humbly thank you, sir. *[To Horatio]* Dost
know this water fly?

HORATIO   No, my good lord.

HAMLET   Thy state is the more gracious, for 'tis a vice to
know him. He hath much land, and fertile. Let a beast   86
be lord of beasts, and his crib shall stand at the King's   87
mess. 'Tis a chuff, but, as I say, spacious in the   88
possession of dirt.

OSRIC   Sweet lord, if Your Lordship were at leisure, I
should impart a thing to you from His Majesty.

HAMLET   I will receive it, sir, with all diligence of spirit.
Put your bonnet to his right use; 'tis for the head.   93

---

20 Larded garnished.   **several** different   **21 Importing** relating to
22 With . . . life i.e., with all sorts of warnings of imaginary dangers if
I were allowed to continue living. (*Bugs* are bugbears, hobgoblins.)
23 That . . . bated that on the reading of this commission, no delay
being allowed   **24 stay** await   **30–1 Ere . . . play** before I could consciously turn my brain to the matter, it had started working on a plan
32 fair in a clear hand.   **33 statists** politicians, men of public affairs
34 A baseness beneath my dignity   **38 conjuration** entreaty
40 palm (An image of health; see Psalm 92:12.)   **41 still** always.
wheaten garland (Symbolic of fruitful agriculture, of peace and
plenty.)   **42 comma** (Indicating continuity, link.)   **43 "as"es** (1) the
"whereases" of a formal document (2) asses.   **charge** (1) import (2)
burden (appropriate to asses)   **47 shriving time** time for confession
and absolution   **48 ordinant** directing.   **49 signet** small seal
50 model replica   **51 writ** writing   **52 Subscribed** signed (with
forged signature).   **impression** i.e., with a wax seal   **53 changeling**
i.e., substituted letter. (Literally, a fairy child substituted for a human
one.)   **54 was sequent** followed

58 defeat destruction   **59 insinuation** intrusive intervention, sticking
their noses in my business   **60 baser** of lower social station   **61 pass**
thrust.   **fell** fierce   **62 opposites** antagonists.   **63 stand me now**
upon become incumbent on me now   **65 th'election** (The Danish
monarch was "elected" by a small number of high-ranking electors.)
66 angle fishhook.   **proper** very   **67 coz'nage** trickery   **68 quit**
requite, pay back   **69 canker** ulcer   **69–70 come In** grow into
74 a man's . . . "one" one's whole life occupies such a short time, only
as long as it takes to count to 1.   **79 bravery** bravado   **86–8 Let . . .**
mess i.e., If a man, no matter how beastlike, is as rich in livestock and
possessions as Osric, he may eat at the King's table.   **87 crib** manger
88 chuff boor, churl. (The Second Quarto spelling, "chough," is a
variant spelling that also suggests the meaning here of "chattering
jackdaw.")   **93 bonnet** any kind of cap or hat.   **his** its

OSRIC   I thank Your Lordship, it is very hot.

HAMLET   No, believe me, 'tis very cold. The wind is northerly.

OSRIC   It is indifferent cold, my lord, indeed.   97

HAMLET   But yet methinks it is very sultry and hot for my complexion.   99

OSRIC   Exceedingly, my lord. It is very sultry, as 'twere—I cannot tell how. My lord, His Majesty bade me signify to you that 'a has laid a great wager on your head. Sir, this is the matter—

HAMLET   I beseech you, remember.

[*Hamlet moves him to put on his hat.*]

OSRIC   Nay, good my lord; for my ease, in good faith.   105 Sir, here is newly come to court Laertes—believe me, an absolute gentleman, full of most excellent differ-   107 ences, of very soft society and great showing. Indeed,   108 to speak feelingly of him, he is the card or calendar of   109 gentry, for you shall find in him the continent of what   110 part a gentleman would see.   111

HAMLET   Sir, his definement suffers no perdition in   112 you, though I know to divide him inventorially would   113 dozy th'arithmetic of memory, and yet but yaw   114 neither in respect of his quick sail. But, in the verity of   115 extolment, I take him to be a soul of great article, and   116 his infusion of such dearth and rareness as, to make   117 true diction of him, his semblable is his mirror and   118 who else would trace him his umbrage, nothing   119 more.   120

OSRIC   Your Lordship speaks most infallibly of him.

HAMLET   The concernancy, sir? Why do we wrap the   122 gentleman in our more rawer breath?   123

OSRIC   Sir?

HORATIO   Is't not possible to understand in another   125 tongue? You will do't, sir, really.   126

HAMLET   What imports the nomination of this gentle-   127 man?

OSRIC   Of Laertes?

HORATIO [*to Hamlet*]   His purse is empty already; all 's golden words are spent.

HAMLET   Of him, sir.

OSRIC   I know you are not ignorant—

HAMLET   I would you did, sir. Yet in faith if you did,   134 it would not much approve me. Well, sir?   135

OSRIC   You are not ignorant of what excellence Laertes is—

HAMLET   I dare not confess that, lest I should compare   138 with him in excellence. But to know a man well were   139 to know himself.   140

OSRIC   I mean, sir, for his weapon; but in the imputation   141 laid on him by them, in his meed he's unfellowed.   142

HAMLET   What's his weapon?

OSRIC   Rapier and dagger.

HAMLET   That's two of his weapons—but well.   145

OSRIC   The King, sir, hath wagered with him six Barbary   147 horses, against the which he has impawned, as I take   147 it, six French rapiers and poniards, with their assigns,   148 as girdle, hangers, and so. Three of the carriages, in   149 faith, are very dear to fancy, very responsive to the   150 hilts, most delicate carriages, and of very liberal con-   151 ceit.   152

HAMLET   What call you the carriages?   153

HORATIO [*to Hamlet*]   I knew you must be edified by the margent ere you had done.   155

OSRIC   The carriages, sir, are the hangers.

HAMLET   The phrase would be more germane to the matter if we could carry a cannon by our sides; I would it might be hangers till then. But, on: six Barbary horses against six French swords, their assigns, and three lib-eral-conceited carriages; that's the French bet against the Danish. Why is this impawned, as you call it?

OSRIC   The King, sir, hath laid, sir, that in a dozen   163 passes between yourself and him, he shall not exceed   164 you three hits. He hath laid on twelve for nine, and it would come to immediate trial, if Your Lordship would vouchsafe the answer.   167

HAMLET   How if I answer no?

---

97 indifferent somewhat   **99 complexion** constitution.   **105 for my ease** (A conventional reply declining the invitation to put the hat back on.)   **107 absolute** perfect   **107–8 differences** special qualities   **108 soft society** agreeable manners.   **great showing** distinguished appearance.   **109 feelingly** with just perception   **109–10 the card . . . gentry** the model or paradigm (literally, a chart or directory) of good breeding   **110–11 the continent . . . see** one who contains in himself all the qualities a gentleman would like to see. (A *continent* is that which contains.)   **112–15 his definement . . . sail** the task of defining Laertes's excellences suffers no diminution in your description of him, though I know that to enumerate all his graces would stupify one's powers of memory, and even so could do no more than veer unsteadily off course in a vain attempt to keep up with his rapid forward motion. (Hamlet mocks Osric by parodying his jargon-filled speeches.)   **115–20 But . . . more** But, in true praise of him, I take him to be a person of remarkable value, and his essence of such rarity and excellence as, to speak truly of him, none can compare with him other than his own mirror; anyone following in his footsteps can only hope to be the shadow to his substance, nothing more.   **122 concernancy** import, relevance   **123 rawer breath** unrefined speech that can only come short in praising him.   **125–6 Is't . . . tongue?** i.e., Is it not possible for you, Osric, to understand and communicate in any other tongue than the overblown rhetoric you have used? (Alternatively, Horatio could be asking Hamlet to speak more plainly.)   **126 You will do't** i.e., You can if you try, or, you may well have to try (to speak plainly).   **127 nomination** naming

134–5 I would . . . approve me (Responding to Osric's incompleted sentence as though it were a complete statement, Hamlet says, with mock politeness, "I wish you did know me to be not ignorant [i.e., to be knowledgeable] about matters," and then turns this into an insult: "But if you did, your recommendation of me would be of little value in any case.")   **138–40 I dare . . . himself** I dare not boast of knowing Laertes's excellence lest I seem to imply a comparable excellence in myself. Certainly, to know another person well, one must know oneself.   **141–2 I mean . . . unfellowed** I mean his excellence with his rapier, not his general excellence; in the reputation he enjoys for use of his weapons, his merit is unequaled.   **145 but well** but never mind.   **147 he** i.e., Laertes.   **impawned** staked, wagered   **148 poniards** daggers.   **assigns** appurtenances   **149 hangers** straps on the sword belt (*girdle*), from which the sword hung.   **and so** and so on.   **149–52 Three . . . conceit** Three of the hangers, truly, are very pleasing to the fancy, decoratively matched with the hilts, delicate in workmanship, and made with elaborate ingenuity.   **153 What call you** What do you refer to when you say   **155 margent** margin of a book, place for explanatory notes   **163 laid** wagered   **164 passes** bouts. (The odds of the betting are hard to explain. Possibly the King bets that Hamlet will win at least five out of twelve, at which point Laertes raises the odds against himself by betting he will win nine.)   **167 vouchsafe the answer** be so good as to accept the challenge. (Hamlet deliberately takes the phrase in its literal sense of replying.)

OSRIC   I mean, my lord, the opposition of your person in trial.

HAMLET   Sir, I will walk here in the hall. If it please His Majesty, it is the breathing time of day with me. Let 172 the foils be brought, the gentleman willing, and the King hold his purpose, I will win for him an I can; if not, I will gain nothing but my shame and the odd hits.

OSRIC   Shall I deliver you so?   177

HAMLET   To this effect, sir—after what flourish your nature will.

OSRIC   I commend my duty to Your Lordship.   180

HAMLET   Yours, yours.   [*Exit Osric.*]
'A does well to commend it himself; there are no tongues else for 's turn.   183

HORATIO   This lapwing runs away with the shell on his 184 head.

HAMLET   'A did comply with his dug before 'a sucked 186 it. Thus has he—and many more of the same breed 187 that I know the drossy age dotes on—only got the 188 tune of the time, and, out of an habit of encounter, a 189 kind of yeasty collection, which carries them through 190 and through the most fanned and winnowed opin- 191 ions; and do but blow them to their trial, the bubbles 192 are out.   193

Enter a Lord.

LORD   My lord, His Majesty commended him to you by young Osric, who brings back to him that you attend him in the hall. He sends to know if your pleasure hold to play with Laertes, or that you will take longer 197 time.

HAMLET   I am constant to my purposes; they follow the King's pleasure. If his fitness speaks, mine is ready; 200 now or whensoever, provided I be so able as now.

LORD   The King and Queen and all are coming down.   203

HAMLET   In happy time.   203

LORD   The Queen desires you to use some gentle enter- 204 tainment to Laertes before you fall to play.   205

HAMLET   She well instructs me.   [*Exit Lord.*]

HORATIO   You will lose, my lord.

HAMLET   I do not think so. Since he went into France, I have been in continual practice; I shall win at the odds.

But thou wouldst not think how ill all's here about my heart; but it is no matter.

HORATIO   Nay, good my lord—

HAMLET   It is but foolery, but it is such a kind of gain- 213 giving as would perhaps trouble a woman.   214

HORATIO   If your mind dislike anything, obey it. I will forestall their repair hither and say you are not fit.   216

HAMLET   Not a whit, we defy augury. There is special 217 providence in the fall of a sparrow. If it be now, 'tis not to come; if it be not to come, it will be now; if it be not now; yet it will come. The readiness is all. Since 220 no man of aught he leaves knows, what is't to leave 221 betimes? Let be.   222

> *A table prepared. [Enter] trumpets, drums, and officers with cushions; King, Queen, [Osric,] and all the state; foils, daggers, [and wine borne in;] and Laertes.*

KING
Come, Hamlet, come and take this hand from me.
> [*The King puts Laertes's hand into Hamlet's.*]

HAMLET [*to Laertes*]
Give me your pardon, sir. I have done you wrong,
But pardon't as you are a gentleman.
This presence knows,   226
And you must needs have heard, how I am punished 227
With a sore distraction. What I have done
That might your nature, honor, and exception   229
Roughly awake, I here proclaim was madness.
Was't Hamlet wronged Laertes? Never Hamlet.
If Hamlet from himself be ta'en away,
And when he's not himself does wrong Laertes,
Then Hamlet does it not, Hamlet denies it.
Who does it, then? His madness. If't be so,
Hamlet is of the faction that is wronged;   236
His madness is poor Hamlet's enemy.
Sir, in this audience
Let my disclaiming from a purposed evil
Free me so far in your most generous thoughts
That I have shot my arrow o'er the house
And hurt my brother.

LAERTES   I am satisfied in nature,   242
Whose motive in this case should stir me most   243
To my revenge. But in my terms of honor
I stand aloof, and will no reconcilement
Till by some elder masters of known honor
I have a voice and precedent of peace   247
To keep my name ungored. But till that time   248
I do receive your offered love like love,

---

172 **breathing time** exercise period.   **Let** i.e., If   177 **deliver you** report what you say   180 **commend** commit to your favor. (A conventional salutation, but Hamlet wryly uses a more literal meaning, "recommend," "praise," in line 182.)   183 **for 's turn** for his purposes, i.e., to do it for him.   184 **lapwing** (A proverbial type of youthful forwardness. Also, a bird that draws intruders away from its nest and was thought to run about with its head in the shell when newly hatched; a seeming reference to Osric's hat.)   186 **comply . . . dug** observe ceremonious formality toward his nurse's or mother's teat   187–93 **Thus . . . are out** Thus has he—and many like him of the sort our frivolous age dotes on—acquired the trendy manner of speech of the time, and, out of habitual conversation with courtiers of their own kind, have collected together a kind of frothy medley of current phrases, which enables such gallants to hold their own among persons of the most select and well-sifted views; and yet do but test them by merely blowing on them, and their bubbles burst.   197 **play** fence.   **that** if   200 **If . . . ready** If he declares his readiness, my convenience waits on his   203 **In happy time** (A phrase of courtesy indicating that the time is convenient.)   204–5 **entertainment** greeting

213–14 **gaingiving** misgiving   216 **repair** coming   217 **augury** the attempt to read signs of future events in order to avoid predicted trouble.   220–2 **Since . . . Let be** Since no one has knowledge of what he is leaving behind, what does an early death matter after all? Enough; forbear.   222.1 *trumpets, drums* trumpeters, drummers 222.3 **all the state** the entire court   226 **presence** royal assembly 227 **punished** afflicted   229 **exception** disapproval   236 **faction** party   242 **in nature** i.e., as to my personal feelings   243 **motive** prompting   247 **voice** authoritative pronouncement.   **of peace** for reconciliation   248 **name ungored** reputation unwounded.

And will not wrong it.

HAMLET   I embrace it freely,
And will this brothers' wager frankly play.—   251
Give us the foils. Come on.

LAERTES   Come, one for me.

HAMLET
I'll be your foil, Laertes. In mine ignorance   253
Your skill shall, like a star i'th' darkest night,
Stick fiery off indeed.

LAERTES   You mock me, sir.   255

HAMLET   No, by this hand.

KING
Give them the foils, young Osric. Cousin Hamlet,
You know the wager?

HAMLET   Very well, my lord.
Your Grace has laid the odds o'th' weaker side.   259

KING
I do not fear it; I have seen you both.
But since he is bettered, we have therefore odds.   261

LAERTES
This is too heavy. Let me see another.
            [He exchanges his foil for another.]

HAMLET
This likes me well. These foils have all a length?   263
                        [They prepare to fence.]

OSRIC   Ay, my good lord.

KING
Set me the stoups of wine upon that table.
If Hamlet give the first or second hit,
Or quit in answer of the third exchange,   267
Let all the battlements their ordnance fire.
The King shall drink to Hamlet's better breath,   269
And in the cup an union shall he throw   270
Richer than that which four successive kings
In Denmark's crown have worn. Give me the cups,
And let the kettle to the trumpet speak,   273
The trumpet to the cannoneer without,
The cannons to the heavens, the heaven to earth,
"Now the King drinks to Hamlet." Come, begin.
                        Trumpets the while.
And you, the judges, bear a wary eye.

HAMLET   Come on, sir.

LAERTES   Come, my lord. [They fence. Hamlet scores a hit.]

HAMLET   One.

LAERTES   No.

HAMLET   Judgment.

OSRIC   A hit, a very palpable hit.   282
                Drum, trumpets, and shot. Flourish.
                              A piece goes off.

LAERTES   Well, again.

KING
Stay, give me drink. Hamlet, this pearl is thine.
        [He drinks, and throws a pearl in Hamlet's cup.]
Here's to thy health. Give him the cup.

HAMLET
I'll play this bout first. Set it by awhile.
Come. [They fence.] Another hit; what say you?

LAERTES   A touch, a touch, I do confess't.

KING
Our son shall win.

QUEEN   He's fat and scant of breath.   289
Here, Hamlet, take my napkin, rub thy brows.   290
The Queen carouses to thy fortune, Hamlet.   291

HAMLET   Good madam!

KING   Gertrude, do not drink.

QUEEN
I will, my lord, I pray you pardon me.   [She drinks.]

KING [aside]
It is the poisoned cup. It is too late.

HAMLET
I dare not drink yet, madam; by and by.

QUEEN   Come, let me wipe thy face.

LAERTES [aside to the King]
My lord, I'll hit him now.

KING   I do not think't.

LAERTES [aside]
And yet it is almost against my conscience.

HAMLET
Come, for the third, Laertes. You do but dally.
I pray you, pass with your best violence;   301
I am afeard you make a wanton of me.   302

LAERTES   Say you so? Come on.   [They fence.]

OSRIC   Nothing neither way.

LAERTES
Have at you now!   305
            [Laertes wounds Hamlet; then, in scuffling,
            they change rapiers, and Hamlet wounds Laertes.]

KING   Part them! They are incensed.

HAMLET
Nay, come, again.   [The Queen falls.]

OSRIC   Look to the Queen there, ho!

HORATIO
They bleed on both sides. How is it, my lord?

OSRIC   How is't, Laertes?

LAERTES
Why, as a woodcock to mine own springe, Osric;   309
I am justly killed with mine own treachery.

HAMLET
How does the Queen?

KING   She swoons to see them bleed.

251 frankly without ill feeling or the burden of rancor   253 foil thin
metal background which sets a jewel off. (With pun on the blunted
rapier for fencing.)   255 Stick fiery off stand out brilliantly
259 laid . . . side backed the weaker side.   261 is bettered is the
odds-on favorite. (Laertes's handicap is the "three hits" specified in
line 165.)   263 likes pleases   267 Or . . . exchange or draws even
with Laertes by winning the third exchange   269 better breath
improved vigor   270 union pearl. (So called, according to Pliny's
Natural History, 9, because pearls are unique, never identical.)
273 kettle kettledrum   282.2 A piece A cannon

289 fat not physically fit, out of training   290 napkin handkerchief
291 carouses drinks a toast   301 pass thrust   302 make . . . me i.e.,
treat me like a spoiled child, trifle with me.   305.1–2 in scuffling, they
change rapiers (This stage direction occurs in the Folio. According to
a widespread stage tradition, Hamlet receives a scratch, realizes that
Laertes's sword is unbated, and accordingly forces an exchange.)
309 woodcock a bird, a type of stupidity or as a decoy.   springe
trap, snare

QUEEN
No, no, the drink, the drink—Oh, my dear Hamlet—
The drink, the drink! I am poisoned.   [*She dies.*]

HAMLET
Oh, villainy! Ho, let the door be locked!
Treachery! Seek it out.   [*Laertes falls. Exit Osric.*]

LAERTES
It is here, Hamlet. Hamlet, thou art slain.
No med'cine in the world can do thee good;
In thee there is not half an hour's life.
The treacherous instrument is in thy hand,
Unbated and envenomed. The foul practice   320
Hath turned itself on me. Lo, here I lie,
Never to rise again. Thy mother's poisoned.
I can no more. The King, the King's to blame.

HAMLET
The point envenomed too? Then, venom, to thy work.
        [*He stabs the King.*]

ALL   Treason! Treason!

KING
Oh, yet defend me, friends! I am but hurt.

HAMLET [*forcing the King to drink*]
Here, thou incestuous, murderous, damnèd Dane,
Drink off this potion. Is thy union here?   328
Follow my mother.   [*The King dies.*]

LAERTES   He is justly served.
It is a poison tempered by himself.   330
Exchange forgiveness with me, noble Hamlet.
Mine and my father's death come not upon thee,
Nor thine on me!   [*He dies.*]

HAMLET
Heaven make thee free of it! I follow thee.
I am dead, Horatio. Wretched Queen, adieu!
You that look pale and tremble at this chance,   336
That are but mutes or audience to this act,   337
Had I but time—as this fell sergeant, Death,   338
Is strict in his arrest—oh, I could tell you—   339
But let it be. Horatio, I am dead;
Thou livest. Report me and my cause aright
To the unsatisfied.

HORATIO   Never believe it.
I am more an antique Roman than a Dane.   343
Here's yet some liquor left.
        [*He attempts to drink from the poisoned cup.
                Hamlet prevents him.*]

HAMLET   As thou'rt a man,
Give me the cup! Let go! By heaven, I'll ha 't.
Oh, God, Horatio, what a wounded name,
Things standing thus unknown, shall I leave behind
        me!
If thou didst ever hold me in thy heart,
Absent thee from felicity awhile,

And in this harsh world draw thy breath in pain
To tell my story. *A march afar off* [*and a volley within*].
        What warlike noise is this?

        Enter Osric.

OSRIC
Young Fortinbras, with conquest come from Poland,
To th'ambassadors of England gives
This warlike volley.

HAMLET   Oh, I die, Horatio!
The potent poison quite o'ercrows my spirit.   355
I cannot live to hear the news from England,
But I do prophesy th'election lights
On Fortinbras. He has my dying voice.   358
So tell him, with th'occurrents more and less   359
Which have solicited. The rest is silence.   [*He dies.*] 360

HORATIO
Now cracks a noble heart. Good night, sweet prince,
And flights of angels sing thee to thy rest!
        [*March within.*]

Why does the drum come hither?

        Enter Fortinbras, with the [*English*] *Ambassadors*
        [*with drum, colors, and attendants*].

FORTINBRAS
Where is this sight?

HORATIO   What is it you would see?
If aught of woe or wonder, cease your search.

FORTINBRAS
This quarry cries on havoc. O proud Death,   366
What feast is toward in thine eternal cell,   367
That thou so many princes at a shot
So bloodily hast struck?

FIRST AMBASSADOR   The sight is dismal,
And our affairs from England come too late.
The ears are senseless that should give us hearing,
To tell him his commandment is fulfilled,
That Rosencrantz and Guildenstern are dead.
Where should we have our thanks?

HORATIO   Not from his mouth,   374
Had it th'ability of life to thank you.
He never gave commandment for their death.
But since, so jump upon this bloody question,   377
You from the Polack wars and you from England
Are here arrived, give order that these bodies
High on a stage be placèd to the view,   380
And let me speak to th' yet unknowing world
How these things came about. So shall you hear
Of carnal, bloody, and unnatural acts,
Of accidental judgments, casual slaughters,   384

---

320 Unbated not blunted with a button.   **practice** plot   **328 union** pearl. (See line 270; with grim puns on the word's other meanings: marriage, shared death.)   **330 tempered** mixed   **336 chance** mischance   **337 mutes** silent observers. (Literally, actors with nonspeaking parts.)   **338 fell sergeant** remorseless arresting officer   **339 strict** (1) severely just (2) unavoidable.   **arrest** (1) taking into custody (2) stopping my speech   **343 Roman** (Suicide was an honorable choice for many Romans as an alternative to a dishonorable life.)

355 o'ercrows triumphs over (like the winner in a cockfight)
358 voice vote.   **359 th'occurrents** the events, incidents
360 solicited moved, urged. (Hamlet doesn't finish saying what the events have prompted—presumably, his acts of vengeance, or his reporting of those events to Fortinbras.)   **366 This . . . havoc** This heap of dead bodies loudly proclaims a general slaughter.   **367 feast** i.e., Death feasting on those who have fallen.   **toward** in preparation
374 his Claudius's   **377 so jump . . . question** so hard on the heels of this bloody business   **380 stage** platform   **384 judgments** retributions.   **casual** occurring by chance

Of deaths put on by cunning and forced cause,   385
And, in this upshot, purposes mistook
Fall'n on th'inventors' heads. All this can I
Truly deliver.
FORTINBRAS   Let us haste to hear it,
And call the noblest to the audience.
For me, with sorrow I embrace my fortune.
I have some rights of memory in this kingdom,   391
Which now to claim my vantage doth invite me.   392
HORATIO
Of that I shall have also cause to speak,
And from his mouth whose voice will draw on more.   394
But let this same be presently performed,   395

Even while men's minds are wild, lest more
    mischance
On plots and errors happen.
FORTINBRAS   Let four captains   397
Bear Hamlet, like a soldier, to the stage,
For he was likely, had he been put on,   399
To have proved most royal; and for his passage,   400
The soldiers' music and the rite of war
Speak loudly for him.   402
Take up the bodies. Such a sight as this
Becomes the field, but here shows much amiss.   404
Go bid the soldiers shoot.
            Exeunt [marching, bearing off the dead bodies;
                        a peal of ordnance is shot off].

385 put on instigated.   **forced cause** contrivance   **391 of memory** traditional, remembered, unforgotten   **392 vantage** favorable opportunity   **394 voice . . . more** vote will influence still others. **395 presently** immediately

397 On on top of   **399 put on** i.e., invested in royal office and so put to the test   **400 for his passage** to mark his passing   **402 Speak** (let them) speak   **404 Becomes the field** suits the field of battle

Othello, the Moor of Venice

Othello differs in several respects from the other three major Shakespearean tragedies with which it is usually ranked. Written seemingly about the time of its performance at court by the King's men (Shakespeare's acting company) on November 1, 1604, after *Hamlet* (c. 1599–1601) and before *King Lear* (1605–1606) and *Macbeth* (c. 1606–1607), *Othello* shares with these other plays a fascination with evil in its most virulent and universal aspect. These plays study the devastating effects of ambitious pride, ingratitude, wrath, jealousy, and vengeful hate—the deadly sins of the spirit—with only a passing interest in the political strife to which Shakespeare's Roman or classical tragedies are generally devoted. Of the four, *Othello* is the most concentrated upon one particular evil. The action concerns sexual jealousy, and, although human sinfulness is such that jealousy ceaselessly touches on other forms of depravity, the center of interest always returns in *Othello* to the destruction of a love through jealousy. *Othello* is a tragic portrait of a marriage. The protagonist is not a king or a prince, as in the tragedies already mentioned, but a general recently married. There are no supernatural visitations, as in *Hamlet* and *Macbeth*. Ideas of divine justice, while essential to *Othello*'s portrayal of a battle between good and evil for the allegiance of the protagonist, do not encompass the wide sweep of *King Lear*, nor do we find here the same broad indictment of humanity. Social order is not seriously shaken by Othello's tragedy. The fair-minded Duke of Venice remains firmly in control, and his deputy Lodovico oversees a just conclusion on Cyprus.

By the same token, *Othello* does not offer the remorseless questioning about humanity's relationship to the cosmos that we find in *King Lear, Hamlet,* and *Macbeth*. The battle of good and evil is, of course, cosmic, but in *Othello* that battle is realized through a taut narrative of jealousy and murder. Its poetic images are accordingly focused to a large extent on the natural world. One cluster of images is domestic and animal, having to do with goats, mon-keys, wolves, baboons, guinea hens, wildcats, spiders, flies, asses, dogs, copulating horses and sheep, serpents, and toads; other images, more wide-ranging in scope, include green-eyed monsters, devils, poisons, money purses, tarnished jewels, music untuned, and light extinguished. The story is immediate and direct, retaining the sensational atmosphere of its Italian prose source by Giovanni Baptista Giraldi Cinthio, in his *Hecatommithi* of 1565 (translated into French in 1584). Events move even more swiftly than in Cinthio's work, for Shakespeare has compressed the story into two or three nights and days (albeit with an intervening sea journey and with an elastic use of stage time to allow for the maturing of long-term plans, as when we learn that Iago has begged Emilia "a hundred times" to steal Desdemona's handkerchief, 3.3.308, or that Iago has accused Cassio of making love to Desdemona "A thousand times," 5.2.219). *Othello* does not have a fully developed double plot, as in *King Lear,* or a comparatively large group of characters serving as foils to the protagonist, as in *Hamlet. Othello*'s cast is small, and the plot is concentrated to an unusual degree on Othello, Desdemona, and Iago. What *Othello* may lose in breadth it gains in dramatic intensity.

Daringly, Shakespeare opens this tragedy of love, not with a direct and sympathetic portrayal of the lovers themselves, but with a scene of vicious insinuation about their marriage. The images employed by Iago to describe the coupling of Othello and Desdemona are revoltingly animalistic, sodomistic. "Even now, now, very now, an old black ram / Is tupping your white ewe," he taunts Desdemona's father, Brabantio. (Tupping is a word used specifically for the copulating of sheep.) "You'll have your daughter covered with a Barbary horse; you'll have your nephews neigh to you"; "your daughter and the Moor are now making the beast with two backs"; "the devil will make a grandsire of you" (1.1.90–3, 113–20). This degraded view reduces the marriage to one of utter carnality, with repeated emphasis on the word "gross": Desdemona has yielded "to the gross clasps of a lascivious Moor" and has made "a gross revolt" against her family and society (lines 129, 137). Iago's second theme, one that is habitual with him, is money. "What ho, Brabantio! Thieves, thieves, thieves! / Look to your house, your daughter, and your bags" (lines 81–2). The implication is of a sinister bond between thievery in sex and thievery in gold. Sex and money are both commodities to be protected by watchful fathers against libidinous and opportunistic children.

We as audience make plentiful allowance for Iago's bias in all this, since he has admitted to Roderigo his knavery and resentment of Othello. Even so, the carnal vision of love we confront is calculatedly disturbing, because it seems so equated with a pejorative image of blackness. Othello is unquestionably a black man, referred to disparagingly by his detractors as the "thick-lips," with a "sooty bosom" (1.1.68; 1.2.71); Elizabethan usage applied the term "Moor" without attempting to distinguish between Arabian and African peoples. From the ugly start of the play, Othello and Desdemona have to prove the worth of their love in the face of preset attitudes against miscegenation. Brabantio takes refuge in the thought that Othello must have bewitched Desdemona. His basic assumption—one to be echoed later by Iago and when Othello's confidence is undermined by Othello himself—is that miscegenation is unnatural by definition. In confronting and accusing Othello, he repeatedly appeals "to all things of sense" (that is, to common sense) and asks if it is not "gross in sense" (self-evident) that Othello has practiced magic on her, since nothing else could prompt human nature so to leave its natural path. "For nature so preposterously to err, / Being not deficient, blind, or lame of sense, / Sans witchcraft could not" (1.2.65, 73; 1.3.64–6). We as audience can perceive the racial bias in Brabantio's view and can recognize also in him the type of imperious father who conventionally opposes romantic love. It is sadly ironic that he should now prefer Roderigo as a son-in-law, evidently concluding that any white Venetian would be preferable to the prince of blacks. Still, Brabantio has been hospitable to the Moor and trusting of his daughter. He is a sorrowful rather than ridiculous figure, and the charge he levels at the married pair, however much it is based on a priori assumptions of what is "natural" in human behavior, remains to be answered.

After all, we find ourselves wondering, what did attract Othello and Desdemona to one another? Even though he certainly did not use witchcraft, may Othello not have employed a subtler kind of enchantment in the exotic character of his travels among "the Cannibals that each other eat, / The Anthropophagi, and men whose heads / Do grow beneath their shoulders" (1.3.145–7)? These "passing strange" events fascinate Desdemona as they do everyone, including the Duke of Venice ("I think

this tale would win my daughter too"). Othello has not practiced unfairly on her—"This only is the witchcraft I have used" (lines 162, 171–3). Yet may he not represent for Desdemona a radical novelty, being a man at once less devious and more interesting than the dissolute Venetian swaggerers, such as Roderigo and the "wealthy curlèd darlings of our nation" (1.2.69), who follow her about? Was her deceiving of her father by means of the elopement a protest, an escape from conventionality? Why has she been attracted to a man older than herself? For his part, Othello gives the impression of being inexperienced with women, at least of Desdemona's rank and complexion, and is both intrigued and flattered by her attentions. "She loved me for the dangers I had passed, / And I loved her that she did pity them" (1.3.169–70). Desdemona fulfills a place in Othello's view of himself. Does she also represent status for him in Venetian society, where he has been employed as a military commander but treated nonetheless as something of an alien?

These subtle but impertinent ways of doubting the motivations of Othello and Desdemona, adding to the difficulties that are inherent in an attempt to understand the mysteries of attraction in any relationship, are thrust upon us by the play's opening and are later crucial to Iago's strategy of breeding mistrust. Just as importantly, however, these insinuations are refuted by Othello and especially by Desdemona. Whatever others may think, she never gives the slightest indication of regarding her husband as different because he is black and old. In fact, the images of blackness and age are significantly reversed during the play's early scenes. Othello has already embraced the Christian faith, whereas Iago, a white Italian in a Christian culture, emerges as innately evil from the very start of the play. Othello's first appearance onstage, when he confronts a party of torch-bearing men coming to arrest him and bids his followers sheathe their swords (1.2.60), is perhaps reminiscent of Christ's arrest in the Garden of Gethsemane; if so, it suggests a fleeting comparison between Othello and the Christian God whose charity and forbearance he seeks to emulate. Othello's blackness may be used in part as an emblem of fallen humanity, but so are we all fallen. His age similarly strengthens our impression of his wisdom, restraint, and leadership. Any suggestions of comic sexual infidelity in the marriage of an older man and an attractive young bride are confuted by what we see in Desdemona's chaste yet sensual regard for the good man she has chosen.

Desdemona is devoted to Othello, admiring, and faithful. We believe her when she says that she does not even know what it means to be unfaithful; the word *whore* is not in her vocabulary. She is defenseless against the charges brought against her, because she does not even comprehend them and cannot believe that anyone would imagine such things. Her love, both erotic and chaste, is of that transcendent wholesomeness common to several late Shakespearean heroines, such as Cordelia in *King Lear* and Hermione in *The Winter's Tale*. Her "preferring" Othello to her father, like Cordelia's placing her duty to a husband before that to a father, is not ungrateful but natural and proper. And Othello, however much he may regard Desdemona in terms of his own identity (he calls her "my fair warrior"), does cherish Desdemona as she deserves. "I cannot speak enough of this content," he exclaims when he rejoins her on Cyprus. "It stops me here; it is too much of joy" (2.1.181, 196–7). The passionate intensity of his love prepares the way for his tragedy; he speaks more truly than he knows in saying, "when I love thee not, / Chaos is come again" (3.3.99–100). Iago speaks truly also when he observes that Othello "Is of a constant, loving, noble nature" (2.1.290). Othello's tragedy is not that he is easily duped, but that his strong faith can be destroyed at such terrible cost. Othello never forgets how much he is losing. The threat to his love is not an initial lack of his being happily married, but rather the insidious assumption that Desdemona cannot love him because such a love might be unnatural. The fear of being unlovable exists in Othello's mind, but the human instrument of this vicious gospel is Iago.

Iago belongs to a select group of villains in Shakespeare who, while plausibly motivated in human terms, also take delight in evil for its own sake: Aaron the Moor in *Titus Andronicus*, Richard III, Don John in *Much Ado About Nothing*, Iago, Edmund in *King Lear*. They are not, like Macbeth or like Claudius in *Hamlet*, men driven by ambition to commit crimes they clearly recognize to be wrong. Although Edmund does belatedly try to make amends, these villains are essentially conscienceless, sinister, and amused by their own cunning. They are related to one another by a stage metaphor of personified evil derived from the Vice of the morality play, whose typical role is to win the Mankind figure away from virtue and to corrupt him with worldly enticements. Like that engaging tempter, Shakespeare's villains in these plays take the audience into their confidence, boast in soliloquy of their cleverness, exult in the triumph of evil, and improvise plans with daring and resourcefulness. They are all superb actors, deceiving virtually every character onstage until late in the action with their protean and hypocritical display. They take pleasure in this "sport" and amaze us by their virtuosity. The role is paradoxically comic in its use of ingenious and resourceful deception—the grim and ironic comedy of vice. We know that we are to condemn morally even while we applaud the skill.

This theatrical tradition of the Vice may best explain a puzzling feature of Iago, noted long ago and memorably phrased by Samuel Taylor Coleridge as "the motive hunting of a motiveless malignity." To be sure, Iago does offer plausible motives for what he does. Despite his resemblance to the morality Vice, he is no allegorized abstraction but an ensign in the army, a junior field officer who

hates being out-ranked by a theoretician or staff officer. As an old-school professional, he also resents that he has not been promoted on the basis of seniority, the "old gradation" (1.1.38). Even his efforts at using influence with Othello have come to naught, and Iago can scarcely be blamed for supposing that Cassio's friendship with Othello has won him special favor. Thus, Iago has reason to plot against Cassio as well as Othello. Nevertheless a further dimension is needed to explain Iago's gloating, his utter lack of moral reflection, his concentration on destroying Desdemona (who has not wronged Iago), his absorption in ingenious methods of plotting, his finesse and style. Hatred precedes any plausible motive in Iago and ultimately does not depend on psychological causality. Probably the tradition of the stage Machiavel (another type of gloating villain based on stereotyped attitudes toward the heretical political ideas of Niccolò Machiavelli), as in Marlowe's *The Jew of Malta*, contributes to the portraiture; this tradition was readily assimilated with that of the Vice.

Iago's machinations yield him both "sport" and "profit" (1.3.387); that is, he enjoys his evildoing, although he is also driven by a motive. This Vice-like behavior in human garb creates a restless sense of a destructive metaphysical reality lying behind his visible exterior. Even his stated motives do not always make sense. When in an outburst of hatred he soliloquizes that "I hate the Moor; / And it is thought abroad that twixt my sheets / He's done my office," Iago goes on to concede the unlikelihood of this charge. "I know not if't be true; / But I, for mere suspicion in that kind, / Will do as if for surety" (lines 387–91). The charge is so absurd, in fact, that we have to look into Iago himself for the origin of this jealous paranoia. The answer may be partly emblematic: as the embodiment and genius of sexual jealousy, Iago suffers with ironic appropriateness from the evil he preaches, and without external cause. Emilia understands that jealousy is not a rational affliction but a self-induced disease of the mind. Jealous persons, she tells Desdemona, "are not ever jealous for the cause, / But jealous for they're jealous. It is a monster / Begot upon itself, born on itself" (3.4.161–3). Iago's own testimonial bears this out, for his jealousy is at once wholly irrational and agonizingly self-destructive. "I do suspect the lusty Moor / Hath leaped into my seat, the thought whereof / Doth, like a poisonous mineral, gnaw my innards" (2.1.296–8). In light of this nightmare, we can see that even his seemingly plausible resentment of Cassio's promotion is jealous envy. The "daily beauty" in Cassio's life makes Iago feel "ugly" by comparison (5.1.19–20), engendering in Iago a profound sense of lack of worth from which he can temporarily find relief only by reducing Othello and others to his own miserable condition. He is adept at provoking self-hatred in others because he suffers from it himself. His declaration to Othello that "I am your own forever"

(3.3.495) is, of course, cynical, but it also signals the extent to which Iago has succeeded in wooing Othello away from Desdemona and Cassio into a murderous union between two women-hating men. The Iago who thus dedicates himself as partner in the fulfillment of Othello's homicidal fantasies is, we learn, capable of fantasizing a bizarre amorous encounter between himself and Cassio (lines 429–41).

Othello comes at last to regard Iago as a "demi-devil" who has tempted Othello to damn himself "beneath all depth in hell"; Lodovico speaks of Iago in the closing lines of the play as a "hellish villain" (5.2.142, 309, 379); and Iago himself boasts that "When devils will the blackest sins put on, / They do suggest at first with heavenly shows, / As I do now" (2.3.345–7). Iago thus bears some affinity to both Vice and the devil, suggesting his relationship both to Othello's inner temptation and to a pre-existent evil force in the universe itself. Conversely, Desdemona is in Emilia's words an "angel," purely chaste; "So come my soul to bliss as I speak true" (5.2.134, 259). When Desdemona lands on Cyprus, she is greeted in words that echo the *Ave Maria:* "Hail to thee, lady! And the grace of heaven . . . Enwheel thee round" (2.1.87–9). These images introduce metaphorically a conflict of good and evil in which Othello, typical of fallen humanity, has chosen evil and destroyed the good at the prompting of a diabolical counselor. Again we see the heritage of the morality play, especially of the later morality play in which the Mankind figure was sometimes damned rather than saved. Even so, to allegorize *Othello* is to obscure and misread its clash of human passion. In fact, we see that the impulse to reduce human complexity to simplistic moral absolutes is a fatal weakness in Othello; by insisting on viewing Desdemona as a type or abstraction, he loses sight of her wonderful humanity. The theological issue of salvation or damnation is not relevant in dramatic terms; the play is not a homily on the dangers of jealousy. The metaphysical dimensions of a homiletic tradition are transmuted into human drama. Acknowledging these limitations, we can notwithstanding see a spiritual analogy in Iago's devil-like method of undoing his victims.

His trick resembles that of the similarly mischief-making Don John in *Much Ado About Nothing:* an optical illusion by which the blameless heroine is impugned as an adulteress. The concealed Othello must watch Cassio boasting of sexual triumphs and believe he is talking about Desdemona. Like the devil, Iago is given power over people's frail senses, especially the eyes. He can create illusions to induce Othello to see what Iago wants him to see, as Don John does with Claudio, but Othello's acceptance of the lie must be his own responsibility, a failure of his corrupted will. Iago practices on Othello with an a priori logic used before on Brabantio and Roderigo, urging the proneness of all mortals to sin and the alleged

unnaturalness of a black-white marriage. All women have appetites; Desdemona is a woman; hence, Desdemona has appetites. "The wine she drinks is made of grapes," he scoffs to Roderigo. "If she had been blessed, she would never have loved the Moor" (2.1.253–5). She is a Venetian, and "In Venice they do let God see the pranks / They dare not show their husbands" (3.3.216–17). Therefore, she, too, is a hypocrite; "She did deceive her father" (line 220). Most of all, it stands to reason that she must long for a man of her own race. Iago succeeds in getting Othello to concur: "And yet, how nature erring from itself—" (line 243). This proposition that Nature teaches all persons, including Desdemona, to seek a harmonious matching of "clime, complexion, and degree" strikes a responsive chord in Othello, since he knows that even though he has authority as a general serving his adopted city he is also black and in some senses a foreigner, an alien. "Haply, for I am black / And have not those soft parts of conversation / That chamberers have." Then, too, he is sensitive that he is older than she, "declined / Into the vale of years" (lines 246, 279–82), "the young affects / In me defunct" (1.3.266–7). And so, if one must conclude from the preceding that Desdemona will seek a lover, the only question is who. "This granted—as it is a most pregnant and unforced position—who stands so eminent in the degree of this fortune as Cassio does?" (2.1.237–9). Once Othello has accepted this syllogistic sequence of proofs, specious not through any lapse in logic but because the axiomatic assumptions about human nature are degraded and do not apply to Desdemona, Othello has arrived at an unshakable conclusion to which all subsequent evidence must be applied. "Villain, be sure thou prove my love a whore," he commissions Iago (3.3.375). Desdemona's innocent pleading for Cassio only makes things look worse. Cassio's reputed muttering while asleep, like the handkerchief seen in his possession or his giddy talk about his mistress Bianca, "speaks against her [Desdemona] with the other proofs" (line 456).

How has Othello fallen so far? His bliss with Desdemona as they are rejoined on Cyprus knows no limit. These two persons represent married love at its very best, erotic and spiritual, she enhancing his manliness, he cherishing her beauty and virtue. His blackness and age are positive images in him, despite earlier insinuations to the contrary. Indeed, we have no reason to suppose that Othello is what we would call "old," despite his worries about being "declined / Into the vale of years" and having lost the "young effects" of sexual desire; he appears to be middle-aged and vigorous, so much so that Desdemona is attracted to him sexually as well as in other ways. He is a man of public worthiness, of command, of self-assurance. Desdemona is the most domestic of Shakespeare's tragic heroines, even while she is also representative of so much that is transcendent. Husband and wife are bound happily in one of Shakespeare's few detailed portraits of serious commitment in marriage. Othello initially has the wisdom to know that Desdemona's feminine attractiveness ought not to be threatening to him: he need not be jealous because she is beautiful, "free of speech," and loves dancing and music, since "Where virtue is, these are more virtuous." Nor does he see any reason at first to fear her "revolt" simply because he is black and older than his wife; "she had eyes, and chose me" (3.3.197–203). Othello's self-assurance through the love he perceives in Desdemona is the strongest sign of his happiness in marriage.

What then gives way? We look at Iago for one important insight, but ultimately the cause must be in Othello himself. Arthur Kirsch has argued persuasively (in *Shakespeare and the Experience of Love*, 1981) that Othello's most grave failing is an insufficient regard for himself. It is in part an inability to counter the effects on him of a culture that regards him as an outsider; he is at last persuaded to see himself with the eyes of Venice, not just of Iago, but of Brabantio (who gladly entertains Othello until he has the presumption to elope with Brabantio's white daughter) and others. The resulting destruction of self-regard is devastating. Othello's jealousy stems from a profound suspicion that others cannot love him because he does not deem himself lovable.

Othello has loved Desdemona as an extention of himself, and, in his moments of greatest contentedness, his marriage is sustained by an idealized vision of himself serving as the object of his exalted romantic passion. When he destroys Desdemona, as he realizes with a terrible clarity, Othello destroys himself; the act is a prelude to his actual suicide. Iago's means of temptation, then, is to persuade Othello to regard himself with the eyes of Venice, to accept the view that Othello is himself alien and that any woman who loves him does so perversely. In Othello's tainted state of mind, Desdemona's very sexuality becomes an unbearable threat to him, her warmth and devotion a "proof" of disloyalty. Othello's most tortured speeches (3.4.57–77, 4.2.49–66) reveal the extent to which he equates the seemingly betraying woman, whom he has so depended on for happiness, with his own mother, who gave Othello's father a handkerchief and threatened him with loss of her love if he should lose it. Othello has briefly learned and then forgotten the precious art of harmonizing erotic passion and spiritual love, and, as these two great aims of love are driven apart in him, he comes to loathe and fear the sexuality that puts him so much in mind of his physical frailty and dependence on woman. The horror and pity of *Othello* rests, above all, in the spectacle of a love that was once so whole and noble made filthy by self-hatred. The tragic flaw thus lies in Othello's maleness, in his fear of betrayal by the innocent woman he loves, and his apparent need to degrade her for the very thing he finds desirable in her—a tendency so common among men that Freud, in the early twentieth century, could declare it to be "the most prevalent form of degradation in erotic life" (in Freud's *Sammlung*, volume 4).

The increasing surrender of Othello's judgment to passion can be measured in three successive trial scenes in the play: the entirely fair trial of Othello himself by the Venetian Senate concerning the elopement, Othello's trial of Cassio for drinking and rioting (when, ominously, Othello's "blood begins my safer guides to rule," 2.3.199), and finally the prejudged sentencing of Desdemona without providing her any opportunity to defend herself. In a corollary decline, Othello falls from the Christian compassion of the opening scenes (he customarily confesses to heaven "the vices of my blood," 1.3.125) to the pagan savagery of his vengeful and ritualistic execution of his wife. "My heart is turned to stone" (4.1.184–5), he vows, and at the play's end he grievingly characterizes himself as a "base Indian" who "threw a pearl away / Richer than all his tribe" (5.2.357–8). Iago knows that he must persuade Othello to sentence and to execute Desdemona himself, for only by active commitment to evil will Othello damn himself. In nothing does Iago so resemble the devil as in his wish to see Othello destroy the innocence and goodness on which his happiness depends.

The fate of some of the lesser characters echoes that of Othello, for Iago's evil intent is to "enmesh them all" (2.3.356). Cassio, in particular, is, like Othello, an attractive man with a single, vulnerable weakness—in his case, a fleshly appetite for wine and women. For him, alternately idolizing and depreciating women as he does, the gap between spiritual and sensual love remains vast, but he is essentially good-natured and trustworthy. His seemingly genial flaws lead to disaster, because they put him at the mercy of a remorseless enemy. Iago is, with fitting irony, the apostle of absolute self-control: "Our bodies are our gardens, to the which our wills are gardeners" (1.3.323–4). Thus, Cassio's tragedy is anything but a straightforward homily on the virtues of temperance. Similarly, Bianca is undone, not through any simple cause-and-effect punishment of her sexual conduct—she is, after all, fond of Cassio and loyal to him, even if he will not marry her—but because Iago is able to turn appearances against her. With his usual appeal to a priori logic, he builds a case that she and Cassio are in cahoots: "I do suspect this trash / To be a party in this injury . . . This is the fruits of whoring" (5.1.86–7, 118). Roderigo is another of Iago's victims, a contemptible one, led by the nose because he, too, has surrendered reason to passion. Emilia cannot escape Iago's evil influence and steals the handkerchief for him, despite knowing its value for Desdemona. Flaws are magnified into disasters by a remorseless evil intelligence. Men and women both must be ceaselessly circumspect; a good reputation is sooner lost than recovered. Emilia is a conventionally decent enough woman—she jests to Desdemona that she would be faithless in marriage only for a very high price—and yet her one small compromise with her conscience contributes to the murder of her mistress. Like Othello, she offers atonement too late, by denouncing her husband in a gesture of defiance toward male authority that says much about the tragic consequences of male mistrust of women. Desdemona is the only person in the play too good to be struck down through some inner flaw, which may explain why Iago is so intent on destroying her along with Othello and Cassio.

As a tragic hero, Othello obtains self-knowledge at a terrible price. He knows finally that what he has destroyed was ineffably good. The discovery is too late for him to make amends, and he dies by his own hand as atonement. The deaths of Othello and Desdemona are, in their separate ways, equally devastating: he is in part the victim of racism, though he nobly refuses to deny his own culpability, and she is the victim of sexism, lapsing sadly into the stereotypical role of passive and silent sufferer that the Venetian world expects of women. Despite the loss, however, Othello's reaffirmation of faith in Desdemona's goodness undoes what the devil-like Iago had most hoped to achieve: the separation of Othello from his loving trust in one who is good. In this important sense, Othello's self-knowledge is cathartic and a compensation for the terrible price he has paid. The very existence of a person as good as Desdemona gives the lie to Iago's creed that everyone has his or her price. She is the sacrificial victim who must die for Othello's loss of faith and, by dying, rekindle that faith. ("My life upon her faith!" Othello prophetically affirms, in response to her father's warning that she may deceive [1.3.297].) She cannot restore him to himself, for self-hatred has done its ugly work, but she is the means by which he understands at last the chimerical and wantonly destructive nature of his jealousy. His greatness appears in his acknowledgment of this truth and in the heroic struggle with which he has confronted an inner darkness we all share.

Onstage and in film and television, *Othello* proves itself to be jarringly relevant to modern concerns about racial conflict and about men's mistreatment of women. Janet Suzman chose to produce the play onstage and subsequently for educational television in Johannesburg, South Africa, at a time when apartheid was soon to be dismantled, even though that surprising if inevitable event was not yet discernible. A racially mixed audience came to see a racially mixed cast, with John Kani, a well-known South African Black actor, as Othello, and a very fair-haired South African actress as Desdemona. Iago unmistakably represented the mindset of a state police officer obsessed with preserving the purity of the White race and therefore venemous in his racial hatred of Othello for his miscegenated marriage with a White woman. The explosively powerful emotions of that production carry over into a memorable film version. Orson Welles's 1951 film version, recently remastered, featured Othello in blackface as the protagonist; so did Laurence Olivier's film of 1965, based on a National Theatre stage production of 1964 with Frank Finlay as Iago and Maggie Smith as Desdemona. Indeed, most Othellos onstage over the centuries have been White actors (including Edmund Kean, John Philip Kemble, Edwin Booth, Charles Macready, Edwin Forrest, Henry Irving, Tommaso Salvini, and Paul Scofield, many of whom also played Iago), with notable exceptions that include Ira Aldridge, Earle Hyman, and Paul Robeson. Robeson's galvanizing performances at the Savoy Theatre in 1930 with Peggy Ashcroft as Desdemona, and then in Margaret Webster's New York production of 1943–1945 with Uta Hagen as Desdemona and José Ferrer as Iago, helped establish the role of Othello as one that great Black actors could perform. Today racially mixed casting allows for all sorts of permutations, though Kenneth Branagh's recent film chooses the more recognizable pattern with Branagh himself as Iago and Laurence Fishburne as Othello. In another recent development, Emilia has stood out in several productions as the raisonneur and heroic figure in the play, speaking as she does on behalf of maltreated women, urging Desdemona to stand up for her rights. One recent Chicago production went so far as to rewrite the ending: Othello and Iago both survive unpunished for what they have done, while Desdemona and Emilia lie dead as their innocent victims. This deliberate and provocative overstatement might seem extreme to some viewers, but unquestionably did signal the direction of recent performance history of this profoundly disturbing play.

Othello, the Moor of Venice

The Names of the Actors

OTHELLO, *the Moor*
BRABANTIO, *[a senator,] father to Desdemona*
CASSIO, *an honorable lieutenant [to Othello]*
IAGO, *[Othello's ancient,] a villain*
RODERIGO, *a gulled gentleman*
DUKE OF VENICE
SENATORS *[of Venice]*
MONTANO, *Governor of Cyprus*
GENTLEMEN *of Cyprus*
LODOVICO *and* GRATIANO, *[kinsmen to Brabantio,] two*
noble Venetians
SAILORS
CLOWN

DESDEMONA, *[daughter to Brabantio and] wife to*
Othello
EMILIA, *wife to Iago*
BIANCA, *a courtesan [and mistress to Cassio]*

[A MESSENGER
A HERALD
A MUSICIAN

Servants, Attendants, Officers, Senators,
Musicians, Gentlemen

SCENE: *Venice; a seaport in Cyprus]*

1.1

Enter Roderigo and Iago.

RODERIGO
Tush, never tell me! I take it much unkindly   1
That thou, Iago, who hast had my purse
As if the strings were thine, shouldst know of this.   3
IAGO   'Sblood, but you'll not hear me.   4
If ever I did dream of such a matter,
Abhor me.
RODERIGO
Thou toldst me thou didst hold him in thy hate.   6
IAGO   Despise me
If I do not. Three great ones of the city,
In personal suit to make me his lieutenant,
Off-capped to him; and by the faith of man,
I know my price, I am worth no worse a place.
But he, as loving his own pride and purposes,
Evades them with a bombast circumstance   14

Horribly stuffed with epithets of war,   15
And, in conclusion,
Nonsuits my mediators. For, "Certes," says he,   17
"I have already chose my officer."
And what was he?
Forsooth, a great arithmetician,   20
One Michael Cassio, a Florentine,
A fellow almost damned in a fair wife,   22
That never set a squadron in the field
Nor the division of a battle knows   24
More than a spinster—unless the bookish theoric,   25
Wherein the togaed consuls can propose   26
As masterly as he. Mere prattle without practice
Is all his soldiership. But he, sir, had th'election;
And I, of whom his eyes had seen the proof   29
At Rhodes, at Cyprus, and on other grounds

1.1 Location: Venice. A street.
1 never tell me (An expression of incredulity, like "tell me another one.")   **3 this** i.e., Desdemona's elopement.   **4 'Sblood** By His (Christ's) blood   **6 him** Othello   **14 bombast circumstance** wordy evasion. (*Bombast* is cotton padding.)

15 epithets of war military expressions   **17 Nonsuits** rejects the petition of.   **Certes** Certainly   **20 arithmetician** i.e., a man whose military knowledge is merely theoretical, based on books of tactics   **22 A . . . wife** (Cassio does not seem to be married, but his counterpart in Shakespeare's source does have a woman in his house. See also 4.1.131.)   **24 division of a battle** disposition of a military unit   **25 a spinster** i.e., a housewife, one whose regular occupation is spinning.   **theoric** theory   **26 togaed consuls** toga-wearing counselors or senators.   **propose** discuss   **29 his** Othello's

Christened and heathen, must be beleed and calmed   31
By debitor and creditor. This countercaster,   32
He, in good time, must his lieutenant be,   33
And I—God bless the mark!—His Moorship's ancient.   34

RODERIGO
By heaven, I rather would have been his hangman.   35

IAGO
Why, there's no remedy. 'Tis the curse of service;
Preferment goes by letter and affection,   37
And not by old gradation, where each second   38
Stood heir to th' first. Now, sir, be judge yourself
Whether I in any just term am affined   40
To love the Moor.

RODERIGO   I would not follow him then.

IAGO   Oh, sir, content you.   43
I follow him to serve my turn upon him.
We cannot all be masters, nor all masters
Cannot be truly followed. You shall mark   46
Many a duteous and knee-crooking knave
That, doting on his own obsequious bondage,
Wears out his time, much like his master's ass,
For naught but provender, and when he's old,
    cashiered.   50
Whip me such honest knaves. Others there are   51
Who, trimmed in forms and visages of duty,   52
Keep yet their hearts attending on themselves,
And, throwing but shows of service on their lords,
Do well thrive by them, and when they have lined
    their coats,   55
Do themselves homage. These fellows have some
    soul,   56
And such a one do I profess myself. For, sir,
It is as sure as you are Roderigo,
Were I the Moor I would not be Iago.   59
In following him, I follow but myself—
Heaven is my judge, not I for love and duty,
But seeming so for my peculiar end.   62
For when my outward action doth demonstrate
The native act and figure of my heart   64
In compliment extern, 'tis not long after   65

But I will wear my heart upon my sleeve
For daws to peck at. I am not what I am.   67

RODERIGO
What a full fortune does the thick-lips owe   68
If he can carry't thus!

IAGO   Call up her father.   69
Rouse him, make after him, poison his delight,
Proclaim him in the streets; incense her kinsmen,
And, though he in a fertile climate dwell,   72
Plague him with flies. Though that his joy be joy,   73
Yet throw such changes of vexation on't   74
As it may lose some color.   75

RODERIGO
Here is her father's house. I'll call aloud.

IAGO
Do, with like timorous accent and dire yell   77
As when, by night and negligence, the fire   78
Is spied in populous cities.

RODERIGO
What ho, Brabantio! Signor Brabantio, ho!

IAGO
Awake! What ho, Brabantio! Thieves, thieves, thieves!
Look to your house, your daughter, and your bags!
Thieves, thieves!   83

Brabantio [enters] above [at a window].

BRABANTIO
What is the reason of this terrible summons?
What is the matter there?

RODERIGO
Signor, is all your family within?

IAGO
Are your doors locked?

BRABANTIO   Why, wherefore ask you this?

IAGO
Zounds, sir, you're robbed. For shame, put on your
    gown!   88
Your heart is burst; you have lost half your soul.
Even now, now, very now, an old black ram
Is tupping your white ewe. Arise, arise!   91
Awake the snorting citizens with the bell,   92
Or else the devil will make a grandsire of you.   93
Arise, I say!

BRABANTIO   What, have you lost your wits?

RODERIGO
Most reverend signor, do you know my voice?

---

31 **beleed and calmed** left to leeward without wind, becalmed. (A sailing metaphor.)   32 **debitor and creditor** (A name for a system of bookkeeping, here used as a contemptuous nickname for Cassio.) **countercaster** i.e., bookkeeper, one who tallies with *counters*, or "metal disks." (Said contemptuously.)   33 **in good time** opportunely, i.e., forsooth   34 **God bless the mark** (Perhaps originally a formula to ward off evil; here an expression of impatience.)   **ancient** standard-bearer, ensign.   35 **his hangman** the executioner of him.   37 **Preferment** promotion.   **letter and affection** personal influence and favoritism   38 **old gradation** step-by-step seniority, the traditional way   40 **term** respect.   **affined** bound   43 **content you** don't you worry about that.   46 **truly** faithfully   50 **cashiered** dismissed from service.   51 **Whip me** Whip, as far as I'm concerned   52 **trimmed . . . duty** dressed up in the mere form and show of dutifulness   55 **lined their coats** i.e., stuffed their purses   56 **Do themselves homage** i.e., attend to self-interest solely.   59 **Were . . . Iago** i.e., if I were able to assume command, I certainly would not choose to remain a subordinate, or, I would keep a suspicious eye on a flattering subordinate.   62 **peculiar** particular, personal   64 **native** innate.   **figure** shape, intent   65 **compliment extern** outward show (conforming in this case to the inner workings and intention of the heart)

67 **daws** small crowlike birds, proverbially stupid and avaricious. **I am not what I am** i.e., I am not one who wears his heart on his sleeve.   68 **full** swelling.   **thick-lips** (Elizabethans often applied the term "Moor" to Negroes.)   **owe** own   69 **carry't thus** carry this off.   72–3 **though . . . flies** though he seems prosperous and happy now, vex him with misery.   73 **Though . . . be joy** Although he seems fortunate and happy. (Repeats the idea of line 72.)   74 **changes of vexation** vexing changes   75 **As . . . color** that may cause it to lose some of its first gloss.   77 **timorous** frightening   78 **As . . . fire** as when a fire, having gained hold by negligence at night   83.1 *at a window* (This stage direction, from the Quarto, probably calls for an appearance on the gallery above and rearstage.)   88 **Zounds** By His (Christ's) wounds   91 **tupping** covering, copulating with. (Said of sheep.)   92 **snorting** snoring   93 **the devil** (The devil was conventionally pictured as black.)

BRABANTIO   Not I. What are you?

RODERIGO   My name is Roderigo.

BRABANTIO   The worser welcome.
I have charged thee not to haunt about my doors.
In honest plainness thou hast heard me say
My daughter is not for thee; and now, in madness,
Being full of supper and distemp'ring drafts,   102
Upon malicious bravery dost thou come   103
To start my quiet.

RODERIGO
Sir, sir, sir—

BRABANTIO   But thou must needs be sure
My spirits and my place have in their power   106
To make this bitter to thee.

RODERIGO   Patience, good sir.

BRABANTIO
What tell'st thou me of robbing? This is Venice;
My house is not a grange.

RODERIGO   Most grave Brabantio,   109
In simple and pure soul I come to you.   110

IAGO   Zounds, sir, you are one of those that will not
serve God if the devil bid you. Because we come to do
you service and you think we are ruffians, you'll have
your daughter covered with a Barbary horse; you'll   114
have your nephews neigh to you; you'll have coursers   115
for cousins and jennets for germans.   116

BRABANTIO   What profane wretch art thou?

IAGO   I am one, sir, that comes to tell you your daughter
and the Moor are now making the beast with two
backs.

BRABANTIO
Thou art a villain.

IAGO   You are—a senator.   121

BRABANTIO
This thou shalt answer. I know thee, Roderigo.   122

RODERIGO
Sir, I will answer anything. But I beseech you,
If't be your pleasure and most wise consent—   124
As partly I find it is—that your fair daughter,
At this odd-even and dull watch o'th' night,   126
Transported with no worse nor better guard   127
But with a knave of common hire, a gondolier,   128
To the gross clasps of a lascivious Moor—
If this be known to you and your allowance   130
We then have done you bold and saucy wrongs.   131
But if you know not this, my manners tell me
We have your wrong rebuke. Do not believe

That, from the sense of all civility,   134
I thus would play and trifle with your reverence.   135
Your daughter, if you have not given her leave,
I say again, hath made a gross revolt,
Tying her duty, beauty, wit, and fortunes   138
In an extravagant and wheeling stranger   139
Of here and everywhere. Straight satisfy yourself.   140
If she be in her chamber or your house,
Let loose on me the justice of the state
For thus deluding you.

BRABANTIO [calling]   Strike on the tinder, ho!   144
Give me a taper! Call up all my people!
This accident is not unlike my dream.   146
Belief of it oppresses me already.
Light, I say, light!   Exit [above].

IAGO   Farewell, for I must leave you.
It seems not meet nor wholesome to my place   149
To be produced—as, if I stay, I shall—   150
Against the Moor. For I do know the state,
However this may gall him with some check,   152
Cannot with safety cast him, for he's embarked   153
With such loud reason to the Cyprus wars,   154
Which even now stands in act, that, for their souls,   155
Another of his fathom they have none   156
To lead their business; in which regard,   157
Though I do hate him as I do hell pains,
Yet for necessity of present life   159
I must show out a flag and sign of love,
Which is indeed but sign. That you shall surely find
him,
Lead to the Sagittary the raisèd search,   162
And there will I be with him. So farewell.   Exit. 163

Enter [below] Brabantio [in his nightgown] with
servants and torches.

BRABANTIO
It is too true an evil. Gone she is;
And what's to come of my despisèd time   165
Is naught but bitterness. Now, Roderigo,
Where didst thou see her?—Oh, unhappy girl!—
With the Moor, say'st thou?—Who would be a father!—
How didst thou know 'twas she?—Oh, she deceives
me
Past thought!—What said she to you?—Get more
tapers.
Raise all my kindred.—Are they married, think you?

---

102 **distemp'ring** intoxicating   103 **Upon malicious bravery** with
hostile intent to defy me   104 **start** startle, disrupt   106 **My . . .
power** my temperament and my authority of office have it in their
power   109 **grange** isolated country house.   110 **simple** sincere
114 **Barbary** from northern Africa (and hence associated with Othello)   115 **nephews** i.e., grandsons   115–16 **you'll . . . germans**
you'll consent to have powerful horses for kinfolks and small Spanish horses for near relatives.   121 **a senator** (Said with mock politeness, as though the word itself were an insult.)   122 **answer** be held
accountable for.   124 **wise** well-informed   126 **At . . . night** at this
hour that is between day and night, neither the one nor the other
127 **with** by   128 **But with a knave** than by a low fellow, a servant
130 **and your allowance** and has your permission   131 **saucy**
insolent

134 **from** contrary to.   **civility** good manners, decency   135 **your
reverence** (1) the respect due to you (2) Your Reverence.   138 **wit**
intelligence   139–40 **In . . . everywhere** to a wandering and
vagabond foreigner of uncertain origins.   140 **Straight** Straightway
144 **tinder** charred linen ignited by a spark from flint and steel, used
to light torches or *tapers* (lines 145, 170)   146 **accident** occurrence,
event   149 **meet** fitting.   **place** position (as ensign)   150 **produced**
produced (as a witness)   152 **gall** rub; oppress.   **check** rebuke
153 **cast** dismiss.   **embarked** engaged   154 **loud** urgent   155 **stands
in act** have started.   **for their souls** to save their souls   156 **fathom**
i.e., ability, depth of experience   157 **in which regard** out of regard
for which   159 **life** livelihood   162 **Sagittary** (An inn or house
where Othello and Desdemona are staying, named for its sign of
Sagittarius, or Centaur.)   **raisèd search** search party roused out of
sleep   163.1 **nightgown** dressing gown. (This costuming is specified
in the Quarto text.)   165 **time** i.e., remainder of life

RODERIGO Truly, I think they are.

BRABANTIO
Oh, heaven! How got she out? Oh, treason of the
  blood!
Fathers, from hence trust not your daughters' minds
By what you see them act. Is there not charms   175
By which the property of youth and maidhood   176
May be abused? Have you not read, Roderigo,   177
Of some such thing?

RODERIGO   Yes, sir, I have indeed.

BRABANTIO
Call up my brother.—Oh, would you had had her!—
Some one way, some another.—Do you know
Where we may apprehend her and the Moor?

RODERIGO
I think I can discover him, if you please   182
To get good guard and go along with me.

BRABANTIO
Pray you, lead on. At every house I'll call;
I may command at most.—Get weapons, ho!   185
And raise some special officers of night.—
On, good Roderigo. I will deserve your pains.   187

Exeunt.

❧

1.2

Enter Othello, Iago, attendants with torches.

IAGO
Though in the trade of war I have slain men,
Yet do I hold it very stuff o'th' conscience
To do no contrived murder. I lack iniquity   2
Sometimes to do me service. Nine or ten times   3
I had thought t'have yerked him here under the ribs.   5

OTHELLO
'Tis better as it is.

IAGO   Nay, but he prated,
And spoke such scurvy and provoking terms
Against your honor
That, with the little godliness I have,
I did full hard forbear him. But, I pray you, sir,   10
Are you fast married? Be assured of this,
That the magnifico is much beloved,   12
And hath in his effect a voice potential   13
As double as the Duke's. He will divorce you,
Or put upon you what restraint or grievance
The law, with all his might to enforce it on,
Will give him cable.

OTHELLO   Let him do his spite.   17
My services which I have done the seigniory   18

Shall out-tongue his complaints. 'Tis yet to know—   19
Which, when I know that boasting is an honor,
I shall promulgate—I fetch my life and being
From men of royal siege, and my demerits   22
May speak unbonneted to as proud a fortune   23
As this that I have reached. For know, Iago,
But that I love the gentle Desdemona,
I would not my unhoused free condition   26
Put into circumscription and confine   27
For the sea's worth. But look, what lights come yond?   28

Enter Cassio [and officers] with torches.

IAGO
Those are the raisèd father and his friends.
You were best go in.

OTHELLO   Not I. I must be found.
My parts, my title, and my perfect soul   31
Shall manifest me rightly. Is it they?

IAGO By Janus, I think no.   33

OTHELLO
The servants of the Duke? And my lieutenant?
The goodness of the night upon you, friends!
What is the news?

CASSIO   The Duke does greet you, General,
And he requires your haste-post-haste appearance
Even on the instant.

OTHELLO   What is the matter, think you?

CASSIO
Something from Cyprus, as I may divine.   39
It is a business of some heat. The galleys   40
Have sent a dozen sequent messengers   41
This very night at one another's heels,
And many of the consuls, raised and met,   43
Are at the Duke's already. You have been hotly called
  for;
When, being not at your lodging to be found,
The Senate hath sent about three several quests   46
To search you out.

OTHELLO   'Tis well I am found by you.
I will but spend a word here in the house
And go with you.   [*Exit.*]

CASSIO   Ancient, what makes he here?   49

IAGO
Faith, he tonight hath boarded a land carrack.   50
If it prove lawful prize, he's made forever.   51

---

175 charms spells   **176 property** special quality, nature   **177 abused** deceived.   **182 discover** reveal, uncover   **185 command** demand assistance   **187 deserve** show gratitude for
1.2. Location: Venice. Another street, before Othello's lodgings.
2 very stuff essence, basic material. (Continuing the metaphor of *trade* from line 1.)   **3 contrived** premeditated   **5 yerked** stabbed.   **him** i.e., Roderigo   **10 I . . . him** I restrained myself with great difficulty from assaulting him.   **12 magnifico** Venetian grandee, i.e., Brabantio   **13 in his effect** at his command.   **potential** powerful   **17 cable** i.e., scope.   **18 seigniory** Venetian government

19 yet to know not yet widely known   **22 siege** i.e., rank. (Literally, a seat used by a person of distinction.)   **demerits** deserts   **23 unbonneted** without removing the hat, i.e., on equal terms (? Or "with hat off," "in all due modesty.")   **26 unhoused** unconfined, undomesticated   **27 circumscription and confine** restriction and confinement   **28 the sea's worth** all the riches at the bottom of the sea.   **28.1** *officers* (The Quarto text specifies, "*Enter* Cassio *with lights, Officers, and torches.*")   **31 My . . . soul** My natural gifts, my position or reputation, and my unflawed conscience   **33 Janus** Roman two-faced god of beginnings   **39 divine** guess.   **40 heat** urgency.   **41 sequent** successive   **43 consuls** senators   **46 about** all over the city.   **several** separate   **49 makes** does   **50 boarded** gone aboard and seized as an act of piracy. (With sexual suggestion.)   **carrack** large merchant ship   **51 prize** booty

CASSIO
    I do not understand.
IAGO   He's married.
CASSIO   To who?

                    [Enter Othello.]

IAGO
    Marry, to—Come, Captain, will you go?   53
OTHELLO   Have with you.   54
CASSIO
    Here comes another troop to seek for you.   55

            Enter Brabantio, Roderigo, with officers and
            torches.

IAGO
    It is Brabantio. General, be advised.   56
    He comes to bad intent.
OTHELLO   Holla! Stand there!
RODERIGO
    Signor, it is the Moor.
BRABANTIO   Down with him, thief!
                    [They draw on both sides.]

IAGO
    You, Roderigo! Come, sir, I am for you.
OTHELLO
    Keep up your bright swords, for the dew will rust
        them.   60
    Good signor, you shall more command with years
    Than with your weapons.
BRABANTIO
    O thou foul thief, where hast thou stowed my
        daughter?
    Damned as thou art, thou hast enchanted her!
    For I'll refer me to all things of sense,   65
    If she in chains of magic were not bound
    Whether a maid so tender, fair, and happy,
    So opposite to marriage that she shunned
    The wealthy curlèd darlings of our nation,
    Would ever have, t'incur a general mock,
    Run from her guardage to the sooty bosom   71
    Of such a thing as thou—to fear, not to delight.
    Judge me the world if 'tis not gross in sense   73
    That thou hast practiced on her with foul charms,
    Abused her delicate youth with drugs or minerals   75
    That weakens motion. I'll have't disputed on;   76
    'Tis probable and palpable to thinking.
    I therefore apprehend and do attach thee   78
    For an abuser of the world, a practicer   79
    Of arts inhibited and out of warrant.—   80
    Lay hold upon him! If he do resist,

Subdue him at his peril.
OTHELLO   Hold your hands,
    Both you of my inclining and the rest.   83
    Were it my cue to fight, I should have known it
    Without a prompter.—Whither will you that I go
    To answer this your charge?
BRABANTIO   To prison, till fit time
    Of law and course of direct session   88
    Call thee to answer.
OTHELLO   What if I do obey?
    How may the Duke be therewith satisfied,
    Whose messengers are here about my side
    Upon some present business of the state
    To bring me to him?
OFFICER   'Tis true, most worthy signor.
    The Duke's in council, and your noble self,
    I am sure, is sent for.
BRABANTIO   How? The Duke in council?
    In this time of the night? Bring him away.   96
    Mine's not an idle cause. The Duke himself,   97
    Or any of my brothers of the state,
    Cannot but feel this wrong as 'twere their own;
    For if such actions may have passage free,   100
    Bondslaves and pagans shall our statesmen be.
                                            Exeunt.

                            ♣

1.3

            Enter Duke [and] Senators [and sit at a table, with
            lights], and Officers. [The Duke and Senators
            are reading dispatches.]

DUKE
    There is no composition in these news   1
    That gives them credit.
FIRST SENATOR   Indeed, they are disproportioned.   3
    My letters say a hundred and seven galleys.
DUKE
    And mine, a hundred forty.
SECOND SENATOR   And mine, two hundred.
    But though they jump not on a just account—   6
    As in these cases, where the aim reports   7
    'Tis oft with difference—yet do they all confirm
    A Turkish fleet, and bearing up to Cyprus.
DUKE
    Nay, it is possible enough to judgment.
    I do not so secure me in the error   11
    But the main article I do approve   12
    In fearful sense.

---

53 **Marry** (An oath, originally "by the Virgin Mary"; here used
with wordplay on *married*.)   54 **Have with you** i.e., Let's go.
55.1–2 *officers and torches* (The Quarto text calls for "*others with lights
and weapons.*")   56 **be advised** be on your guard.   60 **Keep up** Keep
in the sheath   65 **I'll . . . sense** I'll submit my case to one and all
71 **guardage** guardianship   73 **gross in sense** obvious
75 **minerals** i.e., poisons   76 **weakens motion** impair the vital faculties.   **disputed on** argued in court by professional counsel, debated
by experts   78 **attach** arrest   79 **abuser** deceiver   80 **arts inhibited**
prohibited arts, black magic.   **out of warrant** illegal.

83 **inclining** following, party   88 **course of direct session** regular or
specially convened legal proceedings   96 **away** right along.   97 **idle**
trifling   100 **may . . . free** are allowed to go unchecked
1.3. Location: Venice. A council chamber.
0.1–2 *Enter . . . Officers* (The Quarto text calls for the Duke and senators to "*set at a Table with lights and Attendants.*")   1 **composition** consistency   3 **disproportioned** inconsistent.   6 **jump** agree.   **just** exact
7 **the aim** conjecture   11–12 **I do not . . . approve** I do not take such
(false) comfort in the discrepancies that I fail to perceive the main
point, i.e., that the Turkish fleet is threatening

SAILOR (*within*)   What ho, what ho, what ho!

Enter Sailor.

OFFICER   A messenger from the galleys.

DUKE   Now, what's the business?

SAILOR
The Turkish preparation makes for Rhodes.   16
So was I bid report here to the state
By Signor Angelo.

DUKE
How say you by this change?

FIRST SENATOR   This cannot be   19
By no assay of reason. 'Tis a pageant   20
To keep us in false gaze. When we consider   21
Th'importancy of Cyprus to the Turk,
And let ourselves again but understand
That, as it more concerns the Turk than Rhodes,
So may he with more facile question bear it,   25
For that it stands not in such warlike brace,   26
But altogether lacks th'abilities   27
That Rhodes is dressed in—if we make thought of this,   28
We must not think the Turk is so unskillful   29
To leave that latest which concerns him first,   30
Neglecting an attempt of ease and gain
To wake and wage a danger profitless.   32

DUKE
Nay, in all confidence, he's not for Rhodes.

OFFICER   Here is more news.

Enter a Messenger.

MESSENGER
The Ottomites, reverend and gracious,
Steering with due course toward the isle of Rhodes,
Have there injointed them with an after fleet.   37

FIRST SENATOR
Ay, so I thought. How many, as you guess?

MESSENGER
Of thirty sail; and now they do restem   39
Their backward course, bearing with frank
    appearance   40
Their purposes toward Cyprus. Signor Montano,
Your trusty and most valiant servitor,   42
With his free duty recommends you thus,   43
And prays you to believe him.

DUKE   'Tis certain then for Cyprus.
Marcus Luccicos, is not he in town?

FIRST SENATOR   He's now in Florence.

DUKE
Write from us to him, post-post-haste. Dispatch.

FIRST SENATOR
Here comes Brabantio and the valiant Moor.

*Enter Brabantio, Othello, Cassio, Iago,
Roderigo, and officers.*

DUKE
Valiant Othello, we must straight employ you   50
Against the general enemy Ottoman.   51
[*To Brabantio*] I did not see you; welcome, gentle
    signor.   52
We lacked your counsel and your help tonight.

BRABANTIO
So did I yours. Good Your Grace, pardon me;
Neither my place nor aught I heard of business   55
Hath raised me from my bed, nor doth the general
    care
Take hold on me, for my particular grief   57
Is of so floodgate and o'erbearing nature   58
That it engluts and swallows other sorrows   59
And it is still itself.

DUKE   Why, what's the matter?   60

BRABANTIO
My daughter! Oh, my daughter!

DUKE AND SENATORS   Dead?

BRABANTIO   Ay, to me.
She is abused, stol'n from me, and corrupted   62
By spells and medicines bought of mountebanks;
For nature so preposterously to err,
Being not deficient, blind, or lame of sense,   65
Sans witchcraft could not.   66

DUKE
Whoe'er he be that in this foul proceeding
Hath thus beguiled your daughter of herself,
And you of her, the bloody book of law
You shall yourself read in the bitter letter
After your own sense—yea, though our proper son   71
Stood in your action.

BRABANTIO   Humbly I thank Your Grace.   72
Here is the man, this Moor, whom now it seems
Your special mandate for the state affairs
Hath hither brought.

ALL   We are very sorry for't.

DUKE [*to Othello*]
What, in your own part, can you say to this?

BRABANTIO   Nothing, but this is so.

OTHELLO
Most potent, grave, and reverend signors,
My very noble and approved good masters: 79
That I have ta'en away this old man's daughter,
It is most true; true, I have married her.
The very head and front of my offending   82

16 preparation fleet prepared for battle   19 by about   20 assay test.
pageant mere show   21 in false gaze looking the wrong way.   25 So
may . . . it so also he (the Turk) can more easily capture it (Cyprus)
26 For that since.   brace state of defense   27 th'abilities the means
of self-defense   28 dressed in equipped with   29 unskillful deficient in judgment   30 latest last   32 wake and wage stir up and risk
37 injointed them joined themselves.   after second, following
39–40 restem . . . course retrace their original course   40 frank
appearance undisguised intent   42 servitor officer under your command   43 free duty freely given and loyal service.   recommends
commends himself and reports to

50 straight straightway   51 general enemy universal enemy to all
Christendom   52 gentle noble   55 place official position   57 particular personal   58 floodgate i.e., overwhelming (as when floodgates
are opened)   59 engluts engulfs   60 is still itself remains undiminished.   62 abused deceived   65 deficient defective.   lame of sense
deficient in sensory perception   66 Sans without   71 After . . .
sense according to your own interpretation.   our proper my own
72 Stood . . . action were under your accusation.   79 approved
proved, esteemed   82 head and front height and breadth, entire
extent

Hath this extent, no more. Rude am I in my speech,　83
And little blessed with the soft phrase of peace;
For since these arms of mine had seven years' pith,　85
Till now some nine moons wasted, they have used　86
Their dearest action in the tented field;　87
And little of this great world can I speak
More than pertains to feats of broils and battle,
And therefore little shall I grace my cause
In speaking for myself. Yet, by your gracious patience,
I will a round unvarnished tale deliver　92
Of my whole course of love—what drugs, what
　　charms,
What conjuration, and what mighty magic,
For such proceeding I am charged withal,　95
I won his daughter.

BRABANTIO　　　　　　　　A maiden never bold;
Of spirit so still and quiet that her motion　97
Blushed at herself; and she, in spite of nature,　98
Of years, of country, credit, everything,　99
To fall in love with what she feared to look on!
It is a judgment maimed and most imperfect
That will confess perfection so could err　102
Against all rules of nature, and must be driven
To find out practices of cunning hell　104
Why this should be. I therefore vouch again　105
That with some mixtures powerful o'er the blood,　106
Or with some dram conjured to this effect,　107
He wrought upon her.

DUKE　　　　　　　　　To vouch this is no proof,
Without more wider and more overt test　109
Than these thin habits and poor likelihoods　110
Of modern seeming do prefer against him.　111

FIRST SENATOR　But Othello, speak.
Did you by indirect and forcèd courses　113
Subdue and poison this young maid's affections?
Or came it by request and such fair question　115
As soul to soul affordeth?

OTHELLO　　　　　　　　I do beseech you,
Send for the lady to the Sagittary
And let her speak of me before her father.
If you do find me foul in her report,
The trust, the office I do hold of you
Not only take away, but let your sentence
Even fall upon my life.

DUKE　　　　　　　Fetch Desdemona hither.

OTHELLO　[to Iago]
Ancient, conduct them. You best know the place.
　　　　　　　　　[Exeunt Iago and attendants.]

And, till she come, as truly as to heaven
I do confess the vices of my blood,　125
So justly to your grave ears I'll present　126
How I did thrive in this fair lady's love,
And she in mine.

DUKE　Say it, Othello.

OTHELLO
Her father loved me, oft invited me,
Still questioned me the story of my life　131
From year to year—the battles, sieges, fortunes
That I have passed.
I ran it through, even from my boyish days
To th' very moment that he bade me tell it,
Wherein I spoke of most disastrous chances,
Of moving accidents by flood and field,　137
Of hairbreadth scapes i'th'imminent deadly breach,　138
Of being taken by the insolent foe
And sold to slavery, of my redemption thence,
And portance in my travels' history,　141
Wherein of antres vast and deserts idle,　142
Rough quarries, rocks, and hills whose heads touch
　　heaven,　143
It was my hint to speak—such was my process—　144
And of the Cannibals that each other eat,
The Anthropophagi, and men whose heads　146
Do grow beneath their shoulders. These things to hear
Would Desdemona seriously incline;
But still the house affairs would draw her thence,
Which ever as she could with haste dispatch
She'd come again, and with a greedy ear
Devour up my discourse. Which I, observing,
Took once a pliant hour, and found good means　153
To draw from her a prayer of earnest heart
That I would all my pilgrimage dilate,　155
Whereof by parcels she had something heard,　156
But not intentively. I did consent,　157
And often did beguile her of her tears,
When I did speak of some distressful stroke
That my youth suffered. My story being done,
She gave me for my pains a world of sighs.
She swore, in faith, 'twas strange, 'twas passing
　　strange,　162
'Twas pitiful, 'twas wondrous pitiful.
She wished she had not heard it, yet she wished
That heaven had made her such a man. She thanked
　　me,　165
And bade me, if I had a friend that loved her,
I should but teach him how to tell my story,
And that would woo her. Upon this hint I spake.　168
She loved me for the dangers I had passed,

83 Rude Unpolished　85 since . . . pith i.e., since I was seven. (Pith means "strength, vigor.")　86 Till . . . wasted until some nine months ago (since when Othello has evidently not been on active duty, but in Venice)　87 dearest most valuable　92 round plain　95 withal with　97–8 her . . . herself i.e., she blushed easily at herself. (Motion can suggest the impulse of the soul or of the emotions, or physical movement.)　99 years i.e., difference in age.　credit virtuous reputation　102 confess concede (that)　104 practices plots　105 vouch assert　106 blood passions　107 dram . . . effect dose made by magical spells to have this effect　109 more wider fuller.　test testimony　110 habits garments, i.e., appearances.　poor likelihoods weak inferences　111 modern seeming commonplace assumption.　prefer bring forth　113 forcèd courses means used against her will　115 question conversation

125 blood passions, human nature　126 justly truthfully, accurately　131 Still continually　137 moving accidents stirring happenings　138 i'th'imminent . . . breach in death-threatening gaps made in a fortification　141 portance conduct　142 antres caverns.　idle barren, desolate　143 Rough quarries rugged rock formations　144 hint occasion, opportunity　146 Anthropophagi man-eaters. (A term from Pliny's Natural History.)　153 pliant well-suiting　155 dilate relate in detail　156 by parcels piecemeal　157 intentively with full attention, continuously.　162 passing exceedingly　165 made her (1) created her to be (2) made for her　168 hint opportunity. (Othello does not mean that she was dropping hints.)

And I loved her that she did pity them.
This only is the witchcraft I have used.
Here comes the lady. Let her witness it.

Enter Desdemona, Iago, [and] attendants.

DUKE
I think this tale would win my daughter too.
Good Brabantio,
Take up this mangled matter at the best.   175
Men do their broken weapons rather use
Than their bare hands.

BRABANTIO   I pray you, hear her speak.
If she confess that she was half the wooer,
Destruction on my head if my bad blame
Light on the man!—Come hither, gentle mistress.
Do you perceive in all this noble company
Where most you owe obedience?

DESDEMONA   My noble father,
I do perceive here a divided duty.
To you I am bound for life and education;   184
My life and education both do learn me   185
How to respect you. You are the lord of duty;   186
I am hitherto your daughter. But here's my husband,
And so much duty as my mother showed
To you, preferring you before her father,
So much I challenge that I may profess   190
Due to the Moor my lord.

BRABANTIO   God be with you! I have done.
Please it Your Grace, on to the state affairs.
I had rather to adopt a child than get it.   194
Come hither, Moor.   [*He joins the hands of Othello
                                      and Desdemona.*]
I here do give thee that with all my heart   196
Which, but thou hast already, with all my heart   197
I would keep from thee.—For your sake, jewel,   198
I am glad at soul I have no other child,
For thy escape would teach me tyranny,   200
To hang clogs on them.—I have done, my lord.   201

DUKE
Let me speak like yourself, and lay a sentence   202
Which, as a grece or step, may help these lovers   203
Into your favor.
When remedies are past, the griefs are ended   205
By seeing the worst, which late on hopes depended.   206
To mourn a mischief that is past and gone   207
Is the next way to draw new mischief on.   208
What cannot be preserved when fortune takes,   209
Patience her injury a mock'ry makes.   210

The robbed that smiles steals something from the thief;
He robs himself that spends a bootless grief.   212

BRABANTIO
So let the Turk of Cyprus us beguile,
We lose it not, so long as we can smile.
He bears the sentence well that nothing bears   215
But the free comfort which from thence he hears,   216
But he bears both the sentence and the sorrow   217
That, to pay grief, must of poor patience borrow.   218
These sentences, to sugar or to gall,   219
Being strong on both sides, are equivocal.   220
But words are words. I never yet did hear
That the bruisèd heart was piercèd through the ear.   222
I humbly beseech you, proceed to th'affairs of state.

DUKE   The Turk with a most mighty preparation makes
for Cyprus. Othello, the fortitude of the place is best 225
known to you; and though we have there a substitute   226
of most allowed sufficiency, yet opinion, a sovereign 227
mistress of effects, throws a more safer voice on you. 228
You must therefore be content to slubber the gloss of 229
your new fortunes with this more stubborn and   230
boisterous expedition.   231

OTHELLO
The tyrant custom, most grave senators,
Hath made the flinty and steel couch of war
My thrice-driven bed of down. I do agnize   234
A natural and prompt alacrity
I find in hardness, and do undertake   236
These present wars against the Ottomites.
Most humbly therefore bending to your state,   238
I crave fit disposition for my wife,
Due reference of place and exhibition,   240
With such accommodation and besort   241
As levels with her breeding.   242

DUKE
Why, at her father's.

BRABANTIO   I will not have it so.

OTHELLO
Nor I.

DESDEMONA   Nor I. I would not there reside,
To put my father in impatient thoughts
By being in his eye. Most gracious Duke,
To my unfolding lend your prosperous ear,   247

---

175 **Take . . . best** make the best of a bad bargain. 184 **education** upbringing 185 **learn** teach 186 **of duty** to whom duty is due 190 **challenge** claim 194 **get** beget 196 **with all my heart** wherein my whole affection has been engaged 197 **with all my heart** willingly, gladly 198 **For your sake** Because of you 200 **escape** elopement 201 **clogs** (Literally, blocks of wood fastened to the legs of criminals or animals to inhibit escape.) 202 **like yourself** i.e., as you would, in your proper temper. **lay a sentence** apply a maxim 203 **grece** step 205–6 **When . . . depended** When all hope of remedy is past, our sorrows are ended by realizing that the worst has already happened which lately we hoped would not happen. 207 **mischief** misfortune, injury 208 **next** nearest 209–10 **What . . . makes** When fortune takes away what cannot be saved, patience makes a mockery of fortune's wrongdoing.

212 **spends a bootless grief** indulges in unavailing grief. 215–18 **He bears . . . borrow** A person can easily be comforted by your maxim that enjoys its platitudinous comfort without having to experience the misfortune that occasions sorrow, but anyone whose grief bankrupts his poor patience is left with your saying and his sorrow, too. (*Bears the sentence* also plays on the meaning, "receives judicial sentence.") 219–20 **These . . . equivocal** These fine maxims are equivocal, being equally appropriate to happiness or bitterness. 222 **piercèd . . . ear** relieved by mere words reaching it through the ear. 225 **fortitude** strength 226 **substitute** deputy 227 **allowed** acknowledged 227–8 **opinion . . . on you** general opinion, an important determiner of affairs, chooses you as the best man. 229 **slubber** soil, sully 230–1 **stubborn . . . expedition** rough and violent expedition, for which haste is needed. 234 **thrice-driven** thrice sifted, winnowed. **agnize** know in myself, acknowledge 236 **hardness** hardship 238 **bending . . . state** bowing or kneeling to your authority 240–2 **Due . . . breeding** proper respect for her place (as my wife) and maintenance, with such suitable provision and attendance as befits her upbringing. 247 **my unfolding** what I shall unfold or say. **prosperous** favorable

And let me find a charter in your voice,   248
T'assist my simpleness.
DUKE   What would you, Desdemona?
DESDEMONA
That I did love the Moor to live with him,
My downright violence and storm of fortunes   252
May trumpet to the world. My heart's subdued
Even to the very quality of my lord.   254
I saw Othello's visage in his mind,
And to his honors and his valiant parts   256
Did I my soul and fortunes consecrate.
So that, dear lords, if I be left behind
A moth of peace, and he go to the war,   259
The rites for why I love him are bereft me,   260
And I a heavy interim shall support   261
By his dear absence. Let me go with him.   262
OTHELLO   Let her have your voice.   263
Vouch with me, heaven, I therefor beg it not
To please the palate of my appetite,
Nor to comply with heat—the young affects   266
In me defunct—and proper satisfaction,   267
But to be free and bounteous to her mind.   268
And heaven defend your good souls that you think 269
I will your serious and great business scant
When she is with me. No, when light-winged toys
Of feathered Cupid seel with wanton dullness   272
My speculative and officed instruments,   273
That my disports corrupt and taint my business,   274
Let huswives make a skillet of my helm,
And all indign and base adversities   276
Make head against my estimation!   277
DUKE
Be it as you shall privately determine,
Either for her stay or going. Th'affair cries haste,
And speed must answer it.
A SENATOR   You must away tonight.
DESDEMONA
Tonight, my lord?
DUKE   This night.
OTHELLO   With all my heart.
DUKE
At nine i'th' morning here we'll meet again.
Othello, leave some officer behind,
And he shall our commission bring to you,
With such things else of quality and respect   285
As doth import you.
OTHELLO   So please Your Grace, my ancient; 286

A man he is of honesty and trust.
To his conveyance I assign my wife,
With what else needful Your Good Grace shall think
To be sent after me.
DUKE   Let it be so.
Good night to everyone. [To Brabantio] And, noble
   signor,
If virtue no delighted beauty lack,   292
Your son-in-law is far more fair than black.
FIRST SENATOR
Adieu, brave Moor. Use Desdemona well.
BRABANTIO
Look to her, Moor, if thou hast eyes to see.
She has deceived her father, and may thee.
         Exeunt [Duke, Brabantio, Cassio, Senators, and
                                                                    officers].
OTHELLO
My life upon her faith!—Honest Iago,
My Desdemona must I leave to thee.
I prithee, let thy wife attend on her,
And bring them after in the best advantage.   300
Come, Desdemona. I have but an hour
Of love, of worldly matters and direction,   302
To spend with thee. We must obey the time.   303
                                   Exit [with Desdemona].
RODERIGO   Iago—
IAGO   What say'st thou, noble heart?
RODERIGO   What will I do, think'st thou?
IAGO   Why, go to bed and sleep.
RODERIGO   I will incontinently drown myself.   308
IAGO   If thou dost, I shall never love thee after. Why,
   thou silly gentleman?
RODERIGO   It is silliness to live when to live is torment;
   and then have we a prescription to die when death is 312
   our physician.
IAGO   Oh, villainous! I have looked upon the world for 314
   four times seven years, and, since I could distinguish
   betwixt a benefit and an injury, I never found man
   that knew how to love himself. Ere I would say I
   would drown myself for the love of a guinea hen, I   318
   would change my humanity with a baboon.   319
RODERIGO   What should I do? I confess it is my shame
   to be so fond, but it is not in my virtue to amend it.   321
IAGO   Virtue? A fig! 'Tis in ourselves that we are thus or 322
   thus. Our bodies are our gardens, to the which our
   wills are gardeners; so that if we will plant nettles or
   sow lettuce, set hyssop and weed up thyme, supply it 325
   with one gender of herbs or distract it with many,   326
   either to have it sterile with idleness or manured with 327

---

248 **charter** privilege, authorization   252 **My . . . fortunes** my plain
and total breach of social custom   254 **quality** moral and spiritual
identity   256 **parts** qualities   259 **moth** i.e., one who consumes
merely   260 **rites** rites of love. (With a suggestion, too, of "rights,"
sharing.)   261 **heavy** burdensome   262 **dear** grievous   263 **voice**
consent.   266 **heat** sexual passion.   **young affects** passions of youth,
adolescent desires   267 **defunct** done with, at an end.   **proper** personal   268 **free** generous   269 **defend** forbid.   **think** should think
272 **seel** i.e., make blind (as in falconry, by sewing up the eyes of the
hawk during training)   273 **My . . . instruments** my eyes, whose
function is to see   274 **That . . . business** in such a way that my sexual pastimes interfere with my official duties   276 **indign** unworthy,
shameful   277 **Make head** raise an army.   **estimation** reputation.
285 **of quality and respect** of importance and relevance   286 **import**
concern

292 **delighted** capable of delighting   300 **in . . . advantage** at the
most favorable opportunity.   302 **direction** instructions   303 **the
time** the urgency of the present crisis.   308 **incontinently** immediately, without self-restraint   312 **prescription** (1) right based on long-
established custom (2) doctor's prescription   314 **villainous** i.e.,
what perfect nonsense.   318 **guinea hen** (A slang term for a prostitute.)   319 **change** exchange   321 **fond** infatuated.   **virtue** strength,
nature   322 **fig** (To give a fig is to thrust the thumb between the first
and second fingers in a vulgar and insulting gesture.)   325 **hyssop** a
herb of the mint family   326 **gender** kind.   **distract it with** divide it
among   327 **idleness** want of cultivation

industry—why, the power and corrigible authority of 328
this lies in our wills. If the beam of our lives had not 329
one scale of reason to poise another of sensuality, the 330
blood and baseness of our natures would conduct us 331
to most preposterous conclusions. But we have reason
to cool our raging motions, our carnal stings, our 333
unbitted lusts, whereof I take this that you call love to 334
be a sect or scion. 335

RODERIGO   It cannot be.

IAGO   It is merely a lust of the blood and a permission
of the will. Come, be a man. Drown thyself? Drown
cats and blind puppies. I have professed me thy friend, 339
and I confess me knit to thy deserving with cables of
perdurable toughness. I could never better stead thee 341
than now. Put money in thy purse. Follow thou the
wars; defeat thy favor with an usurped beard. I say, 343
put money in thy purse. It cannot be long that Desdemona should continue her love to the Moor—put
money in thy purse—nor he his to her. It was a violent commencement in her, and thou shalt see an an- 347
swerable sequestration—put but money in thy purse. 348
These Moors are changeable in their wills—fill thy 349
purse with money. The food that to him now is as
luscious as locusts shall be to him shortly as bitter as 351
coloquintida. She must change for youth; when she is 352
sated with his body, she will find the error of her
choice. She must have change, she must. Therefore
put money in thy purse. If thou wilt needs damn thyself, do it a more delicate way than drowning. Make 356
all the money thou canst. If sanctimony and a frail vow 357
betwixt an erring barbarian and a supersubtle Vene- 358
tian be not too hard for my wits and all the tribe of
hell, thou shalt enjoy her. Therefore make money. A
pox of drowning thyself! It is clean out of the way. 361
Seek thou rather to be hanged in compassing thy joy 362
than to be drowned and go without her.

RODERIGO   Wilt thou be fast to my hopes if I depend on 364
the issue? 365

IAGO   Thou art sure of me. Go, make money. I have
told thee often, and I retell thee again and again, I hate
the Moor. My cause is hearted; thine hath no less rea- 368
son. Let us be conjunctive in our revenge against him. 369
If thou canst cuckold him, thou dost thyself a pleasure,
me a sport. There are many events in the womb of
time which will be delivered. Traverse, go, provide thy 372
money. We will have more of this tomorrow. Adieu.

RODERIGO   Where shall we meet i'th' morning?
IAGO   At my lodging.
RODERIGO   I'll be with thee betimes. [*He starts to leave.*] 376
IAGO   Go to, farewell.—Do you hear, Roderigo? 377
RODERIGO   What say you?
IAGO   No more of drowning, do you hear?
RODERIGO   I am changed.
IAGO   Go to, farewell. Put money enough in your
purse.
RODERIGO   I'll sell all my land.   *Exit.*
IAGO
Thus do I ever make my fool my purse;
For I mine own gained knowledge should profane
If I would time expend with such a snipe 386
But for my sport and profit. I hate the Moor;
And it is thought abroad that twixt my sheets 388
He's done my office. I know not if't be true; 389
But I, for mere suspicion in that kind,
Will do as if for surety. He holds me well; 391
The better shall my purpose work on him.
Cassio's a proper man. Let me see now: 393
To get his place and to plume up my will 394
In double knavery—How, how?—Let's see:
After some time, to abuse Othello's ear 396
That he is too familiar with his wife. 397
He hath a person and a smooth dispose 398
To be suspected, framed to make women false. 399
The Moor is of a free and open nature, 400
That thinks men honest that but seem to be so,
And will as tenderly be led by the nose 402
As asses are.
I have't. It is engendered. Hell and night
Must bring this monstrous birth to the world's light.
[*Exit.*]

❖

2.1

Enter Montano and two Gentlemen.

MONTANO
What from the cape can you discern at sea?
FIRST GENTLEMAN
Nothing at all. It is a high-wrought flood. 2
I cannot, twixt the heaven and the main, 3
Descry a sail.
MONTANO
Methinks the wind hath spoke aloud at land;
A fuller blast ne'er shook our battlements.
If it hath ruffianed so upon the sea, 7

---

328 corrigible authority power to correct   **329 beam** balance
330 poise counterbalance   **331 blood** natural passions   **333 motions**
appetites   **334 unbitted** unbridled, uncontrolled   **335 sect or scion**
cutting or offshoot.   **339 blind** i.e., newborn and helpless   **341 per-**
durable very durable.   **stead** assist   **343 defeat thy favor** disguise
your face.   **usurped** (The suggestion is that Roderigo is not man
enough to have a beard of his own.)   **347–8 an answerable seques-**
tration a corresponding cutting off or estrangement   **349 wills** carnal
appetites   **351 locusts** fruit of the carob tree (see Matthew 3:4), or
perhaps honeysuckle   **352 coloquintida** colocynth or bitter apple, a
purgative.   **356 Make** Raise, collect   **357 sanctimony** (1) an aura of
goodness (2) love-worship   **358 erring** wandering, vagabond,
unsteady   **361 clean . . . way** entirely unsuitable as a course of action.
362 compassing encompassing, embracing   **364 fast** true   **365 issue**
(successful) outcome.   **368 hearted** fixed in the heart, heartfelt
369 conjunctive united   **372 Traverse** (A military marching term.)

376 betimes early.   **377 Go to** (An expression of impatience or jolly-
ing along others.)   **386 snipe** woodcock, i.e., fool   **388 it is thought**
abroad it is rumored   **389 my office** i.e., my sexual function as husband.   **391 do . . . surety** act as if on certain knowledge.   **holds me**
well regards me favorably   **393 proper** handsome   **394 plume up**
put a feather in the cap of, i.e., glorify, gratify   **396 abuse** deceive
397 he Cassio.   **his** Othello's   **398 dispose** disposition   **399 framed**
formed, made   **400 free and open** frank and unsuspecting   **402 ten-**
derly readily
2.1. Location: A seaport in Cyprus. An open place near the quay.
2 high-wrought flood very agitated sea.   **3 main** ocean. (Also at line
41.)   **7 ruffianed** raged

What ribs of oak, when mountains melt on them,	8
Can hold the mortise? What shall we hear of this?	9

SECOND GENTLEMAN

A segregation of the Turkish fleet.	10
For do but stand upon the foaming shore,	
The chidden billow seems to pelt the clouds;	12
The wind-shaked surge, with high and monstrous	
mane,	13
Seems to cast water on the burning Bear	14
And quench the guards of th'ever-fixèd pole.	
I never did like molestation view	16
On the enchafèd flood.	17

MONTANO   If that the Turkish fleet   18
    Be not ensheltered and embayed, they are drowned;   19
    It is impossible to bear it out.   20

Enter a [Third] Gentleman.

THIRD GENTLEMAN   News, lads! Our wars are done.
    The desperate tempest hath so banged the Turks
    That their designment halts. A noble ship of Venice   23
    Hath seen a grievous wreck and sufferance   24
    On most part of their fleet.

MONTANO   How? Is this true?

THIRD GENTLEMAN   The ship is here put in,
    A Veronesa; Michael Cassio,   28
    Lieutenant to the warlike Moor Othello,
    Is come on shore; the Moor himself at sea,
    And is in full commission here for Cyprus.

MONTANO
    I am glad on't. 'Tis a worthy governor.

THIRD GENTLEMAN
    But this same Cassio, though he speak of comfort
    Touching the Turkish loss, yet he looks sadly   34
    And prays the Moor be safe, for they were parted
    With foul and violent tempest.

MONTANO   Pray heaven he be,
    For I have served him, and the man commands
    Like a full soldier. Let's to the seaside, ho!   38
    As well to see the vessel that's come in
    As to throw out our eyes for brave Othello,
    Even till we make the main and th'aerial blue   41
    An indistinct regard.

THIRD GENTLEMAN   Come, let's do so,   42
    For every minute is expectancy   43

Of more arrivance.	44

Enter Cassio.

CASSIO
    Thanks, you the valiant of this warlike isle,
    That so approve the Moor! Oh, let the heavens   46
    Give him defense against the elements,
    For I have lost him on a dangerous sea.

MONTANO   Is he well shipped?

CASSIO
    His bark is stoutly timbered, and his pilot
    Of very expert and approved allowance;   51
    Therefore my hopes, not surfeited to death,   52
    Stand in bold cure.
                [*A cry*] *within:* "A sail, a sail, a sail!"   53

CASSIO   What noise?

A GENTLEMAN
    The town is empty. On the brow o'th' sea   55
    Stand ranks of people, and they cry "A sail!"

CASSIO
    My hopes do shape him for the governor.   57
                [*A shot within.*]

SECOND GENTLEMAN
    They do discharge their shot of courtesy;   58
    Our friends at least.

CASSIO   I pray you, sir, go forth,
    And give us truth who 'tis that is arrived.

SECOND GENTLEMAN   I shall.   *Exit.*

MONTANO
    But, good Lieutenant, is your general wived?

CASSIO
    Most fortunately. He hath achieved a maid
    That paragons description and wild fame,   64
    One that excels the quirks of blazoning pens,   65
    And in th'essential vesture of creation   66
    Does tire the engineer.

Enter [Second] Gentleman.

    How now? Who has put in?   67

SECOND GENTLEMAN
    'Tis one Iago, ancient to the General.

CASSIO
    He's had most favorable and happy speed.
    Tempests themselves, high seas, and howling winds,
    The guttered rocks and congregated sands—   71
    Traitors ensteeped to clog the guiltless keel—   72
    As having sense of beauty, do omit   73
    Their mortal natures, letting go safely by   74

---

8 **mountains** i.e., of water   9 **hold the mortise** hold their joints together. (A *mortise* is the socket hollowed out in fitting timbers.)
10 **segregation** dispersal   12 **chidden** i.e., rebuked, repelled (by the shore), and thus shot into the air   13 **monstrous mane** (The surf is like the mane of a wild beast.)   14 **the burning Bear** i.e., the constellation Ursa Minor or the Little Bear, which includes the polestar (and hence regarded as the *guards of th'ever-fixèd pole* in the next line; sometimes the term *guards* is applied to the two "pointers" of the Big Bear or Dipper, which may be intended here.)   16 **like molestation** comparable disturbance   17 **enchafèd** angry   18 **If that** If   19 **embayed** sheltered by a bay   20 **bear it out** survive, weather the storm.
23 **designment halts** enterprise is crippled. (Literally, "is lame.")
24 **wreck** shipwreck.   **sufferance** damage, disaster   28 **Veronesa** from Verona (and perhaps in service with Venice)   34 **sadly** gravely
38 **full** perfect   41 **the main . . . blue** the sea and the sky   42 **An indistinct regard** indistinguishable in our view.   43 **is expectancy** gives expectation

44 **arrivance** arrival.   46 **approve** admire, honor   51 **approved allowance** tested reputation   52–3 **not . . . cure** not worn thin through repeated application or delayed fulfillment, strongly persist.
55 **brow o'th' sea** cliff-edge   57 **My . . . governor** I hope and imagine this ship to be Othello's.   58 **discharge . . . courtesy** fire a salute in token of respect and courtesy   64 **paragons** surpasses.   **wild fame** extravagant report   65 **quirks** witty conceits.   **blazoning** setting forth as though in heraldic language   66–7 **And in . . . engineer** and in her real, God-given, beauty, (she) defeats any attempt to praise her. (An *engineer* is one who devises, here a poet.)   67 **put in** i.e., to harbor.   71 **guttered** jagged, trenched   72 **ensteeped** lying under water   73 **As** as if.   **omit** forbear to exercise   74 **mortal** deadly

The divine Desdemona.

MONTANO　　　　　　　　　What is she?

CASSIO

She that I spake of, our great captain's captain,
Left in the conduct of the bold Iago,
Whose footing here anticipates our thoughts　　　78
A sennight's speed. Great Jove, Othello guard,　　79
And swell his sail with thine own powerful breath,
That he may bless this bay with his tall ship,　　81
Make love's quick pants in Desdemona's arms,
Give renewed fire to our extincted spirits,
And bring all Cyprus comfort!

Enter Desdemona, Iago, Roderigo, and Emilia.

　　　　　　　　　　Oh, behold,
The riches of the ship is come on shore!
You men of Cyprus, let her have your knees.
　　　　[*The gentlemen make curtsy to Desdemona.*]
Hail to thee, lady! And the grace of heaven
Before, behind thee, and on every hand
Enwheel thee round!

DESDEMONA　　　　　I thank you, valiant Cassio.
What tidings can you tell me of my lord?

CASSIO

He is not yet arrived, nor know I aught
But that he's well and will be shortly here.

DESDEMONA

Oh, but I fear—How lost you company?

CASSIO

The great contention of the sea and skies
Parted our fellowship.
　　　　　　　(*Within*) "A sail, a sail!" [*A shot.*]
　　　　　　　But hark. A sail!

SECOND GENTLEMAN

They give their greeting to the citadel.
This likewise is a friend.

CASSIO　　　　　　　　See for the news.
　　　　　　　[*Exit Second Gentleman.*]
Good Ancient, you are welcome. [*Kissing Emilia.*]
　Welcome, mistress.
Let it not gall your patience, good Iago,
That I extend my manners; 'tis my breeding　　　100
That gives me this bold show of courtesy.

IAGO

Sir, would she give you so much of her lips
As of her tongue she oft bestows on me,
You would have enough.

DESDEMONA　　　Alas, she has no speech!　　　105

IAGO　　In faith, too much.
I find it still, when I have list to sleep.　　　107
Marry, before Your Ladyship, I grant,
She puts her tongue a little in her heart
And chides with thinking.

EMILIA　　　　　You have little cause to say so.　110

IAGO

Come on, come on. You are pictures out of doors,　111
Bells in your parlors, wildcats in your kitchens,　112
Saints in your injuries, devils being offended,　113
Players in your huswifery, and huswives in your beds.　114

DESDEMONA　　Oh, fie upon thee, slanderer!

IAGO

Nay, it is true, or else I am a Turk.　　　116
You rise to play, and go to bed to work.

EMILIA

You shall not write my praise.

IAGO　　　　　　　　　No, let me not.

DESDEMONA

What wouldst write of me, if thou shouldst praise me?

IAGO

Oh, gentle lady, do not put me to't,
For I am nothing if not critical.　　　121

DESDEMONA

Come on, essay.—There's one gone to the harbor?　122

IAGO　　Ay, madam.

DESDEMONA

I am not merry, but I do beguile
The thing I am by seeming otherwise.　　　125
Come, how wouldst thou praise me?

IAGO

I am about it, but indeed my invention
Comes from my pate as birdlime does from frieze—　128
It plucks out brains and all. But my Muse labors,　129
And thus she is delivered:
If she be fair and wise, fairness and wit,
The one's for use, the other useth it.　　　132

DESDEMONA

Well praised! How if she be black and witty?　133

IAGO

If she be black, and thereto have a wit,
She'll find a white that shall her blackness fit.　135

DESDEMONA

Worse and worse.

EMILIA　　　　　　　How if fair and foolish?

IAGO

She never yet was foolish that was fair,
For even her folly helped her to an heir.　　　138

DESDEMONA　　These are old fond paradoxes to make fools　139

78–9 **Whose . . . speed** whose arrival here has happened a week sooner than we expected.　**81 tall** tall-masted　**100 extend** give scope to.　**breeding** training in the niceties of etiquette　**105 she has no speech** i.e., she's not a chatterbox, as you allege.　**107 still** always.　**list** desire　**110 with thinking** i.e., in her thoughts only.

111 **pictures out of doors** i.e., as pretty as pictures, and silently well-behaved in public　112 **Bells** i.e., jangling, noisy, and brazen.　**in your kitchens** i.e., in domestic affairs. (Ladies would not do the cooking.)　113 **Saints . . . injuries** i.e., putting on airs of sanctity and innocence when wronged by others　114 **Players . . . beds** play-actors at domesticity and truly energetic only as lovers in bed.　116 **a Turk** an infidel, not to be believed.　121 **critical** censorious.　122 **essay** try.　125 **The thing I am** i.e., my anxious self　128 **birdlime** sticky substance used to catch small birds.　**frieze** coarse woolen cloth　129 **labors** (1) exerts herself (2) prepares to deliver a child. (With a following pun on *delivered* in line 130.)　132 **The one's . . . it** i.e., her cleverness will make use of her beauty.　133 **black** dark-complexioned, brunette　135 **She'll . . . fit** she will find a fair-complexioned mate suited to her dark complexion. (Punning on *wight*, person, and contrasting *white* and *black*, with suggestion of sexual coupling.)　138 **folly** (With added meaning of "lechery, wantonness.")　**to an heir** i.e., to bear a child.　139 **fond** foolish

laugh i'th'alehouse. What miserable praise hast thou
for her that's foul and foolish?   141

IAGO
There's none so foul and foolish thereunto,   142
But does foul pranks which fair and wise ones do.   143

DESDEMONA   Oh, heavy ignorance! Thou praisest the worst
best. But what praise couldst thou bestow on a deserving woman indeed, one that, in the authority of her merit, did justly put on the vouch of very malice itself?   147

IAGO
She that was ever fair, and never proud,
Had tongue at will, and yet was never loud,   149
Never lacked gold and yet went never gay,   150
Fled from her wish, and yet said, "Now I may,"   151
She that being angered, her revenge being nigh,
Bade her wrong stay and her displeasure fly,   153
She that in wisdom never was so frail
To change the cod's head for the salmon's tail,   155
She that could think and ne'er disclose her mind,
See suitors following and not look behind,
She was a wight, if ever such wight were—

DESDEMONA   To do what?

IAGO
To suckle fools and chronicle small beer.   160

DESDEMONA   Oh, most lame and impotent conclusion! Do
not learn of him, Emilia, though he be thy husband.
How say you, Cassio? Is he not a most profane and   163
liberal counselor?   164

CASSIO   He speaks home, madam. You may relish him   165
more in the soldier than in the scholar.   166

              [*Cassio and Desdemona stand together,*
                       conversing intimately.]

IAGO [*aside*]   He takes her by the palm. Ay, well said,   167
whisper. With as little a web as this will I ensnare as
great a fly as Cassio. Ay, smile upon her, do; I will
gyve thee in thine own courtship. You say true; 'tis so,   170
indeed. If such tricks as these strip you out of your
lieutenantry, it had been better you had not kissed
your three fingers so oft, which now again you are
most apt to play the sir in. Very good; well kissed! An   174
excellent courtesy! 'Tis so, indeed. Yet again your fingers to your lips? Would they were clyster pipes for   176
your sake! [*Trumpet within.*] The Moor! I know his
trumpet.

CASSIO   'Tis truly so.

DESDEMONA   Let's meet him and receive him.

---

141 **foul** ugly   142 **thereunto** in addition   143 **foul** sluttish   147 **put
. . . vouch** compel the approval   149 **Had . . . will** was never at a loss
for words   150 **gay** extravagantly clothed   151 **Fled . . . may** avoided
temptation where the choice was hers   153 **Bade . . . stay** i.e.,
resolved to put up with her injury and bade her anger to cease
155 **To . . . tail** i.e., to be selfishly demanding and ambitious. (The
fish's lower body, below the rib cage, has fewest bones and is generally the succulent portion. With sexual implication as well: *cod's head*
can be slang for "penis," and *tail* for "pudendum.")   160 **To . . . beer**
i.e., To breastfeed babies and keep petty household accounts.
163–4 **profane and liberal** irreverent and licentious   165 **home** right
to the target. (A term from fencing.)   **relish** appreciate   166 **in** in the
character of   167 **well said** well done   170 **gyve** fetter, shackle.
courtship courtesy, show of courtly manners.   **You say true** i.e.,
That's right, go ahead   174 **the sir** i.e., the fine gentleman
176 **clyster pipes** tubes used for enemas and douches

CASSIO   Lo, where he comes!

              Enter Othello and attendants.

OTHELLO
Oh, my fair warrior!

DESDEMONA   My dear Othello!

OTHELLO
It gives me wonder great as my content
To see you here before me. O my soul's joy,
If after every tempest come such calms,
May the winds blow till they have wakened death,
And let the laboring bark climb hills of seas
Olympus-high, and duck again as low
As hell's from heaven! If it were now to die,
'Twere now to be most happy, for I fear
My soul hath her content so absolute
That not another comfort like to this
Succeeds in unknown fate.

DESDEMONA   The heavens forbid   192
But that our loves and comforts should increase
Even as our days do grow!

OTHELLO   Amen to that, sweet powers!
I cannot speak enough of this content.
It stops me here; it is too much of joy.
And this, and this, the greatest discords be   198
                              [*They kiss.*]
That e'er our hearts shall make!

IAGO [*aside*]   Oh, you are well tuned now!
But I'll set down the pegs that make this music,   201
As honest as I am.   202

OTHELLO   Come, let us to the castle.
News, friends! Our wars are done, the Turks are
    drowned.
How does my old acquaintance of this isle?—
Honey, you shall be well desired in Cyprus;   206
I have found great love amongst them. Oh, my sweet,
I prattle out of fashion, and I dote   208
In mine own comforts.—I prithee, good Iago,
Go to the bay and disembark my coffers.   210
Bring thou the master to the citadel;   211
He is a good one, and his worthiness
Does challenge much respect.—Come, Desdemona.—   213
Once more, well met at Cyprus!

              Exeunt Othello and Desdemona [and all
                       but Iago and Roderigo].

IAGO [*to a departing attendant*]   Do thou meet me presently at
the harbor. [*To Roderigo*] Come hither. If thou be'st
valiant—as, they say, base men being in love have   217
then a nobility in their natures more than is native to
them—list me. The Lieutenant tonight watches on   219
the court of guard. First, I must tell thee this: 220
Desdemona is directly in love with him.

---

192 **Succeeds . . . fate** i.e., can follow in the unknown future.
198.1 *They kiss* (The direction is from the Quarto.)   201 **set down**
loosen (and hence untune the instrument)   202 **As . . . I am** for all my
supposed honesty.   206 **desired** sought after   208 **out of fashion**
indecorously, incoherently   210 **coffers** chests, baggage.   211 **master**
ship's captain   213 **challenge** lay claim to, deserve   217 **base men**
even ignoble men   219 **list** listen to   220 **court of guard** guardhouse.
(Cassio is in charge of the watch.)

RODERIGO   With him? Why, 'tis not possible.

IAGO   Lay thy finger thus, and let thy soul be instructed. 223
Mark me with what violence she first loved the Moor,
but for bragging and telling her fantastical lies. To love 225
him still for prating? Let not thy discreet heart think it.
Her eye must be fed; and what delight shall she have
to look on the devil? When the blood is made dull with
the act of sport, there should be, again to inflame it 229
and to give satiety a fresh appetite, loveliness in favor, 230
sympathy in years, manners, and beauties—all which 231
the Moor is defective in. Now, for want of these
required conveniences, her delicate tenderness will 233
find itself abused, begin to heave the gorge, disrelish 234
and abhor the Moor. Very nature will instruct her in it 235
and compel her to some second choice. Now, sir, this
granted—as it is a most pregnant and unforced 237
position—who stands so eminent in the degree of this 238
fortune as Cassio does? A knave very voluble, no 239
further conscionable than in putting on the mere form 240
of civil and humane seeming for the better compass- 241
ing of his salt and most hidden loose affection. Why, 242
none, why, none. A slipper and subtle knave, a finder 243
out of occasions, that has an eye can stamp and 244
counterfeit advantages, though true advantage never 245
present itself; a devilish knave. Besides, the knave is
handsome, young, and hath all those requisites in him
that folly and green minds look after. A pestilent 248
complete knave, and the woman hath found him 249
already.

RODERIGO   I cannot believe that in her. She's full of
most blessed condition.   252

IAGO   Blessed fig's end! The wine she drinks is made of 253
grapes. If she had been blessed, she would never have
loved the Moor. Blessed pudding! Didst thou not see 255
her paddle with the palm of his hand? Didst not mark
that?

RODERIGO   Yes, that I did; but that was but courtesy.

IAGO   Lechery, by this hand. An index and obscure pro- 259
logue to the history of lust and foul thoughts. They
met so near with their lips that their breaths embraced
together. Villainous thoughts, Roderigo! When these
mutualities so marshal the way, hard at hand comes 263
the master and main exercise, th'incorporate conclu- 264
sion. Pish! But, sir, be you ruled by me. I have brought

you from Venice. Watch you tonight; for the com- 266
mand, I'll lay't upon you. Cassio knows you not. I'll 267
not be far from you. Do you find some occasion to
anger Cassio, either by speaking too loud, or tainting 269
his discipline, or from what other course you please,
which the time shall more favorably minister.   271

RODERIGO   Well.

IAGO   Sir, he's rash and very sudden in choler, and haply 273
may strike at you. Provoke him that he may, for
even out of that will I cause these of Cyprus to mutiny, 275
whose qualification shall come into no true taste again 276
but by the displanting of Cassio. So shall you have a
shorter journey to your desires by the means I shall
then have to prefer them, and the impediment most 279
profitably removed, without the which there were no
expectation of our prosperity.

RODERIGO   I will do this, if you can bring it to any
opportunity.

IAGO   I warrant thee. Meet me by and by at the citadel. 284
I must fetch his necessaries ashore. Farewell.

RODERIGO   Adieu.   *Exit.*

IAGO

That Cassio loves her, I do well believe't;
That she loves him, 'tis apt and of great credit.   288
The Moor, howbeit that I endure him not,
Is of a constant, loving, noble nature,
And I dare think he'll prove to Desdemona
A most dear husband. Now, I do love her too,
Not out of absolute lust—though peradventure
I stand accountant for as great a sin—   294
But partly led to diet my revenge   295
For that I do suspect the lusty Moor
Hath leaped into my seat, the thought whereof
Doth, like a poisonous mineral, gnaw my innards;
And nothing can or shall content my soul
Till I am evened with him, wife for wife,
Or failing so, yet that I put the Moor
At least into a jealousy so strong
That judgment cannot cure. Which thing to do,
If this poor trash of Venice, whom I trace   304
For his quick hunting, stand the putting on,   305
I'll have our Michael Cassio on the hip,   306
Abuse him to the Moor in the rank garb—   307
For I fear Cassio with my nightcap too—   308
Make the Moor thank me, love me, and reward me
For making him egregiously an ass
And practicing upon his peace and quiet   311

---

223 **thus** i.e., on your lips   225 **but** only   229 **the act of sport** sex
230 **favor** appearance   231 **sympathy** correspondence, similarity
233 **required conveniences** things conducive to sexual compatibility
234 **abused** cheated, revolted.   **heave the gorge** experience nausea
235 **Very nature** Her very instincts   237 **pregnant** evident, cogent
238 **in . . . of** as next in line for   239 **voluble** facile, glib   240 **conscionable** conscientious, conscience-bound   241 **humane** polite,
courteous   242 **salt** licentious.   **affection** passion.   243 **slipper** slippery   244 **an eye can stamp** an eye that can coin, create   245 **advantages** favorable opportunities   248 **folly** wantonness.   **green**
immature   249 **found him** sized him up, perceived his intent
252 **condition** disposition.   253 **fig's end** (See 1.3.322 for the vulgar
gesture of the fig.)   255 **pudding** sausage.   259 **index** table of contents.   **obscure** veiled, hidden   263 **mutualities** exchanges, intima-
cies.   **hard at hand** closely following   264 **th'incorporate** the carnal

266 **Watch you** Stand watch   266–7 **for . . . you** I'll arrange for you to
be appointed, given orders; or, I'll put you in charge.   269 **tainting**
disparaging   271 **minister** provide.   273 **choler** wrath.   **haply** perhaps   275 **mutiny** riot   276 **qualification** pacification.   **true taste**
i.e., acceptable state   279 **prefer** advance   284 **warrant** assure.
by and by immediately   288 **apt** probable.   **credit** credibility.
294 **accountant** accountable   295 **diet** feed   304 **trace** i.e., pursue,
dog; or, keep hungry (?) or perhaps *trash*, a hunting term, meaning to
put weights on a hunting dog in order to slow him down   305 **For** to
make more eager for.   **stand . . . on** responds properly when I incite
him to quarrel   306 **on the hip** at my mercy, where I can throw him.
(A wrestling term.)   307 **Abuse** slander.   **rank garb** coarse manner,
gross fashion   308 **with my nightcap** i.e., as a rival in my bed, as one
who gives me cuckold's horns   311 **practicing upon** plotting against

Even to madness. 'Tis here, but yet confused.
Knavery's plain face is never seen till used.   *Exit.*

❖

2.2

Enter Othello's Herald with a proclamation.

HERALD   It is Othello's pleasure, our noble and valiant
general, that, upon certain tidings now arrived, importing the mere perdition of the Turkish fleet, every   3
man put himself into triumph: some to dance, some to   4
make bonfires, each man to what sport and revels his
addiction leads him. For, besides these beneficial   6
news, it is the celebration of his nuptial. So much was
his pleasure should be proclaimed. All offices are open,   8
and there is full liberty of feasting from this present
hour of five till the bell have told eleven. Heaven bless
the isle of Cyprus and our noble general Othello!
                                                              Exit.

❖

[2.3]

*Enter Othello, Desdemona, Cassio, and
attendants.*

OTHELLO
Good Michael, look you to the guard tonight.
Let's teach ourselves that honorable stop   2
Not to outsport discretion.   3
CASSIO
Iago hath direction what to do,
But notwithstanding, with my personal eye
Will I look to't.
OTHELLO   Iago is most honest.
Michael, good night. Tomorrow with your earliest   7
Let me have speech with you. [*To Desdemona*] Come,
my dear love,
The purchase made, the fruits are to ensue;   9
That profit's yet to come 'tween me and you.—   10
Good night.
          Exit [Othello, with Desdemona and attendants].

          Enter Iago.

CASSIO   Welcome, Iago. We must to the watch.
IAGO   Not this hour, Lieutenant; 'tis not yet ten o'th'   13
clock. Our general cast us thus early for the love of his   14
Desdemona; who let us not therefore blame. He hath   15
not yet made wanton the night with her, and she is
sport for Jove.
CASSIO   She's a most exquisite lady.
IAGO   And, I'll warrant her, full of game.

CASSIO   Indeed, she's a most fresh and delicate creature.
IAGO   What an eye she has! Methinks it sounds a parley   21
to provocation.
CASSIO   An inviting eye, and yet methinks right modest.
IAGO   And when she speaks, is it not an alarum to love?   24
CASSIO   She is indeed perfection.
IAGO   Well, happiness to their sheets! Come, Lieutenant,
I have a stoup of wine, and here without are a brace of   27
Cyprus gallants that would fain have a measure to the   28
health of black Othello.
CASSIO   Not tonight, good Iago. I have very poor and
unhappy brains for drinking. I could well wish cour-
tesy would invent some other custom of entertain-
ment.
IAGO   Oh, they are our friends. But one cup! I'll drink for   34
you.   35
CASSIO   I have drunk but one cup tonight, and that was
craftily qualified too, and behold what innovation it   37
makes here. I am unfortunate in the infirmity and   38
dare not task my weakness with any more.
IAGO   What, man? 'Tis a night of revels. The gallants
desire it.
CASSIO   Where are they?
IAGO   Here at the door. I pray you, call them in.
CASSIO   I'll do't, but it dislikes me.   *Exit.*   44
IAGO
If I can fasten but one cup upon him,
With that which he hath drunk tonight already,
He'll be as full of quarrel and offense   47
As my young mistress' dog. Now, my sick fool
Roderigo,
Whom love hath turned almost the wrong side out,
To Desdemona hath tonight caroused   50
Potations pottle-deep; and he's to watch.   51
Three lads of Cyprus—noble swelling spirits,   52
That hold their honors in a wary distance,   53
The very elements of this warlike isle—   54
Have I tonight flustered with flowing cups,
And they watch too. Now, 'mongst this flock of
drunkards   56
Am I to put our Cassio in some action
That may offend the isle.—But here they come.

          *Enter Cassio, Montano, and gentlemen; [servants
          following with wine].*

If consequence do but approve my dream,   59
My boat sails freely both with wind and stream.   60
CASSIO   'Fore God, they have given me a rouse already.   61

2.2. Location: Cyprus.
3 mere perdition complete destruction   **4 triumph** public celebration
6 addiction inclination   **8 offices** rooms where food and drink are kept
2.3. Location: Cyprus. The citadel.
2 stop restraint   **3 outsport** celebrate beyond the bounds of   **7 with
your earliest** at your earliest convenience   **9–10 The purchase . . .
you** i.e., though married, we haven't yet consummated our love.
(Possibly, too, Othello is referring to pregnancy. At all events, his
desire for sexual union is manifest.)   **13 Not this hour** Not for an
hour yet   **14 cast** dismissed   **15 who** i.e., Othello

21 sounds a parley calls for a conference, issues an invitation
24 alarum signal calling men to arms. (Continuing the military
metaphor of *parley*, line 21.)   **27 stoup** measure of liquor, two quarts.
without outside.   **brace** pair   **28 fain have a measure** gladly drink a
toast   **34–5 for you** in your place. (Iago will do the steady drinking
to keep the gallants company while Cassio has only one cup.)
37 qualified diluted.   **innovation** disturbance, insurrection   **38 here**
i.e., in my head.   **44 it dislikes me** i.e., I'm reluctant.   **47 offense**
readiness to give or take offense   **50 caroused** drunk off   **51 pottle-
deep** to the bottom of the tankard.   **watch** stand watch.
52 swelling proud   **53 hold . . . distance** i.e., are extremely sensitive
of their honor   **54 elements** lifeblood   **56 watch** are members of the
guard   **59 If . . . dream** If subsequent events will only confirm my
dreams and hopes   **60 stream** current.   **61 rouse** full draft of liquor

MONTANO   Good faith, a little one; not past a pint, as I
am a soldier.
IAGO   Some wine, ho!
　[*He sings.*]   "And let me the cannikin clink, clink,   65
　　　　And let me the cannikin clink.
　　　　　A soldier's a man,
　　　　　　Oh, man's life's but a span;   68
　　　　Why, then, let a soldier drink."
　Some wine, boys!
CASSIO   'Fore God, an excellent song.
IAGO   I learned it in England, where indeed they are
most potent in potting. Your Dane, your German, and   73
your swag-bellied Hollander—drink, ho!—are noth-
ing to your English.
CASSIO   Is your Englishman so exquisite in his drinking?
IAGO   Why, he drinks you, with facility, your Dane   77
dead drunk; he sweats not to overthrow your Almain;   78
he gives your Hollander a vomit ere the next pottle can
be filled.
CASSIO   To the health of our general!
MONTANO   I am for it, Lieutenant, and I'll do you justice.   82
IAGO   O sweet England! [*He sings.*]

　　"King Stephen was and-a worthy peer,
　　　His breeches cost him but a crown;
　　He held them sixpence all too dear,
　　　With that he called the tailor lown.   87

　　He was a wight of high renown,
　　　And thou art but of low degree.
　　'Tis pride that pulls the country down;   90
　　　Then take thy auld cloak about thee."   91

　Some wine, ho!
CASSIO   'Fore God, this is a more exquisite song than
the other.
IAGO   Will you hear 't again?
CASSIO   No, for I hold him to be unworthy of his place
that does those things. Well, God's above all; and
there be souls must be saved, and there be souls must
not be saved.
IAGO   It's true, good Lieutenant.
CASSIO   For mine own part—no offense to the General,
nor any man of quality—I hope to be saved.   102
IAGO   And so do I too, Lieutenant.
CASSIO   Ay, but, by your leave, not before me; the lieutenant is to be saved before the ancient. Let's have no
more of this; let's to our affairs.—God forgive us our
sins!—Gentlemen, let's look to our business. Do not
think, gentlemen, I am drunk. This is my ancient; this
is my right hand, and this is my left. I am not drunk
now. I can stand well enough, and speak well enough.

GENTLEMEN   Excellent well.
CASSIO   Why, very well then; you must not think then
that I am drunk.   *Exit.*
MONTANO
To th' platform, masters. Come, let's set the watch.   114
　　　　　　　　　　　　　　　[*Exeunt Gentlemen.*]
IAGO
You see this fellow that is gone before.
He's a soldier fit to stand by Caesar
And give direction; and do but see his vice.
'Tis to his virtue a just equinox,   118
The one as long as th'other. 'Tis pity of him.
I fear the trust Othello puts him in,
On some odd time of his infirmity,
Will shake this island.
MONTANO   But is he often thus?
IAGO
'Tis evermore the prologue to his sleep.
He'll watch the horologe a double set,   124
If drink rock not his cradle.
MONTANO   It were well
The General were put in mind of it.
Perhaps he sees it not, or his good nature
Prizes the virtue that appears in Cassio
And looks not on his evils. Is not this true?

　　　　　　Enter Roderigo.

IAGO [*aside to him*]   How now, Roderigo?
I pray you, after the Lieutenant; go.   [*Exit Roderigo.*]
MONTANO
And 'tis great pity that the noble Moor
Should hazard such a place as his own second   133
With one of an engraffed infirmity.   134
It were an honest action to say so
To the Moor.
IAGO   Not I, for this fair island.
I do love Cassio well and would do much
To cure him of this evil.   [*Cry within:* "Help! Help!"]
　　　　　　　　　　　But, hark! What noise?   138

　　　　Enter Cassio, pursuing Roderigo.

CASSIO   Zounds, you rogue! You rascal!
MONTANO   What's the matter, Lieutenant?
CASSIO   A knave teach me my duty? I'll beat the knave
into a twiggen bottle.   142
RODERIGO   Beat me?
CASSIO   Dost thou prate, rogue?   [*He strikes Roderigo.*]
MONTANO   Nay, good Lieutenant. [*Restraining him.*] I
pray you, sir, hold your hand.
CASSIO   Let me go, sir, or I'll knock you o'er the
mazard.   148

---

65 cannikin small drinking vessel   **68 span** brief span of time. (Compare Psalm 39:5 as rendered in the Book of Common Prayer: "Thou
hast made my days as it were a span long.")   **73 potting** drinking.
77 drinks you drinks.   **your Dane** your typical Dane   **78 sweats not**
i.e., need not exert himself.   **Almain** German   **82 I'll . . . justice** i.e.,
I'll drink as much as you.   **87 lown** lout, rascal   **90 pride** i.e.,
extravagance in dress   **91 auld** old   **102 quality** rank

114 set the watch mount the guard.   **118 just equinox** exact counterpart. (*Equinox* is an equal length of days and nights.)   **124 watch . . .
set** stay awake twice around the clock or *horologe*   **133–4 hazard . . .
With** risk giving such an important position as his second in command to   **134 engraffed** engrafted, inveterate   **138.1** *pursuing* (The
Quarto text reads, "*driuing in.*")   **142 twiggen** wicker-covered. (Cassio vows to assail Roderigo until his skin resembles wickerwork or
until he has driven Roderigo through the holes in a wickerwork.)
148 mazard i.e., head. (Literally, a drinking vessel.)

MONTANO Come, come, you're drunk.

CASSIO Drunk?   [*They fight.*]

IAGO [*aside to Roderigo*]

Away, I say. Go out and cry a mutiny.   151

[*Exit Roderigo.*]

Nay, good Lieutenant—God's will, gentlemen—

Help, ho!—Lieutenant—sir—Montano—sir—

Help, masters!—Here's a goodly watch indeed!   154

[*A bell rings.*]

Who's that which rings the bell?—Diablo, ho!   155

The town will rise. God's will, Lieutenant, hold!1   156

You'll be ashamed forever.

Enter Othello and attendants [*with weapons*].

OTHELLO

What is the matter here?

MONTANO   Zounds, I bleed still.

I am hurt to th' death. He dies! [*He thrusts at Cassio.*]

OTHELLO   Hold, for your lives!

IAGO

Hold, ho! Lieutenant—sir—Montano—gentlemen—

Have you forgot all sense of place and duty?

Hold! The General speaks to you. Hold, for shame!

OTHELLO

Why, how now, ho! From whence ariseth this?

Are we turned Turks, and to ourselves do that   164

Which heaven hath forbid the Ottomites?   165

For Christian shame, put by this barbarous brawl!

He that stirs next to carve for his own rage   167

Holds his soul light; he dies upon his motion.   168

Silence that dreadful bell. It frights the isle

From her propriety. What is the matter, masters?   170

Honest Iago, that looks dead with grieving,

Speak. Who began this? On thy love, I charge thee.

IAGO

I do not know. Friends all but now, even now,

In quarter and in terms like bride and groom   174

Devesting them for bed; and then, but now—   175

As if some planet had unwitted men—

Swords out, and tilting one at others' breasts

In opposition bloody. I cannot speak   178

Any beginning to this peevish odds;   179

And would in action glorious I had lost

Those legs that brought me to a part of it!

OTHELLO

How comes it, Michael, you are thus forgot?   182

CASSIO

I pray you, pardon me. I cannot speak.

OTHELLO

Worthy Montano, you were wont be civil;   184

The gravity and stillness of your youth   185

The world hath noted, and your name is great

In mouths of wisest censure. What's the matter   187

That you unlace your reputation thus   188

And spend your rich opinion for the name   189

Of a night-brawler? Give me answer to it.

MONTANO

Worthy Othello, I am hurt to danger.

Your officer, Iago, can inform you—

While I spare speech, which something now offends

me—   193

Of all that I do know; nor know I aught

By me that's said or done amiss this night,

Unless self-charity be sometimes a vice,

And to defend ourselves it be a sin

When violence assails us.

OTHELLO   Now, by heaven,

My blood begins my safer guides to rule,   199

And passion, having my best judgment collied,   200

Essays to lead the way. Zounds, if I stir,   201

Or do but lift this arm, the best of you

Shall sink in my rebuke. Give me to know

How this foul rout began, who set it on;   204

And he that is approved in this offense,   205

Though he had twinned with me, both at a birth,

Shall lose me. What? In a town of war   207

Yet wild, the people's hearts brim full of fear,

To manage private and domestic quarrel?   209

In night, and on the court and guard of safety?   210

'Tis monstrous. Iago, who began't?

MONTANO [*to Iago*]

If partially affined, or leagued in office,   212

Thou dost deliver more or less than truth,

Thou art no soldier.

IAGO   Touch me not so near.

I had rather have this tongue cut from my mouth

Than it should do offense to Michael Cassio;

Yet, I persuade myself, to speak the truth

Shall nothing wrong him. Thus it is, General:

Montano and myself being in speech,

There comes a fellow crying out for help,

And Cassio following him with determined sword

To execute upon him. Sir, this gentleman   222

[*indicating Montano*]

Steps in to Cassio and entreats his pause.   223

Myself the crying fellow did pursue,

Lest by his clamor—as it so fell out—

The town might fall in fright. He, swift of foot,

---

151 **mutiny** riot. 154 **masters** sirs. 154.1 *A bell rings* (This direction is from the Quarto, as are *Exit Roderigo* at line 131, *They fight* at line 150, and *with weapons* at line 157.1.) 155 **Diablo** The devil 156 **rise** grow riotous. 164–5 **to ourselves . . . Ottomites** inflict on ourselves the harm that heaven has prevented the Turks from doing (by destroying their fleet). 167 **carve for** i.e., indulge, satisfy with his sword 168 **Holds . . . light** i.e., places little value on his life. **upon his motion** if he moves. 170 **propriety** proper state or condition. 174 **In quarter . . . terms** in conduct and speech 175 **Devesting them** undressing themselves 178 **speak** explain 179 **peevish odds** childish quarrel 182 **are thus forgot** have forgotten yourself thus.

184 **wont be** accustomed to be 185 **stillness** sobriety 187 **censure** judgment. 188 **unlace** undo, lay open (as one might loose the strings of a purse containing reputation) 189 **opinion** reputation 193 **something** somewhat. **offends** pains 199 **blood** passion (of anger). **guides** i.e., reason 200 **collied** darkened 201 **Essays** undertakes 204 **rout** riot 205 **approved in** found guilty of 207 **town of** town garrisoned for 209 **manage** undertake 210 **on . . . safety** at the main guardhouse or headquarters and on watch. 212 **If . . . office** If made partial by personal relationship or by your being fellow officers 222 **execute upon him** (1) proceed violently against him (2) execute him. 223 **his pause** him to stop.

Outran my purpose, and I returned, the rather   227
For that I heard the clink and fall of swords
And Cassio high in oath, which till tonight
I ne'er might say before. When I came back—
For this was brief—I found them close together
At blow and thrust, even as again they were
When you yourself did part them.
More of this matter cannot I report.
But men are men; the best sometimes forget.   235
Though Cassio did some little wrong to him,
As men in rage strike those that wish them best,   237
Yet surely Cassio, I believe, received
From him that fled some strange indignity,
Which patience could not pass.

OTHELLO   I know, Iago,   240
Thy honesty and love doth mince this matter,
Making it light to Cassio. Cassio, I love thee,
But nevermore be officer of mine.

Enter Desdemona, attended.

Look if my gentle love be not raised up.
I'll make thee an example.

DESDEMONA
What is the matter, dear?

OTHELLO   All's well now, sweeting;
Come away to bed. [*To Montano*] Sir, for your hurts,
Myself will be your surgeon.—Lead him off.   248
                              [*Montano is led off.*]
Iago, look with care about the town
And silence those whom this vile brawl distracted.
Come, Desdemona. 'Tis the soldiers' life
To have their balmy slumbers waked with strife.
                              Exit [*with all but Iago and Cassio*].

IAGO   What, are you hurt, Lieutenant?
CASSIO   Ay, past all surgery.
IAGO   Marry, God forbid!
CASSIO   Reputation, reputation, reputation! Oh, I have
lost my reputation! I have lost the immortal part of
myself, and what remains is bestial. My reputation,
Iago, my reputation!
IAGO   As I am an honest man, I thought you had
received some bodily wound; there is more sense in
that than in reputation. Reputation is an idle and most
false imposition, oft got without merit and lost with-   263
out deserving. You have lost no reputation at all,
unless you repute yourself such a loser. What, man,
there are more ways to recover the General again. You   266
are but now cast in his mood—a punishment more in   267
policy than in malice, even so as one would beat his   268
offenseless dog to affright an imperious lion. Sue to   269
him again and he's yours.

CASSIO   I will rather sue to be despised than to deceive
so good a commander with so slight, so drunken, and   272
so indiscreet an officer. Drunk? And speak parrot?   273
And squabble? Swagger? Swear? And discourse fustian with one's own shadow? O thou invisible spirit
of wine, if thou hast no name to be known by, let us
call thee devil!
IAGO   What was he that you followed with your sword?
What had he done to you?
CASSIO   I know not.
IAGO   Is't possible?
CASSIO   I remember a mass of things, but nothing
distinctly; a quarrel, but nothing wherefore. Oh, God,   283
that men should put an enemy in their mouths to steal
away their brains! That we should, with joy, pleas-
ance, revel, and applause transform ourselves into   286
beasts!
IAGO   Why, but you are now well enough. How came
you thus recovered?
CASSIO   It hath pleased the devil drunkenness to give
place to the devil wrath. One unperfectness shows me
another, to make me frankly despise myself.
IAGO   Come, you are too severe a moraler. As the time,   293
the place, and the condition of this country stands, I
could heartily wish this had not befallen; but since it is
as it is, mend it for your own good.
CASSIO   I will ask him for my place again; he shall tell
me I am a drunkard. Had I as many mouths as Hydra,   298
such an answer would stop them all. To be now a
sensible man, by and by a fool, and presently a beast!
Oh, strange! Every inordinate cup is unblessed, and the   301
ingredient is a devil.
IAGO   Come, come, good wine is a good familiar
creature, if it be well used. Exclaim no more against it.
And, good Lieutenant, I think you think I love you.
CASSIO   I have well approved it, sir. I drunk!   306
IAGO   You or any man living may be drunk at a time,   307
man. I'll tell you what you shall do. Our general's wife
is now the general—I may say so in this respect, for   309
that he hath devoted and given up himself to the   310
contemplation, mark, and denotement of her parts   311
and graces. Confess yourself freely to her; importune
her help to put you in your place again. She is of so
free, so kind, so apt, so blessed a disposition, she   314
holds it a vice in her goodness not to do more than she
is requested. This broken joint between you and her
husband entreat her to splinter; and, my fortunes   317
against any lay worth naming, this crack of your love   318
shall grow stronger than it was before.
CASSIO   You advise me well.

---

227 **rather** sooner   235 **forget** forget themselves.   237 **those . . . best**
i.e., even those who are well disposed toward them   240 **pass** pass
over, overlook.   248 **be your surgeon** i.e., make sure you receive
medical attention.   263 **false imposition** thing artificially imposed
and of no real value   266 **recover** regain favor with   267 **cast in his
mood** dismissed in a moment of anger   267–8 **in policy** done for
expediency's sake and as a public gesture   268–9 **would . . . lion** i.e.,
would make an example of a minor offender in order to deter more
important and dangerous offenders.   269 **Sue** Petition

272 **slight** worthless   273 **speak parrot** talk nonsense, rant. (*Discourse
fustian*, lines 274–5, has much the same meaning.)   283 **wherefore**
why.   286 **applause** desire for applause   293 **moraler** moralizer.
298 **Hydra** the Lernaean Hydra, a monster with many heads and the
ability to grow two heads when one was cut off, slain by Hercules
as the second of his twelve labors   301 **inordinate** immoderate
306 **approved** proved by experience   307 **at a time** at one time or
another   309–10 **for that** that   311 **mark, and denotement** (Both
words mean "observation.")   **parts** qualities   314 **free** generous
317 **splinter** bind with splints   318 **lay** stake, wager

IAGO   I protest, in the sincerity of love and honest 321
kindness.

CASSIO   I think it freely; and betimes in the morning I 323
will beseech the virtuous Desdemona to undertake for
me. I am desperate of my fortunes if they check me 325
here.

IAGO   You are in the right. Good night, Lieutenant. I
must to the watch.

CASSIO   Good night, honest Iago.   *Exit Cassio.*

IAGO
And what's he then that says I play the villain,
When this advice is free I give, and honest,   331
Probal to thinking, and indeed the course   332
To win the Moor again? For 'tis most easy
Th'inclining Desdemona to subdue   334
In any honest suit; she's framed as fruitful   335
As the free elements. And then for her   336
To win the Moor—were't to renounce his baptism,
All seals and symbols of redeemèd sin—   338
His soul is so enfettered to her love
That she may make, unmake, do what she list,
Even as her appetite shall play the god   341
With his weak function. How am I then a villain,   342
To counsel Cassio to this parallel course   343
Directly to his good? Divinity of hell!   344
When devils will the blackest sins put on,   345
They do suggest at first with heavenly shows,   346
As I do now. For whiles this honest fool
Plies Desdemona to repair his fortune,
And she for him pleads strongly to the Moor,
I'll pour this pestilence into his ear,
That she repeals him for her body's lust;   351
And by how much she strives to do him good,
She shall undo her credit with the Moor.
So will I turn her virtue into pitch,   354
And out of her own goodness make the net
That shall enmesh them all.

Enter Roderigo.

How now, Roderigo?

RODERIGO   I do follow here in the chase, not like a
hound that hunts, but one that fills up the cry. My 358
money is almost spent; I have been tonight exceedingly well cudgeled; and I think the issue will be I shall 360
have so much experience for my pains, and so,   361
with no money at all and a little more wit, return again
to Venice.

IAGO
How poor are they that have not patience!
What wound did ever heal but by degrees?
Thou know'st we work by wit, and not by witchcraft,
And wit depends on dilatory time.
Does't not go well? Cassio hath beaten thee,
And thou, by that small hurt, hast cashiered Cassio.   369
Though other things grow fair against the sun,   370
Yet fruits that blossom first will first be ripe.   371
Content thyself awhile. By the Mass, 'tis morning!
Pleasure and action make the hours seem short.
Retire thee; go where thou art billeted.
Away, I say! Thou shalt know more hereafter.
Nay, get thee gone.   *Exit Roderigo.*
                    Two things are to be done.
My wife must move for Cassio to her mistress;   377
I'll set her on;
Myself the while to draw the Moor apart
And bring him jump when he may Cassio find   380
Soliciting his wife. Ay, that's the way.
Dull not device by coldness and delay.   *Exit.* 382

❧

3.1

Enter Cassio [and] Musicians.

CASSIO
Masters, play here—I will content your pains—   1
Something that's brief, and bid "Good morrow,
General."   [*They play.*]

[*Enter*] *Clown.*

CLOWN   Why, masters, have your instruments been in
Naples, that they speak i'th' nose thus?   4

A MUSICIAN   How, sir, how?

CLOWN   Are these, I pray you, wind instruments?

A MUSICIAN   Ay, marry, are they, sir.

CLOWN   Oh, thereby hangs a tail.

A MUSICIAN   Whereby hangs a tale, sir?

CLOWN   Marry, sir, by many a wind instrument that I 10
know. But, masters, here's money for you. [*He gives
money.*] And the General so likes your music that he
desires you, for love's sake, to make no more noise
with it.

A MUSICIAN   Well, sir, we will not.

CLOWN   If you have any music that may not be heard, 16
to't again; but, as they say, to hear music the General
does not greatly care.

A MUSICIAN   We have none such, sir.

---

321 **protest** insist, declare   323 **freely** unreservedly   325 **check**
repulse   331 **free** (1) free from guile (2) freely given   332 **Probal**
probable, reasonable   334 **Th'inclining** the favorably disposed.
subdue persuade   335 **framed as fruitful** created as generous
336 **free elements** i.e., earth, air, fire, and water, unrestrained and
spontaneous.   338 **seals** tokens   341 **her appetite** her desire, or, perhaps, his desire for her   342 **function** exercise of faculties (weakened
by his fondness for her).   343 **parallel** i.e., seemingly in his best interests but at the same time threatening   344 **Divinity of hell!** Inverted
theology of hell (which seduces the soul to its damnation)!   345 **put
on** further, instigate   346 **suggest** tempt   351 **repeals him** attempts
to get him restored   354 **pitch** i.e., (1) foul blackness (2) a snaring
substance   358 **fills up the cry** merely takes part as one of the pack.
360 **issue** outcome   361 **so much** just so much and no more

369 **cashiered** dismissed from service   370–1 **Though . . . ripe** i.e.,
Plans that are well prepared and set expeditiously in motion will
soonest ripen into success.   377 **move** plead   380 **jump** precisely
382 **device** plot.   **coldness** lack of zeal
3.1. Location: Before the chamber of Othello and Desdemona.
1 **Masters** Good sirs.   **content your pains** reward your efforts
4 **speak i'th' nose** (1) sound nasal (2) sound like one whose nose has
been attacked by syphilis. (Naples was popularly supposed to have a
high incidence of venereal disease.)   10 **wind instrument** (With a
joke on flatulence. The *tail*, line 8, that hangs nearby the *wind instrument* suggests the penis.)   16 **may not** cannot

CLOWN   Then put up your pipes in your bag, for I'll
away. Go, vanish into air, away!   *Exeunt Musicians.*
CASSIO   Dost thou hear, mine honest friend?
CLOWN   No, I hear not your honest friend; I hear you.
CASSIO   Prithee, keep up thy quillets. There's a poor   24
piece of gold for thee. [*He gives money.*] If the gentlewoman that attends the General's wife be stirring, tell
her there's one Cassio entreats her a little favor of   27
speech. Wilt thou do this?   28
CLOWN   She is stirring, sir. If she will stir hither, I shall   29
seem to notify unto her.   30
CASSIO
Do, good my friend.   *Exit Clown.*

    Enter Iago.

        In happy time, Iago.   31
IAGO   You have not been abed, then?
CASSIO   Why, no. The day had broke
Before we parted. I have made bold, Iago,
To send in to your wife. My suit to her
Is that she will to virtuous Desdemona
Procure me some access.
IAGO   I'll send her to you presently;
And I'll devise a mean to draw the Moor
Out of the way, that your converse and business
May be more free.
CASSIO
I humbly thank you for't.   *Exit [Iago].*
        I never knew
A Florentine more kind and honest.   43

    Enter Emilia.

EMILIA
Good morrow, good Lieutenant. I am sorry
For your displeasure; but all will sure be well.   45
The General and his wife are talking of it,
And she speaks for you stoutly. The Moor replies   47
That he you hurt is of great fame in Cyprus   48
And great affinity, and that in wholesome wisdom   49
He might not but refuse you; but he protests he loves
you   50
And needs no other suitor but his likings
To take the safest occasion by the front   52
To bring you in again.
CASSIO   Yet I beseech you,
If you think fit, or that it may be done,
Give me advantage of some brief discourse
With Desdemon alone.
EMILIA   Pray you, come in.
I will bestow you where you shall have time
To speak your bosom freely.   58

CASSIO   I am much bound to you.   [*Exeunt.*]

❖

3.2

    Enter Othello, Iago, and Gentlemen.

OTHELLO [*giving letters*]
These letters give, Iago, to the pilot,
And by him do my duties to the Senate.   2
That done, I will be walking on the works;   3
Repair there to me.
IAGO   Well, my good lord, I'll do't.   4
OTHELLO
This fortification, gentlemen, shall we see't?
GENTLEMEN   We'll wait upon Your Lordship.   *Exeunt.*   6

❖

3.3

    Enter Desdemona, Cassio, and Emilia.

DESDEMONA
Be thou assured, good Cassio, I will do
All my abilities in thy behalf.
EMILIA
Good madam, do. I warrant it grieves my husband
As if the cause were his.
DESDEMONA
Oh, that's an honest fellow. Do not doubt, Cassio,
But I will have my lord and you again
As friendly as you were.
CASSIO   Bounteous madam,
Whatever shall become of Michael Cassio,
He's never anything but your true servant.
DESDEMONA
I know't. I thank you. You do love my lord;
You have known him long, and be you well assured
He shall in strangeness stand no farther off   12
Than in a politic distance.
CASSIO   Ay, but, lady,   13
That policy may either last so long,
Or feed upon such nice and waterish diet,   15
Or breed itself so out of circumstance,   16
That, I being absent and my place supplied,   17
My general will forget my love and service.
DESDEMONA
Do not doubt that. Before Emilia here   19
I give thee warrant of thy place. Assure thee,   20
If I do vow a friendship I'll perform it
To the last article. My lord shall never rest.
I'll watch him tame and talk him out of patience;   23

---

24 keep . . . quillets refrain from quibbling.   **27–8 a little . . . speech**
the favor of a brief talk.   **29 stir** bestir herself. (With a play on
stirring, "rousing herself from rest.")   **30 seem** deem it good, think fit
31 In happy time i.e., Well met   **43 Florentine** i.e., even a fellow Florentine. (Iago is a Venetian; Cassio is a Florentine.)   **45 displeasure**
fall from favor   **47 stoutly** spiritedly.   **48 fame** reputation, importance   **49 affinity** kindred, family connection   **50 protests** insists
52 occasion . . . front opportunity by the forelock   **58 bosom** inmost
thoughts

3.2. Location: The citadel.
2 do my duties convey my respects   **3 works** breastworks, fortifications   **4 Repair** return, come   **6 wait upon** attend
3.3. Location: The garden of the citadel.
12 strangeness aloofness   **13 politic** required by wise policy
15 Or . . . diet or sustain itself at length upon such trivial and meager
technicalities   **16 breed . . . circumstance** continually renew itself so
out of chance events, or yield so few chances for my being pardoned
17 supplied filled by another person   **19 doubt** fear   **20 warrant**
guarantee   **23 watch him tame** tame him by keeping him from sleeping. (A term from falconry.)   **out of patience** past his endurance

His bed shall seem a school, his board a shrift;   24
I'll intermingle everything he does
With Cassio's suit. Therefore be merry, Cassio,
For thy solicitor shall rather die   27
Than give thy cause away.   28

Enter Othello and Iago [at a distance].

EMILIA   Madam, here comes my lord.
CASSIO   Madam, I'll take my leave.
DESDEMONA   Why, stay, and hear me speak.
CASSIO
Madam, not now. I am very ill at ease,
Unfit for mine own purposes.
DESDEMONA   Well, do your discretion.   *Exit Cassio.*   34
IAGO   Ha? I like not that.
OTHELLO   What dost thou say?
IAGO
Nothing, my lord; or if—I know not what.
OTHELLO
Was not that Cassio parted from my wife?
IAGO
Cassio, my lord? No, sure, I cannot think it,
That he would steal away so guiltylike,
Seeing you coming.
OTHELLO   I do believe 'twas he.
DESDEMONA *[joining them]*   How now, my lord?
I have been talking with a suitor here,
A man that languishes in your displeasure.
OTHELLO   Who is't you mean?
DESDEMONA
Why, your lieutenant, Cassio. Good my lord,
If I have any grace or power to move you,
His present reconciliation take;   49
For if he be not one that truly loves you,
That errs in ignorance and not in cunning,   51
I have no judgment in an honest face.
I prithee, call him back.
OTHELLO   Went he hence now?
DESDEMONA   Yes, faith, so humbled
That he hath left part of his grief with me
To suffer with him. Good love, call him back.
OTHELLO
Not now, sweet Desdemon. Some other time.
DESDEMONA   But shall't be shortly?
OTHELLO   The sooner, sweet, for you.
DESDEMONA   Shall't be tonight at supper?
OTHELLO   No, not tonight.
DESDEMONA   Tomorrow dinner, then?   63
OTHELLO   I shall not dine at home.
I meet the captains at the citadel.
DESDEMONA
Why, then, tomorrow night, or Tuesday morn,
On Tuesday noon, or night, on Wednesday morn.
I prithee, name the time, but let it not
Exceed three days. In faith, he's penitent;

And yet his trespass, in our common reason—   70
Save that, they say, the wars must make example   71
Out of her best—is not almost a fault   72
T'incur a private check. When shall he come?   73
Tell me, Othello. I wonder in my soul
What you would ask me that I should deny,
Or stand so mamm'ring on. What? Michael Cassio,   76
That came a-wooing with you, and so many a time,
When I have spoke of you dispraisingly,
Hath ta'en your part—to have so much to do
To bring him in! By'r Lady, I could do much—   80
OTHELLO
Prithee, no more. Let him come when he will;
I will deny thee nothing.
DESDEMONA   Why, this is not a boon.
'Tis as I should entreat you wear your gloves,
Or feed on nourishing dishes, or keep you warm,
Or sue to you to do a peculiar profit   86
To your own person. Nay, when I have a suit
Wherein I mean to touch your love indeed,   88
It shall be full of poise and difficult weight,   89
And fearful to be granted.
OTHELLO   I will deny thee nothing.
Whereon, I do beseech thee, grant me this,   92
To leave me but a little to myself.
DESDEMONA
Shall I deny you? No. Farewell, my lord.
OTHELLO
Farewell, my Desdemona. I'll come to thee straight.   95
DESDEMONA
Emilia, come.—Be as your fancies teach you;   96
Whate'er you be, I am obedient.   *Exit [with Emilia].*
OTHELLO
Excellent wretch! Perdition catch my soul   98
But I do love thee! And when I love thee not,   99
Chaos is come again.   100
IAGO   My noble lord—
OTHELLO   What dost thou say, Iago?
IAGO
Did Michael Cassio, when you wooed my lady,
Know of your love?
OTHELLO
He did, from first to last. Why dost thou ask?
IAGO
But for a satisfaction of my thought;
No further harm.
OTHELLO   Why of thy thought, Iago?

---

24 **board** dining table. **shrift** confessional 27 **solicitor** advocate 28 **away** up. 34 **do your discretion** do as you think fit. 49 **His ... take** let him be reconciled to you right away 51 **in cunning** wittingly 63 **dinner** (The noontime meal.)

70 **common reason** everyday judgments 71–2 **Save ... best** were it not that, as the saying goes, military discipline requires making an example of the very best men. (*Her* refers to wars as a singular concept.) 72 **not almost** scarcely 73 **a private check** even a private reprimand. 76 **mamm'ring on** wavering or muttering about. 80 **bring him in** restore him to favor. 86 **peculiar** particular, personal 88 **touch** test 89 **poise ... weight** delicacy and weightiness 92 **Whereon** In return for which 95 **straight** straightway. 96 **fancies** inclinations 98 **wretch** (A term of affectionate endearment.) 99–100 **And ... again** i.e., My love for you will last forever, until the end of time when chaos will return. (But with an unconscious, ironic suggestion that, if anything should induce Othello to cease loving Desdemona, the result would be chaos.)

IAGO
  I did not think he had been acquainted with her.
OTHELLO
  Oh, yes, and went between us very oft.
IAGO Indeed?
OTHELLO
  Indeed? Ay, indeed. Discern'st thou aught in that?
  Is he not honest?
IAGO Honest, my lord?
OTHELLO Honest. Ay, honest.
IAGO My lord, for aught I know.
OTHELLO What dost thou think?
IAGO Think, my lord?
OTHELLO
  "Think, my lord?" By heaven, thou echo'st me,
  As if there were some monster in thy thought
  Too hideous to be shown. Thou dost mean something.
  I heard thee say even now, thou lik'st not that,
  When Cassio left my wife. What didst not like?
  And when I told thee he was of my counsel   123
  In my whole course of wooing, thou criedst "Indeed?"
  And didst contract and purse thy brow together   125
  As if thou then hadst shut up in thy brain
  Some horrible conceit. If thou dost love me,   127
  Show me thy thought.
IAGO My lord, you know I love you.
OTHELLO I think thou dost;
  And, for I know thou'rt full of love and honesty,   131
  And weigh'st thy words before thou giv'st them
    breath,
  Therefore these stops of thine fright me the more;   133
  For such things in a false disloyal knave
  Are tricks of custom, but in a man that's just   135
  They're close dilations, working from the heart   136
  That passion cannot rule.
IAGO For Michael Cassio,   137
  I dare be sworn I think that he is honest.
OTHELLO
  I think so too.
IAGO Men should be what they seem;
  Or those that be not, would they might seem none!   140
OTHELLO
  Certain, men should be what they seem.
IAGO
  Why, then, I think Cassio's an honest man.
OTHELLO Nay, yet there's more in this.
  I prithee, speak to me as to thy thinkings,
  As thou dost ruminate, and give thy worst of thoughts
  The worst of words.
IAGO Good my lord, pardon me.
  Though I am bound to every act of duty,
  I am not bound to that all slaves are free to.   148
  Utter my thoughts? Why, say they are vile and false,
  As where's that palace whereinto foul things

Sometimes intrude not? Who has that breast so pure
But some uncleanly apprehensions
Keep leets and law days, and in sessions sit   153
With meditations lawful?   154
OTHELLO
  Thou dost conspire against thy friend, Iago,   155
  If thou but think'st him wronged and mak'st his ear
  A stranger to thy thoughts.
IAGO I do beseech you,
  Though I perchance am vicious in my guess—   158
  As I confess it is my nature's plague
  To spy into abuses, and oft my jealousy   160
  Shapes faults that are not—that your wisdom then,
  From one that so imperfectly conceits,   162
  Would take no notice, nor build yourself a trouble
  Out of his scattering and unsure observance.   164
  It were not for your quiet nor your good,
  Nor for my manhood, honesty, and wisdom,
  To let you know my thoughts.
OTHELLO What dost thou mean?
IAGO
  Good name in man and woman, dear my lord,
  Is the immediate jewel of their souls.   169
  Who steals my purse steals trash; 'tis something,
    nothing;
  'Twas mine, 'tis his, and has been slave to thousands;
  But he that filches from me my good name
  Robs me of that which not enriches him
  And makes me poor indeed.
OTHELLO By heaven, I'll know thy thoughts.
IAGO
  You cannot, if my heart were in your hand,   176
  Nor shall not, whilst 'tis in my custody.
OTHELLO Ha?
IAGO Oh, beware, my lord, of jealousy.
  It is the green-eyed monster, which doth mock   179
  The meat it feeds on. That cuckold lives in bliss   180
  Who, certain of his fate, loves not his wronger;   181
  But oh, what damnèd minutes tells he o'er   182
  Who dotes, yet doubts, suspects, yet fondly loves!
OTHELLO Oh, misery!
IAGO
  Poor and content is rich, and rich enough,   185
  But riches fineless is as poor as winter   186
  To him that ever fears he shall be poor.

---

123 of my counsel in my confidence   **125 purse** knit   **127 conceit** fancy.   **131 for** because   **133 stops** pauses   **135 of custom** customary   **136–7 They're . . . rule** they are secret or involuntary expressions of feeling that are too strong to be kept back.   **137 For** As for   **140 seem none** not seem at all, not seem to be honest.   **148 that** that which.   **free to** free with respect to.

153 Keep leets and law days i.e., hold court, set up their authority in one's heart. (*Leets* are a kind of manor court; *law days* are the days courts sit in session, or those sessions.)   **153–4 and . . . lawful** i.e., and coexist in a kind of spiritual conflict with virtuous thoughts.   **155 thy friend** i.e., Othello   **158 vicious** wrong   **160 jealousy** suspicious nature   **162 one** i.e., myself, Iago.   **conceits** judges, conjectures   **164 scattering** random   **169 immediate** essential, most precious   **176 if** even if   **179–80 which . . . feeds on** (Jealousy mocks both itself and the sufferer of jealousy; it is self-devouring and is its own punishment.)   **180–1 That . . . wronger** A cuckolded husband who knows his wife to be unfaithful can at least take comfort in knowing the truth, so that he will not continue to love her or to befriend her lover. (Othello echoes this sentiment in lines 204–6, when he vows that he would end uncertainty and cease to love an unfaithful wife.)   **182 tells** counts   **185 Poor . . . enough** To be content with what little one has is the greatest wealth of all. (Proverbial.)   **186 fineless** boundless

Good God, the souls of all my tribe defend
From jealousy!
OTHELLO   Why, why is this?
Think'st thou I'd make a life of jealousy,
To follow still the changes of the moon   192
With fresh suspicions? No! To be once in doubt   193
Is once to be resolved. Exchange me for a goat   194
When I shall turn the business of my soul
To such exsufflicate and blown surmises   196
Matching thy inference. 'Tis not to make me jealous   197
To say my wife is fair, feeds well, loves company,
Is free of speech, sings, plays, and dances well;
Where virtue is, these are more virtuous.
Nor from mine own weak merits will I draw
The smallest fear or doubt of her revolt,   202
For she had eyes, and chose me. No, Iago,
I'll see before I doubt; when I doubt, prove;
And on the proof, there is no more but this—
Away at once with love or jealousy.

IAGO
I am glad of this, for now I shall have reason
To show the love and duty that I bear you
With franker spirit. Therefore, as I am bound,
Receive it from me. I speak not yet of proof.
Look to your wife; observe her well with Cassio.
Wear your eyes thus, not jealous nor secure.   212
I would not have your free and noble nature,
Out of self-bounty, be abused. Look to 't.   214
I know our country disposition well;
In Venice they do let God see the pranks
They dare not show their husbands; their best
      conscience
Is not to leave 't undone, but keep 't unknown.
OTHELLO   Dost thou say so?
IAGO
She did deceive her father, marrying you;
And when she seemed to shake and fear your looks,
She loved them most.
OTHELLO   And so she did.
IAGO   Why, go to, then!   222
She that, so young, could give out such a seeming,   223
To seel her father's eyes up close as oak,   224
He thought 'twas witchcraft! But I am much to blame.
I humbly do beseech you of your pardon
For too much loving you.
OTHELLO   I am bound to thee forever.   228
IAGO
I see this hath a little dashed your spirits.

OTHELLO
Not a jot, not a jot.
IAGO   I'faith, I fear it has.
I hope you will consider what is spoke
Comes from my love. But I do see you're moved.
I am to pray you not to strain my speech
To grosser issues nor to larger reach   234
Than to suspicion.
OTHELLO   I will not.
IAGO   Should you do so, my lord,
My speech should fall into such vile success   238
Which my thoughts aimed not. Cassio's my worthy
      friend.
My lord, I see you're moved.
OTHELLO   No, not much moved.
I do not think but Desdemona's honest.   241
IAGO
Long live she so! And long live you to think so!
OTHELLO
And yet, how nature erring from itself—
IAGO
Ay, there's the point! As—to be bold with you—
Not to affect many proposèd matches   245
Of her own clime, complexion, and degree,   246
Whereto we see in all things nature tends—
Foh! One may smell in such a will most rank,   248
Foul disproportion, thoughts unnatural.   249
But pardon me. I do not in position   250
Distinctly speak of her, though I may fear
Her will, recoiling to her better judgment,   252
May fall to match you with her country forms   253
And happily repent.
OTHELLO   Farewell, farewell!   254
If more thou dost perceive, let me know more.
Set on thy wife to observe. Leave me, Iago.
IAGO [going]   My lord, I take my leave.
OTHELLO
Why did I marry? This honest creature doubtless
Sees and knows more, much more, than he unfolds.
IAGO [returning]
My lord, I would I might entreat Your Honor
To scan this thing no farther. Leave it to time.   261
Although 'tis fit that Cassio have his place—
For, sure, he fills it up with great ability—
Yet, if you please to hold him off awhile,
You shall by that perceive him and his means.   265
Note if your lady strain his entertainment   266
With any strong or vehement importunity;
Much will be seen in that. In the meantime,
Let me be thought too busy in my fears—   269

192–3 To follow . . . suspicions? to be constantly imagining new causes for suspicion, changing incessantly like the moon? **194 once** once and for all. **resolved** free of doubt, having settled the matter. **196 exsufflicate and blown** inflated and blown up or flyblown, hence, loathsome, disgusting **197 inference** description or allegation. **202 doubt . . . revolt** fear of her unfaithfulness **212 not** neither. **secure** free from uncertainty. **214 self-bounty** inherent or natural goodness and generosity. **abused** deceived. **222 go to** (An expression of impatience.) **223 seeming** false appearance **224 seel** blind. (A term from falconry.) **oak** (A close-grained wood.) **228 bound** indebted. (But perhaps with ironic sense of "tied.")

234 issues significances. **reach** meaning, scope **238 success** effect, result **241 honest** chaste. **245 affect** prefer, desire **246 clime . . . degree** country, temperament or skin color, and social position **248 will** sensuality, appetite **249 disproportion** abnormality **250 in position** in making this argument or proposition **252 recoiling** reverting. **better** i.e., more natural and reconsidered **253 fall . . . forms** undertake to compare you with Venetian norms of handsomeness **254 happily repent** haply repent her marriage. **261 scan** scrutinize **265 his means** the method he uses (to regain his post). **266 strain his entertainment** urge his reinstatement **269 busy** officious

As worthy cause I have to fear I am—
And hold her free, I do beseech Your Honor. 271
OTHELLO   Fear not my government. 272
IAGO   I once more take my leave.   *Exit.*
OTHELLO
This fellow's of exceeding honesty,
And knows all qualities, with a learnèd spirit, 275
Of human dealings. If I do prove her haggard, 276
Though that her jesses were my dear heartstrings, 277
I'd whistle her off and let her down the wind 278
To prey at fortune. Haply, for I am black 279
And have not those soft parts of conversation 280
That chamberers have, or for I am declined 281
Into the vale of years—yet that's not much—
She's gone. I am abused, and my relief 283
Must be to loathe her. Oh, curse of marriage,
That we can call these delicate creatures ours
And not their appetites! I had rather be a toad
And live upon the vapor of a dungeon
Than keep a corner in the thing I love
For others' uses. Yet, 'tis the plague of great ones;
Prerogatived are they less than the base. 290
'Tis destiny unshunnable, like death.
Even then this forkèd plague is fated to us 292
When we do quicken. Look where she comes. 293

Enter Desdemona and Emilia.

If she be false, oh, then heaven mocks itself!
I'll not believe't.
DESDEMONA   How now, my dear Othello?
Your dinner, and the generous islanders 296
By you invited do attend your presence. 297
OTHELLO
I am to blame.
DESDEMONA   Why do you speak so faintly?
Are you not well?
OTHELLO
I have a pain upon my forehead here.
DESDEMONA
Faith, that's with watching. 'Twill away again. 301
                      [*She offers her handkerchief.*]
Let me but bind it hard, within this hour
It will be well.
OTHELLO   Your napkin is too little. 303
Let it alone. Come, I'll go in with you. 304
        [*He puts the handkerchief from him, and it drops.*]

DESDEMONA
I am very sorry that you are not well.
                      Exit [with Othello].
EMILIA [*picking up the handkerchief*]
I am glad I have found this napkin.
This was her first remembrance from the Moor.
My wayward husband hath a hundred times 308
Wooed me to steal it, but she so loves the token—
For he conjured her she should ever keep it—
That she reserves it evermore about her
To kiss and talk to. I'll have the work ta'en out, 312
And give't Iago. What he will do with it
Heaven knows, not I;
I nothing but to please his fantasy. 315

Enter Iago.

IAGO
How now? What do you here alone?
EMILIA
Do not you chide. I have a thing for you.
IAGO
You have a thing for me? It is a common thing— 318
EMILIA   Ha?
IAGO   To have a foolish wife.
EMILIA
Oh, is that all? What will you give me now
For that same handkerchief?
IAGO   What handkerchief?
EMILIA   What handkerchief?
Why, that the Moor first gave to Desdemona;
That which so often you did bid me steal.
IAGO   Hast stolen it from her?
EMILIA
No, faith. She let it drop by negligence,
And to th'advantage I, being here, took't up. 329
Look, here 'tis.
IAGO   A good wench! Give it me.
EMILIA
What will you do with't, that you have been so earnest
To have me filch it?
IAGO [*snatching it*]   Why, what is that to you?
EMILIA
If it be not for some purpose of import,
Give't me again. Poor lady, she'll run mad
When she shall lack it.
IAGO   Be not acknown on't. 335
I have use for it. Go, leave me.   *Exit Emilia.*
I will in Cassio's lodging lose this napkin 337
And let him find it. Trifles light as air
Are to the jealous confirmations strong
As proofs of Holy Writ. This may do something.
The Moor already changes with my poison.

---

271 **hold her free** regard her as innocent   272 **government** self-control, conduct.   275 **qualities** natures, types   276 **haggard** wild (like a wild female hawk)   277 **jesses** straps fastened around the legs of a trained hawk   278 **I'd . . . wind** i.e., I'd let her go forever. (To release a hawk downwind was to turn it loose.)   279 **prey at fortune** fend for herself in the wild.   **Haply, for** Perhaps because   280 **soft . . . conversation** pleasing social graces   281 **chamberers** drawing-room gallants   283 **abused** deceived   290 **Prerogatived** privileged (to have honest wives).   **the base** ordinary citizens. (Socially prominent men are especially prone to the common destiny of being cuckolded and to the public shame that goes with it.)   292 **forkèd** (An allusion to the horns of the cuckold.)   293 **quicken** receive life. (*Quicken* may also mean to swarm with maggots as the body festers, as in 4.2.69, in which case lines 292–3 suggest that *even then*, in death, we are cuckolded by *forkèd* worms.)   296 **generous** noble   297 **attend** await   301 **watching** too little sleep.   303 **napkin** handkerchief   304 **Let it alone** i.e., Never mind.

308 **wayward** capricious   312 **work ta'en out** design of the embroidery copied   315 **fantasy** whim.   318 **common thing** (With bawdy suggestion; *common* suggests coarseness and availability to all comers, and *thing* is a slang term for the pudendum.)   329 **to th'advantage** taking the opportunity   335 **lack** miss.   **Be . . . on't** Do not confess knowledge of it; keep out of this.   337 **lose** (The Folio spelling, "loose," is a normal spelling for "lose," but it may also contain the idea of "let go," "release.")

Dangerous conceits are in their natures poisons,   342
Which at the first are scarce found to distaste,   343
But with a little act upon the blood   344
Burn like the mines of sulfur.

    Enter Othello.

                    I did say so.
Look where he comes! Not poppy nor mandragora   346
Nor all the drowsy syrups of the world
Shall ever medicine thee to that sweet sleep
Which thou owed'st yesterday.

OTHELLO   Ha, ha, false to me?   349

IAGO
  Why, how now, General? No more of that.

OTHELLO
  Avaunt! Begone! Thou hast set me on the rack.
  I swear 'tis better to be much abused
  Than but to know't a little.

IAGO   How now, my lord?

OTHELLO
  What sense had I of her stolen hours of lust?
  I saw't not, thought it not, it harmed not me.
  I slept the next night well, fed well, was free and
    merry;   356
  I found not Cassio's kisses on her lips.
  He that is robbed, not wanting what is stolen,   358
  Let him not know't and he's not robbed at all.

IAGO I am sorry to hear this.

OTHELLO
  I had been happy if the general camp,
  Pioneers and all, had tasted her sweet body,   362
  So I had nothing known. Oh, now, forever   363
  Farewell the tranquil mind! Farewell content!
  Farewell the plumèd troops and the big wars   365
  That makes ambition virtue! Oh, farewell!
  Farewell the neighing steed and the shrill trump,
  The spirit-stirring drum, th'ear-piercing fife,
  The royal banner, and all quality,   369
  Pride, pomp, and circumstance of glorious war!   370
  And O you mortal engines, whose rude throats   371
  Th'immortal Jove's dread clamors counterfeit,   372
  Farewell! Othello's occupation's gone.

IAGO Is't possible, my lord?

OTHELLO
  Villain, be sure thou prove my love a whore!
  Be sure of it. Give me the ocular proof,
  Or, by the worth of mine eternal soul,
  Thou hadst been better have been born a dog
  Than answer my waked wrath!

IAGO   Is't come to this?

OTHELLO
  Make me to see't, or at the least so prove it

That the probation bear no hinge nor loop   381
To hang a doubt on, or woe upon thy life!

IAGO My noble lord—

OTHELLO
  If thou dost slander her and torture me,
  Never pray more; abandon all remorse;   385
  On horror's head horrors accumulate;   386
  Do deeds to make heaven weep, all earth amazed;   387
  For nothing canst thou to damnation add
  Greater than that.

IAGO   O grace! O heaven forgive me!
  Are you a man? Have you a soul or sense?
  God b'wi'you; take mine office. O wretched fool,   391
  That lov'st to make thine honesty a vice!   392
  O monstrous world! Take note, take note, O world,
  To be direct and honest is not safe.
  I thank you for this profit, and from hence   395
  I'll love no friend, sith love breeds such offense.   396

OTHELLO Nay, stay. Thou shouldst be honest.   397

IAGO
  I should be wise, for honesty's a fool
  And loses that it works for.

OTHELLO   By the world,   399
  I think my wife be honest and think she is not;
  I think that thou art just and think thou art not.
  I'll have some proof. My name, that was as fresh
  As Dian's visage, is now begrimed and black   403
  As mine own face. If there be cords, or knives,
  Poison, or fire, or suffocating streams,
  I'll not endure it. Would I were satisfied!

IAGO
  I see, sir, you are eaten up with passion.
  I do repent me that I put it to you.
  You would be satisfied?

OTHELLO   Would? Nay, and I will.

IAGO
  And may; but how? How satisfied, my lord?
  Would you, the supervisor, grossly gape on?   411
  Behold her topped?

OTHELLO   Death and damnation! Oh!

IAGO
  It were a tedious difficulty, I think,
  To bring them to that prospect. Damn them then,   414
  If ever mortal eyes do see them bolster   415
  More than their own. What then? How then?   416
  What shall I say? Where's satisfaction?
  It is impossible you should see this,
  Were they as prime as goats, as hot as monkeys,   419

---

342 conceits fancies, ideas   **343 distaste** be distasteful   **344 act** action, working   **346 mandragora** an opiate made of the mandrake root   **349 thou owed'st** you did own   **356 free** carefree   **358 wanting** missing   **362 Pioneers** diggers of mines, the lowest grade of soldiers   **363 So** provided   **365 big** mighty   **369 quality** character, essential nature   **370 Pride** rich display.   **circumstance** pageantry   **371 mortal engines** i.e., cannon. (*Mortal* means "deadly.")   **372 Jove's dread clamors** i.e., thunder

381 probation proof   **385 remorse** pity, penitent hope for salvation   **386 horrors accumulate** add still more horrors   **387 amazed** confounded with horror   **391 O wretched fool** (Iago addresses himself as a fool for having carried honesty too far.)   **392 vice** failing, something overdone.   **395 profit** profitable instruction.   **hence** henceforth   **396 sith** since.   **offense** i.e., harm to the one who offers help and friendship.   **397 Thou shouldst be** It appears that you are. (But Iago replies in the sense of "ought to be.")   **399 that** what   **403 Dian** Diana, goddess of the moon and of chastity   **411 supervisor** onlooker   **414 Damn them then** i.e., They would have to be really incorrigible   **415 bolster** go to bed together, share a bolster   **416 More** other.   **own** own eyes.   **419 prime** lustful

As salt as wolves in pride, and fools as gross 420
As ignorance made drunk. But yet I say,
If imputation and strong circumstances 422
Which lead directly to the door of truth
Will give you satisfaction, you might have't.

OTHELLO
Give me a living reason she's disloyal.

IAGO   I do not like the office.
But sith I am entered in this cause so far, 427
Pricked to't by foolish honesty and love, 428
I will go on. I lay with Cassio lately,
And being troubled with a raging tooth
I could not sleep. There are a kind of men
So loose of soul that in their sleeps will mutter
Their affairs. One of this kind is Cassio.
In sleep I heard him say, "Sweet Desdemona,
Let us be wary, let us hide our loves!"
And then, sir, would he grip and wring my hand,
Cry "O sweet creature!", then kiss me hard,
As if he plucked up kisses by the roots
That grew upon my lips; then laid his leg
Over my thigh, and sighed, and kissed, and then
Cried, "Cursèd fate that gave thee to the Moor!"

OTHELLO
Oh, monstrous! Monstrous!

IAGO   Nay, this was but his dream.

OTHELLO
But this denoted a foregone conclusion. 443
'Tis a shrewd doubt, though it be but a dream. 444

IAGO
And this may help to thicken other proofs
That do demonstrate thinly.

OTHELLO   I'll tear her all to pieces.

IAGO
Nay, but be wise. Yet we see nothing done;
She may be honest yet. Tell me but this:
Have you not sometimes seen a handkerchief
Spotted with strawberries in your wife's hand? 450

OTHELLO
I gave her such a one. 'Twas my first gift.

IAGO
I know not that; but such a handkerchief—
I am sure it was your wife's—did I today
See Cassio wipe his beard with.

OTHELLO   If it be that—

IAGO
If it be that, or any that was hers,
It speaks against her with the other proofs.

OTHELLO
Oh, that the slave had forty thousand lives! 457
One is too poor, too weak for my revenge.
Now do I see 'tis true. Look here, Iago,
All my fond love thus do I blow to heaven. 460

'Tis gone.
Arise, black vengeance, from the hollow hell!
Yield up, O love, thy crown and hearted throne 463
To tyrannous hate! Swell, bosom, with thy freight, 464
For 'tis of aspics' tongues! 465

IAGO   Yet be content. 466

OTHELLO   Oh, blood, blood, blood!

IAGO
Patience, I say. Your mind perhaps may change.

OTHELLO
Never, Iago. Like to the Pontic Sea, 469
Whose icy current and compulsive course
Ne'er feels retiring ebb, but keeps due on
To the Propontic and the Hellespont, 472
Even so my bloody thoughts with violent pace
Shall ne'er look back, ne'er ebb to humble love,
Till that a capable and wide revenge 475
Swallow them up. Now, by yond marble heaven, 476
[Kneeling] In the due reverence of a sacred vow
I here engage my words.

IAGO   Do not rise yet.
[He kneels.] Witness, you ever-burning lights above, 479
You elements that clip us round about, 480
Witness that here Iago doth give up
The execution of his wit, hands, heart, 482
To wronged Othello's service. Let him command,
And to obey shall be in me remorse, 484
What bloody business ever.   [They rise.]

OTHELLO   I greet thy love, 485
Not with vain thanks, but with acceptance bounteous,
And will upon the instant put thee to't. 487
Within these three days let me hear thee say
That Cassio's not alive.

IAGO   My friend is dead;
'Tis done at your request. But let her live.

OTHELLO
Damn her, lewd minx! Oh, damn her, damn her! 491
Come, go with me apart. I will withdraw
To furnish me with some swift means of death
For the fair devil. Now art thou my lieutenant.

IAGO   I am your own forever.   *Exeunt.*

❧

3.4

Enter Desdemona, Emilia, and Clown.

DESDEMONA   Do you know, sirrah, where Lieutenant 1
Cassio lies? 2

---

463 hearted fixed in the heart   **464 freight** burden   **465 aspics'**
venomous serpents'   **466 content** calm.   **469 Pontic Sea** Black Sea
472 Propontic Sea of Marmora, between the Black Sea and the
Aegean.   **Hellespont** Dardanelles, straits where the Sea of Marmora
joins with the Aegean   **475 capable** ample, comprehensive
476 marble i.e., gleaming, polished, and indifferent to human suffering   **479 s.d.** *He kneels* (In the Quarto text, Iago kneels here after
Othello has knelt at line 477.)   **480 clip** encompass   **482 execution**
exercise, action.   **wit** mind   **484 remorse** pity (for Othello's wrongs)
485 ever soever.   **487 to't** to the proof.   **491 minx** wanton.
3.4. Location: Before the citadel.
1 sirrah (A form of address to an inferior.)   **2 lies** lodges. (But the
Clown makes the obvious pun.)

---

420 salt wanton, sensual.   **pride** heat   **422 imputation . . . circumstances** strong circumstantial evidence   **427 sith** since   **428 Pricked**
spurred   **443 foregone conclusion** previous experience or action.
444 shrewd doubt suspicious circumstance   **450 Spotted with strawberries** embroidered with a strawberry pattern   **457 the slave** i.e.,
Cassio   **460 fond** foolish. (But also suggesting "affectionate.")

CLOWN   I dare not say he lies anywhere.

DESDEMONA   Why, man?

CLOWN   He's a soldier, and for me to say a soldier lies, 'tis stabbing.

DESDEMONA   Go to. Where lodges he?

CLOWN   To tell you where he lodges is to tell you where I lie.

DESDEMONA   Can anything be made of this?

CLOWN   I know not where he lodges, and for me to devise a lodging and say he lies here, or he lies there, were to lie in mine own throat.   13

DESDEMONA   Can you inquire him out, and be edified by report?

CLOWN   I will catechize the world for him; that is, make questions, and by them answer.

DESDEMONA   Seek him, bid him come hither. Tell him I have moved my lord on his behalf and hope all will be well.   19

CLOWN   To do this is within the compass of man's wit, and therefore I will attempt the doing it.   *Exit Clown.*

DESDEMONA
Where should I lose that handkerchief, Emilia?

EMILIA   I know not, madam.

DESDEMONA
Believe me, I had rather have lost my purse
Full of crusadoes; and but my noble Moor   26
Is true of mind and made of no such baseness
As jealous creatures are, it were enough
To put him to ill thinking.

EMILIA   Is he not jealous?

DESDEMONA
Who, he? I think the sun where he was born
Drew all such humors from him.

EMILIA   Look where he comes.   31

Enter Othello.

DESDEMONA
I will not leave him now till Cassio
Be called to him.—How is't with you, my lord?

OTHELLO
Well, my good lady. [*Aside*] Oh, hardness to
    dissemble!—
How do you, Desdemona?

DESDEMONA   Well, my good lord.

OTHELLO
Give me your hand. [*She gives her hand.*] This hand is
    moist, my lady.

DESDEMONA
It yet hath felt no age nor known no sorrow.

OTHELLO
This argues fruitfulness and liberal heart.   38
Hot, hot, and moist. This hand of yours requires
A sequester from liberty, fasting and prayer,   40

Much castigation, exercise devout;   41
For here's a young and sweating devil here
That commonly rebels. 'Tis a good hand,
A frank one.

DESDEMONA   You may indeed say so,   44
For 'twas that hand that gave away my heart.

OTHELLO
A liberal hand. The hearts of old gave hands,   46
But our new heraldry is hands, not hearts.   47

DESDEMONA
I cannot speak of this. Come now, your promise.

OTHELLO   What promise, chuck?   49

DESDEMONA
I have sent to bid Cassio come speak with you.

OTHELLO
I have a salt and sorry rheum offends me;   51
Lend me thy handkerchief.

DESDEMONA   Here, my lord.   [*She offers a handkerchief.*]

OTHELLO
That which I gave you.

DESDEMONA   I have it not about me.

OTHELLO   Not?

DESDEMONA   No, faith, my lord.

OTHELLO
That's a fault. That handkerchief
Did an Egyptian to my mother give.
She was a charmer, and could almost read   59
The thoughts of people. She told her, while she kept it
'Twould make her amiable and subdue my father   61
Entirely to her love, but if she lost it
Or made a gift of it, my father's eye
Should hold her loathèd and his spirits should hunt
After new fancies. She, dying, gave it me,   65
And bid me, when my fate would have me wived,
To give it her. I did so; and take heed on't;   67
Make it a darling like your precious eye.
To lose't or give't away were such perdition   69
As nothing else could match.

DESDEMONA   Is't possible?

OTHELLO
'Tis true. There's magic in the web of it.   71
A sibyl, that had numbered in the world
The sun to course two hundred compasses,   73
In her prophetic fury sewed the work;   74
The worms were hallowed that did breed the silk,
And it was dyed in mummy which the skillful   76
Conserved of maidens' hearts.

DESDEMONA   I'faith! Is't true?   77

---

13 lie . . . throat lie egregiously and deliberately.   19 moved my lord petitioned Othello   26 crusadoes Portuguese gold coins   31 humors (Refers to the four bodily fluids thought to determine temperament.)   38 argues gives evidence of.   fruitfulness generosity, amorousness, and fecundity.   liberal generous and sexually free   40 sequester sequestration

41 castigation corrective discipline.   exercise devout i.e., prayer, religious meditation, etc.   44 frank generous, open. (With sexual suggestion.)   46–7 The hearts . . . hands i.e., In former times, people would give their hearts when they gave their hands to something, but in our dedacent present age the joining of hands no longer has that spiritual sense.   49 chuck (A term of endearment.)   51 salt . . . rheum distressful head cold or watering of the eyes   59 charmer sorceress   61 amiable desirable   65 fancies loves.   67 her i.e., to my wife.   69 perdition loss   71 web fabric, weaving   73 compasses annual circlings. (The *sibyl*, or prophetess, was two hundred years old.)   74 prophetic fury frenzy of prophetic inspiration.   work embroidered pattern   76 mummy medicinal or magical preparation drained from mummified bodies   77 Conserved of prepared or preserved out of

OTHELLO
  Most veritable. Therefore look to't well.
DESDEMONA
  Then would to God that I had never seen't!
OTHELLO   Ha? Wherefore?
DESDEMONA
  Why do you speak so startingly and rash?   81
OTHELLO
  Is't lost? Is't gone? Speak, is't out o'th' way?   82
DESDEMONA   Heaven bless us!
OTHELLO   Say you?
DESDEMONA
  It is not lost; but what an if it were?   85
OTHELLO   How?
DESDEMONA
  I say it is not lost.
OTHELLO   Fetch't, let me see't.
DESDEMONA
  Why, so I can, sir, but I will not now.
  This is a trick to put me from my suit.
  Pray you, let Cassio be received again.
OTHELLO
  Fetch me the handkerchief! My mind misgives.
DESDEMONA   Come, come,
  You'll never meet a more sufficient man.   93
OTHELLO
  The handkerchief!
DESDEMONA   I pray, talk me of Cassio.   94
OTHELLO
  The handkerchief!
DESDEMONA   A man that all his time   95
  Hath founded his good fortunes on your love,   96
  Shared dangers with you—
OTHELLO   The handkerchief!
DESDEMONA   I'faith, you are to blame.
OTHELLO   Zounds!   Exit Othello.
EMILIA   Is not this man jealous?
DESDEMONA   I ne'er saw this before.
  Sure, there's some wonder in this handkerchief.
  I am most unhappy in the loss of it.   104
EMILIA
  'Tis not a year or two shows us a man.   105
  They are all but stomachs, and we all but food;   106
  They eat us hungrily, and when they are full   107
  They belch us.

       Enter Iago and Cassio.

             Look you, Cassio and my husband.
IAGO [to Cassio]
  There is no other way; 'tis she must do't.
  And, lo, the happiness! Go and importune her.   110

DESDEMONA
  How now, good Cassio? What's the news with you?
CASSIO
  Madam, my former suit. I do beseech you
  That by your virtuous means I may again   113
  Exist and be a member of his love
  Whom I, with all the office of my heart,   115
  Entirely honor. I would not be delayed.
  If my offense be of such mortal kind   117
  That nor my service past, nor present sorrows,   118
  Nor purposed merit in futurity
  Can ransom me into his love again,
  But to know so must be my benefit;   121
  So shall I clothe me in a forced content,
  And shut myself up in some other course,   123
  To fortune's alms.
DESDEMONA   Alas, thrice-gentle Cassio,   124
  My advocation is not now in tune.   125
  My lord is not my lord; nor should I know him,
  Were he in favor as in humor altered.   127
  So help me every spirit sanctified   128
  As I have spoken for you all my best
  And stood within the blank of his displeasure   130
  For my free speech! You must awhile be patient.   131
  What I can do I will, and more I will
  Than for myself I dare. Let that suffice you.
IAGO
  Is my lord angry?
EMILIA   He went hence but now,
  And certainly in strange unquietness.
IAGO
  Can he be angry? I have seen the cannon
  When it hath blown his ranks into the air,
  And like the devil from his very arm
  Puffed his own brother—and is he angry?
  Something of moment then. I will go meet him.   140
  There's matter in't indeed, if he be angry.
DESDEMONA
  I prithee, do so.   Exit [Iago].
                    Something, sure, of state,   142
  Either from Venice, or some unhatched practice   143
  Made demonstrable here in Cyprus to him,
  Hath puddled his clear spirit; and in such cases   145
  Men's natures wrangle with inferior things,
  Though great ones are their object. 'Tis even so;
  For let our finger ache, and it indues   148
  Our other, healthful members even to a sense
  Of pain. Nay, we must think men are not gods,

---

81 **startingly and rash** disjointedly and impetuously, excitedly.
82 **out o'th' way** lost, misplaced.   85 **an if** if   93 **sufficient** able,
complete   94 **talk** talk to   95–6 **A man . . . love** A man who throughout his career has relied on your favor for his advancement
104 **unhappy** (1) unfortunate (2) sad   105 **'Tis . . . man** A year or two
is not enough time for us women to know what men really are.
106 **but** nothing but   107 **hungrily** hungrily   110 **the happiness** in
happy time, fortunately met.

113 **virtuous** (1) efficacious (2) morally good   115 **office** loyal service
117 **mortal** fatal   118 **nor . . . nor** neither . . . nor   121 **But . . . benefit**
merely to know that my case is hopeless will have to content me (and
will be better than uncertainty)   123 **And shut . . . in** commit myself
to   124 **To fortune's alms** throwing myself on the mercy of fortune.
125 **advocation** advocacy   127 **favor** appearance.   **humor** mood
128 **So . . . sanctified** So help me all the heavenly host   130 **within
the blank** within point-blank range. (The *blank* is the center of the target.)   131 **free** frank   140 **of moment** of immediate importance,
momentous   142 **of state** concerning state affairs   143 **unhatched
practice** as yet unexecuted or undiscovered plot   145 **puddled** muddied   148 **indues** endows, brings to the same condition

Nor of them look for such observancy   151
As fits the bridal. Beshrew me much, Emilia,   152
I was, unhandsome warrior as I am,   153
Arraigning his unkindness with my soul;   154
But now I find I had suborned the witness,   155
And he's indicted falsely.

EMILIA   Pray heaven it be
State matters, as you think, and no conception
Nor no jealous toy concerning you.   158

DESDEMONA
Alas the day! I never gave him cause.

EMILIA
But jealous souls will not be answered so;
They are not ever jealous for the cause,
But jealous for they're jealous. It is a monster   162
Begot upon itself, born on itself.   163

DESDEMONA
Heaven keep that monster from Othello's mind!

EMILIA   Lady, amen.

DESDEMONA
I will go seek him. Cassio, walk hereabout.
If I do find him fit, I'll move your suit
And seek to effect it to my uttermost.

CASSIO
I humbly thank Your Ladyship.
                    Exit [*Desdemona with Emilia*].

                    Enter Bianca.

BIANCA
Save you, friend Cassio!

CASSIO   What make you from home?   170
How is't with you, my most fair Bianca?
I' faith, sweet love, I was coming to your house.

BIANCA
And I was going to your lodging, Cassio.
What, keep a week away? Seven days and nights?
Eightscore-eight hours? And lovers' absent hours   175
More tedious than the dial eightscore times?   176
Oh, weary reck'ning!

CASSIO   Pardon me, Bianca.
I have this while with leaden thoughts been pressed;
But I shall, in a more continuate time,   179
Strike off this score of absence. Sweet Bianca,   180
          [*giving her Desdemona's handkerchief*]
Take me this work out.

BIANCA   Oh, Cassio, whence came this?   181
This is some token from a newer friend.   182
To the felt absence now I feel a cause.
Is't come to this? Well, well.

CASSIO   Go to, woman!
Throw your vile guesses in the devil's teeth,

From whence you have them. You are jealous now
That this is from some mistress, some remembrance.
No, by my faith, Bianca.

BIANCA   Why, whose is it?

CASSIO
I know not, neither. I found it in my chamber.
I like the work well. Ere it be demanded—   190
As like enough it will—I would have it copied   191
Take it and do't, and leave me for this time.

BIANCA   Leave you? Wherefore?

CASSIO
I do attend here on the General,
And think it no addition, nor my wish,   195
To have him see me womaned.

BIANCA   Why, I pray you?

CASSIO   Not that I love you not.

BIANCA   But that you do not love me.
I pray you, bring me on the way a little,   200
And say if I shall see you soon at night.

CASSIO
'Tis but a little way that I can bring you,
For I attend here; but I'll see you soon.

BIANCA
'Tis very good. I must be circumstanced.   204
                    Exeunt omnes.

                              ❖

4.1

                    Enter Othello and Iago.

IAGO
Will you think so?

OTHELLO   Think so, Iago?

IAGO   What,
To kiss in private?

OTHELLO   An unauthorized kiss!

IAGO
Or to be naked with her friend in bed
An hour or more, not meaning any harm?

OTHELLO
Naked in bed, Iago, and not mean harm?
It is hypocrisy against the devil.
They that mean virtuously and yet do so,
The devil their virtue tempts, and they tempt heaven.

IAGO
If they do nothing, 'tis a venial slip.   9
But if I give my wife a handkerchief—

OTHELLO   What then?

IAGO
Why then, 'tis hers, my lord, and being hers,
She may, I think, bestow't on any man.

OTHELLO
She is protectress of her honor too.
May she give that?

151 **observancy** attentiveness   152 **bridal** wedding (when a bride-groom is newly attentive to his bride).   **Beshrew me** (A mild oath.) 153 **unhandsome** insufficient, unskillful   154 **with** before the bar of 155 **suborned the witness** induced the witness to give false testimony 158 **toy** fancy   162 **for** because   163 **Begot upon itself** generated solely from itself   170 **Save** God save.   **make** do   175 **Eightscore-eight** one hundred sixty-eight, the number of hours in a week 176 **the dial** a complete revolution of the clock   179 **continuate** uninterrupted   180 **Strike . . . score** settle this account   181 **Take . . . out** copy this embroidery for me.   182 **friend** mistress.

190 **demanded** inquired for   191 **like** likely   195 **addition** i.e., addition to my reputation   200 **bring** accompany   204 **be circumstanced** be governed by circumstance, yield to your conditions.
4.1. Location: Before the citadel.
9 **venial** pardonable

IAGO
　　Her honor is an essence that's not seen;
　　They have it very oft that have it not.   17
　　But, for the handkerchief—
OTHELLO
　　By heaven, I would most gladly have forgot it.
　　Thou said'st—Oh, it comes o'er my memory
　　As doth the raven o'er the infectious house,   21
　　Boding to all—he had my handkerchief.
IAGO
　　Ay, what of that?
OTHELLO   That's not so good now.
IAGO   What
　　If I had said I had seen him do you wrong?
　　Or heard him say—as knaves be such abroad,   25
　　Who having, by their own importunate suit,   26
　　Or voluntary dotage of some mistress,   27
　　Convincèd or supplied them, cannot choose   28
　　But they must blab—
OTHELLO   Hath he said anything?   29
IAGO
　　He hath, my lord; but, be you well assured,
　　No more than he'll unswear.
OTHELLO   What hath he said?
IAGO
　　Faith, that he did—I know not what he did.
OTHELLO   What? What?
IAGO
　　Lie—
OTHELLO   With her?
IAGO   With her, on her; what you will.
OTHELLO   Lie with her? Lie on her? We say "lie on her"
　　when they belie her. Lie with her? Zounds, that's ful-   36
　　some.—Handkerchief—confessions—handkerchief!   37
　　—To confess and be hanged for his labor—first to be   38
　　hanged and then to confess.—I tremble at it. Nature   39
　　would not invest herself in such shadowing passion   40
　　without some instruction. It is not words that shakes   41
　　me thus. Pish! Noses, ears, and lips.—Is't possible?
　　—Confess—handkerchief!—O devil!

　　　　　　　　　　　　　　　　　　　Falls in a trance.

IAGO   Work on,
　　My medicine, work! Thus credulous fools are caught,
　　And many worthy and chaste dames even thus,
　　All guiltless, meet reproach.—What, ho! My lord!
　　My lord, I say! Othello!

　　　　　　　Enter Cassio.

　　　　　　　How now, Cassio?

CASSIO   What's the matter?
IAGO
　　My lord is fall'n into an epilepsy.
　　This is his second fit. He had one yesterday.
CASSIO
　　Rub him about the temples.
IAGO   No, forbear.
　　The lethargy must have his quiet course.   53
　　If not, he foams at mouth, and by and by
　　Breaks out to savage madness. Look, he stirs.
　　Do you withdraw yourself a little while.
　　He will recover straight. When he is gone,
　　I would on great occasion speak with you.   58

　　　　　　　　　　　　　　　　[Exit Cassio.]

　　How is it, General? Have you not hurt your head?
OTHELLO
　　Dost thou mock me?
IAGO   I mock you not, by heaven.   60
　　Would you would bear your fortune like a man!
OTHELLO
　　A hornèd man's a monster and a beast.
IAGO
　　There's many a beast then in a populous city,
　　And many a civil monster.   64
OTHELLO   Did he confess it?
IAGO   Good sir, be a man.
　　Think every bearded fellow that's but yoked   67
　　May draw with you. There's millions now alive   68
　　That nightly lie in those unproper beds   69
　　Which they dare swear peculiar. Your case is better. 70
　　Oh, 'tis the spite of hell, the fiend's arch-mock,
　　To lip a wanton in a secure couch   72
　　And to suppose her chaste! No, let me know,
　　And knowing what I am, I know what she shall be. 74
OTHELLO   Oh, thou art wise. 'Tis certain.
IAGO   Stand you awhile apart;
　　Confine yourself but in a patient list.   77
　　Whilst you were here o'erwhelmèd with your grief—
　　A passion most unsuiting such a man—
　　Cassio came hither. I shifted him away,   80
　　And laid good 'scuse upon your ecstasy,   81
　　Bade him anon return and here speak with me,
　　The which he promised. Do but encave yourself   83
　　And mark the fleers, the gibes, and notable scorns 84
　　That dwell in every region of his face;
　　For I will make him tell the tale anew,
　　Where, how, how oft, how long ago, and when
　　He hath and is again to cope your wife.   88

I say, but mark his gesture. Marry, patience!
Or I shall say you're all-in-all in spleen,   90
And nothing of a man.

OTHELLO   Dost thou hear, Iago?
I will be found most cunning in my patience;
But—dost thou hear?—most bloody.

IAGO   That's not amiss;
But yet keep time in all. Will you withdraw?   94

[Othello stands apart.]

Now will I question Cassio of Bianca,
A huswife that by selling her desires   96
Buys herself bread and clothes. It is a creature
That dotes on Cassio—as 'tis the strumpet's plague
To beguile many and be beguiled by one.
He, when he hears of her, cannot restrain   100
From the excess of laughter. Here he comes.

Enter Cassio.

As he shall smile, Othello shall go mad;
And his unbookish jealousy must conster   103
Poor Cassio's smiles, gestures, and light behaviors
Quite in the wrong.—How do you now, Lieutenant?

CASSIO
The worser that you give me the addition   106
Whose want even kills me.   107

IAGO
Ply Desdemona well and you are sure on't.
[Speaking lower] Now, if this suit lay in Bianca's power,
How quickly should you speed!

CASSIO *[laughing]*   Alas, poor caitiff!   111

OTHELLO *[aside]*   Look how he laughs already!

IAGO
I never knew a woman love man so.

CASSIO
Alas, poor rogue! I think, i'faith, she loves me.

OTHELLO *[aside]*
Now he denies it faintly, and laughs it out.

IAGO
Do you hear, Cassio?

OTHELLO *[aside]*   Now he importunes him
To tell it o'er. Go to! Well said, well said.   117

IAGO
She gives it out that you shall marry her.
Do you intend it?

CASSIO   Ha, ha, ha!

OTHELLO *[aside]*
Do you triumph, Roman? Do you triumph?   121

CASSIO   I marry her? What? A customer? Prithee, bear   122
some charity to my wit; do not think it so unwhole-   123
some. Ha, ha, ha!

OTHELLO *[aside]*   So, so, so, so! They laugh that win.   125

IAGO   Faith, the cry goes that you shall marry her.   126

CASSIO   Prithee, say true.

IAGO   I am a very villain else.   128

OTHELLO *[aside]*   Have you scored me? Well.   129

CASSIO   This is the monkey's own giving out. She is
persuaded I will marry her out of her own love and
flattery, not out of my promise.   132

OTHELLO *[aside]*   Iago beckons me. Now he begins the   133
story.

CASSIO   She was here even now; she haunts me in every
place. I was the other day talking on the seabank with   136
certain Venetians, and thither comes the bauble, and,   137
by this hand, she falls me thus about my neck—   138

[He embraces Iago.]

OTHELLO *[aside]*   Crying, "Oh, dear Cassio!" as it were; his
gesture imports it.

CASSIO   So hangs and lolls and weeps upon me, so
shakes and pulls me. Ha, ha, ha!

OTHELLO *[aside]*   Now he tells how she plucked him to my
chamber. Oh, I see that nose of yours, but not that dog   144
I shall throw it to.   145

CASSIO   Well, I must leave her company.

IAGO   Before me, look where she comes.   147

Enter Bianca [with Othello's handkerchief].

CASSIO   'Tis such another fitchew! Marry, a perfumed   148
one.—What do you mean by this haunting of me?

BIANCA   Let the devil and his dam haunt you! What did   150
you mean by that same handkerchief you gave me
even now? I was a fine fool to take it. I must take out
the work? A likely piece of work, that you should find   153
it in your chamber and know not who left it there!
This is some minx's token, and I must take out the
work? There; give it your hobbyhorse. *[She gives him   156
the handkerchief.]* Wheresoever you had it, I'll take out
no work on't.

CASSIO   How now, my sweet Bianca? How now? How
now?

OTHELLO *[aside]*   By heaven, that should be my hand-   160
kerchief!

BIANCA   If you'll come to supper tonight, you may; if
you will not, come when you are next prepared for.   163

Exit.

IAGO   After her, after her.

CASSIO   Faith, I must. She'll rail in the streets else.

IAGO   Will you sup there?

CASSIO   Faith, I intend so.

IAGO   Well, I may chance to see you, for I would very
fain speak with you.

---

90 all-in-all in spleen utterly governed by passionate impulses
94 keep time keep yourself steady (as in music)   **96 huswife** hussy
100 restrain refrain   **103 his unbookish** Othello's uninstructed.
conster construe   **106 addition** title   **107 Whose want** the lack of
which   **111 caitiff** wretch.   **117 Go to** (An expression of remonstrance.)   **Well said** Well done. (Sarcastic.)   **121 Roman** (The
Romans were noted for their *triumphs* or triumphal processions.)
122 A customer? Who, I, the whore's customer? (Or, *customer* could
mean "prostitute.")   **122–3 bear . . . wit** be more charitable to my
judgment

125 They . . . win i.e., They that laugh last laugh best.   **126 cry** rumor
128 I . . . else Call me a complete rogue if I'm not telling the truth.
129 scored me scored off me, beaten me, made up my reckoning,
branded me.   **132 flattery** self-flattery, self-deception   **133 beckons**
signals to   **136 seabank** seashore   **137 bauble** plaything   **138 by
this hand** I make my vow   **144–5 not . . . to** (Othello imagines himself cutting off Cassio's nose and throwing it to a dog.)   **147 Before
me** i.e., On my soul   **148 'Tis . . . fitchew!** What a whore she is! Just
like all the others. (*Fitchew* or "polecat" was a common term of contempt for a courtesan or prostitute.)   **150 dam** mother   **153 A likely
. . . work** A fine story   **156 hobbyhorse** harlot.   **160 should be** must
be   **163 when . . . for** when I'm ready for you (i.e., never).

CASSIO   Prithee, come. Will you?

IAGO   Go to. Say no more.   [*Exit Cassio.*] 171

OTHELLO [*advancing*]   How shall I murder him, Iago?

IAGO   Did you perceive how he laughed at his vice?

OTHELLO   Oh, Iago!

IAGO   And did you see the handkerchief?

OTHELLO   Was that mine?

IAGO   Yours, by this hand. And to see how he prizes
the foolish woman your wife! She gave it him, and he
hath given it his whore.

OTHELLO   I would have him nine years a-killing. A fine
woman! A fair woman! A sweet woman!

IAGO   Nay, you must forget that.

OTHELLO   Ay, let her rot and perish, and be damned
tonight, for she shall not live. No, my heart is turned
to stone; I strike it, and it hurts my hand. Oh, the world
hath not a sweeter creature! She might lie by an emperor's side and command him tasks.

IAGO   Nay, that's not your way.   188

OTHELLO   Hang her! I do but say what she is. So delicate
with her needle! An admirable musician! Oh, she will
sing the savageness out of a bear. Of so high and plenteous wit and invention!   192

IAGO   She's the worse for all this.

OTHELLO   Oh, a thousand, a thousand times! And then,
of so gentle a condition!   195

IAGO   Ay, too gentle.   196

OTHELLO   Nay, that's certain. But yet the pity of it, Iago!
Oh, Iago, the pity of it, Iago!

IAGO   If you are so fond over her iniquity, give her patent 199
to offend, for if it touch not you it comes near nobody.

OTHELLO   I will chop her into messes. Cuckold me?   201

IAGO   Oh, 'tis foul in her.

OTHELLO   With mine officer?

IAGO   That's fouler.

OTHELLO   Get me some poison, Iago, this night. I'll not
expostulate with her, lest her body and beauty unpro-   206
vide my mind again. This night, Iago.   207

IAGO   Do it not with poison. Strangle her in her bed,
even the bed she hath contaminated.

OTHELLO   Good, good! The justice of it pleases. Very good.

IAGO   And for Cassio, let me be his undertaker. You   211
shall hear more by midnight.

OTHELLO
Excellent good. [*A trumpet within.*] What trumpet is
that same?

IAGO   I warrant, something from Venice.

Enter Lodovico, Desdemona, and attendants.

'Tis Lodovico. This comes from the Duke.
See, your wife's with him.

LODOVICO
God save you, worthy General!

OTHELLO   With all my heart, sir. 217

LODOVICO [*giving him a letter*]
The Duke and the senators of Venice greet you.

OTHELLO
I kiss the instrument of their pleasures.
                    [*He opens the letter, and reads.*]

DESDEMONA
And what's the news, good cousin Lodovico?

IAGO
I am very glad to see you, signor.
Welcome to Cyprus.

LODOVICO
I thank you. How does Lieutenant Cassio?

IAGO   Lives, sir.

DESDEMONA
Cousin, there's fall'n between him and my lord
An unkind breach; but you shall make all well.   226

OTHELLO   Are you sure of that?

DESDEMONA   My lord?

OTHELLO [*reads*]   "This fail you not to do, as you will—"

LODOVICO
He did not call; he's busy in the paper.
Is there division twixt my lord and Cassio?

DESDEMONA
A most unhappy one. I would do much
T'atone them, for the love I bear to Cassio.   233

OTHELLO   Fire and brimstone!

DESDEMONA   My lord?

OTHELLO   Are you wise?

DESDEMONA
What, is he angry?

LODOVICO   Maybe the letter moved him;
For, as I think, they do command him home,
Deputing Cassio in his government.   239

DESDEMONA   By my troth, I am glad on't.   240

OTHELLO   Indeed?

DESDEMONA   My lord?

OTHELLO   I am glad to see you mad.   243

DESDEMONA   Why, sweet Othello—

OTHELLO [*striking her*]   Devil!

DESDEMONA   I have not deserved this.

LODOVICO
My lord, this would not be believed in Venice,
Though I should swear I saw't. 'Tis very much.   248
Make her amends; she weeps.

OTHELLO   Oh, devil, devil!
If that the earth could teem with woman's tears,   250
Each drop she falls would prove a crocodile.   251
Out of my sight!

DESDEMONA   I will not stay to offend you. [*Going.*]

---

171 Go to (An expression of remonstrance.)   188 your way i.e., the
way you should think of her.   192 invention imagination.   195 gentle a condition wellborn and well-bred.   196 gentle generous, yielding (to other men).   199 fond foolish.   patent license   201 messes
portions of meat, i.e., bits.   206–7 unprovide weaken, disarm
211 be his undertaker undertake to dispatch him.

217 With all my heart i.e., I thank you most heartily   226 unkind
unnatural, contrary to their natures; hurtful   233 T'atone to reconcile
239 government office.   240 on't of it.   243 I am . . . mad i.e., I am
glad to see that you are insane enough to rejoice in Cassio's promotion. (? Othello bitterly plays on Desdemona's I am glad.)   248 very
much too much, outrageous.   250 teem breed, be impregnated
251 falls lets fall.   crocodile (Crocodiles were supposed to weep
hypocritical tears for their victims.)

LODOVICO   Truly, an obedient lady.
I do beseech Your Lordship, call her back.
OTHELLO [*calling*]   Mistress!
DESDEMONA [*returning*]   My lord?
OTHELLO   What would you with her, sir?   257
LODOVICO   Who, I, my lord?
OTHELLO
Ay, you did wish that I would make her turn.
Sir, she can turn, and turn, and yet go on
And turn again; and she can weep, sir, weep;
And she's obedient, as you say, obedient,   262
Very obedient.—Proceed you in your tears.—
Concerning this, sir—Oh, well-painted passion!—   264
I am commanded home.—Get you away;
I'll send for you anon.—Sir, I obey the mandate
And will return to Venice.—Hence, avaunt!
                       [*Exit Desdemona.*]
Cassio shall have my place. And, sir, tonight
I do entreat that we may sup together.
You are welcome, sir, to Cyprus.—Goats and
     monkeys!   *Exit.* 270
LODOVICO
Is this the noble Moor whom our full Senate
Call all in all sufficient? Is this the nature
Whom passion could not shake? Whose solid virtue
The shot of accident nor dart of chance
Could neither graze nor pierce?   He is much changed.
IAGO   He is much changed.
LODOVICO
Are his wits safe? Is he not light of brain?
IAGO
He's that he is. I may not breathe my censure   277
What he might be. If what he might he is not,   278
I would to heaven he were!
LODOVICO   What, strike his wife?   279
IAGO
Faith, that was not so well; yet would I knew
That stroke would prove the worst!
LODOVICO   Is it his use?   281
Or did the letters work upon his blood   282
And new-create his fault?
IAGO   Alas, alas!
It is not honesty in me to speak
What I have seen and known. You shall observe him,
And his own courses will denote him so   286
That I may save my speech. Do but go after,
And mark how he continues.
LODOVICO
I am sorry that I am deceived in him.   *Exeunt.*

❖

4.2

Enter Othello and Emilia.

OTHELLO   You have seen nothing, then?
EMILIA
Nor ever heard, nor ever did suspect.
OTHELLO
Yes, you have seen Cassio and she together.
EMILIA
But then I saw no harm, and then I heard
Each syllable that breath made up between them.
OTHELLO   What, did they never whisper?
EMILIA   Never, my lord.
OTHELLO   Nor send you out o'th' way?
EMILIA   Never.
OTHELLO
To fetch her fan, her gloves, her mask, nor nothing?
EMILIA   Never, my lord.
OTHELLO   That's strange.
EMILIA
I durst, my lord, to wager she is honest,
Lay down my soul at stake. If you think other,   14
Remove your thought; it doth abuse your bosom.   15
If any wretch have put this in your head,
Let heaven requite it with the serpent's curse!   17
For if she be not honest, chaste, and true,
There's no man happy; the purest of their wives
Is foul as slander.
OTHELLO   Bid her come hither. Go.
                          Exit Emilia.
She says enough; yet she's a simple bawd   21
That cannot say as much. This is a subtle whore,   22
A closet lock and key of villainous secrets.   23
And yet she'll kneel and pray; I have seen her do't.

Enter Desdemona and Emilia.

DESDEMONA   My lord, what is your will?
OTHELLO   Pray you, chuck, come hither.
DESDEMONA
What is your pleasure?
OTHELLO   Let me see your eyes.
Look in my face.
DESDEMONA   What horrible fancy's this?
OTHELLO [*to Emilia*]   Some of your function, mistress.   29
Leave procreants alone and shut the door;   30
Cough or cry "hem" if anybody come.
Your mystery, your mystery! Nay, dispatch.   32
                          Exit Emilia.
DESDEMONA [*kneeling*]
Upon my knees, what doth your speech import?

---

257 **What . . . sir?** (Othello implies that Desdemona is pliant and will do a *turn*, lines 257–9, for any man.)   262 **obedient** (With much the same sexual connotation as *turn* in lines 257–9.)   264 **passion** i.e., grief.   270 **Goats and monkeys** (See 3.3.419.)   277–9 **I may . . . were!** I dare not venture an opinion as to whether he's of unsound mind, as you suggest, but, if he isn't, then it might be better to wish he were in fact insane, since only that could excuse his wild behavior!   281 **use** custom.   282 **blood** passions   286 **courses will denote** actions will reveal

---

4.2. **Location: The citadel.**
14 **at stake** as the wager.   15 **abuse your bosom** deceive your breast, your heart.   17 **the serpent's curse** the curse pronounced by God on the serpent for deceiving Eve, just as some man has done to Othello and Desdemona. (See Genesis 3:14.)   21–2 **she's . . . much** i.e., any procuress or go-between who couldn't make up as plausible a story as Emilia's would have to be pretty stupid.   22 **This** i.e., Desdemona   23 **closet lock and key** i.e., concealer   29 **Some . . . function** i.e., Practice your chosen profession, that of bawd (by guarding the door) 30 **procreants** mating couples   32 **mystery** trade, occupation

I understand a fury in your words,
But not the words.

OTHELLO
Why, what art thou?

DESDEMONA   Your wife, my lord, your true
And loyal wife.

OTHELLO   Come, swear it, damn thyself,
Lest, being like one of heaven, the devils themselves   38
Should fear to seize thee. Therefore be double
    damned:
Swear thou art honest.

DESDEMONA   Heaven doth truly know it.

OTHELLO
Heaven truly knows that thou art false as hell.

DESDEMONA
To whom, my lord? With whom? How am I false?

OTHELLO [*weeping*]
Ah, Desdemon! Away, away, away!

DESDEMONA
Alas the heavy day! Why do you weep?
Am I the motive of these tears, my lord?   45
If haply you my father do suspect
An instrument of this your calling back,
Lay not your blame on me. If you have lost him,
I have lost him too.

OTHELLO   Had it pleased heaven
To try me with affliction, had they rained   50
All kinds of sores and shames on my bare head,
Steeped me in poverty to the very lips,
Given to captivity me and my utmost hopes,
I should have found in some place of my soul
A drop of patience. But, alas, to make me
A fixèd figure for the time of scorn   56
To point his slow and moving finger at!   57
Yet could I bear that too, well, very well.
But there where I have garnered up my heart,   59
Where either I must live or bear no life,
The fountain from the which my current runs   61
Or else dries up—to be discarded thence!
Or keep it as a cistern for foul toads   63
To knot and gender in! Turn thy complexion there,   64
Patience, thou young and rose-lipped cherubin—   65
Ay, there look grim as hell!   66

DESDEMONA
I hope my noble lord esteems me honest.   67

OTHELLO
Oh, ay, as summer flies are in the shambles,   68
That quicken even with blowing. O thou weed,   69
Who art so lovely fair and smell'st so sweet
That the sense aches at thee, would thou hadst ne'er
    been born!

DESDEMONA
Alas, what ignorant sin have I committed?   72

OTHELLO
Was this fair paper, this most goodly book,
Made to write "whore" upon? What committed?
Committed? Oh, thou public commoner!   75
I should make very forges of my cheeks,
That would to cinders burn up modesty,
Did I but speak thy deeds. What committed?
Heaven stops the nose at it and the moon winks;   79
The bawdy wind, that kisses all it meets,   80
Is hushed within the hollow mine of earth   81
And will not hear't. What committed?
Impudent strumpet!

DESDEMONA   By heaven, you do me wrong.

OTHELLO
Are not you a strumpet?

DESDEMONA   No, as I am a Christian.
If to preserve this vessel for my lord   86
From any other foul unlawful touch
Be not to be a strumpet, I am none.

OTHELLO   What, not a whore?

DESDEMONA   No, as I shall be saved.

OTHELLO   Is't possible?

DESDEMONA
Oh, heaven forgive us!

OTHELLO   I cry you mercy, then.   92
I took you for that cunning whore of Venice
That married with Othello. [*Calling out*] You, mistress,
That have the office opposite to Saint Peter
And keep the gate of hell!

        Enter Emilia.

                            You, you, ay, you!
We have done our course. There's money for your
    pains.   [*He gives money.*]   97
I pray you, turn the key and keep our counsel.   *Exit.*

EMILIA
Alas, what does this gentleman conceive?   99
How do you, madam? How do you, my good lady?

DESDEMONA   Faith, half asleep.   101

EMILIA
Good madam, what's the matter with my lord?

DESDEMONA   With who?

EMILIA   Why, with my lord, madam.

DESDEMONA
Who is thy lord?

EMILIA   He that is yours, sweet lady.

DESDEMONA
I have none. Do not talk to me, Emilia.
I cannot weep, nor answers have I none
But what should go by water. Prithee, tonight   108

---

38 being . . . heaven looking like an angel   **45 motive** cause   **50 they** the heavenly powers   **56–7 A fixèd . . . finger at** a figure of ridicule to be pointed at scornfully for all of eternity by the slowly moving finger of Time.   **59 garnered** stored   **61 fountain** spring   **63 cistern** cesspool   **64 To . . . gender in** to couple sexually and conceive in. **64–6 Turn . . . hell!** Direct your gaze there, Patience, and your youthful and rosy cherubic countenance will turn grim and pale at this hellish spectacle!   **67 honest** chaste.   **68 shambles** slaughterhouse **69 That . . . blowing** that come to life with the puffing up of the rotten meat on which the flies and their maggots are breeding.

72 ignorant sin sin in ignorance   **75 commoner** prostitute. **79 winks** closes her eyes. (The moon symbolizes chastity.) **80 bawdy** kissing one and all   **81 mine** cave (where the winds were thought to dwell)   **86 vessel** body   **92 cry you mercy** beg your pardon. (Sarcastic.)   **97 course** business. (With an indecent suggestion of "trick," turn at sex.)   **99 conceive** suppose, think.   **101 half asleep** i.e., dazed.   **108 go by water** be conveyed by tears.

Lay on my bed my wedding sheets, remember;
And call thy husband hither.

EMILIA   Here's a change indeed!   *Exit.*

DESDEMONA

'Tis meet I should be used so, very meet.   112
How have I been behaved, that he might stick   113
The small'st opinion on my least misuse?   114

      Enter Iago and Emilia.

IAGO

What is your pleasure, madam? How is't with you?

DESDEMONA

I cannot tell. Those that do teach young babes
Do it with gentle means and easy tasks.
He might have chid me so, for, in good faith,
I am a child to chiding.

IAGO   What is the matter, lady?

EMILIA

Alas, Iago, my lord hath so bewhored her,
Thrown such despite and heavy terms upon her,
That true hearts cannot bear it.

DESDEMONA   Am I that name, Iago?

IAGO   What name, fair lady?

DESDEMONA

Such as she said my lord did say I was.

EMILIA

He called her whore. A beggar in his drink
Could not have laid such terms upon his callet.   128

IAGO   Why did he so?

DESDEMONA   [*weeping*]

I do not know. I am sure I am none such.

IAGO   Do not weep, do not weep. Alas the day!

EMILIA

Hath she forsook so many noble matches,
Her father and her country and her friends,
To be called whore? Would it not make one weep?

DESDEMONA

It is my wretched fortune.

IAGO   Beshrew him for't!   135
How comes this trick upon him?

DESDEMONA   Nay, heaven doth know.   136

EMILIA

I will be hanged if some eternal villain,   137
Some busy and insinuating rogue,   138
Some cogging, cozening slave, to get some office,   139
Have not devised this slander. I will be hanged else.

IAGO

Fie, there is no such man. It is impossible.

DESDEMONA

If any such there be, heaven pardon him!

EMILIA

A halter pardon him! And hell gnaw his bones!   143

Why should he call her whore? Who keeps her
   company?
What place? What time? What form? What
   likelihood?   145
The Moor's abused by some most villainous knave,
Some base notorious knave, some scurvy fellow.
Oh, heavens, that such companions thou'dst unfold,   148
And put in every honest hand a whip
To lash the rascals naked through the world
Even from the east to th' west!

IAGO   Speak within door.   151

EMILIA

Oh, fie upon them! Some such squire he was   152
That turned your wit the seamy side without   153
And made you to suspect me with the Moor.

IAGO

You are a fool. Go to.

DESDEMONA   O God, Iago,   155
What shall I do to win my lord again?
Good friend, go to him; for, by this light of heaven,
I know not how I lost him. Here I kneel.   [*She kneels.*]
If e'er my will did trespass 'gainst his love,
Either in discourse of thought or actual deed,   160
Or that mine eyes, mine ears, or any sense   161
Delighted them in any other form;   162
Or that I do not yet, and ever did,   163
And ever will—though he do shake me off
To beggarly divorcement—love him dearly,
Comfort forswear me! Unkindness may do much,   166
And his unkindness may defeat my life,   167
But never taint my love. I cannot say "whore."
It does abhor me now I speak the word;   169
To do the act that might the addition earn   170
Not the world's mass of vanity could make me.   171
                [*She rises.*]

IAGO

I pray you, be content. 'Tis but his humor.   172
The business of the state does him offense,
And he does chide with you.

DESDEMONA   If 'twere no other—

IAGO   It is but so, I warrant.   [*Trumpets within.*]
Hark, how these instruments summon you to supper!
The messengers of Venice stays the meat.   178
Go in, and weep not. All things shall be well.
      Exeunt Desdemona and Emilia.

     Enter Roderigo.

How now, Roderigo?

RODERIGO   I do not find that thou deal'st justly with me.

IAGO   What in the contrary?

---

112 'Tis . . . very meet i.e., It must be I somehow have deserved this.
113–14 How . . . misuse? What have I done that prompts Othello to
attach even the slightest censure to whatever little fault I may have
committed?   **128 callet** whore.   **135 Beshrew** May evil befall. (An
oath.)   **136 trick** strange behavior, delusion   **137 eternal** inveterate
138 insinuating ingratiating, fawning, wheedling   **139 cogging, cozening** cheating, defrauding   **143 halter** hangman's noose

145 form manner, circumstance.   **148 that . . . unfold** would that you
would expose such fellows   **151 within door** i.e., not so loud.
152 squire fellow   **153 seamy side without** wrong side out   **155 Go
to** i.e., That's enough.   **160 discourse of thought** process of thinking
161 that if. (Also in line 163.)   **162 Delighted them** took delight
163 yet still   **166 Comfort forswear** may heavenly comfort forsake
167 defeat destroy   **169 abhor** (1) fill me with abhorrence (2) make
me whorelike   **170 addition** title   **171 vanity** showy splendor
172 humor mood.   **178 stays the meat** are waiting to dine.

RODERIGO   Every day thou daff'st me with some device, 183
Iago, and rather, as it seems to me now, keep'st
from me all conveniency than suppliest me with the 185
least advantage of hope. I will indeed no longer 186
endure it, nor am I yet persuaded to put up in peace 187
what already I have foolishly suffered.

IAGO   Will you hear me, Roderigo?

RODERIGO   Faith, I have heard too much, for your words
and performances are no kin together.

IAGO   You charge me most unjustly.

RODERIGO   With naught but truth. I have wasted myself
out of my means. The jewels you have had from me to
deliver Desdemona would half have corrupted a vo- 195
tarist. You have told me she hath received them and 196
returned me expectations and comforts of sudden re- 197
spect and acquaintance, but I find none. 198

IAGO   Well, go to, very well.

RODERIGO   "Very well"! "Go to"! I cannot go to, man, 200
nor 'tis not very well. By this hand, I think it is scurvy,
and begin to find myself fopped in it. 202

IAGO   Very well.

RODERIGO   I tell you 'tis not very well. I will make myself 204
known to Desdemona. If she will return me my jewels,
I will give over my suit and repent my unlawful solicitation; if not, assure yourself I will seek satisfaction 207
of you.

IAGO   You have said now? 209

RODERIGO   Ay, and said nothing but what I protest 210
intendment of doing. 211

IAGO   Why, now I see there's mettle in thee, and even
from this instant do build on thee a better opinion
than ever before. Give me thy hand, Roderigo. Thou
hast taken against me a most just exception; but yet I
protest I have dealt most directly in thy affair.

RODERIGO   It hath not appeared.

IAGO   I grant indeed it hath not appeared, and your
suspicion is not without wit and judgment. But,
Roderigo, if thou hast that in thee indeed which I have
greater reason to believe now than ever—I mean
purpose, courage, and valor—this night show it. If
thou the next night following enjoy not Desdemona,
take me from this world with treachery and devise
engines for my life. 225

RODERIGO   Well, what is it? Is it within reason and
compass?

IAGO   Sir, there is especial commission come from
Venice to depute Cassio in Othello's place.

RODERIGO   Is that true? Why, then Othello and Desdemona return again to Venice.

IAGO   Oh, no; he goes into Mauritania and takes away
with him the fair Desdemona, unless his abode be
lingered here by some accident; wherein none can be
so determinate as the removing of Cassio. 235

RODERIGO   How do you mean, removing of him?

IAGO   Why, by making him uncapable of Othello's
place—knocking out his brains.

RODERIGO   And that you would have me to do?

IAGO   Ay, if you dare do yourself a profit and a right.
He sups tonight with a harlotry, and thither will I go to 241
him. He knows not yet of his honorable fortune. If
you will watch his going thence, which I will fashion
to fall out between twelve and one, you may take him 244
at your pleasure. I will be near to second your attempt,
and he shall fall between us. Come, stand not amazed
at it, but go along with me. I will show you such a
necessity in his death that you shall think yourself
bound to put it on him. It is now high suppertime, 249
and the night grows to waste. About it. 250

RODERIGO   I will hear further reason for this.

IAGO   And you shall be satisfied.   *Exeunt.*

❦

4.3

*Enter Othello, Lodovico, Desdemona, Emilia, and
attendants.*

LODOVICO
I do beseech you, sir, trouble yourself no further.

OTHELLO
Oh, pardon me; 'twill do me good to walk.

LODOVICO
Madam, good night. I humbly thank Your Ladyship.

DESDEMONA
Your Honor is most welcome.

OTHELLO   Will you walk, sir?
Oh, Desdemona!

DESDEMONA   My lord?

OTHELLO   Get you to bed on th'instant. I will be returned forthwith. Dismiss your attendant there. Look't
be done.

DESDEMONA   I will, my lord.
Exit [Othello, with Lodovico and attendants].

EMILIA   How goes it now? He looks gentler than he did.

DESDEMONA
He says he will return incontinent,   12
And hath commanded me to go to bed,
And bid me to dismiss you.

EMILIA   Dismiss me?

DESDEMONA
It was his bidding. Therefore, good Emilia,
Give me my nightly wearing, and adieu.
We must not now displease him.

EMILIA   I would you had never seen him!

---

183 thou daff'st me you put me off.   **183–4 device** excuse, trick
185 conveniency advantage, opportunity   **186 advantage** increase
187 put up submit to, tolerate   **195 deliver** deliver to   **195–6 votarist**
nun   **197-8 sudden respect** immediate consideration   **200 I cannot
go to** (Roderigo changes Iago's *go to*, an expression urging patience,
to *I cannot go to*, "I have no opportunity for success in wooing.")
202 fopped fooled, duped   **204 not very well** (Roderigo changes
Iago's *very well*, "all right, then," to *not very well*, "not at all good.")
207 satisfaction repayment. (The term normally means settling of
accounts in a duel.)   **209 You . . . now?** Have you finished?
210–11 protest intendment avow my intention   **225 engines** plots,
snares

235 determinate conclusive, instrumental   **241 harlotry** slut
244 fall out occur   **249 high** fully   **250 grows to waste** wastes away.
4.3 Location: The citadel.
12 incontinent immediately

DESDEMONA
So would not I. My love doth so approve him
That even his stubbornness, his checks, his frowns— 21
Prithee, unpin me—have grace and favor in them.
[*Emilia prepares Desdemona for bed.*]
EMILIA   I have laid those sheets you bade me on the
bed.
DESDEMONA
All's one. Good faith, how foolish are our minds! 25
If I do die before thee, prithee shroud me
In one of these same sheets.
EMILIA   Come, come, you talk. 27
DESDEMONA
My mother had a maid called Barbary.
She was in love, and he she loved proved mad 29
And did forsake her. She had a song of "Willow."
An old thing 'twas, but it expressed her fortune,
And she died singing it. That song tonight
Will not go from my mind; I have much to do 33
But to go hang my head all at one side 34
And sing it like poor Barbary. Prithee, dispatch.
EMILIA   Shall I go fetch your nightgown? 36
DESDEMONA   No, unpin me here.
This Lodovico is a proper man. 38
EMILIA   A very handsome man.
DESDEMONA   He speaks well.
EMILIA   I know a lady in Venice would have walked
barefoot to Palestine for a touch of his nether lip.
DESDEMONA [*singing*]
"The poor soul sat sighing by a sycamore tree,
    Sing all a green willow; 44
Her hand on her bosom, her head on her knee,
    Sing willow, willow, willow.
The fresh streams ran by her and murmured her
        moans;
    Sing willow, willow, willow;
Her salt tears fell from her, and softened the
        stones—"
Lay by these.
[*Singing*] "Sing willow, willow, willow—"
Prithee, hie thee. He'll come anon. 52
[*Singing*] "Sing all a green willow must be my garland.
    Let nobody blame him; his scorn I approve—"
Nay, that's not next.—Hark! Who is't that knocks?
EMILIA   It's the wind.
DESDEMONA [*singing*]
"I called my love false love; but what said he
        then?
    Sing willow, willow, willow;
If I court more women, you'll couch with more
        men."
So, get thee gone. Good night. Mine eyes do itch;
Doth that bode weeping?
EMILIA   'Tis neither here nor there.

DESDEMONA
I have heard it said so. Oh, these men, these men!
Dost thou in conscience think—tell me, Emilia—
That there be women do abuse their husbands 64
In such gross kind?
EMILIA   There be some such, no question.
DESDEMONA
Wouldst thou do such a deed for all the world?
EMILIA
Why, would not you?
DESDEMONA   No, by this heavenly light!
EMILIA
Nor I neither by this heavenly light;
I might do't as well i'th' dark.
DESDEMONA
Wouldst thou do such a deed for all the world?
EMILIA
The world's a huge thing. It is a great price
For a small vice.
DESDEMONA
Good troth, I think thou wouldst not.
EMILIA   By my troth, I think I should, and undo't when
I had done. Marry, I would not do such a thing for a
joint ring, nor for measures of lawn, nor for gowns, 76
petticoats, nor caps, nor any petty exhibition. But for 77
all the whole world! Uds pity, who would not make 78
her husband a cuckold to make him a monarch? I
should venture purgatory for't.
DESDEMONA
Beshrew me if I would do such a wrong
For the whole world.
EMILIA   Why, the wrong is but a wrong i'th' world, and
having the world for your labor, 'tis a wrong in your
own world, and you might quickly make it right.
DESDEMONA
I do not think there is any such woman.
EMILIA   Yes, a dozen, and as many 87
To th' vantage as would store the world they played
        for. 88
But I do think it is their husbands' faults
If wives do fall. Say that they slack their duties 90
And pour our treasures into foreign laps, 91
Or else break out in peevish jealousies,
Throwing restraint upon us? Or say they strike us, 93
Or scant our former having in despite? 94
Why, we have galls, and though we have some grace, 95
Yet have we some revenge. Let husbands know
Their wives have sense like them. They see, and smell, 97
And have their palates both for sweet and sour,
As husbands have. What is it that they do 99

---

21 stubbornness roughness.   **checks** rebukes   **25 All's one** All right. It doesn't really matter.   **27 talk** i.e., prattle.   **29 mad** wild, lunatic   **33–4 I . . . hang** I can scarcely keep myself from hanging   **36 nightgown** dressing gown.   **38 proper** handsome   **44 willow** (A conventional emblem of disappointed love.)   **52 hie thee** hurry. **anon** right away.

64 abuse deceive   **76 joint ring** a ring made in separate halves. **lawn** fine linen   **77 exhibition** gift.   **78 Uds** God's   **87–8 and . . . played for** and enough additionally to stock the world men have gambled and sported sexually for.   **90 they** our husbands.   **duties** marital duties   **91 pour . . . laps** i.e., are unfaithful, give what is rightfully ours (semen) to other women   **93 Throwing . . . us** jealously restricting our freedom.   **94 Or . . . despite** or spitefully take away from us whatever we enjoyed before.   **95 have galls** i.e., are capable of resenting injury and insult.   **grace** inclination to be merciful   **97 sense** sensory perception and appetite   **99 they** husbands

When they change us for others? Is it sport?   100
I think it is. And doth affection breed it?   101
I think it doth. Is't frailty that thus errs?
It is so, too. And have not we affections,
Desires for sport, and frailty, as men have?
Then let them use us well; else let them know,
The ills we do, their ills instruct us so.

DESDEMONA
Good night, good night. God me such uses send   107
Not to pick bad from bad, but by bad mend!   108
                                                           Exeunt.

❖

5.1

Enter Iago and Roderigo.

IAGO
Here stand behind this bulk. Straight will he come.   1
Wear thy good rapier bare, and put it home.   2
Quick, quick! Fear nothing. I'll be at thy elbow.
It makes us or it mars us. Think on that,
And fix most firm thy resolution.

RODERIGO
Be near at hand. I may miscarry in't.

IAGO
Here, at thy hand. Be bold, and take thy stand.
    [*Iago stands aside, Roderigo conceals himself.*]

RODERIGO
I have no great devotion to the deed;
And yet he hath given me satisfying reasons.
'Tis but a man gone. Forth, my sword! He dies.
                                      [*He draws.*]

IAGO
I have rubbed this young quat almost to the sense,   11
And he grows angry. Now, whether he kill Cassio
Or Cassio him, or each do kill the other,
Every way makes my gain. Live Roderigo,   14
He calls me to a restitution large
Of gold and jewels that I bobbed from him   16
As gifts to Desdemona.
It must not be. If Cassio do remain,
He hath a daily beauty in his life
That makes me ugly; and besides, the Moor
May unfold me to him; there stand I in much peril.   21
No, he must die. Be't so. I hear him coming.

Enter Cassio.

RODERIGO [*coming forth*]
I know his gait, 'tis he.—Villain, thou diest!
                              [*He attacks Cassio.*]

CASSIO
That thrust had been mine enemy indeed,
But that my coat is better than thou know'st.   25
I will make proof of thine.
            [*He draws, and wounds Roderigo.*]
RODERIGO   Oh, I am slain!   [*He falls.*   26
                  *Iago, from behind, wounds Cassio
                          in the leg, and exit.*]
CASSIO
I am maimed forever. Help, ho! Murder! Murder!

Enter Othello.

OTHELLO   The voice of Cassio! Iago keeps his word.
RODERIGO   Oh, villain that I am!
OTHELLO   It is even so.
CASSIO   Oh, help, ho! Light! A surgeon!
OTHELLO
'Tis he. O brave Iago, honest and just,
That hast such noble sense of thy friend's wrong!
Thou teachest me.—Minion, your dear lies dead,   34
And your unblest fate hies. Strumpet, I come.   35
Forth of my heart those charms, thine eyes, are blotted;   36
Thy bed, lust-stained, shall with lust's blood be
    spotted.   *Exit Othello.*

Enter Lodovico and Gratiano.

CASSIO
What ho! No watch? No passage? Murder! Murder!   38
GRATIANO
'Tis some mischance. The voice is very direful.
CASSIO   Oh, help!
LODOVICO   Hark!
RODERIGO   Oh, wretched villain!
LODOVICO
Two or three groan. 'Tis heavy night;   43
These may be counterfeits. Let's think't unsafe
To come in to the cry without more help.   45
              [*They remain near the entrance.*]
RODERIGO
Nobody come? Then shall I bleed to death.

Enter Iago [in his shirtsleeves, with a light].

LODOVICO   Hark!
GRATIANO
Here's one comes in his shirt, with light and weapons.
IAGO
Who's there? Whose noise is this that cries on murder?   49
LODOVICO
We do not know.
IAGO   Did not you hear a cry?
CASSIO
Here, here! For heaven's sake, help me!
IAGO   What's the matter?
                      [*He moves toward Cassio.*]

---

100 change exchange. **sport** sexual pastime. **101 affection** passion
107 uses habit, practice **108 Not . . . mend** i.e., not to learn bad conduct from others' badness (as Emilia has suggested women learn
from men), but to mend my ways by perceiving what badness is,
making spiritual benefit out of evil and adversity.
5.1 Location: A street in Cyprus.
1 bulk framework projecting from the front of a shop. **2 bare**
unsheathed. **home** all the way into the target. **11 quat** pimple,
pustule. **to the sense** to the quick **14 Live Roderigo** If Roderigo
lives **16 bobbed** swindled **21 unfold** expose

25 coat (Possibly a garment of mail under the outer clothing, or simply a tougher coat than Roderigo expected.) **26 proof** a test
34 Minion Hussy (i.e., Desdemona) **35 hies** hastens on. **36 Forth
of** From out **38 passage** people passing by. **43 heavy** thick, dark
45 come in to approach **49 cries** cries out

GRATIANO [*to Lodovico*]
This is Othello's ancient, as I take it.

LODOVICO [*to Gratiano*]
The same indeed, a very valiant fellow.

IAGO [*to Cassio*]
What are you here that cry so grievously?   54

CASSIO
Iago? Oh, I am spoiled, undone by villains!   55
Give me some help.

IAGO
Oh, me, Lieutenant! What villains have done this?

CASSIO
I think that one of them is hereabout,
And cannot make away.

IAGO   Oh, treacherous villains!   59
[*To Lodovico and Gratiano*] What are you there? Come
in, and give some help.   [*They advance.*]

RODERIGO   Oh, help me there!

CASSIO
That's one of them.

IAGO   Oh, murderous slave! Oh, villain!
[*He stabs Roderigo.*]

RODERIGO
Oh, damned Iago! Oh, inhuman dog!

IAGO
Kill men i'th' dark?—Where be these bloody thieves?—
How silent is this town!—Ho! Murder, murder!—
[*To Lodovico and Gratiano*] What may you be? Are you
of good or evil?

LODOVICO   As you shall prove us, praise us.   67

IAGO   Signor Lodovico?

LODOVICO   He, sir.

IAGO
I cry you mercy. Here's Cassio hurt by villains.   70

GRATIANO   Cassio?

IAGO   How is't, brother?

CASSIO   My leg is cut in two.

IAGO   Marry, heaven forbid!
Light, gentlemen! I'll bind it with my shirt.
[*He hands them the light, and tends to Cassio's
wound.*]

Enter Bianca.

BIANCA
What is the matter, ho? Who is't that cried?

IAGO   Who is't that cried?

BIANCA   Oh, my dear Cassio!
My sweet Cassio! Oh, Cassio, Cassio, Cassio!

IAGO
Oh, notable strumpet! Cassio, may you suspect
Who they should be that have thus mangled you?

CASSIO   No.

GRATIANO
I am sorry to find you thus. I have been to seek you.

IAGO
Lend me a garter. [*He applies a tourniquet.*] So.—Oh, for
a chair,   83
To bear him easily hence!

BIANCA
Alas, he faints! Oh, Cassio, Cassio, Cassio!

IAGO
Gentlemen all, I do suspect this trash
To be a party in this injury.—
Patience awhile, good Cassio.—Come, come;
Lend me a light. [*He shines the light on Roderigo.*] Know
we this face or no?
Alas, my friend and my dear countryman
Roderigo! No.—Yes, sure.—Oh, heaven! Roderigo!

GRATIANO   What, of Venice?

IAGO   Even he, sir. Did you know him?

GRATIANO   Know him? Ay.

IAGO
Signor Gratiano? I cry your gentle pardon.   95
These bloody accidents must excuse my manners   96
That so neglected you.

GRATIANO   I am glad to see you.

IAGO
How do you, Cassio?—Oh, a chair, a chair!

GRATIANO   Roderigo!

IAGO
He, he, 'tis he. [*A litter is brought in.*] Oh, that's well
said; the chair.   100
Some good man bear him carefully from hence;
I'll fetch the General's surgeon. [*To Bianca*] For you,
mistress,   102
Save you your labor.—He that lies slain here, Cassio,   103
Was my dear friend. What malice was between you?   104

CASSIO
None in the world, nor do I know the man.

IAGO [*to Bianca*]
What, look you pale?—Oh, bear him out o'th' air.   106
[*Cassio and Roderigo are borne off.*]
Stay you, good gentlemen.—Look you pale,
mistress?—   107
Do you perceive the gastness of her eye?—   108
Nay, if you stare, we shall hear more anon.—   109
Behold her well; I pray you, look upon her.
Do you see, gentlemen? Nay, guiltiness
Will speak, though tongues were out of use.

[*Enter Emilia.*]

EMILIA
'Las, what's the matter? What's the matter, husand?

IAGO
Cassio hath here been set on in the dark
By Roderigo and fellows that are scaped.
He's almost slain, and Roderigo dead.

---

83 **chair** litter   95 **gentle** noble   96 **accidents** sudden events
100 **well said** well done   102 **For** As for   103 **Save . . . labor** i.e.,
never you mind tending Cassio.   104 **malice** enmity   106 **bear . . .
air** (Fresh air was thought to be dangerous for a wound.)   107 **Stay
you** (Lodovico and Gratiano are evidently about to leave.)   108 **gastness** terror   109 **stare** (Iago pretends to interpret Bianca's wild looks
as an involuntary confession of guilt.)

---

54 **What** Who. (Also at lines 60 and 66.)   55 **spoiled** ruined, done for
59 **make** get   67 **prove us** prove us to be.   **praise** appraise   70 **I cry
you mercy** I beg your pardon.

EMILIA
Alas, good gentleman! Alas, good Cassio!
IAGO
This is the fruits of whoring. Prithee, Emilia,
Go know of Cassio where he supped tonight.   119
[*To Bianca*] What, do you shake at that?
BIANCA
He supped at my house, but I therefore shake not.
IAGO
Oh, did he so? I charge you go with me.
EMILIA   Oh, fie upon thee, strumpet!
BIANCA
I am no strumpet, but of life as honest   124
As you that thus abuse me.
EMILIA   As I? Faugh! Fie upon thee!
IAGO
Kind gentlemen, let's go see poor Cassio dressed.—   127
Come, mistress, you must tell 's another tale.—
Emilia, run you to the citadel
And tell my lord and lady what hath happed.—
Will you go on afore? [*Aside*] This is the night
That either makes me or fordoes me quite.   *Exeunt.* 132

5.2

*Enter Othello [with a light], and Desdemona in
her bed.*

OTHELLO
It is the cause, it is the cause, my soul.   1
Let me not name it to you, you chaste stars!
It is the cause. Yet I'll not shed her blood,
Nor scar that whiter skin of hers than snow,
And smooth as monumental alabaster.   5
Yet she must die, else she'll betray more men.
Put out the light, and then put out the light.   7
If I quench thee, thou flaming minister,   8
I can again thy former light restore,
Should I repent me; but once put out thy light,   10
Thou cunning'st pattern of excelling nature,   11
I know not where is that Promethean heat   12
That can thy light relume. When I have plucked thy
    rose,   13
I cannot give it vital growth again;
It needs must wither. I'll smell thee on the tree.
                    [*He kisses her.*]
Oh, balmy breath, that dost almost persuade
Justice to break her sword! One more, one more.

Be thus when thou art dead, and I will kill thee,
And love thee after. One more, and that's the last.
                    [*He kisses her.*]
So sweet was ne'er so fatal. I must weep,
But they are cruel tears. This sorrow's heavenly;   21
It strikes where it doth love. She wakes.   22
DESDEMONA   Who's there? Othello?
OTHELLO   Ay, Desdemona.
DESDEMONA   Will you come to bed, my lord?
OTHELLO   Have you prayed tonight, Desdemon?
DESDEMONA   Ay, my lord.
OTHELLO
If you bethink yourself of any crime   28
Unreconciled as yet to heaven and grace,
Solicit for it straight.   30
DESDEMONA
Alack, my lord, what may you mean by that?
OTHELLO
Well, do it, and be brief. I will walk by.
I would not kill thy unpreparèd spirit.
No, heaven forfend! I would not kill thy soul.   34
DESDEMONA
Talk you of killing?
OTHELLO   Ay, I do.
DESDEMONA   Then heaven
Have mercy on me!
OTHELLO   Amen, with all my heart!
DESDEMONA
If you say so, I hope you will not kill me.
OTHELLO   Humh!
DESDEMONA
And yet I fear you; for you're fatal then
When your eyes roll so. Why I should fear I know not,
Since guiltiness I know not; but yet I feel I fear.
OTHELLO
Think on thy sins.
DESDEMONA   They are loves I bear to you.   42
OTHELLO   Ay, and for that thou diest.
DESDEMONA
That death's unnatural that kills for loving.
Alas, why gnaw you so your nether lip?
Some bloody passion shakes your very frame.
These are portents; but yet I hope, I hope,
They do not point on me.
OTHELLO   Peace, and be still!
DESDEMONA   I will so. What's the matter?
OTHELLO
That handkerchief which I so loved and gave thee
Thou gav'st to Cassio.
DESDEMONA   No, by my life and soul!
Send for the man and ask him.
OTHELLO
Sweet soul, take heed, take heed of perjury.
Thou art on thy deathbed.

---

119 **know** learn   124 **honest** chaste   127 **Cassio dressed** Cassio's
wounds dressed.   132 **fordoes** undoes, ruins
5.2. Location: A bedchamber in the citadel.
0.1–2 *in her bed* (Either the curtains are drawn back to reveal the bed
in a recessed area backstage, or the bed is "thrust out" onstage as the
scene begins.)   1 **cause** i.e., cause of justice, the offense itself, which
must be corrected in the name of justice   5 **monumental** i.e., used in
making tombs and funeral monuments   7 **the light . . . light** the
torch or lamp . . . Desdemona's life.   8 **minister** servant   10 **repent
me** change my mind   11 **Thou . . . pattern** you skillfully wrought
perfect example   12 **Promethean heat** (Alludes to two myths: that of
Prometheus stealing fire from heaven for humanity, and that of his
creating humankind.)   13 **relume** rekindle.

21 **they are cruel tears** these tears betoken a sorrowful cruelty, regrettable but just.   22 **It . . . love** (Compare Hebrews 12:6: "For whom the
Lord loveth he chasteneth.")   28 **crime** sin   30 **Solicit** petition, pray.
straight immediately.   34 **forfend** forbid.   42 **They . . . you** i.e., My
only sins are my idolatry of loving you too much.

DESDEMONA
Ay, but not yet to die.

OTHELLO   Yes, presently.   56
Therefore confess thee freely of thy sin;
For to deny each article with oath
Cannot remove nor choke the strong conception   59
That I do groan withal. Thou art to die.   60

DESDEMONA
Then Lord have mercy on me!

OTHELLO   I say, amen.

DESDEMONA
And have you mercy too! I never did
Offend you in my life; never loved Cassio
But with such general warranty of heaven   64
As I might love. I never gave him token.

OTHELLO
By heaven, I saw my handkerchief in 's hand.
Oh, perjured woman! Thou dost stone my heart,   67
And makes me call what I intend to do
A murder, which I thought a sacrifice.
I saw the handkerchief.

DESDEMONA   He found it, then.
I never gave it him. Send for him hither;
Let him confess a truth.

OTHELLO   He hath confessed.

DESDEMONA   What, my lord?

OTHELLO
That he hath used thee.

DESDEMONA   How? Unlawfully?

OTHELLO   Ay.

DESDEMONA
He will not say so.

OTHELLO   No, his mouth is stopped;
Honest Iago hath ta'en order for 't.   76

DESDEMONA
Oh, my fear interprets. What, is he dead?

OTHELLO
Had all his hairs been lives, my great revenge
Had stomach for them all.

DESDEMONA
Alas, he is betrayed and I undone!   [*She weeps.*]

OTHELLO
Out, strumpet! Weep'st thou for him to my face?

DESDEMONA
Oh, banish me, my lord, but kill me not!

OTHELLO   Down, strumpet!

DESDEMONA
Kill me tomorrow; let me live tonight!

OTHELLO   Nay, if you strive—

DESDEMONA
But half an hour!

OTHELLO   Being done, there is no pause.   86

DESDEMONA
But while I say one prayer!

OTHELLO   It is too late.
                                        Smothers her.

EMILIA (*at the door*)
My lord, my lord! What, ho! My lord, my lord!

OTHELLO
What noise is this? Not dead? Not yet quite dead?
I that am cruel am yet merciful;
I would not have thee linger in thy pain.
                          [*He dispatches her.*]
So, so.

EMILIA (*within*)   What, ho! My lord, my lord!

OTHELLO   Who's there?

EMILIA [*within*]
Oh, good my lord, I would speak a word with you!

OTHELLO
Yes, 'tis Emilia.—By and by.—She's dead.
'Tis like she comes to speak of Cassio's death.—   95
The noise was here. Ha! No more moving?   96
Still as the grave. Shall she come in? Were't good?—
I think she stirs again. No. What's best to do?
If she come in, she'll sure speak to my wife.
My wife! My wife! What wife? I have no wife.
Oh, insupportable! Oh, heavy hour!
Methinks it should be now a huge eclipse
Of sun and moon, and that th'affrighted globe
Should yawn at alteration.

EMILIA [*within*]   I do beseech you   104
That I may speak with you, oh, good my lord!

OTHELLO
I had forgot thee. Oh, come in, Emilia.—
Soft, by and by. Let me the curtains draw.—   107
          [*He closes the bedcurtains and opens the door.*]
Where art thou?

                    Enter Emilia.

                          What's the matter with thee now?

EMILIA
Oh, my good lord, yonder's foul murders done!

OTHELLO   What, now?

EMILIA   But now, my lord.

OTHELLO
It is the very error of the moon;   112
She comes more nearer earth than she was wont,   113
And makes men mad.   114

EMILIA
Cassio, my lord, hath killed a young Venetian
Called Roderigo.

OTHELLO   Roderigo killed?

95 like likely that   **96 here** (The Folio's "high" is possible, suggesting that the commotion of the attack on Cassio was loud.)   **104 Should . . . alteration** should gape wide in an earthquake, as if expressing amazement at an eclipse. (According to Pliny, earthquakes often happen during eclipses. The cataclysmic event here is especially terrifying in that it imagines the impossible concurrence of a solar and lunar eclipse—an apocalyptic scenario befitting the horror of Desdemona's death.)   **107 Soft** Wait a minute   **112 error** aberration, irregularity **113 She** Luna, the moon goddess   **114 mad** i.e., "lunatic."

56 presently immediately.   **59 conception** (1) belief in your guilt (2) plan in my mind   **60 groan withal** (1) groan at in sorrow (2) as in giving birth.   **64 warranty** sanction   **67 stone** turn to stone, harden **76 ta'en order** taken measures   **86 Being done** i.e., Since justice has begun its relentless course

And Cassio killed?

EMILIA   No, Cassio is not killed.

OTHELLO
    Not Cassio killed? Then murder's out of tune,
    And sweet revenge grows harsh.

DESDEMONA   Oh, falsely, falsely murdered!

EMILIA   Oh, Lord, what cry is that?

OTHELLO   That? What?

EMILIA
    Out and alas, that was my lady's voice.   123
                    [*She opens the bedcurtains.*]
    Help, help, ho, help! O lady, speak again!
    Sweet Desdemona! O sweet mistress, speak!

DESDEMONA   A guiltless death I die.

EMILIA   Oh, who hath done this deed?

DESDEMONA   Nobody; I myself. Farewell.
    Commend me to my kind lord. Oh, farewell! [*She dies.*]

OTHELLO
    Why, how should she be murdered?

EMILIA   Alas, who knows?

OTHELLO
    You heard her say herself it was not I.

EMILIA
    She said so. I must needs report the truth.

OTHELLO
    She's like a liar gone to burning hell!
    'Twas I that killed her.

EMILIA   Oh, the more angel she,
    And you the blacker devil!

OTHELLO
    She turned to folly, and she was a whore.   136

EMILIA
    Thou dost belie her, and thou art a devil.   137

OTHELLO   She was false as water.

EMILIA   Thou art rash as fire to say
    That she was false. Oh, she was heavenly true!

OTHELLO
    Cassio did top her. Ask thy husband else.   141
    Oh, I were damned beneath all depth in hell
    But that I did proceed upon just grounds
    To this extremity. Thy husband knew it all.

EMILIA   My husband?

OTHELLO   Thy husband.

EMILIA   That she was false to wedlock?

OTHELLO
    Ay, with Cassio. Nay, had she been true,
    If heaven would make me such another world
    Of one entire and perfect chrysolite,   150
    I'd not have sold her for it.

EMILIA   My husband?

OTHELLO
    Ay, 'twas he that told me on her first.
    An honest man he is, and hates the slime
    That sticks on filthy deeds.

EMILIA   My husband?

OTHELLO
    What needs this iterance, woman? I say thy husband.   157

EMILIA
    Oh, mistress, villainy hath made mocks with love!   158
    My husband say she was false?

OTHELLO   He, woman;
    I say thy husband. Dost understand the word?
    My friend, thy husband, honest, honest Iago.

EMILIA
    If he say so, may his pernicious soul
    Rot half a grain a day! He lies to th' heart.
    She was too fond of her most filthy bargain.

OTHELLO   Ha?   [*He draws.*]

EMILIA   Do thy worst!
    This deed of thine is no more worthy heaven
    Than thou wast worthy her.

OTHELLO   Peace, you were best.   168

EMILIA
    Thou hast not half that power to do me harm
    As I have to be hurt. O gull! O dolt!   170
    As ignorant as dirt! Thou hast done a deed—
    I care not for thy sword; I'll make thee known,
    Though I lost twenty lives.—Help! Help, ho, help!
    The Moor hath killed my mistress! Murder, murder!

    Enter Montano, Gratiano, and Iago.

MONTANO
    What is the matter? How now, General?

EMILIA
    Oh, are you come, Iago? You have done well,
    That men must lay their murders on your neck.   177

GRATIANO   What is the matter?

EMILIA [*to Iago*]
    Disprove this villain, if thou be'st a man.
    He says thou told'st him that his wife was false.
    I know thou didst not; thou'rt not such a villain.   181
    Speak, for my heart is full.

IAGO
    I told him what I thought, and told no more
    Than what he found himself was apt and true.   184

EMILIA
    But did you ever tell him she was false?

IAGO   I did.

EMILIA
    You told a lie, an odious, damnèd lie!
    Upon my soul, a lie, a wicked lie.
    She false with Cassio? Did you say with Cassio?

IAGO
    With Cassio, mistress. Go to, charm your tongue.   190

EMILIA
    I will not charm my tongue; I am bound to speak.
    My mistress here lies murdered in her bed—

ALL   Oh, heavens forfend!

EMILIA
    And your reports have set the murder on.

---

123 **Out** (A cry of dismay, intensifying *alas.*)   136 **folly** i.e., wantonness, fleshly sin   137 **belie** slander   141 **else** i.e., if you don't believe me.   150 **chrysolite** precious topaz

157 **iterance** iteration, repetition   158 **made mocks with** made a mockery of   168 **Peace . . . best** You'd better be quiet.   170 **to be hurt** i.e., to endure hurt.   **gull** dupe.   177 **on your neck** to your charge.   181 **such a villain** such a villain as all that.   184 **apt** plausible   190 **charm** control

OTHELLO
Nay, stare not, masters. It is true indeed.
GRATIANO   'Tis a strange truth.
MONTANO
Oh, monstrous act!
EMILIA   Villainy, villainy, villainy!
I think upon't—I think I smell't! O villainy!
I thought so then—I'll kill myself for grief—   199
Oh, villainy, villainy!
IAGO
What, are you mad? I charge you, get you home.
EMILIA
Good gentlemen, let me have leave to speak.
'Tis proper I obey him, but not now.
Perchance, Iago, I will ne'er go home.
OTHELLO
Oh! Oh! Oh!   [Othello falls on the bed.]
EMILIA   Nay, lay thee down and roar,   205
For thou hast killed the sweetest innocent
That e'er did lift up eye.
OTHELLO [rising]   Oh, she was foul!   207
I scarce did know you, uncle. There lies your niece,
Whose breath indeed these hands have newly
    stopped.
I know this act shows horrible and grim.   210
GRATIANO
Poor Desdemon! I am glad thy father's dead.
Thy match was mortal to him, and pure grief
Shore his old thread in twain. Did he live now,   213
This sight would make him do a desperate turn,   214
Yea, curse his better angel from his side,
And fall to reprobance.   216
OTHELLO
'Tis pitiful. But yet Iago knows
That she with Cassio hath the act of shame
A thousand times committed. Cassio confessed it;
And she did gratify his amorous works   220
With that recognizance and pledge of love   221
Which I first gave her. I saw it in his hand;
It was a handkerchief, an antique token
My father gave my mother.
EMILIA   Oh, God! Oh, heavenly God!
IAGO
Zounds, hold your peace.
EMILIA   'Twill out, 'twill out! I peace?
No, I will speak as liberal as the north.   227
Let heaven and men and devils, let them all,
All, all, cry shame against me, yet I'll speak.
IAGO
Be wise, and get you home.
EMILIA   I will not.
                    [Iago threatens Emilia.]
GRATIANO   Fie,

Your sword upon a woman?
EMILIA
Oh, thou dull Moor! That handkerchief thou speak'st of
I found by fortune and did give my husband;
For often, with a solemn earnestness,
More than indeed belonged to such a trifle,   235
He begged of me to steal't.
IAGO   Villainous whore!
EMILIA
She give it Cassio? No, alas! I found it,
And I did give't my husband.
IAGO   Filth, thou liest!
EMILIA
By heaven, I do not, I do not, gentlemen.
Oh, murderous coxcomb! What should such a fool   240
Do with so good a wife?
OTHELLO   Are there no stones in heaven   242
But what serves for the thunder?—Precious villain!   243
         [He runs at Iago; Montano disarms Othello. Iago,
                    from behind, stabs Emilia.]
GRATIANO
The woman falls! Sure he hath killed his wife.
EMILIA
Ay, ay. Oh, lay me by my mistress' side.
                    [Exit Iago.]
GRATIANO   He's gone, but his wife's killed.
MONTANO
'Tis a notorious villain. Take you this weapon,
Which I have here recovered from the Moor.
Come, guard the door without. Let him not pass,
But kill him rather. I'll after that same villain,
For 'tis a damnèd slave.
         Exit [with all but Othello and Emilia,
                    who has been laid by Desdemona's side].
OTHELLO   I am not valiant neither,
But every puny whipster gets my sword.   253
But why should honor outlive honesty?   254
Let it go all.
EMILIA   What did thy song bode, lady?
Hark, canst thou hear me? I will play the swan,
And die in music. [She sings] "Willow, willow, willow."
Moor, she was chaste. She loved thee, cruel Moor.
So come my soul to bliss as I speak true.
So speaking as I think, alas, I die.   [She dies.]
OTHELLO
I have another weapon in this chamber;
It was a sword of Spain, the ice-brook's temper—   262
Oh, here it is. [He finds a sword.] Uncle, I must come
    forth.
GRATIANO [within]
If thou attempt it, it will cost thee dear.

---

199 then (Perhaps at 3.3.331–2 and 4.2.137–54.)   **205 s.d. Othello . . . bed**
(This direction is from the Quarto, as also *He kisses her* at line 19 and *She
dies* at line 129.)   **207 lift up eye** i.e., lift her eyes to heaven.   **210 shows**
looks   **213 Shore . . . thread** sheared the thread of his old age (as Atropos,
one of the three Fates, was thought to do).   **214 turn** deed   **216 reprobance** damnation, i.e., suicide.   **220 gratify** reward   **221 recognizance**
token   **227 liberal as the north** freely as the north wind (blows).

235 belonged was appropriate   **240 coxcomb** fool. (Addressed to
Othello.)   **242 stones** bolts, such as those used for thunderbolts
243 Precious i.e., Arrant, utter.   **243.1–2 He . . . Emilia** (The Quarto
text reads, "*The Moore runnes at Iago. Iago kils his wife.*" The Quarto
also specifies the exit of Iago at line 245 and the death of Emilia at line
260.)   **253 every . . . sword** every whipper-snapper can get the better
of me and my sword.   **254 why . . . honesty?** why should a soldier's
reputation for bravery outlive true integrity?   **262 the icebrook's
temper** tempered in ice-cold water

Thou hast no weapon, and perforce must suffer.

OTHELLO
Look in upon me then and speak with me,
Or, naked as I am, I will assault thee.   267

    [Enter Gratiano.]

GRATIANO
What is the matter?

OTHELLO   Behold, I have a weapon;
A better never did itself sustain
Upon a soldier's thigh. I have seen the day
That, with this little arm and this good sword,
I have made my way through more impediments
Than twenty times your stop. But oh, vain boast!   273
Who can control his fate? 'Tis not so now.
Be not afraid, though you do see me weaponed;
Here is my journey's end, here is my butt   276
And very seamark of my utmost sail.   277
                        [Gratiano steps back.]
Do you go back dismayed? 'Tis a lost fear;   278
Man but a rush against Othello's breast   279
And he retires. Where should Othello go?
                    [He turns to Desdemona.]
Now, how dost thou look now? Oh, ill-starred wench!
Pale as thy smock! When we shall meet at compt,   282
This look of thine will hurl my soul from heaven,
And fiends will snatch at it. Cold, cold, my girl?
Even like thy chastity. Oh, cursèd, cursèd slave!   285
Whip me, ye devils,
From the possession of this heavenly sight!
Blow me about in winds! Roast me in sulfur!
Wash me in steep-down gulfs of liquid fire!
Oh, Desdemon! Dead, Desdemon! Dead! Oh! Oh!   290

    Enter Lodovico, Cassio [carried in a litter],
    Montano, and Iago [prisoner], with officers.

LODOVICO
Where is this rash and most unfortunate man?

OTHELLO
That's he that was Othello. Here I am.

LODOVICO
Where is that viper? Bring the villain forth.
                    [Iago is led forward.]

OTHELLO
I look down towards his feet; but that's a fable.   294
If that thou be'st a devil, I cannot kill thee.
                    [He wounds Iago.]

LODOVICO
Wrench his sword from him.   *[Othello is disarmed.]*

IAGO   I bleed, sir, but not killed.

OTHELLO
I am not sorry neither. I'd have thee live,

For in my sense 'tis happiness to die.   298

LODOVICO
O thou Othello, that was once so good,
Fall'n in the practice of a cursèd slave,   300
What shall be said to thee?

OTHELLO   Why, anything.
An honorable murderer, if you will,
For naught I did in hate, but all in honor.

LODOVICO
This wretch hath part confessed his villainy.
Did you and he consent in Cassio's death?   305

OTHELLO   Ay.

CASSIO
Dear General, I never gave you cause.

OTHELLO
I do believe it, and I ask your pardon.
Will you, I pray, demand that demi-devil
Why he hath thus ensnared my soul and body?

IAGO
Demand me nothing. What you know, you know.
From this time forth I never will speak word.

LODOVICO   What, not to pray?

GRATIANO   Torments will ope your lips.   314

OTHELLO   Well, thou dost best.   315

LODOVICO
Sir, you shall understand what hath befall'n,
Which, as I think, you know not. Here is a letter
Found in the pocket of the slain Roderigo;
And here another. *[He produces letters.]* The one of them
    imports
The death of Cassio, to be undertook
By Roderigo.

OTHELLO
Oh, villain!

CASSIO   Most heathenish and most gross!   322

LODOVICO *[showing another paper]*
Now here's another discontented paper   323
Found in his pocket too. And this, it seems,
Roderigo meant t'have sent this damnèd villain;
But that belike Iago in the interim   326
Came in and satisfied him.   327

OTHELLO *[to Iago]*   Oh, thou pernicious caitiff!—
How came you, Cassio, by that handkerchief
That was my wife's?

CASSIO   I found it in my chamber;
And he himself confessed but even now
That there he dropped it for a special purpose
Which wrought to his desire.

OTHELLO   Oh, fool, fool, fool!   333

CASSIO
There is besides in Roderigo's letter
How he upbraids Iago, that he made him

---

267 **naked** unarmed   273 **your stop** the obstruction you present.
276 **butt** goal, limit. (An archery term.)   277 **seamark** beacon (marking his destination or limit)   278 **lost** groundless   279 **Man . . . rush**
wield no more than a reed   282 **compt** account, judgment day
285 **slave** i.e., Othello himself.   290.1 *in a litter* (The Quarto specifies
that Cassio is *"in a Chaire."*)   294 **towards his feet** i.e., to see if they
are cloven, as the devil's are fabled to be

298 **in my sense** to one who feels as I do   300 **in the practice** through
the plotting, into the snare.   **slave** villain   305 **consent** agree
314 **Torments** Torture   315 **thou dost best** you (Iago) do best not to
talk.   322 **gross** monstrous.   323 **discontented** full of discontent
326 **belike** most likely   327 **Came . . . him** interposed and gave him
satisfactory explanation.   333 **wrought . . . desire** worked out as he
wished, fitted in with his plan.

Brave me upon the watch, whereon it came   336
That I was cast; and even but now he spake,   337
After long seeming dead, Iago hurt him,
Iago set him on.

LODOVICO [*to Othello*]
You must forsake this room and go with us.
Your power and your command is taken off,   341
And Cassio rules in Cyprus. For this slave,
If there be any cunning cruelty
That can torment him much and hold him long,   344
It shall be his. You shall close prisoner rest   345
Till that the nature of your fault be known
To the Venetian state.—Come, bring away.

OTHELLO
Soft you; a word or two before you go.   348
I have done the state some service, and they know't.
No more of that. I pray you, in your letters,
When you shall these unlucky deeds relate,   351
Speak of me as I am; nothing extenuate,
Nor set down aught in malice. Then must you speak
Of one that loved not wisely but too well;
Of one not easily jealous but, being wrought,   355
Perplexed in the extreme; of one whose hand,   356
Like the base Indian, threw a pearl away   357
Richer than all his tribe; of one whose subdued eyes,   358
Albeit unusèd to the melting mood,
Drops tears as fast as the Arabian trees

Their medicinable gum. Set you down this;   361
And say besides that in Aleppo once,
Where a malignant and a turbaned Turk
Beat a Venetian and traduced the state,
I took by th' throat the circumcisèd dog
And smote him, thus.   *[He stabs himself.]*   366
LODOVICO   Oh, bloody period!   367
GRATIANO   All that is spoke is marred.

OTHELLO
I kissed thee ere I killed thee. No way but this,
Killing myself, to die upon a kiss.
                      [He kisses Desdemona and] dies.

CASSIO
This did I fear, but thought he had no weapon;
For he was great of heart.

LODOVICO [*to Iago*]   O Spartan dog,   372
More fell than anguish, hunger, or the sea!   373
Look on the tragic loading of this bed.
This is thy work. The object poisons sight;
Let it be hid. Gratiano, keep the house,   376
                [The bedcurtains are drawn.]
And seize upon the fortunes of the Moor,   377
For they succeed on you. [*To Cassio*] To you, Lord
   Governor,   378
Remains the censure of this hellish villain,   379
The time, the place, the torture. Oh, enforce it!
Myself will straight aboard, and to the state
This heavy act with heavy heart relate.   *Exeunt.*

---

336 **Brave** defy.   **whereon it came** whereof it came about   337 **cast** dismissed   341 **taken off** taken away   344 **hold him long** keep him alive a long time (during his torture)   345 **rest** remain   348 **Soft you** One moment   351 **unlucky** unfortunate   355 **wrought** worked upon, worked into a frenzy   356 **Perplexed** distraught   357 **Indian** (This reading from the Quarto pictures an ignorant savage who cannot recognize the value of a precious jewel. The Folio reading, "Iudean," i.e., infidel or disbeliever, may refer to Herod, who slew Miriamne in a fit of jealousy, or to Judas Iscariot, the betrayer of Christ.)   358 **subdued** i.e., overcome by grief

361 **gum** i.e., myrrh.   366 s.d. *He stabs himself* (This direction is in the Quarto text.)   367 **period** termination, conclusion.   372 **Spartan dog** (Spartan dogs were noted for their savagery and silence.)   373 **fell** cruel   376 **Let it be hid** i.e., draw the bedcurtains. (No stage direction specifies that the dead are to be carried offstage at the end of the play.)   **keep** guard   377 **seize upon** take legal possession of   378 **succeed on** pass as though by inheritance to   379 **censure** sentencing

King Lear

In *King Lear*, Shakespeare pushes to its limit the hypothesis of a malign or at least indifferent universe in which human life is meaningless and brutal. Few plays other than *Hamlet* and *Macbeth* approach *King Lear* in evoking the wretchedness of human existence, and even they cannot match the devastating spectacle of the Earl of Gloucester blinded or Cordelia dead in Lear's arms. The responses of the chief characters are correspondingly searing. "Is man no more than this?" rages Lear. "Unaccommodated man is no more but such a poor, bare, forked animal as thou art" (3.4.101–7). Life he calls a "great stage of fools," an endless torment: "the first time that we smell the air / We wawl and cry" (4.6.179–83). Gloucester's despair takes the form of accusing the gods of gleeful malice toward humanity: "As flies to wanton boys are we to th' gods; / They kill us for their sport" (4.1.36–7). Gloucester's ministering son Edgar can offer him no greater consolation than stoic resolve: "Men must endure / Their going hence, even as their coming hither; / Ripeness is all" (5.2.9–11). These statements need not be read as choric expressions of meaning for the play as a whole, but they do attest to the depth of suffering. In no other Shakespearean play does injustice appear to triumph so ferociously, for so long, and with such impunity. Will the heavens countenance this reign of injustice on earth? Retribution is late in coming and is not certainly the work of the heavens themselves. For, at the last, we must confront the wanton death of the innocent Cordelia—a death no longer willed even by the villain who arranged her execution. "Is this the promised end?" (5.3.268) asks the Earl of Kent, stressing the unparalleled horror of the catastrophe.

Throughout its earlier history, the ancient story of King Lear had always ended happily. In the popular folktale of Cinderella, to which the legend of Lear's daughters bears a significant resemblance, the youngest and virtuous daughter triumphs over her two older wicked sisters and is married to her princely wooer. Geoffrey of Monmouth's *Historia Regum Britanniae* (c. 1136), the ear-

liest known version of the Lear story, records that, after Lear is overthrown by his sons-in-law (more than by his daughters), he is restored to his throne by the intervention of the French King and is allowed to enjoy his kingdom and Cordelia's love until his natural death. (Cordelia, as his successor, is later dethroned and murdered by her wicked nephews, but that is another story.) Sixteenth-century Tudor versions of the Lear story with which Shakespeare was familiar—John Higgins's account in *The First Part of the Mirror for Magistrates* (1574), Raphael Holinshed's *Chronicles* (1587), Edmund Spenser's *The Faerie Queene*, 2.10.27–32, and a play called *The True Chronicle History of King Leir* (by 1594, published 1605)—all retain the happy ending. The tragic pattern may have been suggested instead by Shakespeare's probable source for the Gloucester-Edgar-Edmund plot, Sir Philip Sidney's *Arcadia*, 2.10, in which the Paphlagonian King is the victim of filial ingratitude and deceit.

Yet even Shakespeare's authority was not sufficient to put down the craving for a happy resolution. Nahum Tate's adaptation (1681), which banished the Fool as indecorous for a tragedy and united Edgar and Cordelia in marriage, placing Lear once again on his throne, held the English stage for about 150 years. David Garrick restored some of Shakespeare's lines, and Edmund Kean restored the tragic ending, but it was not until 1838 that *King Lear* was again performed more or less as the dramatist wrote it. One of Shakespeare's editors, Dr. Samuel Johnson, evidently spoke for most eighteenth-century audiences when he confessed that he could hardly bring himself to read Shakespeare's text. Cordelia's slaughter violated that age's longing for "poetic justice." Her death implied a wanton universe and so counseled philosophic despair. Today, Shakespeare's relentless honesty and refusal to accept easy answers convince us that he was right to defy the conventions of his source, though no doubt we, too, distort the play to conform with our supposed toughness of vision.

Shakespeare evidently wrote *King Lear* some time before it was performed at court in December of 1606, probably in 1605 and certainly no earlier than 1603–1604; Edgar's speeches as Tom o' Bedlam contain references to Samuel Harsnett's *Declaration of Egregious Popish Impostures,* which was registered for publication in March of 1603. Thus, *King Lear* was probably written between *Othello* (c. 1603–1604) and *Macbeth* (c. 1606–1607), when Shakespeare was at the height of his literary power in the writing of tragedies.

When we look at the play in formal terms, we are apt to be struck first by its complex double plot. Nowhere else in Shakespearean tragedy do we find anything approaching the rich orchestration of the double plotting in *King Lear.* The links and parallels between the two plots are established on a narrative level early in the play and continue to the end. King Lear misjudges his children and disinherits his loving daughter Cordelia in favor of her duplicitous sisters, whereas Gloucester falls prey to Edmund's deceptions and disinherits his loyal son Edgar; Lear is turned out into the storm by his false daughters, while Gloucester is branded as a traitor by Edmund and deprived of his eyesight; Lear in his madness realizes his fault against Cordelia, while the blind Gloucester "sees" at last the truth about Edgar; and both fathers are cared for by their loving children and are belatedly reconciled to them, but then die brokenhearted. As recent criticism has noted, these narrative parallels are not especially significant in themselves; we are moved, not by the mere repetition of events, but by the enlargement of tragic vision that results from the counterpointing of two such actions. When we see juxtaposed to each other two scenes of trial, Lear's mad arraignment of the absent Goneril and Regan and then the cruel imposition of the mere "form of justice" on the pinioned Gloucester (3.6 and 3.7), we begin to measure the extent to which justice and injustice are inverted by cruelty. When at last the two old men come together, during the storm scenes and especially at Dover, the sad comfort they derive from sharing the wreckage of their lives calls forth piercing eloquence against the stench of mortality. The sight is "most pitiful in the meanest wretch, / Past speaking of in a king" (4.6.204–5).

The play's double structure suggests another duality central to *King Lear:* an opposition of parable and realism, in which "divided and distinguished worlds" are bound together for instructive contrast. (These terms are Maynard Mack's, in his *King Lear in Our Time,* 1965.) To a remarkable degree, this play derives its story from folklore and legend, with many of the wondrous and implausible circumstances of popular romance. A prose rendition might almost begin, "Once upon a time there was a king who had three daughters . . . ." Yet Shakespeare arouses romantic expectation only to crush it by aborting the conventional happy ending, setting up a dramatic tension between an idealized world of make-

believe and the actual world of disappointed hopes. We are aware of artifice and convention, and yet are deeply moved by the "truth" of suffering, love, and hatred. The characters pull us two ways at once; we regard them as types with universalized characteristics—a king and father, his cruel daughters, his loving daughter, and the like—and yet we scrutinize them for psychological motivation because they seem so real and individual.

This duality appears in both the central and the secondary characters. The King of France is in part a hero out of romance, who makes selfless choices and rescues the heroine Cordelia from her distress; yet his motive must also be appraised in the context of a bitter struggle for power. Why does he leave the English court "in choler," and why does he return to England with an army? Is it only to aid his wife and her beleaguered father, or is he negotiating for military advantage? Certainly, a French invasion of England on behalf of Lear complicates the issues of loyalty for the well-meaning Duke of Albany (and perhaps as well for an English Renaissance audience, with its habitual mistrust of the French). The dual focus of the play invites conflicting interpretation. Similarly, Edgar is presented to us on the one hand as the traduced victim in a starkly pessimistic story, dominated by his rationalistic brother, Edmund, who scoffs at religion and undertakes to manipulate those around him for personal gain; on the other hand, Edgar's story grows increasingly improbable as he undertakes a series of disguises and emerges finally as an anonymous champion of chivalry, challenging his brother in the lists like a knight-errant out of Arthurian romance. Edgar's motives are hard to follow. Is he the hero of a fabulous story whose disguises and contriving of illusions for his father are simply part of that storytelling tradition, or is he, in more realistic terms, a man whose disguises are a defensive mask and whose elaborate contrivances defeat themselves? Edmund, his brother, is no less complex. Onstage today he is usually interpreted as smooth and plausible, well-motivated by his father's condescending attitude and by the arbitrariness of the law that has excluded him from legitimacy and inheritance. Yet parable elevates Edmund into something monstrous. He becomes an embodiment of gleeful villainy, like Iago in *Othello,* malignantly evil simply because the evil that is in the universe must find a human form through which to express itself. Edmund's belated attempt to do some good adds to our difficulties in appraising his character, but the restless power of the dual conception supplies a vitality not to be found in pure fable or in realistic literature.

What we see then in Edmund and in others is the union of the universal and the particular, making *King Lear* at once parable and compellingly real. The parable or folktale element is prominent at the beginning of the play and focuses attention on the archetypal situations with which the story is concerned: rivalry between siblings, fear of parental rejection, and, at the same time, parental fear of children's callousness. The "unrealistic" contrast between Cordelia and her wicked sisters, or between Edgar and Edmund, is something we accept as a convention of storytelling, because it expresses vividly the psychic truth of rivalry between brothers and sisters. We identify with Cordelia and Edgar as virtuous children whose worth is misjudged, and who are losing to wicked siblings the contest for parental approval. (In folklore, the rejecting parent is usually a stepparent, which signifies our conviction that he or she is not a true parent at all.) Similarly, we accept as a meaningful convention of storytelling the equally "unrealistic" device by which Lear tests the love of his daughters. Like any parent, he wishes to be loved and appreciated in response to the kindnesses he has performed. The tension between fathers and their marriageable daughters is a recurrent pattern in Shakespeare's late plays, as in *Othello* (in which Brabantio accuses Desdemona of deceiving and deserting him), in *Pericles, Cymbeline,* and *The Winter's Tale,* and in *The Tempest,* in which the pattern is best resolved. In *King Lear,* Shakespeare explores the inherently explosive situation of an imperious father who, having provided for his children and having grown old, assumes he has a right to expect that those children will express their love and gratitude by looking after him.

The difficulty is that the parable of Lear and his children presents two contrasting viewpoints—that of the unappreciated child and that of the unwanted aging parent. Tragic misunderstanding is inevitable, and it outweighs the question of assessing blame. From Lear's point of view, Cordelia's silence is a truculent scanting of obedience. What he has devised is, after all, only a prearranged formality, with Cordelia to receive the richest third of England. Cannot such a ceremony be answered with the conventional hyperbole of courtly language, to which the King's ear is attuned? Don't parents have a right to be verbally reassured of their children's love? How can children be so laconic about such a precious matter? For her part, however, Cordelia senses that Lear is demanding love as payment for his parental kindliness, quid pro quo. Genuine love ought rather to be selfless, as the King of France tells the Duke of Burgundy: "Love's not love / When it is mingled with regards that stands / Aloof from th'entire point" (1.1.242–4). Is Cordelia being asked to prefer Lear before her own husband-to-be? Is this the price she must pay for her upbringing? Lear's ego seems fully capable of demanding this sacrifice from his daughters, especially from his favorite, Cordelia; he has given them his whole kingdom, now let them care for him as befits his royal rank and patriarchal role. The "second childishness" of his old age brings with it a self-centered longing to monopolize the lives of his children and to be a child again. Besides, as king, Lear has long grown accustomed to flattery and absolute obedience. Goneril

and Regan are content to flatter and promise obedience, knowing they will turn him out once he has relinquished his authority. Cordelia refuses to lie in this fashion, but she also will not yield to Lear's implicit request for her undivided affection. Part of her must be loyal to her own husband and her children, in the natural cycle of the generations. "When I shall wed, / That lord whose hand must take my plight shall carry / Half my love with him, half my care and duty" (1.1.100–2). Marriage will not prevent her from obeying, loving, and honoring her father as is fit but will establish for her a new priority. To Lear, as to other fathers contemplating a daughter's marriage in late Shakespearean plays, this savors of desertion.

Lear is sadly deficient in self-knowledge. As Regan dryly observes, "he hath ever but slenderly known himself" (1.1.296–7) and has grown ever more changeable and imperious with age. By dividing his kingdom in three, ostensibly so that "future strife / May be prevented now" (lines 44–5), he instead sets in motion a civil war and French invasion. His intention of putting aside his regal authority while still retaining "The name and all th'addition to a king" (line 136) perhaps betrays a lack of comprehension of the realities of power, although Lear may also have plausible political reasons for what he does, in view of the restive ambitions of the Dukes of Cornwall, Albany, and Burgundy. In any case, he welcomes poisoned flattery but interprets well-intended criticism, whether from Cordelia or Kent, as treason. These failures in no sense justify what Lear's ungrateful children do to him; as he later says, just before going mad, "I am a man / More sinned against than sinning" (3.2.59–60). His failures are, however, tokens of his worldly insolence, for which he must fall. The process is a painful one, but, since it brings self-discovery, it is not without its compensations. Indeed, a central paradox of the play is that by no other way could Lear have learned what human suffering and need are all about.

Lear's Fool is instrumental in elucidating this paradox. The Fool offers Lear advice in palatable form as mere foolery or entertainment and thus obtains a hearing when Kent and Cordelia have been angrily dismissed. Beneath his seemingly innocent jibes, however, are plain warnings of the looming disaster Lear blindly refuses to acknowledge. The Fool knows, as indeed any fool could tell, that Goneril and Regan are remorseless and unnatural. The real fool, therefore, is Lear himself, for having placed himself in their power. In a paradox familiar to Renaissance audiences—as in Erasmus's *In Praise of Folly,* Cervantes's *Don Quixote,* and Shakespeare's own earlier *As You Like It* and *Twelfth Night*—folly and wisdom exchange places. By a similar inversion of logic, the Fool offers his coxcomb to the Earl of Kent for siding with Lear in his exile, "for taking one's part that's out of favor" (1.4.97). Worldly wisdom suggests that we serve those whose fortunes are on the rise, as the obsequious and servile Oswald does.

Indeed, the sinister progress of the first half of the play seems to confirm the Fool's contention that kindness and love are a sure way to exile and poverty. "Let go thy hold when a great wheel runs down a hill lest it break thy neck with following; but the great one that goes upward, let him draw thee after" (2.4.70–3). Yet the Fool resolves to ignore his own sardonic advice; "I would have none but knaves follow it, since a fool gives it" (lines 74–5). Beneath his mocking, the Fool expresses the deeper truth that it is better to be a "fool" and suffer than to win on the cynical world's terms. The greatest fools truly are those who prosper through cruelty and become hardened in sin. As the Fool puts it, deriving a seemingly contrary lesson from Lear's rejection of Cordelia: "Why, this fellow has banished two on 's daughters and did the third a blessing against his will" (1.4.99–101).

These inversions find a parallel in Christian teaching, although the play is nominally pagan in setting. (The lack of explicit Christian reference may be in part the result of a parliamentary order in 1606 banning references to "God" onstage as blasphemous.) Christianity does not hold a monopoly on the idea that one must lose the world in order to win a better world, but its expressions of that idea were plentifully available to Shakespeare: "Blessed are the meek, for they shall inherit the earth" (the Sermon on the Mount); "Go and sell that thou hast, and give to the poor, and thou shalt have treasure in heaven" (Matthew 19:21); "He hath put down the mighty from their seats, and exalted them of low degree" (Luke 1:52). Cordelia's vision of genuine love is of this exalted spiritual order. She is, as the King of France extols her, "most rich being poor, / Most choice, forsaken, and most loved, despised" (1.1.254–5). This is the sense in which Lear has bestowed on her an unintended blessing, by exiling her from a worldly prosperity that is inherently pernicious. Now, with poetic fitness, Lear must learn the same lesson himself. He does so, paradoxically, at the very moment he goes mad, parting ways with the conventional truths of the corrupted world. "My wits begin to turn," he says (3.2.67), and then speaks his first kind words to the Fool, who is his companion in the storm. Lear senses companionship with a fellow mortal who is cold and outcast as he is. In his madness, he perceives both the worth of this insight and the need for suffering to attain it: "The art of our necessities is strange, / And can make vile things precious" (lines 70–1). Misery teaches Lear things he never could know as king about other "Poor naked wretches" who "bide the pelting of this pitiless storm." How are such poor persons to be fed and clothed? "Oh, I have ta'en / Too little care of this! Take physic, pomp; / Expose thyself to feel what wretches feel, / That thou mayst shake the superflux to them / And show the heavens more just" (3.4.28–36). This vision of perfect justice is visionary and utopian, utterly mad, in fact, but it is also spiritual wisdom dearly bought.

Gloucester learns a similar truth and expresses it in much the same way. Like Lear, he has driven into exile a virtuous child and has placed himself in the power of the wicked. Enlightenment comes only through suffering. Just as Lear achieves spiritual wisdom when he goes mad, Gloucester achieves spiritual vision when he is physically blinded. His eyes having been ground out by the heel of Cornwall's boot, Gloucester asks for Edmund only to learn that Edmund has betrayed him in return for siding with Lear in the approaching civil war. Gloucester's response, however, is not to accuse Edmund of treachery but to beg forgiveness of the wronged Edgar. No longer does Gloucester need eyes to see this truth: "I stumbled when I saw." Although the discovery is shattering, Gloucester perceives, as does Lear, that adversity is paradoxically of some benefit, since prosperity had previously caused him to be so spiritually blind. "Full oft 'tis seen / Our means secure us, and our mere defects / Prove our commodities" (4.1.19–21). And this realization leads him, as it does Lear, to express a longing for utopian social justice in which arrogant men will be humbled and the poor raised up by redistributed wealth. "Heavens, deal so still! / Let the superfluous and lust-dieted man, / That slaves your ordinance, that will not see / Because he does not feel, feel your pow'r quickly! / So distribution should undo excess / And each man have enough" (lines 65–70).

To say that Lear and Gloucester learn something precious is not, however, to deny that they are also devastated and broken by their savage humiliation. Indeed, Gloucester is driven to a despairing attempt at suicide, and Lear remains obsessed with the rotten stench of his own mortality, "bound / Upon a wheel of fire" (4.7.47–8). Every decent value that we like to associate with civilization is grotesquely inverted during the storm scenes. Justice, for example, is portrayed in two sharply contrasting scenes: the mere "form of justice" by which Cornwall condemns Gloucester for treason (3.7.26) and the earnestly playacted trial by which the mad Lear arraigns Goneril and Regan of filial ingratitude (3.6). The appearance and the reality of justice have exchanged places, as have folly and wisdom or blindness and seeing. The trial of Gloucester is outwardly correct, for Cornwall possesses the legal authority to try his subjects and at least goes through the motions of interrogating his prisoner. The outcome is, however, cruelly predetermined. In the playacting trial concurrently taking place in a wretched hovel, the outward appearance of justice is pathetically absurd. Here, justice on earth is personified by a madman (Lear), Edgar disguised as another madman (Tom o' Bedlam), and a Fool, of whom the latter two are addressed by Lear as "Thou robèd man of justice" and "thou, his yokefellow of equity" (lines 36–7). They are caught up in a pastime of illusion, using a footstool to represent Lear's ungrateful daughters. Yet true justice is here and not inside the manor house.

Similar contrasts invert the values of loyalty, obedience, and family bonds. Edmund becomes, in the language of the villains, the "loyal" son whose loyalty is demonstrated by turning on his own "traitorous" father. Cornwall becomes a new father to Edmund ("thou shalt find a dearer father in my love," 3.5.25–6). Conversely, a servant who tries to restrain Cornwall from blinding Gloucester is, in Regan's eyes, monstrously insubordinate. "A peasant stand up thus?" (3.7.83). Personal and sexual relationships betray signs of the universal malaise. The explicitly sexual ties in the play, notably those of Goneril, Regan, and Edmund, are grossly carnal and lead to jealousy and murder, while in Cordelia's wifely role the sensual is underplayed. The relationships we are invited to cherish—those of Cordelia, Kent, the Fool, and Gloucester to King Lear, and Edgar to Gloucester—are filial or are characterized by loyal service, both of which are pointedly nonsexual. Nowhere do we find an embodiment of love that is both sensual and spiritual, as in Desdemona in *Othello* or Hermione in *The Winter's Tale*. The Fool's and Tom o' Bedlam's (i.e., Edgar's) gibes about codpieces and plackets (3.2.27–40, 3.4.96) anticipate Lear's towering indictment of carnality, in which his fear of woman's insatiable appetite and his revulsion at her body "Down from the waist" ("there is the sulfurous pit, burning, scalding, stench, consumption. Fie, fie, fie! Pah, pah!") combine with a destructive self-hatred (4.6.124–30).

All these inversions and polarizations are subsumed in the inversion of the word "natural." Edmund is the "natural" son of Gloucester, meaning literally that he is illegitimate. Figuratively, he therefore represents a violation of traditional moral order. In appearance he is smooth and plausible, but in reality he is an archdeceiver like the Vice in a morality play, a superb actor who boasts to the audience in soliloquy of his protean villainy. "Nature" is Edmund's goddess, and by this he means something like a naturalistic universe in which the race goes to the swiftest and in which conscience, morality, and religion are empty myths. Whereas Lear invokes Nature as a goddess who will punish ungrateful daughters and defend rejected fathers (1.4.274–88) and whereas Gloucester believes in a cosmic correspondence between eclipses of the moon or sun and mutinous discords among people (1.2.106–17), Edmund scoffs at all such metaphysical speculations. He spurns, in other words, the Boethian conception of a divine harmony uniting the cosmos and humankind, with humankind at the center of the universe. As a rationalist, Edmund echoes Jacobean disruptions of the older world order in politics and religion as well as in science. He is Machiavellian, an atheist, and Epicurean—everything inimical to traditional Elizabethan ideals of order. To him, "natural" means precisely what Lear and Gloucester call "unnatural."

His creed provides the play with its supreme test. Which definition of "natural" is true? Does heaven exist, and will it let Edmund and the other villainous persons get away with their evil? The question is frequently asked, but the answers are ambiguous. "If you do love old men," Lear implores the gods, "if your sweet sway / Allow obedience, if you yourselves are old, / Make it your cause" (2.4.191–3). His exhortations mount into frenzied rant, until finally the heavens do send down a terrible storm— on Lear himself. Witnesses agree that the absence of divine order in the universe would have the gravest consequences. "If that the heavens do not their visible spirits / Send quickly down to tame these vile offenses," says Albany of Lear's ordeal, "It will come, / Humanity must perforce prey on itself, / Like monsters of the deep" (4.2.47–51). And Cornwall's servants (in a passage missing from the Folio text) have perceived earlier the dire implications of their masters' evil deeds. "I'll never care what wickedness I do, / If this man come to good," says one, and his fellow agrees: "If she [Regan] live long, / And in the end meet the old course of death, / Women will all turn monsters" (3.7.102–5). Yet these servants do, in fact, obey their own best instincts, turning on Cornwall and ministering to Gloucester despite danger to themselves. Similarly, Albany abandons his mild attempts to conciliate his domineering wife and instead uses his power for good. Cordelia's ability to forgive and cherish her father, and Edgar's comparable ministering to Gloucester, give the lie to Edmund's "natural" or amoral view of humanity; a few people, at least, are capable of charity, even when it does not serve their own material self-interest. Conversely, the play suggests that villainy will at last destroy itself, and not simply because the gods are just; Albany's hopeful insistence that "This shows you are above, / You justicers" (4.2.79–80) may be a little more than wishful thinking, to be undercut by some fresh disaster, but at least the insatiable ambitions of Edmund, Goneril, Regan, Cornwall, and Oswald do lead to their violent deaths. Edmund's belated attempt to save the life of Cordelia, though unsuccessful, suggests that this intelligent villain has at last begun to understand the great flaw in his naturalistic creed and to see that, like Goneril and Regan, he has been consumed by his own lust.

Even with such reassurances that villainy will eventually undo itself, the devastation at the end of *King Lear* is so appalling that our questions about justice remain finally unanswered. To ask the question "Who must pay for Lear's self-knowledge?" is to remind ourselves that women must often die in Shakespeare's tragedies so that men may learn, and to perceive even further that, in the absurdist world of *Lear*, the Cartesian logic of cause and effect and poetic justice simply will not account for all that we long to understand. As Roland Barthes well expresses the matter in an essay on Racine, "tragedy is only a means of reclaiming human unhappiness, of subsuming it, thus justifying it under the form of necessity, or wisdom, and purification." Tragedy cannot explain away the death of Cordelia and the heartbreak of her father. The last tableau is a vision of doomsday, with Cordelia strangled, Lear broken and dying, and the "gored state" in such disarray that we cannot be sure what restoration can occur. The very question of political order is dwarfed by the enormity of the personal disaster of Lear and Cordelia. No one wishes longer life for the King: "He hates him / That would upon the rack of this tough world / Stretch him out longer." He is dead; "The wonder is he hath endured so long" (5.3.319–26). Lear's view of life's terrible corruption, pronounced in his madness, seems confirmed in his end. Perhaps the only way in which this tragedy can reclaim so much unhappiness is to suggest that, given the incurable badness of the world, we can at least choose whether to attempt to be like Cordelia and Edgar (knowing what the price may be for such courage) or to settle for being our worst selves, like Edmund, Goneril, and Regan. Overwhelmed as we are by the testimonial before us of humankind's vicious capacity for self-destruction, we are stirred nonetheless by the ability of some men and women to confront their fearful destiny with probity and stoic renunciation, adhering to what they believe to be good and expecting Fortune to give them absolutely nothing. The power of love, though learned too late to avert catastrophe, is at last discovered in its very defeat.

King Lear has become a fable for our times, onstage, in film and television, and in fictional adaptations in novel form. The role of Lear has been a compelling one for so many great Shakespearean actors, including Philip Kemble, Henry Irving, Edwin Forrest, John Gielgud, Donald Wolfit, Donald Sinden, Brian Cox, Michael Gambon, Robert Stephens, and John Wood. Peter Brook's film version of 1970, based on a stage production of 1962, with Paul Scofield as Lear, did much to equate the play's bleak vision with that of our modern existential world. Stimulated by Jan Kott's *Shakespeare Our Contemporary* (translated 1964), a post–World War II apocalyptic interpretation of Shakespeare from the perspective of an ideologically embattled eastern Europe, Brook unfolds a narrative of unrelieved disillusionment. The medium of film enables him to show what it would be like, for example, to have a hundred knights and all their followers descend on Albany's castle at the same time, demanding to be fed and quarreling with the servants of Goneril and Albany; the din and confusion are overwhelming, to such an extent that one can see Goneril's point in wanting to cut back on the King's retinue. A barren, wintry landscape adds visual reinforcement to the savage energies of family and dynastic conflict. Grigori Kozintsev's film of 1971, the work of a great Soviet director, sees the larger movements of the play in Marxist terms as the dialectical imperatives of political and social history; again, the medium of film makes it possible for Kozintsev to do what the stage cannot do, deploy huge casts of anonymous soldiers and workers as both victims and movers of social change. Laurence Olivier's performance of Lear for Grenada Television (directed by Michael Elliott, 1983, Granada Video, 1984) came at the very end of Olivier's life, as his climactic and final role; his interpretation is deeply enhanced by one's perception that the actor is literally dying of cancer. Olivier, weakened but determined, had to be helped through the rigors of the screening, with the result that his Lear is tender, vulnerable, frail, though capable of the outbursts of rage that often come with advanced age. His *King Lear* is about the approach of death. Akira Kurosawa, in his epic *Ran* (1985), chose a more radical adaptation, that of telling a story of a Japanese warlord and his three sons, one of them (like Cordelia) dear but misunderstood, the others treacherous. One of their wives (the Lady Kaede) turns out to be another Edmund, Goneril, Regan, and Lady Macbeth all combined in one, fiercely and murderously determined that her husband succeed by whatever means possible. Kurosawa's vision of evil in the human heart is meant to be terrifying, and it is. The Royal National Theatre production of *King Lear* won several awards for Best Actor (Ian Holm as Lear) and Best Director (Richard Eyre), and is available on video from the BBC and Mobil Masterpiece Theatre (1998). In fiction, Jane Smiley's *A Thousand Acres* (1991) features a similar transposition, in this case to a midwestern American farm run by an aging farmer who transfers his land to his daughters and then sinks into alcoholism and insanity as two daughters squabble over their inheritance and end up losing everything, including their husbands, while their sister Caroline (Cordelia), unwilling to take part in the dividing of the farm, tries unsuccessfully as a lawyer to have the property restored to her father. Edward Bond's stage play called *Lear* (1971) accentuated *King Lear's* already formidable bleakness by adding to its cruelty and violence; in it, war became a never-ending cycle of repression and escalating oppression. In these varied reworkings, we see the remarkable malleability of *King Lear* as an endlessly fascinating subject for new historicist, cultural materialist, deconstructive, and feminist readings that open up topics of misogyny and patriarchy, political ideologies, and philosophical pessimism.

King Lear exists in two early texts, the Quarto of 1608 and the considerably changed Folio version of 1623. Similar disparities appear in *Hamlet, Othello, Troilus and Cressida, Henry IV Part II*, and a number of other plays, but the problem is especially acute in *King Lear*. Shakespeare must have had a hand in the revisions that led to the Folio text. It contains new material. At the same time, the Quarto text contains passages not found in the Folio. The revisions may have resulted from a number of circumstances: cutting for performance (the play as it stands in either version is too long to have been produced in its entirety on the Jacobean stage), censorship, errors in transcription, and still more. The Folio version does alter some matters especially having to do with the French invasion; characters like Albany appear in a different light. The very ending is changed as to which characters speak the concluding lines.

Given these factors, many editions today present two or even three texts for the reader, or mark the text with brackets and other indicators of textual variation. This edition does not do so, though the textual notes do indicate the differences that occur. The reasons for choosing to present here the more traditional composite or eclectic text are these: *King Lear*'s textual variations between Quarto and Folio are more extensive than in some other plays, but are not always different in kind, so that it is a distortion to treat this play alone as a multiple-text play.

To choose either Quarto or Folio is to lose important material that is unquestionably Shakespeare's. To print two or even three versions is to add pages to an already weighty collection. And the presentation of multiple texts, or of a single text that is flagged with bracketed markers, also imposes on the reader a task of sorting out a complex and uncertain textual history that, however important ultimately in studying Shakespeare as a writer and as a reviser, is perhaps best left to subsequent investigation in a full-scale critical edition after one has absorbed the greatness of this play as a piece of writing for the theater. The present composite *King Lear*, based on the Folio text but including the 300 or so lines found only in the First Quarto along with some Quarto readings where the Folio version seems less textually reliable, is in a sense a compromise, but it is one that seems well suited to the purposes of this present edition.

King Lear

[*Dramatis Personae*

KING LEAR
GONERIL,
REGAN, } *Lear's daughters*
CORDELIA,
DUKE OF ALBANY, *Goneril's husband*
DUKE OF CORNWALL, *Regan's husband*
KING OF FRANCE, *Cordelia's suitor and husband*
DUKE OF BURGUNDY, *suitor to Cordelia*

EARL OF KENT, *later disguised as Caius*
EARL OF GLOUCESTER
EDGAR, *Gloucester's son and heir, later disguised as poor Tom*
EDMUND, *Gloucester's bastard son*

OSWALD, *Goneril's steward*
A KNIGHT *serving King Lear*
Lear's FOOL
CURAN, *in Gloucester's household*
GENTLEMEN
Three SERVANTS
OLD MAN, *a tenant of Gloucester*
Three MESSENGERS
A GENTLEMAN *attending Cordelia as a Doctor*
Two CAPTAINS
HERALD

Knights, Gentlemen, Attendants, Servants, Officers, Soldiers, Trumpeters

SCENE: *Britain*]

1.1

Enter Kent, Gloucester, and Edmund.

KENT　I thought the King had more affected the Duke of　1
Albany than Cornwall.　2

GLOUCESTER　It did always seem so to us; but now in
the division of the kingdom it appears not which of
the dukes he values most, for equalities are so weighed　5
that curiosity in neither can make choice of either's　6
moiety.　7

KENT　Is not this your son, my lord?

GLOUCESTER　His breeding, sir, hath been at my charge.　9
I have so often blushed to acknowledge him that now
I am brazed to't.　11

KENT　I cannot conceive you.　12

GLOUCESTER　Sir, this young fellow's mother could;
whereupon she grew round-wombed and had indeed,
sir, a son for her cradle ere she had a husband
for her bed. Do you smell a fault?　16

KENT　I cannot wish the fault undone, the issue of it　17
being so proper.　18

GLOUCESTER　But I have a son, sir, by order of law, some　19
year elder than this, who yet is no dearer in my ac-　20
count. Though this knave came something saucily to　21
the world before he was sent for, yet was his mother
fair, there was good sport at his making, and the
whoreson must be acknowledged.—Do you know this　24
noble gentleman, Edmund?

EDMUND　No, my lord.

GLOUCESTER　My lord of Kent. Remember him hereafter
as my honorable friend.

EDMUND　My services to Your Lordship.　29

KENT　I must love you, and sue to know you better.　30

EDMUND　Sir, I shall study deserving.　31

GLOUCESTER　He hath been out nine years, and away　32
he shall again. The King is coming.　33

Sennet. Enter [*one bearing a coronet, then*] *King
Lear, Cornwall, Albany, Goneril, Regan, Cordelia,
and attendants.*

LEAR

Attend the lords of France and Burgundy, Gloucester.　34

GLOUCESTER　I shall, my liege.　　　　　　　　　　*Exit.*

1.1. Location: King Lear's palace.
1 affected favored　**2 Albany** i.e., Scotland　**5–7 equalities . . .
moiety** the shares balance so equally that close scrutiny cannot find
advantage in either's portion.　**9 breeding** raising, care.　**charge**
expense.　**11 brazed** hardened　**12 conceive** understand. (But
Gloucester puns in the sense of "become pregnant.")　**16 fault** (1) sin
(2) loss of scent by the hounds.　**17 issue** (1) result (2) offspring
18 proper (1) excellent (2) handsome.　**19 by order of law** legitimate
19–20 some year about a year　**20–1 account** estimation.　**21 knave**
young fellow. (Not said disapprovingly, though the word is ironic.)
something somewhat　**24 whoreson** low fellow; suggesting bastardy, but (like *knave* above) used with affectionate condescension
29 services duty　**30 sue** petition, beg　**31 study deserving** strive to
be worthy (of your esteem).　**32 out** i.e., abroad, absent　**33.1** *Sennet*
trumpet signal heralding a procession.　*one . . . then* (This direction
is from the Quarto. The *coronet* is perhaps intended for Cordelia or
her betrothed. A coronet signifies nobility below the rank of king.)
34 Attend Wait upon, usher ceremoniously

LEAR

Meantime we shall express our darker purpose.　36
Give me the map there. [*He takes a map.*] Know that we
have divided
In three our kingdom; and 'tis our fast intent　38
To shake all cares and business from our age,
Conferring them on younger strengths while we
Unburdened crawl toward death. Our son of
Cornwall,
And you, our no less loving son of Albany,
We have this hour a constant will to publish　43
Our daughters' several dowers, that future strife　44
May be prevented now. The princes, France and
Burgundy,
Great rivals in our youngest daughter's love,
Long in our court have made their amorous sojourn
And here are to be answered. Tell me, my
daughters—
Since now we will divest us both of rule,
Interest of territory, cares of state—　50
Which of you shall we say doth love us most,
That we our largest bounty may extend
Where nature doth with merit challenge? Goneril,　53
Our eldest born, speak first.

GONERIL

Sir, I love you more than words can wield the matter,
Dearer than eyesight, space, and liberty,　56
Beyond what can be valued, rich or rare,
No less than life, with grace, health, beauty, honor;
As much as child e'er loved, or father found;　59
A love that makes breath poor and speech unable.　60
Beyond all manner of so much I love you.

CORDELIA [*aside*]

What shall Cordelia speak? Love and be silent.

LEAR [*indicating on map*]

Of all these bounds, even from this line to this,
With shadowy forests and with champains riched,　64
With plenteous rivers and wide-skirted meads,　65
We make thee lady. To thine and Albany's issue
Be this perpetual.—What says our second daughter,
Our dearest Regan, wife of Cornwall? Speak.

REGAN

I am made of that self mettle as my sister,　69
And prize me at her worth. In my true heart　70
I find she names my very deed of love;　71
Only she comes too short, that I profess　72
Myself an enemy to all other joys
Which the most precious square of sense possesses,　74

---

36 we, our (The royal plural; also in lines 37–44, etc.)　**darker purpose** undeclared intention.　**38 fast** firm　**43 constant . . . publish**
firm resolve to proclaim　**44 several** individual　**50 Interest of** right
or title to, possession of　**53 Where . . . challenge** where both natural
affection and merit claim our bounty as its due.　**56 space, and liberty** possession of land, and freedom of action　**59 found** i.e., found
himself to be loved　**60 breath . . . unable** utterance impoverished
and speech inadequate.　**64 shadowy** shady.　**champains riched** fertile plains　**65 plenteous . . . meads** abundant rivers bordered with
wide meadows　**69 that self mettle** that same spirited temperament
70 prize . . . worth value myself as her equal (in love for you). (*Prize*
suggests "price.")　**71 names . . . love** describes my love in action
72 that in that　**74 Which . . . possesses** which the most delicately
sensitive part of my nature can enjoy

And find I am alone felicitate   75
In your dear Highness' love.

CORDELIA [*aside*]   Then poor Cordelia!
And yet not so, since I am sure my love's
More ponderous than my tongue.   78

LEAR
To thee and thine hereditary ever
Remain this ample third of our fair kingdom,
No less in space, validity, and pleasure   81
Than that conferred on Goneril.—Now, our joy,
Although our last and least, to whose young love   83
The vines of France and milk of Burgundy   84
Strive to be interested, what can you say to draw   85
A third more opulent than your sisters'? Speak.

CORDELIA   Nothing, my lord.

LEAR   Nothing?

CORDELIA   Nothing.

LEAR
Nothing will come of nothing. Speak again.

CORDELIA
Unhappy that I am, I cannot heave
My heart into my mouth. I love Your Majesty
According to my bond, no more nor less.   93

LEAR
How, how, Cordelia? Mend your speech a little,
Lest you may mar your fortunes.

CORDELIA   Good my lord,
You have begot me, bred me, loved me. I
Return those duties back as are right fit,   97
Obey you, love you, and most honor you.
Why have my sisters husbands if they say
They love you all? Haply, when I shall wed,   100
That lord whose hand must take my plight shall carry 101
Half my love with him, half my care and duty.
Sure I shall never marry like my sisters,
To love my father all.

LEAR
But goes thy heart with this?

CORDELIA   Ay, my good lord.

LEAR   So young, and so untender?

CORDELIA   So young, my lord, and true.

LEAR
Let it be so! Thy truth then be thy dower!
For, by the sacred radiance of the sun,
The mysteries of Hecate and the night,   110
By all the operation of the orbs   111
From whom we do exist and cease to be,   112
Here I disclaim all my paternal care,
Propinquity, and property of blood,   114
And as a stranger to my heart and me

Hold thee from this forever. The barbarous Scythian,   116
Or he that makes his generation messes   117
To gorge his appetite, shall to my bosom
Be as well neighbored, pitied, and relieved   119
As thou my sometime daughter.

KENT   Good my liege—   120

LEAR   Peace, Kent!
Come not between the dragon and his wrath.
I loved her most, and thought to set my rest   123
On her kind nursery. [*To Cordelia*] Hence, and avoid
    my sight!—   124
So be my grave my peace, as here I give   125
Her father's heart from her. Call France. Who stirs?   126
Call Burgundy.   [*Exit one.*]
              Cornwall and Albany,
With my two daughters' dowers digest the third.   128
Let pride, which she calls plainness, marry her.   129
I do invest you jointly with my power,
Preeminence, and all the large effects   131
That troop with majesty. Ourself by monthly course,   132
With reservation of an hundred knights   133
By you to be sustained, shall our abode
Make with you by due turns. Only we shall retain
The name and all th'addition to a king.   136
The sway, revenue, execution of the rest,   137
Belovèd sons, be yours, which to confirm,
This coronet part between you.

KENT   Royal Lear,   139
Whom I have ever honored as my king,
Loved as my father, as my master followed,
As my great patron thought on in my prayers—

LEAR
The bow is bent and drawn. Make from the shaft.   143

KENT
Let it fall rather, though the fork invade   144
The region of my heart. Be Kent unmannerly
When Lear is mad. What wouldst thou do, old man?
Think'st thou that duty shall have dread to speak
When power to flattery bows?
To plainness honor's bound   149
When majesty falls to folly. Reserve thy state,   150
And in thy best consideration check   151
This hideous rashness. Answer my life my judgment,   152

---

75 felicitate made happy   **78 ponderous** weighty   **81 validity** value. **pleasure** pleasing features   **83 least** youngest   **84 vines** vineyards. **milk** pastures (?)   **85 be interested** be affiliated, establish a claim, be admitted as to a privilege.   **draw** win   **93 bond** filial obligation **97 right fit** proper and fitting   **100 all** exclusively, and with all of themselves.   **Haply** Perhaps, with luck   **101 plight** pledge in marriage   **110 mysteries** secret rites.   **Hecate** goddess of witchcraft and the moon   **111 operation** influence.   **orbs** planets and stars **112 From whom** under whose influence   **114 Propinquity ... blood** close kinship, and rights and duties entailed in blood ties

116 this this time forth.   **Scythian** (Scythians were famous in antiquity for savagery.)   **117 makes ... messes** makes meals of his children or parents   **119 neighbored** helped in a neighborly way **120 sometime** former   **123 set my rest** rely wholly. (A phrase from a game of cards, meaning "to stake all.")   **124 nursery** nursing, care. **avoid** get out of   **125 So ... peace, as** As I hope to rest peacefully in my grave   **126 Who stirs?** i.e., Jump to it; don't just stand there. **128 digest** assimilate, incorporate   **129 Let ... her** Let pride, which she calls plain speaking, be her dowry and get her a husband. **131 effects** outward shows   **132 troop with** accompany, serve. **Ourself** (The royal "we.")   **133 With reservation of** reserving to myself the right to be attended by   **136 th'addition** the honors and prerogatives   **137 sway** sovereign authority   **139 coronet** (Perhaps Lear gestures toward this coronet that was to have symbolized Cordelia's dowry and marriage, hands it to his sons-in-law, or actually attempts to divide it.)   **143 Make from** Get out of the way of **144 fall** strike.   **fork** barbed head of an arrow   **149 To ... bound** Loyalty demands frankness   **150 Reserve thy state** Retain your royal authority   **151 And ... check** and with wise deliberation restrain **152 Answer ... judgment** I wager my life on my judgment that

Thy youngest daughter does not love thee least,
Nor are those emptyhearted whose low sounds
Reverb no hollowness.

LEAR   Kent, on thy life, no more.   155

KENT
My life I never held but as a pawn   156
To wage against thine enemies, nor fear to lose it,   157
Thy safety being motive.

LEAR   Out of my sight!   158

KENT
See better, Lear, and let me still remain
The true blank of thine eye.   160

LEAR   Now, by Apollo—

KENT   Now, by Apollo, King,
Thou swear'st thy gods in vain.

LEAR   Oh, vassal! Miscreant!   164

                 [Laying his hand on his sword.]

ALBANY, CORNWALL   Dear sir, forbear.

KENT
Kill thy physician, and the fee bestow
Upon the foul disease. Revoke thy gift,
Or whilst I can vent clamor from my throat
I'll tell thee thou dost evil.

LEAR
Hear me, recreant, on thine allegiance hear me!   170
That thou hast sought to make us break our vows,   171
Which we durst never yet, and with strained pride   172
To come betwixt our sentence and our power,   173
Which nor our nature nor our place can bear,   174
Our potency made good, take thy reward.   175
Five days we do allot thee for provision
To shield thee from disasters of the world,
And on the sixth to turn thy hated back
Upon our kingdom. If on the tenth day following
Thy banished trunk be found in our dominions,   180
The moment is thy death. Away! By Jupiter,
This shall not be revoked.

KENT
Fare thee well, King. Sith thus thou wilt appear,   183
Freedom lives hence and banishment is here.
[To Cordelia] The gods to their dear shelter take thee,
   maid,
That justly think'st and hast most rightly said!
[To Regan and Goneril] And your large speeches may
   your deeds approve,   187
That good effects may spring from words of love.
Thus Kent, O princes, bids you all adieu.

He'll shape his old course in a country new.   Exit. 190

   Flourish. Enter Gloucester, with France and
   Burgundy; attendants.

GLOUCESTER
Here's France and Burgundy, my noble lord.

LEAR   My lord of Burgundy,
We first address toward you, who with this king   193
Hath rivaled for our daughter. What in the least   194
Will you require in present dower with her
Or cease your quest of love?

BURGUNDY   Most royal Majesty,
I crave no more than hath Your Highness offered,
Nor will you tender less.

LEAR   Right noble Burgundy,   198
When she was dear to us we did hold her so,   199
But now her price is fallen. Sir, there she stands.
If aught within that little-seeming substance,   201
Or all of it, with our displeasure pieced,   202
And nothing more, may fitly like Your Grace,   203
She's there, and she is yours.

BURGUNDY   I know no answer.

LEAR
Will you, with those infirmities she owes,   205
Unfriended, new-adopted to our hate,
Dowered with our curse and strangered with our
   oath,   207
Take her, or leave her?

BURGUNDY   Pardon me, royal sir.
Election makes not up in such conditions.   209

LEAR
Then leave her, sir, for by the power that made me,
I tell you all her wealth. [To France] For you, great King, 211
I would not from your love make such a stray   212
To match you where I hate; therefore beseech you   213
T'avert your liking a more worthier way   214
Than on a wretch whom Nature is ashamed
Almost t'acknowledge hers.

FRANCE   This is most strange,
That she whom even but now was your best object,
The argument of your praise, balm of your age,   218
The best, the dearest, should in this trice of time   219
Commit a thing so monstrous to dismantle   220
So many folds of favor. Sure her offense
Must be of such unnatural degree
That monsters it, or your forevouched affection   223
Fall into taint, which to believe of her

---

155 Reverb no hollowness do not reverberate like a hollow drum,
insincerely. **156–7 My . . . wage** I never regarded my life other than
as a pledge to hazard in warfare **158 motive** that which prompts me
to act. **160 The true . . . eye** i.e., the means to enable you to see better. (*Blank* means "the white center of the target," or, "the true direct
aim," as in "point-blank," traveling in a straight line.) **164 vassal**
i.e., wretch. **Miscreant** (Literally, infidel, heretic; hence, villain, rascal.) **170 recreant** traitor **171 That** In that, since **172 strained**
excessive **173 To . . . power** i.e., to block my power to command and
judge **174 Which . . . place** which neither my temperament nor my
office as king **175 Our . . . good** my power enacted, demonstrated
180 trunk body **183 Sith** Since **187 your . . . approve** may your
deeds confirm your speeches with their vast claims

190 shape . . . course follow his traditional plainspoken ways.
190.1 *Flourish* trumpet fanfare used for the entrance or exit of important persons **193 address** address myself **194 rivaled** competed.
in the least at the lowest **198 tender** offer **199 so** i.e., *dear*, beloved
and valued at a high price **201 little-seeming substance** one who
seems substantial but whose substance is, in fact, little, or, one who
refuses to flatter **202 pieced** added, joined **203 like** please
205 owes owns **207 strangered** disowned **209 Election . . . conditions** No choice is possible under such conditions. **211 tell you**
(1) inform you of (2) enumerate for you. **For** As for **212 make such
a stray** stray so far **213 To** as to. **beseech** I beseech **214 T'avert
your liking** to turn your affections **218 argument** theme **219 trice**
moment **220 to** as to **223 monsters it** makes it monstrous
223–4 or . . . taint or else the affection for her you have hitherto
affirmed must fall into suspicion

Must be a faith that reason without miracle
Should never plant in me.

CORDELIA   I yet beseech Your Majesty—
If for I want that glib and oily art   228
To speak and purpose not, since what I well intend   229
I'll do't before I speak—that you make known
It is no vicious blot, murder, or foulness,   231
No unchaste action or dishonored step
That hath deprived me of your grace and favor,
But even for want of that for which I am richer: 234
A still-soliciting eye and such a tongue   235
That I am glad I have not, though not to have it
Hath lost me in your liking.

LEAR   Better thou
Hadst not been born than not t'have pleased me better.

FRANCE
Is it but this? A tardiness in nature
Which often leaves the history unspoke   240
That it intends to do?—My lord of Burgundy,
What say you to the lady? Love's not love
When it is mingled with regards that stands   243
Aloof from th'entire point. Will you have her?   244
She is herself a dowry.

BURGUNDY [to Lear]   Royal King,
Give but that portion which yourself proposed,
And here I take Cordelia by the hand,
Duchess of Burgundy.

LEAR
Nothing. I have sworn. I am firm.

BURGUNDY [to Cordelia]
I am sorry, then, you have so lost a father
That you must lose a husband.

CORDELIA   Peace be with Burgundy!
Since that respects of fortune are his love,   252
I shall not be his wife.

FRANCE
Fairest Cordelia, that art most rich being poor,
Most choice, forsaken, and most loved, despised,
Thee and thy virtues here I seize upon,
Be it lawful I take up what's cast away.   257
                    [He takes her hand.]
Gods, gods! 'Tis strange that from their cold'st neglect   258
My love should kindle to inflamed respect.—   259
Thy dowerless daughter, King, thrown to my chance,   260
Is queen of us, of ours, and our fair France.
Not all the dukes of wat'rish Burgundy   262
Can buy this unprized precious maid of me.—   263
Bid them farewell, Cordelia, though unkind.   264
Thou losest here, a better where to find.   265

LEAR
Thou hast her, France. Let her be thine, for we
Have no such daughter, nor shall ever see
That face of hers again. Therefore begone
Without our grace, our love, our benison.   269
Come, noble Burgundy.
          Flourish. Exeunt [all but France, Goneril, Regan,
                                      and Cordelia].

FRANCE   Bid farewell to your sisters.

CORDELIA
Ye jewels of our father, with washed eyes   272
Cordelia leaves you. I know you what you are,
And like a sister am most loath to call   274
Your faults as they are named. Love well our father.   275
To your professèd bosoms I commit him.   276
But yet, alas, stood I within his grace,
I would prefer him to a better place.   278
So, farewell to you both.

REGAN
Prescribe not us our duty.

GONERIL   Let your study
Be to content your lord, who hath received you
At Fortune's alms. You have obedience scanted,   282
And well are worth the want that you have wanted.   283

CORDELIA
Time shall unfold what plighted cunning hides;   284
Who covers faults, at last shame them derides.   285
Well may you prosper!

FRANCE   Come, my fair Cordelia.
                    Exeunt France and Cordelia.

GONERIL   Sister, it is not little I have to say of what most
nearly appertains to us both. I think our father will
hence tonight.

REGAN   That's most certain, and with you; next month
with us.

GONERIL   You see how full of changes his age is; the
observation we have made of it hath not been little.
He always loved our sister most, and with what poor
judgment he hath now cast her off appears too grossly.   295

REGAN   'Tis the infirmity of his age. Yet he hath ever
but slenderly known himself.

GONERIL   The best and soundest of his time hath been   298
but rash. Then must we look from his age to receive   299
not alone the imperfections of long-ingraffed condi-   300
tion, but therewithal the unruly waywardness that in-   301
firm and choleric years bring with them.

REGAN   Such unconstant starts are we like to have from   303
him as this of Kent's banishment.

---

228 **for I want** because I lack   229 **purpose not** not intend to do what
I say   231 **foulness** immorality   234 **for which** for lack of which
235 **still-soliciting** ever begging   240 **history** tale, narrative
243–4 **regards . . . point** irrelevant considerations.   252 **Since . . . fortune** Since concern for wealth and position   257 **Be it lawful** if it be
lawful that   258 **from . . . neglect** out of the cold neglect of the gods
259 **inflamed respect** ardent regard.   260 **chance** lot   262 **wat'rish**
(1) well-watered with rivers (2) feeble, watery   263 **unprized** not
appreciated. (With perhaps a sense also of "priceless.")   264 **though
unkind** though they have behaved unnaturally.   265 **here** this place.
where place elsewhere

269 **benison** blessing.   272 **washed** tear-washed   274 **like a sister** i.e.,
because I am your sister   275 **as . . . named** by their true names.
276 **professèd bosoms** publicly avowed love   278 **prefer** advance,
recommend   282 **At . . . alms** as a pittance or dole from Fortune.
283 **And well . . . wanted** i.e., and well deserve to be without the
dowry and the parental affection that you have both lacked and
flouted.   284–5 **Time . . . derides** Time will bring to light what cunning attempts to conceal as if in the folds of a cloak; those who hide
their faults may do so for a while, but in time they will be shamed and
derided.   295 **grossly** obviously.   298–9 **The best . . . rash** Even in the
prime of his life, he was stormy and unpredictable.   300–1 **long-
ingraffed condition** long-implanted habit   301 **therewithal** added
thereto   303 **unconstant starts** impulsive outbursts.   **like** likely

GONERIL   There is further compliment of leave-taking 305
    between France and him. Pray you, let us hit together. 306
    If our father carry authority with such disposition as 307
    he bears, this last surrender of his will but offend us. 308
REGAN   We shall further think of it.
GONERIL   We must do something, and i'th' heat. 310

Exeunt.

❖

1.2

Enter Bastard [Edmund, with a letter].

EDMUND
    Thou, Nature, art my goddess; to thy law   1
    My services are bound. Wherefore should I
    Stand in the plague of custom and permit   3
    The curiosity of nations to deprive me,   4
    For that I am some twelve or fourteen moonshines 5
    Lag of a brother? Why bastard? Wherefore base? 6
    When my dimensions are as well compact,   7
    My mind as generous, and my shape as true,   8
    As honest madam's issue? Why brand they us   9
    With base? With baseness? Bastardy? Base, base?
    Who in the lusty stealth of nature take   11
    More composition and fierce quality   12
    Than doth within a dull, stale, tirèd bed
    Go to th' creating a whole tribe of fops   14
    Got 'tween asleep and wake? Well, then,   15
    Legitimate Edgar, I must have your land.
    Our father's love is to the bastard Edmund
    As to th' legitimate. Fine word, "legitimate"!
    Well, my legitimate, if this letter speed   19
    And my invention thrive, Edmund the base   20
    Shall top th' legitimate. I grow, I prosper.
    Now, gods, stand up for bastards!

Enter Gloucester.

GLOUCESTER
    Kent banished thus? And France in choler parted?
    And the King gone tonight? Prescribed his power, 24
    Confined to exhibition? All this done   25
    Upon the gad? Edmund, how now? What news?   26
EDMUND   So please Your Lordship, none.

[Putting up the letter.]

GLOUCESTER   Why so earnestly seek you to put up that
    letter?
EDMUND   I know no news, my lord.
GLOUCESTER   What paper were you reading?
EDMUND   Nothing, my lord.
GLOUCESTER   No? What needed then that terrible dis- 33
    patch of it into your pocket? The quality of nothing 34
    hath not such need to hide itself. Let's see. Come, if it
    be nothing I shall not need spectacles.
EDMUND   I beseech you, sir, pardon me. It is a letter
    from my brother, that I have not all o'erread; and for 38
    so much as I have perused, I find it not fit for your
    o'erlooking.   40
GLOUCESTER   Give me the letter, sir.
EDMUND   I shall offend either to detain or give it. The
    contents, as in part I understand them, are to blame. 43
GLOUCESTER   Let's see, let's see.

[Edmund gives the letter.]

EDMUND   I hope for my brother's justification he wrote
    this but as an essay or taste of my virtue.   46
GLOUCESTER (*reads*)   "This policy and reverence of age 47
    makes the world bitter to the best of our times, keeps 48
    our fortunes from us till our oldness cannot relish
    them. I begin to find an idle and fond bondage in the 50
    oppression of aged tyranny, who sways not as it hath 51
    power but as it is suffered. Come to me, that of this I 52
    may speak more. If our father would sleep till I waked
    him, you should enjoy half his revenue forever and live
    the beloved of your brother,   Edgar."
    Hum! Conspiracy! "Sleep till I waked him, you should
    enjoy half his revenue." My son Edgar! Had he
    a hand to write this? A heart and brain to breed it
    in? When came you to this? Who brought it?   59
EDMUND   It was not brought me, my lord; there's the
    cunning of it. I found it thrown in at the casement of 61
    my closet.   62
GLOUCESTER   You know the character to be your 63
    brother's?
EDMUND   If the matter were good, my lord, I durst 65
    swear it were his; but in respect of that I would fain 66
    think it were not.
GLOUCESTER   It is his.
EDMUND   It is his hand, my lord, but I hope his heart is
    not in the contents.
GLOUCESTER   Has he never before sounded you in this
    business?
EDMUND   Never, my lord. But I have heard him oft
    maintain it to be fit that, sons at perfect age and fathers 74
    declined, the father should be as ward to the son, and 75
    the son manage his revenue.

---

305 compliment ceremony   **306 hit** agree   **307–8 If . . . offend us** If
our father continues to boss us around with his accustomed imperi-
ousness, this most recent display of willfulness will do us nothing but
harm.   **310 i'th' heat** i.e., while the iron is hot.
1.2. Location: The Earl of Gloucester's house.
1 Nature i.e., the sanction that governs the material world through
mechanistic amoral forces   **3 Stand . . . custom** submit to the vexa-
tious injustice of convention   **4 The curiosity of nations** arbitrary
social gradations   **5 For that** because.   **moonshines** months
6 Lag of lagging behind   **7 dimensions** proportions.   **compact** knit
together, fitted   **8 generous** noble, refined   **9 honest** chaste
11–12 Who . . . quality Whose begetting in the sexual act both
requires and engenders a fuller mixture and more energetic force
14 fops fools   **15 Got** begotten   **19 speed** succeed, prosper
20 invention thrive scheme prosper   **24 tonight** last night.
Prescribed Limited   **25 exhibition** an allowance, pension.
26 Upon the gad suddenly, as if pricked by a gad or spur.

33–4 terrible dispatch fearful quick disposal   **38 for** as for   **40 o'er-**
looking perusal.   **43 to blame** (The Folio reading, "too blame," "too
blameworthy to be shown," may be correct.)   **46 essay or taste** assay,
test   **47 policy and reverence of** policy of reverencing   **48 the best . . .**
times the best years of our lives, i.e., our youth   **50 idle and fond**
useless and foolish   **51 who sways** which rules   **52 suffered** permitted.   **59 to this** upon this (letter).   **61 casement** window   **62 closet**
private room.   **63 character** handwriting   **65 matter** contents   **66 in**
. . . that considering what the contents are.   **fain** gladly   **74 fit** fitting, appropriate.   **perfect age** full maturity   **75 declined** having
become feeble

GLOUCESTER   Oh, villain, villain! His very opinion in the   77
letter! Abhorred villain! Unnatural, detested, brutish   78
villain! Worse than brutish! Go, sirrah, seek him. I'll   79
apprehend him. Abominable villain! Where is he?

EDMUND   I do not well know, my lord. If it shall please
you to suspend your indignation against my brother
till you can derive from him better testimony of his
intent, you should run a certain course; where, if you   84
violently proceed against him, mistaking his purpose,
it would make a great gap in your own honor and
shake in pieces the heart of his obedience. I dare pawn   87
down my life for him that he hath writ this to feel my   88
affection to Your Honor, and to no other pretense of   89
danger.   90

GLOUCESTER   Think you so?

EDMUND   If Your Honor judge it meet, I will place you   92
where you shall hear us confer of this, and by an   93
auricular assurance have your satisfaction, and that   94
without any further delay than this very evening.

GLOUCESTER   He cannot be such a monster—

EDMUND   Nor is not, sure.

GLOUCESTER   To his father, that so tenderly and entirely loves him. Heaven and earth! Edmund, seek
him out; wind me into him, I pray you. Frame the   100
business after your own wisdom. I would unstate   101
myself to be in a due resolution.   102

EDMUND   I will seek him, sir, presently, convey the   103
business as I shall find means, and acquaint you
withal.   105

GLOUCESTER   These late eclipses in the sun and moon   106
portend no good to us. Though the wisdom of nature   107
can reason it thus and thus, yet nature finds itself
scourged by the sequent effects. Love cools, friend-   109
ship falls off, brothers divide; in cities, mutinies; in
countries, discord; in palaces, treason; and the bond
cracked twixt son and father. This villain of mine
comes under the prediction; there's son against father.
The King falls from bias of nature; there's father   114
against child. We have seen the best of our time.
Machinations, hollowness, treachery, and all ruinous
disorders follow us disquietly to our graves. Find out
this villain, Edmund; it shall lose thee nothing. Do it   118
carefully. And the noble and truehearted Kent banished! His offense, honesty! 'Tis strange.   *Exit.*

EDMUND   This is the excellent foppery of the world, that   121

when we are sick in fortune—often the surfeits of our   122
own behavior—we make guilty of our disasters the   123
sun, the moon, and stars, as if we were villains on   124
necessity, fools by heavenly compulsion, knaves,
thieves, and treachers by spherical predominance,   126
drunkards, liars, and adulterers by an enforced obedience of planetary influence, and all that we are evil
in, by a divine thrusting on. An admirable evasion of   129
whoremaster man, to lay his goatish disposition on   130
the charge of a star! My father compounded with my   131
mother under the Dragon's tail and my nativity was   132
under Ursa Major, so that it follows I am rough and   133
lecherous. Fut, I should have been that I am, had the   134
maidenliest star in the firmament twinkled on my
bastardizing. Edgar—

Enter Edgar.

and pat he comes like the catastrophe of the old   137
comedy. My cue is villainous melancholy, with a sigh
like Tom o' Bedlam.—Oh, these eclipses do portend   139
these divisions! Fa, sol, la, mi.   140

EDGAR   How now, brother Edmund, what serious
contemplation are you in?

EDMUND   I am thinking, brother, of a prediction I read
this other day, what should follow these eclipses.   144

EDGAR   Do you busy yourself with that?

EDMUND   I promise you, the effects he writes of succeed   146
unhappily, as of unnaturalness between the child and   147
the parent, death, dearth, dissolutions of ancient amities, divisions in state, menaces and maledictions
against king and nobles, needless diffidences, banish-   150
ment of friends, dissipation of cohorts, nuptial   151
breaches, and I know not what.

EDGAR   How long have you been a sectary astronom-   153
ical?   154

EDMUND   Come, come, when saw you my father last?

EDGAR   The night gone by.

EDMUND   Spake you with him?

EDGAR   Ay, two hours together.

EDMUND   Parted you in good terms? Found you no
displeasure in him by word nor countenance?   160

EDGAR   None at all.

---

77 villain vile wretch, diabolical schemer   **78 Abhorred** Abhorrent.
detested hated and hateful   **79 sirrah** (Form of address used to inferiors or children.)   **84 run a certain course** proceed with safety and
certainty.   **where** whereas   **87–8 pawn down** stake   **88 feel** feel out
89–90 pretense of danger dangerous purpose.   **92 meet** fitting,
proper   **93–4 by an . . . satisfaction** satisfy yourself as to the truth by
what you hear   **100 wind me into him** insinuate yourself into his
confidence. (*Me* is used colloquially.)   **Frame** Arrange   **101 after
your own wisdom** as you think best.   **101–2 I would . . . resolution** I
would give up my wealth and rank to know the truth, have my
doubts resolved.   **103 presently** immediately.   **convey** manage
105 withal therewith.   **106 late** recent   **107 the wisdom of nature**
natural science   **109 sequent effects** i.e., devastating consequences.
114 bias of nature natural inclination   **118 lose thee nothing** i.e.,
earn you a reward.   **121 foppery** foolishness

122–3 surfeits . . . behavior consequences of our own overindulgence
124 on by   **126 treachers** traitors.   **spherical predominance** astrological determinism, because a certain planet was ascendant at the
hour of our birth   **129 divine** supernatural   **130 goatish** lecherous
130–1 on the charge on the responsibility   **131–2 compounded . . .
Dragon's tail** had sex with my mother under the constellation Draco
(not one of the regular signs of the zodiac), or under the descending
point at which the moon's orbit intersects with the ecliptic or apparent orbit of the sun (when an eclipse might occur)   **133 Ursa Major**
the big bear or dipper—not one of the regular signs of the zodiac
134 Fut i.e., 'Sfoot, by Christ's foot.   **that** what   **137 pat** on cue.
catastrophe conclusion, resolution (of a play)   **139 Tom o' Bedlam** a
lunatic patient of Bethlehem Hospital in London turned out to beg for
his bread.   **140 divisions** social and family conflicts. (But with a
musical sense also of florid variations on a theme, thus prompting
Edmund's singing.)   **144 this other day** the other day   **146 promise**
assure   **146–7 succeed unhappily** follow unluckily   **150 needless
diffidences** groundless distrust of others   **151 dissipation of cohorts**
breaking up of military companies, large-scale desertions   **153–4 sectary astronomical** believer in astrology.   **160 countenance** demeanor.

EDMUND   Bethink yourself wherein you may have offended him, and at my entreaty forbear his presence 163
until some little time hath qualified the heat of his 164
displeasure, which at this instant so rageth in him that
with the mischief of your person it would scarcely 166
allay. 167

EDGAR   Some villain hath done me wrong.

EDMUND   That's my fear. I pray you, have a continent 169
forbearance till the speed of his rage goes slower; and, 170
as I say, retire with me to my lodging, from whence I
will fitly bring you to hear my lord speak. Pray ye, go! 172
There's my key. [*He gives a key.*] If you do stir abroad,
go armed.

EDGAR   Armed, brother?

EDMUND   Brother, I advise you to the best. I am no honest man if there be any good meaning toward you. I 177
have told you what I have seen and heard, but faintly, 178
nothing like the image and horror of it. Pray you, 179
away.

EDGAR   Shall I hear from you anon?

EDMUND
I do serve you in this business.   *Exit* [*Edgar*].
A credulous father and a brother noble,
Whose nature is so far from doing harms
That he suspects none; on whose foolish honesty
My practices ride easy. I see the business. 186
Let me, if not by birth, have lands by wit. 187
All with me's meet that I can fashion fit.   *Exit.* 188

❧

1.3

Enter Goneril, and [*Oswald, her*] *steward.*

GONERIL   Did my father strike my gentleman for chiding of his fool?

OSWALD   Ay, madam.

GONERIL   By day and night he wrongs me! Every hour
He flashes into one gross crime or other 5
That sets us all at odds. I'll not endure it.
His knights grow riotous, and himself upbraids us
On every trifle. When he returns from hunting
I will not speak with him. Say I am sick.
If you come slack of former services 10
You shall do well; the fault of it I'll answer. 11
                              [*Horns within.*]

OSWALD   He's coming, madam. I hear him.

GONERIL
Put on what weary negligence you please,
You and your fellows. I'd have it come to question. 14
If he distaste it, let him to my sister, 15

Whose mind and mine, I know, in that are one,
Not to be overruled. Idle old man, 17
That still would manage those authorities 18
That he hath given away! Now, by my life,
Old fools are babes again, and must be used
With checks as flatteries, when they are seen abused. 21
Remember what I have said.

OSWALD   Well, madam.

GONERIL
And let his knights have colder looks among you.
What grows of it, no matter. Advise your fellows so.
I would breed from hence occasions, and I shall, 26
That I may speak. I'll write straight to my sister 27
To hold my very course. Prepare for dinner.   *Exeunt.*

❧

1.4

Enter Kent [*disguised*].

KENT
If but as well I other accents borrow 1
That can my speech diffuse, my good intent 2
May carry through itself to that full issue 3
For which I razed my likeness. Now, banished Kent, 4
If thou canst serve where thou dost stand condemned,
So may it come thy master, whom thou lov'st, 6
Shall find thee full of labors.

            Horns within. Enter Lear, [*Knights,*] *and*
            attendants.

LEAR   Let me not stay a jot for dinner. Go get it ready. 8
                        [*Exit an Attendant.*]
[*To Kent*] How now, what art thou?

KENT   A man, sir.

LEAR   What dost thou profess? What wouldst thou with 11
us?

KENT   I do profess to be no less than I seem: to serve
him truly that will put me in trust, to love him that is
honest, to converse with him that is wise and says 15
little, to fear judgment, to fight when I cannot choose, 16
and to eat no fish. 17

LEAR   What art thou?

KENT   A very honest-hearted fellow, and as poor as the
King.

163 **forbear his presence** avoid meeting him   164 **qualified** moder-
ated   166 **with . . . person** with the harmful effect of your presence;
or, even if there were injury done to you   167 **allay** be allayed.
169–70 **have . . . forbearance** keep a wary distance   172 **fitly** at a fit
time.   **my lord** our father   177 **meaning** intention   178 **but faintly**
only with a faint impression   179 **image and horror** horrid reality
186 **practices** plots.   **the business** i.e., how my plots should proceed.
187 **wit** cleverness.   188 **meet** justifiable.   **fit** to my purpose.
1.3. Location: The Duke of Albany's palace.
5 **crime** offense   10 **come slack** fall short   11 **answer** be answerable
for.   14 **come to question** be made an issue.   15 **distaste** dislike

17 **Idle** Foolish   18 **manage those authorities** exercise those prerogatives   21 **With . . . abused** with rebukes in place of flattering attentiveness, when such flattery is seen to be taken advantage of.
26 **occasions** opportunities for taking offense   27 **speak** speak
bluntly.   **straight** immediately
**1.4. Location: The Duke of Albany's palace still. The sense of time
is virtually continuous.**
1 **as well** i.e., as well as I have disguised myself by means of costume
2 **diffuse** render confused or indistinct   3–4 **May . . . likeness** may
achieve the desired result for which I scraped off my beard and
erased my outward appearance.   6 **come** come to pass that   8 **stay**
wait   8.1 *Attendant* (This attendant may be a knight; certainly the
one who speaks at line 50 is a knight.)   11 **What . . . profess?** What is
your special calling? (But Kent puns in his answer on *profess* meaning
to "claim.")   15 **honest** honorable.   **converse** associate   16 **judgment** i.e., God's judgment.   **choose** i.e., choose but to fight   17 **eat
no fish** i.e., eat a manly diet (?), be a good Protestant (?).

LEAR   If thou be'st as poor for a subject as he's for a
king, thou'rt poor enough. What wouldst thou?
KENT   Service.
LEAR   Who wouldst thou serve?
KENT   You.
LEAR   Dost thou know me, fellow?
KENT   No, sir, but you have that in your countenance 27
which I would fain call master.
LEAR   What's that?
KENT   Authority.
LEAR   What services canst do?
KENT   I can keep honest counsel, ride, run, mar a curi- 32
ous tale in telling it, and deliver a plain message 33
bluntly. That which ordinary men are fit for I am
qualified in, and the best of me is diligence.
LEAR   How old art thou?
KENT   Not so young, sir, to love a woman for singing, 37
nor so old to dote on her for anything. I have years on
my back forty-eight.
LEAR   Follow me; thou shalt serve me. If I like thee no
worse after dinner, I will not part from thee yet.—
Dinner, ho, dinner! Where's my knave, my fool? Go
you and call my fool hither.   [Exit one.]

   Enter steward [Oswald].

You! You, sirrah, where's my daughter?
OSWALD   So please you—   Exit.
LEAR   What says the fellow there? Call the clodpoll back. 46
                                          [Exit a knight.]
Where's my fool, ho? I think the world's asleep.

   [Enter Knight.]

How now? Where's that mongrel?
KNIGHT   He says, my lord, your daughter is not well.
LEAR   Why came not the slave back to me when I called
him?
KNIGHT   Sir, he answered me in the roundest manner, 53
he would not.
LEAR   He would not?
KNIGHT   My lord, I know not what the matter is, but to
my judgment Your Highness is not entertained with 57
that ceremonious affection as you were wont. There's
a great abatement of kindness appears as well in the
general dependents as in the Duke himself also and 60
your daughter.
LEAR   Ha? Say'st thou so?
KNIGHT   I beseech you, pardon me, my lord, if I be
mistaken, for my duty cannot be silent when I think
Your Highness wronged.
LEAR   Thou but rememberest me of mine own concep- 66
tion. I have perceived a most faint neglect of late, 67
which I have rather blamed as mine own jealous 68

curiosity than as a very pretense and purpose of 69
unkindness. I will look further into't. But where's my
fool? I have not seen him this two days.   71
KNIGHT   Since my young lady's going into France, sir,
the Fool hath much pined away.
LEAR   No more of that. I have noted it well. Go you and
tell my daughter I would speak with her. [Exit one.]
Go you call hither my fool.   [Exit one.]

   Enter steward [Oswald].

Oh, you, sir, you, come you hither, sir. Who am I, sir?
OSWALD   My lady's father.
LEAR   "My lady's father"? My lord's knave! You whore-
son dog, you slave, you cur!
OSWALD   I am none of these, my lord, I beseech your
pardon.
LEAR   Do you bandy looks with me, you rascal?   83
                                   [He strikes Oswald.]
OSWALD   I'll not be strucken, my lord.   84
KENT   Nor tripped neither, you base football player. 85
                              [He trips up Oswald's heels.]
LEAR   I thank thee, fellow. Thou serv'st me, and I'll love
thee.
KENT   Come, sir, arise, away! I'll teach you differences. 88
Away, away! If you will measure your lubber's length 89
again, tarry; but away! Go to. Have you wisdom? So. 90
                                  [He pushes Oswald out.]
LEAR   Now, my friendly knave, I thank thee. There's
earnest of thy service.   [He gives Kent money.] 92

   Enter Fool.

FOOL   Let me hire him too. Here's my coxcomb.   93
                              [Offering Kent his cap.]
LEAR   How now, my pretty knave, how dost thou?
FOOL   [to Kent] Sirrah, you were best take my coxcomb. 95
KENT   Why Fool?
FOOL   Why? For taking one's part that's out of favor.
Nay, an thou canst not smile as the wind sits, thou'lt 98
catch cold shortly. There, take my coxcomb. Why, this 99
fellow has banished two on 's daughters and did the 100
third a blessing against his will. If thou follow him, thou 101
must needs wear my coxcomb.—How now, nuncle? 102
Would I had two coxcombs and two daughters.
LEAR   Why, my boy?

---

27 **countenance** face and bearing   32 **keep honest counsel** respect
confidences   32–3 **curious** ornate, elaborate   37 **to love** as to love
46 **clodpoll** blockhead   53 **roundest** bluntest   57 **entertained** treated
60 **general dependents** servants generally   66 **rememberest** remind
66–7 **conception** idea, thought.   67 **faint** halfhearted   68–9 **jealous
curiosity** overscrupulous regard for matters of etiquette

69 **very pretense** true intention   71 **this** these   83 **bandy looks**
exchange glances (in such a way as to imply that Oswald and Lear
are social equals)   84 **strucken** struck   85 **football** (A raucous street
game played by the lower classes.)   88 **differences** distinctions in
rank.   89–90 **If . . . again** i.e., If you want to be laid out flat again, you
clumsy ox   90 **Go to** (An expression of impatience or anger.)   **Have
you wisdom?** i.e., Wise up.   92 **earnest of** a first payment for
93 **coxcomb** fool's cap, crested with a red comb.   95 **you were best**
you had better   98–9 **an . . . shortly** i.e., if you can't play along with
those in power, you'll find yourself out in the cold.   100 **banished**
(Paradoxically, by giving Goneril and Regan his kingdom, Lear has
lost them, given them power over him.)   **on 's** of his   101 **blessing**
i.e., bestowing Cordelia on France and saving her from the curse of
insolent prosperity   102 **nuncle** (Contraction of "mine uncle," the
Fool's way of addressing Lear.)

FOOL　If I gave them all my living, I'd keep my 105
coxcombs myself. There's mine; beg another of thy 106
daughters. 107

LEAR　Take heed, sirrah—the whip.

FOOL　Truth's a dog must to kennel. He must be
whipped out, when the Lady Brach may stand by th' 110
fire and stink.

LEAR　A pestilent gall to me! 112

FOOL　Sirrah, I'll teach thee a speech.

LEAR　Do.

FOOL　Mark it, nuncle:
　Have more than thou showest, 116
　Speak less than thou knowest,
　Lend less than thou owest, 118
　Ride more than thou goest, 119
　Learn more than thou trowest, 120
　Set less than thou throwest; 121
　Leave thy drink and thy whore,
　And keep in-a-door, 123
　And thou shalt have more 124
　Than two tens to a score. 125

KENT　This is nothing, Fool.

FOOL　Then 'tis like the breath of an unfee'd lawyer; you 127
gave me nothing for't. Can you make no use of nothing, nuncle?

LEAR　Why, no, boy. Nothing can be made out of
nothing.

FOOL　[to Kent] Prithee, tell him; so much the rent of his 132
land comes to. He will not believe a fool. 133

LEAR　A bitter fool! 134

FOOL　Dost know the difference, my boy, between a
bitter fool and a sweet one?

LEAR　No, lad. Teach me.

FOOL
　That lord that counseled thee
　　To give away thy land,
　Come place him here by me;
　　Do thou for him stand.
　　　　　　　　　　　　　　　　141
　The sweet and bitter fool
　　Will presently appear: 143
　The one in motley here, 144
　The other found out there. 145

LEAR　Dost thou call me fool, boy?

FOOL　All thy other titles thou hast given away; that
thou wast born with.

KENT　This is not altogether fool, my lord.

FOOL　No, faith, lords and great men will not let me; if 150
I had a monopoly out, they would have part on't. And 151
ladies too, they will not let me have all the fool to myself; they'll be snatching. Nuncle, give me an egg and 153
I'll give thee two crowns.

LEAR　What two crowns shall they be?

FOOL　Why, after I have cut the egg i'th' middle and eat 156
up the meat, the two crowns of the egg. When thou 157
clovest thy crown i'th' middle and gav'st away both
parts, thou bor'st thine ass on thy back o'er the dirt. 159
Thou hadst little wit in thy bald crown when thou
gav'st thy golden one away. If I speak like myself in 161
this, let him be whipped that first finds it so. 162
　[Sings.]　"Fools had ne'er less grace in a year, 163
　　For wise men are grown foppish 164
　And know not how their wits to wear, 165
　　Their manners are so apish." 166

LEAR　When were you wont to be so full of songs,
sirrah?

FOOL　I have used it, nuncle, e'er since thou mad'st thy 169
daughters thy mothers; for when thou gav'st them the
rod and putt'st down thine own breeches,
　[Sings]　"Then they for sudden joy did weep,
　　And I for sorrow sung,
　That such a king should play bo-peep 174
　　And go the fools among."
Prithee, nuncle, keep a schoolmaster that can teach
thy fool to lie. I would fain learn to lie.

LEAR　An you lie, sirrah, we'll have you whipped. 178

FOOL　I marvel what kin thou and thy daughters are.
They'll have me whipped for speaking true, thou'lt
have me whipped for lying, and sometimes I am
whipped for holding my peace. I had rather be any
kind o' thing than a fool. And yet I would not be thee,
nuncle. Thou hast pared thy wit o' both sides and left
nothing i'th' middle. Here comes one o' th' parings.

　　　Enter Goneril.

LEAR
How now, daughter? What makes that frontlet on? 186
You are too much of late i'th' frown.

---

105 living property　**105–6 keep my coxcombs** (as proof of my folly)
106–7 beg . . . daughters i.e., beg for the coxcomb that you deserve for
dealing with your daughters as you did.　**110 Brach** bitch hound
(here likened to Goneril and Regan, who have been given favored
places despite their reeking of dishonest flattery)　**112 gall** irritation,
bitterness—literally, a painful swelling, or bile. (Lear is stung by the
Fool's gibe because it is so true.)　**116 Have . . . showest** don't display your wealth ostentatiously　**118 owest** own　**119 goest** i.e., on
foot. (Travel unostentatiously on horseback, not afoot.)　**120 Learn**
i.e., listen to.　**trowest** believe　**121 Set . . . throwest** don't stake
everything on a single throw　**123 in-a-door** indoors, at home
124–5 And . . . score and you will do better than break even (since a
score equals two tens, or twenty).　**127 'tis . . . lawyer** i.e., it is free—
and useless—advice. (Lawyers, being proverbially mercenary, would
not give good advice unless paid well.)　**132–3 so . . . to** (Because
Lear has given away his land, he can collect no rent.)　**134 bitter**
satirical　**141 Do . . . stand** take his place.　**143 presently** immediately　**144 motley** the parti-colored dress of the professional fool.
(The Fool identifies himself as the sweet fool, Lear as the bitter fool
who counseled himself to give away his kingdom.)　**145 found out
there** discovered there. (The Fool points at Lear.)

150 No . . . let me i.e., Great persons at court will not let me monopolize folly; I am not *altogether fool* in the sense of being "all the fool
there is."　**151 a monopoly out** a corner on the market. (The granting
of monopolies was a common abuse under King James and Queen
Elizabeth.)　**on't** of it.　**153 snatching** seizing their share (including
sexual pleasure).　**156–7 eat . . . meat** and have eaten the edible
part　**159 bor'st . . . dirt** i.e., bore the ass instead of letting the ass
bear you.　**161–2 If . . . so** If I speak like a fool in saying this, let the
first person to discover the truth of this be whipped (since in this corrupt world those who speak truth are punished for doing so).
163–6 "Fools . . . apish" "Fools have never been so out of favor, for
wise men foppishly trade places with the fools and no longer know
how to show off their wit to advantage, they have grown so foolish
in their manners."　**169 used** practiced　**174 bo-peep** (A child's
game.)　**178 An** If　**186 What . . . on?** What is that frown doing on
your forehead?

FOOL   Thou wast a pretty fellow when thou hadst no
need to care for her frowning; now thou art an O with-   189
out a figure. I am better than thou art now; I am a fool,   190
thou art nothing. [*To Goneril*] Yes, forsooth, I will
hold my tongue; so your face bids me, though you say
nothing.
          Mum, mum,
          He that keeps nor crust nor crumb,   195
          Weary of all, shall want some.   196
[*Pointing to Lear*] That's a shelled peascod.   197

GONERIL
Not only, sir, this your all-licensed fool,   198
But other of your insolent retinue
Do hourly carp and quarrel, breaking forth   200
In rank and not-to-be-endurèd riots. Sir,   201
I had thought by making this well known unto you
To have found a safe redress, but now grow fearful,   203
By what yourself too late have spoke and done,   204
That you protect this course and put it on   205
By your allowance; which if you should, the fault   206
Would not scape censure, nor the redresses sleep   207
Which in the tender of a wholesome weal   208
Might in their working do you that offense,   209
Which else were shame, that then necessity   210
Will call discreet proceeding.   211

FOOL   For you know, nuncle,
          "The hedge sparrow fed the cuckoo so long   213
          That it had it head bit off by it young."   214
So, out went the candle, and we were left darkling.   215

LEAR [*to Goneril*]   Are you our daughter?

GONERIL
I would you would make use of your good wisdom,
Whereof I know you are fraught, and put away   218
These dispositions which of late transport you   219
From what you rightly are.

FOOL   May not an ass know when the cart draws the   221
horse? Whoop, Jug! I love thee.   222

LEAR
Does any here know me? This is not Lear.
Does Lear walk thus, speak thus? Where are his eyes?
Either his notion weakens, or his discernings   225
Are lethargied—Ha! Waking? 'Tis not so.   226
Who is it that can tell me who I am?

FOOL   Lear's shadow.

LEAR
I would learn that; for, by the marks of sovereignty,   229
Knowledge, and reason, I should be false persuaded   230
I had daughters.   231

FOOL   Which they will make an obedient father.   232

LEAR   Your name, fair gentlewoman?

GONERIL
This admiration, sir, is much o'th' savor   234
Of other your new pranks. I do beseech you   235
To understand my purposes aright.
As you are old and reverend, should be wise.   237
Here do you keep a hundred knights and squires,
Men so disordered, so debauched and bold   239
That this our court, infected with their manners,
Shows like a riotous inn. Epicurism and lust   241
Makes it more like a tavern or a brothel
Than a graced palace. The shame itself doth speak   243
For instant remedy. Be then desired,   244
By her that else will take the thing she begs,
A little to disquantity your train,   246
And the remainders that shall still depend   247
To be such men as may besort your age,   248
Which know themselves and you.

LEAR   Darkness and devils!   249
Saddle my horses! Call my train together! [*Exit one.*]   250
Degenerate bastard, I'll not trouble thee.
Yet have I left a daughter.

GONERIL
You strike my people, and your disordered rabble
Make servants of their betters.

          Enter Albany.

LEAR
Woe, that too late repents!—Oh, sir, are you come?   255
Is it your will? Speak, sir.—Prepare my horses.
                                    [*Exit one.*]
Ingratitude, thou marble-hearted fiend,
More hideous when thou show'st thee in a child
Than the sea monster!

ALBANY   Pray, sir, be patient.

LEAR [*to Goneril*]   Detested kite, thou liest!   261
My train are men of choice and rarest parts,   262
That all particulars of duty know
And in the most exact regard support   264
The worships of their name. Oh, most small fault,   265

189–90 O without a figure zero, cipher of no value unless preceded by a digit.   195–6 He . . . some i.e., That person who, having grown weary of his possessions, gives all away, will find himself in need of part of what is gone.   196 want lack   197 shelled peascod shelled pea pod, empty of its contents.   198 all-licensed allowed to speak or act as he pleases   200 carp find fault   201 rank gross, excessive   203 safe certain   204 too late all too recently   205 put it on encourage it   206 allowance approval   207–11 nor . . . proceeding nor would the punishments lie dormant which, out of care for the common welfare, might prove unpleasant to you—proceedings that the stern necessity of the times will regard as prudent even if under normal circumstances they might seem shameful.   213 cuckoo a bird that lays its eggs in other birds' nests   214 it its.   it young i.e., the young cuckoo. (A cautionary fable about ungrateful children.)   215 darkling in the dark.   218 fraught freighted, provided   219 dispositions inclinations, moods   221–2 May . . . horse? i.e., May not even a fool see that matters are backwards when a daughter lectures her father?   222 Jug i.e., Joan. (The origin of this phrase is uncertain.)   225 notion intellectual power   225–6 or his . . . lethargied or his faculties are asleep   226 Waking? i.e., Am I really awake?

229 that i.e., who I am.   marks of sovereignty outward and visible evidence of being king   230–1 I should . . . daughters i.e., all these outward signs of sanity and status would seem to suggest (falsely) that I am the king who had obedient daughters.   232 Which Whom   234 admiration (guise of) wonderment   235 other other of   237 should i.e., you should   239 Men . . . bold men so disorderly, so depraved and impudent   241 Shows appears.   Epicurism Excess, hedonism   243 graced dignified   244 desired requested   246 disquantity your train diminish the number of your attendants   247 the remainders . . . depend those who remain to attend you   248 besort befit   249 Which . . . you servants who have proper self-knowledge and an awareness of how they should serve you.   250 train retinue   255 Woe, that Woe to the person who   261 kite bird of prey   262 parts qualities   264 in . . . regard with close attention to detail   264–5 And . . . name and with utter scrupulousness may uphold the honor of their reputation.

How ugly didst thou in Cordelia show!
Which, like an engine, wrenched my frame of nature 267
From the fixed place, drew from my heart all love, 268
And added to the gall. Oh, Lear, Lear, Lear! 269
Beat at this gate [*striking his head*] that let thy folly in
And thy dear judgment out!—Go, go, my people. 271
　　　　　　　　　　　　　[Exeunt some.]

ALBANY
My lord, I am guiltless as I am ignorant
Of what hath moved you.

LEAR　　　　　　　　　It may be so, my lord.—
Hear, Nature, hear! Dear goddess, hear!
Suspend thy purpose if thou didst intend
To make this creature fruitful!
Into her womb convey sterility;
Dry up in her the organs of increase,
And from her derogate body never spring 279
A babe to honor her! If she must teem, 280
Create her child of spleen, that it may live 281
And be a thwart disnatured torment to her! 282
Let it stamp wrinkles in her brow of youth,
With cadent tears fret channels in her cheeks, 284
Turn all her mother's pains and benefits 285
To laughter and contempt, that she may feel
How sharper than a serpent's tooth it is
To have a thankless child! Away, away!
　　　Exit [with Kent and the rest of Lear's followers].

ALBANY
Now, gods that we adore, whereof comes this?

GONERIL
Never afflict yourself to know more of it, 290
But let his disposition have that scope 291
As dotage gives it. 292

　　　　　　Enter Lear.

LEAR
What, fifty of my followers at a clap?
Within a fortnight?

ALBANY　　　　　　What's the matter, sir?

LEAR
I'll tell thee. [*To Goneril*] Life and death! I am ashamed
That thou hast power to shake my manhood thus,
That these hot tears, which break from me perforce,
Should make thee worth them. Blasts and fogs upon
　thee! 298
Th'untented woundings of a father's curse 299
Pierce every sense about thee! Old fond eyes, 300
Beweep this cause again, I'll pluck ye out 301
And cast you, with the waters that you loose, 302

To temper clay. Yea, is't come to this? 303
Ha! Let it be so. I have another daughter,
Who, I am sure, is kind and comfortable. 305
When she shall hear this of thee, with her nails
She'll flay thy wolvish visage. Thou shalt find
That I'll resume the shape which thou dost think 308
I have cast off forever. 　　　　　　　　*Exit.*

GONERIL [*to Albany*]　Do you mark that? 309

ALBANY
I cannot be so partial, Goneril,
To the great love I bear you— 311

GONERIL
Pray you, content.—What, Oswald, ho!
[*To the Fool*] You, sir, more knave than fool, after your
　master.

FOOL　　Nuncle Lear, nuncle Lear! Tarry, take the Fool 314
with thee. 315
　　　A fox, when one has caught her,
　　　And such a daughter
　　　Should sure to the slaughter, 318
　　　If my cap would buy a halter. 319
　　　So the Fool follows after. 　　　*Exit.*

GONERIL
This man hath had good counsel. A hundred knights? 321
'Tis politic and safe to let him keep 322
At point a hundred knights—yes, that on every
　dream, 323
Each buzz, each fancy, each complaint, dislike, 324
He may enguard his dotage with their powers 325
And hold our lives in mercy.—Oswald, I say! 326

ALBANY　　Well, you may fear too far. 327

GONERIL　　Safer than trust too far.
Let me still take away the harms I fear, 329
Not fear still to be taken. I know his heart. 330
What he hath uttered I have writ my sister.
If she sustain him and his hundred knights
When I have showed th'unfitness—

　　　　　Enter steward [Oswald].

　　　　　　　　　　　　　How now, Oswald?
What, have you writ that letter to my sister?

OSWALD　　Ay, madam.

GONERIL
Take you some company and away to horse.
Inform her full of my particular fear,
And thereto add such reasons of your own
As may compact it more. Get you gone, 339

267–8 **Which . . . place** which, like a powerful mechanical contrivance, wrenched my natural affection away from where it belonged　269 **gall** bitterness.　271 **dear** precious　279 **derogate** debased　280 **teem** produce offspring　281 **spleen** violent ill nature 282 **thwart disnatured** obstinate, perverse, and unnatural, unfilial 284 **cadent** cascading.　**fret** wear away　285 **benefits** pleasures of motherhood　290 **Never . . . know** Don't distress yourself by seeking to know　291 **disposition** humor, mood　292 **As that**　298 **Should . . . them** should seem to suggest that you are worth a king's tears. **Blasts and fogs** Infectious blights and disease-bearing fogs 299 **untented** too deep to be probed and cleansed　300 **fond** foolish 301 **Beweep** if you weep for　302 **loose** let loose (in tears)

303 **To temper clay** to mix with earth. (Lear threatens to cast both his eyes and their tears to the ground.)　305 **comfortable** comforting. 308 **the shape** i.e., the kingship　309 **Do . . . that?** i.e., Did you hear his threat to resume royal power?　311 **To** because of　314–15 **take . . . thee** (1) take me with you (2) take the name "fool" with you. (A stock phrase of taunting farewell.)　318 **Should sure** should certainly be sent　319 **halter** (1) rope for leading an animal (2) hangman's noose. 321 **This . . . counsel** (Said sarcastically.)　322 **politic** prudent. (Said ironically.)　323 **At point** armed and ready.　**dream** i.e., imagined wrong　324 **buzz** idle rumor　325 **enguard** protect　326 **in mercy** at his mercy.　327 **fear too far** overestimate the danger.　329 **still take away** always remove　330 **Not . . . taken** rather than dwell continually in the fear of being taken prisoner by such harms.　339 **compact** confirm

And hasten your return.   [*Exit Oswald.*]
                        No, no, my lord,
This milky gentleness and course of yours   341
Though I condemn not, yet, under pardon,   342
You're much more attasked for want of wisdom   343
Than praised for harmful mildness.   344

ALBANY
How far your eyes may pierce I cannot tell.   345
Striving to better, oft we mar what's well.

GONERIL   Nay, then—

ALBANY   Well, well, th'event.   *Exeunt.* 348

❖

1.5

Enter Lear, Kent [disguised as Caius], and Fool.

LEAR [*giving a letter to Kent*]   Go you before to Gloucester   1
with these letters. Acquaint my daughter no further   2
with anything you know than comes from her demand   3
out of the letter. If your diligence be not speedy, I shall   4
be there afore you.

KENT   I will not sleep, my lord, till I have delivered your
letter.   *Exit.*

FOOL   If a man's brains were in 's heels, were't not in   8
danger of kibes?   9

LEAR   Ay, boy.

FOOL   Then, I prithee, be merry. Thy wit shall not go   11
slipshod.   12

LEAR   Ha, ha, ha!

FOOL   Shalt see thy other daughter will use thee kindly,   14
for though she's as like this as a crab's like an apple,   15
yet I can tell what I can tell.

LEAR   What canst tell, boy?

FOOL   She will taste as like this as a crab does to a crab.
Thou canst tell why one's nose stands i'th' middle
on 's face?   20

LEAR   No.

FOOL   Why, to keep one's eyes of either side 's nose,   22
that what a man cannot smell out he may spy into.

LEAR   I did her wrong.   24

FOOL   Canst tell how an oyster makes his shell?

LEAR   No.

FOOL   Nor I neither. But I can tell why a snail has a
house.

LEAR   Why?

FOOL   Why, to put 's head in, not to give it away to his   30
daughters and leave his horns without a case.   31

LEAR   I will forget my nature. So kind a father!—Be my   32
horses ready?

FOOL   Thy asses are gone about 'em. The reason why   34
the seven stars are no more than seven is a pretty   35
reason.

LEAR   Because they are not eight.

FOOL   Yes, indeed. Thou wouldst make a good fool.

LEAR   To take't again perforce! Monster ingratitude!   39

FOOL   If thou wert my fool, nuncle, I'd have thee beaten
for being old before thy time.

LEAR   How's that?

FOOL   Thou shouldst not have been old till thou hadst
been wise.

LEAR
Oh, let me not be mad, not mad, sweet heaven!
Keep me in temper; I would not be mad!   46

[*Enter Gentleman.*]

How now, are the horses ready?

GENTLEMAN   Ready, my lord.

LEAR   Come, boy.   [*Exeunt Lear and Gentleman.*]

FOOL
She that's a maid now, and laughs at my departure,
Shall not be a maid long, unless things be cut
        shorter.   *Exit.* 51

❖

2.1

Enter Bastard [Edmund] and Curan, severally.

EDMUND   Save thee, Curan.   1

CURAN   And you, sir. I have been with your father and
given him notice that the Duke of Cornwall and Regan
his duchess will be here with him this night.

EDMUND   How comes that?

CURAN   Nay, I know not. You have heard of the news
abroad—I mean the whispered ones, for they are yet   7
but ear-kissing arguments?   8

EDMUND   Not I. Pray you, what are they?

CURAN   Have you heard of no likely wars toward twixt   10
the Dukes of Cornwall and Albany?

EDMUND   Not a word.

CURAN   You may do, then, in time. Fare you well, sir.
                                        Exit.

341 **milky . . . course** effeminate and gentle way   342 **under pardon** if you'll excuse my saying so   343 **attasked** taken to task for, blamed   344 **harmful mildness** mildness that causes harm.   345 **pierce** i.e., see into matters   348 **th'event** i.e., time will tell.
1.5. Location: Before Albany's palace.
1 **Gloucester** i.e., the place in Gloucestershire   2 **these letters** this letter.   3 **demand** inquiry   4 **out of** prompted by   8–9 **were't . . . kibes?** wouldn't his brains be in danger of that common affliction of the heel called chilblains?   11–12 **Thy wit . . . slipshod** i.e., Your brains would have no need for slippers to avoid chafing the chilblains, since you have no brains. (Anyone who journeys to Regan in hopes of kind treatment is utterly brainless.)   14 **Shalt** Thou shalt.   **kindly** (1) with filial kindness (2) according to her own nature   15 **crab** crab apple   20 **on 's** of his   22 **of either side 's** on either side of his   24 **her** i.e., Cordelia

30–1 Why, to . . . case i.e., The snail's head and horns are unendangered with its *case* or shell; Lear, conversely, has given away his crown to his daughters, leaving his brows unadorned and vulnerable. (With a suggestion too of the cuckold's horned head, as though Lear's victimization had a sexual dimension.)   **32 nature** natural affection. (Compare line 14 and note.)   **34 Thy . . . 'em** i.e., Your servants (who labor like asses in your service) have gone about readying the horses.   **35 seven stars** Pleiades   **39 To take't . . . perforce!** i.e., To think that Goneril would forcibly take back again the privileges guaranteed to me! (Or perhaps Lear is meditating an armed restoration of his monarchy.)   **46 temper** mental equilibrium   **51 things** i.e., penises.   **cut shorter** (A bawdy joke addressed to the audience.)
2.1 Location: The Earl of Gloucester's house.
0.1 *severally* separately.   **1 Save** God save   **7 abroad** going the rounds.   **ones** i.e., the news, regarded as plural   **8 ear-kissing arguments** lightly whispered topics.   **10 toward** impending

EDMUND
> The Duke be here tonight? The better! Best!   14
> This weaves itself perforce into my business.
> My father hath set guard to take my brother,
> And I have one thing, of a queasy question,   17
> Which I must act. Briefness and fortune, work!—   18
> Brother, a word. Descend. Brother, I say!

> *Enter Edgar.*

> My father watches. Oh, sir, fly this place!
> Intelligence is given where you are hid.
> You have now the good advantage of the night.
> Have you not spoken 'gainst the Duke of Cornwall?
> He's coming hither, now, i'th' night, i'th' haste,   24
> And Regan with him. Have you nothing said
> Upon his party 'gainst the Duke of Albany?   26
> Advise yourself.

EDGAR   I am sure on't, not a word.   27

EDMUND
> I hear my father coming. Pardon me;
> In cunning I must draw my sword upon you.
> Draw. Seem to defend yourself. Now, quit you well.—
> *[They draw.]*   30
> Yield! Come before my father!—Light, ho, here!—   31
> Fly, brother.—Torches, torches!—So, farewell.   32
> *Exit Edgar.*
> Some blood drawn on me would beget opinion   33
> Of my more fierce endeavor. I have seen drunkards   34
> Do more than this in sport. *[He wounds himself in the
> arm.]* Father, father!
> Stop, stop! No help?

> *Enter Gloucester, and servants with torches.*

GLOUCESTER   Now, Edmund, where's the villain?

EDMUND
> Here stood he in the dark, his sharp sword out,
> Mumbling of wicked charms, conjuring the moon
> To stand 's auspicious mistress.

GLOUCESTER   But where is he?   39

EDMUND
> Look, sir, I bleed.

GLOUCESTER   Where is the villain, Edmund?

EDMUND
> Fled this way, sir. When by no means he could—

GLOUCESTER   Pursue him, ho! Go after.
> *[Exeunt some servants.]*
>   By no means what?

EDMUND
> Persuade me to the murder of Your Lordship,
> But that I told him the revenging gods   44

'Gainst parricides did all the thunder bend,   45
Spoke with how manifold and strong a bond
The child was bound to th' father; sir, in fine,   47
Seeing how loathly opposite I stood   48
To his unnatural purpose, in fell motion   49
With his preparèd sword he charges home   50
My unprovided body, latched mine arm;   51
And when he saw my best alarumed spirits,   52
Bold in the quarrel's right, roused to th'encounter,   53
Or whether ghasted by the noise I made,   54
Full suddenly he fled.

GLOUCESTER   Let him fly far.   55
Not in this land shall he remain uncaught;
And found—dispatch. The noble Duke my master,   57
My worthy arch and patron, comes tonight.   58
By his authority I will proclaim it
That he which finds him shall deserve our thanks,
Bringing the murderous coward to the stake;   61
He that conceals him, death.

EDMUND
When I dissuaded him from his intent
And found him pight to do it, with curst speech   64
I threatened to discover him. He replied,   65
"Thou unpossessing bastard, dost thou think,   66
If I would stand against thee, would the reposal   67
Of any trust, virtue, or worth in thee
Make thy words faithed? No. What I should deny—   69
As this I would, ay, though thou didst produce
My very character—I'd turn it all   71
To thy suggestion, plot, and damnèd practice;   72
And thou must make a dullard of the world   73
If they not thought the profits of my death   74
Were very pregnant and potential spirits   75
To make thee seek it."

GLOUCESTER   Oh, strange and fastened villain!   76
Would he deny his letter, said he?
I never got him.   *Tucket within.*   78
Hark, the Duke's trumpets! I know not why he comes.
All ports I'll bar; the villain shall not scape.   80
The Duke must grant me that. Besides, his picture   81
I will send far and near, that all the kingdom
May have due note of him; and of my land,

---

45 bend aim   **47 in fine** in conclusion   **48 loathly opposite**
loathly opposed   **49 fell motion** deadly thrust   **50 preparèd**
unsheathed and ready.   **home** to the very heart   **51 unprovided**
unprotected.   **latched** nicked, lanced   **52 best alarumed** thoroughly
aroused to action, as by a trumpet   **53 quarrel's right** justice of the
cause   **54 ghasted** frightened   **55 Let him fly far** i.e., Any fleeing, no
matter how far, will be in vain.   **57 dispatch** i.e., that will be the end
for him.   **58 arch and patron** chief patron   **61 to the stake** i.e., to
reckoning   **64 pight** determined.   **curst** angry   **65 discover** expose
66 unpossessing unable to inherit, beggarly   **67 reposal** placing
69 faithed believed.   **What** That which, whatever   **71 character**
written testimony, handwriting.   **turn** attribute   **72 suggestion** instigation.   **practice** scheming   **73–6 And . . . seek it** and you must
think everyone slow-witted indeed not to suppose that they would
see how the profits to be gained by my death would be fertile and
potent tempters to make you seek my death.   **76 strange and fastened** unnatural and hardened   **78 got** begot.   **s.d.** *Tucket* series of
notes on the trumpet, here indicating Cornwall's arrival   **80 ports**
seaports, or gateways   **81 picture** description

---

14 The better! Best! So much the better; in fact, the best that could
happen!   **17 queasy question** matter not for queasy stomachs
18 Briefness and fortune Expeditious dispatch and good luck
24 i'th' haste in great haste   **26 Upon his party** i.e., recklessly on
Cornwall's behalf (? It would be dangerous to speak on either side.)
27 Advise yourself Consider your situation.   **on't** of it   **30 quit you**
defend, acquit yourself   **31–2 Yield . . . farewell** (Edmund speaks
loudly as though trying to arrest Edgar, calls for others to help, and
privately bids Edgar to flee.)   **33–4 beget . . . endeavor** create an
impression of my having fought fiercely.   **39 stand 's** stand his, act as
his   **44 that** when

Loyal and natural boy, I'll work the means   84
To make thee capable.   85

Enter Cornwall, Regan, and attendants.

CORNWALL
How now, my noble friend? Since I came hither,
Which I can call but now, I have heard strange news.

REGAN
If it be true, all vengeance comes too short
Which can pursue th'offender. How dost, my lord?

GLOUCESTER
Oh madam, my old heart is cracked, it's cracked!

REGAN
What, did my father's godson seek your life?
He whom my father named? Your Edgar?

GLOUCESTER
Oh, lady, lady, shame would have it hid!

REGAN
Was he not companion with the riotous knights
That tended upon my father?

GLOUCESTER
I know not, madam. 'Tis too bad, too bad.

EDMUND
Yes, madam, he was of that consort.   97

REGAN
No marvel, then, though he were ill affected.   98
'Tis they have put him on the old man's death,   99
To have th'expense and spoil of his revenues.   100
I have this present evening from my sister
Been well informed of them, and with such cautions
That if they come to sojourn at my house
I'll not be there.

CORNWALL   Nor I, assure thee, Regan.
Edmund, I hear that you have shown your father
A childlike office.

EDMUND   It was my duty, sir.   106

GLOUCESTER [*to Cornwall*]
He did bewray his practice, and received   107
This hurt you see striving to apprehend him.   108

CORNWALL   Is he pursued?

GLOUCESTER   Ay, my good lord.

CORNWALL
If he be taken, he shall never more
Be feared of doing harm. Make your own purpose,   112
How in my strength you please. For you, Edmund,   113
Whose virtue and obedience doth this instant
So much commend itself, you shall be ours.
Natures of such deep trust we shall much need;
You we first seize on.

EDMUND   I shall serve you, sir,
Truly, however else.   118

GLOUCESTER   For him I thank Your Grace.

---

84 natural (1) prompted by natural feelings of loyalty and affection (2) bastard   **85 capable** legally able to become the inheritor.   **97 consort** crew.   **98 though** if.   **ill affected** ill-disposed, disloyal.   **99 put him on** incited him to   **100 th'expense and spoil** the squandering   **106 childlike** filial   **107 bewray his practice** expose his (Edgar's) plot   **108 apprehend** arrest   **112–13 Make . . . please** Go about achieving your purpose, making free use of my authority and resources.   **113 For** As for   **118 however else** above all else.

CORNWALL
You know not why we came to visit you—

REGAN
—Thus out of season, threading dark-eyed night:
Occasions, noble Gloucester, of some poise,   122
Wherein we must have use of your advice.
Our father he hath writ, so hath our sister,
Of differences, which I least thought it fit   125
To answer from our home. The several messengers   126
From hence attend dispatch. Our good old friend,   127
Lay comforts to your bosom, and bestow
Your needful counsel to our businesses,
Which craves the instant use.   130

GLOUCESTER   I serve you, madam.
Your Graces are right welcome.   *Flourish. Exeunt.*

❖

2.2

*Enter Kent [disguised as Caius] and steward
[Oswald], severally.*

OSWALD   Good dawning to thee, friend. Art of this   1
house?

KENT   Ay.

OSWALD   Where may we set our horses?

KENT   I'th' mire.

OSWALD   Prithee, if thou lov'st me, tell me.   6

KENT   I love thee not.

OSWALD   Why then, I care not for thee.

KENT   If I had thee in Lipsbury pinfold, I would make   9
thee care for me.   10

OSWALD   Why dost thou use me thus? I know thee not.

KENT   Fellow, I know thee.   12

OSWALD   What dost thou know me for?

KENT   A knave, a rascal, an eater of broken meats;   14
a base, proud, shallow, beggarly, three-suited,   15
hundred-pound, filthy worsted-stocking knave; a   16
lily-livered, action-taking, whoreson, glass-gazing,   17
superserviceable, finical rogue; one-trunk-inheriting   18
slave; one that wouldst be a bawd in way of good ser-   19
vice, and art nothing but the composition of a knave,   20
beggar, coward, pander, and the son and heir of a

---

122 poise weight   **125 differences** quarrels.   **which** which letters   **126 from our home** while still at our palace in Cornwall.   **127 attend dispatch** wait to be dispatched.   **130 the instant use** immediate attention.
2.2 Location: Before Gloucester's house.
0.1 *severally* at separate doors.   **1 dawning** (It is not yet day.)   **6 if thou lov'st me** i.e., if you bear good will toward me. (But Kent deliberately takes the phrase in its literal, not courtly, sense.)   **9 in Lipsbury pinfold** i.e., within the pinfold of the lips, between my teeth. (A *pinfold* is a pound for stray animals.)   **10 care for** i.e., be wary of. (Playing on *care not for*, "do not like," in line 8.)   **12 I know thee not** i.e., I know you for what you are. (Playing on *know thee not*, "am unacquainted with you," in line 11.)   **14 broken meats** scraps of food (such as were passed out to the most lowly)   **15–16 three-suited . . . knave** i.e., a steward of a household, with an allowance of three suits a year and a comfortable income of one hundred pounds, dressed in dirty wool stockings appropriate to the servant class   **16–19 a lily-livered . . . slave** a cowardly, litigious, insufferable, self-infatuated, officious, foppish rogue, whose personal property all fits into one trunk   **19–20 bawd . . . service** i.e., pimp or pander as a way of providing whatever is wanted   **20 composition** compound

mongrel bitch; one whom I will beat into clamorous
whining if thou deny'st the least syllable of thy addi-   23
tion.   24

OSWALD   Why, what a monstrous fellow art thou thus
to rail on one that is neither known of thee nor knows
thee!

KENT   What a brazen-faced varlet art thou to deny thou
knowest me! Is it two days since I tripped up thy heels
and beat thee before the King? Draw, you rogue, for
though it be night, yet the moon shines. I'll make a
sop o'th' moonshine of you, you whoreson, cullionly   32
barbermonger. Draw!   [*He brandishes his sword.*]   33

OSWALD   Away! I have nothing to do with thee.

KENT   Draw, you rascal! You come with letters against
the King, and take Vanity the puppet's part against   36
the royalty of her father. Draw, you rogue, or I'll so
carbonado your shanks—draw, you rascal! Come   38
your ways.   39

OSWALD   Help, ho! Murder! Help!

KENT   Strike, you slave! Stand, rogue, stand, you neat   41
slave, strike!   [*He beats him.*]

OSWALD   Help, ho! Murder! Murder!

*Enter Bastard [Edmund, with his rapier
drawn], Cornwall, Regan, Gloucester, servants.*

EDMUND   How now, what's the matter? Part!   44

KENT   With you, goodman boy, an you please! Come,   45
I'll flesh ye. Come on, young master.   46

GLOUCESTER   Weapons? Arms? What's the matter here?

CORNWALL   Keep peace, upon your lives! [*Kent and
Oswald are parted.*] He dies that strikes again. What is
the matter?

REGAN   The messengers from our sister and the King.

CORNWALL   What's your difference? Speak.   52

OSWALD   I am scarce in breath, my lord.

KENT   No marvel, you have so bestirred your valor.
You cowardly rascal, nature disclaims in thee. A tailor   55
made thee.

CORNWALL   Thou art a strange fellow. A tailor make a
man?

KENT   A tailor, sir. A stonecutter or a painter could not
have made him so ill, though they had been but two
years o'th' trade.

CORNWALL   Speak yet, how grew your quarrel?

OSWALD   This ancient ruffian, sir, whose life I have
spared at suit of his gray beard—

KENT   Thou whoreson zed! Thou unnecessary letter!—   65
My lord, if you'll give me leave, I will tread this un-   66
bolted villain into mortar and daub the wall of a jakes   67
with him.—Spare my gray beard, you wagtail?   68

CORNWALL   Peace, sirrah!
You beastly knave, know you no reverence?

KENT
Yes, sir, but anger hath a privilege.

CORNWALL   Why art thou angry?

KENT
That such a slave as this should wear a sword,
Who wears no honesty. Such smiling rogues as these,
Like rats, oft bite the holy cords atwain   75
Which are too intrinse t'unloose; smooth every
passion   76
That in the natures of their lords rebel,   77
Bring oil to fire, snow to their colder moods,   78
Renege, affirm, and turn their halcyon beaks   79
With every gale and vary of their masters,   80
Knowing naught, like dogs, but following.—   81
A plague upon your epileptic visage!   82
Smile you my speeches, as I were a fool?   83
Goose, an I had you upon Sarum plain,   84
I'd drive ye cackling home to Camelot.   85

CORNWALL   What, art thou mad, old fellow?

GLOUCESTER   How fell you out? Say that.

KENT
No contraries hold more antipathy
Than I and such a knave.

CORNWALL
Why dost thou call him knave? What is his fault?

KENT   His countenance likes me not.   91

CORNWALL
No more, perchance, does mine, nor his, nor hers.

KENT
Sir, 'tis my occupation to be plain:
I have seen better faces in my time
Than stands on any shoulder that I see
Before me at this instant.

CORNWALL   This is some fellow
Who, having been praised for bluntness, doth affect   97

---

65 zed the letter z (regarded as unnecessary and often not included in
dictionaries of the time).   **66–7 unbolted** unsifted; hence, coarse
67 daub plaster.   **jakes** privy   **68 wagtail** i.e., bird wagging its tail
feathers in pert obsequiousness.   **75 holy cords** sacred bonds of loyalty and order   **76 intrinse** intrinsicate, tightly knotted.   **smooth**
flatter, humor   **77 rebel** rebel against reason   **78 Bring . . . moods**
flatteringly fuel the flame of their masters' angry passions, while similarly exacerbating their downward mood swings   **79 Renege,
affirm** nay-say one moment (when their lords are in a denying mood)
and serve as yes-men the next.   **halcyon beaks** (The halcyon or king-
fisher, if hung up, would supposedly turn its beak into the wind.)
80 gale and vary shifting wind   **81 following** fawning and flattery.
82 epileptic i.e., trembling and pale with fright and distorted with a
grin   **83 Smile you** Do you smile at.   **as** as if.   **84–5 Goose . . .
Camelot** (The reference is obscure, but the general sense is that Kent,
if given space and opportunity, would send Oswald packing like a
cackling goose. Camelot, the legendary seat of King Arthur and his
Knights of the Round Table, was thought to have been in the general
vicinity of Salisbury, Sarum, and Gloucester.)   **91 likes** pleases
97 affect adopt the style of

23–4 thy addition the titles I've given you.   **32 sop o'th' moonshine**
something so perforated that it will soak up moonshine as a sop
(floating piece of toast) soaks up liquor   **32–3 cullionly barbermonger** base frequenter of barber shops, fop. (*Cullion* originally meant
"testicle.")   **36 Vanity . . . part** i.e., the part of Goneril (here personified as a character in a morality play)   **38 carbonado** cut crosswise,
like meat for broiling   **38–9 Come your ways** Come on.   **41 neat**
(1) foppish (2) calflike. (*Neat* means "horned cattle.")   **44 matter** i.e.,
trouble. (But Kent takes the meaning "cause for quarrel.")   **45 With
you** I'll fight with you; my quarrel is with you.   **goodman boy** (A
contemptuous epithet, a title of mock respect, addressed seemingly to
Edmund.)   **an** if   **46 flesh** initiate into combat   **52 difference** quarrel.   **55 disclaims in** disowns

A saucy roughness, and constrains the garb   98
Quite from his nature. He cannot flatter, he;   99
An honest mind and plain, he must speak truth!
An they will take't, so; if not, he's plain.   101
These kind of knaves I know, which in this plainness
Harbor more craft and more corrupter ends
Than twenty silly-ducking observants   104
That stretch their duties nicely.   105

KENT
Sir, in good faith, in sincere verity,   106
Under th'allowance of your great aspect,   107
Whose influence, like the wreath of radiant fire   108
On flickering Phoebus' front—
CORNWALL   What mean'st by this? 109
KENT   To go out of my dialect, which you discommend
so much. I know, sir, I am no flatterer. He that be-   111
guiled you in a plain accent was a plain knave, which 112
for my part I will not be, though I should win your   113
displeasure to entreat me to't.   114
CORNWALL [to Oswald] What was th'offense you gave him?
OSWALD   I never gave him any.
It pleased the King his master very late   117
To strike at me, upon his misconstruction;   118
When he, compact, and flattering his displeasure,   119
Tripped me behind; being down, insulted, railed,   120
And put upon him such a deal of man   121
That worthied him, got praises of the King   122
For him attempting who was self-subdued;   123
And, in the fleshment of this dread exploit,   124
Drew on me here again.
KENT   None of these rogues and cowards   126
But Ajax is their fool.
CORNWALL   Fetch forth the stocks! 127

You stubborn, ancient knave, you reverend braggart,   128
We'll teach you.
KENT   Sir, I am too old to learn.
Call not your stocks for me. I serve the King,
On whose employment I was sent to you.
You shall do small respect, show too bold malice
Against the grace and person of my master,   133
Stocking his messenger.
CORNWALL
Fetch forth the stocks! As I have life and honor,
There shall he sit till noon.
REGAN
Till noon? Till night, my lord, and all night too.
KENT
Why, madam, if I were your father's dog
You should not use me so.   139
REGAN   Sir, being his knave, I will.   140
CORNWALL
This is a fellow of the selfsame color   141
Our sister speaks of.—Come, bring away the stocks!   142
                                Stocks brought out.
GLOUCESTER
Let me beseech Your Grace not to do so.
His fault is much, and the good King his master
Will check him for't. Your purposed low correction   145
Is such as basest and contemned'st wretches   146
For pilferings and most common trespasses
Are punished with. The King must take it ill
That he, so slightly valued in his messenger,
Should have him thus restrained.
CORNWALL   I'll answer that.   150
REGAN
My sister may receive it much more worse
To have her gentleman abused, assaulted,
For following her affairs. Put in his legs.
                        [Kent is put in the stocks.]
Come, my good lord, away.
                    Exeunt [all but Gloucester and Kent].
GLOUCESTER
I am sorry for thee, friend. 'Tis the Duke's pleasure,
Whose disposition, all the world well knows,
Will not be rubbed nor stopped. I'll entreat for thee. 157
KENT
Pray, do not, sir. I have watched and traveled hard.   158
Some time I shall sleep out; the rest I'll whistle.
A good man's fortune may grow out at heels.   160
Give you good morrow!   161
GLOUCESTER
The Duke's to blame in this. 'Twill be ill taken.   Exit.

98–9 constrains . . . nature i.e., distorts plainness quite from its true purpose so that it becomes instead a way of deceiving the listener. **99 He . . . he** He professes to be one who abhors the use of flattering speech. (Said sardonically). **101 An . . . plain** If people will take his rudeness, fine; if not, his excuse is that he speaks plain truth. **104–5 Than . . . nicely** than twenty foolishly bowing, obsequious courtiers who outdo themselves in the punctilious performance of their courtly duties. **106 Sir, in good faith.** (Kent assumes the wordy mannerisms of courtly flattery.) **107 th'allowance** the approval. **aspect** (1) countenance (2) astrological position **108 influence** astrological power **109 Phoebus' front** i.e., the sun's forehead **111–14 He . . . to't** The man who used plain speech to you craftily (see lines 102–5) and thereby taught you to suspect plain speakers of being deceitful was in fact a plain rascal, which part I will not play, much as it would please me to incur your displeasure if speaking thus would have that effect. (Kent would prefer to displease Cornwall, since Cornwall is pleased only by flatterers, and Kent has assumed until now that plain speech was the best way to offend, but he now argues mockingly that he can no longer speak plainly, since his honest utterance would be interpreted as duplicity.) **117 late** recently **118 upon his misconstruction** as a result of the King's misunderstanding (me) **119 When . . . displeasure** whereupon Kent, in cahoots with the King and his party, and wishing to gratify the King's anger at me **120 being down, insulted** when I was down, he exulted over me **121–2 And put . . . him** and acted with a bravado that earned him an accolade **123 For . . . self-subdued** for assailing one (i.e., myself) who chose not to resist **124 And . . . exploit** and, in the excitement of his first success in this fearless deed. (Said ironically.) **126–7 None . . . fool** i.e., You never find any rogues and cowards of this sort who do not outdo the blustering Ajax in their boasting.

128 reverend (because old) **133 grace** sovereignty, royal grace **139 should** would **140 being** since you are **141 color** complexion, character **142 away** along **145 check** rebuke, correct **146 contemned'st** most despised **150 answer** be answerable for **157 rubbed** hindered, obstructed. (A term from bowls.) **158 watched** gone sleepless **160 A . . . heels** i.e., Even good men suffer decline in fortune at times. (To be out at heels is literally to be threadbare, coming through one's stockings.) **161 Give you** i.e., God give you

KENT
> Good King, that must approve the common saw, 163
> Thou out of heaven's benediction com'st
> To the warm sun!   [*He takes out a letter.*]
> Approach, thou beacon to this under globe, 166
> That by thy comfortable beams I may 167
> Peruse this letter. Nothing almost sees miracles 168
> But misery. I know 'tis from Cordelia, 169
> Who hath most fortunately been informed
> Of my obscurèd course, "and shall find time 171
> From this enormous state, seeking to give 172
> Losses their remedies." All weary and o'erwatched, 173
> Take vantage, heavy eyes, not to behold 174
> This shameful lodging. 175
> Fortune, good night. Smile once more; turn thy wheel!
> [*He sleeps.*] 176

❖

[2.3]

Enter Edgar.

EDGAR I heard myself proclaimed,
> And by the happy hollow of a tree 2
> Escaped the hunt. No port is free, no place 3
> That guard and most unusual vigilance 4
> Does not attend my taking. Whiles I may scape 5
> I will preserve myself, and am bethought 6
> To take the basest and most poorest shape
> That ever penury, in contempt of man, 8
> Brought near to beast. My face I'll grime with filth,
> Blanket my loins, elf all my hairs in knots, 10
> And with presented nakedness outface 11
> The winds and persecutions of the sky.
> The country gives me proof and precedent 13
> Of Bedlam beggars who with roaring voices 14
> Strike in their numbed and mortifièd arms 15
> Pins, wooden pricks, nails, sprigs of rosemary; 16
> And with this horrible object, from low farms, 17

> Poor pelting villages, sheepcotes, and mills, 18
> Sometimes with lunatic bans, sometimes with prayers, 19
> Enforce their charity. Poor Turlygod! Poor Tom! 20
> That's something yet. Edgar I nothing am. *Exit.* 21

❖

[2.4]

Enter Lear, Fool, and Gentleman.

LEAR
> 'Tis strange that they should so depart from home 1
> And not send back my messenger.
GENTLEMAN   As I learned,
> The night before there was no purpose in them
> Of this remove.
KENT   Hail to thee, noble master! 4
LEAR Ha?
> Mak'st thou this shame thy pastime?
KENT   No, my lord.
FOOL Ha, ha, he wears cruel garters. Horses are tied by 7
> the heads, dogs and bears by th' neck, monkeys by
> th' loins, and men by th' legs. When a man's over- 9
> lusty at legs, then he wears wooden netherstocks. 10
LEAR
> What's he that hath so much thy place mistook
> To set thee here?
KENT   It is both he and she: 12
> Your son and daughter.
LEAR No.
KENT Yes.
LEAR No, I say.
KENT I say yea.
LEAR No, no, they would not.
KENT Yes, they have.
LEAR By Jupiter, I swear no.
KENT
> By Juno, I swear ay.
LEAR   They durst not do't!
> They could not, would not do't. 'Tis worse than
> murder
> To do upon respect such violent outrage. 23
> Resolve me with all modest haste which way 24
> Thou mightst deserve, or they impose, this usage,
> Coming from us.

---

163 **approve** prove true. **saw** proverb (i.e., "To run out of God's blessing into the warm sun," meaning "to go from better to worse," from a state of bliss into the pitiless world. Kent sees Lear as heading for trouble.) 166 **beacon . . . globe** i.e., the sun. (Daylight is coming soon.) 167 **comfortable** comforting 168–9 **Nothing . . . misery** Scarcely anything can make one appreciate miracles like being in a state of misery; to the miserable, any relief seems miraculous.
171 **obscurèd** disguised 171–3 **"and shall . . . remedies"** i.e., "and who, in the fullness of time, will bring relief from the monstrous state of affairs under which we suffer, seeking to remedy what has been destroyed." (The passage may be corrupt. Kent may be reading from his letter.) 173 **o'erwatched** exhausted with staying awake
174 **vantage** advantage (of sleep) 175 **lodging** i.e., the stocks.
176 **wheel** (Since Kent is at the bottom of Fortune's wheel, any turning should improve his situation.)
2.3 Location: Scene continues. Kent is dozing in the stocks.
2 **happy** luckily found 3 **port** (See 2.1.80 and note.) 4 **That** in which 5 **attend my taking** lie in wait to capture me. 6 **bethought** resolved 8 **in . . . man** in order to show how contemptible humankind is 10 **elf** tangle into elflocks 11 **presented** exposed to view, displayed 13 **proof** example 14 **Bedlam** (See the note to 1.2.139.) 15 **Strike** stick. **mortifièd** deadened 16 **wooden pricks** skewers 17 **object** spectacle. **low** lowly

18 **pelting** paltry 19 **bans** curses 20 **Enforce their charity** manage to beg something. **Poor . . . Tom** (Edgar practices the begging role he is about to adopt. Beggars were known as "poor Toms.")
Turlygod (Meaning unknown.) 21 **That's . . . am** There's some kind of existence for me as poor Tom. I am Edgar no longer.
2.4 Location: Scene continues before Gloucester's house. Kent still dozing in the stocks.
1 **they** Cornwall and Regan 4 **remove** change of residence. 7 **cruel** (1) unkind (2) crewel (compare the Quarto spelling, "crewell"), a thin yarn of which hose were made 9–10 **overlusty at legs** given to running away, or overly active sexually 10 **netherstocks** stockings.
12 **To** as to 23 **upon respect** i.e., against my officers (who deserve respect) 24 **Resolve** Enlighten. **modest** moderate

KENT   My lord, when at their home   26
I did commend Your Highness' letters to them,   27
Ere I was risen from the place that showed   28
My duty kneeling, came there a reeking post,   29
Stewed in his haste, half breathless, panting forth   30
From Goneril his mistress salutations;
Delivered letters, spite of intermission,   32
Which presently they read; on whose contents   33
They summoned up their meiny, straight took horse,   34
Commanded me to follow and attend
The leisure of their answer, gave me cold looks;
And meeting here the other messenger,
Whose welcome, I perceived, had poisoned mine—
Being the very fellow which of late
Displayed so saucily against Your Highness—   40
Having more man than wit about me, drew.   41
He raised the house with loud and coward cries.
Your son and daughter found this trespass worth
The shame which here it suffers.

FOOL   Winter's not gone yet if the wild geese fly that   45
way.   46
       Fathers that wear rags
          Do make their children blind,   48
       But fathers that bear bags   49
          Shall see their children kind.
       Fortune, that arrant whore,
          Ne'er turns the key to th' poor.   52
But, for all this, thou shalt have as many dolors for thy   53
daughters as thou canst tell in a year.   54

LEAR
Oh, how this mother swells up toward my heart!   55
Hysterica passio, down, thou climbing sorrow!   56
Thy element's below.—Where is this daughter?   57

KENT   With the Earl, sir, here within.
LEAR   Follow me not. Stay here.   *Exit.*
GENTLEMAN
Made you no more offense but what you speak of?
KENT   None.
How chance the King comes with so small a number?   62
FOOL   An thou hadst been set i'th' stocks for that ques-   63
tion, thou'dst well deserved it.
KENT   Why, Fool?

FOOL   We'll set thee to school to an ant to teach thee   66
there's no laboring i'th' winter. All that follow their   67
noses are led by their eyes but blind men, and there's   68
not a nose among twenty but can smell him that's   69
stinking. Let go thy hold when a great wheel runs   70
down a hill lest it break thy neck with following; but
the great one that goes upward, let him draw thee after. When a wise man gives thee better counsel, give
me mine again. I would have none but knaves follow
it, since a fool gives it.
       That sir which serves and seeks for gain,
          And follows but for form,
       Will pack when it begins to rain   78
          And leave thee in the storm.
       But I will tarry; the fool will stay,
          And let the wise man fly.
       The knave turns fool that runs away;   82
          The fool no knave, pardie.   83

Enter Lear and Gloucester.

KENT   Where learned you this, Fool?
FOOL   Not i'th' stocks, fool.
LEAR
Deny to speak with me? They are sick? They are
weary?
They have traveled all the night? Mere fetches,   87
The images of revolt and flying off.   88
Fetch me a better answer.
GLOUCESTER   My dear lord,
You know the fiery quality of the Duke,
How unremovable and fixed he is
In his own course.
LEAR
Vengeance! Plague! Death! Confusion!   93
Fiery? What quality? Why, Gloucester, Gloucester,
I'd speak with the Duke of Cornwall and his wife.
GLOUCESTER
Well, my good lord, I have informed them so.
LEAR
Informed them? Dost thou understand me, man?
GLOUCESTER   Ay, my good lord.
LEAR
The King would speak with Cornwall. The dear father
Would with his daughter speak, commands, tends
service.   100
Are they informed of this? My breath and blood!   101
Fiery? The fiery Duke? Tell the hot Duke that—
No, but not yet. Maybe he is not well.
Infirmity doth still neglect all office   104
Whereto our health is bound; we are not ourselves   105

When nature, being oppressed, commands the mind
To suffer with the body. I'll forbear,
And am fallen out with my more headier will,   108
To take the indisposed and sickly fit   109
For the sound man. [*Looking at Kent*] Death on my
   state! Wherefore   110
Should he sit here? This act persuades me
That this remotion of the Duke and her   112
Is practice only. Give me my servant forth.   113
Go tell the Duke and 's wife I'd speak with them,
Now, presently. Bid them come forth and hear me,   115
Or at their chamber door I'll beat the drum
Till it cry sleep to death.   117

GLOUCESTER I would have all well betwixt you. *Exit.*

LEAR
Oh, me, my heart, my rising heart! But down!

FOOL   Cry to it, nuncle, as the cockney did to the eels   120
when she put 'em i'th' paste alive. She knapped 'em   121
o'th' coxcombs with a stick and cried, "Down, wan-   122
tons, down!" 'Twas her brother that, in pure kindness   123
to his horse, buttered his hay.   124

    Enter Cornwall, Regan, Gloucester, [and]
    servants.

LEAR   Good morrow to you both.

CORNWALL   Hail to Your Grace!
                            Kent here set at liberty.

REGAN   I am glad to see Your Highness.

LEAR
Regan, I think you are. I know what reason
I have to think so. If thou shouldst not be glad,
I would divorce me from thy mother's tomb,   130
Sepulch'ring an adultress. [*To Kent*] Oh, are you free? 131
Some other time for that.—Belovèd Regan,
Thy sister's naught. Oh, Regan, she hath tied   133
Sharp-toothed unkindness, like a vulture, here.
                [*He lays his hand on his heart.*]
I can scarce speak to thee. Thou'lt not believe
With how depraved a quality—Oh, Regan!   136

REGAN
I pray you, sir, take patience. I have hope   137
You less know how to value her desert   138
Than she to scant her duty.

LEAR   Say? How is that?   139

REGAN
I cannot think my sister in the least
Would fail her obligation. If, sir, perchance
She have restrained the riots of your followers,
'Tis on such ground and to such wholesome end
As clears her from all blame.

LEAR   My curses on her!

REGAN   Oh, sir, you are old;
Nature in you stands on the very verge   147
Of his confine. You should be ruled and led   148
By some discretion that discerns your state   149
Better than you yourself. Therefore, I pray you,
That to our sister you do make return.
Say you have wronged her.

LEAR   Ask her forgiveness?
Do you but mark how this becomes the house: 153
[*Kneeling*] "Dear daughter, I confess that I am old;
Age is unnecessary. On my knees I beg
That you'll vouchsafe me raiment, bed, and food."

REGAN
Good sir, no more. These are unsightly tricks.
Return you to my sister.

LEAR [*rising*]   Never, Regan.
She hath abated me of half my train,   159
Looked black upon me, struck me with her tongue
Most serpentlike upon the very heart.
All the stored vengeances of heaven fall
On her ingrateful top! Strike her young bones,   163
You taking airs, with lameness!

CORNWALL   Fie, sir, fie!   164

LEAR
You nimble lightnings, dart your blinding flames
Into her scornful eyes! Infect her beauty,
You fen-sucked fogs drawn by the powerful sun   167
To fall and blister!   168

REGAN
O the blest gods! So will you wish on me
When the rash mood is on.

LEAR
No, Regan, thou shalt never have my curse.
Thy tender-hafted nature shall not give   172
Thee o'er to harshness. Her eyes are fierce, but thine
Do comfort and not burn. 'Tis not in thee
To grudge my pleasures, to cut off my train,

108–10 And . . . man and now disapprove of my more impetuous will in having rashly supposed that those who are indisposed and sickly were in sound health.   **110 Death . . . state!** (A common oath, here ironically appropriate to a king whose royal authority is dying.) **112 remotion** removal, inaccessibility   **113 practice** deception. **forth** out of the stocks.   **115 presently** at once.   **117 cry sleep to death** i.e., puts an end to sleep by the noise.   **120 cockney** i.e., a Londoner, ignorant of ways of cooking eels   **121 paste** pastry pie. **knapped** rapped   **122 coxcombs** heads   **122–3 wantons** playful creatures, sexy rogues. (A term of affectionate abuse. The cockney wife is trying to coax and wheedle the eels into laying down their lives for the making of the pastry pie—a plea that is about as ineffectual as Lear's imploring his rising heart to subside.)   **123–4 'Twas . . . hay** (Another city ignorance; the act is well intended, but horses do not like greasy hay. As with Lear, good intentions are not enough. The *brother* is related to the cockney wife in that they are both misguidedly tenderhearted.)   **130–1 I would . . . adultress** i.e., I would cease to honor your dead mother's tomb, since it would surely contain the dead body of an adultress. (Only such a fantasy of illegitimacy could explain to Lear filial ingratitude of the monstrous sort that now confronts him.)   **133 naught** wicked. **136 quality** disposition

137–9 I have . . . duty I trust this is more a matter of your undervaluing her merit than of her falling slack in her duty to you.   **139 Say?** Come again?   **147–8 Nature . . . confine** i.e., Your life has almost completed its allotted scope.   **149 By . . . state** by some discreet person who understands your situation and condition   **153 becomes the house** suits domestic decorum and the royal family line. (Said with bitter irony).   **159 abated** deprived   **163 ingrateful top** ungrateful head.   **164 taking** infectious   **167 fen-sucked** (It was supposed that the sun sucked up poisons from fens or marshes.)   **168 To fall and blister** to fall upon her and blister her beauty.   **172 tender-hafted** gentle. (Literally, set in a tender *haft*, i.e., handle or frame.)

To bandy hasty words, to scant my sizes, 176
And, in conclusion, to oppose the bolt 177
Against my coming in. Thou better know'st
The offices of nature, bond of childhood, 179
Effects of courtesy, dues of gratitude. 180
Thy half o'th' kingdom hast thou not forgot,
Wherein I thee endowed.

REGAN   Good sir, to th' purpose. 182
LEAR
Who put my man i'th' stocks?   Tucket within.
CORNWALL   What trumpet's that?
REGAN
I know't—my sister's. This approves her letter, 184
That she would soon be here.

                Enter steward [Oswald].

                          Is your lady come?
LEAR
This is a slave, whose easy-borrowed pride 186
Dwells in the fickle grace of her he follows.— 187
Out, varlet, from my sight!
CORNWALL   What means Your Grace? 188
LEAR
Who stocked my servant? Regan, I have good hope
Thou didst not know on't.

                Enter Goneril.

                        Who comes here? O heavens,
If you do love old men, if your sweet sway
Allow obedience, if you yourselves are old, 192
Make it your cause; send down, and take my part!
[To Goneril] Art not ashamed to look upon this beard?
                [Goneril and Regan join hands.] 194
Oh, Regan, will you take her by the hand?
GONERIL
Why not by th' hand, sir? How have I offended?
All's not offense that indiscretion finds 197
And dotage terms so.
LEAR   O sides, you are too tough! 198
Will you yet hold?—How came my man i'th' stocks?
CORNWALL
I set him there, sir; but his own disorders
Deserved much less advancement.
LEAR   You? Did you? 201
REGAN
I pray you, father, being weak, seem so. 202
If till the expiration of your month
You will return and sojourn with my sister,
Dismissing half your train, come then to me.

I am now from home, and out of that provision 206
Which shall be needful for your entertainment. 207
LEAR
Return to her? And fifty men dismissed?
No! Rather I abjure all roofs, and choose
To wage against the enmity o'th'air, 210
To be a comrade with the wolf and owl—
Necessity's sharp pinch. Return with her?
Why, the hot-blooded France, that dowerless took 213
Our youngest born—I could as well be brought
To knee his throne and, squirelike, pension beg 215
To keep base life afoot. Return with her?
Persuade me rather to be slave and sumpter 217
To this detested groom.   [He points to Oswald.]
GONERIL   At your choice, sir.
LEAR
I prithee, daughter, do not make me mad.
I will not trouble thee, my child. Farewell.
We'll no more meet, no more see one another.
But yet thou art my flesh, my blood, my daughter—
Or rather a disease that's in my flesh,
Which I must needs call mine. Thou art a boil,
A plague-sore, or embossèd carbuncle 225
In my corrupted blood. But I'll not chide thee;
Let shame come when it will, I do not call it. 227
I do not bid the thunder-bearer shoot, 228
Nor tell tales of thee to high-judging Jove. 229
Mend when thou canst; be better at thy leisure.
I can be patient. I can stay with Regan,
I and my hundred knights.
REGAN   Not altogether so.
I looked not for you yet, nor am provided 234
For your fit welcome. Give ear, sir, to my sister;
For those that mingle reason with your passion 236
Must be content to think you old, and so— 237
But she knows what she does.
LEAR   Is this well spoken?
REGAN
I dare avouch it, sir. What, fifty followers? 239
Is it not well? What should you need of more?
Yea, or so many, sith that both charge and danger 241
Speak 'gainst so great a number? How in one house
Should many people under two commands
Hold amity? 'Tis hard, almost impossible.
GONERIL
Why might not you, my lord, receive attendance
From those that she calls servants, or from mine?
REGAN
Why not, my lord? If then they chanced to slack ye, 247
We could control them. If you will come to me— 248
For now I spy a danger—I entreat you

176 bandy volley, exchange. scant my sizes diminish my allowances 177 oppose the bolt lock the door 179 The offices . . . childhood the natural duties and filial obligations due to parents 180 Effects outward manifestations 182 to th' purpose get to the point. 184 approves confirms 186 easy-borrowed easily put on 187 grace favor 188 varlet worthless fellow 192 Allow approve, sanction 194 beard (A sign of age and presumed entitlement to respect.) 197–8 All's . . . so Not everything that the poor judgment and dotage of old age deem offensive is actually so. 198 sides i.e., sides of the chest (stretched by the swelling heart) 201 much less advancement far less honor, i.e., far worse treatment. 202 seem so i.e., don't act as if you were strong.

206 from away from 207 entertainment proper reception. 210 wage wage war 213 hot-blooded spirited, youthful; choleric 215 knee fall on my knees before 217 sumpter packhorse; hence, drudge 225 embossèd swollen, tumid 227 call summon 228 the thunder-bearer i.e., Jove 229 high-judging judging from on high 234 looked not for did not expect 236–7 For . . . old for those who dispassionately consider your intemperate outbursts must conclude that you are old 239 avouch vouch for 241 sith that since. charge expense 247 slack neglect 248 control correct

To bring but five-and-twenty. To no more
Will I give place or notice.   251

LEAR
I gave you all—

REGAN   And in good time you gave it.

LEAR
Made you my guardians, my depositaries,   253
But kept a reservation to be followed   254
With such a number. What, must I come to you
With five-and-twenty? Regan, said you so?

REGAN
And speak't again, my lord. No more with me.

LEAR
Those wicked creatures yet do look well-favored   258
When others are more wicked; not being the worst
Stands in some rank of praise. [*To Goneril*] I'll go with
    thee.   260
Thy fifty yet doth double five-and-twenty,
And thou art twice her love.

GONERIL   Hear me, my lord:
What need you five-and-twenty, ten, or five,
To follow in a house where twice so many   264
Have a command to tend you?

REGAN   What need one?

LEAR
Oh, reason not the need! Our basest beggars   266
Are in the poorest thing superfluous.   267
Allow not nature more than nature needs,   268
Man's life is cheap as beast's. Thou art a lady;
If only to go warm were gorgeous,   270
Why, nature needs not what thou gorgeous wear'st,   271
Which scarcely keeps thee warm. But, for true need—   272
You heavens, give me that patience, patience I need!
You see me here, you gods, a poor old man,
As full of grief as age, wretched in both.
If it be you that stirs these daughters' hearts
Against their father, fool me not so much   277
To bear it tamely; touch me with noble anger,   278
And let not women's weapons, water drops,
Stain my man's cheeks. No, you unnatural hags,
I will have such revenges on you both
That all the world shall—I will do such things—
What they are yet I know not, but they shall be
The terrors of the earth. You think I'll weep;
No, I'll not weep.   *Storm and tempest.*
I have full cause of weeping; but this heart
Shall break into a hundred thousand flaws   287

Or ere I'll weep. Oh, Fool, I shall go mad!   288
       Exeunt [*Lear, Gloucester, Kent, Gentleman,*
                        and Fool].

CORNWALL
Let us withdraw. 'Twill be a storm.

REGAN
This house is little. The old man and 's people
Cannot be well bestowed.   291

GONERIL
'Tis his own blame hath put himself from rest,   292
And must needs taste his folly.   293

REGAN
For his particular, I'll receive him gladly,   294
But not one follower.

GONERIL
So am I purposed. Where is my lord of Gloucester?

CORNWALL
Followed the old man forth.

     Enter Gloucester.

                   He is returned.

GLOUCESTER
The King is in high rage.

CORNWALL   Whither is he going?

GLOUCESTER
He calls to horse, but will I know not whither.

CORNWALL
'Tis best to give him way. He leads himself.   300

GONERIL [*to Gloucester*]
My lord, entreat him by no means to stay.   301

GLOUCESTER
Alack, the night comes on, and the bleak winds
Do sorely ruffle. For many miles about   303
There's scarce a bush.

REGAN   Oh, sir, to willful men
The injuries that they themselves procure
Must be their schoolmasters. Shut up your doors.
He is attended with a desperate train,
And what they may incense him to, being apt   308
To have his ear abused, wisdom bids fear.   309

CORNWALL
Shut up your doors, my lord; 'tis a wild night.
My Regan counsels well. Come out o'th' storm.
                         Exeunt.

❖

3.1

    Storm still. Enter Kent [*disguised as Caius*]
    and a Gentleman, severally.

KENT   Who's there, besides foul weather?

---

251 place or notice houseroom or recognition. **253 depositaries** trustees **254 kept a reservation** reserved a right **258 well-favored** attractive, fair of feature **260 Stands . . . praise** achieves, by necessity, some relative deserving of praise. **264 follow** be your attendants **266 reason not** do not dispassionately analyze. **266–7 Our . . . superfluous** Even our most destitute beggars have some wretched possessions beyond what they absolutely need. **268 Allow not** If you do not allow. **needs** i.e., to survive **270–2 If . . . warm** If fashions in clothes were determined only by the need for warmth, this natural standard wouldn't justify the rich robes you wear to be gorgeous—which don't serve well for warmth in any case. **277–8 fool . . . To** do not make me so foolish as to **287 flaws** fragments

288 Or ere before **291 bestowed** lodged. **292 blame** fault. **hath** that he has, or, that has. **from rest** i.e., out of the house; also, lacking peace of mind **293 taste** experience **294 For his particular** As for him individually **300 give . . . himself** give him his own way. He is guided only by his own willfulness. **301 entreat . . . means** by no means entreat him **303 ruffle** bluster. **308–9 being . . . abused** (he) being inclined to hearken to wild counsel
3.1. Location: An open place in Gloucestershire.
0.2 *severally* at separate doors.

GENTLEMAN
One minded like the weather, most unquietly.
KENT   I know you. Where's the King?
GENTLEMAN
Contending with the fretful elements;
Bids the wind blow the earth into the sea
Or swell the curlèd waters 'bove the main,   6
That things might change or cease; tears his white hair,   7
Which the impetuous blasts with eyeless rage
Catch in their fury and make nothing of;   9
Strives in his little world of man to outstorm   10
The to-and-fro-conflicting wind and rain.
This night, wherein the cub-drawn bear would couch, 12
The lion and the belly-pinchèd wolf
Keep their fur dry, unbonneted he runs
And bids what will take all.
KENT   But who is with him?   15
GENTLEMAN
None but the Fool, who labors to outjest   16
His heart-struck injuries.
KENT   Sir, I do know you,   17
And dare upon the warrant of my note   18
Commend a dear thing to you. There is division,   19
Although as yet the face of it is covered
With mutual cunning, twixt Albany and Cornwall;
Who have—as who have not, that their great stars   22
Throned and set high?—servants, who seem no less, 23
Which are to France the spies and speculations   24
Intelligent of our state. What hath been seen,   25
Either in snuffs and packings of the dukes,   26
Or the hard rein which both of them hath borne   27
Against the old kind King, or something deeper,   28
Whereof perchance these are but furnishings—   29
But true it is, from France there comes a power   30
Into this scattered kingdom, who already,   31
Wise in our negligence, have secret feet   32
In some of our best ports and are at point   33
To show their open banner. Now to you:
If on my credit you dare build so far   35
To make your speed to Dover, you shall find
Some that will thank you, making just report   37
Of how unnatural and bemadding sorrow
The King hath cause to plain.   39
I am a gentleman of blood and breeding,   40

And from some knowledge and assurance offer   41
This office to you.   42
GENTLEMAN
I will talk further with you.
KENT   No, do not.
For confirmation that I am much more
Than my outwall, open this purse and take   45
What it contains. [*He gives a purse and a ring.*] If you
shall see Cordelia—
As fear not but you shall—show her this ring,   47
And she will tell you who that fellow is   48
That yet you do not know. Fie on this storm!
I will go seek the King.
GENTLEMAN
Give me your hand. Have you no more to say?
KENT
Few words, but, to effect, more than all yet: 52
That when we have found the King—in which your
pain   53
That way, I'll this—he that first lights on him   54
Holla the other.   *Exeunt* [*separately*].

❖

3.2

Storm still. Enter Lear and Fool.

LEAR
Blow, winds, and crack your cheeks! Rage, blow!
You cataracts and hurricanoes, spout   2
Till you have drenched our steeples, drowned the
cocks!   3
You sulfurous and thought-executing fires,   4
Vaunt-couriers of oak-cleaving thunderbolts,   5
Singe my white head! And thou, all-shaking thunder,
Strike flat the thick rotundity o'th' world!
Crack nature's molds, all germens spill at once   8
That makes ingrateful man!
FOOL   Oh, nuncle, court holy water in a dry house is bet- 10
ter than this rainwater out o'door. Good nuncle, in,
ask thy daughters blessing. Here's a night pities 12
neither wise men nor fools.
LEAR
Rumble thy bellyful! Spit, fire! Spout, rain!
Nor rain, wind, thunder, fire are my daughters.   15
I tax not you, you elements, with unkindness;   16
I never gave you kingdom, called you children.
You owe me no subscription. Then let fall   18

---

6 main mainland   **7 things** all things   **9 make nothing of** blow about contemptuously   **10 little world of man** i.e., microcosm, which is an epitome of the macrocosm or universe   **12 cub-drawn** famished, with udders sucked dry (and hence ravenous).   **couch** lie close in its den   **15 bids . . . all** (A cry of desperate defiance; "take all" is the cry of a gambler in staking his last.)   **16 outjest** exorcise or relieve by jesting   **17 heart-struck injuries** injuries that strike to the very heart.   **18–19 And . . . to you** and dare, on the strength of what I know about you, entrust a precious undertaking to you.   **22–3 as . . . high** as who does not, among those whom a mighty destiny has enthroned on high   **23 no less** i.e., no other than servants   **24 speculations** scouts, spies   **25 Intelligent of** supplying intelligence pertinent to   **26 snuffs and packings** resentments and intrigues   **27–8 Or . . . King** or the harsh reining in they both have inflicted on King Lear   **29 furnishings** outward shows   **30 power** army   **31 scattered** divided   **32 Wise in** taking advantage of.   **feet** footholds   **33 at point** ready   **35 credit** trustworthiness.   **so far** so far as   **37 making just report** for making an accurate report   **39 plain** complain.   **40 blood and breeding** good family and education

41 assurance confidence, certainty   **42 office** assignment   **45 outwall** exterior appearance   **47 fear not but** be assured that   **48 fellow** i.e., Kent   **52 to effect** in their consequences   **53–4 in which . . . this** in which task, you search in that direction while I go this way
3.2. Location: An open place, as before.
2 hurricanoes waterspouts   **3 drenched** drowned.   **cocks** weathercocks.   **4 thought-executing fires** lightning that acts with the quickness of thought   **5 Vaunt-couriers** forerunners   **8 Crack . . . at once** Crack the molds in which nature makes all life; destroy all seeds at once   **10 court holy water** flattery   **12 ask . . . blessing** (For Lear to do so would be to acknowledge their authority.)   **15 Nor** Neither   **16 tax** accuse.   **with** of   **18 subscription** allegiance.

Your horrible pleasure. Here I stand your slave,
A poor, infirm, weak, and despised old man.
But yet I call you servile ministers,   21
That will with two pernicious daughters join
Your high-engendered battles 'gainst a head   23
So old and white as this. Oho! 'Tis foul.

FOOL   He that has a house to put 's head in has a good
headpiece.   26
    The codpiece that will house   27
      Before the head has any,   28
    The head and he shall louse;   29
      So beggars marry many.   30
    The man that makes his toe   31
      What he his heart should make   32
    Shall of a corn cry woe,   33
      And turn his sleep to wake.   34
For there was never yet fair woman but she made   35
mouths in a glass.   36

LEAR
No, I will be the pattern of all patience;
I will say nothing.

    Enter Kent, [disguised as Caius].

KENT   Who's there?
FOOL   Marry, here's grace and a codpiece; that's a wise   40
man and a fool.
KENT
Alas, sir, are you here? Things that love night
Love not such nights as these. The wrathful skies
Gallow the very wanderers of the dark   44
And make them keep their caves. Since I was man,   45
Such sheets of fire, such bursts of horrid thunder,
Such groans of roaring wind and rain I never
Remember to have heard. Man's nature cannot carry   48
Th'affliction nor the fear.
LEAR   Let the great gods,   49
That keep this dreadful pother o'er our heads,   50
Find out their enemies now. Tremble, thou wretch,
That hast within thee undivulgèd crimes
Unwhipped of justice! Hide thee, thou bloody hand,
Thou perjured, and thou simular of virtue   54
That art incestuous! Caitiff, to pieces shake,   55
That under covert and convenient seeming   56

Has practiced on man's life! Close pent-up guilts,   57
Rive your concealing continents and cry   58
These dreadful summoners grace! I am a man   59
More sinned against than sinning.
FOOL   Alack, bareheaded?
Gracious my lord, hard by here is a hovel;
Some friendship will it lend you 'gainst the tempest.
Repose you there while I to this hard house—
More harder than the stones whereof 'tis raised,
Which even but now, demanding after you,   65
Denied me to come in—return and force
Their scanted courtesy.
LEAR   My wits begin to turn.   67
Come on, my boy. How dost, my boy? Art cold?
I am cold myself.—Where is this straw, my fellow?
The art of our necessities is strange,
And can make vile things precious. Come, your
    hovel.—
Poor fool and knave, I have one part in my heart
That's sorry yet for thee.
FOOL   [*sings*]
    "He that has and a little tiny wit,   74
      With heigh-ho, the wind and the rain,
    Must make content with his fortunes fit,
      Though the rain it raineth every day."   77
LEAR
True, boy.—Come, bring us to this hovel.
                  Exit [with Kent].
FOOL   This is a brave night to cool a courtesan. I'll speak   79
a prophecy ere I go:

    When priests are more in word than matter;   81
    When brewers mar their malt with water;   82
    When nobles are their tailors' tutors,   83
    No heretics burned but wenches' suitors,   84
    Then shall the realm of Albion   85
    Come to great confusion.

    When every case in law is right,   87
    No squire in debt, nor no poor knight;
    When slanders do not live in tongues,   89
    Nor cutpurses come not to throngs;

---

21 ministers agents   **23 high-engendered battles** battalions engendered in the heavens   **26 headpiece** (1) helmetlike covering for the head (2) head for common sense.   **27–34 The codpiece . . . wake** i.e., A man who houses his genitals in a sexual embrace before he has a roof over his head can expect the lice-infested penury of a penniless marriage; and anyone who unwisely places his affection on base things will be afflicted with sorrow and sleeplessness. (The *codpiece* is a covering for the genitals worn by men with their close-fitting hose; here representing the genitals themselves. The *corn* is a bunion on the toe.)   **35–6 made . . . glass** practiced making attractive faces in a mirror.   **40 Marry** (An oath, originally "by the Virgin Mary.")   **grace** royal grace.   **codpiece** (Often prominent in the Fool's costume.)   **44 Gallow . . . dark** frighten the very wild beasts of the night   **45 keep** occupy, remain inside   **48 carry** endure   **49 Th'affliction** the physical affliction   **50 pother** hubbub, turmoil   **54 simular** pretender   **55 Caitiff** Wretch   **56 convenient seeming** deception fitted to the purpose

57 practiced on plotted against.   **57–9 Close . . . grace!** O you secret and buried consciousnesses of guilt, burst open the hiding places that conceal you, and pray for mercy! (*Summoners* are the officers who cited offenders to appear before ecclesiastical courts.)   **65 Which** i.e., the occupants of which.   **demanding** I inquiring   **67 scanted** stinted   **74–7 "He . . . day"** (Derived from the popular song that Feste sings in *Twelfth Night*, 5.1.389 ff.)   **79 This . . . courtesan** i.e., This night is stormy enough to cool even the lust of a courtesan. (*Brave* means "fine, excellent.")   **81 When priests . . . matter** i.e., When priests do not practice what they preach. (This and the next three lines satirize the present state of affairs.)   **82 mar** adulterate   **83 are . . . tutors** can instruct their own tailors about fashion   **84 No heretics . . . suitors** i.e., when the prevailing heresy is lechery (a heresy, in other words, against love rather than against true religion), punished by burning not at the stake but by means of venereal infection   **85 realm of Albion** kingdom of England. (The Fool is parodying a pseudo-Chaucerian prophetic verse.)   **87 right** just. (This and the next five lines offer a utopian vision of justice and charity that will never be realized in this corrupted world.)   **89 When slanders . . . tongues** when no tongues speak slanders

When usurers tell their gold i'th' field,   91
And bawds and whores do churches build,
Then comes the time, who lives to see't,   93
That going shall be used with feet.   94

This prophecy Merlin shall make, for I live before his   95
time.   *Exit.*

3.3

Enter Gloucester and Edmund [with lights].

GLOUCESTER   Alack, alack, Edmund, I like not this unnatural dealing. When I desired their leave that I might
pity him, they took from me the use of mine own   3
house, charged me on pain of perpetual displeasure
neither to speak of him, entreat for him, or any way
sustain him.

EDMUND   Most savage and unnatural!

GLOUCESTER   Go to; say you nothing. There is division   8
between the dukes, and a worse matter than that. I
have received a letter this night; 'tis dangerous to be
spoken; I have locked the letter in my closet. These in-   11
juries the King now bears will be revenged home;   12
there is part of a power already footed. We must in-   13
cline to the King. I will look him and privily relieve   14
him. Go you and maintain talk with the Duke, that
my charity be not of him perceived. If he ask for me,   16
I am ill and gone to bed. If I die for't, as no less is
threatened me, the King my old master must be re-
lieved. There is strange things toward, Edmund. Pray   19
you, be careful.   *Exit.*

EDMUND
This courtesy forbid thee shall the Duke   21
Instantly know, and of that letter too.
This seems a fair deserving, and must draw me   23
That which my father loses—no less than all.   24
The younger rises when the old doth fall.   *Exit.*

*

3.4

Enter Lear, Kent [disguised as Caius], and Fool.

KENT
Here is the place, my lord. Good my lord, enter.

The tyranny of the open night's too rough
For nature to endure.   *Storm still.*
LEAR   Let me alone.   3
KENT
Good my lord, enter here.
LEAR   Wilt break my heart?   4
KENT
I had rather break mine own. Good my lord, enter.
LEAR
Thou think'st 'tis much that this contentious storm
Invades us to the skin. So 'tis to thee,
But where the greater malady is fixed   8
The lesser is scarce felt. Thou'dst shun a bear,
But if thy flight lay toward the roaring sea
Thou'dst meet the bear i'th' mouth. When the mind's
     free,   11
The body's delicate. This tempest in my mind   12
Doth from my senses take all feeling else
Save what beats there. Filial ingratitude!
Is it not as this mouth should tear this hand   15
For lifting food to't? But I will punish home.   16
No, I will weep no more. In such a night
To shut me out? Pour on; I will endure.
In such a night as this? Oh, Regan, Goneril,
Your old kind father, whose frank heart gave all—   20
Oh, that way madness lies; let me shun that!
No more of that.
KENT   Good my lord, enter here.
LEAR
Prithee, go in thyself; seek thine own ease.
This tempest will not give me leave to ponder   24
On things would hurt me more. But I'll go in.   25
[*To the Fool*] In, boy; go first. You houseless poverty—
Nay, get thee in. I'll pray, and then I'll sleep.
                                        Exit [Fool into the hovel].
Poor naked wretches, wheresoe'er you are,
That bide the pelting of this pitiless storm,   29
How shall your houseless heads and unfed sides,   30
Your looped and windowed raggedness, defend you   31
From seasons such as these? Oh, I have ta'en
Too little care of this! Take physic, pomp;   33
Expose thyself to feel what wretches feel,
That thou mayst shake the superflux to them   35
And show the heavens more just.
EDGAR [*within*]   Fathom and half, fathom and half!   37
Poor Tom!

Enter Fool [from the hovel].

---

91 **tell** count.   **i'th' field** i.e., openly, without fear   93 **who** whoever
94 **That . . . feet** that walking will be done on foot. (A comical anticlimax: Nothing will have been changed; don't expect these utopian
dreams to have materialized.)   95 **Merlin** (A great wizard of the
court of King Arthur, who came after Lear. The fool's comical inversion ends his song on a note of paradox and impossibility.)
3.3. Location: Gloucester's house.
3 **pity** be merciful to, relieve   8 **Go to** i.e., No more of that   11 **closet**
private chamber.   12 **home** thoroughly   13 **power** armed force.
footed landed.   13–14 **incline to** side with   14 **look** look for
16 **of** by   19 **toward** impending   21 **courtesy forbid thee** kindess
(to Lear) which you were forbidden to show   23–4 **This . . . all** i.e.,
This betraying by me of my father is something he has brought on
himself, and will surely confer upon me the earldom of Gloucester
and all his wealth.
3.4. Location: An open place. Before a hovel.

3 **nature** human nature   4 **Wilt . . . heart?** i.e., Do you want to relieve
my physical wants and thereby force me to remember my daughters'
ingratitude?   8 **fixed** lodged, implanted   11 **i'th' mouth** i.e., head-
on.   **free** free of anxiety   12 **The body's delicate** i.e., the body's
importunate needs can assert themselves.   15 **as** as if   16 **home**
fully.   20 **frank** liberal   24 **will . . . leave** i.e., keeps me too preoccupied   25 **things would** things (such as filial ingratitude) that would
29 **bide** endure   30 **unfed sides** i.e., lean ribs   31 **looped and windowed** full of openings like windows and loopholes   33 **Take
physic, pomp** Cure yourself, O distempered great ones   35 **superflux** superfluity. (With suggestion of *flux*, "bodily discharge," introduced by *physic*, "purgative," in line 33.)   37 **Fathom and half** (A
sailor's cry while taking soundings, hence appropriate to a deluge.)

FOOL   Come not in here, nuncle; here's a spirit. Help me, help me!

KENT   Give me thy hand. Who's there?

FOOL   A spirit, a spirit! He says his name's poor Tom.

KENT
What art thou that dost grumble there i'th' straw? 43
Come forth.

Enter Edgar [disguised as a madman].

EDGAR   Away! The foul fiend follows me! Through the 45
sharp hawthorn blows the cold wind. Hum! Go to thy 46
bed and warm thee.

LEAR   Didst thou give all to thy daughters? And art thou come to this?

EDGAR   Who gives anything to poor Tom? Whom the foul fiend hath led through fire and through flame, through ford and whirlpool, o'er bog and quagmire; that hath laid knives under his pillow and halters in 53 his pew, set ratsbane by his porridge, made him 54 proud of heart to ride on a bay trotting horse over 55 four-inched bridges to course his own shadow for a 56 traitor. Bless thy five wits! Tom's a-cold. Oh, do de, 57 do de, do de. Bless thee from whirlwinds, star-blast- 58 ing, and taking! Do poor Tom some charity, whom the 59 foul fiend vexes. There could I have him now—and 60 there—and there again—and there.   *Storm still.*

LEAR
Has his daughters brought him to this pass?— 62
Couldst thou save nothing? Wouldst thou give 'em all?

FOOL   Nay, he reserved a blanket, else we had been all 64
shamed.

LEAR
Now, all the plagues that in the pendulous air 66
Hang fated o'er men's faults light on thy daughters! 67

KENT   He hath no daughters, sir.

LEAR
Death, traitor! Nothing could have subdued nature
To such a lowness but his unkind daughters.
Is it the fashion that discarded fathers
Should have thus little mercy on their flesh? 72
Judicious punishment! 'Twas this flesh begot 73
Those pelican daughters. 74

EDGAR   Pillicock sat on Pillicock Hill. Alow, alow, loo, 75
loo!

FOOL   This cold night will turn us all to fools and madmen.

EDGAR   Take heed o'th' foul fiend. Obey thy parents;
keep thy word's justice; swear not; commit not with 80
man's sworn spouse; set not thy sweet heart on proud
array. Tom's a-cold.

LEAR   What hast thou been?

EDGAR   A servingman, proud in heart and mind, that 84
curled my hair, wore gloves in my cap, served the lust 85
of my mistress' heart, and did the act of darkness with
her; swore as many oaths as I spake words, and broke
them in the sweet face of heaven. One that slept in the
contriving of lust and waked to do it. Wine loved I
deeply, dice dearly, and in woman out-paramoured 90
the Turk. False of heart, light of ear, bloody of hand; 91
hog in sloth, fox in stealth, wolf in greediness, dog in
madness, lion in prey. Let not the creaking of shoes 93
nor the rustling of silks betray thy poor heart to 94
woman. Keep thy foot out of brothels, thy hand out of
plackets, thy pen from lenders' books, and defy the 96
foul fiend. Still through the hawthorn blows the cold
wind; says suum, mun, nonny. Dolphin my boy, boy, 98
sessa! Let him trot by.   *Storm still.* 99

LEAR   Thou wert better in a grave than to answer with
thy uncovered body this extremity of the skies. Is man
no more than this? Consider him well. Thou ow'st the 102
worm no silk, the beast no hide, the sheep no wool, 103
the cat no perfume. Ha! Here's three on 's are sophis- 104
ticated; thou art the thing itself. Unaccommodated 105
man is no more but such a poor, bare, forked animal
as thou art. Off, off, you lendings! Come, unbutton
here.   *[Tearing off his clothes.]*

FOOL   Prithee, nuncle, be contented; 'tis a naughty night 109
to swim in. Now a little fire in a wild field were like 110
an old lecher's heart—a small spark, all the rest on 's 111
body cold.

Enter Gloucester, with a torch.

Look, here comes a walking fire.

---

43 **grumble** mutter, mumble   45 **Away!** Keep away!   45–6 **Through ... wind** (Possibly a line from a ballad.)   53–4 **that hath ... porridge** (The fiend has laid in poor Tom's way tempting means to despairing suicide, the most damnable of sins: knives under his pillow when he is asleep, nooses in his church pew when he should be at prayer, and rat poison set beside his soup when he should eat.)   54–7 **made him ... traitor** (The next temptation is a prideful act of great bravado that would be impossible without the devil's aid: riding a horse over bridges only four inches wide in pursuit of one's own shadow.)   57 **five wits** (Either the five physical senses—sight, hearing, etc.—or the five faculties of the mind: common wit, imagination, fantasy, estimation, and memory.)   58–9 **star-blasting** being blighted by influence of the stars   59 **taking** infection, evil influence, enchantment   60 **There** (Perhaps he slaps at lice and other vermin as if they were devils.)   62 **pass** miserable plight.   64 **reserved a blanket** kept a wrap (for his nakedness)   66 **pendulous** suspended, overhanging   67 **fated** having the power of fate   72 **have ... flesh** i.e., punish themselves, as Edgar has done (probably with pins and thorns stuck in his flesh).   73 **Judicious** Appropriate to the crime   74 **pelican** greedy. (Young pelicans supposedly smote their parents and fed on the blood of their mothers' breasts.)

75 **Pillicock** (From an old rhyme, suggested by the sound of *pelican. Pillicock* in nursery rhyme seems to have been a euphemism for penis; *Pillicock Hill,* for the Mount of Venus.)   80 **justice** integrity.   **commit not** i.e., do not commit adultery. (Edgar's mad homily contains fragments of the Ten Commandments.)   84 **servingman** either a "servant" in the language of courtly love or an ambitious servant in a household   85 **gloves** i.e., my mistress's favors   90–1 **out-paramoured the Turk** outdid the Sultan in keeping mistresses.   91 **light of ear** i.e., listening intently for information that can be used criminally   93 **prey** preying.   93–4 **creaking ... silks** (Telltale noises of lovers in a secret assignation.)   96 **plackets** slits in skirts or petticoats.   **thy pen ... books** i.e., do not sign a contract for a loan   98 **suum ... nonny** (Imitative of the wind?)   **Dolphin my boy** (A slang phrase or bit of song?)   99 **sessa** i.e., away, cease (?).   102–4 **Thou ... perfume** Stripped of your finery, you are not indebted to the silkworm for silk, cattle for hide, the sheep for wool, or the civet cat for the perfume derived from its anal pouch.   104–5 **Here ... itself** The three of us here (Kent, the Fool, and Lear) are decked out in the sophistication of supposedly civilized society; you (Edgar) are the unadorned, natural essence, the natural man.   105 **Unaccommodated** Unfurnished with the trappings of civilization, such as clothing   109 **naughty** bad, nasty   110 **wild** barren, uncultivated   111 **on 's** of his

EDGAR   This is the foul fiend Flibbertigibbet! He begins 114
at curfew and walks till the first cock; he gives the web 115
and the pin, squinnies the eye and makes the harelip, 116
mildews the white wheat, and hurts the poor creature 117
of earth.
　　　Swithold footed thrice the 'old; 119
　　　He met the nightmare and her ninefold; 120
　　　　Bid her alight,
　　　　And her troth plight,
　　　And aroint thee, witch, aroint thee! 123
KENT   How fares Your Grace?
LEAR   What's he?
KENT   Who's there? What is't you seek?
GLOUCESTER   What are you there? Your names?
EDGAR   Poor Tom, that eats the swimming frog, the
toad, the tadpole, the wall newt and the water; that in 129
the fury of his heart, when the foul fiend rages, eats
cow dung for salads, swallows the old rat and the
ditch-dog, drinks the green mantle of the standing 132
pool; who is whipped from tithing to tithing and 133
stock-punished and imprisoned; who hath had three 134
suits to his back, six shirts to his body, 135
　　　Horse to ride, and weapon to wear;
　　　But mice and rats and such small deer 137
　　　Have been Tom's food for seven long year.
Beware my follower. Peace, Smulkin! Peace, thou fiend! 139
GLOUCESTER
What, hath Your Grace no better company?
EDGAR   The Prince of Darkness is a gentleman. Modo 141
he's called, and Mahu.
GLOUCESTER [*to Lear*]
Our flesh and blood, my lord, is grown so vile 143
That it doth hate what gets it. 144
EDGAR   Poor Tom's a-cold.
GLOUCESTER
Go in with me. My duty cannot suffer 146
T'obey in all your daughters' hard commands. 147
Though their injunction be to bar my doors
And let this tyrannous night take hold upon you,

Yet have I ventured to come seek you out
And bring you where both fire and food is ready.
LEAR
First let me talk with this philosopher.
[*To Edgar*] What is the cause of thunder?
KENT　　　　　　　　　　　　　　Good my lord,
Take his offer. Go into th' house.
LEAR
I'll talk a word with this same learnèd Theban. 155
[*To Edgar*] What is your study? 156
EDGAR   How to prevent the fiend, and to kill vermin. 157
LEAR   Let me ask you one word in private.
　　　　　　　　　　　[*Lear and Edgar talk apart.*]
KENT [*to Gloucester*]
Importune him once more to go, my lord.
His wits begin t'unsettle.
GLOUCESTER　　　　　　Canst thou blame him?
　　　　　　　　　　　　　　　　Storm still.
His daughters seek his death. Ah, that good Kent!
He said it would be thus, poor banished man.
Thou sayest the King grows mad; I'll tell thee, friend,
I am almost mad myself. I had a son,
Now outlawed from my blood; he sought my life 165
But lately, very late. I loved him, friend,
No father his son dearer. True to tell thee,
The grief hath crazed my wits. What a night's this!—
I do beseech Your Grace—
LEAR   Oh, cry you mercy, sir. 170
[*To Edgar*] Noble philosopher, your company.
EDGAR   Tom's a-cold.
GLOUCESTER [*to Edgar*]
In, fellow, there, in th' hovel. Keep thee warm.
LEAR [*starting toward the hovel*]
Come, let's in all.
KENT　　　　　　　　This way, my lord.
LEAR　　　　　　　　　　　　　　With him!
I will keep still with my philosopher.
KENT [*to Gloucester*]
Good my lord, soothe him. Let him take the fellow. 176
GLOUCESTER [*to Kent*]   Take you him on. 177
KENT [*to Edgar*]
Sirrah, come on. Go along with us.
LEAR   Come, good Athenian. 179
GLOUCESTER   No words, no words! Hush.
EDGAR
Child Rowland to the dark tower came; 181
His word was still, "Fie, foh, and fum, 182
I smell the blood of a British man."　　　*Exeunt.* 183

114 Flibbertigibbet (A devil from Elizabethan folklore whose name appears in Samuel Harsnett's *Declaration of Egregious Popish Impostures*, 1603, and elsewhere.)   114–15 He . . . cock He walks from nightfall till dawn   115–16 web and the pin cataract of the eye 116 squinnies squints   117 white ripening, ready for harvest 119 Swithold Saint Withold, an Anglo-Saxon exorcist, who here provides defense against the *nightmare*, or demon thought to afflict sleepers, by commanding the nightmare to *alight*, i.e., stop riding over the sleeper, and *plight* her *troth*, i.e., vow true faith, promise to do no harm. (Or, an error for *Swithin*.)   footed . . . 'old thrice traversed the wold (tract of hilly upland)   120 ninefold nine offspring. (With possible pun on *fold, foal*.)   123 aroint thee begone   129 water water newt   132 ditch-dog dead dog in a ditch.   mantle scum.   standing stagnant   133 from . . . to tithing from one ward or parish to another 134 stock-punished placed in the stocks   134–5 three suits (Like the menial servant at 2.2.15.)   137 deer animals   139 follower familiar, attendant devil.   Smulkin a devil's name (in Samuel Harsnet's *Declaration*, as are *Modo* and *Mahu* in lines 141–2).   141 The Prince of Darkness The devil   143–4 Our . . . gets it (1) Children have become so hardened in sin that they hate their parents (2) Life is so intolerable that humans cry out at having been born.   146 suffer permit me 147 in all in all matters

155 Theban i.e., one deeply versed in "philosophy" or natural science.   156 study special competence.   157 prevent thwart   165 outlawed . . . blood disowned, disinherited, and legally outlawed 170 cry you mercy I beg your pardon   176 soothe humor   177 Take . . . on i.e., Go on ahead with Edgar.   179 Athenian i.e., philosopher. 181 Child Rowland, etc. (Probably a fragment of a ballad about the hero of the Charlemagne legends. A *child* is a candidate for knighthood.)   182 word watchword   182–3 "Fie . . . man" (This is essentially what the Giant says in "Jack, the Giant Killer.")

3.5

Enter Cornwall and Edmund [with a letter].

CORNWALL   I will have my revenge ere I depart his house.

EDMUND   How, my lord, I may be censured, that nature 3 thus gives way to loyalty, something fears me to 4 think of.

CORNWALL   I now perceive it was not altogether your brother's evil disposition made him seek his death, 7 but a provoking merit set awork by a reprovable 8 badness in himself. 9

EDMUND   How malicious is my fortune, that I must 10 repent to be just! This is the letter he spoke of, which 11 approves him an intelligent party to the advantages 12 of France. Oh, heavens! That this treason were not, or 13 not I the detector!

CORNWALL   Go with me to the Duchess.

EDMUND   If the matter of this paper be certain, you have mighty business in hand.

CORNWALL   True or false, it hath made thee Earl of Gloucester. Seek out where thy father is, that he may be ready for our apprehension. 20

EDMUND   *[aside]*   If I find him comforting the King, it 21 will stuff his suspicion more fully.—I will persevere 22 in my course of loyalty, though the conflict be sore between that and my blood. 24

CORNWALL   I will lay trust upon thee, and thou shalt find a dearer father in my love.   *Exeunt.*

3.6

Enter Kent [disguised as Caius] and Gloucester.

GLOUCESTER   Here is better than the open air; take it thankfully. I will piece out the comfort with what 2 addition I can. I will not be long from you.

KENT   All the power of his wits have given way to his impatience. The gods reward your kindness! 5

        Exit [Gloucester].

Enter Lear, Edgar [as poor Tom], and Fool.

EDGAR   Frateretto calls me, and tells me Nero is an 6 angler in the lake of darkness. Pray, innocent, and 7 beware the foul fiend.

FOOL   Prithee, nuncle, tell me whether a madman be a gentleman or a yeoman? 10

LEAR   A king, a king!

FOOL   No, he's a yeoman that has a gentleman to his son; for he's a mad yeoman that sees his son a gentleman before him.

LEAR

To have a thousand with red burning spits
Come hizzing in upon 'em— 16

EDGAR   The foul fiend bites my back. 17

FOOL   He's mad that trusts in the tameness of a wolf, a 18 horse's health, a boy's love, or a whore's oath. 19

LEAR

It shall be done; I will arraign them straight. 20
[To Edgar] Come, sit thou here, most learnèd justicer. 21
[To the Fool] Thou, sapient sir, sit here. Now, you she-foxes! 22

EDGAR   Look where he stands and glares! Want'st thou 23 eyes at trial, madam? 24
[Sings.] "Come o'er the burn, Bessy, to me—" 25

FOOL   *[sings]*

        Her boat hath a leak,
        And she must not speak
    Why she dares not come over to thee.

EDGAR   The foul fiend haunts poor Tom in the voice of a nightingale. Hoppedance cries in Tom's belly for two 30 white herring. Croak not, black angel; I have no food 31 for thee.

KENT   *[to Lear]*

How do you, sir? Stand you not so amazed. 33
Will you lie down and rest upon the cushions?

LEAR

I'll see their trial first. Bring in their evidence. 35
[To Edgar] Thou robèd man of justice, take thy place; 36
[To the Fool] And thou, his yokefellow of equity, 37

3.5 Location: Gloucester's house.
3 censured judged. **nature** attachment to family **4 something fears** somewhat frightens **7 his** his father's **8–9 but . . . himself** but the promptings of self-worth stimulated by the reprehensible badness of the Earl of Gloucester. **10–11 How . . . just!** i.e., How cruel of fate to oblige me to be upright and loyal by betraying my own father! **11–13 which . . . France** which proves him to be a spy on behalf of the French. **20 for our apprehension** for our arresting of him. **21 If . . . comforting** If I find Gloucester giving aid and comfort to **22 his suspicion** suspicion of him **24 blood** family loyalty, filial instincts.
3.6. Location: Within a building on Gloucester's estate, near or adjoining his house, or part of the house itself. See 3.4.146–54. Cushions are provided, and stools.
2 piece eke **5 impatience** rage, inability to endure more.

6 Frateretto (Another of the fiends from Harsnett.) **6–7 Nero is an angler** (Chaucer's "Monk's Tale," lines 2474–5, tells how Nero fished in the Tiber with nets of gold thread; in Rabelais, 2.30, Nero is described as a hurdy-gurdy player and Trajan an angler for frogs in the underworld.) **7 innocent** simpleton, fool (i.e., the Fool) **10 yeoman** property owner below the rank of gentleman. (The Fool's bitter jest in lines 12–14 is that such a man might go mad to see his son advanced over him.) **16 hizzing** hissing. (Lear imagines his wicked daughters suffering torments in hell or being attacked by enemies.) **17 bites** (i.e., in the shape of a louse) **18–19 tameness . . . health** (Wolves are untamable, and horses are prone to disease.) **20 arraign them** (Lear now imagines the trial of his cruel daughters.) **21 justicer** judge, justice. **22 sapient** wise **23 he** (Probably one of Edgar's devils, or, Lear.) **23–4 Want'st . . . trial** Do you lack spectators at your trial? or, Can't you see who's looking at you? **25 Come . . . me** (First line of a ballad by William Birche, 1558. A *burn* is a brook. The Fool makes a ribald reply, in which the *leaky boat* suggests the woman's easy virtue or perhaps her menstrual period.) **30 nightingale** (Edgar pretends to take the Fool's singing for that of a fiend disguised as a nightingale.) **Hoppedance** (Harsnett mentions "Hoberdidance.") **31 white** unsmoked (contrasted with *black angel*, a demon). **Croak** (Refers to the rumbling in Edgar's stomach, denoting hunger.) **33 amazed** bewildered. **35 their evidence** the witnesses against them. **36 robèd man** i.e., Edgar, with his blanket **37 yokefellow of equity** partner in the law

Bench by his side. [*To Kent*] You are o'th' commission; 38
Sit you, too. [*They sit.*]

EDGAR   Let us deal justly. [*He sings.*]
    Sleepest or wakest thou, jolly shepherd?
      Thy sheep be in the corn; 42
    And for one blast of thy minikin mouth, 43
      Thy sheep shall take no harm. 44
Purr the cat is gray. 45

LEAR   Arraign her first; 'tis Goneril, I here take my oath
before this honorable assembly, kicked the poor King 47
her father.

FOOL   Come hither, mistress. Is your name Goneril?

LEAR   She cannot deny it.

FOOL   Cry you mercy, I took you for a joint stool. 51

LEAR
And here's another, whose warped looks proclaim 52
What store her heart is made on. Stop her there! 53
Arms, arms, sword, fire! Corruption in the place! 54
False justicer, why hast thou let her scape?

EDGAR   Bless thy five wits!

KENT
Oh, pity! Sir, where is the patience now
That you so oft have boasted to retain?

EDGAR [*aside*]
My tears begin to take his part so much
They mar my counterfeiting.

LEAR   The little dogs and all,
Tray, Blanch, and Sweetheart, see, they bark at me.

EDGAR   Tom will throw his head at them.—Avaunt, you 63
curs!
    Be thy mouth or black or white, 65
    Tooth that poisons if it bite,
    Mastiff, greyhound, mongrel grim,
    Hound or spaniel, brach or lym, 68
    Bobtail tike or trundle-tail, 69
    Tom will make him weep and wail;
    For, with throwing thus my head,
    Dogs leap the hatch, and all are fled. 72
Do de, de, de. Sessa! Come, march to wakes and fairs 73
and market towns. Poor Tom, thy horn is dry. 74

LEAR   Then let them anatomize Regan; see what breeds 75
about her heart. Is there any cause in nature that makes
these hard hearts? [*To Edgar*] You, sir, I entertain 77

for one of my hundred; only I do not like the fashion of
your garments. You will say they are Persian; but let 79
them be changed.

KENT
Now, good my lord, lie here and rest awhile.

LEAR [*lying on cushions*]   Make no noise, make no
noise. Draw the curtains. So, so. We'll go to supper 83
i'th' morning. [*He sleeps.*]

FOOL   And I'll go to bed at noon.

    Enter Gloucester.

GLOUCESTER [*to Kent*]
Come hither, friend. Where is the King my master?

KENT
Here, sir, but trouble him not; his wits are gone.

GLOUCESTER
Good friend, I prithee, take him in thy arms.
I have o'erheard a plot of death upon him. 89
There is a litter ready; lay him in't
And drive toward Dover, friend, where thou shalt
    meet
Both welcome and protection. Take up thy master.
If thou shouldst dally half an hour, his life,
With thine and all that offer to defend him,
Stand in assurèd loss. Take up, take up, 95
And follow me, that will to some provision 96
Give thee quick conduct.

KENT   Oppressèd nature sleeps. 97
This rest might yet have balmed thy broken sinews, 98
Which, if convenience will not allow, 99
Stand in hard cure. [*To the Fool*] Come, help to bear thy
    master. 100
Thou must not stay behind. [*They pick up Lear.*]

GLOUCESTER   Come, come, away!
                 Exeunt [*all but Edgar*].

EDGAR
When we our betters see bearing our woes, 102
We scarcely think our miseries our foes. 103
Who alone suffers suffers most i'th' mind, 104
Leaving free things and happy shows behind; 105
But then the mind much sufferance doth o'erskip 106
When grief hath mates, and bearing fellowship. 107
How light and portable my pain seems now, 108
When that which makes me bend makes the King
    bow—
He childed as I fathered. Tom, away! 110

---

38 **Bench** take your place on the bench.   **o'th' commission** one commissioned to be a justice   42 **corn** grainfield   43–4 **And . . . harm** i.e., one shout from your dainty (*minikin*) mouth can recall the sheep from the grainfield and thus save them from dangerous overeating.
45 **Purr the cat** (A devil or familiar from Harsnett; see the note for 3.4.114. *Purr* may be the sound the familiar makes.)   47 **kicked** who kicked   51 **joint stool** low stool made by a joiner, or maker of furniture with joined parts. (Proverbially, the phrase "I took . . . stool" meant "I beg your pardon for failing to notice you." The reference is also presumably to a real stool onstage.)   52 **another** i.e., Regan
53 **store** abundance, material.   **on** of.   54 **Corruption in the place!** i.e., There is iniquity or bribery in this court!   63 **throw his head at** i.e., threaten   65 **or black** either black   68 **brach or lym** bitch-hound or bloodhound   69 **Bobtail . . . trundle-tail** mongrel dog with a docked or bobbed tail, or one that is curly-tailed   72 **hatch** lower half of a divided door   73 **Sessa** i.e., Away, cease.   **wakes** parish festivals
74 **horn** horn-bottle, used by beggars to drink from and to beg for alms   75 **anatomize** dissect   77 **entertain** take into my service

79 **Persian** (Lear madly asks if Edgar's wretched blanket is a rich Persian fabric.)   83 **curtains** bedcurtains. (They presumably exist only in Lear's mad imagination.)   89 **upon** against   95 **Stand . . . loss** will assuredly be lost.   96 **provision** supplies, or, means of providing for safety   97 **conduct** guidance.   98 **balmed** soothed, healed.   **sinews** nerves   99 **convenience** circumstances   100 **Stand . . . cure** will be hard to cure.   102 **our woes** woes like ours   103 **We . . . foes** we almost forget our own miseries (since we see how human suffering afflicts even the great).   104–7 **Who . . . fellowship** Anyone who has no companionship in suffering undergoes the mental anguish of forgetting entirely the carefree ways and happy scenes that were once enjoyed, whereas fellowship in grief enables the mind to rise above such suffering. (I.e., Misery loves company.)   108 **portable** bearable, endurable   110 **He . . . fathered** he suffering cruelty from his children as I from my father.

Mark the high noises, and thyself bewray　　　　　111
When false opinion, whose wrong thoughts defile
　　thee,　　　　　　　　　　　　　　　　　　112
In thy just proof repeals and reconciles thee.　　113
What will hap more tonight, safe scape the King!　114
Lurk, lurk.　　　　　　　　　　　　　*[Exit.]*　115

❧

3.7

Enter Cornwall, Regan, Goneril, Bastard
[Edmund], and Servants.

CORNWALL *[to Goneril]*　Post speedily to my lord your hus-　1
band; show him this letter. *[He gives a letter.]* The army
of France is landed.—Seek out the traitor Gloucester.
　　　　　　　　　　　　　　[Exeunt some Servants.]
REGAN　Hang him instantly.
GONERIL　Pluck out his eyes.
CORNWALL　Leave him to my displeasure. Edmund,
keep you our sister company. The revenges we are　　7
bound to take upon your traitorous father are not fit　8
for your beholding. Advise the Duke, where you are　9
going, to a most festinate preparation; we are bound　10
to the like. Our posts shall be swift and intelligent　11
betwixt us. Farewell, dear sister; farewell, my lord of　12
Gloucester.　　　　　　　　　　　　　　　　　　13

Enter steward [Oswald].

How now? Where's the King?
OSWALD
My lord of Gloucester hath conveyed him hence.
Some five- or six-and-thirty of his knights,　　　　16
Hot questrists after him, met him at gate,　　　　　17
Who, with some other of the lord's dependents,　　18
Are gone with him toward Dover, where they boast
To have well-armèd friends.
CORNWALL　Get horses for your mistress. *[Exit Oswald.]*
GONERIL　Farewell, sweet lord, and sister.
CORNWALL
Edmund, farewell.　　　*Exeunt [Goneril and Edmund].*
　　　　　Go seek the traitor Gloucester.
Pinion him like a thief; bring him before us.
　　　　　　　　　　　　　　[Exeunt Servants.]
Though well we may not pass upon his life　　　　25
Without the form of justice, yet our power

Shall do a court'sy to our wrath, which men　　　27
May blame but not control.

Enter Gloucester, and Servants [leading him].

　　　　　　　　　Who's there? The traitor?
REGAN　Ingrateful fox! 'Tis he.
CORNWALL　Bind fast his corky arms.　　　　　　30
GLOUCESTER
What means Your Graces? Good my friends, consider
You are my guests. Do me no foul play, friends.
CORNWALL
Bind him, I say.　　　　　　　*[Servants bind him.]*
REGAN　　　　　Hard, hard. Oh, filthy traitor!
GLOUCESTER
Unmerciful lady as you are, I'm none.
CORNWALL
To this chair bind him.—Villain, thou shalt find—
　　　　　　　　[Regan plucks Gloucester's beard.]
GLOUCESTER
By the kind gods, 'tis most ignobly done
To pluck me by the beard.
REGAN
So white, and such a traitor?
GLOUCESTER　　　　　　　　Naughty lady,　　38
These hairs which thou dost ravish from my chin
Will quicken and accuse thee. I am your host.　　40
With robbers' hands my hospitable favors　　　　41
You should not ruffle thus. What will you do?　　42
CORNWALL
Come, sir, what letters had you late from France?　43
REGAN
Be simple-answered, for we know the truth.　　　44
CORNWALL
And what confederacy have you with the traitors
Late footed in the kingdom?
REGAN　　　　　　　　　　To whose hands　　46
You have sent the lunatic King. Speak.
GLOUCESTER
I have a letter guessingly set down,　　　　　　48
Which came from one that's of a neutral heart,
And not from one opposed.
CORNWALL　Cunning.
REGAN　And false.
CORNWALL　Where hast thou sent the King?
GLOUCESTER　To Dover.
REGAN
Wherefore to Dover? Wast thou not charged at peril—　55
CORNWALL
Wherefore to Dover? Let him answer that.
GLOUCESTER
I am tied to th' stake, and I must stand the course.　57

111–13 Mark . . . thee Observe what is being said about those in high places or about great events, and reveal your identity only when the general opinion that now slanders you, at length establishing your innocence, recalls you from banishment and restores you to favor. **114 What . . . King!** Whatever else happens tonight, may the King escape safely! **115 Lurk** Keep out of sight
3.7. Location: Gloucester's house.
1 Post speedily Hurry　**7 sister** sister-in-law, Goneril　**8 bound** intending; obliged　**9 the Duke** Albany　**10 festinate** hasty.　**are bound** intend, are committed　**11 posts** messengers.　**intelligent** serviceable in bearing information, knowledgeable　**12–13 my . . . Gloucester** i.e., Edmund, the recipient now of his father's forfeited estate and title. (Two lines later, Oswald uses the same title to refer to Edmund's father.)　**16 his** Lear's　**17 questrists after him** searchers for Lear　**18 the lord's** i.e., Gloucester's　**25 pass upon his life** pass the death sentence upon him

27 do a court'sy i.e., bow before, yield precedence　**30 corky** withered with age　**38 white** white-haired, venerable.　**Naughty** Wicked　**40 quicken** come to life　**41–2 With . . . thus** You should not roughly handle my welcoming face with your hands as though you were robbers.　**43 late** lately　**44 simple-answered** straightforward in your answers　**46 Late footed** recently landed　**48 guessingly set down** conjecturally written　**55 charged at peril** commanded on peril of your life　**57 tied to th' stake** i.e., like a bear to be baited with dogs. **the course** the dogs' attack.

REGAN   Wherefore to Dover?

GLOUCESTER
Because I would not see thy cruel nails
Pluck out his poor old eyes, nor thy fierce sister
In his anointed flesh rash boarish fangs.   61
The sea, with such a storm as his bare head
In hell-black night endured, would have buoyed up   63
And quenched the stellèd fires;   64
Yet, poor old heart, he holp the heavens to rain.   65
If wolves had at thy gate howled that dern time,   66
Thou shouldst have said, "Good porter, turn the key."   67
All cruels else subscribe. But I shall see   68
The wingèd Vengeance overtake such children.   69

CORNWALL
See't shalt thou never.—Fellows, hold the chair.
Upon these eyes of thine I'll set my foot.

GLOUCESTER
He that will think to live till he be old,   72
Give me some help!
          [*Servants hold the chair as Cornwall grinds
          out one of Gloucester's eyes with his boot.*]
                    Oh, cruel! O you gods!

REGAN
One side will mock another. Th'other too.

CORNWALL [*to Gloucester*]
If you see Vengeance—

FIRST SERVANT   Hold your hand, my lord!
I have served you ever since I was a child;
But better service have I never done you
Than now to bid you hold.

REGAN   How now, you dog?

FIRST SERVANT [*to Regan*]
If you did wear a beard upon your chin,
I'd shake it on this quarrel.—What do you mean?   80

CORNWALL   My villain?   [*He draws his sword.*] 81

FIRST SERVANT [*drawing*]
Nay, then, come on, and take the chance of anger.   82
                    [*They fight. Cornwall is wounded.*]

REGAN [*to another Servant*]
Give me thy sword. A peasant stand up thus?   83
          [*She takes a sword and runs at him behind.*]

FIRST SERVANT
Oh, I am slain! My lord, you have one eye left
To see some mischief on him. Oh!   [*He dies.*]   85

CORNWALL
Lest it see more, prevent it. Out, vile jelly!
          [*He puts out Gloucester's other eye.*]

Where is thy luster now?

GLOUCESTER
All dark and comfortless. Where's my son Edmund?
Edmund, enkindle all the sparks of nature   89
To quit this horrid act.

REGAN   Out, treacherous villain!   90
Thou call'st on him that hates thee. It was he
That made the overture of thy treasons to us,   92
Who is too good to pity thee.

GLOUCESTER
Oh, my follies! Then Edgar was abused.   94
Kind gods, forgive me that, and prosper him!

REGAN [*to a Servant*]
Go thrust him out at gates and let him smell
His way to Dover.   *Exit [a Servant] with Gloucester.*
                    How is't, my lord? How look you?   97

CORNWALL
I have received a hurt. Follow me, lady.—
Turn out that eyeless villain. Throw this slave
Upon the dunghill.—Regan, I bleed apace.
Untimely comes this hurt. Give me your arm.
          Exeunt [Cornwall, supported by Regan].

SECOND SERVANT
I'll never care what wickedness I do,
If this man come to good.

THIRD SERVANT   If she live long,
And in the end meet the old course of death,   104
Women will all turn monsters.

SECOND SERVANT
Let's follow the old Earl, and get the Bedlam   106
To lead him where he would. His roguish madness   107
Allows itself to anything.   108

THIRD SERVANT
Go thou. I'll fetch some flax and whites of eggs
To apply to his bleeding face. Now, heaven help him!   110
          Exeunt [with the body].

❧

4.1

Enter Edgar [as poor Tom].

EDGAR
Yet better thus, and known to be contemned,   1
Than still contemned and flattered. To be worst,   2
The lowest and most dejected thing of fortune,   3
Stands still in esperance, lives not in fear.   4

---

61 anointed consecrated with holy oil.   **rash** slash, stick
63–4 would . . . fires would have swelled high enough, like a wave-
lifted buoy, to quench the stars. (*Stellèd* means "starry" or "fixed.")
65 holp helped   **66 dern** dire, dread   **67 turn the key** i.e., let them
in.   **68 All . . . subscribe** All other cruel creatures would show forgiveness except you; this cruelty is unparalleled.   **69 The wingèd
Vengeance** the swift vengeance of the avenging angel of divine wrath
72 will think hopes   **80 I'd . . . quarrel** i.e., I'd pull your beard in
vehement defiance in this cause.   **What do you mean?** i.e., What are
you thinking of, what do you think you're doing? (Said perhaps to
Cornwall.)   **81 villain** servant, bondman. (Cornwall's question
implies, "How dare you do such a thing?")   **82 the chance of anger**
the risks of an angry encounter.   **83.1 She . . . behind** (This stage
direction appears in the Quarto.)   **85 mischief** injury

89 nature i.e., filial love   **90 quit** requite.   **Out** (An exclamation of
anger or impatience.)   **92 overture** disclosure   **94 abused** wronged.
97 How look you? How is it with you?   **104 old** customary, natural
106 Bedlam i.e., lunatic discharged from the insane asylum and
licensed to beg   **107–8 His . . . anything** His being a madman and
derelict allows him to do anything we ask.   **110.1 Exeunt** (At some
point after lines 99–100, the body of the slain First Servant must
be removed.)
4.1. Location: An open place.
1–2 Yet . . . flattered It is better to be openly despised as a beggar than
continually despised behind one's back and flattered to one's face.
3 dejected cast down   **4 Stands . . . fear** gives one some cause for
hope, having nothing to fear (since everything is already lost).

The lamentable change is from the best;   5
The worst returns to laughter. Welcome, then,   6
Thou unsubstantial air that I embrace!
The wretch that thou hast blown unto the worst
Owes nothing to thy blasts.

Enter Gloucester, and an Old Man [leading him].

                                But who comes here?   9
My father, poorly led? World, world, O world!
But that thy strange mutations make us hate thee,   11
Life would not yield to age.   12

OLD MAN
Oh, my good lord, I have been your tenant
And your father's tenant these fourscore years.

GLOUCESTER
Away, get thee away! Good friend, begone.
Thy comforts can do me no good at all;
Thee they may hurt.

OLD MAN   You cannot see your way.

GLOUCESTER
I have no way and therefore want no eyes;
I stumbled when I saw. Full oft 'tis seen
Our means secure us, and our mere defects   20
Prove our commodities. O dear son Edgar,   21
The food of thy abusèd father's wrath!   22
Might I but live to see thee in my touch,   23
I'd say I had eyes again!

OLD MAN   How now? Who's there?

EDGAR *[aside]*
O gods! Who is't can say, "I am at the worst"?
I am worse than e'er I was.

OLD MAN   'Tis poor mad Tom.

EDGAR *[aside]*
And worse I may be yet. The worst is not   27
So long as we can say, "This is the worst."   28

OLD MAN *[to Edgar]*
Fellow, where goest?

GLOUCESTER   Is it a beggar-man?

OLD MAN   Madman and beggar too.

GLOUCESTER
He has some reason, else he could not beg.   31
I'th' last night's storm I such a fellow saw,
Which made me think a man a worm. My son
Came then into my mind, and yet my mind
Was then scarce friends with him. I have heard more
    since.
As flies to wanton boys are we to th' gods;   36

They kill us for their sport.

EDGAR *[aside]*   How should this be?   37
Bad is the trade that must play fool to sorrow,   38
Ang'ring itself and others.—Bless thee, master!   39

GLOUCESTER
Is that the naked fellow?

OLD MAN   Ay, my lord.

GLOUCESTER
Then, prithee, get thee gone. If for my sake
Thou wilt o'ertake us hence a mile or twain   42
I'th' way toward Dover, do it for ancient love,   43
And bring some covering for this naked soul,
Which I'll entreat to lead me.

OLD MAN   Alack, sir, he is mad.

GLOUCESTER
'Tis the time's plague, when madmen lead the blind.   46
Do as I bid thee, or rather do thy pleasure;
Above the rest, begone.   48

OLD MAN
I'll bring him the best 'parel that I have,
Come on't what will.   *Exit.*

GLOUCESTER   Sirrah, naked fellow—   50

EDGAR
Poor Tom's a-cold. *[Aside]* I cannot daub it further.   51

GLOUCESTER   Come hither, fellow.

EDGAR *[aside]*
And yet I must.—Bless thy sweet eyes, they bleed.

GLOUCESTER   Know'st thou the way to Dover?

EDGAR   Both stile and gate, horseway and footpath.
Poor Tom hath been scared out of his good wits. Bless
thee, good man's son, from the foul fiend! Five fiends
have been in poor Tom at once: of lust, as Obidicut;   58
Hobbididance, prince of dumbness; Mahu, of stealing;   59
Modo, of murder; Flibbertigibbet, of mopping   60
and mowing, who since possesses chambermaids and   61
waiting women. So, bless thee, master!

GLOUCESTER *[giving a purse]*
Here, take this purse, thou whom the heavens'
    plagues
Have humbled to all strokes. That I am wretched   64
Makes thee the happier. Heavens, deal so still!
Let the superfluous and lust-dieted man,   66

5–6 The lamentable . . . laughter Any change from the best is grievous, just as any change from the worst is bound to be for the better. **9 Owes nothing** can pay no more, is free of obligation   **11–12 But . . . age** If it were not for your hateful inconstancy, we would never be reconciled to old age and death.   **20–1 Our . . . commodities** Our prosperity makes us proudly overconfident, whereas the sheer afflictions we suffer prove beneficial (by teaching us humility).   **22 The . . . wrath** on whom thy deceived father's wrath fed, the object of his anger.   **23 in** by means of   **27–8 The worst . . . worst** So long as we can speak and act and delude ourselves with false hopes, our fortunes can, in fact, grow worse.   **31 reason** sanity   **36 wanton** childishly cruel

37 How . . . be? i.e., How can he have suffered so much, changed so much?   **38–9 Bad . . . others** It's a bad business to have to play the fool to my sorrowing father, vexing myself and others (with this delay in revealing my true identity).   **42 o'ertake us** catch up to us (after you have found clothing for Tom o' Bedlam)   **43 ancient love** i.e., the mutually trusting relationship of master and tenant that you and I have long enjoyed   **46 'Tis the time's plague** It well expresses the spreading sickness of our present state   **48 the rest** all   **50 Come . . . will** whatever comes of this as regards myself.   **51 I . . . further** i.e., I cannot keep up this pretense any longer. (Literally, "I cannot plaster up the wall.")   **58–60 Obidicut . . . Flibbertigibbet** (Fiends borrowed, as before in 3.4.114 and 139–42, from Harsnett.)   **60–1 mopping and mowing** making grimaces and mouths   **61 since** ever since then   **64 Have . . . strokes** have brought so low as to bear every blow of Fortune.   **66 superfluous and lust-dieted** immoderately gluttonous and luxuriously fed

That slaves your ordinance, that will not see   67
Because he does not feel, feel your pow'r quickly!   68
So distribution should undo excess
And each man have enough. Dost thou know Dover?

EDGAR Ay, master.

GLOUCESTER

There is a cliff, whose high and bending head   72
Looks fearfully in the confinèd deep.   73
Bring me but to the very brim of it
And I'll repair the misery thou dost bear
With something rich about me. From that place   76
I shall no leading need.

EDGAR   Give me thy arm.
Poor Tom shall lead thee.   *Exeunt.*

✤

4.2

Enter Goneril [and] Bastard [Edmund].

GONERIL

Welcome, my lord. I marvel our mild husband   1
Not met us on the way.

[*Enter*] steward [*Oswald*].

                              Now, where's your master?   2

OSWALD

Madam, within, but never man so changed.
I told him of the army that was landed;
He smiled at it. I told him you were coming;
His answer was "The worse." Of Gloucester's
     treachery
And of the loyal service of his son
When I informed him, then he called me sot   8
And told me I had turned the wrong side out.
What most he should dislike seems pleasant to him;
What like, offensive.

GONERIL [*to Edmund*]   Then shall you go no further.
It is the cowish terror of his spirit,   12
That dares not undertake. He'll not feel wrongs   13
Which tie him to an answer. Our wishes on the way   14
May prove effects. Back, Edmund, to my brother;   15
Hasten his musters and conduct his powers.   16
I must change names at home and give the distaff   17

Into my husband's hands. This trusty servant
Shall pass between us. Ere long you are like to hear,   19
If you dare venture in your own behalf,
A mistress's command. Wear this; spare speech.   21
                         [*She gives him a favor.*]
Decline your head. [*She kisses him.*] This kiss, if it durst
     speak,
Would stretch thy spirits up into the air.
Conceive, and fare thee well.   24

EDMUND

Yours in the ranks of death.   *Exit.*

GONERIL   My most dear Gloucester!
Oh, the difference of man and man!
To thee a woman's services are due;
My fool usurps my body.   28

OSWALD   Madam, here comes my lord.   [*Exit.*]   29

Enter Albany.

GONERIL

I have been worth the whistling.

ALBANY   Oh, Goneril,   30
You are not worth the dust which the rude wind
Blows in your face. I fear your disposition;   32
That nature which contemns its origin   33
Cannot be bordered certain in itself.   34
She that herself will sliver and disbranch   35
From her material sap perforce must wither   36
And come to deadly use.   37

GONERIL   No more. The text is foolish.   38

ALBANY

Wisdom and goodness to the vile seem vile;
Filths savor but themselves. What have you done?   40
Tigers, not daughters, what have you performed?
A father, and a gracious agèd man,
Whose reverence even the head-lugged bear would
     lick,   43
Most barbarous, most degenerate, have you madded.   44
Could my good brother suffer you to do it?   45
A man, a prince, by him so benefited?
If that the heavens do not their visible spirits   47
Send quickly down to tame these vile offenses,
It will come,
Humanity must perforce prey on itself,
Like monsters of the deep.

GONERIL   Milk-livered man,   51

---

67 That . . . ordinance who enslaves your divine ordinances to his
own corrupt will   **67–8 that . . . feel** who is resistant to spiritual
insight because, not having suffered himself, he lacks the sympathy
of fellow feeling   **72 bending** overhanging   **73 in . . . deep** i.e., into
the sea below, which is confined by its shores.   **76 about me** on my
person.
4.2. Location: Before the Duke of Albany's palace.
1 Welcome (Goneril, who has just arrived home from Gloucestershire
escorted by Edmund, bids him brief welcome before he must return.)
2 Not met has not met   **8 sot** fool   **12 cowish** cowardly   **13 undertake** venture.   **13–14 He'll . . . answer** He will ignore insults that, if
he took notice, would oblige him to respond, to fight.   **14–15 Our . . .
effects** The hopes we discussed on our journey here (presumably
concerning the supplanting of Albany by Edmund) may come to
pass.   **15 brother** brother-in-law, Cornwall   **16 musters** assembling
of troops.   **powers** armed forces.   **17 change names** i.e., exchange
the roles of master and mistress of the household, and exchange the
insignia of man and woman: the sword and the *distaff*.   **distaff** spinning staff, symbolizing the wife's role

19 like likely   **21 mistress's** (With sexual double meaning.)   **24 Conceive** Understand, take my meaning. (With sexual double entendre,
continuing from *stretch thy spirits* in the previous line and continued in
death, line 25, and *a woman's services*, line 27.)   **28 My fool . . . body** i.e.,
my husband claims possession of me but is unfitted to do so.   **29 s.d.
Exit** (Oswald could exit later with Goneril, at line 88.)   **30 worth the
whistling** i.e., worth the attentions of men. (Alludes to the proverb, "it
is a poor dog that is not worth the whistling.")   **32 fear your disposition** mistrust your nature   **33 contemns** spurns   **34 bordered certain**
safely restrained, kept within bounds   **35 sliver** tear off   **36 material
sap** nourishing substance, the stock from which she grew   **37 to
deadly use** to a bad end, to a destructive purpose.   **38 The text** i.e., on
which you have been preaching   **40 savor but themselves** hunger
only for that which is filthy.   **43 head-lugged** dragged by the head (or
by the ring in its nose) and infuriated   **44 madded** driven mad.
45 brother brother-in-law (Cornwall)   **47 If that** If.   **visible** manifested   **51 Milk-livered** White-livered, cowardly

That bear'st a cheek for blows, a head for wrongs,
Who hast not in thy brows an eye discerning   53
Thine honor from thy suffering, that not know'st   54
Fools do those villains pity who are punished   55
Ere they have done their mischief. Where's thy drum?   56
France spreads his banners in our noiseless land,   57
With plumèd helm thy state begins to threat,   58
Whilst thou, a moral fool, sits still and cries,   59
"Alack, why does he so?"

ALBANY   See thyself, devil!   60
Proper deformity shows not in the fiend   61
So horrid as in woman.

GONERIL   Oh, vain fool!   62

ALBANY
Thou changèd and self-covered thing, for shame,   63
Bemonster not thy feature. Were't my fitness   64
To let these hands obey my blood,   65
They are apt enough to dislocate and tear   66
Thy flesh and bones. Howe'er thou art a fiend,   67
A woman's shape doth shield thee.

GONERIL   Marry, your manhood! Mew!   69

Enter a Messenger.

ALBANY   What news?

MESSENGER
Oh, my good lord, the Duke of Cornwall's dead,
Slain by his servant, going to put out
The other eye of Gloucester.

ALBANY   Gloucester's eyes!

MESSENGER
A servant that he bred, thrilled with remorse,   74
Opposed against the act, bending his sword   75
To his great master, who, thereat enraged,   76
Flew on him and amongst them felled him dead,   77
But not without that harmful stroke which since
Hath plucked him after.

ALBANY   This shows you are above,   79

You justicers, that these our nether crimes   80
So speedily can venge! But, Oh, poor Gloucester!
Lost he his other eye?

MESSENGER   Both, both, my lord.—
This letter, madam, craves a speedy answer;
'Tis from your sister.   [*He gives her a letter.*]

GONERIL [*aside*]   One way I like this well;   84
But being widow, and my Gloucester with her,   85
May all the building in my fancy pluck   86
Upon my hateful life. Another way   87
The news is not so tart.—I'll read, and answer.   88
                              [*Exit.*]

ALBANY
Where was his son when they did take his eyes?   89

MESSENGER
Come with my lady hither.

ALBANY   He is not here.

MESSENGER
No, my good lord. I met him back again.   91

ALBANY   Knows he the wickedness?

MESSENGER
Ay, my good lord. 'Twas he informed against him,
And quit the house on purpose that their punishment
Might have the freer course.

ALBANY   Gloucester, I live   95
To thank thee for the love thou show'dst the King
And to revenge thine eyes.—Come hither, friend.
Tell me what more thou know'st.   *Exeunt.*

❧

4.[3]

Enter Kent [disguised] and a Gentleman.

KENT   Why the King of France is so suddenly gone back
know you no reason?

GENTLEMAN   Something he left imperfect in the state,   3
which since his coming forth is thought of, which im-   4
ports to the kingdom so much fear and danger that his   5
personal return was most required and necessary.

KENT
Who hath he left behind him general?

GENTLEMAN
The Marshal of France, Monsieur la Far.

KENT   Did your letters pierce the Queen to any demonstration of grief?

GENTLEMAN
Ay, sir. She took them, read them in my presence,
And now and then an ample tear trilled down   12
Her delicate cheek. It seemed she was a queen

53–4 **discerning . . . suffering** able to tell the difference between an insult to your honor and something you should tolerate   54–6 **that not . . . mischief** you who fail to understand that only fools like yourself are so tenderhearted as to pity villains (like Gloucester, Lear, and Cordelia) who are apprehended and punished before they have committed a crime.   56 **Where's thy drum?** Where is your military preparedness?   57 **noiseless** peaceful, unprepared for war   58 **thy state . . . threat** (France) begins to threaten your kingdom   59 **moral** moralizing   60 **"Alack . . . so?"** (An utterly ineffectual response to invasion.)   61–2 **Proper . . . woman** The deformity that is appropriate in a fiend's features is even uglier in a woman's (since it is so at variance with her nominally feminine appearance).   63–4 **Thou . . . feature** i.e., You creature whose transformation into a fiend now overwhelms your womanliness, do not, however evil you are, take on the outward form of a monster or fiend.   64 **Were't my fitness** If it were suitable for me   65 **blood** passion   66 **apt** ready   67 **Howe'er . . . fiend** However much you may be a fiend in reality   68 **shield** (Since I, as a gentleman, cannot lay violent hands on a lady.)   69 **Mew** (An exclamation of disgust, a derisive catcall: You speak of manhood in shielding me as a woman. Some manhood!)   74 **bred** kept in his household.   **thrilled with remorse** deeply moved with pity   75 **Opposed** opposed himself   75–6 **bending . . . To** directing his sword against   77 **amongst them** together with the others (?) in their midst (?) out of their number (?)   79 **after** along (to death).

80 **justicers** (heavenly) judges.   **nether** i.e., committed here below, on earth   84 **One way** (i.e., because Edmund is now Duke of Gloucester, and Cornwall, a dangerous rival for the throne, is dead)   85–7 **But . . . life** but she being now a widow, and Edmund in her company, may pull down my imagined happiness (of having the entire kingdom with Edmund), leaving my hopes in ruins.   88 **tart** bitter, sour. (See line 84 and note.)   89 **his son** Edmund.   **his** Gloucester's.   91 **back again** on the way back (from Albany's palace).   95 **Gloucester** The old Earl of Gloucester

4.3. Location: The French camp near Dover.

3 **imperfect in the state** unsettled in state affairs   4–5 **imports** portends   12 **trilled** trickled

Over her passion, who, most rebel-like,   14
Sought to be king o'er her.

KENT   Oh, then it moved her?

GENTLEMAN

Not to a rage. Patience and sorrow strove
Who should express her goodliest. You have seen   17
Sunshine and rain at once. Her smiles and tears
Were like a better way; those happy smilets   19
That played on her ripe lip seemed not to know   20
What guests were in her eyes, which parted thence   21
As pearls from diamonds dropped. In brief,
Sorrow would be a rarity most beloved   23
If all could so become it.   24

KENT   Made she no verbal question?   25

GENTLEMAN

Faith, once or twice she heaved the name of "father"   26
Pantingly forth, as if it pressed her heart;
Cried, "Sisters, sisters! Shame of ladies, sisters!
Kent! Father! Sisters! What, i'th' storm, i'th' night?
Let pity not be believed!" There she shook   30
The holy water from her heavenly eyes,
And, clamor-moistened, then away she started   32
To deal with grief alone.

KENT   It is the stars,
The stars above us, govern our conditions,   34
Else one self mate and make could not beget   35
Such different issues. You spoke not with her since?   36

GENTLEMAN   No.

KENT

Was this before the King returned?

GENTLEMAN   No, since.   38

KENT

Well, sir, the poor distressèd Lear's i'th' town,
Who sometime in his better tune remembers   40
What we are come about, and by no means
Will yield to see his daughter.

GENTLEMAN   Why, good sir?   42

KENT

A sovereign shame so elbows him—his own
    unkindness   43
That stripped her from his benediction, turned her   44
To foreign casualties, gave her dear rights   45
To his dog-hearted daughters—these things sting
His mind so venomously that burning shame
Detains him from Cordelia.   48

GENTLEMAN   Alack, poor gentleman!

KENT

Of Albany's and Cornwall's powers you heard not?   50

GENTLEMAN   'Tis so. They are afoot.   51

KENT

Well, sir, I'll bring you to our master Lear
And leave you to attend him. Some dear cause   53
Will in concealment wrap me up awhile.
When I am known aright, you shall not grieve   55
Lending me this acquaintance. I pray you, go   56
Along with me.   Exeunt.

❧

4.[4]

Enter, with drum and colors, Cordelia,
Gentleman, and soldiers.

CORDELIA

Alack, 'tis he! Why, he was met even now
As mad as the vexed sea, singing aloud,
Crowned with rank fumiter and furrow weeds,   3
With hardocks, hemlock, nettles, cuckooflowers,   4
Darnel, and all the idle weeds that grow   5
In our sustaining corn. A century send forth!   6
Search every acre in the high-grown field
And bring him to our eye.   [*Exit a soldier or soldiers.*]
                                        What can man's wisdom   8
In the restoring his bereavèd sense,
He that helps him take all my outward worth.   10

GENTLEMAN   There is means, madam.
Our foster nurse of nature is repose,
The which he lacks. That to provoke in him   13
Are many simples operative, whose power   14
Will close the eye of anguish.

CORDELIA   All blest secrets,
All you unpublished virtues of the earth,   16
Spring with my tears! Be aidant and remediate   17
In the good man's distress! Seek, seek for him,
Lest his ungoverned rage dissolve the life   19
That wants the means to lead it.

Enter Messenger.

MESSENGER   News, madam.   20
The British powers are marching hitherward.   21

---

14 **who** which   17 **Who . . . goodliest** which of the two could portray
her best.   19 **like a better way** better than that, though similar
20–1 **seemed . . . eyes** seemed oblivious of her tears   23 **a rarity** i.e., a
precious thing, like a jewel   24 **If . . . it** i.e., if all persons were as
attractive in sorrow as she.   25 **verbal** i.e., as distinguished from her
tears and looks   26 **heaved** breathed out with difficulty   30 **Let . . .
believed!** i.e., Let no show of pity be trusted (since they are proved to
be so false)!   32 **clamor-moistened** i.e., her outcry of grief assuaged
by tears.   **started** i.e., went   34 **conditions** characters   35 **Else . . .
make** otherwise, one couple (husband and wife)   36 **issues** offspring.   38 **before . . . returned** before the King of France returned to
his kingdom.   40 **better tune** more composed state of mind
42 **yield** consent   43 **sovereign** overruling.   **elbows him** i.e., prods
his memory, jostles him, thrusts him back   44 **turned her** turned her
out   45 **foreign casualties** chances of fortune abroad   48 **Detains
him from** holds him back from seeing

50 **powers** troops, armies   51 **afoot** on the march.   53 **dear cause**
important purpose   55–6 **grieve . . . acquaintance** regret having
made my acquaintance.
4.4. Location: The French camp.
0.2 **Gentleman** (The Quarto specifies "Doctor" here and at line 11.)
3 **fumiter** fumitory, a weed or herb.   **furrow weeds** weeds growing
in plowed furrows   4 **hardocks** probably burdock, a coarse weedy
plant.   **cuckooflowers** flowers of late spring, when the cuckoo is
heard   5 **Darnel** weed of the grass kind.   **idle** worthless   6 **sustaining corn** sustenance-giving grain.   **A century** (Literally, a troop of
one hundred men.)   8 **What . . . wisdom** i.e., What medical knowledge can accomplish   10 **outward** material   13 **That to provoke** To
induce that   14 **Are . . . operative** many herbal remedies are efficacious; or, there are many effective remedies. (*Simples* are prepared
from a single herb.)   16 **unpublished virtues** little-known benign
herbs   17 **Spring** grow.   **aidant and remediate** helpful and remedial
19 **rage** frenzy   20 **That . . . lead it** that lacks the means to live sanely.
21 **powers** armies

CORDELIA
'Tis known before. Our preparation stands
In expectation of them. O dear father,
It is thy business that I go about;
Therefore great France
My mourning and importuned tears hath pitied.   26
No blown ambition doth our arms incite,   27
But love, dear love, and our aged father's right.
Soon may I hear and see him!   *Exeunt.*

❧

4.[5]

Enter Regan and steward [Oswald].

REGAN   But are my brother's powers set forth?   1
OSWALD   Ay, madam.
REGAN   Himself in person there?
OSWALD   Madam, with much ado.   4
Your sister is the better soldier.
REGAN
Lord Edmund spake not with your lord at home?
OSWALD   No, madam.
REGAN
What might import my sister's letters to him?   8
OSWALD   I know not, lady.
REGAN
Faith, he is posted hence on serious matter.   10
It was great ignorance, Gloucester's eyes being out, 11
To let him live. Where he arrives he moves
All hearts against us. Edmund, I think, is gone,
In pity of his misery, to dispatch   14
His nighted life; moreover to descry   15
The strength o'th'enemy.
OSWALD
I must needs after him, madam, with my letter.
REGAN
Our troops set forth tomorrow. Stay with us;
The ways are dangerous.
OSWALD   I may not, madam.
My lady charged my duty in this business.   20
REGAN
Why should she write to Edmund? Might not you
Transport her purposes by word? Belike   22
Something—I know not what. I'll love thee much;
Let me unseal the letter.
OSWALD   Madam, I had rather—
REGAN
I know your lady does not love her husband,
I am sure of that; and at her late being here   26
She gave strange oeillades and most speaking looks 27
To noble Edmund. I know you are of her bosom.   28
OSWALD   I, madam?

REGAN
I speak in understanding; y'are, I know't.   30
Therefore I do advise you, take this note: 31
My lord is dead; Edmund and I have talked,   32
And more convenient is he for my hand   33
Than for your lady's. You may gather more.   34
If you do find him, pray you, give him this;   35
And when your mistress hears thus much from you, 36
I pray, desire her call her wisdom to her.   37
So, fare you well.
If you do chance to hear of that blind traitor,
Preferment falls on him that cuts him off.   40
OSWALD
Would I could meet him, madam! I should show
What party I do follow.
REGAN   Fare thee well.
Exeunt [separately].

❧

4.[6]

*Enter Gloucester, and Edgar [in peasant's clothes,
leading his father].*

GLOUCESTER
When shall I come to th' top of that same hill?   1
EDGAR
You do climb up it now. Look how we labor.
GLOUCESTER
Methinks the ground is even.
EDGAR   Horrible steep.
Hark, do you hear the sea?
GLOUCESTER   No, truly.
EDGAR
Why, then, your other senses grow imperfect
By your eyes' anguish.
GLOUCESTER   So may it be, indeed.
Methinks thy voice is altered, and thou speak'st
In better phrase and matter than thou didst.
EDGAR
You're much deceived. In nothing am I changed
But in my garments.
GLOUCESTER   Methinks you're better spoken.
EDGAR
Come on, sir, here's the place. Stand still. How fearful
And dizzy 'tis to cast one's eyes so low!
The crows and choughs that wing the midway air   13
Show scarce so gross as beetles. Halfway down   14
Hangs one that gathers samphire—dreadful trade!   15
Methinks he seems no bigger than his head.
The fishermen that walk upon the beach

---

30 y'are you are   **31 take this note** take note of this   **32 have talked**
have come to an understanding   **33 convenient** fitting   **34 gather**
more infer what I am trying to suggest.   **35 this** i.e., this information,
or a love token, or possibly a letter (though only one letter, Goneril's,
is found on his dead body at 4.6.262)   **36 thus much** what I have told
you   **37 call . . . to her** recall herself to her senses   **40 Preferment**
advancement
4.6. Location: Open place near Dover.
1 that same hill i.e., the cliff we talked about (4.1.72–4).   **13 choughs**
jackdaws.   **midway** halfway down   **14 gross** large   **15 samphire** (A
herb used in pickling.)

---

26 importuned importunate   **27 blown** swollen
4.5. Location; Gloucester's house.
1 my brother's powers Albany's forces   **4 with much ado** after much
fuss and persuasion.   **8 import** bear as their purport, express   **10 is**
posted has hurried   **11 ignorance** error, folly   **14 his** Gloucester's
15 nighted benighted, blinded.   **descry** spy out   **20 charged my**
duty laid great stress on my obedience   **22 Belike** It may be   **26 late**
recently   **27 oeillades** amorous glances   **28 of her bosom** in her confidence.

Appear like mice, and yond tall anchoring bark 18
Diminished to her cock; her cock, a buoy 19
Almost too small for sight. The murmuring surge,
That on th'unnumbered idle pebble chafes, 21
Cannot be heard so high. I'll look no more,
Lest my brain turn, and the deficient sight 23
Topple down headlong.

GLOUCESTER   Set me where you stand. 24

EDGAR
Give me your hand. You are now within a foot
Of th'extreme verge. For all beneath the moon 26
Would I not leap upright.

GLOUCESTER   Let go my hand. 27
Here, friend, 's another purse; in it a jewel
Well worth a poor man's taking.   [He gives a purse.]
   Fairies and gods 29
Prosper it with thee! Go thou further off. 30
Bid me farewell, and let me hear thee going.

EDGAR [moving away]
Now fare ye well, good sir.

GLOUCESTER   With all my heart.

EDGAR [aside]
Why I do trifle thus with his despair
Is done to cure it.

GLOUCESTER [kneeling]   O you mighty gods!
This world I do renounce, and in your sights
Shake patiently my great affliction off.
If I could bear it longer and not fall
To quarrel with your great opposeless wills, 38
My snuff and loathèd part of nature should 39
Burn itself out. If Edgar live, oh, bless him!
Now, fellow, fare thee well.   [He falls forward.]

EDGAR   Gone, sir. Farewell.—
And yet I know not how conceit may rob 42
The treasury of life, when life itself
Yields to the theft. Had he been where he thought, 44
By this had thought been past. Alive or dead?— 45
Ho, you, sir! Friend! Hear you, sir! Speak!—
Thus might he pass indeed; yet he revives.— 47
What are you, sir?

GLOUCESTER   Away, and let me die. 48

EDGAR
Hadst thou been aught but gossamer, feathers, air,
So many fathom down precipitating,
Thou'dst shivered like an egg; but thou dost breathe,
Hast heavy substance, bleed'st not, speak'st, art
   sound. 52

Ten masts at each make not the altitude 53
Which thou hast perpendicularly fell.
Thy life's a miracle. Speak yet again.

GLOUCESTER   But have I fall'n or no?

EDGAR
From the dread summit of this chalky bourn. 57
Look up aheight; the shrill-gorged lark so far 58
Cannot be seen or heard. Do but look up.

GLOUCESTER   Alack, I have no eyes.
Is wretchedness deprived that benefit
To end itself by death? 'Twas yet some comfort
When misery could beguile the tyrant's rage 63
And frustrate his proud will.

EDGAR   Give me your arm.
                   [He lifts him up.]
Up—so. How is't? Feel you your legs? You stand.

GLOUCESTER
Too well, too well.

EDGAR   This is above all strangeness.
Upon the crown o'th' cliff what thing was that
Which parted from you?

GLOUCESTER   A poor unfortunate beggar.

EDGAR
As I stood here below, methought his eyes
Were two full moons; he had a thousand noses,
Horns whelked and waved like the enridgèd sea. 71
It was some fiend. Therefore, thou happy father, 72
Think that the clearest gods, who make them honors 73
Of men's impossibilities, have preserved thee. 74

GLOUCESTER
I do remember now. Henceforth I'll bear
Affliction till it do cry out itself 76
"Enough, enough," and die. That thing you speak of, 77
I took it for a man; often 'twould say
"The fiend, the fiend." He led me to that place.

EDGAR
Bear free and patient thoughts.

   Enter Lear [mad, fantastically dressed with wild
      flowers].

                   But who comes here? 80
The safer sense will ne'er accommodate 81
His master thus. 82

LEAR   No, they cannot touch me for coining. I am the 83
King himself. 84

EDGAR   Oh, thou side-piercing sight! 85

---

18 **bark** small sailing vessel   19 **Diminished . . . cock** reduced to the size of her cockboat, small ship's boat   21 **th'unnumbered idle pebble** innumerable, randomly shifting, pebbles   23–4 **Lest . . . headlong** lest I become dizzy, and my failing sight topple me headlong. 26 **For . . . moon** i.e., For the whole world   27 **upright** i.e., up and down, much less forward.   29–30 **Fairies . . . thee!** May the fairies and gods cause this to multiply in your possession!   38 **To quarrel with** into rebellion against.   **opposeless** irresistible   39 **snuff** i.e., useless residue. (Literally, the smoking wick of a candle.)   **of nature** i.e., of my life   42 **conceit** imagination   44 **Yields** consents   45 **By this** by this time   47 **pass** die   48 **What** Who. (Edgar now speaks in a new voice, differing from that of "poor Tom" and also from the "altered" voice he used at the start of this scene; see lines 7–10.) 52 **heavy substance** the substance of the flesh

53 **at each** end to end   57 **bourn** limit, boundary (i.e., the edge of the sea).   58 **aheight** on high.   **shrill-gorged** shrill-throated   63 **beguile** outwit   71 **whelked** twisted, convoluted.   **enridgèd** furrowed (by the wind)   72 **happy father** lucky old man   73 **clearest** purest, most righteous   73–4 **who . . . impossibilities** who win our awe and reverence by doing things impossible to men   76–7 **till . . . die** i.e., until affliction itself has had enough, or until I die.   80 **free** i.e., free from despair   81–2 **The safer . . . thus** i.e., A person in his right senses would never dress himself in such a fashion. (His master is the owner of the safer sense or sane mind. His means "its.")   83–4 **they . . . himself** they cannot prosecute me for minting coins. As king, I enjoy the exclusive royal prerogative for doing so. (Lear goes on to discuss his need for money to pay his imaginary soldiers.)   85 **side-piercing** heartrending. (With a suggestion of Christ's suffering on the cross.)

LEAR   Nature's above art in that respect. There's your 86
press money. That fellow handles his bow like a crow- 87
keeper. Draw me a clothier's yard. Look, look, a 88
mouse! Peace, peace; this piece of toasted cheese will
do't. There's my gauntlet; I'll prove it on a giant. Bring 90
up the brown bills. Oh, well flown, bird! I'th' clout, 91
i'th' clout—hewgh! Give the word. 92

EDGAR   Sweet marjoram. 93

LEAR   Pass.

GLOUCESTER   I know that voice.

LEAR   Ha! Goneril with a white beard? They flattered
me like a dog and told me I had white hairs in my 97
beard ere the black ones were there. To say ay and 98
no to everything that I said ay and no to was 99
no good divinity. When the rain came to wet me 100
once and the wind to make me chatter, when the 101
thunder would not peace at my bidding, there I found 102
'em, there I smelt 'em out. Go to, they are not men o' 103
their words. They told me I was everything. 'Tis a
lie. I am not ague-proof. 105

GLOUCESTER   The trick of that voice I do well remember. 106
Is't not the King?

LEAR   Ay, every inch a king.
When I do stare, see how the subject quakes.
I pardon that man's life. What was thy cause? 109
Adultery?
Thou shalt not die. Die for adultery? No.
The wren goes to't, and the small gilded fly
Does lecher in my sight.
Let copulation thrive; for Gloucester's bastard son
Was kinder to his father than my daughters
Got 'tween the lawful sheets.
To't, luxury, pell-mell, for I lack soldiers. 117
Behold yond simpering dame,
Whose face between her forks presages snow, 119
That minces virtue and does shake the head 120
To hear of pleasure's name; 121
The fitchew nor the soilèd horse goes to't 122

With a more riotous appetite.
Down from the waist they're centaurs, 124
Though women all above.
But to the girdle do the gods inherit; 126
Beneath is all the fiends'.
There's hell, there's darkness, there is the sulfurous pit,
burning, scalding, stench, consumption. Fie, fie, fie!
Pah, pah! Give me an ounce of civet, good apothecary, 130
sweeten my imagination. There's money for thee.

GLOUCESTER   Oh, let me kiss that hand!

LEAR   Let me wipe it first; it smells of mortality.

GLOUCESTER
Oh, ruined piece of nature! This great world 134
Shall so wear out to naught. Dost thou know me? 135

LEAR   I remember thine eyes well enough. Dost thou
squinny at me? No, do thy worst, blind Cupid; I'll not 137
love. Read thou this challenge. Mark but the penning
of it.

GLOUCESTER
Were all thy letters suns, I could not see.

EDGAR [aside]
I would not take this from report. It is, 141
And my heart breaks at it.

LEAR   Read.

GLOUCESTER   What, with the case of eyes? 144

LEAR   Oho, are you there with me? No eyes in your 145
head, nor no money in your purse? Your eyes are in a
heavy case, your purse in a light, yet you see how this 147
world goes.

GLOUCESTER   I see it feelingly. 149

LEAR   What, art mad? A man may see how this world
goes with no eyes. Look with thine ears. See how
yond justice rails upon yond simple thief. Hark in 152
thine ear: change places and, handy-dandy, which is 153
the justice, which is the thief? Thou hast seen a
farmer's dog bark at a beggar?

GLOUCESTER   Ay, sir.

LEAR   And the creature run from the cur? There thou 157
mightst behold the great image of authority: a dog's 158
obeyed in office. 159
Thou rascal beadle, hold thy bloody hand! 160
Why dost thou lash that whore? Strip thine own back;
Thou hotly lusts to use her in that kind 162
For which thou whipp'st her. The usurer hangs the
cozener. 163

---

86 Nature's . . . respect Real life can offer more heart-piercing examples than art.   **87 press money** enlistment bonus.   **87–8 crowkeeper**
laborer hired to scare away the crows.   **88 Draw . . . yard** i.e., Draw
your bow to the full length of the arrow, a cloth-yard long.   **90 do't**
i.e., capture the mouse, an imagined enemy.   **gauntlet** armored glove
thrown down as a challenge.   **prove it on** maintain it against
91 brown bills soldiers carrying pikes (painted brown), or the pikes
themselves.   **well flown, bird** (Lear uses the language of hawking to
describe the flight of an arrow.)   **clout** target, bull's-eye   **92 hewgh**
(The arrow's noise.)   **word** password.   **93 Sweet marjoram** (A herb
used to cure madness.)   **97 like a dog** as a dog fawns   **97–8 told . . .
there** i.e., told me I had the white-haired wisdom of old age before I
had even attained the manliness of a beard.   **98–100 To . . . divinity**
i.e., To agree flatteringly with everything I said was not good theology, since the Bible teaches us to "let your yea be yea and your nay,
nay" (James 5:12; see also Matthew 5:37 and 2 Cor. 1:18).
100–3 When . . . out i.e., Suffering wet, cold, and storm have taught
me about the frailty of the human condition.   **103 Go to** (An expression of impatience.)   **105 ague-proof** immune against illness (literally, fever).   **106 trick** peculiar characteristic   **109 cause** offense.
117 luxury lechery   **119 Whose . . . snow** whose frosty countenance
seems to suggest frigidity between her legs   **120 minces** affects,
mimics   **121 of pleasure's name** the very name of pleasure   **122 The
fitchew . . . to't** neither the polecat nor the well-pastured horse
indulges in sexual pleasure

124 centaurs fabulous creatures with the head, trunk, and arms of a
man joined to the body and legs of a horse   **126 But** Only.   **girdle**
waist.   **inherit** have possession   **130 civet** musk perfume
134 piece (1) fragment (2) masterpiece   **134–5 This . . . naught** Even
so will the whole universe come to an apocalyptic end.   **137 squinny**
squint   **141 take** believe, credit.   **It is** It is taking place, incredibly
enough   **144 case** mere sockets   **145 are . . . me?** is that your meaning, the point you are making?   **147 heavy case** sad plight. (With pun
on *case* in line 144.)   **149 feelingly** (1) by touch (2) keenly, painfully.
152 simple of humble station   **153 handy-dandy** take your choice of
hands (as in a well-known child's game)   **157 creature** poor fellow
158–9 a dog's . . . office i.e., even currish power commands submission.   **160 beadle** parish officer, responsible for giving whippings
162 kind way   **163 The usurer . . . cozener** The moneylender (who
can buy out justice) hangs the con man.

Through tattered clothes small vices do appear;   164
Robes and furred gowns hide all. Plate sin with gold,   165
And the strong lance of justice hurtless breaks;   166
Arm it in rags, a pygmy's straw does pierce it.
None does offend, none, I say, none. I'll able 'em.   168
Take that of me, my friend, who have the power   169
To seal th'accuser's lips. Get thee glass eyes,   170
And like a scurvy politician seem   171
To see the things thou dost not. Now, now, now, now!   172
Pull off my boots. Harder, harder! So.

EDGAR [aside]
Oh, matter and impertinency mixed,   174
Reason in madness!

LEAR
If thou wilt weep my fortunes, take my eyes.
I know thee well enough; thy name is Gloucester.
Thou must be patient. We came crying hither.
Thou know'st the first time that we smell the air
We wawl and cry. I will preach to thee. Mark.

GLOUCESTER   Alack, alack the day!

LEAR
When we are born, we cry that we are come
To this great stage of fools.—This' a good block.   183
It were a delicate stratagem to shoe   184
A troop of horse with felt. I'll put 't in proof,   185
And when I have stol'n upon these son-in-laws,
Then, kill, kill, kill, kill, kill, kill!

Enter a Gentleman [with attendants].

GENTLEMAN
Oh, here he is. Lay hand upon him.—Sir,
Your most dear daughter—

LEAR
No rescue? What, a prisoner? I am even
The natural fool of fortune. Use me well;
You shall have ransom. Let me have surgeons;   191
I am cut to th' brains.

GENTLEMAN   You shall have anything.   193

LEAR   No seconds? All myself?   194
Why, this would make a man a man of salt   195
To use his eyes for garden waterpots,
Ay, and laying autumn's dust.
I will die bravely, like a smug bridegroom. What?   198

I will be jovial. Come, come, I am a king,   199
Masters, know you that?   200

GENTLEMAN
You are a royal one, and we obey you.

LEAR   Then there's life in't. Come, an you get it, you   202
shall get it by running. Sa, sa, sa, sa.   203
Exit [running, followed by attendants].

GENTLEMAN
A sight most pitiful in the meanest wretch,
Past speaking of in a king! Thou hast one daughter
Who redeems nature from the general curse   206
Which twain have brought her to.   207

EDGAR   Hail, gentle sir.   208

GENTLEMAN   Sir, speed you. What's your will?   209

EDGAR
Do you hear aught, sir, of a battle toward?   210

GENTLEMAN
Most sure and vulgar. Everyone hears that   211
Which can distinguish sound.

EDGAR   But, by your favor,   212
How near's the other army?

GENTLEMAN
Near and on speedy foot. The main descry   214
Stands on the hourly thought.   215

EDGAR   I thank you, sir; that's all.

GENTLEMAN
Though that the Queen on special cause is here,   217
Her army is moved on.

EDGAR   I thank you, sir.
Exit [Gentleman].

GLOUCESTER
You ever-gentle gods, take my breath from me;
Let not my worser spirit tempt me again   220
To die before you please!

EDGAR   Well pray you, father.   222

GLOUCESTER   Now, good sir, what are you?   223

EDGAR
A most poor man, made tame to fortune's blows,   224
Who, by the art of known and feeling sorrows,   225
Am pregnant to good pity. Give me your hand.   226
I'll lead you to some biding.   [He offers his arm.]

GLOUCESTER   Hearty thanks.   227

164–5 Through . . . all i.e., Beggars' small vices are apparent for all to see; rich folk, in expensive clothes, succeed in hiding a great deal. **165 Plate** Arm in plate armor   **166 hurtless breaks** splinters harmlessly   **168 able** empower, give warrant to   **169 Take . . . me** (1) Learn that from me (2) Take that protection from me   **170–2 Get . . . dost not** If Gloucester were to fit himself out with spectacles (or perhaps with glass eyeballs, though they are not mentioned elsewhere until later in the seventeenth century), he would look wise like a hypocritical politician.   **174 matter and impertinency** sense and nonsense   **183 This'** This is.   **block** mold for a felt hat. (Lear may refer to the weeds strewn in his hair, which he removes as though doffing a hat before preaching a sermon.)   **184 delicate** subtle   **185 felt** i.e., padding to deaden the sound of the footfall.   **in proof** to the test   **191 natural fool** born plaything   **193 cut** wounded   **194 seconds** supporters.   **195 of salt** of salt tears   **198 bravely** (1) courageously (2) splendidly attired.   **smug** trimly dressed. (*Bridegroom* continues the punning sexual suggestion of *die bravely*, "have sex successfully.")

199 jovial (1) Jovelike, majestic (2) jolly.   **200 Masters** good sirs   **202 life** i.e., hope still.   **an** if   **203 Sa . . . sa** (A hunting cry.)   **206 general curse** fallen condition of the human race   **207 twain** (1) Goneril and Regan (2) Adam and Eve   **208 gentle** noble   **209 speed you** Godspeed, may God prosper you.   **210 toward** imminent.   **211 vulgar** in everyone's mouth, generally known.   **212 Which** who   **214–15 The main . . . thought** The full view of the main body is expected any hour now.   **217 Though that** Although.   **on special cause** for a special reason, i.e., to minister to Lear   **220 worser spirit** bad angel, or ill thoughts   **222 father** (A term of respect to older men, as also in lines 72, 259, and 290, though with ironic double meaning throughout the scene.)   **223 what** who. (Again, Edgar alters his voice to personate a new stranger assisting Gloucester. See line 48, above, and note.)   **224 tame** submissive   **225 known and feeling** personally experienced and heartfelt   **226 pregnant** prone   **227 biding** abode.

The bounty and the benison of heaven   228
To boot, and boot!

Enter steward [Oswald].

OSWALD   A proclaimed prize! Most happy!   229
                    [He draws his sword.]
That eyeless head of thine was first framed flesh   230
To raise my fortunes. Thou old unhappy traitor,
Briefly thyself remember. The sword is out   232
That must destroy thee.
GLOUCESTER   Now let thy friendly hand   233
Put strength enough to't.   *[Edgar intervenes.]*
OSWALD   Wherefore, bold peasant,
Durst thou support a published traitor? Hence,   235
Lest that th'infection of his fortune take   236
Like hold on thee. Let go his arm.   237
EDGAR   'Chill not let go, zir, without vurther 'cagion.   238
OSWALD   Let go, slave, or thou diest!
EDGAR   Good gentleman, go your gait, and let poor volk   240
    pass. An 'chud ha' bin zwaggered out of my life,   241
    'twould not ha' bin zo long as 'tis by a vortnight. Nay,   242
    come not near th' old man; keep out, 'che vor ye, or   243
    Ise try whether your costard or my ballow be the   244
    harder. 'Chill be plain with you.
OSWALD   Out, dunghill!
EDGAR   'Chill pick your teeth, zir. Come, no matter vor
    your foins.   *[They fight. Edgar fells him with his cudgel.]*   248
OSWALD
    Slave, thou hast slain me. Villain, take my purse.   249
    If ever thou wilt thrive, bury my body
    And give the letters which thou find'st about me   251
    To Edmund, Earl of Gloucester. Seek him out
    Upon the English party. Oh, untimely death!   253
    Death!   *[He dies.]*
EDGAR
    I know thee well: a serviceable villain,   255
    As duteous to the vices of thy mistress
    As badness would desire.
GLOUCESTER   What, is he dead?
EDGAR   Sit you down, father. Rest you. *[Gloucester sits.]*
    Let's see these pockets; the letters that he speaks of
    May be my friends. He's dead; I am only sorry
    He had no other deathsman. Let us see.   262
                    [He finds a letter and opens it.]
    Leave, gentle wax, and, manners, blame us not.   263

To know our enemies' minds we rip their hearts;
Their papers is more lawful.   *(Reads the letter.)*
    "Let our reciprocal vows be remembered. You have
many opportunities to cut him off; if your will want   267
not, time and place will be fruitfully offered. There is   268
nothing done if he return the conqueror. Then am I   269
the prisoner, and his bed my jail, from the loathed
warmth whereof deliver me and supply the place for   271
your labor.   272
    Your—wife, so I would say—affectionate servant,
        and for you her own for venture, Goneril."   274
Oh, indistinguished space of woman's will!   275
A plot upon her virtuous husband's life,
And the exchange my brother! Here in the sands
Thee I'll rake up, the post unsanctified   278
Of murderous lechers; and in the mature time   279
With this ungracious paper strike the sight   280
Of the death-practiced Duke. For him 'tis well   281
That of thy death and business I can tell.
                    [Exit with the body.]
GLOUCESTER
The King is mad. How stiff is my vile sense,   283
That I stand up and have ingenious feeling   284
Of my huge sorrows! Better I were distract;   285
So should my thoughts be severed from my griefs,
And woes by wrong imaginations lose   287
The knowledge of themselves.   *Drum afar off.*

    [Enter Edgar.]

EDGAR   Give me your hand.
    Far off, methinks, I hear the beaten drum.
    Come, father, I'll bestow you with a friend.   290
                    Exeunt, [Edgar leading his father].

❖

4.7

*Enter Cordelia, Kent [dressed still in his disguise
costume], and Gentleman.*

CORDELIA
    O thou good Kent, how shall I live and work
    To match thy goodness? My life will be too short,
    And every measure fail me.   3

228–9 **The bounty ... and boot!** In addition to my thanks, I wish you
the bounty and blessings of heaven.   229 **proclaimed prize** one with
a price on his head.   **happy** fortunate.   230 **framed flesh** born
232 **thyself remember** i.e., say your prayers.   233 **friendly** i.e., welcome, since I desire death   235 **published** proclaimed   236 **Lest that**
lest   237 **Like** similar   238 **'Chill** I will. (Literally, a contraction of
Ich will. Edgar adopts Somerset dialect, a stage convention regularly
used for peasants.)   **vurther 'cagion** further occasion.   240 **go your
gait** go your own way   241 **An 'chud** If I could.   **zwaggered** swaggered, bullied   242 **'twould . . . vortnight** it (my life) wouldn't have
lasted a fortnight.   243 **'che vor ye** I warrant you   244 **Ise** I shall.
costard head. (Literally, an apple.)   **ballow** cudgel   248 **foins**
thrusts.   249 **Villain** Serf   251 **letters** letter. (See 4.5.35 and note.)
about me upon my person   253 **Upon** on.   **party** side.   255 **serviceable** officious   262 **deathsman** executioner   263 **Leave** By your
leave.   **wax** wax seal on the letter

267 **him** Albany   267–8 **want not** is not lacking   268 **fruitfully** plentifully and with results   268–9 **There is nothing done** i.e., We will
have accomplished nothing   271 **supply** fill   271–2 **for your labor**
(1) as recompense for your efforts (2) as a place for your amorous
labors.   274 **and for . . . venture** and one ready to venture her own
fortunes for your sake   275 **indistinguished . . . will** limitless and
incalculable expanse of woman's appetite.   278 **rake up** cover up.
post unsanctified unholy messenger   279 **in . . . time** when the time
is ripe   280 **ungracious** wicked.   **strike** blast   281 **Of . . . well** of
Albany, whose death is plotted. It's a good thing for him   283 **How . . .
sense** How obstinate is my deplorable sanity and power of sensation
284 **ingenious** conscious. (Gloucester laments that he remains sane
and hence fully conscious of his troubles, unlike Lear.)   285 **distract**
distracted, crazy   287 **wrong imaginations** delusions   290 **bestow**
lodge. (At the scene's end, Edgar leads off Gloucester; presumably, at
line 282 or else here, he must also dispose of Oswald's body in the
trapdoor or by lugging it offstage.)
4.7. Location: The French camp.
0.2 *Gentleman* ("Doctor" in Q.)   3 **every . . . me** every attempt (to
match your goodness) will fall short.

KENT
  To be acknowledged, madam, is o'erpaid.
  All my reports go with the modest truth,   5
  Nor more nor clipped, but so.
CORDELIA   Be better suited.   6
  These weeds are memories of those worser hours;   7
  I prithee, put them off.
KENT   Pardon, dear madam;
  Yet to be known shortens my made intent.   9
  My boon I make it that you know me not   10
  Till time and I think meet.   11
CORDELIA
  Then be't so, my good lord. [*To the Gentleman*] How
    does the King?
GENTLEMAN   Madam, sleeps still.
CORDELIA   O you kind gods,
  Cure this great breach in his abusèd nature!
  Th'untuned and jarring senses, oh, wind up   16
  Of this child-changèd father!   17
GENTLEMAN   So please Your Majesty
  That we may wake the King? He hath slept long.
CORDELIA
  Be governed by your knowledge, and proceed
  I'th' sway of your own will.—Is he arrayed?   21

        Enter Lear in a chair carried by servants.

GENTLEMAN
  Ay, madam. In the heaviness of sleep
  We put fresh garments on him.
  Be by, good madam, when we do awake him.
  I doubt not of his temperance.
CORDELIA   Very well.   [*Music.*]   25
GENTLEMAN
  Please you, draw near.—Louder the music there!
CORDELIA [*kissing him*]
  O my dear father! Restoration hang
  Thy medicine on my lips, and let this kiss
  Repair those violent harms that my two sisters
  Have in thy reverence made!
KENT   Kind and dear princess!   30
CORDELIA
  Had you not been their father, these white flakes   31
  Did challenge pity of them. Was this a face   32
  To be opposed against the warring winds?
  To stand against the deep dread-bolted thunder   34
  In the most terrible and nimble stroke

Of quick cross lightning? To watch—poor perdu!—   36
With this thin helm? Mine enemy's dog,   37
Though he had bit me, should have stood that night
Against my fire; and wast thou fain, poor father,   39
To hovel thee with swine and rogues forlorn   40
In short and musty straw? Alack, alack!   41
'Tis wonder that thy life and wits at once
Had not concluded all.—He wakes! Speak to him.   43
GENTLEMAN   Madam, do you; 'tis fittest.
CORDELIA
  How does my royal lord? How fares Your Majesty?
LEAR
  You do me wrong to take me out o'th' grave.
  Thou art a soul in bliss; but I am bound
  Upon a wheel of fire, that mine own tears   48
  Do scald like molten lead.
CORDELIA   Sir, do you know me?
LEAR
  You are a spirit, I know. Where did you die?
CORDELIA   Still, still, far wide!   51
GENTLEMAN
  He's scarce awake. Let him alone awhile.
LEAR
  Where have I been? Where am I? Fair daylight?
  I am mightily abused. I should ev'n die with pity   54
  To see another thus. I know not what to say.   55
  I will not swear these are my hands. Let's see;
  I feel this pinprick. Would I were assured
  Of my condition!
CORDELIA [*kneeling*]   Oh, look upon me, sir,
  And hold your hands in benediction o'er me.
                            [*He attempts to kneel.*]
  No, sir, you must not kneel.
LEAR   Pray, do not mock me.
  I am a very foolish fond old man,   61
  Fourscore and upward, not an hour more nor less;
  And, to deal plainly,
  I fear I am not in my perfect mind.
  Methinks I should know you, and know this man,
  Yet I am doubtful; for I am mainly ignorant   66
  What place this is, and all the skill I have
  Remembers not these garments, nor I know not
  Where I did lodge last night. Do not laugh at me,
  For, as I am a man, I think this lady
  To be my child Cordelia.
CORDELIA [*weeping*]   And so I am, I am.
LEAR
  Be your tears wet? Yes, faith. I pray, weep not.
  If you have poison for me I will drink it.
  I know you do not love me, for your sisters
  Have, as I do remember, done me wrong.
  You have some cause, they have not.

---

5 All my reports go All my reports (of my service as Caius to Lear) conform   **6 Nor . . . clipped** i.e., neither more nor less.   **suited** dressed.   **7 weeds** garments.   **memories** remembrances   **9 Yet . . . intent** to reveal my true identity now would alter my carefully made plan.   **10 My . . . it** The favor I seek is.   **know** acknowledge   **11 meet** appropriate.   **16 wind up** tune (as by tightening the slackened string of an instrument)   **17 child-changèd** changed by children's cruelty   **21 I'th' sway** under the direction   **25 temperance** self-control, calm behavior.   **30 reverence** venerable condition   **31 Had you** Even if you had.   **flakes** locks of hair   **32 Did challenge** would have demanded   **34 deep** bass-voiced.   **dread-bolted** furnished with the dreadful thunderbolt

36 cross zigzag.   **watch** stay awake (like a sentry on duty).   **perdu** lost one; a sentinel placed in a position of peculiar danger.   **37 helm** helmet, i.e., scanty hair.   **39 Against** before, in front of.   **fain** constrained   **40 rogues forlorn** abandoned vagabonds   **41 short** broken up and hence uncomfortable   **43 concluded all** come to an end altogether.   **48 wheel of fire** (A hellish torment for the eternally damned.)   **that** so that   **51 wide** wide of the mark, wandering.   **54 abused** confused, deluded.   **55 thus** i.e., thus confused, bewildered.   **61 fond** in my dotage   **66 mainly** entirely

CORDELIA   No cause, no cause.

LEAR   Am I in France?

KENT   In your own kingdom, sir.

LEAR   Do not abuse me.   81

GENTLEMAN
Be comforted, good madam. The great rage,   82
You see, is killed in him, and yet it is danger
To make him even o'er the time he has lost.   84
Desire him to go in. Trouble him no more
Till further settling.   86

CORDELIA   Will't please Your Highness walk?   87

LEAR   You must bear with me.
Pray you now, forget and forgive.
I am old and foolish.

Exeunt [all but Kent and Gentleman].

GENTLEMAN   Holds it true, sir, that the Duke of Corn-   91
wall was so slain?

KENT   Most certain, sir.

GENTLEMAN   Who is conductor of his people?   94

KENT   As 'tis said, the bastard son of Gloucester.

GENTLEMAN   They say Edgar, his banished son, is with
the Earl of Kent in Germany.

KENT   Report is changeable. 'Tis time to look about; the   98
powers of the kingdom approach apace.   99

GENTLEMAN   The arbitrament is like to be bloody. Fare   100
you well, sir.   *[Exit.]*

KENT
My point and period will be throughly wrought,   102
Or well or ill, as this day's battle's fought.   *Exit.*   103

❧

5.1

*Enter, with drum and colors, Edmund, Regan,
Gentlemen, and soldiers.*

EDMUND   *[to a Gentleman]*
Know of the Duke if his last purpose hold,   1
Or whether since he is advised by aught   2
To change the course. He's full of alteration   3
And self-reproving. Bring his constant pleasure.   4

[Exit Gentleman.]

REGAN
Our sister's man is certainly miscarried.   5

EDMUND
'Tis to be doubted, madam.

REGAN   Now, sweet lord,   6
You know the goodness I intend upon you.   7
Tell me, but truly—but then speak the truth—
Do you not love my sister?

EDMUND   In honored love.   9

REGAN
But have you never found my brother's way
To the forfended place?   11

EDMUND   That thought abuses you.   12

REGAN
I am doubtful that you have been conjunct   13
And bosomed with her, as far as we call hers.   14

EDMUND   No, by mine honor, madam.

REGAN
I never shall endure her. Dear my lord,
Be not familiar with her.   17

EDMUND
Fear me not.—She and the Duke her husband!   18

*Enter, with drum and colors, Albany, Goneril,
[and] soldiers.*

GONERIL   *[aside]*
I had rather lose the battle than that sister
Should loosen him and me.

ALBANY   *[to Regan]*
Our very loving sister, well bemet.   21
[To Edmund] Sir, this I heard: the King is come to his
daughter,
With others whom the rigor of our state   23
Forced to cry out. Where I could not be honest,   24
I never yet was valiant. For this business,   25
It touches us as France invades our land,   26
Not bolds the King, with others whom, I fear,   27
Most just and heavy causes make oppose.   28

EDMUND   Sir, you speak nobly.

REGAN   Why is this reasoned?   30

GONERIL
Combine together 'gainst the enemy;
For these domestic and particular broils   32
Are not the question here.

ALBANY   Let's then determine
With th'ancient of war on our proceeding.   34

EDMUND
I shall attend you presently at your tent.

REGAN   Sister, you'll go with us?

GONERIL   No.

---

81 abuse deceive. (Or perhaps Lear feels hurt by the reminder of his having divided the kingdom.)   **82 rage** frenzy   **84 even o'er** fill in, go over in his mind   **86 settling** composing of his mind.   **87 walk** withdraw.   **91 Holds it true** Is it still held to be true   **94 conductor** leader, general   **98 look about** be wary, take stock of the situation   **99 powers of the kingdom** British armies (marching against the French invaders)   **100 arbitrament** decision by arms, decisive encounter   **102 My . . . wrought** i.e., The conclusion of my destiny (literally, the full stop at the end of my life's sentence) will be thoroughly shaped   **103 Or** either.   **as** according as
5.1. Location: The British camp near Dover.
1 Know Inquire.   **last purpose hold** most recent intention (to fight) remains firm   **2 since** since then.   **advised by aught** persuaded by any consideration   **3 alteration** vacillation   **4 constant pleasure** settled decision.   **5 man** i.e., Oswald.   **miscarried** lost, perished.

6 doubted feared   **7 intend** intend to confer   **9 honored** honorable   **11 forfended** forbidden (by the commandment against adultery)   **12 abuses** degrades, wrongs   **13–14 I . . . hers** I fear that you have been sexually intimate with her to the fullest extent possible.   **17 familiar** intimate   **18 Fear me not** Don't worry about me on that score.   **21 bemet** met.   **23 rigor of our state** harshness of our rule   **24 cry out** rebel.   **Where** In a case where.   **honest** honorable   **25 For** As for   **26 touches us as** concerns us insofar as   **27–8 Not . . . oppose** not because the matter emboldens the King and others who, I fear, are driven into opposition by just and weighty grievances.   **30 Why . . . reasoned?** i.e., Why are we arguing about reasons for fighting, instead of fighting?   **32 particular broils** private quarrels   **34 th'ancient of war** the veteran officers

REGAN
  'Tis most convenient. Pray, go with us.   38
GONERIL [*aside*]
  Oho, I know the riddle.—I will go.   39

  [*As they are going out,*] enter Edgar [*disguised*].

EDGAR [*to Albany*]
  If e'er Your Grace had speech with man so poor,
  Hear me one word.
ALBANY [*to the others*]   I'll overtake you.
                                Exeunt both the armies.
                                     Speak.

EDGAR [*giving a letter*]
  Before you fight the battle, ope this letter.   42
  If you have victory, let the trumpet sound   43
  For him that brought it. Wretched though I seem,
  I can produce a champion that will prove   45
  What is avouchèd there. If you miscarry,   46
  Your business of the world hath so an end,
  And machination ceases. Fortune love you!   48
ALBANY   Stay till I have read the letter.
EDGAR   I was forbid it.
  When time shall serve, let but the herald cry
  And I'll appear again.   *Exit* [*Edgar*].
ALBANY
  Why, fare thee well. I will o'erlook thy paper.   53

  Enter Edmund.

EDMUND
  The enemy's in view. Draw up your powers.
                     [*He offers Albany a paper.*]
  Here is the guess of their true strength and forces   55
  By diligent discovery; but your haste   56
  Is now urged on you.
ALBANY   We will greet the time.   *Exit.* 57
EDMUND
  To both these sisters have I sworn my love,
  Each jealous of the other as the stung   59
  Are of the adder. Which of them shall I take?
  Both? One? Or neither? Neither can be enjoyed
  If both remain alive. To take the widow
  Exasperates, makes mad her sister Goneril,
  And hardly shall I carry out my side,   64
  Her husband being alive. Now then, we'll use
  His countenance for the battle, which being done,   66
  Let her who would be rid of him devise
  His speedy taking off. As for the mercy   68
  Which he intends to Lear and to Cordelia,
  The battle done and they within our power,

  Shall never see his pardon, for my state   71
  Stands on me to defend, not to debate.   72
                                              Exit.

❖

5.2

  Alarum within. Enter, with drum and colors, Lear,
  Cordelia, and soldiers, over the stage; and exeunt.

  Enter Edgar and Gloucester.

EDGAR
  Here, father, take the shadow of this tree   1
  For your good host. Pray that the right may thrive.   2
  If ever I return to you again,
  I'll bring you comfort.
GLOUCESTER   Grace go with you, sir!   4
                                         Exit [*Edgar*].

  Alarum and retreat within. Enter Edgar.

EDGAR
  Away, old man! Give me thy hand. Away!
  King Lear hath lost, he and his daughter ta'en.
  Give me thy hand. Come on.
GLOUCESTER
  No further, sir. A man may rot even here.
EDGAR
  What, in ill thoughts again? Men must endure
  Their going hence, even as their coming hither;
  Ripeness is all. Come on.
GLOUCESTER   And that's true too.   11
                                              Exeunt.

♣

5.3

  Enter, in conquest, with drum and colors, Edmund;
  Lear and Cordelia, as prisoners; soldiers, Captain.

EDMUND
  Some officers take them away. Good guard   1
  Until their greater pleasures first be known   2
  That are to censure them.
CORDELIA [*to Lear*]   We are not the first   3
  Who with best meaning have incurred the worst.   4
  For thee, oppressèd King, I am cast down;
  Myself could else outfrown false Fortune's frown.
  Shall we not see these daughters and these sisters?   7

---

38 convenient proper, fitting.   **39 I know the riddle** i.e., I understand the reason for Regan's enigmatic demand that I accompany her, which is that she wants to keep me away from Edmund.   **42 this letter** i.e., Goneril's letter to Edmund found on Oswald's body.
43 sound sound a summons   **45 prove** i.e., in trial by combat
46 avouchèd affirmed.   **miscarry** lose the battle and die   **48 machination** plotting (against your life)   **53 o'erlook** peruse   **55 guess** estimate   **56 discovery** reconnoitering   **57 We . . . time** We will be ready for whatever happens.   **59 jealous** suspicious   **64 carry . . . side** carry out my end of the bargain in our *reciprocal vows* (4.6.266)
66 countenance backing, authority of his name   **68 taking off** killing.

71 Shall they shall   **71–2 my state . . . debate** my position depends upon maintenance by forceful action, not by talk.
5.2. Location: The battlefield.
0.1 *Alarum* trumpet call to arms   **1 father** i.e., reverend old man
2 host shelterer.   **4.2** *retreat* trumpet signal for withdrawal
11 Ripeness (Humans shouldn't die before their time, just as fruit doesn't fall until it's ripe.)
5.3. Location: The British camp.
1 Good guard Guard them well   **2 their greater pleasures** the wishes of those in command   **3 censure** judge   **4 meaning** intentions
7 Shall . . . sisters? i.e., Aren't we even allowed to speak to Goneril and Regan before they order to prison their own father and sister?

LEAR
No, no, no, no! Come, let's away to prison.
We two alone will sing like birds i'th' cage.
When thou dost ask me blessing, I'll kneel down
And ask of thee forgiveness. So we'll live,
And pray, and sing, and tell old tales, and laugh
At gilded butterflies, and hear poor rogues   13
Talk of court news; and we'll talk with them too—
Who loses and who wins; who's in, who's out—
And take upon 's the mystery of things,   16
As if we were God's spies; and we'll wear out,   17
In a walled prison, packs and sects of great ones,   18
That ebb and flow by th' moon.
EDMUND   Take them away.   19
LEAR
Upon such sacrifices, my Cordelia,
The gods themselves throw incense. Have I caught
  thee?   21
He that parts us shall bring a brand from heaven   22
And fire us hence like foxes. Wipe thine eyes;   23
The good years shall devour them, flesh and fell,   24
Ere they shall make us weep. We'll see 'em starved
  first.   25
Come.   Exit [with Cordelia, guarded].
EDMUND   Come hither, Captain. Hark.
Take thou this note. [He gives a paper.] Go follow them
  to prison.
One step I have advanced thee; if thou dost
As this instructs thee, thou dost make thy way
To noble fortunes. Know thou this: that men
Are as the time is. To be tender-minded   32
Does not become a sword. Thy great employment   33
Will not bear question; either say thou'lt do't   34
Or thrive by other means.
CAPTAIN   I'll do't, my lord.
EDMUND   About it, and write "happy" when th' hast done.   36
Mark, I say, instantly, and carry it so   37
As I have set it down.
CAPTAIN
I cannot draw a cart, nor eat dried oats;
If it be man's work, I'll do't.   Exit Captain.

       *Flourish. Enter Albany, Goneril, Regan, [another
       Captain, and] soldiers.*

ALBANY
Sir, you have showed today your valiant strain,
And fortune led you well. You have the captives
Who were the opposites of this day's strife;   43
I do require them of you, so to use them
As we shall find their merits and our safety
May equally determine.
EDMUND   Sir, I thought it fit
To send the old and miserable King
To some retention and appointed guard,   49
Whose age had charms in it, whose title more,   50
To pluck the common bosom on his side   51
And turn our impressed lances in our eyes   52
Which do command them. With him I sent the Queen,   53
My reason all the same; and they are ready
Tomorrow, or at further space, t'appear   55
Where you shall hold your session. At this time
We sweat and bleed; the friend hath lost his friend,
And the best quarrels in the heat are cursed   58
By those that feel their sharpness.   59
The question of Cordelia and her father
Requires a fitter place.
ALBANY   Sir, by your patience,   61
I hold you but a subject of this war,   62
Not as a brother.
REGAN   That's as we list to grace him.   63
Methinks our pleasure might have been demanded   64
Ere you had spoke so far. He led our powers,
Bore the commission of my place and person,
The which immediacy may well stand up   67
And call itself your brother.
GONERIL   Not so hot!
In his own grace he doth exalt himself
More than in your addition.
REGAN   In my rights,   70
By me invested, he compeers the best.   71
GONERIL
That were the most if he should husband you.   72
REGAN
Jesters do oft prove prophets.
GONERIL   Holla, holla!   73
That eye that told you so looked but asquint.   74
REGAN
Lady, I am not well, else I should answer
From a full-flowing stomach. [To Edmund] General,   76

---

13 **gilded butterflies** i.e., gaily dressed courtiers and other ephemeral types, or perhaps actual butterflies 16 **take upon 's** assume the burden of, or profess to understand 17 **God's spies** i.e., detached observers surveying the deeds of humanity from an eternal vantage point. **wear out** outlast 18–19 **packs . . . moon** i.e., followers and cliques attached to persons of high station, whose fortunes change erratically and constantly. 21 **The gods . . . incense** (The gods make offerings to Cordelia instead of receiving them.) 22–3 **He . . . foxes** i.e., Nothing short of a firebrand from heaven will ever part us again. (Firebrands were used to smoke foxes from their lairs; compare also Samson's use of firebrands tied to the tails of foxes in order to punish the Philistines for denying him his wife, in Judges 15:4–5.) 24–5 **The good . . . weep** i.e., the years will be good to us and will utterly foil our enemies' attempts to make us sorrowful as long as we are together (?). 32 **Are . . . is** i.e., must adapt themselves to stern exigencies. 33 **become a sword** i.e., suit a warrior. 34 **bear question** admit of discussion 36 **write "happy"** call yourself fortunate. **th'** thou 37 **carry it** carry it out

43 **opposites** enemies 49 **retention** confinement 50–3 **Whose . . . them** whose advanced age had magic in it, and whose title as king had even more, to win the sympathy of the commoners and turn against us the weapons of those very troops whom we impressed into service. (*In our eyes* may suggest retaliation for the blinding of Gloucester.) 55 **space** interval of time 58–9 **And . . . sharpness** and even the best of causes, at this moment when the passions of battle have not cooled, are viewed with hatred by those who have suffered the painful consequences. (Edmund pretends to worry that Lear and Cordelia would not receive a fair trial.) 61 **by your patience** if you please 62 **subject of** subordinate in 63 **list** please 64 **pleasure** wish. **demanded** asked about 67 **immediacy** nearness of connection 70 **your addition** the titles you confer. 71 **compeers** is equal with 72 **That . . . most** That investiture would be most complete 73 **prove** turn out to be 74 **asquint** (Jealousy proverbially makes the eye look *asquint*, "furtively, suspiciously.") 76 **full-flowing stomach** full tide of angry rejoinder.

Take thou my soldiers, prisoners, patrimony;   77
Dispose of them, of me; the walls is thine.   78
Witness the world that I create thee here
My lord and master.
GONERIL   Mean you to enjoy him?
ALBANY
The let-alone lies not in your good will.   81
EDMUND
Nor in thine, lord.
ALBANY   Half-blooded fellow, yes.   82
REGAN [to Edmund]
Let the drum strike and prove my title thine.
ALBANY
Stay yet; hear reason. Edmund, I arrest thee
On capital treason; and, in thy attaint   85
This gilded serpent. [Pointing to Goneril] For your
   claim, fair sister,
I bar it in the interest of my wife;
'Tis she is subcontracted to this lord,
And I, her husband, contradict your banns.   89
If you will marry, make your loves to me;   90
My lady is bespoke.
GONERIL   An interlude!   91
ALBANY
Thou art armed, Gloucester. Let the trumpet sound.
If none appear to prove upon thy person
Thy heinous, manifest, and many treasons,
There is my pledge. [He throws down a glove.] I'll make
   it on thy heart,   95
Ere I taste bread, thou art in nothing less   96
Than I have here proclaimed thee.
REGAN   Sick, oh, sick!
GONERIL [aside]   If not, I'll ne'er trust medicine. 99
EDMUND [throwing down a glove]
There's my exchange. What in the world he is   100
That names me traitor, villain-like he lies.
Call by the trumpet. He that dares approach,
On him, on you—who not?—I will maintain
My truth and honor firmly.
ALBANY
A herald, ho!
EDMUND   A herald, ho, a herald!

        Enter a Herald.

ALBANY [to Edmund]
Trust to thy single virtue; for thy soldiers,   106
All levied in my name, have in my name
Took their discharge.
REGAN   My sickness grows upon me.

ALBANY [to Soldiers]
She is not well. Convey her to my tent.
                        [Exit Regan, supported.]
Come hither, herald. Let the trumpet sound,
And read out this.   [He gives a paper.]
CAPTAIN   Sound, trumpet!   A trumpet sounds.
HERALD (reads)   "If any man of quality or degree within   113
   the lists of the army will maintain upon Edmund, sup-   114
   posed Earl of Gloucester, that he is a manifold traitor,
   let him appear by the third sound of the trumpet. He
   is bold in his defense."
EDMUND   Sound!   First trumpet.
HERALD   Again!   Second trumpet.
HERALD   Again!   Third trumpet.
                    Trumpet answers within.

        Enter Edgar, armed, [with a trumpeter before
        him].

ALBANY
Ask him his purposes, why he appears
Upon this call o'th' trumpet.
HERALD   What are you?   122
Your name, your quality, and why you answer
This present summons?
EDGAR   Know my name is lost,
By treason's tooth bare-gnawn and canker-bit.   125
Yet am I noble as the adversary
I come to cope.
ALBANY   Which is that adversary?   127
EDGAR
What's he that speaks for Edmund, Earl of
   Gloucester?
EDMUND
Himself. What say'st thou to him?
EDGAR   Draw thy sword,
That, if my speech offend a noble heart,
Thy arm may do thee justice. Here is mine.
                        [He draws his sword.]
Behold, it is the privilege of mine honors,   132
My oath, and my profession. I protest,   133
Maugre thy strength, place, youth, and eminence,   134
Despite thy victor sword and fire-new fortune,   135
Thy valor, and thy heart, thou art a traitor—   136
False to thy gods, thy brother, and thy father,
Conspirant 'gainst this high-illustrious prince,
And from th'extremest upward of thy head   139
To the descent and dust below thy foot   140
A most toad-spotted traitor. Say thou no,   141
This sword, this arm, and my best spirits are bent   142
To prove upon thy heart, whereto I speak,
Thou liest.

---

77 patrimony inheritance   78 the walls is thine i.e., the citadel of my
heart and body surrenders completely to you.   81 let-alone preventing, denying   82 Half-blooded Only partly of noble blood, bastard
85 in thy attaint i.e., as partner in your corruption and as one who
has (unwittingly) provided the *attaint* or impeachment against you
89 banns public announcement of a proposed marriage.   90 make . . .
me i.e., sue to me for permission   91 An interlude! A play; i.e., you
are being melodramatic, or, what a farce this is!   95 make prove
96 in nothing less in no respect less guilty   99 medicine i.e., poison.
100 What Whoever   106 single virtue unaided prowess

113 quality or degree noble birth or rank. (Also in line 123.)
114 lists roster   122 What Who   125 canker-bit eaten as by the
caterpillar.   127 cope encounter.   132 of mine honors i.e., of my
knighthood   133 profession i.e., knighthood.   134 Maugre in spite
of   135 victor victorious.   fire-new newly minted   136 heart
courage   139 upward top   140 descent lowest extreme   141 toad-
spotted venomous, or having spots of infamy.   Say thou If you say
142 bent prepared

EDMUND　In wisdom I should ask thy name.　144
　　But since thy outside looks so fair and warlike,
　　And that thy tongue some say of breeding breathes,　146
　　What safe and nicely I might well delay　147
　　By rule of knighthood, I disdain and spurn.　148
　　Back do I toss those treasons to thy head,　149
　　With the hell-hated lie o'erwhelm thy heart,　150
　　Which—for they yet glance by and scarcely bruise—　151
　　This sword of mine shall give them instant way,　152
　　Where they shall rest forever.—Trumpets, speak!　153
　　　　　　　[He draws.] Alarums. Fight. [Edmund falls.]
ALBANY [to Edgar]
　　Save him, save him!
GONERIL　　　　　　　This is practice, Gloucester.　154
　　By th' law of arms thou wast not bound to answer
　　An unknown opposite. Thou art not vanquished,
　　But cozened and beguiled.
ALBANY　　　　　　　　Shut your mouth, dame,　157
　　Or with this paper shall I stopple it.—Hold, sir.　158
　　Thou worse than any name, read thine own evil.
　　　　　　　　　　　　　[He shows the letter.]
　　[To Goneril] No tearing, lady; I perceive you know it.
GONERIL
　　Say if I do, the laws are mine, not thine.
　　Who can arraign me for't?
ALBANY　　　　　　　　Most monstrous! Oh!
　　Know'st thou this paper?
GONERIL　　　　　　　Ask me not what I know.
　　　　　　　　　　　　　　　　　　Exit.
ALBANY
　　Go after her. She's desperate; govern her.　164
　　　　　　　　　　　　　[Exit a soldier.]
EDMUND
　　What you have charged me with, that have I done,
　　And more, much more. The time will bring it out.
　　'Tis past, and so am I. But what art thou
　　That hast this fortune on me? If thou'rt noble,　168
　　I do forgive thee.
EDGAR　　　　　　Let's exchange charity.　169
　　I am no less in blood than thou art, Edmund;
　　If more, the more th' hast wronged me.　171
　　My name is Edgar, and thy father's son.
　　The gods are just, and of our pleasant vices　173
　　Make instruments to plague us.
　　The dark and vicious place where thee he got　175

Cost him his eyes.
EDMUND　　　　　　Th' hast spoken right. 'Tis true.
　　The wheel is come full circle; I am here.　177
ALBANY [to Edgar]
　　Methought thy very gait did prophesy
　　A royal nobleness. I must embrace thee.
　　　　　　　　　　　　　　[They embrace.]
　　Let sorrow split my heart if ever I
　　Did hate thee or thy father!
EDGAR　Worthy prince, I know't.
ALBANY　Where have you hid yourself?
　　How have you known the miseries of your father?
EDGAR
　　By nursing them, my lord. List a brief tale,　185
　　And when 'tis told, oh, that my heart would burst!
　　The bloody proclamation to escape　187
　　That followed me so near—oh, our lives' sweetness,　188
　　That we the pain of death would hourly die　189
　　Rather than die at once!—taught me to shift　190
　　Into a madman's rags, t'assume a semblance
　　That very dogs disdained; and in this habit　192
　　Met I my father with his bleeding rings,　193
　　Their precious stones new lost; became his guide,　194
　　Led him, begged for him, saved him from despair;
　　Never—oh, fault!—revealed myself unto him
　　Until some half hour past, when I was armed.
　　Not sure, though hoping, of this good success,　198
　　I asked his blessing, and from first to last
　　Told him our pilgrimage. But his flawed heart—　200
　　Alack, too weak the conflict to support—
　　Twixt two extremes of passion, joy and grief,
　　Burst smilingly.
EDMUND　　　　　This speech of yours hath moved me,
　　And shall perchance do good. But speak you on;
　　You look as you had something more to say.
ALBANY
　　If there be more, more woeful, hold it in,
　　For I am almost ready to dissolve,　207
　　Hearing of this.
EDGAR　　　　　This would have seemed a period　208
　　To such as love not sorrow; but another,　209
　　To amplify too much, would make much more　210
　　And top extremity. Whilst I　211
　　Was big in clamor, came there in a man　212
　　Who, having seen me in my worst estate,
　　Shunned my abhorred society; but then, finding
　　Who 'twas that so endured, with his strong arms
　　He fastened on my neck and bellowed out

144 wisdom prudence　146 say smack, taste, indication　147 safe and nicely prudently and punctiliously　148 I . . . spurn i.e., I disdain to insist on my right to refuse combat with one of lower rank. 149 treasons . . . head i.e., accusations of treason in your teeth 150 hell-hated hated as hell is hated　151 Which . . . bruise i.e., which charges of treason—since as yet they merely glance off my armor and do no harm　152 give . . . way provide them an immediate pathway (to your heart)　153 Where . . . forever i.e., my victory in trial by combat will prove forever that the charges of treason apply to you.　154 Save Spare. (Albany wishes to spare Edmund's life so that he may confess and be found guilty.)　practice trickery, or (said sardonically) astute management　157 cozened tricked　158 stopple stop up.　Hold, sir (Addressed to Edgar or, more probably, Edmund.) 164 govern restrain　168 fortune on victory over　169 charity forgiveness (for Edmund's wickedness toward Edgar and Edgar's having slain Edmund).　171 th' hast thou hast　173 pleasant pleasurable　175 got begot

177 The wheel . . . here (Alludes both to the wheel of fortune and to the idea of a completed circle whereby crime meets its appropriate punishment. Edmund sees that everything has at last come around to where it began.)　185 List Listen to　187 The . . . escape In order to escape the death-threatening proclamation　188–90 oh . . . at once! oh, the perversity of our attachment to our lives' sweetness, that we prefer to suffer continually the fear of death rather than die at once and be done with it!　192 habit garb　193 rings sockets　194 stones i.e., eyeballs　198 success outcome　200 flawed cracked　207 dissolve i.e., in tears　208 a period the limit　209–11 but . . . extremity i.e., but another sorrowful circumstance, adding to what is already too much, would increase it and exceed the limit.　212 big in clamor loud in my lamenting

As he'd burst heaven, threw him on my father,   217
Told the most piteous tale of Lear and him
That ever ear received, which in recounting
His grief grew puissant, and the strings of life   220
Began to crack. Twice then the trumpets sounded,
And there I left him tranced.

ALBANY   But who was this?   222

EDGAR
Kent, sir, the banished Kent, who in disguise
Followed his enemy king and did him service   224
Improper for a slave.

            Enter a Gentleman [with a bloody knife].

GENTLEMAN
Help, help, oh, help!

EDGAR   What kind of help?

ALBANY   Speak, man.

EDGAR
What means this bloody knife?

GENTLEMAN   'Tis hot, it smokes.   227
It came even from the heart of—Oh, she's dead!

ALBANY   Who dead? Speak, man.

GENTLEMAN
Your lady, sir, your lady! And her sister
By her is poisoned; she confesses it.

EDMUND
I was contracted to them both. All three
Now marry in an instant.

EDGAR   Here comes Kent.

            Enter Kent.

ALBANY
Produce the bodies, be they alive or dead.
                            [Exit Gentleman.]
This judgment of the heavens, that makes us tremble,
Touches us not with pity.—Oh, is this he?
[To Kent] The time will not allow the compliment   237
Which very manners urges.

KENT   I am come   238
To bid my king and master aye good night.   239
Is he not here?

ALBANY   Great thing of us forgot!
Speak, Edmund, where's the King? And where's
    Cordelia?
            Goneril and Regan's bodies [are] brought out.
See'st thou this object, Kent?   242

KENT   Alack, why thus?

EDMUND   Yet Edmund was beloved.
The one the other poisoned for my sake
And after slew herself.

ALBANY   Even so. Cover their faces.

EDMUND
I pant for life. Some good I mean to do,
Despite of mine own nature. Quickly send—
Be brief in it—to th' castle, for my writ
Is on the life of Lear and on Cordelia.
Nay, send in time.

ALBANY   Run, run, oh, run!

EDGAR
To who, my lord? Who has the office? *[To Edmund]*
    Send   253
Thy token of reprieve.

EDMUND   Well thought on. Take my sword. The captain!
Give it the Captain.

EDGAR   Haste thee, for thy life.
                    [Exit one with Edmund's sword.]

EDMUND
He hath commission from thy wife and me
To hang Cordelia in the prison and
To lay the blame upon her own despair,
That she fordid herself.   260

ALBANY
The gods defend her! Bear him hence awhile.
                            [Edmund is borne off.]

    Enter Lear, with Cordelia in his arms; [Captain].

LEAR
Howl, howl, howl! Oh, you are men of stones!
Had I your tongues and eyes, I'd use them so
That heaven's vault should crack. She's gone forever.
I know when one is dead and when one lives;
She's dead as earth. Lend me a looking glass;
If that her breath will mist or stain the stone,   267
Why, then she lives.

KENT   Is this the promised end?   268

EDGAR
Or image of that horror?

ALBANY   Fall and cease!   269

LEAR
This feather stirs; she lives! If it be so,
It is a chance which does redeem all sorrows
That ever I have felt.

KENT *[kneeling]*   O my good master!

LEAR
Prithee, away.

EDGAR   'Tis noble Kent, your friend.

LEAR
A plague upon you, murderers, traitors all!
I might have saved her; now she's gone forever!
Cordelia, Cordelia! Stay a little. Ha?
What is't thou say'st? Her voice was ever soft,
Gentle, and low, an excellent thing in woman.
I killed the slave that was a-hanging thee.

CAPTAIN
'Tis true, my lords, he did.

LEAR   Did I not, fellow?

---

217 As as if.   **threw . . . father** threw himself on my father's body **220 His** i.e., Kent's.   **puissant** powerful.   **strings of life** heartstrings **222 tranced** entranced, senseless.   **224 his enemy king** i.e., the king who had rejected and banished him   **227 smokes** steams.   **237 compliment** ceremony   **238 Which . . . urges** which common courtesy requires.   **239 aye good night** farewell forever. (Kent believes he himself is near death, his heartstrings having begun to crack.) **242 object** sight

253 office commission.   **260 fordid** destroyed   **267 stone** crystal or polished stone of which the mirror is made   **268 Is . . . end?** (Kent may mean "Is this what all our hopes have come to?" Edgar replies by invoking the Last Judgment.)   **269 image** representation.   **Fall and cease!** i.e., Let all things cease to be!

I have seen the day, with my good biting falchion   281
I would have made them skip. I am old now,
And these same crosses spoil me.—Who are you?   283
Mine eyes are not o'th' best; I'll tell you straight.   284

KENT
If Fortune brag of two she loved and hated,   285
One of them we behold.   286

LEAR
This is a dull sight. Are you not Kent?

KENT   The same,   287
Your servant Kent. Where is your servant Caius?   288

LEAR
He's a good fellow, I can tell you that;
He'll strike, and quickly too. He's dead and rotten.

KENT
No, my good lord, I am the very man—

LEAR   I'll see that straight.   292

KENT
That from your first of difference and decay   293
Have followed your sad steps—

LEAR   You are welcome hither.

KENT
Nor no man else. All's cheerless, dark, and deadly.   295
Your eldest daughters have fordone themselves,   296
And desperately are dead.

LEAR   Ay, so I think.   297

ALBANY
He knows not what he says, and vain is it
That we present us to him.

EDGAR   Very bootless.   299

Enter a Messenger.

MESSENGER   Edmund is dead, my lord.

ALBANY   That's but a trifle here.
You lords and noble friends, know our intent:
What comfort to this great decay may come   303

---

281 falchion light sword   **283 crosses spoil me** adversities take away
my strength.   **284 I'll . . . straight** I'll recognize you in a moment.
285–6 If . . . behold If Fortune were to brag of two persons whom she
has subjected to the greatest fall from her favor into her hatred, Lear
would have to be one of them.   **287 This . . . sight** i.e., My vision is
clouding, or, this is a dismal spectacle.   **288 Caius** (Kent's disguise
name.)   **292 see that straight** attend to that in a moment.   **293 from
. . . decay** from the beginning of your quarrel (with Cordelia) to your
decline of fortune   **295 Nor . . . else** No, not I nor anyone else, or, I
am the *very man* (line 291), him and no one else.   **296 fordone**
destroyed   **297 desperately** in despair   **299 bootless** in vain.
303 What . . . come i.e., whatever means of comforting this ruined
king and state of affairs may present themselves

Shall be applied. For us, we will resign,   304
During the life of this old majesty,
To him our absolute power; [*to Edgar and Kent*] you, to
    your rights,
With boot and such addition as your honors   307
Have more than merited. All friends shall taste
The wages of their virtue, and all foes
The cup of their deservings.—Oh, see, see!

LEAR
And my poor fool is hanged! No, no, no life?   311
Why should a dog, a horse, a rat have life,
And thou no breath at all? Thou'lt come no more,
Never, never, never, never, never!
Pray you, undo this button. Thank you, sir.
Do you see this? Look on her, look, her lips,
Look there, look there!   *He dies.*

EDGAR   He faints.—My lord, my lord!

KENT
Break, heart, I prithee, break!

EDGAR   Look up, my lord.

KENT
Vex not his ghost. Oh, let him pass! He hates him   319
That would upon the rack of this tough world   320
Stretch him out longer.

EDGAR   He is gone indeed.

KENT
The wonder is he hath endured so long.
He but usurped his life.

ALBANY
Bear them from hence. Our present business
Is general woe. [*To Kent and Edgar*] Friends of my soul,
    you twain
Rule in this realm, and the gored state sustain.

KENT
I have a journey, sir, shortly to go.   327
My master calls me; I must not say no.

EDGAR
The weight of this sad time we must obey;
Speak what we feel, not what we ought to say.
The oldest hath borne most; we that are young
Shall never see so much nor live so long.   332

           Exeunt, with a dead march.

---

304 For As for   **307 With . . . honors** with advantage and such further distinctions or titles as your honorable conduct in this war
311 poor fool i.e., Cordelia. (*Fool* is here a term of endearment.)
319 ghost departing spirit.   **320 rack** torture rack. (With suggestion,
in the Folio and Quarto spelling, "wracke," of shipwreck, disaster.)
327 journey i.e., to another world, to death   **332.1 *Exeunt*** (Presumably the dead bodies are borne out in procession.)

Macbeth

Macbeth is seemingly the last of four great Shakespearean tragedies—*Hamlet* (c. 1599–1601), *Othello* (c. 1603–1604), *King Lear* (1605–1606), and *Macbeth* (c. 1606–1607)—that examine the dimensions of spiritual evil, as distinguished from the political strife of Roman tragedies such as *Julius Caesar, Antony* and *Cleopatra,* and *Coriolanus.* Whether or not Shakespeare intended *Macbeth* as a culmination of a series of tragedies on evil, the play does offer a particularly terse and gloomy view of humanity's encounter with the powers of darkness. Macbeth, more consciously than any other of Shakespeare's major tragic protagonists, has to face the temptation of committing what he knows to be a monstrous crime. Like Doctor Faustus in Christopher Marlowe's play, *The Tragedy of Doctor Faustus* (c. 1588–1592), and to a lesser extent like Adam in John Milton's *Paradise Lost* (1667), Macbeth understands the reasons for resisting evil and yet goes ahead with his disastrous plan. His awareness and sensitivity to moral issues, together with his conscious choice of evil, produce an unnerving account of human failure, all the more distressing because Macbeth is so representatively human. He seems to possess freedom of will and accepts personal responsibility for his fate, and yet his tragic doom seems unavoidable. Nor is there eventual salvation to be hoped for, as there is in *Paradise Lost,* since Macbeth's crime is too heinous and his heart too hardened. He is more like Doctor Faustus—damned and in despair.

To an extent not found in the other tragedies, the issue is stated in terms of salvation versus damnation. Macbeth knows before he acts that King Duncan's virtues "Will plead like angels, trumpet-tongued, against / The deep damnation of his taking-off" (1.7.19–20). After the murder, he is equally aware that he has "Put rancors in the vessel of my peace . . . and mine eternal jewel / Given to the common enemy of man" (3.1.68–70). His enemies later describe him as a devil and a "hellhound" (5.8.3). He, like Marlowe's Doctor Faustus before him, has knowingly sold his soul for gain. And, although as a mortal he still has time to repent his crimes, horrible as they are,

Macbeth cannot find the words to be penitent. "Wherefore could not I pronounce 'Amen'?" he implores his wife after they have committed the murder. "I had most need of blessing, and 'Amen' / Stuck in my throat" (2.2.35–7). Macbeth's own answer seems to be that he has committed himself so inexorably to evil that he cannot turn back. Sentence has been pronounced: "Glamis hath murdered sleep, and therefore Cawdor / Shall sleep no more; Macbeth shall sleep no more" (lines 46–7).

Macbeth is not a conventional morality play (even less so than *Doctor Faustus*) and is not concerned primarily with preaching against sinfulness or demonstrating that Macbeth is finally damned for what he does. A tradition of moral and religious drama has been transformed into an intensely human study of the psychological effects of evil on a particular man and, to a lesser extent, on his wife. That moral tradition nevertheless provides as its legacy a perspective on the operation of evil in human affairs. A perverse ambition seemingly inborn in Macbeth himself is abetted by dark forces dwelling in the universe, waiting to catch him off guard. Among Shakespeare's tragedies, indeed, *Macbeth* is remarkable for its focus on evil in the protagonist and on his relationship to the sinister forces tempting him. In no other Shakespearean play is the audience asked to identify to such an extent with the evildoer himself. *Richard III* also focuses on an evil protagonist, but in that play the spectators are distanced by the character's gloating and are not partakers in the introspective soliloquies of a man confronting his own ambition. Macbeth is more representatively human. If he betrays an inclination toward brutality, he also humanely attempts to resist that urge. We witness and struggle to understand his downfall through two phases: the spiritual struggle before he actually commits the crime and the despairing aftermath, with its vain quest for security through continued violence. Evil is thus presented in two aspects: first as an insidious suggestion leading Macbeth on toward an illusory promise of gain and then as a frenzied addiction to the hated thing by which he is possessed.

In the first phase, before the commission of the crime, we wonder to what extent the powers of darkness are a determining factor in what Macbeth does. Can he avoid the fate the witches proclaim? Evidently, he and Lady Macbeth have previously considered murdering Duncan; the witches appear after the thought, not before. Lady Macbeth reminds her wavering husband that he was the first to "break this enterprise" to her, on some previous occasion when "Nor time nor place / Did then adhere, and yet you would make both" (1.7.49–53). Elizabethans would probably understand that evil spirits such as witches appear when summoned, whether by our conscious or unconscious minds. Macbeth is ripe for their insinuations: a mind free of taint would see no sinister invitation in their prophecy of greatness to come. And, in a saner moment, Macbeth knows that his restless desire to interfere with destiny is arrogant and useless. "If chance will have me king, why, chance may crown me / Without my stir" (1.3.145–6). Banquo, his companion, serves as his dramatic opposite by consistently displaying a more stoical attitude toward the witches. "Speak then to me," he addresses them, "who neither beg nor fear / Your favors nor your hate" (lines 60–1). Like Horatio in *Hamlet*, Banquo strongly resists the blandishments of fortune as well as its buffets, though not without an agonizing night of moral struggle. Indeed, promises of success are often more ruinous than setbacks—as in the seemingly paradoxical instance of the farmer, cited by Macbeth's porter, who "hanged himself on th'expectation of plenty" (2.3.4–5). It is by showing Macbeth that he is two-thirds of his way to the throne that the witches tempt him to seize the last third at whatever cost. "Glamis, and Thane of Cawdor! / The greatest is behind" (1.3.116–17).

Banquo comprehends the nature of temptation. "To win us to our harm," he observes, "The instruments of darkness tell us truths, / Win us with honest trifles, to betray 's / In deepest consequence" (1.3.123–6). The devil can speak true, and his strategy is to invite us into a trap we help prepare. Without our active consent in evil (as Othello also learns), we cannot fall. Yet in what sense are the witches trifling with Macbeth or prevaricating? When they address him as one "that shalt be king hereafter" (line 50), they are stating a certainty, for they can "look into the seeds of time / And say which grain will grow and which will not," as Banquo says (lines 58–9). They know that Banquo will be "Lesser than Macbeth, and greater, / Not so happy, yet much happier" (lines 65–6), since Banquo will beget a race of kings and Macbeth will not. How then do they know that Macbeth will be king? If we consider the hypothetical question, what if Macbeth does *not* murder Duncan, we can gain some understanding of the relationship between character and fate; for the only valid answer is that the question remains hypothetical—Macbeth *does* kill Duncan, the witches are right in their prediction. It is idle to speculate that Providence would have found another way to make Macbeth king, for the witches' prophecy is self-fulfilling in the very way they foresee. Character is fate; they know Macbeth's fatal weakness and know they can "enkindle" him to seize the crown by laying irresistible temptations before him. This does not mean that they determine his choice but, rather, that Macbeth's choice is predictable and therefore unvoidable, even though not preordained. He has free choice, but that choice will, in fact, go only one way—as with Adam and Eve in Milton's *Paradise Lost* and in the medieval tradition from which this poem was derived.

Although the powers of evil cannot determine Macbeth's choice, they can influence the external conditions affecting that choice. By a series of apparently circumstantial events, well timed in their effect, they can repeatedly assail him just when he is about to rally to the call of conscience. The witches, armed with supernatural knowledge, inform Macbeth of his new title shortly before the King's ambassadors confirm that he is to be the Thane of Cawdor. Duncan chooses this night to lodge under Macbeth's roof. And, just when Macbeth resolves to abandon even this unparalleled opportunity, his wife intervenes on the side of the witches. Macbeth commits the murder in part to keep his word to her and to prove he is no coward (like Donwald, the slayer of King Duff in one of Shakespeare's chief sources, Raphael Holinshed's *Chronicles*). Not only the opportunities presented to Macbeth, but also the obstacles put in his way are cannily timed to overwhelm his conscience. When King Duncan announces that his son Malcolm is now Prince of Cumberland and official heir to the throne (1.4.36–42), the unintended threat deflects Macbeth's mood from one of gratitude and acceptance to one of hostility. These are mitigating circumstances that affect our judgment of Macbeth, and, even though they cannot excuse him, they certainly increase our sympathetic identification.

We are moved, too, by the poetic intensity of Macbeth's moral vision. His soliloquies are memorable as poetry, not merely because Shakespeare wrote them, but because Macbeth is sensitive and aware. The horror, indeed, of his crime is that his cultivated self is revolted by what he cannot prevent himself from doing. He understands with a terrible clarity, not only the moral wrong of what he is about to do, but also the inescapably destructive consequences for himself. He is as reluctant as we to see the crime committed, and yet he goes to it with a sad and rational deliberateness rather than in a self-blinding fury. For Macbeth, there is no seeming loss of perspective, and yet there is total alienation of the act from his moral consciousness. The arguments for and against murdering Duncan, as Macbeth pictures them in his acutely visual imagination, when weighed, are overwhelmingly opposed to the deed. Duncan is his king and his guest, deserving Macbeth's duty and hospitality. The King is virtuous and able. He has shown every favor to

Macbeth, thereby removing any sane motive for striving after further promotion. All human history shows that murders of this sort "return / To plague th'inventor" (1.7.9–10), that is, provide only guilt and punishment rather than satisfaction. Finally, judgment in "the life to come" includes the prospect of eternal torment. On the other side of the argument is nothing but Macbeth's "Vaulting ambition, which o'erleaps itself" (line 27)—a perverse refusal to be content with his present good fortune because there is more that beckons. Who could weigh the issues so dispassionately and still choose the wrong? Yet the failure is, in fact, predictable; Macbeth is presented to us as typically human, both in his understanding and in his perverse ambition.

Macbeth's clarity of moral imagination is contrasted with his wife's imperceptiveness. He is always seeing visions or hearing voices—a dagger in the air, the ghost of Banquo, a voice crying "Sleep no more!"—and she is always denying them. "The sleeping and the dead / Are but as pictures," she insists. He knows that "all great Neptune's ocean" cannot wash the blood from his hands; "No, this my hand will rather / The multitudinous seas incarnadine, / Making the green one red." To Lady Macbeth, contrastingly, "A little water clears us of this deed. / How easy is it, then!" (2.2.57–72). Macbeth knows that the murder of Duncan is but the beginning: "We have scorched the snake, not killed it." Lady Macbeth would prefer to believe that "What's done is done" (3.2.14–15). Ironically, it is she, finally, who must endure visions of the most agonizing sort, sleepwalking in her madness and trying to rub away the "damned spot" that before seemed so easy to remove. "All the perfumes of Arabia will not sweeten this little hand," she laments (5.1.34–51). This relationship between Macbeth and Lady Macbeth owes much to traditional contrasts between male and female principles. As in the pairing of Adam and Eve, the man is putatively the more rational of the two but knowingly shares his wife's sin through fondness for her. She has failed to foresee the long-range consequences of sinful ambition and so becomes a temptress to her husband. The fall of man and woman into the bondage of sin takes place in an incongruous atmosphere of domestic intimacy and mutual concern; Lady Macbeth is motivated by ambition for her husband in much the same way that he sins to win her approbation.

The fatal disharmony flawing this domestic accord is conveyed through images of sexual inversion. Lady Macbeth prepares for her ordeal with the incantation, "Come, you spirits / That tend on mortal thoughts, unsex me here . . . Come to my woman's breasts / And take my milk for gall" (1.5.40–8). When she accuses her husband of unmanly cowardice and vows she would dash out the brains of her own infant for such effeminacy as he has displayed, he extols her with "Bring forth men-children only! / For thy undaunted mettle should compose / Nothing but males" (1.7.73–5). She takes the initiative,

devising and then carrying out the plan to drug Duncan's chamber-guards with wine. This assumption of the dominant male role by the woman might well remind Elizabethan spectators of numerous biblical, medieval, and classical parallels deploring the ascendancy of passion over reason: Eve choosing for Adam, Noah's wife taking command of the ark, the Wife of Bath dominating her husbands, Venus emasculating Mars, and others.

In *Macbeth*, sexual inversion also allies Lady Macbeth with the witches or weird sisters, the bearded women. Their unnaturalness betokens disorder in nature, for they can sail in a sieve and "look not like th'inhabitants o'th'earth / And yet are on't" (1.3.41–2). Characteristically, they speak in paradoxes: "When the battle's lost and won," "Fair is foul, and foul is fair" (1.1.4,11). Shakespeare probably drew on numerous sources to depict the witches: Holinshed's *Chronicles* (in which he conflated two accounts, one of Duncan and Macbeth, and the other of King Duff slain by Donwald with the help of his wife), King James's writings on witchcraft, Samuel Harsnett's *Declaration of Egregious Popish Impostures* (used also for *King Lear*), and the accounts of the Scottish witch trials published around 1590. In the last, particularly, Shakespeare could have found mention of witches raising storms and sailing in sieves to endanger vessels at sea, performing threefold rituals blaspheming the Trinity, and brewing witches' broth. Holinshed's *Chronicles* refer to the weird sisters as "goddesses of destiny," associating them with the three fates, Clotho, Lachesis, and Atropos, who hold the spinning distaff, draw off the thread of life, and cut it. In *Macbeth*, the weird sisters' power to control fortune is curtailed, and they are portrayed as witches according to popular contemporary understanding, rather than as goddesses of destiny; nonetheless, witches were thought to be servants of the devil (Banquo wonders if the devil can speak true in their utterances, 1.3.107), and through them Macbeth has made an ominous pact with evil itself. His visit to their seething cauldron in 4.1 brings him to the witches' masters, those unknown powers that know his very thought and who tempt him with those equivocations of which Banquo has warned Macbeth. The popularity of witchlore tempted Shakespeare's acting company to expand the witches' scenes with spectacles of song and dance; even the Folio text we have evidently contains interpolations derived in part from Thomas Middleton's *The Witch* (see especially 3.5 and part of 4.1, containing mention of Middleton's songs "Come away" and "Black spirits"). Nevertheless, Shakespeare's original theme of a disharmony in nature remains clearly visible.

The disharmonies of gender relations in *Macbeth* suggest another disturbing dimension of this tragedy. The play is filled with what Janet Adelman (in *Cannibals, Witches, and Divorce*, edited by Marjorie Garber, 1985) aptly calls fantasies of maternal power. Macbeth, like many males, attempts to cope with his imaginings of a destructive maternal power and his fantasies of escape into a world fashioned and controlled solely by himself. Initially, he submits to his wife's idea of manliness and commits murder in order to win her approval, destroying in the process a fatherly figure whose manhood is nonetheless ambivalently presented to us: Duncan is to be sure a nurturing father-king, but he is also too soft and trusting for his own good. Macbeth chooses to side with his masculinized wife against the gentler side of human nature, lauding her as a woman who should "Bring forth men-children only," since her "undaunted mettle should compose / Nothing but males" (1.7.73–5), but, in the longer term, Macbeth finds himself desiccated by his own vulnerability to this masculinized mother. He turns unsuccessfully to the witches for the power he needs to make him author of himself; in the process of attempting to make himself wholly "masculine," he manages instead to strip away from himself "honor, love, obedience, troops of friends," and all the graces that should "accompany old age" (5.3.24–5). His nemesis is appropriately one who was not, in the normal sense, "of woman born," since Macduff "was from his mother's womb / Untimely ripped" (5.8.13–16). Macduff represents, in other words, the self-creating and invulnerable masculinity that Macbeth cannot fashion for himself. The ending of the play is distressingly absolute in its consolidation of male power—a reestablishment of control that seems necessary in view of the virulence of the maternal power the play has dared to unleash.

Patterns of imagery throughout the play point similarly to disorders in nature and in human relationships. The murder of Duncan, like that of Caesar in *Julius Caesar*, is accompanied by signs of the heavens' anger. Various observers report that chimneys blow down during the unruly night, that owls clamor and attack falcons, that the earth shakes, and that Duncan's horses devour each other. (Some of these portents are from Holinshed.) Banquo's ghost returns from the dead to haunt his murderer, prompting Macbeth to speak in metaphors of charnel houses and graves that send back their dead and of birds of prey that devour the corpses. The drunken porter who opens the gate to Macduff and Lennox after the murder (2.3) invokes images of judgment and everlasting bonfire, through which the scene takes on the semblance of hell gate and the Harrowing of Hell. Owls appear repeatedly in the imagery, along with other creatures associated with nighttime and horror: wolves, serpents, scorpions, bats, toads, beetles, crows, rooks. Darkness itself assumes tangible and menacing shapes of hidden stars or extinguished candles, a thick blanket shrouded "in the dunnest smoke of hell" (1.5.51), an entombment of the earth in place of "living light" (2.4.10), a scarf to hoodwink the eye of "pitiful day" (3.2.50), and a bloody and invisible hand to tear to pieces the lives of the virtuous. Sleep is transformed from "great nature's second course" and a "nourisher" of life that "knits up the raveled sleave

of care" (2.2.41–4) into "death's counterfeit" (2.3.77) and a living hell for Lady Macbeth. Life becomes sterile for Macbeth, a denial of harvest, the lees or dregs of the wine and "the sere, the yellow leaf" (5.3.23). In a theatrical metaphor, life becomes for him unreal, "a walking shadow, a poor player / That struts and frets his hour upon the stage / And then is heard no more" (5.5.24–6). This theme of empty illusion carries over into the recurring image of borrowed or ill-fitting garments that belie the wearer. Macbeth is an actor, a hypocrite, whose "False face must hide what the false heart doth know" (1.7.83) and who must "Look like th'innocent flower, / But be the serpent under 't" (1.5.65–6). Even the show of grief is an assumed mask whereby evildoers deceive the virtuous, so much so that Malcolm, Donalbain, and Macduff learn to conceal their true feelings rather than be thought to "show an unfelt sorrow" (2.3.138).

Blood is not only a literal sign of disorder but an emblem of Macbeth's remorseless butchery, a "damned spot" on the conscience, and a promise of divine vengeance: "It will have blood, they say; blood will have blood" (3.4.123). The emphasis on corrupted blood also suggests disease, in which Macbeth's tyranny is a sickness to his country as well as to himself. Scotland bleeds (4.3.32), needing a physician; Macduff and his allies call themselves "the med'cine of the sickly weal" (5.2.27). Lady Macbeth's disease is incurable, something spiritually corrupt wherein "the patient / Must minister to himself" (5.3.47–8). Conversely, the English King Edward is renowned for his divine gift of curing what was called the king's evil, or scrofula. These images are generally paternalistic in their invocation of kings and fathers who heal and unite.

Throughout, the defenders of righteousness are associated with positive images of natural order and with patriarchal control. Duncan rewards his subjects by saying, "I have begun to plant thee, and will labor / To make thee full of growing" (1.4.28–9). His arrival at Inverness Castle is heralded by signs of summer, sweet air, and "the temple-haunting martlet" (1.6.4). He is a fatherly figure, so much so that even Lady Macbeth balks at an act so like patricide. Macduff, too, is a father and husband whose family is butchered. The forest of Birnam marching to confront Macbeth, although rationally explainable as a device of camouflage for Macduff's army, is emblematic of the natural order itself rising up against the monstrosity of Macbeth's crimes. Banquo is, above all, a patriarchal figure, ancestor of the royal line governing Scotland and England at the time the play was written. These harmonies are to an extent restorative. Even the witches' riddling prophecies, "th'equivocation of the fiend" (5.5.43), luring Macbeth into further atrocities with the vain promise of security, anticipate a just retribution.

Nonetheless, the play's vision of evil shakes us deeply. Scotland's peace has been violated, so much so that "to do harm / Is often laudable, to do good sometime /

Accounted dangerous folly" (4.2.76–8). Macduff has been forced to deny his proper manly role of protecting his wife and family; Lady Macduff and her son, along with young Siward, have had to pay with their innocent lives the terrible price of Scotland's tyranny. In his frenzied attempt to prevent the fulfillment of the prophecy about Banquo's lineage inheriting the kingdom, Macbeth has, like King Herod, slaughtered much of the younger generation on whom the future depends. We can only hope that the stability to which Scotland returns after his death will be lasting. Banquo's line is to rule eventually and to produce a line of kings reaching down to the royal occupant to whom Shakespeare will present his play, but, when *Macbeth* ends, it is Malcolm who is king. The killing of a traitor (Macbeth) and the placing of his head on a pole replicate the play's beginning in the treason and beheading of the Thane of Cawdor—a gentleman on whom Duncan built "An absolute trust" (1.4.14). Most troublingly, the humanly representative nature of Macbeth's crime leaves us with little assurance that we could resist his temptation. The most that can be said is that wise and good persons such as Banquo and Macduff have learned to know the evil in themselves and to resist it as nobly as they can.

Along with its timeless interest in murder and the human conscience, *Macbeth* is an intensely political play. It surely was viewed as such when it was first produced in 1606–1607. The drunken porter in 2.3 seemingly refers to the infamous attempt to blow up the houses of Parliament known as the Gunpowder Plot of 1605, and to the subsequent trial of the Jesuit Henry Garnet, the notorious "equivicator," for his part in the conspiracy (2.3.8). Banquo fulfills a historical role as progenitor of the dynastic line that would lead eventually to James VI of Scotland, who had become James I of England in 1603. The pageant of *"eight Kings and Banquo last"* that Macbeth must witness on the occasion of his final visit to the Weird Sisters (4.1.111.1) ends with a *glass* or magic mirror showing many more kings bearing the appurtenances of royal office, including the "twofold balls and treble scepters" that seemingly refer to James's double coronation in 1603 as King of England and Scotland. James was keenly interested in witchcraft. Scotland was a constant worry on England's northern border, aligning itself with France, marauding across the English border, tearing itself apart through clan violence, and, from an English point of view, manifesting the kind of tyranny that the English especially feared. The Scotland of this play thus helps to define, largely by contrast, what is thought to be truly English. The English King who is described as doing "A most miraculous work" in curing "the evil," or scrofula, by his touch (4.3.147–8) suggests a flattering reference to James, who claimed this power of curing. This unnamed English king lends his support to the military attack against Macbeth through which the tyrant is finally over-

thrown. The play simultaneously incorporates an uneasy attitude of hostility toward Scotland along with a vision of union between the two countries that is brought about by the subjugation of Scotland to her southern neighbor. A rough kind of harmony is achieved out of disharmony. Macbeth's act of murderous regicide is answered by another regicide in the name of English law. The quandaries of such a resolution may point to the ambivalence that many English people felt about their odd ruler from the north, the man who came to be known as "the wisest fool in Christendom."

Macbeth is a difficult play to present on stage, at least according to stage tradition: ever since the early twentieth century, actors have referred to it superstitiously as "the Scottish play" as a way of avoiding bad luck that otherwise can hover menacingly over the acting company. Presumably this is a theatrical response to the play's dark probing of irrational magic, fatal determinism, and human frailty. Not coincidentally, perhaps, some of the greatest successes in performance have been on film. Akira Kurosawa's *Throne of Blood* (1957) retells the story of Macbeth, in black and white, as a devastating exploration of ambitious strife among Japanese warlords. Although the dialogue and characters' names of Shakespeare's play are altered throughout, this version captures magnificently the mysterious and malign intent of the prophetic figure Macbeth encounters in a forest, tempting him to evil by the ambiguous promises of future greatness. The forest itself is a striking presence in this film, invested as it is with supernatural terror in the midst of a thunderstorm. The Lady Asaji, wife to Washizu (the Macbeth figure), is horrifyingly obsessed with ambition for her husband; her seeming role as an obedient and decorously aristocratic Japanese wife accentuates the contrast between the surfaces of civilized behavior and the dark inner promptings of competitive self-assertion. A film version with Ian McKellen and Judi Dench as Macbeth and his wife, based on a stage version directed by Trevor Nunn (1976–1978) at Stratford-upon-Avon, London, and Newcastle-upon-Tyne, emphasizes the demonic in such a way as to give the Weird Sisters a real power that is both psychologically plausible and frighteningly irrational. Roman Polanski's film version (1971), though faulted for its sponsorship by Playboy Productions and its consequent flaunting of some grotesque nakedness, does successfully portray Macbeth and Lady Macbeth as a vitally young couple for whom sexuality is integral to their ambition. And of course there have been great stage productions, despite the shibboleth of the bad-luck legend, notably Glen Byam Shaw's production at Stratford-upon-Avon in 1955 starring Laurence Olivier and Vivien Leigh that invited admiration for husband and wife as magnificent, courageous, loyal, and of genuinely tragic stature even if fatally flawed by their hearkening to the voice of evil.

Macbeth

[*Dramatis Personae*

DUNCAN, *King of Scotland*
MALCOLM ⎫
DONALBAIN ⎭ *his sons*

MACBETH, *Thane of Glamis, later of Cawdor, later King of*
   Scotland
LADY MACBETH

BANQUO, *a thane of Scotland*
FLEANCE, *his son*
MACDUFF, *Thane of Fife*
LADY MACDUFF
SON *of Macduff and Lady Macduff*

LENNOX ⎫
ROSS ⎪
MENTEITH ⎬ *thanes and noblemen of Scotland*
ANGUS ⎪
CAITHNESS ⎭

SIWARD, *Earl of Northumberland*
YOUNG SIWARD, *his son*

SEYTON, *an officer attending Macbeth*
Another LORD
ENGLISH DOCTOR
SCOTTISH DOCTOR
GENTLEWOMAN *attending Lady Macbeth*
CAPTAIN *serving Duncan*
PORTER
OLD MAN
Three MURDERERS *of Banquo*
FIRST MURDERER *at Macduff's castle*
MESSENGER *to Lady Macbeth*
MESSENGER *to Lady Macduff*
SERVANT *to Macbeth*
SERVANT *to Lady Macbeth*
Three WITCHES *or* WEIRD SISTERS
HECATE
Three APPARITIONS

Lords, Gentlemen, Officers, Soldiers, Murderers,
   and Attendants

    SCENE: *Scotland; England*]

1.1

Thunder and lightning. Enter three Witches.

FIRST WITCH
  When shall we three meet again?
  In thunder, lightning, or in rain?
SECOND WITCH
  When the hurlyburly's done,
  When the battle's lost and won.
THIRD WITCH
  That will be ere the set of sun.

FIRST WITCH
  Where the place?
SECOND WITCH   Upon the heath.
THIRD WITCH
  There to meet with Macbeth.
FIRST WITCH   I come, Grimalkin!   8
SECOND WITCH   Paddock calls.   9
THIRD WITCH Anon.   10

1.1 Location: An open place.
3 hurlyburly tumult

8 Grimalkin i.e., gray cat, name of the witch's familiar—a demon or evil spirit supposed to answer a witch's call and to allow him or her to perform black magic. **9 Paddock** toad; also a familiar **10 Anon** At once, right away.

715

ALL
Fair is foul, and foul is fair.
Hover through the fog and filthy air.   *Exeunt.*

❖

1.2

Alarum within. Enter King [Duncan], Malcolm,
Donalbain, Lennox, with attendants, meeting a
bleeding Captain.

DUNCAN
What bloody man is that? He can report,
As seemeth by his plight, of the revolt
The newest state.

MALCOLM   This is the sergeant   3
Who like a good and hardy soldier fought
'Gainst my captivity.—Hail, brave friend!
Say to the King the knowledge of the broil   6
As thou didst leave it.

CAPTAIN   Doubtful it stood,
As two spent swimmers that do cling together   8
And choke their art. The merciless Macdonwald—   9
Worthy to be a rebel, for to that   10
The multiplying villainies of nature   11
Do swarm upon him—from the Western Isles   12
Of kerns and gallowglasses is supplied;   13
And Fortune, on his damnèd quarrel smiling,   14
Showed like a rebel's whore. But all's too weak; 15
For brave Macbeth—well he deserves that name—   16
Disdaining Fortune, with his brandished steel,
Which smoked with bloody execution,
Like valor's minion carved out his passage   19
Till he faced the slave,   20
Which ne'er shook hands nor bade farewell to him 21
Till he unseamed him from the nave to th' chops, 22
And fixed his head upon our battlements.

DUNCAN
Oh, valiant cousin, worthy gentleman!   24

CAPTAIN
As whence the sun 'gins his reflection   25
Shipwrecking storms and direful thunders break, 26
So from that spring whence comfort seemed to come 27
Discomfort swells. Mark, King of Scotland, mark. 28
No sooner justice had, with valor armed,
Compelled these skipping kerns to trust their heels 30
But the Norweyan lord, surveying vantage,   31
With furbished arms and new supplies of men,
Began a fresh assault.

DUNCAN
Dismayed not this our captains, Macbeth and
Banquo?

CAPTAIN
Yes, as sparrows eagles, or the hare the lion.   35
If I say sooth, I must report they were   36
As cannons overcharged with double cracks,   37
So they doubly redoubled strokes upon the foe.
Except they meant to bathe in reeking wounds   39
Or memorize another Golgotha,   40
I cannot tell.
But I am faint. My gashes cry for help.

DUNCAN
So well thy words become thee as thy wounds;
They smack of honor both.—Go get him surgeons.
          [Exit Captain, attended.]

Enter Ross and Angus.

Who comes here?

MALCOLM   The worthy Thane of Ross.   45

LENNOX   What a haste looks through his eyes!
So should he look that seems to speak things strange. 47

ROSS   God save the King!

DUNCAN   Whence cam'st thou, worthy thane?

ROSS   From Fife, great King,
Where the Norweyan banners flout the sky   51
And fan our people cold.   52
Norway himself, with terrible numbers,   53
Assisted by that most disloyal traitor,
The Thane of Cawdor, began a dismal conflict,   55
Till that Bellona's bridegroom, lapped in proof, 56
Confronted him with self-comparisons,   57

1.2. Location: A camp near Forres.
0.1 *Alarum* trumpet call to arms   **3 newest state** latest news.
sergeant i.e., staff officer. (There may be no inconsistency with his
rank of "captain" in the stage direction and speech prefixes in the
Folio.)   **6 broil** battle   **8 spent** tired out   **9 choke their art** render
their skill in swimming useless.   **9–13 The merciless . . . supplied**
The merciless Macdonwald—worthy of the hated name of rebel, for
in the cause of rebellion an ever-increasing number of villainous persons and unnatural qualities swarm about him like vermin—is joined
by light-armed Irish footsoldiers and ax-armed horsemen from the
western islands of Scotland (the Hebrides and perhaps Ireland)
14–15 And Fortune . . . whore i.e., Fortune, proverbially a false
strumpet, smiles at first on Macdonwald's damned rebellion but
deserts him in his hour of need.   **16 well . . . name** well he deserves a
name that is synonymous with "brave"   **19 minion** darling. (Macbeth is Valor's darling, not Fortune's.)   **20 the slave** i.e., Macdonwald   **21 Which . . . to him** i.e., Macbeth paused for no ceremonious
greeting or farewell to Macdonwald.   **22 nave** navel.   **chops** jaws
24 cousin kinsman

25–8 As . . . swells Just as terrible storms at sea arise out of the east,
from the place where the sun first shows itself in the seeming comfort
of the dawn, even thus did a new military threat come on the heels of
the seeming good news of Macdonwald's execution.   **30 skipping**
(1) lightly armed, quick at maneuvering (2) skittish   **31 surveying**
vantage seeing an opportunity   **35 Yes . . . eagles** Yes, about as much
as sparrows terrify eagles. (Said ironically.)   **36 say sooth** tell the
truth   **37 cracks** charges of explosive   **39 Except** Unless   **40 memo-**
rize make memorable or famous.   **Golgotha** "place of a skull,"
where Christ was crucified. (Mark 15:22.)   **45 Thane** Scottish title of
honor, roughly equivalent to "Earl"   **47 seems to** seems about to
51 flout mock, insult   **52 fan . . . cold** fan cold fear into our troops.
53 Norway The King of Norway.   **terrible numbers** terrifying numbers of troops   **55 dismal** ominous   **56 Till . . . proof** i.e., until Macbeth, clad in well-tested armor. (Bellona was the Roman goddess of
war.)   **57 him** i.e., the King of Norway.   **self-comparisons** i.e.,
matching counterthrusts

Point against point, rebellious arm 'gainst arm,
Curbing his lavish spirit; and to conclude,
The victory fell on us.

DUNCAN   Great happiness!

ROSS   That now
Sweno, the Norways' king, craves composition;   62
Nor would we deign him burial of his men
Till he disbursèd at Saint Colme's Inch   64
Ten thousand dollars to our general use.   65

DUNCAN
No more that Thane of Cawdor shall deceive
Our bosom interest. Go pronounce his present death,   67
And with his former title greet Macbeth.

ROSS   I'll see it done.

DUNCAN
What he hath lost noble Macbeth hath won.
                                              Exeunt.

❧

1.3

Thunder. Enter the three Witches.

FIRST WITCH   Where hast thou been, sister?

SECOND WITCH   Killing swine.

THIRD WITCH   Sister, where thou?

FIRST WITCH
A sailor's wife had chestnuts in her lap,
And munched, and munched, and munched. "Give
    me," quoth I.
"Aroint thee, witch!" the rump-fed runnion cries.   6
Her husband's to Aleppo gone, master o'th' *Tiger*;   7
But in a sieve I'll thither sail,
And like a rat without a tail   9
I'll do, I'll do, and I'll do.   10

SECOND WITCH
I'll give thee a wind.

FIRST WITCH
Thou'rt kind.

THIRD WITCH
And I another.

FIRST WITCH
I myself have all the other,   14
And the very ports they blow,   15
All the quarters that they know   16
I'th' shipman's card.   17
I'll drain him dry as hay.   18

Sleep shall neither night nor day
Hang upon his penthouse lid.   20
He shall live a man forbid.   21
Weary sev'nnights nine times nine   22
Shall he dwindle, peak, and pine.   23
Though his bark cannot be lost,
Yet it shall be tempest-tossed.
Look what I have.

SECOND WITCH   Show me, show me.

FIRST WITCH
Here I have a pilot's thumb,
Wrecked as homeward he did come.   *Drum within.*

THIRD WITCH
A drum, a drum!
Macbeth doth come.

ALL [*dancing in a circle*]
The Weird Sisters, hand in hand,   32
Posters of the sea and land,   33
Thus do go about, about,
Thrice to thine, and thrice to mine,
And thrice again, to make up nine.
Peace! The charm's wound up.

Enter Macbeth and Banquo.

MACBETH
So foul and fair a day I have not seen.

BANQUO
How far is't called to Forres?—What are these,   39
So withered and so wild in their attire,
That look not like th'inhabitants o'th'earth
And yet are on't?—Live you? Or are you aught
That man may question? You seem to understand me;
By each at once her choppy finger laying   44
Upon her skinny lips. You should be women,
And yet your beards forbid me to interpret
That you are so.

MACBETH   Speak, if you can. What are you?

FIRST WITCH
All hail, Macbeth! Hail to thee, Thane of Glamis!

SECOND WITCH
All hail, Macbeth! Hail to thee, Thane of Cawdor!

THIRD WITCH
All hail, Macbeth, that shalt be king hereafter!

BANQUO
Good sir, why do you start and seem to fear
Things that do sound so fair?—I'th' name of truth,
Are ye fantastical or that indeed   53
Which outwardly ye show? My noble partner   54
You greet with present grace and great prediction   55
Of noble having and of royal hope,
That he seems rapt withal. To me you speak not.   57
If you can look into the seeds of time

---

62 **Norways'** Norwegians'.   **composition** agreement, treaty of peace
64 **Saint Colme's Inch** Inchcolm, the Isle of St. Columba in the Firth
of Forth   65 **dollars** Spanish or Dutch coins   67 **Our** (The royal
"we.")   **bosom** close and intimate.   **present** immediate
1.3. Location: A heath near Forres.
6 **Aroint thee** Begone.   **rump-fed runnion** fat-rumped baggage
7 ***Tiger*** (A ship's name.)   **9–10 like . . . do** (Suggestive of the witches'
deformity and sexual insatiability. Witches were thought to seduce
men sexually. *Do* means (1) act (2) perform sexually.)   **14–17 I . . .
card** I can summon all other winds, wherever they blow and from
whatever *quarter* in the shipman's compass card.   **18 I'll . . . hay**
(With a suggestion of sexually draining the seaman's semen.)

20 **penthouse lid** i.e., eyelid (which projects out over the eye like a
penthouse or slope-roofed structure).   **21 forbid** accursed.   **22 sev'n-
nights** weeks   **23 peak** grow peaked or thin   **32 Weird Sisters**
women connected with fate or destiny; also women having a mysterious or unearthly, uncanny appearance   **33 Posters of** swift travelers
over   **39 is't called** is it said to be   **44 choppy** chapped   **53 fantastical** creatures of fantasy or imagination   **54 show** appear.   **55 grace**
honor   **57 rapt withal** entranced.

And say which grain will grow and which will not,
Speak then to me, who neither beg nor fear   60
Your favors nor your hate.   61

FIRST WITCH   Hail!

SECOND WITCH   Hail!

THIRD WITCH   Hail!

FIRST WITCH
Lesser than Macbeth, and greater.

SECOND WITCH
Not so happy, yet much happier.   66

THIRD WITCH
Thou shalt get kings, though thou be none.   67
So all hail, Macbeth and Banquo!

FIRST WITCH
Banquo and Macbeth, all hail!

MACBETH
Stay, you imperfect speakers, tell me more!   70
By Sinel's death I know I am Thane of Glamis,   71
But how of Cawdor? The Thane of Cawdor lives
A prosperous gentleman; and to be king
Stands not within the prospect of belief,
No more than to be Cawdor. Say from whence   75
You owe this strange intelligence, or why   76
Upon this blasted heath you stop our way   77
With such prophetic greeting? Speak, I charge you.
                                    Witches vanish.

BANQUO
The earth hath bubbles, as the water has,
And these are of them. Whither are they vanished?

MACBETH
Into the air; and what seemed corporal melted,   81
As breath into the wind. Would they had stayed!

BANQUO
Were such things here as we do speak about?
Or have we eaten on the insane root   84
That takes the reason prisoner?

MACBETH
Your children shall be kings.

BANQUO   You shall be king.

MACBETH
And Thane of Cawdor too. Went it not so?

BANQUO
To th' selfsame tune and words.—Who's here?

        Enter Ross and Angus.

ROSS
The King hath happily received, Macbeth,
The news of thy success; and when he reads   90
Thy personal venture in the rebels' fight,   91
His wonders and his praises do contend   92
Which should be thine or his. Silenced with that,   93
In viewing o'er the rest o'th' selfsame day

He finds thee in the stout Norweyan ranks,   95
Nothing afeard of what thyself didst make,   96
Strange images of death. As thick as tale   97
Came post with post, and every one did bear   98
Thy praises in his kingdom's great defense,
And poured them down before him.

ANGUS   We are sent
To give thee from our royal master thanks,
Only to herald thee into his sight,
Not pay thee.

ROSS
And, for an earnest of a greater honor,   104
He bade me, from him, call thee Thane of Cawdor;
In which addition, hail, most worthy thane,   106
For it is thine.

BANQUO   What, can the devil speak true?

MACBETH
The Thane of Cawdor lives. Why do you dress me
In borrowed robes?

ANGUS   Who was the thane lives yet,   109
But under heavy judgment bears that life
Which he deserves to lose. Whether he was combined   111
With those of Norway, or did line the rebel   112
With hidden help and vantage, or that with both
He labored in his country's wrack, I know not;   114
But treasons capital, confessed and proved,   115
Have overthrown him.

MACBETH [*aside*]   Glamis, and Thane of Cawdor!
The greatest is behind. [*To Ross and Angus*] Thanks for
    your pains.   117
[*Aside to Banquo*] Do you not hope your children shall
    be kings
When those that gave the Thane of Cawdor to me
Promised no less to them?

BANQUO [*to Macbeth*]   That, trusted home,   120
Might yet enkindle you unto the crown,
Besides the Thane of Cawdor. But 'tis strange;
And oftentimes to win us to our harm
The instruments of darkness tell us truths,
Win us with honest trifles, to betray 's
In deepest consequence.—   126
Cousins, a word, I pray you.   127
        [*He converses apart with Ross and Angus.*]

MACBETH [*aside*]   Two truths are told,
As happy prologues to the swelling act   129
Of the imperial theme.—I thank you, gentlemen.
[*Aside*] This supernatural soliciting   131
Cannot be ill, cannot be good. If ill,
Why hath it given me earnest of success

60–1 beg . . . hate beg your favors nor fear your hate.   66 happy fortunate   67 get beget   70 imperfect cryptic   71 Sinel's (Sinel was
Macbeth's father.)   75–6 Say . . . intelligence Say from what source
you have this disturbing information   77 blasted blighted   81 corporal corporeal   84 on of.   insane root root causing insanity; variously identified   90–3 and when . . . his and when he reads of your
extraordinary valor in fighting the rebels, he concludes that your
wondrous deeds outdo any praise he could offer.

95 stout haughty, determined, valiant   96 Nothing not at all
97–8 As . . . with post As fast as could be told, i.e., counted, came
messenger after messenger. (Unless the text should be amended to
"As thick as hail.")   104 earnest token payment   106 addition title
109 Who He who   111 combined confederate   112 line the rebel
reinforce Macdonwald   114 in . . . wrack to bring about his country's
ruin   115 capital deserving death   117 The greatest is behind either
(1) Two of the three prophecies (and thus the greatest number of
them) have already been fulfilled, or (2) The greatest one, the kingship, is still to come.   120 home all the way   126 In deepest consequence in the profoundly important sequel.   127 Cousins i.e., Fellow
lords   129 swelling act stately drama   131 soliciting tempting

Commencing in a truth? I am Thane of Cawdor.
If good, why do I yield to that suggestion
Whose horrid image doth unfix my hair   136
And make my seated heart knock at my ribs,
Against the use of nature? Present fears   138
Are less than horrible imaginings.
My thought, whose murder yet is but fantastical,   140
Shakes so my single state of man   141
That function is smothered in surmise,   142
And nothing is but what is not.   143

BANQUO   Look how our partner's rapt.

MACBETH [*aside*]
If chance will have me king, why, chance may crown
    me
Without my stir.

BANQUO   New honors come upon him,   146
Like our strange garments, cleave not to their mold   147
But with the aid of use.

MACBETH [*aside*]   Come what come may,   148
Time and the hour runs through the roughest day.   149

BANQUO
Worthy Macbeth, we stay upon your leisure.   150

MACBETH
Give me your favor. My dull brain was wrought   151
With things forgotten. Kind gentlemen, your pains
Are registered where every day I turn   153
The leaf to read them. Let us toward the King.
[*Aside to Banquo*]   Think upon what hath chanced,
    and at more time,   155
The interim having weighed it, let us speak   156
Our free hearts each to other.   157

BANQUO [*to Macbeth*]   Very gladly.

MACBETH [*to Banquo*]   Till then, enough.—Come, friends.
                                                    Exeunt.

❧

1.4

Flourish. Enter King [Duncan], Lennox, Malcolm,
Donalbain, and attendants.

DUNCAN
Is execution done on Cawdor? Are not
Those in commission yet returned?

MALCOLM   My liege,   2
They are not yet come back. But I have spoke

With one that saw him die, who did report
That very frankly he confessed his treasons,
Implored Your Highness' pardon, and set forth
A deep repentance. Nothing in his life
Became him like the leaving it. He died   8
As one that had been studied in his death   9
To throw away the dearest thing he owed   10
As 'twere a careless trifle.

DUNCAN   There's no art   11
To find the mind's construction in the face.
He was a gentleman on whom I built
An absolute trust.

Enter Macbeth, Banquo, Ross, and Angus.

                    O worthiest cousin!
The sin of my ingratitude even now
Was heavy on me. Thou art so far before   16
That swiftest wing of recompense is slow
To overtake thee. Would thou hadst less deserved,
That the proportion both of thanks and payment   19
Might have been mine! Only I have left to say,   20
More is thy due than more than all can pay.

MACBETH
The service and the loyalty I owe,
In doing it, pays itself. Your Highness' part
Is to receive our duties; and our duties
Are to your throne and state children and servants,   25
Which do but what they should by doing everything
Safe toward your love and honor.

DUNCAN   Welcome hither!   27
I have begun to plant thee, and will labor
To make thee full of growing. Noble Banquo,
That hast no less deserved, nor must be known
No less to have done so, let me infold thee
And hold thee to my heart.

BANQUO   There if I grow,
The harvest is your own.

DUNCAN   My plenteous joys,
Wanton in fullness, seek to hide themselves   34
In drops of sorrow.—Sons, kinsmen, thanes,
And you whose places are the nearest, know
We will establish our estate upon   37
Our eldest, Malcolm, whom we name hereafter
The Prince of Cumberland; which honor must   39
Not unaccompanied invest him only,   40
But signs of nobleness, like stars, shall shine
On all deservers.—From hence to Inverness,   42
And bind us further to you.   43

---

136 **unfix my hair** make my hair stand on end   138 **use** custom.
fears things feared   140 **whose . . . fantastical** in which the conception of murder is merely imaginary at this point   141 **single . . . man**
weak human condition   142 **function** normal power of action.
surmise speculation, imaginings   143 **And . . . not** and nothing else
has any reality for me.   146 **stir** bestirring (myself).   **come** i.e.,
which have come   147–8 **cleave . . . use** do not take the shape of the
wearer until often worn. (Macbeth is often connected in the text with
clothes that don't really fit him.)   149 **Time . . . day** time moves
relentlessly on, no matter what else happens.   150 **stay** wait
151 **favor** pardon.   **wrought** shaped, preoccupied   153 **registered**
recorded (in my memory)   155 **at more time** at a time of greater
leisure   156 **weighed it** given oportunity for reflection on its meaning   157 **Our free hearts** our hearts freely
1.4. Location: Forres. The palace.
2 **in commission** having warrant (to see to the execution of Cawdor)

8 **Became** graced, befitted   9 **been studied** made it his study
10 **owed** owned   11 **careless** uncared for   16 **before** ahead (in
deserving)   19–20 **That . . . mine** that I might have thanked and
rewarded you in ample proportion to your worth.   25 **Are . . . servants** are like children and servants in relation to your throne and
dignity, existing only to serve you   27 **Safe . . . honor** to safeguard
you whom we love and honor.   34 **Wanton** unrestrained   37 **We**
(The royal "we.")   **establish our estate** fix the succession of our state
39 **Prince of Cumberland** title of the heir apparent to the Scottish
throne   40 **Not . . . only** not be bestowed on Malcolm alone; other
deserving nobles are to share honors   42 **Inverness** the seat or location of Macbeth's castle, Dunsinane   43 **bind . . . you** put me further
in your (Macbeth's) obligation by your hospitality.

MACBETH
　　The rest is labor which is not used for you.   44
　　I'll be myself the harbinger and make joyful   45
　　The hearing of my wife with your approach;
　　So humbly take my leave.
DUNCAN   My worthy Cawdor!
MACBETH [aside]
　　The Prince of Cumberland! That is a step
　　On which I must fall down or else o'erleap,
　　For in my way it lies. Stars, hide your fires;   50
　　Let not light see my black and deep desires.
　　The eye wink at the hand; yet let that be   52
　　Which the eye fears, when it is done, to see.   Exit.   53
DUNCAN
　　True, worthy Banquo. He is full so valiant,   54
　　And in his commendations I am fed;   55
　　It is a banquet to me. Let's after him,
　　Whose care is gone before to bid us welcome.
　　It is a peerless kinsman.   Flourish. Exeunt.

♣

1.5

Enter Macbeth's Wife, alone, with a letter.

LADY MACBETH [*reads*] "They met me in the day of success; and I have learned by the perfect'st report they   2
have more in them than mortal knowledge. When I
burnt in desire to question them further, they made
themselves air, into which they vanished. Whiles I
stood rapt in the wonder of it came missives from the   6
King, who all-hailed me 'Thane of Cawdor,' by which
title, before, these Weird Sisters saluted me, and referred me to the coming on of time with 'Hail, king
that shalt be!' This have I thought good to deliver thee,   10
my dearest partner of greatness, that thou mightst not
lose the dues of rejoicing by being ignorant of what
greatness is promised thee. Lay it to thy heart, and
farewell."
　　Glamis thou art, and Cawdor, and shalt be
　　What thou art promised. Yet do I fear thy nature;   16
　　It is too full o'th' milk of human kindness
　　To catch the nearest way. Thou wouldst be great,
　　Art not without ambition, but without
　　The illness should attend it. What thou wouldst
　　　highly,   20
　　That wouldst thou holily; wouldst not play false,

And yet wouldst wrongly win. Thou'dst have, great
　　Glamis,
That which cries "Thus thou must do," if thou have it,   23
And that which rather thou dost fear to do   24
Than wishest should be undone. Hie thee hither,   25
That I may pour my spirits in thine ear
And chastise with the valor of my tongue
All that impedes thee from the golden round   28
Which fate and metaphysical aid doth seem   29
To have thee crowned withal.

Enter [a servant as] Messenger.

　　　　　　　　　What is your tidings?   30
MESSENGER
　　The King comes here tonight.
LADY MACBETH   Thou'rt mad to say it!
　　Is not thy master with him, who, were't so,
　　Would have informed for preparation?   33
MESSENGER
　　So please you, it is true. Our thane is coming.
　　One of my fellows had the speed of him,   35
　　Who, almost dead for breath, had scarcely more
　　Than would make up his message.
LADY MACBETH   Give him tending;   37
　　He brings great news.   *Exit Messenger.*
　　　　　　　　　　The raven himself is hoarse
　　That croaks the fatal entrance of Duncan
　　Under my battlements. Come, you spirits
　　That tend on mortal thoughts, unsex me here   41
　　And fill me from the crown to the toe top-full
　　Of direst cruelty! Make thick my blood;
　　Stop up th'access and passage to remorse,   44
　　That no compunctious visitings of nature   45
　　Shake my fell purpose, nor keep peace between   46
　　Th'effect and it! Come to my woman's breasts   47
　　And take my milk for gall, you murd'ring ministers,   48
　　Wherever in your sightless substances   49
　　You wait on nature's mischief! Come, thick night,   50
　　And pall thee in the dunnest smoke of hell,   51
　　That my keen knife see not the wound it makes,
　　Nor heaven peep through the blanket of the dark
　　To cry "Hold, hold!"   54

Enter Macbeth.

　　　　　　　　Great Glamis! Worthy Cawdor!
　　Greater than both by the all-hail hereafter!
　　Thy letters have transported me beyond   56

---

44 The rest . . . you All activity not devoted to serving you is mere
tediousness and hard work.   **45 harbinger** forerunner, messenger
50 in my way it lies (The monarchy was not hereditary, and Macbeth
had a right to believe that he himself might be chosen as Duncan's
successor; he here questions whether he will interfere with the
course of events.)   **52–3 The eye . . . see** Let the eye shut itself and
not see the hand's deed; yet when the deed is done, let it be fearful to
behold.   **54 full so valiant** fully as valiant as you say. (Apparently,
Duncan and Banquo have been conversing privately on this subject
during Macbeth's soliloquy.)   **55 in . . . fed** it nourishes me to hear
him praised
1.5. Location: Inverness. Macbeth's castle.
2 perfect'st most accurate   **6 missives** messengers   **10 deliver thee**
inform you of   **16 do I fear** I mistrust   **20 illness** evil (that).
highly greatly

23 have are to have, want to have   **24–5 And that . . . undone** i.e.,
and the thing you ambitiously crave frightens you more in terms of
the means needed to achieve it than in the idea of having it; if you
could have it without those means, you certainly wouldn't wish it
undone.   **25 Hie** Hasten   **28 round** crown   **29 metaphysical** supernatural   **30 withal** with.   **33 informed for preparation** i.e., sent me
word so that I might get things ready.   **35 had . . . of** outstripped
37 Give him tending Tend to his needs   **41 tend . . . thoughts** attend
on, act as the instruments of, deadly or murderous thoughts
44 remorse pity   **45 nature** natural feelings   **46 fell** fierce, cruel
46–7 nor . . . and it nor intervene between my *fell purpose* and its
accomplishment.   **48 for gall** in exchange for gall, or perhaps *as* gall.
ministers agents   **49 sightless** invisible   **50 You . . . mischief** you
aid and abet the wickedness of human nature.   **51 pall** envelop.
dunnest darkest   **54 Hold** Stop   **56 letters have** i.e., letter has

This ignorant present, and I feel now
The future in the instant.

MACBETH   My dearest love,
Duncan comes here tonight.

LADY MACBETH   And when goes hence?

MACBETH
Tomorrow, as he purposes.

LADY MACBETH   Oh, never
Shall sun that morrow see!
Your face, my thane, is as a book where men
May read strange matters. To beguile the time,   63
Look like the time; bear welcome in your eye,   64
Your hand, your tongue. Look like th'innocent flower,
But be the serpent under't. He that's coming
Must be provided for; and you shall put
This night's great business into my dispatch,   68
Which shall to all our nights and days to come
Give solely sovereign sway and masterdom.

MACBETH
We will speak further.

LADY MACBETH   Only look up clear.   71
To alter favor ever is to fear.   72
Leave all the rest to me.   *Exeunt.*

❖

1.6

Hautboys and torches. Enter King [Duncan],
Malcolm, Donalbain, Banquo, Lennox, Macduff,
Ross, Angus, and attendants.

DUNCAN
This castle hath a pleasant seat. The air   1
Nimbly and sweetly recommends itself
Unto our gentle senses.

BANQUO   This guest of summer,   3
The temple-haunting martlet, does approve   4
By his loved mansionry that the heaven's breath   5
Smells wooingly here. No jutty, frieze,   6
Buttress, nor coign of vantage but this bird   7
Hath made his pendent bed and procreant cradle.   8
Where they most breed and haunt, I have observed
The air is delicate.

Enter Lady [Macbeth].

DUNCAN   See, see, our honored hostess!
The love that follows us sometime is our trouble,   11
Which still we thank as love. Herein I teach you   12

How you shall bid God 'ild us for your pains,   13
And thank us for your trouble.

LADY MACBETH   All our service
In every point twice done, and then done double,
Were poor and single business to contend   16
Against those honors deep and broad wherewith   17
Your Majesty loads our house. For those of old,   18
And the late dignities heaped up to them,   19
We rest your hermits.

DUNCAN   Where's the Thane of Cawdor?   20
We coursed him at the heels, and had a purpose   21
To be his purveyor; but he rides well,   22
And his great love, sharp as his spur, hath holp him 23
To his home before us. Fair and noble hostess,
We are your guest tonight.

LADY MACBETH   Your servants ever   25
Have theirs, themselves, and what is theirs in compt 26
To make their audit at Your Highness' pleasure,   27
Still to return your own.

DUNCAN   Give me your hand.   28
Conduct me to mine host. We love him highly,
And shall continue our graces towards him.
By your leave, hostess.   *Exeunt.*

❖

1.7

Hautboys. Torches. Enter a sewer, and divers
servants with dishes and service, [and pass] over
the stage. Then enter Macbeth.

MACBETH
If it were done when 'tis done, then 'twere well
It were done quickly. If th'assassination   2
Could trammel up the consequence, and catch   3
With his surcease success—that but this blow   4
Might be the be-all and the end-all!—here,   5
But here, upon this bank and shoal of time,
We'd jump the life to come. But in these cases   7

---

13 bid . . . pains ask God to reward me for the trouble I'm giving you. (This is said in the same gently jocose spirit as lines 11–12.) **'ild** yield, repay **16–17 Were . . . Against** would be poor and small when compared with **18–20 For . . . hermits** In gratitude for the dignities heaped upon us in former days and still others more recently added to them, we are your thankful worshipers who pray for you like hermits or beadsmen. **21 coursed** followed (as in a hunt) **22 purveyor** an officer sent ahead to provide for entertainment; here, forerunner **23 holp** helped **25 We** (the royal "we," also in lines 13–14 and 29) **25–8 Your . . . own** Those who serve you hold their own servants, themselves, and all their possessions in trust from you, and can render an account whenever you wish, ready always to render back to you what is yours. (A feudal concept of obligation.)
1.7. Location: Macbeth's castle; an inner courtyard.
0.1 sewer chief waiter, butler **2–4 If . . . success** i.e., If only the assassination of Duncan could proceed without further consequences and end the matter with the completion of the deed itself. (To *trammel* is to bind up or entangle in a net; *surcease* means "cessation"; *success* means "what succeeds or follows.") **4 that but** so that only **5 here** in this world **7 jump** risk. (But imaging the physical act is characteristic of Macbeth; compare this with line 27.)

63–4 To beguile . . . time To deceive everyone, look the way people expect you to look **68 dispatch** management **71–2 Only . . . fear** Whatever else you do, keep a cheerful countenance. To alter one's countenance is to betray a guilty conscience.
1.6. Location: Before Macbeth's castle.
0.1 Hautboys oboelike instruments **1 seat** site. **3 gentle** (1) noble (2) refined (by the delicate air) **4–5 The . . . mansionry** The house martin, that loves to nest in churches, proves by his devoted nest building **6 jutty** projection of wall or building **7 coign of vantage** convenient corner, i.e., for nesting **8 pendent** hanging, suspended. **procreant** for breeding **11–12 The love . . . love** The love that sometimes forces itself inconveniently upon us we still appreciate, since it is meant as love. (Duncan is graciously suggesting that his visit is a bother, but, he hopes, a welcome one.)

We still have judgment here, that we but teach 8
Bloody instructions, which, being taught, return 9
To plague th'inventor. This evenhanded justice 10
Commends th'ingredience of our poisoned chalice 11
To our own lips. He's here in double trust:
First, as I am his kinsman and his subject,
Strong both against the deed; then, as his host,
Who should against his murderer shut the door,
Not bear the knife myself. Besides, this Duncan
Hath borne his faculties so meek, hath been 17
So clear in his great office, that his virtues 18
Will plead like angels, trumpet-tongued, against
The deep damnation of his taking-off; 20
And Pity, like a naked newborn babe
Striding the blast, or heaven's cherubin, horsed 22
Upon the sightless couriers of the air, 23
Shall blow the horrid deed in every eye,
That tears shall drown the wind. I have no spur 25
To prick the sides of my intent, but only
Vaulting ambition, which o'erleaps itself
And falls on th'other— 28

Enter Lady [Macbeth].

How now, what news?
LADY MACBETH
He has almost supped. Why have you left the
    chamber?
MACBETH
Hath he asked for me?
LADY MACBETH   Know you not he has?
MACBETH
We will proceed no further in this business.
He hath honored me of late, and I have bought 33
Golden opinions from all sorts of people,
Which would be worn now in their newest gloss, 35
Not cast aside so soon.
LADY MACBETH   Was the hope drunk
Wherein you dressed yourself? Hath it slept since?
And wakes it now, to look so green and pale 38
At what it did so freely? From this time
Such I account thy love. Art thou afeard
To be the same in thine own act and valor
As thou art in desire? Wouldst thou have that
Which thou esteem'st the ornament of life, 43
And live a coward in thine own esteem,
Letting "I dare not" wait upon "I would," 45

Like the poor cat i'th'adage?
MACBETH   Prithee, peace! 46
I dare do all that may become a man;
Who dares do more is none.
LADY MACBETH   What beast was't, then,
That made you break this enterprise to me? 49
When you durst do it, then you were a man;
And, to be more than what you were, you would
Be so much more the man. Nor time nor place 52
Did then adhere, and yet you would make both. 53
They have made themselves, and that their fitness
    now 54
Does unmake you. I have given suck, and know
How tender 'tis to love the babe that milks me;
I would, while it was smiling in my face,
Have plucked my nipple from his boneless gums
And dashed the brains out, had I so sworn as you
Have done to this.
MACBETH   If we should fail?
LADY MACBETH   We fail?
But screw your courage to the sticking place 61
And we'll not fail. When Duncan is asleep—
Whereto the rather shall his day's hard journey
Soundly invite him—his two chamberlains 64
Will I with wine and wassail so convince 65
That memory, the warder of the brain, 66
Shall be a fume, and the receipt of reason 67
A limbeck only. When in swinish sleep 68
Their drenchèd natures lies as in a death, 69
What cannot you and I perform upon
Th'unguarded Duncan? What not put upon
His spongy officers, who shall bear the guilt 72
Of our great quell?
MACBETH   Bring forth men-children only! 73
For thy undaunted mettle should compose 74
Nothing but males. Will it not be received, 75
When we have marked with blood those sleepy two
Of his own chamber and used their very daggers,
That they have done't?
LADY MACBETH   Who dares receive it other, 78
As we shall make our griefs and clamor roar 79
Upon his death?
MACBETH   I am settled, and bend up 80
Each corporal agent to this terrible feat. 81

8–10 We . . . th'inventor i.e., we still have punishment for crime in
this world, whereby our bloody acts establish guilty precedents and
thereby invite the just reciprocity of punishing blood with blood.
11 Commends presents.   th'ingredience the contents of a mixture
17 faculties powers of office   18 clear free of taint   20 taking-off
murder   22 Striding the blast bestriding the tempest. (Putti and
cherubs are often portrayed this way in Renaissance graphic arts.)
23 sightless couriers invisible steeds or runners, i.e., the winds
25 tears . . . wind (Showers of rain were popularly supposed to still
the wind.)   28 th'other the other side. (The image is of a horseman
vaulting into his saddle and ignominiously falling on the opposite
side.)   33 bought acquired (by bravery in battle)   35 would ought
to, should   38 green sickly   43 the ornament of life i.e., the crown
45 wait upon accompany, always follow

46 adage (i.e., "The cat would eat fish but she will not wet her feet.")
49 break broach   52 Nor Neither   53 adhere agree, suit.   would
wanted to   54 that their fitness that very suitability of time and
place   61 But Only.   the sticking place the notch into which is fitted
the string of a crossbow cranked taut for shooting   64 chamberlains
attendants on the bedchamber   65 wassail carousal, drink.
convince overpower   66–8 warder . . . only (The brain was thought
to be divided into three ventricles: imagination in front, memory at
the back, and between them the seat of reason. The fumes of wine,
arising from the stomach, would deaden memory and judgment.)
67 receipt receptacle, ventricle   68 limbeck device for distilling liquids   69 drenchèd drowned (in wine)   72 spongy soaked, drunken
73 quell murder.   74 mettle (the same word as *metal*): substance,
temperament   75 received i.e., as truth   78 other otherwise
79 As inasmuch as   80–1 bend up . . . agent harness and direct
every part of me

Away, and mock the time with fairest show.   82

False face must hide what the false heart doth know.

Exeunt.

❧

2.1

Enter Banquo, and Fleance, with a torch before him.

BANQUO   How goes the night, boy?

FLEANCE

The moon is down. I have not heard the clock.

BANQUO

And she goes down at twelve.

FLEANCE   I take't, 'tis later, sir.

BANQUO

Hold, take my sword. [*He gives him his sword.*] There's

husbandry in heaven;   4

Their candles are all out. Take thee that too.

                    [*He gives him his belt and dagger.*]

A heavy summons lies like lead upon me,   6

And yet I would not sleep. Merciful powers,   7

Restrain in me the cursèd thoughts that nature

Gives way to in repose!

Enter Macbeth, and a Servant with a torch.

Give me my sword. Who's there? [*He takes his sword.*]

MACBETH   A friend.

BANQUO

What, sir, not yet at rest? The King's abed.

He hath been in unusual pleasure,

And sent forth great largess to your offices.   14

This diamond he greets your wife withal,

By the name of most kind hostess, and shut up   16

In measureless content.   [*He gives a diamond.*]

MACBETH   Being unprepared,   17

Our will became the servant to defect,   18

Which else should free have wrought.   19

BANQUO   All's well.

I dreamt last night of the three Weird Sisters.

To you they have showed some truth.

MACBETH   I think not of them.

Yet, when we can entreat an hour to serve,

We would spend it in some words upon that business,

If you would grant the time.

BANQUO   At your kind'st leisure.

MACBETH

If you shall cleave to my consent when 'tis,   26

It shall make honor for you.

BANQUO   So I lose none   27

In seeking to augment it, but still keep

My bosom franchised and allegiance clear,   29

I shall be counseled.

MACBETH   Good repose the while!   30

BANQUO   Thanks, sir. The like to you.

Exit Banquo [*with Fleance*].

MACBETH [*to Servant*]

Go bid thy mistress, when my drink is ready,   32

She strike upon the bell. Get thee to bed.

Exit [*Servant*].

Is this a dagger which I see before me,

The handle toward my hand? Come, let me clutch

thee.

I have thee not, and yet I see thee still.

Art thou not, fatal vision, sensible   37

To feeling as to sight? Or art thou but

A dagger of the mind, a false creation,

Proceeding from the heat-oppressèd brain?   40

I see thee yet, in form as palpable

As this which now I draw.   [*He draws a dagger.*]

Thou marshall'st me the way that I was going,   43

And such an instrument I was to use.

Mine eyes are made the fools o'th'other senses,

Or else worth all the rest. I see thee still,

And on thy blade and dudgeon gouts of blood,   47

Which was not so before. There's no such thing.

It is the bloody business which informs

Thus to mine eyes. Now o'er the one half world

Nature seems dead, and wicked dreams abuse   51

The curtained sleep. Witchcraft celebrates   52

Pale Hecate's offerings, and withered Murder,   53

Alarumed by his sentinel, the wolf,   54

Whose howl's his watch, thus with his stealthy pace,   55

With Tarquin's ravishing strides, towards his design   56

Moves like a ghost. Thou sure and firm-set earth,

Hear not my steps which way they walk, for fear

Thy very stones prate of my whereabout

And take the present horror from the time   60

Which now suits with it. Whiles I threat, he lives;   61

---

82 **mock** deceive

2.1 Location: Inner courtyard of Macbeth's castle. Time is virtually continuous from the previous scene.

0.1 *torch* (This may mean "torchbearer," although it does not at line 9.1.)   **4 husbandry** thrift (careful management of resources in the domestic economy)   **6 summons** i.e., to sleep   **7 would not** am reluctant to (owing to my uneasy fears).   **powers** order of angels deputed by God to resist demons   **14 largess** gifts, gratuities. **offices** quarters used for the household work.   **16–17 and shut . . . content** and went to bed professing himself endlessly pleased. **18–19 Our . . . wrought** our good will (to entertain the king) was limited by our meager resources (on such short notice), which otherwise would have poured forth hospitality without restraint.

26 cleave . . . 'tis give me your support, adhere to my view, when the time comes   **27 So** Provided that   **29 franchised** free (from guilt). **clear** unstained   **30 counseled** receptive to suggestion.   **32 drink** i.e., posset or bedtime drink of hot spiced milk curdled with ale or wine, as also in 2.2.6   **37 fatal** ominous.   **sensible** perceivable by the senses   **40 heat-oppressèd** fevered   **43 Thou . . . going** You seem to guide me toward the destiny I intended, toward Duncan's chambers **47 dudgeon** hilt of a dagger.   **gouts** drops   **51 abuse** deceive **52 curtained** curtained by night (and by bedcurtains)   **53 Pale Hecate's offerings** sacrificial offerings to Hecate, the goddess of night and witchcraft. (She is *pale* because she is identified with the pale moon.)   **withered** (Murder is pictured as in images of Death, shrunken and wasted.)   **54 Alarumed** given the signal to action **55 watch** watchword or cry   **56 Tarquin's** (Tarquin was a Roman tyrant who ravished Lucrece.)   **60–1 And take . . . with it** and thus echo and augment the horror which is so suited to this evil hour, or, usurp the present horror by breaking the silence.   **61 threat** i.e., merely threaten to kill Duncan

Words to the heat of deeds too cold breath gives. 62
A bell rings.
I go, and it is done. The bell invites me.
Hear it not, Duncan, for it is a knell
That summons thee to heaven or to hell. *Exit.*

❧

2.2

Enter Lady [Macbeth].

LADY MACBETH
That which hath made them drunk hath made me bold;
What hath quenched them hath given me fire. Hark!
Peace!
It was the owl that shrieked, the fatal bellman, 3
Which gives the stern'st good-night. He is about it. 4
The doors are open; and the surfeited grooms 5
Do mock their charge with snores. I have drugged their possets, 6
That death and nature do contend about them
Whether they live or die.

MACBETH [*within*] Who's there? What, ho!

LADY MACBETH
Alack, I am afraid they have awaked,
And 'tis not done. Th'attempt and not the deed
Confounds us. Hark! I laid their daggers ready; 11
He could not miss 'em. Had he not resembled
My father as he slept, I had done't.

Enter Macbeth, [bearing bloody daggers].

My husband!

MACBETH
I have done the deed. Didst thou not hear a noise?

LADY MACBETH
I heard the owl scream and the crickets cry. 16
Did not you speak?

MACBETH When?

LADY MACBETH Now.

MACBETH As I descended?

LADY MACBETH Ay.

MACBETH Hark! Who lies i'th' second chamber?

LADY MACBETH Donalbain.

MACBETH [*looking at his hands*] This is a sorry sight.

LADY MACBETH
A foolish thought, to say a sorry sight.

MACBETH
There's one did laugh in 's sleep, and one cried "Murder!"
That they did wake each other. I stood and heard them.

But they did say their prayers, and addressed them 28
Again to sleep.

LADY MACBETH There are two lodged together.

MACBETH
One cried "God bless us!" and "Amen!" the other,
As they had seen me with these hangman's hands. 31
List'ning their fear, I could not say "Amen"
When they did say "God bless us!"

LADY MACBETH Consider it not so deeply.

MACBETH
But wherefore could not I pronounce "Amen"?
I had most need of blessing, and "Amen"
Stuck in my throat.

LADY MACBETH These deeds must not be thought 37
After these ways; so, it will make us mad. 38

MACBETH
Methought I heard a voice cry "Sleep no more!
Macbeth does murder sleep," the innocent sleep,
Sleep that knits up the raveled sleave of care, 41
The death of each day's life, sore labor's bath, 42
Balm of hurt minds, great nature's second course, 43
Chief nourisher in life's feast—

LADY MACBETH What do you mean?

MACBETH
Still it cried "Sleep no more!" to all the house;
"Glamis hath murdered sleep, and therefore Cawdor
Shall sleep no more; Macbeth shall sleep no more."

LADY MACBETH
Who was it that thus cried? Why, worthy thane,
You do unbend your noble strength to think 49
So brainsickly of things. Go get some water
And wash this filthy witness from your hand. 51
Why did you bring these daggers from the place?
They must lie there. Go, carry them and smear
The sleepy grooms with blood.

MACBETH I'll go no more.
I am afraid to think what I have done;
Look on't again I dare not.

LADY MACBETH Infirm of purpose!
Give me the daggers. The sleeping and the dead
Are but as pictures. 'Tis the eye of childhood
That fears a painted devil. If he do bleed,
I'll gild the faces of the grooms withal, 60
For it must seem their guilt.
[*She takes the daggers, and*] *exit. Knock within.*

MACBETH Whence is that knocking?
How is't with me, when every noise appalls me?
What hands are here? Ha! They pluck out mine eyes.
Will all great Neptune's ocean wash this blood
Clean from my hand? No, this my hand will rather
The multitudinous seas incarnadine, 66

---

62 Words . . . gives Words give only lifeless expression to live deeds, are no substitute for deeds.
2.2. Location: Scene continues.
3 bellman one who rings a bell to announce a death or to mark the hours of the night **4 Which . . . good-night** i.e., that announces the last good-night, death. **5 grooms** servants **6 mock their charge** make a mockery of their guard duty. **possets** hot bedtime drinks (as in 2.1.32) **11 Confounds** ruins **16 owl, crickets** (The sounds of both could be ominous and prophetic of death.)

28 addressed them settled themselves **31 As** as if. **hangman's hands** bloody hands of the executioner. **37 thought** thought about **38 so** if we do so **41 raveled sleave** tangled skein **42 bath** i.e., to relieve the soreness **43 second course** (Ordinary feasts had two courses, of which the second was the *chief nourisher;* here, sleep is seen as following eating in a restorative process.) **49 unbend** slacken (as one would a bow; contrast with "bend up" in 1.7.80) **51 witness** evidence **60 gild** smear, coat, as if with a thin layer of gold. (Gold was ordinarily spoken of as red.) **66 multitudinous** numerous and teeming. **incarnadine** stain red

Making the green one red. 67

Enter Lady [Macbeth].

LADY MACBETH
My hands are of your color, but I shame
To wear a heart so white. (*Knock.*) I hear a knocking
At the south entry. Retire we to our chamber.
A little water clears us of this deed.
How easy is it, then! Your constancy 72
Hath left you unattended. (*Knock.*) Hark! More
  knocking. 73
Get on your nightgown, lest occasion call us 74
And show us to be watchers. Be not lost 75
So poorly in your thoughts.

MACBETH
To know my deed, 'twere best not know myself. 77

Knock.

Wake Duncan with thy knocking! I would thou
  couldst! *Exeunt.*

❧

2.3

Knocking within. Enter a Porter.

PORTER   Here's a knocking indeed! If a man were porter
of hell gate, he should have old turning the key.
(*Knock.*) Knock, knock, knock! Who's there, i'th' 2
name of Beelzebub? Here's a farmer that hanged 4
himself on th'expectation of plenty. Come in time! 5
Have napkins enough about you; here you'll sweat for't. 6
(*Knock.*) Knock, knock! Who's there, in th'other
devil's name? Faith, here's an equivocator, that could 8
swear in both the scales against either scale, who
committed treason enough for God's sake, yet could
not equivocate to heaven. Oh, come in, equivocator.
(*Knock.*) Knock, knock, knock! Who's there? Faith,
here's an English tailor come hither for stealing out of 13
a French hose. Come in, tailor. Here you may roast 14
your goose. (*Knock.*) Knock, knock! Never at quiet! 15

What are you? But this place is too cold for hell. I'll
devil-porter it no further. I had thought to have let in
some of all professions that go the primrose way to
th'everlasting bonfire. (*Knock.*) Anon, anon! [*He opens the
gate.*] I pray you, remember the porter.

Enter Macduff and Lennox.

MACDUFF
Was it so late, friend, ere you went to bed,
That you do lie so late?

PORTER   Faith, sir, we were carousing till the second 23
cock; and drink, sir, is a great provoker of three things. 24

MACDUFF   What three things does drink especially
provoke?

PORTER   Marry, sir, nose-painting, sleep, and urine. 27
Lechery, sir, it provokes and unprovokes: it provokes
the desire but it takes away the performance. Therefore much drink may be said to be an equivocator
with lechery: it makes him and it mars him; it sets him
on and it takes him off; it persuades him and dis-
heartens him, makes him stand to and not stand to; 33
in conclusion, equivocates him in a sleep and, giving 34
him the lie, leaves him. 35

MACDUFF   I believe drink gave thee the lie last night. 36

PORTER   That it did, sir, i'the very throat on me. But I 37
requited him for his lie, and, I think, being too strong
for him, though he took up my legs sometimes, yet I 39
made a shift to cast him. 40

MACDUFF   Is thy master stirring?

Enter Macbeth.

Our knocking has awaked him. Here he comes.
[*Exit Porter.*]

LENNOX
Good morrow, noble sir.

MACBETH   Good morrow, both.

MACDUFF
Is the King stirring, worthy thane?

MACBETH   Not yet.

MACDUFF
He did command me to call timely on him. 45
I have almost slipped the hour.

MACBETH   I'll bring you to him. 46

MACDUFF
I know this is a joyful trouble to you,
But yet 'tis one.

---

67 one red one all-pervading red. **72–3 Your . . . unattended** Your
preoccupation with yourself has left you inattentive to other matters.
74 nightgown dressing gown **75 to be watchers** to have been awake
and not abed. **77 To know . . . myself** To come to terms with what I
have done, I would do best to shut out the horror entirely and deny
who I am.
**2.3. Location: Scene continues. The knocking at the door has
already been heard in 2.2. It is not necessary to assume literally,
however, that Macbeth and Lady Macbeth have been talking near
the *south entry* (2.2.70) where the knocking is heard.**
2 old plenty of **4 Beelzebub** a devil. **4–5 Here's . . . plenty** i.e., Here's
a farmer who has hoarded in anticipation of a scarcity and will be justly
punished by a crop surplus and low prices. **5 Come in time!** i.e., You
have come in good time! **6 napkins** handkerchiefs or towels (to mop
up the sweat) **8 equivocator** (This is regarded by many editors as an
allusion to the trial of the Jesuit Henry Garnet for treason in the spring of
1606 and to the doctrine of equivocation said to have been presented in
his defense; according to this doctrine, a lie was not a lie if the utterer
had in his mind a different meaning in which the utterance was true.)
13–14 for stealing . . . hose (French fashions, much in demand by style-
conscious courtiers, no doubt provided opportunities for tailors to skimp
in the making of garments while charging customers the full amount.)
14–15 roast your goose heat your tailor's smoothing iron—something
easily done in the flames of hell. (With a pun on the sense, "cook your
goose." A *goose* could also be a long-handled iron, or a prostitute.)

23–4 second cock second crowing of the cock before dawn **27 Marry**
(Originally, an oath, "by the Virgin Mary.") **nose-painting** i.e., red-
dening of the nose through drink **33 makes . . . not stand to** arouses
him sexually but then takes away the ability to perform sexually.
(Repeating the idea of the previous phrases about how it *makes him
and mars him*, etc.) **34 equivocates . . . sleep** (1) lulls him asleep
(2) gives him an erotic experience in dream only **34–5 giving him
the lie** (1) deceiving him (2) laying him out flat **35 leaves him**
(1) dissipates as intoxication (2) is passed off as urine. **36 gave thee
the lie** (1) called you a liar (2) made you unable to stand and put you
to sleep **37 i'the . . . me** (1) giving me the deepest insult imaginable
(2) literally, going down my throat. (*On* means "of.") **39 took . . .
legs** made me unable to stand and threw me to the ground as a
wrestler might do **40 made a shift** managed. **cast** (1) throw, as in
wrestling (2) vomit **45 timely** betimes, early **46 slipped** let slip

MACBETH
The labor we delight in physics pain.
This is the door.   49
MACDUFF   I'll make so bold to call,
For 'tis my limited service.   *Exit Macduff.*   51
LENNOX   Goes the King hence today?
MACBETH   He does; he did appoint so.
LENNOX
The night has been unruly. Where we lay,
Our chimneys were blown down, and, as they say,
Lamentings heard i'th'air, strange screams of death,
And prophesying with accents terrible   57
Of dire combustion and confused events   58
New hatched to the woeful time. The obscure bird 59
Clamored the livelong night. Some say the earth
Was feverous and did shake.
MACBETH   'Twas a rough night.
LENNOX
My young remembrance cannot parallel
A fellow to it.

          Enter Macduff.

MACDUFF   Oh, horror, horror, horror!
Tongue nor heart cannot conceive nor name thee!
MACBETH AND LENNOX   What's the matter?
MACDUFF
Confusion now hath made his masterpiece!   66
Most sacrilegious murder hath broke ope
The Lord's anointed temple and stole thence
The life o'th' building!
MACBETH   What is't you say? The life?
LENNOX   Mean you His Majesty?
MACDUFF
Approach the chamber and destroy your sight
With a new Gorgon. Do not bid me speak;   73
See, and then speak yourselves.
                    Exeunt Macbeth and Lennox.
                    Awake, awake!
Ring the alarum bell. Murder and treason!
Banquo and Donalbain, Malcolm, awake!
Shake off this downy sleep, death's counterfeit,   77
And look on death itself! Up, up, and see
The great doom's image! Malcolm, Banquo,   79
As from your graves rise up and walk like sprites 80
To countenance this horror! Ring the bell. *Bell rings.* 81

          Enter Lady [*Macbeth*].

LADY MACBETH   What's the business,
That such a hideous trumpet calls to parley   83

The sleepers of the house? Speak, speak!
MACDUFF   Oh, gentle lady,
'Tis not for you to hear what I can speak.
The repetition in a woman's ear   87
Would murder as it fell.

          Enter Banquo.

                    Oh, Banquo, Banquo,
Our royal master's murdered!
LADY MACBETH   Woe, alas!
What, in our house?
BANQUO   Too cruel anywhere.
Dear Duff, I prithee, contradict thyself
And say it is not so.

          Enter Macbeth, Lennox, and Ross.

MACBETH
Had I but died an hour before this chance   93
I had lived a blessèd time; for from this instant
There's nothing serious in mortality.   95
All is but toys. Renown and grace is dead;   96
The wine of life is drawn, and the mere lees   97
Is left this vault to brag of.   98

          Enter Malcolm and Donalbain.

DONALBAIN
What is amiss?
MACBETH   You are, and do not know't.
The spring, the head, the fountain of your blood
Is stopped, the very source of it is stopped.
MACDUFF
Your royal father's murdered.
MALCOLM   Oh, by whom?
LENNOX
Those of his chamber, as it seemed, had done't.
Their hands and faces were all badged with blood; 104
So were their daggers, which unwiped we found
Upon their pillows. They stared and were distracted;
No man's life was to be trusted with them.
MACBETH
Oh, yet I do repent me of my fury,
That I did kill them.
MACDUFF   Wherefore did you so?
MACBETH
Who can be wise, amazed, temp'rate and furious,   110
Loyal and neutral, in a moment? No man.
Th'expedition of my violent love   112
Outran the pauser, reason. Here lay Duncan,
His silver skin laced with his golden blood,   114
And his gashed stabs looked like a breach in nature 115
For ruin's wasteful entrance; there the murderers, 116
Steeped in the colors of their trade, their daggers

---

49 **physics pain** i.e., cures that labor of its troublesome aspect.
51 **limited** appointed   57 **accents terrible** terrifying utterances
58 **combustion** tumult   59 **New . . . time** newly born to accompany
the woeful nature of the time.   **obscure bird** owl, the bird of darkness
66 **Confusion** Destruction   73 **Gorgon** one of three monsters with
hideous faces (Medusa was a Gorgon), whose look turned the beholders to stone   77 **downy** feathery, unsubstantial   79 **great doom's
image** simulacrum of the Last Judgment, of Doomsday.   80 **As . . .
rise up** (At the Last Judgment, the dead will rise from their graves to
be judged.)   **sprites** souls, ghosts   81 **countenance** (1) be in keeping
with (2) witness   83 **trumpet** (Another metaphorical suggestion of
the Last Judgment; the *trumpet* here is the shouting and the bell.)

87 **repetition** recital, report   93 **chance** occurrence   95 **serious in
mortality** worthwhile in mortal life.   96 **toys** trifles.   97 **lees** dregs
98 **vault** (1) wine-vault (2) earth, with its vaulted sky   104 **badged**
marked, as with a badge or emblem   110 **amazed** bewildered
112 **Th'expedition** The haste   114 **golden** (See the note for 2.2.60.)
115 **breach in nature** gap in the defenses of life. (A metaphor of military siege.)   116 **wasteful** destructive

Unmannerly breeched with gore. Who could refrain   118
That had a heart to love, and in that heart
Courage to make 's love known?

LADY MACBETH [*fainting*]   Help me hence, ho!   120

MACDUFF
Look to the lady.

MALCOLM [*aside to Donalbain*]
                Why do we hold our tongues,
That most may claim this argument for ours?   122

DONALBAIN [*aside to Malcolm*]
What should be spoken here, where our fate,
Hid in an auger hole, may rush and seize us?   124
Let's away. Our tears are not yet brewed.   125

MALCOLM [*aside to Donalbain*]
Nor our strong sorrow upon the foot of motion.   126

BANQUO   Look to the lady.
                    [*Lady Macbeth is helped out.*]
And when we have our naked frailties hid,   128
That suffer in exposure, let us meet
And question this most bloody piece of work   130
To know it further. Fears and scruples shake us.   131
In the great hand of God I stand, and thence   132
Against the undivulged pretense I fight   133
Of treasonous malice.

MACDUFF   And so do I.

ALL   So all.   134

MACBETH
Let's briefly put on manly readiness   135
And meet i'th' hall together.

ALL   Well contented.
            Exeunt [all but Malcolm and Donalbain].

MALCOLM
What will you do? Let's not consort with them.   137
To show an unfelt sorrow is an office
Which the false man does easy. I'll to England.   139

DONALBAIN
To Ireland, I. Our separated fortune
Shall keep us both the safer. Where we are,
There's daggers in men's smiles; the nea'er in blood,   142
The nearer bloody.

MALCOLM   This murderous shaft that's shot   143
Hath not yet lighted, and our safest way   144
Is to avoid the aim. Therefore to horse,
And let us not be dainty of leave-taking,   146
But shift away. There's warrant in that theft   147

---

118 breeched with gore covered (as with breeches) to the hilts with gore.   **120 make 's love known** make manifest his love.   **122 That . . . ours** to whom this business matters most.   **124 in an auger hole** i.e., in some hiding place, in ambush. (An *auger* is a hole-drilling tool.)   **125 Our . . . brewed** i.e., Our real sorrow has not yet ripened.   **126 upon . . . motion** yet prepared to express itself fully.   **128 our naked frailties hid** clothed our poor, shivering bodies (which remind us of our human frailty)   **130 question** discuss   **131 scruples** doubts, suspicions   **132–4 thence . . . malice** with God's help, I will fight against the as-yet-unknown purpose that prompted this treason.   **133 pretense** design   **134 malice** enmity.   **135 briefly** quickly.   **manly readiness** men's clothing and resolute purpose   **137 consort** keep company, associate   **139 easy** easily.   **142–3 the nea'er . . . bloody** the closer the relationship, the greater the danger to be feared of bloody intent.   **144 lighted** alighted, descended   **146 dainty of** tediously ceremonious in   **147 shift away** disappear by stealth.   **warrant** justification

---

Which steals itself when there's no mercy left.
                            Exeunt.

❧

2.4

Enter Ross with an Old Man.

OLD MAN
Threescore and ten I can remember well,
Within the volume of which time I have seen
Hours dreadful and things strange, but this sore night   3
Hath trifled former knowings.

ROSS   Ha, good father,   4
Thou see'st the heavens, as troubled with man's act,   5
Threatens his bloody stage. By th' clock 'tis day,   6
And yet dark night strangles the traveling lamp.   7
Is't night's predominance or the day's shame
That darkness does the face of earth entomb
When living light should kiss it?

OLD MAN   'Tis unnatural,
Even like the deed that's done. On Tuesday last
A falcon, tow'ring in her pride of place,   12
Was by a mousing owl hawked at and killed.   13

ROSS
And Duncan's horses—a thing most strange and
    certain—
Beauteous and swift, the minions of their race,   15
Turned wild in nature, broke their stalls, flung out,
Contending 'gainst obedience, as they would   17
Make war with mankind.

OLD MAN   'Tis said they eat each other.   18

ROSS
They did so, to th'amazement of mine eyes
That looked upon't.

            Enter Macduff.

                Here comes the good Macduff.—
How goes the world, sir, now?

MACDUFF   Why, see you not?

ROSS
Is't known who did this more than bloody deed?

MACDUFF
Those that Macbeth hath slain.

ROSS   Alas the day,
What good could they pretend?

MACDUFF   They were suborned.   24
Malcolm and Donalbain, the King's two sons,
Are stol'n away and fled, which puts upon them
Suspicion of the deed.

ROSS   'Gainst nature still!

2.4. Location: Outside Macbeth's castle of Inverness.
3 sore dreadful, grievous   **4 trifled former knowings** made trivial all former experiences.   **father** old man   **5–6 the heavens . . . stage** a solar eclipse threatens disapprovingly our human scene of murder. (With a theatrical metaphor in *heavens* [the decorated roof over the stage], *act*, and *stage*.)   **7 traveling lamp** i.e., sun.   **12 tow'ring** circling higher and higher. (A term in falconry.)   **place** pitch, highest point in the falcon's flight   **13 mousing** i.e., ordinarily preying on mice   **15 minions** darlings   **17 as** as if   **18 eat** ate. (Pronounced "et.")   **24 What . . . pretend?** i.e., what could they hope to gain by it?   **suborned** bribed, hired.

Thriftless ambition, that will ravin up   28
    Thine own life's means! Then 'tis most like   29
    The sovereignty will fall upon Macbeth.

MACDUFF
    He is already named and gone to Scone   31
    To be invested.

ROSS   Where is Duncan's body?

MACDUFF   Carried to Colmekill,   33
    The sacred storehouse of his predecessors
    And guardian of their bones.

ROSS   Will you to Scone?

MACDUFF
    No, cousin, I'll to Fife.

ROSS   Well, I will thither.   36

MACDUFF
    Well, may you see things well done there. Adieu,
    Lest our old robes sit easier than our new!

ROSS   Farewell, father.

OLD MAN
    God's benison go with you, and with those
    That would make good of bad, and friends of foes!   40

                                    Exeunt omnes.

❖

3.1

    Enter Banquo.

BANQUO
    Thou hast it now—King, Cawdor, Glamis, all
    As the weird women promised, and I fear
    Thou played'st most foully for't. Yet it was said
    It should not stand in thy posterity,   4
    But that myself should be the root and father
    Of many kings. If there come truth from them—
    As upon thee, Macbeth, their speeches shine—   7
    Why, by the verities on thee made good,
    May they not be my oracles as well
    And set me up in hope? But hush, no more.   10

        Sennet sounded. Enter Macbeth as King, Lady
        [*Macbeth*], *Lennox, Ross, lords, and attendants.*

MACBETH
    Here's our chief guest.

LADY MACBETH   If he had been forgotten,
    It had been as a gap in our great feast
    And all-thing unbecoming.   13

MACBETH
    Tonight we hold a solemn supper, sir,   14
    And I'll request your presence.

BANQUO   Let Your Highness
    Command upon me, to the which my duties   16

Are with a most indissoluble tie
    Forever knit.

MACBETH   Ride you this afternoon?

BANQUO   Ay, my good lord.

MACBETH
    We should have else desired your good advice,
    Which still hath been both grave and prosperous,   22
    In this day's council; but we'll take tomorrow.
    Is't far you ride?

BANQUO
    As far, my lord, as will fill up the time
    Twixt this and supper. Go not my horse the better, 26
    I must become a borrower of the night
    For a dark hour or twain.

MACBETH   Fail not our feast.

BANQUO   My lord, I will not.

MACBETH
    We hear our bloody cousins are bestowed   31
    In England and in Ireland, not confessing
    Their cruel parricide, filling their hearers
    With strange invention. But of that tomorrow,   34
    When therewithal we shall have cause of state   35
    Craving us jointly. Hie you to horse. Adieu,   36
    Till you return at night. Goes Fleance with you?

BANQUO
    Ay, my good lord. Our time does call upon 's.

MACBETH
    I wish your horses swift and sure of foot,
    And so I do commend you to their backs.   40
    Farewell.   *Exit Banquo.*
    Let every man be master of his time
    Till seven at night. To make society
    The sweeter welcome, we will keep ourself   44
    Till suppertime alone. While then, God be with you! 45
        Exeunt Lords [*and all but Macbeth and a Servant*].
    Sirrah, a word with you. Attend those men   46
    Our pleasure?

SERVANT
    They are, my lord, without the palace gate.

MACBETH
    Bring them before us.   *Exit Servant.*
                            To be thus is nothing,   49
    But to be safely thus.—Our fears in Banquo   50
    Stick deep, and in his royalty of nature   51
    Reigns that which would be feared. 'Tis much he
        dares;   52
    And to that dauntless temper of his mind   53
    He hath a wisdom that doth guide his valor
    To act in safety. There is none but he
    Whose being I do fear; and under him
    My genius is rebuked, as it is said   57

---

28 Thriftless Spendthrift.   **ravin up** devour ravenously   **29 like** likely   **31 named** chosen. (See the note for 1.4.50.)   **Scone** ancient royal city of Scotland near Perth   **33 Colmekill** Icolmkill, i.e., Cell of St. Columba, the barren islet of Iona in the Western Islands, a sacred spot where the kings were buried; here, called a *storehouse*   **36 Fife** (Of which Macduff is Thane.)   **40 bension** blessing
3.1. Location: Forres. The palace.
4 stand stay, remain   **7 shine** beam favorably   **10.1** *Sennet* trumpet call   **13 all-thing** in every way   **14 solemn** ceremonious   **16 Command** lay your command

22 still always.   **grave and prosperous** weighty and profitable   **26 this** this present moment.   **Go . . . better** Unless my horse makes better time than I expect   **31 bestowed** lodged   **34 invention** falsehood.   **35 therewithal** besides that   **35–6 cause . . . jointly** questions of state occupying our joint attention.   **40 commend** commit, entrust   **44 we . . . ourself** I will keep to myself   **45 While** Till   **46 Sirrah** (A form of address to a social inferior.)   **49 thus** i.e., king   **50 But** unless.   **in** concerning   **51 royalty of nature** natural kingly bearing   **52 would be** deserves to be   **53 to** added to   **57 My genius is rebuked** my guardian spirit is daunted or abashed

Mark Antony's was by Caesar. He chid the sisters   58
When first they put the name of king upon me,
And bade them speak to him. Then, prophetlike,
They hailed him father to a line of kings.
Upon my head they placed a fruitless crown
And put a barren scepter in my grip,
Thence to be wrenched with an unlineal hand,   64
No son of mine succeeding. If 't be so,
For Banquo's issue have I filed my mind;   66
For them the gracious Duncan have I murdered,
Put rancors in the vessel of my peace   68
Only for them, and mine eternal jewel   69
Given to the common enemy of man   70
To make them kings, the seeds of Banquo kings.
Rather than so, come fate into the list,   72
And champion me to th'utterance!—Who's there?   73

Enter Servant and two Murderers.

Now go to the door, and stay there till we call.
                                                          Exit Servant.
Was it not yesterday we spoke together?
MURDERERS
It was, so please Your Highness.
MACBETH   Well then, now
Have you considered of my speeches? Know
That it was he in the times past which held you
So under fortune, which you thought had been   79
Our innocent self. This I made good to you
In our last conference, passed in probation with you   81
How you were borne in hand, how crossed, the
      instruments,   82
Who wrought with them, and all things else that
      might   83
To half a soul and to a notion crazed   84
Say, "Thus did Banquo."
FIRST MURDERER   You made it known to us.
MACBETH
I did so, and went further, which is now
Our point of second meeting. Do you find
Your patience so predominant in your nature
That you can let this go? Are you so gospeled   89
To pray for this good man and for his issue,
Whose heavy hand hath bowed you to the grave
And beggared yours forever?
FIRST MURDERER   We are men, my liege.   92
MACBETH
Ay, in the catalogue ye go for men,   93
      As hounds and greyhounds, mongrels, spaniels, curs,

Shoughs, water-rugs, and demi-wolves are clept   95
All by the name of dogs. The valued file   96
Distinguishes the swift, the slow, the subtle,
The housekeeper, the hunter, every one   98
According to the gift which bounteous nature
Hath in him closed, whereby he does receive   100
Particular addition from the bill   101
That writes them all alike; and so of men.   102
Now, if you have a station in the file,   103
Not i'th' worst rank of manhood, say't,   104
And I will put that business in your bosoms
Whose execution takes your enemy off,   106
Grapples you to the heart and love of us,
Who wear our health but sickly in his life,   108
Which in his death were perfect.
SECOND MURDERER   I am one, my liege,
Whom the vile blows and buffets of the world
Hath so incensed that I am reckless what
I do to spite the world.
FIRST MURDERER   And I another,
So weary with disasters, tugged with fortune,   113
That I would set my life on any chance   114
To mend it or be rid on 't.
MACBETH   Both of you
Know Banquo was your enemy.
BOTH MURDERERS   True, my lord.
MACBETH
So is he mine, and in such bloody distance   117
That every minute of his being thrusts   118
Against my near'st of life. And though I could   119
With barefaced power sweep him from my sight   120
And bid my will avouch it, yet I must not,   121
For certain friends that are both his and mine,   122
Whose loves I may not drop, but wail his fall   123
Who I myself struck down. And thence it is   124
That I to your assistance do make love,   125
Masking the business from the common eye
For sundry weighty reasons.
SECOND MURDERER   We shall, my lord,
Perform what you command us.
FIRST MURDERER   Though our lives—
MACBETH
Your spirits shine through you. Within this hour at
      most   129
      I will advise you where to plant yourselves,

95 **Shoughs . . . clept** shaggy lap-dogs, long-haired water dogs, and dogs that have been crossbred with wolves are called   96 **valued file** list classified according to value   98 **housekeeper** watchdog   100 **in him closed** enclosed in him   101–2 **Particular . . . alike** particular qualification apart from the catalog that lists them all indiscriminately   103–4 **if . . . manhood** if you occupy not the worst of places in the *rank and file* of men   106 **Whose execution** the doing of which   108 **in his life** while he lives   113 **tugged with** pulled about by (as in wrestling)   114 **set** risk, stake   117 **distance** (1) hostility, enmity (2) interval of distance between fencers   118–19 **thrusts . . . life** stabs me to the heart.   120 **With barefaced power** by open use of my supreme royal authority   121 **And . . . avouch it** and use my mere wish as my justification   122 **For** because of, for the sake of   123–4 **wail . . . Who** I must bewail the death of him who   125 **That . . . love** that I woo your aid   129 **Your . . . you** i.e., Enough; I can see your determination in your faces.

58 **Caesar** Octavius Caesar.   64 **with** by.   **unlineal** not of lineal descent from me   66 **filed** defiled   68 **rancors** malignant enemies (here visualized as a poison added to a vessel full of wholesome drink)   69 **eternal jewel** i.e., soul   70 **common . . . man** i.e., devil   72 **list** lists, place of combat   73 **champion me** fight with me in single combat.   **to th'utterance** to the last extremity (French, *à l'outrance*).   79 **under fortune** down in your fortunes   81–3 **passed . . . with them** went over the proof with you how you were deceived by false promises, how you were thwarted, who the agents were, who directed their activities   84 **To . . . crazed** even to a half-wit of unsound mind   89 **gospeled** imbued with the gospel spirit   92 **yours** your family   93 **go for** pass for, are entered for

Acquaint you with the perfect spy o'th' time,   131
The moment on't, for't must be done tonight,   132
And something from the palace; always thought   133
That I require a clearness. And with him—   134
To leave no rubs nor botches in the work—   135
Fleance his son, that keeps him company,
Whose absence is no less material to me
Than is his father's, must embrace the fate
Of that dark hour. Resolve yourselves apart;   139
I'll come to you anon.

BOTH MURDERERS   We are resolved, my lord.

MACBETH
I'll call upon you straight. Abide within.

                                  Exeunt [*Murderers*].
It is concluded. Banquo, thy soul's flight,
If it find heaven, must find it out tonight.   [*Exit.*]

❖

3.2

Enter Macbeth's Lady and a Servant.

LADY MACBETH   Is Banquo gone from court?

SERVANT
Ay, madam, but returns again tonight.

LADY MACBETH
Say to the King I would attend his leisure
For a few words.

SERVANT   Madam, I will.   *Exit.*

LADY MACBETH   Naught's had, all's spent,
Where our desire is got without content.   7
'Tis safer to be that which we destroy
Than by destruction dwell in doubtful joy.   9

Enter Macbeth.

How now, my lord? Why do you keep alone,
Of sorriest fancies your companions making,   11
Using those thoughts which should indeed have died   12
With them they think on? Things without all remedy
Should be without regard. What's done is done.   14

MACBETH
We have scorched the snake, not killed it.   15
She'll close and be herself, whilst our poor malice   16
Remains in danger of her former tooth.   17
But let the frame of things disjoint, both the worlds
    suffer,   18
Ere we will eat our meal in fear and sleep
In the affliction of these terrible dreams

That shake us nightly. Better be with the dead,
Whom we, to gain our peace, have sent to peace,   22
Than on the torture of the mind to lie   23
In restless ecstasy. Duncan is in his grave;   24
After life's fitful fever he sleeps well.
Treason has done his worst; nor steel, nor poison,   26
Malice domestic, foreign levy, nothing   27
Can touch him further.

LADY MACBETH   Come on,
Gentle my lord, sleek o'er your rugged looks.   30
Be bright and jovial among your guests tonight.

MACBETH
So shall I, love, and so, I pray, be you.
Let your remembrance apply to Banquo;   33
Present him eminence, both with eye and tongue—   34
Unsafe the while, that we   35
Must lave our honors in these flattering streams   36
And make our faces vizards to our hearts,   37
Disguising what they are.

LADY MACBETH   You must leave this.

MACBETH
Oh, full of scorpions is my mind, dear wife!
Thou know'st that Banquo and his Fleance lives.

LADY MACBETH
But in them nature's copy's not eterne.   41

MACBETH
There's comfort yet; they are assailable.
Then be thou jocund. Ere the bat hath flown
His cloistered flight, ere to black Hecate's summons   44
The shard-borne beetle with his drowsy hums   45
Hath rung night's yawning peal, there shall be done   46
A deed of dreadful note.

LADY MACBETH   What's to be done?

MACBETH
Be innocent of the knowledge, dearest chuck,   48
Till thou applaud the deed. Come, seeling night,   49
Scarf up the tender eye of pitiful day,   50
And with thy bloody and invisible hand
Cancel and tear to pieces that great bond   52
Which keeps me pale! Light thickens,   53
And the crow makes wing to th' rooky wood;   54
Good things of day begin to droop and drowse,

131–2 with . . . on't with full and precise instructions as to when it is to be done. (*Spy* means "espial, observation.")   133 something from some distance removed from.   thought being borne in mind   134 clearness freedom from suspicion.   135 rubs defects, rough spots   139 Resolve yourselves apart Make up your minds in private conference
3.2. Location: The palace.
7 content contentedness.   9 Than . . . joy than by destroying achieve only an apprehensive joy.   11 sorriest most despicable or wretched   12 Using keeping company with, entertaining   14 without regard not pondered upon.   15 scorched slashed, cut   16 close heal, close up again.   poor malice feeble hostility   17 her former tooth her fang, just as before.   18 let . . . suffer let the universe itself fall apart, both heaven and earth perish

22 to gain . . . to peace to gain contentedness through satisfied ambition, have sent to eternal rest   23 torture rack   24 ecstasy frenzy.   26 nor steel neither steel   27 Malice domestic civil war.   foreign levy the levying of troops abroad (against Scotland)   30 Gentle . . . looks my noble lord, smooth over your rough looks.   33 Let . . . apply Remember to pay special attention   34 eminence favor   35–6 Unsafe . . . streams we being unsafe at present, we must put on a show of flattering cordiality to make clean our honor. (To *lave* is to wash.)   37 vizards masks   41 nature's . . . eterne nature's pattern will not continue forever.   44 cloistered secluded.   Hecate goddess of night and witchcraft, as in 2.1.53   45 shard-borne borne on shards, or horny wing cases, or, *shard-born*, bred in cow-droppings (shards)   46 yawning drowsy   48 chuck (A term of endearment.)   49 seeling eye-closing. (Night is pictured here as a falconer sewing up the eyes of day lest it should struggle against the deed that is to be done.)   50 Scarf up blindfold.   pitiful compassionate   52 that . . . bond i.e., the bond of natural and moral law (here associated with the full light of day)   53 pale sickly, pallid (like moonlight, contrasted with the full light of day); also, pallid from fear.   Light thickens Darkness is coming on   54 crow rook.   rooky full of rooks

Whiles night's black agents to their preys do rouse.   56
Thou marvel'st at my words, but hold thee still.
Things bad begun make strong themselves by ill.
So, prithee, go with me.   *Exeunt.*

❧

3.3

Enter three Murderers.

FIRST MURDERER [*to the Third Murderer*]
But who did bid thee join with us?
THIRD MURDERER   Macbeth.
SECOND MURDERER [*to the First Murderer*]
He needs not our mistrust, since he delivers   2
Our offices and what we have to do   3
To the direction just.
FIRST MURDERER   Then stand with us.   4
The west yet glimmers with some streaks of day.
Now spurs the lated traveler apace   6
To gain the timely inn, and near approaches   7
The subject of our watch.
THIRD MURDERER   Hark, I hear horses.
BANQUO (*within*) Give us a light there, ho!
SECOND MURDERER   Then 'tis he. The rest
That are within the note of expectation   12
Already are i'th' court.
FIRST MURDERER   His horses go about.   14
THIRD MURDERER
Almost a mile; but he does usually—
So all men do—from hence to th' palace gate
Make it their walk.

Enter Banquo and Fleance, with a torch.

SECOND MURDERER   A light, a light!
THIRD MURDERER   'Tis he.
FIRST MURDERER   Stand to't.
BANQUO   It will be rain tonight.
FIRST MURDERER   Let it come down!
                            [*They attack Banquo.*]
BANQUO
Oh, treachery! Fly, good Fleance, fly, fly, fly!
Thou mayst revenge.—Oh, slave!
                    [*He dies. Fleance escapes.*]
THIRD MURDERER
Who did strike out the light?
FIRST MURDERER   Was't not the way?   25
THIRD MURDERER
There's but one down; the son is fled.
SECOND MURDERER
We have lost best half of our affair.

FIRST MURDERER
Well, let's away and say how much is done.   28
                                    Exeunt.

❧

3.4

*Banquet prepared. Enter Macbeth, Lady
[Macbeth], Ross, Lennox, Lords, and attendants.*

MACBETH
You know your own degrees; sit down. At first   1
And last, the hearty welcome.   [*They sit.*]
LORDS   Thanks to Your Majesty.   2
MACBETH
Ourself will mingle with society   3
And play the humble host.
Our hostess keeps her state, but in best time   5
We will require her welcome.   6
LADY MACBETH
Pronounce it for me, sir, to all our friends,
For my heart speaks they are welcome.

Enter First Murderer [to the door].

MACBETH
See, they encounter thee with their hearts' thanks.   9
Both sides are even. Here I'll sit i'th' midst.   10
Be large in mirth; anon we'll drink a measure   11
The table round. [*He goes to the Murderer.*] There's
    blood upon thy face.
MURDERER   'Tis Banquo's, then.
MACBETH
'Tis better thee without than he within.   14
Is he dispatched?
MURDERER
My lord, his throat is cut. That I did for him.
MACBETH   Thou art the best o'th' cutthroats.
Yet he's good that did the like for Fleance;
If thou didst it, thou art the nonpareil.   19
MURDERER   Most royal sir, Fleance is scaped.
MACBETH
Then comes my fit again. I had else been perfect,
Whole as the marble, founded as the rock,   22
As broad and general as the casing air.   23
But now I am cabined, cribbed, confined, bound in   24
To saucy doubts and fears. But Banquo's safe?   25

---

56 **to . . . rouse** bestir themselves to hunt their prey.
3.3. Location: A park near the palace.
2–4 He . . . just We need not mistrust this man, since the instructions
he brings from Macbeth are so precise.   **6 lated** belated   **7 timely**
arrived at in good time   **12 within . . . expectation** in the list of those
expected   **14 go about** i.e., can be heard as servants take the horses
to the stables (while Banquo and Fleance, provided with a torch, walk
from the palace gate to the castle).   **25 way** i.e., thing to do.

28.1 Exeunt (Presumably, the murderers drag the body of Banquo offstage as they go.)
3.4. Location: A room of state in the palace.
1 degrees ranks (as a determinant of seating)   **1–2 At . . . last** Once
for all   **3 mingle with society** i.e., leave the chair of state and circulate among the guests   **5 keeps her state** remains in her canopied
chair of state.   **in best time** when it is most appropriate   **6 require
her welcome** call upon her to give the welcome.   **9 encounter**
respond to   **10 even** full, with equal numbers on both sides.
11 large liberal, free.   **measure** i.e., cup filled to the brim for a toast
14 'Tis . . . within It is better for you to have his blood on you than he
to have it within him.   **19 the nonpareil** without equal.   **22 founded**
firmly established   **23 broad and general** unconfined.   **casing**
encasing, enveloping   **24 cribbed** shut in   **25 saucy** sharp, impudent, importunate

MURDERER
Ay, my good lord. Safe in a ditch he bides,
With twenty trenchèd gashes on his head,
The least a death to nature.
MACBETH   Thanks for that.
There the grown serpent lies; the worm that's fled   29
Hath nature that in time will venom breed,
No teeth for th' present. Get thee gone. Tomorrow
We'll hear ourselves again.   *Exit Murderer.*
LADY MACBETH   My royal lord,   32
You do not give the cheer. The feast is sold   33
That is not often vouched, while 'tis a-making,   34
'Tis given with welcome. To feed were best at home; 35
From thence, the sauce to meat is ceremony;   36
Meeting were bare without it.

          *Enter the Ghost of Banquo, and sits in Macbeth's
          place.*

MACBETH   Sweet remembrancer!   37
Now, good digestion wait on appetite,   38
And health on both!
LENNOX   May't please Your Highness sit?
MACBETH
Here had we now our country's honor roofed   40
Were the gracèd person of our Banquo present,
Who may I rather challenge for unkindness   42
Than pity for mischance.
ROSS   His absence, sir,
Lays blame upon his promise. Please't Your Highness
To grace us with your royal company?
MACBETH [*seeing his place occupied*]
The table's full.
LENNOX   Here is a place reserved, sir.
MACBETH   Where?
LENNOX
Here, my good lord. What is't that moves Your
     Highness?
MACBETH
Which of you have done this?
LORDS   What, my good lord?
MACBETH
Thou canst not say I did it. Never shake
Thy gory locks at me.
ROSS
Gentlemen, rise. His Highness is not well.
                              [*They start to rise.*]
LADY MACBETH
Sit, worthy friends. My lord is often thus,
And hath been from his youth. Pray you, keep seat.
The fit is momentary; upon a thought   55
He will again be well. If much you note him

You shall offend him and extend his passion.   57
Feed, and regard him not.—[*She confers apart with
     Macbeth.*] Are you a man?
MACBETH
Ay, and a bold one, that dare look on that
Which might appall the devil.
LADY MACBETH   Oh, proper stuff!   60
This is the very painting of your fear.
This is the air-drawn dagger which, you said,   62
Led you to Duncan. Oh, these flaws and starts,   63
Impostors to true fear, would well become   64
A woman's story at a winter's fire,
Authorized by her grandam. Shame itself!   66
Why do you make such faces? When all's done,
You look but on a stool.
MACBETH   Prithee, see there!
Behold, look! Lo, how say you?—
Why, what care I? If thou canst nod, speak too.   70
If charnel houses and our graves must send   71
Those that we bury back, our monuments   72
Shall be the maws of kites.   [*Exit Ghost.*]   73
LADY MACBETH   What, quite unmanned in folly?
MACBETH
If I stand here, I saw him.
LADY MACBETH   Fie, for shame!
MACBETH
Blood hath been shed ere now, i'th'olden time,
Ere humane statute purged the gentle weal;   77
Ay, and since too, murders have been performed
Too terrible for the ear. The time has been
That, when the brains were out, the man would die,
And there an end; but now they rise again
With twenty mortal murders on their crowns,   82
And push us from our stools. This is more strange
Than such a murder is.
LADY MACBETH   My worthy lord,
Your noble friends do lack you.
MACBETH   I do forget.
Do not muse at me, my most worthy friends;
I have a strange infirmity, which is nothing
To those that know me. Come, love and health to all!
Then I'll sit down. Give me some wine. Fill full.
                              [*He is given wine.*]

          Enter Ghost.

I drink to th' general joy o'th' whole table,
And to our dear friend Banquo, whom we miss.
Would he were here! To all, and him, we thirst,   92

---

29 worm small serpent   **32 hear ourselves** personally confer
33 give the cheer welcome your guests.   **33–5 The feast . . . welcome**
A feast seems grudgingly and mercenarily given unless it is repeatedly graced with assurances of welcome.   **35–7 To feed . . . without
it** Plain eating is best done in one's own domestic setting; on more
social occasions, the spice to a feast is ceremony; gatherings are too
unadorned without it.   **38 wait on** attend   **40 roofed** under one roof
42 Who . . . unkindness whom I hope I may reprove for negligence
55 upon a thought in a moment

57 offend him make him worse   **60 Oh, proper stuff!** Oh, nonsense!
62 air-drawn made of thin air, or floating disembodied in space
63 flaws gusts, outbursts   **64 to** compared with.   **become** befit
66 Authorized by told on the authority of   **70 thou** Banquo
71 charnel houses depositories for bones or bodies   **72–3 our . . .
kites** i.e., we will have to leave the unburied bodies to scavenging
birds of prey.   **77 Ere . . . weal** before the institution of law cleansed
the commonwealth of violence and made it civilized. (*Humane*, interchangeable with *human*, means both "appertaining to humankind"
and "benevolent, civilizing.")   **82 mortal murders** deadly wounds.
crowns heads   **92 thirst** desire to drink

And all to all.

LORDS   Our duties and the pledge.   93
                                                  [*They drink.*]

MACBETH [*seeing the Ghost*]
  Avaunt, and quit my sight! Let the earth hide thee!
  Thy bones are marrowless, thy blood is cold;
  Thou hast no speculation in those eyes   96
  Which thou dost glare with!

LADY MACBETH   Think of this, good peers,
  But as a thing of custom. 'Tis no other;
  Only it spoils the pleasure of the time.

MACBETH   What man dare, I dare.
  Approach thou like the rugged Russian bear,
  The armed rhinoceros, or th' Hyrcan tiger;   102
  Take any shape but that, and my firm nerves   103
  Shall never tremble. Or be alive again
  And dare me to the desert with thy sword.   105
  If trembling I inhabit then, protest me   106
  The baby of a girl. Hence, horrible shadow!   107
  Unreal mockery, hence!   [*Exit Ghost.*]
                        Why, so; being gone,
  I am a man again. Pray you, sit still.

LADY MACBETH
  You have displaced the mirth, broke the good meeting
  With most admired disorder.

MACBETH   Can such things be,   111
  And overcome us like a summer's cloud,   112
  Without our special wonder? You make me strange 113
  Even to the disposition that I owe,   114
  When now I think you can behold such sights
  And keep the natural ruby of your cheeks
  When mine is blanched with fear.

ROSS   What sights, my lord?

LADY MACBETH
  I pray you, speak not. He grows worse and worse;
  Question enrages him. At once, good night.   119
  Stand not upon the order of your going,   120
  But go at once.

LENNOX   Good night, and better health
  Attend His Majesty!

LADY MACBETH   A kind good night to all!
                  Exeunt Lords [*and attendants*].

MACBETH
  It will have blood, they say; blood will have blood.
  Stones have been known to move, and trees to speak; 124
  Augurs and understood relations have   125
  By maggotpies and choughs and rooks brought forth 126
  The secret'st man of blood. What is the night?   127

LADY MACBETH
  Almost at odds with morning, which is which.

MACBETH
  How say'st thou, that Macduff denies his person 129
  At our great bidding?

LADY MACBETH   Did you send to him, sir?

MACBETH
  I hear it by the way; but I will send.   131
  There's not a one of them but in his house   132
  I keep a servant fee'd. I will tomorrow—   133
  And betimes I will—to the Weird Sisters.   134
  More shall they speak, for now I am bent to know 135
  By the worst means the worst. For mine own good
  All causes shall give way. I am in blood   137
  Stepped in so far that, should I wade no more,   138
  Returning were as tedious as go o'er.   139
  Strange things I have in head, that will to hand,
  Which must be acted ere they may be scanned.   141

LADY MACBETH
  You lack the season of all natures, sleep.   142

MACBETH
  Come, we'll to sleep. My strange and self-abuse 143
  Is the initiate fear that wants hard use.   144
  We are yet but young in deed.   *Exeunt.*

❖

3.5

Thunder. Enter the three Witches, meeting Hecate.

FIRST WITCH
  Why, how now, Hecate? You look angerly.   1

HECATE
  Have I not reason, beldams as you are?   2
  Saucy and overbold, how did you dare
  To trade and traffic with Macbeth
  In riddles and affairs of death,
  And I, the mistress of your charms,
  The close contriver of all harms,   7
  Was never called to bear my part
  Or show the glory of our art?
  And, which is worse, all you have done
  Hath been but for a wayward son,
  Spiteful and wrathful, who, as others do,
  Loves for his own ends, not for you.
  But make amends now. Get you gone,
  And at the pit of Acheron   15

93 **all to all** all good wishes to all, or, let all drink to everyone else.
96 **speculation** power of sight   102 **armed** armor-plated.   **Hyrcan** of
Hyrcania, in ancient times a region near the Caspian Sea   103 **nerves**
sinews   105 **the desert** some solitary place   106–7 **If . . . girl** If then I
tremble, proclaim me a baby girl, or a girl's doll.   111 **admired disorder**
wondered-at lack of self-control.   112 **overcome** come over   113–14 **You
make . . . owe** You cause me to feel I do not know my own nature (which
I had presumed to be that of a brave man)   119 **At once** now   119 **At once** now
120 **Stand . . . going** Do not take the time to leave in ceremonious order
of rank, as you entered   124 **Stones . . . speak** i.e., Even inanimate
nature speaks in such a way as to reveal the unnatural act of murder
125–7 **Augurs . . . blood** Prophets versed in the interpretation of occult
mysteries have, by reading the signs of magpies and jackdaws, revealed
secret murderers.   127 **the night** i.e., the time of night.

129 **How say'st thou** What do you say to the fact   131 **by the way**
indirectly   132 **them** my Scottish nobles   133 **fee'd** i.e., paid to spy.
134 **betimes** (1) early (2) while there is still time   135 **bent** determined   137 **All causes** all other considerations   138 **should . . . more**
even if I were to wade no farther   139 **were** would be.   **go o'er** to
proceed.   141 **acted . . . scanned** put into performance even before
there is time to scrutinize them.   142 **season** preservative   143–4 **My
. . . use** My strange self-punishing fear is that felt by a novice who
lacks toughening experience.
3.5. Location: A heath. (This scene is probably by another author.)
1 **angerly** angrily, angry.   2 **beldams** hags   7 **close** secret
15 **Acheron** the river of sorrows in Hades; here, hell itself

Meet me i'th' morning. Thither he
Will come to know his destiny.
Your vessels and your spells provide,
Your charms and everything beside.
I am for th'air. This night I'll spend
Unto a dismal and a fatal end.   21
Great business must be wrought ere noon.
Upon the corner of the moon
There hangs a vap'rous drop profound;   24
I'll catch it ere it come to ground,
And that, distilled by magic sleights,
Shall raise such artificial sprites   27
As by the strength of their illusion
Shall draw him on to his confusion.   29
He shall spurn fate, scorn death, and bear
His hopes 'bove wisdom, grace, and fear.
And you all know, security   32
Is mortals' chiefest enemy.   *Music and a song.*
Hark! I am called. My little spirit, see,
Sits in a foggy cloud and stays for me.   [*Exit.*]   35
              Sing within, "Come away, come away," *etc.*

FIRST WITCH
Come, let's make haste. She'll soon be back again.
                                               Exeunt.

                          ❖

3.6

          Enter Lennox and another Lord.

LENNOX
My former speeches have but hit your thoughts,   1
Which can interpret farther. Only I say   2
Things have been strangely borne. The gracious
    Duncan   3
Was pitied of Macbeth; marry, he was dead.   4
And the right valiant Banquo walked too late,
Whom you may say, if't please you, Fleance killed,
For Fleance fled. Men must not walk too late.
Who cannot want the thought how monstrous   8
It was for Malcolm and for Donalbain
To kill their gracious father? Damnèd fact!   10
How it did grieve Macbeth! Did he not straight   11
In pious rage the two delinquents tear
That were the slaves of drink and thralls of sleep?   13
Was not that nobly done? Ay, and wisely too;
For 'twould have angered any heart alive
To hear the men deny't. So that I say

He has borne all things well; and I do think   17
That had he Duncan's sons under his key—
As, an't please heaven, he shall not—they should find   19
What 'twere to kill a father. So should Fleance.
But peace! For from broad words, and 'cause he failed   21
His presence at the tyrant's feast, I hear   22
Macduff lives in disgrace. Sir, can you tell
Where he bestows himself?
LORD   The son of Duncan,   24
From whom this tyrant holds the due of birth,   25
Lives in the English court, and is received
Of the most pious Edward with such grace   27
That the malevolence of fortune nothing
Takes from his high respect. Thither Macduff   29
Is gone to pray the holy king, upon his aid,   30
To wake Northumberland and warlike Siward,   31
That by the help of these—with Him above
To ratify the work—we may again
Give to our tables meat, sleep to our nights,   34
Free from our feasts and banquets bloody knives,   35
Do faithful homage, and receive free honors—   36
All which we pine for now. And this report
Hath so exasperate the King that he   38
Prepares for some attempt of war.
LENNOX   Sent he to Macduff?
LORD
He did; and with an absolute "Sir, not I,"   41
The cloudy messenger turns me his back   42
And hums, as who should say, "You'll rue the time   43
That clogs me with this answer."
LENNOX   And that well might   44
Advise him to a caution, t' hold what distance   45
His wisdom can provide. Some holy angel   46
Fly to the court of England and unfold
His message ere he come, that a swift blessing   48
May soon return to this our suffering country   49
Under a hand accursed!   50
LORD   I'll send my prayers with him.   *Exeunt.*

                          ❖

21 **dismal** disastrous, ill-omened   24 **profound** i.e., heavily pendent, ready to drop off   27 **artificial sprites** spirits produced by magical arts   29 **confusion** ruin.   32 **security** overconfidence   35.1 **"Come away,"** etc. (The song occurs in Thomas Middleton's *The Witch*.)
3.6. Location: Somewhere in Scotland.
1–2 My . . . farther What I've just said has coincided with your own thought. I needn't say more; you can surmise the rest.   3 **borne** carried on.   3–4 **The gracious . . . dead** (Lennox ironically implies that Macbeth's show of sorrow was hypocritical and came only after the murder.)   8 **cannot . . . thought** can help thinking   10 **fact** deed, crime.   11 **straight** straightway, at once   13 **thralls** slaves

17 **borne all things well** managed everything cleverly   19 **an't** if it. **should** would be sure to   21 **from broad words** on account of plain speech   22 **His presence** i.e., to be present   24 **bestows himself** is quartered, has taken refuge. **The son of Duncan** Malcolm   25 **holds . . . birth** withholds the birthright (i.e., the Scottish crown)   27 **Of** by.   **Edward** Edward the Confessor, King of England   29 **his high respect** the high respect paid to him. (Being out of fortune has not lessened the dignity with which Malcolm is received in England.)   30 **upon his aid** in aid of Malcolm   31 **wake Northumberland** rouse the people of Northumberland   34 **meat** food   35 **Free . . . banquets** free our feasts and banquets from   36 **free** freely bestowed, or, pertaining to freemen   38 **exasperate the King** exasperated Macbeth   41 **with . . . I** i.e., when Macduff answered the messenger curtly with a refusal   42 **cloudy** louring, scowling. **turns me** i.e., turns. (*Me* is used colloquially for emphasis.)   43 **hums . . . say** says "umph!" as if to say   44 **clogs** encumbers, loads   45–6 **Advise . . . provide** warn him (Macduff) to keep what safe distance he can (from Macbeth).   48 **His message** i.e., the request for aid against Scotland that Macduff is going to present to King Edward (see lines 29 ff.)   49–50 **suffering country Under** country suffering under

4.1

[A cauldron.] Thunder. Enter the three Witches.

FIRST WITCH
Thrice the brinded cat hath mewed.   1

SECOND WITCH
Thrice, and once the hedgepig whined.   2

THIRD WITCH
Harpier cries. 'Tis time, 'tis time!   3

FIRST WITCH
Round about the cauldron go;
In the poisoned entrails throw.
Toad, that under cold stone
Days and nights has thirty-one   7
Sweltered venom sleeping got,   8
Boil thou first i'th' charmèd pot.

ALL *[as they dance round the cauldron]*
Double, double, toil and trouble;
Fire burn, and cauldron bubble.

SECOND WITCH
Fillet of a fenny snake,   12
In the cauldron boil and bake;
Eye of newt and toe of frog,
Wool of bat and tongue of dog,
Adder's fork and blindworm's sting,   16
Lizard's leg and owlet's wing,
For a charm of powerful trouble,
Like a hell-broth boil and bubble.

ALL
Double, double, toil and trouble;
Fire burn, and cauldron bubble.

THIRD WITCH
Scale of dragon, tooth of wolf,
Witches' mummy, maw and gulf   23
Of the ravined salt-sea shark,   24
Root of hemlock digged i'th' dark,
Liver of blaspheming Jew,
Gall of goat, and slips of yew   27
Slivered in the moon's eclipse,   28
Nose of Turk and Tartar's lips,
Finger of birth-strangled babe
Ditch-delivered by a drab,   31
Make the gruel thick and slab.   32
Add thereto a tiger's chaudron   33
For th'ingredience of our cauldron.   34

ALL
Double, double, toil and trouble;
Fire burn, and cauldron bubble.

SECOND WITCH
Cool it with a baboon's blood,
Then the charm is firm and good.   38

Enter Hecate to the other three Witches.

HECATE
Oh, well done! I commend your pains,   39
And everyone shall share i'th' gains.
And now about the cauldron sing
Like elves and fairies in a ring,
Enchanting all that you put in.   43
          Music and a song: "Black spirits," etc.
                                    [Exit Hecate.]

SECOND WITCH
By the pricking of my thumbs,
Something wicked this way comes.
          Open, locks,
          Whoever knocks!

Enter Macbeth.

MACBETH
How now, you secret, black, and midnight hags?   48
What is't you do?

ALL   A deed without a name.

MACBETH
I conjure you, by that which you profess,
Howe'er you come to know it, answer me.
Though you untie the winds and let them fight
Against the churches, though the yeasty waves   53
Confound and swallow navigation up,   54
Though bladed corn be lodged and trees blown down,   55
Though castles topple on their warders' heads,   56
Though palaces and pyramids do slope   57
Their heads to their foundations, though the treasure
Of nature's germens tumble all together   59
Even till destruction sicken, answer me   60
To what I ask you.

FIRST WITCH   Speak.

SECOND WITCH   Demand.

THIRD WITCH   We'll answer.

FIRST WITCH
Say if thou'dst rather hear it from our mouths
Or from our masters?

MACBETH   Call 'em. Let me see 'em.

FIRST WITCH
Pour in sow's blood, that hath eaten
Her nine farrow; grease that's sweaten   65

4.1. Location: A cavern (see 3.5.15). In the middle, a boiling cauldron (provided presumably by means of the trapdoor; see 4.1.106. The trapdoor must also be used in this scene for the apparitions.) **1 brinded** marked by streaks (as by fire), brindled   **2 hedgepig** hedgehog   **3 Harpier** (The name of a familiar spirit; probably derived from *harpy*.) **cries** i.e., gives the signal to begin   **7–8 Days . . . got** for thirty-one days and nights has exuded venom formed during sleep **12 Fillet** Slice.   **fenny** inhabiting fens or swamps   **16 fork** forked tongue.   **blindworm** slowworm, a harmless burrowing lizard **23 mummy** mummified flesh made into a magical potion.   **maw and gulf** gullet and stomach   **24 ravined** ravenous, or glutted with prey (?) **27 Gall** gall bladder.   **slips** cuttings for grafting or planting.   **yew** (A tree often planted in churchyards and associated with mourning.) **28 Slivered** broken off (as a branch)   **31 Ditch . . . drab** born in a ditch of a harlot   **32 slab** viscous.   **33 chaudron** entrails **34 th'ingredience** the ingredients

38.1 other (Said because Hecate is a witch, too, not because more witches enter.)   **39–43 Oh . . . in** (These lines are universally regarded as non-Shakespearean.)   **43.1 "Black spirits," etc.** (This song is found in Middleton's *The Witch*.)   **48 black** i.e., dealing in black magic **53 yeasty** foamy   **54 Confound** destroy   **55 Though . . . lodged** though unripe grain be laid flat   **56 warders'** guardsmen's   **57 slope** bend   **59 nature's germens** seed or elements from which all nature operates   **60 sicken** be surfeited with its own excess   **65 nine farrow** litter of nine.   **sweaten** sweated

From the murderer's gibbet throw   66
Into the flame.
ALL   Come high or low,   67
Thyself and office deftly show!   68

Thunder. First Apparition, an armed Head.

MACBETH
Tell me, thou unknown power—
FIRST WITCH   He knows thy thought.
Hear his speech, but say thou naught.
FIRST APPARITION
Macbeth! Macbeth! Macbeth! Beware Macduff,
Beware the Thane of Fife. Dismiss me. Enough.   72
                    He descends.

MACBETH
Whate'er thou art, for thy good caution, thanks;
Thou hast harped my fear aright. But one word
    more—   74
FIRST WITCH
He will not be commanded. Here's another,
More potent than the first.   76

Thunder. Second Apparition, a bloody Child.

SECOND APPARITION   Macbeth! Macbeth! Macbeth!
MACBETH   Had I three ears, I'd hear thee.
SECOND APPARITION
Be bloody, bold, and resolute; laugh to scorn
The power of man, for none of woman born
Shall harm Macbeth.   *Descends.*
MACBETH
Then live, Macduff; what need I fear of thee?
But yet I'll make assurance double sure,
And take a bond of fate. Thou shalt not live,   84
That I may tell pale-hearted fear it lies,
And sleep in spite of thunder.   86

*Thunder. Third Apparition, a Child crowned, with
a tree in his hand.*

                    What is this
That rises like the issue of a king   87
And wears upon his baby brow the round   88
And top of sovereignty?
ALL   Listen, but speak not to't.   89
THIRD APPARITION
Be lion-mettled, proud, and take no care
Who chafes, who frets, or where conspirers are.
Macbeth shall never vanquished be until

Great Birnam Wood to high Dunsinane Hill
Shall come against him.   *Descends.*
MACBETH   That will never be.
Who can impress the forest, bid the tree   95
Unfix his earthbound root? Sweet bodements, good!   96
Rebellious dead, rise never till the wood   97
Of Birnam rise, and our high-placed Macbeth   98
Shall live the lease of nature, pay his breath   99
To time and mortal custom. Yet my heart   100
Throbs to know one thing. Tell me, if your art
Can tell so much: shall Banquo's issue ever
Reign in this kingdom?
ALL   Seek to know no more.
MACBETH
I will be satisfied. Deny me this,
And an eternal curse fall on you! Let me know.   105
        [*The cauldron descends.*] *Hautboys.*
Why sinks that cauldron? And what noise is this?   106
FIRST WITCH   Show!
SECOND WITCH   Show!
THIRD WITCH   Show!
ALL
Show his eyes, and grieve his heart;
Come like shadows, so depart!   111

*A show of eight Kings and Banquo last; [the eighth
King] with a glass in his hand.*

MACBETH
Thou art too like the spirit of Banquo. Down!
Thy crown does sear mine eyeballs. And thy hair,
Thou other gold-bound brow, is like the first.   114
A third is like the former. Filthy hags,
Why do you show me this? A fourth? Start, eyes!   116
What, will the line stretch out to th' crack of doom?   117
Another yet? A seventh? I'll see no more.
And yet the eighth appears, who bears a glass
Which shows me many more; and some I see
That twofold balls and treble scepters carry.   121
Horrible sight! Now I see 'tis true,
For the blood-boltered Banquo smiles upon me   123
And points at them for his. [*The apparitions vanish.*]
    What, is this so?   124

95 **impress** press into service, like soldiers   96 **bodements** prophecies   97–8 **Rebellious . . . rise** i.e., May the souls of those I have murdered (Banquo, Duncan) never rise again, since trees themself cannot rise. (An image of the Day of Judgment, when bodies are prophesied to rise again; see *Henry V*, 4.1.135–8.)   99–100 **Shall . . . custom** will live out his full life span until it is time for him to expire (*pay his breath*) in the way of all mortals.   105.1 *Hautboys* oboelike instruments   106 **noise** music   111.1 *eight Kings* (Banquo was the supposed ancestor of the Stuart dynasty, leading forward to King James VI of Scotland and James I of England, the *eighth King* here.)   111.2 *glass* (magic) mirror (also in line 119)   114 **other** i.e., second   116 **Start** Bulge from their sockets   117 **th' crack of doom** the thunder-peal of Doomsday at the end of time.   121 **twofold balls** (A probable reference to the double coronation of James at Scone and Westminster, as King of England and Scotland.)   **treble scepters** (Probably refers to James' assumed title as King of Great Britain, France, and Ireland.)   123 **blood-boltered** having his hair matted with blood   124 **for his** as his descendants.

66 **gibbet** gallows   67 **high or low** of the upper or lower air, from under the earth or in hell; or, one and all   68 **office** function. **68.1** *armed Head* (Perhaps symbolizes the head of Macbeth cut off by Macduff and presented by him to Malcolm, or else the head of Macduff, armed in rebellion against Macbeth.)   72.1 *He descends* (i.e., by means of the trapdoor).   74 **harped** hit, touched (as in touching a harp to make it sound)   76.1 *bloody Child* (Symbolizes Macbeth untimely ripped from his mother's womb; see 5.8.15–16.)   84 **take a bond of** get a guarantee from (i.e., by killing Macduff, to make doubly sure he can do no harm)   86.1-2 *Child . . . hand* (Symbolizes Malcolm, the royal child; the tree anticipates the cutting of boughs in Birnam Wood, 5.4.)   87 **like** in the likeness of   88–9 **round And top** crown

FIRST WITCH
Ay, sir, all this is so. But why   125
Stands Macbeth thus amazedly?   126
Come, sisters, cheer we up his sprites   127
And show the best of our delights.
I'll charm the air to give a sound,
While you perform your antic round,   130
That this great king may kindly say
Our duties did his welcome pay.   132
              Music. The Witches dance, and vanish.

MACBETH
Where are they? Gone? Let this pernicious hour
Stand aye accursèd in the calendar!
Come in, without there!

       Enter Lennox.

LENNOX   What's Your Grace's will?
MACBETH
Saw you the Weird Sisters?
LENNOX   No, my lord.
MACBETH
Came they not by you?
LENNOX   No, indeed, my lord.
MACBETH
Infected be the air whereon they ride,
And damned all those that trust them! I did hear
The galloping of horse. Who was't came by?   140
LENNOX
'Tis two or three, my lord, that bring you word
Macduff is fled to England.
MACBETH   Fled to England!
LENNOX
Ay, my good lord.
MACBETH [*aside*]
Time, thou anticipat'st my dread exploits.   144
The flighty purpose never is o'ertook   145
Unless the deed go with it. From this moment   146
The very firstlings of my heart shall be   147
The firstlings of my hand. And even now,   148
To crown my thoughts with acts, be it thought and
      done:
The castle of Macduff I will surprise,   150
Seize upon Fife, give to th'edge o'th' sword
His wife, his babes, and all unfortunate souls
That trace him in his line. No boasting like a fool;   153
This deed I'll do before this purpose cool.
But no more sights!—Where are these gentlemen?
Come, bring me where they are.   *Exeunt.*

               ♣

4.2

       Enter Macduff's Wife, her Son, and Ross.

LADY MACDUFF
What had he done to make him fly the land?
ROSS
You must have patience, madam.
LADY MACDUFF   He had none.
His flight was madness. When our actions do not,   3
Our fears do make us traitors.
ROSS   You know not   4
Whether it was his wisdom or his fear.
LADY MACDUFF
Wisdom? To leave his wife, to leave his babes,
His mansion, and his titles in a place   7
From whence himself does fly? He loves us not,
He wants the natural touch; for the poor wren,   9
The most diminutive of birds, will fight,
Her young ones in her nest, against the owl.   11
All is the fear and nothing is the love,
As little is the wisdom, where the flight
So runs against all reason.
ROSS   My dearest coz,   14
I pray you, school yourself. But, for your husband,   15
He is noble, wise, judicious, and best knows
The fits o'th' season. I dare not speak much further, 17
But cruel are the times when we are traitors   18
And do not know ourselves, when we hold rumor   19
From what we fear, yet know not what we fear,   20
But float upon a wild and violent sea
Each way and none. I take my leave of you;   22
Shall not be long but I'll be here again.   23
Things at the worst will cease, or else climb upward
To what they were before.—My pretty cousin,
Blessing upon you!
LADY MACDUFF
Fathered he is, and yet he's fatherless.
ROSS
I am so much a fool, should I stay longer
It would be my disgrace and your discomfort.   29
I take my leave at once.   *Exit Ross.*
LADY MACDUFF   Sirrah, your father's dead;   31
And what will you do now? How will you live?
SON
As birds do, mother.
LADY MACDUFF   What, with worms and flies?
SON
With what I get, I mean; and so do they.

4.2. Location: Fife. Macduff's castle.
3–4 When . . . traitors Even when we have committed no treasonous act, our fearful responses make us look guilty.   **7 titles** possessions to which he has title   **9 wants . . . touch** lacks the natural instinct to protect his family   **11 Her . . . nest** when her young ones are in the nest   **14 coz** kinswoman   **15 school** control.   **for** as for   **17 fits o'th' season** violent convulsions of the time.   **18–19 are traitors . . . ourselves** are alienated from one another by a climate of fear and suspected treason   **19–20 hold . . . From what we fear** believe every fearful rumor on the basis of what we fear might be   **22 Each . . . none** this way and that.   **23 Shall** it shall.   **but** before   **29 It . . . discomfort** I should disgrace my manhood by weeping and cause you distress.   **31 Sirrah** (Here, an affectionate form of address to a child.)

125–32 Ay . . . pay (These lines are assumed to have been written by someone other than Shakespeare.)   **126 amazedly** stunned   **127 sprites** spirits   **130 antic round** grotesque dance in a circle   **132 pay** repay.   **140 horse** horses.   **144 thou anticipat'st** you forestall   **145 flighty** fleeting   **146 Unless . . . it** unless the execution of the deed accompanies the conception of it immediately.   **147–8 The very . . . hand** the firstborn promptings of my heart will become my first of deeds.   **150 surprise** attack without warning   **153 trace . . . line** follow him in the line of inheritance.

LADY MACDUFF   Poor bird! Thou'dst never fear   35
The net nor lime, the pitfall nor the gin.   36

SON
Why should I, mother? Poor birds they are not set for.   37
My father is not dead, for all your saying.

LADY MACDUFF
Yes, he is dead. How wilt thou do for a father?

SON   Nay, how will you do for a husband?

LADY MACDUFF   Why, I can buy me twenty at any
market.

SON   Then you'll buy 'em to sell again.

LADY MACDUFF
Thou speak'st with all thy wit,
And yet, i'faith, with wit enough for thee.

SON   Was my father a traitor, mother?

LADY MACDUFF   Ay, that he was.

SON   What is a traitor?

LADY MACDUFF   Why, one that swears and lies.

SON   And be all traitors that do so?

LADY MACDUFF
Every one that does so is a traitor,
And must be hanged.

SON
And must they all be hanged that swear and lie?

LADY MACDUFF   Every one.

SON   Who must hang them?

LADY MACDUFF   Why, the honest men.

SON   Then the liars and swearers are fools, for there are
liars and swearers enough to beat the honest men and
hang up them.

LADY MACDUFF   Now, God help thee, poor monkey!
But how wilt thou do for a father?

SON   If he were dead, you'd weep for him; if you would
not, it were a good sign that I should quickly have a
new father.

LADY MACDUFF   Poor prattler, how thou talk'st!

Enter a Messenger.

MESSENGER
Bless you, fair dame! I am not to you known,
Though in your state of honor I am perfect.   67
I doubt some danger does approach you nearly.   68
If you will take a homely man's advice,   69
Be not found here. Hence with your little ones!
To fright you thus, methinks, I am too savage;
To do worse to you were fell cruelty,   72
Which is too nigh your person. Heaven preserve you!   73
I dare abide no longer.   *Exit Messenger.*

LADY MACDUFF   Whither should I fly?
I have done no harm. But I remember now
I am in this earthly world, where to do harm
Is often laudable, to do good sometime
Accounted dangerous folly. Why then, alas,

Do I put up that womanly defense
To say I have done no harm?

Enter Murderers.

What are these faces?

FIRST MURDERER   Where is your husband?

LADY MACDUFF
I hope in no place so unsanctified
Where such as thou mayst find him.

FIRST MURDERER   He's a traitor.

SON
Thou liest, thou shag-haired villain!

FIRST MURDERER   What, you egg?
[*He stabs him.*]
Young fry of treachery!

SON   He has killed me, mother.   85
Run away, I pray you!   [*He dies.*]
Exit [Lady Macduff] crying "Murder!"
[*followed by the Murderers with the Son's body*].

❦

4.3

Enter Malcolm and Macduff.

MALCOLM
Let us seek out some desolate shade, and there
Weep our sad bosoms empty.

MACDUFF   Let us rather
Hold fast the mortal sword, and like good men   3
Bestride our downfall'n birthdom. Each new morn   4
New widows howl, new orphans cry, new sorrows
Strike heaven on the face, that it resounds   6
As if it felt with Scotland and yelled out   7
Like syllable of dolor.

MALCOLM   What I believe, I'll wail;   8
What know, believe; and what I can redress,   9
As I shall find the time to friend, I will.   10
What you have spoke it may be so, perchance.
This tyrant, whose sole name blisters our tongues,   12
Was once thought honest. You have loved him well;
He hath not touched you yet. I am young; but
something   14
You may deserve of him through me, and wisdom   15
To offer up a weak, poor, innocent lamb
T'appease an angry god.

MACDUFF   I am not treacherous.

MALCOLM   But Macbeth is.

---

85 **fry** spawn, progeny
4.3. Location: England. Before King Edward the Confessor's palace.
3 mortal deadly   **4 Bestride** stand over in defense.   **birthdom** native
land.   **6 that it resounds** so that it echoes   **7–8 As . . . dolor** as if
heaven, feeling itself the blow delivered to Scotland, cried out with a
similar cry of pain.   **8–9 What . . . believe** i.e., What I believe to be
amiss in Scotland I will grieve for, and anything I am certain to be
true I will believe. (But one must be cautious in these duplicitous
times.)   **10 to friend** opportune, congenial   **12 sole** mere   **14 He . . .
yet** i.e., the fact that Macbeth hasn't hurt you yet makes me suspicious of your loyalties.   **young** i.e., inexperienced   **14–15 something
. . . me** i.e., you may win favor with Macbeth by delivering me to him
15 wisdom i.e., it would be worldly-wise

35 **Thou'dst never fear** You are too innocent to be prudently wary of
36 **lime** birdlime (a sticky substance put on branches to snare birds).
gin snare.   37 **Poor . . . for** i.e., Traps are not set for *poor* birds, as you
call me.   67 **Though . . . perfect** though I am perfectly acquainted
with your honorable state.   68 **doubt** fear   69 **homely** plain
72–3 **To . . . person** to do actual harm to you would be savage cruelty,
which cruelty is all too near at hand.

A good and virtuous nature may recoil   20
In an imperial charge. But I shall crave your pardon.   21
That which you are my thoughts cannot transpose;   22
Angels are bright still, though the brightest fell.   23
Though all things foul would wear the brows of grace,   24
Yet grace must still look so.

MACDUFF   I have lost my hopes.   25

MALCOLM
Perchance even there where I did find my doubts.   26
Why in that rawness left you wife and child,   27
Those precious motives, those strong knots of love,
Without leave-taking? I pray you,
Let not my jealousies be your dishonors,   30
But mine own safeties. You may be rightly just,   31
Whatever I shall think.

MACDUFF   Bleed, bleed, poor country!
Great tyranny, lay thou thy basis sure,   33
For goodness dare not check thee; wear thou thy
    wrongs,   34
The title is affeered! Fare thee well, lord.   35
I would not be the villain that thou think'st
For the whole space that's in the tyrant's grasp,
And the rich East to boot.

MALCOLM   Be not offended.   38
I speak not as in absolute fear of you.   39
I think our country sinks beneath the yoke;
It weeps, it bleeds, and each new day a gash
Is added to her wounds. I think withal   42
There would be hands uplifted in my right;   43
And here from gracious England have I offer   44
Of goodly thousands. But, for all this,
When I shall tread upon the tyrant's head,
Or wear it on my sword, yet my poor country
Shall have more vices than it had before,
More suffer, and more sundry ways than ever,   49
By him that shall succeed.

MACDUFF   What should he be?   50

MALCOLM
It is myself I mean, in whom I know

All the particulars of vice so grafted   52
That, when they shall be opened, black Macbeth   53
Will seem as pure as snow, and the poor state
Esteem him as a lamb, being compared
With my confineless harms.

MACDUFF   Not in the legions   56
Of horrid hell can come a devil more damned
In evils to top Macbeth.

MALCOLM   I grant him bloody,   58
Luxurious, avaricious, false, deceitful,   59
Sudden, malicious, smacking of every sin   60
That has a name. But there's no bottom, none,
In my voluptuousness. Your wives, your daughters,
Your matrons, and your maids could not fill up
The cistern of my lust, and my desire
All continent impediments would o'erbear   65
That did oppose my will. Better Macbeth   66
Than such an one to reign.

MACDUFF   Boundless intemperance
In nature is a tyranny; it hath been   68
Th'untimely emptying of the happy throne
And fall of many kings. But fear not yet   70
To take upon you what is yours. You may
Convey your pleasures in a spacious plenty,   72
And yet seem cold; the time you may so hoodwink.   73
We have willing dames enough. There cannot be
That vulture in you to devour so many
As will to greatness dedicate themselves,
Finding it so inclined.

MALCOLM   With this there grows
In my most ill-composed affection such   78
A stanchless avarice that, were I king,   79
I should cut off the nobles for their lands,
Desire his jewels and this other's house,   81
And my more-having would be as a sauce
To make me hunger more, that I should forge   83
Quarrels unjust against the good and loyal,
Destroying them for wealth.

MACDUFF   This avarice
Sticks deeper, grows with more pernicious root
Than summer-seeming lust, and it hath been   87
The sword of our slain kings. Yet do not fear;   88
Scotland hath foisons to fill up your will   89
Of your mere own. All these are portable,   90
With other graces weighed.   91

MALCOLM
But I have none. The king-becoming graces,
As justice, verity, temperance, stableness,

20–1 A good . . . charge i.e., Even as good a virtuous nature as you
have, Macduff, may give way to the insinuations of a royal command
from Macbeth. (With wordplay on the *recoil* of a firearm that is
charged with power and shot.)   22 That . . . transpose My suspicious
thoughts cannot change you from what you are, cannot make you
evil   23 the brightest i.e., Lucifer   24–5 Though . . . so Even though
evil puts on the appearance of good so often as to cast that appearance into deep suspicion, yet goodness must go on looking and acting like itself.   25 hopes i.e., hopes of persuading Malcolm to lead
the cause against Macbeth.   26 Perchance even there i.e., Perhaps in
that same mistrustful frame of mind.   doubts i.e., fears such as that
Macduff may covertly be on Macbeth's side.   27 rawness unprotected condition. (Malcolm suggests that Macduff's leaving his family
unprotected could be construed as more evidence of his not having
anything to fear from Macbeth.)   30–1 Let . . . safeties may it be true
that my suspicions of your lack of honor are founded only in my own
wariness.   33 basis foundation   34 check rebuke, call to account.
wear . . . wrongs continue to enjoy your wrongfully gained powers
35 affeered confirmed, certified.   38 to boot in addition
39 absolute fear complete mistrust   42 withal in addition   43 right
cause   44 England the King of England   49 More . . . ways suffer
more grievously and in more varied ways   50 What . . . be? Whom
could you possibly mean?

52 grafted (1) engrafted, indissolubly mixed (2) grafted like a plant
that will then *open* or unfold   53 opened unfolded (like a bud)
56 confineless limitless   58 top surpass   59 Luxurious lecherous
60 Sudden violent, impetuous   65 continent (1) chaste (2) restraining, containing   66 will lust. (Also in line 89.)   68 nature human
nature   70 yet nevertheless   72 Convey manage with secrecy
73 cold chaste.   the time . . . hoodwink you may thus deceive the
age.   78 ill-composed affection evil disposition   79 stanchless insatiable   81 his one man's.   this other's another's   83 that so that
87 summer-seeming appropriate to youth (and lessening in later
years)   88 sword i.e., cause of overthrow   89 foisons resources,
plenty   90 Of . . . own out of your own royal estates alone.
portable bearable   91 weighed counterbalanced.

Bounty, perseverance, mercy, lowliness,   94
Devotion, patience, courage, fortitude,
I have no relish of them, but abound   96
In the division of each several crime,   97
Acting it many ways. Nay, had I power, I should
Pour the sweet milk of concord into hell,
Uproar the universal peace, confound   100
All unity on earth.
MACDUFF   O Scotland, Scotland!
MALCOLM
If such a one be fit to govern, speak.
I am as I have spoken.
MACDUFF   Fit to govern?
No, not to live. Oh, nation miserable,
With an untitled tyrant bloody-sceptered,   105
When shalt thou see thy wholesome days again,
Since that the truest issue of thy throne
By his own interdiction stands accurst   108
And does blaspheme his breed? Thy royal father   109
Was a most sainted king; the queen that bore thee,
Oft'ner upon her knees than on her feet,
Died every day she lived. Fare thee well.   112
These evils thou repeat'st upon thyself
Hath banished me from Scotland. O my breast,   114
Thy hope ends here!
MALCOLM   Macduff, this noble passion,
Child of integrity, hath from my soul   116
Wiped the black scruples, reconciled my thoughts
To thy good truth and honor. Devilish Macbeth
By many of these trains hath sought to win me   119
Into his power, and modest wisdom plucks me   120
From overcredulous haste. But God above
Deal between thee and me! For even now
I put myself to thy direction and
Unspeak mine own detraction, here abjure   124
The taints and blames I laid upon myself
For strangers to my nature. I am yet   126
Unknown to woman, never was forsworn,   127
Scarcely have coveted what was mine own,
At no time broke my faith, would not betray
The devil to his fellow, and delight
No less in truth than life. My first false speaking
Was this upon myself. What I am truly   132
Is thine and my poor country's to command—
Whither indeed, before thy here-approach,
Old Siward with ten thousand warlike men,
Already at a point, was setting forth.   136

Now we'll together; and the chance of goodness   137
Be like our warranted quarrel!—Why are you silent?   138
MACDUFF
Such welcome and unwelcome things at once
'Tis hard to reconcile.

Enter a Doctor.

MALCOLM
Well, more anon.—Comes the King forth, I pray you?
DOCTOR
Ay, sir. There are a crew of wretched souls
That stay his cure. Their malady convinces   143
The great essay of art; but at his touch—   144
Such sanctity hath heaven given his hand—
They presently amend.
MALCOLM   I thank you, Doctor.   146

Exit [Doctor].

MACDUFF
What's the disease he means?
MALCOLM   'Tis called the evil.   147
A most miraculous work in this good king,
Which often, since my here-remain in England,   149
I have seen him do. How he solicits heaven   150
Himself best knows; but strangely-visited people,   151
All swoll'n and ulcerous, pitiful to the eye,
The mere despair of surgery, he cures,   153
Hanging a golden stamp about their necks   154
Put on with holy prayers; and 'tis spoken,   155
To the succeeding royalty he leaves   156
The healing benediction. With this strange virtue   157
He hath a heavenly gift of prophecy,
And sundry blessings hang about his throne
That speak him full of grace.

Enter Ross.

MACDUFF   See who comes here.
MALCOLM
My countryman, but yet I know him not.   161
MACDUFF
My ever-gentle cousin, welcome hither.   162
MALCOLM
I know him now. Good God betimes remove   163
The means that makes us strangers!
ROSS   Sir, amen.
MACDUFF
Stands Scotland where it did?
ROSS   Alas, poor country,
Almost afraid to know itself. It cannot

---

94 lowliness humility   **96 relish** flavor or trace   **97 division** subdivisions, various possible forms.   **several** separate   **100 Uproar** throw into an uproar   **105 untitled** lacking rightful title, usurping   **108 interdiction** debarring of self   **109 does blaspheme his breed** defames his breeding, i.e., is a disgrace to his royal lineage.   **112 Died . . . lived** lived a life of daily mortification.   **114 breast** heart   **116 Child of integrity** a product of your integrity of spirit; or, you person of perfect integrity   **119 trains** plots, artifices   **120 modest . . . me** wise prudence holds me back   **124 Unspeak . . . detraction** take back all I said in detraction of myself   **126 For** as   **127 Unknown to woman** a virgin   **132 upon** against   **136 at a point** prepared

137–8 the chance . . . quarrel may our chance of success be proportionate to the justice of our cause.   **143 stay** wait for.   **convinces** conquers   **144 essay of art** efforts of medical skill   **146 presently** immediately   **147 evil** i.e., scrofula, supposedly cured by the royal touch; James I claimed this power.   **149 here-remain** stay   **150 solicits** prevails by prayer with   **151 strangely-visited** afflicted by strange diseases   **153 mere** utter   **154 stamp** minted coin   **155–7 and 'tis . . . benediction** it is said that he bequeaths this healing blessedness to his royal progeny.   **157 virtue** healing power   **161 My countryman** (So identified by his dress.)   **know** recognize   **162 gentle** noble   **163 betimes** speedily

Be called our mother, but our grave; where nothing   167
But who knows nothing is once seen to smile;   168
Where sighs and groans and shrieks that rend the air
Are made, not marked; where violent sorrow seems   170
A modern ecstasy. The dead man's knell   171
Is there scarce asked for who, and good men's lives
Expire before the flowers in their caps,   173
Dying or ere they sicken.

MACDUFF   Oh, relation   174
Too nice, and yet too true!

MALCOLM   What's the newest grief?   175

ROSS
That of an hour's age doth hiss the speaker;   176
Each minute teems a new one.

MACDUFF   How does my wife?   177

ROSS
Why, well.

MACDUFF   And all my children?

ROSS   Well too.   178

MACDUFF
The tyrant has not battered at their peace?

ROSS
No, they were well at peace when I did leave 'em.

MACDUFF
Be not a niggard of your speech. How goes't?

ROSS
When I came hither to transport the tidings
Which I have heavily borne, there ran a rumor   183
Of many worthy fellows that were out,   184
Which was to my belief witnessed the rather   185
For that I saw the tyrant's power afoot.   186
Now is the time of help. [*To Malcolm*] Your eye in
     Scotland
Would create soldiers, make our women fight,   188
To doff their dire distresses.

MALCOLM   Be't their comfort   189
We are coming thither. Gracious England hath   190
Lent us good Siward and ten thousand men;
An older and a better soldier none   192
That Christendom gives out.

ROSS   Would I could answer   193
This comfort with the like! But I have words
That would be howled out in the desert air,   195
Where hearing should not latch them.

MACDUFF   What concern they?   196

The general cause? Or is it a fee-grief   197
Due to some single breast?

ROSS   No mind that's honest   198
But in it shares some woe, though the main part
Pertains to you alone.

MACDUFF   If it be mine,
Keep it not from me; quickly let me have it.

ROSS
Let not your ears despise my tongue forever,
Which shall possess them with the heaviest sound   203
That ever yet they heard.

MACDUFF   Hum! I guess at it.

ROSS
Your castle is surprised, your wife and babes
Savagely slaughtered. To relate the manner
Were, on the quarry of these murdered deer,   207
To add the death of you.

MALCOLM   Merciful heaven!
What, man, ne'er pull your hat upon your brows;   209
Give sorrow words. The grief that does not speak
Whispers the o'erfraught heart and bids it break.   211

MACDUFF
My children too?

ROSS   Wife, children, servants, all
That could be found.

MACDUFF   And I must be from thence!   213
My wife killed too?

ROSS   I have said.

MALCOLM   Be comforted.
Let's make us med'cines of our great revenge
To cure this deadly grief.

MACDUFF
He has no children. All my pretty ones?   217
Did you say all? O hell-kite! All?   218
What, all my pretty chickens and their dam
At one fell swoop?   220

MALCOLM   Dispute it like a man.   221

MACDUFF   I shall do so;
But I must also feel it as a man.
I cannot but remember such things were,
That were most precious to me. Did heaven look on
And would not take their part? Sinful Macduff,
They were all struck for thee! Naught that I am,   227
Not for their own demerits, but for mine,
Fell slaughter on their souls. Heaven rest them now!

MALCOLM
Be this the whetstone of your sword. Let grief
Convert to anger; blunt not the heart, enrage it.

167–8 nothing But who nobody except a person who   **168 once** ever
170 marked noticed (because they are so common)   **171 modern
ecstasy** commonplace emotion.   **173 flowers** (Often worn in Elizabethan caps.)   **174 or ere they sicken** before they have had time to
fall ill.   **relation** report   **175 nice** minutely accurate, elaborately
phrased   **176 That . . . speaker** The speaker of news that is scarcely
an hour old is hissed at for reporting stale news   **177 teems** teems
with, yields   **178 well** (Ross quibbles, in his reluctance to tell the bad
news. "The dead are well" means they are at rest.)   **183 heavily**
sadly   **184–6 Of . . . afoot** about many worthy Scots who have been
driven into exile and armed rebellion, which rumor was strengthened
all the more when I saw Macbeth's army on the move (in anticipation
of being attacked).   **188 our women** even our women   **189 doff** put
off, get rid of   **190 Gracious England** i.e., Edward the Confessor
192 none there is none   **193 gives out** tells of, proclaims.   **195 would**
should   **196 latch** catch (the sound of)

197 fee-grief a grief with an individual owner, having absolute ownership   **198 Due to** i.e., owned by   **203 possess them with** put them
in possession of   **207 quarry** heap of slaughtered deer at a hunt.
(With a pun on *dear, deer*.)   **209 pull your hat** (A conventional gesture
of grief.)   **211 Whispers** whispers to.   **o'erfraught** overburdened
213 must had to   **217 He has no children** (Referring either to Macbeth, who must not be a father if he can do such a thing, or, to Malcolm, who speaks comfortingly without knowing what such a loss
feels like to a father.)   **218 hell-kite** (The *kite* is a rapacious bird of
prey; a term of disdain and dislike.)   **220 fell** cruel   **221 Dispute**
Strive against, debate   **227 for thee** i.e., as divine punishment for
your sins.   **Naught** Wicked

MACDUFF
    Oh, I could play the woman with mine eyes
    And braggart with my tongue! But, gentle heavens,
    Cut short all intermission. Front to front   234
    Bring thou this fiend of Scotland and myself;
    Within my sword's length set him. If he scape,   236
    Heaven forgive him too!
MALCOLM   This tune goes manly.   237
    Come, go we to the King. Our power is ready;   238
    Our lack is nothing but our leave. Macbeth   239
    Is ripe for shaking, and the powers above
    Put on their instruments. Receive what cheer you may. 241
    The night is long that never finds the day.   *Exeunt.*

❧

5.1

    Enter a Doctor of Physic and a Waiting-
    Gentlewoman.

DOCTOR   I have two nights watched with you, but can
  perceive no truth in your report. When was it she last
  walked?
GENTLEWOMAN   Since His Majesty went into the field, I
  have seen her rise from her bed, throw her nightgown
  upon her, unlock her closet, take forth paper, fold it,   5
  write upon't, read it, afterwards seal it, and again
  return to bed; yet all this while in a most fast sleep.
DOCTOR   A great perturbation in nature, to receive at
  once the benefit of sleep and do the effects of   9
  watching! In this slumbery agitation, besides her   10
  walking and other actual performances, what, at any
  time, have you heard her say?
GENTLEWOMAN   That, sir, which I will not report after her.
DOCTOR   You may to me, and 'tis most meet you should.   15
GENTLEWOMAN   Neither to you nor anyone, having no
  witness to confirm my speech.

    Enter Lady [Macbeth], with a taper.

    Lo you, here she comes! This is her very guise, and,
  upon my life, fast asleep. Observe her. Stand close.   19
                          [*They stand aside.*]
DOCTOR   How came she by that light?
GENTLEWOMAN   Why, it stood by her. She has light by
  her continually. 'Tis her command.
DOCTOR   You see her eyes are open.
GENTLEWOMAN   Ay, but their sense are shut.
DOCTOR   What is it she does now? Look how she rubs
  her hands.
GENTLEWOMAN   It is an accustomed action with her to
  seem thus washing her hands. I have known her
  continue in this a quarter of an hour.

LADY MACBETH   Yet here's a spot.
DOCTOR   Hark, she speaks. I will set down what comes
  from her, to satisfy my remembrance the more   32
  strongly.
LADY MACBETH   Out, damned spot! Out, I say! One—
  two—why then, 'tis time to do't. Hell is murky.—
  Fie, my lord, fie, a soldier, and afeard? What need we
  fear who knows it, when none can call our power to
  account? Yet who would have thought the old man to
  have had so much blood in him?
DOCTOR   Do you mark that?
LADY MACBETH   The Thane of Fife had a wife. Where is
  she now?—What, will these hands ne'er be
  clean?—No more o'that, my lord, no more o' that;
  you mar all with this starting.   44
DOCTOR   Go to, go to. You have known what you   45
  should not.
GENTLEWOMAN   She has spoke what she should not, I
  am sure of that. Heaven knows what she has known!
LADY MACBETH   Here's the smell of the blood still. All
  the perfumes of Arabia will not sweeten this little
  hand. Oh, oh, oh!
DOCTOR   What a sigh is there! The heart is sorely   52
  charged.   53
GENTLEWOMAN   I would not have such a heart in my
  bosom for the dignity of the whole body.   55
DOCTOR   Well, well, well.
GENTLEWOMAN   Pray God it be, sir.   57
DOCTOR   This disease is beyond my practice. Yet I have
  known those which have walked in their sleep who
  have died holily in their beds.
LADY MACBETH   Wash your hands, put on your night-
  gown; look not so pale! I tell you yet again, Banquo's
  buried. He cannot come out on 's grave.   63
DOCTOR   Even so?
LADY MACBETH   To bed, to bed! There's knocking at the
  gate. Come, come, come, come, give me your hand.
  What's done cannot be undone. To bed, to bed,
  to bed!   *Exit Lady.*
DOCTOR   Will she go now to bed?
GENTLEWOMAN   Directly.
DOCTOR
    Foul whisperings are abroad. Unnatural deeds
    Do breed unnatural troubles. Infected minds
    To their deaf pillows will discharge their secrets.
    More needs she the divine than the physician.
    God, God forgive us all! Look after her;
    Remove from her the means of all annoyance,   76
    And still keep eyes upon her. So, good night.   77
    My mind she has mated, and amazed my sight.   78
    I think, but dare not speak.
GENTLEWOMAN   Good night, good Doctor.
                                    Exeunt.

❧

---

234 intermission delay, interval.   **Front to front** Face to face
236–7 If . . . too! If I let him escape, may he find forgiveness not only
from me but from heaven itself! (This is a condition that Macduff will
not allow to happen.)   **238 power** army   **239 Our . . . leave** we need
only to take our leave (of the English King).   **241 Put . . . instruments**
set us on as their agents, or, arm themselves.
5.1. Location: Dunsinane. Macbeth's castle.
0.1 *Physic* medicine   **5 closet** chest or cabinet   **9–10 do . . . watching**
act as though awake.   **15 meet** suitable   **19 close** concealed.

32 satisfy confirm, support   **44 this starting** these startled movements.
45 Go to (An exclamation of reproof, directed at Lady Macbeth.)
52–3 sorely charged heavily burdened.   **55 dignity** worth, value   **57 Pray
. . . sir** Pray God it will turn out well, as you say, sir. (Playing on the
Doctor's *"Well, well,"* i.e., "Dear, dear.")   **63 on 's** of his   **76 annoyance**
i.e., harming herself   **77 still** constantly   **78 mated** bewildered, stupefied

5.2

Drum and colors. Enter Menteith, Caithness,
Angus, Lennox, [and] soldiers.

MENTEITH
  The English power is near, led on by Malcolm,
  His uncle Siward, and the good Macduff.
  Revenges burn in them, for their dear causes   3
  Would to the bleeding and the grim alarm   4
  Excite the mortified man.
ANGUS   Near Birnam Wood   5
  Shall we well meet them; that way are they coming.   6
CAITHNESS
  Who knows if Donalbain be with his brother?
LENNOX
  For certain, sir, he is not. I have a file   8
  Of all the gentry. There is Siward's son,
  And many unrough youths that even now   10
  Protest their first of manhood.
MENTEITH   What does the tyrant?   11
CAITHNESS
  Great Dunsinane he strongly fortifies.
  Some say he's mad, others that lesser hate him
  Do call it valiant fury; but for certain
  He cannot buckle his distempered cause   15
  Within the belt of rule.
ANGUS   Now does he feel
  His secret murders sticking on his hands;
  Now minutely revolts upbraid his faith-breach.   18
  Those he commands move only in command,   19
  Nothing in love. Now does he feel his title
  Hang loose about him, like a giant's robe
  Upon a dwarfish thief.
MENTEITH   Who then shall blame
  His pestered senses to recoil and start,   23
  When all that is within him does condemn
  Itself for being there?
CAITHNESS   Well, march we on
  To give obedience where 'tis truly owed.
  Meet we the med'cine of the sickly weal,   27
  And with him pour we in our country's purge   28
  Each drop of us.
LENNOX   Or so much as it needs   29
  To dew the sovereign flower and drown the weeds.   30
  Make we our march towards Birnam.
                                Exeunt, marching.

❧

5.3

Enter Macbeth, Doctor, and attendants.

MACBETH
  Bring me no more reports. Let them fly all!   1
  Till Birnam Wood remove to Dunsinane,
  I cannot taint with fear. What's the boy Malcolm?   3
  Was he not born of woman? The spirits that know
  All mortal consequences have pronounced me thus: 5
  "Fear not, Macbeth. No man that's born of woman
  Shall e'er have power upon thee." Then fly, false
    thanes,
  And mingle with the English epicures!   8
  The mind I sway by and the heart I bear   9
  Shall never sag with doubt nor shake with fear.

    Enter Servant.

  The devil damn thee black, thou cream-faced loon!   11
  Where got'st thou that goose look?
SERVANT
  There is ten thousand—
MACBETH   Geese, villain?
SERVANT   Soldiers, sir.
MACBETH
  Go prick thy face and over-red thy fear,   14
  Thou lily-livered boy. What soldiers, patch?   15
  Death of thy soul! Those linen cheeks of thine   16
  Are counselors to fear. What soldiers, whey-face?   17
SERVANT   The English force, so please you.
MACBETH   Take thy face hence.   *[Exit Servant.]*
            [Calling] Seyton!—I am sick at heart
  When I behold—Seyton, I say!—This push   20
  Will cheer me ever, or disseat me now.   21
  I have lived long enough. My way of life   22
  Is fall'n into the sere, the yellow leaf,   23
  And that which should accompany old age,
  As honor, love, obedience, troops of friends,   25
  I must not look to have, but in their stead
  Curses, not loud but deep, mouth-honor, breath
  Which the poor heart would fain deny and dare not.
  Seyton!

    Enter Seyton.

SEYTON
  What's your gracious pleasure?
MACBETH   What news more?

5.2. Location: The country near Dunsinane.
3–5 their . . . man their grievous wrongs would awaken even the
dead to answer the bloody and grim call to battle. **6 well** conveniently **8 file** list, roster **10 unrough** beardless **11 Protest** assert
publicly **15 distempered** disease-swollen, dropsical **18 Now . . .
faith-breach** every minute now, revolts upbraid him for his violation
of all trust and sacred vows. **19 in command** under orders
23 pestered troubled, tormented **27 Meet we . . . weal** i.e., Let us
join forces with Malcolm, the physician of our sick land **28–9 pour
. . . of us** i.e., let us shed all our blood as a bloodletting or *purge* of our
country. **30 dew** bedew, water. **sovereign** (1) royal (2) medically
efficacious

5.3. Location: Dunsinane. Macbeth's castle.
1 Let . . . all! Let all the thanes desert! **3 taint with** become imbued
or infected with, weakened by **5 All . . . consequences** all that happens in this mortal life **8 English epicures** luxury-loving Englishmen. **9 sway** rule myself **11 loon** stupid fellow. **14 Go . . . fear**
i.e., Go prick or pinch your pale cheeks to bring some color into them.
(Current medical theory held that fear caused a retreat of the blood to
the abdominal organs, leaving the countenance pale or *lily-livered*,
line 15.) **15 patch** domestic fool. **16 Death . . . soul!** May your soul
die an eternal death! (An oath.) **linen** i.e., pale, white **17 Are . . .
fear** (The fear is contagious to the rest of the body and to other
observers.) **20 behold** (Macbeth does not finish this thought.)
push effort, crisis **21 cheer** (With a suggestion of "chair.") **disseat**
dethrone **22 way** course **23 sere** dry and withered **25 As** such as

SEYTON
    All is confirmed, my lord, which was reported.
MACBETH
    I'll fight till from my bones my flesh be hacked.
    Give me my armor.
SEYTON   'Tis not needed yet.
MACBETH   I'll put it on.
    Send out more horses. Skirr the country round.   36
    Hang those that talk of fear. Give me mine armor.
    How does your patient, Doctor?
DOCTOR   Not so sick, my lord,
    As she is troubled with thick-coming fancies
    That keep her from her rest.
MACBETH   Cure her of that.
    Canst thou not minister to a mind diseased,
    Pluck from the memory a rooted sorrow,
    Raze out the written troubles of the brain,   44
    And with some sweet oblivious antidote   45
    Cleanse the stuffed bosom of that perilous stuff
    Which weighs upon the heart?
DOCTOR   Therein the patient
    Must minister to himself.
MACBETH
    Throw physic to the dogs! I'll none of it.   49
    Come, put mine armor on. Give me my staff.   50
            [*Attendants arm him.*]
    Seyton, send out. Doctor, the thanes fly from me.—
    Come, sir, dispatch.—If thou couldst, Doctor, cast   52
    The water of my land, find her disease,   53
    And purge it to a sound and pristine health,
    I would applaud thee to the very echo,
    That should applaud again.—Pull't off, I say.—   56
    What rhubarb, senna, or what purgative drug   57
    Would scour these English hence? Hear'st thou of
      them?   58
DOCTOR
    Ay, my good lord. Your royal preparation
    Makes us hear something.
MACBETH   Bring it after me.—   60
    I will not be afraid of death and bane   61
    Till Birnam Forest come to Dunsinane.
            Exeunt [*all but the Doctor*].
DOCTOR
    Were I from Dunsinane away and clear,
    Profit again should hardly draw me here.   [*Exit.*]

❖

5.4

    Drum and colors. Enter Malcolm, Siward,
    Macduff, Siward's Son, Menteith, Caithness,
    Angus, [Lennox, Ross,] and soldiers, marching.

MALCOLM
    Cousins, I hope the days are near at hand   1
    That chambers will be safe.
MENTEITH   We doubt it nothing.   2
SIWARD
    What wood is this before us?
MENTEITH   The wood of Birnam.
MALCOLM
    Let every soldier hew him down a bough
    And bear't before him. Thereby shall we shadow
    The numbers of our host and make discovery   6
    Err in report of us.
SOLDIERS   It shall be done.
SIWARD
    We learn no other but the confident tyrant   8
    Keeps still in Dunsinane and will endure   9
    Our setting down before't.
MALCOLM   'Tis his main hope;   10
    For where there is advantage to be given,   11
    Both more and less have given him the revolt,   12
    And none serve with him but constrainèd things
    Whose hearts are absent too.
MACDUFF   Let our just censures   14
    Attend the true event, and put we on   15
    Industrious soldiership.
SIWARD   The time approaches
    That will with due decision make us know
    What we shall say we have and what we owe.   18
    Thoughts speculative their unsure hopes relate,   19
    But certain issue strokes must arbitrate—   20
    Towards which advance the war.   *Exeunt, marching.*   21

❖

5.5

    Enter Macbeth, Seyton, and soldiers, with drum
    and colors.

MACBETH
    Hang out our banners on the outward walls.
    The cry is still, "They come!" Our castle's strength
    Will laugh a siege to scorn. Here let them lie
    Till famine and the ague eat them up.   4
    Were they not forced with those that should be ours,   5
    We might have met them dareful, beard to beard,   6

36 Skirr Scour   **44 Raze** scrape; erase.   **written troubles of** troubles recorded in   **45 oblivious** causing forgetfulness   **49 physic** medicine   **50 staff** lance or baton of office.   **52 dispatch** hurry.   **52–3 cast The water** diagnose disease by the inspection of urine   **56 Pull't off** (Refers to some part of the armor not properly put on.)   **57 senna** a purgative drug   **58 scour** purge, cleanse, rid   **60 it** i.e., the armor not yet put on   **61 bane** ruin
5.4. Location: Country near Birnam Wood.

1 Cousins Kinsmen, peers   **2 chambers . . . safe** i.e., we may sleep safely in our bedchambers.   **nothing** not at all.   **6 discovery** scouting reports   **8 no other but** no other news but that   **9 Keeps** remains.   **endure** allow, not attempt to prevent   **10 setting down before't** laying siege to it.   **11 advantage** opportunity (i.e., in military operations outside Macbeth's castle in which it is possible for would-be deserters to slip away; in a siege, his forces will be more confined to the castle and under his watchful eye)   **12 more and less** high and low   **14–15 Let . . . event** Let us postpone judgment about these uncertain matters until we've achieved our goal   **18 What . . . owe** what we only claim to have, as distinguished from what we actually have. (*Owe* can mean "own.")   **19–20 Thoughts . . . arbitrate** Speculating can only convey our sense of hope; blows must decide the actual outcome   **21 war** army.
5.5. Location: Dunsinane. Macbeth's castle.
4 the ague fever, disease   **5 forced** reinforced   **6 dareful** boldly, in open battle

And beat them backward home.

A cry within of women.
What is that noise?

SEYTON

It is the cry of women, my good lord.

[*He goes to the door.*]

MACBETH

I have almost forgot the taste of fears.
The time has been my senses would have cooled   10
To hear a night-shriek, and my fell of hair   11
Would at a dismal treatise rouse and stir   12
As life were in't. I have supped full with horrors;   13
Direness, familiar to my slaughterous thoughts,
Cannot once start me.

[*Seyton returns.*]

                    Wherefore was that cry?   15

SEYTON   The Queen, my lord, is dead.

MACBETH   She should have died hereafter;   17
There would have been a time for such a word.
Tomorrow, and tomorrow, and tomorrow   19
Creeps in this petty pace from day to day   20
To the last syllable of recorded time,
And all our yesterdays have lighted fools   22
The way to dusty death. Out, out, brief candle!   23
Life's but a walking shadow, a poor player
That struts and frets his hour upon the stage
And then is heard no more. It is a tale
Told by an idiot, full of sound and fury,
Signifying nothing.   28

Enter a Messenger.

Thou com'st to use thy tongue; thy story quickly.

MESSENGER   Gracious my lord,
I should report that which I say I saw,
But know not how to do't.

MACBETH   Well, say, sir.

MESSENGER

As I did stand my watch upon the hill,
I looked toward Birnam, and anon, methought,
The wood began to move.

MACBETH   Liar and slave!

MESSENGER

Let me endure your wrath if't be not so.
Within this three mile may you see it coming;
I say, a moving grove.

MACBETH   If thou speak'st false,
Upon the next tree shalt thou hang alive
Till famine cling thee. If thy speech be sooth,   40
I care not if thou dost for me as much.

I pull in resolution, and begin   42
To doubt th'equivocation of the fiend
That lies like truth. "Fear not, till Birnam Wood
Do come to Dunsinane," and now a wood
Comes toward Dunsinane. Arm, arm, and out!
If this which he avouches does appear,
There is nor flying hence nor tarrying here.
I 'gin to be aweary of the sun,
And wish th'estate o'th' world were now undone.   50
Ring the alarum bell! Blow wind, come wrack,   51
At least we'll die with harness on our back.   *Exeunt.* 52

❖

5.6

*Drum and colors. Enter Malcolm, Siward,
Macduff, and their army, with boughs.*

MALCOLM

Now near enough. Your leafy screens throw down,
And show like those you are. You, worthy uncle,   2
Shall with my cousin, your right noble son,
Lead our first battle. Worthy Macduff and we   4
Shall take upon 's what else remains to do,
According to our order.

SIWARD   Fare you well.   6
Do we but find the tyrant's power tonight,   7
Let us be beaten, if we cannot fight.

MACDUFF

Make all our trumpets speak! Give them all breath,
Those clamorous harbingers of blood and death!   10

Exeunt. Alarums continued.

❖

5.7

Enter Macbeth.

MACBETH

They have tied me to a stake. I cannot fly,
But bearlike I must fight the course. What's he   2
That was not born of woman? Such a one
Am I to fear, or none.

Enter young Siward.

YOUNG SIWARD   What is thy name?

MACBETH   Thou'lt be afraid to hear it.

YOUNG SIWARD

No, though thou call'st thyself a hotter name
Than any is in hell.

MACBETH   My name's Macbeth.

10 cooled felt the chill of terror   11 my fell of hair the hair of my
scalp   12 dismal treatise sad story   13 As as if   15 start me make
me start.   17 She . . . hereafter She would have died someday, or, she
should have died at some more appropriate time, freed from the
relentless pressures of the moment   19–28 Tomorrow . . . nothing
(For biblical echoes in this speech, see Psalms 18:28, 22:15, 90:9; Job
8:9, 14:1–2, 18:6.)   20 in this in at this   22 lighted (The metaphor is
of a candle used to light one to bed, just as life is a brief transit for
wretched mortals to their deathbeds.)   23 dusty (Since life, made out
of dust, returns to dust.)   40 cling cause to shrivel.   sooth truth

42 pull in resolution can no longer give free rein to my self-confident
determination   50 th'estate the settled order   51 wrack ruin
52 harness armor
5.6. Location: Dunsinane. Before Macbeth's castle.
2 show appear.   uncle i.e., Siward   4 battle battalion.   6 order
plan of battle.   7 Do we If we do.   power army   10 harbingers
forerunners
5.7. Location: Before Macbeth's castle; the battle action is continuous here.
2 course bout or round of bearbaiting, in which the bear was tied to a
stake and dogs were set upon him.

YOUNG SIWARD
    The devil himself could not pronounce a title
    More hateful to mine ear.
MACBETH   No, nor more fearful.
YOUNG SIWARD
    Thou liest, abhorrèd tyrant! With my sword
    I'll prove the lie thou speak'st.
                            Fight, and young Siward slain.
MACBETH   Thou wast born of woman.   12
    But swords I smile at, weapons laugh to scorn,
    Brandished by man that's of a woman born.   *Exit.*

            Alarums. Enter Macduff.

MACDUFF
    That way the noise is. Tyrant, show thy face!
    If thou be'st slain, and with no stroke of mine,
    My wife and children's ghosts will haunt me still.
    I cannot strike at wretched kerns, whose arms   18
    Are hired to bear their staves. Either thou, Macbeth,   19
    Or else my sword with an unbattered edge
    I sheathe again undeeded. There thou shouldst be;   21
    By this great clatter one of greatest note
    Seems bruited. Let me find him, Fortune,   23
    And more I beg not.   *Exit. Alarums.*

            Enter Malcolm and Siward.

SIWARD
    This way, my lord. The castle's gently rendered: 25
    The tyrant's people on both sides do fight,
    The noble thanes do bravely in the war,
    The day almost itself professes yours,   28
    And little is to do.
MALCOLM   We have met with foes
    That strike beside us.
SIWARD   Enter, sir, the castle.   30
                            Exeunt. Alarum.

                        ♣

[5.8]

            Enter Macbeth.

MACBETH
    Why should I play the Roman fool and die   1
    On mine own sword? Whiles I see lives, the gashes   2

Do better upon them.

            Enter Macduff.

MACDUFF   Turn, hellhound, turn!
MACBETH
    Of all men else I have avoided thee.
    But get thee back! My soul is too much charged
    With blood of thine already.
MACDUFF   I have no words;
    My voice is in my sword, thou bloodier villain
    Than terms can give thee out!   *Fight. Alarum.*
MACBETH   Thou losest labor.   8
    As easy mayst thou the intrenchant air   9
    With thy keen sword impress as make me bleed.   10
    Let fall thy blade on vulnerable crests;
    I bear a charmèd life, which must not yield
    To one of woman born.
MACDUFF   Despair thy charm,   13
    And let the angel whom thou still hast served   14
    Tell thee, Macduff was from his mother's womb
    Untimely ripped.   16
MACBETH
    Accursèd be that tongue that tells me so,
    For it hath cowed my better part of man!   18
    And be these juggling fiends no more believed   19
    That palter with us in a double sense,   20
    That keep the word of promise to our ear   21
    And break it to our hope. I'll not fight with thee.   22
MACDUFF   Then yield thee, coward,
    And live to be the show and gaze o'th' time!   24
    We'll have thee, as our rarer monsters are,
    Painted upon a pole, and underwrit,   26
    "Here may you see the tyrant."
MACBETH   I will not yield
    To kiss the ground before young Malcolm's feet
    And to be baited with the rabble's curse.
    Though Birnam Wood be come to Dunsinane,
    And thou opposed, being of no woman born,
    Yet I will try the last. Before my body   32
    I throw my warlike shield. Lay on, Macduff,
    And damned be him that first cries, "Hold, enough!"   34
                    Exeunt, fighting. Alarums.

    *Enter fighting, and Macbeth slain. [Exit Macduff
    with Macbeth's body.] Retreat, and flourish. Enter,
    with drum and colors, Malcolm, Siward, Ross,
    thanes, and soldiers.*

12 s.d. *young Siward slain* (In some unspecified way, young Siward's body must be removed from the stage; his own father enters at line 24.1 and perceives nothing amiss, and in 5.8.38 young Siward is reported *missing* in action. Perhaps Macbeth drags off the body, or perhaps it is removed by soldiers during the alarums.)   **18 kerns** (Properly, Irish foot soldiers; here, applied contemptuously to the rank and file.)
19 staves spears.   **Either thou** i.e., Either I find you and sheathe my sword in you   **21 undeeded** having seen no action.   **shouldst be** ought to be (judging by the noise)   **23 bruited** announced.   **25 gently rendered** surrendered without fighting   **28 professes** declares itself   **30 strike beside us** fight on our side, or miss us deliberately.
5.8. Location: Before Macbeth's castle, as the battle continues; after line 34, within the castle.
1 Roman fool i.e., suicide, like Brutus, Mark Antony, and others
2 Whiles . . . lives i.e., As long as I see any enemy living

8 give thee out name you, describe you.   **9 intrenchant** that cannot be cut, indivisible   **10 impress** make an impression on   **13 Despair** Despair of   **14 angel** evil angel, Macbeth's genius.   **still** always   **16 Untimely** prematurely, i.e., by Caesarian delivery   **18 better . . . man** i.e., courage.   **19 juggling** deceiving   **20 palter . . . sense** equivocate with us   **21–2 That . . . hope** that make promises we hear (and think we understand) but then break promise with what we hoped and expected.   **24 gaze o'th' time** spectacle or sideshow of the age. **26 Painted . . . pole** i.e., painted on a board or cloth and suspended on a pole   **32 the last** i.e., my last resort: my own strength and resolution.   **34.3 *Retreat*** a trumpet call ordering an end to the fighting. **34.3–4 *Enter, with drum and colors, etc.*** (The remainder of the play is perhaps imagined as taking place in Macbeth's castle and could be marked as a separate scene. In Shakespeare's theater, however, the shift is so nonrepresentational and without scenic alteration that the action is virtually continuous.)

MALCOLM
    I would the friends we miss were safe arrived.
SIWARD
    Some must go off; and yet, by these I see   36
    So great a day as this is cheaply bought.
MALCOLM
    Macduff is missing, and your noble son.
ROSS [to Siward]
    Your son, my lord, has paid a soldier's debt.
    He only lived but till he was a man,
    The which no sooner had his prowess confirmed
    In the unshrinking station where he fought,   42
    But like a man he died.
SIWARD   Then he is dead?
ROSS
    Ay, and brought off the field. Your cause of sorrow
    Must not be measured by his worth, for then
    It hath no end.
SIWARD   Had he his hurts before?
ROSS
    Ay, on the front.
SIWARD   Why then, God's soldier be he!
    Had I as many sons as I have hairs
    I would not wish them to a fairer death.
    And so, his knell is knolled.
MALCOLM   He's worth more sorrow,
    And that I'll spend for him.
SIWARD   He's worth no more.
    They say he parted well and paid his score,   52
    And so, God be with him! Here comes newer comfort.

        Enter Macduff, with Macbeth's head.

36 go off die. by these to judge by these (assembled) 42 unshrink-
ing station post from which he did not shrink 52 parted departed,
died. score reckoning

MACDUFF
    Hail, King! For so thou art. Behold where stands   54
    Th'usurper's cursèd head. The time is free.   55
    I see thee compassed with thy kingdom's pearl,   56
    That speak my salutation in their minds,
    Whose voices I desire aloud with mine:
    Hail, King of Scotland!
ALL   Hail, King of Scotland!   Flourish.
MALCOLM
    We shall not spend a large expense of time
    Before we reckon with your several loves   62
    And make us even with you. My thanes and kinsmen,   63
    Henceforth be earls, the first that ever Scotland
    In such an honor named. What's more to do
    Which would be planted newly with the time,   66
    As calling home our exiled friends abroad
    That fled the snares of watchful tyranny,
    Producing forth the cruel ministers   69
    Of this dead butcher and his fiendlike queen—
    Who, as 'tis thought, by self and violent hands   71
    Took off her life—this, and what needful else
    That calls upon us, by the grace of Grace
    We will perform in measure, time, and place.
    So, thanks to all at once and to each one,
    Whom we invite to see us crowned at Scone.   76
                        Flourish. Exeunt omnes.

54 stands i.e., on a pole 55 free released from tyranny. 56 compassed . . . pearl surrounded by the nobles of your kingdom
(literally, the pearls encircling a crown) 62 reckon come to a
reckoning. several individual 63 make . . . you repay your worthiness. 66 would . . . time should be established at the commencement of this new era 69 Producing forth bringing forward to
trial. ministers agents 71 self and violent her own violent
76.1 omnes all.

Antony and Cleopatra

Shakespeare probably wrote *Antony and Cleopatra* in 1606 or 1607; it was registered for publication on May 20, 1608, and apparently influenced a revision of Samuel Daniel's *Cleopatra* that was published "newly altered" in 1607. *Antony and Cleopatra* was thus roughly contemporary with *King Lear* and *Macbeth.* Yet the contrast between those two tragedies and *Antony and Cleopatra* is immense. Unlike *Macbeth,* with its taut focus on a murderer and his wife, *Antony and Cleopatra* moves back and forth across the Mediterranean in its epic survey of characters and events, bringing together the fates of Pompey, Octavius Caesar, Octavia, and Lepidus with those of the protagonists. *King Lear* gives proper names to fourteen characters, *Macbeth* to eighteen, *Antony and Cleopatra* to thirty-one. The Roman play requires no less than forty-two separate scenes, of which most occur in what modern editors label Acts 3 and 4, although no play is less suited to the classical rigors of five-act structure, and these divisions are not found in the reliable Folio text of 1623. Indeed, it is as though Shakespeare resolved at the height of his career to show that he could dispense entirely with the classical "rules," which had never taken serious hold of the English popular stage in any case. The flouting of the unities is so extreme that John Dryden, in his *All for Love or The World Well Lost* (1678), undertook not so much to revise Shakespeare as to start afresh on the same subject. Dryden's play is restricted to the last few hours of the protagonists' lives, at Cleopatra's tomb in Alexandria, with a severely limited cast of characters and much of the narrative revealed through recollection. Although a substantial achievement in its own right, *All for Love* surely demonstrates that Shakespeare knew what he was doing, for Dryden has excised a good deal of the panorama, the excitement, and the "infinite variety" (2.2.246).

Shakespeare departs also from the somber tone of his tragedies of evil. He creates, instead, a world that bears affinities to the ambiguous conflicts of the other Roman plays, to the varying humorous perspectives of the comedies, and to the imaginative reconstructions of the late romances. As protagonists, Antony and Cleopatra lack tragic stature, or so it first appears: she is a tawny gypsy temptress and he a "strumpet's fool," a once-great general now bound in "strong Egyptian fetters" and lost in "dotage" (1.1.13; 1.2.122–3). Several scenes, especially those set in Egypt, are comic and delightfully bawdy: Charmian learning her fortune from the soothsayer, Cleopatra practicing her charms in vain to keep Antony from leaving Egypt or raunchily daydreaming of being Antony's horse "to bear the weight of Antony" (1.5.22), Cleopatra flying into a magnificent rage at the news of Antony's marriage to Octavia and then consoling herself with catty reflections on Octavia's reported low voice and shortness of stature ("I think so, Charmian. Dull of tongue, and dwarfish," 3.3.17). In its comic texture, the play somewhat resembles *Romeo and Juliet,* an earlier play about a younger pair of lovers, although there the bawdry is used chiefly to characterize the lovers' companions and confidants, whereas in *Antony and Cleopatra* it is central to our vision of Cleopatra especially. In any case, the later play is a tragedy about lovers who, despite their quarrels and uncertainties and betrayals of self, are reconciled in a vision of the greatness of their love. In its depiction of two contrasting worlds, also, *Antony and Cleopatra* recalls the movement of several earlier comedies from the realistic world of political conniving to a dreamworld of the romantic and the unexpected. We can endorse neither world fully in *Antony and Cleopatra,* and, accordingly, the vision of life presented is often ambivalent and ironic as much as it is tragic. The contrast of values separating Egypt and Rome underscores the paradox of humanity's quest for seemingly irreconcilable goals. The ending is neither a triumph nor a defeat for the lovers but something of both. If Antony and Cleopatra seem in one way too small to be tragic protagonists, in another way they seem too large, creating imaginative visions of themselves and their union that escape the realm of tragedy altogether. Our attention is focused less on the way in which the protagonists come to understand some meaningful relationship between their character and the fate required of them by a tragic universe than on the almost comic way in which the absurdities of Roman worldly striving and Egyptian dissipation are transfigured in the world of the imagination.

The Roman point of view opens the play and never entirely loses its force. At first, it may seem superior to that of Egypt. Demetrius and Philo, who invite us to view the play's first encounter between Antony and Cleopatra (1.1) from the perspective of the professional Roman soldier, lament the decline of Antony into Circean enslavement. Their tragic concept is of the Fall of Princes, all the more soberly edifying because of the height from which Antony has toppled. "You shall see in him / The triple pillar of the world transformed / Into a strumpet's fool" (1.1.11–13). Egypt is enchanting but clearly enervating— a bizarre assemblage of soothsayers, eunuchs, and waiting-gentlewomen who wish to be "married to three kings in a forenoon and widow them all" (1.2.28–9). Their mirth is all bawdry, tinged with practices, such as transvestitism, that Roman custom views as licentious. The prevailing images are of procreation in various shapes, sleep (mandragora, Lethe), the oriental opulence of Cleopatra's barge (a golden poop, purple sails, silver oars, divers-colored fans), Epicurean feasting, and drinking. As Enobarbus says, "Mine, and most of our fortunes tonight, shall be—drunk to bed" (1.2.47–8).

Antony, for all his reckless defiance of Rome, agrees in his more reflective moments with what Demetrius and Philo have said. "A Roman thought hath struck him," Cleopatra observantly remarks, and Antony has indeed determined that "I must from this enchanting queen break off" (1.2.88, 135). His later return to Cleopatra is at least in part a surrender, a betrayal of his marriage vows to Octavia and his political assurances to Caesar. In the ensuing battles, Antony submits himself dangerously to Cleopatra's governance, and this inversion of dominance in sexual roles, as conventionally understood by the Roman patriarchal world, is emblematic of a deeper disorder within Antony. As Enobarbus concludes bitterly, Antony "would make his will / Lord of his reason" and so has subverted his "judgment" (3.13.3–4, 37) to passion.

From the beginning, Cleopatra has sought dominance over Antony in the war of the sexes. When Antony first came to her on the River Cydnus, we learn, he was so overcome in all his senses that he was "barbered ten times o'er" (2.2.234). Cleopatra boasts that she "angled" for Antony on many occasions, catching him the way fishermen "betray" fish, and that, when she had "drunk him to his bed," she "put my tires and mantles on him, whilst / I wore his sword Philippan" (2.5.10–23). Caesar, affronted by such transvestite debauchery, charges that Antony "is not more manlike / Than Cleopatra, nor the queen of

Ptolemy / More womanly than he" (1.4.5–7). During the battle scenes, Antony's followers complain that "Photinus, an eunuch" (probably Mardian), and Cleopatra's maids manage the war: "So our leader's led, / And we are women's men" (3.7.14–15, 70–1). Antony confesses too late that they were right. He becomes a "doting mallard," one whose heart is "tied by th' strings" to Cleopatra's rudder when her ships retreat in the first naval engagement (3.10.20, 3.11.56). In the mythic images used to raise their relationship to heroic proportions, Antony is like Mars to Cleopatra's Venus (1.5.19), both in a positive and a negative sense. The image has positive connotations of the way in which, as Milton puts it, the "two great sexes animate the world," the masterful soldier and his attractive consort complementing one another in a right relationship of martial prowess and beauty, bravery and love, reason and will; however, to the Renaissance, the myth of Mars and Venus could also be read in a destructive sense, as an adulterous relationship in which reason is subverted to appetite. In another mythic comparison, Antony is like Hercules, not in his prime, but with the shirt of Nessus on his back—a poisoned shirt given to Hercules by his wife in a mistaken hope of thereby assuring his love for her (4.12.43). Antony's soldiers understandably believe that the god Hercules has deserted his reputed descendant and onetime champion (4.3.21–2).

Despite Antony's shameful violation of manhood, honor, attention to duty, self-knowledge, and all that Rome stands for, however, the end of his story is anything but a one-sided endorsement for the Roman point of view. The actual Rome, disfigured by political conniving, falls far short of the ideal. Antony has a point when he protests that "Kingdoms are clay" (1.1.37). Alliances are unstable and are governed by mere political expediency. At first, Antony's wife Fulvia and his brother Lucius have fought one another until forced to unite against the greater threat of Octavius Caesar. Similarly, Antony and Caesar come together only because Pompey has become dangerously powerful at sea and has won the favor of the fickle mob, "Our slippery people" (1.2.192). This detente is not meant to last. As Enobarbus bluntly puts it, "if you borrow one another's love for the instant, you may, when you hear no more words of Pompey, return it again" (2.2.109–11). Enobarbus is rebuked for his unstatesmanlike tone, but no one denies the validity of what he says. In this cynical negotiation, Octavia is a pawn between husband and brother, shabbily treated by both. Caesar coldly bargains away the happiness of the one person of whom he protests that "no brother / Did ever love so dearly" (2.2.159–60). Antony, although hating false promises and resolving to be loyal to Octavia, knows within himself that it won't work. To make matters worse for the fair-minded Antony, he has received great favors from Pompey that he must now uncharitably repudiate in the interests of politics. Pompey does not miss the opportunity to remind Antony of his ingratitude, but the prevailing mood is not so much of bitterness as of ironic futility. Old friendships must be sacrificed; no one seems wholly to blame, and no one can stop the game. Pompey is as much in the wrong as anyone and as powerless. Despite his idealistic hope of restoring republican government to Rome, he has had to ally himself with pirates who offer him sinister temptations. He could be "lord of all the world" (2.7.62) if he would only murder on occasion, but Pompey is destined to be trapped between lofty ends and ignoble means. Lepidus is still another dismaying victim of political callousness, used condescendingly by Caesar and permitted to drink himself into oblivion, until he is cashiered on a trumped-up charge and imprisoned for life.

Octavius Caesar embodies most of all the ironic limits of political ambition. He has avoided enslavement to passion at the very real cost of enslaving himself to his public career as general, triumvir, and future emperor. His ideal warrior is one who, driven by military necessity, would "drink / The stale [urine] of horses and the gilded puddle / Which beasts would cough at" (1.4.62–4). As a general, he is Antony's opposite in every way. He attacks only when he has the advantage and places those who have deserted Antony in his own front lines so "That Antony may seem to spend his fury / Upon himself" (4.6.10–11). He controls his supplies cannily, believing it a "waste" to feast his army (4.1.17). He, of course, declines Antony's offers of single combat. Antony meantime recklessly accepts Caesar's challenge to fight at sea, feasts debauchingly in one "gaudy night" after another (3.13.186), and generously refuses to blame or penalize those who leave him. His sending Enobarbus's belongings after him into Caesar's camp convinces that honest soldier he has made a fatal error, for, however imprudent Antony's chivalry may be, it is unquestionably noble and great-hearted. Caesar is a superb general and political genius, but he is also a military automaton, a logistical reckoner, a Machiavellian pragmatist. In his personal life, he is no less austere and puritanical. He deplores loosening his tongue with alcohol. About women, he is deeply cynical, believing that "want will perjure / The ne'er-touched vestal" (3.12.30–1). Between him and Cleopatra, there is a profound antipathy, based in part on his revulsion at her earlier affair with his namesake and adoptive father, Julius Caesar (3.6.6). Cleopatra may entertain briefly the notion of trying to seduce this new Caesar (3.13.46 ff.), for like Charmian she loves long life "better than figs"(1.2.34), but, if so, she soon discovers that she and Caesar are not compatible. All that he represents she must instead grandly repudiate, choosing death and the fantasy of an eternity with Antony as her way to "call great Caesar ass / Unpolicied" (5.2.307–8).

Cleopatra is a "lass unparalleled" (5.2.316), whose greatness is elusive and all the more enthralling because it is so mysterious. She rises above her counterpart in Shakespeare's source, Plutarch's *Lives of the Noble Grecians and Romans,* in which she is an impressive queenly woman but still essentially a temptress causing the lamentable fall of the hero. Shakespeare's Cleopatra is that but is also something indefinable that can be gotten at only through paradox. Her very character is the essence of contradiction: she knows how "to chide, to laugh, / To weep" (1.1.51–2), to be sullen or violent, like a skillful actor keeping Antony continually off guard. Dispassionately examined, she is a woman no longer young who abuses messengers like an oriental despot, who sends Antony a false report of her death out of fear for her own safety, who will not risk leaving her monument even when Antony lies outside mortally wounded, and who lies about her wealth when captured by Caesar (what is she planning to do with that wealth, anyway?). We cannot be sure that she would not have "packed cards with Caesar" (4.14.19) if she had found him susceptible to her charms. Yet we are not invited to see her dispassionately. Her charm is eternal, and so are the myths surrounding that charm. Observers evoking her splendor do not describe her person directly but, rather, her effects and surroundings: Enobarbus says simply that "For her own person, / It beggared all description" and goes on to catalogue her cloth-of-gold pavilion and her mermaidlike attendants. Most of all, she is a paradox: she makes defect perfection, age cannot wither her, and "vilest things / Become themselves in her, that the holy priests / Bless her when she is riggish" (2.2.207–50). She is both a whore and the Lucretian Venus; both sluttish and holy.

Inspired by Cleopatra, Antony shows himself ready to break down conventional barriers between the sexes and to explore new emotional territory by giving up part of his self-protective masculinity. Antony's embracing of an attractive but sexually dangerous woman is all the more remarkable in a play that follows the harrowing depictions of sexual conflict in *Hamlet, Othello,* and *Lear* and the degrading portrait of erotic enslavement in the "Dark Lady" sonnets, for here the relationship of the lovers, though doomed, is also triumphant. Shakespeare takes a look at something like midlife crisis, conceding freely how ridiculous the male appears to himself and to others in his compulsive tendency to polarize women into saints and whores. Yet Shakespeare also explores ways in which the man and the woman attempt to become increasingly like each other, enabling the man to participate in a vision of union with the feminine principle of generative, erotic, fertile, life-giving vitality, and enabling the woman to join her "husband" in the noble resolve of a Roman suicide.

In Cleopatra, "fancy" exceeds "nature"; the fertility of her Egypt overflows the measure, exceeding the sterility of Rome as her own imaginative fertility exceeds reality itself. When she protests that she will not go to Rome to behold herself in a wretched play and thus see "Some squeaking Cleopatra boy my greatness / I'th' posture of a whore" (5.2.220–1), we realize that Shakespeare is calling attention to his own art as well, pointing out how Elizabethan boy actors on a bare stage can transform reality into a dream that we believe. Cleopatra's mystery is like that of poetry itself. The "real" world pales into insignificance of a "little O, the earth," something "No better than a sty," full of illusory shadows that "mock our eyes with air" (5.2.80, 4.15.64, 4.14.7); and Caesar's triumph vanishes with it. In its place, Antony and Cleopatra raise up a vision of themselves as lovers who, through art, have indeed become eternal. Together they will over-picture Venus and Mars, and will be so renowned that "Dido and her Aeneas shall want troops, / And all the haunt be ours" (4.14.53–4). They are virtually husband and wife—"Husband, I come!" exclaims Cleopatra just before she dies (5.2.287)—united at last in a re-creative vision almost appropriate to comedy; and in their marriage they find a kind of redemption for the defeat that history can inflict. Antony is no longer dying Hercules but the god of Cleopatra's dream whose "legs bestrid the ocean; his reared arm / Crested the world; his voice was propertied / As all the tunèd spheres" (lines 81–3). Through Cleopatra's vision, we realize how all the characteristics that made Antony at once so noble and so sure to fall before Caesar—his generosity amounting to imprudence, his spontaneity, his impatience with the ordinary, his staking his all on love when he hears of Cleopatra's supposed death—have not deserted him. His death serves to reaffirm the magnificence of the very qualities that have brought him down. His essential nobility is confirmed, even if it must be defined in non-Roman ways. He and Cleopatra share the "immortal longings" for which she goes willingly to her death, dressed in her "best attires" like a queen (lines 281, 228), for neither lover will accept anything less than greatness.

Antony and Cleopatra is a daunting play to stage, because the main characters take on a mythic character that seems larger than life, larger than art itself. Michael Goldman imagines what it would be like for an actor to try out for the part of Antony only to be instructed by the casting director, "Now, stand there and be a triple pillar of the world." How can an actor convey the charisma of a man whose very name is legendary? The problem in acting Cleopatra is even more acute. The great actresses who have taken on the assignment have all been praised for many things but also faulted for lacking other dimensions of this amazing character. Vivien Leigh, playing opposite Laurence Olivier's Antony at the St. James Theatre, London, in 1951, was applauded by the critics for her coquettish sexiness and magnetism but perhaps deficient in animal heat and duskiness. Peggy Ashcroft, in Glen Byam Shaw's production at Stratford-upon-Avon in 1953, was lauded as impressively intelligent and capable of huge emotional variation, but was seen as physically small and not as sexually glamorous as Leigh. Margaret Whiting, at the Old Vic in 1957, was regarded by most viewers as simply too young for the part. Vanessa Redgrave, at the Bankside Globe Playhouse in 1973, threw cola bottles at her servants in her fits of temper, and somehow lacked dignity for the final scenes. Glenda Jackson, playing Cleopatra in Peter Brook's de-romanticized version at Stratford-upon-Avon in 1978, was brilliant for her iciness of tone and angularity in wit combat, but at the expense of tenderness and erotic feeling. The role has attracted the greatest of talent, from Janet Suzman to Helen Mirrin to Judi Dench, with similar praise and qualifications. These limits are a tribute to the play itself but a thorny problem for those who are producing the play. Film versions have tended to succumb to the temptations of visual splendor, in the style of Cecil B. DeMille, thus missing the point of the play's verbal and theatrical invocation of the ineffable. One singularly successful production is that on audiotape with Michael Redgrave as Antony and Peggy Ashcroft as Cleopatra; here the listener can imagine the lovers to be as toweringly great as the play's language suggests, magnificently assisted by the voices of two great actors. This is not to say that *Antony and Cleopatra* is unplayable; to the contrary, it shows Shakespeare at the very height of his powers as a professional writer for the theater. At the same time, few plays have ever posed a greater challenge for an acting ensemble.

Antony and Cleopatra

[*Dramatis Personae*

MARK ANTONY,
OCTAVIUS CAESAR, } *triumvirs*
LEPIDUS,

CLEOPATRA,
CHARMIAN,
IRAS,
ALEXAS,
MARDIAN, *a eunuch,* } *Cleopatra's attendants*
DIOMEDES,
SELEUCUS, *Cleopatra's treasurer,*

OCTAVIA, *sister of Octavius Caesar and wife of*
Antony

DEMETRIUS,
PHILO,
DOMITIUS ENOBARBUS,
VENTIDIUS,
SILIUS, } *Antony's friends and followers*
EROS,
CANIDIUS,
SCARUS,
DERCETUS,

A SCHOOLMASTER, *Antony's* AMBASSADOR *to Caesar*

MAECENAS,
AGRIPPA,
TAURUS,
THIDIAS, } *Octavius Caesar's friends and followers*
DOLABELLA,
GALLUS,
PROCULEIUS,

SEXTUS POMPEIUS *or* POMPEY
MENAS,
MENECRATES, } *Pompey's friends*
VARRIUS,

MESSENGERS *to Antony, Octavius, Caesar, and Cleopatra*
A SOOTHSAYER
Two SERVANTS *of Pompey*
SERVANTS *of Antony and Cleopatra*
A BOY
SOLDIERS, SENTRIES, GUARDSMEN *of Antony*
and Octavius Caesar
A CAPTAIN *in Antony's army*
An EGYPTIAN
A CLOWN *with figs*

Ladies attending Cleopatra, Eunuchs, Servants, Sol-
diers, Captains, Officers, silent named characters
(Rannius, Lucillius, Lamprius)

SCENE: *In several parts of the Roman Empire*]

1.1

Enter Demetrius and Philo.

PHILO
Nay, but this dotage of our general's   1
O'erflows the measure. Those his goodly eyes,   2

That o'er the files and musters of the war   3
Have glowed like plated Mars, now bend, now turn   4
The office and devotion of their view   5
Upon a tawny front. His captain's heart,   6
Which in the scuffles of great fights hath burst
The buckles on his breast, reneges all temper   8

1.1. Location: Alexandria. Cleopatra's palace.
1 dotage foolish affection, sometimes associated with old age
2 O'erflows the measure exceeds moderation, exceeds the means of measuring it.

3 files and musters orderly formations **4 plated** clothed in armor
5 office function **6 tawny front** dark face. (Literally, forehead.)
8 reneges all temper renounces all moderation

And is become the bellows and the fan
To cool a gypsy's lust.

Flourish. Enter Antony, Cleopatra, her ladies, the
train, with eunuchs fanning her.

                  Look, where they come.   10
Take but good note, and you shall see in him
The triple pillar of the world transformed   12
Into a strumpet's fool. Behold and see.   13
CLEOPATRA
If it be love indeed, tell me how much.
ANTONY
There's beggary in the love that can be reckoned.   15
CLEOPATRA
I'll set a bourn how far to be beloved.   16
ANTONY
Then must thou needs find out new heaven, new
earth.   17

Enter a Messenger.

MESSENGER   News, my good lord, from Rome.
ANTONY   Grates me! The sum.   19
CLEOPATRA   Nay, hear them, Antony.   20
Fulvia perchance is angry, or who knows   21
If the scarce-bearded Caesar have not sent   22
His powerful mandate to you, "Do this, or this;
Take in that kingdom, and enfranchise that;   24
Perform't, or else we damn thee."   25
ANTONY   How, my love?   26
CLEOPATRA   Perchance? Nay, and most like.   27
You must not stay here longer; your dismission   28
Is come from Caesar. Therefore hear it, Antony.
Where's Fulvia's process? Caesar's, I would say. Both?   30
Call in the messengers. As I am Egypt's queen,
Thou blushest, Antony, and that blood of thine
Is Caesar's homager; else so thy cheek pays shame   33
When shrill-tongued Fulvia scolds. The messengers!
ANTONY
Let Rome in Tiber melt and the wide arch
Of the ranged empire fall! Here is my space.   36
Kingdoms are clay; our dungy earth alike
Feeds beast as man. The nobleness of life

Is to do thus; when such a mutual pair   39
And such a twain can do't, in which I bind,   40
On pain of punishment, the world to weet   41
We stand up peerless.
CLEOPATRA   Excellent falsehood!   42
Why did he marry Fulvia, and not love her?   43
I'll seem the fool I am not. Antony   44
Will be himself.
ANTONY   But stirred by Cleopatra.   45
Now, for the love of Love and her soft hours,
Let's not confound the time with conference harsh.   47
There's not a minute of our lives should stretch   48
Without some pleasure now. What sport tonight?
CLEOPATRA
Hear the ambassadors.
ANTONY   Fie, wrangling queen!
Whom everything becomes—to chide, to laugh,
To weep; whose every passion fully strives
To make itself, in thee, fair and admired!
No messenger but thine; and all alone
Tonight we'll wander through the streets and note
The qualities of people. Come, my queen,
Last night you did desire it.—Speak not to us.
        Exeunt [Antony and Cleopatra] with the train.
DEMETRIUS
Is Caesar with Antonius prized so slight?   58
PHILO
Sir, sometimes when he is not Antony
He comes too short of that great property   60
Which still should go with Antony.
DEMETRIUS   I am full sorry   61
That he approves the common liar, who   62
Thus speaks of him at Rome; but I will hope
Of better deeds tomorrow. Rest you happy!   *Exeunt.*   64

❧

[1.2]

Enter Enobarbus, Lamprius, a Soothsayer, Ran-
nius, Lucillius, Charmian, Iras, Mardian the
eunuch, and Alexas.

CHARMIAN   Lord Alexas, sweet Alexas, most anything
Alexas, almost most absolute Alexas, where's the   2
soothsayer that you praised so to th' Queen? Oh, that

---

10 gypsy's (Gypsies were widely believed to have come from Egypt, to enjoy magical powers, and to be lustful and cunning.) **s.d. Flourish** trumpet fanfare announcing the arrival or departure of important person. **train** retinue **12 triple** one of three. (Alludes to the triumvirate of Antony, Lepidus, and Octavius Caesar; also to tripartite division of the world into Asia, Africa, and Europe.) **13 fool** plaything. **15 There's . . . reckoned** i.e., Love that can be quantified is paltry; ours is infinite. **16 bourn** boundary, limit **17 Then . . . earth** i.e., Only in some new universe could you find a limit to my love. (The language echoes Revelation 21:1 and other biblical passages.) **19 Grates . . . sum** It annoys me! Be brief. **20 them** i.e., the news **21 Fulvia** Antony's wife **22 scarce-bearded Caesar** (Octavius Caesar was twenty-three in 40 B.C., at the time of the play's opening. Antony was forty-three.) **24 Take in** conquer. **enfranchise** set free **25 damn** condemn to death **26 How** i.e., What's that you say? **27 Perchance** (Cleopatra reconsiders what she has said in line 21.) **like** likely. **28 dismission** order to depart **30 process** writ to appear in court. **33 Is . . . shame** is Caesar's vassal, doing homage to him; or else your blushing pays the tribute of shame **36 ranged** well ordered and far-extending

39 thus (May indicate an embrace, or Antony may refer more generally to their way of life.) **40–2 in which . . . peerless** with respect to which I insist that the world, under penalty of punishment if it fails to do so, acknowledge us to be peerless. **43 and not** if he did not **44 I'll . . . not** i.e., I'll pretend to be gullible and believe him, though I know better. **45 be himself** i.e., be the Roman Antony, be the fool and deceiver he always is, etc. **stirred** (1) prompted to noble deeds (2) moved to folly (3) sexually stirred **47 confound** ruin, waste. **conference** conversation **48 should stretch** that should be prolonged **58 prized** valued **60 property** quality, distinction **61 still** always **62 approves** corroborates **64 Of** for **1.2. Location: Alexandria. Cleopatra's palace. 0.1–2 Lamprius . . . Lucillius** (Lamprius may possibly be the soothsayer, but Rannius and Lucillius have no speaking parts here and do not appear again in the play. Mardian is mute here but does speak in later scenes.) **2 absolute** perfect

I knew this husband, which, you say, must charge his   4
horns with garlands!   5

ALEXAS   Soothsayer!

SOOTHSAYER   Your will?

CHARMIAN
Is this the man?—Is't you, sir, that know things?

SOOTHSAYER
In nature's infinite book of secrecy
A little I can read.

ALEXAS [to Charmian]   Show him your hand.

ENOBARBUS [to servants within]
Bring in the banquet quickly; wine enough   12
Cleopatra's health to drink.

CHARMIAN [giving her hand to the Soothsayer]   Good sir,
give me good fortune.

SOOTHSAYER   I make not, but foresee.

CHARMIAN   Pray, then, foresee me one.

SOOTHSAYER
You shall be yet far fairer than you are.

CHARMIAN   He means in flesh.   19

IRAS   No, you shall paint when you are old.   20

CHARMIAN   Wrinkles forbid!

ALEXAS   Vex not his prescience. Be attentive.

CHARMIAN   Hush!

SOOTHSAYER
You shall be more beloving than beloved.

CHARMIAN   I had rather heat my liver with drinking.   25

ALEXAS   Nay, hear him.

CHARMIAN   Good now, some excellent fortune! Let me   27
be married to three kings in a forenoon and widow
them all. Let me have a child at fifty, to whom Herod   29
of Jewry may do homage. Find me to marry me with   30
Octavius Caesar, and companion me with my mis-   31
tress.   32

SOOTHSAYER
You shall outlive the lady whom you serve.

CHARMIAN   Oh, excellent! I love long life better than figs.   34

SOOTHSAYER
You have seen and proved a fairer former fortune   35
Than that which is to approach.

CHARMIAN   Then belike my children shall have no   37
names. Prithee, how many boys and wenches must I   38
have?   39

SOOTHSAYER
If every of your wishes had a womb,
And fertile every wish, a million.

CHARMIAN   Out, fool! I forgive thee for a witch.   42

ALEXAS   You think none but your sheets are privy to   43
your wishes.

CHARMIAN   Nay, come, tell Iras hers.

ALEXAS   We'll know all our fortunes.

ENOBARBUS   Mine, and most of our fortunes tonight,
shall be—drunk to bed.

IRAS [giving her hand to the Soothsayer]   There's a palm
presages chastity, if nothing else.

CHARMIAN   E'en as the o'erflowing Nilus presageth   51
famine.   52

IRAS   Go, you wild bedfellow, you cannot soothsay.   53

CHARMIAN   Nay, if an oily palm be not a fruitful prog-   54
nostication, I cannot scratch mine ear. Prithee, tell her   55
but a workaday fortune.   56

SOOTHSAYER   Your fortunes are alike.

IRAS   But how, but how? Give me particulars.

SOOTHSAYER   I have said.   59

IRAS   Am I not an inch of fortune better than she?

CHARMIAN   Well, if you were but an inch of fortune better than I, where would you choose it?

IRAS   Not in my husband's nose.   63

CHARMIAN   Our worser thoughts heavens mend! Al-   64
exas—come, his fortune, his fortune! Oh, let him marry
a woman that cannot go, sweet Isis, I beseech thee,   66
and let her die too, and give him a worse, and let
worse follow worse till the worst of all follow him
laughing to his grave, fiftyfold a cuckold! Good Isis,
hear me this prayer, though thou deny me a matter of   70
more weight; good Isis, I beseech thee!

IRAS   Amen, dear goddess, hear that prayer of the people! For, as it is a heart-breaking to see a handsome
man loose-wived, so it is a deadly sorrow to behold a   74
foul knave uncuckolded. Therefore, dear Isis, keep de-   75
corum, and fortune him accordingly!   76

CHARMIAN   Amen.

ALEXAS   Lo now, if it lay in their hands to make me a
cuckold, they would make themselves whores but   79
they'd do't.   80

Enter Cleopatra.

ENOBARBUS
Hush! Here comes Antony.

CHARMIAN   Not he. The Queen.

CLEOPATRA   Saw you my lord?

4 this husband (Evidently Alexas has told Charmian that the Sooth-sayer will prophesy a husband for her.)   **4–5 must . . . garlands** i.e., must decorate his cuckold's horns with a garland of flowers, like a sacrificial beast. (Cuckolded men were derisively thought of as grow-ing horns, as a badge of their infamy.)   **12 banquet** light repast, dessert   **19 in flesh** i.e., by putting on weight.   **20 paint** i.e., use makeup   **25 heat . . . drinking** i.e., heat my liver with wine rather than with unrequited love. (The liver was believed to be the seat of sexual desire.)   **27 Good now** Come on, now   **29–30 Herod of Jewry** i.e., even the blustering tyrant who massacred the children of Judea   **30 Find me** i.e., Find in my palm   **31–2 companion . . . mistress** give me equal fortune with Cleopatra; or, perhaps, let Cleopatra become my "companion" or attendant.   **34 better than figs** (Probably a proverbial expression; with genital suggestion.)   **35 proved** experi-enced   **37 belike** probably   **37–8 have no names** be illegitimate.   **38 wenches** girls   **38–9 must I have** am I to have.

42 Out . . . witch (Charmian jokingly says that, since soothsayers, like fools, are allowed to speak freely without penalty, she will forgive him for slander.)   **43 privy to** in on the secret of   **51–2 E'en . . . famine** (Charmian speaks ironically; the overflowing Nile presages abundance. See 2.7.17–23.)   **53 wild** wanton   **54 oily palm** sweaty or moist palm (indicating a sensual disposition)   **54–5 fruitful prognos-tication** omen of fertility   **56 workaday** ordinary   **59 I have said** I have no more to say.   **63 Not . . . nose** (Iras bawdily hints at some place other than in the nose where she would prefer to see her hus-band well endowed.)   **64 Our . . . mend!** (Charmian pretends to be shocked: May heaven improve our dirty minds!)   **66 cannot go** (1) is lame (2) cannot make love satisfactorily or cannot bear children.   **Isis** Egyptian goddess usually identified with fertility and the moon   **70 hear me** hear (on my behalf)   **74 loose-wived** with an unfaithful wife   **75 foul** ugly   **75–6 keep decorum** deal suitably with the case   **76 fortune him** grant him fortune   **79–80 they . . . do't** i.e., they would stop at nothing, even becoming whores, to cuckold me.

ENOBARBUS   No, lady.
CLEOPATRA   Was he not here?
CHARMIAN   No, madam.
CLEOPATRA
    He was disposed to mirth, but on the sudden
    A Roman thought hath struck him. Enobarbus!
ENOBARBUS   Madam?
CLEOPATRA
    Seek him and bring him hither. Where's Alexas?
ALEXAS
    Here at your service.—My lord approaches.

    Enter Antony with a Messenger.

CLEOPATRA
    We will not look upon him. Go with us.
                Exeunt [all but Antony and the Messenger].
FIRST MESSENGER
    Fulvia thy wife first came into the field.   93
ANTONY   Against my brother Lucius?
FIRST MESSENGER   Ay.
    But soon that war had end, and the time's state   96
    Made friends of them, jointing their force 'gainst
        Caesar,   97
    Whose better issue in the war from Italy   98
    Upon the first encounter drave them.   99
ANTONY   Well, what worst?
FIRST MESSENGER
    The nature of bad news infects the teller.   101
ANTONY
    When it concerns the fool or coward. On.
    Things that are past are done with me. 'Tis thus:
    Who tells me true, though in his tale lie death,
    I hear him as he flattered.
FIRST MESSENGER   Labienus—   105
    This is stiff news—hath with his Parthian force
    Extended Asia; from Euphrates   107
    His conquering banner shook, from Syria
    To Lydia and to Ionia,
    Whilst—
ANTONY   Antony, thou wouldst say.
FIRST MESSENGER   Oh, my lord!
ANTONY
    Speak to me home; mince not the general tongue.   111
    Name Cleopatra as she is called in Rome;
    Rail thou in Fulvia's phrase, and taunt my faults   113
    With such full license as both truth and malice
    Have power to utter. Oh, then we bring forth weeds
    When our quick minds lie still, and our ills told us   116
    Is as our earing. Fare thee well awhile.   117

FIRST MESSENGER   At your noble pleasure.
                                    Exit [First] Messenger.

    Enter another Messenger.

ANTONY
    From Sicyon, ho, the news! Speak there.
SECOND MESSENGER
    The man from Sicyon—is there such an one?   120
THIRD MESSENGER [*at the door*]
    He stays upon your will.
ANTONY   Let him appear.—   121
                [Exeunt Second and Third Messengers.]
    These strong Egyptian fetters I must break,
    Or lose myself in dotage.

    Enter another Messenger, with a letter.

                            What are you?
FOURTH MESSENGER   Fulvia thy wife is dead.
ANTONY   Where died she?
FOURTH MESSENGER   In Sicyon.
    Her length of sickness, with what else more serious
    Importeth thee to know, this bears. [*He gives a letter.*]
ANTONY   Forbear me.   128
                            [Exit Fourth Messenger.]
    There's a great spirit gone! Thus did I desire it.
    What our contempts doth often hurl from us
    We wish it ours again. The present pleasure,
    By revolution lowering, does become   132
    The opposite of itself. She's good, being gone;
    The hand could pluck her back that shoved her on.   134
    I must from this enchanting queen break off.
    Ten thousand harms more than the ills I know
    My idleness doth hatch.—How now, Enobarbus!

    Enter Enobarbus.

ENOBARBUS   What's your pleasure, sir?
ANTONY   I must with haste from hence.
ENOBARBUS   Why, then, we kill all our women. We see
    how mortal an unkindness is to them; if they suffer
    our departure, death's the word.
ANTONY   I must be gone.
ENOBARBUS   Under a compelling occasion, let women
    die. It were pity to cast them away for nothing, though
    between them and a great cause they should be es-
    teemed nothing. Cleopatra, catching but the least noise 147
    of this, dies instantly; I have seen her die twenty times 148
    upon far poorer moment. I do think there is mettle in 149

---

93 field battlefield.   **96 time's state** circumstances prevailing at the
moment   **97 jointing** uniting   **98–9 Whose . . . them** whose better
military success drove them from Italy upon the very first encounter.
101 infects the teller i.e., makes the teller seem unwelcome.   **105 as** as
if.   **Labienus** (Brutus and Cassius [see *Julius Caesar*] had sent Quintus
Labienus to Orodes, King of Parthia, to seek aid against Antony and
Octavius Caesar; with a force thus obtained, he is now overrunning the
Roman provinces in the Middle East.)   **107 Extended** seized upon. (A
legal phrase.)   **111 Speak . . . tongue** Speak bluntly; don't minimize the
common report.   **113 Rail . . . phrase** Scold me as Fulvia would   **116 quick**
alive, inventive   **116–17 our ills . . . earing** hearing our faults told to us
improves us, as plowing (*earing*) improves land by rooting out the weeds.

120 The man from Sicyon (The messenger who has just entered, not
being from Sicyon, realizes in some confusion that Antony wants to
hear the news from Sicyon. This second messenger therefore calls out
to ask if the messenger from Sicyon is to be found. Another messenger at the door replies that such a man is indeed waiting, and in a
moment that messenger from Sicyon enters with his report. Some editors change the second and third messengers into attendants.) *Sicyon*
is an ancient city in Greece, where Antony left Fulvia.   **121 stays
upon** awaits   **128 Importeth** concerns.   **Forbear** Leave   **132 By revolution lowering** sinking in our estimation in the course of time and
Fortune's turning wheel   **134 could** would be willing to   **147 noise**
hint, rumor   **148 die** (Playing on a common second meaning of
"achieve sexual orgasm.")   **149 poorer moment** lesser cause.
mettle i.e., sexual vigor

death, which commits some loving act upon her, she
hath such a celerity in dying.

ANTONY   She is cunning past man's thought.

ENOBARBUS   Alack, sir, no, her passions are made of
nothing but the finest part of pure love. We cannot call
her winds and waters sighs and tears; they are greater   155
storms and tempests than almanacs can report. This
cannot be cunning in her; if it be, she makes a shower
of rain as well as Jove.

ANTONY   Would I had never seen her!

ENOBARBUS   Oh, sir, you had then left unseen a wonderful piece of work, which not to have been blessed
withal would have discredited your travel.

ANTONY   Fulvia is dead.

ENOBARBUS   Sir?

ANTONY   Fulvia is dead.

ENOBARBUS   Fulvia?

ANTONY   Dead.

ENOBARBUS   Why, sir, give the gods a thankful sacrifice.
When it pleaseth their deities to take the wife of a man
from him, it shows to man the tailors of the earth;   170
comforting therein, that when old robes are worn out,
there are members to make new. If there were no more   172
women but Fulvia, then had you indeed a cut, and the
case to be lamented. This grief is crowned with consolation; your old smock brings forth a new petticoat,   175
and indeed the tears live in an onion that should water   176
this sorrow.   177

ANTONY
The business she hath broachèd in the state   178
Cannot endure my absence.

ENOBARBUS   And the business you have broached here
cannot be without you, especially that of Cleopatra's,
which wholly depends on your abode.   182

ANTONY
No more light answers. Let our officers   183
Have notice what we purpose. I shall break   184
The cause of our expedience to the Queen   185
And get her leave to part. For not alone   186
The death of Fulvia, with more urgent touches,   187
Do strongly speak to us, but the letters too
Of many our contriving friends in Rome   189
Petition us at home. Sextus Pompeius   190
Hath given the dare to Caesar and commands
The empire of the sea. Our slippery people,   192

Whose love is never linked to the deserver
Till his deserts are past, begin to throw   194
Pompey the Great and all his dignities   195
Upon his son, who—high in name and power,
Higher than both in blood and life—stands up   197
For the main soldier; whose quality, going on,   198
The sides o'th' world may danger. Much is breeding,   199
Which, like the courser's hair, hath yet but life,   200
And not a serpent's poison. Say our pleasure,   201
To such whose place is under us, requires   202
Our quick remove from hence.   203

ENOBARBUS   I shall do't.   [Exeunt separately.]

❖

[1.3]

Enter Cleopatra, Charmian, Alexas, and Iras.

CLEOPATRA
Where is he?

CHARMIAN   I did not see him since.   1

CLEOPATRA [to Alexas]
See where he is, who's with him, what he does.
I did not send you. If you find him sad,   3
Say I am dancing; if in mirth, report
That I am sudden sick. Quick, and return.   5
                                    [Exit Alexas.]

CHARMIAN
Madam, methinks, if you did love him dearly,
You do not hold the method to enforce   7
The like from him.

CLEOPATRA   What should I do I do not?   8

CHARMIAN
In each thing give him way. Cross him in nothing.

CLEOPATRA
Thou teachest like a fool: the way to lose him.

CHARMIAN
Tempt him not so too far. I wish, forbear;   11
In time we hate that which we often fear.

        Enter Antony.

But here comes Antony.

CLEOPATRA   I am sick and sullen.   13

ANTONY
I am sorry to give breathing to my purpose—   14

---

155 sighs i.e., mere sighs   **170 tailors** (The gods can fashion a new
wife for a man, much as a tailor can mend or replace a worn-out garment.)   **172 members** (The word has a bawdy suggestion, pursued
in lines 173–4 and 180 in *cut, case, business,* and *broached; cut* and *case*
suggest the female sexual organs; *broached* suggests something that is
stabbed, pricked, opened.)   **175 smock** undergarment. (Also used
defamatorily of women.)   **176–7 the tears . . . sorrow** i.e., only an
onion could produce tears on this occasion of Fulvia's death.
178 broachèd opened up. (But see the note for line 172.)   **182 abode**
staying.   **183 light** frivolous, indelicate   **184 break** i.e., break the
news of   **185 expedience** haste   **186 leave** consent   **187 urgent
touches** pressing matters   **189 Of . . . friends** from many friends
working in our interest   **190 at home** to come home.   **Sextus Pompeius** son of Pompey the Great, who, though outlawed, has been able
to exploit the division between Antony and Octavius and thereby
gain command of Sicily and the sea; he appears in Act 2
192 slippery fickle

194 throw bestow   **195 Pompey the Great** i.e., the title and honored
status of "Pompey the Great"   **197 blood and life** mettle and vitality
197–8 stands . . . soldier lays claim to being the greatest soldier
198–9 whose . . . danger whose aspiring character and situation, if
allowed to continue unchecked, may endanger the frame of the
Roman world.   **200 like . . . hair** (Allusion to the popular belief that a
horsehair put into water would turn to a snake.)   **200–1 hath . . .
poison** is alive at this point but not yet a poisonous full-grown serpent.   **201–3 Say . . . hence** Tell those who serve me that my wish is
to depart quickly.
1.3 Location: Alexandria. Cleopatra's palace.
1 since lately.   **3 I did . . . you** i.e., Do not let him know I sent you.
sad serious   **5 sudden** suddenly taken   **7 hold the method** follow
the right course   **8 I do not** that I am not doing.   **11 Tempt** Try.
I wish I wish you would   **13 sullen** depressed, melancholy.
14 breathing utterance

CLEOPATRA
Help me away, dear Charmian! I shall fall.
It cannot be thus long; the sides of nature   16
Will not sustain it.

ANTONY   Now, my dearest queen—

CLEOPATRA
Pray you, stand farther from me.

ANTONY   What's the matter?   18

CLEOPATRA
I know by that same eye there's some good news.
What, says the married woman you may go?   20
Would she had never given you leave to come!
Let her not say 'tis I that keep you here.
I have no power upon you; hers you are.

ANTONY
The gods best know—

CLEOPATRA   Oh, never was there queen
So mightily betrayed! Yet at the first
I saw the treasons planted.

ANTONY   Cleopatra—

CLEOPATRA
Why should I think you can be mine, and true—
Though you in swearing shake the thronèd gods—
Who have been false to Fulvia? Riotous madness,   29
To be entangled with those mouth-made vows   30
Which break themselves in swearing!

ANTONY   Most sweet queen—   31

CLEOPATRA
Nay, pray you, seek no color for your going,   32
But bid farewell and go. When you sued staying,   33
Then was the time for words. No going then.
Eternity was in our lips and eyes,   35
Bliss in our brows' bent; none our parts so poor   36
But was a race of heaven. They are so still,   37
Or thou, the greatest soldier of the world,
Art turned the greatest liar.

ANTONY   How now, lady?

CLEOPATRA
I would I had thy inches. Thou shouldst know   40
There were a heart in Egypt.

ANTONY   Hear me, Queen: 41
The strong necessity of time commands
Our services awhile, but my full heart
Remains in use with you. Our Italy   44
Shines o'er with civil swords; Sextus Pompeius   45
Makes his approaches to the port of Rome;

Equality of two domestic powers   47
Breed scrupulous faction; the hated, grown to
    strength,   48
Are newly grown to love; the condemned Pompey,   49
Rich in his father's honor, creeps apace   50
Into the hearts of such as have not thrived
Upon the present state, whose numbers threaten;   52
And quietness, grown sick of rest, would purge   53
By any desperate change. My more particular,   54
And that which most with you should safe my going,   55
Is Fulvia's death.

CLEOPATRA
Though age from folly could not give me freedom,
It does from childishness. Can Fulvia die?

ANTONY   She's dead, my queen.   [*He offers letters.*]
Look here, and at thy sovereign leisure read
The garboils she awaked, at the last, best,   61
See when and where she died.

CLEOPATRA   Oh, most false love!
Where be the sacred vials thou shouldst fill   63
With sorrowful water? Now I see, I see,
In Fulvia's death how mine received shall be.

ANTONY
Quarrel no more, but be prepared to know
The purposes I bear, which are or cease   67
As you shall give th'advice. By the fire   68
That quickens Nilus' slime, I go from hence   69
Thy soldier, servant, making peace or war
As thou affects.

CLEOPATRA   Cut my lace, Charmian, come!   71
But let it be; I am quickly ill, and well,
So Antony loves.

ANTONY   My precious queen, forbear,   73
And give true evidence to his love which stands   74
An honorable trial.

CLEOPATRA   So Fulvia told me.   75
I prithee, turn aside and weep for her;
Then bid adieu to me, and say the tears
Belong to Egypt. Good now, play one scene   78

---

16 **It . . . long** I can't last long at this rate.   **sides of nature** human body, frame   **18 stand farther from me** give me air.   **20 the married woman** Fulvia   **29 Who** you who.   **Riotous madness** What folly on my part   **30 mouth-made** insincerely spoken   **31 in swearing** even while they are being sworn.   **32 color** pretext   **33 sued staying** begged to stay   **35 our** i.e., my. (The royal plural.)   **36 bent** arch, curve.   **none . . . poor** none of my features, however poor   **37 race of heaven** of heavenly origin, or, possibly, of the flavor of heaven.   **40 inches** (1) height (2) manly strength. (With perhaps a bawdy suggestion.)   **41 a heart in Egypt** a mighty courage in the Queen of Egypt.   **44 in use with you** for your use.   **45 Shines . . . swords** glitters everywhere with weapons of civil war

47–8 Equality . . . faction the equal splitting of domestic power between two (Antony and Caesar) breeds petty bickering   **48–9 the hated . . . love** those (like Pompey) who were out of favor, being now strong, have recently come back into popular favor   **49–50 Pompey . . . apace** i.e., Sextus Pompeius, richly inheriting the honor once accorded Pompey the Great, quickly insinuates himself   **52 state** government (of the triumvirate).   **whose** i.e., those supporting Pompey   **53–4 And quietness . . . change** and peace, bored with its own long continuance, longs to purge itself by the violence of war (medically speaking, by vomiting, bowel evacuation, or bloodletting).   **54 particular** personal concern   **55 safe** make safe   **61 garboils** disturbances, commotions.   **best** i.e., best of all   **63 sacred vials** (Alludes to the supposed Roman custom of putting bottles filled with tears in the tombs of the departed.)   **67 which are** which will proceed   **68 fire** i.e., sun   **69 quickens . . . slime** brings to life the mud left by the overflow of the Nile   **71 thou affects** you desire.   **lace** cord or laces fastening the bodice. (Cleopatra pretends she is fainting.)   **73 So** provided that, or, possibly, "in the same way, with changes as sudden as my own"   **74–5 And . . . trial** and bear true witness to the love of one who withstands any honorable test.   **75 So . . . me** i.e., So Fulvia would have said, no doubt. (Said as a taunt.)   **78 Belong to Egypt** are shed for the Queen of Egypt.   **Good now** (An expression of entreaty.)

Of excellent dissembling, and let it look
Like perfect honor.

ANTONY You'll heat my blood. No more. 80

CLEOPATRA
You can do better yet; but this is meetly. 81

ANTONY
Now, by my sword—

CLEOPATRA And target. Still he mends. 82
But this is not the best. Look, prithee, Charmian,
How this Herculean Roman does become 84
The carriage of his chafe. 85

ANTONY I'll leave you, lady.

CLEOPATRA Courteous lord, one word.
Sir, you and I must part, but that's not it;
Sir, you and I have loved, but there's not it;
That you know well. Something it is I would— 90
Oh, my oblivion is a very Antony, 91
And I am all forgotten.

ANTONY But that your royalty 92
Holds idleness your subject, I should take you 93
For idleness itself.

CLEOPATRA 'Tis sweating labor 94
To bear such idleness so near the heart 95
As Cleopatra this. But sir, forgive me, 96
Since my becomings kill me when they do not 97
Eye well to you. Your honor calls you hence; 98
Therefore be deaf to my unpitied folly,
And all the gods go with you! Upon your sword
Sit laurel victory, and smooth success 101
Be strewed before your feet!

ANTONY Let us go. Come;
Our separation so abides and flies 103
That thou, residing here, goes yet with me,
And I, hence fleeting, here remain with thee.
Away! *Exeunt.*

❧

[1.4]

Enter Octavius [Caesar], reading a letter, Lepidus, and their train.

CAESAR
You may see, Lepidus, and henceforth know,
It is not Caesar's natural vice to hate

Our great competitor. From Alexandria 3
This is the news: he fishes, drinks, and wastes
The lamps of night in revel; is not more manlike
Than Cleopatra, nor the queen of Ptolemy 6
More womanly than he; hardly gave audience, or 7
Vouchsafed to think he had partners. You shall find
there
A man who is the abstract of all faults 9
That all men follow.

LEPIDUS I must not think there are
Evils enough to darken all his goodness.
His faults in him seem as the spots of heaven, 12
More fiery by night's blackness, hereditary 13
Rather than purchased, what he cannot change 14
Than what he chooses.

CAESAR
You are too indulgent. Let's grant it is not 16
Amiss to tumble on the bed of Ptolemy,
To give a kingdom for a mirth, to sit 18
And keep the turn of tippling with a slave, 19
To reel the streets at noon, and stand the buffet 20
With knaves that smells of sweat. Say this becomes
him—
As his composure must be rare indeed 22
Whom these things cannot blemish—yet must Antony
No way excuse his foils when we do bear 24
So great weight in his lightness. If he filled 25
His vacancy with his voluptuousness, 26
Full surfeits and the dryness of his bones 27
Call on him for't. But to confound such time 28
That drums him from his sport and speaks as loud 29
As his own state and ours, 'tis to be chid 30
As we rate boys who, being mature in knowledge, 31
Pawn their experience to their present pleasure 32
And so rebel to judgment.

Enter a Messenger.

LEPIDUS Here's more news. 33

FIRST MESSENGER
Thy biddings have been done, and every hour,
Most noble Caesar, shalt thou have report
How 'tis abroad. Pompey is strong at sea,

---

80 heat my blood i.e., anger me. **81 meetly** i.e., fairly well acted. (Said mockingly.) **82 target** shield. **mends** improves (in his "scene / Of excellent dissembling"). **84–5 How . . . chafe** i.e., how Antony, who claims descent from Hercules, plays the role of his enraged ancestor well. (Hercules had become a stock figure of the enraged hero or tyrant.) **chafe** rage. **90 would** wished to say **91 my . . . Antony** my forgetful memory is like Antony (who is now leaving and thus forgetting me) **92 I . . . forgotten** (1) I have forgotten what I was going to say (2) I am entirely forgotten (by Antony). **92–4 But . . . itself** Since you are a queen, your frivolousness must be your subject (i.e., ruled by you); otherwise, I'd think you were frivolousness itself. **94–6 'Tis . . . this** i.e., I am not being frivolous; this is hard for me to bear. (*Sweating, labor,* and *bear* are all associated with pregnancy.) **97 my becomings** (1) those qualities that become me (2) the various roles that I adopt **98 Eye** appear **101 laurel** wreathed with laurel **103 so abides and flies** mingles remaining and going in such a paradoxical fashion
1.4 Location: Rome.

3 competitor partner. (With a suggestion also of "rival.") **6 Ptolemy** (Cleopatra's royal brother, to whom she had been married according to Egyptian custom.) **7 gave audience** i.e., received messengers **9 abstract** epitome **12–13 His . . . blackness** His faults are enhanced by contrast with his virtues, just as the stars in the sky stand out from the darkness **14 purchased** acquired **16 Let's grant** Even if we were to grant **18 mirth** jest, diversion **19 keep . . . of** take turns **20 stand the buffet** exchange blows **22 As his composure** and a man's composition or temperament **24 foils** blemishes **24–5 when . . . lightness** when we have to carry the heavy burden imposed by his levity. **26 His vacancy** his leisure time **27–8 Full . . . for't** the physical disabilities resulting from such voluptuousness (such as venereal disease) would call him to account and would be adequate punishment. **28 confound** waste **29 drums** summons (as by a military drum). **sport** amorous pastime **29–30 speaks . . . ours** summons him urgently in view of his political position and ours as well **30 chid** chided, reprimanded **31 rate** berate. **mature in knowledge** old enough to know better **32 Pawn . . . pleasure** risk for the sake of immediate gratification what experience tells them will be ultimately painful **33 to judgment** against better judgment.

And it appears he is beloved of those   37
That only have feared Caesar. To the ports   38
The discontents repair, and men's reports   39
Give him much wronged.   [*Exit.*]
CAESAR   I should have known no less.   40
It hath been taught us from the primal state   41
That he which is was wished until he were;   42
And the ebbed man, ne'er loved till ne'er worth love,   43
Comes deared by being lacked. This common body,   44
Like to a vagabond flag upon the stream,   45
Goes to and back, lackeying the varying tide   46
To rot itself with motion.

[Enter a Second Messenger.]

SECOND MESSENGER   Caesar, I bring thee word
Menecrates and Menas, famous pirates,   49
Makes the sea serve them, which they ear and wound   50
With keels of every kind. Many hot inroads
They make in Italy. The borders maritime   52
Lack blood to think on't, and flush youth revolt.   53
No vessel can peep forth but 'tis as soon
Taken as seen; for Pompey's name strikes more   55
Than could his war resisted.   [*Exit.*]
CAESAR   Antony,   56
Leave thy lascivious wassails. When thou once   57
Was beaten from Modena, where thou slew'st
Hirtius and Pansa, consuls, at thy heel
Did famine follow, whom thou fought'st against,   60
Though daintily brought up, with patience more
Than savages could suffer. Thou didst drink   62
The stale of horses and the gilded puddle   63
Which beasts would cough at. Thy palate then did
  deign   64
The roughest berry on the rudest hedge.
Yea, like the stag, when snow the pasture sheets,   66
The barks of trees thou browsèd. On the Alps   67
It is reported thou didst eat strange flesh,
Which some did die to look on. And all this—
It wounds thine honor that I speak it now—
Was borne so like a soldier that thy cheek
So much as lanked not.   72
LEPIDUS   'Tis pity of him.   73
CAESAR   Let his shames quickly
Drive him to Rome. 'Tis time we twain
Did show ourselves i'th' field, and to that end

Assemble we immediate council. Pompey
Thrives in our idleness.
LEPIDUS   Tomorrow, Caesar,
I shall be furnished to inform you rightly
Both what by sea and land I can be able   80
To front this present time.
CAESAR   Till which encounter   81
It is my business too. Farewell.
LEPIDUS
Farewell, my lord. What you shall know meantime
Of stirs abroad, I shall beseech you, sir,   84
To let me be partaker.
CAESAR
Doubt not, sir, I knew it for my bond.   86
                          Exeunt [separately].

❖

[1.5]

Enter Cleopatra, Charmian, Iras, and Mardian.

CLEOPATRA   Charmian!
CHARMIAN   Madam?
CLEOPATRA
Ha, ha! Give me to drink mandragora.   3
CHARMIAN   Why, madam?
CLEOPATRA
That I might sleep out this great gap of time
My Antony is away.
CHARMIAN   You think of him too much.
CLEOPATRA
Oh, 'tis treason!
CHARMIAN   Madam, I trust not so.
CLEOPATRA
Thou, eunuch Mardian!
MARDIAN   What's Your Highness' pleasure?
CLEOPATRA
Not now to hear thee sing. I take no pleasure
In aught an eunuch has. 'Tis well for thee   11
That, being unseminared, thy freer thoughts   12
May not fly forth of Egypt. Hast thou affections?   13
MARDIAN   Yes, gracious madam.
CLEOPATRA   Indeed?
MARDIAN
Not in deed, madam, for I can do nothing   16
But what indeed is honest to be done.   17
Yet have I fierce affections, and think
What Venus did with Mars.
CLEOPATRA   Oh, Charmian,
Where think'st thou he is now? Stands he or sits he?
Or does he walk? Or is he on his horse?
Oh, happy horse, to bear the weight of Antony!

---

37 of by   **38 That . . . Caesar** that have obeyed Caesar only through fear.   **39 discontents** discontented. (See 1.3.48–52.)   **40 Give him** represent him as   **41–4 It . . . lacked** It is an ironic lesson of history from the earliest times that the man currently in the public eye is avidly sought after only until he becomes ruler, whereas the public figure whose fortunes have decayed, sought after only when he is no longer worthy of love, becomes loved once he is gone.   **44 common body** populace   **45 vagabond flag** shifting and undependable weeds   **46 lackeying** following in servile fashion, like a lackey   **49 famous** notorious   **50 ear** plow   **52 borders maritime** coastal territories   **53 Lack blood** turn pale.   **flush** vigorous; flushed, ruddy (contrasted with those who *Lack blood*)   **55–6 strikes . . . resisted** inflicts more damage than his forces could against our resistance.   **57 wassails** carousals.   **60 whom** i.e., famine   **62 suffer** show in suffering.   **63 stale** urine.   **gilded** covered with iridescent slime   **64 deign** not disdain   **66 sheets** covers   **67 browsèd** fed upon.   **72 lanked not** did not become thin.   **73 of** about

80 be able be capable of mustering   **81 front** confront, deal with   **84 stirs** commotions   **86 knew** already knew.   **bond** duty, obligation.
1.5 Location: Egypt. Cleopatra's palace.
3 mandragora juice of the mandrake (a narcotic).   **11 aught** (With bawdy suggestion.)   **12 unseminared** castrated   **13 of** from.   **affections** passions.   **16 Not in deed** (Mardian punningly takes the *deed* of *Indeed* in line 15 to mean "physical act.")   **do** (With suggestion of sexual intercourse.)   **17 honest** chaste

Do bravely, horse, for wot'st thou whom thou mov'st? 23
The demi-Atlas of this earth, the arm 24
And burgonet of men. He's speaking now, 25
Or murmuring, "Where's my serpent of old Nile?"
For so he calls me. Now I feed myself
With most delicious poison. Think on me, 28
That am with Phoebus' amorous pinches black 29
And wrinkled deep in time. Broad-fronted Caesar, 30
When thou wast here above the ground, I was
A morsel for a monarch. And great Pompey 32
Would stand and make his eyes grow in my brow; 33
There would he anchor his aspect, and die 34
With looking on his life. 35

Enter Alexas.

ALEXAS   Sovereign of Egypt, hail!
CLEOPATRA
How much unlike art thou Mark Antony!
Yet, coming from him, that great med'cine hath 38
With his tinct gilded thee. 39
How goes it with my brave Mark Antony? 40
ALEXAS   Last thing he did, dear Queen,
He kissed—the last of many doubled kisses—
This orient pearl. [*He gives a pearl.*] His speech sticks in
  my heart. 43
CLEOPATRA
Mine ear must pluck it thence.
ALEXAS   "Good friend," quoth he,
"Say the firm Roman to great Egypt sends 45
This treasure of an oyster; at whose foot,
To mend the petty present, I will piece 47
Her opulent throne with kingdoms. All the East,
Say thou, shall call her mistress." So he nodded,
And soberly did mount an arm-gaunt steed, 50
Who neighed so high that what I would have spoke
Was beastly dumbed by him. 52
CLEOPATRA   What, was he sad, or merry?
ALEXAS
Like to the time o'th' year between the extremes
Of hot and cold, he was nor sad nor merry. 55

CLEOPATRA
Oh, well-divided disposition! Note him, 56
Note him, good Charmian, 'tis the man; but note him. 57
He was not sad, for he would shine on those 58
That make their looks by his; he was not merry, 59
Which seemed to tell them his remembrance lay
In Egypt with his joy; but between both.
Oh, heavenly mingle! Be'st thou sad or merry,
The violence of either thee becomes, 63
So does it no man else.—Met'st thou my posts? 64
ALEXAS
Ay, madam, twenty several messengers. 65
Why do you send so thick?
CLEOPATRA   Who's born that day 66
When I forget to send to Antony
Shall die a beggar. Ink and paper, Charmian. 68
Welcome, my good Alexas. Did I, Charmian,
Ever love Caesar so?
CHARMIAN   Oh, that brave Caesar!
CLEOPATRA
Be choked with such another emphasis! 71
Say, "the brave Antony."
CHARMIAN   The valiant Caesar!
CLEOPATRA
By Isis, I will give thee bloody teeth
If thou with Caesar paragon again 74
My man of men.
CHARMIAN   By your most gracious pardon,
I sing but after you.
CLEOPATRA   My salad days,
When I was green in judgment, cold in blood, 77
To say as I said then. But, come, away,
Get me ink and paper.
He shall have every day a several greeting,
Or I'll unpeople Egypt.   *Exeunt.* 81

❖

[2.1]

Enter Pompey, Menecrates, and Menas, in war-like manner.

POMPEY
If the great gods be just, they shall assist
The deeds of justest men.
MENAS   Know, worthy Pompey, 2
That what they do delay they not deny. 3

---

23 **Do** (With sexual suggestion, as in line 16.)   **wot'st thou** do you know   24 **demi-Atlas** one who (together with Caesar) supports the weight of the whole world, as Atlas did. (Cleopatra disregards Lepidus as a triumvir.)   **arm** strong right arm or weapon   25 **burgonet** light helmet or steel cap, i.e., protector   28–30 **Think . . . time** (Cleopatra reflects on her ability to attract Antony, given the fact that she is dark-skinned [as from the amorous pinches of her lover, the sun] and increasingly wrinkled with age.)   29 **Phoebus'** the sun's   30 **Broad-fronted Caesar** Broad-foreheaded Julius Caesar   32 **great Pompey** Gnaeus Pompey, oldest son of Pompey the Great. (Shakespeare may conflate the two.)   33 **make . . . brow** i.e., rivet his eyes on my face   34 **aspect** look, gaze.   **die** i.e., suffer the extremity of love. (And with suggestion of orgasm, as at 1.2.148.)   35 **his life** that which he lived for.   38 **great med'cine** the philosopher's stone, the supposed substance by which alchemists hoped to turn all baser metals into gold   39 **his tinct** its alchemical potency; also, its color   40 **brave** splendid   43 **orient** shining, bright. (The best pearls were from the East or Orient.)   45 **firm** constant, true.   **Egypt** the Queen of Egypt   47 **piece** augment   50 **arm-gaunt** made trim and hard by warlike service, or hungry for battle   52 **dumbed** drowned out, made inaudible   55 **nor sad** neither sad

56 **well-divided disposition** well-balanced temperament.   57 **the man** i.e., perfectly characteristic of him.   **but** do but, only   58 **would** wished to   59 **make . . . his** model their demeanor on his look   63 **becomes** is becoming to you   64 **posts** messengers.   65 **several** separate, distinct. (Also in line 80.)   66 **Who's** Anyone who is   68 **Shall . . . beggar** (since that day, sure never to come, would be ill-omened)   71 **emphasis** emphatic expression.   74 **paragon** match or compare   77 **green** immature   81 **Or . . . Egypt** Or I will send so many messengers that Egypt will be unpeopled. (Perhaps too with a darker threat of violence.)
2.1 Location: Pompey's camp, probably at Messina, Sicily.
2 MENAS (The Folio assigns the speeches in this scene to "*Mene.*"; some could be for Menecrates, but Pompey ignores him entirely at lines 43–52, and Menecrates never reappears in the play.)   3 **not deny** i.e., do not necessarily deny.

POMPEY

    Whiles we are suitors to their throne, decays   4

    The thing we sue for.

MENAS   We, ignorant of ourselves,   5

    Beg often our own harms, which the wise powers

    Deny us for our good; so find we profit

    By losing of our prayers.

POMPEY   I shall do well.

    The people love me, and the sea is mine;

    My powers are crescent, and my auguring hope   10

    Says it will come to th' full. Mark Antony   11

    In Egypt sits at dinner, and will make

    No wars without doors. Caesar gets money where   13

    He loses hearts. Lepidus flatters both,

    Of both is flattered; but he neither loves,   15

    Nor either cares for him.

MENAS   Caesar and Lepidus

    Are in the field. A mighty strength they carry.   17

POMPEY

    Where have you this? 'Tis false.

MENAS   From Silvius, sir.

POMPEY

    He dreams. I know they are in Rome together

    Looking for Antony. But all the charms of love,   20

    Salt Cleopatra, soften thy waned lip!   21

    Let witchcraft joined with beauty, lust with both,

    Tie up the libertine in a field of feasts,   23

    Keep his brain fuming. Epicurean cooks,   24

    Sharpen with cloyless sauce his appetite,   25

    That sleep and feeding may prorogue his honor   26

    Even till a Lethe'd dullness—

Enter Varrius.

                    How now, Varrius?   27

VARRIUS

    This is most certain that I shall deliver: 28

    Mark Antony is every hour in Rome

    Expected. Since he went from Egypt 'tis

    A space for further travel.   31

POMPEY   I could have given less matter   32

    A better ear. Menas, I did not think

    This amorous surfeiter would have donned his helm   34

    For such a petty war. His soldiership

    Is twice the other twain. But let us rear   36

    The higher our opinion, that our stirring   37

    Can from the lap of Egypt's widow pluck   38

    The ne'er-lust-wearied Antony.

MENAS   I cannot hope   39

    Caesar and Antony shall well greet together.   40

    His wife that's dead did trespasses to Caesar;   41

    His brother warred upon him, although, I think,   42

    Not moved by Antony.

POMPEY   I know not, Menas,   43

    How lesser enmities may give way to greater.

    Were't not that we stand up against them all,

    'Twere pregnant they should square between

        themselves,   46

    For they have entertainèd cause enough   47

    To draw their swords. But how the fear of us

    May cement their divisions and bind up

    The petty difference, we yet not know.

    Be't as our gods will have't! It only stands   51

    Our lives upon to use our strongest hands.   52

    Come, Menas.   *Exeunt.*

❖

[2.2]

Enter Enobarbus and Lepidus.

LEPIDUS

    Good Enobarbus, 'tis a worthy deed,

    And shall become you well, to entreat your captain

    To soft and gentle speech.

ENOBARBUS   I shall entreat him

    To answer like himself. If Caesar move him,   4

    Let Antony look over Caesar's head   5

    And speak as loud as Mars. By Jupiter,

    Were I the wearer of Antonio's beard,

    I would not shave't today.   8

LEPIDUS

    'Tis not a time for private stomaching.

ENOBARBUS   Every time   9

    Serves for the matter that is then born in't.

LEPIDUS

    But small to greater matters must give way.

ENOBARBUS

    Not if the small come first.

LEPIDUS   Your speech is passion;

    But pray you stir no embers up. Here comes

    The noble Antony.

Enter Antony and Ventidius [in conversation].

ENOBARBUS   And yonder, Caesar.

Enter Caesar, Maecenas, and Agrippa, [also in conversation, by another door].

4–5 Whiles . . . for While we are praying, that for which we pray is being destroyed.   **10 My . . . crescent** My armed forces are on the increase.   **auguring** prophesying   **11 it** i.e., my powers or fortune (seen as a crescent moon, becoming full)   **13 without doors** outdoors, i.e., in the battlefield, rather than in the bedroom.   **15 Of** by.   **neither loves** loves neither   **17 A . . . carry** They command a mighty army.   **20 Looking for** Awaiting.   **charms** spells   **21 Salt** lustful.   **waned** faded, withered   **23 Tie . . . feasts** i.e., tether him like an animal in a rich pasture   **24 Epicurean** Let epicurean   **25 cloyless** i.e., which will not satiate   **26 prorogue** defer the operation of   **27 Lethe'd** oblivious. (From the river of the underworld whose waters cause forgetfulness in those who drink.)   **28 deliver** report   **31 space . . . travel** time enough for an even longer journey and labor (travail).   **32 less** less important   **34 helm** helmet   **36 rear** raise   **37 opinion** i.e., of ourselves   **38 Egypt's widow** i.e., Cleopatra, widow of the young King Ptolemy

39 hope expect   **40 well greet** greet one another kindly   **41 did trespasses to** wronged   **42 brother** i.e., Lucius Antonius. (See 1.2.94 ff.)   **43 moved** provoked, incited   **46 pregnant** clear, obvious.   **square** quarrel   **47 entertainèd** maintained   **51–2 It . . . hands** Our very lives depend upon our using our greatest strength.
2.2 Location: Rome. Furniture is put out on which Antony and Caesar are to sit.
4 like himself i.e., in a way befitting his greatness.   **move him** i.e., to anger   **5 look . . . head** i.e., condescend to Caesar as a smaller man   **8 I . . . shave't** i.e., I would continue to wear it and thereby dare Caesar to pluck it (in a symbolic gesture for starting a fight)   **9 private stomaching** personal resentment.

ANTONY
　　If we compose well here, to Parthia.   15
　　Hark, Ventidius.   　　　　　　　[*They confer apart.*]
CAESAR
　　I do not know, Maecenas, ask Agrippa.
LEPIDUS　　Noble friends,
　　That which combined us was most great, and let not
　　A leaner action rend us. What's amiss,   20
　　May it be gently heard. When we debate
　　Our trivial difference loud, we do commit
　　Murder in healing wounds. Then, noble partners,   23
　　The rather for I earnestly beseech,   24
　　Touch you the sourest points with sweetest terms,
　　Nor curstness grow to th' matter.
ANTONY   　　　　　　　　　　　'Tis spoken well.   26
　　Were we before our armies, and to fight,   27
　　I should do thus.   　　　　　　　　　　*Flourish.*
CAESAR　　Welcome to Rome.
ANTONY　　Thank you.
CAESAR　　Sit.
ANTONY　　Sit, sir.
CAESAR　　Nay, then.   　　　　　　　　　　[*They sit.*]
ANTONY
　　I learn you take things ill which are not so,
　　Or being, concern you not.
CAESAR   　　　　　　　　　I must be laughed at   35
　　If, or for nothing or a little, I   36
　　Should say myself offended, and with you
　　Chiefly i'th' world; more laughed at that I should   38
　　Once name you derogately, when to sound your name   39
　　It not concerned me.   40
ANTONY
　　My being in Egypt, Caesar, what was't to you?
CAESAR
　　No more than my residing here at Rome
　　Might be to you in Egypt. Yet if you there
　　Did practice on my state, your being in Egypt   44
　　Might be my question.
ANTONY   　　　　　　　How intend you "practiced"?   45
CAESAR
　　You may be pleased to catch at mine intent   46
　　By what did here befall me. Your wife and brother
　　Made wars upon me, and their contestation
　　Was theme for you. You were the word of war.   49
ANTONY
　　You do mistake your business. My brother never
　　Did urge me in his act. I did inquire it,   51
　　And have my learning from some true reports   52

That drew their swords with you. Did he not rather   53
Discredit my authority with yours,   54
And make the wars alike against my stomach,   55
Having alike your cause? Of this my letters   56
Before did satisfy you. If you'll patch a quarrel,   57
As matter whole you have to make it with,   58
It must not be with this.
CAESAR   　　　　　　　You praise yourself   59
　　By laying defects of judgment to me, but
　　You patched up your excuses.
ANTONY   　　　　　　　　Not so, not so.
　　I know you could not lack—I am certain on't—   62
　　Very necessity of this thought, that I,   63
　　Your partner in the cause 'gainst which he fought,   64
　　Could not with graceful eyes attend those wars   65
　　Which fronted mine own peace. As for my wife,   66
　　I would you had her spirit in such another.   67
　　The third o'th' world is yours, which with a snaffle   68
　　You may pace easy, but not such a wife.   69
ENOBARBUS　　Would we had all such wives, that the men
　　might go to wars with the women!
ANTONY
　　So much uncurbable, her garboils, Caesar,   72
　　Made out of her impatience—which not wanted   73
　　Shrewdness of policy too—I grieving grant   74
　　Did you too much disquiet. For that you must   75
　　But say I could not help it.
CAESAR   　　　　　　　　I wrote to you   76
　　When rioting in Alexandria; you   77
　　Did pocket up my letters and with taunts
　　Did gibe my missive out of audience.
ANTONY   　　　　　　　　　　Sir,   79
　　He fell upon me ere admitted, then.   80
　　Three kings I had newly feasted, and did want   81
　　Of what I was i'th' morning. But next day   82
　　I told him of myself, which was as much   83
　　As to have asked him pardon. Let this fellow
　　Be nothing of our strife; if we contend,   85
　　Out of our question wipe him.
CAESAR   　　　　　　　　　You have broken   86
　　The article of your oath, which you shall never   87
　　Have tongue to charge me with.
LEPIDUS　　Soft, Caesar!   89
ANTONY　　No, Lepidus, let him speak.

---

15 **compose** come to an agreement   20 **leaner** lesser, more trivial.
rend divide.   **What's** Whatever is   23 **healing** i.e., attempting to
heal   24 **The rather for** all the more because   26 **Nor . . . grow** nor
let ill humor be added   27 **to** about to   35 **being** being so, i.e., even
if they are amiss   36 **or . . . or** either . . . or   38 **i'th' world** of all people   39 **Once** under any circumstances.   **derogately** disparagingly
39–40 **when . . . concerned me** i.e., if, as you say, it were none of my
business.   44 **practice on my state** plot against my position
45 **question** business.   **How intend you** What do you mean
46 **catch at** infer   49 **Was . . . war** had you for its theme. They made
war in your name. (*Word* here means "watchword.")   51 **urge . . . act**
claim that he was fighting in my behalf.   **inquire** inquire into
52 **reports** reporters

53 **That . . . you** that fought in your army.   54 **Discredit** injure.   **with**
along with   55 **stomach** desire   56 **Having . . . cause** i.e., I having
just as much reason as you to deplore Lucius's action.   57–9 **If . . .
this** If you insist on manufacturing a quarrel out of shreds and
patches, as if you had substantial material to make it with, you've
chosen a weak matter to use.   62–3 **I know . . . thought** I'm certain
you must have realized   64 **he** i.e., Lucius   65 **with . . . attend** regard
favorably   66 **fronted** confronted, opposed   67 **her . . . another** i.e., a
wife such as she was.   68 **snaffle** bridle bit   69 **pace** put through its
paces, manage   72–5 **So . . . disquiet** I unhappily concede that her
unmanageable commotions, caused by her impatience (at my being
in Egypt) but not lacking in keenness of stratagem, did much to disquiet you, Caesar.   76 **But say** concede that   77 **When** while you
were   79 **Did . . . audience** taunted my messenger out of your presence.   80 **fell** burst in   81–2 **did want . . . morning** was not at my
best as I had been earlier in the day.   83 **of myself** i.e., of my having
had a lot to drink   85 **Be . . . of** have no part in   86 **question** contention   87 **article** terms   89 **Soft** Gently, go easy

The honor is sacred which he talks on now,
Supposing that I lacked it. But, on, Caesar: 92
The article of my oath—

CAESAR
To lend me arms and aid when I required them,   94
The which you both denied.

ANTONY   Neglected, rather;
And then when poisoned hours had bound me up
From mine own knowledge. As nearly as I may   97
I'll play the penitent to you, but mine honesty   98
Shall not make poor my greatness, nor my power   99
Work without it. Truth is that Fulvia,   100
To have me out of Egypt, made wars here,
For which myself, the ignorant motive, do   102
So far ask pardon as befits mine honor
To stoop in such a case.

LEPIDUS   'Tis noble spoken.   104

MAECENAS
If it might please you to enforce no further
The griefs between ye; to forget them quite   106
Were to remember that the present need
Speaks to atone you.

LEPIDUS   Worthily spoken, Maecenas.   108

ENOBARBUS   Or, if you borrow one another's love for the
instant, you may, when you hear no more words of
Pompey, return it again. You shall have time to wrangle in when you have nothing else to do.

ANTONY
Thou art a soldier only. Speak no more.

ENOBARBUS   That truth should be silent I had almost
forgot.

ANTONY
You wrong this presence. Therefore speak no more.   116

ENOBARBUS   Go to, then; your considerate stone.   117

CAESAR
I do not much dislike the matter, but
The manner of his speech; for't cannot be
We shall remain in friendship, our conditions   120
So diff'ring in their acts. Yet, if I knew
What hoop should hold us staunch, from edge to edge   122
O'th' world I would pursue it.

AGRIPPA   Give me leave, Caesar.

CAESAR   Speak, Agrippa.

AGRIPPA
Thou hast a sister by the mother's side,
Admired Octavia. Great Mark Antony
Is now a widower.

CAESAR   Say not so, Agrippa.
If Cleopatra heard you, your reproof
Were well deserved of rashness.   130

ANTONY
I am not married, Caesar. Let me hear
Agrippa further speak.

AGRIPPA
To hold you in perpetual amity,
To make you brothers, and to knit your hearts
With an unslipping knot, take Antony
Octavia to his wife, whose beauty claims
No worse a husband than the best of men,
Whose virtue and whose general graces speak   138
That which none else can utter. By this marriage   139
All little jealousies, which now seem great,   140
And all great fears, which now import their dangers,   141
Would then be nothing. Truths would be tales,   142
Where now half tales be truths. Her love to both   143
Would each to other and all loves to both
Draw after her. Pardon what I have spoke,
For 'tis a studied, not a present thought,
By duty ruminated.

ANTONY   Will Caesar speak?

CAESAR
Not till he hears how Antony is touched   148
With what is spoke already.   149

ANTONY   What power is in Agrippa
If I would say, "Agrippa, be it so,"
To make this good?

CAESAR   The power of Caesar and
His power unto Octavia.

ANTONY   May I never   153
To this good purpose, that so fairly shows,   154
Dream of impediment! Let me have thy hand
Further this act of grace, and from this hour   156
The heart of brothers govern in our loves
And sway our great designs!

CAESAR   There's my hand.
                                            [*They clasp hands.*]
A sister I bequeath you whom no brother
Did ever love so dearly. Let her live
To join our kingdoms and our hearts; and never   161
Fly off our loves again!

LEPIDUS   Happily, amen!   162

ANTONY
I did not think to draw my sword 'gainst Pompey,
For he hath laid strange courtesies and great   164
Of late upon me. I must thank him only,   165
Lest my remembrance suffer ill report;   166
At heel of that, defy him.

LEPIDUS   Time calls upon 's.   167
Of us must Pompey presently be sought,   168
Or else he seeks out us.

---

92 **Supposing** implying   94 **required** requested   97 **From . . .
knowledge** from knowing myself.   98–100 **mine . . . it** my honesty
(in admitting my overindulgence) will not go so far as to dishonor
my greatness, nor, conversely, will my authority be used in a dishonorable way.   102 **motive** moving or inciting cause   104 **noble** nobly
106 **griefs** grievances   108 **atone** reconcile   116 **presence** company.
117 **Go . . . stone** i.e., All right, all right. I'll keep my thoughts to
myself.   120 **conditions** temperaments, dispositions   122 **hoop** barrel hoop.   **staunch** firm, watertight   130 **Were . . . rashness** would
richly deserve the rebuke it would get for such rashness.

138–9 **Whose . . . utter** whose virtues declare themselves better than
any words about them could do.   140 **jealousies** misunderstandings,
suspicions   141 **import** imply; carry with them   142–3 **Truths . . .
truths** True reports (no matter how distressing) would then be dis-
counted as mere rumors, whereas at present half-true reports are
taken for the whole truth.   148–9 **touched With** affected by
153 **unto** over   154 **so fairly shows** looks so promising   156 **Further**
in furtherance of   161–2 **never . . . again** may our amity never desert
us again.   164 **strange** remarkable   165 **only** at least   166 **Lest . . .
report** lest I be accused of ingratitude   167 **At heel of** immediately
after   168 **Of** By.   **presently** at once

ANTONY   Where lies he?

CAESAR
About the mount Misena.

ANTONY   What is his strength   171
By land?

CAESAR   Great and increasing; but by sea
He is an absolute master.

ANTONY   So is the fame.   173
Would we had spoke together! Haste we for it.   174
Yet, ere we put ourselves in arms, dispatch we
The business we have talked of.

CAESAR   With most gladness,   176
And do invite you to my sister's view,   177
Whither straight I'll lead you.   178

ANTONY
Let us, Lepidus, not lack your company.

LEPIDUS
Noble Antony, not sickness should detain me.   180
Flourish. Exeunt. Manent Enobarbus, Agrippa,
Maecenas.

MAECENAS   Welcome from Egypt, sir.

ENOBARBUS   Half the heart of Caesar, worthy Maecenas!   182
My honorable friend, Agrippa!

AGRIPPA   Good Enobarbus!

MAECENAS   We have cause to be glad that matters are so
well digested. You stayed well by't in Egypt.   186

ENOBARBUS   Ay, sir, we did sleep day out of counte-   187
nance and made the night light with drinking.   188

MAECENAS   Eight wild boars roasted whole at a breakfast, and but twelve persons there; is this true?

ENOBARBUS   This was but as a fly by an eagle. We had   191
much more monstrous matter of feast, which worthily
deserved noting.

MAECENAS   She's a most triumphant lady, if report be   194
square to her.   195

ENOBARBUS   When she first met Mark Antony, she
pursed up his heart upon the river of Cydnus.   197

AGRIPPA   There she appeared indeed, or my reporter de-   198
vised well for her.   199

ENOBARBUS   I will tell you.
The barge she sat in, like a burnished throne   201
Burnt on the water. The poop was beaten gold;   202
Purple the sails, and so perfumèd that
The winds were lovesick with them. The oars were
    silver,
Which to the tune of flutes kept stroke, and made
The water which they beat to follow faster,

As amorous of their strokes. For her own person,   207
It beggared all description: she did lie
In her pavilion—cloth-of-gold of tissue—   209
O'erpicturing that Venus where we see
The fancy outwork nature. On each side her   211
Stood pretty dimpled boys, like smiling Cupids,
With divers-colored fans, whose wind did seem   213
To glow the delicate cheeks which they did cool,   214
And what they undid did.

AGRIPPA   Oh, rare for Antony!

ENOBARBUS
Her gentlewomen, like the Nereides,   216
So many mermaids, tended her i'th'eyes   217
And made their bends adornings. At the helm   218
A seeming mermaid steers. The silken tackle
Swell with the touches of those flower-soft hands,
That yarely frame the office. From the barge   221
A strange invisible perfume hits the sense
Of the adjacent wharfs. The city cast   223
Her people out upon her; and Antony,
Enthroned i'th' marketplace, did sit alone,
Whistling to th'air, which, but for vacancy,   226
Had gone to gaze on Cleopatra too,
And made a gap in nature.

AGRIPPA   Rare Egyptian!

ENOBARBUS
Upon her landing, Antony sent to her,
Invited her to supper. She replied
It should be better he became her guest,
Which she entreated. Our courteous Antony,
Whom ne'er the word of "No" woman heard speak,
Being barbered ten times o'er, goes to the feast,
And for his ordinary pays his heart   235
For what his eyes eat only.

AGRIPPA   Royal wench!   236
She made great Caesar lay his sword to bed;   237
He plowed her, and she cropped.

ENOBARBUS   I saw her once   238
Hop forty paces through the public street,
And having lost her breath, she spoke and panted,
That she did make defect perfection,   241
And, breathless, power breathe forth.

MAECENAS
Now Antony must leave her utterly.

ENOBARBUS   Never. He will not.
Age cannot wither her, nor custom stale   245
Her infinite variety. Other women cloy
The appetites they feed, but she makes hungry

Where most she satisfies; for vilest things
Become themselves in her, that the holy priests   249
Bless her when she is riggish.   250

MAECENAS
If beauty, wisdom, modesty can settle
The heart of Antony, Octavia is
A blessèd lottery to him.

AGRIPPA   Let us go.   253
Good Enobarbus, make yourself my guest
Whilst you abide here.

ENOBARBUS   Humbly, sir, I thank you.
                                                    Exeunt.

❧

[2.3]

Enter Antony, Caesar, Octavia between them.

ANTONY
The world and my great office will sometimes
Divide me from your bosom.

OCTAVIA   All which time
Before the gods my knee shall bow my prayers
To them for you.

ANTONY   Good night, sir. My Octavia,
Read not my blemishes in the world's report.   5
I have not kept my square, but that to come   6
Shall all be done by th' rule. Good night, dear lady.
Good night, sir.

CAESAR   Good night.   *Exit [with Octavia].*

        Enter Soothsayer.

ANTONY
Now, sirrah: you do wish yourself in Egypt?   10

SOOTHSAYER   Would I had never come from thence,
nor you thither!   12

ANTONY   If you can, your reason?

SOOTHSAYER   I see it in in my motion, have it not in my   14
tongue; but yet hie you to Egypt again.   15

ANTONY
Say to me, whose fortunes shall rise higher,
Caesar's or mine?

SOOTHSAYER   Caesar's.
Therefore, O Antony, stay not by his side.
Thy daemon—that thy spirit which keeps thee—is   20
Noble, courageous, high unmatchable,   21
Where Caesar's is not; but near him thy angel   22
Becomes afeard, as being o'erpowered. Therefore
Make space enough between you.

ANTONY   Speak this no more.

SOOTHSAYER
To none but thee; no more but when to thee.   25
If thou dost play with him at any game,
Thou art sure to lose; and of that natural luck   27
He beats thee 'gainst the odds. Thy luster thickens   28
When he shines by. I say again, thy spirit   29
Is all afraid to govern thee near him;
But, he away, 'tis noble.

ANTONY   Get thee gone.
Say to Ventidius I would speak with him.
                                    Exit [Soothsayer].
He shall to Parthia.—Be it art or hap,   33
He hath spoken true. The very dice obey him,
And in our sports my better cunning faints   35
Under his chance. If we draw lots, he speeds;   36
His cocks do win the battle still of mine   37
When it is all to naught, and his quails ever   38
Beat mine, inhooped, at odds. I will to Egypt;   39
And though I make this marriage for my peace,
I'th'East my pleasure lies.

        Enter Ventidius.

                            Oh, come, Ventidius.
You must to Parthia. Your commission's ready;
Follow me, and receive't.   *Exeunt.*

❧

[2.4]

Enter Lepidus, Maecenas, and Agrippa.

LEPIDUS
Trouble yourselves no further. Pray you, hasten
Your generals after.

AGRIPPA   Sir, Mark Antony   2
Will e'en but kiss Octavia, and we'll follow.   3

LEPIDUS
Till I shall see you in your soldier's dress,   4
Which will become you both, farewell.

MAECENAS   We shall,   5
As I conceive the journey, be at th' Mount   6
Before you, Lepidus.

LEPIDUS   Your way is shorter;
My purposes do draw me much about.   8
You'll win two days upon me.

MAECENAS, AGRIPPA   Sir, good success!
LEPIDUS   Farewell.   *Exeunt.*

❧

249 **Become themselves** are becoming, attractive.   **that** so that
250 **riggish** lustful.   253 **lottery** prize, gift of fortune
2.3 Location: Rome.
5 **Read** interpret.   **in** according to   6 **kept my square** kept to a
straight course (as guided by a carpenter's square; with pun on *rule,*
"ruler" in next line).   **that** that which is   10 **sirrah** (A form of
address to a social inferior.)   12 **thither** to that place.   14 **in my
motion** intuitively, by inward prompting   15 **hie** hasten   20 **Thy . . .
thee** Your guardian spirit, the spirit that protects you   21 **high
unmatchable** unmatchable in the extreme   22 **Where . . . not** wherever Caesar's spirit is not present (to daunt yours)

25 **no more but when** only when   27 **of** by   28 **thickens** grows dim
29 **by** nearby.   33 **art or hap** skill or luck   35 **cunning** skill
36 **chance** luck.   **speeds** wins   37 **still of** always from   38 **When . . .
naught** when the odds are everything to nothing (in my favor)
39 **inhooped** (The birds were enclosed in hoops to make them fight.)
at odds against the odds.
2.4 Location: Rome.
2 **Your generals after** after your generals.   3 **e'en but** only, just
4 **dress** garb, apparel   5 **become** suit   6 **conceive** understand.
th' Mount i.e., Mount Misenum   8 **about** roundabout.

[2.5]

Enter Cleopatra, Charmian, Iras, and Alexas.

CLEOPATRA
Give me some music; music, moody food
Of us that trade in love.
ALL   The music, ho!

Enter Mardian the eunuch.

CLEOPATRA
Let it alone. Let's to billiards. Come, Charmian.
CHARMIAN
My arm is sore. Best play with Mardian.
CLEOPATRA
As well a woman with an eunuch played
As with a woman. Come, you'll play with me, sir?
MARDIAN   As well as I can, madam.
CLEOPATRA
And when good will is showed, though't come too
    short,   8
The actor may plead pardon. I'll none now.   9
Give me mine angle; we'll to th' river. There,   10
My music playing far off, I will betray
Tawny-finned fishes. My bended hook shall pierce
Their slimy jaws, and as I draw them up
I'll think them every one an Antony,
And say, "Aha! You're caught."
CHARMIAN   'Twas merry when
You wagered on your angling, when your diver
Did hang a salt fish on his hook, which he   17
With fervency drew up.
CLEOPATRA   That time—oh, times!—
I laughed him out of patience; and that night
I laughed him into patience. And next morn,
Ere the ninth hour, I drunk him to his bed,   21
Then put my tires and mantles on him, whilst   22
I wore his sword Philippan.

Enter a Messenger.

                            Oh, from Italy!   23
Ram thou thy fruitful tidings in mine ears,
That long time have been barren.
MESSENGER   Madam, madam—
CLEOPATRA
Antonio's dead! If thou say so, villain,
Thou kill'st thy mistress; but well and free,
If thou so yield him, there is gold, and here   28
My bluest veins to kiss—a hand that kings
Have lipped, and trembled kissing.
    [*She offers him gold, and her hand to kiss.*]
MESSENGER   First, madam, he is well.

CLEOPATRA
Why, there's more gold. But, sirrah, mark, we use
To say the dead are well. Bring it to that,   33
The gold I give thee will I melt and pour
Down thy ill-uttering throat.
MESSENGER   Good madam, hear me.
CLEOPATRA   Well, go to, I will.   37
But there's no goodness in thy face, if Antony
Be free and healthful—so tart a favor   39
To trumpet such good tidings! If not well,
Thou shouldst come like a Fury crowned with snakes, 41
Not like a formal man.
MESSENGER   Will't please you hear me?   42
CLEOPATRA
I have a mind to strike thee ere thou speak'st.
Yet, if thou say Antony lives, is well,
Or friends with Caesar, or not captive to him,
I'll set thee in a shower of gold and hail
Rich pearls upon thee.
MESSENGER   Madam, he's well.
CLEOPATRA   Well said.
MESSENGER
And friends with Caesar.
CLEOPATRA   Thou'rt an honest man.   48
MESSENGER
Caesar and he are greater friends than ever.
CLEOPATRA
Make thee a fortune from me.
MESSENGER   But yet, madam—
CLEOPATRA
I do not like "But yet"; it does allay   51
The good precedence. Fie upon "But yet"!   52
"But yet" is as a jailer to bring forth
Some monstrous malefactor. Prithee, friend,
Pour out the pack of matter to mine ear,   55
The good and bad together. He's friends with Caesar,
In state of health, thou say'st, and, thou say'st, free.
MESSENGER
Free, madam? No, I made no such report.
He's bound unto Octavia.
CLEOPATRA   For what good turn?   59
MESSENGER
For the best turn i'th' bed.
CLEOPATRA   I am pale, Charmian.
MESSENGER
Madam, he's married to Octavia.
CLEOPATRA
The most infectious pestilence upon thee!
                            Strikes him down.
MESSENGER
Good madam, patience.
CLEOPATRA   What say you?   *Strikes him.*
                                                Hence,

2.5 Location: Alexandria. Cleopatra's palace.
8 too short (A bawdy joke on Mardian's being castrated; *will* suggests
"sexual desire"; *come* suggests "reach orgasm.")   **9 I'll none now** i.e.,
I won't play billiards after all.   **10 angle** rod and line   **17 salt** dried,
preserved in salt   **21 ninth hour** i.e., 9 A.M.   **drunk** drank   **22 tires**
headdresses, or perhaps attire.   **mantles** garments   **23 Philippan**
(Named for Antony's victory over Brutus and Cassius at Philippi.)
28 yield (1) grant (2) report

33 well i.e., well out of it, in heaven.   **Bring it to that** If that is your
meaning   **37 go to** i.e., all right, then. (Said remonstratingly.)   **39 tart
a favor** sour a face   **41 Fury** avenging goddess of classical mythology
42 like . . . man in ordinary human form.   **48 honest** worthy
51–2 allay . . . precedence annul the good news that preceded it.
55 pack of matter entire contents (as of a peddler's pack)   **59 turn**
favor, purpose. (But the Messenger replies in the sense of "feat, bout,"
with sexual suggestion.)

Horrible villain, or I'll spurn thine eyes 64
Like balls before me! I'll unhair thy head! 65
　　　　　　　　　　She hales him up and down.
Thou shalt be whipped with wire and stewed in brine,
Smarting in ling'ring pickle!
MESSENGER　　　　　　　　Gracious madam, 67
I that do bring the news made not the match.
CLEOPATRA
Say 'tis not so, a province I will give thee
And make thy fortunes proud. The blow thou hadst
Shall make thy peace for moving me to rage, 71
And I will boot thee with what gift beside 72
Thy modesty can beg.
MESSENGER　　　　　He's married, madam. 73
CLEOPATRA
Rogue, thou hast lived too long!　　*Draw a knife.*
MESSENGER　　　　　　　　Nay then, I'll run.
What mean you, madam? I have made no fault.　*Exit.*
CHARMIAN
Good madam, keep yourself within yourself. 76
The man is innocent.
CLEOPATRA
Some innocents scape not the thunderbolt.
Melt Egypt into Nile, and kindly creatures 79
Turn all to serpents! Call the slave again.
Though I am mad, I will not bite him. Call! 81
CHARMIAN
He is afeard to come.
CLEOPATRA　　　　　　I will not hurt him.
　　　　　　　[The Messenger is sent for.]
These hands do lack nobility, that they strike
A meaner than myself, since I myself 84
Have given myself the cause.

　　　　Enter the Messenger again.

　　　　　　　　　　　Come hither, sir. 85
Though it be honest, it is never good
To bring bad news. Give to a gracious message
An host of tongues, but let ill tidings tell 88
Themselves when they be felt. 89
MESSENGER　　I have done my duty.
CLEOPATRA　　Is he married?
I cannot hate thee worser than I do
If thou again say "Yes."
MESSENGER　　　　　　He's married, madam.
CLEOPATRA
The gods confound thee! Dost thou hold there still? 94
MESSENGER
Should I lie, madam?
CLEOPATRA　　　　　Oh, I would thou didst,

So half my Egypt were submerged and made 96
A cistern for scaled snakes! Go, get thee hence. 97
Hadst thou Narcissus in thy face, to me 98
Thou wouldst appear most ugly. He is married?
MESSENGER
I crave Your Highness' pardon.
CLEOPATRA　　　　　　　He is married?
MESSENGER
Take no offense that I would not offend you. 101
To punish me for what you make me do
Seems much unequal. He's married to Octavia. 103
CLEOPATRA
Oh, that his fault should make a knave of thee, 104
That art not what thou'rt sure of! Get thee hence. 105
The merchandise which thou hast brought from
　　Rome
Are all too dear for me. Lie they upon thy hand, 107
And be undone by 'em!　　*[Exit Messenger.]*
CHARMIAN　　　　　Good Your Highness, patience. 108
CLEOPATRA
In praising Antony, I have dispraised Caesar.
CHARMIAN　　Many times, madam.
CLEOPATRA
I am paid for't now. Lead me from hence;
I faint. Oh, Iras, Charmian! 'Tis no matter.
Go to the fellow, good Alexas. Bid him
Report the feature of Octavia: her years,
Her inclination. Let him not leave out 115
The color of her hair. Bring me word quickly.
　　　　　　　[Exit Alexas.]
Let him forever go!—Let him not, Charmian. 117
Though he be painted one way like a Gorgon, 118
The other way's a Mars. *[To Mardian]* Bid you Alexas 119
Bring me word how tall she is.—Pity me, Charmian,
But do not speak to me. Lead me to my chamber.
　　　　　　　　　　　　　Exeunt.

　　　　　　　❖

[2.6]

*Flourish. Enter Pompey [and] Menas at one
door, with drum and trumpet; at another, Caesar, Lepidus, Antony, Enobarbus, Maecenas,
Agrippa, with soldiers marching.*

---

64 **spurn** kick　65.1 **hales** drags　67 **pickle** pickling solution.
71 **make thy peace** compensate, mollify me　72 **boot thee with** give
you into the bargain, or, make amends with.　**what** whatever
73 **Thy modesty** one of your modest expectations　76 **keep . . .
yourself** i.e., control yourself.　79 **kindly** endowed with innately
good qualities　81 **mad** (1) angry (2) insane, and so apt to bite
84 **A meaner** one of lower social station　84–5 **since . . . cause** since I
am the one I ought to blame.　85 **the cause** i.e., by loving Antony.
88 **host** multitude　89 **when . . . felt** i.e., by being felt rather than spoken aloud. Let bad tidings announce themselves.　94 **confound**
destroy.　**hold there still** stick to your story.

96 **So** even if　97 **cistern** tank.　**scaled** scaly　98 **Narcissus** beautiful
youth of Greek mythology who fell in love with his own reflected
image　101 **Take . . . offend you** Don't be offended that I hesitate to
offend you (by telling bad news), or, don't interpret as offense what is
not meant to offend.　103 **much unequal** most unjust.　104–5 **Oh,
that . . . sure of!** How regrettable that Antony's fault puts you in the
wrong, you who are not yourself hateful even if you have had to
report hateful news as a certain fact!　107 **dear** (1) expensive (2) emotionally precious　107–8 **Lie . . . by 'em** May they remain in your possession unsold, and may you be bankrupt, financially ruined! (i.e.,
May you never profit from your bad tidings!)　115 **inclination** disposition.　117 **him** Antony　118–19 **Though . . . Mars** (Alludes to a
type of picture known as a perspective, which shows different images
when looked at from different angles of vision. A *Gorgon* is a female
monster with serpents in her hair, capable of turning to stone anything that meets her gaze.)
2.6. Location: Near Misenum, in southern Italy near modern
Naples. (But 2.1 perhaps took place in Messina, Sicily.)

POMPEY
    Your hostages I have, so have you mine,
    And we shall talk before we fight.
CAESAR   Most meet   2
    That first we come to words; and therefore have we
    Our written purposes before us sent,   4
    Which if thou hast considered, let us know
    If 'twill tie up thy discontented sword   6
    And carry back to Sicily much tall youth   7
    That else must perish here.
POMPEY   To you all three,
    The senators alone of this great world,   9
    Chief factors for the gods: I do not know   10
    Wherefore my father should revengers want,   11
    Having a son and friends, since Julius Caesar,   12
    Who at Philippi the good Brutus ghosted,   13
    There saw you laboring for him. What was't   14
    That moved pale Cassius to conspire? And what
    Made th'all-honored, honest Roman Brutus,   16
    With the armed rest, courtiers of beauteous freedom,   17
    To drench the Capitol, but that they would   18
    Have one man but a man? And that is it   19
    Hath made me rig my navy, at whose burden
    The angered ocean foams, with which I meant
    To scourge th'ingratitude that despiteful Rome
    Cast on my noble father.
CAESAR   Take your time.
ANTONY
    Thou canst not fear us, Pompey, with thy sails;   24
    We'll speak with thee at sea. At land thou know'st   25
    How much we do o'ercount thee.
POMPEY   At land indeed   26
    Thou dost o'ercount me of my father's house;
    But since the cuckoo builds not for himself,   28
    Remain in't as thou mayst.
LEPIDUS   Be pleased to tell us—   29
    For this is from the present—how you take   30
    The offers we have sent you.
CAESAR   There's the point.

ANTONY
    Which do not be entreated to, but weigh   32
    What it is worth embraced.
CAESAR   And what may follow,   33
    To try a larger fortune.
POMPEY   You have made me offer   34
    Of Sicily, Sardinia; and I must
    Rid all the sea of pirates; then, to send   36
    Measures of wheat to Rome. This 'greed upon,
    To part with unhacked edges and bear back   38
    Our targes undinted.
CAESAR, ANTONY, LEPIDUS   That's our offer.
POMPEY   Know then   39
    I came before you here a man prepared
    To take this offer, but Mark Antony
    Put me to some impatience. Though I lose   42
    The praise of it by telling, you must know,   43
    When Caesar and your brother were at blows,
    Your mother came to Sicily and did find
    Her welcome friendly.
ANTONY   I have heard it, Pompey,
    And am well studied for a liberal thanks   47
    Which I do owe you.
POMPEY   Let me have your hand.
                 [*They shake hands.*]
    I did not think, sir, to have met you here.
ANTONY
    The beds i'th'East are soft; and thanks to you,
    That called me timelier than my purpose hither,   51
    For I have gained by't.
CAESAR   Since I saw you last
    There's a change upon you.
POMPEY   Well, I know not
    What counts harsh Fortune casts upon my face,   54
    But in my bosom shall she never come
    To make my heart her vassal.
LEPIDUS   Well met here.
POMPEY
    I hope so, Lepidus. Thus we are agreed.
    I crave our composition may be written   58
    And sealed between us.
CAESAR   That's the next to do.   59
POMPEY
    We'll feast each other ere we part, and let's
    Draw lots who shall begin.
ANTONY   That will I, Pompey.   61
POMPEY
    No, Antony, take the lot. But, first or last,   62

---

2 meet fitting   **4 purposes** propositions   **6 tie . . . sword** i.e., satisfy your concerns and allow you to forgo a fight   **7 tall** brave   **9 senators alone** i.e., sole rulers of the state (who have thus supplanted the Senate)   **10 factors** agents   **10–14 I do . . . for him** (Julius Caesar defeated Pompey's father, Pompey the Great, and was subsequently assassinated by Brutus and Cassius, among others. Caesar's ghost appeared to Brutus at Philippi, where the combined forces of Antony, Octavius, and Lepidus defeated Brutus and Cassius. [See *Julius Caesar*.] Since Antony, Octavius, and Lepidus thus defeated the avengers of Pompey the Great's death, Pompey the Great's sons and friends should become his avengers by continuing to war on Antony, Octavius, and Lepidus.)   **11 want** lack   **13 ghosted** haunted   **16 honest** honorable   **17 the armed rest** i.e., the rest of those who were armed.   **courtiers . . . freedom** those who serve freedom only   **18 drench** bathe in blood   **19 Have . . . a man** (The republican conspirators acted to keep Julius Caesar from accepting the crown.)   **24 fear** frighten   **25 speak with** confront   **26 o'ercount** outnumber. (But Pompey's use of the word in the next line implies that Antony has cheated him. Plutarch informs us that Antony bought the elder Pompey's house at auction and later refused to pay for it.)   **28 cuckoo** a bird that builds no nest for itself but lays its eggs in other birds' nests.   **29 as thou mayst** as long as you can, or, since you can.   **30 from the present** digressing from the business at hand

32 do . . . to i.e., do not accept merely because we ask   **33 embraced** if accepted by you.   **34 To . . . fortune** i.e., if you decide to risk war with the triumvirs, or, if you join with us to share a greater fortune.   **36 to send** I am to send   **38 To part** we are to part company.   **edges** swords   **39 targes** shields   **42–3 Though . . . telling** i.e., Though I forfeit praise from others by praising myself   **47 well studied for** well prepared to deliver   **51 timelier** earlier   **54 counts** tally marks. (From the practice of casting accounts or reckonings by means of marks or notches on tallies.)   **casts** calculates   **58 composition** agreement   **59 sealed between us** stamped with the official seal of each co-signer.   **61 That will I** I will begin   **62 take the lot** draw lots with the rest of us, accept the results of the lottery.   **first or last** whether you win the lottery to go first or last

Your fine Egyptian cookery shall have
The fame. I have heard that Julius Caesar
Grew fat with feasting there.
ANTONY   You have heard much.
POMPEY   I have fair meanings, sir.   67
ANTONY   And fair words to them.   68
POMPEY   Then so much have I heard.   69
And I have heard Apollodorus carried—   70
ENOBARBUS
No more of that. He did so.
POMPEY   What, I pray you?   71
ENOBARBUS
A certain queen to Caesar in a mattress.   72
POMPEY
I know thee now. How far'st thou, soldier?
ENOBARBUS   Well,
And well am like to do, for I perceive   74
Four feasts are toward.
POMPEY   Let me shake thy hand.   75
                              [*They shake hands.*]
I never hated thee. I have seen thee fight
When I have envied thy behavior.
ENOBARBUS   Sir,
I never loved you much, but I ha' praised ye
When you have well deserved ten times as much
As I have said you did.
POMPEY   Enjoy thy plainness;   80
It nothing ill becomes thee.   81
Aboard my galley I invite you all.
Will you lead, lords?
CAESAR, ANTONY, LEPIDUS   Show 's the way, sir.
POMPEY   Come.   83
              Exeunt. Manent Enobarbus and Menas.
MENAS [*aside*] Thy father, Pompey, would ne'er have
made this treaty.—You and I have known, sir.   85
ENOBARBUS   At sea, I think.
MENAS   We have, sir.
ENOBARBUS   You have done well by water.
MENAS   And you by land.
ENOBARBUS   I will praise any man that will praise me,
though it cannot be denied what I have done by land.
MENAS   Nor what I have done by water.
ENOBARBUS   Yes, something you can deny for your own
safety: you have been a great thief by sea.
MENAS   And you by land.
ENOBARBUS   There I deny my land service. But give me 96
your hand, Menas. [*They shake hands.*] If our eyes had
authority, here they might take two thieves kissing.   98

MENAS   All men's faces are true, whatsome'er their hands
are.
ENOBARBUS   But there is never a fair woman has a true 101
face.
MENAS   No slander; they steal hearts.   103
ENOBARBUS   We came hither to fight with you.
MENAS   For my part, I am sorry it is turned to a drinking. 105
Pompey doth this day laugh away his fortune.
ENOBARBUS   If he do, sure he cannot weep't back
again.
MENAS   You've said, sir. We looked not for Mark 109
Antony here. Pray you, is he married to Cleopatra?
ENOBARBUS   Caesar's sister is called Octavia.
MENAS   True, sir. She was the wife of Caius Marcellus.
ENOBARBUS   But she is now the wife of Marcus Anto-
nius.
MENAS   Pray ye, sir?   115
ENOBARBUS   'Tis true.
MENAS   Then is Caesar and he forever knit together.
ENOBARBUS   If I were bound to divine of this unity, I 118
would not prophesy so.
MENAS   I think the policy of that purpose made more in 120
the marriage than the love of the parties.
ENOBARBUS   I think so too. But you shall find the band
that seems to tie their friendship together will be
the very strangler of their amity. Octavia is of a holy, cold,
and still conversation.   125
MENAS   Who would not have his wife so?
ENOBARBUS   Not he that himself is not so, which is
Mark Antony. He will to his Egyptian dish again.
Then shall the sighs of Octavia blow the fire up in
Caesar, and, as I said before, that which is the strength
of their amity shall prove the immediate author of 131
their variance. Antony will use his affection where it 132
is; he married but his occasion here.   133
MENAS   And thus it may be. Come, sir, will you
aboard? I have a health for you.   135
ENOBARBUS   I shall take it, sir. We have used our
throats in Egypt.
MENAS   Come, let's away.   *Exeunt.*

❧

[2.7]

*Music plays. Enter two or three Servants with a
banquet.*

FIRST SERVANT   Here they'll be, man. Some o' their
plants are ill-rooted already; the least wind i'th' world 2
will blow them down.

---

67 **fair** i.e., friendly   68 **fair** i.e., well-chosen   69 **Then . . . heard** i.e.,
I am not implying more about Antony in Egypt than my words hon-
estly mean.   70–2 **Apollodorus . . . mattress** (Alludes to a tale told by
Plutarch according to which Cleopatra had herself rolled up in a mattress and carried secretly by Apollodorus to meet Julius Caesar.)
74 **like** likely   75 **toward** coming up.   80 **Enjoy thy plainness** Give
free rein to your bluntness   81 **nothing . . . thee** suits you not at all
badly.   83.1 *Manent* They remain onstage   85 **known** known each
other   96 **There** In respect to that   98 **authority** i.e., to make arrests,
like a constable.   **take** arrest.   **two thieves kissing** (1) our two thieving hands shaking (2) two thieves greeting each other.

101 **true** honest (because women use cosmetic art to conceal defects)
103 **No . . . hearts** i.e., You speak true, since women in their own way are
thieves, stealing men's affections.   105 **a drinking** an occasion for drinking.   109 **You've said** You've spoken truly   115 **Pray ye, sir?** Are you in
earnest?   118 **divine** of prophesy about   120 **made more** played more
of a role   125 **conversation** demeanor.   131–2 **author . . . variance** cause
of their falling out.   132–3 **use . . . it is** i.e., satisfy his passion in Egypt
133 **his occasion** what his interests demanded   135 **health** toast
**2.7. Location: On board Pompey's galley, off Misenum in southern
Italy. A table and stools are brought on.**
0.2 *banquet* a course of the feast, probably dessert.   2 **plants**
(1) planted trees (2) soles of the feet

SECOND SERVANT   Lepidus is high-colored.   4

FIRST SERVANT   They have made him drink alms-drink.   5

SECOND SERVANT   As they pinch one another by the   6
disposition, he cries out, "No more," reconciles them   7
to his entreaty, and himself to th' drink.   8

FIRST SERVANT   But it raises the greater war between
him and his discretion.

SECOND SERVANT   Why, this it is to have a name in   11
great men's fellowship. I had as lief have a reed that   12
will do me no service as a partisan I could not heave.   13

FIRST SERVANT   To be called into a huge sphere,   14
and not to be seen to move in't, are the holes where   15
eyes should be, which pitifully disaster the cheeks.   16

A sennet sounded. Enter Caesar, Antony,
Pompey, Lepidus, Agrippa, Maecenas, Enobarbus,
Menas, with other captains [and a Boy].

ANTONY
Thus do they, sir: they take the flow o'th' Nile   17
By certain scales i'th' pyramid. They know   18
By th' height, the lowness, or the mean if dearth   19
Or foison follow. The higher Nilus swells   20
The more it promises; as it ebbs, the seedsman
Upon the slime and ooze scatters his grain,
And shortly comes to harvest.

LEPIDUS   You've strange serpents there.

ANTONY   Ay, Lepidus.

LEPIDUS   Your serpent of Egypt is bred now of your   26
mud by the operation of your sun; so is your crocodile.

ANTONY   They are so.

POMPEY   Sit—and some wine. A health to Lepidus!   29
[They sit and drink.]

LEPIDUS   I am not so well as I should be, but I'll   30
ne'er out.   31

ENOBARBUS   Not till you have slept; I fear me you'll be
in till then.   33

LEPIDUS   Nay, certainly, I have heard the Ptolemies'
pyramises are very goodly things; without contradic-   35
tion I have heard that.

MENAS *[aside to Pompey]*   Pompey, a word.

POMPEY *[to Menas]*   Say in mine ear. What is't?

MENAS *(whispers in 's ear)*
Forsake thy seat, I do beseech thee, captain,
And hear me speak a word.

POMPEY *[to Menas]*
Forbear me till anon.—This wine for Lepidus!   41

LEPIDUS   What manner o' thing is your crocodile?

ANTONY   It is shaped, sir, like itself, and it is as broad as
it hath breadth. It is just so high as it is, and moves
with it own organs. It lives by that which nourisheth   45
it, and, the elements once out of it, it transmigrates.   46

LEPIDUS   What color is it of?

ANTONY   Of it own color too.

LEPIDUS   'Tis a strange serpent.

ANTONY   'Tis so. And the tears of it are wet.   50

CAESAR   Will this description satisfy him?

ANTONY   With the health that Pompey gives him, else
he is a very epicure.   *[Menas whispers again.]*   53

POMPEY *[aside to Menas]*
Go hang, sir, hang! Tell me of that? Away!
Do as I bid you.—Where's this cup I called for?

MENAS *[aside to Pompey]*
If for the sake of merit thou wilt hear me,   56
Rise from thy stool.

POMPEY *[rising]*   I think thou'rt mad. The matter?
[They walk aside.]

MENAS
I have ever held my cap off to thy fortunes.   58

POMPEY
Thou hast served me with much faith. What's else to
say?—   59
Be jolly, lords.

ANTONY   These quicksands, Lepidus,
Keep off them, for you sink.
[Menas and Pompey speak aside.]

MENAS
Wilt thou be lord of all the world?

POMPEY   What say'st thou?

MENAS
Wilt thou be lord of the whole world? That's twice.

POMPEY
How should that be?

MENAS   But entertain it,   64
And, though thou think me poor, I am the man
Will give thee all the world.

POMPEY   Hast thou drunk well?

MENAS
No, Pompey, I have kept me from the cup.
Thou art, if thou dar'st be, the earthly Jove.

---

4 **high-colored** flushed.   5 **alms-drink** i.e., drink charitably consumed in the furtherance of reconciliation. (See next speech and
note.)   6–8 **As . . . drink** As they chafe one another, prompted by
their various temperaments, Lepidus entreats them to stop quarreling, and reconciles himself to the peacemaking business of downing
one drink after another in response to their toasts.   11 **a name** a
name only   12 **had as lief** would just as soon   13 **partisan** long-
bladed spear. (Here, metaphorically, too large a weapon for Lepidus
to wield.)   14–16 **To . . . cheeks** To be summoned by fortune to greatness and yet not be able to fulfill the role greatly is like having eye
sockets with no eyes in them, a defect that will disfigure (*disaster*) the
cheeks. (The underlying image is of a heavenly body that cannot
move properly in its sphere, causing *disaster*, meaning both disfigurement and the evil effects of unfavorable aspect of a planet.)
16.1 *sennet* trumpet call signaling the approach of a procession
17 **sir** (Usually thought to refer to Caesar, but the matter is uncertain.)
take measure   18 **scales** graduated markings   19 **mean** middle
20 **foison** plenty   26 **Your serpent** i.e., This serpent that people talk
about. (The colloquial indefinite *your*.)   29 **health** toast. (Lepidus is
obliged to drink up every time a toast is proposed to him.)   30–1 **I'll
ne'er out** i.e., I'll never refuse a toast, never quit.   33 **in** in drink, in
your cups. (With a play of antitheses between *in* and *out* in line 31.)
35 **pyramises** (Lepidus's drunken error for *pyramides*, plural of
pyramis or *pyramid.*)

41 **Forbear . . . anon** Excuse me for a moment.   45 **it own** its own.
(Also in line 48.)   46 **elements** vital elements   50 **tears** (Alludes to
the ancient belief that the crocodile wept insincere "crocodile tears"
over its victim before devouring it.)   53 **epicure** (1) glutton (2) atheist. (The Epicureans did not believe in an afterlife. Antony's jesting
point is that only an atheist or epicure would be skeptical of such a
satisfying description as Antony has just given of the crocodile.)
56 **merit** i.e., my merits as a loyal follower, or, the merit of my ideas
58 **held . . . off** i.e., been a respectful and faithful servant   59 **faith**
faithfulness.   64 **But entertain it** Only accept the possibility

Whate'er the ocean pales or sky inclips   69
Is thine, if thou wilt ha 't.
POMPEY   Show me which way.
MENAS
These three world-sharers, these competitors,   71
Are in thy vessel. Let me cut the cable,
And, when we are put off, fall to their throats.   73
All there is thine.
POMPEY   Ah, this thou shouldst have done
And not have spoke on 't! In me 'tis villainy;   75
In thee 't had been good service. Thou must know,   76
'Tis not my profit that does lead mine honor;
Mine honor, it. Repent that e'er thy tongue   78
Hath so betrayed thine act. Being done unknown,   79
I should have found it afterwards well done,
But must condemn it now. Desist, and drink.
                              [*He returns to the feast.*]
MENAS [*aside*] For this,
I'll never follow thy palled fortunes more.   83
Who seeks and will not take when once 'tis offered   84
Shall never find it more.
POMPEY   This health to Lepidus!
ANTONY
Bear him ashore. I'll pledge it for him, Pompey.   86
ENOBARBUS
Here's to thee, Menas!   [*They drink.*]
MENAS   Enobarbus, welcome!
POMPEY   Fill till the cup be hid.
ENOBARBUS   There's a strong fellow, Menas.
              [*Pointing to one who carries off Lepidus.*]
MENAS   Why?
ENOBARBUS   'A bears the third part of the world, man;   91
see'st not?
MENAS
The third part, then, is drunk. Would it were all,
That it might go on wheels!   94
ENOBARBUS   Drink thou; increase the reels.   95
MENAS   Come.
POMPEY
This is not yet an Alexandrian feast.
ANTONY
It ripens towards it. Strike the vessels, ho!   98
Here's to Caesar!
CAESAR   I could well forbear 't.
It's monstrous labor when I wash my brain
And it grows fouler.
ANTONY   Be a child o'th' time.
CAESAR   Possess it, I'll make answer.   102
But I had rather fast from all four days   103

Than drink so much in one.
ENOBARBUS [*to Antony*]   Ha, my brave emperor!   104
Shall we dance now the Egyptian Bacchanals   105
And celebrate our drink?   106
POMPEY   Let's ha 't, good soldier.
ANTONY   Come, let's all take hands
Till that the conquering wine hath steeped our sense   109
In soft and delicate Lethe.
ENOBARBUS   All take hands.   110
Make battery to our ears with the loud music,   111
The while I'll place you; then the boy shall sing.
The holding every man shall bear as loud   113
As his strong sides can volley.   114
          Music plays. Enobarbus places them hand in hand.

                    The Song.

BOY [*sings*]
          Come, thou monarch of the vine,
          Plumpy Bacchus with pink eyne!   116
          In thy fats our cares be drowned,   117
          With thy grapes our hairs be crowned.
ALL   Cup us till the world go round,   119
          Cup us till the world go round!
CAESAR
What would you more? Pompey, good night.—Good
    brother,
Let me request you off. Our graver business   122
Frowns at this levity. Gentle lords, let's part;
You see we have burnt our cheeks. Strong Enobarb   124
Is weaker than the wine, and mine own tongue
Splits what it speaks. The wild disguise hath almost   126
Anticked us all. What needs more words? Good night.   127
Good Antony, your hand.
POMPEY   I'll try you on the shore.   128
ANTONY
And shall, sir. Give 's your hand.
POMPEY   Oh, Antony,
You have my father's house. But what? We are
    friends.
Come down into the boat.
ENOBARBUS   Take heed you fall not.   131
              [*Exeunt all but Enobarbus and Menas.*]
Menas, I'll not on shore.
MENAS   No, to my cabin.
These drums, these trumpets, flutes! What!
Let Neptune hear we bid a loud farewell
To these great fellows. Sound and be hanged, sound
    out!   *Sound a flourish, with drums.*

---

69 **pales** impales, fences in. **inclips** embraces 71 **competitors** partners. (With secondary sense of "rivals.") 73 **are put off** have put to sea 75 **on 't** of it. 76 **Thou must know** I must inform you that 78 **Mine honor, it** i.e., my honor comes before my personal profit. **Repent** Regret 79 **unknown** i.e., without my knowledge 83 **palled** decayed, darkened 84 **Who** He who 86 **pledge it** i.e., drink the toast (since Lepidus is too far gone to drink) 91 **'A** He 94 **go on wheels** go fast or easily. (Proverbial.) 95 **reels** (1) revels (2) reeling and whirling of drunkenness. 98 **Strike the vessels** Broach or tap the casks 102 **Possess . . . answer** My answer is, be master of the time; or, possibly, Drink it off, I'll drink in return. 103 **all** all nourishment

104 **brave** splendid 105 **Bacchanals** drunken dance to Bacchus, god of wine 106 **celebrate** consecrate with observances 109 **Till that** until 110 **Lethe** i.e., forgetfulness. (Literally, the river of oblivion in Hades.) 111 **Make battery to** Assault 113 **holding** refrain. **bear** carry, sing 114 **volley** sing in return, answering the stanza with the refrain. 116 **pink eyne** i.e., eyes half-shut, from drinking. 117 **fats** vats, vessels 119 **Cup** Intoxicate 122 **off** to disembark. 124 **we . . . cheeks** our complexions are flushed with drinking. 126 **disguise** (1) masque (2) transforming drunkenness 127 **Anticked us** (1) made dancers of us in a masque (2) made buffoons or fools of us 128 **try you** i.e., take you on in a drinking contest 131 **boat** small boat for taking the party ashore.

ENOBARBUS   Hoo! says 'a. There's my cap.
                              [*He flings it in the air.*]
MENAS   Hoo! Noble captain, come.   *Exeunt.*

❖

[3.1]

*Enter Ventidius as it were in triumph [with Silius,
and other Romans, officers, and soldiers], the dead
body of Pacorus borne before him.*

VENTIDIUS
Now, darting Parthia, art thou struck, and now   1
Pleased fortune does of Marcus Crassus' death   2
Make me revenger. Bear the King's son's body
Before our army. Thy Pacorus, Orodes,   4
Pays this for Marcus Crassus.
SILIUS   Noble Ventidius,
Whilst yet with Parthian blood thy sword is warm,
The fugitive Parthians follow. Spur through Media,   7
Mesopotamia, and the shelters whither
The routed fly. So thy grand captain, Antony,
Shall set thee on triumphant chariots and   10
Put garlands on thy head.
VENTIDIUS   Oh, Silius, Silius,
I have done enough. A lower place, note well,   12
May make too great an act. For learn this, Silius:
Better to leave undone than by our deed
Acquire too high a fame when him we serve's away.
Caesar and Antony have ever won
More in their officer than person. Sossius,   17
One of my place in Syria, his lieutenant,   18
For quick accumulation of renown,
Which he achieved by th' minute, lost his favor.   20
Who does i'th' wars more than his captain can   21
Becomes his captain's captain; and ambition,
The soldier's virtue, rather makes choice of loss   23
Than gain which darkens him.   24
I could do more to do Antonius good,
But 'twould offend him, and in his offense   26
Should my performance perish.
SILIUS   Thou hast, Ventidius, that   28
Without the which a soldier and his sword   29
Grants scarce distinction. Thou wilt write to Antony? 30
VENTIDIUS
I'll humbly signify what in his name,

That magical word of war, we have effected: 32
How with his banners and his well-paid ranks
The ne'er-yet-beaten horse of Parthia   34
We have jaded out o'th' field.
SILIUS   Where is he now?   35
VENTIDIUS
He purposeth to Athens, whither, with what haste
The weight we must convey with 's will permit,   37
We shall appear before him.—On, there. Pass along!
                                          Exeunt.

❖

[3.2]

Enter Agrippa at one door, Enobarbus at another.

AGRIPPA   What, are the brothers parted?   1
ENOBARBUS
They have dispatched with Pompey; he is gone.   2
The other three are sealing. Octavia weeps   3
To part from Rome; Caesar is sad; and Lepidus,   4
Since Pompey's feast, as Menas says, is troubled
With the greensickness.
AGRIPPA   'Tis a noble Lepidus. 6
ENOBARBUS
A very fine one. Oh, how he loves Caesar!   7
AGRIPPA
Nay, but how dearly he adores Mark Antony!
ENOBARBUS
Caesar? Why, he's the Jupiter of men.
AGRIPPA
What's Antony? The god of Jupiter.
ENOBARBUS
Spake you of Caesar? How, the nonpareil!
AGRIPPA
O Antony, O thou Arabian bird!   12
ENOBARBUS
Would you praise Caesar, say "Caesar"; go no further.
AGRIPPA
Indeed, he plied them both with excellent praises.
ENOBARBUS
But he loves Caesar best; yet he loves Antony.
Hoo! Hearts, tongues, figures, scribes, bards, poets,
  cannot   16
Think, speak, cast, write, sing, number, hoo!   17
His love to Antony. But as for Caesar,
Kneel down, kneel down, and wonder.
AGRIPPA   Both he loves.

3.1. Location: The Middle East.
1 darting (The Parthians were famous for archery and for the Parthian
dart which they discharged as they fled.)   **Parthia** i.e., Orodes, King
of Parthia   **2 Crassus' death** (Crassus, member of the first triumvirate with Pompey the Great and Julius Caesar, was overthrown and
treacherously murdered by Orodes in 53 B.C.)   **4 Pacorus, Orodes**
(Pacorus was the son of Orodes.)   **7 The . . . follow** follow the fleeing
Parthians.   **10 triumphant** triumphal   **12 A lower place** One of
lower rank   **17 More . . . person** more through the actions of their
lieutenants than by their own efforts.   **18 of my place** of the same
rank as I.   **his lieutenant** i.e., the commanding officer acting for
Antony   **20 by th' minute** minute by minute, continually   **21 Who**
He who   **23–4 rather . . . him** prefers to lose rather than gain in such
a way as to darken his reputation.   **26 offense** taking offense
28–30 that . . . distinction i.e., discretion, without the which a soldier
can scarcely be distinguished from the sword he uses.

32 word watchword.   **effected** achieved   **34 horse** cavalry   **35 jaded**
driven exhausted like jades, inferior horses   **37 with 's** with us
3.2. Location: Rome.
1 brothers parted brothers-in-law departed.   **2 dispatched** concluded the business   **3 sealing** affixing seals to their agreements, settling matters.   **4 sad** sober   **6 greensickness** a kind of anemia
supposed to affect young women, especially those afflicted with love-
longing. (Used ironically here to refer to Lepidus's hangover and to
his love for Antony and Caesar.)   **7 fine** (*Lepidus* in Latin means
"fine," "elegant.")   **12 Arabian bird** i.e., the fabled phoenix. (Only
one existed at a time; it re-created itself by arising from its ashes.)
16 figures figures of speech   **17 cast** calculate.   **number** write verses

ENOBARBUS
They are his shards, and he their beetle. [*Trumpets
    within.*] So;   20
This is to horse. Adieu, noble Agrippa.   21
AGRIPPA
Good fortune, worthy soldier, and farewell.

        Enter Caesar, Antony, Lepidus, and Octavia.

ANTONY   No further, sir.   23
CAESAR
You take from me a great part of myself;
Use me well in't.—Sister, prove such a wife
As my thoughts make thee, and as my farthest bond   26
Shall pass on thy approof.—Most noble Antony,   27
Let not the piece of virtue which is set   28
Betwixt us as the cement of our love
To keep it builded be the ram to batter
The fortress of it; for better might we
Have loved without this mean, if on both parts   32
This be not cherished.
ANTONY   Make me not offended
In your distrust.
CAESAR   I have said.
ANTONY   You shall not find,   34
Though you be therein curious, the least cause   35
For what you seem to fear. So the gods keep you,
And make the hearts of Romans serve your ends!
We will here part.
CAESAR
Farewell, my dearest sister, fare thee well.
The elements be kind to thee, and make   40
Thy spirits all of comfort! Fare thee well.
OCTAVIA [*weeping*]   My noble brother!
ANTONY
The April's in her eyes; it is love's spring,
And these the showers to bring it on.—Be cheerful.
OCTAVIA [*to Caesar*]
Sir, look well to my husband's house; and—   45
CAESAR
What, Octavia?
OCTAVIA   I'll tell you in your ear.
                        [*She whisper to Caesar.*]
ANTONY
Her tongue will not obey her heart, nor can   47
Her heart inform her tongue—the swan's down
    feather,   48
That stands upon the swell at full of tide,   49
And neither way inclines.   50

ENOBARBUS [*aside to Agrippa*]   Will Caesar weep?
AGRIPPA [*aside to Enobarbus*]   He has a cloud in 's face.
ENOBARBUS [*aside to Agrippa*]
He were the worse for that, were he a horse;   53
So is he, being a man.
AGRIPPA [*aside to Enobarbus*]   Why, Enobarbus,
When Antony found Julius Caesar dead,
He cried almost to roaring; and he wept
When at Philippi he found Brutus slain.
ENOBARBUS [*aside to Agrippa*]
That year indeed he was troubled with a rheum;   58
What willingly he did confound he wailed,   59
Believe't, till I wept too.
CAESAR   No, sweet Octavia,
You shall hear from me still. The time shall not   61
Outgo my thinking on you.
ANTONY   Come, sir, come,   62
I'll wrestle with you in my strength of love.
Look, here I have you [*embracing him*]; thus I let you
    go,
And give you to the gods.
CAESAR   Adieu. Be happy!
LEPIDUS
Let all the number of the stars give light
To thy fair way!
CAESAR   Farewell, farewell!   *Kisses Octavia.*
ANTONY   Farewell!
        Trumpets sound. Exeunt [*in separate groups*].

                        ❧

[3.3]

        Enter Cleopatra, Charmian, Iras, and Alexas.

CLEOPATRA
Where is the fellow?
ALEXAS   Half afeard to come.
CLEOPATRA
Go to, go to.

        Enter the Messenger as before.

                Come hither, sir.
ALEXAS   Good Majesty,   2
Herod of Jewry dare not look upon you   3
But when you are well pleased.
CLEOPATRA   That Herod's head
I'll have; but how, when Antony is gone,
Through whom I might command it?—Come thou
    near.
MESSENGER   Most gracious Majesty!
CLEOPATRA   Didst thou behold Octavia?

---

20 **shards** patches of dung, or, perhaps, wings or wing-cases, i.e., pro-
tectors, patrons   21 **This is to horse** i.e., The trumpet call gives the
signal to depart.   23 **No further** i.e., You need not go on urging your
point, or, you need accompany me no further   26–7 **as . . . approof**
such that my utmost bond shall be justified in certifying what you
will prove to be.   28 **piece** masterpiece   32 **mean** intermediary, or
means   34 **In** by.   **I have said** i.e., I stand by what I've said.
35 **curious** overly inquisitive or touchy   40 **elements** heavens
45 **husband's house** i.e., Antony's house, as at 2.7.130, though
Octavia is also a widow; see 3.3.29   47–50 **Her . . . inclines** i.e., Her
conflicting emotions make her unable to speak aloud, like a swan's
down feather floating at full tide, moving neither up nor down
stream.

53 **He . . . horse** (Alludes to the belief that a horse with a dark spot on
its face was apt to be bad-tempered.)   58 **rheum** i.e., running at the
eyes. (Said of any discharge of secretion from the head.)   59 **What . . .
bewailed** He bewailed what he intentionally destroyed   61 **still** regularly.   61–2 **The time . . . you** Time itself will not outlast my thinking of you.
3.3. Location: Alexandria. Cleopatra's palace.
2 **Go to** (An expression of impatience.)   3 **Herod of Jewry** i.e., Even
the famous tyrant who slaughtered the children. (See 1.2.29–30.)

MESSENGER
Ay, dread Queen.

CLEOPATRA   Where?

MESSENGER   Madam, in Rome.
I looked her in the face, and saw her led
Between her brother and Mark Antony.

CLEOPATRA
Is she as tall as me?

MESSENGER   She is not, madam.

CLEOPATRA
Didst hear her speak? Is she shrill-tongued or low?

MESSENGER
Madam, I heard her speak. She is low-voiced.

CLEOPATRA
That's not so good. He cannot like her long.   15

CHARMIAN
Like her! Oh, Isis, 'tis impossible.

CLEOPATRA
I think so, Charmian. Dull of tongue, and dwarfish.—
What majesty is in her gait? Remember,
If e'er thou looked'st on majesty.

MESSENGER   She creeps:
Her motion and her station are as one.   20
She shows a body rather than a life,   21
A statue than a breather.

CLEOPATRA   Is this certain?   22

MESSENGER
Or I have no observance.

CHARMIAN   Three in Egypt   23
Cannot make better note.

CLEOPATRA   He's very knowing,   24
I do perceive't. There's nothing in her yet.
The fellow has good judgment.

CHARMIAN   Excellent.

CLEOPATRA   Guess at her years, I prithee.

MESSENGER   Madam,
She was a widow—

CLEOPATRA   Widow? Charmian, hark.

MESSENGER   And I do think she's thirty.

CLEOPATRA
Bear'st thou her face in mind? Is't long or round?

MESSENGER   Round, even to faultiness.

CLEOPATRA
For the most part, too, they are foolish that are so.—
Her hair, what color?

MESSENGER   Brown, madam; and her forehead
As low as she would wish it.   36

CLEOPATRA [giving money]   There's gold for thee.
Thou must not take my former sharpness ill.
I will employ thee back again; I find thee   39
Most fit for business. Go make thee ready;

Our letters are prepared.   [Exit Messenger.]

CHARMIAN   A proper man.   41

CLEOPATRA
Indeed, he is so. I repent me much
That so I harried him. Why, methinks, by him,   43
This creature's no such thing.

CHARMIAN   Nothing, madam.   44

CLEOPATRA
The man hath seen some majesty, and should know.

CHARMIAN
Hath he seen majesty? Isis else defend,   46
And serving you so long!   47

CLEOPATRA
I have one thing more to ask him yet, good
    Charmian—
But 'tis no matter; thou shalt bring him to me
Where I will write. All may be well enough

CHARMIAN   I warrant you, madam.   Exeunt.   51

❖

[3.4]

Enter Antony and Octavia.

ANTONY
Nay, nay, Octavia, not only that—
That were excusable, that and thousands more
Of semblable import—but he hath waged   3
New wars 'gainst Pompey; made his will, and read it   4
To public ear;
Spoke scantly of me; when perforce he could not   6
But pay me terms of honor, cold and sickly
He vented them, most narrow measure lent me;   8
When the best hint was given him, he not took't,   9
Or did it from his teeth.

OCTAVIA   Oh, my good lord,   10
Believe not all, or, if you must believe,
Stomach not all. A more unhappy lady,   12
If this division chance, ne'er stood between,   13
Praying for both parts.
The good gods will mock me presently
When I shall pray, "Oh, bless my lord and husband!"
Undo that prayer by crying out as loud,   17
"Oh, bless my brother!" Husband win, win brother,
Prays and destroys the prayer; no midway
Twixt these extremes at all.

ANTONY   Gentle Octavia,
Let your best love draw to that point which seeks   21
Best to preserve it. If I lose mine honor,   22

---

15 **not so good** i.e., not so good for her.   20 **Her . . . one** i.e., she moves with so little animation that it's all the same whether she's moving or standing.   21 **shows** appears as   22 **breather** living being.   23–4 **Three . . . note** There are not three people in Egypt who are better observers.   36 **As . . . it** i.e., such that she wouldn't wish it to be any lower. (A colloquial way of suggesting she is ugly; high foreheads were thought more beautiful.)   39 **employ . . . again** send you back with a message

41 **proper** good   43 **harried** maltreated.   **by** according to   44 **no such thing** nothing much.   46 **else defend** forbid that it be otherwise. (An interjection.)   47 **serving** i.e., he having served   51 **warrant** assure
3.4. Location: Athens.
3 **semblable** similar   4 **read it** (In order to win the populace by showing them what benefits they might expect from him.)   6 **scantly** slightingly   8 **vented** gave vent to, expressed.   **narrow measure lent me** gave me minimal praise   9 **hint** occasion (to praise Antony)   10 **from his teeth** i.e., between clenched teeth, not from the heart.   12 **Stomach** resent   13 **chance** occur   17 **Undo** i.e., and then undo, or, I shall undo   21–2 **Let . . . it** let your warmest love be given to that one of us who seeks to preserve it (your love) best.

I lose myself; better I were not yours
Than yours so branchless. But, as you requested,　　24
Yourself shall go between 's. The meantime, lady,　　25
I'll raise the preparation of a war　　26
Shall stain your brother. Make your soonest haste;　　27
So your desires are yours.

OCTAVIA　　　　　　　　　　Thanks to my lord.　　28
The Jove of power make me, most weak, most weak,
Your reconciler! Wars twixt you twain would be
As if the world should cleave, and that slain men　　31
Should solder up the rift.　　32

ANTONY
When it appears to you where this begins,　　33
Turn your displeasure that way, for our faults　　34
Can never be so equal that your love　　35
Can equally move with them. Provide your going;　　36
Choose your own company and command what cost
Your heart has mind to.　　　　　　　　*Exeunt.*

❧

[3.5]

Enter Enobarbus and Eros, [meeting].

ENOBARBUS　　How now, friend Eros?
EROS　　There's strange news come, sir.
ENOBARBUS　　What, man?
EROS　　Caesar and Lepidus have made wars upon Pompey.
ENOBARBUS　　This is old. What is the success?　　6
EROS　　Caesar, having made use of him in the wars　　7
'gainst Pompey, presently denied him rivality, would　　8
not let him partake in the glory of the action; and, not
resting here, accuses him of letters he had formerly　　10
wrote to Pompey; upon his own appeal seizes him.　　11
So the poor third is up, till death enlarge his confine.　　12
ENOBARBUS
Then, world, thou hast a pair of chops, no more;　　13
And throw between them all the food thou hast,
They'll grind the one the other. Where's Antony?　　15
EROS
He's walking in the garden—thus, and spurns　　16
The rush that lies before him; cries, "Fool Lepidus!"　　17

And threats the throat of that his officer　　18
That murdered Pompey.
ENOBARBUS　　　　　　Our great navy's rigged.　　19
EROS
For Italy and Caesar. More, Domitius:　　20
My lord desires you presently. My news　　21
I might have told hereafter.
ENOBARBUS　　　　　　'Twill be naught,
But let it be. Bring me to Antony.
EROS　　　　　　　　Come, sir.　　*Exeunt.*

❧

[3.6]

Enter Agrippa, Maecenas, and Caesar.

CAESAR
Contemning Rome, he has done all this and more　　1
In Alexandria. Here's the manner of 't:
I'th' marketplace, on a tribunal silvered,　　3
Cleopatra and himself in chairs of gold
Were publicly enthroned. At the feet sat
Caesarion, whom they call my father's son,　　6
And all the unlawful issue that their lust
Since then hath made between them. Unto her
He gave the stablishment of Egypt, made her　　9
Of lower Syria, Cyprus, Lydia,
Absolute queen.
MAECENAS　　　　　　This in the public eye?
CAESAR
I'th' common showplace, where they exercise.　　12
His sons he there proclaimed the kings of kings:
Great Media, Parthia, and Armenia
He gave to Alexander; to Ptolemy he assigned
Syria, Cilicia, and Phoenicia. She
In th' habiliments of the goddess Isis　　17
That day appeared, and oft before gave audience,
As 'tis reported, so.
MAECENAS　　Let Rome be thus informed.
AGRIPPA　　Who, queasy with his insolence already,　　21
Will their good thoughts call from him.　　22
CAESAR
The people knows it, and have now received
His accusations.
AGRIPPA　　　　　　Who does he accuse?
CAESAR
Caesar, and that, having in Sicily
Sextus Pompeius spoiled, we had not rated him　　26
His part o'th'isle. Then does he say he lent me　　27

---

24 **branchless** pruned (of honor).　**25 The meantime** In the meantime　**26–7 I'll . . . brother** I'll raise an army that will deprive your brother of his luster.　**28 So . . . yours** i.e., thus you have obtained your desire (to go). (Or, *so* may mean "as long as.")　**31 cleave** split　**32 Should** would be needed to　**33 where this begins** who started this quarrel　**34 our** i.e., Caesar's and mine　**34–6 our faults . . . them** i.e., you will have to judge between our faults and choose.　**36 Provide** Make arrangements for
3.5. Location: Athens.
6 success outcome, result.　**7 him** i.e., Lepidus　**8 presently** immediately.　**rivality** rights of a partner. (Caesar and Lepidus have newly gone to war against Pompey and have defeated him.)　**10 resting here** stopping with this insult　**11 his own appeal** Caesar's own accusation　**12 up** shut up (in prison).　**enlarge his confine** set him free.　**13 a pair . . . more** a single pair of jaws, with no third partner　**15 They'll . . . other** the jaws will still grind against each other, grind each other down.　**16 thus** (Eros imitates Antony's angry walk.)　**spurns** kicks　**17 rush** strewn rushes

18 And . . . officer and threatens the life of the officer of his
19 Pompey (After his defeat by Caesar and Lepidus, Pompey was murdered—perhaps, according to history, on Antony's orders, but here Antony blames his officer.)　**20 More** I have more to say
21 presently immediately.
3.6. Location: Rome.
1 Contemning Disdaining　**3 tribunal** seat of state, dais　**6 my father's** i.e., Julius Caesar's. (Julius Caesar had adopted his grandnephew Octavius as his son.)　**9 stablishment** settled possession　**12 exercise** put on entertainments and sports.　**17 habiliments** attire　**21 queasy** nauseated, "fed up." (Refers to the Roman people.)　**22 call** withdraw　**26 spoiled** despoiled, plundered.　**rated him** allotted to Antony　**27 th'isle** i.e., Sicily.

Some shipping, unrestored. Lastly, he frets 28
That Lepidus of the triumvirate 29
Should be deposed, and, being, that we detain 30
All his revenue.

AGRIPPA   Sir, this should be answered.

CAESAR
'Tis done already, and the messenger gone.
I have told him Lepidus was grown too cruel,
That he his high authority abused
And did deserve his change. For what I have
    conquered, 35
I grant him part; but then in his Armenia,
And other of his conquered kingdoms, I
Demand the like.

MAECENAS   He'll never yield to that.

CAESAR
Nor must not then be yielded to in this.

Enter Octavia with her train.

OCTAVIA
Hail, Caesar, and my lord! Hail, most dear Caesar!

CAESAR
That ever I should call thee castaway!

OCTAVIA
You have not called me so, nor have you cause.

CAESAR
Why have you stol'n upon us thus? You come not
Like Caesar's sister. The wife of Antony
Should have an army for an usher and
The neighs of horse to tell of her approach 46
Long ere she did appear. The trees by th' way 47
Should have borne men, and expectation fainted,
Longing for what it had not. Nay, the dust
Should have ascended to the roof of heaven,
Raised by your populous troops. But you are come
A market maid to Rome, and have prevented 52
The ostentation of our love, which, left unshown, 53
Is often left unloved. We should have met you 54
By sea and land, supplying every stage 55
With an augmented greeting.

OCTAVIA   Good my lord,
To come thus was I not constrained, but did it
On my free will. My lord, Mark Antony,
Hearing that you prepared for war, acquainted
My grievèd ear withal, whereon I begged
His pardon for return.

CAESAR   Which soon he granted, 61
Being an obstruct 'tween his lust and him. 62

OCTAVIA
Do not say so, my lord.

CAESAR   I have eyes upon him,
And his affairs come to me on the wind.
Where is he now?

OCTAVIA   My lord, in Athens.

CAESAR
No, my most wrongèd sister. Cleopatra
Hath nodded him to her. He hath given his empire
Up to a whore; who now are levying 69
The kings o'th'earth for war. He hath assembled
Bocchus, the King of Libya; Archelaus,
Of Cappadocia; Philadelphos, King
Of Paphlagonia; the Thracian king, Adallas;
King Manchus of Arabia; King of Pont;
Herod of Jewry; Mithridates, King
Of Comagene; Polemon and Amyntas,
The Kings of Mede and Lycaonia,
With a more larger list of scepters. 78

OCTAVIA   Ay me, most wretched,
That have my heart parted betwixt two friends
That does afflict each other!

CAESAR   Welcome hither.
Your letters did withhold our breaking forth 82
Till we perceived both how you were wrong led 83
And we in negligent danger. Cheer your heart. 84
Be you not troubled with the time, which drives 85
O'er your content these strong necessities, 86
But let determined things to destiny 87
Hold unbewailed their way. Welcome to Rome, 88
Nothing more dear to me. You are abused 89
Beyond the mark of thought, and the high gods, 90
To do you justice, makes his ministers 91
Of us and those that love you. Best of comfort, 92
And ever welcome to us.

AGRIPPA   Welcome, lady.

MAECENAS   Welcome, dear madam.
Each heart in Rome does love and pity you.
Only th'adulterous Antony, most large 97
In his abominations, turns you off 98
And gives his potent regiment to a trull 99
That noises it against us.

OCTAVIA   Is it so, sir? 100

CAESAR
Most certain. Sister, welcome. Pray you
Be ever known to patience. My dear'st sister! *Exeunt.* 102

❖

[3.7]

Enter Cleopatra and Enobarbus.

---

28 unrestored that I did not return to him.   **29 of** from   **30 being** having been deposed   **35 For** As for   **46 horse** horses   **47 by** along **52 prevented** forestalled (by your unannounced arrival)   **53 ostentation** ceremonial display   **53–4 which . . . unloved** which, if not made manifest through ceremonious display, often remains unappreciated or ceases to exist.   **55 stage** stage of your journey   **61 pardon** permission   **62 Being . . . him** i.e., since your return to Rome removed the obstacle between him and the gratification of his desires.

69 who i.e., and they   **78 a more larger** an even longer   **82 withhold . . . forth** restrain my advancing to battle   **83 wrong led** wronged, abused   **84 negligent danger** danger through neglect of taking necessary action.   **85 the time** the present state of affairs   **85–6 which . . . necessities** i.e., which tramples your happiness underfoot like a team of animals pulling a wagon   **87–8 let . . . way** allow inevitable events to go unbewailed to their destined conclusion.   **89 Nothing . . . me** i.e., you who are more dear to me than anything.   **90 mark** reach **90–2 the high . . . you** i.e., the high gods (here treated as a singular subject of the verb "makes," and referred to as "his" in line 91) make us and those that love you their ministers of justice in your cause. **97 large** unrestrained   **98 turns you off** rejects you   **99 regiment** government, rule.   **trull** prostitute   **100 noises it** is clamorous **102 Be . . . patience** be patient.
3.7. Location: Near Actium, on the northwestern coast of Greece. Antony's camp.

CLEOPATRA
I will be even with thee, doubt it not.
ENOBARBUS   But why, why, why?
CLEOPATRA
Thou hast forspoke my being in these wars,   3
And say'st it is not fit.
ENOBARBUS   Well, is it, is it?   4
CLEOPATRA
If not denounced against us, why should not we   5
Be there in person?
ENOBARBUS [aside]   Well, I could reply.
If we should serve with horse and mares together,   7
The horse were merely lost; the mares would bear   8
A soldier and his horse.
CLEOPATRA   What is't you say?   9
ENOBARBUS
Your presence needs must puzzle Antony,   10
Take from his heart, take from his brain, from's time
What should not then be spared. He is already
Traduced for levity, and 'tis said in Rome   13
That Photinus, an eunuch, and your maids   14
Manage this war.
CLEOPATRA   Sink Rome, and their tongues rot
That speak against us! A charge we bear i'th' war,   16
And as the president of my kingdom will   17
Appear there for a man. Speak not against it.   18
I will not stay behind.

Enter Antony and Canidius.

ENOBARBUS   Nay, I have done.
Here comes the Emperor.
ANTONY   Is it not strange, Canidius,
That from Tarentum and Brundusium
He could so quickly cut the Ionian sea   22
And take in Toryne?—You have heard on't, sweet?   23
CLEOPATRA
Celerity is never more admired   24
Than by the negligent.
ANTONY   A good rebuke,
Which might have well becomed the best of men,   26
To taunt at slackness. Canidius, we
Will fight with him by sea.
CLEOPATRA   By sea, what else?
CANIDIUS   Why will my lord do so?
ANTONY   For that he dares us to't.   30
ENOBARBUS
So hath my lord dared him to single fight.

CANIDIUS
Ay, and to wage this battle at Pharsalia,
Where Caesar fought with Pompey. But these offers,
Which serve not for his vantage, he shakes off,
And so should you.
ENOBARBUS   Your ships are not well manned;
Your mariners are muleteers, reapers, people   36
Engrossed by swift impress. In Caesar's fleet   37
Are those that often have 'gainst Pompey fought;
Their ships are yare, yours heavy. No disgrace   39
Shall fall you for refusing him at sea,   40
Being prepared for land.
ANTONY   By sea, by sea.
ENOBARBUS
Most worthy sir, you therein throw away
The absolute soldiership you have by land,
Distract your army, which doth most consist   44
Of war-marked footmen, leave unexecuted   45
Your own renownèd knowledge, quite forgo
The way which promises assurance, and
Give up yourself merely to chance and hazard   48
From firm security.
ANTONY   I'll fight at sea.
CLEOPATRA
I have sixty sails, Caesar none better.
ANTONY
Our overplus of shipping will we burn,
And with the rest full-manned, from th' head of
    Actium   52
Beat th'approaching Caesar. But if we fail,
We then can do't at land.

Enter a Messenger.

                                        Thy business?
MESSENGER
The news is true, my lord; he is descried.   55
Caesar has taken Toryne.
ANTONY
Can he be there in person? 'Tis impossible;
Strange that his power should be. Canidius,   58
Our nineteen legions thou shalt hold by land,
And our twelve thousand horse. We'll to our ship.
Away, my Thetis!

Enter a Soldier.

                        How now, worthy soldier?   61
SOLDIER
O noble Emperor, do not fight by sea;
Trust not to rotten planks. Do you misdoubt
This sword and these my wounds? Let th'Egyptians
And the Phoenicians go a-ducking; we   65

---

3 **forspoke** spoken against   4 **fit** appropriate.   5 **If . . . us** i.e., Even if
the war were not declared against me (which it is)   7 **horse** stallions
8 **merely** utterly   8–9 **bear . . . horse** be mounted by a rider and a
stallion.   10 **puzzle** bewilder   13 **Traduced** criticized, censured
14 **an eunuch** (Probably Mardian. In North's Plutarch, Caesar complains that "Mardian the eunuch, Photinus, and Iras . . . and
Charmian . . . ruled the affairs of Antonius' empire." But Photinus
[or Pothinus] was a eunuch, too.)   16 **charge** responsibility, cost
17 **president** ruler   18 **for** in the capacity of   22 **Ionian** (Often applied
to the Aegean, but here the Adriatic. Tarentum and Brundusium or
Brundisium are in the "heel" of Italy, across the Adriatic from Actium
and Toryne.)   23 **take in** conquer   24 **Celerity** Swiftness.   **admired**
wondered at   26 **becomed** become, suited   30 **For that** Because

36 **muleteers** mule-drivers, peasants   37 **Engrossed** collected wholesale.   **impress** impressment, conscription.   39 **yare** quick, maneu-
verable   40 **fall** befall   44 **Distract** divide, divert.   **most** for the
most part   45 **footmen** foot soldiers.   **unexecuted** unused
48 **merely** entirely   52 **head** promontory   55 **he is descried** he has
been sighted.   58 **his power** i.e., his army, let alone himself
61 **Thetis** sea goddess, the mother of Achilles.   65 **go a-ducking**
(1) get drenched (2) cringe

Have used to conquer standing on the earth   66
And fighting foot to foot.
ANTONY   Well, well, away!
  Exeunt Antony, Cleopatra, and Enobarbus.
SOLDIER
By Hercules, I think I am i'th' right.
CANIDIUS
Soldier, thou art; but his whole action grows   69
Not in the power on't. So our leader's led,   70
And we are women's men.
SOLDIER   You keep by land   71
The legions and the horse whole, do you not?   72
CANIDIUS
Marcus Octavius, Marcus Justeius,
Publicola, and Caelius are for sea;
But we keep whole by land. This speed of Caesar's
Carries beyond belief.   76
SOLDIER   While he was yet in Rome
His power went out in such distractions as   78
Beguiled all spies.
CANIDIUS   Who's his lieutenant, hear you?
SOLDIER
They say, one Taurus.
CANIDIUS   Well I know the man.

  Enter a Messenger.

MESSENGER   The Emperor calls Canidius.
CANIDIUS
With news the time's in labor, and throws forth   82
Each minute some.   *Exeunt.*   83

❖

[3.8]

  Enter Caesar [and Taurus] with his army,
  marching.

CAESAR   Taurus!
TAURUS   My lord?
CAESAR
Strike not by land; keep whole. Provoke not battle
Till we have done at sea. Do not exceed
The prescript of this scroll. [*He gives a scroll.*] Our
  fortune lies   5
Upon this jump.   *Exeunt.*   6

❖

[3.9]

  Enter Antony and Enobarbus.

ANTONY
Set we our squadrons on yond side o'th' hill,
In eye of Caesar's battle, from which place   2
We may the number of the ships behold
And so proceed accordingly.   *Exeunt.*

❖

[3.10]

  Canidius marcheth with his land army one way
  over the stage, and Taurus, the lieutenant of
  Caesar, the other way. After their going in is heard
  the noise of a sea fight.

  Alarum. Enter Enobarbus.

ENOBARBUS
Naught, naught, all naught! I can behold no longer.   1
Th'*Antoniad*, the Egyptian admiral,   2
With all their sixty, fly and turn the rudder.
To see't mine eyes are blasted.

  Enter Scarus.

SCARUS   Gods and goddesses,
All the whole synod of them!
ENOBARBUS   What's thy passion?   5
SCARUS
The greater cantle of the world is lost   6
With very ignorance; we have kissed away   7
Kingdoms and provinces.
ENOBARBUS   How appears the fight?
SCARUS
On our side like the tokened pestilence,   9
Where death is sure. Yon ribaudred nag of Egypt—   10
Whom leprosy o'ertake!—i'th' midst o'th' fight,
When vantage like a pair of twins appeared   12
Both as the same, or rather ours the elder,   13
The breeze upon her, like a cow in June,   14
Hoists sails and flies.
ENOBARBUS   That I beheld.
Mine eyes did sicken at the sight, and could not
Endure a further view.
SCARUS   She once being loofed,   18
The noble ruin of her magic, Antony,   19
Claps on his sea wing and, like a doting mallard,   20
Leaving the fight in height, flies after her.   21
I never saw an action of such shame.
Experience, manhood, honor, ne'er before

---

2 **eye** sight. **battle** battle line
3.10 **Location: A field near Actium, as before.**
1 **Naught** All has come to naught   2 **admiral** flagship   5 **synod** assembly   6 **cantle** corner; hence, piece or part   7 **With very ignorance** through utter stupidity   9 **tokened pestilence** (Certain red spots appeared on the bodies of the plague-smitten, called tokens.)   10 **ribaudred** foul, obscene   12–13 **When . . . same** i.e., when the advantage was equal on either side   13 **elder** i.e., more advanced, more likely to inherit   14 **breeze** (1) gadfly (2) light wind   18 **loofed** luffed, with ship's head brought close to the wind. (With a pun on *aloofed*, "becoming distant.")   19 **ruin of** object ruined by   20 **Claps . . . sea wing** i.e., hoists sail, preparing for flight like a water bird.   **mallard** drake   21 **in** at its

66 **Have used** are accustomed.   **standing on the earth** (1) fighting on land (2) standing upright, not *ducking*, or "cringing"   69–70 **his . . . on't** his whole strategy has been developed without regard to where his power really lies.   71 **men** servingmen.   72 **horse** cavalry.   **whole** undivided, held in reserve   76 **Carries** surpasses (like an arrow in archery)   78 **distractions** detachments, divisions
82–3 **With . . . some** More news is born each minute. (*Throws forth* means "gives birth.")
3.8. **Location: A field near Actium, as before.**
5 **prescript** orders   6 **jump** chance, hazard.
3.9. **Location: A field near Actium, as before.**

Did violate so itself.
ENOBARBUS   Alack, alack!

Enter Canidius.

CANIDIUS
Our fortune on the sea is out of breath,
And sinks most lamentably. Had our general
Been what he knew himself, it had gone well.
Oh, he has given example for our flight
Most grossly by his own!
ENOBARBUS
Ay, are you thereabouts? Why then, good night
indeed.   30
CANIDIUS
Toward Peloponnesus are they fled.   31
SCARUS
'Tis easy to't, and there I will attend   32
What further comes.
CANIDIUS   To Caesar will I render   33
My legions and my horse. Six kings already   34
Show me the way of yielding.
ENOBARBUS   I'll yet follow
The wounded chance of Antony, though my reason   36
Sits in the wind against me.   *[Exeunt separately.]* 37

❧

[3.11]

Enter Antony with attendants.

ANTONY
Hark! The land bids me tread no more upon't;
It is ashamed to bear me. Friends, come hither.
I am so lated in the world that I   3
Have lost my way forever. I have a ship
Laden with gold. Take that, divide it; fly,   5
And make your peace with Caesar.
ALL   Fly? Not we.
ANTONY
I have fled myself, and have instructed cowards
To run and show their shoulders. Friends, begone.   8
I have myself resolved upon a course
Which has no need of you. Begone.
My treasure's in the harbor. Take it. Oh,
I followed that I blush to look upon!   12
My very hairs do mutiny, for the white   13
Reprove the brown for rashness, and they them   14

For fear and doting. Friends, begone. You shall
Have letters from me to some friends that will
Sweep your way for you. Pray you, look not sad,   17
Nor make replies of loathness. Take the hint   18
Which my despair proclaims. Let that be left   19
Which leaves itself. To the seaside straightway!   20
I will possess you of that ship and treasure.
Leave me, I pray, a little. Pray you now,
Nay, do so, for indeed I have lost command.   23
Therefore I pray you. I'll see you by and by.   24
[Exeunt attendants. Antony] sits down.

Enter Cleopatra led by Charmian, [Iras,] and Eros.

EROS
Nay, gentle madam, to him, comfort him.
IRAS   Do, most dear Queen.
CHARMIAN   Do; why, what else?
CLEOPATRA   Let me sit down. O Juno!
ANTONY   No, no, no, no, no.
EROS   See you here, sir?
ANTONY   Oh, fie, fie, fie!
CHARMIAN   Madam!
IRAS   Madam, O good Empress!
EROS   Sir, sir!
ANTONY
Yes, my lord, yes. He at Philippi kept   35
His sword e'en like a dancer, while I struck   36
The lean and wrinkled Cassius, and 'twas I
That the mad Brutus ended. He alone   38
Dealt on lieutenantry, and no practice had   39
In the brave squares of war; yet now—no matter.   40
CLEOPATRA
Ah, stand by.
EROS   The Queen, my lord, the Queen.   41
IRAS
Go to him, madam, speak to him.
He's unqualitied with very shame.   43
CLEOPATRA   Well then, sustain me. Oh!
EROS
Most noble sir, arise. The Queen approaches.
Her head's declined, and death will seize her but   46
Your comfort makes the rescue.
ANTONY
I have offended reputation,
A most unnoble swerving.
EROS   Sir, the Queen.   49

---

30 thereabouts i.e., of that mind, thinking of desertion.   **good night indeed** i.e., it's all over.   **31 Peloponnesus** southern Greece (from which Antony then crosses the Mediterranean to Egypt)   **32 to't** to get to it.   **attend** await   **33 render** surrender   **34 horse** cavalry.   **36 wounded chance** broken fortunes   **37 Sits . . . me** i.e., is on my downwind side, tracking me and hunting me down.
3.11. Location: Historically, events such as dispatching the School-master to Caesar took place in Egypt; however, the dramatic impression of this scene is that it occurs soon after the battle.
3 lated belated, like a traveler still journeying when night falls   **5 fly** flee   **8 shoulders** i.e., backs.   **12 that** that which   **13 mutiny** contend among themselves   **14 they them** i.e., the brown hairs reprove the white

17 Sweep your way clear your way (to Caesar)   **18 loathness** unwillingness.   **hint** opportunity   **19 that** i.e., Antony and his cause   **20 leaves** is untrue to, deserts   **23 lost command** i.e., of myself and of my authority.   **24 pray** entreat (as opposed to "command")   **35 Yes . . . yes** (Antony is absorbed in his own bitter thoughts, as also in lines 29 and 31.)   **He** i.e., Octavius.   **kept** kept in its sheath   **36 e'en . . . dancer** i.e., as though for ornament only, in a dance   **38 ended** i.e., defeated. (Not *killed*; Brutus and Cassius committed suicide.)   **He alone** Caesar merely   **39 Dealt on lieutenantry** let his subordinates do the fighting   **40 brave squares** splendid squadrons, bodies of troops drawn up in square formation   **41 stand by** (Cleopatra indicates she is about to faint and needs assistance.)   **43 unqualitied** dispossessed of his own nature, i.e., not himself   **46 but** unless   **49 swerving** lapse, transgression.

ANTONY
    Oh, whither hast thou led me, Egypt? See   50
    How I convey my shame out of thine eyes   51
    By looking back what I have left behind   52
    'Stroyed in dishonor.
CLEOPATRA   Oh, my lord, my lord,   53
    Forgive my fearful sails! I little thought   54
    You would have followed.
ANTONY   Egypt, thou knew'st too well
    My heart was to thy rudder tied by th' strings,   56
    And thou shouldst tow me after. O'er my spirit
    Thy full supremacy thou knew'st, and that
    Thy beck might from the bidding of the gods   59
    Command me.
CLEOPATRA   Oh, my pardon!
ANTONY   Now I must   60
    To the young man send humble treaties, dodge   61
    And palter in the shifts of lowness, who   62
    With half the bulk o'th' world played as I pleased,
    Making and marring fortunes. You did know
    How much you were my conqueror, and that
    My sword, made weak by my affection, would 66
    Obey it on all cause.
CLEOPATRA   Pardon, pardon!   67
ANTONY
    Fall not a tear, I say; one of them rates   68
    All that is won and lost. Give me a kiss.   [*They kiss.*]
    Even this repays me.—We sent our schoolmaster; 70
    Is 'a come back?—Love, I am full of lead.—
    Some wine, within there, and our viands! Fortune
    knows   72
    We scorn her most when most she offers blows.
                               Exeunt.

❧

[3.12]

*Enter Caesar, Agrippa, [Thidias,] and Dolabella,
with others.*

CAESAR
    Let him appear that's come from Antony.
    Know you him?
DOLABELLA   Caesar, 'tis his schoolmaster—
    An argument that he is plucked, when hither   3
    He sends so poor a pinion of his wing,   4
    Which had superfluous kings for messengers 5

    Not many moons gone by.
        Enter Ambassador from Antony.
CAESAR   Approach and speak.
AMBASSADOR
    Such as I am, I come from Antony.
    I was of late as petty to his ends   8
    As is the morn-dew on the myrtle leaf
    To his grand sea.
CAESAR   Be't so. Declare thine office.   10
AMBASSADOR
    Lord of his fortunes he salutes thee, and
    Requires to live in Egypt; which not granted, 12
    He lessens his requests, and to thee sues   13
    To let him breathe between the heavens and earth 14
    A private man in Athens. This for him.
    Next, Cleopatra does confess thy greatness,
    Submits her to thy might, and of thee craves
    The circle of the Ptolemies for her heirs,   18
    Now hazarded to thy grace.
CAESAR   For Antony,   19
    I have no ears to his request. The Queen
    Of audience nor desire shall fail, so she   21
    From Egypt drive her all-disgracèd friend
    Or take his life there. This if she perform
    She shall not sue unheard. So to them both.
AMBASSADOR
    Fortune pursue thee!
CAESAR   Bring him through the bands. 25
        [*Exit Ambassador, attended.*]
    [*To Thidias*] To try thy eloquence now 'tis time.
      Dispatch.
    From Antony win Cleopatra. Promise,
    And in our name, what she requires; add more, 28
    From thine invention, offers. Women are not 29
    In their best fortunes strong, but want will perjure 30
    The ne'er-touched vestal. Try thy cunning, Thidias. 31
    Make thine own edict for thy pains, which we 32
    Will answer as a law.
THIDIAS   Caesar, I go.   33
CAESAR
    Observe how Antony becomes his flaw,   34
    And what thou think'st his very action speaks 35
    In every power that moves.
THIDIAS   Caesar, I shall. *Exeunt.* 36

❧

50–3 See . . . dishonor i.e., See how ashamed I am to have you see me like this, looking back on what I have left behind dishonorably destroyed. **54 fearful** timorous **56 th' strings** (1) the heartstrings (2) towing cable **59–60 Thy . . . Command me** your mere beckoning would command me away from doing the bidding of the gods themselves. **61 treaties** entreaties, propositions for settlement. **dodge** shuffle, cringe **62 palter** use trickery, prevaricate, equivocate. **shifts of lowness** pitiful evasions used by those lacking power **66 affection** passion **67 on all cause** whatever the reason. **68 Fall** Let fall. **rates** equals **70 Even this** This by itself. **schoolmaster** (Identified in Plutarch as Euphronius, tutor to Antony's children by Cleopatra.) **72 viands** food.
3.12 Location: Egypt. Caesar's camp.
3 An argument an indication **4 pinion** i.e., pinion-feather, outer feather **5 Which** who

8 petty to insignificant in terms of **10 To . . . sea** compared to its, the dewdrop's, great source, the sea. **thine office** your official business. **12 Requires** asks. **which not granted** and if that request is not granted **13 sues** petitions **14 breathe** i.e., live **18 circle** crown **19 hazarded . . . grace** dependent on your favor. **For** As for **21 Of audience** neither of hearing. **so** provided that **25 Bring** Escort. **bands** troops on guard, military lines. **28 requires** asks **28–9 add . . . offers** add ideas of your own. **29–31 Women . . . vestal** Women are not strong even at the height of their good fortune, but need will cause even an untouched vestal virgin to break her vows. **31 cunning** skill **32 Make . . . edict** Decree your own reward **33 answer as a law** confirm as if it were a law. **34 becomes his flaw** bears his misfortune and disgrace **35–6 And . . . moves** and what you think his gestures signify in every move he makes.

[3.13]

Enter Cleopatra, Enobarbus, Charmian, and Iras.

CLEOPATRA
What shall we do, Enobarbus?

ENOBARBUS   Think, and die.   1

CLEOPATRA
Is Antony or we in fault for this?   2

ENOBARBUS
Antony only, that would make his will   3
Lord of his reason. What though you fled
From that great face of war, whose several ranges   5
Frighted each other? Why should he follow?
The itch of his affection should not then   7
Have nicked his captainship, at such a point,   8
When half to half the world opposed, he being   9
The merèd question. 'Twas a shame no less   10
Than was his loss, to course your flying flags   11
And leave his navy gazing.

CLEOPATRA   Prithee, peace.

Enter the Ambassador with Antony.

ANTONY   Is that his answer?

AMBASSADOR   Ay, my lord.

ANTONY
The Queen shall then have courtesy, so she   15
Will yield us up.

AMBASSADOR   He says so.

ANTONY   Let her know't.—
To the boy Caesar send this grizzled head,
And he will fill thy wishes to the brim
With principalities.

CLEOPATRA   That head, my lord?

ANTONY [*to the Ambassador*]
To him again. Tell him he wears the rose
Of youth upon him, from which the world should
    note
Something particular. His coin, ships, legions,   22
May be a coward's, whose ministers would prevail   23
Under the service of a child as soon
As i'th' command of Caesar. I dare him therefore
To lay his gay caparisons apart   26
And answer me declined, sword against sword,   27
Ourselves alone. I'll write it. Follow me.
                 [*Exeunt Antony and Ambassador.*]

ENOBARBUS [*aside*]
Yes, like enough, high-battled Caesar will   29

Unstate his happiness and be staged to th' show   30
Against a sworder! I see men's judgments are   31
A parcel of their fortunes, and things outward   32
Do draw the inward quality after them   33
To suffer all alike. That he should dream,   34
Knowing all measures, the full Caesar will   35
Answer his emptiness! Caesar, thou hast subdued   36
His judgment too.

Enter a Servant.

SERVANT   A messenger from Caesar.

CLEOPATRA
What, no more ceremony? See, my women,
Against the blown rose may they stop their nose   39
That kneeled unto the buds.—Admit him, sir.
                    [*Exit Servant.*]

ENOBARBUS [*aside*]
Mine honesty and I begin to square.   41
The loyalty well held to fools does make   42
Our faith mere folly; yet he that can endure   43
To follow with allegiance a fall'n lord
Does conquer him that did his master conquer   45
And earns a place i'th' story.

Enter Thidias.

CLEOPATRA   Caesar's will?

THIDIAS
Hear it apart.

CLEOPATRA   None but friends. Say boldly.   47

THIDIAS
So haply are they friends to Antony.   48

ENOBARBUS
He needs as many, sir, as Caesar has,
Or needs not us. If Caesar please, our master   50
Will leap to be his friend. For us, you know   51
Whose he is we are, and that is Caesar's.

THIDIAS   So.   52
Thus then, thou most renowned: Caesar entreats
Not to consider in what case thou stand'st   54
Further than he is Caesar.

CLEOPATRA   Go on: right royal.   55

3.13. Location: Alexandria. Cleopatra's palace.
1 Think, and die Think despondently, and die of melancholy or by suicide. **2 we** I **3 will** desire (especially sexual) **5 ranges** ranks, lines (of ships) **7 affection** sexual passion **8 nicked** cut short or maimed, or got the better of. **point** crisis **9–10 When . . . question** when the two halves of the world found themselves in conflict, Antony being the sole ground of the quarrel. **11 course** pursue (as in hunting) **15 so** provided that **22 Something particular** some exceptional exploit. **23 May be** could as well be. **ministers** agents, subordinates **26 gay caparisons** resplendent trappings **27 answer me declined** meet me as I am, lowered in fortune and advanced in years **29 like** likely. **high-battled** provided with a mighty army

30–1 Unstate . . . sworder set aside his advantageous fortune and be exhibited publicly in a sword-fight contest with a mere gladiator. **31–4 I see . . . alike** I see that men's judgments are inextricably linked to their fortunes, whereby outward circumstances draw after them inward qualities of character in such a way that both suffer at the same time. **35 Knowing all measures** i.e., having experienced every degree of fortune. **full** at full fortune **36 Answer** (1) meet man to man with (2) correspond with **39 blown** overblown, starting to decay **41 honesty** (With meaning also of "honor.") **square** quarrel. **42–3 The . . . folly** A stubborn loyalty bestowed on fools is folly itself **45 Does . . . conquer** i.e., achieves a moral victory over the very fortune or the person that subdued one's own master **47 apart** in private. **48 haply** perhaps **50 Or . . . us** i.e., or else he doesn't need even us, his case being hopeless. **51 For** As for **52 Whose . . . Caesar's** i.e., we are Antony's friends, and he is Caesar's, so that we, too, are Caesar's. **54–5 Not . . . Caesar** i.e., not to worry about your situation other than to consider that you are dealing with Caesar, the embodiment of magnanimity. **55 right royal** i.e., that is very magnanimous.

THIDIAS
He knows that you embrace not Antony
As you did love, but as you feared him.

CLEOPATRA   Oh!

THIDIAS
The scars upon your honor therefore he
Does pity as constrainèd blemishes,
Not as deserved.

CLEOPATRA   He is a god and knows
What is most right. Mine honor was not yielded,   61
But conquered merely.

ENOBARBUS [aside]   To be sure of that,   62
I will ask Antony. Sir, sir, thou art so leaky
That we must leave thee to thy sinking, for
Thy dearest quit thee.   Exit Enobarbus.

THIDIAS   Shall I say to Caesar
What you require of him? For he partly begs   66
To be desired to give. It much would please him
That of his fortunes you should make a staff
To lean upon; but it would warm his spirits
To hear from me you had left Antony
And put yourself under his shroud,   71
The universal landlord.

CLEOPATRA   What's your name?

THIDIAS
My name is Thidias.

CLEOPATRA   Most kind messenger,
Say to great Caesar this in deputation: 74
I kiss his conquering hand. Tell him I am prompt   75
To lay my crown at 's feet, and there to kneel
Till from his all-obeying breath I hear   77
The doom of Egypt.

THIDIAS   'Tis your noblest course. 78
Wisdom and fortune combating together,   79
If that the former dare but what it can,   80
No chance may shake it. Give me grace to lay   81
My duty on your hand.   [He kisses her hand.]

CLEOPATRA   Your Caesar's father oft,   83
When he hath mused of taking kingdoms in,   84
Bestowed his lips on that unworthy place,
As it rained kisses.

Enter Antony and Enobarbus.

ANTONY   Favors? By Jove that thunders! 86
What art thou, fellow?

THIDIAS   One that but performs
The bidding of the fullest man, and worthiest   88
To have command obeyed.

ENOBARBUS [aside]   You will be whipped.

ANTONY [calling for Servants]
Approach, there!—Ah, you kite!—Now, gods and
devils!   90
Authority melts from me of late. When I cried "Ho!",
Like boys unto a muss kings would start forth   92
And cry, "Your will?"—Have you no ears? I am
Antony yet.

Enter a Servant [followed by others].

                          Take hence this jack and whip him.   94

ENOBARBUS [aside]
'Tis better playing with a lion's whelp   95
Than with an old one dying.

ANTONY   Moon and stars!
Whip him. Were't twenty of the greatest tributaries   97
That do acknowledge Caesar, should I find them
So saucy with the hand of she here—what's her name
Since she was Cleopatra? Whip him, fellows,
Till like a boy you see him cringe his face   101
And whine aloud for mercy. Take him hence.

THIDIAS
Mark Antony—

ANTONY   Tug him away! Being whipped,
Bring him again. This jack of Caesar's shall
Bear us an errand to him.

                          Exeunt [Servants] with Thidias.
[To Cleopatra] You were half blasted ere I knew you.
Ha?   106
Have I my pillow left unpressed in Rome,
Forborne the getting of a lawful race,   108
And by a gem of women, to be abused   109
By one that looks on feeders?   110

CLEOPATRA   Good my lord—

ANTONY   You have been a boggler ever.   112
But when we in our viciousness grow hard—
Oh, misery on't!—the wise gods seel our eyes,   114
In our own filth drop our clear judgments, make us
Adore our errors, laugh at 's while we strut
To our confusion.

CLEOPATRA   Oh, is't come to this?   117

ANTONY
I found you as a morsel cold upon
Dead Caesar's trencher; nay, you were a fragment   119
Of Gnaeus Pompey's, besides what hotter hours,   120
Unregistered in vulgar fame, you have   121
Luxuriously picked out. For I am sure,   122
Though you can guess what temperance should be,

---

61 **right** true.   62 **merely** utterly.   66 **require** ask.   **partly** i.e., as commensurate with his dignity   71 **shroud** shelter. (With suggestion too of a burial cloth.)   74 **in deputation** by you as deputy   75 **prompt** ready   77 **all-obeying** obeyed by all   78 **The doom of Egypt** i.e., my fate.   79–81 **Wisdom . . . shake it** When wisdom and fortune are at odds, if the wise person will have the resolution to desire only what what fortune will allow, then fortune cannot shake that wisdom.   83 **Your Caesar's father** i.e., Julius Caesar, actually Octavius' great-uncle. (See note at 3.6.6.)   84 **mused . . . in** thought about conquering kingdoms   86 **As** as if   88 **fullest** most fortunate, best

90 **kite** a rapacious bird of prey that feeds on ignoble objects, and a slang word for "whore." (Said of Cleopatra.)   92 **muss** game in which small objects are thrown down to be scrambled for   94 **jack** fellow. (Contemptuous.)   95 **whelp** cub   97 **tributaries** rulers paying tribute   101 **cringe** contract in pain   106 **blasted** withered, blighted   108 **getting** begetting.   **lawful** legitimate   109 **abused** deceived, betrayed   110 **feeders** servants.   112 **boggler** waverer, shifty person. (Often used of shying horses.)   114 **seel** blind. (A term in falconry for sewing shut the eyes of wild hawks in order to tame them.)   117 **confusion** destruction.   119 **trencher** wooden plate. **fragment** leftover   120 **Gnaeus Pompey's** (See 1.5.32 and note.)   121 **vulgar fame** common gossip   122 **Luxuriously** lustfully

You know not what it is.

CLEOPATRA   Wherefore is this?   124

ANTONY
To let a fellow that will take rewards
And say "God quit you!" be familiar with   126
My playfellow, your hand, this kingly seal
And plighter of high hearts! Oh, that I were   128
Upon the hill of Basan, to outroar   129
The hornèd herd! For I have savage cause,   130
And to proclaim it civilly were like
A haltered neck which does the hangman thank
For being yare about him.

              Enter a Servant with Thidias.

                            Is he whipped?   133

SERVANT   Soundly, my lord.

ANTONY   Cried he? And begged 'a pardon?

SERVANT   He did ask favor.

ANTONY [*to Thidias*]
If that thy father live, let him repent
Thou wast not made his daughter; and be thou sorry
To follow Caesar in his triumph, since
Thou hast been whipped for following him.
     Henceforth
The white hand of a lady fever thee;   141
Shake thou to look on't. Get thee back to Caesar.
Tell him thy entertainment. Look thou say   143
He makes me angry with him; for he seems
Proud and disdainful, harping on what I am,
Not what he knew I was. He makes me angry,
And at this time most easy 'tis to do't,
When my good stars, that were my former guides,
Have empty left their orbs and shot their fires 149
Into th'abysm of hell. If he mislike   150
My speech and what is done, tell him he has
Hipparchus, my enfranchèd bondman, whom   152
He may at pleasure whip, or hang, or torture,
As he shall like, to quit me. Urge it thou.   154
Hence with thy stripes, begone!
                    Exit [Servant with] Thidias.

CLEOPATRA   Have you done yet?

ANTONY
Alack, our terrene moon is now eclipsed,   156
And it portends alone the fall of Antony.

CLEOPATRA   I must stay his time.   158

ANTONY
To flatter Caesar, would you mingle eyes

With one that ties his points?

CLEOPATRA   Not know me yet?   160

ANTONY
Coldhearted toward me?

CLEOPATRA   Ah, dear, if I be so,
From my cold heart let heaven engender hail,
And poison it in the source, and the first stone
Drop in my neck; as it determines, so   164
Dissolve my life! The next Caesarion smite,
Till by degrees the memory of my womb,   166
Together with my brave Egyptians all,   167
By the discandying of this pelleted storm   168
Lie graveless till the flies and gnats of Nile
Have buried them for prey!

ANTONY   I am satisfied.   170
Caesar sits down in Alexandria, where   171
I will oppose his fate. Our force by land   172
Hath nobly held; our severed navy too
Have knit again, and fleet, threat'ning most sealike. 174
Where hast thou been, my heart? Dost thou hear,
     lady?   175
If from the field I shall return once more
To kiss these lips, I will appear in blood;   177
I and my sword will earn our chronicle.   178
There's hope in't yet.

CLEOPATRA   That's my brave lord!

ANTONY
I will be treble-sinewed, hearted, breathed,   181
And fight maliciously. For when mine hours   182
Were nice and lucky, men did ransom lives   183
Of me for jests; but now I'll set my teeth   184
And send to darkness all that stop me. Come,   185
Let's have one other gaudy night. Call to me   186
All my sad captains. Fill our bowls once more;
Let's mock the midnight bell.

CLEOPATRA   It is my birthday.
I had thought t'have held it poor; but since my lord 189
Is Antony again, I will be Cleopatra.

ANTONY   We will yet do well.

CLEOPATRA [*to attendants*]
Call all his noble captains to my lord.

ANTONY
Do so. We'll speak to them, and tonight I'll force
The wine peep through their scars. Come on, my
     queen,
There's sap in't yet. The next time I do fight   195

---

124 Wherefore is this? i.e., What brought this on? **126 quit** reward. (*God quit you* is said obsequiously to acknowledge a tip.) **128 plighter** pledger **129–30 hill of Basan . . . The hornèd herd** (Allusion to the strong bulls of Bashan, Psalms 22:12 and 68:15. Antony imagines himself as the greatest horned beast, i.e., cuckold, of that herd.) **133 yare** deft, quick **141 fever thee** make you shiver **143 entertainment** reception. **Look** Be sure that **149 orbs** spheres **150 th'abysm** the abyss **152 Hipparchus** (According to Plutarch, the man was a deserter to Caesar's side.) **enfranchèd** enfranchised, freed **154 quit** requite, pay back **156 our . . . eclipsed** i.e., (1) the moon in eclipse portends disaster (2) the waning of the love of Cleopatra (equated with Isis, the moon goddess) spells the end for me **158 stay his time** i.e., be patient until his fury has subsided.

160 ties his points i.e., helps Caesar as a valet with the metal-tipped laces used to fasten articles of clothing. **164 neck** throat or head. **determines** comes to an end, dissolves. (See line 168.) **166 memory of my womb** i.e., my offspring **167 brave** splendid. (Also in line 180.) **168 discandying** melting. **pelleted** falling in pellets **170 for prey** i.e., by eating them. **171 sits down in** lays siege to **172 oppose his fate** confront his (seemingly irresistible) fortune. **174 fleet** float **175 heart** courage. **177 in blood** (1) bloody from battle (2) full-spirited. **178 chronicle** place in history. **181 treble-sinewed . . . breathed** thrice myself in strength, courage, and endurance **182 maliciously** violently, fiercely. **183 nice** delicate, refined **183–4 men . . . jests** I allowed enemies to be ransomed for trifles or as a magnanimous gesture **185 to darkness** i.e., to death, the underworld **186 gaudy** festive **189 held it poor** celebrated it simply **195 sap in't** i.e., life in our enterprise

I'll make Death love me, for I will contend   196
Even with his pestilent scythe.   197
                                    Exeunt [all but Enobarbus].

ENOBARBUS
Now he'll outstare the lightning. To be furious   198
Is to be frighted out of fear, and in that mood
The dove will peck the estridge; and I see still   200
A diminution in our captain's brain
Restores his heart. When valor preys on reason,   202
It eats the sword it fights with. I will seek   203
Some way to leave him.   *Exit.*

❧

[4.1]

*Enter Caesar, Agrippa, and Maecenas, with his
army, Caesar reading a letter.*

CAESAR
He calls me boy, and chides as he had power   1
To beat me out of Egypt. My messenger
He hath whipped with rods, dares me to personal
   combat,
Caesar to Antony. Let the old ruffian know
I have many other ways to die, meantime
Laugh at his challenge.
MAECENAS   Caesar must think,
When one so great begins to rage, he's hunted   8
Even to falling. Give him no breath, but now   9
Make boot of his distraction. Never anger   10
Made good guard for itself.
CAESAR   Let our best heads   11
Know that tomorrow the last of many battles
We mean to fight. Within our files there are,   13
Of those that served Mark Antony but late,   14
Enough to fetch him in. See it done,   15
And feast the army; we have store to do't,   16
And they have earned the waste. Poor Antony!   17
                                                      Exeunt.

❧

[4.2]

*Enter Antony, Cleopatra, Enobarbus,
Charmian, Iras, Alexas, with others.*

ANTONY
He will not fight with me, Domitius?

ENOBARBUS   No.
ANTONY   Why should he not?
ENOBARBUS
He thinks, being twenty times of better fortune,
He is twenty men to one.
ANTONY   Tomorrow, soldier,
By sea and land I'll fight. Or I will live   6
Or bathe my dying honor in the blood
Shall make it live again. Woo't thou fight well?   8
ENOBARBUS
I'll strike, and cry, "Take all."
ANTONY   Well said. Come on!   9
Call forth my household servants. Let's tonight   10

Enter three or four servitors.

Be bounteous at our meal.—Give me thy hand.
Thou hast been rightly honest—so hast thou—   12
Thou—and thou—and thou. You have served me
   well,
And kings have been your fellows.
CLEOPATRA [*aside to Enobarbus*]   What means this?   14
ENOBARBUS [*aside to Cleopatra*]
'Tis one of those odd tricks which sorrow shoots
Out of the mind.
ANTONY   And thou art honest too.
I wish I could be made so many men,   17
And all of you clapped up together in   18
An Antony, that I might do you service
So good as you have done.
ALL   The gods forbid!
ANTONY
Well, my good fellows, wait on me tonight:
Scant not my cups, and make as much of me   22
As when mine empire was your fellow too,   23
And suffered my command.
CLEOPATRA [*aside to Enobarbus*]   What does he mean?   24
ENOBARBUS [*aside to Cleopatra*]
To make his followers weep.
ANTONY   Tend me tonight;
May be it is the period of your duty.   26
Haply you shall not see me more, or if,   27
A mangled shadow. Perchance tomorrow   28
You'll serve another master. I look on you
As one that takes his leave. Mine honest friends,
I turn you not away, but, like a master
Married to your good service, stay till death.
Tend me tonight two hours, I ask no more,
And the gods yield you for't!
ENOBARBUS   What mean you, sir,   34
To give them this discomfort? Look, they weep,

196–7 **I will . . . scythe** i.e., I will outdo even Death himself and his
scythe of *pestilence* or plague.   198 **outstare** stare down.   **furious**
frenzied   200 **estridge** ostrich, or, a kind of hawk.   **still** constantly
202–3 **When . . . with** When valor turns to unreasonable fury, it
destroys the very quality of reasonableness that valor depends on in
battle.
4.1 Location: Before Alexandria. Caesar's camp.
1 **as** as if   8 **rage** rave   9 **breath** breathing space   10 **boot** advantage.
distraction frenzy.   11 **best heads** commanding officers   13 **files** (As
in "rank and file.")   14 **late** lately   15 **fetch him in** surround, capture him.   16 **store** provisions   17 **waste** lavish expenditure.
4.2 Location: Alexandria. Cleopatra's palace.

6 **Or** Either   8 **Shall** that will.   **Woo't** Wilt   9 **strike . . . Take all**
(1) fight to the finish, crying, "Winner take all" (2) strike sail and surrender.   10.1 *servitors* attendants.   12 **honest** true, loyal   14 **fellows** i.e., fellow servants of me.   17 **made . . . men** divided into as
many men as you are   18 **clapped up** combined   22 **Scant not my
cups** i.e., Provide generously   23 **fellow** i.e., fellow servant   24 **suffered** acknowledged, submitted to   26 **period** end   27 **Haply** Perhaps.   **if** if you do   28 **shadow** ghost.   34 **yield** reward

And I, an ass, am onion-eyed. For shame,
Transform us not to women.

ANTONY   Ho, ho, ho!
Now the witch take me if I meant it thus!   38
Grace grow where those drops fall! My hearty friends,   39
You take me in too dolorous a sense,
For I spake to you for your comfort, did desire you
To burn this night with torches. Know, my hearts,   42
I hope well of tomorrow, and will lead you
Where rather I'll expect victorious life
Than death and honor. Let's to supper, come,
And drown consideration.   *Exeunt.*   46

❧

[4.3]

Enter a company of Soldiers.

FIRST SOLDIER
    Brother, good night. Tomorrow is the day.
SECOND SOLDIER
    It will determine one way. Fare you well.   2
    Heard you of nothing strange about the streets?   3
FIRST SOLDIER   Nothing. What news?
SECOND SOLDIER
    Belike 'tis but a rumor. Good night to you.   5
FIRST SOLDIER   Well, sir, good night.

They meet other Soldiers.

SECOND SOLDIER   Soldiers, have careful watch.
THIRD SOLDIER   And you. Good night, good night.
        They place themselves in every corner of the stage.
SECOND SOLDIER   Here we. And if tomorrow   9
    Our navy thrive, I have an absolute hope
    Our landmen will stand up.
FIRST SOLDIER   'Tis a brave army, and full of purpose. 12
        Music of the hautboys is under the stage.
SECOND SOLDIER   Peace! What noise?
FIRST SOLDIER   List, list!   14
SECOND SOLDIER   Hark!
FIRST SOLDIER   Music i'th'air.
THIRD SOLDIER   Under the earth.
FOURTH SOLDIER   It signs well, does it not?   18
THIRD SOLDIER   No.
FIRST SOLDIER   Peace, I say! What should this mean?
SECOND SOLDIER
    'Tis the god Hercules, whom Antony loved,
    Now leaves him.
FIRST SOLDIER   Walk; let's see if other watchmen
    Do hear what we do.
        [They advance toward their fellow watchmen.]
SECOND SOLDIER   How now, masters?   24

ALL [*speak together*]   How now? How now? Do you
    hear this?
FIRST SOLDIER   Ay. Is't not strange?
THIRD SOLDIER   Do you hear, masters? Do you hear?
FIRST SOLDIER
    Follow the noise so far as we have quarter;   29
    Let's see how it will give off.   30
ALL   Content. 'Tis strange.   *Exeunt.*

❧

[4.4]

*Enter Antony and Cleopatra, with [Charmian and]
    others [attending].*

ANTONY
    Eros! Mine armor, Eros!
CLEOPATRA   Sleep a little.
ANTONY
    No, my chuck.—Eros, come, mine armor, Eros!   2

Enter Eros [with armor].

    Come, good fellow, put thine iron on.   3
    If fortune be not ours today, it is
    Because we brave her. Come.
CLEOPATRA   Nay, I'll help too.   5
    What's this for?   [*She helps to arm him.*]
ANTONY   Ah, let be, let be! Thou art
    The armorer of my heart. False, false; this, this. 7
CLEOPATRA
    Sooth, la, I'll help. Thus it must be.
ANTONY   Well, well,   8
    We shall thrive now. See'st thou, my good fellow?
    Go, put on thy defenses.
EROS   Briefly, sir.   10
CLEOPATRA
    Is not this buckled well?
ANTONY   Rarely, rarely.   11
    He that unbuckles this, till we do please   12
    To doff't for our repose, shall hear a storm.   13
    Thou fumblest, Eros, and my queen's a squire   14
    More tight at this than thou. Dispatch. O love,   15
    That thou couldst see my wars today, and knew'st   16
    The royal occupation! Thou shouldst see   17
    A workman in't.

Enter an armed Soldier.

                Good morrow to thee. Welcome.   18
    Thou look'st like him that knows a warlike charge. 19

---

38 the witch take me may I be bewitched   **39 Grace grow** (1) May
rue or herb of grace grow (2) May gracious fortune flourish.   **hearty**
loving   **42 burn . . . torches** i.e., revel through the night.   **46 drown
consideration** drown brooding thought in our winecups.
4.3 Location: Alexandria. Before the palace.
2 determine one way be decided, come to an end one way or the
other.   **3 about** in   **5 Belike** Probably   **9 Here we** Here's our station.   **12 brave** splendid, gallant   **12.1 *hautboys*** oboelike instruments   **14 List** Listen   **18 signs well** is a good sign   **24 masters**
good sirs. (Also in line 28.)

29 as we have quarter as our watch post extends.   **30 give off** cease.
4.4. Location: Alexandria. The palace.
2 chuck (A term of endearment.)   **3 thine iron** i.e., my armor that
you have there. (Or perhaps he is telling Eros to arm.)   **5 brave** defy
7 False You're putting it on wrong   **8 Sooth** In truth   **10 defenses**
armor.   **Briefly** In a moment   **11 Rarely** Excellently   **12–13 He . . .
storm** i.e., Anyone who attempts to burst my armor in the fight,
before I choose myself to unarm and rest, will be greeted by a storm
of blows.   **14 squire** armor-bearer of a knight   **15 tight** deft, skillful.
Dispatch Finish up.   **16–17 knew'st . . . occupation** (would that) you
could appreciate how excellently I carry out the royal art of warfare.
18 workman craftsman, professional   **19 charge** duty, responsibility.

To business that we love we rise betimes   20
And go to't with delight.
SOLDIER   A thousand, sir,
Early though 't be, have on their riveted trim   22
And at the port expect you.   *Shout. Trumpets flourish.* 23

Enter Captains and soldiers.

CAPTAIN
The morn is fair. Good morrow, General.
ALL
Good morrow, General.
ANTONY   'Tis well blown, lads.   25
This morning, like the spirit of a youth
That means to be of note, begins betimes.
So, so. Come, give me that. This way. Well said.   28
Fare thee well, dame. Whate'er becomes of me,
This is a soldier's kiss. [*He kisses her.*] Rebukable,
And worthy shameful check it were, to stand   31
On more mechanic compliment. I'll leave thee   32
Now like a man of steel.—You that will fight,
Follow me close. I'll bring you to't. Adieu.
        Exeunt [Antony, Eros, Captains, and soldiers].
CHARMIAN
Please you, retire to your chamber?
CLEOPATRA   Lead me.
He goes forth gallantly. That he and Caesar might
Determine this great war in single fight!
Then Antony—but now—Well, on.   *Exeunt.*

❖

[4.5]

*Trumpets sound. Enter Antony and Eros; [a
Soldier meeting them].*

SOLDIER
The gods make this a happy day to Antony!   1
ANTONY
Would thou and those thy scars had once prevailed   2
To make me fight at land!
SOLDIER   Hadst thou done so,
The kings that have revolted, and the soldier   4
That has this morning left thee, would have still
Followed thy heels.
ANTONY   Who's gone this morning?
SOLDIER   Who?
One ever near thee. Call for Enobarbus,
He shall not hear thee, or from Caesar's camp
Say, "I am none of thine."
ANTONY   What sayest thou?
SOLDIER   Sir,
He is with Caesar.
EROS   Sir, his chests and treasure

He has not with him.
ANTONY   Is he gone?
SOLDIER   Most certain.
ANTONY
Go, Eros, send his treasure after. Do it.
Detain no jot, I charge thee. Write to him—
I will subscribe—gentle adieus and greetings.   14
Say that I wish he never find more cause
To change a master. Oh, my fortunes have
Corrupted honest men! Dispatch.—Enobarbus!   17
                          Exeunt.

❖

[4.6]

*Flourish. Enter Agrippa, Caesar, with Enobarbus,
and Dolabella.*

CAESAR
Go forth, Agrippa, and begin the fight.
Our will is Antony be took alive;
Make it so known.
AGRIPPA   Caesar, I shall.   [*Exit.*]
CAESAR
The time of universal peace is near.   5
Prove this a prosp'rous day, the three-nooked world   6
Shall bear the olive freely.

Enter a Messenger.

MESSENGER   Antony   7
Is come into the field.
CAESAR   Go charge Agrippa   8
Plant those that have revolted in the van,   9
That Antony may seem to spend his fury
Upon himself.   *Exeunt [all but Enobarbus].*
ENOBARBUS
Alexas did revolt and went to Jewry on   12
Affairs of Antony, there did dissuade   13
Great Herod to incline himself to Caesar
And leave his master Antony. For this pains,
Caesar hath hanged him. Canidius and the rest
That fell away have entertainment but   17
No honorable trust. I have done ill,
Of which I do accuse myself so sorely   19
That I will joy no more.

Enter a Soldier of Caesar's.

SOLDIER   Enobarbus, Antony
Hath after thee sent all thy treasure, with
His bounty overplus. The messenger   22

20 **betimes** early   22 **riveted trim** i.e., armor riveted into place
23 **port** gate   25 **'Tis well blown** i.e., The morning begins well. (Or,
refers to trumpets in line 23 s.d.)   28 **Well said** Well done.   31 **check**
reproof   31–2 **stand . . . compliment** insist on vulgar and routine ceremonies of leavetaking.
4.5. Location: Before Alexandria. Antony's camp.
1 **happy** fortunate   2 **once** formerly   4 **revolted** deserted

14 **subscribe** sign   17 **Dispatch** Make haste, get on with it.
4.6. Location: Before Alexandria. Caesar's camp.
5 **The . . . near** (The Renaissance identified Octavius Caesar, or the
Emperor Augustus as he was subsequently titled, with this *Pax
Romana*, peace under the Roman Empire.)   6 **Prove this** If this prove
to be.   **three-nooked** three-cornered. (Refers to Asia, Europe, and
Africa.)   7 **bear** (1) bring forth (2) wear as a triumphal garland.
olive symbol of peace   8 **charge Agrippa** order Agrippa to   9 **van**
vanguard, front lines   12 **Jewry** Judaea   13 **dissuade** i.e., from following Antony   17 **entertainment** employment, maintenance
19 **sorely** heavily   22 **overplus** in addition.

Came on my guard, and at thy tent is now   23
Unloading of his mules.
ENOBARBUS   I give it you.
SOLDIER   Mock not, Enobarbus,
I tell you true. Best you safed the bringer   27
Out of the host. I must attend mine office,   28
Or would have done't myself. Your emperor
Continues still a Jove.   *Exit.*

ENOBARBUS
I am alone the villain of the earth,   31
And feel I am so most. O Antony,   32
Thou mine of bounty, how wouldst thou have paid   33
My better service, when my turpitude
Thou dost so crown with gold! This blows my heart.   35
If swift thought break it not, a swifter mean   36
Shall outstrike thought; but thought will do't, I feel.   37
I fight against thee? No, I will go seek
Some ditch wherein to die. The foul'st best fits
My latter part of life.   *Exit.*

❧

[4.7]

*Alarum. Drums and trumpets. Enter Agrippa
[and others].*

AGRIPPA
Retire! We have engaged ourselves too far.
Caesar himself has work, and our oppression
Exceeds what we expected.   *Exeunt.*   3

Alarums. Enter Antony, and Scarus wounded.

SCARUS
O my brave Emperor, this is fought indeed!
Had we done so at first, we had droven them home   5
With clouts about their heads.
ANTONY   Thou bleed'st apace.   6
SCARUS
I had a wound here that was like a T,
But now 'tis made an H.   [*Sound retreat*] *far off.*
ANTONY   They do retire.   8
SCARUS
We'll beat 'em into bench holes. I have yet   9
Room for six scotches more.   10

Enter Eros.

EROS
They are beaten, sir, and our advantage serves   11
For a fair victory.
SCARUS   Let us score their backs   12
And snatch 'em up, as we take hares, behind!
'Tis sport to maul a runner.
ANTONY   I will reward thee   14
Once for thy spritely comfort and tenfold
For thy good valor. Come thee on.
SCARUS   I'll halt after.   *Exeunt.*   17

❧

[4.8]

*Alarum. Enter Antony again in a march; Scarus,
with others.*

ANTONY
We have beat him to his camp. Run one before   1
And let the Queen know of our gests. [*Exit a Soldier.*]
                   Tomorrow,   2
Before the sun shall see 's, we'll spill the blood
That has today escaped. I thank you all,
For doughty-handed are you, and have fought   5
Not as you served the cause, but as 't had been   6
Each man's like mine; you have shown all Hectors.   7
Enter the city, clip your wives, your friends,   8
Tell them your feats, whilst they with joyful tears
Wash the congealment from your wounds and kiss
The honored gashes whole.

Enter Cleopatra [attended].

          [*To Scarus*] Give me thy hand;
To this great fairy I'll commend thy acts,   12
Make her thanks bless thee. [*To Cleopatra*] O thou day
o'th' world,   13
Chain mine armed neck; leap thou, attire and all,   14
Through proof of harness to my heart, and there   15
Ride on the pants triumphing!   [*They embrace.*]
CLEOPATRA   Lord of lords,   16
O infinite virtue, com'st thou smiling from   17
The world's great snare uncaught?
ANTONY   My nightingale,
We have beat them to their beds. What, girl, though
gray
Do something mingle with our younger brown, yet
ha' we   20
A brain that nourishes our nerves and can   21

---

23 on my guard while I was standing guard   **27 Best you safed** You would do well to provide safe-conduct for   **28 host** army.   **attend mine office** see to my duties   **31 alone the** the only, the greatest   **32 And . . . most** and am the one who feels it most.   **33 mine** abundant store   **35 blows** causes to swell to the bursting point   **36 mean** i.e., suicide   **37 thought** melancholy.   **do't** i.e., break my heart   **4.7. Location: Field of battle between the camps.**
2 has work is hard pressed.   **our oppression** the heavy attacks against us   **3 s.d.** *Exeunt* (The cleared stage technically marks a new scene, although the alarums provide a sense of continuous action.)   **5 droven** driven   **6 clouts** (1) bandages (2) blows and knocks   **8 H** i.e., the bottom of the T has been cut across to make an H lying on its side. (There is a pun on *ache*, pronounced *aitch*.)   **9 bench holes** the holes of privies, i.e., any desperate place to hide.   **10 scotches** cuts

11–12 our . . . victory i.e., we are in such a favorable position that a complete victory seems in prospect.   **12 score** mark by cuts from a whip   **14 a runner** one in retreat.   **17 halt** limp
4.8. Location: Before Alexandria. The action is virtually continuous.
1 beat driven.   **Run one** Let someone run   **2 gests** deeds.
5 doughty-handed valiant   **6–7 Not . . . mine** not as if you were merely serving the general cause, but as if it were your cause personally   **7 shown** shown yourselves   **8 clip** embrace   **12 fairy** enchantress, dispenser of good fortune   **13 day** light   **14 Chain . . . neck** hang around my neck in an embrace like a medal on a chain   **15 proof of harness** proof-armor, tested armor   **16 pants** heartbeats   **17 virtue** valor   **20 something** somewhat   **21 nerves** sinews, tendons

Get goal for goal of youth. Behold this man;   22
Commend unto his lips thy favoring hand.—   23
Kiss it, my warrior. [*Scarus kisses Cleopatra's hand.*] He
   hath fought today
As if a god, in hate of mankind, had
Destroyed in such a shape.

CLEOPATRA   I'll give thee, friend,
An armor all of gold; it was a king's.

ANTONY
He has deserved it, were it carbuncled   28
Like holy Phoebus' car. Give me thy hand.   29
Through Alexandria make a jolly march;
Bear our hacked targets like the men that owe them.   31
Had our great palace the capacity
To camp this host, we all would sup together   33
And drink carouses to the next day's fate,   34
Which promises royal peril. Trumpeters,   35
With brazen din blast you the city's ear;
Make mingle with our rattling taborins,   37
That heaven and earth may strike their sounds
   together,   38
Applauding our approach. [*Trumpets sound.*] *Exeunt.*

❧

[4.9]

*Enter a Sentry and his company. Enobarbus
follows.*

SENTRY
If we be not relieved within this hour,
We must return to th' court of guard. The night   2
Is shiny, and they say we shall embattle   3
By the second hour i'th' morn.

FIRST WATCH   This last day was a shrewd one to 's.   5
ENOBARBUS   Oh, bear me witness, night—
SECOND WATCH
What man is this?

FIRST WATCH   Stand close, and list him.   8
                          [*They stand aside.*]

ENOBARBUS
Be witness to me, O thou blessèd moon,
When men revolted shall upon record   10
Bear hateful memory: poor Enobarbus did
Before thy face repent.

SENTRY   Enobarbus?
SECOND WATCH   Peace! Hark further.

ENOBARBUS
O sovereign mistress of true melancholy,   15
The poisonous damp of night disponge upon me,   16
That life, a very rebel to my will,
May hang no longer on me. Throw my heart
Against the flint and hardness of my fault,
Which, being dried with grief, will break to powder   20
And finish all foul thoughts. O Antony,
Nobler than my revolt is infamous,
Forgive me in thine own particular,   23
But let the world rank me in register   24
A master-leaver and a fugitive.   25
O Antony! O Antony!   [*He dies.*]

FIRST WATCH   Let's speak to him.
SENTRY
Let's hear him, for the things he speaks
May concern Caesar.

SECOND WATCH   Let's do so. But he sleeps.
SENTRY
Swoons rather, for so bad a prayer as his
Was never yet for sleep.

FIRST WATCH   Go we to him.   31
                 [*They approach Enobarbus.*]

SECOND WATCH   Awake, sir, awake. Speak to us.
FIRST WATCH   Hear you, sir?
SENTRY   The hand of death hath raught him.   34
                         Drums afar off.

Hark, the drums demurely wake the sleepers.   35
Let us bear him to th' court of guard;
He is of note. Our hour is fully out.   37

SECOND WATCH
Come on, then. He may recover yet.
                Exeunt [*with the body*].

❧

[4.10]

Enter Antony and Scarus, with their army.

ANTONY
Their preparation is today by sea;
We please them not by land.

SCARUS   For both, my lord.
ANTONY
I would they'd fight i'th' fire or i'th' air;   3
We'd fight there too. But this it is: our foot   4
Upon the hills adjoining to the city
Shall stay with us—order for sea is given;   6

---

22 Get . . . of i.e., stay competitively equal with.   **this man** i.e., Scarus
23 Commend Entrust, commit   **28 carbuncled** set with jewels
29 Phoebus' car the chariot of the sun.   **31 Bear . . . them** bear our
hacked shields, well suited to the warriors who, like their shields,
have sustained blows. (*Owe* means "own.")   **33 camp this host**
accommodate this army   **34 carouses** toasts   **35 royal peril** i.e., war,
the sport of monarchs.   **37 taborins** drums   **38 That . . . together** i.e.,
that the heavens may echo and augment the loud noise of the drums
4.9 Location: Caesar's camp.
2 court of guard guardroom.   **3 shiny** bright, moonlit.   **embattle**
assemble for the combat   **5 shrewd** unlucky   **8 close** concealed.
list listen to   **10 revolted** who have broken their allegiance.   **upon
record** in the record of history

15 mistress . . . melancholy i.e., the moon, so addressed because of
her supposed influence in causing lunacy   **16 disponge** pour down
(as from a squeezed sponge)   **20 Which** i.e., the heart.   **dried with
grief** (Cold and melancholy blood was thought to strangle and dry
up the heart.)   **23 in . . . particular** in your own person   **24 rank me
in register** put me down in its records   **25 master-leaver** (1) one who
deserts his master (2) nonpareil of deserters.   **fugitive** deserter.
31 for a prelude to   **34 raught** reached   **35 demurely** with solemn
sound   **37 of note** of rank.
4.10 Location: The field of battle.
3 fire . . . air (Along with earth and water, where Antony is already
prepared, fire and air make up the traditional four elements of all
matter.)   **4 foot** foot soldiers   **6 for sea** to fight at sea

They have put forth the haven—   7
Where their appointment we may best discover   8
And look on their endeavor.   *Exeunt.*

❖

[4.11]

Enter Caesar and his army.

CAESAR
But being charged, we will be still by land,   1
Which, as I take't, we shall; for his best force   2
Is forth to man his galleys. To the vales,   3
And hold our best advantage.   *Exeunt.*   4

❖

[4.12]

Enter Antony and Scarus.

ANTONY
Yet they are not joined. Where yond pine does stand,
I shall discover all. I'll bring thee word
Straight how 'tis like to go.   *Exit.*
                    Alarum afar off, as at a sea fight.
SCARUS   Swallows have built   3
In Cleopatra's sails their nests. The augurers   4
Say they know not, they cannot tell, look grimly,
And dare not speak their knowledge. Antony
Is valiant, and dejected, and by starts
His fretted fortunes give him hope and fear   8
Of what he has and has not.

Enter Antony.

ANTONY   All is lost!
This foul Egyptian hath betrayèd me.
My fleet hath yielded to the foe, and yonder
They cast their caps up and carouse together
Like friends long lost. Triple-turned whore! 'Tis thou   13
Hast sold me to this novice, and my heart
Makes only wars on thee. Bid them all fly;
For when I am revenged upon my charm,   16
I have done all. Bid them all fly. Begone!
                                     [Exit Scarus.]

O sun, thy uprise shall I see no more.
Fortune and Antony part here; even here
Do we shake hands. All come to this? The hearts   20
That spanieled me at heels, to whom I gave   21
Their wishes, do discandy, melt their sweets   22

On blossoming Caesar; and this pine is barked   23
That overtopped them all. Betrayed I am.
Oh, this false soul of Egypt! This grave charm,   25
Whose eye becked forth my wars and called them
    home,   26
Whose bosom was my crownet, my chief end,   27
Like a right gypsy hath at fast and loose   28
Beguiled me to the very heart of loss.   29
[Calling] What, Eros, Eros!

Enter Cleopatra.

                    Ah, thou spell! Avaunt!   30
CLEOPATRA
Why is my lord enraged against his love?
ANTONY
Vanish, or I shall give thee thy deserving
And blemish Caesar's triumph. Let him take thee   33
And hoist thee up to the shouting plebeians!
Follow his chariot, like the greatest spot   35
Of all thy sex; most monsterlike be shown   36
For poor'st diminutives, for dolts, and let   37
Patient Octavia plow thy visage up
With her preparèd nails!   *Exit Cleopatra.*
                              'Tis well thou'rt gone,
If it be well to live; but better 'twere
Thou fell'st into my fury, for one death   41
Might have prevented many.—Eros, ho!—   42
The shirt of Nessus is upon me. Teach me,   43
Alcides, thou mine ancestor, thy rage.   44
Let me lodge Lichas on the horns o'th' moon,   45
And with those hands, that grasped the heaviest club,
Subdue my worthiest self. The witch shall die.
To the young Roman boy she hath sold me, and I fall
Under this plot. She dies for't.—Eros, ho!   *Exit.*

❖

[4.13]

Enter Cleopatra, Charmian, Iras, [and] Mardian.

CLEOPATRA
Help me, my women! Oh, he's more mad

---

7 forth forth from   **8 appointment** disposition of forces, equipment.
discover descry
4.11. Location: The field of battle.
1 But being Unless we are.   **still** inactive   **2 we shall** i.e., we will be
left undisturbed   **3 Is forth** has gone forth.   **vales** valleys   **4 hold . . .
advantage** take the most advantageous position.
**4.12 Location: The field of battle at first, though by scene's end the
action appears to be located in Alexandria.**
3 Straight immediately.   **like** likely   **4 augurers** augurs, soothsayers
8 fretted worn away, vexed, checkered   **13 Triple-turned** Three times
faithless (to Julius Caesar, Gnaeus Pompey, and now Antony)
16 charm practicer of charms or spells   **20 shake hands** i.e., in parting.   **hearts** good fellows   **21 spanieled** fawned upon like a spaniel
22 Their wishes whatever they wished.   **discandy** melt, dissolve

23 this pine i.e., Antony.   **barked** stripped of its bark and thus killed
25 This grave charm i.e., This sorceress who casts fatal spells
26 becked beckoned   **27 Whose . . . end** whose embraces were the
crown of my achievement and my goal   **28 right** veritable.   **fast and
loose** a cheating game in which the victim bets that he can make fast
a knot in an ingeniously coiled rope, whereupon the knot is pulled
loose   **29 loss** ruin.   **30 spell** enchantment.   **Avaunt!** Begone!
33 blemish Caesar's triumph i.e., mutilate you and thereby frustrate
Caesar's plan to display you in his triumphal procession into Rome.
35 spot blemish, disgrace   **36 shown** exhibited   **37 diminutives**
underlings, i.e., the populace   **41 Thou fell'st into** you had fallen a
victim to   **42 many** i.e., many other deaths resulting from my rage.
43–5 Nessus . . . Lichas (When Hercules or *Alcides* had fatally
wounded the centaur *Nessus* for trying to rape Hercules's wife
Deianira, Nessus vengefully gave his blood-soaked shirt to Deianira
as a supposed love charm for her husband. The poison gave Hercules
such agony that he cast his page *Lichas* into the air.)
**4.13 Location: Alexandria. This scene appears to follow scene 12
closely. The sense of location is very fluid, and it is not clear where
the end of scene 12 takes place.**

Than Telamon for his shield; the boar of Thessaly   2
Was never so embossed.

CHARMIAN   To th' monument!   3
There lock yourself and send him word you are dead.
The soul and body rive not more in parting   5
Than greatness going off.

CLEOPATRA   To th' monument!   6
Mardian, go tell him I have slain myself.
Say that the last I spoke was "Antony,"
And word it, prithee, piteously. Hence, Mardian,
And bring me how he takes my death. To th'
   monument!   *Exeunt.*

❧

[4.14]

Enter Antony and Eros.

ANTONY
Eros, thou yet behold'st me?

EROS   Ay, noble lord.

ANTONY
Sometime we see a cloud that's dragonish,   2
A vapor sometime like a bear or lion,
A towered citadel, a pendant rock,   4
A forkèd mountain, or blue promontory
With trees upon't that nod unto the world
And mock our eyes with air. Thou hast seen these
   signs;
They are black vesper's pageants.

EROS   Ay, my lord.   8

ANTONY
That which is now a horse, even with a thought
The rack dislimns and makes it indistinct   10
As water is in water.

EROS   It does, my lord.

ANTONY
My good knave Eros, now thy captain is   12
Even such a body. Here I am Antony,
Yet cannot hold this visible shape, my knave.
I made these wars for Egypt, and the Queen,
Whose heart I thought I had, for she had mine—
Which whilst it was mine had annexed unto't
A million more, now lost—she, Eros, has
Packed cards with Caesar and false-played my glory   19
Unto an enemy's triumph.   20

Nay, weep not, gentle Eros. There is left us
Ourselves to end ourselves.

Enter Mardian.

             Oh, thy vile lady!
She has robbed me of my sword.

MARDIAN   No, Antony,   23
My mistress loved thee, and her fortunes mingled
With thine entirely.

ANTONY   Hence, saucy eunuch, peace!
She hath betrayed me and shall die the death.   26

MARDIAN
Death of one person can be paid but once,   27
And that she has discharged. What thou wouldst do   28
Is done unto thy hand. The last she spake   29
Was, "Antony, most noble Antony!"
Then in the midst a tearing groan did break
The name of Antony; it was divided   32
Between her heart and lips. She rendered life   33
Thy name so buried in her.

ANTONY   Dead, then?

MARDIAN   Dead.   34

ANTONY
Unarm, Eros. The long day's task is done,
And we must sleep. [*To Mardian*] That thou depart'st
   hence safe
Does pay thy labor richly; go.   *Exit Mardian.*
       Off, pluck off! [*Eros unarms him.*]
The sevenfold shield of Ajax cannot keep   38
The battery from my heart. Oh, cleave, my sides!   39
Heart, once be stronger than thy continent;   40
Crack thy frail case! Apace, Eros, apace.   41
No more a soldier. Bruisèd pieces, go;
You have been nobly borne.—From me awhile.   43
               Exit Eros.
I will o'ertake thee, Cleopatra, and
Weep for my pardon. So it must be, for now
All length is torture; since the torch is out,   46
Lie down, and stray no farther. Now all labor
Mars what it does; yea, very force entangles   48
Itself with strength. Seal then, and all is done.   49
Eros!—I come, my queen.—Eros!—Stay for me.   50
Where souls do couch on flowers, we'll hand in hand,   51
And with our sprightly port make the ghosts gaze.   52

---

2 Telamon Ajax Telamon, who after the capture of Troy went mad and slew himself when he was not awarded the shield and armor of Achilles.   **the boar of Thessaly** the boar sent by Diana or Artemis to ravage the fields of Calydon, slain by Meleager   **3 embossed** foaming at the mouth from rage and exhaustion.   **monument** tomb presumably built to house Cleopatra's royal remains after her death, like the pyramids.   **5 rive** split, sever   **6 going off** i.e., bidding farewell to its glory.
4.14 Location: Alexandria. (See location of scene 13; again, the sense of time is immediate and the place is fluid.)
2 dragonish shaped like a dragon   **4 pendant** overhanging   **8 black . . . pageants** i.e., the evanescent splendor of a sunset heralding the approach of night.   **10 The rack dislimns** the mass of cloud changes its shape   **12 knave** lad   **19 Packed cards** i.e., stacked the deck.   **false-played** falsely played away   **20 triumph** (1) victory (2) trump card.

23 sword i.e., prowess as a soldier, masculinity.   **26 die the death** be put to death.   **27 of** by   **28 discharged** paid.   **29 unto thy hand** for you, without your having to lift a finger.   **32–3 it . . . lips** i.e., she groaned out half of Antony's name and then died with the unspoken part in her heart only.   **33–4 She . . . in her** She gave back to Nature that part of your name thus buried in her heart.   **38 sevenfold** with seven thicknesses. (The shield of Ajax was of brass reinforced with seven thicknesses of oxhide.)   **39 battery** battering   **40 thy continent** that which contains you   **41 Apace** Quickly   **43 From** Go from   **46 length** prolongation of life.   **the torch** i.e., the life of Cleopatra   **48 very force** any resolute action   **49 with strength** i.e., with its own strength.   **Seal** Finish the business (as in sealing a letter)   **50 Eros** (The meaning of Eros's name, erotic love, is especially apt here.)   **51 couch** lie (here, in the Elysian fields)   **52 sprightly** (1) high-spirited (2) spiritlike, ghostly.   **port** bearing

Dido and her Aeneas shall want troops,   53
And all the haunt be ours.—Come, Eros, Eros!   54

Enter Eros.

EROS
What would my lord?
ANTONY   Since Cleopatra died
I have lived in such dishonor that the gods
Detest my baseness. I, that with my sword
Quartered the world, and o'er green Neptune's back   58
With ships made cities, condemn myself to lack   59
The courage of a woman—less noble mind
Than she which by her death our Caesar tells
"I am conqueror of myself." Thou art sworn, Eros,
That when the exigent should come which now   63
Is come indeed, when I should see behind me
Th'inevitable prosecution of   65
Disgrace and horror, that on my command
Thou then wouldst kill me. Do't. The time is come.
Thou strik'st not me, 'tis Caesar thou defeat'st.
Put color in thy cheek.
EROS   The gods withhold me!   69
Shall I do that which all the Parthian darts,
Though enemy, lost aim and could not?
ANTONY   Eros,
Wouldst thou be windowed in great Rome and see   72
Thy master thus with pleached arms, bending down   73
His corrigible neck, his face subdued   74
To penetrative shame, whilst the wheeled seat   75
Of fortunate Caesar, drawn before him, branded   76
His baseness that ensued?
EROS   I would not see't.   77
ANTONY
Come, then, for with a wound I must be cured.
Draw that thy honest sword, which thou hast worn   79
Most useful for thy country.
EROS   Oh, sir, pardon me!   80
ANTONY
When I did make thee free, swor'st thou not then
To do this when I bade thee? Do it at once,
Or thy precedent services are all   83
But accidents unpurposed. Draw, and come.   84
EROS
Turn from me then that noble countenance

Wherein the worship of the whole world lies.   86
ANTONY   Lo thee!   [*He turns away.*]
EROS [*drawing his sword*]
My sword is drawn.
ANTONY   Then let it do at once
That thing why thou hast drawn it.
EROS   My dear master,
My captain, and my emperor, let me say,
Before I strike this bloody stroke, farewell.
ANTONY   'Tis said, man, and farewell.
EROS
Farewell, great chief. Shall I strike now?
ANTONY   Now, Eros.
EROS (*kills himself*)
Why, there then! Thus I do escape the sorrow
Of Antony's death.   [*He dies.*]
ANTONY   Thrice nobler than myself!
Thou teachest me, O valiant Eros, what
I should, and thou couldst not. My queen and Eros   97
Have by their brave instruction got upon me   98
A nobleness in record. But I will be   99
A bridegroom in my death, and run into't
As to a lover's bed. Come, then, and Eros,
Thy master dies thy scholar. To do thus
I learned of thee.   [*He falls on his sword.*]
                How, not dead? Not dead?
The guard, ho! Oh, dispatch me!   104

Enter [Dercetus and others of] a Guard.

FIRST GUARD   What's the noise?
ANTONY   I have done my work ill, friends.
Oh, make an end of what I have begun!
SECOND GUARD   The star is fallen.
FIRST GUARD   And time is at his period.   109
ALL   Alas, and woe!
ANTONY   Let him that loves me strike me dead.
FIRST GUARD   Not I.
SECOND GUARD   Nor I.
THIRD GUARD   Nor anyone.   *Exeunt [Guard].*
DERCETUS
Thy death and fortunes bid thy followers fly.
This sword but shown to Caesar, with this tidings,
Shall enter me with him. [*He takes up Antony's sword.*]   117

Enter Diomedes.

DIOMEDES   Where's Antony?
DERCETUS   There, Diomed, there.
DIOMEDES
Lives he? Wilt thou not answer, man? [*Exit Dercetus.*]
ANTONY
Art thou there, Diomed? Draw thy sword and give me
Sufficing strokes for death.
DIOMEDES   Most absolute lord,
My mistress Cleopatra sent me to thee.

53 Dido . . . troops We will be the most distinguished lovers in the Elysian fields, outshining even the Queen of Carthage and her famous lover. (In the *Aeneid*, Aeneas deserts Dido in order to found Rome, putting public good ahead of private passion as Antony does not. Dido scorns Aeneas when they meet in the underworld; Antony here imagines himself and Cleopatra in the Elysian fields.) **want troops** lack followers **54 all . . . ours** i.e., we shall be the objects of everyone's attention. **58–9 Quartered . . . cities** divided and conquered the world, and at sea assembled flotillas as dense and populous as cities **59 to lack** for lacking **63 exigent** exigency, time of compelling need **65 prosecution** consequence **69 The gods withhold me!** i.e., God forbid! **72 windowed** placed as in a window **73 pleached** folded or bound **74 corrigible** submissive to correction **75 penetrative** penetrating. **wheeled seat** chariot **76–7 branded . . . ensued** stigmatized, as by a brand, the shame of him that followed. **79 honest** honorable **80 pardon me!** excuse me from doing this! **83 precedent** former **84 accidents unpurposed** events leading to no purpose.

86 worship honor, worth **97 I should . . . not** I should have done for myself and you couldn't do for me. **98–9 got . . . record** won a noble place in history before I have. **104 dispatch** finish **109 his period** its end. **117 enter . . . him** admit me to his service, put me in his good graces.

ANTONY
When did she send thee?
DIOMEDES   Now, my lord.
ANTONY   Where is she?
DIOMEDES
Locked in her monument. She had a prophesying fear
Of what hath come to pass. For when she saw—
Which never shall be found—you did suspect   127
She had disposed with Caesar, and that your rage   128
Would not be purged, she sent you word she was
    dead;
But, fearing since how it might work, hath sent
Me to proclaim the truth, and I am come,
I dread, too late.
ANTONY
Too late, good Diomed. Call my guard, I prithee.
DIOMEDES [*calling*]
What ho, the Emperor's guard! The guard, what ho!
Come, your lord calls.

Enter four or five of the Guard of Antony.

ANTONY
Bear me, good friends, where Cleopatra bides.   136
'Tis the last service that I shall command you.
FIRST GUARD
Woe, woe are we, sir, you may not live to wear   138
All your true followers out.
ALL   Most heavy day!   139
ANTONY
Nay, good my fellows, do not please sharp fate
To grace it with your sorrows. Bid that welcome   141
Which comes to punish us, and we punish it,
Seeming to bear it lightly. Take me up.
I have led you oft; carry me now, good friends,
And have my thanks for all.
              Exeunt, bearing Antony [and Eros].

[4.15]

*Enter Cleopatra and her maids aloft, with
Charmian and Iras.*

CLEOPATRA
Oh, Charmian, I will never go from hence.
CHARMIAN
Be comforted, dear madam.
CLEOPATRA   No, I will not.
All strange and terrible events are welcome,
But comforts we despise. Our size of sorrow,
Proportioned to our cause, must be as great
As that which makes it.

Enter [below] Diomedes.

              How now? Is he dead?

DIOMEDES
His death's upon him, but not dead.
Look out o'th'other side your monument;
His guard have brought him thither.

*Enter [below] Antony, and the Guard
[bearing him].*

CLEOPATRA   O sun,
Burn the great sphere thou mov'st in; darkling stand   11
The varying shore o'th' world! O Antony,
Antony, Antony! Help, Charmian, help, Iras, help!
Help, friends below! Let's draw him hither.
ANTONY   Peace!
Not Caesar's valor hath o'erthrown Antony,
But Antony's hath triumphed on itself.
CLEOPATRA
So it should be, that none but Antony
Should conquer Antony; but woe 'tis so!
ANTONY
I am dying, Egypt, dying. Only
I here importune death awhile, until   20
Of many thousand kisses the poor last
I lay upon thy lips.
CLEOPATRA   I dare not, dear—   22
Dear my lord, pardon—I dare not,
Lest I be taken. Not th'imperious show   24
Of the full-fortuned Caesar ever shall
Be brooched with me. If knife, drugs, serpents, have   26
Edge, sting, or operation, I am safe.   27
Your wife Octavia, with her modest eyes
And still conclusion, shall acquire no honor   29
Demuring upon me. But come, come, Antony—   30
Help me, my women—we must draw thee up.
Assist, good friends.
ANTONY   Oh, quick, or I am gone.
                        [*They begin lifting.*]
CLEOPATRA
Here's sport indeed! How heavy weighs my lord!
Our strength is all gone into heaviness,   34
That makes the weight. Had I great Juno's power,
The strong-winged Mercury should fetch thee up
And set thee by Jove's side. Yet come a little;
Wishers were ever fools. Oh, come, come, come!   38
          They heave Antony aloft to Cleopatra.
And welcome, welcome! Die when thou hast lived;   39
Quicken with kissing. Had my lips that power,   40
Thus would I wear them out.   [*She kisses him.*]
ALL   A heavy sight!   42
ANTONY   I am dying, Egypt, dying.
Give me some wine, and let me speak a little.

---

127 **found** found true   128 **disposed with** come to terms with
136 **bides** abides, dwells.   138–9 **live . . . out** outlive those that serve
you.   141 **To grace** by gracing or honoring
4.15. Location: Alexandria. Cleopatra's monument.
0.1 *aloft* in the gallery above the main stage

11 **sphere** concentric sphere in which, according to Ptolemaic astronomy, the sun moved about the earth as did the planets and stars.
darkling in darkness   20 **importune** i.e., beg a delay of   22 **I dare
not** i.e., I dare not come down   24 **th'imperious show** the imperial
triumphal procession   26 **brooched** adorned (as with a brooch)
27 **operation** power, efficacy   29 **still conclusion** silent judgment
30 **Demuring** looking demurely   34 **heaviness** (1) sadness (2) weight
38 **Wishers . . . fools** Those who wish for things are always fools.
39 **Die . . . lived** i.e., Die after living intensely. (With a pun on *die* suggesting sexual consummation; hence *Quicken* in line 40.)   40 **Quicken**
revive   42 **heavy** doleful

CLEOPATRA
No, let me speak, and let me rail so high
That the false huswife Fortune break her wheel, 46
Provoked by my offense.

ANTONY   One word, sweet Queen: 47
Of Caesar seek your honor, with your safety. Oh! 48

CLEOPATRA
They do not go together.

ANTONY   Gentle, hear me.
None about Caesar trust but Proculeius.

CLEOPATRA
My resolution and my hands I'll trust,
None about Caesar.

ANTONY
The miserable change now at my end
Lament nor sorrow at, but please your thoughts 54
In feeding them with those my former fortunes,
Wherein I lived the greatest prince o'th' world,
The noblest; and do now not basely die,
Not cowardly put off my helmet to
My countryman—a Roman by a Roman
Valiantly vanquished. Now my spirit is going;
I can no more.

CLEOPATRA   Noblest of men, woo't die? 61
Hast thou no care of me? Shall I abide
In this dull world, which in thy absence is
No better than a sty? [Antony dies.] Oh, see, my
    women,
The crown o'th'earth doth melt. My lord!
Oh, withered is the garland of the war;
The soldier's pole is fall'n! Young boys and girls 67
Are level now with men. The odds is gone, 68
And there is nothing left remarkable
Beneath the visiting moon.   [She faints.]

CHARMIAN Oh, quietness, lady!

IRAS She's dead too, our sovereign.

CHARMIAN Lady!

IRAS Madam!

CHARMIAN Oh, madam, madam, madam!

IRAS Royal Egypt, Empress!   [Cleopatra stirs.]

CHARMIAN Peace, peace, Iras.

CLEOPATRA
No more but e'en a woman, and commanded
By such poor passion as the maid that milks
And does the meanest chares. It were for me 80
To throw my scepter at the injurious gods,
To tell them that this world did equal theirs
Till they had stol'n our jewel. All's but naught;
Patience is sottish, and impatience does 84
Become a dog that's mad. Then is it sin 85
To rush into the secret house of death
Ere death dare come to us? How do you, women?

What, what, good cheer! Why, how now, Charmian?
My noble girls! Ah, women, women! Look,
Our lamp is spent, it's out. Good sirs, take heart. 90
We'll bury him; and then, what's brave, what's noble, 91
Let's do't after the high Roman fashion
And make death proud to take us. Come, away.
This case of that huge spirit now is cold.
Ah, women, women! Come. We have no friend
But resolution, and the briefest end. 96
    Exeunt, [those above] bearing off Antony's body.

❧

[5.1]

Enter Caesar, Agrippa, Dolabella, Maecenas,
[Gallus, Proculeius,] with his council of war.

CAESAR
Go to him, Dolabella, bid him yield;
Being so frustrate, tell him, he mocks 2
The pauses that he makes.

DOLABELLA   Caesar, I shall.   [Exit.] 3

Enter Dercetus, with the sword of Antony.

CAESAR
Wherefore is that? And what art thou that dar'st
Appear thus to us?

DERCETUS   I am called Dercetus.
Mark Antony I served, who best was worthy
Best to be served. Whilst he stood up and spoke
He was my master, and I wore my life
To spend upon his haters. If thou please 9
To take me to thee, as I was to him
I'll be to Caesar; if thou pleasest not,
I yield thee up my life.

CAESAR   What is't thou say'st?

DERCETUS
I say, O Caesar, Antony is dead.

CAESAR
The breaking of so great a thing should make 14
A greater crack. The round world 15
Should have shook lions into civil streets 16
And citizens to their dens. The death of Antony 17
Is not a single doom; in the name lay 18
A moiety of the world.

DERCETUS   He is dead, Caesar, 19
Not by a public minister of justice,
Nor by a hirèd knife; but that self hand 21
Which writ his honor in the acts it did
Hath, with the courage which the heart did lend it,

---

46 **false huswife** treacherous hussy   47 **offense** offensive speech.
48 **Of** from   54 **Lament** i.e., neither lament   61 **woo't** wilt thou
67 **pole** polestar or battle standard. (Probably with a suggestion of a
sexual potency now withered and fallen through death.)   68 **The
odds is gone** The distinction between great and small has disappeared   80 **chares** chores, drudgery.   **were** would be fitting
84–5 **Patience … mad** i.e., Patience is for fools, and impatience is for
the mad; both are useless here.

90 **Good sirs** (Addressed to the women.)   91 **brave** fine   96 **briefest**
swiftest
5.1. Location: Alexandria. Caesar's camp.
2 **frustrate** helpless, baffled   2–3 **mocks … makes** makes himself
ridiculous by his delays (in yielding).   9 **spend** expend   14 **breaking** (1) destruction (2) disclosure   15 **crack** (1) cracking apart (2) loud
report.   16 **civil** city   17 **their** i.e., the lions', or else, the citizens
scurry to safety indoors, in their own "dens." (In either case, nature is
inverted in a kind of disorder that earlier accompanied the death of
Julius Caesar.)   18 **Is … doom** i.e., signifies the death and destruction of much more than a single man   19 **moiety** half   21 **self** same

Splitted the heart. This is his sword.
                              [*He offers the sword.*]
I robbed his wound of it. Behold it stained
With his most noble blood.
CAESAR   Look you sad, friends?
The gods rebuke me, but it is tidings   27
To wash the eyes of kings.
AGRIPPA   And strange it is
That nature must compel us to lament
Our most persisted deeds.
MAECENAS   His taints and honors   30
Waged equal with him.
AGRIPPA   A rarer spirit never   31
Did steer humanity; but you gods will give us   32
Some faults to make us men. Caesar is touched.
MAECENAS
When such a spacious mirror's set before him,
He needs must see himself.
CAESAR   O Antony,
I have followed thee to this; but we do launch   36
Diseases in our bodies. I must perforce   37
Have shown to thee such a declining day,   38
Or look on thine; we could not stall together   39
In the whole world. But yet let me lament
With tears as sovereign as the blood of hearts   41
That thou, my brother, my competitor   42
In top of all design, my mate in empire,   43
Friend and companion in the front of war,   44
The arm of mine own body, and the heart   45
Where mine his thoughts did kindle—that our stars,   46
Unreconciliable, should divide   47
Our equalness to this. Hear me, good friends—   48

                    Enter an Egyptian.

But I will tell you at some meeter season.   49
The business of this man looks out of him;   50
We'll hear him what he says.—Whence are you?   51
EGYPTIAN
A poor Egyptian yet, the Queen my mistress,   52
Confined in all she has, her monument,
Of thy intents desires instruction,
That she preparedly may frame herself   55
To th' way she's forced to.
CAESAR   Bid her have good heart.
She soon shall know of us, by some of ours,   57

How honorable and how kindly we
Determine for her; for Caesar cannot live
To be ungentle.
EGYPTIAN   So the gods preserve thee!   *Exit.*
CAESAR
Come hither, Proculeius. Go and say
We purpose her no shame. Give her what comforts   62
The quality of her passion shall require,   63
Lest, in her greatness, by some mortal stroke   64
She do defeat us; for her life in Rome   65
Would be eternal in our triumph. Go,   66
And with your speediest bring us what she says   67
And how you find of her.
PROCULEIUS   Caesar, I shall.   68
                              Exit Proculeius.
CAESAR   Gallus, go you along.   [*Exit Gallus.*]
                              Where's Dolabella,
To second Proculeius?
ALL   Dolabella!
CAESAR
Let him alone, for I remember now   71
How he's employed. He shall in time be ready.
Go with me to my tent, where you shall see
How hardly I was drawn into this war,   74
How calm and gentle I proceeded still   75
In all my writings. Go with me and see   76
What I can show in this.   *Exeunt.*

❧

[5.2]

Enter Cleopatra, Charmian, Iras, and Mardian.

CLEOPATRA
My desolation does begin to make
A better life. 'Tis paltry to be Caesar;   2
Not being Fortune, he's but Fortune's knave,   3
A minister of her will. And it is great
To do that thing that ends all other deeds,   5
Which shackles accidents and bolts up change,   6
Which sleeps and never palates more the dung,   7
The beggar's nurse and Caesar's.   8
          Enter [to the gates of the monument] Proculeius.
PROCULEIUS
Caesar sends greeting to the Queen of Egypt,
And bids thee study on what fair demands   10
Thou mean'st to have him grant thee.
CLEOPATRA   What's thy name?

27 **but it is** if it is not   **30 persisted** persistently desired or pursued
31 Waged equal with battled equally in   **32 steer humanity** govern
any individual.   **will give** insist on giving   **36 followed** pursued
36–7 but . . . bodies i.e., I have hurt you to cure myself, as men lance
diseases in their own bodies   **37 perforce** necessarily   **38 shown to
thee** i.e., suffered myself at your hands   **39 stall** dwell   **41 as sovereign . . . hearts** as precious or efficacious as heart's blood   **42 competitor** associate, partner (and rival)   **43 In . . . design** at the head of
every grand enterprise   **44 front** forehead, face   **45–6 the heart . . .
kindle** the brave heart where my heart kindled its (*his*) thoughts of
courage   **47–8 should . . . this** should divide our equal partnership to
this extreme.   **49 meeter season** more suitable time.   **50 looks . . .
him** reveals itself in his expression   **51 Whence are you?** Where do
you come from?   **52 A . . . yet** i.e., Egyptian Cleopatra, still reduced
in circumstance (and awaiting your will), or, I am a poor Egyptian
still, though subject to Rome's authority   **55 frame herself** shape her
course of action   **57 ours** my people

62 **purpose** intend   **63 passion** grief   **64 greatness** greatness of spirit
65 life in Rome presence in Rome alive   **66 eternal in our triumph**
an eternal glory in my triumphal procession.   **67 with your speediest** as quickly as you can   **68 of** concerning   **71 Let him alone** Don't
bother about him now   **74 hardly** reluctantly   **75 still** always
76 writings i.e., letters to Antony.
5.2. Location: Alexandria. Cleopatra's monument.
2 better i.e., rising above the vicissitudes of fortune   **3 knave** servant
5–8 To do . . . Caesar's i.e., to commit suicide, a sleep that arrests accident and change, and in which the sleeper relishes no more the
dungy earth that sustains both Caesar and the beggar.   **10 study on**
consider carefully

PROCULEIUS
My name is Proculeius.

CLEOPATRA   Antony
Did tell me of you, bade me trust you; but
I do not greatly care to be deceived,   14
That have no use for trusting. If your master   15
Would have a queen his beggar, you must tell him
That majesty, to keep decorum, must
No less beg than a kingdom. If he please
To give me conquered Egypt for my son,
He gives me so much of mine own as I   20
Will kneel to him with thanks.

PROCULEIUS   Be of good cheer;
You're fall'n into a princely hand. Fear nothing.
Make your full reference freely to my lord,   23
Who is so full of grace that it flows over
On all that need. Let me report to him
Your sweet dependency, and you shall find   26
A conqueror that will pray in aid for kindness   27
Where he for grace is kneeled to.

CLEOPATRA   Pray you, tell him
I am his fortune's vassal, and I send him   29
The greatness he has got. I hourly learn   30
A doctrine of obedience, and would gladly
Look him i'th' face.

PROCULEIUS   This I'll report, dear lady.
Have comfort, for I know your plight is pitied
Of him that caused it.   34
         [*Roman soldiers enter from
          behind Cleopatra and take her prisoner.*]
You see how easily she may be surprised.
[*To the soldiers*] Guard her till Caesar come.

IRAS   Royal Queen!

CHARMIAN
Oh, Cleopatra! Thou art taken, Queen.

CLEOPATRA [*drawing a dagger*]
Quick, quick, good hands.

PROCULEIUS   Hold, worthy lady, hold!
            [*He disarms her.*]
Do not yourself such wrong, who are in this
Relieved, but not betrayed.

CLEOPATRA   What, of death too,   40
That rids our dogs of languish?

PROCULEIUS   Cleopatra,   41
Do not abuse my master's bounty by
Th'undoing of yourself. Let the world see
His nobleness well acted, which your death   44
Will never let come forth.

CLEOPATRA   Where art thou, Death?   45
Come hither, come! Come, come, and take a queen

Worth many babes and beggars!

PROCULEIUS   Oh, temperance, lady!   47

CLEOPATRA
Sir, I will eat no meat, I'll not drink, sir;
If idle talk will once be necessary,   49
I'll not sleep, neither. This mortal house I'll ruin,
Do Caesar what he can. Know, sir, that I
Will not wait pinioned at your master's court,   52
Nor once be chastised with the sober eye
Of dull Octavia. Shall they hoist me up
And show me to the shouting varletry   55
Of censuring Rome? Rather a ditch in Egypt
Be gentle grave unto me! Rather on Nilus' mud
Lay me stark nak'd and let the waterflies
Blow me into abhorring! Rather make   59
My country's high pyramides my gibbet   60
And hang me up in chains!

PROCULEIUS   You do extend
These thoughts of horror further than you shall
Find cause in Caesar.

        Enter Dolabella.

DOLABELLA   Proculeius,
What thou hast done thy master Caesar knows,
And he hath sent for thee. For the Queen,   65
I'll take her to my guard.

PROCULEIUS   So, Dolabella,
It shall content me best. Be gentle to her.
[*To Cleopatra*] To Caesar I will speak what you shall
    please,   68
If you'll employ me to him.

CLEOPATRA   Say I would die.
         Exit Proculeius [*with soldiers*].

DOLABELLA
Most noble Empress, you have heard of me?

CLEOPATRA
I cannot tell.

DOLABELLA   Assuredly you know me.

CLEOPATRA
No matter, sir, what I have heard or known.
You laugh when boys or women tell their dreams;
Is't not your trick?

DOLABELLA   I understand not, madam.   74

CLEOPATRA
I dreamt there was an emperor Antony.
Oh, such another sleep, that I might see
But such another man!

DOLABELLA   If it might please ye—

CLEOPATRA
His face was as the heavens, and therein stuck   78
A sun and moon, which kept their course and lighted

---

14 **do . . . to be** am wary of being   15 **That** since I   20 **as** that
23 **Make . . . reference** Refer your case   26 **dependency** submissiveness   27 **pray . . . kindness** beg your assistance to ensure that he may omit no kindness   29–30 **I send . . . got** i.e., I acknowledge his superiority over all he has won, including myself.   34 **Of** by.   0.1 *Roman soldiers* (Perhaps led by Gallus; see 5.1.69. Possibly some speech for him has been omitted.)   40 **Relieved** rescued.   **of death too** i.e., (1) am I *relieved* or deprived even of death (2) am I *betrayed* even of the right to die   41 **our dogs of languish** even our dogs of lingering disease.   44 **acted** accomplished   45 **let come forth** allow to be displayed.

47 **babes and beggars** i.e., those whom death takes easily and often. 49 **If . . . necessary** even if on occasion I must resort to idle talk (to keep myself awake)   52 **wait pinioned** wait in attendance, like a bird with clipped wings, unable to fly   55 **varletry** rabble   59 **Blow . . . abhorring** cause me to swell abhorrently with maggots, or, deposit their eggs on me until I become abhorrent.   60 **gibbet** gallows 65 **For** As for   68 **what** whatever   74 **trick** manner, way.   78 **stuck** were set

The little O, the earth.
DOLABELLA   Most sovereign creature—
CLEOPATRA   His legs bestrid the ocean; his reared arm   81
Crested the world; his voice was propertied   82
As all the tunèd spheres, and that to friends;   83
But when he meant to quail and shake the orb,   84
He was as rattling thunder. For his bounty,   85
There was no winter in't; an autumn 'twas
That grew the more by reaping. His delights   87
Were dolphinlike; they showed his back above   88
The element they lived in. In his livery   89
Walked crowns and crownets; realms and islands
were   90
As plates dropped from his pocket.
DOLABELLA   Cleopatra—   91
CLEOPATRA
Think you there was or might be such a man
As this I dreamt of?
DOLABELLA   Gentle madam, no.
CLEOPATRA
You lie, up to the hearing of the gods.
But if there be nor ever were one such,   95
It's past the size of dreaming. Nature wants stuff   96
To vie strange forms with fancy; yet t'imagine   97
An Antony were nature's piece 'gainst fancy,   98
Condemning shadows quite.
DOLABELLA   Hear me, good madam: 99
Your loss is as yourself, great; and you bear it
As answering to the weight. Would I might never   101
O'ertake pursued success but I do feel,   102
By the rebound of yours, a grief that smites
My very heart at root.
CLEOPATRA   I thank you, sir.
Know you what Caesar means to do with me?
DOLABELLA
I am loath to tell you what I would you knew.
CLEOPATRA
Nay, pray you, sir.
DOLABELLA   Though he be honorable—
CLEOPATRA   He'll lead me, then, in triumph.
DOLABELLA   Madam, he will, I know't.   Flourish.

Enter Proculeius, Caesar, Gallus, Maecenas,
and others of his train.

ALL   Make way there! Caesar!

CAESAR   Which is the Queen of Egypt?
DOLABELLA   It is the Emperor, madam.
                              Cleopatra kneels.
CAESAR   Arise, you shall not kneel. I pray you, rise.
Rise, Egypt.
CLEOPATRA [rising] Sir, the gods will have it thus;
My master and my lord I must obey.
CAESAR   Take to you no hard thoughts.   116
The record of what injuries you did us,
Though written in our flesh, we shall remember
As things but done by chance.
CLEOPATRA   Sole sir o'th' world,   119
I cannot project mine own cause so well   120
To make it clear, but do confess I have   121
Been laden with like frailties which before
Have often shamed our sex.
CAESAR   Cleopatra, know
We will extenuate rather than enforce.   124
If you apply yourself to our intents,   125
Which towards you are most gentle, you shall find
A benefit in this change; but if you seek
To lay on me a cruelty by taking   128
Antony's course, you shall bereave yourself   129
Of my good purposes and put your children
To that destruction which I'll guard them from
If thereon you rely. I'll take my leave.
CLEOPATRA
And may, through all the world! 'Tis yours, and we,   133
Your scutcheons and your signs of conquest, shall   134
Hang in what place you please. Here, my good lord.   135
                    [She gives him a scroll.]
CAESAR
You shall advise me in all for Cleopatra.   136
CLEOPATRA
This is the brief of money, plate, and jewels   137
I am possessed of. 'Tis exactly valued,
Not petty things admitted. Where's Seleucus?   139

[Enter Seleucus.]

SELEUCUS   Here, madam.
CLEOPATRA
This is my treasurer. Let him speak, my lord,
Upon his peril, that I have reserved
To myself nothing.—Speak the truth, Seleucus.
SELEUCUS
Madam, I had rather seal my lips
Than to my peril speak that which is not.
CLEOPATRA   What have I kept back?
SELEUCUS
Enough to purchase what you have made known.

81 bestrid straddled (like the Colossus of Rhodes)   82 Crested sur-mounted   82–3 propertied . . . friends endowed with qualities which, when he spoke to friends, recalled the harmony of the heav-enly bodies in their spheres   84 quail make quail, overawe.   orb world   85 For As for   87–9 His . . . in i.e., Like the dolphin sport-fully rising up out of the sea, his pleasures arose out of the element in which he lived, both glorying in and transcending that element.   89–90 In . . . crownets i.e., Among his retainers (those who would wear his livery) were kings and princes   91 plates coins   95 nor ever were or if there never existed   96 It's . . . dreaming no dream can come up to it, my image of him.   96–9 Nature . . . quite Nature lacks material to equal the remarkable forms produced by fancy or imagination; yet an Antony such as I have pictured forth would him-self be a work of nature, in fact would be Nature's masterpiece in competition with the imagination.   101 As . . . weight commensurate with the weightiness of the loss.   101–2 Would . . . feel May I never succeed at what I desire if I do not feel

116 Take . . . thoughts Don't torment yourself with reproaches.   119 sir master   120 project set forth   121 clear free of blame   124 enforce press home.   125 If . . . intents If you comply with my plans   128 lay . . . cruelty force me to be cruel   129 bereave rob   133 And may i.e., (1) You may leave when you choose (2) You may have your will in anything   134 scutcheons shields showing armor-ial bearings; hence, shields hung up as monuments of victory   135 Hang be hung up in display as your trophies. (But with a hidden suggestion of "be hanged as your captives.")   136 in all for Cleopatra i.e., in all matters pertaining to yourself.   137 brief list   139 Not . . . admitted petty things omitted.

CAESAR

  Nay, blush not, Cleopatra. I approve
  Your wisdom in the deed.

CLEOPATRA   See, Caesar! Oh, behold

  How pomp is followed! Mine will now be yours,   150
  And, should we shift estates, yours would be mine. 151
  The ingratitude of this Seleucus does
  Even make me wild.—Oh, slave, of no more trust
  Than love that's hired! [*Seleucus retreats from her.*]
      What, goest thou back? Thou shalt   154
  Go back, I warrant thee! But I'll catch thine eyes,
  Though they had wings. Slave, soulless villain, dog!
  Oh, rarely base!

CAESAR   Good Queen, let us entreat you.   157

CLEOPATRA

  Oh, Caesar, what a wounding shame is this,
  That thou vouchsafing here to visit me,   159
  Doing the honor of thy lordliness
  To one so meek, that mine own servant should
  Parcel the sum of my disgraces by   162
  Addition of his envy! Say, good Caesar,   163
  That I some lady trifles have reserved,   164
  Immoment toys, things of such dignity   165
  As we greet modern friends withal, and say   166
  Some nobler token I have kept apart
  For Livia and Octavia, to induce   168
  Their mediation; must I be unfolded   169
  With one that I have bred? The gods! It smites me 170
  Beneath the fall I have. [*To Seleucus*] Prithee, go hence,
  Or I shall show the cinders of my spirits   172
  Through th'ashes of my chance. Wert thou a man, 173
  Thou wouldst have mercy on me.

CAESAR   Forbear, Seleucus.   [*Exit Seleucus.*] 175

CLEOPATRA

  Be it known that we, the greatest, are misthought 176
  For things that others do; and when we fall
  We answer others' merits in our name,   178
  Are therefore to be pitied.

CAESAR   Cleopatra,

  Not what you have reserved nor what acknowledged
  Put we i'th' roll of conquest. Still be't yours;
  Bestow it at your pleasure, and believe   182
  Caesar's no merchant, to make prize with you   183
  Of things that merchants sold. Therefore be cheered.
  Make not your thoughts your prisons. No, dear
    Queen,   185
  For we intend so to dispose you as   186

  Yourself shall give us counsel. Feed and sleep.
  Our care and pity is so much upon you
  That we remain your friend; and so adieu.

CLEOPATRA

  My master, and my lord!

CAESAR   Not so. Adieu.
            Flourish. Exeunt Caesar and his train.

CLEOPATRA

  He words me, girls, he words me, that I should not 191
  Be noble to myself. But hark thee, Charmian.   192
          [*She whispers to Charmian.*]

IRAS

  Finish, good lady. The bright day is done,
  And we are for the dark.

CLEOPATRA [*to Charmian*] Hie thee again.   194
  I have spoke already, and it is provided;   195
  Go put it to the haste.

CHARMIAN   Madam, I will.

    Enter Dolabella.

DOLABELLA

  Where's the Queen?

CHARMIAN   Behold, sir.   [*Exit.*]

CLEOPATRA   Dolabella!

DOLABELLA

  Madam, as thereto sworn by your command,
  Which my love makes religion to obey,
  I tell you this: Caesar through Syria
  Intends his journey, and within three days
  You with your children will he send before.
  Make your best use of this. I have performed
  Your pleasure and my promise.

CLEOPATRA   Dolabella,
  I shall remain your debtor.

DOLABELLA   I your servant.
  Adieu, good Queen. I must attend on Caesar.

CLEOPATRA

  Farewell, and thanks.   *Exit* [*Dolabella*].
          Now, Iras, what think'st thou?
  Thou an Egyptian puppet shall be shown
  In Rome as well as I. Mechanic slaves   209
  With greasy aprons, rules, and hammers shall   210
  Uplift us to the view. In their thick breaths,
  Rank of gross diet, shall we be enclouded   212
  And forced to drink their vapor.

IRAS   The gods forbid!   213

CLEOPATRA

  Nay, 'tis most certain, Iras. Saucy lictors   214
  Will catch at us like strumpets, and scald rhymers 215
  Ballad us out o' tune. The quick comedians   216
  Extemporally will stage us and present   217

---

150 **How . . . followed!** how greatness is served! **Mine** All the pomp and following that attends me 151 **shift estates** reverse fortunes, exchange places 154 **hired** paid for. 157 **rarely** exceptionally 159 **vouchsafing** deigning to come 162 **Parcel** particularize 163 **envy** malice. 164 **lady** ladylike, feminine 165 **Immoment toys** trifles of no moment or importance 166 **modern** common. **withal** with 168 **Livia** Octavius Caesar's wife 169–70 **unfolded . . . bred** exposed by one of my household. 172 **cinders** smoldering hot coals 173 **chance** (fallen) fortune. 175 **Forbear** Withdraw 176 **misthought** misjudged 178 **We . . . name** we are accountable for the deeds of others done in our name 182 **Bestow** Use 183 **make prize** haggle 185 **Make . . . prisons** i.e., Don't imprison yourself in your thoughts by misconceiving of your situation. 186 **dispose** dispose of

191–2 **he words . . . myself** he tries to deceive me with mere words to keep me from suicide. 194 **Hie thee again** Return quickly. 195 **spoke** given orders (for the means of suicide) 209 **Mechanic slaves** Common laborers 210 **rules** straight-edged measuring sticks 212 **Rank . . . diet** reeking of coarse food 213 **drink** drink in, breathe deeply 214 **lictors** minor officials in attendance on Roman magistrates 215 **scald** scurvy 216 **Ballad us** sing ballads about us. **quick** quick-witted 217 **Extemporally** in improvised performance

Our Alexandrian revels; Antony
Shall be brought drunken forth, and I shall see
Some squeaking Cleopatra boy my greatness   220
I'th' posture of a whore.

IRAS   O the good gods!

CLEOPATRA   Nay, that's certain.

IRAS
I'll never see't! For I am sure my nails
Are stronger than mine eyes.

CLEOPATRA   Why, that's the way
To fool their preparation and to conquer
Their most absurd intents.

            Enter Charmian.

                        Now, Charmian!
Show me, my women, like a queen. Go fetch   227
My best attires. I am again for Cydnus,
To meet Mark Antony. Sirrah Iras, go—   229
Now, noble Charmian, we'll dispatch indeed—   230
And when thou hast done this chare I'll give thee
leave   231
To play till doomsday. Bring our crown and all.   232
                    [*Exit Iras.*] *A noise within.*
Wherefore's this noise?

            Enter a Guardsman.

GUARDSMAN   Here is a rural fellow
That will not be denied Your Highness' presence.
He brings you figs.

CLEOPATRA
Let him come in.   *Exit Guardsman.*
                        What poor an instrument   236
May do a noble deed! He brings me liberty.
My resolution's placed, and I have nothing   238
Of woman in me. Now from head to foot
I am marble-constant; now the fleeting moon   240
No planet is of mine.

            Enter Guardsman, and Clown [*bringing in a
            basket*].

GUARDSMAN   This is the man.   241

CLEOPATRA   Avoid, and leave him.   *Exit Guardsman.* 242
Hast thou the pretty worm of Nilus there,   243
That kills and pains not?

CLOWN   Truly, I have him, but I would not be the party
that should desire you to touch him, for his biting is
immortal. Those that do die of it do seldom or never   247
recover.

CLEOPATRA   Remember'st thou any that have died on't?

CLOWN   Very many, men and women too. I heard of   250
one of them no longer than yesterday—a very honest
woman, but something given to lie, as a woman   252
should not do but in the way of honesty—how she
died of the biting of it, what pain she felt. Truly, she
makes a very good report o'th' worm. But he that will
believe all that they say shall never be saved by half 256
that they do. But this is most falliable, the worm's an   257
odd worm.

CLEOPATRA   Get thee hence, farewell.

CLOWN   I wish you all joy of the worm.
                    [*He sets down his basket.*]

CLEOPATRA   Farewell.

CLOWN   You must think this, look you, that the worm
will do his kind.   263

CLEOPATRA   Ay, ay; farewell.

CLOWN   Look you, the worm is not to be trusted but in
the keeping of wise people, for indeed there is no
goodness in the worm.

CLEOPATRA   Take thou no care; it shall be heeded.   268

CLOWN   Very good. Give it nothing, I pray you, for it is
not worth the feeding.

CLEOPATRA   Will it eat me?

CLOWN   You must not think I am so simple but I know
the devil himself will not eat a woman. I know that a
woman is a dish for the gods, if the devil dress her   274
not. But truly, these same whoreson devils do the   275
gods great harm in their women, for in every ten that
they make, the devils mar five.

CLEOPATRA   Well, get thee gone. Farewell.

CLOWN   Yes, forsooth. I wish you joy o'th' worm.
                                        Exit.

            [*Enter Iras with royal attire.*]

CLEOPATRA
Give me my robe. Put on my crown. I have
Immortal longings in me. Now no more   281
The juice of Egypt's grape shall moist this lip.
                    [*The women dress her.*]
Yare, yare, good Iras; quick. Methinks I hear   283
Antony call; I see him rouse himself
To praise my noble act. I hear him mock
The luck of Caesar, which the gods give men   286
To excuse their after wrath. Husband, I come!   287
Now to that name my courage prove my title!   288
I am fire and air; my other elements   289

220 **boy** (Allusion to the practice of having women's parts acted by boys on the Elizabethan stage.) 227 **Show** Display 229 **Sirrah** (Compare *sirs*, addressed to the women, in 4.15.90.) 230 **dispatch** (1) finish (2) hasten 231 **chare** task, chore 232.1 *Exit Iras* (It is possible that Charmian leaves, too.) 236 **What** How 238 **placed** fixed 240 **fleeting** inconstant, changing 241 **s.d.** *Clown* rustic 242 **Avoid** Withdraw 243 **worm** snake, serpent. (But elsewhere in this scene with the added connotation of "the male sexual organ" and "earthworm.") 247 **immortal** (Blunder for "mortal.")

250 **heard of** heard from 252 **to lie** (With sexual second meaning hinted at also in *honest*, i.e., "chaste," *die*, i.e., "reach orgasm," and *worm*.) 256 **all . . . half** (The Clown comically reverses the sensible order of these two words.) 257 **falliable** (Blunder for "infallible.") 263 **his kind** its natural function. 268 **Take thou no care** Don't worry 274 **dress** prepare, as in cooking. (With a suggestion also of dressing in alluring clothes.) 275 **whoreson** i.e., rascally, abominable. (A slang expression.) 281 **Immortal longings** longings for immortality 283 **Yare** Quickly 286–7 **which . . . wrath** the luck that the gods give men when they intend to mock and punish them subsequently for their hubris. 288 **to . . . title!** may my courage prove my right to call myself Antony's wife! 289 **other elements** i.e., earth and water, the heavier elements

I give to baser life. So, have you done?
Come then, and take the last warmth of my lips.
Farewell, kind Charmian. Iras, long farewell.
                    [*She kisses them. Iras falls and dies.*]
Have I the aspic in my lips? Dost fall?   293
If thou and nature can so gently part,
The stroke of death is as a lover's pinch,
Which hurts, and is desired. Dost thou lie still?
If thus thou vanishest, thou tell'st the world
It is not worth leave-taking.   298

CHARMIAN
Dissolve, thick cloud, and rain, that I may say
The gods themselves do weep!

CLEOPATRA   This proves me base.
If she first meet the curlèd Antony,   301
He'll make demand of her, and spend that kiss   302
Which is my heaven to have. [*To an asp*] Come, thou
mortal wretch,   303
With thy sharp teeth this knot intrinsicate   304
Of life at once untie. Poor venomous fool,
Be angry, and dispatch. Oh, couldst thou speak,
That I might hear thee call great Caesar ass
Unpolicied!

CHARMIAN   O eastern star!

CLEOPATRA   Peace, peace!   308
Dost thou not see my baby at my breast,
That sucks the nurse asleep?

CHARMIAN   Oh, break! Oh, break!

CLEOPATRA
As sweet as balm, as soft as air, as gentle—
O Antony!—Nay, I will take thee too.
                    [*Applying another asp to her arm.*]
What should I stay—   *Dies.* 313

CHARMIAN
In this wild world? So, fare thee well.   314
Now boast thee, Death, in thy possession lies
A lass unparalleled. Downy windows, close;   316
And golden Phoebus never be beheld
Of eyes again so royal! Your crown's awry;   318
I'll mend it, and then play—   319

        Enter the Guard, rustling in.

FIRST GUARD
Where's the Queen?

CHARMIAN   Speak softly. Wake her not.

FIRST GUARD
Caesar hath sent—

CHARMIAN   Too slow a messenger.
                    [*She applies an asp to herself.*]

Oh, come apace, dispatch! I partly feel thee.

FIRST GUARD
Approach, ho! All's not well. Caesar's beguiled.   323

SECOND GUARD
There's Dolabella sent from Caesar. Call him.
                    [*Exit a guard.*]

FIRST GUARD
What work is here, Charmian? Is this well done?

CHARMIAN
It is well done, and fitting for a princess
Descended of so many royal kings.
Ah, soldier!   *Charmian dies.*

        Enter Dolabella.

DOLABELLA
How goes it here?

SECOND GUARD   All dead.

DOLABELLA   Caesar, thy thoughts
Touch their effects in this. Thyself art coming   330
To see performed the dreaded act which thou
So sought'st to hinder.

        Enter Caesar and all his train, marching.

ALL   A way there, a way for Caesar!   333

DOLABELLA
Oh, sir, you are too sure an augurer;
That you did fear is done.

CAESAR   Bravest at the last,   335
She leveled at our purposes and, being royal,   336
Took her own way. The manner of their deaths?
I do not see them bleed.

DOLABELLA   Who was last with them?

FIRST GUARD
A simple countryman, that brought her figs.   339
This was his basket.

CAESAR   Poisoned, then.

FIRST GUARD   Oh, Caesar,
This Charmian lived but now; she stood and spake.
I found her trimming up the diadem
On her dead mistress; tremblingly she stood,
And on the sudden dropped.

CAESAR   Oh, noble weakness!
If they had swallowed poison, 'twould appear
By external swelling; but she looks like sleep,   346
As she would catch another Antony   347
In her strong toil of grace.

DOLABELLA   Here on her breast   348
There is a vent of blood and something blown;   349
The like is on her arm.

---

293 aspic asp   **298 is . . . leave-taking** does not deserve a ceremonious farewell.   **301 curlèd** with curled hair   **302 make demand** (1) ask questions (2) ask pleasure.   **spend that kiss** expend his desire on her   **303 mortal** deadly.   **wretch** (An affectionate term of abuse, like *fool* in line 305.)   **304 intrinsicate** intricate   **308 Unpolicied** outwitted.   **eastern star** i.e., Venus, the morning star.   **313 What** Why   **314 wild** savage. (Sometimes emended to *vild*, "vile.")   **316 Downy windows** i.e., Soft eyelids   **318 Of** by   **319 mend** fix, straighten

323 beguiled cheated, tricked.   **330 Touch their effects** meet with realization   **333 A way** Make a path   **335 That** that which   **336 leveled at** aimed at, guessed   **339 simple** humbly born   **346 like sleep** as if asleep   **347 As** as if   **348 toil** net   **349 vent** discharge.   **blown** deposited, or, swollen

FIRST GUARD
  This is an aspic's trail, and these fig leaves
  Have slime upon them, such as th'aspic leaves
  Upon the caves of Nile.
CAESAR   Most probable
  That so she died; for her physician tells me
  She hath pursued conclusions infinite   355
  Of easy ways to die. Take up her bed,
  And bear her women from the monument.
  She shall be buried by her Antony.
  No grave upon the earth shall clip in it   359

355 **conclusions** experiments   359 **clip** embrace, clasp

  A pair so famous. High events as these
  Strike those that make them; and their story is   361
  No less in pity than his glory which   362
  Brought them to be lamented. Our army shall   363
  In solemn show attend this funeral,
  And then to Rome. Come, Dolabella, see
  High order in this great solemnity.   366
        Exeunt omnes, [*bearing the dead bodies*].

361 Strike . . . them touch with sorrow those who brought about these deeds   **361–3 their story . . . lamented** the story of these famous lovers is no less pitiable than the fame of him who brought them low is glorious.   **366.1** *omnes* all

The Romances

The Winter's Tale   *The Tempest*

The Winter's Tale

The Winter's Tale (c. 1609–1611), with its almost symmetrical division into two halves of bleak tragedy and comic romance, illustrates perhaps more clearly than any other Shakespearean play the genre of tragicomedy. To be sure, all the late romances feature journeys of separation, apparent deaths, and tearful reconciliations. Marina and Thaisa in *Pericles*, Imogen in *Cymbeline*, and Ferdinand in *The Tempest*, all supposed irrecoverably lost, are brought back to life by apparently miraculous devices. Of the four late romances, however, *The Winter's Tale* uses the most formal structure to evoke the antithesis of tragedy and romance. It is sharply divided into contrasting halves by a gap of sixteen years. The tragic first half takes place almost entirely in Sicilia, whereas the action of the second half is limited for the most part to Bohemia. At the court of Sicilia, we see tyrannical jealousy producing a spiritual climate of "winter / In storm perpetual"; in Bohemia, we witness a pastoral landscape and a sheepshearing evoking "the sweet o'th' year," "When daffodils begin to peer" (3.2.212–13; 4.3.1–3). Paradoxically, the contrast between the two halves is intensified by parallels between the two: both begin with Camillo onstage and proceed to scenes of confrontation and jealousy in which, ironically, the innocent cause of jealousy in the first half, Polixenes, becomes the jealous tyrant of the second half. The mirroring reminds us of the cyclical nature of time and the hope it brings of renewal as we move from tragedy to romantic comedy.

Although this motif of a renewing journey from jaded court to idealized countryside reminds us of *As You Like It* and other early comedies, we sense in the late romances and especially in *The Winter's Tale* a new preoccupation with humanity's tragic folly. The vision of human depravity is world-weary and pessimistic, as though infected by the gloomy spirit of the great tragedies. And because humanity is so bent on destroying itself, the restoration is at once more urgently needed and more miraculous than in the "festive" world of early comedy. Renewal is mythically associated with the seasonal cycle from winter to summer.

King Leontes's tragedy seems at first irreversible and terrifying, like that of Shakespeare's greatest tragic protagonists. He suffers from irrational jealousy, as does Othello, and attempts to destroy the person on whom all his happiness depends. As with Othello, his jealousy stems from a characteristically male fear of inadequacy and rejection. Unlike Othello, however, Leontes needs no diabolical tempter such as Iago to poison his mind against Queen Hermione. Leontes is undone by his own fantasies. No differences in race or age can explain Leontes's fears of estrangement from Hermione. She is not imprudent in her conduct, like her counterpart in Robert Greene's *Pandosto* (1588), the prose romance from which Shakespeare drew his narrative. Although Hermione is graciously fond of Leontes's dear friend Polixenes and urges him to stay longer in Sicilia, she does so only with a hospitable warmth demanded by the occasion and encouraged by her husband. In every way, then, Shakespeare strips away from Leontes the motive and the occasion for plausible doubting of his wife. All observers in the Sicilian court are incredulous and shocked at the King's accusations. Even so, Leontes is neither an unsympathetic nor an unbelievable character. Like Othello, Leontes cherishes his wife and perceives with a horrifying intensity what a fearful cost they both must pay for his suspicions. Not only his marriage, but also his lifelong friendship with Polixenes, his sense of pride in his children, and his enjoyment of his subjects' warm regard, all must be sacrificed to a single overwhelming compulsion.

Whatever may be the psychological cause of this obsession, it manifests itself as a revulsion against all sexual behavior. Like mad Lear, Leontes imagines lechery to be the unavoidable fact of the cosmos and of the human condition, the lowest common denominator to which all persons (including Hermione) must stoop. He is persuaded that "It is a bawdy planet," in which cuck-olded man has "his pond fished by his next neighbor, by / Sir Smile, his neighbor" (1.2.195–201). Leontes's tor-tured soliloquies are laden with sexual images, of unat-tended "gates" letting in and out the enemy "With bag and baggage," and of a "dagger" that must be "muzzled / Lest it should bite its master" (lines 197, 206, 156–7). As in *King Lear*, order is inverted to disorder, sanity to mad-ness, legitimacy to illegitimacy. Sexual misconduct is emblematic of a universal malaise: "Why, then the world and all that's in 't is nothing, / The covering sky is noth-ing, Bohemia nothing, / My wife is nothing" (lines 292–4). Other characters, too, see the trial of Hermione as a testing of humanity's worth: if Hermione proves false, Antigonus promises, he will treat his own wife as a sta-ble horse and will "geld" his three daughters (2.1.148). Prevailing images are of spiders, venom, infection, steril-ity, and the "dungy earth" (line 158).

Cosmic order is never really challenged, however, even though the human suffering is very real and the injustice to women especially apparent. Leontes's fan-tasies of universal disorder are chimerical. His wife is, in fact, chaste, Polixenes true, and the King's courtiers loyal. Camillo refuses to carry out Leontes's order to murder Polixenes, not only because he knows murder to be wrong, but also because history offers not one example of a man "that had struck anointed kings / And flourished after" (1.2.357–8). The cosmos of this play is one in which crimes are invariably and swiftly punished. The Delphic oracle vindicates Hermione and gives Leontes stern warning. When Leontes persists in his madness, his son Mamillius's death follows as an immediate consequence. As Leontes at once perceives, "Apollo's angry, and the heavens themselves / Do strike at my injustice" (3.2.146–7). Leontes paradoxically welcomes the lengthy contrition he must undergo, for it confirms a pattern in the universe of just cause and effect. Although as tragic protagonist he has discovered the truth about Hermione moments too late and so must pay richly for his error, Leontes has at least recovered faith in Hermione's tran-scendent goodness. His nightmare now over, he accepts and embraces suffering as a necessary atonement.

The transition to romance is therefore anticipated to an extent by the play's first half, even though the tone of the last two acts is strikingly different. The old Shepherd signals a momentous change when he speaks to his son of a cataclysmic storm and a ravenous bear set in oppo-sition to the miraculous discovery of a child: "Now bless thyself. Thou mett'st with things dying, I with things newborn" (3.3.110–11). Time comes onstage as Chorus, like Gower in *Pericles*, to remind us of the conscious arti-fice of the dramatist. He can "o'erthrow law" and carry us over sixteen years as if we had merely dreamed out the interim (4.1). Shakespeare flaunts the improbability

of his story by giving Bohemia a seacoast (much to the distress of Ben Jonson) and by bringing onstage either a live bear or an actor costumed as one ("*Exit, pursued by a bear*"; 3.3.57 s.d.). The narrative uses many typical devices of romance: a babe abandoned to the elements, a princess brought up by shepherds, a prince disguised as a swain, a sea voyage, and a recognition scene. Love is threatened, not by the internal psychic obstacle of jeal-ousy, but by the external obstacles of parental opposition and a seeming disparity of social rank between the lovers. Comedy easily finds solutions for such difficul-ties by the unraveling of illusion. This comic world also properly includes clownish shepherds, coy shep-herdesses, and Autolycus, the roguish peddler, whose machinations contribute in an unforeseen manner to the working out of the love plot. Autolycus is in many ways the presiding genius of the play's second half, as domi-nant a character as Leontes in the first half and one whose delightful function is to do good "against my will" (5.2.125). In this paradox of knavery converted sur-prisingly to benign ends, we see how the comic provi-dence of Shakespeare's tragicomic world makes use of the most implausible and outrageous happenings in pur-suit of its own inscrutable design.

The conventional romantic ending is infused, how-ever, with a sadness and a mystery that take the play well beyond what is usual in comedy. Mamillius and Antigonus are really dead, and that irredeemable fact is not forgotten in the play's final happy moments. Hermione, although vindicated by the gods, has suf-fered public shame, the death of one child, separation from her other child, and prolonged isolation from her husband; like Imogen in *Cymbeline*, she has had to endure the consequences of male frailty and thereby redeem her husband through her suffering. Her hus-band, having thrown her aside, must, like Pericles, rediscover and learn to cherish the woman he once chose who now has aged; he must reconfirm his mar-riage to her, even as he learns to accept the marriage of his daughter to a younger man. All of these crucial turn-ings hinge upon Shakespeare's most notable departure from his source, Greene's *Pandosto*: Hermione is brought back to life. All observers regard this event, and the rediscovery of Perdita, as grossly implausible, "so like an old tale that the verity of it is in strong suspicion" (5.2.29–30). The play's very title, *The Winter's Tale*, rein-forces this sense of naive improbability. Why does Shakespeare stress this riddling paradox of an unbe-lievable reality, and why does he deliberately mislead his audience into believing that Hermione has, in fact, died (3.3.15–45), using a kind of theatrical trickery found in no other Shakespearean play? The answer may well be that, in Paulina's words, we must awake our faith, accepting a narrative of death and return to life that cannot ultimately be comprehended by reason. On the rational level, we are told that Hermione has been kept in hiding for sixteen years, in order to fulfill the condition of the oracle that Leontes is to live without an heir (and hence without a wife) until Perdita is found. Such an explanation seems psychologically incomprehensible, however, for it demands that Hermione live in extended isolation and that Paulina serve as the King's conscience for such a long period of time without any way for the participants to know when their suffering will end. Instead, we are drawn toward an emblematic interpretation, bearing in mind that it is more an evocative hint than a complete truth. Throughout the play, Hermione has been repeatedly associated with "Grace" and with the goddess Proserpina, whose return from the underworld, after "Three crabbèd months had soured themselves to death" (1.2.102), signals the coming of spring. Perdita, also associated with Proserpina (4.4.116), is welcomed by her father "As is the spring to th' earth" (5.1.152). The emphasis on the bond of father and daughter, so characteristic of Shakespeare's late plays and especially his romances, goes importantly beyond the patriarchalism of Shakespeare's earlier history plays in its exploration of family relationships. Paulina has a similarly emblematic role, that of Conscience, patiently guiding the King to a divinely appointed renewal of his joy. Paulina speaks of herself as an artist figure, like Prospero in *The Tempest*, performing wonders of illusion, though she rejects the assistance of wicked powers. These emblematic hints do not rob the story of its human drama, but they do lend a transcendent signifi-cance to Leontes's bittersweet story of sinful error, affliction, and an unexpected second happiness.

On stage in recent decades, the play has shown its remarkable dramaturgic effectiveness, especially in the restoration of Hermione to her husband as a living and breathing statue. Peter Brook, at the Phoenix Theatre in London, 1951, chose a permanent set to underscore the play's malleable swift action and its need for the audience to participate imaginatively in the fashioning of theatrical illusion. Trevor Nunn's set at Stratford-upon-Avon in 1969 was a three-sided white box in which nothing was realistically represented. Nunn and John Barton, at Stratford-upon-Avon in 1976, visualized bears everywhere: in motifs of wall hangings and carpets, in a bearskin draped on a couch. The violent irrationality of Ian McKellan's Leontes seemed plausible in such a symbolic and mythic landscape. In Terry Hands's 1986 production also at Stratford-upon-Avon, a huge bear rug on the cool marble floor of Leontes's Regency palace during the play's first half became, in Bohemia, the live bear that tore into the shoulder of Antigonus. Above all, the apparent bringing back to life of Hermione's statue in the final scene has proven again and again to be a masterful *coup de théâtre*. What we see in the theater is of course an illusion, but at what level? Are we to understand that a statue comes to life? Much depends on the actress's skill in appearing motionless and then warm to her husband's touch. The moment is indeed one calculated to awaken our faith in the miracle of renewal and in the power of art to confound illusion and reality. We are led to ponder deeply the mysteries of our own uncertain existence.

The Winter's Tale

The Names of the Actors

LEONTES, *King of Sicilia*
MAMILLIUS, *young prince of Sicilia*
CAMILLO,
ANTIGONUS,
CLEOMENES,
DION,
} *four Lords of Sicilia*

HERMIONE, *Queen to Leontes*
PERDITA, *daughter to Leontes and Hermione*
PAULINA, *wife to Antigonus*
EMILIA, *a lady [attending on Hermione]*

POLIXENES, *King of Bohemia*
FLORIZEL, *Prince of Bohemia*
ARCHIDAMUS, *a lord of Bohemia*
Old SHEPHERD, *reputed father of Perdita*
CLOWN, *his son*
AUTOLYCUS, *a rogue*

[MOPSA,
[DORCAS,
} *Shepherdesses.*]

[A MARINER
A JAILER
Two LADIES *attending Hermione*
Two SERVANTS *attending Leontes*
One or more LORDS *attending Leontes*
An OFFICER *of the court*
A GENTLEMAN *attending Leontes*
Three GENTLEMEN *of the court of Sicilia*
A SERVANT *of the Old Shepherd*

TIME, *as Chorus*]

*Other Lords and Gentlemen, [Ladies, Officers,] and
Servants; Shepherds and Shepherdesses; [Twelve
Countrymen disguised as Satyrs]*

[SCENE: *Sicilia, and Bohemia.*]

1.1

Enter Camillo and Archidamus.

ARCHIDAMUS   If you shall chance, Camillo, to visit Bohemia on the like occasion whereon my services are ²
now on foot, you shall see, as I have said, great ³
difference betwixt our Bohemia and your Sicilia.
CAMILLO   I think this coming summer the King of Sicilia
means to pay Bohemia the visitation which he justly ⁶
owes him.
ARCHIDAMUS   Wherein our entertainment shall shame ⁸
us, we will be justified in our loves; for indeed— ⁹
CAMILLO   Beseech you—

ARCHIDAMUS   Verily, I speak it in the freedom of my ¹¹
knowledge. We cannot with such magnificence—in ¹²
so rare—I know not what to say. We will give you
sleepy drinks, that your senses, unintelligent of our ¹⁴
insufficience, may, though they cannot praise us, as
little accuse us.
CAMILLO   You pay a great deal too dear for what's
given freely.
ARCHIDAMUS   Believe me, I speak as my understanding
instructs me and as mine honesty puts it to utterance.
CAMILLO   Sicilia cannot show himself overkind to Bo- ²¹
hemia. They were trained together in their childhoods,
and there rooted betwixt them then such an affection
which cannot choose but branch now. Since their ²⁴
more mature dignities and royal necessities made
separation of their society, their encounters, though ²⁶

not personal, hath been royally attorneyed with   27
interchange of gifts, letters, loving embassies, that
they have seemed to be together though absent,
shook hands as over a vast, and embraced as it were   30
from the ends of opposed winds. The heavens con-   31
tinue their loves!

ARCHIDAMUS   I think there is not in the world either
malice or matter to alter it. You have an unspeakable
comfort of your young prince Mamillius. It is a   35
gentleman of the greatest promise that ever came into
my note.   37

CAMILLO   I very well agree with you in the hopes of
him. It is a gallant child, one that indeed physics the   39
subject, makes old hearts fresh. They that went on   40
crutches ere he was born desire yet their life to see him   41
a man.

ARCHIDAMUS   Would they else be content to die?

CAMILLO   Yes, if there were no other excuse why they
should desire to live.

ARCHIDAMUS   If the King had no son, they would desire   46
to live on crutches till he had one.   *Exeunt.*   47

1.2

Enter Leontes, Hermione, Mamillius, Polixenes,
Camillo.

POLIXENES
Nine changes of the wat'ry star hath been   1
The shepherd's note since we have left our throne   2
Without a burden. Time as long again   3
Would be filled up, my brother, with our thanks,
And yet we should for perpetuity   5
Go hence in debt. And therefore, like a cipher,   6
Yet standing in rich place, I multiply   7
With one "We thank you" many thousands more
That go before it.

LEONTES   Stay your thanks awhile
And pay them when you part.

POLIXENES   Sir, that's tomorrow.
I am questioned by my fears of what may chance   11
Or breed upon our absence, that may blow   12
No sneaping winds at home to make us say,   13
"This is put forth too truly." Besides, I have stayed   14

To tire your royalty.
LEONTES   We are tougher, brother,
Than you can put us to't.
POLIXENES   No longer stay.   16
LEONTES
One sev'nnight longer.
POLIXENES   Very sooth, tomorrow.   17
LEONTES
We'll part the time between 's, then, and in that   18
I'll no gainsaying.
POLIXENES   Press me not, beseech you, so.   19
There is no tongue that moves, none, none i' th' world
So soon as yours could win me. So it should now,
Were there necessity in your request, although
'Twere needful I denied it. My affairs
Do even drag me homeward, which to hinder
Were in your love a whip to me, my stay   25
To you a charge and trouble. To save both,   26
Farewell, our brother.
LEONTES   Tongue-tied, our Queen? Speak you.
HERMIONE
I had thought, sir, to have held my peace until   28
You had drawn oaths from him not to stay. You, sir,   29
Charge him too coldly. Tell him you are sure
All in Bohemia's well; this satisfaction   31
The bygone day proclaimed. Say this to him,   32
He's beat from his best ward.
LEONTES   Well said, Hermione.   33
HERMIONE
To tell he longs to see his son were strong.   34
But let him say so then, and let him go.
But let him swear so and he shall not stay;   36
We'll thwack him hence with distaffs.   37
[*To Polixenes*] Yet of your royal presence I'll adventure   38
The borrow of a week. When at Bohemia   39
You take my lord, I'll give him my commission
To let him there a month behind the gest   41
Prefixed for 's parting.—Yet, good deed, Leontes,   42
I love thee not a jar o' th' clock behind   43
What lady she her lord.—You'll stay?
POLIXENES   No, madam.   44
HERMIONE
Nay, but you will?
POLIXENES   I may not, verily.
HERMIONE   Verily?

---

27 **personal** in person.   **attorneyed** carried out by deputy   30 **vast** boundless space   31 **ends . . . winds** i.e., opposite ends of the earth. **The heavens** May the heavens   35 **of** in the person of   37 **note** observation.   39–40 **physics the subject** brings health to the subjects of this kingdom   41 **their life** to continue living   46–7 **If . . . one** Even if there were no living heir to the throne, these old people would still wish to go on living in hopes of one.
1.2. Location: The same.   1 **wat'ry star** moon   2 **note** observation. **we** I. (The royal "we.")   3 **burden** occupant.   5 **for perpetuity** forever   6–7 **like . . . place** like a zero at the end of a number, increasing its value by powers of ten, though of itself without value   11–14 **I am . . . truly** I am anxious about what may happen in my absence, especially a stirring up of envy and backbiting that would cause me to say my fears were all too plausible.

16 **Than . . . to't** than anything you can do to try me.   17 **sev'nnight** week.   **Very sooth** Truly   18 **part the time** split the difference, i.e., divide a week in two   19 **I'll no gainsaying** I won't take "no" for an answer.   25 **Were . . . whip** would be a punishment to me, though done through love   26 **charge** expense, burden   28–9 **I . . . to stay** i.e., I almost thought that you were going to get him to swear he *won't* stay, before I got a chance to say anything.   31–2 **this . . . proclaimed** yesterday brought news to satisfy on that score.   32 **Say** If you say   33 **ward** defensive posture. (A fencing term.)   34 **tell** tell us that. **strong** a strong argument.   36 **he shall not stay** i.e., we wouldn't let him stay even if he wanted to.   37 **distaffs** sticks used in spinning, here employed as a domestic kind of weapon.   38 **adventure** risk   39 **borrow** borrowing   41–2 **To . . . parting** to let him stay there a month longer than the originally agreed-upon time for his departure.   42 **good deed** indeed   43–4 **I love . . . lord** I love you not even a tiny bit (literally, a tick of the clock) less than any noble lady loves her husband.

You put me off with limber vows; but I,   47
Though you would seek t'unsphere the stars with
   oaths,
Should yet say, "Sir, no going." Verily,
You shall not go. A lady's "verily" is
As potent as a lord's. Will you go yet?
Force me to keep you as a prisoner,
Not like a guest: so you shall pay your fees   53
When you depart, and save your thanks. How say
   you?
My prisoner or my guest? By your dread "verily,"
One of them you shall be.

POLIXENES   Your guest, then, madam.
To be your prisoner should import offending,   57
Which is for me less easy to commit
Than you to punish.

HERMIONE   Not your jailer, then,
But your kind hostess. Come, I'll question you
Of my lord's tricks and yours when you were boys.
You were pretty lordings then?

POLIXENES   We were, fair Queen,
Two lads that thought there was no more behind   63
But such a day tomorrow as today,
And to be boy eternal.

HERMIONE   Was not my lord
The verier wag o'th' two?   66

POLIXENES
We were as twinned lambs that did frisk i'th' sun
And bleat the one at th'other. What we changed   68
Was innocence for innocence; we knew not
The doctrine of ill-doing, nor dreamed
That any did. Had we pursued that life,
And our weak spirits ne'er been higher reared
With stronger blood, we should have answered
   heaven   73
Boldly "Not guilty," the imposition cleared   74
Hereditary ours.

HERMIONE   By this we gather   75
You have tripped since.

POLIXENES   Oh, my most sacred lady,
Temptations have since then been born to 's, for
In those unfledged days was my wife a girl;   78
Your precious self had then not crossed the eyes
Of my young playfellow.

HERMIONE   Grace to boot!   80
Of this make no conclusion, lest you say   81
Your queen and I are devils. Yet go on.
Th'offenses we have made you do we'll answer,
If you first sinned with us, and that with us
You did continue fault, and that you slipped not

With any but with us.

LEONTES   Is he won yet?   86

HERMIONE
He'll stay, my lord.

LEONTES   At my request he would not.
Hermione, my dearest, thou never spok'st
To better purpose.

HERMIONE   Never?

LEONTES   Never but once.

HERMIONE
What? Have I twice said well? When was 't before?
I prithee, tell me. Cram 's with praise and make 's
As fat as tame things. One good deed dying
   tongueless   92
Slaughters a thousand waiting upon that.   93
Our praises are our wages. You may ride 's
With one soft kiss a thousand furlongs ere
With spur we heat an acre. But to th' goal: 96
My last good deed was to entreat his stay.
What was my first? It has an elder sister,
Or I mistake you. Oh, would her name were Grace!
But once before I spoke to the purpose. When?
Nay, let me have 't; I long.

LEONTES   Why, that was when
Three crabbèd months had soured themselves to
   death
Ere I could make thee open thy white hand
And clap thyself my love. Then didst thou utter,   104
"I am yours forever."

HERMIONE   'Tis grace indeed.
Why, lo you now, I have spoke to th' purpose twice:
The one forever earned a royal husband,
Th'other for some while a friend.

                [She gives her hand to Polixenes.]

LEONTES [aside]   Too hot, too hot!
To mingle friendship far is mingling bloods.   109
I have tremor cordis on me. My heart dances,   110
But not for joy, not joy. This entertainment   111
May a free face put on, derive a liberty   112
From heartiness, from bounty, fertile bosom,   113
And well become the agent. 'T may, I grant.   114
But to be paddling palms and pinching fingers,
As now they are, and making practiced smiles
As in a looking glass, and then to sigh, as 'twere
The mort o'th' deer; oh, that is entertainment   118
My bosom likes not, nor my brows.—Mamillius,   119
Art thou my boy?

MAMILLIUS   Ay, my good lord.

LEONTES   I'fecks,   120

---

47 **limber** limp   53 **fees** payments demanded by jailers of prisoners at the time of their release   57 **import offending** imply my having offended   63 **behind** still to come   66 **The verier wag** truly the more mischievous   68 **changed** exchanged   73 **stronger blood** mature sexual passions   74–5 **the imposition . . . ours** i.e., being freed from original sin itself (if we had continued in that state); or, excepting of course the original sin that is the common condition of all mortals. 78 **unfledged** not yet feathered, i.e., immature   80 **Grace to boot!** Heaven help me!   81 **Of . . . conclusion** Don't follow your implied line of reasoning to its logical conclusion

86 **Is he won yet?** (Leontes has been out of hearing for much of their conversation.)   92 **tongueless** unpraised, unsung   93 **Slaughters . . . that** i.e., will inhibit many other good deeds that would have been inspired by that praise.   96 **heat** traverse as in a race.   **to th' goal** to come to the point   104 **clap** clasp hands, pledge   109 **mingling bloods** (Sexual intercourse was thought to produce a mingling of bloods.)   110 **tremor cordis** fluttering of the heart   111 **entertainment** i.e., of Polixenes by Hermione   112 **free face** innocent appearance   113 **fertile bosom** i.e., generous affection   114 **well . . . agent** do credit to the doer.   118 **mort** note sounded on a horn at the death of the hunted deer   119 **brows** (Alludes to cuckolds' horns, the supposed badge of men whose wives are unfaithful.)   120 **I'fecks** in faith

Why, that's my bawcock. What, hast smutched thy
    nose?   121
They say it is a copy out of mine. Come, captain,
We must be neat; not neat, but cleanly, captain.   123
And yet the steer, the heifer, and the calf
Are all called neat.—Still virginaling   125
Upon his palm?—How now, you wanton calf?   126
Art thou my calf?

MAMILLIUS   Yes, if you will, my lord.

LEONTES
Thou want'st a rough pash and the shoots that I have   128
To be full like me. Yet they say we are   129
Almost as like as eggs. Women say so,
That will say anything. But were they false
As o'erdyed blacks, as wind, as waters, false   132
As dice are to be wished by one that fixes   133
No bourn twixt his and mine, yet were it true   134
To say this boy were like me. Come, sir page,
Look on me with your welkin eye. Sweet villain!   136
Most dear'st! My collop! Can thy dam?—may't be?— 137
Affection, thy intention stabs the center.   138
Thou dost make possible things not so held,   139
Communicat'st with dreams—how can this be?—   140
With what's unreal thou coactive art,   141
And fellow'st nothing. Then 'tis very credent   142
Thou mayst cojoin with something; and thou dost,   143
And that beyond commission, and I find it,   144
And that to the infection of my brains
And hard'ning of my brows.

POLIXENES   What means Sicilia?   146

HERMIONE
He something seems unsettled.

POLIXENES   How, my lord?   147
What cheer? How is't with you, best brother?

HERMIONE   You look
As if you held a brow of much distraction.
Are you moved, my lord?

LEONTES   No, in good earnest.   150
How sometimes nature will betray its folly,   151
Its tenderness, and make itself a pastime   152
To harder bosoms! Looking on the lines   153

Of my boy's face, methoughts I did recoil   154
Twenty-three years, and saw myself unbreeched,   155
In my green velvet coat, my dagger muzzled   156
Lest it should bite its master and so prove,
As ornaments oft do, too dangerous.
How like, methought, I then was to this kernel,
This squash, this gentleman.—Mine honest friend, 160
Will you take eggs for money?   161

MAMILLIUS   No, my lord, I'll fight.

LEONTES
You will? Why, happy man be 's dole!—My brother, 163
Are you so fond of your young prince as we
Do seem to be of ours?

POLIXENES   If at home, sir,
He's all my exercise, my mirth, my matter,   166
Now my sworn friend and then mine enemy,
My parasite, my soldier, statesman, all.
He makes a July's day short as December,
And with his varying childness cures in me   170
Thoughts that would thick my blood.

LEONTES   So stands this squire 171
Officed with me. We two will walk, my lord,   172
And leave you to your graver steps. Hermione,
How thou lov'st us, show in our brother's welcome. 174
Let what is dear in Sicily be cheap.   175
Next to thyself and my young rover, he's
Apparent to my heart.

HERMIONE   If you would seek us,   177
We are yours i'th' garden. Shall 's attend you there? 178

LEONTES
To your own bents dispose you. You'll be found,   179
Be you beneath the sky. [Aside] I am angling now,
Though you perceive me not how I give line.   181
Go to, go to!   182
How she holds up the neb, the bill to him,   183
And arms her with the boldness of a wife   184
To her allowing husband!
                   [Exeunt Polixenes and Hermione.]
                         Gone already!   185
Inch thick, knee-deep, o'er head and ears a forked
    one!—   186
Go play, boy, play. Thy mother plays, and I   187
Play too, but so disgraced a part, whose issue   188

Will hiss me to my grave. Contempt and clamor
Will be my knell. Go play, boy, play. There have been,
Or I am much deceived, cuckolds ere now;
And many a man there is, even at this present,
Now while I speak this, holds his wife by th' arm,
That little thinks she has been sluiced in 's absence   194
And his pond fished by his next neighbor, by
Sir Smile, his neighbor. Nay, there's comfort in't
Whiles other men have gates and those gates opened,   197
As mine, against their will. Should all despair
That have revolted wives, the tenth of mankind   199
Would hang themselves. Physic for't there's none.   200
It is a bawdy planet, that will strike   201
Where 'tis predominant; and 'tis powerful, think it,   202
From east, west, north, and south. Be it concluded,
No barricado for a belly. Know't,   204
It will let in and out the enemy
With bag and baggage. Many thousand on 's   206
Have the disease and feel't not.—How now, boy?

MAMILLIUS
I am like you, they say.

LEONTES   Why, that's some comfort.
What, Camillo there?

CAMILLO [coming forward]   Ay, my good lord.

LEONTES
Go play, Mamillius; thou'rt an honest man.
                                   [Exit Mamillius.]
Camillo, this great sir will yet stay longer.

CAMILLO
You had much ado to make his anchor hold.
When you cast out, it still came home.

LEONTES   Didst note it?   213

CAMILLO
He would not stay at your petitions, made
His business more material.

LEONTES   Didst perceive it?   215
[Aside] They're here with me already, whisp'ring,
  rounding,   216
"Sicilia is a so-forth." 'Tis far gone   217
When I shall gust it last.—How came't, Camillo,   218
That he did stay?

CAMILLO   At the good Queen's entreaty.

LEONTES
"At the Queen's" be't. "Good" should be pertinent,   220
But so it is, it is not. Was this taken   221
By any understanding pate but thine?

For thy conceit is soaking, will draw in   223
More than the common blocks. Not noted, is't,   224
But of the finer natures? By some severals   225
Of headpiece extraordinary? Lower messes   226
Perchance are to this business purblind? Say.   227

CAMILLO
Business, my lord? I think most understand
Bohemia stays here longer.

LEONTES
Ha?

CAMILLO   Stays here longer.

LEONTES   Ay, but why?

CAMILLO
To satisfy Your Highness and the entreaties
Of our most gracious mistress.

LEONTES   Satisfy?   232
Th'entreaties of your mistress? Satisfy?
Let that suffice. I have trusted thee, Camillo,
With all the nearest things to my heart, as well   235
My chamber councils, wherein, priestlike, thou   236
Hast cleansed my bosom. I from thee departed
Thy penitent reformed. But we have been
Deceived in thy integrity, deceived
In that which seems so.

CAMILLO   Be it forbid, my lord!   240

LEONTES
To bide upon't, thou art not honest; or,   241
If thou inclin'st that way, thou art a coward,   242
Which hoxes honesty behind, restraining   243
From course required; or else thou must be counted   244
A servant grafted in my serious trust   245
And therein negligent; or else a fool
That see'st a game played home, the rich stake drawn,   247
And tak'st it all for jest.

CAMILLO   My gracious lord,
I may be negligent, foolish, and fearful;
In every one of these no man is free
But that his negligence, his folly, fear,
Among the infinite doings of the world
Sometime puts forth. In your affairs, my lord,   253
If ever I were willful-negligent,
It was my folly; if industriously   255
I played the fool, it was my negligence,
Not weighing well the end; if ever fearful
To do a thing where I the issue doubted,   258

---

194 **sluiced** drawn off, as by a sluice. (The water in his pond, so to speak, has been drawn off by a cheating neighbor.)   197 **gates** sluice gates, suggestive of the wife's chastity that has been opened and robbed   199 **revolted** unfaithful   200 **Physic** Medicine   201 **It . . . planet** i.e., This unchastity is like the planet Venus.   **strike** blast, destroy by a malign influence   202 **predominant** in the ascendant. (Said of a planet.)   **think it** be assured of this   204 **barricado** barricade.   **Know 't** Be certain of this   206 **bag and baggage** (With sexual suggestion, as earlier in *dagger* [line 156], *sluiced, gates, let in and out,* etc.)   **on 's** of us   213 **still came home** always came back to the ship, failed to hold.   215 **material** important.   216 **They're . . . already** People are already onto my situation.   **rounding** whispering, gossiping   217 **a so-forth** a so-and-so, a you-know-what.   218 **gust** taste, i.e., hear of   220 **pertinent** i.e., appropriately applied   221 **so it is** as things stand.   **taken** perceived

223 **conceit is soaking** understanding is receptive   224 **blocks** blockheads.   225 **But . . . natures** except by those of rarefied intellect.   **severals** individuals   226 **Lower messes** Those who sit lower at table, i.e., inferior persons   227 **purblind** totally blind.   232 **Satisfy?** (Leontes takes the word in a sexual sense.)   235–6 **as well . . . councils** as well as with my private affairs   240 **Be it forbid** i.e., God forbid I should do such a thing   241–4 **To bide . . . required** If you hold back from saying what you think, you are not being honest; or, if you would like to speak but remain silent, you are a coward, allowing frankness to be hamstrung or shackled from carrying out the duty it should perform   245 **grafted . . . trust** taken into my complete confidence. (*Grafted* means "deeply embedded," like a graft.)   247 **home** i.e., for keeps, in earnest. (With perhaps a sexual double meaning, continued in *rich stake drawn*.)   **drawn** won   253 **Sometime puts forth** sometimes shows itself.   255 **industriously** deliberately   258 **the issue doubted** feared the outcome

Whereof the execution did cry out	259
Against the nonperformance, 'twas a fear	260
Which oft infects the wisest. These, my lord,	
Are such allowed infirmities that honesty	262
Is never free of. But, beseech Your Grace,	
Be plainer with me. Let me know my trespass	
By its own visage. If I then deny it,	265
'Tis none of mine.	

LEONTES   Ha' not you seen, Camillo—
But that's past doubt; you have, or your eyeglass   267
Is thicker than a cuckold's horn—or heard—   268
For to a vision so apparent, rumor   269
Cannot be mute—or thought—for cogitation
Resides not in that man that does not think—   271
My wife is slippery? If thou wilt confess,
Or else be impudently negative   273
To have nor eyes nor ears nor thought, then say   274
My wife's a hobbyhorse, deserves a name   275
As rank as any flax-wench that puts to   276
Before her trothplight. Say't and justify't.   277

CAMILLO
I would not be a stander-by to hear
My sovereign mistress clouded so without
My present vengeance taken. 'Shrew my heart,   280
You never spoke what did become you less
Than this, which to reiterate were sin   282
As deep as that, though true.

LEONTES   Is whispering nothing?   283
Is leaning cheek to cheek? Is meeting noses?
Kissing with inside lip? Stopping the career   285
Of laughter with a sigh—a note infallible
Of breaking honesty? Horsing foot on foot?   287
Skulking in corners? Wishing clocks more swift,
Hours minutes, noon midnight? And all eyes   289
Blind with the pin and web but theirs, theirs only,   290
That would unseen be wicked? Is this nothing?
Why, then the world and all that's in't is nothing,
The covering sky is nothing, Bohemia nothing,
My wife is nothing, nor nothing have these nothings,
If this be nothing.

CAMILLO   Good my lord, be cured
Of this diseased opinion, and betimes,   296
For 'tis most dangerous.

LEONTES   Say it be, 'tis true.   297

CAMILLO
No, no, my lord.

LEONTES   It is. You lie, you lie!
I say thou liest, Camillo, and I hate thee,
Pronounce thee a gross lout, a mindless slave,
Or else a hovering temporizer, that   301
Canst with thine eyes at once see good and evil,
Inclining to them both. Were my wife's liver   303
Infected as her life, she would not live   304
The running of one glass.

CAMILLO   Who does infect her?   305

LEONTES
Why, he that wears her like her medal, hanging   306
About his neck, Bohemia—who, if I
Had servants true about me, that bare eyes   308
To see alike mine honor as their profits,
Their own particular thrifts, they would do that   310
Which should undo more doing. Ay, and thou,   311
His cupbearer—whom I from meaner form   312
Have benched and reared to worship, who mayst see   313
Plainly as heaven sees earth and earth sees heaven
How I am galled—mightst bespice a cup   315
To give mine enemy a lasting wink,   316
Which draft to me were cordial.

CAMILLO   Sir, my lord,   317
I could do this, and that with no rash potion,   318
But with a ling'ring dram that should not work
Maliciously like poison. But I cannot   320
Believe this crack to be in my dread mistress,   321
So sovereignly being honorable.   322
I have loved thee—

LEONTES   Make that thy question, and go rot! 323
Dost think I am so muddy, so unsettled,   324
To appoint myself in this vexation, sully   325
The purity and whiteness of my sheets—
Which to preserve is sleep, which being spotted
Is goads, thorns, nettles, tails of wasps—
Give scandal to the blood o' th' prince my son,
Who I do think is mine and love as mine,
Without ripe moving to't? Would I do this?   331
Could man so blench?

CAMILLO   I must believe you, sir.   332
I do, and will fetch off Bohemia for't;   333
Provided that, when he's removed, Your Highness
Will take again your queen as yours at first,

259–60 Whereof . . . nonperformance in which the completion of the task showed how wrong I was in being reluctant to undertake it **262 allowed** acknowledged.   **that** as   **265 visage** face, i.e., plain appearance.   **267 eyeglass** lens of the eye   **268 cuckold's horn** (A thin sheet of horn can be seen through like a lens, though a cuckold's horn is another matter.)   **269 to a vision so apparent** about something so plainly visible   **271 think** i.e., think so   **273–4 Or . . . eyes** or, as the only possible alternative, insist impudently that you have neither eyes   **275 hobbyhorse** wanton woman   **276 flax-wench** common slut.   **puts to** engages in sex   **277 justify't** affirm it. **280 present** immediate.   **'Shrew** Beshrew, curse   **282–3 which . . . true** i.e., to repeat which accusation would be to sin as deeply as her supposed adultery, even if it were true (which it isn't).   **285 career** full gallop   **287 honesty** chastity.   **Horsing foot on foot** Placing one's foot on that of another person and then moving the feet up and down together.   **289 Hours minutes** wishing hours were minutes **290 pin and web** cataract of the eye. (The lovers wish to think themselves unobserved.)   **296 betimes** quickly   **297 Say it be** Even if it is dangerous

301 hovering wavering   **303 Inclining . . . both** being tolerant of evil along with the good.   **304 Infected as her life** as full of disease as is her moral conduct   **305 glass** hourglass.   **306 like her medal** like a miniature portrait of her, worn in a locket   **308 bare** bore, had **310 thrifts** gains   **311 undo** prevent   **312 meaner form** humbler station   **313 benched** placed on the bench of authority.   **worship** dignity, honor   **315 galled** rubbed, chafed   **316 lasting wink** everlasting closing of the eyes (in death)   **317 were cordial** would be restorative.   **318 rash** quick-acting (and therefore easily detected) **320 Maliciously** virulently   **321 crack** flaw.   **dread** worthy of awe **322 sovereignly** supremely   **323 Make . . . rot!** i.e., If you're going to question my accusations, may you rot in hell!   **324 muddy** muddleheaded   **325 To . . . vexation** to give myself this vexation   **331 ripe** ample, urgent   **332 blench** swerve (from sensible conduct). **333 fetch off** do away with; or, with deliberate ambiguity, rescue. (As also in *removed* in the next line.)

Even for your son's sake, and thereby for sealing   336
The injury of tongues in courts and kingdoms
Known and allied to yours.
LEONTES   Thou dost advise me
Even so as I mine own course have set down.
I'll give no blemish to her honor, none.
CAMILLO   My lord,
Go then, and with a countenance as clear
As friendship wears at feasts, keep with Bohemia   343
And with your queen. I am his cupbearer.
If from me he have wholesome beverage,
Account me not your servant.
LEONTES   This is all.
Do't and thou hast the one half of my heart;
Do't not, thou splitt'st thine own.
CAMILLO   I'll do't, my lord.
LEONTES
I will seem friendly, as thou hast advised me.   *Exit.*
CAMILLO
Oh, miserable lady! But, for me,
What case stand I in? I must be the poisoner
Of good Polixenes, and my ground to do't
Is the obedience to a master, one
Who in rebellion with himself will have
All that are his so too. To do this deed,   355
Promotion follows. If I could find example   356
Of thousands that had struck anointed kings
And flourished after, I'd not do't; but since   358
Nor brass, nor stone, nor parchment bears not one,   359
Let villainy itself forswear't. I must
Forsake the court. To do't or no is certain   361
To me a breakneck. Happy star reign now!   362
Here comes Bohemia.

Enter Polixenes.

POLIXENES [*to himself*]   This is strange. Methinks
My favor here begins to warp. Not speak?—   364
Good day, Camillo.
CAMILLO   Hail, most royal sir!
POLIXENES
What is the news i'th' court?
CAMILLO   None rare, my lord.   366
POLIXENES
The King hath on him such a countenance
As he had lost some province and a region   368
Loved as he loves himself. Even now I met him
With customary compliment, when he,
Wafting his eyes to th' contrary and falling   371
A lip of much contempt, speeds from me, and

So leaves me to consider what is breeding   373
That changeth thus his manners.
CAMILLO   I dare not know, my lord.
POLIXENES
How, dare not? Do not? Do you know, and dare not?   376
Be intelligent to me. 'Tis thereabouts,   377
For to yourself what you do know you must,   378
And cannot say you dare not. Good Camillo,   379
Your changed complexions are to me a mirror
Which shows me mine changed too; for I must be   381
A party in this alteration, finding   382
Myself thus altered with't.
CAMILLO   There is a sickness
Which puts some of us in distemper, but
I cannot name the disease; and it is caught
Of you that yet are well.
POLIXENES   How? Caught of me?   386
Make me not sighted like the basilisk.   387
I have looked on thousands who have sped the better   388
By my regard, but killed none so. Camillo,   389
As you are certainly a gentleman, thereto   390
Clerklike experienced, which no less adorns   391
Our gentry than our parents' noble names,   392
In whose success we are gentle, I beseech you,   393
If you know aught which does behoove my
     knowledge
Thereof to be informed, imprison't not
In ignorant concealment.
CAMILLO   I may not answer.   396
POLIXENES
A sickness caught of me, and yet I well?
I must be answered. Dost thou hear, Camillo?
I conjure thee, by all the parts of man   399
Which honor does acknowledge, whereof the least   400
Is not this suit of mine, that thou declare   401
What incidency thou dost guess of harm   402
Is creeping toward me; how far off, how near;
Which way to be prevented, if to be;   404
If not, how best to bear it.
CAMILLO   Sir, I will tell you,
Since I am charged in honor and by him   406
That I think honorable. Therefore mark my counsel,
Which must be even as swiftly followed as
I mean to utter it, or both yourself and me

336 for sealing for the sake of silencing. (Some editors prefer *forsealing*, sealing up tight.)   343 keep remain in company   355 All . . . too i.e., all his followers like him in rebelling against the best in themselves and in obeying his worst self.   To do If I do   356 If Even if   358–9 but . . . one but since recorded history shows no instances of persons who have killed a king and prospered afterwards   361 To do 't or no i.e., Either to kill Polixenes or not to kill him   362 breakneck destruction, ruin.   Happy Propitious, favorable   364 warp change, shrivel, grow askew (as wood warps). (Leontes has just passed by Polixenes without speaking.)   366 rare noteworthy   368 As as if   371 Wafting . . . contrary averting his eyes. falling letting fall

373 breeding hatching   376 Do not? i.e., Or do you mean you don't know?   377 intelligent intelligible.   'Tis thereabouts It must be something of this sort, i.e., that you know and dare not tell   378–9 For . . . dare not i.e., for in your heart, whatever it is you know, you must in fact know, and can't claim it's a matter of not daring to know.   381–2 for . . . alteration i.e., for my looks must have changed, too, reflecting this change in my position   386 Of from   387 sighted provided with a gaze.   basilisk a fabled serpent whose gaze was fatal.   388 sped prospered   389 regard look   390–3 thereto . . . gentle in addition to which you are a cultivated and educated person— something that graces our gentlemanlike condition no less than the worthy name of our ancestors, by succession from whom we are made noble   396 ignorant concealment concealment that would keep me ignorant or that would proceed from pretended ignorance on your part.   399 parts obligations   400–1 whereof . . . not not the least of which is (to answer)   402 incidency likely incident   404 if to be if it can be (prevented)   406 by him i.e., by you yourself

Cry lost, and so good night!

POLIXENES   On, good Camillo.   410

CAMILLO
I am appointed him to murder you.   411

POLIXENES
By whom, Camillo?

CAMILLO   By the King.

POLIXENES   For what?

CAMILLO
He thinks, nay, with all confidence he swears,
As he had seen 't or been an instrument
To vice you to 't, that you have touched his queen   415
Forbiddenly.

POLIXENES   Oh, then my best blood turn
To an infected jelly, and my name
Be yoked with his that did betray the Best!   418
Turn then my freshest reputation to
A savor that may strike the dullest nostril   420
Where I arrive, and my approach be shunned,
Nay, hated too, worse than the great'st infection
That e'er was heard or read!

CAMILLO   Swear his thought over   423
By each particular star in heaven and
By all their influences, you may as well
Forbid the sea for to obey the moon   426
As or by oath remove or counsel shake   427
The fabric of his folly, whose foundation   428
Is piled upon his faith and will continue   429
The standing of his body.

POLIXENES   How should this grow?   430

CAMILLO
I know not. But I am sure 'tis safer to
Avoid what's grown than question how 'tis born.
If therefore you dare trust my honesty,
That lies enclosèd in this trunk which you   434
Shall bear along impawned, away tonight!   435
Your followers I will whisper to the business,   436
And will by twos and threes at several posterns   437
Clear them o'th' city. For myself, I'll put
My fortunes to your service, which are here
By this discovery lost. Be not uncertain,   440
For, by the honor of my parents, I
Have uttered truth, which if you seek to prove,   442
I dare not stand by; nor shall you be safer   443
Than one condemned by the King's own mouth,
    thereon
His execution sworn.

POLIXENES   I do believe thee;

I saw his heart in 's face. Give me thy hand.
Be pilot to me, and thy places shall   447
Still neighbor mine. My ships are ready, and   448
My people did expect my hence departure
Two days ago. This jealousy
Is for a precious creature. As she's rare,
Must it be great; and as his person's mighty,
Must it be violent; and as he does conceive
He is dishonored by a man which ever
Professed to him, why, his revenges must   455
In that be made more bitter. Fear o'ershades me.
Good expedition be my friend, and comfort   457
The gracious Queen, part of his theme, but nothing   458
Of his ill-ta'en suspicion! Come, Camillo,   459
I will respect thee as a father if
Thou bear'st my life off. Hence! Let us avoid.   461

CAMILLO
It is in mine authority to command
The keys of all the posterns. Please Your Highness
To take the urgent hour. Come, sir, away.   *Exeunt.*

❖

2.1

Enter Hermione, Mamillius, [and] Ladies.

HERMIONE
Take the boy to you. He so troubles me,
'Tis past enduring.

FIRST LADY [*taking Mamillius from the Queen*]
                        Come, my gracious lord,
Shall I be your playfellow?

MAMILLIUS
No, I'll none of you.

FIRST LADY   Why, my sweet lord?   4

MAMILLIUS
You'll kiss me hard and speak to me as if
I were a baby still.—I love you better.

SECOND LADY
And why so, my lord?

MAMILLIUS   Not for because   7
Your brows are blacker; yet black brows, they say,
Become some women best, so that there be not   9
Too much hair there, but in a semicircle,
Or a half-moon made with a pen.

SECOND LADY   Who taught' this?   11

MAMILLIUS
I learned it out of women's faces. Pray now,
What color are your eyebrows?

FIRST LADY   Blue, my lord.

MAMILLIUS
Nay, that's a mock. I have seen a lady's nose

---

410 good night i.e., this is the end.   **411 him** by him (Leontes), or, the
one   **415 vice** force, as with a carpenter's tool, or, impel, tempt. (The
Vice was a tempter in the morality play.)   **418 his . . . Best** the name
of him (Judas) who betrayed Christ.   **420 savor** stench   **423 Swear . . .
over** i.e., Even if you should deny his suspicion with oaths   **426 for**
to to   **427 or . . . or** either . . . or   **428 fabric** edifice   **428–30 whose . . .
body** the foundation of which is built upon an unshaken conviction
and which will last as long as his body exists.   **430 How . . . grow?**
How could this suspicion have arisen?   **434 trunk** body. (With a suggestion too of a traveling trunk.)   **435 impawned** i.e., as a pledge of
good faith   **436 whisper to** secretly inform of and urge   **437 posterns**
rear gates   **440 discovery** revelation, disclosure   **442 prove** test
443 stand by affirm publicly; stay

447–8 thy . . . mine your official position will always be near to me.
455 Professed openly professed friendship   **457–9 Good . . . suspicion!** May good speed befriend me, and may my quick departure
ease the predicament of the gracious Queen, who is the object of the
King's suspicions but who is guiltless of them!   **461 bear'st my life
off** can get me out of this alive.   **avoid** depart.
2.1. Location: Sicilia. The royal court.
4 none of you have nothing to do with you.   **7 for because** because
9 so provided   **11 taught'** taught you

That has been blue, but not her eyebrows.
FIRST LADY   Hark ye,
  The Queen your mother rounds apace. We shall
  Present our services to a fine new prince
  One of these days, and then you'd wanton with us,   18
  If we would have you.
SECOND LADY   She is spread of late
  Into a goodly bulk. Good time encounter her!   20
HERMIONE [*calling to her women*]
  What wisdom stirs amongst you?—Come, sir, now
  I am for you again. Pray you, sit by us   22
  And tell 's a tale.
MAMILLIUS   Merry or sad shall 't be?
HERMIONE   As merry as you will.
MAMILLIUS
  A sad tale's best for winter. I have one
  Of sprites and goblins.
HERMIONE   Let's have that, good sir.
  Come on, sit down. Come on, and do your best
  To fright me with your sprites. You're powerful at it.
MAMILLIUS
  There was a man—
HERMIONE   Nay, come sit down, then on.
                                  [*Mamillius sits.*]
MAMILLIUS
  Dwelt by a churchyard. I will tell it softly;
  Yond crickets shall not hear it.   31
HERMIONE
  Come on, then, and give't me in mine ear.
                          [*They converse privately.*]

    [*Enter*] Leontes, Antigonus, Lords, [*and others*].

LEONTES
  Was he met there? His train? Camillo with him?
A LORD
  Behind the tuft of pines I met them. Never
  Saw I men scour so on their way. I eyed them   35
  Even to their ships.
LEONTES   How blest am I
  In my just censure, in my true opinion!   37
  Alack, for lesser knowledge! How accurst   38
  In being so blest! There may be in the cup   39
  A spider steeped, and one may drink, depart,   40
  And yet partake no venom, for his knowledge
  Is not infected; but if one present
  Th'abhorred ingredient to his eye, make known
  How he hath drunk, he cracks his gorge, his sides,   44
  With violent hefts. I have drunk, and seen the spider. 45
  Camillo was his help in this, his pander.
  There is a plot against my life, my crown.
  All's true that is mistrusted. That false villain   48

Whom I employed was pre-employed by him.
  He has discovered my design, and I   50
  Remain a pinched thing, yea, a very trick   51
  For them to play at will. How came the posterns   52
  So easily open?
A LORD   By his great authority,
  Which often hath no less prevailed than so
  On your command.
LEONTES   I know't too well.
  [*To Hermione*] Give me the boy. I am glad you did not
    nurse him.
  Though he does bear some signs of me, yet you
  Have too much blood in him.
HERMIONE   What is this? Sport?   59
LEONTES [*to a Lord*]
  Bear the boy hence; he shall not come about her.
  Away with him! And let her sport herself
  With that she's big with, [*to Hermione*] for 'tis Polixenes
  Has made thee swell thus.   [*Mamillius is led out.*]
HERMIONE   But I'd say he had not,   63
  And I'll be sworn you would believe my saying,
  Howe'er you lean to th' nayward.
LEONTES   You, my lords,   65
  Look on her, mark her well. Be but about
  To say "She is a goodly lady," and   67
  The justice of your hearts will thereto add
  "'Tis pity she's not honest, honorable."   69
  Praise her but for this her without-door form,   70
  Which on my faith deserves high speech, and straight 71
  The shrug, the hum or ha, these petty brands   72
  That calumny doth use—oh, I am out,   73
  That mercy does, for calumny will sear   74
  Virtue itself—these shrugs, these hums and ha's,
  When you have said she's goodly, come between   76
  Ere you can say she's honest. But be't known,
  From him that has most cause to grieve it should be,
  She's an adulteress.
HERMIONE   Should a villain say so,
  The most replenished villain in the world,   80
  He were as much more villain. You, my lord,   81
  Do but mistake.
LEONTES   You have mistook, my lady,   82
  Polixenes for Leontes. Oh, thou thing!
  Which I'll not call a creature of thy place,   84
  Lest barbarism, making me the precedent,
  Should a like language use to all degrees   86
  And mannerly distinguishment leave out   87

---

18 **wanton** sport, play   20 **Good . . . her!** May she have a happy
issue!   22 **for you** ready for you   31 **crickets** i.e., the court ladies, tit-
tering and laughing   35 **scour** scurry   37 **censure** judgment
38 **Alack . . . knowledge!** Would that there were less for me to know!
39 **blest** i.e., with knowledge (that causes unhappiness).   40 **A spider**
(The superstition referred to here is that the drinker is not poisoned
by the spider in the cup unless the spider is known to be there.)
44 **gorge** throat   45 **hefts** heavings, retchings.   48 **mistrusted** suspected.

50 **discovered** disclosed   51 **pinched** tortured, ridiculous.   **trick**
plaything   52 **play** play with   59 **Sport?** A joke?   63 **I'd** I need only
65 **th' nayward** the contrary.   67 **goodly** attractive   69 **honest** chaste
70 **without-door** outward, external   71 **straight** straightaway, at once
72 **brands** i.e., signs, stigmas   73 **out** wrong, in error   74 **does** uses.
(Leontes's point is that no one commits calumny by suggesting with a
shrug that Hermione is unchaste; calumny attacks *virtue itself*, whereas
Hermione has only the false appearance of virtue.)   76 **come between**
interrupt   80 **replenished** complete   81 **He . . . villain** his saying so
would double his villainy.   82 **mistook** taken wrongfully. (Playing
bitterly on *mistake*, "misapprehend.")   84 **Which . . . place** whose
exalted rank I will not desecrate by calling you what you really are
86 **like** similar.   **degrees** social ranks   87 **And . . . out** and leave out
proper distinctions

Betwixt the prince and beggar. I have said
She's an adult'ress; I have said with whom.
More, she's a traitor, and Camillo is
A fedarie with her, and one that knows   91
What she should shame to know herself   92
But with her most vile principal, that she's   93
A bed-swerver, even as bad as those   94
That vulgars give bold'st titles, ay, and privy   95
To this their late escape.

HERMIONE   No, by my life,   96
Privy to none of this. How will this grieve you,
When you shall come to clearer knowledge, that
You thus have published me! Gentle my lord,   99
You scarce can right me throughly then to say   100
You did mistake.

LEONTES   No. If I mistake
In those foundations which I build upon,
The center is not big enough to bear   103
A schoolboy's top.—Away with her to prison!
He who shall speak for her is afar off guilty   105
But that he speaks.

HERMIONE   There's some ill planet reigns. 106
I must be patient till the heavens look
With an aspect more favorable. Good my lords,
I am not prone to weeping, as our sex
Commonly are, the want of which vain dew   110
Perchance shall dry your pities; but I have
That honorable grief lodged here which burns
Worse than tears drown. Beseech you all, my lords,
With thoughts so qualified as your charities   114
Shall best instruct you, measure me; and so   115
The King's will be performed!

LEONTES   Shall I be heard?   116
HERMIONE
Who is't that goes with me? Beseech Your Highness
My women may be with me, for you see
My plight requires it.—Do not weep, good fools;   119
There is no cause. When you shall know your mistress
Has deserved prison, then abound in tears
As I come out. This action I now go on   122
Is for my better grace.—Adieu, my lord.   123
I never wished to see you sorry; now
I trust I shall. My women, come, you have leave.   125
LEONTES   Go, do our bidding. Hence!
                    [*Exit Queen, guarded, with Ladies.*]
A LORD
Beseech Your Highness, call the Queen again.
ANTIGONUS
Be certain what you do, sir, lest your justice

Prove violence, in the which three great ones suffer:
Yourself, your queen, your son.
A LORD   For her, my lord,
I dare my life lay down and will do't, sir,
Please you t'accept it, that the Queen is spotless
I'th'eyes of heaven and to you—I mean
In this which you accuse her.
ANTIGONUS   If it prove
She's otherwise, I'll keep my stables where   135
I lodge my wife. I'll go in couples with her;   136
Than when I feel and see her no farther trust her.   137
For every inch of woman in the world,
Ay, every dram of woman's flesh is false,
If she be.
LEONTES   Hold your peaces.
A LORD   Good my lord—   140
ANTIGONUS
It is for you we speak, not for ourselves.
You are abused, and by some putter-on   142
That will be damned for't. Would I knew the villain;
I would land-damn him. Be she honor-flawed,   144
I have three daughters—the eldest is eleven,
The second and the third, nine and some five—   146
If this prove true, they'll pay for't. By mine honor,
I'll geld 'em all! Fourteen they shall not see   148
To bring false generations. They are co-heirs,   149
And I had rather glib myself than they   150
Should not produce fair issue.
LEONTES   Cease, no more!   151
You smell this business with a sense as cold
As is a dead man's nose; but I do see't and feel't
As you feel doing thus, and see withal   154
The instruments that feel.
ANTIGONUS   If it be so,   155
We need no grave to bury honesty;
There's not a grain of it the face to sweeten
Of the whole dungy earth.
LEONTES   What? Lack I credit?   158
A LORD
I had rather you did lack than I, my lord,
Upon this ground; and more it would content me   160
To have her honor true than your suspicion,
Be blamed for't how you might.
LEONTES   Why, what need we   162
Commune with you of this, but rather follow

---

91 **fedarie** confederate   92–3 **to know . . . principal** to acknowledge
privately even with her contemptible partner   94 **bed-swerver** adulteress   95 **That . . . titles** that common people call by the rudest
names.   **privy** in on the secret   96 **late** recent   99 **published** proclaimed.   **Gentle my** My noble   100 **You . . . say** you scarcely can do
me full justice then merely by saying   103 **center** earth   105 **afar off**
indirectly   106 **But . . . speaks** merely by speaking.   110 **want** lack
114 **qualified** tempered   115 **measure** judge   116 **heard** i.e., obeyed.
119 **fools** (Here, a term of endearment.)   122 **come out** am released
from prison.   122–3 **The action . . . grace** What I now must undergo
will ultimately make me seem more gracious in others' eyes and
ennoble me by suffering.   125 **leave** permission (to attend me).

135–6 **I'll . . . wife** (If Hermione is an adulteress, says Antigonus,
then all women are no better than animals, to be penned up and
guarded suspiciously.)   136 **in couples** i.e., like two hounds leashed
together and hence inseparable   137 **Than . . . her** trust her no further than I can feel her next to me and actually see her.   140 **she** i.e.,
Hermione   142 **abused** deceived.   **putter-on** instigator   144 **land-
damn** lambaste (? Meaning uncertain.)   146 **some** about   148 **geld**
sterilize, de-sex   149 **bring false generations** have illegitimate children.   **They are co-heirs** i.e., They will share my inheritance (since I
have no son to inherit all)   150 **glib** castrate, geld   151 **fair issue** legitimate offspring.   154 **thus** (Leontes presumably grasps Antigonus by
the arm or pinches him or tweaks his nose.)   154–5 **and see . . . feel**
i.e., just as you and I see these fingers that pinch, I see in my mind's
eye the amorous touching of Hermione and Polixenes. (*Withal* means
"in addition.")   158 **credit** credibility.   160 **Upon this ground** in this
matter   162 **we** I. (The royal "we.")

Our forceful instigation? Our prerogative   164
Calls not your counsels, but our natural goodness   165
Imparts this; which if you—or stupefied   166
Or seeming so in skill—cannot or will not   167
Relish a truth like us, inform yourselves   168
We need no more of your advice. The matter,
The loss, the gain, the ordering on't, is all   170
Properly ours.
ANTIGONUS   And I wish, my liege,
You had only in your silent judgment tried it,
Without more overture.
LEONTES   How could that be?   173
Either thou art most ignorant by age,   174
Or thou wert born a fool. Camillo's flight,
Added to their familiarity—
Which was as gross as ever touched conjecture,   177
That lacked sight only, naught for approbation   178
But only seeing, all other circumstances
Made up to th' deed—doth push on this proceeding.   180
Yet, for a greater confirmation—
For in an act of this importance 'twere
Most piteous to be wild—I have dispatched in post   183
To sacred Delphos, to Apollo's temple,   184
Cleomenes and Dion, whom you know
Of stuffed sufficiency. Now from the oracle   186
They will bring all, whose spiritual counsel had   187
Shall stop or spur me. Have I done well?
A LORD   Well done, my lord.
LEONTES
Though I am satisfied, and need no more
Than what I know, yet shall the oracle
Give rest to th' minds of others, such as he   192
Whose ignorant credulity will not
Come up to th' truth. So have we thought it good   194
From our free person she should be confined,   195
Lest that the treachery of the two fled hence
Be left her to perform. Come, follow us.
We are to speak in public, for this business
Will raise us all.
ANTIGONUS [aside]   To laughter, as I take it,   199
If the good truth were known.   Exeunt.

❖

2.2

Enter Paulina, a Gentleman, [and attendants].

PAULINA
The keeper of the prison, call to him.
Let him have knowledge who I am.
                    [The Gentleman goes to the door.]
                              Good lady,   2
No court in Europe is too good for thee;
What dost thou then in prison?

          [Enter] Jailer.

                              Now, good sir,
You know me, do you not?
JAILER   For a worthy lady
And one who much I honor.
PAULINA   Pray you then,
Conduct me to the Queen.
JAILER   I may not, madam.
To the contrary I have express commandment.
PAULINA
Here's ado, to lock up honesty and honor from
Th'access of gentle visitors! Is't lawful, pray you,
To see her women? Any of them? Emilia?
JAILER   So please you, madam,
To put apart these your attendants, I   13
Shall bring Emilia forth.
PAULINA   I pray now, call her.—
Withdraw yourselves.
          [Gentleman and attendants withdraw.]
JAILER   And, madam,
I must be present at your conference.
PAULINA   Well, be't so, prithee.   [Exit Jailer.]
Here's such ado, to make no stain a stain   19
As passes coloring.

          [Enter Jailer, with] Emilia.

                    Dear gentlewoman,   20
How fares our gracious lady?
EMILIA
As well as one so great and so forlorn
May hold together. On her frights and griefs—   23
Which never tender lady hath borne greater—   24
She is something before her time delivered.   25
PAULINA
A boy?
EMILIA   A daughter, and a goodly babe,
Lusty and like to live. The Queen receives   27
Much comfort in't, says, "My poor prisoner,
I am innocent as you."
PAULINA   I dare be sworn.
These dangerous unsafe lunes i'th' King, beshrew
them!   30
He must be told on't, and he shall. The office   31
Becomes a woman best; I'll take't upon me.   32

---

164 Our . . . instigation my own strong inclination.   **164–6 Our pre-**
rogative . . . this My royal prerogative is under no obligation to consult you, but rather out of natural generosity I inform you of the
matter   **166 or** either   **167 Or . . . skill** or pretending to be stupefied
out of cunning   **168 Relish** savor, appreciate   **170 on't** of it
173 overture public disclosure.   **174 by age** through the folly of old
age   **177 as gross . . . conjecture** as palpably evident as any conjecture ever touched upon and verified   **178 approbation** proof
180 Made up added up.   **push on** urge onward   **183 wild** rash.
post haste   **184 Delphos** (See note at 3.1.2.)   **186 Of stuffed suffi-**
ciency abundantly qualified and trustworthy.   **187 all** the whole
truth.   **had** having been obtained   **192 he** any person (such as
Antigonus)   **194 Come up to** face   **195 From** away from.   **free**
accessible   **199 raise** rouse
2.2 Location: Sicilia. A prison.

2 Good lady (Addressed to the absent Hermione.)   **13 put apart** dismiss   **19–20 to make . . . coloring** to make out of no stain at all a
besmirching of honor that surpasses any justification. (Expressed in a
metaphor of dyeing and painting.)   **23 On** In consequence of
24 Which than which   **25 something** somewhat. (Also in line 55.)
27 Lusty vigorous.   **like** likely   **30 lunes** fits of lunacy   **31 on't** of it
32 Becomes suits

If I prove honeymouthed, let my tongue blister   33
And never to my red-looked anger be   34
The trumpet any more. Pray you, Emilia,
Commend my best obedience to the Queen.   36
If she dares trust me with her little babe,
I'll show't the King and undertake to be
Her advocate to th' loud'st. We do not know   39
How he may soften at the sight o'th' child.
The silence often of pure innocence
Persuades when speaking fails.

EMILIA   Most worthy madam,
Your honor and your goodness is so evident
That your free undertaking cannot miss   44
A thriving issue. There is no lady living   45
So meet for this great errand. Please Your Ladyship   46
To visit the next room, I'll presently   47
Acquaint the Queen of your most noble offer,
Who but today hammered of this design,   49
But durst not tempt a minister of honor   50
Lest she should be denied.

PAULINA   Tell her, Emilia,
I'll use that tongue I have. If wit flow from't   52
As boldness from my bosom, let 't not be doubted
I shall do good.

EMILIA   Now be you blest for it!
I'll to the Queen.—Please you, come something nearer.   55

JAILER
Madam, if't please the Queen to send the babe,
I know not what I shall incur to pass it,   57
Having no warrant.

PAULINA   You need not fear it, sir.
This child was prisoner to the womb and is
By law and process of great Nature thence
Freed and enfranchised, not a party to
The anger of the King nor guilty of—
If any be—the trespass of the Queen.

JAILER   I do believe it.

PAULINA
Do not you fear. Upon mine honor, I
Will stand betwixt you and danger.   *Exeunt.*

❧

2.3

Enter Leontes.

LEONTES
Nor night nor day, no rest! It is but weakness
To bear the matter thus, mere weakness. If
The cause were not in being—part o'th' cause,   3
She th'adulteress, for the harlot King   4

Is quite beyond mine arm, out of the blank   5
And level of my brain, plot-proof, but she   6
I can hook to me—say that she were gone,   7
Given to the fire, a moiety of my rest   8
Might come to me again.—Who's there?

[Enter a] Servant.

SERVANT   My lord?
LEONTES   How does the boy?
SERVANT
He took good rest tonight; 'tis hoped   11
His sickness is discharged.
LEONTES   To see his nobleness!
Conceiving the dishonor of his mother,   13
He straight declined, drooped, took it deeply,   14
Fastened and fixed the shame on't in himself,   15
Threw off his spirit, his appetite, his sleep,
And downright languished.—Leave me solely. Go,   17
See how he fares.   *[Exit Servant.]*
                      Fie, fie! No thought of him.   18
The very thought of my revenges that way
Recoil upon me—in himself too mighty,
And in his parties, his alliance. Let him be,   21
Until a time may serve. For present vengeance,
Take it on her. Camillo and Polixenes
Laugh at me, make their pastime at my sorrow.
They should not laugh if I could reach them, nor
Shall she, within my power.

*Enter Paulina [with a baby]; Antigonus and Lords
[trying to hold her back].*

A LORD   You must not enter.
PAULINA
Nay, rather, good my lords, be second to me.   27
Fear you his tryannous passion more, alas,
Than the Queen's life? A gracious innocent soul,
More free than he is jealous.
ANTIGONUS   That's enough.   30
SERVANT
Madam, he hath not slept tonight, commanded
None should come at him.
PAULINA   Not so hot, good sir.
I come to bring him sleep. 'Tis such as you,
That creep like shadows by him and do sigh
At each his needless heavings, such as you   35
Nourish the cause of his awaking. I   36
Do come with words as medicinal as true,
Honest as either, to purge him of that humor   38
That presses him from sleep.
LEONTES   What noise there, ho?

33 blister (It was popularly supposed that lying blistered the tongue.)
34 red-looked red-faced   **36 Commend** deliver   **39 to th' loud'st** as
loudly as I can.   **44 free** generous   **45 thriving issue** successful outcome.   **46 meet** suited.   **Please** If it please   **47 presently** at once
49 hammered of mused upon   **50 tempt** solicit (to serve as ambassador in such a case)   **52 wit** wisdom   **55 come . . . nearer** i.e., come
into the next room (as in lines 46–7).   **57 to pass it** if I let it pass
2.3. Location: Sicilia. The royal court.
3 not in being dead   **4 harlot** lewd. (Originally applied to either sex.)

5–6 out . . . level beyond the range. (Archery terms: *blank* is the center
of the target or the close range needed for a direct shot at it, as in
"point-blank"; *level* is the action of aiming.)   **7 hook** (As with grappling hooks.)   **8 Given to the fire** burned at the stake (as a traitor
conspiring against the King).   **moiety** portion   **11 tonight** last night
13 Conceiving Grasping the enormity of   **14 straight** immediately
15 on't of it   **17 solely** alone.   **18 him** i.e., Polixenes.   **21 his parties
. . . alliance** his supporters and allies.   **27 be second to** aid, second
30 free innocent   **35 heavings** sighs or groans   **36 awaking** inability
to sleep.   **38 humor** distemper

PAULINA
    No noise, my lord, but needful conference
    About some gossips for Your Highness.
LEONTES   How?   41
    Away with that audacious lady! Antigonus,
    I charged thee that she should not come about me.
    I knew she would.
ANTIGONUS   I told her so, my lord,
    On your displeasure's peril and on mine,
    She should not visit you.
LEONTES   What, canst not rule her?
PAULINA
    From all dishonesty he can. In this,
    Unless he take the course that you have done—
    Commit me for committing honor—trust it,   49
    He shall not rule me.
ANTIGONUS   La you now, you hear!   50
    When she will take the rein I let her run,
    But she'll not stumble.
PAULINA   Good my liege, I come—
    And, I beseech you hear me, who professes
    Myself your loyal servant, your physician,
    Your most obedient counselor, yet that dares
    Less appear so in comforting your evils   56
    Than such as most seem yours—I say, I come   57
    From your good queen.
LEONTES   Good queen?
PAULINA
    Good queen, my lord, good queen, I say good queen,
    And would by combat make her good, so were I   61
    A man, the worst about you.
LEONTES [to Lords]   Force her hence.   62
PAULINA
    Let him that makes but trifles of his eyes
    First hand me. On mine own accord I'll off,
    But first I'll do my errand. The good Queen,
    For she is good, hath brought you forth a daughter—
    Here 'tis—commends it to your blessing.
                            [She lays down the baby.]
LEONTES   Out!
    A mankind witch! Hence with her, out o' door!   68
    A most intelligencing bawd!
PAULINA   Not so.   69
    I am as ignorant in that as you
    In so entitling me, and no less honest
    Than you are mad; which is enough, I'll warrant,
    As this world goes, to pass for honest.
LEONTES [to Lords]   Traitors!
    Will you not push her out? [To Antigonus] Give her the
        bastard.
    Thou dotard, thou art woman-tired, unroosted   75

By thy Dame Partlet here. Take up the bastard!   76
    Take't up, I say. Give't to thy crone.
PAULINA [to Antigonus]   Forever
    Unvenerable be thy hands if thou
    Tak'st up the Princess by that forcèd baseness   79
    Which he has put upon't!
LEONTES   He dreads his wife.
PAULINA
    So I would you did. Then 'twere past all doubt
    You'd call your children yours.
LEONTES   A nest of traitors!
ANTIGONUS
    I am none, by this good light.
PAULINA   Nor I, nor any   83
    But one that's here, and that's himself; for he
    The sacred honor of himself, his queen's,
    His hopeful son's, his babe's, betrays to slander,
    Whose sting is sharper than the sword's; and will
        not—
    For, as the case now stands, it is a curse   88
    He cannot be compelled to't—once remove   89
    The root of his opinion, which is rotten   90
    As ever oak or stone was sound.
LEONTES   A callet   91
    Of boundless tongue, who late hath beat her husband   92
    And now baits me! This brat is none of mine;   93
    It is the issue of Polixenes.
    Hence with it, and together with the dam
    Commit them to the fire!
PAULINA   It is yours;
    And, might we lay th'old proverb to your charge,
    So like you, 'tis the worse. Behold, my lords,   98
    Although the print be little, the whole matter
    And copy of the father—eye, nose, lip,
    The trick of 's frown, his forehead, nay, the valley,   101
    The pretty dimples of his chin and cheek, his smiles,
    The very mold and frame of hand, nail, finger.
    And thou, good goddess Nature, which hast made it
    So like to him that got it, if thou hast   105
    The ordering of the mind too, 'mongst all colors
    No yellow in't, lest she suspect, as he does,   107
    Her children not her husband's!
LEONTES   A gross hag!
    And, lozel, thou art worthy to be hanged,   109
    That wilt not stay her tongue.
ANTIGONUS   Hang all the husbands   110
    That cannot do that feat, you'll leave yourself

---

41 **gossips** godparents for the baby at its baptism   49 **Commit** i.e., to prison   50 **La . . . hear!** i.e., There now, you hear how she will go on talking!   56–7 **in comforting . . . yours** when it comes to encouraging your evil courses than those flatterers who seem to be your most loyal servants   61 **by combat** by trial by combat.   **make** prove   62 **worst** least manly, or, lowest in rank   68 **mankind** masculine, behaving like a man   69 **intelligencing bawd** acting as go-between and spy (for the Queen and Polixenes).   75 **woman-tired** henpecked. (From *tire* in falconry, meaning "tear with the beak.")   **unroosted** driven from perch

76 **Partlet** or Pertilote, a common name for a hen (as in *Reynard the Fox* and in Chaucer's "Nun's Priest's Tale")   79 **by that forcèd baseness** under that wrongfully imposed name of bastard   83 **by this good light** by the light of day. (A common oath.)   88–90 **as . . . opinion** i.e., since he is King, he regrettably can't be compelled to change his deeply rooted opinion   91 **callet** scold   92 **late** recently   93 **baits** (With a pun on *beat* in the previous line, pronounced "bate.")   98 **So . . . worse** he's so like you that he fares the worse for it.   101 **trick** characteristic expression.   **valley** cleft above the upper lip   105 **got** begot   107 **No yellow** let there be no yellow, i.e., the color of jealousy. (A chaste woman could hardly expect that her own children are illegitimate, but Paulina may be hyperbolically ridiculing Leontes's suspicions.)   109 **lozel** worthless person, scoundrel. (Addressed to Antigonus.)   110 **stay** restrain

Hardly one subject.

LEONTES   Once more, take her hence.

PAULINA
A most unworthy and unnatural lord
Can do no more.

LEONTES   I'll ha' thee burnt.

PAULINA   I care not.
It is an heretic that makes the fire,   115
Not she which burns in 't. I'll not call you tyrant;   116
But this most cruel usage of your queen,
Not able to produce more accusation   118
Than your own weak-hinged fancy, something savors
Of tyranny and will ignoble make you,
Yea, scandalous to the world.

LEONTES [to Antigonus]   On your allegiance,
Out of the chamber with her! Were I a tyrant,
Where were her life? She durst not call me so   123
If she did know me one. Away with her!

PAULINA
I pray you, do not push me; I'll be gone.
Look to your babe, my lord; 'tis yours. Jove send her
A better guiding spirit!—What needs these hands?   127
You that are thus so tender o'er his follies
Will never do him good, not one of you.
So, so. Farewell, we are gone.   Exit.

LEONTES [to Antigonus]
Thou, traitor, hast set on thy wife to this.
My child? Away with 't! Even thou, that hast
A heart so tender o'er it, take it hence
And see it instantly consumed with fire;
Even thou and none but thou. Take it up straight.
Within this hour bring me word 'tis done,
And by good testimony, or I'll seize thy life,
With what thou else call'st thine. If thou refuse
And wilt encounter with my wrath, say so;
The bastard brains with these my proper hands   140
Shall I dash out. Go, take it to the fire,
For thou set'st on thy wife.

ANTIGONUS   I did not, sir.
These lords, my noble fellows, if they please,
Can clear me in 't.

LORDS   We can. My royal liege,
He is not guilty of her coming hither.

LEONTES   You're liars all.

A LORD
Beseech Your Highness, give us better credit.   147
We have always truly served you, and beseech'   148
So to esteem of us; and on our knees we beg,
As recompense of our dear services   150
Past and to come, that you do change this purpose,
Which being so horrible, so bloody, must
Lead on to some foul issue. We all kneel.

LEONTES
I am a feather for each wind that blows.
Shall I live on to see this bastard kneel
And call me father? Better burn it now
Than curse it then. But be it; let it live.
It shall not neither. [To Antigonus] You, sir, come you
    hither,
You that have been so tenderly officious
With Lady Margery, your midwife there,   160
To save this bastard's life—for 'tis a bastard,
So sure as this beard's gray. What will you adventure 162
To save this brat's life?

ANTIGONUS   Anything, my lord,
That my ability may undergo
And nobleness impose. At least thus much:
I'll pawn the little blood which I have left
To save the innocent—anything possible.

LEONTES [holding his sword]
It shall be possible. Swear by this sword
Thou wilt perform my bidding.

ANTIGONUS [his hand on the hilt]   I will, my lord.

LEONTES
Mark and perform it, see'st thou; for the fail   170
Of any point in't shall not only be
Death to thyself but to thy lewd-tongued wife,
Whom for this time we pardon. We enjoin thee,
As thou art liegeman to us, that thou carry   174
This female bastard hence, and that thou bear it
To some remote and desert place quite out
Of our dominions, and that there thou leave it,
Without more mercy, to it own protection   178
And favor of the climate. As by strange fortune
It came to us, I do in justice charge thee,
On thy soul's peril and thy body's torture,
That thou commend it strangely to some place   182
Where chance may nurse or end it. Take it up.

ANTIGONUS [taking up the baby]
I swear to do this, though a present death
Had been more merciful.—Come on, poor babe.
Some powerful spirit instruct the kites and ravens
To be thy nurses! Wolves and bears, they say,
Casting their savageness aside, have done
Like offices of pity.—Sir, be prosperous
In more than this deed does require!—And blessing 190
Against this cruelty fight on thy side,
Poor thing, condemned to loss!   Exit [with the baby].

LEONTES   No, I'll not rear   192
Another's issue.

                    Enter a Servant.

SERVANT   Please Your Highness, posts   193
From those you sent to th'oracle are come
An hour since. Cleomenes and Dion,

115–16 It is . . . in 't i.e., In burning me, you who would be making or building the fire are the heretic, not me (since loss of faith in innocence is a kind of heresy), or, you can burn a woman if you like, but it's a heretic's fire only if she is, in fact, a heretic.   118 Not able you not being able   123 Where . . . life? how could she escape execution at my command?   127 What . . . hands? What need is there to push me?   140 proper own   147 credit belief.   148 beseech' beseech you   150 dear loyal, heartfelt

Being well arrived from Delphos, are both landed,
Hasting to th' court.

A LORD   So please you, sir, their speed
Hath been beyond account.

LEONTES   Twenty-three days   198
They have been absent. 'Tis good speed, foretells
The great Apollo suddenly will have   200
The truth of this appear. Prepare you, lords.
Summon a session, that we may arraign   202
Our most disloyal lady; for, as she hath
Been publicly accused, so shall she have
A just and open trial. While she lives
My heart will be a burden to me. Leave me,
And think upon my bidding.   *Exeunt [separately].*

❧

3.1

Enter Cleomenes and Dion.

CLEOMENES
The climate's delicate, the air most sweet,
Fertile the isle, the temple much surpassing   2
The common praise it bears.

DION   I shall report,
For most it caught me, the celestial habits—   4
Methinks I so should term them—and the reverence
Of the grave wearers. Oh, the sacrifice!
How ceremonious, solemn, and unearthly
It was i'th'offering!

CLEOMENES   But of all, the burst
And the ear-deaf'ning voice o'th'oracle,
Kin to Jove's thunder, so surprised my sense   10
That I was nothing.

DION   If th'event o'th' journey   11
Prove as successful to the Queen—O, be't so!—
As it hath been to us rare, pleasant, speedy,
The time is worth the use on't.

CLEOMENES   Great Apollo   14
Turn all to th' best! These proclamations,
So forcing faults upon Hermione,
I little like.

DION   The violent carriage of it   17
Will clear or end the business. When the oracle,
Thus by Apollo's great divine sealed up,   19
Shall the contents discover, something rare   20
Even then will rush to knowledge. Go. Fresh horses!
And gracious be the issue!   *Exeunt.*

❧

3.2

Enter Leontes, Lords, [and] Officers.

LEONTES
This sessions, to our great grief we pronounce,
Even pushes 'gainst our heart: the party tried
The daughter of a king, our wife, and one
Of us too much beloved. Let us be cleared   4
Of being tyrannous, since we so openly
Proceed in justice, which shall have due course
Even to the guilt or the purgation.   7
Produce the prisoner.

OFFICER
It is His Highness' pleasure that the Queen
Appear in person here in court. Silence!

*[Enter] Hermione, as to her trial, [Paulina, and]
Ladies.*

LEONTES   Read the indictment.

OFFICER [*reads*] "Hermione, Queen to the worthy
Leontes, King of Sicilia, thou art here accused and ar-
raigned of high treason, in committing adultery with
Polixenes, King of Bohemia, and conspiring with
Camillo to take away the life of our sovereign lord the
King, thy royal husband; the pretense whereof being   17
by circumstances partly laid open, thou, Hermione,
contrary to the faith and allegiance of a true subject,
didst counsel and aid them, for their better safety, to
fly away by night."

HERMIONE
Since what I am to say must be but that
Which contradicts my accusation, and
The testimony on my part no other
But what comes from myself, it shall scarce boot me   25
To say "not guilty." Mine integrity,
Being counted falsehood, shall, as I express it,
Be so received. But thus: if powers divine
Behold our human actions, as they do,
I doubt not then but innocence shall make
False accusation blush and tyranny
Tremble at patience. You, my lord, best know,
Who least will seem to do so, my past life
Hath been as continent, as chaste, as true
As I am now unhappy; which is more
Than history can pattern, though devised   36
And played to take spectators. For behold me—   37
A fellow of the royal bed, which owe   38
A moiety of the throne, a great king's daughter,   39
The mother to a hopeful prince—here standing
To prate and talk for life and honor 'fore

---

198 **beyond account** unprecedented, or, beyond explanation.
200 **suddenly** at once   202 **session** trial
3.1. Location: Sicilia. On the way to Leontes's court.
2 **isle** (Shakespeare follows Greene's *Pandosto* in fictitiously placing
Delphi on an island. Delphi, sometimes known as Delphos [see
2.1.184, 2.3.196, and 3.2.126], was often confused with Delos, the
island birthplace of Apollo and location also of an oracle.)   4 **habits**
vestments   10 **surprised** overwhelmed   11 **th'event** the outcome
14 **is worth . . . on't** has been well employed.   17 **carriage** execution,
management   19 **great divine** chief priest   20 **discover** reveal

3.2. Location: Sicilia. A place of justice, probably at court.
4 **Of us** by me   7 **purgation** acquittal.   17 **pretense** purpose, design
25 **boot** avail   36 **history** story, drama.   **pattern** show a similar
example for   37 **take** please, charm   38 **which owe** who owns
39 **moiety** share

Who please to come and hear. For life, I prize it   42
As I weigh grief, which I would spare. For honor,   43
'Tis a derivative from me to mine,   44
And only that I stand for. I appeal   45
To your own conscience, sir, before Polixenes   46
Came to your court, how I was in your grace,
How merited to be so; since he came,
With what encounter so uncurrent I   49
Have strained t'appear thus; if one jot beyond   50
The bound of honor, or in act or will
That way inclining, hardened be the hearts   52
Of all that hear me, and my near'st of kin
Cry "Fie" upon my grave!

LEONTES   I ne'er heard yet
That any of these bolder vices wanted   55
Less impudence to gainsay what they did   56
Than to perform it first.

HERMIONE   That's true enough,
Though 'tis a saying, sir, not due to me.   58

LEONTES
You will not own it.

HERMIONE   More than mistress of   59
Which comes to me in name of fault, I must not   60
At all acknowledge. For Polixenes,   61
With whom I am accused, I do confess
I loved him as in honor he required;   63
With such a kind of love as might become
A lady like me; with a love even such,
So, and no other, as yourself commanded;
Which not to have done I think had been in me
Both disobedience and ingratitude
To you and toward your friend, whose love had
     spoke,   69
Even since it could speak, from an infant, freely   70
That it was yours. Now, for conspiracy,   71
I know not how it tastes, though it be dished   72
For me to try how. All I know of it
Is that Camillo was an honest man;
And why he left your court, the gods themselves,
Wotting no more than I, are ignorant.   76

LEONTES
You knew of his departure, as you know
What you have underta'en to do in 's absence.

HERMIONE   Sir,
You speak a language that I understand not.
My life stands in the level of your dreams,   81

Which I'll lay down.

LEONTES   Your actions are my dreams.   82
You had a bastard by Polixenes,
And I but dreamed it. As you were past all shame—
Those of your fact are so—so past all truth,   85
Which to deny concerns more than avails; for as   86
Thy brat hath been cast out, like to itself,   87
No father owning it—which is indeed
More criminal in thee than it—so thou
Shalt feel our justice, in whose easiest passage   90
Look for no less than death.

HERMIONE   Sir, spare your threats.   91
The bug which you would fright me with I seek.   92
To me can life be no commodity.   93
The crown and comfort of my life, your favor,
I do give lost, for I do feel it gone,   95
But know not how it went. My second joy
And firstfruits of my body, from his presence
I am barred, like one infectious. My third comfort,
Starred most unluckily, is from my breast,   99
The innocent milk in it most innocent mouth,   100
Haled out to murder; myself on every post   101
Proclaimed a strumpet; with immodest hatred   102
The childbed privilege denied, which longs   103
To women of all fashion; lastly, hurried   104
Here to this place, i'th'open air, before
I have got strength of limit. Now, my liege,   106
Tell me what blessings I have here alive
That I should fear to die? Therefore proceed.
But yet hear this; mistake me not. No life,   109
I prize it not a straw. But for mine honor,
Which I would free, if I shall be condemned   111
Upon surmises, all proofs sleeping else
But what your jealousies awake, I tell you
'Tis rigor and not law. Your Honors all,   114
I do refer me to the oracle.
Apollo be my judge!

A LORD   This your request
Is altogether just. Therefore bring forth,
And in Apollo's name, his oracle.

                         [Exeunt certain Officers.]

HERMIONE
The Emperor of Russia was my father.
Oh, that he were alive and here beholding
His daughter's trial! That he did but see

42 Who please whoever chooses   42–5 For . . . stand for As for life, I value it as I value grief, and would as willingly do without; as for honor, it is transmitted from me to my descendants, and that only I make a stand for.   46 conscience consideration, inward knowledge   49–50 With . . . thus (I ask) by what behavior so unacceptable I have transgressed so that I appear thus (in disgrace and on trial)   52 hardened hardened against me   55–6 wanted Less were more lacking in   58 due applicable   59–61 More . . . acknowledge I must not acknowledge more faults than I actually have.   61 For As for   63 required deserved   69–71 your friend . . . yours i.e., Polixenes, who professed love for you from earliest childhood (as you for him).   71 for as for   72 though . . . dished even if it were to be served up   76 Wotting supposing they know   81 level aim, range

82 Which i.e., my life.   Your . . . dreams i.e., You have performed what I have fantasized, and what you have done preys on my mind.   85 Those of your fact All those who do what you did   86 Which . . . avails your denial of which is understandable, but it won't do you any good   87 like to itself as an outcast, fatherless brat ought to be   90–1 in whose . . . death i.e., which will impose the death sentence at least, perhaps torture also.   92 bug bugbear, bogey, imaginary object of terror   93 commodity asset   95 give reckon as, or give up for   99 Starred most unluckily born under a most unlucky star   100 it its   101 post posting place for public notices   102 immodest immoderate   103 The childbed . . . longs denied the privilege of bedrest after giving birth, something that is the right   104 all fashion every rank   106 got . . . limit regained my strength after having borne a child.   109 No life i.e., I do not ask for life   111 free vindicate   114 rigor tyranny

The flatness of my misery, yet with eyes   122
Of pity, not revenge!

[Enter Officers, with] Cleomenes [and] Dion.

OFFICER *[holding a sword]*
You here shall swear upon this sword of justice
That you, Cleomenes and Dion, have
Been both at Delphos, and from thence have brought
This sealed up oracle, by the hand delivered
Of great Apollo's priest, and that since then
You have not dared to break the holy seal
Nor read the secrets in't.

CLEOMENES, DION   All this we swear.

LEONTES
Break up the seals and read.   131

OFFICER *[reads]*   "Hermione is chaste, Polixenes blameless, Camillo a true subject, Leontes a jealous tyrant,
his innocent babe truly begotten, and the King shall
live without an heir if that which is lost be not
found."

LORDS
Now blessèd be the great Apollo!

HERMIONE   Praised!

LEONTES
Hast thou read truth?

OFFICER   Ay, my lord, even so
As it is here set down.

LEONTES
There is no truth at all i'th'oracle.
The sessions shall proceed. This is mere falsehood.

[Enter a Servant.]

SERVANT
My lord the King, the King!

LEONTES   What is the business?

SERVANT
Oh, sir, I shall be hated to report it!   143
The Prince your son, with mere conceit and fear   144
Of the Queen's speed, is gone.

LEONTES   How? Gone?

SERVANT   Is dead.   145

LEONTES
Apollo's angry, and the heavens themselves
Do strike at my injustice. *[Hermione swoons.]* How now
there?

PAULINA
This news is mortal to the Queen. Look down
And see what death is doing.

LEONTES   Take her hence.
Her heart is but o'ercharged; she will recover.
I have too much believed mine own suspicion.
Beseech you, tenderly apply to her
Some remedies for life.

[Exeunt Paulina and Ladies, with Hermione.]
       Apollo, pardon
My great profaneness 'gainst thine oracle!
I'll reconcile me to Polixenes,

New woo my queen, recall the good Camillo,
Whom I proclaim a man of truth, of mercy;
For, being transported by my jealousies
To bloody thoughts and to revenge, I chose
Camillo for the minister to poison
My friend Polixenes; which had been done,
But that the good mind of Camillo tardied   162
My swift command, though I with death and with
Reward did threaten and encourage him,
Not doing it and being done. He, most humane   165
And filled with honor, to my kingly guest
Unclasped my practice, quit his fortunes here,   167
Which you knew great, and to the hazard
Of all incertainties himself commended,   169
No richer than his honor. How he glisters   170
Through my rust! And how his piety   171
Does my deeds make the blacker!

[Enter Paulina.]

PAULINA   Woe the while!
Oh, cut my lace, lest my heart, cracking it,   173
Break too!

A LORD   What fit is this, good lady?

PAULINA
What studied torments, tyrant, hast for me?   175
What wheels, racks, fires? What flaying, boiling   176
In leads or oils? What old or newer torture
Must I receive, whose every word deserves   178
To taste of thy most worst? Thy tyranny,   179
Together working with thy jealousies—
Fancies too weak for boys, too green and idle   181
For girls of nine—oh, think what they have done,
And then run mad indeed, stark mad! For all
Thy bygone fooleries were but spices of it.   184
That thou betrayed'st Polixenes, 'twas nothing;
That did but show thee, of a fool, inconstant   186
And damnable ingrateful. Nor was 't much
Thou wouldst have poisoned good Camillo's honor,
To have him kill a king—poor trespasses,   189
More monstrous standing by; whereof I reckon   190
The casting forth to crows thy baby daughter   191
To be or none or little, though a devil   192
Would have shed water out of fire ere done't.   193
Nor is't directly laid to thee, the death
Of the young Prince, whose honorable thoughts,
Thoughts high for one so tender, cleft the heart   196
That could conceive a gross and foolish sire   197

---

162 **tardied** delayed   165 **Not . . . done** i.e., death if he did not do it and reward if he did.   167 **Unclasped my practice** disclosed my plot   169 **himself commended** entrusted himself   170 **No richer than** with no riches except   170–1 **How . . . rust!** How he shines in contrast with my fault!   173 **my lace** the lace of my stays   175 **studied** ingeniously devised   176 **wheels . . . flaying** (Various methods of torture: being stretched on a wheel or rack until the bones are broken or pulled apart at the joints, being burned or skinned alive.)   178–9 **whose . . . worst?** I, whose every word seems to invite your severest punishment?   181 **idle** foolish   184 **spices** foretastes, samples   186 **of** for   189 **To have** by having.   **poor** slight   190 **More . . . by** when more monstrous sins are at hand for comparison   191 **crows** carrion birds   192 **or none** either none   193 **shed . . . fire** wept from his fiery eyes or while surrounded by hellfire   196 **tender** young   197 **conceive** apprehend that

---

122 **flatness** boundlessness   131 **up** open   143 **to report** for reporting
144 **conceit and fear** i.e., anxious concern   145 **speed** fate, fortune

Blemished his gracious dam. This is not, no,   198
Laid to thy answer. But the last—Oh, lords,   199
When I have said, cry woe! The Queen, the Queen,   200
The sweet'st, dear'st creature's dead, and vengeance
    for't
Not dropped down yet.

A LORD   The higher powers forbid!

PAULINA
I say she's dead. I'll swear't. If word nor oath
Prevail not, go and see. If you can bring
Tincture or luster in her lip, her eye,   205
Heat outwardly or breath within, I'll serve you
As I would do the gods. But, O thou tyrant!
Do not repent these things, for they are heavier
Than all thy woes can stir. Therefore betake thee   209
To nothing but despair. A thousand knees
Ten thousand years together, naked, fasting,
Upon a barren mountain, and still winter   212
In storm perpetual, could not move the gods
To look that way thou wert.

LEONTES   Go on, go on.   214
Thou canst not speak too much. I have deserved
All tongues to talk their bitt'rest.

A LORD [to Paulina]   Say no more.
Howe'er the business goes, you have made fault
I'th' boldness of your speech.

PAULINA   I am sorry for't.
All faults I make, when I shall come to know them,   219
I do repent. Alas, I have showed too much
The rashness of a woman! He is touched
To th' noble heart. What's gone and what's past help
Should be past grief.—Do not receive affliction   223
At my petition. I beseech you, rather   224
Let me be punished, that have minded you   225
Of what you should forget. Now, good my liege,
Sir, royal sir, forgive a foolish woman.
The love I bore your queen—lo, fool again!
I'll speak of her no more, nor of your children;
I'll not remember you of my own lord,   230
Who is lost too. Take your patience to you,   231
And I'll say nothing.

LEONTES   Thou didst speak but well
When most the truth, which I receive much better
Than to be pitied of thee. Prithee, bring me
To the dead bodies of my queen and son.
One grave shall be for both. Upon them shall
The causes of their death appear, unto
Our shame perpetual. Once a day I'll visit
The chapel where they lie, and tears shed there
Shall be my recreation. So long as nature   240
Will bear up with this exercise, so long

I daily vow to use it. Come and lead me
To these sorrows.   *Exeunt.*

❖

3.3

Enter Antigonus [and] a Mariner, [with a] babe.

ANTIGONUS
Thou art perfect then, our ship hath touched upon   1
The deserts of Bohemia?

MARINER   Ay, my lord, and fear   2
We have landed in ill time. The skies look grimly
And threaten present blusters. In my conscience,   4
The heavens with that we have in hand are angry
And frown upon 's.

ANTIGONUS   Their sacred wills be done! Go, get aboard;
Look to thy bark. I'll not be long before   8
I call upon thee.

MARINER   Make your best haste, and go not
Too far i'th' land. 'Tis like to be loud weather.   10
Besides, this place is famous for the creatures
Of prey that keep upon't.

ANTIGONUS   Go thou away.   12
I'll follow instantly.

MARINER   I am glad at heart
To be so rid o'th' business.   *Exit.*

ANTIGONUS   Come, poor babe.
I have heard, but not believed, the spirits o'th' dead
May walk again. If such thing be, thy mother
Appeared to me last night, for ne'er was dream
So like a waking. To me comes a creature,
Sometimes her head on one side, some another;   19
I never saw a vessel of like sorrow,
So filled and so becoming. In pure white robes,   21
Like very sanctity, she did approach
My cabin where I lay, thrice bowed before me,
And, gasping to begin some speech, her eyes
Became two spouts. The fury spent, anon
Did this break from her: "Good Antigonus,
Since fate, against thy better disposition,
Hath made thy person for the thrower-out
Of my poor babe, according to thine oath,
Places remote enough are in Bohemia;
There weep and leave it crying. And, for the babe   31
Is counted lost forever, Perdita,   32
I prithee, call't. For this ungentle business   33
Put on thee by my lord, thou ne'er shalt see
Thy wife Paulina more." And so, with shrieks,
She melted into air. Affrighted much,
I did in time collect myself and thought
This was so and no slumber. Dreams are toys;   38

---

198 **dam** mother.   199 **Laid ... answer** presented as a charge that
you must answer.   200 **said** finished speaking   205 **Tincture** color
209 **woes can stir** penance can remove.   212 **still** always   214 **To look
... wert** to regard you.   219 **I make** that I make   223–4 **Do ... petition** Do not afflict yourself with remorse at my urging.   225 **minded
you** put you in mind   230 **remember** remind   231 **Take ... you** Arm
yourself with patience   240 **my recreation** (1) my sole diversion (2) my
spiritual regeneration.   **nature** my physical being

3.3 Location: Bohemia. The seacoast.
1 **perfect** certain   2 **deserts of Bohemia** i.e., deserted region on the
coast. (Shakespeare follows Greene's *Pandosto* in giving Bohemia a
seacoast.)   4 **present** immediate.   **conscience** opinion   8 **bark** ship.
10 **like** likely.   **loud** stormy   12 **keep upon't** inhabit it.   19 **some
another** sometimes the other   21 **So ... becoming** i.e., so filled with
sorrow and able to bear it so gracefully.   31 **for** because   32 **Perdita**
i.e., the lost one   33 **ungentle** ignoble   38 **toys** trifles

Yet for this once, yea, superstitiously,
I will be squared by this. I do believe　　　　　40
Hermione hath suffered death, and that
Apollo would, this being indeed the issue
Of King Polixenes, it should here be laid,
Either for life or death, upon the earth
Of its right father. Blossom, speed thee well!
　　　　　　　　　　　[*He lays down the baby.*]
There lie, and there thy character; there these,　　46
　　　　[*He places a box and a fardel beside the baby.*]
Which may, if fortune please, both breed thee, pretty,　47
And still rest thine. [*Thunder.*] The storm begins. Poor
　　wretch,　　　　　48
That for thy mother's fault art thus exposed
To loss and what may follow! Weep I cannot,　　50
But my heart bleeds; and most accurst am I
To be by oath enjoined to this. Farewell!
The day frowns more and more. Thou'rt like to have
A lullaby too rough. I never saw
The heavens so dim by day. A savage clamor!
Well may I get aboard! This is the chase.
I am gone forever!　　　　　*Exit, pursued by a bear.*

　　　　　[Enter a] Shepherd.

SHEPHERD　I would there were no age between ten and
　　three-and-twenty, or that youth would sleep out the
　　rest, for there is nothing in the between but getting
　　wenches with child, wronging the ancientry, stealing,　61
　　fighting—Hark you now, would any but these boiled　62
　　brains of nineteen and two-and-twenty hunt this　63
　　weather? They have scared away two of my best sheep,
　　which I fear the wolf will sooner find than the master.
　　If anywhere I have them, 'tis by the seaside, browsing
　　of ivy. Good luck, an't be his will! [*Seeing the child.*]　67
　　What have we here? Mercy on 's, a bairn, a very pretty　68
　　bairn! A boy or a child, I wonder? A pretty one, a very　69
　　pretty one. Sure some scape. Though I am not bookish,　70
　　yet I can read waiting-gentlewoman in the scape.
　　This has been some stair-work, some trunk-work,　72
　　some behind-door-work. They were warmer that got　73
　　this than the poor thing is here. I'll take it up for pity.
　　Yet I'll tarry till my son come; he hallooed but even
　　now.—Whoa, ho, hoa!　　　　　76

　　　　　Enter Clown.

CLOWN　Hilloa, loa!

SHEPHERD　What, art so near? If thou'lt see a thing to
　　talk on when thou art dead and rotten, come hither.
　　What ail'st thou, man?
CLOWN　I have seen two such sights, by sea and by
　　land! But I am not to say it is a sea, for it is now the sky;
　　betwixt the firmament and it you cannot thrust a
　　bodkin's point.　　　　　84
SHEPHERD　Why, boy, how is it?
CLOWN　I would you did but see how it chafes, how it　87
　　rages, how it takes up the shore! But that's not to the
　　point. Oh, the most piteous cry of the poor souls! Some-
　　times to see 'em, and not to see 'em; now the ship
　　boring the moon with her mainmast, and anon swal-
　　lowed with yeast and froth, as you'd thrust a cork into　91
　　a hogshead. And then for the land service, to see how　92
　　the bear tore out his shoulder bone; how he cried to
　　me for help and said his name was Antigonus, a no-
　　bleman. But to make an end of the ship: to see how
　　the sea flapdragoned it! But first, how the poor souls　96
　　roared and the sea mocked them, and how the poor
　　gentleman roared and the bear mocked him, both
　　roaring louder than the sea or weather.
SHEPHERD　Name of mercy, when was this, boy?
CLOWN　Now, now. I have not winked since I saw these　101
　　sights. The men are not yet cold under water, nor the
　　bear half dined on the gentleman. He's at it now.
SHEPHERD　Would I had been by, to have helped the
　　old man!
CLOWN　I would you had been by the ship side, to have
　　helped her. There your charity would have lacked
　　footing.　　　　　108
SHEPHERD　Heavy matters, heavy matters! But look
　　here, boy. Now bless thyself. Thou met'st with things
　　dying, I with things newborn. Here's a sight for thee;
　　look thee, a bearing cloth for a squire's child! Look　112
　　thee here; take up, take up, boy. Open't. So, let's see.
　　It was told me I should be rich by the fairies. This is
　　some changeling. Open't. What's within, boy?　　115
　　　　　[*The Clown opens the box.*]
CLOWN　You're a made old man. If the sins of your
　　youth are forgiven you, you're well to live. Gold, all　117
　　gold!
SHEPHERD　This is fairy gold, boy, and 'twill prove so.
　　Up with't, keep it close. Home, home, the next way.　120
　　We are lucky, boy, and to be so still requires nothing　121
　　but secrecy. Let my sheep go. Come, good boy, the　122
　　next way home.

---

40 squared directed in my course　**46 thy character** the written account of you (i.e., the one that subsequently will serve to identify Perdita). **these** i.e., the gold and jewels found by the Shepherd, also later used to identify her.　**46.1 box, fardel** (The box, containing gold and jewels, is later produced by the old Shepherd and the Clown; see 4.4.758–9. They also have a *fardel*, or "bundle," consisting evidently of the bearing cloth [3.3.112] and/or mantle [5.2.34] in which the babe was found.)　**47 breed thee** keep you, pay for your support. **pretty** pretty one　**48 And still rest thine** i.e., and still provide a heritage with what is unspent.　**50 Weep I cannot** i.e., I cannot weep as the Queen instructed me (line 31)　**61 ancientry** old people　**62–3 boiled brains** addlepated youths　**67 Good . . . will!** i.e., May God grant me good luck in finding my sheep!　**68 bairn** child　**69 child** i.e., female infant　**70 scape** sexual escapade.　**72–3 stair-work . . . behind-door-work** i.e., sexual liaisons under or behind the stairs or using a room or a trunk for concealment.　**73 got** begot　**76.1 Clown** country fellow, rustic.

84 bodkin's needle's. (A *bodkin* can also be a dagger, awl, etc.)　**87 takes up** (1) contends with, rebukes (2) swallows　**91 yeast** foam　**92 hogshead** large barrel. (The image is of a cork swimming in a turbulent expanse of frothing liquid.)　**land service** (1) dish of food served on land (2) military service on land (as distinguished from naval service); here, the doings on land　**96 flapdragoned** swallowed as one would a flapdragon, i.e., a raisin or the like swallowed out of burning brandy in the game of snapdragon　**101 winked** blinked an eye　**108 footing** (1) foothold (2) establishment of a charitable foundation, one that would provide *charity* (line 107).　**112 bearing cloth** rich cloth or mantle in which a child was carried to its baptism　**115 changeling** child left or taken by fairies.　**117 well to live** well-to-do.　**120 close** secret. **next** nearest　**121–2 to be . . . secrecy** (To talk about fairy gifts would be to insure bad luck.)　**121 still** on a continuing basis

CLOWN   Go you the next way with your findings. I'll go
see if the bear be gone from the gentleman, and how
much he hath eaten. They are never curst but when   126
they are hungry. If there be any of him left, I'll bury it.

SHEPHERD   That's a good deed. If thou mayest discern
by that which is left of him what he is, fetch me to th'   129
sight of him.

CLOWN   Marry, will I; and you shall help to put him i'th'   131
ground.

SHEPHERD   'Tis a lucky day, boy, and we'll do good
deeds on't.   *Exeunt.*

❖

4.1

Enter Time, the Chorus.

TIME
I, that please some, try all, both joy and terror   1
Of good and bad, that makes and unfolds error,   2
Now take upon me, in the name of Time,
To use my wings. Impute it not a crime
To me or my swift passage that I slide
O'er sixteen years and leave the growth untried   6
Of that wide gap, since it is in my power
To o'erthrow law and in one self-born hour   8
To plant and o'erwhelm custom. Let me pass   9
The same I am ere ancient'st order was   10
Or what is now received. I witness to   11
The times that brought them in; so shall I do   12
To th' freshest things now reigning, and make stale
The glistering of this present as my tale   14
Now seems to it. Your patience this allowing,   15
I turn my glass and give my scene such growing   16
As you had slept between. Leontes leaving   17
Th'effects of his fond jealousies, so grieving   18
That he shuts up himself, imagine me,
Gentle spectators, that I now may be
In fair Bohemia. And remember well
I mentioned a son o'th' King's, which Florizel
I now name to you; and with speed so pace   23
To speak of Perdita, now grown in grace   24
Equal with wond'ring. What of her ensues   25
I list not prophesy; but let Time's news   26
Be known when 'tis brought forth. A shepherd's
daughter,

---

126 **curst** mean, fierce   129 **what he is** what is his identity or rank
131 **Marry** i.e., Indeed. (Originally an oath, "by the Virgin Mary.")
4.1.
1 **try** test   2 **that . . . error** i.e., I who make error, thus bringing joy to
the bad and terror to the good, and then at last unfold or disclose error,
thus bringing joy to the good and terror to the bad   6 **growth untried**
developments unexplored   8 **law** any established order (including the
rule of the unity of time in a dramatic performance, conventionally
limiting the action to twenty-four hours).   **self-born** selfsame, or born
of myself (since hours are the creations of Time)   9–11 **Let . . . received**
Let me continue as I have been from before the beginning of time to the
present.   12 **them** i.e., law and custom   14 **glistering** glittering shine
15 **seems to it** seems (stale) when compared with the present.
16 **glass** hourglass   17 **As** as if   18 **fond** foolish   23 **pace** proceed
24–5 **now . . . wondering** now grown so gracious (and graceful) as to
inspire wonderment.   26 **list not** do not care to

And what to her adheres, which follows after,   28
Is th'argument of Time. Of this allow,   29
If ever you have spent time worse ere now;
If never, yet that Time himself doth say   31
He wishes earnestly you never may.   *Exit.*

❖

4.2

Enter Polixenes and Camillo.

POLIXENES   I pray thee, good Camillo, be no more
importunate. 'Tis a sickness denying thee anything, a
death to grant this.

CAMILLO   It is fifteen years since I saw my country.   4
Though I have for the most part been aired abroad, I   5
desire to lay my bones there. Besides, the penitent
King, my master, hath sent for me, to whose feeling   7
sorrows I might be some allay—or I o'erween to think   8
so—which is another spur to my departure.

POLIXENES   As thou lov'st me, Camillo, wipe not out the
rest of thy services by leaving me now. The need I
have of thee thine own goodness hath made. Better
not to have had thee than thus to want thee. Thou,   13
having made me businesses which none without thee
can sufficiently manage, must either stay to execute
them thyself or take away with thee the very services
thou hast done; which if I have not enough
considered—as too much I cannot—to be more thank-   18
ful to thee shall be my study, and my profit therein the
heaping friendships. Of that fatal country, Sicilia,   20
prithee, speak no more, whose very naming punishes
me with the remembrance of that penitent, as thou
call'st him, and reconciled King, my brother, whose
loss of his most precious queen and children are even
now to be afresh lamented. Say to me, when saw'st
thou the Prince Florizel, my son? Kings are no less
unhappy, their issue not being gracious, than they are   27
in losing them when they have approved their virtues.   28

CAMILLO   Sir, it is three days since I saw the Prince.
What his happier affairs may be are to me unknown;
but I have missingly noted he is of late much retired   31
from court and is less frequent to his princely exercises 32
than formerly he hath appeared.

POLIXENES   I have considered so much, Camillo, and   34
with some care, so far that I have eyes under my ser-   35
vice which look upon his removedness; from whom I   36
have this intelligence, that he is seldom from the   37
house of a most homely shepherd—a man, they say,   38

---

28 **to her adheres** concerns her   29 **th'argument** the subject matter
31 **yet that** i.e., yet allow that
4.2. Location: Bohemia. The court of Polixenes.
4 **fifteen** (Compare "sixteen" at 4.1.6.)   5 **been aired abroad** lived
abroad   7 **feeling** heartfelt   8 **allay** means of abatement.   **o'erween**
am presumptuous enough   13 **want** lack   18 **considered** rewarded
20 **heaping friendships** accumulation of your kind services and our
mutual affection.   27 **their . . . gracious** if their children behave ungra-
ciously   28 **approved** proved   31 **missingly** being aware that he is
missing   32 **frequent to** devoted to   34 **so much** as much   35–6 **eyes
. . . removedness** spies who keep an eye on him in his absence
37 **intelligence** news.   **from** away from   38 **homely** simple

that from very nothing, and beyond the imagination
of his neighbors, is grown into an unspeakable estate. 40

CAMILLO I have heard, sir, of such a man, who hath a
daughter of most rare note. The report of her is 42
extended more than can be thought to begin from
such a cottage.

POLIXENES That's likewise part of my intelligence; but,
I fear, the angle that plucks our son thither. Thou shalt 46
accompany us to the place, where we will, not appearing what we are, have some question with the shep- 48
herd; from whose simplicity I think it not uneasy to 49
get the cause of my son's resort thither. Prithee, be my
present partner in this business, and lay aside the
thoughts of Sicilia.

CAMILLO I willingly obey your command.

POLIXENES My best Camillo! We must disguise ourselves. *Exit [with Camillo].*

❧

4.3

Enter Autolycus, singing.

AUTOLYCUS
When daffodils begin to peer, 1
  With heigh, the doxy over the dale! 2
Why, then comes in the sweet o'the year,
  For the red blood reigns in the winter's pale. 4

The white sheet bleaching on the hedge,
  With heigh, the sweet birds, oh, how they
    sing!
Doth set my pugging tooth on edge, 7
  For a quart of ale is a dish for a king. 8

The lark, that tirralirra chants,
  With heigh, with heigh, the thrush and the jay!
Are summer songs for me and my aunts, 11
  While we lie tumbling in the hay.

I have served Prince Florizel and in my time wore
three-pile, but now I am out of service. 14

But shall I go mourn for that, my dear? 15
  The pale moon shines by night,
And when I wander here and there, 17
  I then do most go right. 18

If tinkers may have leave to live, 19
  And bear the sow-skin budget, 20

Then my account I well may give, 21
  And in the stocks avouch it. 22

My traffic is sheets; when the kite builds, look to lesser 23
linen. My father named me Autolycus, who, being, as 24
I am, littered under Mercury, was likewise a snap- 25
per-up of unconsidered trifles. With die and drab I 26
purchased this caparison, and my revenue is the silly 27
cheat. Gallows and knock are too powerful on the 28
highway; beating and hanging are terrors to me. For 29
the life to come, I sleep out the thought of it. A prize, 30
a prize!

Enter Clown.

CLOWN Let me see: every 'leven wether tods; every tod 32
yields pound and odd shilling; fifteen hundred shorn,
what comes the wool to?

AUTOLYCUS [*aside*] If the springe hold, the cock's mine. 35

CLOWN I cannot do't without counters. Let me see; 36
what am I to buy for our sheepshearing feast? Three
pound of sugar, five pound of currants, rice—what
will this sister of mine do with rice? But my father hath
made her mistress of the feast, and she lays it on. She
hath made me four-and-twenty nosegays for the shear- 41
ers—three-man-song men all, and very good ones; 42
but they are most of them means and basses, but one 43
Puritan amongst them, and he sings psalms to horn- 44
pipes. I must have saffron to color the warden pies; 45
mace; dates?—none, that's out of my note; nutmegs, 46
seven; a race or two of ginger, but that I may beg; four 47
pound of prunes, and as many of raisins o'th' sun. 48

AUTOLYCUS Oh, that ever I was born! [*He grovels on the
ground.*]

CLOWN I'th' name of me! 50

AUTOLYCUS Oh, help me, help me! Pluck but off these
rags, and then death, death!

---

40 **unspeakable** beyond description 42 **note** distinction. 46 **angle**
baited fishhook. **our** (The royal plural; also in *us*, line 47.) 48 **question** talk 49 **uneasy** difficult
4.3. Location: Bohemia. A road near the Shepherd's cottage.
1 **peer** peep out, appear 2 **doxy** beggar's wench 4 **pale** (1) paleness
(2) domain, region of authority. (The image is of red blood restoring
vitality to a pale complexion.) 7 **set . . . on edge** i.e., whets the
appetite of my thieving tooth, my taste for thieving. (To *pug* is to
"pull, tug.") 8 **quart of ale** (To be paid for perhaps with profits from
theft of sheets.) 11 **aunts** i.e., whores 14 **three-pile** velvet having
very rich pile or nap 15 **for that** i.e., for being out of service
17 **wander** (i.e., as a thief) 18 **most go right** i.e., live the life that is
meant for me. 19 **leave to live** permission to practice their trade
20 **budget** tool bag

21 **my account** an account of myself 22 **in . . . avouch it** i.e., affirm
that I am a tinker if I find myself sitting in the stocks, where vagabonds
often end up. (Autolycus passes himself off as a tinker to mask his real
calling of thief.) 23–4 **when . . . linen** (The kite, a bird of prey, was
thought to carry off small pieces of linen with which to construct its
nest, whereas Autolycus makes off with larger linen or sheets hung out
to dry.) 24 **Autolycus** (Like his namesake, Ulysses's grandfather, the
son of Mercury, this Autolycus is an expert thief.) **who** (Refers
ambiguously to Autolycus and "My father"; see next note.) 25 **littered under Mercury** (1) sired by Mercury, the god of thieves (2) born
when the planet Mercury was in the ascendant 26 **unconsidered** left
unattended, not worth thinking about 26–8 **With . . . cheat** Gambling
and whoring have brought me to the wearing of these tattered rags,
and my source of income is petty trickery used to cheat simpletons.
28–9 **Gallows . . . to me** i.e., Hanging and being beaten, the ordinary
hazards of being a highwayman, are too much for me; I'll stick to being
a petty thief. 29 **For** As for 30 **sleep . . . it** i.e., don't give a thought to
punishment in the next world. **prize** booty 32 **every . . . tods** every
eleven sheep yield a *tod*, i.e., a bulk of wool weighing twenty-eight
pounds 35 **springe** snare. **cock** woodcock. (A proverbially stupid
bird.) 36 **counters** metal disks used in reckoning. 41 **made me**
made. (*Me* is used colloquially.) **nosegays** bouquets 42 **three-man-
song men** singers of songs for three male voices: bass, tenor, and treble
43 **means** tenors 43–5 **but . . . hornpipes** (Puritans were often laughed
at for their pious singing; this Puritan is imagined as singing hymns
even to the sounds of raucous merriment at a fair.) 45 **warden** made
of the warden pear 46 **out of my note** not on my list 47 **race** root
48 **o'th' sun** dried in the sun. 50 **I'th' name of me!** (An unusual and
perhaps comic oath.)

CLOWN   Alack, poor soul! Thou hast need of more rags to lay on thee, rather than have these off.

AUTOLYCUS   Oh, sir, the loathsomeness of them offend me more than the stripes I have received, which are mighty ones and millions.

CLOWN   Alas, poor man! A million of beating may come to a great matter.

AUTOLYCUS   I am robbed, sir, and beaten; my money and apparel ta'en from me, and these detestable things put upon me.

CLOWN   What, by a horseman or a footman?   63

AUTOLYCUS   A footman, sweet sir, a footman.

CLOWN   Indeed, he should be a footman by the garments he has left with thee. If this be a horseman's coat, it hath seen very hot service. Lend me thy hand; I'll help thee. Come, lend me thy hand. [*He helps him up.*]

AUTOLYCUS   Oh, good sir, tenderly. Oh!

CLOWN   Alas, poor soul!

AUTOLYCUS   Oh, good sir, softly, good sir! I fear, sir, my shoulder blade is out.

CLOWN   How now? Canst stand?

AUTOLYCUS   [*picking his pocket*]   Softly, dear sir; good sir, softly. You ha' done me a charitable office.

CLOWN   [*reaching for his purse*]   Dost lack any money? I   76
have a little money for thee.   77

AUTOLYCUS   No, good sweet sir; no, I beseech you, sir. I have a kinsman not past three quarters of a mile hence, unto whom I was going; I shall there have money or anything I want. Offer me no money, I pray you. That kills my heart.

CLOWN   What manner of fellow was he that robbed you?

AUTOLYCUS   A fellow, sir, that I have known to go about with troll-my-dames. I knew him once a servant of the   85
Prince. I cannot tell, good sir, for which of his virtues it was, but he was certainly whipped out of the court.

CLOWN   His vices, you would say. There's no virtue whipped out of the court. They cherish it to make it stay there; and yet it will no more but abide.   90

AUTOLYCUS   Vices, I would say, sir. I know this man well. He hath been since an ape bearer, then a process   92
server, a bailiff. Then he compassed a motion of   93
the Prodigal Son and married a tinker's wife within a mile where my land and living lies, and, having flown   95
over many knavish professions, he settled only in rogue. Some call him Autolycus.

CLOWN   Out upon him! Prig, for my life, prig! He   98
haunts wakes, fairs, and bearbaitings.   99

AUTOLYCUS   Very true, sir. He, sir, he. That's the rogue that put me into this apparel.

CLOWN   Not a more cowardly rogue in all Bohemia. If you had but looked big and spit at him, he'd have run.

AUTOLYCUS   I must confess to you, sir, I am no fighter. I am false of heart that way, and that he knew, I   106
warrant him.

CLOWN   How do you now?

AUTOLYCUS   Sweet sir, much better than I was. I can stand and walk. I will even take my leave of you and pace softly towards my kinsman's.   111

CLOWN   Shall I bring thee on the way?   112

AUTOLYCUS   No, good-faced sir, no, sweet sir.

CLOWN   Then fare thee well. I must go buy spices for our sheepshearing.   *Exit.*

AUTOLYCUS   Prosper you, sweet sir! Your purse is not   116
hot enough to purchase your spice. I'll be with you at   117
your sheep shearing too. If I make not this cheat bring   118
out another, and the shearers prove sheep, let me be   119
unrolled and my name put in the book of virtue!   120

> *Song.*
>
> Jog on, jog on, the footpath way,
>   And merrily hent the stile-a;   122
> A merry heart goes all the day,
>   Your sad tires in a mile-a.   *Exit.*

❧

4.4

Enter Florizel [in shepherd's garb, and] Perdita [in holiday attire].

FLORIZEL
These your unusual weeds to each part of you   1
Does give a life; no shepherdess, but Flora   2
Peering in April's front. This your sheepshearing   3
Is as a meeting of the petty gods,   4
And you the queen on't.

PERDITA   Sir, my gracious lord,
To chide at your extremes it not becomes me.   6
Oh, pardon that I name them! Your high self,
The gracious mark o'th' land, you have obscured   8
With a swain's wearing, and me, poor lowly maid,   9

63 **horseman** highwayman.   **footman** footpad. (As the Clown observes in line 65, a common robber on foot would have poorer clothes than a mounted highwayman.)   **76–7 I have . . . thee** (The Clown reaches for his money and might have discovered the robbery if Autolycus had not quickly begged him not to bother.)   **85 troll-my-dames** or troll-madams (from the French *trou-madame*), a game in which the object was to *troll* balls through arches set on a board. (Autolycus uses the word to suggest women who *troll* or saunter about.)   **90 no more but abide** make only a temporary or unwilling stay.   **92 ape bearer** one who carries a trained monkey about for exhibition   **92–3 process server** sheriff's officer who serves processes or summonses   **93 compassed a motion** devised a puppet show   **95 living** property

98 Prig Thief   **99 wakes** village festivals   **106 false** cowardly
111 softly slowly   **112 bring . . . way** go part of the way with you.
116 Prosper . . . sir! (Said to the departing Clown.)   **116–17 Your . . . spice** i.e., You'll find but a cold purse to pay for your hot spices; an empty purse is a cold one. (Said after the Clown's departure.)
118–19 cheat bring out swindle lead to   **120 unrolled** taken off the roll (of rogues and vagabonds)   **122 hent** take hold of (as a means of leaping over)
4.4. Location: Bohemia. The Shepherd's cottage. (See lines 181–2, 187, etc.)
1 unusual weeds special, holiday attire   **2 Flora** goddess of flowers
3 Peering . . . front peeping forth in early April, or, in April's countenance or garb.   **4 petty** minor   **6 extremes** extravagant statements
8 mark o'th' land one who is noted and used as a model by everyone
9 wearing garb

Most goddesslike pranked up. But that our feasts   10
In every mess have folly, and the feeders   11
Digest it with a custom, I should blush   12
To see you so attired, swoon, I think,
To show myself a glass.

FLORIZEL   I bless the time   14
When my good falcon made her flight across
Thy father's ground.

PERDITA   Now Jove afford you cause!   16
To me the difference forges dread; your greatness   17
Hath not been used to fear. Even now I tremble
To think thy father by some accident
Should pass this way as you did. Oh, the Fates!
How would he look to see his work, so noble,   21
Vilely bound up? What would he say? Or how   22
Should I, in these my borrowed flaunts, behold   23
The sternness of his presence?

FLORIZEL   Apprehend
Nothing but jollity. The gods themselves,
Humbling their deities to love, have taken
The shapes of beasts upon them. Jupiter   27
Became a bull, and bellowed; the green Neptune   28
A ram, and bleated; and the fire-robed god,   29
Golden Apollo, a poor humble swain,   30
As I seem now. Their transformations
Were never for a piece of beauty rarer,
Nor in a way so chaste, since my desires   33
Run not before mine honor, nor my lusts
Burn hotter than my faith.

PERDITA   Oh, but sir,
Your resolution cannot hold when 'tis
Opposed, as it must be, by th' power of the King.
One of these two must be necessities,
Which then will speak: that you must change this
    purpose
Or I my life.

FLORIZEL   Thou dearest Perdita,   40
With these forced thoughts, I prithee, darken not   41
The mirth o'th' feast. Or I'll be thine, my fair,   42
Or not my father's. For I cannot be
Mine own, nor anything to any, if
I be not thine. To this I am most constant,
Though destiny say no. Be merry, gentle!   46
Strangle such thoughts as these with anything   47
That you behold the while. Your guests are coming.   48

Lift up your countenance as it were the day   49
Of celebration of that nuptial which
We two have sworn shall come.

PERDITA   O Lady Fortune,
Stand you auspicious!

FLORIZEL   See, your guests approach.
Address yourself to entertain them sprightly,   53
And let's be red with mirth.

    [*Enter*] *Shepherd, Clown; Polixenes, Camillo*
    [*disguised*]; *Mopsa, Dorcas; servants.*

SHEPHERD
Fie, daughter! When my old wife lived, upon
This day she was both pantler, butler, cook,   56
Both dame and servant; welcomed all, served all;   57
Would sing her song and dance her turn; now here,
At upper end o'th' table, now i'th' middle;
On his shoulder, and his; her face afire   60
With labor, and the thing she took to quench it   61
She would to each one sip. You are retired,   62
As if you were a feasted one and not
The hostess of the meeting. Pray you, bid
These unknown friends to 's welcome, for it is   65
A way to make us better friends, more known.   66
Come, quench your blushes and present yourself
That which you are, mistress o'th' feast. Come on,
And bid us welcome to your sheepshearing,
As your good flock shall prosper.

PERDITA [*to Polixenes*]   Sir, welcome.
It is my father's will I should take on me
The hostess-ship o'th' day. [*To Camillo*] You're
    welcome, sir.—
Give me those flowers there, Dorcas.—Reverend sirs,
For you there's rosemary and rue; these keep
Seeming and savor all the winter long.   75
Grace and remembrance be to you both,   76
And welcome to our shearing! [*Giving them flowers.*]

POLIXENES   Shepherdess—
A fair one are you—well you fit our ages
With flowers of winter.

PERDITA   Sir, the year growing ancient, 79
Not yet on summer's death nor on the birth
Of trembling winter, the fairest flow'rs o'th' season
Are our carnations and streaked gillyvors,   82
Which some call nature's bastards. Of that kind   83
Our rustic garden's barren, and I care not
To get slips of them.

POLIXENES   Wherefore, gentle maiden,   85
Do you neglect them?

PERDITA   For I have heard it said   86

---

10 pranked up bedecked.   **10–12 But . . . custom** Were it not that whenever folks gather for merry feasting one encounters some folly, which the guests take in their stride as to be expected   **14 To show . . . glass** if I were to see myself in a mirror.   **16 Jove . . . cause!** May Jove grant that you have good reason to be thankful!   **17 To me . . . dread** To me, the difference in our social rank is a source of dread   **21–2 How . . . bound up?** What would he think to see the nobly-born son he created so vilely outfitted? (The *work*, Florizel, is metaphorically a piece of writing, and his garments are the binding of the book.)   **23 flaunts** finery   **27–30 Jupiter . . . swain** (Jupiter in the guise of a bull wooed Europa, Neptune disguised as a ram deceived Bisaltes or Theophane [Ovid, *Metamorphoses*, 6.117], and Apollo took the guise of a humble shepherd to enable Admetus to woo Alcestis.)   **33 in a way** i.e., pursuing a purpose   **40 Or I my life** i.e., or I will be threatened with loss of life (as Polixenes indeed threatens at lines 436–43).   **41 forced** farfetched, unnatural   **42 Or** Either   **46 gentle** i.e., my gentle love.   **47–8 Strangle . . . while** i.e., Put down such thoughts by attending to matters at hand.

49 as as if   **53 Address** Prepare   **56 pantler** pantry servant   **57 dame** mistress of the household   **60 On his . . . his** at one person's . . . another's   **61–2 and . . . sip** and she would toast each one with the drink she took to quench the fire of her labor.   **65 to 's** each to his   **66 more known** better acquainted.   **75 Seeming** outward appearance, color   **76 Grace and remembrance** Divine grace and remembrance after death. (Equated respectively with rue and rosemary.)   **79 the year . . . ancient** i.e., when autumn arrives   **82 gillyvors** gillyflowers, a kind of carnation   **83 nature's bastards** i.e., the result of artificial breeding. (See lines 86–8.)   **85 slips** cuttings   **86 For** Because

There is an art which in their piedness shares 87
With great creating nature.

POLIXENES   Say there be;
Yet nature is made better by no mean 89
But nature makes that mean. So, over that art 90
Which you say adds to nature is an art
That nature makes. You see, sweet maid, we marry
A gentler scion to the wildest stock, 93
And make conceive a bark of baser kind
By bud of nobler race. This is an art
Which does mend nature—change it, rather—but
The art itself is nature.

PERDITA   So it is.

POLIXENES
Then make your garden rich in gillyvors,
And do not call them bastards.

PERDITA   I'll not put
The dibble in earth to set one slip of them, 100
No more than, were I painted, I would wish 101
This youth should say 'twere well, and only therefore
Desire to breed by me. Here's flowers for you:
                      [giving them flowers]
Hot lavender, mints, savory, marjoram, 104
The marigold, that goes to bed wi'th' sun
And with him rises weeping. These are flowers
Of middle summer, and I think they are given 107
To men of middle age. You're very welcome.

CAMILLO
I should leave grazing, were I of your flock,
And only live by gazing.

PERDITA   Out, alas! 110
You'd be so lean that blasts of January
Would blow you through and through. [To Florizel]
      Now, my fair'st friend,
I would I had some flow'rs o'th' spring that might
Become your time of day; [to the Shepherdesses] and
      yours, and yours,
That wear upon your virgin branches yet
Your maidenheads growing. O Proserpina, 116
For the flow'rs now that, frighted, thou let'st fall
From Dis's wagon! Daffodils,
That come before the swallow dares, and take 119
The winds of March with beauty; violets dim, 120
But sweeter than the lids of Juno's eyes
Or Cytherea's breath; pale primroses, 122
That die unmarried ere they can behold

Bright Phoebus in his strength—a malady 124
Most incident to maids; bold oxlips and 125
The crown imperial; lilies of all kinds, 126
The flower-de-luce being one. Oh, these I lack 127
To make you garlands of, and my sweet friend, 128
To strew him o'er and o'er!

FLORIZEL   What, like a corpse?

PERDITA
No, like a bank for Love to lie and play on, 130
Not like a corpse; or if, not to be buried, 131
But quick and in mine arms. Come, take your flowers.
                      [Giving flowers.] 132
Methinks I play as I have seen them do
In Whitsun pastorals. Sure this robe of mine 134
Does change my disposition.

FLORIZEL   What you do
Still betters what is done. When you speak, sweet, 136
I'd have you do it ever. When you sing,
I'd have you buy and sell so, so give alms,
Pray so; and, for the ord'ring your affairs,
To sing them too. When you do dance, I wish you
A wave o'th' sea, that you might ever do
Nothing but that—move still, still so,
And own no other function. Each your doing, 143
So singular in each particular, 144
Crowns what you are doing in the present deeds, 145
That all your acts are queens.

PERDITA   Oh, Doricles, 146
Your praises are too large. But that your youth, 147
And the true blood which peeps fairly through't
Do plainly give you out an unstained shepherd, 149
With wisdom I might fear, my Doricles,
You wooed me the false way.

FLORIZEL   I think you have
As little skill to fear as I have purpose 152
To put you to't. But come, our dance, I pray. 153
Your hand, my Perdita. So turtles pair, 154
That never mean to part.

PERDITA   I'll swear for 'em. 155
                      [They speak apart.]

POLIXENES [to Camillo]
This is the prettiest lowborn lass that ever

---

87 **art** i.e., of crossbreeding.   **piedness** particolored appearance. (Perdita disclaims the art of crossbreeding, since it infringes on what nature itself does so well.)   **89 mean** means   **90 But** unless. (Polixenes's point is that the art of improving on nature is itself natural.) **93 gentler** nobler, more cultivated   **100 dibble** trowel   **101 painted** made artificially beautiful by cosmetics   **104 Hot** eager, ardent, aromatic (?) (Spices were classified as hot or cold.)   **107 middle summer** (Having no autumn flowers in any case [lines 79–82], since it is too early in the season, Perdita flatters her older guests by giving them flowers appropriate to *middle age*.)   **110 Out** (An exclamation of dismay.)   **116 Proserpina** daughter of Ceres, stolen away by Pluto (*Dis*) and taken to Hades when, according to Ovid, she was gathering flowers   **119 take** charm   **120 dim** with hanging heads **122 Cytherea's** Venus's

124 **Phoebus** the sun-god   **124–5 a malady . . . maids** (Young maids, suffering from greensickness, a kind of anemia, are pale like the primrose.)   **126 crown imperial** flower from the Levant, cultivated in English gardens   **127 flower-de-luce** fleur-de-lis.   **I lack** (Because the season is too late for them.)   **128 To . . . friend** to make garlands of them for you (Polixenes and Camillo) and for my sweet friend (Florizel)   **130 like . . . play on** as if one were strewing a bank where Cupid himself might lie in amorous play   **131 or if** or if like a corpse, that is, a living body   **132 quick** alive   **134 Whitsun pastorals** plays (including Robin Hood plays) and English morris dances often performed at Whitsuntide, seven Sundays after Easter. (The part of Maid Marian strikes Perdita as immodest for her usual behavior.) **136 Still . . . done** gets better and better.   **143 Each your doing** Each thing you do and how you do it   **144 singular** unique and peerless **145 Crowns . . . deeds** makes whatever you are doing at the moment seem supremely wonderful   **146 Doricles** (Florizel's disguise name.) **147 large** lavish.   **But that** Were it not that   **149 give you out** proclaim you to be   **152 skill** reason   **153 To . . . to't** i.e., to woo you "the false way," with intent to seduce you.   **154 turtles** turtledoves, as symbols of faithful love   **155 I'll swear for 'em** i.e., I'll be sworn they do.

Ran on the greensward. Nothing she does or seems 157
But smacks of something greater than herself,
Too noble for this place.

CAMILLO   He tells her something
That makes her blood look out. Good sooth, she is 160
The queen of curds and cream.

CLOWN   Come on, strike up!

DORCAS

Mopsa must be your mistress. Marry, garlic, 162
To mend her kissing with!

MOPSA   Now, in good time! 163

CLOWN

Not a word, a word. We stand upon our manners. 164
Come, strike up! 165

> [*Music.*] *Here a dance of shepherds and*
> *shepherdesses.*

POLIXENES

Pray, good shepherd, what fair swain is this
Which dances with your daughter?

SHEPHERD

They call him Doricles, and boasts himself 168
To have a worthy feeding; but I have it 169
Upon his own report and I believe it.
He looks like sooth. He says he loves my daughter. 171
I think so too, for never gazed the moon
Upon the water as he'll stand and read,
As 'twere, my daughter's eyes; and, to be plain,
I think there is not half a kiss to choose
Who loves another best.

POLIXENES   She dances featly. 176

SHEPHERD

So she does anything—though I report it
That should be silent. If young Doricles
Do light upon her, she shall bring him that 179
Which he not dreams of.

> *Enter Servant.*

SERVANT   Oh, master, if you did but hear the peddler at
the door, you would never dance again after a tabor 182
and pipe; no, the bagpipe could not move you. He
sings several tunes faster than you'll tell money. He 184
utters them as he had eaten ballads and all men's ears 185
grew to his tunes.

CLOWN   He could never come better. He shall come in. 187
I love a ballad but even too well, if it be doleful matter 188
merrily set down, or a very pleasant thing indeed and 189
sung lamentably. 190

SERVANT   He hath songs for man or woman, of all sizes. 191
No milliner can so fit his customers with gloves. He 192

has the prettiest love songs for maids, so without
bawdry, which is strange, with such delicate burdens 194
of dildos and fadings, "Jump her and thump her"; and 195
where some stretchmouthed rascal would, as it were, 196
mean mischief and break a foul gap into the matter, 197
he makes the maid to answer, "Whoop, do me no
harm, good man"; puts him off, slights him, with
"Whoop, do me no harm, good man."

POLIXENES   This is a brave fellow. 201

CLOWN   Believe me, thou talkest of an admirable con- 202
ceited fellow. Has he any unbraided wares? 203

SERVANT   He hath ribbons of all the colors i'th'
rainbow; points more than all the lawyers in Bohemia 205
can learnedly handle, though they come to him by th'
gross; inkles, caddisses, cambrics, lawns. Why, he 207
sings 'em over as they were gods or goddesses; you
would think a smock were a she-angel, he so chants to 209
the sleevehand and the work about the square on't. 210

CLOWN   Prithee, bring him in, and let him approach
singing.

PERDITA   Forewarn him that he use no scurrilous words
in 's tunes.   [*The Servant goes to the door.*]

CLOWN   You have of these peddlers that have more in 215
them than you'd think, sister.

PERDITA   Ay, good brother, or go about to think. 217

> *Enter Autolycus, singing.*

AUTOLYCUS

Lawn as white as driven snow,
Cyprus black as e'er was crow, 219
Gloves as sweet as damask roses, 220
Masks for faces and for noses,
Bugle bracelet, necklace amber, 222
Perfume for a lady's chamber,
Golden coifs and stomachers, 224
For my lads to give their dears,
Pins and poking-sticks of steel, 226
What maids lack from head to heel,
Come buy of me, come. Come buy, come buy.
Buy, lads, or else your lasses cry.
Come buy.

CLOWN   If I were not in love with Mopsa, thou shouldst

---

157 greensward grassy turf.   **160 makes . . . out** makes her blush.
162 mistress i.e., partner in the dance.   **163 kissing** i.e., bad breath.
(Dorcas jests that even garlic would improve Mopsa's breath.)   **in
good time** (An expression of indignation.)   **164 stand upon** set store
by   **165.1 dance** (Probably a morris dance.)   **168 and** i.e., and they
say he   **169 feeding** pasturage, lands   **171 He . . . sooth** He appears
to be honest.   **176 another** the other.   **featly** gracefully.   **179 light
upon** choose   **182 tabor** small drum   **184 several** various.   **tell**
count   **185 as** as if. (Also in line 208.)   **187 better** at a better time.
188 but even too well all too well   **189 pleasant** merry   **190 lamentably** mournfully.   **191 sizes** sorts.   **192 milliner** vendor of fancy
ware and apparel, including gloves, ribbons, and bonnets

194 burdens refrains   **195 dildos and fadings** words used as part of
the refrains of ballads. (But with bawdy double meaning unperceived
by the servant, as also in *jump her, thump her, do me no harm,* etc.)
196 stretchmouthed widemouthed, foulmouthed   **197 break . . .
matter** insert some gross obscenity into the song, or, act in a suggestive way   **201 brave** excellent   **202–3 admirable conceited** wonderfully witty and clever   **203 unbraided** not shopworn, new
205 points (1) laces for fastening clothes (2) headings in an argument
207 inkles . . . lawns linen tapes, worsted tape used for garters, fine
heavy linen fabrics, fine sheer linens.   **209 smock** petticoat
210 sleevehand wristband.   **square on't** embroidered bosom or yoke
of the garment.   **215 You . . . peddlers** You'll find peddlers   **217 go
about** intend, wish.   **217.1 Enter Autolycus** (Apparently he is wearing a false beard; later in this scene, he removes it to impersonate a
courtier to the Clown and Shepherd.)   **219 Cyprus** crepe   **220 sweet**
i.e., perfumed. (Also in line 249.)   **222 Bugle bracelet** bracelet of
black glossy beads   **224 coifs** close-fitting caps   **stomachers**
embroidered fronts for ladies' dresses   **226 poking-sticks** rods used
for ironing and stiffening the plaits of ruffs. (With bawdy suggestion.)

take no money of me, but being enthralled as I am, it ²³²
will also be the bondage of certain ribbons and gloves. ²³³

MOPSA   I was promised them against the feast, but they ²³⁴
come not too late now.

DORCAS   He hath promised you more than that, or ²³⁶
there be liars. ²³⁷

MOPSA   He hath paid you all he promised you. Maybe
he has paid you more, which will shame you to give ²³⁹
him again. ²⁴⁰

CLOWN   Is there no manners left among maids? Will ²⁴¹
they wear their plackets where they should bear their ²⁴²
faces? Is there not milking time, when you are going to ²⁴³
bed, or kilnhole, to whistle of these secrets, but you ²⁴⁴
must be tittle-tattling before all our guests? 'Tis well
they are whisp'ring. Clamor your tongues, and not a ²⁴⁶
word more.

MOPSA   I have done. Come, you promised me a tawdry ²⁴⁸
lace and a pair of sweet gloves. ²⁴⁹

CLOWN   Have I not told thee how I was cozened by the ²⁵⁰
way and lost all my money?

AUTOLYCUS   And indeed, sir, there are cozeners abroad;
therefore it behooves men to be wary.

CLOWN   Fear not thou, man, thou shalt lose nothing
here.

AUTOLYCUS   I hope so, sir, for I have about me many
parcels of charge. ²⁵⁷

CLOWN   What hast here? Ballads?

MOPSA   Pray now, buy some. I love a ballad in print
alife, for then we are sure they are true. ²⁶⁰

AUTOLYCUS   Here's one to a very doleful tune, how a
usurer's wife was brought to bed of twenty moneybags at a burden, and how she longed to eat adders' ²⁶³
heads and toads carbonadoed. ²⁶⁴

MOPSA   Is it true, think you?

AUTOLYCUS   Very true, and but a month old.

DORCAS   Bless me from marrying a usurer! ²⁶⁷

AUTOLYCUS   Here's the midwife's name to't, one
Mistress Taleporter, and five or six honest wives that ²⁶⁹
were present. Why should I carry lies abroad?

MOPSA   Pray you now, buy it.

CLOWN   Come on, lay it by, and let's first see more
ballads. We'll buy the other things anon.

AUTOLYCUS   Here's another ballad, of a fish that appeared upon the coast on Wednesday the fourscore of ²⁷⁵
April, forty thousand fathom above water, and sung ²⁷⁶
this ballad against the hard hearts of maids. It was

thought she was a woman and was turned into a cold
fish for she would not exchange flesh with one that ²⁷⁹
loved her. The ballad is very pitiful and as true.

DORCAS   Is it true too, think you?

AUTOLYCUS   Five justices' hands at it, and witnesses ²⁸²
more than my pack will hold.

CLOWN   Lay it by too. Another.

AUTOLYCUS   This is a merry ballad, but a very pretty
one.

MOPSA   Let's have some merry ones.

AUTOLYCUS   Why, this is a passing merry one and goes ²⁸⁸
to the tune of "Two Maids Wooing a Man." There's
scarce a maid westward but she sings it. 'Tis in ²⁹⁰
request, I can tell you.

MOPSA   We can both sing it. If thou'lt bear a part, thou
shalt hear; 'tis in three parts.

DORCAS   We had the tune on't a month ago. ²⁹⁴

AUTOLYCUS   I can bear my part; you must know 'tis my
occupation. Have at it with you. ²⁹⁶

Song.

AUTOLYCUS
Get you hence, for I must go
Where it fits not you to know.
DORCAS
　　　　Whither?
MOPSA　　　　　　Oh, whither?
DORCAS　　　　　　　　　Whither?
MOPSA
It becomes thy oath full well,
Thou to me thy secrets tell.
DORCAS
　　　　Me too. Let me go thither.
MOPSA
Or thou goest to th' grange or mill. ³⁰³
DORCAS
If to either, thou dost ill.
AUTOLYCUS
　　　　Neither.
DORCAS　　　　　　What, neither?
AUTOLYCUS　　　　　　　　　Neither.
DORCAS
Thou hast sworn my love to be.
MOPSA
Thou hast sworn it more to me.
　　Then whither goest? Say, whither?

CLOWN   We'll have this song out anon by ourselves. ³⁰⁹
My father and the gentlemen are in sad talk, and we'll ³¹⁰
not trouble them. Come, bring away thy pack after
me. Wenches, I'll buy for you both. Peddler, let's have
the first choice. Follow me, girls.
　　　　　　　[*Exit with Dorcas and Mopsa.*]
AUTOLYCUS   And you shall pay well for 'em.
　　　　　　　[*He follows singing.*]

232–3 it will . . . bondage it will mean the taking into custody (by
means of purchase and tying up into a parcel)   234 against in anticipation of, in time for   236–7 He . . . liars i.e., He promised to marry
you, too, or else rumor is a liar.   239 paid you more i.e., made you
pregnant   239–40 which . . . again i.e., which will shame you by giving birth to his child.   241–3 Will . . . faces? i.e., Will they always be
talking and revealing personal secrets?   plackets slits in petticoats.
(With bawdy suggestion of the pudendum, as in line 613.)   244 kilnhole fire hole of a baking oven (where maids might gossip).   whistle
whisper   246 Clamor i.e., Silence   248–9 tawdry lace cheap and
showy lace, or, neckerchief. (So called from St. Audrey's Fair.)
250 cozened cheated   257 parcels of charge valuable items.
260 alife on my life   263 at a burden in one childbirth   264 carbonadoed scored across and grilled.   267 Bless God protect, keep
269 Taleporter i.e., talebearer, gossip   275 fourscore eightieth (!)
276 forty thousand fathom 240,000 feet

279 exchange flesh have sex   282 hands at it signatures on it
288 passing surpassingly   290 westward in the West Country
294 on't of it   296 Have at it Here goes   303 Or Either.   grange
farm   309 have this song out finish this song   310 sad serious

Song.

Will you buy any tape,
    Or lace for your cape,
My dainty duck, my dear-a?
    Any silk, any thread,
    And toys for your head,   319
Of the new'st and fin'st, fin'st wear-a?
    Come to the peddler;
    Money's a meddler,   322
That doth utter all men's ware-a.   *Exit.* 323

[*Enter a Servant.*]

SERVANT   Master, there is three carters, three shep- 324
herds, three neatherds, three swineherds, that have 325
made themselves all men of hair. They call themselves 326
saultiers, and they have a dance which the wenches say 327
is a gallimaufry of gambols, because they are not in't; 328
but they themselves are o'th' mind, if it be not too
rough for some that know little but bowling, it will 330
please plentifully.

SHEPHERD   Away! We'll none on't. Here has been too
much   homely   foolery   already.—I know, sir, we 333
weary you.

POLIXENES   You weary those that refresh us. Pray, let's
see these four threes of herdsmen.

SERVANT   One three of them, by their own report, sir, 337
hath danced before the King, and not the worst of the
three but jumps twelve foot and a half by the square. 339

SHEPHERD   Leave your prating. Since these good men 340
are pleased, let them come in; but quickly now.

SERVANT   Why, they stay at door, sir.

[*He goes to the door.*]

Here a dance of twelve Satyrs.

POLIXENES [*to the Shepherd*]
Oh, father, you'll know more of that hereafter.   343
[*To Camillo*] Is it not too far gone? 'Tis time to part
    them.
He's simple and tells much. [*To Florizel*] How now, fair
    shepherd?   345
Your heart is full of something that does take
Your mind from feasting. Sooth, when I was young
And handed love as you do, I was wont   348
To load my she with knacks. I would have ransacked
The peddler's silken treasury and have poured it
To her acceptance; you have let him go,   351
And nothing marted with him. If your lass   352

Interpretation should abuse and call this   353
Your lack of love or bounty, you were straited   354
For a reply, at least if you make a care
Of happy holding her.
FLORIZEL   Old sir, I know   356
She prizes not such trifles as these are.
The gifts she looks from me are packed and locked   358
Up in my heart, which I have given already,
But not delivered. [*To Perdita*] Oh, hear me breathe my
    life   360
Before this ancient sir, who, it should seem,   361
Hath sometime loved! I take thy hand, this hand,
As soft as dove's down and as white as it,
Or Ethiopian's tooth, or the fanned snow that's bolted 364
By th' northern blasts twice o'er.   [*He takes her hand.*]
POLIXENES   What follows this?
How prettily the young swain seems to wash
The hand was fair before! I have put you out.   367
But to your protestation; let me hear   368
What you profess.
FLORIZEL   Do, and be witness to't.
POLIXENES
And this my neighbor too?
FLORIZEL   And he, and more
Than he, and men—the earth, the heavens, and all:
That, were I crowned the most imperial monarch,
Thereof most worthy, were I the fairest youth   373
That ever made eye swerve, had force and knowledge   374
More than was ever man's, I would not prize them
Without her love; for her employ them all,
Commend them and condemn them to her service   377
Or to their own perdition.
POLIXENES   Fairly offered.   378
CAMILLO
This shows a sound affection.
SHEPHERD   But, my daughter,
Say you the like to him?
PERDITA   I cannot speak
So well, nothing so well; no, nor mean better.
By th' pattern of mine own thoughts I cut out   382
The purity of his.
SHEPHERD   Take hands, a bargain!   383
And, friends unknown, you shall bear witness to't:
I give my daughter to him and will make
Her portion equal his.
FLORIZEL   Oh, that must be
I'th' virtue of your daughter. One being dead,   387

---

319 **toys** trifles   322 **meddler** i.e., go-between in commercial transactions   323 **utter** put on the market   324 **carters** cart drivers   325 **neatherds** cowherds   326 **of hair** dressed in skins.   327 **saultiers** leapers or vaulters. (With perhaps a play on *Saltiers* as a blunder for "satyrs.")   328 **gallimaufry** jumble   330 **bowling** (A more gentle sport than the vigorous satyr dancing.)   333 **homely** unpolished   337 **three** threesome   339 **by the square** precisely   343 **Leave** Leave off   343 **Oh, . . . hereafter** (Polixenes completes the conversation he has been having with the old Shepherd during the dance. *Father* is a respectful term of address for older men.)   345 **He's simple** The old Shepherd is guileless   348 **handed** handled, dealt in   351 **To her acceptance** for her to choose   352 **nothing marted with** have done no business with

353 **Interpretation should abuse** should interpret wrongly   354 **were straited** would be hard-pressed   356 **happy holding her** keeping her happy.   358 **looks** looks for   360 **But not delivered** i.e., but I have not confirmed it by a solemn vow before witnesses, making binding the contract.   **breathe my life** i.e., pronounce eternal vows   361 **this ancient sir** Polixenes   364 **fanned** blown.   **bolted** sifted   367 **was** that was.   **put you out** interrupted what you were saying.   368 **to your protestation** on with your public affirmation   373 **Thereof most worthy** the most worthy of monarchs   374 **swerve** turn in my direction (out of awe and respect)   377–8 **Commend . . . perdition** either commend them to her service, or, failing that, condemn them to deserved destruction.   382–3 **By . . . of his** By the purity of my own thoughts I can define the purity of his. (A metaphor of clothes-making; Perdita has formed her own thoughts on the model of his.)   387 **One being dead** When a certain person dies

I shall have more than you can dream of yet;
Enough then for your wonder. But come on: 389
Contract us 'fore these witnesses.
SHEPHERD   Come, your hand;
And, daughter, yours.
POLIXENES   Soft, swain, awhile, beseech you. 391
Have you a father?
FLORIZEL   I have, but what of him?
POLIXENES   Knows he of this?
FLORIZEL   He neither does nor shall.
POLIXENES   Methinks a father
Is at the nuptial of his son a guest
That best becomes the table. Pray you, once more,
Is not your father grown incapable
Of reasonable affairs? Is he not stupid   400
With age and altering rheums? Can he speak? Hear?   401
Know man from man? Dispute his own estate?   402
Lies he not bedrid, and again does nothing
But what he did being childish?
FLORIZEL   No, good sir,   404
He has his health and ampler strength indeed
Than most have of his age.
POLIXENES   By my white beard,
You offer him, if this be so, a wrong
Something unfilial. Reason my son   408
Should choose himself a wife, but as good reason
The father, all whose joy is nothing else
But fair posterity, should hold some counsel   411
In such a business.
FLORIZEL   I yield all this;   412
But for some other reasons, my grave sir,
Which 'tis not fit you know, I not acquaint
My father of this business.
POLIXENES   Let him know't.
FLORIZEL
He shall not.
POLIXENES   Prithee, let him.
FLORIZEL   No, he must not.
SHEPHERD
Let him, my son. He shall not need to grieve
At knowing of thy choice.
FLORIZEL   Come, come, he must not.
Mark our contract.
POLIXENES [discovering himself]   Mark your divorce,
       young sir,
Whom son I dare not call. Thou art too base
To be acknowledged. Thou a scepter's heir,
That thus affects a sheephook?—Thou old traitor,   422
I am sorry that by hanging thee I can
But shorten thy life one week.—And thou, fresh piece

Of excellent witchcraft, who of force must know   425
The royal fool thou cop'st with—
SHEPHERD   Oh, my heart!   426
POLIXENES
I'll have thy beauty scratched with briers and made
More homely than thy state.—For thee, fond boy,   428
If I may ever know thou dost but sigh
That thou no more shalt see this knack—as never   430
I mean thou shalt—we'll bar thee from succession,
Not hold thee of our blood, no, not our kin,
Farre than Deucalion off. Mark thou my words.   433
Follow us to the court.—Thou churl, for this time,   434
Though full of our displeasure, yet we free thee
From the dead blow of it.—And you, enchantment,   436
Worthy enough a herdsman—yea, him too,   437
That makes himself, but for our honor therein,   438
Unworthy thee—if ever henceforth thou   439
These rural latches to his entrance open,
Or hoop his body more with thy embraces,
I will devise a death as cruel for thee
As thou art tender to't.   Exit.
PERDITA   Even here undone!
I was not much afeard; for once or twice
I was about to speak and tell him plainly
The selfsame sun that shines upon his court
Hides not his visage from our cottage, but
Looks on alike. Will't please you, sir, begone?   448
I told you what would come of this. Beseech you,
Of your own state take care. This dream of mine—
Being now awake, I'll queen it no inch farther,
But milk my ewes and weep.
CAMILLO   Why, how now, father?
Speak ere thou diest.   I cannot speak, nor think, 453
SHEPHERD
Nor dare to know that which I know. [To Florizel] Oh,
       sir,
You have undone a man of fourscore three,
That thought to fill his grave in quiet, yea,
To die upon the bed my father died,   457
To lie close by his honest bones; but now
Some hangman must put on my shroud and lay me
Where no priest shovels in dust. [To Perdita] Oh,
       cursed wretch,
That knew'st this was the Prince, and wouldst adven-
       ture
To mingle faith with him! Undone, undone!   462
If I might die within this hour, I have lived
To die when I desire.   Exit.
FLORIZEL [to Perdita]   Why look you so upon me?

389 Enough . . . wonder there will be enough then for you to wonder
at.   391 Soft Wait a minute   400 reasonable affairs matters requiring the use of reason.   401 altering rheums weakening catarrhs or
other diseases.   402 Dispute Discuss.   estate affairs, condition.
404 being childish when he was a child.   408 Something somewhat.
Reason my son It is reasonable that my son. (The disguised Polixenes
seems to be speaking hypothetically, using himself as an example, but
of course the application to Florizel is direct.)   411 hold some counsel be consulted   412 yield concede   422 affects desires, shows
inclination for

425 of force of necessity   426 thou cop'st you deal   428 homely
(1) unattractive (2) humble.   fond foolish   430 knack trifle, schemer
433 Farre . . . off farther in kinship than Deucalion (the Noah of classical legend and hence the primal, distant ancestor of the whole human
race).   434 churl i.e., the Shepherd   436 dead deadly.   enchantment
i.e., Perdita   437–9 him too . . . thee worthy indeed of him (Florizel)
whose behavior renders him unworthy even of you, if we were to set
aside for the moment the question of the dignity of our royal house
448 alike both alike.   453 ere thou diest before you die of grief (?).
(Although Polixenes has relented of his threat to hang the Shepherd,
the Shepherd is gloomily sure it will come to a hanging, lines 459–60.)
457 died died on   462 mingle faith exchange pledges

I am but sorry, not afeard; delayed,
But nothing altered. What I was, I am,
More straining on for plucking back, not following   468
My leash unwillingly.

CAMILLO   Gracious my lord,
You know your father's temper. At this time
He will allow no speech, which I do guess
You do not purpose to him; and as hardly
Will he endure your sight as yet, I fear.
Then, till the fury of His Highness settle,
Come not before him.

FLORIZEL   I not purpose it.
I think Camillo?

CAMILLO   Even he, my lord.

PERDITA
How often have I told you 'twould be thus?
How often said my dignity would last   478
But till 'twere known?

FLORIZEL   It cannot fail but by
The violation of my faith; and then   480
Let nature crush the sides o'th'earth together
And mar the seeds within! Lift up thy looks.   482
From my succession wipe me, father; I   483
Am heir to my affection.

CAMILLO   Be advised.   484

FLORIZEL
I am, and by my fancy. If my reason   485
Will thereto be obedient, I have reason;   486
If not, my senses, better pleased with madness,
Do bid it welcome.

CAMILLO   This is desperate, sir.

FLORIZEL
So call it, but it does fulfill my vow;
I needs must think it honesty. Camillo,
Not for Bohemia nor the pomp that may
Be thereat gleaned, for all the sun sees or
The close earth wombs or the profound seas hides   493
In unknown fathoms, will I break my oath
To this my fair beloved. Therefore, I pray you,
As you have ever been my father's honored friend,
When he shall miss me—as, in faith, I mean not
To see him any more—cast your good counsels
Upon his passion. Let myself and fortune   499
Tug for the time to come. This you may know   500
And so deliver: I am put to sea   501
With her who here I cannot hold on shore;   502
And most opportune to our need I have
A vessel rides fast by, but not prepared   504

For this design. What course I mean to hold
Shall nothing benefit your knowledge nor   506
Concern me the reporting.

CAMILLO   Oh, my lord,   507
I would your spirit were easier for advice,   508
Or stronger for your need.

FLORIZEL   Hark, Perdita.
[To Camillo] I'll hear you by and by.
                    [He draws Perdita aside.]

CAMILLO [aside]   He's irremovable,   510
Resolved for flight. Now were I happy if
His going I could frame to serve my turn,   512
Save him from danger, do him love and honor,
Purchase the sight again of dear Sicilia
And that unhappy king, my master, whom
I so much thirst to see.

FLORIZEL   Now, good Camillo,
I am so fraught with curious business that   517
I leave out ceremony.

CAMILLO   Sir, I think   518
You have heard of my poor services i'th' love
That I have borne your father?

FLORIZEL   Very nobly
Have you deserved. It is my father's music
To speak your deeds, not little of his care
To have them recompensed as thought on.

CAMILLO   Well, my lord,   523
If you may please to think I love the King
And through him what's nearest to him, which is
Your gracious self, embrace but my direction,   526
If your more ponderous and settled project   527
May suffer alteration. On mine honor,   528
I'll point you where you shall have such receiving
As shall become Your Highness, where you may   530
Enjoy your mistress—from the whom I see
There's no disjunction to be made but by,
As heavens forfend, your ruin—marry her,   533
And, with my best endeavors in your absence   534
Your discontenting father strive to qualify   535
And bring him up to liking.

FLORIZEL   How, Camillo,   536
May this, almost a miracle, be done,
That I may call thee something more than man,
And after that trust to thee?

CAMILLO   Have you thought on   539
A place whereto you'll go?

FLORIZEL   Not any yet.
But as th'unthought-on accident is guilty   541
To what we wildly do, so we profess   542

468 More . . . back i.e., like a hound on the leash, all the more eager to go forward for being restrained   478 my dignity i.e., the new status this marriage would have offered   480 then when that happens   482 mar the seeds within i.e., destroy the very sources of life on earth (since all material life was thought to be derived from seeds).   483 From . . . father (Florizel apostrophizes the absent Polixenes.)   483–4 I . . . affection i.e., I will be content with my passionate love for Perdita in place of my inheritance.   Be advised Think carefully, be receptive to wise advice.   485 fancy love.   486 have reason (1) will be reasonable (2) will be sane.   493 wombs encloses, conceals   499 passion anger.   500 Tug contend   501 deliver report   502 who whom   504 rides that rides at anchor.   but though

506–7 Shall . . . reporting would not behoove you to know nor me to report.   508 easier for more open to   510 irremovable immovable   512 frame shape   517 curious demanding care   518 I . . . ceremony (Florizel apologizes for failing to observe proper ceremony toward Camillo under the pressures of the present crisis.)   523 as thought on as deservingly as they merit.   526 embrace . . . direction simply follow my advice   527 ponderous weighty   528 suffer permit   530 become Your Highness suit your royal rank, suit Your Highness   533 forfend forbid   534 with together with   535 discontenting discontented, displeased.   qualify appease, pacify   536 bring . . . liking get him to the point of approval.   539 after ever after   541–2 as . . . wildly do just as the unexpected happening (e.g., of our being discovered by the King) is responsible for what we rashly do at this point

Ourselves to be the slaves of chance and flies   543
Of every wind that blows.

CAMILLO   Then list to me.
This follows, if you will not change your purpose
But undergo this flight: make for Sicilia,
And there present yourself and your fair princess—
For so I see she must be—'fore Leontes.
She shall be habited as it becomes   549
The partner of your bed. Methinks I see
Leontes opening his free arms and weeping   551
His welcomes forth; asks thee there "Son,
    forgiveness!"
As 'twere i'th' father's person; kisses the hands
Of your fresh princess; o'er and o'er divides him   554
Twixt his unkindness and his kindness. Th'one   555
He chides to hell, and bids the other grow
Faster than thought or time.

FLORIZEL   Worthy Camillo,   557
What color for my visitation shall I   558
Hold up before him?

CAMILLO   Sent by the King your father   559
To greet him and to give him comforts. Sir,
The manner of your bearing towards him, with
What you, as from your father, shall deliver—   562
Things known betwixt us three—I'll write you down,
The which shall point you forth at every sitting   564
What you must say, that he shall not perceive
But that you have your father's bosom there   566
And speak his very heart.

FLORIZEL   I am bound to you.
There is some sap in this.

CAMILLO   A course more promising
Than a wild dedication of yourselves
To unpathed waters, undreamed shores, most certain
To miseries enough; no hope to help you,
But as you shake off one to take another;   572
Nothing so certain as your anchors, who   573
Do their best office if they can but stay you   574
Where you'll be loath to be. Besides, you know   575
Prosperity's the very bond of love,   576
Whose fresh complexion and whose heart together   577
Affliction alters.

PERDITA   One of these is true: 578
I think affliction may subdue the cheek,   579
But not take in the mind.

CAMILLO   Yea, say you so?   580

There shall not at your father's house these seven
    years   581
Be born another such.

FLORIZEL   My good Camillo,
She's as forward of her breeding as she is   583
I'th' rear 'our birth.   584

CAMILLO   I cannot say 'tis pity
She lacks instructions, for she seems a mistress   585
To most that teach.

PERDITA   Your pardon, sir; for this
I'll blush you thanks.

FLORIZEL   My prettiest Perdita!
But oh, the thorns we stand upon! Camillo,
Preserver of my father, now of me,
The medicine of our house, how shall we do?
We are not furnished like Bohemia's son,
Nor shall appear so in Sicilia.

CAMILLO   My lord,
Fear none of this. I think you know my fortunes
Do all lie there. It shall be so my care
To have you royally appointed as if   595
The scene you play were mine. For instance, sir,
That you may know you shall not want, one word.

[*They talk aside.*]

Enter Autolycus.

AUTOLYCUS   Ha, ha, what a fool Honesty is! And Trust,
his sworn brother, a very simple gentleman! I have
sold all my trumpery; not a counterfeit stone, not a
ribbon, glass, pomander, brooch, table book, ballad,   601
knife, tape, glove, shoe tie, bracelet, horn ring, to
keep my pack from fasting. They throng who should   603
buy first, as if my trinkets had been hallowed and   604
brought a benediction to the buyer; by which means
I saw whose purse was best in picture, and what I   606
saw, to my good use I remembered. My clown, who
wants but something to be a reasonable man, grew so   608
in love with the wenches' song that he would not stir
his pettitoes till he had both tune and words, which   610
so drew the rest of the herd to me that all their other
senses stuck in ears. You might have pinched a   612
placket, it was senseless. 'Twas nothing to geld a cod-   613
piece of a purse. I could have filed keys off that hung   614
in chains. No hearing, no feeling, but my sir's song,   615
and admiring the nothing of it. So that in this time of   616
lethargy I picked and cut most of their festival purses;
and had not the old man come in with hubbub

---

543 flies i.e., insignificant insects, blown about by the winds of chance
549 habited (richly) dressed   **551 free** generous, noble   **554 fresh**
young and beautiful   **554–5 divides . . . kindness** divides his speech
between his former unkindness (which he condemns) and his present
intention of kindness.   **557 Faster** firmer; also, more swiftly
558 color excuse, pretext   **559 Hold up before** present to.   **Sent** i.e.,
Say you are sent   **562 deliver** say   **564 point you forth** indicate to
you.   **sitting** conference   **566 bosom** inmost thoughts   **572 one** one
misery, one misfortune.   **take** encounter   **573 Nothing** not at all.
573–5 who . . . to be which are doing as well as can be hoped if they
simply hold you in some undesirable place (rather than allowing you
to proceed on toward even greater disaster).   **576–8 Prosperity's . . .
alters** i.e., young love flourishes while things are going well but loses
its fresh complexion and strength of feeling under the test of adversity.   **579 subdue the cheek** make the complexion look pale and
wasted   **580 take in** overcome

581 your father's (Said either to Florizel or Perdita.)   **these seven
years** i.e., for a long time to come. (Camillo's point is that she is a
nonpareil.)   **583 forward . . . breeding** far in advance of her lowly
upbringing   **584 I'th' rear 'our** below me in   **585 instructions** formal
schooling.   **a mistress** a teacher   **595 appointed** equipped, outfitted
601 pomander scent-ball.   **table book** notebook   **603 from fasting**
i.e., from being empty.   **604 hallowed** made sacred, like a relic
606 best in picture i.e., best to look at, most promising   **608 wants
but something** lacks one thing only (i.e., intelligence)   **610 pettitoes**
pig's toes; here, toes   **612 stuck in ears** were occupied with hearing.
613 placket (Literally, slit in a petticoat; with bawdy suggestion.)
senseless insensible.   **613–14 geld . . . purse** cut a purse loose from
the pouch worn at the front of a man's breeches   **615 my sir's** i.e., the
Clown's   **616 nothing** (1) vacuity (2) noting, tune. (*Nothing* and
noting were sounded alike in Elizabethan English.)

against his daughter and the King's son and scared my
choughs from the chaff, I had not left a purse alive in   620
the whole army.

[*Camillo, Florizel, and Perdita come forward.*]

CAMILLO
Nay, but my letters, by this means being there
So soon as you arrive, shall clear that doubt.

FLORIZEL
And those that you'll procure from King Leontes—

CAMILLO
Shall satisfy your father.

PERDITA   Happy be you!
All that you speak shows fair.

CAMILLO [*seeing Autolycus*]   Who have we here?
We'll make an instrument of this, omit
Nothing may give us aid.   628

AUTOLYCUS [*aside*]   If they have overheard me now,
why, hanging.

CAMILLO   How now, good fellow? Why shak'st thou so?
Fear not, man, here's no harm intended to thee.

AUTOLYCUS   I am a poor fellow, sir.

CAMILLO   Why, be so still. Here's nobody will steal that
from thee. Yet for the outside of thy poverty we must   635
make an exchange. Therefore discase thee instantly—   636
thou must think there's a necessity in't—and change   637
garments with this gentleman. Though the penny-   638
worth on his side be the worst, yet hold thee, there's 639
some boot.   [*He gives money.*]   640

AUTOLYCUS   I am a poor fellow, sir. [*Aside*] I know ye
well enough.

CAMILLO   Nay, prithee, dispatch. The gentleman is half 643
flayed already.   644

AUTOLYCUS   Are you in earnest, sir? [*Aside*] I smell the
trick on't.

FLORIZEL   Dispatch, I prithee.

AUTOLYCUS   Indeed, I have had earnest, but I cannot   648
with conscience take it.

CAMILLO   Unbuckle, unbuckle.
        [*Florizel and Autolycus exchange garments.*]
Fortunate mistress—let my prophecy   651
Come home to ye!—you must retire yourself   652
Into some covert. Take your sweetheart's hat   653
And pluck it o'er your brows, muffle your face,
Dismantle you, and, as you can, disliken   655
The truth of your own seeming, that you may—   656
For I do fear eyes—over to shipboard   657
Get undescried.

PERDITA   I see the play so lies
That I must bear a part.

CAMILLO   No remedy.—

Have you done there?

FLORIZEL   Should I now meet my father,
He would not call me son.

CAMILLO   Nay, you shall have no hat.
                            [*He gives it to Perdita.*]
Come, lady, come. Farewell, my friend.

AUTOLYCUS   Adieu, sir.

FLORIZEL
Oh, Perdita, what have we twain forgot?
Pray you, a word.   [*They speak aside.*]

CAMILLO [*aside*]
What I do next shall be to tell the King
Of this escape and whither they are bound;
Wherein my hope is I shall so prevail
To force him after, in whose company
I shall re-view Sicilia, for whose sight   670
I have a woman's longing.

FLORIZEL   Fortune speed us!
Thus we set on, Camillo, to th' seaside.

CAMILLO   The swifter speed the better.
                 Exit [*with Florizel and Perdita*].

AUTOLYCUS   I understand the business; I hear it. To
have an open ear, a quick eye, and a nimble hand is
necessary for a cutpurse; a good nose is requisite also,
to smell out work for th'other senses. I see this is the
time that the unjust man doth thrive. What an
exchange had this been without boot! What a boot is   679
here with this exchange! Sure the gods do this year
connive at us, and we may do anything extempore.   681
The Prince himself is about a piece of iniquity, stealing 682
away from his father with his clog at his heels. If I   683
thought it were a piece of honesty to acquaint the King
withal, I would not do't. I hold it the more knavery to 685
conceal it; and therein am I constant to my profession.

     Enter Clown and Shepherd [*carrying a bundle and
     a box*].

Aside, aside! Here is more matter for a hot brain.
Every lane's end, every shop, church, session, hang-   688
ing, yields a careful man work.   [*He stands aside.*]

CLOWN   See, see, what a man you are now! There is no
other way but to tell the King she's a changeling and   691
none of your flesh and blood.

SHEPHERD   Nay, but hear me.

CLOWN   Nay, but hear me.

SHEPHERD   Go to, then.   695

CLOWN   She being none of your flesh and blood, your
flesh and blood has not offended the King, and so
your flesh and blood is not to be punished by him.
Show those things you found about her, those secret
things, all but what she has with her. This being done,
let the law go whistle, I warrant you.

SHEPHERD   I will tell the King all, every word, yea, and
his son's pranks too; who, I may say, is no honest

---

620 choughs jackdaws   **628 Nothing** nothing that   **635 the outside . . .
poverty** i.e., your ragged clothing   **636 discase** undress   **637 think**
understand   **638–9 pennyworth** i.e., value of the bargain   **640 some
boot** something in addition.   **643 dispatch** hurry. (Also in line 647.)
644 flayed skinned, i.e., undressed   **648 earnest** advance payment.
(Playing on *in earnest* in line 645.)   **651–2 let . . . to ye!** i.e., let my
prophecy that you, Perdita, will be fortunate be fulfilled for you!
653 covert hidden place.   **655–6 as you . . . seeming** as much as you
can, disguise your outward appearance   **657 eyes** spying eyes

670 re-view see again   **679 without boot** i.e., even without added
payment.   **What a boot** What a profit   **681 connive at** look indul-
gently at   **682 about** engaged in   **683 clog** encumbrance (i.e.,
Perdita)   **685 withal** with it   **688 session** court session   **691
changeling** child left by the fairies   **695 Go to** Go ahead. (Or, an
expression of impatience.)

man, neither to his father nor to me, to go about to 704
make me the King's brother-in-law.

CLOWN   Indeed, brother-in-law was the farthest off you could have been to him, and then your blood had been the dearer by I know not how much an ounce.

AUTOLYCUS [aside]   Very wisely, puppies!

SHEPHERD   Well, let us to the King. There is that in this fardel will make him scratch his beard.   711

AUTOLYCUS [aside]   I know not what impediment this complaint may be to the flight of my master.   713

CLOWN   Pray heartily he be at' palace.   714

AUTOLYCUS [aside]   Though I am not naturally honest, I am so sometimes by chance. Let me pocket up my peddler's excrement. [He takes off his false beard.] How 717 now, rustics, whither are you bound?

SHEPHERD   To the palace, an it like Your Worship.   719

AUTOLYCUS   Your affairs there, what, with whom, the condition of that fardel, the place of your dwelling, 721 your names, your ages, of what having, breeding, and 722 anything that is fitting to be known, discover.   723

CLOWN   We are but plain fellows, sir.   724

AUTOLYCUS   A lie; you are rough and hairy. Let me have no lying. It becomes none but tradesmen, and they often give us soldiers the lie, but we pay them for it 727 with stamped coin, not stabbing steel; therefore they do not give us the lie.   729

CLOWN   Your Worship had like to have given us one, if 730 you had not taken yourself with the manner.   731

SHEPHERD   Are you a courtier, an't like you, sir?

AUTOLYCUS   Whether it like me or no, I am a courtier. See'st thou not the air of the court in these enfoldings? 734 Hath not my gait in it the measure of the court? Re- 735 ceives not thy nose court odor from me? Reflect I not on thy baseness court contempt? Think'st thou, for 737 that I insinuate to toze from thee thy business, I am 738 therefore no courtier? I am courtier cap-à-pie, and one 739 that will either push on or pluck back thy business there. Whereupon I command thee to open thy affair. 741

SHEPHERD   My business, sir, is to the King.

AUTOLYCUS   What advocate hast thou to him?

SHEPHERD   I know not, an't like you.

CLOWN [aside to Shepherd]   "Advocate" 's the court word for a pheasant. Say you have none.   746

SHEPHERD   None, sir. I have no pheasant, cock nor hen.

AUTOLYCUS [aside]
How blessed are we that are not simple men!
Yet nature might have made me as these are;
Therefore I will not disdain.

CLOWN [to Shepherd]   This cannot be but a great courtier.

SHEPHERD   His garments are rich, but he wears them not handsomely.

CLOWN   He seems to be the more noble in being fantas- 755 tical. A great man, I'll warrant. I know by the picking 756 on's teeth.   757

AUTOLYCUS   The fardel there? What's i'th' fardel? Wherefore that box?

SHEPHERD   Sir, there lies such secrets in this fardel and box which none must know but the King, and which he shall know within this hour if I may come to the speech of him.

AUTOLYCUS   Age, thou hast lost thy labor.   764

SHEPHERD   Why, sir?

AUTOLYCUS   The King is not at the palace. He is gone aboard a new ship to purge melancholy and air himself; for, if thou be'st capable of things serious, 768 thou must know the King is full of grief.

SHEPHERD   So 'tis said, sir; about his son, that should have married a shepherd's daughter.

AUTOLYCUS   If that shepherd be not in handfast, let him 772 fly. The curses he shall have, the tortures he shall feel, will break the back of man, the heart of monster.

CLOWN   Think you so, sir?

AUTOLYCUS   Not he alone shall suffer what wit can make 776 heavy and vengeance bitter, but those that are ger- 777 mane to him, though removed fifty times, shall all 778 come under the hangman—which, though it be great pity, yet it is necessary. An old sheep-whistling rogue, 780 a ram tender, to offer to have his daughter come into 781 grace? Some say he shall be stoned; but that death is 782 too soft for him, say I. Draw our throne into a sheep- 783 cote? All deaths are too few, the sharpest too easy.   784

CLOWN   Has the old man e'er a son, sir, do you hear, an't like you, sir?

AUTOLYCUS   He has a son, who shall be flayed alive; then, 'nointed over with honey, set on the head of a wasp's nest; then stand till he be three-quarters and a dram 789 dead; then recovered again with aqua vitae or some 790 other hot infusion; then, raw as he is, and in the hot- test day prognostication proclaims, shall he be set 792 against a brick wall, the sun looking with a southward eye upon him, where he is to behold him with flies 794 blown to death. But what talk we of these traitorly ras- 795 cals, whose miseries are to be smiled at, their offenses

---

704 **go about** make it his object   711 **fardel** bundle   713 **my master** i.e., Florizel. (See 4.3.13.)   714 **at'** at the   717 **excrement** outgrowth of hair, beard.   719 **an it like** if it please   721 **condition** nature 722 **having** property   723 **discover** reveal.   724 **plain** simple. (But Autolycus plays on the meaning "smooth.")   727 **give . . . lie** i.e., cheat us. (But *giving the lie* also means to accuse a person to his face of lying, an affront which a soldier would repay with *stabbing steel*.) 729 **give** (Autolycus punningly observes that, since soldiers pay tradesmen for their wares, the tradesmen cannot be said to have *given* the lie, and so a duel is avoided.)   730 **had like** was about   731 **taken . . . manner** i.e., caught yourself in the act, stopped short. (The Clown observes that Autolycus has once again avoided the "giving of the lie" and its consequences in a duel by his clever equivocation. Compare with Touchstone in *As You Like It*, 5.4)   734 **enfoldings** clothes.   735 **measure** stately tread   737–8 **for that . . . business** because I under- take to pry out of you what your business may be   739 **cap-à-pie** from head to foot   741 **open** reveal   746 **pheasant** (The rustics sup- pose that Autolycus has asked them what gift they propose to present as a bribe, as one might do to a judge in a court of law.)

755–6 **fantastical** eccentric.   756–7 **picking on's teeth** (A stylish affectation in Shakespeare's time.)   764 **Age** Old man   768 **be'st capable of** know anything about   772 **handfast** custody. (With a play on "betrothal.")   776 **wit** ingenuity (in devising tortures)   777–8 **ger- mane** related   780 **sheep-whistling** tending sheep by whistling after them   781 **offer** dare   782 **grace** favor.   783–4 **sheepcote** pen for sheep   789 **a dram** i.e., a small amount, a fraction   790 **aqua vitae** brandy   792 **prognostication** forecasting (in the almanac)   794 **he** i.e., the sun   795 **blown** swollen.   **what** i.e., why

being so capital? Tell me, for you seem to be honest
plain men, what you have to the King. Being some- ⁷⁹⁸
thing gently considered, I'll bring you where he is ⁷⁹⁹
aboard, tender your persons to his presence, whisper ⁸⁰⁰
him in your behalfs; and if it be in man besides the
King to effect your suits, here is man shall do it.

CLOWN [*to Shepherd*]　He seems to be of great authority.
Close with him, give him gold; and though authority ⁸⁰⁴
be a stubborn bear, yet he is oft led by the nose
with gold. Show the inside of your purse to the outside of his hand, and no more ado. Remember—
"stoned," and "flayed alive."

SHEPHERD　An't please you, sir, to undertake the
business for us, here is that gold I have. [*He offers
money.*] I'll make it as much more and leave this young
man in pawn till I bring it you.　　　　　　　　⁸¹²

AUTOLYCUS　After I have done what I promised?

SHEPHERD　Ay, sir.

AUTOLYCUS [*taking the money*]　Well, give me the moiety. ⁸¹⁵
[*To the Clown*] Are you a party in this business?

CLOWN　In some sort, sir. But, though my case be a piti- ⁸¹⁷
ful one, I hope I shall not be flayed out of it.

AUTOLYCUS　Oh, that's the case of the shepherd's son.
Hang him, he'll be made an example.

CLOWN [*to Shepherd*]　Comfort, good comfort! We must
to the King and show our strange sights. He must
know 'tis none of your daughter nor my sister; we are
gone else.—Sir, I will give you as much as this old ⁸²⁴
man does when the business is performed, and
remain, as he says, your pawn till it be brought you.

AUTOLYCUS　I will trust you. Walk before toward the
seaside; go on the right hand. I will but look upon the ⁸²⁸
hedge and follow you.　　　　　　　　　　　　⁸²⁹

CLOWN [*to Shepherd*]　We are blessed in this man, as I
may say, even blessed.

SHEPHERD　Let's before, as he bids us. He was provided
to do us good.　　　　　*Exeunt* [*Shepherd and Clown*].

AUTOLYCUS　If I had a mind to be honest, I see Fortune
would not suffer me; she drops booties in my mouth.
I am courted now with a double occasion: gold, and a ⁸³⁶
means to do the Prince my master good, which who
knows how that may turn back to my advancement? I ⁸³⁸
will bring these two moles, these blind ones, aboard ⁸³⁹
him. If he think it fit to shore them again and that the ⁸⁴⁰
complaint they have to the King concerns him noth- ⁸⁴¹
ing, let him call me rogue for being so far officious, for ⁸⁴²
I am proof against that title and what shame else ⁸⁴³
belongs to't. To him will I present them. There may be
matter in it.　　　　　　　　　　　　　　　[*Exit.*]

5.1

*Enter Leontes, Cleomenes, Dion, Paulina, [and]
servants.*

CLEOMENES
Sir, you have done enough, and have performed
A saintlike sorrow. No fault could you make
Which you have not redeemed—indeed, paid down
More penitence than done trespass. At the last,
Do as the heavens have done: forget your evil.
With them, forgive yourself.

LEONTES　　　　　　　　　Whilst I remember
Her and her virtues, I cannot forget
My blemishes in them, and so still think of　　　　8
The wrong I did myself, which was so much
That heirless it hath made my kingdom and
Destroyed the sweet'st companion that e'er man
Bred his hopes out of. True?

PAULINA　　　　　　　　Too true, my lord.
If one by one you wedded all the world,
Or from the all that are took something good　　　14
To make a perfect woman, she you killed
Would be unparalleled.

LEONTES　　　　　　I think so. Killed?
She I killed? I did so, but thou strik'st me
Sorely to say I did. It is as bitter
Upon thy tongue as in my thought. Now, good now, 19
Say so but seldom.

CLEOMENES　　　　Not at all, good lady.
You might have spoken a thousand things that would
Have done the time more benefit and graced
Your kindness better.

PAULINA　　　　　You are one of those
Would have him wed again.

DION　　　　　　　If you would not so,
You pity not the state nor the remembrance　　　25
Of his most sovereign name, consider little　　　26
What dangers by His Highness' fail of issue　　　27
May drop upon his kingdom and devour
Incertain lookers-on. What were more holy　　　29
Than to rejoice the former queen is well?　　　30
What holier than, for royalty's repair,
For present comfort and for future good,
To bless the bed of majesty again
With a sweet fellow to't?

PAULINA　　　　　　There is none worthy,
Respecting her that's gone. Besides, the gods　　　35
Will have fulfilled their secret purposes;　　　36
For has not the divine Apollo said,
Is't not the tenor of his oracle,
That King Leontes shall not have an heir

---

798 what you have to what business you have with　**798–9 Being . . .
considered** i.e., (1) Being a gentleman of some influence (2) If I receive
a gentlemanly consideration, a bribe　**800 tender your persons** introduce you　**804 Close with him** Accept his offer　**812 in pawn** as
security　**815 moiety** half.　**817 case** (1) cause (2) skin　**824 gone
else** undone otherwise.　**828–9 look . . . hedge** i.e., relieve myself
836 occasion opportunity　**838 turn back** redound　**839–40 aboard
him** i.e., to him (Prince Florizel) aboard his ship.　**840 shore** put
ashore　**841–2 nothing** not at all　**843 proof against** invulnerable to

**5.1. Location: Sicilia. The royal court.
8 in them** in comparison with them　**14 the all that are** all the women
that there are　**19 good now** i.e., if you please　**25 nor the remembrance** i.e., nor give consideration to the perpetuation (through bearing a child and heir)　**26 consider** you consider　**27 fail of issue**
failure to produce an heir　**29 Incertain** not knowing what to think or
do (about the royal succession)　**30 well** happy, at rest (in heaven).
35 Respecting in comparison with　**36 Will . . . purposes** are determined to have their secret purposes fulfilled

Till his lost child be found? Which that it shall
Is all as monstrous to our human reason
As my Antigonus to break his grave   42
And come again to me, who, on my life,
Did perish with the infant. 'Tis your counsel   44
My lord should to the heavens be contrary,
Oppose against their wills. [*To Leontes*] Care not for
  issue.   46
The crown will find an heir. Great Alexander
Left his to th' worthiest; so his successor   48
Was like to be the best.

LEONTES   Good Paulina,
Who hast the memory of Hermione,
I know, in honor, oh, that ever I
Had squared me to thy counsel! Then even now   52
I might have looked upon my queen's full eyes,
Have taken treasure from her lips—

PAULINA   And left them
More rich for what they yielded.

LEONTES   Thou speak'st truth.
No more such wives, therefore no wife. One worse,   56
And better used, would make her sainted spirit   57
Again possess her corpse, and on this stage,   58
Where we're offenders now, appear soul-vexed,
And begin, "Why to me?"

PAULINA   Had she such power,   60
She had just cause.

LEONTES   She had, and would incense me   61
To murder her I married.

PAULINA   I should so.   62
Were I the ghost that walked, I'd bid you mark
Her eye and tell me for what dull part in't
You chose her. Then I'd shriek, that even your ears
Should rift to hear me, and the words that followed   66
Should be, "Remember mine."

LEONTES   Stars, stars,   67
And all eyes else dead coals! Fear thou no wife;   68
I'll have no wife, Paulina.

PAULINA   Will you swear
Never to marry but by my free leave?

LEONTES
Never, Paulina, so be blest my spirit!

PAULINA
Then, good my lords, bear witness to his oath.

CLEOMENES
You tempt him overmuch.

PAULINA   Unless another,   73
As like Hermione as is her picture,

Affront his eye.

CLEOMENES   Good madam—

PAULINA   I have done.   75
Yet if my lord will marry—if you will, sir,
No remedy, but you will—give me the office
To choose you a queen. She shall not be so young
As was your former, but she shall be such
As, walked your first queen's ghost, it should take joy   80
To see her in your arms.

LEONTES   My true Paulina,
We shall not marry till thou bidd'st us.

PAULINA   That
Shall be when your first queen's again in breath;
Never till then.   84

Enter a Gentleman.

GENTLEMAN
One that gives out himself Prince Florizel,   85
Son of Polixenes, with his princess—she
The fairest I have yet beheld—desires access
To your high presence.

LEONTES   What with him? He comes not   88
Like to his father's greatness. His approach,   89
So out of circumstance and sudden, tells us   90
'Tis not a visitation framed, but forced   91
By need and accident. What train?

GENTLEMAN   But few,   92
And those but mean.

LEONTES   His princess, say you, with him?   93

GENTLEMAN
Ay, the most peerless piece of earth, I think,
That e'er the sun shone bright on.

PAULINA   Oh, Hermione,
As every present time doth boast itself   96
Above a better gone, so must thy grave   97
Give way to what's seen now! [*To the Gentleman*] Sir,
  you yourself   98
Have said and writ so, but your writing now
Is colder than that theme. She had not been   100
Nor was not to be equaled—thus your verse   101
Flowed with her beauty once. 'Tis shrewdly ebbed   102
To say you have seen a better.

GENTLEMAN   Pardon, madam.
The one I have almost forgot—your pardon!
The other, when she has obtained your eye,
Will have your tongue too. This is a creature,   106
Would she begin a sect, might quench the zeal

42 As as for   **44 'Tis your counsel** It's your advice that   **46 Oppose** oppose himself.   **Care not for** Do not be anxious about   **48 Left . . . worthiest** (When Alexander the Great died in 323 B.C., his son Alexander was yet unborn, necessitating the choice of an heir.)
52 squared me adjusted or regulated myself   **56–7 One . . . used** i.e., If I took a new, less excellent wife and treated her better   **57 her** Hermione's   **58 possess her corpse** i.e., return to earth (*this stage*) in Hermione's human shape   **60 Why to me?** Why this offense to me?   **61 had** would have.   **incense** stir up, incite   **62 should so** would similarly incite you.   **66 rift** rive, split   **67 mine** my eyes.   **Stars** i.e., Her eyes were stars   **68 all eyes else** all other eyes   **73 tempt** bear down on

75 Affront confront   **80 walked . . . ghost** if your first queen's ghost were to walk.   **take joy** be overjoyed   **84.1 *Enter a Gentleman*** (He is called a "Servant" in the Folio text, but his writing poetry in lines 100–4 is more consistent with his being a courtier. Any such person at court is a servant of the king.)   **85 gives out himself** reports himself to be   **88 What** What retinue   **89 Like to** in a manner consistent with   **90 out of circumstance** without ceremony   **91 framed** planned   **92 train** retinue.   **93 mean** lowly.   **96–8 As . . . now!** As every present age boasts its superiority to past times that were in point of fact better, so you, long dead, must give way to present fashion!   **100 that theme** i.e., Hermione, the subject of your verses.   **100–1 She . . . equaled** (Presumably, the poet wrote "She has not been nor is not to be equaled.")   **102 'Tis shrewdly ebbed** i.e., You've egregiously gone back on your word   **106 tongue** i.e., approval

Of all professors else, make proselytes   108
Of who she but bid follow.

PAULINA   How? Not women!   109

GENTLEMAN
Women will love her that she is a woman
More worth than any man; men, that she is
The rarest of all women.

LEONTES   Go, Cleomenes.
Yourself, assisted with your honored friends,
Bring them to our embracement.
                         Exit [Cleomenes with others].
                              Still, 'tis strange
He thus should steal upon us.

PAULINA   Had our prince,
Jewel of children, seen this hour, he had paired
Well with this lord. There was not full a month
Between their births.

LEONTES   Prithee, no more, cease. Thou know'st
He dies to me again when talked of. Sure,
When I shall see this gentleman, thy speeches
Will bring me to consider that which may
Unfurnish me of reason. They are come.   123
         Enter Florizel, Perdita, Cleomenes, and others.
Your mother was most true to wedlock, Prince,
For she did print your royal father off,
Conceiving you. Were I but twenty-one,
Your father's image is so hit in you,   127
His very air, that I should call you brother,
As I did him, and speak of something wildly
By us performed before. Most dearly welcome!
And your fair princess—goddess! Oh! Alas,
I lost a couple that twixt heaven and earth
Might thus have stood begetting wonder as
You, gracious couple, do. And then I lost—
All mine own folly—the society,
Amity too, of your brave father, whom,   136
Though bearing misery, I desire my life   137
Once more to look on him.

FLORIZEL   By his command   138
Have I here touched Sicilia, and from him
Give you all greetings that a king, at friend,   140
Can send his brother; and but infirmity,   141
Which waits upon worn times, hath something seized 142
His wished ability, he had himself   143
The lands and waters twixt your throne and his
Measured to look upon you, whom he loves—   145
He bade me say so—more than all the scepters
And those that bear them living.

LEONTES   O my brother!   147
Good gentleman, the wrongs I have done thee stir

Afresh within me, and these thy offices,   149
So rarely kind, are as interpreters   150
Of my behindhand slackness. Welcome hither,   151
As is the spring to th'earth. And hath he too
Exposed this paragon to th' fearful usage—
At least ungentle—of the dreadful Neptune,   154
To greet a man not worth her pains, much less
Th'adventure of her person?

FLORIZEL   Good my lord,   156
She came from Libya.

LEONTES   Where the warlike Smalus,
That noble honored lord, is feared and loved?

FLORIZEL
Most royal sir, from thence, from him, whose daughter 159
His tears proclaimed his, parting with her. Thence, 160
A prosperous south wind friendly, we have crossed,
To execute the charge my father gave me
For visiting Your Highness. My best train
I have from your Sicilian shores dismissed,
Who for Bohemia bend, to signify   165
Not only my success in Libya, sir,
But my arrival and my wife's in safety
Here where we are.

LEONTES   The blessèd gods
Purge all infection from our air whilst you
Do climate here! You have a holy father,   170
A graceful gentleman, against whose person,   171
So sacred as it is, I have done sin,
For which the heavens, taking angry note,
Have left me issueless; and your father's blest,
As he from heaven merits it, with you,
Worthy his goodness. What might I have been,
Might I a son and daughter now have looked on,
Such goodly things as you?

                    Enter a Lord.

LORD   Most noble sir,
That which I shall report will bear no credit
Were not the proof so nigh. Please you, great sir,
Bohemia greets you from himself by me;
Desires you to attach his son, who has—   182
His dignity and duty both cast off—   183
Fled from his father, from his hopes, and with
A shepherd's daughter.

LEONTES   Where's Bohemia? Speak.

LORD
Here in your city. I now came from him.
I speak amazedly, and it becomes   187
My marvel and my message. To your court   188
Whiles he was hast'ning—in the chase, it seems,
Of this fair couple—meets he on the way

---

108 professors else believers in other sects or deities   **109 Of . . . follow** of all those whom she merely told to follow her.   **How? Not women!** What do you mean? Surely women wouldn't become converts!   **123 Unfurnish** deprive, divest   **127 hit** exactly reproduced   **136 brave** noble   **137 my life** i.e., to live long enough   **138 him** (Redundant in modern syntax.)   **140 at friend** in friendship   **141 but** were it not that   **142 waits . . . times** attends old age   **142–3 something . . . ability** to some extent taken away his ability (to travel) as he wishes   **145 Measured** traversed   **147 those . . . living** those living kings who bear scepters.

149 offices messages of good will, courteous attentions   **150 rarely** exceptionally   **150–1 are . . . slackness** are like commentators on my slowness in greeting you.   **154 Neptune** god of the sea   **156 Th'adventure** the hazard   **159–60 whose . . . her** whose tears, as he parted with her, proclaimed her to be his daughter.   **165 bend** direct their course   **170 climate** dwell, reside (in this clime)   **171 graceful** full of grace, gracious   **182 attach** arrest   **183 dignity and duty** princely dignity and filial duty   **187–8 I . . . message** i.e., I speak perplexedly as befits my perplexity and my astonishing news.

The father of this seeming lady and
Her brother, having both their country quitted
With this young prince.
FLORIZEL   Camillo has betrayed me,
Whose honor and whose honesty till now
Endured all weathers.
LORD   Lay't so to his charge.   195
He's with the King your father.
LEONTES   Who? Camillo?
LORD
Camillo, sir. I spake with him, who now
Has these poor men in question. Never saw I   198
Wretches so quake. They kneel, they kiss the earth,
Forswear themselves as often as they speak.
Bohemia stops his ears and threatens them
With divers deaths in death.
PERDITA   Oh, my poor father!   202
The heaven sets spies upon us, will not have
Our contract celebrated.
LEONTES   You are married?
FLORIZEL
We are not, sir, nor are we like to be.   205
The stars, I see, will kiss the valleys first;
The odds for high and low's alike.
LEONTES   My lord,   207
Is this the daughter of a king?
FLORIZEL   She is,
When once she is my wife.
LEONTES
That "once," I see, by your good father's speed
Will come on very slowly. I am sorry,
Most sorry, you have broken from his liking
Where you were tied in duty, and as sorry
Your choice is not so rich in worth as beauty,   214
That you might well enjoy her.
FLORIZEL [to Perdita]   Dear, look up.
Though Fortune, visible an enemy,   216
Should chase us with my father, power no jot   217
Hath she to change our loves.—Beseech you, sir,
Remember since you owed no more to time   219
Than I do now. With thought of such affections,   220
Step forth mine advocate. At your request
My father will grant precious things as trifles.
LEONTES
Would he do so, I'd beg your precious mistress,
Which he counts but a trifle.
PAULINA   Sir, my liege,
Your eye hath too much youth in't. Not a month
'Fore your queen died, she was more worth such
        gazes
Than what you look on now.
LEONTES   I thought of her

Even in these looks I made. [To Florizel] But your
        petition
Is yet unanswered. I will to your father.
Your honor not o'erthrown by your desires,   230
I am friend to them and you. Upon which errand
I now go toward him. Therefore follow me,
And mark what way I make. Come, good my lord.   233
                                        Exeunt.

❖

5.2

Enter Autolycus and a Gentleman.

AUTOLYCUS   Beseech you, sir, were you present at this
    relation?   2
FIRST GENTLEMAN   I was by at the opening of the fardel,
    heard the old shepherd deliver the manner how he   4
    found it; whereupon, after a little amazedness, we
    were all commanded out of the chamber. Only this,
    methought, I heard the shepherd say: he found the
    child.
AUTOLYCUS   I would most gladly know the issue of it.   9
FIRST GENTLEMAN   I make a broken delivery of the busi-   10
    ness, but the changes I perceived in the King and Cam-   12
    illo were very notes of admiration. They seemed al-   12
    most, with staring on one another, to tear the cases of   13
    their eyes. There was speech in their dumbness, lan-   14
    guage in their very gesture. They looked as they had   15
    heard of a world ransomed, or one destroyed. A notable
    passion of wonder appeared in them, but the wisest
    beholder, that knew no more but seeing, could not say   18
    if th'importance were joy or sorrow; but in the ex-   19
    tremity of the one it must needs be.   20

Enter another Gentleman.

Here comes a gentleman that haply knows more.—   21
The news, Rogero?
SECOND GENTLEMAN   Nothing but bonfires. The oracle
is fulfilled; the King's daughter is found. Such a deal of   24
wonder is broken out within this hour that ballad
makers cannot be able to express it.

Enter another Gentleman.

Here comes the Lady Paulina's steward. He can deliver
you more.—How goes it now, sir? This news which is
called true is so like an old tale that the verity of it is in
strong suspicion. Has the King found his heir?
THIRD GENTLEMAN   Most true, if ever truth were preg-   31
nant by circumstance. That which you hear you'll   32

195 Lay't . . . charge Confront him with it directly.   198 in question
under interrogation.   202 deaths i.e., tortures   205 like likely   207
The odds . . . alike Fortune treats high and low alike.   214 worth
rank   216–17 Though . . . father Though the goddess Fortune herself
were to manifest herself as our enemy and join my father in chasing
us   219–20 since . . . now when you were no older than I am now.
220 With . . . affections Recalling what it was to be in love at that age

230 Your . . . desires If your chaste honor has not been overcome by
sexual desire, or, if what you want in this match is compatible with
your royal honor   233 way progress
5.2. Location: Sicilia. At court.
2 relation narrative, account.   4 deliver report   9 issue outcome
10 broken disjointed, fragmented   12 very notes of admiration veritable marks of wonderment.   13–14 cases of their eyes eyelids.   15 as
as if   18 no . . . seeing nothing except what he could see   19 th'importance the import, meaning   20 of the one of one or the other
21 haply perhaps   24 deal huge quantity   31–2 pregnant by circumstance made apparent by circumstantial evidence.

swear you see, there is such unity in the proofs. The mantle of Queen Hermione's, her jewel about the neck of it, the letters of Antigonus found with it which they know to be his character, the majesty of the creature in 36 resemblance of the mother, the affection of nobleness 37 which nature shows above her breeding, and many 38 other evidences proclaim her with all certainty to be the King's daughter. Did you see the meeting of the two kings?

SECOND GENTLEMAN   No.

THIRD GENTLEMAN   Then have you lost a sight which was to be seen, cannot be spoken of. There might you have beheld one joy crown another, so and in such manner that it seemed Sorrow wept to take leave of them, for their joy waded in tears. There was casting up of eyes, holding up of hands, with countenance of 48 such distraction that they were to be known by garment, not by favor. Our king, being ready to leap 50 out of himself for joy of his found daughter, as if that joy were now become a loss, cries, "Oh, thy mother, thy mother!" then asks Bohemia forgiveness; then embraces his son-in-law; then again worries he his 54 daughter with clipping her; now he thanks the old 55 shepherd, which stands by like a weather-bitten con- 56 duit of many kings' reigns. I never heard of such 57 another encounter, which lames report to follow it and 58 undoes description to do it. 59

SECOND GENTLEMAN   What, pray you, became of Antigonus, that carried hence the child?

THIRD GENTLEMAN   Like an old tale still, which will have matter to rehearse though credit be asleep and not an 63 ear open. He was torn to pieces with a bear. This 64 avouches the shepherd's son, who has not only his 65 innocence, which seems much, to justify him, but a 66 handkerchief and rings of his that Paulina knows. 67

FIRST GENTLEMAN   What became of his bark and his followers?

THIRD GENTLEMAN   Wrecked the same instant of their master's death and in the view of the shepherd; so that all the instruments which aided to expose the child were even then lost when it was found. But oh, the noble combat that twixt joy and sorrow was fought in Paulina! She had one eye declined for the loss of her 75 husband, another elevated that the oracle was fulfilled. 76 She lifted the Princess from the earth, and so locks her in embracing as if she would pin her to her heart, that she might no more be in danger of losing. 79

FIRST GENTLEMAN   The dignity of this act was worth the audience of kings and princes, for by such was it acted.

THIRD GENTLEMAN   One of the prettiest touches of all, and that which angled for mine eyes—caught the water, though not the fish—was when, at the relation of the Queen's death, with the manner how she came to't bravely confessed and lamented by the King, how attentiveness wounded his daughter; till, from 88 one sign of dolor to another, she did, with an "Alas!" I 89 would fain say, bleed tears, for I am sure my heart wept blood. Who was most marble there changed 91 color; some swooned, all sorrowed. If all the world could have seen't, the woe had been universal.

FIRST GENTLEMAN   Are they returned to the court?

THIRD GENTLEMAN   No. The Princess hearing of her mother's statue, which is in the keeping of Paulina—a piece many years in doing and now newly performed 97 by that rare Italian master, Julio Romano, who, had he 98 himself eternity and could put breath into his work, would beguile Nature of her custom, so perfectly he is 100 her ape; he so near to Hermione hath done Hermione 101 that they say one would speak to her and stand in hope of answer—thither with all greediness of affec- 103 tion are they gone, and there they intend to sup. 104

SECOND GENTLEMAN   I thought she had some great matter there in hand, for she hath privately twice or thrice a day, ever since the death of Hermione, visited that removed house. Shall we thither and with our com- 108 pany piece the rejoicing? 109

FIRST GENTLEMAN   Who would be thence that has the benefit of access? Every wink of an eye some new grace will be born. Our absence makes us unthrifty to 112 our knowledge. Let's along.   *Exeunt [Gentlemen].*

AUTOLYCUS   Now, had I not the dash of my former life 114 in me, would preferment drop on my head. I brought 115 the old man and his son aboard the Prince, told him I 116 heard them talk of a fardel and I know not what. But he at that time overfond of the shepherd's daughter—so he then took her to be—who began to be much seasick, and himself little better, extremity of weather continuing, this mystery remained undiscovered. But 'tis all one to me, for had I been the finder 122 out of this secret, it would not have relished among 123 my other discredits.

Enter Shepherd and Clown, [dressed in finery].

Here come those I have done good to against my will, and already appearing in the blossoms of their fortune.

SHEPHERD   Come, boy. I am past more children, but thy sons and daughters will be all gentlemen born.

---

36 character handwriting   **37 affection of** natural disposition to **38 breeding** rearing   **48 countenance** bearing, demeanor   **50 favor** features.   **54 worries he** he pesters   **55 clipping** embracing **56–7 which . . . reigns** who stands by weeping like a weather-beaten fountain that has stood there over the course of many kings' reigns. **58–9 which . . . do it** which makes any account of it seem inadequate and beggars the powers of description in an attempt to do justice to it.   **63 rehearse** relate.   **credit** belief   **64 with** by   **65 avouches** confirms, corroborates   **66 innocence** simplemindedness (such that he would seem unable to invent such a story)   **67 his** Antigonus's **75–6 She . . . fulfilled** i.e., She wept and laughed at the same time. **79 losing** being lost.

88 attentiveness listening to it   **89 dolor** grief   **91 Who . . . marble** Even the most hardhearted   **97 performed** completed   **98 Julio Romano** Italian painter and sculptor of the sixteenth century, better known as a painter (and an anachronism in this play)   **100 beguile** deprive, cheat.   **custom** trade   **101 ape** imitator   **103–4 greediness of affection** eagerness born of love   **104 sup** i.e., feed their hungry eyes (?) or, perhaps, have a commemorative banquet (?). **108 removed** sequestered   **109 piece** add to, augment   **112 unthrifty** to passing up an opportunity to increase   **114–15 had I . . . head** if it weren't for the lingering reputation of petty thievery that hangs about me, royal favor would be sure to fall to my lot.   **116 the Prince** the Prince's ship   **122 'tis all one** it's all the same   **123 relished** tasted well, suited

CLOWN [*to Autolycus*] You are well met, sir. You denied to fight
with me this other day because I was no gentleman 131
born. See you these clothes? Say you see them not and
think me still no gentleman born. You were best say
these robes are not gentlemen born. Give me the lie, 134
do, and try whether I am not now a gentleman born.

AUTOLYCUS   I know you are now, sir, a gentleman born.

CLOWN   Ay, and have been so any time these four
hours.

SHEPHERD   And so have I, boy.

CLOWN   So you have. But I was a gentleman born before
my father; for the King's son took me by the hand
and called me brother; and then the two kings called
my father brother; and then the Prince my brother and
the Princess my sister called my father father; and so
we wept, and there was the first gentlemanlike tears
that ever we shed.

SHEPHERD   We may live, son, to shed many more.

CLOWN   Ay, or else 'twere hard luck, being in so pre- 148
posterous estate as we are. 149

AUTOLYCUS   I humbly beseech you, sir, to pardon me
all the faults I have committed to Your Worship, and to
give me your good report to the Prince my master. 152

SHEPHERD   Prithee, son, do; for we must be gentle, now 153
we are gentlemen.

CLOWN [*to Autolycus*]   Thou wilt amend thy life?

AUTOLYCUS   Ay, an it like Your good Worship. 156

CLOWN   Give me thy hand. I will swear to the Prince
thou art as honest a true fellow as any is in Bohemia. 158

SHEPHERD   You may say it, but not swear it.

CLOWN   Not swear it, now I am a gentleman? Let boors 160
and franklins say it; I'll swear it. 161

SHEPHERD   How if it be false, son?

CLOWN   If it be ne'er so false, a true gentleman may
swear it in the behalf of his friend.—And I'll swear to
the Prince thou art a tall fellow of thy hands and that 165
thou wilt not be drunk; but I know thou art no tall
fellow of thy hands and that thou wilt be drunk. But
I'll swear it, and I would thou wouldst be a tall fellow
of thy hands.

AUTOLYCUS   I will prove so, sir, to my power. 170

CLOWN   Ay, by any means prove a tall fellow. If I do not
wonder how thou dar'st venture to be drunk, not
being a tall fellow, trust me not. Hark, the kings and
the princes, our kindred, are going to see the Queen's
picture. Come, follow us. We'll be thy good masters. 175
Exeunt.

❧

5.3

*Enter Leontes, Polixenes, Florizel, Perdita,
Camillo, Paulina, lords, etc.*

LEONTES
O grave and good Paulina, the great comfort
That I have had of thee!

PAULINA   What, sovereign sir, 2
I did not well, I meant well. All my services
You have paid home. But that you have vouchsafed, 4
With your crowned brother and these your contracted
Heirs of your kingdoms, my poor house to visit,
It is a surplus of your grace which never 7
My life may last to answer.

LEONTES   O Paulina, 8
We honor you with trouble. But we came 9
To see the statue of our queen. Your gallery
Have we passed through, not without much content
In many singularities; but we saw not 12
That which my daughter came to look upon,
The statue of her mother.

PAULINA   As she lived peerless,
So her dead likeness, I do well believe,
Excels whatever yet you looked upon
Or hand of man hath done. Therefore I keep it
Lonely, apart. But here it is. Prepare 18
To see the life as lively mocked as ever 19
Still sleep mocked death. Behold, and say 'tis well. 20
[*Paulina draws a curtain, and discovers*]
Hermione [*standing*] *like a statue.*
I like your silence; it the more shows off
Your wonder. But yet speak; first, you, my liege.
Comes it not something near?

LEONTES   Her natural posture! 23
Chide me, dear stone, that I may say indeed
Thou art Hermione; or rather, thou art she
In thy not chiding, for she was as tender
As infancy and grace. But yet, Paulina,
Hermione was not as much wrinkled, nothing 28
So agèd as this seems.

POLIXENES   Oh, not by much.

PAULINA
So much the more our carver's excellence,
Which lets go by some sixteen years and makes her
As she lived now.

LEONTES   As now she might have done, 32
So much to my good comfort as it is
Now piercing to my soul. Oh, thus she stood,
Even with such life of majesty—warm life,
As now it coldly stands—when first I wooed her!
I am ashamed. Does not the stone rebuke me
For being more stone than it? O royal piece! 38

---

131 **this other** the other   134 **Give me the lie** Accuse me to my face
of lying (an insult that requires a challenge to a duel)   148–9 **preposterous** (Blunder for "prosperous.")   152 **me** on my behalf   153 **gentle** nobly generous   156 **an it like** if it please   158 **honest a true**
worthy an honest   160 **boors** peasants   161 **franklins** farmers owning their own small farms   165 **tall . . . hands** brave fellow   170 **my
power** the best of my ability. (Autolycus slyly promises to use his hands
well—in picking pockets.)   175 **picture** i.e., likeness, painted statue.

5.3. **Location:** Sicilia. Paulina's house.
2 **What** Whatever   4 **home** fully.   7–8 **which . . . answer** which I can
never live long enough to be able to repay.   9 **We . . . trouble** i.e., we
trouble you with the demands of hospitality, though you are kind
enough to call it an honor.   12 **singularities** rarities, curiosities
18 **Lonely** isolated   19 **as lively mocked** as realistically counterfeited
20 **Still** motionless   23 **something** somewhat   28 **nothing** not at all
32 **As she** as if she   38 **piece** work of art.

There's magic in thy majesty, which has
My evils conjured to remembrance and
From thy admiring daughter took the spirits,   41
Standing like stone with thee.

PERDITA   And give me leave,
And do not say 'tis superstition, that
I kneel and then implore her blessing. Lady,
                    [*kneeling*]
Dear Queen, that ended when I but began,
Give me that hand of yours to kiss.

PAULINA   Oh, patience!
The statue is but newly fixed; the color's   47
Not dry.

CAMILLO
My lord, your sorrow was too sore laid on,   49
Which sixteen winters cannot blow away,
So many summers dry. Scarce any joy   51
Did ever so long live; no sorrow
But killed itself much sooner.

POLIXENES   Dear my brother,
Let him that was the cause of this have power   54
To take off so much grief from you as he
Will piece up in himself.

PAULINA   Indeed, my lord,   56
If I had thought the sight of my poor image
Would thus have wrought you—for the stone is
    mine—   58
I'd not have showed it.

LEONTES   Do not draw the curtain.

PAULINA
No longer shall you gaze on't, lest your fancy
May think anon it moves.

LEONTES   Let be, let be.
Would I were dead but that methinks already—
What was he that did make it? See, my lord,
Would you not deem it breathed? And that those veins
Did verily bear blood?

POLIXENES   Masterly done.
The very life seems warm upon her lip.

LEONTES
The fixture of her eye has motion in't,   67
As we are mocked with art.

PAULINA   I'll draw the curtain.   68
My lord's almost so far transported that
He'll think anon it lives.

LEONTES   Oh, sweet Paulina,
Make me to think so twenty years together!
No settled senses of the world can match   72
The pleasure of that madness. Let't alone.

PAULINA
I am sorry, sir, I have thus far stirred you; but

I could afflict you farther.

LEONTES   Do, Paulina;
For this affliction has a taste as sweet
As any cordial comfort. Still methinks   77
There is an air comes from her. What fine chisel
Could ever yet cut breath? Let no man mock me,
For I will kiss her.

PAULINA   Good my lord, forbear.
The ruddiness upon her lip is wet;
You'll mar it if you kiss it, stain your own
With oily painting. Shall I draw the curtain?   83

LEONTES
No, not these twenty years.

PERDITA   So long could I
Stand by, a looker on.

PAULINA   Either forbear,
Quit presently the chapel, or resolve you   86
For more amazement. If you can behold it,
I'll make the statue move indeed, descend
And take you by the hand. But then you'll think—
Which I protest against—I am assisted
By wicked powers.

LEONTES   What you can make her do
I am content to look on, what to speak
I am content to hear; for 'tis as easy
To make her speak as move.

PAULINA   It is required
You do awake your faith. Then all stand still.
On; those that think it is unlawful business   96
I am about, let them depart.

LEONTES   Proceed.
No foot shall stir.

PAULINA   Music, awake her; strike!   [*Music.*]   98
'Tis time. Descend. Be stone no more. Approach.
Strike all that look upon with marvel. Come,   100
I'll fill your grave up. Stir, nay, come away,
Bequeath to death your numbness, for from him   102
Dear life redeems you.—You perceive she stirs.
          [*Hermione comes down.*]
Start not. Her actions shall be holy as
You hear my spell is lawful. Do not shun her   105
Until you see her die again, for then   106
You kill her double. Nay, present your hand.   107
When she was young you wooed her. Now in age
Is she become the suitor?   [*Leontes touches her.*]

LEONTES   Oh, she's warm!
If this be magic, let it be an art
Lawful as eating.

POLIXENES   She embraces him.

CAMILLO   She hangs about his neck.
If she pertain to life, let her speak too.   114

POLIXENES
Ay, and make it manifest where she has lived,
Or how stol'n from the dead.

PAULINA   That she is living,

---

41 admiring filled with wonder.   **spirits** vital spirits   **47 fixed** made
fast in its color   **49 sore** heavily   **51 So . . . dry** i.e., and sixteen summers cannot dry up. (Camillo tells the King that he has imposed too
heavy a sorrow on himself if even sixteen years' time cannot end it.)
54 him i.e., myself (as an innocent cause, but still a cause)   **56 piece
up in himself** add to his own burden.   **58 wrought** affected   **67 The
fixture . . . in't** i.e., Her eye, though motionless, gives the appearance
of motion   **68 As . . . art** in such a way that we are fooled by artistic
illusion.   **72 No settled . . . world** No calm mind in the world

77 cordial restorative, heartwarming   **83 painting** paint.
86 presently immediately   **96 On; those** (Often emended to *Or
those.*)   **98 strike** strike up.   **100 upon** on   **102 him** i.e., death
105–7 Do . . . double i.e., If you ever shun her during the rest of her
life, you will kill her again.   **114 pertain to life** be truly alive

Were it but told you, should be hooted at
Like an old tale; but it appears she lives,
Though yet she speak not. Mark a little while.
[*To Perdita*] Please you to interpose, fair madam. Kneel,   120
And pray your mother's blessing.—Turn, good lady;
Our Perdita is found.

HERMIONE   You gods, look down
And from your sacred vials pour your graces
Upon my daughter's head!—Tell me, mine own,
Where hast thou been preserved? Where lived? How
    found
Thy father's court? For thou shalt hear that I,
Knowing by Paulina that the oracle
Gave hope thou wast in being, have preserved
Myself to see the issue.   129

PAULINA   There's time enough for that,
Lest they desire upon this push to trouble   131
Your joys with like relation. Go together,   132
You precious winners all; your exultation
Partake to everyone. I, an old turtle,   134
Will wing me to some withered bough and there

My mate, that's never to be found again,   136
Lament till I am lost.

LEONTES   Oh, peace, Paulina!   137
Thou shouldst a husband take by my consent,
As I by thine a wife. This is a match,
And made between 's by vows. Thou hast found
    mine,
But how is to be questioned, for I saw her,
As I thought, dead, and have in vain said many
A prayer upon her grave. I'll not seek far—
For him, I partly know his mind—to find thee   144
An honorable husband. Come, Camillo,
And take her by the hand, whose worth and honesty   146
Is richly noted and here justified   147
By us, a pair of kings. Let's from this place.
[*To Hermione*] What? Look upon my brother. Both your
    pardons,
That e'er I put between your holy looks
My ill suspicion. This' your son-in-law   151
And son unto the King, whom, heavens directing,
Is trothplight to your daughter. Good Paulina,   153
Lead us from hence, where we may leisurely
Each one demand and answer to his part
Performed in this wide gap of time since first
We were dissevered. Hastily lead away.   *Exeunt.*

120 madam (Addressed to Perdita as Princess and affianced to be
married.)   **129 the issue** (1) the outcome (2) my child.   **131–2 Lest
. . . relation** lest they (bystanders) insist, at this critical juncture, on
interrupting this moment of joy with your relating of your story or
with their telling what has happened to them.   **134 Partake to** share
with, communicate.   **turtle** turtledove

136–7 My mate . . . lost grieve for my lost mate until I die.   **144 For**
as for   **146 whose** i.e., Camillo's   **147 richly noted** abundantly
acknowledged.   **justified** avouched   **151 This'** This is   **153 trothplight** betrothed

The Tempest

Shakespeare creates in *The Tempest* a world of the imagination, a place of conflict and ultimately of magical rejuvenation, like the forests of *A Midsummer Night's Dream* and *As You Like It*. The journey to Shakespeare's island is to a realm of art where everything is controlled by the artist-figure. Yet the journey is no escape from reality, for the island shows people what they are, as well as what they ought to be. Even its location juxtaposes the "real" world with an idealized landscape: like Plato's New Atlantis or Thomas More's Utopia, Shakespeare's island is to be found both somewhere and nowhere. On the narrative level, it is located in the Mediterranean Sea. Yet there are overtones of the New World, the Western Hemisphere, where Thomas More had situated his island of Utopia. Ariel fetches dew at Prospero's command from the "Bermudas" (1.2.230). Caliban when prostrate reminds Trinculo of a "dead Indian" (2.2.33) who might be displayed before gullible crowds eager to see such a prodigious creature from across the seas, and Caliban's god, Setebos, was, according to Richard Eden's account of Magellan's circumnavigation of the globe (in *History of Travel*, 1577), worshiped by South American natives. An inspiration for Shakespeare's story (for which no direct literary source is known) may well have been various accounts of the shipwreck in the Bermudas in 1609 of the *Sea Venture*, which was carrying settlers to the new Virginian colony. Shakespeare borrowed details from Sylvester Jourdain's *A Discovery of the Bermudas, Otherwise Called the Isle of Devils*, published in 1610, and from William Strachey's *A True Reportory of the Wreck and Redemption . . . from the Islands of the Bermudas*, which Shakespeare must have seen in manuscript since it was not published until after his death. He wrote the play shortly after reading these works, for *The Tempest* was acted at court in 1611. He may also have known or heard of various accounts of Magellan's circumnavigation of the world in 1519–1522 (including Richard Eden's shortened English version, as part of his *History of Travel*,

of an Italian narrative by Antonio Pigafetta), Francis Fletcher's journal of Sir Francis Drake's circumnavigation in 1577–1580, Richard Rich's *News from Virginia* (1610), and still other potential sources of information. Shakespeare's fascination with the Western Hemisphere gave him, not the actual location of his story, which remains Mediterranean, but a state of mind associated with newness and the unfamiliar. From this strange and unknown place, we gain a radical perspective on the old world of European culture. Miranda sees on the island a "new world" in which humankind appears "brave" (5.1.185), and, although her wonder must be tempered by Prospero's rejoinder that "'Tis new to thee" (line 186) and by Aldous Huxley's still more ironic use of her phrase in the title of his satirical novel *Brave New World*, the island endures as a restorative vision. Even though we experience it fleetingly, as in a dream, this nonexistent realm assumes a permanence enjoyed by all great works of art.

Prospero rules autocratically as artist-king and patriarch over this imaginary world, conjuring up trials and visions to test people's intentions and awaken their consciences. To the island come an assortment of persons who, because they require varied ordeals, are separated by Prospero and Ariel into three groups: King Alonso and those accompanying him; Alonso's son, Ferdinand; and Stephano and Trinculo. Prospero's authority over them, though strong, has limits. As Duke of Milan, he was bookishly inattentive to political matters and thus vulnerable to the Machiavellian conniving of his younger brother, Antonio. Only in this world apart, the artist's world, do his powers derived from learning find their proper sphere. Because he cannot control the world beyond his isle, he must wait for "strange, bountiful Fortune, / Now my dear lady" (1.2.179–80) to bring his enemies near his shore. He eschews, moreover, the black arts of diabolism. His is a white magic, devoted ultimately to what he considers moral ends: rescuing Ariel from the spell of the witch Sycorax, curbing the appetite of Caliban, spying on Antonio and Sebastian in the role of Conscience. He thus comes to see Fortune's gift of delivering his enemies into his hands as an opportunity for him to forgive and restore them, not be revenged.

Such an assumption of godlike power is close to arrogance, even blasphemy, for Prospero is no god. His chief power, learned from books and exercised through Ariel, is to control the elements so as to create illusion—of separation, of death, of the gods' blessing. Yet, since he is human, even this power is an immense burden and temptation. Prospero has much to learn, like those whom he controls. He must subdue his anger, his self-pity, his readiness to blame others, his domineering over Miranda. He must overcome the vengeful impulse he experiences toward those who have wronged him, and he must conquer the longing many a father feels to hold on to his daughter when she is desired by another man. He struggles with these problems through his art, devising games and shows in which his angry self-pity and jealousy are transmuted into playacting scenes of divine warning and forgiveness toward his enemies and watchful parental austerity toward Miranda and Ferdinand. Prospero's responsibilities cause him to behave magisterially and to be resented by the spirits of the isle. His authority is problematic to us because he seems so patriarchal, colonialist, even sexist and racist in his arrogating to himself the right and responsibility to control others in the name of values they may not share. Ariel longs to be free of this authority. Perhaps our sympathy for Prospero is greatest when we perceive that he, too, with mixed feelings of genuine relief and melancholy, is ready to lay aside his demanding and self-important role as creative moral intelligence.

Alonso and his court party variously illustrate the unregenerate world left behind in Naples and Milan. We first see them on shipboard, panicky and desperate, their titles and finery mocked by roaring waves. Futile ambition seems destined for a watery demise. Yet death by water in this play is a transfiguration rather than an end, a mystical rebirth, as in the regenerative cycle of the seasons from winter to summer. Ariel suggests as much in his song about a drowned father: "Those are pearls that were his eyes. / Nothing of him that doth fade / But doth suffer a sea change / Into something rich and strange" (1.2.402–5). Still, this miracle is not apparent at first to those who are caught in the illusion of death. As in T. S. Eliot's *The Waste Land*, which repeatedly alludes to *The Tempest,* self-blinded human beings fear a disaster that is ironically the prelude to reawakening.

The illusions created on the island serve to test these imperfect men and to make them reveal their true selves. Only Gonzalo, who long ago aided Prospero and Miranda when they were banished from Milan, responds affirmatively to illusion. In his eyes, their having been saved from drowning is a miracle: they breathe fresh air, the grass is green on the island, and their very garments appear not to have been stained by the salt water. His ideal commonwealth (2.1.150–71), which Shakespeare drew in part from an essay by Montaigne, postulates a natural goodness in humanity and makes no allowance for the darker propensities of human behavior, but at least Gonzalo's cheerfulness is in refreshing contrast to the jaded sneers of some of his companions. Sebastian and Antonio react to the magic isle, as to Gonzalo's commonwealth, by cynically refusing to believe in miracles. They scoff at Gonzalo for insistently looking on the bright side; if he were to examine his supposedly unstained clothes more carefully, they jest, he would discover that his pockets are filled with mud. Confident that they are unobserved, they seize the opportunity afforded by Alonso's being asleep to plot a murder and political coup. This attempt is not only despicable but also madly ludicrous, for they are all shipwrecked and no longer have kingdoms over which to quarrel. Even more ironically, Sebastian and Antonio, despite their insolent belief in their self-sufficiency, are being observed. The villains must be taught that an unseen power keeps track of their misdeeds. However presumptuous Prospero may be to assume through Ariel's means the role of godlike observer, he does awaken conscience and prevent murder. The villains may revert to type when returned to their usual habitat, but even they are at least briefly moved to an awareness of the unseen (3.3.21–7). Alonso, more worthy than they, though burdened, too, with sin, responds to his situation with guilt and despair, for he assumes that his son Ferdinand's death is the just punishment of the gods for Alonso's part in the earlier overthrow of Prospero. Alonso must be led, by means of curative illusions, through the purgative experience of contrition to the reward he thinks impossible and undeserved: reunion with his lost son.

Alonso is thus, like Posthumus in *Cymbeline* or Leontes in *The Winter's Tale,* a tragicomic figure—sinful, contrite, forgiven. Alonso's son Ferdinand must also undergo ordeals and visions devised by Prospero to test his worth, but more on the level of romantic comedy. Ferdinand is young, innocent, and hopeful, well-matched to Miranda. From the start, Prospero obviously approves of his prospective son-in-law. Yet even Prospero, needing to prepare himself for a life in which Miranda will no longer be solely his, is not ready to lay aside at least the comic fiction of parental opposition. He invents difficulties, imposes tasks of logbearing (like those assigned Caliban), and issues stern warnings against premarital lust. In the comic mode, parents are expected to cross their children in matters of the heart. Prospero is so convincing in his role of overbearing parent, insisting on absolute unthinking obedience from his daughter, that we remain unsure whether he is truly like that or whether we are meant to sense in his performance a grappling with his own deepest feelings of possessiveness and autocratic authority, tempered finally by his awareness of the arbitrariness of such a role and his readiness to let Miranda decide for herself. As a teacher of youth, moreover, Prospero is convinced by long experience that prizes too easily won are too lightly esteemed. Manifold are the temptations urging Ferdinand to surrender to the natural rhythms of the isle as Caliban would. In place of ceremonies conducted in civilized societies by the church, Prospero must create the illusion of ceremony by his art. The betrothal of Ferdinand and Miranda accordingly unites the best of both worlds: the natural innocence of the island, which teaches them to avoid the corruptions of civilization at its worst, and the higher law of nature achieved through moral wisdom at its best. To this marriage, the goddesses Iris, Ceres, and Juno bring promises of bounteous harvest, "refreshing showers," celestial harmony, and a springtime brought back to the earth by Proserpina's return from Hades (4.1.76–117). In Ferdinand and Miranda, "nurture" is wedded to "nature." This bond unites spirit and flesh, legitimizing erotic pleasure by incorporating it within Prospero's vision of a cosmic moral order.

At the lowest level of this traditional cosmic and moral framework, in Prospero's view, are Stephano and Trinculo. Their comic scenes juxtapose them with Caliban, for he represents untutored Nature, whereas they represent the unnatural depths to which human beings brought up in civilized society can fall. In this they resemble Sebastian and Antonio, who have learned in supposedly civilized Italy arts of intrigue and political murder. The antics of Stephano and Trinculo burlesque the conduct of their presumed betters, thereby exposing to ridicule the self-deceptions of ambitious men. The clowns desire to exploit the natural wonders of the isle by taking Caliban back to civilization to be shown in carnivals or by plying him with strong drink and whetting his resentment against authority. These plottings are in vain, however, for, like Sebastian and Antonio, the clowns are being watched. The clowns teach Caliban to cry out for "freedom" (2.2.184), by which they mean license to do as one pleases, but are foiled by Ariel as comic nemesis. Because they are degenerate buffoons, Prospero as satirist devises for them an exposure that is appropriately humiliating and satirical.

In contrast with them, Caliban is in many ways a sympathetic character. His sensitivity to natural beauty, as in his descriptions of the "nimble marmoset" or the dreaming music he so often hears (2.2.168; 3.2.137–45), is entirely appropriate to this child of nature. He is, to be sure, the child of a witch and is called many harsh names by Miranda and Prospero, such as "Abhorrèd slave" and "a born devil, on whose nature / Nurture can never stick" (1.2.354; 4.1.188–9). Yet he protests with some justification that the island was his in the first place and that Prospero and Miranda are interlopers. His very existence calls radically into question the value of civilization, which has shown itself capable of limitless depravity. What profit has

Caliban derived from learning Prospero's language other than, as he puts it, to "know how to curse" (1.2.367)? With instinctive cunning, he senses that books are his chief enemy and plots to destroy them first in his attempt at rebellion. The unspoiled natural world does indeed offer civilization a unique perspective on itself. In this it resembles Gonzalo's ideal commonwealth, which, no matter how laughably implausible from the cynic's point of view, does at least question some assumptions—economic, political, and social—common in western societies.

Radical perspectives of this kind invite consideration of many unsettling questions about exploration, colonialist empire building, and sexual imperialism. The fleeting comparison of Caliban to an indigenous native (2.2.33), although ignored in stage productions of the play until the late nineteenth century, suggests a discourse on colonialism in *The Tempest* that anticipates to a remarkable degree a doleful history of exploitation, of providing rum and guns to the natives, and of taking away land through violent expropriation in the name of bringing civilization and God to the New World. Stephano and Trinculo, pouring wine down Caliban's throat and thus reducing him to a worshiping slave, show exploitation at its worst, but surely the play allows us to wonder also if Prospero's enslavement of Caliban, however high-minded in its claims of preventing disorder and rape, is not tainted by the same imperatives of possession and control. The issue is wonderfully complex. Caliban is a projection of both the naturally depraved savage described in many explorers' accounts and the nobly innocent savage described by Montaigne. By dramatizing the conflict without taking sides, Shakespeare leaves open a debate about the worth of Prospero's endeavor to contain Caliban's otherness and produces an ambivalent result in which the apparent victory of colonialism and censorship does not entirely conceal the contradictory struggle through which those values are imposed. The play's many open-ended questions apply not only to the New World but also, nearer at hand, to Ireland—an island on the margins of Britain that was regarded as both savage and threatening.

The play's discourse also raises issues of class and political justice. The battle between Prospero and Caliban is one of "master" and "man" (2.2.183); even if Caliban's cry of "freedom" leads him only into further enslavement by Stephano and Trinculo (who are themselves masterless men), the play does not resolve the conflict by simply reimposing social hierarchy. Caliban, Stephano, and Trinculo are all taught a lesson and are satirically punished for their rebellious behavior, but Caliban at least is pardoned and is left behind on the island at the play's end where presumably he will no longer be a slave. In political terms, Prospero resolves the long-standing hostilities between Milan and Naples by his astute arranging of the betrothal of Miranda to Ferdinand. However much it is idealized as a romantic match presided over harmoniously by the gods, it is also a political union aimed at bringing together the ruling families of those two city states. Prospero's masque, his ultimate vision of the triumph of civilization, transforms the myth of the rape of a daughter (Proserpina) in such a way as to preserve the daughter's chaste honor in a union that will repair the political and social damage done by the ouster of Prospero from his dukedom of Milan. For these reasons, the betrothal of Ferdinand and Miranda must have seemed politically relevant to Shakespeare's audience when *The Tempest* was performed before King James at Whitehall in November of 1611 and then again at court in 1613 in celebration of the marriage of James's daughter Elizabeth to Frederick, the Elector Palatine.

The play's ending is far from perfectly stable. Antonio never repents, and we cannot be sure what the island will be like once Prospero has disappeared from the scene. Since Prospero's occupation of the island replicates in a sense the process by which he himself was overthrown, we cannot know when the cycle of revolution will ever cease. We cannot even be sure of the extent to which Shakespeare is master of his own colonial debate in *The Tempest* or, conversely, the extent to which today we should feel ourselves free to relativize, ironize, or in other ways criticize this play for apparent or probable prejudices. Not even a great author like Shakespeare can escape the limits of his own time, any more than we can escape the limits of our own. Perhaps we can nonetheless project ourselves, as spectators and readers, into Shakespeare's attempt to celebrate humanity's highest achievement in the union of the island with the civilized world. Miranda and Ferdinand have bright hopes for the future, even if those hopes must be qualified by Prospero's melancholic observation that the "brave new world" with "such people in't" is only "new to thee," to those who are young and not yet experienced in the world's vexations. Even Caliban may be at last reconciled to Prospero's insistent idea of a harmony between will and reason, no matter how perilously and delicately achieved. Prospero speaks of Caliban as a "thing of darkness I / Acknowledge mine," and Caliban vows to "be wise hereafter / And seek for grace" (5.1.278–9, 298–9). Prospero's view is that the natural human within is more contented, better understood, and more truly free when harmonized with reason.

Caliban is a part of humanity; Ariel is not. Ariel can comprehend what compassion and forgiveness would be like, "were I human" (5.1.20), and can take good-natured part in Prospero's designs to castigate or reform his fellow mortals, but Ariel longs to be free in quite another sense from that meant by Caliban. Ariel takes no part in the final integration of human society. This spirit belongs to a magic world of song, music, and illusion that the artist borrows for his use but that exists eternally outside of him. Like the elements of air, earth, fire, and water in which it mysteriously dwells, this spirit is morally neutral but incredibly vital. From it the artist achieves powers of imagination, enabling him to bedim the noontide sun or call forth the dead from their graves. These visions are illusory in the profound sense that all life is illusory, an "insubstantial pageant" melted into thin air (4.1.150–5). Prospero the artist cherishes his own humanity, as a promise of surcease from his labors. Yet the artifact created by the artist endures, existing apart from time and place, as does Ariel: "Then to the elements / Be free, and fare thou well!" (5.1.321–2). No doubt it is a romantic fiction to associate the dramatist Shakespeare with Prospero's farewell to his art, but it is an almost irresistible idea, because we are so moved by the sense of completion and yet humility, the exultation and yet the calm contained in this leave-taking.

As though to demonstrate the summation of his artistry as magician-poet in what he may indeed have designed as his farewell to the stage, Shakespeare puts on a dazzling display of the verbal artistry for which he had already become famous. His command of blank verse is, by this time, more flexible and protean than ever before, with a marked increase in run-on lines, caesuras in mid line, the sharing of blank verse lines between two or more speakers, feminine endings, and other features of the late Shakespearean style. (See General Introduction, pp. lxxx-lxxxi). The play is notable for its bravura passages, such as those that begin "Our revels now are ended" (4.1.148–58) and "Ye elves of hills" (5.1.33–57). With its opening storm scene and its solemn shows and masques—the "*several strange shapes*" bringing in a banquet and the appearance of Ariel "*like a harpy*" in 3.3, the masque of Iris, Ceres, and Juno in 4.1, and Prospero's confining the Neapolitans to a charmed circle in 5.1—*The Tempest* presents itself as a tour de force of spectacle and grandeur in which all of these dazzling events are also astutely interrupted by the resurgence of human appetite and by satiric correction. At every turn the drama manifests a deft compression of time and event. The tone is masterfully assured, in prose as in verse. Images of a dreamlike world come together in a remarkable amalgam whereby the characters participate in a fluid world that moves through them even as they move through it, becoming one with the tempest of time.

In performance, *The Tempest* reveals an extraordinary range of interpretive possibilities. Caliban, in nineteenth-century stage versions, was apt to be a grotesque specimen of Darwinian evolution, outfitted with gills, fishy scales, and long fingernails for prying shellfish out of rocks (the long fingernails are in fact mentioned, at 2.2.166). Herbert Beerbohm Tree, in 1904, saw Caliban as hairy from head to foot, with unkempt beard, pointed ears, sinister eyes, and long fingernails. To Frank Benson, at Stratford-upon-Avon in 1891, Caliban (played by Benson himself) was the missing link in an evolutionary chain of monkeys, baboons, and other presumably human ancestors; the Caliban of this production climbed a tree on stage, hung upside down, and gibbered. More recently, in accord with critical interest in the play as a potential critique of colonialism, Caliban has often been seen as a Caribbean native, physically imposing and even handsome, restive under his slavery, a man of immense human dignity. An example is that of David Suchet in Clifford Williams's 1987 production for the Royal Shakespeare Company; Suchet's Caliban, a sympathetic victim of imperialism, evoked unmistable echoes of third-world exploited populations from the West Indies and sub-Saharan Africa. Prospero has undergone no less of a sea change, from the benign authorial stand-in of traditional nineteenth-century productions to a man who can be tyrannical, arbitrary, menacing, close to violence, deeply angry, as in Derek Jarman's 1980 film. Interpretations of Ariel have varied from saccharine sweetness to the punk-haired and drug-inebriated, as in Mark Rylance's Ariel in Ron Daniels's 1982 RSC production. Underlying sexual tensions are evident on all sides in recent productions. Some of the most remarkable versions of the play have abandoned Shakespeare's script to varying degrees, as in Peter Brook's Round House production of 1968 featuring an enormous Sycorax giving birth to Caliban, a takeover of the island and capture of Prospero by Caliban, and a wild orgy. Derek Jarman's film version of 1980 saw the play as dominantly gay, with Caliban as an aging "queen." Giorgio Strehler's *La Tempesta*, Milan, 1977, pictured Ariel as a commedia dell'arte Pierrot attached to a wire, soaring through the air and landing as though on Prospero's raised finger. Peter Greenaway's 1991 film called *Prospero's Books* presented the entire play through Prospero's eyes; John Gielgud, as Prospero, spoke virtually all the lines. The extraordinary range of theatrical innovations that has been brought to this play testifies to the script's own remarkable theatrical self-consciousness and its delight in magic and illusion.

The Tempest

Names of the Actors

ALONSO, *King of Naples*
SEBASTIAN, *his brother*
PROSPERO, *the right Duke of Milan*
ANTONIO, *his brother, the usurping Duke of Milan*
FERDINAND, *son to the King of Naples*
GONZALO, *an honest old counselor*
ADRIAN *and* ⎫
FRANCISCO, ⎬ *lords*
CALIBAN, *a savage and deformed slave*
TRINCULO, *a jester*
STEPHANO, *a drunken butler*
MASTER *of a ship*

BOATSWAIN
MARINERS

MIRANDA, *daughter to Prospero*

ARIEL, *an airy spirit*
IRIS
CERES,
JUNO, ⎬ *[presented by] spirits*
NYMPHS
REAPERS,

[*Other Spirits attending on Prospero*]

THE SCENE: *An island*

1.1

A tempestuous noise of thunder and lightning heard. Enter a Shipmaster and a Boatswain.

MASTER   Boatswain!

BOATSWAIN   Here, Master. What cheer?

MASTER   Good, speak to th' mariners. Fall to't yarely, or we run ourselves aground. Bestir, bestir!   *Exit.*   3

Enter Mariners.

BOATSWAIN   Heigh, my hearts! Cheerly, cheerly, my hearts! Yare, yare! Take in the topsail. Tend to th' Master's whistle.—Blow till thou burst thy wind, if room enough!   6 / 7 / 8

Enter Alonso, Sebastian, Antonio, Ferdinand, Gonzalo, and others.

ALONSO   Good Boatswain, have care. Where's the Master? Play the men.   10

BOATSWAIN   I pray now, keep below.

ANTONIO   Where is the Master, Boatswain?

BOATSWAIN   Do you not hear him? You mar our labor. Keep your cabins! You do assist the storm.   14

GONZALO   Nay, good, be patient.   15

BOATSWAIN   When the sea is. Hence! What cares these roarers for the name of king? To cabin! Silence! Trouble us not.   17

GONZALO   Good, yet remember whom thou hast aboard.

BOATSWAIN   None that I more love than myself. You are a councillor; if you can command these elements to silence and work the peace of the present, we will not hand a rope more. Use your authority. If you cannot, give thanks you have lived so long and make yourself ready in your cabin for the mischance of the hour, if it so hap.—Cheerly, good hearts!—Out of our way, I say.   *Exit.*   23 / 24 / 27

GONZALO   I have great comfort from this fellow. Methinks he hath no drowning mark upon him; his complexion is perfect gallows. Stand fast, good Fate, to his hanging! Make the rope of his destiny our cable, for our own doth little advantage. If he be not born to be   30 / 31 / 33

hanged, our case is miserable.   *Exeunt [courtiers].*   34

Enter Boatswain.

BOATSWAIN   Down with the topmast! Yare! Lower, lower! Bring her to try wi'th' main course. (*A cry within.*) A plague upon this howling! They are louder than the weather or our office.   36 / 38

Enter Sebastian, Antonio, and Gonzalo.

Yet again? What do you here? Shall we give o'er and drown? Have you a mind to sink?   39

SEBASTIAN   A pox o'your throat, you bawling, blasphemous, incharitable dog!

BOATSWAIN   Work you, then.

ANTONIO   Hang, cur! Hang, you whoreson, insolent noisemaker! We are less afraid to be drowned than thou art.

GONZALO   I'll warrant him for drowning, though the ship were no stronger than a nutshell and as leaky as an unstanched wench.   47 / 49

BOATSWAIN   Lay her ahold, ahold! Set her two courses. Off to sea again! Lay her off!   50

Enter Mariners, wet.

MARINERS   All lost! To prayers, to prayers! All lost!
[*The Mariners run about in confusion, exiting at random.*]

BOATSWAIN   What, must our mouths be cold?   53

GONZALO
The King and Prince at prayers! Let's assist them,
For our case is as theirs.

SEBASTIAN   I am out of patience.

ANTONIO
We are merely cheated of our lives by drunkards.   56
This wide-chapped rascal! Would thou mightst lie drowning   57
The washing of ten tides!

GONZALO   He'll be hanged yet,   58
Though every drop of water swear against it
And gape at wid'st to glut him.
(*A confused noise within:*)   "Mercy on us!"—   60
"We split, we split!"—"Farewell my wife and children!"—   61
"Farewell, brother!"—"We split, we split, we split!"
[*Exit Boatswain.*]

ANTONIO   Let's all sink wi'th' King.

SEBASTIAN   Let's take leave of him.

Exit [with Antonio].

GONZALO   Now would I give a thousand furlongs of sea

Names of the Actors This list appears at the end of the play in the First Folio, in this order, with Miranda's name below that of the men, as was conventional in lists of the period.   **PROSPERO**, *the right* the rightful   **CALIBAN ... slave** The Folio reads "*saluage,*" a common alternative spelling of *savage* but perhaps also with a resonance of being salvaged from shipwreck. *Slave* has a range of meanings: wretch, rascal, servile creature, one who is owned by another person, one who is divested of freedom and personal rights.
1.1 Location: On board ship, off the island's coast.
3 Good i.e., It's good you've come, or, my good fellow.   **yarely** nimbly   **6 Tend** Attend   **7 Blow** (Addressed to the wind.)   **7–8 if room enough** as long as we have sea room enough.   **10 Play the men** Act like men, with spirit.   **14 Keep** Remain in   **15 good** good fellow   **17 roarers** waves or winds, or both; spoken to as though they were "bullies" or "blusterers"   **23 work ... present** bring calm to our present circumstances   **24 hand** handle   **27 hap** happen.   **30–1 complexion ... gallows** appearance shows he was born to be hanged (and therefore, according to the proverb, in no danger of drowning)   **33 our ... advantage** our own cable is of little benefit.

34 case is miserable circumstances are desperate.   **36 Bring ... course** Sail her close to the wind by means of the mainsail.   **38 our office** i.e., the noise we make at our work.   **39 give o'er** give up   **47 warrant him for drowning** guarantee that he will never be drowned   **49 unstanched** insatiable, loose, unrestrained. (Suggesting also "incontinent" and "menstrual.")   **50 ahold** ahull, close to the wind.   **courses** sails, i.e., foresail as well as mainsail, set in an attempt to get the ship back out into open water.   **53 must ... cold?** i.e., must we drown in the cold sea?   **56 merely** utterly   **57 widechapped** big-mouthed   **57–8 Would ... tides!** (Pirates were hanged on the shore and left until three tides had come in.)   **60 at wid'st** wide open.   **glut** swallow   **61 split** break apart.

for an acre of barren ground: long heath, brown furze, 66
anything. The wills above be done! But I would fain 67
die a dry death.   *Exit.*

❧

1.2

Enter Prospero [in his magic cloak] and Miranda.

MIRANDA
If by your art, my dearest father, you have   1
Put the wild waters in this roar, allay them.   2
The sky, it seems, would pour down stinking pitch,
But that the sea, mounting to th' welkin's cheek,   4
Dashes the fire out. Oh, I have suffered
With those that I saw suffer! A brave vessel,   6
Who had, no doubt, some noble creature in her,
Dashed all to pieces. Oh, the cry did knock
Against my very heart! Poor souls, they perished.
Had I been any god of power, I would
Have sunk the sea within the earth or ere   11
It should the good ship so have swallowed and
The freighting souls within her.

PROSPERO   Be collected.   13
No more amazement. Tell your piteous heart   14
There's no harm done.

MIRANDA   Oh, woe the day!

PROSPERO   No harm.
I have done nothing but in care of thee,   16
Of thee, my dear one, thee, my daughter, who
Art ignorant of what thou art, naught knowing
Of whence I am, nor that I am more better   19
Than Prospero, master of a full poor cell,   20
And thy no greater father.

MIRANDA   More to know
Did never meddle with my thoughts.

PROSPERO   'Tis time   22
I should inform thee farther. Lend thy hand
And pluck my magic garment from me. So,
        [*laying down his magic cloak and staff*]
Lie there, my art.—Wipe thou thine eyes. Have
    comfort.
The direful spectacle of the wreck, which touched   26
The very virtue of compassion in thee,   27
I have with such provision in mine art
So safely ordered that there is no soul—
No, not so much perdition as an hair   30
Betid to any creature in the vessel   31
Which thou heard'st cry, which thou saw'st sink. Sit
    down,   32

For thou must now know farther.

MIRANDA [*sitting*]   You have often
Begun to tell me what I am, but stopped
And left me to a bootless inquisition,   35
Concluding, "Stay, not yet."

PROSPERO   The hour's now come;
The very minute bids thee ope thine ear.
Obey, and be attentive. Canst thou remember
A time before we came unto this cell?
I do not think thou canst, for then thou wast not
Out three years old.

MIRANDA   Certainly, sir, I can.   41

PROSPERO
By what? By any other house or person?
Of anything the image, tell me, that
Hath kept with thy remembrance.

MIRANDA   'Tis far off,
And rather like a dream than an assurance   45
That my remembrance warrants. Had I not   46
Four or five women once that tended me?

PROSPERO
Thou hadst, and more, Miranda. But how is it
That this lives in thy mind? What see'st thou else
In the dark backward and abysm of time?   50
If thou remem'brest aught ere thou cam'st here,   51
How thou cam'st here thou mayst.

MIRANDA   But that I do not.

PROSPERO
Twelve year since, Miranda, twelve year since,
Thy father was the Duke of Milan and
A prince of power.

MIRANDA   Sir, are not you my father?

PROSPERO
Thy mother was a piece of virtue, and   56
She said thou wast my daughter; and thy father
Was Duke of Milan, and his only heir
And princess no worse issued.

MIRANDA   Oh, the heavens!   59
What foul play had we, that we came from thence?
Or blessèd was't we did?

PROSPERO   Both, both, my girl.
By foul play, as thou say'st, were we heaved thence,
But blessedly holp hither.

MIRANDA   O, my heart bleeds   63
To think o'th' teen that I have turned you to,   64
Which is from my remembrance! Please you, farther.   65

PROSPERO
My brother and thy uncle, called Antonio—
I pray thee mark me—that a brother should
Be so perfidious!—he whom next thyself   68
Of all the world I loved, and to him put
The manage of my state, as at that time   70
Through all the seigniories it was the first,   71

---

66 **heath** heather. **furze** gorse, a weed growing on wasteland
67 **fain** rather
1.2 Location: The island, near Prospero's cell. On the Elizabethan
stage, this cell is implicitly at hand throughout the play, although
in some scenes the convention of flexible distance allows us to
imagine characters in other parts of the island.
1 art magic **2 allay** pacify **4 welkin's cheek** sky's face **6 brave**
gallant, splendid **11 or ere** before **13 freighting souls** cargo of
souls. **collected** calm, composed. **14 amazement** consternation.
piteous pitying **16 but** except **19 more better** of higher rank
20 full very **22 meddle** mingle **26 wreck** shipwreck **27 virtue**
essence **30 perdition** loss **31 Betid** happened **32 Which** whom

---

35 **bootless inquisition** profitless inquiry 41 **Out** fully 45–6 **assurance . . . warrants** certainty that my memory guarantees. 50 **backward
. . . time** abyss of the past. 51 **aught** anything 56 **piece** masterpiece,
exemplar 59 **no worse issued** no less nobly born, descended. 63 **holp**
helped 64 **teen . . . to** trouble I've caused you to remember or put you
to 65 **from** out of 68 **next** next to 70 **manage** management, administration 71 **seigniories** i.e., city-states of northern Italy

And Prospero the prime duke, being so reputed   72
In dignity, and for the liberal arts
Without a parallel; those being all my study,
The government I cast upon my brother
And to my state grew stranger, being transported   76
And rapt in secret studies. Thy false uncle—
Dost thou attend me?

MIRANDA   Sir, most heedfully.

PROSPERO
Being once perfected how to grant suits,   79
How to deny them, who t'advance and who
To trash for overtopping, new created   81
The creatures that were mine, I say, or changed 'em,   82
Or else new formed 'em; having both the key   83
Of officer and office, set all hearts i'th' state   84
To what tune pleased his ear, that now he was   85
The ivy which had hid my princely trunk
And sucked my verdure out on't. Thou attend'st not.   87

MIRANDA
Oh, good sir, I do.

PROSPERO   I pray thee, mark me.
I, thus neglecting worldly ends, all dedicated
To closeness and the bettering of my mind   90
With that which, but by being so retired,   91
O'erprized all popular rate, in my false brother   92
Awaked an evil nature; and my trust,
Like a good parent, did beget of him   94
A falsehood in its contrary as great
As my trust was, which had indeed no limit,
A confidence sans bound. He being thus lorded   97
Not only with what my revenue yielded
But what my power might else exact, like one   99
Who, having into truth by telling of it,   100
Made such a sinner of his memory   101
To credit his own lie, he did believe   102
He was indeed the Duke, out o'th' substitution   103
And executing th'outward face of royalty   104
With all prerogative. Hence his ambition growing—   105
Dost thou hear?

MIRANDA   Your tale, sir, would cure deafness.

PROSPERO
To have no screen between this part he played   107
And him he played it for, he needs will be   108
Absolute Milan. Me, poor man, my library   109
Was dukedom large enough. Of temporal royalties   110
He thinks me now incapable; confederates—   111
So dry he was for sway—wi'th' King of Naples   112
To give him annual tribute, do him homage,   113
Subject his coronet to his crown, and bend   114
The dukedom yet unbowed—alas, poor Milan!—   115
To most ignoble stooping.

MIRANDA   O the heavens!

PROSPERO
Mark his condition and th'event, then tell me   117
If this might be a brother.

MIRANDA   I should sin
To think but nobly of my grandmother.   119
Good wombs have borne bad sons.

PROSPERO   Now the condition.
This King of Naples, being an enemy
To me inveterate, hearkens my brother's suit,   122
Which was that he, in lieu o'th' premises   123
Of homage and I know not how much tribute,
Should presently extirpate me and mine   125
Out of the dukedom and confer fair Milan,
With all the honors, on my brother. Whereon,
A treacherous army levied, one midnight
Fated to th' purpose did Antonio open
The gates of Milan, and, i'th' dead of darkness,
The ministers for th' purpose hurried thence   131
Me and thy crying self.

MIRANDA   Alack, for pity!
I, not remembering how I cried out then,
Will cry it o'er again. It is a hint   134
That wrings mine eyes to 't.

PROSPERO   Hear a little further,   135
And then I'll bring thee to the present business
Which now's upon 's, without the which this story
Were most impertinent.

MIRANDA   Wherefore did they not   138
That hour destroy us?

PROSPERO   Well demanded, wench.   139
My tale provokes that question. Dear, they durst
    not,
So dear the love my people bore me, nor set   141
A mark so bloody on the business, but   142

72 prime first in rank and importance   76 to . . . stranger i.e., withdrew from my responsibilities as duke.   transported carried away   79 perfected grown skillful   81 trash check a hound by tying a cord or weight to its neck.   overtopping running too far ahead of the pack; surmounting, exceeding one's authority   81–3 new . . . formed 'em won the loyalty of my officers by appointing them to new posts, or replaced them with others who would be loyal to Antonio, or else redefined the positions and their occupants   83–5 having . . . ear having now under his control both the officers and the positions, he set a tone for his rule according to his own inclination. (Key is also a metaphor for tuning stringed instruments.)   87 verdure vitality.   on't of it.   90 closeness retirement, seclusion   91–2 but . . . rate i.e., were it not that its private nature caused me to neglect my public responsibilities, had a value far beyond what public opinion could appreciate, or, simply because it was done in such seclusion, had a value not appreciated by popular opinion   94 good parent (Alludes to the proverb that good parents often bear bad children; see also line 120.)   of in   97 sans without.   lorded raised to lordship, with power and wealth   99 else otherwise, additionally   100–2 Who . . . lie i.e., who, by repeatedly telling the lie (that he was indeed Duke of Milan), made his memory such a confirmed sinner against truth that he began to believe his own lie.   103–5 out . . . prerogative as a result of his making himself my substitute and carrying out all the visible functions of royalty with all its rights and privileges.

107–9 To have . . . Milan In order to eliminate all separation between his role and himself, he insisted on becoming the Duke of Milan in name as well as in fact.   110 temporal royalties practical prerogatives and responsibilities of a sovereign   111 confederates conspires, allies himself   112 dry thirsty.   sway power   113 him i.e., the King of Naples   114 his . . . his Antonio's . . . the King of Naples'.   bend make bow down   115 yet hitherto   117 condition pact.   th'event the outcome   119 but other than   122 hearkens listens to   123 he the King of Naples.   in . . . premises in return for the stipulation   125 presently extirpate at once remove   131 ministers . . . purpose agents employed to do this.   thence from there   134 hint prompting   135 wrings (1) constrains (2) wrings tears from   138 impertinent irrelevant.   Wherefore Why   139 demanded asked.   wench (Here a term of endearment.)   141–2 set . . . bloody i.e., make obvious their murderous intent. (From the practice of marking with the blood of the prey those who have participated in a successful hunt.)

With colors fairer painted their foul ends.   143
In few, they hurried us aboard a bark,   144
Bore us some leagues to sea, where they prepared
A rotten carcass of a butt, not rigged,   146
Nor tackle, sail, nor mast; the very rats   147
Instinctively have quit it. There they hoist us,   148
To cry to th' sea that roared to us, to sigh
To th' winds whose pity, sighing back again,
Did us but loving wrong.

MIRANDA   Alack, what trouble   151
Was I then to you!

PROSPERO   Oh, a cherubin
Thou wast that did preserve me. Thou didst smile,
Infusèd with a fortitude from heaven,   154
When I have decked the sea with drops full salt,   155
Under my burden groaned, which raised in me   156
An undergoing stomach, to bear up   157
Against what should ensue.

MIRANDA   How came we ashore?

PROSPERO   By Providence divine.
Some food we had, and some fresh water, that
A noble Neapolitan, Gonzalo,
Out of his charity, who being then appointed
Master of this design, did give us, with
Rich garments, linens, stuffs, and necessaries,   165
Which since have steaded much. So, of his
    gentleness,   166
Knowing I loved my books, he furnished me
From mine own library with volumes that
I prize above my dukedom.

MIRANDA   Would I might   169
But ever see that man!

PROSPERO   Now I arise.   170
    [He puts on his magic cloak.]
Sit still, and hear the last of our sea sorrow.   171
Here in this island we arrived; and here
Have I, thy schoolmaster, made thee more profit   173
Than other princes can, that have more time   174
For vainer hours and tutors not so careful.   175

MIRANDA
Heavens thank you for't! And now, I pray you, sir—
For still 'tis beating in my mind—your reason
For raising this sea storm?

PROSPERO   Know thus far forth:
By accident most strange, bountiful Fortune,
Now my dear lady, hath mine enemies   180
Brought to this shore; and by my prescience
I find my zenith doth depend upon   182

A most auspicious star, whose influence   183
If now I court not, but omit, my fortunes   184
Will ever after droop. Here cease more questions.
Thou art inclined to sleep. 'Tis a good dullness,   186
And give it way. I know thou canst not choose.   187
    [Miranda sleeps.]
Come away, servant, come! I am ready now.   188
Approach, my Ariel, come.

    Enter Ariel.

ARIEL
All hail, great master, grave sir, hail! I come
To answer thy best pleasure; be't to fly,
To swim, to dive into the fire, to ride
On the curled clouds, to thy strong bidding task   193
Ariel and all his quality.

PROSPERO   Hast thou, spirit,   194
Performed to point the tempest that I bade thee?   195

ARIEL   To every article.
I boarded the King's ship. Now on the beak,   197
Now in the waist, the deck, in every cabin,   198
I flamed amazement. Sometime I'd divide   199
And burn in many places; on the topmast,
The yards, and bowsprit would I flame distinctly,   201
Then meet and join. Jove's lightning, the precursors
O'th' dreadful thunderclaps, more momentary
And sight-outrunning were not. The fire and cracks   204
Of sulfurous roaring the most mighty Neptune   205
Seem to besiege and make his bold waves tremble,
Yea, his dread trident shake.

PROSPERO   My brave spirit!   207
Who was so firm, so constant, that this coil   208
Would not infect his reason?

ARIEL   Not a soul
But felt a fever of the mad and played   210
Some tricks of desperation. All but mariners
Plunged in the foaming brine and quit the vessel,
Then all afire with me. The King's son, Ferdinand,
With hair up-staring—then like reeds, not hair—   214
Was the first man that leapt; cried, "Hell is empty,
And all the devils are here!"

PROSPERO   Why, that's my spirit!
But was not this nigh shore?

ARIEL   Close by, my master.

PROSPERO
But are they, Ariel, safe?

ARIEL   Not a hair perished.
On their sustaining garments not a blemish,   219
But fresher than before; and, as thou bad'st me,   220

---

143 **fairer** apparently more attractive   144 **few** few words.   **bark**
ship   146 **butt** cask, tub   147 **Nor tackle** neither rigging   148 **quit**
abandoned   151 **Did . . . wrong** i.e., pitied us even as they drove us
on.   154 **Infusèd** filled, suffused   155 **decked** covered (with salt
tears); adorned   156 **which** i.e., the smile   157 **undergoing stomach**
courage to go on   165 **stuffs** supplies   166 **steaded much** been of
much use.   **So, of** Similarly, out of   169 **Would** I wish   170 **But ever**
i.e., someday   171 **sea sorrow** sorrowful adventure at sea.
173–4 **made . . . can** provided a more valuable education than other
royal children (of either sex) can enjoy   175 **vainer** more foolishly
spent   180 **my dear lady** (Refers to Fortune, not Miranda.)
182 **zenith** height of fortune. (Astrological term.)

183 **influence** astrological power   184 **but omit** but ignore instead
186 **dullness** drowsiness   187 **give it way** let it happen (i.e., don't
fight it).   188 **Come away** Come   193 **task** make demands upon
194 **quality** (1) fellow spirits (2) abilities.   195 **to point** to the smallest
detail   197 **beak** prow   198 **waist** midships.   **deck** poop deck at the
stern   199 **flamed amazement** struck terror in the guise of fire, i.e.,
Saint Elmo's fire.   201 **distinctly** in different places   204 **sight-outrunning** swifter than sight.   **were not** could not have been.
205 **Neptune** Roman god of the sea   207 **trident** three-pronged
weapon   208 **coil** tumult   210 **of the mad** such as madmen feel
214 **up-staring** standing on end   219 **sustaining** protecting
220 **bad'st** ordered

In troops I have dispersed them 'bout the isle.   221
The King's son have I landed by himself,
Whom I left cooling of the air with sighs   223
In an odd angle of the isle, and sitting,   224
His arms in this sad knot.   [*He folds his arms.*]
PROSPERO   Of the King's ship,   225
The mariners, say how thou hast disposed,
And all the rest o'th' fleet.
ARIEL   Safely in harbor
Is the King's ship; in the deep nook, where once   228
Thou called'st me up at midnight to fetch dew   229
From the still-vexed Bermudas, there she's hid;   230
The mariners all under hatches stowed,
Who, with a charm joined to their suffered labor,   232
I have left asleep. And for the rest o'th' fleet,
Which I dispersed, they all have met again
And are upon the Mediterranean float   235
Bound sadly home for Naples,
Supposing that they saw the King's ship wrecked
And his great person perish.
PROSPERO   Ariel, thy charge
Exactly is performed. But there's more work.
What is the time o'th' day?
ARIEL   Past the mid season.   240
PROSPERO
At least two glasses. The time twixt six and now   241
Must by us both be spent most preciously.
ARIEL
Is there more toil? Since thou dost give me pains,   243
Let me remember thee what thou hast promised,   244
Which is not yet performed me.
PROSPERO   How now? Moody?
What is't thou canst demand?
ARIEL   My liberty.
PROSPERO
Before the time be out? No more!
ARIEL   I prithee,
Remember I have done thee worthy service,
Told thee no lies, made thee no mistakings, served
Without or grudge or grumblings. Thou did promise
To bate me a full year.
PROSPERO   Dost thou forget   251
From what a torment I did free thee?
ARIEL   No.
PROSPERO
Thou dost, and think'st it much to tread the ooze
Of the salt deep,
To run upon the sharp wind of the north,
To do me business in the veins o'th' earth   256

When it is baked with frost.
ARIEL   I do not, sir.   257
PROSPERO
Thou liest, malignant thing! Hast thou forgot
The foul witch Sycorax, who with age and envy   259
Was grown into a hoop? Hast thou forgot her?   260
ARIEL   No, sir.
PROSPERO
Thou hast. Where was she born? Speak. Tell me.
ARIEL
Sir, in Argier.
PROSPERO   Oh, was she so? I must   263
Once in a month recount what thou hast been,
Which thou forget'st. This damned witch Sycorax,
For mischiefs manifold and sorceries terrible
To enter human hearing, from Argier,
Thou know'st, was banished. For one thing she did   268
They would not take her life. Is not this true?
ARIEL   Ay, sir.
PROSPERO
This blue-eyed hag was hither brought with child   271
And here was left by th' sailors. Thou, my slave,
As thou report'st thyself, was then her servant;
And, for thou wast a spirit too delicate   274
To act her earthy and abhorred commands,
Refusing her grand hests, she did confine thee,   276
By help of her more potent ministers
And in her most unmitigable rage,
Into a cloven pine, within which rift
Imprisoned thou didst painfully remain
A dozen years; within which space she died
And left thee there, where thou didst vent thy
    groans
As fast as mill wheels strike. Then was this island—   283
Save for the son that she did litter here,   284
A freckled whelp, hag-born—not honored with   285
A human shape.
ARIEL   Yes, Caliban her son.   286
PROSPERO
Dull thing, I say so: he, that Caliban   287
Whom now I keep in service. Thou best know'st
What torment I did find thee in. Thy groans
Did make wolves howl, and penetrate the breasts
Of ever-angry bears. It was a torment
To lay upon the damned, which Sycorax
Could not again undo. It was mine art,
When I arrived and heard thee, that made gape   294
The pine and let thee out.
ARIEL   I thank thee, master.

---

221 troops groups   **223 cooling of** cooling   **224 angle** corner
225 sad knot (Folded arms are indicative of melancholy.)   **228 nook**
bay   **229 dew** (Collected at midnight for magical purposes; compare
with line 324.)   **230 still-vexed Bermudas** ever stormy Bermudas.
(Perhaps refers to the then recent Bermuda shipwreck; see play Introduction. The Folio text reads "*Bermoothes.*")   **232 with . . . labor** by
means of a spell added to all the labor they have undergone
235 float sea   **240 mid season** noon.   **241 glasses** hourglasses.
243 pains labors   **244 remember** remind   **251 bate** remit, deduct
256 do me do for me.   **veins** veins of minerals, or, underground
streams, thought to be analogous to the veins of the human body

257 baked hardened   **259 envy** malice   **260 grown into a hoop** i.e.,
so bent over with age as to resemble a hoop.   **263 Argier** Algiers
268 one . . . did (Perhaps a reference to her pregnancy, for which her
life would be spared.)   **271 blue-eyed** with dark circles under the
eyes or with blue eyelids, implying pregnancy.   **with child** pregnant
274 for because   **276 hests** commands   **283 as mill wheels strike** as
the blades of a mill wheel strike the water.   **284 Save** except.   **litter**
give birth to   **285 whelp** offspring. (Used of animals.)   **hag-born**
born of a female demon   **286 Yes . . . son** (Ariel is probably concur-
ring with Prospero's comment about a "freckled whelp," not contradicting the point about "A human shape.")   **287 Dull . . . so** i.e.,
Exactly, that's what I said, you dullard.   **294 gape** open wide

PROSPERO
If thou more murmur'st, I will rend an oak
And peg thee in his knotty entrails till   297
Thou hast howled away twelve winters.

ARIEL   Pardon, master.
I will be correspondent to command   299
And do my spriting gently.   300

PROSPERO   Do so, and after two days
I will discharge thee.

ARIEL   That's my noble master!
What shall I do? Say what? What shall I do?

PROSPERO
Go make thyself like a nymph o'th' sea. Be subject
To no sight but thine and mine, invisible
To every eyeball else. Go take this shape
And hither come in't. Go, hence with diligence!
                                      Exit [Ariel].

[*To Miranda*] Awake, dear heart, awake! Thou hast
   slept well.
Awake!

MIRANDA   The strangeness of your story put
Heaviness in me.

PROSPERO   Shake it off. Come on,   310
We'll visit Caliban, my slave, who never
Yields us kind answer.

MIRANDA   'Tis a villain, sir,
I do not love to look on.

PROSPERO   But, as 'tis,
We cannot miss him. He does make our fire,   314
Fetch in our wood, and serves in offices   315
That profit us.—What ho! Slave! Caliban!
Thou earth, thou! Speak.

CALIBAN (*within*)   There's wood enough within.

PROSPERO
Come forth, I say! There's other business for thee.
Come, thou tortoise! When?   319

        Enter Ariel like a water nymph.

Fine apparition! My quaint Ariel,   320
Hark in thine ear.   [*He whispers.*]

ARIEL   My lord, it shall be done.   *Exit.*

PROSPERO
Thou poisonous slave, got by the devil himself   322
Upon thy wicked dam, come forth!   323

        Enter Caliban.

CALIBAN
As wicked dew as e'er my mother brushed   324
With raven's feather from unwholesome fen   325
Drop on you both! A southwest blow on ye   326
And blister you all o'er!

PROSPERO
For this, be sure, tonight thou shalt have cramps,

Side-stitches that shall pen thy breath up. Urchins   329
Shall forth at vast of night that they may work   330
All exercise on thee. Thou shalt be pinched
As thick as honeycomb, each pinch more stinging   332
Than bees that made 'em.

CALIBAN   I must eat my dinner.   333
This island's mine, by Sycorax my mother,
Which thou tak'st from me. When thou cam'st first,
Thou strok'st me and made much of me, wouldst give
   me
Water with berries in't, and teach me how
To name the bigger light, and how the less,   338
That burn by day and night. And then I loved thee
And showed thee all the qualities o'th'isle,
The fresh springs, brine pits, barren place and fertile.
Cursed be I that did so! All the charms   342
Of Sycorax, toads, beetles, bats, light on you!
For I am all the subjects that you have,
Which first was mine own king; and here you sty me   345
In this hard rock, whiles you do keep from me
The rest o'th'island.

PROSPERO   Thou most lying slave,
Whom stripes may move, not kindness! I have used
   thee,   348
Filth as thou art, with humane care, and lodged thee 349
In mine own cell, till thou didst seek to violate
The honor of my child.

CALIBAN
Oho, Oho! Would't had been done!
Thou didst prevent me; I had peopled else   353
This isle with Calibans.

MIRANDA   Abhorrèd slave,   354
Which any print of goodness wilt not take,   355
Being capable of all ill! I pitied thee,
Took pains to make thee speak, taught thee each hour
One thing or other. When thou didst not, savage,
Know thine own meaning, but wouldst gabble like
A thing most brutish, I endowed thy purposes   360
With words that made them known. But thy vile race, 361
Though thou didst learn, had that in't which good
   natures
Could not abide to be with; therefore wast thou
Deservedly confined into this rock,
Who hadst deserved more than a prison.   365

CALIBAN
You taught me language, and my profit on't
Is I know how to curse. The red plague rid you   367

297 **his** its   299 **correspondent** responsive, submissive   300 **spriting
gently** duties as a spirit willingly.   310 **Heaviness** drowsiness
314 **miss** do without   315 **offices** functions, duties   319 **When** (An
exclamation of impatience.)   320 **quaint** ingenious   322 **got** begotten, sired   323 **dam** mother. (Used of animals.)   324 **wicked** mischievous, harmful   325 **fen** marsh, bog   326 **southwest** i.e., wind
thought to bring disease

329 **Urchins** Hedgehogs; here, suggesting goblins in the guise of
hedgehogs   330 **vast** lengthy, desolate time. (Malignant spirits were
thought to be restricted to the hours of darkness.)   332 **as honeycomb** i.e., as a honeycomb full of bees   333 **'em** i.e., the honeycomb
338 **the bigger . . . less** i.e., the sun and the moon. (See Genesis 1:16:
"God then made two great lights: the greater light to rule the day, and
the less light to rule the night.")   342 **charms** spells   345 **sty** confine
as in a sty   348 **stripes** lashes   349 **humane** (Not distinguished as a
word from *human*.)   353 **peopled else** otherwise populated   354–65
Abhorrèd . . . prison (Sometimes assigned by editors to Prospero.)
355 **print** imprint, impression   360 **purposes** meanings, desires
361 **race** natural disposition; species, nature   367 **red plague** plague
characterized by red sores and evacuation of blood.   **rid** destroy

For learning me your language!

PROSPERO   Hagseed, hence!   368
Fetch us in fuel, and be quick, thou'rt best,   369
To answer other business. Shrugg'st thou, malice?   370
If thou neglect'st or dost unwillingly
What I command, I'll rack thee with old cramps,   372
Fill all thy bones with aches, make thee roar   373
That beasts shall tremble at thy din.

CALIBAN   No, pray thee.
[Aside]   I must obey. His art is of such power
It would control my dam's god, Setebos,   376
And make a vassal of him.

PROSPERO   So, slave, hence!   377
                              Exit Caliban.

Enter Ferdinand; and Ariel, invisible, playing and
singing. [Ferdinand does not see Prospero and
Miranda.]

Ariel's Song.

ARIEL
Come unto these yellow sands,
    And then take hands;
Curtsied when you have, and kissed   380
    The wild waves whist;   381
Foot it featly here and there,   382
    And, sweet sprites, bear   383
The burden. Hark, hark!   384
        Burden, dispersedly [within].Bow-wow. 385
    The watchdogs bark.
        [Burden, dispersedly within.] Bow-wow.
Hark, hark! I hear
The strain of strutting chanticleer
    Cry Cock-a-diddle-dow.

FERDINAND
Where should this music be? I'th'air or th'earth?
It sounds no more; and sure it waits upon   392
Some god o'th'island. Sitting on a bank,   393
Weeping again the King my father's wreck,
This music crept by me upon the waters,
Allaying both their fury and my passion   396
With its sweet air. Thence I have followed it,   397
Or it hath drawn me rather. But 'tis gone.
No, it begins again.

Ariel's Song.

ARIEL
Full fathom five thy father lies.
    Of his bones are coral made.

Those are pearls that were his eyes.
    Nothing of him that doth fade
But doth suffer a sea change
Into something rich and strange.
Sea nymphs hourly ring his knell.   406
        Burden [within]. Ding dong.
Hark, now I hear them, ding dong bell.

FERDINAND
The ditty does remember my drowned father.   409
This is no mortal business, nor no sound
That the earth owes. I hear it now above me.   411

PROSPERO [to Miranda]
The fringèd curtains of thine eye advance   412
And say what thou see'st yond.

MIRANDA   What is't? A spirit?
Lord, how it looks about! Believe me, sir,
It carries a brave form. But 'tis a spirit.   415

PROSPERO
No, wench, it eats and sleeps and hath such senses
As we have, such. This gallant which thou see'st
Was in the wreck; and, but he's something stained   418
With grief, that's beauty's canker, thou mightst
    call him   419
A goodly person. He hath lost his fellows
And strays about to find 'em.

MIRANDA   I might call him
A thing divine, for nothing natural
I ever saw so noble.

PROSPERO [aside]   It goes on, I see,
As my soul prompts it.—Spirit, fine spirit, I'll free thee
Within two days for this.

FERDINAND [seeing Miranda]   Most sure, the goddess
On whom these airs attend!—Vouchsafe my prayer   426
May know if you remain upon this island,   427
And that you will some good instruction give
How I may bear me here. My prime request,   429
Which I do last pronounce, is—O you wonder!—   430
If you be maid or no?

MIRANDA   No wonder, sir,   431
But certainly a maid.

FERDINAND   My language? Heavens!
I am the best of them that speak this speech,   433
Were I but where 'tis spoken.

PROSPERO [coming forward]   How? The best?
What wert thou if the King of Naples heard thee?

FERDINAND
A single thing, as I am now, that wonders   436
To hear thee speak of Naples. He does hear me,   437

368 learning teaching.   Hagseed Offspring of a female demon
369 thou'rt best you'd be well advised   370 answer other business
perform other tasks.   372 old such as old people suffer, or, plenty of
373 aches (Pronounced "aitches.")   376 Setebos (A god of the Patago-
nians, named in Richard Eden's History of Travel, 1577.)   377.2 Ariel,
invisible (Ariel wears a garment that by convention indicates he is invisible to the other characters.)   380 Curtsied . . . have when you have curtsied   380–1 kissed . . . whist kissed the waves into silence, or, kissed
while the waves are being hushed   382 Foot it featly dance nimbly
383 sprites spirits   384 burden refrain, undersong.   385 s.d. dispersedly i.e., from all directions, not in unison   392 waits upon serves,
attends   393 bank sandbank   396 passion grief   397 Thence i.e.,
From the bank on which I sat

406 knell announcement of a death by the tolling of a bell.
409 remember commemorate   411 owes owns.   412 advance raise
415 brave excellent   418 but . . . stained were it not that his luster is
somewhat darkened   419 canker cankerworm (feeding on buds and
leaves)   426 airs songs.   Vouchsafe Grant   427 remain dwell
429 bear me conduct myself.   prime chief   430 wonder (Miranda's
name means "to be wondered at.")   431 maid (1) a human maiden as
opposed to a goddess (2) unmarried (3) a virgin   433 best i.e., in
birth   436 A single . . . now (1) A single figure who combines into
one person both self and King of Naples (since Ferdinand believes he
has inherited the kingship) (2) A lonely shipwrecked figure
437 Naples the King of Naples.   He . . . me I who hear my own
words am the King of Naples

And that he does I weep. Myself am Naples, 438
Who with mine eyes, never since at ebb, beheld 439
The King my father wrecked.
MIRANDA   Alack, for mercy!
FERDINAND
Yes, faith, and all his lords, the Duke of Milan
And his brave son being twain.
PROSPERO [*aside*]   The Duke of Milan 442
And his more braver daughter could control thee, 443
If now 'twere fit to do't. At the first sight
They have changed eyes.—Delicate Ariel, 445
I'll set thee free for this. [*To Ferdinand*] A word, good
sir.
I fear you have done yourself some wrong. A word! 447
MIRANDA [*aside*]
Why speaks my father so ungently? This
Is the third man that e'er I saw, the first
That e'er I sighed for. Pity move my father
To be inclined my way!
FERDINAND [*to Miranda*]   Oh, if a virgin,
And your affection not gone forth, I'll make you
The Queen of Naples.
PROSPERO   Soft, sir! One word more.
[*Aside*] They are both in either's powers; but this swift
business 454
I must uneasy make, lest too light winning 455
Make the prize light. [*To Ferdinand*] One word more: I
charge thee 456
That thou attend me. Thou dost here usurp 457
The name thou ow'st not, and hast put thyself 458
Upon this island as a spy, to win it
From me, the lord on't.
FERDINAND   No, as I am a man. 460
MIRANDA
There's nothing ill can dwell in such a temple.
If the ill spirit have so fair a house,
Good things will strive to dwell with't.
PROSPERO   Follow me.— 463
Speak not you for him; he's a traitor.—Come,
I'll manacle thy neck and feet together.
Seawater shalt thou drink; thy food shall be
The fresh-brook mussels, withered roots, and husks
Wherein the acorn cradled. Follow.
FERDINAND   No!
I will resist such entertainment till 469
Mine enemy has more pow'r. 470
          He draws, and is charmed from moving.
MIRANDA   O dear father,
Make not too rash a trial of him, for 471

He's gentle, and not fearful.
PROSPERO   What, I say, 472
My foot my tutor?—Put thy sword up, traitor, 473
Who mak'st a show but dar'st not strike, thy
conscience
Is so possessed with guilt. Come, from thy ward, 475
For I can here disarm thee with this stick
And make thy weapon drop. [*He brandishes his staff.*]
MIRANDA [*trying to hinder him*]   Beseech you, father!
PROSPERO
Hence! Hang not on my garments.
MIRANDA   Sir, have pity!
I'll be his surety.
PROSPERO   Silence! One word more 479
Shall make me chide thee, if not hate thee. What,
An advocate for an impostor? Hush!
Thou think'st there is no more such shapes as he,
Having seen but him and Caliban. Foolish wench,
To th' most of men this is a Caliban, 484
And they to him are angels.
MIRANDA   My affections
Are then most humble; I have no ambition
To see a goodlier man.
PROSPERO [*to Ferdinand*]   Come on, obey.
Thy nerves are in their infancy again 488
And have no vigor in them.
FERDINAND   So they are.
My spirits, as in a dream, are all bound up. 490
My father's loss, the weakness which I feel,
The wreck of all my friends, nor this man's threats
To whom I am subdued, are but light to me, 493
Might I but through my prison once a day
Behold this maid. All corners else o'th'earth 495
Let liberty make use of; space enough
Have I in such a prison.
PROSPERO [*aside*]   It works. [*To Ferdinand*] Come on.—
Thou hast done well, fine Ariel! [*To Ferdinand*] Follow
me.
[*To Ariel*] Hark what thou else shalt do me.
MIRANDA [*to Ferdinand*]   Be of comfort. 499
My father's of a better nature, sir,
Than he appears by speech. This is unwonted 501
Which now came from him.
PROSPERO [*to Ariel*]   Thou shalt be as free
As mountain winds; but then exactly do 503
All points of my command.
ARIEL   To th' syllable.
PROSPERO [*to Ferdinand*]
Come, follow. [*To Miranda*] Speak not for him.
                                        Exeunt.

❦

438 **And . . . weep** i.e., and I weep at this reminder that my father is
seemingly dead, leaving me heir.   439 **never . . . ebb** never dry, continually weeping   442 **son** (The only reference in the play to a son of
Antonio.)   443 **more braver** more splendid.   **control** refute
445 **changed eyes** exchanged amorous glances.   447 **done . . . wrong**
i.e., spoken falsely.   454 **both in either's** each in the other's
455 **uneasy** difficult   456 **light** cheap. (Playing on *light*, "easy," in
455.)   457 **attend** follow, obey   458 **ow'st** ownest   460 **on't** of it.
463 **strive . . . with't** i.e., expel the evil and occupy the *temple*, the
body.   469 **entertainment** treatment   470 **s.d.** *charmed* magically
prevented   471 **rash** harsh

472 **gentle** (1) wellborn (2) easily managed.   **fearful** frightening,
dangerous.   473 **My . . . tutor?** i.e., Do you, as my daughter and thus
bound to me by obedience, dare presume to teach me what to do?
475 **ward** defensive posture (in fencing)   479 **surety** guarantee.
484 **To** compared with   488 **nerves** sinews   490 **spirits** vital powers
493 **light** unimportant   495 **corners else** other corners, regions
499 **me** for me.   501 **unwonted** unusual   503 **then** if so, then

2.1

*Enter Alonso, Sebastian, Antonio, Gonzalo,
Adrian, Francisco, and others.*

GONZALO [*to Alonso*]
  Beseech you, sir, be merry. You have cause,
  So have we all, of joy, for our escape
  Is much beyond our loss. Our hint of woe   3
  Is common; every day some sailor's wife,
  The masters of some merchant, and the merchant,   5
  Have just our theme of woe. But for the miracle,   6
  I mean our preservation, few in millions
  Can speak like us. Then wisely, good sir, weigh   8
  Our sorrow with our comfort.
ALONSO   Prithee, peace.   9
SEBASTIAN [*aside to Antonio*]   He receives comfort like
  cold porridge.   11
ANTONIO [*aside to Sebastian*]   The visitor will not give   12
  him o'er so.   13
SEBASTIAN   Look, he's winding up the watch of his wit;
  by and by it will strike.
GONZALO [*to Alonso*]   Sir—
SEBASTIAN [*aside to Antonio*]   One. Tell.   17
GONZALO   When every grief is entertained   18
  That's offered, comes to th'entertainer—   19
SEBASTIAN   A dollar.   20
GONZALO   Dolor comes to him, indeed. You have spo-
  ken truer than you purposed.
SEBASTIAN   You have taken it wiselier than I meant you
  should.
GONZALO [*to Alonso*]   Therefore, my lord—
ANTONIO   Fie, what a spendthrift is he of his tongue!
ALONSO [*to Gonzalo*]   I prithee, spare.   27
GONZALO   Well, I have done. But yet—
SEBASTIAN [*aside to Antonio*]   He will be talking.
ANTONIO [*aside to Sebastian*]   Which, of he or Adrian,   30
  for a good wager, first begins to crow?   31
SEBASTIAN   The old cock.   32
ANTONIO   The cockerel.   33
SEBASTIAN   Done. The wager?
ANTONIO   A laughter.   35

SEBASTIAN   A match!   36
ADRIAN   Though this island seem to be desert—   37
ANTONIO   Ha, ha, ha!
SEBASTIAN   So, you're paid.   39
ADRIAN   Uninhabitable and almost inaccessible—
SEBASTIAN   Yet—
ADRIAN   Yet—
ANTONIO   He could not miss't.   43
ADRIAN   It must needs be of subtle, tender, and delicate   44
  temperance.   45
ANTONIO   Temperance was a delicate wench.   46
SEBASTIAN   Ay, and a subtle, as he most learnedly   47
  delivered.   48
ADRIAN   The air breathes upon us here most sweetly.
SEBASTIAN   As if it had lungs, and rotten ones.
ANTONIO   Or as 'twere perfumed by a fen.   51
GONZALO   Here is everything advantageous to life.
ANTONIO   True, save means to live.   53
SEBASTIAN   Of that there's none, or little.
GONZALO   How lush and lusty the grass looks! How   55
  green!
ANTONIO   The ground indeed is tawny.   57
SEBASTIAN   With an eye of green in't.   58
ANTONIO   He misses not much.
SEBASTIAN   No. He doth but mistake the truth totally.   60
GONZALO   But the rarity of it is—which is indeed
  almost beyond credit—
SEBASTIAN   As many vouched rarities are.   63
GONZALO   That our garments, being, as they were,
  drenched in the sea, hold notwithstanding their fresh-
  ness and glosses, being rather new-dyed than stained
  with salt water.
ANTONIO   If but one of his pockets could speak, would   68
  it not say he lies?   69
SEBASTIAN   Ay, or very falsely pocket up his report.   70
GONZALO   Methinks our garments are now as fresh as
  when we put them on first in Afric, at the marriage of
  the King's fair daughter Claribel to the King of Tunis.
SEBASTIAN   'Twas a sweet marriage, and we prosper
  well in our return.
ADRIAN   Tunis was never graced before with such a
  paragon to their queen.   77

2.1. Location: Another part of the island.
3 hint occasion   **5 The masters . . . the merchant** the officers or owners of some merchant vessel and the merchant who owns the cargo
6 for as for   **8–9 weigh . . . comfort** balance our sorrow against our
comfort.   **11 porridge** (Punningly suggested by *peace*, i.e., "peas" or
"pease," a common ingredient of porridge.)   **12 visitor** one bringing
nourishment and comfort to the sick, as Gonzalo is doing   **12–13 give
him o'er** abandon him   **17 Tell** Keep count.   **18–19 When . . . entertainer** When every sorrow that presents itself is accepted without
resistance, there comes to the recipient   **20 dollar** widely circulated
coin, the German thaler and the Spanish piece of eight. (Sebastian
puns on *entertainer* in the sense of paid performer or innkeeper; to
Gonzalo, *dollar* suggests "dolor," grief.)   **27 spare** forbear, cease.
30–1 Which . . . crow? Which of the two, Gonzalo or Adrian, do you
bet will speak (crow) first?   **32 The old cock** Gonzalo.   **33 The cockerel** Adrian.   **35 laughter** (1) burst of laughter (2) sitting of eggs.
(When Adrian, the *cockerel*, begins to speak two lines later, Sebastian
loses the bet. The Folio speech prefixes in lines 38–9 are here reversed
so that Antonio enjoys his laugh as the prize for winning, as in the
proverb "He who laughs last laughs best" or "He laughs that wins."
The Folio assignment can work in the theater, however, if Sebastian
pays for losing with a sardonic laugh of concession.)

36 A match! A bargain; agreed!.   **37 desert** uninhabited   **39 you're
paid** i.e., you've had your laugh.   **43 miss't** (1) avoid saying "Yet"
(2) miss the island.   **44 must needs be** has to be   **45 temperance**
mildness of climate.   **46 Temperance** a girl's name.   **delicate** (Here
it means "given to pleasure, voluptuous"; in line 44, "pleasant."
Antonio is evidently suggesting that *tender, and delicate temperance*
sounds like a Puritan phrase, which Antonio then mocks by applying
the words to a woman rather than an island. He began this bawdy
comparison with a double entendre on *inaccessible*, line 40.)   **47 subtle** (Here it means "tricky, sexually crafty"; in line 44, "delicate.")
48 delivered uttered. (Sebastian joins Antonio in baiting the Puritans
with his use of the pious cant phrase *learnedly delivered*.)   **51 fen** evil-
smelling marshland.   **53 save** except   **55 lusty** healthy   **57 tawny**
dull brown, yellowish.   **58 eye** tinge, or spot. (Sebastian is mocking
Gonzalo's optimism by saying there's precious little green to see anywhere. Antonio echoes him in line 59 with similar sarcasm.)   **60 He
. . . totally** i.e., He's only a tiny 100% wrong. (Sarcastic.)   **63 As . . . are**
(More sarcasm: Just as many alleged strange sights are doubtful,
including this one.)   **68–70 If . . . report** (More wisecracking: Gonzalo's mud-filled pockets would surely give the lie to his talk of clean
fresh garments, thereby *pocketing up* or tabling the *report*.)   **77 to** for

GONZALO   Not since widow Dido's time.   78

ANTONIO   [*aside to Sebastian*]   Widow? A pox o' that!
How came that "widow" in? Widow Dido!

SEBASTIAN   What if he had said "widower Aeneas"
too? Good Lord, how you take it!   82

ADRIAN   [*to Gonzalo*]   "Widow Dido" said you? You make
me study of that. She was of Carthage, not of Tunis.   84

GONZALO   This Tunis, sir, was Carthage.

ADRIAN   Carthage?

GONZALO   I assure you, Carthage.

ANTONIO   His word is more than the miraculous harp.   88

SEBASTIAN   He hath raised the wall, and houses too.

ANTONIO   What impossible matter will he make easy
next?

SEBASTIAN   I think he will carry this island home in his
pocket and give it his son for an apple.

ANTONIO   And, sowing the kernels of it in the sea,   94
bring forth more islands.

GONZALO   Ay.   96

ANTONIO   Why, in good time.   97

GONZALO   [*to Alonso*]   Sir, we were talking that our
garments seem now as fresh as when we were at
Tunis at the marriage of your daughter, who is now
queen.

ANTONIO   And the rarest that e'er came there.   101

SEBASTIAN   Bate, I beseech you, widow Dido.   102

ANTONIO   Oh, widow Dido? Ay, widow Dido.

GONZALO   Is not, sir, my doublet as fresh as the first   104
day I wore it? I mean, in a sort.   105

ANTONIO   That "sort" was well fished for.   106

GONZALO   When I wore it at your daughter's marriage.

ALONSO
You cram these words into mine ears against
The stomach of my sense. Would I had never   109
Married my daughter there! For, coming thence,   110
My son is lost and, in my rate, she too,   111
Who is so far from Italy removed
I ne'er again shall see her. O thou mine heir
Of Naples and of Milan, what strange fish
Hath made his meal on thee?

FRANCISCO   Sir, he may live.
I saw him beat the surges under him   116
And ride upon their backs. He trod the water,

Whose enmity he flung aside, and breasted
The surge most swoll'n that met him. His bold head
'Bove the contentious waves he kept, and oared   120
Himself with his good arms in lusty stroke   121
To th' shore, that o'er his wave-worn basis bowed,   122
As stooping to relieve him. I not doubt   123
He came alive to land.

ALONSO   No, no, he's gone.

SEBASTIAN   [*to Alonso*]
Sir, you may thank yourself for this great loss,
That would not bless our Europe with your daughter,   126
But rather loose her to an African,   127
Where she at least is banished from your eye,   128
Who hath cause to wet the grief on't.

ALONSO   Prithee, peace.   129

SEBASTIAN
You were kneeled to and importuned otherwise   130
By all of us, and the fair soul herself   131
Weighed between loathness and obedience at   132
Which end o'th' beam should bow. We have lost your
son,   133
I fear, forever. Milan and Naples have
More widows in them of this business' making   135
Than we bring men to comfort them.
The fault's your own.

ALONSO   So is the dear'st o'th' loss.   138

GONZALO   My lord Sebastian,
The truth you speak doth lack some gentleness
And time to speak it in. You rub the sore   141
When you should bring the plaster.

SEBASTIAN   Very well.   142

ANTONIO   And most chirurgeonly.   143

GONZALO   [*to Alonso*]
It is foul weather in us all, good sir,
When you are cloudy.

SEBASTIAN   [*to Antonio*]   Fowl weather?

ANTONIO   [*to Sebastian*]   Very foul.   145

GONZALO
Had I plantation of this isle, my lord—   146

ANTONIO   [*to Sebastian*]
He'd sow't with nettle seed.

SEBASTIAN   Or docks, or mallows.   147

GONZALO
And were the king on't, what would I do?

---

78 widow Dido Queen of Carthage, deserted by Aeneas. (She was, in fact, a widow when Aeneas, a widower, met her, but Antonio may be amused at Gonzalo's prudish use of the term "widow" to describe a woman deserted by her lover.)   **82 take** understand, respond to, interpret   **84 study of** think about   **88 miraculous harp** (Alludes to Amphion's harp, with which he raised the walls of Thebes; Gonzalo has exceeded that deed by recreating ancient Carthage—*wall and houses*—mistakenly on the site of modern-day Tunis. Some Renaissance commentators believed, like Gonzalo, that the two sites were near each other.)   **94 kernels** seeds   **96 Ay** (Gonzalo may be reasserting his point about Carthage, or he may be responding ironically to Antonio, who, in turn, answers sarcastically.)   **97 in good time** (An expression of ironical acquiescence or amazement, i.e., "sure, right away.")   **101 rarest** most remarkable, beautiful   **102 Bate** Abate, except, leave out. (Sebastian says sardonically, surely you should allow widow Dido to be an exception.)   **104 doublet** close-fitting jacket   **105 in a sort** in a way.   **106 sort** (Antonio plays on the idea of drawing lots and on "fishing" for something to say.)   **109 The stomach . . . sense** my appetite for hearing them.   **110 Married** given in marriage   **111 rate** estimation, opinion   **116 surges** waves

120 oared propelled as by an oar   **121 lusty** vigorous   **122 that . . . bowed** that projected out over its (*his*) surf-eroded base, bending down toward the sea   **123 As** as if   **126 That** you who   **127 But . . . her** but would rather turn her loose (or, "lose her")   **128–9 Where . . . on't** where at least she is not a constant reproach in your eye, which has good reason to weep sorrowfully for this unhappy development.   **130 importuned** urged, implored   **131–3 the fair . . . bow** Claribel herself was poised uncertainly, as in a balancing scale, between being unwilling to marry and yet wishing to obey her father.   **135 of . . . making** on account of this marriage and subsequent shipwreck   **138 dear'st** heaviest, most costly   **141 time** appropriate time   **142 plaster** (A medical application.)   **143 chirurgeonly** like a skilled surgeon. (Antonio mocks Gonzalo's medical analogy of a *plaster* applied curatively to a wound.)   **145 Fowl** (With a pun on *foul*, returning to the imagery of lines 30–5.)   **146 plantation** colonial settlement. (With subsequent wordplay on the literal meaning, "planting.")   **147 docks . . . mallows** (Weeds; the first was used as an antidote for nettle stings.)

SEBASTIAN Scape being drunk for want of wine. 149

GONZALO
I'th' commonwealth I would by contraries 150
Execute all things; for no kind of traffic 151
Would I admit; no name of magistrate;
Letters should not be known; riches, poverty, 153
And use of service, none; contract, succession, 154
Bourn, bound of land, tilth, vineyard, none; 155
No use of metal, corn, or wine, or oil; 156
No occupation; all men idle, all,
And women too, but innocent and pure;
No sovereignty—

SEBASTIAN   Yet he would be king on't.

ANTONIO The latter end of his commonwealth forgets
the beginning.

GONZALO
All things in common nature should produce
Without sweat or endeavor. Treason, felony,
Sword, pike, knife, gun, or need of any engine 164
Would I not have; but nature should bring forth,
Of it own kind, all foison, all abundance, 166
To feed my innocent people.

SEBASTIAN No marrying 'mong his subjects?

ANTONIO None, man, all idle—whores and knaves.

GONZALO
I would with such perfection govern, sir,
T'excel the Golden Age.

SEBASTIAN   'Save His Majesty! 171

ANTONIO
Long live Gonzalo!

GONZALO   And—do you mark me, sir?

ALONSO
Prithee, no more. Thou dost talk nothing to me.

GONZALO I do well believe Your Highness, and did it
to minister occasion to these gentlemen, who are of 175
such sensible and nimble lungs that they always use 176
to laugh at nothing.

ANTONIO 'Twas you we laughed at.

GONZALO Who in this kind of merry fooling am nothing
to you; so you may continue, and laugh at nothing
still.

ANTONIO What a blow was there given!

SEBASTIAN An it had not fallen flat-long. 182

GONZALO You are gentlemen of brave mettle; you 183
would lift the moon out of her sphere if she would 184

continue in it five weeks without changing.

Enter Ariel [invisible] playing solemn music.

SEBASTIAN We would so, and then go a-batfowling. 186

ANTONIO Nay, good my lord, be not angry.

GONZALO No, I warrant you, I will not adventure my 188
discretion so weakly. Will you laugh me asleep? For I 189
am very heavy. 190

ANTONIO Go sleep, and hear us. 191
[*All sleep except Alonso, Sebastian, and Antonio.*]

ALONSO
What, all so soon asleep? I wish mine eyes
Would, with themselves, shut up my thoughts. I find 193
They are inclined to do so.

SEBASTIAN   Please you, sir,
Do not omit the heavy offer of it. 195
It seldom visits sorrow; when it doth,
It is a comforter.

ANTONIO   We two, my lord,
Will guard your person while you take your rest,
And watch your safety.

ALONSO   Thank you. Wondrous heavy.
[*Alonso sleeps. Exit Ariel.*]

SEBASTIAN
What a strange drowsiness possesses them!

ANTONIO
It is the quality o'th' climate.

SEBASTIAN   Why
Doth it not then our eyelids sink? I find not
Myself disposed to sleep.

ANTONIO   Nor I. My spirits are nimble.
They fell together all, as by consent; 204
They dropped, as by a thunderstroke. What might,
Worthy Sebastian, oh, what might—? No more.
And yet methinks I see it in thy face
What thou shouldst be. Th'occasion speaks thee, and 208
My strong imagination sees a crown
Dropping upon thy head.

SEBASTIAN   What, art thou waking?

ANTONIO
Do you not hear me speak?

SEBASTIAN   I do, and surely
It is a sleepy language, and thou speak'st 212
Out of thy sleep. What is it thou didst say?
This is a strange repose, to be asleep
With eyes wide open—standing, speaking, moving—
And yet so fast asleep.

ANTONIO   Noble Sebastian,
Thou let'st thy fortune sleep—die, rather; wink'st 217

---

149 **Scape** Escape. **want** lack. (Sebastian jokes sarcastically that this hypothetical ruler would be saved from dissipation only by the barrenness of the island.) **150 by contraries** by what is directly opposite to usual custom **151 traffic** trade **153 Letters** learning **154 use of service** custom of employing servants. **succession** holding of property by right of inheritance **155 Bourn . . . tilth** boundaries, property limits, tillage of soil **156 corn** grain **164 pike** lance. **engine** instrument of warfare **166 it** its. **foison** plenty **171 the Golden Age** an age of prelapsarian abundance and peace; the first of four "ages" of human history, followed by silver, bronze, and lead. **'Save** God save **175 minister occasion** furnish opportunity (for laughter) **176 sensible** sensitive. **use** are accustomed **182 An** If. **flat-long** with the flat of the sword, i.e., ineffectually. **183 mettle** temperament, courage. (The sense of *metal,* indistinguishable as a form from *mettle,* continues the metaphor of the sword. F reads "mettal.") **184 sphere** orbit. (Literally, one of the concentric zones occupied by planets in Ptolemaic astronomy.)

186 **a-batfowling** hunting birds at night with lantern and *bat,* or "stick"; also, gulling a simpleton. (Gonzalo is the simpleton, or fowl, and Sebastian will use the moon as his lantern.) **188–9 adventure . . . weakly** risk my reputation for discretion for so trivial a cause (by getting angry). **190 heavy** sleepy. **191 Go . . . us** i.e., Get ready for sleep, and we'll do our part by laughing. **193 Would . . . thoughts** would shut off my melancholy brooding when they (my eyes) close themselves in sleep. **195 Do . . . it** do not decline the invitation to drowsiness. **204 They . . . consent** The others all fell asleep simultaneously, as if by common agreement **208 Th' occasion . . . thee** The opportunity of the moment calls upon you **212 sleepy** dreamlike, fantastic **217 wink'st** (you) shut your eyes

Whiles thou art waking.

SEBASTIAN   Thou dost snore distinctly;   218
There's meaning in thy snores.

ANTONIO
I am more serious than my custom. You
Must be so too if heed me, which to do   221
Trebles thee o'er.

SEBASTIAN   Well, I am standing water.   222

ANTONIO
I'll teach you how to flow.

SEBASTIAN   Do so. To ebb   223
Hereditary sloth instructs me.

ANTONIO   Oh,   224
If you but knew how you the purpose cherish   225
Whiles thus you mock it! How, in stripping it,   226
You more invest it! Ebbing men, indeed,   227
Most often do so near the bottom run   228
By their own fear or sloth.

SEBASTIAN   Prithee, say on.
The setting of thine eye and cheek proclaim   230
A matter from thee, and a birth indeed   231
Which throes thee much to yield.

ANTONIO   Thus, sir: 232
Although this lord of weak remembrance, this   233
Who shall be of as little memory   234
When he is earthed, hath here almost persuaded—   236
For he's a spirit of persuasion, only   236
Professes to persuade—the King his son's alive,   237
'Tis as impossible that he's undrowned
As he that sleeps here swims.

SEBASTIAN   I have no hope
That he's undrowned.

ANTONIO   Oh, out of that "no hope"
What great hope have you! No hope that way is   241
Another way so high a hope that even   242
Ambition cannot pierce a wink beyond,   243
But doubt discovery there. Will you grant with me   244
That Ferdinand is drowned?

SEBASTIAN   He's gone.

ANTONIO   Then tell me,
Who's the next heir of Naples?

SEBASTIAN   Claribel.

ANTONIO
She that is Queen of Tunis; she that dwells
Ten leagues beyond man's life; she that from Naples   248
Can have no note, unless the sun were post—   249
The Man i'th' Moon's too slow—till newborn chins
Be rough and razorable; she that from whom   251
We all were sea-swallowed, though some cast again,   252
And by that destiny to perform an act
Whereof what's past is prologue, what to come
In yours and my discharge.   255

SEBASTIAN   What stuff is this? How say you?
'Tis true my brother's daughter's Queen of Tunis,
So is she heir of Naples, twixt which regions
There is some space.

ANTONIO   A space whose ev'ry cubit   259
Seems to cry out, "How shall that Claribel
Measure us back to Naples? Keep in Tunis,   261
And let Sebastian wake." Say this were death   262
That now hath seized them, why, they were no worse
Than now they are. There be that can rule Naples   264
As well as he that sleeps, lords that can prate   265
As amply and unnecessarily
As this Gonzalo. I myself could make   267
A chough of as deep chat. Oh, that you bore   268
The mind that I do! What a sleep were this
For your advancement! Do you understand me?

SEBASTIAN
Methinks I do.

ANTONIO   And how does your content   271
Tender your own good fortune?

SEBASTIAN   I remember   272
You did supplant your brother Prospero.

ANTONIO   True.
And look how well my garments sit upon me,
Much feater than before. My brother's servants   275
Were then my fellows. Now they are my men.

SEBASTIAN   But, for your conscience?   277

ANTONIO
Ay, sir, where lies that? If 'twere a kibe,   278
'Twould put me to my slipper; but I feel not   279
This deity in my bosom. Twenty consciences   280
That stand twixt me and Milan, candied be they   281
And melt ere they molest! Here lies your brother,   282
No better than the earth he lies upon,
If he were that which now he's like—that's dead,
Whom I, with this obedient steel, three inches of it,

218 distinctly articulately   221 if heed if you heed   222 Trebles thee o'er makes you three times as great and rich.   standing water water that neither ebbs nor flows, at a standstill.   223 ebb recede, decline   224 Hereditary sloth i.e., natural laziness and the position of younger brother, one who cannot inherit   225–6 If . . . mock it! If you only knew how much you secretly cherish ambition even while your words mock it!   226–7 How . . . invest it! How the more you speak flippantly of ambition, the more you, in effect, affirm it, clothing what you have stripped!   228 the bottom i.e., on which unadventurous men may go aground and miss the tide of fortune   230 setting set expression (of earnestness)   231 matter matter of importance   232 throes causes pain, as in giving birth.   yield give forth, speak about.   233–7 Although . . . alive Although this owner of weak memory, he who will be only weakly remembered when he is dead, has nearly persuaded—since he's a mind or soul devoted solely to persuade—King Alonso that Ferdinand lives   241 that way i.e., in regard to Ferdinand's being saved   242–4 that . . . there that even ambition for high status cannot see anything higher, and even there it doubts the reality of what it sees (because the place is so supremely high). (What then follows is Antonio's analysis of why they can proceed without fear.)

248 Ten . . . life i.e., further than the journey of a lifetime   249 note news, intimation.   post messenger   251 razorable ready for shaving.   from on our voyage from   252 cast were disgorged. (With a pun on casting of parts for a play.)   255 discharge part to play.   259 cubit ancient measure of length of about twenty inches   261 Measure us retrace our journey.   Keep You, Claribel, stay   262 wake i.e., to his good fortune.   264 There be There are those   265 prate speak foolishly   267–8 I . . . chat I could teach a jackdaw to talk as wisely, or, be such a garrulous talker myself.   271–2 And . . . fortune? And how does your contentment with what I've just said further your good fortune?   275 feater more becomingly, fittingly   277 for as for   278 kibe chilblain, here a sore on the heel   279 put me to oblige me to wear   280–2 Twenty . . . molest! Even if there were twenty consciences between me and the dukedom of Milan, may they be lumped together or crystallized like candy and then melted down before I'd let them interfere!

Can lay to bed forever; whiles you, doing thus,   286
To the perpetual wink for aye might put   287
This ancient morsel, this Sir Prudence, who
Should not upbraid our course. For all the rest,   289
They'll take suggestion as a cat laps milk;   290
They'll tell the clock to any business that   291
We say befits the hour.
SEBASTIAN   Thy case, dear friend,
Shall be my precedent. As thou got'st Milan,
I'll come by Naples. Draw thy sword. One stroke
Shall free thee from the tribute which thou payest,   295
And I the king shall love thee.
ANTONIO   Draw together;
And when I rear my hand, do you the like
To fall it on Gonzalo.   [*They draw.*]
SEBASTIAN   Oh, but one word.   298
                                      [*They talk apart.*]

          Enter Ariel [invisible], with music and song.

ARIEL [*to Gonzalo*]
My master through his art foresees the danger
That you, his friend, are in, and sends me forth—
For else his project dies—to keep them living.
                              Sings in Gonzalo's ear.
   While you here do snoring lie,
   Open-eyed conspiracy
      His time doth take.   304
   If of life you keep a care,
   Shake off slumber, and beware.
      Awake, awake!
ANTONIO   Then let us both be sudden.
GONZALO [*waking*]   Now, good angels preserve the King!
                                      [*The others wake.*]
ALONSO
Why, how now, ho, awake? Why are you drawn?
Wherefore this ghastly looking?
GONZALO   What's the matter?
SEBASTIAN
Whiles we stood here securing your repose,   312
Even now, we heard a hollow burst of bellowing
Like bulls, or rather lions. Did 't not wake you?
It struck mine ear most terribly.
ALONSO   I heard nothing.
ANTONIO
Oh, 'twas a din to fright a monster's ear,
To make an earthquake! Sure it was the roar
Of a whole herd of lions.
ALONSO   Heard you this, Gonzalo?
GONZALO
Upon mine honor, sir, I heard a humming,
And that a strange one too, which did awake me.
I shaked you, sir, and cried. As mine eyes opened,   322
I saw their weapons drawn. There was a noise,

That's verily. 'Tis best we stand upon our guard,   324
Or that we quit this place. Let's draw our weapons.
ALONSO
Lead off this ground, and let's make further search
For my poor son.
GONZALO   Heavens keep him from these beasts!
For he is, sure, i'th'island.
ALONSO   Lead away.
ARIEL [*aside*]
Prospero my lord shall know what I have done.
So, King, go safely on to seek thy son.
                              Exeunt [separately].

                              ❖

2.2

     *Enter Caliban with a burden of wood. A noise
     of thunder heard.*

CALIBAN
All the infections that the sun sucks up
From bogs, fens, flats, on Prosper fall, and make him   2
By inchmeal a disease! His spirits hear me,   3
And yet I needs must curse. But they'll nor pinch,   4
Fright me with urchin shows, pitch me i'th' mire,   5
Nor lead me, like a firebrand, in the dark   6
Out of my way, unless he bid 'em. But
For every trifle are they set upon me,
Sometimes like apes, that mow and chatter at me   9
And after bite me; then like hedgehogs, which
Lie tumbling in my barefoot way and mount
Their pricks at my footfall. Sometime am I
All wound with adders, who with cloven tongues   13
Do hiss me into madness.

          Enter Trinculo.

                         Lo, now, lo!
Here comes a spirit of his, and to torment me
For bringing wood in slowly. I'll fall flat.
Perchance he will not mind me.   [*He lies down.*]   17
TRINCULO   Here's neither bush nor shrub to bear off   18
any weather at all. And another storm brewing; I hear
it sing i'th' wind. Yond same black cloud, yond huge
one, looks like a foul bombard that would shed his   21
liquor. If it should thunder as it did before, I know not
where to hide my head. Yond same cloud cannot
choose but fall by pailfuls. [*Seeing Caliban*] What have
we here, a man or a fish? Dead or alive? A fish, he
smells like a fish; a very ancient and fishlike smell; a
kind of not-of-the-newest Poor John. A strange fish!   27
Were I in England now, as once I was, and had but
this fish painted, not a holiday fool there but would   29

---

324 verily true.
2.2. Location: Another part of the island.
2 flats swamps   **3 By inchmeal** inch by inch   **4 needs must** have to.
nor neither   **5 urchin shows** elvish apparitions shaped like hedgehogs   **6 like a firebrand** they in the guise of a will-o'-the-wisp
9 mow make faces   **13 wound with** entwined by   **17 mind** notice
18 bear off keep off   **21 foul bombard** dirty leather jug.   **his** its
27 Poor John salted fish, type of poor fare   **29 painted** i.e., painted
on a sign set up outside a booth or tent at a fair

---

286 thus similarly. (The actor makes a stabbing gesture.)   **287 wink**
sleep, closing of eyes.   **aye** ever   **289 Should not** must not be
allowed to   **290 take suggestion** respond to prompting   **291 tell the
clock** i.e., agree, answer appropriately, chime   **295 tribute** (See
1.2.113–24.)   **298 fall it** let it fall   **304 time** opportunity   **312 securing** standing guard over   **322 cried** called out.

give a piece of silver. There would this monster make 30
a man. Any strange beast there makes a man. When 31
they will not give a doit to relieve a lame beggar, they 32
will lay out ten to see a dead Indian. Legged like a
man, and his fins like arms! Warm, o' my troth! I do 34
now let loose my opinion, hold it no longer: this is no 35
fish, but an islander, that hath lately suffered by a
thunderbolt. [*Thunder.*] Alas, the storm is come again!
My best way is to creep under his gaberdine. There is 38
no other shelter hereabout. Misery acquaints a man
with strange bedfellows. I will here shroud till the 40
dregs of the storm be past. 41

         [*He creeps under Caliban's garment.*]

     Enter Stephano, singing, [a bottle in his hand].

STEPHANO
   "I shall no more to sea, to sea,
     Here shall I die ashore—"
This is a very scurvy tune to sing at a man's funeral.
Well, here's my comfort.   *Drinks.*
(*Sings.*)
   "The master, the swabber, the boatswain, and I, 46
     The gunner and his mate,
   Loved Mall, Meg, and Marian, and Margery,
     But none of us cared for Kate.
   For she had a tongue with a tang, 50
   Would cry to a sailor, 'Go hang!'
   She loved not the savor of tar nor of pitch,
   Yet a tailor might scratch her where'er she did itch. 53
     Then to sea, boys, and let her go hang!"
This is a scurvy tune too. But here's my comfort.
                     Drinks.

CALIBAN   Do not torment me! Oh! 56

STEPHANO   What's the matter? Have we devils here? Do 57
you put tricks upon 's with savages and men of Ind, 58
ha? I have not scaped drowning to be afeard now of
your four legs. For it hath been said, "As proper a man 60
as ever went on four legs cannot make him give 61
ground"; and it shall be said so again while Stephano
breathes at' nostrils. 63

CALIBAN   This spirit torments me! Oh!

STEPHANO   This is some monster of the isle with four
legs, who hath got, as I take it, an ague. Where the 66
devil should he learn our language? I will give him 67
some relief, if it be but for that. If I can recover him 68
and keep him tame and get to Naples with him, he's

a present for any emperor that ever trod on neat's 70
leather. 71

CALIBAN   Do not torment me, prithee. I'll bring my
wood home faster.

STEPHANO   He's in his fit now and does not talk after 74
the wisest. He shall taste of my bottle. If he have never 75
drunk wine afore, it will go near to remove his fit. If I 76
can recover him and keep him tame, I will not take too 77
much for him. He shall pay for him that hath him, and 78
that soundly.

CALIBAN   Thou dost me yet but little hurt; thou wilt
anon, I know it by thy trembling. Now Prosper works
upon thee.

STEPHANO   Come on your ways. Open your mouth. Here
is that which will give language to you, cat. Open your 84
mouth. This will shake your shaking, I can tell you, 85
and that soundly. [*Giving Caliban a drink.*] You cannot 86
tell who's your friend. Open your chaps again. 87

TRINCULO   I should know that voice. It should be—but
he is drowned, and these are devils. Oh, defend me!

STEPHANO   Four legs and two voices—a most delicate 90
monster! His forward voice now is to speak well of his
friend; his backward voice is to utter foul speeches and 92
to detract. If all the wine in my bottle will recover him, 93
I will help his ague. Come. [*Giving a drink.*] Amen! I
will pour some in thy other mouth.

TRINCULO   Stephano!

STEPHANO   Doth thy other mouth call me? Mercy,
mercy! This is a devil, and no monster. I will leave
him. I have no long spoon. 99

TRINCULO   Stephano! If thou be'st Stephano, touch me
and speak to me, for I am Trinculo—be not afeard—
thy good friend Trinculo.

STEPHANO   If thou be'st Trinculo, come forth. I'll pull
thee by the lesser legs. If any be Trinculo's legs, these
are they. [*Pulling him out.*] Thou art very Trinculo
indeed! How cam'st thou to be the siege of this 106
mooncalf? Can he vent Trinculos? 107

TRINCULO   I took him to be killed with a thunderstroke.
But art thou not drowned, Stephano? I hope now thou
art not drowned. Is the storm overblown? I hid me 110
under the dead mooncalf's gaberdine for fear of the
storm. And art thou living, Stephano? Oh, Stephano,
two Neapolitans scaped!   [*He capers with Stephano.*]

30–1 make a man (1) make a man's fortune (2) pass for a human
being. **32 doit** small coin **34 o' my troth** by my faith. **35 hold it**
hold it in **38 gaberdine** cloak, loose upper garment. **40 shroud**
take shelter **41 dregs** i.e., last remains (as in a *bombard* or jug, line 21)
46 swabber crew member whose job is to wash the decks **50 tang**
sting **53 tailor . . . itch** (A dig at tailors for their supposed effeminacy and a bawdy suggestion of satisfying a sexual craving.) **56 Do
. . . me!** (Caliban assumes that one of Prospero's spirits has come to
punish him.) **57 What's the matter?** What's going on here? **58 put
tricks upon 's** trick us with conjuring shows. **Ind** India **60 proper**
handsome **61 four legs** (The conventional phrase would supply *two
legs,* but the creature Stephano thinks he sees has four.) **at** at the
66 ague fever. (Probably both Caliban and Trinculo are quaking; see
lines 56 and 81.) **67 should he learn** could he have learned **68 for
that** i.e., for knowing our language. **recover** revive. (Also in line 77.)

70–1 neat's leather cowhide. **74–5 after the wisest** in the wisest
fashion. **76 afore** before. **go near to** be in a fair way to **77 recover**
restore **77–8 I will . . . much** i.e., no sum can be too much **78 He
shall . . . hath him** Anyone who wants him will have to pay dearly
for him **84–5 cat . . . mouth** (Allusion to the proverb "Good liquor
will make a cat speak.") **85 shake** shake off **86–7 You . . . friend**
i.e., You can't tell who's your friend until someone like me provides
you with a drink. **87 chaps** jaws **90 delicate** ingenious **92 backward voice** (Trinculo and Caliban are facing in opposite directions.
Stephano supposes the monster to have a rear end that can emit *foul
speeches* or foul-smelling wind at the monster's *other mouth,* line 95.)
93 If . . . him Even if it takes all the wine in my bottle to cure him
99 long spoon (Allusion to the proverb "He that sups with the devil
has need of a long spoon.") **106 siege** excrement **107 mooncalf**
monstrous or misshapen creature (whose deformity is caused by the
malignant influence of the moon). **vent** excrete, defecate
110 overblown blown over.

STEPHANO   Prithee, do not turn me about. My stomach
is not constant.   115

CALIBAN
These be fine things, an if they be not spirits.   116
That's a brave god, and bears celestial liquor.   117
I will kneel to him.

STEPHANO   How didst thou scape? How cam'st thou
hither? Swear by this bottle how thou cam'st hither. I
escaped upon a butt of sack which the sailors heaved 121
o'erboard—by this bottle, which I made of the bark of 122
a tree with mine own hands since I was cast ashore.

CALIBAN [kneeling]   I'll swear upon that bottle to be
thy true subject, for the liquor is not earthly.

STEPHANO   Here. Swear then how thou escaped'st.

TRINCULO   Swum ashore, man, like a duck. I can swim
like a duck, I'll be sworn.

STEPHANO   Here, kiss the book. Though thou canst 129
swim like a duck, thou art made like a goose.
                                         [Giving him a drink.]

TRINCULO   Oh, Stephano, hast any more of this?

STEPHANO   The whole butt, man. My cellar is in a rock
by th' seaside, where my wine is hid.—How now,
mooncalf? How does thine ague?

CALIBAN   Hast thou not dropped from heaven?

STEPHANO   Out o'th' moon, I do assure thee. I was the
man i'th' moon when time was.   137

CALIBAN
I have seen thee in her, and I do adore thee.
My mistress showed me thee, and thy dog, and thy
bush.   139

STEPHANO   Come, swear to that. Kiss the book. I will
furnish it anon with new contents. Swear.
                                         [Giving him a drink.]

TRINCULO   By this good light, this is a very shallow 142
monster! I afeard of him? A very weak monster! The
man i'th' moon? A most poor credulous monster!
Well drawn, monster, in good sooth!   145

CALIBAN [to Stephano]
I'll show thee every fertile inch o'th'island,
And I will kiss thy foot. I prithee, be my god.

TRINCULO   By this light, a most perfidious and drunken
monster! When 's god's asleep, he'll rob his bottle. 149

CALIBAN
I'll kiss thy foot. I'll swear myself thy subject.

STEPHANO   Come on then. Down, and swear.
                                         [Caliban kneels.]

TRINCULO   I shall laugh myself to death at this puppy-
headed monster. A most scurvy monster! I could find
in my heart to beat him—

STEPHANO   Come, kiss.

TRINCULO   But that the poor monster's in drink. An 156
abominable monster!

CALIBAN
I'll show thee the best springs. I'll pluck thee berries.
I'll fish for thee and get thee wood enough.
A plague upon the tyrant that I serve!
I'll bear him no more sticks, but follow thee,
Thou wondrous man.

TRINCULO   A most ridiculous monster, to make a
wonder of a poor drunkard!

CALIBAN
I prithee, let me bring thee where crabs grow,   165
And I with my long nails will dig thee pignuts,   166
Show thee a jay's nest, and instruct thee how
To snare the nimble marmoset. I'll bring thee   168
To clust'ring filberts, and sometimes I'll get thee
Young scamels from the rock. Wilt thou go with me? 170

STEPHANO   I prithee now, lead the way without any
more talking.—Trinculo, the King and all our com- 172
pany else being drowned, we will inherit here.— 173
Here, bear my bottle.—Fellow Trinculo, we'll fill him
by and by again.

CALIBAN (sings drunkenly)
Farewell, master, farewell, farewell!

TRINCULO   A howling monster; a drunken monster!

CALIBAN
No more dams I'll make for fish,
    Nor fetch in firing   179
    At requiring,
No more scrape trenchering, nor wash dish.   181
    'Ban, 'Ban, Ca–Caliban
    Has a new master. Get a new man!   183
Freedom, high-day! High-day, freedom! Freedom, 184
high-day, freedom!

STEPHANO   O brave monster! Lead the way.   Exeunt.

❖

3.1

Enter Ferdinand, bearing a log.

FERDINAND
There be some sports are painful, and their labor   1
Delight in them sets off. Some kinds of baseness   2
Are nobly undergone, and most poor matters   3
Point to rich ends. This my mean task   4
Would be as heavy to me as odious, but   5

---

115 constant steady.   **116 an if** if   **117 brave** fine, magnificent
121 butt of sack barrel of Canary wine   **122 by this bottle** i.e., I swear
by this bottle   **129 book** i.e., bottle. (But with ironic reference to the
practice of kissing the Bible in swearing an oath; see *I'll be sworn* in line
128.)   **137 when time was** once upon a time.   **139 dog . . . bush** (The
man in the moon was popularly imagined to have with him a dog and
a bush of thorn.)   **142 By . . . light** By God's light, by this good light
from heaven   **145 Well . . . sooth!** Well pulled on the bottle, truly!
149 When . . . bottle i.e., Caliban wouldn't even stop at robbing his
god (i.e., Stephano) of his bottle if he could catch him asleep.

156 But that were it not that.   **in drink** drunk.   **165 crabs** crab apples,
or crabs   **166 pignuts** earthnuts, edible tuberous roots   **168 marmoset** small monkey.   **170 scamels** (Possibly *seamews*, mentioned in
Strachey's letter, or shellfish, or perhaps from *squamelle*, "furnished
with little scales." Contemporary French and Italian travel accounts
report that the natives of Patagonia in South America ate small fish
described as *fort scameux* and *squame*.)   **172–3 all . . . else** all the rest
of our shipboard companions   **173 inherit** take possession   **179 firing** firewood   **181 trenchering** trenchers, wooden plates   **183 Get a
new man** (Addressed to Prospero.)   **184 high-day** holiday.
3.1. Location: Before Prospero's cell.
1–2 There . . . sets off Some pastimes are laborious, but the pleasure
we get from them compensates for the effort. (Pleasure is *set off* by
labor as a jewel is *set off* by its foil.)   **2 baseness** menial activity
3 undergone undertaken.   **most poor** poorest   **4 mean** lowly   **5 but**
were it not that

The mistress which I serve quickens what's dead　6
And makes my labors pleasures. Oh, she is
Ten times more gentle than her father's crabbed,
And he's composed of harshness. I must remove
Some thousands of these logs and pile them up,
Upon a sore injunction. My sweet mistress　11
Weeps when she sees me work and says such baseness
Had never like executor. I forget;　13
But these sweet thoughts do even refresh my labors,
Most busy lest when I do it.

    Enter Miranda; and Prospero [at a distance,
    unseen].

MIRANDA　　　　　　　　　　　　Alas now, pray you,　15
Work not so hard. I would the lightning had
Burnt up those logs that you are enjoined to pile!　17
Pray, set it down and rest you. When this burns,　18
'Twill weep for having wearied you. My father　19
Is hard at study. Pray now, rest yourself.
He's safe for these three hours.
FERDINAND　　　　　　　　　　　O most dear mistress,　21
The sun will set before I shall discharge　22
What I must strive to do.
MIRANDA　　　　　　　　　　If you'll sit down,
I'll bear your logs the while. Pray, give me that.
I'll carry it to the pile.
FERDINAND　　　　　　　　No, precious creature,
I had rather crack my sinews, break my back,
Than you should such dishonor undergo
While I sit lazy by.
MIRANDA　　　　　　　It would become me
As well as it does you; and I should do it
With much more ease, for my good will is to it,
And yours it is against.
PROSPERO [*aside*]　　　　Poor worm, thou art infected!
This visitation shows it.
MIRANDA　　　　　　　You look wearily.　32
FERDINAND
No, noble mistress, 'tis fresh morning with me
When you are by at night. I do beseech you—　34
Chiefly that I might set it in my prayers—
What is your name?
MIRANDA　　　　　　Miranda.—O my father,
I have broke your hest to say so.
FERDINAND　　　　　　　Admired Miranda!　37
Indeed the top of admiration, worth
What's dearest to the world! Full many a lady　39
I have eyed with best regard, and many a time　40
The harmony of their tongues hath into bondage

Brought my too diligent ear. For several virtues　42
Have I liked several women, never any
With so full soul but some defect in her
Did quarrel with the noblest grace she owed　45
And put it to the foil. But you, oh, you,　46
So perfect and so peerless, are created
Of every creature's best!
MIRANDA　　　　　　　I do not know　48
One of my sex; no woman's face remember,
Save, from my glass, mine own. Nor have I seen
More that I may call men than you, good friend,
And my dear father. How features are abroad　52
I am skilless of; but, by my modesty,　53
The jewel in my dower, I would not wish
Any companion in the world but you;
Nor can imagination form a shape,
Besides yourself, to like of. But I prattle　57
Something too wildly, and my father's precepts　58
I therein do forget.
FERDINAND　　　　　I am in my condition　59
A prince, Miranda; I do think, a king—
I would, not so!—and would no more endure　61
This wooden slavery than to suffer　62
The flesh-fly blow my mouth. Hear my soul speak:　63
The very instant that I saw you did
My heart fly to your service, there resides
To make me slave to it, and for your sake
Am I this patient log-man.
MIRANDA　　　　　　　　Do you love me?
FERDINAND
O heaven, O earth, bear witness to this sound,
And crown what I profess with kind event　69
If I speak true! If hollowly, invert　70
What best is boded me to mischief! I　71
Beyond all limit of what else i'th' world　72
Do love, prize, honor you.
MIRANDA [*weeping*]　　　　　I am a fool
To weep at what I am glad of.
PROSPERO [*aside*]　　　　　Fair encounter
Of two most rare affections! Heavens rain grace
On that which breeds between 'em!
FERDINAND　　　　　　　Wherefore weep you?
MIRANDA
At mine unworthiness, that dare not offer
What I desire to give, and much less take
What I shall die to want. But this is trifling,　79
And all the more it seeks to hide itself
The bigger bulk it shows. Hence, bashful cunning,　81

---

6 **quickens** gives life to　11 **sore injunction** severe command.
13 **Had . . . executor** was never before undertaken by so noble a
being. **I forget** i.e., I forget that I'm supposed to be working
15 **Most . . . do it** (Ferdinand seems to say that the busier he is, the
less likely he is to forget the sweet thoughts that make his labors
pleasant. The line may be in need of emendation.)　17 **enjoined** commanded　18 **this** i.e., the log　19 **weep** i.e., exude resin　21 **these** the
next　22 **discharge** complete　32 **visitation** (1) Miranda's visit to
Ferdinand (2) visitation of the plague, i.e., infection of love　34 **by**
nearby　37 **hest** command. **Admired Miranda** (Her name means
"to be admired or wondered at.")　39 **dearest** most treasured
40 **best regard** thoughtful and approving attention

42 **diligent** attentive. **several** various. (Also in line 43.)　45 **owed**
owned　46 **put . . . foil** (1) overthrew it (as in fencing or wrestling)
(2) served as a *foil*, or "contrast," to set it off.　48 **Of** out of　52 **How . . .**
abroad What people look like in other places　53 **skilless** ignorant.
modesty virginity　57 **like of** be pleased with, be fond of.　58 **Some-**
thing somewhat　59 **condition** rank　61 **I would** I wish it were
62 **wooden slavery** being compelled to carry wood　62–3 **than . . .**
mouth than I would allow flying insects to deposit their eggs in my
mouth as if in decaying flesh.　69 **kind event** favorable outcome
70 **hollowly** insincerely, falsely. **invert** turn　71 **boded** in store for.
mischief harm.　72 **what** whatever　79 **die** (Probably with an
unconscious sexual meaning that underlies all of lines 77–81.)　**to**
want through lacking.　81 **bashful cunning** coyness

And prompt me, plain and holy innocence!
I am your wife, if you will marry me;
If not, I'll die your maid. To be your fellow   84
You may deny me, but I'll be your servant
Whether you will or no.

FERDINAND   My mistress, dearest,   86
And I thus humble ever.

MIRANDA   My husband, then?

FERDINAND   Ay, with a heart as willing   89
As bondage e'er of freedom. Here's my hand.

MIRANDA [clasping his hand]
And mine, with my heart in't. And now farewell
Till half an hour hence.

FERDINAND   A thousand thousand!   92
              Exeunt [Ferdinand and Miranda, separately].

PROSPERO
So glad of this as they I cannot be,
Who are surprised with all; but my rejoicing   94
At nothing can be more. I'll to my book,
For yet ere suppertime must I perform
Much business appertaining.   Exit.   97

3.2

Enter Caliban, Stephano, and Trinculo.

STEPHANO   Tell not me. When the butt is out, we will 1
drink water, not a drop before. Therefore bear up and 2
board 'em. Servant monster, drink to me.   3

TRINCULO   Servant monster? The folly of this island! 4
They say there's but five upon this isle. We are three
of them; if th'other two be brained like us, the state 6
totters.

STEPHANO   Drink, servant monster, when I bid thee.
Thy eyes are almost set in thy head.   [*Giving a drink.*] 9

TRINCULO   Where should they be set else? He were a   10
brave monster indeed if they were set in his tail.   11

STEPHANO   My man-monster hath drowned his tongue
in sack. For my part, the sea cannot drown me. I
swam, ere I could recover the shore, five and thirty   14
leagues off and on. By this light, thou shalt be my   15
lieutenant, monster, or my standard.   16

TRINCULO   Your lieutenant, if you list; he's no standard. 17

STEPHANO   We'll not run, Monsieur Monster.   18

TRINCULO   Nor go neither, but you'll lie like dogs and 19
yet say nothing neither.

STEPHANO   Mooncalf, speak once in thy life, if thou
be'st a good mooncalf.

CALIBAN
How does Thy Honor? Let me lick thy shoe.
I'll not serve him. He is not valiant.

TRINCULO   Thou liest, most ignorant monster, I am in   25
case to jostle a constable. Why, thou deboshed fish,   26
thou, was there ever man a coward that hath drunk so   27
much sack as I today? Wilt thou tell a monstrous lie,   28
being but half a fish and half a monster?

CALIBAN
Lo, how he mocks me! Wilt thou let him, my lord?

TRINCULO   "Lord," quoth he? That a monster should be
such a natural!   32

CALIBAN
Lo, lo, again! Bite him to death, I prithee.

STEPHANO   Trinculo, keep a good tongue in your head.
If you prove a mutineer—the next tree! The poor mon-   35
ster's my subject, and he shall not suffer indignity.

CALIBAN
I thank my noble lord. Wilt thou be pleased
To hearken once again to the suit I made to thee?

STEPHANO   Marry, will I. Kneel and repeat it. I will   39
stand, and so shall Trinculo.   [*Caliban kneels.*]   40

Enter Ariel, invisible.

CALIBAN
As I told thee before, I am subject to a tyrant,
A sorcerer, that by his cunning hath
Cheated me of the island.

ARIEL [mimicking Trinculo]
Thou liest.

CALIBAN   Thou liest, thou jesting monkey, thou!
I would my valiant master would destroy thee.
I do not lie.

STEPHANO   Trinculo, if you trouble him any more in 's
tale, by this hand, I will supplant some of your teeth. 48

TRINCULO   Why, I said nothing.

STEPHANO   Mum, then, and no more.—Proceed.

CALIBAN
I say by sorcery he got this isle;
From me he got it. If Thy Greatness will
Revenge it on him—for I know thou dar'st,
But this thing dare not—   54

STEPHANO   That's most certain.

CALIBAN
Thou shalt be lord of it, and I'll serve thee.

---

84 maid handmaiden, servant.   **fellow** mate   **86 will** desire it.   **My
mistress** i.e., The woman I adore and serve (not an illicit sexual partner)   **89 willing** desirous   **92 A thousand thousand!** A thousand
thousand farewells!   **94 with all** by everything that has happened,
or, *withal*, "by it"   **97 appertaining** related to this.
3.2 Location: Another part of the island.
1 out empty   **2–3 bear . . . 'em** (Stephano uses the terminology of
maneuvering at sea and boarding a vessel under attack as a way of
urging an assault on the liquor supply.)   **4 folly of** i.e., stupidity
found on   **6 be brained** are endowed with intelligence   **9 set . . .
head** fixed in a drunken stare. (But Trinculo answers in a literal
sense.)   **10 set** placed   **11 brave** fine, splendid   **14 recover** gain,
reach   **14–15 five . . . on** i.e., a little over a hundred miles, give or
take, or, off and on, intermittently. (A drunken hyperbole.)   **15 By
this light** (An oath: By the light of the sun.)   **16 standard** standard-
bearer, ensign. (But Trinculo answers in the literal sense: Caliban is *no
standard*, not able to stand up because he's so drunk.)   **17 list** prefer

18 run run away, retreat (as a standard-bearer should not do)
19 Nor . . . dogs i.e., You won't even walk, much less run; you'll lie
down in the field like the proverbial cowardly dog. (With a play on
lie, tell falsehoods.)   **25–6 in case** ready, valiant enough
26 deboshed debauched, drunken   **27 ever . . . coward** ever a coward. (Trinculo appeals to his gargantuan drinking as refutation of the
charge that he is *not valiant*, line 24.)   **28 sack** Spanish white wine
32 natural fool, idiot.   **35 the next tree** i.e., you'll hang.   **39 Marry**
i.e., Indeed. (Originally an oath, "by the Virgin Mary.")
40.1 *invisible* i.e., wearing a garment to connote invisibility, as at
1.2.377.2.   **48 supplant** uproot, displace   **54 this thing** i.e., Trinculo

STEPHANO   How now shall this be compassed? Canst   57
thou bring me to the party?

CALIBAN
Yea, yea, my lord. I'll yield him thee asleep,
Where thou mayst knock a nail into his head.

ARIEL [*mimicking Trinculo*]   Thou liest; thou canst not.

CALIBAN
What a pied ninny's this! Thou scurvy patch!—   62
I do beseech Thy Greatness, give him blows
And take his bottle from him. When that's gone
He shall drink naught but brine, for I'll not show
    him
Where the quick freshes are.   66

STEPHANO   Trinculo, run into no further danger. Interrupt the monster one word further and, by this hand,   69
I'll turn my mercy out o' doors and make a stockfish of
thee.

TRINCULO   Why, what did I? I did nothing. I'll go farther
off.

STEPHANO   Didst thou not say he lied?

ARIEL [*mimicking Trinculo*]   Thou liest.

STEPHANO   Do I so? Take thou that. [*He beats Trinculo.*]
As you like this, give me the lie another time.   76

TRINCULO   I did not give the lie. Out o' your wits and
hearing too? A pox o' your bottle! This can sack and   78
drinking do. A murrain on your monster, and the   79
devil take your fingers!

CALIBAN   Ha, ha, ha!

STEPHANO   Now, forward with your tale. [*To Trinculo*]
Prithee, stand further off.

CALIBAN
Beat him enough. After a little time
I'll beat him too.

STEPHANO   Stand farther.—Come, proceed.

CALIBAN
Why, as I told thee, 'tis a custom with him
I'th'afternoon to sleep. There thou mayst brain him,
Having first seized his books; or with a log
Batter his skull, or paunch him with a stake,   90
Or cut his weasand with thy knife. Remember   91
First to possess his books, for without them
He's but a sot, as I am, nor hath not   93
One spirit to command. They all do hate him
As rootedly as I. Burn but his books.
He has brave utensils—for so he calls them—   96
Which, when he has a house, he'll deck withal.   97
And that most deeply to consider is
The beauty of his daughter. He himself
Calls her a nonpareil. I never saw a woman
But only Sycorax my dam and she;
But she as far surpasseth Sycorax
As great'st does least.

STEPHANO   Is it so brave a lass?   104

CALIBAN
Ay, lord. She will become thy bed, I warrant,   105
And bring thee forth brave brood.

STEPHANO   Monster, I will kill this man. His daughter
and I will be king and queen—save Our Graces!—and
Trinculo and thyself shall be viceroys. Dost thou like
the plot, Trinculo?

TRINCULO   Excellent.

STEPHANO   Give me thy hand. I am sorry I beat thee;
but, while thou liv'st, keep a good tongue in thy head.

CALIBAN
Within this half hour will he be asleep.
Wilt thou destroy him then?

STEPHANO   Ay, on mine honor.

ARIEL [*aside*]   This will I tell my master.

CALIBAN
Thou mak'st me merry; I am full of pleasure.
Let us be jocund. Will you troll the catch   119
You taught me but whilere?   120

STEPHANO   At thy request, monster, I will do reason,   121
any reason.—Come on, Trinculo, let us sing.   *Sings.*   122
    "Flout 'em and scout 'em   123
    And scout 'em and flout 'em!
        Thought is free."

CALIBAN   That's not the tune.   126
        Ariel plays the tune on a tabor and pipe.

STEPHANO   What is this same?

TRINCULO   This is the tune of our catch, played by the
picture of Nobody.   129

STEPHANO   If thou be'st a man, show thyself in thy
likeness. If thou be'st a devil, take't as thou list.   131

TRINCULO   Oh, forgive me my sins!

STEPHANO   He that dies pays all debts. I defy thee.   133
Mercy upon us!

CALIBAN   Art thou afeard?

STEPHANO   No, monster, not I.

CALIBAN
Be not afeard. The isle is full of noises,
Sounds, and sweet airs, that give delight and hurt not.
Sometimes a thousand twangling instruments
Will hum about mine ears, and sometimes voices
That, if I then had waked after long sleep,
Will make me sleep again; and then, in dreaming,
The clouds methought would open and show riches
Ready to drop upon me, that when I waked
I cried to dream again.   145

STEPHANO   This will prove a brave kingdom to me,
where I shall have my music for nothing.

CALIBAN   When Prospero is destroyed.

---

104 brave splendid, attractive   **105 become** suit (sexually)   **119 jocund**
jovial, merry.   **troll the catch** sing the round   **120 but whilere** only a
short time ago.   **121–2 reason, any reason** anything reasonable.
123 Flout Scoff at.   **scout** deride   **126.1** *tabor* small drum   **129 picture of Nobody** (Refers to a familiar figure with head, arms, and legs
but no trunk.)   **131 take't . . . list** (A proverbial formula of bravado
and defiance, as in *Romeo and Juliet*, 1.1.40–1.)   **133 He . . . debts**
(Another proverbial swagger: Death settles all scores, I'm not afraid
to fight.)   **145 to dream** desirous of dreaming

57 compassed achieved.   **62 pied ninny** fool in motley.   **patch** fool.
66 quick freshes running springs   **69 turn . . . o' doors** banish all
merciful feelings.   **stockfish** dried cod beaten before cooking
76 give me the lie call me a liar to my face   **78 A pox** i.e., A plague.
(A curse.)   **79 murrain** plague. (Literally, a cattle disease.)   **90 paunch**
stab in the belly   **91 weasand** windpipe   **93 sot** fool   **96 brave utensils** fine furnishings   **97 deck withal** furnish it with.

STEPHANO   That shall be by and by. I remember the   149
story.

TRINCULO   The sound is going away. Let's follow it,
and after do our work.

STEPHANO   Lead, monster; we'll follow. I would I could
see this taborer! He lays it on.   154

TRINCULO   Wilt come? I'll follow, Stephano.

Exeunt [following Ariel's music].

❖

3.3

*Enter Alonso, Sebastian, Antonio, Gonzalo,
Adrian, Francisco, etc.*

GONZALO
By'r lakin, I can go no further, sir.   1
My old bones aches. Here's a maze trod indeed
Through forthrights and meanders! By your patience,   3
I needs must rest me.

ALONSO   Old lord, I cannot blame thee,
Who am myself attached with weariness,   5
To th' dulling of my spirits. Sit down and rest.   6
Even here I will put off my hope, and keep it
No longer for my flatterer. He is drowned
Whom thus we stray to find, and the sea mocks
Our frustrate search on land. Well, let him go.   10

[Alonso and Gonzalo sit.]

ANTONIO *[aside to Sebastian]*
I am right glad that he's so out of hope.
Do not, for one repulse, forgo the purpose   12
That you resolved t'effect.

SEBASTIAN *[to Antonio]*   The next advantage
Will we take throughly.

ANTONIO *[to Sebastian]*   Let it be tonight,   14
For, now they are oppressed with travel, they   15
Will not, nor cannot, use such vigilance   16
As when they are fresh.

SEBASTIAN *[to Antonio]*   I say tonight. No more.   17

*Solemn and strange music; and Prospero on
the top, invisible.*

ALONSO
What harmony is this? My good friends, hark!

GONZALO   Marvelous sweet music!

*Enter several strange shapes, bringing in a ban-
quet, and dance about it with gentle actions of
salutations; and, inviting the King, etc., to eat,
they depart.*

ALONSO
Give us kind keepers, heavens! What were these?   20

SEBASTIAN
A living drollery. Now I will believe   21
That there are unicorns; that in Arabia
There is one tree, the phoenix' throne, one phoenix   23
At this hour reigning there.

ANTONIO   I'll believe both;
And what does else want credit, come to me   25
And I'll be sworn 'tis true. Travelers ne'er did lie,
Though fools at home condemn 'em.

GONZALO   If in Naples
I should report this now, would they believe me
If I should say I saw such islanders?
For, certes, these are people of the island,   30
Who, though they are of monstrous shape, yet note,
Their manners are more gentle, kind, than of
Our human generation you shall find
Many, nay, almost any.

PROSPERO *[aside]*   Honest lord,
Thou hast said well, for some of you there present
Are worse than devils.

ALONSO   I cannot too much muse   36
Such shapes, such gesture, and such sound,
expressing—
Although they want the use of tongue—a kind   38
Of excellent dumb discourse.

PROSPERO *[aside]*   Praise in departing.   39

FRANCISCO
They vanished strangely.

SEBASTIAN   No matter, since
They have left their viands behind, for we have
stomachs.   41
Will 't please you taste of what is here?

ALONSO   Not I.

GONZALO
Faith, sir, you need not fear. When we were boys,
Who would believe that there were mountaineers   44
Dewlapped like bulls, whose throats had hanging at
'em   45
Wallets of flesh? Or that there were such men   46
Whose heads stood in their breasts? Which now we
find   47
Each putter-out of five for one will bring us   48
Good warrant of.

ALONSO   I will stand to and feed,   49

---

149 **by and by** very soon.   154 **lays it on** i.e., plays the drum vigorously.
3.3. Location: Another part of the island.
1 **By'r lakin** By our Ladykin, by our Lady   3 **forthrights and meanders** paths straight and crooked.   5 **attached with** seized by   6 **To . . .
spirits** to the point of being dull-spirited.   10 **frustrate** frustrated
12 **for** because of   14 **throughly** thoroughly.   15 **now** now that.
travel (Spelled "trauaile" in the Folio and carrying the sense of labor
as well as traveling.)   16 **use such vigilance** be as vigilant   17.1–2 *on
the top* at some high point of the tiring-house or the theater, on a
third level above the gallery

20 **kind keepers** guardian angels   21 **living drollery** comic entertainment, caricature, or puppet show put on by live actors.   23 **phoenix**
mythical bird consumed to ashes every five hundred to six hundred
years, only to be renewed in another cycle   25 **want credit** lack
credibility   30 **certes** certainly   36 **muse** wonder at   38 **want** lack
39 **Praise in departing** i.e., Save your praise until the end of the performance. (Proverbial.)   41 **viands** provisions.   **stomachs** appetites.
44 **mountaineers** mountain dwellers   45 **Dewlapped** having a
dewlap, or fold of skin hanging from the neck, like cattle   46 **Wallets**
pendent folds of skin, wattles   47 **in their breasts** (I.e., like the
Anthropophagi described in *Othello,* 1.3.146.)   48 **putter-out . . . one**
one who invests money or gambles on the risks of travel on the condition that the traveler who returns safely is to receive five times the
amount deposited; hence, any traveler   49 **Good warrant** assurance.
stand to come forward, fall to. (Also in line 52.)

Although my last—no matter, since I feel   50
The best is past. Brother, my lord the Duke,   51
Stand to, and do as we.   [*They approach the table.*]   52

Thunder and lightning. Enter Ariel, like a harpy,
claps his wings upon the table, and with a quaint
device the banquet vanishes.

ARIEL
You are three men of sin, whom Destiny—   53
That hath to instrument this lower world   54
And what is in't—the never-surfeited sea   55
Hath caused to belch up you, and on this island   56
Where man doth not inhabit, you 'mongst men
Being most unfit to live. I have made you mad;
And even with suchlike valor men hang and drown   59
Their proper selves.   [*Alonso, Sebastian, and Antonio*
draw their swords.]
    You fools! I and my fellows   60
Are ministers of Fate. The elements
Of whom your swords are tempered may as well   62
Wound the loud winds, or with bemocked-at stabs   63
Kill the still-closing waters, as diminish   64
One dowl that's in my plume. My fellow ministers   65
Are like invulnerable. If you could hurt,   66
Your swords are now too massy for your strengths   67
And will not be uplifted. But remember—
For that's my business to you—that you three
From Milan did supplant good Prospero;
Exposed unto the sea, which hath requit it,   71
Him and his innocent child; for which foul deed
The powers, delaying, not forgetting, have
Incensed the seas and shores, yea, all the creatures,
Against your peace. Thee of thy son, Alonso,
They have bereft; and do pronounce by me
Ling'ring perdition, worse than any death   77
Can be at once, shall step by step attend
You and your ways; whose wraths to guard you
    from—   79
Which here, in this most desolate isle, else falls   80
Upon your heads—is nothing but heart's sorrow   81
And a clear life ensuing.   82

He vanishes in thunder; then, to soft music,
enter the shapes again, and dance, with mocks
and mows, and carrying out the table.

PROSPERO
Bravely the figure of this harpy hast thou   83
Performed, my Ariel; a grace it had devouring.   84
Of my instruction hast thou nothing bated   85
In what thou hadst to say. So, with good life   86
And observation strange, my meaner ministers   87
Their several kinds have done. My high charms work,   88
And these mine enemies are all knit up
In their distractions. They now are in my power;   90
And in these fits I leave them, while I visit
Young Ferdinand, whom they suppose is drowned,
And his and mine loved darling.   [*Exit above.*]

GONZALO
I'th' name of something holy, sir, why stand you   94
In this strange stare?

ALONSO   Oh, it is monstrous, monstrous!   95
Methought the billows spoke and told me of it;   96
The winds did sing it to me, and the thunder,
That deep and dreadful organ pipe, pronounced
The name of Prosper; it did bass my trespass.   99
Therefor my son i'th'ooze is bedded; and
I'll seek him deeper than e'er plummet sounded,   101
And with him there lie mudded.   *Exit.*

SEBASTIAN   But one fiend at a time,   103
I'll fight their legions o'er.

ANTONIO   I'll be thy second.   104
    Exeunt [*Sebastian and Antonio*].

GONZALO
All three of them are desperate. Their great guilt,   105
Like poison given to work a great time after,   106
Now 'gins to bite the spirits. I do beseech you,   107
That are of suppler joints, follow them swiftly   108
And hinder them from what this ecstasy   109
May now provoke them to.

ADRIAN   Follow, I pray you.
    Exeunt omnes.

❧

4.1

Enter Prospero, Ferdinand, and Miranda.

PROSPERO
If I have too austerely punished you,
Your compensation makes amends, for I

50 Although my last even if this were to be my last meal   **51 best** best part of life   **52.1 harpy** a fabulous monster with a woman's face and breasts and a vulture's body, supposed to be a minister of divine vengeance.   **52.2–3 with . . . vanishes** by means of some ingenious stage contrivance, the food vanishes. (The table remains until line 82.)   **53–6 whom . . . up you** you whom Destiny, acting through this sublunary world as its instrument, has caused the ever-hungry sea to belch up   **59 suchlike valor** i.e., the reckless valor derived from madness   **60 proper** own   **62 whom** which.   **tempered** made hard   **63 bemocked-at** scorned   **64 still-closing** always closing again when parted   **65 dowl** soft, fine feather   **66 like** likewise, similarly.   **If** Even if   **67 massy** heavy   **71 requit** requited, avenged   **77 perdition** ruin, destruction   **79 whose . . . from** to guard you from which heavenly wrath   **80 else** otherwise   **81 is nothing** there is no way   **82 clear** unspotted, innocent   **82.2–3 *mocks and mows*** mocking gestures and grimaces

83 Bravely Finely, dashingly   **84 a grace . . . devouring** your impersonation displayed a ravishing grace. (With a punning suggestion of having caused the banquet to disappear as if by consuming it.)   **85 bated** abated, omitted   **86–8 So . . . done** Similarly, my lesser spirits assisting you have done their various tasks with observant care and attention to detail.   **90 distractions** trancelike state.   **94–5 why . . . stare?** (Gonzalo was not addressed in Ariel's speech to the *three men of sin*, line 53, and is not, as they are, in a maddened state; see lines 105–7.)   **95 it** i.e., my sin. (Also in line 96.)   **96 billows** waves   **99 bass my trespass** proclaim my trespass like a bass note on the music.   **101 than . . . sounded** than ever a lead weight attached to a line tested the depth   **103–4 But . . . o'er** If the demons come at me one at a time, I'll fight them all.   **105 desperate** despairing and reckless.   **106 Like . . . after** like poison, starting to work long after it has been administered   **107 bite the spirits** sap their vital powers through anguish   **107–8 you . . . joints** Adrian, Francisco, and others not under Ariel's numbing spell   **109 ecstasy** mad frenzy
4.1. Location: Before Prospero's cell.

Have given you here a third of mine own life,   3
Or that for which I live; who once again
I tender to thy hand. All thy vexations   5
Were but my trials of thy love, and thou
Hast strangely stood the test. Here, afore heaven,   7
I ratify this my rich gift. O Ferdinand,
Do not smile at me that I boast her off,   9
For thou shalt find she will outstrip all praise
And make it halt behind her.

FERDINAND   I do believe it   11
Against an oracle.   12

PROSPERO
Then, as my gift and thine own acquisition
Worthily purchased, take my daughter. But
If thou dost break her virgin-knot before
All sanctimonious ceremonies may   16
With full and holy rite be ministered,
No sweet aspersion shall the heavens let fall   18
To make this contract grow; but barren hate,
Sour-eyed disdain, and discord shall bestrew
The union of your bed with weeds so loathly   21
That you shall hate it both. Therefore take heed,
As Hymen's lamps shall light you.

FERDINAND   As I hope   23
For quiet days, fair issue, and long life,   24
With such love as 'tis now, the murkiest den,
The most opportune place, the strong'st suggestion   26
Our worser genius can, shall never melt   27
Mine honor into lust, to take away   28
The edge of that day's celebration   29
When I shall think or Phoebus' steeds are foundered 30
Or Night kept chained below.

PROSPERO   Fairly spoke.
Sit then and talk with her. She is thine own.
    [Ferdinand and Miranda sit and talk together.]
What, Ariel! My industrious servant, Ariel!   33

    Enter Ariel.

ARIEL
What would my potent master? Here I am.

PROSPERO
Thou and thy meaner fellows your last service   35
Did worthily perform, and I must use you
In such another trick. Go bring the rabble,   37

O'er whom I give thee power, here to this place.
Incite them to quick motion, for I must
Bestow upon the eyes of this young couple
Some vanity of mine art. It is my promise,   41
And they expect it from me.

ARIEL   Presently?   42

PROSPERO   Ay, with a twink.   43

ARIEL
Before you can say "Come" and "Go,"
And breathe twice, and cry "So, so,"
Each one, tripping on his toe,
Will be here with mop and mow.   47
Do you love me, master? No?

PROSPERO
Dearly, my delicate Ariel. Do not approach
Till thou dost hear me call.

ARIEL   Well; I conceive.   Exit. 50

PROSPERO
Look thou be true; do not give dalliance   51
Too much the rein. The strongest oaths are straw
To th' fire i'th' blood. Be more abstemious,
Or else good night your vow!

FERDINAND   I warrant you, sir, 54
The white cold virgin snow upon my heart   55
Abates the ardor of my liver.

PROSPERO   Well.   56
Now come, my Ariel! Bring a corollary,   57
Rather than want a spirit. Appear, and pertly!—   58
No tongue! All eyes! Be silent.   Soft music.   59

    Enter Iris.

IRIS
Ceres, most bounteous lady, thy rich leas   60
Of wheat, rye, barley, vetches, oats, and peas;   61
Thy turfy mountains, where live nibbling sheep,
And flat meads thatched with stover, them to keep;   63
Thy banks with pionèd and twillèd brims,   64
Which spongy April at thy hest betrims   65
To make cold nymphs chaste crowns; and thy
    broom groves,   66
Whose shadow the dismissèd bachelor loves,   67
Being lass-lorn; thy poll-clipped vineyard;   68
And thy sea marge, sterile and rocky hard,   69
Where thou thyself dost air: the queen o'th' sky,   70

3 a third i.e., Miranda, into whose education I have put a third of my life, or (less precisely) who represents a large part of what I have cared about, along with my dukedom and my magical art   5 tender offer
7 strangely exceptionally   9 boast her off i.e., praise her so, or, perhaps an error for "boast of her"; the Folio reads "boast her of"   11 halt limp   12 Against an oracle even if an oracle should declare otherwise.
16 sanctimonious sacred   18 aspersion dew, shower   21 weeds (In place of the flowers customarily strewn on the marriage bed.)   23 As . . . you i.e., as you long for happiness and concord in your marriage. (Hymen was the Greek and Roman god of marriage; his symbolic torches, the wedding torches, were supposed to burn brightly for a happy marriage and smokily for a troubled one.)   24 issue offspring
26–7 the strong'st . . . can the strongest temptation that the evil spirit within us can propose   28 to so as to   29 edge keen enjoyment, sexual ardor   30 or . . . foundered either that the horses of the sun's chariot have gone lame (thus delaying the night for which I will be so eager)
33 What Now then   35 meaner fellows subordinates   37 trick device.
rabble band, i.e., the meaner fellows of line 35

41 vanity (1) illusion (2) trifle (3) desire for admiration, conceit
42 Presently? Immediately?   43 with a twink in the twinkling of an eye.   47 mop and mow grimaces.   50 conceive understand.
51 true true to your promise   54 good night i.e., say good-bye to.
warrant guarantee   55 The white . . . heart i.e., the chaste ideal to which my heart is devoted   56 liver (The presumed seat of the passions.)   57 corollary surplus, extra supply   58 want lack.   pertly briskly.   59 No tongue! Quiet, everyone!   59.1 Iris goddess of the rainbow and Juno's messenger.   60 Ceres goddess of the generative power of nature.   leas meadows   61 vetches plants for forage, fodder   63 meads meadows.   stover winter fodder for cattle   64 pionèd and twillèd undercut by the swift current and protected by roots and branches that tangle to form a barricade   65 spongy wet.   hest command   66 broom groves clumps of broom, gorse, yellow-flowered shrub   67 dismissèd bachelor rejected male lover   68 poll-clipped pruned, lopped at the top, or pole-clipped, "hedged in with poles"   69 sea marge shore   70 thou . . . air you take the air, go for walks.   queen o'th' sky i.e., Juno

Whose wat'ry arch and messenger am I,   71
Bids thee leave these, and with her sovereign grace,   72
               Juno descends [slowly in her car].
Here on this grass plot, in this very place,
To come and sport. Her peacocks fly amain.   74
Approach, rich Ceres, her to entertain.   75

     Enter Ceres.

CERES
Hail, many-colored messenger, that ne'er
Dost disobey the wife of Jupiter,
Who with thy saffron wings upon my flowers   78
Diffusest honeydrops, refreshing showers,
And with each end of thy blue bow dost crown   80
My bosky acres and my unshrubbed down,   81
Rich scarf to my proud earth. Why hath thy queen   82
Summoned me hither to this short-grassed green?
IRIS
A contract of true love to celebrate,
And some donation freely to estate   85
On the blest lovers.
CERES   Tell me, heavenly bow,
If Venus or her son, as thou dost know,   87
Do now attend the Queen? Since they did plot   88
The means that dusky Dis my daughter got,   89
Her and her blind boy's scandaled company   90
I have forsworn.
IRIS   Of her society   91
Be not afraid. I met Her Deity   92
Cutting the clouds towards Paphos, and her son   93
Dove-drawn with her. Here thought they to have
  done   94
Some wanton charm upon this man and maid,   95
Whose vows are that no bed-right shall be paid   96
Till Hymen's torch be lighted; but in vain.
Mars's hot minion is returned again;   98
Her waspish-headed son has broke his arrows,   99
Swears he will shoot no more, but play with
  sparrows   100
And be a boy right out.

    [Juno alights.]

CERES   Highest Queen of state,   101
Great Juno, comes; I know her by her gait.   102

JUNO
How does my bounteous sister? Go with me   103
To bless this twain, that they may prosperous be,
And honored in their issue.   *They sing:*   105
JUNO
Honor, riches, marriage blessing,
Long continuance, and increasing,
Hourly joys be still upon you!   108
Juno sings her blessings on you.
CERES
Earth's increase, foison plenty,   110
Barns and garners never empty,   111
Vines with clust'ring bunches growing,
Plants with goodly burden bowing;

Spring come to you at the farthest
In the very end of harvest!   115
Scarcity and want shall shun you;
Ceres' blessing so is on you.
FERDINAND
This is a most majestic vision, and
Harmonious charmingly. May I be bold   119
To think these spirits?
PROSPERO   Spirits, which by mine art
I have from their confines called to enact
My present fancies.
FERDINAND   Let me live here ever!
So rare a wondered father and a wife   123
Makes this place Paradise.
    Juno and Ceres whisper, and send
       Iris on employment.
PROSPERO   Sweet now, silence!
Juno and Ceres whisper seriously;
There's something else to do. Hush and be mute,
Or else our spell is marred.
IRIS *[calling offstage]*
You nymphs, called naiads, of the windring brooks,   128
With your sedged crowns and ever-harmless looks,   129
Leave your crisp channels, and on this green land   130
Answer your summons; Juno does command.
Come, temperate nymphs, and help to celebrate   132
A contract of true love. Be not too late.

    Enter certain nymphs.

You sunburned sicklemen, of August weary,   134
Come hither from the furrow and be merry.   135

---

71 **wat'ry arch** rainbow   72.1 *Juno descends* i.e., starts her descent from the "heavens" above the stage   74 **peacocks** birds sacred to Juno and used to pull her chariot. **amain** with full speed.   75 **entertain** receive.   78 **saffron** yellow   80 **bow** rainbow   81 **bosky** wooded. **unshrubbed down** open upland   82 **scarf** (The rainbow is like a colored silk band adorning the earth.)   85 **estate** bestow   87 **son** i.e., Cupid. **as** as far as   88–91 **Since ... forsworn** Since Venus and her blind son Cupid plotted the means by which Dis (Pluto) carried off my daughter Proserpina to be his bride in Hades, I have forsworn their scandalous company.   92 **Her Deity** i.e., Her Highness   93 **Paphos** place on the island of Cyprus, sacred to Venus   94 **Dove-drawn** (Venus's chariot was drawn by doves.)   94–5 **done ... charm** inflicted some lustful spell   96 **that ... paid** that their union will not be sexually consummated   98 **Mars's hot minion** i.e., Venus, the beloved of Mars. **returned** i.e., returned to Paphos   99 **waspish-headed** hotheaded, peevish   100 **sparrows** (Supposed lustful, and sacred to Venus.)   101 **right out** outright. **Highest ... state** Most majestic Queen   102 **gait** i.e., majestic bearing.

103 **sister** i.e., fellow goddess.   105 **issue** offspring.   108 **still** always   110 **foison plenty** plentiful harvest   111 **garners** granaries   115 **In ... harvest** i.e., with no winter in between.   119 **charmingly** enchantingly.   123 **wondered** wonder-performing, wondrous. **wise** (The Folio appears to read "wise" here, but with a tall "s" that resembles an "f," leading to much dispute over this reading. In some copies of the Folio the "s" looks like an "f," perhaps damaged, but evidently as the result of an inkblot, so that the true reading is "s." Even so, an error in transmission would be easy, so that the author's intention is uncertain. The matter bears importantly on whether or not Ferdinand includes Miranda in his vision of paradise.)   128 **naiads** nymphs of springs, rivers, or lakes. **windring** wandering, winding (?)   129 **sedged** made of reeds. **ever-harmless** ever innocent   130 **crisp** curled, rippled   132 **temperate** chaste   134 **sicklemen** harvesters, field workers who cut down grain and grass. **of August weary** i.e., weary of the hard work of the harvest   135 **furrow** i.e., plowed fields

Make holiday; your rye-straw hats put on,
And these fresh nymphs encounter every one   137
In country footing.   138

> *Enter certain reapers, properly habited. They join
> with the nymphs in a graceful dance, towards the
> end whereof Prospero starts suddenly, and speaks;
> after which, to a strange, hollow, and confused
> noise, they heavily vanish.*

PROSPERO [*aside*]
I had forgot that foul conspiracy
Of the beast Caliban and his confederates
Against my life. The minute of their plot
Is almost come. [*To the Spirits*] Well done! Avoid; no
more!   142
FERDINAND [*to Miranda*]
This is strange. Your father's in some passion
That works him strongly.
MIRANDA   Never till this day   144
Saw I him touched with anger so distempered.
PROSPERO
You do look, my son, in a moved sort,   146
As if you were dismayed. Be cheerful, sir.
Our revels now are ended. These our actors,   148
As I foretold you, were all spirits and
Are melted into air, into thin air;
And, like the baseless fabric of this vision,   151
The cloud-capped towers, the gorgeous palaces,
The solemn temples, the great globe itself,   153
Yea, all which it inherit, shall dissolve,   154
And, like this insubstantial pageant faded,
Leave not a rack behind. We are such stuff   156
As dreams are made on, and our little life   157
Is rounded with a sleep. Sir, I am vexed.   158
Bear with my weakness. My old brain is troubled.
Be not disturbed with my infirmity.   160
If you be pleased, retire into my cell   161
And there repose. A turn or two I'll walk
To still my beating mind.
FERDINAND, MIRANDA   We wish your peace.   163
              Exeunt [*Ferdinand and Miranda*].
PROSPERO
Come with a thought! I thank thee, Ariel. Come.   164

          Enter Ariel.

ARIEL
Thy thoughts I cleave to. What's thy pleasure?   165
PROSPERO   Spirit,
We must prepare to meet with Caliban.

ARIEL
Ay, my commander. When I presented Ceres,   167
I thought to have told thee of it, but I feared
Lest I might anger thee.
PROSPERO
Say again, where didst thou leave these varlets?
ARIEL
I told you, sir, they were red-hot with drinking;
So full of valor that they smote the air
For breathing in their faces, beat the ground
For kissing of their feet; yet always bending   174
Towards their project. Then I beat my tabor,
At which, like unbacked colts, they pricked their ears, 176
Advanced their eyelids, lifted up their noses   177
As they smelt music. So I charmed their ears   178
That calflike they my lowing followed through   179
Toothed briers, sharp furzes, pricking gorse, and
thorns,   180
Which entered their frail shins. At last I left them
I'th' filthy-mantled pool beyond your cell,   182
There dancing up to th' chins, that the foul lake
O'erstunk their feet.
PROSPERO   This was well done, my bird.   184
Thy shape invisible retain thou still.
The trumpery in my house, go bring it hither,   186
For stale to catch these thieves.
ARIEL   I go, I go.   *Exit.* 187
PROSPERO
A devil, a born devil, on whose nature
Nurture can never stick; on whom my pains,
Humanely taken, all, all lost, quite lost!
And as with age his body uglier grows,
So his mind cankers. I will plague them all,   192
Even to roaring.

          Enter Ariel, loaden with glistering apparel, etc.

              Come, hang them on this line.   193

          [*Ariel hangs up the showy finery; Prospero and
          Ariel remain, invisible.*] *Enter Caliban, Stephano,
          and Trinculo, all wet.*

CALIBAN
Pray you, tread softly, that the blind mole may
Not hear a foot fall. We now are near his cell.
STEPHANO   Monster, your fairy, which you say is a
harmless fairy, has done little better than played the
jack with us.   198

---

137 encounter join   **138 country footing** country dancing.
138.1 *properly* suitably.   **138.5** *heavily* slowly, dejectedly   **142 Avoid**
Withdraw   **144 works** affects, agitates   **146 moved sort** troubled
state, condition   **148 revels** entertainment, pageant   **151 baseless
fabric** unsubstantial theatrical edifice or contrivance   **153 great
globe** (With a glance at the Globe Theatre.)   **154 which it inherit**
who subsequently occupy it   **156 rack** wisp of cloud   **157 on** of
158 rounded surrounded (before birth and after death), or crowned,
rounded off   **160 with** by   **161 retire** withdraw, go   **163 beating**
agitated   **164 with a thought** i.e., on the instant, or, summoned by
my thought, no sooner thought of than here.   **165 cleave** cling,
adhere

167 presented acted the part of, or, introduced   **174 bending** aiming
176 unbacked unbroken, unridden   **177 Advanced** lifted up   **178 As**
as if   **179 lowing** mooing   **180 furzes . . . gorse** prickly shrubs
182 filthy-mantled covered with a slimy coating   **184 O'erstunk**
smelled worse than, or, caused to stink terribly   **186 trumpery** cheap
goods, the *glistering apparel* mentioned in the following stage direction   **187 stale** (1) decoy (2) out-of-fashion garments. (With possible
further suggestions of "horse piss," as in line 199, and "steal," pronounced like *stale. For stale* could also mean "fit for a prostitute.")
192 cankers festers, grows malignant   **193 line** lime tree or linden.
193.1–2 *Prospero and Ariel remain* (The staging is uncertain. They
may instead exit here and return with the spirits at line 256.)
198 jack (1) knave (2) will-o'-the-wisp

TRINCULO Monster, I do smell all horse piss, at which my nose is in great indignation.

STEPHANO So is mine. Do you hear, monster? If I should take a displeasure against you, look you—

TRINCULO Thou wert but a lost monster.

CALIBAN
Good my lord, give me thy favor still.
Be patient, for the prize I'll bring thee to
Shall hoodwink this mischance. Therefore speak
  softly.   206
All's hushed as midnight yet.

TRINCULO Ay, but to lose our bottles in the pool—

STEPHANO There is not only disgrace and dishonor in that, monster, but an infinite loss.

TRINCULO That's more to me than my wetting. Yet this is your harmless fairy, monster!

STEPHANO I will fetch off my bottle, though I be o'er   213
ears for my labor.   214

CALIBAN
Prithee, my king, be quiet. See'st thou here,
This is the mouth o'th' cell. No noise, and enter.
Do that good mischief which may make this island
Thine own forever, and I thy Caliban
For aye thy footlicker.

STEPHANO Give me thy hand. I do begin to have bloody thoughts.

TRINCULO [seeing the finery] O King Stephano! O peer!   222
O worthy Stephano! Look what a wardrobe here is for thee!

CALIBAN
Let it alone, thou fool, it is but trash.

TRINCULO Oho, monster! We know what belongs to a frippery. O King Stephano!   [He puts on a gown.]   227

STEPHANO Put off that gown, Trinculo. By this hand, I'll have that gown.

TRINCULO Thy Grace shall have it.

CALIBAN
The dropsy drown this fool! What do you mean   231
To dote thus on such luggage? Let't alone   232
And do the murder first. If he awake,
From toe to crown he'll fill our skins with pinches, 234
Make us strange stuff.

STEPHANO Be you quiet, monster.—Mistress line, is   236
not this my jerkin? [He takes it down.] Now is the jerkin 237
under the line. Now, jerkin, you are like to lose your 238
hair and prove a bald jerkin.   239

TRINCULO Do, do! We steal by line and level, an't like 240
Your Grace.

STEPHANO I thank thee for that jest. Here's a garment for't. [He gives a garment.] Wit shall not go unrewarded while I am king of this country. "Steal by line and level" is an excellent pass of pate. There's another 245
garment for't.

TRINCULO Monster, come, put some lime upon your   247
fingers, and away with the rest.

CALIBAN
I will have none on't. We shall lose our time,
And all be turned to barnacles, or to apes   250
With foreheads villainous low.   251

STEPHANO Monster, lay to your fingers. Help to bear 252
this away where my hogshead of wine is, or I'll turn 253
you out of my kingdom. Go to, carry this.   254

TRINCULO And this.

STEPHANO Ay, and this.
   [They load Caliban with more and more garments.]

A noise of hunters heard. Enter divers spirits, in shape of dogs and hounds, hunting them about, Prospero and Ariel setting them on.

PROSPERO Hey, Mountain, hey!

ARIEL Silver! There it goes, Silver!

PROSPERO Fury, Fury! There, Tyrant, there! Hark! Hark!
   [Caliban, Stephano, and Trinculo are driven out.]
Go, charge my goblins that they grind their joints
With dry convulsions, shorten up their sinews   261
With agèd cramps, and more pinch-spotted make
  them   262
Than pard or cat o' mountain.

ARIEL   Hark, they roar!   263

PROSPERO
Let them be hunted soundly. At this hour   264
Lies at my mercy all mine enemies.
Shortly shall all my labors end, and thou
Shalt have the air at freedom. For a little   267
Follow, and do me service.   Exeunt.

❖

5.1

Enter Prospero in his magic robes, [with his staff,] and Ariel.

206 **hoodwink this mischance** cover up (literally, blindfold) this mistake. 213–14 **o'er ears** over my ears in the filthy horse pond (line 182) 222 **King . . . peer** (Alludes to the old ballad beginning, "King Stephen was a worthy peer.") 227 **frippery** second-hand-clothing shop. (Trinculo knows that what they have just found is much finer.) 231 **The dropsy drown** (An oath. *Dropsy* is a disease characterized by the accumulation of fluid in the connective tissue of the body.) 232 **luggage** cumbersome trash. 234 **crown** head 236 **Mistress line** (Addressed to the linden or lime tree upon which, at line 193, Ariel hung the *glistering apparel*.) 237 **jerkin** jacket made of leather 238 **under the line** under the lime tree. (With punning sense of being south of the equinoctial line or equator; sailors on long voyages to the southern regions were popularly supposed to lose their hair from scurvy or other diseases. Stephano also quibbles bawdily on losing hair through syphilis, and puns in *Mistress* and *jerkin*.) **like** likely 239 **bald** (1) hairless, napless (2) meager

240 **Do, do!** i.e., Bravo! (Said in response to the jesting or to the taking of the jerkin, or both.) **steal . . . level** i.e., steal by means of plumb line and carpenter's level, methodically. (With pun on *line*, "lime tree," line 238, and *steal*, pronounced like *stale*, i.e., prostitute, continuing Stephano's bawdy quibble.) **an't like** if it please 245 **pass of pate** sally of wit. (The metaphor is from fencing.) 247 **lime** birdlime, sticky substance (to give Caliban sticky fingers) 250 **barnacles** barnacle geese, formerly supposed to be hatched from barnacles attached to trees or to rotting timber; here, evidently used, like *apes*, as types of simpletons 251 **villainous** vilely 252 **lay to** start using 253 **this** i.e., the *glistering apparel*. **hogshead** large cask 254 **Go to** (An expression of exhortation or remonstrance.) 261 **dry convulsions** racking cramps 262 **agèd** characteristic of old age 263 **pard** panther or leopard. **cat o' mountain** wildcat. 264 **soundly** severely. 267 **little** little while longer
5.1. Location: Before Prospero's cell.

PROSPERO
Now does my project gather to a head.
My charms crack not, my spirits obey, and Time   2
Goes upright with his carriage. How's the day?   3
ARIEL
On the sixth hour, at which time, my lord,   4
You said our work should cease.
PROSPERO   I did say so,
When first I raised the tempest. Say, my spirit,
How fares the King and 's followers?
ARIEL   Confined together
In the same fashion as you gave in charge,
Just as you left them; all prisoners, sir,
In the line grove which weather-fends your cell.   10
They cannot budge till your release. The King,   11
His brother, and yours abide all three distracted,   12
And the remainder mourning over them,
Brim full of sorrow and dismay; but chiefly
Him that you termed, sir, the good old lord,
    Gonzalo.
His tears runs down his beard like winter's drops
From eaves of reeds. Your charm so strongly works
    'em   17
That if you now beheld them your affections   18
Would become tender.
PROSPERO   Dost thou think so, spirit?
ARIEL
Mine would, sir, were I human.
PROSPERO   And mine shall.
Hast thou, which art but air, a touch, a feeling   21
Of their afflictions, and shall not myself,
One of their kind, that relish all as sharply   23
Passion as they, be kindlier moved than thou art?   24
Though with their high wrongs I am struck to th'
    quick,
Yet with my nobler reason 'gainst my fury
Do I take part. The rarer action is   27
In virtue than in vengeance. They being penitent,
The sole drift of my purpose doth extend
Not a frown further. Go release them, Ariel.
My charms I'll break, their senses I'll restore,
And they shall be themselves.
ARIEL   I'll fetch them, sir.
                                        Exit.
[Prospero traces a charmed circle with his staff.]
PROSPERO
Ye elves of hills, brooks, standing lakes, and groves,   33
And ye that on the sands with printless foot
Do chase the ebbing Neptune, and do fly him

When he comes back; you demi-puppets that   36
By moonshine do the green sour ringlets make,   37
Whereof the ewe not bites; and you whose pastime
Is to make midnight mushrooms, that rejoice   39
To hear the solemn curfew; by whose aid,   40
Weak masters though ye be, I have bedimmed   41
The noontide sun, called forth the mutinous winds,
And twixt the green sea and the azured vault   43
Set roaring war; to the dread rattling thunder   44
Have I given fire, and rifted Jove's stout oak   45
With his own bolt; the strong-based promontory   46
Have I made shake, and by the spurs plucked up   47
The pine and cedar; graves at my command
Have waked their sleepers, oped, and let 'em forth
By my so potent art. But this rough magic   50
I here abjure, and when I have required   51
Some heavenly music—which even now I do—
To work mine end upon their senses that   53
This airy charm is for, I'll break my staff,
Bury it certain fathoms in the earth,
And deeper than did ever plummet sound
I'll drown my book.   Solemn music.

    Here enters Ariel before; then Alonso, with a
    frantic gesture, attended by Gonzalo; Sebastian and
    Antonio in like manner, attended by Adrian and
    Francisco. They all enter the circle which Prospero
    had made, and there stand charmed; which
    Prospero observing, speaks:

[*To Alonso*] A solemn air, and the best comforter   58
To an unsettled fancy, cure thy brains,   59
Now useless, boiled within thy skull! [*To Sebastian*
    and Antonio] There stand,   60
For you are spell-stopped.—
Holy Gonzalo, honorable man,
Mine eyes, e'en sociable to the show of thine,   63
Fall fellowly drops. [*Aside*] The charm dissolves
    apace,   64
And as the morning steals upon the night,
Melting the darkness, so their rising senses
Begin to chase the ignorant fumes that mantle   67
Their clearer reason.—O good Gonzalo,   68
My true preserver, and a loyal sir
To him thou follow'st! I will pay thy graces   70
Home both in word and deed.—Most cruelly   71
Didst thou, Alonso, use me and my daughter.
Thy brother was a furtherer in the act.—   73

---

2 **crack** collapse, fail. (The metaphor is probably alchemical, as in *project* and *gather to a head*, line 1.)   3 **his carriage** its burden. (Time is no longer heavily burdened and so can go *upright*, "standing straight and unimpeded.")   4 **On** Approaching   10 **line grove** grove of lime trees.   **weather-fends** protects from the weather   11 **your release** you release them.   12 **distracted** out of their wits   17 **eaves of reeds** thatched roofs.   18 **affections** disposition, feelings   21 **touch** sense, apprehension   23–4 **that . . . they** I who experience human passions as acutely as they   24 **kindlier** (1) more sympathetically (2) more naturally, humanly   27 **rarer** nobler   33 **Ye . . . groves** This passage, down through line 50, is an embellished paraphrase of Golding's translation of Ovid's *Metamorphoses*, 7.197–219.)

36 **demi-puppets** puppets of half size, i.e., elves and fairies   37 **green sour ringlets** fairy rings, circles in grass (actually produced by mushrooms)   39 **midnight mushrooms** mushrooms appearing overnight   40 **curfew** evening bell, usually rung at nine o'clock, ushering in the time when spirits are abroad   41 **Weak masters** i.e., subordinate spirits, as in 4.1.35   43 **the azured vault** i.e., the sky   44–5 **to . . . fire** I have discharged the dread rattling thunderbolt   45 **rifted** riven, split.   **oak** a tree that was sacred to Jove   46 **bolt** thunderbolt   47 **spurs** roots   50 **rough** violent   51 **required** demanded   53 **their senses that** the senses of those whom   58 **air** song.   **and** i.e., which is   59 **fancy** imagination   60 **boiled** i.e., extremely agitated   63 **sociable** sympathetic. **show** appearance   64 **Fall** let fall   67 **ignorant fumes** fumes that render them incapable of comprehension.   **mantle** envelop   68 **clearer** growing clearer   70 **pay thy graces** requite your favors and virtues   71 **Home** fully   73 **furtherer** accomplice

Thou art pinched for't now, Sebastian. [*To Antonio*]
  Flesh and blood,   74
You, brother mine, that entertained ambition,
Expelled remorse and nature, whom, with Sebastian, 76
Whose inward pinches therefore are most strong,
Would here have killed your king, I do forgive thee,
Unnatural though thou art.—Their understanding
Begins to swell, and the approaching tide
Will shortly fill the reasonable shore   81
That now lies foul and muddy. Not one of them
That yet looks on me, or would know me.—Ariel,
Fetch me the hat and rapier in my cell.
        [*Ariel goes to the cell and returns immediately.*]
I will discase me and myself present   85
As I was sometime Milan. Quickly, spirit!   86
Thou shalt ere long be free.
          Ariel sings and helps to attire him.

ARIEL
    Where the bee sucks, there suck I.
    In a cowslip's bell I lie;
    There I couch when owls do cry.   90
    On the bat's back I do fly
    After summer merrily.   92
  Merrily, merrily shall I live now
  Under the blossom that hangs on the bough.

PROSPERO
Why, that's my dainty Ariel! I shall miss thee,
But yet thou shalt have freedom. So, so, so.   96
To the King's ship, invisible as thou art!
There shalt thou find the mariners asleep
Under the hatches. The Master and the Boatswain
Being awake, enforce them to this place,
And presently, I prithee.   101

ARIEL
I drink the air before me, and return
Or ere your pulse twice beat.   *Exit.* 103

GONZALO
All torment, trouble, wonder, and amazement
Inhabits here. Some heavenly power guide us
Out of this fearful country!

PROSPERO   Behold, sir King, 106
The wrongèd Duke of Milan, Prospero.
For more assurance that a living prince
Does now speak to thee, I embrace thy body;
And to thee and thy company I bid
A hearty welcome.   [*Embracing him.*]

ALONSO   Whe'er thou be'st he or no,
Or some enchanted trifle to abuse me, 112
As late I have been, I not know. Thy pulse 113
Beats as of flesh and blood; and, since I saw thee,
Th' affliction of my mind amends, with which

I fear a madness held me. This must crave— 116
An if this be at all—a most strange story. 117
Thy dukedom I resign, and do entreat 118
Thou pardon me my wrongs. But how should
  Prospero 119
Be living, and be here?

PROSPERO [*to Gonzalo*]   First, noble friend,
Let me embrace thine age, whose honor cannot 121
Be measured or confined.   [*Embracing him.*]

GONZALO   Whether this be
Or be not, I'll not swear.

PROSPERO   You do yet taste
Some subtleties o'th'isle, that will not let you 124
Believe things certain. Welcome, my friends all!
[*Aside to Sebastian and Antonio*] But you, my brace of
  lords, were I so minded, 126
I here could pluck His Highness' frown upon you
And justify you traitors. At this time 128
I will tell no tales.

SEBASTIAN   The devil speaks in him.

PROSPERO   No.
[*To Antonio*] For you, most wicked sir, whom to call
  brother
Would even infect my mouth, I do forgive
Thy rankest fault—all of them; and require
My dukedom of thee, which perforce I know
Thou must restore.

ALONSO   If thou be'st Prospero,
Give us particulars of thy preservation,
How thou hast met us here, whom three hours since 136
Were wrecked upon this shore; where I have lost—
How sharp the point of this remembrance is!—
My dear son Ferdinand.

PROSPERO   I am woe for't, sir. 139

ALONSO
Irreparable is the loss, and Patience
Says it is past her cure.

PROSPERO   I rather think
You have not sought her help, of whose soft grace
For the like loss I have her sovereign aid 143
And rest myself content.

ALONSO   You the like loss?

PROSPERO
As great to me as late, and supportable 145
To make the dear loss, have I means much weaker 146
Than you may call to comfort you; for I 147
Have lost my daughter.

ALONSO   A daughter?
O heavens, that they were living both in Naples,

---

74 pinched punished, afflicted **76 remorse and nature** pity and natural feeling. **whom** you who **81 reasonable shore** shores of reason, i.e., minds. (Their reason returns, like the incoming tide.)
85 discase disrobe **86 As . . . Milan** in my former appearance as Duke of Milan. **90 couch** lie **92 After summer** following summer as it moves to various parts of the world **96 So, so, so** (Expresses approval of Ariel's help as valet.) **101 presently** immediately
103 Or ere before **106 fearful** frightening **112 trifle** trick of magic.
abuse deceive **113 late** lately

116 crave require **117 An . . . all** if this is actually happening. **story** i.e., explanation. **118 Thy . . . resign** (Alonso made arrangement with Antonio at the time of Prospero's banishment for Milan to pay tribute to Naples; see 1.2.113–27.) **119 wrongs** wrongdoings.
121 thine age your venerable self **124 subtleties** illusions, magical powers. (Playing on the idea of "pastries, concoctions.") **126 brace** pair **128 justify you** prove you to be **136 whom** we who **139 woe** sorry **143 sovereign** efficacious **145 late** recent **145–7 and supportable . . . you** and I have much weaker means to make my loss supportable than you can call upon to comfort you

The king and queen there! That they were, I wish 151
Myself were mudded in that oozy bed 152
Where my son lies. When did you lose your daughter? 153

PROSPERO
In this last tempest. I perceive these lords
At this encounter do so much admire 155
That they devour their reason and scarce think 156
Their eyes do offices of truth, their words 157
Are natural breath. But, howsoever you have 158
Been jostled from your senses, know for certain
That I am Prospero and that very duke
Which was thrust forth of Milan, who most strangely 161
Upon this shore, where you were wrecked, was
    landed
To be the lord on't. No more yet of this,
For 'tis a chronicle of day by day, 164
Not a relation for a breakfast nor
Befitting this first meeting. Welcome, sir.
This cell's my court. Here have I few attendants,
And subjects none abroad. Pray you, look in. 168
My dukedom since you have given me again,
I will requite you with as good a thing, 170
At least bring forth a wonder to content ye
As much as me my dukedom. 172

Here Prospero discovers Ferdinand and Miranda,
playing at chess.

MIRANDA   Sweet lord, you play me false. 173
FERDINAND   No, my dearest love,
I would not for the world.
MIRANDA
Yes, for a score of kingdoms you should wrangle, 176
And I would call it fair play.
ALONSO   If this prove 177
A vision of the island, one dear son 178
Shall I twice lose.
SEBASTIAN   A most high miracle!
FERDINAND [*approaching his father*]
Though the seas threaten, they are merciful;
I have cursed them without cause.   [*He kneels.*]
ALONSO   Now all the blessings
Of a glad father compass thee about! 182
Arise, and say how thou cam'st here.
                    [*Ferdinand rises.*]
MIRANDA   Oh, wonder!
How many goodly creatures are there here!
How beauteous mankind is! Oh, brave new world 185

That has such people in't!
PROSPERO   'Tis new to thee.
ALONSO
What is this maid with whom thou wast at play?
Your eld'st acquaintance cannot be three hours. 188
Is she the goddess that hath severed us,
And brought us thus together?
FERDINAND   Sir, she is mortal;
But by immortal Providence she's mine.
I chose her when I could not ask my father
For his advice, nor thought I had one. She
Is daughter to this famous Duke of Milan,
Of whom so often I have heard renown,
But never saw before; of whom I have
Received a second life; and second father
This lady makes him to me.
ALONSO   I am hers.
But oh, how oddly will it sound that I
Must ask my child forgiveness!
PROSPERO   There, sir, stop.
Let us not burden our remembrances with
A heaviness that's gone.
GONZALO   I have inly wept, 202
Or should have spoke ere this. Look down, you gods,
And on this couple drop a blessèd crown!
For it is you that have chalked forth the way 205
Which brought us hither.
ALONSO   I say amen, Gonzalo!
GONZALO
Was Milan thrust from Milan, that his issue 207
Should become kings of Naples? Oh, rejoice
Beyond a common joy, and set it down
With gold on lasting pillars: In one voyage
Did Claribel her husband find at Tunis,
And Ferdinand, her brother, found a wife
Where he himself was lost; Prospero his dukedom
In a poor isle; and all of us ourselves 214
When no man was his own.
ALONSO [*to Ferdinand and Miranda*]   Give me your hands. 215
Let grief and sorrow still embrace his heart 216
That doth not wish you joy!
GONZALO   Be it so! Amen!

Enter Ariel, with the Master and Boatswain
amazedly following.

Oh, look, sir, look, sir! Here is more of us.
I prophesied, if a gallows were on land,
This fellow could not drown.—Now, blasphemy, 220
That swear'st grace o'erboard, not an oath on shore? 221
Hast thou no mouth by land? What is the news?
BOATSWAIN
The best news is that we have safely found

151–3 That . . . lies I would wish myself buried in that muddy bed where my son's body lies drowned if that would somehow make them alive and reigning in Naples.   155 admire wonder   156 devour their reason i.e., are openmouthed, dumbfounded   156–8 and scarce . . . breath and scarcely can believe their eyes or their own words. 161 of from   164 of day by day requiring days to tell, or covering a long span of time   168 abroad anywhere else.   170 requite repay 172.1 *discovers* i.e., by opening a curtain, presumably rearstage 173 play me false cheat.   176–7 Yes . . . play i.e., Yes, even if we were playing for twenty kingdoms, something less than the whole world, you would still press your advantage against me, and I would lovingly let you do it as though it were fair play.   178 vision illusion 182 compass encompass, embrace   185 brave splendid, gorgeously appareled, handsome

188 eld'st longest   202 heaviness sadness.   inly inwardly 205 chalked . . . way marked as with a piece of chalk the pathway 207 Was Milan Was the Duke of Milan.   issue child   214–15 all . . . own all of us have found ourselves and our sanity when we all had lost our senses.   216 still always.   his that person's   220 blasphemy i.e., blasphemer   221 That swear'st grace o'erboard i.e., you who expel heavenly grace from the ship by your blasphemies.   not an oath aren't you going to swear an oath

Our King and company; the next, our ship—
Which, but three glasses since, we gave out split—   225
Is tight and yare and bravely rigged as when   226
We first put out to sea.

ARIEL [*aside to Prospero*]   Sir, all this service
Have I done since I went.

PROSPERO [*aside to Ariel*]   My tricksy spirit!   228

ALONSO
These are not natural events; they strengthen   229
From strange to stranger. Say, how came you hither?

BOATSWAIN
If I did think, sir, I were well awake,
I'd strive to tell you. We were dead of sleep,   232
And—how we know not—all clapped under hatches,
Where but even now, with strange and several noises   234
Of roaring, shrieking, howling, jingling chains,
And more diversity of sounds, all horrible,
We were awaked; straightway at liberty;
Where we, in all her trim, freshly beheld
Our royal, good, and gallant ship, our Master
Cap'ring to eye her. On a trice, so please you,   240
Even in a dream, were we divided from them   241
And were brought moping hither.

ARIEL [*aside to Prospero*]   Was't well done?   242

PROSPERO [*aside to Ariel*]
Bravely, my diligence. Thou shalt be free.

ALONSO
This is as strange a maze as e'er men trod,
And there is in this business more than nature
Was ever conduct of. Some oracle   246
Must rectify our knowledge.

PROSPERO   Sir, my liege,
Do not infest your mind with beating on   248
The strangeness of this business. At picked leisure,   249
Which shall be shortly, single I'll resolve you,   250
Which to you shall seem probable, of every   251
These happened accidents; till when, be cheerful   252
And think of each thing well. [*Aside to Ariel*] Come
hither, spirit.   253
Set Caliban and his companions free.
Untie the spell.   [*Exit Ariel.*]
[*To Alonso*]   How fares my gracious sir?
There are yet missing of your company
Some few odd lads that you remember not.   257

*Enter Ariel, driving in Caliban, Stephano, and
Trinculo, in their stolen apparel.*

STEPHANO   Every man shift for all the rest, and let no   258
man take care for himself; for all is but fortune. *Corag-*   259

gio, bully monster, *coraggio!*   260

TRINCULO   If these be true spies which I wear in my   261
head, here's a goodly sight.

CALIBAN
O Setebos, these be brave spirits indeed!   263
How fine my master is! I am afraid   264
He will chastise me.

SEBASTIAN   Ha, ha!
What things are these, my lord Antonio?
Will money buy 'em?

ANTONIO   Very like. One of them
Is a plain fish, and no doubt marketable.

PROSPERO
Mark but the badges of these men, my lords,   270
Then say if they be true. This misshapen knave,   271
His mother was a witch, and one so strong
That could control the moon, make flows and ebbs,
And deal in her command without her power.   274
These three have robbed me, and this demidevil—
For he's a bastard one—had plotted with them   276
To take my life. Two of these fellows you
Must know and own. This thing of darkness I   278
Acknowledge mine.

CALIBAN   I shall be pinched to death.

ALONSO
Is not this Stephano, my drunken butler?

SEBASTIAN   He is drunk now. Where had he wine?

ALONSO
And Trinculo is reeling ripe. Where should they   282
Find this grand liquor that hath gilded 'em?   283
[*To Trinculo*] How cam'st thou in this pickle?   284

TRINCULO   I have been in such a pickle since I saw you
last that, I fear me, will never out of my bones. I shall
not fear flyblowing.   287

SEBASTIAN   Why, how now, Stephano?

STEPHANO   Oh, touch me not! I am not Stephano, but a
cramp.

PROSPERO   You'd be king o'the isle, sirrah?   291

STEPHANO   I should have been a sore one, then.   292

ALONSO [*pointing to Caliban*]
This is a strange thing as e'er I looked on.

PROSPERO
He is as disproportioned in his manners
As in his shape.—Go, sirrah, to my cell.
Take with you your companions. As you look
To have my pardon, trim it handsomely.   297

225 **glasses** hourglasses.   **gave out split** reported shipwrecked, gave up for lost   226 **yare** ready.   **bravely** splendidly   228 **tricksy** ingenious, sportive   229 **strengthen** increase   232 **dead of sleep** deep in sleep   234 **several** diverse   240 **Cap'ring to eye** dancing for joy to see.   **On a trice** In an instant   241 **them** i.e., the other crew members   242 **moping** in a daze   246 **conduct** director   248 **infest** harass, disturb.   **beating on** worrying about   249 **picked** chosen, convenient   250 **single** privately.   **resolve** satisfy, explain to   251 **probable** plausible   251–2 **of every These** about every one of these   252 **accidents** occurrences   253 **well** favorably.   257 **odd** unaccounted for   258–9 **Every . . . himself** (Stephano drunkenly inverts the saying "Every man for himself.")

259–60 *Coraggio* . . . **monster** Have courage, gallant monster   261 **true spies** accurate observers (i.e., sharp eyes)   263 **brave** handsome   264 **fine** splendidly attired   270 **badges** emblems worn by servants to indicate whom they serve   271 **say . . . true** say if they are worthy and loyal servants.   274 **And . . . power** and usurp the moon's command (over tides) without her authority. (Sycorax could control the moon and hence the tides.)   276 **bastard** counterfeit   278 **own** acknowledge.   282 **reeling ripe** staggeringly drunk.   283 **gilded 'em** flushed their complexion (from the drink), giving them a ruddy or gilded appearance.   284 **pickle** (1) fix, predicament (2) pickling brine (in this case, horse urine).   287 **flyblowing** i.e., being fouled by fly eggs (from which he is saved by being pickled).   291 **sirrah** (Standard form of address to an inferior, here expressing reprimand.)   292 **sore** (1) tyrannical (2) sorry, inept (3) wracked by pain   297 **trim** prepare, decorate

CALIBAN
   Ay, that I will; and I'll be wise hereafter
   And seek for grace. What a thrice-double ass   299
   Was I to take this drunkard for a god
   And worship this dull fool!
PROSPERO   Go to. Away!
ALONSO
   Hence, and bestow your luggage where you found it.
SEBASTIAN   Or stole it, rather.
             [*Exeunt Caliban, Stephano, and Trinculo.*]
PROSPERO
   Sir, I invite Your Highness and your train
   To my poor cell, where you shall take your rest
   For this one night; which, part of it, I'll waste   306
   With such discourse as, I not doubt, shall make it
   Go quick away: the story of my life,
   And the particular accidents gone by   309
   Since I came to this isle. And in the morn
   I'll bring you to your ship, and so to Naples,
   Where I have hope to see the nuptial
   Of these our dear-belovèd solemnized;
   And thence retire me to my Milan, where
   Every third thought shall be my grave.
ALONSO   I long
   To hear the story of your life, which must
   Take the ear strangely.
PROSPERO   I'll deliver all;   317
   And promise you calm seas, auspicious gales,
   And sail so expeditious that shall catch   319
   Your royal fleet far off. [*Aside to Ariel*] My Ariel, chick, 320

---

299 **grace** pardon, favor.   306 **waste** spend   309 **accidents** occurrences   317 **Take** take effect upon, enchant.   **deliver** declare, relate
319–20 **catch . . . far off** enable you to catch up with the main part of
your royal fleet, now afar off en route to Naples. (See 1.2.235–6.)

   That is thy charge. Then to the elements
   Be free, and fare thou well!
                [*To the others*] Please you, draw near.   322
                     Exeunt omnes [*except Prospero*].

Epilogue   *Spoken by* PROSPERO.

   Now my charms are all o'erthrown,
   And what strength I have 's mine own,
   Which is most faint. Now, 'tis true,
   I must be here confined by you
   Or sent to Naples. Let me not,
   Since I have my dukedom got
   And pardoned the deceiver, dwell
   In this bare island by your spell,
   But release me from my bands   9
   With the help of your good hands.   10
   Gentle breath of yours my sails   11
   Must fill, or else my project fails,
   Which was to please. Now I want   13
   Spirits to enforce, art to enchant,
   And my ending is despair,
   Unless I be relieved by prayer,   16
   Which pierces so that it assaults   17
   Mercy itself, and frees all faults.   18
   As you from crimes would pardoned be,   19
   Let your indulgence set me free.   *Exit.*   20

---

322 **draw near** i.e., enter my cell.
Epilogue.
9 **bands** bonds   10 **hands** i.e., applause (the noise of which could
break a charm).   11 **Gentle breath** Favorable breeze (produced by
hands clapping or favorable comment)   13 **want** lack   16 **prayer** i.e.,
Prospero's petition to the audience   17 **assaults** penetrates the heart
of   18 **frees** obtains forgiveness for   19 **crimes** sins   20 **indulgence**
(1) humoring, lenient approval (2) remission of punishment for sin

The Poems

Sonnets

Sonnets

Shakespeare seems to have cared more about his reputation as a lyric poet than as a dramatist. He contributed to the major nondramatic genres of his day: to amatory Ovidian narrative in *Venus and Adonis,* to the Complaint in *The Rape of Lucrece,* to philosophical poetry in "The Phoenix and Turtle." He cooperated in the publication of his first two important poems, dedicating them to the young Earl of Southampton with a plea to him for sponsorship. To write poetry in this vein was more fashionable than to write plays, which one did mainly for money.

A poet with ambitions of this sort simply had to write a sonnet sequence. Sonneteering was the rage in England in the early and mid 1590s. Based on the sonneteering tradition of Francesco Petrarch, Sir Thomas Wyatt, and others, and gaining new momentum in 1591 with the publication of Sir Philip Sidney's *Astrophel and Stella,* the vogue ended almost as suddenly as it began, in 1596 or 1597. The sonnet sequences of this brief period bear the names of most well-known and minor poets of the day: *Amoretti* by Edmund Spenser (1595), *Delia* by Samuel Daniel (1591 and 1592), *Caelica* by Fulke Greville (not published until 1633), *Idea's Mirror* by Michael Drayton (1594), *Diana* by Henry Constable (1592), *Phyllis* by Thomas Lodge (1593), and the more imitative sequences of Barnabe Barnes, Giles Fletcher, William Percy, Bartholomew Griffin, William Smith, and Robert Tofte.

Shakespeare wrote sonnets during the heyday of the genre, for in 1598 Francis Meres, in his *Palladis Tamia: Wit's Treasury,* praised Shakespeare's "sugared sonnets among his private friends." Even though they were not printed at the time, we know from Meres's remark that they were circulated in manuscript among the cognoscenti and commanded respect. Shakespeare may actually have preferred to delay the publication of his sonnets, not through indifference to their literary worth, but through a desire not to seem too professional. The "courtly makers" of the English Renaissance, those gentlemen whose chivalric accomplishments were supposed to include versifying, looked on the writing of poetry as an avocation designed to amuse one's peers or to court a lady. Publication was not quite genteel, and many such authors affected dismay when their verses were pirated into print. The young wits about London of the 1590s, whether aristocratic or not, sometimes imitated this fashion. Like young John Donne, they sought the favorable verdict of their fellow wits at the Inns of Court (where young men studied law) and professed not to care about wider recognition. Whether Shakespeare was motivated in this way we do not know, but, in any event, his much-sought-after sonnet sequence was not published until 1609, long after the vogue had passed. The publisher, Thomas Thorpe, seems not to have obtained Shakespeare's authorization. Two sonnets, numbers 138 and 144, had been pirated ten years earlier by William Jaggard in *The Passionate Pilgrim,* 1599, a little anthology with some poems by Shakespeare and some wrongly attributed to him. The sonnets were not reprinted until 1640, either because the sonnet vogue had passed or because Thorpe's edition had been suppressed.

The unexplained circumstances of publication have given rise to a host of vexing and apparently unanswerable questions. Probably no puzzle in all English literature has provoked so much speculation and produced so little agreement. To whom are the sonnets addressed? Do they tell a consistent story, and, if so, do they tell us anything about Shakespeare's life? The basic difficulty is that we cannot be sure that the order in which Thorpe published the sonnets represents Shakespeare's intention, nor can we assume that Thorpe spoke for Shakespeare when he dedicated the sonnets to "Mr. W. H." As they stand, most of the first 126 sonnets appear to be addressed in warm friendship to a handsome young aristocrat, whereas sonnets 127–52 mostly speak of the poet's dark-haired mistress. Yet the last two sonnets, 153–4, seem unrelated to anything previous and cast some doubt on the reliability of the ordering. Within each large grouping of the sonnets, moreover, we find evident inconsistencies: jealousies disappear and suddenly reappear, the poet bewails his absolute rejection by the friend and then speaks a few sonnets later of harmonious affection as though nothing had happened, and so on. Some sonnets are closely linked to their predecessors; some are apparently disconnected (although even here we must allow for the real possibility that Shakespeare intends juxtaposition and contrast). We cannot be sure if the friend of sonnets 1–126 is really one person or several. We can only speculate that the unhappy love triangle described in sonnets 40–2, in which the friend has usurped the poet's mistress, can be identified with the love triangle of the "Dark Lady" sonnets, 127–52. Most readers sense a narrative continuity of the whole yet find blocks of sonnets stubbornly out of place. The temptation to rearrange the order has proved irresistible, but no alternative order has ever won acceptance. The consensus is that Thorpe's order is at times suspect but may have more rationale than at first appears. It is, in any case, the only authoritative order we have.

No less frustrating is Thorpe's dedication "To the Only Begetter of These Ensuing Sonnets, Mr. W. H." Given the late and unauthorized publication, we cannot assume that Thorpe speaks for Shakespeare. Quite possibly he is only thanking the person who obtained the sonnets for him, making publication possible. Mundanely enough, Mr. W. H. could be William Hall, an associate of Thorpe's in the publishing business. Yet Elizabethan usage affords few instances of "begetter" in this sense of "obtainer." Donald Foster has offered new and persuasive arguments for the idea that "Mr. W. H." is only a typographical error of a common sort and that Thorpe meant to say "Mr. W. S.," Master William Shakespeare. In this case, "begetter" would mean simply "creator." This solution has a wonderful neatness about it, but other readers have wondered if it answers the seeming contradiction when Thorpe speaks of "Mr. W. H." and "our ever-living poet" in the dedication as though they are two people. Thorpe offers to Mr. W. H. "that eternity promised by our ever-living poet," as though Mr. W. H. were the very subject of those sonnets whom Shakespeare vows to immortalize.

This interpretation of "begetter" as "inspirer" has prompted many enthusiasts to search for a Mr. W. H. in Shakespeare's life, a nobleman who befriended him. The chief candidates are two. First is the young Earl of Southampton, to whom Shakespeare had dedicated *Venus and Adonis* and *The Rape of Lucrece.* The dedication to the second of these poems bespeaks a warmth and gratitude that had been less evident in the first. The Earl's name, Henry Wriothesley, yields initials that are the reverse of W. H. If this correspondence seems unconvincing, W. H. could stand for Sir William Harvey, third husband of Mary, Lady Southampton, the young Earl's

mother. Some researchers would have us believe that Shakespeare wrote the sonnets for Lady Southampton, especially those urging a young man (her son) to marry and procreate. This entire case is speculative, however, and we have no evidence that Shakespeare had any dealings with Southampton after *The Rape of Lucrece.* The plain ascription "Mr. W. H." seems an oddly uncivil way for Thorpe to have addressed an earl. If meant for Southampton, the sonnets must have been written fairly early in the 1590s, for they give no hint of Southampton's later career: his courtship of Elizabeth Vernon, her pregnancy and their secret marriage in 1598, and his later involvement in Essex's Irish campaign and abortive uprising against Queen Elizabeth. Those literary sleuths who stress similarities to the Southampton relationship are too willing to overlook dissimilarities.

The next chief candidate for Mr. W. H. is William Herbert, third Earl of Pembroke, to whom, along with his brother, Shakespeare's colleagues dedicated the First Folio of 1623. In 1595, Pembroke's parents were attempting to arrange his marriage with Lady Elizabeth Carey, granddaughter of the first Lord Hunsdon, who was Lord Chamberlain and patron of Shakespeare's company. In 1597, another alliance was attempted with Bridget Vere, granddaughter of Lord Burghley. In both negotiations, young Pembroke objected to the girl in question. This hypothesis requires, however, an uncomfortably late date for the sonnets and postulates a gap in age between Shakespeare and Pembroke that would have afforded little opportunity for genuine friendship. Pembroke was only fifteen in 1595; Shakespeare was thirty-one. Besides, no evidence supports the claim other than historical coincidence. The common initials W. H. can be made to produce other candidates as well, such as the Lincolnshire lawyer named William Hatcliffe proposed (to no one's satisfaction) by Leslie Hotson. Hotson wants to date most of the sonnets before 1589, since Hatcliffe came to London in 1587–1588. When such speculations are constructed on the single enigmatic testimonial of the dedication by Thomas Thorpe, who may well have had no connection with Shakespeare, we are left with a case that would not be worth describing had it not captured the imagination of so many researchers.

Biographical identifications have also been proposed for the various personages in the sonnet sequence, predictably with no better success. The rival poet, with "the proud full sail of his great verse" (sonnet 86), has been linked to Christopher Marlowe (who died in 1593), George Chapman, and others. The sequence gives us little to go on, other than that the rival poet possesses a considerable enough talent to intimidate the author of the sonnets and to ingratiate himself with the author's aristocratic friend. No biographical circumstances resembling this rivalry have come to light. Various candidates have also been found for the "Dark Lady." One is Mary

Fitton, a lady-in-waiting at court who bore a child by Pembroke in 1601. Again, we have no evidence that Shakespeare knew her, nor is he likely to have carried on an affair with one of such high rank. A. L. Rowse has proposed Emilia Lanier, wife of Alfonso Lanier and daughter of a court musician named Bassano, a woman of suitably dark complexion perhaps but whose presumed connection with Shakespeare rests only on the reported rumor that she was a mistress of Lord Hunsdon. We are left finally without knowing who any of these people were, or whether indeed Shakespeare was attempting to be biographical at all.

The same irresolution afflicts the dating of the sonnets. Do they give hints of a personal chronicle extending over some years, following Thorpe's arrangement of the sonnets or some alternative order? Sonnet 104 speaks of three years having elapsed since the poet met his friend. Are there other signposts that relate to contemporary events? A line in sonnet 107 ("The mortal moon hath her eclipse endured") is usually linked to the death of Queen Elizabeth (known as Diana or Cynthia) in 1603, though Leslie Hotson prefers to see in it an allusion to the Spanish Armada, shaped for sea battle in a moonlike crescent when it met defeat in 1588. The newly built pyramids in sonnet 123 remind Hotson of the obelisks built by Pope Sixtus V in Rome, 1586–1589; other researchers have discovered pyramids erected on London's streets in 1603 to celebrate the coronation of James I. As these illustrations suggest, speculative dating can be used to support a hypothesis of early or late composition. The wary consensus of most scholars is that the sonnets were written over a number of years; a large number, certainly, before 1598, but some perhaps later and even up to the date of publication in 1609.

However fruitless this quest for nonexistent certainties, it does at least direct us to a meaningful critical question: should we expect sonnets of this "personal" nature to be at least partly autobiographical? Shakespeare's sonnets have struck many readers as cries from the heart, voicing at times fears of rejection, self-hatred, and humiliation, and at other times a serene gratitude for reciprocated affection. This power of expression may, however, be a tribute to Shakespeare's dramatic gift rather than evidence of personal involvement. Earlier sonnet sequences, both Elizabethan and pre-Elizabethan, had established a variety of artistic conventions that tended to displace biography. Petrarch's famous *Rime,* or sonnets, later collected in his *Canzoniere,* though addressed to Laura in two sequences (during her life and after her death), idealized her into the unapproachable lady worshiped by the self-abasing and miserable lover. Petrarch's imitators—Serafino Aquilano, Pietro Bembo, Ludovico Ariosto, and Torquato Tasso among the Italians, Clement Marot, Joachim du Bellay, Pierre de Ronsard, and Philippe Desportes among the French Pléiade—reworked these

conventions in countless variations. In England, the fashion was taken up by Sir Thomas Wyatt, the Earl of Surrey, George Gascoigne, Thomas Watson, and others. Spenser's *Amoretti* and Sidney's *Astrophel and Stella,* though inspired at least in part by real women in the poets' lives, are also deeply concerned with theories of writing poetry. Rejection of the stereotyped attitudes and relationships that had come to dominate the typical Petrarchan sonnet sequence is evidence not of biographical literalism in art but of a new insistence on lifelike emotion in art; as Sidney's muse urges him, "look in thy heart and write." Thus, both the Petrarchan and the anti-Petrarchan schools avoid biographical writing for its own sake. This is essentially true of all Elizabethan sonneteering, from Drayton's serious pursuit of platonic abstraction in his *Idea's Mirror* to the facile chorusing of lesser sonnet writers about Diana, Phyllis, Zepheria, or Fidessa.

The "story" connecting the individual poems of an Elizabethan sonnet sequence is never very important or consistent, even when we can be sure of the order in which the sonnets were written. Dante had used prose links in his *La Vita Nuova* (c. 1282) to stress narrative continuity, and so had Petrarch, but this sturdy framework had been abandoned by the late sixteenth century. Rather than telling a chronological story, the typical Elizabethan sonnet sequence offers a thematically connected series of lyrical meditations, chiefly on love but also on poetic theory, the adversities of fortune, death, or what have you. The narrative events mentioned from time to time are not the substance of the sequence but the occasion for meditative reflection. Attitudes need not be consistent throughout, and the characters need not be consistently motivated like dramatis personae in a play.

Shakespeare's sonnet sequence retains these conventions of Elizabethan sonneteering and employs many archetypal situations and themes that had been explored by his predecessors and contemporaries. His emphasis on friendship seems new, for no other sequence addressed a majority of its sonnets to a friend rather than to a mistress, but even here the anti-Petrarchan quest for spontaneity and candor is in the best Elizabethan tradition of Sidney and Spenser. Besides, the exaltation of friendship over love was itself a widespread Neoplatonic commonplace recently popularized in the writings of John Lyly. Shakespeare's sequence makes use of the structural design found in contemporary models. Even though we cannot reconstruct a rigorously consistent chronological narrative from the sonnets, we can discern overall patterns out of which the poet's emotional crises arise and upon which he constructs his meditative lyrics. Certain groupings, such as the sonnets addressed to the "Dark Lady," 127–52, in which individually they comment on one another through reinforcement or antithetical design and are thus enhanced by their context, achieve a plausible cohesion; a case can be made, in other words, for the order of the poems as Thorpe printed them. Even the last two sonnets, 153 and 154, have their defenders (see Michael J. B. Allen's essay in *Shakespeare Survey*, 1978). Juxtaposition is a favorite technique in Shakespeare's plays, and we must remember that he alone among the major Elizabethan sonneteers wrote for the stage.

Taking note of such considerations, we can account for most of the situations portrayed in Shakespeare's sonnets by postulating four figures: the poet-speaker himself, his friend, his mistress, and a rival poet. The order of events in this tangled relationship is not what the poet wishes to describe; instead, he touches upon this situation from time to time as he explores his own reaction to love in its various aspects.

The poet's relationship to his friend is a vulnerable one. This friend to whom he writes is aristocratic, handsome, and younger than he is. The poet is beholden to this friend as a sponsor and must consider himself as subservient, no matter how deep their mutual affection. Even at its happiest, their relationship is hierarchical. The poet abases himself in order to extol his friend's beauty and virtues (sonnets 52–4, 105–6). He confesses that his love would be idolatry, except that the friend's goodness excels all poetic hyperbole. As the older of the two, the poet sententiously urges his young friend to marry and eternize his beauty through the engendering of children (sonnets 1–17). Such a course, he argues, is the surest way to conquer devouring Time, the enemy of all earthly beauty and love. Yet elsewhere the poet exalts his own art as the surest defense against Time (sonnets 55, 60, 63–5, etc.). These conclusions are nominally contradictory, offering procreation in one instance and poetry in another as the best hope for immortality, but thematically the two are obviously related. In even the happiest of the sonnets, such as those giving thanks for "the marriage of true minds" (116, 123), the consciousness of devouring Time is inescapable. If love and celebratory poetry can sometimes triumph over Time, the victory is all the more precious because it is achieved in the face of such odds.

Love and perfect friendship are a refuge for the poet faced with hostile fortune and an indifferent world. He is too often "in disgrace with fortune and men's eyes" (sonnet 29), oppressed by his own failings, saddened by the facile success of opportunists (sonnets 66–8), ashamed of having sold himself cheap in his own profession (sonnets 110–11). If taken biographically, this could mean that Shakespeare was not happy about his career as actor and playwright, but the motif makes complete sense in the sonnet sequence without resort to biography. A biographical reading also raises the question of homosexual attraction, as urged by Joseph Pequigney in his *Such Is My Love* (University of Chicago Press, 1985). The bawdy reference in sonnet 20.12 to the friend's possession of "one thing to my purpose nothing" would seem to militate against the idea of a consummated homosexual relation-

ship, while conversely many sonnets (such as 138) do point to the poet's consummation with his mistress. Still, the bond between poet and friend is extraordinarily strong, and certainly there is a danger that traditional scholarship has minimized the erotic bond between the poet and his friend out of a distaste for the idea. Occasional absences torture the poet with the physical separation, even though he realizes that pure love of the spirit ought not to be hampered by distance or time (sonnets 43–51). The absence is especially painful when the poet must confess his own disloyalty (sonnets 117–18). The chronology of these absences cannot be worked out satisfactorily, but the haunting theme of separation is incessant and overwhelming. By extension, it includes the fear of separation through death (sonnets 71–3, 126). The concern with absence is closely related to the poet's obsession with devouring Time.

All the poet's misfortunes would be bearable if love were constant, but his dependency on the aristocratic friend leaves him at the mercy of that friend's changeable moods. The poet must not complain when his wellborn friend entertains a rival poet (sonnets 78–86) or forms other emotional attachments, even with the poet's own mistress (sonnets 40–2). These disloyalties evoke outbursts of jealousy. The poet vacillates between forgiveness and recrimination. Sometimes even his forgiveness is self-loathing, in which the poet confesses he would take back the friend on any terms (sonnets 93–5). At times the poet grovels, conceding that he deserves no better treatment (sonnets 57–8), but at other times his stored-up resentment bursts forth (sonnets 93–5). The poet's fears, though presented in no clear chronological order, run the gamut from a fatalistic sense that rejection will come one day (sonnet 49) to an abject and bitter final farewell (sonnet 87). Sometimes he is tormented by jealousy (sonnet 61) and sometimes by self-hate (sonnets 88–9).

The sonnets addressed to the poet's mistress, the "Dark Lady," similarly convey fear, self-abasement, and a panicky awareness of loss of self-control. In rare moments of happiness, the poet praises her dark features as proof of her being a real woman, not a Petrarchan goddess (sonnet 130). Too often, however, her lack of ideal beauty reminds the poet of his irrational enchantment (sonnets 148–50). She is tyrannous, disdainful, spiteful, disloyal, a "female evil" (sonnet 144) who has tempted away from the poet his better self, his friend. The poet is distressed not so much by her perfidy as by his own self-betrayal; he sees bitterly that he offends his nobler reason by his attachment to the rebellious flesh. He worships what others abhor and perjures himself by swearing to what he knows to be false (sonnets 150–2). His only hope for escape is to punish his flesh and renounce the vanity of all worldly striving (sonnet 146), but this solution evades him as he plunges helplessly back into the perverse enslavement of a sickened appetite.

This sketch of only some themes of the sequence may suggest the range and yet the interconnection of Shakespeare's meditations on love, friendship, and poetry. Patterns are visible, even if the exact chronology (never important in the Elizabethan sonnet sequence) cannot be determined. The pattern suggests a pivotal role for the sonnets in Shakespeare's development, as Richard Wheeler has urged in his *Shakespeare's Development* (University of California Press, 1981): the early sonnets about love and marriage pursue relationships central to the comedies, whereas subsequent sonnets move with increasing intensity toward the portrayal of promiscuity and degradation in erotic love and toward new assaults upon the binding power of friendship in such a way as to anticipate the darker vision of the tragedies. The playful and unthreatening heroine of the comedies gives way to a dark lady who inspires in the poet a compulsive and humiliating self-hatred; mutuality in friendship finds itself threatened by a one-sided relationship in which the abasement of the poet is answered by the indifference and infidelity of the friend. It as though in the sonnets Shakespeare opened the Pandora's box of hazardous erotic entanglements he was to dramatize in his late plays.

Shakespeare's concern with patterning is equally evident in matters of versification and imagery. The sonnets are written throughout in the "Shakespearean" or English form, *abab cdcd efef gg.* (Sonnet 126, written entirely in couplets, is an exception, perhaps because it was intended as the envoi to the series addressed to the poet's friend.) This familiar sonnet form, introduced by Wyatt and developed by Sidney, differs markedly from the octave-sestet division of the Petrarchan, or Italian, sonnet. The English form of three quatrains and a concluding couplet lends itself to a step-by-step development of idea and image, culminating in an epigrammatic two-line conclusion that may summarize the thought of the preceding twelve lines or give a sententious interpretation of the images developed up to this point. Sonnet 7 pursues the image of the sun at morning, noon, and evening through three quatrains, one for each phase of the day, and then in the couplet "applies" the image to the friend's unwillingness to beget children. Sonnet 29 moves from resentment of misfortune to a rejoicing in the friend's love and rhetorically mirrors this sudden elevation of mood in the image of the lark "at break of day arising / From sullen earth." Shakespeare's rhetorical and imagistic devices exploit the sonnet structure he inherited and perfected, and remind us again of the strong element of convention and artifice in these supremely "personal" sonnets. The recurring images—the canker on the rose, the pleading of a case at law, the seasonal rhythms of summer and winter, the alternations of day and night, the harmonies and dissonances of music—also testify to the artistic unity of the whole and to the artist's extraordinary discipline in evoking a sense of helpless loss of self-control.

Sonnets

To the Only Begetter of These Ensuing Sonnets

Mr. W. H.

All Happiness and That Eternity Promised
   by Our Ever-living Poet
Wisheth the Well-wishing Adventurer in
   Setting Forth

                                T. T.

1

From fairest creatures we desire increase,
That thereby beauty's rose might never die,
But as the riper should by time decease,
His tender heir might bear his memory;   4
But thou, contracted to thine own bright eyes,
Feed'st thy light's flame with self-substantial fuel,
Making a famine where abundance lies,
Thyself thy foe, to thy sweet self too cruel.   8
Thou that art now the world's fresh ornament
And only herald to the gaudy spring,
Within thine own bud buriest thy content,
And, tender churl, mak'st waste in niggarding.   12
    Pity the world, or else this glutton be:
    To eat the world's due, by the grave and thee.

2

When forty winters shall besiege thy brow
And dig deep trenches in thy beauty's field,

1.1 **increase** procreation   3 **as** just as, while   4 **His** its, the ripening creation (including the young man). **bear his memory** i.e., immortalize it by bearing its features   5 **contracted** (1) engaged, espoused (2) shrunk   6 **self-substantial** of your own substance   10 **only herald to** principal or unique messenger of   11 **thy content** (1) that which is contained in you; potential fatherhood (2) your contentment   12 **mak'st . . . niggarding** squander your substance by being miserly. (An oxymoron, like *tender churl*, "youthful old miser.")   14 **the world's due** i.e., the offspring you owe to posterity. **by . . . thee** (consumed) by death and by your willfully remaining childless.
2.2 **trenches** i.e., wrinkles. **field** (1) meadow (2) battlefield (3) heraldic background

Thy youth's proud livery, so gazed on now,
Will be a tattered weed, of small worth held.   4
Then being asked where all thy beauty lies,
Where all the treasure of thy lusty days,
To say within thine own deep-sunken eyes
Were an all-eating shame and thriftless praise.   8
How much more praise deserved thy beauty's use
If thou couldst answer, "This fair child of mine
Shall sum my count and make my old excuse,"
Proving his beauty by succession thine.   12
    This were to be new made when thou art old,
    And see thy blood warm when thou feel'st it cold.

3

Look in thy glass, and tell the face thou viewest
Now is the time that face should form another,
Whose fresh repair if now thou not renewest
Thou dost beguile the world, unbless some mother.   4
For where is she so fair whose uneared womb
Disdains the tillage of thy husbandry?
Or who is he so fond will be the tomb
Of his self-love, to stop posterity?   8
Thou art thy mother's glass, and she in thee
Calls back the lovely April of her prime;
So thou through windows of thine age shalt see,
Despite of wrinkles, this thy golden time.   12
    But if thou live remembered not to be,
    Die single, and thine image dies with thee.

3 **proud livery** handsome garments   4 **weed** garment. (With a play on a *weed* growing in *beauty's field*, line 2.)   6 **lusty** (1) vigorous (2) lustful   8 **Were . . . praise** would be a shameful admission of gluttony and praise of idle extravagance.   9 **deserved . . . use** would the proper investment and employment of your beauty deserve   11 **Shall . . . excuse** will balance my account and make amends in my old age   12 **thine** derived from you.   13 **were** would be
3.1 **glass** mirror   3 **fresh repair** youthful condition   4 **beguile** cheat. **unbless some mother** withhold the happiness of childbearing from some woman.   5 **uneared** untilled, uncultivated   6 **husbandry** cultivation. (With obvious suggestion of "playing the husband.")   7 **fond** foolish, (self-)loving. **will be** i.e., that he is willing to be   9 **thy mother's glass** the image of your mother   11–12 **So . . . time** in just the same way, you, looking through eyes dimmed by advancing years, and despite your own wrinkles of age, will see in your child an image of your own happy youth.   13 **remembered not to be** in such a way as not to be remembered, without children

4

Unthrifty loveliness, why dost thou spend
Upon thyself thy beauty's legacy?
Nature's bequest gives nothing, but doth lend,
And being frank she lends to those are free.   4
Then, beauteous niggard, why dost thou abuse
The bounteous largess given thee to give?
Profitless usurer, why dost thou use
So great a sum of sums, yet canst not live?   8
For having traffic with thyself alone,
Thou of thyself thy sweet self dost deceive.
Then how, when Nature calls thee to be gone,
What acceptable audit canst thou leave?   12
    Thy unused beauty must be tombed with thee,
    Which, usèd, lives th'executor to be.

5

Those hours, that with gentle work did frame
The lovely gaze where every eye doth dwell,
Will play the tyrants to the very same
And that unfair which fairly doth excel;   4
For never-resting Time leads summer on
To hideous winter and confounds him there,
Sap checked with frost and lusty leaves quite gone,
Beauty o'ersnowed and bareness everywhere.   8
Then, were not summer's distillation left
A liquid prisoner pent in walls of glass,
Beauty's effect with beauty were bereft,
Nor it nor no remembrance what it was.   12
    But flowers distilled, though they with winter meet,
    Leese but their show; their substance still lives sweet.

6

Then let not winter's ragged hand deface
In thee thy summer ere thou be distilled.
Make sweet some vial; treasure thou some place
With beauty's treasure ere it be self-killed.   4
That use is not forbidden usury
Which happies those that pay the willing loan;
That's for thyself to breed another thee,

Or ten times happier, be it ten for one.   8
Ten times thyself were happier than thou art,
If ten of thine ten times refigured thee;
Then what could death do, if thou shouldst depart,
Leaving thee living in posterity?   12
    Be not self-willed, for thou art much too fair
    To be death's conquest and make worms thine heir.

7

Lo, in the orient when the gracious light
Lifts up his burning head, each under eye
Doth homage to his new-appearing sight,
Serving with looks his sacred majesty;   4
And having climbed the steep-up heavenly hill,
Resembling strong youth in his middle age,
Yet mortal looks adore his beauty still,
Attending on his golden pilgrimage;   8
But when from highmost pitch, with weary car,
Like feeble age, he reeleth from the day,
The eyes, 'fore duteous, now converted are
From his low tract and look another way.   12
    So thou, thyself outgoing in thy noon,
    Unlooked on diest, unless thou get a son.

8

Music to hear, why hear'st thou music sadly?
Sweets with sweets war not, joy delights in joy.
Why lov'st thou that which thou receiv'st not gladly,
Or else receiv'st with pleasure thine annoy?   4
If the true concord of well-tunèd sounds,
By unions married, do offend thine ear,
They do but sweetly chide thee, who confounds
In singleness the parts that thou shouldst bear.   8
Mark how one string, sweet husband to another,
Strikes each in each by mutual ordering,
Resembling sire and child and happy mother
Who, all in one, one pleasing note do sing;   12
    Whose speechless song, being many, seeming one,
    Sings this to thee: "Thou single wilt prove none."

4.1 Unthrifty (1) Prodigal (2) Unavailing   **2 thy beauty's legacy** the beauty you inherited (and should pass on to your children).   **4 frank** liberal, bounteous.   **are free** who are generous.   **7 use** (1) use up (2) fail to invest for profit. (See sonnet 6.5 and note.)   **8 live** (1) have a livelihood (2) live in your posterity.   **9 traffic** commerce. (The commercial and financial metaphor hints at sexual self-fascination.) **10 deceive** cheat.   **13 unused** (1) unemployed (2) not invested for profit   **14 lives** would live (in your son)
5.1 frame make   **2 gaze** object of gazes   **3 play . . . to** oppress   **4 unfair** make unlovely.   **fairly** (1) in beauty (2) truly, honestly **5 leads summer on** (1) guides the steps of summer (2) lures summer **6 confounds** destroys   **7 lusty** vigorous   **9 summer's distillation** distilled perfume of flowers   **10 walls of glass** glass containers **11 with . . . bereft** would be lost along with beauty itself   **12 Nor it nor no** (leaving behind) neither it (beauty) nor any   **14 Leese** lose. **still** (1) notwithstanding (2) always
6.1 ragged rough   **3 vial** (With suggestion of a womb.)   **treasure** enrich **5 use** lending money at interest   **6 happies** makes happy.   **pay . . . loan** willingly borrow on these terms and repay the loan   **7 That's . . . thee** i.e., such would be the case if you were to sire a child like you

8 Or . . . one i.e., or indeed the happy mother (of line 6) would be ten times happier were she to bear you ten children instead of one. (*Ten for one* alludes to the highest legal rate of interest, one for ten.) **9 Ten . . . art** i.e., Ten children of yours would be a tenfold blessing and would make you happier   **10 refigured** duplicated, copied (producing one hundred grandchildren)   **13 self-willed** (1) obstinate (2) bequeathed to self
7.1 orient east.   **light** i.e., sun   **2 under** earthly   **9 pitch** highest point (as of a falcon's flight before it attacks).   **car** chariot (of the sungod)   **11 converted** turned away   **12 tract** course   **14 get** beget
8.1 Music to hear i.e., You whom it is music to hear.   **2 Sweets** Sweet things   **3–4 Why . . . annoy?** Why do you not gladly love the sweet things you hear, or find irksome that which is pleasurable?   **6 By unions married** perfectly blended in harmonious chords   **7–8 who . . . bear** you who destroy, by playing a single part only, the harmony (i.e., marriage) that you should sustain.   **9 sweet husband** i.e., paired, as on the double strings of the lute, one string vibrating sympathetically to the other   **10 each in each** i.e., with double resonance, sounding mutually   **13 Whose** i.e., the strings'.   **being . . . one** i.e., making harmony out of several voices   **14 Thou . . . none** (Alludes to the proverb, "One is no number." The single person who dies without posterity leaves nothing of himself behind.)

9

Is it for fear to wet a widow's eye
That thou consum'st thyself in single life?
Ah, if thou issueless shalt hap to die,
The world will wail thee like a makeless wife.   4
The world will be thy widow and still weep
That thou no form of thee hast left behind,
When every private widow well may keep,
By children's eyes, her husband's shape in mind.   8
Look what an unthrift in the world doth spend
Shifts but his place, for still the world enjoys it;
But beauty's waste hath in the world an end,
And, kept unused, the user so destroys it.   12
    No love toward others in that bosom sits
    That on himself such murd'rous shame commits.

10

For shame, deny that thou bear'st love to any,
Who for thyself art so unprovident!
Grant, if thou wilt, thou art beloved of many,
But that thou none lov'st is most evident;   4
For thou art so possessed with murd'rous hate
That 'gainst thyself thou stick'st not to conspire,
Seeking that beauteous roof to ruinate
Which to repair should be thy chief desire.   8
Oh, change thy thought, that I may change my mind!
Shall hate be fairer lodged than gentle love?
Be, as thy presence is, gracious and kind,
Or to thyself at least kindhearted prove: 12
    Make thee another self, for love of me,
    That beauty still may live in thine or thee.

11

As fast as thou shalt wane, so fast thou grow'st
In one of thine from that which thou departest;
And that fresh blood which youngly thou bestow'st
Thou mayst call thine when thou from youth convertest.   4
Herein lives wisdom, beauty, and increase;
Without this, folly, age, and cold decay.
If all were minded so, the times should cease
And threescore year would make the world away.   8
Let those whom Nature hath not made for store,
Harsh, featureless, and rude, barrenly perish;

Look whom she best endowed she gave the more,
Which bounteous gift thou shouldst in bounty cherish.   12
    She carved thee for her seal, and meant thereby
    Thou shouldst print more, not let that copy die.

12

When I do count the clock that tells the time,
And see the brave day sunk in hideous night;
When I behold the violet past prime,
And sable curls all silvered o'er with white;   4
When lofty trees I see barren of leaves
Which erst from heat did canopy the herd,
And summer's green, all girded up in sheaves,
Borne on the bier with white and bristly beard,   8
Then of thy beauty do I question make
That thou among the wastes of time must go,
Since sweets and beauties do themselves forsake
And die as fast as they see others grow;   12
    And nothing 'gainst Time's scythe can make defense
    Save breed, to brave him when he takes thee hence.

13

Oh, that you were yourself! But, love, you are
No longer yours than you yourself here live.
Against this coming end you should prepare,
And your sweet semblance to some other give.   4
So should that beauty which you hold in lease
Find no determination; then you were
Yourself again after yourself's decease,
When your sweet issue your sweet form should bear.   8
Who lets so fair a house fall to decay,
Which husbandry in honor might uphold
Against the stormy gusts of winter's day
And barren rage of death's eternal cold?   12
    Oh, none but unthrifts! Dear my love, you know
    You had a father; let your son say so.

14

Not from the stars do I my judgment pluck,
And yet methinks I have astronomy—
But not to tell of good or evil luck,
Of plagues, of dearths, or seasons' quality;   4
Nor can I fortune to brief minutes tell,
'Pointing to each his thunder, rain, and wind,

9.1 Is . . . eye Is it for fear of eventually leaving some woman a grieving widow when you die   **3 issueless** without offspring   **4 makeless** mateless, widowed   **5 still** constantly, always   **7 private** individual, as distinguished from the whole world   **8 By** by means of   **9 Look what** Whatever.   **unthrift** spendthrift   **10 his** its.
enjoys uses, keeps in circulation   **12 user** i.e., he who should use it. (With a suggestion of a *usurer* who is miserly.)
10.6 thou stick'st you scruple   **7 that . . . roof** i.e., your aristocratic family   **9 thought** intention.   **my mind** my opinion.   **11 presence** appearance, bearing
11.1–2 thou grow'st . . . departest i.e., you survive in a child of your own, though you leave the world behind   **3 youngly** in youth
4 thou . . . convertest you change from youth (to old age).   **7 minded so** sharing your intention (to have no children).   **times** succeeding generations   **8 year** years   **9 for store** for breeding   **10 Harsh . . . rude** ugly, lacking attractive features or appearance, and rudely fashioned

11 Look . . . more to whomever Nature endowed with the greatest gifts, she gave even more   **13 seal** stamp of authority, stamp from which impressions are made
12.1 tells (1) announces (2) counts   **2 brave** splendid   **4 sable** black
6 erst formerly   **7 girded** bundled   **8 bier** i.e., harvest cart. (But with suggestion of funeral bier.)   **beard** i.e., the tufted grain. (But suggesting also a dead man laid out for burial.)   **9 do . . . make** I discuss with myself   **14 breed** begetting offspring.   **brave him** defy Time
13.1 yourself i.e., your eternal self, not vulnerable to Time's decay.
2 here i.e., here on earth   **3 Against** In anticipation of   **6 determination** end   **10 husbandry** careful management. (With a pun on "being a husband.")
14.1 my judgment pluck derive my conclusions   **2 have astronomy** am skilled in astrology   **4 seasons' quality** what the weather of the seasons will be like   **5 fortune . . . tell** foretell events to the precise minute
6 'Pointing appointing, assigning.   **each** each minute.   **his** its

Or say with princes if it shall go well
By oft predict that I in heaven find.
But from thine eyes my knowledge I derive,
And, constant stars, in them I read such art
As truth and beauty shall together thrive
If from thyself to store thou wouldst convert.   12
    Or else of thee this I prognosticate:
    Thy end is truth's and beauty's doom and date.

15

When I consider every thing that grows
Holds in perfection but a little moment,
That this huge stage presenteth naught but shows
Whereon the stars in secret influence comment;   4
When I perceive that men as plants increase,
Cheerèd and checked even by the selfsame sky,
Vaunt in their youthful sap, at height decrease,
And wear their brave state out of memory;   8
Then the conceit of this inconstant stay
Sets you most rich in youth before my sight,
Where wasteful Time debateth with Decay   11
To change your day of youth to sullied night;   12
    And, all in war with Time for love of you,
    As he takes from you I engraft you new.

16

But wherefore do not you a mightier way
Make war upon this bloody tyrant, Time,
And fortify yourself in your decay
With means more blessèd than my barren rhyme?   4
Now stand you on the top of happy hours,
And many maiden gardens yet unset
With virtuous wish would bear your living flowers,
Much liker than your painted counterfeit.   8
So should the lines of life that life repair
Which this time's pencil, or my pupil pen,
Neither in inward worth nor outward fair
Can make you live yourself in eyes of men.   12
    To give away yourself keeps yourself still,
    And you must live, drawn by your own sweet skill.

17

Who will believe my verse in time to come
If it were filled with your most high deserts?
Though yet, heaven knows, it is but as a tomb
Which hides your life and shows not half your parts.   4
If I could write the beauty of your eyes
And in fresh numbers number all your graces,
The age to come would say, "This poet lies;
Such heavenly touches ne'er touched earthly faces."   8
So should my papers, yellowed with their age,
Be scorned like old men of less truth than tongue,
And your true rights be termed a poet's rage
And stretchèd meter of an antique song.   12
    But were some child of yours alive that time,
    You should live twice, in it and in my rhyme.

18

Shall I compare thee to a summer's day?
Thou art more lovely and more temperate.
Rough winds do shake the darling buds of May,
And summer's lease hath all too short a date.   4
Sometime too hot the eye of heaven shines,
And often is his gold complexion dimmed;
And every fair from fair sometimes declines,
By chance or nature's changing course untrimmed.   8
But thy eternal summer shall not fade
Nor lose possession of that fair thou ow'st;
Nor shall Death brag thou wand'r'st in his shade,
When in eternal lines to time thou grow'st.   12
    So long as men can breathe or eyes can see,
    So long lives this, and this gives life to thee.

19

Devouring Time, blunt thou the lion's paws,
And make the earth devour her own sweet brood;
Pluck the keen teeth from the fierce tiger's jaws,
And burn the long-lived phoenix in her blood;   4
Make glad and sorry seasons as thou fleet'st,
And do whate'er thou wilt, swift-footed Time,
To the wide world and all her fading sweets.
But I forbid thee one most heinous crime: 8
Oh, carve not with thy hours my love's fair brow,
Nor draw no lines there with thine antique pen;
Him in thy course untainted do allow
For beauty's pattern to succeeding men.   12

7 Or . . . well or say if things will go well for certain rulers   8 oft predict frequent predictions   10–11 read . . . As gather such learning as, in
effect, that   12 store replenishment (through the begetting of children).
convert turn.   14 doom and date limit of duration, destruction.
15.2 Holds in perfection maintains its prime   3 stage i.e., the world
5 as like   6 Cheerèd and checked (1) urged on, nourished, and held
back, starved (2) applauded and hissed   7 Vaunt boast, exult.   sap
vigor.   at height decrease i.e., no sooner reach full maturity but they
(humans) start to decline   8 brave splendid.   out of memory until
forgotten   9 conceit notion.   inconstant stay mutable brief time (on
earth)   11 debateth competes   13 all in war I, fighting with might
and main   14 engraft you new renew you by grafting, infusing new
life into you (by means of my verse).
16.4 barren (1) unable to produce offspring (2) poetically sterile   6 unset
(1) unplanted (2) unimpregnated   7 virtuous wish desire that is still
chaste   8 liker more resembling you.   painted rendered by art (including poetry), artificial.   counterfeit portrait.   9 lines of life lineage, of
children (whose lineaments are more lifelike than lines of verse or of a
portrait)   10 this time's pencil a portraiture done in this present age.
pupil apprenticed, inexpert   11 fair beauty   12 live survive as   13 give
away yourself i.e., marry and beget children.   keeps preserves   14 skill
i.e., artistry in reproducing yourself, mightier than the poet's pen.

17.3 yet as yet   4 parts qualities.   6 numbers verses   10 of . . .
tongue more garrulous than truthful   11 rage exaggerated inspiration   12 stretchèd meter overstrained poetry, poetic license
18.4 lease allotted time.   date duration.   5 eye i.e., sun   7 fair from
fair beautiful thing from beauty   8 untrimmed stripped of ornament
and beauty.   10 fair thou ow'st beauty you own   12 lines i.e., of
poetry.   to . . . grow'st you become incorporated into time, engrafted
upon it.   14 this i.e., this sonnet
19.4 phoenix legendary bird reputed to live for hundreds of years and
then to be consumed alive (in her blood) in its own ashes, from which
it is then reborn   5 sorry i.e., miserable, uncomfortable.   thou fleet'st
you fleet, hurry   10 antique (1) old (2) antic, capricious, fantastic
11 untainted unsullied; uninjured

Yet, do thy worst, old Time. Despite thy wrong,
My love shall in my verse ever live young.

20

A woman's face with Nature's own hand painted
Hast thou, the master-mistress of my passion;
A woman's gentle heart, but not acquainted
With shifting change, as is false women's fashion;   4
An eye more bright than theirs, less false in rolling,
Gilding the object whereupon it gazeth;
A man in hue, all hues in his controlling,
Which steals men's eyes and women's souls amazeth.   8
And for a woman wert thou first created,
Till Nature, as she wrought thee, fell a-doting,
And by addition me of thee defeated,
By adding one thing to my purpose nothing.   12
　　But since she pricked thee out for women's pleasure,
　　Mine be thy love and thy love's use their treasure.

21

So is it not with me as with that muse,
Stirred by a painted beauty to his verse,
Who heaven itself for ornament doth use
And every fair with his fair doth rehearse,   4
Making a couplement of proud compare
With sun and moon, with earth and sea's rich gems,
With April's firstborn flowers, and all things rare
That heaven's air in this huge rondure hems.   8
Oh, let me, true in love, but truly write,
And then, believe me, my love is as fair
As any mother's child, though not so bright
As those gold candles fixed in heaven's air.   12
　　Let them say more that like of hearsay well;
　　I will not praise that purpose not to sell.

22

My glass shall not persuade me I am old
So long as youth and thou are of one date;
But when in thee Time's furrows I behold,
Then look I death my days should expiate.   4
For all that beauty that doth cover thee
Is but the seemly raiment of my heart,
Which in thy breast doth live, as thine in me.
How can I then be elder than thou art?   8
Oh, therefore, love, be of thyself so wary
As I, not for myself, but for thee will,
Bearing thy heart, which I will keep so chary
As tender nurse her babe from faring ill.   12
　　Presume not on thy heart when mine is slain;
　　Thou gav'st me thine, not to give back again.

23

As an unperfect actor on the stage
Who with his fear is put beside his part,
Or some fierce thing replete with too much rage,
Whose strength's abundance weakens his own heart,   4
So I, for fear of trust, forget to say
The perfect ceremony of love's rite,
And in mine own love's strength seem to decay,
O'ercharged with burden of mine own love's might.   8
Oh, let my books be then the eloquence
And dumb presagers of my speaking breast,
Who plead for love and look for recompense
More than that tongue that more hath more expressed.   12
　　Oh, learn to read what silent love hath writ.
　　To hear with eyes belongs to love's fine wit.

24

Mine eye hath played the painter and hath stelled
Thy beauty's form in table of my heart;
My body is the frame wherein 'tis held,
And perspective it is best painter's art.   4
For through the painter must you see his skill

---

14 My love (1) my beloved (2) my affection for him
20.1 with . . . hand i.e., naturally beautiful   **2 master-mistress** i.e.,
both master and mistress, male and female.   **passion** love   **4 as . . .
fashion** as is the way with women, who are false by nature
5 rolling i.e., roving   **6 Gilding** causing to shine brightly   **7 A man
. . . controlling** one who has a manly appearance surpassing all other
forms. (Suggesting, too, that he captivates all beholders and that his
hue is womanly as well as manly.)   **10 fell a-doting** fell infatuatedly
in love with you and so went mildly crazy   **11 defeated** defrauded,
deprived   **12 to my purpose nothing** out of line with my wishes
13 pricked designated. (With bawdy suggestion; the *thing* in line 12
is a phallus.)   **for women's pleasure** to give (sexual) pleasure to
women   **14 Mine . . . treasure** I will have your love in the truest
sense, while women will enjoy you sexually and bear you children.
(Expressed as a metaphor of financial capital or principal, which
belongs to the poet, versus the *use* or interest, which belongs to
women.)
21.1 muse i.e., poet   **2 Stirred** inspired.   **painted** artificial, created
by cosmetics   **3 Who . . . use** who does not scruple to invoke heaven
itself as an ornament of praise for his mistress   **4 every . . . rehearse**
compares his lady fair with every lovely thing   **5 Making . . . compare** joining (her) in proud comparison   **8 rondure** sphere.   **hems**
encloses, encircles.   **12 gold candles** i.e., stars. (The trite and exaggerated metaphor is of the sort the poet hopes to eschew.)   **13 like . . .
well** like to deal in secondhand or trite expressions   **14 I will . . . sell**
I, who do not intend to sell as a merchant might, will accordingly not
indulge in extravagant and empty praise.

22.1 glass mirror   **2 of one date** of an age, i.e., young   **4 look I** I
foresee that.   **expiate** end.   **5–7 For . . . me** Since my heart dwells in
your breast (and yours in mine), your beauty is in effect a becoming
cover for my heart.   **10 will** i.e., will take wary care of myself for
your sake   **11 Bearing** since I bear.   **chary** carefully   **13 Presume . . .
slain** Do not expect to receive back your heart when mine is slain (as
would happen if you were to stop loving me)
23.1 unperfect one who has not learned his lines sufficiently   **2 is . . .
part** forgets his lines   **3 Or . . . rage** i.e., or some wild creature over-
filled with ungovernable rage   **4 Whose . . . heart** whose excess of
emotion collapses on itself   **5 for . . . trust** mistrusting myself and
fearful of not being trusted.   **forget** forget how   **9 books** (Possibly
refers to the sonnets or to *Venus and Adonis* and *The Rape of Lucrece* or,
more generally, the works of the persona poet.)   **10 dumb presagers**
silent messengers or presenters   **12 that tongue** the tongue of some
rival speaker.   **more hath more expressed** has more often or more
fully said more.   **14 fine wit** sharp intelligence.
24.1 played acted the part of.   **stelled** fixed, installed; or perhaps steeled,
i.e., engraved. (The Quarto reads "steeld.")   **2 table** tablet, wooden panel
used for painting   **3 frame** (1) picture frame (2) bodily frame   **4 perspective** an artist's method of producing a distorted picture that looks
right only from an oblique point of view; or, a painter's technique used
to produce the illusion of reality; or, the science of optics   **5 For . . .
skill** i.e., You must look through the eyes of me, the skillful painter

To find where your true image pictured lies,
Which in my bosom's shop is hanging still,
That hath his windows glazèd with thine eyes. 8
Now see what good turns eyes for eyes have done:
Mine eyes have drawn thy shape, and thine for me
Are windows to my breast, wherethrough the sun
Delights to peep, to gaze therein on thee. 12
    Yet eyes this cunning want to grace their art:
    They draw but what they see, know not the heart.

25

Let those who are in favor with their stars
Of public honor and proud titles boast,
Whilst I, whom fortune of such triumph bars,
Unlooked for joy in that I honor most. 4
Great princes' favorites their fair leaves spread
But as the marigold at the sun's eye,
And in themselves their pride lies burièd,
For at a frown they in their glory die. 8
The painful warrior famousèd for fight,
After a thousand victories once foiled,
Is from the book of honor rasèd quite,
And all the rest forgot for which he toiled. 12
    Then happy I, that love and am beloved
    Where I may not remove nor be removed.

26

Lord of my love, to whom in vassalage
Thy merit hath my duty strongly knit,
To thee I send this written embassage
To witness duty, not to show my wit— 4
Duty so great, which wit so poor as mine
May make seem bare, in wanting words to show it,
But that I hope some good conceit of thine
In thy soul's thought, all naked, will bestow it; 8
Till whatsoever star that guides my moving
Points on me graciously with fair aspect,
And puts apparel on my tattered loving
To show me worthy of thy sweet respect. 12
    Then may I dare to boast how I do love thee;
    Till then not show my head where thou mayst prove
    me.

27

Weary with toil, I haste me to my bed,
The dear repose for limbs with travel tirèd;
But then begins a journey in my head,
To work my mind when body's work's expirèd. 4
For then my thoughts, from far where I abide,
Intend a zealous pilgrimage to thee,
And keep my drooping eyelids open wide,
Looking on darkness which the blind do see; 8
Save that my soul's imaginary sight
Presents thy shadow to my sightless view,
Which, like a jewel hung in ghastly night,
Makes black night beauteous and her old face new. 12
    Lo, thus by day my limbs, by night my mind,
    For thee and for myself no quiet find.

28

How can I then return in happy plight
That am debarred the benefit of rest?
When day's oppression is not eased by night,
But day by night, and night by day, oppressed? 4
And each, though enemies to either's reign,
Do in consent shake hands to torture me,
The one by toil, the other to complain
How far I toil, still farther off from thee. 8
I tell the day, to please him, thou art bright
And dost him grace when clouds do blot the heaven;
So flatter I the swart-complexioned night,
When sparkling stars twire not, thou gild'st th' even. 12
    But day doth daily draw my sorrows longer,
    And night doth nightly make grief's strength seem
    stronger.

29

When, in disgrace with fortune and men's eyes,
I all alone beweep my outcast state,
And trouble deaf heaven with my bootless cries,
And look upon myself and curse my fate, 4
Wishing me like to one more rich in hope,
Featured like him, like him with friends possessed,
Desiring this man's art and that man's scope,

---

7 bosom's shop i.e., heart   **8 his** its.   **glazèd** fitted with glass, paned. (The friend, looking into the poet's eyes where his own eyes are reflected, sees into the poet's heart.)   **13 this cunning want** lack this skill.   **grace** enhance   **14 know not** do not perceive the thoughts of
25.3 of from   **4 Unlooked for** (1) unexpectedly (2) out of the public eye.   **that which**   **5 their . . . spread** i.e., flourish, blossom, prosper   **6 But** only   **7 lies burièd** i.e., will die with the ending of their brief glory   **8 a frown** (1) a prince's frown (2) a cloud obscuring the sun   **9 painful** enduring much, striving.   **famousèd** renowned. **fight** (Reads "worth" in the 1609 Quarto; some editors retain and emend "quite" in line 11 to "forth." Other editors prefer "might.") **11 rasèd** erased (or *razèd*, scraped out)   **12 the rest** i.e., his *thousand victories*   **14 remove** i.e., be unfaithful.   **removed** i.e., removed from favor.
26.1 vassalage allegiance   **4 witness** bear witness to.   **wit** skill, literary ingenuity   **5 wit** intelligence and skill   **6 wanting** lacking **7 good conceit** good conception, favorable opinion   **8 all naked** i.e., poor verse though it is.   **bestow** give lodging to   **9 moving** life and deeds   **10 Points on** directs its rays at.   **aspect** influence (as of a star)   **14 prove** test

27.2 travel (With connotation also of *travail*; spelled "trauaill" in the Quarto.)   **5 from far** i.e., far away from you   **6 Intend** (1) set out upon (2) have purposefully in mind   **8 Looking . . . see** while my thoughts try to peer (toward you) through the darkness, like the blind, who see only darkness   **9 Save** except   **10 thy shadow** the image of you   **14 For** on account of
28.4 But . . . oppressed i.e., but experiencing sleeplessness at night and fatigue during the day.   **6 in . . . hands** i.e., come to a mutual agreement   **7 the other to complain** i.e., the night by causing me to complain   **10 And . . . heaven** i.e., and that you shine in place of the sun when the sun is overclouded   **11 So flatter I** similarly I gratify. **swart** dark   **12 When . . . even** i.e., by saying that, when sparkling stars do not twinkle or peep out, you make bright the evening.
29.3 bootless useless   **4 look upon myself** consider my predicament   **5 more rich in hope** with better prospects of success **6 Featured** formed, i.e., having good looks.   **like him, like him** like a second man, like a third   **7 art** literary skill, learning.   **scope** range of powers

With what I most enjoy contented least;　　　　　8
Yet in these thoughts myself almost despising,
Haply I think on thee, and then my state,
Like to the lark at break of day arising
From sullen earth, sings hymns at heaven's gate;　12
　　For thy sweet love remembered such wealth brings
　　That then I scorn to change my state with kings.

30

When to the sessions of sweet silent thought
I summon up remembrance of things past,
I sigh the lack of many a thing I sought,
And with old woes new wail my dear time's waste.　4
Then can I drown an eye, unused to flow,
For precious friends hid in death's dateless night,
And weep afresh love's long-since-canceled woe,
And moan th'expense of many a vanished sight.　8
Then can I grieve at grievances foregone,
And heavily from woe to woe tell o'er
The sad account of fore-bemoanèd moan,
Which I new pay as if not paid before.　　　　12
　　But if the while I think on thee, dear friend,
　　All losses are restored and sorrows end.

31

Thy bosom is endearèd with all hearts
Which I by lacking have supposèd dead,
And there reigns love and all love's loving parts,
And all those friends which I thought burièd.　4
How many a holy and obsequious tear
Hath dear religious love stol'n from mine eye
As interest of the dead, which now appear
But things removed that hidden in thee lie!　8
Thou art the grave where buried love doth live,
Hung with the trophies of my lovers gone,
Who all their parts of me to thee did give;
That due of many now is thine alone.　　　　12
　　Their images I loved I view in thee,
　　And thou, all they, hast all the all of me.

32

If thou survive my well-contented day
When that churl Death my bones with dust shall cover,
And shalt by fortune once more re-survey
These poor rude lines of thy deceasèd lover,　4
Compare them with the bett'ring of the time,
And though they be outstripped by every pen,
Reserve them for my love, not for their rhyme,
Exceeded by the height of happier men.　　　8
Oh, then vouchsafe me but this loving thought:
"Had my friend's Muse grown with this growing age,
A dearer birth than this his love had brought
To march in ranks of better equipage;　　　12
　　But since he died and poets better prove,
　　Theirs for their style I'll read, his for his love."

33

Full many a glorious morning have I seen
Flatter the mountaintops with sovereign eye,
Kissing with golden face the meadows green,
Gilding pale streams with heavenly alchemy;　4
Anon permit the basest clouds to ride
With ugly rack on his celestial face,
And from the forlorn world his visage hide,
Stealing unseen to west with this disgrace.　8
Even so my sun one early morn did shine
With all-triumphant splendor on my brow.
But out, alack! He was but one hour mine;
The region cloud hath masked him from me now.　12
　　Yet him for this my love no whit disdaineth;
　　Suns of the world may stain when heaven's sun
　　　staineth.

34

Why didst thou promise such a beauteous day
And make me travel forth without my cloak,
To let base clouds o'ertake me in my way,
Hiding thy brav'ry in their rotten smoke?　4
'Tis not enough that through the cloud thou break,
To dry the rain on my storm-beaten face,
For no man well of such a salve can speak
That heals the wound and cures not the disgrace.　8

8 **most enjoy** possess most securely and take greatest pleasure in
10 **Haply** perchance; happily.　**state** state of mind. (Suggesting also
"fortunes.")　14 **change** exchange
30.1 **sessions** (The metaphor is that of a court of law, continued in
summon up, line 2.)　3 **sigh** sigh for　4 **new . . . waste** lament anew
the wasting of precious time or time's erosion of those things held
precious.　5 **unused to flow** not prone to weep　6 **dateless** endless
7 **canceled** paid in full (by grieving)　8 **th'expense** the loss, expenditure　9 **grievances foregone** sorrows past　10 **heavily** sadly.　**tell**
count　11 **account** (1) narrative (2) financial reckoning.　**fore-**
bemoanèd moan previously uttered laments
31.1 **endearèd with all hearts** (1) beloved by all (2) made dear to me
by representing and including those I have loved　2 **lacking** not having　3 **parts** attributes　5 **obsequious** suitable to mourning　6 **reli-**
gious dutiful, reverent　7 **interest of** that which is rightfully due to.
which who　8 **But . . . lie** i.e., no more than absent persons (now
dead), whose best qualities are to be found buried in you.
10 **Hung . . . gone** festooned with symbolic memorials of my past triumphs in being loved by many　11 **parts** shares　12 **That due of**
many that which was both owed by, and paid to, many　13 **I loved**
which I loved　14 **all they** (you) who comprise all of them

32.1 **my . . . day** i.e., the day of my death, which will content me well
3 **And . . . fortune** and if by chance you happen　4 **rude** unpolished.
lover friend　5 **bett'ring** i.e., improved writing, greater cultural
sophistication　7 **Reserve** preserve.　**for my love** (1) out of love for
me (2) for the sake of my love for you.　**rhyme** i.e., poetic skill
8 **height** superiority, highest achievement.　**happier** more gifted or
fortunate　9 **vouchsafe me but** deign to bestow on me just　11 **dearer**
birth i.e., better poem, better artistic creation　12 **better equipage** i.e.,
more finely wrought verse　13 **better prove** turn out to be superior
33.1 **Full** Very　2 **sovereign eye** i.e., morning sunlight　5 **Anon** soon
afterward.　**basest** darkest　6 **rack** mass of cloud scudding before
the wind　11 **out, alack!** (An expression of dismay.)　12 **region** of the
upper air　14 **Suns** i.e., great men. (With a pun on *sons of the world*,
"mortal men.")　**stain** grow dim, be obscured, soiled.　**staineth** is
clouded over.
34.3 **To** only to　4 **brav'ry** finery.　**rotten smoke** foul vapors.　8 **dis-**
grace i.e., the scar, the disfigurement caused by his friend's neglect or
harsh treatment; the *loss* main mentioned in line 10.

Nor can thy shame give physic to my grief;
Though thou repent, yet I have still the loss.
Th'offender's sorrow lends but weak relief
To him that bears the strong offense's cross.   12
　　Ah, but those tears are pearl which thy love sheds,
　　And they are rich, and ransom all ill deeds.

35

No more be grieved at that which thou hast done.
Roses have thorns, and silver fountains mud,
Clouds and eclipses stain both moon and sun,
And loathsome canker lives in sweetest bud.   4
All men make faults, and even I in this,
Authorizing thy trespass with compare,
Myself corrupting, salving thy amiss,
Excusing thy sins more than thy sins are.   8
For to thy sensual fault I bring in sense—
Thy adverse party is thy advocate—
And 'gainst myself a lawful plea commence.
Such civil war is in my love and hate   12
　　That I an accessary needs must be
　　To that sweet thief which sourly robs from me.

36

Let me confess that we two must be twain,
Although our undivided loves are one;
So shall those blots that do with me remain,
Without thy help, by me be borne alone.   4
In our two loves there is but one respect,
Though in our lives a separable spite,
Which, though it alter not love's sole effect,
Yet doth it steal sweet hours from love's delight.   8
I may not evermore acknowledge thee,
Lest my bewailèd guilt should do thee shame,
Nor thou with public kindness honor me
Unless thou take that honor from thy name.   12
　　But do not so; I love thee in such sort
　　As, thou being mine, mine is thy good report.

37

As a decrepit father takes delight
To see his active child do deeds of youth,

So I, made lame by Fortune's dearest spite,
Take all my comfort of thy worth and truth.   4
For whether beauty, birth, or wealth, or wit,
Or any of these all, or all, or more,
Entitled in thy parts do crownèd sit,
I make my love engrafted to this store.   8
So then I am not lame, poor, nor despised,
Whilst that this shadow doth such substance give
That I in thy abundance am sufficed
And by a part of all thy glory live.   12
　　Look what is best, that best I wish in thee.
　　This wish I have; then ten times happy me!

38

How can my Muse want subject to invent
While thou dost breathe, that pour'st into my verse
Thine own sweet argument, too excellent
For every vulgar paper to rehearse?   4
Oh, give thyself the thanks, if aught in me
Worthy perusal stand against thy sight,
For who's so dumb that cannot write to thee,
When thou thyself dost give invention light?   8
Be thou the tenth Muse, ten times more in worth
Than those old nine which rhymers invocate;
And he that calls on thee, let him bring forth
Eternal numbers to outlive long date.   12
　　If my slight Muse do please these curious days,
　　The pain be mine, but thine shall be the praise.

39

Oh, how thy worth with manners may I sing,
When thou art all the better part of me?
What can mine own praise to mine own self bring?
And what is't but mine own when I praise thee?   4
Even for this let us divided live,
And our dear love lose name of single one,
That by this separation I may give
That due to thee which thou deserv'st alone.   8
O absence, what a torment wouldst thou prove,
Were it not thy sour leisure gave sweet leave
To entertain the time with thoughts of love,
Which time and thoughts so sweetly doth deceive,   12

---

9 **shame** repentance for the wrong done.　**physic** remedy　**12 cross** affliction.　**14 ransom** atone for
35.3 stain dim, obscure　**4 canker** cankerworm　**6 Authorizing** sanctioning, justifying.　**compare** comparisons (as in this sonnet)
7 Myself . . . amiss excusing your misdeed, thereby bringing blame on myself　**8 Excusing . . . are** going further to excuse your sins than they warrant, or, excusing you for even worse sins than you have actually committed.　**9 For . . . sense** I reason away your fleshly offenses　**10 Thy . . . advocate** I who profess to be your accuser find myself, instead, pleading your case　**13 That . . . be** that I am compelled (by my love) to be a guilty accomplice
36.1 twain parted　**3 blots** defects, stains of dishonor　**5 but one respect** a mutual regard, singleness of attitude　**6 separable spite** vexing separation　**7 sole effect** unique effect (of making the two of us into one)　**9 not evermore acknowledge** nevermore admit my acquaintance with　**12 Unless . . . from** without consequent loss of honor to　**13 in such sort** in such a way　**14 As . . . report** that since you are mine, your good reputation sustains me also.

37.3 made lame handicapped in life.　**dearest** most bitter　**4 of** in, from　**5 wit** intelligence　**7 Entitled . . . sit** sit enthroned among your qualities　**8 I make . . . store** I add my love to this abundance (and thereby flourish by drawing on their strength).　**10 shadow** idea (in the platonic sense).　**substance** actuality　**13 Look what** Whatever
38.1 want . . . invent lack something to write about　**2 that** you who　**3 Thine . . . argument** yourself as subject　**4 vulgar paper** common piece of writing.　**rehearse** recite, repeat.　**5–6 if . . . sight** if any of my writing strikes you as worthy of perusal　**7 dumb** silent, lacking in subject　**8 When . . . light** when you bring such a light of invention to yourself as poetic subject.　**12 numbers** verses.　**long date** even a very distant limit in time.　**13 curious** finicky　**14 pain** labor
39.1 with manners decently, becomingly　**3–4 What . . . thee?** i.e., Since my better self is entirely yours, what can I gain from praising you but a kind of vainglorious self-praise?　**5 Even for** Precisely because of　**10 not** not that　**11 entertain** pass, occupy　**12 Which . . . deceive** (thoughts of love), which sweetly beguile away time and (sad) thoughts

And that thou teachest how to make one twain
By praising him here who doth hence remain!

40

Take all my loves, my love, yea, take them all;
What hast thou then more than thou hadst before?
No love, my love, that thou mayst true love call;
All mine was thine before thou hadst this more.   4
Then if for my love thou my love receivest,
I cannot blame thee for my love thou usest;
But yet be blamed if thou this self deceivest
By willful taste of what thyself refusest.   8
I do forgive thy robb'ry, gentle thief,
Although thou steal thee all my poverty;
And yet love knows it is a greater grief
To bear love's wrong than hate's known injury.   12
    Lascivious grace, in whom all ill well shows,
    Kill me with spites; yet we must not be foes.

41

Those pretty wrongs that liberty commits
When I am sometime absent from thy heart,
Thy beauty and thy years full well befits,
For still temptation follows where thou art.   4
Gentle thou art, and therefore to be won;
Beauteous thou art, therefore to be assailed;
And when a woman woos, what woman's son
Will sourly leave her till he have prevailed?   8
Ay me, but yet thou mightst my seat forbear,
And chide thy beauty and thy straying youth,
Who lead thee in their riot even there
Where thou art forced to break a twofold truth: 12
    Hers, by thy beauty tempting her to thee,
    Thine, by thy beauty being false to me.

42

That thou hast her, it is not all my grief,
And yet it may be said I loved her dearly;
That she hath thee is of my wailing chief,
A loss in love that touches me more nearly.   4
Loving offenders, thus I will excuse ye:

Thou dost love her because thou know'st I love her,
And for my sake even so doth she abuse me,
Suff'ring my friend for my sake to approve her.   8
If I lose thee, my loss is my love's gain,
And, losing her, my friend hath found that loss;
Both find each other, and I lose both twain,
And both for my sake lay on me this cross.   12
    But here's the joy: my friend and I are one.
    Sweet flattery! Then she loves but me alone.

43

When most I wink, then do mine eyes best see,
For all the day they view things unrespected;
But when I sleep, in dreams they look on thee,
And, darkly bright, are bright in dark directed.   4
Then thou, whose shadow shadows doth make bright,
How would thy shadow's form form happy show
To the clear day with thy much clearer light,
When to unseeing eyes thy shade shines so!   8
How would, I say, mine eyes be blessèd made
By looking on thee in the living day,
When in dead night thy fair imperfect shade
Through heavy sleep on sightless eyes doth stay!   12
    All days are nights to see till I see thee,
    And nights bright days when dreams do show thee
        me.

44

If the dull substance of my flesh were thought,
Injurious distance should not stop my way;
For then despite of space I would be brought,
From limits far remote, where thou dost stay.   4
No matter then although my foot did stand
Upon the farthest earth removed from thee;
For nimble thought can jump both sea and land
As soon as think the place where he would be.   8
But, ah, thought kills me that I am not thought,
To leap large lengths of miles when thou art gone,
But that, so much of earth and water wrought,
I must attend time's leisure with my moan,   12

14 **here** (1) here where I am (2) here in this poem
40.1 all my loves (1) all those whom I love (2) all the love I have. (The young man addressed has taken away the poet's mistress.) **3 No . . . call** i.e., Any love more than you had already—my complete affection—cannot be called true love **5 my love . . . my love** love of me . . . her whom I love **6 for** because. **thou usest** you enjoy (sexually) **7 this self** i.e., me, your other self. (Often emended to "thyself.") **8 By . . . refusest** i.e., by tasting sexual pleasures that your best self would refuse. **10 steal . . . poverty** take for your own the poor little that I have **12 To . . . injury** to endure injuries arising out of a loving relationship than those stemming from calculated hatred. **13 Lascivious grace** i.e., You who are gracious even in your lasciviousness
41.1 pretty graciously committed, sportive. **liberty** licentiousness
3 befits (The subject is *wrongs*, line 1.) **4 still** constantly **7–8 And . . . prevailed** i.e., When a woman woos, what man can resist until he has scored? (*He* is sometimes emended to "she.") **9 seat** place, that which belongs to me (i.e., my mistress) **11 Who** which. **riot** debauchery **12 twofold truth** i.e., her plighted love to me and your plighted friendship to me
42.3 is . . . chief is chief cause of my lamentation

7 abuse betray, wrong **8 Suff'ring** allowing. **approve** try, test (in a sexual sense) **9 my love's** hers whom I love, my mistress's **10 losing her** i.e., I losing her **12 for my sake** as though out of love for me. **cross** torment. **14 flattery** gratifying deception.
43.1 wink close my eyes in sleep **2 unrespected** unnoticed, unregarded; not deserving notice **4 And . . . directed** and, able to see in the darkness (though still shut), are directed toward your brightness in the dark. **5 whose . . . bright** whose image makes darkness bright **6 thy shadow's . . . show** the substance of the shadow, i.e., your presence, make a gladdening sight **8 unseeing eyes** i.e., closed eyes of the dreamer **11 imperfect** unsubstantial, indistinct as in a dream **12 stay** linger, dwell. **13 All . . . to see** All days are gloomy to behold **14 thee me** you to me. (But also suggesting "me to you.")
44.1 dull heavy **4 limits** regions, bounds. **where** to the place where **6 farthest earth removed** that part of the earth farthest removed **8 he** thought **9 ah, thought** ah, the thought **11 so . . . wrought** i.e., I, compounded to such an extent of the heavier elements, earth and water. (The lighter elements are fire and air.)
12 attend time's leisure i.e., wait until time has leisure to reunite us

Receiving naught by elements so slow
But heavy tears, badges of either's woe.

45

The other two, slight air and purging fire,
Are both with thee, wherever I abide;
The first my thought, the other my desire,
These present-absent with swift motion slide. 4
For when these quicker elements are gone
In tender embassy of love to thee,
My life, being made of four, with two alone
Sinks down to death, oppressed with melancholy; 8
Until life's composition be recured
By those swift messengers returned from thee,
Who even but now come back again, assured
Of thy fair health, recounting it to me. 12
    This told, I joy; but then no longer glad,
    I send them back again and straight grow sad.

46

Mine eye and heart are at a mortal war
How to divide the conquest of thy sight;
Mine eye my heart thy picture's sight would bar,
My heart mine eye the freedom of that right. 4
My heart doth plead that thou in him dost lie—
A closet never pierced with crystal eyes—
But the defendant doth that plea deny
And says in him thy fair appearance lies. 8
To 'cide this title is impanelèd
A quest of thoughts, all tenants to the heart,
And by their verdict is determinèd
The clear eye's moiety and the dear heart's part, 12
    As thus: mine eye's due is thy outward part,
    And my heart's right thy inward love of heart.

47

Betwixt mine eye and heart a league is took,
And each doth good turns now unto the other.
When that mine eye is famished for a look,
Or heart in love with sighs himself doth smother, 4

With my love's picture then my eye doth feast
And to the painted banquet bids my heart;
Another time mine eye is my heart's guest
And in his thoughts of love doth share a part. 8
So, either by thy picture or my love,
Thyself, away, are present still with me;
For thou no farther than my thoughts canst move,
And I am still with them and they with thee; 12
    Or, if they sleep, thy picture in my sight
    Awakes my heart to heart's and eye's delight.

48

How careful was I, when I took my way,
Each trifle under truest bars to thrust,
That to my use it might unusèd stay
From hands of falsehood, in sure wards of trust! 4
But thou, to whom my jewels trifles are,
Most worthy comfort, now my greatest grief,
Thou best of dearest and mine only care,
Art left the prey of every vulgar thief. 8
Thee have I not locked up in any chest,
Save where thou art not—though I feel thou art—
Within the gentle closure of my breast,
From whence at pleasure thou mayst come and part; 12
    And even thence thou wilt be stol'n, I fear,
    For truth proves thievish for a prize so dear.

49

Against that time, if ever that time come,
When I shall see thee frown on my defects,
Whenas thy love hath cast his utmost sum,
Called to that audit by advised respects; 4
Against that time when thou shalt strangely pass
And scarcely greet me with that sun, thine eye,
When love, converted from the thing it was,
Shall reasons find of settled gravity— 8
Against that time do I ensconce me here
Within the knowledge of mine own desart,
And this my hand against myself uprear,
To guard the lawful reasons on thy part. 12
    To leave poor me thou hast the strength of laws,
    Since why to love I can allege no cause.

13 **by** from   14 **badges** signs, tokens.   **either's** (1) both earth's and water's, because the earth is heavy and the sea is salt and wet like tears (2) both your and my
45.1 **other two** (i.e., of the four elements discussed in sonnet 44). **slight** insubstantial.   **purging** purifying   4 **present-absent** (1) now here and immediately gone (2) simultaneously both present and absent   7 **two alone** i.e., earth and water   8 **melancholy** a humor thought to be induced by an excess of earth and water   9 **composition** proper balance among the four elements.   **recured** restored   10 **swift messengers** i.e., fire and air, thought and desire   14 **straight** straightway
46.1 **mortal** deadly   2 **How . . . sight** how to divide the spoils of war, namely, the sight of you   3–4 **Mine . . . right** my eye wishes to bar my heart from seeing your image (perhaps a painting), and conversely my heart would like to deny my eye the free enjoyment of that right.   6 **closet** (1) small private room (2) cabinet   7 **the defendant** the eye   9 **'cide** decide   10 **quest** inquest, jury   12 **moiety** portion   13 **mine . . . part** i.e., the eye gets the outward appearance of you. (The jury, composed entirely of those who are loyal to the heart, being its *tenants,* awards true love to the heart.)
47.1 **a league is took** an agreement is reached   3 **When that** When
4 **Or heart** or when my heart.   **himself** itself

5 **With** i.e., on   6 **painted banquet** i.e., visual feast, perhaps an actual picture of the friend   12 **still** constantly
48.1 **took my way** set out on my journey   2 **truest** most trusty   3 **to my use** for my own use and profit   3–4 **stay . . . falsehood** remain out of the hands of thieves   5 **to** compared to   6 **worthy** valuable. **grief** anxiety, cause of sorrow (i.e., because of your absence and likeliness of being stolen)   8 **vulgar** common   12 **part** depart   14 **truth** i.e., even honesty itself
49.1 **Against** In anticipation of   3 **Whenas** when.   **cast . . . sum** added up the sum total. (The metaphor is from closing accounts on a dissolution of partnership.)   4 **advised respects** careful consideration   5 **strangely** as a stranger   8 **of settled gravity** (1) for a dignified reserve or continued coldness (2) of sufficient weight   9 **ensconce** fortify, shelter   10 **desart** i.e., deserving, such as it is. (This Quarto spelling of desert, "desart," indicates the rhyme with *part.*)   11 **this . . . uprear** I raise my own hand (as a witness) against my own interest   12 **To . . . part** i.e., to testify in behalf of the lawful reasons on your side of the case.   14 **Since . . . cause** since I can urge no lawful cause why you should love me.

50

How heavy do I journey on the way,
When what I seek, my weary travel's end,
Doth teach that ease and that repose to say,
"Thus far the miles are measured from thy friend!" 4
The beast that bears me, tirèd with my woe,
Plods dully on, to bear that weight in me,
As if by some instinct the wretch did know
His rider loved not speed being made from thee. 8
The bloody spur cannot provoke him on
That sometimes anger thrusts into his hide,
Which heavily he answers with a groan,
More sharp to me than spurring to his side; 12
    For that same groan doth put this in my mind:
    My grief lies onward and my joy behind.

51

Thus can my love excuse the slow offense
Of my dull bearer when from thee I speed:
From where thou art why should I haste me thence?
Till I return, of posting is no need. 4
Oh, what excuse will my poor beast then find
When swift extremity can seem but slow?
Then should I spur, though mounted on the wind;
In wingèd speed no motion shall I know. 8
Then can no horse with my desire keep pace;
Therefore desire, of perfect'st love being made,
Shall neigh—no dull flesh—in his fiery race.
But love, for love, thus shall excuse my jade: 12
    Since from thee going he went willful slow,
    Towards thee I'll run, and give him leave to go.

52

So am I as the rich whose blessèd key
Can bring him to his sweet up-lockèd treasure,
The which he will not ev'ry hour survey,
For blunting the fine point of seldom pleasure. 4
Therefore are feasts so solemn and so rare,
Since, seldom coming, in the long year set,
Like stones of worth they thinly placèd are,
Or captain jewels in the carcanet. 8
So is the time that keeps you as my chest,
Or as the wardrobe which the robe doth hide,
To make some special instant special blest

By new unfolding his imprisoned pride. 12
    Blessèd are you whose worthiness gives scope,
    Being had, to triumph; being lacked, to hope.

53

What is your substance, whereof are you made,
That millions of strange shadows on you tend?
Since everyone hath, every one, one shade,
And you, but one, can every shadow lend. 4
Describe Adonis, and the counterfeit
Is poorly imitated after you;
On Helen's cheek all art of beauty set,
And you in Grecian tires are painted new. 8
Speak of the spring and foison of the year;
The one doth shadow of your beauty show,
The other as your bounty doth appear,
And you in every blessèd shape we know. 12
    In all external grace you have some part,
    But you like none, none you, for constant heart.

54

Oh, how much more doth beauty beauteous seem
By that sweet ornament which truth doth give!
The rose looks fair, but fairer we it deem
For that sweet odor which doth in it live. 4
The canker blooms have full as deep a dye
As the perfumèd tincture of the roses,
Hang on such thorns, and play as wantonly
When summer's breath their maskèd buds discloses; 8
But, for their virtue only is their show,
They live unwooed and unrespected fade,
Die to themselves. Sweet roses do not so;
Of their sweet deaths are sweetest odors made. 12
    And so of you, beauteous and lovely youth,
    When that shall vade, by verse distills your truth.

55

Not marble nor the gilded monuments
Of princes shall outlive this powerful rhyme,

12 his its. **pride** splendor, proud treasure. **13–14 gives . . . hope** gives me opportunity, when you are with me, to rejoice, and when you are away from me, to hope for reunion.
53.2 strange (1) exotic (2) not belonging to you. **tend** attend.
3 shade shadow (as cast by the sun) **4 And . . . lend** and yet you, being only one person, can cast all sorts of shadowy images or reflections (such as Adonis, Helen, etc.). **5 Adonis** beautiful youth beloved of Venus. **counterfeit** likeness, portrait **7–8 On . . . new** set forth the entire art use to beautify the cheek of Helen of Troy, and the result will be a portrait of you in Grecian attire or headdress.
9 foison abundance, i.e., autumn **12 you . . . know** we recognize you in every beautiful image. **13 But . . . heart** but in the matter of constancy you resemble no one and no one can resemble you.
54.2 By by means of. **truth** (1) constancy (2) substance, integrity
5 canker blooms dog roses (outwardly attractive but not as sweetly scented as the damask rose). **dye** tincture **7 wantonly** sportively
8 discloses causes to open **9 for** because. **their show** in their appearance **10 unrespected** unregarded **11 to themselves** i.e., without profit to others. **12 Of . . . made** i.e., perfumes are made from the crushed petals of these roses. **13 of you** (1) distilled from you (2) with regard to you. **lovely** (1) lovable (2) handsome **14 When . . . truth** when your physical beauty fades, your true substance will be distilled and preserved by (my) verse. (See sonnet 5.) **vade** (1) fade (2) go away

50.1 heavy sadly and slowly **2–4 When . . . friend** when the ease and repose I seek at journey's end will merely remind me that I have gone so many miles from my friend.
51.1 slow offense offense consisting in slowness **2 my dull bearer** i.e., the horse **4 posting** riding swiftly **6 swift extremity** extreme swiftness (in returning to you) **8 In . . . know** even at the speed of flight I won't perceive the motion at all, won't feel as though I'm moving. **11 Shall . . . race** i.e., shall neigh proudly in its fire-swift race, since it, composed like fire of a lighter element, is not held back by the heavy flesh. (See sonnet 45.) **12 for love** for love's sake.
jade nag **14 go** travel on at his own pace.
52.1 as the rich like the rich man **4 For . . . pleasure** lest he blunt the delicacy of pleasure sparingly enjoyed. **5 feasts** feast days. **solemn** ceremonious, festive. **rare** excellent; uncommon **8 captain** principal. **carcanet** necklace of jewels. **9 keeps you** (1) watches over you (2) keeps you from me. **as** like

But you shall shine more bright in these contents
Than unswept stone besmeared with sluttish time.
When wasteful war shall statues overturn,
And broils root out the work of masonry,
Nor Mars his sword nor war's quick fire shall burn   8
The living record of your memory.
'Gainst death and all-oblivious enmity
Shall you pace forth; your praise shall still find room
Even in the eyes of all posterity
That wear this world out to the ending doom.   12
    So, till the judgment that yourself arise,
    You live in this, and dwell in lovers' eyes.

56

Sweet love, renew thy force! Be it not said
Thy edge should blunter be than appetite,
Which but today by feeding is allayed,
Tomorrow sharpened in his former might.   4
So, love, be thou; although today thou fill
Thy hungry eyes even till they wink with fullness,
Tomorrow see again, and do not kill
The spirit of love with a perpetual dullness.   8
Let this sad interim like the ocean be
Which parts the shore where two contracted new
Come daily to the banks, that, when they see
Return of love, more blest may be the view;   12
    As call it winter, which being full of care
    Makes summer's welcome thrice more wished, more
      rare.

57

Being your slave, what should I do but tend
Upon the hours and times of your desire?
I have no precious time at all to spend,
Nor services to do, till you require.   4
Nor dare I chide the world-without-end hour
Whilst I, my sovereign, watch the clock for you,
Nor think the bitterness of absence sour
When you have bid your servant once adieu.   8
Nor dare I question with my jealous thought
Where you may be, or your affairs suppose,

But, like a sad slave, stay and think of naught
Save where you are how happy you make those.   12
    So true a fool is love that in your will,
    Though you do anything, he thinks no ill.

58

That god forbid, that made me first your slave,
I should in thought control your times of pleasure,
Or at your hand th'account of hours to crave,
Being your vassal, bound to stay your leisure!   4
Oh, let me suffer, being at your beck,
Th'imprisoned absence of your liberty,
And, patience-tame to sufferance, bide each check,
Without accusing you of injury.   8
Be where you list, your charter is so strong
That you yourself may privilege your time
To what you will; to you it doth belong
Yourself to pardon of self-doing crime.   12
    I am to wait, though waiting so be hell,
    Not blame your pleasure, be it ill or well.

59

If there be nothing new, but that which is
Hath been before, how are our brains beguiled,
Which, laboring for invention, bear amiss
The second burden of a former child!   4
Oh, that record could with a backward look,
Even of five hundred courses of the sun,
Show me your image in some antique book,
Since mind at first in character was done!   8
That I might see what the old world could say
To this composèd wonder of your frame;
Whether we are mended, or whe'er better they,
Or whether revolution be the same.   12
    Oh, sure I am the wits of former days
    To subjects worse have given admiring praise.

60

Like as the waves make towards the pebbled shore,
So do our minutes hasten to their end,
Each changing place with that which goes before,

55.3 these contents i.e., the contents of my poems written in praise of you   **4 Than unswept stone** than in a memorial stone that has been left unswept, unattended.   **sluttish** neglectful, slovenly, whorish   **5 wasteful** laying waste   **6 broils** uprisings, battles   **7 Nor Mars his sword** Neither Mars's sword (shall destroy)   **9 all-oblivious enmity** oblivion, at enmity with everything   **12 That . . . doom** that will last from now till doomsday. (*That* may refer to *eyes*, *praise*, or *posterity*.)   **13 till . . . arise** until the Judgment Day, when you will arise from the dead
56.1 love i.e., the spirit of love. (The friend is not directly mentioned in this sonnet.)   **1–2 Be . . . appetite** Let no one attempt to argue that true love should be any less sharp-edged in desire than sexual appetite   **3 but** only for   **4 his** its   **6 wink** shut   **9 sad interim** a period of love's abatement or absence   **10 parts the shore** separates the shores.   **contracted new** newly betrothed   **11 banks** shores   **12 love** the loved one   **13 As** just as appropriately
57.1 tend attend   **5 world-without-end** interminable   **6 Whilst . . . you** while I count the minutes, my sovereign, waiting for your command   **7 Nor think** nor dare I think   **9 question with** (1) debate with (2) seek to know by means of   **10 suppose** make conjectures about

13 true (1) constant (2) utter.   **in your will** with regard to your desire (with perhaps an allusion to "Will Shakespeare"; "will" is capitalized in the 1609 Quarto, as in sonnet 135)
58.3 th'account . . . crave should crave an accounting of how you spend your time   **4 stay** await   **6 Th'imprisoned . . . liberty** the lack of freedom I suffer in being absent from you, arising from (*of*) your freedom and licentious behavior   **7 And . . . check** and, trained to endure any suffering, let me put up with each rebuke   **9 list** please.   **charter** privilege   **10 privilege** authorize   **12 self-doing** committed by yourself   **13 am to** must
59.1 that everything   **3–4 laboring . . . child** striving to give birth to a new creation, merely miscarry with the repetition of something created before.   **5 record** memory, especially memory preserved in writing   **6 courses . . . sun** years   **8 Since . . . done** since thought was first expressed in writing.   **10 composèd wonder** wonderful composition   **11 mended** improved.   **whe'er** whether   **12 revolution . . . same** the revolving of the ages brings only repetition.   **13 wits** discerning persons; poets
60.1 Like . . . shore Just as waves move up the shingle beach   **3 changing place with** replacing

In sequent toil all forwards do contend.
Nativity, once in the main of light,
Crawls to maturity, wherewith being crowned,
Crookèd eclipses 'gainst his glory fight,   4
And Time that gave doth now his gift confound.   8
Time doth transfix the flourish set on youth
And delves the parallels in beauty's brow,
Feeds on the rarities of nature's truth,
And nothing stands but for his scythe to mow.   12
    And yet to times in hope my verse shall stand,
    Praising thy worth despite his cruel hand.

61

Is it thy will thy image should keep open
My heavy eyelids to the weary night?
Dost thou desire my slumbers should be broken
While shadows like to thee do mock my sight?   4
Is it thy spirit that thou send'st from thee
So far from home into my deeds to pry,
To find out shames and idle hours in me,
The scope and tenor of thy jealousy?   8
Oh, no, thy love, though much, is not so great;
It is my love that keeps mine eye awake,
Mine own true love that doth my rest defeat,
To play the watchman ever for thy sake.   12
    For thee watch I whilst thou dost wake elsewhere,
    From me far off, with others all too near.

62

Sin of self-love possesseth all mine eye,
And all my soul, and all my every part;
And for this sin there is no remedy,
It is so grounded inward in my heart.   4
Methinks no face so gracious is as mine,
No shape so true, no truth of such account,
And for myself mine own worth do define
As I all other in all worths surmount.   8
But when my glass shows me myself indeed,
Beated and chapped with tanned antiquity,
Mine own self-love quite contrary I read;
Self so self-loving were iniquity.   12
    'Tis thee, my self, that for myself I praise,
    Painting my age with beauty of thy days.

63

Against my love shall be, as I am now,
With Time's injurious hand crushed and o'erworn;
When hours have drained his blood and filled his brow
With lines and wrinkles; when his youthful morn   4
Hath traveled on to age's steepy night,
And all those beauties whereof now he's king
Are vanishing or vanished out of sight,
Stealing away the treasure of his spring;   8
For such a time do I now fortify
Against confounding age's cruel knife,
That he shall never cut from memory
My sweet love's beauty, though my lover's life.   12
    His beauty shall in these black lines be seen,
    And they shall live, and he in them still green.

64

When I have seen by Time's fell hand defaced
The rich proud cost of outworn buried age;
When sometime lofty towers I see down-razed
And brass eternal slave to mortal rage;   4
When I have seen the hungry ocean gain
Advantage on the kingdom of the shore,
And the firm soil win of the wat'ry main,
Increasing store with loss and loss with store;   8
When I have seen such interchange of state,
Or state itself confounded to decay,
Ruin hath taught me thus to ruminate
That Time will come and take my love away.   12
    This thought is as a death, which cannot choose
    But weep to have that which it fears to lose.

65

Since brass, nor stone, nor earth, nor boundless sea,
But sad mortality o'ersways their power,
How with this rage shall beauty hold a plea,
Whose action is no stronger than a flower?   4
Oh, how shall summer's honey breath hold out
Against the wrackful siege of batt'ring days,

---

4 In . . . contend one after another, all struggle onward.   **5 Nativity . . . light** The newborn infant, no sooner born into the broad expanse of this world and the light of day   **7 Crookèd** perverse, malignant **8 doth . . . confound** now destroys what it gave.   **9 doth . . . flourish** pierces through and destroys the ornament, i.e., the physical beauty **10 delves the parallels** digs the wrinkles, furrows   **11 Feeds . . . truth** consumes the most precious things created by the fidelity of nature **12 but . . . mow** that can escape the mowing of Time's scythe. **13 times in hope** times to come
61.4 shadows images. (But also suggesting spirits.)   **8 The scope . . . jealousy** the aim and purport of your suspicion. (Probably in apposition to *shames and idle hours*.)   **62.5 Methinks** It seems to me   **7 for myself** (1) by my own reckoning (2) for my own pleasure   **8 As** as if.   **other** others   **9 glass** mirror. **indeed** as I actually am   **10 Beated** battered, weather-beaten.   **tanned antiquity** i.e., leathery old age   **12 Self . . . iniquity** it would be wicked for the self to love such an aged and unattractive self.   **13 thee, my self** you, with whom I identify myself.   **for** as   **14 days** i.e., youth.

63.1 Against Anticipating the time when.   **love** beloved   **2 crushed and o'erworn** creased and worn threadbare (like a long-used garment) **5 traveled** (1) journeyed (2) labored.   **steepy** precipitous, i.e., descending swiftly toward death   **9 For such a time** (Parallel in construction with *Against* in line 1.)   **fortify** raise works of defense   **10 confounding** destroying   **11 That** so that   **12 though** i.e., though he cut **13 black** (1) inscribed in ink (2) the opposite of fair or beautiful   **14 still** (1) even in death (2) forever.   **green** i.e., as in springtime and youth. **64.1 fell** cruel   **2 The rich . . . age** i.e., those monuments that were the product of proud wealth and magnificent outlay in times now past and forgotten   **3 sometime** formerly   **4 brass . . . rage** i.e., seemingly indestructible brass subdued by the destructive power of decay   **7 of . . . main** at the expense of the ocean   **8 Increasing . . . store** one gaining as the other loses, and losing as the other gains   **9 state** condition **10 state** pomp, greatness; condition in the abstract.   **confounded to decay** destroyed to the point of being in ruins   **12 love** beloved **13 which cannot choose** (Modifies *thought*.)   **14 to have** at having **65.1 Since** i.e., Since there is neither   **3 How . . . plea** how against this destructive force can beauty hope to make its case   **4 action** (1) efficacy (2) case (in law)   **6 wrackful** destructive

When rocks impregnable are not so stout,
Nor gates of steel so strong, but Time decays?   8
Oh, fearful meditation! Where, alack,
Shall Time's best jewel from Time's chest lie hid?
Or what strong hand can hold his swift foot back?
Or who his spoil of beauty can forbid?   12
    Oh, none, unless this miracle have might,
    That in black ink my love may still shine bright.

66

Tired with all these, for restful death I cry:
As, to behold desert a beggar born,
And needy nothing trimmed in jollity,
And purest faith unhappily forsworn,   4
And gilded honor shamefully misplaced,
And maiden virtue rudely strumpeted,
And right perfection wrongfully disgraced,
And strength by limping sway disablèd,   8
And art made tongue-tied by authority,
And folly doctorlike controlling skill,
And simple truth miscalled simplicity,
And captive good attending captain ill.   12
    Tired with all these, from these would I be gone,
    Save that, to die, I leave my love alone.

67

Ah, wherefore with infection should he live,
And with his presence grace impiety,
That sin by him advantage should achieve
And lace itself with his society?   4
Why should false painting imitate his cheek
And steal dead seeming of his living hue?
Why should poor beauty indirectly seek
Roses of shadow, since his rose is true?   8

Why should he live, now Nature bankrupt is,
Beggared of blood to blush through lively veins,
For she hath no exchequer now but his,
And, proud of many, lives upon his gains?   12
    Oh, him she stores, to show what wealth she had
    In days long since, before these last so bad.

68

Thus is his cheek the map of days outworn,
When beauty lived and died as flowers do now,
Before these bastard signs of fair were born,
Or durst inhabit on a living brow;   4
Before the golden tresses of the dead,
The right of sepulchers, were shorn away
To live a second life on second head;
Ere beauty's dead fleece made another gay.   8
In him those holy antique hours are seen
Without all ornament, itself and true,
Making no summer of another's green,
Robbing no old to dress his beauty new;   12
    And him as for a map doth Nature store,
    To show false art what beauty was of yore.

69

Those parts of thee that the world's eye doth view
Want nothing that the thought of hearts can mend;
All tongues, the voice of souls, give thee that due,
Utt'ring bare truth, even so as foes commend.   4
Thy outward thus with outward praise is crowned,
But those same tongues that give thee so thine own
In other accents do this praise confound
By seeing farther than the eye hath shown.   8
They look into the beauty of thy mind,
And that, in guess, they measure by thy deeds;
Then, churls, their thoughts, although their eyes were
    kind,
To thy fair flower add the rank smell of weeds.   12

7 **stout** sturdy, impregnable   8 **decays** brings about their decay.
9–10 **Where . . . hid?** Where, alas, shall the youth and beauty of my
friend (*Time's best jewel*) be hidden away from being deposited by
Time in its repository of forgetfulness?   12 **spoil** despoliation, rav-
aging   14 **my love** (1) my beloved (2) the love I feel for him
66.1 **all these** i.e., the following   2 **As** for instance, namely.   **desert**
one who is deserving   3 **And needy . . . jollity** and empty worthless-
ness adorned in finery   4 **unhappily forsworn** wretchedly and evilly
betrayed   5 **gilded** golden, splendid. (Not here suggesting mere
appearance of splendor.)   6 **strumpeted** accused of profligacy, or violated   7 **right** true.   **disgraced** banished from favor   8 **limping
sway** halting leadership   9 **And art . . . authority** and literature and
learning stifled by censorship   10 **doctorlike** assuming a learned
bearing.   **controlling** dominating, curbing   11 **miscalled simplicity**
slandered as foolishness, naivetè   12 **attending** waiting on, subordinated to   14 **to die** in dying
67.1 **wherefore** why.   **with infection** i.e., with the world's ills, as
enumerated in the preceding sonnet.   **he** i.e., the poet's friend
3 **That . . . achieve** with the result that sin should flourish by being
associated with him   4 **lace . . . society** (1) adorn itself with his company (2) weave its way into his company.   6 **dead seeming of** lifeless
appearance from   7 **poor** inferior.   **indirectly** imitatively, or, falsely
8 **Roses of shadow** i.e., painted roses, cosmetically applied.   **since**
(1) just because (2) since after all

9–12 **Why . . . gains?** Why should he continue to live in this bad
world, seeing that Nature has now squandered all her resources of
beauty on him, with no genuine way left to produce a natural blush
on the cheek, since she has no treasury of natural beauty other than
what is vested in him, and, though (falsely) taking pride in her abundance (of offspring), lives solely on the wealth (of beauty) that he provides?   13 **stores** preserves, keeps in store   14 **last** i.e., recent days,
the present
68.1 **map** embodiment, image   3 **bastard . . . fair** i.e., cosmetics.
born (Suggesting also *borne*, "worn.")   4 **inhabit** dwell   5–7 **Before
. . . head** i.e., before the deplorable current fad of making wigs out of
dead persons' hair   8 **gay** lovely, gaudy.   9 **holy antique hours**
blessed ancient times   10 **all** any   13 **store** stock (with beauty) and
preserve
69.2 **Want** lack.   **mend** improve upon   3–4 **the voice . . . commend**
i.e., uttering heartfelt conviction, allow that as your due, thus saying
what even your enemies would concede to be the bare truth.   5 **outward praise** the kind of praise suited to mere outward qualities
6 **thine own** your due   7 **In other accents** in other terms and with
another emphasis.   **confound** confute, destroy   10 **in guess** at a
guess   12 **To . . . weeds** i.e., to the flower of your outward beauty,
they contrastingly suggest something putrid within.

But why thy odor matcheth not thy show,
The soil is this, that thou dost common grow.

70

That thou art blamed shall not be thy defect,
For slander's mark was ever yet the fair;
The ornament of beauty is suspect,
A crow that flies in heaven's sweetest air. 4
So thou be good, slander doth but approve
Thy worth the greater, being wooed of time,
For canker vice the sweetest buds doth love,
And thou present'st a pure unstainèd prime. 8
Thou hast passed by the ambush of young days,
Either not assailed, or victor being charged;
Yet this thy praise cannot be so thy praise
To tie up envy, evermore enlarged. 12
    If some suspect of ill masked not thy show,
    Then thou alone kingdoms of hearts shouldst owe.

71

No longer mourn for me when I am dead
Than you shall hear the surly sullen bell
Give warning to the world that I am fled
From this vile world, with vilest worms to dwell. 4
Nay, if you read this line, remember not
The hand that writ it, for I love you so
That I in your sweet thoughts would be forgot
If thinking on me then should make you woe. 8
Oh, if, I say, you look upon this verse
When I perhaps compounded am with clay,
Do not so much as my poor name rehearse,
But let your love even with my life decay, 12
    Lest the wise world should look into your moan
    And mock you with me after I am gone.

72

Oh, lest the world should task you to recite
What merit lived in me that you should love,

After my death, dear love, forget me quite;
For you in me can nothing worthy prove— 4
Unless you would devise some virtuous lie
To do more for me than mine own desert,
And hang more praise upon deceasèd I
Than niggard truth would willingly impart. 8
Oh, lest your true love may seem false in this,
That you for love speak well of me untrue,
My name be buried where my body is,
And live no more to shame nor me nor you. 12
    For I am shamed by that which I bring forth,
    And so should you, to love things nothing worth.

73

That time of year thou mayst in me behold
When yellow leaves, or none, or few, do hang
Upon those boughs which shake against the cold,
Bare ruined choirs where late the sweet birds sang. 4
In me thou see'st the twilight of such day
As after sunset fadeth in the west,
Which by and by black night doth take away,
Death's second self, that seals up all in rest. 8
In me thou see'st the glowing of such fire
That on the ashes of his youth doth lie
As the deathbed whereon it must expire,
Consumed with that which it was nourished by. 12
    This thou perceiv'st, which makes thy love more strong,
    To love that well which thou must leave ere long.

74

But be contented when that fell arrest
Without all bail shall carry me away;
My life hath in this line some interest,
Which for memorial still with thee shall stay. 4
When thou reviewest this, thou dost review
The very part was consecrate to thee.
The earth can have but earth, which is his due;
My spirit is thine, the better part of me. 8

13 **odor** i.e., reputation   14 **soil** (1) blemish, fault (2) origin, source, ground.   **common** cheapened by being too familiar and available to all, inferior (like a weed)
70.1 **defect** fault   2 **mark** target   3 **The . . . suspect** i.e., Beauty is always attended by suspicion (*suspect*), as though suspicion were a necessary ornament to beauty   5 **So** Provided that.   **approve** prove   6 **being . . . time** i.e., since it shows you are courted by the world   7 **canker vice** i.e., slander, that is like the cankerworm   8 **unstainèd prime** unspoiled youth (like the pure, unspoiled flower that attracts the cankerworm).   9 **ambush . . . days** temptations of youth   10 **being charged** when you were assailed   11–12 **Yet . . . enlarged** yet the praise you receive cannot be enough to silence malice, which is always at liberty to do its worst.   13 **If . . . show** If some suspicion (*suspect*) of ill doing did not partly obscure your outward attractiveness   14 **owe** own.
71.2 **bell** a passing bell for one who has died, rung once for each year of that person's life   8 **on** of, about.   **make you woe** cause you woe or make you woeful.   10 **compounded** mingled   11 **rehearse** repeat   12 **even with** at the same time as   13 **look . . . moan** investigate the cause of your sorrow   14 **with** because of; for loving; along with
72.1 **recite** tell

7 **hang** (as in hanging trophies on a funeral monument)   10 **of me untrue** (1) about me untruly (2) about me, flawed and inconstant as I am   11 **My name be** let my name be   12 **nor . . . nor** neither . . . nor   13 **that . . . forth** (Perhaps a deprecatory reference to the author's acting and writing of plays, but more probably his verse or his written work generally.)   14 **should you** i.e., you ought to be ashamed
73.4 **Bare . . . sang** (In their arched shape, the bare trees resemble the church choir where the service is sung; with a hint of *quires*, gatherings of *leaves* [see line 2] in a book or manuscript, and evoking memories of church buildings left in ruins by the dissolution of the monasteries in the English Reformation. *Late* means "lately.")   8 **seals** closes   10 **his** its   12 **with** (1) by (2) along with   14 **that** (1) me, your beloved (2) youth and life itself.   **leave** i.e., lose by the speaker's death
74.1 **be contented . . . arrest** do not be distressed when that cruel arrest (carried out by Death)   3 **line** verse.   **interest** legal concern, right, or title   4 **still** (1) always (2) despite death   5 **reviewest this** see this again (and view it with a critical eye)   6 **part was consecrate** part (of me) that was dedicated solemnly (as in a religious service)   7 **his** its

So then thou hast but lost the dregs of life,
The prey of worms, my body being dead,
The coward conquest of a wretch's knife,
Too base of thee to be rememberèd.   12
    The worth of that is that which it contains,
    And that is this, and this with thee remains.

75

So are you to my thoughts as food to life,
Or as sweet-seasoned showers are to the ground.
And for the peace of you I hold such strife
As twixt a miser and his wealth is found: 4
Now proud as an enjoyer, and anon
Doubting the filching age will steal his treasure;
Now counting best to be with you alone,
Then bettered that the world may see my pleasure;   8
Sometime all full with feasting on your sight,
And by and by clean starvèd for a look;
Possessing or pursuing no delight
Save what is had or must from you be took.   12
    Thus do I pine and surfeit day by day,
    Or gluttoning on all, or all away.

76

Why is my verse so barren of new pride?
So far from variation or quick change?
Why with the time do I not glance aside
To newfound methods and to compounds strange?   4
Why write I still all one, ever the same,
And keep invention in a noted weed,
That every word doth almost tell my name,
Showing their birth and where they did proceed?   8
Oh, know, sweet love, I always write of you,
And you and love are still my argument;
So all my best is dressing old words new,
Spending again what is already spent.   12
    For as the sun is daily new and old,
    So is my love still telling what is told.

77

Thy glass will show thee how thy beauties wear,
Thy dial how thy precious minutes waste;
The vacant leaves thy mind's imprint will bear,
And of this book this learning mayst thou taste: 4
The wrinkles which thy glass will truly show
Of mouthèd graves will give thee memory;
Thou by thy dial's shady stealth mayst know
Time's thievish progress to eternity.   8
Look what thy memory cannot contain
Commit to these waste blanks, and thou shalt find
Those children nursed, delivered from thy brain,
To take a new acquaintance of thy mind.   12
    These offices, so oft as thou wilt look,
    Shall profit thee and much enrich thy book.

78

So oft have I invoked thee for my Muse
And found such fair assistance in my verse
As every alien pen hath got my use
And under thee their poesy disperse.   4
Thine eyes, that taught the dumb on high to sing
And heavy ignorance aloft to fly,
Have added feathers to the learnèd's wing
And given grace a double majesty.   8
Yet be most proud of that which I compile,
Whose influence is thine and born of thee.
In others' works thou dost but mend the style,
And arts with thy sweet graces gracèd be;   12
    But thou art all my art, and dost advance
    As high as learning my rude ignorance.

79

Whilst I alone did call upon thy aid,
My verse alone had all thy gentle grace,
But now my gracious numbers are decayed,
And my sick Muse doth give another place.   4

11 **The coward . . . knife** i.e., the cowardly conquest that even such a poor wretch as Mortality, or Death, can make with his scythe   **12 of . . . rememberèd** to be remembered by you.   **13–14 The worth . . . remains** The only worth of my body is the spirit it contains, i.e., this verse, which will remain with you and endure through you.
75.1 as food to life what food is to life   **2 sweet-seasoned** of the sweet season, i.e., spring   **3 of you** to be found in loving you   **6 Doubting** suspecting, fearing that.   **filching** thieving   **7 counting** (1) thinking it (2) reckoning, like a miser   **8 bettered** made happier, better pleased. **see my pleasure** i.e., see me with you, enjoying your company **10 clean** completely, absolutely.   **a look** (1) a glimpse of you (2) an exchange of glances   **12 Save . . . took** except what is had or must be received from you alone.   **13 pine and surfeit** starve and overeat **14 Or . . . or** either . . . or.   **all away** i.e., all food being taken away.
76.1 pride ornament.   **2 quick change** fashionable innovation.
3 time way of the world, fashion   **4 compounds** strange literary inventions, or perhaps, compound words, neologisms.   **5 still all one** continually one way   **6 invention** literary creation.   **noted weed** familiar garment   **8 where** whence   **10 still** always. **argument** subject, theme   **14 telling** (1) retelling (2) counting over. (Continuing the financial wordplay of *Spending* and *spent* in line 12, and in 75.7.)

77.1 glass mirror.   **wear** wear away   **2 dial** sundial   **3 vacant leaves** blank pages. (Apparently these lines accompanied the gift of a book of blank pages, a memorandum book.)   **thy mind's imprint** i.e., your reflections and ideas, to be set down in the memorandum book **4 this learning** i.e., mental profit derived from reflecting and keeping a journal, as explained in lines 9 ff.   **6 mouthèd** all-devouring, gaping.   **memory** reminder   **7 shady stealth** stealthy shadow   **9 Look what** Whatever   **10 waste blanks** blank pages   **10–12 thou . . . mind** you will see those thoughts, the children of your brain, nursed to maturity and ready to be newly reencountered by your mind.
13 offices duties (of meditation and reflection)   **14 thy book** i.e., the memorandum book, where these reflections are to be set down.
78.2 fair favorable   **3 As** that.   **alien** belonging to others.   **got my use** adopted my practice   **4 under thee** i.e., with you as their muse or patron; under your influence.   **disperse** circulate.   **5 on high** aloud. (Also anticipating *aloft*.)   **7 added . . . wing** i.e., enabled learned poets to fly higher still. (A falconry metaphor; birds could be given extra wing feathers.)   **8 And . . . majesty** and have added to the majesty of poets already capable of it.   **9 compile** compose, write **10 influence** inspiration. (With suggestion of astrological meaning.) **11 mend the style** correct or improve the style. (Also with a suggestion of repairing the point of a writing quill or stylus, continuing the metaphor of *pen* and *feathers*.)   **12 arts** learning, literary culture **13 advance** lift up
79.3 numbers verse   **4 doth . . . place** yields place to another.

I grant, sweet love, thy lovely argument
Deserves the travail of a worthier pen,
Yet what of thee thy poet doth invent
He robs thee of and pays it thee again. 8
He lends thee virtue, and he stole that word
From thy behavior; beauty doth he give,
And found it in thy cheek; he can afford
No praise to thee but what in thee doth live. 12
 Then thank him not for that which he doth say,
 Since what he owes thee thou thyself dost pay.

80

Oh, how I faint when I of you do write,
Knowing a better spirit doth use your name,
And in the praise thereof spends all his might
To make me tongue-tied, speaking of your fame! 4
But since your worth, wide as the ocean is,
The humble as the proudest sail doth bear,
My saucy bark, inferior far to his,
On your broad main doth willfully appear. 8
Your shallowest help will hold me up afloat,
Whilst he upon your soundless deep doth ride;
Or, being wrecked, I am a worthless boat,
He of tall building and of goodly pride. 12
 Then if he thrive and I be cast away,
 The worst was this: my love was my decay.

81

Or I shall live your epitaph to make,
Or you survive when I in earth am rotten,
From hence your memory death cannot take,
Although in me each part will be forgotten. 4
Your name from hence immortal life shall have,
Though I, once gone, to all the world must die;
The earth can yield me but a common grave,
When you entombèd in men's eyes shall lie. 8
Your momument shall be my gentle verse,
Which eyes not yet created shall o'erread,
And tongues to be your being shall rehearse
When all the breathers of this world are dead. 12
 You still shall live—such virtue hath my pen—
 Where breath most breathes, even in the mouths of
 men.

82

I grant thou wert not married to my Muse,
And therefore mayst without attaint o'erlook
The dedicated words which writers use
Of their fair subject, blessing every book. 4
Thou art as fair in knowledge as in hue,
Finding thy worth a limit past my praise,
And therefore art enforced to seek anew
Some fresher stamp of these time-bettering days. 8
And do so, love; yet when they have devised
What strainèd touches rhetoric can lend,
Thou, truly fair, wert truly sympathized
In true plain words by thy true-telling friend; 12
 And their gross painting might be better used
 Where cheeks need blood; in thee it is abused.

83

I never saw that you did painting need,
And therefore to your fair no painting set;
I found, or thought I found, you did exceed
The barren tender of a poet's debt; 4
And therefore have I slept in your report,
That you yourself, being extant, well might show
How far a modern quill doth come too short,
Speaking of worth, what worth in you doth grow. 8
This silence for my sin you did impute,
Which shall be most my glory, being dumb;
For I impair not beauty, being mute,
When others would give life and bring a tomb. 12
 There lives more life in one of your fair eyes
 Than both your poets can in praise devise.

84

Who is it that says most which can say more
Than this rich praise: that you alone are you,
In whose confine immurèd is the store
Which should example where your equal grew? 4

5 **thy lovely argument** the theme of your lovable qualities   6 **travail** labor   7–8 **Yet . . . again** yet whatever a poet under your patronage discovers as a literary subject concerning you he merely robs from you and gives you back your own again.   11 **afford** furnish, extend   80.1 **faint** grow weak, falter   2 **better spirit** i.e., rival poet, whom the speaker admires   5 **wide . . . is** as wide as is the ocean   6 **as** as well as   8 **main** ocean.   **willfully** perversely, audaciously   9 **Your . . . afloat** i.e., My genius is so slight that I derive only minimal benefit from the greatness of you as my subject   10 **soundless** unfathomable   11 **wrecked** shipwrecked   12 **tall building** i.e., sturdy construction.   **pride** splendor.   13 **cast away** (1) shipwrecked (2) abandoned   14 **my love** (1) my love for you, which led me to be so reckless in my inferior boat (2) you, my beloved.   **decay** ruin.
81.1 **Or** Whether   3 **hence** (1) this poetry (2) the world   4 **in . . . part** every quality of mine (as distinguished from the poetry)   5 **from hence** (1) from this poetry (2) henceforth   11 **to be** i.e., of persons yet unborn.   **rehearse** recite   12 **breathers** living people.   **this world** this present time   13 **virtue** power   14 **even in the** in the very

82.2 **attaint** blame, discredit.   **o'erlook** look at, peruse   3 **dedicated** devoted. (With suggestion of "dedicatory.")   **writers** i.e., other writers   4 **blessing every book** i.e., you bestowing favor thus on the writings presented to you, or, writers commending their own work.   5 **hue** complexion, appearance   6 **a limit . . . praise** an area extending beyond the capacities of my praise   8 **Some . . . days** some more recently issued imprint, i.e., more up-to-date literary product of this culturally sophisticated age.   11 **wert truly sympathized** would be faithfully matched and described   13 **gross painting** flattery that is heavily laid on, like a cosmetic   14 **abused** misused, misapplied
83.1 **painting** i.e., artificial enhancement of beauty   2 **fair** beauty.   **set** applied   4 **The barren . . . debt** the worthless homage that a poet can offer you   5 **slept . . . report** been neglectful in writing praisingly of you   6 **That** because, so that.   **extant** still alive and much in the public eye   7 **modern** (1) commonplace (2) up-to-date   7–8 **doth come . . . grow** comes too short, in describing your worth, of the actual worth that flourishes in you.   9–10 **This . . . dumb** You imputed my silence to willful failure when, in fact, it will prove most to my credit   11 **being mute** (Modifies *I*.)   12 **bring a tomb** i.e., instead, they bring an inadequate monument that conceals lifelessly rather than enhances.   14 **both your poets** i.e., (probably,) I and the rival poet
84.1–2 **Who . . . praise** What extravagant writer of praise can say more than this in way of praise   3–4 **In . . . grew** in whose person are contained all those rich qualities that would be needed as a model to produce again your equal in beauty.

Lean penury within that pen doth dwell
That to his subject lends not some small glory;
But he that writes of you, if he can tell
That you are you, so dignifies his story.   8
Let him but copy what in you is writ,
Not making worse what nature made so clear,
And such a counterpart shall fame his wit,
Making his style admirèd everywhere.   12
　　You to your beauteous blessings add a curse,
　　Being fond on praise, which makes your praises
　　　　worse.

85

My tongue-tied Muse in manners holds her still,
While comments of your praise, richly compiled,
Reserve thy character with golden quill
And precious phrase by all the Muses filed.   4
I think good thoughts whilst other write good words,
And like unlettered clerk still cry "Amen"
To every hymn that able spirit affords
In polished form of well-refinèd pen.   8
Hearing you praised, I say "'Tis so, 'tis true,"
And to the most of praise add something more;
But that is in my thought, whose love to you,
Though words come hindmost, holds his rank before.   12
　　Then others for the breath of words respect,
　　Me for my dumb thoughts, speaking in effect.

86

Was it the proud full sail of his great verse,
Bound for the prize of all-too-precious you,
That did my ripe thoughts in my brain inhearse,
Making their tomb the womb wherein they grew?   4
Was it his spirit, by spirits taught to write
Above a mortal pitch, that struck me dead?
No, neither he, nor his compeers by night
Giving him aid, my verse astonishèd.   8
He, nor that affable familiar ghost

Which nightly gulls him with intelligence,
As victors of my silence cannot boast;
I was not sick of any fear from thence.   12
　　But when your countenance filled up his line,
　　Then lacked I matter; that enfeebled mine.

87

Farewell! Thou art too dear for my possessing,
And like enough thou know'st thy estimate.
The charter of thy worth gives thee releasing;
My bonds in thee are all determinate.   4
For how do I hold thee but by thy granting,
And for that riches where is my deserving?
The cause of this fair gift in me is wanting,
And so my patent back again is swerving.   8
Thyself thou gav'st, thy own worth then not knowing,
Or me, to whom thou gav'st it, else mistaking;
So thy great gift, upon misprision growing,
Comes home again, on better judgment making.   12
　　Thus have I had thee as a dream doth flatter,
　　In sleep a king, but waking no such matter.

88

When thou shalt be disposed to set me light
And place my merit in the eye of scorn,
Upon thy side against myself I'll fight
And prove thee virtuous, though thou art forsworn.   4
With mine own weakness being best acquainted,
Upon thy part I can set down a story
Of faults concealed, wherein I am attainted,
That thou in losing me shall win much glory.   8
And I by this will be a gainer too;
For, bending all my loving thoughts on thee,
The injuries that to myself I do,
Doing thee vantage, double-vantage me.   12
　　Such is my love, to thee I so belong,
　　That for thy right myself will bear all wrong.

89

Say that thou didst forsake me for some fault,
And I will comment upon that offense;
Speak of my lameness, and I straight will halt,

5–6 Lean . . . glory It is a poor piece of writing indeed that does not confer at least some glory on its subject   8 so sufficiently, thus
10 clear glorious, shining   11 counterpart copy, likeness.   fame endow with fame   13 curse (1) defect in character (2) burden for those seeking to praise you   14 Being fond doting.   which . . .
worse (1) which encourages false flattery (2) which makes all praise seem inadequate in comparison to you.
85.1 in . . . still politely remains silent   2 comments . . . compiled eulogies of you composed in fine language   3 Reserve thy character store up praise of you in their writings.   golden aureate, affected   4 precious affected.   filed polished.   5 other others   6–7 like . . . affords like an illiterate assistant to a priest continually give my approval to every praising verse that the rival poet (and others like him) provides   10 most highmost   11 that . . . thought that which I add is added silently   12 holds . . . before is second to none in love.   13 Then . . . respect Then take notice of others for what they say   14 speaking in effect conveying what speech would say.
86.1 his i.e., an unidentified rival poet's   2 prize capture, booty (as in a seized cargo vessel)   3 inhearse coffin up   5 spirits i.e., literary ancestors or contemporaries. (With a suggestion also of *daemons*, attendant spirits.)   6 pitch height. (A term from falconry.)   dead i.e., dumb, silent.   7 compeers by night spirits (see line 5) visiting and aiding the poet in his dreams or nighttime reading   8 astonishèd struck dumb.   9 ghost spirit (as in lines 5 and 7)

10 gulls misleads.   intelligence information, ideas   12 of with
13 countenance filled up (1) approval repaired any defect in (2) beauty served as subject for   14 lacked I matter I had nothing left to write about
87.1 dear precious   2 like likely, probably.   estimate value.   3 charter of privilege derived from.   releasing i.e., release from obligations of love   4 determinate ended, expired. (A legal term, as throughout this sonnet.)   8 my . . . swerving my rights of possession revert to you.
10 mistaking i.e., overvaluing   11 upon misprision growing arising out of error   12 on . . . making on your forming a more accurate judgment.
88.1 set me light make light of me, value me slightingly   3 Upon thy side supporting your case. (Also *Upon thy part* in line 6.)   7 concealed not publicly known.   attainted dishonored   8 That so that.   losing i.e., separating from. (With a suggestion of "loosing," "setting free," the Quarto spelling.)   12 vantage advantage
89.1 Say Assert, claim   2 comment enlarge   3 Speak . . . halt i.e., If you ascribe to me any kind of handicap, I immediately will limp to show that you are right. (*Halt* also has the suggestion of ceasing to object, remaining silent.)

Against thy reasons making no defense.   4
Thou canst not, love, disgrace me half so ill,
To set a form upon desirèd change,
As I'll myself disgrace, knowing thy will.
I will acquaintance strangle and look strange,   8
Be absent from thy walks, and in my tongue
Thy sweet belovèd name no more shall dwell,
Lest I, too much profane, should do it wrong
And haply of our old acquaintance tell.   12
    For thee against myself I'll vow debate,
    For I must ne'er love him whom thou dost hate.

90

Then hate me when thou wilt; if ever, now;
Now, while the world is bent my deeds to cross,
Join with the spite of fortune, make me bow,
And do not drop in for an after-loss.   4
Ah, do not, when my heart hath scaped this sorrow,
Come in the rearward of a conquered woe;
Give not a windy night a rainy morrow,
To linger out a purposed overthrow.   8
If thou wilt leave me, do not leave me last,
When other petty griefs have done their spite,
But in the onset come; so shall I taste
At first the very worst of fortune's might,   12
    And other strains of woe, which now seem woe,
    Compared with loss of thee will not seem so.

91

Some glory in their birth, some in their skill,
Some in their wealth, some in their body's force,
Some in their garments, though newfangled ill,
Some in their hawks and hounds, some in their horse;   4
And every humor hath his adjunct pleasure,
Wherein it finds a joy above the rest.
But these particulars are not my measure;
All these I better in one general best.   8
Thy love is better than high birth to me,
Richer than wealth, prouder than garments' cost,
Of more delight than hawks or horses be;
And having thee, of all men's pride I boast—   12
    Wretched in this alone, that thou mayst take
    All this away and me most wretched make.

92

But do thy worst to steal thyself away,
For term of life thou art assurèd mine,
And life no longer than thy love will stay,
For it depends upon that love of thine.   4
Then need I not to fear the worst of wrongs,
When in the least of them my life hath end;
I see a better state to me belongs
Than that which on thy humor doth depend.   8
Thou canst not vex me with inconstant mind,
Since that my life on thy revolt doth lie.
Oh, what a happy title do I find,
Happy to have thy love, happy to die!   12
    But what's so blessèd-fair that fears no blot?
    Thou mayst be false, and yet I know it not.

93

So shall I live, supposing thou art true,
Like a deceivèd husband; so love's face
May still seem love to me, though altered new,
Thy looks with me, thy heart in other place.   4
For there can live no hatred in thine eye,
Therefore in that I cannot know thy change.
In many's looks the false heart's history
Is writ in moods and frowns and wrinkles strange,   8
But heaven in thy creation did decree
That in thy face sweet love should ever dwell;
Whate'er thy thoughts or thy heart's workings be,
Thy looks should nothing thence but sweetness tell.   12
    How like Eve's apple doth thy beauty grow,
    If thy sweet virtue answer not thy show!

94

They that have power to hurt and will do none,
That do not do the thing they most do show,
Who, moving others, are themselves as stone,
Unmovèd, cold, and to temptation slow,   4
They rightly do inherit heaven's graces
And husband nature's riches from expense;

---

4 **reasons** charges, arguments   5 **disgrace** discredit   6 **To . . . change** to provide a pretext for (in the interest of justifying) your change of affection and to set it in proper order   7 **As . . . disgrace** as I will disfigure and depreciate myself   8 **acquaintance strangle** put an end to familiarity (with you).   **strange** like a stranger   9 **walks** haunts   12 **haply** perchance   13 **vow debate** declare hostility, quarrel   90.2 **bent** determined.   **cross** thwart   4 **drop . . . after-loss** crushingly add to my sorrow.   5–6 **do not . . . woe** do not, when I have just recovered from my present grief, attack me from the rear   7 **windy, rainy** (Suggestive of sighs and tears.)   8 **linger out** protract.   **purposed** intended, inevitable   11 **in the onset** at the outset   13 **strains** (1) kinds (2) stresses   91.3 **newfangled ill** fashionably unattractive   4 **horse** horses   5 **humor** disposition, temperament.   **his adjunct** its corresponding   7 **measure** standard (of happiness); lot in life   8 **better** surpass, improve upon   10 **prouder** more splendid   12 **of . . . boast** I boast of having the equivalent of all that is a source of pride in other men

92.1 **But do** i.e., But even if you do   2 **term of life** i.e., my lifetime   5–6 **Then . . . end** I need not fear what most people would call the worst of misfortunes, since the seemingly lesser misfortune—loss of your friendship—would prove fatal to me   7–8 **I see . . . depend** i.e., I see that I am happier than most people whose happiness ends when they are cast from favor, since my very existence will cease when I am cast from favor and thus will end my misery.   **humor** whim, fancy   10 **Since . . . lie** since if you desert me it will cost me my life.   11 **happy title** right to be thought happy; fortunate legal right of ownership   13 **that fears** as to fear   14 **Thou . . . not** i.e., My worst fate would be to lose your affection without knowing it and thereby live on in an unloved state, unreleased by the death that certainty of your desertion would bring.
93.1 **So** (Continues the thought of sonnet 92.)   **supposing** I supposing (incorrectly)   2 **face** appearance   3 **new** to something new   5 **For** Since   6 **in . . . change** I won't be able to detect your changed affection from your eyes.   8 **moods** moody looks.   **strange** unfriendly   14 **answer . . . show** does not conform with your outward appearance.   94.1 **and . . . none** and do not willfully try to do hurt   2 **show** i.e., show themselves capable of, or, seem to do   4 **cold** dispassionate   5 **inherit** (1) receive through inheritance (2) enjoy, make use of   6 **husband** carefully manage, preserve.   **expense** waste, expenditure.

They are the lords and owners of their faces,
Others but stewards of their excellence.   8
The summer's flower is to the summer sweet,
Though to itself it only live and die,
But if that flower with base infection meet,
The basest weed outbraves his dignity.   12
    For sweetest things turn sourest by their deeds;
    Lilies that fester smell far worse than weeds.

95

How sweet and lovely dost thou make the shame
Which, like a canker in the fragrant rose,
Doth spot the beauty of thy budding name!
Oh, in what sweets dost thou thy sins enclose!   4
That tongue that tells the story of thy days,
Making lascivious comments on thy sport,
Cannot dispraise, but, in a kind of praise,
Naming thy name, blesses an ill report.   8
Oh, what a mansion have those vices got
Which for their habitation chose out thee,
Where beauty's veil doth cover every blot,
And all things turns to fair that eyes can see!   12
    Take heed, dear heart, of this large privilege;
    The hardest knife ill used doth lose his edge.

96

Some say thy fault is youth, some wantonness;
Some say thy grace is youth and gentle sport;
Both grace and faults are loved of more and less;
Thou mak'st faults graces that to thee resort.   4
As on the finger of a thronèd queen
The basest jewel will be well esteemed,
So are those errors that in thee are seen
To truths translated and for true things deemed.   8
How many lambs might the stern wolf betray,
If like a lamb he could his looks translate!
How many gazers mightst thou lead away,
If thou wouldst use the strength of all thy state!   12
    But do not so; I love thee in such sort
    As, thou being mine, mine is thy good report.

97

How like a winter hath my absence been
From thee, the pleasure of the fleeting year!
What freezings have I felt, what dark days seen!
What old December's bareness everywhere!   4
And yet this time removed was summer's time,
The teeming autumn, big with rich increase,
Bearing the wanton burden of the prime,
Like widowed wombs after their lords' decease.   8
Yet this abundant issue seemed to me
But hope of orphans and unfathered fruit,
For summer and his pleasures wait on thee,
And, thou away, the very birds are mute;   12
    Or, if they sing, 'tis with so dull a cheer
    That leaves look pale, dreading the winter's near.

98

From you have I been absent in the spring,
When proud-pied April, dressed in all his trim,
Hath put a spirit of youth in everything,
That heavy Saturn laughed and leapt with him.   4
Yet nor the lays of birds nor the sweet smell
Of different flowers in odor and in hue
Could make me any summer's story tell,
Or from their proud lap pluck them where they grew.   8
Nor did I wonder at the lily's white,
Nor praise the deep vermilion in the rose;
They were but sweet, but figures of delight
Drawn after you, you pattern of all those.   12
    Yet seemed it winter still, and, you away,
    As with your shadow I with these did play.

99

The forward violet thus did I chide:
"Sweet thief, whence didst thou steal thy sweet that
    smells,
If not from my love's breath? The purple pride
Which on thy soft cheek for complexion dwells   4
In my love's veins thou hast too grossly dyed."
The lily I condemnèd for thy hand,
And buds of marjoram had stol'n thy hair;
The roses fearfully on thorns did stand,   8

---

7 **They . . . faces** they are completely masters of themselves and of the qualities that appear in them   **8 but stewards** are merely custodians or dispensers   **9–10 The . . . die** i.e., Such self-contained persons may seem like flowers that live and die unto themselves, but, in fact, they have much sweetness and beauty to bestow   **12 outbraves his dignity** surpasses in show its worth.   **14 Lilies . . . weeds** (This line appears in the anonymous play *Edward III*, usually dated before 1595 and attributed in part by some editors to Shakespeare.)
95.2 canker cankerworm that destroys buds and leaves   **3 name** reputation.   **6 sport** amours   **8 blesses** graces   **12 all . . . fair** makes everything deceptively beautiful   **13 large** unlimited, licentious   **14 his** its
96.1 wantonness (1) exuberance (2) lechery   **2 gentle sport** gentlemanlike amorousness   **3 of more and less** by high and low   **4 Thou . . . resort** you convert into graces the faults that attend you.   **8 translated** transformed   **9 stern** cruel   **10 like** i.e., unto those of **11 away** astray   **12 the strength . . . state** the full power at your command, i.e., your wealth, charm, and social rank.   **13–14 But . . . report** (The same couplet ends sonnet 36.)   **report** reputation.

97.5 time removed time of separation   **6 big** pregnant   **7 the wanton . . . prime** the fruit or offspring of wanton spring, i.e., the crops planted in springtime   **9 issue** offspring   **10 hope of orphans** orphaned hope   **11 his** its.   **wait on thee** attend on you, are at your disposal   **13 with . . . cheer** in so melancholy a fashion
98.2 proud-pied gorgeously multicolored.   **trim** finery   **4 That** so that. **Saturn** (A planet associated with melancholy, *heavy*.)   **5 nor the lays** neither the songs   **6 different flowers** flowers differing   **7 any summer's story** i.e., any pleasant story   **8 proud lap** i.e., the earth   **11 but sweet . . . delight** mere sweetness, mere delightful forms or emblems **12 after** resembling   **14 shadow** image, portrait.   **these** i.e., the flowers
99.1 forward early and presumptuous. (This sonnet has fifteen lines, the first being introductory.)   **2 thy sweet** your scent   **3 pride** splendor **5 grossly** obviously and heavily   **6 for thy hand** i.e., because it has stolen its whiteness from your hand   **7 And . . . hair** i.e., and I condemned the buds of marjoram for having stolen your hair.   **buds of marjoram** (These are dark purple-red or auburn, and it may be that the reference is to color, although marjoram is noted for its sweet scent.)   **8 on thorns did stand** grew on thorny stems. (With a suggestion of being apprehensive.)

One blushing shame, another white despair;
A third, nor red nor white, had stol'n of both
And to his robbery had annexed thy breath,
But, for his theft, in pride of all his growth 12
A vengeful canker ate him up to death.
    More flowers I noted, yet I none could see
    But sweet or color it had stol'n from thee.

100

Where art thou, Muse, that thou forget'st so long
To speak of that which gives thee all thy might?
Spend'st thou thy fury on some worthless song,
Dark'ning thy pow'r to lend base subjects light? 4
Return, forgetful Muse, and straight redeem
In gentle numbers time so idly spent;
Sing to the ear that doth thy lays esteem
And gives thy pen both skill and argument. 8
Rise, resty Muse, my love's sweet face survey
If Time have any wrinkle graven there;
If any, be a satire to decay,
And make Time's spoils despisèd everywhere. 12
    Give my love fame faster than Time wastes life;
    So thou prevent'st his scythe and crooked knife.

101

O truant Muse, what shall be thy amends
For thy neglect of truth in beauty dyed?
Both truth and beauty on my love depends;
So dost thou too, and therein dignified. 4
Make answer, Muse. Wilt thou not haply say,
"Truth needs no color with his color fixed,
Beauty no pencil, beauty's truth to lay,
But best is best, if never intermixed"? 8
Because he needs no praise, wilt thou be dumb?
Excuse not silence so, for 't lies in thee
To make him much outlive a gilded tomb
And to be praised of ages yet to be. 12
    Then do thy office, Muse; I teach thee how
    To make him seem, long hence, as he shows now.

102

My love is strengthened, though more weak in seeming;
I love not less, though less the show appear.
That love is merchandized whose rich esteeming
The owner's tongue doth publish everywhere. 4
Our love was new and then but in the spring
When I was wont to greet it with my lays,
As Philomel in summer's front doth sing
And stops her pipe in growth of riper days— 8
Not that the summer is less pleasant now
Than when her mournful hymns did hush the night,
But that wild music burdens every bough
And sweets grown common lose their dear delight. 12
    Therefore like her I sometime hold my tongue,
    Because I would not dull you with my song.

103

Alack, what poverty my Muse brings forth,
That, having such a scope to show her pride,
The argument all bare is of more worth
Than when it hath my added praise beside. 4
Oh, blame me not if I no more can write!
Look in your glass, and there appears a face
That overgoes my blunt invention quite,
Dulling my lines and doing me disgrace. 8
Were it not sinful then, striving to mend,
To mar the subject that before was well?
For to no other pass my verses tend
Than of your graces and your gifts to tell; 12
    And more, much more, than in my verse can sit
    Your own glass shows you when you look in it.

104

To me, fair friend, you never can be old,
For, as you were when first your eye I eyed,
Such seems your beauty still. Three winters cold
Have from the forests shook three summers' pride, 4
Three beauteous springs to yellow autumn turned
In process of the seasons have I seen,
Three April perfumes in three hot Junes burned
Since first I saw you fresh, which yet are green. 8

9 **shame** i.e., red for shame   10 **nor red** neither (purely) red   11 **to . . . annexed** to this robbery had added the robbery of   12 **But, for** although, in punishment for.   **in pride . . . growth** in his prime   13 **canker** cankerworm   15 **But** except.   **sweet** scent (as in line 2)
100.3 **fury** poetic inspiration   4 **Dark'ning** debasing   5 **straight** straightway   6 **gentle numbers** noble verses.   **idly** foolishly   7 **lays** songs   8 **argument** subject.   9 **resty** inactive, lazy   10 **If** to see if   11 **If any** if there are any.   **satire to** satirist of, here one composing a satire on Time as a despoiler   12 **spoils** acts of destruction, ravages   13 **faster** (1) more quickly (2) more firmly   14 **thou prevent'st** you forestall, thwart.   **crooked knife** curved blade.
101.1 **what . . . amends** what reparation will you make   2 **truth . . . dyed** truth made integrally a part of the beauty which it inhabits.   3–4 **Both . . . dignified** i.e., Both faith and beauty depend on my love for their proper appreciation and recognition, and you, my Muse, depend for your very office and dignity on that same function.   5 **haply** perhaps   6 **no . . . fixed** no artificial color (with suggestion of *pretense*) added to its natural and permanent color or hue   7 **pencil** paintbrush.   **lay** apply color to, as with a brush   8 **intermixed** adulterated.   9 **dumb** silent.   12 **of** by   13 **office** function   14 **long hence** long in the future.   **shows** appears

102.1 **seeming** outward appearance   3 **merchandized** degraded by being treated as a thing of sale.   **esteeming** valuation   4 **publish** announce, advertise   5 **in the spring** only just beginning   6 **wont . . . lays** accustomed to salute it (our love) with my song   7 **Philomel** the nightingale.   **front** forehead, beginning   8 **stops her pipe** stops singing.   **riper** i.e., those of late summer and autumn   11 **But . . . music** i.e., but because a profusion of wild birds' singing. (Refers to other poets.)   **burdens** weighs down. (But with a musical sense as well; a *burden* is a chorus.)   14 **dull** surfeit
103.1 **poverty** poor stuff   2 **pride** splendor   3 **argument all bare** subject alone, unadorned   5 **no more can write** i.e., (1) am silent (2) cannot go beyond what you yourself are, cannot excel my own poverty of invention.   6 **glass** mirror   7 **overgoes** surpasses; overwhelms.   **blunt invention** unpolished style, writing   8 **Dulling** i.e., making dull by comparison   11 **pass** purpose, issue   13 **sit** reside
104.4 **pride** splendor   6 **process** the progression   8 **which yet** who still

Ah, yet doth beauty, like a dial hand,
Steal from his figure and no pace perceived.
So your sweet hue, which methinks still doth stand,
Hath motion, and mine eye may be deceived,   12
    For fear of which, hear this, thou age unbred:
    Ere you were born was beauty's summer dead.

105

Let not my love be called idolatry,
Nor my belovèd as an idol show,
Since all alike my songs and praises be
To one, of one, still such, and ever so.   4
Kind is my love today, tomorrow kind,
Still constant in a wondrous excellence;
Therefore my verse, to constancy confined,
One thing expressing, leaves out difference.   8
"Fair, kind, and true" is all my argument,
"Fair, kind, and true" varying to other words;
And in this change is my invention spent,
Three themes in one, which wondrous scope affords.   12
    Fair, kind, and true have often lived alone,
    Which three till now never kept seat in one.

106

When in the chronicle of wasted time
I see descriptions of the fairest wights,
And beauty making beautiful old rhyme
In praise of ladies dead and lovely knights,   4
Then, in the blazon of sweet beauty's best,
Of hand, of foot, of lip, of eye, of brow,
I see their antique pen would have expressed
Even such a beauty as you master now.   8
So all their praises are but prophecies
Of this our time, all you prefiguring;
And, for they looked but with divining eyes,
They had not skill enough your worth to sing.   12
    For we, which now behold these present days,
    Have eyes to wonder, but lack tongues to praise.

107

Not mine own fears nor the prophetic soul
Of the wide world dreaming on things to come
Can yet the lease of my true love control,
Supposed as forfeit to a confined doom.   4
The mortal moon hath her eclipse endured,
And the sad augurs mock their own presage;
Incertainties now crown themselves assured,
And peace proclaims olives of endless age.   8
Now with the drops of this most balmy time
My love looks fresh, and Death to me subscribes,
Since, spite of him, I'll live in this poor rhyme,
While he insults o'er dull and speechless tribes;   12
    And thou in this shalt find thy monument,
    When tyrants' crests and tombs of brass are spent.

108

What's in the brain that ink may character
Which hath not figured to thee my true spirit?
What's new to speak, what now to register,
That may express my love or thy dear merit?   4
Nothing, sweet boy; but yet, like prayers divine,
I must each day say o'er the very same,
Counting no old thing old—thou mine, I thine—
Even as when first I hallowed thy fair name.   8
So that eternal love in love's fresh case
Weighs not the dust and injury of age,
Nor gives to necessary wrinkles place,
But makes antiquity for aye his page,   12
    Finding the first conceit of love there bred
    Where time and outward form would show it dead.

109

Oh, never say that I was false of heart,
Though absence seemed my flame to qualify.

9–10 yet . . . perceived yet beauty slips almost imperceptibly away, from you, like the dial hand of a watch making its stealthy progress away from number to number on the dial face.   **11 hue** appearance, complexion.   **still doth stand** remains seemingly unaltered   **13 unbred** not yet born
105.2 show appear   **4 To . . . so** (The poet loves his friend in phrases that recall the paradoxical and mysterious duality of two in one, as in "The Phoenix and Turtle." Such sacred love, by analogy, cannot be idolatry.)   **8 difference** diversity of theme and the seeming diversity of two persons (the poet and his friend) who are essentially one; also the seeming diversity of "Fair, kind, and true" which is also a variation on a single theme.   **11 this change** variations on this theme.   **invention** inventiveness.   **spent** expended   **13 alone** separately (in different people)   **14 kept seat** resided; sat enthroned
106.1 wasted past, used up   **2 wights** persons   **3 beauty** (1) beauty of style and language (2) beauty of the persons described   **5 blazon** i.e., glorification, cataloguing of qualities. (A heraldic metaphor.)
8 master possess, control   **11 for** because.   **divining** guessing or predicting as to the future   **13 For we** For even we   **14 praise** i.e., praise you worthily, sufficiently.

107.1–2 soul . . . world collective consciousness of humanity   **3–4 Can . . . doom** can set a limit to the time allotted to me to love you, though imagined to be destined to expire after a limited term.   **5 mortal moon** (Probably a reference to Queen Elizabeth, ill or deceased, most probably to her death in 1603; she was known as Diana, Cynthia, etc.)
6 And . . . presage and the solemn prophets of disaster now mock their earlier predictions   **7 Incertainties . . . assured** uncertainties have triumphantly given way to certainties. (Probably a reference to the accession and coronation of King James VI of Scotland and I of England.)   **8 olives** (Conventionally associated with peace and probably pointing here to King James I's resolutions of war with Spain and strife in Ireland.)   **of endless age** without foreseen end.   **9 with the drops** i.e., healed as though by a balmy dew. (Balm was employed in the coronation ceremony for James in 1603, as in all such coronations.)
10 subscribes yields   **12 insults . . . tribes** triumphs scornfully over endless generations of dead who have no poet to celebrate them   **14 crests** trophies adorning a tomb.   **spent** expended, wasted away.
108.1 character write   **2 figured** revealed, represented.   **true** constant   **3 register** record   **7 Counting . . . thine** dismissing no old truth as out of date or shopworn, such as the truth that you are mine and I yours   **8 hallowed** (As in "hallowed be thy name" from the Lord's Prayer.)   **9 fresh case** new exterior and circumstance   **10 Weighs not** is unconcerned about   **11 place** consideration, primacy   **12–14 But . . . dead** Love makes age serve its grand purposes, finding in age and antiquity the first stirrings of love, in a place where conventionally one would suppose it to be dead.
109.2 flame passion.   **qualify** temper, moderate.

As easy might I from myself depart
As from my soul, which in thy breast doth lie. 4
That is my home of love; if I have ranged,
Like him that travels I return again,
Just to the time, not with the time exchanged,
So that myself bring water for my stain. 8
Never believe, though in my nature reigned
All frailties that besiege all kinds of blood,
That it could so preposterously be stained
To leave for nothing all thy sum of good; 12
    For nothing this wide universe I call
    Save thou, my rose; in it thou art my all.

110

Alas, 'tis true, I have gone here and there
And made myself a motley to the view,
Gored mine own thoughts, sold cheap what is most dear,
Made old offenses of affections new; 4
Most true it is that I have looked on truth
Askance and strangely. But, by all above,
These blenches gave my heart another youth,
And worse essays proved thee my best of love. 8
Now all is done, have what shall have no end.
Mine appetite I never more will grind
On newer proof, to try an older friend,
A god in love, to whom I am confined. 12
    Then give me welcome, next my heaven the best,
    Even to thy pure and most most loving breast.

111

Oh, for my sake do you with Fortune chide,
The guilty goddess of my harmful deeds,
That did not better for my life provide
Than public means which public manners breeds. 4
Thence comes it that my name receives a brand,
And almost thence my nature is subdued
To what it works in, like the dyer's hand.
Pity me then, and wish I were renewed, 8
Whilst, like a willing patient, I will drink

Potions of eisel 'gainst my strong infection;
No bitterness that I will bitter think,
Nor double penance, to correct correction. 12
    Pity me then, dear friend, and I assure ye
    Even that your pity is enough to cure me.

112

Your love and pity doth th'impression fill
Which vulgar scandal stamped upon my brow;
For what care I who calls me well or ill,
So you o'ergreen my bad, my good allow? 4
You are my all the world, and I must strive
To know my shames and praises from your tongue;
None else to me, nor I to none alive,
That my steeled sense or changes, right or wrong. 8
In so profound abysm I throw all care
Of others' voices that my adder's sense
To critic and to flatterer stoppèd are.
Mark how with my neglect I do dispense: 12
    You are so strongly in my purpose bred
    That all the world besides, methinks, are dead.

113

Since I left you, mine eye is in my mind,
And that which governs me to go about
Doth part his function and is partly blind,
Seems seeing, but effectually is out; 4
For it no form delivers to the heart
Of bird, of flower, or shape, which it doth latch;
Of his quick objects hath the mind no part,
Nor his own vision holds what it doth catch; 8
For if it see the rud'st or gentlest sight,
The most sweet-favor or deformd'st creature,
The mountain or the sea, the day or night,
The crow or dove, it shapes them to your feature. 12

5 **ranged** traveled, wandered 7 **Just . . . exchanged** punctual to the minute, not changed by the period of separation 8 **water for my stain** i.e., repentant tears, to wash away the stain of my offense. 10 **blood** temperament, sensual nature 12 **for** in exchange for 110.2 **motley** jester, fool. **to the view** in the eyes of the world 3 **Gored** wounded 4 **Made . . . new** i.e., repeated old offenses or made offense against old friendship in forming new attachments 5 **truth** constancy 6 **Askance and strangely** disdainfully, obliquely and at a distance. **by all above** by heaven 7 **blenches** swervings. **another youth** i.e., a renewal of true friendship 8 **essays** experiments (in friendship) 9 **Now all** Now that all that. **have what . . . end** take what is eternal (my friendship). 10 **grind** whet, sharpen 11 **newer proof** further experiment, experience. **try** test 13 **next my heaven** you, who are to me second only to heaven itself 111.1 **do you** (A command: "Do") 2 **guilty goddess of** goddess responsible for 3 **life** livelihood 4 **Than . . . breeds** than providing me a means of livelihood that depends on catering to the public. (A probable reference to Shakespeare's career as an actor.) 5 **receives a brand** is disgraced (through prejudice against my occupation) 7 **like the dyer's hand** (The dyer's hand is stained by the dye it handles, just as the dramatist's or actor's nature is almost overpowered by the medium in which he works—the theater.) 8 **renewed** restored to what I was by nature, cleansed

10 **eisel** vinegar, used as an antiseptic against the plague and also as an agent for removing stains 11 **No bitterness** there is no bitterness 12 **Nor . . . correction** nor will I think it bitter to undertake a twofold penance in order to correct what must be doubly corrected. 14 **Even that your pity** that very pity of yours 112.1 **doth th'impression fill** effaces the scar 2 **vulgar scandal** notoriety (for being an actor?) 4 **So you o'ergreen** provided that you cover as with green growth. **allow** approve. 5 **my all the world** everything to me 7–8 **None . . . wrong** no one else but you affects my fixed and hardened sensibilities, whether for better or for worse. 9–11 **In . . . are** Into so deep an abyss do I throw all concern as to what others may think that, adderlike, my ears are deaf to critic and flatterer alike. (Adders were popularly supposed to have no sense of hearing.) 12 **Mark . . . dispense** See how I justify my disregard of the opinion of others 13 **You . . . bred** you are so nurtured in my thoughts and are such a powerful influence over my intentions 113.1 **mine . . . mind** i.e., I'm guided by my mind's eye 2 **that . . . about** i.e., my physical sight 3 **part** (1) divide (2) abandon. **his** its, i.e., the physical eye's. (Also in lines 7 and 8.) 4 **Seems . . . out** seems to be seeing, but in reality is blind 5 **heart** (Here portrayed as capable of receiving sense impressions and of consciousness, as in sonnet 47.) 6 **latch** catch or receive the sight of 7 **Of . . . part** i.e., the mind, attuned to its inner eye, takes no part in the fleeting and lively (*quick*) things seen by the physical sight 8 **Nor . . . holds** nor does the eye itself retain. **catch** see glimpsingly 9 **For . . . sight** for whether it see the most uncouth or most gracious sight 10 **sweet-favor** sweet-featured 12 **shapes . . . feature** makes them resemble you.

Incapable of more, replete with you,
My most true mind thus maketh mine eye untrue.

114

Or whether doth my mind, being crowned with you,
Drink up the monarch's plague, this flattery?
Or whether shall I say mine eye saith true,
And that your love taught it this alchemy, 4
To make of monsters and things indigest
Such cherubins as your sweet self resemble,
Creating every bad a perfect best
As fast as objects to his beams assemble? 8
Oh, 'tis the first, 'tis flatt'ry in my seeing,
And my great mind most kingly drinks it up;
Mine eye well knows what with his gust is greeing,
And to his palate doth prepare the cup. 12
    If it be poisoned, 'tis the lesser sin
    That mine eye loves it and doth first begin.

115

Those lines that I before have writ do lie,
Even those that said I could not love you dearer;
Yet then my judgment knew no reason why
My most full flame should afterwards burn clearer. 4
But reckoning Time, whose millioned accidents
Creep in twixt vows and change decrees of kings,
Tan sacred beauty, blunt the sharp'st intents,
Divert strong minds to th' course of alt'ring things— 8
Alas, why, fearing of Time's tyranny,
Might I not then say, "Now I love you best,"
When I was certain o'er incertainty,
Crowning the present, doubting of the rest? 12
    Love is a babe; then might I not say so,
    To give full growth to that which still doth grow.

116

Let me not to the marriage of true minds
Admit impediments. Love is not love

Which alters when it alteration finds,
Or bends with the remover to remove. 4
Oh, no, it is an ever-fixèd mark
That looks on tempests and is never shaken;
It is the star to every wand'ring bark,
Whose worth's unknown, although his height be taken. 8
Love's not Time's fool, though rosy lips and cheeks
Within his bending sickle's compass come;
Love alters not with his brief hours and weeks,
But bears it out even to the edge of doom. 12
    If this be error and upon me proved,
    I never writ, nor no man ever loved.

117

Accuse me thus: that I have scanted all
Wherein I should your great deserts repay,
Forgot upon your dearest love to call,
Whereto all bonds do tie me day by day; 4
That I have frequent been with unknown minds,
And given to time your own dear-purchased right;
That I have hoisted sail to all the winds
Which should transport me farthest from your sight. 8
Book both my willfulness and errors down,
And on just proof surmise accumulate;
Bring me within the level of your frown,
But shoot not at me in your wakened hate, 12
    Since my appeal says I did strive to prove
    The constancy and virtue of your love.

118

Like as to make our appetites more keen
With eager compounds we our palate urge;
As to prevent our maladies unseen
We sicken to shun sickness when we purge: 4
Even so, being full of your ne'er-cloying sweetness,
To bitter sauces did I frame my feeding
And, sick of welfare, found a kind of meetness

114.1, 3 Or whether (Indicates alternative possibilities.) **1 crowned with you** elevated by possession of you **2 the monarch's . . . flattery** this pleasing delusion to which all monarchs are prone. **4 your love** my love of you. **alchemy** science of transmuting base metals **5 indigest** chaotic, formless **6 cherubins** angelic forms (suggesting the youth and beauty of the friend) **7 Creating** creating out of **8 his beams** its (the eye's) gaze **9 'tis flatt'ry . . . seeing** my eye is flattering my mind (see lines 1–2) **11 what . . . greeing** what agrees with the mind's taste **12 to** to suit **13–14 'tis . . . begin** it extenuates the eye's sinful deed (of misleading the mind) that it tastes of the poison first, like an official taster sampling food before it is given to the king. **115.5 reckoning Time** (1) Time, which we reckon up (2) Time, which demands a reckoning and settles all accounts. **millioned accidents** multitudinous unforeseen occurrences **6 twixt vows** i.e., between the making of vows and their fulfillment **7 Tan** darken, i.e., coarsen **8 Divert . . . things** divert the most resolute of intentions into the current of changing circumstances **9 fearing of** fearing **10 Might . . . say** i.e., wasn't it understandable for me to say then, when I wrote *Those lines* (line 1) **11 certain o'er incertainty** i.e., certain of my love's perfection then, as contrasted with the uncertainty of the future **12 Crowning** exalting. **doubting of** fearing **13 then might . . . so** i.e., therefore it was wrong of me to say then, "Now I love you best" (line 10) **14 To give** thereby giving **116.2 Admit** concede that there might be, allow consideration of. (An echo of the marriage service.)

3 alteration i.e., in age, beauty, affection, health, circumstance **4 Or . . . remove** or changes simply because there is change (by ill health, mental deterioration, death, absence, or inconstancy) in the person loved. **5 mark** seamark, conspicuous object distinguishable at sea as an aid to navigation **7 wand'ring bark** lost ship **8 Whose . . . taken** whose value is beyond estimation, although its altitude above the horizon can be determined (for purposes of navigation). **9 fool** plaything, laughingstock **10 his** i.e., Time's. (Also in line 11.) **bending** curved. **compass** range **12 bears . . . doom** endures or holds out to the very Day of Judgment. **117.1 scanted** come short in **3 Forgot . . . call** forgot to invoke or call upon your most precious love **5 frequent** familiar. **unknown minds** strangers of no consequence **6 And . . . right** and wasted time that should have been devoted to you, to which you had every right **8 should** were likely to **9 Book . . . down** Record both my willful faults and errors **10 on . . . accumulate** to sure proof add surmise, suspicion **11 level** point-blank range, aim **13 appeal** legal appealing of the case. **I . . . prove** my intention was to test **118.1 Like as** Just as **2 eager compounds** pungent, bitter concoctions. **urge** stimulate **3 As** just as. **prevent** anticipate, forestall **4 We . . . purge** we induce a kind of sickness through purging (i.e., evacuation of stomach or bowel), in order to ward off greater sickness **5 Even so** in just the same way **6 bitter sauces** i.e., other loves, undesirable in comparison with you. **frame** adapt, direct **7 sick of welfare** surfeited by health and happiness (in love). **meetness** suitability

To be diseased ere that there was true needing.   8
Thus policy in love, t'anticipate
The ills that were not, grew to faults assured,
And brought to medicine a healthful state
Which, rank of goodness, would by ill be cured.   12
    But thence I learn, and find the lesson true:
    Drugs poison him that so fell sick of you.

119

What potions have I drunk of siren tears,
Distilled from limbecks foul as hell within,
Applying fears to hopes and hopes to fears,
Still losing when I saw myself to win!   4
What wretched errors hath my heart committed,
Whilst it hath thought itself so blessèd never!
How have mine eyes out of their spheres been fitted
In the distraction of this madding fever!   8
Oh, benefit of ill! Now I find true
That better is by evil still made better;
And ruined love, when it is built anew,
Grows fairer than at first, more strong, far greater.   12
    So I return rebuked to my content,
    And gain by ills thrice more than I have spent.

120

That you were once unkind befriends me now,
And for that sorrow which I then did feel
Needs must I under my transgression bow,
Unless my nerves were brass or hammered steel.   4
For if you were by my unkindness shaken
As I by yours, you've passed a hell of time,
And I, a tyrant, have no leisure taken
To weigh how once I suffered in your crime.   8
Oh, that our night of woe might have remembered
My deepest sense how hard true sorrow hits,
And soon to you, as you to me then, tendered

The humble salve which wounded bosoms fits!   12
    But that your trespass now becomes a fee;
    Mine ransoms yours, and yours must ransom me.

121

'Tis better to be vile than vile esteemed
When not to be receives reproach of being,
And the just pleasure lost which is so deemed
Not by our feeling but by others' seeing.   4
For why should others' false adulterate eyes
Give salutation to my sportive blood?
Or on my frailties why are frailer spies,
Which in their wills count bad what I think good?   8
No, I am that I am, and they that level
At my abuses reckon up their own.
I may be straight though they themselves be bevel.
By their rank thoughts my deeds must not be shown,   12
    Unless this general evil they maintain:
    All men are bad, and in their badness reign.

122

Thy gift, thy tables, are within my brain
Full charactered with lasting memory,
Which shall above that idle rank remain
Beyond all date, even to eternity—   4
Or at the least, so long as brain and heart
Have faculty by nature to subsist;
Till each to razed oblivion yield his part
Of thee, thy record never can be missed.   8
That poor retention could not so much hold,
Nor need I tallies thy dear love to score;
Therefore to give them from me was I bold,

12 humble salve i.e., apology and remorse.   **which . . . fits** which is just what wounded hearts need.   **13 that your trespass** that unkindness of yours.   **fee** payment, compensation   **14 ransoms** redeems, excuses   **121.1 vile esteemed** (to be) considered vile   **2 When . . . being** when not to be vile receives the reproach of vileness. (It's even worse to be unjustly accused of wickedness than to be reproved when one's conduct is truly vile.)   **3–4 And . . . seeing** and to lose justifiable pleasure because its justification has to depend not on our feelings but on the censorious attitudes of others.   **5 false adulterate eyes** i.e., the eyes of those whose own wickedness prompts them to misconstrue my innocent love   **6 Give . . . blood** i.e., greet me, in my lusty merriment, with familiarity and with a knowing wink of the eye.   **7 Or . . . spies** Or why should there be persons more faulty than I spying on my fleshly indulgences   **8 Which in their wills** who by the measure of their prurient, licentious minds   **9 am that** am what.   **level** (1) aim (2) guess   **10 abuses** misdoings.   **reckon up their own** i.e., merely enumerate their own misdeeds.   **11 bevel** out of square, crooked.   **12 rank** ugly, foul.   **shown** viewed, interpreted   **14 reign** i.e., prosper. (Only a cynic would interpret my success in love as a paradoxical proof of my sharing in general human depravity.)   **122.1 tables** writing tablet, memorandum book   **2 charactered with** written by   **3 that idle rank** i.e., the relative unimportance of that memorandum book (as compared with the memory itself)   **6 faculty . . . subsist** natural power to survive   **7–8 Till . . . missed** until both heart and brain have given up their memory of you to the ravages of time, what you have written never can be lost. (Hence the memorandum book itself, which the poet has given away, is not essential.)   **9 retention** i.e., the book, an instrument for retaining memoranda.   **so much** i.e., as much as is in my memory   **10 tallies** sticks notched to serve for reckoning. (The notebook is such a mere *tally*.)   **score** reckon   **11 to . . . me** i.e., to give away the writing tablet.   **bold** i.e., bold in taking the liberty

8 ere . . . needing before there was any real necessity for it.   **9 policy** shortsighted calculation.   **t'anticipate** to forestall   **10 assured** actual   **11 to medicine** into a state of needing medical care   **12 rank of goodness** gorged and sickened by good health   **14 Drugs . . . you** a rash and unnecessary course of treatment inflicted true sickness on one (myself) who had thought himself weary of your company.   **119.1 siren** i.e., deceitful. (The poet seems to speak of an affair.)   **2 limbecks** vessels used in distillation.   **foul as hell within** i.e., possessing an inner ugliness and evil contrasted with a beautiful and seductive appearance   **3 Applying . . . fears** trying vainly to control my wild hopes with a sense of fear and to assuage my fears with hope   **4 Still** always.   **saw myself** vainly expected   **6 so blessèd never** never before so fortunate.   **7 How . . . fitted** How my eyes have popped out in convulsive fit   **8 distraction** frenzy.   **madding fever** fever that drives me mad.   **120.1 befriends** benefits (by giving me perspective on what I now need to do)   **2–3 for . . . bow** i.e., realizing the sorrow I felt from your unkindness, I must now acknowledge my own guilt in being unkind to you   **4 nerves** sinews   **6 hell of** hellish   **7 have . . . taken** have not taken the opportunity   **8 weigh** consider.   **in your crime** i.e., from your unkindness; or, from erring as you did. (If I suffered so, I should realize you've suffered, too, from my unkindness.)   **9 that our night of woe** would that the dark and woeful time of our earlier estrangement.   **remembered** reminded   **10 sense** consciousness, apprehension   **11 And . . . tendered** i.e., and would that I had quickly offered to you, as you did to me

To trust those tables that receive thee more.
    To keep an adjunct to remember thee
    Were to import forgetfulness in me.

123

No, Time, thou shalt not boast that I do change.
Thy pyramids built up with newer might
To me are nothing novel, nothing strange;
They are but dressings of a former sight.   4
Our dates are brief, and therefore we admire
What thou dost foist upon us that is old,
And rather make them born to our desire
Than think that we before have heard them told.   8
Thy registers and thee I both defy,
Not wond'ring at the present nor the past,
For thy records and what we see doth lie,
Made more or less by thy continual haste.   12
    This I do vow and this shall ever be:
    I will be true, despite thy scythe and thee.

124

If my dear love were but the child of state,
It might for Fortune's bastard be unfathered,
As subject to Time's love or to Time's hate,
Weeds among weeds, or flowers with flowers gathered.   4
No, it was builded far from accident;
It suffers not in smiling pomp, nor falls
Under the blow of thrallèd discontent,
Whereto th'inviting time our fashion calls.   8
It fears not Policy, that heretic,
Which works on leases of short-numbered hours,
But all alone stands hugely politic,
That it nor grows with heat nor drowns with showers.   12
    To this I witness call the fools of Time,
    Which die for goodness, who have lived for crime.

125

Were't aught to me I bore the canopy,
With my extern the outward honoring,
Or laid great bases for eternity
Which proves more short than waste or ruining?   4
Have I not seen dwellers on form and favor
Lose all, and more, by paying too much rent,
For compound sweet forgoing simple savor,
Pitiful thrivers, in their gazing spent?   8
No, let me be obsequious in thy heart,
And take thou my oblation, poor but free,
Which is not mixed with seconds, knows no art
But mutual render, only me for thee.   12
    Hence, thou suborned informer! A true soul
    When most impeached stands least in thy control.

126

O thou, my lovely boy, who in thy power
Dost hold Time's fickle glass, his sickle hour;
Who hast by waning grown, and therein show'st
Thy lovers withering as thy sweet self grow'st;   4
If Nature, sovereign mistress over wrack,
As thou goest onwards, still will pluck thee back,
She keeps thee to this purpose, that her skill
May Time disgrace and wretched minutes kill.   8
Yet fear her, O thou minion of her pleasure!
She may detain, but not still keep, her treasure.
Her audit, though delayed, answered must be,
And her quietus is to render thee.   12

---

12 those tables i.e., those of memory. **receive thee more** retain more of you. **13 adjunct** aid **14 Were** would be. **import** imply, impute **123.2 pyramids** (May refer to obelisks or other structures erected in Rome in 1586 or in London in 1603.) **3 nothing** not at all **4 dressings . . . sight** reconstructions in new form of things from the past. **5 dates** life spans **7 make . . . desire** consider them newly created to our liking and reinvented by us **8 told** reckoned, told about. **9 registers** visual records, monuments **10 wond'ring** marveling **11 doth lie** deceives us **12 Made . . . haste** i.e., raised one minute and ruined the next (by Time), and alternately overvalued and undervalued by us. **124.1–2 If . . . unfathered** If my love for you were merely the product of circumstances and your high position, we might disavow it as nothing but the bastard child of Fortune **4 Weeds . . . gathered** either despised as worthless like a weed or cherished like a flower as Fortune dictates. **5 accident** chance, fortune **6–8 It . . . calls** it does not grow acquiescent to the dictates of pomp and finery, nor does it weaken under the blows of slavish adversity, both of which the insidious mores of our present age tempt us to regard as fashionable. **9 Policy, that heretic** cunning expediency, false to the spirit of love **10 Which . . . hours** which thinks only shortsightedly of short-term gain and makes only short-term commitments **11 hugely politic** prudent in a long-term sense **12 That . . . showers** so that it neither pins its hopes unrealistically on rising fortunes nor grows desperate in times of adversity. **13–14 To . . . crime** I call as witnesses those creatures of Time who succumb to the moral weaknesses described in this sonnet, and who repent their evil ways only after having lived corruptly.

125.1–4 Were't . . . ruining? Would it mean anything to me if I did public homage to great persons by carrying over their heads a cloth of state as they go in procession, thereby honoring what is external by means of a purely external action, or if I laid foundations for supposedly eternal monuments which then prove to last no longer than the forces of decay and ruin allow? **5 dwellers . . . favor** those who depend on court etiquette and influence peddling; also, in figure and face **6 by paying . . . rent** i.e., by overdoing flattery and depending too much on hopes of obtaining favor **7 For . . . savor** i.e., foregoing wholesome sincerity for the sake of obsequious flattery **8 Pitiful . . . spent** pitiful in their unsuccessful attempts, their means consumed in their ineffectual fawning on greatness. **9 obsequious** (1) courtly (2) devoted **10 oblation** offering. **free** freely offered **11 seconds** inferior matter, adulterants. **art** artifice **12 render** exchange **13 suborned informer** perjured witness, the envious one who has charged the poet with self-interested flattery. **14 impeached** accused **126.1** (This sonnet is made up of six couplets.) **2 Time's . . . hour** Time's treacherous and inexorable hourglass, his reaping time **3 Who . . . grown** you who have grown more youthfully beautiful as you have aged. **show'st** show by way of contrast with yourself **4 Thy lovers** (including the poet) **5 wrack** ruin. (Nature is mistress over decay in that she decays and renews.) **6 onwards** i.e., in life's journey **7 to** for **8 May . . . kill** may put Time to shame and render powerless the passing of the minutes. **9 Yet . . . pleasure!** Yet fear Nature too, you who as her darling are subject to her will! **10 She . . . treasure** i.e., Nature may keep and restore you for a time, but Time will ultimately triumph. **11 Her audit** i.e., The proverbial paying of one's debt to Nature through death; also, Nature's account to Time. **answered** paid **12 quietus** discharge, quittance. **render** surrender

127

In the old age black was not counted fair,
Or if it were, it bore not beauty's name;
But now is black beauty's successive heir,
And beauty slandered with a bastard shame. 4
For since each hand hath put on nature's power,
Fairing the foul with art's false borrowed face,
Sweet beauty hath no name, no holy bower,
But is profaned, if not lives in disgrace. 8
Therefore my mistress' eyes are raven black,
Her brows so suited, and they mourners seem
At such who, not born fair, no beauty lack,
Sland'ring creation with a false esteem. 12
      Yet so they mourn, becoming of their woe,
      That every tongue says beauty should look so.

128

How oft, when thou, my music, music play'st
Upon that blessèd wood whose motion sounds
With thy sweet fingers when thou gently sway'st
The wiry concord that mine ear confounds, 4
Do I envy those jacks that nimble leap
To kiss the tender inward of thy hand,
Whilst my poor lips, which should that harvest reap,
At the wood's boldness by thee blushing stand! 8
To be so tickled, they would change their state
And situation with those dancing chips
O'er whom thy fingers walk with gentle gait,
Making dead wood more blest than living lips. 12
      Since saucy jacks so happy are in this,
      Give them thy fingers, me thy lips to kiss.

129

Th'expense of spirit in a waste of shame
Is lust in action; and, till action, lust

Is perjured, murd'rous, bloody, full of blame,
Savage, extreme, rude, cruel, not to trust, 4
Enjoyed no sooner but despisèd straight,
Past reason hunted, and no sooner had
Past reason hated, as a swallowed bait
On purpose laid to make the taker mad; 8
Mad in pursuit, and in possession so;
Had, having, and in quest to have, extreme;
A bliss in proof, and proved, a very woe;
Before, a joy proposed; behind, a dream. 12
      All this the world well knows; yet none knows well
      To shun the heaven that leads men to this hell.

130

My mistress' eyes are nothing like the sun;
Coral is far more red than her lips' red;
If snow be white, why then her breasts are dun;
If hairs be wires, black wires grow on her head. 4
I have seen roses damasked, red and white,
But no such roses see I in her cheeks;
And in some perfumes is there more delight
Than in the breath that from my mistress reeks. 8
I love to hear her speak, yet well I know
That music hath a far more pleasing sound.
I grant I never saw a goddess go;
My mistress, when she walks, treads on the ground. 12
      And yet, by heaven, I think my love as rare
      As any she belied with false compare.

131

Thou art as tyrannous, so as thou art,
As those whose beauties proudly make them cruel;
For well thou know'st to my dear doting heart
Thou art the fairest and most precious jewel. 4
Yet, in good faith, some say that thee behold
Thy face hath not the power to make love groan;
To say they err I dare not be so bold,
Although I swear it to myself alone. 8
And, to be sure that is not false I swear,
A thousand groans, but thinking on thy face,
One on another's neck, do witness bear
Thy black is fairest in my judgment's place. 12
      In nothing art thou black save in thy deeds,
      And thence this slander, as I think, proceeds.

127.1 old age olden times. **black** darkness of hair and eyes. **fair** (1) beautiful (2) light-complexioned **2 it bore . . . name** i.e., it was not called so **3 now . . . heir** nowadays black has been named lawful successor to the title of beauty **4 beauty . . . shame** i.e., blonde beauty is declared illegitimate, created artificially by cosmetics. **5 put on** assumed **6 Fairing the foul** making the ugly beautiful. **borrowed face** i.e., cosmetics **7 no name . . . bower** no reputation or pride of family, and no sacred abode **8 if not** or even **10 so suited** decked out in the same color and for the same reason **11 At** for. **no beauty lack** i.e., nonetheless make themselves attractive **12 Sland'ring . . . esteem** i.e., dishonoring nature by blurring the distinction between real and false beauty. **13 they** i.e., my mistress' eyes. **becoming of** gracing or being graced by
128.2 wood keys of the spinet or virginal. **motion** mechanism **3 thou gently sway'st** you gently control **4 wiry concord** harmony produced by strings. **confounds** i.e., pleasurably overwhelms **5 jacks** (Literally, upright pieces of wood fixed to the keys and fitted with a quill that plucks the strings of the virginal; here used of the keys and with a pun on *jacks* in the sense of "common fellows," as in line 13.) **8 by** beside, or, with. (The poet stands beside the lady as she plays, blushing to his very lips; he blushes in vexation at the *jacks'* boldness with her hand.) **9 they** i.e., my lips **13 jacks** (With a pun on "knaves, fellows" as in line 5.)
129.1–2 Th'expense . . . action Lust being consummated is the expenditure or dissipation of vital energy in an orgy of shameful extravagance and guilt. (*Spirit* also suggests "sperm.") **2 till action** until it achieves consummation

3 blame (1) guilt (2) recrimination **4 rude** brutal. **to trust** to be trusted **5 straight** immediately **6 Past reason** madly, intemperately **11 in proof** while experienced. **proved** i.e., afterward **12 Before** in prospect **14 the heaven** the seeming bliss of sexual consumation. **hell** (Often equated imagistically with the vagina.)
130.1 nothing not at all **3 dun** dull grayish brown, mouse-colored **5 damasked** mingled red and white **8 reeks** emanates. **11 go** walk **13 rare** extraordinary and unique **14 As . . . compare** as any woman misrepresented with false comparison.
131.1 tyrannous pitiless and domineering. **so as thou art** just as you are (dark, not considered handsome) **3 dear** fond **9 to be sure** as proof. **false I** false that I **10 but thinking on** when I do no more than think of **11 One . . . neck** one rapidly after another **12 black** dark complexion. **my judgment's place** my opinion. **14 this slander** (See lines 5–6.) **proceeds** originates.

132

Thine eyes I love, and they, as pitying me,
Knowing thy heart torment me with disdain,
Have put on black, and loving mourners be,
Looking with pretty ruth upon my pain.   4
And truly not the morning sun of heaven
Better becomes the gray cheeks of the east,
Nor that full star that ushers in the even
Doth half that glory to the sober west   8
As those two mourning eyes become thy face.
Oh, let it then as well beseem thy heart
To mourn for me, since mourning doth thee grace,
And suit thy pity like in every part.   12
    Then will I swear beauty herself is black,
    And all they foul that thy complexion lack.

133

Beshrew that heart that makes my heart to groan
For that deep wound it gives my friend and me!
Is't not enough to torture me alone,
But slave to slavery my sweet'st friend must be?   4
Me from myself thy cruel eye hath taken,
And my next self thou harder hast engrossed.
Of him, myself, and thee I am forsaken—
A torment thrice threefold thus to be crossed.   8
Prison my heart in thy steel bosom's ward,
But then my friend's heart let my poor heart bail;
Whoe'er keeps me, let my heart be his guard;
Thou canst not then use rigor in my jail.   12
    And yet thou wilt; for I, being pent in thee,
    Perforce am thine, and all that is in me.

134

So, now I have confessed that he is thine,
And I myself am mortgaged to thy will,
Myself I'll forfeit, so that other mine
Thou wilt restore to be my comfort still.   4
But thou wilt not, nor he will not be free,
For thou art covetous and he is kind;

He learned but surety-like to write for me
Under that bond that him as fast doth bind.   8
The statute of thy beauty thou wilt take,
Thou usurer, that put'st forth all to use,
And sue a friend came debtor for my sake;
So him I lose through my unkind abuse.   12
    Him have I lost; thou hast both him and me;
    He pays the whole, and yet am I not free.

135

Whoever hath her wish, thou hast thy Will,
And Will to boot, and Will in overplus;
More than enough am I that vex thee still,
To thy sweet will making addition thus.   4
Wilt thou, whose will is large and spacious,
Not once vouchsafe to hide my will in thine?
Shall will in others seem right gracious,
And in my will no fair acceptance shine?   8
The sea, all water, yet receives rain still
And in abundance addeth to his store;
So thou, being rich in Will, add to thy Will
One will of mine, to make thy large Will more.   12
    Let no unkind no fair beseechers kill;
    Think all but one, and me in that one Will.

136

If thy soul check thee that I come so near,
Swear to thy blind soul that I was thy Will,
And will, thy soul knows, is admitted there;
Thus far for love my love suit, sweet, fulfill.   4
Will will fulfill the treasure of thy love,
Ay, fill it full with wills, and my will one.
In things of great receipt with ease we prove
Among a number one is reckoned none.   8
Then in the number let me pass untold,

132.1 **as** as if   **2 Knowing ... torment** knowing that your heart torments   **4 ruth** pity   **6 becomes** adorns.   **cheeks** i.e., clouds   **7 that
full star** the evening star, Hesperus, i.e., Venus.   **even** evening
8 Doth i.e., lends.   **sober** somber, subdued in color   **9 mourning**
black. (Spelled "morning" in the Quarto, suggesting a pun on line 5.)
10 beseem suit   **11 since ... grace** since you look very attractive in
mourning black.   **12 And suit ... part** and dress your pity similarly,
in your heart and eyes.   **14 And ... that** and that all those are ugly
who
133.1 **Beshrew** i.e., A plague upon   **4 slave to slavery** utterly
enslaved   **6 And ... engrossed** i.e., and you have put my dearest
friend, my other self, under even greater restraint.   **engrossed**
(1) driven into obsession (2) bought up wholesale.   **8 crossed**
thwarted, afflicted.   **9 Prison** Imprison.   **thy ... ward** the prison cell
of your hard heart   **10 bail** set free by taking its place   **11 keeps** has
custody of.   **his guard** my friend's guardhouse   **12 rigor** harshness.
my jail i.e., my heart, where my friend is kept (and where I can protect him from your harsh authority).   **13 pent** shut up   **14 and all**
along with everything (including my friend's heart)
134.1 **now** now that   **2 will** (1) wishes (2) fleshly desire   **3 so ...
mine** provided that my other self, my friend   **5 will not** does not
wish to, won't

7 surety-like as security, as guarantor.   **write** sign the bond, endorse
(suggesting that the friend has taken the poet's place with the mistress)   **8 Under ... bind** under that mortgage or bond (of sexual
enslavement) that now binds him as securely as it does me.   **9 statute**
a usurer's security or amount of money secured under his bond.
take call in, invoke. (The lady will exact the full forfeiture specified in
the mortgage as the amount to which her beauty entitles her.)   **10 use**
(1) usury (2) sexual pleasure   **11 sue** (With suggestion also of "woo.")
came i.e., who became   **12 my unkind abuse** your ill usage and
unkind deceiving (of me).   **14 pays** (With sexual suggestion.)
135.1 **Will** (This and the following sonnet and sonnet 143 ring changes
on the word *will*—sexual desire, temper, passion, and the poet's name;
possibly also the friend's name. The word can also suggest the sexual
organs, male and female.)   **3 vex** (by unwelcome wooing).   **still** continually   **6 hide ... thine** (With sexual suggestion.)   **7 will in others**
others' wills   **10 his** its   **13 Let ... kill** Let no unkind word kill any
who seek your favors, or, *Let "no" unkind*, etc., do not kill your wooers
with the word *no*   **14 Think ... Will** i.e., think all your wooers and
their wills to be but one, all comprised in me.
136.1 **check** rebuke.   **come so near** i.e., come so near the truth about
you (in my previous sonnet); with suggestion of physical nearness
also   **2 blind** unperceptive; shut up in the body without sensory
organs   **4 fulfill** grant.   **5 fulfill the treasure** fill full the treasury.
(With suggestion of sexual entry.)   **6 my will** (Suggesting "my
penis.")   **one** one of them.   **7 receipt** capacity. (Suggesting profligacy.)   **8 one ... none** (A variant of the common saying "one is no
number.")   **9 untold** uncounted

Though in thy store's account I one must be;
For nothing hold me, so it please thee hold
That nothing me, a something, sweet, to thee.   12
    Make but my name thy love, and love that still,
    And then thou lovest me for my name is Will.

137

Thou blind fool, Love, what dost thou to mine eyes
That they behold and see not what they see?
They know what beauty is, see where it lies,
Yet what the best is take the worst to be.   4
If eyes corrupt by overpartial looks
Be anchored in the bay where all men ride,
Why of eyes' falsehood hast thou forgèd hooks,
Whereto the judgment of my heart is tied?   8
Why should my heart think that a several plot
Which my heart knows the wide world's common place?
Or mine eyes seeing this, say this is not,
To put fair truth upon so foul a face?   12
    In things right true my heart and eyes have erred,
    And to this false plague are they now transferred.

138

When my love swears that she is made of truth
I do believe her, though I know she lies,
That she might think me some untutored youth,
Unlearnèd in the world's false subtleties.   4
Thus vainly thinking that she thinks me young,
Although she knows my days are past the best,
Simply I credit her false-speaking tongue;
On both sides thus is simple truth suppressed.   8
But wherefore says she not she is unjust?
And wherefore say not I that I am old?
Oh, love's best habit is in seeming trust,
And age in love loves not to have years told.   12

Therefore I lie with her, and she with me,
And in our faults by lies we flattered be.

139

Oh, call not me to justify the wrong
That thy unkindness lays upon my heart;
Wound me not with thine eye but with thy tongue;
Use power with power, and slay me not by art.   4
Tell me thou lov'st elsewhere, but in my sight,
Dear heart, forbear to glance thine eye aside;
What need'st thou wound with cunning when thy might
Is more than my o'erpressed defense can bide?   8
Let me excuse thee: "Ah, my love well knows
Her pretty looks have been mine enemies,
And therefore from my face she turns my foes,
That they elsewhere might dart their injuries."   12
    Yet do not so; but since I am near slain,
    Kill me outright with looks and rid my pain.

140

Be wise as thou art cruel; do not press
My tongue-tied patience with too much disdain,
Lest sorrow lend me words, and words express
The manner of my pity-wanting pain.   4
If I might teach thee wit, better it were,
Though not to love, yet, love, to tell me so,
As testy sick men, when their deaths be near,
No news but health from their physicians know.   8
For if I should despair, I should grow mad,
And in my madness might speak ill of thee.
Now this ill-wresting world is grown so bad,
Mad slanderers by mad ears believèd be.   12
    That I may not be so, nor thou belied,
    Bear thine eyes straight, though thy proud heart go
        wide.

141

In faith, I do not love thee with mine eyes,
For they in thee a thousand errors note;
But 'tis my heart that loves what they despise,
Who in despite of view is pleased to dote.   4
Nor are mine ears with thy tongue's tune delighted,

10 in . . . **account** in your (huge) inventory (of lovers)   **11–12 For . . .
thee** i.e., consider me too insignificant to think of, provided that you
deign to hold insignificant me to you, my sweet, thereby making me
something of worth. (*Something* is sexually suggestive of "some
thing.")   **13 my name** i.e., "will," that is, desire.   **still** continually
14 for because
137.1 Love Cupid, portrayed as blind   **2 see not** do not comprehend
3 lies resides (and deceives through false appearance)   **4 Yet . . . be**
yet take the worst for the best.   **5 corrupt by overpartial looks** corrupted by doting and frankly prejudiced gazing   **6 Be . . . ride** seek
harbor where all men do so, i.e., *ride* in the arms of promiscuous
women   **7 Why . . . hooks** why have you, Love, fashioned snares out
of my eyes' delusion   **9 think . . . plot** think that to be a private field,
i.e., that woman to be the exclusive property of one man   **10 knows**
knows to be.   **common place** (1) a commons, a common pasture
(2) a woman's body that is open, promiscuous.   **11 Or** Or why
should.   **not** not so   **14 false plague** (1) plague of judging falsely
(2) false woman
138.1 (A version of this sonnet appears in *The Passionate Pilgrim*.)
truth fidelity, constancy   **2 believe** i.e., pretend to believe   **5 vainly
thinking** acting as though I thought   **7 Simply** (1) pretending to be
foolish (2) unconditionally.   **credit** give credence to   **9 unjust**
unfaithful, deceitful.   **11 habit** demeanor. (With, however, a suggestion of *garb*, i.e., "something put on.")   **seeming trust** apparent
fidelity   **12 age in love** an aging person in love, or, in matters of love.
told (1) counted (2) divulged.

13 **lie with** (1) deceive (2) have sex with   14 **And . . . be** and so by
lies we flatteringly deceive ourselves about our moral lapses.
139.1 call ask.   **justify the wrong** i.e., condone something actually
taking place under my eyes   **2 unkindness** i.e., flagrant infidelity
3 with thine eye i.e., with a roving eye. (See lines 5–6.)   **4 with
power** i.e., candidly, directly.   **art** artifice, cunning.   **7 What** why
8 bide abide, withstand.   **11 foes** i.e., the *pretty looks*, the beauty and
wanton glances of line 10   **13 near** nearly   **14 rid** end. (*Rid my pain*
also suggests "satiate my craving.")
140.4 pity-wanting (1) unpitied by you (2) pity-craving   **5 wit** wisdom, prudence   **5–6 better . . . so** (I would teach you that) even
though you don't love me, yet, dear friend, it would be better to tell
me that you do   **8 know** i.e., hear.   **11 ill-wresting** misinterpreting
in an evil sense.   **bad** bad (that)   **13 so** i.e., a *mad slanderer* who is
believed.   **belied** slandered   **14 Bear . . . straight** keep your eyes on
me.   **wide** astray.
141.2 errors flaws in beauty   **4 Who . . . view** which (i.e., the heart),
in spite of what the eyes see

Nor tender feeling to base touches prone,
Nor taste, nor smell, desire to be invited
To any sensual feast with thee alone.   8
But my five wits nor my five senses can
Dissuade one foolish heart from serving thee,
Who leaves unswayed the likeness of a man,
Thy proud heart's slave and vassal wretch to be.   12
　　　Only my plague thus far I count my gain,
　　　That she that makes me sin awards me pain.

142

Love is my sin, and thy dear virtue hate,
Hate of my sin, grounded on sinful loving.
Oh, but with mine compare thou thine own state,
And thou shalt find it merits not reproving;   4
Or, if it do, not from those lips of thine
That have profaned their scarlet ornaments
And sealed false bonds of love as oft as mine,
Robbed others' beds' revenues of their rents.   8
Be it lawful I love thee as thou lov'st those
Whom thine eyes woo as mine importune thee.
Root pity in thy heart, that when it grows
Thy pity may deserve to pitied be.   12
　　　If thou dost seek to have what thou dost hide,
　　　By self-example mayst thou be denied.

143

Lo, as a careful huswife runs to catch
One of her feathered creatures broke away,
Sets down her babe and makes all swift dispatch
In pursuit of the thing she would have stay,   4
Whilst her neglected child holds her in chase,
Cries to catch her whose busy care is bent
To follow that which flies before her face,

Not prizing her poor infant's discontent: 8
So run'st thou after that which flies from thee,
Whilst I, thy babe, chase thee afar behind;
But if thou catch thy hope, turn back to me,
And play the mother's part: kiss me, be kind.   12
　　　So will I pray that thou mayst have thy Will,
　　　If thou turn back and my loud crying still.

144

Two loves I have, of comfort and despair,
Which like two spirits do suggest me still:
The better angel is a man right fair,
The worser spirit a woman colored ill.   4
To win me soon to hell, my female evil
Tempteth my better angel from my side,
And would corrupt my saint to be a devil,
Wooing his purity with her foul pride.   8
And whether that my angel be turned fiend
Suspect I may, yet not directly tell;
But being both from me, both to each friend,
I guess one angel in another's hell.   12
　　　Yet this shall I ne'er know, but live in doubt
　　　Till my bad angel fire my good one out.

145

Those lips that Love's own hand did make
Breathed forth the sound that said "I hate"
To me that languished for her sake;
But when she saw my woeful state,   4
Straight in her heart did mercy come,
Chiding that tongue that ever sweet
Was used in giving gentle doom,
And taught it thus anew to greet: 8
"I hate" she altered with an end,
That followed it as gentle day
Doth follow night, who like a fiend
From heaven to hell is flown away.   12
　　　"I hate" from hate away she threw,
　　　And saved my life, saying "not you."

---

6 **Nor . . . prone** nor (is) my delicate sense of touch inclined toward carnal contact (with you)   9 **my five wits** (neither) my five intellectual senses, i.e., the common sense, imagination, fancy, estimation (judgment), and memory   11 **Who . . . man** i.e., which heart abandons the proper government of my person, leaving me the mere likeness of a man   13 **thus far** to the following extent   14 **That . . . pain** i.e., that the sin brings with it its own punishment and contrition, thus presumably shortening my torment after death. (With a suggestion in *pain* of "sexual pleasure"; see sonnet 139.)
142.1–2 Love . . . loving My sin is to love you, and your best virtue is to hate—hate that sin in me, but also because of your uncontrolled sexual longing for other men. (The bitter paradox here is that hatred of sin must be virtue, and yet the lady is herself deeply implicated in this sin; her hatred is more a disdainful rejection of the poet's love than a noble virtue.)   4 **it** i.e., my state   6–7 **That . . . mine** i.e., that have forsworn themselves in love as often as my lips have. (The *scarlet ornaments* are lips and also red wax used to seal documents; they *seal* with a kiss.)   8 **Robbed . . . rents** i.e., and committed adultery with other women's husbands. (The metaphor is of income-yielding estates, *revenues*, whose *rents* or payments made by tenants are not properly paid; the husband does not pay what is owed to the wife in terms of marital affection and the producing of children.)
9–10 **Be . . . thee** i.e., I am as justified in loving you and imploring you with my eyes as you are in pursuing other men. (*Be it lawful* is a legal phrase meaning "Let it be considered lawful that.")   12 **deserve** make you deserving   13 **what . . . hide** what you withhold, i.e., pity
143.1 careful distressed, full of cares, busy.   **huswife** housewife
2 **feathered . . . away** domestic fowl which has broken away from the flock   5 **holds her in chase** chases after her   7 **flies** flees

8 **Not prizing** disregarding   13 **Will** (See sonnets 135, 136.)   14 **still** hush, make quiet.
144.1 (This sonnet appears, somewhat altered, in *The Passionate Pilgrim*.)   2 **suggest** urge, offer counsel, tempt.   **still** continually
3 **right fair** very handsome and blond   4 **ill** i.e., dark of complexion.
11 **from me** away from me. (The poet suspects they are together.)
both . . . friend friends to each other   12 **I . . . hell** I suspect that she (the evil angel) has him in her power (i.e., her sexual embracement; *hell* is slang for the pudenda).   14 **fire . . . out** drive out my good angel, stop seeing him. (With the suggestion of driving him out of the lady's sexual body as one would use fire and smoke to drive an animal out of its burrow, and with the further suggestion that the *fire* is venereal disease. *Bad angel* also hints at bad coinage driving out good money.)
145.1 (This sonnet is in eight-syllable meter.)   5 **Straight** at once
7 **used . . . doom** accustomed to passing a mild sentence   13 **"I hate" . . . threw** i.e., She separated the phrase "I hate" from the hatred I feared it expressed, from hateful meaning   13–14 **hate away . . . And** (Punning perhaps on the name of Shakespeare's wife, Anne Hathaway.)

146

Poor soul, the center of my sinful earth,
Thrall to these rebel powers that thee array,
Why dost thou pine within and suffer dearth,
Painting thy outward walls so costly gay?   4
Why so large cost, having so short a lease,
Dost thou upon thy fading mansion spend?
Shall worms, inheritors of this excess,
Eat up thy charge? Is this thy body's end?   8
Then, soul, live thou upon thy servant's loss,
And let that pine to aggravate thy store;
Buy terms divine in selling hours of dross;
Within be fed, without be rich no more.   12
  So shalt thou feed on Death, that feeds on men,
  And Death once dead, there's no more dying then.

147

My love is as a fever, longing still
For that which longer nurseth the disease,
Feeding on that which doth preserve the ill,
Th'uncertain sickly appetite to please.   4
My reason, the physician to my love,
Angry that his prescriptions are not kept,
Hath left me, and I desperate now approve
Desire is death, which physic did except.   8
Past cure I am, now reason is past care,
And frantic-mad with evermore unrest;
My thoughts and my discourse as madmen's are,
At random from the truth vainly expressed;   12
  For I have sworn thee fair and thought thee bright,
  Who art as black as hell, as dark as night.

148

Oh, me, what eyes hath love put in my head,
Which have no correspondence with true sight!
Or, if they have, where is my judgment fled,
That censures falsely what they see aright?   4
If that be fair whereon my false eyes dote,
What means the world to say it is not so?

If it be not, then love doth well denote
Love's eye is not so true as all men's "no."   8
How can it? Oh, how can love's eye be true,
That is so vexed with watching and with tears?
No marvel then though I mistake my view;
The sun itself sees not till heaven clears.   12
  O cunning love, with tears thou keep'st me blind,
  Lest eyes well-seeing thy foul faults should find.

149

Canst thou, O cruel, say I love thee not,
When I against myself with thee partake?
Do I not think on thee when I forgot
Am of myself, all tyrant for thy sake?   4
Who hateth thee that I do call my friend?
On whom frown'st thou that I do fawn upon?
Nay, if thou lour'st on me, do I not spend
Revenge upon myself with present moan?   8
What merit do I in myself respect
That is so proud thy service to despise,
When all my best doth worship thy defect,
Commanded by the motion of thine eyes?   12
  But, love, hate on, for now I know thy mind:
  Those that can see thou lov'st, and I am blind.

150

Oh, from what power hast thou this powerful might
With insufficiency my heart to sway?
To make me give the lie to my true sight
And swear that brightness doth not grace the day?   4
Whence hast thou this becoming of things ill,
That in the very refuse of thy deeds
There is such strength and warrantise of skill
That, in my mind, thy worst all best exceeds?   8
Who taught thee how to make me love thee more,
The more I hear and see just cause of hate?
Oh, though I love what others do abhor,
With others thou shouldst not abhor my state.   12
  If thy unworthiness raised love in me,
  More worthy I to be beloved of thee.

146.1 **sinful earth** body 2 **Thrall . . . array** made captive by the rebellious flesh that decks you in finery and lines you up in battle array. ("Thrall to" is one of several conjectures; the Quarto repeats "My sinfull earth" from line 1.) 4 **outward walls** i.e., the body, decked out in finery, cosmetics, etc. 5 **having . . . lease** having so brief a period of residence in this world 6 **mansion** dwelling, i.e., the body 8 **charge** expense, outlay. **Is . . . end?** Is this what your body was intended to be used for? 9 **thy servant's** i.e., the body's 10 **let that . . . store** let the body starve to increase your stock of spiritual riches 11 **Buy . . . dross** i.e., purchase eternal life in return for giving up (selling) mere hours of wasteful pleasure; secure *terms* that only God can provide
147.1 **still** always 2 **nurseth** nourishes 3 **preserve the ill** sustain the illness 4 **Th'uncertain** the finicky 7–8 **and I . . . except** and I now, desperately sick and in desperation, discover by experience that desire, which rejected medicine (or, which medical advice warned against), is fatal. 9 **care** medical care. (The line is an inversion of the proverb, "things past cure are past care," i.e., don't worry about what can't be helped. Reason, the physician, has ceased to care for his patient.) 10 **evermore** constant and increasing 12 **vainly** to no sensible purpose
148.4 **censures** judges

7 **love** i.e., the self-deceiving nature of my love. **denote** indicate, demonstrate (that) 8 **eye** (With a pun on "ay," yes.) 10 **vexed** troubled. **watching** remaining awake 11 **I** (Punning on "eye.") **mistake my view** err in what I see
149.2 **partake** take part (against myself). 3–4 **Do . . . sake?** Do I not put consideration of you foremost when I am tyrannously neglectful of, or oblivious of, myself and my best interests on your behalf? 7 **spend** vent 8 **present moan** immediate suffering and lamentation. 9 **respect** value 10 **thy . . . despise** as to think it demeaning to serve you 11 **all my best** all that is best in me. **defect** flaws 14 **Those . . . blind** i.e., you scorn one who loves you in a blind passion, in defiance of reason, and are drawn instead to those who know you for what you are.
150.2 **With insufficiency** by means of all your shortcomings. **sway** rule. 3 **give the lie to** accuse flatly of lying 4 **And . . . day** i.e., and swear that what is so is not so, that what is fair and beautiful is not fair and beautiful, since you are dark. 5 **becoming . . . ill** i.e., ability to show ill things in a becoming light 6 **in . . . deeds** in the most debased of your actions 7 **warrantise of skill** warrant or assurance of expertise 12 **state** i.e., condition of being helplessly in love.

151

Love is too young to know what conscience is;
Yet who knows not conscience is born of love?
Then, gentle cheater, urge not my amiss,
Lest guilty of my faults thy sweet self prove.   4
For, thou betraying me, I do betray
My nobler part to my gross body's treason.
My soul doth tell my body that he may
Triumph in love; flesh stays no farther reason,   8
But, rising at thy name, doth point out thee
As his triumphant prize. Proud of this pride,
He is contented thy poor drudge to be,
To stand in thy affairs, fall by thy side.   12
    No want of conscience hold it that I call
    Her "love" for whose dear love I rise and fall.

152

In loving thee thou know'st I am forsworn,
But thou art twice forsworn, to me love swearing:
In act thy bed-vow broke, and new faith torn
In vowing new hate after new love bearing.   4
But why of two oaths' breach do I accuse thee,
When I break twenty? I am perjured most,
For all my vows are oaths but to misuse thee,
And all my honest faith in thee is lost.   8
For I have sworn deep oaths of thy deep kindness,
Oaths of thy love, thy truth, thy constancy,
And, to enlighten thee, gave eyes to blindness,
Or made them swear against the thing they see;   12

For I have sworn thee fair. More perjured eye,
To swear against the truth so foul a lie!

153

Cupid laid by his brand and fell asleep.
A maid of Dian's this advantage found,
And his love-kindling fire did quickly steep
In a cold valley-fountain of that ground,   4
Which borrowed from this holy fire of Love
A dateless lively heat, still to endure,
And grew a seething bath, which yet men prove
Against strange maladies a sovereign cure.   8
But at my mistress' eye Love's brand new-fired,
The boy for trial needs would touch my breast;
I, sick withal, the help of bath desired,
And thither hied, a sad distempered guest,   12
    But found no cure. The bath for my help lies
    Where Cupid got new fire—my mistress' eyes.

154

The little love god lying once asleep
Laid by his side his heart-inflaming brand,
Whilst many nymphs that vowed chaste life to keep
Came tripping by; but in her maiden hand   4
The fairest votary took up that fire
Which many legions of true hearts had warmed,
And so the general of hot desire
Was, sleeping, by a virgin hand disarmed.   8
This brand she quenchèd in a cool well by,
Which from Love's fire took heat perpetual,
Growing a bath and healthful remedy
For men diseased; but I, my mistress' thrall,   12
    Came there for cure, and this by that I prove:
    Love's fire heats water, water cools not love.

151.1 too young (Love is personified as the young Cupid.)   **2 conscience** guilty knowing, carnal knowledge. (Playing on *conscience,* "moral sense," in line 1.)   **3 urge** stress, invoke.   **amiss** sin   **5 betraying** (1) cheating on (2) leading into temptation   **6 nobler part** i.e., soul   **7–8 that . . . in love** that he, the soul, may triumph in virtuous love. (But ambiguously misinterpretable as urging the flesh to triumph carnally.)   **8 flesh . . . reason** my flesh waits no longer to hear reason's lecture   **9 rising** (With bawdy suggestion of erection, continued in *point, Proud, stand, fall.* Metaphors of conjuration and of the compass needle's point are also invoked.)   **10 triumphant prize** spoils to be enjoyed in victory.   **Proud of** Swelling with.   **pride** splendor; erection   **12 stand** (1) serve, undertake business (2) be erect.   **fall** (as in battle; with sexual suggestion of detumescence)   **13 want** lack
152.1 forsworn i.e., faithless to my vows of love (perhaps marriage vows)   **3 act** sexual act.   **bed-vow** marriage vows to your husband   **3–4 new . . . bearing** i.e., a new contract of fidelity is torn up by your swearing hatred toward me, to whom you have only recently professed love. (Or the *new faith* that is torn up may be that which the lady has sworn to the friend.)   **7 but to misuse** merely to deceive   **8 And . . . lost** i.e., all my professions of honesty are belied when I perjure myself by praising you for loving constancy.   **11 And . . . blindness** i.e., and, to invest you with brightness, I made my eyes testify to things they did not see

13 eye (With a pun on "I.")
153 (This sonnet and the following seemingly have no direct connection with those preceding. They are derived ultimately, through Renaissance adaptations, from an epigram by the fifth-century Byzantine poet Marianus Scholasticus in the Greek Anthology.)   **1 brand** torch. (With phallic suggestion.)   **2 maid** attendant virgin, votaress.   **Dian** Diana, goddess of chastity   **4 of that ground** i.e., nearby. (*Valley-fountain* suggests the female sexual anatomy; compare with 154.9.)   **6 dateless** endless, eternal.   **still** always   **7–8 And grew . . . cure** and became a spring of hot medicinal waters, which even today men discover to be an efficacious cure against strange maladies. (Syphilis was conventionally treated with hot medicinal baths.)   **9 new-fired** having been reignited   **10 for trial** by way of test   **11 withal** from it   **12 hied** hastened.   **distempered** sick. (The bath is suggestive again of the sweating cure for venereal disease.)
154.7 general inspirer and commander, i.e., Cupid   **9 by** nearby   **11 Growing** becoming   **12 thrall** slave, bondman   **13 cure** (With suggestion of treatment for venereal disease, as in 153.7–14.)   **this** i.e., the following proposition.   **that** i.e., my coming, which failed to cure me

Appendix 1

Canon, Dates, and Early Texts

By "canon" we mean a listing of plays that can be ascribed to Shakespeare on the basis of reliable evidence. Such evidence is either "internal," derived from matters of style or poetics in the plays themselves (see General Introduction), or "external," derived from outside the play. The latter includes any reference by Shakespeare's contemporaries to his plays, any allusions in the plays themselves to contemporary events, the entering of Shakespeare's plays for publication in the Stationers' Register (S. R.), actual publication of the plays, and records of early performances. These matters of external evidence are also essential in attempting to date the plays.

The greatest single source of information is the First Folio text of Shakespeare's plays, sponsored by Shakespeare's fellow actors John Heminges and Henry Condell and published in 1623. It contains all the plays included in this present edition of Shakespeare except *Pericles* and *The Two Noble Kinsmen* and offers strong presumptive evidence of being a complete and accurate compilation of Shakespeare's work by men who knew him and cherished his memory. It provides the only texts we have for these eighteen plays: *The Comedy of Errors, The Two Gentlemen of Verona, The Taming of the Shrew, I Henry VI, King John, As You Like It, Twelfth Night, Julius Caesar, All's Well That Ends Well, Measure for Measure, Timon of Athens, Macbeth, Antony and Cleopatra, Coriolanus, Cymbeline, The Winter's Tale, The Tempest,* and *Henry VIII.* This includes nearly half the known canon of Shakespeare's plays. Our debt to the First Folio is incalculable and confirms our impression of its reliability.

The information of the First Folio is further confirmed by contemporary references. In 1598, a cleric and minor writer of the period named Francis Meres wrote in his *Palladis Tamia, Wit's Treasury:*

As the soul of Euphorbus was thought to live in Pythagoras, so the sweet, witty soul of Ovid lives in mellifluous and honey-tongued Shakespeare: witness his *Venus and Adonis,* his *Lucrece,* his sugared sonnets among his private friends, etc.

As Plautus and Seneca are accounted the best for comedy and tragedy among the Latins, so Shakespeare among the English is the most excellent in both kinds for the stage; for comedy, witness his *Gentlemen of Verona,* his *Errors,* his *Love's Labor's Lost,* his *Love's Labor's Won,* his *Midsummer's Night Dream,* and his *Merchant of Venice;* for tragedy his *Richard the II, Richard the III, Henry the IV, King John, Titus Andronicus* and his *Romeo and Juliet.*

Though this list was meant to offer praise, not to be an exhaustive catalogue, it is remarkably full. If the tantalizing *Love's Labor's Won* refers to *The Taming of the Shrew,* Meres's list of comedies is substantially complete down almost to 1598. It does not include the comedies that Shakespeare appears to have written around that date or soon afterward: *Much Ado About Nothing, The Merry Wives of Windsor, As You Like It,* and *Twelfth Night.* Meres correctly names all of Shakespeare's history plays except the *Henry VI* trilogy and of course the later histories, *Henry V* (1599) and *Henry VIII* (1613). He names both of Shakespeare's early tragedies that are not based on English history: *Titus Andronicus* and *Romeo and Juliet.* He tells us about the important nondramatic poems, which did not appear in the First Folio, since that volume is devoted exclusively to plays. Not much can be made of the order in which Meres names the plays, however, for we learn from other sources that *Richard III* clearly precedes *Richard II* in date of composition and that *King John* precedes the *Henry IV* plays.

Other writers of the 1590s add further confirming evidence. John Weever, in an epigram *"Ad Gulielmum Shakespeare,"* published in 1599, refers to "Rose-cheeked Adonis" and "Fair fire-hot Venus," to "Chaste Lucretia" and "Proud lust-stung Tarquin," and to *"Romeo, Richard—* more whose names I know not." Richard Barnfield, in

Poems in Divers Humors (1598), praises Shakespeare for "*Venus*" and "*Lucrece.*" Both Thomas Nashe and Robert Greene seemingly refer to the *Henry VI* plays, missing from Meres's list. Nashe, in his *Pierce Penniless* (1592), speculates how it would "have joyed brave Talbot (the terror of the French) to think that after he had lain two hundred years in his tomb, he should triumph again on the stage." Talbot is the hero of *1 Henry VI*, and we know of no other play on the subject. Greene, in his *Greene's Groats-worth of Wit* (1592), lashes out at an "upstart crow, beautified with our feathers, that with his '*Tiger's heart wrapped in a player's hide*' supposes he is as well able to bombast out a blank verse as the best of you, and, being an absolute *Johannes Factotum*, is in his own conceit the only Shake-scene in a country." The line about "Tiger's heart" is deliberately misquoted from *3 Henry VI*, 1.4.137. (It is possible that this famous attack on Shakespeare was actually written not by Greene himself but by Henry Chettle, his literary executor.)

The Taming of the Shrew (c. 1590–1593)

The Taming of the Shrew was not printed until the First Folio of 1623. Francis Meres does not mention the play in 1598 in his *Palladis Tamia*, unless it is the mysterious "*Loue labours wonne*" on his list. (Meres is not totally accurate, for he omits *Henry VI* from the history plays.) The play must have existed prior to 1598, however, for its style is comparable with that of *The Two Gentlemen of Verona* and other early comedies. Moreover, a play called *The Taming of a Shrew* appeared in print in 1594 (Stationers' Register, 1594). Four theories can be adduced to explain the problematic relationship of *A Shrew* to Shakespeare's play. The two least plausible theories are that Shakespeare, for some reason, reworked someone else's play shortly after its first performance or else wrote *A Shrew* himself as an early version. The third theory is that *A Shrew* represents an imitation of Shakespeare's play by some rival dramatist, who relied chiefly on his memory and who changed characters' names and the location to make the play seem his. Fourth and most plausibly, *A Shrew* may be a somewhat uncharacteristic kind of reported or memorially reconstructed Quarto, "improved" upon by a writer who also borrowed admiringly from Christopher Marlowe and other Elizabethan dramatists. In either of the latter two scenarios, Shakespeare's play would have to be dated earlier than May 1594.

The title page of *A Shrew* proclaims that "it was sundry times acted by the *Right honorable the Earle of Pembrook his seruants.*" Quite possibly this derivative version was merely trying to capitalize on the original's stage success and was, in fact, describing performances of Shakespeare's play. Theater owner and manager Philip Henslowe's record of a performance of "the Tamynge of A Shrowe" in 1594 at Newington Butts, a mile south of London Bridge, may also refer to Shakespeare's play; certainly, the minute distinction between "A Shrew" and "The Shrew" is one that the official records of the time would overlook. The Admiral's men and the Lord Chamberlain's men, acting companies, were playing at Newington Butts at the time, either jointly or alternatingly. Since Shakespeare's company, the Lord Chamberlain's, later owned *The Shrew*, they may well have owned and acted it on this occasion in 1594, having obtained it from the Earl of Pembroke's men when that company disbanded in 1593. Many of Pembroke's leading players joined the Lord Chamberlain's, Shakespeare being quite possibly among them. (The possibility that he came to the Lord Chamberlain's from Lord Strange's men seems less certain today than it once did.) Several echoes of Shakespeare's play in other plays of the early 1590s tend to confirm a date in or before 1593. It is entirely possible, then, that *The Shrew* was acted by Pembroke's men in 1592–1593 and subsequently passed along to the Lord Chamberlain's.

The Folio text of this play is now generally thought to have been printed from Shakespeare's working manuscript or possibly from a transcript of his papers, with perhaps some theatrical annotations as well. Some signs of revision are discernible.

A Midsummer Night's Dream (c. 1595)

A Midsummer Night's Dream was entered on the Stationers' Register, the official record book of the London Company of Stationers (booksellers and printers), by Thomas Fisher on October 8, 1600, and printed by him that same year in Quarto:

A Midsommer nights dreame. As it hath beene sundry times pub*lickely acted, by the Right honoura*ble, the Lord Chamberlaine his *seruants. Written by William Shakespeare.* Imprinted at London, for *Thomas Fisher*, and are to be soulde at his shoppe, at the Signe of the White Hart, in *Fleetestreete*. 1600.

This text appears to have been set from Shakespeare's working manuscript. Its inconsistencies in time scheme and other irregularities may reflect some revision, although the inconsistencies are not noticeable in performance. A Second Quarto appeared in 1619, though falsely dated 1600; it was a reprint of the First Quarto, with some minor corrections and many new errors. A copy of this Second Quarto, evidently with some added stage directions and other minor changes from a theatrical manuscript in the company's possession, served as the basis for the First Folio text of 1623. Changes of speech assignment in the Folio text, especially in Act 5, may reflect a late revival over which Shakespeare had no control. Essentially, the First Quarto remains the author-itative text.

Other than Francis Meres's listing of the play in 1598 in his *Palladis Tamia*, external clues as to date are elusive. Possibly the worry that a lion in a play might frighten the ladies (3.1.24–31) echoes published accounts of a bap-tismal feast at court in August 1594, when a blackamoor was chosen to draw in a chariot in place of a lion for fear of alarming nearby spectators. The description of unruly weather (2.1.88–114) has been related to the bad summer of 1594, but complaints about the weather are perennial. On the assumption that the play celebrates some noble wedding of the period, scholars have come up with a number of suitable marriages. Chief are those of Sir Thomas Heneage to Mary, Countess of Southampton, in 1594; of William Stanley, Earl of Derby, to Elizabeth Vere, daughter of the Earl of Oxford, in 1595; and of Thomas, son of Lord Berkeley, to Elizabeth, daughter of Lord Carey, in 1596. The Countess of Southampton was the widowed mother of the young Earl of Southampton, to whom Shakespeare had dedicated his *Venus and Adonis* and *The Rape of Lucrece*. No one has ever proved convinc-ingly, however, that the play was written for any occasion other than commercial public performance. The play makes sense for a general audience and does not need to depend on references to a private marriage. Shakespeare was, after all, in the business of writing plays for his fel-low actors, who earned their livelihood chiefly by public acting before large paying audiences. In any event, the search for a court marriage is a circular argument in terms of dating; suitable court marriages can be found for any year of the decade. In the last analysis, the play has to be dated on the basis of its stylistic affinity to plays like *Romeo and Juliet* and *Richard II*, works of the "lyric" mid-1590s. The "Pyramus and Thisbe" performance in *A Mid-summer Night's Dream* would seem to bear an obvious relation to *Romeo and Juliet*, although no one can say for sure which came first.

The Merchant of Venice (c. 1596–1597)

The Stationers' Register, the official record book of the Lon-don Company of Stationers (booksellers and printers), for July 22, 1598, contains an entry on behalf of the printer James Roberts for "a booke of the Marchaunt of Venyce, or otherwise called the Iewe of Venyce, Prouided, that yt bee not prynted by the said James Robertes or anye other what-soeuer without lycence first had from the Right honorable the lord Chamberlen." Roberts evidently enjoyed a close connection with the Chamberlain's men (Shakespeare's acting company) and seemingly was granted the special favor of registering the play at this time, even though the company did not wish to see the play published until later (or until they were paid). In 1600, at any rate, Roberts trans-ferred his rights as publisher to Thomas Heyes and print-ed the volume for him with the following title:

The most excellent Historie of the *Merchant of Venice*. VVith the extreame crueltie of *Shylocke* the Iewe towards the sayd Mer-chant, in cutting a iust pound of his flesh: and the obtayning of *Portia* by the choyse of three chests. *As it hath beene diuers times acted by the Lord Chamberlaine his Seruants.* Written by William Shakespeare. AT LONDON, Printed by I. R. [James Roberts] for Thomas Heyes, and are to be sold in Paules Church-yard, at the signe of the Greene Dragon. 1600.

The text of this 1600 Quarto is generally a good one, based seemingly on an accurate copy of Shakespeare's papers by the dramatist himself or some reliable transcriber. It served as copy for the Second Quarto of 1619 (printed by William Jaggard for Thomas Pavier and fraudulently dated 1600) and for the First Folio of 1623. Although some theatrical manuscript seems also to have been consulted in preparation for the Folio text, the Folio variations appear to have little authority.

Francis Meres mentions the play in 1598 in his *Palladis Tamia*. Establishing an earlier limit for dating has proven not so easy. Many scholars have urged a connection with the Roderigo Lopez affair of 1594 (see the Introduction to the play). The supposed allusion to Lopez in the lines about "a wolf, who, hanged for human slaughter" (4.1.134) may simply indicate, however, that wolves were actually hanged for attacking men in Shakespeare's day (as dogs were for killing sheep). Besides, the Lopez case remained so notorious throughout the 1590s that even a proven allusion to it in *The Merchant* would not limit the play to 1594 or 1595. Christopher Marlowe's play, *The Jew of Malta*, was revived in 1594 to exploit anti-Lopez senti-ment but was also revived in 1596. There may be, more-over, an allusion in 1.1.27 to the *St. Andrew*, a Spanish ship captured at Cadiz in 1596, and Shylock's allusion to Jacob and Laban (1.3.69–88) may well echo Miles Mosse's *The Arraignment and Conviction of Usury*, 1595. If so, the likeliest date is 1596–1597.

Much Ado About Nothing (1598–1599)

"The Commedie of muche A doo about nothing a booke" was entered in the Stationers' Register, the official record book of the London Company of Stationers (booksellers and printers), on August 4, 1600, along with *As You Like It*, *Henry V*, and Ben Jonson's *Every Man in His Humor*, all marked as plays of "My lord chamberlens men" (Shake-speare's acting company) and all "to be staied"—that is, not published without further permission. Earlier in the same memorandum, written on a spare page in the Reg-ister, occurs the name of the printer James Roberts, whose registration of *The Merchant of Venice* in 1598 was similarly stayed, pending further permission to publish.

Evidently, the Chamberlain's men were attempting to ensure that they were paid for any plays printed or else to prevent unauthorized publication of these very popular plays. If the latter was their motive, they were too late to forestall the appearance of a bad Quarto of *Henry V* in August 1600, but they did manage to control release of the others. *Much Ado About Nothing* appeared later that same year in a seemingly authorized version:

Much adoe about Nothing. *As it hath been sundrie times publikely* acted by the right honourable, the Lord Chamberlaine his seru-ants. *Written by William Shakespeare.* LONDON Printed by V. S. [Valentine Sims] for Andrew Wise, and William Aspley. 1600.

Once thought to have been set up from a theatrical play-book and then used itself in the theater as a playbook before serving as copy for the First Folio of 1623, this 1600 Quarto text is now generally regarded as having been set from Shakespeare's own manuscript. The names of the actors Will Kempe and Richard Cowley appear among the speech prefixes in 4.2, indicating that Shakespeare had them in mind as he wrote; other irregularities in speech prefixes and scene headings (including "ghost" characters, such as Leonato's wife Innogen) read more like a manu-script in the last stages of revision than a playbook for a finished production. The Folio text was based on this 1600 Quarto, lightly annotated with reference to the playbook but providing little in the way of new readings other than the correction of obvious error.

Francis Meres does not mention the play in September 1598 in his *Palladis Tamia*, unless (and this seems unlikely) it is his "*Loue labours wonne.*" Will Kempe, who played Dogberry, left the Chamberlain's men early in 1599. The likeliest date, then, is the winter of 1598–1599, though pub-lication was not until 1600.

As You Like It (1598–1600)

"As you like yt, a booke" was entered in the Stationers' Register, the official record book of the London Compa-ny of Stationers (booksellers and printers), on August 4, 1600, along with *Much Ado About Nothing, Henry V*, and Ben Jonson's *Every Man in His Humor*, all labeled as "My lord chamberlens mens plaies" and all ordered "to be staied" from publication until further notice. Evidently, the Chamberlain's men (Shakespeare's acting company) were anxious to ensure payment or otherwise protect their rights to these very popular plays. Despite their efforts, *Henry V* appeared in an unauthorized Quarto that same month. *As You Like It* did not appear in print, how-ever, until the First Folio of 1623. The Folio text is a good one, based seemingly on the theatrical playbook that still retained certain authorial features (conceivably, because an autograph fair copy served as the basis for it) or on a

literary transcript either of the playbook or of an author-ial manuscript.

Francis Meres does not mention the play in Septem-ber 1598 in his *Palladis Tamia*. However, the play contains an unusually clear allusion to Christopher Marlowe's *Hero and Leander* ("Who ever loved that loved not at first sight?" 3.5.82), of which the first extant edition appeared in 1598, although Shakespeare may well have known it earlier in manuscript or in some lost edition. Even so, other possible allusions, to the burning of satirical books in June 1599 (see 1.2.85–6) and to the new Globe Theater ("All the world's a stage," 2.7.138), point to a date between late 1598 and the summer of 1600, probably after *Much Ado About Nothing*.

Twelfth Night (1600–1602)

Twelfth Night was registered with the London Company of Stationers (booksellers and printers) in 1623 and was first published in the First Folio of that year in a good text set up from what may have been a scribal transcript of Shakespeare's draft manuscript or possibly the playbook (assuming that the scribe might omit theatrical notations). There was a brief delay in printing *Twelfth Night* in the First Folio, possibly because a transcript was being pre-pared. The play was first mentioned, however, in the *Diary* of a Middle Temple law student or barrister named John Manningham, who describes the festivities for Can-dlemas Day, February 2, 1602, as follows:

At our feast wee had a play called "Twelue Night, or What you Will," much like the Commedy of Errores, or Menechmi in Plau-tus, but most like and neere to that in Italian called *Inganni*. A good practise in it to make the Steward beleeve his Lady wid-dowe was in love with him, by couterfeyting a letter as from his Lady in generall termes, telling him what shee liked best in him, and prescribing his gesture in smiling, his apparaile, & c., and then when he came to practise making him beleeue they tooke him to be mad.

This entry was once suspected to be a forgery perpetrated by John Payne Collier, who published the *Diary* in 1831, but its authenticity is now generally accepted. The date accords with several possible allusions in the play itself. When Fabian jokes about "a pension of thousands to be paid from the Sophy" (2.5.176–7), he seems to be recalling Sir Anthony Shirley's reception by the Shah of Persia (the Sophy) between the summer of 1598 and late 1601. An account of this visit was entered in the Stationers' Register in November 1601. Viola's description of Feste as "wise enough to play the fool" (3.1.60) may recall a poem begin-ning "True it is, he plays the fool indeed," published in 1600–1601 by Robert Armin (who had played the role of Feste). Maria's comparison of Malvolio's smiling face to "the new map with the augmentation of the Indies" (3.2.77–8) refers to new maps published in 1599 in which America (the Indies) was increased in size. Fabian's reference to sailing north and to the icicle on a Dutchman's beard (3.2.25–6) sounds like an allusion to William Barentz's Arctic expedition, first described in English in an account entered in the Stationers' Register on June 13, 1598, though no edition survives before 1609. Leslie Hotson (*The First Night of Twelfth Night*, 1954) has argued for a first performance at court on Twelfth Night in January 1601, when Queen Elizabeth entertained Don Virginio Orsino, Duke of Bracciano, but this hypothesis has not gained general acceptance, partly because the role of Orsino in the play would scarcely flatter such a noble visitor and partly because there is no proof that any of Shakespeare's plays were originally commissioned for private performance. Nevertheless, the episode may have suggested to Shakespeare the name Orsino. All in all, a date between 1600 and early 1602 seems most likely. Francis Meres does not mention the play in 1598 in his *Palladis Tamia*.

Measure for Measure (1603–1604)

Measure for Measure first appeared in the First Folio of 1623. The text was evidently set from scrivener Ralph Crane's copy, possibly of Shakespeare's own draft; the usual inconsistencies of composition have not yet been smoothed away by use in the theater. On the other hand, spellings tend to suggest that Crane was copying a transcript. A recent and controversial hypothesis is that Crane based his copy on a playbook in use after Shakespeare's death, which incorporated some theatrical adaptation by Thomas Middleton and some other reviser, including a song (4.1.1–6) that could have originated in *Rollo, Duke of Normandy* (c. 1617) by John Fletcher and others.

The first recorded performance (according to a Revels account document) was on December 26, 1604, St. Stephen's Night, when "a play Caled Mesur for Mesur" by "Shaxberd" was acted in the banqueting hall at Whitehall "by his Maiesties plaiers." Shakespeare's acting company, previously the Lord Chamberlain's men, had become the King's men after the accession to the throne of James I in 1603. Several allusions in the play seem to point to the summer of 1604, when the theaters, having been closed for a year because of the plague, were reopened. A reference to the King of Hungary (1.2.1–5) may reflect anxieties in England over James's negotiations for a settlement with Spain; censorship would forbid a direct mentioning of Spain. Mistress Overdone's complaint about the war, the "sweat" (plague), the "gallows" (public executions), and poverty (1.2.81–3) are all suggestive of events in 1603–1604,

when war with Spain and the plague were still very much in evidence. Duke Vincentio's reticent habits have been seen as a flattering reference to James's well-known dislike of crowds. Stylistically, the play is clearly later than *Twelfth Night* (1600–1602), so that a date close to the first recorded performance in 1604 is a necessity, even if we cannot be positive about all the supposed allusions to King James.

Richard III (c. 1592–1594)

A Quarto edition of *Richard III*, registered by Andrew Wise on October 20, 1597, appeared later that same year with the following title:

THE TRAGEDY of King Richard the third. Containing, His treacherous Plots against his brother Clarence: the pittiefull murther of his iunocent nephewes: his tyrannicall vsurpation: with the whole course of his detested life, and most deserued death. As it hath beene lately Acted by the Right honourable the Lord Chamberlaine his seruants. AT LONDON Printed by Valentine Sims, for Andrew Wise, dwelling in Paules Chu[r]ch-yard, at the Signe of the Angell. 1597.

This text, one of the most perplexing in all Shakespeare, is sometimes regarded as one that was created when the acting company banded together to reconstruct a play of which the copy was missing. The reconstructed version may have been cut, perhaps for provincial performance. This defective text was the basis of the 1597 Quarto, which was reprinted in 1598, 1602, 1605, 1612, 1622, 1629, and 1634, each of which was successively more error-laden than the previous one. The First Folio text of 1623 seems to have been set mainly from copies of the Third and Sixth Quartos (1602 and 1622), which had been sporadically but heavily corrected against an independent manuscript—possibly Shakespeare's own working manuscript or a copy of it. This manuscript source, some of which may have been interleaved into the printers' copy, represents a generally superior authority to that of the First Quarto. Parts of the Folio text, however, were set from an uncorrected copy of the Third Quarto (1602), and for those passages (3.1.1–158 and 5.3.48 to end of play) the First Quarto, from which the Third Quarto was derived, must serve as copy text. Otherwise, the Folio text is the most authoritative, though it must be approached with caution.

The situation is indeed fraught with unusual uncertainty, since there are many opportunities for the Folio to have perpetuated errors of the earlier Quartos; moreover, its "improvements" over the readings of those Quartos could in some instances be editorial sophistications. The First Quarto offers some readings that demand serious attention. Especially when the Folio's reading differs from those of the First Quarto and is instead derived from Quartos Two through Six, the First Quarto should be preferred unless it is manifestly wrong. At the same time, however, since the First Quarto may reflect adaptation of the original acting text, its changes may not represent Shakespeare's artistic intention either. For these reasons, one must be wary of the First Quarto's assignment of speeches when they vary from the Folio's assignments and also of the First Quarto's cuts, some of which are substantial.

The play is mentioned by Francis Meres in 1598 in his *Palladis Tamia*. John Weever names a *"Richard"* in his *Epigrams*, published in 1599. Most scholars date *Richard III* as 1592–1594, on the basis of its style and its close affinity to the *Henry VI* series (completed probably in 1591–1592). The play may have been influenced by the anonymous *The True Tragedy of Richard III*, registered in June 1594 but probably written in 1590–1592 or even earlier. Shakespeare's play may also have been influenced by Thomas Kyd's *The Spanish Tragedy* (c. 1587) and by Christopher Marlowe's dramas (he died in 1593).

Richard II (c. 1595–1596)

On August 29, 1597, "The Tragedye of Richard the Second" was entered in the Stationers' Register, the official record book of the London Company of Stationers (booksellers and printers), by Andrew Wise, and was published by him later that same year:

THE Tragedie of King Richard the second. *As it hath beene publikely acted by the right Honourable the Lorde Chamberlaine his Seruants.* LONDON Printed by Valentine Simmes for Androw Wise, and are to be sold at his shop in Paules church yard at the signe of the Angel. 1597.

This is a good text, printed evidently from the author's papers or a nontheatrical transcript of them. Wise issued two more quartos of this popular play in 1598, each set from the previous quarto, and then in 1603 transferred his rights to the play to Matthew Law. This publisher issued in 1608 a Fourth Quarto "With new additions of the Parliament Sceane, and the deposing of King Richard" (according to the title page in some copies). The deposition scene has indeed been omitted from the earlier quartos, probably through censorship. A Fifth Quarto appeared in 1615, based on the Fourth Quarto. All the quartos after the first attribute the play to Shakespeare. The added deposition scene in Quartos 4 and 5 seems to have been memorially reconstructed. The First Folio text of 1623 gives a better version of the deposition scene, seemingly because the printers of the Folio had access to the manuscript playbook for this portion of the text. (Some scholars maintain that the Folio text was derived from an earlier quarto or quartos that had been marked up and used as a playbook, but that case has been weak-

ened by recent research.) Most of the Folio text was probably set from an annotated copy of the Third Quarto, and perhaps a leaf in Act 5 from the Fifth Quarto. The annotation was evidently quite uneven, and so the most authoritative text for all but the deposition scene remains the First Quarto; nevertheless, at certain points (especially the first 900 lines, part of 3.2, and much of Act 5), the annotation with reference to the playbook seems to have been more thorough. At such points, the Folio readings deserve serious attention, and the stage directions are often illuminating.

Francis Meres mentions the play in 1598 in his *Palladis Tamia*. Clearly it had been written and performed prior to the Stationers' Register entry in August 1597. Its earliest probable date is 1595, since the play seemingly is indebted to Samuel Daniel's poem, *The First Four Books of the Civil Wars*, published in that year. Shakespeare follows Daniel, for example, in increasing the Queen's age from eleven (according to the chronicles) to maturity, and in other significant details. On December 7, 1595, Sir Edward Hoby invited Sir Robert Cecil to his house in Cannon Row, "where as late as it shall please you a gate for your supper shall be open, and King Richard present himself to your view." Although it is by no means certain that this passage refers to a private performance of Shakespeare's play, stylistic considerations favor a date around 1595 rather than 1597. If, as some scholars contend, Daniel's *Civil Wars* was written after Shakespeare's play rather than before it, the date of *Richard II* might be as early as 1594.

Henry IV, Part I (1596–1597)

On February 25, 1598, "The historye of Henry the IIIJth with his battaile of Shrewsburye against Henry Hottspurre of the Northe with the conceipted mirthe of Sir John Ffalstoff" was entered in the Stationers' Register, the official record book of the London Company of Stationers (booksellers and printers), by Andrew Wise. Later that year appeared the following Quarto:

THE HISTORY OF HENRIE THE FOVRTH; With the battell at Shrewsburie, *betweene the King and Lord* Henry Percy, surnamed Henrie Hotspur of the North. *With the humorous conceits of Sir* Iohn Falstalffe. AT LONDON, Printed by P. S. [Peter Short] for *Andrew Wise*, dwelling in Paules Churchyard, at the signe of the Angell. 1598.

Actually this was not the first quarto, for an earlier fragment of eight pages has survived, part of a text that served as copy for the first complete extant Quarto. Together, these quartos make up an excellent authoritative text, based seemingly on the author's papers or, more probably, a scribal transcript of them. Four more quartos appeared before the First Folio of 1623, each based on the previous quarto. The Folio itself was based on the last of these, perhaps with reference also to some kind of manuscript, although the number of authoritative readings that can be claimed for the Folio is small.

1 Henry IV shows signs of revision in the use of characters' names, most notably that of Falstaff. Plainly, the original version of the play called him Sir John Oldcastle, after one of the prince's companions in the anonymous *Famous Victories of Henry the Fifth* (c. 1588). The name "Oldcastle" was originally intended for *2 Henry IV* as well. The speech prefix "Old." is left standing at 1.2.119 in the Quarto of *2 Henry IV*, one or two lines of verse in *1 Henry IV* are one syllable short, evidently because "Old-castle" has been altered to "Falstaff," and Falstaff is jokingly referred to as "my old lad of the castle" (*1 Henry IV*, 1.2.41). Moreover, there are several contemporary allusions to a play about a fat knight named Oldcastle. Apparently, Henry Brooke, Lord Cobham, a living descendant of the Lollard martyr Oldcastle of Henry V's reign, took umbrage at the profane use Shakespeare had made of this revered name, whereupon Shakespeare's acting company shifted to another less controversial name from the chronicles, Sir John Fastolfe or Falstaff (called "Falstaffe" in the Folio text of Shakespeare's *1 Henry VI* and assigned a cowardly role in the French wars of that play). The revision also changed the names of Oldcastle's cronies from Harvey and Russell to Peto and Bardolph. This edition retains the name "Falstaff," since Shakespeare clearly accepted it as the new name of the character in all his "Falstaff" plays.

Cobham was Lord Chamberlain from July 1596 until his death in March 1597, during which interval Shakespeare's company bore the name of Lord Hunsdon's men. Quite possibly, the difficulty over the name "Oldcastle" erupted during that period, for *1 Henry IV* seems to have been written and performed in late 1596 and early 1597, not long after Shakespeare had finished *Richard II* (c. 1595–1596).

Francis Meres, in his *Palladis Tamia,* 1598, refers to "*Henry the IV*" without specifying one or two parts. Publication of *1 Henry IV* in 1598 confirmed to the Elizabethan public that the changes in names to Falstaff, Peto, and Bardolph had taken place.

Henry V (1599)

An entry in the Stationers' Register, the official record book of the London Company of Stationers (booksellers and printers), for August 4, 1600, provides that "Henry the ffift" and three other plays belonging to the Lord Chamberlain's men (Shakespeare's acting company) are "to be staied" from publication until further permission is granted. Evidently, the Chamberlain's men were anxious to ensure they were paid or to prevent unauthorized publication. They did not succeed, in any event, in preventing the appearance of an unauthorized text of *Henry V*. An entry in the Stationers' Register for August 14 assigns to Thomas Pavier an already

published work entitled "The historye of Henry the Vth with the battell of Agencourt." The Quarto volume to which this entry refers is the following:

THE CHRONICLE History of Henry the fift, With his battell fought at *Agin Court* in *France.* Togither with *Auntient Pistoll. As it hath bene sundry times playd by the Right honorable the Lord Chamberlaine his seruants.* LONDON Printed by *Thomas Creede,* for Tho. Millington, and Iohn Busby. And are to be sold at his house in Carter Lane, next the Powle head. 1600.

The text of this play is manifestly corrupt. It is considerably shorter than the First Folio version and completely omits the choruses and three entire scenes (1.1, 3.1, and 4.2). The remainder seems to have been put together by memorial reconstruction. This unauthorized Quarto served as the basis for a Second Quarto printed by Thomas Creede for Thomas Pavier in 1602 and a third printed by William Jaggard for Thomas Pavier in 1619 but fraudulently dated 1608. The Folio text was printed seemingly from an authorial manuscript, perhaps with occasional reference to the Third Quarto (which contains some potentially troublesome contamination). The Folio text is thus the most reliable version, though the First Quarto is also an interesting witness, especially for visual effects recorded in its stage directions, for a few readings in the text, and for verse lineation of Pistol's speeches.

Francis Meres does not mention the play in 1598 in his *Palladis Tamia,* though he does mention "*Henry the IV.*" The epilogue to *2 Henry IV* (written probably in 1597) promises that "our humble author will continue the story, with Sir John in it, and make you merry with fair Katharine of France"; since the prediction is not really accurate regarding Falstaff, we can be reasonably certain that Shakespeare had not yet begun *Henry V* in 1597. An allusion in the Chorus of Act 5 to "the General of our gracious Empress," who may in good time come home from Ireland with "rebellion broachèd on his sword," has been taken by virtually all editors to refer to the Earl of Essex, who left in March 1599 to quell the Irish rebellion headed by Tyrone. Although Essex returned on September 28 of that same year, having failed utterly in his assignment, the departure of such a charismatic figure could have inspired Shakespeare's praising remark. A minority view holds that the choruses (which do not appear in the unauthorized Quarto of 1600) could have been written later in 1601 for Essex's far more victorious successor, Lord Mountjoy (see Warren D. Smith on *Henry V* in *JEGP,* 1954). Still, Essex was more center stage during those exciting years, more likely to have been the subject of adulation. In any case, the play itself must have been written before August 1600, most probably in 1599. The reference to "this wooden O" in the Chorus of Act 1 is often thought to be Shakespeare's compliment to the company's new theater, the Globe, which was ready for their use probably in 1599; but the play may have been produced at the Curtain instead.

Romeo and Juliet (1594–1596)

A corrupt and unregistered Quarto of *Romeo and Juliet* appeared in 1597 with the following title:

AN excellent conceited Tragedie OF Romeo and Iuliet, As it hath been often (with great applause) plaid publiquely, by the right Honourable the L. of *Hunsdon* his Seruants. LONDON, Printed by Iohn Danter. 1597.

This edition, intended no doubt to capitalize on the play's great popularity, seems to have been memorially reconstructed by two or more actors (probably those playing Romeo and Paris), and possibly thereafter to have been used as a playbook. Its appearance seems to have caused the issuance two years later of a clearly authoritative version:

THE MOST EXcellent and lamentable Tragedie, of Romeo and *Iuliet. Newly corrected, augmented, and amended*: As it hath bene sundry times publiquely acted, by the right Honourable the Lord Chamberlaine his Seruants. LONDON Printed by Thomas Creede, for Cuthbert Burby, and are to be sold at his shop neare the Exchange. 1599.

This text is some 800 lines longer than the first and corrects errors in that earlier version. It seems at one point, however, to have been contaminated by the First Quarto, as though the manuscript source for the Second Quarto (probably the author's rough draft) was defective at some point. A passage from 1.2.53 to 1.3.34 was apparently set directly from the First Quarto. (On this matter, see George W. Williams's old-spelling edition of the play, Duke Univ. Press, 1964.) Q1 may also have influenced Q2 in some other isolated instances. Despite this contamination, however, the Second Quarto is the authoritative text, except for the passage of direct indebtedness to Q1. Q2 served as the basis for the Third Quarto (1609), which in turn served as copy for the Fourth Quarto (undated, but placed in 1622) and the First Folio of 1623. A Fifth Quarto appeared in 1637. The Folio text may embody a few authoritative readings of its own, perhaps by way of reference to a theatrical manuscript.

Francis Meres, in his *Palladis Tamia*, 1598, assigns the play to Shakespeare. So does John Weever in his *Epigrams* of 1599. Internal evidence on dating is not reliable. The Nurse observes that "'Tis since the earthquake now eleven years" (1.3.24); however, it has been discovered that suitable earthquakes occurred in 1580, 1583, 1584, and 1585, giving us a wide choice of dates even if we accept the dubious proposition that the Nurse is speaking accurately. Astronomical reckoning of the position of the moon at the time the play purportedly takes place ("A fortnight and odd days" before Lammastide, August 1, 1.3.16) indicates the year 1596; again, however, we have no reason to assume Shakespeare cared about this sort of internal accuracy. More suggestive perhaps is the argument that Danter's unauthorized publication in 1597 was seeking to exploit a popular new play—one the acting company certainly did not yet wish to see published, since it was a moneymaker. Danter assigns the play to Lord Hunsdon's servants, a name that Shakespeare's company could have used only from July 22, 1596 (when the old Lord Chamberlain, Henry Carey, first Lord Hunsdon, died) to March 17, 1597 (when George Carey, second Lord Hunsdon, was appointed to his father's erstwhile position as Lord Chamberlain). Danter could simply have been using the name of the company at the time he obtained the play, but he may also have indicated performance in late 1596. Danter printed only the first four sheets, but he must have done so by February–March 1597, when his presses were seized. Stylistically, the play is clearly of the "lyric" period of *A Midsummer Night's Dream* and *Richard II*. There are also stylistic affinities to the sonnets and to the narrative poems of 1593–1594. A date between 1594 and 1596 is likely, especially toward the latter end of this period. Whether the play comes before or after *A Midsummer Night's Dream* is, however, a matter of conjecture.

Julius Caesar (1599)

Julius Caesar was first published in the First Folio of 1623. The text is an excellent one, based evidently on a theater playbook or a transcript of it; some theatrical features, such as a provision for the doubling of Cassius and Caius Ligarius, appear to represent a staging configuration that Shakespeare had not anticipated. On the other hand, some stage directions sound authorial, as though Shakespeare's own words had survived into the playbook. Some confusions have survived as well, notably in the handling of Lucilius, Lucius, Titinius, and Pindarus in 4.2. In the Folio, the play is included among the tragedies and entitled *The Tragedy of Julius Caesar*, although the table of contents lists it as *The Life and death of Julius Caesar*.

The play's first performance must have occurred in 1599 or slightly earlier. On September 21, 1599, a Swiss visitor named Thomas Platter crossed the River Thames after lunch with a company of spectators to see "the tragedy of the first Emperor Julius Caesar" performed in a thatched-roofed building. The description fits the Globe, the Rose, and the Swan theaters, but the last of these was not in regular use. The Admiral's men at the Rose are not known to have had a Caesar play, whereas the Chamberlain's men certainly had Shakespeare's play about this time. They had only recently moved from their Theatre in the northeast suburbs of London to the Globe south of the river, and *Julius Caesar* was probably a new play for the occasion.

John Weever, in *The Mirror ofMartyrs* (1601), is surely referring to Shakespeare's play when he describes "the many-headed multitude" listening first to "Brutus' speech, that Caesar was ambitious" and then to "eloquent Mark Antony." (The dedication to Weever's book claims he wrote it "some two years ago," in 1599; however, since this book has been shown to be heavily indebted to a work that first appeared in 1600, Weever's allusion is not as helpful in limiting the date as was once thought.) Ben Jonson's *Every Man in His Humor*, acted in 1599, may also contain allusions to Shakespeare's play. Francis Meres does not mention it in 1598 in his *Palladis Tamia*.

Hamlet (c. 1599–1601)

Like everything else about *Hamlet*, the textual problem is complicated. On July 26, 1602, James Roberts entered in the Stationers' Register, the official record book of the London Company of Stationers (booksellers and printers), "A booke called the Revenge of Hamlett Prince Denmarke as yt was latelie Acted by the Lord Chamberleyne his servantes." For some reason, however, Roberts did not print his copy of *Hamlet* until 1604, by which time the following unauthorized edition had appeared:

THE Tragicall Historie of HAMLET *Prince of Denmarke*. By William Shake-speare. As it hath beene diuerse times acted by his Highnesse seruants in the Cittie of London: as also in the two Vniuersities of Cambridge and Oxford, and else-where. At London printed for N. L. [Nicholas Ling] and Iohn Trundell. 1603.

This edition, the First Quarto of *Hamlet*, seems to have been memorially reconstructed by actors who toured the provinces (note the references to Cambridge, Oxford, and so on), with some recollection of an earlier *Hamlet* play (the *Ur-Hamlet*) written before 1589 and acted during the 1590s. The actors seemingly had no recourse to an authoritative manuscript. One of these actors may have played Marcellus and possibly Lucianus and Voltimand. Their version appears to have been based on an adaptation of the company's original playbook, which itself stood once removed from Shakespeare's working papers by way of an intermediate manuscript. The resulting text is very corrupt, and yet it seems to have affected the more authentic text, because the compositors of the Second Quarto made use of it, especially when they typeset the first act.

The authorized Quarto of *Hamlet* appeared in 1604. Roberts, the printer, seems to have reached some agreement with Ling, one of the publishers of the First Quarto, for their initials are now paired on the title page:

THE Tragicall Historie of HAMLET, *Prince of Denmarke*. By William Shakespeare. Newly imprinted and enlarged to almost as much againe as it was, according to the true and perfect Coppie. AT LONDON, Printed by I. R. [James Roberts] for N. L. [Nicholas Ling] and are to be sold at his shoppe vnder Saint Dunstons Church in Fleetstreet. 1604.

Some copies of this edition are dated 1605. This text was based seemingly on Shakespeare's own papers, with the bookkeeper's annotations, but is marred by printing errors and is at times contaminated by the First Quarto—presumably, when the printers found Shakespeare's manuscript unreadable. This Second Quarto served as copy for a Third Quarto in 1611, Ling having meanwhile transferred his rights in the play to John Smethwick. A Fourth Quarto, undated but before 1623, was based on the Third.

The First Folio text of 1623 omits more than two hundred lines found in the Second Quarto, yet it supplies some clearly authentic passages. It seems to derive from a transcript of Shakespeare's draft, in which cuts made by the author were observed—cuts made by Shakespeare quite possibly because he knew the draft to be too long for performance and which had either not been marked in the Second Quarto copy or had been ignored there by the compositors. The Folio also incorporates other alterations seemingly made for clarity or in anticipation of performance. To this theatrically motivated transcript, Shakespeare apparently contributed some revisions. Subsequently, this version evidently was copied again by a careless scribe who took many liberties with the text. Typesetting from this inferior manuscript, the Folio compositors occasionally consulted the Fourth Quarto, but not often enough. Thus, even though the Folio supplies some genuine readings, as does the First Quarto when both the Folio and the Second Quarto are wrong, the Second Quarto remains the most authentic version of the text.

Since the text of the Second Quarto is too long to be accommodated in the two hours' traffic of the stage and since it becomes even longer when the words found only in the Folio are added, Shakespeare must have known it would have to be cut for performance and probably marked at least some omissions himself. Since he may have consented to such cuts primarily because of the constraints of time, however, this present edition holds to the view that the passages in question should not be excised from the text we read. The *Hamlet* presented here is doubtless longer than any version ever acted in Shakespeare's day and thus does not represent a script for any actual performance, but it may well represent the play as Shakespeare wrote it and then expanded it somewhat while also including passages that he may reluctantly have consented to cut for performance. It is also possible that some cuts were artistically intended, but, in the face of real uncertainty in this matter, an editorial policy of inclusion gives to the reader those passages that would otherwise have to be excised or put in an appendix on questionable grounds of authorial "intent."

Hamlet must have been produced before the Stationers' Register entry of July 26, 1602. Francis Meres does not mention the play in 1598 in his *Palladis Tamia*. Gabriel Harvey attributes the "tragedy of Hamlet, Prince of Denmark" to Shakespeare in a marginal note in Harvey's copy of Speght's Chaucer; Harvey acquired the book in 1598, but he could have written the note any time between then and 1601, or even 1603. More helpful in dating is *Hamlet*'s clear reference to the so-called War of the Theaters, the rivalry between the adult actors and the boy actors whose companies had newly revived in 1598–1599 after nearly a decade of inactivity (see 2.2.337–62). The Children of the Chapel Royal began acting at Blackfriars in 1598 and provided such keen competition in 1599–1601 that the adult actors were at times forced to tour the provinces (see *Hamlet*, 2.2.332–62). *Hamlet*'s reference to the rivalry appears, however, only in the Folio text and could represent a late addition. The reference to an "inhibition" imposed on acting companies "by the means of the late innovation" (2.2.332–3), printed in the 1604 Quarto, may possibly refer to the abortive uprising of the Earl of Essex on February 8, 1601, or to a decree issued by the Privy Council on June 22, 1600, restricting London companies to two performances a week in each of two playhouses. Revenge tragedy was also in fashion during these years: John Marston's *Antonio's Revenge*, for example, dates from 1599–1601, and *The Malcontent* is from about the same time or slightly later, though it is hard to tell who influenced whom. *Hamlet*'s apparent indebtedness to John Florio's translation of Montaigne suggests that Shakespeare had access to that work in manuscript before its publication in 1603; the Florio had been registered for publication in 1595 and 1600.

Othello (c. 1603–1604)

On October 6, 1621, Thomas Walkley entered in the Stationers' Register, the official record book of the London Company of Stationers (booksellers and printers), "The Tragedie of Othello, the moore of Venice," and published the play in the following year:

THE Tragoedy of Othello, The Moore of Venice. *As it hath beene diuerse times acted at the* Globe, and at the Black-Friers, by *his Maiesties Seruants. Written by* VVilliam Shakespeare. LONDON, Printed by N. O. [Nicholas Okes] for *Thomas Walkley*, and are to be sold at his shop, at the Eagle and Child, in Brittans Bursse. 1622.

This text of this Quarto is a good one, based probably on a scribal transcript of Shakespeare's working manuscript, although it is some one hundred and sixty lines shorter than the Folio text of 1623, mostly in scattered small omissions. The Folio text may have been derived (via an intermediate transcript) from a revision of the original authorial manuscript, in which Shakespeare himself copied over his work and made a large number of synonymous or nearly synonymous changes as he did so. These papers, edited by someone else to remove profanity as required by law and introducing other stylistic changes in the process, seemingly became the basis

of the playbook and also of the Folio text. E. A. J. Honigmann (*The Texts of "Othello" and Shakespearian Revision*, 1996) proposes that Ralph Crane prepared a transcript to serve as copy for the Folio text, though not all scholars have agreed.

The textual situation is thus complex. The Folio text appears to contain a significant number of authorial changes, but it was also worked on by one or more sophisticating scribes and by compositors whose changes are sometimes hard to distinguish from those of Shakespeare. The Quarto text was printed by a printing establishment that was not known for careful work but does stand close in some ways to a Shakespearean original. Editorially, then, the Folio is the copy text, and its readings are to be preferred when the Quarto is not clearly correct and especially when the Folio gives us genuinely new words, but the Quarto's readings demand careful consideration when the Folio text may be suspected of mechanical error (e.g., the shortening of words in full lines) or compositorial substitution of alternative forms, normalizations, and easy adjustments of meter. There are times when the Folio's compositor may have been misled by nearby words or letters in his copy. And, because the Folio's stage directions are probably scribal, attention should be paid to those in the Quarto.

According to a Revels account that was suspected of being a forgery soon after its publication in 1842 but is now generally accepted, the earliest mention of the play is on "Hallamas Day, being the first of Nouembar," 1604, when "the Kings Maiesties plaiers" performed "A Play in the Banketinge house att Whit Hall Called The Moor of Venis." Possible echoes of *Othello* in *The Honest Whore, Part I*, by Thomas Dekker and Thomas Middleton (1604) and in Richard Knolles's *History of the Turks* (1603) help fix a forward date of composition. Francis Meres does not list the play in 1598. On stylistic grounds, the play is usually dated in 1603 or 1604, although arguments are sometimes presented for a date as early as 1601 or 1602.

King Lear (c. 1605–1606)

On November 26, 1607, Nathaniel Butter and John Busby entered in the Stationers' Register, the official record book of the London Company of Stationers (booksellers and printers), "A booke called. Master William Shakespeare his historye of Kinge Lear, as yt was played before the Kinges maiestie at Whitehall vppon Sainct Stephens night at Christmas Last, by his maiesties servantes playinge vsually at the Globe on the Banksyde." Next year appeared the following Quarto:

M. William Shak-speare: HIS True Chronicle Historie of the life and death of King LEAR and his three Daughters. *With the vnfortunate life* of Edgar, *sonne* and heire to the Earle of Gloster, and his sullen and assumed humor of Tom of Bedlam: *As it was played before the Kings Maiestie at Whitehall vpon S.* Stephans *night in Christmas Hollidayes.* By his Maiesties seruants playing vsually at the Gloabe on the Bancke-side. LONDON, Printed for *Nathaniel Butter*, and are to be sold at his shop in *Pauls* Church-yard at the signe of the Pide Bull neere St. *Austins* Gate. 1608.

This Quarto is often called the "Pied Bull" Quarto in reference to its place of sale. Twelve copies exist today, in ten different "states," because proofreading was being carried on while the sheets were being run off in the press; the copies variously combine corrected and uncorrected sheets. A Second Quarto, printed in 1619 by William Jaggard for Thomas Pavier with the fraudulent date of 1608, was based on a copy of the First Quarto, combining corrected and uncorrected sheets.

The First Folio text of 1623 may have been typeset from a playbook cut for performance or from a transcript of such a manuscript, and the playbook in its turn appears to have been based on Shakespeare's fair copy (with revisions) of his first draft. The Folio compositors also almost certainly consulted a copy of the Second Quarto from time to time or may have typeset directly from this Quarto as annotated with reference to Shakespeare's fair copy. In writing the fair copy, Shakespeare may have marked some three hundred lines for deletion, but it is possible that he did so chiefly to shorten the time of performance. He also seems to have added some one hundred lines, an apparent contradiction in view of the need for cutting, but possibly dictated by Shakespeare's developing sense of his play. It is also possible that the cuts were carried out by someone else in the preparation of the playbook.

The First Quarto, on the other hand, appears to have been printed from Shakespeare's unrevised and evidently untidy working papers. It is often corrupt, owing in part to type shortages, compositorial uncertainties with the manuscript, and other difficulties in Nicholas Okes's shop. Still, in some matters—especially variants indifferent in meaning (such as *an/if* or *thine/thy*)— the First Quarto may be closer to Shakespeare's preferences than the Folio, behind which are several stages of transmission.

This edition agrees with most recent students of the *Lear* text that the Folio represents a theatrical revision, in which the cuts were devised for performance by Shakespeare's company and quite possibly by Shakespeare himself as a member of that company. The case for artistic preference in the making of those cuts, on the other hand, is less certain and may have been overstated. Many of the cuts have the effect of shortening scenes, especially in the latter half of the play. Some scenes, like 3.6, show open gaps as a result of the cutting: Lear's "Then let them anatomize Regan" (line 75) implies the trial of Goneril as it is dramatized in the First Quarto but cut from the Folio. Other omissions also read like expedients, although they can also be explained by a hypothesis of literary and theatrical rewriting; if Shakespeare himself undertook the

cutting, he would presumably do so as expertly as possible. The fact that the Folio text gives almost no rewritten speeches may suggest that the large cuts were motivated by the need for shortening. This edition holds to the principle that it is unwise to omit the material cut from the Folio text, since we cannot be sure that Shakespeare would have shortened the text had there been no external constraints. At the same time, the added material in the Folio is clearly his and belongs in his conception of the play. The resulting text is a conflation, but one that avoids cutting material that Shakespeare may well have regretted having to excise.

The Stationers' Register entry for November 26, 1607, describes a performance at court on the previous St. Stephen's night, December 26, 1606. The title page of the First Quarto confirms this performance on St. Stephen's night. Such a performance at court was not likely to have been the first, however. Shakespeare's repeated use of Samuel Harsnett's *Declaration of Egregious Popish Impostures*, registered on March 16, 1603, sets an early limit for composition of the play. Other circumstances point to composition of the Quarto text in 1605 or 1606. In May 1605, an old play called *The True Chronicle History of King Leir* was entered in the Stationers' Register as a "Tragecall historie," a phrase possibly suggesting the influence of Shakespeare's play, since the old *King Leir* does not end tragically. Moreover, the title page of the old *King Leir*, issued in 1605, proclaims the text to be "as it hath bene diuers and sundry times lately acted." In view of the unlikelihood that such an old play (written before 1594) would be revived in 1605, scholars have suggested that the title page was the publisher's way of trying to capitalize on the recent popularity of Shakespeare's play. In this case, the likeliest date for the composition of Shakespeare's *King Lear* would be in the winter of 1604–1605. Shakespeare certainly used the old *King Leir* as a chief source, but he need not have waited for its publication in 1605 if, as seems perfectly plausible, his company owned the playbook. This hypothesis of the publication of the old *King Leir* after performances of Shakespeare's play must do battle, however, with indications that Shakespeare did not write *King Lear* until late 1605 or 1606. Gloucester's mentioning of "These late eclipses in the sun and moon" (1.2.106) seems to refer to an eclipse of the moon in September and of the sun in October 1605.

There may be echoes in the First Quarto of *King Lear* of *Eastward Ho!* by George Chapman, Ben Jonson, and John Marston, written in early 1605, and *Miseries of Enforced Marriage*, written by mid-1605. *King Lear* may allude to concerns at court about the King's frequent absences for hunting, about monopolies, the giving away of knighthoods, the King's need of money, and the like, all of which would have seemed pertinent in 1605–1606. The Folio revisions may date from some time around 1610, according to the editors of the Oxford Shakespeare.

Macbeth (*c. 1606–1607*)

Macbeth was first printed in the First Folio of 1623. It was set up from a playbook or a transcript of one. The text is unusually short and seems to have been cut for reasons of censorship or for some special performance. Moreover, all of 3.5 and parts of 4.1 (39–43, 125–32) appear to be interpolations, containing songs from Thomas Middleton's *The Witch* (c.1609–1616). Middleton may have been responsible for other alterations and additions.

Simon Forman, in his manuscript *The Book of Plays and Notes thereof per Formans for Common Policy*, records the first known performance of *Macbeth* on April 20, 1611, at the Globe Theatre. The play must have been in existence by 1607, however, for allusions to it seemingly occur in *Lingua* and *The Puritan* (both published in 1607) and in *The Knight of the Burning Pestle* (probably acted in 1607). On the other hand, the play itself seemingly alludes to James I's royal succession in 1603, to his touching for "the king's evil" (see 4.3.147), and to the trial of the notorious Gunpowder Plot conspirators in March 1606. The interpolations from Middleton's *The Witch* are probably from a later date, perhaps after 1613.

Antony and Cleopatra (*1606–1607*)

On May 20, 1608, Edward Blount entered in the Stationers' Register, the official record book of the London Company of Stationers (booksellers and printers), "A booke Called. Anthony. and Cleopatra," along with "A booke called. The booke of Pericles prynce of Tyre." Blount was friendly with Shakespeare's company, and his entry may have been a "staying entry" designed to forestall unauthorized publication of these texts. If so, the tactic did not succeed with *Pericles*, issued in 1609 by another publisher, but it did succeed with *Antony and Cleopatra*. The play was first printed in the First Folio of 1623. It is a good text, set evidently from Shakespeare's own draft in a more finished state than most of his working papers, or possibly from a transcript of those papers, though not yet prepared to be a playbook.

The year 1608 is thus the latest possible date for *Antony and Cleopatra*. Evidently, it was written in 1606–1607, however, for a "newly altered" edition in 1607 of Samuel Daniel's play *Cleopatra* seems to have been influenced by Shakespeare's play. Shakespeare himself had probably consulted the original edition of *Cleopatra*, published in 1594, or the slightly revised edition of 1599, but Daniel's more thorough revision in 1607 shows signs of his having seen Shakespeare's play in the interim. Also, a play by Barnabe Barnes called *The Devil's Charter* (1607) may contain a parody of Cleopatra's death by asps. Although the printed text of this play advertises corrections and augmentations that could postdate a court performance in February 1607, recent scholarship favors the likelihood that Barnes saw *Antony and Cleopatra* before that—perhaps in late 1606.

The Winter's Tale (*c. 1609–1611*)

The Winter's Tale was first printed in the First Folio of 1623. Its text is a good one, taken evidently from Ralph Crane's transcript of Shakespeare's own well-finished draft or possibly the playbook. As in most other Crane transcriptions, the stage directions are sparse, and the characters' names are grouped at the beginning of each scene. The first recorded performance was on May 15, 1611, when Simon Forman saw the play at the Globe Theater and recorded a summary of it in his commonplace book. Another performance that year at court, on November 5, is recorded in the *Revels Account* and still another, during the winter of 1612–1613. Quite possibly, the play was new at the time Forman saw it. It apparently contains an allusion to the dance of ten or twelve satyrs in Ben Jonson's *Masque of Oberon*, performed at court on January 1, 1611. A 1623 entry in the *Office book* of Sir Henry Herbert, Master of the Revels, refers to *The Winter's Tale* as "an old play . . . formerly allowed of by Sir George Bucke." Bucke (or Buc) was first appointed Master of the Revels in 1610 but had occasionally licensed plays before that date during his predecessor's illness, so that the backward limit of 1610 cannot be considered absolute. Still, matters of style confirm the likelihood that Forman was seeing a new play in 1611.

The Tempest (*c. 1611*)

The Tempest was first printed in the First Folio of 1623. It occupies first place in the volume and is a scrupulously prepared text from a transcript by Ralph Crane of a theater playbook or of Shakespeare's draft after it had been annotated for production; or, Crane may have provided some of the elaboration of stage directions. Shakespeare's colleagues may have placed *The Tempest* first in the Folio because they considered it his most recent complete play. The first recorded performance was at court on November 1, 1611: "Hallomas nyght was presented att Whithall before yᵉ kinges Maiestie a play Called the Tempest." The actors were "the Kings players" (*Revels Account*). The play was again presented at court during the winter of 1612–1613, this time "before the Princes Highnes the Lady Elizabeth and the Prince Pallatyne Elector." The festivities for this important betrothal and wedding were sumptuous and included at least thirteen other plays. Various arguments have been put forward that Shakespeare composed parts of *The Tempest*, especially the masque, for this occasion, but there is absolutely no evidence that the play was singled out for special prominence among the many plays presented, and the masque is integral to the play as it stands. Probably the 1611 production was of a fairly new play. Simon Forman, who saw *Cymbeline* and *The Winter's Tale* in 1611, does not mention *The Tempest*. He died in September 1611. According to every stylistic test, such as run-on and hypermetric lines, the play is very late. Shakespeare probably knew Sylvester Jourdain's *A Discovery of the Bermudas*, published in 1610, and William Strachey's *A True Reportory of the Wreck and Redemption*, dated July 1610, although not published until 1625.

The Sonnets (c. 1593–1603)

On May 20, 1609, "Thomas Thorpe Entred for his copie vnder thandes of master Wilson and master Lownes Warden a Booke called Shakespeares sonnettes." In the same year appeared the following volume:

SHAKE-SPEARES SONNETS. Neuer before Imprinted. AT LONDON By *G. Eld* for *T. T.* [Thomas Thorpe] and are to be solde by *Iohn Wright*, dwelling at Christ Church gate. 1609.

Some copies of this same edition are marked to be sold by William Aspley rather than John Wright; evidently, Thorpe had set up two sellers to distribute the volume. The sonnets were not reprinted until John Benson's rearranged edition of 1640, possibly because the first edition had been suppressed or because sonnets were no longer in vogue. The 1609 edition may rest on a transcript of Shakespeare's sonnets by someone other than the author, and the edition itself is marred by misprints, though Thorpe was a reputable printer. Clearly, the collection was not supervised through the press as were *Venus and Adonis* and *The Rape of Lucrece*. All the evidence suggests that it was obtained without Shakespeare's permission from a manuscript that had been in private circulation (as we know from Francis Meres's 1598 allusion, in his *Palladis Tamia*, to Shakespeare's "sugared sonnets among his private friends"). Two sonnets, 138 and 144, had appeared in 1599 in *The Passionate Pilgrim*. On questions of dating and order of the sonnets, see the Introduction to *The Sonnets* in this volume.

Appendix 2

Sources

The Taming of the Shrew

Scholars do not agree on the relationship of *The Taming of the Shrew* to the play called *The Taming of a Shrew,* published in 1594. *A Shrew* has been argued to be an earlier version of Shakespeare's play, or a memorial reconstruction of it, or derived from a common original. Some recent critics argue that the two versions should be treated as distinct texts. An often-held view is that *A Shrew* is derived from a now-lost earlier version of Shakespeare's play, to which the compiler added original material and borrowed or even plagiarized from other literary sources as well. If so, *A Shrew* would not appear to be a source for Shakespeare's play, as Geoffrey Bullough has argued in his *Narrative and Dramatic Sources of Shakespeare.* Apart from this question, all critics agree that Shakespeare's play consists of three elements, each with its own source: the romantic love plot of Lucentio and Bianca, the wife-taming plot of Petruchio and Kate, and the framing plot, or induction, of Christopher Sly.

The romantic love plot is derived from George Gascoigne's *Supposes,* a neoclassical comedy performed at Gray's Inn (one of the Inns of Court, where young men studied law in London) in 1566. Gascoigne's play was a rather close translation of Ludovico Ariosto's *I Suppositi* (1509), which in turn was based on two classical plays, Terence's *Eunuchus* and Plautus's *Captivi.* The heroine of Gascoigne's version (as of Ariosto's) is Polynesta, the resourceful daughter of Damon, a widower of Ferrara. Two suitors vie for Polynesta's hand: Dr. Cleander, an aged and miserly lawyer, and Erostrato, a Sicilian gentleman who has purportedly come to Ferrara to study. In fact, however, this "Erostrato" is the servant Dulippo in disguise, having changed places with his master. (These disguisings are the "supposes" of the title.) As a servant in Damon's household, "Dulippo" has secretly become

the lover of Polynesta and has made her pregnant. Balia, the nurse or duenna, is their go-between. Meanwhile, "Erostrato" takes great delight in outwitting Dr. Cleander and his unattractive parasite, Pasiphilo. The counterfeit Erostrato's ruse is to produce a rich father who will guarantee a handsome dowry and thereby outbid Cleander in the contest for Polynesta's hand. The "father" he produces, however, is actually an old Sienese stranger, who is persuaded that he is in danger in Ferrara unless he cloaks his identity. Complications arise when Damon learns of his daughter's affair and throws the lover, "Dulippo," into a dungeon. The crafty Pasiphilo overhears this compromising information and resolves to cause mischief for all the principals. Moreover, when Erostrato's real father, Philogano, arrives in Ferrara, he is barred from his son's house by the counterfeit Philogano and resolves to get help. His clever servant, Litio, suggests employing the famous lawyer, Cleander. All is happily resolved when the real Dulippo proves to be the son of Dr. Cleander and the real Erostrato is revealed to be rich and socially eligible for Polynesta's hand in marriage. Cleander is even reconciled to his parasite, Pasiphilo.

Shakespeare, in his play, has almost entirely eliminated the satire of the law that is in his source. Gremio is aged and wealthy, but no shyster. The lover is not imprisoned in a dungeon. The parasite is gone, as also in *The Comedy of Errors.* Bianca does not consummate her affair with Lucentio, as does Polynesta, and hence has no need for a go-between like Balia. Shakespeare adapts a sophisticated neoclassical comedy, racy and cosmopolitan, to the moral standards of his public theater. The witless Hortensio, the tutoring in Latin, and the music lesson are Shakespeare's inventions.

The wife-taming plot of Petruchio and Kate reflects an ancient comic misogynistic tradition, still extant today in the Scottish folksong "The Cooper of Fife" or "The

Wife Wrapped in Wether's Skin" (Francis James Child, *The English and Scottish Popular Ballads* [1888–1898], 5:104). Richard Hosley has argued (in *Huntington Library Quarterly, 27,* 1964) that Shakespeare's likeliest source was *A Merry Jest of a Shrewd and Curst Wife Lapped in Morel's Skin, for her Good Behavior* (printed c. 1550). In this version, the husband beats his shrewish wife with birch rods until she bleeds and faints, whereupon he wraps her in the raw salted skin of an old plow-horse named Morel. Like Kate, this shrewish wife has a gentle younger sister who is their father's favorite. This father warns the man who proposes to marry his older daughter that she is shrewish, but the suitor goes ahead and subsequently tames his wife with Morel's skin. Thereafter, at a celebratory dinner, everyone is impressed by the thoroughness of the taming.

Shakespeare avoids the misogynistic extremes of this story, despite the similarity of the narrative. Instead, he seems to have had in mind the more humanistic spirit of Erasmus's *A Merry Dialogue Declaring the Properties of Shrewd Shrews and Honest Wives* (translated 1557) and Juan Luis Vives's *The Office and Duty of an Husband* (translated 1555). Specific elements of the wife-taming plot have been traced to other possible sources. The scolding of a tailor occurs in Gerard Legh's *Accidence of Armory* (1562); a wife agrees with her husband's assertion of a patent falsehood in Don Juan Manuel's *El Conde Lucanor* (1335); and three husbands wager on the obedience of their wives in *The Book of the Knight of La Tour-Landry* (printed 1484).

The induction story, of the beggar duped into believing himself a rich lord, is an old tale occurring in the *Arabian Nights.* An interesting analogue occurs in P. Heuterus's *De Rebus Burgundicis* (1584), translated into the French of S. Goulart (1606?) and thence into the English of Edward Crimeston (1607). According to Heuterus, in 1440, Philip the Good of Burgundy actually entertained a drunken beggar in his palace "to make trial of the vanity of our life," plying him with fine clothes, bed, a feast, and the performance of "a pleasant comedy."

A Midsummer Night's Dream

No single source has been discovered that unites the various elements that we find in *A Midsummer Night's Dream,* but the four main strands of action can be individually discussed in terms of sources. The four strands are: (1) the marriage of Theseus (Duke of Athens) and Queen Hippolyta, (2) the romantic tribulations and triumphs of the four young lovers, (3) the quarrel of King Oberon and Queen Titania, together with the fairies' manipulations of human affairs, and (4) the "rude mechanicals" and their play of "Pyramus and Thisbe."

For his conception of Theseus, Shakespeare went chiefly to Geoffrey Chaucer's "The Knight's Tale" and to Thomas North's 1579 translation of "The Life of Theseus" in Plutarch's *Lives of the Noble Grecians and Romans.* Chaucer's Theseus is a duke of "wisdom" and "chivalrye," renowned for his conquest of the Amazons and his marriage to Hippolyta. Plutarch provides information concerning Theseus's other conquests (to which Oberon alludes in 2.1.77 ff.), including that of Antiopa. Shakespeare could have learned more about Theseus from Chaucer's *The Legend of Good Women* and from Ovid's *Metamorphoses.* He seems to have blended all or some of these impressions together with his own notion of a noble yet popular Renaissance ruler.

The romantic narrative of the four lovers appears to be original with Shakespeare, although one can find many analogous situations of misunderstanding and rivalry in love. Chaucer's "The Knight's Tale" tells of two friends battling over one woman. Shakespeare's own *The Two Gentlemen of Verona* gives us four lovers, properly matched at first until one of the men shifts his attentions to his friend's ladylove; eventually, all is righted when the false lover recovers his senses. Parallel situations arise in Sir Philip Sidney's *Arcadia* (1590) and in Jorge de Montemayor's *Diana Enamorada* (c. 1559), a source for *The Two Gentlemen.* What Shakespeare adds in *A Midsummer* is the intervention of the fairies in human love affairs.

Shakespeare's knowledge of fairy lore must have been extensive and is hard to trace exactly. Doubtless, much of it was from oral traditions about leprechauns, gremlins, and elves, who were thought to cause such mischief as spoiling fermentation or preventing milk from churning into butter; Puck's tricks mentioned in 2.1.34 ff. are derived from such lore. Some of the oral tales circulating about Robin Goodfellow later reached print, probably somewhat modified, in the prose pamphlet *Robin Good Fellow, His Mad Pranks and Merry Jests* (London, 1628) and a ballad, "The Mad Merry Pranks of Robbin Good-fellow" (c. 1600) in Roxburghe Ballads, vol. 2, ed. William Chappell (Hertford: Stephen Austin for the Ballad Society, 1872), p. 83. Shakespeare seems to have consulted literary sources as well. In Chaucer's "The Merchant's Tale," Pluto and Proserpina as King and Queen of the fairies intervene in the affairs of old January, his young wife May, and her lover Damyan. Fairies appear on stage in John Lyly's *Endymion* (1588), protecting true lovers and tormenting those who are morally tainted. Shakespeare later reflects this tradition in *The Merry Wives of Windsor* (1597–1601). The name Oberon probably comes from the French romance *Huon of Bordeaux* (translated by Lord Berners by about 1540), where Oberon is a dwarfish fairy King from the mysterious East who practices enchantment in a haunted wood. In Edmund Spenser's *The Faerie Queene,* Oberon is the Elfin father of Queen Gloriana (2.10. 75–76). Robert Greene's *James IV* (c. 1591) also features Oberon as the fairy King, and a lost play called *Huon of Bordeaux* was performed by Sussex's men, an acting company, at about this same time. The name "Titania" comes from Ovid's *Metamorphoses*, where it is used as a synonym for both the enchantress Circe and the chaste goddess Diana. The name "Titania" does not appear in Arthur Golding's translation (1567), suggesting that Shakespeare found it in the original. Puck, or Robin Goodfellow, is essentially the product of oral tradition, although Reginald Scot's *The Discovery of Witchcraft* (1584) discusses Robin in pejorative terms as an incubus or hobgoblin in whom intelligent people no longer believe.

Scot also reports the story of a man who finds an ass's head placed on his shoulders by enchantment. Similar legends of transformation occur in Apuleius's *The Golden Ass* (translated by William Adlington, 1566) and in the well-known story of the ass's ears bestowed by Phoebus Apollo on King Midas for his presumption. Perhaps the most suggestive possible source for Shakespeare's clownish actors, however, is Anthony Munday's play *John a Kent and John a Cumber* (c. 1587–1590). In it a group of rude artisans, led by the intrepid Turnop, stage a ludicrous interlude written by their churchwarden in praise of his millhorse. Turnop's prologue is a medley of lofty comparisons. The entertainment is presented before noble spectators, who are graciously amused. *John a Kent* also features a lot of magic trickery, a boy named Shrimp whose role is comparable to that of Puck, and a multiple love plot.

"Pyramus and Thisbe" itself is based on the *Metamorphoses* (4.55 ff.). Other versions that Shakespeare may have known include Chaucer's *The Legend of Good Women*, a poem by William Griffith in 1562, George Pettie's *A Petite Palace of Pettie His Pleasure* (1576), *A Gorgeous Gallery of Gallant Inventions* (1578), and "A New Sonnet of Pyramus and Thisbe" from Clement Robinson's *A Handful of Pleasant Delights* (1584). Several of these, especially the last three, are bad enough to have given Shakespeare materials to lampoon, though the sweep of his parody goes beyond the particular story of Pyramus and Thisbe. The occasionally stilted phraseology of Golding's translation of the *Metamorphoses* contributed to the fun. According to Kenneth Muir (*Shakespeare's Sources*, 1957), Shakespeare must also have known Thomas Mouffet's *Of the Silkworms and Their Flies* (published 1599, but possibly circulated earlier in manuscript), which contains perhaps the most ridiculous of all versions of the Pyramus and Thisbe story. Shakespeare also appears to have been spoofing the inept dramatic style and lame verse of English dramas of the 1560s, 1570s, and 1580s, especially in their treatment of tragic sentiment and high emotion; *Cambises, Damon and Pythias*, and *Appius and Virginia* are examples.

The Merchant of Venice

Shakespeare's probable chief source for *The Merchant of Venice* was the first story of the fourth day of *Il Pecorone*

(The Dunce), by Ser Giovanni Fiorentino. This collection of tales dates from the late fourteenth century but was first published in 1558 at Milan and was not published in English translation in Shakespeare's time. If Shakespeare was unable to read it in Italian, he may conceivably have consulted a translation in some now-lost manuscript; such translations did sometimes circulate. Behind Ser Giovanni's story lies an old tradition of a bond given for human flesh, as found in Persia, India, and the Twelve Tables of Roman Law. This legend first appears in English in the thirteenth-century *Cursor Mundi*, with a Jew as the creditor. A thirteenth-century version of the *Gesta Romanorum* (a popular collection of stories in Latin) adds a romantic love plot; the evil moneylender in this story is not Jewish. The hero pawns his own flesh to a merchant in order to win a lady. He succeeds on his third attempt, having learned to avoid a magic spell that had previously put him to sleep and cost him a large number of florins. When he goes to pay his forfeit, the lady follows him disguised as a knight, and foils the evil merchant by pointing out a quibbling distinction between flesh and blood.

Il Pecorone provided Shakespeare with a number of essential elements, although not all that he has included. Ser Giovanni's story tells of Giannetto, the adventurous youngest son of a Florentine merchant, who goes to live with his father's dearest friend, Ansaldo, in Venice. This worthy merchant gives him money to seek his fortune at sea. Unbeknownst to Ansaldo, Giannetto twice risks everything to woo the lady of Belmont: if he can succeed in sleeping with her, he will win her and her country, but, if he fails, he loses all his wealth. Twice Giannetto is given a sleeping medicine and has to forfeit everything. Returning destitute to Venice twice, he is reunited each time with Ansaldo and given the means to seek his fortune again. For the third such voyage, however, Ansaldo is driven to borrow ten thousand florins from a Jew, using the forfeiture of a pound of flesh as a guarantee. This time, one of the lady's maids warns Giannetto not to drink his wine, and he finally possesses the lady as his wife. Sometime later, remembering that the day of Ansaldo's forfeiture has arrived, Giannetto explains the predicament to his wife and is sent by her to Venice with a hundred thousand florins, but he arrives after the forfeiture has fallen due. The lady, however, following after him in the disguise of a doctor of laws, decrees that the Jew may have no blood and must take no more or no less than one pound of flesh. The Jew is jeered at and receives no money. The "doctor of laws" refuses any payment other than the ring Giannetto was given by his lady. Giving it up unwillingly, he returns to Belmont, where his lady vexes him about the ring but finally relents and tells him all. Shakespeare could thus have found in one source the wooing, the borrowing from a Jewish moneylender, the pound of flesh, the trial, and the business of the rings. The story provides no casket episode, courtship of Nerissa by Gratiano, elopement of Jessica, or clowning of Lancelot Gobbo. The Jew's motive is not prompted by the way he has been treated.

Shakespeare may also have known "The Ballad of Gernutus," a popular English work that seems to be older than the play. It has no love plot but dwells on the unnatural cruelty of a Jewish Venetian usurer who takes a bond of flesh for "a merry jest." Anthony Munday's prose *Zelauto* (1580), though its villain is a Christian rather than a Jewish moneylender, also features a bond of this sort, taken purportedly as a mere sport but with hidden malice. Truculento, the villain, takes the bond of two young men, Rodolfo and his friend Strabino, as surety for a loan. If they forfeit the loan, the young men are to lose their lands and their right eyes as well. The villain has a daughter, Brisana, whom he permits to marry Rodolfo, since Truculento expects to marry Rodolfo's sister Cornelia himself. When Cornelia instead marries Strabino, Truculento angrily takes the young men to court to demand his bond. The two brides disguise themselves as scholars and go to court, where they appeal for mercy and then foil Truculento by means of the legal quibble about blood.

Another possible source for the courtroom scene is *The Orator*, translated into English in 1596 from the French of Alexandre Sylvain. An oration, entitled "Of a Jew, who would for his debt have a pound of the flesh of a Christian," uses many specious arguments also employed by Shylock, and is forthrightly confuted in "The Christian's Answer."

Shylock's relationship to his daughter finds obvious earlier parallels in *Zelauto* and in Christopher Marlowe's play, *The Jew of Malta* (c. 1589), in which Barabas's daughter Abigail loves a Christian and ultimately renounces her faith. The actual elopement, however, is closer to the fourteenth story in Masuccio of Salerno's fifteenth-century *Il Novellino* (not published in English translation in Shakespeare's day).

The casket-choosing episode, not found in *Il Pecorone*, was a widespread legend, occurring, for example, in the story of *Barlaam and Josephat* (ninth-century Greek, translated into Latin by the thirteenth century), in Vincent of Beauvais's *Speculum Historiale*, in the *Legenda Aurea*, in Giovanni Boccaccio's *Decameron* (Day 10, Story 1), in John Gower's *Confessio Amantis*, and—closest to Shakespeare—in the *Gesta Romanorum* (translated into English in 1577 by Richard Robinson and "bettered" by him in 1595). In this last account, the choice is between a gold, silver, and lead casket, each with its own inscription. The first two inscriptions are like Shakespeare's; the third reads, "Thei that chese me, shulle fynde [in] me that God hathe disposid." The chooser, however, is a maiden, and she is not preceded by other contestants.

An old play called *The Jew* is referred to by Stephen Gosson in 1579 as containing "the greediness of worldly choosers, and bloody minds of usurers." Scholars have speculated that this was a source play for Shakespeare, but actually we have too little to go on to make a reliable judgment. Gosson was surely not referring to Robert Wilson's *The Three Ladies of London* (c. 1581) in any case, even though it is sometimes suggested as an analogue to *The Merchant of Venice*, for its Jewish figure, named Gerontus (compare Gernutus in the ballad), is an exemplary person. Besides, the probable date of this play is later than Gosson's remark.

Much Ado About Nothing

Shakespeare's probable chief source for the Hero-Claudio plot of *Much Ado* was the twenty-second story from the *Novelle* of Matteo Bandello (Lucca, 1554). A French translation by François de Belleforest, in his *Histoires Tragiques* (1569 edition), was available to Shakespeare, as was the Italian original. The story of the maiden falsely accused was, however, much older than the story by Bandello. Perhaps the earliest version that has been found is the Greek romance *Chaereas and Callirrhoe*, fourth or fifth century A.D., in which the hero Chaereas, warned by envious rivals of his wife's purported infidelity, watches at dusk while an elegantly attired stranger is admitted by the maid to the house where Callirrhoe lives. Chaereas rushes in and strikes mistakenly at his wife in the dark but is acquitted of murder when the maid confesses her part in a conspiracy to delude Chaereas. Callirrhoe is buried in a deathlike trance but awakens in time to be carried off by pirates. The story reappears in a fifteenth-century Spanish romance, *Tirante el Blanco*, in which the princess Blanche is courted seemingly by a repulsive black man. This Spanish version probably inspired the account in Canto 5 of Ludovico Ariosto's *Orlando Furioso* (1516), to which all subsequent Renaissance versions are ultimately indebted.

In Ariosto's account, as translated into English by Sir John Harington (1591), the narrator is Dalinda, maid to the virtuous Scottish princess Genevra. Dalinda tells how she has fallen guiltily in love with Polynesso, Duke of Albany, an evil man who often makes love to Dalinda in her mistress's rooms but who longs in fact to marry Genevra. Consequently, Polynesso arranges for Genevra's noble Italian suitor, Ariodante, and Ariodante's brother Lurcanio, to witness the Duke's ascent to Genevra's window by a rope ladder. The woman who admits the Duke is, of course, not Genevra but Dalinda disguised as her mistress, having been duped into believing that the Duke merely wishes to satisfy his craving for Genevra by making love to her image. Lurcanio publicly accuses the innocent Genevra and offers to fight anyone who defends her cause (compare Claudio's quarrel with Leonato). The evil Duke tries to get rid of Dalinda, but all is finally put to rights by Rinaldo (the hero of *Orlando Furioso*) and Ariodante. This account gives an unusually vivid motivation for the maid and the villain—a clearer motivation than in Shakespeare's play. A lost dramatic version, *Ariodante and Genevora*, was performed at the English court in 1583.

Shakespeare probably consulted not only Ariosto but also Edmund Spenser's *The Faerie Queene* (2.4), based on Ariosto. Spenser's emphasis is on the blind rage of Phedon, a young squire in love with Claribell. Phedon is tricked by his erstwhile friend Philemon and by Claribell's maid Pryene into believing Claribell false. Pryene's motive in dressing up as Claribell is to prove she is as beautiful as her mistress. When, after having slain Claribell for her supposed perfidy, Phedon learns the truth, he poisons Philemon and furiously pursues Pryene until he is utterly possessed by a mad frenzy.

Shakespeare's greatest debt is, however, to Bandello's story. In a number of details, the story is closer to Shakespeare's play than are those already discussed. Several names are substantially the same as in Shakespeare: the location is Messina, the father of the slandered bride is Lionato di' Lionati (compare Shakespeare's Leonato), and her lover is in the service of King Piero of Aragon (compare Don Pedro of Aragon). As in Shakespeare, a young knight (named Sir Timbreo) seeks the hand in marriage of his beloved (Fenicia) through the matchmaking offices of a noble emissary. The complication of this wooing is somewhat different in that Timbreo's friend Girondo also falls in love with Fenicia, but Girondo then plots with a mischief-loving courtier (resembling Shakespeare's Don John) to poison Timbreo's mind against Fenicia, and Girondo thereupon escorts Timbreo to a garden, where they see Girondo's servant, elegantly dressed, enter Fenicia's window. No maid takes part in the ruse, however, nor indeed is any woman seen at the window. When Fenicia is wrongly accused, she falls into a deathlike trance and is pronounced dead by a doctor, but she is revived. Her father, believing in her innocence, sends her off to a country retreat and circulates the report that she is, in fact, dead. Soon both Timbreo and Girondo are stricken with remorse, Timbreo magnanimously spares his friend's life, and both confess the truth to Fenicia's family. A year later, Timbreo marries a wife chosen for him by Lionato who turns out, of course, to be Fenicia. Girondo marries her sister Belfiore. This account does not provide any equivalent for Beatrice and Benedick. Shakespeare enhances the Friar's role and provides a brother for Leonato. Claudio and Leonato are of comparable social station in Shakespeare, whereas Bandello makes a point of Timbreo's superior social rank.

A lost play, *Panecia* (1574–1575), may have been based on Bandello's work. One other version Shakespeare may have known is George Whetstone's *The Rock of Regard* (1576), based on Ariosto and Bandello. It contains a suggestive parallel to Claudio's rejection of Hero in church. Various Italian plays in the tradition of Luigi Pasqualigo's

Il Fedele (1579), and also a version perhaps by Anthony Munday, *Fedele and Fortunio* (published 1585), are analogous in situation, though Shakespeare need not have known any of them.

For the Beatrice-Benedick plot, no source has been discovered, apart from Shakespeare's own earlier fascination with wit-combat and candid wooing in *Love's Labor's Lost* and *The Taming of the Shrew*. Nor has a plausible source been found for Dogberry and the watch.

As You Like It

Shakespeare's chief source for *As You Like It* was Thomas Lodge's graceful pastoral romance, *Rosalynde: Euphues' Golden Legacy* (1590). Lodge was indebted in turn to *The Tale of Gamelyn*, a fourteenth-century poem wrongly included by some medieval scribes as "The Cook's Tale" in Chaucer's *Canterbury Tales*. *Gamelyn* was not printed until 1721, but Lodge clearly had access to a manuscript of it. Although Shakespeare may not have known *Gamelyn* directly, his play still retains the hearty spirit of this Robin Hood legend. (In later Robin Hood ballads, Gamelyn or Gandelyn is identified with Will Scarlet, a member of Robin Hood's band.)

Even a brief account of *Gamelyn* suggests how greatly the original tale is inspired by Robin Hood legends of outlaws valiantly defying the corrupt social order presided over by the Sheriff and his henchmen. Gamelyn, the youngest of three brothers, is denied his inheritance by his churlish eldest brother John. When Gamelyn demands his rights, John orders his men to beat Gamelyn, but the young man arms himself with a pestle and proves to be a formidable fighter. After defeating the champion wrestler in a local wrestling match (a lower-class sport befitting the social milieu of this story), Gamelyn returns home to find himself locked out by his brother. He kills the porter, flings the man's body down a well, and feasts his companions day and night for a week. John feigns a reconciliation and slyly asks if he can bind Gamelyn hand and foot merely to satisfy an oath he has sworn over the death of the porter. Gamelyn trustingly agrees and is made prisoner. After his bonds have been secretly loosed by Adam the Spencer (the steward), Gamelyn pretends to remain bound until the propitious moment for revenge and escape. The moment arrives during a feast of monks who churlishly refuse to help Gamelyn. With Adam's help, he fells many of them, ties up his brother, and escapes to the woods, where he and Adam are rescued from hunger by a band of merry outlaws. As their chief, Gamelyn becomes a champion of the poor and an enemy of rich churchmen. His brother, now sheriff, brands Gamelyn an outlaw and manages to imprison him, but Gamelyn's second brother, Sir Ote, stands bail for him. On the day of the trial, Gamelyn frees Sir Ote and hangs the sheriff and the jury. Gamelyn finally obtains his inheritance and becomes chief officer of the King's royal forests. This story is uninfluenced by the pastoral tradition and contains no love plot. Its Robin Hood traditions are very much present, nonetheless, in Shakespeare's contrasting portrayal of a tyrannical court and of a just society in banishment.

Lodge retains the primitive vigor of *Gamelyn* but adds generous infusions of pastoral sentiment in the manner of Sir Philip Sidney's *Arcadia* (1590) and sententious moralizing in the manner of John Lyly's *Euphues* (1578). The pastoralism is presented in conventional terms, with none of the genial self-reflexive satire we find in Shakespeare. Psychological motive is intricate, often more so than in Shakespeare's play. The style is also heavily influenced by Lyly's exquisitely balanced, antithetical, and ornamented prose. For his pastoralism, Lodge was indebted not only to Sidney but also to the ancient pastoral tradition that included the Greek Theocritus and the Roman Virgil, the Italian Sannazaro (*Arcadia*), and the Portuguese Jorge de Montemayor (*Diana*). Pastoralism by Lodge's time had become thoroughly imbued with artificial conventions: abject lovers writing sonnets to their disdainful mistresses, princes and princesses in shepherds' disguise, idealized landscapes, stylized debate as to the relative merits of love and friendship, youth and age, city life and country life, and so on. Some of these conventions were derived also from the vogue of sonneteering pioneered by Francesco Petrarch and can thus be described as the stereotypes of "Petrarchism." Lodge accepts these conventions and gives us typical pastoral lovers even in his hero and heroine, although the elements he derived from *Gamelyn* certainly add a contrasting note of violence and danger.

Lodge's account begins much like that of *Gamelyn*. Saladyne, the envious eldest brother, bribes the champion wrestler to do away with Rosader (Orlando) in the wrestling match. Rosader succeeds instead in killing the wrestler and in winning the heart of Rosalynde, daughter of the banished King Gerismond. When she sends him a jewel, Rosader is not at all at a loss for words; indeed, he composes a Petrarchan sonnet on the spot. The usurping King Torismond (no relation to Gerismond), despite his evil nature, is impressed by Rosader's grace and martial prowess. Rosader returns home with friends, breaks open the door, and feasts his company. The wily Saladyne overwhelms Rosader in his sleep and binds him to a post, but Rosader is untied by Adam and makes havoc among the eldest brother's guests, as in *Gamelyn*. In this case, however, the guests are Saladyne's kindred and allies, all of whom have refused to help Rosader. The sheriff tries to arrest Rosader and Adam, but they make good their escape to the Forest of Arden in France. They are saved from starvation by the kindly King Gerismond and his exiled followers. Rosalynde and King Torismond's daughter Alinda meanwhile have been banished from court and have taken abode in the forest under the names of Ganymede and Aliena. They befriend old Corydon (Corin) and young Montanus (Silvius), who is hopelessly in love with the haughty Phoebe. "Ganymede" poses as a woman to test Rosader in his wooing, and they are joined in a mock marriage. Saladyne, now repenting of his evil deeds, comes to the forest, is saved by his brother from a lion, and falls in love with Alinda (whom he helps to rescue from ruffians). The denouement is as in Shakespeare, although the triumphant return to society is more complete: King Torismond is slain, Gerismond is restored to his throne, Rosader is named heir-apparent, and all the friends are appropriately rewarded.

Despite Shakespeare's extensive indebtedness to this charming romance, there is a crucial difference: Lodge's pastoral world is never subjected to a wry or satirical exploration. Lodge offers no equivalent for Touchstone, the fool who sees the absurdity of both country and city; Jaques, the malcontent traveler; William and Audrey, the clownishly simple peasants; or Sir Oliver Martext, the ridiculous hedge-priest. Nor does Lodge tell of Le Beau, the court butterfly. Hymen is a Shakespearean addition, and the conversion of Duke Frederick by a hermit instead of his being overthrown and killed is a characteristically Shakespearean softening touch. Shakespeare's added characters are virtually all foils to the conventional pastoral vision he found in his source.

Twelfth Night

John Manningham's description of a performance of *Twelfth Night* on February 2, 1602, at the Middle Temple (one of the Inns of Court, where young men studied law in London), compares the play to Plautus's *Menaechmi* and to an Italian play called *Inganni*. The comment offers a helpful hint on sources. The *Menaechmi* had been the chief source for Shakespeare's earlier play, *The Comedy of Errors*, and that farce of mistaken identity clearly resembles *Twelfth Night* in the hilarious mix-ups resulting from the confusion of two look-alike twins. Shakespeare certainly profited from his earlier experimenting with this sort of comedy. *Twelfth Night* is not necessarily directly indebted to the *Menaechmi*, however, for Renaissance Italian comedy offered many imitations of Plautus from which Shakespeare could have taken his *Twelfth Night* plot. These include *Gl'Inganni* (1562) by Nicolò Secchi, another *Gl'Inganni* (1592) by Curzio Gonzaga, and, most important, an anonymous *Gl'Ingannati* (published 1537). This last play was translated into French by Charles Estienne as *Les Abusés* (1543) and adapted into Spanish by Lope de Rueda in *Los Engaños* (1567). A Latin version, *Laelia*, based on the French, was performed at Cambridge in the 1590s but never printed. Obviously, *Gl'Ingannati* was widely known, and Manningham was probably referring to it in his diary. To trace Shakespeare's own reading in this matter is difficult, owing to the large number of versions available to him, but we can note the suggestive points of comparison in each.

Both *Inganni* plays feature a brother and a sister mistaken for one another. In the later play (by Gonzaga), the sister uses the disguise name of "Cesare." In Secchi's *Inganni*, the disguised sister is in love with her master, who is told that a woman the exact age of his supposed page is secretly in love with him. Another play by Secchi, *L'Interesse* (1581), has a comic duel involving a disguised heroine. Of the Italian plays considered here, however, *Gl'Ingannati* is closest to Shakespeare's play. A short prefatory entertainment included with it in most editions features the name Malevolti. In the play itself, the heroine, Lelia, disguises herself as a page in the service of Flaminio, whom she secretly loves, and is sent on embassies to Flaminio's disdainful mistress Isabella. This lady falls in love with "Fabio," as Lelia calls herself. Lelia's father, Virginio, learning of her disguise and resolving to marry her to old Gherardo (Isabella's father), seeks out Lelia but instead mistakenly arrests her long-lost twin brother, Fabrizio, who has just arrived in Modena. Fabrizio is locked up as a madman in Isabella's room, whereupon Isabella takes the opportunity to betroth herself to the person she mistakes for "Fabio." A recognition scene clears up everything and leads to the marriages of Fabrizio to Isabella and Flaminio to Lelia. This story lacks the subplot of Malvolio, Sir Toby, *et al.* Nor is there a shipwreck.

Matteo Bandello based one of the stories in his *Novelle* (1554) on *Gl'Ingannati*, and this prose version was then translated into French by François de Belleforest in his *Histoires Tragiques* (1579 edition). Shakespeare may well have read both, for he consulted these collections of stories in writing *Much Ado About Nothing*. His most direct source, however, seems to have been the story of "Apollonius and Silla" by Barnabe Riche (an English soldier and fiction writer), in *Riche His Farewell to Military Profession* (1581), which was derived from Belleforest. Riche involves his characters in more serious moral predicaments than Shakespeare allows in his festive comedy. The plot situation is much the same: Silla (the equivalent of Shakespeare's Viola) is washed ashore near Constantinople, where, disguised as "Silvio," she takes service with a duke, Apollonius (Shakespeare's Orsino), and goes on embassies to the wealthy widow Julina (Shakespeare's Olivia), who proceeds at once to fall in love with "Silvio." When Silla's twin brother, the real Silvio, arrives, he is mistaken by Julina for his twin and is invited to a rendezvous, like Shakespeare's Sebastian. The differences at this point are marked, however, for Silvio becomes Julina's lover and leaves her pregnant when he departs the next day on his quest for Silla. Apollonius is understandably furious to learn of "Silvio's" apparent success with Julina and throws his page into prison. Julina is no less distressed when she learns that the supposed father of her child is in actuality a woman. Only Silvio's eventual return to marry Julina resolves these complications. Shakespeare eschews the pregnancy, the desertion, the imprisonment, and all of Riche's stern moralizing about the bestiality of lust that accompanies this lurid tale. Moreover, he adds the plot of Malvolio, for which Riche provides little suggestion. Shakespeare changes the location to Illyria, with its hint of delirium and illusion, and provides an English flavor in the comic scenes that intensifies the festive character of the play.

Shakespeare's reading may also have included the anonymous play *Sir Clyomon and Sir Clamydes* (c. 1570–1583), Sir Philip Sidney's *Arcadia* (1590), and Emmanuel Forde's prose romance *Parismus* (1598), in which one "Violetta" borrows the disguise of a page. Scholars have suggested that the Malvolio plot may reflect an incident at Queen Elizabeth's court in which the Comptroller of the Household, Sir William Knollys, interrupted a noisy late-night party dressed in only his nightshirt and a pair of spectacles, with a copy of the Italian pornographic writer Aretino's work in his hand. A similar confrontation between revelry and sobriety occurred in 1598: Ambrose Willoughby quieted a disturbance after the Queen had gone to bed and was afterward thanked by her for doing his duty. Such incidents were no doubt common, however, and there is no compelling reason to suppose Shakespeare was sketching from current court gossip.

Measure for Measure

Stories about corrupt magistrates are ancient and universal, but Shakespeare's particular story in *Measure for Measure* seems to go back to an actual incident in the sixteenth-century Italian court of Don Ferdinando de Gonzaga. A Hungarian student named Joseph Macarius, writing from Vienna, tells about an Italian citizen accused of murder whose wife submitted to the embraces of the magistrate in hopes of saving her husband. When the magistrate executed her husband despite her having fulfilled her bargain, she appealed to the Duke, who ordered the magistrate to give her a dowry and marry her. Thereafter, the Duke ordered the magistrate to be executed. This incident seems to have inspired a Senecan drama by Claude Rouillet called *Philanira* (1556), a French translation of this play (1563), a novella in the *Hecatommithi* of G. B. Giraldi Cinthio (1565), and a play by Cinthio called *Epitia* (posthumously published in 1583). Shakespeare may have known both the prose and the dramatic versions by Cinthio.

In Cinthio's story, the wise Emperor Maximian appoints his friend Juriste to govern Innsbruck, warning him to rule justly or expect no mercy from the Emperor. Juriste rules long and well, to the satisfaction of his master and the people of Innsbruck. When a young man named Vico is brought before him for ravishing a virgin, Juriste assigns the mandatory sentence of death. Vico's sister, Epitia, an extraordinarily beautiful virgin of eighteen, pleads for Vico's life, urging that his deed was one of passion and that he stands ready to marry the girl he forced. The judge, secretly inflamed with lust for Epitia, promises to consider the matter carefully. She reports this seemingly encouraging news to Vico, who urges her to persevere. When, however, the judge proposes to take her chastity in return for her brother's life, Epitia is mortified and refuses unless Juriste will marry her. During another interim in these negotiations, Vico begs his sister to save his life at any cost. She then submits to Juriste on the condition that he will both marry her and spare Vico. Next morning, however, the jailer brings her the body of her decapitated brother. She lays her complaint before the Emperor, who confronts Juriste with his guilt. Conscience-stricken, Juriste confesses and begs for mercy. At first, Epitia demands strict justice, but when the Emperor compels Juriste to marry her and then be beheaded, she reveals "her natural kindness" and begs successfully for the life of her wronger. There are several important differences between this account and Shakespeare's play: Vico is actually killed, unlike Claudio, and Epitia sleeps with Juriste and then is married to him. No equivalent to Mariana appears, or to Lucio, Pompey, Mistress Overdone, Elbow, and other characters in the comic scenes of Shakespeare's play. No duke oversees the career of Juriste and ensures that no fatal wrong will occur.

Shakespeare may also have consulted Cinthio's play *Epitia*, but his chief source was George Whetstone's two-part play *Promos and Cassandra* (1578) and a novella on the same subject. In the English play, the corrupt judge is Promos, administrator of the city of Julio under the King of Hungary. The law forbidding adultery has lain in abeyance for some years when a young gentleman named Andrugio is arrested and condemned for "incontinency." His sister Cassandra, like Epitia in Cinthio's play, lays down her precious chastity to Promos in response to her brother's piteous entreaties. Promos gives his assurance that he will marry her and save Andrugio's life. When Promos instead treacherously orders the execution of Andrugio, the jailer secretly substitutes the head of a felon, newly executed and so mutilated as to be unrecognizable even by Cassandra. (This rescue is seen as an intervention "by the providence of God.") The King sentences Promos, just as the Emperor sentences Juriste in Cinthio's play, but in Whetstone's play the King refuses Cassandra's pleas for the life of her new husband until Andrugio reveals himself to be still alive and offers to die for Promos. The King forgives Andrugio on condition that he marry Polina, whom he has wronged. The play also features a courtesan named Lamia and her man, Rosko, who ingratiate themselves with the corrupt officer (Phallax) in charge of investigating their case. Phallax

is ultimately caught and dismissed from office while Lamia is publicly humiliated.

Whetstone wrote a prose novella of this same story in the *Heptameron of Civil Discourses* (1582). Shakespeare appears to have consulted it as well as the play, for the prose version mentions the names of Isabella (as the narrator of the story) and Crassus (compare *Measure for Measure*, 4.5.8), and the King's awarding of measure for measure in his sentencing of Promos—"You shall be measured with the grace you bestowed on Andrugio"—may have given Shakespeare an idea for the title of his play. Shakespeare was also indebted for a few details to a version in Thomas Lupton's *Too Good to Be True* (1581).

Even though Shakespeare's play is closely related to Whetstone's play and novella, Shakespeare has changed much. He adds the motif of the Duke's mysterious disguise. (A not very compelling analogue to this motif occurs in Sir Thomas Elyot's *The Image of Governance*, 1541.) Shakespeare introduces the use of the bed trick, found also in his presumably earlier play *All's Well That Ends Well*. Most important, Shakespeare stresses the moral and legal complexity of his story. Isabella is about to renounce the world by entering a convent. By contrast, Lucio, a Shakespearean addition, is an engaging cynic, hedonist, and slanderer. Claudio, although guilty of fornication, is only technically in violation of the laws against sexual license. Isabella does not surrender her chastity. Her breakdown in the scene with Claudio intensifies her emotional crisis and renders all the more triumphant her final ability to forgive Angelo. Angelo himself is made puritanical in temperament and is spared the actual consequences of his worst intentions so that he can be worthy of being forgiven. Isabella need not marry Angelo, since he has not actually seduced her; she is thus free to marry the Duke. No felon need be executed in Claudio's stead, for Providence provides a natural death in the prison. In the subplot, going well beyond the merest hints in Whetstone, Pompey is a brilliantly original innovation, Elbow a characteristically Shakespearean clown modeled on the earlier Dogberry of *Much Ado About Nothing*, and Escalus a significant spokesman for a moderate and practical course of equity in the law.

Richard III

Richard III, like the *Henry VI* series, is based on Edward Hall's *The Union of the Two Noble and Illustre Families of Lancaster and York* (1542) and on the 1587 edition of Raphael Holinshed's *The Chronicles of England, Scotland, and Ireland*. Both of these historical compilations were deeply indebted for their hostile view of Richard III to Polydore Vergil and Thomas More. Vergil, a papal tax collector who came to England in 1501, spent many years under the patronage of Henry VII writing in Latin his *Anglica Historia* (first published in Basel, 1534). This work portrayed Richard negatively in order to glorify the claim of the Tudor monarch who had deposed Richard in 1485. Vergil argued that England's suffering was a divinely sent scourge, intended to cleanse England of rebelliousness and to prepare the English people for the providential reward of Tudor rule.

Thomas More's *The History of King Richard III*, left unfinished in 1513, was published in two slightly different versions: one in English (1557) and one in Latin (1566). Thomas More obtained much information and possibly an early draft of his narrative from Cardinal Morton, in whose household More lived as a youth. Morton had figured in the struggles of Richard III's reign—he was the Bishop of Ely from whom Richard requested the strawberries (3.4.32–3)—and had become a bitter enemy of the Yorkist king. Thomas More's own purpose in writing the life of Richard III was surely not to glorify Henry VII, with whom More had a strained relationship, but to characterize the evil of political opportunism. His portrait of Richard becomes that of the generic tyrant, behaving as such tyrants behaved in the various literary models from Renaissance Italy with which More was doubtless familiar. The result was, in any case, one-sided. The historical Richard seems to have been no worse than many another late medieval ruler and had indeed some admirable ideas on efficiency in government. More's blackened portrait, because it served the purposes of the Tudor state, became part of the legend and was available to Shakespeare in many versions. Holinshed incorporated verbatim a good deal of More's account.

Apart from Hall's and Holinshed's chronicles, those of Robert Fabyan (first published in 1516) and the *Annals* of John Stow (1580, 1592) may have provided Shakespeare with further details. Another possible source is *A Mirror for Magistrates* (first published in 1559), in which, for example, in "The Complaint of George, Duke of Clarence," we find the riddling prophecy about the letter *G* (see 1.1.39). A second edition of the *Mirror* (1563) contains the Complaints of Edward IV, Anthony Woodville (Lord Rivers), Hastings, Buckingham, Shore's wife, and others. Shakespeare's particular indebtedness to the *Mirror* is not great, though he certainly was familiar with it. The same is probably true of the Latin tragedy *Richardus Tertius* by Thomas Legge (1579) at Cambridge, which contains an interesting scene of Richard's wooing of the Lady Anne not reported in the chronicles. The anonymous *The True Tragedy of Richard III* (published 1594, written c. 1590–1592) may have been useful in its fusing of Senecan revenge motifs with English history and in its focus on the single figure of Richard. The Richard of this anonymous play is an overreacher, a worshiper of Fortune who meets his nemesis in the devoutly Christian Earl of Richmond. Opinion is divided as to whether Shakespeare actually used the play, chiefly because by 1590 he could have found the legend of Richard III set forth in so many works.

Richard II

Shakespeare's primary source for *Richard II* was the 1587 edition of Raphael Holinshed's *Chronicles* covering the years 1398 to 1400. As in his earlier *Henry VI* plays and *Richard III*, Shakespeare departs from historical accuracy in the interests of artistic design. Queen Isabel's part is almost wholly invented, for historically she was a child of eleven at the time the events in this play occurred. Her "Garden Scene" (3.4) is a fine piece of invention, bringing together images of order and disorder that are found in the rest of the play. The Duchess of York's role is entirely original; Holinshed reports the scene in which York's son Aumerle (the Earl of Rutland) rides to the new king and begs for mercy while his father simultaneously denounces him as a traitor, but the Duchess is never mentioned. Shakespeare has added the poignant conflict between husband and wife. Northumberland's role as conspirator against Richard and as hatchet man for Bolingbroke is greatly enlarged; for example, Holinshed never names the persons who engage in the original plotting against Richard. Shakespeare's Bolingbroke returns to England on his own initiative, whereas in Holinshed he does so at the barons' invitation, a change that accentuates the puzzle of Bolingbroke's motive. Another invention is the meeting between John of Gaunt and the Duchess of Gloucester (1.2). In fact, most of Gaunt's character and behavior has no basis in Holinshed at all. Shakespeare creates him to fill the role of thoughtfully conservative statesman, agonized by his son's banishment but doggedly obedient to his monarch. Finally, and most important, Shakespeare has greatly enlarged the role and the poetic nature of King Richard, especially in the final two acts.

Many of these alterations are Shakespeare's own; others derive from his reading in other sources. Samuel Daniel's *The First Four Books of the Civil Wars* (1595) may have had an important influence. Although we cannot discount the possibility that Shakespeare's play may have been written first, the consensus today is that he knew Daniel's poem. It gave him the idea of the Queen's maturity and grief (although not the Garden Scene), and the final meeting of King and Queen. Daniel's Hotspur is unhistorically a young man, as in 2.3 of Shakespeare's play. Like Shakespeare, Daniel sees York as a man of "a mild temperateness." Daniel's Richard and Bolingbroke ride together into London, not separately as in Holinshed. In Daniel's poem, Bolingbroke's indirect manner of insinuating his desire for Richard's death ("And wished that some would so his life esteem / As rid him of these fears wherein he stood") is verbally close to Shakespeare's depiction of this scene. Richard's final soliloquies in these two works show an unmistakable similarity to one another.

Richard II's reign was a controversial subject in the 1590s and produced other plays of varying political col-oration that Shakespeare must have known. *The Life and Death of Jack Straw* (anonymous, 1590–1593) distorts history in its friendly portrayal of Richard's role in the Peasants' Revolt of 1381 and whitewashes government policy. In contrast, the anonymous play *Thomas of Woodstock*, sometimes known as *1 Richard II* (1591–1595), is almost a call for open rebellion against tyranny. Many verbal similarities link this latter play with Shakespeare's *Richard II*, and, although scholars have difficulty in determining which was written first, the wary consensus is that Shakespeare borrowed from *Woodstock*. Such a hypothesis would explain some of the mysterious references to Woodstock's death in the first act of *Richard II*, since the anonymous play deals with historical events preceding those of Shakespeare's play. Shakespeare's debt to *Jack Straw*, on the other hand, is slight, even though he probably knew the play. Christopher Marlowe's *Edward II* (c. 1592), although dealing with another reign, probably taught Shakespeare much about constructing a play in which a weak king gains sympathy in his suffering, while his successor becomes morally tainted by the act of deposition.

Other sources have been proposed—so many, in fact, that Shakespeare's task of writing the play has been compared to that of a historical researcher. More probably he assimilated his wide and varied reading without any formal program of study. He had certainly read Edward Hall's *Union of the Two Noble and Illustre Families of Lancaster and York* (1542), a chief source for his earlier history plays, but in *Richard II* he seems to have recalled little more than its overall thematic pattern. Shakespeare must have known the Complaints of Mowbray and Richard in *A Mirror for Magistrates*, but the verbal echoes are slight in this case. The same is essentially true of *The Chronicles of England* by Jean Froissart, translated by Lord Berners (1525), and two French eyewitness accounts available to Shakespeare only in manuscript: the anonymous *Chronique de la Traïson et Mort de Richard Deux Roi d'Angleterre* and Jean Créton's *Histoire du Roi d'Angleterre Richard*. The Froissart *Chronicles* perhaps gave some hints for Gaunt's refusal to avenge Gloucester's death, for Richard's insensitivity at Gaunt's death, and for Northumberland's role as conspirator. The *Traïson* is notably sympathetic to Richard in his decline, although Shakespeare might also have found this sympathy in Daniel's *Civil Wars*.

Shakespeare's second series of English history plays (*Richard II*, *1* and *2 Henry IV*, *Henry V*) is even freer of the Tudor providential view of history than his first. The second series does not lead forward by any direct link to the reign of the Tudors, as does the first. Henry A. Kelly has shown (*Divine Providence in the England of Shakespeare's Histories*, 1970) that Shakespeare does not follow a single "Tudor myth" but allows spokesmen for both Richard II and his opponents to repeat arguments found in the various chronicles. This practice is especially evident in *Richard II*, in which some spokesmen eloquently warn of the disasters that will follow Bolingbroke's assumption of the throne, while other spokesmen are sympathetic to Bolingbroke's takeover as a political necessity.

Henry IV, Part I

Shakespeare's chief historical source for *1 Henry IV* was the 1587 edition of Raphael Holinshed's *Chronicles*, but he also took some important ideas from Samuel Daniel's *The First Four Books of the Civil Wars* (1595). Following Daniel, Shakespeare readjusts the age of Hotspur (who was historically older than Henry IV) to match that of Prince Hal. Daniel's Hotspur is, like Shakespeare's, dauntless and stubborn, a turbulent yet noble spirit. The theme of a nemesis of rebellion afflicting Henry IV for his usurpation, only touched upon in Shakespeare's play, owes something to Daniel's presentation, although the idea of nemesis is to be found also in Holinshed. Both Holinshed and Daniel err in confusing the Edmund Mortimer whom Glendower captured with his nephew Edmund Mortimer, claimant to the throne; Shakespeare perpetuates this error. Hal's killing of Hotspur is unhistorical, since both Holinshed and Daniel report only that Hal bravely helped rescue his father from attack and that Hotspur was killed in the melee. Daniel does give prominence to Prince Henry in the battle, however, and implies that he and Hotspur will meet face-to-face. Shakespeare invents the scenes in which we see Mortimer as a devoted husband and Hotspur as a fond combatant in wit with his wife Kate; Holinshed merely informs us that these two men were married. Shakespeare greatly expands Glendower's fascination with magic and poetry, changing him from a ruthless barbarian (in Holinshed) into a cranky but charismatic Welshman. Hotspur, despite hints from Daniel and Holinshed, is chiefly Shakespeare's creation.

The most impressive transformations are those of Hal and Falstaff. Shakespeare knew many legends of Hal's wild youth: some from John Stow's *The Chronicles of England* (1580) and *The Annals of England* (1592); others from oral tradition. Many of these stories were also available in Holinshed. Shakespeare's readiest source, however, was a rowdy and chauvinistic play called *The Famous Victories of Henry the Fifth*, registered 1594 but usually ascribed to Richard Tarlton or Samuel Rowley around 1587 or 1588. This play covers all the events of the *Henry IV* plays and *Henry V* in one chaotic sequence. Prince Hal has three companions, Sir John Oldcastle, Tom, and Ned (cf. Ned Poins), in whose company he robs the King's receivers of 1,000 pounds, visits the old tavern in Eastcheap, vexes his father, and strikes the Lord Chief Justice. A crucial difference is that this Hal is truly unregenerate. He not only chases after women and robs, but encourages his companions to look forward to unrestricted license when he is king. Hal seems consciously to desire his father's death. Yet he does reform and banishes his companions beyond a ten-mile limit with a promise to assist them if they amend their conduct. Although Hal's reform is crude and sudden, his popularity aids him when he goes to war against the French. He is followed by a comic crew of London artisans and thieves, who prove invincible against the effete enemy.

Shakespeare owes much to this unsophisticated, vibrant account of Hal's riotous youth, but he has transformed it to his own use. He limits himself in *1 Henry IV* to the action leading up to the Battle of Shrewsbury in order to focus on the coming of age of Prince Henry and the pairing and contrasting of Hotspur, Falstaff, and King Henry IV as alternative models for Hal's behavior. He invents unforgettable comic characters, such as Mistress Quickly, Francis, and Bardolph. Most of all, Shakespeare's portrayal of Falstaff is essentially his own. Sir John Oldcastle of the anonymous play is a minor character, not Hal's closest companion. Falstaff owes something to the tradition of the guileful and inventive Vice of the Tudor morality play (especially when Falstaff is called jestingly "that reverend Vice, that gray Iniquity," 2.4.448), but the influence of the morality play is general rather than specific. To label Falstaff a "Vice" is to reduce him to comic tempter and villain. Falstaff is in part an allowed fool, a parasite, and a *miles gloriosus* or braggart soldier, but he transcends all these conventionalized types with his own unique vitality.

1 Henry IV suggests some acquaintance with the anonymous play *Thomas of Woodstock* (c. 1591–1595), which Shakespeare may also have used for *Richard II*, and with the Complaints of Owen Glendower and Northumberland in *A Mirror for Magistrates* (1559). In neither case is the debt extensive. More suggestive as possible sources are events and social conditions in Shakespeare's England: the Northern Rebellion of 1569 against Queen Elizabeth's government, abuses of military authority by unscrupulous officers, the dangerous state of the highways, the raucous vitality of tavern life in Eastcheap, and the like.

Henry V

Shakespeare's principal historical source for *Henry V*, as for *Richard II* and the *Henry IV* plays, was the 1587 edition of Raphael Holinshed's *Chronicles*. Holinshed's account of Henry V, however, depended so heavily on Edward Hall's *The Union of the Two Noble and Illustre Families of Lancaster and York* (1542) that we sometimes have difficulty knowing whether Shakespeare consulted Holinshed or Hall. He was certainly familiar with both. Shakespeare's sources all acclaim Henry V a hero-king. Samuel Daniel's *The First Four Books of the Civil Wars* (1595), which

Shakespeare may have used for his account of the treasonous plot against Henry (2.2), also praises the King in encomiastic terms.

Shakespeare follows the order of events laid down in Holinshed and Hall: the personal rivalry between Henry and the French Dauphin, Henry's request for reassurance from the clergy as to the legitimacy of the war, the maneuvering of the clergy to forestall a bill in Parliament threatening to seize Church land, the foiling of a plot against Henry's life, the siege of Harfleur, and the glorious victory at Agincourt. Both Holinshed and Hall offer Shakespeare many particulars about the English claim to France: in both accounts, the Archbishop quotes the law—*In terram Salicam mulieres ne succedant*—and goes on at length about King Pharamond, the rivers Elbe and Saale, King Pepin, Hugh Capet, the Book of Numbers, and the rest. On the other hand, Shakespeare omits a three-year campaign that historically intervened between Agincourt and the peace treaty of Troyes. He passes over the Lollard controversy in England, with the execution of Sir John Oldcastle. And, of course, he adds unforgettable characters whom we do not find in the chronicles—Welshmen, Irishmen, Scots, common soldiers, thieves—who show the unity of the British nation under King Henry's charismatic leadership.

For many of his additions to the chronicles, Shakespeare was indebted to the anonymous *The Famous Victories of Henry the Fifth* (c. 1588), a work to which he had turned earlier in writing *1* and *2 Henry IV*. This old play, not registered until 1594 and not printed until 1598, exists today only in a corrupt text; quite possibly Shakespeare knew a fuller and more authentic version that would have given him still more material. Other plays may have existed on the subject, for the Admiral's men (a rival acting company) acted a "harey the v" in 1595 and 1596 that may or may not have been *The Famous Victories*. In any event, the relationship between *Henry V* and *Famous Victories* is at times close. *Famous Victories* omits Henry's long campaign between Agincourt and the final peace treaty, as does Shakespeare's play. The Archbishop of *Famous Victories* discusses the French claim just before the arrival of the French Ambassador with the tennis balls. (In Holinshed, the tennis-ball incident occurs first, at Kenilworth, whereas the Archbishop's lecture occurs sometime later at a meeting of Parliament in Leicester.) Henry assures the French ambassador that he has "free liberty and license to speak." To the Dauphin's insolent gift, taunting Henry about his wild youth, the King suavely replies that "My lord prince Dauphin is very pleasant with me" and promises to repay the insult with balls of brass and iron. (Holinshed mentions this apparently nonhistorical legend only briefly.) When the French noblemen assembled at the French court hear of Henry's arrival on their shores, they tremble with fear, even though the Dauphin recklessly scoffs at so young and prodigal a king. Henry is accompanied to France by a ludicrous assortment of London artisans and thieves, such as John Cobbler, who bids farewell to his wife in a comic scene similar to Pistol's parting from the Hostess, and Derick, who turns the tables on a French soldier much as Pistol deals with Monsieur le Fer. When King Henry woos Katharine of France, he protests to her that he cannot speak flatteringly because he is a plain soldier. She asks in return: "How should I love him, that hath dealt so hardly / With my father?" Despite these resemblances, however, Shakespeare's *Henry V* is incomparably superior to the old play and contains many original scenes and characters, such as King Henry's touring of his camp incognito, the quarrel between Henry and Williams, and above all the scenes involving Fluellen and his fellow captains.

Other possible sources include the *Henrici Quinti Angliae Regis Gesta*, written by a chaplain in Henry V's army; the *Vita et Gesta Henrici Quinti*, erroneously ascribed to Thomas Elmham; the *Vita Henrici Quinti* by "Titus Livius," translated in 1513 (in which the French brag about their horses and armor); a ballad called "The Battle of Agincourt" (c. 1530); and *The Annals of Cornelius Tacitus*, translated in 1598 (in which Germanicus walks disguised through his camp at night "to sound the soldiers' mind," and hears his leadership praised).

Romeo and Juliet

Shakespeare's chief source for *Romeo and Juliet* was a long narrative poem by Arthur Brooke called *The Tragical History of Romeus and Juliet, written first in Italian by Bandell and now in English by Ar. Br.* (1562). Other English versions of this popular legend were available to Shakespeare, in particular William Painter's *The Palace of Pleasure* (1566), but Shakespeare shows only a passing indebtedness to it. Brooke mentions having seen (prior to 1562) a play about the two lovers, but such an old play is not likely to have been of much service to Shakespeare. Nor does he appear to have extensively consulted the various continental versions that lay behind Brooke's poem. Still, these versions help explain the genesis of the story.

The use of a sleeping potion to escape an unwelcome marriage goes back at least to the *Ephesiaca* of Xenophon of Ephesus (by the fifth century A.D.). Masuccio of Salerno, in his *Il Novellino* (1476), seems to have been the first to combine this sleeping potion story with an ironic aftermath of misunderstanding and suicide (as found in the Pyramus and Thisbe story of Ovid's *Metamorphoses*). In Masuccio's account, the lovers Mariotto and Giannozza of Siena are secretly married by a friar. When Mariotto kills a prominent citizen of Siena in a quarrel, he is banished to Alexandria. Giannozza, to avoid marriage with a suitor of her father's choosing, takes a sleeping potion given her by the friar and is buried as though dead. She

is thereupon taken from the tomb by the friar and sent on her way to Alexandria. Mariotto, however, having failed to hear from her because the messenger is intercepted by pirates, returns in disguise to her tomb where he is discovered and executed. Giannozza, hearing this sad news, retires to a Sienese convent and dies of a broken heart.

In Luigi da Porto's *Historia novellamente ritrovata di due Nobili Amanti* (published c. 1530), based on Masuccio's account, the scene shifts to Verona. Despite the feuding of their two families, the Montecchi and the Cappelletti, Romeo and Guilietta meet and fall in love at a carnival ball. Romeo at once forgets his unrequited passion for a scornful lady. Friar Lorenzo, an experimenter in magic, secretly marries the lovers. Romeo tries to avoid brawling with the Cappelletti, but when some of his own kinsmen suffer defeat, he kills Theobaldo Cappelletti. After Romeo's departure for Mantua, Guilietta's family arranges a match for her with the Count of Lodrone. Friar Lorenzo gives Guilietta a sleeping potion and sends a letter to Romeo by a fellow friar, but this messenger is unable to find Romeo in Mantua. Romeo, hearing of Guilietta's supposed death from her servant Peter, returns to Verona with a poison he already possesses. Guilietta awakens in time to converse with Romeo before he dies. Then, refusing the Friar's advice to retire to a convent, she dies by stopping her own breath. This story provides no equivalents for Mercutio and the Nurse, although a young man named Marcuccio appears briefly at the Cappellettis's ball.

Da Porto's version inspired that of Matteo Bandello in his *Novelle* of 1554. Some details are added: Romeo goes to the ball in a vizard (mask), he has a servant named Pietro, a rope ladder is given to the Nurse enabling Romeo to visit Julietta's chamber before their marriage, Romeo obtains a poison from one Spolentino, and so on. The young man at the ball, Marcuccio, is now named Mercutio but is still a minor figure. This Bandello version was translated into French by Pierre Boaistuau in his *Histoires Tragiques* (1559); Boaistuau adds the Apothecary (who is racked and hanged for his part in the tragedy) and has Romeo die before Juliet awakens and slays herself with Romeo's dagger.

Despite Arthur Brooke's implication on the title page that his version is based on Bandello, the narrative poem *Romeus and Juliet* is taken from Boaistuau. Brooke's poem is a severely pious work written in "Poulter's Measure," couplets with alternating lines of six and seven feet. Brooke openly disapproves of the lovers' carnality and haste, although fortunately the story itself remains sympathetic to Romeus and Juliet. Brooke stresses starcrossed fortune and the antithesis of love and hate. He reduces Juliet's age from eighteen (as in Bandello) to sixteen. (Shakespeare further reduces her age to less than fourteen.) Brooke's narrative is generally close to Shakespeare's, though with important exceptions. Shakespeare compresses time from some nine months to a few days. In Brooke, for example, some two weeks elapse between the masked ball and Romeus's encounter with Juliet in her garden, and about two months elapse between the marriage and Tybalt's death. Shakespeare also unifies his play by such devices as introducing Tybalt and Paris early in the story; in Brooke's poem, Tybalt appears only at the time he is slain, and Juliet's proposed marriage to Count Paris emerges as a threat only after Romeus's banishment. Shakespeare's greatest transformation is of the characters. Brooke's Juliet is scheming. His Mercutio remains a shadowy figure, as in Bandello *et al.* Brooke's Nurse is unattractive, although she does occasionally hint at comic greatness: for example, she garrulously confides to Romeus the details of Juliet's infancy and then keeps Juliet on tenterhooks while she prates about Romeus's fine qualities (lines 631–714). Even if Shakespeare's play is incomparably superior to Brooke's drably versified poem, the indebtedness is extensive.

Julius Caesar

Julius Caesar represents Shakespeare's first extensive use of the work of the first-century Greek biographer Plutarch, in Thomas North's translation (based on the French of Jacques Amyot) of *The Lives of the Noble Grecians and Romans* (1579 and 1595). Plutarch was to become Shakespeare's most often used source in the 1600s; prior to 1599 he had consulted it briefly on a number of other occasions. In *Julius Caesar*, he borrows details from three lives: Caesar, Brutus, and Antonius. He uses particular traits of character, such as Caesar's belief that it is "better to die once than always to be afraid of death," Brutus's determination to "frame his manners of life by the rules of virtue and study of philosophy," Cassius's choleric disposition and his "hating Caesar privately more than he did the tyranny openly," and Antonius's inclination to "rioting and banqueting."

The events of the play are substantially present in Plutarch, especially in "The Life of Julius Caesar." Antonius runs the course on the Feast of Lupercal to cure barrenness and offers the diadem to Caesar. Flavius and Marullus despoil the images of Caesar. Caesar observes that he mistrusts pale and lean men such as Brutus and Cassius. Papers are thrown by the conspirators where Brutus can find them, proclaiming "Thou sleepest, Brutus, and art not Brutus indeed." Caesar's death is preceded by prodigies: a slave's hand burns but is unconsumed, a sacrificial beast is found to contain no heart. When Caesar encounters the soothsayer who previously had warned him of his fate and boasts that "the ides of March be come," the soothsayer has the last word: "So they be, but yet are they not past." Brutus's wife Portia complains to him of being treated "like a harlot," not like a partner. Brutus commits what Plutarch calls two serious errors when he forbids his fellow conspirators to kill Antonius and when he permits Antonius to speak at Caesar's funeral. Cinna the Poet is slain by an angry crowd mistaking him for Cinna the conspirator. A ghost appears to Brutus shortly before the last battle saying, "I am thy ill angel, Brutus, and thou shalt see me by the city of Phillippes," to which Brutus replies, "Well, I shall see thee then." Antonius says of the vanquished conspirators that "there was none but Brutus only that was moved to do it, as thinking the act commendable of itself: but that all the other conspirators did conspire his death for some private malice or envy." Shakespeare's debt to Plutarch is greater than these few examples can indicate.

Of course, Shakespeare reshapes and selects, as in his history plays. He compresses into one day Caesar's triumphant procession, the disrobing of the images, and the offer of the crown to Caesar on the Lupercal, when, in fact, these events were chronologically separate. Casca is by and large an invented character, and Octavius's role is considerably enlarged. Brutus's servant Lucius is a minor but effective addition, illustrating Brutus's capacity for warmth and humanity. Brutus's two speeches after the assassination (as mentioned by Plutarch) become one, and Antonius's speech is made to follow immediately after. (In Plutarch, Antonius speaks the following day, after the reading of the will.) Shakespeare accentuates the irrationality and vacillation of the mob, for in Plutarch the people are never much swayed by Brutus's rhetoric, even though they respectfully allow him to speak. The unforgettable speeches of both Brutus and Antonius are not set down at all in Plutarch. More compression of time occurs after the assassination: in Plutarch, Octavius does not arrive in Rome until some six weeks afterward and does not agree to the formation of the Triumvirate until more than a year of quarreling has taken place. The inexorable buildup of tension in Shakespeare's play is the result of careful selection from a vast amount of material. Shakespeare's borrowing from "The Life of Marcus Brutus" is no less extensive and is at the same time reshaped and given new emphasis.

Although Shakespeare depended heavily on Plutarch, he was also aware of later and conflicting traditions about Caesar. On the one hand, Dante's *Divine Comedy* (c. 1310–1321) consigns Brutus and Cassius to the lowest circle of hell, along with Judas Iscariot and other betrayers of their masters. Geoffrey Chaucer's "The Monk's Tale," from the *Canterbury Tales*, similarly portrays Caesar as the manly and uncorruptible victim of envious attackers. On the other hand, Montaigne stresses the hubris of Caesar in aspiring to divinity. (Shakespeare could have read Montaigne in the French original or, if he had access to a manuscript, in John Florio's English translation, published in 1603.) A pro-Brutus view could also be found in the Latin *Julius Caesar* of Marc-Antoine Muret (1553) and the French *César* of Jacques Grévin (1561). That Shakespeare knew these works is unlikely, but they kept alive a tradition with which he was certainly familiar. Possibly he knew such Roman works as Lucan's account of Caesar in the *Pharsalia* and Cicero's letters and orations, which were republican in tenor. Other possible sources include the *Chronicle of the Romans' Wars* by Appian of Alexandria (translated 1578), the anonymous play *Caesar's Revenge* (published 1606–1607, performed in the early 1590s at Oxford), and Thomas Kyd's *Cornelia* (translated from the French Senecan tragedy by Garnier). *Il Cesare* by Orlando Pescetti (1594) is now almost universally rejected as a possible source. The result of Shakespeare's acquaintance with both pro- and anti-Caesar traditions is that he subordinates his own political vision to a balanced presentation of history, showing the significant strengths and disabling weaknesses in both Caesar and the conspirators.

Hamlet

The ultimate source of the *Hamlet* story is Saxo Grammaticus's *Historia Danica* (1180–1208), the saga of one Amlothi or (as Saxo calls him) Amlethus. The outline of the story is essentially that of Shakespeare's play, even though the emphasis of the Danish saga is overwhelmingly on cunning, brutality, and bloody revenge. Amlethus's father is Horwendil, a Governor of Jutland, who bravely kills the King of Norway in single combat and thereby wins the hand in marriage of Gerutha, daughter of the King of Denmark. This good fortune goads the envious Feng into slaying his brother Horwendil and marrying Gerutha, "capping unnatural murder with incest." Though the deed is known to everyone, Feng invents excuses and soon wins the approbation of the fawning courtiers. Young Amlethus vows revenge but, perceiving his uncle's cunning, feigns madness. His mingled words of craft and candor awaken suspicions that he may be playing a game of deception.

Two attempts are made to lure Amlethus into revealing that he is actually sane. The first plan is to tempt him into lechery, on the theory that one who lusts for women cannot be truly insane. Feng causes an attractive woman to be placed in a forest where Amlethus will meet her as though by chance; but Amlethus, secretly warned of the trap by a kindly foster brother, spirits the young lady off to a hideaway where they can make love unobserved by Feng's agents. She confesses the plot to Amlethus. In a second stratagem, a courtier who is reported to be "gifted with more assurance than judgment" hides himself under some straw in the Queen's chamber in order to overhear her private conversations with Amlethus. The hero, suspecting just such a trap, feigns madness and begins crowing like a noisy rooster, bouncing up and down on the straw until he finds the eavesdropper. Amlethus stabs the man to death, drags him forth, cuts

the body into morsels, boils them, and flings the bits "through the mouth of an open sewer for the swine to eat." Thereupon he returns to his mother to accuse her of being an infamous harlot. He wins her over to repentant virtue and even cooperation. When Feng, returning from a journey, looks around for his counselor, Amlethus jestingly (but in part truly) suggests that the man went to the sewer and fell in.

Feng now sends Amlethus to the King of Britain with secret orders for his execution. However, Amlethus finds the letter to the British King in the coffers of the two unnamed retainers accompanying him on the journey and substitutes a new letter ordering their execution instead. The new letter, purportedly written and signed by Feng, goes on to urge that the King of Britain marry his daughter to a young Dane being sent from the Danish court. By this means, Amlethus gains an English wife and rids himself of the escorts. A year later Amlethus returns to Jutland, gets the entire court drunk, flings a tapestry (knitted for him by his mother) over the prostrate courtiers, secures the tapestry with stakes, and then sets fire to the palace. Feng escapes this holocaust, but Amlethus cuts him down with the King's own sword. (Amlethus exchanges swords because his own has been nailed fast into its scabbard by his enemies.) Subsequently, Amlethus convinces the people of the justice of his cause and is chosen King of Jutland. After ruling for several years, he returns to Britain, bigamously marries a Scottish Queen, fights a battle with his first father-in-law, is betrayed by his second wife, and is finally killed in battle.

In Saxo's account, we thus find the prototypes of Hamlet, Claudius, Gertrude, Polonius, Ophelia, Rosencrantz, and Guildenstern. Several episodes are close in narrative detail to Shakespeare's play: the original murder and incestuous marriage, the feigned madness, the woman used as a decoy, the eavesdropping counselor, and especially the trip to England. A translation of Saxo into French by François de Belleforest, in *Histoires Tragiques* (1576 edition), adds a few details, such as Gertrude's adultery before the murder and Hamlet's melancholy. Belleforest's version is longer than Saxo's, with more psychological and moral observation and more dialogue. Shakespeare probably consulted it.

Shakespeare need not have depended extensively on these older versions of his story, however. His main source was almost certainly an old play of *Hamlet*. Much evidence testifies to the existence of such a play. The *Diary* of Philip Henslowe, a theater owner and manager, records a performance, not marked as "new," of a *Hamlet* at Newington Butts on June 11, 1594, by "my Lord Admiral's men" or "my Lord Chamberlain's men," probably the latter. Thomas Lodge's pamphlet, *Wit's Misery, and the World's Madness* (1596), refers to "the visard of the ghost which cried so miserably at the theater, like an oyster wife, 'Hamlet, revenge!' " And Thomas Nashe, in his *Epistle* prefixed to Robert Greene's romance *Menaphon* (1589), offers the following observation:

It is a common practice nowadays amongst a sort of shifting companions, that run through every art and thrive by none, to leave the trade of noverint, whereto they were born, and busy themselves with the endeavors of art, that could scarcely Latinize their neck verse if they should have need; yet English Seneca read by candlelight yields many good sentences, as "Blood is a beggar," and so forth; and if you entreat him fair in a frosty morning, he will afford you whole *Hamlets*, I should say handfuls, of tragical speeches. But O grief! *Tempus edax rerum*, what's that will last always? The sea exhaled by drops will in continuance be dry, and Seneca, let blood line by line and page by page, at length must needs die to our stage; which makes his famished followers to imitate the Kid in Aesop, who, enamored with the Fox's newfangles, forsook all hopes of life to leap into a new occupation; and these men, renouncing all possibilities of credit or estimation, to intermeddle with Italian translations . . .

Nashe's testimonial describes a *Hamlet* play, written in the Senecan style by some person born to the trade of "noverint," or scrivener, who has turned to hack writing and translation. The description has often been fitted to Thomas Kyd, though this identification is not certain. (Nashe could be punning on Kyd's name when he refers to "the Kid in Aesop.") Certainly Thomas Kyd's *The Spanish Tragedy* (c. 1587) shows many affinities with Shakespeare's play and provides many Senecan ingredients missing from Saxo and Belleforest: the ghost, the difficulty in ascertaining whether the ghost's words are believable, the resulting need for delay and a feigning of madness, the moral perplexities afflicting a sensitive man called upon to revenge, the play within the play, the clever reversals and ironically caused deaths in the catastrophe, the rhetoric of tragic passion. Whether or not Kyd, in fact, wrote the *Ur-Hamlet*, his extant play enables us to see more clearly what that lost play must have contained. The unauthorized First Quarto of *Hamlet* (1603) also offers a few seemingly authentic details that are not found in the authoritative Second Quarto but are found in the earlier sources and may have been a part of the *Ur-Hamlet*. For example, after Hamlet has killed Corambis (corresponding to Polonius), the Queen vows to assist Hamlet in his strategies against the King; later, when Hamlet has returned to England, the Queen sends him a message by Horatio warning him to be careful.

One last document sheds light on the *Ur-Hamlet*. A German play, *Der bestrafte Brudermord (Fratricide Punished)*, from a now-lost manuscript dated 1710, seems to have been based on a text used by English actors traveling in Germany in 1586 and afterward. Though changed by translation and manuscript transmission, and too entirely different from Shakespeare's play to have been based on it, this German version may well have been based on Shakespeare's source-play. Polonius's name in

this text, Corambus, is the Corambis of the First Quarto of 1603. (The name may mean "cabbage cooked twice," from *coramblebis*, a proverbially dull dish.)

Der bestrafte Brudermord begins with a prologue in the Senecan manner, followed by the appearance of the ghost to Francisco, Horatio, and sentinels of the watch. Within the palace, meanwhile, the King carouses. Hamlet joins the watch, confiding to Horatio that he is "sick at heart" over his father's death and his mother's hasty remarriage. The ghost appears to Hamlet, tells him how the juice of hebona was poured into his ear, and urges revenge. When Hamlet swears Horatio and Francisco to silence, the ghost (now invisible) says several times "We swear," his voice following the men as they move from place to place. Hamlet reveals to Horatio the entire circumstance of the murder. Later, in a formal session of the court, the new King speaks hypocritically of his brother's death and explains the reasons for his marriage to the Queen. Hamlet is forbidden to return to Wittenberg, though Corambus's son Leonhardus has already set out for France.

Some time afterward, Corambus reports the news of Hamlet's madness to the King and Queen, and presumes on the basis of his own youthful passions to diagnose Hamlet's malady as lovesickness. Concealed, he and the King overhear Hamlet tell Ophelia to "go to a nunnery." When players arrive from Germany, Hamlet instructs them in the natural style of acting and then requests them to perform a play before the King about the murder of King Pyrrus by his brother. (Death is again inflicted by hebona poured in the ear.) After the King's guilty reaction to the play, Hamlet finds him alone at prayers but postpones the killing lest the King's soul be sent to heaven. Hamlet kills Corambus behind the tapestry in the Queen's chamber and is visited again by the ghost (who says nothing, however). Ophelia, her mind deranged, thinks herself in love with a court butterfly named Phantasmo. (This creature is also involved in a comic action to help the clown Jens with a tax problem.)

The King sends Hamlet to England with two unnamed courtiers who are instructed to kill Hamlet after their arrival. A contrary wind takes them instead to an island near Dover, where Hamlet foils his two enemies by kneeling between them and asking them to shoot him on signal; at the proper moment, he ducks and they shoot one another. He finishes them off with their own swords and discovers letter on their persons ordering Hamlet's execution by the English King if the original plot should fail. When Hamlet returns to Denmark, the King arranges a duel between him and Corambus's son Leonhardus. If Leonhardus's poisoned dagger misses its mark, a beaker of wine containing finely ground oriental diamond dust is to do the rest. Hamlet is informed of the impending duel by Phantasmo (compare Osric), whom Hamlet taunts condescendingly and calls "Signora Phantasmo."

Shortly before the duel takes place, Ophelia is reported to have thrown herself off a hill to her death. The other deaths occur much as in Shakespeare's play. The dying Hamlet bids that the crown be conveyed to his cousin, Duke Fortempras of Norway, of whom we have not heard earlier.

From the extensive similarities between *Hamlet* and this German play, we can see that Shakespeare inherited his narrative material almost intact, though in a jumble and so pitifully mangled that the modern reader can only laugh at the contrast. No source study in Shakespeare reveals so clearly the extent of Shakespeare's wholesale borrowing of plot and the incredible transformation he achieved in reordering his materials.

Othello

Shakespeare's main source for *Othello* was the seventh story from the third decade of G. B. Giraldi Cinthio's *Hecatommithi* (1565). Cinthio was available in French but not in English translation during Shakespeare's lifetime. The verbal echoes in Shakespeare's play are usually closer to the Italian original than to Gabriel Chappuys's French version of 1584. Cinthio's account may have been based on an actual incident occurring in Venice around 1508.

Shakespeare is considerably indebted to Cinthio's story for the essentials of the narrative: the marriage of a Moorish captain to a Venetian lady, Disdemona, whose relatives wish her to marry someone else, the mutual attraction to noble qualities of mind in both husband and wife, their happiness together at first, the dispatching of the Moor to Cyprus to take charge of the garrison there, Disdemona's insistence on accompanying her husband through whatever dangers may occur (though the sea voyage, as it turns out, is a very calm one), the ensign's treachery and resolve to destroy the Moor's happiness with Disdemona, her begging her husband to reinstate the squadron leader whom the Moor has demoted for fighting on guard duty (although no mention is made of drunkenness or of the ensign's role in starting the trouble), the ensign's insinuations to the Moor that his wife is cuckolding him because she is becoming weary of her marriage with a black man, the ensign's difficulty in providing ocular proof, his planting of Disdemona's handkerchief in the squadron leader's quarters and his showing the Moor that the handkerchief is now in the squadron leader's possession, his arranging for the Moor to witness at a distance a conversation between the ensign and squadron leader that is, in fact, not about Disdemona, Disdemona's confusion when she is asked to produce the handkerchief, the attack on the squadron leader in the dark, the murder of Disdemona in her bed, the Moor's deep regret at the loss of his wife, the eventual punishment of both the Moor and and the ensign, and the telling of the story publicly by the ensign's wife, who has heretofore kept silent because of her fear of her husband.

Although these correspondences in the story are many, Shakespeare has changed a great deal. He provides Desdemona with a caring and saddened father, Brabantio, out of Cinthio's brief suggestion of family opposition to her marriage, and adds the entire opening scene in which Iago arouses the prejudices of Brabantio. Roderigo is a brilliantly invented character used to reveal Iago's skill in manipulation. Cinthio's ensign, though thoroughly wicked, never expresses a resentment for the squadron leader's promotion and favored treatment by the Moor; instead, the ensign lusts for Disdemona and turns against her and the Moor only when his passion is unrequited. In his complex portrayal of a consuming and irrational jealousy in Iago, Shakespeare goes far beyond his source, making use as well of the inventive villainy of the Vice in the English late medieval morality play. In Cinthio's account, the ensign filches the handkerchief from Disdemona while she is hugging the ensign's three-year-old daughter; the ensign's wife is uninvolved in this mischief, though she does unwillingly learn of her husband's villainy (since he has an idea of using her in his plot) and later feels constrained to hold her tongue when Disdemona asks her if she knows why the Moor is behaving so strangely. (As is usual in prose narrative, the passage of time is much more extended than in Shakespeare's play.)

In the later portions of the story, the changes are more marked. Cinthio relates an episode in which the squadron leader, finding the handkerchief in his room, takes it back to Disdemona while the Moor is out but is interrupted by the Moor's unexpected return home; Shakespeare instead has Cassio approach Desdemona (earlier in the story) to beg her assistance in persuading Othello to reinstate him. Cinthio tells of a woman in the squadron leader's household who copies the embroidery of the handkerchief before it is returned and is seen with it at a window by the Moor; here, Shakespeare finds a suggestion for Bianca, but her role is considerably augmented, partly with the help of a passing remark in Cinthio's account that the squadron leader is attacked and wounded as he leaves the house of a courtesan with whom he occasionally takes his pleasure. In the absence of any character corresponding to Roderigo, the Cinthio narrative assigns to the ensign himself the role of wounding the squadron leader. The manner in which Disdemona is murdered is strikingly different. Cinthio has nothing equivalent to the tender scene between Desdemona and Emilia as Desdemona prepares to go to bed. Cinthio's Moor hides the ensign in a dressing room next to his bedroom and commissions the ensign to bludgeon her to death with a sand-filled stocking, after which the two murderers cause the ceiling of the room to collapse on her and create the impression that a rafter has smashed her skull.

Cinthio also treats the aftermath of the murder in a very different way. The Moor, distracted with grief, turns on the ensign and demotes him, whereupon the ensign persuades the squadron commander to take vengeance on the Moor as his attacker (according to the lying ensign) and killer of Disdemona. When the squadron commander accuses the Moor before the Seigniory, the Moor keeps silent but is banished and eventually killed by Disdemona's relatives. The ensign, returning to his own country, gets in trouble by making a false accusation and dies as the result of torture. Cinthio sees this as God's retribution. The ensign's wife lives to tell her story, unlike Shakespeare's Emilia.

The changed ending is essential to Shakespeare's play. Emilia becomes a more complex figure than the ensign's wife: Shakespeare implicates her in the stealing of the handkerchief but also accentuates her love for Desdemona and her brave denunciation of her husband when at last she knows the full truth. Othello's ritual slaying of Desdemona avoids the appalling butchery of the source story. Shakespeare's ending is more unified, and brings both Othello and Iago to account for the deeds they have committed in this play. Most important, Shakespeare transforms a sensational murder story into a moving tragedy of love.

King Lear

The story of Lear goes back into ancient legend. The motif of two wicked sisters and a virtuous youngest sister reminds us of Cinderella. Lear himself appears to come from Celtic mythology. Geoffrey of Monmouth, a Welshman in close contact with Celtic legend, included a Lear or Leir as one of the pseudo-historical Kings in his *Historia Regum Britanniae* (c. 1136). This fanciful mixture of history and legend traces a supposed line of descent from Brut, great-grandson of Aeneas of Troy, through Locrine, Bladud, Leir, Gorboduc, Ferrex and Porrex, Lud, Cymbeline, Bonduca, Vortigern, Arthur, and so forth, to the historical Kings of England. The Tudor monarchs made much of their purported claim to such an ancient dynasty, and in Shakespeare's day this mythology had a quasi-official status demanding a certain reverential suspension of disbelief.

King Leir, according to Geoffrey, is the father of three daughters, Gonorilla, Regan, and Cordeilla, among whom he intends to divide his kingdom. To determine who deserves most, he asks them who loves him most. The two eldest sisters protest undying devotion, but Cordeilla, perceiving how the others flatter and deceive him, renounces hyperbole and promises only to love him as a daughter should love a father. Furious, the King denies Cordeilla her third of the kingdom but permits her to marry Aganippus, King of the Franks, without dowry. Thereafter, Leir bestows his two eldest daughters on the Dukes of Albania and Cornubia (Albany and Cornwall), together with half the island during his lifetime and the possession of the remainder after his death. In due course, his two sons-in-law rebel against Leir and seize his power. Thereafter Maglaunus, Duke of Albania, agrees to maintain Leir with sixty retainers, but, after two years of chafing at this arrangement, Gonorilla insists that the number be reduced to thirty. Angrily, the King goes to Henvin, Duke of Cornubia, where all goes well for a time; within a year, however, Regan demands that Leir reduce his retinue to five knights. When Gonorilla refuses to take him back with more than one retainer, Leir crosses into France and is generously received by Cordeilla and Aganippus. An invasion restores Leir to his throne. Three years later, he and Aganippus die, after which Cordeilla rules successfully for five years until overthrown by the sons of Maglaunus and Henvin. In prison she commits suicide.

This story, as part of England's mythic genealogy, was repeated in various Tudor versions, such as *The First Part of the Mirror for Magistrates* (1574), William Warner's *Albion's England* (1586), and Raphael Holinshed's *Chronicles* (second edition, 1587). Warner refers to the King's sons-in-law as "the Prince of Albany" and "the Cornish prince"; Holinshed refers to them as "the Duke of Albania" and "the Duke of Cornwall" but reports that it is Cornwall who marries the eldest daughter Gonorilla. *The Mirror*, closer to Shakespeare in these details, speaks of "Gonerell" as married to "Albany" and of "Cordila" as married to "the King of France." Edmund Spenser's *The Faerie Queene* (2.10.27–32) reports that "Cordeill" or "Cordelia" ends her life by hanging herself. Other retellings appear in Gerard Legh's *Accidence of Armory* and William Camden's *Remains*. All of these accounts leave the story virtually unchanged.

Shakespeare's immediate source for *King Lear* was an old play called *The True Chronicle History of King Leir*. It was published in 1605 but plainly is much earlier in style. The Stationers' Register, the official record of the London Company of Stationers (booksellers and printers), for May 14, 1594, lists "A booke called the Tragecall historie of Kinge Leir and his Three Daughters &c.," and a short time earlier Philip Henslowe's *Diary* records the performance of a "Kinge Leare" at the Rose Theatre on April 6 and 8, 1594. The actors were either the Queen's or the Earl of Sussex's men (two acting companies), though probably the Queen's. The play may have been written as early as 1588. George Peele, Robert Greene, Thomas Lodge, and Thomas Kyd have all been suggested as possible authors. Shakespeare probably knew the play before its publication in 1605.

This play of *Leir* ends happily, with the restoration of Leir to his throne. Essentially, the play is a legendary history with a strong element of romance. The two wicked sisters are warned of the King's plans for dividing his kingdom by an obsequious courtier named Skalliger (compare Oswald). It is Skalliger, in fact, who proposes the idea of apportioning the Kingdom in accord with the lovingness of the daughters' responses. Cordella receives the ineffectual support of an honest courtier, Perillus (compare Kent) but is disinherited by her angry father. Trusting herself to God's mercy and setting forth alone to live by her own labor, Cordella is found by the Gallian King and his bluff companion Mumford, who have come to England disguised as palmers to see if the English King's daughters are as beautiful as reported. The King hears Cordella's sad story, falls in love with her, and woos her (still wearing his disguise) in the name of the Gallian King. When she virtuously suggests the palmer woo for himself, he throws off his disguise and marries her forthwith.

Meanwhile the other sons-in-law, Cornwall and Combria (compare Albany), draw lots for their shares of the kingdom. Leir announces that he will sojourn with Cornwall and Gonorill first. Cornwall treats the King with genuine solicitude, but Gonorill, abetted by Skalliger, tauntingly drives her father away. The King acknowledges to his loyal companion Perillus that he has wronged Cordella. Regan, who rules her mild husband as she pleases, receives the King with seeming tenderness but secretly hires an assassin to end his life. (Gonorill is partner in this plot.) The suborned agent, frightened into remorse by a providentially sent thunderstorm, shows his intended victim the letter ordering the assassination.

The Gallian King and Cordella, who have previously sent ambassadors to Leir urging him to come to France, now decide to journey with Mumford into Britain disguised as countryfolk. Before they can do so, however, Leir and Perillus arrive in France, in mariners' garb, where they encounter Cordella and her party dressed as country folk. Cordella recognizes Leir's voice, and father and daughter are tearfully reunited. The Gallian King invades England and restores Leir to his throne.

Shakespeare has changed much in the narrative of his source. He discards not only the happy ending but also the attempted assassination and the numerous romance-like uses of disguise (although Tom o' Bedlam, in an added plot, repeatedly uses disguise). Shakespeare eliminates the humorous Mumford and replaces Perillus with both Kent and the Fool. He turns Cornwall into a villain and Albany into a belated champion of justice. He creates the storm scene out of a mere suggestion of such an event, serving a very different purpose, in his source.

Most of all, he adds the parallel plot of Gloucester, Edgar, and Edmund. Here Shakespeare derived some of his material from Sir Philip Sidney's *Arcadia* (1590). In Book 2, chapter 10 of this greatest of Elizabethan prose romances, the two heroes, Pyrocles and Musidorus, encounter a son leading his blind old father. The old man tells his pitiful tale. He is the deposed King of Paphlago-

nia, father of a bastard son named Plexirtus who, he now bitterly realizes, turned the King against his true son Leonatus—the very son who is now his guide and guardian. The true son, having managed to escape his father's order of execution, has been forced to live poorly as a soldier, while the bastard son has proceeded to usurp his father's throne. In his wretchedness, the King has been succored by his forgiving true son and has been prevented from casting himself off the top of a hill. At the conclusion of this narrative, the villain Plexirtus arrives and attacks Leonatus; reinforcements arrive on both sides, but eventually Plexirtus is driven off, enabling the King to return to his court and bestow the crown on Leonatus. The old King thereupon dies, his heart having been stretched beyond the limits of endurance.

Other parts of the *Arcadia* may have given Shakespeare further suggestions; for example, the disguises adopted by Kent and Edgar are like those of Zelmane and Pyrocles in Sidney's prose work, and Albany's speeches about anarchy and the monstrosity that results from assaults on the rule of law recall one of Sidney's deepest concerns. Edmund is decidedly indebted to the allegorical Vice figure of the late medieval morality play tradition. For Tom o' Bedlam's mad language, Shakespeare consulted Samuel Harsnett's *Declaration of Egregious Popish Impostures*, 1603. (See Kenneth Muir's Arden edition of *King Lear*, pp. 253–6, for an extensive comparison.)

Macbeth

Shakespeare's chief source for *Macbeth* was Raphael Holinshed's *Chronicles* (1587 edition). Holinshed had gone for most of his material to Hector Boece, *Scotorum Historiae* (1526–1527), who in turn was indebted to a fourteenth-century priest named John of Fordun and to a fifteenth-century chronicler, Andrew of Wyntoun. By the time Holinshed found it, the story of Macbeth had become more fiction than fact. The historical Macbeth, who ruled from 1040 to 1057, did take the throne by killing Duncan, but in a civil conflict between two clans contending for the kingship. Contemporary observers credit him with having been a good ruler. Although he was defeated by the Earl of Northumbria (the Siward of Shakespeare's play) at Birnam Wood in 1054, the Earl was forced by his own losses to retire, and Macbeth ruled three years longer before being slain by Duncan's son Malcolm. Banquo and Fleance are fictional characters apparently invented by Boece.

In Holinshed's telling of the story, Duncan is a King with a soft and gentle nature, negligent in punishing his enemies and thereby an unwitting encourager of sedition. It falls to his cousin, Macbeth, a critic of this soft line, and to Banquo, the Thane of Lochaber, to defend Scotland against her enemies: first against Macdowald (Macdonwald in Shakespeare), with his Irish kerns and gallow-glasses, and then against Sueno, King of Norway. (Shakespeare fuses these battles into one.) Shortly thereafter, Macbeth and Banquo encounter "three women in strange and wild apparel, resembling creatures of elder world," who predict their futures as in the play. Although Macbeth and Banquo jest about the matter, common opinion later maintains that "these women were either the Weird Sisters, that is (as ye would say), the goddesses of destiny, or else some nymphs or fairies, endued with knowledge of prophecy." Certainly Macbeth soon becomes the Thane of Cawdor, whereupon, jestingly reminded of the three sisters' promise by Banquo, he resolves to seek the throne. His way is blocked, however, by Duncan's naming of his eldest but still underage son Malcolm to be Prince of Cumberland and heir to the throne. Macbeth's resentment at this is understandable, since Scottish law provides that, until the King's son is of age, the "next of blood unto him"—that is, Macbeth himself, as Duncan's cousin—should reign. Accordingly, Macbeth begins to plot with his associates how to usurp the kingdom by force. His "very ambitious" wife urges him on because of her "unquenchable desire" to be Queen. Banquo is one among many trusted friends with whose support Macbeth slays the King at Inverness or at Bothgowanan. (No mention is made of a visit to Macbeth's castle.) Malcolm and Donald Bane, the dead King's sons, fly for their safety to Cumberland, where Malcolm is well received by Edward the Confessor of England; Donald Bane proceeds on to Ireland.

Holinshed's Macbeth is at first no brutal tyrant, as in Shakespeare. For some ten years he rules well, using great liberality and correcting the laxity of his predecessor's reign. (Holinshed does suggest, to be sure, that his justice is only contrived to court popularity among his subjects.) Inevitably, however, the Weird Sisters' promise of a posterity to Banquo goads Macbeth into ordering the murder of his onetime companion. Fleance escapes Macbeth's henchmen in the dark and afterward founds the lineage of the Stuart Kings. (This genealogy is fictitious.) Macbeth's vain quest for absolute power further causes him to build Dunsinane fortress. When Macduff refuses to help, the King turns against him and would kill him except that "a certain witch, whom he had in great trust," tells the King he need never fear a man born of woman nor any vanquishment till Birnam Wood come to Dunsinane. Macduff flees for his safety into England and joins Malcolm, whereupon Macbeth's agents slaughter Macduff's wife and children at Fife. Malcolm, fearing that Macduff may be an agent of Macbeth, dissemblingly professes to be a voluptuary, miser, and tyrant, but, when Macduff responds as he should in righteous sorrow at Scotland's evil condition, Malcolm reveals his steadfast commitment to the cause of right. These leaders return to Scotland and defeat Macbeth at Birnam Wood, with their soldiers carrying branches before them. Macduff, proclaiming that he is a man born of no woman since he was "ripped out" of his mother's womb, slays Macbeth.

Despite extensive similarities, Shakespeare has made some significant changes. Duncan is no longer an ineffectual king. Macbeth can no longer justify his claim to the throne. Most important, Banquo is no longer partner in a broadly based though secret conspiracy against Duncan. Banquo is, after all, ancestor of James I (at least according to this legendary history), and so his hands must be kept scrupulously clean; King James disapproved of all tyrannicides, whatever the circumstances. Macbeth is no longer a just lawgiver. The return of Banquo's ghost to Macbeth's banqueting table is an added scene. Macbeth hears the prophecy about Birnam Wood and Macduff from the Weird Sisters, not, as in Holinshed, from some witch. Lady Macbeth's role is considerably enhanced, and her sleepwalking scene is original. Shakespeare compresses time, as he usually does.

In making some of these alterations, Shakespeare turned to another story in Holinshed's chronicle of Scotland: the murder of King Duff by Donwald. King Duff, never suspecting any treachery in Donwald, often spends time at the castle of Forres, where Donwald is captain of the castle. On one occasion, Donwald's wife, bearing great malice toward the King, shows Donwald (who already bears a grudge against Duff) "the means whereby he might soonest accomplish" the murder. The husband and wife ply Duff's few chamberlains with much to eat and drink. Donwald abhors the act "greatly in heart" but perseveres "through instigation of his wife." Four of Donwald's servants actually commit the murder under his instruction. Next morning, Donwald breaks into the King's chamber and slays the chamberlains, as though believing them guilty. Donwald is so overzealous in his investigation of the murder that many lords begin to suspect him of having done it. For six months afterward, the sun refuses to appear by day and the moon by night.

The chronicle accounts in Holinshed of Malcolm and Edward the Confessor supplied Shakespeare with further details. A more important supplementary source may have been George Buchanan's *Rerum Scoticarum Historia* (1582), a Latin history not translated in Shakespeare's lifetime, presenting a more complex psychological portrait of the protagonist than in Holinshed. Finally, Shakespeare may have used King James I's *Daemonology* (1597), John Studley's early seventeenth-century version of Seneca's *Medea*, Samuel Harsnett's *Declaration of Egregious Popish Impostures* (1603), and accounts of the Scottish witch trials published around 1590.

Antony and Cleopatra

In writing *Antony* and *Cleopatra*, Shakespeare relied to an unusual extent on his chief source, "The Life of Marcus

Antonius" in the first-century Greek biographer Plutarch's *The Lives of the Noble Grecians and Romans* (in an English version by Sir Thomas North, 1579). Perhaps the best-known example in all Shakespeare of his skillful use of source material is in 2.2.201–36, when Enobarbus describes the first meeting of Antony and Cleopatra on the river Cydnus. Putarch reports the event as follows:

She disdained to set forward otherwise but to take her barge in the river of Cydnus, the poop whereof was of gold, the sails of purple, and the oars of silver, which kept stroke in rowing after the sound of the music of flutes, hautboys, citterns, viols, and such other instruments as they played upon in the barge. And now for the person of herself: she was laid under a pavilion of cloth of gold of tissue, appareled and attired like the goddess Venus, commonly drawn in picture; and hard by her, on either hand of her, pretty fair boys appareled as painters do set forth god Cupid, with little fans in their hands with the which they fanned wind upon her. Her ladies and gentlewomen also, the fairest of them, were appareled like the nymphs Nereides (which are the mermaids of the waters) and like the Graces, some steering the helm, others tending the tackle and ropes of the barge, out of the which there came a wonderful passing sweet savor of perfumes that perfumed the wharf's side, pestered with innumerable multitudes of people. Some of them followed the barge all alongst the river's side; others also ran out of the city to see her coming in. So that in the end, there ran such multitudes of people one after another to see her that Antonius was left post alone in the marketplace, in his imperial seat, to give audience.

Shakespeare retains virtually every detail describing Cleopatra's barge: the poop of gold, the sails of purple, the oars of silver, the flutes, the boys with fans, the gentlewomen like the Nereides, and so on. He borrows phrases and images virtually intact from North, as in the account of Cleopatra's own person. Yet Shakespeare also transforms this scene by putting the description in the mouth of Enobarbus, a largely invented character. Enobarbus's sardonic view derived from military experience, his wry but genuine admiration for Cleopatra, and the prurient curiosity of his Roman listeners—all combine to produce the paradox of cloying appetite and insatiable hunger that helps to define the unforgettable greatness of Cleopatra as a character.

Shakespeare turns to Plutarch for other fabulous stories as well: eight wild boars roasted whole for only twelve guests (2.2.189–90), Cleopatra teasing Antony by causing an old dried salt fish to be placed on his fishing line (2.5.15–18), Menas the pirate suggesting to Pompey that they cut the anchor cable with all their noble guests still aboard (2.7.62–85), Cleopatra's sudden changes from weeping to laughing, and her willingness to be flattered by those who tell her Antony has married Octavia solely out of necessity (3.3), Octavius's tenderness for his sister, the ill-omened nesting of swallows in Cleopatra's sails (4.12.3–4), Antony's disregarding the advice of a valiant

captain not to fight at sea (3.7.62–71), Cleopatra's study of swift means of death (5.2.353–6), Antony's jealous reaction to the embassy of the young Thyreus, or Thidias (3.13.86–170), the suicide of Antony's servant Eros (4.14.85–97), Cleopatra's difficulty in lifting Antony up to her tomb or monument (4.15.30–8), his warning that she should trust none but Proculeius (4.15.50), Cleopatra's deception of Caesar through persuading him that she desires to live (5.2.110–90), the countryman with the basket of figs (5.2.233–5), Cleopatra's death "attired and arrayed in her royal robes" attended by Charmian and Iras, and much more.

Despite these extensive and detailed borrowings, Shakespeare is highly innovative in his use of his sources. He compresses time in order to give a sense of dramatic momentum to the events of many years. He creates vibrant characters like Enobarbus, Charmian, Iras, Mardian, the Soothsayer, Menas, Thidias, Dollabella, and many others for whom the historical sources provide only a sketchy impression or no information at all. In his characterization of the main figures as well, Shakespeare is not content to rely on Plutarch's estimate. To Plutarch, Antony is the tragic victim of infatuation. For all Cleopatra's cultivation and fascination—she knows several languages and rules her country with royal bearing—she is the source of Antony's downfall. Plutarch's attitude is, like Enobarbus's, admiring but ironic. "In the end," he writes, "the horse of the mind, as Plato termeth it, that is so hard of rein (I mean the unreined lust of concupiscence) did put out of Antonius's head all honest and commendable thoughts." This "Roman" view is present in *Antony and Cleopatra*, to be sure, but is counterbalanced by the "Egyptian" view that finds greatness in Antony and Cleopatra's capacity for love. Shakespeare's play sets up a debate among conflicting traditions, as found in various medieval and Renaissance treatments of this famous story. The moralistic perspective condemning vice was popular in medieval texts, such as *De Casibus Virorum Illustrium* and its continuation, John Lydgate's *The Fall of Princes*. The interpretation of Cleopatra as love's martyr was to be found in Geoffrey Chaucer's *The Legend of Good Women*. And, finally, the view of Antony and Cleopatra as heroic protagonists rising above their guilt found expression in several neo-Senecan dramas of the later sixteenth century. Most important for Shakespeare were *The Tragedy of Antony*, translated from Robert Garnier's *Marc Antoine* by Mary Herbert, Countess of Pembroke, in about 1590 (published 1592 and 1595), and *The Tragedy of Cleopatra* by Samuel Daniel (1594), a companion play dealing mainly with the end of Cleopatra's life. Garnier's play had been based on Étienne Jodelle's *Cléopâtre Captive* (1552), the first regular French tragedy. Shakespeare certainly gained from such works as these a sense of tragic greatness in his protagonists. He seems also to have been aware of favorable and unfavorable historical appraisals of Octavius Caesar as both a great ruler and a ruthless and even treacherous politician. One influential work on the more critical side may have been the *Chronicle of the Romans' Wars* by Appian of Alexandria (translated 1578). Virgil's *Aeneid* gave Shakespeare a model for a drama of passion set in the context of Roman history.

The Winter's Tale

Shakespeare based *The Winter's Tale* on Robert Greene's romantic novella called *Pandosto: The Triumph of Time* (1588), or *The History of Dorastus and Fawnia* in its running title. Shakespeare changes the names, reverses the two Kingdoms of Sicilia and Bohemia, and alters the unhappy ending that afflicts King Pandosto and Queen Bellaria of Bohemia (Leontes and Hermione of Sicilia). Otherwise, the narrative outline remains intact. The story begins with the state visit of King Egistus of Sicilia (Polixenes of Bohemia) to his boyhood companion, King Pandosto of Bohemia. Queen Bellaria entertains their guest with such warmth, "oftentimes coming herself into his bedchamber to see that nothing should be amiss to mislike him," that Pandosto grows jealous. He commands his cupbearer Franion (Camillo) to murder Egistus, and the latter seems to agree but instead warns his victim to flee with him. Their hasty departure appears to confirm Pandosto's worst suspicions. He sends the guard to arrest Bellaria as she plays with her young son Garinter (Mamillius). When the Queen gives birth to a daughter in prison, the King orders the child destroyed, but he relents upon the insistence of his courtiers and causes the infant to be set adrift in a small boat. The Queen nobly defends herself at her trial (in language that Shakespeare has copied in some detail). She herself requests that the oracle at Delphos be consulted. The oracle replies in words that Shakespeare has altered only slightly: "Bellaria is chaste, Egistus blameless, Franion a true subject, Pandosto treacherous, his babe an innocent; and the King shall live without an heir if that which is lost be not found." Pandosto is immediately stricken with remorse, and, when Queen Bellaria collapses at the news of her son Garinter's death, she is truly and irrecoverably dead.

A similarly close parallel in the narrative, along with telling changes in a number of details, characterizes the story's second half. The babe is conveyed by a tempest to the coast of Sicilia and is discovered by an impoverished shepherd named Porrus. He and his wife Mopsa adopt the child, naming her Fawnia. By the age of sixteen, Fawnia's natural beauty rivals that of the goddess Flora. At a meeting of the farmers' daughters of Sicilia, where she is chosen mistress of the feast, Fawnia is seen by the King's son Dorastus on his way home from hawking. She counters his importunate suit with the argument that she is too lowly a match for him, but he replies that the gods themselves sometimes take earthly lovers. Her foster father, distressed by the Prince's repeated visits (though he comes in shepherd's costume), resolves to carry the jewels he found with Fawnia to the King and reveal her story, thereby escaping blame for the goings-on. Dorastus escapes with Fawnia to a ship, aided by his servant Capnio (compare Camillo). Capnio also fulfills a role given by Shakespeare to Autolycus, for he manages to trick the shepherd Porrus into thinking he can see the King if he comes aboard Dorastus's ship. A storm drives these voyagers to Bohemia where, because of the ancient enmity between Egistus and Pandosto, they disguise themselves. Pandosto, happening to hear of Fawnia's beauty, orders her and the others to be arrested as spies and summoned to court, whereupon he falls incestuously in love with the disguised Fawnia. He promises to free the young man (who has taken the name of Meleagrus to conceal his identity) only if he will relinquish his claim to Fawnia. King Egistus meanwhile has discovered his son's whereabouts and sends ambassadors to Bohemia demanding the return of Dorastus and the execution of Fawnia, Capnio, and Porrus. Pandosto, his love for Fawnia having turned to hate, is about to comply when Porrus reveals the circumstances of Fawnia's infancy. Overjoyed to rediscover his daughter, Pandosto permits her to marry Dorastus but then falls into a melancholy fit and commits suicide.

Shakespeare has almost entirely created some characters, such as Paulina, Antigonus, the clownish shepherd's son, and Autolycus, though Capnio does perform one of Autolycus's functions by inveigling the old shepherd aboard ship. Antigonus's journey to the seacoast of Bohemia with the infant Perdita and his fatal exit "*pursued by a bear*" are Shakespearean additions. The character of Time is also added, and the shift in tone from tragedy to tragicomedy averts the catastrophe in Greene's novella (in which Pandosto commits suicide). The shepherdesses at the sheepshearing are Shakespearean. The old shepherd has a more substantial and comic role; Camillo is a stronger person than Capnio. Greene's Mopsa, the shrewish wife of old Porrus, disappears from the play. Shakespeare omits the incestuous love of Pandosto for his daughter and brings Hermione back to life. (For this motif of a statue made to breathe, he may well have recalled Ovid's account of Pygmalion in Ovid's *Metamorphoses*, Book 10.) Shakespeare's Leontes is more irrationally jealous than in Greene's account. Leontes's purgative sorrow is more intense and also more restorative than in the source; he is a truly noble and tragicomic figure, the center of a play about forgiveness and renewal.

Shakespeare may also have known Francis Sabie's *The Fisherman's Tale* (1595) and its continuation, *Flora's Fortune* (1595). From Greene's pamphlets, describing in vividly colloquial detail the life of London's underworld, Shakespeare probably derived many of Autolycus's tricks.

The Tempest

No direct literary source for the whole of *The Tempest* has been found. Shakespeare does seem to have drawn material from various accounts of the shipwreck of the *Sea Venture* in the Bermudas, in 1609, although the importance of these materials should not be overstated. Several of the survivors wrote narratives of the shipwreck itself and of their life on the islands for some nine months. Sylvester Jourdain, in *A Discovery of the Bermudas*, published 1610, speaks of miraculous preservation despite the island's reputation for being "a most prodigious and enchanted place." William Strachey's letter, written in July of 1610 and published much later (1625) as *A True Reportory of the Wreck and Redemption . . . from the Islands of the Bermudas*, describes the panic among the passengers and crew, the much feared reputation of the island as the habitation of devils and wicked spirits, the actual beauty and fertility of the place with its abundance of wild life (compare Caliban's descriptions), and the treachery of the Indians they later encounter in Virginia. Shakespeare seems to have read Strachey's letter in manuscript and may have been acquainted with him. The storm scene in Chapter 4 of Laurence Twine's *The Pattern of Painful Adventures*, a major source for *Pericles*, may also have given Shakespeare material for the first scene of *The Tempest*. Shakespeare also kept up with travel accounts of Sir Walter Ralegh and Thomas Harriot, and knew various classical evocations of a New World. The name "Setebos" came from Richard Eden's *History of Travel* (1577), translated from Peter Martyr's *De Novo Orbe* and from other travel accounts of the period. (See the Introduction to *The Tempest* for the potential relevance of various journals of the circumnavigation of the globe.) All these hints are indeed suggestive, but they are scattered and relate more to the setting and general circumstance of Shakespeare's play than to the plot.

Shakespeare certainly consulted Michel de Montaigne's essay "Of the Cannibals," as translated by John Florio in 1603. Gonzalo's reverie on an ideal commonwealth (2.1.150–71) contains many verbal echoes of the essay. Montaigne's point is that supposedly civilized men who condemn as barbarous any society not conforming with their own are simply refusing to examine their own shortcomings. A supposedly primitive society may well embody perfect religion, justice, and harmony; civilized art can never rival the achievements of nature. The ideal commonwealth has no need of magistrates, riches, poverty, and contracts, all of which breed dissimulation and covetousness. The significance of these ideas for *The Tempest* extends well beyond the particular passage in which they are found. And Caliban himself, whose name is an anagram of "cannibal," illustrates (even though he is not an eater of human flesh) the truth of Montaigne's observation apropos of the intense and wanton cruelty he finds so widespread in so-called Western civilization: "I think there is more barbarism in eating men alive than to feed upon them being dead."

Prospero's famous valedictory speech to "Ye elves of hills, brooks, standing lakes, and groves" (5.1.33–57) owes its origin to Medea's similar invocation in Ovid's *Metamorphoses* (Book 7), which Shakespeare knew both in the Latin original and in Golding's translation: "Ye airs and winds, ye elves of hills, of brooks, of woods alone, / Of standing lakes . . . " Medea also anticipates Shakespeare's Sycorax. Medea thus provides material for the representation of both black and white magic in *The Tempest*, so carefully differentiated by Shakespeare. Ariel is part English fairy, like Puck, and part daemon. The pastoral situation in *The Tempest* is perhaps derived from Edmund Spenser's *The Faerie Queene*, Book 6 (with its distinctions between savage lust and true courtesy, between nature and art). Italian pastoral drama as practiced by Guarini and (in England) by John Fletcher may also have been an influence. The masque element in *The Tempest*, prominent as in much late Shakespeare, bears the imprint of the courtly masque tradition of Ben Jonson, Francis Beaumont, and John Fletcher. Virgil's *Aeneid* may have provided Shakespeare with a more indirect source, with its story of wandering in the Mediterranean and storm at sea, love in Carthage, the intervention of the gods, and the fulfillment of destiny in Italy. Donna Hamilton (*Virgil and "The Tempest,"* 1990) contends that Shakespeare "imitated" Virgil so as to argue for a politics of retrenchment.

A German play, *Die Schöne Sidea* by Jacob Ayrer, written before 1605, was once thought to have been based on an earlier version of *The Tempest* as performed by English players traveling in Germany. Today, the similarities between the two plays are generally attributed to conventions found everywhere in romance.

The Sonnets

See the Introduction to *The Sonnets* for a discussion of the sonnet vogue in England of the 1590s, and the previous history of the sonnet in England and on the Continent.

Appendix 3

⌾⌾⌾

Shakespeare in Performance

Lois Potter, University of Delaware

Although we know a good deal about the conditions of performance at the time Shakespeare's plays were first produced, much of this information (summarized in the Introduction, pp. xliv–xlvii) raises as many questions as it answers. We know, for example, that Shakespeare wrote most of his plays for the Lord Chamberlain's men, first formed in 1594 after a period of plague and theater closures, and that the company (officially servants of the courtier whose duties included supervising court entertainments) was honored with the title of the King's men at the accession of James I. Elizabethan acting companies were all male, with boys or young men playing women's roles, but we know almost nothing about how they acted, or who played which parts. We know that the stages of the public, partially roofed playhouses jutted into the yard where the audience stood on three sides, looking up at the actors; the rest of the spectators sat in covered galleries looking down on them. But we are not sure whether the gallery above the stage, pictured in the contemporary illustration of the Swan Theatre interior shown on page xlvi, was meant for musicians, spectators, or both. (And of course we do not know how much the Globe's interior resembled the Swan's.) If, as appears from the illustrations of theater interiors on pages xlvi and lxiv, some spectators normally watched the action from behind the stage, the actors would have had to move a great deal during a scene, as in modern theater-in-the-round productions, to make sure that they were visible and audible to all parts of their audience.

However much information we have, we still cannot know if aspects of the theater that were common then but unusual in our eyes were taken for granted by the spectators who watched the plays in the reigns of Elizabeth and James I. Did they think of the boy actresses as boys or believe in them as women? Those who had traveled to France and Italy would have known that women played women's parts in those countries and were often as famous as the male actors. What was the acting style for love scenes between a man and a cross-dressed boy, and what was the range of responses to it? The players in the open theaters performed by day (normally beginning at 2 P.M.), but used torches and candles to indicate when the action was supposed to be taking place at night. Did audiences find it difficult to accept a convention by which actors, fully visible to the audience, declare that they are unable to see anything? There is probably no single answer. It is likely that then, as always, audience members differed in the extent to which they preferred to believe in the performance or feel superior to it.

To the audiences of Shakespeare's time, the theaters were sumptuous and impressive buildings. Their wooden interiors were painted to look like marble, and the ceiling of the Globe was apparently decorated with the signs of the zodiac (perhaps, when Hamlet and Othello addressed the heavens, they looked at both a real and an artificial sky). Visitors from abroad were taken to see plays; actors traveled with them as far as Prague; versions of them were being translated into German as early as 1618. All this indicates how much English plays and players were respected. By about 1597, the company for which Shakespeare wrote was the one most frequently invited to perform at court, evidence that it was considered the best in London.

The theater in fact offered a great deal of visual and musical pleasure even for those who could not understand the language. Vast sums of money were spent on costumes. The most valuable surviving evidence, an account book of Philip Henslowe, manager of the Rose playhouse, shows that their bright or striking colors (often red and black, with silver and gold) allowed them to stand out on a stage that depended on daylight for most of its illumination. These were not "costumes" but clothes, sometimes bought in secondhand shops and sometimes donated or sold by gentlemen patrons. Characters normally wore contemporary dress, but with some indications of historical costume, like togas for classical characters (see the contemporary drawing, usually taken to be an illustration of *Titus Andronicus*, on p. lxi). Costumes and wigs, as well as false beards, were obviously important for a theater in which twelve to fourteen actors frequently doubled in as many as thirty roles. Music was frequently used in productions and a number of writers, including Shakespeare, incorporated popular contemporary songs into their plays. Robert Johnson, who is credited with the songs to a number of Jacobean plays, may have been the company's in-house composer. Some plays may have had as much music as a modern musical comedy, though very little of it has been identified.

Shakespeare's plays were designed to show off the actors' talents: singing, playing an instrument, dancing, and fencing. Most of his most popular plays end with either a dance or a fight, and nearly all of his tragic heroes (with the interesting exceptions of Othello and Antony) have at least one heroic fight scene. Since memorization and oratory were part of every grammar school education, audiences could recognize the superior memories of the actors who learned the long and complicated speeches that Shakespeare wrote for them. The combination of great actors and a dramatist who wrote great roles for them was attractive to other playwrights, and helped to ensure the company's continuing preeminence.

Shakespeare's practice of writing plays dominated by one very large starring role probably followed Richard Burbage's rise to stardom. Many contemporary references identify him with Richard III (see the anecdote on pp. lxx–lxxi), and he is also known to have played Romeo, Hamlet, Othello, and Lear. John Lowin, who joined the company in 1602–1603, seems to have partnered Burbage in plays with two substantial roles. Shakespeare was unusual in that he wrote equally well for tragic and comic actors, and for the company clown, a type of performer traditionally famous for his ad-libs. Will Kemp, the most famous comedian of his day, certainly created the role of Dogberry—his name accidentally replaces the character's in one quarto of the play. It is not absolutely certain that he played Falstaff, but his departure from the Lord Chamberlain's men in 1599 is often linked with Shakespeare's writing the character out of *Henry V* after having apparently promised (at the end of *2 Henry IV*) to include him in the sequel. Those who think that Shakespeare was in agreement with Hamlet's advice to the players ("Let those that play your clowns speak no more than is set down for them") wonder whether Kemp's inability to refrain from "speaking" led to friction with his leading playwright.

Kemp's successor was Robert Armin, and it is often said that the more literary quality of Shakespeare's later fools resulted from their being tailored for the new actor.

Little is known about the other chief sharers in the company, though attempts have been made to identify them with, for example, references to exceptionally thin or exceptionally fat actors. It is not known whether any particular young actor inspired Shakespeare to write his best female roles, but many boys seem to have been good enough to have a personal following. A spectator who saw *Othello* in Oxford in 1610 mentions how moved the spectators were at the sight of Desdemona after her death.

It has often been suggested that Hamlet's insistence on naturalness, and the First Player's modest claim to have "reformed" the practice of overacting at least to some extent, reflect a perceived difference between the actors for whom Shakespeare wrote and the more melodramatic ones in the company led by Philip Henslowe and its leading actor Edward Alleyn. Yet Alleyn, who created the major Marlowe roles, was no less intelligent and talented than Burbage. It was Alleyn who retired early to live the life of a gentleman (in 1597, when he was only 31), with one brief comeback in 1601–1604. Burbage, on the other hand, went on acting up to his death at the age of 46, a fact that suggests a more theatrical personality than Alleyn's. If there was a movement toward greater naturalism in the 1590s, it probably resulted from greater professionalization and better training of actors, along with greater sophistication of the audiences themselves.

As the Lord Chamberlain's men grew more successful, they looked for a more select location. In 1597 James Burbage, Richard's father, purchased part of the disused monastic site of Blackfriars in the City of London. Protests from the local residents forced him to rent out the building to boys' companies (which performed less frequently) until, early in the reign of James I, times became more favorable. Finally moving into the new premises some time after 1607, the company was able to restrict its public to those who could afford the higher admission prices. In the indoor theaters, all the spectators were seated. Comfortable spectators cause less trouble than uncomfortable ones. The smaller size may have allowed for a more "realistic" style of playing. At the same time, the company continued to use the Globe throughout the period, as well as acting at court and elsewhere, so the actors must have been able to adapt their style to circumstances. In many ways, Shakespeare's last plays are his least "realistic," since they often involve magic, but the technology available in the Blackfriars playhouse may have made the magic convincing.

Besides, if realistic acting means acting that makes one forget that one is watching a play, it is unlikely that the drama was ever truly realistic. Other dramatists' allusions to Shakespeare are obviously meant to break the dramatic illusion: "What, Hamlet, are you mad?" asks a character in *Eastward Ho!* (1605), speaking to a servant who is named Hamlet only so that someone can ask him that question. Shakespeare himself also refers to his own plays. It is likely that the lovers' suicides in "Pyramus and This-be," performed at the end of *A Midsummer Night's Dream*, are meant as an absurd version of the end of *Romeo and Juliet*; Malvolio's madness, in *Twelfth Night*, probably parodies Hamlet's. Perhaps a comedy can make jokes about a tragedy without destroying the atmosphere, but *Hamlet* does the same thing. When Polonius tells Hamlet about playing Julius Caesar "at the university," and being killed by Brutus, many of their audience would remember that, not long before, the two actors speaking these lines had played Caesar and Brutus, respectively, in *Julius Caesar*.

The deaths of Shakespeare in 1616 and of Burbage in 1619 may have temporarily affected Shakespeare's theatrical popularity. Burbage was so much identified with the major roles that, according to one elegy, these characters seemed to have died with him. The Earl of Pembroke may have been typical when, in a letter, he expresses reluctance to go to the theater again. John Taylor, who replaced Burbage in 1619, inherited a number of his roles. He and Lowin led the company for the next twenty years, with first John Fletcher and then Philip Massinger as their leading dramatist. The company had been called the King's men since 1603, but the name was even more appropriate under Charles I than under his father, since the actors were much closer to the court. Taylor even served as acting coach to Queen Henrietta Maria and her ladies when they put on a pastoral tragicomedy in 1633.

Though not all Puritans or parliamentarians were hostile to the theater, and not all of Charles I's courtiers approved of it, the English civil war created a further association between theater and crown. Parliament closed the theaters at the start of the war in 1642, refusing to reopen them even when hostilities had ended. Performances continued nevertheless: professionals acted illegally in the theater buildings that were still usable, or, like amateurs, legally in private houses and inns. Some also went abroad and acted for English royalists in exile. Since the prohibition applied only to plays, scenes involving popular characters (Hamlet and the gravediggers, Falstaff, Bottom) were adapted and disguised as "drolls"—comic sketches—that could be performed in a mixed program of music, dance, and drama. The 1662 frontispiece to a collection of these drolls (p. lxiv) shows how Falstaff and Mrs. Quickly were probably costumed in this period.

The Restoration and the Eighteenth Century (1660–1776)

At the Restoration of 1660, one of Charles II's first acts was to establish two licensed acting companies, one patronized by him, the other by his brother the Duke of York. Each company was assigned a selection of plays from the prewar period. Shakespeare's were among the first to be revived; indeed, actors were already playing them in London before the new theaters had opened. Although one of the speakers in Dryden's dialogue on drama (*An Essay of Dramatic Poesy*, 1665) says that Beaumont and Fletcher's plays were more popular than Shakespeare's or Jonson's, the evidence indicates that Shakespeare went on being a frequently acted dramatist throughout this period. Since the King's company seems to have received preferential treatment, it is likely that the plays awarded to them—*1 Henry IV*, *The Merry Wives of Windsor*, and *Othello*—were the most popular of Shakespeare's works in 1660.

It was natural that Shakespeare's works would need updating; nearly fifty years after their author's death, their language, grammar, and jokes were already becoming obsolete. Audiences saw themselves as too refined for plays with clowns and devils. Both theater managers (Thomas Killigrew and William Davenant) had been playwrights before the war, and both produced the prewar drama with extensive alterations. *The Taming of the Shrew*, as produced in 1667 by the King's company under Killigrew, was called, improbably, *Sauny the Scot*, after the new comic servant who replaced Grumio; the actor John Lacy wrote the title role for himself, exploiting the anti-Scots feeling that had been exacerbated by the Civil War. "Scenes," or scenery, the norm in the theaters of France and Italy, had already been used in prewar masques, and in the 1630s Davenant had already been planning to open a theater equipped to use it for plays. As manager of the Duke's company, he set about revising old plays to create more possibilities for spectacle. His *The Law Against Lovers* (1662) conflated *Measure for Measure* and *Much Ado About Nothing*, neither of which was well known at the period. The result was an emphasis on the romantic part of both plays, as opposed to their low comedy. He added more music and scenery in his adaptations of *Macbeth* (1664) and *The Tempest* (1667); in later revivals, these two works became almost operatic. The new theaters were rather small, and actors still played at the front of the stage, with the wings and backdrop of the new scenery stretching away behind them. Scene changes could be made quickly by rolling away one sliding backdrop to reveal another one behind it, sometimes with a new set of characters already in place. The same painted wings and backdrop were expected to serve for a number of plays, acting as a kind of shorthand to distinguish indoor from outdoor settings. The idea that each play belonged to its own particular visual world did not gain currency until well into the nineteenth century.

Charles II had insisted, in his patent for the new theaters, that the custom of boy actors—unique to England—must end. Most of the women who became actresses during the early years of the Restoration were, inevitably, untrained. The famous Nell Gwyn, mistress of Charles II, was a star of the King's company. She was considered delightful in contemporary comedies, some of which were written especially for her; however, Pepys always insisted that she was disastrous in serious roles, and there is no record of her playing Shakespeare. The new actresses could exploit their natural gifts, their beauty, and their novelty, but no one wanted to see them in character parts, especially those of elderly women. As a result, roles like the witches in *Macbeth* were taken by men, often the company's low comedians, a practice that continued for centuries. The small number of parts for attractive young women in Shakespeare now became a problem. Davenant was skillful at multiplying them. He expanded the part of Lady Macduff; Miranda, no longer the only woman in *The Tempest*, acquired a naïve younger sister, while Caliban and Ariel were likewise paired off with a female monster and spirit respectively.

Some of these changes also had a moral purpose. Davenant balanced the wickedness of Macbeth and his Lady by developing the virtuous Macduffs as foils to them. He also gave Macbeth a death speech (only one line long) to show that the dying man recognized the vanity of his ambition. Later adaptations were still more concerned with "poetic justice." This term meant simply that art ought to reward virtue and punish vice, not because this is what happens in the real world, but because art's duty is to offer virtuous models whenever possible. John Dryden, who had worked with Davenant on *The Tempest*, later wrote free adaptations of both *Antony and Cleopatra* and *Troilus and Cressida*, in which the lovers, far from being unfaithful, are only sympathetic victims of misunderstanding. His version of *Antony and Cleopatra*, called *All for Love, or, the World Well Lost* (1675–1677), largely replaced its model for much of the next century, and was often played under Shakespeare's title. Though Dryden claimed that he had made Antony's wife Octavia a virtuous foil to Cleopatra, the play's success was due less to its superior morality (indeed, its most popular scene was one in which the two women insult each other) than to its simplification of the structure, which subordinated political history to the love story. Shadwell's *Timon of Athens* (1678) provided a faithful woman as well as a faithful steward, to contrast with the mercenary friends and mistress who desert the hero. Thomas Otway's *Caius Marius* (1679) made the suicides of Romeo and Juliet more acceptable by locating them in a classical world. One of Otway's other innovations—letting the heroine revive in time to converse with the hero before they die—was to outlast the adaptation itself. Nahum Tate's *King Lear* (1681) made the virtuous Cordelia a large and dramatic role, worthy of a star actress. He also added a love interest between her and Edgar, and provided a happy ending in which Lear is restored to his throne. The adaptation remained in the repertory for 150 years, and Samuel Johnson defended it in 1765 on the grounds that,

although the unjust tragic ending might be more true to life, "all reasonable beings naturally love justice." Tate's omission of the Fool, a character associated with old-fashioned theater, was not even noticed.

After 1679, the Popish Plot and uncertainty over the royal succession led to Shakespearean adaptations designed to score political points. In 1680, John Crowne wrote *The Misery of Civil War* (1680), the first of two adaptations based on the *Henry VI* plays, while Tate's *The Sicilian Usurper*, adapted from *Richard II*, fell foul of the censor, even though its deposed ruler was more sympathetic than Shakespeare's. In the following year, Tate reversed the order of scenes in *King Lear*, beginning with Edmund's first soliloquy: a bastard son claiming his right to inherit was bound to be topical in the reign of a king who had no legitimate children and whose next heir was a Roman Catholic brother. The turbulent political climate kept audiences away, and the two companies amalgamated in 1682. Very few plays of any kind survive from the last years of Charles II's reign and the three years of James II's leading to the revolution of 1688. In the reign of William and Mary (James's daughter), *King Lear* was once again so topical that it could not be staged. Mary and her sister Anne looked all too much like Lear's daughters, especially since Tate's version ends with the king's abdication in favor of his daughter and son-in-law.

Colley Cibber's *Richard III* (1699), the most successful of all adaptations, benefited from the fact that a number of Shakespeare's history plays had dropped out of the repertory by the end of the century, thus providing a quarry from which the adapter could borrow. Feeling that he had a free hand, Cibber removed Queen Margaret and, since he intended to play Richard himself, gave him some good lines from other histories, including (from 2 *Henry IV*) the death speech that Shakespeare had neglected to write for his hero. This Richard, literally an actor's dream, was more theatrically popular than Shakespeare's had been, a fact that kept the version alive well into the twentieth century (the Olivier film, which also cut Margaret's role, used two recognizable Cibber lines). Cibber had some difficulties with the licenser just before the first performance because it was feared that his opening scene, showing the deposed Henry VI in the Tower, would remind its audiences of the deposed James II. He made sure to show his loyalty in his next adaptation—*King John*, under the title *Papal Tyranny*, coincided with the threatened invasion, in 1715, of James II's exiled Catholic son. As one of the managers of Drury Lane, and as poet laureate (from 1730), Cibber became a popular target for satire, and he is best remembered for Pope's attacks on him in *The Dunciad* (1743). But his entertaining autobiography, *An Apology for the Life of Colley Cibber, Comedian* (1740), is still the best source of information on the early eighteenth-century theater.

Indeed, without Cibber's book, it would be difficult to say much about Shakespearean acting at the turn of the eighteenth century. Though Thomas Betterton was recognized as the greatest actor of his age from the first years of the Restoration, those, like Samuel Pepys, who saw him at this time, praised him highly but in vague terms. Because of the division of the theatrical repertory, Betterton acquired some major Shakespearean roles, like Othello, only after the unification of the two companies in 1682, when senior actors of the King's company took the opportunity to retire. After this, he had virtually a monopoly, and went on playing a much-acclaimed Hamlet until he was seventy, as well as taking the role of Falstaff in what seems to have been his own adaptation of the *Henry IV* plays. Cibber's description of Betterton's Hamlet reacting to the first sight of his father's ghost became a point of comparison for later Hamlets well into the nineteenth century. It is clear that his effects had to do with "presence" rather than with movement—though, of course, Cibber was describing him in his last years, when he was presumably less active.

The early female performers are still more shadowy figures. Women had appeared on stage as singers, or singing actresses, in "operas" performed in the 1650s, and one of these, perhaps Margaret Hughes, may have been the first to play a Shakespearean role (probably Desdemona). Mary Sanderson, who became Mrs. Betterton, was the first Lady Macbeth. Her successor, Elizabeth Barry, was primarily a tragic actress. She is said to have owed her initial success to careful instruction by her lover, the Earl of Rochester, who recognized the importance of constant repetition and, like a modern director, insisted that she should rehearse in the dress that she was going to wear in performance. The best-loved comic actress of Cibber's youth, Anne Bracegirdle, played several Shakespearean comedy heroines alongside the Congreve roles for which she was famous. The popularity of *The Merry Wives of Windsor* may have been due not only to Betterton's playing of Falstaff but also to its two excellent roles for actresses past their first youth, probably the only women in the company experienced enough to do justice to Shakespearean comedy.

Though the history of Shakespeare editing begins in the early eighteenth century, the plays still belonged essentially to the theater; hence, the publication of acting editions, which allowed audiences to read what they were actually going to see in the theater, usually heavily cut and partially modernized. Even so, the first half of the century saw a steady return to original versions, as one role after another was suddenly revealed to be a superb vehicle for a particular actor. Shylock, for instance, had been a not-very-interesting comic miser in a not-very-interesting romantic comedy, often replaced by George Granville's adaptation, *The Jew of Venice* (1701). When Shakespeare's original was revived in 1741, Charles Macklin astonished his fellow-actors as much as the audience by emphasizing Shylock's terrifying malevolence.

Although later actors would play the character more sympathetically, Macklin made him what he has been ever since: a disturbing character who cannot be assimilated into a comic structure. Something of a theorist on acting, Macklin, in teaching other actors, insisted on clear and intelligent diction. Perhaps for that reason, his Iago was the most convincing of the period.

Richard III, in Cibber's version, was the role in which David Garrick made his London debut in 1741. The actor became famous almost instantly and went on to manage the Drury Lane Theatre from 1747 to 1776. Garrick was a self-proclaimed idolater of Shakespeare whose "Jubilee" at Stratford-upon-Avon in 1769 not only inaugurated the practice of celebrations and festivals but also led contemporaries to regard him as almost equal in importance with his author. Despite his reputation for restoring Shakespeare, Garrick was as much of an adapter as his famous predecessors, turning *The Taming of the Shrew* and the last part of *The Winter's Tale* into short three-act plays and making operas out of *A Midsummer Night's Dream* and *The Tempest*. His *Macbeth* had a death speech, much more dramatic and pathetic than the one-line moral that Davenant had given him. His *Romeo and Juliet* had a pathetic farewell scene based on the one in Otway's *Caius Marius*. In response to French criticisms, he even directed a *Hamlet* in 1771 with the low comedy of the gravediggers omitted. Yet he also revived many plays not seen in their Shakespearean form since the Restoration, showing by his acting what superb roles they contained. He was equally gifted at comedy and tragedy. Two of his most popular roles were Benedick and (Tate's) King Lear. *Julius Caesar* and *Othello,* plays in which Betterton had been particularly successful, were better acted by Garrick's chief rival, Spranger Barry, a tall and handsome actor with a beautiful voice. Garrick, shorter and less romantic in appearance, was famous for his mobile and expressive features that allowed him to delineate the transitions between the "passions." It was this grasp of human psychology that he praised in Shakespeare and that others praised in him. His most significant leading lady, Hannah Pritchard, must have been equally versatile, since she was famous both as Rosalind and as Lady Macbeth. It was, however, characteristic of Garrick that he was able to form an excellent company around himself, including a number of fine actresses and low comedians. Without these conditions, it would have been impossible to revive so many of the comedies.

The Romantic Period (1776–1850)

Between Garrick's retirement in 1776 and the end of the century, the theaters changed to the point where a rapid, subtle style like Garrick's was becoming almost impossible. The Licensing Act of 1737 had limited spoken drama to Drury Lane and Covent Garden, the descendents of the two London theaters licensed in 1660 by Charles II. The late eighteenth century saw the rapid growth of a London population in search of entertainment. The two theaters responded by increasing their audience capacity until, at the end of the century, Covent Garden held over 3,000 spectators, and Drury Lane 3,600. When much of the audience was too far from the stage to see facial expressions or hear the softer tones of an actor's voice, the most successful performers were those who could establish themselves through their volume or through visual effects. Two tall and statuesque actors, John Philip Kemble and his more gifted sister, Sarah Siddons, dominated the theater of this period. Siddons's Lady Macbeth was probably the finest performance of the age: when she said that she could smell blood, at least one contemporary spectator declared that he could smell it too. Her other finest Shakespearean roles were Isabella in *Measure for Measure* and Hermione in *The Winter's Tale*, both of them strong women whose sublime moral grandeur dwarfed everyone else. Kemble's attempt to impose greater discipline and unity on theatrical productions, with more historically "correct" sets and costumes, resulted in what must have been the most genuinely classical theater yet seen in Britain. *Coriolanus*, with Kemble in the title role and Siddons as a heroically obsessed Volumnia, was the triumph of their approach. It was ironic that it should have come in an age dominated by the spirit of revolution and of the complex attitudes that are summed up as Romanticism.

It was to this spirit that Edmund Kean appealed. Those who saw him make his famous London debut as Shylock in 1814, wearing a black wig instead of the traditional red one, would have realized at once that he was going to play, not a tragic villain, but a tragic victim. He had been a singer, dancer, and Harlequin before taking London by storm, and his acting benefited from these other skills. Unlike Kemble, who expressed authority and aristocratic dignity, he excelled as Shakespeare's outsiders and outlaws: the hunchbacked Richard III (still in Cibber's softened version), the Moor Othello, and the melancholy Hamlet. Knowing his gift for pathos, he starred in an adaptation of *3 Henry VI* (where York sobs over his murdered son) and attempted to bring back the original ending of *King Lear* (where Lear grieves over the dead Cordelia), but audiences were not yet ready for either. Those who saw him at his best never forgot his haunting delivery of Richard III's forebodings before Bosworth and Othello's farewell to arms, which provided the kind of appreciative, poetic commentary on Shakespeare that characterized the best contemporary criticism.

Kean's career was short, wrecked by drink and scandal. In 1833, just as he had reached his miserable end, another actor, using the stage name of Keane, made his Covent Garden debut in the role of Othello. Ira Aldridge, a black American, may have hoped to announce himself as Kean's successor, but racial prejudice in England prevented him from being accepted as a leading tragedian. He would, however, play Othello all over Europe, and especially in Russia, in bilingual productions with local casts. Like Kean, he sought out the roles of victims and social outcasts: Aaron in his own adaptation of *Titus Andronicus*, as well as (in white make-up) Macbeth, Shylock, and King Lear; like Kean, he was also capable of singing songs in dialect or even a Russian folksong. The excitement that German and Russian spectators felt at the sight of a black actor playing a black character would become an important part of theatrical experience a century later; at this point, it was a novelty. In the 1860s Aldridge finally acted in major London theaters and might have returned to the United States after the Civil War if he had not died unexpectedly while on tour in Poland.

Meanwhile, both of the unruly London theaters were managed, in turn, by William Macready, who, as his diary makes clear, took seriously his responsibility to a dramatist he worshipped. Still more than Kemble, he behaved like a modern director, with a vision of the production as a whole. His revivals of the history plays showed the possibilities of historical reconstruction. He is best known for restoring the Fool to *King Lear* in 1838, though he gave the role to a young woman to ensure that it would be played for pathos rather than low comic effects that might distract from his own scenes. A number of fine actresses played opposite him: Helen Faucit, young, fragile, refined, who would later write a perceptive if sentimental account of her approach to acting some of Shakespeare's female characters; Fanny Kemble, a member of the famous Kemble family, whose memoirs indicate the struggle involved for women in a star-dominated theater; Charlotte Cushman, a powerful visitor from America who sometimes played male roles. The plays were still heavily cut and showed the influence of earlier adaptations, but by the end of his career, Macready could fairly claim to have restored a good deal of Shakespeare's text and to have made the theater more respectable. The repeal of the Licensing Act in 1843, which allowed smaller theaters to cater to different publics, also encouraged gentrification. Samuel Phelps, who managed the working-class Sadler's Wells Theatre from 1844 to 1869, did even more than Macready had, performing thirty-four of Shakespeare's plays; he even restored the original *Richard III*, though other actors continued to prefer the Cibber version. Charles Kean (son of Edmund), at the Princess's Theatre from 1850 to 1859, carried the historicizing process still further; his "archaeological" productions were likely to be accompanied by notes explaining the reason for the choice of period, costumes, and props.

Still, it was only rarely that anyone had the opportunity to impose a concept of Shakespearean production on an acting company in his own theater. Star actors tended to spend much of their time on tour, both in England and America, performing their favorite roles after perhaps one rehearsal with the resident company. Far from seeking new ways to interpret a play, these actors had to rely on standardized stage business (when Mr. Wopsle plays Hamlet in Dickens's *Great Expectations*, an unsympathetic audience comments loudly on each theatrical cliché as it occurs). They naturally tended to conceive of their characters in isolation and to favor tragedy over comedy, which requires ensemble playing. (Similarly, nineteenth-century critics usually focus on the analysis of individual characters.) A common practice was the pitting of one actor against another in a famous role, arguing over which one was the "true" Hamlet or Lear. In one case, the rivalry developed a nationalistic dimension. Macready's visit to America, in 1849, is notorious for the riot at Astor Place in New York, when soldiers fired on and killed some of the crowd outside the theater. The rioters had been trying to drown out Macready's performance of *Macbeth* out of a mistaken loyalty to the American tragedian, Edwin Forrest. On a visit to Britain, Forrest had hissed Macready for some foppish business with a handkerchief that the actor, as Hamlet, had used to illustrate the phrase "I must be idle." Now his personal hostility became a quarrel about effete English acting versus the manly American tradition. In fact, the distinction was largely meaningless: many well-known American actors had begun their careers in England or Ireland. While some American Shakespeareans might have seen themselves as part of the Forrest tradition, and some (like the touring performers depicted by Mark Twain in *Huckleberry Finn*) were of no tradition at all, most American actors continued to look to Europe for models.

The Victorian Era and the Early Twentieth Century (1850–1912)

The greatest American actor of the next generation, Edwin Booth, was a refined and melancholy figure whose readings of the great Shakespearean roles were psychological and poetic. Booth was the son of Junius Brutus Booth, who had acted in London opposite Edmund Kean, and the brother of John Wilkes Booth, the assassin of Abraham Lincoln. (Ironically, all three members of this acting family had once performed together in the great assassination play, *Julius Caesar*.) Though Booth briefly attempted theater management, he spent much of his time in the exhausting business of touring. He clearly thought deeply about his own roles, and about the moments when other characters interacted with him. His correspondence with the New Variorum Shakespeare

editor, H.H. Furness, is quoted in many notes of that edition—an early example of successful communication between the theater and the scholarly world. Yet when Booth was alternating the two leading roles of *Othello* with Henry Irving in 1881, he sent his servant to take notes at rehearsal for him. Nothing in his experience had prepared him for a theater in which the actor-manager expected everyone to fit into a total artistic conception.

It was Irving, the first actor to be knighted, who dominated English Shakespearean acting in the late Victorian era. His pictorial sense was even stronger than that of the actor-managers who preceded him, and the technical means at his disposal in the Lyceum Theatre, which he began to manage in 1878, were much better. The old system of sliding screens in grooves, flanked by a series of wings, had been replaced by the "box set," which was built like a piece of architecture, creating a complete environment. Electric lighting, introduced in the 1880s, provided new, subtle visual effects. The elaborate and beautiful sets often required interminable scene changes and, sometimes, rearrangement of the plays to accommodate them. Irving's own performances were usually controversial. His Malvolio, like his Shylock, was a tragic figure, while his Iago was so witty and likeable that, playing opposite Booth's Othello, he stole all the sympathy from the hero. His theater offered a beautiful dream for the spectator to share: if it also disturbed the spectator, it was through its revelation of the psychological depths of character, never through its comments on social and political issues. Irving's leading lady, Ellen Terry, was both beautiful and brilliant; in most productions she was allowed to be only the former. Bernard Shaw, longing for her to appear in plays about "grownup" topics, by himself or Henrik Ibsen, resented her imprisonment in Irving's world. For Shaw and other modern thinkers, Shakespeare was becoming synonymous with nostalgia and with the moralistic and idealistic thinking that the new drama regarded as a vice. The early twentieth-century theater was finally affected by these critical attempts to reform it, but two kinds of production coexisted for some time. At His Majesty's Theatre, Herbert Beerbohm Tree, like Irving, offered psychologically based character acting in a beautiful scenic environment, recreating Cleopatra's Egypt and Henry VIII's England; having seen his lavish production of *Macbeth*, one critic commented that "Nature put up a pretty feeble imitation of what several barrels of stones and a few sheets of tin could do in His Majesty's." At the Savoy, on the other hand, Harley Granville Barker, a disciple of Bernard Shaw, developed a decorative visual style that was not tied to a specific historical period.

Meanwhile, a more experimental approach to acting was being developed in Germany. The country's unusual political structure, with small dukedoms and cities sponsoring their own theaters, made it possible for the

Duke of Saxe-Meiningen to sponsor his own company of players, sixty-six in all. His leading actors were unremarkable but, when he took them on tour in the 1880s, audiences were impressed by his handling of large groups. The Duke insisted that those who played major roles in one production should be walk-ons in another, so that crowds could be properly rehearsed instead of being assembled from those gathered around the stage door and drilled by the stage manager immediately before each performance.

Frank Benson, a young Oxford graduate, saw the Saxe-Meiningen company at Drury Lane in 1881, and was inspired to develop his own touring company—though, unlike the Duke, he acted in his own productions and consequently shaped them from a star's point of view. From 1886 on, the Bensonians became regular visitors at Stratford-upon-Avon. Shakespeare's birthplace had been briefly famous in 1769, the year of Garrick's Jubilee, but it was only in 1879, when the first Memorial Theatre was built, that tourists had any reason to visit for more than a few hours. Benson essentially created the first Stratford company, though it used the theater only during a short "Festival" season. Having a regular venue and a devoted audience enabled him to revive unusual works, if often drastically cut. In 1901 he inaugurated the new century with a "Grand Cycle" of Shakespeare's histories—the first English production of the plays as a group.

The desire to return to fuller texts and something like the original conditions of Shakespearean performance was initially associated with Germany and then with outsiders like William Poel, who founded the English Stage Society in 1894. Previously, Poel had given an experimental matinee of the First Quarto *Hamlet* at St. George's Hall in 1881. More surprisingly (though his friendship with Bernard Shaw in part explains it), the popular London actor Johnston Forbes-Robertson played an unusually full text of *Hamlet* in 1897, with characters like Reynaldo and Fortinbras appearing for the first time in centuries. Then Benson's company played an uncut *Hamlet* in 1899 and 1900. Poel, who often worked with amateurs, using all-purpose curtains rather than scenery on what was meant to be an Elizabethan stage, revived works previously considered unperformable, by Shakespeare's contemporaries as well as by Shakespeare. For example, he gave the first important *Troilus and Cressida* to be seen in London since 1734, dressing it in Elizabethan rather than classical costume. It was 1912. He had discovered the play's antiwar potential.

The Twentieth Century

World War I drastically curtailed many Shakespearean projects, including those for a gigantic celebration of the anniversary of his death in 1916, which at one point was intended to include the opening of a National Theatre. Although this theater did not come into existence until nearly 100 years after Irving had first suggested it, other developments were creating the conditions that would make Shakespeare plays, with their large casts, commercially viable.

One was the rise of repertory theaters, which could support a large company and a varied range of plays. The most famous of these was London's Royal Victoria, or "Old Vic," founded in 1914. Under a number of gifted directors (notably Robert Atkins, who had directed all the plays in the 1623 Folio by 1923, Harcourt Williams, and Tyrone Guthrie), it was the home to many legendary productions, including John Gielgud's first *Hamlet* (1929) and Olivier's first *Hamlet* (1937). At the Birmingham Repertory Theatre, Barry Jackson had already directed a modern-dress *Hamlet* in 1925. Modern dress had been common practice until the nineteenth century; it now seemed eccentric, but would by the end of the century become almost the norm. The Memorial Theatre at Stratford, after struggling to find its identity, saw some brilliant productions by Peter Brook in the 1940s and 1950s, including three plays traditionally considered minor: *Love's Labor's Lost* (1946), *Measure for Measure* (1948), and a *Titus Andronicus* (1955), starring Olivier, at which audience members regularly fainted at what was then unusual stage violence: the amputation of the hero's hand and the cutting of the villains' throats. Stratford and the Old Vic were becoming rival Shakespeare companies and in the 1960s each achieved a new status. The Memorial Theatre was renamed the Royal Shakespeare Theatre in 1960, with Peter Hall as director, whereas the Old Vic was designated the National Theatre in 1963. Olivier directed its opening production of *Hamlet*, with Peter O'Toole in the title role, and played a famous Othello in 1964. The National Theatre eventually moved into new premises in an arts complex, with three stages, on the South Bank of the Thames.

In the United States, the most exciting Shakespeare productions also occurred during a period of government subsidy: it was depression-era financing that enabled Orson Welles to direct Shakespeare on radio, and, for the Mercury Theatre, his "voodoo" *Macbeth* (1938) with an all-black cast, his anti-Fascist *Julius Caesar* (1937), and his condensation of the major history plays, *Five Kings*, which, although unsuccessful, later influenced his Falstaff film, *Chimes at Midnight* (1966). The other significant development in North America was the growth of summer Shakespeare festivals at outdoor Elizabethan-style theaters, beginning with the Elizabethan Stage at Ashland, Oregon (founded 1935), and the Guthrie-designed Festival Theatre at Stratford, Ontario (1953). Festival seasons allowed juxtapositions of related plays and the yearly performance of successive plays in a history cycle.

It was the English Stratford-upon-Avon, however, that fully seized on the history plays, performing the *Richard II–Henry V* group in 1951, during the Festival of Britain that celebrated the country's emergence from wartime and postwar rationing. For the rest of the century, the "cycle" of history plays would be recognized as a national epic, to be performed for special occasions. For the new Royal Shakespeare Company, Peter Hall and John Barton produced the *Henry VI–Richard III* group of plays—rewritten, reduced to three plays, and called *The Wars of the Roses*. They revived these, along with the other *Henry* plays, for the Shakespeare quatercentenary in 1964. The histories were produced again in 1975 by Terry Hands, with Alan Howard playing all the kings except Henry IV; in 1982 the *Henry IV* plays opened the company's new London theater at the Barbican under Trevor Nunn; and the company, now under Adrian Noble, marked the arrival of the millennium with a freshly conceived production of the *Richard II–Richard III* sequence. Just as the 1951 production showed the influence of Tillyard's essays on the histories as a unified cycle, the plays of the year 2000, deliberately disparate in style and even venue, were the product of a critical movement that emphasized discontinuity and diversity.

Contemporary Critical Approaches

By now, productions might require as much interpretation as plays. In the last half of the twentieth century, the spread of school and university education had created a substantial population that had studied at least one Shakespeare play and a smaller population, including some theater practitioners, that had read not only the plays but also the criticism. Stratford's John Barton, a former Cambridge don, directed *Twelfth Night* (1969) as if it were by Chekhov, encouraging the audience to imagine the unspoken feelings of the characters—not only Viola (Judi Dench), smiling through heartbreak, but Maria, in her apparently hopeless love for Sir Toby, and Sir Andrew in his even more hopeless love for Olivia. This attention to character, often created out of masses of tiny realistic details, informed some of the theater's most highly praised productions. Barton's *Richard II* (1973) worked very differently, externalizing the play's images in ways that were clearly independent of the characters' awareness: for instance, a glimpse of a melting snowman echoed Richard's wish that he were "a mockery king of snow" and linked the fall and rise of kings to a natural cycle of dissolution and renewal.

Other major critical approaches, easier to categorize, quickly found their way onto the stage. Political readings, often influenced by a Brechtian production style, dominated the 1960s and 1970s. These were usually Marxist and anti-authority: lines in which characters expressed high moral sentiments might be juxtaposed (legitimately) with those in which they showed themselves less noble, or (illegitimately) by setting them in a context that undermined them, as when, in Peter Zadek's *Held Henry* (Hero Henry), Henry V delivers the St. Crispin's Day speech to his bored mistress. Even before its first English publication in 1964, *Shakespeare Our Contemporary*, by the Polish critic Jan Kott, had powerfully influenced theater with his comparison of *Hamlet* and the histories to life under a totalitarian regime, *King Lear* to Theater of the Absurd, and the comedies to a Freudian nightmare. Both Brecht and Kott could be recognized behind Peter Brook's *King Lear* (1962), which, in place of the traditional sympathy with the king (a frighteningly harsh Paul Scofield), emphasized his and his followers' brutality toward Goneril's servants, and ruthlessly cut anything that might be cathartic; the Dover cliff meeting between Lear and Gloucester frankly drew on the stage imagery of Samuel Beckett's *Waiting for Godot*. Brook's *A Midsummer Night's Dream* (1970), which based its erotic treatment of Titania and Bottom on Kott's work, found a purely theatrical language for the critical commonplaces about the play's metatheatricality. Without makeup, under bright light, in a white-walled gymnasium that replaced the traditional moonlit forest, Oberon and Puck sat on trapezes and passed the aphrodisiac "flower," a metal plate, from one spinning metallic wand to another. The fact that this operation could, and occasionally did, go wrong was the point: it reminded the audience that the real magic lay in its own willingness to trust the actors. Even the "Pyramus and Thisbe" actors in the final scene were treated as serious artists, representatives of working-class culture who deserved respect. For many of his later productions, Peter Brook went abroad in search of a multilingual, multiethnic cast, searching for ways of escaping the "easy" assumptions about Shakespeare.

It was in fact race and gender rather than class that dominated Shakespeare production in the last quarter of the century. The concern with race began with the great American theatrical event of the 1940s, Margaret Webster's production of *Othello* with the charismatic Paul Robeson in the title role. After the longest run of any Shakespeare play on Broadway, it was taken on tour all over America in 1945, playing only in desegregated theaters. Although Robeson had already played Othello in London (1930), and would do so again at Stratford-upon-Avon, England, in 1959, his long period of disgrace in the politically polarized United States of the 1950s delayed the movement toward race-based casting as a norm. After initial embarrassment about racist language in Shakespeare, the theater began deliberately to explore its implications, as race became a subject for academic study. The range of *Othello* videos available by the 1990s indicates the play's performance history: besides Orson

Welles's film from 1952, these include the National The-atre production of 1964 starring Laurence Olivier and the BBC one with Antony Hopkins (1981), both with white actors in the title role; Trevor Nunn's Chekhovian version originally staged in 1989; the historic South African pro-duction by Janet Suzman, a political act at a time when apartheid still existed; and Oliver Parker's 1994 version, with Laurence Fishburne (opposite Kenneth Branagh's convincingly ordinary Iago), consciously conveying the concentrated power and sensuality associated with black-ness. Confusion between "color-blind casting" (when the audience is supposed to ignore the race of both actor and character) and "race-based casting" (when the audience is being told something about race through the casting) was deliberately cultivated in Jude Kelly's *Othello* (Wash-ington, D.C., 1997). This production enabled Patrick Stewart to achieve his otherwise unrealizable ambition of playing the title role by surrounding a white Othello with African American and Hispanic actors, yet with the play's racial references unaltered.

Just as some critics of racism felt that *Othello* and *The Merchant of Venice* had become theatrically unacceptable, some feminist responses to Shakespeare argued the same about *The Taming of the Shrew*, in which a female charac-ter is made to acquiesce in her humiliation by a husband who uses patriarchal arguments to justify his behavior. The play had usually been directed to soften its final moral, either by making it clear that the protagonists have fallen in love at first sight or by emphasizing its nature as a play within a play, safely distant from real life. A famous production by Michael Bogdanov (Royal Shake-speare Theatre, 1978) doubled the drunken tinker Sly with Petruchio and showed Kate being brutalized into a dazed submission that horrified even her husband. Obvi-ously, the play in this version was no longer a comedy. A less obvious effect of feminism has been the increasing attention paid to Shakespeare's female characters. They tend now to be on stage more than the text directs, as when Ophelia stands appalled while her father reads Hamlet's love letters to the court or Gertrude enters in time to hear Claudius and Laertes plan to poison Ham-let, so that her decision to drink from the cup is recog-nized as a heroic device to save her son's life. The young Elizabeth of York, who does not appear in the text of *Richard III* although she is important to its plot, has fre-quently been seen and even heard in stage versions, as in the 1995 film by Richard Loncraine. The fact that women are often denied speech at crucial moments can be turned to an advantage, as when John Barton and a number of subsequent directors of *Measure for Measure* in the 1980s made Isabella silently refuse the Duke's proposal, which earlier actors and directors had assumed she would eagerly accept.

Still more important, in a theater in which women are far more likely than men to be underemployed, were devices that increased the number of Shakespearean roles for women. Cross-dressed performances, parallel to the productions focused on race, hovered between gen-der based and gender blind. Deborah Warner's *Richard II* in 1995, with Fiona Shaw as the title character (Nation-al Theatre, London), suggested a troubled and potential-ly erotic relationship between Richard and Bolingbroke without defining it further. In the all-male Cheek-by-Jowl production of *As You Like It* (1995), the audience was never certain whether it was meant to be thinking of Ros-alind (Adrian Lester) as male or female. A similar con-fusion was exploited when Michael Kahn's *King Lear* (Washington, D.C., 1999) cast Cordelia as a deaf-mute, signing her lines, which were then interpreted by the Fool. This decision, which would have been meaningless if the audience had not known that the actress (Monique Holt) really was a deaf-mute, might be seen either as a return to the self-conscious theatricality of the Renais-sance stage or as an example of identity politics.

Shakespeare on Film

Of course, the sense of identity between actor and role is strongest in the cinema, where physical appearance mat-ters more and where audiences are particularly likely to bring with them recollections of an actor's previous roles. Films of Shakespeare plays are as old as film itself. Their transfer to videotape and then laserdisc and DVD, a process that began in the 1970s, has given them a much wider circulation and canonized some performances: Olivier's Richard III, for instance, now has much the same iconic status that Cibber gave to Betterton's Hamlet. Orson Welles's film versions of *Macbeth* (1947) and *Othel-lo* (1952), visually remarkable as they were, have benefit-ed from remastering to make their soundtracks more intelligible. The BBC made-for-TV versions of Shake-speare, 1979–1985, often disappointed both film and Shakespeare enthusiasts, though for different reasons, but have been widely used in schools. Kenneth Branagh's films, including a remarkable four-hour uncut *Hamlet* (1996), have been surprisingly successful in making the plays accessible to a popular audience. His *Henry V* (1989) was unfairly praised for being more "real" than Olivier's; both films were star-centered, with Olivier playing a more controlled king, Branagh a more vulnerable one. Where-as Olivier began his film with a view of an idealized Eliz-abethan London, then of a playhouse viewed from a superior perspective as old-fashioned and in some ways comic, Branagh introduced his Chorus (Derek Jacobi) in a room full of movie cameras, though he later allowed him to move among the actors in the film. As often in films, the moments most remembered were visual: Henry's (Branagh's) grief when, in order to enforce prop-er discipline, he is obliged to order the hanging of Bar-dolph, or the long shot, after the Battle of Agincourt, that shows Henry carrying the dead boy in a procession of English soldiers singing *Non nobis Domine*.

Branagh's youth was an asset in bringing Shakespeare to a young audience. Later filmmakers have aimed at a still younger group. *William Shakespeare's Romeo and Juliet* (directed by Baz Luhrmann, 1996), filled as it was with icons of contemporary youth culture, is perhaps the first of these, though it retains Shakespeare's language, juxtaposing it with contradictory images, so that it can be understood either as a complex visual-verbal experience or as a rather simple visual one. The *Hamlet* directed by Michael Almereyda (2000) represents its young characters as college students obsessed with modern technology: Hamlet (Ethan Hawke) is an amateur filmmaker and Ophelia is a photographer; "To be or not to be" is spoken in a video store against a background of videos labeled "Action." For students of the new field of Shakespeare in Popular Culture, Teenage Shakespeare, with the stories rewritten in contemporary language and settings, is becoming a genre in its own right. *Ten Things I Hate About You* (directed by Gil Junger, 1999) and *O* (directed by Tim Blake Nelson, 2001) retell *The Taming of the Shrew* and *Othello* in American high school settings. *The Children's Midsummer Night's Dream* (directed by Christine Edzard, 2001) has a cast of primary school children.

International Contexts and Contemporary Adaptations

Not only have the plays been adapted for every age group, they have turned out to speak an international language. This had not always been true, though English and French actors had visited each other's countries since the seventeenth century: in 1629 French actresses were booed by English audiences, still accustomed to an all-male stage; one group of English actors was booed in the Paris of 1818, but another visiting company in 1827 inspired French writers and actors to try to understand Shakespeare. English and American audiences saw *Othello* with new eyes when the Italian actor Tommaso Salvini, followed by several other famous Italians, performed on tour in the late nineteenth century. Along with the visit of the Berliner Ensemble to London in 1956, the most important influences in the late twentieth century came from Asian, especially Japanese, theater and from central and eastern Europe. Kurosawa's films, *Throne of Blood* (*Macbeth*, 1957) and *Ran* (*King Lear*, 1986), transpose Shakespearean plots into Japanese culture and images. Successful Russian films have ranged from the visually stunning colors of Yan Fried's *Twelfth Night* and Sergei Yutkevitch's *Othello* (both 1955) to Grigori Kozintsev's black-and-white *Hamlet* (1964) and *King Lear* (1971). The opening up of contacts with central and eastern Europe after 1989 has resulted in visits from theater companies of the former eastern bloc countries. When London audiences in 1990 saw *Hamlet* by the Bulandra Theatre of Romania (directed by Alexander Tocilescu), they discovered that plays often regarded in Britain and America as "conservative" tools of the "establishment" had elsewhere been a powerful vehicle for the expression of political dissent. When first produced in 1985, Tocilescu's *Hamlet* was clearly understood to be equating the rottenness of Elsinore with the world created by Nicolae Ceaucescu, the dictator executed in 1989; Ion Caramitru, the actor who played Hamlet, had been one of the leaders of the revolution. In Czech productions of Shakespeare, similarly, actors and audience had gathered in a deliberate act of misreading directed at the occupying Russians: in *Love's Labor's Lost*, of all plays, the princess's suggestion that the courtiers disguised as Muscovites should "be gone" was the high point of the evening.

Western directors have sometimes attempted to deal with a difficult text by interpreting it as "Other," particularly as Japanese: the samurai warrior culture was the background to Barry Kyle's *The Two Noble Kinsmen* (Swan Theatre, Stratford, 1986) and to David Farr's *Coriolanus* (Royal Shakespeare Theatre, 2002), whereas Ron Daniels's *Timon of Athens* (The Other Place, Stratford, 1980) drew on the concept of a society based on gift-giving. Conversely, Yukio Ninagawa's Japanese Shakespeare productions have combined Japanese costumes with a soundtrack of European music (*Macbeth*) and interpreted *The Tempest* through the story of the famous Japanese exile, Shunkan. Such cross-cultural borrowings have sometimes been denigrated as "cultural tourism," by which critics seem to mean that it is illegitimate to appropriate the merely visual aspects of a culture to which one does not belong.

Similarly, the reconstructed "Shakespeare's Globe" in London, which opened in 1997, was accused of attempting to appropriate the emotions of another historical period. Perhaps because the opening production was *Henry V*, the "groundlings" who stood in the yard for only £5 apiece seemed to be modeling themselves on their counterparts in the Globe sequence of Olivier's film, who boo when they hear that Falstaff has been banished. Their willingness to boo the French (and, in the next season, Shylock) at first shocked the critics, and it was suggested that this theater might be suited only to comedies and histories demanding a presentational style, but productions of *Hamlet* (2000) and *King Lear* (2001) showed that it was possible to control audience response to the tragedies. Mark Rylance's *Hamlet* skillfully played his line about groundlings "capable of nothing but inexplicable dumbshow," so that he could respond to their laughter by adding *"and* noise." Whether or not the theater can really tell anyone anything about Elizabethan stage conventions and audience response, it has given considerable pleasure. Other Globes, more and less historically based, now can be found in several countries (the United States, Japan, Poland, and the Czech Republic, among others), while the open stage of Stratford, Canada, remains one of the most successful modifications of the Elizabethan model. In a reversal of the search for authenticity, the Shakespeare Theatre in Washington, D.C., has abandoned its home in the reconstructed Fortune Theatre at the Folger Shakespeare Library for a purpose-built modern auditorium. In fact, the two kinds of theater can coexist. The well-established Shakespeare festivals of Stratford, Ontario; Ashland, Oregon; and Santa Cruz, California, have added well-equipped indoor theaters to their outdoor acting spaces, and an indoor auditorium is projected as an addition to Shakespeare's Globe in London. A reconstruction of the Blackfriars Playhouse opened in Staunton, Virginia, in 2001.

Although it has been impossible to discuss the theatrical fortunes of every Shakespeare play, it may be interesting to end by reflecting how greatly these have fluctuated. If some plays, like *Hamlet* and *Macbeth*, have always been popular, the history of others is more checkered. Some of the comedies most popular today, such as *As You Like It* and *Twelfth Night*, were regarded as insipid in the eighteenth century, redeemed only by their scenes of low comedy and occasional sententious speeches. *The Merry Wives of Windsor* was the most popular comedy during the Restoration; *King John* and *Henry VIII* were more popular in the nineteenth century than *Richard II* or *2 Henry IV*. *Othello* was acted without the "willow scene" (4.3) for most of the eighteenth and nineteenth centuries, and *Troilus and Cressida* and *Titus Andronicus* were performed, if at all, only in heavily adapted versions. It is arguable that the attitude to Shakespeare that Bernard Shaw ridiculed as "Bardolatry" reached its height, not in the Victorian age, but at the end of the twentieth century, a time when any Shakespeare play, however minor, was likely to find a director and an audience. One reason might be that the subsidized theaters had been giving fewer controversial productions since 1980, emphasizing instead what the plays have in common with musical comedies and films. An important American contribution to Shakespeare in performance has taken the form of musicals like *The Boys from Syracuse* (1938), *Kiss Me Kate* (1948), and *West Side Story* (1957), based respectively on *The Comedy of Errors*, *The Taming of the Shrew*, and *Romeo and Juliet*; now, many productions of the comedies followed the Restoration practice of filling them with popular music. What was new was not the practice of adaptation but the attitude toward it. In the mid century, the plays were taken to be fixed quantities: the job of the theater director, as of the critic, was to uncover the "real" work, whether through more authentic staging, a more accurate text, or a better understanding of its meaning. By the end of the millennium, when some theorists were insisting that the text itself was unknowable, it is not surprising to find a much greater tolerance for re-creations and explorations of the plays in other forms.

THE ROYAL GENEALOGY OF ENGLAND, 1154–1625

THE PLANTAGENET KINGS

THE LANCASTRIAN KINGS

In these diagrams, reigning dates are given in parentheses; other dates indicate life span. Abbreviations: P., Prince, D., Duke, E., Earl; b., born, d., died, m., married, r., reigned. English monarchs are printed in boldface type. The spatial arrangement of names in a family indicates order of birth.

In 1 Henry IV, Shakespeare confuses the Edmund Mortimer who married Glendower's daughter and died in 1409 with his nephew Edmund, fifth Earl of March, who asserted a claim to the English throne (see "The Yorkist Kings"). Shakespeare also refers to Henry Percy's (Hotspur's) wife as "Kate," though historically she was named Elizabeth.

Catherine Swynford, third wife of John of Gaunt (see "The Tudor Kings"), bore him children before their eventual marriage. These Beauforts, although later legitimized, were specifically barred from any claim to the English throne.

THE YORKIST KINGS

THE TUDOR KINGS

Maps.

A map of London (below) of Shakespeare's time shows the prominent landmarks, as well as the theaters and other places where plays were performed.
     A map of England and western France (opposite) gives the locations for the scenes of Shakespeare's history plays.

ENGLAND AND WESTERN FRANCE

IRELAND

Dublin

Isle of Man

IRISH SEA

Carnarvon   Conway

Chester

NORTH SEA

Berwick

Carlisle

Durham

Lancaster

York
Towton
Pomfret
Doncaster
Wakefield

Ravenspur
Humber

Derby   Lincoln

0   50   100   150
miles

ATLANTIC

OCEAN

Milford Haven
Pembroke

Shrewsbury

Severn

Hereford
Monmouth

Bosworth
Worcester   Nottingham   Leicester
Coventry
Warwick
Tewkesbury
Gloucester
Berkeley
Bristol

The Wash

Northampton
Bedford

Ely   Norwich
Cambridge

Plymouth

Exeter

Salisbury

Oxford

St. Albans
Barnet

Bury St. Edmunds
Ipswich

Thames

Weymouth   Winchester
Southampton
Isle of
Wight

Guildford

LONDON

Rochester
Lewes   Canterbury
Dover

ENGLISH   CHANNEL

Brest

Cherbourg

Boulogne   Calais
Flushing
Guines   Dunkirk
Ghent
Antwerp

St.-Lô

Fécamp
Harfleur
Caen

Dieppe

Agincourt
Crécy
Abbeville
Lille

Brussels

BRITTANY

NORMANDY

Seine

Rouen

Amiens

Vannes   Rennes

MAINE

Alençon

Évreux
Pontoise

Beauvais

Compiègne
Aisne

Nantes

Loire

Le Mans

ILE DE FRANCE

PARIS

Angiers

ANJOU

Saumur

Chartres
Meaux

Reims

BAY   OF

POITOU

Tours

BERRY

Orleans

Seine

CHAMPAGNE

La Rochelle

Poitiers

Vienne

Troyes

BISCAY

Charente

Cognac

BOURBON

Toul

Angoulême

Limoges

Nevers

BURGUNDY

Bordeaux

Garonne

LIMOUSIN

Loire

Dijon

AQUITAINE

Perigueux

Bayonne
GASCONY

R.J.B.

Bibliography

Abbreviations Used

English Literary History	*ELH*
Publications of the Modern	
Language Association of America	*PMLA*
Shakespeare Quarterly	*SQ*
Shakespeare Studies	*ShakS*
Shakespeare Survey	*ShS*

Works of Reference

Abbott, E. A. *A Shakespearian Grammar.* New ed., London, 1870.

Allen, Michael J. B., and Kenneth Muir, eds. *Shakespeare's Plays in Quarto.* Berkeley, 1981.

Bentley, G. E. *The Jacobean and Caroline Stage.* 7 vols. Oxford, 1941–1968.

Bergeron, David M. *Shakespeare: A Study and Research Guide.* New York, 1975; 2nd ed., rev. David Bergeron and Geraldo de Sousa. Lawrence, Kans., 1987.

Bullough, Geoffrey, ed. *Narrative and Dramatic Sources of Shakespeare.* 8 vols. London, 1957–1975.

Chambers, E.K. *The Elizabethan Stage.* 4 vols. Oxford, 1923; rev., 1945.

———. *The Mediaeval Stage.* 2 vols. Oxford, 1903.

———. *William Shakespeare: A Study of Facts and Problems.* 2 vols. Oxford, 1930.

Dent, R. W. *Shakespeare's Proverbial Language: An Index.* Berkeley, 1981.

Garland Shakespeare Bibliographies, gen. ed. William Godshalk. Published in separate volumes for various plays, at varying dates. Garland: New York.

Greg, W. W. *A Bibliography of the English Printed Drama to the Restoration.* 4 vols. London, 1939–1959.

———, ed. *Shakespeare Quarto Facsimiles.* London, 1939–. (An incomplete set; Greg's work has been supplemented by Charlton Hinman.)

Harbage, Alfred. *Annals of English Drama, 975–1700.* Rev. S. Schoenbaum.

Philadelphia, 1964; 3rd ed., Sylvia Stoler Wagonheim, 1989.

Hinman, Charlton, ed. *The Norton Facsimile: The First Folio of Shakespeare.* New York, 1968.

Hosley, Richard, ed. *Shakespeare's Holinshed.* New York, 1968.

Kökeritz, Helge. *Shakespeare's Names.* New Haven, 1959.

———. *Shakespeare's Pronunciation.* New Haven, 1953.

Long, John. *Shakespeare's Use of Music: Comedies.* Gainesville, Fla., 1955. *Final Comedies,* 1961; *Histories and Tragedies,* 1971.

McDonald, Russ. *The Bedford Companion to Shakespeare: An Introduction with Documents.* Boston, 1996; 2nd ed., 2001.

McManaway, James G., and Jeanne Addison Roberts, compilers. *A Selective Bibliography of Shakespeare.* Charlottesville, Va., 1975.

Muir, Kenneth. *Shakespeare's Sources.* 2 vols. London, 1957.

———, and S. Schoenbaum, eds. *A New Companion to Shakespeare Studies.* London and New York, 1971.

Munro, John, ed. *The Shakespeare Allusion Book.* 2 vols. London and New York, 1909; reissued 1932.

Naylor, Edward W. *Shakespeare and Music.* New ed., London, 1931.

Noble, Richmond. *Shakespeare's Biblical Knowledge.* London, 1935.

———. *Shakespeare's Use of Song.* London, 1923.

Onions, C. T. *A Shakespeare Glossary.* Rev. and enlgd. R. D. Eagleson. Oxford, 1986.

Pegasus Shakespeare Bibliographies. Annotated bibliographies of Shakespeare studies in a 12-volume series, gen. ed. Richard L. Nochimson, including *Love's Labor's Lost, A Midsummer Night's Dream,* and *The Merchant of Venice* (Clifford Chalmers Huffman), *Richard II, Henry IV, I and II,* and *Henry V* (Joseph Candido), *Hamlet* (Michael E. Mooney), *The Rape of Lucrece, Titus Andronicus, Julius Caesar,*

Antony and Cleopatra, and *Coriolanus* (Clifford Chalmers Huffman and John W. Velz), *King Lear* and *Macbeth* (Rebecca W. Bushnell), and *Shakespeare and the Renaissance Stage to 1616* and *Shakespearean Stage History 1616 to 1998* (Hugh Macrae Richmond). Binghamton, N.Y. (1995) and Asheville, N.C., 1996—.

Publications of the Modern Language Association of America (PMLA). Annual Bibliography.

Rothwell, Kenneth S., and Annabelle Henkin Melzer. *Shakespeare on Screen: An International Filmography and Videography.* New York and London, 1990.

Schmidt, Alexander. *Shakespeare-Lexicon.* 5th ed. Berlin, 1962.

Seager, H. W. *Natural History in Shakespeare's Time.* London, 1896.

Seng, Peter J. *The Vocal Songs in the Plays of Shakespeare.* Cambridge, Mass., 1967.

Shakespeare Bulletin.

Shakespeare-Jahrbuch.

Shakespeare Newsletter.

Shakespeare Quarterly. Annual Bibliography.

Shakespeare Studies.

Shakespeare Survey.

Spencer, T. J. B., ed. *Shakespeare's Plutarch.* Harmondsworth, Eng., 1964.

Spevack, Marvin. *The Harvard Concordance to Shakespeare.* Cambridge, Mass., 1973.

Sternfeld, Frederick W. *Music in Shakespearean Tragedy.* London, 1963, 1967.

Thomson, J. A. K. *Shakespeare and the Classics.* London, 1952.

Wells, Stanley, ed. *Shakespeare: Select Bibliographical Guides.* London, 1973.

———, ed. *The Cambridge Companion to Shakespeare Studies.* Cambridge, Eng., 1986.

Life in Shakespeare's England

Allen, Don Cameron. *The Star-Crossed Renaissance.* Durham, N.C., 1941.

Baker, Herschel. *The Image of Man: A Study of the Idea of Human Dignity in Classical Antiquity, the Middle Ages, and the Renaissance.* Cambridge, Mass., 1961. (First published in 1947 as *The Dignity of Man.*)

———. *The Wars of Truth: Studies in the Decay of Christian Humanism in the Earlier Seventeenth Century.* Cambridge, Mass., 1952.

Bakhtin, Mikhail M. *Rabelais and His World,* trans. H. Iswolsky. Cambridge, Mass., 1968.

Barkan, Leonard, *Nature's Work of Art: The Human Body as Image of the World.* New Haven, 1975.

———. *The Gods Made Flesh: Metamorphosis and the Pursuit of Paganism.* New Haven, 1986.

Barroll, J. Leeds. *Politics, Plague, and Shakespeare's Theater: The Stuart Years.* Ithaca, N.Y., 1991.

Bindoff, S. T., et al., eds. *Elizabethan Government and Society.* Essays presented to Sir John Neale. London, 1961.

Bush, Douglas. *The Renaissance and English Humanism.* Toronto, 1939.

Buxton, John. *Elizabethan Taste.* London, 1963.

Byrne, Muriel St. Clare. *Elizabethan Life in Town and Country.* 8th ed. London, 1970.

Camden, Carroll. *The Elizabethan Woman.* Houston, 1952.

Caspari, Fritz. *Humanism and the Social Order in Tudor England.* Chicago, 1954.

Cassirer, Ernst. *The Platonic Renaissance in England,* trans. J. E. Pettegrove. Austin, Tex., 1953.

De Grazia, Margreta, Maureen Quilligan, and Peter Stallybrass, eds. *Subject and Object in Renaissance Culture.* Cambridge, Eng., 1996.

Einstein, Lewis. *Tudor Ideals.* New York, 1921.

Elizabeth I. *Collected Works,* eds. Leah S. Marcus, Janel Mueller, and Mary Beth Rose. Chicago, 2000.

Elton, G. R. *The Tudor Revolution in Government.* Cambridge, Eng., 1959.

Fumerton, Patricia, and Simon Hunt, eds. *Renaissance Culture and the Everyday.* Philadelphia, 1999.

Gallagher, Lowell. *Medusa's Gaze: Casuistry and Conscience in the Renaissance.* Stanford, 1991.

Harrison, G. B. *An Elizabethan Journal.* London, 1928; supplements.

———. *A Jacobean Journal . . . 1603–1606.* London, 1941.

———. *A Second Jacobean Journal . . . 1607 to 1610.* Ann Arbor, Mich., 1958.

Haydn, Hiram. *The Counter-Renaissance.* New York, 1950.

Helgerson, Richard. *Forms of Nationhood: The Elizbethan Writing of England.* Chicago, 1992.

Heninger, S. K., Jr. *A Handbook of Renaissance Meteorology.* Durham, N.C., 1960.

Hirst, Derek. *Authority and Conflict: England, 1603–1658.* Cambridge, Mass., 1986.

Huizinga, Johan. *The Waning of the Middle Ages.* London, 1924; Baltimore, 1955.

Hurstfield, Joel, *Elizabeth I and the Unity of England.* London, 1960.

Jones, Ann Rosalind, and Peter Stallybrass. *Renaissance Clothing and the Materials of Memory.* Cambridge, Eng., 2000.

Jordan, Constance. *Renaissance Feminism: Literary Texts and Political Models.* Ithaca, N.Y., 1990.

Judges, A. V., ed. *The Elizabethan Underworld.* London and New York, 1930. Rpt., London, 1965.

Kewes, Paulina, ed. *Plagiarism in Early Modern England.* Basingstoke, Hampshire, Eng., 2003.

Knights, L. C. *Drama and Society in the Age of Jonson.* London, 1937.

Kocher, Paul. *Science and Religion in Elizabethan England.* San Marino, Calif., 1953.

Lee, Morris. *Great Britain's Solomon: James VI and I in His Three Kingdoms.* Urbana, Ill., 1990.

Lovejoy, A. O. *The Great Chain of Being.* Cambridge, Mass., 1936.

MacCaffrey, Wallace T. *The Shaping of the Elizabethan Regime.* Princeton, 1968.

Marotti, Arthur F., ed. *Catholicism and Anti-Catholicism in Early Modern English Texts.* Basingstoke, Hampshire, Eng., 1999.

Matar, Nabil. *Turks, Moors, and Englishmen in the Age of Discovery.* New York, 1999.

Mattingly, Garrett. *The Armada.* Boston, 1959.

McEachern, Claire, and Debora Shuger, eds. *Religion and Culture in Renaissance England.* Cambridge, Eng., 1997.

McElwee, W. *The Wisest Fool in Christendom.* [About James VI and I.] New York, 1958.

McPeek, James A. S. *The Black Book of Knaves and Unthrifts in Shakespeare and Other Renaissance Authors.* Storrs, Conn., 1969.

Neale, John E. *Elizabeth I and Her Parliaments.* 2 vols. London and New York, 1953–1958.

———. *The Elizabethan House of Commons.* London, 1949.

———. *Queen Elizabeth I.* London, 1934; New York, 1957.

Nichols, John, ed. *The Progresses and Public Processions of Queen Elizabeth.* 3 vols. London, 1823.

Patterson, Annabel M. *Reading Holinshed's Chronicles.* Chicago, 1994.

Peck, Linda Levy. *Court Patronage and Corruption in Early Stuart England.* Boston, 1990.

Penrose, Boies. *Travel and Discovery in the Renaissance, 1420–1620.* Cambridge, Mass., 1955.

Quinones, Ricardo J. *The Renaissance Discovery of Time.* Cambridge, Mass., 1972.

Rowse, A. L. *The England of Elizabeth: The Structure of Society.* London, 1951.

Stallybrass, Peter, and Allon White. *The Politics and Poetics of Transgression.* Ithaca, N.Y., and London, 1986.

Stone, Lawrence. *The Crisis of the Aristocracy,* 1558–1641. Oxford, 1965.

———. *The Family, Sex and Marriage in England, 1500–1800.* London, 1977.

Stow, John. *Survey of London,* ed. C. L. Kingsford. Oxford, 1971.

Targoff, Ramie. *Common Prayer: The Language of Public Devotion in Early Modern England.* Chicago, 2001.

Tawney, R. H. *Religion and the Rise of Capitalism.* New York, 1926, 1962.

Tillyard, E. M. W. *The Elizabethan World Picture.* London, 1943, 1967.

Underdown, David. *Revel, Riot, and Rebellion: Popular Politics and Culture in England, 1603–1660.* Oxford, 1985.

Whigham, Frank. *Ambition and Privilege: The Social Tropes of Elizabethan Courtesy Theory.* Berkeley, 1984.

Willson, David Harris. *King James VI & I.* New York, 1956.

Wilson, F. P. *Elizabethan and Jacobean.* Oxford, 1945.

Wilson, J. Dover, ed. *Life in Shakespeare's England.* Cambridge, Eng., 1911; 2nd ed., 1926.

Woodbridge, Linda. *Women and the English Renaissance.* Urbana, Ill., 1984.

Wright, Louis B. *Middle-Class Culture in Elizabethan England.* Chapel Hill, N.C., 1935.

Wrightson, Keith. *English Society, 1580–1680.* New Brunswick, N.J., 1982.

Zeeveld, W. Gordon. *Foundations of Tudor Policy.* Cambridge, Mass., 1948.

Shakespeare's Predecessors and Contemporaries

See also, under *Works of Reference,* Bentley, Chambers, Greg, and Harbage; under *London Theaters and Dramatic Companies,* McMillin and MacLean; under *Shakespeare Criticism Since 1980,* Dollimore, Garber (*Cannibals*), Goldberg, Greenblatt, Jardine, Loomba, Mullaney, Newman, and Skura; under *The Histories,* Ribner; and under *The Tragedies,* Bushnell.

Altman, Joel B. *The Tudor Play of Mind: Rhetorical Inquiry and the Development of Elizabethan Drama.* Berkeley, 1978.

Bamford, Karen. *Sexual Violence on the Jacobean Stage.* New York, 2000.

Barber, C. L. *Creating Elizabethan Tragedy: The Theater of Kyd and Marlowe.* Chicago, 1988.

Bartels, Emily C. *Spectacles of Strangeness: Imperialism, Alienation, and Marlowe.* Philadelphia, 1993.

Bednarz, James P. *Shakespeare and the Poets' War.* New York, 2001.

Belsey, Catherine. *The Subject of Tragedy: Identity and Difference in Renaissance Drama.* London, 1985.

Berry, Philippa. *Of Chastity and Power: Elizabethan Literature and the Unmarried Queen.* London and New York, 1989.

Bevington, David. *From "Mankind" to Marlowe: Growth of Structure in the Popular Drama of Tudor England.* Cambridge, Mass., 1962.

———. *Tudor Drama and Politics.* Cambridge, Mass., 1968.

———, and Peter Holbrook, eds. *The Politics of the Stuart Court Masque.* Cambridge, Eng., 1991.

Bowers, Fredson T. *Elizabethan Revenge Tragedy, 1587–1642.* Princeton, 1940.

Braden, Gordon. *Renaissance Tragedy and the Senecan Tradition.* New Haven, 1985.

Braunmuller, A. R., and Michael Hattaway, eds. *The Cambridge Companion to English Renaissance Drama.* Cambridge, Eng., 1990.

Bristol, Michael D. *Carnival and Theater: Plebeian Culture and the Structure of Authority in Renaissance England.* London, 1985.

Brooke, C. F. Tucker, ed. *The Shakespeare Apocrypha.* Oxford, 1908.

Brooks, Douglas A. *From Playhouse to Printing House: Drama and Authorship in Early Modern England.* Cambridge, Eng., 2000.

Bruster, Douglas. *Drama and the Market in the Age of Shakespeare.* Cambridge, Eng., 1992.

Burt, Richard. *Licensed by Authority: Ben Jonson and the Discourses of Censorship.* Ithaca, N.Y., 1993.

Bushnell, Rebecca W. *Tragedies of Tyrants: Political Thought and Theater in the English Renaissance.* Ithaca, N.Y., 1990.

Butterworth, Philip. *Theatre of Fire: Special Effects in Early English and Scottish Theatre.* London, 1998.

Caputi, Anthony. *John Marston, Satirist.* Ithaca, N.Y., 1961.

Cohen, Walter. *Drama of a Nation: Public Theater in Renaissance England and Spain.* Ithaca, N.Y., 1985.

Comensoli, Viviana, and Anna Russell, eds. *Enacting Gender on the English Renaissance Stage.* Urbana, Ill., 1999.

Cox, John D., and David Scott Kastan, eds. *A New History of Early English Drama.* New York, 1997.

Craik, T. W. *The Tudor Interlude.* Leicester, 1958, 1962.

Dawson, Anthony B., and Paul Yachnin. *The Culture of Playgoing in Shakespeare's England: A Collaborative Debate.* Cambridge, Eng., 2001.

Deats, Sara Munson. *Sex, Gender, and Desire in the Plays of Christopher Marlowe.* Newark, Del., 1997.

Dessen, Alan C. *Elizabethan Drama and the Viewer's Eye.* Chapel Hill, N.C., 1977.

Diehl, Huston. *Staging Reform, Reforming the Stage: Protestantism and Popular Theater in Early Modern England.* Ithaca, N.Y., 1997.

Dillon, Janette. *Theatre, Court and City, 1595–1610: Drama and Social Space in London.* Cambridge, Eng., 2000.

DiGangi, Mario. *The Homoerotics of Early Modern Drama.* Cambridge, Eng., 1997.

Dolan, Frances E. *Dangerous Familiars: Representations of Domestic Crime in England, 1550–1700.* Ithaca, N.Y., 1994.

Doran, Madeleine. *Endeavors of Art: A Study of Form in Elizabethan Drama.* Madison, Wis., 1954, 1972.

Farley-Hills, David. *Shakespeare and the Rival Playwrights, 1600–1606.* London, 1990.

Findlay, Alison. *A Feminist Perspective on Renaissance Drama.* Oxford, 1999.

———. *Illegitimate Power: Bastards in Renaissance Drama.* Manchester, Eng., 1994.

Finkelpearl, Philip. *John Marston of the Middle Temple.* Cambridge, Mass., 1969.

Freer, Coburn. *The Poetics of Jacobean Drama.* Baltimore, 1981.

Gardiner, H. C. *Mysteries' End.* New Haven, 1946.

Gibbons, Brian. *Jacobean City Comedy.* London, 1968.

Hall, Kim F. *Things of Darkness: Economies of Race and Gender in Early Modern England.* Ithaca, N.Y., 1995.

Hardison, O. B., Jr. *Christian Rite and Christian Drama in the Middle Ages.* Baltimore, 1965.

Hassel, R. Chris. *Renaissance Drama and the English Church Year.* Lincoln, Neb., 1979.

Hattaway, Michael. *Elizabethan Popular Theatre: Plays in Performance.* London, 1982.

Hawkins, Harriett. *Likenesses of Truth in Elizabethan and Restoration Drama.* Oxford, 1972.

Helgerson, Richard. *Adulterous Alliances: Home, State, and History in Early Modern European Drama and Painting.* Chicago, 2000.

Hendricks, Margo, and Patricia Parker, eds. *Women, "Race," and Writing in the Early Modern Period.* London and New York, 1994.

Holbrook, Peter. *Literature and Degree in Renaissance England: Nashe, Bourgeois Tragedy, Shakespeare.* Newark, Del., 1994.

Howard, Jean. *The Stage and Social Struggle in Early Modern England.* London and New York, 1994.

Hunter, G. K. *John Lyly: The Humanist as Courtier.* Cambridge, Mass., 1962.

Kastan, David Scott, and Peter Stallybrass, eds. *Staging the Renaissance: Reinterpretations of Elizabethan and Jacobean Drama.* New York and London, 1991.

Kernan, Alvin. *The Cankered Muse: Satire of the English Renaissance.* New Haven, 1959.

Kiefer, Frederick. *Writing on the Renaissance Stage: Written Words, Printed Pages, Metaphoric Books.* Newark, Del., 1996.

Kirsch, Arthur C. *Jacobean Dramatic Perspectives.* Charlottesville, Va., 1972.

Kolve, V. A. *The Play Called Corpus Christi.* Palo Alto and London, 1966.

Leggatt, Alexander. *Citizen Comedy in the Age of Shakespeare.* Toronto, 1973.

———. *Jacobean Public Theatre.* London, 1992.

Leishman, J. B., ed. *The Three Parnassus Plays (1598–1601).* London, 1949.

Levin, Harry. *The Overreacher: A Study of Christopher Marlowe.* Cambridge, Mass., 1952, 1964.

Levin, Richard. *The Multiple Plot in English Renaissance Drama.* Chicago, 1971.

Margeson, J. M. R. *The Origins of English Tragedy.* Oxford, 1967.

Marrapodi, Michele, ed., with A. J. Hoenselaars. *The Italian World of English Renaissance Drama: Cultural Exchange and Intertextuality.* Newark, Del., 1998.

Maus, Katharine Eisaman. *Inwardness and Theater in the English Renaissance Drama.* Chicago, 1995.

McAlindon, T. *English Renaissance Tragedy.* London, 1986.

McLuskie, Kathleen. *Renaissance Dramatists.* (Feminist Readings.) Atlantic Highlands, N.J., 1989.

Orgel, Stephen. *The Illusion of Power: Political Theater in the English Renaissance.* Berkeley, 1975.

———. *Impersonations: The Performance of Gender in Shakespeare's England.* Cambridge, Eng., 1996.

Orgel, Stephen, and Roy Strong. *Inigo Jones: The Theatre of the Stuart Court.* 2 vols. London and Berkeley, 1973.

Ornstein, Robert. *The Moral Vision of Jacobean Tragedy.* Madison, Wis., 1960.

Rabkin, Norman, ed: *Reinterpretations of Elizabethan Drama.* New York, 1969.

Rasmussen, Mark David, ed. *Renaissance Literature and Its Formal Engagements.* Basingstoke, Hampshire, 2002.

Rose, Mary Beth. *The Expense of Spirit: Love and Sexuality in English Renaissance Drama.* Ithaca, N.Y., 1988.

———. *Gender and Heroism in Early Modern English Literature.* Chicago, 2002.

———. ed. *Renaissance Drama as Cultural History.* Evanston, Ill., 1990.

Sanders, Wilbur. *The Dramatist and the Received Idea: Studies in the Plays of Marlowe and Shakespeare.* Cambridge, Eng., 1968.

Shannon, Laurie. *Sovereign Amity: Figures of Friendship in Shakespearean Contexts.* Chicago, 2002.

Shapiro, James. *Rival Playwrights: Marlowe, Jonson, Shakespeare.* New York, 1991.

Smith, Bruce R. *The Acoustic World of Early Modern England.* Chicago, 1999.

Smith, David L., Richard Strier, and David Bevington, eds. *The Theatrical City: Culture, Theatre and Politics in London, 1567–1649.* Cambridge, Eng., 1995.

Southern, Richard. *The Medieval Theatre in the Round.* London, 1957.

Spivack, Bernard. *Shakespeare and the Allegory of Evil.* New York, 1958.

Traub, Valerie, M. Lindsay Kaplan, and Dympna C. Callaghan, eds. *Feminist Readings of Early Modern Culture: Emerging Subjects.* Cambridge, Eng., 1996.

Vickers, Brian. *"Counterfeiting" Shakespeare: Evidence, Authorship, and John Ford's "Funerall Elegye."* Cambridge, Eng., 2002.

Waith, Eugene M. *The Herculean Hero in Marlowe, Chapman, Shakespeare, and Dryden.* New York, 1962.

Whigham, Frank. *Seizures of the Will in Early Modern English Drama.* Cambridge, Eng., 1996.

White, Paul Whitfield. *Marlowe, History, and Sexuality: New Critical Essays on Christopher Marlowe.* New York, 1998.

———. *Theatre and Reformation: Protestantism, Patronage and Playing in Tudor England.* Cambridge, Eng., 1993.

Wickham, Glynne. *Early English Stages, 1300 to 1660.* 3 vols. London, 1959–1972.

Wilson, F. P. *Marlowe and the Early Shakespeare.* Oxford, 1953.

Woodbridge, Linda. *Women and the English Renaissance: Literature and the Nature of Womankind, 1540–1620.* Urbana, Ill., 1984.

Woolf, Rosemary. *The English Mystery Plays.* Berkeley and Los Angeles, 1972.

Yachnin, Paul. *Stage-Wrights: Shakespeare, Jonson, Middleton, and the Making of Theatrical Value*. Philadelphia, 1997.

Zimmerman, Susan, ed. *Erotic Politics: Desire on the Renaissance Stage*. London and New York, 1992.

London Theaters and Dramatic Companies

See also, under *Works of Reference*, Bentley, and Chambers (*Elizabethan Stage*).

Astington, John H., ed. *The Development of Shakespeare's Theater*. New York, 1992.

Beckerman, Bernard. *Shakespeare at the Globe, 1599–1609*. New York, 1962, 1967.

Bentley, Gerald Eades. *The Profession of Dramatist in Shakespeare's Time, 1590–1642*. Princeton, 1971.

———. *The Profession of Player in Shakespeare's Time, 1590–1642*. Princeton, 1984.

Berry, Herbert. *Shakespeare's Playhouses*. New York, 1987.

Bradley, David. *From Text to Performance in the Elizabethan Theatre: Preparing the Play for the Stage*. Cambridge, Eng., 1992.

Clare, Janet. *"Art Made Tongue-Tied by Authority": Elizabethan and Jacobean Dramatic Censorship*. Manchester, Eng., 1990.

Cook, Ann Jennalie. *The Privileged Playgoers of Shakespeare's London, 1576–1642*. Princeton, 1981.

Dutton, Richard. *Mastering the Revels: The Regulation and Censorship of English Renaissance Drama*. Iowa City, 1991.

Feuillerat, Albert, ed. *Documents Relating to the Office of the Revels in the Time of Queen Elizabeth*. Louvain (Louven), Belgium, 1908.

Foakes, R. A., ed. *The Henslowe Papers: The Diary, Theatre Papers, and Bear Garden Papers. In full and in facsimile*. 3 vols. in 2. London, 1976.

Foakes, R. A., and R. T. Rickert, eds. *Henslowe's Diary*. London, 1961.

Gair, W. Reavley. *The Children of Paul's*. Cambridge, Eng., 1982.

Greg, W. W., ed. *Dramatic Documents from the Elizabethan Playhouses: Stage Plots; Actors' Parts; Prompt Books*. 2 vols. Oxford, 1931.

Gurr, Andrew. *Playgoing in Shakespeare's London*. Cambridge, Eng., 1987; 2nd ed., 1996.

———. *The Shakespearian Playing Companies*. Oxford, 1996.

——— *The Shakespearean Stage, 1574–1642*. Cambridge, Eng., 1970; 2nd ed., 1980.

Gurr, Andrew, and John Orrell. *Rebuilding Shakespeare's Globe*. London and New York, 1989.

Harbage, Alfred. *Shakespeare's Audience*. New York, 1941.

Hodges, C. Walter. *The Globe Restored*. London, 1953; 2nd ed., New York, 1968.

Hosley, Richard. "Was There a Music-room in Shakespeare's Globe?" *ShS 13* (1960), 113–23.

Ingram, William. *The Business of Playing: The Beginnings of the Adult Professional Theater in Elizabethan London*. Ithaca, N.Y., 1992.

King, T. J. *Casting Shakespeare's Plays: London Actors and Their Roles, 1590–1642*. Cambridge, Eng., 1992.

———. *Shakespearean Staging, 1599–1642*. Cambridge, Mass., 1971.

Knutson, Roslyn Lander. *The Repertory of Shakespeare's Company, 1594–1613*. Fayetteville, Ark., 1991.

———. *Playing Companies and Commerce in Shakespeare's Time*. Cambridge, Eng., 2001.

Linthicum, Marie C. *Costume in the Drama of Shakespeare and His Contemporaries*. Oxford, 1936.

Mann, David. *The Elizabethan Player: Contemporary Stage Representation*. London, 1991.

McMillin, Scott. *The Elizabethan Theatre and "The Book of Sir Thomas More."* Ithaca, N.Y., 1987.

McMillin, Scott, and Sally-Beth MacLean. *The Queen's Men and Their Plays*. Cambridge, Eng., 1998.

Nelson, Alan H. *Early Cambridge Theatres: College, University, and Town Stages, 1464–1720*. Cambridge, Eng., 1994.

Nungezer, Edwin. *A Dictionary of Actors*. London and New Haven, 1929.

Shapiro, Michael. *Children of the Revels: The Boys' Companies of Shakespeare's Time and Their Plays*. New York, 1977.

Wickham, Glynne. *Early English Stages, 1300 to 1660*. 3 vols. London, 1959–1972.

Shakespeare's Life and Work

Alexander, Peter. *Shakespeare's Life and Art*. New ed., New York, 1961.

Baldwin, T. W. *William Shakspere's Small Latine and Lesse Greeke*. 2 vols. Urbana, Ill., 1944.

Chambers, E. K. *William Shakespeare: A Study of Facts and Problems*. 2 vols. Oxford, 1930.

Eccles, Mark. *Shakespeare in Warwickshire*. Madison, Wis., 1961.

Honan, Park. *Shakespeare: A Life*. Oxford, 1998.

Matus, Irvin Leigh, *Shakespeare, In Fact*. New York, 1994.

Schoenbaum, S. *Shakespeare's Lives*. Oxford and New York, 1970.

———. *William Shakespeare: A Documentary Life*. Oxford, 1975. Also published with fewer illustrations and a slightly revised text as *A Compact Documentary Life*. 1977.

———. *William Shakespeare: Records and Images*. Oxford, 1981.

Wells, Stanley. *Shakespeare: A Life in Drama*. New York and London, 1995.

Wheeler, Richard P. "Deaths in the Family: The Loss of a Son and the Rise of Shakespearean Comedy," *SQ 51* (2000), 127–53.

Shakespeare's Language: His Development as Poet and Dramatist

See also, under *Works of Reference*, Abbott, Onions, and Schmidt; and under *The Comedies*, Elam.

Barton, Anne. "Shakespeare and the Limits of Language," *ShS 24* (1971), 19–30.

Byrne, Muriel St. Clare. "The Foundations of Elizabethan Language," *ShS 17* (1964), 223–39.

Charney, Maurice. *Shakespeare's Roman Plays: The Function of Imagery in the Drama*. Cambridge, Mass., 1961.

———. *Style in Hamlet*. Princeton, 1969.

Clemen, Wolfgang H. *The Development of Shakespeare's Imagery*. Cambridge, Mass., 1951.

Cruttwell, Patrick. *The Shakespearean Moment and Its Place in the Poetry of the Seventeenth Century*. London, 1954.

Desmet, Christy. *Reading Shakespeare's Characters: Rhetoric, Ethics, and Identity*. Amherst, Mass., 1992.

Dobson, E. J. *English Pronunciation, 1500–1700*. 2 vols. 2nd ed. Oxford, 1968.

Donawerth, Jane. *Shakespeare and the Sixteenth-Century Study of Language*. Urbana, Ill., 1984.

Doran, Madeleine. *Shakespeare's Dramatic Language*. Madison, Wis., 1976.

Empson, William. *The Structure of Complex Words*. London, 1951; 3rd ed., 1977.

Hulme, Hilda M. *Explorations in Shakespeare's Language*. London, 1962.

Kermode, Frank. *Shakespeare's Language*. New York, 2000.

Kökeritz, Helge. *Shakespeare's Names*. New Haven, 1959.

———. *Shakespeare's Pronunciation*. New Haven, 1953.

Lanham, Richard A. *The Motives of Eloquence: Literary Rhetoric in the Renaissance*. New Haven, 1976.

Magnussen, Lynne. *Shakespeare and Social Dialogue: Dramatic Language and Elizabethan Letters*. Cambridge, Eng., 1999.

Mahood, M. M. *Shakespeare's Wordplay*. London, 1957.

Miriam Joseph, Sister. *Shakespeare's Use of the Arts of Language*. New York, 1947. Rpt. in part as *Rhetoric in Shakespeare's Time*. 1962.

Nares, Robert. *A Glossary . . . of Shakespeare and His Contemporaries*. New ed. J. O. Halliwell and Thomas Wright. 2 vols. London, 1859, 1905, Rpt. Detroit, 1966.

Partridge, Eric. *Shakespeare's Bawdy*. London, 1947, 1955.

Spurgeon, Caroline. *Shakespeare's Imagery and What it Tells Us*. Cambridge, Eng., 1935.

Thompson, Ann and John O. *Shakespeare: Meaning and Metaphor*. Iowa City, 1987.

Thorne, Alison. *Vision and Rhetoric in Shakespeare: Looking Through Language*. Basingstoke and New York, 2000.

Vickers, Brian. *The Artistry of Shakespeare's Prose*. London, 1968.

Willbern, David. *Poetic Will: Shakespeare and the Play of Language*. Philadelphia, 1997.

Willcock, Gladys D. "Shakespeare and Elizabethan English," *ShS* 7 (1954), 12–24.

Wright, George T. *Shakespeare's Metrical Art*. Berkeley, 1988.

Textual Criticism and Bibliography

See also under *King Lear*, Urkowitz.

Alexander, Peter. *Shakespeare's "Henry VI" and "Richard III."* Cambridge, Eng., 1929.

Blayney, Peter W. M. *The First Folio of Shakespeare*. Washington D.C., 1991.

———. *The Texts of "King Lear" and Their Origins*. Vol. 1. Cambridge, Eng., 1982.

Bowers, Fredson. *Bibliography and Textual Criticism*. Oxford, 1964.

———. *On Editing Shakespeare*. Charlottesville, Va., 1966.

———. *Principles of Bibliographical Description*. Princeton, 1949.

———. *Textual and Literary Criticism*. Cambridge, Eng., 1959.

Chambers, E. K. *William Shakespeare: A Study of Facts and Problems*. 2 vols. Oxford, 1930.

De Grazia, Margreta. *Shakespeare Verbatim: The Reproduction of Authenticity and the 1790 Apparatus*. Oxford, 1991.

Duthie, G. I. *Elizabethan Shorthand and the First Quarto of "King Lear."* Oxford, 1949.

Gaskell, Philip. *A New Introduction to Bibliography*. New York and Oxford, 1972.

Greg, W. W. *The Editorial Problem in Shakespeare*. 3rd ed. Oxford, 1954.

———. *Principles of Emendation in Shakespeare*. London, 1928.

———. *The Shakespeare First Folio: Its Bibliographical and Textual History*. Oxford, 1955.

Hart, Alfred. *Stolne and Surreptitious Copies: A Comparative Study of Shakespeare's Bad Quartos*. Melbourne and London, 1942.

Hinman, Charlton. *The Printing and Proof-Reading of the First Folio of Shakespeare*. 2 vols. Oxford, 1963.

Honigmann, E. A. J. *The Stability of Shakespeare's Text*. London and Lincoln, Neb., 1965.

Long, William B. " 'A bed for woodstock': A Warning for the Unwary," *Medieval and Renaissance Drama in England* 2 (1985), 91–118.

Maguire, Laurie E., and Thomas L. Berger, eds. *Textual Formations and Reformations*. Newark, Del., 1998.

Masten, Jeffrey. *Textual Intercourse: Collaboration, Authorship, and Sexualities in Renaissance Drama*. Cambridge, Eng., 1997.

McKerrow, Ronald B. *An Introduction to Bibliography for Literary Students*. Oxford, 1927.

———. *Prolegomena for the Oxford Shakespeare*. Oxford, 1939.

McLeod, Randall, ed. *Crisis in Editing: Texts of the English Renaissance*. New York, 1994.

Mowat, Barbara, and Paul Werstine, eds. *The New Folger Library Shakespeare*. New York, 1992–.

Nosworthy, J. M. *Shakespeare's Occasional Plays: Their Origin and Transmission*. London and New York, 1965.

Pechter, Edward, ed. *Textual and Theatrical Shakespeare: Questions of Evidence*. Iowa City, Iowa, 1996.

Pollard, Alfred W. *Shakespeare Folios and Quartos: A Study in the Bibliography of Shakespeare's Plays, 1594–1685*. London, 1909.

———. *Shakespeare's Fight with the Pirates and the Problems of the Transmission of His Text*. Rev. ed. Cambridge, Eng., 1937.

Sisson, C. J. *New Readings in Shakespeare*. 2 vols. Cambridge, Eng., 1956.

Taylor, Gary, and Michael Warren, eds. *The Division of the Kingdoms: Shakespeare's Two Versions of "King Lear."* Oxford, 1983.

Walker, Alice. *Textual Problems of the First Folio*. Cambridge, Eng., 1953.

Wells, Stanley. *Re-editing Shakespeare for the Modern Reader*. Oxford, 1984.

Wells, Stanley, and Gary Taylor. *Modernizing Shakespeare's Spelling*. Oxford, 1979.

Shakespeare Criticism to the 1930s

Badawi, M. M. *Coleridge: Critic of Shakespeare*. Cambridge, Eng., 1973.

Bradby, Anne, ed. *Shakespeare Criticism, 1919–35*. London, 1936.

Coleridge, S. T. *Coleridge on Shakespeare: The Text of the Lectures of 1811–12*, ed. R. A. Foakes. Charlottesville, Va., 1971.

———. *Coleridge's Writings on Shakespeare*, ed. Terence Hawkes. New York, 1959.

Evans, G. Blakemore, ed. *Shakespeare: Aspects of Influence*. Cambridge, Mass., 1976.

Hazlitt, William. *Characters of Shakespear's Plays*. London, 1817.

Johnson, Samuel. *Johnson on Shakespeare*, ed. Arthur Sherbo. Vol. 7 of *The Yale Edition of the Works of Samuel Johnson*. New Haven, 1968.

Kermode, Frank, ed. *Four Centuries of Shakespearean Criticism*. New York, 1965.

Knight, G. Wilson. *The Shakespearian Tempest*. London, 1932, 1953.

Muir, Kenneth. "Fifty Years of Shakespearian Criticism: 1900–1950," *ShS* 4 (1951), 1–25.

Rabkin, Norman, ed. *Approaches to Shakespeare*. New York, 1964.

Ralli, Augustus. *A History of Shakespearian Criticism*. 2 vols. London, 1932.

Raysor, T. M., ed. *Samuel Taylor Coleridge: Shakespearean Criticism*. 2 vols. 2nd ed. London, 1960.

Schlegel, August Wilhelm. *Lectures on Dramatic Art and Literature*, trans. John Black, 1846. Rpt., New York, 1965.

Schücking, Levin L. *Character Problems in Shakespeare's Plays*. London, 1917; trans., 1922.

Shaw, G. B. *Shaw on Shakespeare*, ed. Edwin Wilson. New York, 1961.

Sherbo, Arthur. *Samuel Johnson, Editor of Shakespeare*. Urbana, Ill., 1956.

Smith, David Nichol, ed. *Shakespeare Criticism: A Selection*. World's Classics, Oxford, 1916.

———, ed. *Eighteenth Century Essays on Shakespeare*. 2nd ed. Oxford, 1963.

Stoll, E. E. *Art and Artifice in Shakespeare*. Cambridge, Eng., 1933, 1962.

Vickers, Brian, ed. *Shakespeare: The Critical Heritage*. Several volumes. London and Boston, 1974—.

Welsford, Enid. *The Fool: His Social and Literary History*. London, 1935; rpt. 1966.

Westfall, A. V. *American Shakespearean Criticism, 1607–1865*. New York, 1939.

Shakespeare Criticism from the 1940s to the 1970s

Armstrong, Edward A. *Shakespeare's Imagination: A Study of the Psychology of Association and Inspiration*. London, 1946.

Bethell, S. L. *Shakespeare and the Popular Dramatic Tradition*. London and Durham, N.C., 1944.

Bevington, David, and Jay L. Halio, eds. *Shakespeare: Pattern of Excelling Nature*. Newark, Del., 1978.

Bloom, Allan, with Harry V. Jaffa. *Shakespeare's Politics*. New York and London, 1964.

Brown, John Russell. *Shakespeare's Plays in Performance*. London, 1966.

Bryant, J. A., Jr. *Hippolyta's View: Some Christian Aspects of Shakespeare's Plays*. Lexington, Ky., 1961.

Burckhardt, Sigurd. *Shakespearean Meanings*. Princeton, 1968.

Burke, Kenneth. *Language as Symbolic Action*. Berkeley, 1966.

Calderwood, James L. *Shakespearean Metadrama*. Minneapolis, 1971.

Coghill, Neville. *Shakespeare's Professional Skills*. Cambridge, Eng., 1964.

Colie, Rosalie L. *Shakespeare's Living Art*. Princeton, 1974.

Council, Norman. *When Honour's at the Stake: Ideas of Honour in Shakespeare's Plays*. London, 1973.

Danby, John F. *Poets on Fortune's Hill: Studies in Sidney, Shakespeare, and Beaumont and Fletcher*. London, 1952.

Dean, Leonard F., ed. *Shakespeare: Modern Essays in Criticism*. New York, 1967.

Driver, Tom F. *The Sense of History in Greek and Shakespearean Drama*. New York, 1960.

Dusinberre, Juliet. *Shakespeare and the Nature of Women*. New York, 1975. 2nd ed., 1996.

Eagleton, Terence. *Shakespeare and Society*. New York and London, 1967.

Edwards, Philip. *Shakespeare and the Confines of Art*. London and New York, 1968.

Empson, William. *The Structure of Complex Words*. London, 1951.

Fiedler, Leslie A. *The Stranger in Shakespeare*. New York, 1972.

Fly, Richard. *Shakespeare's Mediated World*. Amherst, Mass., 1976.

Frye, Roland M. *Shakespeare and Christian Doctrine*. Princeton, 1963.

Garber, Marjorie B. *Dream in Shakespeare: From Metaphor to Metamorphosis*. New Haven and London, 1974.

Goddard, Harold C. *The Meaning of Shakespeare*. Chicago, 1951.

Goldman, Michael. *Shakespeare and the Energies of Drama*. Princeton, 1972.

Granville-Barker, Harley. *Prefaces to Shakespeare.* 2 vols. Princeton, 1946–1947.

Harbage, Alfred. *As They Liked it.* New York, 1947.

———. *Shakespeare and the Rival Traditions.* New York, 1952.

Hawkes, Terence. *Shakespeare's Talking Animals: Language and Drama in Society.* London, 1973.

Hawkins, Harriett. *Poetic Freedom and Poetic Truth: Chaucer, Shakespeare, Marlowe, Milton.* Oxford, 1976.

Holland, Norman. *Psychoanalysis and Shakespeare.* New York, 1966.

———. *The Shakespearean Imagination.* New York, 1964.

Jones, Emrys. *The Origins of Shakespeare.* Oxford, 1977.

Jorgensen, Paul A. *Shakespeare's Military World.* Berkeley and Los Angeles, 1956.

Kernan, Alvin B. *The Playwright as Magician: Shakespeare's Image of the Poet in the English Public Theater.* New Haven, 1979.

———, ed. *Modern Shakespearean Criticism.* New York, 1970.

Kettle, Arnold, ed. *Shakespeare in a Changing World.* London and New York, 1964.

Knights, L. C. *Some Shakespearean Themes.* London, 1959.

Kott, Jan. *Shakespeare Our Contemporary.* New York, 1964.

Leavis, F. R. *The Common Pursuit.* London, 1952.

Levin, Richard. *New Readings vs. Old Plays: Recent Trends in the Reinterpretation of English Renaissance Drama.* Chicago, 1979.

McAlindon, T. *Shakespeare and Decorum.* London and New York, 1973.

Rabkin, Norman. *Shakespeare and the Common Understanding.* New York, 1967.

Righter, Anne. *Shakespeare and the Idea of the Play.* London, 1962.

Rossiter, A. P. *Angel with Horns.* London, 1961.

Sanders, Wilbur. *The Dramatist and the Received Idea: Studies in the Plays of Marlowe and Shakespeare.* Cambridge, Eng., 1968.

Sewell, Arthur. *Character and Society in Shakespeare.* London, 1951.

Soellner, Rolf. *Shakespeare's Patterns of Self-Knowledge.* Columbus, Ohio, 1972.

Spencer, Theodore. *Shakespeare and the Nature of Man.* New York, 1942.

Spivack, Bernard. *Shakespeare and the Allegory of Evil.* New York, 1958.

Stewart, J. I. M. *Character and Motive in Shakespeare.* London, 1949.

Stirling, Brents. *The Populace in Shakespeare.* New York, 1949.

Traversi, Derek. *An Approach to Shakespeare.* 2 vols. Rev. ed. London, 1968.

Van Laan, Thomas F. *Role-Playing in Shakespeare.* Toronto, 1978.

Watson, Curtis Brown. *Shakespeare and the Renaissance Concept of Honor.* Princeton, 1960.

Weimann, Robert. *Shakespeare and the Popular Tradition in the Theater*, ed. Robert Schwartz. Baltimore, 1978.

Whitaker, Virgil K. *Shakespeare's Use of Learning.* San Marino, Calif., 1953.

Zeeveld, W. Gordon. *The Temper of Shakespeare's Thought.* New Haven and London, 1974.

Shakespeare Criticism Since 1980, including New Historicism, Gender Studies, and Poststructuralism

See also, under *Shakespeare's Predecessors and Contemporaries*, Bednarz, Belsey, Braden, Bristol, Bruster, Cohen, Dolan, Farley-Hills, Findlay (two items), Freer, McLuskie, Orgel, Rasmussen, Rose, Shannon, and Vickers; and under *Shakespeare Criticism from the 1940s to the 1970s*, Weimann.

Adelman, Janet. *Suffocating Mothers: Fantasies of Maternal Origin in Shakespeare's Plays, "Hamlet" to "The Tempest."* Chicago, 1992.

Alexander, Catherine M. S., and Stanley Wells, eds. *Shakespeare and Race.* Cambridge, Eng., 2000.

Auden, W. H. *Lectures on Shakespeare*, ed. Arthur Kirsch. Princeton, 2000.

Bamber, Linda. *Comic Women, Tragic Men: A Study of Gender and Genre in Shakespeare.* Stanford, 1982.

Barber, C. L. *The Whole Journey: Shakespeare's Power of Development.* Berkeley, 1986.

Bate, Jonathan. *The Genius of Shakespeare.* Oxford, 1997.

Belsey, Catherine. *Shakespeare and the Loss of Eden: The Construction of Family Values in Early Modern Culture.* New Brunswick, N.J., 1999.

Berger, Harry, Jr. *Making Trifles of Terrors: Redistributing Complicities in Shakespeare.* ed. Peter Erickson. Stanford, 1997.

Bergeron, David, ed. *Pageantry in the Shakespearean Theater.* Athens, Ga., 1985.

Bevington, David. *Shakespeare.* Oxford, 2002.

Boose, Lynda E. "The Father and the Bride in Shakespeare," *PMLA* 97 (1982), 325–47.

Bristol, Michael. *Shakespeare's America, America's Shakespeare.* London and New York, 1990.

Bulman, James C., ed. *Shakespeare, Theory, and Performance.* London and New York, 1996.

Calderwood, James. *Shakespeare and the Denial of Death.* Amherst, Mass., 1987.

Callaghan, Dympna C. *Shakespeare Without Women: Representing Gender and Race on the Renaissance Stage.* London and New York, 2000.

———, ed. *A Feminist Companion to Shakespeare.* Oxford, 2000.

Callaghan, Dympna, Lorraine Helms, and Jyotsna Singh. *The Weyward Sisters: Shakespeare and Feminist Politics.* Cambridge, Eng., 1994.

Carey, John, ed. *English Renaissance Studies.* Oxford, 1980.

Cartelli, Thomas. *Repositioning Shakespeare: National Formations, Postcolonial Appropriations.* London and New York, 1999.

Cavell, Stanley. *Disowning Knowledge in Six Plays of Shakespeare.* Cambridge, Eng., 1987.

Charnes, Linda. *Notorious Identity: Materializing the Subject in Shakespeare.* Cambridge, Mass., 1993.

Cook, Ann Jennalie. *Making a Match: Courtship in Shakespeare and His Society.* Princeton, 1991.

Cox, John D. *Shakespeare and the Dramaturgy of Power.* Princeton, 1989.

Daileder, Celia R. *Eroticism on the Renaissance Stage: Transcendence, Desire, and the Limits of the Visible.* Cambridge, Eng., 1998.

Danson, Lawrence. *Shakespeare's Dramatic Genres.* Oxford, 2000.

Dawson, Anthony B. *Indirections: Shakespeare and the Art of Illusion.* Toronto, 1984.

De Grazia, Margreta, Maureen Quilligan, and Peter Stallybrass, eds. *Subject and Object in Renaissance Culture.* Cambridge, Eng., 1996.

Desmet, Christy. *Reading Shakespeare's Characters: Rhetoric, Ethics, and Identity.* Amherst, Mass., 1992.

Desmet, Christy, and Robert Sawyer, eds. *Shakespeare and Appropriation.* London and New York, 1999.

Dobson, Michael. *The Making of the National Poet: Shakespeare, Adaptation, and Authorship, 1660–1769.* Oxford, 1992.

Dolan, Frances E. *Dangerous Familiars: Representations of Domestic Crime in England, 1550–1700.* Ithaca, N.Y., 1994.

Dollimore, Jonathan. *Radical Tragedy: Religion, Ideology and Power in the Drama of Shakespeare and His Contemporaries.* Chicago, 1984; New York, 1989.

Dollimore, Jonathan, and Alan Sinfield. *Political Shakespeare: New Essays in Cultural Materialism.* Manchester, Eng., 1985.

Drakakis, John, ed. *Alternative Shakespeares.* London, 1985.

Dubrow, Heather, and Richard Strier, eds. *The Historical Renaissance: New Essays on Tudor and Stuart Literature and Culture.* Chicago, 1988.

Eagleton, Terence. *William Shakespeare.* Oxford, 1986.

Edwards, Philip, et al., eds. *Shakespeare's Styles.* Cambridge, Eng., 1980.

Engle, Lars. *Shakespearean Pragmatism: Market of His Time.* Chicago, 1993.

Erickson, Peter. *Patriarchal Structures in Shakespeare's Drama.* Berkeley, 1985.

Erickson, Peter, and Coppélia Kahn, eds. *Shakespeare's Rough Magic: Essays in Honor of C. L. Barber.* Newark, Del., 1985.

French, Marilyn. *Shakespeare's Division of Experience.* New York, 1981.

Frye, Northrop. *Northrop Frye on Shakespeare*, ed. Robert Sandler. New Haven, 1986.

Fumerton, Patricia, and Simon Hunt, eds. *Renaissance Culture and the Everyday.* Philadelphia, 1999.

Garber, Marjorie. *Coming of Age in Shakespeare.* London, 1981.

———. *Shakespeare's Ghost Writers: Literature as Uncanny Causality.* London and New York, 1987.

———, ed. *Cannibals, Witches, and Divorce: Estranging the Renaissance.* Baltimore, 1987.

Gibbons, Brian. *Shakespeare and Multiplicity.* Cambridge, Eng., 1993.

Gillies, John. *Shakespeare and the Geography of Difference.* Cambridge, Eng., 1994.

Goldberg, Jonathan. *James I and the Politics of Literature: Jonson, Shakespeare, Donne, and Their Contemporaries.* Baltimore, 1983.

———. *Sodometries: Renaissance Texts, Modern Sexualities.* Stanford, 1992.

Grady, Hugh, ed. *Shakespeare and Modernity: Early Modern to Millennium*. London and New York, 2000.

Greenblatt, Stephen. *Learning to Curse: Essays in Early Modern Culture*. London and New York, 1990.

———. *Marvelous Possessions: The Wonder of the New World*. Chicago, 1991.

———. *Renaissance Self-Fashioning: From More to Shakespeare*. Chicago, 1980.

———. *Shakespearean Negotiations: The Circulation of Social Energy in Renaissance England*. Berkeley, 1988.

Habib, Imtiaz. *Shakespeare and Race: Postcolonial Praxis in the Early Modern Period*. Lanham and Oxford, 2000.

Hall, Kim F. *Things of Darkness: Economies of Race and Gender in Early Modern England*. Ithaca, N.Y., 1994.

Hamilton, Donna B. *Shakespeare and the Politics of Protestant England*. Lexington, Ky., 1992.

Hamlin, William M. *The Image of America in Montaigne, Spenser, and Shakespeare: Renaissance Ethnography and Literary Tradition*. New York, 1995.

Hawkes, Terence. *Meaning by Shakespeare*. London and New York, 1992.

———, ed. *Alternative Shakespeares*. Vol. 2. London and New York, 1996.

Holland, Norman, et al., eds. *Shakespeare's Personality*. Berkeley, 1989.

Howard, Jean E. *Shakespeare's Art of Orchestration: Stage Technique and Audience Response*. Urbana, Ill., 1984.

———. *The Stage and Social Struggle in Early Modern England*. London, 1994.

———, and Marion F. O'Connor, eds. *Shakespeare Reproduced: The Text in History and Ideology*. London and New York, 1987.

———, and Scott Cutler Shershow, eds. *Marxist Shakespeares*. London and New York, 2000.

James, Heather. *Shakespeare's Troy: Drama, Politics, and the Translation of Empire*. Cambridge, Eng., 1997.

Jardine, Lisa. *Reading Shakespeare Historically*. London and New York, 1996.

———. *Still Harping on Daughters: Women and Drama in the Age of Shakespeare*. Sussex and Totowa, N.J., 1983; New York, 1989.

Kahn, Coppélia. *Man's Estate: Masculine Identity in Shakespeare*. Berkeley, 1981.

———. *Roman Shakespeare: Warriors, Wounds, and Women*. London and New York, 1997.

Kamps, Ivo, ed. *Materialist Shakespeare: A History*. London, 1995.

———, ed. *Shakespeare Left and Right*. New York and London, 1991.

Kastan, David Scott. *Shakespeare After Theory*. London, 1999.

———. *Shakespeare and the Book*. Cambridge, Eng., 2001.

———. *Shakespeare and the Shapes of Time*. Hanover, N.H., 1982.

———, ed. *A Companion to Shakespeare*. Oxford, 1999.

Kernan, Alvin. *Shakespeare, the King's Playwright: Theater in the Stuart Court, 1603–1613*. New Haven, 1995.

Kerrigan, William. *Shakespeare's Promises*. Baltimore, 1999.

Kirsch, Arthur. *Shakespeare and the Experience of Love*. Cambridge, Eng., 1981.

Knapp, Robert S. *Shakespeare—The Theater and the Book*. Princeton, 1989.

Knowles, Richard, ed. *Shakespeare and Carnival: After Bakhtin*. London and New York, 1998.

Lenz, Carolyn, et al., eds. *The Woman's Part: Feminist Criticism of Shakespeare*. Urbana, Ill., 1980.

Little, Arthur L., Jr. *Shakespeare Jungle Fever: National-Imperial Re-Visions of Race, Rape, and Sacrifice*. Stanford, 2000.

Loomba, Ania. *Gender, Race, Renaissance Drama*. Manchester, Eng., 1989.

Loomba, Ania, and Martin Orkin, eds. *Post-colonial Shakespeares*. London and New York, 1998.

Mahon, John W., and Thomas A. Pendleton, eds. *"Fanned and Winnowed Opinion": Shakespearean Essays Presented to Harold Jenkins*. London, 1987.

Mallin, Eric. *Inscribing the Time: Shakespeare and the End of Elizabethan England*. Berkeley, 1995.

Marcus, Leah. *Puzzling Shakespeare: Local Reading and its Discontents*. Berkeley, 1988.

Mazzio, Carla, and Douglas Trevor, eds. *Historicism, Psychoanalysis, and Early Modern Culture*. London and New York, 2000.

McDonald, Russ, ed. *Shakespeare Reread: The Texts in New Contexts*. Ithaca, N.Y., 1994.

McMullan, Gordon, and Jonathan Hope, eds. *The Politics of Tragicomedy: Shakespeare and After*. London and New York, 1992.

Melchiori, Giorgio. *Shakespeare's Garter Plays: "Edward III" to "Merry Wives of Windsor."* Newark, Del., 1994.

Miola, Robert S. *Shakespeare's Reading*. Oxford and New York, 2000.

———. *Shakespeare's Rome*. Cambridge, Eng., 1983.

Montrose, Louis. *The Purpose of Playing: Shakespeare and Cultural Politics of the Elizabethan Theatre*. Chicago, 1996.

Mullaney, Steven. *The Place of the Stage: License, Play, and Power in Renaissance England*. Chicago, 1988.

Neely, Carol Thomas. *Broken Nuptials in Shakespeare's Plays*. New Haven, 1985.

Newman, Karen. *Fashioning Femininity and the English Renaissance Drama*. Chicago, 1991.

Novy, Marianne. *Love's Argument: Gender Relations in Shakespeare*. Chapel Hill, N.C., 1984.

———, ed. *Women's Re-Visions of Shakespeare*. Urbana, Ill., 1990.

Nuttall, A. D. *A New Mimesis: Shakespeare and the Representation of Reality*. London, 1983.

Orgel, Stephen. *The Authentic Shakespeare and Other Problems of the Early Modern Stage*. London and New York, 2002.

Orgel, Stephen, and Sean Keilen, eds. *Shakespeare and History; Post-modern Shakespeare; Shakespeare and the Interpretive Tradition; Shakespeare and the Literary Tradition; Shakespeare and Gender; Political Shakespeare*. In separate volumes, New York, 1999.

Parker, Patricia. *Shakespeare from the Margins: Language, Culture, Context*. Chicago, 1996.

———, and Geoffrey Hartman, eds. *Shakespeare and the Question of Theory*. London, 1985.

Paster, Gail Kern. *The Body Embarrassed: Drama and the Disciplines of Shame in Early Modern England*. Ithaca, N.Y., 1993.

Patterson, Annabel. *Shakespeare and the Popular Voice*. Oxford, 1989.

Rabkin, Norman. *Shakespeare and the Problem of Meaning*. Chicago, 1981.

Salingar, Leo. *Dramatic Form in Shakespeare and the Jacobeans*. Cambridge, Eng., 1986.

Schwartz, Murray, and Coppélia Kahn, eds. *Representing Shakespeare: New Psychoanalytic Essays*. Baltimore, 1980.

Siemon, James R. *Shakespearean Iconoclasm*. Berkeley, 1985.

Sinfield, Alan. *Faultlines: Cultural Materialism and the Politics of Dissident Reading*. Berkeley, 1992.

Skura, Meredith Anne. *The Literary Use of the Psychoanalytic Process*. New Haven, 1981.

———. *Shakespeare the Actor and the Purposes of Playing*. Chicago, 1993.

Smith, Bruce R. *Homosexual Desire in Shakespeare's England*. Chicago, 1991.

———. *Shakespeare and Masculinity*. Oxford, 2000.

Stockholder, Kay. *Dream Works: Lovers and Families in Shakespeare's Plays*. Toronto, 1987.

Taylor, Gary. *Reinventing Shakespeare: A Cultural History from the Restoration to the Present*. New York, 1989.

Traub, Valerie. *Desire and Anxiety: Circulations of Sexuality in Shakespearean Drama*. London, 1992.

Vickers, Brian. *Appropriating Shakespeare: Contemporary Critical Quarrels*. New Haven, 1993.

Watson, Robert N. *The Rest is Silence: Death as Annihilation in the English Renaissance*. Berkeley, 1994.

———. *Shakespeare and the Hazards of Ambition*. Cambridge, Mass., 1984.

Wayne, Valerie, ed. *The Matter of Difference: Materialist Feminist Criticism of Shakespeare*. Ithaca, N.Y., 1991.

Weimann, Robert. *Author's Pen and Actor's Voice: Playing and Writing in Shakespeare's Theatre*. Cambridge, Eng., 2000.

Wells, Robin Headlam. *Shakespeare on Masculinity*. Cambridge, Eng., 2000.

———. *Shakespeare, Politics, and the State*. London, 1986.

Wheeler, Richard P. *Shakespeare's Development and the Problem Comedies: Turn and Counter-Turn*. Berkeley, 1981.

White, Paul Whitfield, and Suzanne R. Westfall, eds. *Shakespeare and Theatrical Patronage in Early Modern England*. Cambridge, Eng., 2002.

Williams, Gordon. *Shakespeare, Sex, and the Print Revolution*. London and Atlantic Highlands, N.J., 1996.

Woodbridge, Linda. *The Scythe of Saturn: Shakespeare's Magical Thinking*. Urbana, Ill., 1994.

Woodbridge, Linda, and Edward Berry, eds. *True Rites and Maimed Rites: Ritual and Anti-Ritual in Shakespeare and His Age*. Urbana, Ill., 1992.

Ziegler, Georgianna, ed. *Shakespeare's Unruly Women*. Washington, D.C., 1997.

Shakespeare in Performance; Dramaturgy

See also, under *Shakespeare Criticism from the 1940s to the 1970s*, Goldman and Granville-Barker.

Bartholomeusz, Dennis. *Macbeth and the Players*. Cambridge, Eng., 1969.

Barton, John. *Playing Shakespeare*. London, 1984.

Bevington, David. *Action is Eloquence: Shakespeare's Language of Gesture*. Cambridge, Mass., 1984.

Brockbank, Philip, ed. *Players of Shakespeare*. Cambridge, Eng., 1985.

Brown, Ivor. *Shakespeare and the Actors*. London, 1970.

Brown, John Russell. *Shakespeare's Plays in Performance*. London, 1966.

——. *Shakespeare's Dramatic Style*. London, 1970.

Bulman, J. C., and H. R. Coursen, eds. *Shakespeare on Television*. Hanover, N.H., 1988.

Carlisle, Carol Jones. *Shakespeare from the Greenroom: Actors' Criticisms of Four Major Tragedies*. Chapel Hill, N.C., 1969.

Cohn, Ruby. *Modern Shakespeare Offshoots*. Princeton, 1976.

Cook, Judith. *Shakespeare's Players*. London, 1983.

Davies, Anthony, and Stanley Wells, eds. *Shakespeare and the Moving Image: The Plays on Film and Television*. Cambridge, Eng., 1994.

Dessen, Alan C. *Recovering Shakespeare's Theatrical Vocabulary*. Cambridge, Eng., 1995.

——. *Rescripting Shakespeare: The Text, the Director, and Modern Productions*. Cambridge, Eng., 2002.

——, and Leslie Thomson. *A Dictionary of Stage Directions in English Drama, 1580–1642*. Cambridge, Eng., 1999.

Donohue, Joseph W., Jr. *Dramatic Character in the English Romantic Age*. Princeton, 1970.

Downer, Alan S. *The Eminent Tragedian, William Charles Macready*. Cambridge, Mass., 1966.

Edelman, Charles. *Brawl Ridiculous: Swordfighting in Shakespeare's Plays*. Manchester, Eng., 1992.

Hodgdon, Barbara. *The Shakespeare Trade: Performances and Appropriations*. Philadelphia, 1998.

Hogan, Charles B. *Shakespeare in the Theatre, 1701–1800*. 2 vols. Oxford, 1952–1957.

Jackson, Russell, and Robert Smallwood, eds. *Players of Shakespeare 2*. Cambridge, Eng., 1988. Followed by Vols. 3 (1993); and 4, ed. Smallwood (1998).

Jones, Emrys. *Scenic Form in Shakespeare*. Oxford, 1971.

Jorgens, Jack L. *Shakespeare on Film*. Bloomington, Ind., 1977.

Manvell, Roger. *Shakespeare and the Film*. London and New York, 1971.

McGuire, Philip C. *Speechless Dialect: Shakespeare's Open Silences*. Berkeley, 1985.

McGuire, Philip C., and David A. Samuelson. *Shakespeare: The Theatrical Dimension*. New York, 1979.

Odell, George C. D. *Shakespeare from Betterton to Irving*. 2 vols. New York, 1920, 1966.

Poel, William. *Shakespeare in the Theatre*. London, 1913, 1968.

Price, Joseph G., ed. *The Triple Bond: Plays, Mainly Shakespearean, in Performance*. University Park, Pa., 1975.

Rutter, Carol Chillington, ed. *Documents of the Rose Playhouse*. Manchester, Eng., 1999.

Rutter, Carol, et al. *Clamorous Voices: Shakespeare's Women Today*. New York, 1989.

Shapiro, Michael. *Gender in Play on the Shakespearean Stage: Boy Heroines and Female Pages*. Ann Arbor, Mich., 1994.

Shattuck, Charles H. *The Shakespeare Promptbooks: A Descriptive Catalogue*. Urbana, Ill., 1965.

——. *Shakespeare on the American Stage from the Hallams to Edwin Booth*. Washington, D.C., 1976; *from Booth and Barrett to Sothern and Marlowe*, Washington, D.C., 1987.

Slater, Ann Pasternak. *Shakespeare the Director*. Brighton, Sussex, and Totowa, N.J., 1982.

Speaight, Robert. *William Poel and the Elizabethan Revival*. London, 1954.

Sprague, Arthur Colby. *Shakespeare and the Actors*. Cambridge, Mass., 1944.

——. *Shakespearian Players and Performances*. Cambridge, Mass., 1953.

Styan, J. L. *Shakespeare's Stagecraft*. Cambridge, Eng., 1967.

Wells, Stanley. *Royal Shakespeare: Four Major Productions at Stratford-upon-Avon*. Manchester, Eng., 1977.

The Comedies

See also, under *Shakespeare Criticism Since 1980*, Drakakis (essay by Belsey), Erickson and Kahn (essay by Adelman), and Paster (Chapter 7).

Anderson, Linda. *A Kind of Wild Justice: Revenge in Shakespeare's Comedies*. Newark, Del., 1987.

Barber, C. L. *Shakespeare's Festive Comedy*. Princeton, 1959.

Barton, Anne. *The Names of Comedy*. Toronto, 1990.

Berry, Edward. *Shakespeare's Comic Rites*. Cambridge, Eng., 1984.

Berry, Ralph. *Shakespeare's Comedies: Explorations in Form*. Princeton, 1972.

——. *The Shakespearean Metaphor: Studies in Language and Form*. Totowa, N.J., 1978.

Bloom, Harold, ed., *William Shakespeare: Comedies and Romances*. New York, 1986.

Bradbury, Malcolm, and David Palmer, eds. *Shakespearian Comedy*. London, 1972.

Brown, John Russell. *Shakespeare and His Comedies*. London, 1957, 1968.

Brown, John Russell, and Bernard Harris, eds. *Early Shakespeare*. Stratford-upon-Avon Studies 3. London, 1961. (Including an essay by Frank Kermode on "The Mature Comedies.")

Bryant, J. A., Jr. *Shakespeare and the Uses of Comedy*. Lexington, Ky., 1986.

Burke, William Kenneth. *A New Approach to Shakespeare's Early Comedies: Theoretical Foundations*. New York, 1998.

Carroll, William C. *The Metamorphoses of Shakespearean Comedy*. Princeton, 1985.

Champion, Larry S. *The Evolution of Shakespeare's Comedy*. Cambridge, Mass., 1970.

Charlton, H. B. *Shakespearian Comedy*. London, 1938.

Charney, Maurice, ed. *Shakespearean Comedy*. New York, 1980.

Cody, Richard. *The Landscape of the Mind: Pastoralism and Platonic Theory in Tasso's "Aminta" and Shakespeare's Early Comedies*. Oxford, 1969.

Collins, Michael J., ed. *Shakespeare's Sweet Thunder: Essays on the Early Comedies*. Newark, Del., 1997.

Cook, Ann Jennalie. *Making a Match: Courtship in Shakespeare and His Society*. Princeton, 1991.

Cordner, Michael, Peter Holland, and John Kerrigan, eds. *English Comedy*. Cambridge, Eng., 1994.

Elam, Keir. *Shakespeare's Universe of Discourse: Language-Games in the Comedies*. Cambridge, Eng., 1984.

Evans, Bertrand. *Shakespeare's Comedies*. Oxford, 1960.

Freedman, Barbara. *Staging the Gaze: Postmodernism, Psychoanalysis, and Shakespearean Comedy*. Ithaca, N. Y., 1991.

Friedman, Michael D. "*The World Must Be Peopled*": *Shakespeare's Comedies of Forgiveness*. Madison, N. J., and London, 2002.

Frye, Northrop. "The Argument of Comedy," *English Institute Essays 1948*. New York, 1949.

——. *A Natural Perspective: The Development of Shakespearean Comedy and Romance*. New York, 1965.

Hall, Jonathan. *Anxious Pleasures: Shakespearean Comedy and the Nation-State*. Madison, N. J., 1995.

Hamilton, A. C. *The Early Shakespeare*. San Marino, Calif., 1967.

Hassel, R. Chris. *Faith and Folly in Shakespeare's Romantic Comedies*. Athens, Ga., 1980.

Hawkins, Sherman H. "The Two Worlds of Shakespearean Comedy," *ShakS* 3 (1967), 62–80.

Hunter, Robert G. *Shakespeare and the Comedy of Forgiveness*. New York, 1965.

Huston, J. Dennis. *Shakespeare's Comedies of Play*. New York, 1981.

Leggatt, Alexander. *English Stage Comedy, 1490–1990: Five Centuries of a Genre*. London and New York, 1998.

——. *Shakespeare's Comedy of Love*. London and New York, 1974.

Lerner, Laurence, ed. *Shakespeare's Comedies: An Anthology of Modern Criticism*. Baltimore, 1967.

Levin, Richard A. *Love and Society in Shakespearean Comedy: A Study of Dramatic Form and Content*. Newark, Del., 1985.

Miola, Robert S. *Shakespeare and Classical Comedy: The Influence of Plautus and Terence*. Oxford, 1994.

Nevo, Ruth. *Comic Transformations in Shakespeare*. London, 1980.

Newman, Karen. *Shakespeare's Rhetoric of Comic Character*. New York and London, 1985.

Palmer, David J., and Malcolm Bradbury, eds. *Shakespearian Comedy*. Statford-upon-Avon Studies 1. London, 1972.

Palmer, John. *Comic Characters of Shakespeare*. London, 1946.

Pettet, E. C. *Shakespeare and the Romance Tradition*. London, 1949.

Phialas, Peter G. *Shakespeare's Romantic Comedies*. Chapel Hill, N.C., 1966.

Richmond, Hugh M. *Shakespeare's Sexual Comedy*. Indianapolis, 1971.

Salingar, Leo. *Shakespeare and the Traditions of Comedy*. Cambridge, Eng., 1974.

Shaheen, Naseeb. *Biblical References in Shakespeare's Comedies*. Newark, Del., 1993.

Smidt, Kristian. *Unconformities in Shakespeare's Early Comedies*. London, 1986.

Stevenson, David L. *The Love-Game Comedy*. New York, 1946.

Traversi, Derek. *Shakespeare: The Early Comedies*. London, 1960.

Turner, Robert Y. *Shakespeare's Apprenticeship*. Chicago, 1974.

Westlund, Joseph. *Shakespeare's Reparative Comedies: A Psychoanalytic View of the Middle Plays*. Chicago, 1984.

Wheeler, Richard P. "Deaths in the Family: The Loss of a Son and the Rise of Shakespearean Comedy," *SQ* 51 (2000), 127–53.

Williamson, Marilyn. *The Patriarchy of Shakespeare's Comedies*. Detroit, 1986.

The Problem Plays

Campbell, Oscar James. *Shakespeare's Satire*. London and New York, 1943, 1963.

Foakes, R. A. *Shakespeare, The Dark Comedies to the Last Plays: From Satire to Celebration*. Charlottesville, Va., 1971.

Frye, Northrop. *The Myth of Deliverance: Reflections on Shakespeare's Problem Comedies*. Toronto, 1983.

Jamieson, Michael. "The Problem Plays, 1920–1970: A Retrospect," *ShS* 25 (1972), 1–10.

Lawrence, W. W. *Shakespeare's Problem Comedies*. New York, 1931, 1960.

Maquerlot, Jean-Pierre. *Shakespeare and the Mannerist Tradition: A Reading of Five Problem Plays*. Cambridge, Eng., 1995. (Includes consideration of *Julius Caesar* and *Hamlet*.)

McCandless, David. *Gender and Performance in Shakespeare's Problem Comedies*. Bloomington, Ind., 1997.

Muir, Kenneth, and Stanley Wells, eds. *Aspects of Shakespeare's "Problem Plays": Articles Reprinted from "Shakespeare Survey."* Cambridge, Eng., 1982.

Schanzer, Ernest. *The Problem Plays of Shakespeare*. New York, 1963.

Thomas, Vivian. *The Moral Universe of Shakespeare's Problem Plays*. New York, 1987.

Tillyard, E. M. W. *Shakespeare's Problem Plays*. Toronto, 1949.

Wheeler, Richard P. *Shakespeare's Development and the Problem Comedies: Turn and Counter-Turn*. Berkeley, 1981.

Ure, Peter. *William Shakespeare: The Problem Plays*. London, 1961.

The Taming of the Shrew

See also, under *Shakespeare's Predecessors and Contemporaries*, Marrapodi (essay by Bevington); under *Shakespeare Criticism from the 1940s to the 1970s*, Garber; under *Shakespeare Criticism Since 1980*, Auden, Fumerton and

Hunt (essay by Dolan), Kahn, Lenz et al. (essay by Bean), McDonald (essay by Boose), Novy (*Love's Argument*), and Parker and Hartman (essay by Fineman); under *Shakespeare in Performance*, Rutter; and under *The Comedies*, R. Berry, Charlton, Collins (essays by Dessen and Rutter), Evans, Hawkins, Huston, Leggatt, Nevo, and Stevenson.

Boose, Lynda E. " 'Scolding Brides and Bridling Scolds': Taming the Woman's Unruly Member," *SQ* 42 (1991), 179–213.

Brunvand, Jan Harold. "The Folktale Origin of *The Taming of the Shrew*," *SQ* 17 (1966), 345–59.

Dolan, Frances E., ed. *"The Taming of the Shrew": Text and Contexts*. New York, 1996.

Haring-Smith, Tori. *From Farce to Metadrama: A Stage History of "The Taming of the Shrew," 1594–1983*. Westport, Conn., 1985.

Hosley, Richard. "Was There a 'Dramatic Epilogue' to *The Taming of the Shrew?*" *Studies in English Literature* 1:2 (1961), 17–34.

Hutson, Lorna. *The Usurer's Daughter: Male Friendship and Fictions of Women in Sixteenth-Century England*. London and New York, 1994.

Jayne, Sears. "The Dreaming of *The Shrew*," *SQ* 17 (1966), 41–56.

Korda, Natasha. "Household Kates: Domesticating Commodities in *The Taming of the Shrew*," *SQ* 47 (1996), 109–31.

Maguire, Laurie E. "Cultural Control in *The Taming of the Shrew*," *Renaissance Drama* n.s. 26 (1995), 83–104.

Marcus, Leah. "The Shakespearean Editor as Shrew-Tamer," *English Literary Rennaisance* 22 (1922), 177–200.

Newman, Karen. "Renaissance Family Politics and Shakespeare's *The Taming of the Shrew*," *English Literary Renaissance* 16 (1986), 86–100.

Saccio, Peter. "Shrewd and Kindly Farce," *ShS* 37 (1984), 33–40.

Thompson, Ann, ed., *The Taming of the Shrew*. Cambridge, Eng., 1984.

Thorne, W. B. "Folk Elements in *The Taming of the Shrew*," *Queen's Quarterly* 75 (1968), 482–96.

A Midsummer Night's Dream

See also, under *Life in Shakespeare's England*, De Grazia, Quilligan, and Stallybrass (essay by Parker); under *Shakespeare Criticism from the 1940s to the 1970s*, Calderwood, Coghill, Garber, Granville-Barker, and Kott; under *Shakespeare Criticism Since 1980*, Callaghan (*A Feminist Companion*, essay by Loomba), Mazzio and Trevor (essay by Maus), Montrose, Parker, Paster, and Patterson (Chapter 3); and under *The Comedies*, Barber, Bloom (essay by Girard), Brown and Harris (essays by Kermode and Merchant), Carroll, Collins (essay by Halio), Evans, Huston, Leggatt, Lerner, Palmer and Bradbury (essay by Wells), and Smidt.

Bevington, David. " 'But We Are Spirits of Another Sort': The Dark Side of Love and Magic in *A Midsummer Night's Dream*," *Medieval and Renaissance Studies*, ed. Siegfried Wenzel. Chapel Hill, N.C., 1978.

Donaldson, E. Talbot. *The Swan at the Well: Shakespeare Reads Chaucer*. New Haven, 1985.

Garner, Shirley Nelson. "*A Midsummer Night's Dream*: 'Jack Shall Have Jill; Nought Shall Go Ill,' " *Women's Studies* 9 (1981), 47–63.

Girard, René. "Myth and Ritual in Shakespeare's *A Midsummer Night's Dream*," *Textual Strategies: Perspectives in Post-Structuralist Criticism*, ed. Josué V. Harari. Ithaca, N.Y., 1979.

Howard, Skiles. "Hands, Feet, and Bottoms: Decentering the Cosmic Dance in *A Midsummer Night's Dream*," *SQ* 44 (1993), 325–42.

Lamb, Mary Ellen. "*A Midsummer Night's Dream*: The Myth of Theseus and the Minotaur," *Texas Studies in Literature and Language* 21 (1979), 478–91.

———. " 'Taken by the Fairies': Fairy Practices and the Production of Popular Culture in *A Midsummer Night's Dream*," *SQ* 51 (2000), 277–312.

Montrose, Louis Adrian. " 'Shaping Fantasies': Figurations of Gender and Power in Elizabethan Culture," *Representations* 2 (1.2, Spring 1983), 61–94.

Nuttall, A. D. "*A Midsummer Night's Dream*: Comedy as *Apotrope* of Myth," *ShS* 53 (2000), 49–59.

Olson, Paul A. "*A Midsummer Night's Dream* and the Meaning of Court Marriage," *ELH* 24 (1957), 95–119.

Ormerod, David. "*A Midsummer Night's Dream*: The Monster in the Labyrinth," *ShakS* 11 (1978), 39–52.

Pearson, D'Orsay W. " 'Unkinde' Theseus: A Study in Renaissance Mythography," *English Literary Renaissance* 4 (1974), 276–98.

Wall, Wendy. "Why Does Puck Sweep?: Fairylore, Merry Wives, and Social Struggle," *SQ* 52 (2001), 67–106.

Warren, Roger. *"A Midsummer Night's Dream": Text and Performance*. Text and Performance. London, 1983.

Williams, Gary Jay. *Our Moonlight Revels: "A Midsummer Night's Dream" in the Theatre*. Ames, Iowa, 1997.

Young, David P. *Something of Great Constancy: The Art of "A Midsummer Night's Dream."* New Haven, 1966.

The Merchant of Venice

See also, under *Shakespeare's Predecessors and Contemporaries*, Rose (ed. *Renaissance Drama*, essay by Whigham); under *Shakespeare's Language*, Donawerth; under *Shakespeare Criticism from the 1940s to the 1970s*, Burkhardt, Fiedler, and Granville-Barker; under *Shakespeare Criticism Since 1980*, Auden, Callaghan (*A Feminist Companion*, essay by Singh), Dawson, Erickson and Kahn (essays by Kahn and Wheeler), Garber (*Cannibals*, essay by Mullaney), Grady (essays by Drakakis, Freinkel, and Mallin), Howard and O'Connor (essay by Moisan), Mazzio and Trevor (essay by Siemon), Novy (*Love's Argument*, Chapter 4), Rabkin, and Wayne (essay by Leventen); and under *The Comedies*, Barber, Bradbury and Palmer (essay by Palmer), Brown and Harris (essays by J. R. Brown and Kermode), Evans, Leggatt, Levin, Nevo, and Smidt.

Auden, W. H. "Brothers and Others," *"The Dyer's Hand" and Other Essays*. New York, 1948.

Berger, Harry, Jr. "Marriage and Mercifixion in *The Merchant of Venice:* The Casket Scene Revisited," *SQ* 32 (1981), 155–62.

Boose, Lynda E. "The Comic Contract and Portia's Golden Ring," *ShakS* 20 (1988), 241–54.

Bulman, James C. *The Merchant of Venice*. Shakespeare in Performance. Manchester, Eng., 1991.

Cohen, Walter. "*The Merchant of Venice* and the Possibilities of Historical Criticism," *ELH* 49 (1982), 765–89.

Danson, Lawrence. *The Harmonies of "The Merchant of Venice."* New Haven and London, 1978.

Dessen, Alan C. "The Elizabethan Stage Jew and Christian Example: Gerontus, Barabas, and Shylock," *Modern Language Quarterly* 35 (1974), 231–45.

Edelman, Charles. "Which is the Jew that Shakespeare Knew? Shylock on the Elizabethan Stage," *ShS* 52 (1999), 99–106.

Engle, Lars. " 'Thrift is Blessing': Exchange and Explanation in *The Merchant of Venice*," *SQ* 37 (1986), 20–37.

Freud, Sigmund. "The Theme of the Three Caskets," *Complete Psychological Works of Sigmund Freud*, trans. James Strachey et al. London, 1973–4.

Girard, René. " 'To Entrap the Wisest': A Reading of *The Merchant of Venice*," *Literature and Society*. Selected Papers from the English Institute, 1978, ed. Edward W. Said. Baltimore, 1980.

Hutson, Lorna. *The Usurer's Daughter: Male Friendship and Fictions of Women in Sixteenth-Century England*. London and New York, 1994.

Jardine, Lisa. "Cultural Confusion and Shakespeare's Learned Heroines: 'These Are Old Paradoxes,' " *SQ* 38 (1987), 1–18.

Lever, J. W. "Shylock, Portia, and the Values of Shakespearian Comedy," *SQ* 3 (1952), 383–6.

Lewalski, Barbara K. "Biblical Allusion and Allegory in *The Merchant of Venice*," *SQ* 13 (1962), 327–43.

MacKay, Maxine. "*The Merchant of Venice:* A Reflection of the Early Conflict Between Courts of Law and Courts of Equity," *SQ* 15:4 (1964), 371–5.

Moody, A. D. *Shakespeare: "The Merchant of Venice."* London, 1964.

Newman, Karen. "Portia's Ring: Unruly Women and Structures of Exchange in *The Merchant of Venice*," *SQ* 38 (1987), 19–33.

Normand, Lawrence. "Reading the Body in *The Merchant of Venice*," *Textual Practice* 5 (1991), 55–73.

Overton, Bill. *"The Merchant of Venice": Text and Performance*. Atlantic Highlands, N.J., 1987.

Parten, Anne. "Re-establishing Sexual Order: The Ring Episode in *The Merchant of Venice*," *Women's Studies* 9 (1982), 145–55.

Pettet, E. C. "*The Merchant of Venice* and the Problem of Usury," *English Association Essays and Studies* 31 (1945), 19–33.

Shapiro, James. *Shakespeare and the Jews*. New York, 1996.

Whigham, Frank. "Ideology and Class Conduct in *The Merchant of Venice*," *Renaissance Drama* 10 (1979), 93–115.

Yaffe, Martin D. *Shylock and the Jewish Question*. Baltimore, 1997.

Much Ado About Nothing

See also, under *Shakespeare's Predecessors and Contemporaries*, Marrapodi (essay by Salingar); under *The Comedies*, R. Berry, Brown, Cordner et al. (essay by Everett), Evans, Hunter, Huston, Leggatt, Levin, Nevo, Newman, Salingar, and Stevenson; under *Shakespeare Criticism from the 1940s to the 1970s*, Rossiter; and under *Shakespeare Criticism Since 1980*, Howard and O'Connor (essay by Howard), Kirsch, Lenz et al. (essay by Hays), and Neely.

Barish, Jonas A. "Pattern and Purpose in the Prose of *Much Ado About Nothing*," *Rice U. Studies* 60:2 (1974), 19–30.

Berger, Harry, Jr. "Against the Sink-a-Pace: Sexual and Family Politics in *Much Ado About Nothing*," *SQ* 33 (1982), 302–13.

Cook, Carol. "'The Sign and Semblance of Her Honor': Reading Gender Difference in *Much Ado about Nothing*," *PMLA* 101 (1986), 186–202.

Dawson, Anthony B. "Much Ado about Signifying," *Studies in English Literature* 22 (1982), 211–21.

Dusinberre, Juliet. "Much Ado about Lying," *Shakespeare Readers, Audiences, Players*, eds. R. S. White, Charles Edelman, and Christopher Wortham. Nedlands, Australia, 1998.

Everett, Barbara. "*Much Ado About Nothing*," *Critical Quarterly* 3 (1961), 319–35.

Friedman, Michael D. "Male Bonds and Marriage in *All's Well* and *Much Ado*," *Studies in English Literature* 35 (1995), 231–49.

Jorgensen, Paul A. "*Much Ado About Nothing*," *SQ* 5 (1954), 287–95. Rpt. in *Redeeming Shakespeare's Words*. Berkeley, 1962.

Lane, Robert. " 'Foremost in report': Social Identity and Masculinity in *Much Ado About Nothing*," *Upstart Crow* 16 (1996), 31–47.

Lewalski, Barbara K. "Love, Appearance, and Reality: Much Ado About Something," *Studies in English Literature* 8 (1968), 235–51.

Mason, Pamela. *"Much Ado About Nothing": Text and Performance*. Basingstoke, 1992.

Ormerod, David. "Faith and Fashion in *Much Ado About Nothing*," *ShS* 25 (1972), 93–105.

Taylor, Michael. "*Much Ado About Nothing*: The Individual in Society," *Essays in Criticism* 23 (1973), 146–53.

As You Like It

See also, under *The Comedies*, Barber, R. Berry, Bradbury and Palmer (essay by Anne Barton), Brown, Hunter, Leggatt, Nevo, and Salingar; and under *Shakespeare Criticism Since 1980*, Belsey, Callaghan (*A Feminist Companion*, essay by Neely), Erickson, Lenz et al. (essay by Park), Mahon and Pendleton (essay by Gibbons), and McDonald (essay by Wofford).

Alpers, Paul. *What Is Pastoral?* Chicago, 1996.

Barnet, Sylvan. "Strange Events: Improbability in *As You Like It*," *ShakS* 4 (1968), 119–31.

Bono, Barbara J. "Mixed Gender, Mixed Genre in Shakespeare's *As You Like It*," *Renaissance Genres: Essays on Theory, History, and Interpretation*, ed. Barbara Kiefer Lewalski. Cambridge, Mass., 1986.

Debax, Jean-Paul, and Yves Peyré, eds. *"As You Like It": Essais critiques*. Toulouse, 1998.

Doran, Madeleine. " 'Yet Am I Inland Bred,'" *SQ* 15:2 (1964), 99–114.

Fortin, René E. " 'Tongues in Trees': Symbolic Patterns in *As You Like it*," *Texas Studies in Literature and Language* 14 (1973), 569–82.

Gardner, Helen. "*As You Like It*," *More Talking of Shakespeare*, ed. John Garrett. London and New York, 1959.

Halio, Jay L. " 'No Clock in the Forest': Time in *As You Like It*," *Studies in English Literature* 2 (1962), 197–207.

Hayles, Nancy K. "Sexual Disguise in *As You Like It* and *Twelfth Night*," *ShS* 32 (1979), 63–72.

Howard, Jean E. "Crossdressing, The Theatre, and Gender Struggle in Early Modern England," *SQ* 39 (1988), 418–40.

Kernan, Alvin B. *The Cankered Muse*. New Haven, 1959.

Knowles, Richard. "Myth and Type in *As You Like It*," *ELH* 33 (1966), 1–22.

Marshall, Cynthia. "The Doubled Jaques and Constructions of Negation in *As You Like It*," *SQ* 49 (1998), 375–92.

Montrose, Louis Adrian. " 'The Place of a Brother' in *As You Like It*: Social Process and Comic Form," *SQ* 32 (1981), 28–54.

Ronk, Martha. "Locating the Visual in *As You Like It*," *SQ* 52 (2001), 255–76.

Schleiner, Louise. "Voice, Ideology, and Gendered Subjects: The Case of *As You Like It* and *Two Gentlemen*," *SQ* 50 (1999), 285–309.

Young, David. *The Heart's Forest*. New Haven, 1972.

Twelfth Night

See also, under *The Comedies*, Barber, E. Berry, Bradbury and Palmer (essay by Anne Barton), Brown, Brown and Harris (essay by Kermode), Hunter, Leggatt, Levin, Nevo, and Salingar; and under *Shakespeare Criticism Since 1980*, Callaghan (*A Feminist Companion*, essay by Neely), Erickson and Kahn (essay by Booth), Greenblatt (*Shakespearean Negotiations*, Chapter 3), Hamilton (Chapter 4), Hawkes (essay by Elam), Howard, and Parker and Hartman (essay by Hartman).

Arlidge, Anthony. *Shakespeare and the Prince of Love: The Feast of Misrule in the Middle Temple.* London, 2000.

Auden, W. H. "Music in Shakespeare," *"The Dyer's Hand" and Other Essays.* New York, 1948.

Bloom, Harold, ed. *Modern Critical Interpretations of "Twelfth Night."* New York, 1987.

Booth, Stephen. *Precious Nonsense: The Gettysburg Address, Ben Jonson's Epitaphs on His Children, and "Twelfth Night."* Berkeley, 1998.

Brown, John Russell. "Directions for *Twelfth Night,* or What You Will," *Tulane Drama Review* 5:4 (1961), 77–88.

Downer, Alan S. "Feste's Night," *College English* 13 (1952), 258–65.

Eagleton, Terence. "Language and Reality in *Twelfth Night,*" *Critical Quarterly* 9 (1967), 217–28.

Elam, Keir. "The Fertile Eunuch: *Twelfth Night,* Early Modern Intercourse, and the Fruits of Castration," *SQ* 47 (1996), 1–36.

Hollander, John. *"Twelfth Night* and the Morality of Indulgence," *Sewanee Review* 67 (1959), 220–38.

Hutson, Lorna. "On Not Being Deceived: Rhetoric and the Body in *Twelfth Night,*" *Texas Studies in Literature and Language* 38 (1996), 140–74.

Kerrigan, John. "Secrecy and Gossip in *Twelfth Night,*" *ShS* 50 (1997), 65–80.

Leech, Clifford. *"Twelfth Night" and Shakespearian Comedy.* Toronto, 1965.

Lewalski, Barbara K. "Thematic Patterns in *Twelfth Night,*" *ShakS* 1 (1965), 168–81.

Potter, Lois. *"Twelfth Night": Text and Performance.* London, 1985.

Salingar, L. D. "The Design of *Twelfth Night,*" *SQ* 9 (1958), 117–39.

Shannon, Laurie J. "Nature's Bias: Renaissance Homonormativity and Elizabethan Likeness," *Modern Philology* 98 (2000), 183–210.

Wells, Stanley. *Royal Shakespeare.* Manchester, Eng., 1977. (Includes an account of John Barton's production of *Twelfth Night.*)

Welsford, Enid. *The Fool: His Social and Literary History.* London, 1935.

Williams, Porter, Jr. "Mistakes in *Twelfth Night* and Their Resolution," *PMLA* 76 (1961), 193–9.

Measure for Measure

See also, under *The Comedies,* Hunter and Newman; under *The Problem Plays,* Frye, Schanzer, and Wheeler; under *Shakespeare Criticism from the 1940s to the 1970s,* Empson, Fly, Holland, Levin (pp. 171–93), and Sewell; and under *Shakespeare Criticism Since 1980,* Cox, Dollimore, Dollimore and Sinfield (essays by Dollimore and McLuskie), Drakakis (essay by Rose), Goldberg (Chapter 5), Grady (*Shakespeare and Modernity,* essay by Engle), Hamilton (Chapter 5), Holland et al. (essay by Adelman), Kirsch, Marcus, Mullaney (Chapter 4), and Skura (pp. 243–70).

Bennett, Josephine Waters. *"Measure for Measure" as Royal Entertainment.* New York, 1966.

Bennett, Robert B. *Romance and Reformation: The Erasmian Spirit of Shakespeare's "Measure for Measure."* Newark, Del., 2000.

Brown, Carolyn E. "The Wooing of Duke Vincentio and Isabella of *Measure for Measure:* 'The Image of It Gives [Them] Content,' " *ShakS* 22 (1994), 189–219.

Cacicedo, Alberto. " 'She is fast my wife': Sex, Marriage, and Ducal Authority in *Measure for Measure,*" *ShakS* 23 (1995), 187–209.

Chamberlain, Stephanie. "Defrocking Ecclesiastical Authority: *Measure for Measure* and the Struggle for Matrimonial Reform in Early Modern England," *Ben Jonson Journal* 7 (2000), 115–28.

Chambers, R. W. "The Jacobean Shakespeare and *Measure for Measure,*" *Proceedings of the British Academy* 23 (1937), 135–92.

Coghill, Nevill. "Comic Form in *Measure for Measure,*" *ShS* 8 (1955), 14–27.

Desens, Marliss C. *The Bed-Trick in English Renaissance Drama: Explorations in Gender, Sexuality, and Power.* Newark, Del., 1994.

Fergusson, Francis. *The Human Image in Dramatic Literature.* Garden City, N.Y., 1957.

Gless, Darryl. *"Measure for Measure," the Law, and the Convent.* Princeton, 1979.

Lascelles, Mary. *Shakespeare's "Measure for Measure."* London, 1953.

Leavis, F. R. "The Greatness of *Measure for Measure,*" *Scrutiny* 10 (1942), 234–47.

Leggatt, Alexander. "Substitution in *Measure for Measure,*" *SQ* 39 (1988), 342–59.

Nagarajan, S. *"Measure for Measure* and Elizabethan Betrothals," *SQ* 14 (1963), 115–19.

Shell, Marc. *The End of Kinship: "Measure for Measure," Incest, and the Ideal of Universal Siblinghood.* Stanford, 1988.

Stevenson, David L. *The Achievement of "Measure for Measure."* Ithaca, N.Y., 1966.

Wilson, Harold S. "Action and Symbol in *Measure for Measure* and *The Tempest.*" *SQ* 4 (1953), 375–84.

Wood, Nigel. *"Measure for Measure."* Theory in Practice Series. Buckingham and Philadelphia, 1996.

The Histories

Alexander, Peter. *Shakespeare's, "Henry VI" and "Richard III."* Cambridge, Eng., 1929.

Berry, Edward I. *Patterns of Decay: Shakespeare's Early Histories.* Charlottesville, Va., 1975.

Blanpied, John W. *Time and the Artist in Shakespeare's English Histories.* Newark, Del., 1983.

Calderwood, James L. *Metadrama in Shakespeare's Henriad: "Richard II" to "Henry V."* Berkeley, 1979.

Campbell, Lily B. *Shakespeare's "Histories": Mirrors of Elizabethan Policy.* San Marino, Calif., 1947.

Champion, Larry S. *"The Noise of Threatening Drum": Dramatic Strategy and Political Ideology in Shakespeare and the English Chronicle Plays.* Newark, Del., 1990.

———. *Perspective in Shakespeare's English Histories.* Athens, Ga., 1980.

Dorius, R. J. "A Little More Than a Little," *SQ* 11 (1960), 13–26.

Edwards, Philip. "The Hidden King: Shakespeare's History Plays," *Threshold of a Nation: A Study in English and Irish Drama.* Cambridge, Eng., 1979.

Forker, Charles R. "Shakespeare's Chronicle Plays as Historical-Pastoral," *ShakS* 1 (1965), 85–104.

Hodgdon, Barbara. *The End Crowns All: Closure and Contradiction in Shakespeare's History.* Princeton, 1991.

Holderness, Graham. *Shakespeare's History.* New York, 1985. Largely reprinted in *Shakespeare Recycled: The Making of Historical Drama.* Hempstead, Eng., New York, 1992.

———, ed. *Shakespeare's History Plays: "Richard II" to "Henry V."* London, 1992.

Howard, Jean E., and Phyllis Rackin. *Engendering a Nation: A Feminist Account of Shakespeare's English Histories.* London and New York, 1997.

Jenkins, Harold. "Shakespeare's History Plays: 1900–1951," *ShS* 6 (1953), 1–15.

Jorgensen, Paul A. *Shakespeare's Military World.* Berkeley and Los Angeles, 1956.

Kastan, David Scott. *Shakespeare and the Shapes of Time.* Hanover, N. H., 1982.

Kelly, Henry A. *Divine Providence in the England of Shakespeare's Histories.* Cambridge, Mass., 1970.

Knights, L. C. "Shakespeare's Politics: With Some Reflections on the Nature of Tradition," *Proceedings of the British Academy* 43 (1957), 115–32.

Leggatt, Alexander. *Shakespeare's Political Drama: The History Plays and the Roman Plays.* London, 1988.

Levine, Nina S. *Women's Matters: Politics, Gender, and Nation in Shakespeare's Early History Plays.* Newark, Del., 1998.

Manheim, Michael. *The Weak King Dilemma in the Shakespearean History Play.* Syracuse, N.Y., 1973.

Norwich, John Julius. *Shakespeare's Kings: The Great Plays and the History of England in the Middle Ages: 1337–1485.* London, 1999; New York, 2000.

Ornstein, Robert. *A Kingdom for a Stage.* Cambridge, Mass., 1972.

Palmer, John. *Political Characters of Shakespeare.* London, 1945.

Paris, Bernard J. *Character as a Subversive Force in Shakespeare: The History and Roman Plays.* Rutherford, N.J., and London, 1991.

Patterson, Annabel. *Reading Holinshed's Chronicles.* Chicago, 1994.

Pierce, Robert B. *Shakespeare's History Plays: The Family and the State.* Columbus, Ohio, 1971.

Pilkington, Ace G. *Screening Shakespeare from "Richard II" to "Henry V."* Newark, Del., 1991.

Porter, Joseph. *The Drama of Speech Acts: Shakespeare's Lancastrian Tetralogy.* Berkeley, 1979.

Prior, Moody E. *The Drama of Power: Studies in Shakespeare's History Plays*. Evanston, Ill., 1973.

Pugliatti, Paola. *Shakespeare the Historian*. New York, 1996.

Pye, Christopher. *The Regal Phantasm: Shakespeare and the Politics of Spectacle*. London, 1990.

Rackin, Phyllis. "Anti-Historians: Women's Roles in Shakespeare's Histories," *Theatre Journal* 37 (1985), 329–44.

———. *Stages of History: Shakespeare's English Chronicles*. Ithaca, N.Y., 1990.

Reese, M. M. *The Cease of Majesty*. London and New York, 1961.

Ribner, Irving. *The English History Play in the Age of Shakespeare*, Rev. ed., London, 1965.

Rossiter, A. P. "Ambivalence: The Dialectic of the Histories," *Talking of Shakespeare*, ed. John Garrett. London, 1954.

Saccio, Peter. *Shakespeare's English Kings: History, Chronicle, and Drama*. New York, 1977.

Shaheen, Naseeb. *Biblical References in Shakespeare's History Plays*. Newark, Del., 1989.

Sprague, Arthur Colby. *Shakespeare's Histories: Plays for the Stage*. London, 1964.

Sterling, Eric. *The Movement Towards Subsversion: The English History Play from Skelton to Shakespeare*. Lanham, Md., 1996.

Tillyard, E. M. W. *Shakespeare's History Plays*. London, 1944, 1961.

Traversi, Derek. *Shakespeare from "Richard II" to "Henry V."* London, 1957.

Velz, John W., ed. *Shakespeare's English Histories: A Quest for Form and Genre*. Binghamton, N.Y., 1996.

Winny, James. *The Player King: A Theme of Shakespeare's Histories*. London, 1968.

Yeats, William Butler. "At Stratford-upon-Avon," *Ideas of Good and Evil*. London, 1903.

Richard III

See also, under *The Histories*, Alexander, Berry, Campbell, Kelly, Ornstein, Prior, Ribner, and Saccio; under *Shakespeare's Predecessors and Contemporaries*, Sanders; under *Shakespeare Criticism from the 1940s to the 1970s*, Jones, Rossiter, and Spivack; under *Shakespeare Criticism since 1980*, Dubrow and Strier (essay by Garber), and Lenz et al. (essay by Miner); under *The Tragedies*, Garner and Sprengnether (essay by Rackin), and Hunter; and under *The Henry VI Plays*, Watson.

Anderson, Judith H. "Shakespeare's *Richard III*: The Metamorphosis of Biographical Truth to Fiction," *Biographical Truth: The Representation of Historical Persons in Tudor-Stuart Writing*. New Haven, 1984.

Bevington, David. " 'Why Should Calamity Be Full of Words?' The Efficacy of Cursing in *Richard III*," *Iowa State Journal of Research* 56:1 (1981), 9–21.

Colley, Scott. *"Richard's Himself Again": A Stage History of "Richard III."* New York, 1992.

French, A. L. "The World of *Richard III*," *ShakS* 4 (1968), 25–39.

Hankey, Julie, ed. *Plays in Performance: "Richard III."* Bristol, 1981; 2nd ed., 1988.

Hassel, R. Chris, Jr. *Songs of Death: Performance, Interpretation, and the Text of "Richard III."* Lincoln, Neb., 1987.

Hunter, Robert G. *Shakespeare and the Mystery of God's Judgments*. Athens, Ga., 1976.

Kendall, Paul Murray. *Richard the Third*. New York and London, 1956.

Krieger, Murray. "The Dark Generations of *Richard III*," *Criticism* 1 (1959), 32–48.

Neill, Michael. "Shakespeare's Halle of Mirrors: Play, Politics, and Psychology in *Richard III*," *ShakS* 8 (1975), 99–129.

Sher, Antony. *Year of the King: An Actor's Diary and Sketchbook*. London, 1985.

Torrey, Michael. " 'The plain devil and dissembling looks': Ambivalent Physiognomy and Shakespeare's *Richard III*," *English Literary Renaissance* 30 (2000), 123–53.

Wheeler, Richard P. "History, Character, and Conscience in *Richard III*," *Comparative Drama* 5 (1971–1972), 301–21.

Richard II

See also, under *The Histories*, Calderwood, Campbell, Dorius, Forker, Ornstein, Palmer, Porter, Reese, Ribner, Saccio and Tillyard; under *Shakespeare's Predecessors and Contemporaries*, Sanders; under *Shakespeare's Language*, Mahood; under *Shakespeare Criticism to the 1930s*, Coleridge (*Coleridge's Writings*); under *Shakespeare Criticism from the 1940s to the 1970s*, Bryant, Calderwood, Hawkes, Kernan (essay on the "Major History Plays"), and Rabkin (pp. 81–98); under *Shakespeare Criticism Since 1980*, Bergeron (essay by Black), Parker and Hartman (essay by Berger), and Woodbridge and Berry (essay by Liebler); under *Shakespeare in Performance*, McGuire and Samuelson (essay by McGuire); and under *The Tragedies*, Nevo.

Barkan, Leonard. "The Theatrical Consistency of *Richard II*," *SQ* 29 (1978), 5–19.

Berger, Harry, Jr. "Textual Dramaturgy: Representing the Limits of Theatre in *Richard II*," *Theatre Journal* 39 (1987), 135–55.

Bergeron, David M. "*Richard II*: Internal and External Evidence," *Practicing Renaissance Scholarship: Plays and Pageants, Patrons and Politics*. Pittsburgh, Pa., 2000.

Dorius, R. J. "A Little More Than a Little," *SQ* 11 (1960), 13–26.

Elliott, John R., Jr. "History and Tragedy in *Richard II*," *Studies in English Literature* 8 (1968), 253–71.

Forker, Charles. *Shakespeare: The Critical Tradition: Richard II*. London, 1998.

Gaudet, Paul. "The 'Parasitical' Counselors in Shakespeare's *Richard II*: A Problem in Dramatic Interpretation," *SQ* 33 (1982), 142–54.

Halvorson, John. "The Lamentable Comedy of Richard II," *English Literary Renaissance* 24 (1994), 343–69.

Harris, Kathryn Montgomery. "Sun and Water Imagery in *Richard II*: Its Dramatic Function," *SQ* 21 (1970), 157–65.

Heninger, S. K., Jr. "The Sun-King Analogy in *Richard II*," *SQ* 11 (1960), 319–27.

Humphreys, A. R. *Shakespeare: "Richard II."* London, 1967.

Kantorowicz, Ernst H. *The King's Two Bodies: A Study in Medieval Political Theology*. Princeton, 1957.

Lisak, Catherine. "In Search of *Richard II*: Shakespeare's Use of Eyewitness Accounts of the Revolution (1399–1400); Conflicting Tales and the Dramatic Structure of the Play," *Shakespeare et le Moyen-Âge*. Actes du colloque international de la Société française Shakespeare, gen. ed. Jean-Marie Maguin. Montpellier, France, 2002.

MacKenzie, Clayton G. "Paradise and Paradise Lost in *Richard II*," *SQ* 37 (1986), 318–39.

McMillin, Scott. "Shakespeare's *Richard II*: Eyes of Sorrow, Eyes of Desire," *SQ* 35 (1984), 40–52.

Page, Malcolm. *Text and Performance: "Richard II."* Atlantic Highlands, N.J., 1987.

Potter, Lois. "The Antic Disposition of Richard II," *ShS* 27 (1974), 33–41.

Schoenbaum, S. "*Richard II* and the Realities of Power," *ShS* 28 (1975), 1–13.

Shewring, Margaret. *Shakespeare in Performance: "King Richard II."* Manchester, Eng., 1996.

Stirling, Brents. "Bolingbroke's 'Decision,'" *SQ* 2 (1951), 27–34.

Yeats, W. B. "At Stratford-upon-Avon," *Ideas of Good and Evil*, collected in *Essays and Introductions*. New York, 1961.

Zitner, Sheldon P. "Aumerle's Conspiracy," *Studies in English Literature* 14 (1974), 239–57.

Henry IV, Part I

See also, under *The Histories*, Blanpied, Calderwood, Campbell, Dorius, Kelly, Manheim, Ornstein, Palmer, Porter, Prior, Reese, Saccio, Sprague, Tillyard, and Velz (essay by Rumrich); under *Shakespeare Criticism to the 1930s*, Johnson and Smith (*Eighteenth Century*, essay by Morgann); under *Shakespeare Criticism from the 1940s to the 1970s*, Bevington and Halio (essay by R. G. Hunter), Bryant, Burckhardt, Council, Goldman, Kernan (essay on the "Major History Plays"), Spivack, and Stewart; and under *Shakespeare Criticism Since 1980*, Auden, Dollimore and Sinfield (essay by Greenblatt, originally published by *Glyph 8* and in *Shakespearean Negotiations*), Nuttall, and Watson; and under *The Comedies*, Barber.

Auden, W. H. "The Prince's Dog," *"The Dyer's Hand" and Other Essays*. New York, 1948.

Barber, C. L. "Rule and Misrule in *Henry IV*," *Shakespeare's Festive Comedy*. Princeton, 1959.

Barish, Jonas A. "The Turning Away of Prince Hal," *ShakS* 1 (1965), 9–17.

Bryant, J. A., Jr., "Prince Hal and the Ephesians," *Sewanee Review* 67 (1959), 204–19.

Cohen, Derek. "The Rite of Violence in *1 Henry IV*," *ShS* 38 (1985), 77–84.

Dessen, Alan. "Dual Protagonists in *1 Henry IV*," *Shakespeare and the Late Moral Plays*. Lincoln, Neb., 1986.

Doran, Madeleine. "Imagery in *Richard II* and in *Henry IV*," *Modern Language Review* 37 (1942), 113–22.

Dorius, R. J., ed. *Twentieth Century Interpretations of "Henry IV Part I."* Englewood Cliffs, N.J., 1970.

Empson, William. "Falstaff and Mr. Dover Wilson," *Kenyon Review* 15 (1953), 213–62.

Everett, Barbara. "The Fatness of Falstaff: Shakespeare and Character," *Proceedings of the British Academy* 76 (1990), 109–28.

Gottschalk, Paul A. "Hal and the 'Play Extempore' in *1 Henry IV*," *Texas Studies in Literature and Language* 15 (1974), 605–14.

Hawkins, Sherman H. "Virtue and Kingship in Shakespeare's *Henry IV*," *English Literary Renaissance* 5 (1975), 313–43.

Jenkins, Harold. *The Structural Problem in Shakespeare's "Henry the Fourth."* London, 1956.

Kris, Ernst. "Prince Hal's Conflict," *Psychoanalytic Explorations in Art*. New York, 1964.

Levine, Nina. "Extending Credit in the *Henry IV Plays*," *SQ* 51 (2000), 403–31.

McAlindon, Tom. *Shakespeare's Tudor History: A Study of "Henry IV, Parts 1 and 2."* Aldershot, Eng., 2001.

McLuhan, Herbert Marshall. "*Henry IV*, A Mirror for Magistrates," *University of Toronto Quarterly* 17 (1947–1948), 152–60.

McMillin, Scott. *Shakespeare in Performance: "Henry IV, Part One."* Manchester, Eng., 1991.

Palmer, D. J. "Casting Off the Old Man: History and St. Paul in *Henry IV*," *Critical Quarterly* 12 (1970), 267–83.

Poole, Kristen. "Saints Alive! Falstaff, Martin Marprelate, and the Staging of Puritanism," *SQ* 46 (1995), 47–75.

Toliver, Harold E. "Falstaff, the Prince, and the History Play," *SQ* 16 (1965), 63–80.

Wharton, T. F. "*Henry the Fourth, Parts 1 and 2*": *Text and Performance*. London, 1983.

Wilson, J. Dover. *The Fortunes of Falstaff*. Cambridge, Eng., 1943.

Womersley, David. "Why Is Falstaff Fat?" *Review of English Studies* n.s. 47 (1996), 1–22.

Henry V

See also, under *The Histories*, Calderwood, Campbell, Jorgensen, Kastan, Ornstein, Porter, Prior, Reese, Ribner, Saccio, and Traversi; under *Shakespeare Criticism to the 1930s*, Hazlitt and Schlegel; under *Shakespeare Criticism from the 1940s to the 1970s*, Burckhardt, Goddard, Goldman, and Kernan (essay on the "Major History Plays"); under *Shakespeare Criticism Since 1980*,

Dollimore and Sinfield (essays by Greenblatt and Tennenhouse), Drakakis (essay by Dollimore and Sinfield), Erickson, Mahon and Pendleton (essay by Hammond), Patterson (Chapter 4), and Rabkin (Chapter 2); and under *Shakespeare in Performance*, Price (essay by Barton).

Altman, Joel B. " 'Vile Participation': The Amplification of Violence in the Theater of *Henry V*," *SQ* 42 (1991), 1–32.

Beauman, Sally, ed. *"King Henry V": The Royal Shakespeare Company's Production of "Henry V" for the Centenary Season at the Royal Shakespeare Theatre*. Oxford, 1976. (Includes information on Terry Hands's *Henry V*.)

Cubeta, Paul M. "Falstaff and the Art of Dying," *Studies in English Literature* 27 (1987), 197–211.

Eggert, Katherine. "Nostalgia and the Not Yet Late Queen: Refusing Female Rule in *Henry V*," *ELH* 61 (1994), 523–50.

Granville-Barker, Harley. "From *Henry V* to *Hamlet*," *Proceedings of the British Academy* 11 (1925), 283–309.

Gurr, Andrew. "*Henry V* and the Bees' Commonwealth," *ShS* 30 (1977): 61–72.

Levin, Richard. "Hazlitt on *Henry V*, and the Appropriation of Shakespeare," *SQ* 35 (1984), 134–41.

McEachern, Claire. *The Poetics of English Nationhood, 1590–1612*. Cambridge, Eng., 1996.

The Tragedies

See also, under *Shakespeare's Predecessors and Contemporaries*, Belsey.

Armstrong, Philip. *Shakespeare's Visual Regime: Tragedy, Psychoanalysis, and the Gaze*. Basingstoke and New York, 2000.

Baldo, Jonathan. *The Unmasking of Drama: Contested Representation in Shakespeare's Tragedies*. Detroit, 1996.

Barker, Francis, ed. *The Culture of Violence: Essays on Tragedy and History*. Chicago, 1993.

Barroll, J. Leeds. *Artificial Persons: The Formation of Character in the Tragedies of Shakespeare*. Columbia, S. C., 1974.

Bayley, John. *Shakespeare and Tragedy*. London, 1981.

Bell, Millicent. *Shakespeare's Tragic Skepticism*. New Haven, 2002.

Berry, Philippa. *Shakespeare's Feminine Endings: Disfiguring Death in the Tragedies*. London and New York, 1999.

Berry, Ralph. *Tragic Instance: The Sequence of Shakespeare's Tragedies*. Newark, Del., 1999.

Bradley, A. C. *Shakespearean Tragedy*. London, 1904. (*Hamlet, Othello, King Lear, Macbeth*.)

Brooke, Nicholas. *Shakespeare's Early Tragedies*. London and New York, 1968.

Brown, John Russell, and Bernard Harris, eds. *Early Shakespeare*. London, 1961.

Bulman, James C. *The Heroic Idiom of Shakespearean Tragedy*. Newark, Del., 1985.

Bushnell, Rebecca. *Tragedies of Tyrants: Political Thought and Theater in the English Renaissance*. Ithaca, N.Y., 1990.

Campbell, Lily B. *Shakespeare's Tragic Heroes: Slaves of Passion*. Cambridge, Eng., 1930.

Champion, Larry S. *Shakespeare's Tragic Perspective*. Athens, Ga., 1976.

Charlton, H. B. *Shakespearian Tragedy*. Cambridge, Eng., 1948.

Cunningham, I. V. *Woe or Wonder: The Emotional Effect of Shakespearean Tragedy*. Denver, 1951. Rpt. in *Tradition and Poetic Structure*. Denver, 1960.

Danson, Lawrence. *Tragic Alphabet: Shakespeare's Drama of Language*. New Haven and London, 1974.

Dickey, Franklin M. *Not Wisely But Too Well: Shakespeare's Love Tragedies*. San Marino, Calif., 1957.

Eliot, T. S. "Shakespeare and the Stoicism of Seneca," *Selected Essays, 1917–1932*. London, 1932.

Everett, Barbara. *Young Hamlet: Essays on Shakespeare's Tragedies*. Oxford, 1989.

Falco, Raphael. *Charismatic Authority in Early Modern English Tragedy*. Baltimore, 2000.

Farnham, Willard. *Shakespeare's Tragic Frontier*. Berkeley, 1950.

Frye, Northrop. *Fools of Time: Studies in Shakespearean Tragedy*. Toronto, 1967.

Gajowski, Evelyn. *The Art of Loving: Female Subjectivity and Male Discursive Traditions in Shakespeare's Tragedies*. Newark, Del., 1992.

Garner, Shirley Nelson, and Madelon Sprengnether, eds. *Shakespearean Tragedy and Gender*. Bloomington, Ind., 1996.

Goldman, Michael. *Acting and Action in Shakespearean Tragedy*. Princeton, 1985.

Grene, Nicholas. *Shakespeare's Tragic Imagination*. New York, 1992.

Hawkes, Terence. *Shakespeare and the Reason: A Study of the Tragedies and the Problem Plays*. London, 1964.

Held, George F. *The Good That Lives After Them: A Pattern in Shakespeare's Tragedies*. Heidelberg, 1995.

Holloway, John. *The Story of the Night: Studies in Shakespeare's Major Tragedies*. London and Lincoln, Neb., 1961.

Honigmann, E. A. J. *Myriad-Minded Shakespeare: Essays, Chiefly on the Tragedies and Problem Comedies*. New York, 1989.

———. *Shakespeare: Seven Tragedies Revisited: The Dramatist's Manipulation of Response*. London and New York, 1976. 2nd ed., 2002.

Hunter, Robert Grams. *Shakespeare and the Mystery of God's Judgments*. Athens, Ga., 1976.

Ide, Richard S. *Possessed with Greatness: The Heroic Tragedies of Chapman and Shakespeare*. Chapel Hill, N.C., 1980.

Kiefer, Frederick. *Fortune and Elizabethan Tragedy*. San Marino, Calif., 1983.

Kirsch, Arthur. *The Passions of Shakespeare's Tragic Heroes*. Charlottesville, Va., 1990.

Knight, G. Wilson. *The Wheel of Fire*. London, 1930, 1965.

Lawlor, John. *The Tragic Sense in Shakespeare*. London, 1960.

Leech, Clifford. *Shakespeare's Tragedies and Other Studies in Seventeenth-Century Drama.* London, 1950.

———, ed. *Shakespeare: The Tragedies.* Chicago, 1965.

Liebler, Naomi Conn. *Shakespeare's Festive Tragedy: The Ritual Foundations of Genre.* London and New York, 1995.

Mack, Maynard. *Everybody's Shakespeare: Reflections Chiefly on the Tragedies.* Lincoln, Neb., 1993.

———. "The Jacobean Shakespeare: Some Observations on the Construction of the Tragedies," *Jacobean Theatre,* ed. John Russell Brown and Bernard Harris. Stratford-upon-Avon Studies 1. London, 1960.

Mack, Maynard, Jr. *Killing the King: Three Studies in Shakespeare's Tragic Structure.* New Haven and London, 1973.

Margolies, David. *Monsters of the Deep: Social Dissolution in Shakespeare's Tragedies.* Manchester, Eng., 1992.

McAlindon, T. *Shakespeare's Tragic Cosmos.* Cambridge, Eng., 1991.

Miola, Robert S. *Shakespeare and Classical Tragedy: The Influence of Seneca.* Oxford, 1992.

Neill, Michael. *Issues of Death: Mortality and Identity in English Renaissance Tragedy.* Oxford, 1997.

Nevo, Ruth. *Tragic Form in Shakespeare.* Princeton, 1972.

Proser, Matthew N. *The Heroic Image in Five Shakespearean Tragedies.* Princeton, 1965.

Rackin, Phyllis. *Shakespeare's Tragedies.* New York, 1978.

Reid, Robert Lanier. *Shakespeare's Tragic Form: Spirit in the Wheel.* Newark, Del., 2000.

Ribner, Irving, *Patterns in Shakespearean Tragedy.* New York, 1960.

Rosen, William. *Shakespeare and the Craft of Tragedy.* Cambridge, Mass., 1960.

Sanders, Wilbur, and Howard Jacobson. *Shakespeare's Magnanimity: Four Tragic Heroes, Their Friends and Families.* Oxford, 1978.

Shaheen, Naseeb. *Biblical References in Shakespeare's Tragedies.* Newark, Del., 1987.

Smith, Molly. *The Darker World Within: Evil in the Tragedies of Shakespeare and His Successors.* Newark, Del., 1991.

Snyder, Susan. *The Comic Matrix of Shakespeare's Tragedies.* Princeton, 1979.

Spivack, Bernard. *Shakespeare and the Allegory of Evil.* New York, 1958.

Whitaker, Virgil. *The Mirror up to Nature.* San Marino, Calif., 1965.

Wilson, Harold S. *On the Design of Shakespearian Tragedy.* Toronto, 1957.

Young, David. *The Action to the Word: Structure and Style in Shakespearean Tragedy.* New Haven, 1990.

The Greek and Roman Tragedies

See also, under *Shakespeare Criticism Since 1980,* Paster (Chapter 3).

Brower, Reuben A. *Hero and Saint: Shakespeare and the Graeco-Roman Heroic Tradition.* New York and Oxford, 1971.

Cantor, Paul A. *Shakespeare's Rome: Republic and Empire.* Ithaca, N.Y., 1976.

Charney, Maurice, ed. *Discussions of Shakespeare's Roman Plays.* Boston, 1964.

———. *Shakespeare's Roman Plays: The Function of Imagery in the Drama.* Cambridge, Mass., 1961.

Knight, G. Wilson. *The Imperial Theme: Further Interpretations of Shakespeare's Tragedies Including the Roman Plays.* London, 1931, 1953.

Leggatt, Alexander. *Shakespeare's Political Drama: The History Plays and the Roman Plays.* London and New York, 1988.

MacCallum, M. W. *Shakespeare's Roman Plays and Their Background.* London, 1910.

Maxwell, J. C. "Shakespeare's Roman Plays: 1900–1956," *ShS* 10 (1957), 1–11.

Miles, Geoffrey. *Shakespeare and the Constant Romans.* Oxford, 1996.

Miola, Robert S. *Shakespeare's Rome.* Cambridge, Eng., 1983.

Nicoll, Allardyce, ed. *Shakespeare Survey 10* (1957).

Paris, Bernard J. *Character as a Subversive Force in Shakespeare: The History and Roman Plays.* Rutherford, N.J., and London, 1991.

Phillips, James E., Jr. *The State in Shakespeare's Greek and Roman Plays.* New York, 1940.

Simmons, J. L. *Shakespeare's Pagan World: The Roman Tragedies.* Charlottesville, Va., 1973.

Thomas, Vivian. *Shakespeare's Roman Worlds.* London, 1989.

Thomson, J. A. K. *Shakespeare and the Classics.* London, 1952.

Traversi, Derek. *Shakespeare: The Roman Plays.* Palo Alto, Calif., 1963.

Velz, John W. "The Ancient World in Shakespeare: Authenticity or Anachronism? A Retrospect," *ShS* 31 (1978), 1–12.

———. *Shakespeare and the Classical Tradition: A Critical Guide to Commentary,* 1660–1960. Minneapolis, 1968.

Romeo and Juliet

See also, under *The Tragedies,* Brooke, Brown and Harris (essay by Lawlor), Charlton, Dickey, Nevo, Ribner, and Snyder; under *Shakespeare's Language,* Mahood; under *Shakespeare Criticism to the 1930s,* Hazlitt; under *Shakespeare Criticism from the 1940s to the 1970s,* Calderwood, Granville-Barker, and Rabkin (pp. 162–84); under *Shakespeare Criticism Since 1980,* Callaghan (*A Feminist Companion,* essay by Berry), Daileader, Edwards et al. (essay by Wells), Erickson and Kahn (essay by Snow), Lenz et al. (essay by Kahn), and Novy (*Love's Argument*); and under *Shakespeare in Performance,* Brockbank (essay by Brenda Bruce).

Appelbaum, Robert. " 'Standing to the wall': The Pressures of Masculinity in *Romeo and Juliet,*" *SQ* 48 (1997), 251–72.

Auden, W. H. "Commentary on the Poetry and Tragedy of *Romeo and Juliet.*" The Laurel Shakespeare, gen. ed. Francis Fergusson. New York, 1958.

Evans, Bertrand. "The Brevity of Friar Lawrence," *PMLA* 65 (1950), 841–65.

Evans, Robert O. *The Osier Cage: Rhetorical Devices in "Romeo and Juliet."* Lexington, Ky., 1966.

Everett, Barbara. "*Romeo and Juliet:* The Nurse's Story," *Critical Quarterly* 14 (1972), 129–39.

Halio, Jay, ed. *"Romeo and Juliet": Texts, Contexts, and Interpretation.* Newark, Del., 1995.

Hosley, Richard. "The Use of the Upper Stage in *Romeo and Juliet,*" *SQ* 5 (1954), 371–9.

Levenson, Jill L. *Shakespeare in Performance: "Romeo and Juliet."* Manchester, Eng., 1987.

Melchiori, Giorgio. "Peter, Balthasar, and Shakespeare's Art of Doubling," *Modern Language Review* 78 (1983), 777–92.

Williams, George W., ed. *The Most Excellent and Lamentable Tragedie of Romeo and Juliet.* Durham, N.C., 1964.

Julius Caesar

See also, under *The Greek and Roman Tragedies,* Brower, Charney (both titles), Knight, Miola, and Traversi; under *Shakespeare's Language,* Doran; under *Shakespeare Criticism to the 1930s,* Shaw; under *Shakespeare Criticism from the 1940s to the 1970s,* Burckhardt, Council, Goldman (Chapter 4), Granville-Barker, Kernan (essay by Mack), Rabkin (pp. 105–19), and Stirling; under *Shakespeare Criticism Since 1980,* Kahn; under *The Problem Plays,* Schanzer; and under *The Histories,* Palmer.

Blits, Jan H. *The End of the Ancient Republic: Essays on "Julius Caesar."* Durham, N.C., 1982.

Burke, Kenneth. "Antony in Behalf of the Play," *Southern Review* 1 (1935), 308–19. Rpt. in *The Philosophy of Literary Form.* Baton Rouge, La., 1941.

Knights, L. C. "Shakespeare and Political Wisdom: A Note on the Personalism of *Julius Caesar* and *Coriolanus,*" *Sewanee Review* 61 (1953), 43–55.

Liebler, Naomi Conn. " 'Thou Bleeding Piece of Earth': The Ritual Ground of *Julius Caesar,*" *ShakS* 14 (1981), 175–96.

Miola, Robert S. *"Julius Caesar* and the Tyrannicide Debate," *Renaissance Quarterly* 38 (1985), 271–89.

Ornstein, Robert. "Seneca and the Political Drama of *Julius Caesar,*" *Journal of English and Germanic Philology* 57 (1958), 51–6.

Parker, Barbara L. " 'A Thing Unfirm': Plato's *Republic* and Shakespeare's *Julius Caesar,*" *SQ* 44 (1993), 30–43.

Paster, Gail Kern. " 'In the spirit of men there is no blood': Blood as Trope of Gender in *Julius Caesar,*" *SQ* 40 (1989), 284–98.

Ribner, Irving. "Political Issues in *Julius Caesar,*" *Journal of English and Germanic Philology* 56 (1957), 10–22.

Ripley, John. *"Julius Caesar" on Stage in England and America, 1599–1973*. Cambridge, Eng., 1980.

Rose, Mark. "Conjuring Caesar: Ceremony, History, and Authority in 1599," *English Literary Renaissance* 19 (1989), 291–304.

Velz, John W. "Clemency, Will, and Just Cause in *Julius Caesar*," *ShS* 22 (1969), 109–18.

———. " 'If I Were Brutus Now . . . ': Role-Playing in *Julius Caesar*," *ShakS* 4 (1968), 149–59.

———. "Undular Structure in *Julius Caesar*," *Modern Language Review* 66 (1971), 21–30.

Hamlet

See also, under *Shakespeare's Language*, Donawerth; under *The Tragedies*, Barker, Bradley, Brooke, Goldman, Holloway, Kirsch, Mack, Mack Jr., Rosen, and Whitaker; under *The Greek and Roman Tragedies*, Brower; under *Shakespeare's Predecessors and Contemporaries*, Bowers, and Rabkin (essay by Booth); under *Shakespeare Criticism to the 1930s*, Coleridge (*Coleridge's Writings*); under *Shakespeare Criticism from the 1940s to the 1970s*, Granville-Barker, Hawkes, and Righter; under *Shakespeare Criticism Since 1980*, Cavell (Chapter 5), Drakakis (essay by Rose), Erickson, Garber (*Shakespeare's Ghost Writers*, Chapter 6), Loomba and Orkin (essay by Bertoldi), Mazzio and Trevor (essays by De Grazia and Guillory), McDonald (essay by Parker), Parker and Hartman (essays by Weimann, Ferguson, and Hawkes), Patterson (Chapters 1 and 5), and Schwartz and Kahn (essays by Fineman and Leverenz); under *Shakespeare in Performance*, Bevington; and under *The Problem Plays*, Tillyard.

Bertram, Paul, and Bernice W. Kliman, eds. *The Three-Text "Hamlet": Parallel Texts of the First and Second Quartos and First Folio*. New York, 1991.

Bowers, Fredson T. "Hamlet as Minister and Scourge," *PMLA* 70 (1955), 740–9.

Calderwood, James L. *To Be and Not to Be: Negation and Metadrama in "Hamlet."* New York, 1983.

Charney, Maurice. *Style in "Hamlet."* Princeton, 1969.

Clayton, Thomas, ed. *The "Hamlet" First Published (Q1, 1603): Origin, Form, Intertextualities*. Newark, Del., 1992.

Dawson, Anthony B. *Hamlet*. Shakespeare in Performance. Manchester, Eng., 1995.

Eliot, T. S. "Hamlet and His Problems," *Selected Essays, 1917–1932*. London and New York, 1932.

Erlich, Avi. *Hamlet's Absent Father*. Princeton, 1977.

Ewbank, Inga-Stina. "*Hamlet* and the Power of Words," *ShS* 30 (1977), 85–102.

Fergusson, Francis. *The Idea of a Theater*. Princeton, 1949.

Foakes, R. A. *"Hamlet" versus "Lear": Cultural Politics and Shakespeare's Art*. Cambridge, Eng., 1993.

Frye, Roland Mushat. *The Renaissance "Hamlet": Issues and Responses in 1600*. Princeton, 1984.

Greenblatt, Stephen. *Hamlet in Purgatory*. Princeton, 2001.

Heilbrun, Carolyn G. *Hamlet's Mother and Other Women*. New York, 1990.

James, D. G. *The Dream of Learning*. Oxford, 1951.

Jones, Ernest. *Hamlet and Oedipus*. Rev. ed. New York, 1949, 1954.

Joseph, Bertram. *Conscience and the King*. London, 1953.

Kerrigan, William. *Hamlet's Perfection*. Baltimore, 1994.

Kitto, H. D. F. *Form and Meaning in Drama*. London, 1956.

Knights, L. C. *An Approach to Hamlet*. London, 1960.

Lacan, Jacques. "Desire and the Interpretation of Desire in *Hamlet*," *Yale French Studies* 55/56 (1977), 11–52.

Lee, John. *Shakespeare's "Hamlet" and the Controversies of Self*. Oxford, 2000.

Levin, Harry. *The Question of Hamlet*. New York and London, 1959.

Lewis, C. S. "Hamlet: The Prince or the Poem?" *Proceedings of the British Academy* 28 (1942), 139–54.

Mack, Maynard. "The World of *Hamlet*," *Yale Review* 41 (1952), 502–23.

McCoy, Richard C. "A Wedding and Four Funerals: Conjunction and Commemoration in *Hamlet*," *ShS* 54 (2001), 122–39.

McGee, Arthur. *The Elizabethan Hamlet*. New Haven, 1987.

Muir, Kenneth, and Stanley Wells, eds., *Aspects of "Hamlet": Articles Reprinted from "Shakespeare Survey."* Cambridge, Eng., 1979. (Especially essay by Inga-Stina Ewbank.)

Murray, Gilbert. *Hamlet and Orestes*. Annual Shakespeare Lecture for the British Academy, 1914. London, 1919.

Nicoll, Allardyce, ed. *Shakespeare Survey 9* (1956).

Nietzsche, Friedrich. "The Birth of Tragedy or: Hellenism and Pessimism" (1872), *The Birth of Tragedy and The Case of Wagner*, trans. Walter Kaufmann. New York, 1967.

Rose, Mark. "*Hamlet* and the Shape of Revenge," *English Literary Renaissance* 1 (1971), 132–43.

Rosenberg, Marvin. *The Masks of "Hamlet."* Newark, Del., 1992.

Skulsky, Harold. " 'I Know My Course': Hamlet's Confidence," *PMLA* 89 (1974), 477–86.

States, Bert O. *"Hamlet" and the Concept of Character*. Baltimore, 1992.

Tronch-Pérez, Jesús. *A Synoptic "Hamlet": A Critical-Synoptic Edition of the Second Quarto and First Folio Texts of "Hamlet."* València, Spain, 2002.

Wilson, J. Dover. *What Happens in "Hamlet."* London and New York, 1935, 1951.

Wright, George T. "Hendiadys and *Hamlet*," *PMLA* 96 (1981), 168–93.

Young, David. "Hamlet, Son of Hamlet," *Perspectives on "Hamlet,"* eds. William G. Holzberger and Peter B. Waldock. Lewisburg, Pa., and London, 1975.

Othello

See also, under *The Tragedies*, Philippa Berry, Bradley, Dickey, Garner and Sprengnether (essays by Orlin, Hendricks, and Rose), Goldman, Hawkes, Holloway, Knight, Snyder, and Spivack; under *Shakespeare's Language*, Doran; under *Shakespeare's Predecessors and Contemporaries*, Hendricks and Parker (essays by Boose and Parker); under *Shakespeare Criticism to the 1930s*, Coleridge (*Coleridge's Writings*) and Johnson; under *Shakespeare Criticism from the 1940s to the 1970s*, Empson, Fiedler, Granville-Barker, and Sewell; and under *Shakespeare Criticism Since 1980*, Cavell (Chapter 3), Daileder, Erickson, Erickson and Kahn (essay by Wheeler), Greenblatt (*Renaissance Self-Fashioning*, Chapter 6), Howard and O'Connor (essay by Newman), Kirsch, Lenz et al. (essay by Neely), Loomba and Orkin (essay by Burton), McDonald (essay by Parker), Novy (*Love's Argument*, Chapter 7), and Parker and Hartman (essays by Parker and Showalter).

Adamson, Jane. *"Othello" as Tragedy: Some Problems of Judgment and Feeling*. Cambridge, Eng., 1980.

Altman, Joel B. " 'Preposterous Conclusions': Eros, *Enargeia*, and the Composition of *Othello*," *Representations* 18 (1987), 129–57.

Bartels, Emily C. "Making More of the Moor: Aaron, Othello, and Renaissance Refashionings of Race," *SQ* 41 (1990), 433–54.

Bates, Catherine. "Weaving and Writing in *Othello*," *SQ* 46 (1995), 51–60.

Bayley, John. *The Characters of Love*. London, 1960.

Boose, Lynda E. "Othello's Handkerchief: 'The Recognizance and Pledge of Love'," *English Literary Renaissance* 5 (1975), 360–74.

Calderwood, James L. *The Properties of "Othello."* Amherst, Mass., 1989.

Dean, Leonard F., ed. *A Casebook on "Othello."* New York, 1961.

Evans, Robert C. "Friendship in Shakespeare's *Othello*," *Ben Jonson Journal* 6 (1999), 109–46.

Everett, Barbara. "Inside *Othello*." *ShS* 53 (2000), 184–95.

———. "Reflections on the Sentimentalist's *Othello*," *Critical Quarterly* 3 (1961), 127–39. (A comment on the Leavis article below.)

Garner, S. N. "Shakespeare's Desdemona," *ShakS* 9 (1976), 233–52.

Hankey, Julie, ed. *Plays in Performance: "Othello."* Bristol, 1987.

Heilman, Robert B. *Magic in the Web: Action and Language in "Othello."* Lexington, Ky., 1956.

Honigmann, E. A. J. *The Texts of "Othello" and Shakespearian Revision*. London, 1996.

Hyman, Stanley Edgar. *Iago: Some Approaches to the Illusion of His Motivation*. New York, 1970.

Jones, Eldred. *Othello's Countrymen: The African in English Renaissance Drama*. London, 1965.

Korda, Natasha. *Shakespeare's Domestic Economies: Gender and Property in Early Modern England*. Philadelphia, 2002 (Chapter 4).

Leavis, F. R. "Diabolic Intellect and the Noble Hero: Or The Sentimentalist's Othello," *The Common Pursuit*. London, 1952.

Muir, Kenneth, ed. *Shakespeare Survey 21* (1968).

Nowottny, Winifred M. T. "Justice and Love in *Othello*," *University of Toronto Quarterly* 21 (1952), 330–44.

Orkin, Martin. "Othello and the 'plain face' of Racism," *SQ* 38 (1987), 166–88.

Orlin, Lena Cowen. *Private Matters and Public Culture in Post-Reformation England*. Ithaca, N.Y., 1994.

Rosenberg, Marvin. *The Masks of "Othello."* Berkeley, 1961.

Seltzer, Daniel. "Elizabethan Acting in *Othello*," *SQ* 10 (1959), 201–10.

Snyder, Susan, ed. *"Othello": Critical Essays*. New York, 1988.

Stoll, E. E. *"Othello": An Historical and Comparative Study*. Minneapolis, 1915. Rpt. New York, 1964.

Wine, Martin L. *"Othello": Text and Performance*. London, 1984.

King Lear

See also, under *Life in Shakespeare's England*, De Grazia, Quilligan, and Stallybrass (essay by De Grazia); under *The Tragedies*, Bradley, Cunningham, Frye, Goldman, Holloway, Hunter, Kirsch, Knight, and Rosen; under *The Greek and Roman Tragedies*, Brower; under *Textual Criticism and Bibliography*, Blayney, and Taylor and Warren; under *Shakespeare's Language*, Doran; under *Shakespeare Criticism to the 1930s*, Hazlitt, Johnson, and Stoll; under *Shakespeare Criticism from the 1940s to the 1970s*, Bloom (essay by Jaffa), Burckhardt, Empson, Fly, Granville-Barker, Knights, Kott, and Sewell; under *Shakespeare Criticism Since 1980*, Auden, Boose, Cavell (Chapter 2, identical with the Cavell entry below), Dollimore, Dollimore and Sinfield (essay by McLuskie), Dubrow and Strier (essay by Strier), Erickson, Erickson and Kahn (essay by Berger), Garber (*Shakespeare's Ghost Writers*, Chapter 5), Greenblatt (*Shakespearean Negotiations*, Chapter 4), Loomba and Orkin (essay by Visser), Novy (*Love's Argument*), Patterson (Chapter 5), and Wayne (essay by Thompson); and under *The Romances*, Felperin and Young.

Alpers, Paul J. "*King Lear* and the Theory of the 'Sight Pattern'," *In Defense of Reading*, ed. Reuben A. Brower and Richard Poirier. New York, 1962.

Berger, Harry, Jr. "*King Lear*": The Lear Family Romance," *Centennial Review* 23 (1979), 348–76.

Booth, Stephen. "*King Lear," "Macbeth," Indefinition, and Tragedy*, New Haven, 1983.

Brownlow, F. W. *Shakespeare, Harsnett, and the Devils of Denham*. Newark, Del., 1993.

Cavell, Stanley. "The Avoidance of Love: A Reading of *King Lear," Must We Mean What We Say?* New York, 1969. Rpt. in *Disowning Knowledge in Six Plays of Shakespeare*. Cambridge, Eng., 1987.

Colie, Rosalie L., and F. T. Flahiff, eds. *Some Facets of "King Lear."* Toronto, 1974.

Danby, John F. *Shakespeare's Doctrine of Nature: A Study of "King Lear."* London, 1949.

Delany, Paul, *"King Lear"* and the Decline of Feudalism," *PMLA* 92 (1977), 429–40.

Elton, William R. *King Lear and the Gods*. San Marino, Calif., 1966. Rpt. Lexington, Ky., 1988.

Everett, Barbara. "The New *King Lear," Critical Quarterly* 2 (1960), 325–39.

Foakes, R. A. *"Hamlet" Versus "Lear": Cultural Politics and Shakespeare's Art*. Cambridge, Eng., 1993.

Freud, Sigmund. "The Theme of the Three Caskets," *Complete Psychological Works of Sigmund Freud* 12 (1911–1913), pp. 291–301. London, 1958.

Goldberg, S. L. *An Essay on "King Lear."* Cambridge, Eng., 1974.

Graham, Kenneth J. E. " 'Without the form of justice': Plainness and the Performance of Love in *King Lear," SQ* 42 (1991), 438–61.

Hardison, O. B., Jr. "Myth and History in *King Lear," SQ* 26 (1975), 227–42.

Heilman, Robert B. *This Great Stage: Image and Structure in "King Lear."* Baton Rouge, La., 1948. Rpt. Seattle, 1963.

Heinemann, Margot. " 'Demystifying the Mystery of State': *King Lear* and the World Upside Down," *ShS* 44 (1992), 75–83.

James, D. G. *The Dream of Learning*. Oxford, 1951.

Jorgensen, Paul A. *Lear's Self-Discovery*, Berkeley, 1967.

Kahn, Coppélia. "The Absent Mother in *King Lear," Rewriting the Renaissance: The Discourses of Sexual Difference in Early Modern Europe*, eds. Margaret W. Ferguson et al. Chicago, 1986.

Kernan, Alvin. "Formalism and Realism in Elizabethan Drama: The Miracles in *King Lear," Renaissance Drama* 9 (1966), 59–66.

Kirsch, Arthur. "The Emotional Landscape of *King Lear," SQ* 39 (1988), 154–70.

Kronenfeld, Judy. *King Lear and the Naked Truth: Rethinking the Language of Religion and Resistance*. Durham, N.C., 1998.

Leggatt, Alexander. *King Lear*. Shakespeare in Performance. Manchester, Eng., 1991.

Lothian, J. M. *"King Lear": A Tragic Reading of Life*. Toronto, 1949.

Lusardi, James P., and June Schlueter. *Reading Shakespeare in Performance: "King Lear."* Rutherford, N.J., 1991.

Mack, Maynard. *King Lear in Our Time*. Berkeley, 1965.

Maclean, Norman. "Episode, Scene, Speech, and Word: The Madness of Lear," *Critics and Criticism*, ed. R. S. Crane. Chicago, 1952.

Michie, Donald M., ed. *A Critical Edition of "The True Chronicle History of King Leir and His Three Daughters, Gonorill, Ragan and Cordella."* New York, 1991.

Murphy, John L. *Darkness and Devils: Exorcism and "King Lear."* Athens, Ohio, 1984.

Reibetanz, John. *The "Lear" World: A Study of "King Lear" in Its Dramatic Context*. Toronto, 1977.

Rosenberg, Marvin. *The Masks of "King Lear."* Berkeley, 1972.

Scott, William O. "Contracts of Love and Affection: Lear, Old Age, and Kingship," *ShS* 55 (2002), 36–42.

Sewall, Richard B. *The Vision of Tragedy*. New Haven, 1959.

Snyder, Susan. "*King Lear* and the Psychology of Dying," *SQ* 33 (1982), 449–60.

Soellner, Rolf. "*King Lear* and the Magic of the Wheel," *SQ* 35 (1984), 274–89.

Tate, Nahum. *The History of King Lear* (1681), ed. James Black. Lincoln, Neb. 1975.

Taylor, Gary, and Michael Warren, eds. *The Division of the Kingdoms: Shakespeare's Two Versions of "King Lear."* Oxford, 1983.

Urkowitz, Steven. *Shakespeare's Revision of "King Lear."* Princeton, 1980.

Warren, Michael, preparer. *The Parallel "King Lear," 1608–1623: Parallel Texts of the First Quarto (1608) and the First Folio (1623)*. Berkeley, 1989.

Wittreich, Joseph. *"Image of that Horror": History, Prophecy, and Apocalypse in "King Lear."* San Marino, Calif., 1984.

Macbeth

See also, under *The Tragedies*, Berry, Bradley, Garner and Sprengnether (essay by Adelman), Goldman, Holloway, Hunter, Kirsch, Mack, Mack Jr., and Rosen; under *Shakespeare Criticism to the 1930s*, Smith (essay by De Quincey); under *Shakespeare Criticism from the 1940s to the 1970s*, Sanders and Sewell; under *Shakespeare Criticism Since 1980*, Garber (*Cannibals*, essay by Adelman), Howard and O'Connor (essay by Goldberg), Mullaney (Chapter 5), Schwartz and Kahn (essay by Gohlke), Watson, and Woodbridge and Berry (essay by Willis); and under *The Histories*, Pye.

Bartholomeusz, Dennis. *"Macbeth" and the Players*. Cambridge, Eng., 1969.

Booth, Stephen. *"King Lear," "Macbeth," Indefinition, and Tragedy*. New Haven, 1983.

Brooks, Cleanth. "The Naked Babe and the Cloak of Manliness," *The Well Wrought Urn*. New York, 1947.

Calderwood, James L. *If It Were Done: "Macbeth" and Tragic Action*. Amherst, 1986.

Driver, Tom. *The Sense of History in Greek and Shakespearean Drama*. New York, 1960.

Elliott, G. R. *Dramatic Providence in "Macbeth."* Princeton, 1958.

Fergusson, Francis. "*Macbeth* as the Imitation of an Action," *English Institute Essays 1951* (1952), 31–43.

Freud, Sigmund. "Some Character-Types Met with in Psycho-Analytic Work," trans. E. Cobern Mayne, *Collected Papers*. Vol. 4, pp. 326–32. London, 1925.

Gardner, Helen. "Milton's 'Satan' and the Theme of Damnation in Elizabethan Tragedy," *English Association Essays and Studies* n.s. 1 (1948), 46–66.

Jorgensen, Paul A. *Our Naked Frailties: Sensational Art and Meaning in "Macbeth."* Berkeley, 1971.

Kliman, Bernice W. *Macbeth*. Shakespeare in Performance. Manchester, Eng., 1992.

Knights, L. C. "How Many Children Had Lady Macbeth? An Essay in the Theory and Practice of Shakespeare Criticism," *Explorations*. London, 1946. Rpt. Westport, Conn., 1975.

Norbrook, David. "*Macbeth* and the Politics of Historiography," *Politics of Discourse: The Literature and History of Seventeenth-Century England*, eds. Kevin Sharpe and Steven Zwicker, pp. 78–116. Berkeley, 1987.

Orgel, Stephen. "Macbeth and the Antic Round," *ShS* 52 (1999), 143–53. Rpt. in Orgel, under *Shakespeare Criticism Since 1980*.

Paul, Henry N. *The Royal Play of Macbeth*. New York, 1950.

Purkiss, Diane. *The Witch in History: Early Modern and Twentieth-Century Representations*. London and New York, 1996.

Rosenberg, Marvin. *The Masks of "Macbeth."* Berkeley, 1978.

Sinfield, Alan. "*Macbeth*: History, Ideology and Intellectuals," *Critical Quarterly* 28 (1986), 63–77.

Spender, Stephen. "Time, Violence, and *Macbeth*," *Penguin New Writing*, 3. London, 1940–1941.

Williams, Raymond. "Monologue in *Macbeth*," *Teaching the Text*, eds. Susanne Kappeler and Norman Bryson. London, 1983.

Wills, Garry. *Witches and Jesuits: Shakespeare's "Macbeth."* Oxford, 1995.

Antony and Cleopatra

See also, under *The Tragedies*, Frye, Garner and Sprengnether (essays by Cook and Charnes), Goldman, Holloway, Mack, and Rosen; under *The Greek and Roman Tragedies*, Brower, Cantor, Charney, Miola, and Traversi; under *Shakespeare's Predecessors and Contemporaries*, Comensoli and Russell (essay by Adelman), and Waith; under *Shakespeare's Language*, Doran; under *Shakespeare Criticism to the 1930s*, Coleridge (*Coleridge's Writings*); under *Shakespeare Criticism from the 1940s to the 1970s*, Bethell, Burke, Colie, Granville-Barker, Kettle (essay by Nandy), McAlindon, and Van Laan; under *Shakespeare Criticism Since 1980*, Auden, Bamber, Cavell (pp. 18–37), Charnes, Dollimore (*Radical Tragedy*), Edwards et al. (essay by Hibbard), Erickson (Chapter 4), Holland et al. (essay by Sprengnether), and Neely; under *The Problem Plays*, Schanzer; under *The Histories*, Palmer; and under *The Romances*, Brown and Harris (essay by Ornstein), Danby, and Felperin.

Adelman, Janet. *The Common Liar: An Essay on "Antony and Cleopatra."* New Haven, 1973.

Barroll, J. Leeds. *Shakespearean Tragedy: Genre, Tradition, and Change in "Antony and Cleopatra,"* Washington, D.C., 1984.

Bono, Barbara J. "The Shakespearean Synthesis: *Antony and Cleopatra*," *Literary Transvaluation: From Vergilian Epic to Shakespearean Tragicomedy*. Berkeley, 1984.

Bradley, A. C. *Oxford Lectures on Poetry*. London, 1909, 1961.

Drakakis, John, ed. "*Antony and Cleopatra*." Basingstoke, 1994.

Kaula, David. "The Time Sense of *Antony and Cleopatra*," *SQ* 15:3 (1964), 211–23.

Knights, L. C. *Some Shakespearean Themes*. London, 1959.

Lamb, Margaret. *"Antony and Cleopatra" on the English Stage*. Rutherford, N.J., and London, 1980.

Leavis, F. R. "*Antony and Cleopatra* and *All for Love*: A Critical Exercise," *Scrutiny* 5 (1936–1937), 158–69.

Levine, Laura. *Men in Women's Clothing: Anti-Theatricality and Effeminization, 1579–1642.* Cambridge, Eng., 1994.

Lloyd, Michael. "Cleopatra as Isis," *ShS* 12 (1959), 88–94.

Mack, Maynard. "*Antony and Cleopatra*: The Stillness and the Dance," *Shakespeare's Art: Seven Essays*, ed. Milton Crane. Chicago, 1973.

Madelaine, Richard, ed. *Antony and Cleopatra*. Shakespeare in Production. Cambridge, Eng., 1998.

Markels, Julian. *The Pillar of the World: "Antony and Cleopatra" in Shakespeare's Development*. Columbus, Ohio, 1968.

Mayer, Jean-Christophe, ed. *Lectures de Shakespeare: "Antony and Cleopatra."* Rennes, France, 2000.

Rackin, Phyllis. "Shakespeare's Boy Cleopatra, the Decorum of Nature, and the Golden World of Poetry," *PMLA* 87 (1972), 201–12.

Reimer, A. P. *A Reading of Shakespeare's "Antony and Cleopatra."* Sydney, 1968.

Scott, Michael. *Antony and Cleopatra*. Text and Performance. London, 1983.

Steppat, Michael. *The Critical Reception of Shakespeare's "Antony and Cleopatra" from 1607 to 1905*. Amsterdam, 1980.

Williamson, Marilyn L. *Infinite Variety: "Antony and Cleopatra" in Renaissance Drama and Earlier Tradition*. Mystic, Conn., 1974.

Wood, Nigel, ed. "*Antony and Cleopatra*." Theory in Practice. Buckingham and Philadelphia, 1996.

Yachnin, Paul. "Shakespeare's Politics of Loyalty: Sovereignty and Subjectivity in *Antony and Cleopatra*," *Studies in English Literature* 33 (1993), 343–63.

The Romances

See also, under *Shakespeare Criticism Since 1980*, McMullan and Hope.

Bergeron, David M. *Shakespeare's Romances and the Royal Family*. Lawrence, Kans., 1985.

Brown, John Russell, and Bernard Harris, eds. *Later Shakespeare*. Stratford-upon-Avon Studies 8. London, 1966.

Danby, John F. *Poets on Fortune's Hill*. London, 1952. Reprinted as *Elizabethan and Jacobean Poets*. London, 1964.

Edwards, Philip. "Shakespeare's Romances: 1900–1957," *ShS* 11 (1958), 1–18. See also other articles in this issue.

Fawkner, H. W. *Shakespeare's Miracle Plays: "Pericles," "Cymbeline," and "The Winter's Tale."* Rutherford, N.J., 1992.

Felperin, Howard. *Shakespearean Romance*. Princeton, 1972.

Foakes, R. A. *Shakespeare: From the Dark Comedies to the Last Plays*. London and Charlottesville, Va., 1971.

Frye, Northrop. *Anatomy of Criticism*. Princeton, 1957.

———. *A Natural Perspective: The Development of Shakespearean Comedy and Romance*. New York, 1965.

———. *The Secular Scripture: A Study of the Structure of Romance*. Cambridge, Mass., 1976.

Gesner, Carol. *Shakespeare and the Greek Romance: A Study of Origins*. Lexington, Ky., 1970.

Hartwig, Joan. *Shakespeare's Tragicomic Vision*. Baton Rouge, La., 1972.

Hunter, Robert Grams. *Shakespeare and the Comedy of Forgiveness*. New York, 1965.

James, D. G. "The Failure of the Ballad-Makers," *Scepticism and Poetry*. London, 1937.

Jordan, Constance. *Shakespeare's Monarchies: Ruler and Subject in the Romances*. Ithaca, N.Y., 1997.

Kermode, Frank. *William Shakespeare: The Final Plays*. London, 1963.

Knight, G. Wilson. *The Crown of Life*. London, 1947, 1966.

———. *The Shakespearian Tempest*. London, 1932, 1953.

Leavis, F. R. "A Criticism of Shakespeare's Last Plays," *Scrutiny* 10 (1942), 339–45. Rpt. in *The Common Pursuit*. London, 1952.

Marsh, D. R. C. *The Recurring Miracle: A Study of "Cymbeline" and the Last Plays*. Pietermaritzburg, Natal, 1962, 1964.

Marshall, Cynthia. *Last Things and Last Plays: Shakespearean Eschatology*. Carbondale, Ill., 1991.

Mincoff, Marco. *Things Supernatural and Causeless: Shakespearean Romance*. Newark, Del., 1992.

Mowat, Barbara A. *The Dramaturgy of Shakespeare's Romances*. Athens, Ga., 1976.

Nevo, Ruth. *Shakespeare's Other Language*. New York and London, 1987.

Palfrey, Simon. *Late Shakespeare: A New World of Words*. Oxford, 1997.

Peterson, Douglas L. *Time, Tide, and Tempest: A Study of Shakespeare's Romances*. San Marino, Calif., 1973.

Pettet, E. C. *Shakespeare and the Romance Tradition*. London, 1949.

Platt, Peter G. *Reason Diminished: Shakespeare and the Marvelous*. Lincoln, Neb., 1997.

Richards, Jennifer, and James Knowles, eds. *Shakespeare's Late Plays: New Readings*. Edinburgh, 1999.

Ryan, Kiernan, ed. *Shakespeare: The Late Plays*. New York, 1999.

Smith, Hallett. *Shakespeare's Romances*. San Marino, Calif., 1972.

Strachey, Lytton. "Shakespeare's Final Period," *Books and Characters*. London, 1922.

Traversi, Derek. *Shakespeare: The Last Phase*. New York, 1954.

Yates, Frances A. *Shakespeare's Last Plays: A New Approach*. London, 1975.

Young, David. *The Heart's Forest: A Study of Shakespeare's Pastoral Plays*. New Haven and London, 1972.

The Winter's Tale

See also, under *The Romances*, Felperin, Foakes, Hartwig, Hunter, Knight (*Crown of Life*), Mowat, and Young; and under *Shakespeare Criticism Since 1980*, Cavell (Chapter 6), Erickson, Neely, and Parker and Hartman (essay by Felperin).

Alpers, Paul. *What Is Pastoral?* Chicago, 1996.

Barber, C. L. "'Thou That Beget'st Him That Did Thee Beget': Transformation in *Pericles* and *The Winter's Tale*," *ShS* 22 (1969), 59–67.

Bartholomeusz, Dennis. *"The Winter's Tale" in Performance in England and America, 1611–1976*. Cambridge, Eng., 1982.

Bethell, S. L. *The Winter's Tale: A Study*. London, 1947.

Bishop, T. G. *Shakespeare and the Theatre of Wonder*. Cambridge, Eng., 1996.

Coghill, Nevill. "Six Points of Stage-Craft in *The Winter's Tale*," *ShS* 11 (1958), 31–41.

Draper, R. P. *"The Winter's Tale": Text and Performance*. London, 1985.

Ewbank, Inga-Stina. "The Triumph of Time in *The Winter's Tale*," *Review of English Literature* 5:2 (1964), 83–100.

Frey, Charles. *Shakespeare's Vast Romance: A Study of "The Winter's Tale."* Columbia, Mo., 1980.

Frye, Northrop. "Recognition in *The Winter's Tale*," *Essays on Shakespeare and Elizabethan Drama in Honor of Hardin Craig*, ed. R. Hosley, pp. 235–46. Columbia, Mo., 1962.

Kaplan, Lindsay M., and Katherine Eggert. "'Good queen, my lord, good queen': Sexual Slanders and the Trials of Female Authority in *The Winter's Tale*," *Renaissance Drama* n.s. 25 (1994), 89–118.

Lindenbaum, Peter. "Time, Sexual Love, and the Uses of Pastoral in *The Winter's Tale*," *Modern Language Quarterly* 33 (1972), 3–22.

Matchett, William H. "Some Dramatic Techniques in *The Winter's Tale*," *ShS* 22 (1969), 93–107.

Siemon, James Edward. " 'But It Appears She Lives': Iteration in *The Winter's Tale*," *PMLA* 89 (1974), 10–16.

Snyder, Susan. "Mamillius and Gender Polarization in *The Winter's Tale*," *SQ* 50 (1999), 1–8.

Sokol, B. J. *Art and Illusion in "The Winter's Tale."* Manchester, Eng., 1994.

Tayler, Edward W. *Nature and Art in Renaissance Literature*. New York, 1964.

Wickham, Glynne. "Romance and Emblem: A Study in the Dramatic Structure of *The Winter's Tale*," *The Elizabethan Theatre III*, ed. David Galloway. Hamden, Conn., 1973.

Williams, John Anthony. *The Natural Work of Art: The Experience of Romance in Shakespeare's "Winter's Tale."* Cambridge, Mass., 1967.

The Tempest

See also, under *The Romances*, Brown and Harris (essay by Brockbank), Felperin, Frye (*Natural Perspective*), Hartwig, Kermode, Mowat, Peterson, and Young; under *Shakespeare's Predecessors and Contemporaries*, Bevington and Holbrook (essay by Bevington); under *Shakespeare Criticism to the 1930s*, Coleridge (*Coleridge's Writings*); under *Shakespeare Criticism from the 1940s to the 1970s*, Fiedler, Kernan (*Playwright as Magician*, Chapter 6), and Kott; under *Shakespeare Criticism Since 1980*, Dollimore and Sinfield (essay by Brown), Drakakis (essay by Barker and Hulme), Garber (*Cannibals*, essay by Orgel), Greenblatt (*Shakespearean Negotiations*, Chapter 5), Hamlin, Howard and O'Connor (essay by Cartelli), Lenz et al. (essay by Leininger), Loomba and Orkin (essay by Brotton), McMullan and Hope (essay by Norbrook), and Schwartz and Kahn (essay by Sundelson); and under *The Comedies*, Palmer and Bradbury (essay by Wells).

Auden, W. H. "The Sea and the Mirror: A Commentary on Shakespeare's *The Tempest*," *The Collected Poetry*. New York, 1945.

Berger, Harry, Jr. "Miraculous Harp: A Reading of Shakespeare's *Tempest*," *ShakS* 5 (1969), 253–83.

Demaray, John G. *Shakespeare and the Spectacles of Strangeness: "The Tempest" and the Transformation of Renaissance Theatrical Forms*. Pittsburgh, Pa., 1998.

Frey, Charles. "*The Tempest* and the New World," *SQ* 30 (1979), 29–41.

Hamilton, Donna. *Virgil and "The Tempest": The Politics of Imitation*. Columbus, Ohio, 1990.

Hulme, Peter, and William H. Sherman, eds. *"The Tempest" and Its Travels*. Philadelphia, 2000.

James, D. G. *The Dream of Prospero*. Oxford, 1967.

James, Henry. "Introduction to *The Tempest*." Rpt. in *Henry James: Selected Literary Criticism*, ed. Morris Shapiro. London, 1963.

Mebane, John S. *Renaissance Magic and the Return of the Golden Age: The Occult Tradition and Marlowe, Jonson, and Shakespeare*. Lincoln, Neb., 1989.

Mowat, Barbara A. "Prospero's Book," *SQ* 52 (2001), 1–33.

Orgel, Stephen. "New Uses of Adversity: Tragic Experience in *The Tempest*," *In Defense of Reading*, ed. Reuben A. Brower and Richard Poirier. New York, 1962.

———. "Prospero's Wife," *Representations* 8 (1984), 1–13. Rpt. in Orgel, under *Shakespeare Criticism Since 1980*.

Skura, Meredith Anne. "Discourse and the Individual: The Case of Colonialism in *The Tempest*," *SQ* 40 (1989), 42–69.

Strier, Richard. " 'I am Power': Normal and Magical Politics in *The Tempest*," in *Writing and Political Engagement in Seventeenth-Century England*, ed. Derek Hirst and Richard Strier. Cambridge, Eng., 1999.

Thompson, Ann. " 'Miranda, where's your sister?': Reading Shakespeare's *The Tempest*," *Feminist Criticism: Theory and Practice*, ed. Susan Sellers. New York, 1991.

Vaughan, Alden T. "Shakespeare's Indian: The Americanization of Caliban," *SQ* 39 (1988), 137–53.

Vaughan, Alden T., and Virginia Mason Vaughan. *Shakespeare's Caliban: A Cultural History*. Cambridge, Eng., 1991.

Vaughan, Virginia Mason, and Alden T. Vaughan, eds. *Critical Essays on Shakespeare's "The Tempest."* New York and London, 1998.

William, David. "*The Tempest* on the Stage," *Jacobean Theatre*, eds. John Russell Brown and Bernard Harris, pp. 133–57. Stratford-upon-Avon Studies 1. London, 1960.

Sonnets

See also, under *The Poems*, Dubrow; under *Shakespeare's Predecessors and Contemporaries*, Rasmussen (essay by Alpers); under *Shakespeare Criticism from the 1940s to the 1970s*, Colie, and Kernan (*Playwright as Magician*, Chapter 2); and under *Shakespeare Criticism Since 1980*, Loomba and Orkin (essay by Hall), McDonald (essay by Vendler), Parker and Hartman (essay by Greene), and Wheeler (pp. 179–90).

Allen, Michael J. B. "Shakespeare's Man Descending a Staircase: Sonnets 126 to 154," *ShS* 31 (1978), 127–38.

Booth, Stephen. *An Essay on Shakespeare's Sonnets*. New Haven, 1969.

———. ed. *Shakespeare's Sonnets, Edited with Analytic Commentary*. New Haven, 1977.

Bradley, A. C. *Oxford Lectures on Poetry*. London, 1909, 1961.

Cheney, Patrick. "'O, let my books be . . . dumb presagers': Poetry and Theater in Shakespeare's Sonnets," *SQ* 52 (2001), 222–54.

Clark, S. H. *Sordid Images: The Poetry of Masculine Desire*. London and New York, 1994.

Cousins, A. D. *Shakespeare's Sonnets and Narrative Poems*. Harlow, Eng., 2000.

De Grazia, Margreta. "The Scandal of Shakespeare's Sonnets," *ShS* 46 (1994), 35–49.

Dubrow, Heather. *Echoes of Desire: English Petrarchism and Its Counterdiscourses*. Ithaca, N.Y., 1995.

Fineman, Joel. *Shakespeare's Perjured Eye: The Invention of Poetic Subjectivity in the Sonnets*. Berkeley, 1986.

Giroux, Robert. *The Book Known as Q: A Consideration of Shakespeare's Sonnets*. New York, 1982.

Hubler, Edward, Northrop Frye, Leslie A. Fiedler, Stephen Spender, and R. P. Blackmur. *The Riddle of Shakespeare's Sonnets*. New York, 1962.

Ingram, W. G., and Theodore Redpath, eds. *Shakespeare's Sonnets*. London, 1964.

Innes, Paul. *Shakespeare and the English Renaissance Sonnet: Verses of Feigning Love*. Basingstoke and New York, 1997.

Knight, G. Wilson. *The Mutual Flame: On Shakespeare's Sonnets and "The Phoenix and the Turtle."* London, 1955.

Krieger, Murray. *A Window to Criticism: Shakespeare's Sonnets and Modern Poetics*. Princeton, 1964.

Landry, Hilton. *Interpretations in Shakespeare's Sonnets*. Berkeley, 1963.

———. ed. *New Essays on Shakespeare's Sonnets*. New York, 1976.

Leishman, J. B. *Themes and Variations in Shakespeare's Sonnets*. London, 1961.

Lever, J. W. *The Elizabethan Love Sonnet*. London, 1956.

Melchiori, Giorgio. *Shakespeare's Dramatic Meditations: An Experiment in Criticism*. Oxford, 1976.

Muir, Kenneth. *Shakespeare's Sonnets*. London, 1979.

Pequigney, Joseph. *Such is My Love: A Study of Shakespeare's Sonnets*. Chicago, 1985.

Ramsay, Paul. *The Fickle Glass: A Study of Shakespeare's Sonnets*. New York, 1979.

Ransom, John Crowe. *The World's Body*. New York and London, 1938, 1968.

Schiffer, James, ed. *Shakespeare's Sonnets: Critical Essays*. New York, 1999.

Vendler, Helen. *The Art of Shakespeare's Sonnets*. Cambridge, Mass., 1997.

Textual Notes

These textual notes do not offer an historical collation, either of the early quartos and folios or of more recent editions; they are simply a record of departures in this edition from the copy text. For most plays the notes give the adopted reading of this edition in bold face, followed by the rejected reading in the relevant copy text. Where two substantive early texts are involved, or where a reading from some other earlier edition has been adopted, the notes provide information on the source of the reading in square brackets. In a few texts, adopted readings of editions more recent than the First Folio are indicated by [eds.]. Alterations in lineation are not indicated, nor are some minor and obvious typographical errors; changes in punctuation are indicated when the resulting change in meaning is substantive.

Abbreviations used:

F The First Folio
Q Quarto
O Octavo
s.d. stage direction
s.p. speech prefix

The Taming of the Shrew

Copy Text: The First Folio. The act and scene divisions are missing in the Folio except for Act 1 (before the first Induction), Act 3, Act 4 (at 4.3), and Act 5 (at 5.2).

Ind.1. 0.1 Christopher Sly [printed at the end of the s.d. in F as "Christophero Sly"] **1 [and elsewhere]** SLY *Begger* **10–11 thirdborough** Headborough **16 Breathe** Brach **21 [and elsewhere]** FIRST HUNTSMAN *Hunts.* **81 FIRST PLAYER** *2. Player* **87 SECOND PLAYER** *Sincklo* **99 FIRST PLAYER** *Plai.* **134 peasant.** peasant,
Ind. 2. 2 Lordship Lord **18 Sly's** Sies **26 [and elsewhere]** THIRD SERVINGMAN *3. Man* **27 [and elsewhere]** SECOND SERVINGMAN *2 Man* **47 [and elsewhere]** FIRST SERVINGMAN *1 Man* **53 wi'th'** with **93 Greet** Greece **98 lose** loose **99 [and elsewhere]** PAGE *Lady* **125 SERVINGMAN** *Mes.* **133 it. Is** it is
1.1. 3 fore for **13 Vincentio** *Vincentio's* **14 brought** brough **24 satiety** sacietie **25 Mi perdonate** *Me Pardonato* **33 Ovid be** *Ouid; be* **146 s.d. Manent** *Manet* **163 captum** captam **208 colored** Conlord **227 time.** time **244 your** you **248.2 speak** *speakes*
1.2. 17.1 wrings *rings* **18 masters** mistris **24 Con . . . trovato** *Contutti le core bene trobatto* **25 ben** *bene* **26 Molto** multo **onorato** *honorata* **33 pip** peepe **45 this's** this **51 grows. But** growes but **few,** few. **72 me, were she** me. Were she is **120 me and other more,** me. Other more **171 help me** helpe one **189 Antonio's** *Butonios* **190 his** my **212 ours** yours **265 feat** seeke **280 ben** *Been*

2.1. 8 thee tell tel **75–6 wooing.—Neighbors,** wooing neighbors: **79 unto you** vnto **104 Pisa. By report** *Pisa by report,* **153 struck** stroke **157 rascal fiddler** Rascall, Fidler **168 s.d. Exeunt** *Exit* **186 bonny** bony **244 askance** a sconce **322 s.d. Exeunt** *Exit* **328 in me** me **352 Valance** Vallens **355 pail** pale **373 Marseilles** Marcellus
3.1. 28 Sigeia *sigeria* [also at lines 33 and 42] **43 steterat** staterat **47 [Aside]** *Luc.* **50 BIANCA** [not in F] **51 LUCENTIO** *Bian.* **53 BIANCA** *Hort.* **74 B mi** *Beeme* **76 clef** Cliffe **80 change** charge **odd** old **81 SERVANT** *Nicke*
3.2. 13 behavior. behaviour, **14 man,** man; **29 of thy** of **30 old news** newes **33 hear** heard **54 swayed** Waid **56 cheeked** chekt **60 velour** velure **128 to love** Loue **130 As I** As **150 e'er** ere **182 s.d. Music plays** [after line 183 in F] **199 GREMIO** *Gra.*
4.1. 23 CURTIS *Gru.* **59 Imprimis** Inprimis **81 sleekly** slickely **106 GRUMIO** *Gre.* **168.1. Curtis** *Curtis a Seruant* [after line 169 in F]
4.2. 4 HORTENSIO *Luc.* **6 LUCENTIO** *Hor.* [and at line 8] **7 you? First resolve** you first, resolue **8 read that I profess, The** reade, that I professe the **13 none** me **31 her** them **72 Take . . . alone** [assigned to "Par." in F] **in** me
4.[3] [F has "*Actus Quartus. Scena Prima*" here] **48 to** too **62.1 Enter Haberdasher** [after 61 in F] **63 HABERDASHER** *Fel.* **81 is a** is **88 like a** like **146 where,** where **148 mete-yard** meat-yard **177 account'st** accountedst
4.4. 0.2 [booted] [appears at line 18.2 in F] **1 Sir** Sirs **18.2 bareheaded** booted and bare headed **68.1 Exit** [after line 67 in F; F also adds a s.d., "Enter Peter," after line 68] **78 he's** has **91 except** expect **93 solum** solem
4.5. 14 An And **18 is** in **35 make a** make the **37 Whither** Whether **where** whether **77 she be** she
5.1. 4 [F has "*Exit*" here] **6 master's** mistris **42 brought** brough **50 master's** Mistris **62 copintank** copataine **104.1 Exeunt** *Exit* **139 No** Mo **143 than never** then ueuer
5.[2] [F has "*Actus Quintus*" here] **2 done** come **37 thee, lad** the lad **39 butt** But **40 butt! An** but an **45 bitter** better **two** too **52 TRANIO** *Tri.* **57 Oho** Oh, oh **62 two** too **65 for** sir **93.1 Enter Biondello** [after "Do what you can" in 93 in F] **132 a** fiue **136 you're** your **152 maintenance commits** maintenance. Commits

A Midsummer Night's Dream

Copy text: the First Quarto of 1600. The act and scene divisions are absent from the Quarto; the Folio provides act divisions only.
1.1. 4 wanes waues **10 New** Now **19.1. Lysander** Lysander *and* Helena **24 Stand forth, Demetrius** [printed as s.d. in Q]

26 **Stand forth, Lysander** [printed as s.d. in Q]   74 **their** there   114 **[and elsewhere] lose** loose   132 **Ay** Eigh   133 **hear** here   136 **low** loue   187 **Yours would** Your words   191 **I'd** ile   216 **sweet** sweld   219 **stranger companies** strange companions   224 **s.d. Exit Hermia** [after line 223 in Q]

2.1. 1 **[and elsewhere]** PUCK *Robin*   61 **[and elsewhere]** TITANIA *Qu.*   61 **Fairies** Fairy   79 **Aegles** Eagles   109 **thin** chinne   158 **the west** west   183 **off** of   190 **slay** stay   **slayeth** stayeth   194 **thee** the   201 **not nor** not, not   206 **lose** loose   246.1 [after line 247 in Q]

2.2. 4 **leathern** lethren   9 **FIRST FAIRY** [not in Q; also at line 24]   13 **CHORUS** [not in Q]   44 **comfort** comfor   45 **Be** Bet   49 **good** god   53 **is** it   63 **human** humane   155 **ate** eate

3.1. 52 BOTTOM *Cet.*   72 PUCK *Ro.*   77 BOTTOM *Pyra.* [also at lines 79 and 98]   78 **Odors, odors** Odours, odorous   83 PUCK *Quin.*   84 FLUTE *Thys.* [also at lines 88 and 97]   120 **ousel** Woosell   144 **own** owe   156 **[and elsewhere] Mote** *Moth*   157–8 **Ready . . . go** [assigned to FAIRIES in Q]   170 PEASEBLOSSOM *1. Fai.*   171 COBWEB [not in Q]   172 MOTE *2. Fair.*   173 MUSTARDSEED *3. Fai.*   190 **you** of you   196.1. *Exeunt Exit*

3.2. 0.1 [Q: *Enter King of* Fairies, *and Robin goodfellow*]   **3.1.** [See previous note.]   6–7 **love. / Near . . . bower,** loue, / Neere . . . bower.   15–16 **brake. / When . . . take,** brake, / When . . . take: 19 **mimic** Minnick   38 **[and elsewhere]** PUCK *Rob.*   80 **I so** I   85 **sleep** slippe   213 **like** life   215 **rend** rent   220 **passionate words** words   250 **prayers** praise   260 **off** of   299 **gentlemen** gentleman   313 **too** to   326 **but** hut   344 **s.d. Exit** Exeunt   406 **Speak! In some bush?** Speake in some bush.   426 **shalt** shat   451 **To your** your

4.1. 5 **[and elsewhere]** BOTTOM *Clown*   20 **courtesy** curtsie   24 **marvelous** maruailes   54 **flowerets'** flouriets   64 **off** of   72 **o'er** or   81 **five** fine   82 **ho** howe   116 **Seemed** Seeme   127 **this is** this   132 **rite** right   137.2 *Wind . . . up* they all start vp. *Winde hornes*   171 **saw** see   177 **hear** here   190 **found** fonnd   198 **let us** lets   205 **to expound** expound   208 **a patched** patcht a   213 **ballad** Ballet

4.2. 0.1 [*Snout, and Starveling*] Thisby *and the rabble*   3 STARVELLING *Flut.*   5 FLUTE *Thys.* [and at lines 9, 13, 19]   29 **no** not   34 **ribbons** ribands

5.1. 34 **our** Or   107 **[and elsewhere]** THESEUS *Duk*   122 **his** this   150.1 *Exeunt Exit* [after line 153 in Q]   155 **Snout** *Flute*   190 **up in thee** now vpon   193 **love!** loue   **Thou art my** loue thou art, my   205 **mural down** Moon vsed   209 **[and elsewhere]** HIPPOLYTA *Dutch.*   216 **beasts in, a** beasts, in a   265.1 *Enter Pyramus* [after 267 in Q]   270 **gleams** beames   309 **before** before?   315 **mote** moth   317 **warrant** warnd   325 **tomb** tumbe   347 BOTTOM *Lyon*   363 **gait** gate (also at 411)   366 **lion** Lyons   367 **behowls** beholds   414–15 **And . . . rest** [these lines are transposed in Q]

The Merchant of Venice

Copy text: the First Quarto of 1600 [Q]. The act and scene divisions are absent from the Quarto; the Folio provides act divisions only.

1.1. 0.1 *Salerio Salaryno* [and also elsewhere *Salarino*, and abbreviated *Salar., Sala.,* and *Sal.*]   *Solanio Salanio* [and abbreviated elsewhere *Sola.* and *Sol.*]   19 **Peering** Piring   27 **docked** docks   84 **alabaster** Alablaster   85 **jaundice** Iaundies   112 **tongue** togue   113 **Is** It is   128 **off** of   151 **back** bake

1.2. 44 **Palatine** Palentine [and at line 57]   53 **Bone** *Boune*   58 **throstle** Trassell   119.1 *Enter a Servingman* [after line 120 in Q]

1.3. 28 **[and elsewhere]** SHYLOCK *Iew*   76 **compromised** compremyzd   82 **peeled** pyld   110 **spit** spet [also at lines 124 and 129]   125 **day, another time,** day another time,

2.1. 0.2 *Morocco Morochus*   25 **Sophy . . . prince**, Sophy, and a Persian Prince   31 **thee** the   35 **page** rage

2.2. 1 **[and elsewhere]** LAUNCELOT *Clowne*   3 **[and elsewhere in this scene]** Gobbo *Iobbe*   42 **By** Be   76 **murder** muder   91 **fill horse** philhorse   94 **last** lost   165.1 *Exit Leonardo* [after line 164 in Q]   168 **a suit** sute   180 **[and elsewhere] lose** loose

2.3. 11 **did** doe

2.4. 8 **o'clock** of clocke   9 **s.d.** [after line 9 in Q]   14 **Love news,** Loue, newes   20.1 *Exit clown* [after line 23 in Q]   39 **s.d. Exeunt** Exit

2.5. 44 **Jewess'** Iewes

2.6. 26 **Ho! Who's** Howe whose   35 **night, you** night you   59 **gentlemen** gentleman   61 **Who's** Whose

2.7. 18 **threatens. Men** threatens men   45 **Spits** Spets   69 **tombs** *timber*

2.8. 8 **gondola** Gondylo   39 **Slubber** slumber

2.9. 6 **rites** rights   48 **chaff** chaft   49 **varnished** varnist   64 **judgment** *iudement*   73 [Q provides a s.p.: *Arrag.*]

3.1. 19 **[and elsewhere] lest** least   21.1 *Enter Shylock* [after line 22 in Q]   46 **courtesy** cursie   70 **MAN** [not in Q]   74.1 [Q repeats the s.d. "*Enter Tuball*"]   100 **Heard** heere   114 **turquoise** Turkies

3.2. 23 **eke** ech   61 **live. With** liue with   67 **eyes** *eye*   81 **vice** voyce   84 **stairs** stayers   99 **Veiling** vailing   101 **Therefore** Therefore then   110 **shuddering** shyddring   117 **whether** whither   199 **loved; for intermission** lou'd for intermission,   204 **roof** rough   271.1–2 [after line 219 in Q]   315 BASSANIO [not in Q]   336 **e'er** ere

3.3 0.1 *Solanio Salerio*   24 SOLANIO *Sal.*

3.4. 13 **equal** egall   23 **Hear other things:** heere other things   49 **Padua** Mantua   50 **cousin's** cosin   53 **traject** Tranect   80 **near** nere   81 **my** my my

3.5. 20 **enough** enow   **e'en** in   26 **comes** come   74 **merit it,** meane it, it   81 **a wife** wife   85 **howsome'er** how so mere   87 **s.d. Exeunt** Exit

4.1. 30 **his state** this states   31 **flint** flints   35 **[and elsewhere in this scene]** SHYLOCK *Iewe*   50 **urine; for affection,** vrine for affection.   51 **Mistress** Maisters   73 **You may as well** well   74 **Why he hath made the** the **bleat** bleake   75 **pines** of Pines   81 **more** moe   100 **is** as   123 **sole . . . soul** soule . . . soule   136 **whilst** whilest   228 **No, not** Not not   233 **tenor** tenure   270 **off** of   322 **off** of   396 GRATIANO *Shy.*   405.1 *Exeunt Exit*

5.1. 26 STEPHANO *Messen.* [also *Mess.* at lines 28 and 33]   41 *Lorenzo Lorenzo, &*   49 **Sweet soul** [assigned in Q to Lancelot]   51 *Stephano Stephen*   62 **choiring** quiring   87 **Erebus** *Terebus*   106 **wren** Renne   109 **ho!** how   152 **give it** giue   233 **my** mine

Much Ado About Nothing

Copy text: the Quarto of 1600. The act and scene divisions are missing from the Quarto; the Folio provides act divisions only.

1.1. 0.1. *Messina Messina, Innogen, his wife*   2 **Pedro** Peter [also in line 9]   40 **bird-bolt** Burbolt   84 **Benedick** Benedict   141 **all, Leonato. Signor** all: Leonato, signior   194.1 *Pedro Pedro, Iohn the bastard*   239 **[and elsewhere] loose** loose

1.2. 3 **[and elsewhere]** ANTONIO *Old*   6 **event** euents   25 **skill** shill

1.3. 46 **brother's** bothers   70 **s.d. Exeunt** exit

2.1. 0.1 *Hero his wife, Hero*   0.3 *Ursula* [Q adds "*and a kinsman*"]   2 **[and elsewhere]** ANTONIO *brother*   37 **bearward** Berrord   44 **Peter, for the heavens;** Peter: for the heauens,   50, 53 **curtsy** cursie   67 **hear** here   79.3. *and Don or dumb*   80 **a bout** about   94 BALTHASAR *Bene.* [also at lines 97 and 99]   187 **drover** Drouier   201.2 *Leonato Leonato, Iohn and Borachio, and Conrade*   311 **[and elsewhere]** DON PEDRO *Prince*   369 **s.d. Exeunt** exit

2.3. 7 **s.d.** [at line 5 in Q]   25 **an** and   35.1 *Claudio Claudio, Musicke*   61 BALTHASAR [not in Q]   73–6 **but . . . nonny** &c.   84 **lief** liue   91 **s.d.** [after line 90 in Q]   139 **us of** of vs   171 **doffed** daft

3.1. 0.2. *Ursula Ursley*   23 **s.d.** [after line 25 in Q]   63 **antic** antique   111 **on; I** on I

3.2. 27 **can** cannot   51 DON PEDRO *Bene.*   74 **[and elsewhere]** DON JOHN *Bastard*   75 **e'en** den   91–2 **manifest. For my brother, I . . . heart hath** manifest, for my brother (I . . . heart) hath   108 **her then, tomorrow** her, then to morrow   118 **her, tomorrow** her to morrow

3.3. 17 SEACOAL *Watch 2* [also at line 27]   87 SEACOAL *Watch* [also at lines 95, 105, 125]   134 **reechy** rechie   161 SEACOAL *Watch 1* [also at line 165]   162 FIRST WATCH *Watch 2* [also at line 168]   171 SEACOAL [missing in Q]

3.4. 17 **in** it

3.5. 2 [and elsewhere] DOGBERRY *Const. Dog.*   7 [and elsewhere]
VERGES *Headb.*   9 off of   32 talking. As talking as   50 [Q provides
an "*exit*" at this point]
4.1. 4 FRIAR *Fran.*   28 DON PEDRO *Princn*   167 tenor tenure
202 princes princesse
4.2. 0.1–3 [Q reads "*Enter the Constables, Borachio, and the Towne clearke in
gownes.*"]   1 DOGBERRY *Keeper*   2 [and elsewhere in this scene]
VERGES *Cowley*   4 DOGBERRY *Andrew*   9 [and elsewhere in this
scene] DOGBERRY *Kemp*   18 CONRADE, BORACHIO *Both*   39 SEACOAL
Watch 1 [also at line 53]   47 FIRST WATCH *Watch 2*   51 VERGES *Const.*
67 [and elsewhere] DOGBERRY *Constable*   69 CONRADE [missing in
Q]   Off of   73 CONRADE *Couley*   86.1 *Exeunt exit*
5.1. 16 Bid And   97 anticly antiquely, and   98 off of   116 like likt
167 there's theirs   179 on one   189 Lackbeard there, he
Lacke-beard, there hee   201.1.2 [after line 197 in Q]   251 VERGES *Con. 2*
5.2. 41.1 [after line 42 in Q]   81 myself. So my self so   97 s.d. *Exeunt
exit*
5.3. 2 A LORD *Lord*   3 CLAUDIO [missing in Q]   10 dumb dead   11 [Q
provides a s.p. "*Claudio*" here]   12 BALTHASAR [missing in Q]
22 CLAUDIO *Lo.*   23 rite right   32 speed's speeds
5.4. 53 ANTONIO *Leo.*   96 BENEDICK *Leon.*

As You Like It

Copy text: the First Folio. Act and scene divisions follow the Folio text
throughout.
1.1. 105 she hee   154 OLIVER [not in F]   154 s.d. *Exit* [at line 153 in F]
1.2. 3 I were were   5 [and elsewhere] whither whether   51 goddesses and goddesses   55 [and elsewhere] TOUCHSTONE *Clow.*
56 father farher   80 CELIA *Ros.*   88 Le the   233 love loue;   251.1 [at
line 249 in F]   280 [and occasionally elsewhere] Rosalind *Rosaline*
1.3. 55 likelihood likelihoods   76 her per   87.1 with Lords *&c*
124 be by   135 we in in we   129 travel trauaile   131 [and elsewhere]
woo woe
2.1. 37 antique anticke   49 much must   50 friends friend   59 of the of
2.3. 10 some seeme   16 ORLANDO [not in F]   29 ORLANDO *Ad.*
71 seventeen seauentie
2.4. 1 weary merry   42 thy wound they would   65 you, your
2.5. 1 AMIENS [not in F; also at line 35]   38.1 *All together here* [before
line 35 in F]   41–2 No . . . weather *&c*   46 JAQUES *Amy.*
2.7. 0.1 Lords *Lord*   38 brain braiue   55 Not to seem Seeme   87 comes
come   161 treble, pipes trebble pipes,   173 AMIENS [not in F]
182 Then *The*   190–3 heigh-ho . . . jolly *&c.*   201 master masters
3.2. 26 good pood   115 graft graffe [twice]   123 a desert *Desert*
143 her his   190 whooping hooping   234 such fruit fruite   241 thy
the   254 [and elsewhere] b'wi'you buy you   340 lectures Lectors
354 deifying defying   362 are art
3.3. 52–3 so. Poor men alone? No so poore men alone: No
88 TOUCHSTONE *Ol.*   99 s.d. *Exit Exeunt*
3.4. 29 a lover Louer   41 puny puisny
3.5. 11 pretty, sure pretty sure   65 hear here   105 erewhile yere-while
128 I have Haue
4.1. 1 me be me   18 my by   27 travel trauaile   36 gondola Gundello
44 thousandth thousand   72 warrant warne   148 hyena Hyen
202 it in
4.2. 2 FIRST LORD *Lord*   7 SECOND LORD *Lord*   10 SECOND LORD [not in F]
4.3. 5.1 [after line 3 in F]   8 bid did bid   12 tenor tenure   79–80 bottom; bottom   104–5 itself: it selfe   143 In I   156 his this
5.1. 14 gi' ye   36 sir sit   55 policy police
5.2. 7 nor her nor   31 overcame ouercome
5.3. 15 BOTH PAGES [not in F]   18 In *In the* ring *rang*   24–6 In . . .
spring *In spring time, &c* [also at lines 30–2 and 36–8]   33–8 [this
stanza comes after line 20 in F]
5.4. 25.1. *Exeunt Exit*   34.1 [after line 33 in F]   80 so to the so ro
113 her his   150 JAQUES DE BOYS *2 Bro.* [also at line 182]   163 them
him   170 were vvete   196 rites rights   197 trust they'll end, in
trust, they'l end in   197.1 *Exeunt Exit*

Twelfth Night

Copy text: the First Folio. Act and scene divisions follow the Folio text
throughout.
1.1. 1 [and throughout] ORSINO *Duke*   10–11 capacity capacitie,
11 sea, naught sea. Nought   22 s.d. [after 22 in F]
1.2. 15 Arion Orion
1.3. 51 SIR ANDREW *Ma.*   54 Mary Accost *Mary*, accost   96 curl by
coole my   98 me we   132 dun dam'd   set sit   136 That's That
1.5. 5 [and throughout] FESTE *Clo.*   85 gagged gag'd [also at 5.1. 376]
144 He's Ha's   163.1 *Viola Uiolenta*   296 County's Countes
306 s.d. [F adds "*Finis, Actus primus*"]
2.2. 20 That sure That   31 our O   32 made of, such made, if such
2.3. 3 *diluculo Deliculo*   25 leman Lemon   39 FESTE (sings) *Clowne
sings.*   119 stoop stope   133 a nayword an ayword
2.4. 4 Metal *Mettle*   51 FESTE [not in F]   53 Fly . . . fly *Fye . . . fie*
55 yew *Ew*   88 I It
2.5. 112 staniel stallion   118 portend? portend,   142 born become
achieve atcheeues   156–7 Unhappy." Daylight vnhappy daylight
173 dear *deero*   203 s.d. [F adds "*Finis Actus secundus*"]
3.1. 8 king Kings   68 wise men wisemens   91 all ready already
124 grece grize
3.2. 7 thee the the   64 nine mine
3.4. 15.1–2 s.d. [at line 14 in F, after "hither"]   25 OLIVIA *Mal.*
65.1 *Exeunt exit*   72 tang langer   106 lose loose   175 You Yon
222 thee the   228 sir. I am sure no sir I am sure, no   249 competent
computent   397.1 *Exeunt Exit*
4.1. 34 struck stroke   101 b'wi' buy
4.2. 6 in in in   38 clerestories cleere stores   71 sport to sport
4.3. 1 SEBASTIAN [not in F]   35 s.d. [F adds "*Finis Actus Quartus*"]
5.1. 5 freight fraught   141 Whither Whether   173 He's H'as   190.1 [after
line 187 in F]   195 He's has   200 pavane panyn   205 help? An helpe
an   207 to too   285 He's has   389 tiny tine   406 With hey *hey*

Measure for Measure

Copy text: the First Folio. Act and scene divisions are from the Folio
except as indicated below.
The Names of All the Actors [at the end of the play in F]
1.1. 76 s.d. [at line 75 in F]
1.2. 58 [and elsewhere] MISTRESS OVERDONE *Bawd*   83.1 [after line 84
in F]   85 [and elsewhere] POMPEY *Clo.*   115 [F begins "*Scena Tertia*"
here]   134 morality mortality
1.3. [F labels as "*Scena Quarta*"]   20 steeds weedes   27 Becomes more
More   48 [and elsewhere] More Moe   54.1 *Exeunt Exit*
1.4. [F labels as "*Scena Quinta*"]   0.1 [and elsewhere] *Isabella Isabell*
2 [and throughout] FRANCISCA *Nun*   5 sisterhood Sisterstood
17 stead steed [also at 3.2. 252]   54 givings-out giuing-out
61–2 mind, study, and fast. / He minde: Studie, and fast / He
72 He's Has   78 [and elsewhere] lose loose
2.1. 12 your our   39 breaks brakes   90 [and elsewhere] prunes
prewyns   139.1 [at line 138 in F]
2.2. 63 back again againe   104 ere here
2.3. 31 [and elsewhere] lest least
2.4. 9 sere feard   17 s.d. *Enter Servant* [after line 17 in F]   30 s.d.
Enter Isabella [after line 30 in F]   48 metal mettle   53 or and
75 craftily crafty   76 me be be   94 all-binding all-building
3.1. 29 thee sire, thee, fire   31 serpigo Sapego   52 me to hear them
them to heare me   68 Though Through   91 enew emmew
96 damned'st damnest   131 penury periury   200 advisings. To . . .
good a aduisings, to . . . good; a   216 by oath oath
3.2. 0 [not marked as a new scene in F]   8 law a Law; a   9 on and
26 eat, array eate away   48 it clutched clutch'd   74–5 bondage.
If . . . patiently, why bondage if . . . patiently: Why   109 ungenerative generatiue   147 dearer deare   214 See Sea
4.1. 1 BOY [not in F]   49.1 [after line 48 in F]   61 quests Quest
64 s.d. *Enter . . . Isabella* [after line 64 in F]

4.2. 43–7 If . . . thief [assigned in F to *Clo.*]   **58 yare** y'are   **60.1** [at line 59 in F]   **72 s.d.** *Enter Duke* [after line 72 in F]   **100 This . . . man** [assigned in F to *Duke*]   **Lordship's** Lords   **101 DUKE** *Pro.*   **120 PROVOST** [not in F]

4.3. 92.1 [at line 91 in F]   **93 Varrius** *Angelo*   **100 well** weale
4.4. 6 redeliver reliuer   **15–16 proclaimed. Betimes** proclaim'd betimes   **19 s.d.** [at line 18 in F]
4.5. 6 Flavius' *Flauia's*
5.1. 14 me we   **34 hear!** heere.   **173 s.d.** *Enter Mariana* [after line 173 in F]   **174 her face** your face   **226 promisèd** promis'd   **268 s.d.** [at line 267 in F]   **288.1** [after line 286 in F]   **407 s.d.** *Mariana* Maria   **431 confiscation** confutation   **488.2 Juliet** *Iulietta*   **550 that's** that

Richard III

Copy text: the First Folio, except for two passages, 3.1.1–158 and 5.3.48 to end of play, for which Q1 is copy text. Unless otherwise indicated, the adopted readings are from the First Quarto of 1597 [Q1]. Act and scene divisions are marked in the copy text except as indicated below.

1.1. 1 RICHARD [not in F]   **41.1.** *Enter . . . Brackenbury* [eds.] *Enter Clarence, and Brackenbury, guarded*   **45 the** th'   **52 for** but   **65 tempers him to this** tempts him to this harsh   **75 to her for his** for her   **88 An** 't and   **103 I** I do   **124 the** this   **133 prey** play
1.2. 27 life [eds.] death   **38 HALBERDIER** [eds.] *Gen.*   **39 stand** Stand'st   **78 of a** of   **80 t'accuse** [eds.] to curse   **94 hand** hands   **141 thee** the   **171 words** word   **204 RICHARD** [not in F]   **205** [not in F]   **227.1 Exeunt** [eds.] *Exit* [also at line 229]   **228 RICHARD** Sirs . . . corpse [not in F]   **229.1 Exeunt** Exit
1.3. 17 come comes   **lords** Lord   **19 [and elsewhere] STANLEY** *Der.*   **54 whom** who   **69** [not in F]   **109.1** [after line 110 in F]   **114** [not in F]   **155 Ah, little** A little   **160 of** off   **309 QUEEN ELIZABETH** *Mar.*   **342 FIRST MURDERER** *Vil.* [also at lines 350 and 355]   **351 doers. Be assured** dooers, be assur'd:
1.4. 13 Thence There   **22 waters** water   **22, 23 my** mine   **25 Ten** A   **39 seek** find   **41 Which** Who   **64 my lord** Lord   **99 s.d.** *Exit* [at line 97 in F]   **100 I** we   **122 Faith** [not in F]   **126 Zounds** Come   **147 Zounds** [not in F]   **152 Tut** [not in F]   **192 to have redemption** for any goodnesse   **193** [not in F]   **240** [not in F]   **242 of** on   **269** [in F, printed after line 263]   **272 s.d.** *Stabs him* [after line 272 in F]
2.1. 0.3. Buckingham [eds.] *Buckingham, Wooduill*   **5 in** to   **7 Rivers and Hastings** Dorset and Riuers   **39 God** heauen   **57 unwittingly** vnwillingly   **59 By** To   **68** [F follows with a line: "Of you Lord Wooduill, and Lord *Scales* of you"]   **93 but** and   **108 at** and
2.2. 1 BOY *Edw.*   **3 [and throughout scene] GIRL** [eds.] *Daugh.*   **3 do you** do   **26 his** a   **47 have I** haue   **83 weep** weepes   **84–5 Clarence . . . they** *Clarence* weep, so do not they   **87 Pour** Power   **142 Ludlow** London [also at line 154]   **145** [not in F]   **145.1 Manent** [eds.] *Manet*
2.3. 44 Ensuing Pursuing [but the catchword on page 184 in F is "Ensuing"]
2.4. 1 hear heard   **9 young** good   **21 ARCHBISHOP** *Car.* [Q1] *Yor.* [F]   **65 death** earth
3.1. 1–158 [based on Q1 as copy text]   **2 [and elsewhere] RICHARD** *Glo.*   **60.1** [bracketed s.d. from F]   **111 With all** withall [Q1]   **150.1** [*A sennet*] [from F]   **150.2 Hastings** Hast. Dors.   **Manent** [F2] manet
3.2. 20 councils Councell   **78 as you do** as
3.3. 1 [not in F]
3.4. 9 methinks we thinke   **58** [not in F]   **79.1 Exeunt** [at line 78 in F]   **Manent** Manet   **82 raze** rowse
3.5. 4 wert were   **20 innocence** Innocencie   **34 Look . . . Mayor** [not in F; after line 26 in Q1]   **56 we** I   **hear** heard   **66 cause** case   **74 meet'st advantage** meetest vantage   **104 Penker** [eds.] *Peuker*   **105.1. Exeunt** [eds.] *Exit*   **109 s.d. Exit** Exeunt
3.7. 7 insatiate vnsatiate   **20 mine** my   **33 spake** spoke   **40 wisdoms** wisdome   **43** [not in F]   **44 RICHARD** [not in F]   **54 we'll** we   **83 My lord** [not in F]   **125 her** his [also in lines 126 and 127]   **214 whe'er** where [also in line 229]   **219 Zounds! I'll** we will

220 [not in F]   **224 stone** Stones   **240 Richard** King *Richard*   **241 MAYOR AND CITIZENS** All   **247 cousin** Cousins
4.1. 0.1–5. [F: *Enter the Queene, Anne Duchesse of Gloucester, the Duchesse of Yorke, and Marquesse Dorset*]   **15 BRACKENBURY** *Lieu.* [and at lines 18 and 26]
4.2. 36 My Lord [not in F]   **72 there** then   **87 to** vnto   **90 Hereford** Hertford   **98–118 perhaps . . . today** [not in F]
4.3. 0 [scene division not in F]   **4 whom** who   **5 ruthless** ruthfull   **13 Which** And   **15 once** one   **20 gone; with . . . remorse** gone with . . . Remorse.   **31 at** and   **33 thee** the   **40 Breton** Britaine   **53 leads** leds
4.4. 0 [*Scena Tertia* in F]   **10 unblown** vnblowed   **39** [not in F]   **o'er over** [Q1]   **41 Harry** [eds.] Husband   **45 holp'st** hop'st   **52–3** [lines reversed in F]   **64 Thy** The   **112 weary** wearied   **118 nights . . . days** night . . . day   **128 intestate** intestine   **141 Where** Where't   **225 lanced** [eds.] lanch'd   **239 or** and   **268 would I** I would   **284 This is** this   **324 Of ten** [eds.] Often   **364–5** [lines reversed in F, and the s.p. *Queen Elizabeth* is missing]   **366 KING RICHARD** [not in F]   **377 God** Heauen   **God's** Heauens   **392 in** with   **396 o'erpast** repast   **417 fond** found   **430.1 Exit Queen** [at line 429 in F]   **431.1 Enter Ratcliffe** [below line 432 in F]   **444 Ratcliffe** [eds.] *Catesby*   **498 FIRST MESSENGER** *Mess.*   **503 SECOND MESSENGER** *Mess.*   **506 THIRD MESSENGER** *Mess.* [also at lines 509 and 517]   **518 FOURTH MESSENGER** *Mess.*   **534 tidings** Newes, but
4.5. 0 [*Scena Quarta* in F]
5.1. 11 is, my lord is
5.2. 11 center Centry   **12 Near** Ne're   **17 swords** men
5.3. 0 [scene not marked in F]   **20 track** Tract   **28 you** [eds.] your   **48 ff.** [to the end of the play] [copy text is Q1]   **54 sentinels** [F] centinell [Q1]   **59 CATESBY** [eds.] *Rat.*   **79 sit** [F] set [Q1; also at line 131]   **85 that. The** that the [Q1]   **100 sundered** sundried [Q1]   **107.1** [*Richmond remains*] [substantially from F]   **119 stabbed'st** stabst   **139 GHOST OF RIVERS** *King* [Q1]   **141 GHOST OF GREY** *Gray* [Q1]   **142 GHOST OF VAUGHAN** *Vaugh.* [Q1]   **145 Will** Wel [Q1]   **145.2–150** [after line 158 in Q1]   **151 GHOSTS** [F] *Ghost* [Q1]   **159 GHOST** [not in Q1]   **167 GHOST** [not in Q1]   **176 fall** [F] fals [Q1]   **183 am** and [Q1]   **209 My** Ratcliffe, my   **223 LORDS** *Lo.* [Q1]   **226, 235 A LORD** *Lo.* [Q1]   **243 Richard except** Richard, except   **270.1 Ratcliffe** Rat. & c.   **299 main** [F] matne [Q1]   **301 boot** bootes [Q1]   **304 KING RICHARD** [at line 306 ("King") in Q1]   **324 Brittany** Brittaine   **351 them! Victory** them victorie [Q1]
5.5. 13 STANLEY [not in Q1]   **13 Ferrers** Ferri [Q1]   **15 becomes** become [Q1]   **41 s.d. Exeunt** [F; not in Q1]

Richard II

Copy text: the First Quarto of 1597 as press-corrected in all four extant copies [Q1]; and, for the deposition scene, 4.1. 155–321, the First Folio. Act and scene marking divisions, absent in Q1, are from F except that F provides no scene marking at 5.4 and labels 5.5 and 5.6 as *"Scaena Quarta"* and *"Scaena Quinta,"* respectively.

1.1. 15 presence. Face presence face   **19.1 [and throughout]** *Bolingbroke* Bullingbrooke   **118 by my** [F] by   **139 But** Ah but   **152 gentlemen** [F] gentleman   **162–3 Harry, when? / Obedience bids** Harry? when obedience bids. / Obedience bids   **176 gage. My gage, my**   **178 reputation; that** Reputation that   **192 parle** parlee   **205.1 Exeunt** Exit
1.2. 25 him. Thou him, thou   **42 alas** [not in Q]   **47 sit** [F] set   **48 butcher** [Qb, F] butchers [Qa]   **58 it** [Q2–5, F] is   **59 empty** [Qb, F] emptines, [Qa]   **60 begun** begone   **70 hear** [F] cheere
1.3. 15 thee the   **33 comest** [Q5] comes   **58 thee** the   **104 FIRST HERALD** Herald   **108 his God** [F] God   **128 civil** [Qb, F] cruel [Qa]   **133 Draws** [Qb] Draw [Qa]   **136 wrathful iron** [Qb, F] harsh resounding [Qa]   **172 then but** [F] but   **180 you owe** [F] y'owe   **193 far** fare   **222 night** [Q4–5, F] nightes   **239 had it** had't   **241 sought** ought   **269 world** world:

1.4. 0.1 *Bagot* [F] *Bushie* **20 our cousin,** [F] our Coosens **23 Bagot here, and Green** [Q6; not in Q1] **27 What** [Qb, F] With [Qa] **47 hand. If** hand if **52.1 Enter Bushy** [F] *Enter Bushie with newes* **53 Bushy, what news** [F; not in Q1] **65 ALL** [not in Q1]

2.1. 15 life's liues **18 fond** found **30 [and elsewhere] lose** loose **48 as a** [Q4–5, F] as **68.1–2** [after line 70 in Q1] **70 reined** ragde **102 encagèd** [F] inraged **113 not** not, not **124 brother** brothers **156 kerns** [Qb, F] kerne **161 coin** [Qb, F] coines [Qa] **168 my** [Qb, F] mine **177 the** [F] a **209 seize** cease **239 more** mo **257 King's** [Q3–5, F] King **277 Port le Blanc** le Port Blan **278 Brittany** Brittaine [also in 285] **284 Coint** Coines

2.2. 19 Show [Q6, F] Shows [Qa] **31 though** [Q2–5, F] thought **53 Harry** H.

2.3. 9 Cotswold Cotshall **30 Lordship** Lo: **36 Hereford** [Q3–5, F] Herefords **75 raze** race **99 the lord** [F] Lord **164 [and elsewhere] Bristol** Bristow

2.4. 1 WELSH CAPTAIN *Welsh* [also at line 7]

3.2. 32 succor succors **40 boldly** bouldy **72 O'erthrows** [F] Ouerthrowes **86 name! A** name a **170 through** [Q2–5, F] thorough

3.3. 13 brief with you [F] briefe **31 lord** [F] Lords **59 rain** raigne. **60 waters—on** water's on **100 pastures'** pastors **119 a prince and princesse** **127 ourself** our selues

3.4. 11 joy griefe **26 pins** [F] pines **27 state, for** state for **28 change; woe** change woe **29 apricots** Aphricokes **34 too** [F] two **48 hath htah** **55 seized** ceasde **57 We at** at **80 Cam'st** [Q2–5, F] Canst

4.1. 23 him [Q3–5, F] them **44 Fitzwater** [F] Fitzwaters **55 As** As it **56 sun to sun** sinne to sinne **63 true. You** true you **77 my bond** [Q3–5, F] bond **110 thee** [Q2–5, F] the **146 you** yon **155–321** [This deposition scene is based on the First Folio text; Q1 has only: "Let it be so, and loe on wednesday next, / We solemnly proclaime our Coronation, / Lords be ready all." Unless otherwise indicated all the departures in F from lines 155–321 are taken from Q4.] **184 and on** on **252 and** a **256 Nor** No, nor **297 manners** manner **321.2** *Carlisle Caleil*

5.1. 11 model modle **41 thee** [Q2–5, F] the **84 NORTHUMBERLAND** [F] *King*

5.2. 2 off [F] of **11 thee** [F] the [also at lines 17 and 94] **78 my troth** by my troth **94 thee** the **116 And** An

5.3. 0.1 King *the King* **10 While** Which **31 the** my **36 I may** [Q2–5, F] May **68 And** An **75 shrill-voiced** shril voice **111 KING HENRY** *yorke* **135–6 With . . . him** I pardon him with al my heart

5.4. 0.1 Enter [F] *Manet* **Exton** *Exton, etc.*

5.5. 20 through [F] thorow **22 cannot, die** cannot die **27 sit** [Q3–5, F] set **33 treason makes** treasons make **55 sounds that tell** sound that telles **56 that** which **58 hours, and times** times, and houres

5.6. 8 Salisbury, Spencer [F] Oxford, Salisbury **12.1 Fitzwater** *Fitzwaters* **43 through the** [F] through

1 Henry IV

Copy text: the first complete Quarto of 1598 [Q1]; and, for 1.3.201 through 2.2.110, the fragment of an earlier Quarto [Q0]. The act and scene divisions, missing in Q0 and Q1, are based on F except that F provides no break at 5.3.

1.1. 22 levy leauy **39 Herdfordshire** Herdforshire **62 a dear** deere **69 blood, did** bloud. Did **70 plains. Of** plaines, of **76 In faith, it is** [assigned in Q1 to King]

1.2. 16 king a king **33 proof, now:** proofe. Now **78 similes** smiles **154 thou** the **158 Peto, Bardolph** Haruey, Rossill

1.3. 12 too to, **137 [and throughout] Bolingbroke** Bullingbrooke **194 good night** god-night **201 HOTSPUR** [missing in Q0–Q4] **222 holler** hollow **238 whipped** [Q1] whip [Q0]

2.1. 34 FIRST CARRIER *Car.* **48.1** [below line 47 in Q0] **56 Weald** wild **70 Trojans** Troyans

2.2. 0.1 Poins, Peto, and *Poines, and Peto &c* **12 square** squire **16 two-and-twenty** xxii: **20 Bardolph** Bardol [and thus, or

"Bardoll," throughout the play] **34 mine** [Q1] my [Q0] **42 Go hang** [F] Hang [Q0] **51 BARDOLPH What news** [all assigned as continuation of Poins's speech in line 50] **52 GADSHILL** *Bar.* **78 FIRST TRAVELER** *Trauel.* **82 TRAVELERS** *Trauel.* **86 TRAVELERS** *Tra.*

2.3. 1 HOTSPUR [not in Q1] **4 In** in **48 thee** the **69 A roan** Roane

2.4. 33 precedent present **36 POINS** *Prin.* **121 sun's** soanes **171 PRINCE** *Gad* **172 GADSHILL** *Ross.* [also at lines 174 and 178] **226 keech** catch **242 eel-skin** elsskin **322.1** [after line 321 in Q1] **337 Owen** O **390 tristful** trustfull **398 yet** so **468 lean** lane **518 Good** God [also at line 519] **526 s.d. pockets** pocket **530 PETO** [not in Q1] **535 PRINCE** [not in Q1]

3.1. 55 coz coose [also at line 75] **97 cantle** scantle **126 meter** miter **129 on** an **183 Loseth** Looseth **261 hot Lord** Hot. Lord

3.2. 32 Council counsell **59 won** wan **84 gorged** gordge **96 then** than **145 northern** Northren **161.1** [after line 162 in Q1]

3.3. 35 that's that **57 tithe** tight **119 no thing** nothing **135 owed** ought **173 guests** ghesse **200 o'clock** of clocke

4.1. 1 [and elsewhere] HOTSPUR *Per.* **20 lord** mind **55 is** tis **96 doffed** daft **105 cuisses** cushes **108 dropped** drop **116 altar** altars **123 ne'er** neare **126 cannot** can **127 yet** it **134 merrily** merely

4.2. 3 Coldfield cop-hill **15 yeomen's** Yeomans **31 feazed** fazd **33–4 tattered** tottered **80 s.d. Exit** *Exeunt*

4.3. 23 horse horses **74 heirs . . . followed** heires, as Pages followed **84 country's** Countrey

4.4. 0.1 [and throughout] Michael *Mighell* **18 o'erruled** ouerrulde **36 not, ere** not ere **37 power he** power, he

5.1. 0.2 Lancaster *Lancaster, Earle of Westmerland* **2 bosky** bulky **3 southern** Southren **88 off** of **138 will it** wil

5.2. 3 undone vnder one **8 Suspicion** Supposition **12 merrily** merely **25.1 Hotspur** *Percy* **79 FIRST MESSENGER** *Mes.* **89 SECOND MESSENGER** *Mes.* **94–5 withal / . . . day.** withall. / . . . day,

5.3. 1 in the in **22 A Ah** **35–6 ragamuffins** rag of Muffins

5.4. 4 [and elsewhere] LANCASTER *P. John* **68 Nor** Now **76.1 who he** **92 enough. This** inough, this **thee** the

5.5. 36 bend you bend, you

Henry V

Copy text: the First Folio. Act and scene divisions are for the most part editorially supplied; F marks "*Actus Secundus*" at Act 3, "*Actus Tertius*" at Act 4, "*Actus Quartus*" at 4.7, and "*Actus Quintus*" at Act 5.

Prologue. 1 CHORUS [not in F; also in prologues to other acts]

1.2. 38 succedant succedaul **45 Elbe** Elue [also at line 52] **76 [and elsewhere] Lewis** Lewes **82 Ermengard** *Ermengare* **90–1 day, / Howbeit** day. / Howbeit, **115 ELY** *Bish.* **131 blood** Bloods. **163 her** their **166 A LORD** *Bish. Ely* **197 majesty** Maiesties **212 End** [Q] And **221 [and elsewhere] Dauphin** Dolphin **237 FIRST AMBASSADOR** *Amb.* [also at line 245] **310.1 Flourish** [at the beginning of 2.0 in F]

2.1. 23 mare [Q] name **28 NYM** [Q; not in F] **42, 43 Iceland** Island **73 thee defy** [Q] defie thee **80 enough** enough to **83 you** your **105–6** [Q; not in F] **betting** beating [Q] **116 that's** that

2.2. 29 GREY *Kni.* **87 furnish him** [Q] furnish **107 a** an **108 whoop** hoope **114 All** And **139 mark the** make thee **140 suspicion . . . thee; suspicion, . . . thee.** **147 Henry** [Q] *Thomas* **148 Masham** [Q] *Marsham* **159 Which I** Which **176 have sought** [Q] sought **181.1 Exeunt** *Exit*

2.3. 16–17 'a babbled a Table **24 upward** vp-peer'd **32 HOSTESS** *Woman* **48 word** world

2.4. 0.2 Brittany *Britaine* **1 [and elsewhere] FRENCH KING** *King* **132 Louvre** Louer **146.1 Flourish** [at the beginning of 3.0 in F]

3.0. 6 fanning fayning **17 [and elsewhere] Harfleur** Harflew **35 eke** eech

3.1. 7 conjure commune **17 noblest** Noblish **24 men** me **32 Straining** Straying

3.2. 25 runs wins **67** [and elsewhere in scene] FLUELLEN *Welch*
82 [and elsewhere in scene] JAMY *Scot* **87** [and elsewhere in
scene] MACMORRIS *Irish* **102 quite** quit **112 Chrish** Christ
3.3. 32 heady headly **35 Defile** Desire **43** [here F has s.d. "*Enter
Gouernour*"] **54 all. For** all for
3.4. 2 parles *parlas* [throughout the play, the French has been somewhat
modernized, besides the emendations listed here] **7 Elle** *il* **8 Et les
doigts** [assigned to Alice in F] **9** ALICE *Kat.* **les doigts** *e doyt*
10 souviendrai *souemeray* **12** KATHARINE *Alice* **13 j'ai** *Kath. I'ay*
14 les *le* **16 Nous** [not in F] **40 pas déjà** *y desia* **42 Non** *Nome*
46 Sauf *Sans* **51 les** *le* [also in line 52]
3.5. 11 de *du* **26 "Poor"** may Poore **43 Vaudemont** Vandemont
45 Foix . . . Boucicault *Loys, Lestrale, Bouciquall* **46 knights** Kings
3.6. 31 her [Q] his **37 is make** [Q] makes **111–12 lenity** Leuitie
3.7. 12 pasterns postures **14** *qui a* ches **59 lief** liue **65 et est** *truie
leuye*
4.0. 16 name nam'd **20 cripple** creeple **27 Presenteth** Presented
4.1. 3 Good God **95 Thomas** *Iohn* **158 deaths** [Q] death **propose**
purpose **227 s.d.** *Exeunt Exit* [at line 222 in F] **243 What is** What?
is **adoration** Odoration **273 Hyperion** *Hiperio* **289 reck'ning,
ere . . . numbers** reckning of . . . numbers: **307 friends** friend
4.2. 4 eaux ewes **6 Cieux** *Cein* **11 dout** doubt **47 drooping** dropping
49 gimmaled Iymold **52 all impatient** all, impatient
4.3. 12 [placed after line 14 in F] **48** [Q; not in F] **124 'em** vm
4.4. 15 Or for **36** *à cette heure* asture **37** *couper* couppes **54 l'avez**
layt a **57 remercîments** *remercious* **58 j'ai tombé** Ie intombe
59 très-distingué tres distinie **68 Suivez-vous** *Saaue vous*
4.5. 2 perdu . . . perdu *perdia . . . perdie* **3 Mort de** *Mor Dieu* **16 by a**
[Q] a base **24.1** *Exeunt Exit*
4.6. 34 mistful mixtfull **38 s.d.** *Exeunt Exit*
4.7. 22 e'en in **69** [and elsewhere in this scene] MONTJOY *Her.*
77 the with **109 countryman** Countrymen **114 God** Good **123 'a
live** aliue **126 'a lived** aliue **161** [and elsewhere] **an't** and
4.8. 77 Boucicault *Bouchiquald* **99 Foix** *Foyes* **100 Vaudemont**
Vandemont **Lestrelles** *Lestrale* **104 Keighley** *Ketly* **110–11 loss /
On . . . other?** losse? / On . . . other, **113 we** me **121 in my** [Q] my
122 rites Rights
5.0. 29 but but by
5.1. 39 By Jesu [Q] I say **69 begun** began **88 swear** swore
5.2. 1 [and elsewhere] KING HENRY *King* **12** [and throughout scene]
QUEEN ISABEL *Quee.* **12 England** Ireland **21** [also elsewhere] KING
HENRY *Eng.* **45 fumitory** Femetary **50 all** withall **61 diffused**
defus'd **72 tenors** Tenures **77 cursitory** curselarie **93 Haply**
Happily **98 s.d.** *Manent Manet* **114** [and elsewhere] ALICE *Lady*
190 *meilleur* melieus **255** *grandeur* grandeus **261** *noces* nopcese
264 les *le* **265 baiser** buisse **267 entend** entendre **323 hath** never
hath **332 then in** in **364 paction** Pation
Epilogue CHORUS [not in F]

Romeo and Juliet

Copy text: the Second Quarto of 1599, except for 1.2.53–1.3.34, for which
Q1 (the First Quarto) is the prior authority. Act and scene divisions are
absent from the Second Quarto and the Folio.
1.1. 27 it in [Q1] it **38 side** sides **73** CITIZENS *Offi.* **76** CAPULET'S
WIFE *Wife* **92 Verona's** *Neronas* **120 drave** driue **147 his** is
153 sun same **177 create** [Q1] created **179 well-seeming** [Q1]
welseeing **189 grief to** [Q1] grief, too **192 lovers'** louing **202 Bid
a** [Q1] A **make** [Q1] makes **206 markman** mark man
211 unharmed [Q1] vncharmd **218 makes** make
1.2. 14 The earth Earth **32 on** one **38–9 written here** written. Here
46 One [Q1] on **56 Good e'en** Goddess **57 God gi' good e'en**
Godgigoden **70 and Livia** Liuia [Q2] **79 thee** [Q1] you [Q2]
91 fires fier [Q1]
1.3. 12 an [Q2] a [Q1] **18 shall** [Q1] stal [Q2] **33 wi' th'** [Q1: *with*]
with the [Q2] **50** [and elsewhere] WIFE *Old La.* **66 disposition** [F]

dispositions **67, 68 honor** [Q1] houre **100 it fly** [Q1] flie
105 [and elsewhere] WIFE *Mo.*
1.4. 7–8 [Q1; not in Q2] **23** MERCUTIO *Horatio* **31 quote** cote
39 done [Q1] dum **42 Of** Or **45 like lamps** [Q1] lights lights
47 five fine **57 atomi** [Q1] ottamie **59–61** [these lines follow line 69
in Q2] **66 film** *Philome* **69 maid** [Q1] man **72 O'er** [Q1] On
74 on one **76 breaths** [Q1] breath **80 parson's** Persons **81 dreams
he** [Q1] he dreams **90 elflocks** Elklocks **111 forfeit** [Q1] fofreit
1.5. 0.1 [Q2 adds: "*Enter Romeo*"] **1** FIRST SERVINGMAN *Ser.* [also at
lines 6 and 12] **3** SECOND SERVINGMAN 1 **7 court cupboard**
Courtcubbert **11** THIRD SERVINGMAN 2 **14** FOURTH SERVINGMAN 3
15 longest longer **17** CAPULET 1. *Capu.* [also at lines 35 and 40]
18 a bout about **57 antic** antique **96 ready** [Q1] did readie
2.0. Chorus 1 CHORUS [not in Q2] **4 matched** match
2.1. 7 Nay . . . too [assigned in Q2 to Benvolio] **10 one** [Q1] on
11 Pronounce [Q1] prouaunt **dove** [Q1] day **13 heir** [Q1] her
14 trim [Q1] true **39 open-arse, and** open, or **pop'ring** Poprin
2.2. 16 do [Q1] to **20 eyes** [Q1] eye **41–2 nor any . . . name** ô be some
other name / Belonging to a man **45 were** [Q1] wene **82 pilot** Pylat
83 washed [Q1] washeth **92–3 false . . . They** false at louers periuries.
/ They **99 havior** behauiour **101 more cunning** coying **110 circled**
[Q1] circle **146** [and elsewhere] **rite** right **149, 151** NURSE [not in Q2]
150, 151 JULIET [not in Q2] **163 than mine** then **168 nyas** Neece
180 gyves giues **187 Sleep . . . breast** [Q1; assigned in Q2 to Juliet]
189–90 [preceded in Q2 by an earlier version of lines 1–4 of the next
scene, in which "fleckled darkness" reads "darknesse fleckted" and "and
Titan's fiery wheels" reads "made by *Tytans* wheels"]
2.3. 2 Check'ring [Q1] Checking **22 sometime's** sometime **50 me**
me: **51 wounded. Both our** wounded both, our **85 not. She
whom** [Q1] me not, her
2.4. 18 BENVOLIO [Q1] *Ro.* **28 antic** antique **28–9 phantasimes**
phantacies **33 pardon-me's** pardons mees **40 but a** a **68 Switch
. . . switch** Swits . . . swits **113–14 for himself** [Q1] himself
205 dog's dog **212 s.d.** *Exeunt Exit*
2.5. 11 three there **15 And** *M.* And **26 I had** [Q1] I
2.6. 18 gossamer gossamours **27 music's** musicke
3.1. 2 Capels are *Capels* **67 injured** iniuried **73** *stoccada* stucatho
90 your houses houses **107 soundly too. Your** soundly, to your
121 Alive He gan **123 fire-eyed** [Q1] fier end **136** FIRST CITIZEN
Citti. **138** FIRST CITIZEN *Citi.* **141 all** all: **165 agile** [Q1] aged
183 MONTAGUE *Capu.* **187 hate's** heart's **191 I** [Q1] it
196.1 *Exeunt Exit*
3.2. 1 JULIET [not in Q2] **9 By** And by **12** [and elsewhere] **lose** loose
15 grown grow **47 darting** arting **49 shut** shot **51 Brief sounds**
Briefe, sounds, **of my** my **54** [and elsewhere] **corpse** coarse
60 one on **72 It . . . day** it did [assigned in Q2 to Juliet] **73 O . . .
face** [assigned in Q2 to Nurse] **76 Dove-feathered** Rauenous
doue-featherd **79 damnèd** dimme **143.1** *Exeunt Exit*
3.3. 0.1 [Q2 has "*Enter Friar and Romeo*"] **39** [Q2 follows with a line:
"This may flyes do, when I from this must flie"] **43** [printed in Q2
before line 40] **52 Thou** [Q1] Then **61 madmen** [Q1] mad man
70.1 *Knock Enter Nurse, and knocke* **73 s.d.** *Knock They knocke*
74 Who's whose **75.1** *Knock Slud knock* **80.1** *Enter Nurse* [below
line 78 in Q2] **110 denote** [Q1] deuote **117 lives** [Q1] lies
144 pout'st upon puts vp **168 disguised** disguise
3.4. 10 [and elsewhere] WIFE *La.* **13 be** [Q1] me **23 We'll keep** Well,
keepe
3.5. 13 exhaled exhale **19 the** the the **31 changed** change **36.1** *Enter
Nurse Enter Madame and Nurse* **54** JULIET *Ro.* **67.1** [bracketed s.d.
from Q1] **82 pardon him** padon **130–1 body . . . a bark** body? /
Thou counterfeits. A Barke **133–4 is, . . . flood;** is: . . . floud,
139 gives giue **142 How? Will** How will **151–2 proud . . . Thank**
proud mistresse minion you? / Thanke **160** [and elsewhere] CAPULET
Fa. **172** CAPULET **Oh, God-i'-good-e'en** Father, Godigeden
173 NURSE [not in Q2] **181 liened** liand
4.1. 7 talked [Q1] talke **45 cure** [Q1] care **46 Ah** [Q1] O **72 slay**
[Q1] stay **78 off** [Q1] of **83 chopless** [Q1] chapels **85 his tomb**

his   **98 breath** [Q1] breast   **100 To wanny** Too many   **110 In** Is [Q2 follows with a line: "Be borne to buriall in thy kindreds graue"]   **111 shalt** shall   **115 and he** an he   **116 waking** walking   **126 s.d.** *Exeunt Exit*

4.2. 3, 6 SERVINGMAN *Ser.*   **14 willed** wield   **26 becomèd** becomd   **38 [and elsewhere]** WIFE *Mo.*   **47.1** *Exeunt Exit*

4.3. 20 vial Violl   **49 wake** walke

4.4. 1 [and elsewhere] WIFE *La.*   **12.1** *Exeunt Exit*   **13.1–2** [after line 14 in Q2]   **15 FIRST SERVINGMAN** *Fel.*   **18 SECOND SERVINGMAN** *Fel.*   **21 Thou** Twou   **faith** father   **23 s.d.** [after line 21 in Q2]

4.5. 40 all; life all life   **41 long** loue   **51 behold** bedold   **65 cure** care   **65–6 not . . . Heaven** not, / In these confusions heauen   **82 fond** some   **96 FIRST MUSICIAN** *Musi.*   **98 s.d.** *Exit* Exit omnes [below line 99]   **99, 103 FIRST MUSICIAN** *Fid.*   **99 by** [Q1] my   **99.1** *Enter Peter* Enter Will Kemp   **107 FIRST MUSICIAN** *Minstrels* [and subsequently in this scene indicated by *Minst.* or *Minstrel*]   **123 Then . . . wit** [assigned in Q2 to 2 *M*]   **127 And . . . oppress** [Q1; not in Q2]   **133, 136 Pretty** [Q1] Prates   **145 s.d.** *Exeunt Exit*

5.1. 15 fares my [Q1] doth my Lady   **17, 27, 32 BALTHASAR** *Man*   **24 e'en** in   **defy** [Q1] denie   **33.1** [at line 32, after "good lord," in Q2]   **76 pay** [Q1] pray   **86 s.d.** *Exit Exeunt*

5.3. 3 yew [Q1] young   **21.2** [*Balthasar*] [Q1] Peter   **25 light. Upon** light vpon   **40, 43 BALTHASAR** *Pet.*   **68 conjuration** commiration   **71 PAGE** *Boy* [Q1; s.p. missing in Q2 and line treated as a s.d.]   **102 fair** faire? I will beleeue   **107 palace** pallat   **108** [Q2 has four undeleted lines here: "Depart againe, come lye thou in my arme, / Heer's to thy health, where ere thou tumblest in. / O true Appothecarie! / Thy drugs are quicke. Thus with a kisse I die."]   **123 [and elsewhere]** BALTHASAR *Man*   **137 yew** yong   **168 FIRST WATCH** *Watch* [also at lines 172, 195, 199]   **171 PAGE** *Watch boy*   **182 SECOND WATCH** *Watch*   **183, 187 FIRST WATCH** *Chief. watch*   **187 too** too too   **190 shrieked** shrike   **194 our** your   **199 slaughtered** Slaughter   **201** [Q2 has a s.d. here: "*Enter Capulet and his wife*"]   **209 more early** [Q1] now earling   **232 that** thats   **274–5 place . . . This** place. To this same monument / This   **281 PAGE** *Boy*   **299 raise** raie

Julius Caesar

Copy text: the First Folio. Act divisions are marked in the Folio; scene divisions are editorially supplied.

1.1. 0.1 [and elsewhere] *Marullus* Murellus   **37 Pompey? . . . oft** *Pompey* many a time and oft?   **61 [and elsewhere] whe'er** where

1.2. 0.1 [and elsewhere] *Calpurnia* Calphurnia   **24.1** *Manent* Manet   **124 [and elsewhere] lose** loose   **254 like. He** like he   **301 digest** disgest

1.3. 129 In favor's like Is Fauors, like

2.1. 28 [and elsewhere] lest least   **40 ides** first   **67 of** of a   **83 put** path   **122 women, then,** women. Then   **136 oath, when** Oath. When   **214 eighth** eight   **268 his** hit   **281 the** tho   **310.1** *Enter Lucius and Ligarius* [after "with haste" in line 310 in F]   **314 [and through line 322]** LIGARIUS *Cai.*

2.2. 23 did neigh do neigh   **46 are** heare   **81 Of** And

2.3. 1 ARTEMIDORUS [not in F]   **120 to blame** too blame

3.1. 40 law lane   **114 states** State   **116 lies** lye   **201 [and elsewhere] corpse** Coarse [also Course and Corpes]   **256 ANTONY** [not in F]   **277.1** *Octavius'* Octauio's [also at 5.2.4]   **285 for** from

3.2. 106 art are   **205 ALL** [not in F]   **222 wit** writ   **260 s.d.** *Exeunt Exit*   **262 s.d.** *Enter Servant* [after "fellow" in F]

3.3. 6 Whither Whether

4.2. 34–6 FIRST, SECOND, THIRD SOLDIER [not in F]   **50 Lucius** Lucillius   **52 Lucilius** Lucius   **52.1** *Manent* Manet

4.3. 209–10 off / If off. / If   **230 s.d.** *Enter Lucius* [before line 230 in F]   **244, 246 [and throughout]** Claudius *Claudio*   **246 [and throughout]** Varro *Varrus*   **252 will** it will   **303, 307 VARRO, CLAUDIUS** *Both*

5.1. 42 teeth teethes   **67.1** *Exeunt Exit*   **70** [F has s.d.: "*Lucillius and Messala stand forth*"]   **71 LUCILIUS (stands forth)** *Luc.*   **73 MESSALA (stands forth)** *Messa.*   **99 rest** rests

5.3. 99 fare far   **104 Thasos** *Tharsus*   **108 Flavius** *Flauio*

5.4. 7 LUCILIUS [not in F]   **9 O** *Luc.* O   **12, 15 FIRST SOLDIER** Sold.   **16.1** *Enter Antony* [before line 16 in F]   **17 the news** thee newes

5.5. 33 too, Strato to *Strato*   **77 With all** Withall

Hamlet

Copy text: the Second Quarto of 1604–1605 [Q2]. The First Folio text also represents an independently authoritative text; although seemingly not the correct choice for copy text, the Folio text is considerably less marred by typographical errors than is Q2. The adopted readings in these notes are from F unless otherwise indicated; [eds.] means that the adopted reading was first proposed by some editor since the time of F. Some readings also are supplied from the First Quarto of 1603 [Q1]. Act and scene divisions are missing in Q₁ 1–2; the Folio provides such markings only through 1.3 and at Act 2.

1.1. 1 Who's Whose   **19 soldier** [F, Q1] souldiers   **44 off** [Q1] of   **48 harrows** horrowes   **67 sledded Polacks** [eds.] sleaded pollax   **77 why** [F, Q1] with   **cast** cost   **91 heraldry** [F, Q1] heraldy   **92 those** [F, Q1] these   **95 returned** returne   **97 cov'nant** comart   **98 designed** [eds.] desseigne   **112 e'en so** [eds.] enso   **116 mote** [eds.] moth   **119 tenantless** tennatlesse   **125 feared** [eds.] feare   **142 you** [F, Q1] your   **144 at it** it   **181 conveniently** [F, Q1] conuenient

1.2. 0.2 [and elsewhere] *Gertrude* Gertrad   **1 KING** *Claud.*   **67 so** so much   **77 good** coold   **82 shapes** [Q3] chapes   **83 denote** deuote   **96 a** or   **105 corpse** [eds.] course   **112 you. For** you for   **114 retrograde** retrogard   **129 sullied** [eds.] sallied [Q2] solid [F]   **132 self** seale   **133 weary** wary   **137 to this** thus   **140 satyr** [F4] satire   **143 would** [F, Q1] should   **149 even she** [F; not in Q2]   **175 to drink deep** [F, Q1] for to drinke   **178 to see** [F, Q1] to   **199 waste** [F2] wast [Q2, F]   **206 jelly with . . . fear,** gelly, with . . . feare   **210 Where, as** [Q5] Whereas   **225 Indeed, indeed** [F, Q1] Indeede   **241 Very like, very like** [F, Q1] Very like   **242 hundred** hundreth   **243 MARCELLUS, BERNARDO** [eds.] *Both*   **247 tonight** to nigh   **256 fare** farre   **257 eleven** a leauen   **259.1** *Exeunt* [at line 258 in Q2]   **262 Foul** [F, Q1] fonde

1.3. 3 convoy is conuay, in   **12 bulk** bulkes   **18** [F; not in Q2]   **29 weigh** way   **49 like a** a a   **74 Are** Or   **75 be** boy   **76 loan** loue   **110 Running** [eds.] Wrong [Q2] Roaming [F]   **116 springes** springs   **126 tether** tider   **130 implorators** implorototors   **131 bawds** [eds.] bonds   **132 beguile** beguide

1.4. 2 is a is   **6.1 go off** [eds.] goes of   **17 revel** [Q3] reueale   **19 clepe** clip   **36 evil** [eds.] eale [Q2] ease [Q3]   **37 often dout** [eds.] of a doubt   **49 inurned** interr'd [Q2, Q1]   **61, 79 wafts** waues   **80 off** of   **82 artery** arture   **86.1** *Exeunt Exit*   **87 imagination** [F, Q1] imagion

1.5. 1 Whither [eds.] Whether   **20 on** [eds.] an   **21 fretful porcupine** [F, Q1] fearfull Porpentine   **44 wit** [eds.] wits   **48 what a** what   **56 lust** [F, Q1] but   **angel** Angle   **57 sate** [F] sort   **59 scent** [eds.] sent   **68 alleys** [eds.] allies   **69 posset** possesse   **96 stiffly** swiftly   **119 bird** and   **128 HORATIO, MARCELLUS** *Booth* [also at line 151]   **heaven, my lord** heauen   **138 Look you, I'll** I will   **157 s.d.** *cries Ghost cries*   **179 some'er** so mere   **185 Well** well, well [Q1, Q2]

2.1 0.1 man [eds.] man or two   **3 marvelous** meruiles   **29 Faith, no** Fayth   **41 warrant** wit   **42 sullies** sallies   **43 wi' th'** with   **60 o'ertook** or tooke   **64 takes** take   **76 s.d.** *Exit Reynaldo. Enter Ophelia* [after line 75 in Q2]   **107 passion** passions   **114 quoted** [eds.] coted

2.2. 0.1 [and elsewhere] *Rosencrantz* Rosencraus   **57 o'erhasty** hastie   **73 three** [F, Q1] threescore   **90 since brevity** breuitie   **125 This** [Q2 has a speech prefix: *Pol.* This]   **126 above** about   **137 winking** working   **143 his** her   **148 watch** wath   **149 to a** to   **151 'tis** [F, Q1; not in Q2]   **170.1** [at line 169 in Q2] *Exeunt* [eds.] *Exit*   **210 sanity** sanctity   **212–13 and suddenly . . . him** [F; not in Q2]   **213 honorable lord** Lord   **214 most humbly take** take   **215 cannot, sir** cannot   **216 more** not more   **224 excellent** extent   **228–9 overhappy. / On** euer happy on   **229 cap** lap   **240–70 Let . . . attended** [F; not in Q2]   **267 ROSENCRANTZ, GUILDENSTERN** *Both* [F]   **273 even** euer   **288 could** can   **292 off** of   **304 What a** What   **306–7 admirable, in action how**

...angel, in [F, subst.] admirable in action, how ... Angell in   **310 no,** nor nor   **314 you** yee   **321 of** on   **324–5 the clown ... sear** [F; not in Q2]   **tickle** [eds.] tickled [F]   **326 blank** black   **337–62 How ... too** [F; not in Q2]   **342 berattle** [eds.] be-ratled [F]   **349 most like** [eds.] like most [F]   **373 lest my** let me   **381 too** to   **398–9 tragical-histori-cal, tragical-comical-historical-pastoral** [F; not in Q2]   **401 light ... these** [eds.] light for the lawe of writ, and the liberty: these   **425 By 'r** by   **429 e'en to 't** ento't   **French falconers** friendly Fankners   **433 [and elsewhere]** FIRST PLAYER *Player*   **436–7 caviare** cauiary   **443 affecta-tion** affection   **446 tale** [F, Q1] talke   **456 heraldry** [F, Q1] heraldy   **dismal. Head** dismall head   **474 Then senseless Ilium** [F; not in Q2]   **481 And, like** Like   **495 fellies** [F4] follies [Q2] Fallies [F]   **504 "Mobléd queen" is good** [F; not in Q2; F reads "Inobled"]   **506 bisson** Bison   **514 husband's** [F, Q1] husband   **519 whe'er** where   **540 a** [F; not in Q2]   **541 or** [F, Q1] lines, or   **546 s.d. Exeunt players** [see textual note at line 548.1]   **547 till** tell   **548.1 Exeunt** [F; Q2 has "*Exeunt Pol. and Players*" after line 547]   **554 his** the   **556 and** an   **559 to Hecuba** [F, Q1] to her   **561 the cue** that   **582 Oh, vengeance** [F; not in Q2]   **584 father** [Q1, Q3, Q4; not in Q2, F]   **588 scullion** [F] stallyon [Q2] scalion [Q1]   **600 the devil** a deale the devil the deale

3.1. 1 And An   **28 too** two   **32 lawful espials** [F; not in Q2]   **33 Will** Wee'le   **46 loneliness** lowlines   **to** too   **56 Let's withdraw** with-draw   **56.2 Enter Hamlet** [after line 55 in Q2]   **65 wished. To** wisht to   **73 disprized** despiz'd   **84 of us all** [F, Q1; not in Q2]   **86 sicklied** sickled   **93 well, well, well** well   **100 the** these   **108 your honesty** you   **119 inoculate** euocutat   **122 to a** a   **130 knaves all** knaues   **144 paintings too** [Q1] paintings   **146 jig, you amble** gig & amble   **147 lisp** list   **148 your ignorance** [F, Q1] ignorance   **155 Th'expectancy** Th'expectation   **159 music** musickt   **160 that** what   **161 tune** time   **162 feature** stature   **164** [Q2 has "*Exit*" at the end of this line]   **191 unwatched** vnmatcht

3.2. 10 tatters totters   **split** [F, Q1] spleet   **27 of the** of   **29 praise** praysd   **37 sir** [F; not in Q2]   **45.1 Enter ... Rosencrantz** [after line 47 in Q2]   **88 detecting** detected   **96 now. My lord,** now my Lord.   **107 [and elsewhere]** QUEEN *Ger.*   **108 metal** mettle   **112–13** [F; not in Q2]   **127 devil** deule [Q2] Diuel [F]   **133.1 sound** [eds.] sounds   **133.7 Anon comes** anon come   **135 miching** [F, Q1] munching   **140 keep counsel** [F, Q1] keepe   **153 [and throughout scene]** PLAYER KING *King*   **154 orbèd** orb'd the   **159 [and throughout scene]** PLAYER QUEEN *Quee.*   **162 your** our   **164** [Q2 follows here with an extraneous unrhymed line: "For women feare too much, euen as they loue"]   **165 For** And   **166 In** Eyther none, in   **167 love** Lord   **179 Wormwood, wormwood** That's wormwood   **180 PLAYER QUEEN** [not in Q2]   **188 like** the   **197 joys** joy   **217 An** And   **221 a widow** [F, Q1] I be a widow   **be** [F] be a   **226.1 Exit** [F, Q1] *Exeunt*   **240 wince** [Q1] winch [Q2, F]   **241.1** [after line 242 in Q2]   **254 Confederate** [F, Q1] Considerat   **256 infected** [F, Q1, Q4] inuected   **258 usurp** vsurps   **264** [F; not in Q2]   **274 with two** with   **288.1** [F; after line 293 in Q2]   **308 start** stare   **317 of my** of   **343.1** [after line 341 in Q2]   **357 thumb** the vmber   **366 to the top of** to   **370 can fret me** [F] fret me not [Q2] can fret me, yet [Q1]   **371.1** [after line 372 in Q2]   **385 POLONIUS** [F; not in Q2]   **386 Leave me, friends** [so F; Q2 places before "I will say so," and assigns both to Hamlet]   **388 breathes** breakes   **390 bitter ... day** business as the bitter day   **395 daggers** [F, Q1] dagger

3.3. 19 huge hough   **22 ruin** raine   **23 but with** but   **35.1 Exit** [after "I know" in F]   **50 pardoned** pardon   **58 Offense's** [eds.] Offences   **shove** showe   **73 pat ... a-praying** but now a is a praying   **75 revenged** reuendge   **79 hire and salary** base and silly   **81 With all** Withall

3.4. 5–6 with him ... Mother, Mother, Mother [F; not in Q2]   **7 war-rant** wait   **8.1 Enter Hamlet** [at line 5 in Q2]   **21 inmost** most   **23 Help, ho!** Helpe how   **43 off** of   **51 tristful** heated   **53** [assigned in Q2 to Hamlet]   **60 heaven-kissing** heaue, a kissing   **89 panders** pardons   **91 mine ... soul** my very eyes into my soule   **92 grainèd** greeued   **93 not leave** leaue there   **100 tithe** kyth   **146 Ecstasy** [F;

not in Q2]   **150 I the** the   **165 live** leaue   **172 Refrain tonight** to refraine night   **193 ravel** rouell   **205 to breathe** [eds.] to breath   **222 a** [F, Q1] a most   **224.1 Exeunt** [eds.] *Exit*

4.1. 32.1 [at 31 in Q2]

4.2. 0.1 [Q2: "*Enter Hamlet, Rosencraus, and others.*"]   **2–3** [F; not in Q2; the s.p. in F is "*Gentlemen*"]   **4 HAMLET** [not in Q2]   **5.1** [F; not in Q2]   **7 Compounded** Compound   **18–19 an ape** [not in Q2]   **31–2 Hide ... after** [F; not in Q2]

4.3. 44 With fiery quickness [F; not in Q2]   **56 and so** so   **72 were** will   **begun** begin

4.4. 20–1 name. To name To

4.5. 16 Let ... in [assigned in Q2 to Horatio]   **20.1** [after line 16 in Q2]   **38 with all** with   **52 clothes** close   **57 Indeed, la** Indeede   **62 to** too   **83 in their** in   **98** [F; not in Q2]   **100.1** [below line 97 in Q2]   **103 impetuous** [Q3, F2] impituous [Q2] impittious [F]   **109 They** The   **146 swoopstake** [eds.] soopstake [Q1 reads "Swoop-stake-like"]   **158 Let her come in** [assigned in Q2 to Laertes and placed before "How now, what noyse is that?"]   **s.d. Enter Ophelia** [after line 157 in Q2]   **162 Till** Tell   **165 an old** [F, Q1] a poore   **166–8, 170** [F; not in Q2]   **186 must** [F, Q1] may   **191 affliction** [F, Q1] afflictions   **199 All flaxen** Flaxen   **203 Christian** [F] Christians   **souls, I pray God** [F, Q1] soules   **204 you see** you   **217 trophy, sword** trophe sword

4.6. 7, 9 FIRST SAILOR *Say.*   **9 an't** and   **22 good turn** turne   **26 bore** bord   **30 He** So   **31 will give** will

4.7. 6 proceeded proceede   **7 crimeful** criminall   **15 conjunctive** concliue   **22 gyves** Giues   **23 loud a wind** loued Arm'd   **25 had** haue   **37 How ... Hamlet** [F; not in Q2]   **38 This** These   **46–7 your pardon** you pardon   **48 and more strange** [F; not in Q2]   **Hamlet** [F; not in Q2]   **56 shall live** [F, Q1] liue   **62 checking** the King   **78 ribbon** [eds.] ribaud   **89 my** me   **101 escrimers** [eds.] Scrimures   **116 wick** [eds.] weeke   **123 spendthrift** [Q5] spend thirfts   **135 on** ore   **139 pass** pace   **141 for that** for   **151 shape. If** shape if   **157 ha 't** hate   **160 prepared** prefard   **168 hoar** horry   **172 cold** cull-cold   **192 douts** [F "doubts"] drownes

5.1. 1 [and throughout] FIRST CLOWN *Clowne*   **3 [and throughout]** SECOND CLOWN *Other*   **9 se offendendo** so offended   **12 and to** to   **Argal** or all   **34–7 SECOND CLOWN: Why ... arms?** [F; not in Q2]   **43 that frame** that   **55.1** [before line 65 in Q2]   **60 stoup** soope   **70 daintier** dintier   **85 meant** [Q1, Q3] went   **89 mazard** massene   **106–7 Is ... recoveries** [F; not in Q2]   **107–8 Will his** will   **109 dou-ble ones too** doubles   **120 Oh** or   **121** [F; not in Q2]   **143 Of all** Of   **165 nowadays** [F; not in Q2]   **183 Let me see** [F; not in Q]   **192 chamber** [F, Q1] table   **208–9 As thus** [F; not in Q2]   **216 win-ter's** waters   **226, 235 PRIEST** *Doct.*   **231 Shards, flints** Flints   **246 t' have** haue   **247 treble** double   **262 and rash** rash   **288 thus** this   **296.1** [*Exit*] *Horatio and Horatio*   **301 shortly** thereby   **302 Till** Tell

5.2. 5 Methought my thought   **6 bilboes** bilbo   **9 pall** fall   **17 unseal** vnfold   **19 Ah,** [eds.] A   **29 villainies** villaines   **30 Ere** Or   **43 "as"** es as sir   **52 Subscribed** Subscribe   **57, 68–80** [F; not in Q2]   **73 interim is** [eds.] *interim's* [F]   **78 court** [eds.] count [F]   **81 [and throughout]** OSRIC *Cour.*   **82 humbly** humble   **93 Put your** your   **98 sultry** sully   **for** or   **107 gentleman** [eds.] gentlemen   **109 feel-ingly** [Q4] fellingly   **114 dozy** [eds.] dazzie   **yaw** [eds.] raw   **141 his** [eds.] this   **142 him by them,** him, by them   **149 hangers** hanger   **156 carriages** carriage   **159 might be** be might   **162 impawned, as** [eds.] all [Q2] impon'd, as [F]   **174 purpose, I** purpose; I   **181–2 Yours, yours. 'A does** Yours doo's   **186 comply** so sir   **190 yeasty** histy   **191 fanned** [eds.] prophane [Q2] fond [F]   **winnowed** trennowed   **210 But thou** thou   **218 be now** be   **220 will come** well come   **238** [F; not in Q2]   **248 To keep** To   **till** all   **252 foils. Come on** foiles.   **255 off** of   **261 bettered** better   **270 union** Vnice ["Onixe" in some copies]   **288 A touch, a touch, I** I   **302 afeard** sure   **316 Hamlet. Hamlet** *Hamlet*   **319 thy** [F, Q1] my   **327 murderous** [F; not in Q2]   **328 off** of   **thy union** [F, Q1] the Onixe   **345 ha 't** [eds.] hate [Q2] have 't [F]   **366 proud** prou'd

369 FIRST AMBASSADOR *Embas.*   **381 th' yet** yet   **385 forced** for no
394 on no

Passages contained only in F and omitted from Q2 are noted in the textual notes above. Listed below are the more important instances in which Q2 contains words, lines, and passages omitted in F.

1.1. 112–29 BERNARDO I think . . . countrymen
1.2. 58–60 wrung . . . consent
1.3. 9 perfume and
1.4. 17–38 This heavy-headed . . . scandal   **75–8** The very . . . beneath
2.1. 122 Come
2.2. 17 Whether . . . thus   **217** except my life   **363** very   **366** 'Sblood (and some other profanity passim)   **371** then   **444–5** as wholesome . . . fine   **521–2** of this   **589** Hum
3.2. 169–70 Where . . . there   **216–17** To . . . scope
3.4. 72–7 Sense . . . difference   **79–82** Eyes . . . mope   **168–72** That monster . . . put on   **174–7** the next . . . potency   **187** One word . . . lady   **209–17** There's . . . meet
4.1. 4 Bestow . . . while   **41–4** Whose . . . air
4.2. 4 But soft
4.3. 26–9 KING Alas . . . worm
4.4. 9–67 Enter Hamlet . . . worth
4.5. 33 Oho
4.7. 68–82 LAERTES My lord . . . graveness   **101–3** Th' escrimers . . . them   **115–24** There . . . ulcer
5.1. 154 There
5.2. 106–42 here is . . . unfellowed (replaced in F by "you are not ignorant of what excellence Laertes is at his weapon")   **154–5** HORATIO [*to Hamlet*] I knew . . . done   **193–207** Enter a Lord . . . lose, my lord (replaced in F by "You will lose this wager, my lord")   **222** Let be

Othello

Copy text: the First Folio. The adopted readings are from the Quarto of 1622 [Q1], unless otherwise indicated; [eds.] means that the adopted reading was first proposed by some editor subsequent to the First Folio. Act and scene divisions are marked in the Folio with the exception of 2.3.

1.1. 1 Tush, never Neuer   **4 'Sblood, but** But   **16 And, in conclusion** [Q1; not in F]   **26 togaed** Tongued   **30 other** others   **34 God bless** blesse   **68 full** fall   **thick-lips** Thicks-lips   **74 changes** chances   **75 [and elsewhere] lose** [eds.] loose   **81 Thieves, thieves, thieves** Theeues, Theeues   **83.1** *Brabantio above* [in F, printed as a speech prefix to line 84]   **88 Zounds, sir** Sir [also at line 111]   **103 bravery** knauerie   **119 are now** are   **158 pains** apines   **161 sign. That** [eds.] signe) that   **186 night** might
1.2. 34 Duke Dukes   **50 carrack** Carract   **64 her!** [eds.] her   **69 darlings** Deareling   **89 I do** do
1.3. 1 There is There's   **these** this   **61** DUKE AND SENATORS [*All* Q1] *Sen.*   **101 maimed** main'd   **108 upon** vp on   **DUKE** [Q1; not in F]   **109 overt** ouer   **112 [and elsewhere]** FIRST SENATOR *Sen.*   **124 till** tell   **132 battles** Battaile   **fortunes** Fortune   **141 travels'** Trauellours   **143 rocks, and** Rocks   **heads** head   **145 other** others   **146 Anthropophagi** *Antropophague*   **147 Do grow** Grew   **149 thence** hence   **157 intentively** instinctiuely   **161 sighs** kisses   **203 grece** grise   **204 Into your favor** [Q1; not in F]   **222 piercèd** pierc'd   **ear** eares   **227 sovereign** mere soueraigne   **233 couch** [F] Coach [Q1]   **237 These** [eds.] This   **244 Nor I. I would not** Nor would I   **251 did love** loue   **267 me** [eds.] my   **273 instruments** Instrument   **281** DESDEMONA **Tonight, my lord?** DUKE **This night** [Q1; not in F]   **285 With** And   **294** FIRST SENATOR *Sen.*   **296.1** *Exeunt* Exit   **302 matters** matter   **303 the** the the   **329 beam** [eds.] braine [F] ballance [Q1]   **333–4 our unbitted** or vnbitted   **335 scion** Seyen [F] syen [Q1]   **353 error** errors   **354 She . . . she must** [Q1; not in F]   **358 a supersubtle** super-subtle   **378–82** RODERIGO **What . . . purse** [Q1; not in F]   **386 a snipe** Snpe   **389 He's** [Ha's Q1] She ha's   **396 ear** eares
2.1. 35 prays praye   **36 heaven** Heauens   **42** THIRD GENTLEMAN *Gent.*   **44 arrivance** Arriuancie   **45 this** the   **58** SECOND GENTLEMAN *Gent.*

[also at lines 61, 68, and 95]   **72 clog** enclogge   **84 And . . . comfort** [Q1; not in F]   **90 tell me** tell   **94 the sea** Sea   **96 their** this   **107 list** leaue   **111 doors** doore   **156 [and elsewhere] ne'er** neu'r   **158 such wight** such wightes   **170 gyve** [eds.] giue   **174 An** and   **175 courtesy** Curtsie   **176 clyster pipes** Cluster-pipes   **214.1** *Exeunt* [eds.] *Exit*   **216 hither** thither   **229 again** a game   **239 fortune** Forune   **241–2 compassing** compasse   **243–4 finder out** finder   **244 occasions** occasion   **has** he's   **263 mutualities** mutabilities   **300 for wife** for wift   **307 rank** right   **308 nightcap** Night-Cape
2.2. 6 addiction [eds.] addition   **10 Heaven bless** Blesse
2.3. 27 stoup [eds.] stope   **38 unfortunate** infortunate   **52 lads** else   **57 to put** put to   **61, 71 God** heauen   **76 Englishman** Englishmen   **91 Then . . . auld** [*Then . . . owd* Q1] And take thy awl'd   **93 'Fore God** Why   **97 God's** heau'ns   **106 God forgive** Forgiue   **110 speak** I speake   **123 the** his   **138 s.d. Cry within**: Help! Help! [from Q1: "Helpe, helpe, within"]   **139 Zounds, you** You   **152 God's will** Alas   **153 Montano—sir** *Montano*   **156 God's will, Lieutenant, hold** Fie, fie Lieutenant   **158 Zounds, I** I   **161 sense of place** [eds.] place of sense   **184 wont be** wont to be   **201 Zounds, if I** If I once   **212 leagued** [eds.] league   **218 Thus** This   **227 the** then   **246 well now** well   **255 God** Heauen   **260 thought had** thought   **283 Oh, God** Oh   **308 I'll** I   **311 denotement** [eds.] deuotement   **325–6 me here** me   **337 were't** were   **356 s.d.** *Enter Roderigo* [after line 356 in F]   **369 hast** hath   **372 By the Mass** Introth   **378 on;** [on Q1] on   **379 the while** [eds.] a while
3.1. 1 Musicians [eds.] *Musicians, and Clowne*   **5** [and at lines 7, 9, and 15] A MUSICIAN *Mus.*   **21 s.d. Exeunt** [eds.] *Exit*   **22 hear** heare me   **26 General's wife** Generall   **31** CASSIO **Do, good my friend** [Q1; not in F]   **42 s.d. Exit** [at line 41 in F]   **52 To . . . front** [Q1; not in F]
3.3. 16 circumstance Circumstances   **41 you** your   **55 Yes, faith** I sooth   **66 or** on   **80 By'r Lady** Trust me   **103 you** he   **118 By heaven** Alas   **124 In** Of   **148 that all** that: All   **free to** free   **152 But some** Wherein   **160 oft** of   **161 wisdom then** wisdome   **175 By heaven, I'll** Ile   **183 fondly** [eds.] soundly [F] strongly [Q1]   **188 God** Heauen   **194 Is once** Is   **196 blown** blow'd   **199 dances well** Dances   **216 God** Heauen   **218 keep't** [eds.] keepe [Q1] kept [F]   **225 [and elsewhere] to** too   **230 I'faith** Trust me   **232 my** your   **249 disproportion** disproportions   **264 to hold** to   **275 qualities** Quantities   **276 human** humane   **289 of** to   **294 oh, then heaven mocks** Heauen mock'd   **301 Faith** Why   **305.1 Exit** [at line 304 in F]   **328 faith** but   **345 s.d. Enter Othello** [after "I did say so" in F]   **354 of her** in her   **385 remorse;** [remorce. Q1] remorse   **407 see, sir** see   **411 supervisor** super-vision   **439 then laid** laid   **440 Over** ore   **sighed** sigh   **kissed** kisse   **441 Cried** cry   **455 any that was** [eds.] any, it was   **468 mind perhaps** minde   **471 Ne'er feels** [eds.] Neu'r keepes
3.4. 23 that the   **37 It yet** It   **56 faith indeed** [eds.] Indeed   **77 I'faith** Indeed   **79 God** Heauen   **83 Heaven bless** Blesse   **88 can, sir** can   **94–5** DESDEMONA **I pray . . . Cassio.** OTHELLO **The handkerchief!** [Q1; not in F]   **99 I'faith** Insooth   **100 Zounds** Away   **142 s.d. Exit** [after line 141 in F]   **164 that** the   **169.1 Exit** [after line 168 in F]   **172 I'faith** Indeed   **182 friend.** [eds.] Friend,   **183 absence** [eds.] absence, [Q1] Absence: [F]   **188 by my faith** in good troth
4.1. 32 Faith Why   **36 Zounds, that's** that's   **45 work** workes   **52 No, forbear** [Q1; not in F]   **72 couch** [Coach Q1] Cowch;   **79 unsuiting** [Q1 corrected] vnfitting [Q1 uncorrected] resulting [F]   **81 'scuse** scuses   **97 clothes** Cloath   **103 conster** conserue   **105 you now** you   **109 power** dowre   **113 a woman** woman   **114 i'faith** indeed   **121 Do you triumph, Roman?** Do ye triumph, Romaine?   **122 marry her** marry   **125 win** [eds.] winnes   **126 Faith** Why   **shall marry** marry   **133 beckons** becomes   **138 by this hand, she** [Q1; not in F]   **165 Faith, I** I   **167 Faith** Yes   **214.1** [after line 212 in F]   **217 God save** Saue   **240 By my troth** Trust me   **253 Truly, an** Truely   **286 denote** deonte [F uncorrected] deuote [F corrected]
4.2. 32 Nay May   **33 knees** knee   **35 But not the words** [Q1; not in F]   **51 kinds** kind   **56 A** The   **66 Ay, there** [eds.] I heere   **71 ne'er** neuer   **83 Impudent strumpet** [Q1; not in F]   **96 keep** [eds.] keepes   **s.d.** *Enter Emilia* [after line 94 in F]   **155 O God** Alas   **162 them in**

[eds.] them: or   **174 And . . . you** [Q1; not in F]   **177 you to** to
190 Faith, I I   **for** and   **201 By this hand** Nay   **232 takes** taketh
236 of [Q1; not in F]
4.3. 10.1 *Exit* [after line 9 in F]   **22 favor in them** fauour   **25 faith**
Father   **26 before thee** before   **35 Barbary** *Braberie*   **43 sighing**
[eds.] *singing* [F corrected] *sining* [F uncorrected]   **73 Good troth**
Introth   **74 By my troth** Introth   **78 Uds pity** why   **107 God** Heauen
5.1. 1 bulk Barke   **22 Be't** But   **hear** heard   **36 Forth** For   **50 Did** Do
91 Oh, heaven 'tis   **106 out o'** o'   **113 'Las, what's . . . What's**
Alas, what is . . . What is   **116 dead** quite dead   **126 Faugh! Fie** Fie
5.2. 34 heaven Heauens   **37 say so** say   **56 Yes, presently** Presently
61 Then Lord O Heauen   **96 here** high   **104 Should** Did
108 s.d. *Enter Emilia* [after line 108 in F]   **121 Oh, Lord** Alas
131 heard heare   **148 Nay, had** had   **225 Oh, God! Oh, heavenly**
God Oh Heauen! oh heauenly Powres   **226 Zounds** Come
248 have here haue   **317 not. Here** [not: here Q1] not) heere
357 Indian Iudean

King Lear

Copy text: the First Folio, except for those 300 or so lines found only in
the First Quarto of 1608 [Q1]. Unless otherwise indicated, adopted readings are from the corrected state of Q1. A few readings are supplied from
the Second Quarto of 1619 [Q2]. All readings subsequent to 1619 are
marked as supplied by "eds." Act and scene divisions are as marked in F,
except that F does not mark 2.3 and 2.4, and omits 4.3 entirely, so that
4.4 is marked "*Scena Tertia*" and similarly with 4.5 and 4.6 (though 4.7 is
marked "*Scena Septima*").

1.1. 5 equalities qualities   **20–2 account . . . yet** [eds.] account, though
. . . for: yet   **35 liege** Lord   **55 words** word   **66 issue** issues
68 Speak [Q1; not in F]   **74 possesses** professes   **85 interested**
[eds.] interest   **104** [Q1; not in F]   **110 mysteries** [eds.] miseries [F]
mistresse [Q1]   **135 turns** turne   **156 as a** as   **157 nor** nere
161 LEAR *Kear*   **162** KENT *Lent*   **165** CORNWALL [eds.] *Cor.*   **166 the**
thy   **173 sentence** sentences   **191** GLOUCESTER *Cor.*   **217 best**
object obiect   **229 well** will   **252 respects of fortune** respect and
Fortunes   **272 Ye** [eds.] The   **285 shame them** with shame
286.1 *Exeunt* [eds.] *Exit*   **293 hath not** hath   **306 hit** sit
1.2. 1 [and elsewhere] EDMUND *Bast.*   **21 top** [eds.] to'   **56 waked**
wake   **97–9** EDMUND **Nor . . . earth** [Q1; not in F]   **134 Fut, I** I
136 Edgar [Q1; not in F]   **137 and pat** [eds.] Pat [F] and out [Q1]
147–55 as . . . come, [Q1; not in F]   **182 s.d.** [at line 181 in F]
1.3. 3 [and elsewhere] OSWALD [eds.] *Ste.*   **17–21** [Q1; not in F]
26–7 I would . . . speak [Q1; not in F]   **28 very** [Q1; not in F]
1.4. 1 well will   **31 canst** canst thou   **43.1** *Enter steward* [eds.; after
line 44 in F]   **50 daughter** Daughters   **76.1** *Enter steward* [eds.;
after line 77 in F]   **96** KENT *Lear*   **Fool** my Boy   **135 Dost** Do'st thou
138–53 That . . . snatching [Q1; not in F]   **158 crown** Crownes
175 fools Foole   **195 nor crumb** not crum   **214 it had** it's had
229–32 [Q1; not in F]   **255 Oh . . . come** [Q1; not in F]   **303 Yea . . .**
this [Q1; not in F]   **343 You're** Your are   **attasked** at task
1.5. 0.1 *Kent* Kent, Gentleman   **51 s.d.** *Exit* Exeunt
2.1. 2 you your   **19.1** [after line 18 in F]   **39 stand 's** stand   **69 I should**
should I   **70 ay, though** though   **78 I never got him** [Q1; not in F]
78 s.d. [at line 76 in F, after "seeke it"]   **79 why** wher   **87 strange**
news strangenesse   **100 spoil** wast   **122 poise** prize   **125 least**
thought best though   **132** *Flourish. Exeunt* [eds.] *Exeunt. Flourish*
2.2. 22 clamorous clamours   **45 an** if   **52 What's** What is   **66 you'll**
you will   **78 Bring . . . their** Being . . . the   **79 Renege** Reuenge
80 gale gall   **83 Smile** Smoile   **84 an** if   **101 take't** take it   **109 flick-**
ering flicking   **124 dread** dead   **127 their** there   **132 respect** respects
142.1 [at line 140 in F]   **144–8 His . . . with** [Q1; not in F]   **146 con-**
temned'st [eds.] temnest [Q1]   **148 King** King his Master, needs
153 [Q1; not in F]   **154 Come . . . away** [assigned in F to Cornwall]
good [Q1; not in F]   **154.1** *Exeunt* [eds.] *Exit*   **155 Duke's** Duke

2.3. 18 sheepcotes Sheeps-Coates
2.4. 2 messenger Messengers   **9 man's** man   **18–19** [Q1; not in F]
30 panting painting   **33 whose** those   **56 Hysterica** [eds.] *Historica*
62 the the the   **74 have** hause   **128 you** your   **130 mother's** Mother
183 s.d. [after line 182 in F]   **185.1** [at line 183 in F, after "Stockes"]
187 fickle fickly   **190 s.d.** [after line 188 in F]   **213 hot-blooded**
hot-bloodied   **285 s.d.** [after "weeping" in line 286 in F]   **297 s.d.** [after
line 296 in F]   **298 Whither** Whether [also in line 299]   **302 bleak** high
3.1. 7–15 tears . . . all [Q1; not in F]   **10 outstorm** [eds.] outscorne [Q1]
30–42 [Q1; not in F]
3.2. 3 drowned drown   **38.1** [after line 36 in F]   **50 pother** pudder
85–6 [these lines follow line 92 in F]
3.3. 17 for 't for it
3.4. 7 skin. So 'tis skinso: 'tis   **10 thy** they   **12 This** the   **27 s.d.** [at
line 26 in F]   **31 looped** lop'd   **38.1** *Enter Fool* [F, after line 36:
"*Enter Edgar, and Foole*"]   **44.1** [after line 36 in F]   **46 blows the cold**
wind blow the windes   **51 through fire** though Fire   **52 ford** Sword
57, 58 Bless Blisse   **90 deeply** deerely   **99 sessa** [eds.] *Sesey*
112.1 [after line 108 in F]   **114 fiend** [Q1; not in F]   **115 till the** at
116 squinnies [eds.] squemes [F] squinies [Q1]   **134 stock-punished**
stockt, punish'd   **hath had** hath   **173 in th'** into th'
3.5. 11 he which hee   **26 dearer** deere
3.6. 5.1 *Exit* [at line 3 in F]   **17–55** [Q1; not in F]   **21 justicer** [eds.]
Iustice [Q1]   **22 Now** [Q2] no [Q1]   **24 eyes at trial, madam?** eyes,
at tral madam   **25 burn** [eds.] broome [Q1]   **34 cushions** [eds.]
cushings [Q1]   **36 robèd** robbed   **51 joint** [eds.] ioyne [Q1]   **53 on**
[eds.] an [Q1]   **67 mongrel grim** Mongrill, Grim   **68 lym** [eds.]
Hym   **69 Bobtail tike or trundle-tail** Or Bobtaile tight, or Troudle
taile   **73 Sessa** sese   **76 makes** make   **85.1** [after line 80 in F]
97–101 KENT **Oppressèd . . . behind** [Q1; not in F]   **101** GLOUCESTER
[not in F]   **102–15** [Q1; not in F]
3.7. 10 festinate [eds.] festiuate   **18 lord's dependents** Lords,
dependents   **23 s.d.** *Exeunt* [eds.] *Exit* [at line 22 in F]   **61 rash**
sticke   **66 dern** sterne   **75** FIRST SERVANT *Seru.* [also *Seru.* or *Ser.* at
lines 79, 82, 84]   **83** [F provides a stage direction: "*Killes him*"]
102–10 [Q1; not in F]   **102** SECOND SERVANT *Seruant* [and called "1
Ser" at line 106 in Q1]   **103** THIRD SERVANT 2 *Seruant* [Q1]   **107 Rogu-**
ish [Qa; not in Qb]   **109** THIRD SERVANT 2 *Ser.*   **110.1** *Exeunt* Exit
4.1. 2 flattered. To be worst flattered to be worst,   **41 Then . . . gone**
Get thee away   **57–62 Five . . . master** [Q1; not in F]   **60 Flibberti-**
gibbet [eds.] *Stiberdigebit* [Q1]   **60–1 mopping and mowing** [eds.]
Mobing, & *Mohing* [Q1]
4.2. 0.1 *Bastard* Bastard, and Steward   **2 s.d.** *steward* [Q1; placed at
scene beginning in F]   **30 whistling** whistle   **32–51 I fear . . . deep**
[Q1; not in F]   **33 its** [eds.] ith [Q1]   **48 these** [eds.] this [Q1]
54–60 that . . . so [Q1; not in F]   **58 to threat** threat [Q1 corrected]
61 shows seemes   **63–9, 70** [Q1; not in F]   **76 thereat enraged**
threat-enrag'd   **80 justicers** [Q1 corrected] Iustices
4.3. 1–57 [scene omitted in F]   **11 sir** [eds.] say [Q1]   **16 strove** [eds.]
streme [Q1]   **20 seemed** [eds.] seeme [Q1]   **22 dropped. In** dropt in
32 then her, then   **44 benediction, turned her** benediction turnd
her,   **57 s.d.** *Exeunt* [eds.] *Exit* [Q1]
4.4 [F reads "*Scena Tertia*"]   **3 fumiter** [eds.] femiter [Q1] Fenitar [F]
6 century Centery   **18 distress** desires   **28 right** Rite
4.5 [F reads "*Scena Quarta*"]   **8 letters** Letter   **23 Something** Some
things   **27 oeillades** [eds.] Eliads   **41 meet him** meet
4.6 [F reads "*Scena Quinta*"]   **17 walk** walk'd   **57 summit** Somnet
66–7 strangeness. / Upon . . . cliff what [eds.] strangenesse, / Vpon
. . . Cliffe. What   **71 enridgèd** enraged   **83 coining** crying
97 white the white   **124 they're** they are   **161 thine** thy
164 Through Thorough   **small** great   **165 Plate sin** [eds.] Place
sinnes   **197 Ay . . . dust** [Q1; not in F]   **205 one** a   **218.1** *Exit*
[after "moved on" in line 218 in F]   **235 Durst** Dar'st   **238 'cagion**
'casion   **263–4 not. / To** not / To   **269 done if . . . conqueror. Then**
[eds.] done. If . . . Conqueror then   **274 and . . . venture** [Q1; not in F]

275 indistinguished indinguish'd   **288 s.d. *Drum afar off*** [after line 286 in F]

4.7. 25 doubt not doubt   **25–6 CORDELIA Very . . . there** [Q1; not in F] **33 warring** iarring   **34–7 To stand . . . helm** [Q1; not in F] **59 hands** hand   **60 No, sir** [Q1; not in F]   **83–4 and . . . lost** [Q1; not in F]   **91–103** [Q1; not in F]

5.1. 12–14 [Q1; not in F]   **18 me not** not   **19–20** [Q1; not in F] **24–9 Where . . . nobly** [Q1; not in F]   **35** [Q1; not in F] **41 s.d. *Exeunt . . . armies*** [after line 39 in F]   **48 love** loues

5.3. 13 and hear poor rogues and heare (poore Rogues)   **39–40** [Q1; not in F]   **49 and appointed guard** [Q1 corrected; not in F]   **56–61 At . . . place** [Q1; not in F]   **57 We** [Q1 corrected] mee [Q1 uncorrected] **59 sharpness** [Q1 corrected] sharpes [Q1 uncorrected]   **72 GONERIL** *Alb.*   **85 attaint** arrest   **86 sister** Sisters   **87 bar** [eds.] bare   **100 he is** hes   **105 EDMUND A herald, ho, a herald** [Q1; not in F]   **105.1 *Enter a Herald*** [after line 104 in F]   **106 ALBANY** [not in F]   **112 CAPTAIN Sound, trumpet** [Q1; not in F]   **118 EDMUND Sound** [Q1; not in F] **124–5 lost, / By . . . canker-bit.** lost / By Treasons tooth: bare-gnawne, and Canker-bit,   **132 the** my priuiledge, The   **135 Despite** Despise **146 tongue some say of** tongue (some say) of   **149 those** these **151 scarcely** scarely   **153.1 *Fight*** [eds.] Fights. ["*Alarums. Fights*" is opposite "Saue him, saue him," in line 154 in F.]   **155 arms** Warre **158 stopple** stop   **163 GONERIL** *Bast.*   **163 s.d. *Exit*** [at line 162 after "for 't" in F]   **208–25 This . . . slave** [Q1; not in F]   **217 him** [eds.] me [Q1] **241.1** [after line 234 in F]   **255 The captain** [Q1; not in F]   **262 you** your **280 CAPTAIN** *Gent.*   **282 them** him   **294 You are** [eds.] Your are [F] You'r [Q1]   **299.1** [after "to him" in line 299 in F]   **320 rack** wracke

The above textual notes list all instances in which material not in F is included from Q1. To enable the reader to compare further the F and Q1 texts, a list is provided here of material not in Q1 that is to be found in F. There are some 100 lines in all.

1.1. 40–5 while . . . now   **49–50** Since . . . state   **64–5** and . . . rivers **83–5** to whose . . . interested   **88–9** LEAR Nothing? CORDELIA Nothing **165** ALBANY, CORNWALL Dear sir, forbear.

1.2. 112–17 This . . . graves   **169–75** I pray . . . brother

1.4. 260 ALBANY Pray . . . patient   **273** Of . . . you   **321–33** This . . . unfitness

2.4. 6 KENT No, my lord   **21** KENT By Juno . . . ay   **45–54** FOOL Winter's . . . year   **96–7** GLOUCESTER Well . . . man   **101–2** Are they . . . Fiery? The **139–44** LEAR Say . . . blame   **298–9** CORNWALL Whither . . . horse

3.1. 22–9 Who . . . furnishings

3.2. 79–96 FOOL This . . . time. *Exit*

3.4. 17–18 In . . . endure   **26–7** In . . . sleep   **37–8** Fathom . . . Tom

3.6. 12–14 FOOL No . . . him   **85** FOOL And . . . noon

4.1. 6–9 Welcome . . . blasts

4.2. 26 Oh, the . . . man

4.6. 165–70 Plate . . . lips

5.2. 11 GLOUCESTER And . . . too

5.3. 78 Dispose . . . thine   **91** GONERIL An interlude   **147** What . . . delay **226** ALBANY Speak, man   **316–17** Do you . . . look there

Macbeth

Copy text: the First Folio. Act and scene divisions follow the Folio text, except that 5.8 is not marked in the Folio.

1.1. 9 SECOND WITCH *All*   **10 THIRD WITCH** [not in F]   **11 ALL** [at line 9 in F]

1.2. 1 [and elsewhere] DUNCAN *King*   **13 gallowglasses** Gallowgrosses **14 quarrel** Quarry   **21 ne'er** neu'r   **26 thunders break** Thunders

1.3. 32 Weird weyward [elsewhere in F spelled "weyard"]   **39 Forres** Soris   **97 death. As** death, as   **98 Came** Can   **111 lose** loose

1.4. 1 Are Or

1.5. 1 [and elsewhere] LADY MACBETH Lady   **12 lose** *loose*   **47 it** hit

1.6. 4 martlet Barlet   **9 most** must

1.7. 6 shoal Schoole   **48 do** no

2.1. 56 strides sides   **57 sure** sowre   **58 way they** they may

2.2. 13.1 [at line 8 in F, after "die"]

2.3. 41.1 [after line 40 in F]   **142 nea'er** neere

3.1. 76 MURDERERS *Murth.*   **116 BOTH MURDERERS** *Murth.* [also at line 141]   **142.1 *Exeunt*** [at line 144 in F]

3.3. 7 and end

3.4. 79 time times   **122.1 *Exeunt*** Exit

3.6. 24 son Sonnes   **38 the** their

4.1. 34 cauldron Cawdron   **38.1 *to*** and   **59 germens** Germaine **93 Dunsinane** Dunsmane   **94 s.d. *Descends*** Descend   **98 Birnam** Byrnan [also spelled "Byrnam" at line 93 and "Birnan," "Byrnane," and "Birnane" in Act 5]   **119 eighth** eight

4.2. 1 [and throughout] LADY MACDUFF *Wife*   **22 none** moue **70–1 ones . . . methinks,** ones / To fright you thus. Me thinkes **80 s.d. *Enter Murderers*** [after "What are these faces" in F] **81 [and throughout scene] FIRST MURDERER** *Mur.*   **84 shag-haired** shagge-ear'd

4.3. 4 downfall'n downfall   **15 deserve** discerne   **35 Fare** Far **108 accurst** accust   **124 detraction, here** detraction. Heere   **134 thy** they   **144 essay** assay   **146.1** [after "amend" in F]   **161 not** nor **237 tune** time

5.1. 37 fear who feare? who

5.3. 41 Cure her Cure   **54 pristine** pristiue   **57 senna** Cyme **62.1 *Exeunt*** [at line 64 in F]

5.4. 16 SIWARD *Sey.*

Antony and Cleopatra

Copy text: the First Folio. Act and scene divisions, missing in the Folio, are editorially supplied.

1.1. 41 On One   **52 whose** who

1.2. 4 charge change   **41 fortell** fore-tell   **64–5 Alexas** [printed in F as s.p.]   **83 Saw** Saue   **90 Alexas** *Alexias*   **93 [and through line 118] FIRST MESSENGER** *Messen.* (or *Mess.*)   **116 minds** windes   **119 ho** how   **120 SECOND MESSENGER** 1. *Mes.*   **121 THIRD MESSENGER** 2. *Mes.*   **124 FOURTH MESSENGER** 3. *Mes.*   **126 FOURTH MESSENGER** *Mes.*   **137.1 *Enter Enobarbus*** [after "hatch," line 137, in F]   **144 occasion** an occasion   **162 travel** Trauaile   **186 leave** loue   **191 Hath** Haue   **200 hair** heire   **202 place is** places   **requires** require

1.3. 2 who's Whose   **20 What, says** What sayes   **43 services** Seruicles **63 vials** Violles   **80 blood. No more.** blood no more?   **82 by my** by

1.4. 3 Our One   **8 Vouchsafed** vouchsafe   **9 abstract** abstracts **34 FIRST MESSENGER** *Mes.*   **44 deared** fear'd   **46 lackeying** lacking **48 SECOND MESSENGER** *Mes.*   **57 wassails** Vassailes   **58 Modena** Medena   **59 Pansa** Pausa   **77 we** me

1.5. 3 mandragora *Mandragoru*   **5 time** time: **35.1 *Alexas*** Alexas from Caesar   **52 dumbed** dumbe   **53, What, was** What was **64 man** mans

2.1. 2 [and throughout scene] MENAS Mene.   **22 joined** ioyne **39 ne'er** neere   **42 warred** wan'd   **44–5 greater. . . . all,** greater, . . . all:

2.2. 77 Alexandria; you Alexandria you   **113 soldier only. Speak** Souldier, onely speak   **128 so say** so say   **129 reproof** proofe **180.1 *Exeunt*** Exit omnes   ***Manent*** Manet   **204 lovesick . . . The** Loue-sicke. With them the   **214 glow** gloue   **216 gentlewomen** Gentlewoman   **233 heard** hard

2.3. 23 afeard a feare   **25 thee; . . . to thee.** thee no more but: when to thee,   **31 away** alway   **32 [and elsewhere] Ventidius** *Ventigius* **41 s.d. *Enter Ventidius*** [after "Ventigius," line 41, in F]

2.4. 6 th' Mount Mount   **9 MAECENAS, AGRIPPA** *Both*

2.5. 2 ALL *Omnes*   **10 river. There** Riuer there   **11 off, I** off. I **12 finned** fine   **23 s.d. *Enter a Messenger*** [after "Italy," line 23, in F] **28 him, there** him. / There   **44 is** 'tis   **85 s.d. *Enter . . . again*** [after "sir" line 85, in F]

2.6. 0.1 *Menas* [listed after *Agrippa* in F]   **16 th'all-honored** all-honor'd   **19 is** his   **39 CAESAR, ANTONY, LEPIDUS** *Omnes*   **42–3 impatience. Though . . . telling,** impatience: though . . . telling.   **58 compostion** composion   **67 meanings** meaning   **71 more of** more   **83 CAESAR, ANTONY, LEPIDUS** *All*   **83.1 Manent** *Manet*
2.7. 1 their th'their   **4 colored** *Conlord*   **39 s.d.** *whispers in 's ear* [at line 41 in F]   **93 is** he is   **101 grows** grow   **113 bear** beate   **115 BOY** [not in F]   **119 ALL** [not in F]   **122 off. Our** of our   **126 Splits** Spleet's   **130 father's** Father   **132 MENAS** [not in F]
3.1. 5 [and throughout scene] **SILIUS** *Romaine*   **8** [and elsewhere] **whither** whether
3.2. 10 AGRIPPA *Ant.*   **16 figures** Figure   **49 full** the full   **60 wept** weepe
3.3. 2 s.d. *Enter . . . before* [after "sir," line 2, in F]   **19 looked'st** look'st
3.4. 8 them, then   **9 took't** look't   **24 yours** your   **30 Your** You   **38 has** he's
3.5. 13 world would   **hast** hadst   **chops** chaps   **15 grind the one** grind
3.6. 13 he there hither   **the kings** the King   **30 being, that** being that,   **62 obstruct** abstract   **73 Adallas** *Adullas*   **74 Manchus** *Mauchus*   **76 Comagene** Comageat   **Polemon** *Polemen*   **77 Lycaonia** Licoania
3.7. 4 it is it it   **14 Photinus, an** *Photinus* an   **19 s.d.** *Canidius Camidias* [also spelled "*Camidius*" in this scene and elsewhere]   **21 Brundusium** Brandusium   **23 Toryne** Troine   **29** [and elsewhere] **CANIDIUS** *Cam.*   **36 muleteers** Militers   **52 Actium** Action   **57 impossible;** impossible   **67.1 Exeunt** exit   **70 leader's** led   Leaders leade   **73 CANIDIUS** *Ven.*   **80 Well I** Well, I   **82 in** with
3.8. 6 s.d. *Exeunt* exit
3.9. 4 s.d. *Exeunt* exit
3.10. 0.5. *Enobarbus Enobarbus and Scarus*   **14 June** Inne   **28 he** his
3.11. 6 ALL *Omnes*   **19 that** them   **46 seize** cease   **50 led** lead   **57 tow** stowe   **58 Thy** The
3.12. 0.1. *Dolabella Dollabello*   **13 lessens** Lessons
3.13. 26 caparisons Comparisons   **34 alike. That** alike, that   **55 Caesar** *Caesars*   **74 deputation** disputation   **76 kneel / Till** kneele. / Tell him,   **94 s.d.** *Enter a Servant* [after "him," in line 94, in F]   **104 This** the   **114–15 eyes, / In . . . filth** eyes / In . . . filth,   **133 s.d.** *Enter . . . Thidias* [after "whipped," in line 133, in F]   **140 whipped . . . Henceforth** whipt. For following him, henceforth   **165 smite** smile   **168 discandying** discandering   **171 sits** sets   **202 on** in   **204 s.d.** *Exit* Exeunt
4.2. 1 Domitius *Domitian*   **20 ALL** *Omnes*
4.3. 8 THIRD 1   **25, 31 ALL** *Omnes*
4.4. 5 too too, *Anthony*   **6 ANTONY** [not in F, or mistakenly placed in line 5 as part of Cleopatra's speech]   **8 CLEOPATRA** [not in F]   **24 CAPTAIN** *Alex.*   **32–3 compliment . . . Now** Complement, Ile leaue thee. / Now
4.5. 1, 3, 6 SOLDIER *Eros*   **17 Dispatch.—Enobarbus** Dispatch *Enobarbus*   **17.1 Exeunt** Exit
4.6. 37–8 do 't . . . I doo't. I feele / I
4.7 3 s.d. *Exeunt* Exit   **8 s.d.** [after "heads," line 6, in F]
4.8. 2 gests guests   **18 My** Mine   **23 favoring** sauouring
4.12. 3 s.d. *Alarum . . . fight* [at 0.1 in F]   **4 augurers** Auguries   **21 spanieled** pannelled
4.13. 10 death. To death to'
4.14. 4 towered toward   **10 dislimns** dislimes   **19 Caesar** *Caesars*   **104 ho** how   **119 DERCETUS** *Decre.*   **145.1 Exeunt** Exit
4.15. 26–7 me. If . . . operation, me, if . . . operation.   **56 lived the** liued. The   **78 e'en** in   **96.1** *off of*
5.1 0.1 *Maecenas Menas*   **3.1 Dercetus** *Decretas*   **5, 13, 19 DERCETUS** *Dec.*   **5 Dercetus** *Decretas*   **26 you sad, friends?** you sad Friends,   **28, 31 AGRIPPA** *Dol.*   **48.1** [after "says," line 51, in F]   **54 intents** desires intents, desires,   **59 live** leaue
5.2. 26 dependency dependacie   **35** [F repeats s.p. *Pro.*]   **55 varletry** Varlotarie   **69.1** [after "to him" in F]   **80 O, the** o'th'   **86 autumn 'twas** *Anthony* it was   **102 success but** successe: But   **103 smites** suites   **144 seal** seele   **156 soulless villain** Soule-lesse, Villain   **178 merits in our name,** merits, in our name   **207 s.d.** *Exit* [at line

206 in F]   **216 Ballad** Ballads   **223 my** mine   **228 Cydnus** *Cidrus*   **318 awry** away   **319.1** *in* in, and *Dolabella*   **342–3 diadem . . . mistress**; Diadem; . . . Mistris

The Winter's Tale

Copy text: the First Folio. Characters' names are groups at the heads of scenes throughout the play. Act and scene divisions are as marked in the Folio.

The Names of the Actors [printed in F at the end of the play]   **ARCHIDAMUS** [after *Autoclycus* in F]
1.1. 9 us, we vs: we
1.2. 104 And A   **121 hast** has't   **137–8 be?— / Affection, thy** be / Affection? thy   **148 What . . . brother** [assigned in F to Leontes]   **151–3 its folly, . . . Its tenderness, . . . bosoms!** it's folly? . . . It's tendernesse? . . . bosomes?   **158 do** do's   **202–3 powerful, think it, . . . south. Be** powrefull: thinke it: . . . South, be   **208 you, they** you   **253 forth. In . . . lord,** forth in . . . (my Lord.)   **275 hobbyhorse** Holy-Horse   **386 How? Caught** How caught   **461 off. Hence!** off, hence:
2.1. 2 [and throughout scene] **FIRST LADY** *Lady*   **91 fedarie** Federarie
2.2. 32–3 me. / If . . . blister me, / If . . . blister.
2.3. 2 thus, mere weakness. If thus: meere weaknesse, if   **39 What Who** **61 good, so** good so,
3.2. 10 Silence [printed in F as a s.d.]   **10.1–2 Hermione, as to her trial . . . Ladies** [at start of scene in F, as generally with the s.d. in this play]   **33 Who** Whom   **99 Starred** Star'd   **156 woo** woe
3.3. 64 scar'd scarr'd   **116 made** mad
4.2. 13 thee. Thou, thee, thou
4.3. 1 AUTOLYCUS [not in F]   **7 on** an   **10 With heigh, with heigh** *With heigh*   **38 currants** Currence
4.4. 12 Digest it Digest   **13 swoon** sworne   **60 a fire** o'fire   **83 bastards. Of** bastards) of   **93 scion** Sien   **98 your** you   **160 out** on't   **218 AUTOLYCUS** [not in F]   **244 kilnhole** kill-hole   **297 AUTOLYCUS** [in F, appears at line 298]   **299 Whither** Whether [and similarly throughout song]   **310 gentleman** Gent.   **316 cape** *Crpe*   **339 square** squire   **355 reply, at least** reply at least,   **361 who** whom   **421 acknowledged** acknowledge   **425 who** whom   **430 see** neuer see   **441 hoop** hope   **473 your** my   **473 sight as yet, I fear.** sight, as yet I feare;   **485–6 fancy. If . . . obedient, I** fancie, if . . . obedient: I   **503 our** her   **614 could** would   **filed** fill'd   **off** of   **644 flayed** fled   **708 know not** know   **738 to** at   **833 s.d. Exeunt** [at 845 in F]
5.1. 6 Whilst Whilest [also at line 169]   **59 Where . . . appear** (Where we Offendors now appeare)   **61 just** just such   **75 I have done** [assigned in F to Cleomenes]   **84 s.d. Gentleman Seruant** **85** [and through line 110] **GENTLEMAN,** *Ser.*   **114 s.d. Exit** [after "us" in line 115 in F]   **160 his, parting** his parting
5.2. 113 s.d. *Exeunt* Exit
5.3. 18 Lonely Louely   **67 fixture** fixure

The Tempest

Copy text: the First Folio. Characters' names are groups at the heads of scenes throughout. Act and scene divisions are as marked in the Folio.
Names of the Actors [printed in F at the end of the play]
1.1. 8.1 Ferdinand *Ferdinando*   **34 s.d. Exeunt** Exit   **36** [and elsewhere] **wi' the** with   **38.1** [at line 37 in F]
1.2. 99 exact, like exact. Like   **166 steaded much.** steeded much,   **174 princes** Princesse   **201 bowsprit** Bore-spritt   **213 me. The** me the   **230 Bermudas** *Bermoothes*   **284 she** he   **288 service. Thou** service, thou   **330 forth at** for that   **377.5, 399.1 Ariel's** Ariel (or Ariell)   **385 s.d. Burden, dispersedly** [before "Hark, hark!" in line 384 in F]   **387** [F provides a speech prefix, *Ar.*]   **400 ARIEL** [not in F]
2.1. 38 ANTONIO *Seb.*   **39 SEBASTIAN** *Ant.*   **183 mettle** mettal   **232 throes** throwes
2.2. 9 mow moe   **116 spirits** sprights
3.1. 2 sets set

3.2. 51–2 isle; / From me he Isle / From me, he   **123 scout** *cout*
3.3. 15 travel trauaile   **17.1–2** *Solemn . . . invisible* [after "they are fresh"
in F, and followed by the s.d. at line 19, *Enter . . . depart*]   **28 me** me?
29 islanders? Islands;   **33 human** humaine   **65 plume** plumbe
4.1. 9 off of   **13 gift** guest   **25 love as 'tis now, the** loue, as 'tis now
the   **61 vetches** Fetches   **68 poll-clipped** pole-clipt   **74 Her** here
110 CERES [not in F]   **123 wife** wise   **124.1–2** [after line 127 in F]
163.1 *Exeunt Exit*   **193 s.d.** *Enter Ariel . . . etc.* [after "on this line" in
F, and followed by *Enter Caliban . . . all wet*]   **193 them on** on them
232 Let't let's
5.1. 60 boiled boile   **72 Didst** Did   **75 entertained** entertaine   **82 lies**
ly   **88 ARIEL** [not in F]   **111 Whe'er** Where   **236 horrible,** horrible.
238 her our   **249 business. At** businesse, at   **250 Which . . . single**
(Which shall be shortly single)   **260** *coraggio Corasio*

The Sonnets

Copy text: the Quarto of 1609 [Q].
2.4 tattered totter'd [also at 26.11]   **2.14 cold** could   **6.4 beauty's**
beautits   **8.10 Strikes** Strike [in some copies]   **12.4 all** or
13.7 Yourself You selfe   **15.8 wear** were   **17.12 meter** miter
17.14 twice, in it and twice in it, and   **18.10 [and elsewhere] lose**
loose   **19.3 jaws** yawes   **20.2 Hast** Haste   **22.3 furrows** forrwes
23.6 rite right   **23.14 with** wit   **wit** wiht   **24.1 stelled** steeld
25.9 fight worth   **26.12 thy** their [also at 27.10, 35.8 (twice), 37.7,
43.11, 45.12, 46.3, 46.8, 46.13, 46.14, 69.5, 70.6, 85.3, 128.11, 128.14]
27.2 travel trauaill   **28.12 gild'st** guil'st   **28.14 strength** length
31.8 thee there   **34.2 travel** trauaile   **34.12 cross** losse   **34.13 sheds**

sheeds   **38.2 pour'st** poor'st   **38.3 too** to   **39.12 doth** dost
41.7 woos woes   **42.10 losing** loosing   **44.12 attend time's** attend,
times   **44.13 naught** naughts   **45.9 life's** liues   **46.9 'cide** side
46.12 the he [in some copies]   **47.2 other.** other,   **47.4 smother,**
smother;   **47.11 no** nor   **50.6 dully** duly   **51.10 perfect'st** perfects
55.1 monuments monument   **56.3 [and elsewhere] today** too daie
58.7 patience-tame to suffrance, patience tame, to sufferance
59.6 hundred hundreth   **59.11 whe'er** where   **61.14 off** of   **too** to
62.10 chapped chopt   **63.5 traveled** trauaild   **65.12 of** or
67.6 seeming seeing   **69.3 due** end   **69.14 soil** sole   **71.13 Lest**
Least [also at 72.1, 72.9, and elsewhere]   **73.4 ruined** rn'wd   **choirs**
quiers   **76.7 tell** fel   **77.1 wear** were   **77.10 blanks** blacks
82.8 these the   **83.7 too** to   **88.8 losing** loosing   **90.11 shall** stall
91.9 better bitter   **93.5 there** their   **98.11 were** weare   **99.4 dwells**
dwells?   **99.9 One** Our   **99.13 ate** eate   **102.8 her** his   **106.12 skill**
still   **111.1 with** wish   **112.14 are** y'are   **113.6 latch** lack
113.13 more, replete with more repleat, with   **113.14 mine eye**
mine   **116** [numbered 119 in Q]   **117.10 surmise accumulate;**
surmise, accumulate   **118.5 ne'er-cloying** nere cloying   **118.10 were**
not, grew were, not grew   **119.4 losing** loosing   **121.11 bevel.** beuel
125.6 rent, rent   **125.7 sweet forgoing** sweet; Forgoing   **126.2 sickle**
hour; sickle, hower;   **126.8 minutes** mynuit   **127.2 were** weare
127.10 brows eyes   **129.9 Mad** Made   **129.10 quest to have,** quest,
to haue   **129.11 proved, a** proud and   **132.6 the east** th' East
132.9 mourning morning   **138.12 to have** t' haue   **140.5 were** weare
144.6 side [adopted from *The Passionate Pilgrim*] sight   **144.9 fiend**
[adopted from *The Passionate Pilgrim*] finde   **146.2 Thrall to** My
sinfull earth   **147.7 approve** approoue.   **153.14 eyes** eye

Glossary

Shakespearean Words and Meanings of Frequent Occurrence

A

'A: he (unaccented form).

Abate: lessen, diminish; blunt, reduce; deprive; bar, leave out of account, except; depreciate; humble.

Abuse (N): insult, error, misdeed, offense, crime; imposture, deception; also the modern sense.

Abuse (V): deceive, misapply, put to a bad use; maltreat; frequently the modern sense.

Addition: something added to one's name to denote rank; mark of distinction; title.

Admiration: wonder; object of wonder.

Admire: wonder at.

Advantage (N): profit, convenience, benefit; opportunity, favorable opportunity; pecuniary profit; often shades toward the modern sense.

Advantage (V): profit, be of benefit to, benefit; augment.

Advice: reflection, consideration, deliberation, consultation.

Affect: aim at, aspire to, incline toward; be fond of, be inclined; love; act upon contagiously (as a disease). (PAST PART.) **Affected:** disposed, inclined, in love, loved.

Affection: passion, love; emotion, feeling, mental tendency, disposition; wish, inclination; affectation.

Alarum: signal calling soldiers to arms (in stage directions).

An: if; but; **an if:** if, though, even if.

Anon: at once, soon; presently, by and by.

Answer: return, requite; atone for; render an account of, account for; obey, agree with; also the modern sense.

Apparent: evident, plain; seeming.

Argument: subject, theme, reason, cause; story; excuse.

As: according as; as far as; namely; as if; in the capacity of; that; so that; that is, that they.

Assay: try, attempt; accost, address; challenge.

Atone: reconcile; set at one.

Attach: arrest, seize.

Aweful, awful: commanding reverential fear or respect; profoundly respectful or reverential.

B

Band: bond, fetters, manacle (leash for a dog). **Band** and **bond** are etymologically the same word; **band** was formerly used in both senses.

Basilisk: fabulous reptile said to kill by its look. The basilisk of popular superstition was a creature with legs, wings, a serpentine and winding tail, and a crest or comb somewhat like a cock. It was the offspring of a cock's egg hatched under a toad or serpent.

Bate: blunt, abate, reduce; deduct, except.

Battle: army; division of an army.

Beshrew: curse, blame; used as a mild curse, "Bad or ill luck to."

Bias: tendency, bent, inclination, swaying influence; term in bowling applied to the form of the bowl, the oblique line in which it runs, and the kind of impetus given to cause it to run obliquely.

Blood: nature, vigor; supposed source of emotion; passion; spirit, animation; one of the four humors (see **humor**).

Boot (N): advantage, profit; something given in addition to the bargain; booty, plunder.

Boot (V): profit, avail.

Brave (ADJ.): fine, gallant; splendid, finely arrayed, showy; ostentatiously defiant.

Brave (V): challenge, defy; make splendid.

Brook: tolerate, endure.

C

Can: can do; know; be skilled; sometimes used for *did*.

Capable: comprehensive; sensible, impressible, susceptible; capable of; gifted, intelligent.

Careful: anxious, full of care; provident; attentive.

Carry: manage, execute; be successful, win; conquer; sustain; endure.

Censure (N): judgment, opinion; critical opinion, unfavorable opinion.

Censure (V): judge, estimate; pass sentence or judgment.

Character (N): writing, printing, record; handwriting; cipher; face, features (bespeaking inward qualities).

Character (V): write, engrave, inscribe.

Check (N): reproof; restraint.

Check (V): reprove, restrain, keep from; control.

Circumstance: condition, state of affairs, particulars; adjunct details; detailed narration, argument, or discourse; formality, ceremony.

Clip: embrace; surround.

Close: secret, private; concealed; uncommunicative; enclosed.

Cog: cheat.

Coil: noise, disturbance, turmoil; fuss, to-do, bustle.

Color: appearance; pretext, pretense; excuse.

Companion: fellow (used contemptuously).

Complete: accomplished, fully endowed; perfect, perfect in quality; also frequently the modern sense.

Complexion: external appearance; temperament, disposition; the four complexions—sanguine, choleric, phlegmatic, and melancholy—corresponding to the four humors (see **humor**); also the modern sense.

Composition: compact, agreement, constitution.

Compound: settle, agree.

Conceit: conception, idea, thought; mental faculty, wit; fancy, imagination; opinion, estimate; device, invention, design.

Condition: temperament, disposition; characteristic, property, quality; social or official position, rank or status; covenant, treaty, contract.

Confound: waste, spend, invalidate, destroy; undo, ruin; mingle indistinguishably, mix, blend.

Confusion: destruction, overthrow, ruin; mental agitation.

Continent: that which contains or encloses; earth, globe; sum, summary.

Contrive: plot; plan; spend or pass (time).

Conversation: conduct, deportment; social intercourse, association.

Converse: hold intercourse; associate with, have to do with.

Cope: encounter, meet; have to do with.

Copy: model, pattern; example; minutes or memoranda.

Cousin: any relative not belonging to one's immediate family.

Cry you mercy: beg your pardon.

Cuckold: husband whose wife is unfaithful.

Curious: careful, fastidious; anxious, concerned; made with care, skillfully, intricately, or daintily wrought; particular.

Cursed, curst: shrewish, perverse, spiteful.

D

Dainty: minute; scrupulous, particular; particular about (with **of**); refined, elegant; also the modern sense.

Date: duration, termination, term of existence; limit or end of a term or period, term.

Dear: precious; best; costly; important; affectionate; hearty; grievous, dire; also the modern sense.

Debate: discuss; fight.

Decay (N): downfall, ruin; cause of ruin.

Decay (V): perish, be destroyed; destroy.

Defeat (N): destruction, ruin.

Defeat (V): destroy, disfigure, ruin.

Defy: challenge, challenge to a fight; reject; despise.

Demand (N): inquiry; request.

Demand (V): inquire, question; request.

Deny: refuse (to do something); refuse permission; refuse to accept; refuse admittance; disown.

Depart (N): departure.

Depart (V): part; go away from, leave, quit; take leave (of one another); **depart with, withal:** part with, give up.

Derive: gain, obtain; draw upon, direct (to); descend; pass by descent, be descended or inherited; trace the origin of.

Difference: diversity of opinion, disagreement, dissension, dispute; characteristic or distinguishing feature; alteration or addition to a coat of arms to distinguish a younger or lateral branch of a family.

Digest: arrange, perfect; assimilate, amalgamate; disperse, dissipate; comprehend, understand; put up with (FIG. from the physical sense of digesting food).

Discourse (N): reasoning, reflection; talk, act of conversing, conversation; faculty of conversing; familiar intercourse; relating (as by speech).

Discourse (V): speak, talk, converse; pass (the time) in talk; say, utter, tell, give forth; narrate, relate.

Discover: uncover, expose to view; divulge, reveal, make known; spy out, reconnoiter; betray; distinguish, discern; also the modern sense.

Dispose (N): disposal; temperament, bent of mind, disposition; external manner.

Dispose (V): distribute, manage, make use of; deposit, put or stow away; regulate, order, direct; come to terms. (PAST PART.) **Disposed:** in a good frame of mind; inclined to be merry.

Dispute: discuss, reason; strive against, resist.

Distemper (V): disturb; (N): disorder, ill humor; illness.

Doit: old Dutch coin, one-half an English farthing.

Doubt (N): suspicion, apprehension; fear, danger, risk; also the modern sense.

Doubt (V): suspect, apprehend; fear; also the modern sense.

Doubtful: inclined to suspect, suspicious, apprehensive; not to be relied on; almost certain.

Duty: reverence, respect, expression of respect; submission to authority, obedience; due.

E

Earnest: money paid as an installment to secure a bargain; partial payment; often used with *quibble* in the modern sense.

Ease: comfort, assistance, leisure; idleness, sloth, inactivity; also the modern sense.

Ecstasy: frenzy, madness, state of being beside oneself, excitement, bewilderment; swoon; rapture.

Element: used to refer to the simple substances of which all material bodies were thought to be composed; specifically earth, air, fire, and water, corresponding to the four humors (see **humor**); atmosphere, sky; atmospheric agencies or powers; that one of the four elements which is the natural abode of a creature; hence, natural surroundings, sphere.

Engage: pledge, pawn, mortgage; bind by a promise, swear to; entangle, involve; enlist; embark on an enterprise.

Engine: mechanical contrivance; artifice, device, plot.

Enlarge: give free scope to; set at liberty, release.

Entertain: keep up, maintain, accept; take into one's service; treat; engage (someone's) attention or thought; occupy, while or pass away pleasurably; engage (as an enemy); receive.

Envious: malicious, spiteful, malignant.

Envy: ill-will, malice; hate; also the modern sense.

Even: uniform; direct, straightforward; exact, precise; equable, smooth, comfortable; equal, equally balanced.

Event: outcome; affair, business; also frequently the modern sense.

Exclaim: protest, rail; accuse, blame (with **on**), reproach.

Excursion: stage battle or skirmish (in stage directions).

Excuse: seek to extenuate (a fault); maintain the innocence of; clear oneself, justify or vindicate oneself; decline.

F

Fact: deed, act; crime.

Faction: party, class, group, set (of persons); party strife, dissension; factious quarrel, intrigue.

Fail: die, die out; err, be at fault; omit, leave undone.

Fair (N): fair thing; one of the fair sex; someone beloved; beauty (the abstract concept).

Fair (ADJ.): just; clear, distinct; beautiful; of light complexion or color of hair.

Fair (ADV): fairly.

Fairly: beautifully, handsomely; courteously, civilly; properly, honorably, honestly; becomingly, appropriately; favorably, fortunately; softly, gently, kindly.

Fall: let fall, drop; happen, come to pass; befall; shades frequently toward the modern senses.

Falsely: wrongly; treacherously; improperly.

Fame: report; rumor; reputation.

Familiar (N): intimate friend; familiar or attendant spirit, demon associated with, and obedient to, a person.

Familiar (ADJ.): intimate, friendly; belonging to household or family, domestic; well-known; habitual, ordinary, trivial; plain, easily understood.

Fancy: fantasticalness; imaginative conception, flight of imagination; amorous inclination or passion, love; liking, taste.

Fantasy: fancy, imagination; caprice, whim.

Favor: countenance, face; complexion; aspect, appearance; leave, permission, pardon; attraction, charm, good will; **in favor:** benevolently.

Fear (N): dread, apprehension; dreadfulness; object of dread or fear.

Fear (V): be apprehensive or concerned about, mistrust, doubt; frighten, make afraid.

Fearful: exciting or inspiring fear, terrible, dreadful; timorous, apprehensive, full of fear.

Feature: shape or form of body, figure; shapeliness, comeliness.

Fellow: companion; partaker, sharer (of); equal, match; customary form of address to a servant or an inferior (sometimes used contemptuously or condescendingly).

Fine (N): end, conclusion; **in fine:** finally.

Fine (ADJ.): highly accomplished or skillful; exquisitely fashioned, delicate; refined, subtle; frequently the modern sense.

Flaw: fragment; crack, fissure; tempest, squall, gust of wind; outburst of passion.

Flesh (V): reward a hawk or hound with a piece of flesh of the game killed to excite its eagerness of the chase; hence, to inflame by a foretaste of success; initiate or inure to bloodshed (used for a first time in battle); harden, train.

Flourish: fanfare of trumpets (in stage directions).

Fond: foolish, doting; **fond of:** eager for; also the modern sense.

Fool: term of endearment and pity; frequently the modern sense.

For that, for why: because.

Forfend: forbid, avert.

Free: generous, magnanimous; candid, open; guiltless, innocent.

Front: forehead, face; foremost line of battle; beginning.

Furnish: equip, fit out (furnish forth); endow; dress, decorate, embellish.

G

Gear: apparel, dress; stuff, substance, thing, article; discourse, talk; matter, business, affair.

Get: beget.

Gloss: specious fair appearance; lustrous surface.

Go to: expression of remonstrance, impatience, disapprobation, or derision.

Grace (N): kindness, favor, charm, divine favor; fortune, luck; beneficent virtue; sense of duty or propriety; mercy, pardon; embellish; **do grace:** reflect credit on, do honor to, do a favor for.

Grace (V): gratify, delight; honor, favor.

Groat: coin equal to four pence.

H

Habit: dress, garb, costume; bearing, demeanor, manner; occasionally in the modern sense.

Happily: haply, perchance, perhaps; fortunately.

Hardly: with difficulty.

Have at: I shall come at (you) (i.e., listen to me), I shall attack (a person or thing); let me at.

Have with: I shall go along with; let me go along with; come along.

Having: possession, property, wealth, estate; endowments, accomplishments.

Head: armed force.

Hind: servant, slave; rustic, boor, clown.

His: its. **His** was historically the possessive form of both the masculine and neuter pronouns. **Its,** although not common in Shakespeare's time, occurs in the plays occasionally.

Holp: helped (archaic past tense).

Home: fully, satisfactorily, thoroughly, plainly, effectually; to the quick.

Honest: holding an honorable position, honorable, respectable; decent, kind, seemly, befitting, proper; chaste; genuine; loosely used as an epithet of approbation.

Humor: mood, temper, cast of mind, temperament, disposition; vagary, fancy, whim; moisture (the literal sense); a physiological and, by transference, a psychological term applied to the four chief fluids of the human body—phlegm, blood, bile or choler, and black bile or melancholy. A person's disposition and temporary state of mind were determined according to the relative proportions of these fluids in the body; consequently, a person was said to be phlegmatic, sanguine, choleric, or melancholy.

I

Image: likeness; visible form; representation; embodiment, type; mental picture, creation of the imagination.

Influence: supposed flowing from the stars or heavens of an ethereal fluid, acting upon the characters and destinies of men (used metaphorically).

Inform: take shape, give form to, imbue, inspire; instruct, teach; charge (against).

Instance: evidence, proof, sign, confirmation; motive, cause.

Invention: power of mental creation, the creative faculty; work of the imagination, artistic creation, premeditated design; device, plan, scheme.

J

Jar (N): discord in music; quarrel, discord.

Jar (V): be out of tune; be discordant, quarrel.

Jump: agree, tally, coincide, fit exactly; risk, hazard.

K

Keep: continue, carry on; dwell, lodge, guard, defend, care for, employ, be with; restrain, control; confine in prison.

Kind (N): nature, established order of things; manner, fashion, respect; race, class, kindred, family; **by kind:** naturally.

Kind (ADJ.): natural; favorable; affectionate.

Kindly (ADJ.): natural, appropriate; agreeable; innate; benign.

Kindly (ADV): naturally; gently, courteously.

L

Large: liberal, bounteous, lavish; free, unrestrained; **at large:** at length, in full; in full detail, as a whole, in general.

Late: lately.

Learn: teach; inform (someone of something); also the modern sense.

Let: hinder.

Level: aim; also shades toward the modern sense.

Liberal: possessed of the characteristics and qualities of wellborn persons; genteel, becoming, refined; free in speech; unrestrained by prudence or decorum; licentious.

Lie: be in bed; be still; be confined, be kept in prison; dwell, sojourn, reside, lodge.

Like: please, feel affection; liken, compare.

List (N): strip of cloth, selvedge; limit, boundary; desire.

List (V): choose, desire, please; listen to.

Liver: the seat of love and of violent passions generally (see also **spleen**).

'Long of: owing to, on account of.

Look: power to see; take care, see to it; expect; seek, search for.

M

Make: do; have to do (with); consider; go; be effective, make up, complete; also the modern sense.

Manage: management, conduct, administration; action and paces to which a horse is trained; short gallop at full speed.

Marry: mild interjection equivalent to "Indeed!" Originally, an oath by the Virgin Mary.

May: can; also frequently the modern sense to denote probability; **might** has corresponding meanings and uses.

Mean, means (N): instrument, agency, method; effort; opportunity (for doing something); something interposed or intervening; money, wealth (frequently in the plural form); middle position, medium; tenor or alto part in singing (usually in the singular form).

Mean (ADJ.): average, moderate, middle; of low degree, station, or position; undignified, base.

Measure (N): grave or stately dance, graceful motion; tune, melody, musical accompaniment; treatment meted out; moderation, proportion; limit; distance, reach.

Measure (V): judge, estimate; traverse.

Mere: absolute, sheer; pure, unmixed; downright, sincere.

Mew (up): coop up (as used of a hawk), shut up, imprison, confine.

Mind (N): thoughts, judgment, opinion; message; purpose, intention, desire; disposition; also the modern sense of the mental faculty.

Mind (V): remind; perceive, notice, attend; intend.

Minion: saucy woman, hussy; follower; favorite, favored person, darling (often used contemptuously).

Misdoubt (N): suspicion.

Misdoubt (V): mistrust, suspect.

Model: pattern, replica, likeness.

Modern: ordinary, commonplace, everyday.

Modest: moderate, marked by moderation, becoming; characterized by decency and propriety; chaste.

Moiety: half; share; small part, lesser share; portion, part of.

Mortal: fatal; deadly, of or for death; belonging to mankind; human, pertaining to human affairs.

Motion: power of movement; suggestion, proposal; movement of the soul; impulse, prompting; also the modern sense.

Move: make angry; urge, incite, instigate, arouse, prompt; propose, make a proposal to, apply to, appeal to, suggest; also the modern sense.

Muse: wonder, marvel; grumble, complain.

N

Napkin: handkerchief.

Natural: related by blood; having natural or kindly feeling; also the modern sense.

Naught: useless, worthless; wicked, naughty.

Naughty: wicked; good for nothing, worthless.

Nerves: sinews.

Nice: delicate; fastidious, dainty, particular, scrupulous; minute, subtle; shy, coy; reluctant, unwilling; unimportant, insignificant, trivial; accurate, precise; wanton, lascivious.

Nothing (ADJ.): not at all.

O

Of: from, away from; during; on; by; as regards; instead of; **out of:** compelled by; made from.

Offer: make an attack; menace; venture, dare, presume.

Opinion: censure; reputation or credit; favorable estimate of oneself; self-conceit, arrogance; self-confidence; public opinion, reputation; also the modern sense.

Or: before; also used conjunctively where no alternative is implied; **or . . . or:** either . . . or; whether . . . or.

Out (ADV): without, outside; abroad; fully, quite; at an end, finished; at variance, aligned the wrong way.

Out (INTERJ.): an expression of reproach, impatience, indignation, or anger.

Owe: own; also the modern sense.

P

Pack (V): load; depart, begone; conspire.

Pageant: show, spectacle, spectacular entertainment; device on a moving carriage.

Pain: punishment, penalty; labor, trouble, effort; also frequently the modern sense.

Painted: specious, unreal, counterfeit.

Parle (N): parley, conference, talk; bugle call for parley.

Part (v): depart, part from; divide.

Particular (N): detail; personal interest or concern; details of a private nature; single person.

Party: faction, side, part, cause; partner, ally.

Pass (v): pass through, traverse; exceed; surpass; pledge.

Passing (ADJ. and ADV.): surpassing, surpassingly, exceedingly.

Passion (N): powerful or violent feeling, violent sorrow or grief; painful affection or disorder of the body; sorrow; feelings or desires of love; passionate speech or outburst.

Passion (v): sorrow, grieve.

Peevish: silly, senseless, childish; perverse, obstinate, stubborn; sullen.

Perforce: by violence or compulsion; forcibly; necessarily.

Phoenix: mythical Arabian bird believed to be the only one of its kind; it lived five or six hundred years, after which it burned itself to ashes and reemerged to live through another cycle.

Physic: medical faculty; healing art, medical treatment; remedy, medicine, healing property.

Pitch: height; specifically, the height to which a falcon soars before swooping on its prey (often used figuratively); tarlike substance.

Policy: conduct of affairs (especially public affairs); prudent management; stratagem, trick; contrivance; craft, cunning.

Port: bearing, demeanor; state, style of living, social station; gate.

Possess: have or give possession or command (of something); inform, acquaint; also the modern sense.

Post (N): courier, messenger; post-horse; haste.

Post (v): convey swiftly; hasten, ignore through haste (with **over** or **off**).

Practice (N): execution; exercise (especially for instruction); stratagem, intrigue; conspiracy, plot, treachery.

Practice (v): perform, take part in; use stratagem, craft, or artifice; scheme, plot; play a joke on.

Pregnant: resourceful; disposed, inclined; clear, obvious.

Present (ADJ.): ready, immediate, prompt, instant.

Present (v): represent.

Presently: immediately, at once.

Prevent: forestall, anticipate, foresee; also the modern sense.

Process: drift, tenor, gist; narrative, story; formal command, mandate.

Proof: test, trial, experiment; experience; issue, result; proved or tested strength of armor or arms; also the modern sense.

Proper: (one's or its) own; peculiar, exclusive; excellent; honest, respectable; handsome, elegant, fine, good-looking.

Proportion: symmetry; size; form, carriage, appearance, shape; portion, allotment; rhythm.

Prove: make trial of; put to test; show or find out by experience.

Purchase (N): acquisition; spoil, booty.

Purchase (v): acquire, gain, obtain; strive, exert oneself; redeem, exempt.

Q

Quaint: skilled, clever; pretty, fine, dainty; handsome, elegant; carefully or ingeniously wrought or elaborated.

Quality: that which constitutes (something); essential being; good natural gifts; accomplishment, attainment, property; art, skill; rank, position; profession, occupation, business; party, side; manner, style; cause, occasion.

Quick: living (used substantively to mean "living flesh"); alive; lively, sharp, piercing; hasty, impatient; with child.

Quillets: verbal niceties, subtle distinctions.

Quit: requite, reward; set at liberty; acquit, remit; pay for, clear off.

R

Rack (v): stretch or strain beyond normal extent or capacity to endure; strain oneself; distort.

Rage (N): madness, insanity; vehement pain; angry disposition; violent passion or appetite; poetic enthusiasm; warlike ardor or fury.

Rage (v): behave wantonly or riotously; act with fury or violence; enrage; pursue furiously.

Range: extend or lie in the same plane (with); occupy a position; rove, roam; be inconstant; traverse.

Rank (ADJ.): coarsely luxuriant; puffed up, swollen, fat, abundant; full, copious; rancid; lustful; corrupt, foul.

Rate (N): estimate; value or worth; estimation, consideration; standard, style.

Rate (v): allot; calculate, estimate, compute; reckon, consider; be of equal value (with); chide, scold, berate; drive away by chiding or scolding.

Recreant (N): traitor, coward, cowardly wretch (also as ADJ.).

Remorse: pity, compassion; also the modern sense.

Remove: removal, absence; period of absence; change.

Require: ask, inquire of, request.

Resolve: dissolve, melt, dissipate; answer; free from doubt or uncertainty, convince; inform; decide; also the modern sense.

Respect (N): consideration, reflection, act of seeing, view; attention, notice; decency, modest deportment; also the modern sense.

Respect (v): esteem, value, prize; regard, consider; heed, pay attention to; also the modern sense.

Round: spherical; plain, direct, brusque; fair; honest.

Roundly: plainly, unceremoniously.

Rub: obstacle (a term in the game of bowls); unevenness; inequality.

S

Sack: generic term for Spanish and Canary wines; sweet white wine.

Sad: grave, serious; also the modern sense.

Sadness: seriousness; also the modern sense.

Sans: without (French preposition).

Scope: object, aim, limit; freedom, license; free play.

Seal: bring to completion or conclusion; conclude, confirm, ratify, stamp; also the modern sense.

Sennet: a series of notes sounded on a trumpet to herald the approach or departure of a procession (used in stage directions).

Sense: mental faculty, mind; mental perception, import, rational meaning; physical perception; sensual nature; **common sense:** ordinary or untutored perception, observation or knowledge.

Sensible: capable of physical feeling or perception, sensitive; capable of or exhibiting emotion; rational; capable of being perceived.

Serve: be sufficient; be favorable; succeed; satisfy the need for; serve a turn; answer the purpose.

Several: separate, distinct, different; particular, private; various.

Shadow: shade, shelter; reflection; likeness, image; ghost; representation, picture of the imagination, phantom; also the modern sense.

Shift: change; stratagem, strategy, trick, contrivance, device to serve a purpose; **make shift:** manage.

Shrewd: malicious, mischievous, illnatured; shrewish; bad, of evil import, grievous; severe.

Sirrah: ordinary or customary form of address to inferiors or servants; disrespectful form of address.

Sith: since.

Smock: woman's undergarment; used typically for "a woman."

Something: somewhat.

Sometime: sometimes, from time to time; once, formerly; at times, at one time.

Speed (N): fortune, success; protecting and assisting power; also the modern sense.

Speed (V): fare (well or ill); succeed; be successful; assist, guard, favor.

Spleen: the seat of emotions and passions; violent passion; fiery temper; malice; anger, rage; impulse, fit of passion; caprice; impetuosity (see also **liver**).

Spoil: destruction, ruin; plunder; slaughter, massacre.

Starve: die of cold or hunger; be benumbed with cold; paralyze, disable; allow or cause to die.

State: degree, rank; social position, station; pomp, splendor, outward display, clothes; court, household of a great person; shades into the modern sense.

Stay: wait, wait for; sustain; stand; withhold, withstand; stop.

Stead: assist; be of use to, benefit, help.

Still: always, ever, continuously or continually, constant or constantly; silent, mute; also modern senses.

Stomach: appetite, inclination, disposition; resentment; angry temper, resentful feeling; proud spirit, courage.

Straight: immediately.

Strange: belonging to another country or person, foreign, unfriendly; new, fresh; ignorant; estranged.

Success: issue, outcome (good or bad); sequel, succession, descent (as from father to son).

Suggest: tempt; prompt; seduce.

Suggestion: temptation.

T

Table: memorandum, tablet; surface on which something is written or drawn.

Take: strike; bewitch; charm; infect; destroy; repair to for refuge; modern senses.

Tall: goodly, fine; strong in fight, valiant.

Target: shield.

Tax: censure, blame, accuse.

Tell: count; relate.

Thorough: through.

Throughly: thoroughly.

Toward: in preparation; forthcoming, about to take place; modern senses.

Toy: trifle, idle fancy; folly.

Train: lure, entice, allure, attract.

Trencher: wooden dish or plate.

Trow: think, suppose, believe; know.

U

Undergo: undertake, perform; modern sense.

Undo: ruin.

Unfold: disclose, tell, make known, reveal; communicate.

Unhappy: evil, mischievous; fatal, ill-fated; miserable.

Unjust: untrue, dishonest; unjustified, groundless; faithless, false.

Unkind: unnatural, cruel, faulty; compare **kind.**

Use (N): custom, habit; interest paid.

Use (V): make practice of; be accustomed; put out at interest.

V

Vail: lower, let fall.

Vantage: advantage; opportunity; benefit, profit; superiority.

Virtue: general excellence; valor, bravery; merit, goodness, honor; good accomplishment, excellence in culture; power; essence, essential part.

W

Want: lack; be in need of; be without.

Watch: be awake, lie awake, sit up at night, lose sleep; keep from sleep (TRANS.).

Weed: garment, clothes.

Welkin: sky, heavens.

Wink: close the eyes; close the eyes in sleep; have the eyes closed; seem not to see.

Withal: with; with it, this, or these; together with this; at the same time.

Wot: know.

Index